MODERN BUSINESS LAW AND THE REGULATORY ENVIRONMENT

MODERN BUSINESS LAW AND THE REGULATORY ENVIRONMENT

Third Edition

Thomas W. Dunfee
*University of Pennsylvania,
The Wharton School*

Frank F. Gibson
Ohio State University

John D. Blackburn
Ohio State University

Douglas Whitman
University of Kansas

F. William McCarty
Western Michigan University

Bartley A. Brennan
Bowling Green State University

David Barrett Cohen
California State University, Long Beach

with Contributions by

Robert Wiener
Pace University

Jack Karns
East Carolina University

Nancy Kubasek
Bowling Green State University

McGraw-Hill, Inc.
New York   St. Louis   San Francisco   Auckland   Bogotá   Caracas
Lisbon   London   Madrid   Mexico City   Milan   Montreal   New Delhi
San Juan   Singapore   Sydney   Tokyo   Toronto

MODERN BUSINESS LAW
AND THE REGULATORY ENVIRONMENT

Although care has been taken to provide accurate and current information, the
suggestions, general principles, and conclusions presented in this text are subject to local, state, and federal laws and regulations, court cases, and revisions
of same. The reader is therefore encouraged to consult legal counsel concerning
points of law. This book should not be used as a substitute for competent legal
advice.

This book is printed on acid-free paper.

1 2 3 4 5 6 7 8 9 0 DOW DOW 9 0 9 8 7 6 5

ISBN 0-07-018212-4

This book was set in Century Book by Typographic Sales, Inc.
The editors were Mickey Cox and Terri Varveris;
the design was done by A Good Thing, Inc.;
the production supervisor was Paula Keller.
Project supervision was done by The Total Book.
R. R. Donnelley & Sons Company was printer and binder.

Library of Congress Cataloging-in-Publication Data

Modern business law and the regulatory environment / Thomas W. Dunfee
    . . . [et al.].—3rd ed.
        p.   cm.
    Includes index.
    ISBN 0-07-018212-4
    1. Commercial law—United States.   I. Dunfee, Thomas W.
KF889.M6   1996
346.73'07—dc20
[347.3067]   94-40587

ABOUT THE AUTHORS

Thomas W. Dunfee is the Kolodny Professor of Social Responsibility at The Wharton School of the University of Pennsylvania.

Professor Dunfee served as Chair of the Legal Studies Department at Wharton from 1979 to 1985 and from 1987 to 1991. He was President of the American Business Law Association 1989–1990, served as Editor-in-Chief of the *American Business Law Journal* 1975–1977, and received the Distinguished Senior Faculty Award for Excellence from the ABLA in 1991. He is a member of the Executive Committee of the Society for Business Ethics.

Professor Dunfee has published widely, has been a visiting professor at Georgetown University, the University of Florida, the University of Newcastle (Australia), and Indiana University and has lectured at Reitaku University (Japan), Bocconi University (Milan), Erasmus University (Rotterdam), the London Business School, INSEAD, and many U.S. universities. He has given papers at workshops or conferences at the University of Melbourne, I.E.S.E. (Barcelona), the London School of Economics, the Stockholm School of Economics, the Academy of National Economy of the Government of Russia, and at meetings in Tokyo, Paris, Kingston, Copenhagen, Canberra, and Sydney.

He has published articles in a wide variety of academic journals including *Academy of Management Review*, the *American Business Law Journal*, *Business and Professional Ethics Journal*, *Business Ethics Quarterly*, *California Law Review*, *Journal of Business Ethics*, *Journal of Social Philosophy*, *Northwestern Law Review*, and *Economics and Philosophy*. He also has wide experience acting as consultant to corporations, government agencies, and trade associations.

Frank F. Gibson was a Professor of Business Law and Legal Environment in the College of Business of The Ohio State University. He also served as Chair for the Finance Department. He was formerly Editor-in-Chief of *The American Business Law Journal*, and also served as President of the American Business Law Association. He is now retired.

John D. Blackburn teaches courses in legal environment of business, employment law, and business policy at the Fisher College of Business Administration at The Ohio State University. He has taught at the University of Cincinnati, Indiana University, and the Wharton School of the University of Pennsylvania. He received his B.S. degree from Indiana State University and his J.D. degree from the University of Cincinnati. He was formerly Editor-in-Chief of *The Journal of Legal Studies Education*. He has published articles and books in the field of employment law, including *Labor Relations: Law, Practice and Policy* (Foundation Press) with Julius Getman. Professor Blackburn's article entitled "Restricted Employer Discharge Rights: A Changing Concept of Employment at Will" received the Best Article Award from the *American Business Law Journal*. Professor Blackburn has also written on such topics as worker participation on corporate boards, the Age Discrimination in Employment Act, and privacy rights in employment.

Douglas Whitman is Full Professor at the School of Business Administration of the University of Kansas. He received his B.A. from Knox College, his M.B.A. from the University of Kansas, J.D. from the University of Missouri, and LL.M. from the University of Missouri at Kansas City. He has written articles on advertising law and products liability, and has published in *St. John's Law Review*; *Southwestern Law Journal* (at Southern Methodist Law School); *The University of California, Davis Law Review*; *The University of Pittsburgh Law Review Journal of Product Liability*; and *American Business Law Journal*. His articles have also been reprinted in *The Advertis-*

ing Law Anthology, The Personal Injury Desk Book, The Corporate Counsel's Annual, and by The American Trial Lawyer's Association. He has also written articles for the Advertising Compliance Service.

F. William McCarty is a Professor in the Department of Finance and Commercial Law in the Haworth College of Business at Western Michigan University. Professor McCarty, who was Chair of the Department until 1994, served as a Visiting Scholar at the Japan Center for Michigan Universities while on a 1994–1995 Sabbatical Leave. A specialist in international business law, administrative law, and estate planning, he received a B.A. degree from DePauw University and a J.D. from the University of Michigan. Professor McCarty also received a Diploma from the Europa Institute of the University of Amsterdam. Professor McCarty is the author of articles on international business law and administrative law topics and is the coauthor of several textbooks including *Irwin's Legal and Regulatory Environment of Business, Law and Business, Modern Business Law: Contracts,* and *Modern Business Law: Legal Environment.*

Bartley A. Brennan is a Professor in the Department of Legal Studies at Bowling Green State University. He is a graduate of the School of Foreign Service, Georgetown University (B.S., International Economics) and The College of Law, State University of New York at Buffalo (J.D.). He was a volunteer in the United States Peace Corps, was employed by the Office of Opinions and Review of the Federal Communications Commission, and worked in the General Counsel's office of a private corporation. He has received appointments as a visiting Associate Professor, The Wharton School, University of Pennsylvania, and as a Research Fellow, Ethics Resource Center, Washington, D.C. He is author of articles dealing with government regulation, international law and business, and ethics.

David Barrett Cohen is an attorney in private practice in California. He teaches business law at California State University, Long Beach. He is coauthor of the textbook *Business and Its Legal Environment.* He received a J.D. from the University of Pennsylvania Law School and an M.B.A. from the Wharton School. He also received an M.A., B.A., and B.A.S. from the University of Pennsylvania.

CONTENTS IN BRIEF

APPENDIXES

CONTENTS

APPENDIXES

PREFACE

Modern Business Law and the Regulatory Environment, Third Edition, builds on its tradition of comprehensive, accurate, and up-to-date coverage of important legal topics applicable to business. This edition reflects an expanded team of authors and a broader scope for the book, which contains many new chapters and student learning aids.

David Cohen of California State University, Long Beach, joins the text as a primary author. Jack Karns of East Carolina University, Nancy Kubasek of Bowling Green State University, and Robert Wiener of Pace University contributed new chapters.

All of those involved with the earlier editions express their appreciation and gratitude for the contributions of Frank Gibson. Frank, a former president of the Academy of Legal Studies in Business, significantly influenced the viewpoint of the text and was a congenial and supportive co-author.

Characteristics of the Third Edition

Expanded Topical Coverage: Seven entirely new chapters have been prepared for this edition:

4—Constitutional Law and Business
31—Electronic Fund Transfers
33—Rights of Debtors and Creditors
37—Forms of Business Organization
40—Limited Partnerships
50—Intellectual Property and Computer Law
57—Environmental Law

In addition, several chapters from the second edition have been split into two chapters in order to provide more in-depth treatment for areas where the law is in flux or its influence on business is increasing. As a result, for example, the coverage of commercial transactions and the UCC has expanded from eleven to fifteen chapters. The new chapters provide detailed coverage of areas of law currently so important that they deserve distinct treatment.

Extended Emphasis on Ethics: Business responsibility continues to be an important theme in the business school curriculum. The ALSB has a large business ethics section which reflects the fact that the law course is often the place where ethics is brought into the curriculum. We believe that the interrelatedness of law and ethics supports emphasis on ethical issues within legal studies courses and urge faculty to work in ethical dimensions wherever possible. *Modern Business Law and the Regulatory Environment* supports such coverage in two distinct ways. First, two extensive chapters on individual and corporate responsibility are included together in Part II. They have been substantially rewritten to reflect current developments and new concepts in the business ethics and social responsibility literature. Second, many ethics boxes are scattered throughout the text to challenge students to think about ethics as they encounter various legal topics. Most of the ethics boxes are new and are designed to stimulate student thinking rather than to "preach."

Extended Emphasis on Global Dimensions: As business becomes more globally integrated, even managers of "domestic" companies need to be informed about international dimensions. This is particularly true for the legal environment of a firm. In response to this, the chapter on international law has been significantly revised and updated and global implications have been emphasized, where relevant, throughout the text. For example, the text contains references to the UN Convention on Contracts for the International Sale of Goods.

Cases Integrated into Text: Each chapter has four to five cases integrated into the textual discussion. Cases have been selected on the basis of (1) readability, (2) currency, (3) relevance, and (4) business context. Cases have been carefully edited to achieve the middle ground between cases that are too short, and therefore meaningless, or too long, and therefore tedious for the student. The background for each case is provided in a different color, and the holding of the case has been moved from the background section to the end of the case excerpt.

Boxes and Figures: Boxes are integrated into the text to highlight important issues and trends in the law. Along with the ethics boxes they serve to emphasize important applications and developments. Our experience is that even after taking a business/legal environment course, many students fail to fully appreciate the dynamic nature of the legal system. The issues and trends boxes are designed to emphasize this important dimension. Figures and tables have been added to help the students visualize relationships and to assimilate quickly related information.

Concept Summaries: Each chapter now contains several concept summaries which should help students in self-review. The concept summaries identify and emphasize the key "takeaways" for each of the main topics and may appear as boxes, tables, or figures.

Review Questions and Problems: Each chapter features four types of review questions to help students reinforce what they have learned. First, there is a set of key terms which have been boldfaced in the text. These are followed by a set of discussion questions which ask students questions designed to make sure that they have understood critical distinctions made in the text. Third is a set of hypothetical review problems that have been drafted to provide students experience with applying the legal principles to factual situations. Finally, there is a set of actual case problems, which demonstrate how courts have applied the legal principles, and which give students further experience in thinking about the actual impact of the legal rules that they have studied.

Expanded Appendixes: The Appendixes have been extended and updated. The Appendixes now include The Constitution of the United States of America; Uniform Commercial Code, 1978 Text with 1990 Amendments; Uniform Partnership Act, 1992; Uniform Limited Partnership Act (1976), with 1985 Amendments; and Revised Model Business Corporation Act (1984) (Excerpts).

Supplements: *Modern Business Law and the Regulatory Environment* is accompanied by a complete set of supplements: an instructor's manual and a test bank by Vivica Pierre, California State University, Long Beach; a study guide by Nancy Kubasek, Bowling Green State University; and videotapes by Shepard's/McGraw-Hill. Both the test bank and the instructor's manual are available in computerized form. If you would like information and costs on the supplemental materials, please contact your local McGraw-Hill representative. We value both your interest and our supplements.

Acknowledgments

The authors wish to express their appreciation to Ken MacLeod for his continuing guidance and counsel and to Annette Bodzin for her deft editing and supervision of putting the book into final form.

We have been fortunate to receive helpful and informative reviews from a number of "master" teachers in the field. For their suggestions and insights we thank Robert B. Bennett, Jr., Butler University; Jerald L. Engelman, University of North Dakota; Edward J. Gac, University of Colorado at Boulder; William G. Halm, Ferris State University; James M. Jackman, Oklahoma State University; Deborah S. Kleiner, St. John's University; Paul Lansing, University of Illinois at Urbana–Champaign; Gene Marsh, University of Alabama; Gregory C. Mosier, Oklahoma State University; W. Alfred Mukatis, Oregon State University; Greg

Naples, Marquette University; John Norwood, University of Arkansas; Laura Pincus, DePaul University; Linda Samuels, George Mason University; Larry D. Strate, University of Nevada/Las Vegas; Gary L. Tidwell, College of Charleston; Charles H. Walker, University of Mississippi; and Don Wiesner, University of Miami.

Finally, we would like to thank Sandra Brennan, Ken Marter of Western Michigan University, Nancy Kubasek of Bowling Green State University, and Tia Carter, Wanda Foglia, Stefan Whitwell, and Lauretta Tomasco of The Wharton School for their research and administrative assistance.

Thomas W. Dunfee
Frank F. Gibson
John D. Blackburn
Douglas Whitman
F. William McCarty
Bartley A. Brennan
David Barrett Cohen

MODERN BUSINESS LAW AND THE REGULATORY ENVIRONMENT

PART **I**

LEGAL ENVIRONMENT AND SOURCES OF LAW

1

The Functions and Sources of Law

Legal Systems
Primary Sources of Law
Secondary Sources of Law

Classifications of Law
Reading Cases

Vice President Dan Quayle, in a 1991 speech to the American Bar Association, declared that the ability of the United States to compete in the world economy is threatened by its overabundance of lawyers. The lawyers in the audience gave him a chilly reception and he was roundly rebuked by the ABA president. It was clear, however, that the Vice President had expressed a belief held by many in our society.

In recent years, our legal system has come under attack as never before. The criticisms are many: Our costly propensity to sue one another is harming our competitiveness; excessive jury awards are driving companies out of business; greedy lawyers have encouraged an explosion of lawsuits; our judicial system is overburdened and doesn't function properly; unacceptable delays are the rule rather than the exception.

On the other side, there are those who maintain that the criticisms lack merit or are exaggerated. Many believe that our legal system does a better job than other legal systems in remedying wrongful conduct. Some argue that excessive jury awards aren't as common as critics claim, or that they are effective in deterring outrageous behavior. Some say that lawyers get a bad rap, and

that many devote their lives to protecting the rights of the poor and disenfranchised.

Criticisms of our legal system will be discussed throughout the book, mostly in special boxes devoted to addressing the issues that confront our legal system. These boxes come in four categories: Issues and Trends boxes, which highlight current developments in the law; Ethics boxes, which address the ethical issues raised by our system of law; Preventive Law boxes, which provide practical tips on how business managers can avoid legal trouble in commercial transactions; and Concept Summary boxes, which highlight the major issues described in a section.

But although the book discusses the issues and controversies associated with lawyers and our legal system, it isn't designed to bias your opinion one way or the other. The book *is* designed to teach you how the system works and introduce you to the various areas of law that affect business transactions. Once you understand the legal system, you will be better able to understand and contribute to the debate over whether and how to change it. This book is designed to arm you with some knowledge so that when you have to deal with lawyers and the legal system—and business managers inevitably do—you can do so with more effectiveness and less anxiety.

This chapter introduces the concept of the legal system and then focuses on the legal systems that have developed in the United States.

Legal Systems

Most of us would agree that human beings are social creatures and that we depend upon each other in many ways. This interdependence is the result of both biological and psychological needs; it is also the key to survival in a world in which nature grudgingly provides the requirements for subsistence. On the other hand, difficult problems arise because people live, work, and play together. Over the centuries society has attempted to solve these problems in many ways. One way that has been adopted almost universally is the development of a legal system.

A *legal system* makes the peaceful solution of some of society's problems possible by establishing rules—generally called *laws*—that govern human conduct. In order to be effective, these laws must be enforced by some social institution, generally the government, that has the power to control the manner in which people act.

Legal systems have a variety of functions, including the maintenance of order, the provision of a forum for settling disputes, and the protection of expectations in personal, business, and societal relationships. Legal systems are generally made up of numerous subsystems that create and enforce the law. These include the courts, legislative bodies, law enforcement agencies, and the practicing bar, as well as various types of administrative boards, commissions, and departments.

Primary Sources of Law

Scholars of jurisprudence ponder the sources of law in the metaphysical sense—that is, where does law ultimately come from? Most people are more interested in identifying the sources of law in the practical sense—namely, where does one go to find out what conduct is legal or illegal? These practical sources of law are discussed in the pages that follow.

Constitutions

In most legal systems, the ultimate source of law is the constitution. A **constitution** is a government's basic organizing document. It establishes the framework within which the government must operate. The authority of the constitution is absolute regarding all points that it covers.

Our federal government has a constitution, as does every state government. These constitutions in the American system have three major functions: (1) they guarantee individuals certain basic

---

ETHICS
The Relationship between Law and Ethics

Many of the issues discussed in this chapter involve obligations among persons. The essence of ethics is concern about the impact of actions on others. Thus, law and ethics are closely related. Law defines how people should behave and sanctions those who violate legal proscriptions. Ethical theory identifies how people should behave voluntarily and provides a basis for evaluating the actions of others.

Many people mistakenly believe that law and ethics are essentially the same thing. That is not so, although legal and ethical concepts may interrelate in various ways. Merely complying with the law does not guarantee that one is ethical. Ethics goes beyond the law. The mere fact that the law requires or allows certain conduct does not make it ethical. It is possible to have an unethical law. Slavery was legal in the United States during the first half of the nineteenth century. Slavery was not sanctified as an ethical practice just because it was legal.

Ethical issues are discussed throughout this text. Chapter 8 provides some general background concerning ethical theory and concepts of business ethics. Chapter 9 applies some of these to business firms. Throughout the rest of the text, Ethics boxes, similar to this one, will be used to highlight particular ethical problems and theories.

rights; (2) they allocate power among the legislative, judicial, and executive branches of government; and (3) they allocate power among political subdivisions.

Constitutions derive their authority from the people. In the Constitution of the United States, the people, acting through state governments, grant certain powers to the federal government. In spheres where the federal government has power, its actions are supreme. On the other hand, federal action, such as a congressional enactment, is invalid unless supported by a specific constitutional provision. The U.S. Constitution also restricts actions that Congress, the President, or the federal judiciary can take. For example, Congress cannot pass a law penalizing a person for an action that was legal when committed, nor can a federal agency take a person's property without providing compensation. In addition to limiting actions of government officials, the Constitution ensures that the government will not violate the rights and liberties of individuals.

State constitutions distribute the powers of government within the three branches of state government. They also provide for the distribution of power to political subdivisions, such as counties, cities, townships, and municipalities. For example, a number of state constitutions have "home rule" provisions which allow municipalities the right of self-government in local affairs. Like the U.S. Constitution, most state constitutions declare basic rights and liberties to which people are entitled.

In the legal system operating in the United States the courts have the task of nullifying legislative or executive actions that violate a constitutional provision. In 1934 the U.S. Supreme Court declared unconstitutional the National Recovery Act, which was the cornerstone of President Roosevelt's program to end the Great Depression. When President Truman attempted to seize the steel mills in 1952 in order to end a strike that interfered with the Korean War effort, the Supreme Court determined that he did not have constitutional authority to do so.

Judicial Law

A distinguishing feature of Anglo-American law is its reliance upon previously decided cases as a primary source of law. For many centuries judges and lawyers have looked for past similar cases to determine what the law is in a particular situation. The body of previously decided disputes is known as case law, or **common law,** and the system whereby judges rely on past decisions is known as the common law system. The common law system is founded on the doctrine of *stare decisis* ("to abide by decided cases").

Stare Decisis   The doctrine of **stare decisis** provides that, once a court applies a particular principle of law to a certain set of facts, that same legal principle will govern all future cases in which the facts are substantially the same. Applying the doctrine of *stare decisis* isn't always a straightforward proposition. Rarely are two cases *exactly* alike. The challenge for the attorney comes in finding cases that support his or her client's case, and then convincing the judge that the facts of those cases are "on point"—that is, sufficiently similar to the current case to warrant the same result. The opposing attorney will argue that those cases are *not* relevant to the current case, and will try to find cases which support his or her client's case.

For example, consider a tort case involving a suit by a paying spectator at a recreation-league hockey game in a municipal rink. The spectator is injured by a hockey stick flying into the stands after a player swings at a puck. Let's assume the state is one in which the law indicates that a city, as an agency of the sovereign state, is immune from suit if it is engaged in a governmental function but is not immune and can be held liable if it is engaged in a proprietary or businesslike function. The attorney for the spectator will research previous cases. He or she may find a case in which another city's operation of a municipal football stadium was found to be a businesslike operation, and thus the city could be sued and held liable for negligent operation of the stadium. On the other hand, the attorney representing the city may find a previous case in which a city's operation of a municipal park system, including baseball diamonds, was held to be a part of the recreation program of the city, for the benefit of its citizens, and not a businesslike operation.

Which of those precedent cases would apply to the operation of a hockey rink? Would it make a difference who could use the rink? Does it matter if the city charged admission or made a profit on the operation of the rink? Is it relevant if there are privately owned rinks in or near the city? What basis for comparison or contrast would you find important?

FACTUAL DISTINCTION Even if a statement in a prior case is considered to be precedent for subsequent cases, the facts of a later case may be different from those of the prior case. Even if a similar set of facts is presented in two cases, the legal issues of one case may differ from those previously considered. Thus, the problem of determining whether a hockey rink owned and operated by the city is being run as a "governmental function" or as a "business enterprise" presents different facts from the problem of determining the same question for a city park with baseball diamonds, or a municipal football stadium. While the legal issues in the three cases are the same, significant future distinctions regarding the sport or recreational activity certainly could exist. For example, there might be differences in the degree of supervision exercised by the city over those using the facilities or in the existence of alternative and competing private enterprises engaged in the same activity.

When major factual distinctions exist between a case under consideration and a supposed precedent, the cases are said to be distinguished. *Stare decisis* does not apply to cases that can be distinguished from the relevant precedents. Each attorney must therefore attempt to convince the judge that the cases that support his or her position are on point—and thus must be followed—and that the cases supporting the other side's position should be distinguished—and thus should not be followed.

OVERRULING PRIOR CASE LAW On occasion courts do refuse to follow previous decisions, even though such decisions are based on similar facts, because conditions have changed significantly. The changes may involve new technology or novel economic, social, or political circumstances.

Decisions can also be overruled if, in retrospect, the court deems them to have been plainly wrong or unjust. A famous example is the 1896 U.S. Supreme Court decision in *Plessy v. Ferguson*, which enunciated a "separate but equal" doctrine that allowed public facilities to be segregated on the basis of race. The Supreme Court overruled *Plessy* and the "separate but equal" doctrine in the 1954 case of *Brown v. Board of Education*.

Scope of Precedent Each state has its own sources of law—its own constitution, legislative enactments, administrative rulings, and judge-made precedent. The courts of one state do not have to follow decisions of other states. Of course, external decisions may be consulted for reference, particularly when there are no previous decisions on the point in question in the state where a case is being heard, or when the reasons for adoption of new policies by another state's court may be considered applicable in the state where the case is being heard.

Courts in each jurisdiction—federal or state—are grouped in a particular hierarchy. In this hierarchy appellate courts are generally referred to as higher courts, trial courts as lower courts. Every federal or state trial court is "under" an appellate court. Precedent flows down the hierarchy from higher to lower courts.

All courts are bound by a U.S. Supreme Court decision. In each state the lower trial and appellate courts must abide by precedent established by the highest court of the state.

Courts that are on the same level of the hierarchy are not bound to follow an opinion of a co-equal court. Trial courts need follow only precedent from the appellate court covering their jurisdiction. Thus, the U.S. District Court for the Southern District of New York—a federal trial court—is not bound by a decision of the Ninth Circuit Court of Appeals, whose geographic control is limited to the West Coast.

The doctrine of stare decisis furthers the predictability of the law. If a previous case has been based upon a certain principle, that principle will be used in a subsequent case even though different parties are involved in the latter case. By the principle of stare decisis, judicial decisions thus affect not only the parties to the lawsuit but also people who are involved in later cases that are found to be similar to prior cases. People thus anticipate the legal result of their actions from a consideration of the legal results of similar actions in previous decisions. Courts are legitimately hesitant to renounce or reverse their prior decisions, preferring instead to allow any desired change to be made by the legislature.

Statutes

A **statute** is an act of a legislature that declares, requires, or forbids something. Although for many years cases were the chief source of Anglo-American law, statutes have increased greatly in importance over the past 150 years. Much of the common law from previous centuries has been enacted by legislative bodies into statute. This process is called *codification*. (Codification also refers to the process by which statutes are organized by subject into codes, as discussed below.) Today, a person trying to determine the law in a particular field typically would look first to the appropriate statute and only then to the relevant cases.

Statutes, of course, may not run afoul of the appropriate constitution. In much the same way that constitutions take priority over statutes, statutes can be said to take priority over judicial decisions. When a judicial decision involves an area of law covered by a statute, the court must do its best to interpret the statute even if the court feels that the statute does not reflect wise policy. The exception is when a court finds a statute to be unconstitutional, in which case it may declare the statute to be null and void.

Also, a legislature may overrule a judicial decision by enacting a statute that enunciates a contrary rule. For example, a court might rule in *Smith v. Jones* that, on the basis of common law, a contract made by a person under the age of 21 may be voided by that person. The legislature could then enact a statute providing that any contract executed by a person 18 years of age or older may not be voided because of minority. The statute generally would not apply to *Smith v. Jones* or to other cases arising before the statute's effective date. The statute would, however, cut off the precedential authority that *Smith v. Jones* would have otherwise had.

Given the priority of statutes, then, courts are left to make law in two ways: (1) by interpreting statutes and constitutions and (2) by "filling in gaps" in areas where constitutional and statutory law is silent. The term *statutory law* as used here encompasses not only the enactments of state and federal legislators but also ordinances, administrative rules and regulations, executive decrees, and treaties. An **ordinance** is an enactment of an elected body of local government, such as a city council or a county board of supervisors. Administrative rules and regulations are discussed later in the chapter.

Codes   As statutes are enacted, they are typically incorporated by subject matter into statutory compilations known as **codes.** All federal statutes are included in a general compilation known as the United States Code, which is in turn made up of several codes on various subjects. For example, the Internal Revenue Code is a code within the United States Code that deals with federal taxation. Similarly, state statutes are organized into codes by subject matter. Most states have several codes, including a penal code (which defines crimes under state law) and a revenue and taxation code (which covers state taxation).

THE UNIFORM COMMERCIAL CODE   Most states also have a commercial code, which governs the rights and obligations of parties to commercial transactions. In an effort to promote uniformity in commercial transactions from state to state, the American Law Institute and the National Conference of Commissioners on Uniform State Laws prepared the Uniform Commercial Code (UCC). After the UCC was drafted its sponsors encouraged every state to enact it as its own commercial code. In the several years since it was drafted, the UCC has been adopted in full in forty-nine states and in part by Louisiana. The theory behind having each state enact the same commercial code is that uniform rules and practices facilitate the flow of commerce throughout the country. The desired result is a unified market that is much more prosperous than would have been the case if commercial law had varied widely from state to state. The advantages of a unified market have inspired the European Community to standardize the commercial law of its member countries.

The UCC has a tremendous impact on business law, and will be cited frequently throughout the text. It is set forth in its entirety in Appendix A of this book.

Distinguishing Statutory Law from Case Law   Statutory law, in contrast to judicial law, is usually more directly responsive to political, social, and economic considerations. While judges are clearly cognizant of societal forces that affect and are affected by their case interpretations, their written decisions are usually replete with express references to prior cases and only implicit references to the relative merits of the underlying forces involved in the case.

A statute generally has *prospective* application—that is, it governs conduct from its effective date forward. A judicial decision, on the other hand, has *retrospective* application: it applies to the past conduct that resulted in the lawsuit. As we have learned, of course, judicial decisions also have prospective application to the extent that they set precedent.

Also, statutes tend to have *general* application, meaning that they apply to everyone or to a general class. Examples of statutes that apply to everyone are criminal statutes that forbid murder, theft, and other offenses. Examples of statutes that apply only to a general class are regulatory statutes that govern the conduct of particular types of business entities, such as banks, securities dealers, or electric utility companies. In contrast to statutes, judicial decisions usually have *specific* application, meaning that they apply directly to the parties to the case only. Again, however, judicial decisions indirectly have general application to the extent that they create precedent.

Statutory Interpretation The increasing use of statutes to provide solutions for social problems has not appreciably reduced the importance of cases as a source of law. Most statutes are broadly written, indicating only the outlines of legislative policy. Before the meaning of a statute is established, it often has to be interpreted or, as lawyers say, construed by the courts. Thus, in many situations when a person needs to know what the law is, he or she looks first at the statutory provision and then at cases in which it has been applied. These cases indicate what the statute actually means.

Logically, the process of judicial interpretation at first seems questionable because in effect the courts are explaining what the legislature actually meant. Upon further examination the process makes good sense, for it allows the meaning of the law to be filled in by the courts. They are better equipped than the legislature to respond to specific problems and less affected by the political pressures of the moment. Although having the courts interpret statutes is not without risk, courts in the United States have consistently

stated that, in interpreting statutes, their primary function is to determine and give effect to the intention of the legislature.

Since legislative bodies seldom, if ever, have specific intents, statutory interpretation is, at best, an imperfect science. To add some certainty to the process, courts have developed a number of principles, or canons of statutory interpretation, that they apply to determine legislative intent.

In applying these principles, a court must take into consideration the general purpose of the legislation. This purpose is determined from the entire act in light of its historical background, the evils at which the statute is directed, and its evident objectives. The canons of construction, which include looking at the plain meaning of terms, contextual analysis, and examination of the statute's legislative history, must yield if they conflict with clear evidence of the legislative will.

PLAIN MEANING There may be words or phrases in a statute that can be interpreted in a variety of ways. A basic first step in all statutory interpretations is to look to the plain meaning of the words used to determine what the statute means. As a general rule, the words of a statute will be given their common meaning. Courts presume that the legislature intended to use the words as they are used in everyday communication. In many instances, the plain meaning is obvious and no further interpretative analysis is required.

On occasion, the same word may be used in different contexts by the legislature to mean different things. In some statutes *person* includes a corporation while in others (a rape statute, for example), *person* would not include a corporation. A doctor's or lawyer's practice may be a *business* for some purposes and not for others. For such words, a simple dictionary definition will not suffice. Instead, the courts must consider the context in which the words are used and they must attempt to identify any relevant legislative purpose.

In order to avoid such ambiguity, many statutes include detailed definitions of their key terms. For example, the Uniform Partnership Act (UPA) defines a partnership as "an association of two or more persons." Section 2 of the Act defines *person* as including "individuals, partnerships, corporations, and other associations."

Thus, no one could reasonably argue that *under the provisions of the UPA* a corporation could not be a partner in a partnership.

CONTEXTUAL ANALYSIS   Some legislative enactments are really segments of a larger statutory scheme. In interpreting language that is part of a larger body of legislative provisions, the courts analyze how the specific provision fits into the context of the entire legislative package.

In 1981, for example, Congress passed a series of legislative enactments designed to solve pressing national economic problems. The enactments included an across-the-board reduction in personal tax rates, accelerated depreciation credits for business investment, and numerous provisions to encourage individuals to save. In interpreting a specific section of this legislation, the courts might analyze a provision in the context of the entire package that became law.

LEGISLATIVE HISTORY   In seeking to interpret the meaning of statutory provisions, courts sometimes refer to committee reports, hearings, speeches from the floor of the legislature, prior drafts of the statute, failed amendments, and other aspects of the statute's legislative history. These various components of the statute's history shed light on what the legislature intended.

Dangers, however, exist when a court relies upon legislative history to determine legislative intent. Quite often legislative history is ambiguous. Legislators vote for a statute for different reasons. A statement by one senator in a committee hearing may not represent the majority view. In addition, lawmakers, aware that courts use legislative history to interpret statutes, may be tempted to make statements supporting their own views of what the legislative policy should be, even though they know that this is not the position of the statute's drafters. A further problem with legislative history is that many state legislatures keep few records of the deliberations and discussions leading to the enactment of a statute.

Administrative Rules and Orders

Government regulation of the affairs of individuals and businesses has become quite extensive over the past several years. Much of that regulation is so detailed that it is impractical for it to be imposed by statute. Do we really want Congress, for example, to agonize over the precise level of each mineral that is allowable in drinking water, or the exact minimum height of guard rails in industrial facilities? Because legislatures are ill suited to fill in the minute details that characterize modern regulation, much of that work is left to administrative agencies. An **administrative agency** is a governmental body that is responsible for implementing and administering particular legislation. The Securities and Exchange Commission (SEC), for example, was created in 1934 to administer the Securities Act of 1933 and the Securities Exchange Act of 1934. (The SEC, which will be discussed in greater detail in Chapter 46, has since been charged with implementing other securities statutes as well.) There are scores of agencies in the federal government, including the Environmental Protection Agency, the Federal Trade Commission, the Food and Drug Administration, the Internal Revenue Service, the Immigration and Naturalization Service, the National Labor Relations Board, and the Occupational Health and Safety Administration. Administrative agencies are also found in state governments.

Agencies are created by the legislative branch but are usually housed in the executive branch. They generally have powers that resemble those of all three branches. Most, but not all, agencies have the power to promulgate **rules and regulations,** which are quasi-legislative enactments by an administrative agency designed to implement a particular statute. Typically, the legislature will set the general parameters for regulation in the statute and the agency will "fill in the details" by promulgating rules and regulations with more specific requirements. In order to be valid, administrative rules and regulations must be within the scope of authority granted to the agency by the legislature.

In addition to the authority to promulgate rules and regulations, administrative agencies often have a quasi-judicial authority to adjudicate disputes involving the statute or statutes administered by the agency. The administrative agency decides the dispute by issuing an **order,** which is analogous to a decision rendered by a court. Orders of administrative agencies may generally be reviewed by the courts. Courts typically accord great deference to an agency's interpretation of the statute that it administers. Presumably the administrators have the specialized knowledge and technical skill in their area of expertise that judges do not have.

Secondary Sources of Law

Books, treatises, and other materials that describe and summarize the law are known as *secondary sources*. They are invaluable tools for legal research. There are specialized secondary sources for almost every area of law.

CONCEPT SUMMARY
Sources of Law

Primary Sources

Constitutions	Include the U.S. Constitution and 50 state constitutions; establish framework of government and fundamental legal principles
Judicial cases	Create legal principles through doctrine of precedent, or *stare decisis*; specific and retrospective
Statutes	Enacted by democratically elected legislatures; general and prospective; interpreted by courts
Administrative regulations	Adopted by federal and state agencies such as the Securities Exchange Commission (SEC) and Federal Trade Commission (FTC), as well as by state agencies such as utility rate commissions; rules have force of law; sometimes industry-specific (SEC) or activity-specific (FTC and advertising)

Secondary Sources

Restatements of law	Summaries of judge-made law compiled by legal scholars
Legal encyclopedias and reporters	General summaries of law compiled by legal publishers
Law reviews	Journals published by law schools containing articles discussing legal issues

---

Private companies sponsor reporting services which summarize specific areas of the law and provide updates on changes and new developments each week or each month. Additionally, there are legal encyclopedias which summarize all major areas of the law. Law reviews, another important secondary source of law, are publications edited by law students that include articles on various legal issues. Legal researchers often use these secondary sources to help them find the relevant primary sources of law—that is, constitutions, statutes, cases, and regulations.

Restatements of the law are important secondary sources of law. Restatements are treatises which summarize the common law in a particular field. Restatements are drafted so as to resemble statutes, and are sometimes mistaken for statutes. It is important to keep in mind that restatement provisions are prepared by legal scholars and do not have the legal effect of statutes enacted by legislatures. However, they sometimes serve as models for legislatures that wish to codify certain common law rules into statutory form. Since common law changes, restatements are replaced as necessary. There is thus a *Restatement of Torts, Second* (that is, the second version of the *Restatement of Torts*), a *Restatement of Contracts, Second*, and second and even third restatements for several other topics of law. Restatement provisions are often cited by courts in judicial opinions.

Classifications of Law

There are several different ways to classify law. These classifications involve terms with which you should become familiar.

Civil Law versus Criminal Law

Civil law governs the private rights and obligations that exist between members of society. When a seller sues a buyer for breach of contract, for example, the lawsuit is a civil one. The seller is suing to be compensated for its own private loss, which it alleges was caused by the buyer. Similarly, civil law is involved when a person sues for compensation for injuries allegedly caused by a corporation.

Criminal law, on the other hand, involves infractions against society as a whole. When someone is tried for a crime, he or she is *prosecuted* by a representative of the government. When a case has a title such as *State of Ohio v. Jones* or *U.S. v. Smith*, it is generally (but not always) a criminal case. Federal and state crimes are defined as such by statutes or the common law (although most common law crimes have been codified into statute).

Criminal law can be distinguished from civil law on several counts. In both a civil and a criminal case, the party against whom the suit is brought is known as the **defendant.** But a civil case is brought by the **plaintiff** and a criminal case is brought by a prosecutor, who is an agent of the state.

In a criminal proceeding, it must be determined whether the defendant is *guilty* and should be *convicted.* The concept of guilt is not applicable to civil proceedings. Instead, a civil proceeding is generally designed to determine whether the defendant has incurred **liability** to the plaintiff—that is, whether the defendant has violated the plaintiff's rights in such a manner that entitles the plaintiff to relief. Criminal law is primarily concerned with *punishing* wrongdoers, whereas civil law is primarily geared to *compensating* people whose rights have been violated. Even though defendants in criminal cases may be ordered to pay restitution (compensation for the victims' out-of-pocket losses) and punitive damages may be awarded in civil cases, there is still a difference in emphasis so that forms of punishment are more extensive in criminal cases and the right to compensation more extensive in civil cases. If a criminal defendant is found guilty, he or she may be sentenced to prison, required to pay a fine and/or restitution, or even sentenced to death. If a civil defendant is found liable, however, he or she will generally be made to pay **damages,** or monetary compensation, which can include recovery for intangibles such as pain and suffering not normally allowed in restitution orders. (As we shall see later in the chapter, forms of relief other than damages are sometimes available in civil proceedings.)

A single event can sometimes give rise to both a criminal and civil action. Assume that Fred shoots and wounds Ted with a gun. The state may prosecute Fred for the crimes of attempted murder, assault with a deadly weapon, and battery. If Fred is convicted, he can be sent to jail or be made to pay a fine, but Ted will generally not be compensated for his injuries. Since Ted's private rights have been violated by Fred's actions, Ted may bring a civil suit against Fred. If Ted wins his civil suit, he may be awarded damages in the amount necessary to compensate him for his medical bills, lost wages, pain and suffering, and any other harm that he suffered because of Fred's action. The court may also award Ted punitive damages in order to punish Fred, but the primary object of a civil remedy is supposed to be compensation and not punishment.

Civil Law versus Common Law Systems

The term *civil law* can also have a different meaning from that defined above. The legal systems of Spain, France, and most other European nations are referred to as civil law systems. A civil law system is one in which the most important sources of law are comprehensive statutory codes. The codes are designed to be sufficiently detailed so as to leave judges little room for interpretation. Unlike a common law system, legal doctrine is not shaped and evolved through case law. Louisiana, with its strong French heritage, is the only state in the union with a civil law system. Unless the context suggests otherwise, any reference to civil law in this book is most likely meant to signify the *other* definition of civil law—that is, the law governing the enforcement of private rights.

The civil law systems of continental Europe contrast with the Anglo-American common law system, in which judicial decisions are an important source of law.

Substantive Law versus Procedural Law

Substantive law describes rules which govern the rights and obligations of individuals, businesses, and other organizations. Substantive law tells us what we may and may not do, and, sometimes, what we must do. Most of what we think of as "law" is substantive law: We are not permitted to drive faster than the posted speed limit; if we injure others because of our carelessness or if we violate the terms of a contract, we can be made to pay damages; if we drop litter in a public park, we can be made to pay a fine; we must file income tax returns; if we purposely cause physical harm to another, we can be sent to jail. Substantive law includes any law that governs the conduct of members of society. Substantive law may apply to everyone (no one is allowed to commit murder) or to a specific class within society (corporations whose stock is traded publicly must file reports with the Securities and Exchange Commission).

In our legal system, no one is held responsible for a violation of substantive law until certain procedures are followed to determine if the party really should be held accountable. People who are accused of a crime are entitled to a trial, as are parties to a civil lawsuit. When an administrative agency wishes to take action against a company that it believes is violating a law, the agency generally must give the company the chance to present its side of the story in an administrative tribunal. Certain procedures must be established in order to ensure that these tribunals—be they judicial or administrative—are conducted with fairness and efficiency. That's where procedural law comes in.

Procedural law describes the procedures that must be followed in the adjudication of a case by a court or an administrative agency. The law of *civil procedure* governs the conduct of civil lawsuits, including what types of documents each party must file or may file, deadlines that apply during the litigation process, how each party may elicit information from the other, the circumstances in which the judge may dismiss the case, and how the losing party may appeal. The law of *criminal procedure* applies to the conduct of criminal cases. The law of *evidence* governs how each side may present evidence to prove its case (or rebut the other side's case) at trial. The law of *administrative procedure* sets forth rules for the conduct of administrative agencies, in both their rulemaking and adjudicatory activities.

Law versus Equity

We commonly use the term *law* to mean all the rights, obligations, and procedures laid down by the government. But the term can be used in a more specific sense. Simply put, an action at **law** is one that seeks monetary damages; an action in **equity** is one that seeks some other form of relief.

The distinction between law and equity developed centuries ago in England. Courts of law in the old English system were empowered to grant a plaintiff only one type of relief: requiring the defendant to give the plaintiff money or something else of value. This rigid rule proved to be unsatisfactory because some wrongs could not be properly compensated in this manner. A parallel system thus developed whereby parties who felt that they could not be adequately compensated by monetary damages could petition the king for other types of relief. Such cases were generally decided by a *chancellor*, an agent of the king. Chancellors presided over *courts of equity*, in which they were empowered to fashion nonmonetary forms of relief known as **equitable remedies.**

We will discuss equitable remedies in later chapters, but will introduce two of the more important ones here. An **injunction** is an order that prohibits a party from engaging in some specified conduct. (An injunction may also *require* a party to do something, but this is less common.) Assume, for example, that Jack is in the habit of using the driveway of his neighbor, Zack, without Zack's permission. Monetary damages may be ill suited to protect Zack's interests because Jack is engaging in a continuing pattern of objectionable behavior. It wouldn't be practical for Zack to sue Jack for monetary damages each time that Jack encroached on his driveway. In this case, a court might issue an injunction to prevent Jack from using the driveway.

Specific performance is an equitable remedy that requires the party who has breached a contract to actually perform it. The legal remedy (that is, the remedy *at law*) for breach of contract is the payment of damages. If, for example, a car dealer breaches a contract to sell you a new Dodge Caravan for $15,000, you can sue for damages. You would first be expected to fix your damages by buying a Dodge Caravan elsewhere. If the best price that you could find for an identical model was $18,000, then your damages would be $3,000—the amount that would put you in the same position as you would have been if the original dealer had performed the contract. In this case, the legal remedy is adequate.

But what if the dealer breaches a contract to sell you the last remaining Model-T Ford? You can't go out and buy another one. Even if the dealer was required to pay you the entire purchase price in damages, you still wouldn't be in the position that you contracted to be in because you wouldn't have the Model-T Ford. In such a situation, a court might award specific performance and require the dealer to deliver the car in exchange for the contract price.

Courts of law and courts of equity used to operate on completely separate tracks. Courts of equity even had a different vocabulary from courts of law. The party seeking relief was known as the **petitioner,** because equitable relief was sought by filing a **petition** with the court of equity. (Legal relief, on the other hand, was sought by filing a **complaint** with the court of law.) The party against whom relief was sought was the **respondent.** The chancellor's decision was known as a **decree.**

Today, the systems of law and equity have merged, and courts are empowered to offer both legal remedies (damages) and equitable remedies. A court generally has wide discretion in awarding equitable remedies, but will not grant an equitable remedy when monetary damages are adequate. The court generally will not grant equitable relief to a party that has not behaved fairly and honestly, even if the other party has behaved improperly as well. The object of equitable relief is to fashion a solution that will promote fairness and justice when the legal remedy isn't suited to the task.

The U.S. Constitution grants a right to a trial by jury only in actions "at law." This means that there is no constitutional right to a jury trial when the only relief requested is equitable relief. Petitions for injunctions or other equitable remedies are generally decided by a judge only. Most courts still use the terminology of equity (petitioner, respondent, decree, etc.) in actions for equitable relief.

Reading Cases

Court opinions are an important source of law in our common law system. The opinions are also valuable to demonstrate how courts apply the law to different factual scenarios. Excerpts from court opinions are included throughout this book.

Basic Concepts

Parties   As noted earlier, all civil suits at law have at least one plaintiff (who brings the suit) and at least one defendant (against whom the suit is brought). In actions for equitable relief, the party bringing the suit is usually known as the petitioner and the party against whom the suit is brought is known as the respondent.

Most of the opinions excerpted in this book are from *appellate courts*—that is, courts that review appeals of cases that have been decided by a lower court. (The structure of the court system is discussed in the next chapter.) The party who is appealing the case—that is, the loser in the lower court decision—is known as the **appellant.** The other party, the winner at the lower court level, is known as the **appellee.**

CONCEPT SUMMARY
Classifications of Law

Type	Characteristics	Example
Civil	Governs private rights and obligations	Contract rules governing warranties
	or, a system based on statutory as opposed to judge-made or common law	Commercial law statutes in Louisiana
Criminal	Governs harms against society	Prohibition of assaults with a deadly weapon
Substantive	Governs rights and obligations of individuals, businesses, and other entities	Contract rules governing warranties
Procedural	Procedures for operation of legal system, trials, and other adjudicatory matters	Rules concerning admissibility of evidence
Common	Judge-made law deriving from precedent or *stare decisis*	Contract rules governing offer and acceptance
	or, a system in which judges rely on judge-made law	Commercial law in states other than Louisiana

Some opinions excerpted in this book are from the United States Supreme Court. As we shall see in the next chapter, most parties do not have an automatic right to *appeal* a case to the Supreme Court but rather must *petition* the Supreme Court to hear the case. The party who petitioned the Supreme Court to review the case (i.e., the party who lost the decision at next lower court) is known as the petitioner and the other party is known as the respondent, just as in an equity action.

Judges and Justices   The jurists who preside over court proceedings are known as **judges** or **justices,** depending on the court on which they serve. The members of the U.S. Supreme Court are known as justices, while lower federal court jurists are known as judges. Most, but not all, state judiciaries are similar, with lower court jurists known as judges and members of the state supreme court known as justices.

Decisions   The trial court will enter a **judgment**—that is, a decision—for one party or the other. The court may grant a **dismissal**—that is, rule in favor of the defendant either before the trial begins or during the trial. Chapter 3 provides a more detailed discussion of trial procedure.

An appellate court opinion, as noted above, involves a review of a lower court's decision. If the appellate court chooses to **affirm** the lower court's decision, the decision stands; if the appellate court decides to **reverse** the lower court's decision, the decision is nullified. As we will see in Chapter 2, an appellate court bases its review on the trial record and, unlike a trial court, is not itself equipped to hear evidence. If the appellate court reverses a decision, it may decide that the parties must have the opportunity to present additional evidence in order for a proper decision to be reached. In such a case, the appellate court will **remand** the case—that is, send it back—to the trial court for further proceedings.

Opinions   An **opinion** is a written summary of a case prepared on behalf of one or more members of the court. An opinion includes a statement of the facts of the case, the issues that the court must decide, how the case was decided in any lower court proceedings, the decision that the court is reaching, and the rationale for that decision. Opinions are not issued for all cases, although they are issued for most appellate court cases. A **unanimous opinion** is one on which all judges or justices of the court agree. If the members of the court do not all agree, each may write a **separate opinion.** A separate opinion may be a **dissenting opinion,** in which the judge or justice expresses the view that the court has decided in favor of the wrong party, or a **concurring opinion,** in which the judge or justice supports the decision in favor of the winning party but finds fault with the majority's rationale. A **majority opinion** is an opinion supported by the majority of the judges or justices. The decision set forth in the majority opinion is the official decision of the court, and the majority opinion is the opinion that is given precedential value for *stare decisis* purposes.

Courts and Reporters   The cases excerpted in this book are pulled from various courts around the country. The heading of each case excerpt indicates the court that decided the case.

Cases are published in **reporters,** or collections of cases in roughly chronological order. A reporter includes a series of volumes of cases from a particular court or groups of courts. For example, the *United States Reports* series is the official reporter for U.S. Supreme Court cases. Supreme Court cases are also reported in slightly different formats in the *Supreme Court Reporter,* published by West Publishing Company; the *Lawyers' Edition of the Supreme Court Reports,* published by the Lawyers Cooperative Publishing Company; and by *United States Law Week,* published by the Bureau of National Affairs.

The heading of each case excerpt includes a **citation,** which indicates the exact volume and page of the reporter where the full text of the opinion can be found. The citation also indicates the year in which the case was decided. For example, the citation "470 U.S. 213 (1985)" indicates that the full text of the opinion can be found in Volume 470 of the *United States Reports* (abbreviated "U.S.") on page 213. The citation also tells you that the case was decided in 1985. In this book, we will use the citation to the *United States Reports* for Supreme Court cases whenever possible. The *Supreme Court Reporter* (abbreviated "S.Ct.") publishes cases more quickly than does the *United States Reports;* some of the more recent Supreme Court cases therefore include citations to the *Supreme Court Reporter*, since the *United States Reports* had not published the opinion by the time this book went to press. *United States Law Week* publishes opinions within a week of their release; this book may include some cases that are so recent that only the *Law Week* citation was available.

West Publishing Company also has several other reporters for both federal and state opinions. *Federal Supplement* (abbreviated "F.Supp.") publishes federal trial court opinions, and *Federal Reporter* publishes opinions from the federal courts of appeal. When a sufficient number of volumes accumulates in one reporter, the publisher may decide to start a new series and begin the numbering of volumes all over again. Thus, the *Federal Reporter* has long been into its second series (abbreviated "F.2d").

Other federal reporters are West's *Bankruptcy Reporter*, which includes bankruptcy decisions, and *Federal Rules Decisions*, which collects federal trial court rulings on federal civil procedure.

West also publishes state appellate court opinions in various regional reporters. The *Southern Reporter*, for example, includes opinions from Alabama, Florida, Louisiana, and Mississippi. The citation "579 So.2d 365 (1991)" signifies a 1991 case that can be found in Volume 579, page 365, of the *Southern Reporter, Second Series*. Table 1-1 provides a list of all the major reporters and gives you the information you need to find the full text of any case excerpted in this book.

Table **1-1**

Reporters

	Abbreviation	Coverage
Federal Reporters		
United States Reports	U.S.	U.S. Supreme Court opinions
Supreme Court Reporter	S.Ct.	U.S. Supreme Court opinions
U.S. Law Week	U.S.L.W.	U.S. Supreme Court opinions
Federal Reporter	F., F.2d	Federal appeals court opinions
Federal Supplement	F.Supp.	Federal trial court opinions
Bankruptcy Reporter	Bankr.	Federal bankruptcy opinions
Federal Rules Decisions	F.R.D.	Federal decisions on civil procedure
Regional Reporters		
Atlantic Reporter	A., A.2d	Opinions from Connecticut, Delaware, Maine, Maryland, New Hampshire, New Jersey, Pennsylvania, Rhode Island, Vermont, and the District of Columbia
North Eastern Reporter	N.E., N.E. 2d	Opinions from Illinois, Indiana, Massachussetts, New York, and Ohio
North Western Reporter	N.W., N.W.2d	Opinions from Iowa, Michigan, Minnesota, Nebraska, North Dakota, South Dakota, and Wisconsin
Pacific Reporter	P., P.2d	Opinions from Alaska, Arizona, California, Colorado, Hawaii, Idaho, Kansas, Montana, Nevada, New Mexico, Oklahoma, Oregon, Utah, Washington, and Wyoming
South Eastern Reporter	S.E., S.E.2d	Opinions from Georgia, North Carolina, South Carolina, Virginia, and West Virginia
South Western Reporter	S.W., S.W.2d	Opinions from Arkansas, Kentucky, Missouri, Tennessee, and Texas
Southern Reporter	So., So.2d	Opinions from Alabama, Florida, Louisiana, and Mississippi
California Reporter	Cal. Rptr.	Opinions from California
New York Supplement	N.Y.S., N.Y.S.2d	Opinions from New York

Sample Case

What follows are sample excerpts, from an actual court decision marked to highlight the various features of the format used in this book. Following the *Kelly v. Gwinnell* case is a discussion of the various components of the format.

---

1 **KELLY V. GWINNELL**
2 Supreme Court of New Jersey
3 476 A.2d 1219 (1984)

---

4 **BACKGROUND:** Marie E. Kelly (plaintiff-appellant) was injured in an automobile accident by an automobile driven by Donald Gwinnell. She sued Gwinnell and Joseph and Catherine Zak (defendants-appellees), who had provided liquor to Gwinnell. The Zaks moved to dismiss the case on grounds that a host is not liable for the negligence of an adult social guest. The trial court agreed and dismissed. The dismissal was affirmed by an intermediate appellate court and Kelly appealed to the New Jersey Supreme Court. Additional facts are in the opinion.

5 **Wilentz, Chief Justice**

6 This case raises the issue of whether a social host who enables an adult guest at his home to become drunk is liable to the victim of an automobile accident caused by the drunken driving of the guest.

7 The record . . . discloses that defendant Donald Gwinnell, after driving defendant Joseph Zak home, spent an hour or two at Zak's home before leaving to return to his own home. During that time, according to Gwinnell, Zak, and Zak's wife, Gwinnell consumed two or three drinks of scotch on the rocks. Zak accompanied Gwinnell outside to his car, chatted with him, and watched as Gwinnell then drove off to go home. About twenty-five minutes later Zak telephoned Gwinnell's home to make sure Gwinnell had arrived there safely. The phone was answered by Mrs. Gwinnell, who advised Zak that Gwinnell had been involved in a head-on collision. The collision was with an automobile operated by plaintiff, Marie Kelly, who was seriously injured as a result.

After the accident Gwinnell was subjected to a blood test, which indicated a blood alcohol concentration of 0.286 percent. Kelly's expert concluded from that reading that Gwinnell had consumed not two or three scotches but the equivalent of thirteen drinks; that while at Zak's home Gwinnell must have been showing unmistakable signs of intoxication; and that in fact he was severely intoxicated while at Zak's residence and at the time of the accident.

We therefore hold that a host who serves liquor to an adult social guest, knowing both that the guest is intoxicated and will thereafter be operating a motor vehicle, is liable for injuries inflicted on a third party as a result of the negligent operation of a motor vehicle by the adult guest when such negligence is caused by the intoxication. While we recognize the concern that our ruling will interfere with accepted standards of social behavior; will intrude on and somewhat diminish the enjoyment, relaxation, and camaraderie that accompany social gatherings at which alcohol is served; and that such gatherings and social relationships are not simply tangential benefits of a civilized society but are regarded by many as important, we believe that the added assurance of just compensation to the victims of drunken driving as well as the added deterrent effect of the rule on such driving outweigh the importance of those other values.

Our ruling today will not cause a deluge of lawsuits or spawn an abundance of fraudulent and frivolous claims. Not only do we limit our holding to the situation in which a host directly serves a guest, but we impose liability solely for injuries resulting from the guest's drunken driving.

8   **DECISION:** Reversed and remanded.

9   ## Garibaldi, Judge *(dissenting)*

10   Today, this Court holds that a social host who knowingly enables an adult guest to become intoxicated knowing that the guest will operate a motor vehicle is liable for damages to a third party caused by the intoxicated guest. The imposition of this liability on a social host places upon every citizen of New Jersey who pours a drink for a friend a heavy burden to monitor and regulate guests. It subjects the host to substantial potential financial liability that may be far beyond the host's resources.

My reluctance to join the majority is not based on any exaggerated notion of judicial deference to the Legislature. Rather, it is based on my belief that before this Court plunges into this broad area of liability and imposes high duties of care on social hosts, it should carefully consider the ramifications of its actions.

Whether a guest is or is not intoxicated is not a simple issue. Alcohol affects everyone differently. . . . Experts estimate that it takes alcohol twenty to thirty minutes to reach its highest level in the bloodstream. Thus, a blood alcohol concentration test demonstrating an elevated blood alcohol level after an accident may not mean that the subject was obviously intoxicated when he left the party some time earlier. "Moreover, a state of obvious intoxication is a condition that is very susceptible to after the fact interpretations, i.e., objective review of a subjective decision. Accordingly, to impose on average citizens a duty to comprehend a person's level of intoxication and the effect another drink would ultimately have on such person is to place a very heavy burden on them." (Citations to quoted material omitted.)

The most significant difference between a social host and a commercial licensee, however, is the social host's inability to spread the cost of liability. The commercial establishment spreads the cost of insurance against liability among its customers. The social host must bear the entire cost alone. . . .

I do not propose to fashion a legislative solution. That is for the Legislature. . . . Perhaps, after investigating all the options, the Legislature will determine that the most effective course is to impose the same civil liability on social hosts that the majority has imposed today. I would have no qualms about that legislative decision so long as it was reached after a thorough investigation of its impact on average citizens of New Jersey.

11   ### *CASE NOTE*

The question of whether a social host who furnishes alcoholic beverages to an intoxicated guest may be liable for death or injury caused by the guest's negligent operation of a motor vehicle has been litigated in a number of states. As the principal case indicates, traditionally, the host or hostess had no liability either to the intoxicated driver or to an injured third party. Courts justified this rule on grounds that consumption of the alcohol, and not furnishing it, was the cause of the injury. Additionally, courts held that drunk or sober individuals are responsible for their own actions.

Several state courts have modified this traditional nonliability rule. This occurred initially in states that had enacted "dram shop statutes." These statutes made liquor vendors such as bars, restaurants, taverns, and liquor stores liable for injuries to an obviously intoxicated purchaser or to a third party injured by the purchaser. Unless the dram shop statute limited liability to liquor vendors, state courts generally extended liability to social hosts as well.

A further extension of social host liability occurred in some states, like New Jersey, that did not have dram shop statutes. Beginning in the late 1960s courts in these states began to impose liability on liquor vendors on the basis of negligence if the vendor sold liquor to an obviously intoxicated person who injured another. In New Jersey and at least two other states, Washington and Ohio, liability has been extended to social hosts as well as to liquor vendors, on the basis of negligence.

1. Case title. The title of the case usually lists the parties. Usually, as in this case, the plaintiff is listed first. In some jurisdictions, however, the appellant or respondent is listed first. Thus in some cases, the original defendant can be listed first. In cases where there is more than one plaintiff or defendant, only the first plaintiff or defendant listed on the complaint is generally included in the cited title.

   Certain special types of cases often use titles different from the *Plaintiff v. Defendant* format. A bankruptcy case, for example, might be entitled *Matter of Horton* if Horton is the bankrupt party. *Estate of Brown* might be the title of a probate case in which the court has to decide how to distribute the property of a deceased person named Brown. The designation "In Re" is used to describe a case in which an action is brought concerning a thing, but not in a traditional adversarial manner; for example, *In Re Union Carbide Corporation Gas Plant Disaster*, where the case is just to determine whether a U.S. court has jurisdiction over the the firm.

2. Court. This line indicates the court that has issued the opinion, in this case the Supreme Court of New Jersey.

3. Citation. The case's citation indicates that the full text of *Kelly v. Gwinnell* is found in Volume 476 of *Atlantic Reporter, Second Series* on page 1219. The case was decided in 1984.

4. Background. The authors provide a background summary of each case, including the basic facts and the parties. The background summary also describes the history of the case: who originally brought the suit, who won in the lower court or courts, if applicable, and who is appealing, if applicable.

5. Judge or justice. Although some or all of the members of the court may *join* (that is, subscribe to) an opinion, the opinion is generally delivered by one judge or justice only. An exception is a **per curiam opinion,** which is delivered by all the members of the court.

6. Issue. The opinion excerpt will usually, but not always, include a statement by the court of the issue or issues that it must consider in order to reach a decision in the case.

7. Discussion. After stating the issues of the case, the court goes on to discuss those issues. This discussion generally includes a summary of each side's argument and the court's rationale for finding one side's argument more persuasive than the other's. The opinion typically includes references to prior cases and, often, a discussion of public policy.

8. Decision. The decision is summarized by the authors.

9. Judge or justice issuing separate opinion. If a dissenting or concurring opinion is included, the judge or justice issuing the opinion is identified.

10. Separate opinion. Dissenting or concurring opinions are sometimes excerpted.

11. Case note. In rare cases, the authors include a case note that summarizes subsequent developments regarding the case and/or the issues discussed therein.

The following cases illustrate some of the basic principles introduced in this chapter, for example, the process of appeal, the interpretation of administrative regulations, and the foundational doctrine of the common law system—*stare decisis.*

POWELL V. CALIFORNIA
California Court of Appeal, Second District
232 Cal.App.3d 785 (1991)

BACKGROUND: Laurence Powell, Stacey Koon, and other Los Angeles police officers apprehended and arrested Rodney King after a high-speed chase. King was severely beaten during the arrest. The beating was videotaped by a nearby resident and was played prominently on TV. The police officers were charged with assault. They petitioned to have their criminal trial moved from the County of Los Angeles to another county in California, claiming that they could not receive a fair trial in Los Angeles. The trial court rejected their request and they appealed to the California Court of Appeal, an intermediate appellate court.

The court issued an unsigned "by the court" opinion delivered jointly by all four judges who heard the case.

By the Court

Petitioners Laurence Powell, Theodore J. Briseno, Stacey C. Koon, and Timothy E. Wind (collectively defendants) are police officers charged with specific charges of assault by force likely to produce great bodily injury and with a deadly weapon . . . and an officer unnecessarily assaulting or BEATING any person. . . .

Unbeknownst to the Los Angeles Police Department (LAPD) officers involved, the incident was videotaped by a nearby resident who sold it to a local TV station. The initial showing caused shock, revulsion, outrage and disbelief among viewers. A fire storm immediately developed in the Los Angeles area, so intense and pervasive was the reaction to the videotape.

The defendants were charged with the crimes enumerated above. Questions developed about the integrity of the LAPD and its chief. The mayor of Los Angeles called for the resignation of the chief of POLICE. That action polarized the community. The POLICE Commission became vociferously involved, as did the City Council. . . .

As might be expected, the incident and the resultant political turmoil received massive local media coverage, including newspapers, radio and TV, which has impacted the residents. . . .

On a pretrial petition the appellate court must make an independent determination of the circumstances surrounding a defendant's request for change of venue to determine whether a fair trial is obtainable in the county of original venue.

Section 1033, subdivision (a), requires a change of venue "when it appears that there is a reasonable likelihood that a fair and impartial trial cannot be had in the county."

"[R]easonable likelihood" has been interpreted as requiring something less than "more probable than not," and something more than merely possible. . . .

The question is whether the potential jurors can view the case with the requisite impartiality. Material factors to be considered in resolving the question include the size of the potential jury pool, the nature and extent of the publicity, the status of the accused and the victim, the nature and gravity of the offense, and the existence of political turmoil arising from the incident. . . .

Los Angeles County covers 4,083 square miles. The source list used in the selection of potential jurors in Los Angeles Superior Court includes the list of persons who voted in recent elections and the records of the Department of Motor Vehicles. The potential jury pool in Los Angeles County is 6.526 million according to the Jury Services Division of the Los Angeles County Superior Court. . . .

The People contend the potential jury pool in Los Angeles County is so large that other facts are rendered irrelevant. The trial court apparently based its ruling primarily upon the size of the population in Los Angeles County. That premise has been unacceptable in other cases: Carried to its logical conclusion, the district attorney's argument, if valid, would require that all motions for a change of venue in Los Angeles County must be denied because of its population, regardless of the amount of pretrial publicity which surrounds a notorious criminal case. . . .

In support of the motion for change of venue, defendants rely, in part, on polls of residents of Los Angeles County as reported in the Los Angeles Times. On March 10, 1991, within a week of the incident, the Los Angeles Times reported 86 percent of those surveyed had seen the videotape of the offense and 92 percent believed excessive force had been used. On March 22, 1991, the Los Angeles Times reported 94 percent of all persons surveyed in another poll described themselves as "upset" by the incident and almost two-thirds believed the force used was racially motivated.

Defendants retained experts to conduct a public opinion survey in the community. In a random sample of 1,000 people, 97 percent were aware of the incident. That 97 percent was then broken down into a number of categories: Three percent believed defendants were not guilty of any offense. Fourteen percent had formed no opinion. Eighty-one percent felt defendants were guilty. Seventy percent of the persons from the group who felt defendants were guilty had a "strong" view about the incident. . . .

Important and unusual factors in this case are the status of the defendants as white law enforcement officers and the arrestee as a black, the widespread media usage of the videotape disclosing the nature of the arrest, and the publication of internal POLICE department documents.

It cannot be disputed that difficulty in obtaining a fair trial in Los Angeles County is exacerbated by the fact the defendants are POLICE officers, sworn to protect citizens, to uphold the law and to maintain peace in the community. Their status is the basis of the intense coverage and repeated showing of the videotape. The fact that the videotape depicts local officers in such conduct threatens the community's ability to rely on its police and has caused a high level of indignation, outrage and anxiety.

The record presented before the trial court was sufficient to support defendants' contention they cannot receive a fair trial in Los Angeles County and their contention becomes increasingly more obvious as each day passes. The events of which we have taken judicial notice not only add further support to the defendants' contention but lead us inexorably to conclude there is more than the statutory "reasonable likelihood" standard present here. Under the totality of the circumstances, a change of venue is clearly necessary to assure that defendants have a fair and impartial trial.

We conclude there is a substantial probability Los Angeles County is so saturated with knowledge of the incident, so influenced by the political controversy surrounding the matter and so permeated with preconceived opinions that potential jurors cannot try the case solely upon the evidence presented in the courtroom. Accordingly, we grant the petition for writ of mandate.

DECISION: Petition granted; the trial must be moved to another county.

EDWARDS V. CALIFANO

U.S. Court of Appeals, Tenth Circuit

619 F.2d 865 (1980)

BACKGROUND: Charlotte Edwards and her two children were deserted by John Long, her alcoholic former husband. Long had qualified for social security benefits, and 8 years after he disappeared, Edwards filed for social security benefits for the two children on the grounds that Edwards was presumed dead after 7 years. The Department of Health, Education, and Welfare refused to pay the benefits on the grounds that Long had not been proved to be dead. The federal District Court upheld the ruling and Edwards appealed to the United States Court of Appeals.

Barrett, Circuit Judge

Charlotte Diane Edwards (Edwards) appeals on behalf of her two minor children, Debora A. and Clayton D., from a judgment affirming the decision of the Secretary of Health, Education and Welfare (Secretary) denying a claim for child insurance benefits under Section 202(d) of the Social Security Act.

Section 202(d) provides in pertinent part: for payment of child's insurance benefits for every child of an individual who dies a fully or currently insured individual, if an application for such benefits has been filed, or at the time such application was filed, the child was unmarried, and had not attained the age of 18. . . .

Edwards' former husband, John Richard Long (Long), abandoned her and their two minor children in 1964 and has not contacted Edwards since that time. On November 30, 1972, Edwards filed an application on behalf of her two children for surviving child's insurance benefits based on the earnings record of Long. This application was denied. . . .

. . . [T]he District Court affirmed the ALJ's [Administrative Law Judge, Ed.] denial of benefits. In so doing, the District Court found and concluded, inter alia: The final administrative decision herein is that while John Richard Long has been absent from home for more than seven years, his absence is not unexplained within the meaning of 20 C.F.R. [volumes containing federal regulations, Ed.] s 404.705(a) and he therefore cannot be presumed to be dead. Evidence in the administrative record establishes that John Richard Long was alive after he abandoned his wife and their children in 1964. Wage records show earnings by John Richard Long through the first quarter of 1968. There is also evidence that John lived with his brother James until departing in June of 1967, several months after a state court order . . . imposed a $100.00 per month child support obligation on John. James also stated that he felt John was still alive as late as 1975. The record further establishes that John Richard Long had a drinking problem and had an erratic work record at a variety of jobs through the country.

On the other hand, there is evidence in the record that John Richard Long is dead. Such evidence consists primarily of the statements and testimony of Plaintiff to this effect and the determination of the Oklahoma County District Court that John Richard Long is dead because of his absence of seven years. However, the decree of the Oklahoma County District Court is not binding on either the Secretary or this Court for the purposes of this case. . . .

On appeal to this Court, Edwards contends that she has established that Long was "unexplainedly absent from his residence and unheard of for a period of 7 years" under 20 C.F.R. s 404.705(a), and that the Secretary was accordingly obligated to "presume that such individual has died" and award the benefits requested or otherwise rebut the presumption of death. We hold that Edwards established that Long was "unexplainedly absent" under the regulation, that the presumption of death was not rebutted by the Secretary, and that Edwards was entitled to the benefits requested on behalf of her children. We must therefore reverse. . . .

In reviewing regulations, however, we are reminded that administrative regulations are not absolute rules of law . . . and that an agency's interpretation of its own regulation, which is not based on expertise in its particular field but is rather based on general common law principles, is not entitled to great deference. . . . Neither will we accord substantial weight to an agency's interpretation of a regulation, when, as here, an agency's interpretation is inconsistent with the controlling statute.

Applying these standards we hold that the Secretary's denial of the requested benefits was arbitrary, capricious, and an abuse of discretion, based on the record before us. . . .

Although most prolonged disappearances do not lend themselves to clear-cut explanations, it can be stated with certainty that people do not normally sever all relationships and disappear without a trace for a period of seven years. . . . When a social security applicant presents facts that establish that a wage earner has been absent from his residence and unheard of for a period of seven years, a presumption of death arises under Regulation s 404-705. . . . The burden then shifts to the Secretary to make an affirmative showing either that the "missing person is alive" or that "the anomaly of the disappearance . . . (is) consistent with continued life." . . . The Secretary failed to establish that the disappearance was consistent with continued life. Under these circumstances, the Secretary is bound by his own regulations. . . .

DECISION: Reversed and remanded; the benefits have to be paid.

EQUAL EMPLOYMENT OPPORTUNITY COMMISSION V. TRABUCCO

U.S. Court of Appeals, First Circuit
791 F.2d 1 (1986)

BACKGROUND: The federal Equal Employment Opportunity Commission (EEOC) brought suit against the Commonwealth of Massachusetts, challenging a statute mandating that state police must retire at 50 as a violation of the Age Discrimination Act. In an earlier suit brought by a policeman named Mahoney, who held a desk job, the federal courts upheld the Massachusetts law on the grounds that being under 50 was a bona fide occupational requirement. The District Court rejected the EEOC's challenge to the law on the basis of the ruling in Mahoney's case. The EEOC appealed, arguing that Mahoney's case should not be considered binding precedent for all members of the state police force.

Coffin, Circuit Judge

The question on this appeal is whether the principle of stare decisis forecloses redetermination of an issue raised, considered, and decided in a prior case where the presentation of evidence has been "one-sided," with no proffer of rebuttal expert testimony. Our answer is that stare decisis still applies and, on this record, forecloses redetermination.

This case, brought by the Equal Employment Opportunity Commission (EEOC) against the Commonwealth of Massachusetts, its Commissioner of Public Safety and its Board of Retirement, challenges the Massachusetts statutory mandatory retirement age of 50 for all members of the uniformed branch of the state police, as not being "a bona fide occupational qualification [BFOQ] reasonably necessary to the normal operation of [the branch's] business." Age Discrimination in Employment Act (ADEA).

The action was instituted on January 19, 1984, following a district court decision in *Mahoney v. Trabucco,* 574 F.Supp. 955 (D.Mass. 1983). . . . In *Mahoney,* an officer of the state police who held a desk job as a telecommunications specialist challenged the general mandatory retirement provision and sought injunctive relief from enforcement of the retirement requirement as applied to him. This district court held that age 50 was a BFOQ for most state troopers, but that the Commonwealth had failed to prove that age 50 was a BFOQ for the particular desk job held by officer Mahoney. We reversed, holding that all state troopers should be treated as one occupation. We left in place the district court's holding that age 50 was a BFOQ for that occupation.

The defendants in the case at bar moved for, and the district court granted, summary judgment on the ground that *Mahoney* controlled under the doctrine of stare decisis. EEOC contended that there was a triable issue of material fact because additional "more weighty opinion of the medical community" could be preferred in opposition to the court's decision in *Mahoney.*

Our review of the situations requiring the application of stare decisis indicates that this is a case in which stare decisis should be applied. The essential principles of stare decisis may be described as follows: (1) an issue of law must have been heard and decided, (2) if "an issue is not argued, or though argued is ignored by the court, or is reserved, the decision does not constitute a PRECEDENT to be followed," (3) "a DECISION . . . is STARE decisis despite the contention that the court was not properly instructed by counsel on the legislative history, or that the argument was otherwise insufficient," (4) a decision may properly be overruled if "seriously out of keeping with contemporary views . . . [or] passed by in the development of the law . . . or . . . proved to be unworkable," and (5) there is "a heavy presumption that settled issues of law will not be reexamined."

We have found no case, nor has appellant cited us to any, that supports its contention that a weak or ineffective presentation in a prior case deprives the ruling of precedential effect. Such a contention is directly contrary to the third proposition in the previous paragraph. Indeed, we would not relish the prospect of evaluating the effectiveness of factual presentation and argument as a precondition of our determining whether or not to accord stare decisis effect to an issue that has been raised and decided.

Finally, we conclude from other cases that there is no overpowering trend that indicates that the *Mahoney* ruling is out of sync with the times. A significant number of courts have upheld various mandatory retirement and hiring ages as BFOQ's in police jobs. . . .

On the other hand, some courts have been persuaded by expert testimony that a mandatory retirement age does not meet the BFOQ requirement. . . . At most, this seems to be an issue where experts disagree.

We therefore conclude that appellant has not succeeded in overcoming the heavy presumption that accompanies a ruling on the precise issue in a prior case.

DECISION: Affirmed. Mandatory retirement at 50 is upheld.

Schools of Legal Thought

Legal scholars have long debated the philosophical basis of law. **Jurisprudence** is an academic discipline which attempts to determine the principles on which legal rules are based. Legal philosophers are divided into a number of schools of thought regarding the nature of those underlying principles.

What follows are very brief and simplified descriptions of the major schools of legal thought.

Proponents of the **natural law** school believe that all law derives from a higher authority, be it a supreme being or the natural order of the universe. Natural law scholars believe that the fundamental principles of law, as derived from the higher authority, can be discovered through reason. These fundamental principles, according to this school, are superior to human laws and apply to each society regardless of its particular experience or culture.

Some scholars have used natural law arguments to oppose abortion. According to this line of reasoning, abortion violates a right to life founded in natural law, and any human law is invalid to the extent that it conflicts with this principle. Justice Clarence Thomas, in his 1991 confirmation hearings, was questioned rigorously about praise he once gave to an essay that applied natural law. His questioners on the Senate Judiciary Committee were attempting to determine whether his praise offered any clue as to how he might rule on the abortion issue.

Legal positivism is a school which holds that all law derives from the authority of whatever entity enforces the law—usually the government. Unlike the natural law school, the legal positivism school does not recognize legal authority superior and external to that of the government.

The **historical school** emphasizes the evolution of the law over time. Supporters of this school argue that the best legal principles are those that stand the test of time, and that these principles should not be changed abruptly but rather should be molded gently to suit changing historical circumstances.

The **sociological school** takes the position that legal principles must evolve so as to achieve economic and social justice. The best legal principles, according to this school, are those that best serve the society's needs at any given time.

ISSUES AND TRENDS
Too Many Lawyers?

Have you heard that many scientists have stopped using rats for lab experiments and have started using lawyers instead? Lawyers are more suitable than rats because (1) there are more of them, (2) the scientists don't become attached to them, and (3) there are some things that rats won't do.

That, of course, is a "lawyer joke," one of many that have made the rounds in recent years. The jokes reflect the low regard that some in our society have for lawyers, and perhaps the frustration felt by those who have had unpleasant experiences with our legal system. The popularity of lawyer jokes is fueled by the sentiment expressed by former Vice President Quayle at the start of this chapter: Our country has too many lawyers.

The United States is estimated to have 800,000 lawyers, roughly 70 percent of the world's total. The nation has over 2.5 times the number of lawyers per capita as Britain, almost 3.5 times the number of lawyers per capita as Germany, and over 25 times the number of lawyers per capita as Japan.

Some believe that our overabundance of lawyers encourages an overabundance of lawsuits. The number of new cases filed each year in federal court almost tripled from 1960 to 1990. A 1989 article in *Forbes Magazine* estimated that litigation and related insurance costs this nation $80 billion each year. Others worry that our high number of lawyers hurts competitiveness in other ways: With so many of our best and brightest becoming lawyers (94,000 college graduates applied for law school in 1991), the quality and quantity of our engineers, entrepreneurs, and other wealth-creating members of society are bound to suffer.

On the other hand, some argue that our legal system is more active than those of other countries because we have a greater commitment to protecting the rights of those injured by wrongful conduct. In many societies, some contend, businesses can harm people and the environment with impunity because the legal system offers no redress. These people argue that the costs imposed by our legal system are worth the protection that the system affords to our rights and our quality of life.

Review Questions and Problems

Key Terms

constitution	respondent
common law	decree
common law system	appellant
stare decisis	appellee
statute	judge
ordinance	justice
code	judgment
administrative agency	dismissal
rules and regulations	affirm
order	reverse
civil law	remand
criminal law	opinion
defendant	unanimous opinion
plaintiff	separate opinion
liability	dissenting opinion
damages	concurring opinion
substantive law	majority opinion
procedural law	reporter
law	citation
equity	per curiam opinion
equitable remedies	jurisprudence
injunction	natural law
specific performance	legal positivism
petitioner	historical school
petition	sociological school
complaint	

Discussion Questions

1. What policy is reflected by the concept of *stare decisis*? Does this policy seem logical?
2. Compare and contrast statutory and judge-made or common law.
3. What are the functions of the legal system?
4. Briefly outline the principles that courts apply when interpreting statutes.
5. Explain the purpose and functions of administrative agencies.
6. What is a restatement of the law?
7. Why did courts of equity develop?

Review Problems

1. Smith was involved in litigation in California. She lost her case in the trial court. She appealed to the California appellate court, arguing that the trial court judge had incorrectly excluded certain evidence. To support her argument, she cited rulings by the Supreme Court of North Dakota and the Supreme Court of Ohio. Both the North Dakota and Ohio cases involved facts that were similar to Smith's case. Does the California court have to follow the decisions from North Dakota and Ohio? Support your answer.

2. Business in the downtown area of a large Western city had expanded rapidly. As a result, the area was plagued by traffic problems during the morning rush hour. To alleviate the problem, the city council passed an ordinance that restricted traffic on certain streets to "passenger motor vehicles."

   Swenson, who worked downtown, owned a small truck that he used to drive back and forth to work. When he drove on one of the restricted streets, he was ticketed and forced to pay a substantial fine. He wishes to contest the fine and the interpretation of the ordinance and comes to you for advice. Outline a strategy that might be used to help him.

3. Madison and his adult son lived in a house owned by Madison. At the request of the son, Marshall painted the house. Madison did not authorize the work, but he knew that it was being done and raised no objection. Madison refused to pay Marshall, arguing that he had not contracted to have the house painted.

   Marshall asked his attorney if Madison was legally liable to pay him. The attorney told Marshall that in their state several appellate court opinions had established that when a homeowner allows work to be done on his home by a person who would ordinarily expect to be paid, a duty to pay exists. The attorney stated that on the basis of these precedents, it was advisable for Marshall to bring a suit to collect the reasonable value of the work he had done. Explain what the attorney meant by *precedent* and why the fact that precedent existed was significant.

4. Campbell was driving at 58 mph on interstate highway I-13 passing through Gotham City. She was arrested for violating the 55 mph speed limit. Surveys indicate that the average speed on I-13 at the point where Campbell was arrested is 64 mph. When she was arrested, Campbell was on the inside lane and was being passed by most of the traffic. What arguments could Campbell make as a legal defense? If you were the judge, how would you rule in Campbell's case?

Case Problems

1. Ludenia Howard was charged with violating the Federal Black Bass Act. The Act made unlawful "transportation . . . from any State . . . any black bass . . . if (1) such transportation is contrary to the law of the State . . . from which fish . . . is transported. . . ." The Florida Fish and Game Commission had a rule prohibiting the transportation of black bass out of the state. The commission was a body authorized by the state constitution. Its members were appointed by the governor.

   Howard's attorney argued that the federal act did not apply, since the commission's rule was not a "law of the State." Discuss the validity of this defense. What are the characteristics of a law?

2. Butler and a number of other people organized a corporation ostensibly to assist small business firms to secure loans. They were to be compensated by a finder's fee. The firms for which loans were to be located had to pay an initial membership charge. The firms were solicited by mail. If a firm indicated an interest, it was visited by a salesperson. The entire scheme was a fraud. The corporation retained the membership fees and did nothing to secure loans.

   The corporation, Butler, and twenty-nine others were prosecuted in a single action for mail fraud. Several of the defendants asked to have their cases severed and tried separately because combining this number of defendants in a single case was unfair. Discuss the validity of a government argument based on *stare decisis* that cites numerous cases in which large numbers of defendants had been tried in a single case. Is the trial court bound by these cases?

3. Section 301(a) of the Federal Food, Drug, and Cosmetics Act prohibits the introduction into interstate commerce of any drug that is misbranded. According to Section 502(a), a product is misbranded if its "labeling is false or misleading" and unless the labeling bears "adequate directions for use." The term "labeling" is defined to mean "all labels and other written, printed, or graphic matter (1) upon any article or any of its containers or (2) accompanying such article." Violation of the act is a crime.

   Kordel sells health-food products that are compounds of vitamins, minerals, and herbs. These items are sold to stores. In addition to supplying the product, Kordel separately furnishes pamphlets describing the products. Much of the literature is shipped separately from the drugs and at different times—both before and after drug shipments. Kordel is charged with violating the Food and Drug Act. Based upon the above facts, outline a defense available to him. Explain how the prosecution might overcome this defense.

4. James Good pleaded guilty to promoting a harmful drug when a search of his home uncovered 89 pounds of marijuana along with drug paraphernalia. Four and a half years later, the U.S. government filed an action seizing Good's home and land under a federal forfeiture statute that allowed for the seizure of real property used in the commission of a drug-related crime. The property was seized without prior notice to Good and he didn't appear to contest the seizure. Good subsequently challenged the seizure of his property on the grounds that it violated his constitutional rights to due process of law. The government argued that it had to comply only with the rules concerning search and seizure because its actions were part of the law enforcement process involved with the war on drugs. How do you think the case should be decided?

2

Legal Systems

This chapter examines the structure of the U.S. legal system. In order to help you understand the framework in which the legal system operates, the chapter first explores the relationship between state and federal governments and between branches of government. The discussion examines the doctrine of separation of powers, which determines the manner in which the executive, judicial, and legislative branches carry out their duties. Finally, the chapter outlines the structure of the court system and considers some of the questions involving jurisdiction, which is the power of courts to hear and decide cases.

Relationship between Federal and State Governments

Business administrators today are often concerned and frequently puzzled by the mass of rules, regulations, directives, forms, and reports emanating from both state and federal governments. The cost to business of meeting the demands from these systems is staggering.

In addition to bewilderment caused by the sheer mass of government requirements, confusion results because federal and state laws attempting to achieve different objectives sometimes conflict. Consider the plight of firms faced with the following dilemma:

In 1980 the federal Equal Employment Opportunity Commission adopted a rule prohibiting insurers from using mortality tables that differentiated between males and females. At about the same time, California and New York adopted rules requiring insurers to use mortality tables that differentiated between males and females buying annuity and life insurance contracts. What tables should the firms use?

In spite of the dissatisfaction that sometimes arises from being forced to cope with two major governmental units (federal and state), the business administrator must remember that this system does have some benefits. Many matters are more effectively carried out by local authorities familiar with problems peculiar to their region. At the same time, the diffusion of power between the states and the federal government reduces the authority of each. When power is decentralized, an enduring majority becomes less possible and minority interests have some protection.

The Federal System

The dual nature of government in the United States is attributable to **federalism.** Although the term is not mentioned in the Constitution and has seldom been defined by the judiciary, the concept is basic to understanding U.S. political and legal systems. In essence, U.S. federalism is a system that allocates the powers of sovereignty between the state and federal governments.

The basis of federalism is the U.S. Constitution, which is a compact between the states and the federal government. This compact was created by the people when they ratified the Constitution. The Constitution delegates certain powers of the states—which are sovereign—to the federal government; however, it also states that all powers that are not delegated to the federal government are retained by the states. Thus, state powers are known as *retained powers* while those of the federal government are known as *delegated powers.*

The principal delegated powers are the power to tax, borrow money, regulate commerce, coin money, create a federal judicial system, declare war, and provide for an army and navy. In addition to the delegated powers, the Constitution granted Congress the power to make all laws that "shall be necessary and proper" for carrying out the delegated powers. For example, Congress under its constitutional power to regulate commerce has the power to prohibit racial discrimination in hotels, motels, and restaurants. Powers that are "necessary and proper" to carry out the delegated powers are called *implied powers.*

Article IV of the Constitution provides that when the federal government acts within the framework of its delegated powers, its actions are supreme. Similarly, the actions of each state are supreme when the state acts on the basis of a retained power. At the same time, there are some powers that are *concurrent*, since they can be asserted by both state and federal governments. The power to tax is an example. Both state and federal governments have this power.

Relationship between Branches of Government

Government officials at all levels must act within limits prescribed by law. This principle, which is vital to the continuance of U.S. democracy, is often referred to as the "rule of law" or "supremacy of law." Simultaneously, many of these same officials whose actions are circumscribed by law play major roles in the development of law and in the administration of the legal system. The following material discusses actions of officials in different branches of government as these actions influence the legal system.

Separation of Powers

The **separation-of-powers doctrine** involves the division of the authority of government among legislative, judicial, and executive branches and contemplates that none of the three shall exercise any of the powers belonging to the others. Early in the nineteenth century, Chief Justice John Marshall described the end result of the doctrine as follows: "The difference between the departments undoubtedly is, that the legislature makes, the executive executes, and the judiciary construes the law."

Making, executing, and interpreting the law do not have to be independent of one another for a legal system to function effectively. These three services might well be performed by a single entity. Since the adoption of the Constitution, however, a cardinal principle of U.S. political life has been to separate the three branches of government. Separation is intended to prevent the domination of one branch by another and to protect the liberties of the people by preventing the accumulation of power in a single source.

In spite of the well-known principle reflected in Chief Justice Marshall's statement, the business or public administrator viewing the legal environment might decide that the separation-of-powers principle is more honored in the breach than in the observance. It is certainly true that the U.S. legal system has never embodied complete separation of powers. This would be inefficient even if it were possible. In fact, the checks-and-balances system, which is integral to the federal Constitution and those of most states, is based upon the concept that each of the three constituent elements of government has a substantial influence on the others. There is enough influence to ensure that power to some extent will be balanced. Although nothing requires state governments to adhere to the separation-of-powers principle, most state constitutions follow the federal pattern. Even when not especially provided for by a state constitution, the concept is usually maintained in practice or required by judicial decision.

Numerous illustrations of the intermixture of functions can be cited. Congress, if it does not violate constitutional mandates, can modify much of the jurisdiction of federal courts. Congress can restrict the power of the President to remove certain federal officials, investigate the executive departments, and remove the President from office. The judiciary can determine if legislative enactments are constitutional, and the President can veto bills passed by Congress.

During the 1970s and 1980s the separation-of-powers principle was the subject of considerable

national discussion and concern. In the early 1970s much of the legal controversy surrounding the Watergate investigation revolved around the separation of powers. In that controversy, President Nixon unsuccessfully contended that the separation of powers allowed him as President to ignore requests from Congress for information and orders from federal courts that he produce the famous "Watergate tapes" (recordings Nixon made of himself which included references to cover-ups of law violations).

Doe v. Sullivan, the case that follows, required the court to sort out the authority of all three branches of government.

DOE V. SULLIVAN
U.S. Court of Appeals, D.C. Circuit
938 F.2d 1370 (1991)

BACKGROUND: After Iraq invaded Kuwait in 1990, the United States deployed hundreds of thousands of troops to the Persian Gulf. The Department of Defense (DOD) was concerned about Iraq's chemical weapons arsenal and wanted to use two drugs that it believed would be effective to protect soldiers who might be exposed to chemical attack. The problem was that the drugs had not yet been approved by the federal Food and Drug Administration (FDA). The FDA was responsible for implementing the Food, Drug and Cosmetic Act (the FDC Act), which governed the use of drugs that had not yet been approved. A regulation promulgated by the FDA would have required the military to get prior consent from each soldier before using the drugs on that soldier, or else go through a laborious process to demonstrate that the soldier was unable to give his or her consent. The DOD, believing that it would be impractical to follow the FDA regulation in the event of chemical warfare, lobbied the FDA to revise the regulation. The FDA agreed, and issued Rule 23(d), which allowed the agency to waive the consent requirement for certain unapproved drugs in combat-related situations.

John Doe (not his real name) was a soldier stationed in the Persian Gulf. He did not want the military to be able to use unapproved drugs on him without his permission. He brought a class action (a suit brought by a representative party on behalf of a large group of people holding equivalent legal claims) on behalf of military personnel stationed in the Persian Gulf challenging Rule 23(d). The government argued that the judiciary was not empowered to review Rule 23(d), because only the legislative and executive branches had authority over the military's actions in times of war. The federal district court ruled for the government, and Doe appealed.

Ginsburg, Circuit Judge

The district court held, initially, that Doe's claims were not amenable to judicial review. Only the electoral branches—Congress and the President—that court indicated, are competent authorities in matters of military discipline and strategy. With respect to Doe's challenge to the FDA's authority to promulage Rule 23(d), the district judge noted:

Plaintiffs' claim against the Secretary of Health and Human Services regarding the FDA's interim rule arguably does not implicate military discipline and strategy. Whether the fact that the interim rule was adopted at the DOD's request in preparing for possible war insulates it from the ordinary scope of judicial review is not clear. However, Congress delegated rulemaking authority regarding unapproved drugs to the FDA, which is part of the executive branch. . . .

The Supreme Court has cast the principle of judicial deference to the electoral branches in military matters in broad terms. . . .

On balance, therefore, the Court believes that [Rule 23(d)] is not reviewable.

We agree that deference is owed to the political branches in military matters, but do not agree that judicial review of the matter here at issue is out of order.

In contrast to the turbulent background of this litigation, Doe's facial challenge to Rule 23(d) is a straightforward one with a commonplace cast. Doe contends that, in promulgating Rule 23(d), the FDA stepped outside its statutory authority and adopted an exception to its informed consent regulations that is "not in accordance with law." Doe therefore seeks a court order setting aside the FDA's action. We see no "military action" bar to the brand of review Doe now requests.

From the main rule that administrative acts are reviewable in court on the complaint of a person adversely affected . . . the Administrative Procedure Act (APA) excepts . . . "military authority exercised in the field in time of war or in occupied territory." The government emphasizes that exception. We think the "military authority" exception is not on point.

Doe currently does not ask us to review military commands made in combat zones or in preparation for, or in the aftermath of, battle. His claim, as now advanced, entails no judicial interference with the relationship between soldiers and their military superiors.

We confront at this time not a dispute over military strategy or discipline, not one between soldiers and their superiors, but one over the scope of the authority Congress has entrusted to the FDA. . . .

The FDA's Rule 23(d), we recognize, unquestionably involves a military matter: it allows the FDA to grant the Department of Defense a waiver of informed consent requirements in certain battlefield or combat-related situations. But the judgment Doe asks the court to make does not entail judicial review of the existence of a military exigency. Rather, Doe's facial attack asks simply whether the law that governs FDA action permits the measure which that non-military agency has taken. The question thus presented is meet for judicial review. . . .

DECISION: The Circuit Court of Appeals ruled that the judiciary did have the power to review Rule 23(d). The court then went on to hold that Rule 23(d) was within the scope of the FDC Act and therefore valid.

The Dual Court Structure

As a result of the federal system, a dual structure of courts prevails in the United States. Each person not only is subject to the laws of a particular state, which generally are interpreted by the courts of that state, but is also subject to the laws of the United States, which are generally interpreted by the federal courts. Before we examine some of the effects of the dual nature of government in the United States, a brief survey of the general structure of U. S. courts is in order.

The division of authority among the various court systems operating in the United States is accomplished by defining each court's **jurisdiction,** or its power of court to hear and decide cases. As we shall see, jurisdiction can vary from court system to court system as well as among different types of courts within a single system.

FIGURE 2-1

Ohio Judicial Structure

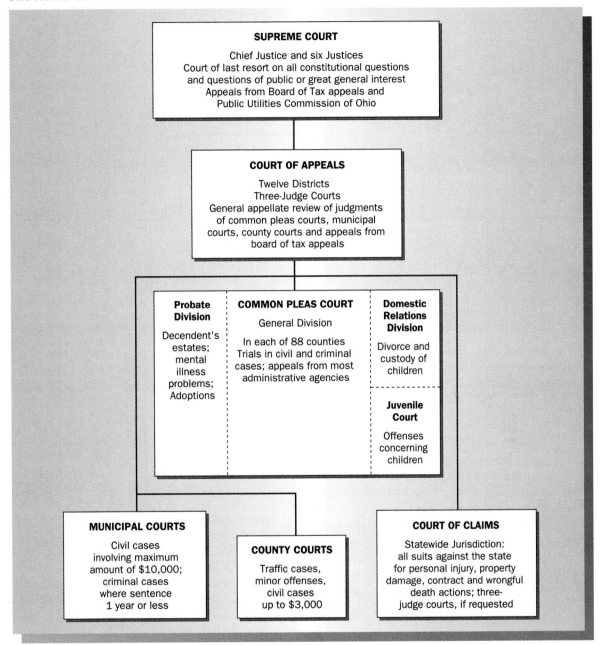

In view of the fifty-one independent court systems that operate within the United States, this might seem an impossible task. The task, however, is simplified by a common structural pattern that exists for most states. This structure can be understood if each state system and the federal system are envisioned as pyramids with two or sometimes three levels. A typical state judicial structure and the federal judicial structure are shown in Figures 2-1 and 2-2.

FIGURE 2-2

U.S. Judicial Structure

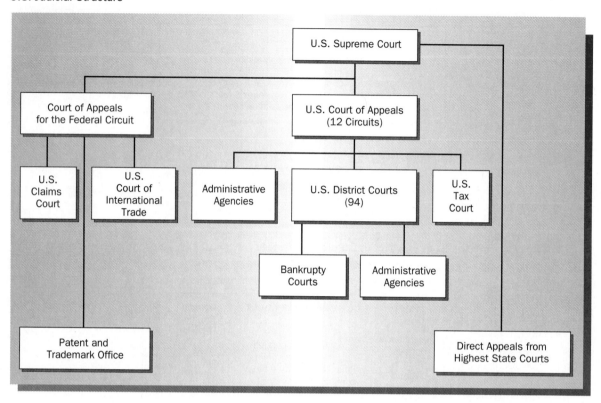

Trial Courts

Trial courts are courts in which lawsuits are first filed. As such, they are referred to as courts of **original jurisdiction.** Some trial courts are also described as courts of **general jurisdiction.** They have the power to hear most types of cases. Other trial courts have **limited jurisdiction.** This is because the types of cases that these courts can hear are limited. Usually the limitation involves a monetary amount or subject matter. For example, a court might be limited to hearing cases in which the amount in dispute is less than $10,000, or it might have the power only to hear cases involving juveniles.

Federal Trial Courts In the federal system the trial courts are called **U.S. District Courts.** The United States is divided into over ninety districts, and each has a single district court. U.S. District Courts have the power to hear almost all types of federal cases except those that

Congress has assigned by statute to a special court such as the U.S. Court of Claims or the U.S. Court of International Trade.

State Trial Courts In the states the trial-court base of the structural pyramid is complicated by the existence of both courts of general jurisdiction and courts of limited jurisdiction. Each state has trial courts of general jurisdiction throughout the state. In Ohio they are called courts of common pleas; New York refers to them as supreme courts. Probably the most common designation is county court.

Although the titles differ from state to state, these general trial courts have some common characteristics. Usually they are organized on a county basis. They have the power to hear a wide variety of cases, both criminal and civil, and there are ordinarily no upper limits on their monetary jurisdiction.

Especially in heavily populated areas, many courts of general jurisdiction have specialized divisions to hear cases that involve domestic relations, juveniles, and decedent estates. In some states an independent probate or surrogate court handles decedent estate matters. In a number of states the specialized courts are set up independently of the statewide trial courts. It is also a common practice to separate courts with criminal jurisdiction from those that hear civil cases.

All states have a number of trial courts of limited jurisdiction. These courts can decide only those cases in which the plaintiff is seeking monetary damages of a limited amount. Frequently they have no power to issue injunctions or to order specific performance, and their criminal jurisdiction is limited to petty offenses and minor misdemeanors. It is impossible to make general statements about these courts because of the wide variety of tasks that have been assigned to them in different states. In some areas these lower trial courts have extensive monetary jurisdiction and consist of a number of full-time, legally trained judges with large staffs. These courts often play significant roles in the administration of justice. In other states these courts hear only the most trivial cases and are presided over by part-time judges, sometimes with no legal training. Courts of this latter kind often exist only because state legislatures have failed to modernize local judicial administration.

Intermediate Appellate Courts

An **appellate court** is a court which reviews the decisions of lower courts. Many states have only trial courts and a supreme court; in those states the supreme court is the only appellate court. However, the federal system and those of heavily populated states have intermediate appellate courts—courts that review decisions of trial courts. Appellate decisions may in turn be reviewed by the highest court in the system.

Federal Intermediate Appellate Courts

The federal intermediate appellate courts are called **U.S. Circuit Courts of Appeals.** The United States is currently divided into twelve geographic circuits, with a court of appeals for each. These courts hear appeals from the federal district courts and from actions taken by many federal administrative agencies.

State Intermediate Appellate Courts

State intermediate appellate courts are found only in the heavily populated states. In half the states no intermediate level of review exists. Often the reason is that the highest court of the state can handle all cases that are appealed. In some states a need for an intermediate level of review exists, but neither the state constitution nor the legislature has authorized the creation of such a court.

The purpose of intermediate appellate courts is to improve the administration of justice by reducing the burden on the state's supreme court. Their presence both speeds up the judicial process and allows the high court to concentrate on cases that it considers significant for the administration of the state's judicial system.

State intermediate appellate courts have broad appellate jurisdiction. They hear appeals from trial courts of general jurisdiction and, frequently, from trial courts of limited jurisdiction and/or specialized courts. In many states the intermediate appellate courts also hear appeals from administrative agency determinations. Like the trial courts, these courts have a variety of names. A number of states call them courts of appeals; superior court is also a common designation. In New York these courts are the appellate division of the supreme court.

Although these courts are not the highest appellate court, for most appeals they are the court of last resort. There are two principal reasons for this. First, an appeal is a very expensive process. Most litigants cannot afford even an initial review, much less the cost of the two appeals necessary to argue their case before the highest appellate court. Second, in most states with an intermediate level of review, the highest court has the discretion to review only those cases that it considers to be necessary. A person appealing from the intermediate level must petition the high court. Ordinarily, these petitions are rejected because the high court is satisfied that justice has been accorded by the intermediate appellate court's review.

Courts of Last Resort

The federal government and each state has a supreme appellate court that sits at the top of the judicial system. At the federal level, this court is known as the **U.S. Supreme Court.** Most states also call their highest court the supreme court; in New York the highest court is called the court of appeals. Ordinarily a party whose case is heard at this level in a state system can appeal the case no further. In some few instances, however, a case appealed to the highest court of a state can be reviewed by the U.S. Supreme Court. This is true only if the case involves a substantial federal question, such as the interpretation of the U.S. Constitution or of a federal statute, and if the U.S. Supreme Court agrees to consider the state court judgment.

Only a few cases are appealable to the U.S. Supreme Court as a matter of right. In all other circumstances the party unhappy with the federal circuit court decision must first ask the Supreme Court to hear the case by petitioning for a **writ of certiorari.** If the Supreme Court wants to hear the case, it will grant the petition. Most petitions for certiorari are denied.

Jurisdiction

A court generally may not adjudicate a case unless it has jurisdiction over both the *subject matter* of and the *parties* to the case. Jurisdiction over the subject matter is known as **subject-matter jurisdiction.** Jurisdiction over the parties is known as **personal jurisdiction** (or in personam jurisdiction). Each is discussed below.

Subject-Matter Jurisdiction

The subject-matter jurisdiction of federal courts is limited by the Constitution. There are certain types of cases that can be heard only in federal court; federal courts are said to have **exclusive jurisdiction** over such cases, which include those involving bankruptcy, immigration, patents, copyrights, and federal crimes. State courts have exclusive jurisdiction over certain matters, including divorce and other types of family law. Matters not subject to the exclusive jurisdiction of the federal or state courts are matters of **concurrent jurisdiction**—they may be adjudicated in either federal or state court.

Federal Subject-Matter Jurisdiction
Federal courts have subject-matter jurisdiction over two types of cases: those involving a federal question and those between citizens of different states. These are discussed in turn. Keep in mind that if a case meets the requirements for federal subject-matter jurisdiction, it does not mean that the case could not be brought in state court. Unless the case involves a matter subject to the exclusive jurisdiction of the federal courts, it may be heard in state court as well.

FEDERAL QUESTIONS   Federal courts have jurisdiction when the decision depends upon the interpretation of the Constitution of the United States, a federal statute, or a treaty. These cases are said to involve a **federal question.** A large percentage of federal litigation consists of federal question cases. These cases include those based upon statutes such as the Sherman Act, the Securities Exchange Act, and the National Labor Relations Act, or regulation developed thereunder.

DIVERSITY OF CITIZENSHIP   A second important source of jurisdiction in the federal courts arises from the constitutional provision permitting Congress to grant jurisdiction to the federal courts in "controversies between citizens of different states."

Federal jurisdiction founded on the fact that the parties are citizens of different states is known as **diversity of citizenship** jurisdiction (sometimes shortened to diversity jurisdiction). In order to limit the number of diversity cases that the federal courts have to decide, legislation requires that the amount in controversy must exceed $50,000. Additional limitations require that each plaintiff's claim in a multiple-party action exceed $50,000 and that no plaintiff or defendant be a citizen of the same state. A corporation is defined to be a citizen both of the state of incorporation and of the state in which it has its principal place of business.

The original purpose of diversity jurisdiction was to protect a citizen of one state from possible bias in favor of a party whose case was being heard in his or her home state. It is generally believed that the need for diversity jurisdiction was greater in the early years of the republic, when people identified more strongly with their states. Now, it is probably less likely that a state court would be biased against an out-of-state citizen. As a result, many people are critical of diversity jurisdiction. They argue that it unduly complicates litigation, increases the cost of the federal judicial system, and forces the federal courts to hear cases that might more effectively be decided by state courts, since the cases involve state law.

The *Gafford* case, which follows, discusses two important issues concerning federal diversity jurisdiction. First, how do you determine what the actual amount in controversy is when it would seem very easy for an interested party to just make an unsupported claim that $50,000 is involved? Second, how is a large corporation's principal place of business to be determined? A large company, such as General Electric, has major operations in many states. Which of those states is its "principal place of business"?

GAFFORD V. GENERAL ELECTRIC
U.S. Court of Appeals, Sixth Circuit
997 F.2d 150 (1993)

BACKGROUND: Gafford was an aspiring meeting planner at General Electric. On two separate occasions she was passed over for advanced positions. She sued GE in Kentucky state court, claiming that she had been discriminated against on the basis of her gender. GE successfully moved to have the case tried in federal court on the basis of diversity jurisdiction. GE won the case before the federal district court and Gafford appealed, arguing among other things that the federal court did not have proper diversity jurisdiction.

Jones, Circuit Judge

Returning to the instant case, Gafford contends that GE never met its burden of proving that the amount in controversy exceeded $50,000 once she set that issue in controversy. GE responds that Earl F. Jones, Senior Counsel for Labor and Employment at GE's Appliance Park facility in Louisville, Kentucky, testified at the pretrial hearing on jurisdiction that, should Gafford prevail on her claims, she would be entitled to a sum greater than $50,000 for backpay, as well as additional amounts for attorney fees and other damages. Gafford did not offer any rebuttal witnesses at the jurisdiction hearing. Nor were any affidavits filed to contradict Jones' testimony. Given GE's burden of proof settled upon above, we find that the district court did not err in finding that the amount in controversy exceeded $50,000.

Gafford also takes issue with the district court's determination that diversity of citizenship among the parties was complete. Gafford is a citizen of Kentucky. This is undisputed. For purposes of determining diversity jurisdiction, a corporation can be a citizen of two states: (1) its state of incorporation; and (2) the state of its principal place of business. GE is incorporated in New York. This is also undisputed. What is disputed is whether GE's principal place of business is in Kentucky. Gafford basically argues that, given the size of the GE facility in Kentucky, which encompasses over 9000 employees, "it would be reasonable to conclude that Jefferson County, Kentucky is a principal place of business for General Electric." . . .

By common sense and by law, a corporation can have only one principal place of business for purposes of establishing its state of citizenship. . . . At the pretrial hearing on jurisdiction, and in an affidavit submitted before this hearing took place, GE submitted evidence to the court that Schenectady, New York is its principal place of business, where basic corporate and personnel records are maintained. . . .

In making this determination, courts have followed various approaches, or "tests." The "nerve center" test emphasizes the situs of corporate decision-making authority and overall control. . . . The "corporate activities"/"place of activity" test emphasizes the location of production activities or service activities. . . . We take this opportunity to direct courts in this circuit to employ the total activity test, taking into consideration all relevant factors and weighing them in light of the facts of each case.

Given the test to be applied, we find that the district court did not clearly err in determining GE's principal place of business to be New York. There was enough evidence before the district court for it to determine that GE's . . . operations were dispersed, and that GE's basic corporate and personnel records were maintained in New York.

Plaintiff-appellant Carol L. Kirchner Gafford appeals the unfavorable disposition of her sex discrimination suit on a veritable plethora of multifarious grounds. We find no merit in Gafford's contentions and thus affirm. . . .

Gafford graduated from high school in 1951. In November 1952, she began working for the General Electric Company ("GE") in Louisville, Kentucky as a general clerk in its maintenance office. In the years that followed, she worked in various GE offices at various secretarial/receptionist jobs. She left GE on two different occasions, once from February 1958 to May 1959, and once from August 1969 to March 1971. While employed at GE, she took courses in advanced typing, shorthand, and English.

In April 1973, she began working for GE's Meetings and Conventions Operation as a "Grade 8" Secretary to Hal Kendle, Manager of the Meetings and Conventions Operation. Through time, her responsibilities increased. Her compensation and title increased accordingly. In September 1973, she was raised to a "Grade 9" Clerk; in November 1979, she became a "Grade 11" Coordinator. . . .

In October 1986, a Meeting Planner died unexpectedly. Gafford filled out self-nomination papers for the position. . . . When she returned from her vacation, she was told that the job had not been posted. The job had, however, been given to Joe Schoettmer. . . .

In October 1988, GE decided to hire a new Manager of the Meetings and Conventions Operation. They chose Bill Fochtman, a GE employee with thirty years of experience, who was losing his former position due to corporate reorganization. . . .

On September 27, 1989, Gafford sued GE in the Jefferson Circuit Court of the Commonwealth of Kentucky. Her claims arose under Kentucky's civil rights statute. . . . Her basic contention was that she did not get the Manager position or the Meeting Planner position because of her gender. . . .

On October 18, 1989, GE filed a petition for removal in the United States District Court for the Western District of Kentucky based on diversity of citizenship. . . . In removing this case, GE asserted federal subject matter jurisdiction on the basis of diversity of citizenship and satisfaction of the amount-in-controversy requirement. . . . A defendant desiring to remove a case has the burden of proving the diversity jurisdiction requirements. . . .

Section 311 [enacted in 1988] amends 28 U.S.C. 1332 to provide for an increase in the amount in controversy required for federal diversity of citizenship cases from $10,000 to $50,000. . . . The last time the amount in controversy was revised was in 1958. That upward revision produced at least a short-term reduction in the number of diversity cases. . . .

The increase in the amount in controversy to $50,000 should reduce the federal diversity caseload by up to 40%, according to the proponents of reform.

DECISION: The decision of the District Court was upheld and Gafford lost.

State Subject Matter Jurisdiction The Tenth Amendment provides that each state retains the powers not delegated to the United States by the Constitution. This means that state courts have jurisdiction over all cases involving the constitution of the state, its statutes, and its common law. Federal courts cannot interfere with state courts unless a controversy involves an area in which the U.S. Constitution grants power to the federal government. For example, if a person is charged with violating a state criminal statute, a federal court is not involved unless the defendant raises a question under the U.S. Constitution or a federal statute. A similar result would follow if a business firm were being sued for breach of contract. A state court would have exclusive jurisdiction, unless the requirements for diversity jurisdiction exist or an issue under the U.S. Constitution or federal law was involved.

PERSONAL JURISDICTION In order to adjudicate a case, a court must not only have jurisdiction over the subject matter. It must also have jurisdiction over the parties to the case. (There are certain exceptions to this rule that apply in cases involving property located within the state where the court sits.)

The due process clauses of the Constitution are important factors in deciding whether a court may exercise jurisdiction over a particular person. The Constitution forbids the federal government or any state government from depriving any person of life, liberty, or property without due process of law. The upshot of this requirement is that any time the government proposes to require someone to give up life, liberty, or property—as is the case when the person is a defendant in a civil or criminal case—it may do so only after conducting a fair trial or other appropriate proceeding. There are numerous factors to consider in determining whether a proceeding is "fair." For now, we are concerned with only two:

1. Has the defendant received proper notice of the proceeding?
2. Is it fair to haul the defendant before this particular court?

Least problematic is when a defendant is sued in a federal or state court sitting in his or her home state. In order for the court to establish jurisdiction, the defendant simply needs to be served with the proper papers within the state. Alternatively, if the defendant is a resident of the state but is outside of the state at the time, the court may assert jurisdiction if it follows procedures for service designed to give the absent defendant notice of the action. The court may also assert jurisdiction over a nonresident defendant if the defendant can be served within the state where the court sits (if he or she is visiting the state, for example). The problem arises when a federal or state court wishes to assert jurisdiction over a nonresident defendant who is not within the state. The state's power to assert jurisdiction in such a case is known as its **long-arm jurisdiction.**

LONG-ARM JURISDICTION During the past 70 years, the development of the automobile and the expansion of business enterprises into national markets have led to rules that extend the jurisdiction of state courts beyond state boundaries. These rules are a good example of the manner in which the legal system adapts to a changing environment. In view of the traditional requirement that the defendant be served personally, consider the difficulties of the plaintiff in each of the following situations:

1. Plaintiff is an Ohio resident injured in Ohio by a Missouri driver who returns home immediately after the accident.
2. Plaintiff is a California resident injured in California by a defective lathe manufactured by a New York firm.

In both instances, the plaintiff might bring suit in the court of the state in which the defendant resides or, if the amount involved is over $50,000, in a federal court. Although these possibilities exist, very likely they would be both inconvenient and expensive, and the plaintiff ordinarily would prefer to sue in his or her home state.

To permit injured plaintiffs to bring suit against nonresident drivers, a number of states in the 1920s adopted legislation that gave local courts jurisdiction over nonresidents driving within the state. Later, this long-arm theory was extended to cover not only nonresidents driving on the state's highways but also various business-related activities carried on within the state. The Supreme Court has ruled that, as long as the defendant has certain minimum contacts with a state that make it fair for plaintiff to sue in that state, due process is not violated and the courts of the plaintiff's state have jurisdiction.

Determination of whether a federal court sitting in a given state may exercise jurisdiction over a party involves the exact same analysis that would apply if a state court were attempting to assert jurisdiction. If, for example, a state court in California would not be permitted to assert personal jurisdiction over a particular party, a federal court sitting in California also would not be able to assert jurisdiction over that party.

The limits of long-arm jurisdiction are discussed in the landmark case of *World-Wide Volkswagen Corp. v. Woodson,* which follows.

WORLD-WIDE VOLKSWAGEN CORP. v. WOODSON

U.S. Supreme Court
444 U.S. 286 (1980)

BACKGROUND: Plaintiffs Harry and Kay Robinson (respondents below) bought an Audi from Seaway Volkswagen in New York. On a drive through Oklahoma, the Audi was involved in an accident and caught fire. Mrs. Robinson and her two children were burned. The Robinsons sued Seaway, World-Wide Volkswagen (the wholesale dealer), Audi (the manufacturer), and Volkswagen (the importer). Seaway and World-Wide Volkswagen (petitioners below), which did not have operations in Oklahoma, argued that the Oklahoma court did not have personal jurisdiction over them. The Oklahoma trial court ruled that an Oklahoma court could assert jurisdiction over Seaway and World-Wide Volkswagen, and the Supreme Court of Oklahoma affirmed. The U.S. Supreme Court agreed to review the case.

White, Justice

As has long been settled, and as we reaffirm today, a state court may exercise personal jurisdiction over a nonresident defendant only so long as there exist "minimum contacts" between the defendant and the forum State. The concept of minimum contacts, in turn, can be seen to perform two related, but distinguishable, functions. It protects the defendant against the burdens of litigating in a distant or inconvenient forum. And it acts to ensure that the States, through their courts, do not reach out beyond the limits imposed on them by their status as coequal sovereigns in a federal system.

The protection against inconvenient litigation is typically described in terms of "reasonableness" or "fairness." We have said that the defendant's contacts with the forum State must be such that maintenance of the suit "does not offend 'traditional notions of fair play and substantial justice.'" *International Shoe Co. v. Washington.* The relationship between the defendant and the forum must be such that it is "reasonable . . . to require the corporation to defend the particular suit which is brought there."

Implicit in this emphasis on reasonableness is the understanding that the burden on the defendant, while always a primary concern, will in an appropriate case be considered in light of other relevant factors, including the forum State's interest in adjudicating the dispute; the plaintiff's interest in obtaining convenient and effective relief, at least when that interest is not adequately protected by the plaintiff's power to choose the forum; the interstate judicial system's interest in obtaining the most efficient resolution of controversies; and the shared interest of the several States in furthering fundamental substantive social policies. . . .

Applying these principles to the case at hand, we find in the record before us a total absence of those affiliating circumstances that are a necessary predicate to any exercise of state-court jurisdiction. Petitioners carry on no activity whatsoever in Oklahoma. They close no sales and perform no services there. They avail themselves of none of the privileges and benefits of Oklahoma law. They solicit no business there either through salespersons or through advertising reasonably calculated to reach the State. Nor does the record show that they regularly sell cars at wholesale or retail to Oklahoma customers or residents or that they indirectly, through others, serve or seek to serve the Oklahoma market. In short, respondents seek to base jurisdiction on one, isolated occurrence and whatever inferences can be drawn therefrom: the fortuitous circumstance that a single Audi automobile, sold in New York to New York residents, happened to suffer an accident while passing through Oklahoma.

It is argued, however, that because an automobile is mobile by its very design and purpose it was "foreseeable" that the Robinsons' Audi would cause injury in Oklahoma. Yet "foreseeability" alone has never been a sufficient benchmark for personal jurisdiction under the Due Process Clause. . . .

If foreseeability were the criterion, a local California tire retailer could be forced to defend in Pennsylvania when a blowout occurs there, a Wisconsin seller of a defective automobile jack could be haled before a distant court for damage caused in New Jersey, or a Florida soft-drink concessionaire could be summoned to Alaska to account for injuries happening there. Every seller of chattels would in effect appoint the chattel his agent for service of process. His amenability to suit would travel with the chattel.

DECISION: Reversed. The Supreme Court held that the Oklahoma courts did not have personal jurisdiction over Seaway and World-Wide Volkswagen.

CONCEPT SUMMARY
Jurisdiction

Definition: The power of a court over a person, thing, or cause of action

Element	Example
Subject-Matter Jurisdiction	
Power to hear the type of case	Domestic-relations court can hear a custody case; probate court cannot
Federal Courts	
Federal question	Suit under U.S. antitrust laws
Diversity	Citizen of Maryland sues citizen of West Virginia alleging breach of a $75,000 contract
Personal Jurisdiction	
Power over the parties (when properly served with legal process):	
Over own citizens	Can sue a New Jersey resident in New Jersey
Through long-arm statutes	Can sue in New Jersey someone who has committed a tort there
Someone who voluntarily appears	New Jersey Court has power over someone who consents to suit in New Jersey, or who is served with process while in New Jersey

Coordinating Court Systems

The dual court system gives rise to some potential problems of coordination. One of these results from the fact that the courts of one state have no authority over the courts of the other states. Thus, a state court might ignore the valid judicial acts of another state's courts, unless compelled to recognize them by the Constitution. A second problem exists in that state courts often must decide disputes that have substantial connections with other states. For example, if a contract made in Kansas is to be performed in Colorado, which state's law should apply if the contract is breached? The problems are discussed below.

Full Faith and Credit Clause

Imagine the problems that people in the United States would face if the judgments, public acts, and public records of each of the states could be ignored by the courts and other official bodies in another state. A business firm that won a contract case in one state might have to fight the same battle in each of the other states in which it was necessary to enforce the judgment. A person validly married in Ohio might not be recognized as married in New York. A divorce granted in California might not be recognized in any other state. The problems both to business and to the community at large would be endless and frustrating. The framers of the Constitution fortunately anticipated these difficulties and included in the Constitution sections designed to reduce the impact of state sovereignty.

Article IV, Section 1, of the Constitution states as follows: "Full Faith and Credit shall be given in each state to the public Acts, Records and judicial Proceedings of every other State." The intention of this sentence was to prevent states from refusing to recognize the judgments, public acts, and records of another state. In adopting the Constitution, each of the states surrendered this portion of its sovereign power.

The full faith and credit clause permits a litigant who wins a judgment in one state to take this judgment into the courts of another state, which must accept it as binding. Of course, a litigant who loses a case in the courts of one state is also denied an opportunity to bring it in another state.

As a result of the full faith and credit clause, a business firm winning a judgment for damages in Ohio can have this judgment enforced in any of the other states. This is true even though the cause of action is not recognized in the other state, the Ohio judgment is the result of legal error, or the Ohio judgment contravenes the public policy of the second state. The full faith and credit clause does not, however, require the courts of the second state to recognize a judgment rendered by a court that does not have jurisdiction. Nor does the enforcing state have to recognize a judgment obtained in violation of due process.

The full faith and credit clause is not applicable to criminal cases. A state does not have to enforce the criminal law of other states. The criminal defendant is entitled to be tried by the courts in the state where the crime was committed. Defendants who flee to another state can be extradited and returned for trial to the state where the crime was committed.

Conflict of Laws

Today, business and most other significant human activities cut across state boundaries. Conversely, these same state boundaries are important to the structure of the U.S. legal system. As we have seen, each state makes and enforces its own laws within its boundaries. There is no indication at this time that the legal importance of state boundaries will decrease, but it is clear that technological advances in communication and transportation will further reduce the importance of these boundaries in most other areas of American life.

The dichotomy between the limited importance of state boundaries in human activity generally and their continued importance in legal administration creates numerous problems for the business community. The following is a small sample of the many important legal questions that the business administrator should consider if business is carried on in more than one state:

1. Are the provisions of all legal documents such as contracts, promissory notes, and bills of exchange valid in each state where used?
2. Do the same time limitations for bringing suit exist in other states where the firm is doing business?
3. If employees based in one state are assigned temporarily to jobs in another, which state's workers' compensation laws apply?
4. Is income taxable in the state where earned also taxable in the firm's home state?
5. How does the firm's responsibility for defective merchandise vary in the states where its products are marketed?

The fact that much activity, both commercial and otherwise, ignores state lines also creates a major problem for judicial administration. In many instances state courts will be called upon to settle disputes with a substantial out-of-state dimension. In these situations a question that frequently must be answered is: What state law applies?

Although we would expect that a state court would apply its own state's law in all litigation, it doesn't always do so. Many instances exist in which state courts apply the laws of a sister state instead of its own state's laws. Public-policy considerations underlie this choice. Both statutes and cases recognize that in a legal dispute the controlling law should be that which the parties reasonably would expect it to be. Results in litigation should not depend upon fortuitous circumstances that determine the forum. In addition, the U.S. Supreme Court has held that due process is violated if a state court applies its own laws to transactions that have more substantial contacts with other states. Since even small businesses often operate across state lines, the business administrator must be aware of the law that applies to actions taken not only at home but in other states as well.

The decision as to which state's law may govern will often make all the difference in litigation. Thus, state choice of law principles are very important, and they may be tested under constitutional doctrines of due process of law and full faith and credit, as indicated in the *Allstate Insurance Company* case, which follows.

ALLSTATE INSURANCE COMPANY V. HAGUE
U.S. Supreme Court
450 U.S. 971 (1981)

BACKGROUND: Ralph Hague died when his motorcycle was struck by un uninsured driver. The accident happened in Wisconsin, both parties to the accident were citizens of Wisconsin, and three Allstate Insurance policies held by Hague had been delivered in Wisconsin. The three insurance policies were for $15,000 each. Minnesota law would allow the three to be "stacked" so that Hague's widow could recover $45,000. Wisconsin law would not allow stacking so that she only could recover $15,000. Hague's widow sued in Minnesota to recover on the insurance policies. The Minnesota trial court applied Minnesota law to allow stacking, and the ruling was upheld by the Minnesota Supreme Court. Allstate appealed to the U.S. Supreme Court.

Brennan, Justice

The Minnesota state court, therefore, examined the conflict-of-laws issue in terms of (1) predictability of result, (2) maintenance of interstate order, (3) simplification of the judicial task, (4) advancement of the forum's governmental interests, and (5) application of the better rule of law. Although stating that the Minnesota contacts might not be "in themselves, sufficient to mandate application of [Minnesota] law," under the first four factors, the court concluded that the fifth factor—application of the better rule of law—favored selection of Minnesota law.

The court emphasized that a majority of States allow stacking and that legal decisions allowing stacking "are fairly recent and well considered in light of current uses of automobiles." In addition, the court found the Minnesota rule superior to Wisconsin's "because it requires the cost of accidents with uninsured motorists to be spread more broadly through insurance premiums than does the Wisconsin rule." Finally, the court buttressed its initial opinion by indicating "that contracts of insurance on motor vehicles are in a class by themselves" since an insurance company "knows the automobile is a movable item which will be driven from state to state." From this premise the court concluded that application of Minnesota laws was "not so arbitrary and unreasonable as to violate due process." . . .

In deciding constitutional choice-of-law questions, whether under the Due Process Clause or the Full Faith and Credit Clause, this Court has traditionally examined the contacts of the State, whose law was applied, with the parties and with the occurrence or transaction giving rise to the litigation. In order to ensure that the choice of law is neither arbitrary nor fundamentally unfair, the Court has invalidated the choice of law of a State which has had no significant contact or significant aggregation of contacts, creating state interests, with the parties and the occurrence or transaction. . . .

Minnesota has three contacts with the parties and the occurrence giving rise to the litigation. In the aggregate, these contacts permit selection by the Minnesota Supreme Court of Minnesota law allowing the stacking of Mr. Hague's uninsured motorist coverages.

First, and for our purposes a very important contact, Mr. Hague was a member of Minnesota's work force, having been employed by a Red Wing, Minn., enterprise for the 15 years preceding his death. While employment status may implicate a state interest less substantial than does resident status, that interest is nevertheless important. The State of employment has police power responsibilities towards the nonresident employee that are analogous, if somewhat less profound, than towards residents. Thus, such employees use state services and amenities and may call upon state facilities in appropriate circumstances.

In addition, Mr. Hague commuted to work in Minnesota. . . . The State's interest in its commuting nonresident employees reflects a state concern for the safety and well-being of its work force and the concomitant effect on Minnesota employers. Second, Allstate was at all times present and doing business in Minnesota. By virtue of its presence, Allstate can hardly claim unfamiliarity with the laws of the host jurisdiction. . . .

Third, respondent became a Minnesota resident prior to institution of this litigation. The stipulated facts reveal that she first settled in Red Wing, Minn., the town in which her late husband had worked. She subsequently moved to Savage, Minn., after marrying a Minnesota resident who operated an automobile service station in Bloomington, Minn. Her move to Savage occurred "almost concurrently," with the initiation of the instant case. There is no suggestion that Mrs. Hague moved to Minnesota in anticipation of this litigation or for the purpose of finding a legal climate especially hospitable to her claim. . . .

In sum, Minnesota had a significant aggregation of contacts with the parties and the occurrence, creating state interests, such that application of its law was neither arbitrary nor fundamentally unfair. Accordingly, the choice of Minnesota law by the Minnesota Supreme Court did not violate the Due Process Clause or the Full Faith and Credit Clause.

DECISION: Affirmed. Hague's widow was entitled to have the insurance policies stacked.

Review Questions and Problems

Key Terms

federalism	U.S. Supreme Court
separation-of-powers doctrine	writ of certiorari
trial court	subject-matter jurisdiction
original jurisdiction	personal jurisdiction
general jurisdiction	exclusive jurisdiction
limited jurisdiction	concurrent jurisdiction
U.S. District Court	federal question
appellate court	diversity of citizenship
U.S. Circuit Court of Appeals	long-arm jurisdiction

Discussion Questions

1. Are there circumstances in which a suit may be brought either in federal court or in state court? Explain.

2. For many years, a suit could be brought in federal court on the basis of diversity of citizenship if at least $10,000 was at stake. Congress recently raised this minimum amount to $50,000. Why do you think Congress raised the minimum amount?

3. May a suit involving a corporation reach the federal courts on the basis of diversity of citizenship? If so, how is a corporation's citizenship determined?

4. What is the minimum amount in controversy for a suit brought in federal court on the basis of a federal question?

5. Discuss the limits on a state's power to exercise long-arm jurisdiction.

Review Problems

1. Wedgeco is incorporated in Delaware but does business exclusively in California. Myron, a citizen of Delaware, is injured by one of Wedgeco's products. Myron sues Wedgeco in Delaware state court. Wedgeco argues that the Delaware court may not assert jurisdiction over the corporation. Wedgeco argues that it is incorporated in Delaware for legal purposes only, and that it otherwise transacts no business within the state. Should the court accept Wedgeco's argument? Discuss.

2. Acme Corp., which manufactures blenders and other household appliances, is incorporated in Cal-

ifornia and does business exclusively in that state. Dan, a resident of California, moves to Maine and takes his Acme blender with him. In Maine, Dan's blender catches fire and injures him. In what courts may Dan sue Acme? Discuss.

3. Donald Yee, who resides in Pennsylvania, enters into an agreement to construct a building for Malone Company, a New York corporation. The contract price is $125,000. The building is to be built on land owned by Malone Company in Pennsylvania. The agreement is signed in Yee's office in Philadelphia. Yee defaults and Malone sues in federal court. Does the federal court have jurisdiction? Discuss.

4. Clements sued Signa Corporation for breach of warranty in the Illinois courts. Clements purchased a boat from Barney's Sporting Goods, an Illinois corporation. Signa, the manufacturer of the boat, was an Indiana corporation with no offices in Illinois. Signa advertised in boating magazines that Clements received, and Signa's boat was displayed at a Chicago boating show. Barney's Sporting Goods, which was located in Illinois, also displayed the boat. Barney's furnished Clements with a written warranty issued by Signa. Do the Illinois courts have jurisdiction over Signa? Discuss.

Case Problems

1. The U.S. Constitution grants Congress the authority to pass budgets. The President is given the authority to either sign a budget into law or veto it; once the budget is enacted, the President is responsible for implementing it. On December 12, 1985, President Reagan signed into law the Gramm-Rudman-Hollings Act. The purpose of the Act was to eliminate the federal budget deficit. The Act set up a "maximum deficit amount" for federal spending for each year from 1986 to 1991. The Act required across-the-board federal spending cuts to reach the targeted deficit levels. The calculation of the required deductions was to be made by the Comptroller General, an officer of the legislative branch. The Act required the President, in the event that a budget passed by Congress exceeded the "maximum deficit amount," to issue an order mandating spending reductions specified by the Comptroller General. Congressman Synar, who voted against the Act, wished to challenge it in court. On what basis might you advise him to challenge the Act? Discuss.

2. Ferens lost his right hand in Pennsylvania when it allegedly became caught in a harvester manufactured by John Deere Co. Pennsylvania law (statute of limitations) requires that this kind of personal injury claim be brought within two years. After the two years had elapsed, Ferens, a Pennsylvania resident, filed (1) a proper diversity suit in Pennsylvania District Court for breach of contract (the statute of limitations is longer for breach of contract claims), and (2) a personal injury claim in the District Court in Mississippi, where John Deere does business (Mississippi has a six year statute of limitations for personal injury claims). Ferens now wants to transfer the Mississippi case to Pennsylvania under a federal statute allowing transfers for the convenience of the parties, and he argues that the Mississippi statute of limitations must be applied. Should this be allowed? Discuss.

3. Rudzewicz, a Michigan resident, entered into a franchise agreement with Burger King, a Florida corporation whose principal offices are in Miami. Under this agreement Rudzewicz was authorized to use Burger King's trademarks and operate a Burger King restaurant in Michigan. The contract stated that the franchise relationship is established in Miami and governed by Florida law, and requires that all monthly payments and correspondence be sent to Miami. When Rudzewicz fell behind in his payments, Burger King brought a diversity action for breach of contract in the Florida Federal District Court and won. However, the Court of Appeals reversed holding that the District Court could not exercise personal jurisdiction over Rudzewicz under the Florida long-arm statute because it would "offend fundamental fairness which is the touchstone of due process." Do you agree with the Court of Appeals? Discuss.

4. Finley's husband was killed when his plane struck electrical power lines on its approach to a city-run airfield in San Diego. She claimed the Federal Aviation Administration was negligent in performing their air traffic control functions and sued the United States in Federal District Court under the Federal Tort Claims Act. She subsequently tried to add state law claims against both the city and the utility company that maintained the power lines. All the parties are residents of California. Should Finley be allowed to sue the city and the utility company in Federal District Court? Discuss.

3

Civil Litigation and Alternative Dispute Resolution

The previous chapter described the structure of court systems in the United States. This chapter focuses on how those systems are supposed to function. The pages that follow will describe the steps of the civil litigation process. While the volume of litigation in this country continues to increase, more and more businesses are looking to resolve their disputes outside the judicial system. The chapter also examines arbitration, mediation, and other alternative methods of dispute resolution.

The Adversary Principle

In the United States litigation is characterized by the **adversary principle**. This principle places the responsibility for developing and proving cases upon the parties rather than upon some designated legal official, with the court serving primarily as a referee. Because of the complexi-

ties of litigation, ordinarily the parties hire lawyers to represent them and to argue for them.

The rationale for the adversary principle is that truth and justice will be most effectively attained by making each litigant responsible for his or her case. Those directly involved have more incentive than outsiders to see the evidence, the legal arguments, and other factors in their favor presented in the best light.

The adversary principle is not without its critics. Some argue that under the adversary system, winning or losing often depends upon the skill of the attorneys instead of the merits of the case.

Settlement

Before we examine the litigation process, it is important to note that the overwhelming majority of cases are settled. **Settlement** occurs when the parties to a lawsuit agree, at some point in the litigation process, on terms under which a lawsuit will be terminated. In a settlement agreement, the defendant generally agrees to pay the plaintiff some amount of money and in return the plaintiff drops the suit. Since litigation is so costly, both sides typically can save money by settling. The parties especially have an incentive to settle when both sides have a similar perception of the case's merits. As you study the litigation process in the pages that follow, keep in mind that the parties generally may settle at any point in that process.

Issues of Fact and Issues of Law

There are two types of issues that may be presented in any litigation: issues of *fact* and issues of *law*. An issue of fact is a disagreement between

---

ISSUES AND TRENDS
Too Many Lawsuits?

The United States is said to be the most litigious society on earth—that is, Americans are more prone than any other people to take their disputes to court. Nearly 94 million new cases were filed in state courts in 1992. The majority of those involved traffic violations or violations of other ordinances, but 19.7 million of those filings were civil lawsuits. The federal court caseload also has continued to climb: Over 276,000 new cases were filed in federal district courts in 1993, up from just over 89,000 in 1960. The rate of increase in new federal filings has actually started to decline in recent years, at least in part because Congress raised the dollar-value threshold for diversity actions from $10,000 to $50,000; new filings in federal court had almost reached 300,000 in 1985. Congress may have slowed the growth in federal lawsuits, but litigants shut out of federal court are presumably taking their cases to state courts.

The judicial system has been hard-pressed to keep pace with the growth in lawsuits. In some systems, it is common for cases to take 5 years to get to trial. The problem has led many potential litigants to seek out alternative means of dispute resolution, such as arbitration. Some court systems require disputes to be sent to arbitration if the amount in controversy is less than a certain amount.

ETHICS
The Lawyer's Dilemma

The adversary principle sometimes puts lawyers into awkward situations. A lawyer is considered an officer of the court who has a general duty to see that justice is done. But a lawyer also is the advocate for his or her client and must vigorously pursue the client's best interests—within the law.

Consider the following case. An attorney is representing a client who was a by-stander struck by a car as a result of a collision. The two drivers involved had insurance policies with limits of $100,000 and $50,000 for paying such claims. But one of the drivers also had an umbrella policy that would pay an additional $1 million after the first policy was exhausted. The client had incurred hospital expenses of over $112,000 and the lawyer negotiated the settlement of the claim with the hospital. During the negotiation, the lawyer realized that the representative of the hospital knew about the two smaller policies but did not know about the $1 million policy.

What would you do? Would you mention the $1 million policy?

The Code of Ethics for lawyers states that, "In his representation of a client a lawyer shall not . . . knowingly make a false statement of law or fact."

You may be surprised to learn that the lawyer who actually faced this choice and didn't tell about the policy was suspended from practicing law for 6 months. The failure to speak was considered the equivalent of a false statement. *Nebraska State Bar Association v. Addison*, 412 N.W.2d 855 (Neb. 1987).

the parties as to the facts of the case. For example, a plaintiff may allege that the defendant breached an oral agreement to hire her. The defendant may answer that he never made such an oral agreement. Both sides can't be right. One of the functions of a trial is to resolve issues of fact—that is, to determine what the facts really are. In a jury trial, the jury is the "finder of fact." It is thus for the jury to decide which side's witnesses seem more credible and which party's other evidence is more convincing. In cases tried without a jury, the judge acts as the finder of fact.

An issue of law is a question of how the law applies to a given set of facts. Assume from our last example that the defendant *did* orally agree to hire the plaintiff. Is the oral agreement enforceable? That is an issue of law, because the answer depends not on what the facts are but on what the law provides. At trial, the judge decides issues of law. Depending on the circumstances, the judge decides legal issues either directly or through his or her instructions to the jury (discussed later in the chapter).

Pretrial Procedures

The Summons

A lawsuit actually begins when the defendant is served with a summons. The **summons** is a document that informs the defendant that action is being brought and that a judgment against the defendant will be entered by default if no appropriate response is made. The summons tells the defendant little or nothing about the nature of the plaintiff's claim. Traditionally, the law has required that the summons be handed to the defendant, but most states today allow service by a variety of methods, including publication, mailing, or delivery to the defendant's residence.

Pleadings

The **pleadings** are documents exchanged by the parties that outline their respective claims and defenses. The basic pleadings are the complaint and the answer. Copies of each document of the pleadings are filed with the court.

The Complaint The **complaint**, which is the initial pleading, spells out in some detail the nature of the claim. In practice, in many jurisdictions the summons and the complaint are served together. The statements in the complaint as well as the other pleadings are statements of fact. The procedural rules of one state direct that the statements be "plain and concise" and "sufficiently particular to give the court and parties notice of the transactions, occurrences . . . intended to be proved. . . ."

United States District Court for the Southern District of Ohio

Civil Action, File Number 94/1234

John D. Smith, Plaintiff
v.   Complaint
Douglas Jones, Defendant

1. Plaintiff is a citizen of the State of Ohio and defendant is a citizen of the State of Kansas. The matter in controversy exceeds, exclusive of interest and costs, the sum of fifty thousand dollars.
2. On August 31, 1985, in Mountain View, a public park in Portland, Oregon, defendant negligently drove a bicycle against plaintiff, who was jogging on a public way in said park. As a result, plaintiff was thrown to the ground and had his arm and leg broken and was otherwise injured, was prevented from carrying out his business, suffered great pain in body and mind, and incurred expenses for medical attention and hospitalization in the sum of $5,000.
3. Wherefore plaintiff demands judgment against defendant in the sum of $70,000 and costs.

Signed: *Frank F. Johnson*
Attorney for Plaintiff
Address: Mulberry Building
Newark, Ohio 43201

FIGURE 3-1

Complaint

The Answer   The **answer** is the pleading in which the defendant responds to the allegations set forth in the complaint. Typically, the answer takes each allegation in the complaint and *admits* it, *denies* it, or states that the defendant is without sufficient knowledge to either admit or deny it. When the defendant states that he or she is without sufficient knowledge to either admit or deny an allegation, it is treated as a denial of the allegation. Most jurisdictions allow the defendant to issue a general denial, which is a blanket denial of all the allegations set forth in the complaint.

The answer may also include **affirmative defenses**, which are additional facts that would tend to exonerate the defendant. For example, if a seller sues a buyer for failure to pay for goods delivered, the buyer might assert as an affirmative defense that the goods arrived severely damaged.

Finally, the defendant may also include a counterclaim in the answer. A **counterclaim** is an assertion by the defendant that he or she has a claim against the plaintiff that could be the basis for an independent action. A counterclaim is treated in the same way that a claim is treated, but with the roles reversed. The plaintiff, in a separate pleading known as a **reply**, must respond to the counterclaim by admitting, denying, or pleading insufficient knowledge with respect to the allegations in the counterclaim. If the defendant wins the counterclaim, he or she will generally be entitled to damages from the plaintiff.

A sample compliant and sample answer are shown in Figures 3-1 and 3-2.

Functions of Pleadings   The pleadings serve different purposes. They provide notice to the parties of the opposition's claims. In many jurisdictions this is their chief purpose. When notice is the function of the pleadings, the aim is to provide for fairness in the litigation. A second purpose of the pleadings is to determine what differences exist between the parties as each sees the facts and understands the law. In answering, if the defendant does not deny a statement that the plaintiff has made in the complaint, (recall that pleading insufficient knowledge is treated as a denial), the court assumes that no dispute exists regarding that particular fact. If the defendant does deny an allegation made in the complaint, an issue of fact exists that must be resolved in some manner. Similarly, if the defendant makes a motion to dismiss on the ground of legal insufficiency, then an issue of law—a dispute as to what the law is—exists that also must be resolved.

United States District Court for the Southern District of Ohio

Civil Action, File Number 94/1234

John D. Smith, Plaintiff
v.
Douglas Jones, Defendant

Answer

1. Defendant admits the allegation contained in paragraph 1 of the complaint.
2. Defendant alleges that he is without knowledge or information sufficient to form a belief as to the allegations contained in paragraph 2 of the complaint; and denies each and every other allegation contained in the complaint.

Signed: *Barbara A. Brown*
Attorney for Defendant
Address: 81 Main Street
Bowling Green, Ohio 43264

FIGURE 3-2
Answer

DIOGUARDI V. DURNING

U.S. Court of Appeals, Second Circuit

139 F. 2d 774 (1944)

BACKGROUND: Plaintiff Dioguardi attempted to import certain bottles of "tonic" from Italy. The bottles were seized by U.S. customs officials at the Port of New York and sold at auction. Dioguardi sued Durning, the collector of customs for the Port of New York. Durning moved to dismiss the case for failure to state a claim for which relief could be granted, and the federal District Court granted the motion. Dioguardi appealed.

Clark, Circuit Judge

In his complaint, obviously home drawn, plaintiff attempts to assert a series of grievances against the Collector of Customs at the Port of New York growing out of his endeavors to import merchandise from Italy "of great value," consisting of bottles of "tonics." We may pass certain of his claims as either inadequate or inadequately stated and consider only these two: (1) that on the auction day, October 9, 1940, when defendant sold the merchandise at "public custom," "he sold my merchandise to another bidder with my price of $110, and not of his price of $120," and (2) "that three weeks before the sale, two cases, of 19 bottles each case, disappeared." . . .

This complaint was dismissed by the District Court, with leave, however, to plaintiff to amend, on motion of the United States Attorney, appearing for the defendant, on the ground that it "fails to state facts sufficient to constitute a cause of action."

Thereupon plaintiff filed an amended complaint, wherein, with an obviously heightened conviction that he was being unjustly treated, he vigorously reiterates his claims, including those quoted above and now stated as that his "medicinal extracts" were given to the Springdale Distilling Company "with my betting [bidding?] price of $110: and not their price of $120," and "It isn't so easy to do away with two cases with 37 bottles of one quart. Being protected, they can take this chance." An earlier paragraph suggests that defendant had explained the loss of the two cases by "saying that they had leaked, which could never be true in the mauner they were bottled." On defendant's motion for dismissal on the same ground as before, the court made a final judgment dismissing the complaint, and plaintiff now comes to us with increased volubility, if not clarity.

It would seem, however, that he has stated enough to withstand a mere formal motion, directed only to the face of the complaint, and that here is another instance of judicial haste which in the long run makes waste. Under the new rules of civil procedure, there is no pleading requirement of stating "facts sufficient to constitute a cause of action," but only that there be "a short and plain statement of the claim showing that the pleader is entitled to relief," and the motion for dismissal under Rule 12(b) is for failure to state "a claim upon which relief can be granted." . . .

We think that, however inartistically they may be stated, the plaintiff has disclosed his claims that the collector has converted or otherwise done away with two of his cases of medicinal tonics and has sold the rest in a manner incompatible with the public auction he had announced. . . .

In view of plaintiff's limited ability to write and speak English, it will be difficult for the District Court to arrive at justice unless he consents to receive legal assistance in the presentation of his case. The record indicates that he refused further help from a lawyer suggested by the court, and his brief (which was a recital of facts, rather than an argument of law) shows distrust of a lawyer of standing at this bar. It is the plaintiff's privilege to decline all legal help, but we fear that he will be indeed ill advised to attempt to meet a motion for summary judgment or other similar presentation of the merits without competent advice and assistance.

DECISION: The Circuit Court of Appeals reversed the District Court's decision and remanded the case for a new trial.

There are other pretrial motions that may be made, some of which are designed to correct defects in the pleadings. After all the pleadings have been filed, either party may make a **motion for judgment on the pleadings**. Such a motion may be granted if the parties, in their pleadings, do not disagree about the material facts of the case and if the pleadings indicate that one party is entitled to win.

Other important motions may be made at later stages in the process. They will be described at appropriate points in the discussion.

Discovery

Once the pleadings have been made, each side will generally need information from the other side in order to prepare for trial. Assume, for example, that Fred gets violently ill after eating a doughnut that he bought from Dominic's Doughnuts. In order to prepare his case against Dominic's, Fred might want to know, for example, what ingredients were used in the doughnuts, where and when the ingredients were purchased, how the doughnuts were kept, who was on duty at the time of the sale, and whether that person was properly trained. Similarly, Dominic's will want to obtain information from Fred—what else he ate that day, whether he had a preexisting medical condition that could have been the actual cause of his illness, whether he actually bought the doughnut from Dominic's, and so on.

Discovery procedures are the methods by which each side is permitted to elicit information from the other side prior to trial. The law gives each side a fairly broad right to discovery, so that each side can find out as much as possible about the other side's case. There are several reasons this is desirable. First, broad discovery lessens the possibility that one side or the other will be surprised at trial; the desire is to have the outcome be determined on the merits and not be influenced by one side's ability to spring surprises on the other.

Second, discovery enables the sides to narrow the issues. The parties may disagree about certain facts at the pleadings stage but, upon further investigation, it may become apparent that one side or the other is correct. When as many issues as possible are dispensed with prior to trial, the trial can be conducted more quickly and efficiently. If all the disputes as to the facts of the case can be resolved through discovery, then a trial can be avoided; the judge can decide the case by granting a motion for summary judgment (discussed below).

Third, discovery can encourage the parties to settle their dispute out of court. As each side gets more information from the other side, it can become apparent how strong each side's case is. Discovery can help move the parties toward a settlement, and therefore save everyone the time and expense of a trial.

Because discovery is such an important part of the litigation process, trial judges may generally levy stiff sanctions against parties who needlessly obstruct their opponent's discovery.

Depositions A **deposition** is the oral testimony of a witness taken under oath outside the courtroom, usually in the office of one of the attorneys. A court reporter records the testimony, and the attorneys for both sides may question the witness. The transcript of the deposition may be used under limited circumstances at trial. If the testimony of the witness at trial conflicts with the deposition, then the deposition may be introduced to highlight the discrepancy. If the witness is unavailable at trial, the deposition generally can be introduced in lieu of the testimony.

A **deponent**—the person testifying at a deposition—need only testify as to matters within his or her personal knowledge and memory; there is no requirement that the deponent "brush up" on the information that the opposing side will want to elicit from him or her. However, the deponent can generally be required to produce certain documents at the deposition to ensure that the other side will be able to obtain the information that it needs.

Business managers stand a fairly good chance of being deposed at some point in their careers.

Interrogatories **Interrogatories** are written questions submitted to the opposing party, who then must respond to the questions in a sworn written statement. Unlike a deposition, which can be taken of any witness, an interrogatory may be submitted only to a party to the suit. A party responding to an interrogatory is responsible for consulting all information within that party's control—files, records, and so on—in order to ensure that the answers are complete and accurate. Judges are likely to impose sanctions on parties who leave pertinent information out of their responses to interrogatories.

Interrogatories are generally cheaper than depositions and are often used to obtain background information.

Inspection of Documents and Property
A party can require the opposing party to produce certain documents for inspection. Alternatively, a party may gain the right of access to the other party's property in order to inspect documents or otherwise inspect the premises.

Physical or Mental Examination When a party's physical or mental condition is relevant to the case, the judge may grant the opposing party's request to compel a physical or mental examination. The other party will be allowed to obtain the results of the examination. The examination will generally be limited to areas that are relevant to the case.

Requests for Admission A **request for admission** is a request from one party to another to admit to certain facts in writing. The party who receives the request may admit the statements, deny them, or declare that he or she is without sufficient knowledge to admit or deny. If a fact is admitted, it is considered to be established for the

purpose of the trial. A request for admission can thus serve to narrow the issues of a case.

Problems Arising During Discovery
Courts generally monitor discovery to ensure that the process isn't abused. Although parties are granted a very broad right of discovery, there are limits. For example, a competitor may not use discovery as a pretext to gain access to trade secrets. And the tools of discovery, which can sometimes impose substantial costs on the parties to whom they are directed, may not be used for the purpose of harassing an opposing party. If the court feels that a party is using discovery for improper purposes, it may issue a **protective order** that declares certain matters to be off limits to the opposing party.

On the other hand, courts must often deal with parties who fail to cooperate with legitimate discovery requests. In such a case, a party may file a **motion to compel** the other party's response to the discovery request. If the motion is granted, the information requested will have to be furnished.

Summary Judgment Disagreements between the parties as to the relevant facts of the case can sometimes be resolved through discovery. Either party in such case may bring a **motion for summary judgment**, which, if granted, results in the judge deciding the case without trial. The party making the motion is contending that there is no genuine issue of fact that needs to be resolved. Ordinarily, a motion for summary judgment will be supported by one party's affidavits and documentary evidence to show that the other party's factual claims have no merit. The party opposing the motion may also submit affidavits and other evidence, and both parties are generally permitted to argue for their respective positions at a hearing before the judge. This distinguishes a motion for summary judgment from a motion for judgment on the pleadings, in which the judge bases his or her ruling exclusively on the pleadings.

The judge should not grant the motion unless he or she is convinced that no material issue of fact exists. Issues of fact must be decided at trial. If the judge is convinced that no material issue of fact exists, there is no need for a trial. In such a case, the judge may simply apply the law to the facts and decide the case.

Pretrial Conference

A **pretrial conference** is a meeting prior to trial called by the judge with the attorneys from both sides. Most jurisdictions provide for pretrial conferences, which are designed to narrow and simplify the factual and legal issues. If possible, admissions of fact and of documents that will avoid unnecessary proof are obtained. The parties may consider other items such as the number of expert witnesses who will testify, the need to amend the pleadings, and the date for the trial.

The format of pretrial conferences varies from one jurisdiction to another. In some courts, the pretrial conference is a formal affair; in others, there is considerable informality. Often the parties themselves attend the conference, but in some jurisdictions only the opposing counsel and the conferring judge meet. In large metropolitan courts one or two judges will be assigned to supervise the pretrial calendar, but in rural areas the judge assigned the case will usually direct the conference.

Exploring the issues at a pretrial conference helps to eliminate surprise at the trial. Thus, the outcome is more likely to reflect a fair resolution of the issues between the parties. In many instances the pretrial conference is used to consider the possibility of settling the case. If the parties are not too far apart, the conferring judge may try to persuade them to reach a settlement. Under no circumstances, however, should the parties be forced to settle, since a forced settlement denies them their right to trial. In some areas the pretrial conference has been criticized as a device used by the court to force settlements in order to reduce the number of cases pending on the court dockets.

The Trial

In many instances litigation results because the parties are unable to agree about what actually happened—what the facts are. The purpose of the trial is to process the information that will be used to determine the facts. For most civil litigation, the U.S. legal system uses the *petit jury*—a group of laypersons—to decide these important questions. Parties, however, may waive their right to have a jury determine the facts. If the right is waived or the case is one in which the parties do not have the right to a jury trial, the trial judge decides the facts.

The Jury System

Although the jury system has many critics, it continues to be important in American law because of strong historic support. For many decades Americans have looked upon the jury as a bulwark of democracy. It is an institution in which citizens participate directly, and it is often seen as a protection against the power of government. These sentiments stem primarily from the use of juries in criminal cases, but parties in civil cases generally feel more satisfied when their claims are determined by juries rather than by judges. Today, the history and tradition of trial by jury are so ingrained in our legal system that many would raise strong objections to proposals to limit further the right to trial by jury.

Traditionally, the civil jury consisted of twelve persons. Over the past three decades there has been a trend toward smaller trial juries, and many jurisdictions now allow juries of fewer than twelve in most civil cases. Historically, the civil jury's verdict was required to be unanimous, but here again change has taken place, and in more than half the states unanimous verdicts are no longer required. These changes have been made primarily to shorten trials and make it possible for the courts to try more cases with less delay.

One of the first steps in the jury trial is the selection of the jurors. Lists of prospective jurors are made from various sources, depending upon the jurisdiction. The names should be chosen at random from these sources, and the lists should represent a fair cross section of the community.

In the *Ramseur* case, which follows, the judge attempted to come up with a jury panel which closely reflected the local community in terms of its composition by race, gender, and other factors. The case involves selection of a grand jury (see Chapter 5), which is a special type of jury used to determine whether individuals should be indicted for criminal offenses. The membership of the grand jury is selected from a larger group of prospective jurors called a venire. The selection process involves questioning of the prospective jurors through a process known as voir dire.

RAMSEUR V. BEYER

U.S. Court of Appeals, Third Circuit
983 F.2d 1215 (1993)

BACKGROUND: In 1983, Thomas Ramseur was convicted for the murder of Asaline Stokes, his former girlfriend. He had stabbed her repeatedly in front of six witnesses. Ramseur had been indicted by a grand jury that was set up by the judge in such a way as to ensure that it reflected the diversity of Essex County, New Jersey. Ramseur appealed his conviction, arguing that the selection process for the grand jury violated his constitutional right to equal protection of the laws.

Roth, Circuit Judge

The assignment judge who empaneled Ramseur's grand jury used the following procedure once the venire was assembled: First, the judge briefly interviewed each juror. Then he did one of three things: excused the juror for cause, asked the juror to take a seat in the body of the courtroom for the time being, or asked the juror to take a seat on the panel. Those he asked to sit in the body of the courtroom fell into one of two groups. The first group consisted of those persons who had asked to be excused but whose excuses had been denied. They were asked to sit in the body of the courtroom with the understanding that they might be called upon to serve later, after all of the other prospective jurors had been questioned. The second group consisted of persons who proffered no excuse, stated they were willing to serve, but were nonetheless asked to sit aside.

In the course of empaneling Ramseur's grand jury, the judge announced that he was attempting to "pick a cross section of the community" to serve on the grand jury. . . . I don't mind telling you, ladies and gentlemen of the jury or the panel of the grand jury, I am trying to get a cross section; and as you've probably noticed, I have asked two of the blacks who have indicated a willingness to serve to sit in the body of the courtroom. I am deliberately trying to get an even mix of people from background and races, and things like that. And if any of you think that I am in any way being sneaky about it, please understand that I am not. . . .

After panel members one through twenty-two had been selected, but prior to voir dire, the assignment judge asked Ms. Catagen to come up from the body of the courtroom and take seat number twenty-three. The judge then embarked on voir dire of the jurors assembled. One of the jurors explained that she was "prejudiced against certain people, certain races." The judge excused that juror, explaining, "I appreciate your honesty, and we don't want people like you to serve on the Grand Jury." . . . At a hearing regarding Ramseur's allegations in 1983, one assignment judge stated that rather than selecting jurors randomly "it may be on the basis of my observation of them that I feel that they should not be selected."

Q. Now, you said that you also look for a cross section. What is a cross section? And what does a cross section consist of?

A. My concept of Essex County is that Essex County is made up of black, white, Hispanic, Oriental men and women, people who have different vocations or not vocations, people who have advocation [sic] retired, executives, assembly line workers, people who perform ministerial tasks on a day-to-day basis, housewives, mothers. I could go on and on I guess. . . .

Discrimination in the jury selection process harms the defendant, prospective and actual jurors, and the community as a whole. The defendant has an "interest in neutral jury selection procedures . . . because racial discrimination in the selection of jurors casts doubt on the integrity of the judicial process, and places the fairness of a criminal proceeding in doubt. . . .

In order to establish an equal protection violation, a party must show that there has been some actual "purposeful discrimination" in the jury selection process. . . . The crucial question at issue in the present case is whether such purposeful discrimination has been demonstrated. . . . It is necessary to establish three elements to raise an inference of discrimination in the context of grand jury selection. First, the prospective juror allegedly discriminated against must be a member of a cognizable racial group. Second, there must be a jury selection practice that permits those to discriminate who are of a mind to discriminate. . . . Finally, the defendant must show that the "opportunity for discrimination" was utilized (citations to quoted material omitted). . . .

In the present case, the first criterion is clearly met. The assignment judge's statement, after three jurors were passed over for service, that he had asked two African-Americans to sit in the body of the courtroom in his effort to create a cross section of the community on the grand jury panel demonstrates that two prospective jurors, treated in this manner, were members of a cognizable racial group. Moreover, the second criterion is met. The practices employed by the assignment judges in the Essex County grand jury selection processes provided an opportunity for discrimination. . . . The real problem here is whether that opportunity for discrimination was utilized absent the actual exclusion of a juror from the panel on the basis of race. . . .

Viewing the facts of the present case in the light of precedent, we conclude that the statements and actions of the assignment judge in the present case did not impermissibly infect the proceedings at issue and do not comprise an equal protection violation. First, there was no actual exclusion of a prospective juror on account of her race. The two jurors who were initially passed over based upon their race were eventually empaneled.

Second, we do not believe that the assignment judge's statements and actions short of actual exclusion comprised an equal protection violation. The assignment judge mentioned that he employed race as a factor in his effort to "pick a cross section of the community" and "get an even mix of people from background and races, and things like that." He also temporarily asked two African-American prospective jurors to sit in the body of the courtroom until they were belatedly empaneled. While we find objectionable this subjective sorting of the jury members and the judge's statements about balancing the jury according to race, we cannot conclude that these activities violated the Equal Protection Clause. While subjectively rigging the jury to represent his vision of the appropriate representation of Essex County's population was ill-conceived, it apparently was not motivated by a desire to discriminate purposefully against African-Americans, nor was it apparently an attempt expressly to limit the number of African-Americans who could serve on an Essex County grand jury.

DECISION: Affirmed. The conviction was upheld.

IN RE JAPANESE ELECTRONIC PRODUCTS ANTITRUST LITIGATION

U.S. Court of Appeals, Third Circuit
631 F. 2d 1069 (1980)

BACKGROUND: Two American electronics manufacturers sued seventeen Japanese competitors alleging violations of U.S. antitrust and antidumping laws. The plaintiffs demanded a trial by jury, but fourteen of the defendants (appellants below) objected on the ground that the issues presented in the case were too complex. The defendants pointed out that the jury would be called upon to make technical comparisons of thousands of products and to evaluate the impact of complex financial conditions and marketing approaches. The federal District Court ruled that the plaintiffs were entitled to a jury trial, and the defendants appealed.

Seitz, Chief Judge

Appellants . . . contend that the due process clause of the fifth amendment prohibits trial by jury of a suit that is too complex for a jury. They further contend that this due process limitation prevails over the seventh amendment's preservation of the right to jury trial. The primary value promoted by due process in factfinding procedures is "to minimize the risk of erroneous decisions." *Greenholtz v. Inmates of the Nebraska Penal and Correctional Complex.* A jury that cannot understand the evidence and the legal rules to be applied provides no reliable safeguard against erroneous decisions. Moreover, in the context of a completely adversary proceeding, like a civil trial, due process requires that "the decisionmaker's conclusion . . . rest solely on the legal rules and evidence adduced at the hearing." *Goldberg v. Kelly.* Unless the jury can understand the legal rules and evidence, we cannot realistically expect that the jury will rest its decision on them.

If a particular lawsuit is so complex that a jury cannot satisfy this requirement of due process but is nonetheless an action at law, we face a conflict between the requirements of the fifth and seventh amendments. . . .

The due process objections to jury trial of a complex case implicate values of fundamental importance. If judicial decisions are not based on factual determinations bearing some reliable degree of accuracy, legal remedies will not be applied consistently with the purposes of the laws. There is a danger that jury verdicts will be erratic and completely unpredictable, which would be inconsistent with evenhanded justice. Finally, unless the jury can understand the evidence and the legal rules sufficiently to rest its decision on them, the objective of most rules of evidence and procedure in promoting a fair trial will be lost entirely. We believe that when a jury is unable to perform its decisionmaking task with a reasonable understanding of the evidence and legal rules, it undermines the ability of a district court to render basic justice.

The loss of the right to jury trial in a suit found too complex for a jury does not implicate the same fundamental concerns. The absence of a jury trial requirement in equitable and maritime actions indicates that federal courts can provide fair trials and can grant relief in accordance with the principles of basic justice without the aid of a jury. . . .

The district court asserted that the due process argument fails to account for the special benefits that juries bring to civil litigation. Because the jury is a representative of the community and can call upon the community's wisdom and values, the legal system has relied on it to perform two important functions. The first is "black box" decisionmaking. The jury issues a verdict without an opinion to explain or justify its decision. This feature allows juries to perform a type of "jury equity," modifying harsh results of law to conform to community values in cases where a judge would have to apply the law rigidly. The second function is to accord a greater measure of legitimacy to decisions that depend upon determinations of degree rather than of absolutes, such as whether particular conduct constitutes negligence. Certain decisions of this "line-drawing" nature seem less arbitrary when made by a representative body like the jury.

In the context of a lawsuit of the complexity that we have posited, however, these features do not produce real benefits of substantial value. The function of "jury equity" may be legitimate when the jury actually modifies the law to conform to community values. However, when the jury is unable to determine the normal application of the law to the facts of a case and reaches a verdict on the basis of nothing more than its own determination of community wisdom and values, its operation is indistinguishable from arbitrary and unprincipled decisionmaking. Similarly, the "line-drawing" function is difficult to justify when the jury cannot understand the evidence or legal rules relevant to the issue of where to draw a line.

The district court also noted that preservation of the right to jury trial is important because the jury "provides a needed check on judicial power."

A jury unable to understand the evidence and legal rules is hardly a reliable and effective check on judicial power. Our liberties are more secure when judicial decisionmakers proceed rationally, consistently with the law, and on the basis of evidence produced at trial. If the jury is unable to function in this manner, it has the capacity of becoming itself a tool of arbitrary and erratic judicial power.

DECISION: The Circuit Court of Appeals ruled that the plaintiffs were not entitled to a jury trial.

Burden of Proof

It is commonly said that the plaintiff bears the "burden of proof" in civil litigation, just as the government has the burden of proof in a criminal prosecution. This means that if the plaintiff does not prove all the essential elements of his or her case, he or she is not entitled to win regardless of how weak the defense is. The plaintiff must cross the threshold of establishing a **prima facie case**, which means that the plaintiff must present evidence on each essential element in his or her own case to the degree that would entitle the plaintiff to win assuming that the evidence is not contradicted. Once the plaintiff has established a prima facie case, the burden shifts to the defendant to rebut the plaintiff's evidence and/or to establish affirmative defenses that would excuse the defendant from liability.

Burden of proof also refers to the level of certainty with which the plaintiff must establish his or her case. In civil cases, the plaintiff generally must prove his or her case by a **preponderance of the evidence**, which means that the plaintiff must establish in the factfinder's mind that it is more likely than not that each essential element of the plaintiff's case is present. Assume that a case turns on whether the defendant was speeding. Witnesses for the plaintiff have testified that the defendant was speeding, and witnesses for the defendant have testified that the defendant was traveling within the legal speed limit. In order to find for the plaintiff, the jury must be more convinced by the plaintiff's evidence than by the defendant's evidence—if only by the slightest degree. This is a much easier burden than that faced at a criminal trial, in which the prosecution must prove the defendant's guilt beyond a reasonable doubt. At a criminal trial, a jury should not convict if it has a reasonable doubt as to the defendant's guilt, even if the jury finds the prosecution's case to be substantially more convincing than that of the defendant.

Some civil cases must be proved by *clear and convincing evidence*, which is a standard that is tougher than the preponderance standard but not as demanding as the criminal standard.

In the *J.C. Penney Insurance Company* case, which follows, the court discusses whether the test of clear and convincing evidence should be applied in a case in which an insurance claim was denied because the claimant was suspected of setting the fire himself.

J.C. PENNEY INSURANCE COMPANY V. VARNEY

U.S. Court of Appeals, Sixth Circuit
853 F. 2d 926 (1988)

BACKGROUND: Varney's home burned on March 9, 1985 as the result of arson. Suits were filed in which J.C. Penney sought a determination that it did not have to pay a claim for loss on Varney's homeowner's policy, which had been issued by J.C. Penney Insurance. The case was heard by a jury, which found that the insurance claim did not have to be paid. Varney appealed.

Lively, Circuit Judge

The parties stipulated that J.C. Penney Casualty Insurance Co. (Penney) issued a homeowner's insurance policy to Varney on November 16, 1984. The policy which covered Varney's residence in Hardy, Kentucky, was in force on March 9, 1985, when the property was destroyed by fire. The parties stipulated that the fire which destroyed the property "was incendiary in origin and intentionally set by some person," but there was no agreement as to who was responsible for the fire. One of Penney's affirmative defenses to Varney's claim was that the fire "was caused by the Defendant, or others as agent of the Defendant acting by or at the direction of or with the knowledge and consent of the Defendant. . . ." Since this was the only contested issue of liability, the district court properly placed the burden of proof on Penney.

One of Varney's requested jury instructions read as follows:

> The burden of the plaintiff/insurance company is to show by clear and convincing proof that either the defendant, Varney, burned his home or conspired with some unknown third party to have his home and contents destroyed by fire.
>
> By clear and convincing evidence, the Court means that you should be fully satisfied, satisfied to a moral certainty, and be clearly convinced that the defendant, Varney, burned his home, or had it burned, in order to return a verdict for the plaintiff/insurance company. You should not find for the plaintiff/insurance company on mere surmise, conjecture or suspicion of Varney's involvement in the destruction of his house and contents.

The district court refused to give the requested instruction. . . . Thereafter, the court charged the jury in accordance with its previous rulings:

> At the beginning of the case, I told you that the plaintiff has the burden of proving the case by a preponderance of the evidence. That means that the plaintiff has to produce evidence which, considered in the light of all the facts, lead you to believe that what the plaintiff claims is more likely true than not. To put it differently, if you were to put the plaintiff's and the defendant's evidence on opposite sides of the scales, plaintiff's would have to make the scales tip slightly on that side. If plaintiff fails to meet this burden, your verdict must be for the defendant.

It appears that the Kentucky Supreme Court has never decided between the PREPONDERANCE of the EVIDENCE standard and the CLEAR and CONVINCING evidence standard in a case of this kind. However, Kentucky courts have consistently applied the preponderance standard when the issue has arisen. The CLEAR and CONVINCING evidence standard has been applied in cases where a party seeks to prove an oral modification or rescission of a written agreement, seeks to establish a lost will, or seeks relief or recovery on a claim of fraud or mutual mistake. . . . No Kentucky case has held that an insurer must establish an arson defense by clear and convincing evidence. We are not completely comfortable deciding a diversity case principally upon the authority of a state decision rendered more than 100 years ago. However, insurers frequently defend by asserting that one claiming the proceeds of a fire policy caused the insured premises to be burned.

. . . While the precedent may not be as firmly established in Kentucky, the decided cases indicate that Kentucky courts will continue to treat the arson defense as an ordinary issue in a civil case and apply the preponderance of the evidence standard.

DECISION: Affirmed. The insurance claim did not have to be paid.

With a counterclaim, the roles are switched: The defendant generally has the burden of proving a counterclaim by a preponderance of the evidence.

Trial Stages

The principal steps in the trial after jury selection are described below.

Opening Statements   Each side is given the opportunity to summarize the case that it intends to present. The plaintiff's attorney generally goes first.

Presentation of Evidence   After the opening statements, each side is given the opportunity to present its case. The plaintiff's attorney generally goes first. Each side builds its case by presenting evidence, which may be in the form of oral testimony, documents, physical exhibits, and demonstrations.

Oral testimony may be taken from the ordinary witnesses and from expert witnesses. The testimony is prompted by questions from the attorneys for both sides. Generally, an attorney will call his or her witness to the stand and ask questions. The initial questioning by an attorney of his or her own witness is known as **direct examination**. The opposing attorney then has the right to **cross examination**, in which he or she may question the witness on matters raised in direct examination. The attorney who originally called the witness then generally may retain the witness for **redirect examination**, which is limited to matters raised in cross-examination. Matters raised in redirect examination may be the subject of the opposing side's **recross examination**. The process generally is allowed to continue until both sides are satisfied.

The examination of witnesses and the presentation of other evidence must comply with the rules of evidence, which are designed to ensure that the jury isn't influenced by irrelevant, speculative, or redundant matters. We've all seen television and movie dramatizations of courtroom proceedings in which an attorney shouts, "I object!" An objection during testimony is usually prompted by the attorney's belief that the other side's line of questioning has strayed outside the bounds permitted by the rules of evidence.

After the plaintiff's witnesses have testified, the defendant frequently moves to dismiss on the grounds that the plaintiff has failed to prove all the facts necessary to establish a case. If the court agrees, it can terminate the case at this point. A similar motion is often made by one or both of the parties after all the evidence has been presented. In many jurisdictions this motion is referred to as a **motion for a directed verdict**. If it is granted, the case is in effect taken from the jury and determined by the judge.

Closing Arguments   After both sides have rested their respective cases, each side may present a closing argument to urge the jury to return a verdict in its favor.

Instructions to the Jury   After all the evidence has been submitted and the attorneys for both sides have summed up their cases, the judge explains to the jury the law that applies to the case. This process, which is called *instructing* or *charging* the jury, presents the jury with information about the essential facts that each party must prove to support its position as well as the relationships between the evidence presented and the legal issues involved.

Instructions given by the court are ordinarily based upon the requests made by opposing counsel. The instructions are read to the jury in open court, and in many jurisdictions they are furnished to the jury in writing as well.

Basically, the instructions present alternatives indicating the legal result of each possible factual finding the jury might make. Suppose that in litigation involving Joe, a defendant, and Mary, a plaintiff, the single contested fact is whether Joe made a statement to Mary with the intention of deceiving her. Legally, if he did intend to deceive, he will be liable; if he did not, the case against him will be dismissed. The judge might charge the jury as follows: "If you determine that the defendant made the statement with the intention of deceiving the plaintiff, you must find for the plaintiff. If, however, you determine that the defendant's statement was made with no intention of deceiving the plaintiff, you must find for the defendant."

Another important function of the judge's instructions is to explain to the jury the rules regarding which side has the burden of proof on each issue in the case.

Although the basic concept underlying the charge to the jury is quite simple, in most cases there are numerous factual differences that can influence the outcome of the case. The result is that instructions, unless carefully drafted, can confuse the jury. In addition, determining proper instructions in many cases is a complicated, argumentative process that delays litigation and frequently results in appeal. Because of these problems, a number of jurisdictions now either encourage or require the use of standard or patterned instructions. These instructions are developed by bar associations and courts to explain the law to the jury adequately and simply.

THE VERDICT   A trial is usually concluded when the jury brings in a **verdict**, an answer to the questions that the court has submitted to it. In a civil action the verdict will be either general or special. A **general verdict** is one in which the jurors comprehensively determine the issues for either the plaintiff or the defendant. If the jury finds for the plaintiff, the amount of damages will also be stated. In a **special verdict** the jury will provide written answers to specific questions of fact that the court submitted to it. The court, using these answers, then applies the law and resolves the issues in dispute between the parties.

The losing side might make a motion for a judgment notwithstanding the verdict, also known as a **motion for judgment n.o.v.** The judge may grant this motion if, on the basis of the evidence presented, no reasonable jury could possibly have ruled in the way that the jury has ruled. For example, a judge might grant a motion for judgment n.o.v. to overturn a verdict for the plaintiff if the plaintiff has not presented credible evidence to prove each essential element of his or her case.

Judgment and Execution

The **judgment** establishes the relief to which the parties are entitled. If the jury finds for the defendant, the judgment will dismiss the plaintiff's suit. If the plaintiff wins the case, ordinarily the judgment will award him or her a sum of money. When a monetary award does not furnish the plaintiff adequate relief, the court may order relief of another sort.

If the plaintiff has won a monetary judgment, the court provides machinery for locating the defendant's assets, for preventing the defendant from disposing of these assets, and finally for selling the assets with proceeds of the sale being used to satisfy the judgment. The defendant is often referred to as a **judgment debtor**. The final

step is accomplished by a sheriff who seizes and then sells the assets. If the judgment debtor's assets are in the hands of a third party, the court can order the third party to turn the property over to the plaintiff. This procedure, referred to as **garnishment**, is sometimes used to require an employer to turn over to a creditor a portion of the wages of an employee who is a judgment debtor.

Sometimes a judgment debtor has assets that are income producing. Under these circumstances the court can appoint a receiver who will operate the property and pay the proceeds to the creditor after deducting operating expenses. Often the receiver will be empowered to negotiate the sale of the property and apply the net proceeds to the debt instead of having the property seized by the sheriff and auctioned off at what might be an inopportune time.

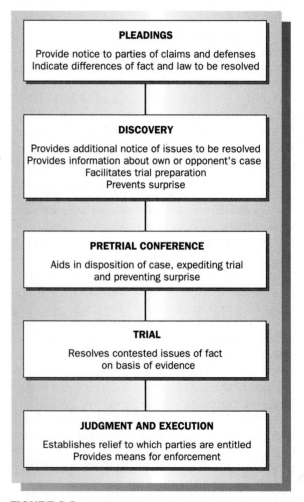

FIGURE 3-3

The Litigation Process

The Appellate Process

The function of an appellate court is to review the legal rulings that one or both of the parties think the trial court judge made incorrectly. This is a different function from that of the trial court, which is charged primarily with deciding differences between the parties about the facts. Because of this difference in function, the appellate process differs substantially from the trial process.

In an appeal, a determination of facts is unnecessary, since all factual issues have already been decided at the trial. Because the oral testimony of witnesses and other types of evidence are not needed, the direct and cross examination of witnesses and the rules of evidence, which are designed to help the finders of fact make a correct determination, are eliminated. Interim procedures such as discovery and motions for summary judgment also have no place in an appellate court, since these procedures exist to help resolve factual issues.

When deciding if a legal error has been committed, the appellate court gets considerable information. This includes a record of the trial. Additional input is supplied by the parties, who, in our adversary system, are responsible for either pointing out the errors or supporting the rulings of the lower court. In fact, if one or both of the parties does not argue that some substantial legal error has been made, the appellate court has no power to review the trial.

The input from the parties generally consists of oral arguments before the court supported by written presentations called **briefs**. The appellate court judges, especially in the higher courts, make their decisions on the basis of the oral arguments of the parties, the briefs, and their own research and group discussion. For many cases the appellate court decision then is supported by a published written opinion.

Another difference between the trial and appellate process is the number of judges involved. Appeals are heard by a number of judges, whereas in a trial a single judge presides.

Alternative Dispute Resolution

Litigation is a costly and time-consuming endeavor. Our judicial system has been overburdened with a tremendous caseload. As a result,

---

ISSUES AND TRENDS
Using the Judicial System to Intimidate the Public

Developers planning major projects often encounter opposition from homeowners' associations, environmental groups, citizens' groups, and private citizens. In recent years, developers have discovered a weapon to discourage such opposition: SLAPP suits (strategic lawsuits against public participation). SLAPP works like this: A developer sues citizens and groups who publicly criticize the developer's project, alleging defamation and conspiracy. The lawsuit seeks some inflated amount in damages—the average amount asked in SLAPP suits was reported in 1992 to be about $9 million. Although the suit is unlikely to ultimately succeed—the defendants, after all, have merely exercised their First Amendment right to free speech—the defendants often are unable to bear the financial burden of protracted litigation. SLAPP suits typically go on for years. Some individual defendants are forced to spend life savings, and some homeowners' associations are forced to deplete their treasuries, to pay their lawyers.

Legislation has been introduced in some states to restrict SLAPP suits. One proposal would allow a court to block a suit unless the plaintiff could show that it was substantially likely to prevail. Some have criticized such proposals as denying parties their day in court, but others contend that such restrictions are necessary to keep the judicial system from being abused by those who would use it to intimidate the public.

---

some cases don't make it to trial until years after they're filed. More and more businesses are looking for cheaper, quicker ways to resolve disputes.

Alternative dispute resolution (ADR) is a term that describes a number of procedures that have become popular in recent years as alternatives to litigation. ADR procedures are less formal than litigation, and are therefore cheaper and less time-consuming. Some of the more popular ADR procedures are discussed below.

Arbitration

Arbitration is a process in which a dispute is submitted to a third party who is chosen by the parties to the dispute. The arbitrator, who usually has some expertise in the subject matter of the dispute, hears arguments, reviews evidence, and renders a decision (known as an **award**). The process is much less formal than a trial. It also takes less time: many arbitration proceedings can be completed in an hour or two. Some arbitrations are conducted by a three-member panel—each party chooses one member of the panel and those members jointly select a third member.

An arbitrator, unlike a judge, is not bound by precedent. An arbitrator is likely to rely more heavily on his or her own experience and is given wide latitude to fashion an award that he or she believes to be fair.

A party who is not satisfied with an arbitration award generally may turn to the judicial system for relief. In **binding arbitration**, however, the arbitration award is final. Binding arbitration is sometimes required by statute, but in most cases arbitration is binding only if both parties agree in advance to be bound by it. Another special form of arbitration is **last-offer arbitration**, in which the arbitrator must choose between the final positions of the two parties. Last-offer arbitration is used in major league baseball when a player and club owner cannot agree on the player's salary.

Arbitration is probably the most heavily utilized and well-established ADR technique. It has long been used for labor-management disputes and for disputes between businesses, but today it is also used for consumer complaints, personal injury cases, and a wide variety of other situations.

Some courts now require that certain disputes be sent to arbitration. As part of an experimental arbitration program set up by Congress in 1988, federal courts in some districts may compel arbitration in any case in which the monetary award in controversy is less than a certain amount. A party who is not satisfied with the award in a compulsory arbitration may generally seek a **trial de novo**, a regular judicial trial in which the prior arbitration proceedings are not considered. Compulsory arbitration programs have also been adopted by California and several other states.

Private Courts

Private courts, also known as "rent a judge" systems, offer the parties the opportunity to pay a third party to judge their dispute. Retired judges generally preside over private courts. Procedures for private court proceedings vary, but the process can be similar to arbitration. The television show *People's Court* is a private court system.

Mediation

Mediation is the utilization of a neutral third party to attempt to bring the parties to settlement. Mediation is usually an informal, voluntary process that is designed to move the parties toward a mutually satisfactory agreement. Although the mediator participates in the negotiations, he or she does not decide the dispute. Mediation is often used in labor negotiations, but has also been used in landlord-tenant disagreements, domestic disputes, and disagreements between neighbors.

Minitrial

A **minitrial** is a proceeding in which the lawyers for both parties present a brief version of their case before a panel made up of representatives from both sides (typically managers of business organizations). The process is sometimes presided over by a neutral third party approved by both sides. No decision is rendered by the tribunal; rather, after each side makes its presentation, the party representatives attempt to negotiate a settlement. Minitrial proceedings are generally kept confidential.

Summary Jury Trial

A **summary jury trial** is an expedited proceeding that takes place before a judge and jury after the discovery phase of litigation. After each party presents a summarized version of its case, the jury renders a verdict. Unless the parties have agreed otherwise in advance, the verdict is not binding. The verdict is generally used to drive the parties toward settlement.

Fact-Finding

Fact-finding is another alternative mechanism for dispute resolution. This process is primarily used in public sector collective bargaining. The

TABLE 3-1

Concept Summary	Alternative Dispute Resolution
Arbitration	Dispute decided by arbitrator or panel of arbitrators chosen by parties
	Arbitrators often have expertise in subject matter of dispute
	Presentations are less formal than court proceedings
Private courts	Parties hire neutral third party to decide dispute, typically a retired judge
Mediation	Third party participates in negotiations and attempts to bridge gaps in parties' positions, but does not decide dispute
Minitrial	Lawyers for each side present summary version of case to tribunal made up of management from both sides
	Tribunal does not decide dispute
	After presentations, both sides retire to attempt to settle case without their lawyers
Summary jury trial	After discovery, both sides present summary version of case before judge and jury
	Jury returns a verdict
	Unless parties have agreed to be bound by verdict, verdict is used as basis for settlement discussions
Fact-finding	Neutral fact finder, drawing on information from parties and independent research, recommends solutions to each unresolved issue
	Used primarily in public sector collective bargaining
Conciliation	Informal process in which third party attempts to bring together parties not yet ready to come to the table

fact finder, drawing on information provided by the interested parties and independent research, recommends a written solution to each outstanding issue. The recommended solution is never binding, but often it paves the way for further negotiation and mediation.

Conciliation

Conciliation is an informal process in which the third party tries to bring the disputing parties together in hopes of lowering tensions, improving communication, helping to interpret issues, providing technical assistance, exploring potential solutions, and bringing about a negotiated settlement, either informally or, in a subsequent step, through formal mediation. Conciliation frequently is used in volatile conflicts and in disputes where the parties are unable, unwilling, or unprepared to come to the table to negotiate their differences.

Table 3-1 is a Concept Summary that describes the various alternative dispute resolution techniques.

Review Questions and Problems

Key Terms

adversary principle
settlement
pleadings
summons
complaint
answer
affirmative defenses
counterclaim
reply
motion
demurrer
motion for judgment on the pleadings
discovery
deposition
deponent
interrogatories

request for admission
protective order
motion to compel
motion for summary judgment
pretrial conference
prima facie case
preponderance of the evidence
direct examination
cross examination
redirect examination
recross examination
motion for a directed verdict
verdict
general verdict
special verdict

motion for judgment n.o.v. last-offer arbitration
judgment trial de novo
judgment debtor private court
garnishment mediation
briefs minitrial
arbitration summary jury trial
award fact-finding
binding arbitration conciliation

Discussion Questions

1. Explain the purpose of the following in civil litigation: (a) pleadings, (b) long-arm statutes, (c) motion for a directed verdict, (d) full faith and credit clause, and (e) peremptory challenge.

2. What is the adversary principle?

3. What is the function of a jury in a civil trial?

4. Under what circumstances should a motion for summary judgment be granted?

5. Why have alternative dispute resolution procedures become more popular in recent years?

6. Compare and contrast the various alternative dispute resolution procedures.

Review Problems

1. Taylor was a party to litigation involving a real estate problem. Taylor's friend Bennett testified in Taylor's behalf at the trial. Bennett's testimony was critical to the outcome of the case. Taylor lost the case and decided to appeal. When Taylor informed Bennett of his intention to appeal, Bennett told him that he could not testify a second time, since the experience had drained him emotionally. Taylor told Bennett that it would not be necessary for him to testify again. Explain why.

2. Smith and Barney were involved in a dispute involving the legal meaning of a clause in their contract. Smith's attorney stated that the only difference that the parties had was a difference of law. Neither party would concede, and Barney contemplated litigation. Would his case be brought in a court with original jurisdiction or in a court with appellate jurisdiction? Support your answer.

3. Sam Falcone owns a house in a predominately Italian neighborhood. His neighbor, Tony Fatio, tells Falcone that the Fatios are going to sell their home. Believing that the ethnic character of the area is changing, Sam contracts to sell his home. Tony than tells Sam that the Fatios have decided not to sell. Sam is upset and hires an attorney to sue Fatio. What legal steps should Fatio's attorney take if Fatio is served with a complaint? Why?

4. Smith is suing Harris for personal injuries arising as a result of an auto accident involving the two.

Smith plans to call a witness to testify that Harris ran a red light. Harris plans to call a witness to testify that it was Smith, not Harris, who ran the red light. After both witnesses have been deposed, Harris moves for summary judgment. What should the court consider in deciding whether to grant the motion? Without assuming additional facts, do you think the court should grant the motion?

5. Grant sues Lee for breach of contract. An essential element of Grant's claim is that a contract between the parties existed, but Grant fails to produce any evidence of a contract at trial. What motion should Lee's attorney make when Grant rests his case? If the motion is denied and the jury returns a verdict for Grant, what motion should Lee make at that point? What might Lee do if that motion is denied?

6. Yummy Foods is sued by Barker, who claims that she became severely ill after eating a Yummy Foods frozen dinner. Yummy Foods' attorney answers the complaint with a general denial, but knows little about the case. What information would Yummy Foods' attorney like to obtain in order to prepare for the case, and what specific discovery tools should the attorney utilize in order to obtain the information?

Case Problems

1. Thiel sued Southern Pacific for injuries he sustained after falling from a train. The jury returned a verdict for Southern Pacific. Thiel appealed, claiming that the method for selecting the jury had been improper. The attorney for Southern Pacific testified that he had deliberately excluded anyone who worked for a daily or hourly wage. Do you think that Thiel has grounds to challenge the verdict?

2. Schaffer sued Donegan, his medical expert from a previous malpractice suit, because Schaffer was forced to settle his malpractice claim when Donegan informed him during the malpractice trial that he had changed his mind about causation and could no longer testify that the treating doctors' negligence caused Schaffer's injuries and losses. In the trial against the medical expert, the deciding issue was whether Donegan changed his testimony for valid medical reasons. After losing in the lower court, Schaffer appealed on the grounds that Donegan should have had the burden of proving he changed his testimony for valid medical reasons; thus, the court erred by placing the burden on him to prove that Donegan changed his testimony for invalid medical reasons. Who had the burden of proving why the expert changed his testimony?

3. In a will contest, Crain claimed that Brown used undue influence to compel their father to draft a new will which left less to Crain. At the jury trial there was conflicting evidence as to whether at the time of writing the new will the father was feeble, blind, and deaf, or whether he was active and independent with only moderately impaired

sight and hearing. After losing in the lower court, Crain appealed, alleging that the trial court should have instructed the jury to consider the father's physical or mental deterioration and his blindness and deafness in determining whether there were sufficient suspicious circumstances to presume undue influence. Would such instructions be proper?

4. A dispute arose between employer Christensen and the union association SCCC over whether the master labor agreement negotiated by SCCC and a multiemployer bargaining association applied in San Diego County, a county not listed in the original agreement but added by amendment. The SCCC claimed it applied because the short-form memorandum agreement Christiansen signed provides that short-form signatories are bound by the master agreement and any renewal or amendments. The short form also includes a broad arbitration provision stating that the parties agree to submit all disputes to arbitration, pursuant to which SCCC filed a grievance. Christiansen instituted an action in federal court and obtained an order stating that the arbitration provision did not apply to this dispute and the agreement did not apply to San Diego County. SCCC appealed, claiming that the dispute should have been decided by the arbitrators. Should the question of whether the labor agreement applies in San Diego County be decided by arbitration or by the courts?

4

Constitutional Law and Business

Business in the United States is conducted in a legal environment over which the U.S. Constitution rules supreme. Most of the states have constitutions, but usually, and all the time in this chapter, when we say "constitutional law" or "the Constitution" we mean the U.S. Constitution.

Business in other countries is often not governed by a constitution. England, the principal source of our legal heritage, has never had a constitution. In fact, the thirteen colonies did not create the Constitution immediately upon independence. A Continental Congress adopted the Articles of Confederation in 1778. When it was felt that a stronger central government was needed, the Constitutional Convention met in Philadelphia and drafted the Articles of the U.S. Constitution, which have been in effect, largely unchanged, since 1788.

Important constitutional issues affecting business are also discussed in other chapters of this book. The commerce clause, the legal basis for most federal legislation concerning business, was explained in Chapter 2. There you also learned that the Constitution separates the powers of the federal government in a tripartite, or three-part, framework. The legislative, executive, and judicial branches check and balance each other. In Chapter 5, you will read about constitutional issues in criminal procedure, such as Fourth Amendment search-and-seizure law, self-incrimination under the Fifth Amendment, and the Sixth Amendment right to counsel. The governmental power of eminent domain granted by the Fifth and Fourteenth Amendments is examined in Chapter 40. In this chapter, you will see how the

Constitution provides fundamental rules for business to follow under our legal system.

Federalism

What right does the government have to govern business? What is the source of its power? The Preamble to the Constitution begins "We the People" to make it clear that government power comes from the people. In our system of **federalism,** this power is shared by the federal, state, and local governments. The people delegate specifically identified powers to the federal government. Any government power not granted to the federal government in the Constitution is kept by the state and local governments.

The limited enumerated powers of the federal government have grown over time, largely through actions of the federal government itself. For example, Congress, the federal legislature, has the power "[t]o make all Laws which shall be necessary and proper for carrying out" the Constitution. And Congress has made many laws. As federal government power has grown, the power of the states has shrunk. The Constitution itself has also developed, through amendment and interpretation. As a result, especially since the Civil War, states have lost much of their right to do things differently from each other.

Federal Supremacy and the Preemption Doctrine

Federal law is supreme—so says the Constitution. "This Constitution, and the Laws of the United States which shall be made in Pursuance thereof . . . shall be the supreme Law of the Land." This supremacy clause establishes the **preemption doctrine** that all law must comply with federal law. If constitutional federal law expressly or impliedly shows the intent to regulate an area of law, it preempts the field; that is, it overrides state and local laws. If a conflict exists between them, federal law prevails. This is the principle of **federal supremacy.**

Federal supremacy results in a limitation of state and local governing authority over business. In the case of *Bonito Boats, Inc. v. Thunder Craft Boats, Inc.*, Thunder Craft Boats copied a Bonito Boats unpatented fiberglass recreational boat without permission and in violation of a Florida

statute. The Supreme Court decided that the state law was unenforceable because it conflicted with and was preempted by federal patent law authorized by the patent clause of the Constitution, a field of regulation reserved to Congress.

Judicial Review

What happens if a legislative or executive act affecting business conflicts with the Constitution itself? The Constitution is our ultimate legal authority, and no act that contradicts it can stand. The Constitution rules supreme over all law in the United States. But the Constitution is often written in broad terms. Who decides what it means? The courts interpret the Constitution and the U.S. Supreme Court has the final say.

Under our system of checks and balances, the judiciary has the power of **judicial review.** The authority of courts to determine the constitutionality of legally challenged governmental acts has been accepted since 1803 when it was asserted by the first Chief Justice of the Supreme Court, John Marshall, in the case of *Marbury v. Madison.* Any federal, state, or local law that violates the Constitution is unconstitutional—invalid and unenforceable. Even laws passed by the Congress must pass this constitutionality test if contested. In 1989 Congress passed a Flag Protection Act criminalizing burning of the United States flag. Shawn D. Eichman and others burned several flags on the steps of the Capitol to protest United States foreign and domestic policy and they were prosecuted. The Court decided in *United States v. Eichman* that the Flag Protection Act unconstitutionally violated the freedom of speech rights of the defendants.

The Constitution also rules supreme over the executive branch. As John Marshall observed in *Marbury v. Madison,* the United States "has been emphatically termed a government of laws, and not of men." Even presidential acts are subject to judicial review. During the Watergate investigation President Richard Nixon claimed executive privilege and withheld documents from the judiciary. The Supreme Court declared his act unconstitutional, and Nixon acquiesced.

The federal legislative branch also has some review power over the federal judiciary based on the Constitution. Although federal judges interpret the Constitution, they too are subordinate to its rules. Congress may remove from office a federal judge who violates the Constitution, for example, by taking bribes.

The Evolution of the Constitution

The Constitution is a living document. It was intended to last a long time. It is, as the preamble says, for "ourselves and our Posterity." And the Constitution has lasted, mainly because it has evolved.

The Constitution of 1788 was quite different from the Constitution of today: it has been amended twenty-six times. The Bill of Rights, declaring the freedoms of religion, speech, and the press, freedom from unreasonable search and seizure, and the right to due process of law, was not adopted until 1791. Slavery was not prohibited until the Thirteenth Amendment in 1865; federal income tax was first permitted in 1913 by the Sixteenth Amendment; and only white men who were at least 21 years old could vote in 1788. African Americans were given the right to vote in 1870 by the Fifteenth Amendment, female suffrage came in 1920 with the Nineteenth Amendment, and the voting age became 18 years old in 1971 with the most recent amendment, the Twenty-Sixth.

But amendment is not the only way the Constitution has changed. The meaning of the Constitution has developed through interpretation by courts, especially the Supreme Court. The basic principles of the Constitution are written broadly enough for judges to understand it differently as our society and economy change. Courts face new problems they must decide based on a Constitution mostly written over 200 years ago. And it is the miracle of the Constitution that it is resilient enough to have survived all those years.

Sometimes the Supreme Court reinterprets the Constitution; that is, it changes its mind about what the Constitution means. In 1896, the Court decided in *Plessy v. Ferguson* that public segregation was constitutional as long as facilities were equal. In 1954, the Court decided in *Brown v. Board of Education* that separate public school facilities are inherently unequal. Such changes are rare, partly because of the respect of Supreme Court Justices for their predecessors and the doctrine of stare decisis. The slow evolution of constitutional law helps businesses predict the legal consequences of their actions. While judicial opinions often lag behind actions of the legislative and executive branches, they also tend to be longer lasting.

State Action

The Constitution applies to **state action,** that is, the public actions of governments and, except for slavery, not to the private actions of individuals and organizations. If the Senate Ethics Committee subpoenas a senator for delivery of his diaries to investigate sexual harassment charges, state action occurs and constitutional issues are raised. On the other hand, if a purely private business takes an employee's diary from an office desk, no constitutional right is violated. Federal, state, or local legislation may apply constitutional principles to private action. But state action, governmental action through one of its branches or through an agent, is generally a prerequisite for the application of the Constitution.

When the government acts directly, state action has clearly taken place. What if a private person or organization acts like a government? Such action may be treated as state action and trigger constitutional rights. The test is whether the functions involved are traditionally exclusive to the state, in other words a duck test: if it walks like a duck and quacks like a duck, it is treated like a duck. If a company creates a company town and provides all public functions and activities, its actions are state action. But a shopping mall is not the "functional equivalent" of a town. The action of a privately owned electric utility granted a monopoly by the state is not state action, and, therefore, its customers are not entitled to the Constitutional right of due process from the company. The same conclusion results with nursing homes and specialized private schools, even if they are heavily regulated and almost completely state-funded, because such functions are not "the exclusive province of the state."

Governments necessarily act through people and their actions are state action. But what if the government hires a private person or organization to act for it? As we reinvent government, it is increasingly common that public functions are contracted out to private businesses. In the United States, there has already been privatization of public parking lots and airports, building inspection, waste management (garbage collection and disposal), public education, and prisons. Does the Constitution apply in these cases? Must such businesses abide by constitutional law? In many cases the line between state and private action is blurred.

Does privatization result in a loss of constitutional protections because there is no state action? *West v. Atkins*, a case in which a private person is hired to work for the government, addresses this question.

WEST V. ATKINS

U.S. Supreme Court
487 U.S. 42 (1988)

BACKGROUND: Quincy West, a North Carolina state prison inmate, tore an Achilles tendon playing volleyball. Samuel Atkins, a private physician contracted by the state to provide orthopedic services to inmates, was assigned to West. West, a prisoner in "close custody," was not free to choose another doctor. West was treated with casts for several months, but his medical care ended while West's ankle was still swollen and painful and without surgery he alleged the doctor said was necessary. West sued Atkins under federal law (42 U.S.C. §1983) for violation of his constitutional Eighth Amendment right to be free from cruel and unusual punishment through inadequate treatment. Under this federal law, individuals may be liable for loss of constitutional rights "under color of state law," that is, through state action. The district court held by summary judgment that a "contract physician" does not act "under color of state law." The circuit court of appeals affirmed.

Blackmun, Justice

This case presents the question whether a physician who is under contract with the State to provide medical services to inmates at a state-prison hospital on a part-time basis acts "under color of state law," . . . when he treats an inmate. . . .

To state a claim under §1983, a plaintiff must allege the violation of a right secured by the Constitution and laws of the United States, and must show that the alleged deprivation was committed by a person acting under color of state law. . . .

[D]eliberate indifference to a prisoner's serious medical needs, whether by a prison doctor or a prison guard, is prohibited by the Eighth Amendment. . . . The only issue before us is whether . . . respondent [Atkins] acted under color of state law in treating West's injury.

The traditional definition of acting under color of state law requires that the defendant . . . have exercised power "possessed by virtue of state law and made possible only because the wrongdoer is clothed with the authority of state law." . . . To constitute state action, . . . "the party charged with the deprivation must be a person who may fairly be said to be a state actor." "[S]tate employment is generally sufficient to render the defendant a state actor.". . . Thus, generally, a public employee acts under color of state law while acting in his official capacity or while exercising his responsibilities pursuant to state law. . . .

Respondent [Atkins], as a physician employed by North Carolina to provide medical services to state prison inmates, acted under color of state law for purposes of §1983 when undertaking his duties in treating petitioner's injury. Such conduct is fairly attributable to the State. . . .

"An inmate must rely on prison authorities to treat his medical needs; if the authorities fail to do so, those needs will not be met." In light of this, . . . the State has a constitutional obligation, under the Eighth Amendment, to provide adequate medical care to those whom it has incarcerated. North Carolina employs physicians, such as respondent [Atkins], and defers to their professional judgment, in order to fulfill this obligation. By virtue of this relationship, effected by state law, Doctor Atkins is authorized and obliged to treat prison inmates, such as West. He does so "clothed with the authority of state law." . . .

Contracting out prison medical care does not relieve the State of its constitutional duty to provide adequate medical treatment to those in its custody, and it does not deprive the State's prisoners of the means to vindicate their Eighth Amendment rights. . . .

Scalia, Justice (concurring)

I do not believe that a doctor who lacks supervisory or other penological duties can inflict "punishment" within the meaning of that term in the Eighth Amendment. . . .

Decision: The circuit court of appeals decision was reversed and remanded. West got a trial on the merits of his case.

Constitutional Rights

The Constitution protects certain personal rights. Some of these rights are expressed either as freedom from state action ("Congress shall make no law respecting" or "No State shall deprive") or as rights not to be infringed ("the right of the people"). Other fundamental rights are implied either by enumerated rights such as a right to liberty under the due process clause or by the Ninth Amendment reference to other rights "retained by the people" including rights to interstate travel, vote, and marry, and a general right of privacy.

Whether expressed or implied, personal rights limit governmental powers. But although Constitutional rights are often stated in absolute terms, in practice they are not absolute. Sometimes personal rights and governmental powers conflict. When this happens, the courts use legal tests to weigh the legal interests and achieve an appropriate balance. Which test is used depends on the rights involved. The more important the right, the less the power of government to encroach on them.

Whose rights are protected from prohibited state action? Except for privileges and immunities (discussed later in this chapter) and participation in the political process (such as voting and holding federal office), constitutional rights refer to people or persons and not citizens. Therefore, all natural persons, including illegal aliens, are constitutionally protected from prohibited governmental action. Corporations are artificial persons, but as legal persons that can sue and be sued they have constitutional rights, although these rights are often less than those of natural persons.

The rights stated in the first ten amendments, adopted in 1791 and collectively known as the Bill of Rights, applied at first only to federal state action. However, the Supreme Court has ruled that most of these rights are incorporated by the Fourteenth Amendment of 1868 under its due process clause and these rights now apply to state state action as well. Through this incorporation doctrine, the "war between the states" has resulted in a union of shared fundamental rights not to be infringed upon by any government, be it federal, state, or local.

First Amendment

The Constitution means what the Supreme Court says it means. No better example of this principle can be found than the cases interpreting the rights expressed in the First Amendment to the Constitution. This amendment states that "Congress shall make no law" limiting the freedoms of religion, speech, the press, and peaceable assembly. The wording seems unambiguous, allowing for *no* law limiting these rights. However, even these enumerated freedoms are not absolute in our legal system. They must be balanced against any conflicting governmental interests or constitutional rights and do not always prevail.

Freedom from and of Religion

Business does not take place in a cultural vacuum. Religion is a strong element in our culture. The First Amendment provides for freedom from and of religion. If government wants to legislate the relationship between religion and business, it must be aware that, according to the Supreme

TABLE 4-1

Freedom from and of Religion			
Classification	**Test**	**State Action**	**State Interest**
Establishment and free exercise clauses	Strict scrutiny	Necessary	Compelling

Court, "a statute must not only have a secular purpose and not foster excessive entanglement of government with religion, its primary effect must not advance or inhibit religion." How should government respond to our religiously diverse work force? What rights do workers have concerning religion? What are the rights of corporations?

Establishment Clause

Congress is directed in the First Amendment to "make no law respecting an establishment of religion." Under this **establishment clause**, can government make "blue laws" establishing Sunday, the Christian Sabbath, as a uniform day of rest and tranquility? What then of Muslims, Jews, and Seventh-day Adventists who observe other days as their Sabbaths? What of the right of atheists and agnostics to be free from religion? Does the establishment clause, as incorporated by the Fourteenth Amendment, prohibit a state from requiring businesses to close on Sunday? The Court said no. Does it bar a state from requiring businesses to permit workers to observe the Sabbath of their religion? The Court said yes. Donald Thornton, a Presbyterian, was a department manager at a Caldor department store. He told his boss that he would not be able to work on the Presbyterian Sabbath, Sunday. Caldor demoted Thornton to a clerical position. Thornton sued Caldor based on a Connecticut statute that absolutely prohibited employers from requiring employees to work on their Sabbath. The Court, in *Thornton v. Caldor*, decided that the state statute was unconstitutional under the establishment clause because it advanced Sabbath religious observance disregarding the interests of the employer and other nonobservant employees.

Free Exercise Clause

The First Amendment also directs Congress to "make no law . . . prohibiting the free exercise" of religion. This **free exercise clause** raises the flip side of the establishment-of-religion question. When is state action an unconstitutional prohibition of the free exercise of religion? State action that inhibits Sabbath observance may violate the First Amendment. Consider the business law case of *Hobbie v. Unemployment Appeals Commission of Florida*. After working for the Lawton jewelry store for 2 1/2 years, Paula Hobbie converted to Seventh-Day Adventism. She told her boss that she would not be able to work on the Seventh-Day Adventist Sabbath, from sundown on Friday to sundown on Saturday. Lawton not only discharged Hobbie but successfully opposed her claim for unemployment compensation. The Court found that denial of unemployment compensation unconstitutionally burdened Hobbie's free exercise of religion.

In both establishment clause and free exercise clause cases, that is, cases which concern freedom from and of religion, the Court uses a strict scrutiny constitutionality test: Does the state action taken (legislative or executive or both) have a *necessary* relationship to a *compelling* state interest? If it does, the action is constitutional. If it doesn't, it isn't. (See Table 4-1.)

Freedom of Speech

For our society to continue free, we must have freedom of speech and "free trade in ideas." So observed Supreme Court Justice Oliver Wendell Holmes Jr. in adopting a business metaphor for a concept that often affects business. The First Amendment asserts that "Congress shall make no law . . . abridging the freedom of speech." The speech protected may be spoken, written, or symbolic gestures, such as the flag burning in the Eichman case. But as precious as it is, the right of free speech is also not absolute. Justice Holmes also observed that "The most stringent protection of free speech would not protect a man in falsely

TABLE 4-2

Freedom of Speech

Classification	Test	State Action	State Interest
Ordinary speech	Strict scrutiny	Necessary	Compelling
Commercial speech	Intermediate	Reasonable	Substantial

shouting fire in a theatre and causing a panic." Fighting words or speech that is fraudulent, defamatory, or obscene competes with other important interests and may be legally restricted. (See Chapters 6 and 55.)

Commercial Speech

Commercial speech, that is, speech concerning business interests, has societal value and is protected by the First Amendment. But because that interest is balanced against governmental interests in the regulation of commerce, state action concerning commercial speech is subject to a lower level of scrutiny than the strict scrutiny constitutionality test used in ordinary speech cases. (See Table 4-2.)

Political Speech   Freedom of speech is fundamental to our political process, but does it extend to corporations? That question was presented to the Supreme Court in the case of *First National Bank v. Bellotti.* Massachusetts had made it a crime for corporations to contribute to campaigns on referenda. The Court decided that this statute was an unconstitutional limitation on speech. Corporations, as legal persons, have a First Amendment right to participate in the political process. That includes inserting a corporation's views on public policy issues along with its bills. Corporations can also hire lobbyists to per-

suade members of Congress—for example, insurance companies seeking to influence the national health care plan.

Nonpolitical Speech   What of commercial speech that does not concern political issues? Businesses have an interest in communicating the advantages of their goods and services and consumers have an interest in truthful information about them to help make their purchasing decisions. Therefore, advertisements of prescription drug prices, as in *Virginia State Board of Pharmacy v. Virginia Citizens Consumer Council, Inc.,* cannot be constitutionally banned. But the government has a great interest in protecting consumers from deceptive speech and preventing illegal activity. Laws may limit protected commercial speech, but such laws must pass an intermediate standard of review.

As the Court decided in the *Central Hudson Gas and Electric Corp. v. Public Service Commission* case, statutes restricting commercial speech are enforceable only if (1) the governmental interest in preventing the speech is substantial, (2) the restriction directly and materially advances that interest, and (3) the restriction is reasonably proportionate and narrowly tailored to the interest.

Is advertising by professionals of their services protected by the First Amendment? If so, to what extent? The *Fane* case considers these questions.

EDENFIELD V. FANE
U.S. Supreme Court
113 S.Ct. 1792 (1993)

BACKGROUND: Scott Fane, a licensed certified public accountant (CPA), moved from New Jersey to Florida. In New Jersey, he had built a tax practice by telephoning and meeting with executives of small and mid-sized businesses. The Florida Board of Accountancy prohibited uninvited, personal solicitation of prospective clients. Fane sued the officers of the board, including Fred H. Edenfield Jr., arguing that his First Amendment right to freedom of commercial speech had been violated. Both the federal district court and the Eleventh Circuit Court of Appeals ruled in Fane's favor. The board appealed asserting, among other things, concern for the effect of solicitation of business clients on the ethics of auditors.

Kennedy, Justice

In the case now before us, we consider a solicitation ban applicable to Certified Public Accountants (CPAs) enacted by the State of Florida. We hold that, as applied to CPA solicitation in the business context, Florida's prohibition is inconsistent with the free speech guarantees of the First . . . [Amendment]. . . .

The rule [prohibiting solicitation], . . . presented a serious obstacle [to Fane], because most businesses are willing to rely for advice on the accountants or CPAs already serving them. In Fane's experience, persuading a business to sever its existing accounting relations or alter them to include a new CPA on particular assignments requires the new CPA to contact the business and explain the advantages of a change. This entails a detailed discussion of the client's needs and the CPA's expertise, services and fees. . . .

Whatever ambiguities may exist at the margins of the category of commercial speech, it is clear that this type of personal solicitation is commercial expression to which the protections of the First Amendment apply. . . .

In the commercial context, solicitation may have considerable value. . . . In particular, with respect to nonstandard products like the professional services offered by CPAs, these benefits are significant.

In denying CPAs and their clients these advantages, Florida's law threatens societal interests in broad access to complete and accurate commercial information that First Amendment coverage of commercial speech is designed to safeguard. . . .

Commercial speech, however, is "linked inextricably" with the commercial arrangement that it proposes, so the State's interest in regulating the underlying transaction may give it a concomitant interest in the expression itself. For this reason, laws restricting commercial speech, unlike laws burdening other forms of protected expression, need only be tailored in a reasonable manner to serve a substantial state interest in order to survive First Amendment scrutiny. Even under this intermediate standard of review, however, Florida's blanket ban on direct, in-person, uninvited solicitation by CPAs cannot be sustained as applied to Fane's proposed speech.

To determine whether personal solicitation by CPAs may be proscribed under the test set forth in Central Hudson we must ask whether the State's interests in proscribing it are substantial; whether the challenged regulation advances these interests in a direct and material way; and whether the extent of the restriction on protected speech is in reasonable proportion to the interests served. Though we conclude that the Board's asserted interests are substantial, the Board has failed to demonstrate that its solicitation ban advances those interests. . . .

To justify its ban on personal solicitation by CPAs, the Board proffers two interests. First, the Board asserts an interest in protecting consumers from fraud or overreaching by CPAs. Second, the Board claims that its ban is necessary to maintain both the fact and appearance of CPA independence in auditing a business and attesting to its financial statements.

The State's first interest encompasses two distinct purposes: to prevent fraud and other forms of deception, and to protect privacy. As to the first purpose, . . . the State may ban commercial expression that is fraudulent or deceptive without further justification. . . .

Likewise, the protection of potential clients' privacy is a substantial state interest. Even solicitation that is neither fraudulent nor deceptive may be pressed with such frequency or vehemence as to intimidate, vex, or harass the recipient. . . .

The Board's second justification for its ban—the need to maintain the fact and appearance of CPA independence and to guard against conflicts of interest—is related to the audit and attest functions of a CPA. . . .

Although the State's interest in obscuring the commercial nature of public accounting practice is open to doubt, the Board's asserted interest in maintaining CPA independence and ensuring against conflicts of interest is not. We acknowledge that this is substantial.

That the Board's asserted interests are substantial in the abstract does not mean, however, that its blanket prohibition on solicitation serves them. . . .

The Board has not demonstrated that, as applied in the business context, the ban on CPA solicitation advances its asserted interests in any direct and material way. It presents no studies that suggest personal solicitation of prospective business clients by CPAs creates the dangers of fraud, overreaching, or compromised independence that the Board claims to fear. . . .

We reject the Board's argument and hold that, as applied in this context, the solicitation ban cannot be justified as a prophylactic rule. . . .

"Broad prophylactic rules in the area of free expression are suspect. Precision of regulation must be the touchstone in an area so closely touching our most precious freedoms." Even under the First Amendment's somewhat more forgiving standards for restrictions on commercial speech, a State may not curb protected expression without advancing a substantial governmental interest. Here, the ends sought by the State are not advanced by the speech restriction, and legitimate commercial speech is suppressed. For this reason, the Board's rule infringes upon Fane's right to speak, as guaranteed by the Constitution.

O'Connor, Justice (Dissenting)

In my view, the States have the broader authority to prohibit commercial speech that, albeit not directly harmful to the listener, is inconsistent with the speaker's membership in a learned profession and therefore damaging to the profession and society at large. . . . Commercialization has an incremental, indirect, yet profound effect on professional culture, as lawyers know all too well. . . .

DECISION: Affirmed in favor of Scott Fane.

Can government prohibit truthful advertisement of legal business activities? Yes, if the restriction passes the Central Hudson test. In *Posadas de Puerto Rico Associates v. Tourism Company of Puerto Rico*, Puerto Rico licensed casinos for gambling but prevented them from advertising this activity. The Court decided that even though gambling in these casinos was legal, the restriction was constitutional because of the public interest in limiting gambling.

Marketing of legal products can also be constitutionally restricted. Cigarette commercials are banned from television and radio. Hard liquor may not be promoted on television and advertisers are prohibited from showing beer drinking.

Government can also require commercial speech. Cigarette packages must have health warnings, and, in some places, bars must warn pregnant patrons of the dangers of alcohol use to their fetus and restaurants must post first-aid directions for choking.

Offensive Speech

Offensive speech may be obscene or only indecent. Obscene language is not constitutionally protected and may be banned. What is obscene? Supreme Court Justice Potter Stewart said simply, "I know it when I see it." But the legal definition of obscene speech is as follows: speech that, by contemporary community standards, appeals to a prurient interest, is patently offensive, and, according to expert witnesses, lacks serious literary, artistic, political, or scientific value.

Indecent speech is speech that is offensive by contemporary community standards but not obscene, and has limited First Amendment protection. Indecent speech may be restricted by time, place, and manner, but no more than is necessary. The government has an interest in the general well-being of young minors and parent supervision of their children's watching of indecent television programs. But this interest must be balanced against the First Amendment right of older minors and adults in watching such entertainment. In the *Action for Children's Television v. Federal Communications Commission* case, the District of Columbia Circuit Court of Appeals decided that limiting indecent programming to between midnight and 6 a.m. was too restrictive and unconstitutional.

Freedom of the Press

Freedom of the press receives special mention in the First Amendment. The press's constitutional protection is strong, but not absolute. Can the Federal Communications Commission compel cable broadcasting companies to reserve channels for public broadcasting? This "must carry" rule is at issue in the *Turner Broadcasting v. Federal Communications* case.

TURNER BROADCASTING SYSTEM V. FEDERAL COMMUNICATIONS COMMISSION

U.S. Supreme Court
113 S. Ct. 1806 (1993)

BACKGROUND: The Federal Communications Commission required cable broadcasting companies to reserve channels for public broadcasting. Turner Broadcasting lost in the Federal District of Columbia District Court and appealed to the Supreme Court which granted a writ of certiorari. Turner also asked Chief Justice William H. Rehnquist to prevent enforcement of the rule until the case was decided by the Supreme Court.

Rehnquist, Chief Justice

Applicants [Turner Broadcasting System et al.] have asked me, as Circuit Justice for the District of Columbia Circuit, to enjoin enforcement of §§4 and 5 of the Cable Television Consumer Protection and Competition Act of 1992 . . . which require cable operators to reserve a portion of their channel capacity for carrying local commercial and noncommercial educational broadcast stations. Applicants, cable operators and programmers, contend that these "must-carry" provisions violate the First Amendment because (1) they ten [sic] cable operators what speakers they must carry, thereby controlling the content of the operator's speech and shrinking the number of channels available for programming they might prefer to carry; (2) they inhibit the operators' editorial discretion to determine what programming messages to provide to subscribers; and (3) they give local broadcast "speakers" a preferred status. . . .

An injunction is appropriate only if . . . the legal rights at issue are "indisputably clear." . . . [It is not] "indisputably clear" that applicants have a First Amendment right to be free of the must-carry provisions. In *Miami Herald Publishing Co. v. Tornillo,* we struck down Florida's right of reply statute, holding that the State may not compel "editors or publishers to publish that which reason tells them should not be published." Under Tornillo, Congress plainly could not impose the must-carry provisions on privately owned newspapers. In *Red Lion Broadcasting Co. v. FCC,* however, we upheld the Federal Communications Commission's requirement that broadcasters cover public issues, and give each side of the issue fair coverage. Noting that there is a finite number of frequencies available, we stated that "it is the purpose of the First Amendment to preserve an uninhibited marketplace of ideas in

---

which truth will ultimately prevail, rather than to countenance monopolization of that market, whether it be by the Government itself or a private licensee." Although we have recognized that cable operators engage in speech protected by the First Amendment, we have not decided whether the activities of cable operators are more akin to that of newspapers ore [sic] wireless broadcasters.

In light of these two lines of authority, it simply is not indisputably clear that applicants have a First Amendment right to be free from government regulation. . . .

DECISION: Injunction denied.

In 1994, the Supreme Court decided by 5-to-4 in the *Turner Broadcasting System v. Federal Communications Commission*, case that the large number of cable broadcasting channels makes the First Amendment commercial speech rights of cable companies more like those of newspapers than television broadcasters. However, the FCC's must-carry rules are content-neutral and therefore constitutional if they serve an important or substantial governmental interest and restrict no more speech than necessary. The governmental interest here is the preservation of the First Amendment right of the 40 percent of U.S. households without cable television to receive free broadcast television. This right is put at risk by the power of cable television to exercise bottleneck or gatekeeper monopoly power over broadcast television in households with cable television. The danger is that cable companies may drop television broadcasters and force them out of business. Therefore, the Court remanded the case for review of the economic effect of the must-carry rule on broadcast television. The Court's efforts to balance these competing First Amendment interests will continue. In the meantime, the must-carry rule survives.

Freedom of Peaceable Assembly

The First Amendment also protects "the right of the people peaceably to assemble." This right too can affect business. The National Association for the Advancement of Colored People, the sponsor of nonviolent boycotting of white merchants to achieve equality and racial justice in Claiborne County, Mississippi, from 1966 to 1972, could not be held liable for economic losses. However, violence, such as in 1992 in Los Angeles, even for the same objectives, is not constitutionally protected.

Equal Protection

Persons are guaranteed **equal protection** in actions by the federal government (through interpretation of the Fifth Amendment's due process clause) and state and local governments (as stated in the Fourteenth Amendment: "No State shall . . . deny to any person within its jurisdiction the equal protection of the laws"). Equal protection means that similar natural and legal persons such as corporations must be treated in the same way by the state. The Constitution does not provide for equal treatment by private action.

Laws are full of distinctions based on differences. Incomes are taxed at different rates, and not everyone is entitled to food stamps, welfare, and social security. The question is not whether state action separates people according to their characteristics. The question is whether a classification is permitted by the Constitution, that is, whether the government can adequately justify such distinctions.

Determination of the constitutionality of differential treatment by state action begins with the kind of classification made. Next, the court applies the appropriate test or review. There are three kinds of classification, each with its own level of scrutiny: suspect, quasi-suspect, and other classes. (See Table 4-3.)

Suspect Classes

Intentional governmental classifications based on race, religion, or citizenship are **suspect classes** and subject to a **strict scrutiny test.** These distinctions are unconstitutional unless the government can show that its action is *necessary* to achieve a *compelling* state interest. The word *discrimination* is often used in equal protection cases, especially those involving suspect classes. Often discrimination means only that a group is

TABLE 4-3

Equal Protection

Classifications	Review/test	State Action	State Interest
Suspect (e.g.,race,citizenship, religion)	Strict scrutiny	Necessary	Compelling
Quasi-suspect (e.g., gender, age)	Intermediate scrutiny	Substantial	Important
Other (i.e., neither suspect nor quasi-suspect)	Rationality	Reasonable	Legitimate

disadvantaged through classification, not necessarily that the classification violates the principle of equal protection. However, under strict scrutiny review, intentional governmental discrimination based on suspect classification is, nearly always, unconstitutional. (See affirmative action in Chapter 56.) As we have seen, the strict scrutiny test is also applied in cases concerning fundamental rights, such as freedom of speech and association and the rights to interstate travel, privacy, and voting, but not to education.

Discrimination comes in different forms. State action may discriminate on its face, that is, in legislation. Or it may discriminate only in its executive application as in the 1886 case of *Yick Wo v. Hopkins.* San Francisco required permits for laundries to operate in wooden buildings. All but one of non-Chinese laundries were granted permits, but all 200 Chinese applicants were denied. The Court called this a "practical denial by the State of ... equal protection of the laws." In a Texas county where 11 percent of eligible jurors had Spanish surnames, not one of over 6,000 jurors selected over 25 years was Mexican American. The Court decided in *Hernandez v. Texas,* that Pete Hernandez was constitutionally entitled to a jury "from which all members of his class are not systematically excluded." And segregation of black and white public school students in the landmark 1954 *Brown v. Board of Education of Topeka* case led the Court to observe that "Separate educational facilities are inherently unequal." Discrimination against members of minority races, including aboriginal Americans, is nearly always fatal. Only in two cases during World War II, in which persons of Japanese ancestry were relocated to detention camps and subjected to curfews, has overt racial discrimination been upheld by the Court.

Are aliens—that is, noncitizens—a suspect class? The equal protection clause refers to "persons" and not "citizens." Only constitutional rights such as voting and holding high public office are reserved to citizens. For the purpose of state and local state action, noncitizens are a suspect class. A state cannot deny aliens the right to compete for all state civil service jobs. Nor can a state deny resident aliens financial aid for higher education.

Quasi-Suspect Classes

Distinctions based on gender and illegitimacy are **quasi-suspect** classifications subject to a heightened, **intermediate scrutiny.** The question here is whether the state action bears a *substantial* relationship to an *important* state interest.

Governmental gender discrimination may violate equal protection. A law requiring alimony only from husbands to wives upon divorce did not pass the intermediate scrutiny test. Nor did a preference of males over females as estate administrators. But a statutory rape law under which only males could be criminally liable was found to bear a substantial relationship to the important state interest of deterring unwanted pregnancies. And requiring only males to register for the draft was held constitutional because women are excluded from combat duty.

Other Classes

The **rationality test,** or rational-basis review, is applied in all other cases, that is, those that do not concern suspect or quasi-suspect protected classes. Under this lowest standard, the government only has to show that its action was *reasonably* related to a *legitimate* state interest and is not arbitrary. In these cases, courts generally defer to the government regulation. To win, a challenger must prove that there is no conceivable rational basis to the law.

Economic and social legislation often discriminates against one class of persons, goods, or services and may be subjected to rationality review. Minnesota banned plastic nonreturnable milk containers to protect the environment. Plastic manufacturers presented impressive evidence that this legislation would encourage the use of paperboard cartons and do more ecological harm than good. The Court decided in *Minnesota v. Clover Leaf Creamery Co.* that under rationality review the statute was constitutional because the Minnesota legislature could have rationally concluded that its law would help.

Discrimination on the basis of wealth, mental or physical disability, and age is in this category.

The Court has decided that the forced retirement of police officers at age 50 and judges at age 70 is not irrational.

Are homosexuals members of a protected class and entitled to heightened scrutiny of government action against them? Or is rationality review the appropriate standard? This question has not yet been answered by the Supreme Court, but the following case shows that, in the case of homosexual government employees, the rational-basis test has gums if not teeth.

STEFFAN V. ASPIN

U.S. Court of Appeals, D.C. Circuit
8 F.3d 57 (1993)

BACKGROUND: Joseph Steffan was an outstanding midshipman, in the top ten in leadership and military performance at the United States Naval Academy. He was a battalion commander and sang the National Anthem at the Army-Navy football game. In 1987, Steffan was forced to resign his commission because he answered "Yes, sir" when a superior officer asked him whether he was a homosexual.

Steffan argued in the District of Columbia District Court that forcing him to resign solely on the basis of his homosexual orientation denied him his constitutional right to equal protection. That court decided in favor of the defendants, including Les Aspin, then the secretary of defense. It held that homosexuals are not a suspect class. Using rational-basis review, the court said that the military's gay ban was constitutional because it was rationally related to the legitimate goals of "maintenance of discipline, morale, good order, a respected system of rank and command, . . . morality and respect for the privacy interests of both officers and the enlisted" and to the goal of preventing the spread of AIDS in the armed forces. Steffan appealed.

Mikva, Chief Judge

II. Discussion

Mr. Steffan argues that the Navy constructively discharged him in violation of the equal protection component of the Fifth Amendment's Due Process Clause. The equal protection component imposes the same restrictions upon the federal Government that the Fourteenth Amendment's Equal Protection Clause places upon the States. . . .

Mr. Steffan was forced to leave the Navy because of the . . . [Department of Defense Directives]: he truthfully stated that he was a homosexual. . . . Therefore, the constitutionality of the Directives is the central issue in this case.

The Secretary's brief relies heavily upon the concept of "military deference" to sustain its Directives. And not without reason—for it is surely true that we accord great independence to decisions of the military branches in their areas of expertise. . . .

But . . . [t]here is no "military exception" to the Constitution. This is particularly true for equal protection cases. When the military fails to accord individuals the equal protection of the laws, it treads upon an area of expertise that has long been conceded to the courts. In deciding such cases, therefore, courts should not stray from the boundaries of ordinary equal protection review. For example, faced with a claim that the military discriminates against African-Americans or women, the court should not fail to apply strict or intermediate scrutiny to the military's action. . . .

In this case, . . . we decline to rule on whether a "compelling" or "important" state interest is necessary. This would depend, of course, on whether homosexuals, defined by their sexual orientation, are a "suspect" or "quasi-suspect" class accorded "heightened scrutiny" under equal protection review. . . .

We find it unnecessary to inquire whether homosexuals, as defined solely by orientation, comprise a "suspect" or "quasi-suspect" class. We need not decide, because we find that even if homosexuals are not accorded suspect status, the DOD Directives cannot survive constitutional scrutiny.

A. Rationality Review

Any governmental action that burdens individuals unequally but does not burden a "suspect class" need only survive "rationality," or "rational-basis" review. Rationality review requires that the action be "rationally related to a legitimate governmental purpose." This is not an exacting standard. . . . Absent a burden upon a suspect class, the court's role is merely to ensure: (1) that the government has a legitimate purpose for distinguishing among the individuals affected; and (2) that the means chosen to effect that purpose bear some reasonable relation to it, and thus are not wholly arbitrary. . . .

B. Propensity to Engage in Illegal Conduct

[T]he primary purpose of the regulations is to exclude from the military those individuals who have a propensity to engage in unlawful conduct. . . .Those "homosexual acts" are forbidden to military servicemembers, and there is no dispute that laws forbidding such conduct are constitutional. . . .

The Secretary's asserted rationale for the Directives can thus be stated as follows: a person who, by his own admission, "desires" to engage in homosexual conduct . . .and that person must be dismissed from the military as a prophylactic measure. . . . [U]nder rationality review, the Secretary need not show a perfect means-ends fit, but only a reasonable relation between the means (excluding persons of homosexual orientation) and the end (preventing homosexual conduct).

But there is no such rational relation here. Homosexual conduct is more than a practice discouraged by the military: it is grounds for discipline and sometimes (in the case of sodomy) a criminal act. Therefore, the Secretary's justification for the gay ban presumes that a certain class of persons will break the law or the rules solely because of their thoughts and desires. This is inherently unreasonable. . . .

[T]he Secretary has accorded Mr. Steffan differential treatment solely because of the content of his thoughts. . . . We think this is repugnant to the various common law and constitutional principles that guard the sanctity of a person's thoughts against government control. . . . Accordingly, we find that the Secretary's "propensity" argument . . . is illegitimate as a matter of law. It cannot provide a rational basis for the DOD Directives.

C. Effect on Morale, Discipline, and Recruitment of Heterosexuals

The Secretary does not claim that homosexual servicemembers themselves will have poor morale or discipline, nor does he assert that they will intentionally sabotage the interests of the military. Instead, the Secretary fears that these grievous consequences will arise because heterosexual soldiers will be appalled at the requirement that they serve alongside homosexuals. Under rationality review, the court must presume that the Secretary's fears are well-founded, even though we may have a higher opinion of the maturity of members of the armed forces than do their policymakers. . . . Similar objections were voiced by opponents of President Truman's 1948 executive order requiring racial integration of the armed forces. But a cardinal principle of equal protection law holds that the government cannot discriminate against a certain class in order to give effect to the prejudice of others. . . . Such discrimination plays directly into the hands of the bigots; it ratifies and encourages their prejudice. . . .

D. Privacy

The Secretary also argues, . . . that the presence of homosexuals in the military will invade the privacy of heterosexual servicemen. . . .

This argument can mean one of two things: either (1) that homosexual servicemembers will ogle and stare at their heterosexual counterparts in the shower or other close quarters; or (2) that heterosexuals will fear such staring and feel an invasion of privacy. This argument that homosexuals will stare is very similar to the argument that they will engage in homosexual acts. Again, it equates thoughts and desires with propensity to engage in misconduct. The argument that heterosexuals will fear such staring is, in turn, a version of the argument that government should be allowed to give effect to the irrational fears and stereotypes of third parties.

E. Rationales Not Offered by the Secretary

[P]reventing the spread of AIDS in the armed forces. We do not agree that this could be a rational basis for the Directives. Homosexual orientation cannot spread the AIDS virus. Homosexual, or heterosexual, conduct can—and then only if one of the participants carries the virus. Even if AIDS happens to be more prevalent today among homosexuals than among heterosexuals, justifying the Directives on this basis requires the illegitimate assumption that persons of homosexual orientation will break the rules by engaging in homosexual conduct as members of the armed forces.

Finally, another rationale . . . is homosexuals' alleged susceptibility to blackmail. . . . But . . . the military's policy only increases the risk of blackmail by making gays and lesbians remain in the closet for fear of forfeiting their careers. . . . If there is a risk to military security from homosexuality, then, the Directives themselves are to blame for it.

III. Conclusion

The DOD Directives . . . are not rationally related to any legitimate goal. . . . The constitutional requirement of equal protection forbids the government to disadvantage a class based solely upon irrational prejudice, whatever the standard of review. We find that the Directives violate the equal protection component of the Fifth Amendment's Due Process Clause. . . .

DECISION: The circuit court reversed the district court's decision. It ordered the defendants to grant Mr. Steffan his diploma from the United States Naval Academy, reinstate him to military service, and commission him as an officer.

CASE NOTE

The armed forces "don't ask, don't tell, don't pursue" policy concerning homosexuals was not controlling in this case, but this example of equal protection rationality review has precedential value. The Clinton administration did not appeal the equal protection analysis of this case, but did appeal the court order to commission Steffan.

Due Process

The state may constitutionally deprive a person of life, liberty, or property, but not without due process of law, a fair and reasonable procedure. This requirement applies to the federal (Fifth Amendment) and state and local (Fourteenth Amendment) governments through their **due process clauses**. There is due process protection only against state action, not against private action. Aside from slavery, private deprivations of life, liberty, or property are constitutional, although they are often illegal.

Life, Liberty, or Property

What does the Constitution mean by life, liberty, and property and how is one deprived of them? Life means being alive and the government may take it from you through capital punishment. Liberty is freedom from physical confinement such as imprisonment and involuntary commitment of an adult to a mental institution. And property includes all kinds of real and personal property which the government can take through taxation, eminent domain (see Chapter 49), and forfeiture law (as you will read in the *Good* case). But the due process definition of liberty and property also embraces entitlements, that is, legitimate claims to benefits created by statute. Required public high school education is such an entitlement, and therefore, disciplinary suspension requires due process. Other examples of entitlements include a driver's license, continued employment at a state university of a teacher with "implied" tenure, and utility service from a government company when it may only be terminated for cause. Even a state statutory right against employment discrimination may be protected by the due process clause for "The hallmark of property . . . is an individual entitlement grounded in state law which cannot be removed except 'for cause.'" And because persons are entitled to constitutional rights, much of the Bill of Rights has been applied to the states by the doctrine of incorporation through the due process clause of the Fourteenth Amendment.

Procedural and Substantive Due Process

To deprive a person of life, liberty, or property by state action, due process is constitutionally re-quired. What is due process? As interpreted by the Supreme Court, the due process clause includes two components, a procedural part and a substantive part.

Procedural Due Process   Under the due process clause, persons are constitutionally entitled to procedural due process; that is, they are due or owed a fair procedure before being deprived of life, liberty, or property by state action. More procedural due process is required for explicit constitutional rights than for state-created entitlements.

What are the elements of procedural due process? Adequate notice, that is, notification to the party to be deprived and adequate hearing of that party's defense. The amount of notice and hearing the Constitution requires depends on the facts. The more serious the deprivation, the more process is due. A summons on a car windshield may be enough notice for a parking violation, but a defendant in a murder trial is entitled to quite a bit more notice. Repeated failing grades from teachers and outside physicians is sufficient notice to a medical school student that she may not graduate.

The hearings constitutionally mandated for $25 fines and death penalty cases are also significantly different. Must the hearing take place before deprivation? What if the deprivation is temporary or it is an emergency situation, for example, taking an unconscious homeless person out of the cold? An informal complaint procedure may be constitutionally adequate for the termination of a state employee. But a full adversary hearing, including a right to counsel under the Sixth Amendment and a right to appeal up to the Supreme Court, is required in a capital case.

If you are convicted of a crime, are you entitled to full due process rights before being deprived of life, liberty, or property? Or does a convicted criminal enter a legal wonderland in which it is "Sentence first—verdict afterwards"?* Capital punishment is irreversible, so notice and hearing must come first. But a person may be deprived of liberty and even held without bail based solely on an indictment. And what of deprivation of property? This question is discussed in the case of *United States v. Good*.

---

* Lewis Carroll, *Alice in Wonderland*, Chapter 12 (1865).

UNITED STATES V. GOOD

U. S. Supreme Court
114 S. Ct. 492 (1993)

BACKGROUND: In 1985 , police found 89 pounds of marijuana and drug paraphernalia in the house of James Daniel Good. Good pleaded guilty to promoting a harmful drug in violation of Hawaii law. He was sentenced to 1 year in jail and 5 years' probation; he was also fined $1,000 and forfeited to Hawaii $3,187 in cash found on his property.

Four and one-half years after the police search, a U. S. magistrate judge granted the government a warrant to seize Good's house and 4 acres of land under federal forfeiture law because the property had been used in the commission of a federal drug offense. The warrant was based on Good's conviction and the evidence discovered during the search. The government seized Good's property without prior notice to Good or an adversary hearing and began to collect rent from his tenants.

Good argued that the seizure deprived him of property without Fifth Amendment due process. The district court granted the government's motion for summary judgment. The Court of Appeals for the Ninth Circuit unanimously held that depriving Good of his property without prior notice or hearing violated the due process clause.

Kennedy, Justice

The principal question presented is whether, in the absence of exigent circumstances, the Due Process Clause of the Fifth Amendment prohibits the Government in a civil forfeiture case from seizing real property without first affording the owner notice and an opportunity to be heard. We hold that it does. . . .

The Due Process Clause of the Fifth Amendment guarantees that "no person shall . . . be deprived of life, liberty, or property, without due process of law." Our precedents establish the general rule that individuals must receive notice and an opportunity to be heard before the Government deprives them of property.

The Government does not, and could not, dispute that the seizure of Good's home and four-acre parcel deprived him of property interests protected by the Due Process Clause. By the Government's own submission, the seizure gave it the right to charge rent, to condition occupancy, and even to evict the occupants. Instead, the Government argues that it afforded Good all the process the Constitution requires. The Government. . . . argues that the seizure of real property under the drug forfeiture laws justifies an exception to the usual due process requirement of preseizure notice and hearing. . . .

Whether ex parte seizures of forfeitable property satisfy the Due Process Clause is a question we last confronted in *Calero-Toledo v. Pearson Yacht Leasing Co.*, which held that the Government could seize a yacht subject to civil forfeiture without affording prior notice or hearing. Central to our analysis in *Calero-Toledo* was the fact that a yacht was the "sort [of property] that could be removed to another jurisdiction, destroyed, or concealed, if advance warning of confiscation were given." The ease with which an owner could frustrate the Government's interests in the forfeitable property created a "'special need for very prompt action'" that justified the postponement of notice and hearing until after the seizure.

We had no occasion in *Calero-Toledo* to decide whether the same considerations apply to the forfeiture of real property, which, by its very nature, can be neither moved nor concealed. . . .

The right to prior notice and a hearing is central to the Constitution's command of due process. "The purpose of this requirement is not only to ensure abstract fair play to the individual. Its purpose, more particularly, is to protect his use and possession of property from arbitrary encroachment—to minimize substantively unfair or mistaken deprivations of property. . . ."

We tolerate some exceptions to the general rule requiring predeprivation notice and hearing, but only in "'extraordinary situations where some valid governmental interest is at stake that justifies postponing the hearing until after the event.'" Whether the seizure of real property for purposes of civil forfeiture justifies such an exception requires an examination of the competing interests at stake, along with the promptness and adequacy of later proceedings. . . .

Good's right to maintain control over his home, and to be free from governmental interference, is a private interest of historic and continuing importance. . . .

The ex parte preseizure proceeding affords little or no protection to the innocent owner. . . . "Fairness can rarely be obtained by secret, one-sided determination of facts decisive of rights. . . . No better instrument has been devised for arriving at truth than to give a person in jeopardy of serious loss notice of the case against him and opportunity to meet it."

The purpose of an adversary hearing is to ensure the requisite neutrality that must inform all governmental decisionmaking. That protection is of particular importance here, where the Government has a direct pecuniary interest in the outcome of the proceeding. Moreover, the availability of a postseizure hearing may be no recompense for losses caused by erroneous seizure. Given the congested civil dockets in federal courts, a claimant may not receive an adversary hearing until many months after the seizure. And even if the ultimate judicial decision is that the claimant was an innocent owner, or that the Government lacked probable cause, this determination, coming months after the seizure, "would not cure the temporary deprivation that an earlier hearing might have prevented." . . .

The question in the civil forfeiture context is whether ex parte seizure is justified by a pressing need for prompt action. We find no pressing need here. . . .

Requiring the Government to postpone seizure until after an adversary hearing creates no significant administrative burden. . . . From an administrative standpoint it makes little difference whether that hearing is held before or after the seizure. And any harm that results from delay is minimal in comparison to the injury occasioned by erroneous seizure. . . .

The constitutional limitations we enforce in this case apply to real property in general, not simply to residences. That said, the case before us well illustrates an essential principle: Individual freedom finds tangible expression in property rights. At stake in this and many other forfeiture cases are the security and privacy of the home and those who take shelter within it. . . .

In sum, based upon the importance of the private interests at risk and the absence of countervailing Government needs, we hold that the seizure of real property under [federal civil forfeiture law] is not one of those extraordinary instances that justify the postponement of notice and hearing. Unless exigent circumstances are present, the Due Process Clause requires the Government to afford notice and a meaningful opportunity to be heard before seizing real property subject to civil forfeiture. . . .

Thomas, Justice (concurring in part and dissenting in part)

What convinces me that Good's due process rights were not violated are the facts of this case—facts that are disregarded by the Court in its well-intentioned effort to protect "innocent owners" from mistaken Government seizures. . . . Good is not an "innocent owner"; he is a convicted drug offender. . . .

Wherever the due process line properly should be drawn, in circumstances such as these, a preseizure hearing is not required as a matter of constitutional law. Moreover, such a hearing would be unhelpful to the property owner. As a practical matter, it is difficult to see what purpose it would serve. Notice, of course, is provided by the conviction itself. In my view, seizure of the property without more formalized notice and an opportunity to be heard is simply one of the many unpleasant collateral consequences that follows from conviction of a serious drug offense. . . .

DECISION: The Court decided in favor of Good and remanded the case for further proceedings consistent with the opinion.

Substantive Due Process The due process clause also contains a substantive component. Substantive due process concerns the substance of legislation and the legislative process. Most of the Bill of Rights is applied to the states through incorporation by the Fourteenth Amendment due process clause. For example, First Amendment freedom of speech principles were applied in the commercial speech *Fane* case.

A hot substantive due process issue is punitive damages. In business fraud and other civil intentional tort cases (see Chapter 6), punitive monetary damages may be awarded to the plaintiff in addition to damages for actual injury. Punitive damages, like fines, are intended to punish and deter the defendant, but whereas fines go to the government, punitive damages go to the plaintiff. Therefore, the excessive fines clause of the Eighth Amendment does not apply to punitive damages because they are not fines. Punitive damages may exceed all other damages combined and businesses that pay these sizable, hard to predict costs argue that fairness compels tort reform by Congress or the courts.

Do punitive damages violate substantive due process? They may. The Court has stated that the due process clause imposes substantive limits "beyond which penalties may not go." In the insurance fraud case of *Pacific Mutual Life Insurance Company v. Haslip*, the trial court assessed damages of $4,000 for medical expenses, $196,000 for emotional distress, and $840,000 for punitive damages, four times the amount of all other damages. Although the Supreme Court affirmed, it observed that the due process clause would be violated by "extreme results that jar one's constitutional sensibilities" and that this award "may be close to the line." The Court acknowledged that it is difficult to determine whether a particular award is so "grossly excessive" as to violate substantive due process. "We need not, and indeed we cannot, draw a mathematical bright line between the con-

stitutionally acceptable and the constitutionally unacceptable that would fit every case. We can say, however, that [a] general concern of reasonableness . . . properly enters into the constitutional calculus."

In the 1993 case of *TXO Production Corp. v. Alliance Resources Corp.*, TXO tried to cut Alliance out of its share of a West Virginia oil and gas deal. Alliance sued and was awarded $19,000 in damages for legal fees and 526 times that amount, $10 million, in punitive damages. TXO argued that the punitive damages award was so excessive that it was an unconstitutional arbitrary deprivation of property without due process of law. The Court decided for Alliance, saying that these punitive damages were a reasonable punishment for TXO's reprehensible conduct and a proper deterrent of potential harm.

Taxing and Spending Powers

The federal government has the general power to tax and spend based on Article I, Section 8, and to tax incomes based on the Sixteenth Amendment. Federal courts uphold tax statutes "so long as the motive of Congress and the effect of its legislative action are to secure revenue for the benefit of the general government. The taxing and spending powers may be used to achieve public policy objectives. For example, cigarettes may be taxed to generate revenue for a national health care plan and tax credits may subsidize farmers and oil companies. But the taxing power may not be used to violate another part of the Constitution. Taxation of selected types of publications unconstitutionally limits freedom of the press. Also, the equal protection clause bars a state from taxing foreign (i.e., out-of-state) corporations at a higher rate than domestic (i.e., in-state) corporations without a reasonable relationship to a legitimate state interest. And taxing foreign insurance companies at 4 percent while domestic insurance companies are taxed at only 1 percent in order to benefit the state economy is not a legitimate state interest.

International Trade

Article I, Section 8, of the Constitution also gives Congress the power "To regulate Commerce with foreign Nations." Congress affects international trade unilaterally through tariffs (taxes) on and quotas of imported goods, and bilaterally and multilaterally through treaties and agreements with other countries such as the North American Free Trade Agreement (NAFTA) and the General Agreement on Tariffs and Trade (GATT).

Contract Clause

The **contract clause** declares that "No state shall . . . pass any . . . Law impairing the Obligation of Contracts" (Article I, Section 10). A state legislature may not substantially weaken existing contract rights created by agreements with the state or between private parties. This prohibition is not absolute. The job of government is to govern. "No legislature can bargain away the public health or the public morals." Therefore, a law can constitutionally modify contracts, but only if it is reasonable and necessary to serve an important public purpose.

In 1962, New Jersey and New York sold to private investors (the Port Authority) state bonds containing a financial security covenant. In 1974, both states totally repealed this covenant by statute to release funds in order to improve mass transit and discourage car use. The Court, in *United States Trust Company of New York v. New Jersey*, observed that there were other ways to serve these important public purposes. Therefore, this impairment of state contractual obligations was not reasonable and necessary and violated the contract clause.

Privileges and Immunities Clause

To achieve the Constitution's objective of making one nation out of several states, the **privileges and immunities clause** (in Article IV, Section 2, and the Fourteenth Amendment) protects the basic rights of U.S. citizens even when they travel to other states. Nonresidents must be treated the same as residents unless there are substantial reasons for discrimination.

A state cannot require residency for an attorney to practice law. Nor can residents be preferentially hired for construction projects such as the Trans-Alaska Pipeline. But state public universities can charge nonresidents higher tuitions. The privileges and immunities clause does not apply to nonresident corporations and aliens because they are not citizens. But corporations have rights under the commerce clause (see Chapter 2), and corporations and aliens have rights under the equal protection clause (discussed earlier in this chapter).

State Immunity

Under the Eleventh Amendment (1798), states are generally immune from suits in federal court. This legal protection is based on the principle of sovereign immunity, that the state cannot be sued unless it consents. In *Atascadero State Hospital v. Scanlon*, Douglas James Scanlon argued that, in violation of the federal Rehabilitation Act, he was refused a California state hospital graduate student assistantship due to his physical disabilities. California claimed Eleventh Amendment immunity, which the Court granted.

Review Questions and Problems

Key Terms

federalism	suspect class
preemption doctrine	strict scrutiny test
federal supremacy	quasi-suspect class
judicial review	intermediate scrutiny
state action	rationality test
establishment clause	due process clause
free exercise clause	contract clause
commercial speech	privileges and
equal protection	immunities clause

Discussion Questions

1. Should non-Christian, non-Sunday Sabbath observers be allowed to open for business on Sunday in a county with a Sunday blue law?

2. Would the taxation of commercial enterprises by religions such as the Church of Scientology violate the free exercise clause?

3. Should the Amish who refuse Social Security benefits on religious grounds be exempt from paying Social Security taxes?

4. Can violent movies, video games, or music be indecent or obscene and restricted or banned by the government?

5. Does the constitutional right of privacy protect one's computer E-mail?

6. Does discrimination against children, such as excluding them from R-rated movies and buying alcoholic beverages, violate equal protection?

7. Would the federal subsidy of tobacco farmers pass rationality review?

8. Do punitive damages encourage economical behavior? Without punitive damages, would businesses find it more cost efficient to injure others than to avoid injury? Consider the difficulty of assessing actual damages and the possibility of concealment of civil injuries.

Review Problems

1. Ju Hua is a recent Chinese immigrant who works as a translator for the California state government. She observes the Chinese New Year (which falls between January 10 and February 19) as her most important holiday. In November, Ju explains to her supervisor that she would be happy to work on January 1, the Christian New Year, but would like to have the Chinese New Year as a day off. Her request is denied. Ju does not come to work on the Chinese New Year and is fired. Ju argues that January 1 commemorates Jesus' circumcision and, therefore, observing it as a legal holiday violates the establishment clause. She also claims the right to observe the Chinese New Year under the free exercise clause. Lastly, Ju contends that the equal protection clause protects her right to celebrate her cultural heritage. Is she correct? Would the argument be stronger if she worked on Christmas Eve and Christmas Day instead, noting that they celebrate Jesus's birth?

2. The executive branch of the government has proposed a health care plan for every person in the United States. The Health Insurance Association of America, representing 270 small and medium-sized insurance companies, opposes this plan. Its members agree to spend millions of dollars in a television ad campaign to defeat the government proposal. It also decides to enclose antiplan literature in every mailing to its customers. The insurance industry is heavily regulated by the states. Can government (local, state, or federal) constitutionally prohibit these ads or mailings in opposition to government policy? Can government compel the insurance companies to distribute an informational booklet on the health care plan?

3. The Municipal Securities Rulemaking Board, a private organization in New York City, is concerned over the influence peddling of bond dealers. Therefore, it bans political contributions from member bond dealers to local officials and candidates who could reciprocate with lucrative underwriting business. Is this action constitutional? Would it be constitutional to put a cap on contributions by bond dealers? By all corporations? Would these acts be constitutional if this were a public agency?

4. A racist article targeted at African Americans is published in the University of Pennsylvania newspaper and distributed on campus. African American students are apprehended while destroying all of the copies of the newspaper on public display. Have they violated the First Amendment freedom of the press provision?

5. WBLS-FM is a popular black-oriented New York City radio station licensed by the Federal Communications Commission. It has announced its plan not to play songs with lyrics about sex, drugs, and gangs that advocate violence, especially against women and homosexuals. The target of this policy was hard-core rap music. "Gangsta rappers" complain that this censorship denies them access to the public airwaves and violates their freedom of speech.

6. New Jersey passes a law restricting computer-generated phone calls by telemarketers to potential clients. Does this law violate the businesses' commercial speech rights? Is it a constitutional protection of the potential clients' right of privacy?

7. The New York City Human Rights Commission rules that children under the age of 4 years old, even if accompanied by an adult, cannot go to movies that are not G or PG rated if it is after 5:30 p.m. It says that such children often distract other movie viewers when they cry or are otherwise disruptive. Rolando Acosta, a poor single father, claims that this policy unconstitutionally discriminates against his 2-year-old's freedom of hearing speech right. He also contends that he cannot afford a baby-sitter so this ruling discriminates against the poor. Does the ruling violate the equal protection rights of Rolando or infant Acosta?

8. Maria Hernandez owns a bodega in San Juan, Puerto Rico. One night three men enter her store and instruct her to empty the cash register. Instead, Ms. Hernandez takes out her unlicensed 38-caliber gun and starts firing, wounding one of the robbers. The district attorney charges her with possession of an illegal firearm in violation of the Brady Gun Licensing Law. Does Ms. Hernandez have a defense based on her Second Amendment right "to keep and bear Arms"? Is the Brady law clause requiring a 5-day waiting period and background check before purchasing a handgun constitutional?

9. According to a study, half of drunk drivers killed in 1990 had blood alcohol content of .20 percent, showing that they had consumed about eight drinks in an hour. A local Texas magistrate requires

those found guilty of driving under the influence of that much alcohol to have license plates with scarlet markings. This program is intended to protect them and other drivers from possible injury and to deter people from driving while intoxicated. Does this policy violate the due process, equal protection, or cruel and unusual punishment clauses?

10. Robin Umphrey, who works for a telemarketing firm that makes interstate phone calls, discovers that the parent company has been monitoring her phone conversations, both work-related and private, without notifying her.

11. Andres Espinosa manages a clothing factory in Southern California. A news magazine has recently reported that employers in the area employ illegal aliens in sweatshops at below-minimum-wage salaries. Agents of the Immigration and Naturalization Service arrive at Mr. Espinosa's factory and insist on being let in to confirm the immigration status of the employees. Does Mr. Espinosa have a constitutional right under the Fourth Amendment to keep the agents out?

12. Teresa Harris is a manager at Forklift Systems, Inc., an equipment rental company. Charles Hardy, the president of the company, tells Harris, in front of others, "You're a woman, what do you know," "We need a man as the rental manager," called her "a dumb ass woman," and suggested that they "go to the Holiday Inn to negotiate [your] raise." Harris files a suit for sexual harassment due to an abusive work environment.

Hardy defends noting that he is the president of a private company so there is no state action here and the government cannot interfere. He also argues that he has a constitutional right to say whatever he wants to say. Who wins and why? Would the result be different if Harris were a government employee?

Case Problems

1. The National Association of Attorneys General (NAAG) represents all the attorneys general of all the states. It adopted consumer protection guidelines setting standards governing the content and format of airline advertising, frequent flyer plans, and compensation to passengers who give up their seats on overbooked flights. Trans World Airlines (TWA) is notified by Dan Morales, the attorney general of Texas, of his intent to act, based on these guidelines, against allegedly deceptive fare advertisements. TWA argues that the NAAG guidelines are preempted by the 1978 Airline Deregulation Act (ADA). The ADA prohibits the states from enforcing any law "relating to rates, routes, or services" of any air carrier. Deceptive trade practices are under the jurisdiction of the federal Department of Transportation. Can Don Morales take action against TWA if its fare advertisements are deceptive?

2. Eddie C. Thomas, a Jehovah's Witness whose religion forbade making of implements of war, worked for a steel mill. His department closed and he was assigned to manufacture tank turrets. Thomas quit, but his application for unemployment insurance was denied. Was the free exercise clause violated here?

3. A local ordinance in Azusa, California, banned astrology, card or tea reading, fortune telling, hypnotism, mediumship, palmistry, and spiritual reading for a fee. Fatima Stevens, minister of the Spiritual Psychic Science Church of Truth, asked for an injunction against enforcement of this ordinance so that she can engage in the business of telling fortunes. Is fortunetelling a commercial activity or speech? If it is speech, is it commercial or noncommercial speech? Is the ordinance constitutional?

4. The Kitty Kat Lounge in South Bend, Indiana, and Darlene Miller wanted to provide patrons with nonobscene totally nude dancing as entertainment. Indiana required pasties and a G-string. The Lounge and Miller argued that their First Amendment free-speech rights were violated. Is Miller's dancing expressive speech? Is it protected by the First Amendment? If it is protected, can Indiana still constitutionally restrict it on the basis of important or substantial government interests?

5. Willie Warren Sr. and others operated agricultural labor camps. They hired people in Atlanta, Georgia, for a day of work, but instead, took them to North Carolina and Florida farms to work for weeks and months. These field workers worked long hours for little ($5 every other week) or no pay. Sometimes they were told that they owed more money for their housing, clothes, and single meal a day than they had earned. The migrant workers were kept from leaving by their poverty (they had no money for transportation), alcohol, threats that they would be brought back, and acts of violence (such as beatings with a stick). Did these acts violate the Constitution? Would the result be different if the migrant farm workers were illegal aliens?

5

Introduction to Criminal Law

The Basis of Criminal Law

Punishment

Classification of Crimes

Criminal Act and Intent

Regulatory Crimes

Steps in the Criminal Justice Process

Defenses

Criminal Procedure

Corporate Criminal Liability

White-Collar Crime

RICO

Criminal law is increasingly an area of concern for business managers. The scope of business activity prohibited by criminal statutes has broadened considerably over the years, and a growing number of business managers are being convicted of crimes. This chapter provides an introduction to criminal law and procedure, with a focus on white-collar crime. The chapter devotes special attention to the federal Racketeer Influenced and Corrupt Organizations (RICO) Act, which since 1970 has developed into an enormous potential source of liability for businesses.

The Basis of Criminal Law

A **crime** is an offense against society. Local, state, and federal statutes prohibit certain acts because they are antisocial or deviate from established social norms. In some instances it is the failure to act that society considers wrong. These acts of either commission or omission are crimes.

A person who commits a crime is prosecuted by a public official, generally called a prosecuting or district attorney. The prosecution is brought on behalf of the state that is representing the interests of society. One difference between criminal and civil litigation is that in a criminal case the state is always the plaintiff.

As the state is the plaintiff in a criminal case, the victim of a criminal act recovers nothing even if the prosecution is successful. However, the victim may pursue a civil action against the wrongdoer in order to recover damages. In most cases this is not very effective, as the defendant is incarcerated or is financially unable to pay damages. Therefore, some states have statutes that provide compensation for victims of criminal acts.

Punishment

Punishment is the principal means that society employs to accomplish the objectives of the criminal law. The punishments that can be imposed on those who violate the law vary widely depending upon the crime, but the punishment may be severe. It can be a fine, imprisonment, or even execution. Often the guilty person is both fined and imprisoned. Also, for many crimes conviction involves the loss of important civil rights such as the right to vote, hold public office, or serve as a juror. An additional punishment, but one that is not established by statute, is the stigma that is attached to the person convicted of a crime.

Purposes of Punishment

Two very different views exist as to the purpose of punishment. Many people believe that the purpose of punishment is deterrence. Because of punishment the criminal will not repeat the act, and the threat of punishment will deter others from doing it. Others believe that retribution is the ultimate reason for criminal punishment. They feel that because most people are capable of choosing between right and wrong, a person who violates an accepted social norm must be made to "pay" his or her debt to society. Because violating some social norms provides a greater threat to society than violating other social norms, the punishment for some criminal acts is more extensive than it is for other criminal acts.

Classification of Crimes

Crimes are commonly classified as either felonies or misdemeanors. Many state statutes define a crime as a **felony** if it is punishable by death or imprisonment in a state penitentiary. Federal law defines a felony as a crime that is punishable by death or imprisonment in a federal prison. The significant factor determining a felony is the punishment that is authorized by statute, not that which is imposed upon the offender.

A **misdemeanor** is an offense that is less serious than a felony. Some states define a misdemeanor as a crime punishable by incarceration in a place other than a state penitentiary. Some jurisdictions recognize a third classification called **petty offenses**. These are usually traffic violations and are not really considered crimes.

Both felonies and misdemeanors are divided into classes so that sentencing will be more uniform. As an illustration, the *Model Penal Code* classifies felonies as (1) felonies of the first degree, (2) felonies of the second degree, and (3) felonies of the third degree. The first- and second-degree felonies are subject to greater punishment because they apply to more serious criminal acts.

Although the distinction between felonies and misdemeanors developed at common law, in many situations it continues to be important today. For example, for most felony convictions the person who is convicted loses certain civil rights, such as the right to vote or hold public office. This is not true if the individual is convicted of a misdemeanor.

Criminal Act and Intent

In order to convict a person of a crime, the state traditionally has had to prove that the defendant committed a *criminal act* and, additionally, that the defendant had *criminal intent* when he or she committed the criminal act. In criminal law, these two elements of a crime are known by their Latin names. The criminal act is known as **actus reus**, and criminal intent is known as **mens rea**.

Actus Reus

In order to be convicted of a crime, one generally must commit a criminal act. Assume, for example, that William is president of a bank and diverts funds from his customers' accounts to his personal account. The act of diverting the funds is a criminal act, and thus satisfies the actus reus requirement; if William diverted the funds with criminal intent, then he has committed a crime.

Assume, on the other hand, that William intends to steal funds from his customers' accounts but does not act on his intention. Although William in this case clearly has criminal intent, he has not committed a criminal act and hence is not guilty of a crime.

Although actus reus has traditionally been a requirement for criminal liability, there are some crimes that are predicted not upon a criminal act but rather upon the *failure* to act. For example, federal money laundering law makes it a crime for financial institutions to fail to file reports of certain large financial transactions.

Mens Rea

In addition to proving that the defendant committed a criminal act, the state generally must, in order to convict the defendant, prove that he or she acted with criminal intent—mens rea. This is sometimes thought of as the "guilty mind" requirement. For example, if A were to take a coat from a restaurant genuinely believing it to be her own, she would not be guilty of a crime. She did not have a guilty mind.

The guilty mind requirement is readily established by the state if it can prove that a person planned or intended to do a wrongful act, but lesser degrees of awareness of wrongdoing are also sufficient to establish mens rea. Consider the following situation involving bribery of a public official. The XYZ Co. needs a government license to export a product that it manufactures. The company is having difficulty obtaining the license. The company's independent sales agent states that he can get a license for $10,000, as he "knows certain people in politics." If the firm gives the agent $10,000, its conduct is such that in all probability a bribe will occur. Although the firm did not bribe anyone, the mens rea of the offense is established, as it acted knowing that its actions would cause this result.

Mens rea can also be established if a person acts recklessly or negligently, as the following case illustrates.

STATE V. WHEAT

Court of Appeals of Louisiana
471 So.2d 1027 (1985)

BACKGROUND: Deborah Wheat was convicted of negligent homicide under Louisiana law and was sentenced to four years imprisonment at hard labor. She appealed, arguing that the record contained no evidence proving "criminal negligence," an essential element of the crime of negligent homicide. Additional facts are in the opinion.

Edwards, Judge

In a non-jury trial the court found the following facts. At approximately 10:30 p.m. on April 30, 1983, Deborah Wheat was driving a 1969 Cadillac on Union Avenue, a well lighted residential area in Bogalusa, Louisiana. She made a turn at a high rate of speed onto Wilmuth Street and proceeded south. She accelerated steadily for about 180 yards with no slowing or braking, weaving all the while back and forth across the road. Farther along on Wilmuth Street, Peter Voltolina had parked his Ford automobile along the northbound lane of travel, partially in the roadway, with its headlights on. Two men were standing out in the street beside the car, speaking with Voltolina who was seated behind the wheel. The Cadillac struck both men and the Ford, killing one man and severely injuring the other.

Deborah Wheat had been seen earlier in the evening at a barroom where she was observed to be unsteady on her feet, but no one saw her actually drinking. Police at the accident scene smelled alcohol on her breath, and they found several empty beer cans in her car. No sobriety test was performed on defendant at any time. There was conflicting testimony as to whether she actually drank anything that night, since her mother and her friend, Rhonda Pierce, both testified that Deborah Wheat had remained sober.

The trial court evaluated the record and held that defendant had been drinking heavily, was drunk, had no business driving a vehicle, and consequently failed to maintain control of her automobile.

LSA-R.S. 14:32 provides in part, "[N]egligent homicide is the killing of a human being by criminal negligence." LSA-R.S. 14:12 goes on to say, "[C]riminal negligence exists when, although neither specific nor general criminal intent is present, there is such disregard of the interest of others that the offender's conduct amounts to a gross deviation below the standard of care expected to be maintained by a reasonably careful man under like circumstances."

The applicable standard for reviewing sufficiency is whether, after viewing the evidence in the light most favorable to the prosecution, any rational trier of fact could have found that the essential elements of the crime were proven beyond a reasonable doubt.

In *State v. Fontenot,* the supreme court set forth the essential elements of negligent homicide which the State must prove:

(1) that defendant was criminally negligent, i.e., that there was such disregard of the interest of others that the offender's conduct amounted to a gross deviation below the standard of care expected to be maintained by a reasonably careful man under like circumstances; and (2) that a killing resulted from this conduct.

Defendant argues on appeal that the State proved only ordinary negligence as opposed to the required criminal negligence. She denies being drunk, citing the conflicting testimony. She argues that the speed of her vehicle was never firmly established and that the victim was negligently standing in the roadway next to a car that was improperly parked in the street. Lastly, she claims that her vehicle was weaving due to her own efforts to avoid an accident.

There is ample evidence in the record to sustain a holding that Deborah Wheat was drunk at the time of the accident. The trial judge stated that the helpful testimony on defendant's behalf by her mother and by Rhonda Pierce was actually prevarication and could not be accepted.

Likewise, the record justifies the finding that Deborah Wheat was speeding in a residential neighborhood. Several witnesses testified that they heard squealing tires as she turned onto Wilmuth Street and that the car's motor was running much too fast for moderate travel. Some witnesses saw the car approaching and noticed that its speed was too great for that particular street. Another witness seated in the parked Ford cried out in warning as the Cadillac approached on its collision course.

Defendant's contention that she was weaving to avoid an accident is hardly credible when considered in proper context. She was on an unobstructed residential street with adequate lighting and dry pavement. Even though the Ford which she struck was parked partially in the street, defendant's lane was completely open and accessible. No weaving was necessary since there was nothing for her to avoid.

This court agrees with the trial court that the test for criminal negligence was adequately met. Drunk driving at an excessive speed in a residential neighborhood constitutes a gross deviation below the standard of care expected to be maintained by a reasonable person.

DECISION: The appellate court affirmed the trail court's judgment.

Regulatory Crimes

There are a limited number of crimes that do not require mens rea. These are often referred to as "strict liability" crimes. Several of them are of particular importance to business. They apply to industries that are closely regulated by government. These industries involve the sale of potentially harmful products such as drugs and alcohol. Examples of strict liability offenses are actions such as the mislabeling of drugs or the sale of liquor to minors. In both of these situations many states provide that the person who committed the act will be liable even if he or she has acted in error.

When a legislature creates a regulatory crime, it has decided that the need to protect the public outweighs the traditional requirement that a person in order to be guilty of a criminal act must have a guilty mind. Because mens rea is not required, most regulatory crimes do not have punishments that are as severe as those for other crimes. Some states have made a fine the maximum penalty for regulatory crimes.

Steps in the Criminal Justice Process

The criminal justice system is complex. Criminal law involves both state and federal constitutions, state and federal legislation, and state and federal cases interpreting both constitutions and legislation. Variations in procedures for dealing with crimes exist from jurisdiction to jurisdiction. In the following paragraphs, if a substantial number of jurisdictions handle an issue one way and a substantial number handle it another way, both methods are mentioned. If only one method is mentioned, that is the manner in which the majority of states treat it.

Report of the Crime and Prearrest Investigation

The criminal justice system usually starts when the police receive information concerning the possible commission of a crime. The police may obtain this information from an outside source or through their own investigation. If it appears likely that a crime has been committed, the offense will be recorded as a "reported" crime. The officer must then determine whether the crime actually was committed and whether there is sufficient information indicating the guilt of a particular person to justify arresting and charging that person.

A variety of investigatory techniques may be used. The suspect could be questioned, potential witnesses interviewed, and the scene of the crime examined. The examination of the scene often involves collection of physical evidence.

Arrest

Arrest is taking a person into custody in a lawful manner and charging him or her with a crime. In order to make a lawful arrest, an officer must have probable cause to believe that a crime has been committed. **Probable cause** requires that the officer have reasonable grounds based upon more evidence for than against that an accused has committed a crime. The evidence must be such that it would convince an ordinarily prudent person.

Most arrests are made on the basis of a warrant. To obtain a warrant, a law enforcement officer must file a sworn complaint with the court alleging that a crime has been committed. If the court is convinced that probable cause exists and that a crime has been committed, it issues a warrant.

A law enforcement officer may also obtain a warrant on the basis of a grand jury indictment. A **grand jury** is a body of citizens that hears evidence from a prosecutor concerning criminal activities. An **indictment** is an instrument that charges the accused with committing a crime. The grand jury decides whether there is sufficient evidence to indict someone for the crime. It does not decide whether the person is guilty; it merely decides that there is sufficient evidence to indict. When it does decide that there is sufficient evidence, a judge issues a warrant for the person's arrest based upon the indictment.

In some situations an officer may make an arrest without a warrant. The general rule is that an officer may make a warrantless arrest for a felony if probable cause exists and the officer believes that the suspect may not easily be located again. Ordinarily warrantless arrests for misdemeanors may be made only if the misdemeanor is committed in the officer's presence.

Booking

After arrest the accused is taken to the stationhouse for recording the arrest and the offense that motivated it. This part of the process is called "booking." If the arrest is for a misdemeanor, the person arrested may be released by paying "stationhouse bail." To effect release, the accused must put up cash as security and promise to appear before a magistrate on a given day. If arrested for a more serious offense, the person will be put in a holding cell until he or she is presented before a magistrate. Before bringing the accused before a magistrate, the arresting officer must write a report as to what occurred and have it reviewed by a superior officer. The superior officer may decide that charging the individual arrested with criminal activity would not be the best way to handle the case. The officer may reduce the charges or give the accused a warning and release him or her from custody.

First Appearance

If the higher-ranking officer decides to continue the process, most states require that the arrested suspect be taken promptly before a magistrate, commissioner, or justice of the peace. This public official informs the suspect of the charges and of the suspect's constitutional rights. If the charges involve only misdemeanors, the accused may elect to plead guilty. At that time a sentence may be imposed on the accused without any further proceedings. If the accused pleads not guilty or if the charges involve a felony, the public officer will set the bail.

Preliminary Hearing   During the preliminary hearing before the magistrate the prosecutor must introduce enough evidence to convince a magistrate that there is probable cause to believe that the accused committed the crime. If the magistrate believes that the probable cause exists, he or she will "bind the case over" to the next stage in the proceedings. In some jurisdictions the case is "bound over" to a grand jury. If the grand jury agrees with the decision of the magistrate that probable cause exists, the grand jury returns an indictment, which is designed to notify the person of the charges so that he or she can prepare a defense. Some jurisdictions do not provide a grand jury review. They have the magistrate issue an *information*. Like the indictment, an information notifies the accused of the charges against him or her so that a defense can be prepared.

Charges and Plea

Once charges have been filed with a trial court, the defendant is informed of them and asked to enter a plea. If the individual is charged with a serious crime, he or she can elect whether to have a jury trial or to be tried by a judge. A serious crime is usually defined as one for which incarceration of more than six months is possible. The defendant may enter a plea of guilty, not guilty, or nolo contendere. *Nolo contendere* is a plea in which the defendant does not admit guilt but agrees not to contest the charges. Some courts treat this the same as a guilty plea; however, the nolo contendere plea cannot be used against the defendant in a civil case.

In this stage of the judicial process **plea bargaining** often occurs. The use of plea bargaining varies from jurisdiction to jurisdiction. The purpose of plea bargaining is to get the defendant to plead guilty. This substantially reduces the prosecutor's task as a trial is no longer necessary.

In plea bargaining the prosecutor and the accused negotiate as to the particular criminal violation with which the accused will be charged. Some students of the criminal justice system are critical of plea bargaining because it allows the accused to accept responsibility for a less serious crime. Many different reasons exist for a defendant to plea-bargain. Probably the most significant is to substitute a less serious offense in place of the one for which the accused is charged. This reduces uncertainty and almost always means a lesser sentence.

There are two types of plea bargains: those that reduce the seriousness of the charges and those that reduce the severity of the sentence. For example, a defendant might agree to plead guilty to a charge of manslaughter to avoid a possible conviction for murder, which in many states carries the death penalty. Although it is the prosecutor, not the judge, who participates in plea bargaining, the recommendation of the prosecutor as to what the sentence should be usually greatly influences the sentence.

ETHICS
Plea Bargain

Jack attempted to murder his employer. The government filed first degree murder charges against Jack and the police arrested him. After the preliminary hearing, it became evident to the prosecutor that the state lacked enough evidence to be certain of obtaining a conviction at trial. Rather than risk the possibility of losing at trial, the prosecutor proposed to Jack's attorney that Jack plead guilty to a reduced charge—manslaughter. The reduced charge carried a maximum penalty of 10 years in jail. First degree murder carried a maximum penalty of life in prison.

Taking into consideration that there is good evidence to suggest Jack was guilty of first degree murder, is it ethical to propose such a plea to Jack? If the state failed to convince the jury, Jack would be released from jail. He might harm other persons. Taking this into consideration, one could at least argue that it would be in the best interest of society at large to remove him from society, at least for some time. The experience of jail might also discourage Jack from violating the law in the future.

FIGURE 5-1

Steps in a Criminal
Proceeding

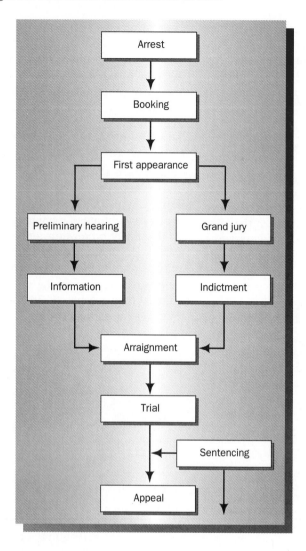

Trial: Standards of Proof

The final basic stage of the criminal judicial process, excluding appeals, is the trial. The prosecution has the entire burden of proof. The defendant does not have to prove anything. The standard of proof required to judge a person guilty in a criminal proceeding is not the probable cause standard that applied earlier in the criminal judicial process; it is proof beyond a reasonable doubt.

If convicted, the criminal will be sentenced. The punishment will vary from case to case, depending on the statutes that define the crimes and their punishment, and on the degree of latitude the judge is allowed in sentencing from one case to another.

Figure 5-1 lists the steps in a criminal proceeding.

Defenses

Even if a criminal defendant has committed the acts that he or she has been accused of, the defendant may avoid liability if he or she has a valid *defense*. Some of the more important criminal defenses are discussed below.

Entrapment

Entrapment occurs when a law enforcement officer or other government official induces someone to commit a crime that he or she otherwise would not have committed. For the defense of entrapment to apply, the idea for the crime must originate with the law enforcement official and not the accused. Assume, for example, that an undercover police officer chooses a teenager at random and induces him to deliver illegal narcotics to a certain address in exchange for cash. If the teenager is arrested for trafficking in illegal narcotics, he might be able to escape liability by raising the entrapment defense.

The defense of entrapment does not, however, prohibit the police from mounting "sting" operations to trap criminals. If the prosecution can prove the defendant was *predisposed* to commit the crime, then the defense will not be applied. For example, assume that an undercover vice squad officer poses as a prostitute and is propositioned by a would-be customer. If the would-be customer is arrested for soliciting a prostitute, he would not be entitled to assert the defense of entrapment.

Mistake

A mistake of fact may negate the mens rea requirement for criminal liability. Assume that Joe, at an airport baggage-claim area, mistakenly picks up someone else's suitcase, which is of the same color, size, and make as Joe's suitcase. In a prosecution for theft, Joe would be able to assert the defense of mistake.

While a mistake of fact can absolve one of criminal liability, a mistake of law, except in certain very limited circumstances, cannot. A person thus cannot escape criminal liability for failing to file a tax return by claiming that he didn't know it was required. As the saying goes, "Ignorance of the law is no excuse."

Duress

The defense of **duress** is available when someone is forced to commit a crime to escape an immediate threat of serious physical harm or death. Assume that Fred is waiting in line at a bank when a robber bursts in. The robber puts a gun to Fred's head and demands that Fred assist him in the robbery. If Fred complies, he will probably be able to absolve himself of criminal liability by asserting the defense of duress. Duress traditionally has not been recognized as a defense to murder, but some jurisdictions have abolished this limitation.

Incapacity

The defense of **incapacity** is available when one does not have the mental capacity to understand the moral consequences of one's acts. Incapacity thus negates the mens rea that is generally re-

quired to establish criminal liability. Three types of incapacity are infancy, insanity, and intoxication, which are discussed below.

Infancy   Under the common law, a child younger than 7 years old could not be convicted of a crime. It was presumed conclusively that a child of that age was incapable of distinguishing between right and wrong. Children between 7 and 14 years of age were *presumed* under the common law to lack the capacity to form mens rea; that presumption could be rebutted, however, by evidence that the child understood the moral consequences of his or her acts. The law in most states is derived from the common law rule, although the age ranges vary from state to state.

Insanity   An insane person may lack the capacity to form the mens rea necessary to convict the person of a crime. According to the traditional rule, insanity may be used as a defense if the defendant's mental illness prevented him or her from appreciating the wrongful nature of the criminal act or from distinguishing between right and wrong. Some states also allow the insanity defense for a defendant whose mental illness created an "irresistible impulse" to commit the criminal act, even if the defendant knew it was wrong.

Intoxication   Intoxication through the voluntary consumption of drugs or alcohol generally is not a defense to a crime. However, intoxication can serve as a defense if the crime requires proof of some *specific intent* and the defendant's intoxication made it impossible for the defendant to form that specific intent. For example, a person may not be convicted of first degree murder in most states unless the killing was premeditated and performed with malice. If Mel kills someone while intoxicated, he may be able to argue that his intoxication prevented him from forming the state of mind necessary for murder. However, Mel's intoxication would not be a defense to a lesser offense requiring mere recklessness, such as manslaughter.

Justifiable Use of Force

One may use reasonable force to protect one's property. Deadly force is never justified to protect property only. Deadly force may be used, however, in circumstances where one reasonably believes that such force is necessary to protect oneself from the immediate threat of great bodily harm or death.

Criminal Procedure

As noted in Chapter 3, the United States has an adversarial system of justice. In an adversarial system each party is responsible for developing and proving its own case. As the state with its extensive resources seems to have an advantage in a criminal case, a fundamental goal of criminal procedure is to ensure that the accused, who must defend against the state, is not convicted erroneously. Society prefers that some guilty individuals escape conviction rather than have an innocent person convicted of a crime.

Although protecting the innocent person is a primary goal of criminal procedure, other goals are also important. These other goals include minimizing the burden placed upon the person who is accused of a crime and must stand trial, maintaining the appearance as well as the reality of fairness, and achieving equality in the application of the law. The combination of these goals has played a significant role in shaping the procedures in the criminal justice system of the United States.

Procedural Protections: The Bill of Rights

A defendant in a criminal case benefits from a number of procedural protections. Several of these are contained in the Bill of Rights of the Constitution. Although the Bill of Rights expressly limits the power of the federal government only, the U.S. Supreme Court has determined that most of the important guarantees of the Bill of Rights bind state governments as well. A brief summary of the provisions of the Bill of Rights that apply to criminal procedure follows.

The Fourth Amendment   The Fourth Amendment states, "The right of the people to be secure in their persons, houses, papers, and effects, against unreasonable searches and seizures, shall not be violated, and no Warrants shall issue, but upon probable cause, supported by Oath or affirmation, and particularly describing the place to

be searched, and the persons or things to be seized." Probable cause is thus required before a warrant is issued.

There are certain situations in which a police officer may conduct a search without first obtaining a valid search warrant. These include situations in which the party voluntarily consents to the search, where the police officer is in hot pursuit of the suspect or where incriminating evidence is in the police officer's plain view from a public place.

In order to protect citizens from unlawful searches and seizures, the Supreme Court has developed the **exclusionary rule.** According to the exclusionary rule, any evidence obtained as a direct or indirect result of a Fourth Amendment violation will not be admissible against the defendant in court. Assume, for example, that the police, acting on a tip, search Bob's house for drugs without first obtaining a search warrant. The search turns up large amounts of illegal drugs and Bob is arrested. Because the warrantless search was a violation of Bob's Fourth Amend-

---

ISSUES AND TRENDS
Exclusionary Rule

For many years, particularly in the 1950s and 1960s, the U.S. Supreme Court favored a broad interpretation of the exclusionary rule. This of course resulted in the state not having enough evidence in some cases to convict persons who had in fact perpetrated the crime in question. The philosophical attitudes of new justices appointed to the Supreme Court after that time differed with that of the justices on the Court in the 1950s and 1960s. The new justices were more responsive to the criticism that this rule sometimes allows persons to escape conviction.

In more recent years, the Supreme Court has narrowed the application of the exclusionary rule. For example, the Supreme Court has recognized a "good faith" exception to the rule which allows prosecutors to present evidence obtained pursuant to an invalid search warrant as long as the police relied on the warrant in good faith.

Ethics
Defending Controversial Criminals

We are accustomed to seeing attorneys represent highly controversial or unpopular parties. Think of your reaction when you saw attorneys representing the defendants charged with bombing the World Trade Center, or the government of Iraq in disputes with the United States. Or think of local stories in which people were charged with crimes and you felt the individual was guilty. Yet you see an attorney aggressively defending them on the television news.

Assume even further that the attorney personally believes that the client is guilty. Does that mean that the attorney is acting unethically? The role obligation of lawyers is an important consideration in such situations. Lawyers are expected to represent their clients' interests. The Model Rules of Professional Conduct (adopted with some variations in many states) provide: "A lawyer's representation of a client . . . does not constitute an endorsement of the client's political, economic, social or moral views or activities," and: "A lawyer shall not counsel a client to engage, or assist a client, in conduct that the lawyer knows is criminal. . . ." The comments to the Model Rules further provide "A criminal accused has a right to the assistance of an advocate, a right to testify and a right of confidential communication with counsel."

Even guilty criminals have a right to counsel to ensure that their legal rights are protected and to provide assistance in all stages of a criminal proceeding, including the sentencing process if the accused is convicted. In what circumstances, if any, would you want to limit the actions of counsel for those accused of criminal violations?

ment rights, the prosecution will not be permitted to introduce any evidence that drugs were found in Bob's house during the search. If the illegal search had turned up a clue that led the police to additional incriminating evidence against Bob (for example, an address where Bob processed drugs), the prosecution would not be able to introduce that additional evidence either. The exclusionary rule prevents prosecutors from enjoying the "fruit of a poisonous tree." In this case, the state would probably not be left with enough evidence to convict Bob.

The Fifth Amendment The Fifth Amendment provides that no one can be deprived of "life, liberty, or property" without due process of the law. *Due process*, as discussed in Chapter 4, means that the procedures in litigation—either civil or criminal—must be fair. The person must have adequate notice of the charges being brought against him or her and an opportunity to defend before an impartial court. Fairness means also that the proceedings in a particular case must be the same as those in similar cases and the parties must have the same responsibilities and privileges as parties in similar cases.

The prohibition against double jeopardy is also in the Fifth Amendment. **Double jeopardy** means trying someone more than once for a single offense. This may occur when more than one person is victimized in a particular crime, but only one victim is involved in the criminal suit. After the defendant is tried for that alleged crime, the victim not involved in the original court case cannot initiate another trial.

The prohibition against double jeopardy means that the state may not appeal an acquittal.

The Sixth Amendment The Sixth Amendment states: "In all criminal prosecutions, the accused shall enjoy the right to a speedy and public trial, by an impartial jury of the State and district wherein the crime shall have been committed, which district shall have been previously ascertained by law, and to be informed of the nature and cause of the accusation; to be confronted with the witnesses against him; to have compulsory process for obtaining witnesses in his favor, and to have the Assistance of Counsel for his defence." This amendment contains many protections for the defendant in a criminal action, including the right to an impartial jury.

The Sixth Amendment right to fair trial before an impartial jury can sometimes conflict with the First Amendment guarantee of press freedom. When a sensational case has received extensive news coverage, it can be difficult to find potential jurors who do not bring some preexisting bias to the case. The tension between the First and Sixth Amendments is explored in the case that follows.

IN RE APPLICATION OF DOW JONES & COMPANY

U.S. Court of Appeals, Second Circuit

842 F.2d 603 (1988)

BACKGROUND: A major scandal erupted when Wedtech, a military contractor, was charged with fraudulently obtaining federal contracts that were set aside for minority-owned businesses. A number of prominent government officials, including former Congressman Mario Biaggi and former Bronx Borough President Stanley Simon, were charged with fraud, racketeering, bribery, and other crimes. The case received much publicity, and details from the grand jury proceedings—which were supposed to be secret—were leaked to the news media before indictments were returned. The district court issued a "gag order" which prohibited the parties to the case from talking to the media. A number of news organizations, including the *Wall Street Journal,* NBC, and the Associated Press, appealed the order.

Cardamone, Circuit Judge

The record reflects a plethora of publicity concerning the Wedtech investigation since October 1986. From then until the April 1, 1987 indictment, articles appeared in all of the region's major newspapers detailing the joint federal-state investigation and the grand jury proceedings relating to Stanley Simon. Although the attribution to sources and the facts vary in their specificity, and perhaps accuracy, the net effect clearly translated secret grand jury proceedings into matters of public knowledge. In late May 1987, news articles again described in detail the targets, charges, negotiations, and timing of the superseding June 3 indictment. The news stories revealed what was being investigated, what the grand jury was hearing, what witnesses were being called or about to be called, and what they would say. This apparently accurate information was often ascribed to "law enforcement sources," "law enforcement officials," and "prosecutors."

In these and other flurries of publicity, the prosecutors, defendants, and defense counsel participated in the escalating publicity duels. As a result, on April 10, 1987—nine days after the original indictment was filed against Stanley Simon—his defense counsel orally proposed in open court before Judge Cannella that the parties agree to a "gag" order restraining extrajudicial speech by all trial participants. Simon's counsel asserted that media publicity resulting from state and federal prosecutors' violation of grand jury secrecy required a blanket order to insure that his client received a fair trial. . . .

On April 23, 1987 the district court nonetheless entered a broad restraining order directed to the prosecutors, defendants, and defense counsel. . . . On July 10 the district court modified its April 23 order so that it provides

Ordered, that the United States Attorney and the District Attorney for Bronx County, their representatives and agents, defendants Stanley Simon, Mario Biaggi, John Mariotta, Peter Neglia, Bernard Ehrlich, Richard Biaggi and Ronald Betso, and their counsel and representatives SHALL NOT MAKE ANY extrajudicial statement concerning this case (1) to any person associated with a public communications media, or

(2) that a reasonable person would expect to be communicated to a public communications media, except that nothing in this Order shall prohibit any individual from:

(A) Stating, without elaboration or characterization—

    (1) the general nature of an allegation or defense;

    (2) information contained in the public record;

    (3) the scheduling or result of any step in the proceedings; or

(B) Explaining, without characterization, the contents or substance of any motion or step in the proceedings, to the extent such motion or step is a matter of public record.

This Order supersedes all previous orders.

As appears from its terms, this order does not impinge on the full reporting of courtroom and other public proceedings. It prohibits virtually all other extrajudicial speech relating to the pending Wedtech case. . . . The impact of the subject order implicates press freedom, even though it does so indirectly. There is tension between the media's First Amendment right to publish and an accused person's Sixth Amendment right to a fair trial before an impartial jury.

Each right is crucial to the maintenance of a free society. Without freedom of the press a free society will not long endure. A free press is particularly important when public officials face criminal charges relating to their use of office. Although often appearing unfair in the eyes of the public, pretrial publicity, "even pervasive, adverse publicity—does not inevitably lead to an unfair trial." *Nebraska Press Ass'n v. Stuart.* It should not be overlooked that a jury need not consist of persons entirely ignorant of the case they are about to hear; all that the Constitution requires is a jury that is impartial, one that is capable of fairly deciding on the evidence before it whether defendants are innocent or guilty.

At the same time the proper administration of criminal justice must protect an accused's Sixth Amendment rights. "[T]he theory of our system," as Justice Holmes explained 80 years ago, "is that the conclusions to be reached in a case will be induced only by evidence and argument in open court, and not by any outside influence, whether of private talk or public print." *Patterson v. Colorado.* Aware of this inherent tension between freedom of the press and the right to trial by an impartial jury, the framers of our Constitution did not assign priorities between them. When the exercise of free press rights actually tramples upon Sixth Amendment rights, the former must nonetheless yield to the latter. . . .

To decide whether the pretrial publicity justified the order, the standard by which to measure justification is whether there is a "reasonable likelihood" that pretrial publicity will prejudice a fair trial. . . .

DECISION: The Court of Appeals affirmed the gag order.

The Eighth Amendment The Eighth Amendment prohibits excessive bail, excessive fines, and cruel and unusual punishment. Some have argued that punitive damages, which are awarded in civil cases to punish particularly offensive behavior, should be subject to the Eighth Amendment limit on excessive fines. Many businesses favor this view because a growing number of businesses have been required to pay extremely large amounts in punitive damages. The Eighth Amendment has traditionally been interpreted to apply to criminal fines only, and not to civil damages. However, those who favor applying the Eighth

Amendment to punitive damages note that since punitive damages are designed to punish wrong-doers rather than compensate victims, such damages bear more resemblance to criminal fines than to civil damages. The Supreme Court has yet to adopt this view.

Corporate Criminal Liability

Until the 1850s American law generally held that a corporation could not be guilty of a crime. The law rejected corporate criminal liability primarily on two grounds. First, as a corporation was not a living person, it could not have the guilty mind that the law required for a criminal conviction. In addition, as the corporation was an artificial person, it could not be physically punished. As corporations began to play a more significant role in the economy, the judicial system reexamined the reasons underlying corporate criminal immunity and rejected them.

The first successful cases against corporations involved strict liability offenses. An example is the mislabeling of drugs. This type of offense did not require the government to prove that the defendant had a guilty mind. All it had to prove was that the defendant did the act. As the criminal law evolved, courts also began to convict corporations of crimes that required criminal intent. Courts looked at the conduct of the corporation's agents and employees to establish this necessary element. Courts also concluded that although a corporation could not be physically punished, fining a corporation that had benefited through its employees' illegal acts was an appropriate sanction.

As corporate criminal liability expanded, corporations argued that fining the organization for the illegal acts of its employees was unfair. They contended that the punishment was really being inflicted upon the shareholders, who had done nothing wrong. Of course, if the board of directors authorized the employees' action, the corporation would be responsible. However, proving corporate authorization is very difficult.

Courts have usually rejected the argument that punishing the corporation for its employees' illegal act is unfair on public-policy grounds. As the corporation benefits from the illegal acts of its employees—both legal and illegal—it should be responsible for what they do within the scope of their authority.

As the criminal liability of corporations is based upon a determination that the acts and intent of its employees are the acts of the corporation, the status of the employee who commits the act is sometimes a question in criminal litigation involving corporations. Today, the majority rule in the United States is that acts of employees at most levels will be imputed to the corporate employer as long as the employee intended to benefit the organization.

White-Collar Crime

White-collar crime is a term commonly used to describe nonviolent criminal acts committed in a commercial context by members of the managerial or professional class. The term includes offenses committed by employees against their employers as well as offenses that business firms commit against the general public. Specific examples of white-collar crime are embezzlement, employee theft, bribery, antitrust violations, income tax evasion, bankruptcy fraud, and securities fraud.

White-collar crimes cost society billions of dollars. Criminal acts by employees may bankrupt a business, but even if they do not, they reduce profitability. The losses that are a result of criminal activity result in higher prices for goods and services, as firms must cover these losses to remain in business. Criminal offenses committed by business firms are an even greater burden on society. These acts not only add to the substantial cost of crime, but they also increase distrust of both business and government.

Almost all criminal acts can be committed in a commercial setting; however, some occur much more frequently in business than others. Some examples follow.

Bribery

Bribery is the offering, giving, receiving, or soliciting of money or anything else of value for the purpose of influencing governmental action. Bribery is one of the principal crimes that cause many people to be critical of business. Incidents of bribery appear frequently in the news. People are often familiar with major bribery scandals that involve business, such as the payment of millions of dollars to the president of Honduras to eliminate an unfavorable export tax on bananas. Another well-known example is the payment that Lockheed made to the prime minister of Japan to secure government contracts. During the 1980s bribery scandals involved high public officials of both the Carter and Reagan administrations.

Legal Principles   The primary focus of the law of bribery has been on payments to public officials. The classic example of an illegal bribe is a payment to a judge to obtain a favorable ruling in litigation. The typical statute might condemn "offering or giving or promising to give something of value with the corrupt intent to induce or influence the action, vote, or opinion of a person in any public or official capacity." Although most statutes require "corrupt" intent on the part of the payor, a few do not require intent and condemn outright certain payments to judges, jurors, witnesses, and others. The reasons generally given for condemning public bribes are to protect the public interest and to ensure the efficient and fair operation of governmental institutions.

Commercial bribes are treated more leniently under the law, with relatively few instances resulting in legal challenges. Although several federal and state statutes apply to commercial bribes in special circumstances, few laws deal specifically or solely with commercial bribes. Some state criminal antibribery statutes apply by their literal terms to commercial bribes. The New York Penal Code is an example. It provides as follows:

> A person is guilty of commercial bribing when he confers, or offers or agrees to confer any benefit upon any employee, agent, or fiduciary without the consent of the latter's employer or principal; with intent to influence his conduct in relation to his employer's or principal's affairs.

Approximately half the states condemn commercial bribery. The statutes generally require that there be an intent to influence the bribe-taker's conduct. The bribe-taker must be influenced in regard to some discretionary activity. Many statutes follow the lead of New York and condemn the soliciting of a bribe equally with the offering of one. About a dozen states prohibit a purchasing agent receiving something of value from a seller.

Larceny

Larceny is another crime frequently associated with business. **Larceny** involves the physical taking of another's property with the wrongful intent of depriving the owner of the property or its value. Statutes generally divide larceny into two grades according to the value of the property. **Grand larceny** involves property of substantial value and is a felony. **Petit larceny** involves less valuable property, usually less than $50, and is a misdemeanor.

In order to be larceny, the property must be taken without the owner's consent, but not by violence. If a person takes another's property by violence, the offense is **robbery.** Usually statutes make punishment for robbery more severe than punishment for larceny.

Some common law courts had difficulty applying larceny principles to a scam in which the wrongdoer tricked the owner into voluntarily giving up the property. They reasoned that the property was taken with the owner's consent. As a result, many states enacted "false pretenses" statutes. These statutes made it a crime for someone to obtain another's property by a statement that intentionally deceives the victim. Computer fraud and the fraudulent use of credit cards are other forms of larceny that legislatures often treat specifically by statutes.

Embezzlement

Business firms often are the victims of embezzlement. **Embezzlement** is the misappropriation of property, usually money, by one to whom it has been entrusted. The classic examples are bank employees or accountants who take for themselves money entrusted to them as part of their jobs.

Embezzlement and larceny differ. Embezzlement is committed when a person who legitimately has possession of someone else's property deprives that person of the property or its value. For example, if A rents an automobile intending not to return it and does not do so, the crime is larceny. On the other hand, if after renting the automobile A decides to keep it, the offense is embezzlement. An embezzlement is committed even if a person who is entrusted with property takes it intending to restore it before the loss is discovered and even if the property is actually returned.

UNITED STATES V. COIN

Court of Appeals, Ninth Circuit
753 F.2d 1510 (1985)

BACKGROUND: Raymond Coin (defendant-appellant) was convicted in U.S. District Court of embezzling tribal funds. He appealed, contending that the District Court had erred in refusing to give a jury instruction which stated that restitution, while not a defense to the crime, may be considered as evidence bearing on intent.

Per Curiam

Appellant Raymond Joseph Coin appeals his conviction by a jury for embezzling tribal funds in violation of 18 U.S.C. § 1163. He claims that the district court erred in refusing to give a jury instruction which stated that restitution, while not a defense to the crime, may be considered as evidence bearing on intent. We affirm.

Coin was elected vice-chairman of the Hopi Tribe in December 1981. As part of his duties, he was to run the Hopi Civic Center. In November of 1982, Coin obtained some blank requisitions, ostensibly to pay some bills for the Center. Coin's secretary subsequently picked up checks in the amount of the requisitions from the tribal treasurer's office, including one for $20,000 made out to Northern Arizona Theatre. The next day, Coin deposited the $20,000 check in a bank account he opened for Northern Arizona Theatre. From this account he made one payment of $12,258.59 to purchase movie equipment, and used the remainder for his personal benefit.

After Coin was indicted for embezzling tribal funds, but before trial, the Hopi Tribal Council demanded that he repay the embezzled funds with interest. Coin repaid the money without interest. At trial, Coin denied intending to embezzle, steal or convert funds to his own use, claiming that because the funds had been paid to his company, Northern Arizona Theatre, he could use some of the money for his own purposes. The district court refused to give Coin's restitution jury instruction, which stated that:

> You have heard evidence that the Defendant returned monies to the Hope [sic] tribe upon demand. While restitution is not a defense to the crimes with which the Defendant is charged, you may consider such payment as evidence bearing on intent.

The intent to return property is not a defense to embezzlement, nor to misapplication of funds. Such crimes are complete when the misapplication or embezzlement occurs. The victim of the crime is deprived of its right to make decisions about how its property or funds are to be used.

Some courts, however, have declared that restitution may be relevant on the issue of intent, primarily when restitution is contemporaneous with the crime.

Here, contemporaneity was lacking. Rather, Coin's offer to repay came months later, and repayment did not occur until after he was indicted. The crime occurred and was complete when funds were misapplied; whatever occurred later as to repayment was neither material nor a defense.

The district court correctly rejected Coin's proposed jury instruction. The instruction given was more favorable than was required.

DECISION: Affirmed.

Forgery

A person commits **forgery** when, with the intent to defraud, the person alters another's writing without authority or passes off an unauthentic document as genuine. If Sam adds a zero to his paycheck and attempts to cash it for $5,000 instead of $500, he has committed forgery.

Mail and Wire Fraud

Federal law makes it a crime to use the mails in connection with any scheme to defraud. Thus if Sleazeco mails brochures to advertise "genuine antique coins" which are really counterfeits, it will have violated the federal mail fraud statute.

Normally, a violation of the mail fraud statute can be punished by a fine of up to $1,000, a prison term of up to 5 years, or both. In the wake of the savings and loan scandal of the late 1980s, Congress added especially tough penalties for mail fraud violations that affect a financial institution. The maximum penalties in such a case are a fine of $1 million, a jail term of 30 years, or both.

Similarly, the federal wire fraud statute prohibits the use of wire, television, or radio communications in connection with a scheme to defraud. Telephone communications are considered "wire" communications and are thus covered by the statute. In the example above, Sleazeco would be guilty of wire fraud if it advertised its "genuine antique" counterfeit coins on radio or television. It would also be guilty of violating the statute if it conducted any business with respect to the coins over the phone. The penalties for wire fraud are identical to those for mail fraud, including the more severe punishment for violations that affect a financial institution.

Bankruptcy Fraud

Businesses that have accumulated too much debt may generally dissolve or reorganize themselves under the protection of the federal bankruptcy statutes. In the bankruptcy process, discussed in greater detail in Chapter 34, the court supervises the distribution of the debtor's assets among its creditors. The debtor is required to disclose all of its assets; the concealment of assets for the purpose of protecting them from creditors constitutes criminal bankruptcy fraud. Bankruptcy fraud may also be committed by creditors, who are required to file claims for amounts that they are owed by the debtor. It is a crime for a creditor to file a false claim.

Money Laundering

Parties who derive income from an illegal source, such as drug dealing, often attempt to make it appear as if the funds were generated from a legitimate source. This is known as **money laundering.** The federal Money Laundering Control Act makes it a crime to enter into a financial transaction with the intent to conceal an illegal source of funds. Suppose that Jim has made $100,000 from the sale of illegal drugs. He wants to make it appear that he received the $100,000 by borrowing it from a legitimate source, so he prepares false loan documents to evidence a $100,000 loan. Jim has engaged in criminal money laundering.

Conspiracy

When two or more people agree to cooperate in the commission of a crime, they have each committed the separate crime of **conspiracy.** Conspirators may be punished for conspiracy in addition to the crime that they have conspired to commit. In most jurisdictions, criminal liability for conspiracy does not accrue until one of the conspirators performs some overt act in furtherance of the criminal purpose. Once one conspirator performs such an overt act, all of the conspirators become criminally liable for the conspiracy. This is true even if the conspirators do not ultimately commit the crime that they had planned to commit.

Other White-Collar Crimes

During the past 75 years Congress and the states have enacted numerous laws that expand the criminal liability of business firms. In some instances these acts prohibit actions that were previously lawful. Often these acts provide both criminal and civil penalties. Because of the importance of these statutes to business, several of them are discussed in later chapters. They include the Sherman Act, which is the subject of Chapter 54, and the 1933 and 1934 securities acts, which are discussed in Chapter 46.

TABLE 5-1

Concept Summary	Common White-Collar Crimes
Bribery	Offering, giving, receiving, or soliciting anything of value for the purpose of influencing governmental action
Larceny	Physical taking of another's property with the intent of depriving the owner of it
Embezzlement	Wrongful taking of another's property by a person legitimately in possession of the property
Forgery	Altering another's writing without authority or passing off an unauthentic document as genuine, in either case with the intent to defraud
Mail fraud	Using the mails in connection with any scheme to defraud
Wire fraud	Communicating any message or image with the intent to defraud over the telephone, wire, television, or radio
Bankruptcy fraud	Among other examples, concealing assets (debtor) or filing a false claim (creditor)
Money laundering	Concealing the source of funds derived through illegal activity
Conspiracy	Agreeing with another to cooperate in the commission of a crime; in most jurisdictions, at least one conspirator must perform at least one act in furtherance of the conspiracy

Persons convicted of violating the Sherman Act, the securities acts, or the Foreign Corrupt Practices Act, as well as numerous other federal and state acts, are subject to substantial fines and imprisonment. For example, an individual convicted of a Sherman Act violation can be fined up to $350,000 and sentenced up to 3 years in jail. A corporation is subject to a maximum fine of $10 million. Many violations of federal securities laws are also subject to criminal prosecution.

RICO

In 1970 Congress enacted the Racketeer Influenced and Corrupt Organizations Act, commonly known as **RICO.** Although the original purpose of the Act was to fight organized crime, RICO's broad sweep has enabled it to be used against legitimate businesses with no ties to gangsters. Indeed, RICO has fast become one of the most feared statutes in the business community.

RICO was passed in response to a growing concern that gangsters were taking over legitimate businesses. In enacting RICO, Congress attempted to provide a weapon that could be used to limit the infiltration of business by organized crime. RICO has both criminal and civil provisions, both of which are discussed below. The civil provisions of RICO (often referred to as "Civil RICO") are a major concern to legitimate businesses. Civil RICO is discussed in this chapter because civil liability under RICO must be predicated on the defendant's criminal activity.

Basic Provisions

Section 1962 of RICO prohibits any person from using a "pattern of racketeering activity" to invest in, maintain an interest in, or participate in an "enterprise." Since RICO is a federal act, it applies only to enterprises that affect interstate commerce.

RICO defines both "enterprise" and "racketeering activity" very broadly. An enterprise under RICO includes "any partnership, corporation, association, or other legal entity, and any union or group of individuals associated in fact although not a legal entity." Racketeering encompasses a broad range of activities, including bankruptcy fraud, embezzlement from pension and union funds, mail and wire fraud, securities law violations, and money laundering.

In order to violate Section 1962, the defendant must engage in a *pattern* of racketeering activity. In order to establish a pattern, the defendant must engage in at least two acts of racketeering. Furthermore, there must be some relationship and continuity between those acts—isolated acts do not constitute a "pattern." An act that can serve as the basis of a RICO violation is known as a **predicate offense.**

Criminal Sanctions

A person who violates RICO Section 1962 is subject to stiff criminal sanctions. A convicted violator may be fined in an amount up to $25,000, jailed for up to 20 years, or both. Perhaps more importantly, RICO provides for the forfeiture of the gains that the defendant acquired through the illegal activity. As a result, the government in a successful prosecution can seize the legitimate business interests acquired by "racketeering" profits. This deprives the individual of the ability to continue to control business and weakens the hold that organized crime has over legitimate business.

Civil RICO

Although the stated purpose of RICO is to combat organized crime, RICO is a major source of potential civil liability for legitimate business firms. Section 1964(c) of RICO allows any person whose business or property has been injured as a result of a Section 1962 violation to collect treble damages (three times the amount actually lost), court costs, and attorney's fees.

Significantly, a defendant need not have been convicted of the predicate offenses in order to incur civil RICO liability—it is sufficient that the defendant *could be* convicted of each of the required predicate offenses. Recall our example from earlier in the chapter in which Sleazeco advertises "genuine antique coins"—which are really counterfeit—through mailed brochures and television commercials. In doing so, Sleazeco could be charged with violating the federal mail fraud and wire fraud statutes. A violation of either statute is a predicate offense under RICO. Therefore, Sleazeco can be held liable for a RICO violation if the mail fraud violation and the wire fraud violation form a "pattern." The two offenses most likely would be deemed to form a pattern in this case, since they are not isolated, unconnected events. Assume, though, that Sleazeco is never convicted of these offenses. Now assume that Sam has purchased $100,000 worth of Sleazeco's coins and later learns that

they are fake. Sam then brings a civil RICO action against Sleazeco for treble damages. In order to prevail, Sam must show by a mere *preponderance of the evidence* that Sleazeco committed the predicate offenses, that they constituted a pattern, and that Sam was injured as a result. Note that if Sleazeco were being prosecuted for either of the predicate offenses or for a criminal violation of RICO, the state would have to prove that the violations occurred *beyond a reasonable doubt.* It is thus easier to prove a civil RICO claim than to win a criminal RICO prosecution on the basis of the exact same behavior.

Many business managers worry about the prospect of being stained with the label of "racketeer" by losing a civil RICO case, even if they are never convicted of any criminal wrongdoing. Because of the threat of triple damages and adverse public relations resulting from a charge of racketeering, a business firm will often settle a civil RICO claim even if the case against the firm is very weak.

One of the major complaints about RICO is that even though it was designed to fight organized crime, its terms don't appear to distinguish between violations that are characteristic of organized crime and those that aren't. As a result, "garden variety" fraud and breach-of-contract claims—the type that many legitimate businesses are forced to defend—can subject a business with no mob ties to RICO's severe sanctions.

In the 1980s, once attorneys began to recognize that RICO could be used in civil suits, a tremendous upsurge in the number of civil RICO suits began to swamp the courts. Many civil suits routinely included a RICO claim. Some of these suits resulted in enormous judgments against people and businesses that had only the most distant relationship to the operation of the alleged criminal enterprise.

The following case represents an attempt by the U.S. Supreme Court to curtail the use of RICO in suits against persons who were not actively engaged in managing or operating a business. This case curtails abuse by limiting the potential defendants to those actually running the enterprise. Even so, it should be noted that an outsider associated with the operation and management of an enterprise still can be subject to damages under civil RICO.

REVES V. ERNST & YOUNG

U.S. Supreme Court
1993 U.S. Lexis 1940 (1993)

BACKGROUND: Jack White, the general manager of the Farmer's Cooperative of Arkansas and Oklahoma, Inc. (the Co-Op) began taking loans from the Co-Op to finance the construction of a gasohol plant by his company, White Flame Fuels, Inc. In 1980, White proposed that the Co-Op purchase White Flame. Thereafter, White and the Co-Op entered into a consent decree relieving White of his debts and providing that the Co-Op had owned White Flame since February 15, 1980.

The Co-Op retained Joe Drozal of Russell Brown to perform its 1981 financial audit. In 1982, Russell Brown was merged with Arthur Young and Company, which later became Ernst & Young. In the course of the audit, Drozal concluded that White Flame's 1981 fixed-asset value was approximately $4.5 million. Drozal had to determine how that value should be treated for accounting purposes. Suffice it to say that he chose to value it at $4.5 million, rather than a lower figure which would have indicated the Co-Op was insolvent.

On April 22, 1982, Arthur Young presented its 1981 audit report to the Co-Op's board. In that audit's note 9, Arthur Young expressed doubt whether the investment in White Flame could ever be recovered. Arthur Young did not tell the board of its conclusion that the Co-Op had always owned White Flame or that without that conclusion the Co-Op was insolvent. At the Co-Op's 1982 annual meeting, Arthur Young distributed to the Co-Op's members condensed financial statements. These included White Flame's $4.5 million asset value among its total assets but omitted the information contained in the audit's note 9.

In February 1984, the Co-Op filed for bankruptcy. The trustee in bankruptcy filed suit against 40 individuals and entities including Arthur Young on behalf of the Co-Op and certain noteholders. The Court of Appeals applied a "manage or operate" test in arriving at its conclusion that Arthur Young was not liable under RICO. The United States Supreme Court affirmed the decision of the Court of Appeals on behalf of Arthur Young.

Blackmun, Justice

In determining the scope of a statute, we look first to its language. If the statutory language is unambiguous, in the absence of a clearly expressed legislative intent to the contrary, that language must ordinarily be regarded as conclusive. Section 1962(c) makes it unlawful "for any person employed by or associated with any enterprise . . . to conduct or participate, directly or indirectly, in the conduct of such enterprise's affairs through a pattern of racketeering activity. . . ."

The narrow question in this case is the meaning of the phrase "to conduct or participate, directly or indirectly, in the conduct of such enterprise's affairs." As a verb, "conduct" means to lead, run, manage, or direct. Congress could easily have written "participate, directly or indirectly, in an enterprise's affairs," but it chose to repeat the word "conduct." We conclude therefore that "conduct" requires an element of direction.

The more difficult question is what to make of the word "participate." Petitioners argue that Congress used "participate" as a synonym for "aid and abet." Within the meaning of section 1962(c) "participate" appears to have a narrower meaning. It seems that Congress chose a middle ground, consistent with a common understanding of the word "participate"—to take part in.

Once we understand the word "conduct" to require some degree of direction and the word "participate" to require some part in that direction, the meaning of section 1962(c) comes into focus. In order to "participate, directly or indirectly, in the conduct of such enterprise's affairs," one must have some part in directing those affairs. The "operation or management" test expresses this requirement in a formulation that is easy to apply.

Of course, "outsiders" may be liable under section 1962(c) if they are "associated with" an enterprise and participate in the conduct of its affairs—that is, participate in the operation or management of the enterprise itself.

In sum, we hold that "to conduct or participate, directly or indirectly, in the conduct of such enterprise's affairs," one must participate in the operation or management of the enterprise itself.

In the existing case, it is undisputed that Arthur Young relied upon existing Co-Op records in preparing the 1981 and 1982 audit reports. The AICPA's professional standards state that an auditor may draft financial statements in whole or in part based on information from management's accounting system. It is also undisputed that Arthur Young's audit reports revealed to the Co-Op's board that the value of the gasohol plant had been calculated based on the Co-Op's investment in the plant. Thus, we only could conclude that Arthur Young participated in the operation or management of the Co-Op itself if Arthur Young's failure to tell the Co-Op's board that the plant should have been given its fair market value constituted such participation. We think that Arthur Young's failure in this respect is not sufficient to give rise to liability under section 1962(c).

DECISION: The judgment of the Court of Appeals is affirmed.

Review Questions and Problems

Key Terms

crime	exclusionary rule
felony	double jeopardy
misdemeanor	bribery
petty offense	larceny
actus reus	grand larceny
mens rea	petit larceny
arrest	robbery
probable cause	embezzlement
grand jury	forgery
indictment	money laundering
plea bargaining	conspiracy
entrapment	RICO
duress	predicate offense
incapacity	

Discussion Questions

1. People have different ideas as to why someone who violates the criminal law should be punished. What are these ideas?

2. Explain mens rea and indicate situations in which mens rea is not required as an element of criminal conduct.

3. Describe the procedural protections provided defendants in a criminal case by the Fourth, Fifth, and Sixth amendments to the U.S. Constitution.

4. List the differences that exist between civil litigation and criminal litigation.

5. Explain the difference between larceny and embezzlement.

Review Problems

1. White was a sheriff in a rural area. An anonymous caller informed White that Lehman, a local farmer, was promoting dog fights on his farm. Without getting a warrant, White searched several of the farm buildings. He found a number of dogs penned in a barn. Three of them were scarred and had injuries that could have been caused only by fighting. White arrested Lehman for promoting dog fights, a misdemeanor. Lehman's attorney moved that the case be dismissed on the grounds that the search was illegal. Would the attorney be successful? Support your answer.

2. Carbone was a licensed electrician. One day while rewiring a residence, he decided to leave for lunch before finishing a connection. He made a temporary connection that he knew was dangerous.

While he was at lunch the connection caused a short and the building caught fire. A woman who was in the building was killed. Carbone was criminally charged for her death. His attorney argued that as Carbone lacked intent, he could not be guilty. Was the attorney correct? Support your answer.

3. Lacey was killed by an automobile driven by Cantrell, who was charged and convicted of manslaughter. Lacey's estate sued Cantrell for damages. Cantrell defended on grounds that a person cannot be tried twice for the same act. Will Cantrell's defense succeed? Support your answer.

4. Ayer is the office manager for a plumbing contractor. The company receives small amounts of cash from time to time through the mail. Ayer is responsible for depositing these funds. She always does this, but often when she is short of cash she uses the funds for her personal needs and replaces them when she is paid. Has Ayer committed a crime? Discuss.

Case Problems

1. A confidential informant of unproven reliability informed the Burbank police that Sanchez and Stewart were selling drugs from their home. On the basis of this information the police launched an investigation. During the course of this investigation, one of the people seen leaving the home of Sanchez and Stewart was identified as a confidant of Leon, who was under investigation for drug-related activ-

ities. As a result of police observations, the Burbank police obtained a warrant to search the home. The search turned up large quantities of illegal drugs. The defendants filed a motion to exclude the evidence seized on the grounds that the police observations were insufficient to establish probable cause. The defendants argued that the warrant was thus defective and the ensuing search illegal. Assume that the warrant *was* defective but that the police relied upon it in good faith. What should be the result?

2. Wayne Schmuck sold used cars after he rolled back their odometer readings. He then sold these vehicles to retail dealers at inflated prices. Schmuck contended that the government could not convict him of mail fraud because he never mailed anything to anyone. The items mailed in this case were title application forms. However, the retail dealers, not Schmuck, mailed these to the Wisconsin Department of Transportation on behalf of its customers. The government contended that the mailing of the title applications by the dealers could serve as a basis for the mail fraud conviction. Is the government correct?

3. G.M. Leasing Corporation owed the IRS money. The IRS made a warrantless forced entry into a building owned by the corporation. Does such a search, in the absence of a warrant, violate the Fourth Amendment?

4. LeRoy was vice president of Local 214, a labor union. LeRoy was placed on the payroll of several contractors in order to maintain labor peace. Are his actions a violation of RICO

6

Intentional Torts

Torts against the Person

Torts against Property Interests

There are countless ways in which a business or individual can, intentionally or unintentionally, violate the private rights of others. A business might violate a competitor's rights by spreading untrue, damaging rumors about the competitor. A manufacturer may violate the rights of consumers by putting unsafe products on the market. An individual might drive carelessly and collide with another car, thus violating the rights of the other car's occupants. An individual might violate another person's rights by stealing from him or her. All these wrongs are covered by the law of torts.

A person commits a **tort** when he or she breaches a duty owed to another party in a manner that gives the other party a right to compensation. Torts do *not* include breach of contract (which we'll study later in the book), but torts do include every other type of wrong that gives a private party the legal right to seek compensation.

Tort actions are brought in civil lawsuits, not criminal prosecutions; they are therefore brought by private plaintiffs on their own behalf rather than by public prosecutors on behalf of society. The same act, however, can give rise to both criminal and civil tort liability. For example, if John intentionally hits Tom over the head with a baseball bat, John can be prosecuted by the state for the crimes of assault and battery. Additionally, Tom can bring a civil lawsuit against John for assault and battery, which also happen to be torts. The criminal action might result in John's being imprisoned by the state; the civil action might result in John's being required to compensate Tom monetarily for the injuries caused by John's behavior.

In order to sustain a tort action, the plaintiff must at minimum show that the defendant has caused some injury to the plaintiff's person or property.

Torts can be divided into three categories: intentional torts, negligence, and strict liability. A person commits an **intentional tort** by purposefully engaging in conduct that violates the plaintiff's rights. The example above, in which John intentionally hit Tom with a baseball bat, is an illustration of an intentional tort. Intentional torts are the focus of this chapter. The next chapter focuses on negligence (which involves failure to exercise reasonable care rather than wrongful intent) and strict liability (which is imposed in the absence of fault).

Intentional torts are distinguished from other torts by the presence of voluntary intent to bring about results that the law does not sanction. The required element of intention does not necessarily mean an evil motive or desire to harm, for an actor may be liable for the consequences of a practical joke or for the consequences of an act he or she did not believe would cause injury. Rather, the actor does something knowingly, and his or her responsibility extends not only to desired consequences, such as bruises from a baseball bat, but also to those that the actor believes or should believe are likely to follow. Several intentional torts are discussed here. For convenience, they are classified into two categories: torts against the person and torts against property interests.

Torts against the Person

Several torts protect an individual from intentional interference with his or her body and mind. Starting with the tort of battery, this section discusses the torts that provide redress for the intentional infliction of bodily or mental harm.

Battery

Battery is the intentional touching of another without justification and without consent. The touching need not be direct; the defendant need only have intentionally *caused* the wrongful contact. Thus, shooting someone constitutes a battery. *Justification*, a term of art (a word with a special meaning to a particular profession or trade—in this case, law), is usually the key to whether a battery has been committed. Obviously, minimal or social touching is not considered battery, but justification is not established merely because onlookers approve of the action. *Reasonableness* is the standard. Generally, courts hold that a person can meet force or the threat of force with similar force without liability. However, if the perceived threat is to a third party or if the threat is to property, the chance of establishing justification is less. Consider the following case.

KATKO V. BRINEY

Supreme Court of Iowa
183 N.W.2d 657 (1971)

BACKGROUND: Katko (plaintiff) was injured when a spring gun discharged and shot him in the leg while he was trespassing in an unoccupied farmhouse owned by the Brineys (defendants). Katko sued the Brineys for battery, and the jury returned a verdict for Katko for $20,000 in actual damages and $10,000 in punitive damages. The trial judge denied the Brineys' motion for a new trial. The Brineys appealed to the Supreme Court of Iowa.

Moore, Chief Justice

The primary issue presented here is whether an owner may protect personal property in an unoccupied boarded-up farmhouse against trespassers and thieves by a spring gun capable of inflicting death or serious injury.

We are not here concerned with a man's right to protect his home and members of his family. Defendants' home was several miles from the scene of the incident.

Plaintiff's action is for damages resulting from serious injury caused by a shot from a 20-gauge spring shotgun set by defendants in a bedroom of an old farm house which had been uninhabited for several years. Plaintiff and his companion, Marvin McDonough, had broken and entered the house to find and steal old bottles and dated fruit jars which they considered antiques.

The main thrust of defendants' defense in the trial court and on this appeal is that "the law permits use of a spring gun in a dwelling or warehouse for the purpose of preventing the unlawful entry of a burglar or thief."

Prosser on Torts, third edition, pages 116–18, states:

> [T]he law has always placed a higher value upon human safety than upon mere rights in property. It is the accepted rule that there is no privilege to use any force calculated to cause death or serious bodily injury to repel the threat to land or chattels, unless there is also such a threat to the defendant's personal safety as to justify a self-defense. . . . Spring guns and other man-killing devices are not justifiable against a mere trespasser, or even a petty thief. They are privileged only against those upon whom the landowner, if he were present in person, would be free to inflict injury of the same kind.

Defendants' motions were properly overruled.

DECISION: The Supreme Court of Iowa affirmed the trial judge and ruled in favor of Katko.

Assault

Assault is the intentional act of putting someone in immediate apprehension of a battery. The victim need not necessarily be "frightened"; apprehension is used to mean "expectation." For example, words alone typically do not constitute an assault, because they usually are not sufficient to put an ordinary person in apprehension of immediate harm. On the other hand, if the words are coupled with a threat of immediate physical harm—for example, a menacing gesture—an assault could be established.

One should note that an assault still occurs if the defendant goes beyond the mere threat of battery and actually commits the battery. Persons liable for battery are thus often liable for assault as well.

False Imprisonment

False imprisonment is the intentional confinement of a nonconsenting individual within boundaries fixed by the defendant for an appreciable time. The tort protects an individual's freedom of movement or liberty. The tort arises in business contexts from attempts to deal with suspected shoplifters or with employees suspected of dishonest behavior. Here the customer's or employee's interest in unrestrained movement conflicts with the storeowner's or employer's interest in protecting his or her property. At common law, a storekeeper is liable in tort for false imprisonment if he or she detains a suspected shoplifter who ultimately is found innocent. This places the storekeeper in a dilemma: If the storekeeper suspects a person of shoplifting, has the individual arrested, and then discovers that the person did not steal anything, the storekeeper is liable for false imprisonment; if the storekeeper does nothing and permits the suspected shoplifter to leave the store, all hope of proof is lost forever. The result is that, in most cases, unless he or she is absolutely sure, the storekeeper will let the suspected shoplifter go and will pass on the loss to the consuming public.

Because shoplifting is a major social problem, costing the consuming public billions of dollars through inflated prices, the law in most states resolves the conflict between the storekeeper's property interest and the consumer's liberty interest by conferring a limited or qualified privilege upon the storekeeper to reasonably detain those he or she reasonably suspects of shoplifting.

Defamation

Defamation is the communication of untrue statements about someone to a third party. The statements in question must injure the victim's reputation or character. For example, if Jack tells his friends that Mary is a prostitute, when in fact she is not, Jack has defamed Mary.

There are two categories of defamation: **slander,** or oral defamation, and **libel,** or written defamation. In most states today, plaintiffs must establish that they have been damaged—for example, by a loss of customers, business, or a particular contract.

One form of defamation, **defamation per se,** eliminates the necessity of establishing such damages. Four categories of defamation fall under the per se rule. Defamation per se exists when the plaintiff alleges that the defendant:

- Accused the plaintiff of having committed a serious crime, such as murder
- Stated that the plaintiff had a loathsome disease, such as a venereal disease
- Asserted that the plaintiff was professionally incompetent, such as calling a surgeon "a butcher"
- Stated that the plaintiff was an unchaste woman

Several defenses may be asserted in a defamation case. *Truth* is an absolute defense. Thus, if Jack calls Mary a prostitute and Mary in fact is a prostitute, Jack has a good defense. It is also necessary that someone other than the person defamed hear the defamatory statement. If someone angrily shouts a defamatory remark about someone else, but no one hears it, there can be no liability for defamation. Another defense against a charge of defamation is *privilege.* If defamation occurs in a privileged context, no legal relief is available to the victim of the defamation. A privilege may be either an absolute privilege or a qualified privilege. An absolute privilege exists for judges, legislators, lawyers, and parties and witnesses acting in their official capacities or in the roles for which the privilege exists. A qualified privilege exists for communications where it is in the public interest to promote the communication. For example, if one employer asks another to comment on the character of a former employee, the former employer enjoys a qualified privilege to do so. The qualified privilege is lost if the plaintiff can establish malice on the part of the speaker.

Invasion of Privacy

A person's dignity and the right to be let alone are protected by the tort of **invasion of privacy.** The courts have recognized four types of invasion of privacy: (1) intrusion upon the plaintiff's physical solitude (for example, illegal searches of persons, eavesdropping, peering into windows); (2) appropriation of the plaintiff's name or likeness (using a picture of the plaintiff in an advertisement); (3) placement of the plaintiff in a false light in the public eye (falsely attributing authorship of a poem to a well-known poet); and (4) public disclosure of private facts (disclosing an employee's illness to a third party).

Intentional Infliction of Emotional Distress

A person's interest in emotional tranquility is protected as a result of a recent trend to recognize **intentional infliction of emotional distress** as a separate tort. The tort may be defined as the intentional causing of severe mental suffering in another by means of extreme and outrageous conduct. Liability is limited to outrageous acts that cause bona fide emotional injury. The defendant's conduct must be what the average community member would consider extremely outrageous. The plaintiff's emotional distress must in fact exist and it must be severe. Minor offenses, such as name calling, are not actionable, although they may wound the feelings of the victim and cause some degree of mental upset. The

---

ETHICS
E-Mail, Scanners, and Privacy

Employee privacy has been an important concern in the workplace for several decades. Questions pertaining to the right of employers to conduct random drug testing, to listen in on employee telephone conversations, or to search employee lockers arise on a regular basis. Now a new area of concern for employee privacy has arisen. Many companies have E-mail systems through which employees receive and send messages. The systems are often set up so that managers and others have the ability to go into the system and read the messages that employees have sent to others, or to look at the "private" files that employees have set up for themselves. Employer accessing of the private files of employees has resulted in the discovery of employee abuse of firm computer systems to handicap races, to run a private Amway distributorship, or to send anonymous sexually suggestive messages to co-workers.

The scanners that have become so familiar at supermarkets present marketers with the ability to trace individual consumer purchases that are made by credit card or by check. The information concerning purchasing habits can then be sold to advertisers, which can target the individual's personal purchasing habits. Thus, if a particular consumer buys denture adhesive, he or she may be sent direct-mail advertising by denture adhesive sellers.

As a manager responsible for information technology in your firm, what policies would you implement concerning privacy?

---

plaintiff cannot recover merely because of hurt feelings; the law is not concerned with trifles and cannot provide a civil remedy for every personal conflict in a crowded world. Previously, the acts had to result in direct physical injury for there to be recovery for mental distress. Even the more liberalized modern standard is difficult to sustain in most instances. Consider the following case.

GOLDFARB V. BAKER

Supreme Court of Tennessee
547 S.W.2d 567 (1977)

BACKGROUND: Mark Goldfarb (plaintiff), a Memphis State University student, was enrolled in a course taught by Professor Arthur Baker (defendant). During a class meeting, an unidentified prankster entered the classroom, threw a pie, which struck the professor, and ran away. Baker immediately accused Goldfarb of the assault. The next day, Baker forbade Goldfarb from attending class, had him ejected from the building when he attempted to take his seat, and, in the presence of others, accused Goldfarb of attempting to blackmail him.

Goldfarb sued Baker for the tort of intentional infliction of emotional distress. Goldfarb, a former state prisoner, claimed that because of this episode he was falsely portrayed as a lawless individual whose attempted rehabilitation had failed, he lost the confidence of his associates, and he was frustrated in his effort to reform his life. He claimed that Baker's actions caused him extreme mental anguish, humiliation, depression, and distress. The trial judge found Baker's alleged conduct not sufficiently outrageous to be actionable and dismissed Goldfarb's complaint for failure to state a claim. Goldfarb appealed to the Supreme Court of Tennessee.

Brock, Justice

It has proven to be difficult to formulate an objective legal standard for determining whether or not particular unseemly conduct is so intolerable as to be tortious. The *Restatement (2d) of Torts* informs us that it is not enough, according to the cases, ". . . that the defendant has acted with an intent which is tortious or even criminal, or that he has intended to inflict emotional distress, or even that his conduct has been characterized by 'malice,' or a degree of aggravation which would entitle the plaintiff to punitive damages for another tort." It has been held that the defendant's conduct must be so outrageous in character and extreme in degree as to be beyond the pale of decency and that it must have caused serious mental injury to the plaintiff. The conduct must be "atrocious," "utterly intolerable," and "beyond all bounds of decency."

Moreover, conduct which would be intolerable if unprovoked may be excused if it results from circumstances of annoyance or stress.

This complaint shows that the defendant acted under provocation. The plaintiff claims that he was innocent of any wrong doing in the pie-throwing episode but not that the defendant knew, or that he should have known, that he was making a false accusation. Although the accusation of blackmail was excessive, still it was the product of a sudden, unjustified, and humiliating attack by someone upon the defendant. The plaintiff was warned that he would be excluded from class because of his supposed conduct and apparently did not protest his innocence at that point. With no reason to believe he was acting against the wrong person, the defendant apparently was justified in taking measures to prevent further disorder in his classroom. We hold that the facts alleged do not state a cause of action. The facts alleged in the complaint do, indeed, constitute a misfortune for the plaintiff. However, against a large part of the frictions and irritations and clashing of temperaments incident to participating in community life, a certain toughening of the mental hide is a better protection than the law could ever be. The present case is among those frictions and irritations.

DECISION: The Supreme Court of Tennessee affirmed the trial judge's decision in favor of Baker.

Wrongful Death

Surviving family members may bring a **wrongful death** action against a defendant whose willful or negligent behavior caused their relative's death. Most states have wrongful death statutes that specify which relatives are entitled to recover. Generally, spouses, parents, and children are entitled to recover for loss of financial support and companionship. Manufacturing firms are often sued in wrongful death actions when a death arises from defective products or workplace accidents. The following case is an interesting illustration of a wrongful death action outside the business context.

GEORGE V. INTERNATIONAL SOCIETY FOR KRISHNA CONSCIOUSNESS OF CALIFORNIA

California Court of Appeal, Fourth District
4 Cal.Rptr.2d 473 (1992)

BACKGROUND: Robin George was 14 years old in 1974 when she became involved with the Hare Krishna movement in Orange County, California. Her parents, Jim and Marcia George, became concerned when she started to practice her Hare Krishna faith. Rsabadeva, president of the local Hare Krishna temple, encouraged Robin to run away from home so that she could practice her faith. Rsabadeva and other Hare Krishna devotees hatched a plan whereby Robin would run away from home and take refuge with Hare Krishna members in San Diego. When Robin's parents tracked her down to San Diego, Hare Krishna members arranged for Robin to be secretly flown to New Orleans. During the several months in which Robin stayed in New Orleans, her parents tried persistently to find out where she was. They enlisted the help of Jayatirtha, another Hare Krishna devotee, who pretended to be sympathetic to the Georges' plight but who actually assisted in the scheme to keep Robin's whereabouts a secret.

After Robin was discovered in New Orleans by local police, she returned home with her father. After 3 weeks at home, Robin ran away again with the assistance of Hare Krishna members. Robin was sent to live at the Hare Krishna temple in Ottawa, Canada, and Hare Krishna members throughout the country engaged in an elaborate plan to deceive the Georges and law enforcement officials as to Robin's whereabouts. Robin was eventually found in Ottawa and returned home again. This time, she decided to stay home and not to rejoin the Hare Krishna movement. Four months after Robin returned home, her father, Jim, suffered a heart attack. Jim died several months later after suffering several strokes.

Marcia and Robin George sued the Hare Krishna movement for several torts, including Jim's wrongful death. The jury awarded Robin $75,000 on her wrongful death cause of action, and the Hare Krishnas appealed.

Wiener, Justice

Defendants argue there is no evidence to support the jury verdict in favor of Robin because their conduct could not have been the cause of Jim George's death and his death was not reasonably foreseeable. They also assert the compensatory damage award was excessive. . . . Here the jurors accepted the testimony of the Georges' expert, Dr. William Pitt, a cardiologist who had reviewed Jim George's medical records; they rejected the testimony of defendants' expert.

Dr. Pitt testified that stress is considered to be one of the "basic risk factors" of coronary artery disease. Stressful events raise the level of adrenaline in the blood which, in turn, increases the heart rate and changes the way the heart contracts.

Dr. Pitt then described how the stress resulting from Jim George's encounters with the Krishna organization contributed to his death in 1976. Pitt said that Jim George had led a relatively normal life. He developed coronary artery disease, but "had no particularly outstanding aggravating circumstances to make it much worse." In the middle of this relatively average existence, he suffered the severe impact of losing his daughter and directed virtually all of his energies toward retrieving her. "[T]he trouble he had, trying to locate her, the blind alley that he went up, the contact that he had with the Krishna organization and with the police department, et cetera, continued to aggravate his coronary disease."

Dr. Pitt concluded these events significantly accelerated Jim George's illness. In the normal course of the disease and without optimal treatment Jim George's life expectancy should have been at least five years from the onset of the disease. With optimal treatment it would have been "substantially longer." Dr. Pitt also testified that Jim George's delayed response to the stress—his suffering a heart attack nearly four months after Robin's return home—was a relatively common occurrence.

The jury resolved conflicts in expert testimony in favor of Robin and we may not disturb its implied findings on the question of causation.

There is also ample evidence to support the jury's implied finding that Jim George's death was reasonably foreseeable by the defendants. The foreseeability required is the *risk of harm*, not of the particular intervening act. If the defendant's conduct was a substantial factor in bringing about the harm, the defendant need not have foreseen the extent of the harm or the precise manner in which it occurred.

Marcia explained to Rsabadeva on at least two occasions that her husband had a weak heart, was taking Robin's absence badly, and that she was afraid this would kill him. Marcia reported that Rsabadeva snickered and told her that another devotee's father had a heart attack but did not die. Marcia also informed Jayatirtha about her husband's weak heart and explained that the inability to find Robin would kill her husband because of the terrible stress it was causing him. In spite of defendants' knowledge of Jim George's weak heart, they persisted in concealing Robin's whereabouts and subjected the Georges to verbal and physical abuse.

Defendants argue the compensatory damage award was excessive because it represented more than Jim George's entire earnings for a period longer than he was expected to live. However, the plaintiff in a wrongful death action may recover for damages arising from loss of society, comfort, care and protection afforded by the decedent in addition to damages for pecuniary loss of a parent. Here there is sufficient evidence to establish the close relationship between Robin and her father that would give rise to this type of loss. Although Jim George had a limited earning capacity, viewing the entire record we cannot say the $75,000 wrongful death verdict is so large that it shocks the conscience and suggests passion, prejudice or corruption on the part of the jury.

DECISION: The court affirmed the jury's award in favor of Robin on the wrongful death claim.

Torts against Property Interests

Tort claims exist to redress intentional interference with property rights, including contract rights. Some of these are discussed below. Claims to redress interference with *intellectual* property rights, such as patents and trademarks, are discussed later in the book.

Trespass

The tort of trespass is really two torts: trespass to land and trespass to personal property.

Trespass to land may be defined as intentionally entering upon another's land or causing an object or a third person to do so. Trespass to land may also occur when a person intentionally remains on another's land or fails to remove from the land an object that he or she is under a duty to remove. Liability exists for trespass to land even when no harm results from the trespass. The major defenses to trespass to land are *consent* and unavoidable *accidental intrusion.*

Trespass to personal property may be defined as intentionally taking or damaging the personal property of another. An example of trespass to personal property is a creditor who, in an attempt to repossess a car held as collateral for a loan to a debtor, mistakenly takes someone else's car. The defenses of consent and unavoidable accident apply also to the tort of trespass to personal property.

Conversion

Conversion is the intentional exercise of control over personal property, thereby seriously interfering with another person's right of possession. The difference between the tort of trespass to personal property and the tort of conversion lies in the measure of damages. For trespass to personal property, recovery is limited to the diminished value of the personal property because of any injury to it. For conversion, the measure of damages is the full value of the property at the time it was converted. Because of the larger recovery, conversion is limited to serious interferences with the right of possession that justify requiring the defendant to pay the full value of the property. Thus, in the preceding example of the creditor who repossessed the wrong car, there would be no conversion if the creditor immediately returned the car. He or she would, however, be liable for trespass to personal property and could be required to pay costs, such as gasoline and depreciation. If the creditor totally wrecked the car while driving it away, he or she would be liable for the full value of the car to the car's owner for the tort of conversion.

Nuisance

A **nuisance** is an unlawful interference with a person's use or enjoyment of his or her land. It includes any use of property that gives offense to or endangers life or health—for example, by unreasonably polluting the air. The interference with the landowner's interest must be substantial. The standard is similar to the test for the tort of intentional infliction of emotional distress: a definite and substantial offensiveness, inconvenience, or annoyance to the normal person in the community.

In nuisance cases, the interference must not only be substantial; it must also be unreasonable. This involves weighing the gravity and probability of harm resulting from the defendant's conduct against its social utility. Thus, a defendant may engage in a reasonable use of his or her property at the expense of the neighbors.

Although most nuisance cases are brought as intentional tort claims, the basis of liability is the nature of the interference with the plaintiff's use and enjoyment of property, not the intent of the defendant. Liability may extend to negligent interferences and, when the interference results from an abnormally offensive activity, to strict liability.

Interference with Contractual Relations

An individual who intentionally and without justification causes a third person not to perform a contract with another is liable for the resulting harm. The elements of the business tort of **interference with contractual relations** are (1) an existing contract between the plaintiff and a third party; (2) the defendant's knowledge of this contract; (3) intentional and improper interference inducing or causing a breach of the contract; and (4) resulting damage. The following case considers the third element: what constitutes intentional and improper inducement to breach a contract.

EDWARD VANTINE STUDIOS, INC. V. FRATERNAL COMPOSITE SERVICE, INC.

Court of Appeals of Iowa
373 N.W.2d 512 (1985)

BACKGROUND: Edward Vantine Studios, Inc. (plaintiff) sued Fraternal Composite Services, Inc. (defendant) for the tort of interference with contracts. The two companies were involved in the business of photographing composites of fraternities and sororities on various campuses throughout the country. Vantine's booking agent completed signed contracts with several fraternities and sororities at Iowa State University for the 1982–83 school year.

In the summer of 1981, a sales manager for Fraternal Composite visited all the fraternities and sororities at Iowa State, but signed no new contracts. In the spring of 1982, the sales manager visited fifteen houses on campus and again signed no new contracts. In the summer of 1982, the sales manager talked with officers at all the fraternities and sororities. He returned to many of these houses, and was told that the organizations had existing contracts with Vantine. The sales manager suggested that the houses investigate the legality of these contracts. On later visits, the sales manager signed contracts with twelve houses that had previous contracts with Vantine. All but one of those contracts contained an indemnity clause—a provision stating that Fraternal Composites would pay any legal costs or fees incurred in breaking the contracts that were already held with Vantine.

Members of the fraternities and sororities expressed dissatisfaction with previous service provided by Vantine. Fraternal Composites attempted to capitalize on these objections by offering a lower price and an earlier delivery date than Vantine. However, the fraternity and sorority members indicated that they would not have terminated Vantine's contract except for the insertion of the indemnity clause in Fraternal Composite's contract. They testified that they were not subjected to any undue pressure from the actions of Fraternal Composite's sales manager. Vantine was notified that its contracts were terminated when its photographer appeared at the fraternity and sorority houses for scheduled photography sessions. Fraternal Composites later provided the desired services and all customers were satisfied.

The trial court determined that Fraternal Composites committed the tort of interference with contracts. Fraternal Composites appealed to the Iowa Court of Appeals.

Hayden, Judge

Defendant's primary contention is that its actions in interfering with plaintiff's contracts were not intentional or improper and hence were not actionable. We disagree.

There can be little question but that defendant intentionally interfered with plaintiff's contracts. Defendant concedes its awareness of those contracts during the course of its attempts to obtain its own contracts with the twelve houses. Defendant advised the houses to investigate the validity of their contracts with plaintiff and then suggested or at least agreed to insert a clause in its own contracts to indemnify the houses for any legal costs or fees incurred by reason of their breach of their contracts with plaintiff. This is certainly an intentional course of conduct which induced the houses not to perform their contracts with plaintiff.

We also believe and agree with the trial court that defendant's interference was improper to the extent that it agreed to indemnify the houses for any legal costs or fees resulting from their breach of plaintiff's contracts. We concede defendant's point that the business of photographing composites for college fraternities and sororities is very competitive and that the various individual companies in that business will seek to expand their own share of the market, very often at the expense of their competitors. We do not, however, believe that this competitive factor gives defendant free rein to use whatever inducements it can think of to lure potential customers away from already existing valid and binding contracts. We adopt the trial court's language on this point: If the contracts had been terminated by reason of better price, better service, or better quality alone, . . . the Court would not have determined there was a tortious interference with the contracts. It may have caused some claim or cause of action between [plaintiff] and the breaching fraternity and sorority, but it would not have created an actionable tort against the Defendant herein. The Defendant, however, by the insertion, or the encouragement of the insertion, of the indemnity clause has crossed over the line of legitimate competition. It has committed an actionable tort by such activity.

Representatives from five of the fraternities involved testified that they would not have breached their agreements with plaintiff and contracted with defendant without the indemnity clause agreed to by the defendant. The importance of this clause to defendant is thus obvious. Our acceptance of such a tactic would render the notion of sanctity of contract a nullity and would indicate that a contract could be breached with impunity merely by having the party inducing the breach assume the financial consequences of such breach.

DECISION: The Iowa Court of Appeals affirmed the trial court's decision in favor of Vantine.

TABLE 6-1

Concept Summary	Selected Intentional Torts
Torts against the Person	
Battery	Intentional touching of another without justification or consent
Assault	Intentional act of putting someone in immediate apprehension of a battery
False imprisonment	Intentional confinement of a nonconsenting individual
Defamation	Communication of an untrue, injurious statement about someone to a third party
Invasion of privacy	Intrusion on someone's physical solitude; appropriation of someone's name or likeness; placement of someone in false light in public eye; *or* public disclosure of private facts
Intentional infliction of emotional distress	Intentional causing of mental suffering through extreme and outrageous conduct
Wrongful death	Intentional (or negligent) behavior which causes the death of another
Torts against Property Interests	
Trespass to land	Intentional entry upon another's land or causing an object or third person to do so
Trespass to personal property	Intentional taking or damaging of another's personal property
Conversion	Intentional exercise of control over another's personal property
Nuisance	Unlawful interference with another's use or enjoyment of his or her land
Interference with contractual relations	Intentional and improper interference with a contract between others, causing breach

Review Questions and Problems

Key Terms

tort

intentional tort

battery

assault

false imprisonment

defamation

slander

libel

defamation per se

invasion of privacy

intentional infliction of emotional distress

wrongful death

trespass to land

trespass to personal property

conversion

nuisance

interference with contractual relations

Discussion Questions

1. What are the three classifications of tort law?

2. What kind of intent is required for an intentional tort?

3. What two defenses are available for most intentional torts?

Review Problems

1. Arnie, a self-described "ladies' man," has a secretary named Millie. On one occasion, Arnie slapped Millie hard on the buttocks. Arnie claims that he was "just horsing around," but the incident made Millie very upset. The next day, when Arnie and Millie were alone in his office, Arnie said to Millie, "I'm gonna slap your butt again!" Millie again became very upset. Has Arnie committed any of the torts discussed in this chapter? If so, which one or ones? Discuss.

2. An employer suspected that one of ten employees had stolen company property. The employer called a meeting of the suspected employees and told them that if the guilty employee did not come forward and confess the act within 5 minutes, the employer would commence to fire the employees in alphabetical order during each successive minute thereafter. Amy Able was the first employee fired after the initial 5-minute period had elapsed. Upon being told that she was fired, Amy started crying and immediately left the employer's premises and returned home. At home, Amy's husband consoled her, saying, "Don't worry, Amy. We'll sue the employer for all he is worth for the tort of intentional infliction of emotional distress." If Amy sues the employer, will she win? Explain.

3. A. L. Stephens and Carl Stephens had arranged to bury their brother, George Stephens, at the Goodby Cemetery, with the permission of the owners of the cemetery. At 7:30 a.m. on the day of the burial, Bud Waits came to the cemetery and informed A. L. Stephens that Stephens was trespassing on his lot. Bud Waits went home to get some papers that would prove his ownership of the lot, and he sent his wife, Ora Waits, to the cemetery to prevent the burial. At 12:30 p.m., the vault in which George Stephens' casket was to be placed was brought to the cemetery. Mrs. Waits seated herself on the vault, took up an iron pick, and threatened to strike anyone who attempted to place the vault in the grave. From 2:30 p.m. until 3:30 p.m., funeral services were held in the church adjoining the cemetery. When the body was brought to the grave, Ora Waits refused to allow anyone to move the vault on which she was seated or to place it in the grave. A. L. Stephens sought out a justice of the peace, who finally persuaded Ora Waits to get off the vault so that George Stephens could be put in it. A. L. and Carl Stephens sued Bud and Ora Waits, alleging that the Waitses committed the tort of intentional infliction of emotional distress. Who wins and why?

4. Dun & Bradstreet, Inc., a credit-reporting agency, sent a report to five subscribers indicating that Greenmoss Builders, Inc., a construction contractor, had filed a voluntary petition for bankruptcy. The report was false and grossly misrepresented Greenmoss Builders' assets and liabilities. Thereafter Dun & Bradstreet issued a corrective notice, but Greenmoss Builders was dissatisfied with this notice and brought a defamation lawsuit against Dun & Bradstreet, alleging that the report had injured its reputation and seeking damages. What must Greenmoss Builders prove in order to recover damages from Dun & Bradstreet? Explain.

Case Problems

1. Marion Bonkowski, accompanied by her husband, left Arlan's Department Store in Saginaw, Michigan, about 10:00 p.m. on December 18, 1992, after making several purchases. Earl Reinhardt, a private policeman on duty that night in Arlan's, called to her as she was walking toward her car, which was parked about 30 feet away in the adjacent parking lot. Reinhardt motioned to Mrs. Bonkowski to return toward the store. When she had done so, Reinhardt said that someone in the store had told him that Mrs. Bonkowski had put three pieces of jewelry into her purse without having paid for them. Mrs. Bonkowski denied she had taken anything unlawfully, but Reinhardt told her that he wanted to see the contents of her purse. On a cement step in front of the store, Mrs. Bonkowski emptied the contents of her purse into her husband's hands. Mr.

Bonkowski produced sales slips for the items she had purchased, and Reinhardt, satisfied that she had not committed larceny, returned to the store. Mrs. Bonkowski brought suit against Earl Reinhardt and Arlan's Department Store, claiming that, as a result of defendants' tortious acts, she suffered numerous psychosomatic symptoms, including headaches, nervousness, and depression. Who wins? Explain.

2. On leaving a restaurant, X by mistake takes Y's hat from the rack, believing it to be his own. When he reaches the sidewalk, X puts on the hat, discovers his mistake, and immediately reenters the restaurant and returns the hat to the rack. Has X committed either trespass to personal property or conversion?

3. H obtained a credit card in his name only from Slick Oil Company and used it in making purchases at Slick gas stations. W, a secretary at Cow College, handled family finances. W informed H (but not Slick) that she would not make further payments on the account, and the account became delinquent in the amount of $200. Slick sent a letter to the personnel director at Cow College seeking assistance. The letter claimed that W was Slick's customer and had incurred expenses and it requested Cow College's assistance in interviewing W. Did Slick commit any intentional torts?

4. Morgan owned a tract of 9 acres of land on which he had his dwelling, a restaurant, and accommodations for thirty-two trailers. High Penn Oil Co. owned an adjacent tract on which it operated an oil refinery, at a distance of 1,000 feet from Morgan's dwelling. Morgan sued High Penn to recover damages for a nuisance and to abate such nuisance by injunction. Morgan's evidence was that for some hours on 2 or 3 different days each week the refinery emitted nauseating gases and odors in great quantities, which invaded Morgan's land and other tracts of land. High Penn failed to put an end to this atmospheric pollution after receiving notice and demand from Morgan to abate it.

High Penn's evidence was that the oil refinery was a modern plant of the type approved, known, and in general use for renovating used lubricating oils; that it was not so constructed or operated as to give out noxious gases or odors in annoying quantities; and that it had not annoyed Morgan or other persons save on a single occasion when it suffered a brief mechanical breakdown. Who should win? Explain.

5. Brents, an exasperated creditor, put a placard in the show window of his garage, on a public street, which stated that "Dr. W. R. Morgan owes an account here for $49.67. This account will be advertised as long as it remains unpaid." Morgan sued Brents for the tort of invasion of privacy. Who wins? Explain.

7

Negligence
and Strict Liability

Negligence   Strict Liability

This chapter considers two classifications of tort law concerned with civil redress for unintentional injuries: (1) negligence and (2) strict liability.

Negligence

Negligence is conduct that creates an unreasonable risk of foreseeable harm to another.

Elements of Negligence

In order to establish a case of negligence, the plaintiff must satisfy five elements. These are:

1. That the defendant owed a *duty of care* to the plaintiff. The plaintiff must establish that the law recognizes an obligation of the defendant to conform to a certain standard of conduct for the protection of the plaintiff against an unreasonable risk of foreseeable harm.

2. That the defendant *breached this duty.*

3. That the plaintiff sustained an *injury.*

4. That the defendant caused the plaintiff's injury. This is known as *cause in fact* or *actual cause.*

5. That the defendant's conduct was the *proximate or legal cause* of the plaintiff's injury.

That is, the plaintiff must show a reasonably close causal connection between the defendant's conduct and the resulting injury to the plaintiff. Not every injury actually caused by the defendant is compensable—only those that are the foreseeable and probable consequences of the defendant's conduct. Thus, in addition to showing that the defendant actually caused the plaintiff's injury, the plaintiff must establish that the injury was a foreseeable consequence of the defendant's conduct.

Duty of Care   The first element of a plaintiff's prima facie case of negligence is the existence of a duty on the part of the defendant to protect the plaintiff from injury resulting from the defendant's conduct. It is not enough for the plaintiff to show that he or she was injured by the defendant's conduct. The plaintiff must also show that the law imposed a duty on the defendant to protect the plaintiff from the consequences of the defendant's conduct.

The determination of whether a duty of care is to be imposed upon the defendant is a question of law that is decided by the judge. The judge must determine whether there is any "law" that would require the defendant to bear the risk or whether the plaintiff must bear his or her own loss.

Several factors may influence the court's decision. The factors that are considered in determining whether the law should impose a duty are the risk, foreseeability, and likelihood of injury weighed against the social utility of the actor's conduct, the extent of the burden of guarding against the injury, and the consequences of placing the burden on the actor.

As illustrated by the following case, the question of whether the defendant owes a duty to the plaintiff sometimes depends on whether the plaintiff's injury was foreseeable.

DOE V. BRITISH UNIVERSITIES NORTH AMERICA CLUB

U.S. District Court, D. Connecticut
788 F. Supp. 1286 (1992)

BACKGROUND: Drummond, a counselor at a summer camp operated by the Boy Scouts of America, allegedly sexually assaulted a 14-year-old camper. Drummond, a British citizen, was hired after being recommended for the position by British Universities North America Club (BUNAC). Under an arrangement with a local council of the Boy Scouts, British citizens wishing to work as camp counselors in the United States could apply through BUNAC, which would then screen the applicants and recommend suitable candidates to work at Boy Scout camps. The final hiring decision, however, was made by the camp itself. The assaulted camper, referred to in the opinion as "John Doe," filed suit through his guardian, "Richard Doe." Doe contended that BUNAC had been negligent in screening Drummond's application. BUNAC moved for summary judgment.

Nevas, District Judge

Negligence is often defined as a breach of duty. It is axiomatic, therefore, that where there is no legal duty, there can be no actionable negligence. Unless some relationship exists between the person injured and the defendant, by which the latter owes a duty to the former, there can be no liability for negligence.

Doe contends that judged against the standard for determining the existence of a duty under Connecticut law, BUNAC fails to meet its burden of showing that no duty exists as a matter of law. Specifically, Doe contends that the harm that came to John Doe was a foreseeable result of BUNAC's failure to properly screen Drummond's sexual orientation. Doe argues that BUNAC should have known that Drummond was a homosexual and that it was likely that Drummond would practice homosexuality in the all-male environment of Camp Workcoeman. Doe concludes that in light of what BUNAC knew or should have known about Drummond's sexual orientation and the possibility that Drummond would practice homosexuality at the Camp, BUNAC should have anticipated the risk of the type of harm suffered by John Doe and, thus, a clear duty was owed to Doe by BUNAC. . . .

Under Connecticut law, the ultimate test of the existence of a duty to use care is found in the foreseeability that harm may result if it is not exercised. The test is, would the ordinary man in the defendant's position, knowing what he knew or should have known, anticipate that harm of the general nature of that suffered was likely to result? Doe does not allege that Drummond was an applicant with a documented or even discoverable history of child molestation or sexual deviancy. Rather, the crux of Doe's claim is that because Drummond admits to being a homosexual, BUNAC should or could have anticipated that he would molest male campers while working at the Camp. Assuming that BUNAC should or could have discovered the full scope of Drummond's homosexuality, an assumption adopted only for the purposes of considering the sufficiency of BUNAC's motion for summary judgment,

Drummond's molestation of John Doe cannot be characterized as a foreseeable consequence of Drummond's sexual orientation even under the most liberal reading of Doe's claim. Drummond had no prior criminal record or history of sexual misconduct. Doe, moreover, offers not one scintilla of credible evidence to suggest that homosexuals pose a greater risk of committing sexual molestation, assault, or criminal conduct than heterosexuals in a summer camp environment.

Absent any tangible evidence of Drummond's predisposition toward deviant sexual conduct, it is impossible to see how the "ordinary person" in BUNAC's position could have anticipated the harm that Drummond caused John Doe. While the sexual molestation of campers by counselors is always a possibility, moreover, there is no justifiable reason for BUNAC to anticipate that Drummond was more of a risk to campers than any other Camp employee even if it had known about Drummond's homosexual orientation. To find otherwise would be to hold that homosexuals are predisposed towards molesting or sexually assaulting minor males simply by virtue of their sexual orientation. The court cannot and will not adopt such a position absent sufficient evidentiary support.

DECISION: The District Court granted BUNAC's motion for summary judgment.

Breach of Duty   The plaintiff must satisfy the judge or the jury that the defendant breached his or her duty to exercise due care. The courts have established a standard of behavior to determine breach of duty. The standard is that of the hypothetical "reasonable and prudent person under the same or similar circumstances." The judge or jury compares the defendant's conduct with the presumed conduct of the reasonably prudent person under the same or similar circumstances. If the defendant's conduct does not conform to this ideal standard of conduct, the defendant will be deemed to have breached his or her duty to exercise due care.

In the following case the court considers whether the manufacturer of an elevator breached its duty to design a reasonably safe elevator.

WESTINGHOUSE ELECTRIC CORP. V. NUTT

Court of Appeals of District of Columbia
407 A.2d 606 (1979)

BACKGROUND: During lunch break at Henley Elementary School in Washington, D.C., sixth grader Dirickson Nutt left the school grounds with several friends and went to a nearby apartment building. There, they boarded a self-service freight elevator that had been designed, manufactured, and installed by Westinghouse Electric Corp. (defendant). Under a service contract, Westinghouse was responsible for the maintenance and repair of the elevator.

After boarding the elevator, one of the boys pushed the fifth-floor button, and the elevator ascended. At the fifth floor, the doors opened, but no one got off. As the elevator left the fifth floor, moving upward, one of the boys forced open the doors, bringing the elevator to an immediate stop between the fifth and sixth floors.

The passengers jumped out of the immobilized elevator through the door opening, landing in the hall corridor four feet below. In leaving the elevator, Dirickson Nutt slipped down the elevator shaft through the open space underneath the car. As a result of his fall, he sustained a wound to his left arm, requiring amputation above the wrist. He also suffered facial injuries, requiring plastic surgery.

Dirickson Nutt, through his father, sued Westinghouse, claiming negligence in the design and maintenance of the elevator. They presented an expert witness, Frederick

Foote, who suggested alternative design features that he considered feasible. The jury found in favor of the Nutts (plaintiffs or appellees), awarding a verdict of $150,000. Westinghouse appealed to the District of Columbia Court of Appeals.

Gallagher, Associate Justice

Essentially, the issue is whether the Nutts established a prima facie case of negligent design. Westinghouse alleges a failure by the Nutts, as plaintiffs, to prove a departure by Westinghouse from the applicable standard of care. A breach of duty by the defendant is, of course, a prerequisite of liability; negligent conduct, by definition, "falls below the standard established by law for the protection of others against unreasonably great risk or harm."

Without question Westinghouse, as manufacturer, was under a duty to design a reasonably safe elevator.

As this court recently stated, the manufacturer of a [product] will be liable for injuries to others expected to use the [product] when the injuries are caused by the lack of reasonable care in adopting a safe plan or design. This duty of care includes the adoption of reasonable safety devices. What constitutes "reasonable care" will vary with the circumstances, and involves a balancing of the likelihood of harm, and the gravity of harm if it happens, against the burden of precaution which would be effective to avoid the harm.

Westinghouse points to its compliance with existing industry-wide standards as dispositive of the question of due care. Two professional engineers, experts in elevator design, testified at trial that the elevator complied with all applicable safety codes and regulations. An elevator inspector for the District of Columbia government established conformance with the local elevator code. It is axiomatic, however, that compliance with legislative or industry standards does not prevent a finding of negligence where a reasonable man would take additional precautions.

Similarly, industry-wide custom influences, but does not conclusively determine, the applicable standard of care. As Justice Holmes put it, "What usually is done may be evidence of what ought to be done, but what ought to be done is fixed by a standard of reasonable prudence, whether it is usually complied with or not." Evidence of industry custom, however, may be conclusive when a plaintiff fails to introduce any evidence that the product was not reasonably safe for its intended use. Thus, the elevator's conformity to industry and legal standards established Westinghouse's due care unless the Nutts proffered contrary evidence that the product, as designed, created an unreasonable danger.

The sole evidence produced by the Nutts to establish a departure from the standard of care was the testimony of Mr. Foote. In effect, Mr. Foote gave his opinion that a longer toe guard or a different latch placement would have prevented the accident. However, evidence of a design alternative, by itself, is not sufficient to impose liability on the manufacturer.

It is one thing to show that the defendant might have designed a safer product; quite another to show that the product he did design was unreasonably dangerous. The defendant is not obliged to design the safest possible product, or one as safe as others make or a safer product than the one he has designed, so long as the design he has adopted is reasonably safe.

A finding of unreasonable danger most often turns on the absence of a safety device that was available at the time of manufacture. Evidence of available safety mechanisms illustrates what is feasible, and suggests a body of knowledge of which the defendant should be aware.

Here, testimony of customary safety features was not introduced. In addition, appellees' evidence failed to establish that an elongated toe guard is known to be feasible, even though not utilized by other manufacturers. This would seem to be the furthest courts have gone in imposing a duty on the manufacturer to keep abreast of recent scientific developments. Mr. Foote admitted on cross-examination that he had no knowledge of the feasibility of his suggestions.

Against Westinghouse's evidence that the equipment was reasonably safe as designed, the Nutts mustered little contrary evidence. Mr. Foote's safety suggestions were not competent evidence that Westinghouse, the manufacturer, created an unreasonable danger. Thus appellees failed to prove Westinghouse's deviation from the applicable standard of care in designing the elevator.

Since the facts, viewed most favorably to [appellees], permit but one reasonable conclusion as to the proper judgment, the trial court erred in submitting the question of negligent design to the jury.

DECISION: The District of Columbia Court of Appeals reversed the lower court decision and ordered the lower court to enter judgment for Westinghouse.

Injury   The plaintiff must establish that he or she sustained an injury. The injury incurred by the plaintiff is typically a physical injury to the plaintiff's person or property. The courts are reluctant to allow liability to extend to mental injuries because they are difficult to establish. In most states, the plaintiff may recover damages for negligent infliction of mental distress only if the defendant causes immediate physical injury to the plaintiff or causes mental distress that is followed by physical harm.

Actual Cause   The plaintiff must establish a causal relationship between the injury and the defendant's act. The defendant's conduct is a cause of the event if it was a material element and a substantial factor in bringing that event about. If the defendant's conduct was a substantial factor in causing the plaintiff's injury, the defendant will not be absolved from liability merely because other causes contributed to the result.

Proximate Cause   Suppose that Bartles drives carelessly and "rear ends" James' car on the freeway. Bartles and James pull their cars over to the side of the road and get out to inspect the damage. James is then struck by a car driven by Ernest, who is drunk. James suffers a broken leg. In this example, Bartles' careless driving can be said to be the actual cause of James' broken leg: If Bartles had not caused the initial accident, James would not have been struck by Ernest's car. It certainly seems fair to hold Bartles responsible for the damage to James' car caused by the initial collision with Bartles. But is it fair to hold Bartles responsible for James' broken leg?

Establishing that the defendant's conduct was the actual cause of the plaintiff's injury is *necessary*, but not *sufficient*, to hold the defendant li-

able for negligence. The plaintiff must also prove that the defendant's conduct was the *proximate cause* of the plaintiff's injury. We'll return to the Bartles and James example after we examine the concept of proximate cause.

Because one act of negligence should not subject a defendant to unlimited liability for all the consequences that could possibly result, tort law has developed the doctrine of proximate cause to limit the defendant's liability to only those events that are reasonably foreseeable. Under the doctrine of **proximate cause,** a defendant is liable only for the natural, probable, foreseeable, and thus avoidable consequences of his or her conduct, not for all consequences, however remote. The need for the doctrine arises because it is theoretically possible to trace the causal effects of some events through a number of ever-more-distant occurrences. In such situations, it may be theoretically possible to say that the defendant actually caused the injury by setting forth a chain of events that resulted in injury to the plaintiff. However, it is another thing to say that the defendant should be liable for the plaintiff's loss where the likelihood of injury was not foreseeable. Underlying the proximate cause requirement is recognition of the fact that a particular wrong may set off a chain of events so completely unforeseeable, and resulting in an injury so remotely related to the wrong itself, that common sense suggests that the defendant should not be liable for it. Thus, the doctrine of proximate cause should be viewed as a principle of law and policy that limits liability to foreseeable injuries.

Let's return to the auto accident involving Bartles and James. Even if Bartles' careless driving is found to be the *actual* cause of James' broken leg, is it the *proximate* cause of the personal injury? Was it a natural, probable, and foreseeable consequence of Bartles' conduct that Ernest would

---

PREVENTIVE LAW
Tort Liability in Manufacturing

Practices that often lead to tort liability with regard to the manufacture of products include the following:

- Placing a low priority on product safety
- Having the attitude that "it's the consumer's responsibility"
- Having an inadequate understanding of the consumer (for example, failing to anticipate foreseeable product misuse)
- Failure to consider total product life (for example, failing to consider product deterioration in marketing plans)
- Relying on industry or government standards, which frequently represent *minimum* standards, not state-of-the-art research
- Insufficient communication to and from customers (for example, inadequate warning labels and user manuals, and inadequate procedures for field representatives to send information about consumer product use to upper management)

Manufacturers concerned about tort liability should do the following:

- Put organizational strength into the program. For example, product safety committees—staffed by employees from engineering, manufacturing, quality control, and marketing—are needed if company strategy is to be implemented.
- Establish an insurance program. In addition to providing financial protection, insurance companies often perform "safety audits" and give advice on safety measures—a valuable service to smaller companies.
- Stay in touch. Companies need to stay in touch with legal developments, consumer expectations, and technological change in order to respond effectively to the environment.
- Develop disaster plans. When disaster strikes, sound management has anticipated it and has a plan for responding to it. The plan may include procedures for handling a product recall, communicating with the consuming public, and dealing with lawsuits.

---

strike James with his car? Probably not. In this case, James could recover from Bartles the cost of repairing any damage caused by the initial accident, but he would probably have to look to Ernest to compensate him for his broken leg.

Some courts and commentators see the doctrine of proximate cause as a variant of the duty question. Consider the following case.

KIMBLE V. MACKINTOSH HEMPHILL CO.
Supreme Court of Pennsylvania
59 A.2d 68 (1948)

BACKGROUND: Harry Kimble was killed when the roof of the MacKintosh Hemphill foundry fell on him as he worked below. His wife, Virginia Kimble (plaintiff), sued MacKintosh Hemphill Co. (defendant) to recover the loss of her deceased husband's future earnings. The jury returned a verdict in her favor in the sum of $5,823.20. Mackintosh Hemphill moved the trial court to grant judgment in favor of MacKintosh Hemphill, notwithstanding the jury verdict. The trial judge refused this request, and MacKintosh Hemphill appealed the trial judge's decision to the Supreme Court of Pennsylvania.

Maxey, Chief Justice

Defendant's liability is predicated upon its failure to maintain the roof in a safe condition and in failing to inspect, discover and correct its faulty condition.

Defendant disclaims liability alleging (1) that the proximate cause of the fatality was a cyclonic wind of an extraordinary intensity and (2) that this relieved defendant from liability irrespective of whether or not its claimed antecedent negligence was a substantial factor in bringing about the harm.

Plaintiff's witnesses contradicted the evidence with regard to the severity of the wind on the date of the accident.

Defendant contends that the court erred in submitting the question of negligence to the jury and should have declared as a matter of law that an act of God was responsible for Kimble's death. Whether or not the fatal injury to plaintiff's decedent was due to an act of God or to defendant's negligence was a question of fact for the jury. The condition of the roof, the intensity of the wind on the date of the accident and on previous occasions at the same place were factual questions. The charge of the court was comprehensive and accurate. The trial judge charged:

> It is the law that no person is answerable for what is termed an act of Providence, that is, if some visitation of Providence comes along that in our ordinary experience we are not anticipating, then no one can be held to answer for that act, so that if the wind on this day was of such severity that it could not be reasonably anticipated by the Defendant, and that by reason of the wind, a part of the roof was blown off, then the Defendant would not be liable. However, if the storm were not of that severity, if it were only such a storm as occasionally happens, but is reasonably to be anticipated on occasions of every year or two, then that would not be an act of Providence. If they were such as were reasonably to be expected to occur occasionally, then such storms would be guarded against. An act of Providence as related to cases of injurious negligence is one against which ordinary skill and foresight is not expected to provide. Whether the injury in this case is attributable to such a cause or is the consequence of negligence is a question of fact for you to determine. Even if, with an extraordinary wind or storm there is concurring negligence, the party chargeable with it will be relieved from liability if the wind or storm is so overwhelming in character that it would of itself have produced the injury complained of, independently of negligence if there were negligence.

In the instant case, defendant by using ordinary diligence and attention could have prevented the serious consequences which resulted from its failure to inspect and correct the faulty condition of the foundry roof. We said in Fitzpatrick v. Penfield . . . :

> High winds are not of infrequent occurrence, and this particular wind was termed an ordinary wind occurring three or four times in a year. It was not an unusual one, and it was for the jury to find under all the evidence whether it was likely to have occurred, and should have been provided against. One who fails in his duty to remedy a defective or dangerous condition is liable for injuries resulting therefrom, although the immediate cause of the injury is the wind. The causal connection is not broken, and the original wrong doer is liable for the injury sustained.

DECISION: The Supreme Court of Pennsylvania affirmed the trial judge's decision.

Procedural Doctrines

The plaintiff has the burden of persuading the trier of fact that he or she is entitled to recovery. This burden of proving the defendant's negligence is placed upon the plaintiff because it is the plaintiff who is asking the court for relief. In certain cases, the plaintiff may have the burden of proof lightened by two procedural doctrines: negligence per se and *res ipsa loquitur*.

Negligence Per Se Under the doctrine of **negligence per se**, a plaintiff may use the defendant's violation of a criminal statute to establish the defendant's negligence. Thus, a criminal statute may become a measure of civil liability. If a statute proscribes certain behavior and the defendant violates the statute, most states hold that the violation of the statute is negligence itself. That is, the violation of the statute creates a conclusive presumption that the defendant was negligent. In a few states, the court admits the information of the defendant's violation of the statute as evidence of negligence.

In order for the doctrine of negligence per se to apply, the statute must be relevant to the case; that is, the court must determine that the statute was intended to apply as a standard of civil liability. Thus, the court must examine the legislative purpose in enacting the statute. Since most state statutes do not contain any expression of the legislative purpose, this must be surmised by the court. Courts determine whether a statute was intended to apply in the case at hand by determining whether the plaintiff falls within the class of individuals that the statute was intended to protect and whether the injury sustained by the plaintiff was of the type that the statute was intended to prevent. If these two factors are present, the plaintiff may invoke the doctrine of negligence per se.

As an example, assume that a California statute requires that all swimming pools must have a lifeguard present if children are permitted to swim there. Assume that the Jonco apartment complex has an unsupervised swimming pool that all residents, including children, are permitted to use. Assume further that 8-year-old Macauley drowns while using the pool. Can Macauley's family invoke the doctrine of negligence per se in a suit against Jonco? Yes. The statute was clearly aimed at protecting children against injuries that might be suffered in a swim-ming pool. Macauley, as a child, was a member of the class that the statute intended to protect and his injury, drowning, was almost certainly one that the statute was intended to prevent.

Now assume that Ebert is trying to escape with a VCR stolen from a Jonco apartment. He cuts through the swimming pool area where, as in the previous example, children are allowed to swim without the supervision of a lifeguard. He accidently falls into the pool and, because there is no lifeguard there to save him, he drowns. Ebert's family sues Jonco and attempts to invoke the negligence per se doctrine. The family argues that if Jonco had followed the law, there would have been a lifeguard posted at the scene and Ebert would have been rescued. Should the court accept this argument? Probably not. Ebert, as an adult, is not a member of the class that the statute was intended to protect.

Res Ipsa Loquitur The doctrine of **res ipsa loquitur** ("the thing speaks for itself") uses circumstantial evidence to establish a prima facie case of negligence. The doctrine is designed for cases in which the plaintiff cannot know the exact negligent act. For example, if someone walking alongside a factory is hit by a crate that fell from a second-story window, the practical difficulty of proving who was at fault is obvious. Yet it is just as obvious that, on its face, the act itself indicates the existence of negligence on the part of the company. Under the doctrine of *res ipsa loquitur*, it is inferred that the defendant's negligence is the cause of the plaintiff's injury when (1) the event is the kind that usually does not happen without negligence and (2) other responsible causes, including conduct by the plaintiff, are sufficiently eliminated by the evidence. Such proof is sufficient to support a jury verdict for the plaintiff. Because the prima facie case is based on inferences, however, the defendant is allowed to come forward with some explanation of the situation other than negligence. The doctrine of *res ipsa loquitur* is frequently used in cases of product liability, surgical malpractice, and negligent construction of buildings.

Defenses

There are two basic defenses to a negligence action: contributory negligence and assumption of risk. The burden of pleading and proving these defenses is on the defendant. Current trends with regard to these defenses have undercut their utility.

Contributory Negligence Contributory negligence is conduct by the plaintiff that contributes as a legal cause to the harm he or she has suffered and that falls below the standard to which the plaintiff is required to conform for his or her own protection. In other words, the plaintiff's failure to exercise due care for his or her own safety constitutes a contributing cause to his or her own injury. Contributory negligence, raised by the defendant, alleges that, although the defendant may have been negligent, the plaintiff was also negligent in some way directly related to the plaintiff's injury. The existence of contributory negligence is an issue of fact, governed by the same tests and rules as the negligence of the defendant. The plaintiff is required to conform to the standard of conduct of the reasonable and prudent person under the same or similar circumstances.

Assume that Ernest, on the way home from his accident described earlier with Bartles and James, continues to drive carelessly and strikes and injures Alicia, a jogger. But assume that Alicia was jogging carelessly down the middle of a busy street, wearing a "Walkman" that prevented her from hearing approaching vehicles. If Ernest can establish that Alicia's own negligence was a contributing cause to Alicia's injuries, then Ernest can invoke the defense of contributory negligence.

The case that follows illustrates how the plaintiff's own carelessness can act as a bar to his or her recovery.

CRENSHAW V. HOGAN

Court of Appeals of Georgia
416 S.E.2d 147 (1992)

BACKGROUND: A woman (appellant) tripped, fell, and injured herself while visiting the property of the defendant (appellee). The woman sued, and the trial court granted the defendant's motion for summary judgment. She appealed.

Shulman, Judge

The appellant lost her footing when the heel of her shoe got caught in what she described as a "hole" at the edge of the appellee's driveway, where is adjoined a walkway leading to the front door of the house. She described this hole as being about 14 inches long, three inches wide, and less than half an inch deep. The sun was out at the time, and the appellant acknowledged that there was nothing to obscure her view of the hole.

The appellant's purpose in coming onto the premises was to engage in a social visit with appellee's nephew, who lived there with the appellee. The appellant contends that the nephew was the appellee's paying tenant and that because she (the appellant) was there as his guest, she stood in his shoes and enjoyed the status of an invitee.

Based on the photographic evidence included in the record and on the appellant's own deposition testimony, we conclude that the asserted defect which caused her to fall was so open and obvious that it could not be considered actionable. . . . It is common knowledge that small cracks, holes and uneven spots often develop in pavement; and it has been held that where there is nothing to obstruct or interfere with one's ability to see such a "static" defect, the owner or occupier of the premises is justified in assuming that a visitor will see it and realize the risk involved. The appellant's reliance on *Pinkney v. VMS Realty* as authority . . . is misplaced. The plaintiff there had fallen a distance of about a foot from one ramp of an enclosed, multi-level parking garage onto an adjacent ramp. On the basis of her testimony that the two levels appeared to blend together due to a combination of poor lighting and the absence of railing or warning markers, the court held that a fact issue existed as to

> whether her failure to see the ledge barred her from recovery. Whereas the accident in *Pinkney* occurred inside an enclosed structure at night, under lighting conditions which may have created an optical illusion, the accident in the present case occurred outdoors, in broad daylight; and the appellant acknowledged that there was nothing to interfere with her ability to see the asserted defect.
>
> **DECISION:** The Court of Appeals affirmed the decision in favor of the defendant.

Since the tort of negligence bases liability upon fault, proof of contributory negligence was formerly an absolute bar to recovery by the plaintiff. Because of the harshness of this rule, the concept of comparative negligence was developed. Under the doctrine of **comparative negligence**, the plaintiff's recovery is reduced by the percentage of responsibility that the plaintiff bears for the accident. Let's assume, from our previous example, that Ernest is found to be 70 percent at fault for Alicia's injuries and Alicia is found to bear 30 percent of the blame. If Alicia suffers injuries amounting to $1 million, then she will be able to recover only $700,000, or 70 percent, from Ernest. In some states, a plaintiff found to be more than 50 percent at fault is completely barred from recovery.

In those states that have comparative negligence statutes (now a majority), a plaintiff's contributory negligence is no longer a complete bar to recovery. Comparative negligence removes the "all or nothing" rule of contributory negligence and replaces it with a rule that allows the jury to apportion damages to reflect the relative fault of the parties.

TABLE 7-1

Concept Summary   Negligence

Elements of Negligence

Duty	Defendant must have owed a duty to the plaintiff.
Breach of duty	Defendant must have breached that duty by failing to exercise the degree of care that a reasonable and prudent person would have exercised under the circumstances.
Injury	Plaintiff must have sustained some injury to person, property, or (with certain limitations) psyche.
Actual cause	Defendant's breach of duty must have been a material element and substantial factor in causing plaintiff's injury.
Proximate cause	Plaintiff's injury must have been a natural, probable, and foreseeable consequence of defendant's breach of duty.

Defenses to Negligence

Contributory negligence	In strict contributory negligence jurisdictions, plaintiff is completely barred from recovery if his or her own failure to exercise proper care contributed to his or her own injury.
Comparative negligence	In comparative negligence jurisdictions, plaintiff may generally recover even if his or her failure to exercise proper care contributed to his or her own injury. However, plaintiff's recovery is reduced by the percentage of fault attributable to him or her. In some states, plaintiff cannot recover anything if he or she is more than 50 percent at fault.
Assumption of risk	Plaintiff is barred from recovery if he or she knowingly and voluntarily accepted risk of injury.

Assumption of Risk The defense of **assumption of risk** exists when the plaintiff actually had or should have had knowledge of the risk and voluntarily exposed himself or herself to it. In such a situation the defendant, although negligent, is not responsible for the resulting injury. This is similar to consent to an intentional tort, which also denies recovery.

Therefore, when the plaintiff voluntarily enters into some relationship with the defendant, with knowledge that the defendant will not protect him or her against the risk, the plaintiff is regarded as tacitly or impliedly consenting to the possible negligence and agreeing to take a chance. For example, the plaintiff may accept employment knowing that he or she is expected to work in a dangerous area; or ride in a car with knowledge that the brakes are defective; or enter a baseball park, sit in an unscreened seat, and thereby consent that the players proceed with the game without taking any precautions to protect the plaintiff from being hit by the ball. In effect, the defendant is simply relieved of the duty that would otherwise exist.

Strict Liability

Up to this point, the discussion of tort law has focused on situations in which liability is based on fault. That is, a defendant's liability depends either on some intentional wrongdoing (see Chapter 6) or on the defendant's unreasonable conduct (negligence). However, the law imposes liability in some situations even if the defendant is not guilty of intentional wrongdoing and even if the defendant has exercised reasonable care. This is known as **strict liability**. The strict liability standard has been applied in situations where the defendant's conduct creates an unusually high risk of harm even if due care is exercised. In such situations injury is highly probable, and to require the plaintiff to prove negligence is to require him or her to bear the risk inherent in the defendant's dangerous conduct. Although the law could simply prohibit such conduct on the part of the defendant, there is some hazardous conduct that is socially beneficial, such as blasting done during the construction of buildings. The strict liability standard reflects a social policy that the defendant may engage in the activity but must bear the inherent risk of loss. The result of the strict liability standard is that the injured plaintiff is compensated for his or her injury by the party who caused it; that party in turn must consider such liability as a cost of undertaking a certain type of activity.

Strict liability was early applied to the keepers of dangerous animals. A dangerous animal is one that is known by its keeper to be likely to inflict injury—for example, a lion, a tiger, or a poisonous snake. For strict liability to apply, the keeper must know or have reason to know of the animal's dangerous propensities.

Strict liability was later applied to ultrahazardous activities. Common examples are blasting operations, public fireworks, and storing gasoline in dangerous proximity to nearby property. Consider the following case.

SPANO V. PERINI CORP.
Court of Appeals of New York
250 N.E.2d (1969)

BACKGROUND: Spano (plaintiff) was the owner of a garage in Brooklyn, which was wrecked by a blast occurring on November 27, 1962. Also damaged by the blast was an automobile owned by Davis (plaintiff), who had left his car in the garage for repairs. Spano and Davis each sued the Perini Corp. (defendant), which was engaged in constructing a tunnel in the vicinity. The two cases were tried together, and judgments were rendered in favor of Spano and Davis. Perini appealed, and an intermediate appellate court reversed the judgment, declaring that the established rule in New York required proof of negligence. Spano and Davis appealed to the Court of Appeals of New York, which is the highest court of that state.

Fuld, Chief Judge

The principal question posed on this appeal is whether a person who has sustained property damage caused by blasting on nearby property can maintain an action for damages without showing that the blaster was negligent. Since 1893, when this court decided the case of *Booth v. Rome, W. & O.T.R.R. Co.,* it has been the law of this State that proof of negligence was required unless the blast was accompanied by an actual physical invasion of the damaged property—for example, by rocks or other material being cast upon the premises. We are now asked to reconsider that rule.

The Appellate Division observed that "[i]f *Booth* is to be overruled, the announcement thereof should come from the authoritative source and not in the form of interpretation or prediction by an intermediate appellate court."

In our view, the time has come for this court to make that "announcement" and declare that one who engages in blasting must assume responsibility, and be liable without fault, for any injury he causes to neighboring property.

The concept of absolute liability in blasting cases is hardly a novel one. The overwhelming majority of American jurisdictions have adopted such a rule. Indeed, this court itself, several years ago, noted that a change in our law would conform to the more widely (indeed almost universally) approved doctrine that a blaster is absolutely liable for any damages he causes, with or without trespass.

However, the court in the *Booth* case rejected such an extension of liability for the reason that "[t]o exclude the defendant from blasting to adapt its lot to the contemplated uses, at the instance of the plaintiff, would not be a compromise between conflicting rights, but an extinguishment of the right of the one for the benefit of the other." The court expanded on this by stating, "This sacrifice, we think, the law does not exact. Public policy is sustained by the building up of towns and cities and the improvement of property. Any unnecessary restraint on freedom of action of a property owner hinders this."

This rationale cannot withstand analysis. The plaintiff in *Booth* was not seeking, as the court implied, to "exclude the defendant from blasting" and thus prevent desirable improvements to the latter's property. Rather, he was merely seeking compensation for the damage which was inflicted upon his own property as a result of that blasting. The question, in other words, was not whether it was lawful or proper to engage in blasting but who should bear the cost of any resulting damage—the person who engaged in the dangerous activity or the innocent neighbor injured thereby. Viewed in such a light, it clearly appears that Booth was wrongly decided and should be forthrightly overruled.

DECISION: The Court of Appeals of New York reversed the lower-level intermediate appellate court's decision and reinstated the trial court judgment in favor of Spano and Davis.

Vicarious Liability

Under the doctrine of **vicarious liability,** an employer is liable for the negligence committed by an employee within the scope of his or her employment. The doctrine is also known as *imputed negligence,* or **respondeat superior** ("let the superior respond"). It is an application of strict liability theory, meaning that for policy reasons liability is imposed regardless of the employer's fault or blame. Unlike other applications of strict liability, however, the employer's liability is based upon some fault of the employee.

It may seem odd that courts recognize a rule imposing liability upon an otherwise innocent employer for the employee's wrongdoing. Liability could be limited only to instances in which the employer knowingly hires a careless agent or commands the agent's tortious conduct. Although several justifications for the doctrine have been offered throughout its history, *respondeat superior* may be seen as simple allocation of risk: Between two innocent persons, the employer and the injured party, society has decided that the employer is more likely to be in a better position to bear the burden of injury.

Scope of Employment Limitation The employer is not, however, made responsible for each and every tort that the employee commits. Only when the employee commits a tort in the scope of employment—that is, when the injury is caused by the employee's wrongdoing incidental to the employment purposes—is the employer liable under *respondeat superior*. To make the employer responsible for acts that are in no way connected with employment goals would be unfair. The employer can be expected to bear only those costs that are closely associated with the business.

This limit on the employer's liability is easier to state than to apply. Determining if the employee is acting within the scope of employment often is difficult because the employee may temporarily be performing a personal errand, or doing the employer's work while also serving a personal purpose, or performing the employer's work in a forbidden manner. No precise formula exists to solve the problem of whether, at a particular moment, a particular employee is engaged in the employer's business. Whether the employee is inside or outside the scope of employment often is a matter of degree. Since the scope-of-employment test determines whether *respondeat superior* applies as a guide in close cases, reference should be made to the larger policy purposes that the doctrine is supposed to serve.

No-Fault Insurance Systems

In two areas, state-mandated insurance compensation systems have replaced the traditional tort litigation system as a means of loss allocation. These areas are workers' compensation and no-fault automobile insurance.

Workers' Compensation In the nineteenth century, the defenses of contributory negligence and assumption of risk, along with the fellow-servant rule (which provided that an employer was not liable for a worker's injury when the injury resulted from the negligence of a fellow worker), made it extremely unlikely that an employee could hold the employer liable for on-the-job injuries. In response to the growing number of job-related injuries and the political pressure generated by labor groups, state legislatures in the early twentieth century enacted workers' compensation statutes. By 1949, every state had some form of workers' compensation system. Although the laws vary, they have certain common features.

Workers' compensation statutes substitute a strict liability standard for negligence with regard to job-related injuries. Fault is immaterial. Employees are entitled to benefits whether or not they were negligent and whether or not their employer was free from fault.

Injuries that arise out of and during the course of employment are compensable under workers' compensation statutes. This standard is similar to the scope-of-employment test of the *respondeat superior* doctrine, discussed previously. Under workers' compensation, employers are required either to contribute to a state-administered workers' compensation fund or, as in most states, to procure workers' compensation insurance from private insurers.

Claims for workers' compensation benefits are administered by a state agency, usually called the Industrial Commission or Workers' Compensation Bureau. If the employer contests the claim, the agency holds a hearing and determines if the injury is compensable under the statute. Because an employer's contribution to the state fund or the employer's insurance premiums depends upon the employer's experience rating, there is an economic incentive for the employer to contest doubtful claims.

Workers' compensation benefits are computed according to a schedule of compensation. The schedule establishes the financial amount that an injured employee is entitled to according to the type of injury or disability that the employee suffered.

No-Fault Automobile Insurance Many negligence cases involve automobile accidents. Because of the amount of court time devoted to these cases, states have enacted statutes that, to varying degrees, remove recovery for automobile accident injuries from the courts to administrative agencies. The purpose of these statutes is to provide an injured party with an automatic but minimal amount of recovery rather than a day in court with its potential for a greater recovery. The laws differ from state to state. Basically, they provide that the injured party need not prove negligence in the traditional way but only that the no-fault insurance statute is applicable to the case. As long as the amount claimed by the injured party is below a prescribed maximum, his

ISSUES AND TRENDS
Tort Reform

Tort law, once limited to debate in the nation's courtrooms, has become a matter of intense public debate. To date, the debate has been among lawyers and representatives of the business community and insurers.

Pointing to freakish lawsuits, multi-million-dollar damage awards, and soaring insurance costs, business groups and insurers have urged Congress and state legislatures to undertake "tort reform" by passing laws that would repudiate many court-made legal doctrines. Proponents of tort reform argue that many of these judge-made rules were made only in the last 20 years and represent judicial activism that must be rebuked by legislation.

Plaintiff's lawyers and consumer advocates argue that what insurers and business groups want is special-interest protection. They assert that to take the few "freak" cases among the thousands of tort cases decided each year and suggest that they are typical of the mass of cases misrepresents the tort system. Most tort reform proposals, they contend, are designed to rob injured persons of their right to compensation or, at least, to discourage them from pursuing their rights.

Some tort reform proposals are summarized below.

Limit Pain and Suffering Awards   Put a cap ($100,000 has been proposed) on damages for intangible injuries such as pain and suffering, emotional distress, and loss of companionship.

Limit Punitive Damages   Limit punitive damages to some percentage of compensatory damages, or grant the judge, rather than the jury, exclusive authority to award punitive damages.

Adopt the "English Rule"   Require the loser in a civil suit to pay the winner's legal bills.

or her own insurance pays the claim without regard to fault. This process is analogous to the change from negligence claims to workers' compensation insurance for recovery by injured employees.

Review Questions and Problems

Key Terms

negligence	comparative negligence
proximate cause	assumption of risk
negligence per se	strict liability
res ipsa loquitur	vicarious liability
contributory negligence	*respondeat superior*

Discussion Questions

1. Describe each of the elements of negligence.
2. What procedural doctrines are available to plaintiffs in a negligence case, and what defenses are available to defendants?
3. In what types of cases has strict liability been applied?
4. When is vicarious liability applied?

Review Problems

1. Dickerson drives negligently and runs down Victor, a bicyclist. Although Victor's bicycle is severely damaged, Victor himself sustains no injuries. Victor takes his bicycle to the shop to be repaired. While he is in the shop, an arsonist sets fire to the shop. Victor is injured in the ensuing blaze. Can Victor hold Dickerson responsible for his personal injuries? Specifically, which elements of negligence, if any, can Victor prove against Dickerson with respect to his personal injury and which, if any, can he not establish?

2. Ace Construction Co. is hired to build a gymnasium for State University. One week after the gymnasium is completed, the roof collapses in the middle of the night when no one is around. Clues are difficult to find amid the rubble, and State University is unable to provide any direct evidence to establish that Ace Construction built the facility in a negligent manner. Might State University still be able to win a negligence suit against Ace? Discuss.

3. Myron, a student at San Diego State, is returning from a night of carousing in the bordertown of Tijuana, Mexico. Myron, who is drunk, drives back across the border into the United States. Shortly

after crossing the border, Myron's car strikes Javier, an illegal alien who is running across Interstate Highway 5. Javier's wife sues Myron. What is the result? Discuss.

4. A fireman developed lung cancer after some years of inhaling smoke while fighting fires and also smoking cigarettes. The fireman filed a claim for workers' compensation benefits. Will the fireman recover benefits? Explain.

Case Problems

1. The Chasms Portland Cement Co. failed to clean petroleum residue out of an oil barge, which was tied to a dock. Lightning struck the barge, the vapor inside it exploded, and workers on the dock were injured. Is Chasms liable to the workers for their injuries? Explain.

2. Breisig operated an automobile repair shop. Roberts took his car to Breisig's shop for repairs. When Roberts asked when the car would be ready, Breisig said that he hoped the repairs would be completed by the end of the day. If they were, Breisig said, he would park the car in his shop's parking lot so Roberts could pick it up that evening. About 7:00 p.m. Breisig finished the work and parked the car in the lot, leaving the keys in the ignition. Soon thereafter two teenagers stole the car and drove it around town. They picked up two friends and left the car on a street overnight. The next day one of the friends, Williams, returned to the car and, while driving it negligently, struck George, who suffered serious injuries. George sued Breisig, claiming that leaving the keys in an unattended car was negligence, particularly since Breisig's shop was located in a deteriorating neighborhood. Breisig denied liability. Who wins? Explain.

3. A passenger was running to catch one of the Long Island Railroad Company's trains. A railroad employee, trying to assist the passenger to board the train, dislodged a package from the passenger's arms, and it fell upon the rails. The package contained fireworks, which exploded with some violence. The concussion overturned some scales, many feet away on the platform, and they fell upon Palsgraf and injured her. Palsgraf sued the Long Island Railroad Company, claiming that it was liable for her injuries as a result of its employee's negligence. Long Island Railroad disclaimed any liability. Who wins? Explain.

4. A driver for the Coca-Cola Bottling Company delivered several cases of Coca-Cola to the restaurant where Escola worked as a waitress. She placed the cases on the floor, one on top of the other, under and behind the counter, where they remained for over 36 hours. Later Escola picked up the top case and set it upon an ice cream cabinet in front of and about 3 feet away from the refrigerator. She then proceeded to take the bottles from the case, one at a time, and put them into the refrigerator. After she had placed three bottles in the refrigerator and had moved the fourth bottle about 18 inches from the case, it exploded in her right hand. The bottle broke into two jagged pieces and inflicted a deep 5-inch cut, severing blood vessels, nerves, and muscles of the thumb and palm of her hand. Escola sued Coca-Cola, relying on the doctrine of *res ipsa loquitur* and strict product liability theory. Will Escola succeed under this approach? Explain.

5. A dead mouse is found baked inside a loaf of bread from the Continental Baking Co., and Doyle is injured by eating the bread. Continental introduces many witnesses who testify that all possible care was used in the bakery, and that such precautions made it impossible for mice to get into the product. Continental makes a motion for a directed verdict in its favor. Will the court grant the motion?

6. On a stormy night the owner of a tractor truck left it parked without lights in the middle of the road. The driver of a car in which Hill was a passenger saw the truck in time to turn and avoid hitting it, but negligently failed to do so. Hill is injured. Who is liable to her?

7. Anthony and Jeannette Luth were driving south on the Seward Highway in Alaska when their car collided with another driven by Wayne Jack. The accident occurred when Jack attempted to pass another vehicle going north. On the day of the accident, and for the previous 6 weeks, Jack was employed by Rogers and Babler Construction Company as a flagman on a road construction project. At the time of the accident, he was returning home to Anchorage from his job site, having completed a 7:00 a.m. to 5:30 p.m. workday. Jack did not live near the job site and commuted approximately 25 miles to work by car every day. The Master Union Agreement under which Jack worked provided for additional remuneration of $8.50 a day, since the job site was located a considerable distance from Anchorage. However, all the firm's employees on this particular construction project received the $8.50 additional remuneration whether they commuted from Anchorage or lived near the job site. The Luths sued Rogers and Babler Construction, claiming the company was responsible under the doctrine of *respondeat superior* for their injuries. Is the company liable? Explain.

8

Business and Ethics

Today, the media are reporting a never-ending litany of stories about corruption, conflicts of interest, insider trading, environmental pollution, deadly hazards in the workplace, sexual harassment, overbilling on government contracts, check kiting, and banking, savings and loan, and consumer frauds. The list goes on, ad infinitum. Concurrently, there has been a revival of interest in business ethics. Many basic questions are raised. How does one determine what constitutes right conduct in business? For example, is it ever acceptable to lie in a negotiation? What is the trend in business ethics? Is behavior in the business world worse than it was 10 years ago? Are there general principles of business ethics that apply to all forms of commercial activity? This chapter will shed light on these timely and important questions.

Ethics and Law

The relationship between ethics and law needs to be clarified, particularly prior to a discussion of ethics in a law book. Ethics is a discipline dealing with what is right and wrong in human conduct. As such, it may be viewed as a set of principles of conduct governing an individual or a profession.

In Western thought there are at least three widely accepted approaches to determining what is ethical: (1) consequential or utilitarian approaches, (2) deontological or duty-based approaches, of which Kantian ethics is an example, and (3) contractarian approaches with emphasis on consent. In addition, there are concepts such as stakeholders and virtue ethics which help us understand business ethics.

Some managers appear to believe that obeying the law is sufficient to be considered ethical. Although there may be an ethical obligation to obey most laws, it is incorrect to think that all ethical responsibilities can be satisfied by meticulous law compliance. For one thing, some laws are unethical. Slavery was once the law of the United States, yet a very strong case can be made that slavery is unethical. Secondly, ethical obligations often go beyond the law. It may be unethical, yet legal, to lie or to dishonor a promise. The law cannot, and should not, be used to ensure that every person lives up to every single ethical obligation.

In many cases it can be argued that there is an ethical obligation to obey the law. This obligation extends to acting in compliance with the spirit of the law, and not acting to seek loopholes or defeat the obvious purpose of the law. There appears to be a growing trend toward looking to "marketplace morality" as a means of defining what certain legal terms mean. Many statutes or common law principles contain terms or depend on concepts such as "good faith," "bad faith," "unfair," and "reckless disregard." The meaning of these terms in the marketplace helps to define their legal scope. In addition, juries may be influenced by whether the actions in a particular lawsuit appear consistent with commonplace conceptions of morality.

Ethics in Business

Ethics involves formal consideration of the interests of others in deciding how to behave or act. All businesses impact outsiders in their operations. Consider the decision by an owner to close a small glass-blowing plant that has been vital to the well-being of a small rural community and that has always been reasonably profitable. What questions must be answered in order to determine whether the plant-closing decision is ethical? Does motive make a difference? Should the focus be solely on the outcome from the viewpoint of the decision maker? Do local attitudes and customs primarily determine the ethical course of action? Is every case unique, or are there certain fundamental principles that apply regardless of the situation?

These basic questions have been the subject of much debate and formal analysis, particularly among philosophers. However, before exploring how they might be answered, we must first deal with the fundamental issue of whether ethical analysis is even possible in business. We will first discuss arguments, based upon relativism and egoism, that ethical analysis is not possible or legitimate in the business world, then proceed to a discussion of some of the fundamental Western theories of ethics, and finally present some principles of professional business ethics.

Relativism and Egoism

Relativism

Is ethical analysis dependent upon the social-economic context in which it occurs? The argument of **relativism** lies at the heart of the current debates about the propriety of paying bribes in foreign markets, setting lower standards for plant safety overseas, or discriminating on the basis of

sex in Muslim countries. Relativists who defend such actions argue that local custom makes it mandatory that international firms follow the local rules. When in Rome, one *must* do what the Romans do. Paying bribes is justified by arguing that (1) they are required by local custom and it is arrogance to impose American values upon other societies, (2) they are necessary to compete against foreign firms willing to pay bribes to get business, and (3) whatever harm results will affect only the foreign country (which after all has permitted bribery to flourish).

Similar explanations are given by those who follow different safety standards at foreign locations or who operate in Saudi Arabia. Is there anything wrong with following local practice? Certainly, there are circumstances in which people would defer to local preferences. Many businesspeople would not drink alcohol at a Muslim gathering, tip in an Australian restaurant, or insist on wearing shoes in a Buddhist temple.

The issue is of a different magnitude when it involves situations such as plant safety in less-developed countries. The local government may clearly prefer to have lower safety standards as a way to attract foreign investment. In Bhopal, the Union Carbide plant which had a gas explosion, killing several thousand people, was producing an agricultural product important to India and other developing countries with chronic food shortages. The plant was partly owned by India, and therefore could also generate foreign trade earnings that are critical to the development of the Indian economy.

The fact that one might defer to local custom does not mean that local custom can *always* determine what constitutes right conduct. No one would accept bizarre local practices, such as requiring the human sacrifice of a member of the firm in order to get a license to do business, as ethical. Relativism as an ethical theory would reduce ethical analysis to nothing more than conducting a proper survey of local customs and laws.

The counterpoint to relativism is the view that there are certain universal principles that transcend local custom or practice. These universal principles may be based upon fundamental human rights such as life, liberty, and physical well-being, or upon practices that improve human welfare. Under this view, a society as a whole can be considered to be immoral if its generally accepted practices violate universal norms.

If one accepts the notion of universal principles, then the relativism argument cannot be used to dispense with a consideration of ethical issues in business. A decision to practice apartheid in South Africa or to pay a bribe in Indonesia must be justified on grounds other than local practice.

Egoism

Egoism is acting solely to maximize one's self-interest. The egoist considers the interests of others solely to determine how they affect his or her own self-interest. There are two types of egoism which serve as counterpoints to formal ethical theory. The first, **psychological egoism**, assumes that humans are incapable of genuinely considering the interests of others. Seemingly altruistic acts such as charity and caring for the sick and disabled are dismissed as actually based upon selfish motivations. Charitable persons are considered to be getting kicks from a power trip or by having others become dependent upon them. The concept of psychological egoism is contrary to the basic assumptions about humankind that are found in the major religions and is counterintuitive. If psychological egoism is accepted as accurately descriptive of human nature, then there would be no point to the study of ethics.

Ethical egoism takes the normative position that everyone has the right to act in his or her own self-interest. This form has some serious defenders in the business world, who not only advocate it as a human right, but who also see it as an extension of Adam Smith's invisible hand. They claim that society is best off when people act as they selfishly desire. It is the responsibility of government to impose any necessary limits on their behavior. The "ethical" egoist will act to maximize self-interest subject only to compliance with the law. In a contract negotiation, if it is possible to lie, be undetected, and benefit, the ethical egoist will do so. The egoist would breach a contract whenever the damages to be paid are less than the benefit of the breach, so long as breaching would not produce additional offsetting costs such as the loss of reputation. Under this view the plant owner would only consider his or her own interests in deciding whether to close the plant. Society would have the responsibility for providing any necessary social safety net.

Ultimately, egoism as a theory of ethics can be criticized on the basis of its impact on society. A society made up of ethical egoists would be dominated by opportunistic behavior. Opportunistic behavior may include theft, fraud, double-dealing, treachery, and other similar actions. Negotiators anticipating opportunistic behavior enter into more costly contracts, while actual opportunism directly reduces economic efficiency. One is likely to be much more careful when contracting with someone who is considered untrustworthy, and the extra care will translate into increased costs, including greater use of elaborate contracts, monitoring, and extensive background data gathering. When these costs occur differentially among firms or industries, they may result in the misallocation of resources. Because egoism legitimizes opportunism and may sanction actions harming other human beings, it is not satisfying as an ethical theory. The argument that egoism is a basic human right is subject to challenge on grounds that it is incompatible with human nature and that most people would not choose to recognize such a right on a universal basis.

Rejection of egoism does not require adoption of a principle of ethical altruism whereby it is considered inappropriate for an individual to consider his or her own interest in evaluating the morality of a proposed course of action. That, of course, is not the case. The standard methods of ethical analysis that are relevant to business incorporate the interest of the actor in the ultimate consideration of the nature or impact of the proposed action. The actor is a member of society, and as such his or her interests do count.

Theories and Concepts of Moral Responsibility

Three theories of moral responsibility particularly relevant to business practice have been propounded by Western moral philosophers: (1) deontology, (2) utilitarianism, and (3) social contract. **Deontological theory** is founded upon concepts of duty which serve as guidelines to moral behavior. In contrast, **utilitarian theory** is outcome-oriented. **Social contract** is concerned with specific procedures or principles for allocating wealth, rights and responsibilities among the members of society.

A social contract is an implied, informal understanding concerning norms of behavior that will be followed in certain contexts. It has been suggested, for example, by Donaldson[1] that there is an implied social contract between society and the business organizations that operate within the society. As part of the implied contract, society promises to provide an environment conducive for business operations, while in turn business agrees to operate by the rules established by society.

In addition to the formal ethical theories, various concepts or ideas are associated with business ethics. The best known of these is the **stakeholder** concept. The stakeholder concept requires that business firms consider the interests of stakeholders in making decisions. Stakeholders include all of those who might be affected in a significant way by the decisions of the firm. Thus, a list of stakeholders for a major corporation would include creditors, residents living near a plant, local governments, unions, distributors, and so on. Under a stakeholder analysis, ethical firms must identify the interests of significant stakeholders and then incorporate those interests into the ultimate decision.

Another idea associated with business ethics is that of virtue. Often based upon Aristotle, the key idea is that individuals are self-fulfilled by practicing key virtues in all dimensions of life, including their jobs. In the words of Robert Solomon:[2]

> The bottom line of the Aristotelian approach to business ethics is that we have to get away from "bottom line" thinking and conceive of business as an essential part of the good life, living well, getting along with others, having a sense of self-respect, and being part of something one can be proud of. Aristotle argued that what I have called "abstract greed" ("the profit motive") was a kind of pathology, a defect of character, an "unnatural" and antisocial vice.

Duty-Based Ethics

Immanuel Kant (1724–1804) was a profound and influential duty-based philosopher. Kant identified several general guiding principles for moral behavior based upon the fundamental nature of human beings. Kant formulated several versions of a categorical imperative of duty—an obligation existing as an affirmative duty in all circumstances and contexts.

In his most famous statement of the categorical imperative, Kant identified a duty requiring each individual to act in such a manner that the individual could will that the action be a universal rule followed by all. Individuals must refrain from any action that would be problematic if everyone were to do it. One cannot make an unfair exception for himself or herself. Cutting into waiting lines or putting slugs into honor system newspaper vending machines are immoral acts. One cannot expect others to wait in line or pay fares and then assert that one has a special privilege to violate the principle.

In another characterization of the categorical imperative, Kant cautioned that it is immoral to treat other human beings merely as means. The treatment of human beings as merely means is the equivalent of treating people as objects, a denial of their basic humanity. Intention is always important in judging whether an individual has acted ethically.

Kant's principles provide general guidance, but they need to be systematically applied to a business context. In that context, the disagreements are likely to begin. Is there an absolute duty not to lie in a business negotiation? Some would dispute such a concept of duty. How, then, are duties to be derived?

To begin with, it could be postulated that there are certain basic *general* duties such as treating others on a nondiscriminatory basis, acting in good faith, dealing with subordinates through fair procedures, avoiding physical harm to others, eschewing conflicts of interest, and obeying the law that apply to everyone. Such fundamental duties form the core of business ethics and are applicable to all businesspeople in all contexts.

These general duties are supplemented by specific duties that apply to certain individuals in certain contexts. Specific duties could arise from personal promises, professional codes of behavior, or role obligations. The following are examples of specific duties:

- A corporate lawyer has a duty to keep confidential the proprietary information of his or her employer.

- A real estate agent representing a seller must not purchase the property for his or her own account without notifying the seller.

- A corporate manager must not compete secretly with his or her own firm.
- An automobile engineer with responsibility for design safety must hold paramount the physical well-being of users.
- An arbitrator must not delegate decision making to someone else without the consent of the disputing parties.
- An accountant cannot agree to a contingent fee arrangement dependent upon a particular finding or result.
- Bank employees should not reveal information relating to their customers to unauthorized persons, nor should confidential information of clients be used to benefit the bank financially.

For a given individual, then, it may be possible to come up with a list of specific ethical duties that should be observed. But the task does not end at that point. One of the most difficult problems for duty-based ethical theorists arises when duties come into conflict. For example, a corporate lawyer has an obligation to maintain the confidentiality of client confidences. But suppose that the lawyer discovers a corporate plan to steal millions through computer fraud. The lawyer is aware of the implications of the plan and is certain that crimes will be committed. What should the lawyer do?

The lawyer is a member of the legal system and is charged with upholding the law. The lawyer also owes duties of confidentiality to the corporate client. Revealing the confidential information would prevent the commission of a major economic crime. In many states, the lawyers' rules of professional responsibility would only provide that a lawyer *may* resign after trying various ways to blow the whistle inside the corporation.

The lawyer is thus faced with a conflict between the duty of confidentiality and the duty to uphold the law. Universalizing the action alternatives fails to provide clear-cut guidance. Widespread breaching of confidentiality may cause clients to become reluctant to disclose information to their attorneys, thus restricting their ability to provide proper representation. On the other hand failing to disclose may result in much higher levels of crime, assisted by the passiveness of lawyers.

The case that follows presents another dimension of the problem of conflicting duties for lawyers—the client who announces that he intends to lie on the witness stand.

NIX v. WHITESIDE

U.S. Supreme Court
54 L.W. 4194 (1986)

BACKGROUND: Whiteside (petitioner-respondent), a convicted felon, sued Nix, the warden of the state prison in which he was held, alleging that he should be released because he had been denied his constitutionally protected rights to a fair trial and representation by counsel when he was convicted.

Emanuel Whiteside fatally stabbed Calvin Love in the course of an argument over the sale of marijuana. Whiteside was charged with murder, and Gary Robinson was appointed to defend him. Whiteside told Robinson that he stabbed Love because he thought Love was reaching for a gun ("piece") hidden under a pillow. No gun was found during the police search of the premises after the stabbing. Although Whiteside had repeatedly told Robinson that he had not actually seen a gun, as the trial date drew closer, he grew nervous and told Robinson that he was going to testify that he saw something "metallic" because "if I don't say I saw a gun, I'm dead." Robinson responded by telling Whiteside that testifying to seeing something metallic would constitute perjury. Robinson further warned that if Whiteside committed perjury during the trial, Robinson would withdraw as counsel and advise the judge about the reason.

Whiteside heeded Robinson's warning and testified that he thought Love was reaching for a gun and that he acted in self-defense. He was convicted of second-degree murder.

Whiteside then went into federal court and argued that the actions of Robinson had denied him his rights to representation by counsel and a fair trial guaranteed by the U.S. Constitution. The federal trial court ruled against Whiteside, but the federal court of appeals reversed and found that Whiteside's constitutional rights had been violated.

Burger, Chief Justice

We granted certiorari to decide whether the Sixth Amendment right of a criminal defendant to assistance of counsel is violated when an attorney refuses to cooperate with the defendant in presenting perjured testimony at his trial. . . .

In *Strickland,* we recognized counsel's duty of loyalty and his "overarching duty to advocate the defendant's cause." Plainly, that duty is limited to legitimate, lawful conduct compatible with the very nature of a trial as a search for truth. Although counsel must take all reasonable lawful means to attain the objectives of the client, counsel is precluded from taking steps or in any way assisting the client in presenting false evidence or otherwise violating the law. . . .

It is universally agreed that at a minimum the attorney's first duty when confronted with a proposal for perjurious testimony is to attempt to dissuade the client from the unlawful course of conduct. . . .

The essence of the brief *amicus* of the American Bar Association reviewing practices long accepted by ethical lawyers, is that under no circumstance may a lawyer either advocate or passively tolerate a client's giving false testimony. This, of course, is consistent with the governance of trial conduct in what we have long called "a search for truth." The suggestion sometimes made that "a lawyer must believe his client not judge him" in no sense means a lawyer can honorably be a party to or in any way give aid to presenting known perjury. . . .

Whatever the scope of a constitutional right to testify, it is elementary that such a right does not extend to testifying *falsely.* . . .

Robinson's admonitions to his client can in no sense be said to have forced respondent into an *impermissible* choice between his right to counsel and his right to testify as he proposed for there was no *permissible* choice to testify falsely. For defense counsel to take steps to persuade a criminal defendant to testify truthfully, or to withdraw, deprives the defendant of neither his right to counsel nor the right to testify truthfully. . . .

Similarly, we can discern no breach of professional duty in Robinson's admonition to respondent that he would disclose respondent's perjury to the court. The crime of perjury in this setting is indistinguishable in substance from the crime of threatening or tampering with a witness or a juror. A defendant who informed his counsel that he was arranging to bribe or threaten witnesses or members of the jury would have no "right" to insist on counsel's assistance or silence. Counsel would not be limited to advising against that conduct. An attorney's duty of confidentiality, which totally covers the client's admission of guilt, does not extend to a client's announced plans to engage in future criminal conduct. In short, the responsibility of an ethical lawyer, as an officer of the court and a key component of a system of justice, dedicated to a search for truth, is essentially the same whether the client announces an intention to bribe or threaten witnesses or jurors or to commit or procure perjury. No system of justice worthy of the name can tolerate a lesser standard. . . .

DECISION: The Supreme Court reversed, ruling that Whiteside must remain in jail.

The basic concept of a mandatory duty runs into trouble when a decision maker is confronted with conflicting obligations. Some additional methodology is required to establish priorities for dealing with instances of conflicting duties. Duty-based theorists have responded to this problem by constructing hierarchical systems of duties and proposing decision techniques based upon concepts of procedural justice. The hierarchical systems never seem to eliminate completely the problem of conflicting duties; instead, they just refine the conflict to a consideration of competing comparable duties. Systems which rely solely upon standards of procedural justice similarly beg the issue. Without some method of assigning relative weights to principles of duty, the individual businessperson is left with little guidance as to how to act in the many situations that involve conflicting duties.

The idea that a profession may set its own ethical rules is a form of relativism. Although representatives of a profession may have special insights into the daily practice and social role of the profession, they cannot be the final arbiters, in an ultimate sense, of what is "right" in professional practice. Instead, their actions developing professional ethical standards must always be subject to testing under general ethical theory. Many professions over the years have developed ethical standards that limit competition among their members or that set minimum fees. This dark side of formal professional standards is reflected in the following case.

NATIONAL SOCIETY OF PROFESSIONAL ENGINEERS V. UNITED STATES

U.S. Supreme Court
435 U.S. 679 (1978)

BACKGROUND: The U.S. government (plaintiff) filed a civil suit under the Sherman Antitrust Act against the National Society of Professional Engineers (defendant, Society) alleging that the provision of their code of ethics preventing competitive bidding for jobs was illegal. The Society argued that the restriction was necessary in order to ensure safety. The District Court rejected that justification without even making a factual determination of the validity of the safety argument. The Court of Appeals for the District of Columbia affirmed.

Stevens, Justice

The National Society of Professional Engineers (Society) was organized in 1935 to deal with the nontechnical aspects of engineering practice, including the promotion of the professional, social, and economic interests of its members. Its present membership of 69,000 resides throughout the United States and in some foreign countries. Approximately 12,000 members are consulting engineers who offer their services to governmental, industrial, and private clients. Some Society members are principals or chief executive officers of some of the largest engineering firms in the country.

The charges of a consulting engineer may be computed in different ways. He may charge the client a percentage of the cost of the project, may set his fee at his actual cost plus overhead plus a reasonable profit, may charge fixed rates per hour for different types of work, may perform an assignment for a specific sum, or he may combine one or more of these approaches. Suggested fee schedules for particular types of services in certain areas have been promulgated from time to time by various local societies. This case does not, however, involve any claim that the National Society has tried to fix specific fees, or even a specific method of calculating fees. It involves a charge that the members of the Society have unlawfully agreed to refuse to negotiate or even to discuss the question of fees until after a prospective client has selected the engineer for a particular project. Evidence of this agreement is found in § 11(c) of the Society's Code of Ethics, adopted in July 1964.[1]. . .

In its answer, the Society averred that the standard set out in the Code of Ethics was reasonable because competition among professional engineers was contrary to the public interest. It was averred that it would be cheaper and easier for an engineer "to design and specify inefficient and unnecessarily expensive structures and methods of construction." Accordingly, competitive pressure to offer engineering services at the lowest possible price would adversely affect the quality of engineering. Moreover, the practice of awarding engineering contracts to the lowest bidder, regardless of quality, would be dangerous to the public health, safety, and welfare. For these reasons, the Society claimed that its Code of Ethics was not an "unreasonable restraint of interstate trade or commerce."

The Sherman Act does not require competitive bidding; it prohibits unreasonable restraints on competition. Petitioner's ban on competitive bidding prevents all customers from making price comparisons in the initial selection of an engineer, and imposes the Society's views of the costs and benefits of competition on the entire marketplace. It is this restraint that must be justified, and petitioner's attempt to do so on the basis of the potential threat that competition poses to the public safety and the ethics of its profession is nothing less than a frontal assault on the basic policy of the Sherman Act.

. . . The assumption that competition is the best method of allocating resources in a free market recognizes that all elements of a bargain—quality, service, safety, and durability—and not just the immediate cost, are favorably affected by the free opportunity to select among alternative offers. Even assuming occasional exceptions to the presumed consequences of competition, the statutory policy precludes inquiry into the question whether competition is good or bad.

DECISION: The Supreme Court affirmed; a code of ethics cannot override the procompetitive principles of the Sherman Act.

[1]That section, which remained in effect at the time of trial, provided: "Section 11—The Engineer will not compete unfairly with another engineer by attempting to obtain employment or advancement or professional engagements by competitive bidding. . . ."

Utilitarianism

Utilitarianism constitutes an alternative to a duty-based approach. Utilitarians are concerned with the ultimate impact of actions on the welfare of society as a whole. The emphasis is on the greatest good for the greatest number. Recall the example of the use of newspaper vending machines and waiting lines. A utilitarian would evaluate the practice of cutting into lines or of putting slugs into the machines on the basis of the overall effect on society. If such behaviors were common, the queuing effect of the lines would disappear, resulting in physical strength determining position in line; and the convenience of newspaper vending machines would be lost. Thus, such actions would also be found unethical under a utilitarian view.

The utilitarian calculation is made from the viewpoint of society as a whole, not just from the perspective of the actor. An individual cannot calculate what would be best for him or her and claim a utilitarian justification for the action. That would be an example of egoism.

By its emphasis on final outcomes, utilitarianism appears to avoid some of the problems encountered by the duty-based approach. Closer observation, however, reveals that utilitarians also encounter significant difficulties. A fundamental question for the utilitarian is how society's interest should be calculated. The question can be approached in very different ways. Under one approach, happiness and freedom from pain is the primary good to be used in evaluating the morality of actions. Others emphasize principles of intrinsic worth, for example, health.

A quite different approach is to evaluate an action on whether its outcome serves to maximize the preferences of individuals within society, whatever those preferences happen to be. Individuals are assumed to have very different individual preferences: some prefer the beach, some prefer the mountains, some like self-denial, others like to consume conspicuously. Advocates of maximizing personal utility argue that an action is ethical when it tends to allow other individuals the opportunity to realize their own personal preferences. Under a liberty-as-key utility approach actions that significantly interfere with the liberties of others would be characterized as unethical. Marketplace decisions and voting are the two primary ways in which individuals indicate their preferences.

There are two forms of utilitarianism: act and rule utilitarianism. **Act utilitarianism** requires an ad hoc analysis of each and every action that may have moral consequences. Once agreement is reached on the ultimate criteria to use in evaluating outcomes (happiness, health, maximization of personal utilities), the difficult task of measuring the probable impact must be faced. The problem is similar to that faced in any sort of cost-benefit type of analysis. How can the various costs and benefits be put into equivalent terms?

The second form of utilitarianism is called **rule utilitarianism.** Rule utilitarians avoid making an independent judgment for every proposed act. Instead, rules are identified that are assumed to maximize utility. A probability judgment is made that if certain behavior predominates—for example, businesspeople always try to act in good faith—then maximum utility will result. Although rule utilitarianism may seem similar to a duty-based analysis, it differs in a fundamental regard. The rule utilitarian devises the rules solely on the basis of whether they are likely to contribute to right outcomes. Further information about a rule's effectiveness or a change in patterns of behavior that alter the likely outcomes produced by a rule should result in remodeling the rule. In contrast, duty-based rules are understood as more fundamental and unchangeable, and such duties are to be observed even when they impose net costs on society.

Pareto superiority, a principle of public choice, involves related principles and can be applied to a utilitarian analysis. An action is Pareto superior if it improves the situation of a person or group and no one else is harmed by it. Pareto superiority is concerned with outcomes and involves evaluating the impact of an action upon others, and thus is consistent with a utilitarian analysis.

One major problem with Pareto superiority is that it takes the status quo as given. Major inequities may be preserved as actions are evaluated on the basis of whether they produce benefit on their own accord. Pareto superiority cannot be used to condemn the status quo. Thus, actions supporting apartheid could be characterized as ethical using a standard of Pareto superiority so long as some white South-Africans are better off and no blacks are worse off. Another problem is that few important policies or actions can ever meet the stringent requirement that no one be made worse off. Thus, Pareto superiority is irrelevant to most of the tough decisions involving business ethics.

Social Contract

The classical social contract theories are based upon a hypothetical contract among the members of a society, or between the members of a society and a sovereign or government. The parties agree to the terms of the contract because, as rational people, they understand that the only way to solve a particular problem (avoiding anarchy or establishing a productive business environment) is to have an unwritten agreement establishing certain standards of behavior and rights. The theories of social contract often generate fundamental justice principles pertaining to the division of wealth, rights and responsibilities within a society.

Several social contract theories are directly related to business ethics. In his influential book, *Morals by Agreement*,[3] David Gauthier bases a social contract upon an assumption that people are rational egoists. He claims that self-interested people will cooperate in order to maximize their own well-being, and would agree to a social contract based upon self-restraint.

Thomas Donaldson has worked out social contract theories directly relevant to business ethics. In his 1989 book, *The Ethics of International Business*,[4] Donaldson uses the metaphor of a global social contract as a device for determining what constitutes ethical behavior in international business transactions. Donaldson engages in a "thought experiment" and asks what type of arrangement would rational people enter into if they were required to design a new world of international business. Donaldson concludes that people would want to establish a minimal floor of responsibility for global corporations. All corporations would be required to respect a set of fundamental rights. His list (p. 81) includes the following:

1. The right to freedom of physical movement
2. The right to ownership of property
3. The right to freedom from torture
4. The right to a fair trial
5. The right to nondiscriminatory treatment (based on race or sex)

6. The right to physical security
7. The right to freedom of speech and association
8. The right to minimal education
9. The right to political participation
10. The right to subsistence

Real Social Contracts?   Business litera-ture is filled with references to real, existing so-cial contracts. It is common to find managers and labor leaders referring to "the" social contract which is thought to exist between employers and employees. Such real social contracts can be a source of specific ethical obligations. Identifiable ethical norms can be found within such diverse groups in business as corporations, real estate brokers, travel agents, purchasing executives, and so on. Individuals who become members of such groups, or who engage in transactions where widely accepted ethical norms exist will be expected to conform to those norms.

Integrative Social Contracts Theory
Thomas Donaldson and Thomas Dunfee have en-visioned a hypothetical social contract which takes into account the ethical standards devel-oped by groups through real social contracts. They envision global humanity coming together to work out a rational arrangement for ethics in eco-nomic life. The rational humans at this global con-vention would recognize that moral rationality is bounded in the same way that economic rational-ity is bounded. Moral agents, when attempting to decide the right thing to do, are constrained by a lack of information and a limited amount of time for making the decision. Consider the manager who must decide whether to hold up the Chal-lenger space shuttle to replace the O-ring seal. If the manager is a utilitarian the manager must somehow estimate the probabilities that the seal will fail, and the voluminous consequences that would attend to a decision to hold up the launch. Although after the fact the decision may seem ob-vious, at the time it was made it was virtually im-possible to make a true utilitarian decision.

Similarly, ethical theorists are limited in their ability to design an ethical calculus applicable to all humanity in all contexts. This is particularly the case with regard to business decision-making. What is the ethical decision for a travel agent whose large corporate client wants the agent to use fare loopholes to reduce costs and whose

suppliers (airlines in this case) state they don't want travel agents to use loopholes? Before an Immanuel Kant, or any other ethical theorist could respond to this question, he (or she) would have to have a full understanding of the business environment in which the decision will be made.

Thus, the global conventioneers charged with designing a system for economic ethics would recognize the constraints imposed by bounded moral rationality. But they would also want to have a moral fabric in business in order to pro-vide a conducive environment for wealth genera-tion. How can they do this? A plausible solution is for them to agree to allow people to form into economic groupings as they wish, and to generate binding ethical norms for members of the groups. Thus, Donaldson and Dunfee conclude that they would want business communities or groups to have **moral free space.** People, including man-agers, would want to have moral free space be-cause they want to keep their moral options open until they confront the full context and environ-ment of a decision. Further, they would want to retain the freedom to specify norms of economic interaction consistent with their own cultural, ideological, and/or religious preferences. Thus, "(m)uslim managers may wish to participate in systems of economic ethics compatible with the teachings of Mohammed; European and Ameri-can managers may wish to participate in systems of economic ethics giving due respect to individ-ual liberty; and Japanese managers may prefer systems showing respect for the value of the col-lective."

Local norms, based upon social contracts among groups of people, could be identified by determining what the members of the group be-lieve to be right and wrong behaviors, and by also noting the actual behavior of the group. When a substantial majority of a group, be it a corpora-tion, trade association, bar association, or any other community of individuals, believe that a particular action is wrong, and eschew such be-havior, then it can be said that a norm exists au-thentic to that group.

However, the humans designing an ethical sys-tem would not want to allow all such norms to be considered ethical norms. There may be norms that condone murder as a method of enforcing contracts, or that endorse coarse racial or sexual discrimination. As a consequence, it can be as-sumed that they would want to restrict the moral free space of communities by requiring that before any community norms become ethically obligatory, they must be found to be compatible with **hypernorms.** Hypernorms (the norms by which all other norms are to be judged) entail principles so fundamental to human existence that we would expect them to be reflected in a convergence of religious, philosophical and cultural beliefs. A list of hypernorms would include such things as:

- An obligation to respect the dignity of each human person
- Core human rights, such as personal freedom, physical security and well being, the ownership of property, etc.

Thus, in order to be found ethically obligatory, a norm generated in moral free space must be compatible with hypernorms. But before we can say that a particular norm must be followed, another problem must be resolved. There are literally millions of communities generating millions of norms. Individuals simultaneously belong to different communities which may have directly contradictory norms. Many transactions cross communities (e.g., a U.S. firm doing business in Indonesia) where there are directly conflicting norms. These circumstances require a determination of which community's norms are to prevail.

Donaldson and Dunfee propose a set of six priority rules for sorting among mutually exclusive norms. These are particularly important in global business transactions. The rules are as follows:

1. Transactions solely within a single community, which do not have significant adverse effects on other humans or communities, should be governed by the host community's norms.
2. Community norms indicating a preference for how conflict of norms situations should be resolved should be applied, so long as they do not have significant adverse effects on other humans or communities.
3. The more extensive or more global the community which is the source of the norm, the greater the priority which should be given to the norm.
4. Norms essential to the maintenance of the economic environment in which the transac-

tion occurs should have priority over norms potentially damaging to that environment.
5. Where multiple conflicting norms are involved, patterns of consistency among the alternative norms provides a basis for prioritization.
6. Well-defined norms should ordinarily have priority over more general, less precise norms.

The priority rules are to be applied in a manner consistent with the letter and spirit of the macro social contract and are not intended as theoretically precise principles. The six rules are to be weighed and applied in combination. Similar to the process of statutory interpretation, there is no precise hierarchy for the six rules, and instead, emphasis should be on the fit of the particular ethical principle with one or two of the principles, or with a convergence of the rules toward a particular result.

Integrative Social Contracts Theory "establishes a means for displaying the ethical relevance of existing norms in industries, corporations, and other economic communities, even as it limits the acceptable range of such norms. . . . It . . . advocates much closer scrutiny of existing ethical beliefs and practices in institutions as dissimilar as the EC, the Sony Corporation, the international rubber market, and Muslim banks."[5]

CONCEPT SUMMARY
Business Ethics

1. Utilitarianism—do that which produces the best consequences
2. Duty-based ethics—act with the intention to honor fundamental duties—act as though you could will that your action be a general rule for humankind
3. Social contract—act consistent with the standards that all rational humans would agree to, honor generally understood agreements
4. Stakeholder analysis—consider the interests of those who have a significant stake in your decisions
5. Virtue—live with honor and self-respect, exercise self-restraint

Rule-of-Thumb Principles of Business Ethics

The individual businessperson, confronted with an ethical dilemma (e.g., whether to accept a case of Scotch from a supplier), faces a daunting array of sources of information concerning the right choice. His or her firm may have a code of ethics that states either very general principles (e.g., always put the customer's interests first, be loyal to the firm) or establishes specific rules (e.g., don't accept gifts from any supplier worth $25 or more). He or she may belong to a professional society that has a suggested code (e.g., never accept anything from a supplier). His or her peers may have established practices (e.g., okay to take a gift worth more than $25 from a long-time supplier), and friends may have a different view (e.g., it's none of the firm's business if it is a holiday gift).

The general theories discussed previously seem rather abstract in such a context. How is the overall interest of society involved? Is there some fundamental human right or duty at issue? Such discussions raise the issue of whether there are any generic principles of business ethics that can serve as a foundation for everyday decision making.

Such principles would have to be consistent with the basic functions of business, would have to be defensible under general ethical theory, and would have to be meaningful. Seven possible general principles will be presented below. Although generally consistent with utilitarian and duty-based ethical theories, the main support for this type of list comes from social contract. The claim would be made that these principles are supported by existing social contracts in business and in the broader society, even at the global level.

Honor Confidentiality Much business information is made available with the express or implied understanding that it is to be used only for certain purposes. When a firm discloses financial information as part of a merger negotiation, it expects that the data will only be used in the context of that negotiation. A fast-food franchise which discloses its "secret recipe" to a supplier expects the supplier to keep the confidence. Many employees know proprietary information about their firm: new designs, marketing plans, competitors' weaknesses. Researchers working on new products may know critically important information. Some of the information may be of great value and could capture a high price if wrongfully disclosed. The efficiency of the business system depends upon the honoring of confidentiality. Individual privacy rights are also an important basis for confidentiality.

However, none of these principles are to be taken as absolutes. They all require judgment in their application. If, for example, a manager is aware of confidential information that indicates that her firm is endangering people in its disposal of toxic wastes, it may be permissible for her to disclose that information in order to prevent human injury. In that case, a right to blow the whistle may override the principle of confidentiality. Critical factors include the nature of the information, the manner in which it was obtained, whether a confidentiality agreement exists, and so on.

Avoid Even the Appearance of a Conflict of Interest A conflict of interest arises when someone has a personal interest that contrasts with a duty owed to another, or mutually exclusive duties are owed to two or more people. A duty arises out of an obligation that comes from a promise, a contractual obligation, a role (trustee, agent, guardian . . .), a personal or family relationship, or by law. A simple example is when a purchasing agent for a corporation selects a close relative as a supplier, or an agent represents both the buyer and the seller in the same transaction.

Conflicts of interest can be resolved in several ways, so that it is not always necessary to refrain when there is a conflicting self-interest or a competing obligation. The standard ways to make sure that one has not given into a conflict of interest are to (1) disclose fully to all affected parties, (2) have a truly independent party certify the fairness of the transaction, or (3) refrain personally and have someone else, who is totally independent, make the decision. The stress on avoiding the "appearance" of a conflict is to make sure that, at the least, there is full disclosure.

Willingly Comply with the Law Some businesspeople appear to think that they are sufficiently ethical if they just comply with the law. Although there is some relationship, ethics and the law are not the same thing. Ethics goes beyond the law; merely complying with the law does not constitute, per se, the satisfaction of all ethical obligations. Ethics involves voluntary behavior that reflects concern about others; compliance with the law may occur merely out of a fear of being caught and punished. Compliance with a law that violates universal ethical principles (e.g., a law requiring human sacrifice) is unethical behavior.

Willing compliance with the law goes beyond employing a cost-benefit analysis of complying with a particular legal rule. It also mitigates against too easy an acceptance of excuses such as (1) the law is not enforced, (2) the law is bad law, (3) the boundaries of the law are vague, or (4) the law is something different from its literal statement, for example, the speed limit is sixty-five rather than fifty-five miles per hour. Although civil disobedience may be sanctioned in certain, very limited circumstances, in almost all business contexts ethical analysis supports obeying the law.

Exercise Due Care   This principle is one of professional competency. A businessperson who has special training or experience can be expected to perform at a level that reflects that training and experience. The principle of due care distinguishes professionals from laypeople. Although the principle is easily understood in the context of a doctor or lawyer, it has applicability to businesspeople also. A marketing manager should be expected to demonstrate special abilities in carrying out his or her job. A financial analyst would be expected to notice certain things in a financial report that might escape someone who is not trained or experienced in finance. The principle constitutes an ethical duty in that others rely upon and are affected by the quality of work performed by the businessperson.

Act in Good Faith   A fundamental obligation, rooted in both American and international commercial law, is to act in good faith. Good faith incorporates a number of attributes, including honoring promises, avoiding deceit, and living up to the reasonable expectations that others have concerning behavior. One way to think of what good faith means is to act as though you expect the business relationship to be long term. If you know that you will encounter the other person again and again, how would you act?

The essence of good faith is fairness. Treating others fairly includes following just procedures in addition to recognizing the legitimate claims of others. Consider the case of an oil company that decides to terminate an independent dealer who has operated one of their service stations for many years. Good faith would require that the dealer's expectations based upon prior promises and actions be considered, and that the dealer be given a chance to respond to the reasons for the termination. Ultimately, any termination should be for just reasons and carried out in a fair manner.

Respect the Liberty and Rights of Others   Other humans are entitled to be treated with respect. Managers are often in a position where they can greatly influence the way in which people are treated. A common problem that younger lower-level managers report is that they perceive a conflict between their values and those of their firm. In a famous survey in 1979, 40 percent of the middle managers reported that they had been asked by a superior to do something they were sure was unethical; and 10 percent had been asked to do something illegal! Being put into a compromising position constitutes a denial of their right to respect.

Employers who consider restricting the rights of political access, privacy, and speech of their employees should consider the full consequences of the restrictions. Although it is legal to impose limits on such employee rights (not without limit), and there may be times when the greater social good requires some limitation; far-reaching limits, imposed by enough firms, may have a significantly detrimental impact on the viability of basic rights in our society. At the individual level, businesspeople should limit restrictions to those that are clearly business justified. The current debate concerning drug or AIDS testing of employees is at the heart of this principle.

Respect Human Well-Being   A fundamental ethical principle is to do no harm. The concept of harm is necessarily a relative one. Selling drugs that constitute powerful cures for serious diseases, but that also produce harmful side effects, is not per se unethical. The ethicality of the action will depend upon appropriate disclosure of the side effects and the relationship between the harm caused and the good achieved.

This principle applies to hazards in the workplace, inherently harmful substances, and hidden defects in products. It lies at the heart of much of product liability and tort law. This principle is very fundamental and, in many instances, can be seen as trumping the other principles. Thus, if a businessperson faces a choice between observing confidentiality and disclosing information that would prevent harm to human well-being, the information should be disclosed.

CONCEPT SUMMARY

Seven Rule-of-Thumb Principles of Business Ethics

1. Honor confidentiality
2. Avoid conflicts of interest
3. Willingly comply with the law
4. Exercise due care
5. Act in good faith
6. Respect the liberty and rights of others
7. Respect human well-being

Libertarianism and Equalitarianism

A controversial theory of social justice that has important ramifications for business is **libertarianism**. Libertarians emphasize individual free-

dom based upon property rights and a minimal role for government. The wealth of society is to be distributed on the basis of market transactions. Thus, it is just for a rock star to receive much greater financial rewards than a first violinist of a symphony orchestra or a Nobel laureate scientist working on a cancer cure. The uneducated person whose talents are not in demand is justly given little. Redistribution of wealth by government fiat, seen as arbitrarily benefiting the least productive, is an infringement of the basic libertarian principle: "From each as they choose, to each as they are chosen." Of course, it is perfectly okay for one individual to freely choose to give charity to another. The severely handicapped who cannot care for themselves would be left to fend for themselves unless there was sufficient individual charity to provide for their needs. It is difficult to imagine characterizing a society as "just" that fails to provide for the needs of the severely disadvantaged.

This issue is picked up in American law in the context of imposing affirmative duties to act to assist those in need. The general rule of tort law has been that one cannot be sued for failing to go to the aid of another, even when the rescue would surely succeed without danger to the rescuer. An ethical obligation to attempt a rescue can be supported by both duty-based and utilitarian analyses. The case that follows provides an interesting legal dimension to this issue.

SOLDANO V. O'DANIELS

Court of Appeals of California, Fifth District
141 Cal. App.3d 443 (1983)

BACKGROUND Soldano (plaintiff) sued O'Daniels (defendant) for denying access to a telephone in an emergency situation. The incident arose when Soldano's father got into a fight in a saloon. A witness ran across the street to the defendant's restaurant and asked to be allowed either to use the phone or to have the restaurant call the police. The defendant's employee denied all help and the father was shot to death. The son filed suit alleging that the refusal to provide help contributed to the father's wrongful death. The trial court gave summary judgment against the son.

Andreen, Judge

Does a business establishment incur liability for wrongful death if it denies use of its telephone to a good samaritan who explains an emergency situation occurring without and wishes to call the police? . . .

There is a distinction, well rooted in the common law, between action and nonaction. It has found its way into the prestigious Restatement Second of Tots (hereafter cited as Restatement), which provides in section 314: "The fact that the actor realizes or should realize that action on his part is necessary for another's aid or protection does not of itself impose upon him a duty to take such action." Comment c of section 314 is instructive on the basis and limits of the rule and is set forth in the footnote.[1] The distinction between malfeasance and nonfeasance, between active misconduct working positive injury and failure to act to prevent mischief not brought on by the defendant, is founded on "that attitude of extreme individualism so typical of anglo-saxon legal thought."

Defendant argues that the request that its employee call the police is a request that it *do* something. He points to the established rule that one who has not created a peril ordinarily does not have a duty to take affirmative action to assist an imperiled person. . . .

Here there was no special relationship between the defendant and the deceased. It would be stretching the concept beyond recognition to assert there was a relationship between the defendant and the patron from Happy Jack's Saloon who wished to summon aid. But this does not end the matter.

It is time to reexamine the common law rule of nonliability for nonfeasance in the special circumstances of the instant case. . . .

Crime is a blight on our society and a matter of great citizen concern. The President's Commission on Law Enforcement and the Administration of Justice, Task Force Report: The police (1967) recognized the importance of citizen involvement in crime prevention: "[C]rime is not the business of the police alone. . . . The police need help from citizens, . . ." The commission identified citizen crime reporting programs in some cities. These have proliferated in recent years.

The Legislature has recognized the importance of the telephone system in reporting crime and in summoning emergency aid. Penal Code section 384 makes it a misdemeanor to refuse to relinquish a party line when informed that it is needed to call a police department or obtain other specified emergency services. This requirement, which the Legislature has mandated to be printed in virtually every telephone book in this state, may have wider printed distribution in this state than even the Ten Commandments. It creates an affirmative duty to do something—to clear the line for another use of the party line—in certain circumstances. . . .

We turn now to the concept of duty in a tort case. The Supreme Court has identified certain factors to be considered in determining whether a duty is owed to third persons.

We examine those factors in reference to this case. (1) The harm to the decedent was abundantly foreseeable; it was imminent. The employee was expressly told that a man had been threatened. The employee was a bartender. As such he knew it is foreseeable that some people who drink alcohol in the milieu of a bar setting are prone to violence. (2) The certainty of decedent's injury is undisputed. (3) There is arguably a close connection between the employee's conduct and the injury: the patron wanted to use the phone to summon the

---

[1]The rule stated in this Section is applicable irrespective of the gravity of the danger to which the other is subjected and the insignificance of the trouble, effort, or expense of giving him aid or protection.

The origin of the rule lay in the early common law distinction between action and inaction, or "misfeasance" and "nonfeasance.". . .

Liability for nonfeasance was slow to receive any recognition in the law. It appeared first in, and is still largely confined to, situations in which there was some special relation between the parties, on the basis of which the defendant was found to have a duty to take action for the aid or protection of the plaintiff.

The result of the rule has been a series of older decisions to the effect that one human being, seeing a fellow man in dire peril, is under no legal obligation to aid him, but may sit on the dock, smoke his cigar, and watch the other drown. Such decisions have been condemned by legal writers as revolting to any moral sense, but thus far they remain the law. It appears inevitable that, sooner or later, such extreme cases of morally outrageous and indefensible conduct will arise that there will be further inroads upon the older rule.

police to intervene. The employee's refusal to allow the use of the phone prevented this anticipated intervention. If permitted to go to trial, the plaintiff may be able to show that the probable response time of the police would have been shorter than the time between the prohibited telephone call and the fatal shot. (4) The employee's conduct displayed a disregard for human life that can be characterized as morally wrong: he was callously indifferent to the possibility that Darrell Soldano would die as the result of his refusal to allow a person to use the telephone. Under the circumstances before us the bartender's burden was minimal and exposed him to no risk: all he had to do was allow the use of the telephone. It would have cost him or his employer nothing. It could have saved a life. (5) Finding a duty in these circumstances would promote a policy of preventing future harm. A citizen would not be required to summon the police but would be required, in circumstances such as those before us, not to impede another who has chosen to summon aid. (6) We have no information on the question of the availability, cost, and prevalence of insurance for the risk, but note that the liability which is sought to be imposed here is that of employee negligence, which is covered by many insurance policies. (7) The extent of the burden of the defendant was minimal, as noted. . . .

A business establishment such as the Circle Inn is open for profit. The owner encourages the public to enter, for his earnings depend on it. A telephone is a necessary adjunct to such a place. It is not unusual in such circumstances for patrons to use the telephone to call a taxicab or family member. . . .

We conclude that the bartender owed a duty to the plaintiff's decedent to permit the patron from Happy Jack's to place a call to the police or to place the call himself.

Decision: Held, reversed; summary judgment should not have been rendered in favor of the defendant.

In contrast to libertarianism, **equalitarianism** treats all individuals alike regardless of market preferences or even productive effort. Even though the Declaration of Independence declares that all men are created equal, there are obvious ways in which people differ. Some are more diligent, more intelligent, or more talented. Nonetheless, equalitarians argue that all are alike in their basic humanity. Therefore, everyone has a right to start from the same point.

An obvious problem with equalitarianism is that few would choose to work hard if everyone benefited equally from their labor. Everyone would have an incentive to be a free rider, or to try to conceal what he or she was producing. The amount of cheating that has existed with our income tax system, which has been designed to bring about limited redistributions of wealth, demonstrates that many people would not willingly accept an equalitarian system.

Many surveys ask individuals how they behave and then ask them how they think their peers generally behave. Most of these studies indicate that individual businesspeople tend to think that they are more ethical than the average person. Stated oppositely, most managers tend to believe that the general level of ethical behavior is below the standard that they set for themselves. A persistent assumption that others are unethical should be a source of concern. If individuals misperceive that general ethical practice is lower than their own, and then conclude that they will be at a competitive disadvantage by continuing a high standard of behavior, they may shift their own behavior toward conformity with what they think others do.

Moral Development and Individual Ethics

Moral psychologist Lawrence Kohlberg spent many years observing how young boys reasoned about moral issues. Kohlberg studied the manner in which moral reasoning evolved and ultimately developed an influential framework based upon six stages of human moral development. Kohlberg concluded that all humans begin at a very selfish stage and then as a result of experience evolve more sophisticated ways of thinking about moral

TABLE 8-1

Kohlberg's Model of Levels and Stages of Moral Development

Level		Stage
Pre-conventional level (Self-interest)	Stage 1: Stage 2:	Avoid pain, get reward Naive instrumental hedonism; back scratching
Conventional level (Group orientation)	Stage 3: Stage 4:	Good boy—good girl; approval of peers, family Law and order, recognize duty to society, obey legitimate authority
Post-conventional (Moral autonomy)	Stage 5: Stage 6:	Obey good laws, recognize a social contract, recognize individual rights Act in accord with logical, consistent, universal moral principles

dilemmas. Kohlberg claimed that the process of moral development was invariable in that individuals didn't skip stages, but instead, went through the stages in sequence. He also concluded that one would never regress from a higher stage to a lower stage. The progress that he observed is from a self-oriented thinking to a second level he described as a conventional or social level in which the primary reference is to social norms, peer opinion and law. Almost all the subjects studied ended up at one of these two levels. A few advanced to a third level of moral autonomy in which their reasoning was based upon universal ethical concepts. Table 8–1 summarizes Kohlberg's framework.

A primary value of the Kohlberg framework is as a device to characterize arguments. A cost-benefit calculation whether to obey the law (what are the chances of my getting caught and what will it cost me?) is stage 1 reasoning. A decision to obey the law, because it is the law and it is socially desirable for people to obey the law, is stage 4 reasoning. Note that the stage 1 thinker and the stage 4 thinker may come to the same decision, but their reasoning is vastly different.

The Kohlberg framework has been roundly criticized. Carol Gilligan, noting that Kohlberg's studies were limited to males, has presented an alternative view. Gilligan is concerned that a formal social justice framework such as Kohlberg's fails to be sufficiently open to relational and caring dimensions of ethics. Gilligan's studies of young girls found that they tended to think quite differently about certain types of moral issues. Others have challenged the hierarchal implica-

tions of Kohlberg's work, arguing that the framework lacks philosophical justification when it implies that a duty-based approach is superior to social contract, or that a law-and-order orientation is superior to recognizing duties to family and close friends.

Studies of managers have found that they tend to vary the stage of moral reasoning used depending upon the context of the decision. Most managers appear to be at stage 3 or stage 4 and are therefore similar to the population as a whole. Yet at the same time, surveys indicate that there is a significant amount of questionable behavior on the part of managers. A major issue is whether the behavior of managers is getting less ethical over time. Unfortunately, good time-series studies have yet to be conducted to provide a definitive answer to that important question. The replicated studies that do exist do not show a dramatic trend toward less ethical behavior.

It is common to hear statements to the effect that modern society has lost its moral compass and, particularly that young people are less ethical than used to be the case. Consider the information in Tables 8–2 and 8–3 which report data taken from a massive study undertaken by Donald McCabe and Linda Trevino.

Do you agree with the findings reported in the two tables? Are they consistent with your experience? If so, why do you think so much cheating occurs? What kind of changes could be made to bring about a lowering in the amount of cheating? Why would you think that studying business or planning a business career would be associated with a greater amount of cheating?

TABLE 8-2

Self-Reported Cheaters by Intended Occupation*

	N	% Self-Reported Cheaters		N	% Self-Reported Cheaters
Arts	484	65	Law	552	63
Business	1,090	76	Medicine	623	68
Education	967	58	Public/govt. service	444	67
Engineering/science	861	72	Other	551	66

*Comparisons of business with other occupations using a simple *t* test are significant at $p<0.05$ or better.

TABLE 8-3

Self-Reported Cheating by Undergraduate Major*

	Student Reports N	%	Faculty Reports N	%
Business	274	87	32	69
Engineering/science	1,608	72	238	84
Humanities/social sciences	3,912	64	469	82
Other	234	67	45	76

*Student comparisons of business majors with other majors using a simple *t* test are significant at $p<0.001$. Faculty comparisons of business with other majors are significant at $p<0.01$.

From Donald L. McCabe and Linda Klebe Trevino, "Cheating among Business Students: A Challenge for Business Leaders and Educators," Working Paper, 1992.

Specific Issues in Business Ethics

Business ethics encompasses a wide range of activities. The next sections present a few specific issues of business ethics in greater detail.

Ethics in Negotiation

The process of negotiation is replete with moral issues. Many consider lying a necessary if not a sophisticated negotiating technique. Few would reveal their true price when asked at the beginning of a negotiation ("Although I'm asking $500, I'll take $350"), or volunteer information about all the shortcomings of the item they are selling ("I assume that you are aware that the prices of 1950s baseball cards have been falling and will probably continue to do so").

An ethical principle of honesty (good faith) can be based upon the premise that we all expect honesty in others and that those who are dishonest make unfair exceptions of themselves. A duty-based approach founded upon principles of strict honesty would recognize exceptions in only exceptional circumstances. An outcome-based analysis may be more flexible. If there are circumstances in which the economic system and thus society generally benefits from certain forms of falsehood (it sounds outrageous—but stay with the argument), then those forms would be considered ethical.

How might such an argument be made? Albert Carr argued such a position in 1968 in a controversial article in the *Harvard Business Review*.[6] Carr argues that business is a game, similar to sports, and that certain types of dishonesty are completely compatible with the rules of the business game. The use of deception is justified on two implicit grounds. First, he argues that business is more efficient when appropriate dishonesty is employed. Deception is treated as an inherent element of negotiation. Carr justifies this by analogies to playing poker and military strategy. The very nature of such activities requires deception. The same would hold true for sports when a quarterback changes a play at the line of scrimmage or a baseball coach gives signals to his ball players. Both will attempt deception and the better they are at deceiving, the greater will be their chances of success in their roles.

The second justification put forward is based upon implied consent. Carr assumes that knowledgeable business practitioners realize that deception is essential in negotiation, so they anticipate that those with whom they deal will act deceptively. Those who are not aware of the standard practice have a duty to educate themselves before engaging in serious negotiations.

The following case appears to reflect the type of attitude advocated by Carr as sound business practice. Do you agree?

VOKES V. ARTHUR MURRAY, INC.

Florida District Court of Appeals, Second District
212 So.2d 906 (1968)

BACKGROUND: Vokes (plaintiff), a fifty-one-year-old widow, brought this action against Arthur Murray, Inc. (defendant), a dance-instruction corporation, to recover damages caused by the defendant's fraud. The defendant argued that there was no fraud or misrepresentation on its part, that its statements were mere "trade puffing." The trial court found for the defendant and dismissed the plaintiff's amended complaint; from that decision, the plaintiff appealed.

Pierce, Judge

Plaintiff Mrs. Audrey E. Vokes, a widow of 51 years and without family, had a yen to be "an accomplished dancer" with the hopes of finding "new interest in life." So, on February 10, 1961, a dubious fate, with the assist of a motivated acquaintance, procured her to attend a "dance party" at Davenport's "School of Dancing" where she whiled away the pleasant hours, sometimes in a private room, absorbing his accomplished sales technique, during which her grace and poise were elaborated upon and her rosy future as "an excellent dancer" was painted for her in vivid and glowing colors. As an incident to this interlude, he sold her eight 1/2-hour dance lessons to be utilized within one calendar month therefrom, for the sum of $14.50 cash in hand paid, obviously a baited "come-on."

Thus she embarked upon an almost endless pursuit of the terpsichorean art during which, over a period of less than sixteen months, she was sold fourteen "dance courses" totalling in the aggregate 2302 hours of dancing lessons for a total cash outlay of $31,090.45, all at Davenport's dance emporium. All of these fourteen courses were evidenced by execution of a written "Enrollment Agreement—Arthur Murray's School of Dancing" with the addendum in heavy black print, "No one will be informed that you are taking dancing lessons. Your relations with us are held in strict confidence," setting forth the number of "dancing lessons" and the "lessons in rhythm sessions" currently sold to her from time to time, and always of course accompanied by payment of cash of the realm.

All the foregoing sales promotions, illustrative of the entire fourteen separate contracts, were procured by defendant Davenport and Arthur Murray, Inc., by false representations to her that she was improving in her dancing ability, that she had excellent potential, that she was responding to instructions in dancing grace, and that they were developing her into a beautiful dancer, whereas in truth and in fact she did not develop in her dancing ability, she had no "dance aptitude," and in fact had difficulty in "hearing the musical beat." The complaint alleged that such representations to her "were in fact false and known by the defendant to be false and contrary to the plaintiff's true ability, the truth of plaintiff's ability being fully known to the defendants, but withheld from the plaintiff for the sole and specific intent to deceive and defraud the plaintiff and to induce her in the purchasing of additional hours of dance lessons." It was averred that the lessons were sold to her "in total disregard to the true physical, rhythm, and mental ability of the plaintiff." In other words, while she first exulted that she was entering the "spring of her life," she finally was awakened to the fact there was "spring" neither in her life nor in her feet.

It is true that "generally a misrepresentation, to be actionable, must be one of fact rather than of opinion." . . . But this rule has significant qualifications, applicable here. It does not apply where there is a fiduciary relationship between the parties, or where there has been some artifice or trick employed by the representor, or where the parties do not in general deal at "arm's length" as we understand the phrase, or where the representee does not have equal opportunity to become apprised of the truth or falsity of the fact represented.

DECISION: The Court of Appeals found the statements made by the plaintiff in her complaint could be the basis for finding that the defendant committed fraud. Accordingly, it reversed the trial court's dismissal of the plaintiff's complaint.

As demonstrated in the *Vokes* case, one problem with Carr's analysis is that both sides may not be playing by the same rules. One side thinks that deception is understood, the other party assumes that honesty will be strictly adhered to. Carr's analysis also fails to provide any guidelines concerning what the limits are. Although a baseball manager will disguise signals and try to confuse the other team concerning whether a sacrifice bunt has been called, there are clear rules that one doesn't breach. It is not okay to bribe the umpire for favorable rulings.

The ultimate shortcoming of Carr's analysis is that it fails to consider the costs directly imposed by deception. If everyone acted completely opportunistically in negotiations by lying and refusing to honor promises, all negotiators would take steps to protect themselves. Defensive strategies that could be employed include insisting upon more elaborate and detailed contract terms and the use of monitoring or control mechanisms. These purely defensive strategies would raise the costs of negotiation and implementation and would reduce the flexibility of contracts. The cost of contracting would increase in society as a whole, and society would be worse off.

The problem is likely to be a serious one only if a significant percentage of people behave opportunistically. So long as only a few behave that way, and costs are neither high nor widespread, can opportunistic behavior be considered acceptable on moral grounds? The answer is no, because an individual can get away with deception without imposing a major cost on society only if most other people don't do it. Individuals taking advantage of this situation would be making an exception of themselves and would be violating the generally accepted ethical principles described earlier in the chapter.

Bribery

Bribery appears endemic in our modern world. Scanning *The Wall Street Journal* or major newspapers for articles describing incidents of bribing will produce major scandal almost daily. As widely as bribery is practiced, it is also condemned. Defenses of bribery as moral are infrequent. Those who bribe do so secretly. Few people brag publicly about successful bribes and even fewer about having been the recipient of large bribes. Yet, there are many ambiguities that must be dealt with in evaluating the ethical nature of a bribe. Consider the following situations:

1. A wealthy patron gives $20 to the maître d' of an exclusive restaurant in order to get preferred seating.

2. You tip a waitress 15 percent (or 25 percent) of the check in a restaurant where you eat once a week.

3. A banker pays $10,000 to a state legislator for a 20-minute speech to bank employees with the expectation that the legislator will meet

personally with the banker on occasion and generally support the positions of the banking industry.

4. The legislator accepts the payment and assumes that there are no strings attached, that the banker is just trying to insure general "good will," and that $10,000 is a reasonable payment for the speech. The legislator plans to consider the interests of all of his or her constituents in deciding how to vote on legislation and assumes this is understood by the banker.

5. A cola manufacturer pays $10,000 to a state government official to get a license to do business in that state. The license should be granted under state law, but the goverment official requires the payments in order to supplement his own income.

6. A cola manufacturer pays $10,000 to a state official in return for a promise that a competitor will be denied a license to do business in that state.

7. A salesperson gives a Christmas present of a $50 bottle of single malt Scotch to the purchasing agent of a potential buyer.

8. A salesperson gives a Christmas present of a $15,000 sports car to the purchasing agent of a potential buyer.

Numerous questions are raised by these examples. How relevant is intent? It is often stated that it takes two to have a bribe. Must both the payor and the payee be thinking "bribe" in order to consider the transaction to be one? Or, a closely related question, do certain words of expectancy have to be used in order to call an arrangement a bribe? Does it make any difference if the payor avoids stating any specific quid pro quo or if the payee avoids consenting to any requested quid pro quo? Does the status of the payee make a difference? Examples 7 and 8 involve commercial bribes rather than payments to public officials. Should commercial payments be seen as part of the market system, or are they bribes just as much as payments to public officials? A *bribe* is a payment or offering of something of value to another, in return for a promised or actual breach of an obligation owed to the general public or to another individual. Thus, the essence of a bribe is a conflict of interest—a payment for breaching a duty to another. This definition does not distin-

guish between public and commercial bribes. It includes commercial bribes because they may involve the breach of a duty the recipient owes to an employer, partner, or business associate. A bribe need not necessarily involve the use of "magic words" or require a detailed statement of the quid pro quo required. An implied understanding of what is expected is enough. Generally, one can assume that large sums are not given in a context where current or future business dealings are involved without some expectancy of a return. Further, one can generally assume that large sums are not paid merely to ensure the normal performance of one's duty.

Trivial sums may be given as a result of custom and may not involve an expected quid pro quo (except at an equally trivial level). The relative value of the payment, its nature (concealed, purely personal to the payee, etc.), and the relative roles of the payor and payee are all important in determining whether a morally condemnable bribe has taken place.

Why condemn bribes? There are three major arguments to consider. The first is that they involve, by definition, a breach of trust or duty. There are two basic ways by which a bribe may originate— one is that the payor offers the payment to the payee for a quid pro quo; the other is that the payee solicits the payment from the payor as a form of selling his or her office or position.

The problem when the payor initiates the transaction is relatively straightforward. Assuming that the payor is acting efficiently and is paying for an outcome that would not otherwise occur, it is clear that the payee is breaching a duty to the public or to another individual. The payor is morally culpable because the payor's purpose is to induce the breach of duty.

Moral culpability is even more obvious when the payee initiates (extorts) the payment. The payee is selling his or her position or office and by requesting the payment is implying that the outcome would be otherwise if the payment is not made. By initiating the transaction, the payee is proposing a blatant breach of duty or trust.

What about the payor in a case of extortion? Is the payor excused from moral culpability because the payment is forced upon him or her by the payee? On a number of occasions business-people have found themselves in the awkward position of having to make a payment in order to get a vitally needed license or inspection certificate. The payment is made and then several years later there is disclosure that the particular public official had taken bribes. An investigation ensues to determine who has paid bribes to the official and at that time the businessperson's payments are discovered. The businessperson's defense is that the payments were extorted and that there was really no choice. That argument will not constitute a legal defense if a criminal case is filed, but it will often cause the prosecutor to use discretion and decide not to prosecute. The question may reasonably be asked, If the businessperson thought that extortion was occurring, why wasn't it reported to the appropriate authorities at the time? In some unfortunate communities the answer may well be that the local law enforcement officials were part of the bribery scheme.

The second argument against bribery is that it often is a form of theft in that the payee is selling assets or resources that are not his or hers to sell. The benefit of the bribe goes to the payee who in turn directs either public or corporate assets toward the payor. Consider a typical case involving a purchasing agent. The agent in the normal performance of his or her duties would buy supplies from ABC corporation at a price of $70,000. Instead, the agent accepts a cash bribe of $5,000 from a representative of XYZ and causes his firm to buy the identical supplies from XYZ for $80,000. The agent has effectively stolen $10,000 from his company and has directly benefited in the amount of $5,000. In many circumstances involving a bribe, both the payor and the payee may be seen as stealing the object of value that is transferred to the payor (the $80,000 contract).

The final argument against bribery is that it is unfair. When a bribe is paid to a public official, that official is induced to act contrary to a politically established public policy establishing how goods and rights are to be distributed. When the payee acts contrary to that mandate, the public interest is harmed. Similarly, in a commercial bribe, the more efficient supplier is defeated, not on the merits, but because of the payment of a bribe. This outcome is both inefficient and unfair.

Justifications for Bribes   Various justifications may be offered by the parties to a bribe. We have already discussed one common payor defense, that the bribe was extorted by the payee. Other justifications include (1) the bribe is efficient in that it overcomes irrational regulation or corruption, (2) the bribe is necessary to the survival of the firm in a competitive environment, and (3) the action is really innocent because it is impossible to determine what constitutes a bribe as distinguished from a gift.

The efficiency justification has civil disobedience overtones. Corrupt or inefficient government regulation (or corporate rules) must be overcome by a payment to a representative of the obstructionist organization. There are several defects in this argument. First, the bribery serves to foster the corruption or inefficiency, and it will not by itself correct the alleged evils. Second, civil disobedience requires a public stand to bring attention to unfair or inefficient rules. Covert bribery does not encourage public pressure or awareness and serves only to benefit the payor and/or payee. The efficiency argument is of little help in absolving the payee. If the payee recognizes impropriety and has the power to override it, the payee should not require payment in order to exercise his or her authority.

The necessity argument has been extended to the conclusion that bribes "are an essential feature of the free enterprise system and as such should be of no concern to regulatory systems."[7] The argument has often been advanced in criticism of the Foreign Corrupt Practices Act. American managers have alleged that they are at a competitive disadvantage in competing with foreign firms because of limits on their ability to bribe ascribed to the Foreign Corrupt Practices Act.

Remember, however, that our definition of a bribe involves a payment personally benefiting the payee which requires a breach of duty on the part of the payee. The efficiency of such a system is highly questionable. In contrast to the statement that the marketplace requires bribes is the following quote from a committee report on the Foreign Corrupt Practices Act, concluding that bribery ". . . short-circuits the marketplace by limiting business to those companies too inefficient to compete in terms of price, quality or service or too lazy to engage in honest salesmanship, or too intent upon unloading marginal products."[8]

The final argument justifies bribery because of the sheer uncertainty of what constitutes an illegal or immoral bribe. This "claimed uncertainty" argument is used by miscreants in many areas including the antitrust and securities laws. The accused professes that he or she didn't understand the issues and concludes that proper lines are impossible to draw. In more refined terms, the argument is that bribes are difficult to distinguish from real gifts, and that reciprocity or quid pro quo is a basic and proper component of human relationships. Reciprocity is valued in personal relationships and is a required element of an enforceable contract (the doctrine of consideration). Therefore, one should be cautious about condemning it, even in the case of a seeming bribe. The main flaw in this argument is that it fails to consider the breach of duty that is an essential part of a bribe. The reciprocity is not of something possessed by the payee personally, but instead, is of property or rights of someone else, to whom the payee owes a duty. The reciprocity is therefore not a true exchange and is not analogous to contract.

Although there are some hard "gray-area" cases in which bribes are hard to distinguish, this is also true of most other ethical issues. The ultimate question is whether or not there is a principled basis upon which to distinguish bribes. There is, and most cases will be relatively clearcut. There should be little question that situations 3, 4, 5, 6, and 8 involved bribes.

Review Questions and Problems

Key Terms

ethics	stakeholder
relativism	utilitarianism
egoism	act utilitarianism
psychological egoism	Pareto superiority
ethical egoism	moral free space
rule utilitarianism	hypernorms
deontological theory	equalitarianism
social contract	libertarianism

Discussion Questions

1. Describe the difference between an egoistic and an utilitarian analysis. Explain how each might lead to the same result when employed by a drug company trying to decide whether to pull a tainted prescription drug off the market.

2. Describe the difference between a rule utilitarian and a deontological approach to business ethics. Explain how a principle of honoring confidentiality can be justified under each approach.

Review Problems

1. You are hiring a new manager for your department. You have several good applicants. Assume that the one that is most suited for the job in training and experience has also been found to have done one of the things listed here. How would that affect your decision whether to hire the individual?

    (a) The individual listed on his résumé that he had an MBA from Rutgers. In fact, he does not have an MBA.

    (b) The individual listed that his prior salary was $40,000. In fact, the prior salary was $32,000.

    (c) The individual had put in false claims on expense account forms on several occasions.

    (d) The individual had been convicted of embezzlement and put on probation.

    (e) The individual had gone to a reporter about misdealings at his prior firm. The ensuing controversy had attracted considerable publicity and resulted in lawsuits being filed against the firm. The employee had been fired because of the whistle-blowing.

2. You have been asked to give an evaluation on an employee who is at your level and with whom you have worked. You only know the employee through work. How likely would you be to reveal the following information about the employee? Assume that there is no question at all about the truth of what you would say.

    (a) That the employee is racist.

    (b) That the employee has admitted to you about cheating on tax returns.

    (c) That the employee has admitted to you about making personal long-distance calls on company lines.

    (d) That the employee has admitted to you about double billing on expense account charges.

    (e) That the employee has admitted to you about stealing company property.

    Would it make any difference whether the party asking for your assessment was (1) your boss, (2) another supervisor in the same firm, or (3) a manager from another firm?

3. An elderly lady who now lives in a nursing home hires you to sell her old house for her. She suggests she would take $40,000 for it. She owned the house for forty years but has not seen it for several years. She is unaware that it is now located by a new shopping center near a new expressway where similar properties have been selling for $75,000.

    Assume you are a friend of the owner but are not a realtor. You know she trusts you a great deal. You also know of several possible buyers, one of whom is a close friend of yours. What would you do?

    Suppose you wanted to buy the house as an investment for your church/fraternity/social club. Would you? How much would you pay?

Suppose you face the situation described here not as a friend but as a realtor employed by the lady. Would your answers be different? What if you weren't assisting her but were a buyer who was recently transferred to the city looking for residential property. Would you take advantage of the lady's ignorance? Is this a question of law or ethics?

4. Desperate Air Corporation (DAC) flies routes along the U.S. East Coast. DAC acquired a number of hotels and undeveloped properties five years ago as part of a short-lived diversification strategy. DAC has recently experienced substantial losses, has a negative cash flow, and bankruptcy looms as a possibility unless high labor costs can be reduced and consumer confidence restored.

Benton Williams has just been brought in as CEO to revitalize DAC. Williams began by cutting back on middle management positions and by placing a one year moratorium on hiring MBAs. Middle managers terminated by DAC and other airlines have had a tough time finding equivalent jobs.

DAC owns a large underdeveloped ocean front property on the east coast of Florida. Williams directed George Nash, DAC's Vice President of Real Estate, to find a buyer for the property in order to generate badly needed cash. After some effort, Nash identified Fledgling Industries, a relatively new developer of retirement villas as a good prospect. Fledgling is interested in finding a property on which it could build a complex of high rise retirement condos featuring elaborate walking trails and outside recreational facilities.

DAC had conducted a full environmental audit of the property 6 months previously and had discovered no problems with the property. A copy of the report was given to the Fledgling representative who also walked over the property and discovered no problems. The representative asked "Anything I should know about?" Nash replied, "No problems."

As the negotiations progressed with Fledgling, Nash was approached by a long time friend at the firm who told him that there was some highly toxic waste on the property. The friend said that she learned about it through the rumor mill at the firm and that she had checked it out by going over the property, and after some difficulty, she discovered several buried metal containers which were marked "Danger! Biohazard. Radioactive medical waste." The containers were cracked and liquid contents had seeped out into the ground. She said she wanted Nash to know because she was concerned that innocent people could be hurt if the sale went through.

Nash contacted Williams, but before he could mention the containers to him, Williams interrupted and told him it was vital that the sale be closed and that it be done as soon as possible. Nash consulted with a DAC lawyer who told him that Florida law does not require the disclosure of hazardous substances on commercial property so long as there hasn't been a fraudulent misstatement about the condition of the property.

Nash was troubled about whether he should mention the hazardous materials to the Fledgling representative before he closed the sale. He knew that Fledgling was considering some other similar properties and Nash thought that if he mentioned the toxic spill problem that Fledgling would probably not go through with the sale. At the least, it could delay the sale for months while the spill was investigated and potential liability problems considered. Nash figured that he would be unlikely ever to deal with Fledgling again regarding future real estate sales as DAC did not own any other properties that fit Fledgling's business.

The question of whether to close the sale immediately bothered Nash enough that he talked with his wife about it, and then prayed about what to do. After taking those steps, Nash decided that he should go ahead and close the sale.

Did Nash do the right thing? Justify your conclusion.

Footnotes

[1] Thomas Donaldson, *Corporations and Morality*, Prentice-Hall, 1982.

[2] Robert Solomon, *Ethics and Excellence*, Oxford University Press, 1993, p. 104.

[3] David Gauthier, *Morals by Agreement*, Oxford University Press, 1986.

[4] Thomas Donaldson, *The Ethics of International Business*, Oxford University Press, 1989.

[5] Thomas Donaldson and Thomas W. Dunfee, "Toward a Unified Conception of Business Ethics: Integrative Social Contracts Theory," *Academy of Management Review* 19(2), 1994, p. 279.

[6] Albert Carr, *Harvard Business Review*, 64(1) 1968.

[7] John Danley, "Towards a Theory of Bribery," *Business and Professional Ethics Journal*, 1983, p. 19.

[8] Ibid, p. 33.

9

Social Responsibility of Business

The Modern Debate Concerning
Corporate Social Responsibility

The Limited View: Profit Making as
Social Responsibility

The Broader View: Corporations Have
Plural Responsibilities

Evaluation of the Debate

Implementing Social Responsibility

External Incentives for Social
Responsibility

Most major business firms at one time or another have been accused of unethical practices or have been charged with criminal offenses. The media are full of stories of controversial and irresponsible actions by corporations. Chemical plants leak toxic gases, defense contractors put in false claims or produce faulty parts, major banks launder money, brokerage houses employ fraudulent practices in dealing with banks or their customers, investment banking firms abuse client confidences, firms incur debt in fighting off corporate raiders and then have to lay off employees, firms produce dangerous products that kill or maim their customers—the list seems endless. Critics of business seize upon incidents like these and argue that business firms are irresponsible by their very nature.

This chapter summarizes the current diversity of viewpoints concerning the proper extent of business responsibility. The core question is whether business can fairly be expected to do more than just seek to maximize profits. If the answer is found to be that there are greater expectations for business, then the next question

becomes: How can those additional responsibilities be determined and implemented? This chapter summarizes strategies that a business can use to implement social responsiveness, and then, consistent with the theme of the text, describes how the legal system provides incentives for responsible behavior.

The Modern Debate Concerning Corporate Social Responsibility

Some readers may be surprised to learn that there has been a long-standing debate concerning the nature and extent of the social responsibility of corporations. The debate evolves from the fact that corporations are established to operate primarily to further the interests of their owners. For publicly held corporations, the **owners** are the shareholders, who expect the corporation to earn profits. **Shareholders** buy stock because they expect to benefit from some combination of an increased share price and the payment of dividends. The long-term shareholder benefits directly only when management is successful in its duty to earn profits. The debate is whether corporations should go beyond that duty and consider the interests of other parties—often referred to as stakeholders.

Stakeholders (see Chapter 8) are those people outside the firm who are directly affected by its actions. Stakeholders may include suppliers, distributors, creditors, neighbors, local or state governments, and so on. There are many ways in which stakeholders can be affected by decisions made by a firm's managers. A decision to forgo installing a device that masks noxious odors in a plant's emissions can greatly affect the quality of life of neighbors living near the plant. The decision to lay off workers or close plants can affect the infrastructure in the local community, threatening the quality of schools, medical care, and other basic community services.

In many instances, shareholders and stakeholders will have directly competing interests, making it impossible for management to serve both interests simultaneously. Installing expensive emission control equipment that goes beyond what the law requires may use funds that otherwise could be distributed to shareholders in a dividend. Keeping an unprofitable plant in operation may benefit the community while having a negative impact on the long-run profitability of the firm.

The Limited View: Profit Making as Social Responsibility

The basic challenge to the idea of social responsibility has been closely identified with Milton Friedman, the well-known conservative economist and Nobel laureate. Some of his arguments against social responsibility follow:

- There is no such thing as *corporate* social responsibility because only individuals have responsibilities.

- In an economic system based upon private property, the corporate executive is employed by the owners (shareholders) to make as much money as possible while conforming to the basic rules in society, both those embodied in law and those embodied in ethical custom.

- The corporate executive acting as an agent for the stockholders should not make decisions about social responsibilities and social investment because those represent tax decisions, and the imposition of taxes and the expenditure of tax proceeds are governmental functions.

- The doctrine of social responsibility involves the acceptance of the socialist view that political mechanisms, not market mechanisms, are the appropriate way to determine the allocation of scarce resources to alternative uses.

Milton Friedman goes so far as to characterize the concept of social responsibility as "subversive doctrine." He sees it as inconsistent with the basic tenets of a capitalistic society. Friedman fears that even when managers use claims of being responsible as a subterfuge for maximizing profits, they unwittingly encourage an environment in which social responsibility will be forced upon firms by government fiat.

There is good reason to believe that many, but not all, shareholders would agree with Friedman. Suppose that Exxon is considering giving a donation of $10 million to your university. The money would come from operating revenues. If Exxon did not give the money to your university, it could be used for capital improvements, to pay off debt, to support employee raises, or to increase dividends. If Exxon were to poll its shareholders asking whether it should give the money or increase its dividend, how do you think the majority would respond? How would you respond if a company in which you held shares asked you whether you would like an extra $10 in dividends or, instead, would prefer that they give the money to a charity that you disfavor?

Shareholders invest in companies because they expect a financial return over time. They do not expect a business corporation to be primarily involved in social activities. If they wish to distribute their wealth to others, they will do so by giving directly to an organization such as the United Way. That way, they can choose the objects of their beneficence. It is reasonable to assume that most shareholders would have a different priority for charitable contributions than the company's managers.

There are two basic types of corporate socially responsive acts: (1) actions that are designed to avoid or lessen harm to others, such as spending for safety or pollution control, and (2) actions that are designed to bring about additional social benefits, such as charitable contributions or building community day-care centers. Actions in the second category are particularly likely to involve questions of legitimacy. For example, what gives executives the right to prefer one charity over another in dispensing corporate assets? Managers of corporate philanthropic programs are often besieged by senior executives on behalf of the latters' favorite charities. Is it appropriate for a CEO (chief executive officer) to make sure that her company gives large sums of money to her alma mater and her favorite charity, particularly when, as a consequence of the gift, the CEO has a building named for her or receives a high-profile appointment to the board of the charity? It happens all the time. Many companies would defend the donation saying that it is for a worthy cause and that the recognition received by the CEO benefits the firm. Generally, the donation will be approved through standardized procedures which involve other managers in the decision process.

The Broader View: Corporations Have Plural Responsibilities

Many executives and commentators reject the singular-purpose view that firms must act solely in the furtherance of shareholder interests and advocate that firms engage in actions that go beyond maximizing profits. Although conceding that profits are the most important goal of a business firm, they also recognize a responsibility to respond to the critical needs of stakeholders and to play a broader role in society.

Defenders of this plural-mission view see business as having a symbiotic relationship with its social environment. Business contributes to the material wealth of society. Business, in turn, requires a stable, structured, market-oriented environment based upon the protection of property and the rule of law. In order to ensure a conducive environment in which to operate, business must respond to unmet social needs. Further, it is assumed that society desires and welcomes such responsiveness.

Professionalism

Many managers accept the concept of *professionalism* as further support for the plural concept. Professionals, such as doctors or lawyers, have well-established public service obligations. These are specified by professional bar associations or medical societies. Certainly business management is not a profession in the traditional sense of having educational requirements, licensing procedures, and enforced codes of ethical behavior. But senior managers are entrusted with the management of important resources that can affect society in dramatic ways. They are often individuals with substantial financial and technical acumen and may belong to organizations that set or endorse ethical standards, for example, the Public Affairs Council, the American Management Association, or the Business Roundtable. Although the standards or positions of these organizations may be informal, they may still have a significant effect on their members.

Corporations as Moral Agents

Another justification for plural responsibilities is based upon the claim that corporations have moral duties to give effect to the interests of stakeholders. Such claims are based upon an assumption that a corporation can be treated as a moral agent. If a corporation is a moral agent, then it is possible to point a finger of blame at the entity itself when the organization produces an immoral outcome. By investing Ford Motor Company with moral agency, one can hold the organization responsible for the defective design of the Pinto gas tanks.

But what does it mean to hold a corporation responsible for the actions of its employees? Is everyone who is associated with the corporation culpable? Such an expansive principle of guilt by association would certainly be awkward. It seems unfair to say that a maintenance employee in a business office in Los Angeles who never had any ability to influence design decisions at Ford is somehow morally accountable for the defective design. And what about an engineer who unsuccessfully protested the design but was overruled by his superiors?

Critics of the concept of **moral accountability** argue that a corporation, as a lifeless entity, cannot generate an immoral intention. A corporation only can act through human agents. It is those agents, and not the corporate entity, that should be considered responsible. Finally, the critics worry that if blame is fixed solely upon a legal entity, the human perpetrators may escape discovery and punishment. The corporate entity could thus become a shield protecting the real wrongdoers from judgment.

Advocates of the moral accountability of corporations, such as Peter French and Kenneth Goodpaster, counter that corporations are human collectives that are capable of actions attributable directly to the collective entity. Many corporations appear to have evolved policies that are the output of corporate processes which cannot be attributed to any particular individuals. This characteristic is consistent with the evolving concept of corporate culture, which views companies as having discernible cultures resulting from company history, heroes, practices, and traditions. For example, collective attitudes regarding the treatment of minorities may become institutionalized in a firm. Senior managers desiring to change these attitudes may find the strong corporate culture nearly impossible to alter.

French would attribute to the corporate entity those actions resulting from the firm's formal policies and procedures. Thus, Ford as an entity would be held accountable for the Pinto because its design resulted from the standard processes and policies of Ford. The responsibility would attach to the entity and not to any particular Ford employees. Employees who are not involved in a direct role would not have individual responsibility. Those employees who were responsible for the design would be morally accountable on the basis of their personal actions.

The issue of **corporate moral accountability** has several ramifications in law. One is the question of whether corporations can be charged with human-type crimes such as homicide or manslaughter, discussed later in this chapter. As a moral agent, a corporation is capable of the intent required to establish that a crime was committed. If not viewed as a moral agent, then the case for applying the criminal law to corporations is weakened.

The second context relates to the complex issue of **successor liability** for corporations. The problem can be demonstrated best by an example. Suppose that in 1985 Acme Space Heater produced a defective space heater that could cause fires when placed close to fabric furniture.

The next year Acme changed the design of its heaters and corrected the problem. The Acme line of space heaters was quite profitable. In 1990, Conglomerate Corporation purchased the current line of space heaters from Acme by a contract that specified that Conglomerate would not assume any liability, and that Acme remained responsible for any claims. Acme tried to stay in business with some other products but failed and filed for bankruptcy in 1992. In 1994 Veronica was badly injured by one of the 1985 model heaters and sued Conglomerate Corporation. Conglomerate had made very substantial profits off the Acme line of space heaters since 1985.

Such an issue is a troublesome one for the courts. Contract law would support a conclusion that Conglomerate is not liable because of the limitation-of-liability clause in the sales contract. Nor has Conglomerate actively engaged in committing a wrong: it did not design the defective product. On the other hand, it might be possible to argue that Conglomerate should have been aware of the problems with the space heater and therefore should bear responsibility because it is profiting from the same line of products. Our moral sense might be particularly affected if it were revealed that the primary purpose of the transaction between Acme and Conglomerate was to limit potential liability by leaving behind a corporation with limited assets, which was unable to pay large claims. Ultimately, the resolution of this problem depends in part on how the corporate entity is viewed. If the entity is seen as morally accountable, then there is less justification for transferring liability to a successor corporation; when the first corporation ceases to exist, liability ends. Only Acme, the responsible entity, should be held accountable. If this situation is considered unjust to prospective plaintiffs, then state governments must find a way to set up contingency funds to deal with this common situation.

A corporation, considered morally accountable, becomes a candidate for reform whenever it engages in immoral actions. Reform might be achieved by changing managers, adopting new policies, formalizing ethics through company codes, or changing the composition of the board of directors. For example, E. F. Hutton pled guilty in 1985 to over 2,000 counts of mail and wire fraud based upon manipulations of financial accounts in banks that resulted in Hutton collecting interest or gaining credit on phantom money. In response, an outside study was conducted that led to changes in the board of directors and in Hutton's internal management system. By bringing outside directors into a majority position on the board and changing its internal management of financial responsibility, Hutton hoped to ensure that it would never again engage in similar practices. Ultimately, Hutton underwent the most dramatic type of transformation; it was acquired by the much larger firm of Shearson Lehman Bros. There was considerable speculation at the time that one reason for the merger was that Hutton had never fully recovered from the loss of reputation associated with its various scandals.

Corporate reputations can change significantly over time, indicating public acceptance of the concept of reform. In the 1970s, Ford was plagued with a negative reputation for safety and quality problems; by the mid-1980s Ford management had dramatically turned around the public perception of the firm.

Society's Expectations

Proponents of the limited view of profit making as social responsibility suggest that government should not expect corporations to do more than obey the law and maximize profits. That view has not been followed in practice. The probusiness Reagan administration of the 1980s explicitly called on business to increase charitable contributions and to engage in social activities under a rubric of "voluntarism." The courts have rejected shareholder suits challenging corporate contributions to charities and educational institutions, and the federal tax law allows corporations to deduct such disbursements within generous limits.

The argument that managers should respond only to the desires of the owner/shareholders is also not supported by current interpretations of corporate law. The actual, legally enforceable ownership rights given to shareholders are quite limited. Shareholders have only limited rights to corporate information and have no specific rights to any corporate buildings, equipment, or products. They do not have a right to demand that management listen to their preferences: they can act only through formal processes such as shareholder resolutions. In fact, management often opposes shareholder proposals by which shareholder groups seek to change bylaws or

otherwise make their views known. Shareholders are investors, not property owners. As investors they have a right to expect that corporate management will give primacy to their interest in financial returns. But they cannot expect that a corporation will forgo all activities that cannot demonstrably be shown to increase investor wealth. Of course, unhappy shareholders can sell their stock, and they can sue whenever management has breached its fiduciary duties to them, for example, using corporate assets for the managers' own benefit.

Ethics as Good Business

Managers often defend social responsibility as good business in the long run. They see it generally enhancing goodwill and the firm's reputation, and even may identify socially responsible actions that they believe directly benefit the firm. For example, by contributing to local education or artistic programs, a firm may help ensure a better quality of life in the community which will aid them in recruiting or retaining employees and make employees happier and more productive. Although the firm's managers would be hard pressed to demonstrate empirically a real benefit to the firm, the argument seems valid on intuitive grounds. The social fabric of the society in which the firm operates must be maintained and that occurs only if the firm, in common with the other members of society, satisfies its obligation to contribute to strong social institutions.

A related argument is that by acting responsibly, the firm forestalls government regulation that would probably be less efficient than private action. This argument is based upon an assumption that private firms can perform certain social activities more efficiently than government agencies. For example, a private firm might be able to provide a day-care center that is open to the entire community and would operate with lower costs than one established by the public sector. The lower costs could be due to the fact that the firm is responding to a competitive environment, is forced to control costs, and has superior management. If the center is operated at a loss, the firm is sustaining the operation as a contribution to society from its operating revenues.

In the safety area, failure by firms to take adequate precautions may result in substantial public demand for direct regulation, or for prohibitions

---

CONCEPT SUMMARY
The Social Responsibility Debate

Friedman View: Profit-Making as Social Responsibility	Pluralist View: Firms Have Social Responsibility
Only individuals have social responsibilities	Corporations are moral agents
Violates legal duty as agent of shareholders	Legal duties extend to stakeholders
Social responsibility is a function of government	Society (and government) wants firms to be socially responsible
Interferes with profit-making function	Being socially responsible is good business

---

on the sale or advertising of certain products. Although the government can promulgate standards and set up procedures that firms must follow in new product development, there is invariably an information lag that handicaps such regulation. Often significant costs are associated with such government intervention. Progressive, responsible management can reduce the need for direct regulation by giving safety aspects considerable priority.

Evaluation of the Debate

The debate over the scope and nature of corporate responsibility is apolitical in the sense that political conservatives and liberals may be found uncomfortably together supporting the same side in a particular debate. Ethics is not a particular political perspective; it is not the case that "ethics is only for Democrats" (or Republicans). Some conservatives support private social action as a means of forestalling public action, whereas some liberals think that corporations should stay away from a social agenda because they lack true legitimacy and will only push conservative viewpoints.

Secondly, the debate is one-sided in that few practicing managers advocate the narrow view. Instead, most managers practice the plural concept by undertaking a wide range of socially responsive actions. The contrary position is argued formally by only a few academics. However, much of the literature in finance and economics is based upon assumptions that firms act solely to maximize shareholder wealth.

Few firms eschew all forms of socially responsible behavior. When asked to justify socially responsive actions, managers give many explanations. The list would include all the arguments discussed in this chapter, plus more personal responses based upon religious beliefs or individual conscience.

Implementing Social Responsibility

Although there are numerous supporters of the idea that business firms must be socially responsible, there is no universally agreed upon method for deciding exactly what firms should do. Managers constantly confront difficult questions in directing a firm's social agenda. Should a firm make charitable contributions in a year in which it is laying off employees or closing plants? Should a firm spend more on the safety of its products or give money to feed the homeless or sponsor medical research?

Methods of Implementation

Table 9-1 summarizes the major ways by which corporations attempt to incorporate ethical values into their cultures.

Although the use of formal codes dominates the methods used, employee training in ethics is rapidly becoming more common as firms search for ways to make ethics real for their employees. Approaches vary. Some firms have a few sessions on ethics in the general programs required for entering managerial and professional employees.

TABLE 9-1

Implementing Ethics in Corporations

Codes of ethics

Ethics committee on board of directors

Ethics committee of senior executives

Ethics hot line

Ethics officer

Ethics ombudsman

Ethics coverage in management training

Ethics games/video

Others have developed games or problems based upon the firm's experience. In a typical game, teams of new employees are presented with case problems that have been drafted by managers of the firm. The discussions are led by corporate personnel and tied into the company code of ethics. Some programs feature senior executives of the firm who address the employees and explain the firm's ethical values, stressing the importance of ethical behavior by everyone associated with the firm.

Ethics committees, comprised of board members or senior executives, generally have responsibility for overall policy statements. Common responsibilities include setting general policies such as limits on doing business in South Africa or drafting or modifying a code of ethics. Some firms have ombudsmen or judiciary committees that are actively involved in enforcing the provisions of the code. Such officers may also hear complaints concerning the violation of employee rights and be the first contact for a potential whistle-blower.

Many firms now have **ethics hot lines** which employees may call, often on an anonymous basis, when they have a question pertaining to ethics. A rapidly increasing approach is for a firm to designate a senior executive as the ethics officer for the firm. This executive has the ultimate responsibility to ensure that the employees of the firm act in accordance with the firm's ethical principles and values. The use of ethics officers has increased so rapidly that in 1993 a newly formed organization, The Ethics Officers Association, held its first annual meeting in Waltham, MA.

Some major firms issue an annual report of their social activities. Although critics may view such reports as public relations puffery, they can have a very positive effect upon the operations of the firm. The very process of compiling and issuing the report will likely influence management practices. When a firm publicly reports its philanthropic ventures each year, it may be unlikely to cut back without sound reasons for doing so.

Codes of Ethics

Well over 90 percent of major companies have implemented a formal code of ethics. The widespread adoption of codes is a relatively recent phenomenon. They are usually intended as a basic code of conduct for employees and provide guidance concerning how the employee should treat the firm (for example, treat proprietary information as confidential) and deal with the firm's stakeholders (for example, no giving or receiving of business-related gifts above a certain amount). Most firms have a regularized method by which employees are informed of the code. The most formal approach is to require an annual signed statement that the employee is familiar with the provisions of the code and intends to comply. Although they vary greatly in their formality, most codes are enforced. Sanctions employed include negative performance ratings, salary reductions, and, in extreme cases, termination.

Historically, corporate codes have been criticized for emphasizing unethical behavior that might hurt the firm while paying less attention to unethical actions that might benefit the firm.

Stakeholder Management

Stakeholder management is a relatively recent formal concept emphasizing corporate responsiveness to the external environment. The term "stakeholder" is contrasted with "stockholder" to demonstrate that management has responsibilities that transcend its obligations to the share owners of the corporation. In stakeholder management the firm's executives undertake an obligation to identify and respond to the legitimate interests of the company's stakeholders.

A stakeholder has been defined by Freeman as "any group of individuals who can affect or is affected by the achievement of an organization's purpose."[1] This definition is the broadest possible and would incorporate diverse groups such as employees, shareholders, consumer activists, government regulators, and terrorist groups. For our purposes, it will help to limit the definition to those individuals or organizations that have a real economic interest in corporate decisions but are not directly subject to the authority of corporate management. A more reasonable, limited definition is more likely to be accepted as a viable management tool. The modified definition excludes employees (but not unions because they are not under management's authority); radical political groups concerned about noneconomic issues, who are themselves unaffected by the firm's operations; and those who have very minimal economic interests which would be difficult for management to incorporate, for example, the interest of a push-cart hot dog vendor in the shade provided by trees that the firm intends to transplant.

The Process of Stakeholder Management

Stakeholder management is the process by which stakeholders and their interests are identified and then incorporated into the operating and planning functions of the firm. A firm that is constantly incorporating stakeholder concerns into its management process is far more likely to anticipate developing strategic issues that represent attractive opportunities or foreboding threats. Firms that spot strategic issues as they evolve are far more likely to respond successfully.

The process of stakeholder management involves the following steps:

- Identifying present and prospective stakeholders
- Identifying stakeholder interests
- Prioritizing interests according to immediacy and likely significance
- Responding to important interests by incorporating them in (1) the strategic planning process, (2) ongoing business decisions, and (3) public affairs management strategy.

The first step in stakeholder management is to identify the present and prospective stakeholders

of the firm. The list may vary significantly from firm to firm but will typically include governments (local, state, federal, foreign), creditors, suppliers, consumer groups, and shareholders. Depending on the nature of a firm's business, stakeholders may also include trade associations, special interest groups (for example, groups concerned about nuclear power or advertising to children), distributors, professional associations, and unions.

Figure 9-1 shows what a map of the stakeholders of a multinational consumer product company might look like.

The connecting lines between the firm and the stakeholders point both ways in order to emphasize that each of them has the power to affect the other. Stakeholders can employ a variety of strategies to influence a firm's actions that affect them, including the exercise of economic, political, and legal power.

Economic power can be exercised through employing a boycott or a strike, or by limiting the credit available to the firm. The exercise of economic power is often used in conjunction with negotiations between the firm and representatives of the stakeholder group. A well-publicized example was the consumer boycott initiated by INFACT (a consumer advocate group) to protest the marketing practices followed by Nestlé in selling infant formula in developing countries. If economic power fails, then stakeholders can turn to political or legal power. A dramatic example of the exercise of **political power** was the successful effort of independent gasoline dealers in getting state legislation passed prohibiting oil companies from competing with them by operating company-owned stations. The dealers turned to the political arena after they felt they were treated unfairly in the allocation of gasoline during the first OPEC (Organization of Petroleum Exporting Countries) oil crisis, and were thereafter frustrated in their attempts to work out the problem directly with their own suppliers.

Legal power would include filing suit under product liability or discrimination law, enforcing claims, or even causing the corporation to sue itself under what is known as a shareholders' derivative suit. Construction unions employed a mixed strategy of boycotts, political intervention, and lawsuits in forcing Toyota to use union labor in building an auto plant in Georgetown, Kentucky. The union boycotted the initial construction, suc-

FIGURE 9-1

Stakeholder Map

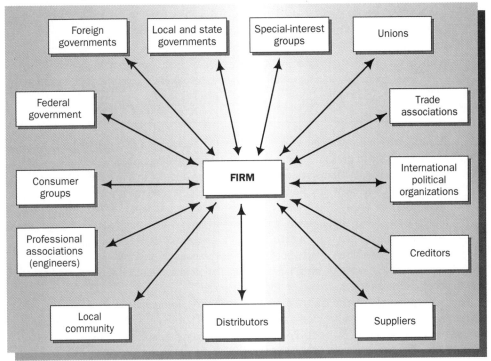

cessfully lobbied against a $32 million federal tax break for Toyota, and filed suits against the proposed plant under environmental laws.

Of course, stakeholders don't always win when they engage in legal proceedings. But even unsuccessful lawsuits can impose a cost on a firm. The *General Motors* case which follows generated a great deal of publicity in 1993. General Motors was losing market share, its net worth was declining and it had substantial intermittent losses. In response, General Motors announced it was closing a number of plants and was consolidating operations. This provoked a sea of negative press and the lawsuit described in the following case.

CHARTER TOWNSHIP OF YPSILANTI, COUNTY OF WASHTENAW AND STATE OF MICHIGAN VS. GENERAL MOTORS CORPORATION

State of Michigan Court of Appeals (1993)

506 N. W. 2d 556

BACKGROUND: The defendant has operated two plants in Ypsilanti for a number of years. The first is known as the Hydra-Matic plant and employs 9,000; the second, known as Willow Run, employs 4,000. Over the years, the township granted the defendant a total of 11 tax abatements; three for Willow Run. For example, on July 17, 1984, the township approved defendant's application for a twelve-year 50 percent abatement of personal property taxes on the corporation's $175 million investment for the introduction of a new car.

On December 18, 1991, defendant announced that it had decided to consolidate the work being done at Willow Run and Arlington, Texas, at Arlington.

Ypsilanti Township, the County of Washtenaw and the State of Michigan sued to enjoin General Motors "from transferring the production of its Caprice Sedan, and Buick and Cadillac (sic, Chevrolet) station wagons, from the Willow Run plant to any other facility."

The trial court found that the abatement statute and application did not create a contract between the township and the corporation; however, in favor of the plaintiff, the court found that the defendant was bound by promissory estoppel to retain production of the Caprice line in Willow Run as long as the company produces that model.

Per Curiam

The trial court found that a promise was made from the background of defendant's negotiations for abatements and principally from Willow Run plant manager Harvey Williams' statement at a public hearing. Williams stated that "upon completion of this project and favorable market demand, it will allow Willow Run to continue production and maintain continuous employment for our employees.". . .

The trial court's finding that defendant promised to keep Caprice and station wagon production at Willow Run is clearly erroneous. First, the mere fact that a corporation solicits a tax abatement and persuades a municipality with assurances of jobs cannot be evidence of a promise. The very purpose of tax abatement legislation is to induce companies to locate and to continue business enterprises in the municipality. . . .

Second, representations of job creation are a statutory prerequisite. . . .

Third, the fact that a manufacturer uses hyperbole and puffery in seeking an advantage or concession does not necessarily create a promise. For example, statements such as "we're partners" and "we look forward to growing together" were not found to constitute a promise to keep a collective bargaining agreement in force for the foreseeable future so as to create by promissory estoppel a continuing duty of the employer to honor an expired agreement. . . .

Even if the finding of promise could be sustained, reliance on the promise would not have been reasonable. . . .

It has never been held that an abatement carries a promise of continued employment. Indeed, the history of this case shows that persons involved in the 1988 Willow Run abatement understood that defendant was not promising continued employment. . . .

At a township board meeting in November 1988, Dillard Craiger, chairman of the Washtenaw County Board of Commissioners, opposed a tax break for Willow Run "unless a commitment was made thereby securing employment for the community.". . .

Other speakers then took the floor, several of whom specifically pointed out that defendant had not committed itself to continue operating the Willow Run plant for any particular period of time. . . .

Defendant's representatives were not asked to respond to these comments, and no member of the township board took issue with them. Instead, Supervisor Prater urged the board to approve defendant's application. The township board then voted unanimously to approve a twelve-year abatement at Willow Run; the resolution contained no suggestion that approval was conditioned on a commitment to operate the plant for any particular period. . . .

In short, defendant made no promises.

DECISION: Reversed. General Motors can shut down the Ypsilanti plant.

CASE NOTE

In an ironic twist to this case, General Motors promised Arlington, Texas, that if it closed its plant there within the first five years, it would give back the abated taxes it received as part of the deal. Presumably, the General Motors commitment to Arlington was indeed a legally enforceable promise.

Once the firm's stakeholders have been identified, the next step is to identify their specific claims or interests. A good starting point is to determine how the stakeholders themselves perceive their interests in the firm. Many firms employ a continuous environmental scanning system to identify emerging social issues. Corporate staff, consultants, and outside counsel monitor the media, administrative proceedings, and other activities for events that have present or future significance for the firm. One focus of such an environmental scanning system could be to monitor known stakeholders.

Strategies for identifying stakeholder interests include (1) direct communications with representatives of stakeholder organizations (for example, setting up an organization of distributors that meets regularly), (2) employing consultants who are able to deal directly with designated stakeholders, (3) hiring new managers from the ranks of important stakeholders (for example, former employees of a state or federal regulatory agency), and (4) regularly scanning the publications and formal statements of stakeholder organizations. Through this process, a firm can anticipate the concerns of stakeholder groups. It is often difficult for a firm's management to identify accurately stakeholder priorities without employing some formal scanning method. The values and objectives of managers and stakeholders often differ significantly regarding an appropriate strategic plan for the firm. Managers often have difficulty accepting stakeholder viewpoints as valid because of the extreme variances in perspective.

The process of identifying stakeholder concerns may produce a lengthy list. The list given in Table 9-2, which is based upon a hypothetical consumer products company, is representative.

The lengthy (although incomplete) listing of possible stakeholder issues makes it abundantly clear that a large firm may face dozens of stakeholder groups that are concerned about hundreds of issues. Multiple stakeholders may be interested in the same issue. And, on a particular issue, stakeholders may be at odds with one another. An employees' union and suppliers may wish to see a marginally profitable plant with a pollution control problem kept going, whereas lenders and state government regulators may prefer that the plant be closed. Another important stakeholder, the local community, may find its constituent parts in heated disagreement over the issue. Citizens concerned about the quality of the environment may wish to see the plant closed, whereas those dependent economically upon the plant may want to see it survive. The process by which a firm's management prioritizes issues is critical to the development of an effective response to complex multidimensional stakeholder issues.

Once stakeholder issues have been identified, they can be prioritized in terms of immediacy and likely impact on both the firm and the affected stakeholders. This requires a subjective judgment that is based upon prior experience with strategic issues. Line managers should be involved in the judgment process because they are likely to have direct involvement with the consequences of the strategic issues. The longer a system of stakeholder management has been in place, the greater is the likelihood of an accurate assessment of the importance of an issue because of similar prior experiences.

Once an issue is identified and prioritized, there are a variety of ways in which a firm can respond. The fundamental principle guiding response strategies is that the stakeholder interest must be valued in equivalent economic terms with the firm's interests in the operating decision. If relevant, the stakeholder interest should be incorporated into the corporate planning process on a similar basis.

On many occasions, a firm's management may conclude that it should not give in to the pressures exerted by a particular stakeholder group. Strategies that can be employed to respond to opposing stakeholder groups are briefly described in Table 9-3.

Although public affairs managers often feel that they are swimming with one arm against a powerful current in trying to influence major social trends, the strategies listed in Table 9-3 can have significant cumulative impacts. Faced with the boycott of its products in the United States over its marketing of infant formula in developing countries, Nestlé eventually used many of the strategies listed, and ultimately the boycott was lifted. Nestlé had some success in responding to the problems even though many religious groups had endorsed the boycott and the consumer groups were well organized. By becoming more aware of the concerns of the stakeholder groups, Nestlé came to realize that it should make some changes in its marketing strategies.

TABLE 9-2

Concerns of Stakeholders in a Multinational Consumer Products Firm

Stakeholder	Interests
Federal government	Solid waste disposal Air pollution Fair employment practices
Foreign governments	Conservation of their natural resources Currency fluctuations Plant safety Local employment
State governments	Plant safety Water conservation
Unions	Runaway plants Plant closings Grievance procedures
Consumer groups	Advertising to children Dangerous products Misleading ads or advertising harmful products
Creditors	Conservation of financial resources
Suppliers	Continuity of business relationships
Distributors	Competition through dual distribution Promotional support Pricing freedom
Professional association	Observance of profession's ethical standards
Special interest groups	Advertising to children Trading in South Africa
Local community	Air pollution Plant safety Layoffs Plant closings/relocation

Use of some public affairs management (PAM) strategies may raise serious ethical questions. The phrase "public affairs management" carries with it overtones of manipulation. Firms should always consider the interests of stakeholders and, where relevant, the interest of society generally in employing PAM techniques. Applying these techniques without consideration of their ethical consequences may produce perverse results.

Beyond the ethical constraints on PAM, there are legal constraints. Corporations should make sure that they are not violating the legal rights of others and are acting within the permissible bounds of their authority. Many states and administrative agencies have sought to limit corporate power to engage in various public affairs strategies. Limiting regulations are often based upon a fear that corporations will come to dominate the public affairs process because of their wealth, access to media, and ability to engage the efforts of thousands of supporters.

Corporations have certain rights that must be respected by regulators. Corporations are "persons" entitled to equal protection and due process of law under the Constitution. That means, for example, that corporate property cannot be taken without appropriate notice and compensation. On the other hand, just because corporations have certain basic legal rights does not mean that they are entitled to every right that applies to human citizens. Corporations may not assert a right of privacy or the Fifth Amendment privilege against self-incrimination.

TABLE 9-3

Public Affairs Management Strategies

Strategy	Description
Issue advertising	Develop and place ads in media advocating a particular policy position or social viewpoint
Invoke independent authority	Where creditability is at issue, involve independent authority with perceived integrity, for example, Nestlé establishing the Muskie Commission to review complaints about marketing infant formula overseas
Coalition building	Seek out and involve stakeholders having interests compatible with those of the firm
Recruitment from key stakeholders	In compliance with law, hire managers who have formerly worked for key stakeholders, for example, defense contractors hiring former military personnel (after the mandatory waiting period), regulated firms hiring former regulators
Lobbying	Sponsor and support favorable legislation; oppose harmful legislation; use company or consulting lobbyists
Establish formal communication modes	Provide access to significant stakeholders, for example, a consumer hot line for complaints
Administrative process	Scan developing regulations; comment on pending developments
Litigation	Sue as plaintiffs asserting valid causes of action (should be used as a strategy of last resort); engage in preventive legal actions to reduce exposure as a defendant
Trade associations	Join and participate actively to influence their lobbying and public positions
Political involvement	Sponsor corporate political action committees (PACs); advocate positions on referenda and other political issues
Cultivate grassroots support	Contact firm's consumers/stockholders and inform regarding the firm's position on social/public issues

Freedom of speech and free access to government are very important rights for corporations because they pertain to very important PAM strategies, such as participating in electoral politics or engaging in advocacy advertising. In these areas, corporations have qualified rather than absolute rights. The *Bellotti* case that follows demonstrates some of the parameters of those rights.

FIRST NATIONAL BANK OF BOSTON V. BELLOTTI

U.S. Supreme Court
435 U.S. 765 (1978)

BACKGROUND: The First National Bank of Boston (plaintiff-appellant) sued the Massachusetts Attorney General (defendant-appellee) to prevent the enforcement of a statute limiting corporate lobbying on state referenda. The Bank wanted to spend money to publicize its opposition to a pending Massachusetts ballot question that, if successful, would permit the state legislature to impose a graduated personal income tax. A Massachusetts statute made it a crime for a corporation to spend money to influence votes on state referendum proposals pertaining to a personal income tax or other matters not materially affecting the corporation. The Bank challenged the constitutionality of the law. The Supreme Judicial Court of Massachusetts upheld the law and the Bank appealed to the U.S. Supreme Court.

Powell, Justice

. . . If the speakers here were not corporations, no one would suggest that the State could silence their proposed speech. It is the type of speech indispensable to decision-making in a democracy, and this is no less true because the speech comes from a corporation rather than an individual. The inherent worth of the speech in terms of its capacity for informing the public does not depend upon the identity of its source, whether corporation, association, union, or individual.

. . . Appellee . . . advances two principal justifications for the prohibition of corporate speech. The first is the State's interest in sustaining the active role of the individual citizen in the electoral process and thereby preventing diminution of the citizen's confidence in government. The second is the interest in protecting the rights of shareholders whose views differ from those expressed by management on behalf of the corporation. However weighty these interests may be in the context of partisan candidate elections, they either are not implicated in this case or are not served at all, or in other than a random manner, by the prohibition in §8.

. . . Appellee advances a number of arguments in support of his view that these interests are endangered by corporate participation in discussion of a referendum issue. They hinge upon the assumption that such participation would exert an undue influence on the outcome of a referendum vote, and—in the end—destroy the confidence of the people in the democratic process and the integrity of government. According to appellee, corporations are wealthy and powerful and their views may drown out other points of view. If appellee's arguments were supported by record or legislative findings that corporate advocacy threatened imminently to undermine democratic processes, thereby denigrating rather than serving First Amendment interests, these arguments would merit our consideration. . . . But there has been no showing that the relative voice of corporations has been overwhelming or even significant in influencing referenda in Massachusetts, or that there has been any threat to the confidence of the citizenry in government. . . . To be sure, corporate advertising may influence the outcome of the vote; this would be its purpose. But the fact that advocacy may persuade the electorate is hardly a reason to suppress it: The Constitution "protects expression which is eloquent no less than that which is unconvincing." . . . Finally, appellee argues that §8 protects corporate shareholders, an interest that is both legitimate and traditionally within the province of state law. . . . The statute is said to serve this interest by preventing the use of corporate resources in furtherance of views with which some shareholders may disagree. This purpose is belied, however, by the provisions of the statute, which are both underinclusive and overinclusive.

. . . The underinclusiveness of the statute is self-evident. Corporate expenditures with respect to a referendum are prohibited, while corporate activity with respect to the passage or defeat of legislation is permitted, . . . even though corporations may engage in lobbying more often than they take positions on ballot questions submitted to the voters. Nor does §8 prohibit a corporation from expressing its views, by the expenditure of corporate funds, on any public issue until it becomes the subject of a referendum, though the displeasure of disapproving shareholders is unlikely to be any less.

The fact that a particular kind of ballot question has been singled out for special treatment undermines the likelihood of a genuine state interest in protecting shareholders. It suggests instead that the legislature may have been concerned with silencing corporations on a particular subject. Indeed, appellee has conceded that "the legislative and judicial history of the statute indicates . . . that . . . [it] was 'tailor-made' to prohibit corporate campaign contributions to oppose a graduated income tax amendment.". . .

. . . The overinclusiveness of the statute is demonstrated by the fact that §8 would prohibit a corporation from supporting or opposing a referendum proposal even if its shareholders unanimously authorized the contribution or expenditure. Ultimately shareholders may decide, through the procedures of corporate democracy, whether their corporation should engage in debate on public issues. Acting through their power to elect the board of directors or to insist upon protective provisions in the corporation's charter, shareholders normally are presumed competent to protect their own interests. In addition to intracorporate remedies, minority shareholders generally have access to the judicial remedy of a derivative suit to challenge corporate disbursements alleged to have been made for improper corporate purposes or merely to further the personal interests of management.

DECISION: The Supreme Court reversed and struck down the statute on constitutional grounds.

> **CONCEPT SUMMARY**
> ### Steps in Stakeholder Management
>
> - Identify stakeholders
> - Determine the interests of affected stakeholders
> - Prioritize stakeholder interests
> - Account for stakeholder interests in
>   strategic planning
>   operations
>   public affairs management

External Incentives for Social Responsibility

So far, we have considered the justifications for social responsiveness on the part of corporate management and the types of strategies used to foster an environment of responsiveness. The rationale for such actions has, up to this point, been limited to general concepts of professionalism and societal obligation and assertions of capability for enhancing profits. In this section, we encounter sources of more direct pressure on corporations to be responsible. An important, at times undervalued, incentive is the response of the market to perceived irresponsibility in the safety of products. Demand for the products can be lessened and the stock price of the company can fall in response. There are many ways by which government, at all levels, can intervene. State governments, through their chartering functions, can change the legal structure of corporations with the idea that organizational redesign will alter manager behavior. Or state legislatures and courts can modify the civil liability systems to increase their deterrence effect for irresponsible behavior. Corporations as entities and managers as individuals can be exposed to criminal liability. Or firms can be subjected to direct regulation by administrative agencies.

Market Incentives for Safety

In certain circumstances the market may provide a strong incentive for corporations to act responsibly. Even though a firm's actions may be legal, public perception that the firm has acted irresponsibly can have a strong negative impact upon the firm. This is particularly the case for dangerous consumer products, especially those bought with discretionary income and for which there are ready substitutes.

The publicity generated by product liability cases, or administrative actions such as recalls, may result in heavy costs for the firms associated with the dangerous products or services. The Great Adventure Amusement Park suffered a significant falloff in business the year after a fire in its Haunted Castle killed eight youths. The sales of Ford Pintos, Firestone 500 radials, Tylenol, and Rely tampons all fell off dramatically after publicity about potential dangers. Even more limited actions, such as compulsory product repairs, have been found to depress the sales of the brands affected.[2]

The market losses associated with negative publicity surrounding legal proceedings cannot be covered by insurance. One study of recalls of automobiles and drugs found that substantial capital market penalties, reflected in lower stock prices, are also imposed upon those producing defective products.[3] In fact, capital market losses associated with the firms studied exceeded estimates of both the direct costs of the recalls and the total social costs of the defective product. Relying on these and similar studies, some commentators conclude that the market is more effective in bringing about safe products than government regulation.[4]

There are, however, many circumstances in which government regulation should be more effective than the market. If consumers cannot discover the harms associated with products, or have no alternative even though they are aware of the risk, the market incentive for safety is substantially reduced.

Structural Change

One of the best-known advocates of structural change is Christopher Stone, who wrote *Where the Law Ends* (New York: Harper & Row, 1975). Stone argues that corporations must be encouraged to study the social and human repercussions of their proposed actions so that they can always be prepared to present justifications for their conduct. Stone proposes a number of changes in the form of corporate organization that would, he reasons, bring about positive changes in corporate behavior. He would eliminate the use of inside directors (directors who hold management positions in the firm), require that a designated percentage of directors be financially disinterested, and, most importantly, define by law the precise functions that directors must perform. A director breaching these requirements would be subjected to unindemnifiable liability and would be ineligible to serve in a major corporate post for a designated term of years.

Stone would further extend the principles applied to directors to the operating officers of the firm. He would require by law that corporations have certain designated management positions, filled by individuals who meet legally established specifications, who would be required to carry out specifically designated tasks. Thus, a steel company might be required to have a vice-president of environmental compliance who is trained in the technical aspects of pollution control, who would oversee tests of air emission, sign such reports, and see that corrective measures were implemented when necessary.

Stone has also advocated requiring corporations to gather and review certain data, such as the drug use experience of customers of a pharmaceutical firm. To insure proper review, certain internal written reports to designated officers might be required. The data in raw form would have to be retained for a designated period of time, and the government would have the right to inspect the data at any time. This would presumably open up corporations and make sure that stakeholder interests are considered at the proper points.

Stone's critics argue that his approach would increase costs and discourage competent people from entering management positions. After all, who would want to undertake a job where they might be subjected to a substantial uninsurable liability? Many problems arise with the proposals that corporate procedures and positions be determined by governmental fiat. There are many forms of corporate organization and behavior. To force all companies to fit a particular mold, even for only a small part of their operations, could produce substantial inefficiencies. Emphasis on government inspections may compromise trade secrets and product development, and might even stimulate bribery. Many of the record-keeping requirements would be difficult to enforce and might just result in higher costs.

Beyond Stone, a number of other proposals have been aimed at changing corporate behavior through structural alterations. Some have been geared to changing the role and nature of the board of directors. The argument is that a more independent board of directors will do a better job of watching over management.

Opponents of such reform proposals claim that a more independent board will be less efficient. Each director should represent the entire firm. Purposefully developing adversarial relationships can only provoke counterproductive conflict.

A second focus of reform has been to strengthen shareholders' rights. The assumption is that shareholders are a diverse lot, representative of a wide range of societal interests, and that if individual shareholders have real authority, they can effectively limit the discretionary powers of the professional managers.

A major shareholder movement emerged in the 1990s, largely through the efforts of large institutional shareholders such as CALPERS, the pension fund of the state of California. These large shareholders brought pressure to have management compensation closely tied to performance and were particularly critical of highly paid senior managers whose companies underperformed financially. They also launched campaigns to get firms to drop "poison pills" and other devices used to make it difficult for outsiders to take over the company and displace existing management.

Incentives Through the Tort Law

A major debate today is whether the tort law, particularly in the area of product liability, provides appropriate incentives for socially responsible behavior on the part of firms. Proponents of expansive tort liability argue that it is one of the most effective ways of insuring that firms consider social interests. They reason that the anticipation of potentially large judgments makes management very careful in dealing with products having the potential for harming humans. Opponents claim that the current system overdeters. In support they advance a number of arguments to the effect that the current law produces negative incentives. The potential for large claims may become so high that firms respond by holding back on product improvements, thereby causing products to be less safe than they might be. Assessing large judgments against manufacturers has the negative effect of increasing the costs of products, which tends to hurt poorer people. Opponents further argue that the system is out of control in that the large sums paid by defendants often fail to benefit the injured parties. In some cases over half of all the money paid has gone to lawyers and those responsible for administering the claims.

The awarding of punitive damages against corporations highlights the issues involved in using the court system to reform corporate behavior. The state courts in the United States have differed in their approach to the question of whether a corporation should be liable for punitive damages. Some will allow punitive damages only when the tortious act was expressly authorized (or subsequently ratified) by the corporation. Others will impose punitive damages whenever malice or recklessness is present so long as the act was committed by an employee acting within the scope of employment. Still another line of cases will impose liability when the act was authorized or committed by someone at the general management level.

As would be expected, this diversity of approaches produces inconsistent results. When Richardson-Merrell defrauded the FDA (Federal Drug Administration) in the distribution of MER/29, an anticholesterol drug, both Toole and Roginsky developed cataracts from taking the drug. Their claims were based upon the exact same actions by Richardson-Merrell, yet Toole was awarded $250,000 in punitive damages in California,[5] whereas Roginsky was denied punitive damages in New York.[6]

Which of the approaches represents better policy? Courts limiting the application of punitive damages to instances of actual authority do so for the following reasons:

1. Concern that recurring assessments of punitive damages, in which the amounts are essentially pulled out of a hat, may endanger the financial viability of the affected corporation.

2. The cost of punitive damages is ultimately borne by the shareholders, who are without fault.

3. It is unfair to impose extra damages on a company for unauthorized acts committed by its employees.

Courts imposing punitive damages more broadly find support among the following arguments:

1. The action is outrageous and is attributable to the corporation.

2. The action was undertaken for the benefit of the corporation.

3. Threats of real financial harm are necessary in order to have an impact upon the behavior of others.

4. It is unfair for an individual to receive punitive damages when an act is committed by an individual but not to be able to recover when the act is attributable to a corporation.

Punitive damage awards have been attacked by defendants as unconstitutional because they constitute "excessive fines" or "cruel and unusual punishment," which are forbidden by the Constitution. None of the attacks have been successful to date but it seems certain that more challenges will occur.

Incentives Through the Criminal Law

The imposition of criminal sanctions upon corporations or individual managers may have a significant impact upon business behavior. The prospect of jail sentences or the kind of widespread notoriety that accompanies criminal trials should make managers especially cautious about complying with the law. In 1991, sentencing guidelines for corporations convicted of criminal actions under federal law were established. The guidelines focused on means by which criminally convicted corporations could be directed to remedy the harm they had caused. The guidelines set up a point system for determining the size of fines judges can impose.

Fines are dependent upon the type of offense and the actions of the firm relating to the crime. The seriousness of the offense is determined by assessing the highest total amount among the pecuniary gain realized by the defendant, the loss imposed upon victims or the fine assessable under a table provided in the guidelines. The fines in the table run from $5,000 to $72,500,000. This amount can be reduced or increased by a determination of the steps taken by the firm to prevent and detect criminal conduct, the level and extent of involvement by senior managers and the organization's response after it discovers that the offense has been committed. For example, a firm would receive a lower fine if it could show that it had implemented an "effective program" to prevent and detect violations of law. To qualify as effective, such a program would have to be reasonably designed, implemented, and enforced. Among other things, "high-level" managers of the firm must have overall responsibility to oversee compliance with such standards.

Review Questions and Problems

Key Terms

owner

shareholder

stakeholder

professionalism

moral accountability

corporate moral accountability

successor liability

ethics hot line

stakeholder management

economic power

political power

legal power

corporate ethics officer

public affairs management

federal corporate sentencing guidelines

Discussion Questions

1. Describe a process for General Motors to follow in its decision to close the plant in Ypsilanti that would ensure a sufficient consideration of stakeholder interests.

2. Describe how a code of ethics of academic integrity could be developed at your institution that would be responsive to the problem of student cheating.

3. Which of the following are stakeholders of General Motors (GM)? Ford Motor Company? The Detroit Tigers baseball team? The Goodyear tire company? The National Tire Dealers and Retreaders Association? The United Auto Workers? The City of Detroit? The GM Dealers Association?

Review Problems

1. In 1993, Marriott corporation announced that they were going to divide the firm into two major components. One unit, the "good firm" would operate the hotels and receive management fees. The good firm was expected to have a strong positive cash flow. The other unit, the "bad firm", would own most of the unsold hotels and other problem real estate. Shortly after the reorganization was announced the price of some of the Marriott bonds which were secured against the bad firm fell about 25-30%. The stock price increased, but not by a large margin. Marriott management were quoted as saying that their sole obligation was to their shareholders and that they intended to honor all contractual commitments to their bond holders. Discuss in the context of the social responsibility debate.

2. In May 1984, a fire erupted in the Haunted Castle at the Great Adventure Amusement Park in central New Jersey. The fire apparently started when a young man held a cigarette lighter against the wall. Eight young people died of asphyxiation in the fire.

There were no sprinklers in the Haunted Castle and it was not hooked into a central alarm system. The attraction was comprised of a series of truck trailers and people walked through it under the direction of Great Adventure employees. One or more employees, known as Rovers, constantly walked through the Castle.

The local government fire inspectors had classified the building as a temporary structure and thus had exempted it from the fire code's mandate that public buildings have sprinklers. There had been a number of studies conducted by risk consultants who had recommended, among many other things, that sprinklers be installed in the Haunted Castle. In the aftermath of the fire, the State of New Jersey brought charges of aggravated manslaughter against the corporation, Great Adventure, Inc., and against two executives, including the general manager of Great Adventure. The families of the victims also filed civil tort suits seeking damages from Great Adventure, Inc., for wrongful death. How should responsibility be allocated?

3. You have been elected as the chairman of the contributions committee at ABC Steel Company, where in addition to planning and administrating corporate contributions, you are responsible for preparing an annual contributions budget.

ABC Steel is a major producer of steel and steel products with its primary mill located in an economically depressed city in the Northeast. Unemployment due to layoffs and a low-skilled work force is running high, crime rates are higher than the national average, and living conditions in the inner city are well below national standards. Cultural activity is slowly dying.

As chairman, you may spend any amount up to 1 percent of total net income (this year's income is approximately $100 million) on corporate contributions. This year top management at ABC Steel can agree upon only seven possible areas of contribution. They are:

1. the nearby college of engineering.
2. the United Way federated drive.
3. the local cultural center for the performing arts.
4. the Harvard Business School.
5. neighborhood revitalization projects.
6. the local Unemployment Services Bureau.
7. the Worldwide Famine Relief Society.

Your job is to determine how large the corporate contributions budget should be and what amounts, if any, should be allocated among the seven alternatives.

Just a few months earlier, in a speech to the American Council for the Arts, the CEO underscored the importance of corporate philanthropy in American life and reemphasized that ABC Steel's profits were continuing to decline for the third straight year due to competition from overseas and low productivity at home. The outlook for the U.S. steel industry is not promising. ABC Steel laid off 500 employees for an indefinite period two months ago. None has been recalled to work.

As chairman, you must present your annual budget to top management with supporting arguments for your selections. You have also been asked to draft a statement to the shareholders describing the rationale behind the contributions.

4. In 1974, Classic Container Corporation decided to follow the lead of Royal Cork and Seal, National Can, and Canadian Can in developing its operations in international markets. The container and packaging industry, in searching for new fields in which to grow, had sought opportunities in international markets for their canning and bottling operations. Classic, recognized as one of the top ten firms in the industry with approximately a 9 percent U.S. market share in the canning and bottling of consumer products, felt that it must follow the lead of others in the industry in the hope that new markets would bring the sales growth it so desperately needed without having to rely on technological breakthroughs.

Classic's management determined that its major competitors had overwhelming advantages in most of the European countries because of earlier entrance into those markets. Consequently, Classic's management concluded that its best strategic move would be the establishment of manufacturing and marketing operations for cans and bottles in developing countries, especially in Africa. By not having to compete with the giants of the industry on a head-to-head basis in the international markets and by maintaining its own manufacturing operation in the underdeveloped countries, it seemed reasonable that Classic could make a significant market penetration.

Responsibility for entry into African markets was assigned to the International Division of Classic. The head of that department was William Taylor, who had a reputation for exceeding performance targets, and who was considered the leading candidate eventually to succeed Thomas Hahn as CEO. The operating responsibility for Eastern Africa fell to Reginald More.

When More approached the government of East Zamia (Zamia) through diplomatic channels late in 1974, the idea of the establishment of manufacturing operations was warmly received. As negotiations proceeded with the Secretary of Commerce of Zamia, however, it became clear that Classic would not be hiring as many citizens of that country as its government desired. Because its operations were so highly mechanized, Classic required skilled American workers and managers for its operations and could employ Zamians in small numbers and only then as menial laborers. Still, the Zamian government was anxious to attract industry from the West and encouraged Classic to begin construction of a plant. All of the initial permissions were quickly granted by the appropriate Zamian officials.

By late 1976, Classic had completed the land clearing and external construction for a large plant operation in Zamia. Shipments of machinery from its U.S. operations were due to arrive by early 1977. Then, in what More considered to be a surprise move, the Commerce officials of Zamia informed More that the Classic plant operation could not begin as planned in mid-1977. The Zamian officials cited a myriad of regulations that were not previously mentioned and the failure to hire natives as reasons for the holdup. The officials explained to More that all of these matters could be resolved immediately and operations could begin as scheduled if certain payments were made to both the officials themselves and the Secretary's staff. These payments were to be in U.S. dollars and would be a one-time payment. Unfortunately, the Zamians would not allow these "payments for administrative costs" to be publicly recorded.

More was very troubled by these developments. Delays in starting the plant operation could have a dramatic influence on its ultimate profitability. There were rumors that Royal was negotiating to build a plant in neighboring Kenya. Any significant delay would probably cause the International Division to fall short of its performance target for 1977.

On the one hand, More could not ascertain whether or not the requested payments constituted official policy of the Zamian government. Personally, More considered such payments unethical and contrary to his personal values. Classic Container had implemented a Code of Ethics in 1976. The Code had a provision that prohibited "making any payments on behalf of the Corporation that are contrary to the law of the United States or of the country in which they are made." The Code further contained a formal procedure by which an employee could whistle-blow about violations. On the other hand, the Code provided that an employee could be terminated for willful abuse of the whistle-blowing system.

More discussed the problem with Taylor. Taylor's first question was, "How much do they want?" When More mentioned the amount, Taylor said, "That sounds reasonable. Pay it." More then stated his reservations and mentioned the Code. Taylor then became somewhat irritated and said, "Look, there are big sums involved here. You can be doggoned sure that Royal will make similar payments if they go into Kenya. Pay the blankety-blank bribe!"

What should More do?

Footnotes

[1] R. Edward Freeman, *Strategic Management: A Stakeholder Approach* (Boston: Pitman, 1984), p. 53.

[2] Crafton, Hoffer, and Reilly, "Testing the Impact of Recalls on the Demand for Automobiles," 19 *Economic Inquiry*, 694 (1981).

[3] Jarrell and Peltzman, "The Impact of Product Recalls on the Wealth of Sellers," 93:3 *Journal of Political Economy*, 512 (1985).

[4] Viscusi, "Market Incentives for Safety," *Harvard Business Review*, 133 (July–August, 1985).

[5] Toole v. Richardson-Merrell, 60 Cal.Rptr. 398 (Cal.App. 1967).

[6] Roginsky v. Richardson-Merrell, 378 F.2d 832 (2d Cir. 1967).

10

Introduction to the Law of Contracts

The Utility of Contracts

Contract Defined

Source of Contract Law

Classification of Contracts

Contracts are all-pervasive in our daily lives. Contracts govern a boarding agreement with the university, renting an apartment, buying books at the bookstore, agreeing to lend a roommate money, and buying beer at the local store. The law of contracts establishes the parameters of permissible business and individual transactions.

The Utility of Contracts

Contract law can be viewed in several ways. Some see the freedom of individuals and organizations to contract as fundamental to our basic free enterprise system. Viewed in this manner, the law of supply and demand learned in economics is implemented every day by innumerable contracts between sellers and buyers. Contract law facilitates exchanges between the parties by protecting both seller and buyer against the possible bad-faith conduct of the other. Without this protection, the parties could breach contracts at will. If the law of contracts did not provide a remedy for the breach of an agreement, buyers and sellers would have to take extraordinary and costly steps to protect themselves. For example, sellers might be forced to require buyers to pay the entire purchase price before agreeing to sell or ship

goods. Buyers, on the other hand, might not be willing to pay the seller until the goods are received. Buyers and sellers would lose almost all of the flexibility that they enjoy in commercial dealings, and the cost of doing business would increase drastically.

Another view of a contract is that it is a tool by which people—often, but not always, assisted by their lawyers—establish a private set of rules to govern a particular business or personal relationship. Under this perspective, a contract is a device by which a situation may be defined and controlled. The expectations of the contracting parties are made known and serve as guides for future behavior.

For example, by use of a real-estate purchase contract, a seller promises to sell a house and lot to a buyer. In the contract, a number of the parties' expectations are spelled out. Such expectations include (1) when the buyer may take possession, (2) what kind of document of title the seller is to provide the buyer, (3) what articles the seller may remove from the house and yard, (4) how the taxes owing are to be split among the parties, (5) how the risk of unexpected future damage is to be allocated among the parties, etc.

By virtue of this contractual agreement, the buyer and seller have created their own set of rules to govern the house-sale transaction. In a sense, their agreement embodies a private legal system. Not surprisingly, many of the questions that arise concerning the operation of a governmental legal system also come up in the context of private agreements. For example, what is to be done if the parties in the agreement just described fail to provide for responsibility in case of loss and the house is destroyed by an earthquake after the contract is signed but before the buyer takes possession? Or what happens if one of the parties blatantly disregards one of the clearly established private rules—for example, by refusing to provide the required evidence of title?

In the first case (loss of a house due to an earthquake) the basic expectations of at least one of the parties cannot be met. Either the buyer will be required to purchase damaged property or the seller will be required to give up a sale he or she thought was closed and final. How can this issue be resolved when the parties have not dealt with the problem themselves and insurance does not cover the loss? For commonly occurring situations of this sort, the courts and legislatures have established guidelines. In addition, general legal principles have been promulgated determining how contractual provisions should be interpreted when issues such as this arise.

The second case (refusing to provide required evidence of title) goes to the heart of contract law. From a public-policy perspective, it would not be desirable for the parties to attempt to enforce their contract by private means. Our legal system does not tolerate the use of threats or force to induce faithful observance of the terms of private agreements. (An ironic use of the term "contract" is to speak of "putting out a contract" on someone when describing the criminal procurement of violence against a designated victim.) Instead, it allows the parties to a contract to enforce its terms through civil suits.

A number of questions are immediately posed by the intervention of the legal system when private parties disagree. Should all private agreements be enforced—for example, an agreement by two bank robbers to split the proceeds of a holdup 55/45? What type of relief should be provided for the party injured as a result of the other's failure to observe the terms of the agreement? Could a university obtain a court order compelling a professor who has just won a million-dollar lottery to teach the last academic year of a 3-year teaching contract? Should the legal system enforce only "fair" contracts? If so, what constitutes a fair contract? Should unwritten contracts be enforceable?

Because the case that follows involved actor Lee Marvin and received extensive media coverage, it provides an interesting introduction to the law of contracts. The reader should try to determine what policy issues the court considered in determining whether a private agreement should be enforced.

MARVIN V. MARVIN
Supreme Court of California
557 P.2d 106 (1976)

BACKGROUND: Michelle Treola Marvin (plaintiff) lived with actor Lee Marvin (defendant) from October 1964 to May 1970, when he compelled her to leave. She sued Mr. Marvin, claiming that they had entered into an oral contract in 1964 in which both parties agreed they would share equally their earnings and property no matter who earned them. She claimed that they agreed to represent themselves as husband and wife and that she would be a homemaker and companion, giving up her career as an entertainer and singer. Mr. Marvin in his defense claimed that this was not an enforceable contract because it was made between nonmarital partners, involved in an illicit relationship, and thus was contrary to public policy. A lower court ruled in favor of Mr. Marvin, leaving all property accumulated by the couple with him. Ms. Marvin appealed.

Tobriner, Justice

During the past 15 years, there has been a substantial increase in the number of couples living together without marrying. Such nonmarital relationships lead to legal controversy when one partner dies or the couple separates. . . .

Defendant first and principally relies on the contention that the alleged contract is so closely related to the supposed "immoral" character of the relationship between plaintiff and himself that the enforcement of the contract would violate public policy. He points to cases asserting that a contract between nonmarital partners is unenforceable if it is "involved in" an illicit relationship . . . or made in "contemplation" of such a relationship. A review of the numerous California decisions concerning contracts between nonmarital partners, however, reveals that the courts have not employed such broad and uncertain standards to strike down contracts. The decisions instead disclose a narrower and more precise standard: a contract between nonmarital partners is unenforceable *only to the extent* that it *explicitly* rests upon the immoral and illicit consideration of meretricious sexual services.

In *Bridges v. Bridges* (1954), both parties were in the process of obtaining divorces from their erstwhile respective spouses. The two parties agreed to live together, to share equally in property acquired, and to marry when their divorces became final. The man worked as a salesman and used his savings to purchase properties. The woman kept house, cared for seven children, three from each former marriage and one from the nonmarital relationship, and helped construct improvements on the properties. When they separated, without marrying, the court awarded the woman one-half the value of the property. Rejecting the man's contention that the contract was illegal, the court stated that: "Nowhere is it expressly testified to by anyone that there was anything in the agreement for the pooling of assets and the sharing of accumulations that contemplated meretricious relations as any part of the consideration or as any object of the agreement." . . .

Defendant's [next] contention is noteworthy for the lack of authority advanced in its support. He contends that enforcement of the oral agreement between plaintiff and himself is barred by Civil Code section 5134, which provides that "All contracts for marriage settlements must be in writing. . . ." A marriage settlement, however, is an agreement in contemplation of marriage in which each party agrees to release or modify the property rights which would otherwise arise from the marriage. The contract at issue here does not conceivably fall within that definition, and thus is beyond compass of section 5134.

Defendant finally argues that enforcement of the contract is barred by Civil Code section 43.5, subdivision (d), which provides that "No cause of action arises for . . . [b]reach of a promise of marriage." This rather strained contention proceeds from the premise that a promise of marriage impliedly includes a promise to support and to pool property acquired after marriage to the conclusion that pooling and support agreements not part of or accompanied by promise of marriage are barred by the section. We conclude that section 43.5 is not reasonably susceptible to the interpretation advanced by defendant, a conclusion demonstrated by the fact that since section 43.5 was enacted in 1939, numerous cases have enforced pooling agreements between nonmarital partners, and in none did court or counsel refer to section 43.5.

In summary, we base our opinion on the principle that adults who voluntarily live together and engage in sexual relations are nonetheless as competent as any other persons to contract respecting their earnings and property rights. Of course, they cannot lawfully contract to pay for the performance of sexual services, for such a contract is, in essence, an agreement for prostitution and unlawful for that reason. But they may agree to pool their earnings and to hold all property acquired during the relationship in accord with the law governing community property; conversely they may agree that each partner's earnings and the property acquired from those earnings remains the separate property of the earnings partner. So long as the agreement does not rest upon illicit meretricious consideration, the parties may order their economic affairs as they choose, and no policy precludes the courts from enforcing such agreements.

In the present instance, plaintiff alleges that the parties agreed to pool their earnings, that they contracted to share equally in all property acquired, and that defendant agreed to support plaintiff. The terms of the contract as alleged do not rest upon any unlawful consideration. We therefore conclude that the complaint furnishes a suitable basis upon which the trial court can render declaratory relief. The trial court consequently erred in granting defendant's motion for judgment on the pleadings.

DECISION: The lower court decision for Lee Marvin was reversed and remanded for new trial.

CASE NOTE

The trial court, upon remand, found that the evidence did not show that Ms. Marvin gave up her career at Mr. Marvin's request or for his benefit. Further, the court found that the couple's words and conduct showed neither an express nor implied contract to share property. The court found that performance of "homemaking" services for a paramour does not of itself imply a contract to share property since such things are frequently done for other reasons, such as shared affection. Having found no expressed or implied contract, the court, in equity, awarded $104,000 to Ms. Marvin for rehabilitation purposes. (See Case No. C-23303, Memorandum Opinion, Superior Court of the State of California, County of Los Angeles, April 18, 1979, reprinted in 5FLR 3077, 3983–3085 [1979].)

Mr. Marvin appealed this decision, and the California Court of Appeals reversed the trial court, stating that there was no basis in equity or in law for awarding Ms. Marvin $104,000 to rehabilitate herself (122 Cal. App. 3d.871 [1981]).

In states where *Marvin* is followed, unmarried couples may enter into enforceable cohabitation agreements as long as they are not based on the provision of sexual services. Such agreements generally outline how expenses will be shared during the relationship and how the couple's property will be divided in the event of a breakup. In many states, cohabitation agreements are not enforced on the grounds that they violate the public policy in favor of promoting marriage and traditional families.

When a court refuses to enforce a contract on public-policy grounds, it is essentially saying that the enforcement of the contract would violate the community's sense of right and wrong. There is no formal procedure for a court to determine what public policy is. This determination is generally made by the judge based on his or her personal understanding of community morality. The case that follows, *In the Matter of Baby M,* is another highly publicized case that turned on the court's understanding of public policy. The effect that public policy considerations have on the enforceability of contracts will be discussed in greater detail in Chapter 16.

IN THE MATTER OF BABY M

Supreme Court of New Jersey
537 A.2d 1227 (1988)

BACKGROUND: William Stern entered into a surrogate parenting contract with Mary Beth Whitehead. The contract provided that Whitehead would be artificially inseminated with Mr. Stern's sperm and would carry his child to term. The contract called for Whitehead, upon the birth of the child, to hand the child over to William Stern and his wife, Elizabeth, and to take whatever steps were necessary to terminate her rights to the child. The child was then to be adopted by Elizabeth Stern and raised by the Sterns. Whitehead was to receive $10,000 for her services.

During her pregnancy, Whitehead developed a very strong emotional attachment to the child. Whitehead gave birth to a girl and delivered her to the Sterns. Having become despondent about her separation from the child, Whitehead pleaded with the Sterns to allow the child to stay with Whitehead for 1 week. The Sterns agreed, fearing that Whitehead would commit suicide if they refused. Whitehead subsequently refused to return the child and eventually fled her home in New Jersey with the child. The child was recovered 4 months later at Whitehead's parents' home in Florida. The Sterns sued to enforce the surrogacy agreement and to obtain exclusive custody of the child. The trial court ruled in the Sterns' favor and terminated Whitehead's parental rights. Whitehead appealed.

Wilentz, Chief Justice

The point is made that Mrs. Whitehead *agreed* to the surrogacy arrangement, supposedly fully understanding the consequences. Putting aside the issue of how compelling her need for money may have been, and how significant her understanding of the consequences, we suggest that her consent is irrelevant. There are, in a civilized society, some things that money cannot buy. In America, we decided long ago that merely because conduct purchased by money was "voluntary" did not mean that it was good or beyond regulation and prohibition. Employers can no longer buy labor at the lowest price they can bargain for, even though that labor is "voluntary," or buy women's labor for less money than paid to men for the same job, or purchase the agreement of children to perform oppressive labor, or purchase the agreement of workers to subject themselves to unsafe or unhealthful working conditions. There are, in short, values that society deems more important than granting to wealth whatever it can buy, be it labor, love, or life. Whether this principle recommends prohibition of surrogacy, which presumably sometimes results in great satisfaction to all of the parties, is not for us to say. We note here only that, under existing law, the fact that Mrs. Whitehead "agreed" to the arrangement is not dispositive.

The long-term effects of surrogacy contracts are not known, but feared—the impact on the child who learns her life was bought, that she is the offspring of someone who gave birth to her only to obtain money; the impact on the natural mother as the full weight of her isolation is felt along with the full reality of the sale of her body and her child; the impact on the natural father and adoptive mother once they realize the consequences of their conduct. Literature in related areas suggests these are substantial considerations, although, given the newness of surrogacy, there is little information.

The surrogacy contract is based on principles that are directly contrary to the objectives of our laws. It guarantees the separation of a child from its mother; it looks to adoption regardless of suitability; it totally ignores the child; it takes the child from the mother regardless of her wishes and her maternal fitness; and it does all of this, it accomplishes all of its goals, through the use of money.

Beyond that is the potential degradation of some women that may result from this arrangement. In many cases, of course, surrogacy may bring satisfaction, not only to the infertile couple, but to the surrogate mother herself. The fact, however, that many women may not perceive surrogacy negatively but rather see it as an opportunity does not diminish its potential for devastation to other women.

DECISION: The Supreme Court of New Jersey ruled that Whitehead's contractual agreement to give up her child was null and void because it violated public policy. The court affirmed the award of custody to the Sterns but reversed the termination of Whitehead's parental rights. The court ruled that Whitehead was entitled to visitation rights.

FIGURE 10-1

Forming a Binding Contract

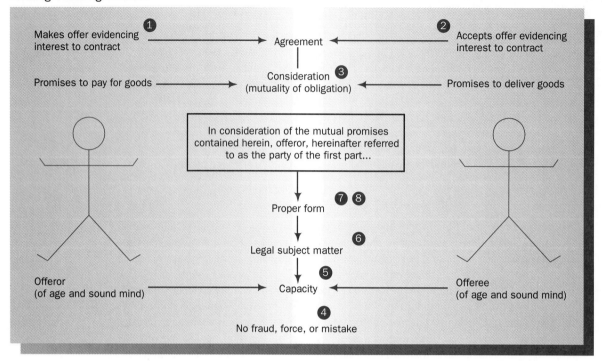

Contract Defined

The issues posed earlier in this chapter will be discussed in the following chapters as the basic outline of the law of contracts is presented. For now, we need to define a *contract*. A **contract** is an agreement that the courts will recognize and enforce. What do the courts require before an agreement will be recognized and enforced? The following list represents the elements of enforceability for most types of contracts in most jurisdictions. In parentheses the reader will find the chapter in this text that discusses each element.

1. A valid offer (Chapter 11)
2. A proper acceptance (Chapter 12)
3. Sufficiency of consideration (Chapter 13)
4. Absence of fraud, force, or legally significant mistake (Chapter 14)
5. Legal capacity of parties (Chapter 15)
6. Consistency with general public policy (Chapter 16)
7. Observance of proper legal form (Chapter 17)
8. Consistency with special rules governing the type of agreement involved (throughout Part III).

The relationship between the eight requirements is dramatized in Figure 10-1. This figure, which captures the various requirements for an enforceable contract, is intended as a reference and will be more meaningful as you progress through this part of the text. We recommend that you refer back to it as you study contract law.

Source of Contract Law

General contract law has a common law basis. This means that the principles of contract law are to be found in judicial decisions of cases involving contractual disputes. Under the doctrine of precedent, or *stare decisis*, courts will follow their earlier decisions involving similar situations. This principle of consistency in judicial decision making produces fields of judicially made law, such as contracts, torts, and agency. With the exception of Louisiana, no state has a comprehensive statute promulgating contract law.

There are, however, a number of statutes that spell out special rules for certain types of contracts. For example, state statutes regulate the use of insurance contracts. The most important of the state statutes affecting contract law is the Uniform

Commercial Code (UCC). The UCC, which has been adopted at least in part by the legislatures of all fifty states, established a series of rules dealing with all aspects of commercial transactions. One part of the UCC, Article 2, contains rules governing sales contracts. (Article 2 of the UCC is included in full in the Appendix.) If the UCC does not provide a rule covering an aspect of a sales contract, the general common law of contracts controls. If there is a UCC rule, it governs sales contracts even when the common law rule is to the contrary. This relationship is spelled out in Figure 10-2.

Many international transactions involving the sale of goods are governed by the UN Convention on Contracts for the International Sale of Goods (CISG), which went into effect in 1988. At least twenty-five countries, including the United States and many of its major trading partners, are party to the CISG. The CISG applies to any sales transaction where the buyer's and seller's respective places of business are in different signatory countries, unless the parties provide otherwise. Thus, a French company's sale of wine to a U.S. importer would be governed by the CISG (unless the parties provide otherwise), since both France and the U.S. are parties to the CISG. The CISG does not apply to transactions between a company in the United States and a company whose place of business is in a nonsignatory country. However, the applicability of the CISG depends on the party's *place of business*, not its national-ity. So if a corporation chartered by and based in the Republic of Utopia, which is not a CISG signatory, has a plant in France, sales transactions between the French plant and companies located in other signatory countries would be governed by the CISG.

The CISG includes many provisions similar to those found in Article 2 of the UCC, but it also reflects trading practices favored by various countries other than the United States.

Several basic points regarding the true nature of contracts must now be made. First, almost all contracts are voluntarily carried out by the parties to their mutual satisfaction, so the judicial system never becomes involved. This is due in part to the fear of legal sanctions, but also results from observance of the ethical duty to act in good faith in business transactions.

Second, the mere fact that one has a legal right to sue for breach of contract does not mean that it is a sound business decision to do so. Before a suit is filed, factors such as likelihood of again doing business with the other party, industry attitudes about litigious businesses, relative economic strength of the parties, and alternative private means of resolving the dispute should be considered. Third, although we will be discussing basic rules pertaining to contracts in general, there are many specific categories of contracts that have certain individualized rules of law pertaining to them.

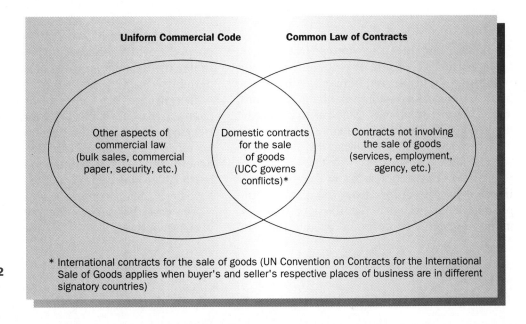

FIGURE 10-2

Sources of Contract Law

* International contracts for the sale of goods (UN Convention on Contracts for the International Sale of Goods applies when buyer's and seller's respective places of business are in different signatory countries)

Classification of Contracts

The following classification of contracts seeks to aid the reader in analyzing problems related to contracts as they are covered in subsequent chapters. It will be assumed there that the reader is familiar with these categories of contracts and the terminology involved.

Express, Implied, and Quasi Contracts

An **express contract** is one formed by the words of the parties, either oral or written. A **contract implied-in-fact** is derived from the actions of the parties. Going to a doctor, describing symptoms, and accepting treatment establishes a contract implied-in-fact. The test is whether a reasonable person would intend to contract by engaging in such actions.

A **quasi contract**, also known as a **contract implied-in-law**, differs from express and implied-in-fact contracts in that the parties did not intend to make a contract. In creating the legal fiction of a quasi contract, the courts are not trying to fathom the intentions of the parties; they are simply trying to be fair. Suppose, for example, that a doctor performed expensive and valuable services upon a patient who had suddenly become unconscious in the doctor's waiting room. There is clearly no express contract. Further, many courts would refuse to recognize a contract implied-in-fact because no intention could be inferred regarding any actions of the patient. A quasi contract could be posited, however, that would require the patient to pay the reasonable value of the services rendered.

In order for the courts to recognize a quasi contract, there must be (1) a benefit or unjust enrichment retained by the benefited party and (2) no other legal recourse for the "victim" of the benefit. The victim is entitled to recover only the reasonable value of the benefit—not what would have been a likely contract price.

The case that follows illustrates the doctrine of quasi contract.

U.S. v. Summit General Contracting Corp.

U.S. District Court, Eastern District of New York

760 F.Supp. 1004 (1991)

Background: Summit was the general contractor chosen to construct the Naval Telecommunications Center (NTCC) for the U.S. Navy. Falco was a subcontractor hired by Summit to do pile-driving work for the project. After Falco had completed its work, the Navy revised the project's design in a manner that required additional pile-driving work to be performed. Summit requested Falco to perform the additional work, but Summit and Falco never agreed on a price for it. Falco did the additional work but did not receive additional compensation. Falco sued.

Bartels, District Judge

The defendants' claim that there was no separate oral arrangement between Summit and Falco for Falco to return to drive additional piles on July 13, 1989 is belied by the evidence, and the Court has so found. The uncontroverted evidence adduced at trial was that Falco was advised by Summit, on or about May 19, 1989 to dismantle and remove its rig from the construction site because the pile driving phase of the project was complete and the piles were acceptable. Approximately five weeks later, Vrettos, Summit's project manager, contacted KK, Falco's engineer, and advised him that due to pile cap redesign additional piles had to be driven. Inasmuch as the sub-contract specifically excluded any additional work due to redesign of this nature it is obvious that Falco remobilized its crew and equipment and returned to the NTCC because of a separate and distinct arrangement between itself and Summit to enable Summit to comply with the Navy's directive, and not because of any duty Falco owed Summit under the sub-contract.

Under New York law no contract can be formed where the parties have not agreed on an essential term, such as price. The undisputed evidence was that the parties had not agreed on the price Summit would pay Falco to return to the NTCC. Therefore, the oral arrangement is unenforceable and fails to supply the basis for Falco's claim to costs associated with the work it performed on July 13, 1989.

This, however, does not end the Court's inquiry. Since the Court is guided by equitable as well as legal principles Falco may recover for the additional work it performed in July under the theory of quasi contract. "A 'quasi contract' only applies in the absence of an express agreement, and it is not really a contract at all, but rather a legal obligation imposed in order to prevent a party's unjust enrichment." *Clark–Fitzpatrick v. Long Island R.R. Co.* The sub-contract did not encompass the relationship between the parties with respect to the work performed on July 13, 1989 and there is no other enforceable agreement between the parties for that work. Moreover, it is obvious that Summit derived a substantial benefit from the work Falco performed on July 13, 1989. Therefore, since Summit requested that Falco return to the NTCC to do additional work for which Falco would receive additional monies, and Falco in fact rendered services in accordance with that request, Falco should recover the reasonable costs associated with the work it performed on July 13, 1989.

Decision: The federal district court ruled in favor of Falco.

Executed and Executory Contracts

An **executed contract** is one in which all required performances have been rendered. A goes to B's garage, picks up a new tire, and pays B. The contract has been fully performed. Nothing remains to be done by either party. An **executory contract** is one in which some of the required performance remains to be done. A and B enter

---

ISSUES AND TRENDS
An International Comparison of Contracting

Contracting is more formal in the United States than in many other countries. The classical or formal approach to contracting involves relatively elaborate contracts which are subject to stringent tests before they will be enforced by the courts. In using formal contracts, the parties try to anticipate most of the problems that are likely to arise in the future. Thus, the contract will contain many clauses that deal with potential risks of loss, or the ability of the parties subsequently to transfer interests under the contract to someone else.

Japan is an example of a less formal system of contracting. There, a relational approach is taken. The parties from a relationship based on the mutual understanding that they will work out problems as they arise in the future. The initial agreement is less elaborate because there is no attempt to anticipate many future developments.

Many international transactions involving agreements between firms from different countries depend upon arbitration as a way of resolving disputes. The disparate legal rules and varying expectations often involved in international business produce a need for specialized expertise when disagreements occur. There is a system of international arbitration that responds to the need for dispute resolution.

Each approach has its advantages. Formal contracting reduces the chances that a party's basic expectancies under the contract will be defeated. Relational contracting is less expensive and time-consuming in the first instance because the agreement is more basic and simple. Further, the mindset of the parties may make it more likely that they can work out problems as they inevitably arise in the future. Arbitration takes the problem out of the hands of the parties and yet can provide a quick resolution that is sensitive to the special requirements of the disputing firms.

---

an agreement whereby B agrees to repair A's car in 2 weeks and A agrees to pay B $100 upon completion. Since neither party has performed his or her part of the agreement, it is executory in nature. This distinction is significant, because the courts will be influenced by the performance status of an executory contract in determining the relief to be given to the victim of a breach of contract. Remedies are discussed in Chapter 16.

Valid, Void, and Voidable Contracts

A **valid contract** is one that is perfectly good and that may be enforced by all parties to it. A **void contract**, on the other hand, is not good; it is not enforceable by anyone. A void contract is a contradiction in terms in that it is not really a contract under our definition. For example, if A contracts with B to kill C, who is A's wife, the failure of B to perform will not be grounds for a suit by A because a legally enforceable contract never existed. A **voidable contract** has an in-between status. It is currently valid, but one or more of the

parties has the power to render the contract unenforceable. A, a minor, contracts with B, who is of legal age, to paint B's house. The contract is voidable by A. As explained in Chapter 15, A has the right to disaffirm the agreement anytime before reaching majority and shortly thereafter.

Bilateral and Unilateral Contracts

A contract may involve an exchange of promises in which two parties agree that each will perform in a certain way in the future. Player promises to abide by the team rules and be available to play baseball for the coming season. Team promises to pay Player $85,000 for the year. At the moment the contract is signed, neither party starts performing. Instead, the agreed-upon performance will take place in the future. The exchange of a promise for a promise is known as a **bilateral contract**.

Suppose Team promises to pay Player $2,000 for every home run over thirty during the season. Player has not promised to hit more than thirty home runs and will not be in breach of contract

---

CONCEPT SUMMARY
Classification of Contracts

Context	Terms	Distinctions
Manifestation of intent	Express	Formed by the words of the parties, either oral or written.
	Implied-in-fact	Derived from the action of the parties. Test: Would a reasonable person intend to contract by engaging in the act?
	Implied-in-law	A legal fiction wherein contractual rights are imputed in an attempt to be fair. No actual agreement exists.
Enforceability	Valid	Enforceable by all parties.
	Void	Not enforceable by anyone.
	Voidable	Currently valid, but may be rendered unenforceable by one or more parties.
Manner of acceptance	Bilateral	Offer seeks acceptance by promise.
	Unilateral	Offer seeks acceptance by performance.

---

for failing to do so. Instead, Team has made a promise that performance will be forthcoming in exchange for an act. This is an offer of a **unilateral contract** that can be accepted only by performance of the act. Most commercial contracts are bilateral. The various definitions are diagrammed in the accompanying Concept Summary.

Review Questions and Problems

Key Terms

contract

express contract

contract implied-in-fact

quasi contract

contract implied-in-law

executed contract

executory contract

valid contract

void contract

voidable contract

bilateral contract

unilateral contract

Discussion Questions

1. What elements must be present before the courts will enforce a contract?

2. What is meant by the statement that contracts is a "common law field"?

3. What contracts are governed by the UCC?

4. How does a contract implied-in-law differ from one implied-in-fact?

Review Problems

1. Cone has a house in a development that looks very similar to his neighbor's house. The neighbor orders landscaping done. The landscaper arrives and starts working on Cone's house. Cone sees the landscaper and does nothing until the lawn has been leveled and several attractive bushes have been planted. Landscaper sues Cone. Result?

2. Suppose that Cone had been gone all day and that Cone did not like the work done. Would that change the outcome in the case?

3. A seller "lists" a house for sale with a real estate broker, thereby promising to pay a 7 percent commission if the broker finds a buyer ready, willing, and able to buy for $75,000. What kind of contract is this?

4. John Doe requests that Jack Maverick paint his house, promising that he will pay him $1,200 when Maverick finishes. Maverick paints the house. What type of contract is this?

Case Problems

1. On December 20, Johnson wrote Cook and offered to pay Cook for cleaning out a drainage ditch and doing some other odd jobs. Cook replied in a letter on December 23 and promised to do the work.

Meantime Johnson sold the ranch to Fink on January 22. A heavy frost prevented Cook from doing the work until April. When he finally finished the work, Cook sent a bill to Johnson for $1,790. Must Johnson pay the bill? Would it make any difference in your answer if Cook was aware of the sale to Fink before he did the job?

2. The Millers had several marital disputes and ultimately tried to resolve them by signing a contract among themselves. Under the contract, Mr. Miller agreed to pay Mrs. Miller $200 a year and provide for "the necessary expenses of the family." Mrs. Miller agreed to "keep her home and family in a comfortable and reasonably good condition" and both agreed to "refrain from scolding, fault-finding, and anger, insofar as relates to the future, and to use every means within their power to promote peace and harmony." Mr. Miller stopped making the payments and Mrs. Miller sued to enforce the contract. Decision?

3. Richardson asked the J.C. Flood Company to clear a clogged sewer line. The snake cable used in clearing the line became stuck, and when the line was excavated to free the cable, it was discovered that an adjacent water line was leaking. Local laws required that a certain quality water line be used. The J.C. Flood Company replaced the water line while they had the ground opened up. Richardson had been informed of the necessity to excavate and to do additional work to clear the sewer line, and that there was a problem with the water line. When Richardson received a bill for the work done, she refused to pay for the work on the water line. Must Richardson pay the full bill?

4. McCall met rock star Peter Frampton while she was still married to someone else. They moved in together. After they broke up, McCall sued Frampton for breach of an oral agreement. McCall claimed that under their agreement, McCall was to leave her husband, move in with Frampton, and devote herself to promoting Frampton's career. In return, Frampton was to share his income with McCall. Should this contract, if proven, be enforceable? Discuss.

5. Andrews was a Seventh Day Adventist who was forbidden by his religion from working on his Sabbath (sundown Friday to sundown Saturday). Before applying for a job as a bus driver for the New York City Transit Authority, he advised the authority that he could not work on his Sabbath. Andrews was nonetheless hired. When he was scheduled to work on Saturday, he tried to get another driver to change shifts with him. He was unable to find a substitute and didn't show up for work, after which he was suspended without pay. Andrews sued, claiming that the Transit Authority had a quasi-contractual obligation to allow him not to work on his Sabbath because they allowed him to be tested and trained for his job with the full knowledge of his religious requirements. The Transit Authority argued that it made every effort to accommodate Andrews' schedule, but that when they were unable to do so it was Andrews' responsibility to either show up for work or find a replacement. What result?

11

The Offer

Requirements for an Offer   Termination of the Offer

I t is important for parties negotiating an agreement to know if that agreement will be enforced by the legal system. Usually, neither party envisions the need to resort to legal action to enforce their agreement (or to recover monetary damages) if the other party has not performed as agreed. Yet each party wants the assurance that, if it becomes necessary, he or she can reasonably expect the law and its institutions to stand behind the agreement.

The law of contracts defines and determines which agreements will be recognized and enforced. Since contract law requires a valid offer to have been made in order for an agreement to be recognized as an enforceable contract, we begin our study of contract law with this requirement.

Requirements for an Offer

An **offer** is a proposal that manifests intent to enter into a contract. The offer is made by the **offeror** to the **offeree.** If the offer is valid and still in force, then the offeree's acceptance of the offer creates a valid contract and binds both parties to the terms of the offer.

In order for a valid offer to exist, contract law requires the offer to:

1. Manifest the intent to enter into a contract
2. Be definite and certain regarding the essential terms of the proposed contract
3. Be communicated to the offeree.

Each of these requirements is discussed in detail in this chapter.

Once the existence of an offer has been determined, the question of whether the offer still exists at the time of its acceptance may arise. Has the offer terminated? How long do offers last before they expire? What brings about the termination of an offer? Questions related to the termination of an offer are discussed at the end of this chapter.

Intent to Contract

Determining Intent How should a person's intent be determined? Consider the following situations. Suppose you are at a used-car dealer's lot. The price of a car you like is listed as $3,995. You ask the salesperson what he'd take for the car; he doesn't answer you, but responds by asking you what you would offer. If you then say, "I wouldn't pay the list price, but I might pay $3,000 if I could finance it," have you made an offer? Did you intend by that statement to commit to a contract?

An auctioneer selling home furnishings announces at the start of the auction that anyone who wants to bid on an item should simply raise his or her hand when he asks for a certain price. If you, in gesturing to a friend with whom you are talking, raise your hand while the auctioneer is asking for a $500 bid for a couch, have you offered to buy it? Are you intending to contract?

Suppose you receive an advertisement in the mail listing the prices of hundreds of items the local department store wants to sell. Have you received an offer? Did the store intend to make an offer to any person receiving or reading its advertisement? To answer these questions, we must first consider how a person's intent is ascertained.

Is intent determined by examining what a person was thinking when he or she said something? Does the law look into a person's mind to determine his or her thoughts? Do we simply ask the person what his or her intentions were? A person's actual intentions are very difficult to determine. In fact, a person's subjective state is not susceptible to discovery or verification.

Instead, the law seeks to determine intent entirely by objective standards. What would a reasonable person observing the actions and hearing the statements of the offeror conclude about the offeror's intentions of entering into a contract? The evidence of the offeror's intent is determined not by examining that person's inner feelings, but by reviewing the offeror's actions and words as perceived by a reasonable person.

Social Invitation, Excitement, or Jest

The law presumes that there is no objective manifestation of intent to contract in situations involving social invitations. Thus, an invitation to a wedding, even one requesting an RSVP, would not be considered an offer to contract. Similarly, an invitation to attend the movies or to come for dinner is not an offer to contract. Therefore, an acceptance does not impose a contractual obligation on the inviter.

Suppose that someone makes a statement in the midst of an exciting event. As I watch my favorite basketball team fall behind in a play-off game, I exclaim to you and to everyone else who can hear me, "These bums are worthless! I'd sell my tickets to the finals for 2 cents!" Should the law treat my statement as an offer that invites your acceptance?

If it was apparent to you that I was upset and you should have known that I did not really in-

tend to contract, there will not be the requisite manifestation of intent. Factors to be considered in determining whether I manifested contractual intent include the correlation between the "offer" price and the value of the object, whether from an objective viewpoint I appeared excited and upset, and whether we had discussed the sale of the tickets at some previous time.

Sometimes, a statement will be made in jest; there is no manifestation of the intent to contract because the offeror was only kidding. Informal bets often fall into this category: "I'll bet you $100 you can't throw the ball through the hoop." Similarly, the prankster who says, "I'd pay $1,000 to anyone who gives my boss an exploding cigar," cannot be taken seriously. Yet the jester must be careful if the joke relates to a situation where the other party might take the joke seriously. If a reasonable person would interpret an offeror's words and acts as the expression of intent to enter a contract, there will be a binding agreement even if the offeror was joking.

Advertisement of Goods for Sale Do advertisements in the newspaper constitute offers? If they do, the reader can go into the store and say "I accept" and thereby create a contractual obligation for the store. If 5 people or 50 or 5,000 accept, the store would have to fulfill all acceptances or else be liable for breach of contract.

Courts have interpreted the law as not imposing such an unfair burden on each business advertiser. Thus, as a general principle, advertisements do not constitute offers. However, if the advertiser uses language in the advertisement that, to the reasonable reader, expresses a commitment to contract, the courts will enforce a contract resulting from the offeree's acceptance of the seller's advertisement. While the *Lefkowitz* case is thus an illustration of the application of the exception to the general rule of law, it has become a classic involving the possible interpretation of advertisements as offers.

LEFKOWITZ V. GREAT MINNEAPOLIS SURPLUS STORE

Supreme Court of Minnesota
86 N.W.2d 689 (1957)

BACKGROUND: Lefkowitz (plaintiff) brought suit against the Great Minneapolis Surplus Store (defendant) to enforce a contract he had made to purchase a fur offered for sale by the defendant in a newspaper advertisement. The defendant responded that its advertisement was not an offer, and therefore no contract had been made between it and the plaintiff. The trial court found that a contract did exist and ordered a judgment for the plaintiff in the amount of $138.50. The defendant's request to the trial court for a new trial was denied and the defendant then appealed for review by the Minnesota Supreme Court.

Murphy, Justice

This case grows out of the alleged refusal of the defendant to sell to the plaintiff a certain fur piece which it had offered for sale in a newspaper advertisement. It appears from the record that on April 6, 1956, the defendant published the following advertisement in a Minneapolis newspaper:

> Saturday 9 A.M. Sharp
> 3 Brand New
> Fur
> Coats
> Worth to $100.00
> First Come
> First Served
> $1
> Each

On April 13, the defendant again published an advertisement in the same newspaper as follows:

> Saturday 9 A.M.
> 2 Brand New Pastel
> Mink 3-Skin Scarfs
> Selling for $89.50
> Out they go
> Saturday. Each. . . . $1.00
> 1 Black Lapin Stole
> Beautiful
> Worth $139.50. . . . $1.00
> First Come
> First Served

The record supports the findings of the court that on each of the Saturdays following the publication of the above-described ads the plaintiff was the first to present himself at the appropriate counter in the defendant's store and on each occasion demanded the coat and the stole so advertised and indicated his readiness to pay the sale price of $1. On both occasions, the defendant refused to sell the merchandise to the plaintiff, stating on the first occasion that by a "house rule" the offer was intended for women only and sales would not be made to men, and on the second visit that plaintiff knew defendant's house rules.

The trial court properly disallowed plaintiff's claim for the value of the fur coats since the value of these articles was speculative and uncertain. The only evidence of value was the advertisement itself to the effect that the coats were "Worth to $100.00," how much less being speculative especially in view of the price for which they were offered for sale. With reference to the offer of the defendant on April 13, 1956, to sell the "1 Black Lapin Stole . . . worth $139.50 . . ." the trial court held that the value of this article was established and granted judgment in favor of the plaintiff for that amount less the $1 quoted purchase price.

The defendant contends that a newspaper advertisement offering items of merchandise for sale at a named price is a "unilateral offer" which may be withdrawn without notice. He relies upon authorities which hold that, where an advertiser publishes in a newspaper that he has a certain quantity or quality of goods which he wants to dispose of at certain prices and on certain terms, such advertisements are not offers which become contracts as soon as any person to whose notice they may come signifies his acceptance by notifying the other that he will take a certain quantity of them. Such advertisements instead have been construed as an invitation for an offer of sale on the terms stated, which offer, when received, may be accepted or rejected by the seller and which therefore does not become a contract of sale until such acceptance. Thus, until a contract has been so made, the seller may modify or revoke such prices or terms as it has advertised.

However, there are numerous authorities which hold that a particular advertisement in a newspaper or circular letter relating to a sale of articles may be construed by the court as constituting an offer, the acceptance of which would complete a contract. The test of whether a binding obligation may originate in advertisements addressed to the general public is whether the facts show that some performance was promised in positive terms in return for something requested. . . .

Whether in any individual instance a newspaper advertisement is an offer rather than an invitation to make an offer depends on the legal intention of the parties and the surrounding circumstances. We are of the view on the facts before us that the offer by the defendant of the sale of the Lapin fur was clear, definite, and explicit, and left nothing open for negotiation. The plaintiff having successfully managed to be the first one to appear at the seller's place of business to be served, as requested by the advertisement, and having offered the stated purchase price of the article, he was entitled to performance on the part of the defendant. . . .

The defendant contends that the offer was modified by a "house rule" to the effect that only women were qualified to receive the bargains advertised. The advertisement contained no such restriction. This objection may be disposed of briefly by stating that, while an advertiser has the right at any time before acceptance to modify his offer, he does not have the right, after acceptance, to impose new or arbitrary conditions not contained in the published offer.

DECISION: The trial court's decision was affirmed. Lefkowitz accepted a valid offer and Great Minneapolis must perform or pay damages.

Definite and Certain Terms

The second requirement of an offer is that it be definite and certain regarding the essential terms of the proposed contract. As the court in the *Lefkowitz* case concluded, where the offeror's statement is clear, definite, and explicit and leaves nothing open for negotiation, an offer (not merely an invitation to make an offer) has been made. What terms must be expressed in order for a statement to be construed as an offer?

If I offer to sell you my 1994 Honda Accord and you agree, do we have a contract? We have omitted the most basic element of an agreement—the price. Would a court seek to complete our agreement for us? How would it do so? Reference to a standard used car price or a trade price such as is found in a Blue Book wouldn't be of much help. My car could have been driven 5,000 miles or 50,000 miles. It could have been well cared for or poorly cared for. Thus, there is no ready reference point that a court could use to enforce this agreement. Since a court does not wish to make a contract where the parties themselves have failed to do so, it would conclude that no offer was made by me when I proposed to sell you my car. Therefore, your agreement in response was not an acceptance of an offer. Obviously, no contract resulted from our expressions.

The general legal principle requires that an offer define the essential terms of performance by both the offeror and the offeree. One of the essential terms that an offer must contain is the subject matter of the proposed transaction. Is the offeror going to sell a car? What car? Does the sale of the car include the sale of the ski rack on top of the car? The spare tire in the trunk? The offer must reasonably identify the subject matter.

A second essential term that an offer must include is the quantity of items being offered. A farmer proposing to sell wheat to a bakery must specify how much wheat he wants to sell. A furni-

ture dealer's agreement to sell you "bedroom furniture" for $500 would be too vague unless it specified how many items were included in the offer.

Finally, as the first example regarding the used car sale illustrates, the price of the item offered for sale must be specified. The price is specified if it is either fixed or easily determinable. My offer to lend you $1,000 at the prime interest rate in effect at the Chase Manhattan Bank is specific. While the offer doesn't state exactly what that rate of interest actually is, the rate is determinable.

The case that follows, *Simmons v. All American Life Insurance*, illustrates the need for definite terms in a contract. When multiple written communications are exchanged, it is sometimes unclear when the contract is actually formed. In this case, a young man's unexpected death required the resolution of the question of when a valid offer to contract was accepted.

SIMMONS V. ALL AMERICAN LIFE INSURANCE
Court of Appeals of Oregon
838 P.2d 1088 (1992)

BACKGROUND: Plaintiffs are beneficiaries under a $25,000 life insurance policy they claim their deceased son had with the defendant. The University of Utah Alumni Association (Association) had bought $5,000, nine month policies from the defendant as gifts for alumni who wished to enroll. In May, 1989, plaintiff's son (decedent) enrolled in this $5,000 program by returning a certificate sent to him by the Association, and the Association paid the premium for this initial coverage. That certificate of insurance indicated that when this nine month policy expired, he had the "guaranteed option to continue to be insured" for an additional $25,000, without taking a medical exam or answering any health questions, as long as he paid the first premium. The Association acknowledged the decedent's enrollment in October, 1989, and confirmed the availability of the $25,000 coverage. According to the letter, all he had to do was "verify [his] beneficiary and pay the premium."

On March 8, 1990, the following documents (mailed March 5th) were received at decedent's address: a letter, a brochure, a certificate of insurance for a $25,000 group term life insurance policy, and a continuation form for a "Graduate Gift Term Life Insurance Plan-Phase 2." Unfortunately, plaintiffs' son had been injured in an accident the day before, March 7, 1990, and did not regain consciousness before dying on April 3, 1990. Ten days after decedent's death, plaintiffs' attorney mailed a check for $26.75 to cover the first premium, enclosed a continuation form which the attorney signed "for [decedent]," and asked for the forms needed to claim the $25,000 policy proceeds. When the insurance company refused to pay, the plaintiffs brought an action in the County Court and were awarded the $25,000 in benefits. The insurance company then appealed the trial court's decision to the Court of Appeals of Oregon.

Edmonds, Judge

Defendant argues that decedent did not accept its offer to insure his life for $25,000 before he died. Plaintiffs contend that a binding contract for the $25,000 occurred when decedent accepted Association's offer by enrolling in the program in May, 1989.

An offer must be certain so that, when an unqualified acceptance occurs, there will be a meeting of the minds as to the obligations that each assumes under the contract (citations omitted). In order to have a valid contract of insurance, the amount of the premium must be agreed on, expressly or impliedly. None of the documents decedent received from Association in May, 1989, included information about the amount of the premium that he would be required to pay for the $25,000 policy. The first reference to the premium was in Association's October, 1989, letter that was mailed to decedent after he had purportedly accepted the offer. The amount of the premium was an essential term in the agreement to insure decedent's life for $25,000. Until decedent was aware of the amount and had agreed to pay it, he could not have entered into an enforceable agreement to purchase the $25,000 insurance policy. When he sent in the certificate for the $5,000 coverage in May, 1989, he did not have that information. Accordingly, the correspondence could not constitute an offer, because it was too indefinite.

DECISION: The trial court was reversed and the insurance company did not have to pay the $25,000 life insurance benefits.

The Uniform Commercial Code has substantially liberalized the definite-and-certain-terms requirement as it applies to the sale of goods. Most contracts covered by the UCC involve business transactions between experienced parties. The business world has many established reference points for value, such as organized trading exchanges and arms-length private sales transactions involving goods identical to the ones in question.

In recognition of these facts Section 2-204(3) of the UCC provides that a sales contract is valid even though it leaves open essential terms if (1) the parties nevertheless intended to make a contract *and* (2) there is a "reasonably certain basis for giving an appropriate remedy." Further, Section 2-305 provides that purposefully leaving open the price term is not fatal and that in such cases the price is to be a reasonable price. Note that under Section 2-305 we would have made a contract for the sale of my used Honda *if* we had intended to leave the price open while binding ourselves to a contract. Sections 2-308 and 309 also specify how the terms are to be filled in if nothing is said as to place of delivery or time for delivery. Under the UCC, however, it is still necessary to specify the quantity term in order for an offer to form the basis of an enforceable agreement.

Communication of the Offer

General Rule   The third requirement that must be met for a valid offer to exist is that the offer be communicated to the party for whom the offer is intended. The communication may be expressed or implied. For example, if the offeree learns of an offer from a third person who is not the offeror and the offer is a general offer susceptible of acceptance by anyone who learns of it, the offeree has the power to accept the communicated offer. Communication is usually not a problem with offers. Two recurring situations, however, present legal problems regarding the effect to be given to the communication of an offer.

The Reward Offer   The first of these is the case of a reward. A reward is an offer for a unilateral contract. It is not unusual for someone to perform the act bargained for in the reward offer without knowing about the reward. If this occurs, then under the technical rules of contract law the party performing the act is not entitled to the reward. But that does not represent sound policy when viewed in the context of the reasonable expectations of our society. Most people expect that rewards will be paid if their terms are met. As a consequence, many states provide by statute that rewards will be enforceable regardless of whether the person performing the act called for in the offer first received a communication of the offer of a reward.

The Fine-Print Offer   The second situation involves what might be called the fine-print problem. Consumers may often be asked to sign contracts that contain a myriad of fine-print provisions, many of which are quite harsh. For example, a price-adjustment clause may increase the price of a car over the contract price before delivery, or a waiver clause may surrender the consumer's rights to resist the entering of a legal judgment against him upon default of an installment payment. Most consumers signing such contracts are unaware of the existence or the legal effect of such clauses. Some courts have refused to enforce them on the theory that they were not really communicated to the consumer.

CONCEPT SUMMARY
Formation of Offers

In order to create a power of acceptance, an offer must:

1. Manifest intent to enter into a contract. This intention must be apparent to an objective observer.
2. Contain definite and certain terms. The parties, subject matter, and quantity term of the contract must be indicated, plus whatever else is necessary to identify the basic terms of the agreement.
3. Be communicated. Communication may actually take place, or it may be implied in certain circumstances.

Termination of the Offer

If the requirements for an offer have been met, the offeree has a chance to accept and enter into a contract with the offeror. Yet the offer may be terminated prior to its acceptance. The termination of an offer may occur in a variety of ways; through lapse of time, revocation, rejection, death, and destruction of subject matter.

Lapse of Time

The offer itself may provide that it will terminate within a specified period. Once that period expires the offer is terminated. Thus an offer that states "This offer is good until May 30" would terminate after that date. It should be noted that the offeror should be specific regarding the duration of the offer. Consider the following situation. On March 1, the offeror mails a letter dated February 27 stating that "this offer expires in 10 days." The offeree receives the letter on March 4. Does the offer expire 10 days from February 27 or from March 4? What policy should the courts follow in interpreting this language? The courts that have

considered this problem have reached different decisions.

Even if the offeror does not provide for a specific termination date, the offer will lapse after a "reasonable time." How long is a reasonable time? The answer must vary with the circumstances surrounding the offer. An offer to sell real estate such as a home or an office building will probably last for weeks or months. An offer to buy stocks or commodities, which can fluctuate rapidly in price, may be open for acceptance for only minutes.

Further, the definition of "reasonable time" is affected by the context in which an offer is made. If you seek to buy souvenir pennants to sell outside the Super Bowl, your offer to the supplier would terminate no later than the day of the game. The timing of any prior dealings between the offeror and offeree will be relevant in determining what is a reasonable time for an offer to remain open.

The *Drouin* case involves an offer whose expiration date was set by statute. The case also deals with the proper manner of acceptance, a subject which will be discussed in greater detail in Chapter 12.

DROUIN V. FLEETWOOD ENTERPRISES
California Court of Appeal
209 Cal.Rptr. 623 (1985)

BACKGROUND: Drouin bought a motor home manufactured by Fleetwood. She had to have the motor home repaired several times. After the motor home finally broke down for good, Drouin sued Fleetwood for damages. Prior to trial, Drouin's attorney made a settlement offer pursuant to California Code of Civil Procedure Section 998. According to Section 998, a settlement offer expires unless it is accepted prior to trial or within 30 days after it is made, whichever occurs first. On July 14, 30 days after Drouin's settlement offer was made, a document was filed with the court on behalf of Fleetwood stating Fleetwood's acceptance of the settlement offer. However, Drouin was not notified of the acceptance until August 6. The parties continued to litigate and went to trial. Drouin won a judgment of $23,574.51, which was more than Fleetwood would have had to pay under the settlement offer. Fleetwood appealed, challenging, among other things, the court's failure to recognize its acceptance of Drouin's settlement offer.

Sims, Associate Justice

Defendant contends the court erred in failing to enter judgment upon its purported acceptance of plaintiff's offer of compromise pursuant to section 998. The trial court ruled the offer was revoked by an oral counteroffer at a settlement conference. . . . [E]ven assuming arguendo Fleetwood's capacity to accept plaintiff's 998 offer was not terminated by its counteroffer, the 998 offer was withdrawn by operation of law before it was accepted. Consequently, Fleetwood's counteroffer is ultimately immaterial. Section 998, subdivision (b) provides in pertinent part: "If such offer is not accepted prior to trial or within 30 days after it is made, whichever occurs first, it shall be deemed withdrawn. . . ." This language plainly means that the offeree must accept the offer within the prescribed time. The statute also provides, "If such offer is accepted, the offer with proof of acceptance shall be filed and the clerk or the judge shall enter judgment accordingly." This language contemplates that there must be an acceptance and that proof of the acceptance must be filed in the action.

Unless section 998 requires a different rule, operation of section 998 is governed by principles of classic contract law. It is, according to a hackneyed expression, hornbook law that an acceptance of an offer must be communicated to the offeror to become effective. The record in this case discloses that no acceptance of plaintiff's offer of June 14 was communicated to her within the 30 day limit. This "Notice of Acceptance" was not served on plaintiff until August 6, 1982, well beyond the statutory period. Because Fleetwood never communicated its acceptance of plaintiff's 998 offer to plaintiff within the 30 day period, no valid acceptance was effected before the offer was withdrawn by operation of law.

We note that a contrary conclusion—allowing acceptance of a 998 offer without communication to the offeror—would often result in a waste of time, effort, and costs. Indeed, that is precisely what happened here: despite the filing in the action of the "notice of acceptance" on July 14, the parties continued to litigate until the purported acceptance was served on plaintiff on August 6. Had the "notice of acceptance" been effective as an acceptance, this litigation effort would have occurred after the effective settlement of the case and, therefore, would have been futile.

DECISION: The appeals court affirmed the decision in Drouin's favor.

Revocation by the Offeror

General Rule   A **revocation** is a withdrawal of the offer by the offeror. The law requires that, in order to be effective, a revocation, like the original offer, must be communicated to the offeree. Generally, the revocation must be received by the offeree before the offeree has effectively accepted the offer. While an offeror generally has the power to revoke the offer at any time prior to its acceptance, there are several exceptions to this rule.

Even if the offer states that it will remain open for a specified time, the rule allowing the offeror to revoke at any time prior to acceptance usually applies. Thus, in the preceding example the offeror wrote on February 27 that the offer would expire in 10 days. Suppose the offeror decides on March 2 that he wants to revoke the offer prior to the end of the 10-day period. Can he do that when he has already committed himself to holding the offer open for 10 days? The general answer is "Yes" as long as no acceptance of the offer has been made by the offeree. There are, however, several situations in which the offeror is not permitted to revoke an offer.

Limitations   There are a number of exceptions to the rule that an offer may be revoked at any time prior to acceptance.

First, the parties may execute an option contract. An **option contract** is a contract whereby the offeror, in exchange for something of value, agrees with the offeree to keep an offer open for a certain time. With an option contract, the offer cannot be revoked for the period specified in the contract. For example, a school board offers to sell for $100,000 to Acme Development Company a school that it no longer uses. Acme is thinking of buying the school if it can interest several businesses in renting space there after the building has been remodeled. Acme might agree with the school board to enter into an option contract, by which, in consideration of a payment of $5,000, the school board gives Acme 90 days to accept or reject the offer. During those 90 days, the school board cannot sell to someone else, nor can it revoke its offer to Acme.

Second, the Uniform Commercial Code (Section 2-205) provides that if an offer to buy or sell goods contains a promise that it will be held open for a specific time, it cannot be revoked by the offeror during that time. An offer held open pur-

---

Issues and Trends
International Sales Contracts

With the growing importance of international trade, more and more transactions will be governed by the UN Convention on Contracts for the International Sale of Goods (CISG). The United States and several of its major trading partners are party to the CISG, which went into effect in 1988. As discussed in the last chapter, the CISG applies to any transaction that involves the sale of goods from a seller located in a signatory country to a buyer located in another signatory country (unless the parties choose otherwise).

Article 16 of the CISG essentially incorporates the UCC concept of the firm offer. It provides that an offer may not be revoked "if it indicates, by stating a fixed time for acceptance or otherwise, that it is irrevocable." Unlike the UCC, the CISG doesn't impose a 3-month limit on the duration of an irrevocable offer. Article 16 also provides that an offer is irrevocable "if it was reasonable for the offeree to rely on the offer as being irrevocable and the offeree has acted in reliance on the offer." This concept is very similar to the doctrine of promissory estoppel.

Recall our discussion of the problem that arises when an offeree receives by mail an offer which "expires in 10 days." U.S. law hasn't entirely settled whether the 10 days starts on the date the offeror sends the offer, on the date the offeree receives it, or on the date of the letter. Article 20 of the CISG addresses this issue directly: "A period of time for acceptance fixed by the offeror in a telegram or a letter begins to run from the moment the telegram is handed in for dispatch or from the date shown on the letter or, if no such date is shown, from the date shown on the envelope."

FIGURE 11-1

Bidding on Construction Jobs

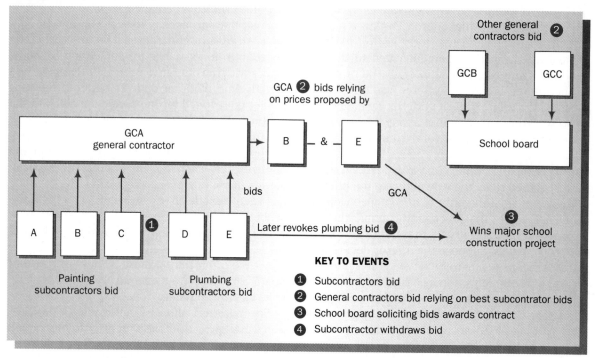

KEY TO EVENTS

1. Subcontractors bid
2. General contractors bid relying on best subcontrator bids
3. School board soliciting bids awards contract
4. Subcontractor withdraws bid

suant to UCC Section 2-205 is known as a **firm offer**. Section 2-205 requires that the offeror be a merchant in the kind of goods being offered and that the offer must be in writing and signed by the offeror. Finally, the time during which the offer is irrevocable is limited to three months. This rule does not apply to offers that are not made by merchants or that do not involve the sale of goods. Nevertheless, most commercial transactions (other than those for services or for real estate) fall within the terms of the firm-offer rule.

Third, if the offer requires an act to be performed in order to accept the offer (i.e., the offer seeks to have the offeree enter into a unilateral contract), the law limits the offeror's power to revoke the offer while the offeree is in the process of performing the requested act of acceptance. While traditionally the offeree's act must be fully completed before an acceptance and a contract result, in recent years the trend of many decisions has been to suspend the offeror's right of revocation until the offeree has had a reasonable time to complete the act called for in the offer.

Fourth, in order to avoid unfairness, courts will usually limit an offeror's right to revoke if an offer is made in such a way that the offeree reasonably expects that the offer will not be re-

voked. This exception to the general rule is known as the doctrine of **promissory estoppel.** It requires (1) that the statement of offer is one that the offeror should anticipate would be relied on by the offeree, (2) that the offeree in fact does rely on the statement, and (3) that the offeree is harmed by relying on the offer's irrevocability.

Typical of the application of the doctrine of promissory estoppel in limiting the right to revoke an offer is in the context of the standard relationship between a general building contractor and various subcontractors. The general contractor requests bids (offers) from potential subcontractors to do specialized work such as heating, plumbing, electrical, and carpentry. The general contractor relies on some of these bids in making its own bid to the building owner. Suppose that the general contractor finds that the building owner has accepted its offer to do the required work, but before the general contractor informs the subcontractor that the subcontractor's bid (offer) is accepted, the subcontractor revokes it. The basic situation is dramatized in Figure 11-1.

The following case provides an example from another context of what must be proved under the doctrine of promissory estoppel.

WERNER V. NORWEST BANK SOUTH DAKOTA

Supreme Court of South Dakota
499 N.W.2d 138 (1993)

BACKGROUND: The plaintiff, a manufacturer of picture frames, brought this action against defendant bank alleging that it failed to fulfill a promise to finance the cost of materials needed to fill an order for 10,000 to 20,000 frames ("the order"). The bank's refusal to loan $75,000 for the purchase of materials and supplies for the order caused Werner to fail to complete it because he ran out of money. Plaintiff had obtained numerous business loans from the bank from 1979 to 1982 (but had defaulted on a note due in 1981 and another due in May, 1982). In June of 1982, plaintiff met with one of defendant's loan officers and discussed a loan of somewhere between $60,000 and $80,000 to finance the order. Defendant's loan officer indicated that the bank could handle a loan in that range, but at no time did they discuss a specific amount, interest rate, term, or collateral.

When the bank refused to loan the money in October, and several other banks similarly denied plaintiff's loan applications, plaintiff was able to get $50,000 in advance payments from the customer who ordered the frames. In the meantime, defendant bank did loan plaintiff lesser amounts totaling $19,000, to cover various expenses. Werner still did not have enough money to complete the order, and filed this action claiming breach of an oral contract. The trial court granted summary judgment for the bank, and the plaintiff appealed to the Supreme Court of South Dakota. After the Supreme Court affirmed the trial court's finding that there was no valid express contract because essential terms were left open, it discussed plaintiff's argument based on justifiable reliance and promissory estoppel.

Henderson, Justice

Due to the lack of contractual certainty as previously indicated, Werner could not have reasonably relied on Norwest to grant him a loan in excess of $60,000. According to Werner, when he asked if Norwest could handle a $70,000 to $80,000 loan, [the loan officer] responded, "No problem." Even so, this affirmation does not constitute mutual assent to an oral contract. The agreement upon which Werner allegedly relied is too "vague, uncertain and unsettled" to support an estoppel claim.

Under a promissory estoppel argument, Werner would have to show where he altered his position to his detriment in the reasonable belief that a promise would be performed. For the reasons justifiable reliance was denied, we also fail to find promissory estoppel. Werner was able to secure funds from (other sources), as well as smaller loans from Norwest, after Norwest rejected the large loan. Furthermore, there is no reason to believe that the purchase of materials would not have been done except for the alleged loan agreement.

DECISION: The appellate court affirmed the trial court's finding in favor of the defendant because the plaintiff did not establish promissory estoppel.

Rejection by the Offeree

An offer terminates when the offeree responds with a **rejection**—that is, an expression of the offeree's unwillingness to accept the offer. An offeree may also respond to an offer with a **counteroffer,** which is an offer by the original offeree that pertains to the same subject matter as the original offer, but which in some way changes the terms of the original offer. A counteroffer is treated as a rejection coupled with a new offer.

For example, Sam may offer to sell his car to Joe for $1,000. If Joe responds, "I'll buy your car for

---

PREVENTIVE LAW
Ambiguities in Negotiations

Many of the problems described in this chapter result from the parties using ambiguous language in their negotiations. Although ambiguity is inherent in negotiations as to the terms of an agreement, you should be very careful to make sure that you don't use language that could be interpreted as a formal offer or acceptance before you are ready to agree. Otherwise you may be stuck with terms that you didn't intend to agree to. When the contract is valuable or involves a long-term relationship, it is wise to consult with an attorney even during preliminary stages of negotiation. Don't wait until you are ready to have a formal document drafted. An attorney can offer important advice about terms and negotiation strategies.

Even if the importance of the contract does not justify consulting with an attorney, you should be extremely careful in the language that you use. For example, if you are responding to an offer and are seeking additional information, make very clear that you are not counteroffering and thus rejecting the offer. When you make offers be clear in your own mind whether you want the other party to promise or to act. And so on.

$800," then Joe has rejected Sam's offer and made a counteroffer. With respect to this new counteroffer, Joe, the original offeree, is now the offeror, and Sam, the original offeror, is now the offeree. Sam is now in the position to bind both parties to a contract by accepting Joe's counteroffer.

Let's say that Sam rejects Joe's counteroffer, and Joe is now willing to buy the car for the original $1,000 asking price. Since Joe has already rejected—and thus terminated—Sam's original offer, Joe no longer has the power to create a contract automatically by accepting the terms of the original offer. Either Sam must reinstate his original offer (which would again give Joe the power to bind both parties by accepting it), or *Joe* must offer to buy the car for $1,000 (giving Sam the power to bind both parties by accepting it).

An offeree who merely seeks information about the terms of the offer (Must I pay cash? What credit terms are available? Is that your lowest price?) is making an inquiry that is neither an acceptance nor a rejection of the offer.

It is sometimes difficult to determine how to categorize the response of the offeree to an offer. If the response is an acceptance, the parties have made a contract. If the response is a rejection, the offer is terminated and the parties must begin their negotiations anew. If the response is neither an acceptance nor a rejection, but instead is an inquiry, then the original offer is not terminated but remains for the offeree's review.

Death of a Party

The death of either the offeror or the offeree will terminate an ordinary offer. Assume that the offeree, not knowing about the offeror's death, accepts the offer after the offeror dies but during a reasonable time after the offer has been received. No contract will be formed. The offeree need not have notice of the offeror's death for the offer to be terminated; the death itself terminates the offer.

An exception to the general rule that the death of either party terminates the offer can occur with the option contract that the parties make to keep the offer irrevocable. In the case of an option contract, there is a contractual obligation to hold an offer open for a set period. The effect of the offeror's death in this case depends upon whether the contractual obligations involved are ordinarily considered to survive the death of the offeror. This issue is discussed in Chapter 16, which deals with the discharge of contractual obligations.

Illegality

Contracts that are contrary to public policy will not be enforced. The concept of illegality as it affects contracts is discussed in detail in Chapter 13. For present purposes, it is important to note that an offer that is legal when made is terminated if it subsequently becomes illegal; the offer then cannot be accepted. If a state makes illegal the

ETHICS
Ethics in Offers

Intention is important in certain ethical theories, particularly those which identify principles or duties that people are expected to follow. In contrast are theories which are just concerned with the consequences of actions. How would you judge the following practices?

1. You have a summer job as a desk clerk at a hotel. You are instructed to quote (offer) a set price of $100 a night for a basic room. But if anyone asks for lower price, you are to offer $90 for the same room. You notice that businesspeople often ask for the lower rate but that guests who appear to be less well off rarely ask about discounts. You have been told never to volunteer a discount.

2. You see a new Sanyo compact disk player advertised in the newspaper at 25 percent off the best price that you have seen in other stores. You go to the store and they tell you they are sold out of the model that you want, but they have other models for sale.

3. Scott, a negotiator for a local group of warehouse workers at a discount retailer, has been told that although the membership wants an extra holiday and an 8 percent raise, they will settle for no more holidays and a 5 percent raise. The strike fund is nearly depleted and the union wants to avoid a strike. A major sale is scheduled in 2 weeks and Scott thinks that if he forces the issue he may get it all. Scott tells the representative for the firm: "This is my final offer, I have to get 10 percent or its equivalent in days off. The union is pushing to strike, and I doubt if I can prevent them from going out if I don't get results right now."

CONCEPT SUMMARY
Termination of Offers

Method	By	Communication Required	Limitation
Lapse of time	Expiration of stated or reasonable time	No	
Revocation	Act of offeror	Yes	Option contracts Firm offers by merchants Prior to acceptance Detrimental reliance by offeree
Rejection	Act of offeree May occur through counteroffer	Yes	
Death	Of either party	No, in most cases	Option contracts in certain cases
Destruction of subject matter	By unforeseen event	No	

sale of a certain drug as of January 1, an offer to sell it, legally made the prior December 15, terminates on January 1 if it has not been accepted prior to that date.

Destruction of the Subject Matter

Hoper offers to sell his Porsche to Allen, who is familiar with the car. Although neither knew it, 5 minutes after the offer was made a landslide destroyed Hoper's garage and the car. Such destruction of the subject matter of the offer by an "act of God" will terminate the offer.

Suppose, instead, that Farmer offers to sell 10,000 bushels of apples to Processor and that Farmer's apples are subsequently destroyed by an act of God, such as a tornado. Your immediate reaction is very likely to be that, of course, the offer is terminated because the subject matter of the offer (Farmer's apples) has been destroyed. In fact, that is probably what a court would conclude; it is impossible for the offer to be performed. However, if Processor could prove that Farmer had offered to sell 10,000 bushels of apples in general rather than apples raised specifically from Farmer's property, then the offer would still be valid. In that case, Farmer could purchase the needed apples from someone else; the fact that Farmer's apples were destroyed would not mean that all apples were unavailable. Thus, it is necessary to determine whether the subject matter of Farmer's offer was 10,000 bushels of apples from his particular farm property or merely 10,000 bushels of apples. A tornado destroying Farmer's apples would terminate the offer to sell apples from his farm but would not affect the offer to sell apples in general.

Questions and Review Problems

Key Terms

offer	firm offer
offeror	promissory estoppel
offeree	rejection
revocation	counteroffer
option contract	

Discussion Questions

1. What terms must be specified in a valid offer at common law? Under the UCC?
2. List five ways in which an offer can terminate.
3. Describe the effect of a counteroffer.

Review Problems

1. Owner put a sign in front of her house stating that an antique swing was "For Sale by Owner." Buyer saw owner in the front yard and said, "How much do you want for the swing." Owner answered, "I expect to get $125." Buyer held out his hand, which Owner shook, and while the handshaking was going on, said "It's a deal." Did Owner make an offer?

2. Studious graduates from college and takes a job with a consumer goods company. As part of the interviewing process, Studious is told that he will receive an "impressive bonus" if the company increases profits by 10 percent by the end of the year. The firm has a 14 percent increase in profits. Is Studious entitled to a bonus?

3. Seller mails a letter to Buyer in which Seller offers to sell 1,000 bushels of grain at a set price. The letter is dated April 10. The letter states: "This offer must be accepted within 5 days." The letter is postmarked April 12. The letter is received on April 16. On what date does the offer expire? What would be the best policy regarding this issue?

4. General Contractor is seeking bids for parts of a major contract that the General Contractor intends to bid on. General gets a bid from Small Company to do the plumbing for $15,000. That is the lowest bid that General has, and General lists $15,000 for the plumbing work. General does not list Small Company by name. General wins the main contract and then calls several other plumbing companies. One of them agrees to do the job for $14,000. Should Small Company have a claim against General? What is the best way to deal with this type of problem?

Case Problems

1. Rofra, Inc., bid for plumbing work to be done for the Board of Education. The bid was sent in response to a "Solicitation for Connection of Building Sewer to the Public Sewer at Sunatsville Senior High School." Attached to that solicitation notice was a statement of "Contract General Provisions" that included a section reserving to the board the right "to reject any and all bids, in whole or in part. . . ." Plaintiff Rofra was the second lowest bid-

der for the work; the lowest bidder did not have in its employ a "master plumber" as the solicitation terms required. The plaintiff sues to enforce the contract, which it claims exists as a result of the school board's solicitation offer and its own bid, which was the lowest bid conforming to the offer. The defendant claims no contract exists. Is the plaintiff right?

2. Sokol made a written offer dated March 10 to purchase a house owned by Hill. At the same time, Sokol delivered to Nash, who was the real-estate broker representing Hill, a check for $500 as earnest money. The offer stated that the defendants had 3 days to accept. Hill signed on March 12. On the same day Sokol called Nash and orally withdrew his offer. Nash deposited the check on March 14. On March 15, Nash hand-delivered the contract form signed by Hill and dated March 12 to Sokol. Sokol sues for the $500. What is the result?

3. Smith owned a storefront property that Shelton was interested in leasing. After having several conversations with Shelton, Smith's real estate agent sent Shelton a letter dated July 15 stating the terms discussed by the parties for leasing the premises. The letter concluded with the following paragraph: "A lease is being drawn and will be forwarded to you soon. Please execute the copy of this letter as your agreement to these terms and conditions and return to us so we can take the space off the market and hold same for you." Shelton signed an acceptance at the bottom of the letter and returned it to Smith's agent. Two weeks later, Smith's agent sent a lease to Shelton. Differences between the parties arose and the lease was never signed. Unable to find a substitute tenant, Smith sued Shelton. Smith argued that by signing the acceptance at the bottom of the July 15 letter, Shelton had agreed to enter into a lease agreement according to the terms of the letter. Shelton argued that the letter could

not form the basis of a contract because it left out essential terms. For example, even though the letter stated the rent at $400 per month, the letter did not state when the rent would be payable. The draft lease also called for Shelton to pay the first and last month's rent at the beginning of the rental period, a requirement that Shelton had not agreed to. What result?

4. Mrs. Green, an elderly woman, owned a car which she stored at a garage owned by Smith. According to a contractual arrangement between Mrs. Green and Smith, Smith would have one of his employees drive the car to Mrs. Green's house whenever she asked for it and then drive it back to the garage when she was through with it. Mrs. Green was billed monthly for this service. After the arrangement had continued for 2 years, Smith started sending a folder with the monthly bill. The outside of the folder listed rates for automobile service offered by Smith's garage. The inside of the folder contained a provision that the car owner agreed to be responsible for any damage or liability arising when the car was in the hands of one of Smith's employees. While one of Smith's employees was driving the car back to Smith's garage, he collided with Mr. Moore. After Smith compensated Mr. Moore for his injuries, he sued Mrs. Green for reimbursement. Smith argued that according to the provision printed on the inside of the folder, Mrs. Green was responsible for the cost of the accident. Smith argued that Mrs. Green had impliedly agreed to the provision by not objecting to it and continuing to store her car at Smith's garage. Mrs. Green argued that the provision was part of an offer that had never properly been communicated to her. She claimed that there was nothing on the outside of the folder to indicate that such a provision would be on the inside, and that she had never read the inside of the folder. What result?

12

The Acceptance

Intent to Accept

Communication of Acceptance

Satisfying Terms of the Offer

Acceptance Problems

Cancellation of Acceptance

I n the last chapter we learned about the offer, the initial step in the formation of a contract. This chapter focuses on the other side of the coin: the acceptance. An **acceptance** is an offeree's manifestation of intent to enter into a contract according to the terms of the offer. Whether the offeree must agree to be bound *exactly* to the terms of the offer is one of the many issues that we will discuss in this chapter.

A valid offer that has not been terminated creates the power of acceptance in the offeree. If the offeree properly accepts the offer and if the other requirements for a valid contract are met (we will discuss these other requirements in the chapters that follow), then the offeree's acceptance creates a contract that binds both parties.

In order to be valid, an acceptance must meet certain criteria. First, like the offer itself, the acceptance must be made with the intent to contract. Second, the acceptance by the offeree must also be communicated to the offeror. Third, the acceptance must usually satisfy all the conditions and terms established by the offer. As was noted in the previous chapter, a change in the terms of an offer usually results not in an acceptance but in a rejection that terminates the offer. This chapter will discuss each of these elements required of an acceptance. Several special situations in which ac-

ceptance problems arise, and the cancellation of an acceptance, will also be discussed. Figure 12-1 demonstrates the basic process of agreement.

Intent to Accept

The courts generally look for the same evidence of intent on the part of the offeree as is required of the offeror. Was the acceptance made with the intent to commit the offeree to enter into a contract? If the offeree replies to an offer by stating "Your offer looks good" or "I will give immediate consideration to your request," there is no manifestation of intent to enter into a contract.

The offeree must show a commitment. "I might accept your offer" leaves open the possibility that the offer will be rejected. Similarly, a response that leaves for the future the commitment of the offeree, such as "I'll let you know next week if the proposal is satisfactory," does not constitute an acceptance.

As with intent on the part of the offeror, it is the objective manifestation of the offeree's intent, not its subjective basis, that is critical. The law is not concerned with the offeree's state of mind; instead, it asks what the offeree's words or actions would indicate to a reasonable person about his or her intent to accept an offer.

FIGURE 12-1

The Process of Agreement

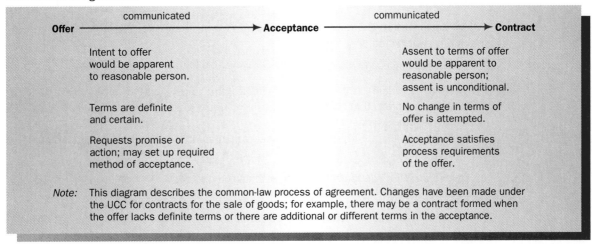

Note: This diagram describes the common-law process of agreement. Changes have been made under the UCC for contracts for the sale of goods; for example, there may be a contract formed when the offer lacks definite terms or there are additional or different terms in the acceptance.

Unless so required by the offer, the acceptance need not be expressed in words. Actions on the part of the offeree can constitute an acceptance. Thus, if a widget manufacturer sends a potential buyer five dozen widgets, with an invoice stating their purchase price, the buyer who says nothing but uses the widgets will have manifested by her action an intent to accept the manufacturer's offer to sell.

The *Crouch* case provides an example of a court determining that a person's actions can constitute an acceptance of an offer, even where the offeree argues that he did not "express" any acceptance.

CROUCH V. MARRS

Supreme Court of Kansas

430 P.2d 204 (1967)

BACKGROUND: This was an action brought by Crouch (plaintiff) against Marrs (defendant), the current possessor of a building and its contents, seeking a determination from the court that an agreement to purchase the property that Crouch made with the Purex Corporation resulted in a contract. Purex Corporation claimed it made no contract with Crouch, but instead had contracted to sell said property to Martin Asche. Asche then responded and stated he sold part of the property to Roy Marrs. When Crouch sought to take some of the property which he claimed was purchased from Purex Corporation, Marrs prevented Crouch from getting at the property. Crouch then brought this action against Marrs, seeking to prevent Marrs from interfering with the property claimed by Crouch. The other parties involved were then made parties to the suit filed by Crouch. The trial court found against Crouch and in favor of Marrs.

Hatcher, Commissioner

The facts of the controversy do not appear to be in dispute. Six miles north of Meade, Kansas, was an old silica processing plant which was owned by the Purex Corporation of Lakewood, California. The plant had not been used for many years.

On February 26, 1964, the plaintiff, Crouch, wrote to the Purex Corporation asking for their lowest price if they were interested in selling the building and its contents. The letter read in part:

I would be interested in buying the old building that housed the plant and what other items that are still left.

On March 4, 1964, Crouch received a letter of reply from Purex Corporation signed by Frank Knox which stated:

We will sell this building and the equipment in and about that building for a total of $500.

On March 19, 1964, Crouch wrote to Frank Knox, Purex Corporation, stating that the building was in "pretty bad condition" and asking "would you consider taking $300 for what is left?" This letter was not answered.

Later, on April 16, 1964, Crouch addressed another letter to Frank Knox, Purex Corporation, which read:

I guess we will try the building for the amount you quoted, $500. I am sending you a personal check for this amount.

It is conceded that this letter constituted a new offer and was not a continuation of the previous negotiations.

The record discloses the check signed by Phillip Crouch and made payable to Frank Knox was endorsed by Knox and then was paid and cancelled by several banks, including the Piqua Bank at which Crouch maintained his checking account.

On April 17, 1964, the Purex Corporation, through Frank Knox, wrote a letter to Martin Asche which stated:

In answer to your inquiry about our property approximately six miles north of Meade, Kansas.

We will sell for $500 the mine building and whatever machinery and equipment which remains in or about that building. A condition of sale will require that the property purchased be removed from the premises within forty-five days.

If this price is acceptable, we will be pleased to receive a cashier's check to cover.

On April 24, 1964, Asche wrote a letter accepting the offer of April 17, which reads:

We are enclosing a cashier's check for $500 and the bill of sale of mine buildings with the agreement of option to purchase property.

On April 27, 1964, Frank Knox sent Crouch the following telegram:

Your counter offer received April 23 is unacceptable. Your check mistakenly deposited by Purex will be recovered and returned to you or Purex check will be issued to you if your check cannot be located.

There followed a letter dated May 16, 1964, which read:

This is a follow-up to our telegram to you of April 27, advising you that your check which we received on April 23 was not acceptable, but that it had been deposited by mistake. Since we were unable to recover your check, we herewith enclose our check for $500 to reimburse you.

In the meantime, Martin Asche had entered into a contract to sell the building to Roy Marrs who owned the land surrounding the building site for $500 and had entered into a contract to sell the equipment to the C. & D. Used Truck Parts for $800. Crouch commenced salvage of the building but Roy Marrs put a lock on the gate and would not allow Crouch to enter.

Appellant Crouch contends that on the basis of the prior negotiations the acceptance and endorsing appellant's check by the Purex Corporation constituted the formation of a contract of sale. The question is whether the endorsing and depositing appellant's check constituted an acceptance of his offer to buy? We think it did.

The endorsing and depositing a check constitutes an acceptance of the offer to buy which accompanies it because the act itself indicates acceptance. An offer may be accepted by performing a specified act as well as by an affirmative answer. Also, where the offeree exercised dominion over the thing offered him—in this instance the check—such exercise constitutes an acceptance of the offer. It is elementary that an offer may be accepted by performing or refraining from performing a specified act as well as by an affirmative answer.

We are forced to conclude that the acceptance and endorsement of the check accompanying the offer to purchase the property in controversy constituted an acceptance of the offer.

DECISION: The trial court decision was reversed and title to the property was awarded to the plaintiff Crouch.

Communication of Acceptance

An acceptance must be communicated in order to be effective. What action must be taken in order to communicate an acceptance depends on whether the offeror seeks a unilateral or a bilateral contract.

Bilateral or Unilateral Agreement

If the offer is one to enter into a unilateral contract (a promise for an act or an act for a promise), the offeree must either perform the requested act or respond with the requested promise. Thus, a promise for an act ("I'll pay you $10 if you type my paper by tomorrow night") requires the offeree to perform the act (type the paper by tomorrow night) in order to accept the offer to pay $10. However, if the offer requires a promise in exchange for an act ("I'll lend you $10 right now if you promise to repay me $11 a week from tomorrow"), the offeree must make the promise to repay (either expressly by stating a promise or impliedly by taking the offered $10) in order to accept the offer. An offeror may also seek the offeree's forbearance, an agreement to refrain from doing something that the offeree might otherwise do. Thus, the statement "I promise to pay you $100 if you don't smoke cigarettes for a year" is also an offer to enter into a unilateral contract. The offeree is asked to forbear from an act that he or she might otherwise do.

In the case where the offer requires an act from the offeree ("I'll pay you $10 if you type my paper by tomorrow night"), only the act need be performed in order to accept the offer. The offeree need not first communicate to the offeror that he or she intends to perform the requested act. On the other hand, if the offer requires a promise from the offeree ("I'll lend you $10 now if you *promise* to repay me $11 next Friday") the offeree must of course communicate that promise to the offeror.

Similarly, if the offer is one to enter into a bilateral contract, one in which each party makes a promise ("I'll promise to sell you my 1986 Ford if you promise to pay me $800 cash"), the offeree must also communicate his or her promise in order to accept the offer. In the event of uncertainty as to what the offer requires of an offeree, most courts will interpret an agreement as consisting of bilateral promises, thus requiring a communication from the offeree rather than a requested act of acceptance in exchange for the offeror's promise.

Means of Communication

Usually, any means of communication that gives the offeror notice of the offeree's intent to accept the offer is effective. However, as the third requirement of an acceptance suggests, the offeree must also comply with all the terms of the offer. Thus, if the offer dictates that the acceptance be communicated by certain means or occur at a certain time or place, the offeree generally must comply with those provisions. An acceptance made in a different manner or at a different time or place would be ineffective.

If the offer does not require the offeree to use a specific means of communication, problems can arise concerning the time at which an acceptance by an offeree would be effective. While the time of acceptance is not critical to most contracts, where the offeror has attempted a revocation or where the intended acceptance is delayed or lost, an analysis of the method or time of acceptance is necessary.

Generally, if the means of communication used by the offeree in communicating acceptance is authorized by the offer, the acceptance is effective when delivered by the offeree to the communication agency.

This rule is known as the **mailbox rule** because it provides, for example, that an acceptance that may properly be communicated by mail becomes effective as soon as it is deposited in the mailbox. The mailbox rule can also be applied to other forms of communication. For example, an acceptance that may be made by telegram becomes effective as soon as the message is delivered or otherwise communicated to the company that will transmit the telegram. The offeror may expressly or impliedly authorize the offeree to use a particular means of communication. Thus, if the offer states, "You may use the mail for your acceptance," the offeree's acceptance is effective at the moment a letter of acceptance is deposited with the postal service even if the letter is delayed in reaching the offeror or is lost. The offeree has effectively communicated acceptance by delivering it to the "agent" (post office) authorized by the offeror. Even if the offer does not expressly authorize the use of a particular means of communication, the law holds that an offer made by one means of communication can be accepted by the same means. Thus, a mailed offer implies authorization to the offeree to use the mail for acceptance.

In fact, the modern rule in most jurisdictions is that the offeree may use any "reasonable means of communication" in accepting the offer. What constitutes a reasonable means of communication depends on the subject matter of the offer, the custom and usage in a particular trade or business, and the prior conduct or dealings of the parties. If, for example, it is customary in the industry or trade for acceptances to be sent by mail or if the parties in prior transactions had used the mail to enter into contracts, an acceptance would be effective when mailed. An acceptance sent by a means not recognized as an implied or express agent of the offeror will be effective only upon receipt.

The following case demonstrates the application of the mailbox rule.

PRIBIL V. RUTHER
Supreme Court of Nebraska
262 N.W.2d 460 (1978)

BACKGROUND: Pribil (plaintiff) brought this action against Ruther (defendant), seeking to enforce a contract whereby Pribil agreed to buy real estate owned by Ruther. The defendant claimed she verbally rejected the plaintiff's offer to purchase the property before he received her written acceptance of it. The trial court found for the plaintiff and the defendant appealed.

Boslaugh, Justice

This is an appeal in an action for specific performance of a real estate contract. The defendant Bertha Ruther owns a quarter section of land in Holt County, Nebraska. The defendant listed this property for sale with John Thor, a real estate broker, on January 20, 1976.

On April 12, 1976, the plaintiff Lawrence Pribil executed a written offer to purchase the property for $68,000. The offer to purchase was on a form known as a Uniform Purchase Agreement, which included a space for a written acceptance of the offer. The defendant and her husband signed the acceptance on the same day and handed an executed copy of the agreement to Thor for delivery to the plaintiff.

Thor returned to his office in Norfolk, Nebraska, and asked an office employee, Mrs. Kasebaum, to send a copy of the agreement to the plaintiff. Mrs. Kasebaum wrote a letter to the plaintiff, dated April 14, 1976, with a copy of the agreement enclosed, which was sent to the plaintiff by certified mail. The letter was postmarked "April 15, 1976 p.m." and was received by the plaintiff on April 16, 1976.

The defendant became dissatisfied with the transaction the day after she had signed the acceptance when she discovered a test well had been drilled on the property at the plaintiff's request and the driller had estimated a well would produce 500 to 800 gallons of water per minute. The defendant testified that she called the plaintiff's home at about 5 P.M. on April 13, 1976, and told the plaintiff's wife that she, the defendant, would not sell the property. The plaintiff's wife testified this conversation did not take place until some ten days later, near the end of April 1976.

The defendant further testified that she called Thor the next morning, April 14, 1976, and said that she was going to "terminate the contract," because Thor had lied to her. According to Thor this conversation took place at 11:42 a.m. on April 15, 1976. Thor testified that immediately after receiving the call from the defendant, he called the plaintiff and told the plaintiff that the defendant was not going to sell the farm.

The principal issue in this case is whether the defendant had effectively rejected the plaintiff's offer and revoked her acceptance of the offer before the acceptance had been communicated to the plaintiff. Since the plaintiff sought to enforce the contract, the burden was on the plaintiff to establish that there was a contract. A party who seeks to compel specific performance of a written contract has the burden of proving the contract.

An express contract is proved by evidence of a definite offer and unconditional acceptance. Where the offer requires a promise on the part of the offeree, a communicated acceptance is essential.

The signing of the acceptance on the Uniform Purchase Agreement by the defendant did not make the contract effective. It was necessary that there be some communication of the acceptance to the plaintiff. There must be some irrevocable element such as depositing the acceptance in the mail so that it is placed beyond the power or control of the sender before the acceptance becomes effective and the contract is made. Delivery to the agent of the defendant was not delivery to the plaintiff as it did not put the acceptance beyond the control of the defendant.

The plaintiff contends that the deposit of the acceptance in the mail by Thor satisfied the requirement that the acceptance be communicated. Where transmission by mail is authorized, the deposit of the signed agreement in the mail with the proper address and postage will complete the contract. The difficulty in this case is that there is no evidence that the acceptance was deposited in the mail before Thor called the plaintiff and informed him that the defendant would not sell the property.

The evidence is that Thor handed the purchase agreement to Mrs. Kasebaum with instructions to send a copy to the plaintiff. Mrs. Kasebaum did not testify. Thor testified, "I can't testify when she mailed it, except by reading the postmarks on the envelope and the return receipts." The postmark indicates only that the postage was canceled sometime during the afternoon of April 15, 1976. The telephone call from the defendant was received at 11:42 A.M. on that same date. The call from Thor to the plaintiff was made immediately afterward.

If we assume that transmission by mail was authorized in this case, there is no evidence to show that the acceptance was deposited in the mail before the defendant's call to Thor's, and Thor's call to the plaintiff notifying him that the defendant had rejected his offer. The evidence does not show that the acceptance was communicated to the plaintiff and thus became effective before the defendant changed her mind and rejected the offer.

DECISION: The trial court's decision was reversed and the Supreme Court ruled in favor of defendant Ruther.

Satisfying Terms of the Offer

A well-known maxim of contract law is that "the offeror is the master of his or her offer." This means that in order for an acceptance to be effective, it must generally satisfy the terms and requirements imposed by the offer. This principle is illustrated in the following case.

NEWMAN V. SCHIFF

U.S. Court of Appeals, Eighth Circuit
778 F.2d 460 (1985)

BACKGROUND: Irwin Schiff, a self-styled "tax rebel," is the author of several books and other materials espousing the view that people are not really required to pay federal income tax. While appearing live on the CBS news show Nightwatch, Schiff said: "[T]here is nothing in the Internal Revenue Code . . . which says anybody is legally required to pay the tax. . . . If anybody calls this show . . . and cites any section of this Code that says an individual is required to file a tax return, I will pay them $100,000." The next morning, John Newman saw the offer rebroadcast on CBS Morning News. After researching the Internal Revenue Code, he found a number of sections that he believed required individuals to file tax returns. He sent a letter to Schiff demanding the $100,000. Schiff refused, contending that Newman's acceptance wasn't timely. Newman sued in federal district court and lost. Newman appealed.

Bright, Senior Circuit Judge

The present case concerns a special type of offer: an offer for a reward. At least since the time of Lilli Carlill's unfortunate experience with the Carbolic Smoke Ball, courts have enforced public offers to pay rewards. *Carlill v. Carbolic Smoke Ball Co.*

In that case, frequently excerpted and discussed in student lawbooks, the Carbolic Smoke Ball Company advertised that it would pay a "100£ reward" to anyone who contracted "the increasing epidemic influenza, colds, or any disease caused by taking cold, after having used the Carbolic Smoke Ball three times daily for two weeks according to the printed directions supplied with each ball."

Ms. Carlill, relying upon this promise, purchased and used a Carbolic Smoke Ball. It did not, however, prevent her from catching the flu. The court held that the advertised reward constituted a valid offer which Ms. Carlill had accepted, thereby entitling her to recovery.

The Missouri courts enforced a public reward offer in a case concerning the notorious desperado Jesse James. Rudy Turilli, operator of the "Jesse James Museum," appeared before a nationwide televised audience and offered $10,000 to anyone who could disprove his contention that Jesse James was not murdered in 1882, but in fact lived for many years thereafter under the alias J. Frank Dalton and last resided with Turilli at his museum into the 1950s. Stella James, a relative of Jesse James, accepted the challenge and produced affidavits of persons who had identified Jesse James' body after the shooting in 1882. Turilli denied that the evidence satisfied the requisite degree of proof and refused to pay the $10,000. The trial court ruled that Ms. James was entitled to the reward, and the Missouri Court of Appeals upheld this judgment.

In the present case, Schiff's statement on Nightwatch that he would pay $100,000 to anyone who called the show and cited any section of the Internal Revenue Code "that says an individual is required to file a tax return" constituted a valid offer for a reward. In our view, if anyone had called the show and cited the code sections that Newman produced, a contract would have been formed and Schiff would have been obligated to pay the $100,000 reward, for his bluff would have been properly called.

Newman, however, never saw the live CBS Nightwatch program upon which Schiff appeared and this lawsuit is not predicated on Schiff's Nightwatch offer. Newman saw the CBS Morning News rebroadcast of Schiff's Nightwatch appearance. This rebroadcast served not to renew or extend Schiff's offer, but rather only to inform viewers that Schiff had made an offer on Nightwatch. The rebroadcast constituted a newsreport and not a renewal of the original offer. An offeror is the master of his offer and it is clear that Schiff by his words, "If anybody calls this show. . ." limited his offer in time to remain open only until the conclusion of the live Nightwatch broadcast. A reasonable person listening to the news rebroadcast could not conclude that the above language—"calls this show"—constituted a new offer; rather than what it actually was, a newsreport of the offer previously made, which had already expired.

Schiff's claim that there is nothing in the Internal Revenue Code that requires an individual to file a federal income tax return demands comment. The kindest thing that can be said about Schiff's promotion of this idea is that he is grossly mistaken or a mere pretender to knowledge in income taxation. We have nothing but praise for Mr. Newman's efforts which have helped bring this to light.

Section 6012 of the Internal Revenue Code is entitled "Persons required to make returns of income," and provides that individuals having a gross income in excess of a certain amount "shall" file tax returns for the taxable year. 26 U.S.C. § 6012. Thus, section 6012 requires certian individuals to file tax returns.

The district court stated that Schiff's argument is "blatant nonsense." Schiff did not challenge this ruling. . . .

Although Newman has not "won" his lawsuit in the traditional sense of recovering a reward that he sought, he has accomplished an important goal in the public interest of unmasking the "blatant nonsense" dispensed by Schiff. For that he deserves great commendation from the public. Perhaps now CBS and other communication media who have given Schiff's mistaken views widespread publicity, *see supra*, pp. 461–62, will give John Newman equal time in the public interest.

DECISION: The Circuit Court of Appeals affirmed the decision for Schiff.

Acceptance Varying Offer

According to the traditional common law rule, an acceptance must precisely mirror the terms of the offer. A variation in terms or an addition of new conditions causes the response of the offeree to be considered a rejection coupled with a counteroffer.

There are some situations where the law or facts imply terms that may not have been expressed in the offer. In these cases, the expression of those terms by the offeree in accepting is not considered to add to or vary the terms of the offer.

For example, if you offer to sell me your house for $75,000 and in response I state, "I accept your offer, subject to my attorney checking that you have good title to the property," my response would be considered an acceptance. It is implied by law that the person offering to sell a house guarantees that he or she has a good title to it. My response has not changed the terms of your offer. Similarly, suppose it is customary in an industry (according to trade usage) that an offer to sell goods for a stated price implies that the buyer has "30 days, same as cash" to pay for them. The buyer who expresses in an acceptance "I'll accept your offer if the normal credit terms are extended" is not varying the terms of the offer; those credit terms were a part of the original offer, even though not expressed by the offeror.

Battle of the Forms   The general rule that any response that varies the terms of an offer cannot be considered an acceptance has proved unworkable in commercial transactions where each party has form documents that it sends in response to inquiries. The problem of the "battle of the forms" arises because each party desires to be the one whose form controls the transaction.

For example, the buyer's form to the seller might say:

> We offer to buy *500 widgets* from you at *$100* each. The goods are to be shipped to us *by June 1st.* They must be packaged in cartons of 50 each. Payment will be due from us 60 days after receipt of the widgets. No arbitration. No variation in the terms of this offer can be made without our written consent.

Seller has received a definite offer. It wants to sell the widgets, but on slightly different terms, and responds with its own form:

> We have received your offer to buy 500 widgets and are glad to contract with you. Our goods will be shipped to you packaged in cartons of 100 each. Disputes will be submitted to arbitration. Payment will be due from you 30 days after receipt of the widgets. Thank you for your order.

Do the parties have a contract? Clearly, there is an offer, but have the terms of the offer been accepted? Under common law, if the terms of the offer are not mirrored by the terms of the acceptance, no contract results. But suppose the parties act as if there is a contract, sending and accepting the goods without protest. Later a dispute arises over the terms of payment. The seller argues that the dispute must be submitted to arbitration.

Whether the seller is correct that the dispute must be submitted to arbitration depends upon how the forms are treated. Under common law, the seller's form would be considered a counteroffer that was accepted by the buyer's actions in taking the goods. This is called the last-shot doctrine because the last document exchanged before the parties perform controls the transaction. Under that rule, the seller's form controls, and arbitration is required.

The typical problematic exchange of forms by merchants is dramatized in Figure 12-2. Sellers typically want to restrict warranties and damages. They also tend to prefer arbitration because the system may be a familiar one to sellers who sponsor arbitration through their industry associations. Buyers, not surprisingly, want warranties and special damages and may be resistant to arbitration because they think that it may unfairly favor the sellers. Note that the crossing-of-forms problem is rarely a consumer problem because consumers are not very likely to use form documents.

The UCC and Acceptance Varying Offer The Uniform Commercial Code has sought to deal with problems that arise because of the battle of forms. Section 2-207 provides that, in certain situations, the terms of an acceptance can add to or differ from those proposed in the offer. This provision of the UCC reads as follows:

(1) A definite and seasonable expression of acceptance or a written confirmation which is sent within a reasonable time operates as an

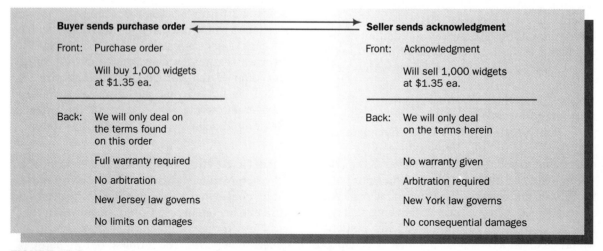

Buyer sends purchase order	Seller sends acknowledgment
Front: Purchase order	Front: Acknowledgment
Will buy 1,000 widgets at $1.35 ea.	Will sell 1,000 widgets at $1.35 ea.
Back: We will only deal on the terms found on this order	Back: We will only deal on the terms herein
Full warranty required	No warranty given
No arbitration	Arbitration required
New Jersey law governs	New York law governs
No limits on damages	No consequential damages

FIGURE 12-2

The Crossing of Forms

acceptance even though it states terms additional to or different from those offered or agreed upon, unless acceptance is expressly made conditional on assent to the additional or different terms.

(2) The additional terms are to be construed as proposals for addition to the contract. Between merchants such terms become part of the contract unless:

    (a) the offer expressly limits acceptance to the terms of the offer;

    (b) they materially alter it; or

    (c) notification of objection to them has already been given or is given within a reasonable time after notice of them is received.

(3) Conduct by both parties which recognizes the existence of a contract is sufficient to establish a contract for sale although the writings of the parties do not otherwise establish a contract. In such case, the terms of the particular contract consist of those terms on which the writings of the parties agree, together with any supplementary terms incorporated under any other provisions of this Act.

In the typical battle-of-the-forms scenario, the parties don't focus on the differences between their respective forms until a problem arises. Only when a problem does arise do the parties start to argue about whose terms govern the transaction. Must the dispute be sent to arbitration, as provided in the seller's form? Did the seller bear the risk of loss during shipment, as provided in the buyer's form? Section 2-207 is designed to settle such disputes.

The operation of Section 2-207 is easier to understand if it's broken down into components. The basic questions that Section 2-207 answers with respect to any battle-of-the-forms scenario are:

1. Was a contract created by the exchange of documents?

2. If a contract *was* created by the exchange of documents, what terms are included in the contract?

3. If a contract was *not* created by the exchange of documents, was a contract created by the subsequent conduct of the parties? If so, what are the terms of that contract?

These issues will be discussed in turn.

Was a Contract Created by the Exchange of Documents? Under Section 2-207, there are two ways for a contract to be created: (1) by the exchange of documents between the parties and (2) by the conduct of the parties. Subsection (1) determines whether a contract is created as a result of the exchange of documents. The general rule is that a definite and seasonable (that is, timely) expression of acceptance is effective as an acceptance, even if the acceptance contains additional or different terms. The UCC thus abandons the common-law mirror-image rule, which treats a purported acceptance with additional or different terms as a rejection and counteroffer. The UCC approach is more likely to result in a contract being recognized, and better reflects the commercial understanding of when a "deal" has been made.

There is an exception to the rule that a definite and seasonable expression of acceptance is effective as an acceptance. When the acceptance is expressly made conditional on the offeror's assent to the offeree's additional or different terms, then a contract is *not* created by the exchange of documents. Let's return to the original example where the buyer offered to purchase 500 widgets for $100 each. Recall that the seller sent back a form which purported to accept the offer, but which contained terms that were inconsistent with those of the offer. (The seller's form called for shipment in packages of 100 rather than 50, for disputes to be submitted to arbitration and for payment to be due 30, rather than 60, days after delivery.)

If the seller's form had stated that the seller's acceptance was *conditional* upon the buyer's assent to the buyer's new terms—that is, that the seller's acceptance was good only if the buyer agreed to the seller's terms—then *no contract would have been created by the exchange of forms*. Keep in mind that even if no contract is created by the exchange of forms, it is still possible for a contract to be created later by conduct if the parties behave as if they have a contract. Contracts created by conduct are discussed later.

If the seller's form had *not* stated that seller's acceptance was conditional upon the buyer's assent to the new terms, then a contract *would* have been created by the exchange of forms. The next question is which terms are included in that contract: the buyer's terms, the seller's terms, or a combination?

What Terms of a Contract Are Created by Exchange of Documents? Once we determine that a contract has been created by the exchange of documents pursuant to Section 2-207(1) we must turn to Section 2-207(2) to determine whether the contract will incorporate the additional or different terms included in the acceptance. Subsection (2) creates a two-track approach to this issue: if both parties are merchants, then one set of rules applies; if at least one party is not a merchant, then another set of rules applies. A **merchant** is generally defined in UCC Section 2-104 as a person who deals in goods of the kind involved in the transaction. If Acme, Inc. is a retail shoe company, then Acme would be a merchant in any transaction in which it bought or sold shoes. If Acme makes a one-time-only sale of one of its used trucks to one of its employees, however, Acme would not be a merchant for the purposes of that transaction.

If at least one party is not a merchant, then the additional or different terms included in the acceptance are treated as mere proposals for addition to the contract. If the offeror doesn't agree to them, then they are not included in the contract.

If both parties are merchants, then the additional or different terms become part of the contract unless one or more of these conditions apply:

1. The offeror has stated in his or her offer that he or she will agree only on the basis of the offer's terms,

2. The additional or different terms will materially alter the contract,

3. The offeror has already objected to the additional terms or thereafter objects to them within a reasonable time

The effect of this provision is to prevent the offeree unilaterally making major changes in the contract. Only nonmaterial changes by the offeree are incorporated into the contract, and even nonmaterial changes are excluded if the offeror objects to them. The UCC thus rejects the common law last-shot doctrine.

What constitutes a "material" alteration of the contract? That is for courts to decide on a case-by-case basis. Courts will generally consider material any attempt by the seller to disclaim liability for any defect in the product. Also, courts generally treat provisions calling for arbitration as being material.

Was the Contract Created by Conduct? Even if a contract isn't created pursuant to Section 2-207(1)—that is, through the exchange of documents—a contract can still be created under Section 2-207(3) if *both* parties behave as if they have a contract. Thus, if the parties start to perform (i.e., if the seller starts to make delivery and the buyer makes at least partial payment), the UCC will treat their arrangement as a valid contract. What are the terms of the contract? Under Section 2-207(3), the terms are all terms on which the parties' respective documents agree plus any supplementary terms provided by the UCC. These supplementary terms, commonly referred to as "gap fillers," are terms that the UCC automatically incorporates into sales contracts that are silent on price, method of delivery, place of delivery or other important matters. The gap-filler terms are set forth in Article 2, Part 3 of the UCC.

Figure 12-3 illustrates how UCC Section 2-207 operates with regard to the creation of a contract in cases where the acceptance varies from the offer. Figure 12-4 outlines how to determine what terms will be included in a contract created pursuant to Section 2-207. The concepts illustrated in these figures provide a framework for analyzing Section 2-207 problems, such as those posed by the case that follows.

AIR PRODUCTS & CHEM., INC. V. FAIRBANKS MORSE, INC.

Supreme Court of Wisconsin
206 N.W.2d 414 (1973)

BACKGROUND: Air Products (plaintiff), a buyer of large electric motors, brought this action against Fairbanks (defendant), the manufacturer, alleging that the motors, which were manufactured by the defendant and sold to the plaintiff, contained defective parts unreasonably dangerous to parts of other motors that caused damage to those motors and economic loss to the plaintiff.

The contract was created in a classic battle-of-the-forms sequence. Air Products first sent a purchase order form setting forth its terms and conditions. Fairbanks responded with its own acknowledgment-of-order form that included, among other things, a provision limiting Fairbanks's liability to Air Products.

The trial court said the acknowledgment form could limit the plaintiff's right to recover damages against the defendant. The plaintiff appealed.

Hanley, Justice

On the reverse side of the "acknowledgment of order" there are printed six separate provisions. . . .

Provision #6 which is the subject of the dispute between the parties provides that:

6.—The Company nowise assumes any responsibility or liability with respect to use, purpose, or suitability, and shall not be liable for damages of any character, whether direct or consequential, for defect, delay, or otherwise, its sole liability and obligation being confined to the replacement in the manner aforesaid of defectively manufactured guaranteed parts failing within the time stated.

Fairbanks contends that provision #6 contained on the reverse side of their "acknowledgment of order" became part of the contract between it and Air Products while Air Products contends that its right to rely on implied [warranties] . . . and consequential damages has in no way been limited because it never assented to the exclusion of any warranties or damages. Both parties are in agreement that sec. 2-207, of the Uniform Commercial Code (12A Pennsylvania Statutes Ann. sec. 2-207) is the appropriate standard by which their rights must be determined. . . .

One commentator has aptly stated the threshold questions involved in subsection (1) of 2-207:

Thus, under subsection (1), there are two instances in which a contract may not have been formed. First, if the offeror could not reasonably treat the response of the offeree as an acceptance there is no contract. Second, if the offeree's acceptance is made expressly conditional on the offeror's assent to variant provisions, the offeree has made a counter-offer. However, under section 2-207(3) either situation may result in contract formation by subsequent conduct of the parties.

Because the reverse side of Fairbanks' Acknowledgment of Order states that the provisions contained there ". . . form part of the order acknowledged and accepted on the face hereof . . ." it would seem that Air Products could have "reasonably" assumed that the parties "had a deal."

Since there is no express provision in the purchase orders making assent to different or additional terms conditioned upon Air Products' assent to them, the second requirement of coming under U.C.C. 2-207 is also met.

Air Products . . . contend[s] that if the added terms of the "acknowledgment of order" were "additional" terms they still do not become part of the contract because the prerequisite to their becoming a part of the contract which are contained in subsection (2) were not satisfied. Section 2-207(2) required that:

The additional terms are to be construed as proposals for addition to the contract. Between merchants such terms become part of the contract unless:

(a) the offer expressly limits acceptance to the terms of the offer;

(b) they materially alter it; or

(c) notification of objection to them has already been given or is given within a reasonable time after notice of them is received.

The language employed by Air Products in its "terms and conditions" was not express enough to bring into play the provisions of either subsection 2-207(a) or (c). The ultimate question to be determined, therefore, is whether the disclaimer contained in Fairbanks' "acknowledgment of order" materially altered the agreement between the parties pursuant to sec. 2-207(2)(b). If they materially alter what would otherwise be firmed by the acceptance of an offer, they will not become terms unless the buyer expressly agrees thereto. "If, however, they are terms which would not so change the bargain they will be incorporated unless notice of objection to them has already been given or is given within a reasonable time." . . .

Air Products contend[s] that the eradication of a multi-million dollar damage exposure is *per se* material. Fairbanks bases its argument on the ground that consequential damages may not be recovered except in "special circumstances" or in a "proper case." 2-714(2), (3).

We agree with plaintiffs . . . Air Products and conclude that the disclaimer for consequential loss was sufficiently material to require express conversation between the parties over its inclusion or exclusion in the contract.

DECISION: The trial court's decision was reversed and the Supreme Court ruled in favor of plaintiff Air Products.

International Approach The UN Convention on Contracts for the International Sale of Goods (CISG), discussed in the previous two chapters, deals with acceptances varying from offers in a manner that borrows from both the common law mirror-image rule and UCC Section 2-207. Under CISG Article 19, a purported acceptance that contains "additions, limitations and other modifications" of the offer's terms is generally deemed to be a rejection and a counteroffer. However, if the purported acceptance contains additional or different terms that don't materially alter the terms of the offer, then those terms become part of the contract unless the offeror sends

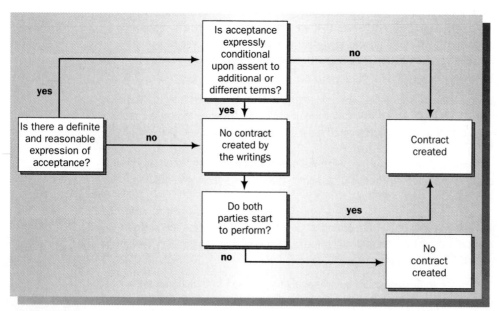

FIGURE 12-3

Creation of Contract under UCC Where Acceptance Varies from Offer

FIGURE 12-4

Inclusion and Exclusion of Terms in Contracts Created under UCC 2-207

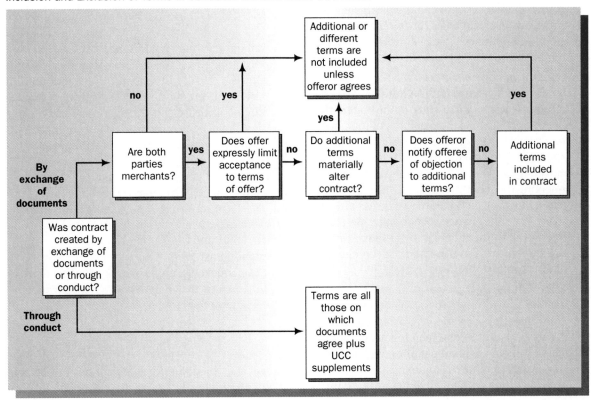

a notice of objection to the offeree within a reasonable time. Among the terms that are always considered material under the CISG are those relating to price, payment, quality and quantity of goods, place and time of delivery, liability, and the settlement of disputes.

Acceptance Problems

At the outset of the chapter, we noted the three requirements that must be met in order for an acceptance to result: there must be an intent to contract, an effective communication, and a response that generally satisfies all the terms and requirements imposed by the offer. It should be noted that, in many situations, it is generally the offeror, not the offeree, who controls the form and manner of the acceptance. This is because of the third requirement—that the acceptance conform to the terms and requirements imposed by the offer. Thus, the offeror often has the power to change the general rule applied in many of the situations this chapter has discussed. All the offeror must

do is to add to the offer the requirements that it seeks to obtain from the offeree. Several unusual acceptance problems arise because of the offeror's control of the acceptance.

Silence as Acceptance

Generally, the offeree who responds silently to the offer is not considered to be accepting the offer. Mere inaction and silence are usually not regarded as manifestations of intent to agree on a contract. However, some exceptions to this rule occur, usually because of the terms suggested in the offer. Book clubs, record clubs, wine clubs, and gourmet clubs often make agreements under which the club "members" will be considered to have accepted the "monthly offer" if they are silent and do not inform the club that the merchandise offered is not desired. The exceptions recognized by the law usually occur in one of three situations.

1. If the transactions the parties have entered into in the past show their intent to regard si-

lence as an acceptance, that intent becomes a part of their future transactions. Here, the *course of dealing* between the parties in past transactions is the basis for finding their present intent to have silence constitute acceptance.

2. The *initial agreement* between the parties constitutes the basis for treating silence by the offeree as acceptance. Thus, at the beginning of the transactions, the members of the book, record, or wine club sign a written agreement stating that they agree to pay for the items received if they do not send in the card or notice rejecting the monthly offering. The members agree that they do not have to express affirmatively their acceptance each month; silence on the part of the members is, by virtue of the initial agreement, also a method of accepting the club's monthly offering.

3. If the offeree *uses the goods* and treats them as if he had accepted them, the courts consider the offeree's actions and silence as together constituting the required acceptance. This problem occurs most often with regard to magazines or newspapers mistakenly being sent to people who didn't order them. Courts usually consider that, since the offeror is in business and did not intend a gift, the person who receives them and reads them is assumed to have agreed to pay for them. Most states now have statutes that allow the recipient of unsolicited merchandise, particularly where sent through the mail, to treat such items as gifts. The Postal Reorganization Act provides that mailing unsolicited merchandise is an unfair method of competition unless the product is marked "sample" or is sent by a charity. The Act also provides that the recipient may treat the received merchandise as a gift. Silence and use of such products will not be construed as acceptance of an implied offer to sell.

The Auction

An auction is a sales device whereby members of the public or a designated group come together to compete, by means of bids, for the purchase of goods or realty. Auctions are usually conducted by professional auctioneers or by public officials and may be of two types. In an **auction with re-**

---

serve, the object bid for does not have to be sold if the auctioneer is dissatisfied with the level of the bidding. In an **auction without reserve**, the object must be sold to the highest bidder.

Under UCC Section 2-328, an auction is considered to be with reserve unless it is expressly stated to be without reserve. Because at least one court has held that the phrase "will sell to highest bidder" is insufficient to make an auction without reserve, the actual words "without reserve" should be used in an announcement to insure that the auction is of that type.

In an auction with reserve, each bid is considered an offer. Acceptance is signaled by the fall of the hammer or some other symbolic act that is customary for the type of auction involved. In an auction without reserve, the announcement is considered the offer and each bid is an acceptance subject to the condition that no higher bid is made. This is illustrated in Figure 12-5.

Cancellation of Acceptance

We have discussed the problems that occur in determining whether there has been an acceptance of the offer. If an acceptance has been made, the

FIGURE 12-5

Two Types of Auctions

	Offer	Acceptance
With reserve	Each bid	Fall of the hammer following highest bid
Without reserve	Announcement that an item is up for auction	Each bid, subject to condition that no higher bid is made

offer can no longer be revoked by the offeror because it has now become part of a contract. Similarly, the offeree who has accepted the offer generally is not free to reject the offer subsequently. Neither party can reverse its original position. While contract law generally follows this interpretation, statutes in many states allow one of the contracting parties to cancel an acceptance (or to terminate an offer) in certain circumstances.

Typical of these statutes is Michigan's Home Solicitation Sales Act (M.C.L.A. 445.111 et. seq.). The law grants to the buyer of goods or services costing more than $25 who has made an offer or who has accepted an offer the right to revoke the offer or cancel the acceptance within 3 business days from the date of the transaction. The law applies only to a home solicitation sale made at the residence of the buyer and only the buyer, not the seller, is given the right to revoke the offer or cancel the acceptance. The law is intended to protect the consumer from high-pressured salespeople who force the consumer to act in a way he or she might not if given more time and less pressure. The 3-day period is often referred to as a "cooling-off period" since the buyer has this time to reconsider the transaction.

Review Questions and Problems

Key Terms

acceptance	merchant
mailbox rule	auction with reserve
last-shot doctrine	auction without reserve

Discussion Questions

1. When can acceptance occur without some written or spoken manifestation?

2. What is the difference between a bilateral and a unilateral agreement?

3. To what extent must an acceptance match the terms of an offer under common law? Under the UCC?

4. When can silence act as acceptance of an offer?

Review Problems

1. A seller offered equipment to a buyer at a specified price, stating that a 25 percent down payment was required with any order. The seller further required that the purchaser submit a signed order to be accepted by the seller. The buyer telephoned the seller, stating that the offer was accepted, and asking that the seller commence delivery immediately. The seller responded, "We'll get on it immediately." Subsequently, the seller discovered an error in the price that was originally quoted. The buyer insists that a valid contract at the quoted price exists. Do you agree?

2. A purchaser, responding in writing by letter, asked a vendor to sell two railroad cars of steel products at $15 per ton. The vendor wrote back, "We can't sell at that price, but would accept a price on two cars at $17.50 per ton." The purchaser then responded in writing, "We will purchase from you two carloads at $17.50 per ton. Our inspector will inspect the shipment for parts to be accepted or rejected." The vendor replied, "We do not agree with inspection; we are not selling subject to inspection." Is there a contract? If so, does it include the right of inspection?

3. Just prior to his policy lapsing, the insured received a renewal notice from the insurer, stating that if the insured did not wish to renew, he must

return the renewal notice or be liable for the renewal premium. The insured threw the notice in the trash, as he did with subsequent identical notices from the insurer. Will the insured be liable for the renewal premium?

4. Sally Student joined a compact disk club. She sent in $1 and received six CDs of her choice. The terms of the club required her to buy six CDs at the reduced club membership prices for the next 2 years. Each month the club sends its members a form that must be returned or the "CD of the Month" will be sent. Sally doesn't return the first form and receives the new Crash Test Dummies CD. Sally copies the CD and then returns it and refuses to pay for the CD. Does Sally have to pay for the CD?

Case Problems

1. A subcontractor made a contract with a general contractor that allowed the general contractor to use the subcontractor's machine for a specified time period while it was doing construction work on the landowner's property. When the time for the use of the subcontractor's machine expired, the subcontractor sent a bill to the landowner for rental due on the machine and an invoice stating the rental rate for the continued use of the machine. The landowner responded to the bill and informed the subcontractor that the equipment needs for future construction work on his property were being examined by the general contractor and that all future rental payments for the use of the subcontractor's machine would be the responsibility of the general contractor. The subcontractor's machine remained on the property of the landowner, but was not used by him or by the general contractor. Is there a contract between the landowner and the subcontractor for the rental of the subcontractor's machine?

2. Westside and Hurble entered into an option agreement on April 5, 1963, wherein Hurble, for $50, was given a 60-day option to purchase certain real estate. The option provided that the offer by Westside to sell the real estate at an agreed-upon price was irrevocable. On May 2, 1963, Hurble sent Westside a letter stating that Hurble exercised its option and also noting that "as additional inducement for Hurble to exercise its option, you have agreed that all utilities, gas, water, sewer, and electricity, will be extended to the property prior to the closing date. The contract of sale is hereby amended to provide that the seller shall extend all utility lines to the property before the closing date. Please sign this letter to indicate your acceptance of the amendment." On May 14, Hurble sent Westside another letter instructing it to disregard the proposed amendment in the letter of May 2 and that it now was exercising its option without amendment. Has Hurble accepted Westside's offer so as to create a contract?

3. Farley solicited a bid from Clark whereby the latter agreed to fabricate 100 trailers at a designated price. Farley considered other bids and decided to award the job to another firm. Farley prepared a check for the other firm and sent it by mistake to Clark. The check was for $18 less per unit than the offer. Clark deposited the check and began production. Farley sued to recover the proceeds of the check. What result?

4. Over a series of transactions occurring during a 2-year period, the plaintiff, Carpet Mart, purchased a variety of carpeting from the defendant, Collins & Aikman. After checking that the terms agreed to in oral conversations were met, the defendant sent an acknowledgment form to the plaintiff for each of its orders. The following provision was printed on the acknowledgment form:

> The acceptance of your order is subject to all of the terms and conditions on the face and reverse side hereof, including arbitration, all of which are accepted by buyer; it supersedes buyer's order form, if any. It shall become a contract either (a) when signed and delivered by buyer to seller and accepted in writing by seller, or (b) at seller's option, when buyer shall have given to seller specification of assortments, delivery dates, shipping instructions, . . . or instructions to bill and hold as to all or any part of the merchandise herein described, or when buyer has received delivery of the whole or any part thereof, or when buyer has otherwise assented to the terms and conditions hereof.

Is the arbitration agreement appearing on the back of the acknowledgment form sent to the Carpet Mart by Collins & Aikman a part of the contract between them?

13

Consideration

Legal Detriment
Bargained Exchange

Promissory Estoppel

No legal system enforces all promises. For example, a promise to undertake a social obligation—to come for dinner or to attend a wedding—would not be enforced by any court. The mere fact that one person promises something to another creates no legal duty and makes no remedy available if the person does not carry out the promise. The problem before the courts has been to determine which promises should be enforced and which should not.

The preceding chapters examined the requirements of a valid offer and acceptance as the essential elements of an agreement. Although agreement is essential to the formation of a contract, not all agreements are contracts. This chapter focuses on the additional element that is generally necessary if an agreement is to rise to the level of a contract. This element is the consideration.

Consideration is the exchange element of a contract. It is what induces the parties' agreement. It is what one party must give to another to make the other party legally obligated to perform its promise, the quid pro quo of the agreement. If there is no consideration there is no contract, and this is true even if there has been a valid offer and acceptance.

Consideration is the legal obligation that a person takes on. This person is a *promisee*. A promisee bargains with someone who makes a promise—the *promisor*. This bargained exchange is the consideration.

Society benefits from the fair enforcement of promises. A society that refused to enforce any promise would place people in risky positions. A promisor's word would be only as good as his or her reputation for performance. But no society can enforce all promises. Some promises are unreasonable or harmful. The existence of consideration is treated as evidence that the promisee's expectation is reasonable and that nonperformance would injure the community.

The concept of consideration can be illustrated by a simple example. John carelessly drives his car into David's. David's car is damaged and he has a right to sue John. John promises to pay David $500, and David promises that he will not sue over the car accident. The contract is supported by consideration. John has undertaken a new obligation—to pay David. David has given up a legal right—to sue John.

The following discussion examines two components of consideration: the legal detriment of the promisee and the bargained exchange for the promise.

Legal Detriment

A person incurs *legal detriment* by voluntarily agreeing to assume a duty or to give up a right. A person must do or promise to do what he or she is not legally obligated to do, or the person must promise not do do what he or she has a right to do.

227

A *legal* detriment is not the same as real detriment or loss. In deciding whether someone has incurred a legal detriment, the courts do not focus on whether that person suffered economic or physical loss. The courts focus on whether the person agreed either to assume a *duty* or to relinquish a *right*. The following case illustrates the distinction between the two kinds of detriments.

HAMER V. SIDWAY

Court of Appeals of New York, Second Division

27 N.E. 256 (1891)

BACKGROUND: In March 1869, William E. Story, Sr., promised his nephew, William E. Story, 2d, the sum of $5,000 if the nephew would refrain from drinking, smoking, swearing, and gambling until his twenty-first birthday. In January 1875, the nephew had reached his twenty-first birthday. Having satisfied all of the necessary conditions, he wrote to his uncle claiming the $5,000. The uncle replied that the nephew would get the money. But he asked to be allowed to hold it in the bank until he felt that the nephew was capable of taking care of it. In 1879, the nephew turned over his claim to the $5,000 to his wife. In turn, she turned it over to Hamer (plaintiff). When the uncle died, Hamer claimed the $5,000. But the executor of the estate, Sidway (defendant), denied the claim. The executor argued that the $5,000 was without consideration, because the nephew had benefited from the actions that were necessary to receive the reward. Hamer recovered at trial, but the judgment was reversed on appeal. Hamer then appealed to the Court of Appeals of New York, that state's highest court.

Parker, Judge

The question which provoked the most discussion by counsel on this appeal, and which lies at the foundation of plaintiff's asserted right of recovery, is whether by virtue of a contract defendant's testator, William E. Story, became indebted to his nephew, William E. Story, 2d, on his twenty-first birthday in the sum of $5,000. The trial court found as a fact that "on the 20th day of March, 1869, . . . William E. Story agreed to and with William E. Story, 2d, that if he would refrain from drinking liquor, using tobacco, swearing and playing cards or billiards for money until he should become twenty-one years of age, then he, the said William E. Story, would at that time pay him, the said William E. Story, 2d, the sum of $5,000 for such refraining, to which the said William E. Story, 2d, agreed," and that he "in all things fully performed his part of said agreement." The defendant contends that the contract was without consideration to support it, and therefore invalid. He asserts that the promisee, by refraining from the use of liquor and tobacco, was not harmed, but benefited; that that which he did was best for him to do, independently of his uncle's promise—and insists that it follows that, unless the promisor was benefited, the contract was without consideration—a contention which, if well founded, would seem to leave open for controversy in many cases whether that which the promisee did or omitted to do was in fact of such benefit to him as to leave no consideration to support the enforcement of the promisor's agreement. Such a rule could not be tolerated, and is without foundation in the law. The exchequer chamber in 1875 defined "consideration" as follows: "A valuable consideration, in the sense of the law, may consist either in some right, interest, profit or benefit accruing to the one party, or some forbearance, detriment, loss, or responsibility given, suffered, or undertaken by the other." Courts "will not ask whether the thing which forms the consideration does in fact benefit the promisee or a third party, or is of any substantial value to any one. It is enough that something is promised, done, forborne, or suffered by the party to whom the promise is made as consideration for the promise made to him." Anson, Cont. 63. "In general a waiver of any legal right at the request of another party is a sufficient consideration for a promise." Pars. Cont. *444. "Any damage, or suspension, or forbearance of a right will be sufficient to sustain a promise." 2 Kent, Comm. (12th Ed.) *465. Pollock in his work on Contracts, (page 166) after citing the definition given by the exchequer chamber, already quoted, says: "The second branch of this judicial description is really the most important one. 'Consideration' means not so much that one party is profiting as that the other abandons some legal right to the present, or limits his legal freedom of action in the future, as an inducement for the promise of the first." Now, applying this rule to the facts before us, the promisee used tobacco, occasionally drank liquor, and he had a legal right to do so. That right he abandoned for a period of years upon the strength of the promise of the testator that for such forbearance he would give him $5,000. We need not speculate on the effort which may have been required to give up the use of those stimulants. It is sufficient that he restricted his lawful freedom of action within certain prescribed limits upon the faith of his uncle's agreement, and now, having fully performed the conditions imposed, it is of no moment whether such performance actually proved a benefit to the promisor, and the court will not inquire into it; but, were it a proper subject of inquiry, we see nothing in this record that would permit a determination that the uncle was not benefited in a legal sense.

Decision: The Court of Appeals found in favor of Hamer, the plaintiff, and reversed the lower appellate court ruling and affirmed the judgment of the trial court.

Adequacy vs. Sufficiency of Consideration

When deciding whether a contract is supported by consideration, it is important to distinguish between the *adequacy* of the consideration and the *sufficiency* of the consideration. Although the semantic distinction between these terms is small, the legal distinction between them is significant. So watch your language!

The term *adequacy* refers to the quantity or value of the consideration. Courts do not generally inquire into the adequacy of the consideration; they are concerned only that there is a legally sufficient consideration, meaning that the promisee incurred a legal detriment in exchange for the promise. Thus, any legal detriment constitutes valuable consideration no matter how economically inadequate it may be.

For example, suppose that for $1 Penelope gave to Ring Telephone Company the right to install and maintain telephone wire over her land. Later Penelope finds out that other property owners have received much more money for giving the same rights to Ring. Penelope cannot later refuse to allow Ring on her land by arguing that she received an inadequate consideration for her promise to Ring. For Ring to obtain enforcement of Penelope's promise, Ring must show that Penelope received sufficient consideration for her promise. Ring would be able to obtain enforcement because, by paying $1 to Penelope, Ring relinquished the right it had to keep its money. Thus Ring incurred a legal detriment in exchange for Penelope's promise. A court would enforce her promise because the economic value of the consideration is not relevant in determining whether there is a valid consideration.

Courts do not inquire into the adequacy of consideration, because they should not be required to police the marketplace to protect people from their own imprudence. This policy of judicial self-restraint in dealing with economic matters is consistent with the common law notion that the courts do not make contracts for people. However, the rule assumes that the parties have freely entered into their agreement. Where this assumption is questioned, the courts *do* take into account the adequacy of consideration. If someone argues that a contract was made through fraud, misrepresentation, duress, undue influence, or mistake, a court will examine the adequacy of the consideration as evidence of the existence of those factors. A court might also find evidence of fraud if the consideration is so grossly inadequate that it shocks the conscience of the court. The case that follows is an illustration of this point.

AHERN V. KNECHT

Appellate Court of Illinois
563 N.E.2d 787 (1990)

BACKGROUND: Mrs. Ahern's air conditioner stopped working properly during a heat wave. On June 23, 1989, she called defendant Knecht out to repair the unit. Knecht charged Ahern $762 for his work. Unbeknownst to Ahern at the time, Knecht unnecessarily repeated repair work that had been done on the unit by another contractor 2 months earlier. The unit still wasn't operating properly after Knecht left, and Ahern hired someone else to fix the air conditioner for $72. Ahern brought an action to recover excessive charges from Knecht. The trial court found that Knecht's work was worth $150, minus the $72 that Ahern was required to pay the other repairman. The trial court therefore awarded Ahern a judgment of $684. Knecht appealed, arguing that the court was not entitled to inquire into the adequacy of consideration supporting his contract with Ahern.

Woodward, Justice

Because plaintiff complained that defendant's prices were outrageously exorbitant in relation to the value of the services received, our examination of the evidence focuses first on the adequacy of consideration to support the contract. Consideration is any act or promise which is of benefit to one party or disadvantageous to the other. Generally, courts will not inquire into the adequacy of the consideration to support a contract. However, where the amount of consideration is so grossly inadequate as to shock the conscience of the court, the contract will fail. Evidence of gross inadequacy of consideration has been considered by some Illinois courts as tantamount to fraud. . . . Thus, where there is a substantial failure of consideration for a contract, particularly where the inadequacy is accompanied by other inequitable or unconscionable features, a court of equity may rescind or cancel the contract. Alternatively, substantial nonperformance or breach of contract warrants rescission where the matter, in respect to which the failure of performance occurs, is of such a nature and of such importance that the contract would not have been made without it. A plaintiff desiring to rescind a contract must merely show the nonperformance or the inability to perform by defendant and offer to return the value of the consideration received or otherwise return the other party to the status quo *ante*.

A contract may be treated as unconscionable when it is improvident, oppressive, or totally one-sided. Even where there is no actual fraud, courts of equity will relieve against hard and unconscionable contracts which have been procured by taking advantage of the condition, circumstances or necessity of the other parties. Factors relevant to finding a contract unconscionable include gross disparity in the values exchanged or gross inequality in the bargaining positions of the parties together with terms unreasonably favorable to the stronger party. Courts will also look to such factors as the age and education of the contracting parties, their commercial experience, and whether the aggrieved party had a meaningful choice when faced with unreasonably unfavorable terms.

The circumstances existing when the contract was entered into in this case were such that the terms of the contract should be set aside as unconscionable. It is clear that the services rendered were of little or no value in contrast to the price paid to defendant. Gross excessiveness of price alone can make an agreement unconscionable. Defendant performed services that had been performed a few weeks prior to June 23, including raising and levelling the condenser slab in less than 20 minutes with plaintiff's patio gravel for $210 and wet washing the condenser and coils for $138. Furthermore, he was to check, clean, and tighten the electrical connections for $69, fix the leak for $72, and add freon for another

$119. In these last three tasks, defendant not only failed to perform substantially, but the unit was further disabled during defendant's service call whereas it had been mechanically operating prior to defendant's work on it. It is quite evident that the crux of the problem was a freon leak which was easily corrected by yet another service company for only $72. In addition, defendant required the payment of $154 just to answer the service call and "diagnose" or, more properly, misdiagnose, the problem. We have no difficulty in concluding that there was a grossly disparate exchange of values here which may be due to defendant's incompetence or his sharp business practices.

The bargaining power of the parties was similarly disproportionate. Mrs. Ahern professed her ignorance of procedures for repairing an air conditioner, and she was obviously relying on defendant's purported expertise. The cooling failure occurred during a heat wave, and she was already liable for the $154 service call even before agreeing to the remaining repair charges. Mrs. Ahern testified that she felt intimidated by defendant. It is clear that defendant was in a superior bargaining position. Freedom to contract is enhanced by a requirement that both parties be aware of the burdens they are assuming; however, the notion of free will has little meaning as applied to one who is ignorant of the consequences of her acts. Courts must be realistic in examining the true nature of a consumer transaction such as this one where the complexity of the technology involved is such that it would be unconscionable to expect the ordinary consumer to have skill equal to that of the expert in dealing at arm's length. In view of the consumer's lack of experience in this type of transaction, the defendant's substantial charge for travel and diagnosis, his representations that the services were all necessary, and his insistence on immediate payment suggesting urgency, we conclude that this consumer had no meaningful choice and the agreement was not voluntarily and understandingly entered into.

DECISION: The appeals court affirmed the decision in favor of Ahern.

Another circumstance in which a court examines the adequacy of consideration is in the equal exchange of interchangeable goods or the equal exchange of money. Goods that are *fungible* are indistinguishable and interchangeable. One carload of wheat cannot be distinguished from another; the carloads of wheat are thus fungible goods. Under the *fungible goods* doctrine, a contract calling for an exchange of equal amounts of wheat is not supported by consideration. Similarly, people who put a clause in their agreement that each has given the other $1 as consideration for the agreement will find that they have no contract because there is no consideration.

Unlike adequacy of consideration, sufficiency of consideration is readily examined by the courts. If what was given in exchange for a promise is insufficient to constitute consideration, there is no contract. In order for sufficient consideration to exist, there must be a legal detriment bargained for and given in exchange for a promise. When what is given is not a legal detriment, then it is not sufficient to constitute consideration and no contract is formed.

Illusory Promises

Any promise that leaves it up to the promisor whether to perform is *illusory*. A person who promises to do something "if I feel like it" has not promised anything at all and has incurred no legal detriment. Even though people use promissory language, if the person making the promise is not required to do anything, the promise is illusory. An illusory promise is not sufficient consideration because nothing has been promised.

Although the rule that an illusory promise cannot serve as sufficient consideration is logical, the result of such a rule can be harsh. Two categories of promises illustrate this problem: cancellation or termination clauses and output and requirements contracts. We turn to those now.

Cancellation or Termination Clauses

Contracts often let one or both parties cancel obligations under certain circumstances. Suppose that two enter into a contract in which one promises to buy and the other promises to sell 500 widgets a month. The buyer has the right to cancel "at any time without notice." That clause means that there is no contract. Lack of consideration makes the buyer's promise illusory. Because the buyer has the right to terminate the agreement at will and is not required to perform, the buyer has not actually assumed a duty to buy. If a cancellation clause allows a party to avoid an obligation at will, the contract is voidable. A contract that is voidable at the will of one of the parties is illusory.

However, the situation is different if the buyer is required to notify the seller that he or she is terminating the contract. Most courts hold that with a termination clause requiring notice ahead of time, the promisor incurs a legal detriment.

Additionally, many courts have held that when a termination clause contains no notice requirement, the requirement of a reasonable notice of termination is assumed. This assumption is made when it is clear that both parties intended to enter into a binding contract. This approach seeks to preserve the intent of the parties and reflects legislative and judicial reluctance to strike down an otherwise valid agreement on a technicality.

Output and Requirements Contracts

An **output contract** is an agreement to sell one's entire production of goods during the term of the contract to a purchaser. A **requirements contract** is an agreement to purchase all one's requirements for a given product during the term of the contract from the seller. Such contracts are useful, especially for new businesses. However, many courts once held that such agreements are illusory because they provide no specifications of how much of the product is to be sold or bought. The seller might choose not to produce all of the product that it is capable of producing, and the buyer might choose not to buy the product.

The UCC (Section 2-306) has legitimized output and requirements contracts by providing standards required for enforcement. It imposes an obligation to act in good faith on the party who determines the quantity. This good-faith obligation constitutes a sufficient consideration for any output or requirements contract.

The Pre-existing Duty Rule

When people promise to do something that they are already obligated to do, they have not incurred a legal detriment. This is known as the **pre-existing duty rule**.

For example, people cannot promise not to commit crimes in return for payment because they have a pre-existing duty not to commit crimes or torts. Thus, some pre-existing duties are created by law. Similarly, public officials cannot collect rewards for performing their duty. If a shopkeeper offers a $5,000 reward for the arrest and conviction of the person who burglarized his or her store, the police officer who diligently pursues and jails the offender may not collect that reward. The officer is already required by law to catch criminals and therefore has incurred no new legal detriment that would entitle him or her to enforcement of the promise of reward.

A pre-existing duty also may be created by contract. When the promise of one party is merely a repetition of an existing promise and no additional duties are imposed, the promise does not constitute consideration. For example, suppose that Penelope hires Julius to repair her garage door. Julius and Penelope agree that the price of the repair will be $150. However, after starting work, Julius reconsidered his costs and asks Penelope to pay him $200. She agrees. Upon completion of the repair, Julius is entitled to only $150. Because Julius was already under contract to repair Penelope's door for $150, he has incurred no legal detriment in exchange for her promise to pay $50 more. Julius has merely agreed to finish the repair, which he was under a contractual duty to do already.

The pre-existing duty rule is often criticized as illogical. In the preceding example, Penelope appears able to avoid the enforcement of her promise. But the reason for the rule is the concern that enforcement of the second promise would encourage coercion. In most of the cases where the pre-existing duty rule is invoked, the second bargain was coerced. For example, a contractor might threaten a homeowner that unless she pays an extra $150, he will leave her roof half fixed. Where the facts do not show coercion, the courts have stretched doctrine to reach a more desired result.

For example, if in consideration for Penelope's promise to pay $50 more, Julius had agreed to do something, however slight, that was not called for in the original contract, Julius would have incurred a legal detriment. The addition of a new duty in exchange for Penelope's promise makes the promise enforceable.

Another device for getting around the pre-existing duty rule is for the parties to agree to rescind their old contract and make a new one. Contracts may be canceled and new ones made when the people involved mutually consent to the cancellation of the contracts. Furthermore, the cancellation itself is a contract and must be supported by consideration. In this case, the consideration usually takes the form of the parties' agreement to release each other from their obligations. When people rescind their earlier agreement and enter into a new one, there are actually three contracts: the original contract, the rescission contract, and the new contract.

Some courts recognize an exception to the pre-existing duty rule in cases where the second promise results from substantial *unforeseen difficulties* in performance. For example, if a contractor agreed to build a house and a tornado destroyed the half-built house, some courts would hold that an owner's subsequent promise to pay the contractor more is binding, even though the contractor has not agreed to do anything more than was called for by the original contract. The suspicion of coercion by the contractor is not present, the owner might be criticized for promising to pay more to induce the contractor to continue but later disavowing the promise.

The following case illustrates some of the issues in the pre-existing duty rule.

LEVINE V. BLUMENTHAL

Supreme Court of New Jersey
186 A. 457 (1936)

BACKGROUND: On April 16, 1931, William Levine (respondent) agreed to lease a business site to Anne Blumenthal (appellant). Rent for the first year was to be $2,100, payable in monthly installments of $175 in advance. The second year the rent was scheduled to increase to $2,400, payable in monthly installments of $200. In April 1932, approximately 1 year into the lease term, Blumenthal told Levine that, due to adverse business conditions generally resulting from the Great Depression, she would be unable to pay the increased rent of $200. She asserted that if Levine insisted on the extra $25 a month, she would have to leave the building and perhaps go out of business altogether. Blumenthal claimed that Levine agreed not to demand the extra $25 a month until business improved. Levine claimed that he agreed to accept the reduced rent "on account." Blumenthal paid rent of $175 for 11 months of the second year of the lease and then vacated the premises. Levine sued to recover the unpaid rent for the last month of the lease and the unpaid balance of $25 per month for the preceding 11 months. The trial court ruled in favor of Levine, and Blumenthal appealed the judgment.

Heher, Justice

The district court judge found, as a fact, that "a subsequent oral agreement had been made to change and alter the terms of the written lease, with respect to the rent paid," but that it was not supported by "a lawful consideration," and therefore was wholly ineffective.

The insistence is that the current trade depression had disabled the lessees in respect to the payment of the full rent reserved, and a full consideration sufficient to support the secondary agreement arose out of these special circumstances; and that, in any event, the execution of the substituted performance therein provided is a defense of law, notwithstanding the want of consideration. It is said also that, "insofar as the oral agreement has become executed as to the payments which had fallen due and had been paid and accepted in full as per the oral agreement" the remission of the balance of the rent is sustainable on the theory of gift, if not of accord and satisfaction.

The point made by respondent is that the subsequent oral agreement to reduce the rent . . . created no binding obligation.

It is elementary that the subsequent agreement, to impose the obligation of a contract, must rest upon a new and independent consideration. The rule was laid down in very early times that even though a part of a matured liquidated debt or demand has been given and received in full satisfaction thereof, the creditor may yet recover the remainder. The payment of a part was not regarded in law as a satisfaction of the whole, unless it was in virtue of an agreement supported by a consideration. The principle is firmly imbedded in our jurisprudence that a promise to do what the promisor is already legally bound to do is an unreal consideration. It has been criticized, at least in some of its special applications, as "medieval" and wholly artificial—one that operates to defeat the "reasonable bargains of businessmen." But these strictures are not well grounded. They reject the basic principle that a consideration, to support a contract, consists either of a benefit to the promisor or a detriment to the promisee—a doctrine that has always been fundamental in our conception of consideration. It is a principle, almost universally accepted, that an act or forbearance required by a legal duty owing to the promisor that is neither doubtful nor the subject of honest and reasonable dispute is not a sufficient consideration.

Yet any consideration for the new undertaking, however insignificant, satisfies this rule. . . . For instance, an undertaking to pay part of the debt before maturity, or at a place other than where the obligor was legally bound to pay, or to pay in property, regardless of its value, or to effect a composition with creditors by the payment of less than the sum due, has been held to constitute a consideration sufficient in law. The test is whether there is an additional consideration adequate to support an ordinary contract, and consists of something which the debtor was not legally bound to do or give.

And there is authority for the view that, where there is no illegal preference, a payment of part of a debt, "accompanied by an agreement of the debtor to refrain from voluntary bankruptcy," is a sufficient consideration for the creditor's promise to remit the balance of the debt. But the mere fact that the creditor "fears that the debtor will go into bankruptcy, and that the debtor contemplates bankruptcy proceedings," is not enough; that alone does not prove that the creditor requested the debtor to refrain from such proceedings.

The cases to the contrary either create arbitrary exceptions to the rule, or profess to find a consideration in the form of a new undertaking which in essence was not a tangible new obligation or a duty not imposed by the lease, or, in any event, was not the price "bargained for as the exchange for the promise," and therefore do violence to the fundamental principle. They exhibit the modern tendency, especially in the matter of rent reductions, to depart from the strictness of the basic common-law rule and give effect to what has been termed a "reasonable" modification of the primary contract.

So tested, the secondary agreement at issue is not supported by a valid consideration; and it therefore created no legal obligation. General economic adversity, however disastrous it may be in its individual consequences, is never a warrant for judicial abrogation of this primary principle of the law of contracts.

It remains to consider the second contention that, in so far as the agreement has been executed by the payment and acceptance of rent at the reduced rate, the substituted performance stands, regardless of the want of consideration. This is likewise untenable. Ordinarily, the actual performance of that which one is legally bound to do stands on the same footing as his promise to do that which he is legally compellable to do. This is a corollary of the basic principle. Of course, a different rule prevails where bona fide disputes have arisen respecting the relative rights and duties of the parties to a contract, or the debt or demand is unliquidated, or the contract is wholly executory on both sides.

It is settled in this jurisdiction that, as in the case of other contracts, a consideration is essential to the validity of an accord and satisfaction. On reason and principle, it could not be otherwise. This is the general rule. The cases cited by appellant are not in point. It results that the issue was correctly determined.

DECISION: The Supreme Court of New Jersey affirmed the trial court judgment in favor of Levine.

The drafters of the UCC cut through the maze of the common law and established a different rule for goods transactions. The UCC (Section 2-209) states simply: "An agreement modifying a contract within this Article needs no consideration to be binding." For example, suppose that a supplier agrees to deliver goods at $1 a unit. Later, due to market conditions, the supplier calls the buyer and asks if the buyer will agree to pay $2 a unit for the same goods. Under the preexisting duty rule, the buyer's promise to pay the higher price would not be enforceable for lack of consideration. However, under the UCC, if the buyer agrees to pay the higher price, the promise is enforceable. Note that the buyer still has to *agree* to pay the higher price. The buyer can refuse to accept the price change and hold the supplier to the original contract or recover for its breach. Once they have agreed to the modification, they cannot later disavow their promise.

Compromise of Debts   The pre-existing duty rule also comes into play in agreements between debtors and creditors to compromise on payments of debts. The delinquent debtor is a perennial problem for creditors. On the theory that a bird in the hand is worth two in the bush, creditors often accept less than the amount owed on the debt. But sometimes such arrangements are not enforceable for lack of consideration. If a creditor later seeks to recover full payment on the original debt, a debtor may not be able to enforce the creditor's promise to accept only partial payment. If the creditor's promise is not supported by consideration, because the debtor has not incurred any new legal detriment, the debtor may not be able to enforce the promise.

For example, suppose that a student owes State College $1,000. State College agrees to accept $300 as full payment. State College's promise to release the student from all claims is not supported by consideration. Because the student is already under a duty to pay $300, plus an additional $700, the student has not incurred any additional legal detriment.

However, to avoid causing people severe hardship or discouraging honesty and fair dealing, the courts have tried to find new consideration of some kind to support such compromises. Thus, when a debtor gives partial payment on a loan before the loan is due, or when a debtor gives a combination of money and property as satisfaction of the debt, courts may hold that the new consideration supports a modification of the original contract.

Under bankruptcy laws, once someone is declared bankrupt, the person is no longer required to pay his or her creditors. The debts are discharged by court order. But in some circumstances, it is advantageous to the bankrupt debtor to reaffirm some old debts and keep paying them. The courts usually hold that the consideration is the refusal of the debtor to use the defense of bankruptcy to avoid the creditor. Debtor and creditor then are free to reach a settlement in which the debtor satisfies the debt with only partial payment.

A slight variation of this device involves what are called **composition agreements**. These are used when debtors are in financial difficulties and fear being unable to pay their creditors in full. To avoid bankruptcy, one creditor may call other creditors to convince them to accept less than what is owed. The expenses of declaring bankruptcy and the likelihood that some creditors may wind up with nothing sometimes are enough incentive for creditors to consent to such an agreement. For example, if Julius thinks that he can pay 40 percent of his total debts, he may seek to enter into a composition agreement with his creditors. In such a case, each creditor may agree to accept 40 percent of the amount due from Julius.

The consideration in such agreements is the promises of the creditors to forgo part of their claims, the debtor's payment to the assenting creditors in equal proportions, the debtor's securing the assent of the creditors, or the part payment made to other creditors. Courts want to encourage these agreements between creditors and debtors, because they discourage litigation.

Accord and Satisfaction When a legitimate dispute exists about the existence or size of a debt, the pre-existing duty rule gives way to the doctrine of *accord and satisfaction.*

An **accord and satisfaction** is the offer of something different from what was provided for in the original contract (the accord) and an agreement to accept it (the satisfaction). Partial payment of an unliquidated debt, offered as full satisfaction of the obligation, is supported by consideration and discharges the obligation.

For example, suppose that Julius hires Penelope, a marketing consultant, to advise him about where to locate his business. Penelope performs the service and delivers a bill for $10,000. Julius believes that her fee is much too high for the services rendered. He maintains that a more reasonable fee would be $3,000. Together they settle their dispute by agreeing on a fee of $4,000. Here, the debt is in dispute; the amount owed is uncertain; the debt is unliquidated. By agreeing to pay $4,000, Julius is assuming a duty to pay $1,000 more than he in good faith believes is owed. By agreeing to take $4,000, Penelope is relinquishing her right to collect $6,000 more, which she in good faith believes is owed her. Each party has incurred a legal detriment in exchange for the other's promise. Their agreement is supported by consideration.

Forbearance to Pursue a Legal Right If people bargain, and one side agrees to give up a legal right, that surrender is adequate consideration to support a contract. This situation arises most frequently in insurance cases, when an insurance company promises to pay an agreed upon settlement amount in return for a claimant's promise not to file suit to recover for the alleged injury. If the insurance company refuses to make the payment after it has agreed to do so, the claimant is no longer bound by the contract and may file suit. However, the claimant may choose instead to file suit against the insurance company for breach of contract, seeking the promised settlement and any other damages.

The law in this area becomes muddied when the insurance company responds that the claimant did not have a valid claim from the outset. Because one cannot surrender what one does not have a right to in the first place, the insurance company argues that in surrendering or not asserting an invalid claim, the claimant has suffered no legal detriment and therefore any promise of settlement made in return by the insurance company is not supported by consideration.

Courts have generally not accepted this argument. Many courts have held that if the claim was made in good faith and a reasonable person could believe that the claim was well founded, surren-

---

PREVENTIVE LAW
Accord and Satisfaction

The precise mechanics of an accord and satisfaction vary among the states. The most common approach requires, as the first step, that the debtor notify the creditor of the disputed claim. Then, assuming that the debt is acknowledged but the amount is disputed, the debtor may write a check for the amount the debtor believes is due, indicate on the check itself that it is being tendered as payment in full, and then send it to the creditor along with a note indicating that the amount of liability is disputed. Once the creditor receives the check, the creditor has three options: (1) to cash the check, in which case the creditor accepts the debtor's offer of settlement and the debt is discharged; (2) to return the check, refusing the debtor's offer, and proceed as the creditor would in any collection case; or (3) to cash the check in defiance of the conditions upon which it was tendered, but only after first notifying the debtor that acceptance of the check is under protest. This last option is expressly allowed by Section 1-207 of the UCC. It should be noted that the accord-and-satisfaction doctrine applies only when there is a good-faith dispute. A bad-faith dispute will result in the debt being classified as a liquidated claim, in which case the pre-existing duty rule would apply and the debt would not be discharged by the attempted settlement.

der or forbearance would provide sufficient consideration. Other courts have held that good faith alone is sufficient. Still other courts have accepted claims when there is objective uncertainty as to the validity of the claim. The trend appears to be that if the claim is neither patently ridiculous nor corruptly asserted, then the court will view surrender or forbearance as adequate consideration.

This area of law resembles the doctrine of accord and satisfaction. Agreeing not to pursue a legal claim constitutes a legal detriment, because a person is relinquishing a right to bring suit. The requirement that the claimant believe in good faith that the claim is valid is similar to the requirement of a good-faith dispute for an accord and satisfaction.

Bargained Exchange

A person who receives a promise can incur all kinds of legal detriment, and even much real detriment for good measure, but it will not serve as sufficient consideration unless it is the bargained exchange for the promisor's promise.

Bargain

The requirement that the parties bargain is not so much a requirement that they actually sit down and dicker over the consideration as it is a requirement that the consideration be something that the promisor requested in return for being bound by the promise. An example of an unbargained for promise is a promise to make a gift. Sometimes a person attaches conditions to making a gift, things that the promisee must do to accept the gift. For example, Jennifer promises to give her tape collection to her sister, Shannon, if Shannon will come over to pick up the tapes. Jennifer is not bargaining for Shannon to come over, and there is no consideration for the promise to give the tapes. The critical factor in distinguishing a promise to make a gift on condition from a promise that is supported by consideration is the motive of the promisor.

Another example of a promise that is not supported by bargained-for consideration is a promise to do something because of something the promisee has done in the past. *Past consideration* is no consideration because it was not bar-

gained for in exchange for the promisor's promise. Past consideration cannot be used to support a new promise, because the legal detriment was neither bargained for nor given in exchange for the promise. Because every new contract requires new consideration, past consideration cannot be used to create an enforceable obligation.

The reasoning of the courts in refusing to enforce promises based upon past consideration stems not so much from a lack of legal detriment as from a lack of bargained exchange. The present promise is induced by a past consideration; the past consideration was not given in exchange for the present promise.

Likewise, a promise by one party made to another that is based on only a moral duty generally does not constitute consideration. Technically speaking, if the promisor has received a material benefit that prompts the making of a promise, there is no consideration. For example, if A pulls B from a burning building, saving B's life, and a week later B promises to give A $5,000 "in consideration for saving my life," B's promise is not enforceable because A's conduct was not induced by B's promise.

Exchange

Two parties may sign a written agreement in which one party agrees to do something in exchange for the other party's promise to pay a sum. For example, one person may promise something in exchange for "$1 in hand paid, receipt of which is acknowledged." The dollar is what is bargained for and given over in exchange for the promise.

If the stated consideration is a pretense, there is no consideration. If the stated consideration is not actually exchanged, there is no consideration. Just saying that they have agreed to a price of $1 does not constitute consideration. If the consideration is nominal, perhaps $1 in exchange for a valuable promise, courts examine whether that $1 was bargained for and given in exchange for the promise. The dollar must be both bargained for and actually exchanged for the promise to be supported by sufficient consideration. In some courts, an untrue *recital of consideration* operates as an implied promise to pay the recited sum and this implied promise satisfies the consideration requirement.

Promissory Estoppel

The requirement that a contract be supported by consideration is part of classic contract law. However, many courts have criticized the results of this requirement. Legislative dissatisfaction with the doctrine has been expressed in the UCC. The courts have established a substitute for consideration, the doctrine of *promissory estoppel*.

The doctrine permits a remedy based on reliance upon a promise. Under the doctrine of **promissory estoppel**, someone who makes a promise is "estopped" (meaning "made to stop") from denying the existence of the promise in cases where the promisee has justifiably relied upon the promise and has suffered harm. Thus, a promise that induces detrimental reliance upon the part of the promisee may be sufficient to bind the promisor, even though the detriment was not bargained for and given in exchange for the promise, so long as the promisor had reason to expect some act of reliance by the promisee.

Four elements must be established by the promisee. These elements are:

1. A promise. Not just any promise will do. The promise must be the type of promise that the promisor should reasonably expect the promisee will rely upon. The promise must generally be expressed. However, silence may constitute an implied promise where the promisor is under a duty to speak.

2. The promisee must in fact rely upon the promise. The reliance must be justifiable.

3. Substantial economic detriment to the promisee is necessary.

4. Injustice can be avoided only by the enforcement of the promise.

For example, consider the case of an employer who promises to pay an employee an annuity for the rest of the employee's life. The employee resigns from a profitable job, as the employer expected the employee would. The employee receives the annuity for several years. In the meantime, the employee becomes disqualified from working. The employer's promise would be enforced under the doctrine of promissory estoppel. Now suppose that the employee had been able to work. In that event, third and fourth elements of promissory estoppel would not be met. The following case illustrates the application of promissory estoppel.

ALLEN M. CAMPBELL CO. V. VIRGINIA METAL INDUSTRIES, INC.

U.S. Court of Appeals, Fourth Circuit
708 F.2d 930 (1983)

BACKGROUND: Allen M. Campbell Co. (plaintiff), in August 1981, intended to bid on a Department of Navy contract to construct housing for enlisted personnel at Camp LeJeune, North Carolina. The deadline for submission of bids was 2:00 P.M. on August 11, 1981. At about 1:30 P.M., Virginia Metal Industries, Inc. (defendant), telephoned Campbell and quoted a price to supply all hollow metal doors and frames required by the plans and specifications. The price quoted was $193,121, plus applicable taxes. Campbell based the computation for its bid for the Navy project upon the quoted price for the hollow metal doors and frames of $193,121 and taxes. Campbell was the successful bidder and was awarded the Navy contract. Virginia Metal backed out of its promise, and as a consequence, Campbell had to obtain the items covered by the quoted price of $193,121 from another supplier, at a cost $45,562 greater than what it had been led to expect Virginia Metal would charge. Campbell sued Virginia Metal Industries, Inc. for the $45,562. The trial court dismissed Campbell's complaint, and Campbell appealed to the Fourth Circuit Court of Appeals.

Murnaghan, Circuit Judge

In carrying out the functions of a judge, one comes to realize that there are very few cases indeed in which ultimately the facts do not control the outcome. Arguments impeccable in their abstract reliance upon broadly phrased principles of law tend to evaporate when the equities point to a different result. Purely linguistic considerations should not be permitted to outweigh substance.

Virginia Metal's rejoinder to Campbell's suit for the difference of $45,562 is that there had been no promise by Campbell that, should it prove the successful bidder for the Navy contract, it would purchase doors and frames from Virginia Metal. Absent the consideration that such an undertaking would have provided, the argument runs, there was no contract, Campbell was legally free to shop around and purchase from someone other than Virginia Metal, and hence there existed no obligation on Virginia Metal's part to abide by the promise to sell for $193,121 plus taxes.

As a consequence of the gigantic achievements in the field of contracts law by Samuel Williston and others, we have on rare occasions to confront situations posing some difficulty because they do not fit precisely into the patterned concepts laid down and accumulated by Williston and his followers. Nothing, not even the law of contracts, however, is altogether perfect.

We are not the first court to encounter the situation where there has been a promise unsupported by consideration which has occasioned reliance and change of position so that the promisor who backs away from his undertaking visits a real hardship on the promisee. An absence of consideration in such cases should not permit an unjust result. Rather, the law has developed the concept of promissory estoppel which allows recovery even in the absence of consideration where reliance and change of position to the detriment of the promisee make it unconscionable not to enforce the promise or to award damages for its breach.

As the case was argued to us, a great deal of attention was devoted to whether or not the doctrine of promissory estoppel applies in North Carolina. Both parties proceeded on the assumption that there was no direct authority one way or the other. However, the recent North Carolina case of *Wachovia Bank & Trust Company, N.A. v. Rubish* addressed the question and explicitly held that the law of North Carolina includes, and where appropriate applies, the doctrine of promissory estoppel. [T]he court stated:

> In order to prove a waiver by estoppel [a promisee] . . . need only prove an express or implied promise . . . and [his] detrimental reliance on that promise.

At the present stage of the case, action in reliance on the promise to sell doors and frames for $193,121 plus taxes cannot be disputed. It was alleged in the amended complaint: "Plaintiff submitted its bid for the entire project to the Government in reliance upon Defendant's quoted price for the hollow metal doors and frames."

In the case as pleaded by Campbell, the elements of a promissory estoppel are clearly present. Under the well-pleaded allegations of fact, even in the absence of consideration, there was a sufficiently binding promise by Virginia Metal.

DECISION: Ruling for Campbell, the Fourth Circuit Court of Appeals reversed the trial court decision and sent the case back to the trial court for trial.

ETHICS
Policy and Ethical Considerations in Enforcing Promises

Knee deep into the study of contract law as we are, it is easy for the reader to see contract law as a web of rules to be mastered for the next exam. However, as abstract and mysterious as the material in this chapter is, it brings us face to face with the policy tensions at odds in this area of law. If you have thought of contract law as just so much doctrine, this chapter, when viewed critically, forces you to face some basic questions about contract law and policy.

The basic question that contract law seeks to answer is: When should a promise be enforced? For example, which of the following promises do you think should be enforced?

- A promise to come to dinner
- A promise by your uncle to leave you $5,000 in his will
- A promise by your uncle to leave you $5,000 in his will if you promise to take care of him in his old age
- A promise by a customer to order as much of your merchandise as the customer "chooses to order"
- A promise by your landlord to reduce your rent so long as you remain in your apartment, as you previously promised, under the existing lease
- A seller's quoted price for supplies that you have used to compute a bid for a government contract

Review Questions and Problems

Key Terms

consideration

output contract

requirements contract

pre-existing duty rule

composition agreements

accord and satisfaction

promissory estoppel

Discussion Questions

1. Explain the difference between adequacy and sufficiency of consideration.
2. List three types of situations in which the pre-existing duty rule creates legal difficulties.
3. Briefly explain the two basic components of consideration.
4. Explain the doctrine of promissory estoppel.

Review Problems

1. Gill had performed plumbing work for Black Canyon Construction but had not been paid fully. In October 1971, the stockholders of Black Canyon sold the company and agreed to assume various liabilities that the company then had. Gill sued the stockholders in March 1972 for his accumulated debt, but he agreed to dismiss his suit in return for continued work and total payment due. Gill completed the new work and soon found himself back in court trying to collect his money. The court ruled that he was not a beneficiary of the October sale and could not collect for work done prior to then. Could he enforce the rest of the later agreement?

2. Carmichael, a shoe store owner, owed International Shoe Company $5,318.92 for shoes sold to him. When his debt had earlier been $12,272.51, Carmichael had agreed to pay International Shoe $8,000 immediately and the balance at $50 a week in return for receipt on account of an additional $2,000 worth of shoes. Carmichael was making payment according to this schedule when suddenly International Shoe Company brought suit for the balance of money owed. Result?

3. Polinger pledged $200,000 to the United Jewish Appeal (UJA), a nonprofit group that raises funds for various charities. He died shortly afterward, leaving an unpaid balance of $133,500.   The UJA sued to recover the unpaid balance from Polinger's estate. UJA used Polinger's announcement of his pledge to induce others to pledge large amounts, although the effect of Polinger's pledge on the decisions of other solicited contributors was not known. What additional information would you require to determine

whether the UJA should recover, and how should this information affect the outcome?

4. Plaintiffs each had put down a $1,000 deposit toward the purchase of condominium units. Each receipt contained an agreement providing that the deposit was to insure the buyer the "first option" to purchase a specified unit at a specified price, and if the sales contract eventually drawn up by the seller proved unacceptable to the buyer, the deposit would be refunded with interest. The seller later notified each buyer that the units would be priced 16 percent above the agreed-upon price. Plaintiffs sued for breach of contract. Were the contracts to give the buyers the option of buying their units at the original price that was supported by sufficient consideration?

5. Buyer signed an order for the purchase of three sprinklers to be installed before May 1, 1974. The sprinklers were to be paid for upon delivery. The agreement permitted the buyer to cancel by notifying the seller 30 days before the delivery date. Seller delivered only two of the three sprinklers. Buyer paid for them and sued for breach of contract for failure to deliver the third. Seller argued that buyer's option to cancel the order rendered buyer's promise to pay for the sprinklers illusory and that there was thus no consideration for the seller's promise to deliver the sprinklers. What was the result and why?

Case Problems

1. The Boston Redevelopment Authority (BRA) took over the buildings owned and operated by the Graphic Arts Finish Company. Graphic's president agreed with BRA that Graphic would receive its "total certified actual moving expenses" from BRA in return for leaving the premises peacefully and quickly and relocating elsewhere. Graphic alleges it performed these promises and demands the $54,069.11 still owed by BRA for moving expenses. Result?

2. While Hurley worked for Marine Contractors, he accumulated $12,000 in a retirement trust plan. The plan provided that when an employee left the company for reasons other than disability or retirement at age 65, the employee's share would be held by Marine for 5 years before distribution to the employee. Marine's president agreed to pay Hurley his $12,000 share immediately if Hurley would not compete with Marine within 100 miles for five years. Hurley agreed and received his money. But less than a year later Hurley was in active competition with Marine. Was the agreement valid?

3. Keen's mother died, leaving Keen an interest in property that the mother had owned jointly with her husband, Keen's stepfather. Keen agreed not to claim her mother's interest in return for a promise from her stepfather that he would leave the entire property to her upon his death. He died without a will, and the state claimed that it was the rightful owner as there had been inadequate consideration in the contract between Keen and her stepfather. Result?

4. Sons, Inc., had leased premises from W&T for over 3½ years and wished, contrary to the terms of the lease, to leave. W&T was bound by the terms of the lease at least until April 30 of the year following its execution. It could terminate after that on 90 days' notice to Sons. Sons had no such option, and W&T intended to enforce the lease against it for the full 10-year term. Could Sons terminate?

14

Genuine Assent

Fraud	Undue Influence
Duress	Mistake

In the preceding chapters, the elements that are necessary for the formation of a contract were discussed. Almost all agreements that include those elements will be enforced as contracts. In some situations, however, the elements required for a valid and enforceable contract appear to be present but in reality are not. For example, if a store owner accepts a gang leader's offer to protect his property from gang violence if he agrees to pay the gang $100 per month, the store owner is not genuinely assenting to the terms of the contract. Similarly, if a used car salesperson falsely states that the car has a rebuilt engine and has never been in an accident, the buyer who relies on that information and signs a purchase contract has not genuinely assented. Assent to a contract must be given voluntarily and knowingly by each of the parties; if it is not, there is no genuine assent and thus no contract between them.

This chapter discusses situations involving agreements that lack genuine assent. *Fraud, duress, undue influence,* or even *mistake* may nullify a party's assent to a contract and entitle that party to relief. The relief granted will vary with the circumstances.

Fraud

Fraud exists where there is:

1. A misrepresentation of fact
2. That is material
3. That is made with knowledge of its falsity and with intent to deceive the other party
4. Who reasonably relies on the misrepresented statement
5. Causing injury as a consequence of the reliance

A simple case of fraud is diagrammed in Table 14-1.

TABLE 14-1

A Case of Fraud

Intent	Jones, knowing her car has been seriously damaged in an accident and rebuilt in the auto shop, . . .
Misrepresentation of a material fact	Tells Smith that the car has never required repairs beyond ordinary maintenance.
Reasonable reliance	Smith chooses Jones's car over another car he has considered buying because he knew the other car had once been wrecked and repaired.
Injury resulting from reliance	One week after purchase, the defect becomes obvious and Smith must spend $500 to replace the fender, which has rusted prematurely.

The essence of fraud is misrepresentation. One party intentionally misrepresents certain facts to the second party, who, relying on the misrepresentations, changes his or her legal position in assenting to enter into a contract. If the party who misrepresents the facts clearly intends the misrepresentation and the resulting deception of the second party, fraud results. On the other hand, a misrepresentation of facts may be unintentional; in that case, there is no fraud. It is important to note, however, that a person who has assented to a contract as a result of a misrepresentation of fact, whether intentional and fraudulent or unintentional and innocent, is allowed to rescind or cancel a contract entered into as a result of the misrepresentation. The difference between the two misrepresentations is that the intentional misrepresentation constituting fraud is also a tort. The victim of such a tort may not only rescind or cancel the contract but also sue for damages to compensate for any loss incurred. The victim of unintentional misrepresentation has the right only to rescind or cancel the contract; no relief for loss will be granted to that party.

A person who has been induced by fraud to enter into a contract will be allowed to cancel or rescind the contract. In addition, since fraud is an intentional tort, the victim of fraud can sue for damages to compensate for any loss. Punitive damages are also allowed if it can be proved that the fraud was committed with malicious intent. Additionally, if the victim of fraud can establish injury by a pattern of violations of federal mail fraud, wire fraud, bankruptcy fraud, or securities fraud statutes, the victim may be able to recover triple damages under the Racketeer Influenced and Corrupt Organizations Act (RICO) provisions discussed in Chapter 5.

Misrepresentation of Fact

A misrepresentation is active concealment of a material fact or partial disclosure of information that is represented as the full truth. A misrepresentation may be expressed or implied; it may be made in writing, orally, or through conduct. Silence can constitute a misrepresentation in situations where the law imposes a duty to speak.

Active Concealment of Fact   An active concealment of a fact is the most obvious type of misrepresentation. If the seller of a used car turns back the odometer to conceal the number of miles the car has been driven, fraud has occurred. Of course, an express statement of fact that is a lie also constitutes fraud.

Fraud applies to a partially misleading statement as well as to an outright lie. If a company supplies a balance sheet and profit-and-loss statement to a bank from which it seeks to borrow money and fails to disclose important information about its liabilities or the true nature of its assets, the partial disclosure of the truth constitutes a misrepresentation.

Silence and the Duty to Disclose Information   In order to find a misrepresentation the law generally requires either an affirmative act or an express statement, but on occasion silence may constitute a misrepresentation of fact leading to fraud. In order for silence to be the basis for fraud, the silence must be interpreted as an intentional misrepresentation.

Generally, mere failure to disclose information to the other party does not constitute even an unintentional and innocent misrepresentation because the law does not impose a duty of disclosure.

There are, however, a number of exceptions to this rule. Statutes such as the Truth-in-Lending Act require disclosure regarding finance charges in contracts where money is being lent. Similarly, many jurisdictions recognize an implied warranty, and thus a duty to disclose known defects, in the sale of a new house.

Suppose one party knows certain material facts, knows the other party does not know them, and knows that if those facts were known there would be no contract. A prospective seller of land, for example, may know of a hidden defect in the property, one that could not be observed through inspection. If the seller fails to inform the purchaser of the defect, the seller could be held liable for fraud because the silence was intended to mislead the purchaser into assuming there was no defect.

A person in a fiduciary relationship with another must disclose all known information concerning the subject of that special relationship. An agent owes this duty to a principal, a partner owes it to another partner, and an attorney owes it to a client. The disclosure by a physician to a patient of the risk of surgery is a necessary precondition of the patient's ability to consent to the surgery. Silence and nondisclosure in the face of such a duty may be the basis for a finding of fraud.

ETHICS
Creative Resume Writing

The best jobs in any field are highly competitive. All applicants search for creative ways to signal their special talents and capabilities. Employers offering the best jobs may be overwhelmed by a flood of resumes and find it very difficult to pick out the best candidates. The resume becomes all important.

Many universities offer assistance in writing resumes, as they want their graduates to get good jobs. Students may be advised to state their prior work experience as positively as possible and to emphasize their success as students.

Some law schools have been sufficiently concerned about resume inaccuracy to set up resume verification procedures to monitor student resumes. In a recent study [24 *Arizona State Law Journal* 1181 (1992)] 62 percent of the law schools surveyed reported uncovering at least one case of resume inaccuracy. The most common problem areas involve false statements pertaining to grade point average and class rank.

Examples of problematic resumes include a student who "rounded off" his grades and reported a 2.76 grade point as a 3.0. Another student listed rank as 25 percent, when in fact he ranked in the bottom 25 percent of his law school class.

What factors determine when creative resume writing goes too far and becomes unethical behavior?

A Fact Must Be Misrepresented False statements that are merely opinions cannot be considered the basis for fraud since an opinion is not a fact. Whether a statement is one of fact or opinion is a matter that must be determined in each particular case. In general, an opinion is a statement of one's expectations concerning future events or one's personal beliefs. A merchant who sells goods may state that the product will last "a long time" or that the "sale price is reasonable" or that the manufacturer of the goods has "an excellent reputation." Usually, such a statement is known as "puffing" and constitutes a mat-

ter of opinion. On the other hand, the car dealer's statement that a used car has been driven only 25,000 miles and was purchased by the present seller from the original owner for $3,000 are statements of fact. Such statements relate to events that either did or did not take place. Their truth or falsity can be proven.

Although statements of opinion are not generally regarded as statements of fact, the opinion of an expert is treated as a statement of fact. When an accountant states that in his or her opinion the books and records of a corporation were kept in a manner consistent with generally accepted accounting procedures, he or she speaks as an expert. If there was proof that the accountant actually did not hold that opinion, the statement would constitute a misrepresentation that could be the basis for a finding of fraud.

Materiality

The question of whether a fact is a material fact is determined on a case-by-case basis. The test usually seeks to ascertain whether the person would have entered into a contract if he or she had known of the misrepresentation. The policy of the law is to distinguish between insignificant facts and those that are significant, or material. One cannot simply review a contract with numerous complex clauses, find one minor misrepresentation of fact made by the other party, and then sue for fraud. There is a misrepresentation of a material fact only if the fact in question was one of the important reasons for entering into the contract.

Knowledge of Falsity and Intent to Deceive

The third requirement for fraud is that the misrepresentation of a material fact be made with knowledge of the falsity and with intent to deceive. Knowledge of the falsity and the intent to deceive are often referred to as **scienter**, a Latin word meaning "knowingly." The law does not require proof that the person who committed fraud had an evil or malicious motive. The question is whether that person knew the facts and then misrepresented them. As with other areas of the law in which intent must be determined, a person is deemed to have intended the natural consequences of an action. It is no excuse for the person making a misrepresentation of a material fact to say that he or she did not intend to take advantage of the other party. Nor can a person merely say that he or she did not know the true facts if he or she recklessly disregarded those facts that were available. Knowledge of the facts will be inferred if a person makes a statement with reckless disregard for their truth.

The intent to deceive is found in the intent to create a false impression. Since fraud requires this intent, mere negligence or carelessness cannot constitute fraud. The professional accountant, lawyer, or doctor who fails to disclose certain facts or makes half-true statements is clearly negligent because he or she is not acting as a professional. In order to find fraud, however, the crucial element of *scienter* also must exist. There must be an active intent to deceive, essentially a cover-up of known facts.

Reliance

The fourth element to be proved in a case of fraud is that the misrepresentation of a material fact that was made knowingly and with intent to deceive was relied upon by the party to whom it was made. A person who does not pay attention to a misrepresented fact, or who conducts his or her own investigation to determine whether a fact is true, is not relying upon what the other party has said or done. In that case, even if there is a misrepresentation of a material fact, since there is no reliance there is no fraud.

Suppose a person acts foolishly in relying on a fraudulent statement. Will the law protect that person? While there is some conflict among court decisions as to what constitutes "unreasonable" reliance, where there is an intentional misrepresentation relief will generally be granted even though the defrauded party was foolish or negligent. In balancing the interests of the foolish person against those of the person intentionally misrepresenting a material fact, the law generally seeks to protect the victim of the fraud. As the next case illustrates, this rule sometimes is applied even if the victim of fraud is a sophisticated insurance company that should know better.

KORAL INDUSTRIES V. SECURITY-CONNECTICUT LIFE INSURANCE CO.

Supreme Court of Texas
802 S.W.2d 651 (1990)

BACKGROUND: Koral applied to Security for a life insurance policy for Lewis Lindsey, one of its key employees. In the application, Lindsey did not disclose that he had been hospitalized several times in recent years and that he had been treated for alcohol abuse and depression. Relying on the information provided, Security issued a policy that would pay $1 million to Koral in the event of Lindsey's death. Lindsey died, and Security had the claim investigated. The investigation revealed the prior medical problems that Lindsey did not disclose on the application. Security refused to pay the $1 million to Koral, and instead refunded Koral's premiums with interest. Koral sued Security for breach of contract and won. The appeals court reversed in favor of Security, however, and Koral appealed to the Supreme Court of Texas.

Per Curiam

The jury found that Lindsey had knowingly made false representation to Security to induce Security to issue the policy; that Security had relied on those representations; that Security was aware of facts that would have caused a prudent person to make an inquiry; and that such an inquiry, if made with due diligence, would have uncovered Lindsey's fraud. . . . The general rule was stated in *Isenhower v. Bell*, and dates back to 1888:

When one has been induced to enter into a contract by fraudulent representations, the person committing the fraud cannot defeat a claim for damages based upon a plea that the party defrauded might have discovered the truth by the exercise of proper care. An affirmative answer to the requested special issue based upon what Isenhower should have known would not, therefore, have constituted a defense to the alleged fraud.

Failure to use due diligence to suspect or discover someone's fraud will not act to bar the defense of fraud to the contract. The concept of precluding a cause of action based on fraudulent misrepresentation was eloquently stated in *Western Cottage Piano & Organ Co. v. Anderson*:

It is not the rule that a person injured by the fraudulent and false representations of another is held to the exercise of diligence to suspect and discover the falsity of such statements. In the absence of knowledge to the contrary, he would have a right to rely and act upon such statements, and certainly the wrongdoer in such a case cannot be heard to complain that the other should have disbelieved his solemn statements.

Therefore, only the insurer's actual knowledge of the misrepresentations would have destroyed its defense of fraud. "The test always is, to avoid the defense of fraud as to a material fact upon the score of waiver, the company must know the identical statement as made is untrue." *Dossett v. Franklin Life Ins. Co.*

We agree with the court of appeals that Security's defense of fraudulent inducement and misrepresentation was a valid defense to Koral's breach of contract claims.

DECISION: The Supreme Court of Texas affirmed the decision in favor of Security.

Injury or Damage

The fifth element required to prove fraud is that an injury occurred as a result of the fraud. The party who relied upon a misrepresentation of a material fact that was knowingly and intentionally made must prove that some damage was caused by the fraud. What loss was suffered? If the purchaser of a car relies on a statement that a car has been driven only 30,000 miles and it is later proved to have been driven 60,000 miles, what damage has the purchaser suffered? The basic standard is the difference in value between that which was promised and relied upon and that which in fact was received. If there is no difference, there is no injury; but if there is a difference, the defrauded party will be compensated for the injury suffered. If the fraudulent statement was made maliciously or with extreme carelessness or recklessness, the defrauded party can recover punitive as well as compensatory damages.

Duress

A second factor nullifying a party's assent to a contract is duress. Few areas of the law of contracts have undergone such radical changes in the twentieth century as has the law governing duress. Relief from an agreement on the grounds of duress is clearly available if a person is deprived of liberty or property through physical force. Even the threat of physical force, although not carried out, constitutes duress. Yet duress is not limited to these situations.

Duress includes any wrongful act or threat that overcomes the free will of the consenting party. The essence of duress is lack of free will or voluntary consent. Economic coercion, threats to a person's family and loved ones, and other uses of moral or social force to put a person in such fear that his or her act is not voluntary constitute duress.

In determining whether a contract can be avoided on account of duress, one must ascertain (1) whether the acts or threats were wrongful and (2) whether it was the acts or threats, and not the free will of the party, that induced the required contractual assent.

Duress cannot be limited to the fear that might overcome an ordinary person. If a contracting party, whether brave or timid, is actually coerced into assenting to the contract, duress has occurred. Thus, the state of mind of the person who is being threatened must be examined. Did one party involuntarily accept the terms of the other party? Were the circumstances such that there was no practicable alternative? Were those circumstances due to the coercive acts of the other party? Read carefully the *Totem Marine* case, which discusses the requirements of economic duress or business compulsion.

TOTEM MARINE T. & B. V. ALYESKA PIPELINE, ETC.

Supreme Court of Alaska
584 P.2d 15 (1978)

BACKGROUND: Totem (plaintiff), under a contract with Alyeska (defendant), was required to transport pipeline construction materials to Alyeska by ship from Texas to Alaska. Because of delays caused by Alyeska, Totem's ship was unable to make it to Alaska by the contract deadline. Totem's ship had gotten as far as California when Alyeska terminated the contract and took the freight off the ship.

Totem then sent Alyeska invoices between $260,000 and $300,000, the costs and charges it had incurred in its attempt to perform the contract. Totem was in urgent need of cash and was close to bankruptcy. Alyeska delayed making payment and advised Totem it might have to wait months to be paid. Six or seven weeks after Alyeska had terminated the contract, it offered to pay Totem slightly less than $100,000 in exchange for a release by Totem of all claims against Alyeska for further payment.

Totem agreed to the terms, signed the release, and 6 months later filed suit. It claimed its agreement to accept the partial payment due it and the release of all claims against Alyeska had been made because of the economic duress it was subjected to by Alyeska. Alyeska asserted that, as a matter of law, there was no basis for Totem's claim of economic duress and asked the court to grant a summary judgment in its favor. The trial court agreed with Alyeska and granted its request for a dismissal judgment. Totem appealed to the Alaska Supreme Court.

Burke, Justice

At the outset, it is helpful to acknowledge the various policy considerations which are involved in cases involving economic duress. Typically, those claiming such coercion are attempting to avoid the consequences of a modification of an original contract or of a settlement and release agreement. On the one hand, courts are reluctant to set aside agreements because of the notion of freedom of contract and because of the desirability of having private dispute resolutions be final. On the other hand, there is an increasing recognition of the law's role in correcting inequitable or unequal exchanges between parties of disproportionate bargaining power and a greater willingness to not enforce agreements which were entered into under coercive circumstances.

Section 392 (b) of the *Restatement of Contracts* defines duress as: any wrongful threat of one person by words or other conduct that induces another to enter into a transaction under the influence of such fear as precluded him from exercising free will and judgment, if the threat was intended or should reasonably have been expected to operate as an inducement.

Many courts state the test somewhat differently, eliminating use of the vague term "free will," but retaining the same basic idea. Under this standard, duress exists where: (1) one party involuntarily accepted the terms of another, (2) circumstances permitted no other alternative, and (3) such circumstances were the result of coercive acts of the other party. The third element is further explained as follows:

In order to substantiate the allegation of economic duress or business compulsion, the plaintiff must go beyond the mere showing of reluctance to accept and of financial embarrassment. There must be a showing of acts on the part of the defendant which produced these two factors. The assertion of duress must be proven by evidence that the duress resulted from defendant's wrongful and oppressive conduct and not by the plaintiff's necessities.

Economic duress does not exist merely because a person has been the victim of a wrongful act; in addition, the victim must have no choice but to agree to the other party's terms or face serious financial hardship. Thus, in order to avoid a contract, a party must also show that he had no reasonable alternative to agreeing to the other party's terms, or as it is often stated, that he had no adequate remedy if the threat were to be carried out. An available alternative or remedy may not be adequate where the delay involved in pursuing that remedy would cause immediate and irreparable loss to one's economic or business interest.

Professor Dalzell, in *Duress by Economic Pressure II*, 20 N. Carolina L. Rev. 340, 370 (1942), notes the following with regard to the adequacy of legal remedies where one party refuses to pay a contract claim:

Nowadays, a wait of even a few weeks in collecting on a contract claim is sometimes serious or fatal for an enterprise at a crisis in its history. The business of a creditor in financial straits is at the mercy of an unscrupulous debtor, who need only suggest that if the creditor does not care to settle on the debtor's own hard terms, he can sue. This situation, in which promptness in payment is vastly more important than even approximate justice in the settlement terms, is too common in modern business relations to be ignored by society and the courts.

Turning to the instant case, we believe that Totem's allegations, if proved, would support a finding that it executed a release of its contract claims against Alyeska under economic duress. Totem has alleged that Alyeska deliberately withheld payment of an acknowledged debt, knowing that Totem had no choice but to accept an inadequate sum in settlement of that debt; that Totem was faced with impending bankruptcy; that Totem was unable to meet its pressing debts other than by accepting the immediate cash payment offer by Alyeska; and that through necessity, Totem thus involuntarily accepted an inadequate settlement offer from Alyeska and executed a release of all claims under the contract. If the release was in fact executed under these circumstances, we think that under the legal principles discussed above that this would constitute the type of wrongful conduct and lack of alternatives that would render the release voidable by Totem on the ground of economic duress. Therefore, we hold that the superior court erred in granting summary judgment for appellant and remand the case to the superior court for trial in accordance with the legal principles set forth above.

DECISION: The court found in plaintiff Totem's favor, reversing the trial court's decision.

Undue Influence

Undue influence exists when one person exercises mental coercion over another. The cases frequently involve an elderly, sick, and senile person as the coerced victim of another person's undue influence. The essence of undue influence is that the influenced person's own judgment and free will are subjected to those of the dominating person. Thus, the assent given by the influenced person is not that person's genuine assent.

In examining a case involving undue influence, the courts usually follow a two-step approach. First, they seek to determine if there has been a dominant-subservient relationship between the two parties. For example, certain fiduciary relationships, such as those between attorney and client, banker and customer, and doctor and patient, involve a high degree of trust by one party in the other. Second, once the relationship is determined to have been one in which one party could by his or her influence dominate the other, the courts shift the presumption of lack of undue influence to a presumption that such undue influence did exist when a contract between the two benefited the dominant party. Unless the dominant party can then prove a lack of undue influence, the subservient party is allowed to avoid the contract. The case that follows illustrates the doctrine of undue influence.

Odorizzi v. Bloomfield School District
Court of Appeals of California
54 Cal. Rptr. 533 (1966)

BACKGROUND: Odorizzi (plaintiff) sued Bloomfield School District (defendant) to be reinstated as a teacher. Odorizzi was employed during 1964 as an elementary school teacher by the defendant Bloomfield School District and was under contract with the district to continue to teach school the following year as a permanent employee. On June 10, he was arrested on criminal charges [relating to homosexual conduct] and on June 11, he signed and delivered to his superiors his written resignation as a teacher, which the district accepted on June 13. In July, the criminal charges against Odorizzi were dismissed and in September he sought to resume his employment with the district. When the district refused to reinstate him, he filed suit asserting that his resignation was invalid because he lacked the capacity to make a valid contract.

Odorizzi asserted that his resignation was invalid because it was obtained through undue influence. Specifically, Odorizzi declared that he had been under such severe mental and emotional strain at the time he signed his resignation, having just completed the process of arrest, questioning by the police, booking, and release on bail, and having gone for 40 hours without sleep, that he was incapable of rational thought or action.

While he was in this condition and unable to think clearly, the superintendent of the district and the principal of his school came to his apartment. They said that they were trying to help him and had his best interests at heart, that he should take their advice and immediately resign his position with the district, that there was no time to consult an attorney, that if he did not resign immediately the district would suspend and dismiss him from his position and publicize his arrest and cause him "to suffer extreme embarrassment and humiliation"; but that if he resigned at once, the incident would not be publicized and would not jeopardize his chances of securing employment as a teacher elsewhere. Odorizzi pleaded that because of his faith and confidence in their representations they were able to substitute their will and judgment for his own and thus obtain his signature to his purported resignation. The trial court dismissed the complaint and Odorizzi appealed.

Fleming, Justice

Undue influence, in the sense we are concerned with here, is a shorthand legal phrase used to describe persuasion which tends to be coercive in nature, persuasion which overcomes the will without convincing the judgment. The hallmark of such persuasion is high pressure, a pressure which works on mental, moral, or emotional weakness to such an extent that it approaches the boundaries of coercion. In this sense, undue influence has been called overpersuasion.

Misrepresentation of law or fact are not essential to the charge, for a person's will may be overborne without misrepresentation. In essence, undue influence involves the use of excessive pressure to persuade one vulnerable to such pressure, pressure applied by a dominant subject to a servient object. In combination, the elements of undue susceptibility in the servient person and excessive pressure by the dominating person makes the latter's influence undue, for it results in the apparent will of the servient person being in fact the will of the dominant person. . . .

The difficulty, of course, lies in determining when the forces of persuasion have overflowed their normal banks and become oppressive flood waters. There are second thoughts to every bargain, and hindsight is still better than foresight. Undue influence cannot be used as a pretext to avoid bad bargains or escape from bargains which refuse to come up to expectations. A man who buys a tract of desert land in the expectation that it is in the immediate path of the city's growth and will become another Palm Springs, an expectation cultivated in glowing terms by the seller, cannot rescind his bargain when things turn out differently. If we are temporarily persuaded against our better judgment to do something about which we later have second thoughts, we must abide the consequences of the risks inherent in managing our own affairs.

However, overpersuasion is generally accompanied by certain characteristics which tend to create a pattern. The pattern usually involves several of the following elements: (1) discussion of the transaction at an unusual or inappropriate time, (2) consummation of the transaction in an unusual place, (3) insistent demand that the business be finished at once, (4) extreme emphasis on untoward consequences of delay, (5) the use of multiple persuaders by the dominant side against a single servient party, (6) absence of third-party advisers to the servient party, (7) statements that there is no time to consult financial advisers or attorneys. If a number of these elements are simultaneously present, the persuasion may be characterized as excessive. . . .

The difference between legitimate persuasion and excessive pressure, like the difference between seduction and rape, rests to a considerable extent in the manner in which the parties go about their business. For example, if a day or two after Odorizzi's release on bail the superintendent of the school district had called him into his office during business hours and directed his attention to those provisions of the Education Code compelling his leave of absence and authorizing his suspension on the filing of written charges, had told him that the District contemplated filing written charges against him, had pointed out the alternative of resignation available to him, had informed him he was free to consult counsel or any adviser he wished and to consider the matter overnight and return with his decision the next day, it is extremely unlikely that any complaint about the use of excessive pressure could ever have been made against the school district.

But, according to the allegations of the complaint, this is not the way it happened, and if it had happened that way, plaintiff would never have resigned. Rather, the representatives of the school board undertook to achieve their objective by overpersuasion and imposition to secure plaintiff's signature but not his consent to his resignation through a high-pressure carrot-and-stick technique—under which they assured plaintiff they were trying to assist him, he should rely on their advice, there wasn't time to consult an attorney, if he didn't resign at once the school district would suspend and dismiss him from his position and publicize the proceedings, but if he did resign the incident wouldn't jeopardize his chances of securing a teaching post elsewhere.

Plaintiff has thus pleaded both subjective and objective elements entering the undue influence equation and stated sufficient facts to put in issue the question whether his free will had been overborne by defendant's agents at a time when he was unable to function in a normal manner.

DECISION: The appeals court reversed the dismissal of Odorizzi's complaint.

Mistake

Mistake is generally defined as a state of mind not in accord with the facts. The term "mistake," when used in contract law, refers to a mental attitude coupled with an act having legal significance (such as the execution of a contract). There are many different kinds of mistakes that can be made by parties to a contract. They can make a mistake in the performance or execution of the contract. One party can make a mistake in judgment; another can make a mistaken assumption concerning the subject matter of the contract. Mistakes in typing a written contract can occur, as can mistakes concerning the presumed legality or tax effect of a particular transaction. In most situations in which mistakes are made, the law grants no relief to the mistaken party. If legal relief is to be given when a mistake has occurred, a number of factors must be examined.

The legal significance of any mistake must be determined by answering several questions. Among these are the following:

1. Did one or both have a mistaken thought?
2. Did the mistake induce a mutual expression of agreement or merely induce action by one party?
3. Should one or both parties have had reason to know of the mistake?
4. Was the fact as to which a mistake occurred of substantial importance and one that was not part of the risk assumed by either of the parties?

These questions seek to determine not only who made the mistake but also what kind of mistake was made and what effect it had on the contract. Did both parties make a mistake that induced action by only one party, or did one party make a mistake that induced action by both parties? Was it a serious mistake? If a serious mistake was made by one party, does that mean that the other party should have known of the mistake? If a mistake was made by both parties to a contract, it is referred to as a **bilateral mistake**. If only one of the parties was mistaken, then a **unilateral mistake** occurred.

Bilateral Mistake

There are several contexts in which contracting parties can make bilateral mistakes. Both parties can make a mistake concerning an important material fact on which the contract is based. Typical cases involving such mistakes are those in which the subject matter of the contract has, unknown to both parties, been destroyed prior to the agreement of the parties. Suppose you agreed to buy my lakefront summer cottage in northern Michigan and I agreed to sell it. We decided to enter into a contract for purchase and sale on our return from the cottage to the city. However, unknown to us, before we got there, a fire destroyed the cottage. Mistakenly believing the cottage was still standing, we contracted for its purchase and sale. Our mistake was a bilateral mistake of an important material fact; we both believed that the cottage still existed. When a bilateral mistake concerning the subject matter of the contract occurs, the courts grant relief to the parties and allow the contract to be rescinded. It was not the fault of either party that their assumptions were mistaken. If the parties actually had known the true facts, they would not have entered into their contract.

An issue of mistake may often arise because the parties have a different understanding of what key words in the contract mean. In a classic British case from 1864, Wichelhaus agreed to purchase from Raffles cotton to be transported from India on a ship named *Peerless*. Unbeknownst to the parties, there were actually two ships named *Peerless* and both were scheduled to sail from India to London that season. Raffles transported the cotton on a ship named *Peerless*, which set sail in October. Wichelhaus refused to purchase the cotton, claiming that the *Peerless* identified in the contract was a second ship scheduled to set sail in December. Raffles sued, but the court held that Wichelhaus was not required to purchase the cotton. Because of the parties' mutual mistake of fact, no contract existed.

A U.S. court confronted with the facts of the *Peerless* case today might decide the case differently. The case provides a good illustration, however, of the problems that arise when parties attach different meanings to the language of the contract. This is particularly likely to happen in international transactions in which the words used in one language may have a slightly different meaning when translated into another language. The dispositive issue often becomes what constitutes a reasonable interpretation of the words used. Relevant references include industry trade usage, government regulations, statutory defini-tions and even basic dictionaries. Ultimately, however, the question is one of the reasonable-ness of the behavior of the parties and their par-ticular expectations. The interesting case that follows demonstrates the manner in which courts try to resolve such disputes.

FRIGALIMENT IMPORTING CO., LTD. v. B.N.S.
U.S. District Court, Southern District of New York
190 F.Supp. 116 (1960)

BACKGROUND: B.N.S. (defendant) entered into two contracts to sell 200,000 pounds of "U.S. fresh frozen chicken, grade A, government-inspected, eviscerate" of certain weight per chicken at between 33 and 37 cents a pound. Frigaliment (plaintiff) ex-pected broiling or frying chicken and instead received stewing chicken. The plaintiff sued for breach of warranty on the grounds that the chickens did not conform to their description in the contract.

Friendly, Circuit Judge

The issue is, what is chicken? Plaintiff says, "chicken" means a young chicken, suitable for broiling and frying. Defendant says "chicken" means any bird of that genus that meets con-tract specifications on weight and quality, including what it calls "stewing chicken" and plain-tiff pejoratively terms "fowl." Dictionaries give both meanings, as well as some others not relevant here. To support its, plaintiff sends a number of volleys over the net; defendant es-says to return them and adds a few serves of its own. Assuming that both parties were act-ing in good faith, the case nicely illustrates Holmes' remark "that the making of a contract depend not on the agreement of two minds in intention, but on the agreement of two sets of external signs—not on the parties' having *meant* the same thing but on their having *said* the same thing." I have concluded that plaintiff has not sustained its burden of persuasion that the contract used "chicken" in the narrower sense.

Since the word "chicken" standing alone is ambiguous, I turn first to see whether the contract itself offers any aid to its interpretation. Plaintiff says that 1½–2 lbs. birds neces-sarily had to be young chicken since the older birds do not come in that size, hence the 2 ½–3 lbs. birds must likewise be young. This is unpersuasive—a contract for "apples" of two different sizes could be filled with different kinds of apples even though only one species came in both sizes.

Plaintiff's next contention is that there was a definite trade usage that "chicken" meant "young chicken." Defendant showed that it was only beginning in the poultry trade in 1957, thereby bringing itself within the principle that "when one of the parties is not a member of the trade or other circle, his acceptance of the standard must be made to appear" by prov-ing either that he had actual knowledge of the usage or that the usage is "so generally known in the community that his actual individual knowledge of it may be inferred." Here there was not proof of actual knowledge of the alleged usage; indeed, it is quite plain that defendant's belief was to the contrary. In order to meet the alternative requirement, the law of New York demands a showing that "the usage is of so long continuance, so well estab-lished, so notorious, so universal and so reasonable in itself, as that the presumption is vi-olent that the parties contracted with reference to it, and made it a part of their agreement.

Defendant's witness Weininger, who operates a chicken eviscerating plant in New Jersey, testified "Chicken is everything except a goose, a duck, and a turkey. Everything is a chicken, but then you have to say, you have to specify which category you want or that you are talking about." Its witness Fox said that in the trade "chicken" would encompass all the various classifications. Sadina, who conducts a food inspection service, testified that he would consider any bird coming within the classes of "chicken" in the Department of Agriculture's regulations to be a chicken. The specifications approved by the General Services Administration include fowl as well as broilers and fryers under the classification "chickens." Statistics of the Institute of American Poultry Industries uses the phrases "Young chickens" and "Mature chickens," under the general heading "Total chickens." And the Department of Agriculture's daily and weekly price reports avoid use of the word "chicken" without specification.

When all the evidence is reviewed, it is clear that defendant believed it could comply with the contracts by delivering stewing chicken in the 2½–3 lbs. size. Defendant's subjective intent would not be significant if this did not coincide with an objective meaning of "chicken." Here it did coincide with one of the dictionary meanings, with the definition in the Department of Agriculture Regulations to which the contract made at least oblique reference, with at least some usage in the trade, with the realities of the market, and with what plaintiff's spokesman had said. Plaintiff asserts it to be equally plain that plaintiff's own subjective intent was to obtain broilers and fryers; the only evidence against this is the material as to market prices and this may not have been sufficiently brought home. In any event it is unnecessary to determine that issue. For plaintiff has the burden of showing that "chicken" was used in the narrower rather than in the broader sense, and this has not been sustained.

DECISION: The court found in favor of defendant B.N.S.

Unilateral Mistake

A unilateral mistake is a mistake made by only one of the contracting parties. If one party makes a careless or negligent mistake in negotiating or in performing a contract, the law generally will not grant that party relief from the mistake. There are, however, several exceptions to this rule. Even when a mistake is made by only one party, courts generally grant relief if refusing to do so would impose undue hardship or expense on the mistaken party. In other words, the courts seek to balance the scales of justice. In doing so, the courts examine the relative consequences to both parties of a decision to grant or deny relief for a unilateral mistake. What is the burden that will be imposed on the other party if relief is granted to the mistaken party? What is the hardship suffered by the mistaken party if no relief is granted? Either a slight burden on the innocent party or a great burden on the mistaken party generally will be grounds for granting relief even where only one party has made a mistake.

Knowledge of Mistake

If a mistake was made by only one of the contracting parties, but the other party knew or should have known of the mistake, the courts generally will not allow the other party to take advantage of the mistake by enforcing the contract. Suppose several contractors were asked to submit bids for construction work on a hospital addition and the bid submitted by one of the contractors was significantly lower than all the other bids. If the bid was lower because of the contractor's unilateral mistake in calculation and the error was so great that the hospital has reason to know of the mistake prior to its acceptance of the contractor's bid, the contractor would be granted relief from the obligation. The *McGough* case presented below exemplifies this type of mistake.

Another type of unilateral mistake is one concerning a person's identity. We have seen in the chapters on offer and acceptance that an offer may be accepted only by the person to whom it is made. But what if the offeror receives an acceptance from one whom he mistakenly believes to be the offeree?

If offeror A intends to deal only with party B, but party C accepts the offer, there is no contract between C and A even if A mistakenly believes that party C is party B. A's mistake in identifying party C as party B is a unilateral mistake about which party C knew or should have known. Party C never received an offer from A and thus must have known that A was mistaken in identifying C as a person who could accept his offer.

A mistake as to the identity of a person can also be made as a result of fraud. A person can forge identification papers and pass as someone else. Such a situation would be a combination of fraud and mistake. Consequently, there would be double reason to allow the person who was both the victim of fraud and the party who had made a unilateral mistake that was known to the other party to avoid the contract.

However, if a person makes an offer to someone who occupies a certain capacity—for example, the manager of the ABC store—any person who is in that capacity can accept it. If, unknown to the offeror, a new manager has been appointed, the offeror cannot plead mistake because he thought his friend, the former manager, was still there. In this case, the offer is made to any person in the position, not to the individual who was mistakenly thought to be there. There is no mistaken identity in this situation, only a mistaken assumption.

M. J. McGough Company v. Jane Lamb Memorial Hospital

U.S. District Court S.D. Iowa
302 F.Supp. 482 (1969)

BACKGROUND: McGough (plaintiff), a contractor, sued Jane Lamb Memorial Hospital (defendant) to have his bid declared rescinded and his surety released from liability. The hospital that received the bid filed suit to recover damages for the contractor's refusal to execute the contract and other documents in accordance with the original bid. Upon a consolidated trial of the cases, the District Court held that the contractor was entitled to have its bid rescinded and its surety released from liability on bond, since because of a clerical error, the bid was low by $199,800, or approximately 10 percent of the bid.

Stephenson, Chief Judge

The bid of M. J. McGough was submitted shortly before the opening time of 2:00 P.M., on February 16, 1968. The bids were opened by the Chairman of the Board of Trustees of Jane Lamb Memorial Hospital, Mr. Clark Depue III, at 2:00 P.M., and recorded as follows:

M. J. McGough Co., St. Paul	$1,957,000
Knutson Construction Co., Minneapolis	2,123,643
Steenberg Construction Co., St. Paul	2,185,000
Rinderknecht Construction Co., Cedar Rapids	2,264,000
O. Jorgensen & Sons Construction Co., Clinton	2,322,064
Lovering Construction Co., St. Paul	2,326,380
Universal Construction Co., Kansas City, Mo.	2,500,000
Ringland-Johnson-Crowley Co., Inc., Clinton	2,577,837
Priester Construction Co., Davenport	2,611,000

These figures were relayed to Mr. J. H. McGough, President of M. J. McGough Company, by a representative present at the opening. Mr. McGough was immediately concerned over the ten percent (10%) difference between his low bid and the next lowest bid of Knutson Construction Company. (By his testimony at trial, Mc. McGough explained that Knutson Construction Company was known in the trade as a notoriously low bidder.) Feeling a serious mistake had been made in the compilation of his bid, Mr. McGough called his representative at the opening and instructed him to request that he be allowed to withdraw his bid. This request was transmitted to Mr. Depue at approximately 2:45 p.m., while the Board was still analyzing the bids received. Shortly thereafter, Mr. McGough spoke with Mr. Depue by telephone and Mr. Depue requested a letter explaining the circumstances of the mistake and a written request to withdraw. Mr. McGough and his staff then began checking the papers relating to this bid and discovered an error in the amount of $199,800. The circumstances surrounded the error were set out in a letter dated February 16, 1968, directed to Milton Holmgrain, the hospital administrator. In the letter, McGough offered to "submit to you immediately all of our records relating to this project for verification of this error." In spite of this, the Board of Trustees, without further communication with M. J. McGough Company, at its meeting on February 22, 1968, passed a "Resolution of Intent" to the effect that the Board intended to accept the bid of M. J. McGough Company subject to obtaining the approval of the Division of Hospital Services of the Iowa State Department of Health and the U.S. Public Health Service. . . .

The circumstances surrounding the mistake in the bid of M. J. McGough Company are not seriously disputed. The majority of the subcontractor bids used in computing the bid of M. J. McGough Company were received on February 16, 1968. The sub-bids were recorded as they were phoned in on a slip of paper. Mr. McGough received the sub-bid of Artcraft Interiors, Inc., during this period of frenzied activity, and although he correctly recorded it on the slip of paper as $222,000, he verbally called it to an employee who recorded it as $22,000. This erroneous figure was, subsequently, transposed by the employee on the recapitulation sheet and used in computing the final bid of M. J. McGough Company. It was not until after the opening of bids, when Mr. McGough sought to check their figures, that the mistake was discovered.

By the overwhelming weight of authority a contractor may be relieved from a unilateral mistake in his bid by rescission under the proper circumstances. The prerequisites for obtaining such relief are: (1) the mistake is of such consequence that enforcement would be unconscionable; (2) the mistake must relate to the substance of the consideration; (3) the mistake must have occurred regardless of the exercise of ordinary care; (4) it must be possible to place the other party in status quo.

Applying the criteria for rescission for a unilateral mistake to the circumstances in this case, it is clear that M. J. McGough Company and his surety, the Continental Insurance Company, are entitled to equitable relief. The notification of mistake was promptly made, and Mr. McGough made every possible effort to explain the circumstances of the mistake to the authorities of Jane Lamb Memorial Hospital. Although Jane Lamb Hospital argues to the contrary, the Court finds that notification of the mistake was received before acceptance of the bid. The mere opening of the bids did not constitute the acceptance of the lowest bid. Likewise, the acceptance by the Board of Trustees on February 22, 1968, being conditional, was not effective. Furthermore, it is generally held that acceptance prior to notification does not bar the right to equitable relief from a mistake in the bid.

The mistake in this case was an honest error made in good faith. While a mistake in and of itself indicates some degree of lack of care or negligence, under the circumstances here there was not such a lack of care as to bar relief. The mistake here was a simple clerical error. To allow Jane Lamb Memorial Hospital to take advantage of this mistake would be unconscionable.

DECISION: The court found in favor of plaintiff McGough.

TABLE 14-2

CONCEPT SUMMARY	**Genuine Assent**

There is no genuine assent if there is:

Fraud	A material fact has been misrepresented, with knowledge and intent to deceive. Reasonable reliance on the misrepresentation has caused injury to the deceived party.
Duress	A wrongful act or threat, rather than the free will of the party, has induced contractual assent.
Undue Influence	A dominant-subservient relationship exists. The dominant party has induced the subservient party to enter an agreement.
Unilateral mistake	When one party entered the agreement, he or she mistook some fact of substantial importance. The other party knew or should have known of this mistake.

Mistake of Material Fact

Finally, in determining the legal significance of a mistake, a court seeks to evaluate the performance of the mistake. Was the fact which resulted in the mistake of substantial importance? Would the party seeking relief from the mistake have entered into the contract even if no mistake had been made? The court must find that it was the mistaken fact that, at least in part, induced the party seeking relief to enter into the contract. The law is reluctant to undo a contract. Only the most significant and important mistakes of facts are grounds for contract rescission.

Related to the determination of the importance of the mistake is the question of the assumption of risk made by the parties. If a mistake of judgment regarding a risk assumed by either of the contracting parties has been made, the court will not grant relief. In many business situations, a contract is made conditional upon an uncertain event. Both parties exchange promises based on their assumptions concerning the likelihood of that event occurring. What is the likelihood of lightning striking your home in the next year? Do you and your insurance company have different assumptions about such an event? What is the value of property located on the outskirts of town? Do seller and purchaser have the same assumptions as to the likelihood of the proposed shopping center locating on or near the property? Certainly, if the parties disagree, one of the parties will be mistaken in its assumption; but no relief will be given if both parties have assumed the risk. The "value" of many items is by nature uncertain because of business custom, prevailing mores, social policy, and existing law.

A Concept Summary of the basic principles of genuine assent is provided in Table 14-2.

Review Questions and Problems

Key Terms

fraud	undue influence
scienter	bilateral mistake
duress	unilateral mistake

Discussion

1. What are the essential elements of fraud?
2. Why do the courts refuse to enforce agreements made under duress?
3. How does undue influence differ from duress?
4. When does a mistake justify the rescission of an agreement?

Review Problems

1. Jones, who had recently purchased waterfront land, hired the Suntree Construction Company to build a home on his newly purchased property. The project was suspended when a county building inspector found evidence of soil slippage. The inspector issued an order suspending construction until a soil expert certified the land as sufficiently stable for construction. Jones discharged the home contractor and brought action to rescind the land sale. Will he succeed? Does Suntree have recourse?

2. A beauty salon employee's plans to open her own salon next door came to the attention of her employer. The employee was summoned to headquar-

ters ostensibly to discuss new hair dyes. When she arrived, she was confronted with questions about her plans, which she denied. Upon management's request, she signed an employment agreement which included a clause restricting her from competing with her employer. Later, the employee brought suit to rescind the contract owing to duress. What is the result?

3. Ted, aged 42, has been the legal guardian of Frank, aged 19, since Frank's childhood. Frank has always trusted Ted and relied on Ted's advice in making important decisions. When Frank inherits $100,000 from his Uncle Mortimer, Ted advises Frank to enter the following agreement: For an annual fee of $10,000, Ted will invest Frank's inheritance for him. Frank is uncertain of the wisdom of this agreement, but concurs when Ted assures him, "I am doing this solely for your welfare." Is there any way Frank can nullify the agreement?

Case Problems

1. Greber suffered from a weight problem. After trying a complimentary treatment at the local Slenderella Salon, she immediately agreed to take a weight-reducing course consisting of 150 treatments at a total cost of $300. Greber also had long suffered a back ailment and informed the Slenderella Salon manager of this before signing the agreement. The manager did not discourage Greber from entering into the contract; she in fact thought that the treatments would do her back some good. Several days later, prior to engaging in any of the paid treatments, Greber's back hurt so much that she consulted a doctor, who advised her against taking the Slenderella program. Now Slenderella is suing for the money Greber agreed to pay, but she wants to rescind the contract. What result?

2. Oliver and Argo leased property and equipment to Gilreath and Johnson for use as a retail oyster and seafood business. The lease provided in pertinent part: "The lessees agree to make at their own expense, and without expense to the lessor . . . all of the necessary and needful repairs to said premises." Soon after agreeing to take the property, Gilreath and Johnson were assured by Oliver that if the equipment needed repairs, he would have Basham fix it at no charge to them. Six months later, various refrigeration equipment broke down, causing other damage and rendering the business inoperable. Gilreath and Johnson called Basham for repairs and he refused to help them. They then vacated the building and claimed Oliver fraudulently induced them to sign the lease. Is their claim justified?

3. Usry leased two ice-making machines from Poag, an agent for Granite Management Services (GMS).

Prior to the execution of the contract, Poag drew up a separate purchase order, signed by Usry, that contained the following: "Customer own[s] equipment at end of lease" and "free service until lease ends." The lease agreement itself contained no such language, but said: "the contract constitutes the entire agreement between the lessor and lessee and . . . no representation or statement made by any representative of lessor or the supplier not stated herein shall be binding." When the machines failed to perform properly and Usry was refused free service, he stopped making lease payments. GMS brought suit, but Usry claimed he was induced into signing the agreement by the fraudulent misrepresentation of Poag. Will Usry be able to rescind the contract?

4. Robinson, a young married man, was employed as the assistant manager in one of the Gallaher Drug Company stores. After 18 months on the job, he was accused of theft and embezzlement. Robinson admitted his guilt and was discharged from employment. The following day, he was invited to corporate headquarters to discuss restitution of the funds involved. After some discussion, Robinson entered into a written agreement to pay Gallaher Drug the sum of $2,000. He thereafter made payments totaling $741.64 and then refused to continue. The company seeks to enforce the contract, but Robinson says it was procured under duress and is therefore voidable. Is Robinson's defense a good one?

5. Sorrell was considering buying vacant land owned by Young. Young told Sorrell that he "could build a house on the lot." After buying the land, Sorrell prepared to build a house on the property. Sorell's contractor discovered that the land was too unstable to support a house because a great deal of fill dirt had been added to the lot. Young had not told Sorrell that the lot had been filled. Young contended that he was not aware that the land wasn't suitable for building a home, and that Sorrell should have examined the land more closely before buying it. Sorrell sued Young to rescind the land sale contract. What result?

6. The Beierles bought a motel from the Taylors. Before buying the motel, the Beierles were aware that the motel had been losing money. The Taylors, however, provided the Beierles with an analysis of projected income and expense which indicated that, under the right circumstances, the motel could earn over $27,000 per year. After taking over the motel, the Beierles failed to make a profit. They defaulted on a loan that the Taylors had made to them in connection with the sale of the property. The Beierles sued the Taylors to rescind the motel sale agreement on the grounds that the Taylor's income projection had been fraudulent. What result?

15

Capacity to Contract

Contractual Capacity and Mental Incompetency

Contractual Capacity of Minors

Contract law makes it clear that not all agreements are enforceable. The contracting parties must mutually consent to a contract by making an offer and acceptance. One party's acts or promises generally must be supported by consideration from the other party to be enforceable. The consent of each of the parties must be genuine; if it is forced, it will not be acceptable.

It follows then that a person who is unable to voluntarily consent to a contract would not have the capacity to contract. **Contractual capacity** is concerned with a person's ability to understand that a contract is being made and to understand its general terms. A person who is too immature or mentally incapable of appreciating the nature of a contractual obligation lacks the capacity to contract. This chapter reviews a number of situations in which a person's contractual capacity is at issue. Today, these situations generally involve people suffering from mental illness, intoxicated persons, and minors. The chapter first considers capacity problems due to possible mental incompetence, whether due to mental illness or to intoxication. It then reviews the special problems which arise when a minor, a person under the age of majority, makes a contract. Although in the past, married women, convicts, and aliens were sometimes found to lack the capacity to make certain contracts, recent court decisions and statutory revisions have eliminated these capacity concerns.

Persons who lack the capacity to contract are protected by the law. These people, who may be unable to effectively bargain with their counterparts in making contracts, are allowed to avoid or escape their commitments. The contracts they make are not valid; they may either be avoided by that person, **a voidable contract**, or they are absolutely void, **a void contract**, and without effect. While the law seeks to protect the person who lacks the capacity to contract, it also presumes that anyone making a contract has the capacity to do so. Thus, the burden of proving a lack of capacity is on the person asserting it. The person who acts senile or who is clearly under age is presumed to be capable of making a valid contract. To make the contract void, that person must do something to indicate that he or she wants to exercise the option that the law allows.

The test of capacity to make a contract is not whether a person's mind is impaired or whether the person has understood all the terms of a contract. Instead, capacity to contract is determined by whether a person has the ability to understand the nature of the transaction (does the person know he or she is making a contract?) and to understand its consequences (does the person know that he or she is agreeing to pay money in exchange for the other person's promise to deliver goods?).

As Table 15-1 illustrates, there are varying degrees of capacity. The presumption is that all people making contracts have contractual capacity. If they do and there are no capacity problems, their contract is *valid*. At the other extreme, a person who is unconscious or very young (such as a typi-

TABLE 15-1

Capacity to Contract, from Valid to Void

Valid Contract	Voidable Contract	Void Contract
Both parties have full contractual capacity	One or both parties lacks capacity and is protected from his or her contractual commitments; that party can avoid the contract if desired.	One or both parties is so unable to consent to a contract that the law says their attempt to contract is not effective.

cal 3-year-old), or a person who has been determined by a court to be mentally incompetent, is unable to consent to any contract. If one of these persons should make a contract, that contract is *void*; it is without any legal effect. In the middle are contracts that are *voidable*; these are contracts made by people who the law will protect by allowing them to avoid or disaffirm the contract. When a contract is voidable because one of the parties lacked the capacity to contract, only the party who lacks the capacity may disaffirm it. **Disaffirmance** is the act of avoiding or repudiating a contract. If that party does not want to disaffirm the contract or does not do so in the way the law requires, the contract is valid. If, however, that party does effectively avoid or disaffirm the contract, he or she is not obligated to fulfill its terms.

Contractual Capacity and Mental Incompetency

Mental Illness and Capacity to Contract

Sometimes the law is concerned with contracts made by people who have been legally determined to be insane. Contracts these people make are considered void. Suppose a court has determined Martha is incompetent; it has appointed a guardian, conservator, or other representative to act for her in buying groceries, paying bills, and making other contracts. If Martha and Alice make a contract whereby Martha agrees to pay Alice $25 if Alice will give Martha a book and both Martha and Alice want to enforce the contract, the law will still consider the contract void. Martha has no capacity to contract.

On the other hand, a person may be suffering from a mental illness or defect. If that person has not been legally determined to be incompetent or

insane, the presumption is that the person does have the capacity to contract. Incapacity due to mental illness may involve a diagnosed mental illness such as schizophrenia, brain damage, mental retardation, or senility. People with a mental illness or defect may have the capacity to make valid contracts during certain times, when they are lucid and can understand the consequences of a specific contract. If they make a contract when they are not lucid, the contract is voidable. That person then has the option of either treating the contract as valid or of making it void. Table 15-2 depicts the effect of mental illness on contractual capacity.

The test for mental incapacity generally examines whether a person understands the nature and general consequences of the contract. Thus, the capacity to contract of a person suffering from a mental illness generally is concerned with what a person knows and understands. The Restatement of Contracts (Second) provides that a person's contracts are voidable if the person is un-

TABLE 15-2

Mental Illness and Capacity to Contract

Determination of Mental Illness	Affect on Contractual Capacity
Person has been legally determined to be incompetent or insane	Loses capacity to contract; any contract is void
Person suffers from mental illness	Contract may be valid if made while lucid; Contract is voidable if made while not lucid; fairness of avoiding contract affects right to disaffirm

able to *act* in a reasonable manner in relation to the transaction and the other person has reason to know of his condition.[1] This standard is broader than the test that focuses only on a person's understanding. It provides protection to people who do understand the transaction, but, due to a mental defect or illness, are unable to control their actions.

Although courts from several states are considering the Restatement standard, as the Pennsylvania case that follows illustrates, some states are reluctant to adopt a new standard. In any case where the capacity to contract is challenged, the burden of proving that the contract is voidable is on the party seeking the right to disaffirm. When that burden is not met, as is the situation in the *McGovern* case that follows, the court will not allow a contract to be avoided, even if it was entered into as a result of poor judgment.

McGOVERN v. COMMONWEALTH STATE EMPLOYEES' RETIREMENT BOARD

Supreme Court of Pennsylvania (1986)
517 A. 2d 523

BACKGROUND: Francis McGovern retired from the Delaware Joint Toll Bridge Commission on January 9, 1981, after working there for thirty years. In December, 1980, just prior to his retirement, he selected two of several options for payout of retirement benefits due him under his retirement plan. The option he selected provided for a payment to him and, if he died before his wife, to his wife. Mrs. McGovern had been ill with Hodgkins disease since 1979. If McGovern had selected options that did not guarantee some payment to his wife if he were to die first, his estate would have received over $150,000.

Mrs. McGovern died on January 23, 1981 and Mr. McGovern died five days later. Accordingly, Mr. McGovern's estate received approximately $28,000 from his pension benefits. The heirs of Mr. McGovern's estate claim that he was not mentally competent when he signed the retirement papers. The Retirement Board found that McGovern did not lack the capacity to contract, but the trial court, adopting a new standard for determining mental competency to contract, reversed and ruled for the McGovern heirs. The Retirement Board appealed to the Supreme Court.

Flaherty, Justice

According to the testimony of McGovern's son, daughter and friends, McGovern suffered during the last year of his life from alcoholism and apparent distress at the state of his wife's health. Although Mrs. McGovern was told in March of 1980 that she was terminally ill, Mr. McGovern refused to acknowledge that his wife was going to die. . . . Mrs. McGovern's friends testified that he was so sensitive to any conversation concerning his wife's health that they would never mention it unless he introduced the subject.

When Mrs. McGovern was hospitalized for almost two months during the last year of her life, Mr. McGovern visited her only once, for five minutes, and would sometimes insist that his wife was malingering, or that she had a bleeding ulcer. Additionally, although Mr. McGovern had an alcohol problem for many years, when his wife's illness became apparent, he drank more heavily, even to the point of missing work and being too drunk to keep appointments. Finally, there was some evidence that Mr. McGovern was not always attuned to reality in other ways: after he retired, he would, on occasion, dress in his uniform and demand to be taken to work, and after his wife died, Mr. McGovern refused to eat and was heard having conversations with his dead father.

The board advised the junior Mr. McGovern that his father's retirement documents were binding and could not be changed. On November 25, 1981, an administrative hearing was

[1]Restatement (Second) of Contracts, s 15.

conducted at which Mr. McGovern contended that on December 17, 1980, the day his father completed his retirement application forms, his father did not have the requisite mental capacity to execute a retirement application. After hearing testimony from Mr. McGovern's friends and family, including a letter from the family doctor, and evidence from the retirement official who dealt with Mr. McGovern, a hearing examiner rejected this claim. The Board affirmed the hearing officer, based on its conclusion that Mr. McGovern did, in fact, possess the requisite mental capacity on the day in question and that he understood the nature of the transaction.

In support of this adjudication, the Board found that although Mr. McGovern had an alcohol problem and was distressed about his wife's illness with cancer, Mr. McGovern, some two months before his retirement, executed a will which even his son believed to be competently executed; he conducted his job over the years in a controlled and responsible fashion; he sometimes admitted and sometimes denied the seriousness of his wife's illness; he appeared coherent and responsive to the retirement official on December 27, 1980, during the meeting at which he selected his retirement options; and after the meeting of December 17, he sent a check to the retirement fund, as discussed at that meeting, to purchase his military buy-back retirement time.

Whether these facts support a conclusion that Mr. McGovern was legally competent to execute his retirement papers on the day in question will depend on the legal definition of competence. . . . Under Pennsylvania law, it is presumed that an adult is competent to enter into an agreement, and a signed document gives rise to the "the presumption that it accurately expresses the state of mind of the signing party." To rebut this presumption, the challenger must present evidence of mental incompetency which is clear, precise and convincing.

This Court has held that where mental capacity to execute an instrument is at issue, "the real question is the condition of the person at the very time he executed the instrument or made the gift in question. . . . We further held that a person's mental capacity is best determined by his spoken words and his conduct, and that the testimony of persons who observed such conduct on the date in question outranks testimony as to observations made prior to and subsequent to that date. Mere mental weakness, if it does not amount to inability to comprehend the contract, and is unaccompanied by evidence of imposition or undue influence," is insufficient to set aside a contract. Finally, a presumption of mental incapacity does not arise merely because of an unreasonable or unnatural disposition of property.

Contrary to these principles concerning the Pennsylvania law of competence, Commonwealth Court in this case adopted a new standard of competence based on the Restatement of Contracts, 2d. Section 15 of the Restatement, relied on by the court below, states:

Mental Illness or Defect

(1) A person incurs only voidable contractual duties by entering into a transaction if by reason of mental illness or defect

  (a) he is unable to understand in a reasonable manner the nature and consequences of the transaction, or

  (b) he is unable to act in a reasonable manner in relation to the transaction and the other party has reason to know of his condition.

(2) Where the contract is made on fair terms and the other party is without knowledge of the mental illness or defect, the power of avoidance under Subsection (1) terminates to the extent that the contract has been so performed in whole or in part or the circumstances have so changed that avoidance would be unjust. In such a case a court may grant relief as Justice requires.

This Court has never adopted Section 15 of the Restatement, which requires a post-hoc determination of reasonableness, and we decline to do so now. In fact, because the provisions of

Section 15 establish new tests for incompetence which conflict with those previously established by this Court, Commonwealth Court exceeded its authority in purporting to adopt Section 15 of the Restatement.

Accepting, as we do, that the common law of incompetence as it has been articulated in our prior cases is the law that controls this case, even if it were conceded that Mr. McGovern may have been incompetent to execute any legal document at certain intervals of time within months of his wife's death, substantial evidence also supports the conclusion that on December 17, 1980, he was lucid and understood the terms of the retirement contract.

It is our conclusion, therefore, that Commonwealth Court was in error in reversing the Board's determination, which properly applied the law of incompetency and which was supported by substantial evidence. . . . The real thrust of Mr. McGovern's claim in this case is that his father's designation of his mother as a secondary beneficiary was unreasonable and unwise. From some points of view, that may be true, but no one can say that belief that another will overcome a terrible disease and live is lunatic; no one can successfully assert that such a belief, even against the medical evidence, renders one incompetent. Such a belief may be, from some points of view, thoughtless, against scientific probabilities, irrational, and. . . it may even be said to be selfish and heedless of the needs of others. But whatever may be said about it, it cannot, without more, be said to prove incompetence. Thus, the claim that is made here in the name of incompetence is in reality a challenge to the wisdom, the desirability, the thoughtfulness and the rationality of the disposition. But such a challenge may not succeed, for neither courts nor disappointed heirs may alter the disposition of the property of a deceased person merely on the grounds that person acted in a way that the challenger believes to be irrational.

DECISION: The Order of Commonwealth Court is reversed and the determination of the Pennsylvania State Employee's Retirement Board is reinstated.

Generally, in the absence of fraud or special circumstances, if a person is slightly under the influence of alcohol or is partially intoxicated, contracts made by that person will be considered valid. Intoxication that causes some impairment of a person's judgment or a feeling of exhilaration generally is not sufficient to render contracts voidable. Instead there must be intoxication to such a degree that a person is deprived of reason and unable to understand the consequences of his or her actions.

If a person is so intoxicated as to lack the capacity to contract, he or she will usually be allowed to disaffirm and avoid its obligations. If, however, the intoxicated person cannot return the consideration he or she has received, in the absence of fraud by the other party, he or she will generally not be granted the right to disaffirm the contract. Furthermore, if the contract was for necessaries, the intoxicated person, like the minor, will be held liable for the reasonable value of the furnished items. Figure 15-1 depicts the questions to be considered in determining if there is a lack of contractual capacity due to intoxication.

Contractual Capacity

Overview

The legal capacity to enter into contracts is not the same as the capacity to commit a crime or a tort. The law often holds a minor responsible for criminal or tortious acts, but a minor is not generally liable for contracts. The higher standard applied to contracts is due in part to the fact that contracts generally involve bargaining with another person. A minor contracting with an adult needs to be protected from making unwise or foolish contracts. Similarly, the standard of capacity is also generally higher for contracting than for making a gift or a will. Neither of those methods of disposing of property involves bargaining with other parties, as is the case with contracts.

Historically, the law has provided special protection to minors who enter into contracts. This privileged contractual status has been based on their assumed immaturity and inexperience regarding commercial transactions. Historically the

FIGURE 15-1

Intoxication and Lack of Contractual Capacity

1. Has the person claiming a lack of capacity been legally determined to be incompetent due to habitual drunkenness?

   If **yes**, there is a lack of contractual capacity.
   If **no**, go to question 2.

2. Was the person claiming a lack of contractual capacity under the influence of drugs or alcohol?

   If **no**, there is **no** lack of contractual capacity.
   If **yes**, go to question 3.

3. Did the other contracting party cause that person's capacity?

   If **yes**, there is a lack of contractual capacity.
   If **no**, go to question 4.

4. Did the other contracting party know of that person's intoxication and seek to take advantage of it?

   If **yes**, there is a lack of contractual capacity.
   If **no**, go to question 5.

5. Is the person who is intoxicated only partially intoxicated?

   If **yes**, there is **no** lack of contractual capacity.
   If **no**, go to question 6.

6. Is the intoxicated person able to understand the consequences of his or her action?

   If **yes**, there is **no** lack of contractual capacity.
   If **no**, go to question 7.

7. Is the intoxicated person able to return the consideration he or she received?

   If **yes**, there is a lack of contractual capacity.
   If **no**, the person will not be able to disaffirm the contract.

common law has treated people under the age of 21 as minors, but since the enactment of the Twenty-sixth Amendment to the U.S. Constitution, which lowered the voting age to 18, most states have lowered the age of majority from 21 to 18. Accordingly, although most of the cases that follow concern individuals who are minors because they are under 21, in most states now only persons under 18 are considered minors.

The protection extended by the law allows the minor the choice of either carrying out and enforcing the contract or seeking to avoid its provisions. Avoidance of the contract is done by any act that manifests the minor's intent to no longer be bound by the contract. Most contracts entered into by minors are voidable contracts. The contracts are valid unless the minor, by disaffirming them, seeks to avoid their provisions. There are a number of contracts, however, that a minor is not allowed to disaffirm. Examples of such contracts are the following:

1. A contract by a minor to enlist in the armed forces

2. A contract by a minor to borrow money from an institutional lender or the government for the purpose of financing some portion of the minor's postsecondary education

3. A contract by a minor consenting to the adoption of a child

4. A contract of a minor to participate in a professional sport

5. A contract of a minor that includes a provision where the minor as an employee or purchaser of a business agrees not to compete with the business of the employer or seller

6. A contract to borrow money from a lender which is secured by a mortgage

The contracts that are not voidable by minors vary from state to state. Statutes in each state have to be examined to ascertain exactly which contracts of minors are not subject to disaffirmance.

In addition to enforcing contracts that state statutes declare not subject to disaffirmance, contracts for necessaries are also usually excepted from the general rule allowing minors to avoid their contracts. The law generally holds the minor liable for the reasonable value of the necessaries furnished to him. Thus, if a minor has contracted to pay $100 for necessary and suitable clothes whose reasonable value is only $70, the minor's liability would be $70, not $100. Minors' contracts for necessaries are discussed in greater detail later in this chapter.

Although the general presumption is that a minor's contract is subject to disaffirmance, a court deciding whether a minor is liable on his contract must determine the answers to several questions:

1. Do any statutes specify that this particular type of contract should not be subject to disaffirmance?

2. Does the law (statutes or court decisions) consider that the subject of this particular contract constitutes a necessary, so that the minor would not be liable for the contract price but only for the reasonable value of the necessary?

3. If the contract is subject to disaffirmance, has the minor done something that in fact amounts to disaffirmance?

Disaffirmance of Contracts by Minors

Contracts Subject to Disaffirmance As has been noted, some contracts that minors make are not subject to disaffirmance. Thus, the first question that must be answered concerning the minor's act of disaffirmance is whether the contract is one that cannot be disaffirmed. Unless state statutes expressly exempt the particular contract, or its subject matter is considered a necessary, the law generally will treat any contract made by a minor as subject to disaffirmance.

Time of Disaffirmance Generally a minor may avoid any contract that is subject to disaffirmance during the time of his or her minority and for a reasonable period of time after attaining the age of majority. The law thus gives the minor a period of time to review and reflect on the contractual agreements made during minority. What constitutes a reasonable time depends on the complexity of the transaction, its subject matter, and the circumstances peculiar to each agreement.

Methods of Disaffirmance Disaffirmance occurs by the minor manifesting an unwillingness to be bound by the contract. The minor can simply inform the other party (whether an adult or minor) that he or she intends to disaffirm their contractual agreement. Or the minor can do some other act that clearly indicates that he or she has such an intent. Thus, the minor who has agreed to sell goods to one purchaser but instead sells them to a third party has by such an act disaffirmed the contract with the original purchaser. Similarly, a minor who sues to avoid his or her responsibility for a contract's obligation manifests his or her intent to disaffirm that contract.

Disaffirmance and Restitution of Property by the Minor

While the law seeks to protect the minor from unwise or imprudent contracts, there is disagreement among court decisions as to the rights of the parties if a minor cannot return the property he or she received. The majority of the decisions hold that a minor may disaffirm a contract and receive back any consideration given even if the minor is unable to return to the other party that which the minor has received. The rule that restitution is not required in order for the minor to avoid the contract is intended to protect the minor by discouraging adults from contracting with minors.

A minority of decisions require the minor to return the consideration received from the other party in order to be able to disaffirm the contract. If the minor is unable to return the property received (or its equivalent value), the minor will not be allowed to disaffirm the contract. These courts assert that the minor's right to disaffirm can be used only to protect the minor (as a shield), but not to allow the minor to unfairly benefit at the other party's expense (as a sword). Figure 15-2 illustrates these rules.

The case that follows Figure 15-2 involves a discussion of this concept as applied to a child star who seeks to disaffirm a contract made with a management company that acted as his agent.

FIGURE 15-2

Minor's Right to Disaffirm and Duty to Return Consideration Received

Majority rule: Right to disaffirm is not dependent on return of consideration.

DEFENSIVE

A minor can disaffirm defensively when disaffirmance protects minor from a bad bargain. If a minor purchases a car and the brakes become defective in 20 days, the minor can protect herself by returning the car and getting back all the money paid, even though the car is not in the same condition as when it was purchased.

OFFENSIVE

A minor can disaffirm offensively when disaffirmance is desired, regardless of consequences. Assume a minor purchases a car and drives it across the country. After using it, he may disaffirm his contract obligation to pay the remainder of the purchase price. If the minor returns the car, he may get back the money he paid for the car. (Sometime depreciation is deducted.)

Minority rule: Minor can disaffirm only if minor returns the consideration or its equivalent value.

If the minor purchases a car and causes major damage to it, he or she can't get any money back by returning the junked car, since its value is not equivalent to what was paid.

Scott Eden Management v. Kavovit

Supreme Court, Westchester County

563 N.Y.S.2d 1001 (1990)

BACKGROUND: Andrew Kavovit, a child actor, signed a contract when he was 12 to have Scott Eden Management manage his career in the entertainment industry. The contract entitled Scott Eden to a 15 percent commission on Andrew's gross earnings. Andrew landed a number of parts, including a continuing role on the soap-opera *As the World Turns*. Andrew's attorney notified Scott Eden of Andrew's intention to disaffirm the contract "on the grounds of infancy" as of February 8, 1989. Scott Eden sued Andrew for the right to collect its commission on Andrew's future income derived from contracts signed before February 8, 1989.

Coppola, Justice

An infant's contract is voidable and the infant has an absolute right to disaffirm. This aspect of the law of contracts was well entrenched in the common law as early as the fifteenth century. In bringing this action, and defending the motion, plaintiffs fully recognize the principle of law involved here and in no way challenge the infant's right to disaffirm. Rather, plaintiffs rely upon a corollary to the main rule, which also evolved early in the Common Law:

"After disaffirmance, the infant is not entitled to be put in a position superior to such a one as he would have occupied if he had never entered into his voidable agreement. He is not entitled to retain an advantage from a transaction which he repudiates. 'The privilege of infancy is to be used as a shield and not as a sword.'. . .

The restoration of consideration principle, as interpreted by the courts, has resulted in the infant being responsible for wear and tear on the goods returned by him. In the event that the minor cannot return the benefits obtained, he is effectively precluded from disaffirming the contract in order to get back the consideration he has given. In *Vichnes v. Transcontinental & Western Air,* the infant paid the air fare from New York to Los Angeles. On returning to New York she demanded the return of her money. Appellate Term granted summary judgment to defendant because "there is no basis for rescission here in view of the concession that the reasonable value of the transportation was the sum paid by plaintiff." . . .

Here, the position adopted by defendants is no different than that advanced on behalf of the infant who had taken the airplane ride and wanted her money back. . . . In each case, the infant consumed the fruits of the contract and refused to pay for that fruit, to the clear prejudice of the other party. In this case, the infant will continue to reap the benefits of his contract with plaintiff but is using his infancy as an excuse not to honor the promise made in return for that benefit.

If the argument asserted by defendants were adopted by the Court, the infant would be put in a position superior to that which he would have occupied had he never entered into the contract with plaintiff. He would be retaining an advantage from the repudiated transaction, i.e., using the privilege of infancy as a sword rather than a shield. Not only is this manifestly unfair, but it would undermine the policy underlying the rule allowing disaffirmance. If the infant may rescind the contract with the manager immediately after a lucrative performance contract is signed, yet still retain the benefits of the performance contract, no reputable manager will expend any efforts on behalf of an infant.

DECISION: The court ruled that Andrew was required to continue to pay Scott Eden 15 percent of his gross earnings on contracts signed prior to February 8, 1989.

ETHICS
Fair Treatment of Minors

Courts disagree on the legal question of whether emancipated minors should legally be held responsible for their contracts. The ethical question is whether it is fair for a minor to sign a contract that says "I represent that I am 21 years of age or over and recognize that this sale is based on this representation," and then be able to disaffirm. The question for legal policy is somewhat different—at what age is it just to hold young people accountable for their agreements, particularly when they are emancipated from their parents—16, 18, 21?

In one case *Kiefer v. Howell Motors, Inc.,* the minor was nearly 21 and was even represented by a lawyer. Essentially the case involved a consumer dispute and the "minor" decided to use his minority as a sword to achieve a favorable outcome. If a minor intentionally and purposefully misrepresents his or her age with the intention of keeping options open, do you think the minor has acted unethically?

From the viewpoint of the law, a different question is involved. The policy question is, What is the best way to protect minors overall? A rule that a few may abuse, but that protects a lot of minors who need protection, may be considered efficient, although a few people get away with acts that are inconsistent with the purpose of the law.

Disaffirmance and Misrepresentation of Age

A minor's right to disaffirm a contract is also often influenced by misrepresentations the minor makes. When a minor misrepresents his or her age and such misrepresentation is relied on by the other party, who is then induced to enter into a contract, a conflict between legal policies results. On the one hand, the law seeks to protect the minor and allow the minor to disaffirm contracts made while he or she was under the age of majority. The law wants to insure that the minor is not victimized by wiser and more mature adults. On the other hand, if a person is the victim of fraud, the law generally allows the victim to rescind the contract that resulted from the fraud.

What should be done if the minor commits the fraud and the adult is the victim? The responses of the courts have not been uniform; the court decisions are split. Figure 15-3 poses the questions which courts usually ask in determining if a minor does have the right to disaffirm his or her contract and avoid its obligations.

A Minor's Contract for Necessaries and Parent's Liability for Minor's Contracts

As we have noted, a minor is generally liable for the reasonable value of necessary items for which he or she has contracted. That liability is limited to the reasonable value of the items, which may be less than their contracted price. What constitutes necessary items varies with the needs of the individual concerned. Generally, food, clothing, and shelter, suitable to the minor's station in life, will be regarded as necessaries. The court looks to see whether the contracted items are essential to the minor's general welfare.

What about the purchase of a stereo set? A car? The contract for the payment of college tuition? Only an analysis of the needs of the individual minor can provide the answer to these questions.

Since the law often protects the minor by allowing contracts to be disaffirmed, those contracting with minors will seek to hold other parties liable for the minor's contracts. With the

1. Is the contract one which is **not** subject to disaffirmance?

    A. If **yes**, it is valid.
    B. If **no**, it is voidable.

2. Is the contract for necessaries?

    A. If **yes**, the minor is liable for the reasonable value.
    B. If **no**, the contract is voidable.

3. If the contract is voidable, has the minor done something that amounts to disaffirmance?

    A. (1) Did the act occur within a reasonable time after reaching the age of majority?
       (2) Was there an express act or inaction that clearly shows the intent **not** to ratify?
    B. If **no** to either question, the contract is valid.
       If **yes** to both questions, the contract is voidable.

4. Did the minor return the consideration received, or its fair value, to the other party?

    A. If **no**, a majority of states say the contract can still be disaffirmed but a minority of states says the contract becomes valid.
    B. If **yes**, the contract is voidable.

5. Did the minor misrepresent his or her age?

    A. If **yes**, a majority of states say the contract is valid as misrepresentation prevents disaffirmance; a minority of states say the contract is still voidable by the minor.
    B. If **no**, the contract is voidable.

FIGURE 15-3

Contracts by Minors: Questions Affecting Capacity

lowering of the age of majority in most states to 18, those who are minors are less likely to be emancipated, self-supporting, or totally independent from their parents or guardians. Businesspeople contracting with 16- or 17-year-olds are likely to do so only if the parent or another adult is expressly committed to perform the minor's contractual obligations. Banks will require an adult cosignor for any loan made to a minor. Merchants will check to confirm that charge cards are issued in the name of an adult and that the minor child has the express permission of that adult to make purchases. School authorities will require parental permission and approval, as well as the child's consent, prior to participation by the child in extracurricular activities or special programs. Most businesses are aware of the law's desire to protect the minor; they therefore seek to make contracts with adults whose contracts are not subject to disaffirmance.

Even in situations where the merchant does not have an express contract with the parent of a minor, a merchant who furnishes necessary items to a minor may be able to hold one or both of the minor's parents liable. By statute in most states, the law requires a parent to furnish necessary items to his or her minor children. If the merchant can prove that the items the minor agreed to purchase were necessary for the minor, and were not being—but could be—furnished by a parent, the parent can be held liable. The contract between the parent and the merchant is not an express contract, created by the parties; it is implied by the provisions of the law.

Where a merchant furnishes necessary items to a minor, the merchant may hold either the parent or the minor liable for the reasonable value (not the contract price) of those items. If the minor is emancipated and is not dependent for financial support on his or her parents, the merchant can hold the minor liable. A contract for necessaries by a minor is valid; it is not subject to disaffirmance by the minor. If the minor is dependent on one or more parents for financial support and for furnishing his or her necessaries, and if a parent is able to furnish those necessaries, then the merchant can hold the parent liable. In either case, the merchant can recover the reasonable value of necessary items furnished to a minor. The case that follows puts an interesting twist on the issues discussed above. What if a minor's *parents* enter into a contract for the minor's necessaries, but they are unable to pay for them? Does this give rise to an *implied* contract with the minor so that the minor could be required to pay under the necessaries doctrine?

NORTH CAROLINA BAPTIST HOSPITALS, INC. V. FRANKLIN

Court of Appeals of North Carolina
405 S.E. 2d 814 (1991)

BACKGROUND: Nine-year old Melanie Beth Franklin was injured in an automobile accident and was treated at plaintiff's hospital. Melanie's parents signed papers accepting responsibility for Melanie's medical costs. When Melanie's parents failed to fully pay Melanie's hospital bill, the hospital sued Melanie. The trial court ruled in the hospital's favor. The court reasoned that Melanie had impliedly contracted to receive treatment and, since the hospital's services qualified as "necessaries," Melanie could not avoid the contract. Melanie appealed.

Phillips, Judge

The dispositive issue in this case is whether under the circumstances established defendant child is liable under the necessaries doctrine for the hospital services furnished her by plaintiff. The following legal principles apply: The necessaries doctrine, under which infants, lunatics and others generally incapable of entering into enforceable contracts may be held liable for necessaries, one of which is medical and hospital care when ill or injured, has been a part of Anglo-American jurisprudence since before the time of Lord Coke. Under the doctrine an infant who contracts for or obtains necessaries that are not being supplied by his parents or guardian may not disavow the agreement and can be held liable for their fair value, and when an infant or lunatic receives necessaries at the request of others, but not upon their credit, the law will imply a promise by the recipient to pay their reasonable value under *quantum meruit*. But a child living with its parents cannot be held liable even for necessaries "unless it be proved that the parent was unable or unwilling to furnish the child with such clothes, . . . as the parent considers necessary." *Freeman v. Bridger* "[T]he mere fact that an infant has a father, mother, or guardian does not prevent his being bound to pay what was actually necessary for him when furnished, if neither his parents nor guardian did anything toward his care or support." *Cole v. Wagner*. The best view according to one authority is that the necessaries doctrine is *quasi* contractual in nature, since an infant's contract for necessaries, whether express or implied, is enforceable only to the extent that the amount charged is reasonable. The general law appears to be that "to render the infant liable, the necessaries must have been furnished to him on his own credit and not on the credit of others." 43 C.J.S. *Infants* Sec. 180 (1978). . . .

Since the record clearly shows that plaintiff's admittedly necessary services for the child were not furnished upon her credit or at her request, but were furnished at the request of the parents, who agreed to pay for them, the judgment holding the defendant child liable has no basis under the foregoing authorities. . . .

Plaintiff relies, as did the court, upon the statement in *Cole v. Wagner,* as to a child being liable for necessaries when the parents do nothing to obtain them, but the parents here, unlike those in *Cole,* did do something. They did everything that any parent could possibly do for its child in regard to the necessaries except pay for them after the debt was incurred. They were living with, caring for and supporting the child; they arranged for the child to obtain the necessary hospital care both in Morganton and Winston-Salem; they assumed responsibility for the charges and contracted to make small monthly payments on them; and they submitted to the entry of a default judgment against them. Sifted down, the question really is did the inability of the parents to pay their debt to the hospital make the child liable for it under the necessaries doctrine? No authority of which we are aware holds that it did; and we hold that it did not. To hold otherwise, as the court in effect did, would make children the guarantors of their parents' debts for clothes, lodging, schooling, medical care and other necessaries. Heretofore the necessaries doctrine has not had that scope, and guaranties have not been established in that manner.

DECISION: The Court of Appeals reversed and ruled in Melanie's favor.

Ratification of Contracts by Minors

In general, a minor can avoid any contract by exercising the power of disaffirmance. The effective surrender of the power of disaffirmance is known as **ratification**. Since contracts entered into by a minor are subject to disaffirmance, ratification cannot take place until after the minor attains the age of majority.

A ratification by a minor can occur in any of three ways. First, the minor may fail to make a timely disaffirmance. Since the minor has the right to disaffirm only for the period of his or her minority, plus a reasonable period of time after attaining the age of majority, the minor who does not disaffirm within that time ratifies by such action (or inaction) the contract made during minority. Second, the minor can expressly state, orally or in writing, that he or she intends to ratify the contract. If the express statement is clear and unambiguous and is made after attainment of the age of majority, ratification of the contract has occurred. Once such ratification occurs, the power to disaffirm terminates. Finally, after attaining the age of majority, the minor may by his or her conduct manifest an intent to ratify the contract made while a minor.

CONCEPT SUMMARY
Lack of Capacity and Incompetency

Incompetency due to mental illness	Traditionally resulted in *void*, rather than *voidable*, contract.
	Modern approach is to treat contracts made by possible incompetents (those not legally adjudged incompetent) as *voidable*.
	Alleged incompetent has burden of proving incompetency (unless he or she has been legally adjudged incompetent).
Incompetency due to intoxication	Some jurisdictions allow disaffirmance when other party knew of intoxication and took unfair advantage of it.
	Intoxication must be to a degree that the person is deprived of reason or is unable to understand the consequences of his or her actions.
	If the intoxicated party is unable to return consideration, he or she may lose the right to disaffirm.
	Intoxicated person may be held liable for reasonable value of necessaries.
Incompetency due to minority	Contract voidable, with several exceptions (e.g., contracts for necessaries, contracts to enlist in the armed forces, contracts to finance postsecondary education, contracts consenting to adoption, professional sports contracts, contracts not to compete and loans secured by a mortgage).
	Some jurisdictions prohibit disaffirmance when minor has received consideration and is unable to return it (or its equal value).
	Minor may be deemed to ratify contract by failing to disaffirm within a reasonable time after reaching majority or through conduct which manifests an intent to ratify.

In the Smith case, a car dealer argued that Smith, a minor, had ratified a contract because he failed to disaffirm it within a reasonable time after reaching the age of majority.

BOBBY FLOARS TOYOTA INC. V. SMITH
Court of Appeals of North Carolina
269 S.E.2d 320 (1980)

BACKGROUND: When Charles Smith (defendant) was 17 years, 11 months, he bought a car from Bobby Floars Toyota (plaintiff). He signed an installment agreement to pay the balance in thirty monthly installments. Age 18 was the year of majority for executing contracts in North Carolina. At age 18 years, 10 months, he returned the car to the plaintiff and stopped making car payments. The plaintiff sold the car at public auction, and sued Smith for the balance that was not obtained at auction. The trial court granted the defendant's motion for dismissal. The plaintiff appealed.

Morris, Justice

The only question is whether Smith's voluntarily relinquishing the automobile 10 months after attaining the age of majority constitutes a timely disaffirmance of his contract with Floars. The rule is that the contracts of an infant may be disaffirmed by the infant during minority or within a reasonable time after reaching majority. What is a reasonable time depends on the circumstances of each case. In the instant case, we believe that 10 months is an unreasonable time within which to elect between disaffirmance and ratification, in that this case involves an automobile, an item of personal property which is constantly depreciating in value. Modern commercial transactions require that both buyers and sellers be responsible and prompt.

We are of the further opinion that Smith waived his right to avoid the contract. The privilege of disaffirmance may be lost where the infant affirms or ratifies the contract after reaching majority. Certain affirmations or conduct evidencing ratification is sufficient to bind the infant, regardless of whether a reasonable time for disaffirmance had passed. In the present case, it is clear that Smith recognized as binding the installment note evidencing the debt owed from his purchase of an automobile. He continued to possess and operate the automobile after his 18th birthday, and he continued to make monthly installments as required by the note for 10 months after becoming 18. We hold, therefore, that Smith's acceptance of the benefits and continuance of payments under the contract constituted a ratification of the contract, precluding subsequent disaffirmance.

DECISION: The Court of Appeals reversed in favor of plaintiff Floars.

Review Questions and Problems

Key Terms

contractual capacity   ratification
disaffirmance

Discussion Questions

1. What is the test of a person's capacity to make a contract?

2. Are all contracts for minors voidable? Explain.

3. Are most contracts made by people who are intoxicated voidable by them?

Review Problems

1. Pelham, 17-year-old, bought a car from Howard Motors for $2,075.60, paying $500 down. In the bill of sale, Pelham certified that he was 18 or older, and he told the salesman he was 20. Pelham took the car home but brought it back the next day for repairs. When Howard failed to correct the problems, Pelham had his attorney write the company, repudiating the contract and demanding return of the down payment. Should Pelham prevail?

2. Horton, age 17, rented three furnished rooms from Johnson. He and his wife occupied the rooms for 5 months. When Horton moved out, Johnson brought suit for one week's rent, "one week of notice in lieu of intent to terminate tenancy," and damages to furnishings. Could Horton be held responsible?

3. Stewart and Curry were partners in a paving contracting business. Curry began to drink heavily and on one occasion was hospitalized for alcoholism.

During this time, Curry contributed very little to the paving business. For several months Stewart and Curry talked about their business problems. Stewart prepared an agreement dissolving the partnership and gave it to Curry. Two weeks later Curry and Stewart signed the agreement and several other documents relating to the dissolution of the partnership. Three months later Curry filed suit. He claimed that he was still recovering from his alcoholism, under the influence of sedatives, and therefore was entitled to avoid the dissolution agreement because he lacked the capacity to contract. Do you agree?

4. Bowling, age 16, bought a used car from Sperry for several hundred dollars. He paid the full amount in cash. After 1 week, he found the main bearing had burned out. He returned the car to Sperry and asked that it be repaired; Sperry said the repair would cost Bowling $80. Bowling said he wouldn't pay $80 and left the car with Sperry. The next week he wrote to Sperry that he wanted to disaffirm his purchase contract. He asked for his money back. Sperry refused, and Bowling sued. Can Bowling disaffirm this contract? How would you decide if this car is a necessity for Bowling?

5. Jack Jones, a 16-year-old high school student, lives with his parents. He works part time but depends on his parents for most of his support. Jack buys a number of items and then notifies each of the sellers that he is a minor, is renouncing his contract, and will not return the merchandise. Further, he wants his money back. What should happen regarding his purchase of the following items?

   (a) Drugs at a drugstore that were prescribed for his asthma

   (b) Food at a local restaurant bought after school and before going to his part-time job

   (c) A winter jacket costing $60 to keep him warm in the Michigan winter

(d) $400 in photography equipment for his hobby of three years

6. James Taylor, a minor, bought a used car when he was 1 year under the age of majority and began making payments on it to the bank that financed it. Then he went into the service and made no more payments on the car. He told his father to have the bank pick up the car. It did so and sold it for salvage. When Taylor returned from the service, the bank claimed that he had not disaffirmed his contract because he did not ask for the return of his payments. Do you agree? Why?

7. Pat, a minor, made a compromise settlement with Mazurek, an adjuster representing the insurance company that underwrote Workmen's Compensation for the state. The agreement was based upon compensation due Pat for a back injury he sustained while employed at Midway Toyota. Mazurek represented Midway Toyota during the settlement negotiations and negotiated directly with Pat and his mother, who was present when he signed the agreement. Pat's mother did not object to the signing. Neither she nor any other adult cosigned the agreement. Since Pat was the sole contracting party with Mazurek while his mother was present at the agreement, is he now entitled to disaffirm the agreement? Why or why not?

Case Problems

1. Williamson wanted to sell her home because her mortgage was in default and the mortgagee was threatening foreclosure. Williamson had a history of excessive drinking. Her mother and other witnesses testified that she still had the problem at the time she executed a contract to sell her equity in her home to Matthews for $1,700 even though it was worth almost ten times that amount. At the trial, Dr. Feist provided expert testimony that she showed signs of early organic brain syndrome due to excessive drinking, that some of her brain cells were destroyed, and that her ability to transact business had been impaired. Several witnesses testified she had several drinks before going to the attorney's office to sign the contract of sale. Matthews noted that when the parties first went to the attorney's office, the attorney read the contract terms to each party. A few hours after completing the sale, Williamson said she didn't have an attorney who represented her and that the contract should be voidable due to her lack of capacity. Do you agree?

2. In 1974, Brenda Butler inherited land on C Street. In 1982, she deeded the property to herself and her husband Charles. After Brenda died in 1984, her husband became the sole owner of the property and at his death a year later, Charles's brother and sister owned the land. Brenda's son, David, claimed Brenda lacked the capacity to deed the property to Charles in 1982. David and Brenda's granddaughters testified that Brenda started to become confused in 1980 and that the periods of her confusion would come and go. Brenda's doctor testified that when Brenda was hospitalized in 1982, five months after she signed the deed, her condition prevented her from thinking in an analytical, coordinated fashion and that she suffered from a memory loss. A CAT scan at that time showed some atrophy of her brain and a deteriorating mental condition. Charles's brother testified that he visited Brenda several times in 1982 while she was hospitalized and she always knew him. The attorney who prepared Brenda's 1982 deed testified that she was unaware of any unusual behavior by Brenda on the day she prepared the deed. Did Brenda lack the capacity to contract?

3. In September 1986, Edith Hatchel deeded four parcels of land in the city of Virginia Beach, Virginia, to Resort Development. Less than 2 months later, on a petition filed by the Department of Social Services, a court found Edith to be incapacitated by reason of mental illness. Edith's niece, Beth Brown, who was named by the court to act on Edith's behalf, claimed the September 1986 deed was made while Edith lacked the capacity to contract. Brown testified that her aunt was distorted, confused, and unable to understand any written document. A psychologist who talked with the grantor in October 1986 said, "I don't think there is any way this lady could have understood what she was doing at the time the deed was executed." Resort Development presented several witnesses who were present at the real estate closing when the property was sold. Her attorney testified she "knew what was going on" and her mental awareness was good. The real estate agent testified that she understood she was signing a deed to property that included her home. Did Ethel Hatchel lack the capacity to contract?

4. In September 1963, Darwin Cundick sold his livestock, equipment, development company, and range land in Wyoming to Broadbent. At the end of 1960, Cundick was diagnosed by his physician as having "depressive psychosis" and was referred to a psychiatrist. During the next 2 years, Cundick was treated by his own physician for a heart condition and minor illnesses. After Cundick's wife filed suit to set aside the sale of his property, he was examined by two neurosurgeons who testified that based on their March 1964 examination of Cundick, their opinion was that on the very date of his sale he "was a confused and befuddled man with very poor judgment." Cundick and Broadbent had negotiated their contract and then met to sign a paper summarizing its terms. Cundick's lawyer rewrote that one-page agreement into an eleven-page contract. The lawyer testified he had explained the terms of the sale to all parties, including Cundick and his wife, and all apparently understood it. There was no testimony from Cundick's friends, neighbors, or family that supported the allegation that he was mentally incompetent in 1963. Do you think there is enough proof to show that Cundick lacked the capacity to contract?

16

Illegality

Statutes and Illegal Contracts

The Common Law and Illegal
    Contracts

Effects of Illegality

Although an agreement may include all the elements necessary to constitute a valid contract, if its purpose or object is illegal the contract may not be enforced. The most obvious example of an illegal contract is an agreement to commit a crime. Television detective shows have made us all familiar with the expression "to put a contract out on someone." No one would argue that the person performing that "contract" should be aided by the courts in securing the agreed contract price.

In most jurisdictions, legislatures have declared certain transactions involving either criminal acts or tortious wrongs to be illegal. Contractual agreements that violate these statutes generally cannot be enforced. Some states prohibit the sale of firecrackers, others do not. Some states proscribe gambling, whereas other states allow and in fact promote certain kinds of gambling.

Since the public policy of a state may be declared by the legislature or pronounced by the courts, both statutory and common law sources must be examined to determine which contractual agreements are illegal and unenforceable. While the lists of such contracts vary from state to state, this chapter examines a few of the most common regulations of illegal agreements. The first section of the chapter focuses on typical statutory provisions that make certain contracts illegal. The second section concerns court decisions based on common law principles rather than statutory language that determine particular contracts to be illegal. The final section examines the effect of a statute or court decision declaring a contract to be illegal. While illegal contracts cannot generally be enforced by either party, some exceptions do exist because of special public policy concerns. Consequently, not all illegal contracts are unenforceable. Furthermore, where only a portion of a contract is illegal and unenforceable, in certain cases the remainder of the contract can be enforced.

Statutes and Illegal Contracts

Statutes make a variety of contracts illegal. As contracts are regulated more by state law than federal law, our focus here is on state statutes. Although there is significant variation from state to state in areas of contract regulation, at least four areas are frequently the concern of state statutes. These include wagering, usury, Sunday laws, and licensing laws.

Wagering Agreements

A wagering contract is one in which the parties promise to pay a designated sum of money or to transfer property upon the determination of an uncertain event or a fact in dispute. Bets on a horse race, football game, or roll of the dice are all wagers. The public policy regarding wagering agreements varies from state to state. While most states prohibit many wagering agreements, generally schemes such as raffles, bingo, or the awarding of door prizes are permitted under certain conditions.

A number of states have recognized that substantial revenues can be obtained from gambling and have instituted state-operated lotteries. At least thirty-four states sponsor some type of lottery games. Similarly, charitable organizations may be licensed under certain conditions to conduct raffles, to give millionaires' parties, or to sponsor bingo games. In a few states, wagering agreements that do not involve substantial amounts of money are permitted. Thus, a friendly bet on the local football game might be permitted in some states while prohibited in others. A poker game among senior citizens in Florida received national attention in 1982 when a local prosecutor decided to enforce the state's gambling laws. Although the enforcement of these laws is usually sporadic, it is wise to check the statutes in each state and to be aware of the possibility (if not the probability) that not only might contracts violating these statutes be unenforceable but also they might result in criminal sanctions.

Not all contracts that reward each party differently depending on a future event are wagers. An insurance policy, for example, is such a contract. Contracts for the sale or purchase of commodities that will be harvested in the future are similarly speculative. These agreements, however, involve items of value that are being sold and purchased. The parties are not merely speculating on the outcome of a future event. The insured has a substantial interest in his life or property, and the commodity purchaser agrees to accept the commodity being bargained for. Since these agreements are not wagers, they are not illegal and unenforceable.

Usury Contracts

Most states have **usury** laws that limit the amount of interest that may be charged by a lender. Any contract by which the lender receives more than the permitted interest is illegal. There usually are civil consequences as well as criminal penalties placed upon those who lend money at usurious rates. In most states, the lender is denied the right to collect any interest on a usurious contract. Some states also prohibit the lender from collecting the principal due on the loan as well as the in-

terest. A few states allow the lender to collect the interest permitted by law and prohibit only the excess "illegal" interest. Lenders are usually permitted to recover expenses incurred in preparing loan documents. Similarly, they may be able to assess fees as a cost of obtaining a loan. These expenses and fees are not generally considered interest.

There often are many different usury statutes in the same state. Some statutes apply only to small loan associations, while others are aimed at installment loans such as credit card transactions. Loans made to businesses are often totally exempt from usury statutes. Most states permit interest rates charged by those who issue credit cards to exceed the statutory rate. Similarly, interest charged to finance a home or a car may usually exceed the basic rate. Finally, almost all states permit small loan companies to charge rates up to 36 percent. These rates are permitted so that the borrower who can't go to conventional financial institutions will have a legitimate place from which to borrow.

The primary objective of usury statutes is to protect the borrower from being forced to pay an excessive amount for the use of money. Usury has been illegal since biblical times, and the usurious lender has often been a moral outcast. Yet, frequently, the effect of a usury statute penalizes the people most in need of funds. Whenever inflation pushes the market price for the use of money higher than the maximum rate allowed by law, some lenders stop making loans. Borrowers in need of funds can then turn only to unregulated lenders, whose interest rates generally reflect the increased demand for their money. Some financial institutions once located in New York transferred some of their operations to other states because of the effect of New York's usury laws on their business.

Sunday Laws

Some states have **Sunday laws** (also called "blue laws") that forbid "all secular labor and business on the Sabbath." In these states, it would seem that all contracts made on Sunday are illegal and unenforceable, at least as long as they remain executory. Other states prohibit only certain types of transactions or the sale of certain goods on Sunday. Frequently, a state statute or municipal ordinance will prohibit the sale of alcoholic beverages on Sunday. The sale of automobiles or certain other consumer products on Sunday is also prohibited in some communities in order to regulate competition among sellers and to provide a day of rest from commercial activity.

In interpreting these statutes, courts typically seek to avoid the harsh effects that could result if the agreements were totally unenforceable. Instead, if some part of the agreement is made or performed on some day other than Sunday, the contract is usually enforced. Thus, a contract that would have been illegal because it was entered into on a Sunday will be legal if the parties later negotiate or in any way approve their earlier illegal agreement. Active enforcement of these laws, however, varies significantly from state to state and even among communities within the same state.

The Sunday laws raise questions pertaining to both the establishment of a state religion and interference with the freedom of religion. The establishment argument is that the laws are part of an effort to legislate particular religious practices. The freedom of religion argument is based upon the impact of Sunday laws. If a particular businessperson is forbidden by his or her religion to work on a sabbath other than Sunday, and is forbidden by law from working on Sunday, that person can only work 5 days a week. A competitor who either is an atheist or observes a Sunday sabbath can work 6 days a week. The Supreme Court has rejected these arguments, finding a secular basis for Sunday laws, which are seen as enhancing community life by providing for rest and quiet and protecting employees from having to work 7-day weeks.

The following case which was brought against Sears Roebuck is typical of the court decisions upholding Sunday laws.

POYER V. SEARS ROEBUCK CO., INC.

U.S. District Court
741 F.Supp. 98 (D. Md. 1990)

BACKGROUND: Poyer, an office clerk at Sears, quit her job after Sears announced a policy of requiring office clerks to work on Saturday or Sunday. Poyer says that the Maryland statute requiring wholesalers and retailers to give a Sabbath to its employees states a public policy that any discharge of an employee because he or she will not work on the Sabbath is illegal and requires the employer to compensate the employee for the wrongful discharge. Sears claims it can fire Poyer for violating its policy because the Sunday law violates the U.S. Constitution.

Smalkin, District Judge

This removed diversity case, involving the discharge of a retail employee who refused to work in a Sears store on Sundays and setting forth causes of action for wrongful discharge and intentional infliction of emotional distress, is before the Court on the defendant's motion for summary judgment. That motion raises . . . the issue of the constitutionality of Md.Ann.Code art. 27, § 493 (1987 Repl.Vol.), which provides for the mandatory allowance, by wholesalers and retailers, of a day of rest to any employee on Sunday or "his Sabbath." The defendant claims that the statute is unconstitutional under the First and Fourteenth Amendments, and both the plaintiff and the Attorney General of Maryland . . . contend that the statute is constitutional. . . .

The Court is of the opinion, although the question is a close one, that the statute is constitutional. Unlike the Connecticut statute held unconstitutional in *Thornton v. Caldor, Inc.*, the Maryland statute specifically refers to an employee's "day of rest," and, more significantly, unlike the Connecticut law, the Maryland statute does not prescribe any religious test (of sincerity of belief or otherwise) against which the employee's selection of his or her day of rest is to be measured. Taken against the background of previous Maryland cases that have not given the Maryland sabbath laws an exclusively religious interpretation, it is the opinion of this Court that the sabbath reference in the statute is not to be confined to its religious meaning, *viz.*, that of a religiously-required or -inspired day of rest, but is to be given its figurative meaning, simply a day of rest. The *Oxford English Dictionary* (OED) (1971) gives both a religious definition and a figurative, secular definition for the word *sabbath*. The latter definition is "a time or period of rest; a cessation from labour, trouble, pain, and the like." The OED gives literary illustrations for this usage going back to the Fourteenth Century. In this secular sense, which is the one in which it is used in the Maryland statute, the sabbath provision does not run afoul of the First Amendment.

In light of the factors recited above, the Court is of the opinion that the statute in question does not violate the Establishment Clause of the First Amendment to the Constitution of the United States.

Next, the Court has decided that the statute does not violate the Equal Protection Clause of the Fourteenth Amendment. The limitation of the statute's coverage to retail and wholesale establishments is a rational distinction drawn between such operations, which directly or indirectly serve the consumer, and such enterprises as manufacturing, construction, agriculture, and the professions, which either do not directly serve the consumer or do not require for their conduct a fixed place of carrying on business, with set hours. The Court cannot say that the Maryland Legislature acted irrationally in confining the operation of §493 to retail and wholesale establishments.

Turning to the remaining issues, the Court assumes, for purposes of this motion, that the statute in question states a valid public policy of Maryland, and that, if plaintiff was in fact discharged in violation of that policy, she would have an action against her former employer under the rule in *Adler v. American Standard Corp.,* . . . The difficulty in applying the *Adler* rule to this case, though, is that under the undisputed facts, there is no triable issue as to plaintiff's *discharge.* Obviously, no *Adler* action lies unless the employee has been discharged. The undisputed facts here show that the store manager, in response to a need for office clerks (and plaintiff was one of four office clerks in the store) to work Saturdays and Sundays, scheduled them *all* for duty on a weekend rota. This action was not solely directed at plaintiff, but applied to all persons in her job category, and all four of them were dissatisfied with the new policy. To mollify the clerks, Sears offered them reassignment to jobs that would not require Sunday work. . . . Instead of being reassigned (at a pay loss of 37 cents per hour), plaintiff quit. In this case, the Court need proceed no farther than to point out that there is *no* evidence that the employer's conduct in requiring Sunday work was directed especially at the plaintiff (in an effort to get her to resign), as opposed to all employees similarly situated. This requirement of individual targeting was recognized in Judge Wilkinson's dissent in *Paroline v. Unisys Corp.,* which the Fourth Circuit has recently adopted *en banc* as the opinion of the court on the issue of constructive discharge. Because this Court believes that the Court of Appeals of Maryland would adopt the Fourth Circuit's targeted action requirement for constructive discharge, this Court holds that plaintiff can make out no case of constructive discharge, a *sine qua non* of her *Adler* claim.

Finally, the facts, no matter how liberally taken in plaintiff's favor, fail to make out the kind of *extreme* or *outrageous* conduct needed to sustain a Maryland claim of intentional infliction of emotional distress. In this case, the Court concludes as a matter of law that Sears simply made a legitimate business decision, which, although obviously personally distasteful and even hurtful to the plaintiff, because of her sincere desire to "[r]emember the sabbath day, to keep it holy," *Exodus* 20:8 (King James), was not conduct so atrocious and extreme as to be intolerable among civilized persons.

DECISION: The court granted judgment for defendant Sears.

ETHICS

Using Sunday Blue Laws as a Competitive Tool

Sunday blue laws are found throughout Europe and North America and are omnipresent in Australia, where few items can be bought on a weekend after noon on Saturdays. Although seemingly innocuous, such laws may have a very substantial impact on the competitive position of firms. There have been cases where blue laws have been enacted which have resulted in a firm losing 30 to 40 percent of its sales.

In 1990, the Great Atlantic & Pacific Tea Co. (A&P) spent $250 million to acquire seventy Miracle Food Mart supermarkets in Ontario, Canada. Soon after, Ontario's provincial government reinstated some Sunday blue laws that prohibited supermarkets, as well as some other retail firms, from doing business on Sundays. Partially as a result, A&P's overall earnings decreased from $150 million in 1990 to $100 million in 1991.

In some instances, particularly in the United States, the advocates of Sunday laws are merchants who have most of their sales during the week and who lose business to discounters who do a large volume weekend business. Certainly one of the most effective ways to compete is to use the power of lawmaking to have the competition seriously constrained by law. Is it unethical for the weekday merchants to make arguments supporting blue laws based upon protecting people from having to work on weekends and providing for a day of rest when their real intent is to hamper their competitors? If their sole intent to benefit themselves is concealed and they do not believe the arguments that they put forward, they are not acting in good faith. Sunday blue laws deny choice to consumers (who by voting with their dollars indicate that they prefer to shop on weekends) and should only be enacted when there is an overwhelming public support and valid justification for the restrictions.

Licensing Regulations

Statutes in all states require that licenses, certificates, permits, or registrations be obtained by people planning to perform certain acts. A state will typically have boards and commissions that license accountants, architects, attorneys, beauticians, builders, chiropractors, community planners, dentists, foresters, land surveyors, nurses, physicians, realtors, and many other practitioners. Each board and commission is charged with regulating some activity of interest to the state, frequently by issuing licenses or permits to those persons who meet qualifications established for the regulated activity.

In some cases, state statutes merely require a fee to be paid in order to obtain the needed license. These licensing laws are known as *revenue statutes* since they are primarily concerned with raising revenue, even though there may be some application procedure that also must be completed. Usually, anyone can obtain a fishing license or a bait dealer's license. Such licensing laws do not usually subject the licensee to any significant regulation by the state.

On the other hand, the primary purpose of *regulatory statutes* is to regulate those obtaining a license. The state wants to ensure that its nurses, doctors, real estate brokers, plumbers, lawyers, and others who serve the public are competent to engage in the profession or business being licensed. While regulatory statutes are concerned chiefly with the protection of the public, a fee is often assessed to cover administrative costs. There are several consequences for persons who do not comply with the requirements of state licensing statutes. In some cases, the violation of a state licensing law can lead to criminal charges. In other cases, a special panel, board, or professional association may be authorized to take disciplinary action against the person who has not complied with the state's licensing provisions.

ISSUES AND TRENDS
Regulatory Licensing Statutes: Pro and Con

The following editorial excerpted from *The Wall Street Journal*, June 18, 1993, discusses the negative effect of licensing boards. Proponents of licensing statutes that are intended to regulate conduct argue that the statutes protect the public from unscrupulous people whose advertisements lure the public into contracting for services from unqualified practitioners. The opponents suggest the statutes restrict competition from new entrants, such as Monique. Is it time for an overhaul of licensing statutes? Many states are reviewing their laws to see if some of their regulatory statutes are unnecessary.

Monique in Tangles

Monique Landers is a 15-year-old high school student who already has her own small African hair-braiding business. That is she *did* until six weeks ago when the state of Kansas shut her down because she didn't have a cosmetology license.

Monique learned she had to close her business just after she returned from New York, where she had been honored as one of five Outstanding High School Entrepreneurs. An official at the Kansas Cosmetology Board read about her award and promptly demanded that she desist. . . .

Monique started "A Touch of Class," and began braiding and washing the hair of friends and family members. She made a profit of about $100 a month.

This was too much for the Kansas Cosmetology Board, which warned her it was illegal for her to in any way touch hair for profit without a license. If she didn't stop, they wrote the youngster, she was subject to "a fine or imprisonment in the county jail or both." . . .

Last year, we reported on Taalib-Dan Uqdah, a Washington, D.C.., hair-braider, who was almost shut down because he posed a threat to other salons. John Stossel, a reporter for ABC's "20/20," says his 20 years of consumer reporting have taught him that licensing board "rules can end up hurting more people than they protect.". . .

Perhaps Monique has technically violated Kansas's cosmetology statute. If so , it's time it and the licensing laws in other states that regulate 500 occupations, covering 10% of the nation's work force, were overhauled. A valuable program . . . has enough trouble turning at-risk youth around without having to battle petty bureaucrats at the same time.

Our primary concern in this chapter is not, however, with these criminal or disciplinary consequences to the violator of a state licensing law. Instead, our focus is on the civil law consequences to the parties who have made a contract that does not comply with the licensing requirements. If, like Kansas, a state requires you to have a license in order to be a cosmetologist, can you contract with people to braid their hair if you do not have the required license? Will the state enforce your contract? If you are not paid by the other contracting party, can you bring suit to recover the money you were to be paid? The answer to these questions depends on the wording of the applicable licensing statute.

Frequently, the statute itself will specify that any agreements made by persons who do not comply with its terms will be unenforceable. When the statute is silent concerning the enforceability of such agreements, the courts frequently look to the purpose of the statute.

Contracts made without a license in violation of a revenue statute are usually enforceable. Thus, a farmer who should but does not have a license to sell her produce at a city market can enforce contracts with those who purchase the

TABLE 16-1

Contracts and Licensing Statutes

Type	Purpose	Examples	Violation of Statute
Regulatory	Protect the public	Professional licensing for attorneys, architects, nurses, plumbers, realtors	Contract is void; possible administrative proceedings; possible criminal case
Revenue-raising	Raise money for the state	Bait-dealer's license; fishing license	Contract is valid; possible minor penalty for noncompliance

products. While the farmer has violated a licensing statute that is intended to raise revenue for the city, that violation does not affect contracts made by the farmer. If the purpose of the licensing statute is primarily regulatory, however, the person who performs services or delivers goods without complying with the licensing provisions will be denied the court's aid in enforcing contracts he has made with the purchasers of his goods of services. Table 16-1 summarizes the differences between regulatory and revenue-raising statutes. The *Silver* case exemplifies the approach of the courts to enforcement of contracts that violate these types of licensing statutes.

SILVER V. A.O.C. CORPORATION
Court of Appeals of Michigan
187 N.W.2d 532 (1971)

BACKGROUND: Silver (plaintiff), a handyman, sued A.O.C. Corporation (defendant) to collect a fee incurred when Silver replaced electrical wiring for the defendant. Plaintiff Silver was a journeyman electrician who had been employed by defendant's predecessor to repair lights at an apartment building in Detroit. He was not licensed as an electrical contractor under state law or city ordinance. Defendant A.O.C. Corporation was an apartment management company that had become the manager of the apartment building in question. When the plaintiff met the caretakers at the apartment building, he gave them his card so they could "call him in an emergency if the caretakers could not get ahold of the management company."

In 1967, the caretaker's wife called the plaintiff to repair a short circuit in the caretaker's apartment. Subsequently, he was asked by her to fix one or two hallway lights. The plaintiff found the wires in the hallway were burned by oversized bulbs and he undertook to replace all the defective wiring. His work was accomplished over a 4-month period, and he submitted a bill to defendant for $893. It was defendant's first notice that the work had been done.

The defendant refused to pay the plaintiff, and the plaintiff sued in the common pleas court. That court found the plaintiff's work was a "minor repair" exempt from the licensing statute and awarded judgment for the plaintiff. The circuit court affirmed and the defendant was granted leave to appeal to the court of appeals.

Per Curiam

Defendant claims the trial courts erred in holding that plaintiff was exempt from the licensing statute because the work done was minor repair work.

The electrical administrative act was an act "to safeguard persons and property" and "to provide for licensing of electricians and electrical contractors and the inspection of electrical wiring."

The act, in effect, is to insure that persons who do electrical work are duly licensed. Section 7 of the act provides that no person, firm, or corporation shall engage in a business of electrical contracting unless duly licensed as an electrical contractor. An exception to this section is minor repair work, Section 7(a), which is defined as "electrical wiring not in excess of a valuation of $50."

There appears to be little doubt that what plaintiff was doing would be considered to be electrical contracting. Section 1(b) defines electrical contracting as "any person, firm or corporation engaged in the business of erecting, installing, altering, repairing, servicing or maintaining electrical wiring devices, appliances or equipment." One of defendant's witnesses, a senior assistant electrical engineer and supervisor of the Detroit electrical inspection bureau, testified that the type of work done "was required to have been contracted for by a licensed electrical contractor."

Thus, unless the work fell under the "minor repair work" exception it could only be done by a licensed electrical contractor, which plaintiff wasn't.

As stated earlier, "minor repair work" is that which in value is worth $50 or less. Included in this figure must be the material as well as labor necessary to complete the repair and restore the item to good working order. It was stipulated below that the value of the work done was $893. Since this is well in excess of $50, this work would not come under the "minor repair work" exception to the licensing requirement.

Plaintiff was in violation of the licensing act when he did the work. Therefore, his action to recover on the contract should be barred from the courts. When one enters into a contract to perform services or furnish materials in violation of a statute which is enacted to protect the public health, morals, and safety, and which contains a penal provision, as this statute does, he cannot maintain an action to recover thereon.

DECISION: The court of appeals found the plaintiff had violated the state's licensing requirements since his work was not merely minor repairs. The court reversed the lower court and found in favor of defendant A.O.C. Corporation.

The Common Law and Illegal Contracts

In addition to contracts prohibited by statute, the courts have from time to time determined that certain agreements violate public policy and are to be considered illegal. In some instances, a court has initially declared certain classes of contracts illegal and the state legislature has subsequently endorsed that action by enacting a statute to the same effect. The contracts discussed in this section are those that courts at common law initially condemned even if in some states they are now regulated by statute. The contracts covered in this section include those that restrain trade, relieve one party from some liability to another party, include unconscionable provisions, or involve other acts that conflict with public policy.

Agreements in Restraint of Trade

The law disfavors agreements where one person agrees not to compete with another. Such agreements impose too great a restraint on the individual and adversely affect competition within our society. Unless such agreements are incidental to other lawful contracts and are limited to reasonable terms, the courts will not enforce them.

Agreements not to compete are often found in contracts in which a business is being purchased and sold. The purchaser wants to ensure that the seller, who has built up the good will of the business, will not continue to be in competition with the purchased business. Noncompetitive agreements are also found in employer–employee contracts. An employee may be working in a vital segment of the employer's business. The employer wants to ensure that the employee does not establish a competing business based in part upon the valuable information learned from the employer.

A noncompetitive agreement must be reasonable to the concerned parties and to the public. Agreements that restrain trade by restricting competition between the seller and purchaser of a business are generally viewed in a favorable light by the courts. A court's inquiry will usually focus on whether a contract provision restraining the seller is reasonable in time and space. A provision restricting the seller from being employed in a similar business or opening up a new business that is competitive with the purchaser will be reasonable for several years but not for 10 or 20 years. The restraint ordinarily cannot prohibit the seller from opening a similar business in the next state or in a distant community. Instead, the geographic area of the restraint must be the area in which the need for protection by the purchaser is most dominant.

Agreements made between an employer and employee that restrict the employee's right to compete with the employer are usually examined more closely by the courts than are agreements between the seller and purchaser. Unlike the purchaser of a business, the employee generally is not in an equal bargaining position with the other contracting party. In the sale of a business, there almost always is a recognized need for the purchaser to be able to protect the goodwill of the business. Frequently, the goodwill is the primary asset being purchased, and the purchaser will not be able to protect it if the seller can compete with the business being sold. The employer, on the other hand, does not have as great a need to protect the business' goodwill against the employee. Usually, an employee is less likely to be able to leave the employer's business and to take the employer's goodwill to his or her own use as the seller of a business could do. In these employment cases, the courts will examine not only the need for protection by the employer from the employee but also the relative hardship imposed on the employee. The employee's lack of bargaining power can be a decisive factor in many cases. The public interest, served or defeated by the restraint, also will be examined, particularly when vital services or goods might be withheld from the community if the restraint is enforced.

There are, however, certain circumstances in which an employee may possess valuable information that could harm the employer if it was revealed to a competitor. Employees who are working in new product design, or drug research, or who know key client lists and confidential

PREVENTIVE LAW
Noncompetition Clauses

There are many businesses in which the enforceability of noncompetition clauses is critical to the long-run success of the business. In many hightech fields, competitors may purposely hire away key employees to obtain information about new products and processes. Sales firms such as manufacturer' representatives and wholesalers may also be vulnerable to employees leaving and taking clients they have cultivated while working for the firm. This problem is particularly severe in the financial services industry where brokers and investment bankers often jump from one firm to another.

There is a natural tendency when drafting clauses to make them as far-reaching as possible to protect all potential interests of the firm. An aggressive strategy may backfire in this area because if the court finds that the clause is unreasonable in its reach, it may throw out the entire provision leaving the firm with no protection at all.

The noncompetition clause may be a part of an employee handbook or some other general document. As a consequence, many employees may not actually know about the clause and how it applies. New employees should check out the nature of any restrictions and be sure that they understand the rules of the game. Concurrently, the firm should make sure that employees understand what is considered trade secret material and what restrictions will be imposed upon them when they leave the firm. This will prevent unpleasant surprises later on.

TABLE 16-2

Determining the Enforceability of Noncompetitive Agreements

Type of Agreement	Court Focus	Presumption
General agreements	Compare burden and benefits for each party	Only those agreements with small burden and/or great benefit will be enforced
Purchaser–seller agreement restricting seller from competing	Is restraint reasonable in time (duration) and space (geographic area)?	If the restraint is reasonable, agreement is usually enforced
Employer–employee agreement restricting employee from competing	Will the employer be clearly affected by competition from this employee?	Burden is on employer to demonstrate need
	Did the employee have any bargaining power?	Court often concerned with protecting employee
	Will enforcing the agreement adversely affect the community?	If vital services are lost (doctor in small town), agreement will not be enforced

information relating to compensation or cost, may be in a position to damage seriously their former employer.

It is not uncommon for an employer to ask a successful employee to sign a noncompetition agreement after the employee has been working for the firm for several years. In those cases, there is an issue of sufficient consideration in addition to the question of the basic enforceability of the clause. Prior to the enactment of legislation restricting limitations on the vesting of pension plans, employers would try to tie observance of a noncompetition clause into the right to receive pension or other severance payments. If an employee went to work for a near competitor, the promised payments were cut off. Such "self-help" measures are still possible to the extent that they don't violate pension plan legislation.

Ultimately, the courts must balance these various competing equities in determining whether a restrictive clause should be enforced. A critical dimension is always the determination of the reasonableness of the restraint itself.

After the reasonableness of the restraint has been determined, the court must then decide several questions related to the agreement's enforceability. If the parties have made an unreasonable restraint, should the court rewrite the restraint so that it is reasonable and enforce it under those terms or should it leave the one party free from any restraint? Similarly, if a business sale and purchase agreement contains a provision that unreasonably restrains the seller, is that provision one that can be separated from other provisions in the agreement? Is the contract divisible into separate sections? If one part of a contract is illegal and unenforceable, can any part of the remaining contract be meaningfully enforced?

Table 16-2 depicts the concerns usually addressed by courts examining contracts with noncompetition provisions.

The *Gomez* case addresses some of these issues in the context of an employment agreement. The court in *Gomez* didn't rely on common law principles because there was a statute on the books that applied directly to case. The Texas statute interpreted in *Gomez*, however, reflects common law principles that have been applied to restrictive covenants in several jurisdictions.

GOMEZ V. ZAMORA
Court of Appeals of Texas
814 S.W.2d 114 (1991)

BACKGROUND: Gomez worked for TAMSS, a service that helped hospitals to recover money from the government for medical services provided to indigent patients. Over the years, TAMSS had developed unique computer software, forms, procedures, and expertise that gave it a big advantage over its competitors. Its forms and procedures were easily transferable to others wishing to use them to compete against TAMSS, so TAMSS was particularly vulnerable to employees wishing to steal trade secrets and use their training to start competing businesses. Upon receiving a promotion at TAMSS, Gomez signed an employment agreement that included a restrictive covenant forbidding Gomez from competing against TAMSS in its "existing market area" and in any "future market area begun during employment." Gomez was fired from TAMSS when it was discovered that he was planning to start a competing business. Gomez did indeed start a competing business, MAPA. TAMSS and Zamora, TAMSS's owner, sued Gomez and MAPA for violating the restrictive covenant. The trial court granted a temporary injunction against Gomez and MAPA, prohibiting them from competing against TAMSS in a certain geographical area. Gomez appealed.

Hinojosa, Justice

In 1989, the Texas Legislature enacted legislation establishing the enforceability of a covenant not to compete when such a covenant:

(1) is ancillary to an otherwise enforceable agreement but, if the covenant not to compete is executed on a date other than the date on which the underlined agreement is executed, such covenant must be supported by independent valuable considerations; and
(2) contains reasonable limitations as to time, geographical area, and scope of activity to be restrained that do not impose a greater restraint than is necessary to protect the goodwill or other business interest of the promisee.

The covenant barred appellant from competing in an "existing marketing area" and a "future marketing area of the employer begun during employment". Attachment A, which described the "Future Marketing Area Of Employer" listed thirty seven Texas cities, including all major metropolitan areas and several minor cities. Thus, the geographic area covered by the covenant encompasses the thirty seven cities listed in "Attachment A," as well as the "existing marketing area."

Except for the attachment to the covenant not to compete, TAMSS at no time offered evidence clearly defining its existing or future marketing area. . . .

After reviewing the evidence, we hold that TAMSS failed to establish that the covenant not to compete contained reasonable limitations on geographic area because the record does not reflect the geographic area intended to be covered by the covenant. Moreover, the covenant as written fails to accurately specify the geographic scope covered by covenant. Indefinite descriptions of the area covered by a non-competition covenant render them unenforceable as written. . . .Thus, we conclude that the covenant is unenforceable not only because no evidence defined the geographic scope of the agreement, but also because it was indefinite as written. Thus, the covenant is incapable of supporting injunctive relief without reformation.

Moreover, if we look only to those cities listed on Attachment A, the covenant not to compete would cover virtually every major metropolitan area in the State of Texas. Non-competition covenants with such a broad geographic scope have generally been held unenforceable, particularly when no evidence establishes that the employee actually worked in all areas covered by the covenant.

Appellee requests reformation of the injunction in the event that we find the injunction overbroad; however, we cannot do so. Section 15.51(c) specifies the procedure for enforcement of overbroad non-competition covenants. First, the promisee must request that the trial court reform the covenant. Second, the trial court shall reform the covenant so that it is reasonable as set forth in § 15.50(2). Then, the promisee may seek enforcement through injunction. We have previously stated that the failure to request reformation in the trial court operates as a waiver of the right of reformation.

There is nothing in the record reflecting that TAMSS requested the trial court to reform the covenant. Appellee's statutory right to reformation is therefore waived.

DECISION: The court of appeals reversed and dissolved the temporary injunction against Gomez and MAPA.

Contracts with Exculpatory Clauses

Exculpatory clauses in a contract relieve or limit the liability of one of the parties in the event that the party does not perform his or her part of the contract. Such clauses are viewed with disfavor by the law. The policy of the law is that damages caused by one party's nonperformance of contract terms should be recoverable by the injured party. An exculpatory clause that relieves one party of liability thus may be contrary to legal policy. While it has generally been the courts that have declared such contract provisions to be unenforceable as contrary to public policy, statutes in many states declare some of these clauses to be unenforceable and illegal. For example, in most jurisdictions there are statutes that deny the enforceability of at least some part of exculpatory clauses found in apartment leases prepared by landlords for tenants.

Exculpatory clauses that are unenforceable can be classified under two main headings: (1) those limiting liability of a dealer who sells goods or services to the public and (2) those limiting an employer's liability for negligence that causes injury to an employee. As to clauses of the first type, the law notes that there rarely is equality of bargaining power between the consumer and the dealer. It is in the public interest that those people who serve the public and whose contracts with the public are usually not the subject of bargaining and negotiation not be allowed to relieve themselves of liability for their own negligence. As to clauses of the second type, the policy of the law is to discourage negligence by making wrongdoers pay damages. If an employer or its agent causes injury to anyone, even an employee, the injured party should be able to recover damages.

Furthermore, an employee too is generally not in an equal bargaining position with an employer. Thus, such clauses are not favored and will not be enforced.

Some exculpatory clauses that limit the liability of one of the contracting parties in the event of nonperformance by that party will be enforced. Some states allow contracting parties the freedom to contract under the broadest possible terms. In these states, freedom of contract outweighs concern over exculpatory clauses. Two factors are particularly important in these instances: the bargaining power of the parties and the degree to which the law otherwise regulates the concerned agreement. If both parties are business firms that have negotiated the terms of their agreement with each other, the courts are more likely to allow one of the parties to limit its liability. Similarly, if one of the businesses is already subject to significant regulatory control by the state, the rules, regulations, and policies of the state regulatory agencies may permit the business to limit its liability in certain contracts.

One of the most common situations in which one of the parties to a contract seeks to limit his or her liability concerns the bailee of property. A bailee is someone who has been given the right to possess personal property. The restaurant checkroom, the downtown parking lot, the airport baggage counter, the warehouse storing your out-of-season snowmobile are all bailees. These bailees usually have signs on their property, statements on the backs of receipts, or identification tickets that limit their liability, even for their own negligence, in the event your property is lost or damaged. While such clauses are generally enforceable, in some cases courts will not enforce them because to do so would violate public policy. While it is impossible to define what constitutes public policy, it is clear that social forces play major roles in shaping this concept. The public policy implications of exculpatory clauses are discussed in the *Morgan* case.

MORGAN v. SOUTH CENTRAL BELL TELEPHONE COMPANY
Supreme Court of Alabama
466 So.2d 107 (1985)

BACKGROUND: Morgan was a periodontist (a dentist who treats gum disease). Upon expanding his practice into Bessemer in 1980, Morgan contracted to have his practice advertised in the Bessemer Yellow Pages. It was important for Morgan to be listed in the Yellow Pages, because a Yellow Pages listing was the only permanent form of advertising permitted by the State Board of Dental Examiners. Morgan's name was omitted from the 1980 Bessemer Yellow Pages, and he sued South Central Bell Telephone Company for damages. Morgan's contract with the phone company included an exculpatory clause that purported to protect the phone company from liability for its errors and omissions. After the trial court ruled for Morgan, the phone company appealed.

Embry, Justice

The trial court held that exculpatory clause in the 1980 contract valid and enforceable. Plaintiffs contend the clause was not freely bargained for, is unconscionable in nature, and should not be enforced by this court.

The instant case illustrates the need for a more comprehensive rule concerning exculpatory clauses. A review of the various methods by which other states have dealt with exculpatory clauses and their refusal to enforce them convinces us that the best rule, and the simplest in application, is that exculpatory clauses affecting the public interest are invalid. That rule was set forth by the California Supreme Court in *Tunkl v. Regents of the University of California*. Six criteria were established to identify the kind of agreement in which an exculpatory clause is invalid as contrary to public policy.

[1] It concerns a business of a type generally thought suitable for public regulation. [2] The party seeking exculpation is engaged in performing a service of great importance to the public, which is often a matter of practical necessity for some member of the public. [3] The party holds himself out as willing to perform this service for any member of the public who seeks it, or at least any member coming within certain established standards. [4] As a result of the essential nature of the service, in the economic setting of the transaction, the party invoking exculpation possesses a decisive advantage of bargaining strength against any member of the public who seeks his services. [5] In exercising a superior bargaining power the party confronts the public with a standardized adhesion contract or exculpation, and makes no provision whereby a purchaser may pay additional fees and obtain protection against negligence. [6] Finally, as a result of the transaction, the person or property of the purchaser is placed under the control of the seller, subject to the risk of carelessness by the seller or his agents.

The transaction before this court clearly meets the *Tunkl* criteria. The contract arises out of a private business transaction of the telephone company which in all other respects is regulated by the Public Service Commission in performing its services. Certainly, the telephone company would not argue that it is engaged in a business other than one which performs a service of great importance to the public when it distributes a Yellow Pages book without cost to every telephone customer. The telephone company without question holds itself out as willing to give reasonable public service to all who apply for an advertisement in the Yellow Pages.

As to whether the telephone company, which is invoking exculpation, possesses a decisive advantage of bargaining strength, the courts have differed. Some courts hold that there are many other modes of advertising which the businessman may employ if the contract offered him by the telephone company is not attractive.

The issue, however, is not whether there are other forms of advertising available, but whether such other modes are tied directly to the telephone service enjoyed by almost every home and business in the state. The telephone company has an exclusive private advertising business which is tied to its public utility service of providing telephone service and which reaches almost every home and office in the state. Therefore, the telephone company can state to a customer that an ad will be published but name its own terms, including a limitation of its own liability for negligence.

We are satisfied that the plaintiffs did not have a meaningful choice relative to the inclusion of an exculpatory clause in the 1980 Bessemer contract and that the defendants had the bargaining power in a gross and unbalanced manner in determining the terms and conditions in the directory advertisement.

Therefore, the exculpatory clause is unenforceable because, under the criteria above established, it is invalid as contrary to public policy.

DECISION: The Supreme Court of Alabama affirmed the decision in favor of Morgan.

Unconscionable Contracts

A court may refuse to enforce a contract on the grounds of **unconscionability** if it finds the contract is too oppressive or one-sided. While a court may refuse to enforce unconscionable contracts even in the absence of express legislative authority, the basis for most of the litigated cases today

---

ETHICS
Unconscionability

The test of unconscionability comes as close to applying a principle of ethics directly as any part of our commercial law. The test is one of fairness, whether or not a practice would be seen as improper by one of good conscience.

Critics of the principle of unconscionability have argued that it produces a wild hare—an unpredictable, unstructured standard that could be used to set aside contracts willy-nilly and that would reduce certainty, make planning more difficult, and thereby increase transaction costs.

In addition, the critics claim that a principle of unconscionability is unnecessary. They note that the legal doctrines of fraud, duress, undue influence, consideration, lack of capacity and mistake all are available to deal with problems of coercion or gross unfairness. These doctrines are seen as preferable to unconscionability because they have definite parameters and can be applied without the danger of establishing a precedent for second guessing bargains. As it has turned out, however, the courts have been very reasonable in the way in which they have applied the principle and it appears clear that only the more outrageous practices have been condemned as unconscionable.

The doctrine of unconscionability can be seen as inconsistent with the concept of freedom of contract. An underlying premise of freedom of contract is that society should not act to set aside the outcomes of freely bargained agreements, regardless of how harsh (or unconscionable) they may seem to outsiders.

is the Uniform Commercial Code. Section 2-302 of the code provides:

1. If the court as a matter of law finds the contract or any clause of the contract to have been unconscionable at the time it was made, the court may refuse to enforce the contract, or it may enforce the remainder of the contract without the unconscionable clause, or it may so limit the application of any unconscionable clause as to avoid any unconscionable result.

2. When it is claimed or appears to the court that the contract or any clause thereof may be unconscionable, the parties shall be afforded a reasonable opportunity to present evidence as to its commercial setting, purpose and effect to aid the court in making the determination.

What makes a contract unconscionable is of course for court determination. Several factors seem important. What is the relative bargaining power of the parties? Is one party economically stronger than the other? Does each party have options? Can the seller sell to others or is there only one source of supply from which the buyer can purchase the desired goods? How reasonable are the terms which are claimed to be unconscionable?

According to the Official Comment to UCC Section 2-302, the basic test of unconscionability is whether, in the light of the general commercial background and the commercial needs of the particular trade or case, the clauses involved are so one-sided as to be unconscionable under the circumstances existing at the time of the making of the contract.

The object is to prevent oppression and unfair surprise and not to disturb the allocation of risk arising because of one party's superior bargaining power.

The *Meredith* case that follows concerns several interrelated problems. The "waiver of defense clause" contained in the contract specifies that the purchaser will waive defenses against the seller (perhaps if he's unsatisfied with the quality of the product) and that any of those defenses will also be waived against the seller's assignee (in this case the Personal Finance Company) who has now stepped into the seller's place and stead. Such a clause is similar to the exculpatory clauses just noted since it limits the claims or defenses that one party can use against the other party.

The court's analysis of unconscionability thus is often affected by the same factors as would be its analysis of an exculpatory clause.

PERSONAL FINANCE COMPANY V. MEREDITH

Court of Appeals of Illinois
350 N.E.2d 781 (1976)

BACKGROUND: Personal Finance Company (plaintiff) sued the Merediths (defendants) to collect money owed pursuant to a sales contract. The plaintiff, Personal Finance Company, was the assignee of two retail installment sales contracts under which the defendants, Bennie and Joyce Meredith, purchased a food freezer, notions, staples, and frozen meat from Tri-State Foods Company. One contract provided for the purchase by the defendants of a food freezer at a cash price of $748.00, credit life insurance of $12.91, and a finance charge of $232.69, payable in twenty-four monthly installments of $41.40. The other contract was for "notions, staples, and frozen meat" at a cash price of $552.06, credit life insurance of $1.94, and a finance charge of $43.66, payable in six monthly installments of $99.61. The contracts were assigned to the plaintiff approximately a month after their execution.

Defendants made eight payments totaling $339.63 on the food freezer contract and payments of $493.03 on the other contract. The plaintiff brought suit in circuit court to collect the amounts owed on the contracts in the sum of $758.60, plus attorneys' fees, totaling $253.30 and $1.31 as interest accrued since maturity of the second contract. The defendants asserted that the contracts were unconscionable. The trial court awarded judgment to plaintiff for the full amount requested, and defendant appealed.

Karns, Presiding Justice

The record discloses that the defendants were induced to purchase these items by a salesman of Tri-State Foods who appeared at their home one evening while they were preparing to go bowling. They asked him to come back another night, but when he told them he was in town just that day they agreed to listen to him. The defendants testified that they agreed to purchase the food freezer and the frozen meats because the salesman made it sound "like a really good deal." They stated that at that time they did not receive a copy of the contract and the payment terms were not filled in on the contracts. Nor apparently were they furnished with a notice that they had three days to rescind the agreement as required by section 2B of the Consumer Fraud Act.

The defendants also maintained that the contract price of the food freezer ($748.00) was about $300.00 more than the price quoted them by the salesman and that they thought they were only purchasing the freezer and the meat. The salesman did not testify, as neither the assignee nor the defendants knew his whereabouts. The record discloses that when the contracts were executed defendants were both employed but at the time of the suit they were not. . . .

Defendants argue that the instant contracts are harsh and oppressive; that they did not know that a waiver of defense clause existed since the clause was inconspicuous; that they are persons of little formal education; [and] that they did not "bargain for" these clauses. . . .

An unconscionable contract was unenforceable at common law in Illinois as were individual clauses to the extent they produced an unconscionable result. An unconscionable contract has been described as a one-sided contract or one which no man in his senses and not under delusion would make and no honest and fair man would accept. Other courts have stated that where the aggrieved party reasonably did not know that a certain clause was in the contract or had no meaningful choice but to have that clause included in the contract, that the clause is unconscionable. A clause may also be unconscionable if it purports to eliminate or limit the other party's right to assert and recover for a breach of contract or for a tort arising from the transaction. . . .

We are well aware of the disparity of sophistication and bargaining power that frequently exists in the consumer retail installment sales market and the abuses of the mechanism of judicial enforcement which can result from automatic enforcement of these "agreements." Courts have refused to bind a person who has little education, does not speak or read English, or who has been the victim of deceptive sales techniques, resulting in lack of knowledge or notice of the contract terms. Proof of these objective indications of an aggrieved party's ignorance of the contract are exceptions to the general rule, well-established in Illinois, that a person who signs a contract has manifested his intention to be bound by the terms of that contract and cannot claim he was ignorant of those provisions.

Here the appellants claimed that they did not have an opportunity to read the contracts when they agreed to purchase the freezer and the meat. Nevertheless they signed the contracts and had them in their possession for several months before defaulting. Joyce Meredith testified that they received the contracts when the food and the freezer were delivered while Bennie Meredith stated that the contracts were not received until after that date. By either version, they paid on the contracts for more than four months after the contracts and the merchandise were delivered. While it was alleged that the appellants had little formal education, no proof of this allegation was offered. The record does not indicate that appellants were precluded from examining the contract before they signed. Although their decision to purchase the freezer and food was induced by the salesman's representations, their failure to examine the contract, by their own testimony, was not caused by the salesman's alleged unfair techniques but by their haste to get to their bowling game.

Defendants did not lack a meaningful choice since there is no indication in the record that the items purchased were necessities to defendants or that defendants could not have purchased these same items on credit without these clauses from other sources.

As discussed earlier, the contracts contained an admonition to the defendant-buyers, prominently placed on the face of the contracts above the space for defendants' signatures and in readable type, that unless the defendants notified the person to whom the contracts were assigned within five days of the date they received the merchandise of any claim they had against the seller, they could not assert a claim against the assignee later. Because from the face of the contracts we believe that the defendants should have been aware of the clauses they now challenge and have failed to demonstrate that when they signed the contracts and after they received the contracts they were precluded from reading and understanding their rights under the clause or that they could not discover defects in the merchandise or notify the assignee of their complaints within the five day period, we must conclude that the instant waiver of defense clauses are not unconscionable.

DECISION: While the court agreed with the trial court that the terms of the contract were not unconscionable and could be enforced, it reversed and remanded the trial court's decision on other grounds.

Contracts against Public Policy

A contract or a provision in a contract may be declared contrary to public policy if it injures the interest of the public or tends to interfere with the public's general welfare, health, safety, or morals. But what constitutes public policy? The term itself is vague and uncertain. Today's public policy may be repudiated by tomorrow's generation. In *Henningsen v. Bloomfield Motors*, the New Jersey Supreme Court held that a disclaimer of warranties in a printed form contract used by all large automobile companies was contrary to public policy. The court stated:

Public Policy is a term not easily defined. Its significance varies as the habits and needs of a people may vary. It is not static and the field of application is an ever increasing one. A contract, or a particular provision therein, valid in one era may be wholly opposed to the public policy of another. Public policy statements can be found in constitutional provisions, legislative enactments, and judicial opinions. As those policies stem from political, economic, social, and historical factors, there is really no limit as to what sources a court may use in determining public policy. An analysis of public policy–based court decisions invariably produces conflicting results from jurisdiction to jurisdiction.

For a summary of contracts frequently found to be illegal, see Table 16-3.

Effects of Illegality

The general policy of the law is to refuse to enforce an illegal agreement. Note that refusing to enforce an agreement is not the same as determining that no agreement has been made. Usually, if a contract is unenforceable, the law leaves the parties alone. It will not assist either party in enforcing the contract against the other. However, what if one party to an unenforceable agreement has done something illegal while the other party has acted legally? Shouldn't the law aid the party who acted legally? Should the law seek to have the party that acted illegally return to the other party anything he or she received?

What about an agreement that has both legal and illegal provisions? Can the legal provisions be enforced while still denying enforcement to the illegal portions of the contract? The answer to this question depends on the degree to which the terms of and consideration paid for the contract are separate and divisible. If the essence of the entire contract is illegal, probably none of its provisions can be enforced. On the other hand, if a seller and purchaser agree to sell and buy a business and the contract terms also illegally provide that the seller will not compete with the purchaser in any business in any location for a lengthy period of time, the fact that the restraint on the seller

TABLE 16-3

Concept Summary	Typical Illegal Contracts
Wagering agreements	Prohibited in most states, typically with limited exceptions for raffles, bingo, state lotteries, and other activities.
Usury provisions	Prohibit lenders from charging interest at a rate in excess of the legal limit. Most usury statutes have several exemptions, most commonly for loans made to businesses and credit card loans. Some states prohibit lender from collecting any interest on usurious loan; others prohibit lender from collecting interest *or principal* on usurious loan; a few states allow lender to collect interest up to the legal limits.
Sunday laws	Prohibit the transaction of commerce (or certain types of transactions) on Sunday.
Licensing violations	Contracts made in violation of a *revenue* statute are generally enforceable; in the case of contracts made in violation of a *regulatory* license requirement, the party lacking the required license generally may not enforce the contract.
Noncompetition clauses	Generally unenforceable; such provisions in sale of business contracts and in some employment contracts will be enforced if reasonable in duration (time) and geographic scope (space).
Exculpatory clauses	Generally unenforceable, but court examines the bargaining power of parties and degree of other regulation of affected activity.
Unconscionable agreements or clauses	Court may refuse to enforce a contract or clause if it is so one-sided and oppressive that it "shocks the conscience" of the court.
Contracts against public policy	General explanation given for court determination that some expressed or implied legal policy requires the court to refuse to enforce the contract; often seems based on political, social, or historical reasons.

is unreasonable and unenforceable probably would not make illegal and unenforceable the remaining terms for the transfer of the business.

There are also some other very limited circumstances in which the courts will provide relief to a party who has been caught in an illegal contract. If the public policy involved is designed to protect a class of persons and the party suing is of that class, then the courts may allow the contract to be enforced to the benefit of that party. Or, if the plaintiff

---

ETHICS
You Be the Judge

How would you decide in each of these cases? Why?

1. Defendant pays a judge a $20,000 bribe to find for the defendant. The judge keeps the $20,000 and decides in favor of the plaintiff. The defendant sues the judge seeking to have the $20,000 returned (as the judge didn't decide as agreed).

2. Johnson needs to borrow $10,000 to put a new furnace in his house before winter comes; he can't find anyone to lend him the money. McDonald agrees to lend Johnson $10,000 if Johnson will pay 30 percent interest and waive the effect of the state's usury law. Johnson agrees. Johnson refuses to pay any interest and in fact pays only $1,000 of the principal amount due. McDonald sues.

3. Washington contracts to deliver $100,000 worth of milk to Yoshida in Chicago. Washington delivers milk that meets all federal and state standards. Yoshida does not have a license to sell the milk in Chicago. Yoshida takes delivery of the milk but refuses to pay Washington. Washington sues Yoshida.

is not *in pari delicto* (in equal fault) with the defendant, some relief may be granted. Thus, if the plaintiff is not aware that a regulatory-type license has not been obtained by the defendant, and the plaintiff would be injured if both parties are left where they are, the courts may provide some remedy.

Nevertheless, the instances in which the courts provide relief are quite limited. More typical is the view reflected in the common law decision at the turn of the century in *Woodson*. Even though one of the partners will receive a windfall from the court's unwillingness to provide a remedy, the court emphasizes its desire to take a complete hands-off approach to enforcing illegal contracts.

WOODSON V. HOPKINS
Supreme Court of Mississippi
37 So.Rptr. 1000 (1905)

BACKGROUND: Woodson (plaintiff) and Hopkins (defendant) entered into a usurious business together. Hopkins successfully sued Woodson at the trial court level for an accounting of money allegedly due and for an injunction preventing Woodson from further participation in the business. Woodson appealed.

Whitfield, Chief Justice

We hold, without hesitation, that no such robbing contracts as this record discloses can be other than against the public policy of the state, on account of their extortionate character. "While the chief sources for determining the public policy of a nation are its constitution, laws, and judicial decisions, still, however, these are not the sole criteria, and the courts should not hesitate to declare a contract illegal merely because no statute or precedent prohibiting it can be found." . . .

"Where illegal contracts are executed by the parties, then the same principle of public policy which leads courts to refuse to act when called upon to enforce them will prevent the court from acting to relieve either party from the consequence of the illegal transactions. In such cases the defense of illegality prevails, not as a protection to the defendant, but as a disability in the plaintiff." . . . "The fact that the party seeking to enforce executory provisions of an illegal contract, though they consist only of promises to pay money, has performed the contract on his part, and that, unless the other party is compelled to perform, he will derive a benefit therefrom, will not induce the court to enforce such provisions. Nor can the party performing, on his part, the provisions of an illegal contract, recover on the ground of an implied promise on the part of the party receiving the benefits therefrom to pay therefor, as the law will imply no promise to pay for benefits received under an illegal contract by reason of the performance thereof by the other party." . . .

The courts leave violators of the law, as they ought to be left, in the condition where it finds them. They are repelled by the courts because of the great supervening principle of public policy involved, without reference to the attitude which one of the parties may occupy to the other, where both are in pari delicto. As pungently put in *Hoffman v. McMullen,* supra: "Courts are not organized to enforce the saying that 'there is honor among wrongdoers,' and the desire to punish the man that fails to observe this rule must not lead the court to a decision that such persons are entitled to the aid of courts to adjust their differences arising out of, and requiring an investigation of, their illegal transactions."

And the principle is universal that one party to an illegal contract can have no accounting from the other, where he must call in the aid, directly or indirectly, of the illegal contract to make out his case.

DECISION: The court dismissed the suit and reversed the lower court on the grounds that the courts leave parties to an illegal contract in the position in which the court finds them.

Review Questions and Problems

Key Terms

usury

Sunday laws

exculpatory clauses

unconscionability

Discussion Questions

1. Why do usury statutes exist? Would it be a good idea to enact a statute that requires that every sale be at a just price?

2. Under what circumstances will agreements in restraint of trade be enforced?

3. In what situations is an exculpatory clause most likely to be enforced?

4. Under the UCC, who decides what may be done with an unconscionable contract?

Review Problems

1. The telephone company in the region of Atlantis charges all customers a one-time hookup charge of $25 for the connection of telephone service. This charge is in addition to all itemized expenses, which are also passed on to the customer, and is labeled a "service fee." It appears on the form contracts supplied by the phone company to all customers, and phone connection is not possible without the payment of such fee. Does the service fee render the contract unconscionable?

2. Edward parked his car in a garage where the keys are left with the car. The garage had large signs at all exits stating that the garage was not liable for any damage to cars left on the premises. Edward's car disappeared. The car was worth $20,000 and had $30,000 worth of jewelry in the trunk. Edward sues the garage claiming $50,000. What is the best result?

3. Tovar, a physician practicing in the state of Kansas, wrote the Paxton Hospital in Illinois to inquire about obtaining a position as a full-time resident. In his letter and in a subsequent personal interview, Tovar fully described the nature and extent of his education, training, and licensing as a physician. The hospital assured him that his professional credentials were satisfactory and hired him. Soon thereafter Tovar, who had relocated to Illinois, was discharged by Paxton Hospital for failure to hold a license to practice medicine in Illinois as required by a state statute. Tovar claimed illegal breach of employment by the hospital. Result?

4. Weaver, a high school dropout, signed a service station lease with American Oil Company containing a clause in fine print that released the oil company from liability for its negligence and compelled him, as lessee, to indemnify American for any damage or loss thus incurred. Weaver never read the lease, nor was it ever explained to him. During the course of business, a visiting American Oil employee negligently sprayed gasoline over Weaver and his assistant, causing them to be burned and injured on the leased premises. American disclaimed liability on the basis of the contract clause. Is this correct?

Case Problems

1. Mayfair Fabrics leased commercial premises from Natell upon the condition that Mayfair absolve Natell of all liability for loss or damage to Mayfair's property by fire, explosion, or otherwise. Natell subsequently was negligent in causing a fire that resulted in considerable damage to Mayfair's operations. Mayfair seeks to recover damages on the basis of the landlord's negligence, but Natell urges he is protected under the lease from any liability. Which way would you rule?

2. Hiyanne worked as a contact lens grinder and fitter for the House of Vision from 1959 until 1964 in branch stores, several in different cities. His employment contract said that upon the termination of his relationship with the employer, he would never engage in the same or similar business anywhere within a 30-mile radius of any of the branch stores in which he had rendered services. Hiyanne resigned his position in 1964 and began working for a competitor just 150 feet from one of those House of Vision stores. The House of Vision seeks to enforce the restrictive covenant in the original employment contract. What result?

3. Boardwalk Regency Corporation planned to sponsor a backgammon tournament in which players would post a fee and prizes would be paid out of these fees and an additional amount contributed by the sponsor. The tournament was to be held at the Boardwalk Regency Casino and Hotel in Atlantic City. The New Jersey Constitution states that, "No gambling of any kind shall be authorized by the Legislature unless approved by a majority of state voters." Boardwalk argues that backgammon is not a "game of chance" as defined in the state's gambling laws because skill and strategy is so important in determining the outcome of the game. The Attorney General argues that because the roll of dice plays such a material role in the game, the backgammon tournament would be gambling, in violation of the state's constitution unless it is first approved by vote of the people. Who is correct?

4. Sweazea, a building owner, contracted with Measday for water and gas plumbing work. A local statute requires that a permit be applied for before plumbing work is begun—the intent of the regulation being that work done for which a permit is required is to be inspected for compliance with professional standards. Measday failed to apply for

a permit until he had substantially completed the job. Now Sweazea has refused to finish paying him and Measday claims a breach of their contract. Sweazea says the contract cannot be enforced because it is illegal due to the statutory violation. Does the violation make the contract illegal?

5. Siders was employed as a salesman for Knoebel Mercantile Company in the candy and tobacco distributing business. Siders's assigned territory was Colorado Springs, Colorado, a small territory with about 150 customers. According to an employment contract signed by Siders, Siders would be prohibited for 2 years after termination from working for any of Knoebel's competitors in any state in which Knoebel was transacting business—namely Colorado, Wyoming, Montana, New Mexico, Nebraska, Kansas, and South Dakota. After 2 years on the job, Siders went to work for John Sexton & Co. Although Sexton was in competition with Knoebel, there was a considerable difference in their scope of operations: Knoebel dealt in 10,000 items, all manufactured by others, and Sexton dealt in only 1,600 items, many of which it manufactured. Knoebel sued Siders to enforce the restrictive covenant. What result?

6. Henrioulle was injured when he tripped on a rock in the stairway of his apartment complex. He sued his landlord for his injuries. The landlord's defense was based on an exculpatory clause in the lease that relieved the landlord from liability for injuries sustained on the premises "or in the common areas thereof" (including the stairway). What result?

7. Schroeder parked his car in a lot owned by Allright, Inc. and left his keys with the attendant. Schroeder was given a claim ticket which stated, in large print, that the lot closed at 6:00 P.M. The ticket also included, in smaller print, a clause limiting Allright's liability in the event that the car was damaged or stolen. Signs in the lot directed customers returning after 6:00 P.M. to pick up their keys at another lot operated by Allright. Schroeder came back for his car around midnight and found that it was gone. The car was recovered several days later, but it had been damaged. The keys were found in the trunk. Schroeder sued Allright for damages to his car. Allright's defense was based on the limitation-of-liability clause printed on the ticket. Schroeder claims that he never read the clause and that the clause was never pointed out to him by the attendant. What result?

17

Legal Form

Statute of Frauds

Contracts within the Statute of Frauds

Equitable Estoppel and Promissory Estoppel

The Parol Evidence Rule

Interpretation of Contractual Provisions

Many people assume that contracts must be written to be enforceable. In fact, most oral contracts are valid; only a few types of contracts must be written. This chapter first identifies the contracts that must be written to be enforced. The legal principles governing the interpretation of contracts, whether in oral or written form, are then examined.

Statute of Frauds

Contracts Required to Be in Writing

The law requiring certain contracts to be in writing is derived from an English statute. In 1677, the English Parliament enacted a law, the Statute for the Prevention of Frauds and Perjuries, known today as the **statute of frauds**. The law sought to prevent fraud concerning the existence of contracts by requiring that certain contracts be written and signed before they could be enforced. Today, all of the states in the United States have enacted similar statutes requiring that certain contracts be in writing to be enforceable. These contracts, discussed in detail later, include:

1. Contracts in consideration of marriage (prenuptial agreements)
2. Personal representative's promise to pay for the debts of the deceased
3. Promises to pay for the debt of another
4. Sale of land or an interest in land
5. Promises not performable in one year
6. Sale of goods for $500 or more

Internationally, the convention on Contracts for the International Sale of Goods has been adopted by most of the world's major trading nations. Under the CISG, contracts for the sale of goods do not have to be in writing. No written requirement is imposed by the law of most of the civil law countries. Thus, whether common law, civil law, or the CISG applies, most contracts for the sale of goods do not have to be in writing. Of course, prudent business practice usually dictates that most contractual commitments be evidenced by signed written agreements.

Some U.S. states require that certain other contracts—for example, real estate brokerage agreements—be written to be enforceable. Although the statutes were designed for the broad purpose of preventing fraud and perjury, they serve three more specific purposes.

First, the presence of a written contract reduces the chance that a court and jury will be misled about the existence or terms of the contract. Second, people are more likely to think about what they are committing themselves to do if they are required to sign something. They are less likely to act rashly. Finally, requiring a written agreement serves as a channeling device, distinguishing between those contracts that are enforceable and those that are not.

What Constitutes a Writing?

If a contract must be in writing, it is said to be *within the statute.* If it does not have to be in writing, it is *without the statute.* Oral contracts that are required to be in writing are considered unenforceable in most states, although the party seeking to avoid such a contract must raise the statute-of-frauds defense or else be legally bound by the contract.

What must a written contract include? To be enforced, such a contract must be evidenced by a document describing the basic agreement signed by the person being sued on the contract. In general, the document must identify the parties, the subject matter of the contract, and the performance obligations of the parties.

Problems with the Rule

The rule that certain contracts must be written has on occasion worked to the disadvantage of consumers. The experience of a former student provides a ready example. The student signed a contract for the purchase of a motorcycle for $1,200. The merchant then contacted the student and told him that the dealership could not sell the cycle for less than $1,350. The student produced the contract form. It had never been signed by the merchant. The student could not sue to enforce the agreement.

In similar situations, a contract may be signed by a salesperson who does not have the appropriate authority to sign for the merchant. Thus, even when there is a written contract, there are several hurdles that must be overcome before it is enforceable. A consumer who reviews a written agreement may believe that he or she has made a valid deal; however, if there is a statute-of-frauds

problem, the unwary consumer may have no legal recourse.

The example of the student and the motorcycle also demonstrates a second problem with the statute. The student could not sue the merchant. But could the merchant sue the student? The surprising answer is yes—because the student had signed the contract. Because of this problem of one-way enforceability, the statute has been partially modified by section 2-201(2) of the UCC in regard to agreements between merchants. Even greater strides have been made with the recent development of consumer protection laws at both state and federal levels. These laws will be discussed later in this chapter.

A final problem arises from the technical application of the rule. The purpose of the statute is to ensure that there is in fact an underlying contract between the parties. Yet some courts have refused to enforce oral agreements that fall within the scope of the statute and that everyone concedes were made. Modern courts have responded to this unfortunate tendency by emphasizing the rule's exceptions. When it comes to applying the statute, it is important to recognize that the exceptions are as important as the rule.

Contracts within the Statute of Frauds

Contracts in Consideration of Marriage

Contracts in consideration of marriage involve property settlements in exchange for a promise to marry. Such prenuptial agreements are commonly used when two well-to-do people, both with children of their own, decide to marry late in life. Mutual promises to marry do not have to be written.

Personal Representative's Promise to Pay for the Debts of the Deceased

When a person dies, it is normal for some bills to be left unpaid. Certainly, the creditors of the deceased will seek to be paid from the deceased's assets before they are distributed to heirs. To wind up the estate of a decedent, the personal representative (sometimes referred to as the executor) of the estate must pay the outstanding bills. Generally, the representative pays them from the assets of the decedent. If the decedent did not leave sufficient assets, some creditors may go unpaid. The personal representative need not pay the creditors from his or her own assets.

In some situations, such as when the personal representative is a close relative of the decedent, the personal representative may promise to personally pay the decedent's creditors. Perhaps the relative does not want heirloom property to be seized by the creditors to pay their bills. As the relative who serves as a personal representative is often in a vulnerable emotional state, the law requires that his or her promise to personally be responsible for the decedent's debt must be in writing to be enforceable.

Promises to Pay for the Debt of Another

The promise by the personal representative to pay for the debts of the decedent is one example of one person's promise to pay for another person's debts. Other examples may involve a parent promising a merchant to pay for an adult child's debts or an adult child promising to pay the medical expenses of his or her parent. Similarly, a president of a small corporation may be asked by a bank to pay for the debts of the corporation. In such cases, it is important to determine if the promisor is agreeing to be primarily or secondarily liable for the other person's debts.

Primary and Secondary Liability The basic way to determine whether a person's promise to pay another's debt must be written is to ask whether the person making the promise is primarily or secondarily liable. **Primary liability** exist when the creditor can proceed directly against the person making the promise. **Secondary liability** exists when the creditor must look first to the original debtor before proceeding against the promisor. Promises involving secondary liability are within the statute and must be in writing to be enforced.

For example, Charles is the owner of a local hardware store. Martin, a recent college graduate, has gone into business for himself as a building contractor. Martin comes into Charles's store seeking building supplies because he has just landed his first building contract. Charles, however, is unwilling to let Martin have the goods on credit, essentially because Martin hasn't had time to establish a credit rating. Martin was prepared for this and had his father, James, a well-known local businessman, call Charles and guarantee Martin's creditworthiness. James promises that if Martin defaults, James will cover Charles's losses. James's promise is covered by the statute of frauds. James has not made an absolute promise to pay Martin's debts; rather, he has made a *conditional* promise to pay only if Martin defaults. Charles must *first* look to Martin, not to James, for payment. James is secondarily liable. His promise must be in writing.

However, assume that Martin has won the building contract from James, his father. This time, when James calls Charles, he tell Charles to give Martin all the supplies he needs and to send the bill to him, James. In this case, the father is primarily liable. His oral promise is enforceable and Charles can look directly to the father for payment.

Main-Purpose Doctrine In addition to the primary-secondary liability distinction, the courts also limit the application of the statute with the **main-purpose doctrine.** Under this doctrine, an oral promise creating secondary liability is nonetheless enforceable if it is made mainly to benefit the person making the promise. Assume, for example, that a franchisor of a tool rental business learns that one of her franchisees in a key location is about to be evicted for not paying rent on time. Franchisor calls the landlord and says, "I'll pay the rent if Franchisee doesn't pay you what he owes you. Don't evict him right now." That oral promise would be enforceable, because Franchisor's main purpose in making the promise is for her own benefit. The franchise system depends for its success upon a strong distribution system, and the franchisor usually receives direct periodic payments from each operating franchisee. Thus, Franchisor has a personal motive for promising to keep the franchised outlets operating effectively.

Sale of Land or an Interest in Land

For our purposes, land is considered earth and the things permanently attached to it. The most common real estate transactions, such as the sale of residential or commercial property, clearly fall under this rule and must be written. But what constitutes an *interest* in land?

Assume that I promise to sell to you the right to cross my property for a particular purpose. This is known as an *easement*, and it constitutes an interest in land. Thus my promise, if only oral, is not enforceable. An option to buy is considered an interest in land, as is a lien or security interest given against the land. In many states, leases are within the statute, although some states require that only leases for an extended term (for example, more than 1 year) must be in writing.

A generally recognized exception to the provision about real estate is the **doctrine of part performance.** This doctrine is used in circumstances where one party promises to sell land in return for certain actions by the buyer. For example, Owner of real property may promise to sell part of it to Tenant if Tenant improves the entire property and works it for Owner. After Tenant does the work, Owner refuses to sell and raises the statute of frauds as a defense. If the parties have acted as though they had entered into a contract for the sale of certain land and if failing to recognize an oral agreement would defraud Tenant, the courts enforce the oral agreement. The part performance must be substantial and in reliance on the oral promise to sell. The following case shows the application of the part-performance doctrine.

MARTIN V. SCHOLL

Supreme Court of Utah

678 P. 2d 274 (1983)

BACKGROUND: Rodney Martin (plaintiff) began work as a ranch laborer for George Chaffin in 1936. He became foreman of the farm and ranch properties in 1947 and continued in that capacity until after Chaffin's death almost 30 years later. In 1947, Chaffin orally agreed to convey to Martin 120 acres of land referred to as the "home place" if Martin would continue to work as his foreman. Martin remained as foreman, receiving a salary and occasional raises. He labored long and unusual hours and with his wife rendered personal services to Chaffin in reliance on the agreement. In 1968, as part of his estate plan, Chaffin formed the George Chaffin Investment Company (Company) and conveyed all of his real estate, including the 120-acre ranch, to it. Martin had no notice of the conveyance. When Chaffin died some 7 years later, Martin first learned that the ranch had been transferred to the Company. He sued the Company and Scholl, the representative of Chaffin's estate, seeking specific performance of the agreement he had made. The trial court agreed with Martin and ordered the contract specifically performed. The Company and Chaffin's estate appealed to the Supreme Court of Utah.

Howe, Justice

Ordinarily a verbal gift of land or an oral agreement to convey land is within the statute of frauds. However, the doctrine of part performance allows a court of equity to enforce an oral agreement, if it has been partially performed, notwithstanding the statute:

> Part performance to be sufficient to take a case out of the statute must consist of clear, definite, and unequivocal acts of the party relying thereon, strictly referable to the contract, and of such character that it is impossible or impracticable to place the parties in status quo, mere nonaction being insufficient.

. . . In the case at bar the court found evidence to support a contract between Martin and Chaffin which was based upon the testimony of Martin's witnesses. The court also found that Martin relied upon the oral agreement. The court concluded that Martin would not have continued to work for and provided personal services to Chaffin except for the agreement between them.

[R]eviewing the court's application of our law to those findings, we can only conclude that the court erred in its holding that there was sufficient part performance. The trial court drew one conclusion from Martin's services, but that is legally insufficient since they admit of another equally valid and consonant conclusion against his claim of contract.

The fact that Martin worked for Chaffin as his foreman is not an exclusively referable act of reliance on the alleged oral agreement since it was consonant with Martin's employment. Martin's long hours, not atypical of a ranch foreman's life, were remunerated by salary. Martin's wife's driving Chaffin to various locations on occasion and asking him to stay for dinner when he was at the Martin house during mealtime were not inconsistent with good relations between an employer and an employee and his family. . . .

Martin's claim that he declined other and better offers of employment elsewhere to remain with Chaffin is also unavailing to prove reliance since, as we quoted earlier, mere nonaction is insufficient to constitute part performance.

We have no quarrel with the argument in the dissenting opinion that the statute of frauds should not be used to perpetrate a fraud upon an innocent and unsuspecting person such as an employee who renders services in good faith upon a promised expectation. Such a rule would be easy to apply if there were some magical way of determining in each case whether a contract was in fact made. There being no sure-proof method of determining whether a contract was made, the Legislature has made it the policy in this state that oral contracts for the conveyance of land will not be enforced except where there is sufficient part performance to provide a high evidentiary basis for their existence. This policy which the Legislature has translated into the statute of frauds may well result, in some cases, in the denial of a benefit to a well-deserving employee or servant. We are helpless to prevent that result where the evidence of part performance of the claimed contract falls below the high evidentiary standard required by courts of equity—regardless of the precise words which they may use in describing that standard. As unfortunate as it would be to deprive a man who had worked his life in reliance upon the expectation of receiving property, it would be equally serious to take property from an owner after his death (when he cannot be heard) on the strength of a questionable oral agreement supposedly made many years prior. If the statute of frauds is to be given any force, we cannot affirm the trial court.

DECISION: The Supreme Court of Utah ruled in favor of Scholl and the Chaffin Investment Company and reversed the trial court decision.

Stewart, Justice (dissenting)

By its rigid application of the "exclusively referable test," the majority raises the standard of proof in cases such as the instant case to a level that is unnecessarily high. In cases where the existence of the contract has already been proved by independent evidence, as in the instant case, the exclusively referable test in effect requires that the plaintiff "reprove" the existence of the contract by part performance. Concededly, where there is *no* other evidence of the contract, the "exclusively referable" test is an appropriate test. However, in this case there is other evidence of the contract. . . .

What is critical, and is clear in the record, is that the plaintiff devoted his whole life to maintaining the deceased's farm as if it were the plaintiff's own farm. The trial court's finding that the plaintiff would not have spent "his lifetime but for" the existence of the contract should be dispositive.

I respectfully submit that the doctrine of part performance in this case has been construed so narrowly that it has failed to achieve its intended purpose of avoiding application of the statute of frauds with such rigor as to produce the very kind of fraud that the statute was intended to prevent.

Promises Not Performable in One Year

If a contract cannot be performed within a year, it must be put in writing. For example, a 3-year contract for the services of a professional athlete must be written.

Assume, however, that no date is set in a contract. Instead, the arrangement is to continue until some event occurs or until one of the parties cancels the agreement. Such contracts do not have to be written if the event could possibly occur within one year or if there is no limitation on the right to cancel during the first year. For example, an agreement to provide service to a person until death usually need not be written because death could occur within one year.

One problem arises with contracts involving construction projects. Determining whether these contracts must be written becomes a question of fact. Is there any possibility that if everything goes perfectly (no strikes, good weather), the job can be completed within a year? If so, the contract need not be written.

The case that follows provides a good discussion of the 1-year rule.

SHERWIN V. AULT

Appellate Court of Illinois
579 N.E. 2d 425 (1991)

BACKGROUND: Plaintiffs Sherwin and Murphy owned farmland. During the 1987 crop year, defendant Ault farmed their land pursuant to a written agreement. The agreement provided that the term of the agreement expired on December 31, 1987. On October 13, 1987, Ault asked Sherwin if they could renew their agreement for the 1988 crop year. Sherwin said "Okay," and that she would forward the paperwork later. According to Ault, Sherwin indicated that the new agreement would be identical to the 1987 agreement (except, of course, for the dates). In March 1988, although Sherwin still had not forwarded a new agreement to Ault, Ault attempted to enter the land with his tractors. Sherwin and Murphy brought an action to enjoin Ault from entering their land. The trial court ruled for Sherwin and Murphy, finding that the October 13 agreement was within the statute of frauds. Ault appealed.

Barry, Justice

Defendant initially challenges the trial court's determination that the Statute of Frauds applies on these facts. Defendant argues under *Martin v. Federal Life Insurance Company,* that the Statute of Frauds applies to oral contracts which are not to be performed within the space of one year from the making thereof. Defendant, citing *Martin,* states that the test is whether it appears from a reasonable interpretation of the terms of the agreement that it is capable of performance within a year, not whether such occurrence is likely. Defendant requests the court take judicial notice of the fact that many farmers in central Illinois and particularly in Warren County have the vast majority of their crops harvested by October 13th of each year. Plaintiff, in response, argues that it is clear by a review of the 1987 written contract that the "Term" of the operating agreement ended on December 31 of the crop year. Plaintiff further states that the section "Storage facilities" of the agreement provides for the defendant to use one-half of plaintiff's storage facilities until September 15 of the year following the crop year. Since both December 31, 1988 and September 1989 were more than a year after October 13, 1987, the plaintiff's argument is that any agreement entered into on October 13, 1987, which incorporates by reference the terms of the prior year's agreement, must have been in writing. . . .

The test for determining whether the statute bars a particular agreement is "whether the contract by its terms is capable of full performance within a year, not whether such occurrence is likely." (*Martin v. Federal Life Ins. Co.*) The one-year period is measured from the time of the making of the agreement. Thus, in an employment contract where the parties orally agreed on May 31, 1960 to plaintiff's employment for a one-year period beginning June 6, 1960, the contract was held unenforceable by virtue of the Statute of Frauds. *Sinclair v. Sullivan Chevrolet Co.*

In the case before us, although the February, 1987 written agreement expressly states that it was not intended as a lease of land, it has characteristics of both a farm lease and an employment agreement. . . .

The written agreement extends by its terms from March 1 to December 31, 1987. An oral renewal of the agreement, to be enforceable as a contract by its terms capable of full performance within a year, would have to have been made after December 31, 1987. Any agreement for the March through December, 1988 crop year which was made prior to December 31, 1987 would have to have been in some written form to avoid the bar of the Statute of Frauds. . . .

We do not subscribe to defendant's position that the Statute of Frauds does not control since it was *possible* that the oral contractual agreement could have been fully performed by completing the crop harvest for the 1988 season before October 13, 1988. . . .

Defendant cites *Stein v. Malden Mills* in support of his argument that it was not impossible to complete the agreement within a year. In *Stein,* unlike here, the parties' agreement did not contain a specific date for the completion of performance. Rather, a contingency event was the only provision marking the end date. The parties agreed to plaintiff's employment "as long as the customer reordered the same style number of fabric." On review, the court noted that that event might never materialize or could happen at any time before the expiration of a year. Consequently, because it was possible pursuant to the terms of the agreement that performance could be fully completed within a year, the Statute of Frauds was no bar to its enforcement.

In this case, we need not speculate about the likelihood or possibility of completing harvest, storing grain or marketing it within any particular time period because the contract contained a specific date by which it would be considered fully performed.

DECISION: The appellate court affirmed the trial court decision in favor of the plaintiff landowners because the October oral agreement was within the statute of frauds.

Sale of Goods for $500 or More

The UCC statute of frauds (Section 2-201) states:

1. Except as otherwise provided in this section a contract for the sale of goods for the price of $500 or more is not enforceable by way of action or defense unless there is some writing sufficient to indicate that a contract for sale has been made between the parties and signed by the party against whom enforcement is sought or by his authorized agent or broker. A writing is not insufficient because it omits or incorrectly states a term agreed upon but the contract is not enforceable under this paragraph beyond the quantity of goods shown in such writing.

2. Between merchants if within a reasonable time a writing in confirmation of the contract and sufficient against the sender is received and the party receiving it has reason to know its contents, it satisfies the requirements of Subsection 1 against such party unless written notice of objection to its contents is given within ten days after it is received.

3. A contract which does not satisfy the requirements of Subsection 1 but which is valid in other respects is enforceable

   a. if the goods are to be specially manufactured for the buyer and are not suitable for sale to others in the ordinary course of the seller's business and the seller, before notice of repudiation is received and under circumstances which reasonably indicate that the goods are for the buyer, has made either a substantial beginning of their manufacture or commitments for their procurement; or

b. if the party against whom enforcement is sought admits in his pleading, testimony or otherwise in court that a contract for sale was made, but the contract is not enforceable under the provision beyond the quantity of goods admitted; or

c. with respect to goods for which payment has been made and accepted or which have been received and accepted.

Subsection 1 establishes the general rule that a contract for the sale of goods for $500 or more must be evidenced by "some writing" to be enforceable. The writing must be signed by the party against whom enforcement is sought. The writing requirement may be satisfied by more than one document. One case has held that a signed memo *without* terms referring to an unsigned document with terms established an enforceable contract.

The rest of the section limits the general rule. Subsection 2 modifies the one-way enforceability result in the case of merchants. Assume that Jones and Smith, both merchants, orally agree to a contract. The next day Jones sends a signed letter to Smith detailing the terms of the agreement. Smith does not respond for 10 days. The contract is enforceable against Smith on the basis of Jones's letter even though Smith has never signed anything.

The three exceptions established in Subsection 3 have a common element: in the situations defined, there is persuasive evidence that a contract has in fact been made. Under (b) there is an outright admission by the defendant that a contract exists. It would be contrary to the basic purpose of the statute to allow a defense in such a circumstance. Under (c), one can assume that a buyer will not accept goods unless a contract is intended. Note that the contract is enforceable only in regard to the quantity of goods that has been accepted. Similarly, a seller will not accept payment unless a contract is intended. A down payment may satisfy the exception in Subsection 3, paragraph c. This is simply a version of the part-performance exception to the statute of frauds, which, until the UCC, applied only to contracts involving an interest in land. The specially manufactured goods in (a) must be shown to have a reasonable connection with the buyer. Again there is external evidence that a contract has been made.

The case that follows involves the application of the UCC statute of frauds.

SOUTHWEST ENGINEERING COMPANY V. MARTIN TRACTOR COMPANY

Supreme Court of Kansas
473 P.2d 18 (1970)

BACKGROUND: Southwest Engineering Company (plaintiff) was preparing to submit a bid to the U.S. Army Corps of Engineers for construction of runway lighting facilities. On April 28, 1966, Southwest's construction superintendent, R. E. Cloepfil, met with Ken Hurt, manager of Martin Tractor Company's (defendant) engine department, in the town of Springfield to negotiate the price of a standby generator and accessory equipment to be used for the project. At this meeting, the agent for Martin Tractor noted each required item and its price on a memorandum but hand-printed his name and that of his company in the upper left-hand corner. On May 24, 1966, Martin Tractor wrote to Southwest refusing to supply the generator and equipment. Southwest repeatedly tried to convince Martin Tractor to supply the equipment, until September 6, 1966, when it got the required items from another supplier at a cost of $6,041 more than the figures listed by Martin Tractor on the memorandum. Southwest sued Martin Tractor for breach of contract. The trial court entered judgment for Southwest in the amount of $6,041. Martin appealed to the Supreme Court of Kansas.

Fontron, Justice

The basic disagreement centers on whether the meeting between Hurt and Cloepfil at Springfield resulted in an agreement which was enforceable under the provisions of the Uniform Commercial Code (sometimes referred to as the Code), which was enacted by the Kansas Legislature at its 1965 session. . . .

Southwest takes the position that the memorandum prepared by Hurt at Springfield supplies the essential elements of a contract required by the foregoing statute, *i.e.*, that it is (1) a writing signed by the party sought to be charged, (2) that it is for the sale of goods and (3) that quantity is shown. In addition, the reader will have noted that the memorandum sets forth the prices of the several items listed. . . .

[D]efendant . . . maintains . . . that the writing in question does not measure up to the stature of a signed memorandum within the purview of the Code; that the instrument simply sets forth verbal quotations for future consideration in continuing negotiations.

But on this point the trial court found there *was* an agreement reached between Hurt and Cloepfil at Springfield; that the formal requirements of K.S.A. 84-2-201 *were* satisfied; and that the memorandum prepared by Hurt contains the three essentials of the statute in that it evidences a sale of goods, was authenticated by Hurt and specifies quantity. . . .

We believe the record supports all the above findings. With particular reference to the preparation and sufficiency of the written memorandum, the following evidence is pertinent:

Mr. Cloepfil testified that he and Hurt sat down at a restaurant table and spread out the plans which Hurt had brought with him; that they went through the specifications item by item and Hurt wrote each item down, together with the price thereof; that while the specifications called for a D353 generator, Hurt thought the D343 model might be an acceptable substitute, so he gave prices on both of them and Southwest could take either one of the two which the Corps of Engineers would approve; that Hurt gave him (Cloepfil) the memorandum "as a record of what he had done, the agreement we had arrived at at our meeting in the restaurant at the airport."

We digress at this point to note Martin's contention that the memorandum is not signed within the meaning of 84-2-201. The sole authentication appears in handprinted form at the top left-hand corner in these words: "Ken Hurt, Martin Tractor, Topeka, Caterpillar." The court found this sufficient, and we believe correctly so. K.S.A. 84-1-201(39) provides as follows:

Signed includes any symbol executed or adopted by a party with present intention to authenticate a writing. . . .

It is quite true, as the trial court found, that terms of payment were not agreed upon at the Springfield meeting. Hurt testified that as the memorandum was being made out, he said they wanted 10 percent with the order, 50 percent on delivery and the balance on acceptance, but he did not recall Cloepfil's response. Cloepfil's version was somewhat different. He stated that after the two had shaken hands in the lobby preparing to leave, Hurt said their terms usually were 20 percent down and the balance on delivery; while he (Cloepfil) said the way they generally paid was 90 percent on the tenth of the month following delivery and the balance on final acceptance. It is obvious the parties reached no agreement on this point.

However, a failure on the part of Messrs. Hurt and Cloepfil to agree on terms of payment would not, of itself, defeat an otherwise valid agreement reached by them. K.S.A. 84-2-204(3) reads:

Even though one or more terms are left open a contract for sale does not fail for indefiniteness if the parties have intended to make a contract and there is a reasonably certain basis for giving an appropriate remedy. . . .

In our view, the language of the two Code provisions is clear and positive. Considered together, we take the two sections to mean that where parties have reached an enforceable agreement for the sale of goods, but omit therefrom the terms of payment, the law will imply, as part of the agreement, that payment is to be made at time of delivery. In this respect the law does not greatly differ from the rule this court laid down years ago. . . .

We do not mean to infer that terms of payment are not of importance under many circumstances, or that parties may not condition an agreement on their being included. However, the facts before us hardly indicate that Hurt and Cloepfil considered the terms of payments to be significant, or of more than passing interest. Hurt testified that while he stated his terms he did not recall Cloepfil's response, while Cloepfil stated that as the two were on the point of leaving, each stated their usual terms and that was as far as it went. The trial court found that only a brief and casual conversation ensued as to payment, and we think that is a valid summation of what took place.

DECISION: The Supreme Court of Kansas affirmed the trial court judgment in favor of Southwest.

Equitable Estoppel and Promissory Estoppel

As we have noted, courts have become increasingly sensitive to the use of the statute of frauds to perpetrate fraud. They have tried to minimize fraud by using the doctrines of equitable estoppel and promissory estoppel.

Equitable estoppel, a doctrine as old as the statute itself, is used in situations where applying the statute would result in a substantial injustice. The part-performance exception to the statute discussed earlier in this chapter is basically an application of the doctrine of equitable estoppel.

Promissory estoppel is a more specific application of the principles of equitable estoppel. As indicated in Chapter 13, *promissory estoppel* has been used primarily to make exceptions to the rule that all contracts be supported by consideration.

If the person making the promise should have known that the promise would induce the person being promised something to rely on the promise to his or her detriment, the doctrine of promissory estoppel may require the promisor to comply with the contract even if the contract does not satisfy the statute of frauds.

For example, consider how promissory estoppel might apply to a contract governed by the statute of frauds in the following case. Assume that Rogers is a police captain who will be eligible for retirement in 2 years. The retirement package includes a pension of full salary, paid medical insurance, life insurance, and other benefits. In ad-

dition, the city's contract with the police union provides that no one, union member or not, may be discharged except for cause. Sullivan, chair of the board of a large corporation, induces Rogers to quit his job as a police officer in exchange for an extremely lucrative 10-year employment contract with Sullivan's company. Sullivan further promises to put the contract in writing when she returns from Europe. Unfortunately, Sullivan is killed while traveling, and the other board members are reluctant to honor Sullivan's promise of employment to Rogers.

Under traditional statute-of-frauds principles, the contract would be unenforceable. Because it is an offer of employment for 10 years, the contract falls within the requirement that it be put in writing. Rogers, having already quit his job as a police captain, would be without a remedy and without a job. Fortunately for Rogers, most courts today do not tolerate such an inequitable result. It is apparent that Sullivan knew and intended that her promise of employment would induce Rogers to quit his current job in reliance on the promise. Because he has been induced to quit his prior job, and because injustice cannot otherwise be avoided, Sullivan's fellow board members are bound by the contract. They are, in essence, "estopped" from asserting the statute of frauds as a defense.

The result would have been different had the policeman not yet quit his job at the time of Sullivan's death and the refusal of the other board members to honor the contract. All jurisdictions have required that the promisee be in danger of suffering "unconscionable injury" if the contract is not enforced. When people have relied to their detriment on other people's promises, and when enforcing a contract is the only way to prevent either substantial injury or injustice, the contract is to be enforced.

When deciding whether to use promissory estoppel as a means for avoiding the statute of frauds, it is important to consider the aspect of damages. In an action for breach of contract, a plaintiff can generally recover compensatory damages to the extent that they can be proven. However, this is not true when recovery is based upon promissory estoppel. The courts have held uniformly that when promissory estoppel is used as a means of avoiding the statute of frauds, only restitutional damages (i.e., out-of-pocket expenses) can be recovered. In these cases, the plaintiff generally is not entitled to the benefit of the bargain; instead, he or she will only be restored to the position he or she was in before acting in reliance on the defendant's promise.

In the following case, the court considers whether the doctrine of promissory estoppel ap-

---

PREVENTIVE LAW
Complying with the Statute of Frauds

"Get it in writing!" These four words are well worth remembering when it comes to making contracts. Most of the problems discussed in this chapter can be avoided by observing this simple rule. Even if you are sure that a contract is not within the statute of frauds, a written agreement, signed by the party you are contracting with, containing the essential terms will always be excellent evidence of your contract.

---

plies to take an oral promise outside the statute of frauds. Excerpts of the case appeared in Chapter 13 with regard to the application of the doctrine of promissory estoppel in connection with promises that are not supported by consideration. The following is the remainder of the court's opinion.

ALLEN M. CAMPBELL CO. V. VIRGINIA METAL INDUSTRIES, INC.

U.S. Court of Appeals, Fourth Circuit
708 F.2d 930 (1983)

BACKGROUND: Allen M. Campbell Co. (plaintiff), in August 1981, intended to bid on a Department of Navy contract to construct housing for enlisted personnel at Camp LeJeune, North Carolina. The deadline for submission of bids was 2:00 P.M. on August 11, 1981. At about 1:30 P.M., Virginia Metal Industries, Inc. (defendant), telephoned Campbell and quoted a price to supply all hollow metal doors and frames that were required by the plans and specifications. The price promised was $193,121, plus applicable taxes. Campbell based the computation for its bid for the Navy project upon the quoted price for the hollow metal doors and frames of $193,121 and taxes. Campbell was the successful bidder and was awarded the Navy contract. Virginia Metal backed out of its promise, and as a consequence, Campbell had to obtain the items covered by the quoted price of $193,121 from another supplier, at a cost $45,562 greater than what it had been led to expect Virginia Metal would charge. Campbell sued Virginia Metal Industries, Inc. for the $45,562. The trial court dismissed Campbell's complaint, and Campbell appealed.

Murnaghan, Circuit Judge

[W]e must next deal with the contention of Virginia Metal that it cannot be held liable since its promise was not in writing. The Uniform Commercial Code has been adopted in North Carolina and N.C.Gen.Stat.Sec. 25-2-201 requires that a contract for the sale of goods involving more than $500 must be in writing. The answer, however, lies in the language of N.C.Gen.Stat.Sec. 25-1-103:

> Unless displaced by the particular provisions of this chapter, the principles of law and equity, including . . . the law relevant to . . . estoppel . . . or other validating or invalidating cause shall supplement its provisions.

The question then becomes whether North Carolina's doctrine of promissory estoppel creates an exception to or is displaced by the statute of frauds. There is a split of authority in decisions from states other than North Carolina on the question of whether promissory estoppel is to be deemed an exception to the statute of frauds. . . . North Carolina . . . has expressed approval of the position taken in Restatement (Second) of Contracts, Section 139, the cornerstone of the rationale adopted by the courts which have held that promissory estoppel will, in circumstances like those here presented, render inapplicable the U.C.C. statute of frauds. Thus in the *Wachovia* case the court observed that:

> Furthermore, "[a] promise which the promisor should reasonably expect to induce action or forbearance on the part of the promisee . . . and which does induce the action or forbearance is enforceable notwithstanding the Statute of Frauds if injustice can be avoided only by enforcement of the promise. The remedy granted for breach is to be limited as justice requires." Restatement (Second) of Contracts, Section 139 (1981). This view is consistent with that found in cases in which this Court has recognized exceptions to the Statute of Frauds.

In light of the status of what we perceive to be the law that North Carolina courts would apply to the facts of this case, the fact that the promise was entirely oral would not bar recovery. Consequently, the grant to Virginia Metal of judgment on the pleadings for failure to state a claim upon which relief can be granted was erroneous.

DECISION: Ruling for Campbell, the Fourth Circuit Court of Appeals reversed the trial court decision and sent the case back to the trial court for trial.

ETHICS
Raising the Defense of the Statute of Frauds

The British judge, James Stephens, wrote that "The cases in which a man of honour would condescend to avail himself of [the statute of frauds] must, I should think, be very rare indeed." By that he meant that usually when a contract is subject to the defense of the statute of frauds, there is little question but that a real contract exists. Thus, the party seeking to avoid enforcement is doing so on a legal technicality, a failure of legal form, not on the basis of a genuine dispute that no contract was made. There has been some debate whether a lawyer can act ethically in asserting the statute-of-frauds claim even though the lawyer believes that the underlying contract is valid. In the United States, that issue has been resolved in favor of the lawyer asserting the claim unless there is knowledge of fraud or some disqualifying conduct.

The client has the legal right to raise the defense even if the client does not appreciate the broader policies of the law. What pro and con arguments could be used to determine if a client consenting to use the statute of frauds defense acts ethically? Who do you think is likely to be the most influential in deciding whether to use a defense of this sort—the lawyer or the client?

The Parol Evidence Rule

Even if people have to reduce an agreement between them to writing, and even if the writing satisfies all the requirements of the statute of frauds, some disputes will occur as to the meaning of the language in the contract or allegations that the contract has been modified or does not include *all* the terms of the agreement. To solve these problems, it is often helpful to turn to what is known as the parol evidence rule. The **parol evidence rule** provides that when a provision in a written contract is unambiguous, a party generally may not offer evidence of any prior or contemporaneous agreement outside of the contract which contradicts any contract provision. **Parol evidence** refers to statements or writings that do not appear in the written contract document. Parol evidence can be either written or oral.

The parol evidence rule is based upon a simple principle. When contracting parties draw up a document of their agreement that appears both complete and final on its face, it is appropriate to conclude that the parties have put everything into that document. Thus, the contracting parties may not use earlier or concurrent agreements to contradict the written document. In essence, the rule says "enough already." If the parties have negotiated an agreement, have concluded that the written document includes all the terms they agreed to, then that document, and only that document, can be used as evidence of their contract.

Like the statute of frauds, the parol evidence rule imposes a technical formal requirement on the way the parties write their agreements. Sometimes, the effect of the parol evidence rule is similar to the statute of frauds rule; consumers and small businesspeople who are unaware of it may be harmed. For example, if a consumer buys a television from a clerk in an electronics store, the consumer may intend to rely both on the written warranty for the product and the oral statement of the clerk that extends or adds to that warranty. The parol evidence rule often makes unenforceable those oral promises that were not written into the contract.

Requirements

The parol evidence rule applies only to written contracts that are final and apparently complete. If the written contract is obviously incomplete or states that certain terms are to be filled in later,

the rule does not apply. The parol evidence rule does not require that the parties use a writing; only the statute of frauds provisions do that. Instead, the parol evidence rule determines that if there is a written agreement, one that is final and complete, it cannot be altered or added to except by a proper written document.

Attorneys have responded to the parol evidence rule by putting clauses similar to the following in written contracts:

> This contract is the final and complete agreement between the parties. All prior negotiations and/or agreements are merged into this contract and all additions to or alterations or changes in this contract must be in writing and signed by both parties.

Such clauses, known as *integration agreements*, are intended to integrate all earlier agreements of the parties into the contract document. The hope is that an integration agreement will make it extremely difficult to introduce evidence of earlier agreements, whether written or oral. Whether the final document integrates earlier documents is really a question of fact that must be resolved by considering the particular circumstances of the contract negotiations. In addition, an ambiguous provision of a written contract may be cleared up by parol evidence. But parol evidence that *contradicts* the written agreement is inadmissible.

These two issues—whether the document is a final integration and whether its terms are ambiguous—give the courts leeway to limit the application of the parol evidence rule. Many courts have used this opportunity to make rulings hostile to the rule. Why such hostility? Doesn't the basic principle underlying the parol evidence rule make sense? The answer is that the principle is flawed and often produces an unfair result.

The parol evidence principle assumes a contract fully negotiated between equals or near equals. But, as we have seen, many written contracts, particularly those entered into by consumers, do not meet that standard. Instead, consumers are handed form contracts to sign. Invariably these contain a clause stating that the form represents the final agreement between the parties and that there are no other understandings between them. It is not uncommon for a salesperson to make oral statements such as, "We'll extend the warranty 30 extra days," or "Of course, we'll provide free service for a year," or "Although it's not our usual policy, we will deliver your purchase free of charge." Relying on these statements, consumers sign contracts and then are prevented by the parol evidence rule from trying to show the "other understandings" that the consumer assumed were part of the deal.

Further, form contracts are drafted for the standard or typical deal. Any customized deal causes problems with the form. Salespeople, office managers, and consumers are not likely to be familiar with the legal consequences described in legal jargon in the form. In these cases, a merchant may use the parol evidence rule as a shield against liability.

The case that follows shows how courts have tried to soften the effect of the parol evidence rule.

MASTERSON V. SINE

Supreme Court of California
436 P.2d 561 (1968)

BACKGROUND: Rebecca Masterson and her husband, Dallas (plaintiffs), together owned a ranch. On February 25, 1958, they deeded it to Medora and Lu Sine (defendants). The deed "reserved unto grantors herein [the Mastersons] an option to purchase the above described property on or before February 15, 1968." Medora Sine was Dallas Masterson's sister. After the deed was given, Dallas became bankrupt. Rebecca and his trustee (the person in the bankruptcy proceeding who was responsible for collecting assets and paying claims) sued to enforce the option to purchase the ranch. The Sines offered evidence showing that the parties wanted the property kept in the Masterson family, and because the option was personal, it could not be exercised by the trustee in bankruptcy. The trial court found that the parol evidence rule prevented admission of the new information from the Sines and ruled that the option could be exercised. Defendants Medora and Lu Sine appealed to the Supreme Court of California.

Traynor, Chief Justice

When the parties to a written contract have agreed to it as an "integration"—a complete and final embodiment of the terms of an agreement—parol evidence cannot be used to add to or vary its terms. . . . When only part of the agreement is integrated, the same rule applies to that part, but parol evidence may be used to prove elements of the agreement not reduced to writing. . . .

The crucial issue in determining whether there has been an integration is whether the parties intended their writing to serve as the exclusive embodiment of their agreement. The instrument itself may help to resolve that issue. It may state, for example, that "there are no previous understandings or agreements not contained in the writing," and thus express the parties' "intention to nullify antecedent understandings or agreements." Any such collateral agreement itself must be examined, however, to determine whether the parties intended the subjects of negotiation it deals with to be included in, excluded from, or otherwise affected by the writing. Circumstances at the time of the writing may also aid in the determination of such integration. . . .

California cases have stated that whether there was an integration is to be determined solely from the face of the instrument and that the question for the court is whether it "appears to be a complete . . . agreement." . . .

Neither of these strict formulations of the rule, however, has been consistently applied. The requirement that the writing must appear incomplete on its face has been repudiated in many cases where parol evidence was admitted "to prove the existence of a separate oral agreement as to any matter on which the document is silent and which is not inconsistent with its terms"—even though the instrument appeared to state a complete agreement. . . .

In formulating the rule governing parol evidence, several policies must be accommodated. One policy is based on the assumption that written evidence is more accurate than human memory. This policy, however, can be adequately served by excluding parol evidence of agreements that directly contradict the writing. Another policy is based on the fear that fraud or unintentional invention by witnesses interested in the outcome of the litigation will mislead the finder of facts. . . . McCormick has suggested that the party urging the spoken as against the written word is most often the economic underdog, threatened by severe hardship if the writing is enforced. In his view the parol evidence rule arose to allow the court to control the tendency of the jury to find through sympathy and without a dispassionate assessment of the probability of fraud or faulty memory that the parties made an oral agreement collateral to the written contract, or that preliminary tentative agreements were not abandoned when omitted from the writing. He recognizes, however, that if this theory were adopted in disregard of all other considerations, it would lead to the exclusion of testimony concerning oral agreements whenever there is a writing and thereby often defeat the true intent of the parties.

Evidence of oral collateral agreements should be excluded only when the fact finder is likely to be misled. The rule must therefore be based on the credibility of the evidence. One such standard, adopted by section 240(1)(b) of the Restatement of Contracts, permits proof of a collateral agreement if it "is such an agreement as might *naturally* be made as a separate agreement by parties situated as were the parties to the written contract." . . .

The option clause in the deed in the present case does not explicitly provide that it contains the complete agreement, and the deed is silent on the question of assignability. Moreover, the difficulty of accommodating the formalized structure of a deed to the insertion of collateral agreements makes it less likely that all the terms of such an agreement were included. . . . This case is one, therefore, in which it can be said that a collateral agreement such as that alleged "might naturally be made as a separate agreement." . . . The case is not one in which the parties "would certainly" have included the collateral agreement in the deed. . . .

It is contended, however, that an option agreement is ordinarily presumed to be assignable if it contains no provisions forbidding its transfer or indicating that its performance involves elements personal to the parties. The fact that there is a written memorandum, however, does not necessarily preclude parol evidence rebutting a term that the law would otherwise presume. . . . In the present case defendants offered evidence that the parties agreed that the option was not assignable in order to keep the property in the Masterson family. The trial court erred in excluding that evidence.

DECISION: The Supreme Court of California ruled in favor of the Sines and reversed the trial court judgment.

Exceptions

A number of logical exceptions follow directly from the basic premise of the parol evidence rule. The fact that on a particular day two people sign a formal agreement does not mean that they have intended to bind themselves forever to those particular terms. As a consequence, parol evidence is always admissible to prove a *later modification* of the contract. The major legal problem with modification, as discussed in Chapter 13, is with the sufficiency of consideration.

Parol evidence is admissible to clear up an *ambiguity* in the contract terms. It is also admissible to prove fraud, alteration, mistake, illegality, duress, undue influence, or lack of capacity. If any of these things can be shown, then the document does not represent a valid contract. It would be very poor legal policy to allow the parol evidence rule to protect a defrauding party or to prevent the showing of duress or mistake. For example, fraud may be perpetrated when one party alters the document or signs it after inserting another page with different terms. Similarly, a typing mistake may occur as the document is prepared. These occurrences may be proved by parol evidence.

UCC Parol Evidence Rule

The UCC (Section 2-202) has a special parol evidence rule applicable to the sale of goods. This rule is more liberal than the common law rule. Usage of trade and course of dealing or performance are always admissible, whether or not the contract terms are found to be ambiguous. The only way by which such factors would be inadmissible would be by an express contract term to that effect.

Further, unless it is quite clear that the document represents an exclusive statement, non-contradictory *additional* terms may be admitted into evidence. There is no presumption that a written document is considered by the parties as a complete, exclusive statement of their agreement.

The Effect of Consumer Protection Statutes

Consumer protection laws can affect the use of the parol evidence rule. Most states have adopted such laws, and they add an interesting twist to the rule. Many such laws make it illegal for suppliers to *fail* to integrate all earlier agreements, oral or otherwise, into the final contract document. Thus, if a car salesman makes a variety of performance and warranty guarantees to a car buyer, but the manufacturer's warranty that comes with the car or the bill of sale does not reflect these guarantees, the salesman has violated such consumer laws. Further, because of these laws, the salesman may not argue his guarantees should not be binding because of the parol evidence rule.

Interpretation of Contractual Provisions

When people who have made a contract dispute its terms, the courts use specific, established rules of interpretation to resolve the disputes.

Problems typically arise because:

1. In using prepared form documents, the parties:
   a. Add language that contradicts other provisions in the form
   b. Do not intend that all of the form provisions apply to their agreement, or
   c. Add ambiguous language
2. In using negotiated, specially prepared documents, the parties:
   a. Use ambiguous language,
   b. Fail to anticipate a problem that arises during performance, or
   c. Compromise without coming to precise understanding of certain terms

In interpreting the particular language used in a written contract, the courts are primarily concerned with correctly learning the intention of the contracting parties. The intentions of the parties cannot be learned by simply asking the people what they intended because, obviously, if they had agreed on the issue in question they would not be in court. Consequently, the courts use the following specific rules designed to ascertain the objectively viewed intention of the parties:

1. Words are to be given their plain and ordinary meanings so long as such an interpretation does not result in a clearly unique or strange result.
   a. The meaning of words may be varied by the prior usage between the parties. The parties are governed by their course of dealing.
   b. Technical words and terms are to be given technical meanings unless it is clear that the parties intend some other definition. (This rule tends to be important in contracts for the sale of land because of the large number of technical terms used in real property law.)
   c. Trade usage may supply a basis for the interpretation of terms.
2. Writings are to be interpreted as a whole, and language is not to be taken out of context.
3. Special circumstances under which a con-

PREVENTIVE LAW
Contract Law and the Written Word

The material in this chapter should alert you to the need to give careful attention to written contracts. The statute of frauds, the parol evidence rule, and the rules regarding contract interpretation have all been created to carry out sound public policies. However, contracting parties that neglect to consider the impact of these rules on their contracting obligations run grave risks that their dealings will not be given their intended effect in court.

Although the statute of frauds requires that certain contracts be evidenced by a writing, there are occasions when this is not immediately possible. Sellers and buyers frequently do business over the phone. Under UCC Section 2-201, merchants can satisfy the statute's requirements by sending confirmatory memoranda of their transactions. One common way that sellers satisfy this requirement is by sending an invoice evidencing that an order has been received from a buyer. Buyers frequently send their own purchase orders confirming their phone orders.

Often in negotiations, the parties arrive at certain preliminary understandings before they finally enter into an agreement. Later, the parties may disagree over the "intent" of their written contract. It is here that the parol evidence rule can be used to provide finality to the written word. This is particularly important for businesses that need to control the potential liability that they are exposed to by their sales agents. The use of an integration clause can serve to limit a court's treatment of a dispute to what the parties have provided in their writing.

Finally, businesspeople who are in a hurry to "close the deal" are often too quick to leave the hard task of hammering out the precise language of a contract to "the obvious intent of the document." This is often captured in expressions such as, "Well, let's not worry about all that, we know what we intend here." Such an attitude can be a lawyer's dream, since what at one time seemed "obvious" to the parties often becomes the subject of litigation. Astute businesspeople know when not to cut costs. Paying a lawyer to draft a contract that expresses the parties' intent, while appearing to be an unnecessary expense, can save future costs by avoiding litigation. When memories fade and arguments arise, a carefully written contract can go a long way in settling an argument.

---

tract was made may be used to show the actual understanding of the parties.

4. Legal and reasonable interpretations are preferred over illegal and unreasonable alternatives.

5. Specific provisions control general provisions.

6. Generally, handwritten provisions prevail over typed provisions, and typed provisions prevail over printed provisions. In applying this rule, the courts assume that the material most recently added by the parties represents their true intention.

7. In commercial contracts, the UCC supplies many implied terms. Usually the UCC terms are applicable unless the parties provide otherwise in their agreement.

Review Questions and Problems

Key Terms

statute of frauds

primary liability

secondary liability

main-purpose doctrine

doctrine of part performance

equitable estoppel

parol evidence rule

parol evidence

Discussion Questions

1. List the types of contracts that must be in writing.

2. Explain how the doctrines of equitable estoppel and promissory estoppel minimize possibly unjust results of the statute of frauds.

3. Describe the general circumstances under which the parol evidence rule does *not* apply.

4. How may the statute of frauds and the parol evidence rule work to the detriment of consumers?

Review Problems

1. Cohen bought a farm jointly owned by Luca Rienzo and his eight brothers and sisters. After the Cohen purchase, Luca, who had lived there for 30 years, made improvements on the buildings, rented part of the farm, and cultivated the rest. After 11 months Cohen asserted his interest in the property. Luca's wife claims that there was an oral agreement between her and Cohen that, after Cohen acquired the property, he would reconvey it to her. Decision?

2. Cohn advertised in the *New York Post* that his 30-foot sloop was for sale. Fisher checked over the boat, phoned Cohn, and they agreed to the sale of the boat for $4,650. They met the next day. Fisher gave Cohn a check for $2,325 and wrote on it "deposit on sloop, *D'Arc Wind*, full amount $4,650." Fisher then contacted Cohn and said he would not close the deal. Fisher stopped payment on the check. Cohn then sold the boat for $3,000 to another and sued to enforce the contract with Fisher. Is Fisher liable for damages for breach of contract?

3. Williams entered into a home construction contract with the Johnsons. The Johnsons signed the contract that had an integration clause and further stated, "There are no verbal agreements or representations in connection therewith." Williams sought to enforce the contract against the Johnsons, and they defended that they had signed thinking that it was an estimate and that they had told Williams that their signing was contingent upon the approval of financing by their bank. Can Williams enforce the contract?

Case Problems

1. Pope & Cottle sold lumber to Blakely, to be used in building a garage for Wheelwright. Blakely failed to pay, and Wheelwright told Pope & Cottle that he would pay Blakely's debt "from such funds as might be in his hands due the said Blakely." Pope & Cottle then formally released Blakely and demanded payment of the $1,478.63 from Wheelwright, who refused to pay. Pope & Cottle sued Wheelwright on the promise. Decision?

2. Barney Sorrenson owed Security $1,400. Barney's mother, Ragnhild Sorrenson, wanted to borrow $200 from Security. Security agreed to make the loan if Ragnhild "would secure up the debts of Barney." Security made the loan and the question arose whether Ragnhild's estate was liable for Barney's debts. Is it?

3. A representative of Mid-South, a plastic supplier, and Fortune Furniture Manufacturing entered into an oral agreement by which Mid-South would provide Fortune with plastic needed in the latter's manufacturing process. As a consequence, the following letter was sent and received:

Mr. Sidney Whitlock, President
Fortune Furniture Manufacturers, Inc.
Okolona, Mississippi 38860

Dear Sid:
   This is to confirm the agreement entered into this date between myself and Phil Stillpass on behalf of Mid-South Plastic Co. Inc. and you on behalf of Fortune Manufacturing Co. Inc.
   We agree to maintain expanded and 21 oz. plastic in the warehouse of Mid-South Furniture Suppliers, Inc. in sufficient amounts to supply all of the plastic for your plant's use, and if for any reason we do not have the necessary plastic you will be at liberty to purchase the plastic from any other source and we will pay the difference in price between that paid the other source and our current price.
   We also agree to pay Fortune 2% rebate on the gross sale price of our plastic as an advertisement aid to your Company which rebate to be paid at your request.
   We assure you that all fabrics you need will be in our warehouse at all times and we appreciate your agreeing to buy all of your plastics from us.

Very truly yours,

W.E. Walker, President
(Mid-South)

Mid-South was unable to supply all of Fortune's needs and Fortune had to buy from other suppliers at a higher price. Does Fortune have a cause of action against Mid-South?

4. Mitchell agreed by a written contract to purchase a farm from Lath. Mitchell contended that in return for her agreement to purchase the farm, Lath agreed to remove an icehouse that she found objectionable. The icehouse was not removed, and Mitchell sued to compel its removal. Decision?

5. Harris contracted to sell cotton to Hine Cotton Co., and both signed the following document:

This agreement is entered into this date wherein Hine Cotton Company, 103 East Third Street, Rome, Georgia agrees to buy from H. E. Harris and Sons, Route 1, Taylorsville, Georgia all the cotton produced on their 825 acres. The rate of payment shall be as follows:

1. All cotton ginned prior to December 20, 1973, and meeting official U.S.D.A. Class will be paid for at 30¢ per pound. Below Grade Cotton at 24 ½¢ per pound.

2. All cotton ginned on or after December 20, 1973,

will be paid for at the rate of 1,000 over the CCC Loan Rate with Below Grades being paid for at 24 1/2¢ per pound. Settlement will be made on net weights on Commercial Bonded Warehouse Receipts with U.S.D.A. Class cards attached with $1 per bale being deducted from the proceeds of each bale.

During the time that the cotton was growing its market value more than doubled, and Hine wrote and asked assurance of Harris that he would perform. Harris repudiated by return letter. Hine sued for the $140,000 difference between the contract price and the market price. Result?

6. Beanblossom sold 1,000 bushels of soybeans to Lippold at $4.42 per bushel. Lippold then brought suit claiming that the 1,000-bushel transaction was partial performance of an oral contract by which Beanblossom was to sell 7,000 bushels of soybeans at $4.42 per bushel. Beanblossom denies that any oral contract was ever made. Decision?

7. Draggage Co. contracted with Pacific Gas to remove and replace the cover of a steam turbine. Draggage agreed "to indemnify Pacific against all losses, damage, expense, and liability resulting from . . . injury to property, arising out of or in any way connected with the performance of this contract." During the work, the cover fell and damaged the turbine. Pacific sued Draggage for the $25,144.51 it spent on repairs. Draggage offered to prove by the testimony of employees of both firms that the parties had understood that the indemnity clause was meant to cover only third parties. Is such proof allowable?

18

Rights of Third Parties

Assignment
Delegation of Duties

Contracts for the Benefit
of a Third Party

Originally, a plaintiff could maintain a contract action only against the party with whom the contract had been made. Over the years this limiting doctrine, which is referred to as **privity of contract** or privity, has lost most of its importance. Today, there are several situations in which a person who is not a party to a contract can use the contract as the basis for suit. The following are some examples:

1. The person suing, often called the third party, has acquired another's contract right by purchase or gift. For example, Smith agrees to sell his house to Jones. Jones decides she does not want the house. She transfers her right to Martin. In most cases, Martin would have a right to sue Smith if Smith refused to perform.

2. The original contract was made for the benefit of a noncontracting third party who is the plaintiff. For example, Brown insures his life with Capital Insurance Company. He names Green as beneficiary. If the company refuses to honor the agreement, Green ordinarily has a right to sue.

This chapter deals with these two situations.

Assignment

In an executory contract each party acquires rights as a result of the agreement. Each party also has obligations or duties because of the agreement. An **assignment** occurs when a person who has contract rights transfers them to someone else. In example 1, Jones, who has a right to buy a house, transfers the right to Martin. Jones is said to have assigned her right to Martin.

A person or firm transferring contract rights is called an **assignor**. The recipient of these rights is the **assignee**. The party responsible for performance is the **obligor**. Consider the following example. A mill promises to deliver 1,000 bushels of wheat to a food processor for $2,000, payable in 60 days. The mill has a duty to transfer title to the wheat to the food processor. On the other hand, the food processor has a duty to pay the mill $2,000. The food processor's duty is the mill's right. Conversely, the mill's duty is the food processor's right. (See Figure 18-1.)

If the mill needed cash immediately, it might transfer its right to the $2,000 to its bank. This could be done by an assignment. The mill would be the assignor, the bank the assignee, and the

FIGURE 18-1

Rights and Duties in an Executory Contract

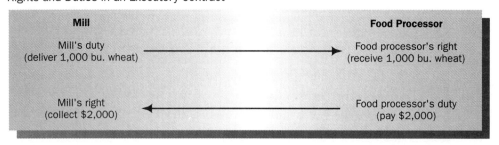

food processor the obligor. Of course, the food processor could assign its right to the wheat to someone as well. The food processor would be the assignor, the recipient of the right the assignee, and the mill the obligor. This is illustrated in Figure 18-2.

Assignment of Monetary Rights

In this credit-oriented society, the contract right most frequently assigned is the right to receive a sum of money. The transfer of rights to receive a monetary payment is an integral part of the American economic system. It is the legal basis for several types of financing. An example would be financing automobile sales. In a large percentage of cases, the buyer of a new automobile purchases on "time." The dealer, however, in order to maintain its inventory and to pay business expenses, must often have cash immediately. In order to obtain this cash, the dealer might assign its contract right to the buyer's payment to a financial institution. The financial institution, now the owner of the right, would notify the buyer and order the buyer to make payments to it.

Accounts Receivable and Factoring The assignment is also the basis for accounts receivable financing and factoring. In **accounts receivable financing**, a lender advances funds to a business and the loan is secured by the accounts receivable of the business. This means that if the business does not repay the loan, the lender will be entitled to satisfy the debt with the business's accounts receivable. In **accounts receivable factoring**, the party advancing the funds (known as the **factor**) makes an absolute purchase of outstanding accounts that are assigned to it. The debtor is instructed to pay the factor directly. If the factor is unable to collect, it ordinarily suffers the loss. In accounts receivable financing, the debtor usually continues to pay the original creditor who has guaranteed payment of the account to the financing agency.

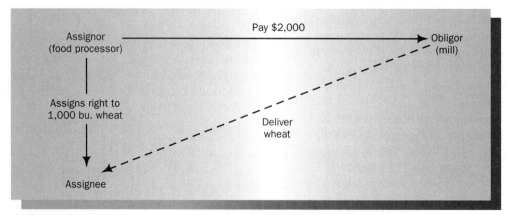

FIGURE 18-2

Assignment of Food Processor's Right to Wheat

For example, Fretter Appliances sells some of its appliances on credit, allowing purchasers to make installment payments. Fretter's right to receive these payments is an account receivable. If it wants the purchasers to pay the installments to Fretter, it could use the accounts receivable to borrow money from First Bank. The bank would have a security interest in the accounts to insure that its loan is repaid. If Fretter didn't repay the loan, the bank could order the purchasers to pay it directly. In this accounts receivable financing, Fretter owns the accounts and is paid by the purchasers. On the other hand, Fretter may sell the accounts to First Bank, which would then own them. The purchaser would make payments directly to the bank, which in this case is called a factor. In factoring, the risk of nonpayment by the purchaser is on the bank, whereas in accounts receivable financing, the risk is on Fretter Appliances.

Because of the economic importance of free transferability of rights to receive money, and because the assignment of a monetary obligation does not materially alter the obligor's responsibility, few limitations have been placed upon assignment of money rights. In fact, Section 9-318(4) of the Uniform Commercial Code provides that a contractual term limiting the right to assign a monetary right is ineffective. However, for public policy reasons, a number of states either prohibit or limit wage assignments.

Wage Assignments   States may regulate and restrict the assignment of wages. Legislatures hope to protect wage earners through such statutes. Some states have prohibited the assignment of future wages. In other states, statutes limit the right to make assignments of future earnings to a specific time period.

In the absence of statutes such as these, the general rule is that future earnings under an existing contract of employment may be assigned. On the other hand, if the assignor is not employed at the time of the assignment, the assignment normally is invalid at law.

Generally, an employee need not obtain the consent of his or her employer before making an assignment of wages under an existing contract of employment.

Assignment of Nonmonetary Rights

Monetary rights are almost always assignable because it really does not make much difference to whom the debtor pays the money.

In determining whether other types of rights are assignable, the guiding principle is whether the transfer materially changes the obligor's duty. The payment of money, the obligation to sell goods or land, and the obligation to do a job to a particular specification are usually freely assignable. If, however, the nature of the assignment or the circumstances are such that the obligor's responsibilities are materially changed, an assignment will be ineffective. Consider the following two examples:

1. Montgomery, an architect, has contracted to design an office building for the ABC Co. The building is to be constructed in New York City. The company decides not to build and assigns the contract to the XYZ Co., which plans to build an apartment house in Chicago.

2. Smith Co., a manufacturer of fine furniture, has contracted to sell a large quantity to Johnson & Sons. The buyer is a major department store with an excellent credit rating. Payment for the furniture is to be made over a 12-month period. Johnson & Sons assigns the contract to Pepper Inc., a discount house that has been in business less than a year.

In both of these cases the assignments would probably be unenforceable as they materially change the obligor's duties under the contracts.

Prohibition of Assignment

Sometimes the parties to a contract attempt to prohibit assignment by a provision in the agreement restricting it. Most courts will enforce provisions restricting assignment. However, a number of courts have refused to recognize such restrictions on the ground that a contract right is property and the owner should be free to transfer it if he or she wishes to do so.

In the following case, the plaintiff argues that the assignment of the contract is prohibited as the assignor's duty to him cannot be effectively performed by an assignee.

HURST V. WEST

Court of Appeals of North Carolina
272 S.E.2d 378 (1980)

BACKGROUND: A client, William F. Hurst (plaintiff), brought an action for breach of contract against his attorneys, West and Groome (defendants). The law firm had entered into a contract with Hurst to represent him on a criminal case. In return, Hurst gave the attorneys an interest in some property he owned. The contract between the parties permitted the attorneys to sell the property and apply the proceeds against their fees. The attorneys succeeded in getting the criminal charges against Hurst dropped. Thereafter, they assigned their interest in the contract to J. D. Hurst and Hurst Distributors, Inc. William Hurst claimed it was a breach of contract for West and Groome to assign the contract. The trial court directed a verdict in favor of the attorneys.

Martin, Judge

The general rule is that contracts may be assigned. The principle is firmly established in this jurisdiction that, unless expressly prohibited by statute or in contravention of some principle of public policy, all ordinary business contracts are assignable, and that a contract for money to become due in the future may be assigned.

The Supreme Court has stated:

> A valid assignment may be made by any contract between the assignor and the assignee which manifests an intention to make the assignee the present owner of the debt. The assignment operates as a binding transfer of the title to the debt as between the assignor and the assignee regardless of whether notice of the transfer is given to the debtor.

Exceptions to the rule that contracts are freely assignable are when the contract expressly provides that it is not assignable, or when performance of some term of the contract involves an element of personal skill or credit. "Whether or not a contractual duty requires personal performance by a specific individual can be determined only by interpreting the words used in the light of experience."

The contract between William F. Hurst and West and Groome contained no express prohibition against assignment. Although the duty of defendant attorneys to defend plaintiff William Hurst on the charges then pending against him involved an element of personal skill and would not have been assignable to a third party, those obligations were fulfilled and discharged when the criminal charges against Hurst were dismissed. The remaining obligation of defendants under the contract, that they sell the property at a reasonable market value if the option to purchase were not exercised, was not personal in nature, as such a performance can be rendered with equal effectiveness by an assignee of the contract. Thus it is clear that no breach occurred merely by West and Groome's assignment of the contract to J. D. Hurst and Hurst Distributors, Inc.

Traditionally the assignment of a contract did not operate to cast upon the assignee the duties and obligations or the liabilities of the contract if the assignee did not assume such liabilities. But in *Rose v. Materials Co.*, our Supreme Court held that unless a contrary intention is apparent, an assignee under a general assignment of an executory bilateral contract becomes the delegatee of the assignor's duties and impliedly promises to perform them. The Court adopted and reaffirmed as the more reasonable rule:

> The assignment on its face indicates an intent to do more than simply to transfer the benefits assured by the contract. It purports to transfer the contract as a whole, and

since the contract is made up of both benefits and burdens both must be intended to be included. It is true the assignor has power only to delegate and not to transfer the performance of duties as against the other party to the contract assigned, but this does not prevent the assignor and the assignee from shifting the burden of performance as between themselves. Moreover, common sense tells us that the assignor, after making such an assignment, usually regards himself as no longer a party to the contract. He does not and, from the nature of things, cannot easily keep in touch with what is being done in order properly to protect his interests if he alone is to be liable for non-performance. Not infrequently the assignor makes an assignment because he is unable to perform further or because he intends to disable himself for further performance. The assignee on the other hand understands that he is to carry out the terms of the contract, as is shown by the fact that he usually does. . . .

In the present case, J. D. Hurst and Hurst Distributors, Inc. expressly agreed to assume all liabilities and responsibilities under the original contract and to hold defendants harmless "from any liability or responsibility under said contract and particularly from any liability or claim of any kind or description William Hurst may now or hereafter make against the Seller [defendants] for accounting or sale of property." J. D. Hurst and Hurst Distributors, Inc., as assignees of the contract, could take by transfer only what rights and interests the assignor had at the time of the assignment, and took subject to any setoffs and defenses available to plaintiffs against the assignor.

Because plaintiff's evidence did not establish the necessary elements of breach of contract, we hold that the directed verdict in favor of defendants was proper.

DECISION: The court of appeals affirmed the verdict of the trial court.

Rights of the Assignee

Defenses Good against Assignor and Assignee   Although assignment is an integral element of much business financing, the assignee, ordinarily a financial institution advancing funds, is subject to some legal risk. All that the assignee acquires are the rights possessed by the original assignor. If the obligor has defenses that can be asserted against the assignor, these same defenses can be asserted against the assignee. For example, if the original transaction was voidable because of fraud or failure of consideration, the obligor can assert these defenses against the assignee to the same extent that it could have asserted them against the assignor. If the underlying transaction is voidable because the obligor lacked the capacity to contract, this defense can also be asserted by the obligor against the assignee. The following case illustrates the risk to a transferee who takes a contract right by assignment.

CHIMNEY HILL OWNERS ASSOCIATION V. ANTIGNANI
Supreme Court of Vermont
392 A.2d 423 (1978)

BACKGROUND: In 1966, the Chimney Hill Corporation (Corporation) developed a 900-lot tract for vacation homes known as Chimney Hill. In addition to the lots, there was a 300-to-500-acre area of common land that contained a clubhouse, pools, tennis courts, roads, and a water system. A standard deed provided that each lot was to be assessed an annual charge for use and maintenance of the common land and facilities. The Corporation and its "successors and assigns" had the right to collect the annual charge. The duty to pay the annual charge was imposed upon each lot owner.

In 1968, the Eastern Woodworking Company (defendant) acquired eleven lots. At the time the Corporation agreed in writing to charge Eastern only a single assessment on one lot rather than eleven separate assessments "until one or more of the lots have been improved." The same agreement was made with defendants Antignani and Keatinge, both of whom also purchased several lots.

In 1975, the Corporation conveyed the common land and facilities to the Chimney Hill Owners Association (Association). The Association collectively represented all property owners in Chimney Hill. The Corporation assigned to the Association the right to collect the assessments on each lot. Subsequently, the Association billed the defendants for a separate assessment on each lot they owned. The defendants refused to pay based upon the agreement with the Corporation. The Association sued and the trial court entered judgment in favor of the defendant lot owners. The Association appealed.

Hill, Justice

A Declaration of Protective Covenants, Restrictions and Reservations pertaining to Chimney Hill was executed by Chimney Hill Corporation and recorded in the Town Clerk's office in Wilmington. The Declaration was included in each purchase and sales agreement and each deed executed for lots in Chimney Hill. Paragraph 10 of the Declaration is the focus of the dispute in these actions.

Paragraph 10 states that an annual charge shall be assessed against each lot in Chimney Hill and paid "to the grantor, its successors and assigns" for the right to use the common lands, facilities and services maintained and provided by the "grantor, its successors and assigns." The charge is made a debt collectible by suit in a court of competent jurisdiction and a lien on the lot conveyed until paid. Paragraph 10 further provides that acceptance of a deed bound by the Declaration shall be construed to be a covenant by the grantee, his heirs, successors and assigns to pay the charge to the grantor, its successors and assigns. Lastly, Paragraph 10(E) states:

> That this charge shall run with and bind the land hereby conveyed, and shall be binding upon the grantee or grantees, his, her, their, or its heirs, executors, administrators, successors and assigns, until May 31, 1988, unless earlier terminated by written release of the grantor, its successors or assigns.

The plaintiff seeks to recover the assessments, in its own right, under the assignment from Chimney Hill Corporation. In the assignment, the Corporation assigned to the plaintiff the right to collect from each owner in Chimney Hill the annual charge. As assignee, however, the plaintiff takes the right to collect subject to all defenses of the obligor against the assignor that have not been acquired or set up in fraud of the rights of the assignee after notice has been given of their existence.

As to defendant Eastern, the trial court concluded that it possessed a valid release from Chimney Hill Corporation concerning the ten unimproved lots, which was a valid defense to the plaintiff's claim. Paragraph 10(E) of the Declarations reserves to the grantor, Chimney Hill Corporation, its successors and assigns, the right to terminate the annual charge on any of the lots. Eastern's sales agreement, executed by both Eastern and Chimney Hill Corporation, provides that one annual charge only will be assessed on Eastern's eleven lots until one or more have been improved. The sales agreement contains just the release contemplated by Paragraph 10(E).

Eastern's defense based on the release is valid against the plaintiff as assignee of Chimney Hill Corporation.

Defendant Eastern has a valid written release signed by Chimney Hill Corporation, which unequivocally waives the right to annual charges on ten unimproved lots and which is binding on Chimney Hill Corporation. The court found at the time the plaintiff acquired the common lands and facilities it was aware that some multiple lot owners were being charged one assessment. The issue is whether with this knowledge the plaintiff is charged with the duty to inquire further as to when and why such single assessments were made. We think such inquiry should have been made. If such inquiry had been made of the Chimney Hill Corporation, the existence of Eastern's written release would have been revealed.

DECISION: The Supreme Court of Vermont affirmed the judgment of the trial court.

As the *Chimney Hill* case illustrates, the value of what an assignee acquires is determined by the underlying contract. This is true even when the assignee takes in good faith and has no knowledge of what took place in the underlying transaction. An assignee can protect itself from this risk to a degree by asking the obligor if it has defenses against performance. If the obligor gives assurances that no defenses exist, the obligor may not at a later time assert defenses that are inconsistent with these assurances.

Suppose that First National Bank wishes to purchase a note signed by a homeowner. The homeowner agreed to pay Acme Home Improvement $500 for work done on the home. If the bank, prior to taking the note, asks the homeowner (the obligor on the note) if Acme did the work, and the homeowner says yes, the homeowner may not assert the failure of Acme to do the work as a reason to refuse to pay the bank after it takes the note.

With and Without Recourse   An assignee can also protect itself by extracting from the assignor a commitment to repurchase a claim that is uncollectible. This is usually referred to as an **assignment with recourse**. In an **assignment without recourse**, the assignee assumes the risks of collection.

Guarantees Made to Assignee   Even in situations in which an assignment is made without recourse, the assignor by the very act of assigning makes certain warranties to the assignee. Although collection is not guaranteed, the assignor does guarantee that any document evidencing the right is genuine and that the right is not subject to any undisclosed defenses of which he or she is aware. In addition, the assignor guarantees that he or she will do nothing to defeat or impair the assignment. If the assignor were to personally collect the debt, he or she would thus violate this last guarantee.

Notice to the Obligor

For several reasons the assignee should notify the obligor of the assignment as soon as possible.

Assignment to One Person   Suppose that Mary owes $100 to Betty. Betty then assigns her right to receive $100 to John. Betty is thus the assignor and John the assignee of a contractual right to receive money. What if John never instructs Mary to pay him rather than Betty? In that situation because Mary is unaware of the assignment, she could pay the entire sum to Betty. This would completely discharge Mary of any obligation under the contract. John's only recourse in this situation would be against Betty. John could sue Betty for not observing the implied warranty that she would do nothing to prevent John from obtaining performance from Mary.

In most states, after proper notice is given, the person who must perform can no longer assert counterclaims or defenses against the person getting the contract rights unless these arise out of the transaction that gave rise to the assignment. Additionally, until the person who must perform gets notice of the assignment, he or she may perform to the assignor. Once the person who must perform has notice of the assignment, however, he or she can honor the contract only by performing to the assignee. If the right assigned is a debt, the debtor is discharged only by payment to the assignee. A debtor who pays the original creditor after notice of assignment would have to make a second payment to the assignee.

Assignment to Two or More People   Notice is also important if the assignor fraudulently or mistakenly assigns the same right to two different parties. For example, Mary owes $100 to Betty, and Betty assigns her right to receive the $100 to John. If John fails to notify Mary, this would give Betty the opportunity to assign this same debt to Tom. In most states, because John was the first assignee, he has the right to collect. However, in some states, if Tom notified Mary of the assignment before John did, Tom would be entitled to collect. John's only recourse in that situation would be against Betty.

Form of Assignment

Although people may validly assign rights orally, for a number of reasons they should do so in a writing and sign the document. The principal reason is to provide the clear evidence that a transfer of the right has taken place. In addition, many states have statutes that require certain types of assignments to be in writing in order to be effective. One common example is the wage assignment. The UCC also requires that certain commercial assignments must be in writing in order to be effective.

The document should describe the right that is being transferred and identify who has the duty to perform. A typical assignment of a contract right might be worded as follows:

> For value received, receipt of which is hereby acknowledged, Betty Blaine does hereby assign to John Smith all her right, title, and interest in a contract between Mary Morris and Betty Blaine, dated February 28, 1995, which contract obligates Mary Morris to pay the undersigned $10,000 on or before October 31, 1995.
>
> The undersigned further guarantees payment of and agrees that if default be made, she, Betty Blaine, will pay the full amount to John Smith upon demand.
>
> Dated July 20, 1995.
> Signed by ————————————
>   Betty Blaine

Delegation of Duties

Up to this point we have been looking primarily at situations in which a person who owns a contract right wishes to transfer it. A party to a contract who has an obligation to perform may wish to transfer that obligation to another party. This is permissible as long as the obligation is not personal in nature and transferring it does not violate a public policy. A transfer of contractual duties or

obligations is referred to as a **delegation**.

We have seen that when a party to a contract assigns a right, generally no guarantee is given that the new owner of the right will be able to collect. The obligor who transfers his duty makes a different commitment. He or she continues to be liable for performance except in those situations in which the party for whom the obligation must be performed releases the obligor from responsibility. This is called a **novation**. If a novation is carried out properly, the original obligor is released from a duty to perform, and the third party now has the entire obligation.

Delegable Duties

The delegation of a duty is an attempt to extinguish a duty in the assignor and create a similar duty in the assignee. Generally, duties are delegable, although a delegation does not extinguish the duty or relieve the assignor of the duty to perform in the event that the delegate fails to perform. The obligations incurred as a result of most business contracts can be transferred.

Construction contracts are good examples of the type of contract in which the obligor's duties are delegable. Ordinarily the parties understand that the general contractor will not perform all the work. Much will be done by subcontractors, although the general contractor is responsible for their performance. A typical delegation involving a construction contract is shown in Figure 18-3.

Nondelegable Duties

A duty may not be delegated under these conditions:

1. The performance by the person to whom the duty is delegated would be significantly different from that of the person bound by contract to perform. Garth Brooks may not honor Madonna's singing contracts.

2. The person who originally made the contract has a substantial interest in using the personal services of the other contracting party. Even though another designer or apprentice might be able to do just as good a job for me in designing a chair, if I contract with a master craftsman to do it for me, I don't want the craftsman to delegate his duty to an apprentice.

PREVENTIVE LAW
Assignment of Lease

A commercial or residential lease often contains a provision prohibiting the lessee from assigning the lease or subletting the premises. (The differences between assignment and subletting are discussed in Chapter 48.) Provisions limiting assignment or subletting reduce the value of the lease to the tenant, and they can cause the tenant a number of problems. For example, a business firm might need to move for a good reason. If it has signed a long-term lease with a provision limiting assignment or subletting, it might have to wait until the lease terminates in order to make this move.

Lease provisions that limit assignment or subletting are written in a variety of ways. Some of them are absolute prohibitions. Others restrict assignment or subletting without the lessor's consent. Usually these provisions provide that the lease terminates if the tenant assigns or sublets. The tenant, however, remains responsible for the rent until the lessor again leases the property. If the lessor cannot lease at the rental in the original lease, the original tenant remains liable for the difference.

Traditionally, in most states, if a lease provided that it could not be assigned without the lessor's consent, the lessor could withhold its consent without explanation or reason. Although a number of states still follow this rule, case law in some states and statute in a few states require that the lessor's consent cannot be withheld without reason.

In order to prevent misunderstanding and to limit litigation, both commercial and residential tenants should examine the lease for provisions limiting assignment or subletting. As a minimum, the tenant should insist that the provision be worded in such a way that the lessor can only withhold consent for a valid reason. Many leases are worded in this manner, and a number of states apply a rule-of-reason standard when the lease requires the tenant to obtain the lessor's written consent before assigning or subletting. A rule-of-reason standard means that the lessor can refuse its consent only upon reasonable grounds. These would include factors such as the credit rating of the proposed assignee or sublessee, its business record, and the legality of the proposed lease. In a commercial lease, both lessor and lessee would be well advised to spell out in the lease the grounds upon which the lessor can refuse to consent to an assignment or sublease.

Even in the states that follow a rule-of-reason standard, the lease may contain a provision giving the lessor absolute discretion to accept a replacement tenant. Hardship, ill-feeling, and litigation can be avoided if, when a provision of this nature is included in the lease, the tenant is aware of restrictions on the transfer of the leasehold.

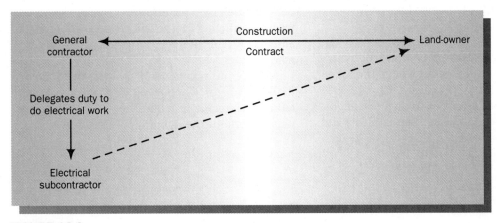

FIGURE 18-3

Delegation of Duties

What if, in a contract between Smith and Jones, Jones delegates his duties to Brown, and informs Smith that he will no longer be responsible for the performance of the contract? Smith may treat Jones's action as a breach of contract. However, if Brown does perform and Smith accepts Brown's performance, Jones's obligation to perform is extinguished. In this case, a novation has occurred. The person for whom the third party performs no longer has any obligation under the original contract.

In a situation such as that among Smith, Jones, and Brown, the courts disagree as to whether Jones can force such an agreement on Smith without Smith's consent. Some courts permit Smith to take Brown's services, and still sue Jones for breach of contract. Other courts treat Smith's acceptance of Brown's services as a consent by Smith to extinguish Jones's liability under the contract.

Contracts for the Benefit of a Third Party

In many instances, a third party will benefit from the performance of a contract. In some cases, the contracting parties have actually made the agreement for the benefit of the third party. The third party in such a case is known as a **third-party beneficiary**. In other situations, an outsider will benefit even though the parties to the agreement did not plan to benefit the third party. A common example of a contract made primarily to benefit a third party is the life insurance policy. Its primary purpose is to provide benefits for a third party upon the insured's death. The contract, however, is between the insured and the insuring company.

A question that the courts have frequently had to face is whether a third party who will benefit from an agreement has a right to sue if the agreement is not carried out. This question is especially troublesome when the parties to the contract did not contemplate benefiting another; or if they did,

this was not their primary concern. What they were interested in doing was benefiting themselves.

Although the law varies from state to state, most jurisdictions allow third parties to sue if they are **intended beneficiaries**—that is, third parties whom the parties to the contract intended to benefit from the contract. An **incidental beneficiary**, or a party who benefits from a contract even though the parties to the contract did not contract for the purpose of conferring such a benefit, generally is not permitted to sue to enforce the contract.

Intended Beneficiary

As an intended beneficiary has the right to sue the promisor but an incidental beneficiary does not, determining if a person is an intended beneficiary is a critical question. The fact that a person benefits from a contract between two others is not enough. The intention of the parties to benefit the third party must be clear. This intention may be evidenced by the terms of the contract, the circumstances under which it was made, and what the parties were trying to accomplish.

The contract does not have to identify or refer to a third party by name in order for the third party to enforce it. For example, in *United States v. Ogden Technology Laboratories*, the United States sued successfully as a third-party beneficiary of a contract between two private firms. Although the United States was not named in the contract, the contract provisions indicated that certain tests were being conducted for its benefit. The laboratory conducting the tests was assured of a defense contract priority, the testing was to be witnessed by a government inspector, and the party contracting for the tests could terminate the agreement if in the best interests of the government.

As the court points out in the case that follows, the question of whether a third party is an intended beneficiary is a question of fact. The court must determine the intention of the parties.

CONCORDIA COLLEGE V. SALVATION ARMY

Court of Appeals of Minnesota

470 N.W.2d 542 (1991)

BACKGROUND: George and Phyllis Engh, husband and wife, each executed wills in 1980. In connection with the execution of George's will, George and Phyllis executed a contract whereby each agreed not to change his or her will. George's 1980 will provided that some of his money would be left to Concordia College. In spite of the contract, George amended his will, and in 1985, three years after Phyllis' death, he executed a new will. George amended his new will several times prior to his death in 1988. The version of George's will in effect at the time of his death left no money to Concordia College. Concordia College and others who were cut out of George's will sued to enforce the 1980 contract between the Enghs not to amend their respective wills. The trial court dismissed, and the plaintiffs (referred to as the appellants in the opinion below) appealed.

Norton, Judge

Whether parties to a contract intend to benefit a third party is a question of fact. . . .

The Minnesota Supreme Court has adopted the intended beneficiary approach in the Restatement (Second) of Contracts § 302. Under Section 302, a third party can recover as an intended beneficiary where: (1) recognition of third-party beneficiary rights is appropriate and (2) a duty is owed to the beneficiary or the promisee intends to benefit the beneficiary.

> If, by the terms of the contract, performance is directly rendered to a third party, he is intended by the promisee to be benefited. Otherwise, if the performance is directly rendered to the promisee, the third party who also may be benefited is an incidental beneficiary with no right of action. *Buchman Plumbing Co. v. Regents of the University of Minn.* (1974).

Any intent to benefit the third party must be found in the contract as read in light of all the circumstances at the time of contracting.

Appellants contend that, as intended beneficiaries, they have standing to bring this action to enforce the agreement. That is, as residual legatees under the 1980 will of George Engh, they are intended beneficiaries of the 1980 agreement between George and Phyllis Engh not to revoke or change their wills.

The 1980 agreement stated in pertinent part:

> The parties hereto are husband and wife and they each, on the 3rd day of October, 1980, made and executed Wills, copies of which are attached hereto and incorporated herein by reference.
>
> In consideration of their mutual agreements herein, each of the parties hereto do hereby agree that during the lifetime of each of the parties, neither party will revoke or change the Will executed by each of the parties on the 3rd day of October, 1980, copies of which Wills are attached hereto as heretofore stated.

This contract language states that neither party will revoke or change their 1980 wills. The wills were attached to the agreement and incorporated therein by reference. . . . The language of the agreement with the incorporation of George's 1980 will illustrates George's intent to benefit appellants. Additionally, George and Phyllis were both present during his attorney's explanation of their wills and the consequences of signing the agreement. The attorney testified that George and Phyllis both understood the significance of the agreement.

The attorney testified that George wanted the agreement so that he could be absolutely sure that his will could not be changed by Phyllis following his death. George wanted to maintain control of his estate by having it distributed according to his 1980 will after his death. The attorney testified that George assured Phyllis at the time of the signing of the agreement that he would not change his will and that his family and her family would be beneficiaries. George's primary concern was the protection of the residual legatees. . . .

In this case, the trial court's finding that appellants were not intended beneficiaries was clearly erroneous. Appellants do have standing to commence an action seeking enforcement of the terms of the 1980 agreement between George and Phyllis Engh. . . . The language of the agreement, the incorporation of the wills into the agreement, testimony of the significance of the wills and agreement to George and Phyllis, and testimony that George did not want Phyllis to be able to change the beneficiaries of his 1980 will at the time of the making of the will and agreement support appellants' contention that they are intended third-party beneficiaries of the 1980 agreement between George and Phyllis.

Decision: The court of appeals reversed the trial court decision and remanded the case to trial court.

Donee Beneficiary If a contract is primarily for the benefit of a third party and the promisee's intent is to confer a gift upon the third party, the intended beneficiary is a **donee beneficiary**.

Life insurance is a good example of a situation involving a donee beneficiary. (See Figure 18-4.) The typical policy requires the insurance company to pay a certain amount of money in the event of the death of the insured. The insured purchased this policy with the intent to benefit the third party. If the insurance company refuses to pay, the donee beneficiary may sue the company for the amount of the insurance policy. The donee beneficiary is permitted to sue even though he or she is not in privity of contract with the company and has not given anything to the insurance company.

Creditor Beneficiary If the purpose of the contract is to discharge an obligation that the promisee owes or believes he or she owes to the third party, the third party is a **creditor beneficiary**. In the case of a donee beneficiary, the promisee intends to make a gift. In the case of a creditor beneficiary, the promisee wishes to discharge an obligation owed to the creditor beneficiary.

Suppose that Tina owes Cindy $1,000. Tina sells her automobile to Sam, who promises to pay $1,000 to Cindy in order to discharge the debt between Tina and Cindy. Cindy is a creditor beneficiary of Sam's promise and has an enforceable claim against Sam for $1,000. (See Figure 18-5.)

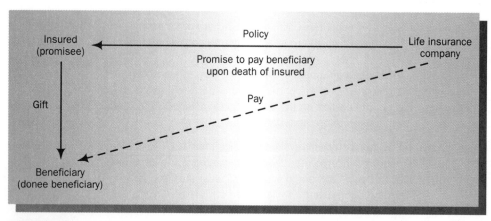

FIGURE 18-4

Donee Beneficiary

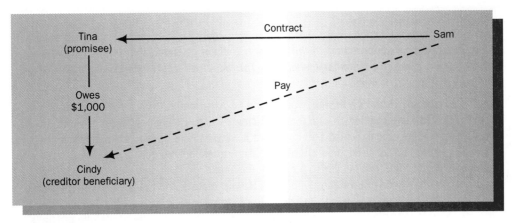

FIGURE 18-5
Creditor Beneficiary

Incidental Beneficiary

If a promisee neither intends to confer a gift on the third party nor is trying to discharge an obligation to the third party, the third party is an incidental beneficiary. He or she has no rights under the contract. Suppose that McDonald's contracted to build a store next to Louise's dress shop. Because the McDonald's would attract many people to the area, Louise anticipated she would do more business than ever. The contract between McDonald's and the builder was not intended to benefit Louise. If the builder breaches the contract and the McDonald's is never built, does Louise have a cause of action against the builder? No. This contract was not intended to benefit Louise in any way. She would have no cause of action against the builder even though, had the store been built, her business might have increased.

In the case that follows, the court had to decide whether the plaintiff was an incidental beneficiary.

BAIN V. GILLISPIE
Court of Appeals of Iowa
357 N.W.2d 47 (1984)

BACKGROUND: Jim Bain (plaintiff-appellee) refereed a basketball game between the University of Iowa and Purdue University. As the game was ending, Bain called a foul on an Iowa player. The Purdue player scored the point and Purdue won the game. John and Karen Gillispie (defendants-appellants) operate a novelty store known as Hawkeye John's Trading Post. The store specializes in University of Iowa sports memorabilia. A few days after the game, the Gillispies began marketing T-shirts showing a man with a rope around his neck and captioned "Jim Bain Fan Club."

On learning of this, Bain sought injunctive relief and damages. The Gillispies counterclaimed, alleging that Bain's conduct in officiating at the game was below the standard required of a professional referee. They asked for $175,000 in damages on grounds that Iowa's loss had deprived it of the Big Ten championship, destroying a potential market for their memorabilia. Bain moved for summary judgment on the counterclaim. The trial court sustained this motion.

The Gillispies appealed. They argued that summary judgment should not have been granted as two triable issues of fact existed. They were (1) Bain's action as a referee was negligent and (2) they were third-party beneficiaries of an employment contract between Bain and the Big Ten Athletic Conference.

Snell, Presiding Judge

[The appellate court first dealt with the negligence claim. It stated that the trial court was correct when it granted summary judgment. The appellate court approved the following statement by the trial court.]

This is a case where the undisputed facts are of such a nature that a rational fact finder could only reach one conclusion—no foreseeability, no duty, no liability. Heaven knows what uncharted morass a court would find itself in if it were to hold that an athletic official subjects himself to liability every time he might make a questionable call. The possibilities are mind boggling. If there is a liability to a merchandiser like the Gillispies, why not to the thousands upon thousands of Iowa fans who bleed Hawkeye black and gold every time the whistle blows? It is bad enough when Iowa loses without transforming a loss into a litigation field day for "Monday Morning Quarterbacks." There is no tortious doctrine of athletic official's malpractice that would give credence to Gillispies' counterclaim.

The trial court also found that there was no issue of material fact on the Gillispies' claim that they were beneficiaries under Bain's contract with the Big 10. Gillispies argue that until the contract is produced, there exists a question of whether they are beneficiaries. There is some question of whether there is a contract between Bain and the Big 10. In his response to interrogatories, Bain stated that he had no written contract with the Big 10, but that there was a letter which defined "working relationship." Although this letter was never produced and ordinarily we would not decide an issue without the benefit of examining the letter's contents, we nevertheless find the issue presently capable of determination. By deposition Gillispies answered that there was no contract between them and Bain, the Big 10 Athletic Conference, the University of Iowa, the players, coaches, or with anybody regarding this issue. Thus, even if the letter were considered a contract, Gillispies would be considered third-party beneficiaries. Because Gillispies would not be privy to the contract, they must be direct beneficiaries to maintain a cause of action, and not merely incidental beneficiaries.

A direct beneficiary is either a donee beneficiary or a creditor beneficiary. In *Olney v. Hutt,* the Iowa Supreme Court defined these terms as follows:

> (1) Where performance of a promise in a contract will benefit a person other than the promisee that person is, . . . (a) a donee beneficiary if it appears from the terms of the promise in view of the accompanying circumstances that the purpose of the promisee in obtaining the promise of all or part of the performance thereof is to make a gift to the beneficiary or to confer upon him a right against the promisor to some performance neither due nor supposed or asserted to be due from the promisee to the beneficiary; (b) a creditor beneficiary if no purpose to make a gift appears from the terms of the promise in view of the accompanying circumstances and performance of the promise will satisfy an actual or supposed or asserted duty of the promisee to the beneficiary.

Gillispies make no claim that they are creditor beneficiaries of Bain, the Big 10 Athletic Conference, or the University of Iowa. "The real test is said to be whether the contracting parties intended that a third person should receive a benefit which might be enforced in the courts." It is clear that the purpose of any promise which Bain might have made was not to confer a gift on Gillispies. Likewise, the Big 10 did not owe any duty to the Gillispies such that they would have been creditor beneficiaries. If a contract did exist between Bain and the Big 10, Gillispies can be considered nothing more than incidental beneficiaries and as such are unable to maintain a cause of action.

Consequently, there was no genuine issue for trial which could result in Gillispies obtaining a judgment under a contract theory of recovery. The ruling of the trial court sustaining the summary judgment motion and dismissing the counterclaim is affirmed.

DECISION: The trial court ruling for Bain was affirmed.

Review Questions and Problems

Key Terms

privity of contract

assignment

assignor

assignee

obligor

accounts receivable financing

accounts receivable factoring

factor

assignment with recourse

assignment without recourse

delegation

novation

third-party beneficiary

intended beneficiary

incidental beneficiary

donee beneficiary

creditor beneficiary

Discussion Questions

1. Explain why it is important for an assignee to immediately notify the obligor of the assignment.

2. In situations in which an assignor has assigned the same right twice, law in some states gives priority to the assignment first made. Present arguments in support of this rule. Other states give priority to the assignee who first notifies the obligor. Present arguments in support of this rule.

3. How do you determine if an intended beneficiary is a creditor or a donee beneficiary?

Review Problems

1. Lenox Homes built a house for the Buengers in 1972. In 1974, the Buengers sold the house to the Coburns. The Coburns occupied the house and found that the septic system installed by Lenox was faulty. The Coburns sued Lenox and claimed that they were beneficiaries of the contract made between Lenox and the Buengers. Do you agree?

2. Mrs. Lara entered the Kern County hospital to give birth. She died shortly after her child was born, and the hospital was not paid for the medical services it provided to her child. Under state law, her husband, a part-time farmworker, was billed by the hospital. Can the hospital assign its right to receive money from Mr. Lara to a collection service?

3. Smith purchases a new automobile from the Warren Oldsmobile dealer. One of the terms of the purchase is that the dealer perform certain specified warranty work on the car for 2 years without further charge. A year after Smith's purchase, the chief mechanic at Warren quits, and Warren notifies Smith that all future warranty work will be performed by the Ace Garage. Warren contracts with the Ace Garage to provide this service to Smith. May Warren do this? Explain.

4. Asphalt Paving Company contracted with the city of Flint to pave certain streets. A clause in that contract provided that Asphalt would be liable for damages to any property resulting from the paving work. In moving one of its bulldozers, Asphalt struck a gas main, which exploded and seriously damaged the house of Leo Stevenson. Stevenson sued Asphalt and relied on the contract between Asphalt and the city of Flint. Can Stevenson use that contract in his case?

Case Problems

1. Rosier was a frequent purchaser of large quantities of oil on open account from Chanute Refining. A federal statute required inspection of oil before shipment; Chanute Refining had been doing this for Rosier, charging him an inspection fee. The statute was declared invalid and Rosier demanded a refund of the inspection fees that had been paid to Chanute Refining.

   On June 19, Rosier purchased additional oil from Chanute Refining for $3,500. On June 29, Chanute assigned Rosier's account along with several others to Sinclair Co. When Rosier refused to pay, he was sued by Sinclair. At the trial Sinclair offered to present evidence to prove that it did not know of the dispute regarding the inspection fees. Is this evidence admissible? Why or why not?

2. In the preceding case, what are Sinclair's rights, if any, against Chanute Refining?

3. Bull Dog Insurance issued a policy of insurance to D'Alassano against loss by theft of an automobile. The automobile was stolen and never recovered. D'Alassano assigned his claim under the policy to Ginsberg. The policy provided that "no assignment of interest under this policy shall be or become binding upon the association unless the written consent . . . is endorsed thereon and an additional membership fee is paid." Present arguments supporting Ginsberg's right to collect under the policy.

4. Dooley contracted with Rose to provide enough stone to meet Rose's business requirements for ten years at favorable listed prices. In return, Rose promised not to compete with Dooley in the rock-crushing business. Later, Dooley assigned the contract to Vulcan Materials Co. Is Vulcan required to supply stone to Rose at the original contract prices?

5. MGM contracted to pay Selznick royalties upon the first TV broadcast of "Gone with the Wind." Later, Selznick obtained a large loan from Haas by assigning his right to payment of the royalties to Haas as security for the loan. Selznick notified MGM of the assignment and asked that Haas be notified in advance of any royalty payments to be made to Selznick. MGM refused but neither Selznick nor Haas pursued the matter. Haas died, Selznick defaulted on the loan, and Haas's estate obtained a judgment against Selznick. When the movie was broadcast, MGM paid Selznick, but Haas did not receive notice or a payment. Haas's estate sued MGM

to recover the royalty payment. Was the royalty payment effectively assigned by Selznick to Haas under the UCC?

6. McDonald's granted a franchise in the Omaha-Council Bluffs area to Copeland, a reputable and highly successful businessman. *In a separate agreement*, Copeland was granted a right of first refusal, that is, the right to receive the first offer of additional McDonald's franchises to be developed in the area. Subsequently, Copeland assigned his franchise contracts to Shupack, with McDonald's consent. When McDonald's later offered a new area franchise to someone else, Shupack sued, claiming that the right of first refusal was included in the assignment from Copeland so that he should have been offered the new restaurant first. McDonald's had previously written Shupack stating that the right was personal to Copeland and had not passed to Shupack. Was the right assignable? How can you determine whether it was personal to Copeland?

7. Cunningham played basketball for the Cougars, a professional team owned by Southern Sports Corp. His contract prohibited assignment to another club without his consent. When Southern Sports assigned the Cougars franchise and Cunningham's contract to Munchak Corp., Cunningham protested, claiming that his contract was personal and therefore not assignable. Is the assignment of Cunningham's contract effective?

8. Simpson was president and minority shareholder of Skyuka Mining. JOC entered into an agreement with the majority shareholders of Skyuka to buy Skyuka. Simpson was not a party to the agreement, but the agreement stated that JOC would undertake to conclude a similar agreement with Simpson to purchase his shares. JOC and Simpson never entered into such an agreement, and JOC refused to purchase Simpson's shares. Simpson sued to require JOC to purchase his shares for their fair market value. What result? Discuss.

19

Performance, Discharge, and Remedies

Performance Dependent upon
Conditions

Substantial Performance and
Material Breach

Discharge of Contractual
Obligations

Remedies

The discussion of contract law to this point has been concerned with the issue of whether or not a valid contract has been entered into by the parties. Now the focus shifts to what happens after the contract has been made: the consequences of performance and nonperformance of the contractual obligations. Some contracts are made and performed simultaneously—for example, when someone buys a newspaper from a street vendor. However, other contracts are entered into by the parties with a view to performance by one or both of them sometime in the future. Between the making of the contract and its time of performance, changed circumstances may make performance no longer desirable for one of the parties. For example, if a building contractor agrees to build a house for a buyer and the costs of supplies and labor increase significantly between the time the contract is made and the time the house is to be built, the builder may have second thoughts about the deal, particularly if another buyer is willing to pay the builder more than the current contract provides.

Under these circumstances, the level of performance by the builder may be something less than was anticipated by the first buyer. Suppose the builder uses lower-grade materials and hires other than journeymen workers to construct the building. What are the buyer's rights? Can the buyer require the contractor to fire the workers, tear down the construction, and rebuild the house using quality materials and journeymen workers? Suppose the builder, having laid the foundation, learns of the other buyer who is willing to pay more. Can the builder stop work on the first house and start work on the second buyer's house with a view to finishing the first house after he has built the second? The contract may or may not deal explicitly with such possibilities. Where it does not, or if the parties disagree about their interpretations of how the contract is to resolve such issues, litigation may result. The practice of the courts is to place a commonsense construction on the intention of the parties respecting performance of a contract and to fashion a reasonable and just remedy for the breach of a duty to perform.

Performance Dependent upon Conditions

Conditional Promises

Sometimes the parties to a contract will condition their respective performances upon the occurrence of an event. For example, a seller may condition its duty to deliver ordered goods upon the buyer's making a specified down payment. Similarly, the buyer may condition its obligation to pay the remainder of the price owed upon its being able to obtain financing for the purchase or upon its satisfaction with the delivered merchandise, or both. In these examples, the contract does not create a duty to perform unless and until some event occurs. Such promises are termed conditional.

Similarly, a duty of performance may be conditioned upon the nonoccurrence of an event. An example is a promise to cut a lawn if it does not rain on Saturday.

An event may create or extinguish a present duty of performance. For example, the making of the down payment by the buyer in the preceding example gives rise to a present duty in the seller to deliver the merchandise. On the other hand, in the lawn-mowing example, rain on Saturday extinguishes the mower's present duty to cut the lawn.

An event that must first occur in order to give rise to a duty of performance is called a **condition precedent**. An event that extinguishes a duty of performance is called a **condition subsequent**. The nonoccurrence of a condition precedent excuses nonperformance by the party whose duty of performance was to arise only after the condition precedent materialized. The occurrence of a condition subsequent excuses the nonperformance of a party whose duty of performance was extinguished by the condition subsequent. In both cases, the party relying upon the condition is not liable to the other party for breach of contract because the nonperformance was excused. If the condition precedent, however, happens to be the other party's performance, the nonoccurrence of the condition precedent gives the party relying upon that condition a claim against the other for breach of contract. In such a case, the party relying upon the condition has its nonperformance excused, whereas the other nonperforming party remains liable for breach of contract.

Approval or Satisfaction

Contracts sometimes contain provisions requiring that a party's performance be approved by the other party or by a third person who is not a party to the contract. In such cases, the approval of the other party or the third person is a condition to the performance of one of the parties to the contract. For example, a contract for the sale of real estate may require that title be approved by an attorney. The attorney's approval is a condition precedent to the buyer's duty to purchase the property. If the attorney concludes that the seller does not have title to the property, the buyer's obligation to purchase is excused by virtue of the failure of the condition (the attorney's approval) to materialize.

A common example of a contract requiring the approval of a third party is the typical construction contract. Construction contracts frequently require outside approval of the work before the owner is obligated to pay. Usually the job must be inspected by an architect or an engineer who issues a certificate if the construction has met the specifications contained in the building plans. Until this certificate is issued, the owner has no obligation to make payment, because the certificate is a condition precedent to performance by the owner.

Just as a party's duty of performance may be conditioned upon the other party's performance being approved by a third person, so can a party's duty to perform be conditioned upon its own satisfaction with the other party's performance. That is, one of the parties may bargain that its performance will personally satisfy the other party. Although there is considerable risk to the person or firm making this kind of commitment, it is relatively common. Contracts for the sale of goods often give the purchaser the right to return the goods if not satisfied. Employment contracts for a specific period of time sometimes allow the employer to terminate employment if the employee's service is not personally satisfactory to the employer.

Because of the potential danger of forfeiture in a contract in which one party or a third party must be satisfied, courts have generally interpreted these provisions narrowly. They have consistently held that the dissatisfaction or refusal to approve must be in good faith and not left to the whim or idiosyncrasies of the interested party.

This means that the dissatisfaction is not to be feigned and must be based upon some valid reason.

For example, suppose that an artist agrees to paint a portrait of Penelope to her satisfaction. Any dissatisfaction expressed by Penelope must be made in good faith—that is, it must be an honest dissatisfaction. Proving Penelope's bad faith may be difficult because her dissatisfaction is a subjective state involving artistic taste and personal feeling. But suppose that the artist can show that Penelope expressed dissatisfaction with the portrait only after she had suffered severe financial reversals. The artist might succeed in arguing that Penelope was really responding to her changed financial condition rather than to the quality of the artist's work.

When performance can be measured against an objective standard—for example, if a reasonable person would be satisfied—the party to the contract must also be satisfied. Suppose that Bigdome, Inc. contracts to buy certain tools from Ace Tool that are to be satisfactory to Bigdome. If Ace can establish that the tools meet certain standards in Bigdome's industry—for example, that they have been calibrated according to industry standards—Bigdome's dissatisfaction will not excuse its nonpayment for the tools.

Substantial Performance and Material Breach

The normal manner in which the parties' contractual expectations will be satisfied is through complete and exact performance of the contract. This, of course, is the purpose of the bargain. As a factual matter, most contracts are fully performed and the relationships end. However, there may be a failure of performance, and the injured party must determine what remedy is available.

Substantial Performance

The most satisfactory manner of performance of contractual obligations is for both parties to perform exactly as promised. However, this is not always what happens. One party may perform erroneously as a result of misinterpreting the contract. Or exact performance may be prevented by circumstances that cannot be controlled. Clearly,

a party is entitled to the promised performance. Just as clearly, justice dictates that the injured party should not be unjustly enriched by the penalty imposed on the defaulting party.

When one party fails to render a part of the promised performance, the following questions may arise:

1. Is the other party privileged to refuse to render a reciprocal promised performance?
2. Is the other party discharged from its contractual duty?
3. Can the other party sue for damages, regarding the breach as "total"?
4. Can the other party sue for damages for a "partial" breach?

Under the older common law, an express contract had to be completed to the last detail before a party could enforce the performance of the other party. Under the newer concept of **substantial performance**, a party who has failed to provide exact performance may nevertheless enforce the performance of the other party if (1) there was substantial performance of the contract, (2) there was an honest effort to comply fully to the contract's requirements, and (3) there was no willful or intentional departure from the terms of the contract. The rationale for the substantial-performance doctrine is that justice does not demand full, literal fulfillment of contractual obligations but only substantial fulfillment.

Where one of the contracting parties has substantially performed its contractual duties, it is entitled to enforce performance by the other party. That is, the injured party may not refuse to render a reciprocal promised performance; it is not discharged from its contractual duties. However, the party that rendered substantial performance rather than exact performance is in breach of contract. The breach is a partial breach, not a material breach; nevertheless, it remains a breach of contract. Where there has been a breach of contract the injured party may sue and recover damages for the breach. Thus, although the injured party is not excused from its promised reciprocal performance, it is entitled to recover damages for the other party's failure to perform exactly as promised. If the injured party's promised performance is payment, it would be entitled to deduct from the contract price the amount that will compensate for the damages sustained.

The doctrine of substantial performance arises most commonly in construction cases. In such cases, the owner generally refuses to pay the builder full price for construction work on the ground that the building doesn't conform exactly to contract specifications. *Plante v. Jacobs*, excerpted later in the chapter, is an example of such a case. The case that follows, however, illustrates that the substantial-performance doctrine can be applied to a wide variety of situations.

RUSSELL V. SALVE REGINA COLLEGE

U.S. Court of Appeals, First Circuit
938 F.2d 315 (1991)

BACKGROUND: Sharon Russell was admitted to Salve Regina College to study nursing. She weighed 280 pounds. At the start of Russell's junior year, the college started to pressure her to lose weight. At the insistence of college officials, she joined Weight Watchers. However, she did not lose a significant amount of weight. She failed a nursing course during her junior year, for reasons, she claimed, that had to do with her weight and not her performance. Failing a course would normally have resulted in her expulsion from the nursing program, but college officials offered her a deal by which she could remain in the program if she signed a weight-loss contract. Russell signed the contract, which required her to attend Weight Watchers meetings weekly and to lose at least 2 pounds per week. Russell attended the meetings, but did not lose 2 pounds per week. In the summer after her junior year, Russell was asked to withdraw from the nursing program and did so. She sued Salve Regina, claiming that the college had breached its contractual obligation to provide her with an education. The federal district court held for Russell, and Salve Regina appealed. In the opinion excerpt below, the federal circuit court applies the law of Rhode Island.

Timbers, Circuit Judge

The district court, in its jury charge, had boiled the agreement between the parties down to one in which Russell was required to abide by disciplinary rules, pay tuition and maintain good academic standards, and the College was required to provide her with an education until graduation. The court also informed the jury that the agreement was modified by the weight-loss contract the parties signed during Russell's junior year. The jury was told that if Russell "substantially performed" her side of the bargain, the College's actions constituted a breach. The district court held that the Rhode Island Supreme Court would apply the substantial performance standard to the contract in question.

The jury found that Salve Regina had breached its contract with Russell by expelling her. . . .

On its . . . appeal to this court, Salve Regina challenged the court's application of the substantial performance doctrine to the contract between Russell and the College. . . .

The doctrine of substantial performance "is one that has played a part in the enforcement of contracts and in the statement of contract law." *Corbin on Contracts* "When a contract has been made for an agreed exchange of two performances, one of which is to be rendered first, the rendition of one substantially in full is a constructive condition precedent to the duty of the other party to render his part of the exchange."

The Rhode Island Supreme Court specifically has applied this doctrine in the construction contract context. *DiMario v. Heeks* In that case, quoting Corbin, the court explained that "the evaluation of a contractor's performance as substantial or unsubstantial is not simple but rather is 'a matter of degree,' and should be made 'relatively to all the other complex factors' in a case." . . .

In the instant case, after receiving a "substantial performance" instruction from the trial court, the jury apparently found that Russell had substantially performed her part of both the underlying matriculation agreement as well as the "side agreement" relating to her weight loss. Our task is to determine whether it was proper for the court to give the substantial performance instruction to the jury in the first instance. . . .

The facts of this case are novel. We find it unremarkable that neither the Rhode Island Supreme Court—nor, indeed, any court of which we are aware—has been confronted with a fact pattern like this one. Our plenary review of Rhode Island law, however, as well as the law of other jurisdictions, convinces us that the Rhode Island Supreme Court would have applied the doctrine of substantial performance to the instant case.

The College's arguments notwithstanding, we find no evidence that the Rhode Island Supreme Court has evinced a particularly begrudging attitude toward the doctrine of substantial performance. . . . Furthermore, although the Rhode Island Supreme Court to date has not spoken on the doctrine's applicability much beyond the building contract context, that silence reflects only the fact that the court apparently has not been faced squarely with the issue. Salve Regina can point to no case in which the Rhode Island Supreme Court has *rejected* the doctrine on the ground that its applicability is limited to construction contracts nor any language so suggesting in any of the cases where the doctrine has been applied. We have no reason to believe that that court would disagree with Professor Corbin that "[t]his problem of 'substantial performance' is involved in contracts of all kinds, contracts for the sale of land or of goods, contracts for the rendering of personal services, and contracts for manufacture and transportation, as well as for contracts for the building of buildings or for other creative construction."

The weight of authority indicates that the doctrine of substantial performance has wide applicability. Our review of Rhode Island contract law suggests that the Rhode Island Supreme Court would be inclined to follow the weight of authority.

DECISION: The circuit court of appeals affirmed the decision in favor of Russell.

Material Breach

The antithesis of substantial performance is a level of nonperformance tantamount to a material breach of contract. That is, a party who fails to perform its contractual obligation substantially is deemed to have materially breached the contract, and thereby is liable to the injured party for damages. However, a material breach carries with it a further legal consequence. The injured party is excused from rendering any reciprocal promised performance. That is, a material breach of contract by one party entitles the injured party to treat its contractual duties as discharged—any nonperformance by the innocent party is excused—and further entitles the injured party to sue and recover damages resulting from the material breach.

Whether a party's failure to perform a contractual duty exactly amounts to a material breach or substantial performance is an issue of considerable importance. The test of substantial performance is whether the performance met the essential purpose of the contract and whether the nonperformance was willful. Thus, a party who relies on the substantial-performance doctrine must show that its departure from the contract was slight and unintentional.

In the following case, the court wrestled with the problem of balancing a policy against unjust enrichment with a policy of ensuring that a party gets what the contract promises. While reading the case, keep in mind that a business firm should never enter a contract with the intention of providing only a substantial performance. That is an unethical strategy that could easily destroy the firm's reputation.

PLANTE V. JACOBS

Supreme Court of Wisconsin

103 N.W.2d 296 (1960)

BACKGROUND: Eugene Plante (plaintiff) contracted with Frank and Carol Jacobs (defendants) to construct a house according to plans and specifications. The specifications were standard printed forms with some modifications and additions written in by the parties. Although the house had essentially been completed, Jacobs refused to pay the full price because Plante had misplaced the wall between the kitchen and the living room, thus narrowing the living room by more than 1 foot. Plante sued Jacobs to recover the unpaid balance of the contract price. The trial court entered judgment for Plante in the sum of $4,152.90. The Jacobses appealed to the Supreme Court of Wisconsin.

Hallows, Justice

The defendants argue the plaintiff cannot recover any amount because he has failed to substantially perform the contract. The plaintiff conceded he failed to furnish the kitchen cabinets, gutters and down-spouts, sidewalk, closed clothes poles, and entrance seat amounting to $1,601.95. This amount was allowed to the defendants. The defendants claim some 20 other items of incomplete or faulty performance by the plaintiff and no substantial performance because the cost of completing the house in strict compliance with the plans and specifications would amount to 25 or 30 per cent of the contract price. The defendants especially stress the misplacing of the wall between the living room and the kitchen, which narrowed the living room in excess of one foot. The cost of tearing down this wall and rebuilding it would be approximately $4,000. The record is not clear why and when this wall was misplaced, but the wall is completely built and the house decorated and the defendants are living therein. Real estate experts testified that the smaller width of the living room would not affect the market price of the house.

The defendants rely on *Manitowoc Steam Boiler Works v. Manitowoc Glue Co.* for the proposition there can be no recovery on the contract unless there is substantial performance. . . . The test of what amounts to substantial performance seems to be whether the performance meets the essential purpose of the contract.

Substantial performance as applied to construction of a house does not mean that every detail must be in strict compliance with the specifications and the plans. Something less than perfection is the test of specific performance unless all details are made the essence of the contract. This was not done here. There may be situations in which features or details of construction of special or of great personal importance, which if not performed, would prevent a finding of substantial performance of the contract. In this case the plan was a stock floor plan. No detailed construction of the house was shown on the plan. There were no blueprints. The specifications were standard printed forms with some modifications and additions written in by the parties. Many of the problems that arose during the construction had to be solved on the basis of practical experience. No mathematical rule relating to the percentage of the price, of cost of completion or of completeness can be laid down to determine substantial performance of a building contract. Although the defendants received a house with which they are dissatisfied in many respects, the trial court was not in error in finding the contract was substantially performed.

The next question is what is the amount of recovery when the plaintiff has substantially, but incompletely, performed. For substantial performance the plaintiff should recover the contract price less the damages caused the defendant by the incomplete performance.

Both parties agree *Venzke v. Magdanz* states the correct rule for damages due to faulty construction amounting to such incomplete performance, which is the difference between the value of the house [with the defects and its value] if it had been constructed in strict accordance with the plans and specifications. This is the diminished-value rule. The cost of replacement or repair is not the measure of such damage, but is an element to take into consideration in arriving at value under some circumstances. The cost of replacement or the cost to make whole the omissions may equal or be less than the difference in value in some cases and, likewise, the cost to rectify a defect may greatly exceed the added value to the structure as corrected. The defendants argue that under the *Venzke* rule their damages are $10,000. The plaintiff on review argues the defendants' damages are only $650. . . .

The trial court applied the cost-of-repair or replacement rule as to several items, relying on *Stern v. Schlafer,* wherein it was stated that when there are a number of small items of defect or omission which can be remedied without the reconstruction of a substantial part of the building or a great sacrifice of work or material already wrought in the building, the reasonable cost of correcting the defect should be allowed. However, in *Mohs v. Quarton* the court held when the separation of defects would lead to confusion, the rule of diminished value could apply to all defects.

In this case no such confusion arises in separating the defects. The trial court disallowed certain claimed defects because they were not proven. This finding was not against the great weight and clear preponderance of the evidence and will not be disturbed on appeal. Of the remaining defects claimed by the defendants, the court allowed the cost of replacement or repair except as to the misplacement of the living room wall. Whether a defect should fall under the cost-of-replacement rule or be considered under the diminished-value rule depends upon the nature and magnitude of the defect. This court has not allowed items of such magnitude under the cost-of-repair rule as the trial court did. Viewing the construction of the house as a whole and its cost we cannot say, however, that the trial court was in error in allowing the cost of repairing the plaster cracks in the ceilings, the cost of mud jacking and repairing the patio floor, and the cost of reconstructing the non-weight-bearing and nonstructural patio wall. Such reconstruction did not involve an unreasonable economic waste.

The item of misplacing the living room wall under the facts of this case was clearly under the diminished-value rule. . . . To tear down the wall now and rebuild it in the proper place would involve a substantial destruction of the work, if not all of it, which was put into the wall and would cause additional damage to other parts of the house and require replastering and redecorating the walls and ceilings of at least two rooms. Such economic waste is unreasonable and unjustified.

DECISION: The Supreme Court of Wisconsin affirmed the trial court judgment in favor of Plante.

Sale of Goods

In contracts for the sale of goods, the doctrine of substantial performance is not applicable. Both case law and statute require the seller to make what is often referred to as "perfect tender." In one case, a federal court stated that "there is no room in commercial contracts for the doctrine of substantial performance." Section 2-601 of the Uniform Commercial Code states that "if the goods or the tender of delivery fail in any respect to conform to the contract, the buyer may (a) reject the whole; or (b) accept the whole; or (c) accept any commercial unit or units and reject the rest."

Several other provisions of the UCC, however, ameliorate the harsh effect of the perfect-tender rule. The buyer who rejects goods as nonconforming must disclose the nature of the defect to the seller. The seller is then entitled to a reasonable time to "cure the defect." If the buyer accepts a tender of goods, it cannot revoke that acceptance if there has been substantial performance in good faith. A similar rule applies in installment contracts, where the buyer may reject any installment only "if the non-conformity substantially impairs the value of that installment and cannot be cured."

Time of Performance

Contracts often stipulate a time by which performance must be completed. A common example is a contract for goods that states the date upon which delivery will be made. Sometimes the time of performance is important to the parties. In other instances, performance by a particular time, even though stated in the agreement, really does not make much difference.

Ordinarily, unless the nature of a contract is such as to make performance by an exact date vital, failure of a party to perform on or before the agreed-upon day does not discharge the duty of the other party. This rule may be viewed as simply an application of the substantial-performance doctrine to the time-of-performance issue. Contracts for the sale of real estate usually come within this rule. If a real estate contract sets a closing date of February 15, the inability of the buyer to close because the necessary financing has not been approved does not excuse the seller from performing. The buyer would be able to enforce the contract later, but the seller would be entitled to interest on the purchase price from the originally scheduled closing date as well as actual damages, if any, that could be proved.

Some courts say that time is always of the essence in contracts for the sale of goods. This means that if a seller misses the date upon which delivery has been promised even by a day or two, the buyer has the right to refuse delivery and sue for damages. Although it is true that delay is more apt to be fatal in contracts for the sale of goods, not every delay will discharge the other party of its contractual duties. In most jurisdictions, the courts will weigh all aspects of the situation before determining whether time was of the essence even in a contract for the sale of goods.

If performance on or before a particular time is important to one or both parties, they should include a provision in the contract that clearly indicates this. Ordinarily this is indicated by the words "time is of the essence." A statement of this kind is often included in contracts. To be of any value, the statement must indicate clearly which part of the performance is of the essence of the agreement.

If the parties do not agree specifically that time is of the essence, then determining whether it is in a particular situation requires consideration of the circumstances. A wholesaler who promises delivery to a retailer before April 1 and knows that the retailer plans a major advertising campaign to begin April 1 would have to perform on or before that date, even though the contract did not include a "time is of the essence" clause. If the situation, the subject matter of the contract, or a clearly written provision that time is of the essence makes time a material factor, performance by that time is essential. Late performance can be rejected even though benefit has been conferred, and the injured party can refuse to meet its own commitment as well as sue for damages.

Discharge of Contractual Obligations

One question that managers must frequently deal with is whether a contractual obligation has terminated. Sometimes management is concerned with this question because it believes that a performance to which the firm is entitled has not been completed. In other situations, the question is whether the firm has met its own contractual commitments.

When a contract is said to be *discharged*, one or more of the legal relations of the parties have been terminated. Most commonly this means that the legal duty of one of the parties has been terminated. A party who is under a legal duty by virtue of his or her contract may assert that the duty has been "discharged" by some event that has occurred since the making of the contract.

Seldom are all the legal relations of the contracting parties terminated at the same time. A party may be discharged from further contractual duty, by an act of the other party or some other event, and continue to retain all the rights, powers, and privileges that he or she possessed. It is indeed possible for all the contractual obligations to be terminated at once, as where contract duties are discharged by the agreement of the parties.

Contract duties may be discharged in a variety of ways. Some of these have already been discussed, although not in the context of discharge. The following discussion focuses on the primary methods of discharge.

Discharge by Complete Performance

The most obvious method of discharge of a contractual duty is by complete performance. Most contracts are discharged in this way. Complete performance means full and exact performance—not only of the character, quality, and amount required, but also within the time agreed upon.

Discharge by Occurrence of a Condition Subsequent

As mentioned earlier, a condition subsequent is an event that terminates a present duty of performance. If a condition subsequent occurs, it discharges a duty of performance. Because of their potentially harsh effect, conditions subsequent expressed in a contract are narrowly construed by the courts.

Discharge by Mutual Agreement

Rescission   A contract still executory on both sides may be discharged by an express agreement that it shall no longer bind either party. Such an agreement, called **mutual rescission**, is itself a contract to discharge a prior contract. Its purpose is to restore the parties to the positions they occupied before entering into the first contract.

Substitution of New Contract   A contract may be discharged by the substitution of a new contract. The difference between discharge by a substituted contract and discharge by rescission is that a rescission is a total obliteration of the contract, whereas a substitution provides a new contract in place of the old one. Discharge by substitution results by expressly substituting a new contract for the old one or by making a new contract inconsistent with the old one, with new terms agreed upon by both sides.

Novation   A contract duty of a party may be discharged by the substitution of a new party for one of the original parties. Such a substitution is known as a **novation**. In a novation a new contract is created whose terms are the same as the old contract's but whose parties are different. For a novation to be valid, all three parties must agree to the substitution. A novation need not be of express agreement. It may arise from the conduct of the parties indicating acquiescence in a change of liability.

Discharge by Impossibility of Performance

After a contract has been formed, but prior to full performance, an event may occur that makes performance by one of the parties difficult, unprofitable, impracticable, or impossible or that frustrates the very purpose for which one of parties entered into the contract. Given this state of affairs, the party who views its own performance as no longer desirable may be expected not to perform its contractual obligation, and the other party may be expected to sue, claiming such nonperformance to be a breach of contract. When a party is sued for nonperformance, it may defend on the basis that supervening events made its performance impossible or that the purpose for which it made the contract had become frustrated. Before examining what constitutes discharge by impossibility or frustration of purpose, it may prove helpful to view the question as one of how the risks of loss should be distributed. That is, when some supervening event makes a party's performance impossible, the legal and policy problem that is presented is: Who should bear the risk of loss occasioned by the occurrence of the unexpected event? Thus, the role of the contract in society may be seen as an allocation of the risks of loss, and the rules regarding discharge by reason of impossibility provide an example of how the courts fashion rules allocating the risks of loss in a manner that best serves society and reflects the presumed intent of the parties where the parties have failed to state their intent precisely.

Risk of Loss   Fundamental questions of public policy are involved in many cases in which the issue of discharge of contractual obligation and its relationship to performance are considered. These policies, although often at the root of the problem as well as the solution, are generally not discussed in the opinions. A basic premise of Anglo-American contract law is that competent adults should be allowed freely to enter contracts for legitimate purposes. Connected to this premise of freedom of contract is the notion that a person should not be discharged from contractual obligations unless these commitments have been carried out exactly as promised. The emphasis given to freedom of contract and the attendant obligation to perform are reasons that contracting is used as a means of allocating many types of risks. The possibility of fluctuating price is a risk involved in many contracts. Consider a typical business agreement, tens of thousands of which are made each year. The manager of the student dining service contracts with National Dairy to have delivered to the main dining hall at the university 1,500 pints of milk each day during October at $0.08 per pint. She has accepted the risk that the market price of milk will decrease as well as numerous other risks incident to disposing of the milk. The dairy has accepted the risk of a price increase and numerous risks incident to delivery.

The bargaining underlying decisions to assume particular risks is influenced by factors such as economic power, friendship, persuasiveness, and habit. Although these and other considerations are important, the major element in arm's-length negotiations is the decision makers' anticipation and evaluation of events that might affect their ability to perform. In some transactions, however, events occur that neither were anticipated by the parties nor could reasonably have been contemplated when they made the agreement. These events often create new or different risks that materially affect the ability of a party to perform.

This can be illustrated by the oil embargo imposed by Arab nations in 1973. Manufacturers dependent upon oil found costs of production substantially increased. Many were parties to contracts made when the price of oil was low. In agreeing to sell at a particular price, they had assumed a risk under conditions that were reasonably well known. The new conditions were not only different but were also unexpected.

If performance is prevented or becomes more costly because of unexpected new conditions, what should the law's position be? Must a promise be fulfilled insofar as possible even if the result is a crushing loss to one party and a windfall profit to the other? Or should the party who will suffer because of the unexpected new conditions be allowed to avoid performance at the expense of the other who has relied upon the promised performance and given something in exchange for it? This question arises in many cases and is frequently answered only with great difficulty. The court must balance the desirability of enforcing agreements freely made against the injustice of requiring a party to suffer losses of which the risks could not have been foreseen.

Strict or Objective Impossibility The early common law of contract disregarded unanticipated events and required a party to carry out a promised performance in spite of the fact that it was more difficult, expensive, or demanding than either party had contemplated when the agreement was made. A promise was considered absolute. If it was impossible to perform, the defaulting party was required to pay damages.

This doctrine was so harsh that in a number of common situations the courts began to excuse a promisor on grounds that performance had literally become impossible. This became known as the **doctrine of impossibility**. Although this interfered with voluntarily assumed risk allocations, justice and fair play clearly supported the courts' position.

Thus, the rule developed that if, after a contract has been formed but before full performance, some unforeseeable event occurs that makes performance objectively impossible, the promisor's duty to perform is discharged. By "objectively impossible" the courts mean that no person could legally or physically perform the contract. If the event that arises makes performance impossible only for the particular promisor, it is merely a subjective impossibility and is insufficient to discharge the promisor's duty of performance. Objective impossibility has been found in the following three circumstances: (1) the death or serious illness of a promisor whose personal performance is required, (2) a change of law making the promised performance illegal, and (3) the destruction of the subject matter of the contract.

Commercial Impracticability and Frustration of Purpose The trend in the law is toward an enlargement of the definition of impossibility. As a result, a fourth circumstance has been frequently allowed in recent years: where impossibility is due to the existence of a certain state of affairs, the nonoccurrence of which was a basic assumption on which the contract was made. "Impossibility" is probably an inappropriate word to use in such circumstances. Thus, courts have used the terms *commercial impracticability* and *frustration of purpose* to describe such a circumstance. The two concepts are different but closely related.

The concept of **commercial impracticability** describes a situation where a party claims that some circumstance has made its own performance impracticable. Performance may be impracticable because extreme and unreasonable difficulty, expense, injury, or loss to one of the parties will occur. A severe shortage of raw materials or of supplies, due to war, embargo, local crop failure, unforeseen shutdown of major sources of supply, or the like, which either causes a marked increase in cost or prevents performance altogether may constitute impracticability.

The concept of **frustration of purpose** deals with a situation that arises when a change in circumstances makes one party's performance virtually worthless to the other, frustrating its purpose in making the contract. Frustration of purpose differs from commercial impracticability in that there is no impediment to performance by either party. For the concept of frustration of purpose to excuse a party's nonperformance, the purpose that is frustrated must have been a principal purpose of the party in making the contract, the frustration must be substantial, and the nonoccurrence of the frustrating event must have been a basic assumption on which the contract was made.

The *Second Restatement of Contracts* has endorsed both the concept of commercial impracticability (Section 261) and the concept of frustration of purpose (Section 265). The revisers of the *Restatement* were influenced by UCC Section 2-615, which excuses a seller from making timely delivery when the seller's performance has become commercially impracticable "by the occurrence of a contingency the nonoccurrence of which was a basic assumption on which the contract was made. . . ."

The following case concerns the application of UCC 2-615.

MISHARA CONSTRUCTION CO. V. TRANSIT MIXED CONCRETE CO.

Supreme Judicial Court of Massachusetts
310 N.E.2d 363 (1974)

BACKGROUND: Mishara Construction Co. (plaintiff) was the general contractor for a construction project. It contracted with the Transit Mixed Concrete Co. (defendant) to supply all the ready-mixed concrete needed for the project. Under the contract, Mishara was to specify the dates and amounts of deliveries. In April 1967, a labor dispute stopped work on the project. Work resumed in June, but the workers maintained their picket line for 2 more years. Transit Mixed Concrete made few deliveries during the 2-year period, and Mishara had to obtain concrete from other sources. Mishara sued for damages as a result of Transit's delays and the higher cost of purchasing concrete elsewhere. Transit defended on the basis of impossibility of performance. The trial court entered judgment for Transit. Mishara appealed to the Supreme Judicial Court of Massachusetts.

Reardon, Justice

We are asked to decide as matter of law and without reference to individual facts and circumstances that "picket lines, strikes or labor difficulties" provide no excuse for nonperformance by way of impossibility. This is too sweeping a statement of the law and we decline to adopt it.

The excuse of impossibility in contracts for the sale of goods is controlled by the appropriate section of the Uniform Commercial Code, §2-615. That section sets up two requirements before performance may be excused. First, the performance must have become "impracticable." Second, the impracticability must have been caused "by the occurrence of a contingency the non-occurrence of which was a basic assumption on which the contract was made." This section of the Uniform Commercial Code has not yet been interpreted by this court. Therefore it is appropriate to discuss briefly the significance of these two criteria.

With respect to the requirement that performance must have been impracticable, the official Code comment to the section stresses that the reference is to "commercial impracticability" as opposed to strict impossibility. This is not a radical departure from the common law of contracts as interpreted by this court. Although a strict rule was originally followed denying any excuse for accident of "inevitable necessity," it has long been assumed that circumstances drastically increasing the difficulty and expense of the contemplated performance may be within the compass of "impossibility." By adopting the term "impracticability" rather than "impossibility" the drafters of the Code appear to be in accord with Professor Williston who stated that "the essence of the modern defense of impossibility is that the promised performance was at the making of the contract, or thereafter became, impracticable owing to some extreme or unreasonable difficulty, expense, injury, or loss involved, rather than it is scientifically or actually impossible."

The second criterion of the excuse, that the intervening circumstance be one which the parties assumed would not occur, is also familiar to the law of Massachusetts. The rule is essentially aimed at the distribution of certain kinds of risks in the contractual relationship. By directing the inquiry to the time when the contract was first made, we really seek to determine whether the risk of the intervening circumstance was one which the parties may be taken to have assigned between themselves. It is, of course, the very essence of contract that it is directed at the elimination of some risks for each party in exchange for others. Each receives the certainty of price, quantity, and time, and assumes the risk of changing market prices, superior opportunity, or added costs. It is implicit in the doctrine of impossibility (and the companion rule of "frustration of purpose") that certain risks are so unusual and have such severe consequences that they must have been beyond the scope of the assignment of risks inherent in the contract, that is, beyond the agreement made by the parties. To require performance in that case would be to grant the promisee an advantage for which he could not be said to have bargained in making the contract. "The important question is whether an unanticipated circumstance has made performance of the promise vitally different from what should reasonably have been within the contemplation of both parties when they entered into the contract. If so, the risk should not fairly be thrown upon the promisor." . . .

With this backdrop, we consider Mishara's contention that a labor dispute which makes performance more difficult never constitutes an excuse for nonperformance. We think it is evident that in some situations a labor dispute would not meet the requirements for impossibility discussed above. A picket line might constitute a mere inconvenience and hardly make performance "impracticable." Likewise, in certain industries with a long record of labor difficulties, the nonoccurrence of strikes and picket lines could not fairly be said to be a basic assumption of the agreement. Certainly, in general, labor disputes cannot be considered extraordinary in the course of modern commerce. Admitting this, however, we are still far from the proposition implicit in the plaintiff's requests. Much must depend on the facts known to the parties at the time of contracting with respect to the history of and prospects for labor difficulties during the period of performance of the contract, as well as the likely severity of the effect of such disputes on the ability to perform. From these facts it is possible to draw an inference as to whether or not the parties intended performance to be carried out even in the face of the labor difficulty. Where the probability of a labor dispute appears to be practically nil, and where the occurrence of such a dispute provides unusual difficulty, the excuse of impracticability might well be applicable. Thus in discussing the defense of impossibility, then Chief Judge Cardozo noted an excuse would be provided "conceivably in some circumstances by unavoidable strikes." The many variables which may bear on the question in individual cases were canvassed by Professor Williston in Williston, Contracts (Rev. ed.) § 1951A (1938), and he concluded that the trend of the law is toward recognizing strikes as excuses for nonperformance. We agree with the statement of the judge in Badhwar v. Colorado Fuel & Iron Corp. on the same question: "Rather than mechanically apply any fixed rule of law, where the parties themselves have not allocated responsibility, justice is better served by appraising all of the circumstances, the part the various parties played, and thereon determining liability."

DECISION: The Supreme Judicial Court of Massachusetts affirmed the trial court judgment for Transit.

Discharge by Breach of Contract

A contract is breached when a party under a present duty of performance fails to perform. As already discussed, a material breach of contract by one party discharges the injured party from any further duty of performance. A partial or minor breach of contract does not operate as a discharge but does render the breaching party liable for the injuries sustained by the innocent party as a result of the breach.

Anticipatory Breach   In most instances, breach of contract occurs only after performance is due. Sometimes, however, a party to a contract repudiates a commitment to perform before the time that performance is required. This is known as an **anticipatory breach**. An anticipatory breach raises the questions whether the other party is immediately discharged from its contractual obligations and whether it can seek a remedy immediately.

Most courts allow immediate action as if the entire contract had been broken. This is justified upon the grounds that the repudiation has destroyed the good-faith relationship upon which successful performance of the contract is based and that simple justice should allow a party to take immediate action to protect its expectations.

Repudiation must be clear and unequivocal. A statement by one of the parties indicating doubt as to ability to perform or even doubt as to whether it wants to is not an anticipatory breach. Repudiation does not have to be verbal. An act is sufficient if it clearly indicates an intent not to perform in the future. A party who prevents another from performing an act that is necessary to carrying out the agreement has committed an anticipatory breach. Some courts have held that voluntary or involuntary bankruptcy is the equivalent of anticipatory breach.

When the other party to a contract has repudiated prior to performance, a firm has several options. It may treat the entire contract as broken and sue immediately for damages without complying further with its own obligations. Assume A and B have entered into an agreement in which A agrees to move a house for B. B has promised to

---

PREVENTIVE LAW
Dealing with the "Impossible" Situation

As seen by the discussion of the defense of impossibility earlier, the trend recently has been toward a liberal definition of the term "impossibility." The concept of commercial impracticability has been recognized by many jurisdictions and is included in the Uniform Commercial Code.

Despite the trend toward expanding the situations that give rise to a discharge due to impossibility or impracticability, it is better to address this issue in a written contract than let a court determine whether a given situation will result in the discharge of a contractual duty. When a party to a contract anticipates a risk, its consequences can be limited by contractual provisions. For example, the parties might agree to excuse a late delivery if delivery is prevented by a railroad strike or by inclement weather. Many types of insurance are also used by firms to protect themselves from some of the risks incident to contract.

pay A $3,000 for the job and obtain all necessary permits and road clearances. If A repudiates the agreement, it is not necessary for B to obtain the permits and clearances prior to bringing suit.

The firm may choose to ignore the repudiation and wait until performance is due before taking any action, or it may rescind the agreement and sue to recover anything it has furnished under the contract.

In goods transactions, reasonable grounds for insecurity give rise to the right to demand assurance of performance, and the failure to give such assurance is a repudiation according to Section 2-609 of the UCC. Under Section 2-610, repudiation may be treated as an immediate breach.

Remedies

As we noted in earlier chapters, a major function of contract law is to assure that people's expectations based upon commitments made by others are met. Businesses must be able to plan future operations effectively. Private individuals also, in our complicated world, must plan for the future if they are to live satisfactory lives. Because both business and personal planning often are based upon commitments from others, methods of inducing people to honor their agreements are of major importance to society.

Legal remedies are available to enforce legal promises. Even if the parties pay little conscious attention to what will happen if a promise is broken, the underlying threat of legal recourse has an impact. In this section, we explore some of the remedies provided by the law to induce contractual performance and list them in Table 19-1.

The courts usually do not require a party actually to perform a breached promise. They offer several reasons for this reluctance. First, because agreements often are for long periods of time, the courts feel that continuous supervision of performance would be a difficult, if not impossible, burden. Second, the courts fear that they would become involved in disputes over whether the terms of the agreement were being met. A party ordered to perform might do as little as it could get away with. The other party would raise objections to this minimal performance, with the court being required to settle recurring differences. Finally, in some cases, a court decree ordering a person to perform would verge on involuntary servitude.

Dollar Damages

As a result of judicial reluctance to order actual performance, contract law attempts to compensate the injured party by requiring monetary damages from defaulting parties. The general objective of damages is to place the injured party in the position it would have been in had the agreement been carried out. For example, if a firm has contracted to buy 1,000 units at $6 for delivery on January 15, and the units are not delivered, the buyer has a right to obtain the units elsewhere. If the market price is now $6.50, the buyer may be awarded damages of $500, the additional amount that had to be paid to obtain 1,000 units. Then the buyer is placed in the position it would have been in under the contract. In both instances, the buyer has to pay at least $6,000, so this amount is not part of its damages.

TABLE **19-1**

Concept Summary	Remedies for Breach of Contract
Contractual Remedies	**When Available**
Money	Generally available
Specific performance	Only if the payment of monetary damages is not an adequate remedy
Injunction	In personal service contracts, if a person agreed to exclusively serve the plaintiff and to enforce ancillary agreements
Rescission	In cases involving fraud, duress, undue influence, and mistake
Restitution	If a contract has been canceled, a party has been unjustly enriched or benefited from an unenforceable contract, and if there has been mistaken payment of money

In most cases, damages cover reasonably anticipated losses and expenses as well as any gains and profits that might have been made. This rule, although easily stated, is often complex in application and leads to many legal problems.

The Reasonable Anticipation Standard The defaulting party is responsible for those damages that a reasonable person could foresee at the time the contract was made. In the often cited English case of *Hadley v. Baxendale*, a mill was shut down because of a broken shaft. The mill owner delivered the shaft to a cartage (transportation) company that promised to return it in 3 days. When the shaft was not returned in 3 days as promised, the mill owner sued for the profits lost during the additional period that the mill was closed. The appellate court refused to allow the plaintiff to recover the lost profits, contending that it was not reasonable to anticipate that a mill would be closed completely because of a broken shaft.

Although the defendant is responsible only for reasonably foreseeable losses, anticipation of a *particular* loss is unnecessary. Responsibility extends to that which a reasonable person would know in the ordinary course of events. It also extends to knowledge of special circumstances that could result in larger than ordinary loss.

Certainty Closely related and often overlapping the rule that an injured party is entitled to compensation only for losses that could reasonably have been foreseen is the additional requirement that damages be certain, not speculative nor uncertain. The plaintiff must establish that a particular loss was caused by the breach and that the amount lost actually can be calculated.

A problem about the certainty of the relationship between breach and loss arises when the defendant can show that intervening factors might have been responsible for plaintiff's loss. Ordinarily, the relationship is a known fact. If a jury finds that the breach was the "primary" or "chief" cause of the loss, the loss is part of the damage award.

Difficult problems also arise out of the need for certainty in the actual calculation of damages. Courts generally have not equated *certainty* with *absolute exactness*. In fact, they appear to have been more concerned with the need for certainty in allowing an award of damages than they are with certainty in calculating the actual amount to be awarded. Over the years, courts in commercial cases have increasingly admitted the testimony of expert witnesses who analyze business records and market summaries to satisfy the certainty requirement. One difficult question for the courts has been whether a defaulting defendant should be responsible for the loss of future profits stemming from a particular contract. Although most jurisdictions allow an injured party to collect anticipated profits if a contract is breached with a business in operation, the rule appears to be different when the business is new or being planned. In these cases, the plaintiff is not entitled to anticipated profits.

The following case illustrates the application of the reasonable anticipation standard.

STIFFT'S JEWELERS V. OLIVER
Supreme Court of Arkansas
678 S.W.2d 372 (1984)

BACKGROUND: Charles and Mary Oliver, a married couple, and their daughter Grace (plaintiffs-appellees) lived in Batesville, Arkansas; and Stifft's Jewelers (defendant-appellant) was a Little Rock company engaged in the business of selling and repairing jewelry. On June 26, 1982, Mrs. Oliver brought three rings to Stifft's to be repaired. The rings were a .70 carat marquise diamond, which was Mrs. Oliver's engagement ring; a one-third carat diamond, which Mr. Oliver's mother had willed to Grace Oliver; and a one-fourth carat garnet, which had originally belonged to Mrs. Oliver's grandmother. The value of the three rings was approximately $3,800.

On the same day, Mr. Oliver purchased a 1-carat diamond ring as an anniversary gift for Mrs. Oliver. Stifft's agreed to mail all four rings after the repairs and proper cleaning were completed. The Olivers received a package in the mail from Stifft's that only contained the anniversary ring. When contacted by the Olivers, Stifft's maintained that all four rings were placed in the same box.

The Olivers sued Stifft's, seeking the replacement cost of the rings plus $50,000 in sentimental value. At trial, the jury returned a verdict in favor of the Olivers for $4,000 replacement cost and $4,000 for sentimental value. Stifft's Jewelers appealed the award of $4,000 for sentimental value to the Supreme Court of Arkansas.

Hollingsworth, Justice

This appeal is from the judgment of $4,000 in sentimental value in favor of the Olivers.

The question here is the amount of damages that can be established with reasonable certainty under the facts of this case. Since there was a market value established for the rings, we must now determine whether a special or sentimental value is greater than the market value, and what the parties understood their obligations to be. We look to our holding in *Morrow, et al v. First National Bank of Hot Springs,* for guidance. There we reaffirmed the adoption of the "tacit agreement test" for the recovery of special damages for a breach of contract. We stated: "By that test the plaintiff must prove more than the defendant's mere knowledge that a breach of contract will entail special damages to the plaintiff. It must also appear that the defendant at least tacitly agreed to assume responsibility."

Here the appellees have not pointed out where the appellant company was made aware of the sentimental value of the rings. Neither do they show any tacit agreement by appellant to assume responsibility.

There could be circumstances where the value of the property is primarily sentimental and the jury could determine that value, provided there was a tacit agreement by the parties. However, the circumstances do not exist here because no tacit agreement was made and the alleged sentimental value of the lost rings is so highly speculative in this case that it was not a proper element of damages for consideration by the jury.

DECISION: The Supreme Court of Arkansas ruled in favor of Stifft's Jewelers and struck the award of $4,000 for sentimental value.

Mitigation of Damages A person injured by breach of contract has a right to recover losses that are reasonably predictable and relatively certain. The injured party, however, must limit these losses as much as possible. An injured party cannot allow damages to accumulate and then collect all that has been lost. The injured party cannot continue to perform when the other party is in default and then recover the full contract price.

The obligation of the injured party to keep losses as low as possible is known as **mitigation of damages**. If opportunities to mitigate damages are available and plaintiff has not taken advantage of them, the court subtracts from any award the amount by which the plaintiff could have minimized his or her own losses.

The mitigation requirement forces the injured party to make many decisions if the contract is breached. An employee who has a contract but is fired must secure comparable employment elsewhere if possible. This requirement raises several questions. Is any employment paying the same amount comparable? Suppose a potential job involves moving to an area that the injured party does not like. Is the employment comparable?

A difficult mitigation decision for a manufacturer occurs when a buyer repudiates an agreement during the manufacturing of special items. The manufacturer-seller may have invested heavily in parts and materials necessary for the job. Managers must decide if the buyer's losses will be less if the firm immediately halts production and sells the partially completed merchandise for salvage or if it completes the contract and sells the finished merchandise on the market. The UCC allows the manufacturer to do either as long as it uses "reasonable commercial judgment."

The following case illustrates some of the possible ramifications of mitigation decisions.

PARKER V. TWENTIETH CENTURY FOX FILM CORPORATION

Supreme Court of California

474 P.2d 689 (1970)

BACKGROUND: Shirley MacLaine Parker (plaintiff), a well-known actress, was under contract with Twentieth Century Fox Film Corporation (defendant) to play the female lead in the film company's musical, *Bloomer Girl*. Parker was to be paid a minimum "guaranteed compensation" of $53,571.42 per week for 14 weeks for a total of $750,000. Before beginning production, Twentieth Century Fox notified Parker of its decision not to produce the movie and offered her instead the lead role in a western, *Big Country, Big Man*. Unlike *Bloomer Girl*, which was to be filmed in California, *Big Country, Big Man* was to be filmed in Australia. Additionally, the right of approval over the director and screenplay, which was granted to Parker under her original contract, was to be omitted from any contract that she would sign to work in *Big Country, Big Man*. Parker refused the offer and sued to recover the agreed compensation. The trial court awarded judgment for Parker. Twentieth Century Fox appealed to the Supreme Court of California.

Burke, Justice

[D]efendant's sole defense to this action which resulted from its deliberate breach of contract is that in rejecting defendant's substitute offer of employment plaintiff unreasonably refused to mitigate damages.

The general rule is that the measure of recovery by a wrongfully discharged employee is the amount of salary agreed upon for the period of service, less the amount which the employer affirmatively proves the employee has earned or with reasonable effort might have earned from other employment. However, before projected earnings from other employment opportunities not sought or accepted by the discharged employee can be applied in mitigation, the employer must show that the other employment was comparable, or substantially similar, to that of which the employee has been deprived; the employee's rejection of or failure to seek other available employment of a different or inferior kind may not be resorted to in order to mitigate damages.

In the present case defendant has raised no issue of *reasonableness of efforts* by plaintiff to obtain other employment; the sole issue is whether plaintiff's refusal of defendant's substitute offer of "Big Country" may be used in mitigation. Nor, if the "Big Country" offer was of employment different or inferior when compared with the original "Bloomer Girl" employment, is there an issue as to whether or not plaintiff acted reasonably in refusing the substitute offer. Despite defendant's arguments to the contrary, no case cited or which our research has discovered holds or suggests that reasonableness is an element of a wrongfully discharged employee's option to reject, or fail to seek, different or inferior employment lest the possible earnings therefrom be charged against him in mitigation of damages.

Applying the foregoing rules to the record in the present case, with all intendments in favor of the party opposing the summary judgment motion—here, defendant—it is clear that the trial court correctly ruled that plaintiff's failure to accept defendant's tendered substitute employment could not be applied in mitigation of damages because the offer of the "Big Country" lead was of employment both different and inferior, and that no factual dispute was presented on that issue. The mere circumstances that "Bloomer Girl" was to be a musical revue calling upon plaintiff's talents as a dancer as well as an actress, and was to be produced in the City of Los Angeles, whereas "Big Country" was a straight dramatic role in a "Western Type" story taking place in an opal mine in Australia, demonstrates the difference in kind between the two employments; the female lead as a dramatic actress in a western style motion picture can by no stretch of imagination be considered the equivalent of or substantially similar to the lead in a song-and-dance production.

Additionally, the substitute "Big Country" offer proposed to eliminate or impair the director and screenplay approvals accorded to plaintiff under the original "Bloomer Girl" contract, and thus constituted an offer of inferior employment. No expertise or judicial notice is required in order to hold that the deprivation or infringement of an employee's rights held under an original employment contract converts the available "other employment" relied upon by the employer to mitigate damages, into inferior employment which the employee need not seek or accept.

DECISION: The Supreme Court of California affirmed the trial court judgment in favor of Parker.

Liquidated Damages Some contracts include a provision in which the parties agree on an amount of compensation for the injured party if there is a breach. This is known as a **liquidated damages clause**. Generally, when negotiating, the parties do not concern themselves with the effects of a breach. They are primarily interested in performance and its costs and benefits. But in some instances, the results of a breach are an important part of the bargain. This consideration often is important in contracts involving large sums of money, in which the time of completion is highly important, or when the amount of loss in the event of breach is unclear.

In other cases, one of the parties may think that liquidated damages will force the other to perform. If that party has superior bargaining power, the other party might agree to pay damages that would exceed any likely loss. When liquidated damages are not reasonably related to loss, they are not damages, but rather a penalty that violates the underlying concept of damages—that is, to place the injured party in the position it would have been in had the contract been performed. Courts therefore have been unwilling to accept liquidated damage provisions that penalize the defaulting party. They do not recognize a provision that is not reasonably related to losses.

The UCC (Section 2-718) provides:

Damages for breach by either party may be liquidated in the agreement but only at an amount which is reasonable in the light of the anticipated or actual harm caused by

the breach, the difficulties of proof of loss, and the inconvenience or *nonfeasibility* of otherwise obtaining an adequate remedy. A term fixing unreasonably large liquidated damages is void as a penalty.

Punitive Damages **Punitive damage**, or exemplary damages are those that exceed the injured party's loss. In tort cases, they are often a substantial portion of the plaintiff's recovery. The primary purpose of punitive damages is to deter the defendant and others from the type of act that caused the loss. Punitive damages are seldom awarded in contract cases. In those few instances in which they have been awarded, plaintiffs have been able to prove something akin to fraud, recklessness, or malice.

Recently some courts have allowed punitive awards in contract cases in which the plaintiff was a consumer, or at least a "little guy" with limited bargaining power, and the defendant, a party with greater bargaining power, acted outrageously or oppressively.

Specific Performance

Although Anglo-American law generally awards damages to a party against whom there has been a breach, under some circumstances, the courts require the defaulting party actually to perform the promised act. This remedy for breach is referred to as **specific performance**. The governing principle is that specific performance is required when payment of damages would not adequately or completely compensate the injured party. A contract promise to pay money ordinarily is not enforced specifically because the damage remedy is considered adequate.

Whether the damage remedy is adequate depends to a large extent upon the facts of the particular case. The courts generally have held that damages are inadequate in two types of cases. First are those cases in which the subject matter of the contract is unique. Unusual items of personal property, such as antiques and original paintings, clearly fall into this category. Money is not considered an adequate replacement for a prized heirloom. Second are cases involving the sale of real estate. Because of land's economic importance, the courts historically have assumed that every piece of land is unique. As a result, contracts for the sale of real estate almost inevitably can be enforced specifically. Real estate agreements are the subject matter that is most commonly involved in actions for specific performance.

Other types of agreements that courts have considered unique pervade economic activity. They include contracts to sell a business, to issue a policy of insurance, to repurchase corporate stock, to act as a surety, to execute a written instrument, and even, in some instances, to lend money. In these and similar cases, if the defendant can show that the plaintiff has an adequate remedy at law, specific performance is not granted.

The UCC (Section 2-716) provides that in goods transactions, "Specific performance may be decreed where the goods are unique or in other proper circumstances." The Official Comment on this section states:

> The present section continues in general prior policy as to specific performance. . . . However, without intending to impair in any way the exercise of the court's sound discretion in the matter, this article seeks to further a more liberal attitude than some courts have shown in connection with the specific performance of contracts of sale.

Under the UCC, if a buyer cannot readily find substitute goods in the market, the buyer is entitled to an award of specific performance, although the goods may not be "unique." The code allows a court to award specific performance "in other proper circumstances."

Injunction

An **injunction** is an order by the court which forbids a party from committing some specified act. The remedy of injunction is granted at the court's discretion when the defendant's continued behavior or threatened behavior will result in irreparable harm to the plaintiff and when monetary damages thus would not be adequate to compensate the plaintiff.

Injunctions have been used in employment contracts to prevent a party from performing the contract service for someone else. In a leading English case, an opera singer had contracted to sing exclusively for a particular company. When she refused to do so, the court forbade her from singing for any other company. The court felt that it could not compel her specifically to perform her contractual obligation but that economic pressure might move her to honor it.

American courts generally follow a similar rule in personal service contracts where the defendant refuses to perform. If the defendant's services expressly or by clear implication have been promised exclusively to the plaintiff, the courts forbid service for anyone else. An injunction, however, is not to be granted if the injured plaintiff could be compensated adequately by damages. As a result, injunctions are granted in personal service contracts only if the individual is a person with unique skills. Professional athletes who refuse to honor their contracts with one employer are often forbidden to perform for another.

The injunction is also used to enforce ancillary agreements not to compete. As discussed in Chapter 16, this type of agreement is permissible under certain circumstances. These generally involve the sale of a business and its accompanying goodwill, an employment contract in which the employee agrees not to work for a competitor or compete with the employer after leaving the job, or an employment contract in which the employee has access to customer lists or trade secrets that could be used by a business rival. Injunctions are also used to enforce covenants that limit land use. A rental or ownership agreement may contain a provision limiting the premises to residential use. If the tenant or owner uses the property for some other purpose, someone injured by the improper use may get an injunction.

Rescission and Restitution

Many situations exist in which a party has the right to rescind or cancel a contract. Rescission (see Chapter 12) is available in cases involving fraud, duress, undue influence, and mistake. During the past decade, many laws have given consumers the right to cancel contracts under certain circumstances. One example is the home solicitation or door-to-door sales contract. Many states and a Federal Trade Commission rule allow a buyer 3 days to cancel certain types of agreements that have been solicited and made in the buyer's home. These laws also generally require the seller to notify the buyer in writing of this right. The 3-day period does not start until notification is given. The right to cancel a home solicitation sales contract does not depend upon any wrongdoing by the seller.

When a contract is canceled, both parties must, if possible, return any benefits received under the agreement. This return is known as making **restitution**. Restitution may involve returning specific items or compensating for benefits conferred. The principle of restitution applies even for cancellation

---

PREVENTIVE LAW
Allocating Risk with Contracts

Perhaps no chapter better illustrates the strategic importance of a well-written contract than this chapter on performance, discharge, and remedies. In an uncertain commercial world, the contract is the tool that businesses use to allocate risks. Thus, an electric utility may enter into a long-term supply contract with a coal company in an effort to fix the cost of coal and to protect itself against future fluctuations in coal prices.

The contract rules contained in this chapter should be viewed as the legal framework surrounding a negotiated transaction. Some of the rules can serve as useful tools during contract negotiations. Most of the rules can be altered or avoided by the parties simply by addressing them in their contracts.

For example, the inclusion of conditions in a contract by a party may permit that party to avoid a contractual duty when circumstances change to make the contractual undertaking no longer attractive. Thus, during times of rising interest rates, offers to purchase real estate frequently condition the buyer's duty to purchase to the availability of a mortgage at a specified interest rate. Depending upon one's negotiating power, a contracting party could artfully draft a contract that would reduce the risk of financial loss on a contractual undertaking.

Another example of how the law discussed in this chapter can serve as a useful tool for contracting parties can be seen in the concept of liquidated damages. By including a valid liquidated damages clause in a contract, a party can limit the liability resulting from its nonperformance of a contractual duty.

The substantial-performance doctrine illustrates a rule of contract law that may be avoided by careful contract drafting. It is the substantial-performance doctrine that left the Jacobses with a dream home that was less than what they had dreamed of in the case of *Plante v. Jacobs*. Notice that very little was covered in the contract. The contract did not include blueprints for the house. The parties relied on "standard forms." The Jacobses could have avoided the problems they encountered by making the items that they considered important the "essence" of the contract. This, of course, would depend upon the bargaining power that they brought to the negotiation of their contract. It is the substantial-performance doctrine that also accounts for the rule that failure to comply exactly with a contract's deadline will not result in a forfeiture. This too, however, can be avoided by including a provision in the contract that "time is of the essence."

At this point in the discussion of contract law, it should not come as a surprise that a carefully written contract can serve to avoid many of the problems that parties may encounter in their business relations.

due to fraud. The defrauded plaintiff is entitled to the return of benefits conferred because of fraud; but the law requires the defrauded plaintiff, if possible, to return the wrongdoer to the status quo. The defrauded plaintiff may, of course, choose to enforce the contract and sue for damages.

Restitution is a remedy also available in cases in which one person has been unjustly enriched at another's expense. Unjust enrichment is a fundamental concept affecting several legal areas, the theory being that justice is violated if a person is allowed to retain benefits that enrich him or her unfairly at another's expense. As a result, the courts may order restitution of those benefits or their value. Before the courts order restitution, they must to be convinced that retention of the benefits not only enriches the person but that the enrichment is unjust.

Restitution is ordered by the courts when money has been paid by mistake or when a person has benefited from a contract that turns out to be unenforceable. The restitution rule applies if one party keeps the benefits from a broken contract when these could have been returned easily.

Review Questions and Problems

Key Terms

condition precedent	frustration of purpose
condition subsequent	anticipatory breach
substantial performance	mitigation of damages
discharge	liquidated damages
mutual rescission	clause
novation	punitive damages
doctrine of impossibility	specific performance
commercial	injunction
impracticability	restitution

Discussion Questions

1. Under what circumstances will performance qualify as substantial under the substantial performance doctrine?
2. What is meant by "impossibility of performance"?
3. What is the standard a court uses to award dollar damages when lost profits are involved?
4. Why should a party who has not breached a contract be required to mitigate the damages of the breaching party?

Review Problems

1. Ace contracted with Jones to do certain remodeling work on the building owned by Jones. Jones supplied the specifications for the work. The contract price was $70,000. After the work was completed, Jones was dissatisfied and had Clay, an expert, compare the work done to the specifications provided. Clay testified that the work had been done improperly by Ace and that it would cost about $6,000 to correct the mistakes of Ace. If Jones refuses to pay any amount to Ace, what recourse, if any, does Ace have against Jones? Explain.

2. On January 4, General Contractors, Inc. entered into a contract with Julius and Penelope Jones to construct a house fit for occupancy by June 1. What is the legal consequence if General Contractors fails to complete the house by June 1, but does finish it by June 20? What would be the consequence if the contract stated that with regard to the June 1 deadline, "time is of the essence"? Suppose further that by May 10 no work has yet been started by General Contractors. When contacted by Julius, General Contractors' president states that due to other projects still pending, he is unable to build the house until late November. What legal recourse, if any, do Julius and Penelope have against General Contractors?

3. Frank and Flo Gibson enter into a contract with Ace Home Builders for the construction of a house. After construction was completed, the Gibsons discovered several cracks in the foundation which caused flooding in the basement. What recourse do the Gibsons have against Ace, if any?

4. A contractor agreed to build a skating rink for the plaintiff at a price of $180,000. The rink was to be completed by December 1 and was designed to replace a similar but older rink that the plaintiff rented for $800 per month. A clause in the contract awarded the plaintiff "$100 per day in liquidated damages" for each day after December 1 that the rink was not completed. Was this a valid liquidated damages clause? Explain.

5. On April 15, Don Construction contracted to build a house for Jessup. The contract price was $55,000. The agreement contained a provision stating that the builder would deduct $1,000 a day from the contract price for each day the house was not completed after August 15. It was not completed until September 15. Don Construction refused to deduct $30,000 from the contract price. Jessup refused to sue. Don Construction sued, claiming the $1,000 a day was a penalty clause, not a liquidated damages clause. What result? Explain.

6. Julius W. Erving ("Dr. J") entered into a 4-year contract to play exclusively for the Virginia Squires of the American Basketball Association. After 1 year, he left the Squires to play for the Atlanta Hawks of the National Basketball Association. The contract signed with the Squires provided that the team

could apply for an injunction to prohibit Erving from playing for any other team. Erving sued to have his contract set aside for fraud. The Squires counterclaimed seeking injunctive relief pending arbitration. Who won? Explain.

7. Berke entered into an employment contract with Bettinger to become a sales manager. The contract provided that if Berke terminated employment he could not work for any employment agency for at least 1 year within 55 miles of Philadelphia. Berke left Bettinger and opened his business immediately within a 50-mile radius. Bettinger seeks an injunction claiming irreparable harm. What result?

Case Problem

1. The Aluminum Company of America (ALCOA) sued for relief from a burdensome toll conversion contract under which it converted alumina into molten aluminum for the Essex Group, Inc. (Essex), the supplier of the raw material. ALCOA sought a declaratory judgment that its nonperformance of the contract was excused as a result of commercial impracticability and frustration of purpose. For relief, it sought a reformation or modification of the contract.

   Under the terms of the contract, entered into December 26, 1967, and labeled the Molten Metal Agreement, Essex would supply ALCOA with alumina, which ALCOA would convert into molten aluminum at its Warrick, Indiana plant. Essex then would pick up the aluminum for further processing into aluminum wire products. The contract contained a complex price formula, with escalators pegged to the Wholesale Price Index–Industrial Commodities (WPI-IC), a government price index, and on the average hourly labor rates paid to ALCOA employees at the Warrick plant. The adjusted price was subject to an overall ceiling of 65 percent of the price of a specified type of aluminum sold on specified terms as published in a trade journal.

   The price formula was designed to reflect changes in nonlabor and labor costs. The indexing system was evolved by ALCOA with the aid of the eminent economist Alan Greenspan. ALCOA selected the WPI-IC as a pricing element after assuring itself that the index had closely tracked ALCOA's nonlabor production costs for many years in the past and was highly likely to continue to do so in the future. The formula, however, had failed to account for burgeoning energy costs. Beginning in 1973, OPEC's actions to increase oil prices and unanticipated pollution control costs greatly increased ALCOA's electricity costs. Electrical power is the principal nonlabor cost factor in aluminum conversion, and the electrical power rates rose much more rapidly than did the WPI-IC. ALCOA complained that if it were compelled to perform the unexpired term of the 16-year contract, it would lose over $75 million. Essex counterclaimed for damages and specific performance of the contract, arguing that ALCOA had breached the contract. Who wins? Explain. If you decide in favor of ALCOA, should the court be allowed to reform the contract by writing a wholly new price term for the parties? If so, how would you reform the price formula? If you decide in favor of Essex, should the court award the remedy of specific performance?

20

Introduction to Sales Contracts

Good Faith

Scope of Article 2

Merchants

Creation of Sales Contracts

Acceptance

Leases

Billions of transactions involving the sale of goods occur across the country each day, ranging from an airline's major aircraft order all the way down to the countertop mint that you might buy from a convenience store to get change. The next several chapters deal with the sale of goods, which specifically excludes the sale of real property.

Sales law had traditionally been governed by the common law, which had come to embody principles that reflected the actual practices of merchants. Around the turn of the twentieth century, efforts were made in both England and the United States to codify the common law on sales into a statute. In the United States, that effort resulted in the Uniform Sales Act, a statute that was enacted by several states.

Over the next several decades, commercial activity in the United States developed dramatically. Thanks to advances in technology, old methods of manufacturing and marketing goods gave way to mass production and distribution. The Uniform Sales Act came to be viewed by many as a relic from an earlier era.

In 1951, the National Conference of Commis-sioners on Uniform State Laws completed its draft of the Uniform Commercial Code. The UCC was designed not only to replace the Uniform Sales Act but to replace the various and sundry state laws covering commercial paper, secured transactions, and every other area of commercial law. In short, the UCC was designed to cover every aspect of most commercial trans-actions.

The UCC, like the Uniform Sales Act, was also designed to make commercial law substantially uniform in every state. In this respect the UCC has been quite successful: It has been fully adopted in forty-nine states and partially adopted in Louisiana.

In earlier chapters on contract law, we learned how the UCC differs from traditional common law in areas such as the statute of frauds, modifi-cation of contracts without consideration, and the battle-of-the-forms problem. But where our study of contract law covered both traditional common law and the UCC, our study of commer-cial law will rely almost exclusively on the UCC. The case law of commercial transactions is made up mostly of cases interpreting the UCC.

Good Faith

Article 1 of the UCC contains provisions that are generally applicable to the entire UCC. Article 1 includes most of the definitions that apply to various provisions of the code.

One of the most important Article 1 provisions is Section 1-203, which provides that "Every contract or duty within this Act imposes an obligation of good faith in its performance or enforcement."

Subsection 1-201(19) defines **good faith** as "honesty in fact in the conduct or transaction concerned." No direct sanction is imposed for failure to act in good faith. Instead, it is a general principle available to the courts that may be followed in dealing with other issues arising under the UCC. For example, Section 2-302 expressly provides for judicial modification or nullification of unconscionable contracts and contract terms. The good faith provision complements the concept of unconscionability, and good faith may be used as a guideline in determining whether certain aspects of a commercial transaction may be considered unconscionable. The good faith principle can also be used on its own—for example, to disallow an extortionate modification of a contract when the buyer has become so dependent on the seller for the supply of a commodity that the buyer cannot effectively resist the seller's demand for a higher price.

Scope of Article 2

Article 2 of the UCC applies generally to *transactions* in goods (Section 2-102), but many of its provisions apply specifically to the *sale* of goods. This chapter and those that follow will focus on the sale of goods, the most common transaction governed by Article 2. In order to more specifically define what is meant by the term "sale of goods," we must discuss the terms "sale" and "goods."

Sale

Section 2-106(1) defines a **sale** as a transaction which involves the passing of title from the seller to the buyer for a price. (The passing of title will be discussed in Chapter 21.) Article 2 also uses the term **contracts for sale**, which includes both present sales and a contract to sell at a future time. In a **present sale** the making of a contract and the completion of the sale (passing of title) occur at the same time. For example, Smith signs a contract to purchase a car at an auto dealership and immediately drives off with the car. A **future sale** is a contract for sale in which the making of the contract and the completion of the sale occur at different times. For example, Acme Co. signs a contract to purchase 1,000 widgets from Widgetco for $1,000, with delivery in 30 days.

Goods

Unless the sale involves the sale of "goods," the contract is not controlled by Article 2. Section 2-105(1) of the UCC defines **goods** as "all things . . . which are movable at the time of identification to the contract for sale." In order for an item to qualify as a good, two requirements must be met: (1) the item must be tangible (have a physical existence); and (2) it must be movable.

ETHICS

Good Faith in Commercial Transactions

In Chapter 8, "Business and Ethics," good faith was identified as one of seven basic principles of business ethics. Most businesspeople can describe what is meant by "good faith" in their industry. Further, the concept of "bad faith" is coming to have a more precise meaning to contract law, where actions falling under the standard are more likely to be sanctioned by punitive damages.

Did the drafters of the code intend to require that all sales contracts be consistent with an *ethical* standard of good faith in their formation and performance? The courts have not adopted that approach to date, and the principle of good faith has been used more as a general admonition than as a separate legal doctrine. The language is there, however, and someday the courts may use it to bring certain ethical standards into the commercial law on a more explicit basis.

The UCC definition of goods also includes the unborn of young animals, growing crops, and other things attached to realty that are to be severed. A contract for the sale of growing crops, timber to be cut, or other severables is a contract for the sale of goods.

If a contract covers goods that are not yet existing and identified, the goods are **future goods**, and the sale of future goods operates as a contract to sell. For example, assume that Jones and a pool table manufacturer sign a contract under which the manufacturer is to deliver 100 specifically designed pool tables to Jones in 6 months. If the pool tables are not yet manufactured at the time the contract is signed, then they are future goods.

Contracts Not Covered

Contracts that are not covered by Article 2 are those involving the sale of real property, personal property other than goods (e.g., the contract for the sale of an investment security), or services.

Where a contract involves both goods and services, the court may apply Article 2 even though the contract is not a pure goods contract. The sale of mixed goods and services has created a number of complex cases. If the dentist fills one of your teeth with silver, is the transaction a sale of goods? If a plumber comes to your house and installs a new pipe, is the transaction a sale of goods? It is most likely, in both of these examples, that a court would construe the transaction as a service contract because goods are only incidentally involved in the performance of the service contract. In other words, because the service aspect of the transaction predominates, the transaction is not covered by Article 2.

Conversely, an item might be sold along with a minor service. Suppose you went to a restaurant at which a waiter or waitress brought food to the table. Courts are likely to construe the situation as predominately a sale of goods and therefore covered by Article 2. Obviously, not all situations are this clear-cut, and the mixture of goods and services gives courts some trouble in deciding whether Article 2 or the common law of contracts should control a situation.

Merchants

Merchants are generally held to different standards under the UCC from those of nonmerchants. The implied warranty of merchantability applies only to merchants. (Implied warranties are discussed in the chapter on warranties.) Only merchants are bound by firm offers, and only merchants may be bound, without agreement, by additional terms in an acceptance. There are other examples of the higher standards applied to merchants.

Why discriminate between merchants and nonmerchants? Several justifications can be given. Merchants can reasonably be expected to be more sophisticated regarding the legal rules pertaining to their profession. They should know when to seek the advice of counsel and are, in fact, often guided by legal advice. Many merchants enter into sales transactions day after day. A nonmerchant seller, on the other hand, may make one major sale every 2 or 3 years. If we view the special rules for merchants from a consumer perspective, it seems appropriate that consumers should be held to a less rigorous standard.

Who is a merchant? The UCC defines a merchant in three different ways. A **merchant** may be a person who deals in goods of the kind in question. If a person in the hardware business sells a hammer, he or she is a merchant for purposes of the sale of the hammer because a hardware store regularly deals in goods such as hammers. A second person classified by the UCC as a merchant is one who by his or her occupation represents himself or herself as having knowledge or skill peculiar to the practices or goods involved in the transaction. Suppose a mechanical contracting firm installed cooling equipment; with respect to the sale of the cooling equipment, it would be regarded as a merchant. Finally, a person may be classified as a merchant if he or she employs someone who qualifies as a merchant, under the first two definitions, to act on his or her behalf. If Mary hired a jeweler to represent her in the sale of her diamonds, the UCC treats *her* as a merchant because she employed a merchant.

The *Decatur* case discusses the problem of when a farmer is a merchant. Some courts view farmers as merchants but others reject this view, as the following case illustrates.

DECATUR COOPERATIVE ASSOCIATION V. URBAN

Supreme Court of Kansas
547 P.2d 323 (1976)

BACKGROUND: Decatur Cooperative (plaintiff) sued Urban (defendant). Urban allegedly entered into an oral contract for sale of 10,000 bushels of wheat with the plaintiff, a grain elevator cooperative. The lower court ruled for Urban.

Harman, C., Justice

Urban is a resident of Decatur County and was a member of the cooperative throughout the year 1973. He has been engaged in the wheat farming business for about twenty years. He owns about 2,000 acres of his total farmed acreage of 2,320 acres. He is engaged solely in the farming business. Decatur contends the parties entered into an oral contract by phone whereby Urban agreed to sell to the cooperative 10,000 bushels of wheat at $2.86 per bushel, to be delivered on or before September 30, 1973. Urban denies that any contract sale was made.

During the phone conversation there was discussion of a written memorandum of sale to be prepared and sent to Urban later. A confirmation was signed by Decatur's assistant manager and was binding as against Decatur. Urban received the confirmation within a reasonable time, read it, and gave no written notice of objection to its contents within ten days after it was received.

On August 13, 1973, Urban notified Decatur that he would not deliver the wheat. The price of wheat at the cooperative on that date was $4.50 per bushel.

Under Subsection (2) of 2-201 a "merchant" is deprived of the defense of the Statute of Frauds as against an oral contract with another merchant if he fails to object to the terms of a written confirmation within ten days of its receipt. The issue presently here is whether or not appellee is, under the facts, also a "merchant." If he is not, Section 2-201 acts as a bar to the enforcement of the alleged contract. Professionalism, special knowledge and commercial experience are to be used in determining whether a person in a particular situation is to be held to the standards of a merchant.

The writers of the official UCC comment virtually equate professionals with merchants—the casual or inexperienced buyer or seller is not to be held to the standard set for the professional in business. The defined term "between merchants," used in the exception proviso to the Statute of Frauds, contemplates the knowledge and skill of professionals on each side of the transaction. The transaction in question here was the sale of wheat. Urban as a farmer undoubtedly had special knowledge or skill in raising wheat but we do not think this factor, coupled with annual sales of a wheat crop and purchases of seed wheat, qualified him as a merchant in that field. The parties' stipulation states Urban has sold only the products he raised. There is no indication any of these sales were other than cash sales to local grain elevators, where conceivably an expertise reaching professional status could be said to be involved.

We think the trial court correctly ruled under the particular facts that Urban was not a merchant for the purpose of avoiding the operation of the Statute of Frauds pursuant to K.S.A. 84-2-201(1).

DECISION: The Kansas Supreme Court affirmed. It ruled that Urban was not a merchant for purposes of the sale of the wheat.

Creation of Sales Contracts

The UCC makes it much easier for a court to find that a contract for the sale of goods has been made. If the court determines that the parties intended an agreement because of something they wrote or said, or because of their conduct, it can find that a contract for sale of goods has been made even though the moment of its making is uncertain. Section 2-204(3) states the principle pertaining to "open terms" adopted in the UCC. The contract will not be set aside for indefiniteness merely because one or more terms have been left open, as long as the parties intended to make a contract and there is a reasonably certain basis for giving an appropriate remedy. The more terms the parties have left open, the more difficult it will be for a court to conclude that the parties intended to make a binding agreement. For the court to have a reasonably certain basis for giving an appropriate remedy, the parties must specify in the contract the quantity of goods sold.

Indefiniteness

Prior to the adoption of the UCC, a court would sometimes refuse to enforce a contract because parties either intentionally or unintentionally failed to cover all the terms necessary for the contract to be considered valid and enforceable. The contract might not have clearly specified the price to be paid or certain delivery or payment terms. Rather than fill in the missing terms for the parties, the courts simply refused to enforce the agreement. The UCC, in Part 3 of Article 2, provides a number of statutory terms that may be used by a court in the event the contract fails to specify particular terms.

Price   Section 2-304 states that the price can be made payable "in money or otherwise." Thus a contract will not fail simply because it does not make the price payable in money. The price can be paid in money, goods, realty, or "otherwise."

But what if the parties leave the price term open? Section 2-305 covers this situation. It is not necessary for the contract to include the price term. If it has not been agreed upon at the time the contract is executed, then the price will be whatever a reasonable price is at the time of delivery. Any price set at a later date must be done in "good faith." If the buyer has the right to set the price at a later time, and he or she sets an unreasonably low price in light of the market conditions and surrounding circumstances, then the price declared will not be controlling because the buyer acted in bad faith. If one of the parties to a contract has the duty to fix a price and he or she fails to do so, the other party may cancel the contract or may set a reasonable price.

However, a contract will fail for indefiniteness if the price term is left out and if the contract clearly states that the parties do not intend to be bound by the agreement if the price is not subsequently fixed and agreed upon. Unless the contract very clearly indicates that the parties do not wish to be bound if the price cannot be agreed upon, the court may end up setting a price for them.

Delivery   The contract may also not contain directions for the time, place, or method of delivery. Even so, the contract will not fail for indefiniteness. If the time for delivery has not been specified in the contract, Subsection 2-309(1) states that the time for shipment or delivery shall be a reasonable time. What is reasonable depends on the circumstances. If the contract calls for successive performances but does not specify when the contract terminates, it is valid for a reasonable time but may be terminated at any time by either party upon reasonable notice. If the contract does not specify whether the delivery is to be in one lot or in several lots, the goods must be tendered in a single delivery and payment is due at that time.

Section 2-308 makes the seller's place of business or, if he or she has no place of business, the seller's residence the appropriate place for delivery of goods in the absence of a specified place of delivery. If the contract is for the sale of identified goods that the parties know are located at some place other than the seller's place of business or residence, the place where the goods are located is the place for delivery.

Quantity   The only term that absolutely must be stated in a contract for the sale of goods is the quantity term. Section 2-201 of the statute of frauds states: "a writing is not insufficient because it omits or incorrectly states a term agreed upon but the contract is not enforceable . . . beyond the quantity of goods shown in such writing." If the contract is one that must be in writing in order to be enforceable, and the writing omits the quantity term, there is no enforceable contract. If the writing incorrectly states the quantity term, there may be an enforceable contract—at least to the extent of the quantity stated in the writing.

Thus the UCC reflects the philosophy that a contract for the sale of goods should not fail, even though one or more terms have been left open, as long as the parties intended to enter into a contract and "there is a reasonably certain basis for giving an appropriate remedy" (Section 2-204[3]).

Parol Evidence

Recall from Chapter 14 that the UCC has liberalized the common law parol evidence rule with respect to the sale of goods. Section 2-202 provides that unless the court finds that a written agreement was intended to constitute the complete and exclusive statement of the terms of the agreement, evidence of *consistent* additional terms may be introduced to explain or supplement the written agreement.

Even in such a situation, it still may be possible to bring suit in *tort*, as opposed to a *contractual* theory of recovery, a point which is discussed in the following case.

KELLER V. A. O. SMITH HARVESTORE PRODUCTS, INC.

Colorado Supreme Court
15 UCC Rep. Serv. 2d (1991)

BACKGROUND: Alfred and Martha Keller (plaintiffs) purchased two Harvestore grain storage systems manufactured by A. O. Smith Harvestore (defendant). These silos were specifically constructed to prevent oxygen from coming into contact with feed stored in the silos, thus enabling ranchers to store feed indefinitely and cut feed losses. The company provided videotapes, brochures, and extensive literature to promote sales of Harvestore Silos. Based on this information, the Kellers purchased two Harvestore systems. The agreement they signed contained the following provision:

> This order form is the entire and only agreement between the Seller and Buyer; and no oral statements or agreements not confirmed herein, or by a subsequent written agreement, shall be binding on either the Seller or Buyer.

After the Kellers began to use the Harvestore systems, they began to experience serious problems with their cattle. The Kellers brought suit based on negligent misrepresentation. Negligent misrepresentation is defined in Section 552(1) of the Restatement of Torts (Second) as

> One who, in the course of his business, profession or employment, or in any other transaction in which he has a pecuniary interest, supplies false information for the guidance of others in their business transactions, is subject to liability for pecuniary loss caused to them by their justifiable reliance upon the information, if he fails to exercise reasonable care or competence in obtaining or communicating the information.

The seller argued that such a claim was barred by the terms of the written purchase agreement. The trial court ruled for the Kellers.

Kirshbaum, Justice

[Does] a cause of action for negligent misrepresentation lie against the manufacturer of a product for representations made during the course of the sale of that product despite the execution of a fully integrated sales agreement[?]

It is well established that in some circumstances a claim of negligent misrepresentation based on principles of tort law, independent of any principle of contract law, may be available to a party to a contract. In addition, as we have observed, section 552(1) contains a definition of negligent misrepresentation. It is thus clear that a contracting party's negligent misrepresentation of material facts prior to the execution of an agreement may provide the basis for an independent tort claim asserted by a party detrimentally relying on such negligent misrepresentations.

AOSHPI argues that, assuming the availability of a negligent misrepresentation claim in the circumstances of this case, the Kellers' execution of a fully integrated sales agreement precludes their assertion of such a claim. We disagree.

Integration clauses generally permit contracting parties to limit future contractual disputes to issues relating to the reciprocal obligations expressly set forth in the executed document. Thus the terms of a contract intended to represent a final and complete integration of the parties' agreement are enforceable and parol evidence offered to establish the existence of prior or contemporaneous agreements is inadmissible to vary the terms of such contract. However, as we have noted, claims of negligent misrepresentation are based not on principles of contractual obligation but on principles of duty and reasonable conduct. The parol evidence rule does not bar the admission of evidence to establish tort claims not specifically prohibited by the terms of an agreement. We recognized this distinction in Bill Dreiling Motor Co., wherein we concluded that the parol evidence rule applicable to contract disputes had no force in a tort action alleging fraudulent misrepresentation in the inducement to execute an agreement.

Many other courts have also concluded that the mere presence of a general integration clause in an agreement does not bar a claim for negligent or fraudulent misrepresentation.

We conclude that a general integration clause does not effect a waiver of a claim of negligent misrepresentation not specifically prohibited by the terms of the agreement. The general language of the integration provisions of the purchase agreements here at issue does not specifically preclude negligent misrepresentation claims.

The policy of encouraging honesty and candor in contract negotiations, which policy is reflected in the recognition of an implied covenant of good faith and fair dealing, supports this result. The implied covenant of good faith and fair dealing would virtually be eliminated if a contracting party could escape liability for negligent conduct simply by inserting a general integration clause into the agreement. As the court in Formento stated, "a seller should not be allowed to hide behind an integration clause to avoid the consequences of a misrepresentation, whether fraudulent or negligent."

DECISION: The Colorado Supreme Court affirmed the decision for the Kellers.

It should be noted that the UCC parol evidence rule permits an agreement to be explained or supplemented by course of performance, course of dealing, or usage of trade. These concepts are discussed below.

Course of Performance, Course of Dealing, Usage of Trade

In interpreting a contract, the court must take into consideration more than the literal language of the contract and the meaning that is normally associated with the words used in the contract. The UCC requires the court to examine the course of dealing, usage of trade, or course of performance between the parties.

Whenever possible, the express terms of the agreement and any course of dealing, usage of trade, and course of performance must be construed as consistent with one another. When such a construction is unreasonable, the written terms control the situation. Sections 2-208(2) and 1-205(4) make it apparent that conflicts between the express and implied terms are to be resolved in the following manner:

1. Express terms prevail over course of dealing, usage of trade, and course of performance if they cannot be reasonably construed together.
2. Course of performance prevails over both course of dealing and usage of trade.
3. Course of dealing prevails over usage of trade.

Course of Performance   Section 2-208(1) states:

ISSUES AND TRENDS
Terms in an Incomplete Contract Will Be Supplied

Larry and Ralph are having lunch at a restaurant. Larry is a salesman and his company supplies Ralph's store with sunglasses. Over lunch they agreed that Ralph needed 200 pairs of sunglasses from Larry's company. The terms of the agreement such as price, time of shipment, and place of shipment were not agreed upon at that time. In order to have some written proof of the agreement, Ralph wrote on a napkin, "I order 200 pairs of sunglasses (signed) Ralph." Ralph gave the napkin to Larry.

Prior to the adoption of the Uniform Commercial Code such a contract would have been unenforceable because of indefiniteness. The drafters of the UCC wrote the code so that any contract would be upheld so long as there was an intent to contract. If the parties intended to contract, the UCC will assist the parties by filling in the omitted terms. The only term that the UCC will not supply is the quantity term.

Where the contract for sale involves repeated occasions for performance by either party with knowledge of the nature of the performance and opportunity for objection to it by the other, any course of performance accepted or acquiesced in without objection shall be relevant to determine the meaning of the agreement.

Course of performance involves situations where more than one performance is contemplated by the contract.

Consider, for example, a contract that required the buyer to pay for sand at a certain price per ton, "truck measure." In determining the meaning of the phrase "truck measure," the court noted the seller's practice, after entering into the contract, of determining the quantity delivered by referring to the capacity of the truck in which the sand was delivered. The buyer never objected to this practice of the seller. Thus, the behavior of the seller and the buyer *after* entering into the contract was examined in order to determine the meaning of the phrase "truck measure."

The following case illustrates how course of performance can be used to interpret the terms of a contract.

LANCASTER GLASS CORP. V. PHILIPS ECG, INC.
U. S. Court of Appeals, Sixth Circuit
835 F. 2d 652 (1987)

BACKGROUND: Philips ordered over 100,000 LEA-1015B bulbs from Lancaster in February 1980. The bulbs were to be released to Philips in batches over the course of several months. The LEA-1015B bulb is essentially an empty television picture tube. Philips used the bulbs to manufacture cathode ray tubes, which would eventually be used as computer screens. As part of that manufacturing process, Philips would "T-band" the bulbs—a process by which a steel strip is placed around the perimeter of the bulb in order to prevent the bulb from shattering.

One month after the first group of bulbs was released, Philips was notified by one of its customers that the T-bands on a shipment of cathode ray tubes had slipped. Such slippage rendered the T-bands ineffective to prevent tubes from shattering. After investigating the matter, Philips found that the slippage might have been caused by the fact that the dimensions of Lancaster's bulbs were somewhat different from the dimensions indicated on the engineering drawings that Lancaster had supplied to Philips. Notwithstanding this discovery, Philips continued to accept bulbs from Lancaster.

Citing economic difficulties, Philips requested a renegotiation of some of the terms of its contract with Philips. The parties executed a modified agreement on January 29, 1981. The agreement did not call for Lancaster to revise the dimensions of its bulbs to prevent the T-bands from slipping. Philips continued to accept bulbs from Lancaster for several weeks, but then sought to renegotiate the contract again because of the "poor market situation." In April 1981, Philips presented Lancaster with evidence that the T-band slippage problem was caused by the improper dimensions of Lancaster's bulbs. Philips contended that the slippage problem made the bulbs unusable and demanded credit for the bulbs Philips had in inventory. Lancaster refused, and Philips sued. Lancaster counterclaimed for the price of bulbs that Philips had accepted but not paid for and for the bulbs that Philips had refused to accept. The trial court awarded Lancaster $714,511.23 plus interest. Philips appealed.

Martin, Judge

Under UCC § 2-208(1), when "the contract for sale involves repeated occasions for performance by either party with knowledge of the nature of the performance and opportunity for objection to it by the other, any course of performance accepted or acquiesced in without objection shall be relevant to determine the meaning of the agreement." As comment 1 explains, "[t]he parties themselves know best what they have meant by their words of agreement and their action under that agreement is the best indication of what that meaning was."

The contract in dispute here clearly satisfies the prerequisites of section 2-208(1). Under the February 1980 contract, Lancaster released the LEA-1015B bulbs in incremental quantities designated by Philips. Further, beginning in August 1980, . . .Philips knew that some of the diagonal angles on many of the bulbs were exceeding the one-and-one-half degrees called for on the drawing, and Philips had numerous opportunities to object to this course of performance. Therefore, if we find that Philips accepted or acquiesced in this course of performance without objection, Philips' conduct will help us determine what the parties intended the language "conform to the drawing" to mean with respect to the critical non-toleranced dimension, the diagonal panel skirt taper angle.

We believe Philips acquiesced, without objection, in Lancaster's repeated tendering of bulbs which had diagonal angles exceeding the . . . dimension indicated on the engineering drawing. Philips first became aware of the T-band slippage problem in April 1980, and, by August, it had learned that the diagonal angle on some of the Lancaster bulbs were exceeding the dimension indicated on the engineering drawing. Although it strongly suspected the excessive slope was contributing to, if not causing, the slippage problem, Philips continued to accept several releases of bulbs under the February 1980 contract "without objection" despite numerous opportunities to voice its concern. Granted, Philips raised the issue in discussions with Lancaster, but it never did so in a way that can be considered as an objection that the tendered bulbs did not conform to the contract. For example, when Philips first discussed the problem with Lancaster in August 1980, Philips did not object to Lancaster's response that it could only change the slope of the diagonal angle on future production runs, after Philips completed the February 1980 order. Similarly, when Philips raised the T-band slippage issue during the January 1981 negotiations, by its own admission it did so merely as a "negotiating ploy" in an effort to obtain price concessions during a period when its sales were slow. Moreover, during this crucial period, Philips drafted an agreement which purportedly settled "all matters" pertaining to the February 1980 contract. Pursuant to that agreement, Philips subsequently accepted releases of LEA-1015B bulbs, bulbs which it knew would be in the same condition as those which Philips knew were not T-banding satisfactorily.

Therefore, because Philips, without objection, acquiesced in Lancaster's tendering of bulbs with excessive angles, we conclude that the bulbs conformed to the drawing, as Philips understood that phrase. Thus, the tendered bulbs conformed to the contract, and Philips was not justified in cancelling the February 1980 contract.

DECISION: The court of appeals affirmed the judgment for Lancaster.

Course of Dealing "A course of dealing is a sequence of previous conduct between the parties to a particular transaction which is fairly to be regarded as establishing a common basis of understanding for interpreting those expressions and other conduct" (Section 1-205[1]).

For example, in the past a seller may have permitted the buyer to take 5 percent off the invoice price if the buyer paid within 30 days of the billing date. By permitting the buyer to take a 5 percent discount, the seller over a period of time has created a course of dealing between the parties that would be relevant in determining whether the buyer could take a 5 percent discount in the future for paying within 30 days of the billing date.

Course of performance relates to conduct *after* the execution of an agreement, whereas course of dealing relates to conduct between the parties *prior* to the execution of an agreement. Because the conduct that is material to a course of dealing occurs prior to the execution of an agreement, course of dealing cannot be used to modify or waive a written contract.

Usage of Trade Section 1-205(2) states:

(2) A usage of trade is any practice or method of dealing having such regularity of observance in a place, vocation or trade as to justify an expectation that it will be observed with respect to the transaction in question. The existence and scope of such a usage are to be proved as facts. If it is established that such a usage is embodied in a written trade code or similar writing the interpretation of the writing is for the court.

Usage of trade is not the same as custom because the practice or method of dealing may be of recent origin or may be followed only in a particular part of the country. It simply must be observed with such regularity "as to justify an expectation that it will be observed with respect to the transaction in question." Like course of dealing, usage of trade can be used to give meaning to the particular language selected by the parties in their contract.

An oil company agreed to sell asphalt to a paving contractor, with the price specified as "Oil Company's posted price at time of delivery." At a later time the oil company raised its price for asphalt. The contractor contended that a usage of trade existed in the industry that sellers must deliver all asphalt at the preincrease prices if the contractor already had sold the asphalt to a third party. According to the contractor, the price increase, by trade custom, should apply only to future sales made by the contractor. This custom in the industry is a usage of trade that should be taken into consideration in determining the price the oil company could charge for its asphalt. The oil company should not be able to raise the price for asphalt delivered to the contractor that the contractor had already sold to a third party.

Filling in Terms The UCC sets up a system to fill in the missing terms in an agreement between parties. Where a term is fully expressed in writing or by a valid oral statement, this term will control the agreement unless it conflicts with a mandatory provision of the UCC. In the absence of a particular term in a written agreement, the court will fill it in by first looking to course of performance, then to course of dealing, and finally to usage of trade to supply the missing information. If none of these enables the court to fill in a missing term, the court will examine the statutory "gap-filling" terms in Part 3 of Article 2 of the UCC to fill in the missing information. If the UCC does not specify the term to be filled in, then the contract is enforced even though the court is unable to fill in the missing term—as long as the contract indicates that the parties intended to be bound and there is a reasonably certain basis for giving an appropriate remedy.

Statute of Frauds

Recall from Chapter 14 that Section 2-201 of the UCC sets forth a special statute of frauds applicable to the sale of goods. The general rule is that a contract for the sale of goods for $500 or more must be evidenced by "some writing" in order to be enforceable. Additionally, that writing must generally be signed by the party against whom enforcement is sought. Between merchants, however, an oral contract is enforceable if it is followed up by a written confirmation and the party receiving the confirmation does not object in writing within 10 days. A more complete discussion of Section 2-201 can be found in Chapter 14.

The following case deals with the question of whether the parties had entered into an agreement evidenced by some writing.

POLLACK V. NEMET MOTORS, INC.

New York Supreme Court, Appellate Division, First Department

561 N. Y. S. 2d 457 (1990)

BACKGROUND: Pollack alleged that he purchased a new 1976 Triumph TR6 Roadster for $13,000 from Nemet Motors. Nemet Motors argued that the UCC's statute of frauds requires some writing in order for an agreement to be enforceable and no such writing existed. The trial court ruled for Pollack.

Memorandum Decision

In support of his motion for summary judgment, plaintiff submitted a cancelled check in the amount of $455.00, made payable to "Nemet Motors." On the face of the check was typed "Deposit 1976 TR6" and the notation "Agreement to purchase and deposit subject to inspection of vehicle Financing." On the reverse side was typed, "Agreement to purchase of deposit subject to vehicle inspection, application of all manufacturer's and Dealer warranties, and ability to obtain financing. Purchase Price $13,000.00." The IAS court correctly determined that the check evinces a binding agreement between plaintiff and defendant, sufficient to the statute of frauds (UCC § 2-201). Further, the provision that the agreement was "subject to inspection of vehicle & Financing" constitutes nothing more than a condition precedent to performance which, pursuant to CPLR § 3015(a), plaintiff was not required to plead. Defendants' argument that the language constituted a condition precedent to the formation of the contract itself is unsupported by the record, and no issue of fact has been raised with respect thereto based upon the conclusory affidavit of Thomas Nemet, who, in any event, was not a party to the negotiations between plaintiff and Nemet Motors, Inc. Nor is there any evidence to support the conclusion that the attempts by defendants to increase the purchase price subsequent to the endorsement of the check by Nemet Motors, Inc., constituted anything more than additional and post-contractual negotiations, and do not suffice to raise material issues of fact with respect to any of the elements necessary to demonstrate an oral modification of the contract.

DECISION: The appellate court affirmed the judgment for Pollack.

Acceptance

Method of Acceptance

Several important changes from the common law rules of offer and acceptance appear in the UCC. For example, the authors of the UCC adopted Subsection 2-206(1) to make it easier for offerees to determine in what manner they must accept an offer when they feel that the offer itself does not make clear how it must be accepted. The code provides that "unless otherwise unambiguously indicated by the language or circumstances, . . . an offer to make a contract shall be construed as inviting acceptance in any manner and by any medium reasonable in the circumstances." For example, one might, when faced with an offer made by telegram, accept by mail unless the circumstances warranted a more immediate reply. If the offeror has specified a particular mode of acceptance, however, even under the UCC the offeree must accept in that manner.

Shipment   Subsection (b) of Section 2-206(1) permits a seller to accept an order or offer to buy goods "either by a prompt or current shipment of conforming or nonconforming goods." This in effect allows for both bilateral and unilateral contracts. If the seller chooses to accept the offer by the prompt shipment of goods, an acceptance occurs whether conforming or nonconforming goods are shipped. This means the seller no longer can argue when the buyer receives nonconforming goods that there has been no acceptance of the offer, and therefore no breach of contract, because nonconforming goods were shipped in response to the buyer's order. When there has been a shipment of nonconforming goods in response to an order, there is both an acceptance of the offer and a breach of contract.

Accommodating Shipment   Of course, situations may arise where the seller is unable to supply the exact item ordered by the buyer but is in the position to ship something very similar and perhaps equally acceptable to the buyer. If the seller wishes to ship the goods to the buyer on the condition that the buyer may return them if he or she does not want them, the seller may ship nonconforming goods to accommodate a buyer. Section 2-206(1)(b) provides that "such a shipment of nonconforming goods does not constitute an acceptance if the seller seasonably notifies the buyer that the shipment is offered only as an accommodation to the buyer." If the buyer finds the goods unacceptable, he or she may return them, but the accommodating shipment will *not* be treated as a breach of contract.

Beginning Performance   It is also possible under the UCC to accept an offer by beginning performance. The offeree, rather than responding

to an offer with an acceptance, might choose to perform the requested act. The UCC recognizes this as a method of acceptance where it is "a reasonable mode of acceptance," but it places an important limitation on the offeree's power to accept in this manner: "an offeror who is not notified of acceptance within a reasonable time may treat the offer as having lapsed before acceptance." Where the offeror in New York offers to purchase lawn mowers from a company in Los Angeles, the company in Los Angeles may begin to produce the mowers, but it must also notify the New York purchaser of its acceptance. If it fails to do so, the New York company may treat the offer as having been rejected. The Los Angeles company has only a reasonable time from the time it commences performance to notify the buyer of the acceptance. If the offeror doesn't hear from the offeree within a reasonable time, he may safely make other arrangements to obtain the lawn mowers without fear of being held to the contract.

Form of Acceptance

The common law requirement that the acceptance be a mirror image of the offer and the resulting battle-of-forms problem were discussed in Chapter 9. The explanation of the UCC modification of the common law rule in Section 2-207 that is supplied in Chapter 9 should be reviewed at this point.

Leases

In the last several years, leasing transactions have become very popular. This is true in both the consumer context, where many automobiles and household items are leased, as well as in the commercial context, where equipment is frequently leased. The value of personal property leasing transactions has grown into the billions of dollars annually.

Until recently, personal property lease transactions were governed by a mish-mash of common law principles relating to both personal property and real estate leases and, by analogy, to UCC provisions governing sales and secured transactions. In 1987, the National Conference of Commissioners on Uniform State Laws completed

---

CONCEPT SUMMARY
Sales Law

Good faith involves honesty in fact in the conduct or transaction involved.

A **sale** is the passing of title from the seller to the buyer for a price.

Goods are tangible, movable items at the time of identification to the contract of sale.

A **merchant** is one who deals in goods of the kind in question; or one who by his or her occupation represents himself or herself as having knowledge or skill peculiar to the practices or goods involved in the transaction; or one who employs a merchant to act on his or her behalf.

The **creation of sales contract** involves the following elements:

- If the parties intended to make a contract, and there is a reasonably certain basis for giving a remedy, the contract will not be set aside based on indefiniteness.
- Generally a writing can be explained or supplemented by consistent additional terms.
- Generally, a writing can be explained or supplemented by course of dealing, usage of trade, or course of performance.
- A contract for the sale of goods for $500 or more must be in writing.

An **acceptance** includes an offer in any manner and by any medium reasonable in the circumstances. This includes acceptance by the shipment of goods and by beginning performance.

The **lease of personal property** is covered in Article 2A of the UCC, which embodies most of the general principles in Article 2.

---

work on Article 2A of the Uniform Commercial Code, which governs personal property leasing transactions. Article 2A has been adopted in several states, and several more are expected to adopt it.

Most of the general principles embodied in Article 2 have been incorporated into Article 2A. This should not be surprising, because most personal property lease transactions bear a strong resemblance to sales transactions. In both types of transactions, rules are needed to determine, among other things, if goods conform to the contract, how to supply missing contractual terms, how to interpret express and implied warranties, and what remedies each party has in the event of a breach. Because of these similarities, the provisions of Article 2A often appear to be identical to Article 2 provisions except that the "lessor" and "lessee" have been substituted for the "seller" and "buyer."

Because of the strong similarity between Article 2 and Article 2A, we will not cover Article 2A in any detail in this book. But it should be noted that many of the principles in Article 2 now apply, through Article 2A, to personal property lease transactions as well as to sales transactions.

Review Questions And Problems

Key Terms

good faith	future sale
sale	goods
contracts for sale	future goods
present sale	merchant

Discussion Questions

1. What contracts are not covered by Article 2 of the UCC?
2. What is the difference between a "course of performance" and a "course of dealing"?
3. What is the one term that absolutely must be stated in a contract for the sale of goods?
4. Why does the UCC distinguish between "merchants" and "nonmerchants"?

Review Problems

1. Weaver's contracts with Casual Slacks for the sale of teenage clothing, the order calling for delivery during "June–August." The shipment is made in August and is incomplete. Weaver's refuses to pay the full invoice price, since the shipment is received so late as to miss the major part of the preschool marketing period, making it necessary to mark the clothing one-third to one-half off the usual retail price in order to sell it. Weaver's contends that the use of the term "June–August" has a trade meaning of delivery of a substantial portion of the goods in June, a similar delivery in July, and the balance in August. Casual Slacks, on the other hand, contends that the use of the terminology "June–August" is unambiguous and means that delivery may be made at any time during the period from June 1 to August 31. Weaver's introduces parol evidence of the meaning in the trade of "June–August" at trial.

   Does the term "June–August" have a meaning given it by a usage in the trade so as to explain or supplement the express terms of the written agreement? Is this testimony admissible?

2. Dravo and Key enter into an oral contract for Key to sell Dravo up to 143,000 pounds of 2-inch or smaller steel punchings. No price is specified. Key provides part of the goods under the contract but Dravo refuses to pay. Dravo now contends that the contract is invalid for lack of a specified price term. What result?

3. Acme orders 10,000 perforated widgets from Widgetco, to be delivered in ten monthly shipments of 1,000 widgets each. Each widget contains fifteen perforations. Acme accepts the first eight monthly shipments of widgets, but refuses to accept the ninth shipment because the widgets "don't have enough perforations." The contract does not indicate how many perforations each widget should have, but Acme contends that in the widget trade, the term "perforated widget" refers to a widget with twenty perforations. Widgetco sues Acme for breach of contract. What result?

4. Schubert agreed to sell Kipp ten lawnmowers at a price of $300 each. Kipp agreed to buy the mowers at this price. At a later date, Kipp argues that because the parties have left a number of terms open, such as the time for delivery, the contract is too indefinite to be enforced. Is Kipp correct?

Case Problems

1. Koenen, a classic car collector, learned that Royal Buick would receive one of 500 specially manufactured, limited-edition Buick Regal Grand National automobiles. Koenen and Royal Buick executed a purchase order which left out the price term. Koenen agreed orally with the Royal Buick salesperson that he would pay the sticker price for the car, which had not yet been determined at the time the purchase order was executed. Koenen had purchased two limited-edition Grand Nationals from Royal Buick in prior years and had paid the sticker price each time. When the car arrived, Royal Buick attempted to sell it to someone else. Koenen sued. Royal Buick argued that its purchase order with Koenen was not a contract because it lacked a price term and that parol evidence regarding the price should not be admitted. Should the court admit evidence that Koenen had agreed to pay the sticker price? How should the case be decided?

2. Harbach, a farmer, orally contracts in February with Continental to sell 25,000 bushels of soybeans at $3.81 per bushel, delivery and payment deferred until October, November, and December. There is some question about whether Continental sent Harbach written confirmation of the contract. Harbach contends he did not receive such a confirmation. Harbach then refuses to make delivery, contending that no contract exists and, even if there is a contract, that the statute of frauds prevents enforcement. Further, Harbach claims that he, as a farmer, was not a merchant at the time of the transaction and therefore the merchant exception to Section 2-201 does not apply. At trial, evidence is admitted tending to show that Harbach has been engaged in agricultural pursuits for over 25 years and, in particular, has raised and sold grain, primarily corn, but including some small quantities of soybeans, on the type of contract here in issue for several years. It is known that Harbach is familiar with the operations of the grain market on which both corn and soybeans are traded. Is Harbach, who is a farmer, also a merchant?

3. Ratzlaff entered into a contract to sell his total crop of popcorn to Baker. The contract permitted Ratzlaff to cancel the contract if Baker failed to pay upon delivery. Ratzlaff made two deliveries to Baker, but Baker failed to pay at that time. Ratzlaff did not demand payment. Instead, he attempted to cancel the agreement with Baker. Ratzlaff thereafter sold the popcorn to another buyer at double the price Baker had agreed to pay. Is Ratzlaff obligated to act in good faith in deciding whether to terminate or not?

4. Smith-Scharff Paper Company manufactured paper bags. Bernard Mayer orally agreed to purchase all of the bags the company had in stock. Smith-Scharff sent him a bill for $20,000. Mayer now argues that such a contract must be in writing to be enforceable. Is he correct?

21

Sales: Title, Risk of Loss, and Insurable Interests

Title	Insurable Interest
Risk of Loss	Article 6

In transactions involving the sale of goods, as with everything in life, things don't always go as planned. Transactions can go wrong even if no one is at fault. For example, assume that a buyer in Oklahoma City orders a shipment of lawnmowers from a manufacturer in Chicago. If the lawnmowers are destroyed in a truck accident while they're being shipped to Oklahoma City, should the seller or the buyer bear the loss? What if the lawnmowers are destroyed by fire at the seller's plant? What if they're destroyed by fire after they're dropped off in Oklahoma City but before the buyer has had the chance to pick them up? This chapter will discuss how the Uniform Commercial Code approaches such problems.

Prior to the adoption of the UCC, the question of who bore the risk of loss in any transaction depended solely on who had *title* to the goods at the time of the loss. Other important issues, such as whether a party had an insurable interest in goods, were also determined by who had title. The UCC has essentially separated the concepts of title, risk of loss, and insurable interest; a party can bear the risk of loss of goods, or have an insurable interest in them, even if another party has title. The UCC has thus deemphasized the importance of title in determining the rights and obligations of parties to sales contracts.

The material that follows will discuss the UCC definitions of title, risk of loss, and insurable interest and outline how these concepts interrelate.

Title

Title under the Uniform Commercial Code

Section 2-401 determines when the buyer obtains title to goods covered by a contract. Title may not pass prior to identification of the goods. When the goods are identified to the contract, the buyer acquires certain rights in them, called a special property interest in the goods. **Identification** means that specific goods are somehow identified (by a mark or by being set aside or described) as the object of the particular transaction. For example, a buyer agrees to purchase a color TV. When a seller selects a particular TV in the warehouse as the one that the buyer is to get, that TV becomes identified in the contract. In a sense, prior to identification of specific goods, there is nothing on which a title can be passed.

Generally, the parties are free to arrange by explicit agreement for the transfer of title to existing goods in any manner and on any conditions. If the parties fail to specify when title is to pass, it passes at the time and place when the seller has delivered the goods. The point at which the seller has completed his or her obligations as to delivery is discussed in the following material.

Origin Contract   If the seller intends to send the goods to the buyer, but the contract does not require the seller to deliver the goods to a destination, title to the goods passes to the buyer at the time and place of shipment. This is called an **origin contract**. It operates as follows:

Suppose that a buyer in Oklahoma City has entered into an origin contract to purchase lawnmowers from a seller in Chicago. The seller's only obligation under the contract is to put the mowers on board a truck in Chicago bound for Oklahoma City. Title to the mowers remains in the seller only until the seller delivers the goods to the trucking company.

Destination Contract   If the seller is obligated under the contract actually to deliver the goods to the buyer, the title to the goods does not pass to the buyer until they are tendered to the buyer at the destination specified in the contract. This is called a **destination contract**. In the last example, suppose the contract required the seller to actually deliver the lawnmowers to the buyer in Oklahoma City, as opposed to merely delivering them to the trucking company in Chicago. In this situation, title to the mowers remains in the seller until he or she tenders it to the buyer. This means that if the goods arrive in Oklahoma City, and the shipper, at a reasonable time, offers to deliver the mowers to the buyer's place of business, a tender has been made and title passes to the buyer—whether or not the buyer actually takes delivery of the goods.

The comments on Section 2-503 make it clear that the seller is not obligated to deliver to a named destination unless he or she has specifically agreed to such a delivery. In other words, there is a presumption that the parties intended an origin contract, not a destination contract. Unless the contract calls for the seller to deliver goods at a particular destination, his or her only obligation will be to deliver them to a carrier.

Documents of Title   Goods are often transferred through the use of *documents of title*, documents which give the party holding them the legal right to take the goods covered by the document. For example, a *warehouse receipt* is a document of title that gives the proper holder the right to goods stored in a warehouse. A *bill of lading* is a document of title that gives the proper holder the right to goods in the possession of a carrier. Documents of title are discussed in detail in Chapter 23.

If a document of title is *negotiable*, it can be transferred from one party to another. For example, title to goods stored in a warehouse can be transferred through the seller's transfer of its negotiable warehouse receipt to the buyer. Section 2-401(3) provides that if goods are to be delivered in this manner (and note that the goods are "delivered" in this case without being moved), title passes when the negotiable document of title is delivered from the seller to the buyer.

Suppose that the lawnmowers in the previous example had been stored in a public warehouse. When the seller deposited the mowers at the warehouse, the seller should have received a warehouse receipt entitling the seller to take the mowers back. If the contract calls for the goods to be delivered without being moved, then the seller could effectively deliver the mowers to the buyer by delivering the warehouse receipt (assuming that it is negotiable) to the buyer. Title would pass at the time that the warehouse receipt is delivered to the buyer.

No Documents   If the goods are already identified to the contract (the seller has specified certain goods will be given to the buyer), no delivery is called for under the contract and no documents are to be delivered, then title to the goods passes at the time and place of contracting. In the earlier example, suppose the seller had the mowers in his or her own plant. The seller intended for the buyer to pick up the mowers at the seller's plant. He or she identified certain mowers as the buyer's prior to signing the contract. In this situation, title to the mowers passes to the buyer at the time of contracting.

When a seller sells goods to a buyer, the seller may not retain title to the goods. Any attempt to retain title in the contract of sale will be construed by the court as a mere reservation of a security interest in the goods.

Transfer of Title to Third Persons

Section 2-401 determines when the buyer receives title to goods from the seller. Once the buyer receives goods, he or she may choose to convey them to a third party. Section 2-403 determines the title of the third person who receives goods from the original buyer.

If the buyer receives title to the goods pursuant to Section 2-401, he or she has the power to transfer the good title to goods to a third person. But what if the buyer, for example, gives the seller a bad check—does the buyer have the power to transfer good title to a third person? Section 2-403 answers this question.

Void Title   Section 2-403 gives a purchaser all title that his or her transferor had or had power to transfer. Suppose a person steals goods from someone, and the thief sells the goods to an innocent third party who knows nothing of the theft. The third party in this situation acquires a **void title**; that is, if the original owner demands the goods back from him or her, the third party must surrender the goods. The thief had no title to the goods, nor did he or she have any power to transfer title to the goods to anyone else. Figure 21-1 illustrates how a void title operates.

Voidable Title   Certain persons acquire a mere **voidable title**. As between the original owner and the buyer with a mere voidable title, the owner may reclaim his or her goods. Suppose Mary gave Alice a bad check in return for Alice's

dress. As long as Mary had the dress, Alice could get it back from Mary because Mary had acquired a mere voidable title by giving a bad check.

However, if the buyer with voidable title transfers the goods to a third person, in certain instances the third person may retain possession of goods even as against the original owner. The third person must establish several things in order to keep the goods. This person must prove that he or she was a good faith purchaser for value. Essentially, this means that the third person must establish that he or she acquired the goods by paying a reasonable price and that, in doing so, the person acted in good faith. Assuming the third person establishes that he or she is a good faith purchaser for value, he or she also must establish that the person from whom the third party acquired the goods had a voidable title. Figure 21-2 illustrates how a voidable title operates.

The UCC sets out several transactions that give rise to a voidable title. If a case does not fit in one of these four transactions, the court must refer to the cases and statutes to determine whether the third person's title is voidable. The four transactions giving rise to a voidable title are:

1. When the transferor of the goods was deceived as to the identity of the purchaser
2. When the purchaser acquired the goods by giving a check that is later dishonored
3. When the transaction was one in which title was not to pass until the seller was paid

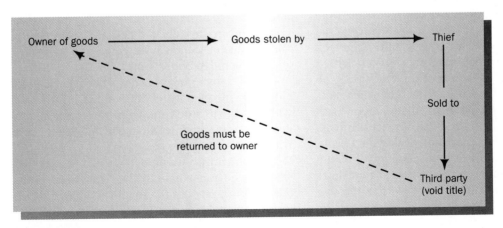

FIGURE 21-1

Void Title. The third party must return the goods to the owner.

FIGURE 21-2

Voidable Title. The third party does not have to return the goods to the original owner.

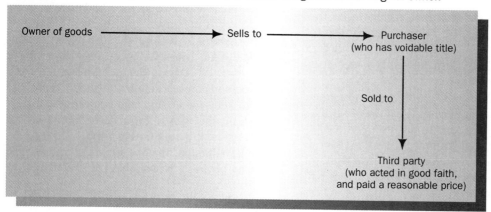

4. When the goods were procured through criminal fraud

This provision works as follows. Suppose Alfred is in the business of selling typewriters. Sam robs Alfred and takes a typewriter. Sam sells this typewriter to Alice. Alice acquires a void title. Alfred may reclaim the typewriter from Alice even if she took the typewriter in good faith, without any knowledge of the theft, and paid a reasonable price for the typewriter.

Let's change these facts somewhat so that Sam gives Alfred a check that later bounces. He sells the typewriter to Alice, who purchases it for a reasonable price and is unaware of the bad check. Alfred now demands the typewriter back from Alice. May Alice keep the typewriter? The answer is yes, because she acquired the typewriter from Sam, a person with a *voidable* title. Sam acquired a voidable title because he gave Alfred a check that subsequently bounced. As between Alfred and Sam, as long as Sam kept the typewriter, Alfred was able to get it back from Sam. Once Sam transferred the typewriter to Alice, a good faith purchaser for value, Alfred lost his right to reacquire the typewriter. The same result would occur if Sam deceives Alfred as to his identity, or if Sam agrees to pay cash for the typewriter at some later date, or if Sam acquires the typewriter through criminal fraud. If Sam acquires a voidable title by any of these devices, or any other transfer recognized as voidable by state law, Sam has the power to transfer a title good against the original seller to a good faith purchaser for value.

Purchases from Someone with Good Title The UCC protects anyone who purchases from a person who acquires good title. In the case noted earlier, suppose Sam gives a check to Alfred that subsequently bounces, and Sam resells the goods to Alice, a good faith purchaser for value. Alice now has the power to transfer all title she has. As she has a title good against even Alfred, she can transfer a good title to Linda—even if Linda knows that Sam acquired the goods from Alfred by passing a bad check! Linda cannot qualify as a good faith purchaser, but she still acquires a good title since she takes it through Alice.

Entrustment It is also possible for a merchant who deals in goods of the kind entrusted to him or her to transfer all title of the entruster to a buyer in the ordinary course of business. **Entrustment** is broadly defined as "any delivery and any acquiescence in retention of possession" and is covered in Subsection 2-403(2) and (3).

Such a transfer might occur when a jeweler accidentally mixes a watch left with him for repair with his regular stock and sells it to a customer by mistake. Another situation in which this applies is when a manufacturer sells goods to a retailer. If the manufacturer attempts to take a security interest in the goods held by the retailer for resale, this does not prevent the retailer from cutting off the manufacturer's security interest by selling the goods to a customer. The buyer acquires a clear title if he or she qualifies as a "buyer in the ordinary course of business" (as defined below).

To obtain a title superior to that of the previ-

FIGURE 21-3

Entrustment. The third party may keep the goods because the owner entrusted the painting to a merchant who dealt in goods of this kind (paintings) and the buyer is a buyer in the ordinary course of business.

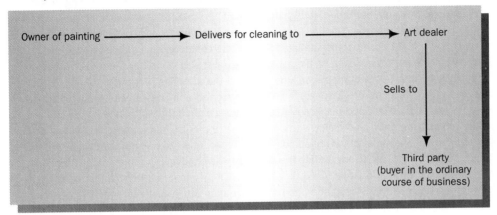

ous owner of the goods, the buyer must establish several facts. The goods must have been entrusted to a merchant regularly dealing in goods of that kind. In the case of the jeweler, the jeweler regularly deals in watches so he qualifies as a merchant. (Note that the definition of merchant here is narrower than under Section 2-104.) The jeweler has the power to transfer all rights of the entruster to a buyer in the ordinary course of business. A **buyer in the ordinary course of business** is a person who, in good faith and without knowledge that the sale to him or her is in violation of the own-

ership rights or security interest of a third party, buys in ordinary course from a person in the business of selling goods of this kind. Whether a person is a buyer in the ordinary course depends on the facts and circumstances of the case. In the case of the jeweler who mixes the watch with his other stock, the jeweler has the power to transfer good title to a person who purchases the watch from him. See Figure 21-3.

The case that follows provides a good discussion of when the UCC rules regarding entrustment apply.

KAHR V. MARKLAND

Appellate Court of Illinois, Fourth District
543 N.E. 2d 579 (1989)

BACKGROUND: Rita and Toby Kahr (plaintiffs) donated sacks of clothing to defendant Goodwill, but mistakenly included sterling silver and Mr. Kahr's wallet with the clothes. Goodwill put the silver on sale, and it was almost immediately purchased by defendant Karon Markland. The Kahrs sued to have the silver returned and won at trial court. Markland and Goodwill appealed.

McCullough, Presiding Judge

At trial, Rita Kahr testified regarding how the silver was mistakenly included with the donation for Goodwill. She stated that the silver was put in bags to be put in her attic along with jewelry and credit cards when she and Toby went on vacation. After returning from vacation, the bags of valuables were put on the dining room table with sacks of clothes for Goodwill.

When Toby took the bags of clothes to Goodwill, he mistakenly picked up the bags containing the silver. Approximately two hours after Toby returned from Goodwill, Rita asked where the silver was and then Rita and Toby realized it was taken to Goodwill. That same day, Toby called Goodwill and was told the pieces had been sold. Rita stated the silver was a wedding present 27 years previous from her father. Rita stated that no one told the Goodwill employees not to sell the silver but her husband did tell Goodwill the donation was clothing only. Toby's testimony in court and in his deposition substantiated Rita's statements. He also stated he knew the donation would be resold; however, he did not know the silver was in the bags with the clothing.

Judy Taylor, the Goodwill employee who received the plaintiffs' donations in April 1983, testified that she priced the silver after it was discovered and knew it was a bit nicer than other silver received by Goodwill. Taylor stated she discovered the wallet among the clothing after Toby left the store and called someone at the plaintiffs' home about the wallet. She did not mention the silver in the phone conversation because she had not yet discovered the silver. Taylor did not recall Toby stating the donation was clothing but remembered he did not want a receipt for the donation. According to Taylor, Toby became irate when he called concerning the items. Taylor stated she had no conversation with Markland regarding the silver. Taylor testified it was not uncommon for Goodwill to receive nice things in donations but she did not recognize the silver to be sterling.

Taylor testified in her deposition that Markland shopped at Goodwill almost everyday and on April 5 bought the silver within five minutes after it was received. Deborah Neese, Director of Operations for Goodwill, testified that Taylor had authority to price donations immediately and display them for resale.

Markland testified in her deposition that she worked for Goodwill for a short time in 1972 through 1973 as a sales clerk receiving donations. When she purchased the silver, Markland stated she knew it was not stainless steel but was uncertain whether the silver was sterling or silver plate. Markland stated she purchased the silver because of the monogram "K" on each piece and realized when she arrived at home that the silver was sterling. Markland stated she received a telephone call from Taylor and Neese asking her to return the silver but she refused. . . .

Markland urges this case is governed entirely by section 2-403 of the UCC. Markland urges the plaintiffs "entrusted" the silver to Goodwill, whether intentionally or otherwise, and under sections 2-403(2) and (3), she acquired title to the silver from the plaintiffs. Therefore, Markland maintains the trial court's emphasis on lost property is erroneous. . . .

Goodwill . . . maintains that public policy requires this court to reverse the trial court and find Goodwill had good title to transfer to Markland. Goodwill states that an affirmance by this court in this case would place an unreasonable burden on Goodwill and a seriously hamper its ability to provide a valuable community service. Goodwill also insists it was not "put on notice," after the discovery of the plaintiff's wallet, that plaintiffs did not intend to donate the silver.

Sections 2-403(2) and (3) of the UCC provide:

"(2) Any entrusting of possession of goods to a merchant who deals in goods of that kind gives him power to transfer all rights of the entruster to a buyer in ordinary course of business.
(3) 'Entrusting' includes any delivery and any acquiescence in retention of possession regardless of any condition expressed between the parties to the delivery or acquiescence and regardless of whether the procurement of the entrusting or the possessor's disposition of the goods have been such as to be larcenous under the criminal law."

The UCC defines "delivery" as follows:

"'Delivery' with respect to instruments, document of title, chattel paper or certificated securities means voluntary transfer of possession."

The above definition does not extend to goods. However, the comments on subsection (3) of section 2-403, as adopted in Illinois, state:

"This subsection, in defining the term 'entrusting' as used in subsection (2), combines and extends the policy set forth in [Uniform Sales Act] § 25 and [Uniform Trust Recipients Act] § 9. It includes *any voluntary transfer of possession by or with the consent of the entrustor.*" (Emphasis added.)

An entrustment requires four essential elements: (1) an actual entrustment of the goods by the delivery of possession of those goods to a merchant; (2) the party receiving the goods must be a merchant who deals in goods of that kind; (3) the merchant must sell the entrusted goods; and (4) the sale must be to a buyer in the ordinary course of business. The record establishes there was no delivery or voluntary transfer of the sterling silver because plaintiffs were unaware of its place in the bags of clothes. Markland does not dispute this fact but dismisses it as immaterial.

Before the entrustment provisions of the UCC can be applied, a delivery is required. Plaintiff's act of unknowingly leaving the sterling silver with Goodwill is not equivalent to a voluntary transfer. The term "voluntary" is defined as: "proceeding from the will or from one's own choice or consent" and "done by design or intention." (Webster's Third New International Dictionary 2564 (1981).) We conclude the entrustment provisions of the UCC did not apply to this case.

DECISION: The appeals court affirmed the trial court's ruling in favor of the Kahrs.

Risk of Loss

The UCC creates several methods for allocating the risk of loss between the parties:

1. By express agreement
2. By the use of mercantile terms
3. By Sections 2-509 and 2-510
4. By Section 2-326

Terms

When contracting, merchants frequently use mercantile terms or symbols as abbreviated methods of stating the delivery duties of the seller. The UCC defines these mercantile terms in Sections 2-319 to 2-325. Unless the parties to a contract specify another meaning, the UCC definitions of these terms control.

FOB and FAS   The terms **FOB** (free on board a carrier, typically a truck or train) and **FAS** (free alongside a ship) are defined in Section 2-319. Where the contract states "FOB St. Louis" and the seller is in St. Louis, then by Section 2-319(1)(a) the seller has the expense and risk of putting the goods into the possession of a carrier

and shipping the goods in accordance with the provisions of Section 2-504. This is a shipment or *origin contract.* This section requires the seller, unless otherwise agreed:

1. To put the goods in the possession of the carrier
2. To make a proper contract for transportation of the goods (e.g., meat must be refrigerated)
3. To obtain and deliver or tender to the buyer any documents necessary for the buyer to obtain possession of the goods
4. To promptly notify the buyer of the shipment

If the contract states "FOB New York" and the seller is in St. Louis and the buyer in New York, then the seller pays the freight and bears the risk of loss under Section 2-319(1)(b). This is a *destination contract.* The seller must at his or her own risk and expense transport the goods to New York and tender them to the buyer in New York. Section 2-503 requires the seller to put and hold conforming goods at the buyer's disposition and to give the buyer reasonable notification in order to enable him or her to take delivery. The tender must be at a reasonable hour and the goods must be available for a reasonable period of time.

Table 21-1 summarizes the various UCC rules that govern risk of loss. The left hand column states various possible agreements the parties may have with respect to risk of loss. In the corresponding right hand column Table 21-1 indicates whether the buyer or the seller bears the risk of loss in each given situation listed in the left hand column.

TABLE 21-1 **Risk of Loss**

Situation	Risk of Loss
Parties use a written agreement on risk of loss.	The agreement determines whether the buyer or the seller bears the risk of loss.
Parties use terms in order to allocate risk of loss.	
FOB origin	Buyer bears the risk of loss after the goods are delivered to the carrier.
FOB destination	Seller bears the risk of loss until the goods are tendered to the buyer.
The parties do not use a written agreement or terms to allocate risk of loss and there has been no breach of contract by either party (UCC 2-509 controls) *and*	
The parties ship by carrier using a destination contract	Seller bears the risk of loss until the goods are tendered to the buyer.
The parties ship by carrier using an origin contract	Buyer bears the risk of loss after the goods are delivered to the carrier.
The goods are held by a bailee and the parties use a negotiable document of title	Seller bears the the risk of loss until the buyer receives the documents.
The goods are held by a bailee and the parties use a nonnegotiable document of title	Seller bears the risk of loss until the bailee acknowledges the buyer's right to the goods.
The seller is to deliver the goods itself or the buyer is to pick up the goods itself and the seller is a merchant	Seller bears the risk of loss until the goods are delivered to the buyer.
The seller is to deliver the goods itself or the buyer is to pick up the goods itself and the seller is not a merchant.	Seller bears the risk of loss until the goods are tendered to the buyer.
The parties do not use a written agreement or terms to allocate risk of loss and there has been a breach of contract by either party (UCC 2-510 controls) *and*	
The seller breached the contract and the buyer rejected the goods	Risk of loss is on the seller until the buyer accepts the goods.
The seller breached the contract and the buyer revoked its acceptance of the goods	Risk of loss is on the seller to the extent of any deficiency in buyer's insurance.
The buyer breached the contract	Risk of loss is on the buyer to the extent of any deficiency in the seller's insurance.
Parties use a sale on approval contract (UCC 2-327 controls).	Risk of loss is on the seller until the goods are delivered to the buyer and the buyer accepts the goods. If the buyer rejects the goods, the return is at the seller's risk.
Parties use a sale or return contract (UCC 2-327 controls).	Risk of loss does not pass until the goods are delivered to the buyer and are accepted by the buyer. Once the goods have been accepted, if the buyer returns the goods to the seller, the risk of loss is on the buyer.

Presumption-of-Origin Contract   By means of an examination of the contract and the surrounding circumstances, it generally will be possible to determine whether the seller must send the goods to the buyer and whether the parties contemplated an origin or a destination contract. If the contract fails to cover this point clearly, the presumption is that the parties intended an origin contract. Suppose a contract read as follows: "Ship to ABC Corp., 1321 Redbud Lane, Mobile, Alabama." The seller's business is in Houston, Texas, and the buyer is located in Mobile. The mere fact that the label indicates where the package is to be shipped does not overcome the presumption that this is an origin contract. However, the statement "FOB ABC Corp., 1321 Redbud Lane, Mobile, Alabama" creates a destination contract. The seller must at his or her own risk and expense transport the goods to Mobile and tender them to the buyer in Mobile.

If the contract specifies "FOB vessel *St. Louis*" or "FOB car or other vehicle," the seller must, in addition to bearing the expense and risk of transportation, load the goods on board.

CIF   The term **CIF** stands for cost, insurance, and freight. When this term is used, it means that the price includes the cost of the goods, the cost of insuring the goods, and freight to a named destination. The seller must at his or her own expense put the goods into the possession of a carrier at the port for shipment and obtain a negotiable bill of lading covering the entire transportation to the named destination.

C & F   According to Section 2-320 (1 and 3), when a contract includes the term **C & F**, the price includes cost and freight to the named destination. The seller need not obtain insurance under a C & F term. The term has the same effect and imposes upon the seller the same obligations and risks as a CIF term, except for the obligation to insure. The risk of loss under CIF or C & F is on the buyer once the seller has delivered the goods to the carrier.

Ex-Ship   In a sale **ex-ship**, the seller must cause the goods to be delivered to the buyer from a ship that has arrived at the port of delivery. The seller must pay freight to the named port, release the ship owner's lien, and furnish the buyer with a direction that puts the ship under a duty to deliver the goods. The risk of loss does not pass until the goods are properly unloaded from the ship.

No Arrival, No Sale   The term **no arrival, no sale** is used when the parties execute a destination contract by which the risk of loss remains on the seller during shipment. Under this term, however, the seller is not liable for breach of contract if the goods are not delivered through no fault of the seller. The parties may arrive at a different understanding, but the seller is generally free of liability if goods conforming to the contract fail to arrive due to the hazards of transportation. If the seller fails to ship the goods or if he ships nonconforming goods, Section 2-324 does not relieve the seller of liability.

Risk of Loss in the Absence of Terms

The Uniform Sales Act, which governed the law of sales prior to the adoption of the UCC, forced the courts to struggle with the question of who held title to the goods in order to determine which party bore the risk of loss. The UCC greatly simplifies the determination of who bears the risk of loss by treating risk of loss separately from the issue of the title.

Voluntary Agreement   In general the UCC reflects the philosophy that the parties may determine the details of a contract. The parties may arrive at an agreement on risk of loss contrary to that specified in the UCC. The agreement may shift the allocation of risk of loss, or it may divide the risk between the parties. The only restraints on the modification of the risk-of-loss provisions in the UCC are that such modifications be made in good faith and are not unconscionable.

If a seller intends to shift the risk of loss to the buyer, the contract must clearly state the manner in which risk of loss will be allocated. This is especially true when the seller tries to shift the risk of loss to the buyer before he or she takes possession of the goods. In *Hayward v. Postma*, 188 N.W.2d 31 (1971), the seller argued that the risk of loss for a 30-foot Revel Craft Playmate Yacht worth $10,000 that was destroyed by fire while it was still at the seller's premises should fall on the buyer. Neither the seller nor the buyer had an insurance policy covering the boat. The seller claimed that he had transferred the risk of loss to the buyer by a clause in the security agreement signed by the parties.

(See Chapter 29 for an explanation of security agreements.) The court acknowledged that a risk of loss could be transferred to the buyer in this fashion, but it observed that the agreement in this case was not sufficiently clear and prominent to apprise the buyer that he bore the risk of loss on the yacht. The court noted that the usual rule in such cases was for the risk of loss to fall on the merchant-seller unless he or she had physically delivered the goods to the buyer. The rationale for this rule was that the buyer had no control over the goods and that it would be extremely unlikely that the buyer would carry insurance on goods not yet in his possession. The seller might transfer this risk to the buyer only if he or she clearly brought this matter to the buyer's attention.

Risk of loss may be specifically allocated by a clause in a contract, or the parties may allocate risk of loss through the use of a mercantile term, such as FOB.

No Agreement If the contract between the buyer and the seller fails to specify how risk of loss will be allocated between the parties, Section 2-509 controls if there is a loss but no breach of contract. Section 2-510 applies if there has been a loss and a breach of contract.

The policy underlying these provisions is to place the loss on the party most likely to have insured against the loss. The person in possession of the goods normally is able to prevent a loss from occurring in the first place. For this reason the risk of loss usually falls on the party in possession of the goods.

Section 2-509 divides risk of loss into three categories: (1) goods shipped by carrier, (2) goods held by a bailee that are to be delivered without being moved, and (3) all other cases.

Identification Risk of loss cannot pass to the buyer until the goods are identified to the contract. Section 2-501 states that, in the absence of a contrary agreement, identification occurs: when the contract is made if the goods are existing and identified; or if the goods are future goods, when the goods are shipped, marked, or otherwise designated by the seller as goods to which the contract refers.

Shipment by Carrier When the parties enter into an origin contract and agree to delivery by carrier, risk of loss shifts to the buyer when the seller puts the goods in the possession of a carrier, makes a reasonable contract for their transportation, obtains all documents necessary for the buyer to obtain possession of the goods, and notifies the buyer of the shipment.

If a destination contract is involved, whereby the seller agrees to ship the goods to the buyer by carrier, risk passes to the buyer when the seller has put and held conforming goods at the buyer's disposition at the destination point and given the buyer any notification and documents reasonably necessary to take delivery of the goods.

Suppose a paint manufacturer sells 500 cans of paint to a retail paint store. If the parties agree for the seller to ship the goods to the buyer's store at 1011 Main, Oklahoma City, and the goods are lost in transit after the seller loads them on a common carrier (e.g., a railroad, truck, or airline), who bears the risk of loss? It must first be determined if the parties entered into an origin contract or a destination contract. Bear in mind that the UCC views an origin contract as the typical contract. The seller does not bear the risk of loss after placing the goods on the carrier unless he has specifically agreed to bear the risk of loss to the destination point. In this case the courts probably would treat the agreement as an origin contract and place the risk of loss on the buyer. The term "ship to," attached to the goods with an address, has no significance in determining who bears the risk of loss. On the other hand, language such as "FOB buyer's plant" or "Ship to buyer, risk of loss remains on seller until tender by carrier to buyer" clearly contemplates a destination contract, and the risk does not pass to the buyer until the goods are tendered to the buyer at the place of destination.

The risk of loss will not pass unless the seller makes a proper contract for transportation and ships conforming goods.

Goods Held by a Bailee If the goods are not to be shipped by carrier but are in possession of a bailee and are to be delivered without being moved, Section 2-509(2) controls. If the bailee has issued a negotiable document of title, the risk of loss passes to the buyer when he or she receives the negotiable document of title. Risk of loss also passes to the buyer after his or her receipt of a nonnegotiable document of title, but not until the buyer has had a reasonable opportunity to present the document to the bailee. If the bailee refuses to honor the nonnegotiable document of title, risk of loss does not pass. If a nonnegotiable document of title has been issued, risk of loss passes to the buyer when the bailee acknowledges the buyer's right to the possession of the goods.

The following case discusses how risk of loss operates when goods are stored in a warehouse.

JASON'S FOODS, INC. V. PETER ECKRICH & SONS, INC.

U.S. Court of Appeals, Seventh Circuit
41 UCC Rep. Serv. 1287 (1985)

BACKGROUND: Jason's (plaintiff) sued Eckrich (defendant). Around December 20, 1982, Jason's Foods contracted to sell 38,000 pounds of "St. Louis style" pork ribs to Peter Eckrich & Sons, delivery to be effected by a transfer of the ribs from Jason's account in an independent warehouse to Eckrich's account in the same warehouse—a transfer on paper. Jason's notified Eckrich that the transfer would be made between January 10 and January 14, 1983. On January 13 Jason's phoned the warehouse and requested that the ribs be transferred to Eckrich's account. A clerk at the warehouse noted the transfer on its books immediately but did not mail a warehouse receipt to Eckrich until January 17 or 18, and it was not until January 24, when Eckrich received the receipt, that it knew the transfer had taken place.

In the meantime, on January 17 there was a fire at the warehouse and the ribs were destroyed. Jason's sued Eckrich for the price of the ribs.

Posner, Circuit Judge

Section 2-509(2) of the Uniform Commercial Code provides that where the "goods are held by a bailee to be delivered without being moved, the risk of loss passes to the buyer . . . (b) on acknowledgment by the bailee of the buyer's right to possession of the goods." We must decide whether acknowledgment to the *seller* complies with the statute.

Jason's argues that when the warehouse transferred the ribs to Eckrich's account, Jason's lost all rights over the ribs, and it should not bear the risk of loss of goods it did not own or have any right to control.

. . . Section 2-509(2) separates title from risk of loss. Title to the ribs passed to Eckrich when the warehouse made the transfer on its books from Jason's account to Eckrich's, but the risk of loss did not pass until the transfer was "acknowledged."

. . . Since whoever will be liable for the loss can insure against it, the court must determine who is liable before knowing who can insure, rather than vice versa. If acknowledgment to the seller is enough to place the risk of loss on the buyer, then Eckrich should have bought insurance against any losses that occurred afterward. If acknowledgment to the buyer is necessary (we need not decide whether acknowledgment to a third party may ever suffice), Jason's should have bought insurance against any losses occurring until then.

A related section of the Uniform Commercial Code, § 2-503(4)(a), makes acknowledgment by the bailee (the warehouse here) a method of tendering goods that are sold without being physically moved; but, like §2-509(2)(b), it does not indicate to whom acknowledgment must be made. . . . Rules on tender have, it is true, a different function from rules on risk of loss; they determine at what point the seller has completed the performance of his side of the bargain. He may have completed performance, but if the goods are still in transit the risk of loss does not shift until the buyer receives them, if the seller is a merchant. In the case of warehouse transfers, however, the draftsmen apparently wanted risk of loss to conform to the rules for tender. And those provisions apparently require (in the case where no document of title passes) acknowledgment to the buyer. Jason's could have instructed the warehouse to call Eckrich when the transfer was complete on the warehouse books.

. . . If one party is in a better position than the other to prevent a loss, this is a reason for placing the risk of loss on him, to give him an incentive to prevent it. It would be a reason for placing liability on a seller who still had possession of the goods, even though title had passed. But between the moment of transfer of title by Jason's and the moment of receipt of the warehouse receipt by Eckrich, neither party to the sale had effective control over the ribs.

When did the risk of loss pass? Does "acknowledgment" mean receipt, as in the surrounding subsections of § 2-509(2), or mailing? Since the evidence was in conflict over whether the acknowledgment was mailed on January 17 (and at what hour), which was the day of the fire, or on January 18, this could be an important question—but in another case. Jason's waived it. The only theory it tendered to the district court, or briefed and argued in this court, was that the risk of loss passed either on January 13, when the transfer of title was made on the books of the warehouse, or at the latest on January 14, because Eckrich knew the ribs would be transferred at the warehouse sometime between January 10 and 14. We have discussed the immateriality of the passage of title on January 13; we add that the alternative argument, that Eckrich knew by January 14 that it owned the ribs, exaggerates what Eckrich knew. By the close of business on January 14 Eckrich had a well-founded expectation that the ribs had been transferred to its account; but considering the many slips that are possible between cup and lips, we do not think that this expectation should fix the point at which the risk shifts.

DECISION: The court decided that as there had been no acknowledgment by the bailee to Eckrich, the buyer, of Eckrich's right to the ribs, risk of loss had not passed to the buyer at the time of the fire, and therefore it remained on Jason's.

Other Cases   All other cases *not* involving a breach of contract are covered by Section 2-509(3). This section covers the situation where the seller intends to deliver the goods to the buyer in the seller's truck or the buyer intends to pick up the goods at the seller's place of business. Subsection (3) sets out two rules, one of which covers a merchant-seller and the other applies to a nonmerchant-seller. In the case of the merchant-seller, risk of loss remains on the seller until the buyer actually takes physical possession of the goods. If the seller is not a merchant, risk of loss passes to the buyer on tender of delivery. Tender means putting and holding conforming goods at the buyer's disposition and giving the buyer any notification reasonably necessary to enable him to take delivery. The tender must be at a reasonable hour and kept available long enough for the buyer to take possession.

Suppose Acme Glass agrees to sell fifteen panels of glass to a building contractor. Nothing is said about who bears the risk of loss in the contract. If the glass is destroyed prior to the time the contractor picks up the glass, who bears the risk of loss? As Acme Glass deals in goods of this kind, it is a merchant under Section 2-104. Acme must actually deliver physical possession of the glass to the contractor. The risk of loss is on Acme.

But suppose Elmo sells fifteen panels of glass to his next-door neighbor and tenders them to his neighbor. The neighbor fails to pick up the glass, and after a week passes a fire destroys Elmo's home and the glass. Who bears the risk of loss? Because Elmo is not a merchant, and he tendered the glass to his neighbor, the risk of loss falls on his neighbor.

Note that a merchant-seller who retains physical possession of goods after selling them retains the risk of loss. This is true even after title has passed and the seller has received his or her money for the goods, as is illustrated by the following case.

MARTIN V. MELLAND'S INC.
Supreme Court of North Dakota
283 N.W.2d 76 (1979)

BACKGROUND: Israel Martin (plaintiff) purchased a hay-moving machine from Melland's (defendant). Martin traded in his old haystack mover on the new one, but he retained possession of it. The old haystack mover was destroyed while in Martin's possession.

Erickstad, Chief Justice

The narrow issue on this appeal is who should bear the loss of a truck and an attached haystack mover that was destroyed by fire while in the possession of the plaintiff, Israel Martin (Martin), but after the certificate of title had been delivered to the defendant, Melland's Inc. (Melland's). The destroyed haymoving unit was to be used as a trade-in for a new haymoving unit that Martin ultimately purchased from Melland's.

On June 11, 1974, Martin entered into a written agreement with Melland's, a farm implement dealer, to purchase a truck and attached haystack mover for the total purchase price of $35,389. Martin was given a trade-in allowance of $17,389 on his old unit, leaving a balance owing of $18,000 plus sales tax of $720 or a total balance of $18,720. The agreement provided that Martin "mail or bring title" to the old unit to Melland's "this week." Martin mailed the certificate of title to Melland's pursuant to the agreement, but he was allowed to retain the use and possession of the old unit "until they had the new one ready."

Fire destroyed the truck and the haymoving unit in early August, 1974, while Martin was moving hay. The parties did not have any agreement regarding insurance or risk of loss on the unit.

The district court found "that although the Plaintiff [Martin] executed the title to the . . . [haymoving unit], he did not relinquish possession of the same and therefore the Plaintiff was the owner of said truck at the time the fire occurred."

The position that the Code has taken, divorcing the question of risk of loss from a determination of title, is summed up by Professor Nordstrom in his hornbook on sales:

> No longer is the question of title of any importance in determining whether a buyer or a seller bears the risk of loss. It is true that the person with title will also (and incidentally) often bear the risk that the goods may be destroyed or lost; but the seller may have title and the buyer the risk, or the seller may have the risk and the buyer the title. In short, title is not a relevant consideration in deciding whether the risk has shifted to the buyer. R. Nordstrom, Handbook of the Law of Sales, 393 (1970).

It is clear that a barter or trade-in is considered a sale and is therefore subject to the Uniform Commercial Code. It is also clear that the party who owns the trade-in is considered the seller. Subsection 3 of Section 2-509 is applicable in this case.

Martin admits that he is not a merchant; therefore, it is necessary to determine if Martin tendered delivery of the trade-in unit to Melland's. Tender is defined in Section 2-503 UCC, as follows:

> (2-503) Manner of seller's tender of delivery.—
> 1. Tender of delivery requires that the seller put and hold conforming goods at the buyer's disposition and give the buyer any notification reasonably necessary to enable him to take delivery. The manner, time and place for tender are determined by the agreement and this chapter, and in particular
>   a. tender must be at a reasonable hour, and if it is of goods they must be kept available for the period reasonably necessary to enable the buyer to take possession; but

b. unless otherwise agreed the buyer must furnish facilities reasonably suited to the receipt of the goods.

It is clear that the trade-in unit was not tendered to Melland's in this case. The parties agreed that Martin would keep the old unit "until they had the new one ready."

We hold that Martin did not tender delivery of the trade-in truck and haystack mover to Melland's pursuant to Section 2-509 UCC; consequently, Martin must bear the loss.

DECISION: The court affirmed a decision for Melland's.

Risk of Loss When Contract Is Breached

Section 2-510 addresses the problem of risk of loss when there has been a breach of contract by either the seller or the buyer. If for any reason the goods delivered by the seller fail to live up to the requirements of the contract, the risk of loss does not pass to the buyer.

The examples given in the sections that follow invariably involve goods being destroyed. These examples assume, of course, that the destruction of the goods is not the fault of the buyer or the seller.

Breach by Seller—Buyer Rejects   Section 2-510(1) covers the situation where the seller tenders or delivers goods that do not conform to the contract under circumstances that give the buyer the right to reject (refuse to accept) the goods. In this case the risk of loss remains on the seller until the buyer accepts the goods or the seller replaces the nonconforming goods with conforming goods (referred to as a "cure" by the seller).

Suppose a seller ships paper goods to the buyer. Because the goods fail to meet the standards set forth in the contract, the buyer rejects the goods. The buyer holds the goods, and while in her possession they are destroyed by fire. In this case, the seller bears the risk of loss. What if the buyer accepts the paper in spite of its nonconformity? The risk of loss is then on the buyer. Likewise, if the seller takes back the nonconforming paper and substitutes conforming paper, and then the paper is destroyed, the risk of loss is on the buyer since the seller has "cured" his defective performance.

Breach by Seller—Buyer Revokes   Section 2-510(2) sets forth the buyer's rights when he or she revokes an acceptance. When the buyer rightfully revokes an acceptance, the risk of loss is treated as having remained on the seller from the beginning, to the extent of any deficiency in the buyer's insurance.

Suppose a seller ships groceries, which the buyer accepts. Thereafter, the buyer finds some defect in the groceries that gives him grounds to revoke the acceptance. When the buyer revokes his acceptance, the risk of loss is treated as having been on the seller from the beginning. If the goods are destroyed while in the buyer's possession, after the buyer's revocation, the loss falls on the seller entirely if the buyer has no insurance. What if the buyer has $500 worth of insurance, but the fire destroys $2,000 worth of groceries? Five hundred dollars of the loss falls on the buyer's insurance company, and the other $1,500 falls on the seller.

Breach by Buyer   The final subsection of 2-510 puts the risk of loss on the buyer when she breaches the contract before the risk of loss passes to the buyer. In this case the seller may, to the extent of any deficiency in his or her insurance coverage, treat the risk of loss as resting on the buyer for a commercially reasonable time. The seller must meet several conditions to put the loss on the buyer:

1. The seller must have had conforming goods.
2. The goods must have been identified to the contract.
3. The buyer must have breached the contract before the loss passed to the buyer.
4. The loss must not have been covered, at least in part, by the seller's insurance.
5. The loss must have occurred within a commercially reasonable time.

Suppose on June 1 the parties enter into a contract for a delivery scheduled for June 15. On June 10 the seller segregates conforming goods and identifies them to the contract. Normally the risk of loss remains on a merchant-seller, assuming the buyer plans to pick up the goods at the seller's place of business, until she delivers the goods to the buyer (Subsection 2-509[3]). On June 12 the buyer repudiates the contract. On June 14 the goods are destroyed while in possession of the seller. If the seller has no insurance, the whole loss falls on the buyer. If the seller has $500 worth of insurance and the loss is greater than $500, then the seller's insurance company will be responsible for $500 and the buyer will be responsible for the remaining loss.

What if the seller keeps the goods in storage until March of the next year, at which time they are destroyed? The buyer might argue that the loss did not occur within a commercially reasonable time. Such an argument probably would be successful.

Sale or Return and Sale on Approval

Section 2-326(1) states that if goods are delivered primarily for use and may be returned by the buyer to the seller even though they conform to the contract, the transaction is a **sale on approval**. If the goods are delivered to a buyer who is entitled to return conforming goods and the buyer intends to resell the goods, the transaction is a **sale or return**.

In order to determine whether conforming goods that may be returned to the seller have been sold on sale-or-return or sale-on-approval terms, the court must examine whether the buyer intended to use the goods or to resell them.

When goods are purchased on sale on approval, the buyer may wish to try out the goods before accepting them. If she uses the goods in order to try them out, this does not constitute acceptance. The risk of loss and title remain with the seller until the buyer accepts the goods. Acceptance can occur automatically if the buyer fails to notify the seller of her election to return the goods within a reasonable time. Acceptance of any part of the goods is acceptance of the whole—if the goods conform to the contract. If the buyer elects to return the goods, the return is at the seller's risk and expense. If the buyer is a merchant, she must follow any instructions provided by the seller.

Under sale-or-return terms, the buyer can return all or part of the goods shipped to her as long as they are substantially in their original condition. The buyer, however, must elect to return them within a reasonable time, and she must return them at her own risk and expense.

The following case illustrates the sale-on-approval rule.

PREWITT V. NUMISMATIC FUNDING CORP.

U.S. Court of Appeals, Eighth Circuit
39 UCC Rep. Serv. 797 (1984)

BACKGROUND: Numismatic (defendant) sells rare and collector coins by mail. Prewitt (plaintiff) responded to Numismatic's advertisement in a December 1981 issue of *The Wall Street Journal* offering six Morgan silver dollars. Shortly thereafter, a salesman from Numismatic called Prewitt and Prewitt agreed to receive several coins on an "approval basis." Two weeks later, Prewitt received in the mail fifteen Morgan silver dollars. The literature enclosed with the coins stated "Everything is available to you on a fourteen-day approval basis." The invoice stated that title did not pass until the buyer paid the account in full and that the buyer had 14 days from the date of receipt in which to settle the account. The literature gave no directions as to how to return unwanted coins.

Prewitt immediately returned the coins via Federal Express and enclosed a letter expressing his disapproval of the shipment of coins. When Numismatic contacted him again, however, he agreed to review several additional coins on an approval basis. The second shipment, containing fifty-two coins valued in excess of $20,000, was sent on the same terms as the first. Prewitt selected seven coins and returned the remaining coins via either the U.S. Postal Service or Federal Express.

On February 10, 1982, Numismatic mailed Prewitt twenty-eight gold and silver coins in two packages valued at $61,975. As with earlier shipments, the coins were sent on a 14-day approval basis with no instructions for the return of unwanted coins. Prewitt instructed his wife to return them via certified mail for the maximum amount of insurance available—$400 per package. She mailed the coins February 23, 1982, but Numismatic never received them. Prewitt then brought this action seeking a declaration of his nonliability for the coins.

Bright, Circuit Judge

In awarding Prewitt a declaratory judgment of nonliability, the district court determined, and the parties do not dispute, that the delivery of coins between seller Numismatic and buyer Prewitt constituted a sale "on approval." Under the provisions of the Uniform Commercial Code relating to risk of loss, as adopted in Missouri, the court held that the risk of loss remained with the seller.

A. Course of Dealing and Course of Performance Arguments

Appellant Numismatic advances two theories in which it contends that the parties impliedly agreed to shift the risk of loss to Prewitt. First, it argues that an agreement by Prewitt to assume the risk of loss arose by implication from the prior course of dealings between the parties in which Prewitt had returned coins fully insured via Federal Express. . . .

The code defines "course of dealing" as "a sequence of previous conduct between the parties to a particular transaction which is fairly to be regarded as establishing a common basis of understanding for interpreting their expressions and other conduct." A court should look to course of dealing to supplement or qualify the terms of an agreement where the parties are or should be aware of that course of dealing. . . .

No instructions were provided prescribing a method of return on any of the shipments. Thus, we conclude that the evidence is insufficient to show "a sequence of previous conduct" establishing a course of dealing between the parties.

Numismatic's second contention is that an agreement to shift the risk of loss from the seller to the buyer may be implied from Prewitt's conduct in obtaining some, albeit inadequate, insurance on the packages in question. Under the Missouri parol evidence rule, course of performance may also be used to explain or supplement the terms of a written agreement. Course of performance is defined, and its applicability prescribed in [Mo Rev Stat] § 400.2-208(1):

> (1) Where the contract for sale involves repeated occasions for performance by either party with knowledge of the nature of the performance and opportunity for objection to it by the other, any course of performance accepted or acquiesced in without objection shall be relevant to determine the meaning of the agreement.

There is simply no basis upon which we can identify any course of performance in this case. It is undisputed that Prewitt purchased insurance on and returned the coins all in one large shipment. The official comments to [Mo Rev Stat] § 400.2-208 note that the section has no application to cases involving only a single occasion of conduct.

B. Seasonable Notification

Numismatic also contends that the buyer assumed the risk of loss under the "sale on approval" provisions of the Uniform Commercial Code because he did not seasonably notify the seller of his election to return the goods and did not seasonably return the goods.

> The district court rejected Numismatic's contention because the sale on approval contract gave Prewitt fourteen days to decide whether to accept or reject the coins. Numismatic does not dispute that Prewitt placed the coins in the mail for return within the fourteen day period.
>
> In our view of the record, we find no error in the district court's findings of fact and its conclusions of law logically follow from those findings. In sum, Numismatic failed to produce evidence sufficient to establish any basis upon which the district court could have found that the risk of loss shifted to the buyer in a "sale on approval" transaction. Accordingly, we affirm.
>
> **DECISION:** The court affirmed the lower court's ruling for Prewitt.

Insurable Interest

The UCC, in Section 2-501, specifies who has an insurable interest in goods. The buyer obtains an insurable interest in existing goods as soon as they are identified to the contract. The buyer obtains an insurable interest even though the goods identified are nonconforming.

However, if the contract is for the sale of future goods, that is, goods that are not yet in existence and identified, the buyer obtains an insurable interest in the future goods when they are shipped, mailed, or otherwise designated by the seller as goods to which the contract refers.

The seller has an insurable interest in goods so long as he or she has title to the goods or any security interest in the goods.

Article 6

Article 6 of the UCC was drafted to prevent a particular type of fraud by merchants. The fraud that Arti-

PREVENTIVE LAW

After examining the material in the text on the question of risk of loss, it should be evident that there are many ways that a person may end up bearing the risk of loss. One way to avoid bearing the risk of loss is to include a specific contractual provision dealing with risk of loss. Another possibility is to purchase insurance. In such a case, if a person ends up bearing the loss, this loss will be paid by the insurance company.

cle 6 addressed is best illustrated by an example. Suppose that Mark is starting up a shoe store. In order to acquire inventory, Mark takes out a loan from First Bank. Without notifying First Bank, Mark then sells all of his inventory in bulk to Brian, who knows nothing about the First Bank loan. Mark then absconds with the proceeds of the sale. First Bank may not be entitled under the law to recover the inventory from Brian, an innocent purchaser. In that event, First Bank will suffer a loss unless it can find Mark—and, more importantly, his money.

Article 6 attempted to deal with this "bulk-sale risk" by requiring the buyer in bulk to obtain a list of the seller's creditors and to notify those creditors of the impending sale. Creditors not receiving such notice were generally given the right to nullify the sale.

Many criticized Article 6 on the grounds that it imposed too great a burden on the buyer in bulk to protect the interests of the seller's creditors. Over time, it has become easier for potential buyers to check the credit standing of a seller and to discover any liens on the seller's property. Given that a buyer is bound to honor any lien filed in the public records, critics of Article 6 contended that it was needlessly burdensome on buyers to make them comply with the detailed disclosure requirements set forth in the article. These requirements, according to the critics, have impeded good faith sales of businesses.

The National Conference of Commissioners on Uniform State Laws, the body responsible for drafting the UCC, joined the chorus of criticism in 1989 and recommended that Article 6 be repealed. In the alternative, the commissioners suggested that states adopt a modified version of Article 6 that would apply only to sellers whose principal business is the sale of inventory from stock. It remains to be seen whether the majority of states will eventually repeal Article 6 or adopt the modified version.

Review Questions and Problems

Key Terms

identification	FOB
origin contract	FAS
destination contract	CIF
void title	C & F
voidable title	ex-ship
entrustment	no arrival, no sale
buyer in the ordinary course of business	sale on approval
	sale on return

Discussion Questions

1. If a seller in New York and a buyer in St. Louis execute a contract with the term "FOB St. Louis," what type of contract is it?

2. What four types of transactions give rise to voidable title?

3. What is a document of title?

4. Can both the seller and the buyer have an insurable interest in the same goods at the same time?

Review Problems

1. Detwiller purchases a new truck from Stevens Dodge. The truck is then shipped to Bob, a dealer closer to Detwiller's hometown, for a pickup. After Detwiller pays Stevens Dodge, documents of title are sent to Detwiller. Prior to the receipt thereof, the truck is destroyed by fire while sitting on Bob's lot. Detwiller and Stevens Dodge have no agreement regarding the risk of loss. Where does the risk of loss lie?

2. Eberhard agrees to sell and ship certain goods to Brown. The contract does not contain any FOB terms, nor is there any agreement on who bears the risk of loss. Certain goods are placed on board a common carrier by Eberhard but are apparently lost in transit. Eberhard now sues Brown for the price of the goods. Brown contends that the risk of loss remains with Eberhard. Is Brown's contention correct?

3. Mitchell Lumber Co. contracts to sell lumber to Home Builders, Inc. The lumber delivered does not meet the specifications called for in the contract, and Home Builders prepares to return the lumber. Before the lumber can be returned, it is destroyed by fire. Who bears the risk of loss?

4. Radio World purchases 1,000 radios from Electronics Manufacturers, Inc. Soon after accepting the radios, Radio World discovers that at least some of them contain a hidden defect and fail to conform to contract specifications. Radio World revokes its acceptance of the radios and prepares to return them to Electronics Manufacturers. Before Radio World can return the radios, they are stolen. Do you need any additional information to determine who bears the risk of loss? If so, what? Describe how the risk of loss would be determined in this case.

5. The Mudville Nine baseball team orders twenty specially designed bats from Sluggerco. After Sluggerco manufactures the bats, but just before they are scheduled to be delivered, the buyer repudiates the contract. The next day, the bats are destroyed in a fire at Sluggerco's plant. The loss is fully covered by Sluggerco's insurance. Who must bear the expense of the loss? Why?

Case Problems

1. The Jetts purchased an organ from Menchey Music Service. The store attempted to retain title to the organ after delivery of it to the Jetts. Before paying for the organ, the Jetts sold the organ to another person. A criminal action was brought against the Jetts based on the theory that they had committed a crime by selling the organ. The prosecution had to prove that title was in Menchey Music Service to establish the crime of fraudulent conversion. Who had title to the organ—Menchey Music Service or the Jetts?

2. Vineyard Wine Company, the buyer, bought wine from Rheinberg-Kellerei, the seller, a West German wine producer and exporter. While en route to the United States, the wine was lost at sea. The buyer did not receive prompt notice of the shipment, and in fact did not learn of the shipment until after the wine was lost at sea. Was the risk of loss on the buyer or the seller?

3. Lane was in the business of selling boats. He sold a boat to John Willis. Willis paid for the boat with a check that was later dishonored. Willis thereafter sold the boat to Jimmy Honeycutt. Willis had nothing to indicate that he was the owner of the boat. He sold the boat to Honeycutt that was worth over $6,500 for $2,500. Did Honeycutt get good title to the boat?

4. Karinol Corporation agreed to ship watches to Pestana. The goods were loaded on a carrier but were lost in transit. Does the risk of loss fall on Karinol or Pestana?

22

Sales: Performance

Terms

Acceptance

Rejection

Revocation

Installment Contracts

Assurance of Performance

Anticipatory Repudiation

Impossibility

The formation and interpretation of sales contracts were discussed in the preceding chapter. This chapter focuses on the performance obligations of the parties to a sales contract.

Terms

The basic duty of the seller is to deliver or make available the goods purchased by the buyer. The buyer's basic responsibility is to pay for the goods purchased. The obligations of the seller and buyer are discussed in turn.

Delivery

Section 2-307 of the Uniform Commercial Code makes it the duty of the seller to transfer and deliver goods in accordance with the terms of the contract. But in what manner must the seller deliver the goods? Must he or she deliver all the goods at one time? The answer to this question is found in Section 2-307: all the goods must be delivered at one time, unless the contract states otherwise. The buyer may reject a delivery that has been improperly delivered in lots—subject to the seller's right to cure the improper tender. The seller cures an improper delivery by subsequently delivering the goods in the proper manner.

Delivery in Lots Sometimes, however, delivery in a single lot will not be possible. Suppose, for example, that the buyer does not have sufficient storage space to take delivery of the entire order at one time. Must the buyer take it anyway? Section 2-307 provides that "where the circumstances give either party the right to make or demand delivery in lots the price if it can be apportioned may be demanded for each lot." Thus the seller can, in certain circumstances, deliver the goods in separate lots. For example, if the seller is unable to find enough trucks or railroad cars to deliver the goods in a single lot, delivery may be made in lots and the seller may demand payment for each lot.

Place for Delivery The next question is: What is the proper place for delivery? Section 2-308 makes the seller's place of business the proper place for delivery in most cases. If the contract is for the sale of identified goods that are known by both parties to be at some other place, that place is the proper place for delivery of the goods. If the parties have agreed to delivery by carrier or have authorized delivery by carrier, the seller's duties with respect to delivery are governed by Sections 2-503 and 2-504. Keep in mind that the UCC rules on place of delivery do not apply if the parties agree in the contract to another place of delivery.

Time for Delivery If the time for shipment or delivery has not been agreed upon, the time for shipment or delivery is a reasonable time. What is reasonable depends on the nature, purpose, and circumstances of the action to be taken. Where a time has been left open for delivery, neither party may demand delivery or offer delivery at an unreasonably early time. The performance requirements of destination and shipment contracts were described in Chapter 21.

Delivery of Nonconforming Goods What happens if the seller delivers at the proper place and time, but the goods he or she delivers do not conform to the contract? Section 2-508(1) makes it clear that, although a tender or delivery has been rejected by the buyer because it is nonconforming, the buyer does not necessarily have a right to sue for breach of contract. If the time for performance has not yet expired, the seller may "seasonably" notify the buyer of his or her intention to cure and may then make a conforming delivery within the contract time. What is seasonable notice? Section 1-204(3) states: "An action is taken 'seasonably' when it is taken at or within the time agreed or if no time is agreed at or within a reasonable time." Thus if the seller is to deliver goods on December 1, and she delivers nonconforming goods that the buyer rejects on November 1, the seller may notify the buyer of her intention to cure and deliver conforming goods anytime up through December 1. What if the seller delivers nonconforming goods on November 29 and notifies the buyer that she will attempt to cure? May she do so at that late date? Two days is probably not seasonable notice.

What if the seller sends a nonconforming tender that she reasonably believes will be acceptable to the buyer? If the seller did not anticipate at the time of sending the nonconforming goods that the buyer would reject them, and if the seller lacks the time to deliver conforming goods before the time for performance elapses, the seller has a "reasonable time" to substitute performance. Suppose a seller has agreed to deliver green, red, and blue swimsuits by December 1 and, because she has no blue suits in stock, sends yellow, green, and red suits. The buyer may be able to reject the goods as nonconforming. If the goods arrive on November 29 the seller will not have time to cure, so she may try to rely on Section 2-508(2) to obtain extra time to cure. Reasonable grounds to believe that the buyer will accept the goods may be found in the prior course of dealing, course of performance, or usage of trade, as well as in the circumstances surrounding the making of the contract. If the buyer has accepted a substitute color on swimsuits in the past, that is reasonable grounds for believing that the buyer will accept a substitute color now. The buyer may protect himself by including a "no replacement" clause in the contract.

The following case, *T. W. Oil, Inc. v. Consolidated Edison Co.*, illustrates one reason why the UCC gives the seller the right to cure. Suppose that you have contracted to purchase a commodity—let's say oil—at a certain price. Suppose further that by the time the oil is to be delivered, the market price of oil has fallen and you can buy it more cheaply from another supplier. If the seller delivers oil that in some way doesn't conform to the contract, might you not be tempted to use the nonconformity as an excuse to get out of the contract? As *T. W. Oil* illustrates, Section 2-508(2) limits the ability of the buyer in such a situation to escape the terms of his bargain.

T. W. OIL, INC. v. CONSOLIDATED EDISON CO.
Court of Appeals of New York
35 UCC Rep. 12 (1982)

BACKGROUND: T. W. Oil, Inc. (plaintiff) sued Con Edison (defendant) for breach of contract after Con Ed refused to accept what it claimed to be nonconforming oil and refused to allow the plaintiff to seasonably cure. The lower court awarded the plaintiff $1,385,512.83, the difference between the original price and the amount it received in the open market upon selling the oil Con Ed had refused. The appellate division affirmed, and the defendant appealed.

Fuchsberg, Judge

In January 1974, midst the fuel shortage produced by the oil embargo, the plaintiff purchased a cargo of fuel oil whose sulfur content was represented to it as no greater than 1%. While the oil was still at sea en route to the United States in the tanker *MT Khamsin*, plaintiff received a certificate from the foreign refinery at which it had been processed informing it that the sulfur content in fact was .52%. Thereafter, on January 24, the plaintiff entered into a written contract with the defendant (Con Ed) for the sale of this oil. The agreement was for delivery to take place between January 24 and January 30, payment being subject to a named independent testing agency's confirmation of quality and quantity. The contract, following a trade custom to round off specifications of sulfur content at, for instance, 1%, .5% or .3%, described that of the *Khamsin* oil as .5%. In the course of the negotiations, the plaintiff learned that Con Ed was then authorized to buy and burn oil with a sulfur content of up to 1% and would even mix oils containing more and less to maintain that figure.

When the vessel arrived on January 25, its cargo was discharged into Con Ed storage tanks in Bayonne, New Jersey. In due course, the independent testing people reported a sulfur content of .92%. On this basis, acting within a time frame whose reasonableness is not in question, on February 14 Con Ed rejected the shipment. Prompt negotiations to adjust the price failed; by February 20, plaintiff had offered a price reduction roughly responsive to the difference in sulfur reading, but Con Ed, though it could use the oil, rejected this proposition out of hand. It was insistent on paying no more than the latest prevailing price, which, in the volatile market that then existed, was some 25% below the level which prevailed when it agreed to buy the oil.

The very next day, February 21, plaintiff offered to cure the defect with a substitute shipment of conforming oil scheduled to arrive on the SS *Appolonian Victory* on February 28. Nevertheless, on February 22, the very day after the cure was proffered, Con Ed, adamant in its intention to avail itself of the intervening drop in prices, summarily rejected this proposal too. The two cargos were subsequently sold to third parties at the best price obtainable, first that of the *Appolonian* and, sometime later, after extraction from the tanks had been accomplished, that of the *Khamsin*.

We turn to the central issue on this appeal: Fairly interpreted, did subdivision 2 of Section 2-508 of the Uniform Commercial Code require Con Ed to accept the substitute shipment plaintiff tendered? In approaching this question, we, of course, must remember that a seller's right to cure a defective tender, as allowed by both subdivisions of Section 2-508, was intended to act as a meaningful limitation on the absolutism of the old perfect tender rule, under which no leeway was allowed for any imperfections.

Since we here confront circumstances in which the conforming tender came after the time of performance, we focus on subdivision 2-508(2). On its face, taking its conditions in the order in which they appear, for the statute to apply (1) a buyer must have rejected a nonconforming tender, (2) the seller must have had reasonable grounds to believe this tender would be acceptable (with or without money allowance) and (3) the seller must have "seasonably" notified the buyer of the intention to substitute a conforming tender within a reasonable time.

In the present case, none of these presented a problem. The first one was easily met for it is unquestioned that, at .92%, the sulfur content of the *Khamsin* oil did not conform to the .5% specified in the contract and that it was rejected by Con Ed. The second, the reasonableness of the seller's belief that the original tender would be acceptable, was supported not only by proof that the contract's .5% and the refinery certificate's .52% were trade equivalents, but by testimony that, by the time the contract was made, the plaintiff knew Con Ed burned fuel with a content of up to 1%, so that, with appropriate price adjustment, the *Khamsin* oil would have suited its needs even if, at delivery, it was, to the plaintiff's surprise, to test out at .92%. Further, the matter seems to have been put beyond dispute by the defendant's readiness to take the oil at the reduced market price on February 20.

As to the third, the conforming state of the *Appolonian* oil is undisputed, the offer to tender it took place on February 21, only a day after Con Ed finally had rejected the *Khamsin* delivery and the *Appolonian* substitute then already was en route to the United States. It is almost impossible, given the flexibility of the Uniform Commercial Code definitions of "seasonable" and "reasonable" to quarrel with the finding that the remaining requirements of the statute also had been met.

In dealing with the application of Section 2-508 (subd [2]), courts have been concerned with the reasonableness of the seller's belief that the goods would be acceptable rather than with the seller's pre-tender knowledge or lack of knowledge of the defect.

A seller should have recourse to the relief afforded by the Uniform Commercial Code, Section 2-508 (subd [2]) as long as it can establish that it had reasonable grounds, tested objectively, for its belief that the goods would be accepted. It goes without saying that the test of reasonableness, in this context, must encompass the concepts of "good faith" and "commercial standards of fair dealing" which permeate the Code.

DECISION: The New York Court of Appeals affirmed the judgment in favor of T. W. Oil, finding that T. W. Oil had reasonable grounds to believe that its nonconforming shipment of oil would be accepted by Con Edison and that T. W. Oil seasonably notified Con Edison of its intention to cure.

Payment

Cash or Check Unless the parties have agreed to the contrary or the goods are sold on credit, payment is due at the time and place at which the buyer is to receive the goods (Section 2-310[a]). Tender of payment is sufficient when it is made by any means or in any manner current in the ordinary course of business unless the seller demands payment in legal tender (Section 2-511[2]). The buyer usually may pay by check, unless the seller demands cash. If the seller demands cash, he or she must give the buyer a reasonable time to obtain the cash. The purpose of giving the buyer additional time to collect the cash is to prevent the buyer from being unprepared at the time for payment because he or she planned to pay by check or some other instrument. This provision prevents the seller from treating the buyer's inability to pay in cash at the time for payment as a breach of contract. In the event the seller accepts the buyer's check, the payment is conditional on the check being paid by the bank when it is presented for payment (Section 2-511[3]). If the bank dishonors the check, the buyer still must pay for the goods.

Right to Inspect The buyer generally has a right before payment or acceptance to inspect the goods at any reasonable place and time and in any reasonable manner, unless the contract provides for delivery COD or for payment against documents of title. If the seller ships COD, the buyer must pay for the goods even if they do not conform to the contract unless the nonconformity appears without inspection (Section 2-512[1]). However, the buyer will have other remedies, discussed later, if the goods are nonconforming. Although the buyer must pay under these circumstances before he inspects the goods, the buyer may still inspect the goods after payment. The buyer is not considered to have accepted the goods until he has had a reasonable opportunity to inspect them. Whether or not the buyer has accepted affects the type of remedies that are available to him.

If the buyer chooses to inspect the goods the buyer must bear the cost of inspection unless the inspection reveals that the goods do not conform to the contract. In such case, the buyer may recover expenses from the seller if he rejects the goods.

Where the parties have specified a particular place or method of inspection, that place or method will be presumed to be the exclusive one.

Delivery by Documents of Title If delivery is authorized and made by means of documents of title, payment is generally due at the time and place at which the buyer is to receive the documents, regardless of where the goods are to be received. The buyer must pay for the goods when he is tendered the appropriate documents. He still retains the right to inspect the goods. No acceptance occurs until the buyer has had the opportunity to inspect them. Thus if a buyer purchased the goods COD and receives the proper documents, he must pay for the goods even though they are still in transit. When the goods arrive, he may then inspect them and exercise the right to accept or reject.

Suppose a seller in Illinois ships goods to a buyer in California. The seller receives a bearer-negotiable bill of lading from the shipper. This document permits the person in possession of it to pick up the goods from the carrier. The seller gives this bill of lading to her bank, which in turn transfers the document to a California bank for collection. The California bank calls in the buyer, receives payment from her, and releases the bill of lading to the buyer. The bank then transfers the money back to the seller's bank. The buyer may now pick up the goods from the carrier when they arrive in California. If he inspects the goods and finds that they do not conform to the contract, the buyer may at that point reject the goods—even though the buyer has already paid for them—and demand a refund from the seller.

Acceptance

Acceptance may occur in one of three ways under Section 2-606 of the UCC. Acceptance is unrelated to the question of who has title to the goods, which is governed by Section 2-401.

Express Statement of Acceptance

The buyer accepts the goods if, after a reasonable opportunity to inspect them, she indicates that the goods are conforming or that she will take the goods even though they are not conforming. Suppose a buyer orders 100 blue and red swimsuits. If the seller delivers 100 blue and green swimsuits, the buyer, after inspecting them, accepts the goods by indicating that she will take them even though they are not blue and red. Bear in mind that because this delivery was not conforming, the buyer could have rejected the swimsuits. The consequences of an acceptance are as follows:

1. Buyer must pay contract rate for the goods accepted.
2. Buyer forfeits the right to reject.

3. Buyer must, within a reasonable time after he or she discovers the breach, notify the seller of the breach or be barred from any remedy.
4. Burden shifts to buyer to establish the breach of contract.

Inaction

An acceptance may also occur as a result of inaction by the buyer—that is, by the buyer's failure to reject the goods effectively after he has had a reasonable opportunity to inspect them. Suppose the blue and green swimsuits arrive on January 1 but, rather than opening the box immediately to inspect the goods, the buyer puts the box in the storeroom. The buyer could have inspected the goods on January 1, determined that they were not conforming, and rejected them. On April 15 the buyer opens the box. The buyer now wants to reject the suits. Because of the buyer's inaction, however, it may be too late to reject them.

Act Inconsistent with Seller's Ownership

The third method of acceptance is the buyer's commission of any act that is inconsistent with the seller's ownership. Suppose the buyer receives the blue and green swimsuits, puts them on the shelves in the store, and sells a number to the public. Selling the suits amounts to an act inconsistent with the seller's ownership.

Knowledge of Defects In considering Section 2-606(1), which provides that a buyer has accepted when he or she has done "any act inconsistent with the seller's ownership," the courts should distinguish cases where the buyer knows of a defect from those where he or she is unaware of it. In the example in the preceding paragraph the buyer knew the goods were nonconforming, made no attempt to reject them, and sold them to third parties. This is an act inconsistent with the seller's ownership. The same would be true if the buyer attempted to reject the suits but then sold them to third persons.

Sometimes it is impossible for the buyer to avoid using the product even after rejecting it. Suppose a homeowner purchases a wall-to-wall carpet that is glued to the floor. In this situation the homeowner may call the seller, reject the carpet, and continue to use it.

PREVENTIVE LAW
Inspect Goods at Once

Johnson Fence Company receives a shipment of fencing on April 1. It places the fencing in storage and does not inspect it until August 1. At that time it determines the fencing is not in conformity with the contract. By its failure to act Johnson has probably accepted the fencing.

This situation illustrates the importance of instructing all employees to inspect immediately each shipment to make certain that it conforms to the buyer's order. If the fencing does not conform, the buyer should immediately notify the seller that it is rejecting the shipment.

PREVENTIVE LAW
Rejecting Goods

Payless Carpet receives a truckload of carpet. The trucker unloads the carpet in the Payless warehouse. A Payless employee immediately determines that the carpet does not conform to the contract with the seller and notifies the seller the same day of the nonconformity. In the meantime some of the Payless salesmen sell part of the carpet to customers because they did not realize Payless had rejected the carpet. By selling the carpet, Payless has accepted the goods.

Employees should be instructed to somehow mark goods that have been rejected so that other employees will not accidentally sell such goods. Everyone should also be instructed never to sell goods that have been rejected.

A more difficult case is the continued use of a car or mobile home after a rejection. Whether the continued use constitutes acceptance under Section 2-606(1)(c) is not easy for the courts to resolve. In general it is dangerous to use the goods after a rejection because a court may construe this as an acceptance. This matter is discussed later in this chapter.

Another difficult situation arises when the buyer uses the goods prior to rejecting them although the buyer is aware of a defect. If the buyer and the seller are attempting to straighten the problem out, and this is why the buyer has delayed rejecting the goods, the use of the product at this time should not be regarded as an acceptance. The policy of the UCC is to encourage parties to work out their differences.

Similarly, the buyer's use of a product while unaware of a defect should not constitute an

acceptance under Section 2-606(1)(c). Suppose the buyer purchases a car and drives it 2 days, and then the transmission fails. One could argue that the UCC gives the buyer the right to inspect goods and a reasonable time to reject them. Therefore use of the car for 2 days, prior to learning of the defect, should not constitute an acceptance.

J. L. Clark Manufacturing Co. v. Gold Bond Pharmaceutical Corporation, which follows, provides a good discussion of what constitutes an "act inconsistent with the seller's ownership" under Section 2-606(1)(c). The buyer in *J. L. Clark* cites a number of cases where a buyer's acts were *not* judged to be inconsistent with the seller's ownership. As you read *J. L. Clark*, think of reasons why the cases cited by the buyer would or would not be applicable to this case.

J. L. CLARK MANUFACTURING CO. V. GOLD BOND PHARMACEUTICAL CORP.

U.S. District Court, District of Rhode Island

669 F. Supp. 40 (1987)

BACKGROUND: Gold Bond (defendant) bought several thousand metal powder containers from Clark (plaintiff), which it used to package its pharmaceutical products. Gold Bond claimed that the containers were defective and refused to pay for them, but continued to use them until it was able to find substitute packaging. Clark sued Gold Bond for the purchase price of the containers.

Lagueux, District Judge

On or about November 9, 1984, Gold Bond ordered 250,000 four ounce powder bodies and covers and 250,000 ten ounce powder bodies and covers for a total contract price of $172,523.09. It is undisputed that Gold Bond received delivery of the containers and began to use them in the packaging and distribution of its product. Invoices for the goods were issued by Clark in February 1985. Gold Bond, alleging that the containers were defective, refused to remit payment.

In a letter to Clark's sales representative, dated April 18, 1985, William Garey, president of Gold Bond, identified certain problems which defendant had allegedly encountered with the cans. First, jagged edges on some covers and bodies inhibited proper attachment of the two components. Second, the bottoms of some cans were improperly attached, permitting powder leakage. Garey stated that not all defects could be detected prior to filling. As a result, filled containers were shipped to retailers, only to be subsequently returned to Gold Bond for credit and reimbursement of shipping charges. Third, the color of the covers did not match those of the bodies.

By letter dated May 8, 1985 and hand-delivered to Garey on May 9, 1985, Clark's president, William O. Nelson, requested that Gold Bond either immediately cease use of the containers and return them to Clark or pay all outstanding invoices. Gold Bond, however, while refusing to remit payment, continued to utilize the cans in the distribution and sale of its product. In fact, it is undisputed that Gold Bond continued to use the cans in its production process until at least February 1986. Defendant contends that such continued use was necessitated by the unavailability of alternative containers in which to market its powder. . . .

Pursuant to § 2-607 of the Uniform Commercial Code as adopted by Pennsylvania, a buyer must pay at the contract rate for any goods accepted. Section 2-606(1) provides that "[a]cceptance of goods occurs when the buyer * * * (c) does any act inconsistent with the seller's ownership." Under this subsection, any action taken by the buyer which is inconsistent with its claim that it has rejected the goods constitutes an acceptance. U.C.C. § 2-606 comment 4. Having examined the undisputed, material facts in view of § 2-606(1)(c), this Court concludes that, as a matter of law, Gold Bond accepted the containers.

Gold Bond continued to fill and sell the containers until at least February 1986. Defendant ceased use of the cans when plastic packaging became available. Gold Bond's continued use of the containers for approximately one year after its purported rejection and in contravention of Clark's May 1985 request that the cans be returned is patently inconsistent with the seller's ownership.

Defendant's contention that business considerations mandated continued use of the containers does not require a different conclusion. In substance, Gold Bond argues that, upon encountering difficulties with Clark's product, it had no alternative, if Gold Bond was to remain in business, but to continue to utilize the the metal containers until substitute packaging, in this case plastic containers, was designed and manufactured. It is undisputed that Gold Bond ceased use of Clark's cans once this alternative packaging became available. Gold Bond contends that, in view of the lack of an alternative means of maintaining production, continued use of the metal containers was reasonable and did not invalidate its alleged earlier rejection.

Assuming, *arguendo*, that earlier discontinuation of use of Clark's containers would have resulted in the cessation of defendant's business activities, such a predicament does not legitimate the equivocal rejection attempted in the instant matter by Gold Bond. The cases cited by defendant in support of its argument are factually distinguishable from the instant matter and are thus unpersuasive here.

In *Yates v. Clifford Motors*, the court held that a buyer's continued use of a truck for approximately two months after communication of his rejection of the vehicle was not inconsistent with rejection. Although the buyer had used the vehicle frequently prior to notifying the seller of his rejection, following that date the vehicle was used only sparingly and only for essential purposes. The vehicle served as the buyer's only means of transportation. The court concluded that the ends of justice would not be served by penalizing a consumer who had exercised his right to reject by prohibiting the consumer from even the slightest use of the goods involved until the conclusion of the litigation. The court found that such reasoning was particularly applicable when, as in that case, the goods involved, such as motor vehicles, were essential to modern life.

In *Cardwell v. International Housing*, the court, although ultimately determining that the buyers had reaccepted a mobile home despite their earlier revocation, held that the buyers' continued residence in the home was not conclusive in determining whether they intended to abide by their revocation. The court cited with approval *Fablok Mills v. Cocker Machine & Foundry Co.*

In *Fablok*, a buyer revoked acceptance of ten manufacturing machines. After revocation, the buyer continued to use some of the machines. The court held that such conduct did not preclude successful assertion of buyer's claim of revocation. The court stated that, under the circumstances, such actions were not unreasonable as a matter of law. Specifically, the lack of availability of alternative machinery left the buyer "with the grim choice of either continuing to use some of the machines or going out of business."

Although the above-cited cases demonstrate that, under certain circumstances, an otherwise valid and timely rejection or revocation of acceptance will not be rendered ineffective by a buyer's continued use of the goods, all three cases are distinguishable from the instant matter in that they did not involve use of disposable goods. In *Yates*, *Cardwell*, and *Fablok*, despite some delay, and possibly depreciation, the goods remained available for eventual return to the seller. In fact, in *Fablok*, in holding that the buyer's continued use of the machinery did not negate its claim of revocation, the court relied, *inter alia*, on the seller's failure to contact the buyer concerning return of the goods and its failure to demonstrate that it had been prejudiced by the buyer's continued use of the machines. In the instant matter, defendant's continued use of the containers in distributing its powder products to its retailers permanently deprived Clark of any opportunity to reacquire possession of the goods. Such conduct is unreasonable and inconsistent with both Clark's ownership and Gold Bond's purported rejection of the goods and therefore constitutes an acceptance of the containers.

DECISION: The district court ruled that Clark was entitled to recover the purchase price of the containers from Gold Bond. The court refused, however, to dismiss a counterclaim by Gold Bond for damages resulting from the defects in Clark's containers. Gold Bond was thus given a chance to prove that Clark should pay Gold Bond damages to offset damages that Gold Bond owed to Clark.

Notice of Rejection Assuming the buyer wants to reject a nonconforming delivery of goods, he or she must notify the seller and specify the grounds for rejection, thereby giving the seller a chance to deliver conforming goods. Should the buyer accept nonconforming goods, the buyer retains the right to sue for damages.

Suppose that Acme Lawn Equipment sends a lawn-sprinkler system on March 1 to Johnson's Lawn Supply. When the sprinkler system arrives, Johnson determines that the system fails to conform to the contract description. Johnson must reject the goods within a reasonable time after he receives them, and he must notify Acme within a reasonable time that he has done so. Suppose he receives the sprinkler system on March 5. If Johnson sends a letter to Acme on March 10 rejecting the system and specifying his reasons, he has probably complied with the requirements of Section 2-602. Since Johnson is a merchant, he must follow any instructions he receives from Acme with respect to the sprinkler system. After rejecting the goods, Johnson must be careful not to take any action inconsistent with Acme's ownership, such as selling the sprinkler to a customer. If Johnson sells the sprinkler, the courts would find he has accepted the sprinkler, even though he rejected it earlier.

Commercial Units If the buyer chooses to accept part of a commercial unit, he or she must accept the entire unit (Section 2-606). However, the buyer does not need to accept goods that do not conform to the contract. Section 2-601 gives him or her three options if the seller tenders delivery of nonconforming goods: the buyer may (1) reject all the goods; (2) accept all the goods; or (3) accept any commercial unit or units and reject the rest. Commercial unit is defined in Section 2-105(b):

> "Commercial unit" means such a unit of goods as by commercial usage is a single whole for purposes of sale and division of which materially impairs its character or value on the market or in use. A commercial unit may be a single article (as a machine) or a set of articles (as a suite of furniture or an assortment of sizes) or a quantity (as a bale, gross, or carload) or any other unit treated in use or in the relevant market as a single whole.

Let's say that a buyer orders 100 pairs of men's shoes and 100 pairs of women's shoes, but the seller instead delivers 200 pairs of men's shoes. Let's also say that a commercial unit in this case is 100 pairs of shoes. The buyer can (1) reject all 200 pairs of shoes; (2) accept all 200 pairs of shoes, or (3) accept one commercial unit (100 pairs) of shoes. If the buyer elects to accept the commercial unit of 100 pairs of shoes, he or she must pay at the contract rate for the shoes accepted. Section 2-717 allows the buyer to recover from the seller for the breach of contract or, as an alternative, to deduct damages from the purchase price.

Rejection

Perfect-Tender Rule

Section 2-601 of the UCC gives the buyer of goods who has received an improper delivery the right to reject goods "if the goods or the tender of delivery fail in any respect to conform to the contract." This is called the "perfect-tender rule." It does not apply to installment contracts, which are discussed later in this chapter, and it is limited by the seller's right to cure.

As a practical matter, the perfect-tender rule is not very significant because of the manner in which the courts interpret Section 2-601. A buyer will be able to reject goods, as a practical matter, only where the goods or tender fail in a substantial respect to conform to the contract. Trivial defects in the tender will not give the buyer a right to reject.

To Reject

As indicated earlier, failure to make an effective rejection may constitute an acceptance. To make certain that a buyer does not unintentionally accept goods, he or she must follow the provisions of Section 2-602. The goods delivered must have been nonconforming and the seller must have failed to cure the nonconformity. The buyer must then (1) reject the goods within a reasonable time after their delivery or tender, and (2) seasonably notify the seller of the rejection.

Timing of Notice Actions are taken seasonably if they are taken at or within the time agreed or, if no time is agreed, within a reasonable time (Section 1-204[3]). If the buyer acts too slowly in rejecting the goods, he or she will be deemed to have accepted them. In order to determine whether the buyer acted within a reasonable time, the court will consider the surrounding circumstances.

Duties after Rejection   Once the buyer has given the requisite notice of rejection within a reasonable time, she must take care not to give the appearance of exercising ownership over the goods. If the goods are in the possession of a buyer who is not a merchant, her only duty is to hold them with reasonable care for a sufficient time for the seller to take possession.

If the buyer is a merchant, her duties with respect to rejected goods are set out in Section 2-603. If the seller has no agent or place of business at the market of rejection, the merchant-buyer who has the goods in her possession or control must follow any reasonable instructions received from the seller with respect to the goods.

In the absence of such instructions the merchant-buyer must make reasonable efforts to resell the goods for the seller if they are perishable or threaten to decline in value speedily. If the seller chooses to have the buyer resell the goods, the buyer must act in good faith. The buyer is entitled to reimbursement from the seller for caring for and selling the goods, or she may deduct expenses from the proceeds of the sale.

A buyer in possession of rejected goods that will not decline rapidly in value has several options if the seller fails to give instructions within a reasonable time. Section 2-604 provides that the buyer may (1) store the goods, (2) reship them to the seller, or (3) resell the goods at the seller's expense.

State the Defect   It is not sufficient for the buyer merely to tell the seller that he or she rejects the goods. To be safe, the buyer must specifically state the particular defect on which he or she is basing the rejection to give the seller an opportunity to cure it. If the buyer rejects the goods but fails to specify the defect, and the defect is of a nature that the seller could have cured, the buyer cannot rely on this unstated defect as a basis for rejection or to establish a breach of contract.

It is not necessary that the buyer be absolutely precise—a quick informal notice of the defects will suffice. Section 2-605(1)(b) says that a buyer must state the particular defect if both the buyer and the seller are merchants and if the seller has made a written request for a full and final written statement of all defects on which the buyer proposes to rely as justification to reject the goods. If the buyer fails to list certain defects in the written statement, he or she cannot cite these defects as grounds for rejection in a subsequent trial.

Once the buyer accepts goods, he or she loses the right to reject them. Whether the goods have been rejected or whether an acceptance has been revoked is important in establishing the remedies available to the buyer.

Figure 22-1 illustrates the various ways in which the actions of the buyer and seller can result in the acceptance or rejection of goods. Keep in mind that the story doesn't always end with an effective acceptance or rejection of the goods. As noted earlier, the seller may have the right to cure following a rejection. And as we shall see in the next section, an acceptance can sometimes be revoked.

Revocation

As indicated above, once a buyer accepts goods, he or she loses the right to reject them. However, it still may be possible for the buyer to revoke his or her acceptance and compel the seller to take the goods back.

A buyer cannot revoke unless he or she meets one of three conditions listed in Section 2-608:

- The buyer knew of the defect but accepted because he or she reasonably believed the nonconformity would be cured and it was not seasonably cured

- The buyer did not discover the defect prior to his or her acceptance because the defect was difficult to discover

- The buyer did not discover the defect prior to his or her acceptance because the seller assured the buyer there were no defects

If any of these three conditions applies, and the nonconformity substantially impairs the value of the goods to the buyer, the buyer may revoke the acceptance.

The question of whether a nonconformity substantially impairs the value of goods to the buyer depends on the specific circumstances of the

FIGURE 22-1

Acceptance and Rejection

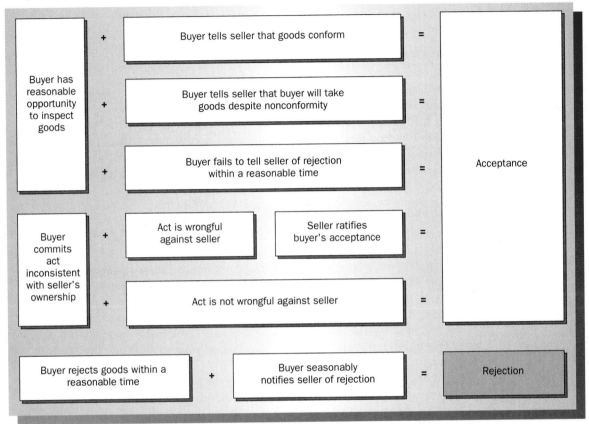

buyer. A buyer may revoke his acceptance if a nonconformity substantially impairs the value of the goods to him, even if most people would consider the nonconformity to be inconsequential.

Would this give someone the right to revoke his acceptance of a car just because the spare tire was missing? Read *Colonial Dodge, Inc. v. Miller* and find out.

COLONIAL DODGE, INC. V. MILLER
Supreme Court of Michigan
362 N.W.2d 704 (1984)

BACKGROUND: On April 19, 1976, Clarence Miller (defendant) ordered a 1976 Dodge station wagon from Colonial Dodge (plaintiff), which included a heavy-duty trailer package with extra wide tires. On May 28, 1976, Miller picked up the car. His wife then inspected it and noticed it did not have a spare tire. The next morning Miller notified Colonial Dodge, and he insisted on having the tire he ordered immediately. He was told there were no spare tires available at that time. Miller then informed the salesman that he would stop payment on the two checks that were tendered as the purchase price and that the vehicle could be picked up from in front of his home. Miller parked the car in front of his home, where it remained until the temporary 10-day registration sticker had expired, whereupon the car was towed away by the police department.

Colonial sued Miller for the purchase price of the car. The trial court entered a judgment for Colonial. It found that Miller had wrongfully revoked his acceptance of the vehicle. Miller appealed.

Kavanagh, Justice

This case requires the court to decide whether the failure to include a spare tire with a new automobile can constitute a substantial impairment in the value of that automobile entitling the buyer to revoke his acceptance of the vehicle under MCL 440.-2608; MSA 19.2608. . . .

Defendant argues that he never accepted the vehicle under MCL 440.2606; MSA 19.2606, claiming mere possession of the vehicle is not sufficient according to the UCC. Plaintiff contends defendant did accept the vehicle by executing an application for Michigan title and driving the vehicle away from the dealership. The trial court stated "[t]he parties agree that defendant Miller made a valid acceptance of the station wagon under § 2.606 of the Uniform Commercial Code." . . .

Plaintiff argues the missing spare tire did not constitute a substantial impairment in the value of the automobile, within the meaning of MCL 440.2608(1); MSA 19.2608(1). Plaintiff claims a missing spare tire is a trivial defect, and a proper construction of this section of the UCC would not permit defendant to revoke under these circumstances. It maintains that since the spare tire is easy to replace and the cost of curing the nonconformity very small compared to the total contract price, there is no substantial impairment in value.

However, MCL 440.2608(1); MSA 19.2608(1) says "[t]he buyer may revoke his acceptance of a lot or commercial unit whose nonconformity substantially impairs its value *to him*." . . . (Emphasis added.)

We cannot accept plaintiff's interpretation of MCL 440.2608(1); MSA 19.2608(1). In order to give effect to the statute, a buyer must show the nonconformity has a special devaluing effect on him and that the buyer's assessment of it is factually correct. In this case, the defendant's concern with safety is evidenced by the fact that he ordered the special package which included special tires. The defendant's occupation demanded that he travel extensively, sometimes in excess of 150 miles per day on Detroit freeways, and often in the early morning hours. Mr. Miller testified that he was afraid of a tire going flat on a Detroit freeway at 3 A.M. Without a spare tire, he testified, he would be helpless until morning business hours. The dangers attendant upon a stranded motorist are common knowledge, and Mr. Miller's fears are not unreasonable.

We hold that under the circumstances the failure to include the spare tire as ordered constituted a substantial impairment in value to Mr. Miller, and that he could properly revoke his acceptance under the UCC.

That defendant did not discover this nonconformity before he accepted the vehicle does not preclude his revocation. There was testimony that the space for the spare tire was under a fastened panel, concealed from view. This out-of-sight location satisfies the requirement of MCL 440.2608(1)(b); MSA 19.2608(1)(b) that the nonconformity be difficult to discover. . . .

Defendant's notice to plaintiff and holding of the car pending seller's disposition was sufficient under the statute, at least in the absence of evidence that defendant refused a request by the plaintiff to sign over title.

Plaintiff contends defendant abandoned the vehicle, denying it any opportunity to cure the nonconforming tender as prescribed in MCL 440.2508; MSA 19.2508. We find that defendant's behavior did not prevent plaintiff from curing the nonconformity. Defendant held the vehicle and gave notice to the plaintiff in a proper fashion; he had no further duties.

Decision: The Supreme Court of Michigan reversed and entered a judgment for Miller.

Reasonable Time

For the revocation of acceptance to be effective, it must occur within a reasonable time after the buyer discovers or should have discovered grounds for revocation. The buyer must notify the seller within a reasonable time to give the seller a chance to cure and to help minimize the buyer's losses. There are   many cases dealing with whether the buyer's actions were taken within a reasonable time.

Substantial Change

The buyer must revoke his or her acceptance before the condition of the goods has changed substantially. An exception to this rule is where the goods have changed substantially because of their own defects.

Suppose, for example, that Ms. Smith purchases a trailer home from the Lemon Corporation. A week after moving in, she discovers a hidden plumbing defect. The next day, the trailer is heavily damaged by flooding. If the flooding was caused by the hidden plumbing defect, then Ms. Smith will be able to revoke her acceptance even though the trailer's condition has deteriorated. If, however, the damage occurred because Ms. Smith ruptured her waterbed, she will probably have to repair the water damage if she wants to revoke her acceptance.

Suppose now that Ms. Smith puts that unpleasant experience behind her and purchases a brand new trailer. She inspects the unit prior to moving in and finds no defects. Soon after moving in, she realizes that the hat rack that's supposed to be in the closet is missing. Can she revoke her acceptance? No, because the missing hat rack does not substantially impair the value of the trailer. Ms. Smith is, however, entitled to recover from the seller the value of the hat rack.

In the following case, *Schumaker v. Ivers*, the court considers an attempt to revoke acceptance of an organ after several attempts by the seller to repair it.

SCHUMAKER V. IVERS

Supreme Court of South Dakota
238 N.W.2d 284 (1976)

BACKGROUND: The Schumakers (plaintiffs) purchased an electric organ from Ivers (defendant). After accepting the organ, the Schumakers experienced considerable difficulties with it and attempted to rescind. Although several months passed before the plaintiffs had attempted to rescind their acceptance, the trial court found the Schumakers had properly revoked their acceptance of the organ. Therefore it ruled for the plaintiffs. Defendant appealed.

Wollman, Justice

On November 30, 1972, plaintiffs went to defendant's music store for the purpose of looking at electric organs. Plaintiffs looked at several models and discussed the matter with defendant, who recommended the organ in question, described in the testimony as a Story Clark Magi model. Defendant suggested that plaintiffs permit him to deliver the organ to their home on a trial basis. Plaintiffs agreed that defendant could do so, and the organ was delivered to plaintiffs' home on December 7, 1972. Mrs. Schumaker played the organ on the day it was delivered and noticed nothing unusual.

On December 11, 1972, Mrs. Schumaker went to defendant's store and paid in full the purchase price of the organ in the amount of $1,119.71. According to her testimony, she asked defendant about the warranty and service on the organ and was assured by defendant that it would all be taken care of and that he had a man who serviced organs.

Approximately two weeks after the organ was delivered, one of the bass pedals failed to play. Shortly thereafter another bass pedal also failed to play, as did two keys on the keyboard. Mrs. Schumaker called defendant on or about December 27, 1972, and told him about the problems she had been having with the organ. Defendant said that he would send out a serviceman. Nothing was done, however, until March 13, 1973, when defendant and his serviceman came to plaintiffs' home and worked on the organ. Following their visit—and here the record is rather vague with regard to dates—plaintiffs again experienced difficulty with the organ in that one key in every octave in both keyboards failed to play. Mrs. Schumaker called defendant on May 11, 1973, and told him that she was still having difficulty with the organ and that she was unhappy with it and wanted a refund of the purchase price. Defendant and his serviceman came to plaintiffs' home and after some discussion, during which defendant refused to accede to Mrs. Schumaker's request that he take back the organ and refund the purchase price, plaintiffs agreed to permit defendant to bring out a replacement organ on the condition that if it did not work, defendant would take it back and refund the purchase price of the first organ. On or about May 22, 1973, defendant brought out a replacement organ. Shortly thereafter the rhythm system on the second organ began to malfunction. In response to plaintiffs' call, defendant's serviceman attempted to repair the organ on several occasions during the period from May 24 to June 1, 1973, but was unable to remedy the problem. During his last service call the serviceman removed the rhythm system component from the organ. Following this visit the lower keyboard failed to play.

Sometime after June 1, 1973, defendant's employees attempted to return the original organ, which defendant claimed had been put into proper operating condition, to plaintiffs' home but were prevented from doing so by plaintiffs. Plaintiffs sought the advice of an attorney, who wrote to defendant on or about June 15, 1973, regarding the organ. On August 3, 1973, plaintiffs filed suit against defendant in the nature of a rescission action praying for the return of the purchase price of the organ.

Defendant contends that because the record reveals that he at all times stood ready to honor the one-year free parts and service warranty on the organ, plaintiffs should not have been permitted to summarily refuse him the opportunity to do so by revoking their acceptance of the organ. In view of the numerous unsuccessful attempts by defendant to satisfactorily repair the original organ, we conclude that the trial court did not err in holding that plaintiffs had rightfully revoked their acceptance.

As far as the adequacy of the notice is concerned, defendant acknowledged that Mrs. Schumaker had told him that plaintiffs wanted him to take the organ back and refund the purchase price. If this revocation of acceptance was in any way waived by plaintiffs' accepting delivery of the second organ, such waiver was clearly based upon the condition that the replacement organ would operate satisfactorily, a condition that failed to materialize. Plaintiffs moved promptly to send notice through their legal counsel shortly after the second organ became completely inoperable.

DECISION: The Supreme Court of South Dakota affirmed the decision for the Schumakers, ruling that they had properly revoked their acceptance of the organ.

Lemon Laws

As the *Schumaker* case illustrates, consumers sometimes have a great deal of difficulty with products they purchase. This can be highly frustrating, particularly if the product in question is expensive and something a person relies on daily. Problems with automobiles have given consumers some of the biggest headaches because people need some means of transportation to get to work, buy groceries, and do a host of other activities.

UCC Section 2-608 gives a person a right to revoke his or her acceptance, but as previously noted, the buyer must comply with a number of requirements before he or she can exercise this right.

To minimize some of the problems associated with defective vehicles many state legislatures have passed what have popularly been dubbed lemon laws. **Lemon laws** are laws designed to help consumers obtain replacements or refunds when they have purchased a defective vehicle.

CONCEPT SUMMARY
Acceptance, Rejection, and Revocation of Goods

Acceptance is indicated by express statement of acceptance, inaction, or an act inconsistent with the seller's ownership.

Rejection is indicated if the goods are rejected within a reasonable time after their delivery or tender, and if the seller is notified of rejection:

Revocation takes place if these conditions are met.
1. Buyer must have known of the defect in the goods but accepted, thinking the defect would be cured; or buyer did not discover the defect prior to acceptance because the defect was difficult to discover; or buyer did not discover the defect prior to acceptance because the seller assured the buyer there were no defects; and
2. The nonconformity substantially impairs the value of the goods to the buyer; and
3. The buyer revokes within a reasonable time after the buyer discovers or should have discovered grounds for revocation; and
4. The buyer revokes his acceptance before the condition of the goods has changed substantially.

These laws require a manufacturer, its dealers, and agents to attempt to correct any vehicle problem reported by a consumer during the period the vehicle is under a warranty. If the defects are such that they cannot be repaired within a reasonable number of attempts, lemon laws generally require the manufacturer to provide either a replacement vehicle or a full refund. Significantly, unlike the UCC, these laws define what a "reasonable number of attempts" at repairing a vehicle are. Generally, they specify that a reasonable number of attempts to repair have been made after four or more repair attempts have failed to correct the problem or after the vehicle has been out of service for a cumulative total of thirty or more working days. These laws tend to give the manufacturer, rather than the consumer, the right to choose between a replacement and a refund. This approach differs from that taken in the UCC, which does not require a person to take a replacement if he or she revokes his or her acceptance.

The threshold question in these statutes is, When does a consumer who has purchased a defective vehicle have a right to demand a refund or a replacement? Lemon laws follow the UCC Section 2-608 "substantial impairment of value" standard. A fairly common requirement is that a defect must exist that substantially impairs the use and value of the vehicle to the consumer.

Assuming there is a substantial impairment of value, the consumer generally must notify the manufacturer within the warranty period or 1 year after delivery, whichever comes first. This means, for example, that a consumer might make a claim for a replacement or refund 12 months after making a purchase. If the consumer were to proceed under UCC Section 2-608 instead, there would always be the risk that a court might find the revocation did not take place "before any substantial change in the condition of the goods which is not caused by the defect." Thus the lemon laws focus on whether the consumer acted within the time specified in the statute as opposed to whether he or she acted before a substantial change in the value of the goods occurred.

The type of vehicles covered varies from state to state. Some apply to all motor vehicles, whereas others may exclude vehicles such as motorcycles or motor homes. The emphasis is generally on vehicles for personal or household use rather than for commercial use. Unlike suits filed under the UCC, consumers are permitted to recover their attorney fees.

Installment Contracts

As noted earlier, where goods are tendered to the buyer that do not conform to the contract, the buyer has three options under Section 2-601. However, a different rule applies when the parties enter into an installment contract. Section 2-612(1) defines an installment contract as "one which requires or authorizes the delivery of goods in separate lots to be separately accepted, even though the contract contains a clause, 'each delivery is a separate contract' or its equivalent." Assuming that the parties entered into an installment contract, what is the effect of a nonconforming delivery on one of the installments? Section 2-612(2) and (3) set out the rules governing this situation. In general the standard applied when one of the parties breaches an installment contract is not so rigorous as the standard applied when there has been a breach of contract requiring delivery to take place at one time. The reason for this is that it would be unfair if a breach on an installment could always be used as grounds for canceling the entire contract.

Rejection of an Installment

Under Section 2-612, the buyer must accept an installment delivery of nonconforming goods if the nonconformity is curable and if the seller gives adequate assurance that it will be cured. However, a buyer may reject a nonconforming installment if the nonconformity substantially impairs the value of that installment and cannot be cured. Unlike rejections, which can occur if the goods fail to conform in any respect, for both revoca-tions and rejections of installments the buyer must show that the goods are substantially nonconforming.

Cancellation of Entire Contract

In certain circumstances the nonconformity or default with respect to one or more installments may be so great that the entire contract has been substantially impaired in value. If this is the case, the entire contract may be canceled. If the buyer wishes to cancel the contract, he or she must not accept a nonconforming installment without notifying the seller seasonably of the cancellation. If the buyer fails to give the required notice, the contract is reinstated. Likewise, the contract is reinstated if the aggrieved party "brings an action with respect only to past installments or demands performance as to future installments."

Assurance of Performance

What type of assurance must the seller give under Section 2-612(2) to force the buyer to accept a nonconforming installment? The standard is the same as that under Section 2-609, which deals with the right to adequate assurance of perfor-

---

ETHICS
Duty to Perform

John C. Melon, a farmer, planted a wheat crop and contracted with the local grain elevator to sell his crop at a price of $2.20 per bushel when harvested. When actually harvested the market price had risen to $4.00 per bushel due to a severe drought. John had to borrow additional money from a bank, and selling his crop at $2.20 would not be enough to keep current on the loan. John's failure to make loan payments would in turn allow the bank to take the farm and dispossess John and his family. The grain elevator contract has a liquidated damages clause that would help John come out ahead by selling to another buyer for $4.00 and paying the damages owed to the elevator.

Some people argue that contract law allows one to choose between performing and paying damages. They reason that if one is willing to pay the damages, then one is ethically entitled to breach. As seen in preceding chapters, others argue that promises have moral force and cannot be ethically broken except under special circumstances. Here two dramatic changes have occurred since the contract was formed: (1) John's financial condition has changed dramatically and (2) there has been a dramatic market upheaval. Although John's hardship seems important, we don't know the impact of his failing to pay on the operator of the grain elevator. Perhaps the operator might go bankrupt if John doesn't honor the contract. Important factors in this case could include whether the parties did or should have anticipated the volatile market, their relative financial positions, and the duties that they owe to other parties affected by the transaction.

mance in all sales contracts. Because one of the parties to a contract may become unwilling or unable to perform a contract after entering into it, this section allows the other party to demand an assurance of performance.

Basically, Section 2-609 allows the aggrieved party to do three things:

- Suspend his or her own performance and all preparatory action
- Require adequate assurance of performance
- Treat the contract as broken if the grounds for insecurity are not cleared up within a reasonable time, not to exceed 30 days

What constitutes "adequate" assurance of performance depends on the facts. If a seller of good repute promises that a defective delivery will be straightened out, this will normally be sufficient. But if an untrustworthy seller makes the same statement, the statement alone might be insufficient.

When merchants have contracted, the question of insecurity and adequacy of any assurance offered is judged by commercial standards rather than by legal standards. For example, if a reasonable merchant would believe that a buyer will not pay, this will be regarded as reasonable grounds for insecurity.

Anticipatory Repudiation

Rather than a situation involving uncertain ability or willingness to perform, one of the parties to a contract may be faced with a direct repudiation of the contract. If one of the parties to a contract has indicated that he or she will not perform at some date in the future, must the other party wait until that date to find out if the other party actually performs?

Suppose two persons enter into a contract to be performed on August 1. If the seller says on June 1 that he or she will not deliver on August 1, what can the buyer do? This matter is covered by Sections 2-610 and 2-611. If either party to the contract indicates that he or she will not perform at some time in the future, and the failure to perform would substantially impair the value of the contract, the aggrieved party may (1) simply wait a commercially reasonable time for per-

formance or (2) treat the contract as broken and seek any available remedy. This is true even if the aggrieved party has urged the other party to retract his or her repudiation. In any event, the aggrieved party's own performance may be suspended.

If the aggrieved party chooses the first option, Section 2-611 permits the repudiating party to retract his or her repudiation unless the aggrieved party has canceled the contract, materially changed his or her position, or indicated that he or she considers the repudiation final. Although a retraction may be made by "any method which clearly indicates to the aggrieved party that the repudiating party intends to perform," the repudiating party must give the aggrieved party whatever assurances of performance are demanded, consistent with Section 2-609.

What if two parties enter into a contract calling for delivery of goods on May 15, and on January 1 the seller tells the buyer he will not deliver the goods pursuant to the contract? The buyer may treat the contract as having been breached on January 1, acquire the goods elsewhere, and bring a suit for damages against the seller. The buyer need not wait until May 15 to see if the seller changes his mind. Alternatively, the buyer may wait a commercially reasonable time for the seller to perform.

Impossibility

In certain instances a party to a contract may be unable to perform because the goods have been destroyed. The UCC in Section 2-613 allows both parties to escape from the contract when goods identified to the contract have been totally destroyed without fault of either party before the risk of loss passes to the buyer. If the goods have been only partially destroyed, or have deteriorated so as no longer to conform to the contract, Section 2-613(b) gives the buyer the option to either treat the contract as avoided or accept the goods with due allowance for the deterioration or the deficiency in quantity but without further right against the seller.

Goods Must be Identified

For Section 2-613 to apply the goods must be identified when the contract is made. If particular goods are not specified in the contract, then Section 2-613 does not apply. A seller who simply promises to deliver 100 lawnmowers to the buyer cannot rely on Section 2-613, but a seller who specifies 100 lawnmowers *from his or her plant*, which then burns to the ground along with all the mowers, may rely on the defense of impossibility (assuming that he or she was not responsible for the destruction). Section 2-613 applies even though the goods were already destroyed at the time of contracting if neither party knew of the loss.

Impracticability

Sometimes performance will not be impossible, but will nonetheless be very difficult. Section 2-615 excuses the seller from a timely delivery of goods where unforeseen supervening circumstances make performance impracticable. The mere fact that costs go up does not excuse performance; that is the type of business risk assumed in signing a contract. On the other hand, a severe shortage of raw materials or supplies due to a contingency such as war, embargo, or unforeseen shutdown of major sources of supply, which causes the goods to be significantly more expensive or impossible to obtain, is the type of situation covered.

Partial Performance

The seller is excused from the contract completely if she can establish that she is absolutely unable to perform due to the occurrence of a contingency not contemplated by the parties, but the seller must fulfill the contract to the extent possible if she can only partially perform. Section 2-615(b) states that when a seller can partially perform, she must allocate production and deliveries among the customers in a fair and reasonable manner. If the seller chooses to allocate goods, or if there will be a delay or nondelivery of goods, the seller must notify the buyer seasonably.

Section 2-616 states that a buyer, upon receipt of notification of a material or indefinite delay or of an allocation, may by written notification to the seller terminate the contract or agree to take the available allocation. The buyer must agree to this modification within a reasonable time, not to exceed 30 days, or the contract will lapse as to any deliveries affected.

Although a buyer does not have to accept the allocated goods, he must accept substituted performance if the agreed manner of delivery becomes commercially impossible. Likewise, if the agreed means of payment fails because of domestic or foreign government regulation, the seller under certain conditions must accept a substantially equivalent manner of payment.

Review Questions and Problems

Key Terms

cure
seasonable
commercial unit
lemon law
installment contract

Discussion Questions

1. What must a buyer do to effectively reject nonconforming goods under the UCC?
2. Describe the difference between rejection and revocation.
3. What test of impossibility is adopted by the UCC?
4. When must the buyer pay for the goods if the contract is silent concerning the time, place, and method of payment?

Review Problems

1. United Airlines ordered a flight simulator from Conductron Corporation. The contract provided that the simulator would not be deemed "accepted" by United unless and until it met the specifications of United and the Federal Aviation Administration (FAA). The contract provided that title to the simulator would nonetheless pass to United upon delivery. Because of delays in the completion of the simulator, the parties modified the contract to provide for testing of the simulator at United's flight training center rather than at Conductron's plant. Before the simulator was delivered to United, United employees notified Conductron of over 600 deficiencies in the device. The modified contract entitled United to cancel the agreement if all of the deficiencies were not corrected by November 1, 1969. Conductron subsequently delivered the simulator, which United used for training purposes. United could not use the machine as an aircraft flight simulator because it had not yet been approved by the FAA. On April 18, 1969, after the simulator had been tested for 10 hours by United test pilots, it was destroyed by a fire of unknown origin. United sued Conductron for breach of contract, claiming that Conductron had failed to deliver an

acceptable simulator by the agreed-upon date. Conductron claimed that United had accepted the simulator through its use and possession of it, and thus had waived its right to object to the nonconformities it had noted before delivery. What result? See UCC Sections 2-606 and 1-102.

2. In February 1980 Wickliffe Farms signed a contract with Owensboro Grain Company by which it agreed to deliver 35,000 bushels of white corn to Owensboro between December 15, 1980, and January 31, 1981. The contract said nothing about where the corn was to be grown, although there was evidence that the parties expected Wickliffe to grow the corn on its own farmland. A severe drought made it impossible for Wickliffe to grow and deliver the full 35,000 bushels. If Owensboro were to sue Wickliffe for damages resulting from the failure to deliver the full 35,000 bushels, should Wickliffe be able to raise the defense of impracticability under UCC Section 2-615?

3. Earl Gallin, who owned an electronics components business, purchased several materials from Surplus Electronics Corporation between July and September 1977. Surplus guaranteed the usability of its products and provided that unacceptable items could be returned for full refund. Gallin had not paid for any of the aforementioned purchases by January 1978, and Surplus sued for the adjusted purchase price of $6,170. Gallin admitted to owing $2,656, but claimed that he was in the process of testing the balance of the components for usability and would, when he was finished, return the unacceptable goods in one shipment. This testing process had apparently not been completed when the trial commenced in April 1980. What result?

4. Robertson Manufacturing brought an action against Jefferson Tile concerning payment for 13,500 tiles delivered by Robertson to Jefferson. Jefferson received the tiles and discovered they were defective. Rather than allowing the seller to attempt to correct the defect, Jefferson corrected the tiles itself and installed them on a building. Robertson now brings suit for the cost of the tiles. Jefferson argues it should be compensated for the extra expense it incurred in correcting the defects. Is Jefferson correct?

Case Problems

1. Harper entered into a contract with Tri-County Ford Tractor Sales to purchase a tractor. The tractor broke down a number of times. Tri-County unsuccessfully tried to repair the tractor a number of times. Harper revoked his acceptance of the tractor 17 months after he contracted to purchase it. He seeks to cancel the contract and obtain his money back. Can Harper revoke his acceptance?

2. Holiday agreed to manufacture and sell to B.A.S.F. 6 million cassettes with delivery to begin April 1970 at 500,000 cassettes per month until completed. Many of the cassettes delivered were defective, but Holiday managed to correct the defects. Under what circumstances, if any, could B.A.S.F. cancel the entire contract?

3. McDonald's ordered some computerized cash registers from AMF. A number of months passed and AMF was unable to deliver the cash registers. AMF was forced to delay the date for shipment. In May McDonald's and AMF met to discuss the machines. At that time AMF did not have a working machine and could not produce one within a reasonable time because its personnel were too inexperienced. McDonald's demanded a reasonable assurance of performance, and when it did not receive one, it canceled the contract on July 29. Was McDonald's entitled to cancel the contract?

4. Gulf entered into a contract with Eastern for the sale of jet fuel in the early 1970s. The parties knew the price of crude oil would fluctuate so they specified West Texas Sour, a crude oil, as an indicator of the price of crude oil to Gulf. Eastern would be obligated to pay for the oil it purchased according to the price of West Texas Sour. During the period of the contract the U.S. government imposed controls on the price of West Texas Sour. Certain other oil purchased by Gulf was not controlled, especially imported oil, and Gulf felt it should be entitled to charge more for the oil delivered than the price it paid for West Texas Sour. Gulf viewed the purpose of the contract as frustrated. It argued the contract should be set aside based on the theory of commercial impracticability. Is Gulf correct?

23

Sales: Remedies

Statute of Limitations

Seller's Remedies

Buyer's Remedies

Limitation or Alteration of Remedies

We now have examined some of the important principles related to the creation and performance of a contract. This chapter discusses the remedies available to sellers and to buyers when a contract is breached. We will briefly examine the rules for filing a suit for breach of contract.

Statute of Limitations

The victim of a breach in a sales transaction will often have more than one form of relief available. Some of the remedies are mutually exclusive and others involve limiting factors such as a specific number of days within which one must act. When a breach of a sales contract occurs, the victim should immediately contact a lawyer to insure that the right to seek a remedy is not inadvertently lost.

Time Limit

Uniform Commercial Code Section 2-725 provides that a person who wishes to bring an action for breach of a sales contract must bring suit within 4 years after the cause of action has occurred—unless the parties have agreed to a shorter period of time. The statute of limitations can be reduced to not less than 1 year by agreement. If a party to a contract fails to bring suit within the time stipulated in the agreement (or, if no time is stipulated, within 4 years), he or she is barred from ever bringing suit even though he or she may have an otherwise perfectly valid claim.

Time Statute Starts to Run

The 4-year period starts to run from the date the breach of contract occurs, whether or not the aggrieved party knows of the breach, except in the case of a breach of warranty. The time limit for a breach of warranty begins to run when tender of delivery is made. If a warranty *explicitly* extends to the future performance of goods *and* discovery of the breach *must* await the time of such performance, the cause of action accrues when the breach is or should have been discovered.

Thus there are two statute-of-limitation rules that apply to warranties—the *normal warranty*, on which the time limit for filing suit begins to run when tender of delivery is made, and the *prospective warranty*, on which the time limit for filing suit begins not on delivery but when the breach is or should have been discovered.

At first blush one would suppose that most warranties are prospective in character; however, the courts *very* seldom find a warranty to be prospective.

Consider, for example, a clause worded as follows: "Seller will repair any defects discovered during the warranty period." You might think that this is a prospective warranty, because the seller

404

undertakes to do something in the future. However, courts have found such a warranty to be a normal warranty: The seller doesn't actually guarantee that the product will perform properly in the future; the seller simply promises to repair any defects that may be found. The statute of limitations for such a warranty would therefore expire 4 years from the date of delivery.

On the other hand, a contract stating: "Seller hereby warrants that the product will operate free from material defects during the warranty period" probably will create a prospective warranty. In this case, the seller is actually warranting that the future condition of the goods will conform to a certain standard.

Because of the subtle and seemingly technical differences between a normal warranty and a prospective warranty, it is probably safest to assume that suit must be filed within 4 years of the date of delivery in a breach-of-warranty suit.

Diligence in reporting defects is important because it permits the seller to attempt to remedy the defect and helps to minimize the buyer's damages.

Seller's Remedies

If the buyer wrongfully rejects goods, improperly revokes his or her acceptance, fails to make a payment due, or repudiates part or all of the contract, the aggrieved seller has a number of remedies.

Election of Remedies

The UCC rejects the idea that a seller must elect only one remedy. Instead, whether one remedy bars another will depend on the circumstances of a particular case.

The purpose of the remedies provided for in the UCC is not to punish the wrongdoer, but simply to put the aggrieved party in the position that he or she would have been in had the contract been performed.

Remedies Available

Section 2-703 gives the aggrieved seller a number of remedies:

1. Withhold delivery of goods
2. Stop delivery of goods held by a bailee
3. Resell the goods and recover damages
4. Recover damages for nonacceptance as provided in Section 2-708
5. Recover the price
6. Cancel the contract

What if the buyer breaches the contract before all of the goods are ready to be delivered? In such case, the seller can identify any finished goods that conform to the contract—that is, designate such goods as goods that were to have been sold to the buyer. As for the unfinished goods, the seller may either stop work on them and sell them for scrap or salvage value or, in the exercise of reasonable commercial judgment, complete the goods and identify them to the contract.

The reason the seller is allowed this option is to minimize the damages sustained by the buyer. If the seller chooses to complete the work on unfinished goods, the burden is on the buyer to show that it was unreasonable for the seller to complete the goods. The seller may then proceed to resell under Section 2-706 or, where resale is not practicable, bring an action for the price under Section 2-709.

Resale

The UCC contemplates the seller's principal remedy as resale. When the buyer has wrongfully rejected goods, revoked his acceptance improperly, failed to make a payment, or repudiated all or part of a contract, the seller may resell the goods in question. The seller is not obligated to resell the goods, but this is the usual manner of establishing damages since the seller is in the business of selling goods. If the seller resells the goods in good faith and in a commercially reasonable manner, she may recover the difference between the resale price and the contract price together with any incidental damages, but minus any expenses saved as a result of the buyer's breach.

Incidental Damages   Section 2-710 states that **incidental damages** to the seller include "any commercially reasonable charges, expenses or commissions incurred in stopping delivery, in the transportation, care and custody of the goods after the buyer's breach, in connection with return or resale of the goods or otherwise resulting from the breach." These are the typical expenses a seller might incur; however, the UCC allows for all commercially reasonable expenditures made by the seller. Suppose the seller had entered into a contract for $4,650, and the buyer breached. If the seller incurred $29.50 in expenses in reselling the goods, and they were sold in good faith and in a commercially reasonable manner for $3,000, the seller would be entitled to recover from the buyer a total of $1,679.50—$1,650 representing the difference between the contract price and actual resale price, plus $29.50 in incidental damages.

Manner of Resale To assure that the resale takes place in a fair manner, Section 2-706 sets out provisions for conducting the resale. Of course, the parties may agree between themselves as to the details of the resale, but the method of resale still must be fair. In the absence of such an agreement, the resale may be at a public or private sale, as long as every aspect of the sale is commercially reasonable. In choosing whether to have a public or private sale, the character of the goods must be considered and relevant trade practices and usages must be observed. If the seller elects a private sale, she must give the buyer reasonable notification of her intent to resell. It is not necessary to give the buyer notification of the time and place of the private sale.

At a public sale only identified goods can be sold unless their seller is able to sell them as futures in goods—that is, agreements to deliver goods at some future date—at a recognized market for public sale of future goods. These identified goods must be sold at a usual place or market for public sale if one is available. Before selling the goods, the seller must give the buyer reasonable notice of the time and place of the resale unless the goods are perishable or threaten to decline rapidly in value. This means the sale must be at a place or market where potential buyers may reasonably be expected to attend and the buyer has an opportunity to bid or notify others of the sale. In order to assure the best possible price, prospective bidders must be given an opportunity to inspect the goods. The seller is permitted to buy the goods. These measures are included to benefit the original buyer by tending to increase the resale price.

If the goods are resold improperly to a purchaser who buys in good faith at the resale, the purchaser takes title free of any rights of the original buyer.

Suppose our seller in the earlier example resold the goods for $5,000. Must she account to the buyer for the $350 above the original contract price of $4,650? The seller is not accountable to the buyer for any profit she makes. The seller in this situation may keep the profit.

The code also requires that the resale be conducted in a timely manner. The reason for this requirement is that a resale as soon as possible after the buyer's breach is likely to bring the market price for the goods.

Failure to Comply What happens if the seller fails to comply with the restrictions placed on the resale of goods? Does this bar her from any remedy? If she fails to comply with the provisions for resale in Section 2-706, the resale price cannot be used in calculating damages. However, the seller can still collect something. If the seller acts improperly, she must establish damages under Section 2-708.

Damages

Market Price Section 2-708(1) makes the seller's damages for nonacceptance or repudiation by the buyer the "difference between the market price at the time and place for tender and the unpaid contract price." In addition to this amount, the seller may recover for any incidental damages incurred, but he must deduct from the damages any expenses saved as a result of the buyer's breach. A seller might utilize this section to keep the goods that the buyer has refused to accept. It is not mandatory that the seller resell the goods in order to establish his damages although, as noted earlier, most sellers will attempt to resell the goods.

The market price is measured at the time and place for tender. To take an obvious case, if the buyer agreed by contract to pick up the goods at the seller's place of business on June 15 and the buyer breaches, the seller may be able to collect the difference between the contract price and the market price at which the goods are selling in the town where the seller's business is located. If the buyer agreed to pay $1,000 for the goods, and they are now selling for $800 in the seller's town, the seller collects $1,000 minus $800, or $200, plus incidental damages and minus any expenses saved. In this case, the seller would presumably receive the same amount of damages whether the seller resold the goods and sued under 2-706 or collected under 2-708(1).

Madsen v. Murrey & Sons Company, Inc. illustrates that a market price can be determined for goods even if they are custom-made for the breaching buyer. *Madsen* also discusses the commercial reasonableness of a seller's decision to dismantle goods and sell them for salvage value.

MADSEN V. MURREY & SONS COMPANY, INC.
Supreme Court of Utah
743 P.2d 1212 (1987)

BACKGROUND: Erik Madsen was trying to develop a pool table which, like a pinball machine, would produce light and sound effects. Madsen contracted with Murrey & Sons, a pool table manufacturer, to purchase 100 pool tables specially designed to accommodate electronic lighting and sound effects to be designed and installed by Madsen. The total contract price was $55,000, of which $42,500 was paid by Madsen in advance. Madsen was unable to develop a proper design for the electronic components and advised Murrey & Sons that he would be unable to take delivery of the 100 custom-designed tables. Murrey & Sons, which had already completed the tables, dismantled them and sold them for salvage and firewood. Madsen sued to recover his advance payment.

Howe, Justice

Seller [Murrey & Sons] asserts that it sufficiently mitigated its damages by dismantling the pool tables and salvaging various components that could be used to manufacture other pool tables. The salvage value to seller was claimed to be $7,448. It presented testimony that selling the tables as "seconds" would damage its reputation for quality and that the various holes, notches, and routings placed in the tables to accommodate the electrical components to be installed by buyer [Madsen] weakened the structure of the tables so as to submit seller to potential liability if they were sold on the market.

On the other hand, Ronald Baker, who had been involved with the manufacturing and marketing of pool tables for 25 years, testified on behalf of the buyer that the notches, holes, and routings made in the frame to accommodate electrical wiring would not adversely affect the quality or marketability of the 100 pool tables. According to Baker, the tables could have been sold at full value or at a discounted price. In addition to this testimony, the trial court had the opportunity to view the experimental table developed by buyer and his associates and observe the holes, notches, and routings necessary for the electrical components.

The trial court found that seller's action in dismantling the tables and using the materials for salvage and firewood, rather than attempting to sell or market the tables at full or a discounted price, was not commercially reasonable. The court then concluded that seller had a duty to mitigate its damages and failed to do so. The finding is supported by competent evidence. We find no clear error. . . . As a result of buyer's breach, seller justifiably withheld delivery of the 100 pool tables. Still, buyer is entitled to recover the $42,500 paid on the contract less the damages suffered by seller. . . . Our review of the record reveals that the trial court neglected pertinent elements of Utah's commercial code in assessing seller's damages.

The applicable statute to be used in determining seller's damages for nonacceptance or repudiation is Utah Code Ann. § 70A-2-708 (1980), which provides:

(1) Subject to subsection (2) and to the provisions of this chapter with respect to proof of market price (section 70A-2-723), the measure of damages for nonacceptance or repudiation by the buyer is the difference between the market price at the time and place for tender and the unpaid contract price together with any incidental damages provided in this chapter (section 70A-2-710), but less expenses saved in consequence of the buyer's breach.

(2) If the measure of damages provided in subsection (1) is inadequate to put the seller in as good a position as performance would have done then the measure of damages is the profit (including reasonable overhead) which the seller would have made from full performance by the buyer, together with any incidental damages provided in this chapter (section 70A-2-710), due allowance for costs reasonably incurred and due credit for payments or proceeds of resale.

Seller argues that section 70A-2-708(2) is the proper formula for assessing its damages. That, however, would be inconsistent with the general rule that requires application of section 70A-2-708(1) where the trial court finds that a reasonably accessible market exists wherein the aggrieved seller can market its goods. "By market, we mean a market which, if availed of, would have substantially mitigated [seller's] damages." *Timber Access Industries Co. v. U.S. Plywood-Champion Papers, Inc.* The trial court concluded that seller failed to perform its duty to mitigate its damages by not marketing or attempting to sell the pool tables on the open market. Having found that a market existed, seller's damages must be determined under section 70A-2-708(1).

Applying the trial court's finding that the pool tables if completed could have been sold for at least $21,250, seller's damages are the difference between the market price ($21,250) and the contract price ($55,000), or $33,750. The trial court found that seller was not entitled to any incidental damages. Buyer is not entitled to any further credit for expenses saved by seller in consequence of buyer's breach. Since the $21,250 which the trial court charged seller with was for completed tables, no savings would have occurred. Under section 70A-2-718(2), (3), buyer's right to restitution of advance payments on the contract ($42,500) is subject to offset to the extent that seller establishes damages ($33,750), for a total recovery of $8,750.

DECISION: The Supreme Court of Utah affirmed the judgment in favor of Madsen but reduced his damages from $21,250 to $8,750.

Profit   In *Madsen*, the court refused to allow the seller to recover its expected profit because the amount it could recover under Section 2-708(1)—contract price minus market price—was sufficient to put the seller in as good a position as performance would have done. If the measure of damages provided by Section 2-708(1) is inadequate to put the seller in as good a position, the seller may collect the profit (including overhead) that he would have recovered had the contract been performed plus any incidental damages. One case where the seller would not be in the same position as performance would have put him is that of the **lost-volume seller**.

Suppose a retailer agrees to sell a couch for $500 to Ms. Jones. If Ms. Jones breaches the contract, the retailer would be entitled to the difference between the contract price ($500) and the market price ($500). This would leave the retailer with no damages as long as he is able to sell all the couches in stock. But what if the supply of couches exceeds the demand? In that case, because Ms. Jones breached the contract, the seller will sell one less couch. In this situation the seller should be able to receive the profit (including overhead) that he would have made on Ms. Jones's contract.

Bill's Coal Co., Inc. v. Board of Public Utilities of Springfield illustrates the analysis that a court must undertake to determine whether a seller is a lost-volume seller and thus entitled to recover lost profits from a breaching buyer.

BILL'S COAL CO., INC. V. BOARD OF PUBLIC UTILITIES OF SPRINGFIELD

United States Court of Appeals, Tenth Circuit
9 UCC Rep. Serv. 2d 1238 (1989)

BACKGROUND: Bill's Coal and Cherokee Coal (the sellers) were under contract with the Board of Public Utilities of Springfield, Missouri (the purchaser) to supply the purchaser with all the coal that it required until the expiration date of the contract. The contract enabled the purchaser to terminate the contract early if it could find another supplier that could provide the coal at at price 15 to 20 percent lower than the contract price. Citing this provision, the purchaser tried to terminate the contract. The sellers disputed the purchaser's right to terminate and sued. The purchaser was eventually judged to have breached the contract, and the sellers were awarded the difference between the contract price and the market price. Despite this victory, the sellers appealed, claiming that they were lost-volume sellers and hence entitled to recover their lost profits.

McKay, Circuit Judge

The district court determined that UCC §2-708(1) applied in determining the proper measure of damages. The damages provided in §2-708(1) are the difference between the market price and the contract price of the goods. UCC §2-708(2) provides for damages up to the amount of the lost profits from the contract which has been breached. Sellers fall into §2-708(2) only if they can demonstrate that they would receive inadequate damages under §2-708(1). Section 2-708(2) is basically designed for specific categories of sellers, such as lost volume sellers, component sellers, and jobber sellers. Sellers here argued that they were entitled to receive §2-708(2) damages. Sellers have the burden of proving that they are lost volume sellers and thus fall under §2-708(2). A lost volume seller is one who has the capacity to perform the contract which was breached as well as other potential contracts, due to their unlimited resources or production capacity. Although sellers seek to portray the analysis of lost volume seller as a question of law subject to de novo review (sellers characterize their appeal as being limited to "questions of law"), it is a decision dictated by the underlying facts and thus ultimately a question of fact reviewed under the clearly erroneous standard. Even where there is a mixed question of law and fact that involves primarily a factual inquiry, the "clearly erroneous" standard is appropriate.

Evidence presented at trial indicated that sellers did not have the production capacity to perform purchaser's contract as well as to sell to other potential purchasers. During the years following 1980, sellers often fell behind in shipping to purchaser the amount of coal required under the contract. In fact, one of the two principal mines on which sellers relied for shipments to purchaser was out of production for several months during this period. In order to meet purchaser's needs, sellers found it necessary to purchase coal from other suppliers. In addition, sellers claimed in the district court that they had lost sales to other customers because it was necessary to ship coal to purchaser from the Porter and Chetopa mines. This contention is in direct conflict with sellers' position that it had the capacity to perform the contract in dispute and also to sell to third parties. Mr. Hirlinger, sellers' president, admitted that sellers were able to make the sale of 11,609 tons of coal to another customer only because purchaser ceased accepting coal from sellers. Based on this evidence, the trial court found that the sellers did not have the ability to perform the contract in dispute and sell to potential third parties at the same time. Based on our review of the evidence, the district court was not clearly erroneous in its finding that sellers were not lost volume sellers, and thus §2-708(1) was the proper measure of damages.

> **DECISION:** The court of appeals upheld the district court's ruling that the sellers were entitled to the difference between the contract and market prices of the coal, rather than their lost profits.

Price The seller can recover the price of goods sold only under certain circumstances. Price actions may be maintained when resale of the goods is impracticable, when the buyer has accepted the goods, or when the goods were destroyed or lost within a reasonable time after the risk of loss had passed to the buyer. If the seller wishes to obtain the contract price, the goods that have been earmarked for the contract and are still in his possession must be held for the buyer. If the seller is able to resell them prior to collecting a judgment, he may do so and the proceeds will be credited to the buyer.

Once the buyer has accepted goods, the UCC permits the seller to recover the price of the goods. Whether a buyer has accepted does not depend on the passing of title or on the date set for payment. Suppose the seller delivers goods to the buyer, and the buyer states that she will take the goods. The buyer's statement constitutes an acceptance and renders her liable for the price.

Likewise, if goods are lost or damaged within a commercially reasonable time after the risk of loss has passed to the buyer, the buyer is liable for the price. A seller who ships goods "FOB seller's plant" needs only to deliver the goods to the carrier. Once the goods are in the possession of the carrier, the risk of loss passes to the buyer. In the event the goods are destroyed while in possession of the carrier, the buyer is liable for the price of the goods.

If the goods have not been accepted by the buyer or destroyed after the risk of loss has passed, an action for the price can be maintained for goods identified to the contract only after a "reasonable effort to resell" them at a reasonable price. The seller need not try to resell, however, if circumstances indicate that it would not be possible to resell them at a reasonable price. Suppose a manufacturer custom-designed a rolling steel door for a buyer. If the steel door does not fit any other building because it was custom-designed, the buyer is liable for the price of the door. Figure 23-1 summarizes the remedies available to a seller.

Withhold Delivery

In the event the buyer becomes insolvent, the seller's ability to collect damages from the buyer under the sections previously discussed will be impaired. If the buyer has no money, a judgment against him will be of little practical value to the seller. For this reason the UCC provides special remedies where the buyer becomes insolvent.

When the seller discovers that a buyer has become insolvent, she may refuse to deliver the goods to the buyer except for cash. If the buyer owes the seller for goods delivered before the seller learned of the buyer's insolvency, the seller may also demand payment for all goods previously delivered before making any further deliveries. The mere fact that the seller withholds delivery of goods does not mean that she is barred from exercising any remedy available for damages.

Goods in Possession of Buyer If the buyer received the goods on credit while he was insolvent, the seller has 10 days to demand their return. Receiving goods on credit amounts to a misrepresentation of solvency by the buyer and therefore is fraudulent against the seller. If the seller learns of the buyer's insolvency and actually demands return of the goods within 10 days, the seller is entitled to the goods. If the buyer misrepresented his solvency to the seller in writing within 3 months of the time the buyer received the goods, the 10-day limit does not apply. In that event the seller may claim actual fraud by the buyer and, if she can establish fraud, may reclaim the goods.

Goods Held by Carrier or Bailee If the goods have already been delivered to a carrier or other bailee, the seller may wish to stop delivery upon discovering that the buyer is insolvent. It is not necessary for the buyer to be insolvent in all cases for the seller to stop delivery; however, if the seller wishes to stop shipments of less than a carload, the buyer must be insolvent. For the seller to stop delivery when the buyer breaches the contract, the amount must be a delivery as large as a carload if the buyer is solvent. This pro-

FIGURE 23-1

Seller's Remedies

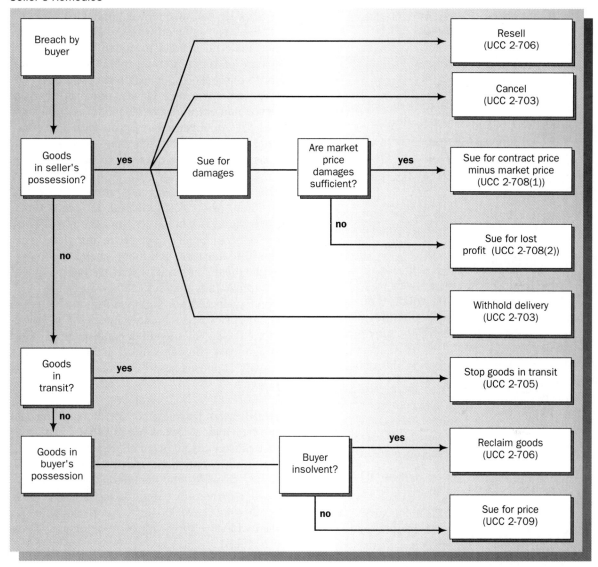

vision was adopted because it is a burden on the carriers to stop delivery. If a seller of a smaller-than-carload lot had doubts about the buyer's capacity to pay, she can ship COD. There is, of course, risk in stopping any shipment because improper stoppage is a breach by the seller.

The seller can stop delivery until the buyer has received the goods, until the documents of title have been negotiated to the buyer, or until the carrier or other bailee gives notice that the goods are being held for the buyer. The seller must give notice to the bailee with sufficient time to enable the bailee by reasonable diligence to stop delivery

of the goods. Assuming notice arrives in time for the bailee to act diligently, the bailee must hold and deliver the goods according to the seller's directions. If a negotiable document of title was issued, however, this must be surrendered before the bailee must obey the stop order.

Buyer's Remedies

When the seller fails to make delivery or repudiates or the buyer rightfully rejects or revokes acceptance of goods, the buyer has several remedies:

1. Cancel the contract and recover any amounts
   paid to seller
2. Cover (discussed below)
3. Recover damages pursuant to Section 2-713
4. Gain possession of goods identified to the
   contract pursuant to Section 2-502
5. Obtain specific performance or replevy the
   goods pursuant to Section 2-716
6. Resell goods in his or her possession pursuant in certain circumstances

Cover

When the seller fails to make a delivery or indicates that he will not deliver pursuant to a contract, the buyer is faced with the situation of not
having material needed to conduct business. To
take care of this situation, the UCC allows the
buyer to purchase goods in substitution for those
covered in the contract. This is known as the right
to **cover** and is the most frequently used buyer's
remedy. If the buyer acts in good faith and without unreasonable delay, she may establish damages as the difference between the cost of cover
and the contract price.

The court will not second-guess the buyer in
determining the reasonableness of her actions
but will merely examine whether the buyer's actions were reasonable at the time and places she
acted. If it later turns out that a cheaper or more
effective means of cover was available, this does
not automatically mean that the buyer acted unreasonably. In addition to the difference between
the cover price and the contract price, the buyer
is entitled to any incidental or consequential damages incurred, but she must deduct from the
claim any expenses saved as a result of the seller's breach.

Incidental Damages   Incidental damages
to the buyer include, but are not limited to, "expenses reasonably incurred in inspection, receipt,
transportation and care and custody of goods
rightfully rejected, any commercially reasonable
charges, expenses or commissions in connection
with effecting cover and any other reasonable expense incident to the delay or other breach" (Section 2-715[1]).

**Consequential Damages   Consequen-
tial damages** include all losses resulting from the
general or particular requirements and needs of
the buyer that the seller had reason to know of at
the time of contracting and that could not *reasonably* have been prevented by cover or otherwise.

For example, assume that a Christmas tree
merchant purchases trees from a lumber company. If the lumber company fails to deliver the
trees, the merchant could, as discussed above,
buy the trees elsewhere and sue the lumber company for the amount it had to pay in excess of the
contract price. But what if the merchant can't obtain substitute trees until just before Christmas,
when most people have already bought their

trees? Clearly, the Christmas tree merchant will earn much less profit than would have been earned had the lumber company delivered the trees on time. This lost profit represents consequential damages to the merchant, damages not included in the merchant's cover remedy.

It is not necessary that the buyer establish damages with mathematical precision, but the buyer does bear the burden of proving the loss. Consequential damages also include an injury to a person or property if it proximately results from a breach of warranty.

Section 2-719(3) allows the seller to limit or exclude consequential damages, unless to do so would be unconscionable under the circumstances. A limitation of consequential damages for personal injuries in the case of consumer goods is presumed to be unconscionable. No such presumption exists for commercial losses.

Damages

If the seller has failed to deliver goods in accordance with a contract or has repudiated the contract, the buyer may establish damages by covering, although it is not mandatory to cover. The buyer may instead elect to establish damages under Section 2-713, which makes the measure of damages the difference between the market price at the time the buyer learned of the breach and the contract price. The buyer also can collect any incidental and consequential damages incurred, but he must credit the seller with any expenses saved as a result of the seller's breach. The market price will be determined by examining the current market price (when the buyer learned of the breach) at the place for tender or, if the buyer rejected the goods after they arrived or revoked acceptance, by examining the current market price (when the buyer learned of the breach) at the place of arrival. Thus the UCC uses as a guideline the market in which the buyer would have obtained cover had he attempted to cover.

If the seller was to have tendered goods to the buyer in Los Angeles, the market price to be used would be the prevailing price in the Los Angeles market at the time the buyer learned of the breach. If the buyer had attempted to cover, presumably this would have been the price he would have paid.

In certain circumstances, the measure of damages provided by Section 2-713 can greatly exceed the buyer's actual loss. Such was the case in *Allied Canners & Packers v. Victor Packing Co. of California*, in which the court had to decide whether to award damages based on the difference between a greatly inflated market price and the contract price.

ALLIED CANNERS & PACKERS V. VICTOR PACKING CO. OF CALIFORNIA

Court of Appeals, First District
209 Cal. Rptr. 60 (1984)

BACKGROUND: Allied (plaintiff) sued Victor (defendant). Allied was a corporation engaged in the business of exporting dry, canned, and frozen fruit products. Victor was engaged in the business of packing and processing fruit. On September 3, 1976, Allied entered into a contract with Victor whereby Victor was to sell and deliver five containers (each holding 37,500 pounds) of raisins during the month of October 1976. On September 8, 1976, the parties entered into a second contract whereby Victor agreed to sell and deliver an additional five containers of raisins on the same terms. The contracts provided for Victor to sell the raisins at 29.75 cents per pound with a discount of 4 percent.

On September 9, 1976, heavy rains severely damaged the raisin crop, adversely affecting Victor's supply of raisins. On September 15 Victor notified Allied that it would not deliver the raisins as required by the contracts. Allied did not cover by purchasing raisins on the open market. The earliest either party could have bought raisins was October 1976, when the price of raisins was between 80 and 87 cents per pound.

Allied had earlier contracted to export to two buyers the raisins that Allied was to have received from Victor. One of Allied's buyers agreed to rescind its contract to purchase three containers of raisins, but the other buyer demanded delivery of seven containers of raisins. However, Allied's contract with the second buyer contained a clause that relieved Allied of any liability caused by developments beyond its control. Allied sued Victor for damages due to its breach of contract.

Rouse, Judge

Allied argued at trial, and contends on appeal, that it was the buyer under its contracts with Victor and therefore entitled to damages pursuant to Commercial Code § 2713, subdivision (1). . . .

Allied contends that pursuant to § 2713, subdivision (1), it is entitled to damages in the amount of $150,281.25, representing the difference between the contract price of 29.75 cents per pound and a market price of 87 cents per pound for 262,500 pounds (seven containers) of NTS raisins. . . .

It has been recognized that the use of the market price-contract price formula under § 2-713 does not, absent pure accident, result in a damage award reflecting the buyer's actual loss.

For example, in this case it is agreed that Allied's actual lost profit on the transaction was $4,462.50, while application of the market-contract price formula would yield damages of approximately $150,000.

Viewing § 2-713 as, in effect, a statutory provision for liquidated damages, it is necessary for us to determine whether a damage award to a buyer who has not covered is ever appropriately limited to the buyer's actual economic loss which is below the damages produced by the market-contract formula, and, if so, whether the present case presents a situation in which the damages should be so limited.

We conclude that in the circumstances of this case—in which the seller knew that the buyer had a resale contract . . . the buyer has not been able to show that it will be liable in damages to the buyer on its forward contract, and there has been no finding of bad faith on the part of the seller–the policy of § 1106, subdivision (1), that the aggrieved party be put in as good a position as if the other party had performed requires that the award of damages to the buyer be limited to its actual loss, the amount it expected to make on the transaction.

Decision: The California Court of Appeals ruled for Allied. But the court held Victor was liable for $4,462.50—not the $150,281.25 Allied had demanded.

When the buyer has accepted goods and the time for revocation has passed, he is still entitled to damages if the seller fails to perform properly. The buyer's damages are the difference between the value of the goods accepted and the value they would have had if they had been as warranted. The buyer may also collect incidental and consequential damages. For example, if the purchaser of an automobile determines that the car has a defective horn, a court might award her as damages the cost of repairing or replacing the defective horn.

Specific Performance and Replevin

Specific Performance The buyer may in some cases wish to actually obtain the goods rather than recover monetary damages, especially when the buyer is unable to find substitute goods elsewhere. Section 2-716 provides that the buyer may obtain specific performance of the contract when the goods are unique or in other proper circumstances. (see Chapter 19.) What is unique depends on the circumstances. In any event, if a buyer is unable to cover, this is good evidence of other proper circumstances that merit specific performance of the contract.

Replevin The buyer has a right under section 2-716 to recover goods specifically earmarked for the contract if after a reasonable effort he is unable to find substitute goods or if the circumstances indicate that he will be unable to find them. This is known as the right to **replevin**.

Right to Resell   If the buyer rightfully rejects goods or properly revokes acceptance of them, the buyer has a security interest in the goods in his possession or control. The buyer may hold and resell these goods if he has paid a part of the price or has incurred expenses for the inspection, receipt, transportation, care, or custody of the goods. If the buyer resells, he must comply with Section 2-706 and must forward the balance of the amount received (beyond what was paid on the goods and expenses) to the seller.

Liquidated Damages

Rather than leave the determination of damages to the court, the parties may agree in advance what the measure of damages will be in the event that one of the parties to the contract breaches. When damages have been specified in the contract they are referred to as **liquidated damages**. A court will enforce the amount set by the parties only if it is a reasonable amount in light of all the circumstances. If it is unreasonably large, it is void as a penalty. This leaves the court free to award damages as seem appropriate under the circumstances. If the buyer would normally sustain $500 a day in damages in the event the seller fails to deliver on time, a provision awarding the buyer $10,000 a day for every day the seller is late in delivering the goods would be void as a penalty.

The buyer's remedies are summarized in Figure 23-2.

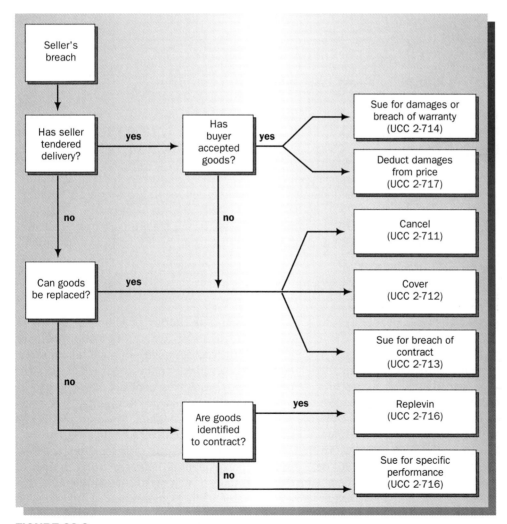

FIGURE 23-2

Buyer's Remedies

CONCEPT SUMMARY
Remedies Available to an Aggrieved Buyer

If the seller fails to deliver the goods or the buyer rightfully rejects the goods, the buyer may

- Cancel the contract and recover any money paid to the seller
- Cover as provided for in Section 2-706
- Recover damages pursuant to Section 2-713

If the buyer rejects or revokes, the buyer has a security interest in goods to the extent that he or she has paid part of price or has incurred expenses. The buyer may therefore resell the goods.

If the buyer accepts nonconforming goods delivered by the seller, the buyer may obtain the difference between the value of the goods accepted and the value they would have had if they had been as warranted pursuant to Section 2-714.

If the buyer wants the goods still in seller's possession, the buyer may obtain specific performance of contract pursuant to Section 2-716 or replevy the goods pursuant to Section 2-716.

ISSUES AND TRENDS
Computer Law: Limitation of Remedies

A problem that is becoming more widespread as more and more businesses and professionals use computer software is the failure of the software to perform as expected by the user. A user may experience very large losses when its software fails to perform properly. In such a case the purchaser may wish to sue for consequential damages. Many software sellers come with "as is" warranties. They do not even promise to correct flaws in the software. The position of the software makers has been that when a buyer opens the software, the buyer agrees to the conditions of the limited warranty.

It is quite likely this area of the law will continue to develop. In the meantime buyers should bear in mind they may be unable to collect damages for losses caused by the failure of the software to perform correctly.

Limitation or Alteration of Remedies

The UCC does not require parties to a contract to follow these rules on remedies. The parties to a contract are free to shape their own remedies. They may add remedies not covered in the UCC, or they may choose to substitute different remedies for those provided in Article 2. Damages recoverable under Article 2 may be limited or altered. If the parties to a contract wish to specify one particular remedy to be employed exclusively, the contract must clearly indicate that the remedy is the sole remedy available to the aggrieved party.

All attempts to modify or eliminate the remedies provided under Article 2 are subject to the charge of unconscionability. Some minimum remedy must be available to the aggrieved party. If the remedy provisions in a contract are found to be unconscionable or to deprive either party of a substantial value of the bargain, the court may strike them and apply the remedies found in Article 2.

As noted in the chapter on warranties, the UCC permits consequential damages to be limited or excluded unless such an exclusion would be unconscionable. Where consumer goods are involved, however, a limitation of consequential damages for injury to a person is prima facie unconscionable.

Review Questions and Problems

Key Terms

incidental damages

lost-volume seller

cover

consequential damages

replevin

liquidated damages

Discussion Questions

1. What is considered to be the seller's principal remedy under the UCC?

2. What is meant by "cover" as that term is used in the UCC?

3. How is the "market price" determined in a suit for breach of contract under the UCC?

4. When will a buyer be entitled to specific performance under the UCC?

5. Describe the difference between incidental and consequential damages.

Review Problems

1. Perry was injured while working on scaffolding. He intends to file suit for breach of warranty. The manufacturer of the scaffolding in its warranty agreed to make repairs to the equipment should they be needed. When does the statute of limitations begin to run on this equipment—on the tender of delivery or when the breach is or should have been discovered?

2. Sun Maid contracted to buy 1,800 tons of raisins from Victor Packing Company and Pyramid Packing Company. The packing companies should have been aware that Sun Maid's practice was to resell the raisins at a profit. The packers repudiated their contracts by refusing to deliver the last 610 tons of raisins. Is Sun Maid entitled to recover from the packers the profit it would have made on the resale of the 610 tons of raisins? How would these damages be characterized under the UCC? What section, if any, grants such a remedy?

3. The Sedmaks orally contracted with Charlie's Chevrolet in Missouri to buy a certain Corvette for $15,000. The car was a limited edition manufactured by Chevrolet to commemorate the Corvette's selection as the Indianapolis 500 pace car. Six thousand such special cars were manufactured and each dealer was allotted only one. The Sedmaks ordered specific options on the car which differentiated it from most others in the limited edition.

Charlie's subsequently received offers for the car of $24,000 and $28,000 from Hawaii and Florida, respectively. When the car arrived, Charlie's notified the Sedmaks that they could not have it for $15,000, but would have to bid for it. The Sedmaks, alleging that they could only acquire an identical car, if at all, at great difficulty, expense, and inconvenience, sued Charlie's for specific performance of the contract. Do you think that the Sedmaks are entitled to specific performance under UCC Section 2-716?

4. Acme Lawn Mowers agrees to sell 50 Acme mowers to Bill's Lawn & Garden Supply. Without any reason, Bill refused to accept or pay for the mowers when they were delivered. Acme had a contract price of $300 per mower. It resold the mowers after giving Bill notice of the time and place of the sale, for $250. What damages can Acme receive?

Case Problems

1. Hays entered into an oral contract by which Wilson agreed to sell to Hays at a sale price of 1 cent per brick for 600,000 used uncleaned bricks. Hays paid Wilson $6,000 in advance. Wilson delivered 400,000 bricks. Hays sued for a return of the proportionate part of the sale price he did not receive—$2,000. May Hays recover $2,000?

2. Publicker entered into a 3-year requirements-type contract with Union Carbide in which Union Carbide agreed to supply Publicker with ethanol. During the 3-year period Union Carbide indicated that it would no longer supply Publicker with ethanol unless Publicker agreed to pay Union Carbide an increased purchase price. Union Carbide contended that unforeseen increased costs entitled it to receive a higher price. Publicker refused and filed suit. Did Union Carbide breach the contract? If so, what damages, if any, is Publicker entitled to recover?

3. Thorstenon contracted to purchase a Case 730 tractor and mounted F-11 Farmland loader from Mobridge for $3,900. No delivery date was specified. In the fall of the next year Mobridge notified Thorstenon that there would be no delivery of the tractor. Thorstenon then purchased at a price of $1,000 more than the contract price the same tractor and loader. May Thorstenon recover the $1,000 extra cost?

4. McMillan agreed to purchase a bulldozer from Meuser. McMillan agreed to pay a purchase price of $9,825. When the time for delivery came, December 24, 1973, McMillan refused to accept or pay for the bulldozer. About 14 months later Meuser sold the bulldozer for $7,230 at a price sale. Can Meuser use the resale price in calculating his damages?

24

Warranties

When the seller of goods makes a representation as to the character, quality, or title of the goods as part of the contract of sale, and promises that certain facts are as represented, a warranty has been made. A seller who assures or guarantees the buyer that the goods will conform to certain standards may be liable for damages if the goods fail to meet those standards.

Types of Warranties

Express Warranties

Sometimes a seller, through words or actions, creates an **express warranty**. In a written document, or sometimes orally, the seller specifies precisely the terms of his or her guarantees to the buyer. Suppose Acme Machines states in literature provided with a lifting device that the machine will lift loads of up to 1,000 pounds. This is a representation of fact—either the machine will lift up to 1,000 pounds or it will not. A seller who makes such a statement creates an express war-

ranty that the machine will lift up to 1,000 pounds. If a buyer purchases the machine and later learns that its lifting capacity does not exceed 400 pounds, the buyer can bring an action for breach of an express warranty.

Figure 24-1 is an example of a typical consumer product warranty.

Implied Warranties of Quality

Not every warranty arises out of the words or actions of the seller. Sometimes a warranty as to the quality of the goods arises by operation of law. Two warranties arise out of a sale automatically by operation of law—the **implied warranty of merchantability** and the **implied warranty of fitness for a particular purpose.**

In the example mentioned earlier, suppose the manufacturer designed and sold the lifting device for use in loading railroad boxcars. If the machine fails to function properly when used in loading boxcars, the manufacturer has breached the implied warranty of merchantability. This warranty arose, not out of any words or actions of the

418

FIGURE 24-1

A Typical Consumer Product Warranty

LIMITED WARRANTY

Touch Control by Moen products have been manufactured under the highest standards of quality and workmanship. We warrant to the **consumer** all parts of your Touch Control by Moen products against defects in material and workmanship for TEN (10) YEARS from date of purchase. Any defective part will be replaced FREE OF CHARGE, excluding labor or service charges. We will not be responsible for any product damage due to installation error, product abuse, or product misuse whether performed by a contractor, service company, or yourself. Use of other than genuine Moen factory parts may void this warranty.

This warranty applies **only to the consumer use** of the product and any inquiries regarding warranty claims are to be directed to:

Stanadyne/Moen Division
377 Woodland Avenue
Elyria, Ohio 44036.

This warranty gives you specific legal rights and you may also have other rights which vary from state to state.

seller, but merely as a result of making the sale. The machine was not merchantable because it was not fit for the purposes for which such goods are sold.

Assume instead that the purchaser of this machine told the seller what his requirements were. The buyer stated that he needed a machine capable of lifting very dense packages weighing around 2,000 pounds. The buyer relied on the seller's skill and judgment to select a suitable machine for him. These facts create an implied warranty of fitness for a particular purpose.

Implied Warranty of Title

A third warranty also automatically arises from a sale—the **warranty of title.** What if the buyer in this example learned after purchasing the lifting device that it had been stolen? In this case, by selling stolen merchandise, the seller has breached the implied warranty of title.

These warranties are discussed in greater detail in the following material.

Warranty Law

Development of the Law

Warranty cases are one of the most common types of cases arising out of the sale of a product. Sometimes a person or company who purchases a product experiences problems with it. Then the question arises, Whose responsibility is it to repair the product? The buyer naturally hopes the seller will repair the product. The actual rights of the buyer are in part governed by the wording of the warranty, if any, and in part by statutes.

For many years the law favored the seller—the law followed the doctrine of caveat emptor (let the buyer beware). Starting with the twentieth century the law slowly moved in the direction of recognizing more rights for the buyer. More recently, really starting in the late 1960s, the consumer movement has pressed the courts and legislatures to strengthen the rights of purchasers. The doctrine of caveat emptor does not govern the law of sales today.

Source of Warranty Law

The law governing all aspects of sales law, including warranties, developed on a case-by-case basis. For many centuries the law of sales was found in the decisions of judges dealing with real cases.

Toward the end of the nineteenth century, scholars and practitioners became increasingly dissatisfied with the case-law approach. Many people advocated more uniformity in the law. This movement gave rise to the Uniform Sales Act (1906), a suggested model for state legislatures, which some states eventually adopted. After a number of years, the Uniform Sales Act was superseded by the Uniform Commercial Code, which has been adopted by every state except Louisiana. Louisiana has enacted some parts of the UCC, but not Article 2. Article 2 of the UCC covers the law of sales, including the rules relating to warranties.

While the UCC rules generally govern in the area of warranties, bear in mind that other statutes have been passed that have an impact on these rules. The discussion in the text is largely confined to the UCC rules.

Sale of Goods

In order to determine whether Article 2 of the UCC applies to a given case, one must determine if the facts involve a sale of goods. A *sale* is defined in Section 2-106 of the UCC as "the passing of title from the seller to the buyer for a price." *Goods* are tangible (having a physical existence) property that is movable at the time of identification to the contract (Section 2-105).

Suppose Margaret agrees to sell her watch to Penelope. A watch is a tangible, movable article. If the parties intend to pass title to the watch for a price, this transaction constitutes a sale under Section 2-106.

What if Margaret *gives* the watch to Penelope? No sale is involved in such a transaction and the principles of Article 2 do not control. A gift is not a sale of property for a price.

Other Situations

The mood of the courts in the 1970s, as earlier indicated, shifted in the direction of consumer rights. Many courts were confronted with cases in which the plaintiff wished to claim some warranty protection under the UCC but had not purchased goods.

Such cases often arose with leases. Technically, Article 2 does not apply to leases because the parties to the transaction do not intend a transfer of title.

In 1987, the National Conference of Commissioners on Uniform State Laws completed work on Article 2A of the Uniform Commercial Code, which governs the leasing of personal property. A number of states have adopted Article 2A, and more are expected to follow suit. The warranty provisions that benefit lessees under Article 2A are virtually identical to those that protect buyers of goods under Article 2. This chapter will discuss the Article 2 warranties only, but keep in mind that very similar provisions apply to lease transactions.

Even before Article 2A was drafted, some courts extended the warranty provisions of Article 2 to leases and other transactions not involving the sale of goods. Courts have, for example, found implied warranties in the sale of homes and in personal service contracts.

The point to bear in mind is that a plaintiff should not give up pursuing a case based on warranties simply because the transaction does not appear to be a sale or lease of goods. If a court feels there is good reason to extend the protection of the UCC beyond a pure sale or lease of goods, it may elect to do so.

Warranty of Title

Provisions

When a purchaser buys goods, receipt of good title to the goods is expected. This belief is reflected in the provisions of Section 2-312(1), which states that the seller of goods warrants (1) the title conveyed is good and its transfer rightful and (2) the goods are free of any security interest or other encumbrance of which the buyer at the time of contracting has no knowledge. This warranty arises automatically by operation of law.

Exposing Buyer to a Suit

The first provision—that the title conveyed is good and its transfer rightful—assures the buyer of a good title. Certainly, if a seller conveys stolen property to a buyer, the seller has breached the warranty of title. Suppose, however, that a seller, believing he owns an automobile, sells this automobile to a buyer. After the sale, a third party informs the buyer that he, the third party, is the one who lawfully holds title to the automobile. A title is not good if it unreasonably exposes the buyer to a lawsuit. In this case the buyer may be forced to litigate the issue of title in court with the third party. Whatever the resolution of the case—that is, whether or not the third party establishes that he or she is the lawful owner of the automobile— if the third party's claim is not frivolous, the buyer may sue the seller for breach of the implied warranty of title. The seller's questionable title wrongfully exposed the buyer to a suit.

Free of Encumbrance

The seller also warrants to the buyer that the goods are free of any security interest or other encumbrance of which the buyer at the time of contracting has no knowledge. If the seller conveys mortgaged property to the buyer without informing the buyer of this fact, this violates the warranty of title.

Goods Do Not Infringe

A merchant-seller also warrants that the goods sold do not infringe upon the patent, trademark, or copyright of a third party. This is true unless the seller has manufactured the goods according to the buyer's specifications.

Circumstances Indicating No Warranty of Title

There is no warranty of title in a contract for sale when the circumstances give the buyer reason to know that the person selling does not claim title in himself or herself or that he or she is purporting to sell only such right or title as he or she or a third person may have. This means that when the buyer purchases goods at a sheriff's sale, or from an executor or foreclosing creditor, the seller is not warranting the title.

Express Warranties

Provisions

The UCC (Section 2-313) states that express warranties are created as follows:

(a) Any affirmation of fact or promise made by the seller to the buyer which relates to the goods and becomes part of the basis of the bargain creates an express warranty that the goods shall conform to the affirmation or promise.

(b) Any description of the goods which is made part of the basis of the bargain creates an express warranty that the goods shall conform to the description.

(c) Any sample or model which is made part of the basis of the bargain creates an express warranty that the whole of the goods shall conform to the sample or model.

Affirmation of Fact

Although a specific factual statement will create a warranty, a statement as to the value of goods or a statement of the seller's opinion or commendation of the goods does not create a warranty (Section 2-313[a]). It is reasonable to expect that a person selling goods will make favorable statements about the product being sold. For this reason statements as to value or mere opinions do not create an express warranty under the UCC.

Suppose the salesman at Al's Used Car Lot states to a person looking at a 1984 Ford, "That car is the best deal in town." Such a statement is the typical positive statement a buyer expects of a seller. No one expects a seller to run his or her products down. Because the average purchaser expects these favorable comments from a seller, a buyer may not rely upon a statement like the one here dealing with the 1984 Ford. It may not be relied upon in a breach-of-warranty case.

Basis of the Bargain   An affirmation of fact, like a description or sample or model, must become "part of the basis of the bargain" in order to give rise to an express warranty. When does an affirmation of fact become part of the basis of the bargain? All the statements of the seller are part of the basis of the bargain unless good reason is shown to the contrary.

A statement becomes part of the "basis of the bargain" when it helps to induce the buyer to make the purchase. Suppose a buyer orders a new Corvette at Al's New Car Lot, and Al tells the buyer "Your Corvette will be in that sexy shiny red color that's so popular these days." Suppose that the Corvette that actually arrives is blue. Has the seller breached an express warranty?

If the buyer had indicated to the seller that the

color of the car was important to him, then the color would have certainly become part of the basis of the bargain. As such, the seller's statement regarding the red color would have created an express warranty that the seller would have breached by delivering a blue car. Even if the buyer had not responded to the seller's statement regarding color, the statement would have become part of the basis of the bargain. Since each statement by the seller is presumed to become a part of the basis of the bargain, the buyer needn't respond to each of the seller's statements in order for such statements to give rise to express warranties.

Suppose the buyer had responded to the seller's statement by saying, "I don't care about the color. I just want the first new Corvette you can deliver." In this case, the seller's statement about the red color appears not to have contributed to the buyer's decision to purchase the car. The seller's statement on color would thus *not* have become part of the basis of the bargain, and the seller would not have breached an express warranty by delivering a blue car.

Puffing   If the seller of a dining-room set says, "This is the best dining room set in town," a buyer would not reasonably use this statement as part of the basis of the bargain between the parties. This type of language is commonly referred to as "puffing." To create an express warranty under the UCC more than mere puffing by the seller is required. If the seller instead says, "This table is solid oak," an express warranty that the table is solid oak is created. Either the table is oak or it is not; whether it is oak is a question of fact, not of opinion. If it turns out that the table is pine stained an oak color, and the buyer wanted an oak table, the buyer may bring an action for breach of an express warranty created by the seller's statement.

Many of the cases dealing with puffing do not cite a clear rule. The more specific the statement is, the more likely that a court will call it one of fact and not opinion. Whether the statement is oral or written is also important. The most commonly cited rule could be called the fact-opinion rule as stated by the court in *Royal Business Machines v. Lorraine Corp.*, 633 F.2d 34 (1980):

The decisive test for whether a given representation is a warranty or merely an expres-

sion of the seller's opinion is whether the seller asserts a fact of which the buyer is ignorant or merely states an opinion or judgment on a matter of which the seller has no special knowledge and on which the buyer may be expected also to have an opinion and to exercise his judgment. . . . General statements to the effect that goods are "the best" . . . or are "of good quality," or will "last a lifetime" and be "in perfect condition" . . . are generally regarded as expressions of the seller's opinion or "the puffing of his wares" and do not create an express warranty.

Some cases following this test have failed to find an express warranty. For example, in *Carpenter v. Alberto Culver Co.* the plaintiff brought suit because she suffered an adverse skin reaction after using a hair dye manufactured by Alberto Culver. The plaintiff argued that an express warranty was created by the City Drug Store through a clerk who stated to her that several of the clerk's friends used the dye and that her own "hair came out very nice" and the plaintiff "would get very fine results." The court found these rather vague statements were not express warranties. Other courts, however, have found such statements to be express warranties. In *General Supply & Equipment Co. v. Phillips*, the plaintiff brought suit over some plastic paneling sold by the defendant to the plaintiff to cover the plaintiff's greenhouses as roofing material. The paneling had been advertised as follows: "Tests show no deterioration in 5 years normal use" and "It won't turn black or discolor . . . even after years of exposure." The paneling darkened and turned black about 2 years after it was installed. The court noted that the plaintiff had knowledge of the facts asserted in the advertising and would not have bought the paneling had he not seen the advertisement. It found that these statements appearing in the advertising constituted an express warranty. Other cases in the warranty area seem to follow different tests for determining if a statement is or is not puffing.

When a seller describes a Doberman pinscher as a "docile dobe," is that an express warranty that the dog will not bite? Or is it mere puffing? The court in the case which follows sank its teeth into these and other issues.

WHITMER V. SCHNEBLE V. HOUSE OF HOYT, INC.

Appellate Court of Illinois, Second District
331 N.E.2d 115 (1975)

BACKGROUND: The Schnebles (plaintiffs) filed suit against House of Hoyt (defendant). On July 26, 1968, Robert and Frances Schneble bought a female Doberman pinscher from the House of Hoyt. They alleged that the dog was represented to them as a "docile dobe" appropriate for one "who is in need of a dog for companionship and friendship but wants very little aggressiveness in him." However, the bill of sale, signed by the Schnebles, described the dog as "medium aggressive," which was further described in the literature given to them as a dobe that "can love and fight with equal zeal" and was suitable "for people who want true protection."

Some 2 1/2 years later the dog was bred and had puppies. On January 9, 1971, Sherry Whitney, a neighbor's child, was looking at the puppies when she was bitten by the mother. The parents of Sherry Whitney sued the Schnebles. The Schnebles then filed a third-party complaint against the House of Hoyt on the theory of breach of express warranty. The trial court dismissed the Schnebles' complaint against the House of Hoyt. The Schnebles appealed.

Hallett, Judge

The Schnebles contend that Hoyt is liable to them because of the breach of an express warranty that the "dobe" was "docile," etc.

It is very doubtful whether any of the language alleged in Count 1 amounted to an express warranty. Statements merely of the seller's opinion or sales talk do not constitute express warranties. Furthermore, as we have indicated, the bill of sale and brochure, which the Schnebles concede, destroy their claim.

But even if there were an express warranty, it would not appear that there was a breach. Nowhere do the Schnebles allege that Hoyt stated that the dog would not bite. Even a docile dog is known and expected to bite under certain circumstances. And this court will not infer a warranty that the dog will never bite from the language which was used. "[T]he law will not lend itself to the creation of an implied warranty which patently runs counter to the experience of mankind or known forces of nature. It will not read into any sale or bailment a condition or proviso which is unreasonable, impossible, or absurd." *Meester v. Roose* (1966), 259 Iowa 357, 144 NW2d 274, 276.

In addition, the statements complained of only describe the personality of the dog at the time it was sold. There is no warranty by the seller that the dog's personality will not change in the future. Yet the plaintiff did not allege that there had been a breach of the warranty on the date of the sale or that the condition of the dog had remained unchanged during the 2 1/2 years since the sale. Indeed, it would be difficult for the plaintiffs to so allege since the dog had new masters, gotten older and had puppies.

We therefore conclude that there is no merit to this contention.

DECISION: The appellate court affirmed the decision for House of Hoyt.

Advertising A statement need not be made specifically to the buyer in order to create an express warranty in the buyer's favor. Statements made to the general public by way of brochures, catalogues, and other advertising can also give rise to express warranties. Note, however, that a buyer must have actually read the advertisement in order to recover for breach of warranty. *Interco. Inc. v. Randustrial Corp.*, which is excerpted below, provides a good discussion of how advertising can become part of the basis of a bargain.

INTERCO, INC. V. RANDUSTRIAL CORP.

Court of Appeals of Missouri

533 S.W.2d 257 (1976)

BACKGROUND: Suit was brought against Randustrial Corp. (defendant) by Interco (plaintiff) for breach of warranty. Interco claimed that Randustrial's Sylox flooring, which Interco had installed in Building No. 1 of its St. Louis facility, failed to live up to the description provided in Randustrial's catalog. The jury found for Randustrial. Interco appealed.

Gunn, Judge

Interco maintains that it was entitled to judgment as a matter of law based on a breach of express warranty by Randustrial. Interco argues that the purchase of Sylox was based on the following Randustrial catalogue description of the material and asserts an express warranty thereby:

> Sylox is a hard yet malleable material which bonds firm to wood floors for smooth and easy hand-trucking. Sylox will absorb considerable flex without cracking and is not softened by spillage of oil, grease or solvents.

We have noted that Interco claims the existence of a warranty as to Sylox, and Randustrial argues the absence of a warranty. We disagree with Randustrial's contentions in this regard. Although Randustrial contends its reference to Sylox in its sales catalogue did not constitute an express warranty, if the words used in the catalogue constitute a description or an affirmation of fact or promise about Sylox and became a part of the basis of the bargain, an express warranty was created. The catalogue stated that "Sylox will absorb considerable flex." Thus, there was a description or affirmation of fact or "warranty" regarding Sylox giving rise to the purpose for which it was purchased by Interco. This was not mere puffing of a product. Interco was entitled to take the catalogue description of Sylox at its face value and plain meaning. All the buyers are required to establish is that the express warranties were made and that they were false, thereby establishing a breach of the contract.

Randustrial's argument that Interco failed to prove reliance on any warranty is also not felicitous. There is no mention of reliance in 2-313.

The fact that the language read by Interco was contained in a catalogue and was basically an advertisement does not preclude a finding that it is a warranty. A brochure, catalogue, or advertisement may constitute an express warranty. . . . However, the catalogue advertisement or brochure must have at least been read, as the UCC requires the proposed express warranty be part of the basis of the bargain. Randustrial does not dispute the fact that Interco had read the catalogue.

Randustrial relies on the pre-UCC case of *Turner v. Central Hardware Co.* (1964), arguing that the statement that Sylox "will absorb considerable flex" merely reflects the seller's opinion of the goods and creates no warranty. In the Central Hardware Co. case, a ladder advertised as "mighty strong and durable" collapsed under use causing injury to the plaintiff. In discussing the use of factual information vis-à-vis mere "sales talk" in advertising, the court said:

> The seller's privilege to puff his wares, enhance their quality and recommend their value, even to the point of exaggeration, is unquestionable, so long as his salesmanship remains in the field of "dealer's talk," commendation or mere expressions of opinion. . . .

We believe that the foregoing pre-UCC law continues under 2-313, which specifically excludes a seller's mere opinion or commendation from being interpreted as an express warranty. The Central Hardware Co. case does make clear, though, that the language chosen by the seller in his advertising must be interpreted in favor of the buyer in order to restrict "untruthful puffing of wares." We believe that this is the same type of approach desired by the draftsmen of the UCC. . . . An important factor is whether the seller assumes to assert a fact of which the buyer may be expected to have an opinion and be able to express his own judgment.

Although Randustrial is pertinacious in its contention that the catalogue content regarding absorbability of considerable flex is merely a reflection of opinion, we must disagree. It is manifest that the words so used were meant to induce purchases through the assurance that considerable flex would be absorbed and were not mere opinion. The words were an affirmation of fact within the meaning of 2-313.

But having determined that an express warranty as to Sylox did exist, we reach the crux of this case—whether there was a breach of that warranty by Randustrial as a matter of fact. Ordinarily—and this case is no exception—the question of whether there has been a breach of warranty is a factual matter to be determined by the trier of fact.

The keystone of this case and the basis for Randustrial's triumph before the jury and affirmation by this court continues to be the phrase "absorb considerable flex." That phrase is too imprecise to be defined as a matter of law. It was for the jury to determine as a matter of fact whether Sylox conformed to the promise to absorb considerable flex. The jury could have reasonably found on the basis of the evidence presented to it that the flex or movement in the second floor of Building No. 1 was more than considerable and more than Sylox was designed to accommodate. The fact issue as to what amounted to considerable flex in this case was proper for the jury to determine.

DECISION: The court of appeals affirmed the jury verdict, although it found that the statement in question was not puffing. The court thus held that the statement was an express warranty. However, the court let stand the jury's finding that Randustrial's warranty was not breached by the floor's failure to withstand the considerable punishment that Interco inflicted on it.

Description

An express warranty can also be created by describing goods if the description is part of the basis of the bargain between the parties. The seller need not use the word "warranty," nor is it necessary that the buyer rely on the seller's affirmation of fact or promise in order to find that the seller made an express warranty. Comment 3 to Section 2-313 states: "In actual practice affirmations of fact made by the seller about the goods during a bargain are regarded as part of the description of those goods; hence no particular reliance on such statements need be shown in order to weave them into the fabric of the agreement." The description need not be by words. Technical specifications, blueprints, or the like, if made part of the basis of the bargain between the parties, can create an express warranty.

Sample or Model

An express warranty also can be made by a sample or model that is made part of the basis of the bargain between the parties. When the seller actually draws an item from the bulk of goods that is the subject matter of the sale, the item is referred to as a sample; when a demonstration item is offered for inspection, it is called a model.

Creation after Contracting

It is possible for an express warranty to be created after the contract has been executed by the parties. If the buyer asks the seller, for example, whether the plastic just bought will withstand freezing temperatures and the seller replies "yes," this might constitute an express warranty. Section 2-209(2) of the UCC permits modification of a contract without consideration. However, the statute of frauds must be complied with.

If the parties orally agree upon an express warranty, but the final executed contract fails to reflect this agreement, the party wishing to assert the warranty may encounter difficulties in establishing its existence. The parol evidence rule found in Section 2-202 prohibits any evidence that contradicts a writing intended by the parties as a final expression of their agreement.

Implied Warranty of Merchantability

Provisions

Section 2-314 of the UCC states:

(1) Unless excluded or modified (Section 2-316), a warranty that the goods shall be merchantable is implied in a contract for their sale if the seller is a merchant with respect to goods of that kind. Under this section the serving for value of food or drink to be consumed either on the premises or elsewhere is a sale.

(2) Goods to be merchantable must be at least such as

(a) pass without objection in the trade under the contract description; and

(b) in the case of fungible goods, are of fair average quality within the description; and

(c) are fit for the ordinary purposes for which such goods are used; and

(d) run, within the variations permitted by the agreement, of even kind, quality and quantity within each unit and among all units involved; and

(e) are adequately contained, packaged, and labeled as the agreement may require; and

(f) conform to the promises or affirmations of fact made on the container or label if any.

(3) Unless excluded or modified (Section 2-316) other implied warranties may arise from course of dealing or usage of trade.

Thus the implied warranty of merchantability arises by operation of law—not as a result of any warranty expressly stated in the contract. The re-

quirements stated in Section 2-314(2) are *cumulative*, but subsection (b) deals only with fungible, or interchangeable, goods. This is not an exhaustive list of what is "merchantable" but merely states that the goods must at least comply with these requirements.

Generally the court will try to determine if the goods are fit for the ordinary purposes for which such goods are used. In making this determination, the court will consider the manner in which such goods are used. A seller who delivers shoes that come apart when the buyer walks around in them has breached the warranty of merchantability because shoes certainly should be fit for ordinary walking.

Merchants

It should be noted that Section 2-314 applies only when the seller is a merchant. If the seller is not a merchant, no such warranty arises. For example, Siemen brought suit for breach of the implied warranty of merchantability. He had purchased an old multirip saw from a man in the sawmill business. While operating the machine, Siemen was injured. Siemen cannot recover based on the implied warranty of merchantability because the defendant was not in the business of selling saws and therefore was not a merchant pursuant to Section 2-104.

If a seller is a nonmerchant, there is no implied warranty of merchantability. Nonetheless, these provisions may serve as guidelines when the nonmerchant-seller states that the goods are guaranteed.

Fungible Goods

If the sale involves fungible goods, the court will examine whether the goods are of "fair average quality." This means that the goods must be roughly of the same type as specified in the contract. Some of the lowest quality goods could be included in the delivery, but the mix must average out to be close to the standard in the contract.

Food

In determining whether or not food is merchantable, some courts follow the "foreign-natural distinction"—that is, a given food is merchantable if it contains elements that are natural to the product. A consumer who breaks his tooth on a cherry pit while eating a piece of cherry pie would be unable to recover in a jurisdiction following this test. Other jurisdictions follow the "reasonable expectation" test—that is, only those things that we reasonably expect to be in the food should be in it. In a jurisdiction following the "reasonable expectation" test the consumer who breaks a tooth on a cherry pit in a piece of pie might be able to recover.

In a famous case involving breach of the implied warranty of merchantability, *Webster v. Blue Ship Tea Room, Inc.*, the plaintiff brought suit because, while she was eating fish chowder at the Blue Ship Tea Room, a fish bone became lodged in her throat. This led to two esophagoscopies and the eventual extraction of the fish bone. The question in this case was whether there had been a breach of the implied warranty of merchantability. The court delved into the culinary traditions of New England and determined that fish chowder normally contains large chunks of fish in which a consumer ought to expect bones. The court ruled that the occasional presence of fish bones should be anticipated by a customer, and therefore it decided for the Tea Room.

Implied Warranty of Fitness for a Particular Purpose

Particular Purpose

If the seller knows at the time of contracting the particular purpose for which the buyer wants the goods and the buyer relies on the seller's skill or judgment to select or furnish suitable goods, there is an implied warranty that the goods will be fit for the purpose the buyer specifies at the time of contracting (Section 2-315).

A particular purpose differs from the ordinary purpose for which goods are used. If a buyer wishes to purchase climbing shoes and asks the seller to select a pair for him or her, the seller breaches this warranty if he or she sells the buyer shoes used only for ordinary walking. The shoes might be suitable for walking and therefore merchantable, but they would not be suitable for the particular purpose the buyer specified. It is not necessary that the buyer state how he or she intends to use the product as long as the circumstances should make the seller aware of the needs of the buyer.

Simply because the goods are merchantable does not mean they are fit for the buyer's particular purpose. If the buyer wishes to purchase a furnace for use at home and tells the seller that he or she wants to heat a house of 2,000 square feet, the seller has breached the implied warranty of fitness for a particular purpose if the heater is inadequate to heat the buyer's house, even though it operates properly and would heat a much smaller house quite nicely.

Unlike the implied warranty of merchantability, this warranty applies to both merchants and nonmerchants.

Reliance

Reliance is critical under Section 2-315. If the buyer supplies specifications to the seller, there is no reliance and hence no breach of the warranty, even if the seller knows the purpose for which the goods are to be used.

The implied warranty of fitness for a particular purpose is discussed in *Gates v. Abernathy*. The case should give comfort to anyone who has ever been faced with the bewildering predicament of having to buy clothes for a wife or girlfriend.

GATES V. ABERNATHY
Court of Appeals of Oklahoma
11 UCC 491 (1972)

BACKGROUND: Gates (plaintiff) brought suit against Abernathy (defendant), the owner of the shop, Penelope's. Gates purchased a dress for his wife. He was assured that the dress was suitable for his wife. It was not, and Gates sued to receive his money back. The trial court decided for Gates, and Abernathy appealed.

Neptune, Justice

One of the plaintiffs, Dr. Paul Gates, wished to purchase some clothes to give his wife (the other plaintiff) as a Christmas present. Dr. Gates had never before bought any clothing for his wife and was ignorant of what size she wore. He was aware, however, that his wife had frequently shopped at "Penelope's," a shop owned by defendant, and that she had been waited on there by the store manager, Penny. Therefore, he went to "Penelope's," spoke to Penny and explained to her that he wished to buy some clothes to give to his wife as a Christmas present. Penny showed Dr. Gates certain items in sizes that she said she was certain would be proper for Mrs. Gates. Dr. Gates picked out three pant suits in the size that Penny had recommended and purchased them. It was understood that if the suits did not fit or if there "was any problem" they could be returned.

When she received the gifts, Mrs. Gates tried them on and discovered that they were much too big. Shortly after Christmas, Dr. Gates returned the pant suits to "Penelope's" and received a credit slip. When Mrs. Gates came to the shop with the credit slip she was unable to find anything in her size. She was directed to another store owned by defendant but found nothing acceptable in her size. She demanded the money back but this was refused. Dr. and Mrs. Gates brought this action to recover the purchase price of the suits plus attorney fees.

Plaintiffs sued under section 2-315 claiming breach of an implied warranty of fitness for a particular purpose. Defendant entered a general denial. The trial court sitting without a jury entered judgment for plaintiff in the sum of $192.62 plus an attorney's fee of $50 plus $4 for costs. Defendant appeals.

Appellant asserts that this is not a situation where appellees could recover on an implied warranty of fitness. There is no merit in this contention. The statute upon which the action is based, section 2-315, states:

> Where the seller at the time of contracting has reason to know any particular purpose for which the goods are required and that the buyer is relying on the seller's skill or judgment to select or furnish suitable goods, there is unless excluded or modified under the next section an implied warranty that the goods shall be fit for such purpose.

It is hard to imagine a case which fits into the outline of the statute as well as this one. It is uncontested that the buyer here was relying on the judgment of the seller to furnish the kind of goods he wanted, nor is there any question that the seller was aware that the seller's expertise was being relied on by the buyer. Appellees did not sue on the basis that the clothes were not merchantable or useable as clothes. Rather, appellees claimed that they were not useable for the particular purpose for which they were bought, that is, for Mrs. Gates to wear.

The statute gives relief to a buyer who relies on a seller's expertise to buy a product to be used in a particular manner. Even before the statute was enacted the Oklahoma Supreme Court gave relief in analogous circumstances. In *Ransom v. Robinson Packer Co.* (1926), the court said:

> Where an article of personal property is sold for a definite purpose made known to the seller, and the seller represents that the article will perform that particular purpose, there is a warranty of fitness which protects the purchaser and for which the seller is liable, in the event the article fails to do what it was sold to do.

In that case, pumps sold to the buyer operated in the manner expected, but they did not perform the job that the seller had promised. In the case at bar, the clothes were good clothes but they did not fit Mrs. Gates as the seller had represented. We conclude that the instant case is controlled by section 2-315.

DECISION: The appeals court affirmed the decision for Gates.

Table 24-1 lists the express and implied warranties discussed thus far and summarizes how each such warranty is created.

Conflict of Warranties

When a purchaser buys a product, it may have only one warranty or it may have several warranties. Warranties on a product should be construed by the court in such a fashion as to give effect to every warranty. On the other hand, if it is impossible to give effect to all warranties, the intention of the parties will determine which warranty is controlling. Section 2-317 sets forth three rules to determine the intention of the parties:

(a) Exact or technical specifications displace an inconsistent sample or model or general language of description.
(b) A sample from an existing bulk displaces inconsistent general language of description.
(c) Express warranties displace inconsistent implied warranties other than an implied warranty of fitness for a particular purpose.

These rules control unless one of the parties introduces evidence indicating that the rules would lead to an unreasonable result. It should be noted that if the seller misleads the buyer by implying that all the warranties can be performed, and they cannot all be performed, the seller will be stopped from setting up the inconsistency of the warranties as a defense.

Exclusion or Modification of Warranties

Express Warranties

Express warranties, as noted earlier, can be created by an affirmation of fact or promise made by the seller, or by a description, or by a sample or model that is made part of the basis of the bargain between the parties. Once an express warranty has been created, it is very difficult to disclaim. Section 2-316(1) states:

> Words or conduct relevant to the creation of an express warranty and words or conduct tending to negate or limit warranty shall be construed wherever reasonable as consistent with each other; but subject to the provisions of the Article on parol or extrinsic evidence (Section 2-202) negation or limitation is inoperative to the extent that such construction is unreasonable.

Conflict between Warranty and Disclaimer Once an express warranty comes into existence, any language in the contract suggesting that express warranties have been disclaimed will create a conflict between the warranty and the disclaimer. If it is possible to read the warranty and disclaimer as consistent, the court must do so, but if such a reading is unreasonable, then the express warranty prevails over the disclaimer. The drafters of the UCC were trying to protect the buyer from hidden disclaimers by making any language inconsistent with the express warranty ineffective. In this way the buyer is not misled.

TABLE $24\text{-}1$

Concept Summary	Types of Warranties
Type	**How Created**
Express warranties	By affirmation of fact or promise; by description of the goods; by sample or model
Implied warranty of merchantability	If the seller is a merchant, automatically created by operation of law
Implied warranty of fitness for a particular purpose	Created by operation of law when seller knows or should know of buyer's purpose and where buyer relies on seller's judgment
Warranty of title	Automatically created by operation of law

Thus any contract that uses language excluding "all warranties, express or implied," but that also contains an express warranty in direct conflict with this attempted disclaimer, will not succeed in eliminating the express warranty. If the seller provides the buyer with a sample but tries to exclude all express warranties in the contract, it is unlikely that the express warranty created by the sample can be disclaimed through use of such language.

Suppose a person signs a contract for the purchase of steel pipe. The contract explicitly states that the pipe will withstand temperatures down to 30 degrees below zero. This statement is an affirmation of fact and constitutes an express warranty. The contract also attempts to exclude "all warranties, express and implied." Is such a clause effective to eliminate the warranty that the pipe will withstand temperatures at least as low as 30 degrees below zero? The court must read the warranty and disclaimer as consistent if possible. Here such a reading would not be possible. If the buyer purchases the pipe, and it fails to withstand a temperature of 30 degrees below zero, he or she has a cause of action against the seller for breach of warranty. The express warranty and the exclusion directly conflict. The express warranty has not been effectively excluded.

Problems of Proof Section 2-316(1) is subject to the provisions on parol or extrinsic evidence (Section 2-202). These relate to the problem of proving an express warranty. Although the parties may have in fact agreed upon a particular express warranty, they may not have incorporated it into the final written contract. The question then becomes, Can the person asserting the existence of an express warranty introduce evidence of an oral agreement arrived at before the contract was signed (but not expressed in the contract) when the contract disclaims the existence of any express warranties? The parol evidence rule, found in Section 2-202, may prevent this evidence from being introduced at trial because it contradicts the written terms of the contract.

Suppose in our pipe example the salesperson tells the purchaser orally that the pipe will withstand temperatures at least as low as 30 degrees below zero. However, the contract the buyer signs explicitly states that the seller will not guarantee the performance of the pipe in temperatures below zero. The contract states that it is intended as the final agreement of the parties and is a complete and exclusive statement of the terms of the agreement. Clearly, this contract is not silent or ambiguous on the question of the pipe's ability to withstand temperatures. The court will not permit introduction of the salesperson's statement to alter or vary the explicit terms of this written contract.

Implied Warranties

Implied Warranty of Merchantability The implied warranty of merchantability may be disclaimed if the disclaimer mentions the word "merchantability" and, in case of a writing, is conspicuous. Explicitly stating in a written contract "There is no implied warranty of merchantability," in larger type than the rest of the contract, will call the buyer's attention to the exclusion of this warranty. This may also be excluded by other language, as is discussed below.

Implied Warranty of Fitness for a Particular Purpose To exclude the implied warranty of fitness for a particular purpose, the exclusion must be in writing and conspicuous. It can be disclaimed by the language: "There are no warranties which extend beyond the description on the face hereof." Note that subsection (2) of 2-316 does not specifically require that language excluding the implied warranty of fitness must use the phrase "implied warranty of fitness." A seller might state in a written contract "There is no implied warranty of fitness." If this appears in larger type than the rest of the contract, it will call the buyer's attention to the exclusion of this warranty. This warranty may also be excluded by other language, as discussed in the next paragraph.

Language That Excludes All Implied Warranties Excluding or modifying either of the implied warranties of quality can easily be accomplished by using the language specified in Section 2-316(2), as discussed above.

Phrases such as "as is" or "with all faults" can exclude all implied warranties (Section 2-316[3]).

The seller need not use these exact phrases as long as the language used "in common understanding calls the buyer's attention to the exclusion of warranties and makes plain that there is no implied warranty." By using the phrases provided, a seller can be certain of protection. It should be noted that subsection (3)(a) says nothing about the phrase being conspicuous. Because there are differing court decisions on this point, a prudent seller will make such a disclaimer conspicuous.

Conspicuous Language   To make certain that disclaimer language is conspicuous, the seller probably should use type larger and darker than that of the rest of the contract and the disclaimer should appear on the first page of the contract. An extremely careful seller might use a different color type for the disclaimer and have the buyer initial the paragraph containing the disclaimer. If this course is followed, there will be little doubt that the buyer was aware of the disclaimer of all warranties.

Examination of Goods   Section 2-316(3)(b) permits a seller to exclude the implied warranties by giving the buyer an opportunity to examine the goods or a sample or model. If a seller wishes to rely upon subsection (3)(b), he or she must demand that the buyer examine the goods and give the buyer the opportunity to inspect the goods before entering into the contract; and the buyer must have examined the goods as fully as he or she desires. The seller, by demanding that the buyer examine the goods, puts the buyer on notice that he or she is assuming the risk of defects that an examination would reveal. Merely telling the buyer the goods are available for inspection is not sufficient; the seller must demand that the buyer examine them.

When the buyer examines the goods, a sample, or a model, the buyer's skill and method of examining will determine what defects are excluded by the examination. Defects that the buyer is unable to discover because they are latent or beyond his or her power of discovery through reasonable examination will not be excluded. *Tarulli v. Birds in Paradise* is a famous illustration of the consequences of a failure to examine the goods after a demand has been made on the buyer.

TARULLI V. BIRDS IN PARADISE
Civil Court of New York, Queens County
417 N.Y.S.2d 854 (1979)

> **BACKGROUND:** Tarulli (plaintiff) brought suit for the death of an exotic bird he had bought from Birds in Paradise (defendant).

Posner, Justice

This is a small claims action which involves a defendant doing business as Birds in Paradise and a plaintiff whose purchase of an exotic bird turned into a veritable Miltonian "Paradise Lost."

On Dec. 18, 1978, the plaintiff, Bart Tarulli signed an agreement with the defendant, a dealer in birds, for the sale of one Moluccan Cockatoo. The agreed upon consideration was $400 cash and one Mexican Yellow Head Parrot. The agreement of sale, specifically signed and agreed to by plaintiff, Tarulli, stated as follows:

> This bird is guaranteed to be in good health, to the best of our knowledge, at the time of sale. The customer has a health guarantee extending to close of business 12-20-78, in which to have the bird checked by a licensed veterinarian and is urged to do so. If the veterinarian finds anything seriously wrong with the bird, it will be exchanged for another bird of equal value of the customer's choice, at once or when available, provided a letter from the examining veterinarian is offered as evidence of the bird's illness, and the bird is returned within the guarantee period. No exchange will be made after this period.

Plaintiff testified during trial that he never took the cockatoo to a veterinarian during the period permitted in the agreement. On or about Jan. 12, 1979 the cockatoo showed symptoms of illness and plaintiff brought said bird to Dr. B. J. Schiller, a veterinarian. Despite the extensive care and treatment administered by Dr. Schiller, the cockatoo died that same evening.

Dr. Schiller, as an expert witness for the plaintiff, testified that a post-mortem examination revealed the cause of death as anemia which she would guess existed for more than three weeks, but wasn't sure how long.

It is the plaintiff's contention that the defendant breached the implied warranty of merchantability under the Uniform Commercial Code section 2-314, and [that plaintiff] should be entitled to the sum of $800 ($400 plus the value of the Mexican Yellow Head Parrot), and $50 for veterinary fees.

The plaintiff bolsters this contention by arguing that birds fall within the definition of "goods" as contained in UCC section 2-105(1). Furthermore, the defendant satisfied the definition of a "merchant" under the UCC section 2-104. Thus, the plaintiff maintains that he bought "goods" from a "merchant" and said goods were defective at the time of sale, thereby breaching the implied warranty of merchantability, which was not excluded or modified as per UCC section 2-316. The plaintiff emphasizes UCC section 2-316(2) that to exclude or modify the implied warranty of merchantability, there must be specific mention of the word "merchantability" and the writing must be conspicuous. The plaintiff argues that the defendant failed expressly to exclude the implied warranty of merchantability by failing to specifically mention merchantability in the conditions of sale.

However, subsection 2 of UCC section 2-316 is not the exclusive mechanism to exclude or modify the implied warranty of merchantability. Subsection (3) provides as follows:

> Notwithstanding subsection (2)
>
> (b) when the buyer before entering into the contract has examined the goods or the sample or model as fully as he desired or has refused to examine the goods there is no

implied warranty with regard to defects which an examination ought in the circumstances to have revealed to him.

The Official Comment 8 of section 2-316 of the Code states that this subsection goes to the nature of the responsibility assumed by the seller at the time of the making of the contract.

Of course if the buyer discovers the defect and uses the goods anyway, or if he unreasonably fails to examine the goods before he uses them, resulting injuries may be found to result from his own action, rather than proximately from a breach of warranty.

In order to bring the transaction within the scope of "refused to examine" in paragraph (b), it is not sufficient that the goods are available for inspection. There must in addition be a demand by the seller that the buyer examine the goods fully. The seller by the demand puts the buyer on notice that he is assuming the risk of defects which the examination ought to reveal.

This court finds that the defendant did in fact make such a demand upon the plaintiff to have the cockatoo checked by a licensed veterinarian before Dec. 20, 1978, and it was specifically for the purpose of having the veterinarian determine whether there is "anything seriously wrong with the bird," which only then would entitle the plaintiff to certain relief.

Here, the defendant by the demand for an examination of the cockatoo by a veterinarian put the plaintiff on notice that he is assuming the risk of defects which the examination ought to reveal. Not only was there testimony by the plaintiff that he never took the cockatoo to a veterinarian within the designated period; in effect, bringing the transaction within the scope of a refusal to examine, as per section 2-316(3)(b). But, there is also plaintiff's expert testimony of Dr. Schiller, who on cross-examination was asked: "If the bird had been brought in during the guarantee period, could the anemia have been detected?" And in answer to that question, Dr. Schiller stated unequivocally "yes." In other words, the burden of examination was on the plaintiff, who by not exercising his obligation which would have uncovered the anemia, forfeited any claim for damages based on discoverable defects.

DECISION: The court ruled in favor of Birds in Paradise.

Implied Warranty of Title   The warranty of title may be excluded or modified by specific language that makes the buyer aware that the seller is not claiming title in himself or herself or that the seller is selling only whatever right or title he or she or a third person may have. This is the only manner in which a warranty of title can be excluded or modified. Specific language must be included in the contract for sale beyond that specified in Section 2-316, which deals with exclusion of express and implied warranties, to make clear to the buyer that the seller does not warrant the title to the goods. The reason for this requirement is that the buyer normally may expect a seller to warrant the title even though the seller is excluding all other warranties.

Limitation of Remedies

The reader should distinguish the attempt to exclude or modify a warranty from an attempt by the seller to limit the remedies of the buyer under Section 2-718 or 2-719. Section 2-316(4) states that remedies for breach of warranty can be limited in accordance with these two sections.

Liquidated-Damages Clauses   A liquidated-damages clause provides for the payment of a particular sum by a party if he or she breaches the contract. Section 2-718 deals with an attempt by the parties to provide for liquidated damages. Such agreements will be enforceable only if the contract provides for an amount that is reasonable in the light of the anticipated or actual harm caused by the breach, the difficulties of proving loss, and the inconvenience or nonfeasibility of otherwise obtaining an adequate remedy. A term fixing unreasonably large liquidated damages is void as a penalty. Section 2-718 allows the parties to agree in advance that the seller will pay the buyer a particular sum if there is a breach of warranty, as long as the sum is reasonable.

Limitation or Modification of Remedies Section 2-719 allows the parties (subject to certain limitations) to modify or limit the remedies provided in Article 2. Subsection 3 recognizes the validity of clauses limiting or excluding consequential damages, unless the limitation or exclusion is unconscionable. If the seller attempts to limit consequential damages for injury to a person by consumer goods, the clause is prima facie unconscionable.

Consequential damages include any loss resulting from general or particular requirements and needs of the buyer that the seller had reason to know about at the time of contracting and that could not reasonably have been prevented by the buyer's obtaining the goods elsewhere or otherwise, and injury to person or property proximately resulting from any breach of warranty (Section 2-715[a]).

Even though an attempt to limit consequential damages for injury to a person is prima facie unconscionable, any limitation on damages when the loss is commercial is not prima facie unconscionable. The seller can still attempt to disclaim all warranties, as provided in Section 2-316. In this respect, note the limitations placed on a seller's power to disclaim under the Magnuson-Moss Act discussed later in this chapter.

Consider *Posttape Associates v. Eastman Kodak Co.* Posttape Associates produced a documentary film using Kodak film. Each cannister and box bore the legend:

> READ THIS NOTICE This film will be replaced if defective in manufacture, labeling or packaging, or if damaged or lost by us or any subsidiary company even though by negligence or other fault. Except for such replacement, the sale, processing, or other handling of this film for any purpose is without warranty or liability.

Posttape used the film but, because it turned out to be defective, the movie had to be reshot. Posttape wished to recover consequential damages to compensate it for the cost of the second filming of the documentary.

The court noted that an agreement that limits damages in this fashion must clearly indicate that no other damages are available to the buyer other than those listed on the cannister. It remanded the case for retrial on the issue of whether the cannister provided for an exclusive remedy. In making the determination whether the remedy provided by Kodak eliminated consequential damages of this nature, the circuit court instructed the lower court to take into consideration the trade practices in the film industry and the nature of the agreements.

Federal Trade Commission Warranty Rules

In the Magnuson-Moss Warranty–Federal Trade Commission Act, which became effective in July 1975, Congress expanded the power of the Federal Trade Commission (FTC), specified minimum disclosure standards for written consumer product warranties, and set certain minimum standards for those warranties. The act can be enforced by the FTC, by the U.S. Attorney General, or by a private party. The act gives consumers an opportunity to learn in advance of a purchase the nature of the warranty and to provide for effective enforcement of the warranty in case of breach. However, the act does not *require* warranties on consumer products.

Products Covered

The act applies to any consumer product accompanied by a written warranty. A consumer product is any tangible personal property normally used for personal, family, or household purposes, including personal property intended to be attached to real estate. Service contracts are also covered by the act. Goods that are purchased for commercial or industrial purposes or for resale in the ordinary course of business are not covered by the FTC warranty rules.

The FTC warranty rules require compliance only if the consumer product costs $15 or more and is accompanied by a written warranty. If a company does not wish to be bound by the act or the FTC rules, it should not offer a written warranty on its consumer products. Oral warranties are not covered by the act.

Information That Must Be Disclosed

A written warranty must be in terms easily understood by the average consumer. It must disclose to consumers before the sale of the product such information as:

1. The name and address of the warrantor
2. The products or parts covered
3. A statement of what the warrantor will do, at whose expense, and for what period of time
4. The step-by-step procedure that the consumer should follow to enforce the warranty

Full or Limited Warranty

The act requires that a product be labeled as having either a "limited" or a "full" warranty. This labeling system allows a consumer to compare products before making a final purchase. Prior to the act, the consumer frequently did not even know what type of warranty the product carried until arriving home, opening the box, and finding the warranty.

A written full warranty must provide the following:

1. Any defects, malfunctions, or inability to conform to the terms of a written warranty must be corrected by the warrantor without charge and within a reasonable length of time.
2. The warrantor cannot limit the period within which the implied warranties will be effective with respect to the consumer product.
3. The warrantor cannot limit or exclude consequential damages on a consumer product unless noted conspicuously on the face of the warranty.
4. The warrantor must allow the consumer to choose between a refund of the purchase price or replacement of the defective product or part after a reasonable number of attempts to remedy the defect or malfunction.

A limited warranty does not give the consumer these guarantees. A product must be clearly and conspicuously labeled as having a limited warranty if a written warranty is provided and the full warranty conditions are not met. Figure 24-2 is a typical limited warranty.

Disclaimer of Implied Warranty

The provision that a warrantor cannot disclaim any implied warranty is important. The act prohibits the disclaimer or modification of an implied warranty if a written warranty is given or if a service contract is entered into with the purchaser within 90 days after the sale. A "full" warranty cannot disclaim, modify, or even limit the basic implied warranties. The purchaser of a consumer product with a "limited" warranty also is assured that the implied warranties cannot be disclaimed or modified. But the implied warranties can be limited in duration to that of the written warranty—as long as the limitation is reasonable, conscionable, and conspicuous.

This product has been manufactured under the highest standards of quality and workmanship. We warrant to the **consumer** all parts of this product against defects in material and workmanship for **ten** (10) **years** from date of purchase. Any defective part will be replaced **free of charge**, excluding labor or service charges. We will not be responsible for any product damage due to installation error, product abuse, or product misuse whether performed by a contractor, service company, or yourself. Use of other than Acme factory parts may void this warranty.

This warranty applies only **to the consumer use** of the product and any inquiries regarding warranty claims are to be directed to

Acme Corporation
100 Main Street
Anytown, Missouri 66066

This warranty gives you specific legal rights and you may also have other rights which vary from state to state.

FIGURE 24-2

Acme Corporation: Limited Warranty

ISSUES AND TRENDS
Federal Trade Commission Used Car Rule

The Federal Trade Commission has adopted a rule designed to protect consumers who want to purchase a used automobile. In the past such people were to a great extent at the mercy of the seller.

The FTC used car rule requires dealers to place window stickers on all used cars offered for sale. This window sticker either spells out a warranty or indicates the vehicle in question is being offered "as is." If the seller does not offer a warranty, the sticker must state that the buyer is responsible for any repairs should the car fail to operate properly. The sticker must urge prospective buyers to seek an independent inspection before making a purchase. The sticker must also warn customers that since spoken promises are difficult to enforce, any promises given by the dealer should be reduced to a written form.

The FTC used car rule provides protection to persons who need protection. In the past many purchasers of used cars have ended up with a pile of repair bills. Yet these people quite often are the persons least able to afford such bills. The FTC used car rule has helped such persons by informing them in advance of their rights. Such a rule helps purchasers make informed decisions whether or not to purchase used cars.

The passage of the Magnuson-Moss Act creates yet another source of law that must be consulted in resolving warranty disputes. The following case illustrates how the Magnuson-Moss Act works to restrict the ability of sellers to use disclaimers of the implied warranty of merchantability.

ISMAEL V. GOODMAN TOYOTA
North Carolina Court of Appeals
417 S.E.2d 290 (1992)

BACKGROUND: Ismael purchased a used 1985 Ford Tempo from Goodman Toyota. Additionally, he simultaneously purchased from Goodman a vehicle service agreement for $695. He testified that the car "shook" during the test drive prior to his purchase. The salesman assured them that the car "probably just needed a tune-up and that Goodman would repair anything that was found wrong with the car at no charge." Ismael purchased the car "as is." Immediately after the purchase he experienced problems with the car. From the date of purchase to the time of trial, he was able to drive the car only 700 miles.

The trial court ruled that the dealer bore no responsibility for subsequent repair of the vehicle because it was purchased in an "as is" condition.

Wells, Justice

The underlying premise of plaintiff's contention is that defendant violated the Magnuson-Moss Warranty Act and is therefore liable for damages plaintiff suffered as a result of that violation.

In order for this plaintiff to have established his entitlement to relief under the Act, he must have shown he was damaged by the defendant's failure to comply with an obligation under the Act, the service contract, and/or an implied warranty. 15 U.S.C.A. § 2310(d)(1).

Defendant contends that since the uncontradicted evidence proved the car was sold "as is," all express and implied warranties were effectively disclaimed pursuant to our Uniform Commercial Code, . . . and therefore plaintiff had no claim for breach of an implied warranty. Defendant also contends that since no express or implied warranties were given, the Act does not apply in this case. We disagree.

Defendant correctly contends that, as a general rule, the implied warranty of merchantability is excluded by an "as is" sale. However, the Act significantly limits a supplier's ability to modify or disclaim implied warranties. If, at the time of sale or within 90 days thereafter, a supplier enters into a service contract with the consumer which applies to such consumer product, the supplier may not disclaim or modify any implied warranty with respect to that product. Furthermore, a disclaimer made in violation of §2308(a) is ineffective for purposes of the Act *and* state law.

In this case, the evidence that plaintiff and defendant, at the time of sale, entered into a written service contract for repair of the Tempo was undisputed. The agreement was a service contract within the meaning of the Act because it was in writing and defendant agreed to perform certain repairs for a specified duration (24,000 miles) or fixed period of time (24 months). Further, the plaintiff paid defendant an additional $695.00 for the contract. Therefore, under §2308(a)(2) of the Act, defendant was prohibited from disclaiming the implied warranty of merchantability which arose in the contract of sale under State law and the "as is" sale was ineffective as a disclaimer of this warranty. . . .

We conclude that plaintiff's evidence conclusively established the necessary requirements to recover damages from defendant for breach of the implied warranty of merchantability. Thus, the trial court improperly concluded that defendant was not liable to plaintiff for breach of warranty.

DECISION: The court of appeals reversed the judgment of the trial court and entered a judgment on behalf of Ismael.

Consequential Damages

A full warranty may limit consequential damages. The Magnuson-Moss Act permits such a limitation, although UCC Section 2-719 states that the consequential damages may be limited or excluded only as long as the limitation is conscionable. The limitation of consequential damages for injury caused by consumer goods is prima facie unconscionable under Section 2-719(3).

Warranties and Personal-Injury Claims

Warranties may be used by a person injured by a product to establish a personal-injury claim. If an injured party is able to establish that the defendant made a warranty, failed to live up to the warranty, and as a result of the breach of warranty the plaintiff was injured by the product, he or she may be able to collect damages based on breach of warranty. One of the major problems associated with warranties was the absence of privity of contract, as discussed in the next section.

Privity of Contract and Section 2-318

Today the trend is away from requiring the plaintiff to establish privity of contract with the defendant. *Privity* is a direct contractual relationship between the parties. Section 2-318 states the UCC's limited rule on privity. The drafters of the UCC presented three alternative sections for the states to consider adopting.

Alternative A. Many states have adopted Alternative A, which states:

A seller's warranty whether express or implied extends to any natural person who is in the family or household of his buyer or who is a guest in his home if it is reasonable to expect that such person may use, consume or be affected by the goods and who is injured in person by breach of the warranty. A seller may not exclude or limit the operation of this section.

Any natural person in the buyer's family or household, or one who is a guest in his or her home, may sue the seller directly for injuries sustained. This provision does not help all persons injured by a defective product, for example, a bystander. If a man is mowing his lawn, and the mower blade flies off and strikes his neighbor, the neighbor may not avail himself of Section 2-318 in states that have adopted only Alternative A.

Alternative B. Alternative B extends to "all natural persons who may reasonably be expected to use, consume or be affected by the goods and who are injured in person by breach of the warranty." A number of states have adopted this alternative. Both A and B limit the damages recoverable as a result of a breach of warranty to personal damages.

Alternative C. Alternative C extends the warranty protection to "any person, natural or otherwise." This would include damage to a corporation. Thus Alternative C covers injury of any type, not just personal injuries.

Suits against Someone Other Than the Buyer's Seller The UCC does not take a direct position on suits against someone more remote in the distributive chain than the buyer's immediate seller. If a man is injured by his defective mower, he can clearly bring suit against the retail merchant from whom he purchased the mower. The UCC does not take a position whether the man can sue the wholesaler or manufacturer of the mower. However, most courts today allow suit to be brought under Section 2-318 against the manufacturer and wholesaler, and thus privity does not pose a serious problem to an injured party who wishes to bring suit for breach of warranty. Injured parties typically try to sue the manufacturer because the manufacturer is often in a better position to pay than a local retailer.

Notice

There can be a problem under the UCC, however, if notice is not given of the breach of warranty. Section 2-607(3) clearly states that the buyer must, in a reasonable time after he or she discovers or should have discovered any breach of war-

ranty, notify the seller of the breach or be barred from any remedy. Therefore notice must be given to the seller and everyone in the distributive chain for the injured party to sue under the UCC.

Assuming that the plaintiff establishes a warranty and a breach of that warranty, and that as a result of the breach he or she was injured, a successful case may be pursued against the seller. Today many personal-injury suits arising out of the use of a defective product are based on warranty theory. The area of law dealing with defective products is called "products liability." The other theories on which suit may be brought are discussed in Chapter 25.

Review Questions and Problems

Key Terms

express warranty

implied warranty of merchantability

implied warranty of fitness for a particular purpose

warranty of title

Discussion Questions

1. What are the three implied warranties that automatically arise out of the sale of a good?

2. List the ways in which an express warranty may be created.

3. If you were a merchant who wanted to exclude all implied warranties in your transaction with a consumer, what would you do to make sure the exclusion would hold up in court?

Review Problems

1. Autzen contracted to purchase a used 50-foot boat from Taylor for $100,000. After agreeing on the price, but during the process of negotiating, Autzen was assured that the boat was in good condition. Taylor's agent had the boat inspected for dry rot prior to Autzen's purchase, although Autzen felt it was unnecessary to do so. Upon completion of the inspection, the inspector concluded that the hull was very sound "and that the boat should be well suited for its intended purpose." Autzen then gave Taylor's agent $10,000 and took possession. Approximately 2 months later, Autzen discovered that parts of the boat's flying bridge had been weakened by dry rot. A further inspection of the boat revealed that there was an enormous amount of dry rot and insect infestation. Was there an express warranty made as to the condition of the boat?

2. Louis orders a quantity of enamel-lined steel pipe from Key for an Alaskan construction project. The pipe as ordered was delivered in March, a time of extremely low temperatures. In April, Louis began laying the pipe. By early May, some 5,000 feet of the pipe had been installed. An inspection of the pipe at this time revealed that portions of the interior enamel lining had cracked away from the steel outer casing and were hanging down in sheets. Louis brought suit for breach of the implied warranty of fitness for a particular purpose under Section 2-315. Was there an implied warranty of fitness for a particular purpose?

3. Christopher purchased a motor home from Larson for $16,000. Christopher was assured by Larson's salesman that the motor home would meet the requirements Christopher expressed to the salesman. This all led to Christopher's purchasing the motor home. On the backside of the contract was a disclaimer of warranties, including the implied warranty of merchantability among other fine-print provisions. This disclaimer was never called to Christopher's attention. Christopher and his family took a trip in the motor home, which proved to be defective in a number of ways. Some repairs were needed to make it back home. Was the disclaimer of warranties effective?

4. George is the owner of a 1971 Mustang, purchased from Pettigrew, a retail Ford dealer. Browder, George's mother-in-law, is injured when the right front wheel of the Mustang collapses. Ford Motor Company, the manufacturer of the Mustang, validly disclaims all implied warranties made to George. Browder sues Pettigrew and Ford for, among other things, breach of the implied warranties, alleging her status as a third-party beneficiary. Is Browder a third-party beneficiary of any implied warranties?

Case Problems

1. Plaintiff Cantrell was injured while using a ladder that had come in a cardboard box bearing the following message:

GOOD QUALITY; LIGHT-STRONG-SAFE; RATED LOAD 200 LBS; FOR SAFETY'S SAKE BUY ME. I'M LIGHT AND STRONG; FIVE YEAR GUARANTEE. . . . The manufacturer guarantees the ladder, under normal use and service to be free from defects in material and workmanship, for five years from the date of purchase.

Cantrell weighed only 165 pounds. The ladder had not been misused or abused, and at the time it collapsed it was being used on a clean cement floor with all braces properly extended and locked. The front legs of the ladder buckled inward, throwing the plaintiff to the cement floor. Cantrell sued Amarillo Hardware (the wholesaler) and Werner (the manufacturer) for breach of warranty. The defendants argued that there was no evidence indicating that any component, design feature, or material used in the ladder was defective, and without product defect they were not liable. Do you agree?

2. Ricklefs purchased an automobile from Clemens. Clemens gave Ricklets a certificate of title that warranted the title to be free of all liens. Ricklefs was subsequently notified by the FBI that the automobile was stolen. Has Clemens breached the warranty of title?

3. Terry Drayton was with her father while he was attempting to clear a clogged sink in the bathroom. Mr. Drayton was using a bottle of Liquid Plumr that he had purchased. After he poured half a bottle down the drain, he placed a towel over the drain. At that moment Terry screamed. She had been doused with drain cleaner. This product had been advertised as "safe." Did this create an express warranty which was breached as a result of the injury Terry sustained?

4. Levondosky ordered a drink while gambling at a casino. The casino's cocktail server served the drink free of charge, in accordance with the casino's common practice in connection with gambling customers. Levondosky swallowed a few thin chips of glass from the rim of the glass in which the beverage was served. Can Levondosky recover from the casino for a breach of implied warranty? If so, which one?

25

Product Liability

Negligence
Strict Liability

Innocent Misrepresentation

The term **product liability** refers to the liability of manufacturers and other sellers of products for injuries caused by their products. Product liability is not a single theory of law. Rather, it encompasses a number of legal theories that we have already studied—negligence, strict liability, and misrepresentation. This chapter will review these subjects in the specific context of product liability. Warranty law, to which the last chapter was devoted and which will not be discussed again here, is also included within product liability when the warranty in question relates to a product.

Negligence

Recall from Chapter 7 that in order to establish a prima facie case for **negligence**, the plaintiff must establish that (1) the defendant owed a *duty* to the plaintiff, (2) the defendant *breached* that duty by failing to exercise that degree of care that a prudent person would have exercised under the circumstances, (3) the defendant's breach of duty caused an *injury* to the plaintiff, and (4) the defendant's breach of duty was the *proximate cause* of the plaintiff's injury. Keep these factors in mind as we discuss ways in which manufacturers and other parties can incur negligence liability in the product liability context.

Today it is not necessary for the plaintiff to establish privity of contract in a product liability negligence case. In other words, the plaintiff need not have purchased the product directly from the defendant.

Negligence of Manufacturer in Assembly

Section 395 of the *Restatement of Torts Second* sets forth a standard by which the courts may judge the actions of a manufacturer. It states:

> A manufacturer who fails to exercise reasonable care in the manufacture of a chattel which, unless carefully made, he should recognize as involving an unreasonable risk of causing physical harm to those who use it for a purpose for which the manufacturer should expect it to be used and those whom he should expect to be endangered by its probable use, is subject to liability for physical harm caused to them by its lawful use in a manner and for a purpose for which it is supplied.

The *Restatement* in this section covers the problem of a product that for one reason or another leaves the manufacturer's premises in an unsafe condition because reasonable care was not taken in assembling it. For example, a manufacturer of automobiles fails to inspect a vehicle carefully and so does not notice that one of two bolts necessary to the safe operation of the car is missing. As a result, while the automobile's purchaser is driving it down the highway the car veers out of control and crashes into a lamppost.

In this case the manufacturer's failure to exercise reasonable care in manufacturing the automobile created an *unreasonable* risk of physical harm to persons using the automobile. The purchaser in this example used the car in a lawful manner and for its rightful purpose—that is, driving. The manufacturer is liable to the purchaser for his or her injuries that resulted from negligence in the manufacture of the automobile.

Bear in mind that if the manufacturer is able to convince a court that it exercised reasonable care in manufacturing its product, no liability arises under Section 395 of the *Restatement*.

Contrast this example with one involving an automobile that should have had a second bolt but did not because the company failed to provide for it in the design. In this situation, if the vehicle ends up in a collision, the manufacturer is not liable for negligence in *assembling* the automobile. Instead, it may be liable for negligence in *designing* the automobile, as discussed in the next section.

A great number of cases today involve the issue of defective design.

Manufacturer's Negligent Design

An important aspect of the current law of product liability relates to the manufacturer's liability for a defectively designed product. Unlike negligence in production, which may affect one or a few products, defective design may affect an entire class of products and involve potential liability to thousands of individuals. Several federal agencies charged with regulating certain types of products are increasingly using mandatory recall as a corrective device.

A manufacturer can be held liable for injuries to a person caused by a product that is defective because of poor design or improper construction or assembly. Section 398 of the *Restatement of Torts Second* announces a standard for the design of products:

> A manufacturer of a chattel made under a plan or design which makes it dangerous for the uses for which it is manufactured is subject to liability to others whom he should expect to use the chattel or to be endangered by its

probable use for physical harm caused by his failure to exercise reasonable care in the adoption of a safe plan or design.

This means that a manufacturer must exercise due care in the design of all products. Putting a product on the market that later is determined to be unsafe for normal use may result in liability for physical injuries caused by the product.

Suppose a manufacturer adopts a design for its product that is obviously unsafe—for example, an electric fan that does not have a screen to protect users from the rotating metal blade. A young child, unable to comprehend the danger involved, sticks her hand into the path of the blade and the blade clips off a finger. The manufacturer may be liable for the child's injury because it failed to exercise reasonable care in the adoption of a safe design for the fan.

Manufacturer's Duty to Inspect, Test, and Warn

Testing and Inspecting   The manufacturer generally must exercise due care to make certain a product placed on the market is safe. This includes reasonable tests and inspections to discover present or latent defects in a product before putting it on the market. For example, the manufacturer of a chair was held liable when it failed to discover a defect that it could have ascertained by inspecting the chair.

Suppose a manufacturer of lamps exercises reasonable care with respect to the design and assembly of its lamps. Will this be sufficient to relieve it of any legal liability to someone injured by a lamp? What if the cord on the lamp was frayed when manufactured and as a result the purchaser was electrocuted when he plugged the lamp cord into a socket? One could argue that the manufacturer had failed to exercise due care in inspecting the lamp cord.

Warning   It is not sufficient for a manufacturer merely to test and inspect a product. Sometimes the manufacturer also has a duty to warn the public of the potential danger of a product. Section 388 of the *Restatement* suggests the following standard with respect to a duty to warn:

> One who supplies directly or through a third person a chattel for another to use is subject

to liability to those whom the supplier should expect to use the chattel with the consent of the other or to be endangered by its probable use, for physical harm caused by the use of the chattel in the manner for which and by a person for whose use it is supplied, if the supplier

(a) knows or has reason to know that the chattel is or is likely to be dangerous for the use for which it is supplied, and

(b) has no reason to believe that those for whose use the chattel is supplied will realize its dangerous condition, and

(c) fails to exercise reasonable care to inform them of its dangerous condition or of the facts which make it likely to be dangerous.

Suppose the manufacturer of a chemical knows that the chemical is highly caustic and that users may not be aware of that fact. In this situation the manufacturer should exercise reasonable care to inform users of the chemical of its causticity. This might be accomplished by putting a prominent warning on the containers in which the chemical is supplied. If the manufacturer fails to supply any warning, it will be liable to any person injured by the chemical whom the manufacturer could expect to use or be endangered by the probable use of the product—for example, someone transferring the chemical to another container. The manufacturer must exercise reasonable care to inform such a person of the caustic nature of the chemical. If it fails to give such a warning and the person is injured, the manufacturer will be liable for the injuries that person sustains.

The defect in the product must be the *proximate cause* of the injury—that is, there must be a connection between the defect in the product and the injury sustained. If a chemical in a drum explodes when exposed to heat, but the specific injury was caused by the drum's falling on a worker's foot, it would not be possible to say that failure to warn of the chemical's flammability was the proximate cause of the worker's injury.

Subsection (a) of the *Restatement* indicates that the manufacturer must be able to *foresee* that the product may be dangerous if used improperly. Foreseeability is very important in duty-to-warn

cases. The phrase "for which it is supplied" can be a problem where the injured party misuses the product. Must the manufacturer warn consumers not only of dangers inherent in the proper use of the product but also of dangers inherent in its misuse? Many courts have required this of a manufacturer.

A warning must be clear and intelligible. Even if a warning makes clear the dangers inherent in using or misusing the product, there is still the problem of who should be warned. Suppose, for example, that a warning appears in literature supplied by the manufacturer to purchasers of its products but not directly on the dangerous article itself. In *Griggs v. Firestone Tire and Rubber Co.*[1] the court held that even under these circumstances the jury could have found that Firestone did not properly discharge its duty to warn because, although it provided a warning with literature that accompanied a dangerous tire rim, it could have put the warning directly on the rim. Although courts in other jurisdictions may or may not rule as the *Griggs* court ruled, it is probably prudent for a manufacturer to put a warning in a place where it will be seen by all persons who might be endangered by the product. For example, if the seller of a lawnmower wants to warn purchasers not to put their hands in the mower's exhaust chute while the mower is in operation, it could put such a warning in the instructions for operating the mower. A warning decal on the exhaust chute, however, would more likely be seen by users of the mower.

Subsection (b) of Section 388 deals with the obviousness of the defect. If the chattel is in an obviously dangerous condition, it may be unnecessary to warn of the danger. On the other hand, if the danger is not likely to be discovered by persons using the product (in other words, if the danger is *latent*), a duty to warn exists. The manufacturer should then exercise reasonable care to inform users of the latent danger.

In addition, a number of other statutes and regulations—for example, the Food, Drug, and Cosmetic Act and the Federal Hazardous Substances Act—require warnings on certain products.

The case that follows discusses whether a manufacturer has a duty to warn of dangers that might arise not only in connection with the use of a product, but also in connection with the storage, handling, and disposal of a product.

RICHMOND, FREDERICKSBURG & POTOMAC RAILROAD CO. V. CARRIER CORPORATION INDUSTRIES, INC.

U.S. District Court, E. D. Virginia

787 F. Supp. 572 (1992)

BACKGROUND: Richmond, Fredericksburg & Potomac Railroad sued several parties for dumping hazardous waste at its scrap recycling and disposal site. One of the defendants, Washington Gas, allegedly sent air conditioners that leaked toxic PCBs while being stored, handled, and destroyed for recycling at the site. Washington Gas, in turn, brought a third-party complaint against Carrier, the manufacturer of the air conditioners. (A third-party complaint is brought by a defendant against a third party who may be liable for all or part of the damages that the original defendant may be required to pay the original plaintiff.) Washington Gas claimed, among other things, that Carrier was negligent in failing to warn Washington Gas that PCBs might leak from the air conditioners while they were being stored, handled, or destroyed. Carrier moved to dismiss the third-party complaint.

Ellis, District Judge

In Virginia, a manufacturer's duty to warn about dangers associated with a product's use is governed by § 388 of the Restatement (Second) of Torts. Under § 388, liability exists for a negligent failure to warn only if an injury occurs during a use of the product that is reasonably foreseeable to the manufacturer. Manufacturers are expected reasonably to foresee (i) that a person may be injured while the product is being used for the purposes for which it was manufactured and sold and (ii) that a person may be injured while the product is being used in surroundings which are normal for the use of the product.

Virginia has not squarely addressed whether a manufacturer's duty to warn under § 388 applies to the storage, handling, and disposal of products after their useful lives. Thus, this Court must determine whether the Supreme Court of Virginia would conclude that a manufacturer must reasonably foresee that storage, handling, and disposal are possible uses of its product that must be taken into account in determining the necessity for, and nature of, any warning. In making this determination, the Court concludes that the Supreme Court of Virginia would find persuasive the two decisions that have addressed the specific issue of negligent failure to warn to the dangers of storing, handling, and disposing of scrap metal containing hazardous substances. See *High v. Westinghouse Elec. Corp.* (1989); *Kalik v. Allis-Chalmers Corp.* (1987). Significantly, both decisions hold that manufacturers have no duty to warn about hazardous substances that may be released from a product during the product's destruction or disposal for recycling because such destruction substantially changes the product and is not a reasonably foreseeable use. In *Kalik*, however, the court distinguished between storage and handling on the one hand and disposal by destruction on the other. The court allowed the jury to decide whether storage and handling was a reasonably foreseeable use of the manufacturer's product for which the manufacturer had a duty to warn about the possible release of hazardous substances. Although not explained fully by the Court, presumably this question went to the jury because storage and handling after a product's serviceable life is a use of the product that a manufacturer should reasonably foresee.

Accordingly, this Court concludes that the Supreme Court of Virginia would find, as a matter of law, that the destruction of Carrier's air conditioners for recycling purposes was not a use of the air conditioners that Carrier should have reasonably foreseen. Dismantling or destroying an air conditioner changes the product and any possible intended use of the product as originally manufactured. Thus, Carrier had no duty to warn of the possible release of hazardous substances that might arise from this unforeseeable use of the product. But storage and handling stand on a different footing from destructive disposal. The Supreme Court of Virginia, in this Court's view, would not find, as a matter of law, that the storage and handling of Carrier's air conditioners was an unforeseeable use. Instead, it would allow this question to be decided by the jury. Because the air conditioners were still in their originally manufactured form at the time of storage and handling, a jury could find that Carrier reasonably should have foreseen that the air conditioners would normally be handled and stored after their serviceable lives and that Carrier had a duty to warn of the possible release of hazardous substances during such handling and storage.

DECISION: Washington Gas's negligence claim against Carrier was dismissed to the extent that it related to the disposal of the air conditioners, but was not dismissed to the extent that it related to their storage and handling.

Negligence of Assemblers and Submanufacturers

Many products are composed of parts manufactured by several companies. To what extent is a company that uses the products of another company in making its own product liable if a component part malfunctions? Take the case of an airplane company. If a malfunctioning altimeter causes the plane to crash, can the manufacturer escape liability by pointing to the altimeter manufacturer?

Assemblers An assembler generally must make reasonable tests and inspections to discover latent defects. In *MacPherson v. Buick Motor Co.*,[2] Buick, the manufacturer, was held liable for a defective wheel used on the automobile even though Buick bought the wheel from another company. The court held Buick liable because the defect could have been discovered if Buick had made a reasonable inspection of the wheel. Thus an assembler must make reasonable inspections and tests of parts to be incorporated into the finished product to protect itself from liability.

Makers of Component Parts The manufacturer of a component part can also be liable for negligence if the part is so negligently made as to render the product in which it is incorporated unreasonably dangerous for use. Similarly, the manufacturer of materials to be used in products that would be dangerous unless the materials are carefully made is also liable if it fails to exercise reasonable care.

Retailer's Negligence

Design and Construction If a plaintiff wishes to recover from the retailer for injuries sustained in using a defective product, negligence will not be an effective theory of recovery in most instances. (See however, the discussion of strict liability.) When a retailer receives a product from a manufacturer, he or she knows very little about it beyond what the buyer may know. Quite frequently the product is packaged when the retailer receives and sells it. As the retailer actually has very little control over the product's design or fabrication, it makes sense not to hold him or her liable for negligence. The retailer's duty with regard to design or construction of products is minimal.

Inspections, Tests, Warnings Normally a retailer does not need to inspect or test the items sold if he or she neither knows nor has reason to know that the product is dangerous. The courts tend to impose a duty to inspect or test under these circumstances. On the other hand, if the retailer should have known that the product was dangerous and could have inspected or tested the item, he or she may be liable. Two classes of retailers who must pay special attention to the products they sell are food retailers and druggists.

Suppose a grocery store received a shipment of frozen TV dinners. When the trucker delivered the load, he informed the manager that the truck's refrigeration unit failed to function properly during part of the trip. The truck driver believed that the dinners may have thawed although they were frozen at the time of delivery. Without inspecting them, the manager ordered the stock boys to load the dinners in the store's freezers. In such a case, although a grocery store would generally not be expected to inspect the TV dinners, the store might be liable for its failure to inspect.

The same is true of the duty to warn. If the retailer should know that a product is dangerous, and that the danger is of a type the purchaser is not likely to discover, the retailer should warn the purchaser.

In the earlier example, the grocery store should at the very least warn purchasers that the TV dinners had defrosted in transit. (The most prudent course of action, of course, would be to simply not sell the TV dinners.)

Representing Products as Own

If the retailer advertises, labels, or packages a product in such a fashion that it appears that the retailer is the manufacturer, the retailer will be held to the same standards as the manufacturer.

Many companies market under their own name products manufactured by someone else. Sears, Roebuck, for example, sells floor scrubbers manufactured by another company but labeled "Kenmore"—the Sears trade name.

The *Restatement of Torts Second*, Section 400, states: "One who puts out as his own product a chattel manufactured by another is subject to the same liability as though he were its manufacturer." In other words, if a company puts his or her name, trade name, or trademark on a product, the company is putting the product out as its own. If the seller marks the goods as "made for" the seller, this rule still applies unless the real manufacturer is clearly indicated.

Statutory Violations of Proof of Negligence

Some federal and state statutes, such as the Federal Food, Drug, and Cosmetic Act, specify a certain standard of conduct. If a party injured by a product is able to point to a statute or regulation that has not been complied with, this may create a statutory right of action that is independent of the common law action. If a manufacturer ignores safety standards promulgated by a government agency, the company may be held liable. For this reason a company must keep well informed of

governmental statutes and regulations pertaining to the products it manufactures.

Defenses Available in Negligence

Recall from Chapter 7 that there are a number of defenses to negligence. These defenses apply in the product liability context as well.

Contributory or Comparative Negligence

Contributory negligence is any conduct on the part of the plaintiff that (1) falls below the standard of care that a reasonably prudent person would use to protect his or her own safety, and (2) contributes to the plaintiff's injury. In jurisdictions that apply the doctrine of contributory negligence strictly, the plaintiff's contributory negligence is a complete bar to his or her recovery.

Many states have replaced the doctrine of contributory negligence with that of **comparative negligence**, which also applies in product liability cases. While contributory negligence bars recovery by the plaintiff, comparative negligence does not.

When a court applies the *comparative negligence doctrine*, the court or jury weighs the relative negligence of the parties and reduces the amount of recovery in proportion to the plaintiff's negligence.

For example, suppose a jury decided that the employer was 80 percent responsible for a given injury but that the employee was 20 percent responsible. If the court followed the doctrine of contributory negligence, the plaintiff would recover nothing. If, however, the court applied the doctrine of comparative negligence, the jury would determine how much the plaintiff's injuries were worth (for example, $100,000) and then reduce this amount by 20 percent—the extent of the plaintiff's responsibility for the accident. The plaintiff would therefore receive $80,000.

In some comparative negligence jurisdictions, the plaintiff is completely barred from recovery if he or she is judged to be more than 50 percent responsible for his or her own injury.

The case that follows discusses whether an injured passenger's failure to wear a seatbelt can serve as a defense in a product liability suit against an automobile manufacturer.

McElyea v. Navistar International Transportation Corp.

U.S. District Court, E. D. of Pennsylvania
788 F. Supp. 1366 (1991)

BACKGROUND: Jerry McElyea was driving a vehicle manufactured by Navistar when he drove off the road, struck a tree stump, and was ejected from the vehicle. He became paralyzed. McElyea sued Navistar for failing to design a crashworthy vehicle. McElyea did not claim that Navistar's design of the vehicle caused the accident, but rather that Navistar's failure to design a crashworthy vehicle enhanced his injuries resulting from the accident. Navistar moved for summary judgment, arguing that McElyea would not have been injured if he had been wearing a seatbelt.

Troutman, Senior District Judge

The essential elements of the claim in a crashworthiness case, which plaintiffs are required to prove, are "(1) an alternative, safer design, practicable under the circumstances; (2) the resulting injuries if the safer design had been used; and, as a corollary to second element, (3) the extent of the enhanced injuries attributable to the defective design." Here plaintiffs have alleged that a design defect in the vehicle which Navistar manufactured permitted McElyea to be ejected from the vehicle. They further asserted, in order to meet the second element of a crashworthiness claim, that McElyea's injuries would have been slight had a safer design prevented his ejection from the vehicle. Finally, plaintiffs have consistently maintained that the severe injury, resulting in paralysis, which McElyea sustained is attributable entirely to the allegedly defective design which permitted his ejection from the vehicle. Plaintiffs have never asserted that the slight injuries which McElyea may have sustained in the accident would have been attributable to any other design defect in the vehicle.

In arguing that application of the seatbelt defense supports summary judgment in light of the facts of this case and plaintiffs' claim, defendant Navistar is relying upon the doctrine of "avoidable consequences," as well as upon the elements of a strict liability crashworthiness case. Application of the avoidable consequences doctrine denies recovery to a plaintiff for that portion of the loss which could have been avoided by his own reasonable efforts. It is the defendant's burden to show that plaintiffs unreasonably failed to minimize their damages.

The facts of record in this case, specifically, McElyea's failure to wear his seatbelt, as well as the undisputed evidence that he would not have been ejected from the vehicle had he been wearing it, viewed in conjunction with the elements which plaintiffs are required to establish in order to support a crashworthiness case and the claim of enhanced injury made by plaintiffs here, clearly demonstrate that plaintiffs would not have sustained any damages had McElyea been wearing his seatbelt at the time of the accident. Because plaintiffs cannot recover from defendant for damages which reasonably could have been avoided, we conclude, therefore, that McElyea's failure to take reasonable precaution of wearing his seatbelt, and thus, to eliminate his injuries, precludes plaintiffs from seeking recovery from Navistar in this case. Hence, defendant Navistar is entitled to judgment as a matter of law based upon the unchallenged proof that the enhanced injuries which plaintiffs claim resulted from the allegedly defective design of the vehicle were entirely avoidable.

DECISION: The district court granted Navistar's motion for summary judgment.

ETHICS
Manufacture of Dangerous Products

Willie Watson acquired from an acquaintance a handgun manufactured by Charter Arms Corporation. Willie used the gun to kidnap, rob, rape, and murder Kathy Newman, who was a third-year medical student at Tulane University. Willie was tried and convicted of the crimes he committed. He was incapable of paying any monetary judgments that might be awarded against him.

Kathy Newman's mother filed suit against Charter Arms Corporation, alleging that the wrongful death of her daughter was caused by the defendant's designing, manufacturing, and marketing an unreasonably dangerous product. Mrs. Newman argued that use of the product to cause death was foreseeable, citing U.S. Justice Department estimates that 22,000 deaths, including suicides are caused by handguns each year.

Charter Arms countered that it is legal to manufacture and sell handguns and that the corporation should not be held responsible for the criminal acts of others that could not be specifically foreseen. Charter also argued that the typical gun consumer buys a gun with full knowledge that it can be used as a murder weapon. Therefore, Charter reasoned, the general public does not consider the marketing of handguns to be unreasonably dangerous and would not support significant restrictions on their sale.

Difficult ethical problems are presented in the distribution of dangerous products. If the products do not have a positive utility or are illegal, then their manufacture and distribution would be unethical. But if the products do have a positive utility, are legal, and are desired by many individuals, then the ethical duty of the manufacturer is transformed into an obligation to warn and to take reasonable steps to make the product as safe as practicable.

When a product is addictive, yet another issue is presented. Certainly distributing a product in such a way as to maximize addiction, or directing the sale of the product toward young people, is ethically problematic. Ultimately it must be the responsibility of government, reflecting the national will, to decide whether certain categories of products should be banned altogether.

Assumption of Risk In *assumption of risk* the defendant asserts that the plaintiff acted voluntarily with full knowledge and appreciation of the risk involved. In general, contributory negligence and assumption of risk are available to defendants in product liability suits based on negligence. This makes negligence a less appealing doctrine for the plaintiff than other theories discussed later in this chapter.

Obvious Danger and Abnormal Use
Some courts have also denied relief to the plaintiff on the theory that the danger presented to the plaintiff was obvious, and other courts have denied recovery on the theory that the plaintiff made an abnormal use of the product.

Strict Liability

As we learned in Chapter 7, the doctrine of **strict liability** allows liability to be imposed in certain cases even if the defendant exercised reasonable care—that is, even if the defendant was not "at fault." Strict liability has long applied to ultrahazardous activities. Thus, if a company engages in an ultrahazardous activity such as blasting, the company can be held liable for injuries caused by its blasting even if the company did everything reasonably possible to prevent such injuries from occurring.

In the 1960s, the doctrine of strict liability was expanded to product liability. Today, most states will hold sellers of defective products strictly liable for injuries if certain conditions apply. The most commonly followed rule is set forth in *Restatement of Torts, Second*, Section 402A, which provides as follows:

(1) One who sells any product in a defective condition unreasonably dangerous to the user or consumer or to his property is subject to liability for physical harm thereby caused to the ultimate user or consumer, or to his property, if

    (a) the seller is engaged in the business of selling such a product, and

    (b) it is expected to and does reach the user or consumer without substantial change in the condition in which it is sold.

(2) The rule stated in Subsection (1) applies although

    (a) the seller has exercised all possible care in the preparation and sale of his product, and

    (b) the user or consumer has not bought the product from or entered into any contractual relation with the seller.

Section 402A then requires the plaintiff to establish each of the following:

(1) The defendant is in the business of selling the product.

(2) The product was expected to and in fact reached the injured party without substantial change in the condition in which it was sold.

(3) The product was in a defective condition.

(4) This defective condition rendered the product unreasonably dangerous to the user or consumer or his or her property.

(5) There was a casual relationship between the defect and the damage done to the plaintiff.

(6) This resulted in physical harm to his or her person or property.

If the plaintiff succeeds in establishing all these elements, the plaintiff will prevail at trial.

The plaintiff must establish the existence of a defect in the product and prove that the defect caused his or her injuries. If there is no defect in the product, the plaintiff may not recover. Furthermore, if there is a defect but the injury sustained by the plaintiff was not related to the defect, the plaintiff will not win at trial.

The following case illustrates the application of strict liability in an automobile accident case.

BUEHLER V. WHALEN

Court of Appeals of Illinois
355 N. E. 2d 99 (1976)

BACKGROUND: Buehler (plaintiff) brought an action against the driver of a vehicle, Whalen (defendant), for injuries sustained in an automobile accident. Buehler also sued Ford Motor Company, another defendant in this case, based on the contention that the design of the vehicle rendered it unreasonably dangerous to a user. The trial court decided for Buehler against Ford. Ford appealed.

Eberspacher, Justice

The vehicle driven by the Buehlers was a 1966 Ford Fairlane. This vehicle was one of several Ford cars that, since 1960, had been equipped with a flange mounted fuel tank. The flange mounted tank is different from the strap mounted fuel tanks used on other cars in that the top of the flange mounted tank serves as the floor of the trunk whereas the strap mounted tank is placed beneath the floor of the trunk and is therefore separated from the trunk compartment. The flange mounted tank is also screwed into place and it is held rigidly to the car structure, whereas the strap mounted tank is held by metal bands which allow it to be displaced to some extent under stress.

The tank's nonflexible gas filler spout runs through the luggage compartment to a license plate bracket above the bumper. The flange of the tank is about two and one-half inches from the bumper while the rear of the tank itself is four inches from the bumper.

The flange mounted tank was not used in American cars prior to 1960. In that year Ford began using that type of tank in some of its cars. General Motors and Chrysler stayed with the strap mounted tank. Since 1970 Ford changed back to strap mounted tanks for all its automobiles.

In the 1966 Ford Fairlane, the only shield separating the trunk compartment, where the fuel tank and filler spout are located, from the passenger compartment, is a fiberboard panel and the rear seat padding. It was undisputed that neither of these materials significantly limits the passage of fire.

After the collision, the gas cap to the Buehler auto was found near the scene of impact. The ears to the cap, which secure it to the filler spout, were missing. Similar ears were found inside the Buehler's fuel tank. The filler spout was found to be no longer extending through the opening in the license bracket area, but was instead below the bumper or about flush with it.

For the reasons enunciated in *Suvada v. White Motor Co.*, strict liability is imposed against a manufacturer in cases involving products where a defective condition makes them unreasonably dangerous to a user. Defectively designed products are unreasonably dangerous because they fail to perform in a manner reasonably to be expected in light of their nature and intended functions.

A manufacturer's duty to design a product which is reasonably fit for its intended use encompasses foreseeable ancillary consequences of normal use, which in the case of automobiles includes collisions. The environment in which an automobile is used must be taken into consideration by a manufacturer when designing its product. In an automobile dependent society, involving extensive usage, crowded highways, heavy loads, and high speeds, the statistically inevitable consequences of normal use of an auto entail the proven hazard of injury producing collisions of different kinds. Since injury-producing impacts are foreseeable, the manufacturer is under a duty to design its vehicle to avoid subjecting the user to an unreasonable risk of injury in the event of a collision.

Viewing the evidence in its aspect most favorable to the plaintiffs, it appears clear that an impact to the trunk of the Buehlers' 1966 Ford Fairlane was an occurrence that was objectively reasonable to expect. In the event of such an impact it is also reasonable to expect that fire could develop in the trunk where the fuel system was located and could spread to the passenger compartment. In such a situation there would exist a high probability of serious burns or death resulting from an intense gasoline fed fire originating in the trunk. Testimony showed that Ford could have used a strap mounted tank that would have greatly reduced the risk of fire upon a rear-end impact. This type of tank was in fact used by Ford in prior as well as subsequent comparable models. Chrysler and General Motors had always used the strap mounted fuel tank. Moreover, there was testimony that the cost of placing a shield, in the 1966 Ford Fairlane, between the passenger compartment and the fuel containing system would only be one dollar plus one-half hour of labor time. Such a shield would have substantially reduced the risk of injury to the plaintiffs by providing additional time to effectuate an escape. We note that in the instant case it took less than one minute for the occupants to be removed from the burning vehicle. We are therefore of the opinion that the risks of harm to the plaintiffs were not so improbable or extraordinary as to be unforeseeable to Ford and that Ford owed the plaintiffs a duty to design its vehicles so as to reduce the probability of the injuries suffered.

We are now led to determine if the plaintiffs made a *prima facie* case that one or any design defect proximately caused the plaintiffs' injuries. Ford contends that the plaintiffs failed to sustain their burden of proof. Causation is primarily a question of fact for a jury to determine. If there was sufficient evidence from which a jury could find that an unreasonably dangerous condition existed in the Ford Fairlane by reason of its design and that the fire or the instantaneous spread of fire into the passenger compartment resulted from that condition, then the jury's verdict must be left undisturbed.

The evidence viewed in the light most favorable to the plaintiffs shows that upon impact the Buehler auto immediately burst into flame from a gasoline source in the interior of the car. Expert testimony showed that the location of the fuel tank, filler spout, and gas cap in the trunk made them extremely vulnerable in the event of a rear-end impact; that the flange mounted tank was susceptible to stress; and that the filler spout tended to be displaced into the trunk and the gas cap could break off in the event of a rear-end impact. In addition, the lack of any shielding device between the passenger compartment and the trunk permitted any fire that would develop in the trunk to spread without resistance into the passenger compartment. In the experts' opinion these conditions were unreasonably dangerous and were causally related to plaintiffs' burns. They believed that upon impact the spout was displayed into the trunk and that the configuration change of the fuel tank broke the gas cap off and forced gasoline to spray into the trunk. The fire that resulted from a spark from the impact instantly spread into the passenger compartment because no barrier protected that compartment and therefore the plaintiffs suffered serious burns, even though they were extracted in one minute or less.

We are satisfied that there was sufficient evidence to support the jury's verdict.

DECISION: The appeals court affirmed the judgment for Buehler.

Manufacturers, Distributors, and Retailers

Under Section 402A, any "seller" may be held liable for injuries resulting from a defective product. This would generally include any party on the distribution chain for a product: the manufacturer, the retailer, and any intermediate wholesaler or distributor. States that have not adopted Section 402A tend not to impose liability on distributors who merely send the product on to someone else. Note that the term "seller," for the purposes of Section 402A, applies only to those in the business of selling the particular product. If, for example, Acme is in the business of manufacturing microwave ovens, it can be held strictly liable for injuries suffered by a consumer as a result of a defect in one of its ovens. Suppose, however, that Acme keeps a coffee machine on its premises for employees to use. When its existing machine becomes old and Acme intends to replace it, an employee offers to buy the old machine from Acme. Acme would not be considered a "seller" under Section 402A with respect to the sale of its coffee machine, since it is not in the business of selling coffee machines. Acme would thus not be held strictly liable if the employee were injured on account of a defect in the coffee machine.

The following case deals with the liability of a distributor under Section 402A.

KONOWAL V. HEINRICH BAUMGARDEN CO.
1983 WL 4202 (Ohio App.)

BACKGROUND: Konowal (plaintiffs) sued Heinrich (defendant) and other companies. Vitrex was a Spanish corporation that manufactured pots and pans. Easterling Company was an Illinois corporation that purchased sets of pots and pans manufactured by Vitrex and sold them to Betsy Ross Foods. Betsy Ross Foods in turn sold the pots and pans sets to Amherst Sparkle Market. Mrs. James Camera purchased one of these sets from Amherst Sparkle Market as a gift for her daughter, Kathleen Konowal. Mrs. Konowal used one of these pots to boil water. As she picked up the pot, one of its handles came off and boiling water spilled on Mrs. Konowal's son, Jeff, who was severely burned.

The Konowals brought suit to recover damages for Jeff's injuries. Named in the suit were Heinrich Baumgarden Company, the corporation that manufactured the handle; Vitrex; Easterling; and Amherst Sparkle Market.

The trial court dismissed the complaint against Heinrich Baumgarden and Vitrex and granted summary judgments in favor of Amherst Sparkle Market and Easterling.

Baird, Judge

The trial court concluded that the imposition of strict tort liability upon one of the distributors would be unjust where the commodity was packaged in Spain and passed to plaintiffs through a chain of distributors which had no notice that the commodity was defective. The court found persuasive the cases cited by the defendant that a middleman distributor who neither modifies nor alters a product in its original container should be held to a different standard than the manufacturer-assembler.

We are of the opinion that the determinative case on this issue is *Temple v. Wean United, Inc.* That opinion specifically approved Section 402 (A) of the Restatement of Torts 2d.

We find illustration 1 of the Restatement of Torts 2d particularly pertinent to the instant case:

> A manufactures and packs a can of beans, which he sells to B, a wholesaler. B sells the beans to C, a jobber, who resells it to D, a retail grocer. E buys the can of beans from D, and gives it to F. F serves the beans at lunch to G, his guest. While eating the beans, G breaks a tooth, on a pebble of the size, shape, and color of a bean, which no reasonable inspection could possibly have discovered. There is satisfactory evidence that the pebble was in the can of beans when it was opened. Although there is no negligence on the part of A, B, C, or D, each of them is subject to liability to G. On the other hand E and F, who have not sold the beans, are not liable to G in the absence of some negligence on their part.

As noted in the reporter's notes to Section 402 (A), public policy requires that the burden of accidental injuries caused by defective products intended for consumption be placed on those who market them, regardless of fault, so as to afford maximum protection for the consumer. We conclude, therefore, that the Supreme Court did not intend to limit the strict liability of *Temple v. Wean United* only to the manufacturer of products, but intended to apply strict liability to distributors and retailers as well.

To prevail on the theory of strict liability plaintiffs must prove that:

> (1) There was, in fact, a defect in the product manufactured and sold by the defendant; (2) such defect existed at the time the product left the hands of the defendant; and (3) the defect was the direct and proximate cause of the plaintiff's injuries or loss.

A defect is considered to exist in a product which is not of good and merchantable quality, fit and safe for its ordinary intended use.

In its motion for summary judgment defendant did not provide any evidence that the pot was not defective. There is evidence, by way of depositions and affidavits, that the product was in a sealed package and remained unopened from the time it left the manufacturer until it was opened by the user. There is also evidence that the pot handle broke while being used for boiling water, an ordinary intended use, and that the handle broke the second or third time the pot was so used. Under these facts and the law as already stated, we conclude that summary judgment for Easterling was not proper and reverse the judgment of the trial court.

DECISION: The appeals court reversed the decision that granted summary judgment in Easterling's favor.

Manufacturers of Component Parts

Not only may an injured party sue the manufacturer of a product under strict liability in tort, but in many jurisdictions he or she may also sue the manufacturer for any defective part incorporated into the finished product.

Bystanders

Bystanders   Suppose the injured person did not purchase the product or qualify as a member of the buyer's household or a guest. Such a person is nevertheless able to collect under the theory of strict liability in tort. Section 402A of the *Restatement* makes the seller liable "to the ultimate user or consumer, or to his property." The American Law Institute, which wrote the Restatement, did not express an opinion on whether the rule should be extended to persons other than users or consumers, but a number of court decisions have extended strict liability to bystanders.

Duty to Warn

What if a manufacturer produces a product that, although carefully manufactured, could cause injury to a person because of some latent danger? For example, suppose a drain cleaner could not safely be used with liquid bleach—two articles a person might commonly use in housecleaning—but the manufacturer failed to warn users of this fact. Under the *Restatement*, such a manufacturer could be held liable because the product was in a "defective condition unreasonably dangerous to the user or consumer."

One cannot escape liability under Section 402A by giving an incomplete or inadequate warning of the dangers inherent in using a product.

Defective Condition

In strict liability cases a plaintiff must establish that the product was defective, that the defect caused the injury in question, and that the defendant is the party responsible for the defect.

The problem of establishing what the term *defect* means has been a difficult one for the courts. One of several tests used by the courts is to examine what the expectations of the consumer were with respect to a product, and then to determine whether the injured party was surprised by the danger associated with the product. This area is likely to continue to create problems for the courts, and other tests for what a defect is will undoubtedly be adopted.

Unreasonable Danger

Not only must there be a defect in the product that caused injuries to a consumer, the plaintiff must also establish that the danger posed by the product was unreasonable—that is, more dangerous than would be contemplated by an ordinary consumer.

Some products are obviously defective but still not unreasonably dangerous. A stove that gets foods too hot may be defective but not necessarily unreasonably dangerous. A new car delivered with grease on its upholstery is defective but not dangerous. Some courts do not require the plaintiff to establish unreasonable danger in order to recover.

Defenses

Contributory negligence is generally not available as a defense in a strict liability suit: since the defendant's failure to exercise reasonable care is not an issue in strict liability, neither is the plaintiff's failure to exercise reasonable care. Most courts, however, do recognize assumption of risk as a defense to a strict liability claim.

Table 25-1 is a Concept Summary listing the product liability causes of action covered in this chapter as well as defenses to each of them.

TABLE 25-1

Product Liability Theories and Defenses	
Negligence	Contributory negligence; assumption of risk; obvious danger; abnormal use
Strict liability	Assumption of risk; product changed condition substantially after leaving seller's hands
Misrepresentation	Puffing; no reliance

ISSUES AND TRENDS
Proposals for Product Liability Reform

Many businesses have become alarmed at the number of product liability lawsuits that have been brought in recent years, and at the large awards plaintiffs have won in some of those suits. Business leaders have offered a number of product liability reform proposals which would, in their opinion, limit the damage that product liability lawsuits can do to the competitiveness of U.S. companies. Many consumer groups oppose these proposals, believing them to be an attempt by business to saddle consumers with an unfair amount of the risk that products will cause injury. Some of these proposals are listed below:

Uniform federal law. Replace the patchwork of state laws with a single federal code.

Limit punitive damages. Limit the amount of punitive damages that a plaintiff could collect in any one case to the amount of compensatory damages awarded or to some percentage thereof. Limit the amount of punitive damages that can be awarded against a company in a related series of cases (for example, asbestos cases). Absolute bar to punitive damages in cases involving medical devices, drugs, and aircraft that meet federal standards.

Compliance with government standards. Provide that the defendant's compliance with government standards creates a rebuttable presumption that the product is not unreasonably dangerous; failure to comply with government standards gives rise to the presumption that the product *is* unreasonably dangerous.

Limit liability for design defects. Limit liability for design defects to cases where the manufacturer knew or should have known of the danger. Also, do not allow evidence of subsequent safety improvements to a product to be used as evidence that the product wasn't safe prior to the change.

Statute of repose. Create a deadline after the introduction of a product after which no products liability suit could be filed with respect to that product.

Limit joint and several damages. Provide that each defendant is liable only to the extent that it caused the plaintiff's injury.

Innocent Misrepresentation

Sometimes by oral statements or through advertising, brochures, catalogs, and the like, a seller may incorrectly state something about its product. When a seller misrepresents its product, and a buyer relies upon the misrepresentation, the buyer who is injured by the product may have a cause of action based on the misrepresentation. Innocent **misrepresentation** is defined by the *Restatement of Torts Second*, Section 402B:

One engaged in the business of selling chattels who, by advertising, labels or otherwise, makes to the public a misrepresentation of a material fact concerning the character or quality of a chattel sold by him is subject to liability for physical harm to a consumer of the chattel caused by justifiable reliance upon the misrepresentation, even though

(a) it is not made fraudulently or negligently, and

(b) the consumer has not bought the chattel from or entered into any contractual relation with the seller.

A material fact, for the misrepresentation of which the *Restatement* holds a seller accountable, is one that was taken into consideration by the buyer in deciding to purchase the product. Note that a seller may be held liable under Section 402B even if the misrepresentation is not made fraudulently or even negligently. Section

402B thus imposes strict liability on sellers for misrepresentations that result in physical harm.

Defenses

Two defenses frequently asserted by defendants in innocent-misrepresentation cases are puffing and absence of reliance.

Puffing Puffing is a statement of mere opinion or loose general praise. If a statement is mere puffery, the plaintiff will not recover. Determining which statements are puffing and which are not is often difficult. Courts differ in their willingness to characterize statements as puffing.

Reliance To recover on grounds of innocent misrepresentation, not only must the manufacturer's misrepresentation of a material fact not be puffing but the buyer must prove that he or she *justifiably relied upon* the misrepresentation. If the buyer was unaware of the misrepresentation or indifferent to it, or if the statement did not influence his or her purchase or subsequent conduct, the buyer may not recover. The misrepresentation must have been a *substantial* factor in inducing the purchase or use of the product.

The following case provides an example of innocent misrepresentation.

KLAGES V. GENERAL ORDNANCE EQUIPMENT CORPORATION

Superior Court of Pennsylvania
367 A. 2d 304 (1976)

BACKGROUND: Klages (plaintiff) sued General Ordnance (defendant). John R. Klages was employed as a night auditor at Conley's Motel. After once being held up by armed robbers, Klages purchased General Ordnance's Mace pen for protection. The promotional literature for the weapon stated in part: "Rapidly vaporizes on face of assailant effecting 'instantaneous incapacitation' . . . an attacker is 'subdued—instantly' . . . An advertisement in Time Magazine stated that Chemical Mace is 'a weapon that disables as effectively as a gun yet does no permanent injury.'" When Klages was again held up soon thereafter, he removed the Mace pen from the cash register where it was stored. Using the cash register as a shield, he squirted the Mace, hitting the intruder right beside the nose. He immediately ducked below the register, but the intruder shot him in the head. As a result of the injury, Klages suffered complete loss of sight in his right eye. He later instituted suit against the retailer and manufacturer of the Mace pen. The lower court submitted the case to a jury based on innocent misrepresentation, and the jury decided for the plaintiff. The defendant appealed.

Hoffman, Judge

Having adopted section 402B of the Restatement (Second) of Torts as the law of this Commonwealth, we must determine whether the appellant misrepresented "a material fact concerning the character or quality of a chattel sold by him."

The comments to section 402B are helpful in this regard. First, Comment f states that "[t]he fact misrepresented must be a material one, upon which the consumer may be expected to rely in making his purchase." Comment g states that section 402B "does not apply to statements of opinion, and in particular it does not apply to the kind of loose general praise of wares sold which, on the part of the seller, is considered to be 'sales talk,' and is commonly called 'puffing'—as, for example, a statement that an automobile is the best on the market for the price . . . In addition, the fact misrepresented must be a material one, of importance to the normal purchaser by which the ultimate buyer may justifiably be expected to be influenced in buying the chattel."

The facts and circumstances surrounding the purchase of a product are helpful in determining whether the representation is of a material fact. In this case, the appellant sold a product designed as a tool to deter violence. Its sole anticipated use was to protect the purchaser from harm under extremely dangerous circumstances and the appellee specifically purchased the product with these explicit purposes in mind. Specific representations about the effectiveness of the weapon under such dangerous circumstances are clearly material. The mace weapons were described as effecting an instantaneous, immediate, complete incapacitation of an assailant. This is not "loose, general praise"; rather it is specific data on the capability of a product. The lower court, therefore, properly submitted the issue of liability under section 402B to the jury.

DECISION: The superior court affirmed the decision for Klages.

Review Questions and Problems

Key Terms

product liability

negligence

contributory negligence

comparative negligence

strict liability

misrepresentation

Discussion Questions

1. Explain the differences and similarities between a product liability action based on negligence and one based on strict liability in tort.

2. Must a manufacturer warn of every danger associated with a product?

3. What is meant by the term *contributory negligence*?

4. What are two defenses often asserted in a misrepresentation case?

5. What elements must be established for a plaintiff to recover under strict liability in tort?

Review Problems

1. Floyd Roysdon claimed that he suffered from severe peripheral vascular disease as a result of many years of smoking cigarettes manufactured by R. J. Reynolds Tobacco Company. He argued that the cigarettes are defective and unreasonably dangerous to the health of users and that the warnings on cigarette packages and in their advertising are inadequate to apprise users fully of the medical risks involved in smoking. Should Roysdon prevail on either argument?

2. Brown bought a helicopter from Brantly Corporation for use in his business. The promotional literature accompanying the helicopter described it as "safe, dependable, not tricky to operate" and one that "beginners and professional pilots alike agree is easy to fly." Although Brown had his airplane pilot's license, he had never flown a helicopter. Nevertheless, he purchased the Brantly helicopter and began to use it for some of his business trips. The third time he used it he flew in fairly heavy wind. When he was unable to control it, the helicopter crashed to the ground and Brown did not survive the crash. Brown's heirs sued on the basis of the "misrepresentations made by the Brantly Corporation in its literature." Should Brown's heirs recover?

3. Myron buys a helmet at an Army-Navy surplus store. The helmet comes in a box labeled "Police Riot Protection Helmet." The box features a picture of a policeman riding a motorcycle while wearing the helmet. Myron uses the helmet as a motorcycle helmet and suffers head injuries after he is involved in the accident. Myron sues the helmet manufacturer for misrepresentation, claiming that the picture on the box improperly implied that the helmet was suitable for use as a motorcycle helmet. The manufacturer contends that the helmet was marketed as a riot protection helmet and not as a motorcycle helmet. What result?

Case Problems

1. Waterson was severely injured when the rear axle of her GM car broke, causing her to run into a utility pole. There was testimony that Waterson could have "walked away" from the accident had she been wearing a seatbelt. GM claimed that Waterson's failure to wear a seatbelt should bar or at least limit her recovery. Waterson claims that since a defect in the GM vehicle caused the accident, her failure to wear a seatbelt should not be taken into account. What result?

2. David Mello purchased a hydraulic jack at K-Mart. The jack bore the K-Mart label and its container stated "Manufactured in Taiwan, Republic of

China, for K-Mart Corporation." David was injured when he was using the jack to repair an automobile. He brought suit against K-Mart alleging negligent design and manufacturing of the jack. K-Mart moved for summary judgment, stating that it did not design or manufacture the jack and that it was not designed specifically for K-Mart. Is K-Mart correct?

3. J. H. Horne was a 300-pound furniture store employee. He injured his back when the chair he was occupying in the employees' lounge collapsed. Mr. Horne brought a strict product liability suit against the manufacturer, alleging that the chair had been improperly glued and that the manufacturer had failed to test the chair for defects. The defendant argued that the chair was designed for home use and was not intended for use in commercial establishments and that such commercial use consti-

tuted a misuse and negated liability for injury. Does this argument relieve the defendant of liability?

4. After the plaintiff had complained of mosquito bites his sister applied Union Carbide's "6-12" insect spray to his skin and clothing. Before the spray dried, the plaintiff walked across a carpeted room and turned on a television set. As he touched the set, a spark from static electricity ignited the spray, inflicting severe burns to his upper body. The plaintiff's suit alleges that the warning label was inadequate. Does he win?

Footnotes

[1] 513 F. 2d 851 (8th Cir. 1975).

[2] 111 N. E. 1050 (N. S. 1916).

26

Introduction to Negotiable Instruments and Documents of Title

Documents of Title
Letter of Credit
Negotiable Instruments

Types of Negotiable Instruments
Parties to Negotiable Instruments
Using Negotiable Instruments

I n earlier chapters, we learned how the Uniform Commercial Code had standardized state law relating to the sale of goods. Our discussion of sales law focused primarily on issues relating to the goods themselves: delivery, title, conformity to the contract, warranties, and defects. In this chapter and in the chapters that follow, we will concentrate on the other side of the equation: the means of paying for goods and other property. The UCC has standardized the law in this area as well.

Documents of Title

According to UCC Section 1-201 (15), a **document of title** is any document that:

> in the regular course of business or financing is treated as adequately evidencing that the person in possession of it is entitled to re-

ceive, hold and dispose of the document and the goods it covers. To be a document of title, a document must purport to be issued by or addressed to a bailee and purport to cover goods in the bailee's possession which are either identified or are fungible portions of an identified mass.

These documents are usually issued by professional bailees who are in the business of either delivering or storing goods. A **bailee** is one who takes temporary possession of the property of another for a particular purpose.

Warehouse Receipts

Definition   If a seller wishes to store goods temporarily, he or she may deliver the goods to a "warehouseman." A **warehouseman** is a bailee in the business of storing goods for hire. The seller

FIGURE 26-1

Warehouse Receipt

ACME WAREHOUSE
A PUBLIC WAREHOUSE

Date of Issue:

This is to certify that we have received in our warehouse located at 100 Tree Street in the city of Kansas City, Kansas for the account of _____

_____ in apparent good order except as noted hereon the following property, subject to all terms and conditions contained herein and on the reverse side hereof, such property to be delivered to the order of _____

_____ upon payment of all storage, handling and other charges and the surrender of this document bearing proper indorsement.

Lot #	Quantity	Said to Be or Contain	Storage per Month		Handling In and Out	
			Rate	Per	Rate	Per

ACME Warehouse Company claims a lien for all lawful charges for storage and preservation of the goods described above, as well as for all lawful claims for monies advanced, interest, insurance, transportation, labor, weighing, and all other charges and expenses in connection with the goods. Except as may otherwise be required by law, the ACME Warehouse Company has not insured the goods described above for the benefit of the depositor against fire or other casualty.

ACME WAREHOUSE COMPANY

By: _____

Its:

The goods listed below are hereby released from this receipt for delivery. Any unreleased balance of the goods is subject to lien for any unpaid charges and advances on the released portion, in addition to the lien as aforedescribed.

Date	Lot #	Quantity Released	Signature	Quantity Due on Receipt

[*Source:* Douglas Whitman, F. William McCarty, Frank F. Gibson, Thomas W. Dunfee, Bartley A. Brennan, and John D. Blackburn, *Law and Business* (New York: Random House, 1987), p. 332. Copyright © 1987 by Thomas W. Dunfee, F. William McCarty, Frank F. Gibson, Douglas Whitman, John D. Blackburn, and Bartley A. Brennan.]

receives a **warehouse receipt**. (See Figure 26-1.) This receipt enables the seller, or anyone to whom the seller transfers the document, to pick up the goods from the warehouseman. A seller might decide to ship goods instead of storing them. When the seller delivers the goods to a **carrier** (a bailee who transports goods rather than merely storing them) for purposes of delivery, the carrier will give the seller a **bill of lading**. (See Figure 26-2.) This document enables its possessor to receive the goods from the carrier. Warehouse receipts and bills of lading are the most familiar documents of title.

Form A warehouse receipt need not be in any particular form, but it must contain certain information. Among other things, the warehouse receipt must contain information about the location of the warehouse, the date of issue of the receipt, to whom the goods are to be delivered, the storage or handling charges, a description of the goods or their containers, and a statement that

FIGURE 26-2

Order Bill of Lading

ORDER BILL OF LADING
ACME TRANSPORT COMPANY

Received, subject to the classifications and tariffs in effect on the date of issue of this Bill of Lading, the property described below, in apparent good order (except as noted) marked, consigned, and destined as indicated below, which company agrees to carry to its place of delivery at said destination. It is mutually agreed that every service to be performed hereunder shall be subject to all the conditions not prohibited by law herein contained, which are hereby agreed to by the shipper and accepted for himself and his assigns. The surrender of this ORIGINAL ORDER BILL OF LADING properly indorsed shall be required before the delivery of the property.

Car Initial	Car Number	Length/Capacity of Car		Weight in Tons		Waybill Date	Waybill No.
		Ordered	Furnished	Gross	Tare		

STOP THIS CAR AT	FOR	CONSIGNEE AND ADDRESS AT STOP
AT	FOR	

ORIGIN	STATE

FULL NAME OF SHIPPER

ADDRESS:

Bill of Lading Date	Bill of Lading No.	Invoice No.

CONSIGNED TO THE ORDER OF:

Destination:

Shippers Special Instruction (Include Icing, Ventilation, Heating, Weighing, Etc.)

No. Pkgs.	Description of Articles	Weight	Rate	Freight	Advances	Prepaid

[*Source:* Douglas Whitman, F. William McCarty, Frank F. Gibson, Thomas W. Dunfee, Bartley A. Brennan, and John D. Blackburn, *Law and Business* (New York: Random House, 1987), p. 332. Copyright © 1987 by Thomas W. Dunfee, F. William McCarty, Frank F. Gibson, Douglas Whitman, John D. Blackburn, and Bartley A. Brennan.]

advances have been made or liabilities incurred for which the warehouseman claims a lien or security interest.

In the event the warehouseman improperly prepares the warehouse receipt, he or she may be liable—to anyone who purchases the document for value and in good faith—for any damages caused by the nonreceipt or misdescription of the goods.

Duties of Warehouseman   A warehouseman must exercise such care with respect to goods in his or her possession as a reasonably careful person would exercise under like circumstances.

Absent a contrary agreement, a warehouseman must keep separate the goods covered by each receipt so as to permit at all times identification and delivery of those goods, except that different lots of fungible goods may be commingled. **Fungible goods** are interchangeable goods—goods such as wheat or corn—of which any unit is treated as the equivalent of any other unit.

Rights of Warehouseman   On notifying the person on whose account the goods are held and any other person known to claim an interest in the goods, a warehouseman may require payment of any charges and the removal of the goods from the warehouse at the termination of the period of storage fixed by the document. If no period is fixed in the warehouse receipt for the removal of the goods, the notice may specify their removal at a certain time after the lapse of 30 days. If the goods are not removed by such date, the warehouseman may sell the goods in accordance with UCC Section 7-210.

The warehouseman has a lien on any goods stored in his or her possession for charges for storage, transportation, insurance, labor, or other expenses relating to the goods, and for expenses necessary for preservation of the goods or reasonably incurred in their sale.

A warehouseman's lien may be enforced by public or private sale of the goods in blocks or in parcels, at any time or place and on any terms that are commercially reasonable, after notifying all persons known to claim an interest in the goods (Section 7-210).

Bills of Lading

Definition   When a shipper puts goods in the hands of a carrier, he or she receives a receipt called a bill of lading. The **bill of lading** is a document between the carrier and the shipper covering the terms and conditions of the arrangement between them. It is a document issued by the carrier to transport the goods. Thus the parties contemplate some movement of the goods from one place to another, whereas parties using a warehouse receipt plan to store the goods. UCC Section 1-201(6) defines bill of lading as follows:

"Bill of lading" means a document evidencing the receipt of goods for shipment issued by a person engaged in the business of transporting or forwarding goods and includes an airbill. "Airbill" means a document serving for air transportation as a bill of lading does for marine or rail transportation, and includes an air consignment note or air waybill.

Duties of Carrier   A carrier who issues a bill of lading must exercise the degree of care in relation to the goods that a reasonably careful person would exercise under the circumstances.

The warehouseman and carrier generally have a duty to deliver the goods to the person entitled to them under the document. Before the goods are delivered, the bailee's lien must generally be satisfied and the document of title must be surrendered for cancellation or notation of partial deliveries. A bailee has no liability if he or she delivers goods in good faith and if there has been compliance with the provisions of Article 7 of the UCC and the terms of the document. The UCC in Section 1-201(19) defines good faith as "honesty in fact in the conduct or transaction concerned."

Transferability   Documents of title may, under certain circumstances, be *negotiated*—that is, transferred to a third party in a manner that could give the transferee certain valuable rights. The concept of negotiability will be examined in greater detail as part of the discussion of negotiable instruments. But keep in mind that Article 3 of the UCC, which governs the negotiability of negotiable instruments, does not apply to documents of title.

A document of title is negotiable if it provides that the goods are to be delivered to the unspecified *bearer*—that is, whoever bears or possesses the document at any given time—or to the *order* of a named person. The concepts of bearer instruments and order instruments will be explained more fully below in the context of negotiable instruments.

A bill of lading is both a contract and a receipt and is usually transferable to another party. The person who ships goods may transfer the document to a third person. The third person may present the document to the carrier at the destination and obtain the goods.

A seller who wishes to deliver goods to a buyer in a distant location may arrange for the goods to be shipped by carrier. The carrier will deliver a bill of lading to the seller. It would be possible merely to mail the bill of lading to the purchaser. Assuming that the bill of lading is negotiable and made out to bearer, the buyer could receive delivery of the goods merely by presenting the bill of lading to the carrier. This is fine when the buyer has already paid for the goods. What if the buyer has not yet paid the seller, and the seller wants to be paid in full before he or she delivers the goods? The seller may deliver the bill of lading to his or her bank, along with a commercial instrument called a draft. The draft and the bill of lading are

---

PREVENTIVE LAW
Documentary Credits

One situation in which documentary credits are very commonly used is international transactions. If the buyer is in the United States and the seller is in Europe, a buyer in this situation may have doubts about whether the seller will actually deliver the goods in question. Likewise, the seller may be concerned that if it ships the goods, the buyer might never pay for them. In order to overcome the natural reluctance on the part of parties that are far apart to enter into a contract, parties will use a documentary credit combined with a bill of lading and a draft.

Simply put, the process is as follows. The buyer goes to its bank and requests from the bank a documentary credit (in effect, a promise by the buyer's bank to pay the seller for the goods). The seller then delivers the goods to a shipper and receives a bill of lading from the shipper indicating that the goods in question are in possession of the shipper. The seller gives this document, as well as any other documents specified by the parties, to its bank. The European bank transfers these documents to the buyer's bank. The buyer may then give its bank a draft for the amount in question, and the U.S. bank gives the buyer the bill of lading. The U.S. bank pays the obligation and this money is forwarded to the seller in Europe.

---

forwarded by the seller's bank to a bank in the buyer's town. The bank in the buyer's town requires the buyer to pay the draft (in essence, to pay for the goods) and then turns over the bill of lading to the buyer. The bank then sends the buyer's money to the seller's bank. In this manner a seller receives payment prior to the time the buyer receives the goods. The buyer, having paid for the goods and received the bill of lading, may now claim the goods from the carrier.

Letter of Credit

Another document used by businesspeople is a letter of credit. The UCC defines a **letter of credit** as an engagement by a bank or other person made at the request of a customer that the issuer will honor drafts or other demands for payment upon compliance with the conditions specified in the credit.

A buyer in one country may wish to purchase goods from a seller in another country. The seller may not be willing to extend credit to the buyer. In order to receive the goods, the buyer may arrange for a letter of credit from a bank. The bank agrees to pay the seller when the bank is presented the appropriate documents. This agreement makes the bank, rather than the buyer, the party obligated to pay. By using a letter of credit, the buyer may obtain goods from the seller be-

cause the seller is assured of payment from the buyer's bank.

In certain instances, the bank will be forced to pay even though the buyer is unhappy with the goods delivered under the contract. The bank's obligation to pay under the letter of credit is independent of its customer's obligations under the contract of sale.

Negotiable Instruments

The law of negotiable instruments dates back hundreds of years. The states first adopted the Negotiable Instruments Law in 1896. The drafters of the Negotiable Instruments Law based their work on the British Bill of Exchange Act of 1882, which was a codification of eighteenth- and nineteenth-century British case law. The drafters of the Uniform Commercial Code proposed that Articles 3 and 4 replace the Negotiable Instruments Law in 1951, and every state eventually adopted some form of the code.

While in 1951 the UCC seemed very up to date, by the 1980s the American Law Institute recognized the need to make changes in it to make it consistent with modern banking practices. In 1896 people dealt on a face-to-face basis and used paper to record their agreements. Today, many people deal with one another without ever seeing or speaking to each other. We use fax machines, telephones, electronic terminals, and computers—technology completely unknown at that time. Where once banks manually examined every check, today they rely on automated check processing. They are required by law to rapidly make funds available to depositors.

Section 3-102(a) UCC states that Article 3 applies to negotiable instruments.

To make the code consistent with modern business practices and technology, every section of Article 3 was rewritten in 1990. Article 4 was also revised to conform to the extensive changes in Article 3. Revised Articles 3 and 4 have been adopted in a majority of the states.

Unlike in the past, Articles 3 and 4 have their own statutes of limitation (Sections 3-118 and 4-111).

A **negotiable instrument** is any written promise or obligation to pay certain sums of money. Drafts and notes are examples of negotiable instruments.

A negotiable instrument differs from an ordinary obligation to pay money. The principle difference is that the negotiable instrument's **payee**—the party to whom the instrument is payable—can, in certain circumstances, transfer to a third party rights which are greater than the rights of the payee. This concept will be illustrated in the sections which follow. An instrument becomes negotiable by satisfying certain requirements, discussed in Chapter 27.

Contracts and Commercial Paper

A person may enter into a contract with another person for the payment of money. Suppose Smith agrees to pay Jones $100, and they enter into a contract that reflects Smith's obligation to pay $100 to Jones. In general, Jones's right to receive $100 may be assigned by Jones to a third person. Jones in this case is referred to as the *assignor* or

transferor, and the person to whom he has transferred this right to receive money is referred to as the *assignee* or *transferee*. There is nothing improper about assigning a contractual right to receive money to a third party.

Rather than sign a contract to pay $100, Jones might instead ask Smith to sign a negotiable instrument in which Smith agrees to pay the $100 to Jones. Jones may then transfer the instrument to a third person. When a negotiable instrument is given by Smith to Jones, the UCC refers to the transfer as an *issuance* of the instrument. If Jones properly transfers the instrument to a third party, the UCC calls this a **negotiation**.

A right to receive money may be created by contract and *assigned* to a third party, or it may be created by a negotiable instrument and *negotiated* to a third party. In either case the third party may collect. Why would a person enter into a negotiable instrument rather than a contract to pay money?

Advantages of Negotiable Instruments

There are a number of advantages associated with a negotiable instrument as opposed to a simple contract to receive money. A person in possession of a negotiable instrument may actually be in a better legal position than the person from whom he or she took the instrument. On the other hand, an assignee of a simple contractual right to receive money is never in any better position than his or her assignor. The courts often state that the assignee "steps into the shoes" of the assignor. By this, the courts mean that the assignee is in the same position with respect to enforcing the contract as was the assignor. (See Figure 26-3.)

Let us take a look at how this might occur. Suppose Smith agrees to pay Jones $100. Jones then assigns his right to receive $100 to Robinson.

Contractual Right to Receive Money	Negotiable Instrument
1. A agrees to pay B (assignor) 2. B assigns to C (assignee) 3. C steps into the shoes of the assignor, B	1. A agrees to pay B (transferor) 2. B negotiates to C (transferee) 3. If C is a holder in due course, C takes free of certain defenses A has against B

FIGURE 26-3

Robinson has the same rights as her transferor or assignor, Jones. If Jones agreed to deliver a 1970 Chevrolet in return for the $100, but he never delivered it, Robinson would be subject to the defense that the car was never delivered. Because Smith could assert the failure to deliver the car against Jones, he may assert it against Robinson. But what if Smith signed a negotiable instrument and issued it to Jones instead of a contract and Jones then negotiated it to Robinson? If Robinson qualified as a holder in due course (discussed in Chapter 27), she would take the instrument free of the defense that Jones never delivered the automobile to Smith.

Another situation in which the holder in due course of a negotiable instrument stands in a better position than an assignee of a contractual right to receive money is when a thief transfers the instrument. Suppose in the prior example that a thief steals the negotiable instrument from Robinson. If the instrument qualifies as *bearer paper*—that is, a negotiable instrument payable to whatever person happens to hold it at the time—the thief has the power to transfer good title to the instrument, under certain circumstances, to an innocent third party who gives value for the instrument and is unaware that he or she is dealing with a thief. If the thief in this example transfers the instrument to Moore, Moore may receive good title to the instrument. In this case she may enforce the instrument against the original person obligated to pay, that is, Smith. Smith may not assert against Moore the defense that the instrument was stolen if Moore qualifies as a holder in due course of a bearer-negotiable instrument. Had Moore taken a contractual right to receive money from the thief, rather than a negotiable instrument, she would be subject to Smith's claim that the contract was stolen. The as-signee of a contractual right to receive money steps into the shoes of the assignor. Whatever defenses could be asserted against the assignor may be asserted against the assignee. Because the thief (the assignor) had no interest in the contract, he or she could not transfer any interest in the contract to Moore (the assignee). (See Figure 26-4.) The same rules apply if a finder, rather than a thief, transfers a bearer-negotiable instrument or a contractual right to receive money.

There are a number of other advantages to holding a negotiable instrument rather than a contractual right to receive money. For this reason people prefer to acquire negotiable instruments rather than take a contractual right to receive money.

Why does the law permit certain persons in possession of negotiable instruments to enforce them when their transferors could not enforce the instruments? The UCC reflects the policy that negotiable instruments should be freely transferable. By giving a holder in due course these additional rights, the UCC encourages the transfer and acceptability of negotiable instruments.

Types of Negotiable Instruments

There are two basic types of negotiable instruments: promissory notes and drafts.

Promissory Notes

A **promissory note** is a written *promise* to pay money. It must contain an unconditional promise to pay a fixed amount—that is, a definite, specified amount—of money. It must be payable on demand or at a definite time. It must be payable

Contractual Right to Receive Money	Negotiable Instrument
1. A agrees to pay B (assignor)	1. A agrees to pay B (transferor) (by bearer instrument)
2. B assigns to C (assignee)	2. B negotiates to C (transferee) (bearer instrument)
3. Stolen by D who sells it to E	3. Stolen by D who sells it to E
4. E is subject to the defense the contract was stolen	4. E is a holder in due course (if E holds bearer paper, he or she takes free of defense that instrument was stolen)

FIGURE 26-4

simply to "bearer" (which makes it bearer paper) or "to the order of" a named party (as when a check is made payable to the order of John Smith). And it must be signed by the person making the promise.

There are two parties to the instrument: the **maker** who agrees to pay a certain sum of money, and the *payee*, the person the maker promises to pay.

A **demand note** is one that is payable on demand. A **time note** is one that is payable at some definite time. If a note states that it is payable on demand, the person in possession of the instrument knows that he or she may collect on the instrument immediately by demanding payment from the maker. If the note states that it is payable 90 days after date, the person in possession of the instrument knows that the maker must pay 90 days from the date on the note.

In the note in Figure 26-5, Douglas Whitman, the maker, promises to pay a fixed amount of money to Thomas Dunfee, the payee. The payee knows he will be able to demand payment on this instrument 2 years from January 1, 1995. Because this instrument is not payable on demand, it is a time note.

Suppose that Thomas Dunfee wishes to negoti-ate this instrument to Bartley Brennan. Dunfee may transfer his rights under this note to Brennan by indorsing it, usually on the back of the instrument, and delivering it to Brennan. In this case Dunfee is called the **indorser** (or transferor) and Brennan is referred to as the **indorsee** (or transferee).

Drafts

A **draft** (also called a bill of exchange) is a written *order* to pay money. It is a written, unconditional order by one person addressed to another person, signed by the person giving the order, requiring the person to whom it is addressed to pay a fixed amount in money, on demand or at some specific time, to the order of bearer or some specific person. The person giving the order is called the **drawer**. The person to whom the order is addressed is the **drawee**. The person who is to receive the money is the *payee*. The drawer may name himself or herself as the payee.

In the draft shown in Figure 26-6 John Blackburn, the drawer, orders William McCarty, the drawee, to pay a sum of money to Frank Gibson, the payee. It is an unconditional order, in writing, signed by John Blackburn (the party who gives

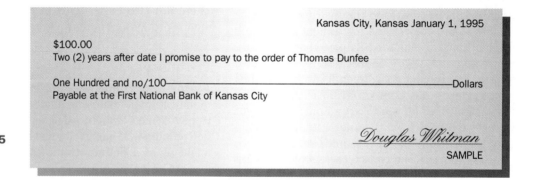

FIGURE 26-5
Promissory
Note

FIGURE 26-6
Draft

FIGURE 26-7

Check

SAMPLE

No. 101
January 1, 1995

Pay to the order of Douglas Whitman $100.00
One Hundred and no/100————————————————————————————Dollars

The First National Bank of Chicago

Bartley Brennan

the order), to William McCarty. It orders William McCarty to pay a fixed amount in money ($100) to the order of a specific person, Frank Gibson. The draft in this case is not payable immediately, as it would be in the case of a demand instrument. This draft is a time instrument, as opposed to a demand instrument, since it is not payable until thirty days after January 1, 1995.

While John Blackburn has ordered William McCarty to pay $100, McCarty is not obligated to pay anything until McCarty agrees to pay this draft. If he agrees to pay the draft, he becomes an **acceptor**. A drawee becomes an acceptor of a draft by signing his or her name across the face of the draft. The acceptor may also write on the instrument the date on which he or she accepted the instrument as well as the place where it will be paid. Once the drawee has accepted the draft, he or she is obligated to pay it when it becomes due.

As was the case for the note, if Frank Gibson, the payee, wants to transfer this instrument to Tom Dunfee, he may do so. Gibson may transfer his rights under this draft to Dunfee by indorsing the draft and delivering it to Dunfee. In this case Gibson is called the indorser (transferor) and Dunfee is called the indorsee (or transferee).

Checks

A **check** is a special form of draft that is written by a depositor (drawer) directing a bank (drawee) to pay a designated sum of money on demand to a third party (payee) (UCC 1990, Section 3-104 [f]).

The check in Figure 26-7 is payable on demand. Whenever the person named on the check presents it for payment, he or she is entitled to

payment of the $100. (See Chapter 28 for an extensive discussion of the law relating to checks.) The drawer of the check is Bartley Brennan, who signed it. The drawee is the First National Bank of Chicago. The payee is Douglas Whitman. Clearly, this check contains an unconditional order directed to the bank to pay a fixed amount of money at a definite time to the order of a specific person.

In addition to the ordinary check, the UCC recognizes several special types of checks. Section 3-104 of the UCC treats a **money order** as a check even though it bears the words *"money order"* on its face. A **cashier's check** is a draft drawn by a bank on itself. A **teller's check** is a draft drawn by a bank on another bank. A **traveler's check** is an instrument that is payable on demand which requires a countersignature by a person whose specimen signature appears on the instrument. A **certificate of deposit** represents an acknowledgement by a bank of the receipt of a designated sum of money plus a promise to repay this sum at an agreed rate of interest. A certificate of deposit is a note of the bank.

The various types of negotiable instruments are summarized in Table 26-1.

TABLE 26-1

Types of Negotiable Instruments

Promissory note	Written, unconditional promise to pay a fixed amount of money; maker agrees to pay payee
Draft	Written, unconditional order to pay a fixed amount of money; drawer orders drawee to pay payee

Parties to Negotiable Instruments

Accommodation Party

A person may become a party to a negotiable instrument by signing it. If a person signs an instrument for the purpose of lending his or her name and credit to another party to the instrument, but the person signing does not directly benefit from any value given for the instrument, the person signing is called an **accommodation party** and that person is said to sign *for accommodation* (Section 3-419 [a]). The person for whose benefit the instrument was issued for value is called the *accommodated party*. Assume, for example, that Junior wants to buy a car but does not have the credit history to qualify for a car loan. The lender might nonetheless loan the money to Junior if his father also signs the promissory note as an accommodation party to Junior. In this case Junior would be the accommodated party and his father would be the accommodation party.

The liability of an accommodation party depends on the liability of the party accommodated. An accommodation party is liable in the capacity in which he or she signed the instrument. An accommodation party may sign as a maker, drawer, acceptor, or indorser (Section 3-419 [b]). If the accommodated party has primary liability on the instrument, then the accommodation party will have primary liability as well. Suppose in the prior example that Junior signed the note as the maker of the note. The maker of a note has primary liability on the note—that is, the maker is the primary party obligated to pay a note. If the father signs Junior's note, the father will have primary liability as well. The accommodated party might instead have secondary liability on the instrument—such as an indorser of an instrument. If the accommodation party signs this instrument, he or she will have secondary liability on the instrument; that is, the secondary party must pay the instrument if the party primarily obligated to pay fails to pay it.

According to Section 3-419 (e), an accommodation party is never liable to the accommodated party. However, if the accommodation party pays the instrument, he or she has a right of recourse against the accommodated party. Suppose in the prior example that Junior signed as a maker of the note and the father signed as an accommodation party. If Junior pays the note, he cannot attempt to collect the amount paid from his father. On the other hand, if the father ends up paying the note, then he has a right to attempt to collect the amount owed from Junior. This is a common occurrence. If Junior is unable to pay the note, it is unlikely that the father will be able to collect from him either. For this reason, a person should be very careful about signing instruments as an accommodation party.

Guarantors   If an accommodation party signs in such a fashion that he or she unambiguously indicates he or she is *guaranteeing collection*, the accommodation party need not pay until after the holder has attempted to collect from the accommodated party and has been unable to collect from that party (Section 3-419 (d)). Thus, a person who guarantees *collection* is not obligated to pay an instrument until the holder has fully pursued his remedies against the party primarily obligated to pay. Suppose that Anderson signs a note in order to purchase an automobile. Anderson's mother also signed the note but added words to the note indicating unambiguously that she was merely guaranteeing collection of the note. If Anderson fails to pay the note, the bank to whom the note is payable must first attempt to collect the note from Anderson before proceeding against her mother.

If an accommodation party signs in such a fashion that he or she *guarantees payment* of the obligation, the accommodation party in effect is saying he or she will pay the instrument when it is due. In this situation, the accommodation party has the same liability on the instrument as the original debtor. It is not necessary to attempt to collect first from the party accommodated before attempting to collect from the accommodation party. For example, suppose that Phillips signs a note in order to purchase a boat. His father also signs the note and guarantees payment of it. If Phillips fails to pay the note, the bank to whom the note is payable may file suit against Phillips's father without first suing Phillips.

The following case discusses the question of whether a guaranty agreement signed by Billy Huff was a negotiable instrument and therefore governed by Article 3 of the Uniform Commercial Code.

GUARANTOR PARTNERS V. HUFF

Tennessee Courts of Appeals, Middle Section

830 S. W. 2d 73 (1992)

BACKGROUND: On the advice of his accountant, in November 1985 Billy C. Huff purchased an interest in a limited partnership. The limited partnership was formed for the purpose of acquiring and operating a 132-unit apartment complex in Little Rock, Arkansas. In order to acquire the financing for this acquisition, Huff provided a guaranty to the lender. The guaranty agreement was on a form separate from the note signed by the limited partnership. When the limited partnership defaulted on a note, the lender called upon the various guarantors, including Mr. Huff. The other members of the limited partnership paid off the note and then brought suit against Huff based on his guaranty. The trial court ruled that the guaranty agreement was controlled by Article 3 and it ruled on behalf of the limited partnership.

Koch, Justice

The outcome of this appeal hinges on which body of law defines the parties' rights and obligations. The trial court, finding Mr. Huff's guaranty agreement to be a negotiable instrument, determined that Article 3 of the Uniform Commercial Code was controlling. We have determined that the trial court erred as a matter of law and, therefore, that Guarantor Partners was not entitled to a summary judgment.

The courts of this state have never directly addressed the question of whether a separate continuing guaranty is a negotiable instrument. However, of the courts that have addressed the question, a vast majority have held that a separate continuing guaranty is not a negotiable instrument for the purpose of the U.C.C.

The theoretical basis for the majority rule is that a separate continuing guaranty is not an "instrument" as the U.C.C. defines the term. As with other states, Tenn. Code Ann. provides that the term "means a negotiable instrument." Many types of documents calling for the payment of money are "negotiable." However, they are not "negotiable instruments" subject to the rules in Article 3 unless they contain all the elements required by Tenn. Code Ann.

Guaranties, by their very nature, are conditional promises to pay because guarantors promise to pay only on the condition that the principal debtor fails to pay.

A guaranty is not payable at a definite time or on demand since it is payable only when the principal debtor defaults. Continuing guaranties may be payable on numerous occasions.

There is one exception to the general rule that a separate continuing guaranty is not a negotiable instrument. This is when the guaranty, although on a separate form, is so firmly affixed to a negotiable instrument that it becomes part of the instrument itself. Mere descriptive references in a note to a separate guaranty do not have the same effect. However, under this exception, the guaranty itself is not a separate negotiable instrument. It becomes an undistinguishable part of the negotiable instrument to which it is attached. This exception does not apply to this case . Mr. Huff's guaranty was on a separate form and was not affixed or incorporated into the note. SInce Guarantor Partners is not entitled to a judgment as a matter of law under either theory, it was not entitled to a summary judgment.

DECISION: The court reversed the judgment for the limited partnership and remanded the case to the trial court.

Using Negotiable Instruments

Negotiable instruments generally are used in several ways: to borrow money, as a substitute for money, as a credit device, or to create some evidence of a debt.

To Borrow Money

If Brown goes to the bank to borrow money, the bank will probably ask Brown to sign a note in which he promises to repay the money over a certain period of time at a stated rate of interest. Suppose Brown wants to purchase an automobile with the proceeds of the loan. The bank will ask him to sign a note and a security agreement. (See Chapter 30 for a discussion of security agreements.) The note obligates Brown to repay the money to the bank over a period of time or on a fixed maturity date. The security agreement gives the bank an interest in the automobile Brown intends to purchase. In the event Brown fails to comply with his obligations under the note, the bank will exercise its rights under the security agreement. The bank may repossess the automobile, resell it, and pay off the note with the proceeds of the sale.

To Create Evidence of a Debt

In the example discussed in the previous paragraph the note signed by Brown serves as written evidence of Brown's obligation to the bank. The note constitutes proof that Brown in fact owes the bank a certain amount of money, which must be repaid at a certain time.

As a Substitute for Money

Negotiable instruments also serve as a substitute for money. When a person goes into a store to purchase an item, she might pay for it by presenting a check to the store. If she is purchasing a very expensive item, she will probably prefer to use a check because it eliminates the need to carry a large sum of money. It also provides a record of payment.

As a Credit Device

Negotiable instruments may also be used as a credit device. Suppose a seller wanted to sell goods to a buyer in another part of the country.

The seller could insist that the buyer send a certified check before it ships the goods. In this way the seller would be certain of payment. Alternatively, the seller might sell the goods to the buyer on credit. The seller would bill the buyer for the goods at a later date. Of course, if the buyer does not pay at that time, the seller may have to sue. In the suit the seller would have to prove that the buyer owed him or her money. If the buyer had signed a negotiable instrument, it would greatly simplify the case since the seller would have evidence of the obligation.

Another possibility open to the seller is to utilize a draft. The draft may be utilized to finance a sale. A draft is an order by the drawer to the drawee to pay a certain sum of money. Suppose an Ohio seller wishes to ship goods to a buyer in Kansas. The seller will load the goods on a carrier, such as a truck, and the trucking company will provide him or her with a bill of lading—a document giving the person holding it the power to claim the goods. The seller then ships the goods to the buyer in Kansas. At the same time the seller prepares a draft. If the seller wants to be paid at once, he or she will prepare a demand draft. The seller (the drawer of the draft) draws a draft ordering the buyer (the drawee) to pay a certain sum of money to the seller's bank (the payee). As noted earlier, at this point the buyer has no obligation on the draft. Only when he or she *accepts* the draft does the drawee incur any obligation to pay the draft. The seller will then give the draft and the bill of lading to its bank for collection. The seller's bank transfers the draft through banking channels to the buyer's bank in Kansas. The Kansas bank presents the draft to the buyer, and the buyer accepts and pays it. The buyer then receives from the bank the bill of lading, which enables the buyer to receive the goods from the carrier. The Kansas bank forwards the money back to the Ohio bank through banking channels.

When a seller uses a draft with an attached bill of lading, it is called a **documentary draft**. If a draft alone is utilized, the draft is called a **clean draft**.

The seller may also use a time draft, called a **trade acceptance**. It serves as a credit device to enable the buyer to receive the goods immediately without paying for them at once. In this instance the seller follows the same procedure outlined earlier. The seller names himself or herself on the draft as the payee and sets a time at which the draft is payable. The bank in Kansas asks the buyer to accept the draft, which he or she does by signing his or her name across the face of the instrument or in a space provided for the acceptor's signature. At this point the drawee buyer becomes an acceptor of the draft. This obligates the buyer to pay the draft at whatever date it becomes due. The bank releases the bill of lading to the buyer. It then returns the draft to the seller. The seller may retain the draft until its due date, then present the draft to the buyer for payment at that time. If the seller uses a time draft payable June 1, which the buyer signs on January 1, he or she then waits until June 1. On June 1 the seller presents the draft to the buyer for payment. Alternatively, the seller may want cash at once. In this case the seller takes the draft to a third party, such as a bank, and negotiates it to the bank. The bank pays the seller its money at once. The bank then waits until June 1 to collect the draft. On June 1 the bank presents the draft to the buyer for payment.

Drafts, notes, and checks may be used in other ways. But in general they are used as credit extension devices, to borrow money and to create some evidence of a debt.

Negotiability

The UCC seeks to encourage the free transferability of negotiable instruments. The holder-in-due-course device is the basic method by which such transferability is encouraged. A **holder in due course** is a person with good title to an instrument, who took the instrument in good faith, for value, and without notice of any claims or defenses against it. A holder in due course of a negotiable instrument is given preferred status.

For example, Merchant purchases goods from Manufacturer and signs a negotiable promissory note. Manufacturer negotiates the note to Financial Institution. Merchant never receives the goods and raises the fact as a defense against Financial Institution. Because Financial Institution is a holder in due course, Merchant cannot successfully raise the defense of failure of consideration and refuse to pay Financial Institution. Instead, Merchant's only recourse is to sue Manufacturer for breach of contract.

Some modifications of the rule relating to the holder-in-due-course doctrine have been made in the area of consumer transactions. Some states have adopted the Uniform Consumer Credit Code, which prohibits the use of promissory notes when consumer goods are purchased. A major modification of the holder-in-due-course device in consumer transactions was created by a Trade Regulation Rule adopted by the Federal Trade Commission. This rule is discussed in Chapter 28.

Review Questions and Problems

Key Terms

document of title	indorsee
bailee	draft
warehouseman	drawer
warehouse receipt	drawee
carrier	acceptor
fungible goods	check
bill of lading	cashier's check
letter of credit	certificate of deposit
negotiable instrument	accommodation party
payee	documentary draft
negotiation	clean draft
promissory note	trade acceptance
maker	holder in due course
demand note	teller's check
time note	traveler's check
indorser	money order

Discussion Questions

1. Explain how a letter of credit can be used to facilitate foreign trade.

2. What advantages are associated with taking a negotiable instrument as opposed to a simple contract to receive money?

3. Give an example of how commercial paper can be used in each of the following ways:

   a. To borrow money

   b. To create evidence of a debt

   c. As a substitute for money

   d. As a credit device

Review Problems

1. An instrument contains the following information: "January 1, 1995, Thirty (30) days after date I promise to pay to the order of John Frank the sum

of One Hundred and no/100 Dollars (signed) Peter Graves." Identify what type of instrument this is.

2. An instrument reads as follows: "January 1, 1995, On demand, Pay to the order of Alice Smith the sum of One Hundred and no/100 Dollars (signed) Jack Jones." In the lower left-hand corner it also states "To Bill Ford, Kansas City, Missouri." What type of instrument is this?

3. Martha's Restaurant ordered several pieces of restaurant equipment from Restaurant Supply Company. Restaurant Supply intends to ship these goods by Acme Trucking Company. Martha's has not paid for the goods yet. How can a bill of lading be used to make certain Restaurant Supply is paid before Martha's receives the goods? What is a bill of lading?

4. Kelly agrees to sell her motorboat to Young. Young agrees to pay Kelly $1,200 for the boat. The $1,200 is to be paid over 12 months in twelve equal installments of $100 each. Kelly intends to resell this contractual right to receive money to Anderson. Why might it be somewhat risky for Anderson to purchase this contractual right to receive money from Kelly?

5. Swinson wants to purchase a $12,000 boat. Owing to his poor credit history, the lender refuses to loan him any money unless a creditworthy person also signs the note as an accommodation party. Swinson asks his best friend, Case, to sign the note and Case agrees to sign as an accommodation party.

Case signs the instrument in such a fashion as to guarantee collection. Swinson defaults on the note. Can the lender require Case to pay before it attempts to collect on the note from Swinson?

Case Problem

1. Kelly, an aluminum siding salesman, visited Mr. and Mrs. Burchett. Kelly offered to have aluminum siding installed on their home for a certain price and proposed that if they would agree to have their house used as a "show house" for other potential customers they would receive $100 credit off the purchase price for every aluminum siding contract sold in their area. In this way, the Burchetts were led to believe that they would receive the aluminum siding for free. After agreeing to the deal, the Burchetts were each given a contract to read. They were then asked to sign forms, which they assumed were identical to the contracts they had read. What they actually signed, without reading, were notes and mortgages covering the cost of the contract with no provision made for the "show house" credit. The aluminum siding was installed but the Burchetts found it unsatisfactory. Allied purchased the notes with no knowledge that they may have been fraudulently procured. Assuming that no consumer protection statutes apply, can Allied recover on the notes?

27

Negotiable Instruments: Negotiability

Requirements of Negotiable
Instruments

Rules of Construction

I n the last chapter, we learned about the different types of negotiable instruments and introduced the concept of negotiability. We learned that the *negotiation* of an instrument to a third party can potentially leave that third party with greater rights than he or she would have had under a mere assignment of the right to receive money.

We learned that a *holder in due course* of a negotiable instrument—that is, one who took the instrument in good faith, for value, and without notice of any claims of defenses against it—can collect on the instrument in many cases even if the person the instrument was purchased from is legally barred from collecting.

In order to become a holder in due course, one must hold a negotiable instrument. What makes an instrument a *negotiable* instrument? This will be the focus of this chapter.

Requirements of Negotiable Instruments

The requirements of a negotiable instrument are formal, and considerable emphasis is placed upon the use of special words. The courts will

look to the document itself to determine whether it is negotiable. The UCC requires that the document be (1) a signed (2) writing (3) containing a promise or order to pay (4) that is unconditional (5) relating to a fixed amount (6) of money. Further, it must (7) contain no other undertaking or instruction, (8) be payable on demand or at a definite time, and (9) be payable to order or to bearer (or words of similar meaning). Section 3–104(c) of the 1990 UCC states a check may be negotiable even though it is not payable to order or bearer.

The instrument must then be duly negotiated in order for the transferee to obtain the status of a holder in due course. Negotiation requires that (1) the instrument be transferred (2) to a proper holder (3) with any required proper indorsement.

Transfer may be achieved through either physical delivery or, more rarely, a constructive delivery of the instrument. Constructive delivery occurs when the transferee, with intent to effect a transfer, performs a symbolic act representing the transfer. For example, delivery of the keys to a safe containing the instrument may constitute a constructive transfer.

FIGURE 27-1

Promissory
Note

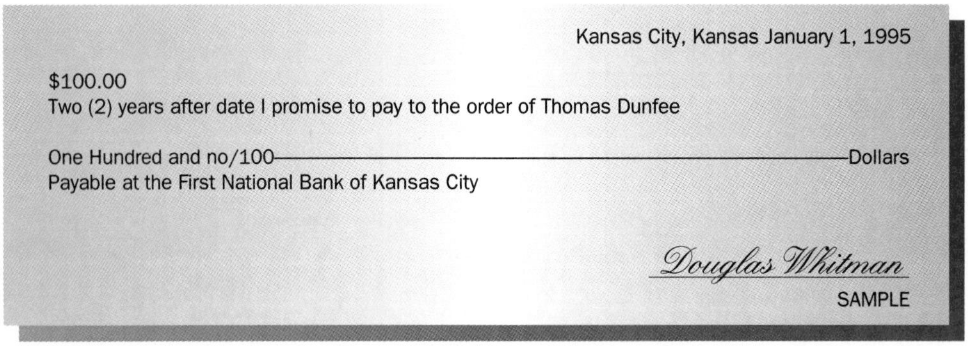

Kansas City, Kansas January 1, 1995

$100.00

Two (2) years after date I promise to pay to the order of Thomas Dunfee

One Hundred and no/100————————————————————————Dollars

Payable at the First National Bank of Kansas City

Douglas Whitman

SAMPLE

Examine the promissory note in Figure 27-1. Does it meet all the requirements of negotiability?

Run through the checklist provided in Table 27-1 to see if it passes the test. You'll find that:

1. The instrument is signed by the maker (Doug Whitman).
2. The instrument is in writing.
3. The instrument contains a promise to pay.
4. The promise is unconditional.
5. The maker promises to pay a fixed amount.
6. The amount of this note is in money.
7. The instrument contains no other undertaking or instruction.
8. The instrument is payable at a definite time.
9. The instrument is payable to order.

Certain instruments may be very similar to a negotiable instrument. For example, a contract for the sale of goods might contain an unconditional promise to pay a fixed amount of money. The most distinguishing characteristic of a negotiable instrument is that it is payable to order or bearer; this is often referred to as "words of negotiability."

If an instrument is missing one or more of the requirements of a negotiable instrument, the instrument could still be transferred but it would *not* be governed by the rules in Article 3 of the UCC. While one cannot agree by contract that such an instrument is a negotiable instrument, nothing keeps a court from applying the provisions of Article 3 to a writing by analogy. Furthermore, the immediate parties to a contract may provide that the provisions of Article 3 determine their rights and obligations and this agreement may be binding on transferees as well (Section 3-104[Comment 2]).

Signed

To be negotiable, an instrument must be signed by the maker or drawer or by an agent acting on behalf of the maker or drawer. (Section 3-401[a]).

TABLE **27-1**

Requirements for Negotiability

An instrument is negotiable if

- The obligation is *in writing*
- The document is *signed*
- The document contains a *promise or order to pay*
- The promise or order relates to a *fixed amount*
- The fixed amount is in *money*

- The promise or order is *unconditional*
- The document contains *no other undertaking or instruction*
- The instrument is payable *on demand or at a definite time*
- The instrument is effectively *payable to order or to bearer*

Note: A check does not need to be payable to order or bearer.

It is not necessary actually to sign an instrument by handwriting; a signature may be made by printing, stamping, writing, or initialing. The question is whether the symbol on the instrument was executed or adopted by the party signing the instrument with the present intention of authenticating the writing.

Agent   It is not necessary to sign an instrument personally. The principal may designate an agent or representative to sign for him or her (Section 3-403[a]). When an agent has authority to sign documents, he or she has the power to bind the principal.

Capacity of Signer   A person may sign an instrument in a number of capacities—as a drawer of a draft, as an acceptor of a draft, as a maker of a note, or as an indorser of an instrument. To be enforceable, a note must be signed by the maker. A draft must be signed by the drawer to be enforceable.

It is necessary to determine in what capacity a person signed an instrument. Unless a signature is obviously not an indorsement, any signature on an instrument will be treated as an indorsement (Section 3-204[a]).

Signature of a Representative   A person's signature may be made by someone on behalf of someone else. If an agent authorized to sign on another's behalf signs a negotiable instrument, this binds the principal. A person who is incapacitated might appoint a person to sign documents on his or her behalf. Likewise, an agent of a corporation (such as the treasurer or president) may sign a negotiable instrument on behalf of the corporation if that agent is authorized to do so.

The power to sign for another may be an express authority granted to the agent, or it may be implied in law or in fact, or it may rest merely upon apparent authority. It is not necessary for there to be any particular form of appointment in order to establish such appointment.

An agent must sign an instrument properly, otherwise he or she may be liable under certain circumstances for the face amount of the instrument. A good way for a person to sign an instrument in a representative capacity on behalf of another is as follows:

Peter Pringle
by Arthur Adams, Agent

A signature in this manner clearly indicates to any person taking it that the agent signed on behalf of the principal and did not intend to incur any personal liability on the instrument. If an officer of the corporation is signing on behalf of the corporation, he or she should sign the instrument as follows:

Book Corporation
by Doug Whitman, President

This signature clearly indicates that Whitman signed on behalf of the corporation and intended to bind *only* the corporation and not himself. This becomes significant when a corporation is unable to pay its debts. Normally shareholders and officers are not liable for the debts of the corporation. However, when a corporation is unable to pay its debts, the holders of instruments may attempt to enforce the instruments against anyone whose signature is on them. A small corporation owned by the person who signed a note might go bankrupt. In that case the holder of the note may sue the officer who signed the note. If that person failed to sign the note in the manner suggested previously, he or she might end up paying a debt of the corporation.

If an agent signs an instrument on behalf of someone else, the represented person will be liable to the same extent that the represented person would be bound if the signature were on a simple contract (Section 3-402[a]). In other words, ordinary agency rules control in this situation. Consider the following two situations:

1. John Blackburn signs an instrument on behalf of Thomas Dunfee, but the only signature appearing on the instrument is "John Blackburn."

2. John Blackburn signs an instrument on behalf of Thomas Dunfee, but the only signature on the instrument is "Thomas Dunfee."

In both of these cases, Thomas Dunfee is bound on the instrument because Thomas Dunfee authorized John Blackburn to sign the instrument on his behalf. The UCC thus reverses the old rule that no one is liable on an instrument unless his or her signature appears on the instrument.

The question then arises, To what extent is a representative who signs an instrument liable on that instrument? Unlike the old version of the UCC, the 1990 code does not specify specific signatures that avoid or impose liability. Instead, the code states a general rule that a representative must use a signature that unambiguously indicates the signature was made on behalf of a person identified in the instrument (Section 3-402[b] [1]).

This general rule suggests that it would not be good for an agent to sign an instrument but fail to name the person represented or note that the agent signed in a representative capacity. Consider the following two examples:

1. John Blackburn signs an instrument on behalf of Thomas Dunfee, but the only signature appearing on the instrument is "John Blackburn."

2. The name "Thomas Dunfee" is written on the instrument and immediately below that name John Blackburn signs "John Blackburn" without indicating that Blackburn signed as an agent.

In each of these cases, both John Blackburn and Thomas Dunfee would be liable on the instrument to a holder in due course because John Blackburn fails to show unambiguously that he is signing in a representative capacity only. If the person who is attempting to enforce the instrument does not qualify as a holder in due course, then John Blackburn may escape liability by proving that the original parties to the instrument did not intend for Blackburn to be held liable on the instrument (Section 3-402[b] [2]).

The 1990 UCC also adopts a new rule for checks. If a person signs a check in a representative capacity, but fails to indicate his or her representative capacity on the check, the agent will *not* be liable on the check if the signature was an authorized signature of the represented person and the check is payable from the account of the represented person who is identified on the check.

Suppose that Mary Anderson, the treasurer of Colonial Baking Corporation, signed a check written on the Colonial bank account "Mary Anderson." She did not include her title "treasurer" on the check nor did she sign "Colonial Baking Corporation." In this situation, only Colonial is liable on the check and *not* Mary Anderson. Even so, it is probably clearer to sign a check as follows:

Colonial Baking Corporation
Mary Anderson, Treasurer

Unconditional Promise or Order

An instrument, in order to be negotiable, must contain an unconditional promise or order to pay. Notes and certificates of deposit must contain an unconditional *promise* to pay. Drafts must include an unconditional *order* to pay. (Checks need not be payable to order or bearer.) If the language in an instrument states that the obligor *promises* to pay someone, the instrument cannot be a draft or check.

Suppose John Doe wrote out the following statement on a piece of paper: "IOU $100 (signed) John Doe." This piece of paper obviously has some characteristics of a negotiable instrument. But it lacks one important element: a promise or an order to pay. While John Doe acknowledges his obligation to pay a debt of $100, he does not promise to pay it or order someone else to pay it. This missing element renders the IOU nonnegotiable. In the typical note a statement appears such as "I promise to pay." In the case of a draft some language must appear that orders someone or some institution to pay. In the draft in Figure 27-2 this requirement is fulfilled by placing the drawee's name after the word "To," or as it appears in that

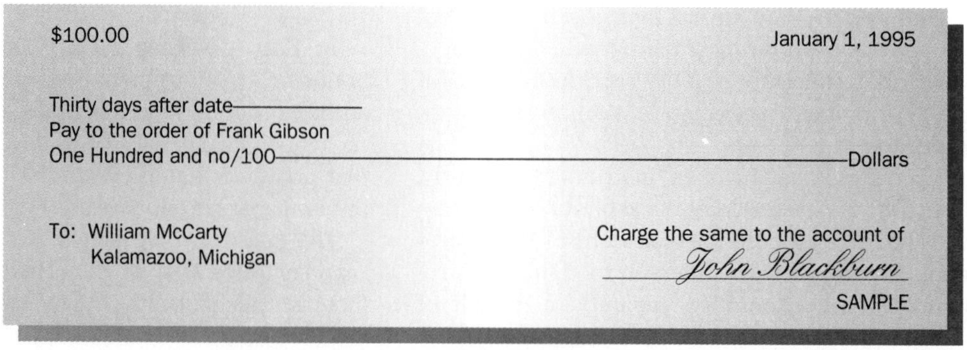

$100.00   January 1, 1995

Thirty days after date————————
Pay to the order of Frank Gibson
One Hundred and no/100——————————————————————————Dollars

To: William McCarty   Charge the same to the account of
    Kalamazoo, Michigan   *John Blackburn*
                                                   SAMPLE

FIGURE 27-2
Draft

FIGURE 27-3

Check

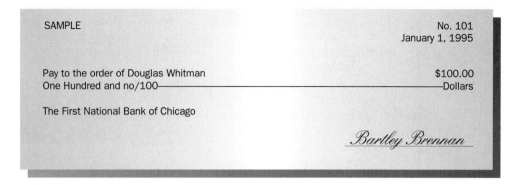

```
SAMPLE                                                    No. 101
                                                   January 1, 1995


      Pay to the order of Douglas Whitman                 $100.00
      One Hundred and no/100——————————————————————————Dollars

      The First National Bank of Chicago

                                                  Bartley Brennan
```

instrument: "To: William McCarty." On a check the name of the drawee bank will appear on the face of the check. The check illustrated in Figure 27-3 has the words "The First National Bank" in the lower left-hand corner of the check.

The negotiability of an instrument must be determinable by an examination of the face of the instrument itself. It must not be necessary for anyone who wishes to take the instrument to refer to any other document in order to determine if an instrument is negotiable.

The following case discusses the question of whether the Resolution Trust Corporation acquired a negotiable instrument.

RESOLUTION TRUST CORPORATION V. 1601 PARTNERS, LTD.

U.S. District Court, N.D. Tex.
796 F. Supp. 238 (1992)

BACKGROUND: 1601 Partners (Defendant) executed a note, along with an accompanying deed of trust as security, on October 2, 1984, in the amount of $1,650,000 payable to Southmark Corporation. This note was assigned to San Jacinto Savings Association, which subsequently failed and was taken over by the Resolution Trust Corporation (plaintiff). The partners failed to pay the note in question, and San Jacinto foreclosed on the property. The RTC now seeks to recover the balance owed on the note, $1.9 million, from 1601 Partners. The partners wanted to assert as a defense that they were released from liability on the note by the original lender, Southmark Corporation. The RTC contends that as a holder in due course it was not subject to such a defense.

Sanders, Chief Judge

Defendants Phillips and Friedman respond that Southmark released them from any liability to Southmark on the note in question. That defense, they contend, is effective against Southmark's transferees—SJSA and plaintiff RTC—because those entities are not holders in due course of the note. Phillips and Friedman cite to §3.302 of the Texas Business & Commerce Code ("UCC"), which provides that, if a note is not a "negotiable instrument," its holder cannot qualify as a holder in due course which takes free of personal defenses. Phillips and Friedman insist that the note is not a negotiable instrument under UCC 3.104 because it does not contain an unconditional promise.

The UCC provides that a promise is not unconditional if the instrument "states that it is subject to or governed by any other agreement." Here, the note states that "the terms, agreements and conditions of [the Deed of Trust] are by reference made a part of this instrument." Courts hold that when an instrument incorporates by reference the terms of another document the instrument becomes "subject to or governed by" another agreement for purposes of §3.105(b), and the promise contained within the instrument, therefore, is rendered conditional.

Mere reference to a note being secured by a mortgage, of course, is common commercial practice and does not affect the negotiability of the note. The language within the note executed by 1601 Partners, however, exceeds the outer bounds of "mere reference," as it explicitly purports to incorporate the terms of the Deed of Trust. Accordingly, the note is not a negotiable instrument under Texas law.

The RTC's reliance on the federal holder in due course doctrine is misplaced. The RTC contends that, because it took the note in good faith and for value, the RTC is entitled to protection as a holder in due course, even though the note is non-negotiable. In Campbell Leasing, Inc. v. FDIC, the Fifth Circuit held that the FDIC may be a federal holder in due course without meeting the technical state law requirements for holder in due course status. Negotiability, however, is not a requirement the Fifth Circuit has been willing to relax. In Sunbelt Saving, the court expressly refused to extend federal holder in due course status to the FDIC or its successor in cases in which it acquires non-negotiable instruments through purchase and assumption transactions. Accordingly, the non-negotiability of the note in this case prevents the RTC from qualifying as a holder in due course. Defendants' release is effective against the RTC.

DECISION: The trial court ruled that the note was not negotiable.

If the instrument states it is subject to or governed by any other agreement, it is not negotiable. If the instrument merely refers to a separate agreement or states that it arises out of such an agreement, it is negotiable.

For example, if a note contains the statement "Payment is subject to the terms of the contract entered into between the parties," it is not negotiable. In order to determine the terms of the note, a person who wishes to take it would need to examine a document other than the instrument, the contract. On the other hand, a simple notation such as "A contract was entered into at the time of executing this note" is a mere reference to the contract and does not make the note subject to the terms of the contract. A note with such a notation is negotiable.

Oral statements do not affect the negotiable character of an instrument. Suppose that McGrew tells Allison at the time she executes a promissory note that she will pay the note only if Allison delivers a 1989 Ford to her. This statement has no effect on the negotiable character of the instrument. A party examining the face of the instrument would be unaware of the oral condition put on the instrument by McGrew at the time she executed the note.

In a change from the old code, the 1990 code states that a promise is not conditional because payment is limited to a particular source or fund (Section 3-106[b]). For example, if the language in an instrument states "Pay only out of the Acme account," the instrument is still treated as a negotiable instrument.

Articles 3 and 4 do not make clear the effect of a legend on a check such as "Void after 90 days" or "Void over $100." If a depositor wishes to use such legends, the agreement between a bank and its depositor must provide for the use of such provisions.

Fixed Amount

Section 3-104(a) of the 1990 code requires that a negotiable instrument be payable in a fixed amount of money. The requirement of a "fixed amount" refers only to principal. Section 3-112 permits an instrument to specify a certain amount of interest, but if it is not possible to determine the amount of interest, interest is payable at the judgment rate.

The code now recognizes the negotiability of instruments such as variable rate notes in which the interest rate fluctuates from time to time according to some formula or index described in the instrument. For example, suppose that Jane Adams agrees to borrow $2,000 from the First National Bank to be repaid in monthly installments over a 1-year period at a rate of interest adjusted monthly according to the 1-year Treasury bill rate. Although it is necessary to check what the current Treasury bill rate is every month, the code nonetheless recognizes the negotiability of such instruments.

In Money

Section 1-201(24) defines money as a medium of exchange adopted or authorized by the government, a foreign government, or an intergovernmental organization. Section 3-107 permits this instrument, in the absence of a contrary agreement, to be paid in foreign money or in dollars.

Payable on Demand or at Certain Time

To be negotiable, an instrument must be payable on demand or at a definite time. An instrument is payable on demand if it is payable at sight or on presentation or if it contains no time for payment (Section 3-108). It must be paid whenever the holder presents it for payment.

An instrument payable at a definite time must state the date on which it is payable. Suppose an instrument is payable 2 years after its date—that is, 2 years after January 1, 1995. If the maker of this note failed to insert a date, the note would not be negotiable because it would not be payable at a definite time. However, Section 3-115 permits a holder of an instrument to fill in the date agreed to by the parties before negotiating the instrument. If an instrument is undated, its date is the day it is issued to the payee (Section 3-113[b]). Not all instruments are this simple, but they may

still be payable at a definite time.

According to Section 3-108 an instrument is payable at a definite time if by its terms it is payable:

1. On demand or at sight
2. On elapse of a definite period of time after sight or acceptance
3. At a fixed date or time ascertainable at the time the instrument is issued
4. At a fixed time or date subject to the right to prepay
5. At a fixed time or date subject to the right to acceleration
6. At a fixed time or date subject to the right to extension at the option of the holder
7. At a fixed time or date subject to the right extension to a further definite time at the option of the maker or acceptor or automatically upon or after a specified act or event

The instrument in Figure 27-4 is payable at a fixed period after a stated date. A draft payable "30 days after sight" is also payable at a definite time. When the holder presents the draft to the drawee and the drawee accepts it (thereby becoming the acceptor of the draft), the 30-day period begins to run.

The time for payment must be determinable from the face of the instrument. An instrument may contain an **acceleration clause**, which, in an instrument payable at a definite time, permits the entire draft to become due immediately upon the option of one of the parties or the occurrence of some specified event. A clause in an instrument that reads "payable June 1, 1995, but the entire sum is due and payable immediately in the event the maker dies" is a valid acceleration clause. The payee of this instrument knows he or

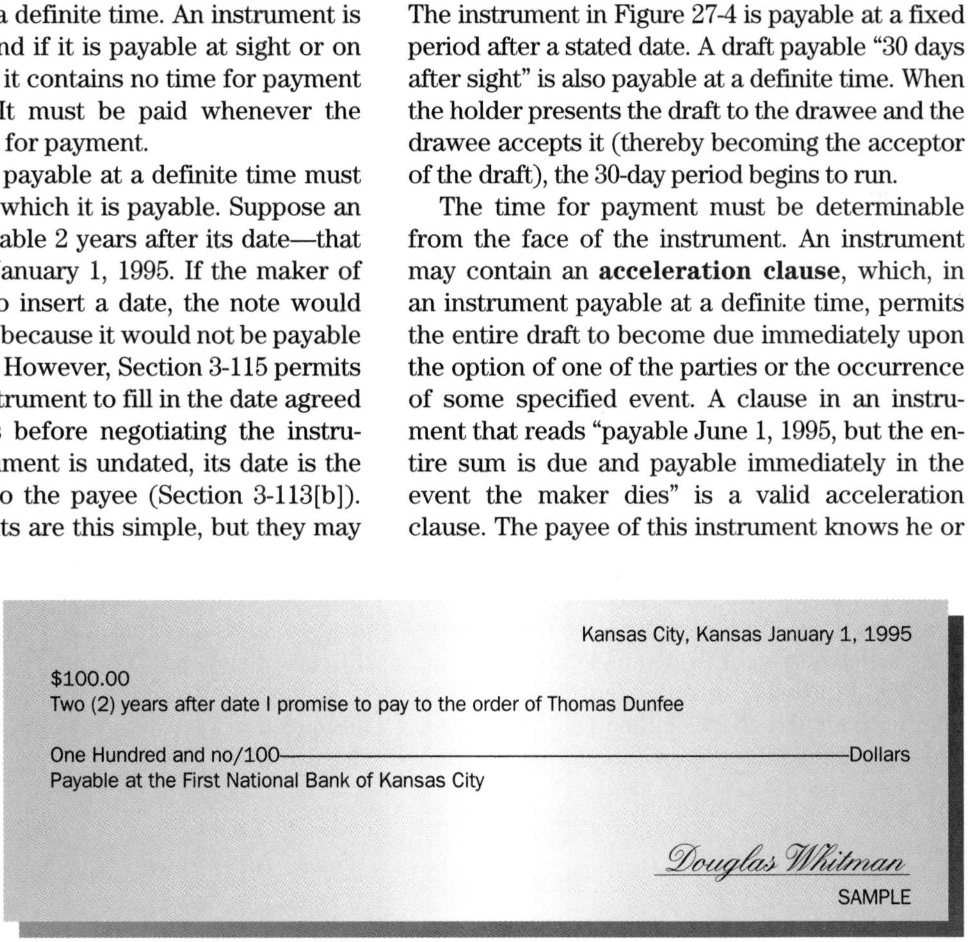

Kansas City, Kansas January 1, 1995

$100.00
Two (2) years after date I promise to pay to the order of Thomas Dunfee

One Hundred and no/100————————————————————Dollars
Payable at the First National Bank of Kansas City

Douglas Whitman
SAMPLE

FIGURE 27-4

Promissory Note

she will be paid on June 1, 1995, at the latest, or earlier if the maker dies before that time. An instrument can also be written in such a fashion that the holder can accelerate the time for payment. However, as noted before, the holder must reasonably believe that the prospect of payment or performance has been impaired.

The instrument also may be made payable at a definite time subject to extension at the option of the holder, or subject to extension to a further definite time at the option of the maker or acceptor, or subject to extension automatically upon the occurrence of an act or event.

If the instrument is payable only upon an act or event whose occurrence is uncertain, the instrument is not payable at a definite time even though the act or event has occurred. For instance, if the note is payable "upon the marriage of my daughter," and the daughter has now married, the note is still not payable at a definite time. It must be possible to determine, at the time the acceptor takes the instrument, whether the instrument is payable at a definite time or on demand. The specified event (the daughter's marriage) may never occur. She may never marry, or she may die before the note comes due. In such cases the instrument would never be payable. No one would want to take an instrument unless he or she was certain that it would be paid either immediately or at some definite time in the future.

To Order or to Bearer

To be negotiable, an instrument must be payable to order or to bearer. "Order" and "bearer" are *words of negotiability*. An instrument payable to order is known as **order paper**; an instrument payable to bearer is known as **bearer paper**. These concepts are explained below.

To Order UCC Section 3-109(b) states: "A promise or order that is not payable to bearer is payable to order if it is payable (i) to the order of an identified person or (ii) to an identified person or order. A promise or order that is payable to order is payable to the identified person." Thus a note payable "to the order of John Jones" is nego-

tiable. When an instrument is payable "to the order of John Jones," it is payable to John Jones *or whomever else that John Jones designates.* The phrase "to the order of" thus indicates that the instrument is meant to be freely transferable.

On the other hand, a note "payable to John Jones" is *not* negotiable because it does not say "to the order of." The phrase "payable to John Jones" means that it is payable to John Jones *only*, and not to anyone else that John Jones may designate. The phrase does not indicate that the instrument was meant to be freely transferable as a negotiable instrument.

The courts strictly interpret the requirement that an order instrument use the *language* of an order instrument.

An order instrument must specify a particular person or organization so that it will be clear who is entitled to payment. It can be made payable to more than one person. For example, an instrument can be "payable to the order of John Doe and Acme Car Repair." In this case the instrument may be properly negotiated to a third party only if *both* parties to the instrument indorse it. An instrument made payable to two parties in this fashion may not be properly negotiated if only John Doe or Acme Car Repair indorses it. People often use this device when they want to make certain that all parties to whom they are obligated have been paid. On the other hand, if an instrument is made payable to the order of "John Doe *or* Acme Car Repair," the signature of *either* party as an indorser, along with a delivery of the instrument, will result in a proper negotiation (Section 3-110[d]).

If it is not clear whether an instrument is payable to either payee or both payees, the signature of *either* payee along with a delivery of the instrument will be sufficient to negotiate the instrument (Section 3-110[d]). Obviously if a person wanted to make certain that all parties to whom he or she is obligated are paid, using unclear language defeats this goal. The code in effect places the risk of ambiguity on the issuer.

In the following case the court grapples with the question of whether an indorsement with a virgule is ambiguous.

MUMMA V. RAINIER NATIONAL BANK
Washington Court of Appeals, Div. 1
808 P.2d 767 (1991)

BACKGROUND: Jan Mumma received a check from Mutual of Enumclaw representing a partial annuity withdrawal of $13,904.48. She met with James H. Liddell, an investment advisor doing business under the corporate name JHL & Associates. Liddell agreed to invest her money in Fidelity, a nationally traded mutual fund management company. At Liddell's direction, Mumma indorsed the check to "Fidelity/JHL & Associates." Liddell deposited the check into an account at Rainier National Bank with the indorsement "JHL & Associates." The check did not have Fidelity's indorsement. The Rainier National Bank collected the check.

Mumma was unable to collect from JHL & Associates, which was insolvent or from Liddell, who was serving jail time for fraud stemming from this incident and others like it. Mumma filed suit against Rainier National Bank. She argued that the bank converted the check because the check did not have the indorsement of both JHL and Fidelity. The trial court dismissed her claims.

Baker, Justice

The resolution of this case depends upon whether the slash or "virgule" symbol ("/") used by Mumma in endorsing her check is interpreted to mean "and" or "or". Mumma contends the slash is ambiguous and therefore, her check was not payable in the alternative. Rainier contends that the common meaning of the slash is "or", and thus the check was payable in the alternative either to Fidelity or JHL.

Mumma contends that ambiguous checks—checks "not in the alternative"—are payable jointly and must have the endorsement of all payees. She argues that a slash is often used to connote something other than "or", citing as examples: miles/hour, 7/20/90, 3/4, and d/b/a. In addition, Mumma herself worked in the travel industry, where she alleges "M/M" is used to mean Mr. and Mrs. Since the slash can have many different meanings depending on its context, she argues that the symbol is ambiguous and the trial court's holding creates a trap for the unwary check writer.

Each of appellant's arguments assumes that an ambiguity exists. She disregards the plain meaning of the slash symbol, which two federal courts and courts in two other states have unanimously held to mean "or" in the same context presented here.

These decisions rely on dictionary definitions of "virgule", which state that the symbol connotes disjunctive, or alternative, construction: "'a short slanting stroke drawn between two words, usually *and* and *or* (thus, and/or), and indicating that either may be used by the reader to interpret the sense.'" Ryland Group, Inc., at 148 (quoting Webster's New International Dictionary [2d ed. 1961]); "'[a] short oblique stroke (/) between two words indicating that whichever is appropriate may be chosen to complete the sense of the text in which they occur'". L.B. Smith, Inc., at 497 n.2 (quoting The Random House Dictionary [1967]).

While Mumma is correct that the virgule or diagonal symbol has many uses in modern language, she cites none outside of the travel industry that involve the conjunctive ("and") meaning. We are not inclined to transport the peculiarities of a particular business usage into the code of commercial law. In the absence of a more general showing that the virgule means "and" in common usage, we choose to put our own law in accordance with previously decided cases on the same issue.

DECISION: The court of appeals affirmed the decision of the trial court and ruled for Rainier.

A person might name as a payee of a check a corporation or the officer of a corporation. Suppose that John Smith makes a check payable "to the order of Joe Doaks, President of Acme Corporation." Either Doaks, or Doaks's successor in office, or Acme Corporation can be a holder of the instrument and may negotiate the instrument (Section 3-110[c][2][ii]).

Instruments payable to public offices may be made payable to the officeholder. Suppose that Mary Adams pays the property taxes on her office building by writing a check made payable to the order of "Susan Smith, County Treasurer." This instrument may be negotiated by Susan Smith or whomever is the county treasurer at the time the county receives Adams's check (Section 3-110[c][2][iv]).

It should be noted that the 1990 code makes a check a negotiable instrument even though it is not payable to order or the bearer. Therefore all instruments other than checks must be payable to either order or to bearer in order to be negotiable instruments.

To Bearer UCC Section 3-109 (a) states the rule with respect to instruments payable to bearer. Even though an instrument fails to qualify as an order instrument, it is negotiable if it is payable to bearer. An instrument is payable to bearer if

1. It is payable to bearer or to the order of bearer
2. It indicates that the person in possession of it is entitled to payment
3. It does not state a payee
4. It is payable to cash or to the order of cash or otherwise indicates it is not payable to an identified person

If an instrument is bearer paper, anyone who obtains possession of the instrument has the power to negotiate it. Suppose that Anderson issues a draft to Taylor and makes the draft "payable to bearer" and not to the order of Taylor. Taylor thereafter misplaces the draft and Wilson finds it. Because it is bearer paper, Wilson has the power to negotiate the draft to a bank.

In a change from the prior rules, if there is confusion as to whether an instrument is order paper or bearer paper, it is presumed to be bearer paper. Suppose that a person obtains a check on which the words "Pay to the order of" are printed on the

check. The person fills out the words "John Doe or bearer." Section 3-109(a)(1) indicates that if an instrument uses ambiguous terms like this, the instrument is payable to bearer.

No Other Undertaking or Instruction to Do Any Act in Addition to the Payment of Money

Even if an instrument is a signed writing containing an unconditional promise or order to pay a fixed amount of money, payable on demand or at a definite time, and payable to order or to bearer, it still may not be negotiable if the maker or drawer agrees to any other undertaking or instruction in addition to the payment of money (Section 3-104[a]).

Certain additional information may be given in an instrument without impairing its negotiability:

1. A statement that collateral has been given to secure the obligation
2. An authorization to confess judgment or dispose of the collateral
3. A waiver of the benefit of any law intended for the advantage or protection of a person who owes a debt

Date

Section 3-113(a) states that an instrument may be antedated (dated at sometime in the past) or postdated (dated at some time in the future). For example, suppose that Alice Jones on June 1 gives an instrument to a bank dated June 15. This would be a postdated instrument. If this instrument is payable at a fixed period after the date, such as payable 6 months after date, the stated date determines when it is payable. In this case, it would be payable 6 months after June 15—not 6 months after June 1.

Demand instruments are *not* payable before the date of the instrument. It should be noted that Section 4-401(c) carves an exception out of this rule with respect to checks. A bank *may* pay a postdated check before the date on the check unless the drawer has notified the bank of the postdating.

An instrument is not affected by the fact that it is undated. The date of such an instrument is the date of its issue, or if it has not been issued, then the date it first comes into possession of a holder (Section 3-113[b]).

FIGURE 27-5

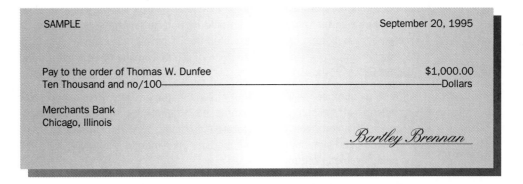

SAMPLE   September 20, 1995

Pay to the order of Thomas W. Dunfee $1,000.00
Ten Thousand and no/100——————————————————————————————Dollars

Merchants Bank
Chicago, Illinois

Bartley Brennan

Rules of Construction

Section 3-114 states that if an instrument has contradictory terms,

1. Typewritten terms prevail over printed terms
2. Handwritten terms prevail over both typewritten and printed terms
3. Words prevail over numbers

See, for example, Figure 27-5. There is a conflict between the words and the numbers. The code states that the words control; therefore, this is a check for $10,000—not for $1,000.

Not all situations are crystal-clear. In the following case the court grapples with the question of how to treat a conflict between an impression made on the center line of the check and the numbers appearing in the right-hand side of the check.

GALATIA COMMUNITY STATE BANK V. KINDY

Arkansas Supreme Court
16 UCC Rep. Serv. 2d 710 (1991)

BACKGROUND: Kindy buys and sells diesel engine parts. He agreed to purchase four diesel engines from Tony Hicks, who was to deliver them. Kindy agreed to give Hicks a check for $5,500. The check which he actually delivered was imprinted by a check-writing machine for $5,500 in the center underline section of the check commonly used for stating the amount of the check in words. The impression made by the check-writing machine could be felt on the front and back of the check. In the box on the right-hand side of the check commonly used for numbers appears the number $6,500. The bank honored the check for $5,500.

Thereafter, because Hicks had not delivered the engines, Kindy stopped payment on the check. Kindy's bank refused to honor the check when the Galatia Bank presented it to his bank for payment. The bank then brought suit against him for $5,500. The trial court ruled for Kindy.

Newbern, Justice

One question is whether imprinted numbers located where words are customarily placed on a check control numbers placed where numbers are customarily placed. . . .

We find [this] question satisfactorily answered in St. Paul Fire & Marine Ins. Co. v. State Bank of Salem, 412 N.E.2d 103 [30 UCC Rep Serv 557] (Ind. App. 1980). In that case, there was a conflict between an amount imprinted by a check imprinting machine and numbers expressed in typewritten figures. The court recognized the imprinted amount was not expressed in words, but held "the purposes of the U.C.C. are best served by considering an amount imprinted by a checkwriting machine as 'words' for the purpose of resolving an ambiguity between that amount and an amount entered upon the line usually used to express the amount in figures." The court quoted from a pre- U.C.C. case, United States Fidelity and Guaranty Company v. First National Bank of South Carolina of Columbia, 244 S.C. 436, 137 S.E.2d 582 (1964), as follows:

> A prime purpose, as we see it, of making a sum payable when expressed in words controlling over the sum payable expressed in numbers is the very fact that words are much more difficult to alter. The perforated imprinting by a check-writing machine, while expressing the sum payable in numbers, is even more difficult to successfully alter than a sum payable in written words.

Because a check imprinting machine's purpose is to protect against alterations, the amount shown on the imprint should control whether the number is in words or numbers. As Professor Hawkland has written:

> A purchaser does not obtain notice of a claim or defense solely because there is a conflict among handwritten, printed and typewritten terms. Although a purchaser might question whether some irregularity has occurred, the premise of section 3-114 seems to be that any conflict is a mere mistake and therefore should be ignored.

DECISION: The Arkansas Supreme Court entered a verdict for $5,500 on behalf of the Galatia Community State Bank.

Review Questions and Problems

Key Terms

acceleration clause   bearer paper
order paper

Discussion Questions

1. What are the requirements for an instrument to be negotiable?
2. List three different phrases that would make an instrument bearer paper.

Review Problems

1. Ross agrees to pay his cousin Mary $300. He signs a piece of paper that states: "IOU $300 (signed) Ross James." Is this a negotiable instrument?
2. Anderson signs a demand note for $200 payable to the order of Bailey. The note states that it was given in exchange for the sale of a bicycle by Bailey to Anderson. The note also states that it is governed by the terms of the contract entered into between Bailey and Anderson for the sale of the bicycle. Do either of these provisions render the note nonnegotiable?

3. Erwin enters into a contract with Singer for the purchase of some machinery. Erwin promises to pay Singer $2,000 for the machinery. Erwin signs a note that specifies, among other things, that the note will be paid by Erwin in British pounds. The note also states that it is "payable six months after sight, but the entire sum is due and payable immediately if Erwin dies." Is this instrument negotiable?
4. Prentice entered into a contract with Moore. Prentice signed the following note: "January 1, 1986, Thirty days after date, Pay to Bill Moore the sum of One Hundred and no/100 Dollars (signed) Mary Prentice." Is this instrument negotiable?
5. Michelle Clark was asked by her brother, David Clark, to act as his representative while he was out of the country. David gave Michelle the authority to sign instruments on his behalf until he returned to the United States. Michelle was asked to sign a note on behalf of David. What is the proper way for her to sign this note?

Case Problems

1. The president and sole stockholder of Fred Dowie Enterprises, Inc. ordered 325,000 hot dog buns from Colonial Baking. He paid for the buns with a check for $28,640. The check showed the name of the corporation and its address in the upper left-hand corner. The signature on the check was "Frederick J. Dowie." Dowie did not sign the corporation's name,

nor write the word "President" after his name. Colonial sued Dowie in his personal capacity as the signer of the check. Dowie did not introduce any evidence of an agreement, understanding, or course of dealing between the parties that when he signed he did so as a representative of the corporation. Is Dowie personally liable on this check in light of the fact that the corporation's name was imprinted on the check?

2. Cook, a corporate treasurer, signed two corporate checks, but she failed to indicate her representative capacity, that is, "Corporate Treasurer." The checks carried the imprinted name of the corporation at the top and on the lower right-hand corner just above the place for signing. Is Cook personally liable on this check?

3. Davis Aircraft Engineering, Inc., entered into a loan agreement with Bank A. On the face of each note was printed: "This note evidences a borrowing made under, and is subject to, the terms of the loan agreement." There is nothing in the loan agreement that would impose any contingency upon the obligation to pay. Davis contends that the notes are nonnegotiable because there is not an unconditional promise to pay. Will Davis win?

4. Hotel Evans contracted with A. Alport & Son to construct a hotel and in return gave Alport certain promissory notes. The notes contained the notation "with interest at bank rates." At the time of payment, the bank wrote "8½%" above the words "bank rates." Are the notes negotiable?

28

Negotiable Instruments: Transfer, Negotiation, and Holder in Due Course

Transfer and Negotiation

Indorsements

Holder in Due Course

Payee as Holder in Due Course

As noted in the preceding chapter, several conditions must be met in order for a person to qualify as a holder in due course:

1. He or she must be in possession of a *negotiable* instrument (as explained in Chapter 27).
2. The instrument must be issued or *negotiated* to the holder.
3. The person in possession of the negotiable instrument validly issued or negotiated to him or her must also *comply with Section 3-302* of the Uniform Commercial Code.

When these three conditions are met, the person in possession of a negotiable instrument attains the preferred status of a holder in due course. This chapter examines the concepts of negotiation and holder in due course.

Transfer and Negotiation

Issuance of Instrument

When a negotiable instrument has been drawn up and signed by the parties, one more step must take place for the instrument to become enforceable: It must be *issued* by the maker or drawer to the holder. In the typical transaction, issuance occurs when the maker or drawer of the instrument hands the instrument to the payee. This delivery of the instrument by the drawer or maker to the payee is called an *issuance* of the instrument.

The maker or drawer of an instrument is generally *not* liable on an instrument until he or she delivers or issues the instrument. Delivery of an instrument simply means the voluntary transfer of the instrument. Transfer may be achieved either by physical delivery or, in rare instances, by constructive delivery of the instrument. Constructive delivery occurs when the maker or drawer, with the intent to effect a transfer, performs a symbolic act representing the transfer. For example, delivery of the keys to a safe containing the instrument may constitute a constructive transfer.

In determining whether a delivery took place, the courts must examine the *intent* of the parties. However, if someone other than the assignee of the instrument has physical possession of it, there is a rebuttable presumption that delivery has occurred. If the maker or drawee still has physical possession of the instrument, there is a rebuttable presumption that delivery was not intended.

Suppose John Smith signed a note payable to Grace Jones, and he placed it on his desk. If Jones burglarized Smith's office and took the instrument, may she enforce it against Smith? No. Clearly, although he signed the instrument, Smith did not issue (voluntarily deliver) it to Jones. If a thief stole the note, however, and transferred it to a holder in due course, the holder in due course could enforce the note against Smith—even though Smith never voluntarily transferred it to Jones. This is because the absence of delivery is a *personal defense*. A **personal defense** is a defense which may *not* be asserted against a holder in due course. Personal defenses are generally defenses that arise out of the transaction in which the instrument was originally issued. Such defenses include breach of contract, lack of consideration, failure of a condition precedent, and mistake. Personal defenses, as well as those defenses which *are* available against a holder in due course, will be discussed more fully in Chapter 29.

Returning to our example with John Smith, assume now that the person who ultimately ends up in possession of the stolen note is *not* a holder in due course. In this case, Smith could assert the personal defense that the note had never been voluntarily delivered. Smith would not have to pay the note.

This example illustrates the chief benefit of holder-in-due-course status: the right to take instruments free from all personal defenses. Anyone who is not a holder in due course, on the other hand, takes the instrument subject to all defenses or claims by any party. A holder in due course has rights that are much greater than those of a mere transferee.

Transfer of Instrument

Once the original maker or drawer of an instrument has signed and issued the instrument, the instrument may be transferred to a third party. If the transfer constitutes a *negotiation*, the person to whom the instrument is transferred becomes a *holder* of the instrument. If the transfer fails to qualify as a negotiation, the person to whom the instrument is transferred (the assignee) will never attain the status of a holder in due course. Such a person takes the instrument by *assignment* (as opposed to taking it by negotiation), and therefore may not become a holder of the instrument. A person must be a holder of an instrument in order to qualify as a holder in due course. This is true even if the instrument assigned qualifies as a negotiable instrument under Section 3-104(a).

If a person in possession of an instrument takes it by *assignment*, the transaction is governed by the law of contracts rather than Article 3 of the UCC. The person to whom the instrument is assigned is a mere *assignee* of a contractual right to receive money. The transfer gives the assignee all the rights of the *assignor* (the person who transferred the instrument to the assignee). However, the assignee also takes the instrument subject to any defenses or claims that might have been asserted against his or her assignor or any prior party to the instrument.

A person who takes a nonnegotiable instrument also is governed by the law of contracts rather than Article 3 of the UCC. Article 3 applies only to negotiable instruments.

To take an example, suppose John Smith signs a note payable to Jones and issues it to her. Grace Jones wishes to transfer the note to her daughter, Mary Jones. If Jones fails to transfer the note properly (as discussed later in this chapter), her daughter becomes a mere assignee of a contractual right to receive money from Smith. This means that Mary acquires all the rights her mother had (the right to receive money from Smith) but takes the instrument subject to any claims or defenses Smith might have against Jones. Suppose Jones acquired the note from Smith in return for her promise to give Smith a 1989 Ford. After acquiring the note, Jones refuses to transfer the title to the Ford to Smith. So long as the note was in Jones's hands, Smith had a defense on the instrument—breach of contract. If sued by Jones on the instrument, he could refuse to pay the note because Jones failed to live up to her part of the bargain. Because Mary "steps into the shoes of her assignor," she takes the note subject to the defense of breach of contract. If Mary sues Smith on the note, Smith may assert against Mary the failure of her mother to deliver the Ford as a reason for his refusal to pay the note.

Negotiation

Section 3-201 of the 1990 code defines **negotiation** as "a transfer of possession, whether voluntary or involuntary, of an instrument by a person other than the issuer to a person who thereby becomes its holder."

Section 1-201(20) defines a **holder** as the "person in possession if the instrument is payable to bearer, or, in the case of an instrument payable to an identified person, if the identified person is in possession."

How does one become a holder? The person in possession of the instrument must in some cases have (1) the indorsement of the prior holder of the instrument and (2) a *transfer of possession* (Section 3-201[a]). It should be noted that the transfer of possession can occur by an *involuntary* transfer of possession. In other cases a transfer of possession alone will be sufficient to negotiate the instrument. If the instrument qualifies as an *order instrument* the former is required, but a *bearer instrument* may be negotiated by transfer of possession alone. As explained in the preceding chapter, an order instrument generally is one made payable to the order of someone. A bearer instrument is one made payable to "bearer" or "cash."

Suppose John Smith writes a note, but makes it payable to bearer as shown in Figure 28-1. Smith now physically transfers possession of the note to Grace Jones. The act of transferring the note to Jones is an *issuance* of the instrument. What if Jones now wants to transfer this note to her daughter Mary Jones? What must she do to validly negotiate the note so that Mary becomes a holder of the instrument? All Jones must do is to transfer possession of the note to Mary because this is a bearer instrument, which may be negotiated by a transfer of possession alone.

Suppose instead that this note was made payable to the order of Grace Jones, as in Figure 28-2. If Jones merely transfers possession of this instrument to Mary, there has not been a negotiation of the instrument. This note must be indorsed on the back by Jones and delivered to Mary to negotiate it because it is an *order instrument*.

Let us reexamine the definition of holder in

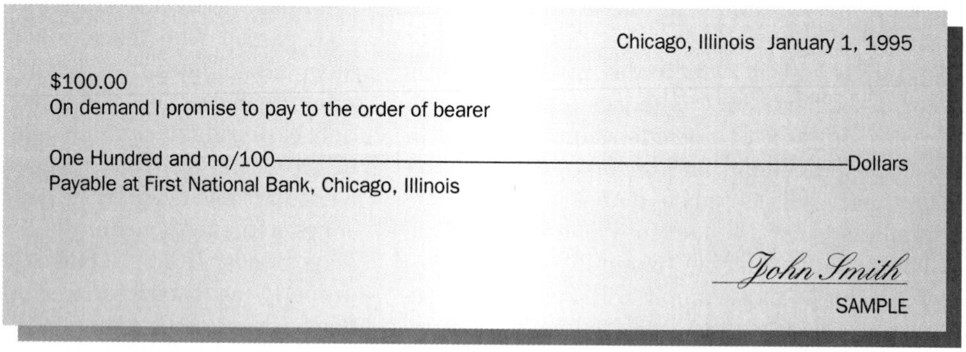

Chicago, Illinois   January 1, 1995

$100.00
On demand I promise to pay to the order of bearer

One Hundred and no/100————————————————————————Dollars
Payable at First National Bank, Chicago, Illinois

John Smith
SAMPLE

FIGURE 28-1

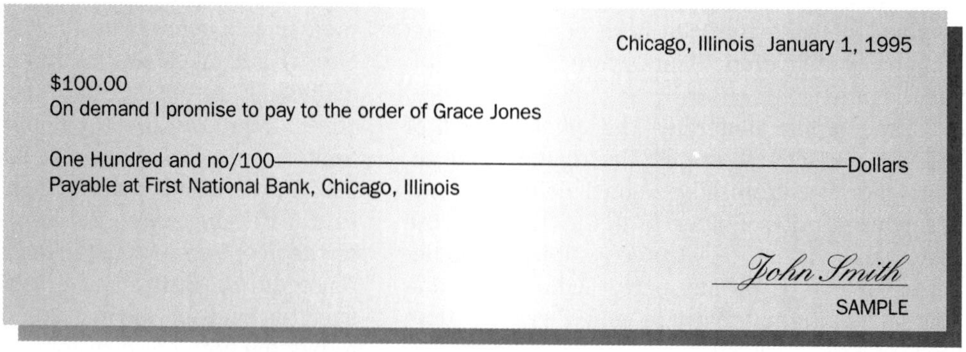

Chicago, Illinois   January 1, 1995

$100.00
On demand I promise to pay to the order of Grace Jones

One Hundred and no/100————————————————————————Dollars
Payable at First National Bank, Chicago, Illinois

John Smith
SAMPLE

FIGURE 28-2

Section 1-201(20). In the two notes appearing earlier, once Jones takes possession of either note she is a holder. The first note is drawn "to bearer." All she need do to become a holder is to take possession of the note. To become holder of the second note, she again only needs to take possession because the second note was drawn payable to her order. Mary becomes a holder of the first note when she got possession of it because it was drawn "to bearer." To become a holder of the second note, Mary must not only take possession but must also obtain her mother's indorsement, because the instrument originally was drawn "to the order of" Jones. As it was not originally drawn to Mary's order, she must first obtain her mother's signature to negotiate the instrument effectively.

Because they may be negotiated by a transfer of possession alone, whether the transfer is voluntary or *involuntary*, there is some risk in creating instruments that are payable to bearer. What if Smith signed the first note, which was payable to bearer, and a thief stole it? A thief becomes the holder of the instrument when possession is obtained. There is an *involuntary* transfer of possession that results in negotiation to the thief (Section 3-201[a] [Comment 1]). The thief then may negotiate the instrument to a third party who can enforce the instrument against the original party.

The same rules apply if a person *finds* a bearer instrument. A finder becomes the holder of the instrument through an involuntary transfer of possession. The finder then may negotiate the instrument to a third party, who can enforce the instrument against the original party. Bearer instruments must be handled very carefully because an involuntary transfer of possession can result in the negotiation of the instrument to a thief or the finder of a bearer instrument.

While bearer instruments expose the maker or drawer to some risks, the same is not true of order instruments. Take the note illustrated in Figure 28-2. It is payable to the order of Jones and therefore qualifies as an order instrument. Suppose a thief or finder comes into possession of this instrument. If the thief signs Jones's name and transfers the instrument to an innocent third party, Quinn, does Quinn become a holder of the instrument? No. This instrument was drawn payable to the order of Jones. To negotiate it, there must be a transfer of possession of the instrument, and the instrument must be indorsed by Jones. The forged *indorsement by the thief* is ineffective. No title to

the instrument passes to Quinn; she does not become a holder. The note has not been negotiated to Quinn because she lacks Jones's indorsement. Because Quinn holds the instrument through a forged indorsement, when she presents it to Smith for payment, Smith may refuse to pay the instrument if he detects that Jones did not sign it. Not only does Quinn not qualify as a holder of the instrument, but anyone to whom Quinn transfers the instrument also will not become a holder. Generally one may not qualify as a holder under a forged indorsement of an order instrument.

To review negotiation, (1) if the instrument is a bearer instrument, transfer of possession alone is sufficient to negotiate the instrument and (2) if the instrument is an order instrument, to negotiate it the appropriate party must indorse and transfer possession of it to someone.

Indorsements

The 1952 code did not define an *indorsement*. The 1990 code defines an indorsement as a signature, other than that of a signer as maker, drawer, or acceptor, made on an instrument for the purpose of

1. Negotiating the instrument
2. Restricting payment of the instrument, or
3. Incurring indorser's liability on an instrument

The general rule is that a signature is an indorsement if the instrument does not indicate an unambiguous intent of the signer not to sign as an indorser (Section 3-204[a]). Intent is determined by looking at the words and terms of the instrument, the place of the signature, custom, and other circumstances.

The indorser is the person who makes an indorsement. An indorsement must be written by or on behalf of the holder. In most cases the indorsement is written on the back of an instrument.

If for some reason there is no space on the reverse side of the instrument, the indorsement may appear on a paper firmly affixed to the instrument. Such a paper is called an **allonge**. It will not be sufficient to pin or clip the allonge to the instrument. The allonge must be firmly attached in such a manner that it will not become separated from the instrument—as by gluing the allonge to the instrument.

When a person transfers an order instrument for value, he or she has an obligation (absent a

FIGURE 28-3

Blank
Indorsement

contrary agreement) to indorse the instrument. However, a negotiation of the instrument does not take place until the instrument has been indorsed. When a person receives an order instrument that lacks the indorsement of the transferor, the transferee may require the transferor to indorse the instrument. The transferee of an order instrument without the requisite indorsement is not a holder (Section 3-203[c]).

Sometimes an instrument may be made payable to a person, but the person who wrote the instrument failed to correctly spell the name of the payee. For example, suppose that a drawer of a check made the check payable to the order of "Douglas Whiteman" intending to pay Douglas Whitman. In such a situation, Douglas Whitman may indorse in the name stated in the instrument (Douglas Whiteman), or in the holder's name (Douglas Whitman), or both (Douglas Whiteman, Douglas Whitman). A signature in both names may be required by a person taking the instrument (Section 3-204[d]).

Negotiable instruments are indorsed for two reasons: (1) the indorsement may be necessary to negotiate the instrument and (2) the indorsement may be required to obligate the indorsee to pay the instrument under certain circumstances discussed in the next chapter.

Blank Indorsements

A **blank indorsement** specifies no particular indorsee and may consist of a mere signature (Section 3-205[b]). This is the most common type of indorsement. How would Grace Jones indorse in blank the note in Figure 28-2 that was payable to her order? On the reverse side of the note she would sign it as shown in Figure 28-3.

When Jones signs the instrument in this fashion and transfers possession of it to another person, there has been a negotiation of the note. The person to whom she transfers the note becomes a holder of the note. Jones has transferred title to the instrument to the third person. By indorsing the instrument in this fashion, she also promises to pay the instrument, under certain circumstances, if John Smith fails to pay.

When an instrument is payable to order and it is indorsed in blank, it becomes payable to bearer and may be negotiated by transfer of possession alone. Just as in the case of an instrument originally payable to bearer, an instrument that is indorsed in blank may be negotiated by transfer of possession alone. This means that the same risks associated with an instrument that is originally payable to bearer also apply to an instrument that is indorsed in blank. A thief or finder has the power to negotiate the instrument indorsed in blank to an innocent third party so that the third person becomes a holder of the instrument.

M. G. Sales, Inc. v. Chemical Bank, the case that follows, suggests a motto for anyone who endorses a negotiable instrument in blank: Be careful!

M. G. SALES, INC. V. CHEMICAL BANK

Supreme Court of New York, Appellate Division, First Department
554 N.Y.S.2d 863 (1990)

BACKGROUND: Gardner, the president of M. G. Sales, Inc. (plaintiff), made out two $6,000 corporate checks payable to himself. Gardner indorsed both checks in blank and then apparently lost them. Gardner went to the corporation's bank, Chemical Bank (defendant), and obtained stop-payment orders for the checks. The stop-payment orders, however, expired by their terms after 6 months, and Gardner did not renew them. More than 1 year later, Leon Fried surfaced with the checks. He added his indorsement to each check and deposited them into his account at another Chemical Bank branch. Chemical Bank paid the proceeds of the check to Fried. M. G. Sales sued Chemical Bank, claiming that its payment of the checks was improper. Chemical Bank moved for a summary judgment dismissing plaintiff's complaint against it. The trial court refused Chemical Bank's motion, and the bank appealed.

Memorandum Decision

The two checks were bearer paper when lost by Mr. Gardner, as they were signed, payable to, and endorsed in blank by him. . . . UCC 4-404 provides that "[a] bank is under no obligation to a customer having a checking account to pay a check, other than a certified check, which is presented more than six months after its date, but it may charge its customer's account for a payment made thereafter in good faith". Thus, the bank committed no error in accepting and paying out on the checks.

The [lower] court found a question of fact existed as to whether the bank paid the checks in violation of its own directive against acceptance of double-endorsed checks. However, the only evidence presented that such a policy existed was a sign from an unidentified Chemical Bank branch stating that the bank did not accept double-endorsed checks, without any indication as to when the sign was posted or obtained. Chemical, however, submitted the affidavit of an officer responsible for the branch that accepted the checks. He stated that the bank's policy limiting the acceptance of double-endorsed checks for deposit commenced in 1984 and that signs to that effect were put up in August of 1984. This affidavit was uncontradicted by the plaintiff and conclusively established that Chemical had no policy against the acceptance of double-endorsed checks when the checks were presented in 1983. Further, as the UCC contains no prohibition against the acceptance of double-endorsed checks, it was not error for the bank to accept the checks here in question (*see, e.g.,* UCC 3-204 *et seq.*).

DECISION: The complaint against Chemical Bank was dismissed.

Special Indorsements

A **special indorsement** specifies the person to whom or to whose order the instrument is payable (Section 3-205[a]). Jones could indorse the note discussed earlier as shown in Figure 28-4. The note in question was originally payable to the order of Grace Jones and therefore was an order instrument. When Jones indorsed the note in this manner it became payable to the order of the special indorsee (Mary Jones) and may be further negotiated only by Mary Jones's indorsement and transfer of possession of the note to a third person. A note remains an order instrument when it is indorsed with a special indorsement.

Jones could also have indorsed the note with the words "Pay to the order of Mary Jones, (signed) Grace Jones" or "Pay to Mary Jones or order, (signed) Grace Jones." In other words, it is not necessary to include the words of negotiability in the special indorsement. While it is true than an instrument originally must be payable to order or to bearer for it to be negotiable, the special indorsement need not include the words of negotiability.

FIGURE 28-4

Special Indorsement

It is possible to convert an instrument indorsed in blank into a special indorsement by writing over the signature of the indorser in blank words such as "Pay to Mary Jones." If Mary's mother simply indorsed the note over to Mary by signing "Grace Jones" on the reverse side, Mary could convert the indorsement into a special indorsement by writing the words "Pay to Mary Jones" above her mother's signature. The instrument would then need to be indorsed by Mary Jones, and Mary Jones would need to transfer possession of the note to someone in order for there to be a valid negotiation of the instrument.

By specially indorsing bearer paper, and thereby converting it to order paper, the person taking possession of the instrument avoids the risks associated with bearer paper. If a thief then steals the instrument, the thief must forge the signature of the special indorsee to whose order the instrument is payable. Because a forged indorsement will be ineffective, the special indorsee has protected himself or herself.

The following case illustrates the use of special indorsements.

KLOMANN V. SOL K. GRAFF & SONS

Appellate Court of Illinois

317 N.E.2d 608 (1974)

BACKGROUND: Georgia Klomann (plaintiff) sued the partnership Sol K. Graff & Sons (defendant). Robert Graff executed three notes for the defendant partnership, Sol K. Graff & Sons. The notes were made payable to Fred Klomann. Klomann specially indorsed the notes to his daughter, Candace Klomann, and handed them to her. She looked at the notes, then returned them to Fred. At a later date Fred scratched out Candace's name in the special indorsement and inserted the name of his wife, Georgia Klomann, and delivered the notes to Georgia. Georgia Klomann then brought suit to enforce these notes. The lower court ruled Georgia Klomann could enforce these notes and receive payment on them from Sol K. Graff & Sons.

Dieringer, Justice

The defendant contends the plaintiff has no right, title or interest in the promissory notes, thereby raising an issue of fact which precluded the entry of summary judgment in favor of the plaintiff.

The plaintiff maintains the defense of whether Georgia Klomann has an interest in the notes is not available to the defendant. In support of her contention, the plaintiff relies on Section 3-306(d) of the Uniform Commercial Code which provides:

Unless he has the rights of a holder in due course any person takes the instrument subject to (d) the defense that he or a person through whom he holds the instrument acquired it by theft or that payment or satisfaction to such holder would be inconsistent with the terms of a restrictive indorsement. *The claim of any third person to the instrument is not otherwise available as a defense to any party liable thereon unless the third person himself defends the action for such party* [emphasis added].

We believe that the plaintiff has no right, title or interest in the promissory notes. Section 3-204 of the Uniform Commercial Code provides:

(1) A special indorsement specifies the person to whom or to whose order it makes the instrument payable. Any instrument specially indorsed becomes payable to the order of the special indorsee and may be further negotiated only by his indorsement.

A review of the record in the instant case reveals Fred Klomann specially indorsed the promissory notes to his daughter, Candace, in August, 1967. The notes, therefore, could only be further negotiated by Candace. Examination of the record further reveals Candace, the special indorsee, has never negotiated the notes. Fred Klomann, in April, 1970, improperly scratched out Candace's name in the special indorsement and inserted the name of his wife Georgia. Section 3-201 of the Uniform Commercial Code provides in pertinent part:

(1) Transfer of an instrument vests in the transferee such rights as the transferor has therein . . .

When Fred Klomann signed the notes in question to his daughter he no longer had any interest in them. His attempted assignment to Georgia approximately three years later conveyed only that interest which he had in the notes, which was nothing. Plaintiff, therefore, has no interest in the notes sued on in the instant case. We do not believe, as the plaintiff contends, that the Uniform Commercial Code intends to not allow the maker of the note to look into the situation and see where title really lies.

DECISION: The appellate court ruled Georgia Klomann could not enforce the notes against the defendant, Sol K. Graff & Sons, because the instruments had not been properly indorsed to Georgia Klomann.

Qualified Indorsements

The two indorsements discussed earlier, in blank and special, are also **unqualified indorsements**. This means that the in-blank or special indorser is promising to pay the holder of the instrument under certain circumstances.

For example, suppose Grace Jones received the $100 note from Smith and then indorsed the note in blank and transferred possession of it to Mary Jones. If Mary Jones attempts to collect from Smith when the note comes due, but Smith refuses to pay, Mary Jones could sue Grace Jones for the $100 because Grace Jones indorsed with an unqualified indorsement.

The unqualified indorser in effect guarantees payment of the instrument if the holder is unable to collect from the maker, drawer, or acceptor when the instrument comes due.

A person who wishes to negotiate an instrument through a **qualified indorsement** does so by adding "without recourse" or similar words to the indorsement as in Figures 28-5 and 28-6. The indorsement in Figure 28-5 is a qualified, in-blank indorsement. The indorsement in Figure 28-6 is a qualified, special indorsement. When Grace Jones signs in either of these ways, she eliminates her

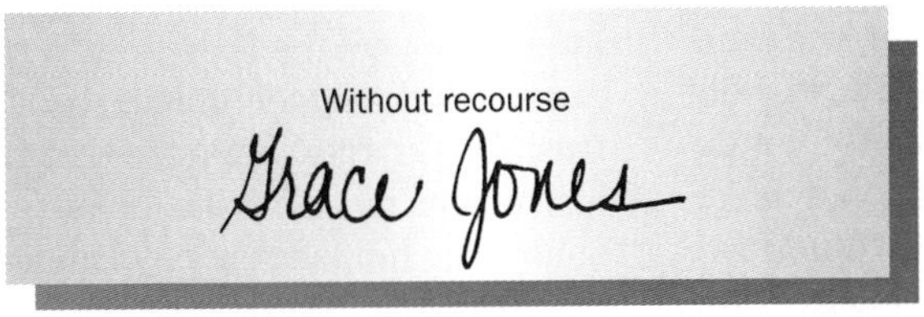

FIGURE 28-5

Qualified,
In-Blank
Indorsement

Without recourse

Grace Jones

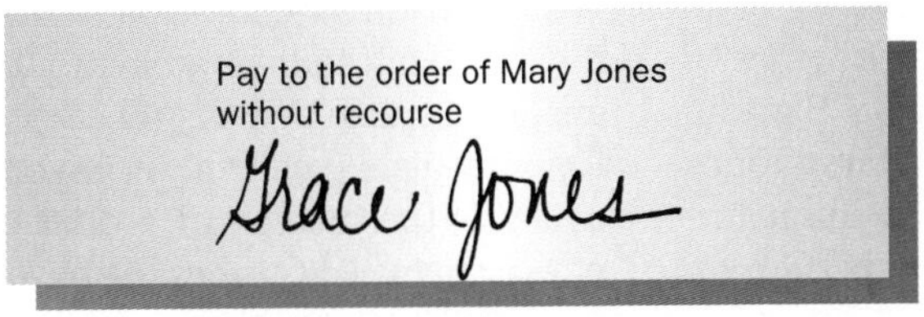

FIGURE 28-6

Qualified,
Special
Indorsement

Pay to the order of Mary Jones
without recourse

Grace Jones

secondary or conditional liability as an indorser. The secondary or conditional liability is the agreement of an unqualified indorser to pay the instrument if the party primarily obligated to pay fails to pay the instrument when it comes due. The concept of secondary liability is discussed in greater depth in the next chapter.

Both a qualified and an unqualified indorser, however, give certain warranties to the persons to whom they transfer their instruments. This warranty liability, which will be discussed in greater detail in the next chapter, is not excluded by signing an instrument with a qualified indorsement (Section 3-415[c]).

Restrictive Indorsements

In addition to in-blank, special, and qualified indorsements, the UCC also creates a category of indorsements called **restrictive indorsements.** The UCC creates several types of restrictive indorsements.

In a departure from the 1952 code, Section 3-206(b) of the 1990 code no longer recognizes a conditional indorsement as a restrictive indorsement. (A conditional indorsement states a condition to the right of the indorsee to receive payment on the instrument.) Such an indorsement is ineffective with respect to *all* parties except the indorser and the indorsee. (The *indorsee* is the party to whom the indorser transfers possession of the instrument.) Suppose that Grace Jones draws a check payable to the order of Annette O'Neil. O'Neil then indorses the check over to Sandra Benson in the following fashion: "Pay to Sandra Benson when she delivers her 1989 Ford to me, (signed) Annette O'Neil." O'Neil then transfers possession of the note to Benson. If Benson presents the check for payment, the bank on which it is written may pay the check without regard to the condition. If Benson has not yet delivered the Ford to O'Neil, but Benson has received payment on the check, O'Neil would have a suit against Benson for her failure to deliver the Ford to O'Neil.

Prohibit Further Transfer Indorsements that attempt to prohibit further transfer of an instrument also are highly uncommon. Such an indorsement might read: "Pay to Mary Jones only." The indorser is attempting to prohibit further transfer of the instrument through such an indorsement. But such an indorsement does not prevent the further transfer or negotiation of the instrument. It is treated as if it were an unrestrictive indorsement.

For Deposit or Collection The most common restrictive indorsement is the indorsement that includes words such as "for collection," "for deposit," "pay any bank," or like terms signifying a purpose of deposit or collection. For example, if Smith gave Jones a check for $100, Jones might indorse the check "For deposit, (signed) Grace Jones." This is an in-blank, restrictive, unqualified indorsement.

The indorsement "pay any bank" specifies that only banks are to receive the proceeds of the instrument. When a person deposits a check to his or her bank account, the bank may restrictively indorse the check in this manner. Only a bank could then become a holder of an instrument so indorsed, unless a bank specially indorsed the check to someone who is not a bank. A bank might use such an indorsement when putting a check through the collection process.

Suppose that a thief steals the check that Jones, in the example above, indorsed "for deposit." The thief cashes the check at a store. The store then deposits the check in an account at the store's bank. As Jones did not receive the amount paid for the check, both the bank and the store are liable for converting the check (Section 3-206[c][1] and [2]). On the other hand, if Jones deposits the check to an account at her bank and her bank credits her account, Jones's bank becomes a holder of the check.

Trust Indorsements A restrictive indorsement that states that it is for the benefit or use of the indorser or another person is a *trust indorsement.* Such an indorsement might read "Pay Lance only in trust for George." Suppose that Lance indorses the instrument in blank and delivers it to a holder for value. The holder may pay Lance without incurring any liability unless the holder has notice of a breach of fiduciary duty as provided in Section 3-307. The same rule applies if Lance delivers the check to a depositary bank for collection. (A **depositary bank** is the first bank to take an item.) The same rule also applies if Lance delivers the check to a *payor* bank for immediate payment. (A **payor bank** is the bank which is the drawee of a draft. If a drawee bank pays a check, it becomes the payor bank.)

Subsequent transferees of the check from a holder or a depositary bank are not affected by the trust indorsement unless they have knowledge that Lance dealt with the check in breach of trust (Section 3-206[d][1]).

Anomalous Indorsement   A person who makes an indorsement who is not a holder of the instrument is an anomalous indorser. Such indorsements are generally made to accommodate a party to an instrument. An anomalous indorsement does not affect the manner in which the instrument may be negotiated (Section 3-205[d]). This means that order paper remains order paper even if someone signs it with an in-blank anomalous indorsement.

Holder in Due Course

In order for a holder of a negotiable instrument to become a holder in due course of the instrument, Section 3-302 requires that:

- The holder must not have taken an instrument that had obviously been forged or altered
- The holder must not have taken an instrument that was obviously irregular or incomplete

Furthermore, the holder must have taken the instrument

- For value
- In good faith
- Without notice the instrument is overdue, has been dishonored, or there was an uncured default
- Without notice the instrument contains an unauthorized signature or has been altered
- Without notice of any defense against the instrument or claim in recoupment
- Without notice of any claim to the instrument

Even if a person in possession of an instrument fulfills the requirements of Section 3-302, he or she still may not qualify as a holder in due course. A person claiming the status of a holder in due course must also establish that he or she holds a *negotiable* instrument and that he or she is a *holder* of the instrument.

The mere fact that a person holds a nonnegotiable instrument does not mean that he or she will not recover. As we noted earlier, the right to receive money is generally assignable to third persons. The only problem for the assignee is that he or she steps into the shoes of the assignor—that is, the assignee acquires only the rights the assignor had. If a defense existed between the original parties to a contract to pay money, that defense may be asserted against the assignee of the contractual right to receive money.

In the event the party originally obligated to pay has no defenses that could have been asserted against the assignor, he or she must pay the assignee. The mere fact that the assignee is in possession of a nonnegotiable instrument is not a defense. If John Smith gives Grace Jones a $100 bearer note, but it in some respect fails to comply with Section 3-104, it is nonnegotiable. Suppose that Jones transferred the note to her daughter Mary. Under these facts it appears that Smith must pay Mary when the note comes due even though the instrument is not negotiable. But what if Jones defrauded Smith? Because John Smith could assert the defense of fraud against Jones (the assignor), he may assert fraud to avoid paying the note against Mary (the assignee).

Instead of a nonnegotiable instrument, suppose the parties were dealing with a negotiable instrument. Smith could refuse to pay Mary, even if the instrument was negotiable, if he could establish that Mary was not a holder of the instrument. Once again, a holder is a person in possession if the instrument is payable to bearer, or in the case of an instrument payable to an identified person, if the identified person is in possession (Section 1-201[20]). If the instrument was not properly negotiated to Mary, she would not qualify as a holder of the instrument. Suppose the original note was negotiable and was payable to the order of Grace Jones (rather than payable to bearer) and Jones delivered the note to Mary but failed to indorse it. Mary is not a holder of the note. In order to negotiate an order instrument, the holder must indorse it and deliver it to someone. Jones failed to indorse the note. (Mary may be able to require Jones to indorse the note but, until Jones indorses it, Mary may not qualify as a holder of the note.)

Assuming that the note is negotiable, and the person attempting to enforce it is a holder, that person may qualify as a holder in due course if he or she otherwise complies with Section 3-302. The following material discusses these requirements.

Forged, Altered, Irregular, and Incomplete Instruments

Section 3-302(a)(1) of the 1990 code makes it clear that a person who takes an instrument that is so irregular or incomplete as to call into question its authenticity is not a holder in due course. A person who takes an instrument that was obviously forged or altered also cannot qualify as a holder in due course. This provision means that a person taking such an instrument takes it subject to the defenses of the obligor or the claims of prior owners.

For Value

According to Section 3-303, a holder satisfies the requirement that he or she takes the instrument for value under the following circumstances:

1. The instrument is issued or transferred for a promise of performance, to the extent the promise has been performed.
2. The transferee acquires a security interest in or lien on the instrument (other than by legal process).
3. The instrument is issued or transferred as payment of or as security for a preexisting claim.
4. The instrument is issued or transferred in exchange for a negotiable instrument.
5. The instrument is issued or transferred in exchange for an irrevocable commitment to a third person by the person taking the negotiable instrument.

Promise of Performance   The issue of a promise of performance is related to whether an instrument was issued for *consideration*. Section 3-303(b) states that an instrument was issued for consideration if it was issued for a promise of performance. For example, suppose that an attorney promises to perform $100,000 in legal services in 1997. The note is issued in January of 1996 and is payable in 1996. The attorney may attempt to enforce the note in 1996 because the note was issued for consideration. The maker of the note does not have a defense in this case because the services need not be performed until 1997.

If an instrument was issued for a promise of performance and the date for performance has passed and the promise has not been performed, the issuer has a defense (Section 3-303[b]). Suppose that the attorney does not perform the services promised in 1997. The attorney then attempts to enforce the instrument in 1998. In this case, the maker of the note has a defense even though the note was issued for consideration.

On the other hand, a holder gives *value* for an instrument to the extent he or she *actually performs* the promise given to the other party (Section 3-303[a][1]). Suppose that an attorney performs $100,000 in legal services and her client gives her a note for $100,000. As the attorney has actually performed the promise given to the client, the attorney has given full value for the instrument and she is a holder in due course for the full amount of the instrument—$100,000.

Suppose that John Smith issues a $100 note payable to the order of Grace Jones. Jones in turn gives the note to Mary, who promises to pay Jones $100 in return for the note. Mary is not a holder in due course of this note because she has not given Jones value in exchange for the note. This is a mere promise to give value. Until Mary pays the $100, she has not given value.

If the holder has only *partly* performed, the holder has the rights of a holder in due course only "to the fraction of the amount payable under the instrument equal to the value of the partial performance divided by the value of the promised performance" (Section 3-302[d]). In other words, the holder has a pro rata right as a holder in due course. Suppose that Anderson negotiates a $1,000 note to Calvin. Calvin promises to pay $900 for the note. Calvin pays $500 to Anderson. Calvin has the rights of a holder in due course to the extent of the *fraction* of the amount payable under the instrument ($1,000) equal to the value of the partial performance ($500) divided by the value of the promised performance ($900). ($500 divided by $900 = .555 × $1,000 = $555.55.) This rather complex formula rewards Calvin, the holder, with a portion of the profit he originally bargained for.

Banks and Value   The mere fact that a person deposits a check in her account and is given a credit by her bank does not mean the bank has given the depositor value. The mere crediting of an account by a bank does not constitute the giving of value.

Under UCC Section 4-211, a bank has given value to the extent it has a security interest in an item if a bank has otherwise complied with the requirements of what constitutes a holder in due course. A bank has a security interest in an item to the extent credit given for an item has been withdrawn (Section 4-210[a][1]).

There may be some question as to whether a depositor has drawn against a particular instrument in light of the fact the depositor may already have some funds in her account when a check is deposited. When the depositor makes a withdrawal from the account, how do we know if the depositor has drawn against the newly deposited check, and not against the funds that were already in the account? Section 4-210(b) adopts a rule that "credits first given are first withdrawn." In other words, the UCC adopts a "first in, first out" rule.

Suppose that Alice gives Frank a check for $100. Frank takes the check to his bank and deposits it on June 1. At that time Frank already has $200 in his account. On June 2 Frank receives another $100 check from Alice, which he deposits to his account that day. On June 3 Frank withdraws $200 from his account. At this point, has the bank given value for either of Alice's checks? No. Because the UCC applies a first-in-first-out rule, the $200 is treated as a withdrawal of the $200 initially in Frank's account. On June 4 Frank withdraws another $100. In this case the bank has now given full value for Alice's first check, which was deposited to Frank's account on June 1. If the bank otherwise complies with Section 3-302, it will be treated as a holder in due course of Alice's first check, which was deposited June 1. On June 5 Alice notifies the bank of a defense on the second check. On June 6 the bank permits Frank to withdraw the final $100 from his account. Has the bank given value for Alice's second check? No. Applying the first in, first out rule, Frank's final $100 withdrawal is treated as a withdrawal against Alice's second check. Because the bank gave value *after* it learned of Alice's defense, it has not given value for the second check and can-

not qualify as a holder in due course of the second check.

Security Interest in Instrument   If a person acquires a security interest in or a lien on an instrument (other than by legal process), he or she takes the instrument for value. Security interests and liens are interests that one has in an obligor's property in order to secure the payment or performance of an obligation. If an obligee has a security interest in or lien on a negotiable instrument, and if the obligor doesn't pay or perform the obligation as agreed, then the obligee may use the negotiable instrument to satisfy the obligation.

Suppose Jane agrees to purchase some goods from a business. The business has some doubts about Jane's capacity to pay for the goods. Jane has a note from Linda in which Linda agrees to pay her $100. If the business sells goods to Jane on credit for $100 and takes the note from Linda to Jane as security for the debt, it has given value for Linda's note. If Jane does not pay for the goods, the business may collect the $100 from Linda since it gave value for Linda's note by taking the note as security for the debt owed by Jane.

It should be noted that Section 3-302(e) states that if the person obliged to pay the instrument has a defense or claim that could be asserted against the person who granted the security interest, "the person entitled to enforce the instrument may assert rights as a holder in due course only to an amount payable under the instrument which, at the time of enforcement of the instrument, does not exceed the amount of the unpaid obligation secured."

For example, suppose that Gibson negotiates a note of Clark's for $1,000 to Anderson as security for payment of Gibson's debt to Anderson of $600. Gibson may be treated as a holder in due course only to the extent of $600. With respect to the other $400, Clark may assert any defense he has against Gibson.

Instrument as Payment or Security for Preexisting Claim   Under UCC Section 3-303(a)(3), a holder is treated as having given value when the holder takes the instrument in payment of or as security for an antecedent (that is, preexisting) claim, whether or not the claim is then due.

Suppose Alice purchases some goods from Jane in March for $100. Several months elapse. In May, Alice gives Jane a $100 note. Jane is treated as having given value for the note. But what if Jane merely asked for some security in May, and Alice gave a $100 note executed by Tom? The UCC treats Jane as having given value for Tom's note. If Alice fails to pay Jane, Jane might attempt to collect on the note from Tom. Jane will be treated as having given value for Tom's note even though she took it as security for an antecedent claim against Alice, and even though she made no additional concessions to Alice at the time she took Tom's note. If Jane otherwise has complied with Section 3-302, she will be treated as a holder in due course of Tom's note and will take the note free of certain defenses Tom might have been able to assert against Alice.

Holder Who Gives a Negotiable Instrument A holder who has given a negotiable instrument in exchange for a second negotiable instrument has, under UCC Section 3-303(a)(4), given value for the second negotiable instrument.

If, for example, Fastbuck Finance Company purchases a pool of consumer installment notes from Short-Circuit City Appliances, Fastbuck will be able to satisfy the "value" requirement if it pays for the notes by check. However, as we shall discuss later in the chapter, certain consumer loans are subject to special rules that substantially erode the standard holder-in-due-course protections.

Irrevocable Commitment to Third Person Section 3-303(a)(5) also provides that a holder has given value if the holder has made an irrevocable commitment to a third person on the basis of the instrument. Suppose Short-Circuit City Appliances gives its bank a $1,000 promissory note. In return, the bank issues a letter of credit in which the bank promises to pay a supplier for goods shipped to Short-Circuit City. Because a letter of credit constitutes an irrevocable commitment by the bank to the supplier, the bank has given value for the $1,000 note.

Note that an irrevocable commitment to a third person satisfies the value requirement even if that

---

ETHICS
Taking an Instrument from a Merchant

Sleazy Appliances sells appliances on an installment payment basis. Sleazy has the buyer sign a sales contract and a promissory note. It then sells the promissory note to a local bank. Sleazy has a reputation for selling broken-down appliances and for being unwilling to uphold its warranties. Sleazy has just sold a full set of appliances to Carla Consumer and has brought Carla's promissory note to National Bank. National has heard about Sleazy's poor reputation.

Is it ethical for National Bank to purchase the note from Sleazy?

In order to acquire the status of a holder in due course a holder must take the note in good faith. One might question whether the bank is acting in good faith. Good faith is a subjective standard that requires honesty in fact in the transaction concerned. Since National Bank knew of no problem with the contract between Carla and Sleazy, it could be said to have acted in good faith. Thus National Bank could take this note as a holder in due course even though it knew of Sleazy's poor reputation. Whether the bank acts ethically in taking such a note is another question. If National has good grounds for believing that Sleazy engages in unethical practices, then it has a professional duty to check out Sleazy before handling promissory notes from Sleazy on a regular basis. The fact that it has some information about Sleazy can be seen as triggering an ethical obligation to look further. Some cautious lawyers might advise the bank not to investigate, because if an investigation turned up specific evidence of improper practices, the bank might lose its ability to be a holder in due course in future transactions. What advice would you give National Bank?

commitment is in the form of an executory promise. Section 3-303(a)(5) thus provides an exception to the general rule that an executory promise does not constitute value.

Good Faith

In a major departure from the 1952 code, the 1990 code redefines *good faith* in Section 3-103(a)(4) as "honesty in fact *and the observance of reasonable commercial standards of fair dealing."* This *objective* test applies to the performance of all duties under Articles 3 and 4. The code thus no longer applies a subjective test for determining whether a person acted in good faith.

Whether an individual took an instrument in good faith is determined at the time of taking the instrument.

Without Notice

We now know that a person, to qualify as a holder in due course, must be the holder of a negotiable instrument who took the instrument for value and in good faith. In order to qualify as a holder in due course, this person must also take the instrument

1. Without notice the instrument is overdue, has been dishonored, or there was an uncured default
2. Without notice the instrument contains an unauthorized signature or has been altered
3. Without notice of any defense or claim in recoupment as described in Section 3-305(a)
4. Without notice of any claim to the instrument as described in Section 3-306

Overdue   A person who acquires an instrument once it is overdue cannot qualify as a holder in due course. A check is overdue 90 days after its date. Other demand instruments are overdue if they have been outstanding for more than a reasonable time. All demand instruments can be overdue at an earlier date if a demand for payment was made. In this case, the instrument is overdue the day after a demand for payment was made (Section 3-304[a]). Suppose that Mark acquires a check 120 days after the date on the check. In this case, Mark has taken the check with notice it is overdue. Mark cannot qualify as a holder in due course of the check.

If an instrument is payable at a definite time, in general, unless the payment of *principal* has been accelerated, it does not become overdue unless there was a default in payment of principal (Section 3-304[c]). Assuming that is not the case, an instrument payable at a definite time is overdue the day after its due date. Suppose that Alice signs a note that is payable on March 1, 2000. Mark acquires this instrument on April 1, 2001. Mark has taken the note with notice it is overdue. Mark cannot qualify as a holder in due course of this note.

Dishonored   In general a dishonor of an instrument occurs when a demand for payment or acceptance has been made and the party expected to pay or accept refuses to do so. Suppose a note payable September 1, 1999, is presented by the payee to the maker on that date. If the maker refuses to pay at that time, there has been a dishonor of the instrument. Anyone who takes the instrument after this date cannot qualify as a holder in due course.

Unauthorized Signature or Alteration   If a person is aware that an instrument contains an unauthorized signature or has been altered, he or she cannot qualify as a holder in due course. Suppose that Mark, at the time he acquires a check, knows that the signature of the drawer was forged. Because Mark has notice of an unauthorized signature, Mark cannot qualify as a holder in due course of the check.

Defenses   Many defenses can be asserted against an instrument. A defense to an instrument is typically something that is asserted as a reason not to pay the instrument. For example, if a person taking a note is aware that the payee defrauded the maker of the note, such a person cannot qualify as a holder in due course.

Claim in Recoupment   One cannot be a holder in due course if one has notice of a claim in recoupment; that is, a claim for damages caused by a breach of contract by the original payee on the instrument. Claims in recoupment are discussed in greater detail in Chapter 29.

Claims   A claim to an instrument is a claim of a property or possession right to the instrument (Section 3-306). A person cannot be aware of such a claim and still qualify as a holder in due course. An example of a claim would be when a person feels he or she has the right to rescind a negotiation and reclaim the instrument.

Discharge Section 3-302(b) states that notice of a discharge of a party, other than a discharge in bankruptcy, is not notice of a defense. However, if a person became a holder in due course of the instrument with notice of the discharge, the discharge may be asserted against the person who became a holder in due course with knowledge of the discharge. The filing of a public notice does not constitute notice of a defense or claim.

Suppose that Mark signed a note for $25,000 payable to the First National Bank. Mark thereafter was discharged from his obligations under this note by the bankruptcy court. A person who has knowledge of this fact is aware of a defense on the instrument. This defense is good even against a holder in due course.

Security Interest in Instrument Suppose that Anderson negotiates a note of Williams for $1,000 to Smith as security for payment of Anderson's debt to Smith of $600. Williams has a defense that is good against Anderson but Smith was unaware of this defense at the time he took the note. Because Williams has a defense that is good

against Anderson, if Smith attempts to enforce Williams's note, Smith can only avail himself of the rights of a holder in due course for the amount Anderson owes to Smith—$600. With respect to the other $400, Williams may assert any defenses that he has against Anderson as a basis for not paying the additional $400 (Section 3-302[e]).

Other Situations Even if all other elements necessary to become a holder in due course have been satisfied, a person will not be treated as a holder in due course if he or she has acquired rights in an instrument by legal process or by purchase in an execution, bankruptcy, or creditor's sale; by purchase in a bulk transaction; or as successor in interest to an estate (Section 3-302[c]).

Contrary State Laws Section 3-302(g) states that the rules with respect to the holder in due course doctrine are subordinate to the many state laws restricting the use of the holder in due course doctrine in consumer transactions as well as certain business transactions.

The following case illustrates the types of factors a court will consider in determining whether a holder has notice of any defense against an instrument. As you read the case, consider the relationship between the good-faith and notice requirements.

SCHWEGMANN BANK & TRUST CO. OF JEFFERSON V. SIMMONS

U.S. Court of Appeals, Fifth Circuit
880 F.2d 838 (1989)

BACKGROUND: Simmons (defendant) invested in the East Pointe Land Partners 1985 Limited Partnership, which was formed to purchase real estate in Texas. Simmons made his investment by executing a promissory note payable to Q-L Investments, the general partner of the East Pointe partnership. Q-L negotiated the note to its related company, Quinn-L Capital Corporation, which in turn negotiated the note to the Bank of Commerce to secure a loan to Quinn-L. Finally, Simmons's note was negotiated by Bank of Commerce to Schwegmann Bank (plaintiff), which had helped to fund certain loans arranged by Bank of Commerce to Quinn-L and related companies. The East Pointe partnership was not fully subscribed; that is, it did not attract the amount of money that it had planned to attract from investors. Two weeks after the Simmons note was negotiated to Schwegmann, Quinn-L filed for bankruptcy. Schwegmann sued Simmons to collect on the note. The federal district court held for Schwegmann, and Simmons appealed.

Jones, Circuit Judge

[W]e begin with the findings of the district court based on uncontroverted summary judgment evidence:

[T]he Simmons note was not overdue and, thus, there could not have been notice to that effect, on April 1, 1986. It is undisputed that there was nothing on the face of the Simmons note to indicate a defense or claim of validity. Moreover, there was no information concerning the business practices of either [Bank of Commerce] or Quinn-L to indicate that the Simmons note was subject to a defense. As indicated above, Sneed [Schwegmann's President] believed that the history of Quinn-L in repaying loans on a short term basis had been good.

Yet, Simmons alleges that Schwegmann knew certain facts which provided Schwegmann with notice of Simmons's three defenses to the note: failure of consideration; federal securities law violations; and fraud. We disagree; the facts alleged could not alert Schwegmann to any such defenses nor do they create a material fact issue as to whether Schwegmann acted in bad faith.

The facts that Schwegmann was supposed to have known fall into one or more of three categories: (1) the fruition of a known investment risk; (2) contingencies contemplated and disclosed in the East Pointe Prospectus; or (3) evidence that Q-L or Quinn-L was in a poor economic condition. None of these facts, individually or together, raise an inference that Dr. Simmons was defrauded, that the securities laws had been violated, or that there had been a failure of consideration. We shall discuss each fact in turn.

That the East Pointe limited partnership might never be fully subscribed was a known investment risk disclosed in the East Pointe Prospectus. The fact that it was not fully subscribed at the time Schwegmann Bank assumed the Simmons note, or that there were plans to refinance the East Pointe project, yields no notice of fraud and no defense to payment of the note. Schwegmann had no duty to inquire further into why this project was not yet fully subscribed.

Even assuming that the Quinn-L note and other Quinn-L loans funded by the Bank of Commerce were delinquent when Schwegmann purchased Simmons's note, that provides no notice of defenses Simmons may have had on his note. At most, that is some indication that Quinn-L may have been experiencing financial difficulties. As the district court stated, "[m]ere knowledge of poor financial health of the debtor does not preclude a subsequent debtor from obtaining holder in due course status." The same analysis applies to the alleged fact that the Bank of Commerce president believed that "Quinn-L had not adequately responded to his inquiries regarding the use of the funds loaned under the Quinn-L note." Schwegmann Bank did investigate these matters, and Simmons does not dispute that Schwegmann was satisfied at the time it acquired his note that most of the proceeds of the loan were on deposit at the Texas American Bank.

The fact that the note of one limited partner (Sirbasku) was delinquent in another limited partnership which jointly secured the Quinn-L note would not alert Schwegmann that Simmons had any defenses to his note for the East Pointe partnership.

The East Pointe Prospectus provided that outside financing might be required and that mortgages and liens might have to be granted in exchange for the outside financing. The East Pointe Prospectus also provided that entities related to Quinn-L had the right to borrow funds from the partnership. The fact that these contingencies came to pass does not indicate failure of consideration, securities law violation, or fraud.

Finally, Simmons alleges that Schwegmann knew that the Bank of Commerce had filed a $2.5 million suit against the Ricou-Brewster partnership run by the same promoters. This is, again, notice that another Quinn-L related company was having financial difficulty. The relationship, if any, to the Simmons note and any potential defenses to its payment is extremely tenuous and is not developed in the record by Simmons. If knowledge of Quinn-L's financial condition is insufficient to constitute actual knowledge of Simmons's claimed defenses, then knowledge of a related company's financial difficulty is equally insufficient.

Besides these facts, Simmons alleges that the Bank of Commerce President sent a letter to Schwegmann asserting that the Simmons note was not in default. Simmons claims that this is evidence of bad faith on the part of Schwegmann since the representations were drafted in large part by a Schwegmann attorney with the intention of whitewashing Simmons's defenses and creating a fraudulent impression of good faith. Yet, the letter only recites three uncontested representations, and the only reference to the Simmons note is that none of "the notes serving as collateral for the [loan are] in default," with the exception of the Sirbasku note. That statement is true; its inclusion cannot serve as evidence of bad faith. The author of the letter is immaterial.

There is simply no evidence that Schwegmann acted in bad faith or had any notice of Simmons's claimed defenses. Schwegmann did investigate the use of funds advanced to Quinn-L, and there are no facts that should have led Schwegmann to inquire further than it did. The facts, moreover, do not suggest that Schwegmann deliberately evaded learning information that would have supplied claims or defenses by Simmons against payment of his note. We conclude that there is no genuine issue of material fact concerning Schwegmann's holder in due course status.

DECISION: The court of appeals affirmed the decision for Schwegmann.

Shelter Provision

While a person who holds an instrument may not qualify as a holder in due course, he or she may have all the rights of a holder in due course. The so-called **shelter provision** of the UCC, found in Section 3-203(b), states that the "transfer of an instrument vests in the transferee such rights as the transferor had therein." The drafters of the UCC adopted this provision to encourage the free transferability of negotiable instruments.

The result of the shelter provision is that a person who for one reason or another does not qualify as a holder in due course may nonetheless acquire the *rights* of a holder in due course. Such a person can acquire the rights of a holder in due course if the party that transferred the note to such person was a holder in due course, or if someone else further back in the chain of possession was a holder in due course.

TABLE 28-1

Requirements for Holder-in-Due-Course Status

1. Holder must take the instrument *for value*. This can be accomplished by:
   - Performing the agreed performance
   - Acquiring a security interest in or lien on the instrument (other than by legal process)
   - Taking the instrument as payment of or security for a preexisting claim
   - Giving a negotiable instrument
   - Making an irrevocable commitment to a third party
2. Holder must take the instrument in *good faith*. An objective standard is used.

3. Holder must take the instrument *without notice*.
   - That instrument is overdue
   - That that instrument has been dishonored or there was an uncured default
   - That the instrument contains an unauthorized signature or has been altered
   - Of any defense against it or claim in recoupment
   - Of any claim to it
4. The instrument must not have been obviously forged or altered.
5. The instrument must not have been obviously irregular or incomplete.

For example, assume that Millard accepts a $20,000 promissory note from Monroe as payment for Millard's BMW. Rather than deliver the BMW to Monroe as agreed, Millard drives it to his new home in southern Mexico. Before fleeing, however, Millard negotiates the note to Simpson, who qualifies as a holder in due course. Simpson negotiates the note to Millard's brother, Carlyle, who is aware of (but did not participate in) Millard's misdeed. Because Carlyle has notice of a defense against the note, he cannot qualify as a holder in due course. But Carlyle *does* acquire all of the rights that his transferee, Simpson, had in the note. Since Simpson was a holder in due course, Carlyle, under the shelter principle, acquires the *rights* of a holder in due course. Carlyle will therefore take the note free of Monroe's defense, even though Carlyle knew of the defense. Furthermore, anyone to whom Carlyle negotiates the note will acquire all of the rights that Carlyle had—the rights of a holder in due course.

There are limits to the shelter principle. A person who was actually a party to any fraud or illegality affecting the instrument cannot acquire the rights of a holder in due course.

Payee As a Holder in Due Course

A holder in due course occupies a very special position: He or she takes an instrument free of any claim of legal title or liens. Furthermore, the holder in due course generally takes the instrument free from all defenses of any party to the instrument (excluding a limited set of defenses discussed in the next chapter).

The original payee of a negotiable instrument can qualify as a holder in due course, as illustrated in the case that follows. This case also illustrates the benefits of holder-in-due-course status.

AMERICAN FEDERAL BANK, FSB v. PARKER

Court of Appeals of South Carolina
392 S.E.2d 798 (1990)

BACKGROUND: American Federal entrusted Kirkman, a horse dealer, with blank promissory notes. Kirkman was to use the notes to enable his customers to finance purchases of horses. Kirkman deceived Parker into signing an American Federal promissory note in blank. Parker thought that he and Kirkman were together borrowing $35,000 to finance their purchase of a horse. But once Kirkman had obtained Parker's signature on the note, he filled it in for $85,000, pocketed the extra $50,000 and disappeared. Contrary to his promise to Parker, Kirkman did not cosign the note. Parker was thus left as the sole obligor on an $85,000 note payable to American Federal. Parker repaid $35,000, the amount he thought he was borrowing, but refused to pay the additional $50,000. American Federal sued Parker to collect the balance. The trial court ruled in favor of American Federal, and Parker appealed.

Cureton, Judge

Parker executed a promissory note in blank. Under the Uniform Commercial Code the maker of a note agrees to pay the instrument according to its tenor at the time of engagement or as completed pursuant to Section 36-3-115 on incomplete instruments. . . . If the completion of an instrument is unauthorized the rules as to material alteration apply. . . . The completion of an incomplete instrument otherwise than as authorized is considered an alteration. A subsequent holder in due course may enforce an incomplete instrument as completed. . . . Where blanks are filled or an incomplete instrument is otherwise completed the loss is placed upon the party who left the instrument incomplete and the holder is permitted to enforce it according to its completed form.

We agree with the trial court that no jury issue is created and the bank was entitled to the directed verdicts. The responsibility for the situation rests with Parker. He and Kirkman negotiated their deal. Parker signed a blank promissory note. He relied upon Kirkman to co-sign the note and fill it in for $35,000. Parker's negligence substantially contributed to the material alteration as a matter of law. *Cf. Burwell v. South Carolina National Bank* (experienced businessman had responsibility to be aware of contents of documents before he signed them). Parker argues it was not reasonable commercial practice for American Federal to give Kirkman possession of blank promissory notes. After the fact, Parker argues the bank should have contacted him or checked to be sure everything was correct before disbursing the proceeds of the loan to Kirkman. There is no evidence in the record to establish the bank had any reason to inquire into the facial validity of the note. The note was complete when presented to the bank and there were no obvious alterations on it. The bank loan officer had known Kirkman for several years. He also had met Parker in the past and knew Parker was in the horse business. Further, there was testimony that banking practices do not prohibit execution of promissory notes outside of the bank in some cases although it is not a routine practice.

The record establishes American Federal took the note in good faith and without notice of any defense to it by Parker. American Federal gave value for the note when it disbursed the funds to Kirkman. As a holder in due course, American Federal may enforce the note against Parker as completed.

DECISION: The court of appeals affirmed the decision in favor of American Federal.

Breach of Fiduciary Duty

A *fiduciary* is a representative of another party, such as a trustee of a trust or the officer of a corporation, who owes a duty of trust and confidence to the represented person who may be the beneficiary of a trust or a corporation or someone to whom a duty of trust and confidence is owed (Sections 3-307[a][1] and [2]).

An important issue with respect to the breach of fiduciary duty relates to the question of whether the taker of an instrument who takes an instrument from a fiduciary takes the instrument as a holder in due course. If the taker qualifies as a holder in due course, the taker is not subject to any claims or defenses of the represented party. Section 3-307 attempts to clarify the issue of when a party has notice of a breach of fiduciary duty and thus does not qualify as a holder in due course.

The typical scenario involves a fiduciary who embezzles money that belongs to the represented person. The fiduciary takes an instrument that belongs to the represented person and uses the proceeds of the instrument for the personal benefit of the fiduciary. When the represented person discovers this breach of fiduciary duty the fiduciary is replaced. A suit is then brought against the bank that took the instrument for collection or paid value for the instrument. If it can be established that the party taking the instrument was aware of the breach of the fiduciary duty owed to the represented person, the taker of the instrument is subject to any defenses that can be asserted by the represented person. Notice to the taker of the fiduciary's breach is considered to be notice of the claim of the represented person (Section 3-307[b][1]).

Section 3-307(b)(2) states that if the instrument was either payable to the represented person or was payable to the fiduciary, then the taker is presumed to have notice of the breach of the fiduciary duty if

1. The instrument was taken in payment of or as security for a debt known by the taker to be a personal debt of the fiduciary
2. The instrument was taken in a transaction known by the taker to be for the personal benefit of the fiduciary
3. The instrument was deposited in an account other than an account of the fiduciary, as such, or an account of the represented person

Suppose that a guardian takes an instrument made payable to the person as guardian for the represented person. The guardian then deposits the check to his personal account. One would not normally expect an instrument of this character to be used for the personal benefit of the guardian. A bank which takes this check cannot qualify as a holder in due course and thus is subject to any claim of the represented person (Section 3-307[b][2]).

The following case deals with just such an abuse of power by a father who was a guardian for his son.

SMITH V. OLYMPIC BANK

The Supreme Court of Washington
969 P.2d 92 (1985)

BACKGROUND: Charles Alcombrack was appointed guardian for his son Chad Alcombrack who was then 7 years old and the beneficiary of his grandfather's life insurance policy. The insurance company issued a check for $30,588.39 payable to "Charles Alcombrack, Guardian of the Estate of Chad Stephen Alcombrack, a Minor." The attorney for the son's estate directed the father to open up a guardianship checking account. Instead, the father opened up a personal checking account at the bank. The following was printed on the back of the check:

> By endorsement of this check the payee acknowledges receipt of the amount thereof in full settlement of all claims resulting from the death of Roy Alcombrack, certificate holder under Group Life Policy No. 9,745,632 /s/ Charles Alcombrack Guardian of the Estate of Chad Stepen Alcombrack, a minor

In spite of this written notice on the check, the bank allowed the father to place the entire amount in a personal checking account. The father and his new wife used all but $320.60 of the trust money for their own personal benefit.

After the depletion of the son's estate, J. David Smith was appointed successor guardian. He received a judgment against the father and instituted suit against the bank. The trial court granted a judgment for the bank.

Dore, Justice

Olympic Bank claims that it is a holder in due course (HIDC) and, as such, is not subject to the claims of the petitioner.

The issue raised by this case is whether the bank had knowledge that the guardian was breaching his fiduciary duty when it allowed him to deposit a check, made payable to him in his guardianship capacity, into his personal accounts. As to this issue, *Von Gohren v. Pacific Nat'l Bank* is persuasive and controlling. In *Von Gohren*, it was held that a bank had notice that an employee was breaching her fiduciary duty when it allowed her to deposit third-party checks payable to her employer in her personal account. The bank was put on notice despite the fact that the employer had authorized the employee to draw checks against his account and also to endorse checks made payable to him and deposit such checks into his account. The court held that notice need not always consist of actual knowledge of a breach of a fiduciary duty, but can be predicated upon reasonable commercial standards. The court concluded by stating:

> It is our view that since defendant had notice of the claim . . . and since it is undisputed that defendant did nothing to investigate Mrs. Martin's authority to negotiate checks payable to her employer, we must hold as a matter of law it did not act in accordance with reasonable commercial standards. The same conclusion is mandated in the present case.

Here, the bank knew it was dealing with guardianship funds. The check was payable to the father as guardian and not to him personally. The father endorsed it in his guardianship capacity. The bank received a call from the guardian's attorney inquiring about the fee the bank charged for guardianship accounts, and a trust officer for the bank replied in a letter referring to the "Estate of Chad Alcombrack".

While this is the first time, under the Uniform Commercial Code, that we have held a bank liable for allowing a guardian to deposit trust funds in a personal account, we have held a bank liable in a pre-Code case for allowing a trustee to breach his fiduciary duty.

The Court of Appeals 37 Wash.App. 117, 678 P.2d 845 is reversed and this case is remanded to the trial court to render a judgment in favor of the guardian in the amount of $30,267.79 plus prejudgment interest at the rate of 6 percent per annum from October 28, 1975 to July 21, 1981; commencing July 22, 1981 such judgment shall accrue interest at the rate of 12 percent per annum.

DECISION: The Supreme Court of Washington reversed and entered a judgment for the guardian.

The taker is also presumed to have notice of the breach of fiduciary duty if the instrument was issued by the fiduciary or the represented party to the taker as payee and one of the three points listed above occurs (Section 3-307[b][4]).

For example, suppose that the fiduciary takes a corporate check and makes the check payable to the taker as payee. The fiduciary uses the check to pay a personal debt. The taker cannot qualify as a holder in due course.

Suppose that an instrument is issued by the represented person or issued by the fiduciary, and is made payable to the fiduciary personally. This is a common situation. For example, businesses often do this to pay money they owe to their employees. Therefore, if the president of Smith Corporation makes a check payable to himself and he deposits the check in his personal account, these facts do *not* put the bank on notice of a breach of fiduciary duty unless the bank has notice of the wrongdoing (Section 3-307[b][3]).

Modification of the HDC Doctrine

The holder-in-due-course doctrine has largely succeeded in promoting the free transfer of negotiable instruments, but it caused unwanted side-effects in the area of consumer finance.

Consumers typically finance the purchase of major items by executing consumer credit contracts, which are actually installment promissory notes payable to the dealer. The dealer will then typically "discount" the note to a finance company or bank—that is, sell the note for a lump

sum price that reflects the present value of the expected stream of payments from the consumer. Alternatively, the dealer may arrange for the bank or finance company to loan the purchase money directly to the consumer.

Problems often arose in cases where the goods were defective, and the dealer was unwilling or unable to repair or replace the goods. The finance company or bank holding the consumer's installment note would typically be a holder in due course, entitled to payment regardless of any defenses that the consumer might have had against the dealer. And in the worst cases, the dealer would, by the time the consumer could get around to bringing a legal action, be "judgment-proof"—bankrupt or even disappeared without a trace. The consumer might then be stuck having to pay in full for goods of no value.

In order to remedy this situation, the Federal Trade Commission (FTC) in the mid-1970s promulgated a rule that substantially erodes the holder-in-due-course doctrine in the area of consumer finance. Several states have enacted consumer protection legislation that similarly limits the doctrine.

The FTC rule requires each *seller* (but not the lender) of consumer goods to print on each consumer credit contract, in large, bold-faced type, a notice that states in part that "any holder of this consumer credit contract is subject to all claims and defenses which the debtor could assert against the seller of goods or services obtained pursuant hereto or with the proceeds hereof." A *seller* is required to ensure that a similar notice is printed on

---

ISSUES AND TRENDS
Destruction of Holder-in-Due-Course Doctrine

The abuses of the holder-in-due-course doctrine and the resulting injury to consumers have led to modification of the holder-in-due-course doctrine by the Federal Trade Commission. Another effective means of contesting the status of a holder is to utilize the provisions of the Uniform Consumer Credit Code (UCCC)—if it has been adopted in the state in question. At the present time the UCCC has been adopted in a small number of states. The scope of the act extends only to consumer credit transactions.

In the states that have adopted the UCCC there is a virtual elimination of the holder-in-due-course doctrine as it applies to consumer credit transactions. This is accomplished by two sections of the UCCC, Sections 3-307 and 3-404. Section 3-307 states that in consumer credit sales or consumer leases, the seller may not take a negotiable instrument other than a check dated not later than 10 days after its issuance. Section 3-404 states that an assignee of the rights of the seller or lessor is subject to all claims and defenses of the consumer against the seller, notwithstanding the fact that the assignee has the status of a holder in due course. In UCCC states a consumer's claims and defenses are not avoided by transferring the instrument to a third party who qualifies as a holder in due course.

---

the credit contract in cases where the seller is paid from the proceeds of a loan made directly by the bank or finance company to the consumer. However, this notice is required only if there is an affiliation between the seller and the lender.

The effect of the FTC requirement, of course, is to prevent the holder of a consumer credit contract from enjoying the rights of a holder in due course. If the consumer has a legitimate defense against the seller, the consumer can assert that defense against the bank or finance company as well.

Keep in mind that the FTC rule, as well as most state consumer protection laws, apply only to the purchase of goods intended for personal, family, or household use.

The FTC puts the onus on the *seller* to ensure that required notice is properly printed on (1) any consumer credit contract that the seller requires a consumer to sign, and (2) any consumer credit

contract the proceeds of which are used to reimburse the seller for goods sold to a consumer. A seller's failure to ensure that the notice is printed as required constitutes an unfair trade practice under the Federal Trade Commission Act.

What would happen if a consumer were to execute a consumer credit contract that did *not* contain the required legend and the contract was negotiated to a holder in due course? Clearly, the seller would be subject to sanction by the FTC.

It should be noted that the FTC language does not make a promise or order conditional. Therefore, an instrument with this language can be a negotiable instrument. Consequently, the rules of Article 3 govern the interpretation of an instrument with this language (Section 3-106 [d]). However, holders of such instruments *cannot* be holders in due course of the instruments. The following case discusses how the FTC rule operates.

TINKER V. DE MARIA PORSCHE AUDI, INC.

District Court of Appeal of Florida
459 So.2d 487 (1984)

BACKGROUND: Gerald Tinker (plaintiff) commenced this action against De Maria Porsche Audi, Inc. and Central National Bank of Miami (defendants). He alleged fraud and misrepresentation on the part of De Maria in connection with his purchase of a used Jaguar sports car. The bank counterclaimed for the unpaid balance due on the installment loan contract executed by Tinker for the purchase of the vehicle.

In 1976 Tinker purchased a 1972 Jaguar from De Maria. A salesman verbally represented to Tinker, prior to the sale, that the car was in good operating condition, was powered by its original engine, and had never been in a major collision. Tinker had problems with the car immediately after he purchased it. The car operated poorly and Tinker soon discovered that it was not powered by its original engine and had previously been "totaled" in a major collision.

In connection with the purchase of the vehicle Tinker executed a retail installment contract and note with De Maria. The Central National Bank provided financing for De Maria on a floor-plan basis and the installment contract and note were assigned to the bank pursuant to a preprinted assignment clause contained in the contract. Tinker never dealt with the bank prior to delivery of the car. The installment sales contract contained the following legend:

NOTICE

ANY HOLDER OF THIS CONSUMER CREDIT CONTRACT IS SUBJECT TO ALL CLAIMS AND DEFENSES WHICH THE DEBTOR COULD ASSERT AGAINST THE SELLER OF THE GOODS OR SERVICES OBTAINED PURSUANT HERETO OR WITH THE PROCEEDS HEREOF. RECOVERY HEREUNDER BY THE DEBTOR SHALL NOT EXCEED AMOUNTS PAID BY THE DEBTOR HEREUNDER.

When De Maria failed to replace or successfully repair the car after it became totally inoperable, Tinker ceased making payments to the bank and sued to recover. The trial court found for the defendants De Maria Porsche Audi and Central National Bank of Miami. Tinker appealed.

Ferguson, Judge

Whether the jury's finding of fraud by De Maria is, as contended by Tinker, an absolute defense to the Bank's counterclaim for the balance owed on the contract, depends on the legal efficacy of the "Notice" provision which was included. Appellant expressed some uncertainty at trial as to how the provision operates. . . .

The Notice is required by federal law in all consumer credit contracts made in connection with purchase money loans, such as installment sales contracts where the consumer executes the sales agreement together with a promissory note, both of which are, through a preprinted assignment clause, assigned to a bank which is closely affiliated with the seller. The effect of the federal rule is to defeat the holder in due course status of the assignee institutional lender, thus removing the lender's insulation from claims and defenses which could be asserted against the seller by the consumer.

Prior to the passage of the rule, consumers were caught in a "no-win" situation when the seller failed to remedy the defect either because of its unwillingness or its disappearance from the market. The institutional lenders then took advantage of protections under the holder in due course doctrine when the consumer sought to assert seller misconduct as a defense to the creditor's suit for payment on the note. The rule is expressly designed to compel creditors to either absorb seller misconduct costs or seek reimbursement of those costs from sellers.

DECISION: The court of appeal ruled for Tinker.

It is clear that not only does the FTC notice clause entitle the buyer to withhold the balance of the purchase price owed to the creditor when the seller's contractual duties are not fulfilled, but it gives the buyer a complete defense should the creditor sue for payment.

Review Questions and Problems

Key Terms

personal defense	unqualified indorsement
negotiation	qualified indorsement
holder	restrictive indorsement
allonge	indorsement
blank indorsement	depositary bank
special indorsement	payor bank
anomalous indorsement	shelter provision
good faith	

Discussion Questions

1. What must a person do to negotiate an order-negotiable instrument? If the negotiable instrument is a bearer instrument, what must the person do to negotiate it?

2. What is a special indorsement? How does a person negotiate an instrument with a special indorsement?

3. In what respect, if any, has the FTC altered the holder-in-due-course doctrine?

Review Problems

1. On June 1 Morris takes a note that was payable to the order of Katz. Katz, a holder in due course of the note, indorsed and delivered the note to Morris. At that time Morris was aware that the note was overdue. Is Morris a holder in due course?

2. If a person takes an instrument under suspicious circumstances, does this mean that he cannot be a holder in due course of that instrument?

3. Talbot has $500 in his checking account at the First National Bank as of July 1. Talbot deposits a check from Smith for $250 to his account on July 2. On July 7 the bank permits Talbot to withdraw $200 from his account. On July 8 the bank allows him to withdraw $300 from his account. On July 9 it allows Talbot to withdraw the remaining $250 from his account. When, if ever, did the bank give value for Smith's check?

4. Scott Smith signed a note for $1,000 payable to the order of Yvonne Kennedy. Yvonne in turn transferred the note to Renee Clark, who gave Yvonne a check for $1,000 in return for the note. Has Renee given value for the note?

5. Christian Hughes indorsed the back of an instrument that was payable to his order as follows: "Without recourse, Christian Hughes." What type of indorsement is this, and why would a person indorse an instrument in this fashion?

6. A note was executed as follows: "Boston, Massachusetts, January 1, 1995. On demand I promise to pay to the order of Randy Davidson One Hundred and no/100 Dollars. Payable at the First National Bank of Boston (signed) Pamela Hyde." Pamela issued this note to Randy. Randy in turn indorsed the note on the back as follows: "Pay to the order of Rose Davidson (signed) Randy Davidson." He then delivered the note to his wife, Rose Davidson. Identify this indorsement and explain the consequences of using such an indorsement.

Case Problems

1. Yvonne Lowe signed the following note: "San Antonio, Texas, January 1, 1995. On demand I promise to pay to the order of Donna Sylvester One Hundred and no/100 Dollars. Payable at the First National Bank of San Antonio (signed) Yvonne Lowe." Yvonne issued this note to Donna. Soon thereafter a thief stole the note and sold it to an innocent purchaser. Did the innocent purchaser get a good title to this instrument? Would it make any difference if the note had been payable to bearer rather than to the order of Donna Sylvester?

2. Pazol drew a check on Fulton National Bank for payment to Eidson. Eidson deposited the check into his account at Sandy Springs Bank. On the same day Eidson withdrew the amount of the check from his account. On the next day Sandy Springs discovered the dishonorment of this check. Sandy Springs claims it is a holder in due course and demands payment from Pazol. Pazol claims Sandy Springs does not qualify as a holder in due course because it gave no value for the check. Is Sandy Springs a holder in due course?

3. Murphy gave a $15,000 check on September 27 to Brownsworth. Murphy thereafter decided Brownsworth had defrauded him, and Murphy on September 28 stopped payment on the check. Brownsworth on the morning of September 28 went to a branch bank of Manufacturers. The manager vaguely knew Brownsworth, but he still called Murphy's bank to verify that the money was in the account. This transaction took place prior to Murphy stopping payment on the check. Manufacturers cashed the check. When Manufacturers was unable to collect, because of the stop-payment order, Manufacturers brought suit on the check. Murphy

argued that the bank was not a holder in due course because of a lack of good faith. By cashing the check for a person who was not a regular customer, Murphy argued, Manufacturers was not acting in good faith. Is Murphy correct?

4. Pappas purchased a carpet from Allo. Allo held up the delivery of the carpet. Allo asked Pappas to contact Jaeger. Based on the phone call, it became apparent that Allo owed Jaeger some money. In order to get the carpet released, Pappas sent a check for $6,500 to Allo, who indorsed it and forwarded the check to Jaeger. Pappas at no time stated he was placing any conditions on the check. The next day, because of a dispute with Allo, Pappas stopped payment on the check. The carpet in the meantime was released to Pappas. Pappas's check was returned to Jaeger marked "payment stopped." Pappas claimed that someone who takes a negotiable instrument cannot ignore facts which indicate the possibility of a defense good against it. Did Pappas have a good defense for stopping payment on the check?

29

Negotiable Instruments: Liability, Defenses, and Discharge

Liability
Warranty Liability

Defenses
Discharge

C hapters 27 and 28 discussed the different types of negotiable instruments as well as the significant legal doctrines that support negotiable instruments as a vital component of the economy of the United States. This chapter investigates further the liability of parties who use negotiable instruments in business transactions and the defenses available against honoring them. This chapter concludes with a discussion of the ways in which an obligation on a negotiable instrument may be discharged.

Liability

Section 3-401(a) of the 1990 code provides that no person is liable on an instrument unless (1) he or she signed the instrument or (2) the instrument was signed on behalf of a person by an agent or representative and the signature of the agent was binding on the person represented.

A signature may be made manually or with any symbol executed with an intention to authenti-

cate the writing (Section 3-401 [b]). A signature thus need not be the handwritten name of a natural person. It can be typed, printed, marked, or made in any other manner, so long as the signing party has, at the time, the intention to authenticate the writing.

Assume that Joe Bleau receives his paycheck and takes it to his bank. Bleau may indorse the check by affixing his thumbprint to it, provided that he does so with the intention of indorsing it. The bank, of course, may as a matter of policy refuse to accept a check indorsed in that manner. The point is that Bleau's thumbprint in this case makes him as liable on the instrument as he would have been had he signed his name on it.

Types of Signature

Signature by an Authorized Representative In commercial transactions, it is frequently necessary for authorized representatives to sign instruments on behalf of others. This is always true in the case of a corporation, which is not a natural person and can only act through its officers, directors, and other authorized representatives. Chapter 27 included a detailed discussion of the rules that apply when an authorized representative signs a negotiable instrument on behalf of his or her principle. A person intending to sign an instrument in a representative capacity must be careful to not inadvertently make himself or herself liable on the instrument.

Forged or Unauthorized Signatures

An unauthorized signature, according to Section 3-403 (a), is not treated as the valid signature of the person whose name is signed. This general rule is subject to certain exceptions. Before discussing the exceptions, let us look at some examples of unauthorized signatures.

The most obvious type of unauthorized signature is a forged signature. Assume, for example, that Fred Smith receives a check made payable to George Bush. Fred cashes the check and forges George Bush's name. Fred's forged signature will not be effective to bind the real George Bush to the check. In fact, Section 3-403 (a) provides that "an unauthorized signature is ineffective except as the signature of the unauthorized signer in favor of a person who in good faith pays the instrument or takes it for value." By paying the check the bank has given value for the check. The bank can enforce the check against Fred.

Another type of unauthorized signature is one in which the signer does not actually have the authority that he or she purports to have. Suppose, for example, that Gene Jones impersonates the president of Widgetco, Inc. and applies for a loan from Gullible Bank. If Gene signs a promissory note "Gene Jones, as president of Widgetco, Inc.," his signature is not effective to bind Widgetco to the terms of the note. And if Gullible Bank gave value for the instrument in good faith, it would be entitled to treat the note as if Jones had signed it on his own behalf. Section 1-201 (43) also defines an "unauthorized" signature as one that includes a signature made by one exceeding actual or apparent authority.

If an organization requires that more than one person sign in its name and one of the requisite signatures is lacking, the signature of the organization is unauthorized (Section 3-403 [b]. For example, suppose that Acme Corporation requires the signature of Paul Adams, the president of Acme, and June Smith, the vice president, on every check. If a corporate check has only Paul Adams's signature on it, the signature of the *corporation* is unauthorized. Likewise, if Paul Adams signs the check, then forges the signature of June Smith on the check, the signature of the *corporation* is unauthorized.

Section 3-403 (b) refers to the authorized signature of an organization. Section 1-208 (28) defines the term "organization" as, among other things, "two or more persons having a joint or common interest." Therefore, if the signature of both a husband and a wife are required on an instrument, the signature is unauthorized if either of their signatures is lacking.

The following case deals with the question of whether a corporate check which is missing one of the required signatures is unauthorized.

KNIGHT COMMUNICATIONS V. BOATMEN'S NATIONAL BANK

Missouri Court of Appeals, Eastern District
805 S.W. 2d 199 (1991)

BACKGROUND: In 1985 two couples, the Browns and the Knights, formed a business called Knight Communications. The signature card agreement for the corporate checking account required the signature of one of the Browns and one of the Knights. In spite of this fact, the bank began honoring checks with the signatures of only one or both of the Knights, but without the signature of either of the Browns. When this was discovered, the Knights brought suit against Boatmen's Bank. The trial court ruled that the signature on these checks was authorized.

Carl R. Gaertner, Judge

No Missouri cases have determined whether the absence of a required signature constitutes an unauthorized signature. A majority of jurisdictions addressing the issue conclude that when a check requires two or more signatures, the lack of any one of them is an unauthorized signature.

The contract between the corporation and the bank authorized payment of a check containing two signatures. Therefore, anything less than the required combination was an "unauthorized" signature.

We hold that a missing but necessary drawer signature constitutes an "unauthorized signature."

DECISION: The Missouri Court of Appeals ruled that the signatures on these checks were unauthorized.

Effective or Operative Unauthorized Signatures

There are exceptions to the general rule that a forged or unauthorized signature is inoperative.

Ratification If the person whose name has been signed without authority later *ratifies* the unauthorized signature, then the signature becomes an effective signature (Section 3-403[a]).

A ratification can be express, as in the case where the person tells the holder that he or she retroactively approves of the signature even though it was made without authorization. Ratification can also occur through conduct, such as retaining the benefits of the transaction knowing that the signature was unauthorized.

If an unauthorized signature is ratified, the person whose name is signed incurs whatever liability that person would have had on the instrument if the signature had been authorized in the first place.

The ratification relieves the unauthorized signer of any liability *on the instrument*. However, the unauthorized signer might still be held liable in a separate tort action to the person whose name was signed without authority; and the person might still be held criminally liable for forgery or other offenses.

Imposter Rule The **imposter rule**, set forth in Section 3-404(a), is another exception to the rule that unauthorized signatures are inoperative. This rule holds that if a person pretends to be someone else and convinces a drawer or maker to issue an instrument to the person being impersonated, the imposter has the power to indorse the instrument in the name of the impersonated person.

For example, suppose a construction business owes a debt to a subcontractor, Mike Adams. Bill, after learning of this debt, goes to the company's bookkeeper posing as Mike Adams. The bookkeeper makes out a check to Mike Adams and gives it to Bill. Bill takes the check to a bank, indorses it as "Mike Adams," and collects the amount of the check from the bank. Under the imposter rule, Bill's phony indorsement is nonetheless effective. The company will not be able to recover the funds from the bank. Additionally, the 1990 code recognizes as valid the indorsement of an imposter who impersonates an agent authorized to act for the payee (Section 3-404[a]). Suppose that Pierson is the President of Acme Corporation. An imposter impersonates Pierson and takes a check from a drawer payable to the order of Acme Corporation. The imposter can negotiate the check.

The rationale for the imposter rule is that the loss should be placed on the party in the best position to avoid it in the first place: the drawer of the draft or the maker of the note. The drawer or maker is in a better position to spot the imposter than is a later holder of the instrument. Therefore the UCC treats the indorsement of the imposter just as if the rightful payee had indorsed the instrument.

Clients' Security Fund v. Allstate Insurance Company provides a good discussion of what the imposter rule is—and what it is not.

CLIENTS' SECURITY FUND V. ALLSTATE INSURANCE COMPANY

Superior Court of New Jersey, Appellate Division
530 A.2d 357 (1987)

BACKGROUND: New Jersey attorney Samuel K. Yucht represented a number of clients who settled personal injury claims with Allstate. For each client, Yucht delivered a forged release authorizing a settlement draft to be issued jointly to his client and himself. Yucht would then take the draft, forge his client's signature, add his own signature, and deposit the proceeds of the draft into his trust account at First Fidelity Bank. Yucht would thereafter withdraw the funds for his personal use. When Yucht's clients learned of their losses, they filed claims with Clients' Security Fund of the Bar of New Jersey (plaintiff). The plaintiff paid the claims and then sued Allstate and First Fidelity. First Fidelity cross-claimed against co-defendant Allstate, asserting that the imposter rule made the forged signatures effective and hence relieved First Fidelity of any liability. First Fidelity's cross-claim against Allstate was dismissed, and First Fidelity appealed.

Havey, Judge

N.J.S.A. 12A:3-405, the so-called "impostor rule", is an exception to the general rule that a forged instrument is ineffective to pass title.

If *N.J.S.A.* 12A:3-405 applies, the indorsement is deemed effective . . . with the result that the loss is shifted to the drawer.

The rationale of the rule is at least in part predicated on a negligence or estoppel theory. As between two innocent persons, the one whose act was the cause of the loss should bear the consequences. The loss should fall ". . . on the person who dealt with the impostor, and presumably, had the best opportunity to take precautions that would have detected the fraud, rather than on a subsequent holder who had no similar opportunity." *Fair Park National Bank v. South Western Investment Co.,* 541 *S.W.* 2d 266 (1976). Thus, since it is the drawer who deals with the impostor, he should bear the loss. In effect, *N.J.S.A.* 12A:3-405 ". . . conclusively presumes that the drawer was negligent in not requiring identification." *White & Summers,* § 16-8 at 631.

White & Summers characterize the "impostor rule" as ". . . a banker's provision intended to narrow the liability of banks and broaden the responsibility of their customers." *Id.* at 639. The commentators caution against expansion of application of the rule:

[W]e believe the courts should be hesitant to expand 3-405 beyond its explicit limits, for 3-405 is an exception to the general obligation of a bank to pay only according to the order of its customer and it is in derogation of one of the main protections customers believe they are buying, namely protection from theft by one who forges the indorsement of the intended payee. [*Ibid.*]

So viewed, § 3-405 must be limited to the clear case where there has been an imposture which induces the issuance and delivery of an instrument to the impostor or his confederate. The term "impostor" refers to "impersonation" and does not extend to a false representation that the party is the authorized agent of the principal. *Uniform Commercial Code* Comment § 2, *N.J.S.A.* 12A:3-405. The drawer who takes the precaution of making the instrument payable to the principal is entitled to have his indorsement. Ibid. "Impersonation" is the act of pretending or representing oneself to be another. Such impersonation is of an identity, either real or fictitious, with which the drawer believes he is dealing. "Impersonation" is distinguishable from forgery, which involves alteration of a writing without authorization or the execution of a writing ". . . so that it purports to be the act of another who did not authorize that act or of a fictitious person[.]" *N.J.S.A.* 2C:21-1a(1) and (2).

To accept First Fidelity's claim that Yucht was an impersonator would effectively negate the general rule that a forged instrument is ineffective to pass title. Virtually every forger would be an "impersonator." Every forged instrument would thus be rendered effective, thereby immunizing the depository bank from liability.

DECISION: The court affirmed the dismissal of First Fidelity's cross-claim against Allstate.

Fictitious Payee Rule   The **fictitious payee rule** of Section 3-404 deals with an instrument drawn by an employee on behalf of the employer. Any person in possession of the instrument may indorse the instrument to a person who takes the instrument in good faith and for value or collection if

1. A person whose intent determines to whom an instrument is payable does not intend the payee of an instrument to have an interest in the instrument (Section 3-404[b] [i]) or

2. The payee of an instrument was a fictitious person (Section 3-404[b] [ii]).

Section 4-404, for the most part, applies in cases of employee fraud involving checks of corporations and other organizations.

Suppose that the treasurer of International Corporation, a person authorized to draw checks on behalf of the company, makes a check payable to Acme Corporation, a company that does business with International. Acme is thus a real company rather than a fictitious company. The treasurer knows that International does not owe any money to Acme. The treasurer makes a check payable to Acme Corporation *intending that Acme will not have an interest in the check.* The treasurer may take the check and may negotiate it to another party by indorsing it in the name "Acme Corporation."

Alternatively, suppose the treasurer instead fraudulently drew a check payable to a *nonexistent* company—the May Corporation. In this situation, the treasurer may take the check and negotiate it to another party by indorsing it in the name "May Corporation."

Double Forgeries   In both of these examples, as the treasurer had the power to draw checks on behalf of International, there has been no forgery of the drawer's signature. If the party taking the check acted in good faith, the loss will fall on International.

It sometimes occurs that both the signature of the drawer was forged and the indorsement was forged. For example, a thief steals Acme's checks, forges the name of the treasurer, and makes the check payable to Joe Doe with the intention of *stealing it.* The thief becomes a holder of the instrument and is entitled to enforce the instrument (Section 3-404[b] [1]). The thief forges the indorsement of Joe Doe and passes the check on to another party. The thief's indorsement in the name of Joe Doe is an effective indorsement in so far as a person who in good faith pays the instrument or takes it for value or for collection (Section 3-404[b][2]). Thus the taker becomes a holder of the instrument and a person entitled to enforce it. However, absent some sort of negligence by the drawer (Acme), if the drawee bank pays this check, the loss will fall on the drawee. It is not entitled to charge its customer's account because the drawer's signature was forged (Section 3-404, Comment 2, Case 5).

Substantially Similar   The 1990 code creates a new rule in Section 3-404(c) by stating that an indorsement that is substantially similar to that of the payee, or the deposit of an instrument in an account in a name substantially similar to that of the payee is an effective indorsement. For example, suppose that the treasurer of Acme Corporation makes a check payable to May Corporation. When the treasurer negotiates this check, he indorses it "Mae Corporation." As the name on the indorsement is substantially similar to that of the payee, the indorsement is effective even though it is not exactly correct.

Responsibility for Fraudulent Indorsements by Employee

Unlike the fictitious payee rule of Section 3-404, which deals with an instrument drawn by an employee on behalf of the employer, Section 3-405 does not involve an instrument drawn by an employee. Section 3-405 deals with instruments that were drawn by someone other than the employee who fraudulently indorses the instrument. Cases falling under this code section involve an employee who was entrusted with responsibility (as defined in Section 3-405[a] [3]) with respect to an employer's checks and this employee fraudulently indorsed a check.

What if a faithless employee forges the employer's indorsement to a check that is (1) made payable to the employer or (2) fraudulently indorses the name of a payee on a check issued by the employee's employer? In these cases Section 3-405(b) controls. In general, this section places the risk of loss *on the employer* for fraudulent indorsements by employees who are entrusted with responsibility with respect to instruments. The rationale for placing the loss on the employer is that the employer is in the best position to avoid the loss in the first place by taking care in hiring, training, and supervising its employees.

Suppose that a bookkeeper working for International Corporation receives a check made payable to International. The bookkeeper steals the check and forges International's indorsement. The indorsement by the bookkeeper is effective because the employer entrusted the bookkeeper with responsibility with respect to the check. The loss here falls on International.

Alternatively, suppose that the accounts payable clerk caused a check payable to Acme Corporation to be sent to the clerk's home. The clerk takes the check and indorses it to another party. This is an effective negotiation of the check to the other party because the employee was *entrusted with responsibility* with respect to the check. International will be liable for this check.

Substantially Similar Like Section 3-404, Section 3-405(c) does not require an indorsement of the payee's name to be exactly the same as the name listed on the instrument as the payee.

Comparative Fault It should be noted that both Sections 3-404 and 3-405 now contain a provision that may result in the shifting of the loss to the party who takes an instrument if that party fails to exercise ordinary care and the failure to exercise ordinary care substantially contributes to the loss (Sections 3-404[d] and 3-405[b]). The drafters of the code have essentially shifted from a contributory-negligence standard to a **comparative-fault** approach. Loss is allocated based upon the relative fault of the parties as determined by the trier of fact. **Ordinary care** is defined for a person engaged in business as "observance of reasonable commercial standards, prevailing in the area in which the person is located" (Section 3-103[a] [7]).

As an example of how this comparative-fault standard might result in a shifting of the loss for an item from the drawer to another party, consider the following situation. The accounts payable clerk for International Corporation mentioned earlier takes a check made payable by her employer to the order of IBM. The check is for $300,000. Before depositing the check, the clerk opens an account at First National Bank in the name of IBM. The bank opens the account without requiring any proof that the clerk was authorized to act on behalf of IBM. A few days later, the clerk deposits the stolen check to the account at First National. First National receives payment for the check and thereafter permits the clerk to withdraw the money in the account by a wire transfer to another country. The trier of fact could find in this case that First National Bank failed to exercise ordinary care—it did not observe reasonable commercial standards—and its failure to exercise ordinary care contributed to the loss experienced by International Corporation. In this case, the trier of fact may apportion some or all of the loss suffered by International Corporation to the First National Bank.

NEGLIGENCE If a person fails to exercise ordinary care and this failure to exercise ordinary care substantially contributes to (1) an alteration of an instrument or (2) the making of a forged signature on an instrument, the person who failed to exercise ordinary care may not use the alternation or the forged signature as a defense against a person who in good faith paid the instrument or took it for value or for collection (Section 3-406). For example, suppose that an employer uses a rubber stamp to sign his name. The stamp as well as the employer's checks were left in an unlocked drawer. Someone stole a check and signed the check with the rubber stamp. The employer's bank deducted the amount of the check from his account. If the employer demands that his bank recredit his account in light of the forgery of his signature, the bank may argue under Section 3-406 that the employer is precluded from asserting forgery against it because the employer failed to exercise ordinary care with respect to his checks and the rubber stamp and this failure to exercise ordinary care substantially contributed to the forgery of the employer's signature.

Section 3-406(b) also includes a comparative-fault standard. Thus, if the employer can show that the bank in the example above failed to exercise ordinary care in paying the item, the loss will be allocated between the parties.

KID GLOVES, INC. v. FIRST NATIONAL BANK OF JEFFERSON PARISH

Louisiana Court of Appeals, Fifth Circuit
600 S. 2d 779 (1992)

BACKGROUND: Kid Gloves, Inc. is a corporation solely owned by Peter Sather. An acquaintance, Lawrence E. Andrews, expressed an interest in buying the company. Andrews began working for Sather to familiarize himself with the business. Thereafter they went to the First National Bank of Jefferson Parish to open a commercial checking account. Sather introduced Andrews to a bank officer as the "chief financial officer" of the corporation. The signatures of both men were required on all checks.

Andrews thereafter cashed two checks made out to himself, both of which appeared to have the required two signatures. Sather soon thereafter discovered the checks. He alleged his signature had been forged. Sather asked to have his account recredited for $5,000. The trial court ruled for the bank.

Gothard, Justice

Kid Gloves, Inc. argues that, since Sather's signature was required and not on the checks (having been forged), the bank was negligent in cashing the checks.

Where the plaintiff has made a prima facie case that the bank paid a forged check, the bank must show that the customer negligently managed his account, that the negligence substantially contributed to the forgery, and that the bank used reasonable commercial standards in the way it handled the account.

As outlined above, the bank has shown through the testimony of an assistant vice president that it used reasonable commercial standards in opening the account and in handling the cashing of checks.

Sather testified that Larry Andrews had approached him as an ex-officer of the bank he had been using. Sather gave no information as to how long or how well he knew Andrews or whether he made any inquiries as to his trustworthiness; nevertheless, he gave him full access to the company checkbook. Either Sather or Andrews performed the daily banking errands. "[Banking] was done by basically whoever was headed in that direction at the time doing deliveries, or whatever." . . .

The facts of this case are similar to those of Ashley-Hall, Etc. v. Bank of New Orleans, where the bookkeeper had forged checks. The court found that the general manager's failure to exercise adequate supervision or review of the bookkeeper's actions while allowing unrestricted access to the company's checks constituted negligence that contributed substantially to the forgery.

DECISION: The court of appeals affirmed the decision on behalf of the bank.

Primary Versus Secondary Liability

Knowing merely that a person's authorized signature appears on an instrument is not enough to determine the *nature* of the person's liability on the instrument. As we shall see, the nature of a person's liability depends upon the capacity in which that person signs the instrument—as maker, drawer, drawee, or indorser. The capacity of the person whose signature appears on the instrument determines whether that person incurs primary or secondary liability on the instrument. These types of liability are discussed below.

Primary or Unconditional Liability A person with **primary liability** (also known as unconditional liability) on an instrument assumes an unconditional responsibility to pay the instrument according to its terms. A person with primary liability is not excused from paying the instrument even if the holder presents the instrument long after it becomes due. This obligation continues until the statute of limitations prevents the holder from recovering.

The *maker* of a promissory note has primary liability on the note. Under Section 3-414(b) the liability of the *drawer* on an unaccepted draft is treated as a primary liability. The issuer of a cashier's check also has primary liability on the cashier's check under Section 3-412.

The *drawee* of a draft can also incur primary liability, but only under certain circumstances. Recall that a draft is a three-party instrument in which the drawer orders the drawee to pay a payee. When the drawee accepts this order, the drawee becomes the **acceptor,** assuming primary liability on the draft (Section 3-413[a]).

Until the drawee's acceptance—that is, his or her signed engagement to honor the draft as presented (Section 3-409[a])—the drawee has no liability on the instrument; upon acceptance, unconditional liability is established. By accepting, the drawee agrees to honor the instrument according to its terms as presented. The mechanics of acceptance were discussed in Chapter 26.

Section 3-413(b) provides some protection for acceptors of drafts (or banks that certify a check). If the acceptor states the amount certified or accepted, it will only be liable to pay the amount stated.

On the other hand, if an instrument does not state the amount certified or accepted, and the amount of the instrument is subsequently raised, a holder in due course can enforce it for the amount of the instrument at the time it was raised.

Secondary Liability A party that incurs **secondary liability** on an instrument does not assume an absolute obligation to pay the instrument according to its terms. Rather, such a party can only be required to pay the instrument if certain conditions are satisfied.

Indorsers of any type of negotiable instrument generally have secondary liability. If a draft has *not* been accepted, the drawer of the draft is primarily liable (Section 3-414[b]). However, a drawer of a draft that was accepted by a party *other than a bank* must pay the draft if the acceptor subsequently dishonors it; thus the drawer is secondarily liable in this situation (Section 3-414[d]). If a *bank* accepts a draft, the drawer is discharged (Section 3-414[c]).

Prerequisites for Establishing Secondary Liability

Generally the following must occur to establish the secondary liability of an indorser or of a drawer in those cases in which a drawer has secondary liability on an instrument:

- Presentment
- Dishonor
- Notice of Dishonor

A fourth step, protest, *may* be used in some situations but is no longer required.

Presentment The maker of a note and the acceptor of a draft have unconditional liability on an instrument. It is not necessary for a holder of an instrument first to present the instrument to the maker or acceptor before commencing suit against either of them.

On the other hand, before a party with secondary liability on an instrument can be required to pay the instrument, under certain circumstances, it is necessary to present the instrument to the party expected to pay or accept it. When presentment is required, it must take place before any party has secondary liability on an instrument. Unless presentment is accomplished correctly, all indorsers are discharged completely. If a check was not presented within *30 days after its date*, the drawer is discharged to a limited extent if the drawee becomes insolvent during any delay in presentment (Section 3-414[f]).

Section 3-501 requires the presentment take place at the place specified in the instrument. It may be done orally or in writing. The UCC also recognizes that the parties may agree that an electronic presentment be made on a bank, in which case an electronic transfer of the pertinent information takes place rather than an actual physical delivery of the item itself. If such means are used, the presentation takes place when the presentment notice is received (Section 4-110).

Dishonor   A **dishonor** of an instrument occurs if the instrument is properly presented for acceptance or payment and the party upon whom presentment is made refuses to accept or pay the instrument (Section 3-502). A draft is dishonored if the drawee either refuses to accept or pay it. A note is dishonored only if the maker refuses to pay.

Payment of an instrument may be deferred without dishonor to provide the person upon whom presentment is made an opportunity to examine it to determine if it is properly payable.

As a general rule, an instrument must be paid on the date of presentment (Section 3-502). Subject to any required notice of dishonor, a holder, upon dishonor, has an immediate right of recourse against any party with secondary liability on the instrument.

Notice of Dishonor   In most cases the final step in establishing the liability of secondary parties is to provide **notice of dishonor**, that is, notice that the instrument has been dishonored. Notice is given by the holder who has been unable to obtain either acceptance or payment of an instrument. The most common type of notice of dishonor is the check that has been returned because the drawer of the check had insufficient funds or has stopped payment on the check for some reason.

A collecting bank (that is, a bank that takes an item for collection) must give notice of dishonor before midnight of the next banking day following the banking day on which the bank receives notice of dishonor of the instrument. Any other person must give notice of dishonor within 30 days following the day on which the person re-

ceives notice of dishonor (Section 3-503[c]). Section 3-504 recognizes that presentment and notice of dishonor may in certain circumstances be excused.

Protest   At one point in time protest was mandatory under certain circumstances. It is no longer mandatory. **Protest** is an official certificate of dishonor given by a consular officer of the United States, a notary public, or other person authorized to certify dishonor by the law of the country in which the dishonor takes place (Section 3-505[b]).

Liability of the Drawer

Contrary to the 1952 code, the 1990 code, under Section 3-414(b), stipulates that the drawer of an *unaccepted* draft has primary liability on the draft. This means that the drawer is no longer entitled to notice of dishonor before being obligated to pay an unaccepted draft. Suppose that Donald sent a check for $70 to Southwestern Bell in payment of his monthly telephone bill. Donald's bank refused to accept the check or pay it. Southwestern Bell may immediately attempt to collect from Donald without first providing him notice of the dishonor.

On the other hand, if a *bank* accepts a draft, the drawer is discharged (Section 3-414[c]). This means that if the bank accepts Donald's check, then for some reason Southwestern Bell is unable to collect on the instrument from the bank, Southwestern Bell *cannot* hold Donald liable on the check.

A drawer *does* remain liable on a draft if it was accepted by a drawee who was *not* a bank (Section 3-414[d]). When a drawee of such a draft accepts, the drawee/acceptor becomes primarily liable on the draft. The drawer is secondarily liable should the drawee/acceptor fail to pay. The drawer's liability is identical to that of an indorser of such a draft. In this situation, the holder must provide a timely notice of dishonor in order to hold the drawer liable on the instrument.

A drawer may avoid such secondary liability by drawing the instrument "without recourse" or otherwise disclaiming liability to pay the draft. However, the UCC no longer permits the *drawer* of a *check* to disclaim secondary liability (Section 3-414[e]).

Liability of the Indorser

The undertaking of an indorser is set forth in Section 3-415. The indorser is required, upon dishonor and any necessary notice of dishonor, to pay the instrument. This duty is owed to any person entitled to enforce the instrument or any subsequent indorser who paid the instrument.

Suppose that Al repays a debt owed to Cindy by writing Cindy a check on Al's account at First National Bank. Cindy indorses the check over to Susan, who in turn indorses the check over to Dan. Dan duly presents the check for payment to the bank. The bank dishonors the check. According to Section 3-415(a), each indorser is required to pay the instrument to any person entitled to enforce the instrument or to a subsequent indorser who paid the instrument. This means that Dan may require Susan to pay the check after giving notice of dishonor to Susan. If Susan pays the check, she can turn around and require Cindy to pay the check after giving the requisite notice of dishonor to Cindy. Cindy can then require Al to pay the check as the check was dishonored because it was never accepted by the bank (Section 3-414[b]). It is possible to short-circuit this process by Dan demanding payment from the drawer of the check, Al, directly. Dan could also demand payment from any of the prior indorsers. Suppose that Dan required Cindy to pay the instrument. Cindy could then demand payment from Al.

Section 3-415(b) permits an indorser to avoid liability on an instrument by indorsing it "without recourse." Such an indorsement is a qualified indorsement. Essentially the indorser who uses a "without recourse" indorsement is saying that he or she will *not* pay the instrument if the party primarily obligated to pay the instrument fails to do so.

If a proper notice of dishonor is not given to an indorser, the liability of the indorser is discharged. Once a bank accepts a draft, the liability of the indorser is discharged. An indorser is also discharged if a check is not presented for payment or deposited for collection within 30 days of the date the indorsement was made. (Section 3-415[e]).

Warranty Liability

Regardless of whether a person signs an instrument, the person is deemed to make certain warranties when he or she transfers the instrument to another person. These warranties are known as **transfer warranties**. A person is also deemed to make certain warranties when he or she obtains payment or acceptance of the instrument after presenting it. These warranties are known as **presentment warranties**.

A person can be held liable for breaching transfer or presentment warranties even if he or she has not signed the instrument. The ability to recover on the basis of these warranties does not depend upon whether there has been proper presentment, dishonor, notice of dishonor, or protest.

Transfer Warranties

Section 3-416(a) (1990) states that a person who transfers an instrument *by indorsement* and receives consideration for it makes five separate warranties to the indorsee and to all subsequent holders. (The transferor who does not indorse makes these warranties only to his or her immediate transferee.) The five warranties are:

1. The transferor is entitled to enforce the instrument.
2. All signatures on the instrument are genuine and authorized.
3. The instrument has not been altered.
4. The instrument is not subject to any defense or claim of any party that could be asserted against the transferor.
5. The transferor has no knowledge of any insolvency proceedings against the maker, acceptor, or drawer of an unaccepted draft.

By making the first warranty, the transferor in effect is saying that there are no unauthorized or missing indorsements that would prevent the transferee from becoming a person entitled to enforce the instrument.

Suppose Jack issues a check to Mary. A thief steals the check from Mary, forges her indorsement and transfers it to Jane. Jane in turn transfers it to Nick. When Nick presents the check to the bank, the bank refuses to pay it because Mary, who by that time had learned of the theft, had stopped payment on the check. As Mary's indorsement was forged, Nick cannot enforce the check. Even so, Nick can hold Jane liable for breach of the implied warranty of title.

The implied warranty that all signatures are genuine and authorized might be breached, for example, in the following way. Suppose in the earlier example Jack's signature was a forgery. Therefore when Nick attempted to collect on the check, the bank refused because it detected that Jack's signature had been forged. In this situation Nick can hold Jane liable for breach of her promise that all signatures were genuine.

Suppose a person acquires an instrument that has been altered and, because the person is a mere holder as opposed to a holder in due course, is unable to recover anything on the instrument. Such a person may sue the person he or she took the instrument from for breach of the implied warranty that the instrument has not been altered.

An illustration of the fourth warranty would be if Mark tricks Dan into signing a negotiable instrument for $200 when in fact Dan owed Mark nothing. Mark then negotiated this instrument to Bill. When Bill attempted to recover he was unable to collect. In this case Bill can sue Mark because Mark breached the warranty that no defense existed against him.

The fifth warranty reflects the fact that the transferor does not guarantee that an instrument will be collectable. The transferee should determine the collectability of an instrument before acquiring it. On the other hand, if the transferor knew that the party primarily liable on an instrument was bankrupt, the failure to disclose this amounts to a fraud upon the transferee.

In order to avail oneself of these warranties, Section 3-416(c) states that notice of a claim for a breach of warranty must be given within 30 days of the time a person has reason to know of a breach of warranty and the identity of the indorser. If a timely notice is not given, the amount of liability of the indorser will be reduced by the amount of the loss that could have been avoided had a timely notice been given.

The transfer warranties *cannot be disclaimed* with respect to checks (Section 3-416([c])). The transfer warranties may be disclaimed for all other instruments.

Presentment Warranties

The presentment warranties dealt with in Section 3-417(a) are given to drawees of uncertified checks and other unaccepted drafts. Any person who obtains payment or acceptance of a draft from a drawee making payment or accepting the draft in good faith warrants to the drawee that

1. The transferor is, or was at the time the transferor transferred the draft, a person entitled to enforce the draft or authorized to obtain payment or acceptance of the draft on behalf of a person entitled to enforce the draft.

2. The draft has not been altered.

3. The transferor has no knowledge that the signature of the drawer of the draft is unauthorized.

When a drawee pays or accepts an instrument in good faith, the drawee receives presentment warranties not only from the party who obtains payment or acceptance, but also from *any* prior transferor of the instrument (Section 3-417[a] [ii]).

The first warranty in effect is a warranty that there are no unauthorized or missing indorsements. The second warranty is a guarantee that the draft has not been altered. The final warranty guarantees the drawee that the transferor does not know the drawer's signature was forged. The code thus follows the rule of *Price v. Neal*: The drawee takes the risk that the drawer's signature is unauthorized.

Suppose the drawee wants to assert a claim that the instrument in question contains an unauthorized indorsement against the person who obtained payment of the instrument. Section 3-417(c) gives a defense to the warrantor that the indorsement was effective because of the actions of a fictitious payee, an imposter, a faithless employee, or the negligence of the drawer. In effect, this rule keeps the drawee from shifting the loss from its customer (the drawer) to the warrantor in these situations.

Section 3-417 (d) states the presentment warranties that are made in all cases not covered in Section 3-417 (a). Thus, a different set of presentment warranties applies if a person obtains payment from a drawer with respect to a dishonored draft or payment from an indorser with respect to a dishonored draft or any other instrument is presented for payment to a party obliged to pay the instrument (e.g., when a note is presented to a maker for payment or when an accepted draft is presented to the acceptor for payment). In this case the transferor makes only one warranty: The transferor is, or was, at the time of the transfer of the instrument, a person entitled to enforce the instrument or authorized to obtain payment on behalf of a person entitled to enforce the instrument. In effect, the transferor is stating that there are no unauthorized or missing indorsements and that the transferor has good title to the instrument.

It is not possible for these warranties to be disclaimed with respect to checks (Section 3-417 [e]).

Notice of a claim for breach of warranty must be given to the warrantor within 30 days after the claimant has reason to know of the breach and the identity of the warrantor.

Defenses

As we learned in the last chapter, holders in due course are not subject to several defenses that can be asserted against an ordinary holder. This is one of the chief benefits of holder-in-due-course status. Certain defenses, however, apply to all holders, even holders in due course and those who receive the rights of a holder in due course through the shelter principle. These defenses are popularly known as **real defenses**. **Personal defenses** is the term for those defenses to which an ordinary holder is subject but to which a holder in due course—or one with the rights of a holder in due course—is not.

Real Defenses

All holders, including holders in due course and those with the rights of a holder in due course, are subject to the real defenses discussed below.

Forgery A person whose signature is used on a negotiable instrument without authority is not liable on the instrument.

Alteration Section 3-407 states that alteration means either (1) an unauthorized change in an instrument that purports to modify in any respect the obligation of a party, or (2) an unauthorized addition of words or numbers or other change to an incomplete instrument relating to the obligation of a party.

The mere alteration of an instrument does not necessarily result in the discharge of anyone's obligation on an instrument. The alteration must have been fraudulently made to discharge a party. For example, there is no discharge if a party holding an instrument fills a blank space in an instrument believing that he is entitled to do so.

Section 3-407 (c) states that a person who takes an instrument for value, in good faith, and without notice of the alteration may enforce the instrument according to its original terms. For example, if a holder of a $100 instrument altered the instrument to make it payable for $1,000, a subsequent party that acquired the instrument for value, in good faith and without notice of the alteration could enforce it for $100.

In the case of an incomplete instrument, a person who takes the instrument for value, in good faith, and without notice of the unauthorized completion, may enforce the instrument for the amount as completed. Suppose that a drawer signs a check but fails to fill out the amount. A thief acquires the instrument, fills it out for $1,000, and transfers it to another party. If that party acquired it for value, in good faith, and without notice of the unauthorized completion, the person may enforce the instrument for $1,000.

The following case deals with an incomplete instrument that was improperly completed.

NATIONAL LOAN INVESTORS, L. P. v. MARTIN

Supreme Court of Iowa
488 S.W. 2d 163 (1992)

BACKGROUND: The National Loan Investors purchased the assets of insolvent Pisgah Savings Bank. Two of the assets were notes signed by William Martin. Martin was a business customer of the bank from 1975 until he quit farming in 1984. Martin would sign a blank note when he purchased cattle and then rely on the bank officials to fill in the correct amount later when the check came in for the cattle. Someone without authority filled in the dates and amounts on the two notes that were signed by Martin with the loan amounts left blank. The notes were completed in 1987. They do not represent Martin's debt to the bank. The trial court found for Martin.

Louis W. Schultz, Justice

[W]e find William signed the notes, his signatures are not "'unauthorized' signature[s] or endorsement[s]" which could constitute forgery under our commercial code, Iowa Code §554.1201(43). Notwithstanding our finding that the loan amounts on the notes were inappropriately filled in later, a holder in due course "may enforce [the notes] as completed." Iowa Code §554.3407(3).

Martin asserts the defense of fraud in factum. Fraud in factum is incorporated in Iowa's commercial code at Iowa Code §554.3305(2)(c) as follows:

> such misrepresentation as has induced the party to sign the instrument with neither knowledge nor reasonable opportunity to obtain knowledge of its character or its essential terms.

The commentary to this Code section provides as follows:

> The common illustration is that of the maker who is tricked into signing a note in the belief that it is merely a receipt or some other document. The theory of the defense is that his signature on the instrument is ineffective because he did not intend to sign such an instrument at all. Under this provision the defense extends to an instrument signed with knowledge that it is a negotiable instrument, but without knowledge of its essential terms.
>
> The test of the defense here stated is that of excusable ignorance of the contents of the writing signed. The party must not only have been in ignorance, but must also have had no reasonable opportunity to obtain knowledge. In determining what is a reasonable opportunity all relevant factors are to be taken into account, including the age and sex of the party, his intelligence, education and business experience; his ability to read or to understand English, the representations made to him and his reason to rely on them or to have confidence in the person making them; the presence or absence of any third person who might read or explain the instrument to him, or any other possibility of obtaining independent information; and the apparent necessity, or lack of it, for acting without delay.
>
> Unless the misrepresentation meets this test, the defense is cut off by a holder in due course. Iowa Code Ann. §554.3305 cmt. 7 (1967)

William was a farmer and businessman. He was obviously literate and had signed many notes previously. In a similar case, a maker who signed a blank note was not allowed to assert a fraud in factum defense. FDIC v. Culver. The court emphasized that the note maker was literate and rejected his argument that he had no opportunity to learn of the essential terms which were left blank at the time he signed the note. Id.

Based on the foregoing, we conclude that plaintiff has a right to enforce the two promissory notes as completed. Consequently, we must reverse that portion of the trial court's ruling which voids the promissory notes.

DECISION: The court ruled the note was enforceable as completed.

Fraud in the Execution   The basis of this defense is similar to that underlying forgery and material alteration. A holder in due course attempting to recover on a forged instrument is not allowed to recover because the defendant never agreed to be bound. Where a material alteration has occurred, the defendant's liability is limited because he or she did not agree to the instrument's terms as they now appear. In **fraud in the execution**, also called fraud in the factum, the party defending escapes liability because he or she was misled as to what was being signed.

This might happen in a number of ways. Extreme cases exist in which a promissory note was cleverly hidden under another document that a person supposedly signed. Upon removal of the cover document, the signature is on the note, which the payee then negotiates. The more usual situation is one in which a buyer signs a promissory note or some other type of negotiable instrument, being assured by the seller that the instrument is merely an authorization to conduct a credit investigation or a receipt. In these situations, because the signer never intended to make a promise, no liability exists. For this defense to be successful, the defendant must be able to show that no reasonable opportunity existed to discover what was actually being signed. If the defendant acted carelessly either in not reading the instrument being signed or in some other manner, the defense will fail. The dangers of failing to read what one signs are illustrated in the case that follows.

FEDERAL DEPOSIT INSURANCE CORPORATION V. CULVER

U.S. District Court, District of Kansas
640 F. Supp. 725 (1986)

BACKGROUND: Culver (defendant) entered into a business relationship with Kalliel whereby Kalliel would control the financial aspects of Culver's farm while Culver would manage the farming operation. Culver informed Kalliel that he urgently needed money to stave off foreclosure. Kalliel arranged for $30,000 to be be wired from Rexford State Bank to Culver's bank. Culver assumed that Kalliel would be responsible for repaying the money. Shortly thereafter, Culver was visited by one Gilbert, whom Culver believed was working for Kalliel. Gilbert asked Culver to sign a document which Gilbert told Culver was merely a receipt for the $30,000 that Culver had received. Actually, the document that Culver signed was a promissory note payable to Rexford State Bank. Rexford State Bank eventually became insolvent, and Culver's note was purchased by the Federal Deposit Insurance Corporation (plaintiff). The FDIC sued Culver to collect on the note.

O'Connor, Chief Judge

To determine whether these facts fit the definition of fraud in the factum, we look . . . in the Kansas Uniform Commercial Code. For instance, Official UCC comment 7 to section 3-305 provides this advice:

Paragraph (c) of subsection (2) is new. It follows the great majority of the decisions under the original Act in recognizing the defense of "real" or "essential" fraud, sometimes called fraud in the essence or fraud in the factum, as effective against a holder in due course. The common illustration is that of the maker who is tricked into signing a note in the belief that it is merely a receipt or some other document. The theory of the defense is that his signature on the instrument is ineffective because he did not intend to sign such an instrument at all. Under this provision the defense extends to an instrument signed with knowledge that it is a negotiable instrument, but without knowledge of its essential terms.

The test of the defense here stated is that of excusable ignorance of the contents of the writing signed. The party must not only have been in ignorance, but must also have had no reasonable opportunity to obtain knowledge. (Emphasis added.)

A portion of the 1983 Kansas Comment to this same section offers guidance as to the proper construction of the term "excusable ignorance." The Comment provides as follows:

> Kansas decisional law would seem to be in accord on the possibility of fraud in the factum as a real defense, the decision in Ort v. Fowler, 31 K. 478, 2 P. 580 (1884), being a good example of facts not satisfying the defense because of the failure of the maker to satisfy a standard of conduct comparable to that required by this subsection.

Given this Kansas Comment's reference to *Ort*, an examination of the facts and the holding in that case should be useful in determining whether defendant showed "excusable ignorance" in mistaking the note at issue here for a receipt.

In *Ort*, a farmer was working alone in his field. A stranger came up to him and represented himself to be the state agent for a manufacturer of iron posts and wire fence. After some conversation, the stranger persuaded the farmer to accept a township-wide agency for the same manufacturer. The stranger then completed two documents which he represented to be identical versions of an agency contract. Because the farmer did not have his glasses with him and, in any event, "could not read without spelling out every word," the stranger purported to read the document to the farmer. No mention was made of any note. Both men signed each document, with the farmer not intending to sign anything but a contract of agency. Ultimately, it was established that a least one of those documents was a promissory note. A *bona fide* purchaser of that note brought suit against the farmer, and the farmer attempted to defend the action on the basis of fraud in the factum. After the trial court rejected that defense, the farmer appealed.

The Kansas Supreme Court, in an opinion by Justice David Brewer (later a United States Supreme Court Associate Justice), phrased the issue on appeal as follows: "A party is betrayed into signing a bill or note by the assurance that it is an instrument of a different kind. Under what circumstances ought he to be liable thereon?" Three alternative answers were then suggested:

> One view entertained is, that as he never intended to execute a bill or note, it cannot be considered his act, and he should not be held liable thereon any more than if his name had been forged to such an instrument. A second view is, that it is always a question of fact for the jury whether under the circumstances the party was guilty of negligence. A third is the view adopted by the trial court, that as [a] matter of law, one must be adjudged guilty of such negligence as to render him liable who, possessed of all his faculties and able to read, signs a bill or note, relying upon the assurance or the reading of a stranger that it is a different instrument.

Defendant herein would obviously prefer either the first or second alternative. The court, however, made its decision clear:

> We approve of the latter doctrine. It presents a case, of course, of which one of two innocent parties must suffer, but the bona fide holder is not only innocent, but free from all negligence. He has done only that which a prudent, careful man might properly do, while on the other hand the maker of the note has omitted ordinary care and prudence. A party cannot guard against forgery; but if in possession of his faculties and able to read, he can know the character of every instrument to which he puts his signature; and it is a duty which he owes to any party who may be subsequently affected by his act, to know what it is which he signs. By his signature he invites the credence of the world to every statement and promise which is in the instrument he has subscribed; and he is guilty of negligence if he omits to use the ordinary means of ascertaining what those provisions and statements are. If he has eyes and can see, he ought to examine; if he can read, he ought to read; and he has no right to send his signature out into the world affixed to an instrument of whose contents he is ignorant. If he relies upon the word of a stranger, he makes that stranger his agent. He adopts his reading as his own knowledge. What his agent knows, he knows; and he cannot disaffirm the acts of that agent done within the scope of the authority he has intrusted to him.

It is obvious from reading defendant's deposition that he is able to read and understand the English language. Thus, under the rule announced in Ort, defendant was negligent in relying on Gilbert's assurance that the note was only a receipt. Given the 1983 Kansas Comment referring to the Ort absence-of-negligence standard as "comparable to that required by [K.S.A. 84-3-305(2)(c)]," we must also conclude that defendant has failed to show the "excusable ignorance" necessary to establish fraud in the factum. In the words of the statute, we conclude as a matter of law that defendant had a "reasonable opportunity to obtain knowledge of [the document's] character" before he signed it.

DECISION: The district court granted the FDIC's motion for summary judgment.

Fraud in the execution differs from the false statement made to induce a person to enter into a contract. This is called **fraud in the inducement**. Fraud in the inducement is a personal defense discussed later in this chapter.

Infancy As indicated in Chapter 15, a minor has the right to rescind most contractual obligations. The extent to which this right exists depends on state law. Under the UCC a minor may raise the defense of infancy against a holder in due course to the same extent that infancy is a contractual defense according to state law governing the transaction. For example, in most states a minor purchasing a stereo is allowed to disaffirm the contract since the item is not a necessity. If the minor signs a note as payment for the stereo, the note is not enforceable even if transferred to a holder in due course who has no knowledge of the maker's minority.

Other Incapacity Mental incapacity and incapacity as a result of intoxication can be used as defenses against a holder in due course in limited instances. Incapacity other than infancy is available against a holder in due course if applicable state laws render the underlying obligation a nullity. In effect this means that the underlying contract must be void, not just voidable, if incapacity is to be used successfully against a holder in due course. In most states contracts by mental incompetents are void only if the incompetent has been adjudicated insane. A similar rule applies to intoxication. If the promisor's intoxication was so extreme that he or she could not have intended to contract, the agreement is void. In a similar situation a person obligated on commercial paper has a good defense against the holder in due course.

Duress and Illegality Duress and illegality are treated by the UCC in a manner similar to incapacity other than infancy. In both instances, if applicable state law renders the contract void, duress or illegality can be asserted against a holder in due course. In most states a contract secured by duress is voidable, not void; thus duress is generally unavailable as a defense against a holder in due course. If, however, the duress is so extreme that the agreement is void from the beginning, duress is a good defense. Illegality is treated in a comparable manner, as the following case indicates.

NEW JERSEY MORTGAGE & INVESTMENT CORP. V. BERENYI

Superior Court of New Jersey, Appellate Division
356 A.2d 421 (1976)

BACKGROUND: New Jersey Mortgage and Investment Corp. (plaintiff-respondent) was the holder in due course of a negotiable promissory note. Andrew and Anna Berenyi (defendants-appellants), the makers, refused to pay and the holder in due course sued on the note. Berenyi argued that no liability existed because the transaction was illegal. The trial court entered judgment for the plaintiff. Defendant appealed.

Before Judges Kolovsky, Bischoff, and Botter
Per Curiam

Defendant Anna Berenyi appeals from a judgment for plaintiff based on the following stipulated facts:

1. On May 25, 1964, in a proceeding brought by Arthur J. Sills, Attorney General of the State of New Jersey, against Kroyden Industries, Inc., a corporation of the State of New Jersey, in the Superior Court of New Jersey, Chancery Division, Essex County, a Consent Order was made by Honorable Ward J. Herbert, J.S.C., which Order enjoined the said Kroyden Industries, Inc. from committing certain acts or making certain representations with its customers in connection with the sale of carpeting.

2. In August, 1964, the defendants, Andrew Berenyi (now deceased) and Anna Berenyi, were referred from a participant in a sales scheme of Kroyden Industries, Inc., for the purchase of carpeting.

3. An employee of Kroyden Industries, Inc. offered, in violation of the injunction aforesaid, to give to the defendants carpeting which, if the contract price of $1,100.00 was paid, was worth $44.00 per square yard without making any payments as long as they referred prospective buyers to Kroyden Industries, Inc.

4. The defendants agreed to this plan since the carpeting would not cost them anything as long as they made the required referrals.

5. The defendants, relying upon the above offer and representations, signed a negotiable promissory note for $1,521.00. Said instrument was negotiated to the plaintiff herein.

6. The plaintiff is a holder in due course for value of the negotiable promissory note sued upon and had no knowledge or notice of the proceedings brought against Kroyden Industries, Inc.; and had no knowledge or notice of the entry of the Order in the Chancery Division by Judge Herbert; and had no knowledge or notice that Kroyden Industries, Inc., violated the aforementioned injunctive Order.

The trial judge ruled that the fact that the note was obtained as part of a transaction entered into by Kroyden Industries, Inc. (Kroyden) in violation of the injunctive order was not a defense in an action brought by plaintiff, whose status as a holder in due course, with no knowledge or notice of the injunctive order, was admitted.

The controlling issue presented is whether the defense here asserted is a "real" defense or a "personal" defense. Real defenses are available against even a holder in due course of a negotiable instrument; personal defenses are not available against such a holder. We affirm since we are satisfied that the defense presented is not a "real" defense.

Defendant argues that since the transaction which resulted in the execution and delivery of defendant's note was engaged in by Kroyden in violation of the injunctive order, the transaction was "illegal and thus a nullity under N.J.S.A. 12A:3-305," which provides in pertinent part as follows:

> To the extent that a holder is a holder in due course takes the instrument free from . . .
> (2) all defenses of any party to the instrument with whom the holder has not dealt except . . .
> (b) such other incapacity, or duress, or illegality of the transaction, as renders the obligation of the party a nullity; and . . .

However, the fact that it was illegal for Kroyden to enter into the transaction did not by reason of that fact render defendant's obligation under the note she executed a nullity.

On the contrary, as noted in the New Jersey Study Comment on N.J.S.A. 12A:3-305(2)(b):

In New Jersey, a holder in due course takes free and clear of the defense of illegality, unless the statute which declares the act illegal also indicates that payment thereunder is void. . . . (See e.g., N.J.S.A. 2A:40-3 which specifically provides that notes given in payment of a gambling debt "shall be utterly void and of no effect.") . . . where no such statute is involved, it has been held that a negotiable instrument which is rooted in an illegal transaction or stems from a transaction prohibited by statute or public policy is no reason for refusing to enforce the instrument in the hands of a holder in due course.

There being no statute ordaining that a note obtained in violation of an injunction is void and unenforceable, the illegality involved is not a "real" defense; the note is enforceable in the hands of a holder in due course who had no knowledge or notice of the injunction.

DECISION: The appellate division ruled for New Jersey Mortgage.

CASE NOTE

This case is an example of the manner in which negotiable instruments used in consumer transactions can injure unsophisticated buyers. As noted in Chapter 28, a substantial number of states have adopted statutes and the Federal Trade Commission has adopted a rule limiting the use of negotiable instruments in consumer transactions.

Discharge in Bankruptcy Providing individuals and firms that are insolvent with an opportunity to make a fresh start has long been an important public policy. Where a holder in due course is a creditor of the bankrupt and for one reason or another the claim of the holder in due course is not asserted until the bankrupt is discharged, the discharge provides a good defense.

Personal Defenses

While the new code is quite helpful with respect to real defenses, it recognizes personal defenses in Section 3-305(a)(2) but does not define them. Discussed below is a partial list of personal defenses. Ordinary holders are subject to these defenses; those with the rights of holders in due course are not.

For most of the personal defenses listed below, examples are given of how the personal defense could be asserted against the original named payee of the instrument. As you read each example, remember that the personal defense will be of no avail if a person with the rights of a holder in due course comes into possession of the instrument and tries to enforce it.

The Absence of Consideration to Support the Contract Under Sections 3-303 (b) and 3-305 (a) (2) the absence of consideration sufficient to support a contract is a defense against a holder who does not have the rights of a holder in due course. Thus, if Fred executes a $500 promissory note payable to Tom and receives nothing in exchange for the note, Fred could assert the lack of consideration as a defense if Tom sued Fred to collect on the note.

Nonissuance The nonissuance of a negotiable instrument is a personal defense. Recall the example from the beginning of the last chapter, in which Smith signs a note payable to Jones and leaves it on Smith's desk. Jones burglarizes Smith's office and takes the note. If Jones attempts to require Smith to pay the note, Smith could assert the personal defense of nonissuance of the instrument.

Fraud in the Inducement Earlier in the chapter, we learned that fraud in the execution is a real defense. Fraud in the execution occurs when someone is tricked into signing a negotiable instrument that he or she did not intend to sign. But what if someone is tricked into entering into the transaction itself and then voluntarily signs a negotiable instrument pursuant to the transaction? The latter scenario describes fraud in the inducement, a personal defense.

Assume that Sam Sucker buys a "nearly new" Yugo from Al's Used Car Lot, financing the purchase by signing a promissory note payable to Al's. Sam thought he was buying a car with 3,000 miles on it. That's what the odometer and the salesman had assured him. Actually, as a disgruntled former employee of Al's would later reveal, the Yugo's odometer was rolled back from 60,000 miles.

Since Sam voluntarily signed the promissory note with the intention of taking out a loan, he may not assert the real defense of fraud in the execution. But since he was fraudulently induced to buy the car, Sam may assert the personal defense of fraud in the inducement against Al's.

Incapacity   We learned earlier in the chapter that mental incapacity and incapacity due to intoxication can be real defenses if such incapacity renders the underlying contract *void*, and not just *voidable*. The converse is that when either type of incapacity renders a contract voidable, but not automatically void, such incapacity gives rise to a personal defense. Whether a contract made by a person lacking capacity is void or merely voidable is a matter of state law. The issue is discussed in greater detail in Chapter 15.

Duress and Illegality   As noted above, duress and illegality are treated in a manner similar to the way that mental incapacity and capacity due to intoxication are treated. If the duress or illegality is sufficient to make the contract void, and not merely voidable, then it will give rise to a real defense. Otherwise, the duress or illegality will merely provide the basis for a personal defense. Duress is discussed in Chapter 14; illegality in Chapter 16.

Claim in Recoupment   An attempt was made in the 1990 code to distinguish situations in which one of the parties received nothing in exchange for his or her promise (the absence of consideration to support a contract) and situations in which a party received something from the other party but now wishes to sue because the performance rendered by the other party was in some way less than satisfactory. A claim in recoupment refers to the latter situation.

Section 3-305(a)(3) deals with claims in recoupment. A **claim in recoupment** as used in this context essentially is a claim for *damages* caused by a breach of contract by the original payee of the instrument—if the claim in question arose from the transaction that gave rise to the instrument. On the other hand, wholly unrelated claims (those that do not relate to the transaction

that gave rise to the instrument) cannot be asserted against a holder.

Suppose that Joe's Sporting Goods, Inc. orders 1,000 hot-pink sweatbands from Sam's Sweatbands, Inc. Joe's sends Sam's a promissory note for the purchase price prior to delivery. Sam's breaches the contract by delivering sweatbands which are a drab shade of olive green, rather than the popular hot-pink color that Joe's ordered. Joe's has a claim in recoupment against Sam's. The claim arose from the transaction that gave rise to the instrument.

Suppose instead that Joe's is also Sam's landlord. Sam's failed to pay several months rent. As the claim for back rent did not arise from the transaction that gave rise to the negotiable instrument, the claim for back rent is *not* a claim in recoupment.

The code states that the original obligor on an instrument may assert a claim in recoupment that the obligor had against the original payee of the instrument. In the sweatbands example, therefore, if Sam's is still in possession of the note, Joe's may assert its claim for damages against Sam's should Sam's bring suit based on the note.

If the instrument is negotiated to a holder in due course, however, the holder in due course is *not* subject to a claim in recoupment (Section 3-305 [b]). Suppose that a buyer negotiates a note to a payee in return for the sale of goods worth $500. The payee delivers the goods, but it subsequently develops that the goods were defective in some respect. In the meantime, payee transferred the instrument to a person who qualifies as a holder in due course. The claim of breach of warranty *cannot* be asserted against a subsequent holder who qualifies as a holder in due course.

If the person who acquires the instrument is not a holder in due course, the claim for breach of warranty can only be used to reduce the amount owed on the instrument (Section 3-305 [b]). If the buyer's claim for breach of warranty in the above example was worth $50, the buyer would have to pay the holder $450 on the note. If the buyer's claim was for $1,000, the buyer would owe the transferee of the instrument nothing if the transferee failed to qualify as a holder in due course. The buyer cannot recover the other $500 of his claim from the holder.

Table 29-1 is a Concept Summary designed to help you review real and personal defenses.

TABLE **29-1**

Concept Summary	Real and Personal Defenses	
Real defenses (defenses to which all holders are subject)	Personal defenses (defenses to which holders with the rights of a holder in due course are not subject)	Real defenses (if they render the underlying agreement void) and personal defenses (if they render the underlying agreement voidable)
• Forgery	• Breach of Contract	
• Alteration	• Lack of Consideration	• Mental Incapacity
• Fraud in the Execution	• Nonissuance of Instrument	• Incapacity Due to Intoxication
• Infancy	• Fraud in the Inducement	• Duress
• Discharge in Bankruptcy	• Claim in Recoupment	• Illegality

Discharge

It should be noted that no discharge of any party under UCC Article 3 is effective against a subsequent holder in due course unless the holder in due course has notice of the discharge when he or she takes the instrument (Section 3-601[b]), except discharge in bankruptcy (Section 3-305 [a][1]). A party might thus incur liability on an instrument even after he or she has been "discharged" from liability.

Payment or Satisfaction

A party who pays an instrument discharges his or her liability on the instrument (Section 3-602). A party who partially pays an instrument discharges his liability to the extent of his payment.

The obligation of a party to pay an instrument is not discharged under certain circumstances specified in Section 3-602(b)(1). For example, if a party pays an instrument in violation of a court order, that party is not discharged. Additionally, suppose that Anderson has a valid claim of ownership against an instrument. Anderson thereafter indemnifies the party obligated to pay the instrument (the bank in this case) against a loss resulting from a refusal to pay the instrument. If the bank ignores the indemnity agreement with Anderson and pays the instrument, the bank is not discharged.

Cancellation and Renunciation

Under Section 3-604, the holder of an instrument can discharge any party to the instrument through cancellation or renunciation. Cancellation can be accomplished by stamping words such as "canceled," "paid," or "satisfied" across the face of the instrument or over the party's signature, by otherwise striking out the party's signature, or by purposely destroying or mutilating the instrument with the intention of canceling it.

The holder can also discharge any party by renouncing his or her rights in the instrument. This can be accomplished by surrendering the instrument to the party to be discharged or by delivering a signed writing to such party which renounces the holder's rights in the instrument.

Review Questions and Problems

Key Terms

impostor rule	notice of dishonor
fictitious payee rule	protest
ordinary care	transfer warranties
comparative fault	presentment warranties
primary liability	real defenses
acceptor	personal defenses
secondary liability	fraud in the execution
presentment	fraud in the inducement
dishonor	claim in recoupment

Discussion Questions

1. What events must occur to establish the secondary liability of indorsers?

2. What warranties does a person who transfers an instrument by indorsement make?

3. What real defenses is a holder in due course subject to?

Review Problems

1. Jim, as maker, signs a promissory note payable to the order of Tim. Tim negotiates the note to Tom. Tom negotiates the note to Harry, who is a holder in due course. Under what circumstances can Harry hold Tom liable on the note?

2. Jack wrote a check made payable to Mike Prosser. A thief stole this check and transferred it to John Collins. If the thief indorsed the check with an unqualified indorsement at the time he signed it, has the thief any warranty liability to Collins?

3. Roberson obtained Smith's checkbook. Roberson wrote out a check for $5,000 payable to himself, and he signed Smith's name as the drawer of the check. Does Smith have any liability on this instrument?

Case Problems

1. Henry Jaroszewski and his wife agreed to purchase frozen food from Merit Food Corporation to be delivered in three deliveries. The note they signed authorized the bank to pay $1,850 to Merit. The purchasers became dissatisfied with the food after receiving $200 worth, and they refused to accept further deliveries. The bank in the meantime had paid Merit the $1,850. The purchasers now claim Merit's representatives fraudulently represented the nature of the forms they were signing. They also claim the bank knew of Merit's misconduct because it had dealt with Merit on similar transactions in the past. Must Jaroszewski pay the bank?

2. Mrs. Heastie bought a satellite dish from U.S. Satellite Systems for $4,000. Since she did not have the funds to purchase it, U.S. Satellite found financing for her. The Community Bank agreed to provide credit for her. The note she signed had the requisite FTC notice. However, she also signed a document that said that she would not raise any defense that she had concerning the work performed by U.S. Satellite against the bank. The dish proved to be defective. If the bank sues Mrs. Heastie, can she assert the defenses she has against U.S. Satellite against the bank?

3. Brazil entered into a contract with the payee of a check under consideration to make improvements on his home. Brazil gave a check to the contractor based on the contractor's false representation that he had already purchased certain materials to be used in making the improvements on Brazil's home. After Brazil discovered no material had been purchased, he stopped payment on the check. By this time a holder in due course had acquired the check. Does Brazil have a defense that is good against a holder in due course?

30

Negotiable Instruments: Checks

The Bank and Its Customers

Checks Generally

Stop Payment

Unauthorized Signatures and
   Alterations

Forged Signature of the Drawer

Payment on a Forged Indorsement

Full Payment Checks

This chapter deals with the most common form of commercial paper: checks. Checks and electronic funds transfers, which are discussed in the next chapter, are the most important means of transfering funds in our economy.

Recall from Chapter 26 that a check is a specialized type of draft. In the case of a check, the drawer of the check orders a bank to pay someone on the drawer's behalf. Thus a check is a draft drawn on a bank and payable on demand. Transactions involving checks are governed by Articles 3 and 4 of the Uniform Commercial Code.

This chapter will first outline some basic principles of a relationship central to all checking transactions: the relationship between a bank and its customer. The chapter will go on to discuss the rights and duties of all parties to a transaction involving a check.

The Bank and Its Customers

Everyone knows today that many other institutions in addition to banks use checks. In order to make the UCC consistent with modern practices,

the code now gives a broader definition to the word "bank." Section 4-105(1) defines a bank as "a person engaged in the business of banking, including a savings bank, savings and loan association, credit union or trust company." This means, for example, that for purposes of Article 4, if a person writes a check on her account at Acme Savings and Loan, the provisions of Article 4 relating to banks also apply to this transaction.

Additionally, the definition of "account" in Section 4-104(a)(1) refers to, among other things, a "credit account with a bank." This means that if a customer has a line of credit, and the account is with a bank, a check written on the line of credit, as well as a check written on an asset account, is governed by the rules in Article 4. Suppose that Jan Smith has a line of credit for $10,000 with American Express. She is permitted at any time to write checks until she reaches her limit—$10,000. The checks provided to her are written on an account with the American Express Centurion Bank. Article 4 controls this relationship as well.

The relationship between a bank and its customer depends on the status of the customer. Section 4-104(a)(5) defines a customer as "a person having an account with a bank or for whom a bank has agreed to collect items, including a bank that maintains an account at another bank." Thus a customer can be someone other than a depositor. Generally, though, a customer is thought of as a depositor.

In light of the principal-agent relationship between a bank and its customer, one might conclude from agency law that the bank's authority to act terminates upon the death or declaration of incompetency of the principal. Because of the large number of items handled by a bank, and the possible liability of the bank for a wrongful dishonor, the UCC instead relieves a bank of liability for payment of any instrument before it has notice of the death or incompetency of the drawer. The bank may pay (and another bank consequently may accept) an item until it knows of the death or of the adjudicated incompetence and has a reasonable opportunity to act on it (Section 4-405).

Even if the bank knows of the death of a customer, the UCC permits the bank to pay or certify a check drawn on it for 10 days after it receives notice. The bank may pay or certify a check unless a person claiming an interest in the account orders the bank to stop payment during this 10-day period. Suppose Smith writes a check on March 10 and someone presents it for payment on March 15. Even if Smith dies on March 11, and the bank knows it, the bank may honor the check. On the other hand, if an heir notifies the bank to stop payment of the check, the bank must comply.

Checks Generally

Types of Checks

As noted above, a check is a specialized type of draft that is drawn on a bank and payable on demand. In addition to the normal checks most commonly used, there are specialized types of checks: certified checks, cashier's checks, traveler's checks, and teller's checks.

Certified Checks   A **certified check** means a check accepted by the bank on which it is drawn (Section 3-409[d]). A bank's certification of a check constitutes acceptance of the check. Recall from the previous chapter that when a drawee accepts an instrument it becomes primarily liable on the instrument. Thus, once a bank certifies a check, it becomes obligated to honor it. Also, the drawer of a certified check has no right to stop payment on it. (Stop-payment orders will be discussed later in the chapter.)

Certification of a check is most commonly obtained by the drawer. A bank has no obligation to certify a check in the absence of a specific agreement to do so. Typically, a bank certifies a check by placing on the face of the check a "certified" stamp, the date, the amount certified and the signature of the bank's authorized representative.

A check may also be indorsed after it has been certified. In this case the certification remains effective and the indorser will have all of the duties and liabilities that an indorser normally has (see Chapter 29).

Cashier's Checks   A **cashier's check** is a draft with respect to which the drawer and drawee are the same bank or branches of the same bank (Section 3-104[g]). Cashier's checks are typically purchased from a bank in cases where the purchaser wishes to substitute the bank's credit for his or her own credit.

As an example, suppose that Shady Electronics, a retail outlet, wishes to purchase some compact disk players from the manufacturer for a total price of $10,000. The manufacturer is unwilling to take a Shady Electronics check as payment because it is unfamiliar with Shady's credit history (or perhaps because it *is* familiar with Shady's credit history). The manufacturer therefore requires that payment be made with a cashier's check. To obtain one, Shady will pay a bank $10,000 plus a fee. In return, the bank will issue a check drawn on itself, payable to the manufacturer and signed on behalf of the bank itself. With a cashier's check in hand, the manufacturer need not worry about Shady's creditworthiness.

Note that a bank's certification of a check also has the effect of substituting the bank's credit for that of another party. Certified checks are commonly used in commercial transactions.

Traveler's Checks   Section 3-104(i) defines a **traveler's check** as an instrument that is (1) payable on demand; (2) drawn on or payable at or through a bank; (3) designated by the term "traveler's check" or by a substantially similar term, and (4) requires as a condition of payment a countersignature by a person whose specimen signature appears on the instrument.

The purchaser of a traveler's check is required to sign the check both when it is purchased from the bank and when it is used. Traveler's checks, as the name implies, are typically used by travelers who do not wish to carry large amounts of cash. Traveler's checks, as the television commercials point out, are safer to carry than cash because it is more difficult for an unauthorized person to use them. The authorized signature for a traveler's check is already on the face of the check. When a party wishes to use a traveler's check, he or she must sign the check again in the presence of the party taking the check. This makes it easier to spot an unauthorized signature thus making it safer to take than a mere personal check.

Teller's Check   Section 3-104(h) defines a **teller's check** as "a draft drawn by a bank (i) on another bank, or (ii) payable at or through a bank."

When a bank draws a check on another bank, the question sometimes comes up: Can the drawer/bank stop payment on its check written on another bank? This question is addressed in the following case.

SPECIALTY FLOORING CO. V. PALMETTO FEDERAL SAVINGS BANK OF SOUTH CAROLINA
South Carolina Court of Appeals
394 S.E.2d 13 (1990)

BACKGROUND: John Wingo, president of Specialty Flooring, deposited a check for $67,371.32 at Palmetto Federal Savings Bank of South Carolina. The check was written by USA Construction Company on an account at Palmetto. On March 9, 1987, prior to the bank opening for business, an officer of USA Construction Company called Palmetto and informed the bank it was going to stop payment on the check to Specialty Flooring.

Soon thereafter, Palmetto issued a bank check in the amount of $70,000 drawn on Palmetto's account with Citibank (a teller's check) to Specialty Flooring in return for a $70,000 check drawn on Specialty's account at Palmetto. Later that same day, USA stopped payment on its check to Specialty Flooring. On March 12, the clearing house notified Palmetto that payment had been stopped on the check issued by USA to Specialty.

Palmetto revoked a provisional credit given to Specialty. It also stopped payment on its teller's check because Specialty's account lacked funds sufficient to cover the $70,000 check Specialty had issued to Palmetto in exchange for the teller's check (referred to as a bank check by the court).

The trial court ruled that Palmetto could stop payment on the teller's check.

Shaw, Judge

Specialty contends the trial judge erred in concluding Palmetto was entitled to stop payment on the bank check. We disagree.

Specialty argues that the check issued by Palmetto should be considered a cashier's check which generally cannot be countermanded. Where a bank is both the drawer and drawee of a cashier's check, the check is the primary obligation of the bank and the bank promises to pay a sum which cannot be countermanded. Generally, a bank is not entitled to stop payment or countermand a check drawn upon itself. However, if the bank draws a check upon a different bank, the bank generally has the right to stop payment.

In the case at hand, the check issued by Palmetto was drawn upon its account with another bank. Therefore, Palmetto was entitled to stop payment on the check.

Specialty further contends the trial judge erred in failing to find Palmetto breached its contract as drawer of the check. We disagree. The drawer of a check generally has the right to stop payment on the check, but remains liable on the instrument to a holder in due course. The question thus becomes whether Specialty is a holder in due course of the bank check. We agree with the trial judge that Specialty does not meet the criteria of a holder in due course and therefore takes the instrument subject to the defense of want or failure of consideration. . . . The purchaser has notice of a claim or defense if the purchaser has notice that the obligation of any party is voidable in whole or in part. A person has notice of a fact when he has actual knowledge or notice or, from all the facts and circumstances known to him at the time in question, he has reason to know that it exists.

Given the uncontroverted fact that Specialty requested the instrument from Palmetto with the knowledge that U.S.A. intended to stop payment on its check leaving an inadequate balance in its account to cover the check issued in consideration of the bank check, we find the trial judge properly concluded Specialty was not a holder in due course of the bank check. It thus took the instrument subject to the defense of failure of consideration and Palmetto thus is not liable on the instrument.

DECISION: The court ruled that Palmetto could stop payment on its teller's check.

Money Order   Both banks and nonbanks sell money orders. The form of the money order determines how it is treated under Article 3. The most common form of **money order** is an ordinary check on which the seller bank is the drawee. The amount is machine impressed. The drawer dates it and fills in the name of the payee. It is possible for a drawer to stop payment on such a check.

Sometimes a money order takes the form of a teller's check. If so, it is treated for Article 3 purposes as a teller's check. Postal money orders sold by the U.S. Post Office are governed by federal law (Section 3-104, comment 4).

Effect on Obligation

Section 3-310(a) states that if a certified, cashier's, or teller's check is taken as payment, the obligation is discharged absent a contrary agreement. Suppose that Acme Corporation owes $1,000 to Smith Corporation. Acme sends a $1,000 cashier's check to Smith Corporation. This discharges the debt owing between Acme and Smith.

Wrongfully Stopping Payment or Refusing to Pay

In the past banks sometimes created lawsuits by wrongfully stopping payment on a certified, teller's, or cashier's check in order to please good customers. Such instruments are often used between parties when one of the parties does not want to accept a personal check from the other party. Suppose that Acme Corporation wanted Smith Corporation to sell some goods to Acme. Smith was unsatisfied with Acme's financial situation, therefore Smith insisted upon receiving a cashier's check from Acme in exchange for the goods. Acme obtained a cashier's check from its bank, First National Bank. First National was both drawer and drawee of this check and Smith Corporation was the payee of the cashier's check. In this case, Acme is called a *remitter*—a person who purchases an instrument from its issuer which is payable to someone other than the purchaser (Section 3-103[11]). Naturally, Smith Corporation felt quite confident about being paid in this situation, so it delivered the goods to Acme. Soon thereafter, Acme discovered a serious defect in the goods. Acme, a very good customer of the First National Bank, asked a bank officer to refuse to pay the cashier's check when it was presented for payment. When Smith presented the check for payment, the bank refused to pay it.

A remitter cannot stop payment on a check. To permit such instruments not to be paid would undercut the commercial utility of such instruments. But a bank can wrongfully stop payment as the above example illustrates.

In order to discourage banks from engaging in this practice, revised Article 3 provides enhanced penalties for wrongfully dishonoring such an instrument. Section 3-411(b) states that if a bank wrongfully refuses to pay or stops payment on such instruments it can be liable to the person attempting to enforce the check for compensation for expenses, loss of interest and in some cases, consequential damages. Expenses include attorney fees.

While it is true that a bank cannot refuse to pay such an instrument based on the *remitter's* defenses, a bank can refuse to pay based on its own defense. A bank is *not* liable for expenses or consequential damages if it refuses to pay or stop payment because

1. The bank suspends payments
2. The bank has reasonable grounds to believe it has a claim or defense against the person entitled to enforce the instrument
3. The bank has reasonable doubt whether the person demanding payment is the person entitled to enforce the instrument
4. Payment is prohibited by law

For example, suppose that the bank issued a cashier's check to Acme Corporation which was payable to Smith Corporation. The bank expected to be paid for the check by Acme (the remitter), but Acme failed to pay the bank. In this case, the bank can refuse to pay the instrument and can use the defense of failure of consideration as a basis for its refusal to pay the check—as long as a holder in due course is not in possession of the instrument.

Lost, Destroyed, or Stolen Cashier's, Teller's, or Certified Checks

Suppose that Acme Corporation (the remitter) obtains a $1,000 cashier's check from its bank, First National Bank, which is payable to the order of Smith Corporation. Acme delivers this check to Smith. Thereafter, the check is stolen from Smith Corporation.

Revised Article 3 creates a rule to deal with this situation in Section 3-312. This rule permits a claimant of the cashier's check to request the bank to reissue the cashier's check. The claimant must also submit a "declaration of loss" explaining what happened to the check. The bank must pay or reissue the cashier's check on the ninetieth day following the date the cashier's check was issued. A bank *may* pay the person submitting the claim before this date if it wishes to do so. Once this occurs, the bank is no longer liable on the original certified check.

Up to this point in time, however, the bank may pay the original certified check. If it pays a person entitled to enforce the original certified check, payment to this person discharges all liability of the bank on the certified check.

Unfortunately for the person who submitted the claim, if the bank pays the claimant, and thereafter the original certified check shows up in the hands of a holder in due course, the person who submitted the claim must pay the holder in due course (Section 3-312[c]).

Check Collection

Figure 30-1 illustrates how a check is processed in the banking system. The check's payee or holder will typically deposit the check in his or her own bank, which then becomes known as the depositary bank. A **depositary bank** is defined as "the first bank to take an item even though it is also the payor bank, unless the item is presented for immediate payment over the counter" (Section 4-105[2]).

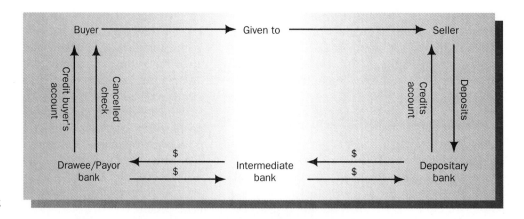

FIGURE 30-1

Life of a Check

The depositary bank will then typically give the depositor provisional credit on the check. **Provisional credit** is credit that can be revoked within a certain period of time if the check is not ultimately paid by the drawee bank. The depositary bank will then attempt to obtain payment on the check from the bank on which the check is drawn, which, if it pays the check, becomes known as the payor bank. A **payor bank** is defined as "a bank that is the drawee of a draft" (Section 4-105[3]). However, if the depositary bank does not have an account with the payor bank (banks have accounts with one another to facilitate the collection process), the depositary bank will transfer the check to the drawee bank indirectly through one or more intermediary banks—that is, banks in the chain of collection other than the depositary bank and the payor bank. An **intermediary bank** is defined as "a bank to which an item is transferred in course of collection except the depositary or payor bank" (Section 4-105[4]).

As an example, assume that Ricky in New York sends Micky, his brother in Los Angeles, a $100 check for his birthday. The check is drawn on Ricky's account in MegaBank of New York. Micky deposits the check into his account at MellowBank of Los Angeles. MellowBank gives Micky's account provisional credit in the amount of $100. MellowBank does not have an account at MegaBank, but it does have an account at San Francisco's MiddleBank, which in turn has an account at MegaBank. MellowBank thus transfers the check to MiddleBank, which gives MellowBank provisional credit in the amount of $100. MiddleBank then sends the check on to MegaBank, which pays it. MiddleBank's provisional credit to MellowBank's account with it then becomes final, as does MellowBank's provisional credit to Micky's account at MellowBank.

In this example, MellowBank is the depositary bank and MegaBank is the payor bank. MiddleBank is the only intermediary bank, although often more than one intermediary bank is needed to form a chain of collection from the depositary bank to the payor bank. Also, both MellowBank and MiddleBank are collecting banks. **Collecting banks** include all banks in the chain of collection other than the payor bank—in other words, the depositary bank and the intermediary banks. Section 4-105(5) defines it as "a bank handling an item for collection except the payor bank."

In the above example, all of the banks in the chain of collection were private-sector banks. Checks are also commonly cleared through the Federal Reserve System. MellowBank thus might have deposited the check in its account at the Federal Reserve Bank of San Francisco, which would then send the check onto the Federal Reserve Bank of New York, which would then obtain payment from MegaBank.

Expedited Funds Availability Act Banks have traditionally adopted policies under which they place "holds" on deposited checks—that is, a customer who deposits a check may not withdraw some or all of the funds (either directly or by check) until a certain period of time has passed. These hold periods were justified, at least in theory, by the check collection process outlined above. Since the Expedited Funds Availability Act of 1987 has gone into effect, banks have been subject to strict guidelines on the amount of time that they can put holds on most checks. The checks require that funds deposited in the form of a "local check"—that is, a check drawn on a bank in the same region as the depositary bank as defined by the act—be available to the depositor within 1 business day. Funds deposited in the form of a nonlocal check must be made available within 4 business days.

The act also generally requires funds deposited by certain types of checks to be made available on the next business day after deposit. Such types of checks generally include checks drawn on the U.S. Treasury, checks drawn on a state or local government (when deposited within the state), checks drawn on a different branches of the depositary bank (unless they're located in different states or check processing regions), cashier's checks, and certified checks. The act also provides that the first $100 of checks deposited on any one business day be available for withdrawal by the next business day.

Electronic Presentation The Expedited Funds Availability Act makes it essential for banks to move in the direction of faster check collection. In fact, many financial institutions had already moved in the direction of presenting information concerning an item rather than actually presenting the item itself to the drawee bank (referred to as "truncation"). The revised code expressly recognizes that parties may agree to the electronic presentation of information concerning the item in Section 4-110(a). Electronic presentation encourages truncation, which speeds up the check collection process.

Warranty Liability In Chapter 29, we learned that anyone who transfers an instrument and receives value for it is deemed to make certain *transfer warranties* to the transferee and to all subsequent transferees or holders who take the instrument in good faith. Additionally, anyone who presents an instrument and obtains payment or acceptance of it is deemed to make certain *presentment warranties* to the party that pays or accepts the instrument in good faith; any prior transferor of the instrument is also deemed to make these presentment warranties to the party that pays or accepts the instrument. These transfer and presentment warranties are set forth in Sections 3-417 and 3-416.

Section 4-207 sets forth transfer warranties that are virtually identical to those of Section 3-416, except it adds another warranty. Section 4-207(b) provides that customers or collecting banks that transfer items, whether by indorsement or not, agree to pay the item if it is dishonored. This obligation cannot be disclaimed. Section 4-208 sets forth presentment warranties. It conforms to Section 3-417.

Encoding and Retention Warranties

In addition to other warranties, anyone who encodes information on or with respect to an item after issue warrants to later banks dealing with the item that the information is correctly encoded (Section 4-209[a]).

A person who retains an item pursuant to an agreement for electronic presentation warrants to later banks dealing with the item that the retention and presentment of the item comply with the agreement (Section 4-209[b]).

Failure to Indorse

What if the customer fails to indorse the check? Normally, an order instrument must be indorsed in order for a proper negotiation to occur. The UCC has a special provision to speed up the collection process. Section 4-205(1) makes the depositary bank a holder of an item which it received for collection whether its customer indorsed the item or not. It is *not* necessary for the depositary bank to put an indorsement on an instrument in order for it to be a holder of the instrument.

Not an Assignment of Funds

Merely because one receives a check from someone else does not mean that one is entitled to the funds in the other's account. A check does not operate as an assignment of funds in the hands of the drawee (Section 3-408). A bank is not liable on a check until it accepts it. As for the holder of the check, he or she has no recourse against the bank when it fails to accept a check. The holder of a check that has been dishonored must attempt to collect from the drawer of the check or from one of the indorsers.

Overdrafts

If a bank decides to honor a check, it may do so even though the charge creates an overdraft (Section 4-401[a]). A customer who writes a check for $550 but who has deposited only $500 in his or her account, has in effect authorized the bank to pay $550 to the payee. By implication, the customer has agreed to reimburse the bank for the other $50. The bank has no obligation to honor such a check because it creates an overdraft. At most banks the customer will soon discover that his or her check has bounced.

Section 4-401(b) provides some protection for the individual who neither signed the item nor benefited from the proceeds of the item. Suppose that son is authorized to draw checks on mom's account. Mom writes a check for $550 to pay for a dress which she purchased. This rule makes only mom liable for the extra $50 and not son because he neither signed the check nor benefited from the overdraft.

The following case involves an unusual situation. The bank did not bounce the check, but instead honored it even though this created an overdraft.

PULASKI STATE BANK V. KALBE

Wisconsin Court of Appeals
364 N.W.2d 162 (1985)

BACKGROUND: Pulaski State Bank (plaintiff) sued Kalbe (defendant). Kalbe signed a check for $7,260 on her account at Pulaski State Bank. Thereafter, it was stolen and cashed at a Florida bank. Pulaski State Bank received the check on Thursday, January 8, 1982, and paid it on Monday, January 12, 1982. The check created an overdraft of $6,542.12. The bank commenced this action to recover $7,260. The trial court awarded the bank the amount of the check. Kalbe appealed.

Dean, Judge

The bank could properly pay the check even though it created an overdraft. Section 404.401(1), Stats, unambiguously states that a bank may charge a customer's account for an item otherwise properly payable even though the charge creates an overdraft. The bank's payment of an overdraft check is treated as a loan to the depositor, which may be recovered. Kalbe argues that checks creating unusually large overdrafts are not properly payable. She relies on the definition of properly payable, which "includes the availability of funds for payment at the time of decision to pay or dishonor." Section 404.104(1)(i), Stats. Section 404.104(1)(i), however, is a source of bank discretion and does not limit the bank's power to pay overdrafts. The statute gives banks the option of dishonoring checks when sufficient funds are not available. The bank may consider the check to be not properly payable and refuse to pay without risk of liability for wrongful dishonor. This does not prevent the bank from alternatively paying the overdraft check and, if it is otherwise properly payable, charging the customer's account. Section 404.401(1) places no limit on the size of the overdraft or the bank's reason for payment. Construing the statutes together, "otherwise properly payable" refers to those requirements other than availability of funds.

It is undisputed that in all other respects the check was properly payable. Kalbe does not argue that the bank honored an altered check or a check bearing a forged or unauthorized maker's signature. The check was therefore otherwise properly payable and Kalbe's liability is complete. The check creating the overdraft carried Kalbe's implied promise to reimburse the bank.

A duty of good faith, however, is imposed on the bank because it charged Kalbe's account according to the tenor of a completed item. Moreover, every contract or duty within ch 404 imposes an obligation of good faith in its performance or enforcement. . . .

We cannot say that the bank's conduct evidences bad faith. The bank attempted to contact Kalbe before the midnight deadline. The bank also confirmed the check with the Florida bank. Kalbe did not report the check's loss or theft until finally contacted by the bank.

DECISION: The court of appeals also ruled for the Pulaski State Bank.

Postdating

The 1990 code adopts a somewhat modified rule with respect to postdated checks. Section 4-401(c) permits a bank to charge a customer's account for a check even though payment was made before the date of the check. If a customer wishes to prevent a bank from honoring its check before the date specified on the check, the customer must notify the bank of the postdated check and must give such notice far enough ahead of time so as to give the bank a reasonable opportunity to act on the check. If this is the case, and the bank fails to act on the customer's timely notice, the bank may be liable for damages for loss resulting from its failure to observe the customer's notice.

Suppose that a customer writes a check on March 1 to his landlord that is dated March 15. The landlord could deposit this check for collection on March 1. The customer's bank could honor this check when it is presented to the bank for payment even though the check is presented before March 15. To protect himself, the tenant should notify the bank well in advance that he has written a postdated check and the bank should not honor the check before March 15.

It should be noted that the Fair Debt Collection Practices Act makes it illegal for a debt collector to take a postdated check.

Failure of the Bank to Honor a Check

What if the bank fails to pay a check written by the drawer when it ought to have done so? The bank will be liable to the drawer for any damages proximately caused by a wrongful dishonor of the check. If the bank merely made a mistake, its liability is limited to actual damages proved. The UCC explicitly recognizes damages for arrest and prosecution and other consequential damages proximately caused by the wrongful dishonor. If a drawer wrote a check that the bank wrongfully failed to honor, he or she could be prosecuted. (In most states the drawer probably would not be arrested. Most states require that notice of the dishonor be given to the drawer and an opportunity to make the check good. During this period the drawer probably would be able to straighten the matter out with the bank.)

Stale Checks

A bank also has no obligation to its checking-account customers to honor uncertified checks presented more than 6 months after date. Such a check is referred to as a **stale check** (Section 4-404). On the other hand, the bank may honor such a check if it acts in good faith. If one receives a dividend check from GM on August 1 but neglects to cash it until March 1 of the following year, the check is stale. Nonetheless, it would seem reasonable to cash such a check, as GM presumably would not object if the check were paid.

Prior to cashing a check that is more than 6 months old, a bank probably should consult with the drawer concerning the check. The drawer could argue that if the bank fails to check first with him or her, then a failure to make such a con-

sultation prior to cashing the check violates the bank's obligation to act in good faith.

Stop Payment

Right to Stop

Section 4-403 of the UCC gives a bank customer the right to stop payment of a check. Subsection (a) requires the customer to notify the bank in such time and manner as to give the bank a reasonable opportunity to act on the stop-payment order. The order must be received by the bank before it has paid a check in cash, accepted the check, or certified it.

Under Section 4-403(b) an oral order is effective for fourteen days; a written order is effective for six months. A written stop-payment order can be renewed for additional periods of 6 months. In the event a check is paid over a binding stop-payment order the burden is on the bank's customer to establish any loss incurred as a result of paying the check.

Section 4-405(b) provides that when a bank's customer has died, any person claiming an interest in the account of the deceased may stop payment on checks drawn on his or her account.

Defenses

Even though the drawer of the check has the right to stop payment, he or she remains liable to any holder of the instrument unless the drawer has a defense good against the holder. The drawer of a check cannot issue a check to a payee and expect to escape liability simply by stopping payment on the check. The drawer must establish a defense that can be successfully asserted against the holder of the instrument—for example, failure of consideration. If one writes a $450 check to an appliance store for a refrigerator, but the store never delivers the refrigerator, one would be able to stop payment on the check. If the store sued, one could successfully assert failure of consideration as a defense against the store. The store may not proceed against the bank for refusing to honor the check because a check is not an assignment of funds in the account of the drawer.

If the drawer of a check is so unfortunate as to write a check like the drawer in the previous example, and it is transferred to a holder in due course, or someone having the rights of a holder in due course, he or she may be liable on the check even if he or she stopped payment on it. The defense of failure of consideration is a personal defense and therefore may not be asserted successfully against a holder in due course. On the other hand, a real defense, like adjudicated insanity, may be asserted against a holder in due course.

The written agreement between a bank and its customer sometimes purports to waive or limit the bank's liability for improper payment over a stop-payment order. Such agreements are not enforceable in some states, but the majority rule is that they are enforceable so long as they don't excuse a bank's lack of ordinary care or good faith.

Questions sometimes arise when a customer provides information to the bank that is not entirely accurate. Considering the fact that the bank probably uses an automated system, it may create problems if the customer, for example, does not indicate the correct amount of the check on which he or she wishes the bank to stop payment. The system may simply ignore the stop-payment order because it was not provided correct information. In describing an item, a customer must provide the information that allows the bank's system to identify the item with reasonable certainty (Section 4-403, comment 5). This issue probably will be dealt with in the agreement between the bank and its customer.

It should be recognized that Article 4 gives banks a considerable degree of freedom in drafting their deposit agreements with customers. Section 4-103(a) states "[T]he parties may determine by agreement the standards by which the bank's responsibility is to be measured if those standards are not manifestly unreasonable." This provision recognizes the concept of freedom of contract between a bank and its customer.

Bank's Right of Subrogation

When a bank pays a check over a stop-payment order, then, in order to avoid unjust enrichment and to the extent necessary to prevent a loss by the bank, the bank is given a right of subrogation (Section 4-407). A party with the right of **subrogation** acquires the rights that some other party had with respect to an instrument or underlying transaction. When the bank is subrogated to the rights of another party, the bank essentially steps into the shoes of that other party and may pursue

or defend a claim to the same extent that that other party could have done. Into whose shoes may the bank step? That depends on the circumstances, which will be discussed below.

Bank Subrogated to Rights of Holder in Due Course   When a bank pays a check to a holder in due course over a stop-payment order, the bank may generally step into the shoes of the holder in due course against the customer.

As an example, suppose that Harry is a holder in due course of a check written by Seymour on his account at First Bank. Seymour issues a stop-payment order on the check, but First Bank pays the check anyway.

Recall from previous chapters that Harry, as a holder in due course, would have been entitled to payment on the check assuming that no real defense could be asserted against him. Seymour would thus be unjustly enriched if he could stop payment on the check and then force First Bank, after having paid the check, to recredit his account.

To avoid this unjust enrichment, Section 4-407 allows the bank, after paying the check to the holder in due course, to step into the shoes of the holder in due course in a dispute with the drawer. That means that if Seymour would not have had grounds to prevent Harry from receiving payment on the check, Seymour will similarly not have grounds to require First Bank to recredit his account.

Bank Subrogated to Rights of Payee or Other Holder   Section 4-407 provides that a bank, after paying a check over a stop-payment order, is generally subrogated to the rights of the payee or any other holder against the drawer with respect to the check or the underlying transaction.

For example, assume that Sam's Shoe Store orders 100 identical pairs of shoes from Fred's Factory. Sam's pays for the shoes with a $1,000 check drawn on Sam's account at First Bank. Fred's delivers only 80 pairs of shoes, and Sam's issues a stop-payment order on the check. If Sam's accepts the 80 pairs of shoes delivered, Fred's would be entitled to $800. If First Bank pays the $1,000 check over the stop-payment order, then First Bank is subrogated to the rights of Fred's— that is, First Bank will not be required to recredit to Sam's account the $800 that Sam's would have been required to pay Fred's. First Bank would, however, be required to recredit the remaining $200. As we shall see in the next section, however, the bank would then be entitled to recover the $200 from Fred's.

Bank Subrogated to Rights of Drawer

Section 4-407 provides that a bank that has paid a check over a stop-payment order is generally subrogated to the rights of the drawer against the payee or any other holder with respect to the underlying transaction. Returning to our previous example, recall that Fred's Factory received full payment on a $1,000 check. But since Fred's only delivered 80 pairs of shoes out of the required 100, Fred's was only entitled to receive $800. Sam's Shoe Store, the buyer, would be entitled to recover the remaining $200. But if First Bank, after paying the check, makes Sam's whole by recrediting $200 to Sam's account, then the bank can step into Sam's' shoes and recover the $200 windfall from Fred's Factory.

Unauthorized Signatures and Alterations

Customer's Duty to Discover and Report

The revised Section 4-406 in the 1990 code reflects the ongoing changes within the banking industry. Billions of checks are written every year. Returning those checks to the customer has become a substantial burden.

Section 4-406(a) gives the bank the option of returning the checks paid or alternatively providing information in the statement of account sufficient to allow the customer to identify which checks have been paid. Such a statement should indicate the check number, the amount of the check, and the date of payment. It is sufficient to send the customer an image of the check.

If the checks are not returned to the customer, the person retaining the checks must either keep them or, alternatively, keep legible copies of the checks for 7 years after receipt of the checks. The person keeping the checks must be able to provide either the check or, if the check has been destroyed, a legible copy of the check (Section 4-406[b]).

Once the checks or a statement of the account have been provided to a customer, the customer must exercise reasonable promptness in examining the statement or checks to determine if any payment was not authorized because of an alteration of a check or because the drawer's signature was not authorized. The customer must promptly report an unauthorized payment to the bank (Section 4-406[c]). This duty arises only if a bank sends the checks or a statement of account to its customer. A bank is not required by these rules to send the checks or a statement of the account to the customer.

A Single Item

If a customer fails to promptly report any unauthorized signature or alteration to the bank, the loss for this check will fall on the customer if the bank establishes that it suffered a loss as a result of the customer's failure to provide this information to the bank (Section 4-406[d][1]).

Several Items by the Same Wrongdoer

Sometimes a single individual will write a series of forged checks or alterations on a drawer's account. The initial loss for any forged or altered checks will fall on the bank. But after the customer has had a reasonable time period (not exceeding 30 days) in which to examine the checks or the statement of account and to notify the bank of any unauthorized signatures or alterations, the loss for any future unauthorized payments will fall on the customer. The loss for any unauthorized signatures and alterations will remain on the customer until it notifies the bank. Thereafter, if the bank honors any more such checks written by the same wrongdoer, the loss will fall on the bank (Section 4-406[d][2]).

Consider the following case. Mary receives her checks on June 1. Her signature had been forged on a check that had been returned to her on June 1. Susan, an acquaintance of Mary, forged the check. Susan then forges another check on Mary's account on June 5. Mary receives the second check along with her statement and other checks on July 1. Susan then forges another check on July 18. The third check is returned to Mary on August 1.

On August 3 Mary discovers all the checks forged by Susan. She notifies the bank that day and asks the bank to recredit her account.

The UCC gives Mary a maximum of 30 days from the time she should have reasonably discovered the unauthorized payment to notify the bank. Mary thus had 30 days from the date she received the first forged check (June 1) in which to notify the bank. The bank must recredit her account for the first two checks; however, it need not recredit her account for the third check because it was honored after the date by which Mary was obligated to notify the bank of the forgery—June 30. The bank may charge Mary's account for any check honored by the bank after June 30 up to the time it receives notice of the forgeries from Mary.

If the bank honors a forgery by Susan after Mary notifies the bank on August 3, the bank is not acting with reasonable care and it will not be able to charge her account for any check it honors after August 3.

Comparative Fault

In line with several other new provisions of the code adopting the concept of comparative fault, Section 4-406(e) also adopts this concept. If the customer who failed to provide a timely notice to the bank of a forgery or alteration is able to establish that the bank failed to exercise ordinary care in paying the check and that the failure substantially contributed to the loss, the loss will be allocated between the customer and the bank according to the degree of fault of each party.

A customer has 1 year from the date the customer receives a disputed check or the statement of the account in which to notify the bank the check was improperly paid. After 1 year, the customer cannot ask for the bank to recredit his or her account even if the bank failed to exercise ordinary care (Section 4-406[f]).

The question has come up whether it is a reasonable banking practice for a bank to fail to examine every check to determine the authenticity of each drawer's signature. In fact, banks today do not examine every signature.

Section 3-103(a)(7) defines the term *ordinary care*. It specifically notes that reasonable commercial standards do not require a bank to examine an instrument so long as this procedure is consistent with the bank's prescribed procedures and does not vary unreasonably from general banking practices.

The following case deals with this issue in the context of Section 4-406.

RHODE ISLAND HOSPITAL TRUST NATIONAL BANK V. ZAPATA CORPORATION

U.S. Court of Appeals, First Circuit
848 F.2d 291 (1988)

BACKGROUND: A Zapata employee stole some checks from Zapata and wrote a large number of forged checks. Zapata argued that even if it was negligent in failing to notify the bank of the forgeries after receiving its checks and statements, the bank failed to exercise ordinary care because it failed to examine every check to determine if Zapata's name had been forged on the checks.

The trial court ruled for the bank. Zapata appealed.

Breyer, Circuit Judge

The record convinces us that Zapata failed to carry its burden of establishing "lack of ordinary care" on the part of the Bank. First, the Bank described its ordinary practices as follows: The Bank examines all signatures on checks for more than $1,000. It examines signatures on checks between $100 and $1,000 (those at issue here) if it has reason to suspect a problem, *e.g.*, if a customer has warned it of a possible forgery or if the check was drawn on an account with insufficient funds. It examines the signatures of a randomly chosen one percent of all other checks between $100 and $1,000. But, it does not examine the signatures on other checks between $100 and $1,000. Through expert testimony, the

Bank also established that most other banks in the nation follow this practice and that banking industry experts recommend it. Indeed, Trust National Bank's practices are conservative in this regard, as most banks set $2500 or more, not $1,000, as the limit beneath which they will not examine each signature.

Second, both bank officials and industry experts pointed out that this industry practice, in general and in the particular case of the Trust National Bank, saved considerable expense, compared with the Bank's pre–1981 practice of examining each check by hand. To be specific, the change saved the Bank about $125,000 annually. Zapata accepts this testimony as accurate.

Third, both a Bank official and an industry expert testified that changing from an "individual signature examination" system to the new "bulk-filing" system led to *no* significant increase in the number of forgeries that went undetected.

Fourth, even if one assumes, contrary to this uncontradicted evidence, that the new system meant *some* increase in the number of undetected forged checks, Zapata still could not prevail, for it presented *no* evidence tending to show any such increased loss unreasonable in light of the costs that the new practice would save. Instead, it relied simply upon the assertion that costs saved the bank are irrelevant. But, that is not so, for what is reasonable or unreasonable insofar as "ordinary care" or "due care" or "negligence" (and the like) are concerned is often a matter of costs of prevention compared with correlative risks of loss.

DECISION: The court of appeals ruled that the bank had not failed to exercise ordinary care.

Forged Signature of the Drawer

Signature of the Drawer Required

For an instrument to be negotiable, either a person must have signed the instrument or someone acting in his or her behalf must have signed the instrument intending to bind the drawer (Section 3-401[a]). Thus, if someone forges the signature of the drawer on his or her checks, the drawer is not liable (unless he or she subsequently ratifies the signature).

It should be noted that in some instances an organization requires more than one signature on an instrument. Section 3-403(b) states that if one of the required signatures is missing or forged, the signature of the organization is unauthorized.

The UCC assumes that the bank will recognize the signatures of its customers and will not honor forgeries. For example, Stan manages to steal one of Robert's checks without Robert learning of the theft. Stan makes the check payable to himself and forges Robert's signature. The bank charges Robert's account. When Robert receives his checks and statement, he discovers the forgery. Robert immediately notifies the bank. Assuming Robert was not negligent, the bank must recredit his account.

Other Persons Liable

Assuming that the bank paid a check, and the customer establishes that his or her signature was unauthorized, the bank may not charge his or her account. It may be, however, that the bank can collect from someone other than its customer.

Liability of Forger

Section 3-403(a) states that, even though an unauthorized signature does not bind a customer of the bank, it operates as the signature of the unauthorized signer in favor of any person who in good faith pays the instrument or takes it for value.

Payment on a Forged Indorsement

In order for a drawee bank to charge a drawer's account properly when it honors one of his or her checks, the bank must pay only a person entitled to enforce the instrument. With respect to bearer paper, this does not create a problem. But what if the drawer wrote a check to a specific payee, whose indorsement was forged or unauthorized? No one who comes into possession of the check can be a holder because of the forged indorsement. (As no one could become a holder of the check, no one could become a holder in due course with respect to the check.) That being the case, it would be improper for the bank to charge its customer's account.

In the event a bank charges its customer's (the drawer's) account in this situation, it must recredit the customer's account for the amount of the check. The bank, in turn, could sue the person who presented the instrument for payment for breach of the presentment warranty that there were no unauthorized indorsements (Section 3-417[a][1]).

For example, suppose that Bill writes a check to Martha and makes it payable to Martha. Bill issues the check to Martha. Thereafter, a thief steals the check from Martha. The thief forges Martha's indorsement and cashes the check at Bill's bank. The bank charges Bill's account. As the check had an unauthorized indorsement on it, the bank was not a holder of the check and therefore was not a party entitled to charge Bill for the check.

In addition to a suit by the drawer against the drawee (payor) bank, there is also a possibility of a suit by the intended payee when a bank has paid an instrument bearing a forged indorsement. Section 3-420(a) recognizes that an instrument is *converted* when any person takes an instrument from a person not entitled to enforce the instrument or a bank pays an instrument to a person not entitled to enforce the instrument or receive payment. The intended payee of an instrument cannot bring an action for conversion unless the payee initially received delivery of the instrument.

The following case deals with an instrument paid by a bank to a person who was not entitled to enforce the instrument. The First Pennsylvania Bank held the check through a forged indorsement.

LEVY V. FIRST PENNSYLVANIA BANK, N.A.

Superior Court of Pennsylvania
36 UCC Rep. Serv. 184 (1985)

BACKGROUND: The Levys (plaintiffs) filed suit against First Pennsylvania Bank (defendant-appellant). The Levys were clients of the law firm of Bolger & Picker. When they sold their business, Novelty Printing, in February 1978 the Levys instructed Richard Robinson, a partner at Bolger & Picker, to open an account for them in the name of B&J Corp. at a local brokerage firm. When the treasury bills purchased by the broker matured, Robinson was directed to deposit checks sent to him by the broker into the Levys' bank accounts at Girard Bank and Industrial Valley Bank.

Robinson received three checks in the sums of $75,000, $75,000, and $72,776.87 from the broker. Instead of depositing them in the Levys' bank accounts, he deposited them in his own personal account at First Pennsylvania. Robinson accomplished this by signing the back of the checks with the names of the payees, B&J Corp. and Novelty Printing Company Profit Sharing Trust, and the notations "deposit to account No. 773-784-4." This was Robinson's personal account. He later withdrew the money and disposed of it. When the scheme was discovered, the law firm's insurer paid to the Levys the amount of the checks.

The Levys then brought this action against First Pennsylvania for conversion. The bank joined Bolger & Picker and Robinson as codefendants. At a nonjury trial the Levys were awarded $222,776.87 with interest from September 14, 1979, the date upon which the insurer reimbursed the Levys. The bank appealed.

Olszewski, Justice

Appellant assigns a number of errors to the lower court's opinion; we address them seriatim. Appellant first argues that it cannot be held liable for making final payment on the instruments because Robinson's endorsements were not forgeries.

Appellant avers that the endorsement was not forged because Robinson had the authority to endorse the checks. If he did have the authority to endorse, appellant claims Robinson's writing of the payees' names constituted an endorsement in blank, and then the checks were properly payable to anyone under 13 Pa CS § 3204. What subsequently happened to the checks would be irrelevant to the bank's liability, in appellant's view.

The trial court found that Robinson's authority was limited to endorsing checks for deposit into the Levys' accounts at Girard and IVB. It found that neither expressed nor implied authority to endorse in blank existed, and that the endorsements were unauthorized.

Under Pennsylvania law, the issue of agency is for the finder of fact. Here, the court, as finder of fact, concluded that Robinson had no authority to endorse the checks as he did. When a finding of fact is adequately supported by the record, we will not overrule the trial court. The record indicates that the Levys told Robinson to deposit the checks in their accounts. Accordingly, we do not disturb the court's finding.

DECISION: The Superior Court of Pennsylvania ruled for the Levys.

Recall from Chapter 29 that in certain instances there can be a valid negotiation of a check even if an imposter forges the indorsement of the payee (the imposter rule) or someone indorses the check with the signature of a fictitious payee (the fictitious payee rule). In such cases, the preceding rules concerning forgery do not control.

Full Payment Checks

Another problem relating to the use of checks has to do with the relationship between the Code and the contract doctrine of accord and satisfaction. As a matter of contract law, if A owes B a debt and there is no dispute concerning the amount due, a promise of B to discharge A's debt in return for payment of an amount less than that due is unenforceable for lack of consideration. This is because by promising to pay a portion of the total debt already owed B, A is incurring no legal obligation that did not already exist. However, if the amount A owes B is subject to dispute, an agreement by B to accept a compromise sum to discharge A's indebtedness constitutes consideration for the promise to pay. An accord and satisfaction has been achieved.

The 1990 code changes the law with respect to accord and satisfaction. At one point, it was possible for the payee to receive a check marked "paid in full" and indorse the check "with reservation of rights"—thus attempting to preserve his or her rights against the person submitting the paid in full check. Revised Section 1-207(2) explicitly states that "reservation of rights" language does

not apply to an accord and satisfaction.

A common way for a person who owes money to effect an accord and satisfaction is to tender a **full payment check**—that is, a check marked "paid in full" or in some similar manner. For example, suppose that Myron charges Byron $2,000 for legal services rendered. Byron thinks that the bill is inflated, and agrees to pay only $1,500. Byron sends Myron a check for $1,500, marked "paid in full." If Myron cashes the check, an accord and satisfaction will have occurred.

Section 3-311 now governs full payment checks. If the drawer in good faith tendered a check in full payment of a bill subject to a bona fide dispute (an unliquidated debt), and the payee

TABLE 30-1

Examples of Checks Not Properly Payable	
Check	**Is It Properly Payable?**
Check without a drawer's signature or a signature of an agent authorized to bind the drawer	No
Check dated 1/17 and paid 1/18	Yes
Check with a forged indorsement	No
Check that would create an overdraft	Yes

CONCEPT SUMMARY
Checks

Types of check

1. Certified check is a check accepted by the bank on which it is drawn.
2. Cashier's check is a draft with respect to which the drawer and the drawee are the same bank or branches of the same bank.
3. Traveler's check is a check payable on demand; drawn or payable at or through a bank; is designated as a traveler's check and requires a countersignature by a person whose name appears on the instrument.
4. Teller's check is a draft drawn by a bank on another bank or payable at or through a bank.
5. Money order is generally a check on which the seller bank is the drawee, the amount is machine impressed, and the drawer dates, signs, and fills in the name of the payee.

Check collection

1. Depositary bank is the bank in which a check is initially deposited for collection.
2. Payor bank is a bank which pays a check.
3. Intermediary bank is a bank in the chain of collection.
4. Collecting bank is any bank in the chain of collection that is not a payor bank.

Stop payment

1. Oral stop-payment orders are effective for 14 days.
2. Written stop-payment orders are effective for 6 months.
3. If a bank fails to honor a stop-payment order it may be liable.

Unauthorized signatures and alterations

1. Customer has a duty to examine his or her statement and the items honored and notify the bank promptly of any unauthorized signatures or alterations.
2. A special rule applies to checks presented by the same wrongdoer. Customer must report unauthorized signatures and alterations within 30 days.

Forged signature of the drawer

1. If the drawer's signature has been forged on an instrument, the drawer is not liable.
2. Negligence of the drawer may be a defense for a bank which has paid a check.

Payment on a forged indorsement

If a bank charges its customer's account, and a check has a forged indorsement, the bank must recredit the customer's account.

Full payment checks

Cashing a check marked paid in full will result in an accord and satisfaction.

PREVENTIVE LAW

Frank visits his dentist. The dentist performs some work and 2 weeks later sends Frank a bill for $800. Frank thinks this amount is totally out of line. He writes the dentist a letter to that effect and encloses a check for $500, an amount Frank believes is reasonable. On the check, Frank writes "Paid in Full." The dentist's bookkeeper indorses the check on behalf of the dentist and deposits the check to the dentist's account.

If the dentist does nothing, the cashing of the check will discharge Frank from this debt. On the other hand, if within 90 days the dentist discovers what happened, he can tender repayment of the $500 to Frank. The dentist may then bring suit for the full amount of the check.

---

cashes the check, an accord and satisfaction results. The payee is *not* free to bring suit for the balance of the debt the payee feels the debtor owes him or her. A claim is discharged if the party receiving the in full payment check knew that the instrument was tendered in full satisfaction of a claim or an agent (of the payee) having responsibility for such checks knew that the instrument was tendered in full satisfaction of a claim (Section 3-311[d]).

Section 3-311(c) provides some protections for the person or business receiving an in full payment check. A claim will not be discharged if (1) the person receiving the check attempted to return the amount of the instrument within 90 days of payment of the instrument, or (2) the party receiving the check required that in full payment checks be sent to a particular office and the check in question was not sent to that office.

Suppose that on June 1 Acme Construction mailed a notice to all of the businesses with whom it dealt stating that if they wished to submit a full payment check to Acme, the check must be sent to Doris Smith, the treasurer of Acme Construction. In September, a dispute arose between a customer and Acme. The customer sent a full payment check to the accounting department rather than directly to Doris Smith. The person handling the check failed to note the fact that the check was marked in full payment and he deposited the check for collection. Acme still retains a right to sue its customer for whatever additional funds it feels it is entitled to receive because, under these circumstances, the cashing of the in full payment check did not work as a discharge of the debt owing between Acme and its customer.

Review Questions and Problems

Key Terms

certified check	payor bank
cashier's check	intermediary bank
traveler's check	collecting bank
money order	stale check
teller's check	subrogation
depositary bank	full payment check
provisional credit	

Discussion Questions

1. What, if anything, should a customer do when he or she receives his or her statement and checks from the bank?

2. Under what circumstances, if any, might a person be liable for a check when his or her signature, as the drawer of the check, has been forged?

3. Under what circumstances, if any, could a bank charge its customer's account for a check it honored even though the customer had given the bank a stop-payment order on the check?

4. If a bank certifies a check, how does this affect the drawer's obligation on the check?

Review Problems

1. Mark Wade wrote a check for $250 on September 30 in payment of his rent for October. The check was dated October 10. He gave the check to the manager at the Villa Apartments. The manager assured Mark that he would not deposit the check until October 10. Mark did not have enough money in his account on September 30 to cover the check, but he planned to deposit his paycheck on October 1. Mark's employer

failed to pay him on October 1. In the meantime the manager of the Villa Apartments accidentally deposited the check to the Villa account. If the check is presented to Mark's bank, could it honor the check?

2. Ron Mather wrote a check on his account on July 1, 1986. This check was presented for payment on February 1, 1987. What type of check is one that is presented so long after it was written? Can the bank honor it?

3. Amy Gardner wrote a check out and made it payable to the order of Andrew Clark. This check was stolen from Andrew, and the thief cashed the check. The thief forged Andrew Clark's signature on the back of the check. Amy's bank then honored the check and charged her account. Soon thereafter Andrew informed Amy of the theft. When Amy notified the bank of the forgery, must the bank recredit her account, if she informed the bank immediately?

4. Murphy operated a restaurant. His bookkeeper wrote a series of checks on his account by forging his name on the checks. When the checks were returned to the restaurant, the bookkeeper reviewed the checks and the statement. Several months later Murphy learned of the forgeries and notified his bank. He demanded that the bank recredit his account. Must the bank recredit his account?

Case Problems

1. Smith, Whalley's bookkeeper, forged and cashed a series of checks, drawn on Whalley's business account with Bank. This occurred between January and May. Smith was in complete charge of Whalley's books and records. Whalley's president routinely examined the bank statements to determine the account balance but did not examine any of the canceled checks. After examining the statements, the president returned the statements and checks to Smith. No one reported the forgeries to Bank until Smith was discharged in June, when irregularities were found. Bank acted in good faith in paying the forged checks. May Whalley recover the amount of the forged checks from Bank? Was Whalley's procedure with respect to the canceled checks and bank statement an exercise of reasonable care?

2. Kidwell had a checking account with Exchange Bank, upon which the president of Kidwell was authorized to draw. Smith, the corporate secretary of Kidwell, forged the president's signature on sixty-five checks made payable to her. This occurred over a three-year period. These forgeries were not reported by Kidwell to Exchange Bank until after the end of the three-year period. The facts disclose that the quality of the forgeries ranged from crude to fair; that Exchange Bank handled a large volume of checks compared to other banks; and that Exchange Bank may not have compared all the signatures on the checks against the signature card bearing the signature of Kidwell's president. Will Kidwell's failure to report the forgeries to Exchange Bank excuse any liability of the bank for improper payment?

3. Zenith maintained an account with Marine Midland Bank on which either the president or vice-president of Zenith was authorized to sign checks. In 1972, between February and November, Zenith's bookkeeper drew twenty fraudulently signed checks. Marine Midland paid these checks and charged them to Zenith's account. Each month Marine Midland sent the statements and checks from the account to Zenith for inspection. Each month, the bookkeeper received the statements and canceled checks and approved the debits. In November the subterfuge was discovered. Marine Midland was unable to recover $4,297 of the amounts paid on the checks and refused to recredit Zenith's account for this loss. Zenith sued Marine Midland to compel such action. Must Marine Midland recredit Zenith's account?

4. On December 8, Thomas gave Ralph Gallo a check for a rug. On December 10, Thomas ordered his bank to stop payment on the check. On the afternoon of the next day, the bank cashed the check. Is the bank responsible for its failure to honor the stop payment order?

31

Electronic Fund Transfers

Consumer Electronic Fund
 Transfers

Commercial Electronic Fund
 Transfers

Technology has revolutionized the way in which money is exchanged in our society. In the olden days, money could only be transferred through the physical exchange of coins and, later, paper currency. Later, commercial paper—especially checks—emerged as a primary vehicle for making payments. Today, the volume of funds transfered electronically exceeds that exchanged by checks or bank credit cards.* The amount of money transfered through electronic wire systems is staggering, sometimes reaching $2 trillion on a single day.[†] The importance of electronic fund transfers continues to grow as more and more human bank tellers lose their jobs to automated tellers and as more and more customers become accustomed to banking from home by using their telephones and personal computers.

This chapter will discuss the emerging body of law that is designed to deal with electronic fund transfers. First, we will cover the law relating to the various systems that are revolutionizing the ways in which consumers bank and make payments. Then, we will discuss the regulation of electronic fund transfer systems typically used in large commercial transactions.

*Fry, "Basic Concepts in Article 4A: Scope and Definitions," *Business Lawyer.* 45:1401 (1990).

†French, "Unauthorized and Erroneous Payment Orders," *Business Lawyer.* 45:1425 (1990).

Consumer Electronic Fund Transfers

Types of Consumer Electronic Fund Transfers

There are several types of electronic fund transfers (EFTs) currently in use for consumers. Typically, in order to initiate a transaction on any of the machines involved, the consumer has a card that gives him or her access to the machine. Often, the consumer also has a secret number to prevent others from using the card should it fall into the wrong hands.

Point-of-Sale Terminals In some places around the country point-of-sale (POS) terminals are utilized. Typically, these terminals are located in a business. This permits the business to transfer funds from an individual's account to the account maintained by the business. Thus a point-of-sale terminal might be found in a grocery store. When a customer purchases groceries, the terminal at the grocery store permits the customer to transfer money from his or her account to the store account.

Automated Tellers and Cash Dispensers A second type of EFT device is the automated-teller machine (ATM) or the cash dispenser (CD). The automated-teller machine permits the user to withdraw cash, make deposits, and transfer money from one account to another without dealing with bank personnel. Automated-teller machines provide a number of benefits for consumers, the foremost of which is 24-hour banking. A card holder may make deposits or withdrawals, for example, at any time of day or night.

The cash dispenser merely dispenses cash. These machines may be either on-line or off-line. If they are on-line, the machine is connected to a central processing computer that has access to the consumer's account. Thus the entire transaction may be completed immediately. In off-line machines the machine stores the data for collection at a later time. This means that the on-line system is much more complex, but it completes all transactions at the time a consumer initiates them.

Pay-by-Phone Systems A third EFT device is the pay-by-phone system. Here, the consumer calls his or her bank and orders the bank to pay the persons or businesses he or she specifies, thereby eliminating the need for writing a check. This system is frequently used to pay utility bills.

Preauthorized Direct Deposits and Automatic Payments Finally, there are preauthorized direct deposits and automatic payments. An employer might enter into an agreement with its employee to deposit his or her wages periodically in the employee's account at a bank. This is a preauthorized direct deposit. Such a deposit saves a trip to the bank for the employee.

Conversely, the buyer of a product might agree with a seller to have monthly payments automatically withdrawn from the buyer's account and transferred to the seller's. Such an arrangement is frequently made between the buyer of a house and the mortgage company. The buyer need not worry about forgetting to make a payment because each payment is withdrawn from the buyer's account automatically.

The Electronic Fund Transfer Act

Congress in 1978 passed the Financial Institutions Regulatory and Interest Rate Control Act. One part of this legislation is the Electronic Fund Transfer Act (EFTA), which regulates financial institutions that offer electronic fund transfers involving an account held by a consumer. The act, which became effective in 1980, establishes some rules by which the parties to these transactions will be governed.

Definitions The primary objective of the Electronic Fund Transfer Act (EFTA) is to protect certain rights of consumers dealing with such electronic systems. A consumer under the act is any *natural* person. The term *electronic fund transfer* under the act means "any transfer of funds, other than a transaction originated by check, draft, or similar paper instrument, which is initiated through an electronic terminal, telephonic instrument, or computer or magnetic tape so as to order, instruct, or authorize a financial institution to debit or credit an account."

The following case discusses the scope of the Electronic Fund Transfer Act.

WACHTER V. DENVER NATIONAL BANK

U.S. District Court, District of Colorado
751 F. Supp. 906 (1990)

BACKGROUND: Pro se plaintiff June Elga Wachter arranged for the Denver National Bank to make a wire transfer of $143.42 to California. The bank confirmed that the transfer had been received. Wachter thereafter brought suit against the bank for alleged damages arising out of the wire transfer. She alleged that the bank violated the Electronic Fund Transfer Act. The bank argued that this act did not apply to the transaction in question. This court agreed with the bank.

Carrigan, District Judge

Plaintiff's allegations and claim for relief are based solely on alleged violations of the Electronic Fund Transfer Act ("the Act"), 15 U.S.C. § 1693 *et seq.* Therefore, the question whether the Act applies here to provide the plaintiff grounds for relief controls my decision.

The act defines "electronic fund transfer," in relevant part, as:

"any transfer of funds, other than a transaction originated by check, draft, or similar paper instrument, which is initiated through an electronic terminal, telephonic instrument, or computer or magnetic tape so as to order, instruct, or authorize a financial institution to debit or credit an account. Such term includes, but is not limited to, point-of-sale transfers, automated teller machine transactions, direct deposits or withdrawals of funds, and transfers initiated by telephone." 15 U.S.C. § 1693a(6).

Thus, two requirements must be met to qualify a transaction as an electronic fund transfer: (1) it must be initiated through an electronic terminal, telephonic instrument, or computer or magnetic tape, and (2) it must order, instruct or authorize a financial institution to debit or credit an account.

Whether the first requirement is satisfied depends in part on who initiated the transfer, the financial institution or the consumer.

A bank's use of an electronic device merely to process a transaction internally does not constitute an electronic funds transfer within the Act's meaning. Rather, the Act's focus is upon consumer-initiated or consumer-authorized transfers where electronic devices are utilized in place of face-to-face banking transactions. The presence of personal contact with bank personnel who intercede between a consumer and the electronic device used to facilitate a transaction removes that transaction from the scope of the Act.

The transfer here does not fit the definition of "electronic fund transfer." First, the transfer was not initiated through an electronic device as defined by the Act. Instead, the plaintiff initiated her wire transfer through contact with the bank's personnel. The face-to-face nature of this personal banking transaction removes it from the scope of the Act's coverage. The fact that the bank used an electronic device to process the transfer internally does not change the result.

Second, the plaintiff's transfer did not order, instruct or authorize the bank to debit or credit an account. Because the Act was designed to protect consumers, the only reasonable interpretation would apply it only to debits or credits of the *consumer's* accounts. Here the plaintiff paid for her wire transfer with cash. Her account at the bank, if any, was not debited, and the account at the California bank credited with the wire transfer was not the plaintiff's.

For the reasons stated, I find and conclude that the Act does not apply to the instant wire transfer. Plaintiff's claims are based solely on alleged violations of the Act. While the plaintiff may complain about the way her transfer was handled, it appears to a certainty that no relief can be granted under any set of facts that could be proven in support [of] her complaint's allegations. Therefore, the plaintiff has failed to state a claim upon which relief can be granted and this suit must be dismissed.

DECISION: The court ruled that this transaction was not covered by the Electronic Fund Transfer Act and therefore dismissed the case.

Disclosure of Terms and Conditions
The EFTA requires that the terms and conditions of electronic fund transfers be disclosed at the time a customer contracts for such services. The financial institution must disclose matters such as the consumer's liability for an unauthorized transfer, what charges may be imposed, the right of the consumer to stop payment of a preauthorized electronic fund transfer, and the liability of the institution to the consumer.

Documentation   Each time a customer initiates an electronic fund transfer, the financial institution must make available to the customer written documentation of the transfer.

The documentation must indicate the amount involved and the date of the transfer, the type of transfer, the identity of the customer's account from which or to which funds are transferred, the identity of any third party to whom or from whom funds are transferred, and the location or identification of the electronic terminal involved.

The financial institution must provide each customer with a periodic statement for each account that may be accessed by electronic means.

Preauthorized Transfers   A preauthorized electronic fund transfer is an electronic fund transfer authorized in advance to recur at substantially regular intervals.

A preauthorized electronic fund transfer that debits a customer's account may be utilized only if the customer agrees in writing and is furnished a copy of the authorization. The customer can stop payment on such preauthorized transfers if he or she notifies the financial institution orally or in writing at any time up to 3 business days preceding the scheduled date of such transfer. If the financial institution requests it when the oral notice is given, the customer must provide written confirmation of the oral notice within 14 days of an oral notification.

In the event the preauthorized transfers vary in amount the financial institution or the payee must give the customer reasonable advance notice of the amount to be transferred and the scheduled date of the transfer.

Error Resolution   Within 60 days after receiving a financial statement, a customer may notify his or her financial institution of any errors in the report. Such notice obligates the financial institution to investigate the alleged error and report the results of the investigation to the customer within 10 business days. (If notice of error is given to the financial institution orally, the institution may require the customer to provide written confirmation within 10 business days.)

In the event the results of the investigation reveal that an error occurred the financial institution must promptly correct the error. This must be done within 1 business day after such an error is discovered.

Alternatively, the financial institution may provisionally recredit the customer's account pending an investigation of the account. This must be done within 10 business days after receiving notice of error. The financial institution then has 45 days after receipt of the notice to conclude the investigation. If during this period it determines that an error did not occur, the financial institution has 3 business days after arriving at this conclusion to deliver or mail an explanation to the customer.

If the financial institution fails to follow this procedure, or if contrary to the evidence it knowingly and willfully concludes that the customer's account was not in error, the customer is entitled to treble damages.

Customer Liability for Unauthorized Transfers   Once the customer is in possession of means of access such as a card and a secret number, his or her liability, in the event of an unauthorized transfer, will not exceed the lesser of $50 or the amount obtained prior to the time the financial institution becomes aware that an unauthorized electronic fund transfer has been or may be effected. However, the customer must notify the financial institution of the loss or theft within 2 days after discovering the loss or theft of a card or other means of access.

If a bank learns on June 1 that an unauthorized transfer from a customer's account on May 31 has occurred, the maximum that the customer can lose is $50. If the transfer was for $25, the customer loses $25. But if the transfer was for $75, the customer loses only $50.

If the customer fails to report the loss or theft within 2 days, the customer's liability in this situation is limited to the lesser of $500 or the amount of unauthorized transfers that occur after 2 business days following the customer's discovery of the loss or theft but prior to his or her notifying the financial institution.

Suppose the customer loses his card on June 1 but fails to report the loss until June 10. If a thief manages to make a withdrawal from the customer's account on June 2 for $100 and another withdrawal on June 8 for $300, the customer would owe the bank $300, if the bank can establish that the customer learned of the loss on June 1.

If the customer fails to report an unauthorized use within 60 days of receiving a periodic statement, he or she is liable for losses resulting from *any* unauthorized transfer that appeared on the statement if the financial institution can show the loss would not have occurred but for the failure of the customer to report the loss within 60 days. This provision is similar to UCC Section 4-406, which puts the burden on customers to examine their statements in a timely fashion.

A transfer from a consumer's account will not be deemed to be unauthorized if the person making the transfer obtained the card, code, or other means of access to the account from the consumer.

Liability of the Financial Institution
Under the EFTA a financial institution is liable to a customer for all damages proximately caused by its failure to make an electronic fund transfer, in accordance with the terms and conditions of an account, in the correct amount or in a timely manner when properly instructed to do so by the customer.

There are certain exceptions to this rule—for example, if the electronic terminal does not have sufficient cash to complete the transaction or the customer does not have sufficient funds in his or her account. If the failure was not intentional and resulted from a bona fide error, the financial institution is liable for the actual damages proved. *Feinman*, the case that follows, illustrates these principles—and also illustrates how litigious our society has become.

FEINMAN v. BANK OF DELAWARE

U.S. District Court, D. Delaware
728 F. Supp. 1105 (1990)

BACKGROUND: Jeff and Consuela Feinman (plaintiffs) maintained an account with Bank of Delaware (defendant) that could be accessed through ATMs. From January 1987 to February 1988, the Feinmans had overdrawn their checking account eight times. In February 1988, the Feinmans caused their account to be overdrawn once again through a combination of checks and ATM withdrawals. Without notifying the Feinmans, the bank then placed a "deny cash" restriction on the account. The temporary restriction prevented the Feinmans from withdrawing cash through ATMs; they could still, however, withdraw funds by check or by dealing directly with the bank's human tellers, provided that they returned their account to a positive balance. After learning of the restriction on their ATM privileges, the Feinmans attempted to have the privileges restored. The bank attempted to remove the restriction on February 28, by which time the Feinmans had restored their account to a positive balance. For some reason, the bank's attempt to remove the restriction wasn't properly processed, and the Feinmans found that they were still unable to withdraw funds through ATMs. The Feinmans complained again on March 2 and the restriction was removed. The Feinmans sued, claiming that the bank had wrongfully denied them access to their funds in violation of the EFTA.

Longobardi, Chief Judge

On Saturday, February 27th, the Feinmans drove to Philadelphia from their home in Newark, Delaware, to take their two children out for dinner. When they arrived in Philadelphia, they testified that the ATM from which they attempted to withdraw funds denied them access. Already having made plans for their night out and having already driven to Philadelphia, the Feinmans decided that the only alternative left to them was to drive over to Jeff Feinman's brother's (the "brother") house to borrow money from him. The Plaintiffs testified they considered their financial matters personal and had never had to borrow money from the brother before. They testified they were embarrassed and humiliated to unexpectedly show up at his house to borrow money despite the fact that Jeff Feinman said he and his brother shared a close relationship and were "good friends." The Plaintiffs testified they had to suffer the jokes and teasing of the brother at their own expense. The next day, after they all spent the night at his brother's house, Mr. Feinman attempted to withdraw funds from several other ATM's in the area. All denied him access due to the "deny cash" restriction. Upon returning to his brother's house, the Plaintiffs allegedly endured further teasing because of the inability to obtain the funds. The brother did not testify to corroborate the Plaintiffs' testimony. As previously indicated, Mr. Feinman contacted the Defendant on February 29th and again on March 2nd to remove the restriction from the Plaintiffs' Account.

The Act addresses the financial institution's responsibility to notify the consumer with respect to certain changes to the consumer's account.

> A financial institution shall notify a consumer in writing at least twenty-one days prior to the effective date of any change in any term or condition of the consumer's account required to be disclosed under subsection (a) of this section if such change would result in greater cost or liability for such consumer or decreased access to the consumer's account. A financial institution may, however, implement a change in the terms or conditions of an account *without prior notice* when such change is immediately necessary to maintain or restore the *security* of an electronic fund transfer system or a consumer's account. 15 U.S.C. § 1693c(b) (emphasis added).

The security reason given by the Defendant for the restriction on the Plaintiffs' Account was, *inter alia*, that the Plaintiffs had overdrawn their Account by the use of ATMs in the past and presented a risk to do so in the future. Indeed, the reason for the February 19th overdraft was, in part, caused by the Plaintiffs' use of an ATM to withdraw cash. The fact that the Plaintiffs had overdraft protection on their Account would have allowed them to withdraw up to $500 in funds from an ATM per day even though their Account did not have a positive asset balance. Furthermore, the Plaintiffs were aware of this capability. Unlike an overdrawn check, the Defendant could not "return" the transaction to restore a positive balance. Because of this very real possibility of future attempts at overdrawing their Account by way of ATM withdrawals, as well as the other factors in the Defendant's decision, the Court finds that the Defendant reasonably concluded that there was a security risk at the time it decided to place the deny cash restriction on the Account. . . .

The Act provides for the liability of financial institutions, such as the Defendant, in certain instances. Section 1693h provides that "a financial institution shall be liable to a consumer for all damages proximately caused by . . . the financial institution's failure to make an electronic fund transfer, *in accordance with the terms and conditions of an account*, in the correct amount or in a timely manner when *properly* instructed to do so by the consumer. . . ." 15 U.S.C. § 1693h(a)(1) (emphasis added). The liability of a financial institution under section 1693h is expressly limited by the "terms and conditions" of the account. . . .

On February 29th, Plaintiffs contacted the Defendant and requested that the restriction on their Account be removed. The ATM Department was instructed to remove the restriction on that day. The Court finds, by a preponderance of the evidence, that the restriction was not removed at that time due to either unintentional human error or a computer error. The restriction was subsequently removed on March 2nd when the Plaintiffs again complained and requested its removal. This failure to remove the restriction coupled with the Plaintiffs' attempts to withdraw cash from the Account through an ATM, constitute a violation of section 1693h(a)(1). The Plaintiffs were denied access to their funds by way of electronic transfer due to the Defendant's failure to comply with the terms and conditions of the Account agreement. During this time period, the Defendant's security risk had been removed. There was a positive Account balance and the Defendant had the opportunity to counsel the Plaintiffs on the proper use of their ATM privileges.

Section 1693h(c) provides that "[i]n the case of a failure described in subsection (a) of this section which was not intentional and which resulted from a bona fide error, notwithstanding the maintenance of procedures reasonably adapted to avoid any such error, the financial institution shall be liable for actual damages proved." The Court finds that the failure of the Defendant to remove the restriction timely was a bona fide error and was not intentional in spite of procedures reasonably adapted to avoid any such error. Accordingly, the Defendant is only liable to the Plaintiffs for actual damages proved during this time period.

At trial, the attorney for the Plaintiffs stated: "Your Honor, the only evidence we have offered as to actual damages occurred in Philadelphia." The evidence also indicated that the Plaintiffs had to contact the Defendant to remove the restriction on two occasions (February 29th and March 2nd). There were no actual damages proved with respect to the short time period that the Plaintiffs took to contact the Defendant. Furthermore, the Plaintiffs retained the ability to access their funds by writing checks or through human teller withdrawals. The Court finds that the Plaintiffs have failed to prove actual damages for the time period from February 29th to March 2nd.

DECISION: The court ruled that the bank was justified in restricting the Feinmans' account without notice, but had violated the EFTA by failing to remove the restriction on February 29. The court ruled, however, that the Feinmans had proven no damages, and were hence not entitled to recover anything.

The financial institution is also liable for damages proximately caused by its failure to credit a deposit of funds and to fail to stop payment of a preauthorized transfer from a customer's account.

Other than the failure to stop payment, a financial institution is not liable if it shows that its failure to act resulted from an act of God or other circumstances beyond its control or from a technical malfunction that was known to the customer at the time he or she attempted to initiate an electronic fund transfer or, in the case of a preauthorized transfer, at the time such transfer should have occurred.

Commercial Electronic Fund Transfers

Checks, discussed in the last chapter, are a convenient way to transfer money—but not the fastest way. Because of the check-clearing process, it can take several days for the transfer of funds from the payor to the payee to become final. For many commercial transactions today, that's just not good enough—businesses increasingly demand "same-day funds;" or payments that become final on the same day that they're initiated. That's why more and more payments are being made through electronic wire transfer systems that can finalize transfers within a day. Hundreds of trillions of dollars are exchanged through wire transfers each year.

The largest wire transfer system is **FedWire,** owned and operated by the twelve regional Federal Reserve Banks. The FedWire system utilizes the accounts that banks are required to maintain with their respective district Federal Reserve Banks. When a bank sends a payment order on FedWire on behalf of its customer, funds are moved from that bank's account at its district Federal Reserve Bank to the account of the payee's bank at *its* district Federal Reserve Bank.

A typical FedWire transaction is best described by an example. Suppose that MegaCorp is required to make a $1 million payment to Bilko Industries by wire transfer. MegaCorp instructs its bank, AppleBank of New York, to make the payment to Bilko's account at OrangeBank of California. AppleBank is required to maintain an account at the Federal Reserve Bank of New York, OrangeBank at the Federal Reserve Bank of San Francisco. AppleBank first debits $1 million from MegaCorp's account and sends the payment order over FedWire. The Federal Reserve System then moves the $1 million from AppleBank's account at the Federal Reserve Bank of New York to OrangeBank's account at the Federal Reserve Bank of San Francisco. OrangeBank receives the funds on behalf of Bilko and credits Bilko's account at OrangeBank in the amount of $1 million. If the payment order is issued early enough in the day, final payment will occur on the same day that the order was placed on the wire.

FedWire isn't the only wire transfer system. The most notable system other than FedWire is the New York Clearinghouse Interbank Payments System, commonly known as **CHIPS.** The primary players in the CHIPS system are a limited number of "settling banks" chosen by the Federal Reserve Bank of New York. (Prior to 1979, all of the CHIPS settling banks were New York banks; others have since been allowed to join.) Throughout the day, the settling banks place orders on the CHIPS computer system on behalf of their customers, directing payments to be made to other settling banks on behalf of *their* customers. The CHIPS computer network doesn't actually transfer money; it merely keeps track of how much each settling bank owes and is owed for the day. At the end of the day, those settling banks with negative balances (that is, those that owe more than they are owed) make FedWire payments to those settling banks with positive balances until each settling bank has paid (or has been paid) the correct amount.

In addition to the CHIPS settling banks, there is a larger number of "participating banks" that can use CHIPS by running payments through the settling banks. Each participating bank must have an account at a settling bank in order to use CHIPS. For example, assume that ShallowBank of Los Angeles is a CHIPS participating bank with an account at ObnoxiousBank of New York, a CHIPS settling bank. If ShallowBank wishes to send a wire transfer over CHIPS on behalf of its customer, the bank will send the funds to ObnoxiousBank, which will then send the appropriate payment order over the CHIPS network. If the ultimate payee has an account at a CHIPS settling bank, ObnoxiousBank will direct the payment to that bank. If the ultimate payee has an account at a CHIPS *participating* bank, then ObnoxiousBank will direct the payment order to the settling bank at which the participating bank has an account. That settling bank will in turn send the funds on to the participating bank.

The EFTA doesn't cover FedWire or CHIPS transactions. In fact, the EFTA only covers transactions involving accounts held by natural persons for personal, family, or household purposes. For many years, the large number of electronic fund transfers that fell outside the scope of the EFTA was governed by a hodgepodge of federal regulations and system regulations—and, in many cases, no regulations at all.

FedWire is operated in accordance with Regulation J, promulgated by the board of governors of the Federal Reserve System, and with Federal Reserve Bank Operating Circulars that are issued from time to time. CHIPS has its own internal rules of governance. Taken as a whole, these rules and regulations don't come close to providing a comprehensive framework for regulating commercial electronic fund transfers. No such framework existed prior to 1989, when Article 4A of the Uniform Commercial Code (UCC) was introduced.

UCC Article 4A

Scope of Article 4A   Article 4A of the UCC is an attempt to create a uniform body of law in the fifty states to regulate electronic fund transfers not covered by the EFTA. Article 4A and the EFTA are mutually exclusive: Section 4A-108 provides that Article 4A does not apply to a funds transfer any part of which is subject to the EFTA, as that act may be amended from time to time. Article 4A does, however, cover consumer transactions that are not subject to the EFTA. (A discussion of those consumer transactions not governed by the EFTA is beyond the scope of this book.)

Article 4A is not technically limited to *electronic* fund transfers; fund transfers by any means, including mail, are covered. It is clear, however, that the article was inspired primarily by the need to establish rules for electronic fund transfers.

Fund transfers made by check are covered by Articles 3 and 4, and not by Article 4A. Article 4A applies only to "credit transfers"—that is, transfers where the instruction to pay is given by the party who is to *make* the payment, and not the party who is to *receive* the payment. Checks do not involve credit transfers because the instruction to pay a check is given, through presentment, by the party who is to *receive* the payment. Wire transfers, on the other hand, are credit transfers, because the party who initiates the transfer is the party making the payment.

Basic Parties to an Article 4A Transaction   An Article 4A transaction invariably involves the following: A party wishing to make a payment instructs its bank either to pay an amount of money to another party or to cause that other party to be paid. The party wishing to make payment is known as the **originator** (Section 4A-104[c]). The party who is ultimately to be paid is known as the **beneficiary** (Section 4A-103[a][2]).

Note that in an Article 4A transaction, payment is never made directly by the originator to the beneficiary, but always through their respective banks. **Originator's bank** is a defined term in Article 4A, meaning, as one might expect, the bank to whom the originator gives the initial payment instruction (Section 4A-104[d]). Similarly, **beneficiary's bank** is defined as the bank which ultimately pays the beneficiary or credits the amount of the payment to the beneficiary's account.

Transactions Covered by Article 4A

According to Section 4A-102, Article 4A applies generally to "funds transfers." A **funds transfer** is defined in Section 4A-104(a) as a series of transactions made for the purpose of paying the beneficiary.

A funds transfer is made up of one or more *payment orders*. A **payment order** is an instruction by a party to a bank to pay (or cause another bank to pay) an amount of money to a beneficiary. The party who gives the instruction is known as the **sender** of the payment order (Section 4A-103[a][5]); the bank that receives the sender's instruction is known as the **receiving bank** (Section 4A-103[a][4]).

An instruction must satisfy certain conditions in order to qualify as a payment order. First, the payment order must either state an amount to be paid which is either fixed or which can be determined by the receiving bank (Section 4A-103[a][1]). Second, the instruction must not state any condition to payment other than the time that payment is to be made (Section 4A-103[a][1][i]). Third, the receiving bank must be reimbursed either by debiting the sender's account or by otherwise receiving payment from the sender.

The sender's instruction to the receiving bank may be given orally, electronically, or in writing.

To illustrate the application of these terms and some additional concepts, let us return to the example where MegaCorp pays Bilko $1 million by wire transfer. The *funds transfer* will be the entire set of transactions made to move the $1 million from MegaCorp to Bilko. MegaCorp is the *originator*, and Bilko the *beneficiary*.

First, MegaCorp instructs its bank, AppleBank of New York, to wire transfer $1 million to Bilko's account at OrangeBank of California. AppleBank is the *originator's bank*, OrangeBank the *beneficiary's bank*. MegaCorp's instruction to Apple-

Bank is a *payment order*—the first payment order of the funds transfer. With respect to this payment order, MegaCorp is the *sender* and AppleBank the *receiving bank*. The parties, then, wear different hats over the course of the transaction, depending on whether we're referring to their role in a particular payment order or in the fund transfer as a whole.

At this point, AppleBank isn't obligated to do anything under Article 4A. In order for AppleBank to incur an obligation with respect to the payment order under Article 4A, it must *accept* the payment order (Section 4A-212). If, for example, MegaCorp doesn't have $1 million in its account to cover the wire transfer, AppleBank may *reject* the payment order by notifying MegaCorp orally, electronically, or in writing (Section 4A-210[a]). If the receiving bank rejects a payment order, it may not later accept the same payment order; similarly, a receiving bank may not later reject a payment order that it has already accepted (Section 4A-210[d]).

It should be noted that even though *Article 4A* doesn't require a receiving bank to accept a payment order, the bank may have a separate agreement in effect with the sender that would require the bank to accept the order. If the bank fails to accept a payment order in violation of such an agreement, then the bank could be held liable for breach of its agreement with the sender. But liability in such a situation would be founded on general contract law, and not on Article 4A.

If AppleBank decides to go ahead with the transaction, it will *execute* MegaCorp's payment order. A receiving bank **executes** a payment order when it issues a payment order of its own intended to carry out the payment order that it has received (Section 4A-301). Execution of a payment order is the manner in which a receiving bank (other than the beneficiary's bank) accepts the payment order (Section 4A-209).

Let's assume that AppleBank puts the $1 million payment order onto FedWire. What AppleBank is doing, essentially, is instructing the Federal Reserve Bank of New York to pay $1 million to the Federal Reserve Bank of San Francisco, which can then credit the funds to OrangeBank on behalf of Bilko. AppleBank's instruction to the Federal Reserve Bank of New York is itself a payment order, the second payment order of this funds transfer. By issuing this second payment order, AppleBank has **executed**, and hence *accepted,* the original payment order that it received from MegaCorp.

Now let's look at the second payment order. AppleBank is the sender of this payment order and the Federal Reserve Bank of New York is the receiving bank. Note that Federal Reserve Banks are treated as a "banks" for the purposes of Article 4A (Section 4A-105, comment 1), as are savings banks, savings and loan associations, credit unions, and other institutions that are similar to banks (Section 4A-105[a][2]).

The Federal Reserve Bank of New York in this example is an *intermediary bank.* An **intermediary bank** is defined in Section 4A-104(b) as a receiving bank other than the originator's bank or the beneficiary's bank. Thus, an intermediary bank is a bank somewhere in middle of the chain of banks— not at the very beginning and not at the very end.

The next step in the funds transfer is for the Federal Reserve Bank of New York to request the Federal Reserve Bank of San Francisco to pay $1 million to OrangeBank. This is the third payment order of our funds transfer, with the Federal Reserve Bank of New York acting as sender and the Federal Reserve Bank of San Francisco, another intermediary bank, acting as receiving bank. By issuing this third payment order, the Federal Reserve Bank of New York has executed and accepted the second payment order.

The fourth and final payment order occurs when the Federal Reserve Bank of San Francisco requests OrangeBank to credit the $1 million to Bilko's account. In this payment order, the Federal Reserve Bank of San Francisco is the sender and OrangeBank is the receiving bank.

Note that OrangeBank cannot *execute* this last payment order, because a bank can only execute a payment order by turning around and issuing another payment order. A payment order can only be made to a bank, and OrangeBank, as the beneficiary's bank, is the last bank in the chain. The way in which the beneficiary's bank accepts a payment order is different from the way in which other receiving banks accept a payment order. One way for the beneficiary's bank to accept the payment order is simply to credit the beneficiary's account and notify the beneficiary of the right to withdraw the funds (Sections 4A-209[b][1] and 4A-405[a]).

In the preceding example, the intermediary banks were Federal Reserve Banks. That need not be the case, however. If, for example, the wire transfer had been made through CHIPS or some other private network, the intermediary banks would be private-sector commercial banks. Figure 31-1 illustrates a sample funds transfer. Note again how each party (other than the beneficiary) has more than one label, depending on whether we focus on their role in a particular payment order or in the overall funds transfer.

Proper Time for Execution and Payment   The **execution date** of a payment order is the date on which the receiving bank must execute the payment order (Sections 4A-301[b] and

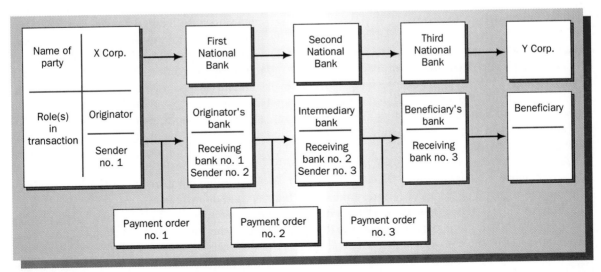

FIGURE 31-1

Sample Funds Transfer

4A-302). Generally, the execution date is specified by the sender in the payment order. However, the execution date may not be earlier than the day on which the receiving bank receives the payment order. Furthermore, the bank may establish a "cut-off" time after which incoming payment orders are deemed to be received on the next business day (Section 4A-106[a]). If the sender does not specify an execution date, the execution date is the date that the payment order is received (Section 4A-301[b]).

The sender may also specify a **payment date**, which is the day on which the beneficiary is properly payable by the beneficiary's bank (Section 4A-401). The payment date cannot be earlier than the day the beneficiary's bank receives its payment order. If no payment date is specified, the payment date is the day on which the beneficiary's bank receives the payment order.

If the sender *does* indicate a payment date, then the *execution* date is the payment date or an earlier date that is reasonably necessary to allow the beneficiary to be paid on the payment date. Assume, for example, that First Bank receives a payment order which specifies that the beneficiary, John Deaux, is to be paid on March 4. If First Bank decides to accept the payment order, it must execute it in time to allow the ultimate payment to John Deaux to occur on March 4. If several additional payment orders are required to get the funds to John Deaux, First Bank must take this into account. First Bank will not, however, be held responsible if it receives the payment order too late to allow it to get the funds to John Deaux by the payment date.

If the sender specifies that the funds transfer should be made by wire transfer or telephone, or otherwise indicates that the most expeditious means should be used, then the receiving bank must transmit its payment order in the most expeditious means possible and instruct its intermediary bank, if it used one, to do the same (Section 4A-302[a][2]).

Section 4A-305 imposes liability on receiving banks that cause a delay in a funds transfer either by failing to execute payment orders on time or by failing to choose the proper means of execution. If the funds transfer is completed despite the receiving bank's delay, then the bank must pay interest either to the originator or the beneficiary for the period of the delay. If the delay prevents the funds transfer from being completed, then the bank is liable to the originator for expenses and interest losses. Consequential damages may not be recovered unless otherwise provided in an express written agreement of the receiving bank.

Sender's Obligation to Pay Receiving Bank   The receiving bank's acceptance of a payment order generally gives rise to the sender's obligation to pay the receiving bank the amount of the order (Section 4A-402). If the receiving bank is the beneficiary's bank, the sender's payment is not due until the payment date. If the receiving bank is a bank other than the beneficiary's bank, the sender's payment is not due until the execution date.

If the funds transfer is not ultimately completed—that is, if the beneficiary's bank does not ultimately accept the order to pay the beneficiary—then the obligation of each sender is excused. Each sender that has already paid its receiving bank in such a situation is generally entitled to a refund with interest (Section 4A-402[d]).

Failure to Follow Instructions in Payment Order   If a receiving bank accepts a payment order, it is generally obligated to execute it in accordance with any instructions that the order may contain. If the sender specifies a particular intermediary bank that should be used or a particular funds-transfer system (such as Fed-Wire or CHIPS) be utilized, then the sender's instruction must be followed (Section 4A-302[a][1]). An exception exists where the bank determines in good faith that using the funds-transfer system designated by the sender is not feasible or would unduly delay the funds transfer's completion (Section 4A-302[b]).

If the receiving bank executes a payment order by issuing its own payment order to an intermediary bank, the latter payment order should include any special instructions or requirements contained in the first payment order (Section 4A-302[a]). Thus, if the first payment order specified that the funds should be transmitted by wire transfer, the payment order to the intermediary bank should do the same.

If a receiving bank fails to follow or properly pass along the instructions of its payment order, and if the originator's instructions aren't followed as a result, then the receiving bank is liable to the originator for the originator's expenses. For example, assume that Ted wishes to send a wire transfer to Ed. Ted issues a payment order to First Bank and instructs First Bank to use Second Bank as an intermediary bank. Ted pays First Bank $10 as a service charge for the funds transfer. If First Bank disobeys Ted's instructions and uses some other intermediary bank to effect the transfer, then Ted will be entitled to a refund of his $10.

Errors in Executing Payment Orders

If a receiving bank attempts to execute a payment order by erroneously issuing a payment order in an amount greater than the amount of sender's order, then the sender is only obligated to pay the receiving bank the amount of the sender's order (Section 4A-303[a]). The same rule applies if the receiving bank mistakenly issues a duplicate of a payment order already sent.

When the beneficiary receives a windfall because of the receiving bank's mistake, the bank can recover that beneficiary's windfall to the extent allowed by the law governing mistake and restitution (Section 4A-303[a]). (See Chapter 14 for a discussion of mistake and restitution.)

If a receiving bank erroneously issues a payment order in an amount *less* than the sender's order, then the receiving bank may correct the mistake by issuing a new payment order to cover the shortfall (Section 4A-303[b]). In order for the correction to be effective, however, the new payment order must be issued by the execution date. If the receiving bank does not correct the shortfall, then the sender is only required to pay the receiving bank the amount of the receiving bank's erroneous payment order.

Wrong Beneficiary

If the receiving bank executes a payment order by issuing its own payment order to the wrong beneficiary, then the sender and all previous senders are not required to pay for their orders (Section 4A-303[c]).

When a payment order has been directed to the wrong beneficiary, then the bank that made the mistake can recover that beneficiary's windfall to the extent allowed by the law governing mistake and restitution (Section 4A-303[c]).

Unauthorized Payment Orders

As noted earlier, the volume of funds transfers covered by Article 4A is enormous. Fraudulent or erroneous payment orders can have disastrous consequences. For this reason, Article 4A encourages banks and customers to adopt *security procedures* to make sure that each payment order is properly authorized and is not issued in error. A **security procedure** is defined in Section 4A-201 as

> a procedure established by agreement of a customer and a receiving bank for the purpose of (i) verifying that a payment order or communication amending or cancelling a payment order is that of the customer, or (ii) detecting error in the transmission or the content of the payment order or communication.

Note that a procedure, in order to qualify as a security procedure, need only be designed to verify authorization *or* detect errors. However, in order to fully protect itself from liability under Article 4A, the bank should adopt and follow procedures that do both. Note also that the security procedure cannot be instituted unilaterally by the bank; it must be agreed to by the bank and the customer.

Examples of security procedures are codes, passwords, and call-back procedures. The comparison of the signature on a payment order with an authorized specimen signature does *not*, in and of itself, qualify as a security procedure (Section 4A-201).

If the receiving bank follows a security procedure designed to verify authorization, then the risk of an unauthorized transfer is generally borne by the sender. If the procedure is followed, then any unauthorized payment order will generally be treated as a valid payment order of the customer—and hence the customer will have to pay for it—so long as (1) the security procedure is a commercially reasonable method to verify authorization and (2) the bank proves that it accepted the order in good faith (Section 4A-202[b]).

There is an exception to the foregoing rule if the customer can essentially prove that the unauthorized payment order did not result from a lapse or shortcoming in the customer's internal security procedures. The details for satisfying this exception are set forth in Section 4A-203(a).

Payment Order Erroneously Transmitted by Sender

Section 4A-205 deals with the situation where a sender erroneously transmits a payment order in an amount greater than the

TABLE 31-1

Concept Summary	Resolution of Funds Transfer Problems under Article 4A
Problem	**Resolution**
Receiving bank rejects payment order	No resolution under Article 4A, but sender may have remedy under contract law (Section 4A-212).
Receiving bank delays execution, and hence delays payment	Receiving bank must pay interest either to originator or beneficiary (Section 4A-305).
Receiving bank causes payment delay by choosing inappropriate means of executing payment order	Receiving bank must pay interest to either originator or beneficiary (Section 4A-305).
Funds transfer is not completed	Obligation of each sender is excused (Section 4A-402).
Receiving bank issues payment order in amount greater than that of sender's order	Sender must only pay amount ordered; receiving bank may attempt to recover from beneficiary under law of mistake or restitution (Section 4A-303[a]).
Receiving bank issues payment order in amount less than that of sender's order	Sender must only pay amount sent by receiving bank; receiving bank may issue additional order on or before execution date (Section 4A-303[b]).
Receiving bank issues payment order to wrong beneficiary	Previous senders not obligated to pay; receiving bank may attempt to recover from wrong beneficiary under law of mistake and restitution (Section 4A-303[c]).
Originator's bank executes unauthorized payment order	Originator bears loss as long as beneficiary is in good faith and follows commercially reasonable security procedure for verifying authorization (Section 4A-202[b]). (See exception, Section 4A-203[a])
Originator transmits erroneous payment order	If receiving bank follows security procedure for errors, originator bears loss unless originator proves that (1) it complied with security procedure and (2) bank would have detected error had it complied (Section 4A-205). Loss shifts back to originator if originator fails to inform bank of error within reasonable time after receiving notice (Section 4A-205[b]).

amount intended, or a payment order that is a duplicate of one already sent. Even though the sender has made the error, a receiving bank who accepts an erroneous order must, in order to protect itself from bearing the loss, follow a security procedure designed to detect errors. The sender will not be required to pay any excess amount sent in error if it can prove that (1) it complied with the security procedure and (2) the error would have been detected if the receiving bank had also complied with the security procedure. The sender thus bears the burden of proving that the receiving bank failed to follow the security procedure.

Even if the sender can prove that the receiving bank didn't follow the security procedure, the sender still must show that it acted with proper diligence to detect the error. If the bank notifies the sender that has accepted the erroneous payment order (or that it has debited the amount of the order from the sender's account), then the sender has a duty to discover the error and inform the bank of it. If the sender fails to tell the bank of the error within a reasonable time, not to exceed 90 days after the sender received the bank's notice, then the sender is liable for any resulting loss to the bank (Section 4A-205[b]). The sender's liability may not exceed the amount of the erroneous order.

Table 31-1 summarizes how Article 4A deals with these and other problems.

The following case deals with a sender's order which specified the wrong account number.

SHAWMUT WORCESTER COUNTY BANK V. FIRST AMERICAN BANK & TRUST

U.S. District Court, D. Mass.
731 F. Supp. 57 (1990)

BACKGROUND: Shawmut Worcester County Bank mistakenly transferred $10,000 from the account of American Optical Corporation to First American Bank & Trust in West Palm Beach, Florida, purportedly for the benefit of Fernando Degan by means of an electronic funds transfer system known as FedWire. The payment order issued from Shawmut to First American, which was a duplicate of an earlier transfer which is not in question, specified the wrong account number. Shawmut discovered the error 106 days after the mistaken transfer. Shawmut asked First American to reverse the transfer. Since First American's customer refused to authorize the reversal, First American also refused to do so.

Young, District Judge

Fedwire rules do not permit a cancellation, "revocation," or "reversal" of a previous day's funds transfer without permission of the receiving bank. The transferee or receiving bank is under no obligation under Regulation J to comply with a request, even if the transferor provides indemnity. Both the ALI Article 4A and the Fedwire rules recognize that even with indemnity, the beneficiary's bank may be reluctant to alienate its customer, the beneficiary, by denying the customer the funds. See UCC §4A-211 Comment 5. The language of UCC §4A-211 is permissive, not mandatory, where, as here, the funds transfer system rules do not permit cancellation without the permission of a receiving bank. Even if a receiving bank is the sender's "agent" on the day of the transfer, the regulatory framework that undergirds the parties' relationship cannot support the conclusion that the receiving bank is an agent for the sender charged with a duty broader than simply to credit promptly the beneficiary's account. The policies underlying this arrangement are even more compelling where a sending bank requests cancellation of a payment order three and one half months after the receiving bank has credited its customer's account. This court rules that, as matter of law, a receiving bank is not negligent where it credits a payment order to the account as set out in the order.

Shawmut next argues that First American should have acted to prevent the reasonably foreseeable harm that proximately resulted from its negligent failure to notice that Shawmut's second payment order was a mistake and duplicative. The issue before the court, thus, is whether First American was somehow put on notice that the transaction was so irregular that it should have investigated the circumstances prior to crediting the account a second time.

If Shawmut's own contributory negligence is put to one side for a moment, this last argument has some appeal. As a practical matter, the receiving bank probably is in a better position to recover the funds from the beneficiary, especially where the beneficiary is a customer of that bank. It thus makes sense that the risk of loss for duplicative payment orders such as the one involved in the instant case be shifted in some instances to a bank which blithely executes payment orders without exercising even ordinary care. The American Law Institute is considering this matter. See ALI Article 4A-205 permitting such a shift of the risk of loss where the sender can show that it complied with applicable security procedures and that the error would have been detected by the receiving bank had that bank complied with similar security procedures. Here, however, there is no evidence before the court that First American failed to comply with one of its own security procedures and no evidence that the lack of a reasonable security procedure may have caused the error to have gone undetected.

DECISION: The court ruled for First American that the transfer would not be reversed.

Review Questions and Problems

Key Terms

FedWire	sender
CHIPS	receiving bank
originator	execution
beneficiary	intermediary bank
originator's bank	execution date
beneficiary's bank	payment date
funds transfer	security procedure
payment order	

Discussion Questions

1. What are four types of consumer electronic fund transfer services?

2. How does the coverage of the Electronic Fund Transfer Act differ from that of Article 4A of the Uniform Commercial Code?

3. Why should a bank offer security procedures designed both to verify authorization *and* detect errors?

4. Compare the operation of FedWire to that of CHIPS.

Review Problems

1. On March 1, Roger issues a payment order to First Bank, directing it to transfer $100,000 to James' account at Second Bank. The payment order does not specify when payment is to be made. What is the execution date for the payment order?

2. Miles issues a payment order to Infidelity Bank, directing it to transfer $1 million to Jiles' account at MetroBank. Infidelity mistakenly issues a payment order for $2 million, which is eventually transferred to Jiles. Miles pays Infidelity Bank $1 million for the wire transfer. Is Infidelity entitled to recover the remaining $1 million? If so, from whom?

3. Mickey is the treasurer of Grubco and is authorized to issue payment orders on Grubco's behalf. Mickey intends to issue a payment order directing Local Bank to transfer $1000 to Stubco's account at State Bank. Mickey mistakenly includes too many zeros on the payment order and faxes a $100,000 payment order to Local Bank. Local Bank executes the payment order in the amount of $100,000. Assume that Grubco and Local Bank have established a security procedure by agreement. Under what circumstances could Grubco avoid having to pay the full $100,000 to Local Bank? Even if those circumstances exist, are there additional circumstances that could shift the loss back onto Grubco? If so, what are those additional circumstances?

4. William is fired as vice president of Interco, but not before he manages to obtain the secret codes used for the wire transfer security procedure that Interco has established with National Bank. William, purportedly on behalf of Interco, issues a payment order directing National Bank to transfer $10 million to his account at BCCI. National Bank executes the payment order and William receives the money. What will National Bank have to prove in order to avoid having to bear the loss?

5. David forges a payment order in which Giantco purportedly instructs CountryBank to transfer $1 million to David's account. An expert at duplicating signatures, David makes a perfect replica of the signature of Giantco's treasurer and faxes the payment order to CountryBank. A CountryBank employee receives the fax, compares the signature to the treasurer's specimen signature, and immediately executes the payment order. David receives the money. Giantco refuses to pay CountryBank for the payment order, and CountryBank sues. What result?

Case Problem

1. Frederick Ognibene used his Citibank ATM card to make a cash withdrawal. Upon completing the transaction, he was approached by someone posing as a Citibank employee. The "employee" pretended to be testing an adjacent Citibank ATM; he asked Ognibene if he could use his card to test the machine. Unbeknownst to Ognibene, the "employee" used the card to withdraw $400 from Ognibene's account. Ognibene sued Citibank to recover the $400. What result?

32

Secured Transactions

M uch of the nation's economy is based on transactions involving credit. Credit is often provided to buyers by manufacturers, wholesalers, and retailers who are willing to accept payment in the future in order to market their products. In addition, institutions such as commercial banks, factors, and finance companies make loans to finance business inventories, business operations, and consumer sales.

Sometimes providing credit for individuals or business firms subjects the lender to considerable risk because of the possibility that the debt will not be paid. This risk is reduced if the lender can obtain an interest in property as assurance that the debtor will meet his or her obligation. When a creditor establishes a valid security interest and the debtor fails or refuses to pay, the creditor can take the property or have it sold and the proceeds applied against the debt. A creditor who acquires a security interest in personal property is known as a **secured creditor**. The property providing the security is called **collateral**.

This chapter discusses the nature and scope of security interests in personal property and fixtures. Chapter 49 deals with transactions in which real property is the collateral. Much of the law dealing with secured transactions in which

personal property is the collateral is based on Article 9 of the Uniform Commercial Code (UCC).

Article 9

Background of Article 9

Article 9 of the UCC provides a comprehensive scheme for administering the many different types of financing using personal property as security.

One of the major objectives of the drafters of Article 9 was to provide a uniform and simple system for creditors to establish a security interest. Thus, Article 9 supersedes prior legislation dealing with such security devices as chattel mortgages, conditional sales, trust receipts, factor's liens, and assignments of accounts receivable. For these devices the drafters substituted the single term **security interest**.

Terminology of Article 9

In addition to security interest, a number of other terms have specific meanings as they are used in Article 9. The following are important for understanding how a creditor protects an interest in particular personal property or fixtures. Most of these will be discussed in greater detail as they relate to particular provisions of Article 9.

Secured Party   A lender, seller, or other person in whose favor there is a security interest, including a person to whom accounts or chattel paper have been sold, is known as a **secured party** (Section 9-105[m]).

Security Agreement   A **security agreement** is an agreement that creates or provides a security interest (Section 9-105[2]).

Financing Statement   The **financing statement** is the document that gives notice to all persons searching the records that the secured party claims an interest in certain collateral owned by the debtor (Section 9-402). Subject to certain requirements to be discussed later, the security agreement may be filed instead of a separate financing statement.

Although the UCC no longer retains distinctions based on form, for purposes of filing the financing statement in the appropriate place it is extremely important to understand what type of collateral is involved. If the secured party improperly classifies the collateral, he or she may file the financing statement in the wrong place and lose whatever protection he or she might have had against other creditors of the debtor.

Goods   **Goods** are defined in Section 9-105(h) as all things that are movable at the time the security interest attaches. Goods are **fixtures** when they become so related to particular real estate that an interest in them arises under real estate law (Section 9-313[1][a]). Goods are classified in one of four categories: **consumer goods, equipment, farm products,** or **inventory**. The classification of goods depends on their use, but goods cannot be classified in more than one category in any single transaction.

Goods are **consumer goods** if they are used or bought for use primarily for personal, family, or household purposes (Section 9-109[1]). A TV bought from a retail merchant for use in the home is a consumer good.

Goods are **equipment** when they are used primarily in business if they are not inventory, farm products, or consumer goods (Section 9-102[2]). A machine used in operating a plant is considered equipment.

Goods are **farm products** if they are crops, livestock, or supplies used or produced in farming operations, or if they are products, crops, or livestock in their unmanufactured states (for example, maple syrup), and if they are in possession of a debtor engaged in raising, fattening, grazing, or other farming operations. When crops or livestock or their products come into the hands of someone not engaged in farming operations, they cease to be farm products. Eggs in the hands of a farmer are farm products, but when the farmer sells those eggs to a dairy company, they become inventory in the hands of the dairy company.

Goods are **inventory** if they are held by a person for sale or lease or to be furnished under service contracts or if they are raw materials, work in process, or materials used or consumed in business (Section 9-109[4]). If materials used or consumed in a business have a long life span, they are equipment; but if they are consumed in the manufacture of a product, they are inventory. For example, bolts used in manufacturing a car are inventory, but a drill used in manufacturing a car is equipment.

Purchase-Money Security Interest   A security interest taken by a seller in items sold to a buyer to secure all or part of the price is a **purchase-money security interest** (PMSI). This term also encompasses a security interest taken by a person who gives value to a debtor to acquire rights in or the use of collateral if the collateral is so used (Section 9-107). If a retail merchant sells goods to a purchaser and retains a security interest in these goods, it is a PMSI. Similarly, if a bank makes a loan to a man to purchase a boat and he buys a boat with the money, a PMSI in the boat may have been created. Under the UCC, purchase-money obligations often have priority over other obligations.

Instrument   According to Section 9-105(i), **instrument** means a negotiable instrument (as defined in Section 3-104, for example, a note) or a security (as defined in Section 8-102, for example, stocks) or any other writing that evidences a right to the payment of money and is not itself a security agreement or lease and is of a type that is, in the ordinary course of business, transferred by delivery with any necessary indorsement or assignment.

Document of Title   A **document of title** is a written instrument issued by or addressed to a person who holds goods for another. It identifies those goods unless they are fungible, that is, part of an identifiable mass (Section 1-201[15]). For example, an order from a farmer who has stored corn addressed to the storage facility to deliver 10,000 bushels of the corn to a railroad is a document of title. Other documents of title are bills of lading, dock warrants, dock receipts, and warehouse receipts.

Chattel Paper   A writing or writings that evidence both a monetary obligation and a security interest in or a lease of specific goods are **chattel paper**. If the transaction consists of a security agreement or a lease and an instrument or a series of instruments, the *group* of writings taken together constitutes chattel paper.

When a merchant sells goods to a consumer, the merchant may retain a security interest in the goods sold. Suppose a retail merchant sells a television set to a consumer and retains a security interest in it. The contract by which the merchant retains a security interest in the TV is a security agreement: the merchant is the secured party; the buyer is the debtor; and the TV is the collateral. If the merchant wishes to finance his operations, he or she may sell a number of such contracts to a bank. With respect to the bank, these contracts are collectively referred to as *chattel paper*. The retail dealer is a debtor with respect to the bank, and the bank is the secured party. The customers are referred to as *account debtors*. Figure 32-1 illustrates a transaction involving the use of chattel paper and the creation of a purchase-money security interest.

Account   An **account** is any right to payment for goods sold or leased or for services rendered that is not evidenced by an instrument or chattel paper, whether or not it has been earned by performance (Section 9-106). Accounts are not evidenced by writing. This term covers the ordinary account receivable. If a clothing store sells clothes to customers on an open account and gives them 30 days to pay, the accounts of the customers can be sold to a financer. The financer would be a secured party, the clothing store the debtor, and the customers the account debtors.

General Intangibles   The term **general intangibles** refers to any personal property other than goods, accounts, chattel paper, documents, and money (Section 9-106). The term covers the various contractual rights and personal property that are used as commercial security—for example, goodwill, trademarks, and patents.

Scope of Article 9

Article 9 applies primarily to security interests in personal property and fixtures arising out of agreements. The article does not apply to statutory liens such as the mechanic's or artisan's lien. These liens are created by legislation to protect contractors and others who provide improvements to real property. Article 9 does, however, cover priority problems between statutory liens and secured transactions (Section 9-310). Additionally, the article applies to transactions involving the sale of accounts and chattel paper.

Although Article 9 applies to consumer transactions, its provisions do not replace other state legislation such as small loan acts, retail installment sales statutes, and other regulatory measures applicable to consumer financing.

The major exclusion from Article 9 coverage is security interests in real estate. Fixtures, however, are covered, and in some circumstances real estate and Article 9 transactions are connected. For example, if Jones owns a promissory note and a real estate mortgage securing funds he has advanced to Smith, Jones may use them as collateral when borrowing from Brown. Article 9 also applies to transactions in which the collateral is minerals, standing timber, or growing crops.

Establishing an Enforceable Security Interest

The secured party wishing to protect his or her rights in the collateral must first establish an enforceable security interest in the collateral. Establishing a security interest gives the creditor rights in the collateral that the creditor can enforce against the *debtor*. A security interest in and of itself is *not* sufficient to protect the creditor against other secured parties who may have rights in the same collateral. We will learn later in the chapter how a creditor who establishes a security interest may protect himself or herself against the claims of other creditors.

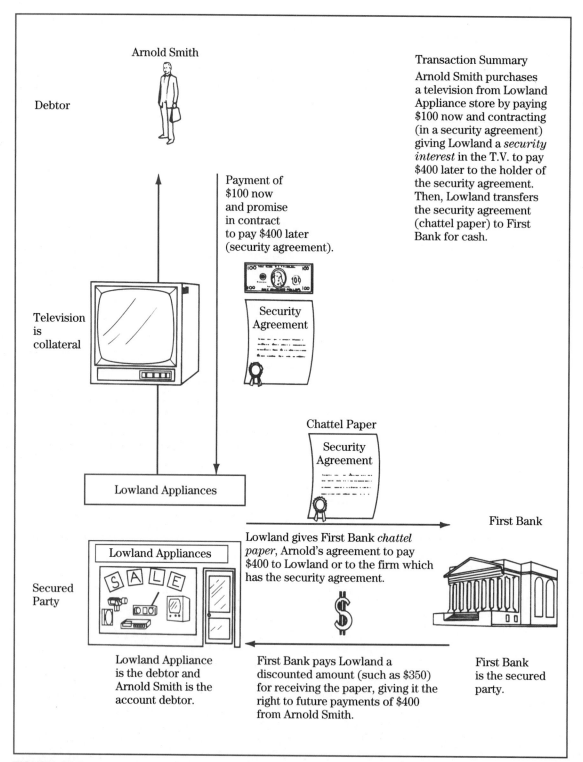

Arnold Smith

Debtor

Television
is
collateral

Payment of
$100 now
and promise
in contract
to pay $400 later
(security agreement).

Security
Agreement

Lowland Appliances

Chattel Paper

Security
Agreement

First Bank

Lowland gives First Bank *chattel
paper*, Arnold's agreement to pay
$400 to Lowland or to the firm which
has the security agreement.

Secured
Party

Lowland Appliances

SALE

Lowland Appliance
is the debtor and
Arnold Smith is the
account debtor.

First Bank pays Lowland a
discounted amount (such as $350)
for receiving the paper, giving it the
right to future payments of $400
from Arnold Smith.

First Bank
is the secured
party.

Transaction Summary

Arnold Smith purchases
a television from Lowland
Appliance store by paying
$100 now and contracting
(in a security agreement)
giving Lowland a *security
interest* in the T.V. to pay
$400 later to the holder of
the security agreement.
Then, Lowland transfers
the security agreement
(chattel paper) to First
Bank for cash.

FIGURE 32-1

A Purchase-Money Security Interest

Attachment of a security interest is said to occur when the security interest becomes effective. Three conditions must be satisfied in order for a creditor's security interest to attach (Section 9-203). These conditions, which need not occur simultaneously or in any particular order, are as follows:

1. The debtor has signed a valid *security agreement* (unless the collateral is in the second party's possession pursuant to an agreement of the parties).
2. The secured party has given *value* to the debtor.
3. The debtor has *rights in the collateral.*

The Security Agreement

A **security agreement** creates or provides a security interest (Section 9-105[1]). Unless the collateral is in the possession of the secured party, the security agreement must be in writing. The agreement must contain a description of the collateral and be signed by the debtor. A description that reasonably identifies the collateral is sufficient; however, care should be taken to describe the collateral since insufficient identification can lead to litigation.

Although the formal requirements of a security agreement are minimal, most also contain references to the following items:

After-Acquired Property   **After-acquired property** is collateral that becomes the subject of a security interest after the parties have reached an initial agreement. One example would be a retailer's inventory purchased to replace goods subject to the original security agreement. When an after-acquired property clause is included in a security agreement, the secured party acquires a "continuing general lien" in property acquired to replace the original inventory.

Future Advances   Security agreements may include a clause covering advances of credit made by the secured party after the agreement is signed. This is necessary if the advance is to be secured by the original agreement. The clause might read: "This security agreement shall include future advances or other indebtedness that debtor may owe to secured party during the time that the security agreement is in force, whenever incurred." Rights of the debtor established by an after-acquired property clause and a future advance clause are often referred to as a **floating lien**. Combining the after-acquired property and future advances clauses facilitates the financing of inventory and accounts receivable where the collateral is goods being retailed or raw materials being manufactured.

A number of other subjects are covered in most security agreements. They include, but are not limited to, the following:

1. Amount of the debt
2. Terms of payment
3. Responsibility for care and maintenance of the collateral
4. Acceleration of payment rights
5. Right to additional collateral

Value Given to Debtor

The second requirement for a security interest to attach is that value be given by the secured party to the debtor. This requirement is generally satisfied when the secured party extends credit to the debtor, or enters into a binding commitment to do so. According to UCC Section 1-201(44), "value" includes "any consideration sufficient to support a simple contract." A preexisting claim by the secured party can also satisfy the value requirement.

Debtor Has Rights in the Collateral

The final requirement for the attachment of a security interest is that the debtor have rights in the collateral. The debtor need not have title to the collateral. A purchaser acquiring property under an agreement in which the seller retains title has rights in the collateral sufficient to support a creditor's security interest.

Perfection of a Security Interest

A security interest that has attached may be enforced by the secured party against the debtor. However, a security interest alone does not protect the secured party against the rest of the world. The secured party, in order to protect his or her rights to the collateral against other secured parties, must *perfect* his or her security interest. **Perfection** of a security interest occurs when the secured party satisfies Article 9 requirements designed to put the rest of the world on notice of the security interest. A secured party who perfects his or her security interest will generally have rights in the collateral superior to those of a subsequent secured party with rights in the same collateral.

Methods of Perfecting a Security Interest

The secured party may perfect a security interest by either of the following methods:

1. Filing a financing statement in the appropriate public office
2. Taking possession of the collateral

In some transactions security interests are automatically perfected when they attach to the collateral. Whether the secured party may perfect by filing, by taking possession, or by relying upon automatically obtaining a perfected security interest depends to a large extent upon the classification of the collateral involved.

In certain instances the secured party automatically obtains a perfected security interest without taking possession of the collateral or filing. Article 9 provides that a merchant who sells consumer goods to a buyer on credit does not need to file a financing statement or take possession of the goods to perfect interest in the items sold. With the exception of motor vehicles and fixtures, a perfected security interest arises automatically when the merchant's security interest in the collateral attaches (Section 9-302[d]). The merchant's security interest is a purchase-money security interest.

Additionally, Article 9 establishes temporary automatic security interests in two situations. The most important is a 10-day security interest in any proceeds a debtor receives from the sale of the collateral. A 21-day security interest measured from the time of attachment is automatically perfected in certain negotiable documents and stocks in the debtor's possession (Section 9-304).

Perfection by Filing

The most common method of perfecting a security interest is by filing a financing statement. This document, when properly filed, gives the public notice of the secured party's interest in the collateral. Public notice needs to be provided so other creditors or transferees of the debtor may learn of the creditor's claims to the collateral.

The Financing Statement A financing statement must:

1. Give the names of the debtor and the secured party and their respective addresses
2. Be signed by the debtor
3. Contain a statement indicating the types—or describing the items—of collateral

A financing statement is effective even if it contains minor errors. When the financing statement covers crops, timber to be cut, minerals, or goods that are to become fixtures, the financing statement must describe the real estate involved. Normally a standard form is used for the financing statement (see Figure 32-2); however, under the UCC a copy of the security agreement may be used if it contains all of the preceding information and is signed by the debtor. Parties usually do not file the security agreement. If the parties wish to amend the financing statement, the UCC requires filing of a writing signed by both debtor and secured party.

Many financing statements are filed incorrectly because the wrong name is used for the debtor. Section 9-402(7) provides that the name on a financing statement is sufficient if it gives the individual, partnership, or corporate name of the debtor, whether or not it adds other trade names or names of partners. Suppose that Alfred Zimmer operates a business under the name Southern Pit Barbeque. Should the statement be filed under Z or S? Here, it should be filed under the name of the debtor—Zimmer. If Zimmer changed his name, or if he were operating a corporation that changed its name, must the secured party refile its financing statement? Yes; if the filed financing statement becomes seriously misleading, it will not be effective to perfect a security interest in collateral acquired by the debtor more than four months after the name change.

Place of Filing The place of filing depends on the type of collateral covered by the security agreement. If the secured party improperly classifies the collateral and files in the wrong of-

FIGURE 32-2

Financing
Statement
(Approved Form
UCC Sec. 9-402)

This financing statement is presented to a filing
officer for filing pursuant to the Uniform
Commercial Code.

Name of Debtor (or Assignor) _____
Address _____
Name of Secured Party (or Assignee)

_____

Address _____

1. This financing statement covers the following types
   (or items) of property:
   (Describe) _____

2. (If collateral is crops) The above described crops
   are growing or are to be grown on:
   (Describe Real Estate and specify Name
   of Record Owner) _____

3. (If collateral is goods which are or are to become
   fixtures) The above described goods are affixed
   or to be affixed to:
   (Describe Real Estate and specify Name
   of Record Owner) _____

4. (If proceeds or products of collateral are claimed)
   Proceeds—Products of the collateral are also
   covered.
Signature of Debtor (or Assignor)

_____

Signature of Secured Party (or Assignee)

_____

fice, the financing statement is ineffective as to
the described collateral.

For collateral related to land such as fixtures,
goods that are to become fixtures, timber to be
cut, or minerals, filing generally is required in the
county where the land is located. For other types
of collateral the states have different rules concerning the proper place to file. A number of
states direct that filing take place in the county of
the debtor's residence or, if the debtor is not a resident of the state, in the county where the goods
are kept. Other states take the position that filing
is most effective when centralized on a statewide
basis. This reduces costs and facilitates the acquisition of credit information. These states generally require that filing, except for land-related
collateral, be done in the office of the Secretary of
State, located in the state capital.

Time and Duration of Filing   A financing statement can be filed at any time—even before a security agreement is made or before a
security interest attaches to the collateral (Section 9-402[1]). A secured party might want to file
before attachment because this may aid in getting

a higher priority than other parties claiming an interest in the same collateral by filing.

A filed financing statement is effective for 5
years from the date of filing. To ensure its continuing validity after 5 years, the secured party must
file a **continuation statement**; otherwise, the
security interest becomes unperfected. A continuation statement may be filed by the secured party
within 6 months prior to the expiration of the 5-
year period. The continuation statement makes
the original statement valid for an additional 5
years. Succeeding continuation statements may
be filed. The continuation statement need be
signed by only the secured party.

What if the secured party allows the financing
statement to lapse at the end of 5 years, although
the debtor is still obligated to him, and an intervening creditor files an effective financing statement? Section 9-403(2) states that the security
interest "is deemed to have been unperfected as
against a person who became a purchaser or lien
creditor before lapse." Suppose a bank lends
money to A and properly perfects a security interest in A's collateral; then 4 years later a finance
company also lends money to A and perfects its

security interest in the same equipment. If the bank allows the filing to lapse, the finance company is entitled to priority over the bank's security interest, which became unperfected by the lapse.

Sometimes judges give a *very* strict interpretation to statutory provisions. In the following case, the court holds that the UCC requires a continuation statement to be filed *within* 6 months prior to the expiration of the 5-year period.

BANQUE WORMS V. DAVIS CONSTRUCTION CO., INC.

Kentucky Court of Appeals
831 S.W.2d 921 (1992)

BACKGROUND: A New York bank lent $11,750,000 to the Dollar Branch Coal Company. The bank took a security interest in the mining equipment of the company, including a Euclid R-25 rock truck. On October 12, 1982 the bank filed a financing statement. On April 10, 1987, the bank filed a continuation statement.

On November 23, 1987, the Dollar company sold the R-25 rock truck to Davis for $36,192. The bank claimed to have a security interest in the truck. The lower court ruled that the bank's security interest in the truck was unperfected on the date it was transferred to Davis. Hence Davis acquired a clear title to the truck. The bank appealed.

Gudgel, Justice

This statute provides, in effect, that if a security agreement which retains a security interest in collateral has been perfected by the filing of a financing statement, the statement lapses at the expiration of a five-year period unless a continuation statement is filed prior to the lapse. Further, if the security interest becomes unperfected by lapse, it is deemed to have become unperfected as against a person who became a purchaser before the lapse. To be timely, a continuation statement must be filed within six months prior to the expiration of the five-year period during which the original financing statement is effective. Only if the continuation statement is timely filed is the effectiveness of the original financing statement continued.

Here, it is uncontroverted that appellant's continuation statement was filed with the clerk on April 10, 1987, which was six months and two days before the expiration of the financing statement's five-year effective period. Because the continuation statement was not filed within six months prior to the lapse of the financing statement's effective period, appellant's security interest in the rock truck became unperfected on October 12, 1987, which was five years after the date on which the financing statement was filed.

In re Hubka, 64 B.R. 473, 2 UCC Rep.Serv.2d 740 (Bankr.D.Neb.1986), the reviewing court specifically quoted and discussed Professor Gilmore's statement that the filing of a premature continuation statement should not have the effect of invalidating the statement. In rejecting this view, the court stated:

> It is obvious to this court that the commentators don't think the law should mean what it says. However, the matter has been discussed enough times by the attorneys general of various states and by enough courts, that if the legislatures of the various states and the drafting committee of the Uniform Commercial Code wanted to change the plain language of the statute, there has been plenty of time to do it. Since it has not been changed, this court interprets the language to be mandatory and finds that a filing of a continuation statement outside the last six months of life of a financing statement causes the perfection of a security interest to lapse.

We hold that appellant's continuation statement was invalid because it was not filed within the six-month period indicated by KRS 355.9–403(3). Hence, appellant's underlying security interest in the rock truck had lapsed and was unperfected on the date Davis acquired title to the vehicle.

Next, we must determine whether Davis acquired a title to the rock truck which is free and clear of appellant's unperfected security interest in the vehicle. The court adjudged that it did. We perceive no error in this ruling.

True enough, KRS 355.9–201 states that except as otherwise provided, a security agreement is effective against purchasers of the collateral. If the security agreement is unperfected, however, the agreement is subordinate to the rights of certain specified persons. KRS 355.9–301. Among the persons protected is a purchaser who is not a secured party and who is not a buyer in the ordinary course of business, to the extent that the purchaser "gives value and receives delivery of the collateral without knowledge of the security interest and before it is perfected." KRS 355.9–301(1)(c). Appellant acknowledges that for purposes of this statute Davis (1) is not a secured party, (2) did not buy the truck in the ordinary course of business, and (3) gave value for the truck. However, appellant contends that Davis is not entitled to avail itself of the protection afforded by KRS 355.9–301(1)(c) because Davis is chargeable with constructive knowledge of the unperfected security interest since both the financing statement and the continuation statement respecting the truck were on file in the Harlan County Clerk's office. We are constrained to disagree.

The general definition section of the code states that a person "knows" or has "knowledge" of a fact when he or she has actual knowledge of it. KRS 355.1-201(25). Actual knowledge is not defined as including the concept of constructive knowledge. For purposes of KRS 355.9–301(1)(c), therefore, Davis cannot be deemed to have had knowledge of appellant's security agreement merely because it arguably should have known of it. Since appellant's security agreement was unperfected and it is undisputed that Davis acquired the rock truck under circumstances described in KRS 355.9–301(1)(c) without actual knowledge of the security interest, the court did not err by adjudging that Davis' interest in the vehicle is superior to appellant's.

DECISION: The Kentucky Court of Appeals affirmed the ruling for Davis.

Perfection by Possession

For most types of collateral, an alternative to perfection by filing is for the secured party to take possession of the property. Article 9 permits a secured party to perfect a security interest in goods, negotiable documents, or chattel paper by taking possession of them. The secured party may choose, however, to perfect an interest in these items by filing a financial statement.

A security interest in money or negotiable instruments can generally be perfected only by the secured party's taking possession. The same is generally true for a security evidenced by a certificate (such as a stock certificate that represents shares of stock). For instance, if A puts up 100 shares of General Motors stock as security for a bank loan, and if the shares are represented by certificates, then the bank must hold the certificates in order to have a perfected security interest.

A security interest in general intangibles or (in most cases) accounts must be perfected by filing.

A secured party in possession of collateral is under a duty to use reasonable care in its custody and preservation. The secured party must keep the collateral identifiable unless it is fungible, in which case it may be commingled. The secured party responsible for a loss to the collateral through failure to use reasonable care bears that loss, but the security interest is retained. Reasonable expenses incurred to preserve the collateral and insurance costs are borne by the debtor.

CONCEPT SUMMARY
Methods of Perfection

1. Collateral for which security interest is perfected *automatically* upon attachment:
   Consumer goods subject to a purchase-money security interest
2. Collateral for which security interest is perfected by *filing only:*
   Fixtures
   Accounts*
   General intangibles
3. Collateral for which security interest is perfected by *taking possession only:*
   Money
   Negotiable instruments*
   Securities evidenced by certificates*
4. Collateral for which security interest is perfected by *filing or taking possession:*
   Equipment
   Inventory
   Farm products
   Chattel paper
   Documents of title
   Consumer goods (other than goods subject to a purchase-money security interest or a certificate of title statute)
5. Collateral for which security interest is perfected by compliance with *certificate of title statute* and/or *filing:*
   Motor vehicles

*Subject to certain exceptions.

Priority

In some situations other people besides the secured creditor claim an interest in the collateral. A secured creditor may have to compete with someone who has purchased the collateral from the debtor, holders of statutory liens, general creditors, a trustee in bankruptcy, other secured creditors, and even the government. Because of the different interests involved, numerous state and federal statutes influence the solution to these conflicts.

Article 9 of the UCC does, however, provide the rules for resolving many of them.

The Unperfected Security Interest

As a general rule, Article 9 establishes a priority for the holder of a perfected security interest against other creditors and transferees from the debtor. Although the key to the secured creditor's protection is perfection of the security interest, limited protection is afforded an unperfected security interest. The unperfected security interest does enjoy priority over general creditors of the debtor who have established no lien on the collateral.

General creditors, however, have little difficulty in overcoming this priority. The general creditor may obtain a judgment against the debtor and have the sheriff levy on the property the creditor wishes to claim, even though the creditor knew of the secured party's interest in the collateral. Because of the relative ease with which a general creditor can establish a priority over an unperfected security interest, the prudent secured creditor will always perfect to obtain maximum safety.

Conflicting Security Interests

When two or more persons claim security interests in the same collateral, the general rule of priority is stated in Section 9-312(5)(a) as follows:

conflicting security interests rank according to priority in time of filing or perfection—*Priority dates from the time a filing is first made covering the collateral or the time the security interest is first perfected, whichever is earlier, provided that there is no period thereafter when there is neither filing nor perfection* [emphasis added].

Under Article 9 a party may file with respect to particular collateral before it comes into existence. A security interest cannot be perfected, however, until the security interest attaches to the collateral. A secured party must take possession of the collateral or the debtor must sign a security agreement and receive value from the secured party and acquire rights in the collateral for the perfection of the security interest to occur.

Section 9-312(5)(a) specifies that priority occurs when a filing is first made covering the collateral *or* when the security interest is first perfected, whichever is earlier. This rule makes it advantageous for a secured party to file its financing statement as soon as possible. The date of the filing will control if the security interest is subsequently perfected. It is also possible to perfect by taking possession of certain types of collateral. In this case the perfection is effective from the time the secured party takes possession of the collateral.

Taking into consideration the times at which perfection is effective and the rules stated in Section 9-312(5), consider the following examples: A perfects his security agreement against collateral held by X on January 1. B perfects a security interest in the same collateral on February 1. Because A perfected his interest on January 1, A has priority (Section 9-312[5][a]). Suppose that A's security interest in X's collateral attaches on January 1 and B's security interest in X's collateral attaches on February 1, but neither secured party perfects his interest. Whichever secured party first perfects his interest (by taking possession of the collateral or by filing) takes priority, and it makes no difference whether or not he knows of the other interest at the time he perfects his own. Thus if B perfects by filing before A, his interest has priority over A's. Section 9-312(5)(b) states the rule where neither party perfects. This rule is somewhat theoretical, but if neither perfects, the first interest to attach wins—this would be A, whose interest attached on January 1.

Suppose instead that a secured party files a financing statement on June 1 but fails to perfect his or her security interest at that time because the security interest has not yet attached to the collateral. On July 1 a second secured party perfects an interest in the same collateral. On August 1 the first secured party's interest attaches to the collateral, and the security interest is thus perfected on August 1. In this situation the first secured party has priority because the filing was on June 1 and this was before the second secured party's interest became effective on July 1. Once again, there is an advantage under the UCC to filing as soon as possible.

Purchase-Money Security Interest

The UCC places the holder of a purchase-money security interest (PMSI) in a beneficial position. Article 9 provides a claimant with a PMSI priority over a conflicting security interest in the same collateral if the PMSI is perfected within ten days of the time the debtor takes possession of the collateral (Section 9-312[4]). Priority for a PMSI may be justified on grounds that the party enabling property to be purchased deserves to be protected.

A PMSI provides protection for the seller in the following situation, although a perfected security interest already exists in the collateral: First State Bank advances funds to Jones Manufacturing and perfects a security interest in all the firm's equipment. The security agreement contains a provision extending the bank's interest to any after-acquired equipment. At a later date Jones purchases a new machine on credit from Smith Machine Company. As long as Smith Machine files a financing statement within ten days of the machine's delivery, its security interest has priority over that of First State Bank.

Consumer Goods   The holder of a PMSI in most types of consumer goods has extensive protection. Perfection is automatic for the retailer who obtains a security agreement from a customer. No filing is necessary to establish the seller's priority (Section 9-302[1][d]). One exception to this rule is motor vehicle financing. To perfect a security interest in a motor vehicle, the secured party must file a security agreement or comply with a state's certificate of title law.

Inventory   A PMSI in inventory has priority even though another creditor has previously perfected a security interest in the debtor's inventory if the following events occur (Section 9-312[3]):

1. The PMSI is perfected at the time the debtor receives possession of the inventory.

2. The purchase-money secured party gives notification in writing to the holder of the conflicting security interest who has filed a financing statement covering the same types of inventory (i) before the date of the filing made by the purchase-money secured party or (ii) before the beginning of the twenty-one-day period where the PMSI is temporarily perfected without filing or possession.

3. The holder of the conflicting interest receives notice within 5 years *before* the debtor receives possession of the inventory.

4. The notification states that the person giving notice has or expects to acquire a PMSI in inventory of the debtor, describing such inventory by item or type.

It is not necessary to notify secured creditors who have not filed financing statements, even if the person claiming a PMSI has knowledge of their interests.

Problems arising under Section 9-312(3) usually involve a conflict between a secured party claiming interest in certain collateral under an after-acquired property clause and a person claiming a PMSI in the same collateral. The rationale for this section is that a secured party typically will make advances on new inventory or releases of old inventory as new inventory is received. If the inventory financer learns of the PMSI in particular inventory, he or she may not make an advance against it (Section 9-312[3][b]).

The priority of the PMSI in inventory extends only to *identifiable cash proceeds* received on or before the inventory is delivered to the buyer. If the goods are sold to a buyer on account, the PMSI priority does not extend to these proceeds. Suppose a secured party makes a loan to a retailer to finance his or her operations and retains a security interest in after-acquired accounts receivable. After this a manufacturer sells goods to the retailer and perfects a PMSI in this inventory and the proceeds from their sale. Between the two parties, whose security interest has priority if the only assets of the retailer are accounts receivable generated by the sale of merchandise sold by the manufacturer? The secured party claiming a security interest in after-required accounts receivable has priority because accounts are not cash proceeds.

Collateral Other Than Inventory   UCC Section 9-312(4) provides that a PMSI in collateral other than inventory has priority over another security interest in the same collateral or its proceeds, so long as the PMSI is perfected at the time the debtor receives possession of the collateral or within 10 days thereafter. Recall that a PMSI in consumer goods (other than motor vehicles) is automatically perfected, and thus automatically takes priority over conflicting security interests.

For collateral that qualifies neither as consumer goods nor as inventory, the secured party with a PMSI must, in order to protect his or her priority, perfect his or her security interest within the 10-day grace period. In the *Ivie* case, which follows, the court was called upon to resolve an ambiguity as to when the secured party's grace period started. Note that Georgia, where *Ivie* was decided, has adopted a slightly modified version of Section 9-312(4): The secured party in Georgia has *15* days, rather than 10 days, to perfect once the debtor receives possession of the collateral.

IN RE IVIE & ASSOCIATES, INC.

U.S. Bankruptcy Court, N.D. Georgia
84 B.R. 882 (1988)

BACKGROUND: The Chattahoochee Bank filed a financing statement to perfect its security interest in all equipment owned by Ivie, including after-acquired property. Thereafter, in May and June of 1985, IPI delivered to Ivie three pieces of equipment known as "scrapers." At the time each scraper was delivered, no written agreement existed between Ivie and IPI. On July 31, 1985, the parties executed lease agreements for each of the three scrapers, and each agreement was back-dated to the date the scraper was delivered. IPI also filed financing statements for each of the three scrapers, but only one of the financing statements was filed within 15 days after the scraper was delivered.

Ivie went bankrupt. IPI filed a motion with Ivie's bankruptcy court to allow IPI to exercise its rights to the scrapers, arguing that IPI had perfected PMSI's on each scraper that had priority over the interests of any other creditor. IPI argued that its grace period to file financing statements should be measured from July 31, 1985, when the lease agreements were executed, and not from the respective dates of actual delivery. The Chattahoochee Bank opposed IPI's motion, arguing that IPI did not perfect its security interests within the applicable grace periods and that the bank preexisting security interest had priority over that of IPI.

Cotton, Bankruptcy Judge

The key question is when did Ivie obtain "possession" of the scrapers within the meaning of O.C.G.A. Section 11-9-312(4). The Bank argues that Ivie obtained possession when IPI delivered the scrapers to Ivie. On the other hand, IPI argues that, although Ivie obtained technical possession of the scrapers on delivery, Ivie obtained possession within the meaning of O.C.G.A. Section 11-9-312(4) when the parties entered into the respective lease agreements.

The Bank contends that *James Talcott, Inc. v. Assocs. Capital Co.,* 491 F.2d 879 (6th Cir.1974) controls in determining this issue while IPI counters and argues that *United States v. Hooks (In re Hooks),* 40 B.R. 715 (Bankr.M.D.Ga.1984) governs. The court has examined the law on this matter and has determined that *Talcott* is controlling in the case at bar.

In *Talcott,* the debtor granted Talcott, Inc. a security interest in "all fixtures, equipment, chattels, machinery . . . and collateral of every kind, *now or hereafter owned*" (emphasis in original). Talcott, Inc. perfected its security interest by properly filing its financing statement.

Thereafter, Highway Equipment Company ("Highway") delivered equipment to the debtor. Subsequent to delivery, Highway entered into two separate equipment lease agreements with the debtor. An option to purchase addendum was attached to the lease agreements. Highway filed financing statements on this equipment within ten days of the execution of each agreement, but more than ten days after delivery to the debtor.[1] Both agreements dated back to the time of delivery.

Highway eventually assigned its security interest to Associates Capital Company, Inc. ("Associates"). The debtor later failed to make the required payments and Associates repossessed the equipment. Prior to a public sale of the equipment, Talcott, Inc. filed suit claiming priority in the equipment.

The District Court found that Talcott, Inc. had priority in the equipment and granted summary judgment in their favor. On appeal, the Sixth Circuit stated that the only question was "when did Getz [the debtor] receive possession of the collateral as a 'debtor'." The Sixth Circuit found the lower court's analysis most convincing and affirmed the District Court's holding, which stated:

[1] The creditor in that case was required to perfect his interest within ten days from the time that debtor received possession of the collateral in order to have priority over a conflicting security interest in the same collateral. In the case at bar, the Georgia statute provides for a fifteen day period to perfect. [O.C.G.A. Section 11-9-312(4)].

It would be a frustration of this purpose [certainty in commercial transactions under the U.C.C.] to hold that a purchase money secured party can deliver goods to his debtor, delay indefinitely before entering into a security agreement which binds the debtor retroactively as of the delivery date, and still obtain a perfected security interest by filing within ten days of the agreement.

The Sixth Circuit found the critical fact was that the agreements provided that the rent began as of the dates of delivery. They agreed with the District Court that debtor obtained possession on delivery and thus, in order to perfect a purchase money security interest in the equipment, Associates had to perfect within ten days of delivery.

* * *

Of critical import to the court in *Talcott* were the lease agreements which specified that rent would begin as of the date of delivery to the debtor. Likewise, in the subject case, the lease agreements specifically dated back to the time of delivery when Ivie took possession. Accordingly, this court determines that Ivie acquired possession of the three scrapers for purposes of O.C.G.A. Section 11-9-312(4) at the time they were delivered by IPI, rather than the time that Ivie and IPI entered into the lease agreements for the three scrapers. In the present case, the facts are virtually identical to *Talcott*. Scraper #1 was delivered to Ivie on May 23, 1985 and a financing statement was filed on June 27, 1985. Scraper #2 was delivered to Ivie on June 12, 1985 and a financing statement was filed on June 27, 1985. Scraper #3 was delivered to Ivie on June 17, 1985 and a financing statement was filed on August 5, 1985.

Because IPI did not file its financing statement on Scrapers #1 and #3 within 15 days of the time debtor took possession, as required by O.C.G.A. Section 11-9-312(4), IPI failed to timely perfect its purchase money security interest ("PMSI") in these scrapers. Thus, the Bank's prior security interest in equipment, including after-acquired property, has priority over IPI's purchase money security interest in Scrapers #1 and #3 pursuant to O.C.G.A. Section 11-9-312(5)(a). . . .

On the other hand, Ivie obtained possession of Scraper #2 on June 12, 1987. IPI filed a financing statement to perfect its interest in that scraper within fifteen days therefrom on June 27, 1987. Because it timely perfected its purchase money security interest in Scraper #2, IPI has priority over the Bank pursuant to O.C.G.A. Section 11-9-312(4).

Decision: The court ruled in favor of IPI with respect to Scraper #2 only, and in favor of the bank with respect to the other two scrapers.

Chattel Paper and Instruments

When chattel paper is sold by the seller to a secured party, the secured party may choose to have the retail merchant collect the accounts, or the secured party may collect the accounts. The secured party may leave the chattel paper with the dealer, or the secured party may take possession of the paper. As noted previously, an interest in chattel paper may be perfected by either filing or taking possession of it.

Leaving it in the hands of the retail merchant is dangerous: If the secured party leaves the paper in the hands of the merchant and perfects an interest by filing, a subsequent secured party who takes possession of this chattel paper may gain priority over the secured party who merely files to perfect. Certain purchasers of chattel paper left in the debtor's possession take free of the security interest that has been perfected by filing. This is one of the limitations on the otherwise protected status of a party with a perfected security interest.

In general the rules applicable to chattel paper also apply to the purchase of instruments. Recall, however, that a security interest in instruments generally can be perfected only by possession. The only types of perfected nonpossessory security interest that can arise in an instrument are the temporary twenty-one-day perfection provided for in Section 9-304(4) and (5) or the 10-day perfection in proceeds of Section 9-306. If a security interest is temporarily perfected under either of these sections, a person taking possession of an instrument during this period without knowledge that it is subject to a security interest has priority over the conflicting security interest (Section 9-308[a]). Figure 32-3 illustrates the steps to be taken to create and perfect a security interest that will have priority over other secured creditors.

Protection of Buyers of Goods

Buyers in the Ordinary Course of Business   The UCC gives some buyers of goods protection against perfected security inter-

ests. When a person in "good faith and without knowledge that the sale to him or her is in violation of the ownership rights or security interest of a third party in the goods buys in ordinary course from a person in the business of selling goods of that kind" (excluding pawnbrokers), he or she qualifies as a **buyer in ordinary course of business.** Under Section 9-307(1) a buyer in the ordinary course of business takes free of a security interest created by his or her seller even if it is perfected and the buyer knows this.

This section permits the ordinary consumer to buy goods from a retail merchant without

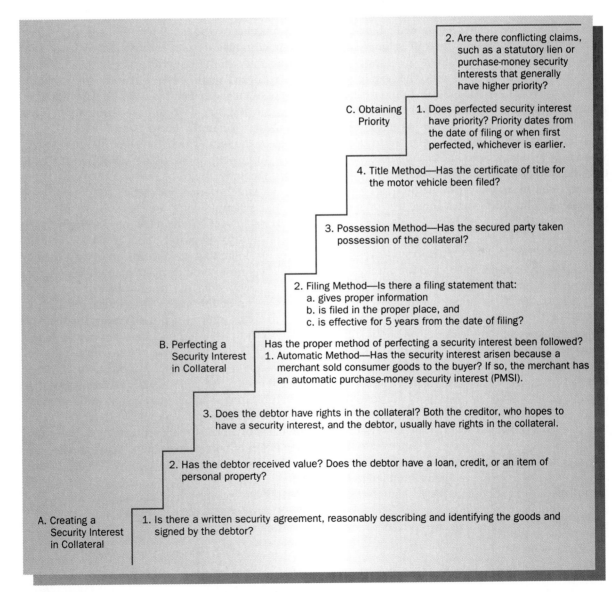

2. Are there conflicting claims, such as a statutory lien or purchase-money security interests that generally have higher priority?

C. Obtaining Priority

1. Does perfected security interest have priority? Priority dates from the date of filing or when first perfected, whichever is earlier.

4. Title Method—Has the certificate of title for the motor vehicle been filed?

3. Possession Method—Has the secured party taken possession of the collateral?

2. Filing Method—Is there a filing statement that:
   a. gives proper information
   b. is filed in the proper place, and
   c. is effective for 5 years from the date of filing?

B. Perfecting a Security Interest in Collateral

Has the proper method of perfecting a security interest been followed?
1. Automatic Method—Has the security interest arisen because a merchant sold consumer goods to the buyer? If so, the merchant has an automatic purchase-money security interest (PMSI).

3. Does the debtor have rights in the collateral? Both the creditor, who hopes to have a security interest, and the debtor, usually have rights in the collateral.

2. Has the debtor received value? Does the debtor have a loan, credit, or an item of personal property?

A. Creating a Security Interest in Collateral

1. Is there a written security agreement, reasonably describing and identifying the goods and signed by the debtor?

FIGURE 32-3

Creating a Valid Security Interest

being liable to a secured party of the merchant who claims a security interest in the goods purchased by the buyer. Normally, of course, a security agreement permits a merchant to sell from inventory. This section therefore applies to the situation in which the security agreement between the seller and the secured party does not permit such sales.

If a buyer buys goods from someone not in the business of selling goods of that kind, he or she is *not* a buyer in ordinary course of business. This means that the buyer-in-the-ordinary-course-of-business rule stated in Section 9-307(1) does not apply. Suppose a finance company lends money to a retail merchant and obtains a perfected security interest in the merchant's equipment. Since the merchant is not in the business of selling equipment, but rather is in the business of selling inventory, someone who purchases this equipment from the merchant is *not* a buyer in the ordinary course of business. On the other hand, a person buying consumer goods, such as an automobile, from a seller who ordinarily sells those goods, when buying in good faith and without knowledge that the sale of goods to him violates an existing security interest, is a buyer in the ordinary course of business. That buyer takes goods free of even a perfected security interest in the goods.

Buyers *Not* in the Ordinary Course of Business A special rule exists for purchase of consumer goods—that is, goods used primarily for personal, family, or household purposes (Section 9-109[1]). Remember that a PMSI in consumer goods can be perfected without filing (other security interests in consumer goods must be filed). As long as the buyer buys without knowledge of the security interest for his or her own personal, family, or household purposes before a financing statement is filed, he or she takes free of even a perfected security interest (Section 9-307[2]).

Suppose that Linda purchased a refrigerator on a secured basis from Acme. Linda intended to use the refrigerator in her home. Because the refrigerator was a consumer good in this case, Acme's interest in it was automatically perfected even

though it did not file a financing statement. After the retailer delivered it to her home, Linda decided she really wanted another color appliance. Linda called her next door neighbor, Alice. Alice agreed to purchase the refrigerator for $50 less than Linda paid for it. Alice was unaware of the security agreement between Acme and Linda, and Alice intended to use the refrigerator in her home. If Alice makes the purchase before Acme files a financing statement, Alice takes the refrigerator free of Acme's security interest. Alice is what is called a buyer *not* in the ordinary course of business.

Protection of Other Buyers A buyer who purchases goods subject to a security interest may, under certain circumstances, take the goods free of the security interest even if the buyer doesn't qualify as a buyer in the ordinary course of business. Section 9-307(3) provides that a buyer other than a buyer in the ordinary course of business generally takes free of a security interest to the extent that the security interest secures future advances made after the secured party becomes aware of the purchase—or after 45 days, whichever comes earlier.

As an example, suppose that a bank makes a revolving line of credit available to Higby. The line of credit is secured by all Higby's personal property, including his tractor. At a time when Higby has no outstanding balance on his line of credit, Higby sells his tractor to Wigby. If the bank learns of the sale and thereafter makes a loan to Higby under the line of credit, the tractor will *not* be part of the collateral for the loan. Similarly, if the bank does *not* learn of the sale and makes a loan to Higby more than 45 days after the sale, the tractor will not be part of the collateral for the loan. The upshot of this provision is that a creditor making future advances on the basis of a preexisting security agreement (1) may not rely on collateral that he or she knows has been sold and (2) has 45 days to learn of the sale.

The case that follows illustrates how Section 9-307(3) works and also discusses how a person qualifies as a "buyer."

DAVIS COUNTY SAVINGS BANK V. PRODUCTION CREDIT ASSOCIATION

Supreme Court of Iowa
419 N.W.2d 384 (1988)

BACKGROUND: Dale and Shirley Hendricks owned certain farm equipment which was used as collateral for a series of loans made by Davis County Savings Bank. The security agreement between the Hendrickses and the bank provided that the collateral would secure future advances. In 1979, Dale and Shirley transferred the equipment to Dan and Amber Hendricks, their son and daughter-in-law. Dan and Amber obtained the equipment pursuant to a lease/purchase agreement whereby the couple would pay the purchase price of the equipment over a 10-year period. The agreement provided that Dan and Amber would take possession of the equipment immediately, but Dale and Shirley would retain title until the purchase price was paid. Dan and Amber granted a security interest in the equipment to PCA, which perfected its interest by filing.

In 1980, Dale and Shirley paid off all their outstanding debts to Davis County Savings Bank. Later that year, the bank began making additional loans to Dale and Shirley on the same security agreement. In 1982, the equipment was sold by PCA (Dan and Amber's secured party) at a public sale. The bank, claiming that it was entitled to the proceeds because it was a prior perfected secured party, sued PCA. The trial court ruled in favor of the bank, and PCA appealed.

Schultz, Presiding Judge

Section 554.9307(3) provides protection to "buyers" of collateral who are not entitled to the protection afforded buyers in the ordinary course of business under section 554.9307(1). Due to their knowledge of the bank's security interest, Dan and Amber are not buyers in the ordinary course of business. Thus, the issue is whether they are "buyers" entitled to protection under subsection (3).

* * *

The transaction between Dale and Shirley and Dan and Amber, although designated a "lease/purchase" agreement, was a transfer of interest with reservation of title as security. Although Dale and Shirley retained title, Iowa Code section 554.1201(87) (definition of security interest) states that "retention or reservation of title by a seller of goods notwithstanding shipment or delivery to the buyer (section 554.2401) is limited in effect to a reservation of a 'security interest'." . . . Consequently, under the Code Dale and Shirley are left with only a security interest in the equipment. The remainder of their interest was transferred to Dan and Amber.

* * *

Although the term "buyer" is not defined in the Code, the term "purchase" is. A "purchase" is "any voluntary transaction creating an interest in property, including taking by sale, discount, negotiation, mortgage, pledge, voluntary lien, issue, reissue or gift." Iowa Code § 554.1201(32). Under this broad definition, Dan and Amber clearly "purchased" an interest in the farm equipment. As used in section 554.9307(3) the terms "purchase" and "buyer" refer to the same transaction and so, because Dan and Amber "purchased" the equipment they are entitled to the protection provided.

* * *

Because Dan and Amber are "buyers" entitled to protection under section 554.9307(3), application of the statute to these facts is fairly easy. The bank claims a security interest under a future advance clause for funds advanced more than forty-five days after the purchase by Dan and Amber. Because the advances were not made pursuant to a commitment entered into within the forty-five day period, the plain words of the statute mean that Dan and Amber took the equipment free of the bank's claimed interest. As successor to Dan and Amber's interest, the PCA also takes free. This is precisely the type of situation at which the statute is aimed.

* * *

While future advance clauses are allowed under our law, *see* Iowa Code § 554.9204(3), the drafters of the Code and our legislature found it prudent to limit the effect of a future advance clause after transfer of the collateral to a buyer. Section 554.9307(3) strikes a balance between the interests of a creditor who has obtained an interest in collateral to secure future advances and the interests of one who buys the collateral.

The provision proceeds on the assumption that, after an appropriate grace period, a creditor should know whether the collateral has been sold before making another advance or committing himself to one. Unless he has knowledge to the contrary, the secured party is allowed for 45 days to assume that the debtor still owns the collateral. Advances made with knowledge, or after the 45–day period, may not be secured by the sold collateral.

DECISION: The Supreme Court of Iowa ruled in favor of PCA, reversing the lower court's decision.

Statutory Liens

If a person furnishes services or materials in the ordinary course of business, any lien upon goods in his or her possession given by state law for such materials or services takes priority over a perfected security interest (Section 9-310). This means that when a mechanic repairs a vehicle, if state law gives him or her a mechanic's lien on the car for services rendered, this interest is superior to that of a bank that has a security interest in the car.

Security Interest in Fixtures

Goods are fixtures, as noted earlier, when they become so attached to a particular piece of real estate that an interest in them arises under real-estate law (Section 9-313[1]). Article 9 recognizes three categories of goods in relation to fixtures:

1. Those that retain their *chattel* character entirely and are not part of the real estate, which should be perfected by filing in accordance with the rules on personal property
2. *Ordinary building materials* that have become an integral part of the real estate, which should be perfected by recording a real estate mortgage
3. *Fixtures* that are perfected by making a **fixture filing**, a financing statement filed in the office where a mortgage on the real estate would be filed or recorded, covering goods that are or are to become fixtures (Section 9-313[1][b])

The financing statement for a fixture filing must contain a description of the real estate sufficient to identify it. Applying this test, a description is adequate if a person searching the real-estate records would discover the filing. In some states the description is adequate if it sufficiently describes real estate for purposes of a mortgage.

A fixture filing gives to the fixture security interest priority as against other real estate interests based on the principle that the first to file or record prevails. This is the usual rule with respect to conflicting real estate interests. An additional requirement is that the debtor must have an interest of record in the real estate or be in possession (such as a tenant). This later requirement restricts a valid fixture filing where the creditor is a contractor.

There are three exceptions to the first-to-file rule. The first exception to the rule exists for a PMSI in a fixture. This interest has priority over previously recorded real estate interests as long as the security interest is perfected by a fixture filing before the goods become fixtures or within 10 days thereafter (Section 9-314[4][a]).

Another exception to the rule covers readily removable factory or office machines or readily removable replacements of domestic appliances that are consumer goods. If an interest in these goods is perfected by any method in Article 9 before they become fixtures, the fixture filing prevails over a conflicting interest of most claims that are acquired in the real estate or the conflicting interest of the owners.

The final exception to the first-to-file rule for filing gives a perfected security interest in fixtures priority over a conflicting interest that is a lien on the real estate obtained by legal or equitable proceedings after the security interest was perfected (Section 9-313[4][c]).

Accessions and Commingled or Processed Goods

A secured party who claims an interest in **accessions**, which are goods installed or affixed to other goods, is entitled to priority with certain exceptions over anyone else claiming an interest in the whole goods if the security interest attaches before the goods become accessions (Section 9-314[1]).

If a security interest in goods is perfected and the goods subsequently become part of a product

or mass and their identity is lost in the product or goods, the security interest continues in the product or mass (Section 9-315).

As the Preventive Law box indicates, the creditor seeking to minimize the risk of nonpayment by the debtor must, among other things, perfect the security interest in the debtor's goods.

Assignment

A common business practice is for a seller of goods holding an installment contract with an accompanying security interest to transfer these to a finance company. In return the finance company advances funds that the seller uses in the operation of its business.

Rights of an Assignee

When an installment contract and security interest are sold to a finance company, the finance company becomes the secured party. Since this transaction is usually an assignment, the finance company is often referred to as the *assignee*. The original seller, who is the assignor, is now a *debtor* since it has received an advance from the finance company. The original purchaser is referred to as an **account debtor**. In general the UCC does not permit the original purchaser to restrict the assignment of an installment contract (Section 9-318[4]). Even if the parties include a provision restricting assignment in the installment contract, the contract may be assigned.

In the absence of a contrary provision the rights of an assignee are subject to all terms of the contract between the account debtor and assignor and any defense or claim arising therefrom. The assignee takes the contract subject to any claims the account debtor has against the as-signor that arise independently of the contract and accrue *before* the account debtor receives notification of the assignment (Section 9-318[1][a] and [b]).

Suppose that Acme sold some goods to International on open account. Acme borrowed money from Financial and put this account up as collateral for the loan. Financial then notified International, the account debtor, to pay Financial rather than Acme. Who should International pay? This question is discussed in the following case.

CAPITAL FACTORS, INC. V. CALDOR, INC.

New York Supreme Court, Appellate Division
582 N.Y.S.2d 1012 (1992)

BACKGROUND: A supplier sold goods to Caldor. Caldor continued to make payments to the supplier rather than to Capital Factors even though Capital Factors had taken a security interest in the supplier's accounts and had notified Caldor to pay it rather than the supplier. Capital Factors sued Caldor because it had not received any money from Caldor. The lower court ruled that Caldor must pay Capital Factors. Caldor appealed.

Memorandum Decision

We agree that the notice stamped on the assignor's invoices—"PAYABLE TO: CAPITAL FACTORS, INC. P.O. BOX 9413, DEERFIELD BEACH, FL 33443, REMITTANCE IS TO BE MADE ONLY TO THEM IN PAR FUNDS. ANY OBJECTION TO THIS BILL, OR ITS TERMS, MUST BE REPORTED TO THEM WITH TEN DAYS AFTER ITS RECEIPT"—apprised defendant account debtor that the account had been assigned, that payment was to be made to the plaintiff-as-signee, and that the rights assigned were those contained on the invoice itself. Specifically demanding that payment was to be made to a person other than the assignor and reasonably referring to the goods reflected on the invoices, the stamp satisfied the notice requirements of UCC § 9-318(3). Since "no particular form of notice is required by the [Uniform Commercial Code] and actual knowledge of a fact is notice thereof" defendant should have inferred from the stamp that the account had been assigned.

DECISION: The appellate court affirmed the ruling for Capital Factors.

Waiver of Defenses

Quite often a seller, anticipating the documents will be used in financing, asks the buyer to sign an installment contract and security agreement containing words similar to the following:

Buyer hereby agrees to waive as against any assignee of this contract all claims or defenses buyer may have against secured party to the full extent permitted by law.

This clause facilitates the seller's assignment of the installment contract to a financer, for the buyer has waived its rights to sue and set up defenses against the financer (assignee). If a buyer accepts this terminology, it must settle any dispute arising over the goods with the seller, although the seller has transferred all its rights to a finance company. The UCC permits waiver-of-defense clauses as long as the assignee takes the assignment for value, in good faith, and without notice of a claim or defense.

A waiver-of-defense clause is effective against the account debtor unless his or her defense is one that could be asserted against a holder in due course of a negotiable instrument (see Chapter 28) or a statute or decision establishes a different rule for consumer goods. A Federal Trade Commission rule, discussed in Chapter 28, abolishes the use of such clauses in consumer contracts everywhere in the United States, but the clause is still effective in business transactions that do not involve sales to a consumer.

Default

When the debtor defaults under a security agreement, a secured party has the rights and remedies provided in Article 9 and whatever rights and remedies the security agreement itself gives the secured party—subject to certain limitations specified in Section 9-501(3). In general the secured party may reduce the claim to a judgment, foreclose, or otherwise enforce the security interest by any available judicial procedure. The secured party may elect to reduce the claim to a judgment and then levy on the collateral. In this case the judgment lien relates back to the date of perfection of the security interest (Section 9-501[5]). When there is a judicial sale following judgment, execution, and levy, the judicial sale is a foreclosure of the security interest, but the sale is not governed by Article 9.

Secured Party's Right to Possession After Default

In the absence of a contrary agreement, if the debtor defaults, the secured party has a right to possession of the collateral. Section 9-503 permits a secured party to take possession of the collateral if it may be done without breach of the peace. This means the secured party may go to the place where the collateral is and take possession of it. Although the UCC permits self-help repossession, the process is not without legal risk.

One problem involves the meaning of the term "breach of peace," which is used in the statute but not defined. If the secured party commits a breach of the peace in repossessing the collateral, he or she is subject to tort liability.

Suppose that a secured party decides to hire a third party to retrieve the goods from the debtor. If the third party breaches the peace in the course of obtaining the goods, does the secured party have any liability? The following case addresses this question.

MBANK EL PASO, N.A. V. SANCHEZ

Texas Supreme Court
17 UCC Rep.Serv.2d 1358 (1992)

BACKGROUND: Yvonne Sanchez failed to pay the note on her automobile. MBank therefore decided to repossess her car. The bank hired El Paso Recovery Services to perform this task for it. In the course of repossessing the car, El Paso breached the peace. Sanchez sued the MBank and the trial court ruled in favor of MBank. Sanchez appealed.

Mauzy, Justice

The issue in this case is whether a secured creditor may avoid liability for breaches of the peace by using an independent contractor to carry out repossession. The court of appeals, applying § 9.503, held that a creditor cannot delegate the duty of peaceable repossession to an independent contractor. We agree.

MBank El Paso hired El Paso Recovery Service to repossess Yvonne Sanchez's automobile because of her default on a note. Two men dispatched to Sanchez's home found the car parked in the driveway, and hooked it to a tow truck. Sanchez demanded that they cease their efforts and leave the premises; but the men nonetheless continued with the repossession. Before the men could tow the automobile into the street, Sanchez jumped into the car, locked the doors, and refused to leave. The men then towed the car at a high rate of speed, with Sanchez inside, to the repossession yard. They parked the car in the fenced repossession yard and padlocked the gate. Sanchez was left in the repossession lot, with a Doberman pinscher guard dog loose in the yard, until later rescued by her husband and police.

Sanchez filed suit against MBank, alleging that it was liable for the tortious acts of El Paso Recovery Service. MBank moved for summary judgment on the ground that El Paso Recovery Service was an independent contractor for whom MBank bore no responsibility.

As a general rule, when a duty is imposed by law on the basis of concerns for public safety, the party bearing the duty cannot escape it by delegating it to an independent contractor. Section 424 of the *Restatement (Second) of Torts* (1965) provides:

> One who by statute or by administrative regulation is under a duty to provide specified safeguards or precautions for the safety of others is subject to liability to the others for whose protection the duty is imposed for harm caused by the failure of a contractor employed by him to provide such safeguards or precautions.

Comment a to §424 further explains that a duty to take safety precautions cannot be delegated to an independent contractor:

> The rule stated in this Section applies whenever a statute or an administrative regulation imposes a duty upon one doing particular work to provide safeguards or precautions for the safety of others. In such a case the employer cannot delegate his duty to provide such safeguards or precautions to an independent contractor.

We believe that §9-503 of the UCC imposes a duty on secured creditors pursuing nonjudicial repossession to take precautions for public safety.

Other jurisdictions agree that a creditor cannot escape the duty of peaceable repossession by delegating it to an independent contractor.

A secured creditor certainly has a strong interest in obtaining collateral from a defaulting debtor. That interest, however, must be balanced against society's interest in the public peace. If a creditor chooses to pursue self-help, it must be expected to take precautions in doing so. If this burden is too heavy, the creditor may seek relief by turning to the courts.

Because the Bank chose to pursue nonjudicial repossession, it assumed the risk that a breach of the peace might occur. ("[T]he bank having chosen its remedy must stand by the attendant duties and liabilities thereof.") Under §424 of the *Restatement (Second) of Torts*, the Bank remains liable for breaches of the peace committed by its independent contractor. We therefore affirm the judgment of the court of appeals.

DECISION: The Texas Supreme Court reversed the judgment and ruled for Yvonne Sanchez.

Disposition of Collateral

After default the secured party may sell, lease, or otherwise dispose of the collateral. The disposition may be by public or private proceedings—but every aspect of the disposition, including the method, manner, time, place, and terms, must be commercially reasonable. Prior to public sale, the secured party usually must notify the debtor of the time and place of the sale or, if it is a private sale, the debtor must be notified of the time. If nonconsumer goods are involved, the secured party must also notify any other secured party from whom he or she has received written notice of a claim of an interest in the collateral. If any one aspect of the disposition is not commercially reasonable, the sale can be set aside.

The purchaser of the collateral generally takes free of any security interest or lien subordinate to that of the secured party. If the purchaser bought at a public sale, he or she must not have had knowledge of any defects in the sale and must not have bought in collusion with the secured party, other bidders, or anyone else conducting the sale. In any other case the purchaser must simply act in good faith.

As a general rule, the secured party may retain the collateral in satisfaction of the obligation. If a secured party wishes to do this, the debtor and other appropriate parties, such as those with security interests in the collateral, must be notified. In the absence of objections within 21 days from the date of notification, the secured party may keep the collateral. If objections are received, he or she must dispose of the collateral as directed by the UCC.

If the collateral is sold, the proceeds are distributed in the following order: The reasonable expenses incurred in repossessing and disposing of the collateral are deducted. Next, the secured party collects the unpaid debt and other lawful charges agreed to in the security agreement. Finally, if the secured party receives written demand from any subordinate security interests, these are paid. Any remaining funds go to the debtor.

For example, if the debtor owed the secured party $50,000 and put up his or her equipment as collateral for a loan, the distribution would be as follows if the secured party got $90,000 for the equipment: The secured party's reasonable administrative expenses would first be deducted (suppose they were $2,000), leaving $88,000. Then the $50,000 would be deducted, leaving $38,000. If he or she had received a written demand from a subordinate party who also claimed that the debtor owed him or her $50,000, the subordinate party would get the balance of $38,000.

In the *Gulf Homes* case, which follows, the court examines whether the sale of a mobile home was commercially reasonable. Which aspects of the disposition of the collateral most concern the court?

GULF HOMES, INC. v. GOUBEAUX

Supreme Court of Arizona
602 P.2d 810 (1980)

BACKGROUND: Gulf Homes (plaintiff-appellee) sold a mobile home to Goubeaux (defendant-appellant) for approximately $9,500 in Tucson, Arizona. Goubeaux made a $550 down payment but made no other payments. He subsequently abandoned the home. After the default by Goubeaux, Gulf Homes repossessed it and sought to sell it. It sent a notice to him, posted a notice on the home and in three places in Phoenix, Arizona. It also advertised the sale in a Phoenix paper. The place of the sale was at Gulf Home's Phoenix office. When no one appeared at the sale, Gulf Home purchased it for $7,000. It then sued Goubeaux for the balance due it under its sales contract. Goubeaux claimed the sale was not commercially reasonable. The trial court and Court of Appeals found for the seller.

Holohan, Justice

The UCC has provided a broad, rather than a per se, rule to test the validity of a disposition. The test is whether every aspect of the disposition is commercially reasonable. . . . Some approved methods of conducting a sale of collateral are set forth in A.R.S.sec.44–3153(B) which provides that if the secured party has "sold in conformity with reasonable commercial practices among dealers in the type of property sold he has sold in a commercially reasonable manner."

* * *

. . . We find no authority which makes it mandatory for a secured party to conduct a repossession sale in the same manner as an original sale.

The distance between the place of sale and the location of the collateral presents a more difficult issue. The sale was held approximately 125 miles from the location of the mobile home. At the time of the repossession sale, the appellee had an office in Tucson, from which the mobile home was originally sold to the appellants. In selling mobile homes in Tucson, the appellee would advertise in two major Tucson newspapers. In conducting its repossession sale, however, the appellee posted notice of the sale in Phoenix; advertised the sale in one issue of the Arizona Weekly Gazette, a weekly newspaper published in Phoenix; and then held the sale at its Phoenix office, while the mobile home remained on a lot in Tucson.

When suing for a deficiency, the burden of proof is upon the secured party, who must prove that disposition of the collateral was conducted in a commercially reasonable manner. . . . There was no evidence presented by appellee which showed that holding a repossession sale, as well as advertising and posting notice of such, a substantial distance from the location of the mobile home, was in conformity with reasonable commercial practices of mobile home dealers. The only evidence at trial bearing on this issue consisted of the following exchange on cross-examination of appellee's president by appellants' counsel:

Q: I believe at the time of this sale, the sale was held in your—excuse me, at the time of the repossession auction the auction itself was held in your office in Phoenix, is that correct?

A: That is correct.

Q: At that time, the mobile home itself was in a mobile home park here in Tucson, is that not correct?

A: That's correct.

Q: Could you tell me why the sale was held in your Phoenix office instead of next to the mobile home down here?

A: Well, this particular mobile home is a two-part mobile home, it's a double-wide.

Q: Yes.

A: If you tear it apart and move it, you run into a lot of expense, and of course that expense would have had to have been borne by Mr. Goubeaux; furthermore incur a lot more expense, and so for elimination of expense and convenience, that was the way it was done, probably save him—Mr. Goubeaux—probably about a thousand dollars or better.

Q: Rather than moving the mobile home to Phoenix to sell it, did you consider moving the sale to the mobile home in Tucson?

A: Well, I think this was done for convenience all the way around.

Q: That being your convenience, I take it?

A: Well, it's convenience of saving the trip, saving money, and it was properly advertised and noted and offered to people to look at, and then we didn't even have one call on it.

The decision of reasonableness is usually one of fact to be resolved by the trier of fact. No evidence was presented showing that a sale of a mobile home located a substantial distance from the place of sale was consistent with reasonable commercial practices of mobile home dealers. Absent a showing of commercial practices to the contrary, the circumstances indicate that the sale should have been advertised, noticed, and sold in Tucson where the mobile home was available for inspection. The location of the chattel was in a metropolitan area with a population in excess of 350,000 people. The area is a major trade center for the southern part of the state. Notices and advertising in Phoenix some 125 miles away would not have much efficacy in producing buyers in Tucson. As the testimony shows, any buyer in Phoenix would be faced with an additional expense of "probably about a thousand dollars or better" to move the mobile home from Tucson to Phoenix.

DECISION: The Supreme Court held that the seller had not established that the collateral it sold had been disposed of in a commercially reasonable manner. Accordingly, it remanded the case to the trial court for further proceedings consistent with its opinion.

Right of Redemption

Although rarely done in actual practice, the collateral may be redeemed by the debtor or any other secured party any time before the secured party has disposed of it, or entered into a contract to dispose of it, or completed the process for retaining the collateral under Section 9-505(2). The party redeeming, however, must pay all money owed and perform all obligations owing at the time he or she attempts to redeem the property.

Liability of Secured Party for Noncompliance

Clearly, if the secured party is not performing as required by the UCC, he or she may be restrained from disposing of the collateral. If the disposition has already occurred, the secured party is liable for any loss caused by a failure to comply with Part 5 of Article 9. Where the disposition of the collateral is not carried out in a commercially reasonable manner, the secured party cannot use the proceeds from the sale of the collateral to cover the debtor's payment deficiencies.

Termination

Once the debtor's obligation has been satisfied, the secured party generally must file a termination statement with each officer with whom a financing statement was filed. A **termination statement** is a document which serves notice that the secured interest perfected by a particular financing statement is no longer in effect.

If consumer goods are involved, the termination statement must be filed within 1 month of the debt's repayment, or within 10 days following a written demand by the debtor. If the collateral is not consumer goods, and the debtor demands in writing a termination statement, then the secured party must furnish a termination statement for each filing officer with whom a financing statement was filed. If the secured party fails to file as required by Article 9 or to furnish a termination statement 10 days after a proper demand, then he or she will be liable to the debtor for $100 and for any resulting loss caused thereby (UCC Section 9-404).

Review Questions and Problems

Key Terms

secured creditor
collateral
security interest
secured party
security agreement
financing statement
goods
fixtures
consumer goods
equipment
farm products
inventory
purchase-money security interest
instrument
document of title
chattel paper
account
general intangibles
attachment
after-acquired property
floating lien
perfection
continuation statement
buyer in the ordinary course of business
fixture filing
accessions
account debtor

Discussion Questions

1. Explain how goods are classified and give an example of each type of goods. Can goods become fixtures?
2. How can a retailer seller be both a creditor and a debtor with respect to security interests in the property once in the seller's store and then sold to a consumer or other business?
3. Why is it necessary to perfect a security interest? How does perfection of a security interest occur?

Review Problems

1. Stryker manufacturers medical equipment for sale to medical institutions and retailers. It also sells directly to consumers in its wholly owned retail outlets. Stryker has created a subsidiary, Styk Corporation, for the purpose of financing the purchase of its products by various customers. In which of the following situations does Styk not have to file a financing statement to perfect its security interest against competing creditors in the equipment sold by Stryker?
   a. Sales made to consumers who purchase for their own personal use
   b. Sales made to medical institutions
   c. Sales made to retailers who in turn sell to buyers in the ordinary course of business
   d. Sales made to any buyer who uses the equipment as a fixture

2. Gilmore, an automobile dealer, had an inventory of forty cars and ten trucks. He financed the purchase of this inventory with First Bank under an agreement dated January 5, which gave the bank a security interest in all vehicles on Gilmore's premises, all future acquired vehicles, and the proceeds from their sale. On January 10 the bank properly filed a financing statement that identified the collateral in the same way that it was identified in the agreement. On April 1 Gilmore sold a passenger car to Todd for family use and a truck to Diamond Company for its hardware business. Does the bank have a perfected security interest? If so, when was it perfected? Does it matter whether the property being secured is inventory? Is the car subject to the security interest of the bank after it is sold?

3. Lowland Appliances, Inc. sells various brand-name appliances at discount prices. Lowland maintains a large inventory that it obtains from various manufacturers on credit. These manufacturer-creditors have all filed and taken secured interests in the appliances and proceeds therefrom that they have sold to Lowland on credit. Lowland in turn sells to hundreds of ultimate consumers; some pay cash but most pay on credit. Lowland takes a security interest but does not file a financing statement for credit. Does Lowland have a perfected security interest in the goods sold on credit? Are the appliances considered consumer goods or inventory?

4. Mary Morris is the owner of a computer store. She has borrowed money from First Bank to finance her inventory of computers. First Bank and Mary have entered into a security agreement that gives First Bank a security interest in Mary's present and after-acquired inventory and all proceeds therefrom. Suppose Mary now needs money to buy additional inventory—computers that she has never stocked before. If Second Bank were to lend Mary $25,000, could it have priority over First Bank with regard to its loan?

5. Central Air Conditioner, Inc. went to the First National Bank on February 1. The bank agreed to loan Central $100,000. Central signed a note, a security agreement, and a financing statement. On February 15, First National filed the financing statement, which claimed a security interest in Central's equipment. At this point, however, First National had not actually loaned any money to Central.

   On March 1, Central went to the Merchant's Bank. Central again signed a note, a security agreement, and a financingment. Central gave Merchant's a security interest in its equipment. On March 10, Merchant's filed the financing statement—and on that date it gave Central $50,000.

   On March 30, First National completed its loan to Central and gave Central $100,000 on that date. Which party, First National or Merchant's, has the first claim to Central's equipment?

6. Appliance Store, a retailer, financed itself with a loan from First National Bank. First National took a perfected security interest in all the equipment currently owned by Appliance Store. The security agreement included an after-acquired property clause. The bank filed a financing statement covering its interest in Appliance Store's equipment on February 1.

   On March 1 of that same year, Appliance Store decided to purchase one refrigerator from International Refrigerators. International intends to take a purchase money security interest in the refrigerator it intends to sell to Appliance Store. What precautions, if any, should International take with respect to giving possession of the refrigerator to Appliance Store in light of First National's perfected position?

7. Betty purchased a Steinway piano for her home. The seller took a perfected security interest in the piano, but it did not file a financing statement. A week later an unexpected financial crisis caused Betty to need cash. She called her next-door neighbor, Adele. Adele was unaware of the security agreement between Betty and the seller. Adele paid Betty $200 less for the piano than Betty paid for it. Adele bought the piano for use in her home. Did Adele take the piano subject to the seller's security interest?

Case Problems

1. Cunningham purchased a Triumph from Camelot Motors. He paid cash for the car. United Bank had a perfected security interest in all of Camelot's inventory. When Camelot sold a vehicle, the security agreement required it to pay the proceeds of the sale to the bank. Camelot failed to do this. Under these circumstances, did Cunningham take the car free of the perfected security interest of United Bank in his automobile?

2. Butler defaulted on a loan from Ford Motor Credit Company. The loan was secured by Butler's truck. A towing company hired by Ford towed the unlocked truck from Butler's open driveway in the middle of the night. No one saw or confronted the towing company employees at the time. Butler sued Ford, claiming that the repossession breached the peace and was therefore illegal. Is Butler correct?

3. Timbrook became delinquent in her payments on a mobile home purchased from Winchester Mobile Home Sales. Although she tried to work out an agreeable payment schedule, she was unable to do so. Thereafter, while Timbrook was at work, representatives of the creditor broke the lock to release a pet and removed her home and all her possessions. Did the actions of the creditor's representative breach the peace?

33

Rights of Debtors and Creditors

Liens on Real and Personal Property
Suretyship

Lender Liability
Debtor Protection Statutes

The early history of debtor-creditor law was heavily weighted in favor of creditors. Debtors were subjected to harsh penalties, including jail sentences, for failure to make timely payment of debts. Interest rates and debt collection practices were not subject to rigorous regulation by state or federal government. This trend gave way to a philosophy aimed at protecting the rights of debtors, and is evidenced by the wide variety of federal statutes enacted during the last 25 years.

Although this recent era of consumer protection was viewed as long overdue, there is developing criticism that the pendulum has swung too far in the debtor direction. Creditors attempting to collect debts face what they consider to be a number of procedural obstacles that unnecessarily delay the ultimate result, which is the seizing of the debtor's property so that it can be sold to satisfy the outstanding debt. This chapter reviews the various rights of creditors and debtors in debt collection disputes, as well as the remedies that are available to achieve a resolution short of filing a bankruptcy petition. The bankruptcy solution will be discussed in the following chapter.

Liens on Real and Personal Property

Chapter 32 dealt with special protection afforded to creditors that achieve secured status pursuant to the Uniform Commercial Code. Although it is preferable from a creditor viewpoint to hold a perfected security interest in the debtor's personal property, many creditors are not in a position to claim this status. Likewise, Chapter 48 indicates that a bank which holds the mortgage on real estate is in a similar secured position in the event that there is a default on the underlying promissory note. In these two instances, the debtor has agreed to a **consensual lien**—that is, to the creation of the encumbrance that places the creditor in a preferred position relative to competing creditors.

A lien represents a claim against the debtor's property that requires satisfaction before the property can be made available to other creditors. This means that the property, or any proceeds received from its sale, must be paid over to the creditor holding the lien before any other creditors without liens are paid. Further, liens that are attached to a debtor's property are accounted for chronologically, so that an earlier recorded lien takes precedence over later recorded competing liens. If a creditor cannot hold a secured position against certain property or collateral, his or her second choice is to have the lien recognized and attached to the debtor's real and personal property as soon as possible. This will allow the creditor to take precedence over all other unperfected security interests.

As mentioned previously, real and personal property liens can be created by consensual agreement of debtor and creditor. However, liens also can arise by virtue of the common law or judicial proceedings. Common law liens include liens created in favor of individuals providing services, such as artisans, laborers, innkeepers, and common carriers. Judicial liens are those liens recognized by the courts which facilitate the creditor's efforts to hold and possibly seize the debtor's property, either prior to or immediately following the conclusion of a collection lawsuit.

Common Law Possessory Liens

The common law provides for a variety of liens that are available to service providers, such as innkeepers and laborers. These liens are referred to as "possessory" because the common law requires that the service provider continue to hold possession of the customer's personal property following the completion of all services agreed upon between the parties. Most importantly, possessory liens cease to exist if the service provider voluntarily gives up possession of the personal property. Common law possessory liens have been recognized by statute in many states, and are more appropriately referred to as statutory liens in those jurisdictions.

Artisan's Lien The common law provides an **artisan's lien** for a creditor who delivers services for labor and materials used to repair the debtor's personal property. This lien allows the artisan to keep the personal property pending payment by the debtor for the services rendered. For example, Tom takes five business dress suits to a tailor for alterations. Assuming no agreement to the contrary, the tailor can keep the suits until Tom provides payment. If the amount charged by the tailor is reasonable, the tailor may sell the suits after passage of a reasonable time.

The artisan's lien applies only as long as the service provider has possession of the personal property. An artisan lien is lost in most cases when possession of the property is transferred, unless the lienholder records the lien. State law also generally requires that the agreement provide for a cash payment as opposed to a credit transaction. Although statutes usually permit the artisan to sell the property after a reasonable time, notice must be given to the debtor before a formal foreclosure process is undertaken.

Innkeeper's Lien Common law also recognized a lien on a guest's luggage for the benefit of the innkeeper for unpaid room charges. The value of the **innkeeper's lien** is limited to the amount of the agreed upon charge unless there was no such agreement, in which case the lien will be valued at the reasonable value of the lodging provided. As with the artisan's lien, the innkeeper has a valid lien only so long as she has possession of the guest's luggage, and any transfer of possession, other than for a temporary period, will serve to terminate the innkeeper's lien. The foreclosure process allows the innkeeper to dispose of the luggage in an attempt to recover the cost of the unpaid charges.

Statutory Liens

Mechanic's Lien There are essentially three types of statutory liens. First, most states have enacted statutes recognizing the common law liens for service providers, as discussed above. Second, state law provides for a **mechanic's lien** when an individual has performed services and used materials in making repairs or improvements of real property, and the owner does not make payment. Obviously, the creditor in this case cannot maintain possession of the real property, so the lien is statutory and nonpossessory. In this case, the creditor takes a security interest in the real property since the lien is attached to it.

For example, Jerry and Beth agree to have an in-ground swimming pool put in their backyard. At completion, they are able to make only a partial payment or no payment at all to the contractor. The materialman in this case has a mechanic's lien against the real property benefited by the work performed. The lien will be effective when notice is filed within a specified period of time following the last date that materials or labor was supplied. The encumbrance remains with the property until the debt is paid in full, and the contractor ultimately has the right to have the property sold to satisfy the debt. Jerry and Beth would face an additional problem if they decided to sell the real property prior to paying the debt in full. The contractor's recording of the mechanic's lien would give constructive notice to a potential buyer that the property was subject to a lien, and thereby make the property less attractive to the buyer.

In the following case the operator of an ambulance and wrecker service argued that a lien attached to a car which had been towed from the scene of the accident for all necessary charges. The operator also had provided ambulance services to those individuals injured in the accident.

ALABAMA FARM BUREAU MUTUAL CASUALTY COMPANY V. LYLE SERVICE AMBULANCE-WRECKER
Alabama Court of Appeals
395 So. 2d 90 (Ala. Civ. App. 1981)

BACKGROUND: On November 11, 1978, an insured of Farm Bureau had an accident in the insured's automobile. Defendant Lyle responded to a report of an accident with wrecker and ambulance. Several passengers in the automobile were injured in addition to the insured. Lyle's ambulance transported all to a hospital. Lyle also was directed by the insured to remove the automobile from the scene by wrecker and to hold it until further notice. The ambulance service charge was $376. The fee for towing and storage until the date of the trial amounted to $632. Although the trial court did not find that Lyle had a lien against the car, it ruled that Lyle had a claim superior to that of plaintiff Farm Bureau with regard to the subject vehicle. On appeal by Farm Bureau, Lyle argued that the automobile was subject to a mechanic's lien and a common law lien for the services which he had provided.

Wright, Judge

There can be no question that Lyle had no statutory lien. [The Alabama Code Section] by its terms does not apply to one providing towing or storing of an automobile. It applies only to a workman who contributes his labor or material to the "production, manufacture or repair" of a vehicle. Lyle did none of these things. The statute by its terms is supplementary to the common-law lien.

The principle upon which the common-law lien arose was that every bailee for hire, who, by his labor, material or skill, has imparted an additional value to the property placed in his hands had a lien thereon for the agreed or reasonable charges and the right to hold the property until paid. Such lien attached only to the specific property. . . . It has been held generally that a common-law lien is not applicable to towage and storage charges on an automobile.

We have found no Alabama cases holding that either a common-law lien or a statutory lien may be acquired by a garageman for towing or storage charges. We believe it clear, as previously stated, that by its terms, [the Alabama Code Section] fails to provide a lien for such charges. As the statute is derived from and is merely supplementary to the common law, it logically follows that there is not a common-law lien for such charges.

There being no lien, the trial court erred in its judgment granting Lyle a superior claim to and the right to hold the automobile of Farm Bureau and charge additional storage until the judgment is paid.

The evidence discloses that Farm Bureau, through an agent, demanded possession of the vehicle within two days after Lyle towed it in. Lyle wrongfully withheld possession and may not recover storage charges after that demand.

DECISION: The trial court's ruling for Lyle was reversed.

UCC Article 7.   The third type of statutory lien is provided in Article 7 of the Uniform Commercial Code and involves common carriers and warehouse operators. Article 7 sets forth the rules governing formation, methods of perfection, and foreclosure process for these common carrier and warehouse liens. Common carriers and warehouse operators often find themselves unable to collect payment for unpaid shipping or storage charges; however, they remain in possession of the debtor's goods. A **UCC Article 7 lien** allows them to issue notice of foreclosure, and if the debtor does not redeem the property, the lienholder can proceed with a sale. The lienholder can record an Article 7 lien but, unlike the common law possessory lien, the security interest is retained even when the property is transferred to a third party or the debtor.

Tax Liens

When the Internal Revenue Service (IRS) makes a tax assessment, it is required by law to provide notice and demand for payment to the taxpayer within 60 days. Assuming that the required notice and payment demand are issued, the government is entitled to an automatic **tax lien** against all the taxpayer's property owned at the time of assessment or acquired thereafter. A tax lien is viewed as coming into existence as of the date of the assessment and remains intact until the entire tax liability is paid; otherwise, it becomes unenforceable owing to a lapse of time. The tax lien is valid for 10 years unless the IRS reduces its lien to judgment.

To enforce its tax lien, the IRS has the option of seeking a lien foreclosure, an action similar to that described above with respect to other creditor liens. However, unless the IRS has filed a Notice of Federal Tax Lien (NFTL) with the state, county, or local government office designated by state law, it will not be accorded secured creditor status. In effect, the filing of an NFTL is comparable to the perfection process that other secured creditors must satisfy in order to receive priority over other competing creditors seeking to claim the same property. The absence of NFTL means that the tax lien will not take priority over a previously established mechanic's lien or judgment lien.

Judicial Liens and Prejudgment Remedies

A creditor has the option of seeking a **judicial lien**, or collection of the debt through the judicial process, if the debtor does not voluntarily pay. In a collection action the creditor seeks a judgment by the court against the debtor stating exactly how much is owed, including principal and interest. A judgment may also provide for attorney's fees if the underlying credit contract provides for them. However, prior to bringing a formal lawsuit or pending the outcome of a case that has already been filed, the creditor may look for prejudgment remedies to either preclude the need for going to court or to ensure that the debtor does not dispose of assets that may be needed to satisfy a judgment.

CONCEPT SUMMARY
Types of Liens

Types	How Created
Artisan's lien	Services for labor and materials to repair personal property
Innkeeper's lien	Unpaid lodging charges
Mechanic's lien	Services for labor and materials to repair real property
UCC Article 7 lien	Unpaid shipping or storage charges
Tax lien	Assessment of tax is made by IRS followed by notice and demand for payment within 60 days
Judicial lien	Recognized by a court judgment

Attachment   **Attachment** is perhaps the best known and most used prejudgment remedy. This process permits the creditor to seize the debtor's property pending the outcome of litigation and is accomplished by procuring a writ of attachment from the court. Strict procedures govern the issuance of a writ of attachment, since there is no absolute certainty that the creditor will prevail. Generally, the creditor is required to post a bond as security in the event that the debtor should win the lawsuit. The bond money is available to cover court costs as well as the costs incurred by the debtor as a result of having lost the use of his or her property for a period of time. Most attachment statutes require an affidavit from the creditor indicating that there is a bona fide concern that the debtor will dispose of or secrete away the assets necessary to cover any judgment that the court might enter.

The writ of attachment directs the sheriff to take control and custody of the debtor's nonexempt property and to hold it until the lawsuit is resolved. This is known as a *levy*, and means that if the creditor prevails in court the property can be sold and the proceeds used to pay the creditor all costs owed. Any excess money from the sale is then turned over to the debtor.

Replevin   **Replevin** is similar to attachment except that it permits secured creditors to reach only the property that is the security or collateral for the loan. The creditor can use attachment to seize any property owned by the debtor except that which is classified as exempt by

---

ISSUES AND TRENDS
Prejudgment Attachment

The question of whether a state prejudgment attachment statute violated a debtor's due process rights was addressed in the Supreme Court case *Connecticut v. Doehr*, 11 S. Ct. 2105 (1991). In March 1988, John DiGiovanni made an application to a Connecticut state court for a prejudgment attachment order against Brian Doehr's home in the amount of $75,000. DiGiovanni stated in his supporting affidavit that he had been maliciously assaulted in a physical altercation with Doehr and had suffered serious bodily injuries sufficient to establish probable cause that a decision would be rendered in his favor in a subsequent civil lawsuit. The court issued a $75,000 attachment order against Doehr's home.

Doehr filed suit in federal district court, challenging Connecticut's prejudgment attachment statute and arguing that it violated the due process clause of the Fourteenth Amendment to the U.S. Constitution. The Connecticut statute in question provided: "The court or a judge of the court may allow the prejudgment remedy to be issued by an attorney without a hearing upon verification by oath of the plaintiff or of some competent affiant [person who swears an oath] that there is probable cause to sustain the validity of the plaintiff's claims and that the prejudgment remedy requested is requested for an attachment of real property."

The U.S. Supreme Court held the Connecticut statute unconstitutional on due process grounds, since it did not provide for notice to the defendant and the right to a hearing prior to issuance of the attachment order. Only if a hearing was held could the court evaluate both sides of the case. Otherwise, Doehr faced a strictly one-sided determination by the court that would undoubtedly place significant restrictions and impairments on his real property.

The Supreme Court also stated that notice and hearing would not necessarily be required if the affiant could demonstrate exigent circumstances, such as an emergency situation where it was believed that the defendant was about to move, transfer, or impair property so as to make the real property unavailable for execution of a judgment. State statutes providing for this emergency circumstance also had to provide for a postattachment hearing for the defendant in order to comply with due process requirements. In the *Doehr* case, the Court held that although DiGiovanni's affidavit was in compliance with the Connecticut statute, there was no showing of exigent circumstances sufficient to meet the emergency circumstances test.

statute. In a replevin action the sheriff replevies the secured collateral in the same manner that a writ of attachment would be effected. For example, a savings and loan association lends money to a debtor to purchase an expensive boat and files a financing statement perfecting its security interest. Upon default by the debtor, the savings and loan could seek a writ of replevin by posting a bond and filing an affidavit with the court. The boat would be seized and, unlike in an attachment case, it would be turned over to the plaintiff savings and loan association pending the completion of the lawsuit.

Garnishment   **Garnishment** is both a prejudgment and postjudgment remedy that permits the creditor to reach the debtor's cash assets typically held by a financial institution. In a prejudgment garnishment action the court will order the garnishee holding the debtor's cash assets not to pay the debtor until the creditor's suit is concluded. The garnishment order will stand following the resolution of the case if the creditor wins, and will be valid for whatever period necessary for the debtor to satisfy the judgment. Whether prejudgment or postjudgment, a garnishment creates a lien on the garnished assets effective on the date that the action is served on the garnishee. However, the federal Consumer Credit Protection Act limits a garnishment action by allowing the debtor to retain either 75 percent of his weekly after-tax, disposable income, or an amount equal to 30 hours' paid work at the federal minimum wage level, whichever is greater. Similarly, most states provide statutory limits on the amount of wages subject to a writ of garnishment.

Receivership   One other prejudgment and postjudgment remedy that is used in exceptional cases is **receivership**. It is an equitable remedy whereby the party seeking it asks the court to appoint a neutral third party to take control over the assets. The duties and powers of the receiver are prescribed by the court, and the receiver will act as the representative of the court until the litigation is concluded. One example of effective use of a receivership arises when a partnership is deteriorating and the individual partners do not trust each other to properly operate the entity's business. A partner could ask that the court appoint a receiver to run the partnership pending resolution of the partners' dispute.

CONCEPT SUMMARY
Prejudgment Remedies

Type	How Created
Attachment	Creditor posts bond and court issues a writ to seize secured and/or unsecured property
Replevin	Secured creditor posts bond and court issues a writ to seize secured property (collateral) only
Garnishment	Court orders garnishee to hold debtor's cash assets pending conclusion of creditor's lawsuit
Receivership	Court appoints a third party to take control of debtor's assets pending conclusion of creditor's debt collection lawsuit

---

Judicial Liens and Postjudgment Remedies

A debt collection lawsuit generally results in default judgment, since the debtor often does not have any adequate defense. However, acquiring the judgment against the debtor is much easier than actually collecting the debt. In most states the judgment creditor can obtain a judicial lien against the debtor's real property merely by recording the judgment. The judgment creditor's priority is determined on the basis of how many other creditors have properly filed and recorded against the same real property.

Execution and Exempt Property   To satisfy a judgment the creditor has several postjudgment remedies available. The first is **execution**, which is a separate judicial process permitting the creditor to seize the assets of the debtor. It is similar to attachment in that the creditor petitions the clerk of court to issue a writ of execution whereby the sheriff is directed to levy or seize the debtor's real and personal property. From the date that a writ of execution is served, the debtor generally has a period of about 10 days to claim certain real and personal property as exempt.

State statutes generally provide a listing of debtor property that will be exempt from the creditor's execution action. Prior to the implementation of a writ of execution by the sheriff, the debtor must be given written notice of his or her right to claim **exempt property** and afforded an opportunity to notify the court. The debtor must file a written list of exempt property with the court prior to the expiration of the 10 day period or risk losing this protection. Exempt property statutes generally provide protection to property items most needed by the debtor, such as clothing, trade tools, vehicles, and a personal residence. However, statutory protection in nearly all states permits protection of only a certain dollar amount and not the entire value of particular property.

For example, the most common allowance is for a **homestead exemption**, which permits the debtor either to protect his or her home entirely or to exempt at least a portion of the equity in the home. Assume that Jonas has a $50,000 judgment being executed against him, and that he has a home with a fair market value of $175,000 and an outstanding mortgage on the home of $75,000. If state law allows for a 100 percent homestead exemption, Jonas as debtor could keep the home. However, if the state allowed for only a $50,000 exemption in the home, the residence would be sold by the sheriff for $175,000. The proceeds would be divided as follows: (1) $75,000 to the holder of the first mortgage, (2) $50,000 of equity to the debtor as exempt property, and (3) the remaining $50,000 to the judgment creditor.

Statutory protection of the homestead varies widely among states. Without question, the most favorable state homestead statute is found in Florida. Long before Florida became a popular destination for vacationers and retirees, the state legislature felt that action was necessary in order to prompt people to become permanent residents. Consequently, the legislature included in the state's constitution a 100 percent homestead exemption.

By comparison, most other states statutorily limit debtors to protecting anywhere from $10,000 to $50,000 of equity in their homes. This homestead protection extends to all debtors, regardless of whether they have filed for bankruptcy. As a result, debtors from other states often establish Florida residency and then sink as much of their liquid assets as possible into a personal residence. The residence is then protected from either an in-state or out-of-state judgment creditor. Much publicity has resulted from wealthy individuals acting to take advantage of this constitutional protection, and there is considerable pressure building to change the law. However, since the Florida homestead law is included in the state's constitution, the matter cannot be handled by legislative amendment. A statewide voter referendum is required in order to make the change.

In the following case, a debtor sold his homestead property only to have a judgment creditor make a claim against the cash proceeds from the sale. The Arizona court addressed the question of whether the homestead exemption should be extended to cover not only the real property, but also the money proceeds received from its sale.

McLAWS v. KRUGER

Arizona Supreme Court
636 P 2d 95 (Ariz. 1981)

BACKGROUND: On November 25, 1977, Kruger sold a piece of real property in which he later claimed a homestead exemption. The trial court granted McLaws a writ of garnishment against the sale's proceeds in order to satisfy a judgment he had obtained in an unrelated contract action against Kruger. On appeal Kruger claimed that the cash proceeds from the voluntary sale of his homestead were exempt from garnishment by his judgment creditor, since he intended to reinvest the proceeds in a new homestead at the time of the sale of the original homestead. The Arizona Court of Appeals affirmed the trial court's issuance of the writ of garnishment and Kruger appealed.

Gordon, Justice

The Arizona homestead exemption provides that any state resident over eighteen years of age, whether married or single, may hold a house or a mobile home as a homestead. . . . Furthermore, [Arizona law] provides that '[t]he homestead, from the date of recording the claim, is exempt from attachment, execution and forced sale, and from the sale under a judgment or lien existing prior to recording the claim. . . .' Pursuant to these statutes, then, the Krugers were entitled to declare a homestead on their property; had they not sold it, the property would be exempt from attachment.

The sale of the property, however, brings into play the statutes relating to personal property exemptions. Those statutes specifically delineate what forms of personal property are exempt from attachment by judgment creditors. [The Arizona statute] deals specifically with exempted money proceeds but nowhere includes proceeds from the voluntary sale of homesteaded real property.

We agree with the trial court, which believed that if the Legislature wished to include the proceeds of voluntary sales of homesteaded property, it would have done so in its 1976 revision of the homestead and personal property exemptions.

Accordingly, we affirm the holding of the trial court denying [Kruger's] motion to quash the writ of garnishment.

DECISION: The Arizona Supreme Court held for McLaws in affirming the decision by the appellate court.

Right of Redemption Following service of a writ of execution, the debtor is allowed a brief period during which she can exercise a **right of redemption**. This permits her to buy back the property by paying the creditor the amount that is owed according to the judgment lien. Failure to exercise this right within the period fixed by statute means that the debtor can reacquire property only by bidding against any other potential purchasers who appear at the sheriff's sale. At these sales any purchaser is on notice that he or she is buying only the debtor's interest in the property, and that the property is being purchased subject to any other bona fide claims against it. As a result of this inherent risk, it is quite common for these auctions to be referred to as "fire sales," with the property usually being sold for far less than its market value.

Supplementary Proceeding If the creditor's judgment lien is not satisfied by the writ of execution, he can choose to employ a **supplementary proceeding**. In this action, the creditor undertakes the equivalent of an investigation to determine if the debtor has any assets that escaped the execution process. Interested parties are questioned as to their knowledge regarding the debtor's property and any attempts on his part to secrete away or shield the property from the execution process. Should the creditor discover any assets, he or she can petition the court to appoint a receiver to take control and preserve the assets pending the issuance of a court order to sell the property.

Garnishment As mentioned above, garnishment is both a prejudgment and postjudgment remedy. The distinguishing feature of garnishment as a postjudgment remedy is that the debtor is ordered to turn the assets over so that they can be sold to satisfy the judgment lien. The purpose of prejudgment garnishment is simply to have the debtor hold the assets and preserve them pending resolution of the collection lawsuit.

Receivership As stated previously, receivership is both a prejudgment and postjudgment creditor remedy. The process for requesting this remedy is the same except that in postjudgment cases the action is initiated after the court has recognized by an order that a debt is properly owed to the creditor. This remedy would still be attractive in a postjudgment situation where, for example, the assets of a partnership had to be

CONCEPT SUMMARY
Postjudgment Remedies

Type	How Created
Execution	Judgment creditor petitions clerk of court to issue a writ allowing sheriff to seize debtor's real or personal property
Garnishment	Court issues a postjudgment writ directing garnishee to turn over debtor's cash assets to creditor
Receivership	Court orders a third party to take control of debtor's assets

managed despite a court order recognizing that a debt was owed to a particular partner. It would be unlikely that feuding partners could resolve their differences following a court judgment such that they could continue to operate the firm together.

Debtor's Alternative Remedies

Assignment for the Benefit of Creditors Many states allow through either common law or statute the option of a debtor's assignment for the benefit of creditors. The debtor voluntarily assigns property title to an assignee or a trustee who assumes responsibility for the assets. Most often the value of the assets will be less than the total debt outstanding, and those creditors who accept the assignment will receive an equal share of proceeds once the assets are sold by the trustee. Although the creditor is not obligated to accept the assignment, if he or she does it works to discharge the debtor. Any creditor who rejects the assignment is free to proceed with a formal collection action against all nonexempt property owned by the debtor. A more drastic alternative is for creditors to file an involuntary bankruptcy petition against the debtor. This forced bankruptcy is valuable to the creditor who refuses to accept the assignment, since the petition imposes an automatic stay. An automatic stay is an order issued by the court that halts any effort by the bankruptcy trustee to dispose of the assets and also stops all other legal and debt collection ac-

tions directed against the debtor. The subject of bankruptcy is discussed in more detail in the following chapter.

Composition Agreement Another alternative for the overextended debtor is to enter into a **composition agreement**. Under this arrangement the creditors agree to accept less than the full amount that is owed as complete satisfaction and to give the debtor a discharge from the remaining unpaid balance. This agreement is a contract not only between debtor and creditors but also among the creditors themselves. Those creditors joining in the composition agreement are bound by its terms, while other, dissenting creditors are free to seek other remedies against the debtor. Failure on the part of the debtor to fully perform the composition agreement gives the creditor parties the right to seek specific performance of the contract, or to seek enforcement of the original debt.

Consider the following example, which differentiates between an assignment for the benefit of creditors and a composition agreement. To avoid filing bankruptcy, Whirlpools, Inc. voluntarily files an assignment for the benefit of its creditors with Thomas Spaulding acting as assignee. Spaulding later learns about a bank account of Whirlpools, Inc. at First Union Bank. However, before the assignee can obtain the funds, one of the corporation's creditors—who obtained a judgment against Whirlpools 4 days after the assignment for the benefit of creditors—serves a writ of execution against the bank. The creditor, Hardware, Inc., did not agree to the assignment and subsequently obtains the entire $5,000 in Whirlpools' bank account. In a lawsuit by Spaulding against Hardware, Inc., the question is who will prevail. Since Hardware, Inc. did not agree to the assignment for the benefit of creditors, it was free to exhaust its collection remedies against all the debtor's nonexempt property, and it will prevail over Spaulding.

However, assume that instead of an assignment for the benefit of creditors, Whirlpools, Inc. enters into a composition agreement with all its creditors, including Hardware, Inc. A composition agreement is an agreement not only between the debtor and the creditors but also among the creditors, binding them to its terms. In the present case, if Hardware, Inc. is a judgment creditor and 2 days after signing the composition agreement becomes aware of the bank account, it cannot take action to execute a writ against the account. Hardware, Inc. is bound by the composition agreement, and any unilateral collection action can be construed by Whirlpools, Inc., and more importantly by the other creditors, as a breach of contract.

Extension of Repayment Period   In an effort to avoid either an assignment for the benefit of creditors or a composition agreement, the debtor may attempt to negotiate a separate contractual settlement with an individual creditor. This settlement requires creditor consent and may provide for an extension of the time in which the debtor can repay the debt. The consideration for this arrangement is that the creditor agrees not to file a collection action in return for the debtor's promise to pay the debt within the extension period. This separate contract, which is similar to the composition agreement, can then be enforced by a court following breach by the debtor.

Suretyship

When a creditor is uncertain as to whether credit should be extended to a debtor, he or she can seek some additional protection by requiring that a third party agree to accept liability for the debt.

The creditor has the security of knowing that the third party will be available to satisfy the debt. Such a creditor/third-party relationship can be structured as a surety or a guaranty arrangement. Although there are important differences between these two approaches, both surety and guaranty agreements are governed by contract law.

Surety Versus Guarantor and Indemnity

In a suretyship agreement a third person, the **surety**, agrees to be responsible for the debtor's obligation. The surety accepts primary liability and can be called upon to satisfy the debt on the due date. It is not required that the creditor seek payment from the debtor prior to demanding that the surety fulfill the contract obligation, nor is the creditor required to exhaust all debt collection remedies against the debtor prior to requiring payment from the surety. For all practical purposes, it is as though the surety were the party borrowing the money from the creditor. Finally, surety contracts are not required to be in writing; however, they are governed by the Statute of Frauds. A prudent businessperson will attempt to have a surety agreement reduced to writing in

---

CONCEPT SUMMARY
Debtor Rights

Type	Protection Afforded
Exempt property	Debtor property not available to satisfy creditor's debt claim or judgment
Homestead exemption	Exempt property consisting of all or a portion of debtor's equity in a personal residence
Right of redemption	Debtor can buy back seized property from the creditor within a brief period following service of a writ of execution
Assignment for the benefit of creditors	Subject to acceptance by each creditor, debtor assigns property title to assignee or trustee who pays creditors an equal share of cash proceeds following asset liquidation. Creditor usually receives less than total debt owed
Composition agreement	Contract by debtor with and between creditors to accept less than the full amount owed as complete satisfaction
Extension of repayment period	Creditor agrees to give debtor more time to repay and not to institute a debt collection action during that period

order to avoid any problems in having a court enforce the contract.

For example, assume that Jill has just graduated from college and wants to buy a car. Since she does not have a job, the bank is concerned about her ability to make the monthly payments. The loan officer asks that Jill have her parents cosign the promissory note as cosureties. This agreement will make Jill and her parents primarily liable, and the bank will be able to hold them jointly and severally liable for the performance obligation.

A guaranty agreement is slightly different in that a third party, the **guarantor**, promises to pay the debt of the principal debtor only after default. In the suretyship example above, Jill and her parents were all principal debtors, but in a guaranty contract the third person making the promise to pay the debt is not primarily liable. The principal debtor remains primarily liable based upon his or her original promise with the creditor, while the guarantor is secondarily liable by virtue of her secondary or collateral promise to the creditor. The arrangement normally requires that the creditor exhaust all collection efforts and remedies against the principal debtor before the guarantor becomes liable. Even though the principal debtor may have failed to make payments as required, the creditor will have to take legal action to get a ruling that the promissory note is in default. It is this formal default by the principal debtor that triggers the guarantor's secondary liability.

In the surety example explained earlier, assume that Jill had a job but wanted to buy a more expensive automobile. Even though Jill tries to convince the bank that she has a steady income and is a very prudent money manager, the bank is unwilling to loan her the amount needed to buy the car she wants. Jill's parents, on the other hand, know that their daughter manages her financial affairs wisely and are willing to sign the promissory note as guarantors. If the bank is willing to accept this arrangement, Jill's parents will become liable for making good on the payments after Jill is deemed to be in default. Until that time, the bank must seek payment from Jill only.

Unlike suretyship agreements, guaranty contracts must generally be in writing to be enforceable. The major exception to this general rule is when an oral guaranty promise to pay the principal debtor's obligation has as its "main purpose" the conferring of a benefit upon the guarantor.

Assume that Contractor builds homes pursuant to contracts that he signs with each individual future homeowner. Contractor also has an agreement with the local Building Supply Company allowing him to purchase bulk raw materials on credit, materials which are then used in the construction of the homes that are being built at any given time. Homeowner makes progress payments to Contractor as construction continues, and Contractor in turn pays his labor costs as well as raw materials costs to Building Supply Company. Unknown to Homeowner, Contractor is in financial difficulty and fails to make the payments to Building Supply. The Company subsequently terminates his right to purchase materials on credit, requiring cash payment for all transactions. Homeowner becomes aware of this problem, but remains very satisfied with Contractor's quality of work.

Homeowner telephones Building Supply Company and tells the firm president to go ahead and extend credit to Contractor only for those materials necessary to build Homeowner's house. Further, Homeowner states that he will personally guarantee the debt in the event Contractor does not pay. Homeowner makes a progress payment to Contractor, who uses the money to pay a personal credit card debt, not Building Supply Company. The Company then seeks to have Homeowner make good on his oral promise to pay the debt. Although Homeowner could argue that any such guaranty promise had to be in writing to be enforceable under the Statute of Frauds, Building Supply will be able to claim that the promise falls under the "main purpose" exception. This does not mean that the Company automatically will be able to enforce payment against Homeowner. It simply means that the Company will be permitted to introduce evidence at trial tending to establish that Homeowner made the oral promise. Figure 33-1 illustrates this example.

In a judicial proceeding the trier of fact will determine whether the evidence sustains the claim that the oral, secondary promise was in fact made. If so, Homeowner will be held to his obligation under the oral promise. The policy behind this exception is clear. In the above example, Homeowner could have advantaged himself by knowing that guaranty contracts have to be in writing to be enforceable, and purposefully ensuring that his communications with Building Supply Company were oral. When the Company

FIGURE 33-1

Guaranty
Contracts: Main
Purpose Doctrine

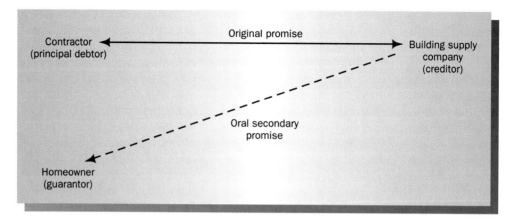

later sought payment from Homeowner, he could deny that an oral contract was made and demand that a writing be produced to establish that a guaranty agreement exists. It is also important that should Homeowner openly admit that he made the oral promise, evidence of this admission would be relevant in the lawsuit brought by Building Supply Company to enforce the guaranty promise.

Under current law in some states the distinctions between surety and guaranty contracts are not significant. This view was presented by the *Restatement of Security* and has been followed by a number of courts. The *Restatement* takes the position that the terms "surety" and "guarantor" are synonymous and can be used interchangeably. In jurisdictions that follow this view, the distinctions mentioned earlier are not material.

Finally, there is a difference between a suretyship contract and a contract of **indemnity**. In a suretyship contract the surety makes a promise to the creditor who is to benefit from the performance of the debtor. In a contract of indemnity

the party that promises to ensure performance makes the promise to the principal debtor who is required to perform the act of making payment. In essence, a suretyship contract protects the creditor from nonpayment by the debtor, while an indemnity agreement protects the principal debtor from any loss incurred as a result of being forced to pay the debt owed to the creditor. The indemnifying party will become liable only after the principal debtor has suffered an actual loss by having to pay the amount owed to the creditor; a mere threat of loss is insufficient.

Surety and Guarantor Rights

The rights and defenses available to the surety and guarantor are similar. Absent an agreement to the contrary, sureties and guarantors who have paid the debtor's obligation have rights to reimbursement, contribution, and subrogation. The **right of reimbursement** permits recovery of expenses that are incurred as a result of performance that is in compliance with the agreement.

CONCEPT SUMMARY	
Surety and Guarantor Rights	
Type	**Protection Afforded**
Reimbursement	Permits recovery of expenses incurred by surety or guarantor in performing agreement
Contribution	Permits cosurety or coguarantor who has paid the creditor to seek payment from cosureties or coguarantors of their share of the debt
Subrogation	Permits cosurety or coguarantor who has paid the debt to seek payment from the principal debtor

These expenses are typically related to the efforts of the surety or guarantor in instituting legal action against the debtor for repayment, such as court costs and legal fees. The **right of contribution** is applicable when there are cosureties or coguarantors but only one of them actually has paid the creditor. Contribution requires that the other cosureties or coguarantors pay their share of the amount paid to the creditor. The agreement will determine the extent of the share, but usually it is an equal or proportionate amount. Finally, the **right of subrogation** provides that when a surety or guarantor has paid the debt owed the creditor, the surety or guaran-

tor is entitled to all the rights that the creditor had against the debtor. This permits action against the debtor to collect the amount of money that was paid to the creditor.

The general rule is that a coguarantor can seek contribution after he or she has been required to make any payment on the underlying obligation. In the following case, the coguarantors agreed specifically in their contract that the entire indebtedness had to be paid before the right of contribution could be enforced. Garner, a coguarantor, made a partial payment of the indebtedness and then sought contribution.

LAYNE V. GARDNER
Alabama Supreme Court
612 So. 2d 404 (Ala. 1992)

BACKGROUND: In the summer of 1988, Delbert and Charlotte Layne, Michael and Patricia Moses, and Robert Garner formed LGM Fun Enterprises, Inc. (LGM) to develop, build, and operate a miniature golf course in Perdido Key, Florida. The Laynes, the Moseses, and Garner were one-third shareholders in the company. To finance the project, LGM borrowed $280,000 from Peoples Savings Bank (Bank). The Bank took a mortgage on the miniature golf course site to secure the loan. As additional security, the Bank required all the corporate shareholders to sign a personal guaranty agreement. Section 5 of this agreement provided that a coguarantor could not enforce his or her right of contribution "unless and until all of the indebtedness shall have been fully paid and discharged." The Bank also held a $125,000 certificate of deposit owned by Garner.

Sometime in 1989, LGM experienced financial difficulties. Garner lent the corporation money to make the payments on the bank loan and to fund the day-to-day operation of the golf course. In early 1990, LGM defaulted on the bank loan and the Bank applied the balance of Garner's certificate of deposit toward the debt.

Anticipating the corporation's default and the Bank's application of his certificate of deposit toward the debt, Garner sued the Laynes, seeking contribution from them of their pro rata share of the debt. The trial court ruled in favor of Garner and awarded a $62,848.85 judgment against the Laynes. On appeal to the Supreme Court of Alabama, the Laynes argued that they were not liable, since the coguarantor agreement required that the debt be fully discharged and since Alabama law similarly required full payment before a coguarantor's liability would be triggered.

Maddox, Justice

The Laynes argue (1) that the trial court erred, as a matter of law, in entering the judgment against them for contribution on the corporate debt when the guaranty agreement prohibits a suit for contribution until all of the debt is "fully paid and discharged" and (2) that the law of contribution among cosureties requires complete satisfaction of the debt by one party before that party can seek contribution from his cosureties. We agree with the Laynes that Garner's suit was premature, based on the express terms of the guaranty agreement. . . .

However, we disagree with the Laynes' argument that Alabama law requires that the entire debt be paid before contribution among cosureties would be required.

Section 5 of the guaranty agreement is clear and unambiguous. It states, in clear and simple terms, that no cosurety or coguarantor can "exercise . . . any right of contribution against . . . any person liable" on the debt "unless and until" the indebtedness has been "fully paid." The obvious import of Section 5 is that a coguarantor or cosurety cannot seek contribution against other coguarantors or cosureties unless the entire debt has been paid.

Garner argues in response that Section 5 was intended to benefit only the Bank, that it was not bargained for by the parties, and that it would be unconscionable to enforce the provision among the coguarantors.

The clear language of Section 5 states that the coguarantors will not enforce any right of contribution against "any person liable to payment of the indebtedness" before full payment has been made. . . . The Laynes fall within the meaning of this phrase. Thus, Garner's argument that the guaranty agreement should only benefit the Bank is unfounded, based on the unambiguous language of the guaranty agreement itself.

Based on the foregoing, the judgment entered in favor of Garner against the Laynes is reversed, and the cause is remanded to the trial court with instructions to dismiss the claim for contribution. [W]e emphasize that Garner is free to sue the Laynes under the express terms of the guaranty agreement when the debt has been fully paid and discharged.

DECISION: The Alabama Supreme Court held for the Laynes and reversed the trial court decision.

Surety and Guarantor Defenses

A surety or guarantor may be able to avoid paying the creditor by raising certain defenses. The general rule is that defenses available to the debtor are also available to the surety or guarantor. For example, in a sale-of-goods contract, a defense could be raised that the quality of the goods was deficient so as to permit the debtor the opportunity to reject them in accordance with the perfect tender rule. The surety or guarantor will certainly want to consider all possible defenses prior to making payment to the creditor. However, they cannot raise traditional contract law questions concerning the legal capacity of the debtor. If the debtor is under 18 years of age or was insane at the time the debtor-creditor contract was formed, the surety or guarantor will not be able to avoid his or her obligation to the creditor. However, if the surety or guarantor can establish that he or she lacked capacity, this defense can be raised to avoid payment.

In certain instances the surety or guarantor can establish that he or she has been discharged from the obligation to pay the creditor. If the debt is paid either by the debtor or by a third party, any surety or guarantor is discharged from liability. A similar situation occurs when the principal debtor is discharged from liability by the creditor, or the debtor and creditor enter into an agreement without the consent of the surety that changes the debtor's performance obligation. Assume that a debtor enters in a sales contract with a creditor manufacturer for specially made goods, and the contract has a guarantor. During the production process it becomes apparent that the contract specifications regarding the product need to be modified, and that this modification will require an agreement to increase the per unit price. The debtor and creditor enter into a contract modification without the guarantor's consent, since they are anxious to complete the production process. Because of the change in the terms of the underlying contract, the guarantor's obligation has been discharged.

Lender Liability

Until 15 years ago, the typical lawsuit involving a lending institution and a debtor usually meant that the lender was suing for nonpayment or nonperformance of a contract obligation. Debtor defendants rarely asserted counterclaims in their answers, and when they did, the courts rarely ruled against the lending institution. In the last 10 years this trend has been dramatically altered as debtors began to raise a wide variety of claims against banks following the breakdown of the debtor-creditor relationship. This developing area of law is referred to as **lender liability** and involves claims ranging from common law fraud and negligence to violations of environmental statutes.

The basis for most of the common law claims revolves around the debtor's contentions that the lender acted or failed to act in a manner which put the debtor's business entity or operation in financial jeopardy. For example, a standard arrangement for borrowing money from a bank consists of establishing a line of credit for a dollar limit sufficient to meet the debtor's needs. The debtor takes draws or advances on the line of credit as needed, but does not receive a lump-sum payment, as is the case with a standard promissory note. Creditors are able to monitor the business and can make decisions as to whether to approve advances for a variety of reasons. Sales by a real estate developer might go down significantly in a recessionary market, as happened during 1990 to 1992, and the lender might feel that the projected sales of developed lots and homes will be inadequate to cover the line of credit debt. In any event, when the debtor is denied access to the line of credit, the cash flow to the business is extinguished, and very often, the entity will fail. In other situations, the debtor has operated by having the lender approve a number of short-term loans. As the debtor's overall financial condition worsens, the lender fails to approve another loan.

Another consideration is the change taking place in the banking industry. Lending institutions are aggressively seeking out new markets by testing the strength of state branch banking laws, and by pushing for federal approval of mergers between former competitors. Banks are looking for opportunities to participate in the selling of securities by having their financial loan officers pass federal licensing examinations. Simply stated, the nature of the banking business has changed dramatically, and as a part of this change the institutions are shedding their local identities. This new posture made banks much more aggressive in recruiting new business, and in the late 1980s lending institutions fueled the development of commercial office space by lending large amounts of money to corporations without the personal guaranties of the primary officers and shareholders involved. As the developers were unable to rent the office units and the loans were defaulted, banks realized that their lending policies had to be tightened. This led to increased scrutiny of all real estate loans and decisions to cut off short-term and credit-line financing to certain customers. These actions were certainly a contributing factor leading to the lender liability cases filed by debtors during the last 10 years.

Common Law Claims

Negotiation and Breach of Contract The debtor-lender relationship is established formally when a contractual agreement is reached to lend money. However, a legal relationship is often established much sooner during the contract negotiation process. During the mid- to late 1980s banks had surplus funds to lend and actively sought out potential borrowers. In some instances, the prize customers of competing lending institutions were targeted by a lender in an effort to create new business. This aggressive recruitment, coupled with an active contract negotiation process, creates an environment in which a relationship is established well before any formal agreement is reached by the parties. Lenders that incorrectly state what they can provide or that inflate the benefits the debtor will receive by doing business with them are subject to potential claims of contract breach. There is a distinction drawn between the creditor stating an "opinion" through mere sales talk and making a commitment that ultimately will become part of the loan contract.

Statute of Frauds Although it obviously is preferable for the parties to reduce their agreement to writing, loan agreements may be negotiated without this formality. In many states the common law Statute of Frauds may be applicable, especially when the contract involves real estate or concerns a project that will not be completed within 1 year. State statutes may also require that loan agreements in excess of an established amount be in writing to be enforceable. When agreements are informal and not reduced to writing, either party is in a position to argue that they are unenforceable.

This can be a particular problem for debtors who rely on an oral agreement to renew a loan contract for several additional periods. For example, a real estate firm has plans to develop a tract of land into a residential community. The project is expected to take 36 months to complete, but the lender claims that its current loan policy permits loan agreements of this type for a maximum of only 12 months. In order to placate the debtor, a bank officer gives oral assurances that the loan commitment will be extended twice to cover the period of development. Prior to the expiration of the first loan contract, the lender determines that the project is not likely to be successful and is a bad investment for the bank. The debtor is informed that the loan will not be renewed and now faces the prospect of having to prove that the oral commitments were made. Proof will be difficult given the effect of the Statute of Frauds rule. Additionally, even if the debtor is able to overcome this obstacle, at trial the lender may also contend that evidence of the oral agreements must be precluded under the parol evidence rule.

Acceleration Clauses and Demand Notes   Another contract issue is presented if the promissory note contains an **acceleration clause** which permits the lender to issue a **demand note** upon the happening of a certain event—usually failure to make a payment of principal and/or interest. The event places the debtor in technical default, and permits the lender to foreclose on the property, securing the loan if the default is material. However, the debtor generally is provided an opportunity to correct a minor breach rather than face the prospect of having the property taken away. Despite the fact that such an option is available to the debtor, creditors will often attempt to use a technical breach as an opportunity to close down a loan commitment considered to be risky and not worth any future investment. In these cases, a lender choosing this course of action must follow strict procedures in terms of providing notice of default to the debtor and taking action to foreclose against the secured property.

Fraud and Negligence   It is common for lender liability lawsuits to combine tort claims with a breach-of-contract cause of action. The debtor argues that the creditor committed misrepresentation or fraud in the loan negotiation process. Fraud is more difficult to prove, since an intention to deceive on the part of the lender must be established. As a result, the debtor may include an allegation of negligence in the complaint. Negligence claims are based on a breach of the lender's duty of care owed to the debtor. This theory has become increasingly important in lender liability cases, especially when the formal rules of evidence mentioned previously prevent proof of oral commitments and possible fraudulent acts on the part of the lender.

Economic Duress, Control, and Good Faith   Debtors also rely on a number of other tort theories. Economic duress and wrongful con-

---

ISSUES AND TRENDS
How Bank Policies Are Changing

One of the most difficult problems facing banks in this era of lender liability cases is the allegation by debtors that bank officials made oral promises regarding loan terms despite the language contained in the written agreement. Although such oral agreements are generally unenforceable under the common law Statute of Frauds or an appropriate state statute, some courts have created exceptions allowing the debtor the opportunity to present evidence of the oral agreement at trial. Banks are well aware that once this type of evidence is presented to a jury there may be a significant sympathy factor created for the plaintiff-debtor.

  Lenders have responded to this potential problem by including mandatory arbitration provisions in loan documents. These binding arbitration clauses provide that the debtor waive the right to a jury trial and that all disputes concerning the loan arrangement be turned over to a professional arbitrator. The advantages to the lender are obvious and significant. Arbitrators generally award lower damages to plaintiffs than do juries, and the decisions cannot be appealed to a court of law. Finally, unlike in a jury trial, punitive damages are not available in the arbitration setting.

trol may be alleged where the lender has used a superior bargaining position to dictate managerial and policy decisions to the debtor company. The more influence the lender has in determining courses of action taken by the debtor, the greater likelihood the court will view the relationship as one more closely resembling a partnership. In this situation the court will impose a fiduciary responsibility on the lender to act in the best interest of not only itself but the "debtor-partner" as well. Finally, the concept of good faith from the Uniform Commercial Code has become a part of the common law of contracts in most states. This means that every contract contains an implied understanding that the parties will act in good faith in executing their performance obligations, and any failure to do so can be treated as a breach of contract. Debtors also rely on this theory to establish that the lender acted negligently by violating its implied duty to act in good faith.

Statutory Claims

State Consumer Protection Acts   The plaintiff-debtor's complaint usually will include some causes of action based on federal or state statutes. One of the most common is a claim based on a state's consumer protection act (CPA). Every state has a CPA, and these statutes provide consumers with the right to sue when they are victimized by unfair and deceptive trade practices. About half of the state CPAs consider a business practice to be deceptive if it has the "tendency or capacity to deceive." This deception standard was developed from decisions by the Federal Trade Commission and the federal courts as they enforced Section 5 of the Federal Trade Commission Act. In general, the remaining state CPAs provide a listing of activities that will constitute an unfair or deceptive trade practice. State courts have recognized that the lender-debtor

relationship established with a bank is generally covered by state CPAs, since the statutes were intended to provide broad protection to consumers engaged in a range of business and commercial activities.

Toxic Waste   Lending institutions that become actively involved in the borrower's business operations can be held liable under a variety of federal and state statutes, including securities, racketeering, and environmental laws. A high-profile statutory claim is the federal Comprehensive Environmental Response, Compensation, and Liability Act (CERCLA) of 1980. Lenders foreclosing on real property that served as collateral for a loan may find that they are liable for the cleanup costs associated with toxic or chemical waste on the property. This can be a serious problem for the lender, since the cleanup costs often far exceed the value of the loan made to the borrower. Another major concern for lenders is the development of state statutes that mirror CERCLA in terms of providing for comparable liability.

Although CERCLA provides an exemption for lending institutions that have made loans to parties responsible for polluting the real property, the Environmental Protection Agency (EPA) has argued successfully that such exemptions must be restricted. In the following case, the Maryland Bank and Trust Company foreclosed on real estate it held as security for a loan, and subsequently purchased the real property at the foreclosure sale. An EPA investigation revealed toxic waste on the property, and the government filed an action claiming that the bank should be viewed as the owner or operator of the real property. The EPA sought to exercise its right under CERCLA to bill the costs of cleanup to the owner or operator of the land, and claimed that this liability should be borne by Maryland Bank and Trust Company.

▍ UNITED STATES V. MARYLAND BANK AND TRUST CO.

Maryland Federal District Court
632 F. Supp. 573 (D.Md. 1986)

BACKGROUND: McLeod owned a 117-acre parcel of real property in Maryland where he operated a trash and garbage business. Maryland Bank & Trust (MB&T) held a mortgage on the property, and the money that was loaned to McLeod was used to operate the business enterprise. During 1972 or 1973 McLeod allowed hazardous

---

materials to be dumped on the land. MB&T subsequently initiated a foreclosure action and took title to the property. The Environmental Protection Agency became aware of the existence of the toxic waste and directed MB&T to remove it from the site. The bank president refused, and the EPA undertook action to remove the hazardous materials. The U.S. government filed this lawsuit against MB&T pursuant to CERCLA to recover the $551,713.50 spent by the EPA to clean up the land.

Northrop, Judge

Section 107(a) of CERCLA provides:

Notwithstanding any other provision or rule of law, . . .

(1) the owner and operator of a vessel . . . or a facility, . . .

(4) . . . shall be liable, for

(A) All costs of removal or remedial action incurred by the United States Government or a State [in removing hazardous waste from the vessel or facility].

The Court initially turns to the question of whether MB&T falls within section 107(a)(1). That section holds liable "the owner and operator" of the facility. It is undisputed that MB&T has been the owner of the facility since May 1982. . . . Notwithstanding the language "owner and operator," a party need not be both an owner and operator to incur liability under this subsection. . . .

The definition of "owner and operator" contained in section 101(20)(A) . . . excludes from liability "a person, who, without participating in the management of a vessel or facility, holds indicia of ownership primarily to protect his security interest in the . . . facility." MB&T disclaims liability on the basis of this exemption. . . .

The interpretation of section 101(20)(A) urged upon the Court by MB&T runs counter to the policies underlying CERCLA. Under the scenario put forward by the bank, the federal government alone would shoulder the cost of cleaning up the site, while the former mortgagee-turned owner, would benefit from the clean-up by the increased value of the now unpolluted land. At the foreclosure sale, the mortgagee could acquire the property cheaply. All other prospective purchasers would be faced with potential CERCLA liability, and would shy away from the sale. Yet once the property has been cleared at the taxpayers' expense and becomes marketable, the mortgagee-turned owner would be in a position to sell the site at a profit.

In essence, the [bank's] position would convert CERCLA into an insurance scheme for financial institutions, protecting them against possible losses due to the security of loans with polluted properties. Mortgagees, however, already have the means to protect themselves, by making prudent loans. Financial institutions are in a position to investigate and discover potential problems in their secured properties. For many lending institutions, such research is routine. CERCLA will not absolve them from responsibility for their mistakes of judgment.

DECISION: The federal trial court held that Maryland Bank & Trust was the owner of the land and was required to reimburse the United States for the cost of hazardous waste cleanup as provided in CERCLA.

Following the *Maryland Bank and Trust Co.* case, the Eleventh Circuit Court of Appeals issued a ruling that greatly expanded the liability of lending institutions in situations where it could be demonstrated that they had the potential for affecting decisions made by the borrower relative to the handling of toxic waste. In *United States v. Fleet Factors Corp.*, 901 F.2d 1550 (11th Cir. 1990), the lender had become actively involved in the management of the debtor's business operation to the point of approving layoff of employees and controlling access to the business facility by third parties. The court ruled that:

> . . . a secured creditor may incur [CERCLA] liability, without being an operator, by participating in the financial management of a facility to a degree indicating a capacity to influence the corporation's treatment of hazardous wastes. It is not necessary for the secured creditor actually to involve itself in the day-to-day operations of the facility in order to be liable—although such conduct will certainly lead to the loss of the protection of the statutory exemption. Nor is it necessary for the secured creditor to participate in management decisions relating to hazardous waste. Rather, a secured creditor will be liable if its involvement with the management of the facility is sufficiently broad to support the inference that it could affect hazardous waste disposal decisions if it so chose.

The effect of the *Fleet Factors* decision was to expand the potential liability of the lending institution in situations where it simply could have had an impact on hazardous waste decisions, rather than in situations where actual participation could be proved. The reaction of banks and lending institutions to this decision resulted in the issuance of a rule by the Environmental Protection Agency on April 29, 1992, which rejected the *Fleet Factors* approach. The EPA rule utilizes a two-part test to define participation in management as "actual participation in the management or operational affairs of the . . . facility by the holder, and does not include the mere capacity to influence, or ability to influence, or the unexercised right to control facility operations."

Remedies

Traditional Contract Remedies The range of contract remedies is discussed in detail in Chapter 19. However, a brief mention of these remedies is appropriate here in order to emphasize what the debtor is seeking in a lender liability action. Debtors who initiate lender liability lawsuits generally seek damages under traditional contract and tort law, as well as any appropriate statutory claims. When breach of contract is proved the debtor seeks to recover an amount sufficient to compensate for losses sustained as a result of the lender's actions. Damages that result directly from the breach are considered "compensatory," while other, "consequential" damages may be recoverable if the debtor can prove that they were foreseeable at the time the contract was formed.

Punitive Damages Whether or not punitive damages will be awarded depends upon the level of tortious misconduct by the lender as judged by the trier of fact. Debtors attempt to establish that the lender's intentional or unintentional torts combined with the contract breach so as to justify a damage award well above traditional compensatory damages. Generally, punitive damages are allowed in contract cases only when there is a showing of fraud or other intentional conduct that rises to a level the court feels should be subject to special treatment. A nonbreaching party is generally entitled to any damages that are necessary to put him or her in the position he or she would have been in had the contract breach not occurred. With respect to punitive damages, this concept is expanded, since the court often wants to set an example that will persuade other lenders not to engage in similar activity.

Equitable Remedies Specific performance is typically not directed by a court unless there are unique circumstances warranting such a remedy. This is because of the court's hesitancy to keep two parties together in a contractual relationship which has deteriorated and in which there is almost certain to be continued animosity between the parties.

For example, a real estate developer has several companies, each of which has a separate line of credit with the same bank to develop different residential and commercial office projects. Given an economic downturn in the economy, the bank concludes that the developments will not be successful in that customers will not be waiting to purchase the homes and business tenants will not be available to rent the offices. The bank decides to freeze advances on the lines of credit, and the developer sues, arguing traditional lender liability claims and requesting the court to order specific performance of the credit agreement. Assuming there are no contractual provisions on which the bank could base its decision to halt funding, the court would be hesitant to order that the parties be forced to continue their relationship so as to afford the developer an opportunity to complete the projects.

The strained relationship between the parties would invite future disagreements that might lead to additional litigation. However, in certain instances the court will consider specific performance when the plaintiff can demonstrate that traditional contract remedies are not adequate to compensate the loss. The following case involves two banks that made loan commitments to the same debtor and illustrates when a court will agree to enter an order of specific performance.

FIRST NATIONAL STATE BANK OF NEW JERSEY V. COMMONWEALTH SAVINGS AND LOAN ASSOCIATION OF NORRISTOWN

U.S. Court of Appeals, Third Circuit
610 F.2d 164 (3d Cir. 1979)

BACKGROUND: Mathema Developers undertook to build a shopping mall in Camden County, New Jersey. Mathema needed a short-term construction loan and a long-term permanent loan in order to complete the project. On May 21, 1974, Commonwealth Savings and Loan Association of Norristown executed a standby commitment to make a permanent loan of $3.5 million to Mathema prior to July 23, 1975. The loan agreement provided that Mathema immediately would pay 1 percent of the loan amount, and could extend the commitment date by 6 months by paying another .5 percent of the loan amount.

Concurrently with negotiating the loan agreement with Commonwealth, Mathema entered into a $3.6 million construction loan agreement with First National State Bank of New Jersey. First National investigated Commonwealth's commitment to make the long-term loan, and among the conditions imposed by First National was the requirement that Mathema consent to an assignment of the Commonwealth permanent loan agreement. Mathema assigned the Commonwealth loan agreement to First National, and Commonwealth provided a written approval of the assignment.

Prior to July 23, 1975, both Mathema and First National requested in writing that the Commonwealth permanent loan be closed. Commonwealth rejected the requests, claiming that the project was incomplete relative to the building plans and specifications of the loan agreement. On July 22, 1975, First National decided to exercise its right under the assignment to extend the Commonwealth loan commitment by 6 months. First National delivered a check to Commonwealth, protesting its refusal to close the original loan agreement.

Without the cash flow from the permanent loan agreement, Mathema defaulted on the First National construction loan, and First National foreclosed on the property. Mathema and First National filed suit requesting an order of specific performance that required Commonwealth to provide the permanent loan monies as previously agreed. The federal district trial court granted First National's request for specific performance and ordered Commonwealth to close the permanent loan agreement. Commonwealth appealed.

Adams, Circuit Judge

Since both parties agree that the shopping mall is a financial failure, it would appear paradoxical for Commonwealth to insist that First National should have attempted to persuade some other mortgage lender to take over a bad investment. We therefore reject Commonwealth's assertion that specific performance was improper because First National should have attempted to mitigate its damages by obtaining substitute performance at a higher interest rate.

There is ample evidence in the record to support the district court's conclusion that accurate calculation of damages was impracticable in this case. The basic measure of such damages would be to subtract from the amount of the permanent loan the estimated value of the shopping mall. However, the distinct qualities of such a property preclude a definitive estimate. The trial judge would have been forced to choose among widely disparate appraisals of the value of the mall. . . .

As between the construction lender and the permanent lender, it does not appear unreasonable to place the risk of the success or failure of a real estate venture on the latter. Real estate developments generally are riskier than other business investments, and therefore mortgage rates are significantly higher than interest rates on most other loans. If the permanent lender can escape its commitment when a project seems to have failed, that party will have achieved a significant shifting of risks without a corresponding shift in the returns on successful ventures. A permanent lender's primary security on such a venture is the capitalized value of the project, and so it is the permanent lender, not the construction lender, that has the responsibility and presumably the expertise to analyze the business risks. It is therefore appropriate to place the risk of the project's nonviability on the permanent lender.

DECISION: The Third Circuit Court of Appeals affirmed the judgment of the trial court.

Statutory Treble Damages and Workouts   Statutory remedies are often available to the debtor depending on his or her ability to establish a cause of action as prescribed by the law. Debtors are drawn to these statutes because they typically provide for recovery of treble damages, as is the case with many state consumer protection acts. Consequently, given the complexity of proving claims in a lender liability case, as well as the broad range of remedies available to the debtor, attorneys often will endeavor to reach a settlement referred to as a **workout**. The parties weigh the hazards of litigation as well as other considerations such as whether the debtor is insolvent and may consider filing bankruptcy. Lenders are well aware that a bankruptcy petition will necessarily prolong the ultimate resolution of the dispute. Furthermore, since most lender liability cases involve real estate used as collateral to secure the loan, a workout arrangement may be reached in which the lender will take some but not all of the real property. This type of arrangement is usually achieved when the lender believes that it has some vulnerability should the case go to trial.

Fraudulent Transfers

Proof of Fraud   Debtors attempting to prevent creditors from locating and seizing their assets may make a **fraudulent transfer** of the property to a third person, such as a close relative or friend. The purpose of these transfers is quite clear, and the common law of fraudulent conveyances makes them voidable by the transferor's creditors. To establish a case against the debtor, the creditor must demonstrate "badges of fraud" so as to indicate that the true purpose of the transfer was to avoid the payment of a bona fide debt. Courts accept circumstantial evidence to establish a case, since intent to defraud is often difficult to prove. In a fraudulent conveyance lawsuit, the plaintiff-creditor will typically offer the following types of evidence where applicable: (1) that the debtor maintained control over the property despite alleged transfer to another person, (2) that the transfer was made to a close family member, (3) that the transfer was not the result of an arm's-length bargain and lacked consideration, or (4) that the debtor transferred substantially all his or her assets just prior to legal action being taken by the creditor.

Although fraudulent conveyance common law can be traced to the English Statute of Elizabeth enacted in 1570, the National Conference of Commissioners on Uniform State Laws drafted a uniform law to attempt to deal with the wide disparities developing in state law. The predecessor to the Uniform Fraudulent Transfer Act (UFTA) was issued first in 1918 and then significantly revised and renamed the UFTA in 1984. The purpose of the later revision was to bring the uniform law into conformance with commercial practices as reflected in the Uniform Commercial Code and the federal Bankruptcy Code.

Creditor Remedies   As a result, creditors in states that have adopted the uniform law can rely on both the common law and statutory provisions to establish a fraudulent conveyance cause of action. However, the most important issue to the creditor is the range of remedies afforded under state law for laying claim to the improperly transferred property. Creditors can seek to have the transfer avoided and set aside, or they can attempt to execute against the property in the hands of the transferee. It also may be necessary to consider filing a motion for injunction if there is any indication that the transferee may dispose of the property once it becomes clear that his or her ownership has been challenged. In this instance the creditor would consider the prejudgment remedies discussed above to ensure that the property was available pending the outcome of the fraudulent conveyance lawsuit against the debtor-transferor.

Bulk Transfers

Background   A common type of fraudulent conveyance occurs when a merchant sells all or a significant part of inventory in a transaction that would be characterized as outside the ordinary course of business. In a typical case the merchant is deep in debt to inventory suppliers and other unsecured creditors, and decides to make a **bulk transfer** of inventory to a good faith purchaser who is unaware of the seller's scheme to defraud creditors. Since the buyer is innocent by virtue of having no knowledge of the seller's motives, the transaction is not covered by fraudulent conveyance laws. Additionally, the creditors generally cannot levy or reach the inventory assets being held by the bona fide purchaser.

Uniform Commercial Code   Article 6 of the UCC was drafted with the intention of providing a uniform law for dealing with these bulk transfers (see Chapter 21). The essence of the protection afforded to creditors by Article 6 centers around disclosure requirements. By requiring that the seller disclose the identity of all creditors to the buyer and also inform the creditors of the intended bulk sale, the purchaser and creditors are on notice as to the seller's intentions. Failure to provide this notice means that the transfer will be ineffective as to the seller's creditors. The

practical effect is that the buyer is not protected as an innocent purchaser, and the creditors can take action against the inventory assets held by the buyer.

UCC Revision   In 1988 the National Conference of Commissioners on Uniform State Laws (NCCUSL) and the American Law Institute (ALI) issued a report which stated that it was no longer necessary to regulate bulk transfers. Both organizations openly encouraged states that had adopted Article 6 to repeal it. The report supported this recommendation with the argument that innocent purchasers should not be held responsible for a dishonest seller's failure to pay creditors, along with the fact that statutes now make it easier for creditors to pursue these debtors and to enforce judgments against them. Since states had already enacted the original Article 6 and had developed a substantial history of regulating bulk transfers, the NCCUSL and ALI recognized that some state legislatures would be hesitant to adopt their recommendation. In fact, these organizations understood that some states would continue to regulate bulk transfers despite the report's recommendation, and that it was necessary to adopt a Revised Article 6, entitled "Bulk Sales," which would afford reasonable protection to creditors in light of modern jurisdictional laws.

Revised Article 6 restricts coverage to bulk sales transactions where the seller's "principal business is the sale of inventory from stock," and further defines a bulk sale as

> a sale not in the ordinary course of seller's business of more than half the seller's inventory, as measured by value on the date of the bulk sale agreement, if on that date the buyer has notice, or after reasonable inquiry would have had notice, that the seller will not continue to operate the same or a similar kind of business after the sale.

Revised Article 6 also covers bulk sales only when the equity of transferred assets is valued between $10,000 and $25 million. Sales outside these limits are regarded as having little risk, since a buyer would be more likely to investigate a large inventory value before consummating the transaction, and would similarly be less concerned if the inventory value was small.

Compliance with state bulk transfer laws is likely to become increasingly complex as legislatures deal with amending statutes or repealing them entirely. Some of the consistency that had been gained by having many states adopt much of the UCC verbatim will be lost. Sellers will have to assume the responsibility for seeking out the current status of bulk transfer law in their state, or risk having the transaction be ruled ineffective as to their creditors.

Debtor Protection Statutes

There are several federal statutes which provide additional protection to consumer debtors. The Equal Credit Opportunity Act makes it unlawful to discriminate on the basis of sex or marital status in determining whether to extend credit to a consumer. The Truth-in-Lending Act requires creditors to make certain disclosures in the loan negotiation process. The Fair Debt Collection Practices Act regulates the activities of debt collectors and prohibits certain conduct considered to be abusive. These consumer-oriented statutes are discussed in more detail in Chapter 55.

Review Questions and Problems

Key Terms

consensual lien
possessory lien
artisan's lien
innkeeper's lien
statutory lien
mechanic's lien
UCC Article 7 lien
tax lien
judicial lien
attachment
replevin
garnishment
receivership
execution
exempt property
homestead exemption

right of redemption
supplementary proceeding
composition agreement
surety
guarantor
indemnity
right of reimbursement
right of contribution
right of subrogation
lender liability
acceleration clause
demand note
workout
fraudulent transfer
bulk transfer

Discussion Questions

1. What options are available to the creditor if it appears that the debtor is going to transfer assets in order to avoid paying the debt?

2. Is there any difference between prejudgment and postjudgment garnishment?

3. Under what circumstances would a debtor choose to enter into an assignment for the benefit of creditors or a composition agreement?

4. What is exempt property?

5. What is the difference between a surety and a guaranty?

6. Why is the Statute of Frauds important in a lender liability action?

7. When are punitive damages typically awarded in a lender liability case?

8. What is a bulk transfer?

Review Problems

1. Beth takes her television set to Acme Service for repairs. She has taken the set to Acme in the past and still owes $150 for repairs done previously. When Beth arrives to pick up the television, she is informed that the current repair bill is $78, which she pays in cash. The Acme representative then informs her that the television set will not be released unless she pays the remaining $150 bill. Does Acme have a lien on Beth's television set that will prevent Beth from taking possession?

2. Jerry regularly parks his car in a downtown vacant lot while he is at work. There are no signs indicating that parking is prohibited on the lot. At the end of a workday Jerry finds his car missing and notices numerous signs prohibiting parking. He later learns that Wilson Towing Service has possession of his car and is demanding $95 to cover its charges before the automobile will be returned. Is there a lien against the car sufficient to allow Wilson Towing to retain possession?

3. Jim and Laura own an appliance store and sell a wide variety of products. The business has recently experienced some financial difficulty, and its primary supplier refuses to sell any more merchandise on credit without a surety. Laura's parents agree to cosign a contract for the purchase of twenty microwave ovens. After the ovens are delivered, Jim discovers that at least half of them have a serious defect. Jim notifies the supplier that the shipment is rejected and that all the ovens will be returned. The supplier immediately brings an action against the cosureties for payment. What defense, if any, do the cosureties have against the supplier?

4. Rick Watson is the president and sole shareholder of Ocean Bay Village, Inc., a real estate development firm. Ocean Bay is engaged in the business of improving raw real estate so that local permits for sewer, water, and other utilities can be acquired. The company then sells the improved land and permit rights to a construction developer to build a residential community or commercial properties. Watson negotiates with Union Bank for a $150,000 line of credit to be used to prepare a real estate parcel for development. In discussions with the bank, Watson makes it clear that the improvement and permitting process will take approximately 3 years. Bank officials state that the internal policy allows them to sign only a 12-month credit line, but they also give Watson oral assurances that the line will be extended or renewed as necessary. Because of a slumping real estate market, 10 months later the bank freezes Ocean Bay's credit line, allowing no more advances. Subsequently, the bank initiates foreclosure against the real property securing the line of credit. Does Ocean Bay Village, Inc. have a valid lender liability claim against Union Bank?

Case Problems

1. While driving his car, Younger collides with another vehicle. The police and a tow truck from the West End Towing Service arrive simultaneously at the scene of the accident. Without securing Younger's permission, the tow truck driver removes Younger's automobile from the scene and takes it to West End's place of business. West End demands that Younger pay $68 for the return of his car, claiming that the police ordered the truck driver to remove the automobile from the highway. Does West End have a lien on the car for the towing and storage charges?

2. In 1981 Jetco entered into a contract to make roof repairs to the Spizmans' home for $15,272. In August 1981, after the work was completed, the Spizmans made a partial payment of $5,000 to Jetco. At that time they made no complaints about the quality of the work. The Spizmans also explained that they wanted to withhold the remainder of the money to wait for rain to see if there were any leaks. Jetco agreed to accept the $5,000 partial payment on condition that the balance be paid within 30 days. During a subsequent rainstorm the Spizmans experienced water leakage attributable to the repairs, and they refused to pay Jetco the balance due. Does Jetco have a valid mechanic's lien?

3. Keeling purchased a pickup truck with financing provided by Chrysler Credit Corporation. The corporation held a perfected security interest in the truck, and when Kneeling defaulted on the note, the company attempted to repossess the vehicle. Unknown to Chrysler, the manager of the apartment complex where Keeling lived had requested that the Highway Towing Service tow the vehicle to its lot. Highway had stored the vehicle for approximately 2 months when Chrysler located it. Chrysler then demanded that Highway turn over possession of the car, but Highway refused until it was paid a $50 towing fee plus $1,235 in storage fees. Chrysler filed suit against Highway, which claimed that it had an artisan's lien on the truck that took priority over Chrysler's perfected security interest. Did Highway Towing Service have an artisan's lien on the truck?

4. John Daniels contracted to buy a used car from Lindsay Cadillac Company in 1981. Seymoure, John's brother, agreed to act as a cosigner and signed the purchase contract on the line marked "Co-Buyer." Lindsay assigned the contract to General Motors Acceptance Corporation (GMAC). In 1982 the loan was in default, and without notifying Seymoure, GMAC brought an action against both brothers for the balance due on the note. Seymoure contended that he had signed as a guarantor, not as a surety, and that GMAC had to proceed against John before Seymoure's secondary liability would be triggered. Was Seymoure a guarantor or a surety as to this contract?

34

Bankruptcy

The use of credit for the purchase of property, goods, and services has become common for both consumers and businesses. In difficult economic times, when interest rates soar and unemployment and loss of income are experienced by consumers and businesses alike, many borrowers are forced into bankruptcy. Hundreds of thousands of bankruptcies are filed each year in the United States, the overwhelming majority of them personal bankruptcies.

Bankruptcy laws provide relief and protection to the debtor while fairly distributing the debtor's assets among creditors. Bankruptcy laws are provided for in Article I, Section 8 of the U.S. Constitution: "The Congress shall have the power . . . to establish . . . uniform laws on the subject of bankruptcies throughout the United States." Thus bankruptcy laws are entirely federal; states do not have the power to enact bankruptcy laws. State laws do, however, play a role in bankruptcy proceedings in defining the nature of liens, secured transactions, and other property interests.

Background of Today's Bankruptcy Law

In the last several decades, numerous landmark changes have occurred in bankruptcy laws. In 1978, Congress passed the Bankruptcy Reform Act. Known as the Bankruptcy Code, this law became effective on October 1, 1979.

The 1978 Act also introduced a new court structure. Bankruptcy courts were introduced into each federal district and were made adjuncts to the federal district courts. Unlike the judges of the district courts, who are given lifetime tenure, bankruptcy judges are appointed for a term of 14 years. The bankruptcy courts were given broad jurisdictional powers so that they could hear and decide all cases affecting the debtor or the debtor's estate.

However, in a 1982 case, *Northern Pipeline Construction Co. v. Marathon*, the U.S. Supreme Court held that the statute's grant of broad jurisdiction to the bankruptcy courts violated Article 3 of the U.S. Constitution.

In July of 1984 the Bankruptcy Amendments and Federal Judgeship Act were passed into law. The 1984 Act was divided into three sections or titles. Title I created a new bankruptcy court arrangement to replace the provisions found unconstitutional by the Supreme Court. This section, which now controls the jurisdiction of bankruptcy courts, gives original and exclusive jurisdiction of bankruptcy cases to the federal district courts. The newly created bankruptcy courts were organized as units of the district court and given only jurisdiction over proceedings arising under or related to bankruptcy laws. The bankruptcy judge's decision was also made reviewable by the district court judge.

The second section or title of the new law created additional federal district and Court of Appeals judges. The third title of the 1984 Act made several substantive changes in the 1978 Bankruptcy Code. For example, the law limits the right of a debtor who files a Chapter 11 bankruptcy reorganization (discussed at the end of the chapter) to reject unilaterally a collective bargaining labor contract.

Another change in the bankruptcy laws came in October 1986. Congress added a new chapter, Chapter 12, to the bankruptcy laws to provide special treatment for the family farmer. The Bankruptcy Judges, United States Trustees, and Family Farmer Bankruptcy Act of 1986 was intended to aid the family farmer who was facing severe economic conditions. Some of the special provisions of Chapter 12 are briefly discussed at the end of the chapter.

While a bankruptcy judge has broad powers, he or she does not in fact administer the debtor's estate. That power is given to a trustee in bankruptcy. A temporary trustee is initially appointed by the bankruptcy judge; later the creditors are allowed to select a permanent trustee of their own at their initial meeting. The trustee represents the debtor's estate and administers it by collecting the property, investigating the financial status of the debtor, and making reports to the court concerning the distribution of the estate.

Types of Bankruptcy Proceedings

The bankruptcy laws provide for four kinds of proceedings.

Liquidation In a **liquidation**, the debtor's assets—or the proceeds of those assets after they have been sold—are distributed to the creditors. Liquidation, also known as straight bankruptcy, is the most common type of bankruptcy proceeding and will be the primary focus of our discussion.

Reorganization A **reorganization**, a type of bankruptcy proceeding frequently used by corporate debtors, allows the debtor to stay in business rather than liquidate. In the reorganization, the debtor and creditors agree on a plan that provides for the debtor to pay some portion of its debts while being discharged from paying the remaining portion. The main features of this form of

bankruptcy will be noted and compared with liquidation proceedings near the end of the chapter.

Regular Income A third type of bankruptcy proceeding, provided for in Chapter 13 of the bankruptcy laws, permits the adjustment of debts of an individual with a regular income. This proceeding is often referred to as either a Chapter 13 or **regular-income plan**, since it provides relief for an individual who has a regular income but does not result in the debtor becoming bankrupt. The regular-income plan will be briefly discussed near the end of this chapter.

Family Farmer A fourth type of bankruptcy proceeding is available to the family farmer. Its provisions, found in Chapter 13, are very similar to those for the individual with a regular income. The farmer, and his or her family, is entitled to remain in possession of the farm and prepares a plan to reorganize. Neither Chapter 12 nor Chapter 13 proceedings result in bankruptcy.

The Bankruptcy Proceeding

The liquidation or straight bankruptcy proceeding is either a **voluntary proceeding** (initiated by the debtor) or an **involuntary proceeding** (initiated by the creditors). The debtor can be an individual, a corporation, or a partnership that has a residence, domicile, place of business, or property in the United States. Corporations that are subject to extensive regulation by administrative agencies are not subject to the bankruptcy law. The financial failures of insurance companies, banks, savings and loan associations, and similar institutions are subject to special regulatory proceedings rather than to the bankruptcy laws. Railroads and municipal corporations are not subject to the liquidation or straight bankruptcy proceedings. Railroads are subject to the reorganizations referred to at the end of this chapter, while municipal corporations can seek adjustment of their debts under another section of the bankruptcy laws if state laws authorize such action.

Commencement of the Proceeding

Voluntary Proceeding The filing of a voluntary proceeding automatically subjects the debtor and its property to the jurisdiction and supervision of the bankruptcy court. Once the petition is filed,

CONCEPT SUMMARY
Types of Bankruptcy Proceedings and Eligible Debtors

	Chapter 7 Liquidation*	Chapter 11 Reorganization*	Chapter 12 Family Farmer	Chapter 13 Regular Income[†]
Eligible debtors	Individual Partnership Corporation	Individual Partnership Corporation	Individual (and spouse) Partnership Corporation	Individual
Ineligible debtors	Municipalities Railroads Insurance companies Banks, savings and loans, and credit unions	Stockbrokers Commodity brokers Insurance companies Banks, savings and loans, and credit unions	Debtor with less than 50% of gross income from farming Debtor with more than $1.5 million in debts Corporate debtor with less than 50% of stock held by family, *or* with some stock that has been publicly issued	Stockbrokers Commodity brokers

*Farmers, nonprofit corporations, and municipalities are not eligible for involuntary cases.

[†]There can be no involuntary Chapter 13 cases.

creditors cannot start a suit or seek the enforcement of an existing judgment against the debtor.

Involuntary Proceeding Creditors can file an involuntary proceeding against any debtor who could have filed a voluntary proceeding, with two exceptions: An involuntary proceeding cannot be filed against farmers or nonprofit corporations. If the debtor has twelve or more creditors, at least three of the creditors must join in filing the petition. If there are fewer than twelve creditors, any one of them can file the petition. Regardless of how many creditors file, their unsecured claims against the debtor must total at least $5,000. Thus two irate creditors, with claims against a debtor totaling $3,000, cannot force the debtor into involuntary bankruptcy; neither can 200 such creditors having a total of less than $5,000 in claims.

If the debtor does not challenge the creditors' petition, the debtor's property is subjected to the jurisdiction and supervision of the bankruptcy court. However, if the debtor does challenge the petition, the creditors must prove that the debtor has not been paying his or her debts as they become due or that the debtor's property has been placed in receivership or assignment for the benefit of the creditors within 120 days before the petition was filed. Once the creditors prove either requirement, the debtor's property is subjected to the court's supervision. But if neither requirement is proved, the creditors' petition is dismissed.

Automatic Stay As soon as a voluntary or involuntary bankruptcy petition is filed, an **automatic stay** comes into effect. This means that all litigation between the debtor and any of the creditors is suspended, including all legal actions by the creditors to collect their respective debts. Secured creditors may petition for relief from the automatic stay in certain circumstances, such as when the inability to sell the secured party's collateral immediately will result in irreparable harm to the secured party. For example, a court might allow a creditor with a security interest in perishable meat products to sell those meats, even though the debtor has filed for bankruptcy. Some actions, such as criminal proceedings and the collection of alimony or child support, are not subject to the automatic stay.

The case that follows, which involves the highly publicized bankruptcy reorganization of the Johns-Manville Corporation, illustrates how the automatic stay issue can become complicated when the litigation becomes complex.

IN RE JOHNS-MANVILLE CORPORATION

U.S. District Court, S.D. New York

40 B.R. 219 (1984)

BACKGROUND: Johns-Manville Corporation filed a Chapter 11 reorganization petition because claims and lawsuits filed against it for injuries caused by the asbestos it manufactured totaled more than the company's net worth. Since Johns-Manville's petition stayed the cases brought against it, Lake, a Quebec company that was also a defendant in many of those cases, sought to determine the effect of that stay on its defense in those cases. GAF, the insurance company for Johns-Manville, also sought a ruling regarding the effect of the stay order on cases brought against it.

Brieant, Judge

Three separate appeals from decisions and orders of the Honorable Burton Lifland, Bankruptcy Judge, are before this Court for determination. They arise out of the proceedings pursuant to Chapter 11 of the Bankruptcy Code, initiated by Johns-Manville Corporation ("Manville"). Since these are related matters, we consider them together.

After more than a century of use of asbestos containing products, in residences, schools, ships, automobiles, factories, and in a vast number of applications, it was suddenly discovered that asbestos is dangerous and that inhalation of the dust is carcinogenic and debilitating. A litigation explosion ensued with a vast number of cases brought by persons claiming injury in plants where the product was used, or otherwise. The financial threat and the disruption of its business flowing from the litigation caused the Debtor Manville, a large manufacturer of asbestos, to seek the protection of the Bankruptcy Court in this district, which it did on August 26, 1982, treating those claiming to have been injured as its contingent creditors in the amounts set forth in their pleadings, making a total of claims in excess of Two Billion Dollars, more than the net worth of the Debtor.

As of 1982, appellant Lac D'Amiante duQuebec, Ltee. (hereinafter "Lake") was an original or impleaded defendant in several hundred asbestos-related tort cases pending in various jurisdictions throughout the United States. Manville was also a defendant in many of these suits. Among the proceedings against Manville which were stayed under the Bankruptcy Code following the filing of its Chapter 11 proceedings on August 26, 1982 are approximately 80 cases (the "plantworker cases") pending in New Jersey relating to claims arising from exposure to asbestos suffered at a Manville plant located at Manville, New Jersey. Lake is one of Manville's co-defendants in these cases.

In November 1982 Lake applied for an order clarifying the extent of the stays issued by the Bankruptcy Court pursuant to §§ 105 and 362 of the Bankruptcy Code. Lake sought a ruling from Judge Lifland that neither the statutory stay nor the accompanying stay order issued by the Bankruptcy Court prohibit it from obtaining pretrial discovery of documents and by deposition, as well as trial testimony from Manville, for its own use in those suits from which Manville has been severed.

On January 10, 1983 Judge Lifland issued two decisions determining the Lake application, the Manville proceeding, and several additional consolidated proceedings involving interpretation of the stay and stay order. . . . Appellants contend that the automatic stay provision simply does not apply to the testimony or discovery sought here. They argue that since they do not seek discovery by Manville as a party opponent, discovery from its employees as non-party witnesses cannot be construed as "proceedings against the debtor" which are subject to stay. . . .

This Court recognizes, as does the Bankruptcy Court, that stays of proceedings of the sort present here are not intended to be permanent. They must be reasonable as to scope and duration. Eventually, as a part of some plan of reorganization, and by some judicial process, either in this Court or in the Bankruptcy Court, or in the many state and federal courts where asbestos related cases are now pending, the liability of the Debtor's estate to respond to these claims and cross-claims must be adjudicated in accordance with due process, as must be its obligations for indemnification or contribution to other possible joint tort-feasors. Thereafter, whatever Manville owes, it must pay, either as part of its plan of reorganization pursuant to Chapter 11 of the Code, or as a disposition of its assets to claimants in order of their priority pursuant to Chapter 7 of the Code, or as a judgment debtor if these proceedings be dismissed.

Not withstanding any impressions to the contrary, neither the reorganization proceedings nor the stay can last forever.

At least as of the present, which is the only time as of which this Court may speak, the determination of the Bankruptcy Court to continue the stay is entirely reasonable, and absolutely necessary if there shall be any hope of reorganizing the Debtor in accordance with the statutory goal. Manville cannot be reorganized while its management is chasing around the country preparing for pre-trial discovery and protecting its legitimate interests in the scope and conduct of deposition testimony. To suggest otherwise, as noted above, would be to ignore the realities of modern litigation.

In light of the statutory purpose of the stay in bankruptcy, which "does more than prevent claims against the assets of the debtor," but gives "the debtor a breathing period in which to organize his or her affairs," the court below was fully justified in protecting the debtor for a reasonable time from the attempts to remove the stay.

DECISION: The court held that the stay order against Johns-Manville also applied to Lake's attempt to obtain from Johns-Manville information that would be useful to Lake in its own defense.

The Role of Creditors

Within a reasonable time after a petition in bankruptcy has been filed, the debtor must file with the court a schedule of assets and liabilities, a statement of financial affairs, and a list of creditors. The creditors listed by the debtor are then notified of the bankruptcy petition. Those who have claims against the debtor file proofs of claims with the court. The court generally allows the claims unless they are objected to by the debtor or other creditors. The creditors who are claimants in the bankruptcy proceeding are generally unsecured creditors.

If a creditor has a claim secured by a security interest or other lien on specific property of the debtor, that creditor, and only that creditor, can use the property to pay off the debt. If the value of that property is equal to the value of the debt, the creditor need not be concerned with the debtor's remaining assets and liabilities. An unsecured creditor is a person whose claim must be paid from the general property of the debtor; this creditor has no right or legal interest to any specific property of the debtor. It is this creditor who usually is most affected by the debtor's bankruptcy.

After the claims of the creditors have been filed and allowed, the court calls a meeting of the unsecured creditors. The judge cannot appear at the creditors' meeting, but a temporary trustee appointed by the judge does attend. At their first meeting the creditors normally do several things. First, they usually elect a permanent trustee. The permanent trustee may be the person appointed by the court to serve on a temporary basis or it may be someone else. At least 20 percent of the total amount of unsecured claims that have been filed and allowed must be represented at the meeting. The vote of creditors holding more than half of the total value of the unsecured claims represented at the meeting elects the trustee.

The second function performed by the creditors at their first meeting is the examination of the debtor. The debtor is placed under oath and is asked questions by the creditors and the trustee. The questions usually concern the nature of the debtor's assets and matters relevant to the potential discharge of the debts listed by the debtor.

Trustee in Bankruptcy

The **trustee in bankruptcy** is the party responsible for administering the debtor's estate in a liquidation. An interim trustee is named by the federal office of the United States Trustee shortly after the bankruptcy petition is filed. The creditors, at their first meeting, elect either the interim trustee or some other party as the permanent trustee.

The Debtor's Estate

Property in the Estate

The trustee collects all the property in the estate, reduces the property to money, and closes the estate after distributing the money according to the priorities established by the bankruptcy law. The debtor's estate consists of all property owned by or on behalf of the debtor as of the date of the filing of the bankruptcy petition.

Property Added to the Estate

After-Acquired Property Certain property acquired by the debtor after the petition has been filed—known as **after-acquired property**—will be added to the debtor's estate. Specifically, property acquired within 180 days after the date of the filing of the petition is added to the estate if the debtor acquired the property by inheritance, as a result of a property settlement or divorce decree with the debtor's spouse, or as a beneficiary on a life insurance policy.

Preference Property The trustee has the right under some circumstances to void or recall certain transfers of property made by the debtor. If the debtor transferred property to one creditor in prejudice to other creditors at a time when the debtor was insolvent, the property transferred may, under certain circumstances, be recovered and added to the debtor's estate.

Such transfers are known as **preferences** and, because they can be avoided by the trustee, they are part of a larger category of transfers known as **voidable transfers**. In order to constitute a preference, the transfer must have been made by the debtor within 90 days prior to the filing of the bankruptcy petition. It must have been made at a time when the debtor was insolvent, that is, when his or her debts were greater than assets. The transfer must have given the creditor more than the creditor would have received through the bankruptcy proceeding in order to constitute a preference. Thus not all transfers of property to creditors prior to the filing of the petition constitute preferences; however, if the transfer does constitute a preference, it can be added to the debtor's estate.

One type of transfer that may not be avoided by the trustee in bankruptcy is a "**contemporaneous exchange**"—that is, an exchange in which the debtor receives something of value and pays for it immediately or within the billing cycle. An example of a contemporaneous exchange is when Acme Hardware buys 100 hammers from HammerTime, Inc. and pays cash for them immediately upon delivery. Contemporaneous exchanges are allowed because no business could operate without the ability to make them. If a troubled business is allowed some breathing room to operate, there is the chance that it will be able to pull itself out of its troubles and avoid bankruptcy. If contemporaneous exchanges could be avoided by the trustee, no one would do business with a struggling company because any money received from the debtor within 90 days before a bankruptcy filing could be taken back by the trustee.

The case that follows discusses the applicability of the contemporaneous exchange exception.

IN THE MATTER OF CHG INTERNATIONAL, INC.

U.S. Court of Appeals, Ninth Circuit

897 F.2d 1479 (1990)

BACKGROUND: CHG filed a voluntary petition to reorganize under Chapter 11. One of its creditors, Barclays Bank, had made long-term loans to CHG. CHG filed an additional complaint alleging that two interest payments that it made on those loans within 90 days before the filing were voidable preferences and should be returned by Barclays Bank to the estate. The bankruptcy court held that the payments were voidable preferences and ordered Barclays Bank to return them to the estate. The U.S. District Court reversed this decision on appeal, and CHG appealed that decision to the U.S. Court of Appeals.

Hall, Circuit Judge

The bankruptcy court found that the interest payments on the CD and real estate loans were preferential as a matter of law and could thus be avoided under 11 U.S.C. § 547(b), which provides:

(b) Except as provided in subsection (c) of this section, the trustee may avoid any transfer of an interest of the debtor in property—

(1) to or for the benefit of a creditor;

(2) for or on account of an antecedent debt owed by the debtor before such transfer was made;

(3) made while the debtor was insolvent;

(4) made on or within 90 days before the date of the filing of the petition. . . .

(5) that enables such creditor to receive more than such creditor would receive if the case were a case under chapter 7 of this title. . . .

Barclays did not controvert that the interest payments it received from CHG fall within this section, but established to the district court's satisfaction an affirmative defense under section 547(c)(2), which provides:

(c) The trustee may not avoid under this section a transfer—
*   *   *

(2) to the extent that such transfer was—

(A) in payment of a debt incurred by the debtor in the ordinary course of business or financial affairs of the debtor and the transferee;

(B) made in the ordinary course of business or financial affairs of the debtor and the transferee; and

(C) made according to ordinary business terms;
*   *   *

A brief exposition of the history of and policies behind section 547 is necessary to properly resolve the issues in this case. The foremost purpose behind the voidable-preference provision is to assure fair or equal treatment of all creditors within the same class. Thus, if a debtor "prefers" a certain creditor by making payments on an antecedent debt to him shortly before filing for bankruptcy, the trustee can avoid or undo that preference. Such a payment would necessarily hurt other similarly situated creditors by depleting the estate.

A second policy behind section 547 is to discourage a race by the creditor to collect payment while the debtor is still marginally solvent, or a race to the courthouse to force the debtor into bankruptcy, when waiting might allow the debtor to regain his financial footing and not have to declare bankruptcy at all. Were there no rule allowing avoidance of preferences, a creditor would have a strong incentive to hound the debtor with demands for collection or petition the debtor into involuntary bankruptcy immediately so that the debtor could not deplete his assets trying to keep afloat.

The section 547(b) provision on voidable preference does not force a debtor out of business by making his suppliers wary of trading with him, knowing he might be able to recall all recent payments made to them. Under section 547(c)(1), a trustee may not avoid a transfer made as a "contemporaneous exchange" for new value given to the debtor, such as, for example, a cash purchase of goods or services. This creates a problem for a debtor who does not want to pay cash, because his later payments for goods and services provided on credit may be deemed payment of antecedent rather than current debt, and his suppliers would be reluctant to deal other than on a cash basis if they suspect him of being insolvent. Section 547(c)(2) was intended to complement the contemporaneous exchange section. As originally enacted in 1979, section 547(c)(2) required that the debtor's payment to the creditor be made within 45 days after the debt was incurred. "Payments made within the 45-day credit cycle were so close to 'contemporaneous' that they were not to be treated as payments on 'antecedent' debts." *In re RDC Corp.*

The rationale for both the old "current expense" rule and for the section 547(c)(2) exception is the same: the payment does not diminish the estate, is not for an antecedent debt, and allows the debtor to remain in business.

The Bankruptcy Amendment and Federal Judgeship Act ("BAFJA") amended the Code in 1984 to eliminate the 45-day limit. Prior to this amendment, the 45-day limitation very clearly precluded long-term loans from coming within the exception. The issue we must decide in this case is whether Congress intended to fundamentally change the scope of the ordinary course exception by including more than transactions which are substantially contemporaneous exchanges. Cases and scholarly commentary have gone both ways, but the better view is that the amendment was intended to eliminate an artificial time limit, and nothing more.

There is little legislative history accompanying the 1984 Amendment. Congress had initially settled on the 45-day limitation because it perceived that 45 days reflected the typical billing cycle of transactions intended to fall within that exception. This 45-day limitation had been the subject of numerous complaints by consumer lenders, trade creditors, and commercial paper issuers. Trade creditors complained that the trade credit periods in many industries were longer than 45 days, and commercial paper issuers were required to artificially shorten the maturity dates of commercial paper. . . . In answer to these complaints, Congress eliminated the 45-day limitation. Long-term lenders had not been active in seeking this change in preference law, but a literal and superficial reading of the new section 547(c)(2) appears to remove the primary obstacle which excluded these loans from the exception.

However, most cases interpreting this section hold that it does not cover payments on long-term loans. They do this by finding either that Congress did not intend section 547(c)(2) to except long-term debt from avoidance, that long-term debt is not incurred in a debtor's ordinary course of business, or both.

In *In re Bourgeois*, the first case to squarely address this issue in its holding, the court held that principal and interest payments by the debtor to a bank on long-term loans were not intended by the 1984 Amendment to fall within the section 547(c)(2) exception to avoidance of preferential transfers. The court noted that Congress did not intend to change the spirit of the section, i.e., the exemption from avoidance of trade credit transactions which are substantially contemporaneous exchanges.

To hold such payments on long term loans to be in the ordinary course of business within the meaning of 547(c)(2) would be to flout the clear intent of that subsection, and the entire policy of the preference provisions as a whole. Such a holding would virtually denude the preference provisions of the Code of any meaning at all. *Id.*

This argument is very persuasive. If the exception were to include long-term debt, this would neutralize the effect of the preference section by excepting almost every kind of payment a debtor makes during the 90-day period. Essentially there would be nothing left for the debtor's trustee to avoid. Such a significant shift in the congressional policy behind preference law favoring equality of distribution should not be presumed given the lack of legislative history demonstrating that such a shift was intended.

Decision: The Court of Appeals reversed the District Court's decision and ruled that Barclays Bank had to return the interest payments to the estate.

Lien Creditor's Property A third type of property that may be added to the debtor's estate is the property obtained by the trustee acting as a lien creditor. Thus if the debtor had given to a creditor a lien on certain property and if that lien had not been perfected or had not become effective as of the date of the filing of the petition, the trustee could add that property to the debtor's estate. The trustee, as of the date of the filing of the petition, has the status of a lien creditor, and if that status gives the trustee a better claim on certain property than the claims of other creditors, the property that those creditors thought they had an interest in can be added to the debtor's estate. Those creditors would then not have any preference on the specific property added to the debtor's estate. Instead, they would become unsecured creditors who would file a claim and receive whatever portion of their debt that is eventually distributed to them by the trustee.

Other Voidable Transfers The trustee also has the power to restore to the debtor's estate certain property transferred by or on behalf of the debtor to third parties. First, any transfer made *after* the filing of the bankruptcy petition, whether by or on behalf of the debtor, can be voided by the trustee within 2 years after the transfer or before the bankruptcy case is concluded, whichever occurs first. Second, the trustee may void any transfer made by the debtor within 1 year prior to the filing of the petition if the transfer was a fraudulent transfer or was made with the intent of hindering, delaying, or defrauding a creditor. Finally, since the trustee administers the property of the debtor, any property

that can be returned to the debtor due to someone else's fraud, mistake, duress, or undue influence can be reached by the trustee and added to the estate.

Exemptions from the Estate

An individual debtor can claim certain exemptions that are not available to corporations or partnerships. While the exempt property is brought into the estate when the bankruptcy petition is filed, if the debtor properly claims an exemption the exempt property will be removed from the estate. Thus it will not be subject to distribution to the creditors, but can be retained by the debtor. He or she is allowed to keep the exempt property and still be discharged from listed debts and liabilities.

The Bankruptcy Reform Act of 1978 made available to all debtors a list of properties exempt under federal bankruptcy laws. However, the debtor need not rely on that list if he or she desires instead to select the exemptions available under the law of the state where the debtor lives. Furthermore, the bankruptcy laws permit a state to require that the debtor use the exemptions listed under the state law. Thus the debtor has the choice of following either the state or the federal exemption list unless the law of the state where the debtor lives requires the debtor to follow the state list. Over one-half of the states require debtors in those states to follow the state's exemption laws.

Federal Exemptions The list of properties exempted by federal law from the debtor's estate in bankruptcy includes:

The debtor's residence, up to a value of $7,500

The debtor's interest in a motor vehicle, up to $1,200 in value

The debtor's interest in household furnishings, wearing apparel, appliances, books, musical instruments, animals, or crops held for personal, family, or household use up to $200 in value for each item

Up to $500 jewelry

The debtor's interest in any property, up to $400, plus up to $3,750 of any amount unused under Section 1

The debtor's interest, up to $750, in implements, tools of the trade, or professional books

Any unmatured life insurance policy owned by the debtor, except for credit life policies

The debtor's interest, not exceeding $4,000, in the accrued interest or dividends from life insurance policies

Prescribed health aids

The debtor's right to certain public benefits, including unemployment compensation, social security, veteran's benefits, and disability benefits

The debtor's interest in any other kind of property, up to a value of $400, plus any amount not used under the first exemption listed (thus if a debtor does not own a residence, he or she can exempt $7,900 of the property under this exemption)

State Exemptions The properties exempt for a debtor under state law vary, depending on the state of the debtor's residence. Some state laws do not place a dollar limit on the amount of certain exemptions. Such a law exists in Kansas and is discussed in the *Belcher v. Turner* case below. Other states do limit the amount of most exemptions.

BELCHER V. TURNER
U.S. Court of Appeals, Tenth Circuit
579 F.2d 73 (1978)

BACKGROUND: Carl and Esther Belcher (appellants) filed a voluntary petition for bankruptcy. They claimed that the duplex in which they lived was exempt property under the Kansas homestead exemption law. Turner, the trustee in bankruptcy, argued that only one-half of their duplex was exempt. The bankruptcy judge and District Court agreed with the trustee; the Belchers then appealed to the Court of Appeals.

Lewis, Circuit Judge

This appeal arises out of bankruptcy proceedings in the district court for the District of Kansas. Appellants Carl and Esther Belcher filed a voluntary petition for bankruptcy in which they claimed as exempt property a side-by-side duplex which they own. The claim was made under the homestead exemption set out in the Kansas Constitution, art. 15, § 9 and Kan.Stat.Ann. §60-2301.

In a memorandum decision the bankruptcy judge found that each unit in the duplex has a separate entrance, driveway, garage, and address. There is no common entrance except through an unfinished attic. The Belchers had resided in one unit since purchasing the property and had always leased the other unit. After finding the above facts the bankruptcy judge discussed the applicable law and determined that only the half occupied by the Belchers was exempt. The district court affirmed.

. . . (T)he Bankruptcy Act makes available to bankrupts those exemptions prescribed by state law. The scope and application of such exemptions are defined by the state courts and we are bound by their interpretations.

The Kansas cases which are most analogous on their facts are those considering an application of the exemption to property used by an owner partly as a residence and partly for business purposes. The most recent statement of the general rule [is] that

[t]he test for determining whether a structure is a homestead is determined by its use or occupancy as a residence, and an incidental departure for business purposes does not deprive it of its homestead character. . . .

Of course, if [the building] should practically become a business house rather than a home, it would then cease to be exempt.

Appellants argue the overriding purpose of this duplex was to provide them with a home. They suggest the rental of half the building was consistent with this purpose because the rent was used to pay the mortgage on the entire property. We believe these arguments ignore the underlying fact that half of the duplex has always been rented out and was never intended or expected to serve as appellants' residence. The unit was intended to produce income. Reduced to its essential, appellants' claim of Kan.Stat.Ann. §60-2301 provides in pertinent part:

A homestead to the extent of one hundred and sixty (160) acres of farming land, or of one acre within the limits of an incorporated town or city, occupied as a residence by the family of the owner, together with all the improvements on the same, shall be exempted from forced sale under any process of law. . . .

The above exemption is made applicable to bankruptcy proceedings by 11 U.S.C. § 24. The exemption is based only on the fact that the two units are part of the same physical structure. This one factor is not and should not be dispositive. The Kansas cases cited by appellants which inferentially support exempting the entire duplex did not involve bankruptcy. The purpose and intent of the Bankruptcy Act and its allowance of the homestead exemption counsel a different result. The aim is to protect and preserve the residence of the debtor; exempting the half of the duplex in which appellants reside will fully achieve that purpose.

DECISION: The Court of Appeals affirmed the judgment of the District Court.

CASE NOTE

Under present law, if the debtor elects to use state exemptions rather than federal exemptions as the Belchers did in this case, the law of the state where the debtor resided for the greater part of the preceding 6 months would be considered.

Distribution of Debtor's Estate

Priority Claims

After the trustee has collected all the debtor's property and reduced it to money, the money is distributed to the creditors. (Secured creditors can proceed against the property with which their debt is secured. If any portion of their debt is unsecured, that portion must be considered along with other unsecured claims.) Some claims are given a higher priority than others. Claims are paid in order of their priority. Thus each class of claims is paid in full before any payment is made of claims of lower priority. If there is not enough money to pay fully all claims in any class, the money available is prorated among the creditors in that class.

A claim that is given some sort of priority is known as a **priority claim**. A claim that is not given priority is known as a **general claim**. General claims are paid only if and to the extent that there is anything left in the estate after all priority claims have been satisfied.

The highest priority is assigned to the costs and expenses involved in administering the bankruptcy proceeding. These include legal fees, accountants' fees, trustee fees, and court costs. The second class of claims pertains only to involuntary proceedings: expenses occurring in the ordinary course of the debtor's business or financial affairs after filing of the case but prior to appointment of the trustee. The third class consists of claims for wages, salaries, or commissions earned by employees within 90 days before the filing of the petition or the cessation of the debtor's business, whichever occurs first. Claims in this class are given priority up to $2,000 per individual.

Three other categories of claims have some priority over general claims. The fourth class consists of claims for contributions to an employee benefit plan arising from services rendered within 180 days before the filing of the petition or the cessation of the debtor's business. The limit per claimant in this category is also $2,000, and no individual can receive more than $2,000 from a combination of claims falling in the third and fourth priority classes. The fifth class is for claims for deposits made on consumer goods or services that were not received; the limit for claims in this class is $900. The sixth and last class consists of tax claims submitted by governmental units.

General Claims If a claim exceeds the amount allowed as a priority, the excess becomes a general claim. After all classes of priority have been paid, any remaining property is distributed on a pro rata basis to all unsecured creditors with general claims against the debtor's estate. Often, as Figure 34-1 illustrates, there will be little, if any, distribution to other unsecured creditors who have only a general claim against the debtor. Thus it is important to creditors who can do so to have their claims classified as priority claims.

Discharge of Debts

After the debtor's estate has been liquidated and distributed among the creditors, the bankruptcy court conducts a hearing to determine if the debtor should be discharged from the remaining debts. A **discharge**, which relieves the debtor of the obligation to repay his or her remaining debts, can be granted to an individual petitioner but not a partnership or a corporation. Those business

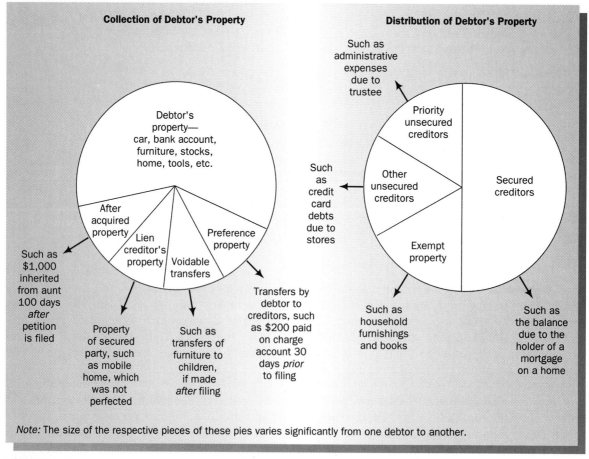

Note: The size of the respective pieces of these pies varies significantly from one debtor to another.

FIGURE 34-1

Collection and Distribution of Debtor's Estate for a Chapter 7 Liquidation Proceeding entities may seek to reorganize under Chapter 11 or they may seek liquidation.

Exceptions to Discharge

Under certain circumstances the court will deny a discharge to a debtor. If this occurs, the debtor remains liable for the unpaid portion of the creditors' claims. A debtor will be denied a discharge if a prior discharge was granted within 6 years of the filing of the petition. A discharge will not be granted if the debtor, within 1 year before the filing of the petition, or at any time thereafter, intentionally concealed or transferred assets with the intent to hinder, delay, or defraud creditors.

Other reasons for refusing a discharge to a debtor include the debtor's concealment, destruction, falsification, or failure to keep records related to the debtor's financial condition or business transactions. A debtor who fails to explain the loss of assets adequately or who refuses to obey a lawful order of the bankruptcy court or who makes any fraudulent statement or claim in connection with the bankruptcy case can be denied the discharge of unpaid debts, as the *Horton* case indicates below. Since the new bankruptcy law has virtually the same provisions as those of the old law referred to in the *Horton* case, the determination made in *Horton* would probably be followed by courts reviewing the new law.

MATTER OF HORTON

U.S. Court of Appeals, Ninth Circuit
621 F.2d 968 (1980)

BACKGROUND: Horton, the defendant debtor, filed a bankruptcy petition but was denied a discharge by the bankruptcy judge because the debtor failed to keep adequate records or accounts from which his financial condition and business transactions could be determined. The debtor dealt in cash in all his business transactions and kept few records. The bankruptcy judge's decision was affirmed by the U.S. District Court and Horton appealed to the Court of Appeals.

Grant, District Judge

The defendant, Robert Jackson Horton, sought a discharge of his debts in bankruptcy. This was refused by the bankruptcy judge in December 1974. The reason for refusing discharge was "Horton's unjustified failure to keep adequate books of accounts or records from which his financial condition and business transactions could be discerned." Maintaining such records is required. This decision was affirmed by the district court, which entered judgment against Horton after a consideration of the merits of his claim. Horton now appeals to this court, contending that the lower courts erred in not granting him relief.

Horton is no stranger to the Bankruptcy Court. He has made his appearance there like clockwork every seven years. He was first granted a discharge in 1960 and again in 1967. This latest petition in bankruptcy was filed in 1973. At that time the case was routinely assigned to Judge Downey. The judge immediately disqualified himself, however, since he had presided over the previous discharges and felt he did not have the requisite impartiality in Horton's latest cause. The case was accordingly assigned to Judge Hughes.

The Bankruptcy Act provides that a discharge cannot be granted if the bankrupt has failed to keep sufficient records of his financial transactions. Although this failure may be deemed justifiable under the particular circumstances of the bankrupt, in this case the failure was found unjustified. Horton alleges that the findings of fact and law were insufficient under the requirements of Bankruptcy Rule 752(a).

The record reveals that the bankruptcy judge filed a five-page memorandum in which he reduced a convoluted and often contradictory factual record into findings of law and fact. This memorandum assessed (1) the records Horton kept, (2) the sufficiency of those records, and (3) once the records were found to be insufficient, whether the keeping of insufficient records was excusable in this particular case. The memorandum is more than sufficient to satisfy the requirements of Rule 752(a).

Horton's essential disagreement is not with the sufficiency of the findings, but with their correctness and the appropriateness of the legal standard applied. Therefore, we turn our attention to determining whether these findings are supported by the record. Unless they are clearly erroneous, they will not be disturbed on appeal.

Using these standards, we have assessed the record in this case. It shows that Horton dealt almost exclusively in cash during all his business transactions, keeping little or no verifiable records. He was unable to show where his salary was spent. As the bankruptcy judge and the district court concluded, his dislike of banks did not absolve him from keeping records. These fact findings are not clearly erroneous.

Against this general backdrop of scanty record keeping, we have examined Horton's contention that certain of his daughter's records provide the information Horton cannot supply. Horton built a house for his daughter, acting as a general contractor and paying suppliers and builders over Twenty Thousand Dollars in cash payments, without keeping any financial records of these dealings. Horton alleges that his daughter's records should be substituted for his own, to satisfy the provisions of Section 14(c)(2).

Legally, however, Horton had a duty to maintain his own records of such a transaction, even if his daughter's records were complete.

Even if we accepted the dubious contention that Horton could rely upon his daughter's records, they are not sufficient for that purpose. The transcript reveals that these records do not differentiate between payments made to Horton to reimburse him and those which were made directly to suppliers for the materials. Therefore, even if they are considered, they do not clarify Horton's financial position. Furthermore, the testimony of Horton and his daughter and her roommate [was] found to be "incredible" and replete with inconsistencies and contradiction.

Once the Trustee has shown that the bankrupt's records are inadequate, the burden shifts to the bankrupt to justify the nonexistence of these records. The record explicitly and implicitly indicates that the bankruptcy judge correctly applied these presumptions and burden of proof. Horton's argument to the contrary is without merit.

DECISION: The Court of Appeals affirmed the District Court judgment denying a discharge to Horton.

Nondischargeable Claims

If none of the exceptions applies, the discharge relieves the debtor from any obligation for the payment of the debts that arose prior to the filing of the petition. A judgment entered by a court on a debt that is discharged becomes void; no action can be taken to collect that debt. Nevertheless, there are some claims for which the debtor continues to be liable; these are known as **nondischargeable claims**. Claims that are not dischargeable include:

- Claims for back taxes accrued within 3 years prior to the bankruptcy
- Claims arising out of the debtor's embezzlement, fraud, or larceny
- Claims based on the debtor's willful or malicious torts
- Claims for alimony or child support
- Certain fines and penalties payable to governmental units
- Educational loans that became due and payable less than 5 years prior to the filing of the bankruptcy petition

Reaffirmations

While the discharge of debts owed by the debtor to creditors relieves the debtor of any legal obligation to pay those debts, the debtor may make a **reaffirmation** of a debt. That is, after the discharge the debtor may undertake to pay off the debt anyway. However, since the debtor may be under a great deal of pressure from former creditors to reaffirm the discharged debts, the bankruptcy laws make the reaffirmation of debts somewhat difficult.

A simple promise by the debtor, even in writing, is not sufficient for a valid reaffirmation. First, the court must conduct a hearing at which the debtor is informed of the consequences of such action. Second, the debt must usually be approved by the court as not imposing an undue hardship on the debtor and being in the debtor's best interest. If these conditions are not met, the reaffirmation of the debt is not valid and its discharge is effective.

Business Reorganization

Instead of filing a petition for liquidation, an individual or business may elect to file for reorganization under Chapter 11 of the Bankruptcy Act. As in a liquidation proceeding, a petition for reorganization may also be filed by the creditors. Most of the rules that apply to the liquidation proceeding also apply to the reorganization. Railroads, however, are not subject to liquidation because of the public's dependence on their services. Reorganization allows a financially troubled firm or railroad to continue to operate while its financial resources and obligations are put in order.

Under Chapter 11 reorganizations the court must appoint a **creditors' committee**. This committee usually consists of the seven largest unsecured creditors and is appointed as soon as practicable after the order for relief has been entered by the court. The task of the creditors' committee is to examine the affairs of the business and decide whether the business should continue in operation. The committee also usually determines whether to request that a trustee should take over the management of the business. If necessary, the committee may employ attorneys, accountants, and other agents to assist it in performing these tasks. Generally, the debtor or any other interested party may file a plan for reorganization. While only the debtor may file a plan during the first 120 days after the petition has been filed (unless a trustee has been appointed), the debtor's plan is usually developed in consultation with the creditors. A debtor who files a plan within the 120 days has an additional 60 days to have the plan approved by the creditors. The court can extend or reduce these time periods for good cause. If the debtor does not meet the deadline or is unable to obtain the consent of the creditors, any party in interest (a creditor or the trustee) may propose a plan.

The plan that is proposed must classify claims and ownership interests. It must specify the treatment of each class of claims and must provide for the same treatment for all persons in the same class unless the holder of a particular claim agrees to less favorable treatment. The plan must also provide adequate means for carrying out the plan's payment terms. If the debtor

---

ETHICS
Any Ethical Obligation after Discharge?

Lauretta T. goes through a bankruptcy proceeding and is fully discharged from all remaining debts after her unsecured creditors are paid 25 cents on the dollar. Several of the creditors are small business owners who are hurt by their inability to collect 100 percent of the money Lauretta owes them. One month after the discharge Lauretta wins $5 million in the state lottery.

Under the law Lauretta does not have to pay her former creditors, but does she have an ethical obligation? If there had been a voluntary resolution of the debts between Lauretta and her creditors, then one might conclude that Lauretta has no obligation to go back and make good her former debts. However, if the transaction was involuntary, and had a negative impact upon some of her creditors, do you think that Lauretta should pay off the debts which have been legally discharged?

is a corporation, the plan must also protect stockholder voting rights, ensure that nonvoting stock will not be issued, and provide that in the selection of officers and directors the interests of creditors and stockholders will be protected.

The plan may modify the rights of some of the creditors. It may specify that some property be transferred to other creditors, that some creditors be partially paid over an extended time, and even that some creditors not be paid. The only requirement is that all the debtor's claimants must receive as much as they would have received in a liquidation proceeding.

Those who hold claims or interests in the debtor's property are allowed to vote on the proposed plan. If creditors representing more than one-half of the number of claimants and at least two-thirds of the value of the claims in a class vote in favor of the plan, that class of creditors has accepted the plan.

Normally a plan will not be approved unless all those whose claims or interests have been impaired—those whose rights have been altered or who are to receive less than the full value of their claims or interests—have agreed to it. The court, however, may possibly confirm a plan even when those with impaired claims don't consent if the court determines that all persons in a particular class are treated fairly and equitably. Confirmation of the plan binds debtor and creditors. The property of the debtor is released from the claims of the creditors, and the debtor is given a Chapter 11 discharge. The process followed in a Chapter 11 reorganization proceeding is illustrated in Figure 34-2, while Figure 34-3 depicts a court's order for a recent reorganization.

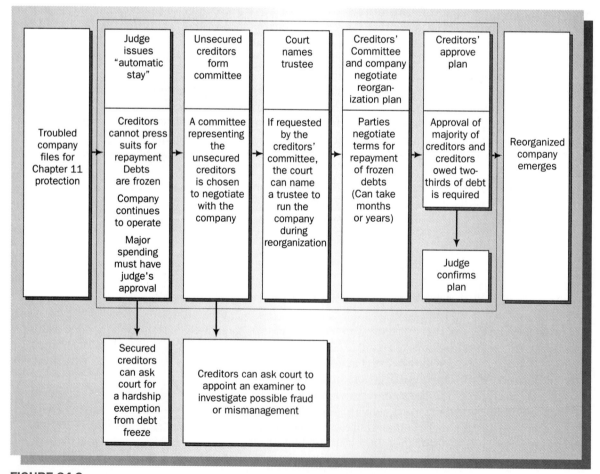

FIGURE 34-2

The Chapter 11 Reorganization Process

FIGURE 34-3

Confirmation of Chapter 11
Reorganization Plan

**UNITED STATES BANKRUPTCY COURT
FOR THE WESTERN DISTRICT OF LOUISIANA
SHREVEPORT DIVISION**

IN RE:

CRYSTAL OIL COMPANY,   CASE NO. 586-02834

DEBTOR   CHAPTER 11 PROCEEDING

**NOTICE OF ENTRY OF ORDER CONFIRMING
PLAN OF REORGANIZATION OF CRYSTAL OIL COMPANY**

TO: The Creditors and Shareholders of Crystal Oil Company and all Other Parties in Interest.

PLEASE TAKE NOTICE that on December 31, 1986, the Second Amended and Restated Plan of Reorganization (the "Plan") of Crystal Oil Company, debtor and debtor-in-possession in the above referenced case (the "Company"), was confirmed by the United States Bankruptcy Court for the Western District of Louisiana, Shreveport Division, and an Order Confirming Plan (the "Confirmation Order") was entered on the docket by the Clerk of the Bankruptcy Court which, among other things, provided:

(1) that the provisions of the Plan shall bind all the Company's creditors and interest holders, whether or not they have accepted the Plan, and shall discharge the Company from all debts that arose before October 1, 1986, the petition date, and that the distributions provided for under the Plan shall be in exchange for and in complete satisfaction, discharge, and release of all claims against and interest in the Company or any of its assets or properties, including any claim or interest accruing after October 1, 1986, and prior to the Effective Date (as defined herein);

(2) that the property of the Company's estate shall revest in the Company on the Effective Date and after the Effective Date, except as provided in the Plan, the Company may operate its business and buy, use, acquire, and dispose of its property, free of any restrictions contained in the Bankruptcy Code;

(3) that as of the Effective Date, all property of the Company shall be free and clear of all claims and interest of creditors and equity security holders, except for the obligations that are imposed in the Plan; and

(4) that as a condition to the receipt of the distributions to be provided under the Plan, all creditors and interest holders of the Company shall be required to surrender such creditor's or interest holder's securities and related documents as required under the Plan.

PLEASE TAKE FURTHER NOTICE that the New Securities (as defined in the Plan) that are to be issued to the holders of the 15% Senior Notes, the Debentures and the Common Stock (as such terms are defined in the Plan) shall be deemed to have been issued as of December 31, 1986, and the sole and exclusive right of such holders against the Company with respect to such securities shall be to exchange such securities for the New Securities to be issued to them pursuant to the Plan.

PLEASE TAKE FURTHER NOTICE that the Plan shall become effective (i) on January 30, 1987, if the Confirmation Order has not been stayed on appeal by a court of competent jurisdiction and (ii) if the Confirmation Order is stayed on appeal by a court of competent jurisdiction 15 days after such stay is resolved by final order (the "Effective Date").

December 31, 1986.

                              BY ORDER OF STEPHEN V. CALLAWAY,
                              UNITED STATES BANKRUPTCY JUDGE

FULBRIGHT & JAWORSKI
51st Floor
1301 McKinney Street
Houston, TX 77010
(713) 651-5350

COOK, YANCEY, KING & GALLOWAY
Suite 400, American Tower
401 Market Street
Shreveport, LA 71101
(318) 221-6277

COUNSEL FOR CRYSTAL OIL COMPANY

[Source: *The Wall Street Journal*, January 9, 1987, page 31. Reprinted with permission]

PREVENTIVE LAW

Actions To Be Taken by a Creditor of a Chapter 11 Bankruptcy Reorganization

What can creditors do if a business firm they deal with is considering a Chapter 11 reorganization?

1. First and foremost, make critical decisions before a filing occurs.

   a. Monitor accounts closely. If a debtor falls behind on payments, seek additional collateral for your account. A creditor is in a stronger position if its claim is secured.

   b. Review the debtor's business. If you think you will not receive much under a reorganization, consider making a deal to cancel the debt for immediate but partial payment. (Bankruptcy laws do allow the trustee to set aside such deals if they are made just prior to the filing.)

2. Once a petition is filed, your first step should be to file a proof of claim—find out the date by which all claims must be filed and be sure all your claims are filed before that date.

3. You may be able to reclaim property—you have until 10 days after the filing to reclaim any goods supplied up to 10 days before the filing.

4. Talk to other creditors—the more information you have about the debtor's assets, the better position you can be in. Obtain the list of creditors and amount owed from the bankruptcy clerk.

5. Keep tabs on what is happening.

   a. Consider filing a notice of appearance. Unless your claim is for a small amount and there are many other large claims, you probably will want to receive notice of the proceedings.

   b. Make a personal visit to court to help establish contact and to find out whom to call if you need quick information.

   c. Look after your own interest. If the debtor doesn't file a plan within 120 days, the creditors can file their own plan, although this doesn't often occur.

Chapter 13—Regular Income Plans

Chapter 13 proceedings are used by individuals with regular incomes who owe debts and want to pay them without harassment by creditors. While the prior law made this bankruptcy proceeding available only to wage earners, under the present law any individual (except a stockbroker or commodity broker) who has a regular income (whether from wages, investments, social security, or pensions) and unsecured debts of less than $100,000 and secured debts of less than $350,000 may use Chapter 13. Unlike liquidation or reorganization, Chapter 13 proceedings can be begun only by a voluntary petition filed by the debtor.

Upon the filing by the debtor of a Chapter 13 proceeding, an automatic stay stops creditors from taking action against the debtor. The debtor then proposes a plan providing for the use of future income for the payment of creditors. That income will be subject to control by a trustee, and the plan must ensure that all claims entitled to priority are paid in full. Unsecured claims may be divided into classes, but all claims within any class must be treated the same. Claimants may be paid in full or paid an amount not less than what they would receive in a liquidation proceeding. Usually, the plan provides for the payment of creditors over 3 years or less; however, the court may extend the period of payment to 5 years.

In order for the plan to be confirmed by the court, priority claimants must be paid in full, to the extent that money is available, unless they agree to accept less than the full amounts of their claims. Secured creditors vote on whether to accept the plan. If these creditors do not accept the plan, but either retain their liens or receive the properties securing their claims, the court will still confirm the plan. Unsecured creditors do not vote on the plan, but they must receive at least the amounts they would have received in a liquidation proceeding.

A court will not confirm a Chapter 13 plan unless it is satisfied that the plan was submitted in good faith. The *Doersam* case, which follows, discusses this good faith requirement in a context that could soon become very familiar to some of you: the repayment of student loans.

IN RE DOERSAM

U.S. Court of Appeals, Sixth Circuit
849 F.2d 237 (1988)

BACKGROUND: Winifred Doersam used a $10,000 student loan guaranteed by the Ohio Student Loan Commission (OSLC) to finance her graduate education in computer science at the University of Dayton. She was also the cosigner on a $5,000 student loan, also guaranteed by OSLC, to finance her daughter's education. Prior to receiving her master's degree, Doersam took a $24,000-per-year position with the NCR Corporation. She completed the requirements for her degree, and 6 weeks prior to graduation she filed a petition and plan under Chapter 13. She proposed to pay off only 19 percent of her unsecured debt, most of which consisted of student loans. Doersam listed as dependents her 23-year-old daughter, who was employed at the time, and her 1-year-old granddaughter. OSLC objected to the confirmation of Doersam's plan, and the bankruptcy court ruled in OSLC's favor. The federal district court affirmed in favor of OSLC, ruling that Doersam's plan had been filed in bad faith. Doersam appealed.

Keith, Circuit Judge

In evaluating good faith in specific situations, we find helpful, as did the district court, the factors enumerated in *In re Kitchens*:

1. the amount of debtor's income from all sources;
2. the living expenses of the debtor and his dependents;
3. the amount of attorney's fees;
4. the probable or expected duration of the debtor's Chapter 13 plan;
5. the motivations of the debtor and his sincerity in seeking relief under the provisions of Chapter 13;
6. the debtor's degree of effort;
7. the debtor's ability to earn and the likelihood of fluctuation in his earnings;
8. special circumstances such as inordinate medical expenses;
9. the frequency with which the debtor has sought relief under the Bankruptcy Reform Act and its predecessors;
10. the circumstances under which the debtor has contracted his debts and his demonstrated bona fides, or lack of same, in dealing with his creditors;
11. the burden which the plan's administration would place on the trustee.

These factors should not be viewed as exclusive; in the final analysis, good faith should be evaluated on a case-by-case basis in light of the structure and general purpose of Chapter 13.

The fact that all or part of the debt consists of educational loans presents special problems. Ordinarily, such loans are not dischargeable under Chapter 7. The mere fact that a debtor attempts to discharge a debt that would be nondischargeable under Chapter 7 is not sufficient in itself to warrant a finding that the plan was not proposed in good faith. However, whether the debt would be nondischargeable under Chapter 7 is a factor which is relevant to the determination of good faith.

Moreover, the debt which the debtor seeks to discharge is also germane to the question of good faith. Here, the repayment structure of educational loans is of particular relevance:

Unlike most commercial loans which are granted only upon a showing of credit worthiness and ability to make repayment, guaranteed student loans, on the other hand are granted only upon a debtor establishing need. Unlike most loans, guaranteed student loans do not require a borrower to commence repayment until the borrower has completed his or her education. It is therefore most questionable when a debtor accepts a student loan and then, prior to its maturity, attempts to extinguish the debt in bankruptcy without ever making an attempt to repay it. It stretches credulity to say that the debtor made an honest effort to pay these debts as required by 11 U.S.C. § 1325(a)(3).*State Education Assistance Authority v. Johnson.*

Based on the foregoing considerations, the district court correctly found that Doersam's plan had not been proposed in good faith. The bulk of Doersam's unsecured indebtedness consists of student loans which would not have been dischargeable under Chapter 7. Doersam made absolutely no effort to repay these loans despite their long-term character, and despite the fact that they were instrumental in her securing a position paying approximately $24,000.00 per year. Indeed, her student loans had not yet become due at the time that she submitted her plan. Moreover, as both the bankruptcy court and district court noted, the listing of a working daughter and a minor grandchild for whom Doersam is not legally responsible, and the budgeting of $400.00 per month for food based on those questionable listings, are further grounds for finding that the plan was not filed in good faith.

DECISION: The Court of Appeals affirmed the decision in favor of OSLC.

CONCEPT SUMMARY
Summary of Four Types of Bankruptcy Proceedings

	Chapter 7 Liquidation	Chapter 11 Reorganization	Chapter 12 Family Farmer	Chapter 13 Regular Income
Who initiates the case?	Debtor—voluntary or creditor—involuntary	Debtor	Debtor	Debtor
What happens to debtor's property?	It is liquidated to pay creditors (except for exempt property of individual)	It is preserved	It is preserved	It is preserved
How are creditors paid?	From property of debtor	From debtor's future income	From debtor's future income	From debtor's future income
What happens to unpaid debts?	They are eliminated by the discharge	They may be reduced but not below amount creditor would have received under Chapter 7 liquidation	Priority claimants are paid in full; others may be reduced or eliminated	Priority claimants are paid in full; others may be reduced or eliminated

Chapter 12—Relief for the Family Farmer

As noted at the beginning of the chapter, this recent section of the bankruptcy law was intended to provide relief for family farmers who had been and were facing some very difficult economic conditions. Only a family farmer with regular annual income can be a debtor under Chapter 12. Over 50 percent of the annual gross income of the debtor must be from farming operations.

Essentially, Chapter 12 allows a debtor to reorganize, much like the small businesses and individuals who can use the provisions of Chapter 13. The farmer is allowed to remain in possession of the property and is required to file a plan for reorganization within 90 days (the time can be extended by the court). The plan is quite similar to plans that are to be filed in Chapter 13 proceedings. The farmer's future income is to be subject to control by the trustee. All priority claims are to be paid in full and the repayment period is to be no longer than 3 years (the court can extend it to 5 years). Finally, the plan is to provide for the same treatment for all claims and interests within a particular class, unless the holder agrees to accept less (this is a little different from the comparable Chapter 13 provision).

Review Questions and Problems

Key Terms

liquidation

reorganization

regular-income plan

voluntary proceeding

involuntary proceeding

automatic stay

trustee in bankruptcy

after-acquired property

preference

voidable transfer

contemporaneous exchange

priority claim

general claim

discharge

nondischargeable claim

reaffirmation

creditors' committee

Discussion Questions

1. Compare and contrast the uses and consequences of the three kinds of bankruptcy proceedings.
2. What is the purpose of the bankruptcy law?

3. What are exemptions? Give several examples of exemptions in bankruptcy.
4. Who receives the property of the debtor who is not exempt?

Review Problems

1. Assume that an individual debtor has a regular income, owns a small ($20,000) business, and has $30,000 of property, $75,000 of unsecured debts, and $225,000 of secured debts. The debtor wants to stay in business but cannot pay her debts. Which of the bankruptcy proceedings is available for and might help this debtor?
2. Review the federal exemptions in bankruptcy listed in this chapter. Assume Belcher's duplex is valued at $75,000—$40,000 for the portion he resides in and $35,000 for the rental portion (it is not maintained as well as his residence). If the court followed federal law rather than state law in the debtor's use of exemptions, how would the court's decision in this case differ from the version presented in the text?
3. Brenda purchased a refrigerator, stove, and air conditioner from Freddie's Appliance Store. She paid Freddie $1,000 and signed a contract to take delivery of the appliances in 2 weeks. One week after her purchase of the appliances, Freddie filed a straight bankruptcy. What will be Brenda's status as a claimant? Is she entitled to any priority?
4. Nancy is a debtor considering bankruptcy. She does not own a home but does own a car (valued at $5,000, on which she still owes $4,000), jewelry valued at $1,000, six items of household goods, three of which are valued at $400 each and three of which are valued at $200 each, and $8,000 in the bank. How much of this property would be exempt under the federal exemptions?
5. Bob Smith filed a petition for a Chapter 13 regular income adjustment. His plan proposed paying $6,000 to the unsecured creditors, who were owed $20,000. The trustee determined that the sale of the debtor's nonexempt property in a Chapter 7 proceeding would provide $12,000 for the unsecured creditors. Should Smith's plan be confirmed?

Case Problems

1. Kapela and Brovenick were the sole shareholders of a corporation that borrowed money from a bank. Each personally guaranteed to the bank the loan made to the corporation. Later the corporation lent money to Brovenick, one of the shareholders; he gave the corporation a promissory note for that loan. The corporation assigned that note to the bank.

   One week prior to the corporation's filing for bankruptcy, Brovenick paid money to the bank; he claimed that payment reduced his debt to the corporation and also reduced his guarantor obligation to the bank. Five months after the bankruptcy petition was filed by the corporation, Newman, the corporation's trustee in bankruptcy, brought suit against both shareholders and sought to recover for the corporation the money paid by Brovenick to the bank. The trustee claimed the payment constituted a voidable preference, benefiting the shareholder-guarantors at the expense of other creditors of the same class. Do you agree?

2. Keidel borrowed $3,500 from the bank to finance the purchase of a mobile home she was buying from its seller, Mitchell. She signed a security agreement with the bank and gave it her promissory note. The bank gave her a check, issued to her and to Olin Employees' Credit Union, the prior lienholder. The bankrupt was advised to get a new certificate of title showing that she, instead of seller Mitchell, had the title to the mobile home.

Keidel began to apply for a certificate of title, but didn't complete her application. Five months later she filed a petition in bankruptcy. One month after that date the bank applied for and obtained a new certificate of title, showing Keidel's ownership of the mobile home and the bank's lien interest. Under the state law the bank had a security interest in the mobile home as of the date of its loan to Keidel, but that security interest was not perfected until the date the bank applied for the new certificate of title. Does the trustee in bankruptcy, standing in the position of a lien creditor, prevail over the bank that had a security interest created prior to the date of the petition in bankruptcy, but perfected after that date?

3. Emily Westhem's original engagement ring had belonged to Andrew Westhem's grandmother. A number of years ago it was stolen and the insurance proceeds were used to purchase the ring here in question. The present ring is a diamond ring having a fair market value of more than $3,000 and described as one emerald-cut diamond of approximately four carats with two side diamonds.

The present California Code of Civil Procedure exempts "[n]ecessary household furnishings and appliances and wearing apparel, ordinarily and reasonably necessary to, and personally used by, the debtor and his resident family." The bankrupt claims the ring is exempt as wearing apparel, reasonably necessary to and personally used by his wife. The trustee claims it is not exempt. Who is correct?

4. The defendant filed a voluntary proceeding in bankruptcy. Six weeks later his mother died and he became entitled to money from a trust fund that had been created by the defendant's father. After his mother's death, the debtor filed a disclaimer, which under state law disclaimed his interest in that money and passed it instead to his children. The trustee in bankruptcy claims that the property that the debtor was entitled to was part of his estate and that the state law allowing him to disclaim it is inconsistent with and subject to the federal bankruptcy law. Is the trustee correct?

5. Petitioners are claims adjusters and attorneys who provided professional services to an insurance company that has been liquidated under state law. The statutory scheme for distributing assets of an insolvent insurance company gives priority status, after expenses of administration are paid, to claims owed to employees. The language of the state law is very similar to that in the federal bankruptcy statutory provision. The other general creditors claim that the attorneys and claims adjusters are not employees, but rather, are independent contractors. Thus amounts owed to them are not due as "wages" and are not entitled to priority status. Assume that this provision in the state law is interpreted in the same way as is the provision in the federal bankruptcy laws. Should the claims adjusters' and attorneys' claims, or a part of them, be granted priority status?

6. Bruce Clark, a football player for the New Orleans Saints, filed for relief under Chapter 11 after the seventh game of the 1988 season. His annual salary of $575,000 was payable in sixteen installments during each week of the regular season. Clark's contract with the Saints required him to pass a physical at the beginning of the season, which he did. The contract also provided that if his play fell below a level of quality acceptable to the team, he could be released and not be compensated for the remainder of the season. Although Clark was not released, the latter clause became important, because it raised an issue as to whether Clark earned his entire salary upon passing the preseason physical (even though he would actually be paid over the course of the regular season) or whether he earned it week by week, subject to the team's right to release him. If Clark earned his salary week by week, then any money that he earned after filing the petition would not be part of the estate. If he earned his entire salary at the start of the season, then the entire salary would have been earned prior to filing and would hence have been part of the estate. Should Clark's entire salary for the year be included in the estate?

PART **VI**

AGENCY LAW

35

The Agency Relationship

Agency Defined
Creation of Agency Relations

Rights and Duties between Principal
and Agent

The purpose of an agency is to allow one person to accomplish results through another person's activities. Despite modern advances in communication and transportation, a person has only one pair of hands to work with, has one mouth to speak from, and can be in only one place at a time. When the time arrives that more hands and mouths are needed, or when it becomes necessary to transact business at the same time in various and remote places, the businessperson must turn to someone for assistance and representation. That someone is the agent.

Agency Defined

Agency is the legal relationship created when two people agree that one of them, called the **agent**, is to represent the other, called the **principal**, subject to the principal's right to control the agent's conduct in the delegated activity. Agency relates to commercial or business transactions conducted between the principals and third parties through the agent. In agency relations the principal confides to the agent the management of some business that the principal may lawfully do in person. The result is to bind the principal legally to third persons as though the principal personally transacted the business. The agent is merely the medium. When the dealings are com-

pleted and the dust finally clears, it is the principal and the third person who are legally bound to each other. It is the agent who ties the bond.

Types of Agents

Agents are classified as either general agents or special agents. The **general agent** is more or less continuously employed by the principal to conduct a series of transactions. He or she may be the manager of the principal's business or the lowliest of clerks. The **special agent** is hired for one particular transaction or occasion. There is no continuity in the special agent's employment. He or she is hired on a one-shot basis. Realtors and investment brokers are examples of special agents. The distinction between general and special agents is primarily a matter of degree, depending on the agent's continuity of employment.

Types of Principals

Principals are classified as either disclosed or undisclosed. In the usual agency transaction the third person knows that the agent is acting for a principal and the principal's identity. The principal's identity may be important because the third person may be relying on the principal's credit and reputation. The agent's identity is unimportant because the transaction is between the principal and the third person, and the agent is not a party to the deal. When the third person knows the principal's identity, the principal is referred to as a **disclosed principal**.

Sometimes a principal may not wish to reveal his or her identity and the existence of the agency relation to the third person. When the third person has no knowledge that the agent is working for the particular principal, the principal is called an **undisclosed principal**. In these situations the agent's identity becomes more important than the principal's identity. Because the agent purports to be acting on his or her own, the agent is a party to the contract along with the principal.

Agency Distinguished

There are many relationships in which one person acts for the benefit of another that are distinguished from agency. It is important to distinguish an agency relationship from other arrangements. If it is an agency, certain legal consequences attach. If it is some other relation, significantly different legal consequences may attach.

In determining whether a relationship is an agency, the name the parties give it is not controlling. The *substance* of the relationship is controlling. Whether a relationship is an agency does not depend on clever draftsmanship. Otherwise people could label their relationships to avoid liability.

What distinguishes agency from other similar relations is the power of control retained by the principal over the agent's activities. Relations usually distinguished from agency may become agency relations if this power of control is present.

Because they render services while pursuing independent occupations, *independent contractors* usually are not agents. When working for employers, these contractors agree to accomplish only certain results and are responsible only for their final products. Employers hire them by the job and do not control the details of performance. This relationship differs from the principal-agent relationships, because principals control their agents' contractual dealings. Because independent contractors usually are not agents, their employers are not liable to the contractors' creditors nor to persons harmed by the contractors' negligence. But an individual contractor may become an agent or servant if the employer retains control over the details of performance. Whether an independent contractor becomes an agent depends on the degree and character of the control retained by the employer over the work done, and no absolute dividing line can be drawn between the two. An employer who hires an independent contractor to perform dangerous work or to take on duties which by law cannot be delegated to others remains liable for injuries caused by the contractor.

Creation of Agency Relations

Capacity

Any person having capacity to consent can become a principal or an agent. A principal has capacity only to appoint an agent to perform activities that the principal may lawfully perform. A person is not allowed to accomplish through an agent what he or she is not allowed to accomplish alone. A statute may restrict a person's capacity to be an agent. Licensing statutes may limit the capacity of someone to act as an agent by requiring a license to engage in a particular business. For example, most states require real-estate brokers to be licensed before they may lawfully engage in the practice of buying and selling real estate for others.

Formalities

Generally, no formalities are required to create an agency. Payment need not be promised or made to the agent for representing the principal. Uncompensated agents are called *gratuitous* agents. The transactions they conduct are as binding on their principals as dealings conducted by *paid* agents. For example, if Penelope, knowing that her roommate is going by the bookstore after classes, asks her roommate to stop and buy a book on Penelope's account, the bookstore is entitled to payment from Penelope.

Usually it is not necessary to create an agency relation in writing. But written authorization often is desirable. Prudent businesspeople spell out their agency relations in carefully drafted written instruments. Written authorization, sometimes called a *power of attorney*, is necessary in a few situations. (For more on power of attorney, see Chapter 36.)

Rights and Duties between Principal and Agent

Agent's Right to Compensation

Unless it appears that the agent's services are intended to be gratuitous, the agent is entitled to compensation for the general value of his or her services. The agent's right to compensation usually is provided by contract, with matters of interpretation determined according to the ordinary rules of contract law.

In the absence of an agreement, there is an implied obligation on a principal to pay for services rendered by the agent when the services are customarily paid for. If the agency contract does not provide compensation, a promise to pay is inferred from the fact that the agent's services are rendered at the principal's request or have been accepted by the principal.

When customary and practical, the principal is obligated to keep and render accounts of the compensation owed to the agent. This allows the agent to know what he or she is entitled to and serves to implement the agent's right to compensation. Like the right to compensation, this right to an accounting depends on custom and usage. For example, principals employing traveling sales agents whose compensation is based on completed sales are in the better position to maintain sales records. Therefore they customarily keep the accounts. When this custom exists, an individual principal is required to maintain the records. But agents such as real-estate brokers and lawyers, who own their own businesses and have complete knowledge of all transactions, ordinarily keep their own accounts. Principals employing them are relieved of accounting responsibilities. But principals may be required to maintain certain records for tax purposes. The parties also may state in their agency contract who is to maintain and render accounts.

As another incident of the principal's obligation to compensate the agent, the principal is obligated to assist and cooperate with the agent and to do nothing that unreasonably prevents the agent's performance. This duty of the principal to refrain from unreasonably interfering with the agent's work allows the agent to render performance and be compensated. If the principal unreasonably interferes with the agent's performance, the agent is entitled to the compensation that would have been earned if he or she had been permitted to perform as originally requested. Only the principal's unreasonable interference is prohibited, and what is "unreasonable" depends on the circumstances. Unreasonable interference may be improper commands to the agent or the principal's conduct toward third persons. The parties also may specify what constitutes an unreasonable interference.

For example, ordinarily nothing is said by the parties about competition by the principal, and the principal is allowed to compete with the agent because competition is not considered unreasonable. But if the parties provide that the principal is not to compete either directly or by hiring other agents, competition by the principal is an unreasonable interference and constitutes a material breach of the agency agreement. An example of this type of agency contract is an exclusive real-estate listing contract between a homeowner and a real-estate broker, providing that the owner not compete against the broker by attempting to sell the property through his or her own efforts or by listing the property with other brokers.

In addition to compensating the agent for services rendered, the principal is obligated to indemnify or reimburse the agent for any authorized expenses or losses suffered by the agent while acting for the principal. An **indemnity** is an obligation or duty resting on one person to make good any loss or damage incurred by another while acting for his or her benefit. It is simply the shifting of an economic loss to the person primarily responsible for it. The guiding principle is that the true benefactor should bear the burden of payment. In agency relations the agent customarily incurs expenses on behalf of the principal. The agent is exposed to claims as a result of being designated an agent by the principal. Because the principal originally put the agent in this position, the principal bears the financial burden.

The agent's right to indemnity usually is provided in the agency agreement, and the parties may provide that the agent bears the risk of loss and the expenses of performance of his or her duties. But if no provision is made for indemnity, the right is inferred when the agent incurs an expense, suffers a loss, or assumes a liability while acting in an authorized manner. For example, the agent is entitled to reimbursement from the principal for any authorized payment that is necessary to the agent's performance. This right to reimbursement does not arise until payment is made.

When the principal is liable to the agent for compensation, reimbursement, or indemnity, the agent is permitted a lien or security interest in the principal's goods or money lawfully possessed by the agent. This lien only extends to the amount of the agent's compensation or indemnity and entitles the agent to retain possession of the property or the proceeds from its sale until the agent is paid what is owed. (See Figure 35-1.)

Agent's Fiduciary Duty of Loyalty

Because the agent acts solely for the principal's benefit in all matters connected with the agency, the principal-agent relation is called a *fiduciary relationship*, and the agent is referred to as the principal's fiduciary. A **fiduciary** is simply someone who acts for someone else or holds property for the benefit of another. An agency relation is just one form of fiduciary relation. Other examples are executors and administrators of estates as well as trustees.

The important element of the fiduciary relation is that the fiduciary acts for another person. Because someone else puts trust and confidence in the fiduciary, the fiduciary is held to very high standards of conduct. Certain fiduciary duties are imposed for the protection of the other person's property and interests, and the courts do not tolerate any change of these duties without the consent of the other person. A fiduciary is under a general duty to act for the other person's benefit on matters within the relationship. The agent,

therefore, is under a fiduciary obligation to act solely for the principal's benefit in all matters affecting the agency relation.

As part of the fiduciary duty, the agent must give undivided loyalty to the principal. Such fidelity is fundamental to the agency relation, because without it there would be no assurance that the principal's interests would be promoted. The agent must act with the utmost good faith solely for the principal's benefit with no adverse or competing interests on his or her part. The agent must not allow his or her personal interests to conflict with the principal's. He or she may not compete directly with the principal without permission or indirectly by working for the principal's compensation without the principal's consent.

Because the agent is bound to act solely for the principal, the agent must forward all agency profits to the principle. All benefits resulting from the agency relation belong to the principal. The agent may not secretly profit from his or her performance. All profits belong to the principal. The agent may not use the principal's property for his or her own benefit without the principal's consent. Furthermore, the agent may not take advantage of an opportunity rightfully belonging to the principal. For example, a purchasing agent, authorized to buy property for the principal, cannot buy for himself or herself any property that the principal would be interested in buying. Any such property bought belongs to the principal even though held by the agent.

It follows that the agent cannot deal with the principal as an adverse party, unless the principal consents to such a transaction. For example, a

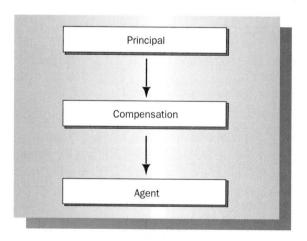

FIGURE 35-1

Principal's Duty Toward the Agent

sales agent authorized to sell the principal's property to third persons cannot buy the property for himself or herself with out the principal's consent. Even if the agent pays a fair price, the principal may cancel the sale and recover the property or obtain any profits made by the agent in any resale of the property to an innocent purchaser.

Because the agent cannot deal with the principal as an adverse party, the agent also cannot represent an adverse party in a transaction with the principal unless both parties are fully informed and agree to the arrangement. Such dual agencies, involving the agent representing two adverse parties, have a great potential for fraud. Any transaction negotiated by a double agent is voidable at the option of the party having no knowledge of the agency.

The agent's duty of loyalty also extends to the use of confidential information, such as the principals' trade secrets and customer lists. The agent may not use or communicate information confidentially given to him or her by the principal.

The following case illustrates the application of an agent's fiduciary duty of loyalty.

DOUGLAS V. AZTEC PETROLEUM CORP.
Court of Appeals of Texas
695 S.W.2d 312 (1985)

BACKGROUND: In February 1980 Richard Seib, president of Aztec Petroleum Corporation (defendant-appellee), engaged Donnie Douglas (plaintiff-appellant) to buy a 4,900-acre block of oil and gas leases for Aztec in Anderson County, Texas. For his services Douglas was to receive $5,000, together with an assignment of an overriding royalty interest in the leases obtained.

On February 23, 1980 Aztec sent Douglas a $5,000 payment in advance for buying the leases, and two other checks totaling $124,180 to pay for leases. Douglas immediately went to work getting the block together. By the end of March all but a few tracts had been leased.

Douglas had a $60 personal checkbook balance when he made the agreement with Aztec. As soon as Aztec's money arrived, Douglas put it in his own account and embarked on a spending spree. He bought two cars and a boat, paid numerous personal expenses, and retired two bank notes out of the account recently filled with Aztec money. Later a photocopy of each check was sent to Aztec with the payee altered to show that a lessor had received the money actually spent on personal items.

Douglas did not put all of Aztec's money in the bank. During the acquisition period Aztec sent Douglas $343,557.36. Forty-two thousand dollars was kept as cash by Douglas and never deposited. When he made the final accounting to Aztec in June 1980, Douglas sent bogus receipts to show that the cash went to lessors. He later admitted at trial that he did not really obtain receipts for cash payments but that his wife had forged all of those sent to Aztec by transposing signatures of lessors from other documents.

Once most of the leases were obtained, Douglas became very anxious to receive his override royalty. However, Seib kept badgering Douglas for an accounting. Douglas concocted a false account by using forged receipts and altering the amount and payee of the checks to plug in whatever figure was necessary to come to $338,557.35, the amount committed to his charge. He then took the false account, together with the forged receipts and altered checks supporting it, to Aztec's Dallas headquarters.

Upon receipt of the account, Seib contacted some of the lessors and discovered several who were not paid the amounts reported. With this knowledge he refused to convey the override royalty to Douglas.

Douglas sued Aztec for the override royalty. Aztec denied liability and counterclaimed for actual and exemplary damages. A jury verdict resulted in a judgment denying Douglas the override royalty and awarding Aztec $107,834.57 in actual damages and $100,000 in exemplary damages. Douglas appealed to the Texas Court of Appeals.

Bass, Justice

[B]oth Aztec's defensive pleadings and counterclaim state facts sufficient to allege Douglas' breach of fiduciary duty. Breach of fiduciary duty is a tort.

It is uncontroverted that Douglas was Aztec's agent. An agency is a fiduciary relationship. The law requires more of a fiduciary than arms-length marketplace ethics. He owes his principal loyalty and good faith; integrity of the strictest kind; fair, honest dealing; and the duty not to conceal matters which might influence his actions to his principal's prejudice. He is obligated to exercise a high degree of care to conserve his principal's money and to pay it only to those entitled to receive it. He must keep his principal's funds as a separate and identifiable account. The agent must make an accounting to his principal of any money that has come into his possession because of his agency. A fiduciary has no right to make merchandise of the confidence reposed in him.

Douglas' own testimony is a startling catalogue of violations of almost every fiduciary duty.

The evidence in this case overwhelmingly and conclusively demonstrates Douglas' breach of trust. Douglas' own testimony establishes it. We therefore conclude that Douglas' breach of fiduciary duty is established as a matter of law. It is a fundamental principle of our law that an agent who acts adversely to his principal or otherwise breaches his fiduciary obligation is not entitled to compensation for his services. In *Jackson v. Williams*, the court cited with approval sec. 469 Restatement of Agency which states:

An agent is entitled to no compensation for conduct which is disobedient or which is a breach of this duty of loyalty; if such conduct constitutes a willful and deliberate breach of his contract of service, he is not entitled to compensation even for properly performed services for which no compensation is apportioned.

The override represented compensation due Douglas for "honest and forthright" performance of his agency, a duty imposed on every fiduciary. The court's judgment that Douglas is not entitled to the overriding royalty interest is based upon conclusive evidence of his willful breach of fiduciary duty. The court's denial of the override to Douglas is a proper legal consequence of his established infidelity.

Honest and forthright performance is a covenant implied in every contract. But the fiduciary relationship imposes an even more rigorous standard on the agent—loyalty, good faith and integrity of the strictest kind. Douglas admits diverting large amounts of Aztec money to his personal use. He acknowledges preparing a bogus account. Aztec's accountant testified that, excluding Douglas' $5,000 compensation and $2,903.34 legitimate leasing expense, $107,874.57 out of the $343,557.36 did not go for the purchase of oil leases. There is ample legally sufficient evidence from which the jury could decide that Douglas willfully misappropriated that sum. The evidence is uncontroverted that he failed to account for it.

Douglas seeks to set aside the jury's award of exemplary damages arguing that exemplary damages are not recoverable for breach of contract. However, punitive damages are proper when a coincident tort is pleaded and proven. We should not say to defaulting fiduciaries that the most for which they can be held accountable in equity are the profits which would have remained theirs had they not been called to account.

Aztec alleged and conclusively proved breach of fiduciary duty, a tort justifying the award of exemplary damages. Therefore we hold the trial court did not err in awarding exemplary damages as found by the jury.

DECISION: The Texas Court of Appeals affirmed the trial court judgment against Douglas.

Agent's Duty to Obey

Because the principal's control over the agent's activity is an important element of the agency relation, the agent must obey any reasonable instruction from the principal regarding the agent's performance. The "reasonableness" of an instruction depends on ethical and legal considerations. For example, a sales agent need not obey an order to misrepresent the quality of merchandise, for such an order is illegal and unethical.

If the principal issues an ambiguous instruction, the agent should seek clarification while giving it a reasonable interpretation consistent with trade practice and prior dealings. Reasonable instructions that are clear, precise, and imperative must be strictly followed, or the agent is liable for any losses resulting from disobedience. Any violation of such a clear directive is not excused by custom or usage in the business. Furthermore, the agent's motives are immaterial to his or her liability. The fact that the agent disobeys in good faith, intending to benefit the principal, does not relieve the agent of liability for any resulting loss. But the agent may disobey instructions to respond to an emergency that the agent did not create, if communication with the principal is impractical.

Agent's Duty to Use Skill and Care

The agent must use whatever skill and care is required to perform the principal's business. If the agent fails to exercise reasonable skill and care, the principal may recover for any loss or damage resulting from the agent's negligence. The principal is permitted to rely on the agent to perform the assigned responsibilities properly, and the agent is in the better position to know whether he or she possesses the qualifications to perform the job. The duty of skill and care arises from what is commonly accepted as the customs and experience in everyday living. If someone hires another to perform a job, he or she usually expects that the job will be done skillfully and carefully. Thus the agent should possess and exercise the necessary skill and care to perform the principal's business. For example, an insurance broker should know something of the trade, the form of policy, the nature of the risk, the solvency of the underwriter, and all general matters affecting the contract, or the broker is liable for negligently failing to provide adequate insurance protection for the insured.

The agent is only required to exercise reasonable and ordinary skill and care in the performance of the agency objectives. He or she is held to a standard of skill and care ordinarily possessed by persons engaged in the same business or occupation. However, if the agent claims certain special skills, he or she is held to a higher standard of care that is commensurate with the claimed specialization.

The following case shows the duty of diligence in a contemporary setting.

MARKLAND V. TRAVEL TRAVEL SOUTHFIELD, INC.

Missouri Court of Appeals
810 S.W.2d 81 (1991)

BACKGROUND: The Marklands requested a travel agent, Travel Travel, to arrange a vacation for them in St. Croix. Travel Travel made travel arrangements for the Marklands on Eastern Airlines and Flyfaire Vacations, a subsidiary of Eastern. Included in the package were vouchers supplied by the airlines that could be used to pay for the Marklands' hotel accommodations. The Marklands paid Travel Travel $6,548, which included the cost of airfare and accommodations plus a 10 percent commission. Ten days into their stay in St. Croix, the Marklands were informed by their hotel that their vouchers were no longer good because Eastern and Flyfaire had gone bankrupt. The Marklands were thus required to pay an additional $4,900 for their accommodations. Also, they had to spend an additional $1,756 so that they could return to the United States on another airline.

The Marklands sued Travel Travel for $6,656, the amount of damages they claim to have suffered. Travel Travel, which had used the Marklands' money to pay Eastern and Flyfaire, argued that it was not responsible for the Marklands' loss. Travel Travel pointed to a provision in its contract stating that the agency was not responsible for any breach of contract by the airlines, and urging the customer to purchase travel insurance. The trial court awarded the Marklands only $654.80, the amount of Travel Travel's commission. The Marklands appealed.

Pudlowski, Presiding Judge

The weight of authority in the United States holds that a travel agent who arranges vacation plans and therefore acts as more than a "ticket agent" is a special agent of the traveler for the purposes of that one transaction between the parties. As agent, a travel agency has a duty to use reasonable efforts to apprise a customer of information material to the agency which the travel agency has notice the customer would desire. However, "[t]he scope of this duty of disclosure will be limited, naturally, to what is reasonable on any given instance." *Rookard v. Mexicoach.*

In *United Airlines, Inc. v. Lerner*, the court determined that "[w]hile there is not duty of investigation, the travel agent must disclose all information the agent learns which is material to the object of the agency." The court held that the travel agency did not breach a duty by failing to warn the traveler of the potential for weather conditions causing temporary road closures thereby interrupting the traveler's ski vacation. The court reasoned that "[t]he law requires that agents be loyal not prescient." Also, where the travel agency is unaware that the vacation is not an impossibility, the travel agency is not required to inform its clients of potential danger ahead. Based upon this analysis, the Court concluded that a travel agent has a duty to disclose reasonably obtainable relevant information to the traveler unless that information is so clearly obvious and apparent to the traveler, that as a matter of law, the travel agent would not be negligent in failing to disclose it.

In the case at bar, the evidence revealed that the agent, Travel Travel, derived its information about Eastern's problem from the same sources as the Marklands. It had no "inside information." The threat of either a labor strike or bankruptcy of Eastern Airlines or its subsidiary, Flyfaire, was only a potential occurrence possibility. Both the principal and the agent were aware of this likelihood. In addition, the agent advised the principals, although in very small print, that they could protect themselves from loss by purchasing travel insurance. In addition, Travel Travel, in strict compliance with the requests of the Marklands, performed all of its duties. The Marklands requested air transportation to and from St. Croix and specific hotel accommodations. Within three or four days the travel agent had made such arrangements. In connection with the arrangements, the Marklands received the confirmation of the plan, which enumerated the airline and the hotel, the time of arrival and departure. The principals were obviously satisfied with the arrangements and sent their check to the agency some ten days later. They had approximately six weeks to change their accommodations but did not and they fetched the documents one week prior to their departure.

DECISION: The appeals court affirmed the trial court decision.

Agent's Duty to Inform and Account

It makes sense that parties in agency relations should communicate with each other. Therefore a duty is imposed on the agent to communicate to the principal on anything affecting the principal's interests. The agent must make a reasonable attempt to inform the principal of matters relating to any agency transaction about which the agent should realize the principal would want to know.

For example, a real estate agent who is authorized to sell the principal's property at a specified price and on specified terms should inform the principal if he or she knows of someone who will pay a higher price or agree to better terms. Furthermore, the agent should disclose any information that disqualifies the agent from effectively promoting the principal's interests. If the agent is unable to undertake the principal's interests, he or she must

---

ETHICS
The Agent in the Middle

Agents are expected to act on behalf of the principal and to put the principal's interests first. But sometimes the scope of duties is not so clear. Consider the case of a travel agent who is the "agent" of the airlines, but who also serves a large corporate client. The corporate client may demand that the agent make use of so-called fare loopholes such as back-to-back ticketing or hidden city ticketing. Hidden city ticketing operates in the following way. You want to fly from Chicago to Boston. The price of the ticket one way is $400. But you discover that the same airline has a flight from Chicago to Bangor, Maine with a stop in Boston. The cost of the ticket to Bangor is $300. You buy the ticket to Bangor and get off in Boston and don't use the rest of the ticket. The rules of the airlines prohibit the use of fare loopholes.

Assume that the travel manager for your university has determined that if the university travel agency uses hidden city ticketing it will save the university $500,000 in travel costs each year. The travel manager then demands that the agency use the loophole. What should the agency do? How would you handle this problem?

FIGURE 35-2

Agent's Duties toward the Principal

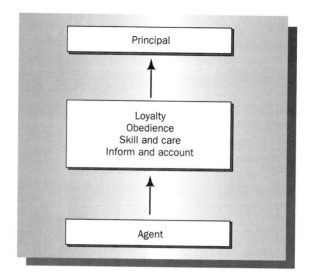

inform the principal. Even if the agent is merely ill for a day, the agent's duty to inform requires the agent to notify the principal of the fact so that the principal may make other arrangements.

It follows that if the agent must communicate with the principal, he or she also must keep and render an account of money or other property that the agent receives. This account includes anything received from the principal as well as anything obtained from third persons for the principal. The agent is liable to the principal if he or she does not properly account for all funds coming into the agent's possession during the agency relation.

Although it is ordinarily the principal's duty to keep his or her own accounts, the duty shifts to the agent if the agent is entrusted with funds or property or is required to make collections and expenditures. The manner of accounting need not be formal or meet technical accounting requirements. The method of bookkeeping depends on what is normally done in the business or is accepted by the principal.

Implicit in the duty to account is the agent's duty not to mix the principal's money or property with his or her own. The reason for this requirement is to make any accounting more accurate. Thus the agent may not put the principal's money in his or her own bank account or in a joint account unless the principal agrees to such an arrangement. To allow otherwise would make it difficult to determine whether it was the principal's or the agent's money that was deposited. (See Figure 35-2.)

The following case illustrates the judicial approach to disclosure within the context of the broker-investor relationship. The case is also included because it brings together many of the agent's fiduciary duties.

McKEEHAN V. WITTELS

Court of Appeals of Missouri

508 S.W.2d 277 (1977)

BACKGROUND: Dorothy McKeehan (plaintiff), looking for investment opportunities, dealt directly with Malcolm and Jacob Wittels Investment Company (defendants). In response to the Wittelses' urging, McKeehan entrusted $28,813 to them. The Wittelses invested this money in a type of investment security known as a deed of trust in property. After the investments matured, McKeehan repeatedly demanded that her funds be returned. The Wittelses, who knew of McKeehan's instructions, disregarded them. The Wittelses renewed the investments without her consent and against her expressed wishes. Additionally, tax liens existed on all properties in the investments, and there was strong evidence that the Wittelses were aware of these tax liens. McKeehan sued the Wittelses for damages, alleging that they breached their fiduciary duties to her. The trial court entered judgment in favor of McKeehan in the amount of $29,942.65 actual damages and $25,000 punitive damages. The Wittelses appealed to the Missouri Court of Appeals.

McMillian, Judge

[P]laintiff pleads that defendants breached their fiduciary duty by deliberately failing to follow her instructions, failing to disclose essential information affecting the security of her investments, and misrepresenting certain facts for the purpose of furthering their own financial position.

Loyalty to their trust is firmly exacted of all agents by law, and when one uses his position for his own ends, regardless of the welfare of his principal, he becomes responsible for a resultant loss, as if he unscrupulously handles money or property confided to him to benefit himself. An agent cannot ignore the directions given to him as to how the business put in to his hands shall be transacted, and cannot use his agency for his own advantage, to the detriment of the principal. Likewise, a fiduciary relationship between principal and agent obligates the agent to fully disclose all material facts to the principal, to strictly avoid misrepresentation and in all respects to act with utmost good faith.

[The] evidence is sufficient to sustain a finding that defendants Malcolm Wittels and Wittels Investment Co., knowingly failed to follow plaintiff's explicit instructions regarding the handling of her investments.

We also find ample evidence to sustain a finding that Malcolm and Jacob Wittels and Wittels Investment Co. breached their fiduciary duty to plaintiff by failing to disclose material facts regarding her investments. It is the established law in this jurisdiction that the existence of a confidential or fiduciary relationship between principal and agent obligates the agent to make a complete and full disclosure of all material facts concerning the transaction which might affect the principal's decision regarding his or her investments. Similarly, it is a breach of fiduciary duty for an agent to occupy a position antagonistic to his principal.

Plaintiff's evidence strongly supports the trial court's finding that the defendants Malcolm and Jacob Wittels and Wittels Investment Company did occupy a position antagonistic to plaintiff and consequently failed to disclose all necessary facts to plaintiff regarding her investments. The record is clear that as to certain parcels of property, defendants sold the first deed of trust to plaintiff and held on to the more profitable second deed themselves. Plaintiff also introduced exhibits and testimony that tax liens existed on all of the parcels of property held under the deeds of trust purchased from defendants. Malcolm Wittels testified that he knew that a tax lien was considered to be a first lien on the property. There is strong evidence that Malcolm and Jacob Wittels were aware of the existence and accrual of tax liens on the properties at the time plaintiff purchased and held the deed of trust. When the deed of trust was given to Dorothy McKeehan under the circumstances shown in the evidence, she was justified in believing she was purchasing a first deed of trust constituting a first lien on the property and not subject to any prior tax liens. The record clearly reflects the extreme unlikelihood that defendants Malcolm and Jacob Wittels were unaware of these tax liens. Their failure to disclose the tax liens to plaintiff at the time of sale and the failure to disclose the accrual of these tax liens is more than sufficient evidence to sustain the trial court's finding and judgment with respect to these defendants.

We have carefully read the record and have concluded that there is substantial evidence to support the trial court's finding that defendants Malcolm and Jacob Wittels and Wittels Investment Company breached their fiduciary duty to plaintiff.

DECISION: The Missouri Court of Appeals ruled in favor of McKeehan and affirmed the trial court judgment.

CONCEPT SUMMARY
The Agent's Rights and Duties

The agent's right to compensation requires the principal to:

- Pay the agent for services
- Keep records
- Render an accounting
- Not interfere with the agent's performance
- Indemnify agent for expenses

To enforce this right, the agent is permitted a lien on the principal's goods or money.
The agent's fiduciary duty requires the agent to:

- Be loyal to the principal
- Avoid conflicts of interest
- Not compete with the principal
- Not deal with the principal as an adverse party
- Not represent an adverse party in dealings with the principal
- Not disclose confidential information

If the agent violates this duty, the agent forfeits all right to compensation.
The agent's duty to obey requires the agent to:

- Follow reasonable instructions of the principal

The agent's duty to use skill and care requires the agent to:

- Use reasonable skill and care

The agent's duty to inform and account requires the agent to:

- Communicate with the principal on matters affecting the agency
- Disclose information to the principal
- Account for property and funds entrusted to the agent
- Not commingle the principal's funds with those of the agent

Review Questions and Problems

Key Terms

agency	disclosed principal
agent	undisclosed principal
principal	indemnity
general agent	fiduciary
special agent	

Discussion Questions

1. What is an agency relationship? Who is the principal and who is the agent?

2. What distinguishes an agent from an independent contractor?

3. Why is an agency relationship a fiduciary relationship?

4. What duties does a principal owe an agent? What duties does an agent owe a principal?

Review Problems

1. Penelope had inspected equipment to be sold at an auction. She planned to go to the auction and try to buy three pieces of equipment. On the day of the auction her friend Andrew gratuitously offered to go to the auction for Penelope and to bid on the equipment for her. Penelope authorized Andrew to bid up to $10,000 for each of the three pieces she wanted. Andrew acquired the first piece for Pene-

lope for $9,000. He bid on the second piece on his own behalf and bought it for $9,500. Andrew left the auction before the third piece was offered. It was sold for $7,000. Is Andrew the agent of Penelope? Explain. If so, has Andrew violated any of the duties that an agent owes a principal? Explain.

2. Owner orally authorized Agent to sell his house. Agent completed a sale of the house to Buyer. When Buyer attempted to enforce the contract against Owner, Buyer was told that the contract was not enforceable because Owner's agency relation with the Agent was not in writing. Must Owner have given Agent written authorization?

3. Owner listed his house with Penelope, a real-estate broker, granting Penelope an exclusive right to sell Owner's house. Penelope entered negotiations with Buyer, who seemed interested in purchasing the property. Buyer found the price agreeable. But he insisted on including a clause in the sales contract giving him the right to cancel the contract if he could not get a loan to finance his purchase. At the closing, Buyer exercised his right to cancel, giving as his reason the inability to procure a loan. Penelope turned to Owner and claimed that she was entitled to her commission even though the sale did not go through. Must Owner pay Penelope a commission?

4. Peter authorized Arnon, a grain broker, to buy for Peter at the market 20,000 bushels of wheat. Arnon had in storage at the time 5,000 bushels belonging to John, who had authorized Arnon to sell for him. Arnon also had 15,000 bushels which she owned. Arnon transferred these 20,000 bushels to Peter's name and charged Peter the current market price. Shortly thereafter and before Peter had used or sold the wheat, the market price declined sharply. Peter refused to pay for the wheat and tried to cancel the contract. Can Peter do this? Explain.

Case Problems

1. Julius and Olga Sylvester owned an unimproved piece of land near King of Prussia, Pennsylvania. They were approached by Beck, a real-estate broker, who asked if they were willing to sell their land, stating that an oil company was interested in buying, renting, or leasing the property. The Sylvesters said that they were only interested in selling, and they authorized Beck to sell the property for $15,000. Several weeks later Beck phoned the Sylvesters and offered to buy the property for himself for $14,000. Olga asked, "What happened to the oil company?" and Beck responded, "They are not interested. You want too much money for it." The Sylvesters sold the property to Beck, who sold it to Epstein for $25,000. When the Sylvesters learned that Beck had realized a huge profit in a quick resale of the property, they sued Beck claiming that he owed them the $9,000 profit. Does Beck owe the Sylvesters the money?

2. Bucholtz engaged Sirotkin Travel to arrange a trip for herself and her husband to Las Vegas. The agency advised her that they would stay at the Aladdin Hotel. Changes were made in the arrival and departure time of their flight from that originally stated. At the airport the tags on the Bucholtz's baggage were switched so that the baggage was not directed to the Aladdin Hotel. They were required to take alternative accommodations at a motel located about a half mile out of town. This created additional expense and inconvenience for Bucholtz and her husband in traveling to places of interest in town. Bucholtz sued Sirotkin for damages resulting from the Bucholtzs' inconvenience and discomfort.

3. Roberto was the administrator of Brown County General Hospital. Pursuant to his employment contract, the hospital established a "deferred compensation" savings account into which the hospital was required to make periodic deposits. Roberto's employment contract provided that he would be entitled to the funds in the account immediately upon the termination of his employment. Roberto was fired for allegedly embezzling over $54,000 from the hospital. Roberto admitted some of the charges and paid over $54,000 to the court pending a determination of whether the hospital was entitled to the money. Roberto claimed, however, that he was still entitled to the funds in the deferred compensation account. The hospital refused to pay. Is Roberto entitled to the money in the account?

36

The Effect of Agency Relations

Contractual Dealings: Principal and
   Third Parties
Contractual Dealings: Agents and
   Third Parties

Agent's Tortious Activity
Termination of Agency

Chapter 35 examined the nature of the principal-agent relation by focusing on how the two parties create their relation and the rights and duties they owe each other. But there is more to the agency relation. The principal hires the agent to interact with others as the principal's representative. This interaction is the essence of the agency. It is the reason the agent is hired. The agent's interactions with others affect the principal's legal obligations when the agent (1) makes contracts for the principal with third persons or (2) commits torts during the agent's employment that harm others. When the agent acts in these ways, the legal picture adds a third dimension. The legal consequences of this interaction attach not only to the principal and the agent, but to the third person, affecting the rights and duties of each person toward the others. This chapter explores how these legal consequences affect all three individuals. The chapter also examines the ending of the agency relation and how it affects the rights of the parties.

Contractual Dealings: Principal and Third Parties

The contracts made by any authorized agent for a principal are as binding on the principal as they would have been had the principal entered into them in person.

An agent's authority is conferred by various methods. The principal may expressly authorize the agent's action. The principal may indicate to the agent by conduct that the agent has authority to undertake certain transactions. Authority is established also if others can reasonably infer from the principal's conduct that the principal authorizes the agent's activity. Even when the principal does not authorize someone to act as an agent, a third party may establish authority if the principal later authorizes transactions done for him or her.

Actual Authority

Actual authority is the power of an agent to affect the principal's legal relations by acts done according to the principal's show of consent to the agent. The principal may consent by any means that causes the agent to understand what the principal wants the agent to do. If the agent's actual authority is stated in words, it is referred to as **express authority**. If the agent's actual authority is communicated by the principal's conduct toward the agent, it is called **implied authority**. The legal effect of the two is the same: The agent is empowered to change the principal's legal relations with third persons. For example, if a businessperson tells a secretary to accept customer payments, the secretary has express authority to collect payments as instructed. If the secretary also buys office supplies and the principal pays without objection, the secretary or the seller may reasonably infer that the principal authorizes continued purchases of office supplies. In both situations the principal is obligated to others by the secretary's actions.

Express Authority   The clearest example of express authority is the *power of attorney*. A **power of attorney** is a formal written instrument conferring authority upon an agent. Powers of attorney often are used because a third person entering into a specific, major transaction with an agent may require evidence of the agent's authority. In these situations the authority may be set forth in a form that is familiar and convenient to people in the business. The acts authorized usually require the execution of specifically described documents. For example, banks and other professional lenders that deal regularly with borrowers' agents have standard forms for the purpose of assuring themselves of the authority of agents to borrow on their principals' credit. Because of absence, sickness, age, or lack of interest, people widely delegate the management of their affairs to others. Interpretation of the activities included in these powers often is a problem.

Informal written expressions of authority often are included in standard-form contracts that the agent negotiates with third persons. Known as merger clauses, integration clauses, or exculpatory clauses, these statements serve explicitly to limit an agent's authority to make only those agreements contained in the standard-form contract. Figure 36-1 is an example of a merger clause.

Unauthorized transactions made by the agent with a third person, who has notice of this limitation on the agent's authority, are not binding on the principal. Obligations undertaken in violation of this express limitation of authority are the agent's.

Implied Authority   In most agency relations it is impossible to express every detail of the agent's authority. For example, if a storeowner hires someone to manage the business, it is impossible to describe every single management function. For the sake of flexibility, the agent is allowed additional implied authority to perform activities that he or she or a third party might reasonably infer are incidental or necessary to carry out the principal's instructions.

Several factors determine whether implied authority exists. The circumstances generally considered by courts are customary trade usages, the principal's practices with other agents in similar situations, and earlier experiences of the principal and the particular agent. For example, a question of whether a particular salesperson has the implied authority to extend warranties on merchandise sold to third persons may be answered by examining what similar salespeople in the trade usually do, what other salespeople employed by the principal usually do, and what the principal has permitted that particular salesperson to do in the past.

Although the principal implicitly authorizes the agent to do whatever is ordinarily required to accomplish the job, sometimes as the job progresses the agent confronts an emergency. In such an emergency, the agent can reasonably infer that the principal consents to the agent's

---

It is hereby further agreed that there are no prior writings, verbal negotiations, understandings, representations, or agreements between the parties not hererin expressed, and no agent of Seller is authorized to make or enter into on Seller's behalf any writings, verbal negotiations, understandings, representations, or agreements not here expressed.

FIGURE 36-1

A Typical Merger Clause

undertaking whatever is required to protect the principal's interests. Authorization of the agent's activity is implied in these situations. This implied authority exists only when the threat to the principal's business is sudden and unexpected and when contract with the principal or superior officer is impractical. It extends only to activities that the emergency makes necessary.

Apparent Authority

Authority also exists if the principal's conduct causes third persons reasonably to believe that the agent is authorized. This rule permits third parties to rely on the principal's manifestation in dealing with an agent. This type of authority is called **apparent authority**. Its effect on the principal's liability to third persons is the same as actual authority, because both types empower the agent to affect the principal's legal relations with others. The adjectives "actual" and "apparent" denote only the viewpoints used in interpreting the principal's conduct. Actual authority is determined from the agent's viewpoint. Apparent authority is determined from the third person's viewpoint.

The agent's apparent authority may arise in various ways. It may result from the principal's statement to a third person or from the principal's allowance of the agent's activities. It may be established from the principal's permission to the agent to do something under circumstances creating a reputation of authority in the area in which the agent acts. Earlier dealings between the agent and third persons might lead a third person reasonably to infer that the agent is authorized. For example, a customer might reasonably believe that a salesper-

---

CONCEPT SUMMARY
Types of Authority

Actual Authority	Principal actually consents to agent's authority in advance.
• Express authority	Principal communicates authority to agent expressly, either orally or in writing.
	Example: Principal exercises power of attorney that expressly grants agent authority to perform certain acts on principal's behalf.
• Implied authority	Agent's authority to perform certain acts on principal's behalf is implied from principal's conduct or from the circumstances.
	Example: Store owner hires employee to manage store. Employee's implied authority might include acts reasonably necessary to manage store, including ordering equipment, supplies, and inventory and hiring employees.
Apparent Authority	Principal's conduct to *third party* gives third party reasonable impression that agent has authority to perform certain acts on principal's behalf. Principal is estopped from denying that purported agent had actual authority to perform such acts.
	Example: Store owner hires employee to manage store, and orders business cards for the employee that identify him as the store's "manager." It is customary in the business for managers to be able to order equipment, although the manager's contract specifically requires him to get the owner's approval for any equipment order. The manager signs a contract ordering equipment from a supplier who is not aware that the manager does not have the authority to execute the order. If the owner disapproves of the order, he will still be bound by it. Because of the custom in the trade, he will be estopped from denying that the manager had the authority to order the equipment.

---

son in a department store is authorized to transact business in an adjacent department. But apparent authority cannot be established by the agent's statements alone. If it could, anyone might confer upon himself or herself authority to obligate others simply by acting and talking like an agent.

The doctrine of apparent authority is discussed and illustrated in the case that follows.

STATE SECURITY INSURANCE CO. V. BURGOS
Supreme Court of Illinois
583 N.E.2d 547 (1991)

BACKGROUND: Mr. and Mrs. Burgos purchased an insurance policy from plaintiff State Security Insurance Co. to protect them from liability arising in connection with the operation of their liquor store. The Burgoses never dealt directly with the plaintiff insurer; they purchased their policy through Patis, their insurance broker. In 1981, a customer was shot and killed outside the Burgoses' store by the Burgoses' son, who was also a store employee. The Burgoses notified Patis about the incident immediately, but did not notify the plaintiff directly. Patis did not notify the plaintiff about the shooting. Upon learning of the incident 2 years later, the plaintiff brought a declaratory action to seek a ruling that it was not liable on the insurance policy. The plaintiff argued that the policy required the Burgoses to inform the plaintiff "as soon as practicable" of any occurrence covered by the policy. The Burgoses argued that they satisfied that requirement by notifying Patis. The issue, then, was whether Patis had the authority to accept notification on the plaintiff's behalf. The trial court granted summary judgment against the plaintiff, and the appeals court affirmed. The plaintiff appealed to the Supreme Court of Illinois.

Bilandic, Justice

It is undisputed that the Burgoses informed the broker immediately following the occurrence. The policy requires that notice be given to plaintiff or any of its "authorized agents." It is generally recognized that an insurance broker acts as an agent of the insured, rather than as an agent of the insurer. However, a broker can act as the agent of the insurer, or as the agent of both the insurer and the insured. Further, a broker may have apparent authority to act as the insurer's agent. It is a well-established precept of agency law that a principal will be bound by the authority he appears to give to another, as well as that authority which he actually gives. Apparent authority arises where a principal creates, through words or conduct, the reasonable impression that the putative agent has been granted authority to perform certain acts. Apparent authority is that authority which a reasonably prudent person, in view of the principal's conduct, would naturally suppose the agent to possess. The principal, having created the appearance of authority, is estopped to deny it to the detriment of a third party.

A broker's apparent authority to act as an agent of an insurer may be established by the course of dealings between the broker and the insurer. Where an insurer's manner of dealing with the broker in regard to the insured would lead the insured to believe that the broker had the authority to perform the acts in question, the insurer is estopped to deny the broker's authority to perform those acts. Apparent authority in the broker thus arises where the insurer knowingly *causes* or *permits* the broker to act so as to justify the insured in believing that the broker possesses the authority exercised.

Acquiescence by the insurer in the broker's conduct is sufficient to establish the broker's apparent authority. It is not necessary that the insurer be aware of the particular acts being performed by the broker; once the insurer has created the appearance of authority, the insurer is estopped to deny it, even though the insurer may be ignorant of its exercise. Fairness mandates such a result because, where the insurer has created the appearance of authority in the broker, the loss must fall upon the insurer, rather than upon the innocent insured.

In the case at bar, we find that plaintiff's manner of dealing with Patis and the Burgoses created the appearance that Patis had authority to accept notice of occurrences. The deposition and affidavits in the record demonstrate that plaintiff used Patis as its intermediary in all of its dealings with the Burgoses. Plaintiff used Patis to deliver the policy to the Burgoses, rather than sending the policy to the Burgoses directly. Patis was used by plaintiff to bill the Burgoses for premiums on plaintiff's behalf and Patis collected all premiums from the Burgoses to be forwarded to plaintiff. All notices from plaintiff to the Burgoses regarding cancellation, renewals or premium changes were sent by plaintiff, through Guild, to Patis, who forwarded them to the Burgoses. It is true, as plaintiff points out, that Patis never submitted a prior notice of occurrence to plaintiff on the Burgoses' behalf. Therefore, plaintiff argues, it could not be deemed to have clothed the broker with apparent authority to accept such a notice. However, the record reveals that the Burgoses did not have any prior "occurrences" to report while covered under a policy issued by plaintiff.

> In sum, the Burgoses had no contact whatsoever with plaintiff, except through Patis. It is apparent that nothing prohibited plaintiff from contacting the Burgoses directly. Rather, this lack of direct contact was due primarily to plaintiff's decision to use Patis as its intermediary for every aspect of its transactions with the Burgoses. Plaintiff's choice to deal with the Burgoses in this manner made it reasonable for the Burgoses to believe that Patis was authorized to receive notice on plaintiff's behalf. Plaintiff caused Patis to act so as to justify a belief in the Burgoses that Patis was plaintiff's "authorized agent" for notice purposes.
>
> **DECISION:** The Illinois Supreme Court affirmed the judgment against the insurer.

Ratification of Unauthorized Activity

Authorization of the agent need not occur before the agent transacts the principal's business. If the principal earlier has not authorized someone to act as an agent, the principal may supply the authority later by *ratifying* the transaction. **Ratification** is the later approval by the principal of an earlier, unauthorized act by someone claiming to act as an agent. Ratification may occur when the agent exceeds his or her original authority and enters into unauthorized transactions or when a stranger supposedly acts as another's agent. The difference between the principal's liability created by ratification rather than earlier authorization is the timing of the principal's consent to be bound. In actual or apparent authority, the principal shows consent before the agent conducts any business. In ratification, the principal's consent comes after the business is conducted.

Because ratification treats the transaction as if it had been originally authorized, only those acts that could have been authorized originally may later be ratified. For this reason the ratifier must have been competent to be a principal at the time the transaction took place. Only those acts undertaken for the principal may be ratified. No ratification can occur for acts done by someone acting on his or her own.

Any act of a principal that shows complete, knowledgeable affirmation of the agent's acts can constitute a ratification. Any acts, words, or conduct reasonably indicating an intent to ratify may constitute a ratification. For example, a principal who benefits by an agent's unauthorized bargain or sues to enforce a contract made by a false agent may constitute a ratification. But the principal's affirmation must be complete. He or she cannot affirm part of a transaction but disaffirm the rest. The following case shows a court applying the concepts of express authority, implied authority, apparent authority, and ratification.

PAILET V. GUILLORY
Louisiana Court of Appeals
315 S.2d 893 (1975)

BACKGROUND: Cella Equipment Company entered into a 5-year lease with Ra Abramson and her sister, Ruth Pailet (appellee), for the lease of office space. Ruth and Ra had inherited the property from their mother's estate. In the lease Richard Michel and Twyman Guillory (appellants) personally guaranteed Cella rental payments. Later the lease was assigned (transferred) to Twyman Guillory with the lessor's approval.

All matters concerning the leased property were handled for the lessors by Ra Abramson's husband, Dr. Albert Abramson. Michel and Guillory first contacted Dr. Abramson about leasing the property. They sent Dr. Abramson the rent checks made out to the lessors. And Dr. Abramson handled minor repairs on the property. Michel and Guillory never had any direct contact with the lessors; their only contact was with

Dr. Abramson. Dr. Abramson made it clear to Michel and Guillory that he did not own the leased property and that in certain matters he could act only with the permission of the lessors. For instance, he made it clear that he did not have authority to lease the property. The lease was made only after Ruth and Ra had approved the lease terms and signed the lease themselves. Also, the assignment of the lease from Cella to Guillory was approved in writing by the lessors.

In March of 1973 Guillory and Michel approached Dr. Abramson and asked that the lease be canceled. Dr. Abramson told them that he would have to check with the lessors, because he did not have the authority to cancel. A few days later Dr. Abramson notified Guillory that the lessors had agreed to cancel the lease. Later Ra admitted that she had consented to the cancellation, but Ruth vigorously denied that she had been contacted by Dr. Abramson and denied that she had agreed to the cancellation.

Guillory vacated the property in 1973, and the building was not rented until after 1974. In 1975 Pailet sued Guillory and Michel for her half of the rents due to her, which she claimed was $82.50 per month for 24 months for a total of $1,980. The trial court entered judgment for Pailet. Guillory and Michel appealed to the Louisiana Court of Appeals.

Fruge, Judge

Appellants contend that even if Mrs Pailet did not agree to cancellation of the lease, she is bound by the act of Dr. Abramson, who was vested with the implied authority to cancel the lease.

An agency relationship may be created through either express or implied authority. Like an express agency, an implied agency is an actual agency. Apparent authority, on the other hand, creates no actual agency relationship. However, where the principal clothes an agent with apparent authority to perform certain acts and a third party who has no knowledge of or reason to believe that there are limitations on that authority, deals with the agent, then the principal is bound by the acts of the agent, which although beyond the actual power delegated to him, are within his apparent authority.

In the case before us, although there was never any express agency relationship between Mrs. Pailet and Dr. Abramson, he clearly had the authority to act as her agent in some matters concerning the leased property. Dr. Abramson was given the authority to collect rents, to make minor repairs, and to represent the lessors in preliminary negotiations regarding the lease.

However, the question before us is whether he had the implied authority to cancel the lease. Implied authority is actual authority which is inferred from the circumstances and nature of the agency itself. An agent is vested with the implied authority to do all of those things necessary or incidental to the agency assignment. In this case, Dr. Abramson's agency authority included collecting the rent and making minor repairs. Certainly the authority to cancel the lease is not incidental or necessary to his authority to collect rent and make minor repairs. No such authority can be inferred in these circumstances, particularly where the authority to lease or permit assignment was not given.

We turn now to the issue of apparent authority. The concern here is whether the principal did anything to clothe the agent with apparent authority to perform the act though no actual authority was given. Because third persons are not privy to the actual terms of the agency agreement, they may rely upon the indicia of authority with which the agent is vested.

We do not find that the lessors in this case clothed Dr. Abramson with the apparent authority to cancel the lease. Dr. Abramson himself denied that he had any authority to do so. The lease agreement and permission for the assignment to Twyman Guillory were signed by the lessors and not by Dr. Abramson. Thus all the indications were that Dr. Abramson did not have authority to cancel.

Appellants rely on the fact that all of their communications with the lessors concerning the leased property were through Dr. Abramson. This alone is not enough. The fact that Dr. Abramson failed to secure cancellation of the lease from Mrs. Pailet is not imputable to her, but rather to the appellants since they relied on Dr. Abramson to secure cancellation.

Appellants' final argument is that because Mrs. Pailet waited nine months before making any claim to the rent, she ratified the cancellation made by Dr. Abramson. However, for ratification to occur the facts must indicate a clear and absolute intent to ratify the act. In this case, there is no evidence that Mrs. Pailet even had any knowledge that Dr. Abramson told the defendants that the lease was cancelled. In these circumstances there could be no intent to ratify.

DECISION: The Louisiana Court of Appeals ruled in favor of Pailet and affirmed the trial court decision in her favor.

Effect of Agent's Knowledge

An important consequence of the agency relation is that the principal is charged with knowing everything about the agency that the agent knows. The agent must communicate to the principal information about agency matters. Presumably the agent tells the principal everything relating to the agent's performance. Whether this actually is done is unimportant, because the reason for imputing the agent's knowledge to the principal is to protect innocent third persons. When determining the principal's liability to innocent third persons, the principal and not the third person bears the risk of the agent's failure to inform.

Notification is the act of informing an agent, which has the same legal effect as if the principal had received it. For example, filing a claim with an insurance company's claims agent is a form of notification to the company. To be effective, notification must be made to an agent authorized to receive it. Frequently the terms of a contract specify the person authorized to receive notice, but the agent also may be implicitly or apparently authorized to receive notification. Notice to an agent who is not authorized to receive it is not effective notification to the principal unless the principal later ratifies its receipt.

A principal is not assumed to know what an agent knows when the agent and a third party conspire to cheat or defraud the principal or when the agent otherwise acts against the principal's interests. In these situations the principal's knowledge is not assured because it cannot be presumed that the agent communicates the information to the principal. For example, an insur-

ance company may rescind an insurance contract when there is collusion between the insured and the company's agent to defraud the company.

Contractual Dealings: Agents and Third Parties

Contractual liability depends on whether a person is a party to the contract. Generally an agent who negotiates an authorized contract for a principal is not a party to the agreement and therefore is neither liable on the contract nor able to enforce it against the third person. The agent may agree to become a party, but in most situations the agent acts only for the principal. But even if not a party to the agreement, an agent is responsible for unauthorized dealings, based on an implied warranty of authorization to act for the principal.

Undisclosed Agency

When the agent acts for an undisclosed principal, the third person has no notice of the agency relation or the principal's identity. From the third person's viewpoint the person negotiating the contract is the party to the contract. For this reason an agent purporting to act alone, but in fact acting for an undisclosed principal, becomes a party to the contract, along with the principal. However, while outwardly appearing to be a party, in reality the agent is still acting for another. This relationship transforms the agent into a peculiar form of contracting party with special rights and duties. For example, if the agent enforces the contract against the third party, the principal is entitled to any proceeds or performance, because that is what the principal and agent originally agreed. Once the undisclosed principal's identity is revealed, the agent may force the third person to choose which party is responsible for performance. If the agent is forced to perform, he or she is entitled to reimbursement from the principal.

Disclosed Agency

The agent who contracts in the name of a disclosed principal does not become a party to the contract unless he or she personally agrees to do so. The principal and third person are directly liable to each other, and the agent is not involved. An agent seeking to avoid personal liability under a contract must fully disclose the principal's identity.

Agent's Warranty Liability

The agent for a disclosed principal may be liable to a third person even without becoming a party to the contract. If the agent purports to act with authority but actually exceeds this authorization, the principal is not bound on the transaction unless it is ratified. However, the agent is not a party to the contract because he or she purported to contract for someone else. While not liable as a contracting party, the agent is responsible for damages to the third person for breach of an implied warranty of authority. The agent is better able to know the limits of his or her authorization, and a third person is permitted reasonably to rely on the agent's representation of authority. The agent may avoid liability by informing the third person that he or she makes no warranty or is unsure of his or her authority.

Agent's Tortious Activity

Agents sometimes commit torts against third parties in the course of their employment. Such torts may be intentional or negligent. Either way, the innocent victim may recover damages for the resulting injury. Damages may be recovered from the agent, because every person generally is responsible for his or her own torts. The principal also is sometimes financially responsible for the agent's torts.

Doctrine of *Respondeat Superior*

The principal is liable for any torts the agent commits during the agent's employment. This concept, called the doctrine of **respondeat superior** ("let the superior respond"), is imposed regardless of the principal's fault or blame. Strict liability is used in other areas of tort law where significant policy reasons require discarding traditional fault ideas in favor of no-fault liability. However, unlike other applications of strict liability, the principal's liability is based on some original fault of the agent. Thus the principal's responsibility is often referred to as *vicarious*.

Scope of Vicarious Liability

While *respondeat superior* is recognized because it is believed desirable and expedient to make the principal responsible for injuries inflicted by the agent, the principal is not made responsible for every tort the agent commits. Only when the agent commits a tort in the scope of employment is the principal liable under *respondeat superior*. The phrase "scope of employment" indicates the limits of the principal's liability for another's wrongdoing. The principal is liable only for accidents that are incidental to agency purposes. To make the principal responsible for acts that are in no way connected with agency goals would be unfair. The principal can be expected to bear only those costs that are closely associated with the business.

This limit on the principal's liability is easier to state than to apply. Determining if the agent is act-ing within the scope of employment often is difficult because the agent may temporarily be performing a personal errand or doing the principal's work while also serving a personal purpose, or the agent may be performing the principal's work in a forbidden manner. No precise formula exists to determine whether at a particular moment a particular agent is engaged in the principal's business. Whether the agent is inside or outside the scope of employment is often a matter of degree. Since the scope-of-employment test determines whether *respondeat superior* applies, as a guide courts often refer to the policy purposes that *respondeat superior* is supposed to serve.

The following case shows just how far an agent's scope of employment may extend.

MAUK V. WRIGHT

U.S. District Court, Middle District of Pennsylvania
367 F.Supp. 961 (1973)

BACKGROUND: Denise Mauk (plaintiff) was driving her 1969 Volkswagen shortly after midnight on July 21, 1971, when she was involved in an accident with a 1968 Lincoln Continental driven by Stephen Wright (defendant), a professional football player for the Washington Redskins (defendant). Wright had just picked up a girlfriend to give her a ride from her place of work to her home in Carlisle, Pennsylvania. Carlisle was the site of the Redskins' annual training camp, operated from July 10 until Labor Day.

Wright had spent the day before the accident in football training exercises. After dinner the team members viewed training films until midevening. Then they watched the annual College All Star football game, which began at 9:00 p.m. on July 20. That night the players were given a curfew of 30 minutes after the end of the televised game.

Wright watched the game at a local "beer joint," then went to a local cocktail lounge where his girlfriend worked. Several minutes after midnight, Wright and his girlfriend left the cocktail lounge and were shortly thereafter involved in the collision.

Mauk sued the Washington Redskins as well as Wright, seeking compensation for her injuries. In the U.S. District Court (trial court), the defendant Washington Redskins requested that the trial judge grant a summary judgment in its favor. The Washington Redskins argued that Wright's leisure-time activity fell outside the scope of his employment with the Redskins.

Herman, District Judge

The entire National Football League provides a unique backdrop to the employment situation. The standard player contract has clauses which if violated effectively bar the player from joining any other team. As a general provision of employment, the Redskins' rules for training camp provide: "The Club reserves the right to impose and require observance of reasonable standards of personal conduct, regardless of whether these situations are directly connected with the team."

According to Coach Allen, the players average two free hours per day between the end of the evening meeting and curfew. The issue is whether that recreation time, in the context of training camp, comes within the course and scope of employment.

In order to establish the Redskins' liability via *respondeat superior* the plaintiff must establish that Wright was acting within the scope of his employment. The concept requires that the employee's action benefit the employer in his business relation.

[T]his court sees the primary potential benefit to be the morale of the players during a time when the club must build "players mentally and physically ready to play in the NFL season." The training camp, albeit brief, is all-important to establishing a cohesive mental unity amongst the team members, a unity apparently not possible were the players free of close contact and scrutiny.

This court finds the employment relationship between Wright and the Redskins to be so unique as to be without parallel. For the fixed period of the football training camp the players' time is accounted for seven days per week and all but two or three hours per day. During the limited "free time" the conduct, dress and associates of the players are circumscribed to the extent that the player can be barred from employment for improper conduct "regardless of whether [it is] . . . directly connected with the team."

Although the fact of employment is not seriously at issue, the nature of that relationship is. The parties have not agreed on the type nor import of any "free time" controls which might exist over the players. The tone, temper and character of training camp, though in dispute, are such that a jury could find recreation beneficial to player and team alike. Taking plaintiff's evidence at face value, there is sufficient evidence that the Redskins did "control" the players during the free time to deny the Redskins' motion for summary judgment and require a complete exposition of evidence from all sides. Given the jury's role and the disputed facts, this court is of the view that summary judgment would be inappropriate at this juncture.

DECISION: The District Court judge refused to grant the Washington Redskins' request for a summary judgment in its favor.

Agent's Liability to Third Parties

In conducting the principal's business, the agent may, of course, harm third persons. The fact that the agent acts in a representative capacity does not make the agent immune from tort liability to third persons. Although the doctrine of *respondeat superior* extends the principal's liability by making the principal liable to third persons for the agents' torts, the doctrine does not affect the agent's liability. An agent's tort liability to another is the same as if the agent were not employed. The doctrine of *respondeat superior* does not repeal the law of torts, which makes individuals liable for the torts they commit. *Respondeat superior* makes both the principal and the agent liable to the victim. Thus the agent's tort liability differs from the agent's usual liability in contract. Because the agent for a disclosed principal usually is not a party to the agreement, the agent is not liable on the contract.

Termination of Agency

Probably a majority of agencies end when the objective for which the agency was created is met or when the time allotted for completing performance expires. But the agency can end in many other ways. It may be ended by events or conditions that destroy the agent's power to act for the principal. An example is the bankruptcy of the principal or of the agent, if the agent's financial status is important to the relationship. Another example is the destruction of the subject matter. In addition, because the agency relationship is consensual, either party may end the agency at any time by withdrawing his or her consent. The death or incompetence of the principal also ends the agency. But some states permit the relationship to continue after the principal's incompetence if a power of attorney expressly so provides or if the power of attorney is approved by the court.

Notifying Agent of Termination

Before an attempted termination is effective, the other party to the relation ordinarily must be notified of the termination. Thus if the principal wishes to fire the agent, notice to the agent of the termination is required to revoke the agent's authority. Notification may be made in any way that tells the agent that his or her services are no longer desired. For example, if a realtor who has been hired by a homeowner to sell the owner's house hears that the owner has sold the house on his or her own, the realtor should realize the agency relation has been terminated. In this way revocation of an agent's authority is like revocation of an offeror's contract offer. Actual notice is needed, but no particular form of notice is required. All that is needed is for the agent to realize that the agency is over.

Notifying Third Parties of Termination

Although revocation of the agent's real authority may be accomplished by notifying the agent, third parties also must be notified. If they do not know of the termination, they may think that the agency still exists and continue to transact business with the agent and hold the principal responsible. To revoke the agent's apparent authority, the principal must give suitable notice of the agent's termination to third parties.

What constitutes "suitable" notice depends on the circumstances. In some cases no notice need be given at all. Generally no notice need be given to third parties when the principal ends the employment of a special agent, such as a realtor, because this type of agency gives notice to third parties of its limited authority. People dealing with special agents should seek assurance of the agent's continued authority. Usually this may be done by seeking written authorization. Principals giving their agents written authority should invalidate the writing upon ending the agency.

When the principal ends a general agency, the principal normally must actually notify everyone whom the principal has dealt with through the agent. This may require consulting appropriate records for determining the agent's customers, although sometimes it is impossible to notify every person who has dealt with the agent. Others who might rely upon the agency relationship deserve to know that the agency has ended. In these situations reasonable notice requires some compromise between the principal's duty to notify third parties and the difficulty of doing so. Suitable notice is any means reasonably designed to reach all third parties. Publication in a newspaper is a typical method. After publication, all persons except those who dealt with the agent on a regular basis are considered to have been notified of the termination.

A number of changes in circumstances automatically terminate the agent's authority. These include events such as the loss or destruction of the subject matter, the bankruptcy of the principal or, under some circumstances, the bankruptcy of the agent, and the death or incompetence of the principal. When the agency is terminated because of change of this nature, generally neither the agent nor the third party need be notified of the termination. The courts entertain the fiction that these events are facts known to all. Because everybody in the world knows about the event all at once, its occurrence automatically revokes the agent's authority. This results in excusing the principal from being liable to the third party for breach of the agent's warranty of authority.

A sizable minority of states allow the agent's authority to continue after the principal dies or is declared incompetent until the agent or the third party learns of the death or incompetence. In these states the agent can bind the estate of a dead or incompetent principal and can avoid any warranty liability. In the case of banks the Uniform Commercial Code (UCC) provides that neither the death nor the incompetence of the customer revokes a bank's authority to accept, pay, or collect an item until the bank knows of the death or the judgment of incompetency and has a reasonable opportunity to act on it.

Irrevocable Agency

In some agency relations the principal cannot revoke the agent's authority because the agent has an interest in continuing the relation. Courts sometimes say the agent possesses a property right in the relation or has an **agency coupled with an interest**. Actually these are not true agencies. Usually an agency exists to allow the principal to accomplish something through the agent. An **irrevocable agency** is designed to allow the agent to do something for himself or herself.

An irrevocable agency is like a contract that must be specifically performed. Someone breaching a contract must perform the agreed undertaking if money is no substitute for performance. Similarly, if the agent must continue performing as an agent to protect an interest because money will not pay for the principal's breach of a promise not to revoke, the agency is irrevocable. An example of an irrevocable agency is when a debtor borrows money, giving property as collateral by granting the creditor authority to sell the property in the event of default. The creditor is the debtor's agent. Money cannot substitute for continuing the agency relation, because the agency has been created to protect the creditor against the debtor's financial default.

The following case discusses some of the issues involved in termination of an agency relation as a result of the death of the principal.

CHARLES WEBSTER REAL ESTATE V. RICKARD

Court of Appeals of California
98 Cal. Rptr. 559 (1971)

BACKGROUND: On May 26, 1967 Dr. Moore and his wife executed an exclusive listing contract with Warde D. Watson Realty Company, giving the broker an exclusive and irrevocable right to sell a 156-acre vineyard at a stated price of $234,000 for a term ending December 31, 1968. The agreed commission was to be 5 percent of the selling price, to be paid to the broker if the property was sold during the term of the listing by the broker, by the owner, or through any other source. The agreement also provided that if the owner withdrew the property from sale or if it was transferred or leased during the term, he would pay the specified commission to the broker.

On March 18, 1968, the listing was transferred from Warde D. Watson Realty to Charles Webster Real Estate (plaintiff). Dr. Moore and his wife consented in writing to the transfer. The stated price was reduced to $187,200. Dr. Moore died on June 19, 1968, and the probate court appointed H. E. Rickard (defendant) as executor of Dr. Moore's estate. (An executor manages the affairs of a dead person's estate in order to carry out, or "execute," the terms of the will.) In November 1968 Rickard sold the vineyard for $152,000 independently of any efforts by Webster Real Estate. Upon learning of the sale, Webster Real Estate demanded $7,600, representing a 5 percent commission on the sale price of $152,000. When payment was not made, Webster Real Estate sued Rickard for the $7,600. After a trial before a judge without a jury, judgment was entered in favor of Webster Real Estate. Rickard appealed to the California Court of Appeals.

Franson, Judge

A real estate listing creates an agency between the broker and the owner.

Because of its personal and fiduciary character, the agency is terminated by the death of or renunciation by the agent or by the death of or revocation by the principal, unless the agent has an interest in the subject of the agency. Respondent concedes that under the listing he was not vested with an interest in the agency. Upon termination of the agency, the authority of the agent ceases except as to bona fide transactions entered into with third parties prior to actual notice of termination.

Death is a fortuitous event beyond the control of the decedent. It cannot be deemed to be a wrongful act and ordinarily is not even a breach of contract by the deceased. Death terminates the agency by operation of law, and the authority of the broker to represent the owner in seeking a buyer for the property is ended.

In the *Restatement Second of Agency*, section 120, "Death of Principal," Comment a, the following is stated:

> *Rationale.* Agency is a personal relation, necessarily ending with the death of the principal; the former principal is no longer a legal person with whom there can be legal relations. One cannot act on behalf of a nonexistent person. Further, to the extent that agency is a consensual relation, it cannot exist after the death or incapacity of the principal or the agent . . . [A]n agreement that an agency should continue after death is a legal impossibility.

The *Restatement* gives the following example: P employs A as a salesman at a specified commission, the agreement stating that the employment is to continue for one year and is not to terminate if P dies—the authority ends.

The owner-broker relationship is a personal one based on mutual confidence and requires not only diligence by the broker in seeking a buyer but, necessarily, the cooperation of the owner in giving the broker information concerning the property, in showing the property, and in negotiating the terms of sale to a prospective buyer. We believe that it is reasonable to assume that both the broker and the owner intended that the listing would terminate on the death of either party. In the absence of an expression of intention to the contrary, the continued life of both reasonably must be deemed an implied condition of the contract. In such a case the death of either renders impossible the performance contemplated and the contract is discharged.

We recognize that there may be situations where a representative may be liable for a commission to a broker if he has ratified or affirmed the contract of his decedent. Also, where the representative has accepted the benefit of the efforts of the broker he may be liable for the reasonable value of the services; for example, if he sells the property to a buyer procured by the broker. Neither of these situations is before us. The record shows that respondent never procured a buyer at the price stated in the listing, nor was he responsible for securing the buyer for the ultimate sale.

We conclude that the contractual obligation of Dr. Moore under the listing terminated on his death rather than devolving upon his executor, and that the judgment for a commission based upon the contract cannot stand.

DECISION: The California Court of Appeals reversed the trial court judgment and found in favor of Rickard, Dr. Moore's executor.

ETHICS
The Opportunistic Agent

There is a growing literature in management and finance that stresses certain inherent problems in the agency relationship. The agent is expected to act on behalf of the principal, but the agent may have certain expertise or possess certain exclusive information that will make it hard for the principal to monitor the agent's activities. Knowing this, the unethical agent may take advantage of the principal and either shirk on the job, if the agent is being paid by the hour, or divert resources to his or her own use.

The agent who shirks or diverts is giving in to an actual conflict of interest. The agent owes a duty to the principal to put the principal's interests first. But the agent may have a personal financial interest that is at odds with the obligation to the principal. The agent who gives in to this temptation violates standards of professional business ethics.

Review Questions and Problems

Key terms

actual authority

express authority

implied authority

power of attorney

apparent authority

ratification

respondeat superior

agency coupled with an interest

irrevocable agency

Discussion Questions

1. How can an agent affect a principal's liability to third parties in contractual transactions?

2. How can an agent affect the principal's tort liability to third parties?

3. When does an agent who negotiates contracts on behalf of a principal become liable to the third party?

4. Why is notification important in ending agency relations?

Review Problems

1. Profit Corporation authorized Anderson, an employee, to find a buyer for used equipment that Profit intended to sell. Anderson believed that he had authority to contract for the sale of the equipment, but in fact he did not have such authority. Anderson found a prospective buyer, Caveat Corporation, and contracted with Caveat on behalf of Profit for the sale of the equipment to Caveat. In this contract Anderson warranted that the equipment was fit for Caveat's particular needs. A responsible officer of Profit read the contract and directed that the equipment be shipped to Caveat. The equipment did not meet the special needs of Caveat, and Caveat refused to pay for it. Profit sued Caveat for the contract price. Who wins and why?

2. Mrs. Terry, dealing with Alice, a clerk in Peters Department Store, sees a cashmere sweater she likes, but she notices that it is slightly soiled. Alice, pushing for a sale, agrees to mark it down from $55 to $40, which she has no authority to do. Mrs. Terry consents, asks that the sweater be delivered, and promises to pay COD. The manager of Peters sees the item being wrapped, corrects the bill, and sends it out to Mrs. Terry. On seeing her sweater accompanied by a bill for $55, Mrs. Terry calls and is told by Peters that Alice had no authority to knock down the price. Mrs. Terry is told that she should either pay the bill or return the sweater. Is Mrs. Terry entitled to the bargain? Why or why not?

3. Anderson and Boyd planned to form Capable Corporation to market a new product. Anderson told Portaro that he was president of Capable Corporation and contracted with Portaro to lease a retail store building. Anderson signed the lease as follows: "Capable Corporation by Anderson, President." When Capable Corporation was chartered (given legal existence), it did not ratify the contract. Portaro sued Capable Corporation, Anderson, and Boyd for breach of contract to lease. What result and why?

4. Principal Corporation owns a chain of jewelry stores. All stores are owned completely by Principal, but each store is operated under the name of the person who is the store manager. Ambrose manages one of Principal's stores. Xenia sold merchandise to Ambrose for sale in the store. The merchandise was to be delivered within 10 days, and payment was to be made 30 days after delivery. Ambrose signed the contract in his own name. Xenia did not know of the agency relationship between Principal and Ambrose. If Xenia fails to perform the contract, what are the rights and liabilities of Principal, Ambrose, and Xenia among themselves? Explain. If Xenia delivers the merchandise and is not paid within 30 days, what are the rights and liabilities of Principal, Ambrose, and Xenia among themselves? Explain.

5. Harold, the owner of Harold's Department Store, directed Julius, his stock handler, to arrange a display containing light bulbs. Julius arranged the display in a negligent manner. Penelope, a purchaser, was injured when the display fell over, causing the light bulbs to explode. Penelope brought suit against both Harold and Julius for damages. Harold went bankrupt before the case went to court. Julius claimed that he should not be liable because he had acted under Harold's direction. Is Julius right? Explain.

6. Paul, the sole owner of a small manufacturing plant producing special equipment, employed Arnon as a traveling sales representative. On March 1 Paul's plant was damaged by fire. On March 2 Arnon contracted with Terry for the sale of certain equipment to be manufactured at Paul's plant. Neither Arnon nor Terry knew of the fire. On March 3 Paul died of a heart attack. On March 4 Arnon contracted with Frank for the sale of equipment to be manufactured at Paul's plant. Neither Arnon nor Frank knew of the fire or Paul's death. What are the rights and liability of Paul, Arnon, Terry, and Frank among themselves? Explain.

Case Problems

1. All-Pro Reps, Inc., is engaged in the business of representing professional athletes in contractual dealings and in providing financial management services to athletes. John Jones contacted basketball player Nate Archibald to make a one-day appearance at Jones' boys' camp and was told by Archibald to contact All-Pro. All-Pro informed

Jones that Archibald would appear at the camp on August 15, 1973. A timely payment of the agreed compensation was made by Jones. On August 10, 5 days before the scheduled appearance, All-Pro, which had been notified by Archibald on the night of August 9 that circumstances prevented him from making the appearance, sent this information by mail to Jones and refunded the consideration paid by Jones. This letter was received by Jones on August 14. Jones filed suit against All-Pro. His complaint alleged that All-Pro was Archibald's authorized agent in the transaction, that Archibald willfully breached the contract, that All-Pro knew or should have known that Archibald would not appear, that All-Pro knew or should have known that its method of communication would not allow sufficient time to secure a replacement, that All-Pro breached its duty to supply to Jones a replacement of a person of equal stature and reputation as Archibald and to give timely notice of Archibald's nonappearance, and that the consequence of all this was that Jones incurred damages in the amount of $200,000 for loss of reputation. Who wins and why?

2. Central Construction Company, which was in the home improvement business, employed sales agents on a commission basis. One of Central's agents called on the Dembrowskis and induced them to sign a contract to buy new siding, doors, and windows. The Dembrowskis agreed to let their home be used as a model, because the agent said that a percentage of other sales made by Central as a result of using the Dembrowskis' home as a model would be credited to the Dembrowskis in sufficient amounts to pay the contract in full. In other words, the agent led the Dembrowskis to believe that allowing their home to be used as a model would earn them enough in commissions to pay for the entire contract. The contract, which was Central's standard contract, clearly stated that the agent was not authorized to make any agreement with the customer regarding the use of the customer's home as a model or the payment of commissions to the customer for referring additional business. The Dembrowskis were aware of this provision, but the agent assured them that the provision did not apply to them. Central had no knowledge of its agent's fraudulent conduct. The Dembrowskis sued Central to reform the contract to incorporate the agent's statements regarding commissions that the Dembrowskis would be entitled to. What is the result and why?

3. Harvey, while employed by the Magnolia Health Center as a laboratory technician, ordered laboratory testing services from Bio-Chem Medical Laboratories. Harvey failed to disclose that he was ordering the services on behalf of Magnolia. After he left Magnolia, Harvey was billed by Bio-Chem for the services. Harvey claimed that he ordered the services in a representative capacity and refused to pay. Bio-Chem sued Harvey. What is the result and why?

PART VII

BUSINESS

ORGANIZATIONS

37

Forms of Business Organization

When entering today's world of business, the selection of a form of business by the entrepreneur has both short- and long-term implications. While some factors like cash flow and bottom-line profile are obvious, others, such as tax and management control might not be so readily apparent. This chapter highlights three major forms of business: single proprietorship, partnership, and corporation; the factors to be weighed in selecting one of the forms, and the advantages of each. It closes with an overview of some specialized forms of business which are frequently used today.

Single Proprietorship

A **single proprietorship** is usually a small business operated and controlled by one or two people. Usually the owner receives all the profits and assumes full liability for the debts of the business. The owner's personal property or estate (upon death) is liable for all the business debts.

Partnership

A **partnership** is a form of business organization in which two or more individuals agree, either implicitly or through an expressed agreement, to carry on a business as co-owners for the purpose of making profits. The partners are held personally liable. If there is not an expressed agreement between the partners, the Uniform Partnership Act (UPA), which has been adopted in forty-eight states, determines the responsibilities and liability of the partnership. A partner's share of the profit from the partnership is taxed as ordinary income both at the federal and state levels. The partnership's profit, in contrast, is taxed only at the state level in the state in which it is doing business. Law firms, accounting firms, and engineering firms take the form of partnerships.

A **limited partnership** is an agreement between two or more people to operate a business as follows: One partner is a general partner who actively runs the business and usually has contributed the largest amount of investment capital.

671

Usually one or more limited partners play no active role in the management of the business and have contributed smaller amounts of investment capital. Limited partners usually are responsible for losses up to the amount of their capital contributions unless otherwise specified in the agreement. General partners are personally liable for all debts. Limited partnerships are usually involved in risk-taking ventures that require large sums of capital. For example, natural gas and oil exploration ventures are often limited partnerships. See Chapters 38–40 for discussion of partnerships in greater detail.

Corporation

A **corporation** is a business entity created for the primary purpose of making profits. A certificate of incorporation must be registered with the Secretary of State of the state in which the entity is to be incorporated. A corporation requires one or more officers, a board of directors, and shareholders. The shareholders invest money in a business and receive certificates of ownership in return. They elect boards of directors, who in turn elect officers or management to carry on the daily operation of the corporation. Shareholders usually are liable only to the extent of the money they have invested. The directors usually are not liable for the debts of the corporation unless they can be shown to have exercised bad business judgment on the basis of a reasonably prudent person's standard for people in their positions. Shareholder derivative suits are more frequent today. These suits request courts to order directors or officers to return funds to the corporations from their personal assets because they have violated the business judgment rule. Corporations are discussed in greater detail in Chapters 41–45.

Factors to Be Weighed in Selecting a Form of Business Organization

Managerial Control

One of the major factors to be considered by an individual in choosing a form of business organization is how much control he or she wants over the business entity. For a family-owned or closely held business that needs to raise capital to expand and compete, the decision about degree of control is an important one. If owners intend to incorporate and sell shares, they must weigh the degree of control over operations that they will give up and also the possibility of a takeover by shareholders (see Chapters 44 and 45).

Extent of Personal Liability

When choosing a form of business organization, the extent of personal liability for a sole proprietorship or a limited partnership is likely to be greater than that for a corporation. This matter of liability is significant, because even if an individual dies, his or her estate is liable for the debts of a partnership or single proprietorship. As discussed in Chapters 38 and 39, partners are liable personally for the debts of a partnership. Shareholders in a corporation are not.

Transferability of Interest

As discussed in Chapters 38 and 39, a partnership interest may be assigned (transferred to another), but assignees generally do not have the same partnership rights as parties to the partnership agreement. Shares in a corporation generally are transferable by shareholders.

Taxation

A single proprietorship pays federal and state taxes on the business profits as ordinary income. Each partner is taxed on his or her proportional share of the partnership's income, whether distributed or not. Only state taxes are paid by the partnership. A corporation pays state and federal tax on net profits. Shareholders also pay federal and state tax on dividends they receive.

Legal Status

In most states, a single proprietorship is not a separate legal entity divorced from its owners, and thus the business is dissolved when the owner dies. In the case of a corporation, even if the officers, directors, or a shareholder dies, the corporation continues in legal existence. See Table 37-1 for a comparison of business organizations according to the five factors discussed here.

TABLE 37-1

Comparison of Major Business Organizations

Characteristics	Single Proprietorship	Partnership	Corporation
Managerial control	Controlled by single individual only	Controlled by partners each with equal vote, unless partnership agreement directs otherwise	Controlled by shareholders, who elect directors, who appoint managers
Extent of personal liability	Unlimited personal liability	Unlimited liability except in case of limited partnerships, in which only general partners have unlimited liability	Limited liability of shareholders for debts of corporation as well as managers and directors, unless corporate veil is "pierced"
Transferability of interest	Interest can be sold or assigned at any time	Interest of partnership can be assigned but not partnership rights unless approved by partners	Shares of stock in a corporation can be transferred
Taxation	Owner's profits taxed as personal income	Partners pay pro rata share of income taxes on net profits of partnership, whether distributed or not; partnership does not pay federal income tax, but some states levy taxes	Corporation income tax paid at federal and state levels; dividends of shareholders taxed at federal and state levels
Legal status	Not a separate legal entity; terminated upon death of owner	Not a separate legal entity in most states; dissolved upon death of a partner unless partnership agreement states otherwise	A separate legal entity with perpetual existence in the event of death of a shareholder, an officer, or a director

Advantages and Disadvantages of Each Major Form of Business Organization

Single Proprietorship

Advantages   Managerial control in a single proprietorship is kept in the hands of a single owner, and all profits are retained by him or her. It is the easiest form of business to start, because it does not require a partnership agreement or incorporation papers. The sole proprietor pays only ordinary personal income taxes and does not pay corporate income taxes. As discussed in Chapter 43, corporate income taxes may be lower than those on a single proprietorship because of a lower rate of taxation and tax breaks that reduce the taxable income of a corporation.

Disadvantages   A sole proprietorship has unlimited personal liability for all debts of the business. All the owner's personal assets and those of the family are subject to contractual, tort, and other forms of liability. Sole proprietors can expand operations only with their personal wealth or with what can be borrowed.

Partnership

Advantages An expressed or implied agreement between two or more individuals to carry on a business for the purpose of making a profit enables each to raise capital more easily than one can do and to spread liability among a greater number of individuals. There are certain tax advantages for partnerships. Partners do not pay social security taxes but do pay a self-employment tax. In some states, the partnership's net profits are not subject to state income taxes, although each partner pays a pro rata share of income taxes on his or her share.

Disadvantages A partnership is mainly disadvantaged by the fact that a creditor may hold each partner personally liable. Even if a partner has not personally signed a contract, he or she may be held liable, because all partners in a partnership generally become legal agents of the partnership. Further, a partnership is dissolved when one of the partner dies, unless the partnership agreement states otherwise. Managerial control and profits are spread among all the partners in proportion to their investment or according to the terms of the partnership agreement. Lawyers, doctors, engineers, and retail establishments that formerly chose the partnership form of doing business now are incorporating to obtain federal tax advantages (lower rate of taxation) and tax-exempt pension and profit-sharing plans.

Corporation

Advantages A corporation's major advantage is that it can raise capital and expand by selling shares (stocks). There is no personal liability for its shareholders. Its shares are easily transferable on the stock market if it is a publicly owned corporation (see Chapter 43). The corporation has a separate legal status divorced from its ownership, and so its owners, managers, and directors are protected from personal liability unless the corporate "veil is pierced." A court may hold managers and officers personally liable if the corporate form is a fiction and is being used to avoid the law.

Disadvantages When a business entity is incorporated, original owners lose control over the corporation's policy decisions, and often the entity's direction. Individual and institutional shareholders (pension funds, mutual funds, insurance companies) become the owners of the corporation and elect boards of directors to make these decisions. Management can also be removed by the board. If shareholders disagree with their return on investment (dividends) or the direction of the corporation, they will request the board to make such changes. Institutional investors have been responsible for changes in the management of Eastman Kodak, General Motors, and International Business Machines (IBM).

Specialized Forms of Business Organization

In addition to the three major forms of business organizations discussed thus far in this chapter, there has been a growth in several less well-known ways of operating a business. They include: joint ventures, cooperatives, syndicates, joint stock companies, and franchising. For businesses involved in retailing of food or shoes (McDonald's or Athlete's Foot) franchising may be the best method of organization and marketing. For two corporations, such as General Motors and Toyota, a joint venture may be the best means of pooling resources to compete in the marketplace. The major goals of these special forms of business organization are to raise capital quickly, mass-produce goods and services, and market them in the least costly manner. Although corporations and partnerships are founded on state law, most specialized forms of business are based on private contractual arrangements.

Joint Venture

A **joint venture** exists when individuals or corporations agree to pool their capital and labor for the purpose of producing and selling goods, securities, or commodities for a limited period of time. The joint venture agreement, unlike that of a partnership, generally is limited to a definite period or to a defined number of transactions. Major joint venture agreements like that of General Motors and Toyota spell out in considerable detail the rights and duties of each party, the nature of the decision-making process, and how labor relations will be carried on.

In some states, joint ventures may sue and be sued. In most states, the lack of a legal status means that both corporations and individuals involved in joint ventures may be sued as individuals.

Cooperative

A **cooperative** is a nonprofit business organization formed by individuals in a private agreement. Its aim is to market products at the best prices. The most common form of cooperative is a farmers' cooperative in which farmers agree to pool their crops to obtain the best market prices. Any profits made by the cooperative are returned to its members in the form of dividends. Unlike a corporations's dividends, which are paid out according to the amount of capital shareholders have invested, dividends of a cooperative are paid out in proportion to the amount of business the members have conducted with the organization yearly.

Unincorporated cooperatives are generally treated as partnerships in most states. In contrast, an incorporated cooperative is governed by separate state statutes enacted to cover nonprofit corporations.

Syndicate

Syndicates, often referred to as *investment groups*, are individuals, partnerships, or corporations who make a private agreement to associate with each other to finance a purchase which individual members could not make alone. Syndicates usually are involved in commercial transactions such as buying hotels or sports teams. The advantage of this type of business association is that it can quickly raise large amounts of capital. The disadvantage is that members of a syndicate may later find themselves held individually liable for a breach of contract or tort if a third-party plaintiff is successful in a suit against them.

Joint Stock Company

A **joint stock company** generally is a partnership arrangement in which partners agree to stock ownership in exchange for partnership liability. It resembles a corporation in that members own transferable stock shares. But it is usually treated as a partnership in that all goods or property owned are held in the name of the members, and each partner is held personally liable when successfully sued by a third party. Unlike a partnership, each member is not an agent for the other in terms of making enforceable contracts.

Franchising

Franchising is often referred to as a method of marketing goods whereby a corporation, partnership, or individual (franchisor) enters into a private contractual agreement with another individual, corporation, or partnership (franchisee) giving the franchisee the right to use a trademark or copyright for a specific purpose for a limited period of time. McDonald's Corporation allows its franchisees to use its trademark and logo, under the conditions outlined in its agreement, for the purpose of selling specific types of foods provided by McDonald's.

Terms and conditions of the franchisor's agreement may include:

- The hours a franchisee's store will be open
- The products to be sold
- The percentage of gross profits to go to the franchisor
- The health and sanitary conditions that will prevail
- The grounds for terminating the franchisor-franchisee relationship

TABLE **37-2**

Specialized Forms of Business

Type	Characteristics
Joint venture	A group of people or businesses that pool capital and labor
Cooperative	A nonprofit business created to market products
Syndicate	An investment group created for the purpose of financing a purchase
Joint stock	A partnership in which partners agree to stock ownership in exchange for partnership liability
Franchising	A method of marketing goods in which the franchisee is given the right to use the franchisor's trademark or copyright

Further, when involved in a franchisor-franchisee agreement, the franchisor may require the franchisee to buy only its own product in exchange for the use of its brand name. These provisions are often referred to as tying or *tie-in agreements*. They have been scrutinized by courts for possible restraints of trade (Section 1 of the Sherman Antitrust Act), because the franchisor is refusing to allow its franchisee to buy from any competitors of the franchisor. The case below illustrates an unsuccessful defense by a franchisor when an antitrust complaint was filed by one of its franchisees.

SIEGEL V. CHICKEN DELIGHT, INC.

U.S. Court of Appeals, Ninth Circuit
448 F.2d 43 (9th Cir., 1974)

BACKGROUND: Siegel and other franchisees (plaintiffs-appellees) are suing the franchisor, Chicken Delight, Inc. (defendant-appellant), for injury resulting from illegal restraints imposed by a franchise contract that was signed by both parties. The restraints in question are Chicken Delight's contractual requirements that franchisees purchase certain essential cooking equipment, dry-mix food items, and trademark-bearing packaging exclusively from Chicken Delight as a condition of obtaining a Chicken Delight trademark license. These requirements are asserted to constitute a tying arrangement, unlawful per se under Section 1 of the Sherman Act (15 U.S.C. § 1). The U.S. District Court ruled in favor of the plaintiff on all issues except one justification by the defendant. Chicken Delight appealed.

Merrill, Judge

In order to establish that there exists an unlawful tying arrangement plaintiffs must demonstrate: *First*, that the scheme in question involves two distinct items and provides that one (the tying product—the trademark of Chicken Delight) may not be obtained unless the other (the tied product—cooking item) is also purchased. *Second*, that the tying product possesses sufficient economic power appreciably to restrain competition in the tied product market. *Third*, that a "not insubstantial" amount of commerce is affected by the arrangement. Chicken Delight concedes that the third requirement has been satisfied. It disputes the existence of the first two. Further it asserts that, even if plaintiffs should prevail with respect to the first two requirements, there is a *fourth* issue: whether there exists a special justification for the particular tying arrangement in question.

The District Court ruled . . . that Chicken Delight's unique registered trade-mark, in combination with its demonstrated power to impose a tie-in, established as matter of law the existence of sufficient market power to bring the case within the Sherman Act.

It can hardly be denied that the Chicken Delight trade-mark is distinctive; that it possesses goodwill and public acceptance unique to it and not enjoyed by other fast food chains.

It is now clear that sufficient economic power is to be presumed where the tying product is patented or copyrighted.

* * *

Chicken Delight maintains that, even if its contractual arrangements are held to constitute a tying arrangement, it was not an unreasonable restraint under the Sherman Act. Three different bases for justification are urged.

* * *

The third justification Chicken Delight offers is the "marketing identity" purpose, the franchisor's preservation of the distinctiveness, uniformity and quality of its product.

In the case of a trade-mark this purpose cannot be lightly dismissed. Not only protection of the franchisor's goodwill is involved. The licensor owes an affirmative duty to the public to assure that in the hands of his licensee the trade-mark continues to represent that which it purports to represent. For a licensor, through relaxation of quality control, to permit inferior products to be presented to the public under his licensed mark might well constitute a misuse of the mark.

However, to recognize that such a duty exists is not to say that every means of meeting it is justified. Restraint of trade can be justified only in the absence of less restrictive alternatives. . . .

The District Court found factual issues to exist as to whether effective quality control could be achieved by specification in the case of the cooking machinery and the dip and spice mixes. These questions were given to the jury under instructions; and the jury, in response to special interrogatories, found against Chicken Delight.

We agree. One cannot immunize a tie-in from the antitrust laws by simply stamping a trade-mark symbol on the tied product—at least where the tied product is not itself the product represented by the mark.

DECISION: Affirmed. The Court of Appeals ruled in favor of Siegel and the other franchisees.

Government Regulation of Franchising
Because many franchisors overpromised potential sales to franchisees and did not disclose fairly all the terms of their agreement, the Federal Trade Commission enacted regulations that provided that certain franchisors must disclose details of their operation to franchisees 10 days before entering into an agreement. In addition, if the franchisor makes any earning predictions, it must show the basis of the predictions. Violations of these rules may lead to civil fines of up to $10,000.

Limited Liability Company

In recent years, states have created a new kind of business organization, the **limited liability company** (LLC). It is a hybrid entity which offers en-

CONCEPT SUMMARY
Types of Business Organizations

Single proprietorship	An entity which one or more people carry on for profit
Partnership	An entity in which two or more people agree to carry on a business as co-owners for the purpose of making a profit
Corporation	An entity which does business for profit and is incorporated by registering with the Secretary of State in one of the states where it does business
Joint venture	An entity in which individuals pool their capital and labor for producing goods and services for sale for a limited period of time, and share profits
Syndicate	Individuals, partners, or corporations that by agreement associate with each other to finance large commercial ventures for profit
Joint stock company	An entity in which partners agree to stock ownership in exchange for partnership liability
Franchising	A marketing arrangement whereby a franchisor agrees to give the franchisee a right to use a trademark for a limited period of time in exchange for a lump-sum payment and a percentage of the profits made by the franchisee

trepreneurs and small businesses some important advantages. It allows them to limit liability, similar to the status of a shareholder in a corporation, while enjoying the top status of a partner in a partnership. That is, the LLC itself will be federally taxed not as a corporation but as a partnership. Also, there are few restrictions involved in the number of individuals or entities that may participate in an LLC. Members of the LLC share in the profits from the business and have a right to manage and exercise control without affecting their profit share or limited liability status.

Some disadvantages are that because LLC statutes are new, a large number of cases have not come before state courts for the purpose of interpreting such laws. A very small (but growing) body of case law exists to advise individuals. Further, the securities departments of states and the federal Securities Exchange Commission (SEC) are investigating and filing legal actions (at the end of 1993) as to whether ownership interests in LLCs are securities and thus must be registered under the federal and state securities laws.

LLCs have become attractive for start-up entrepreneurs in such fields as "wireless cable" and related communications technology. They may replace partnerships and joint ventures in the future.

Review Questions and Problems

Key Terms

single proprietorship	syndicate
partnership	cooperative
limited partnership	joint stock company
corporation	franchising
joint venture	limited liability company

Discussion Questions

1. What are the advantages of a corporate form of organization?
2. What factors should be weighed in determining whether a partnership or corporation is the better form of business organization in a particular case?
3. What features does a joint stock company have that make it like a partnership?
4. What advantage does a single proprietorship have over a corporation?

5. Why do individuals enter into limited liability company arrangements?

Review Problems

1. A, the owner of a brokerage house, signed a limited partnership agreement with B, C, and D, who contributed $10,000 each. When a client sued A for mishandling her investment portfolio, causing a $500,000 loss, and won, A's assets and those of the partnership could not cover the loss. Do B, C, and D have to cover what A and the partnership assets cannot? Explain.

2. A franchisor of ice cream stores requires its franchisees to buy only from approved suppliers. A franchisee sues, claiming that this requirement is a tying agreement which violates Section 1 of the Sherman Antitrust Act. Does it? Explain.

3. A was the owner of a scrap iron business. B loaned A money to purchase scrap under an informal agreement that when A sold the scrap, B would be repaid with interest. A dispute arose, and B claimed that this was a joint venture, and he should receive a portion of A's profits. What is the result? Explain.

4. A and B entered into an agreement to buy a professional baseball club and share profits and losses equally. A was to be the only active party to the agreement. What form of business organization had they formed? Explain.

Case Problems

1. In 1984, Wright Furniture Mills (Wright) sold furniture to the Bedtime Sleep Shop. The shop was incorporated in 1983 and purchased by Sherill in 1985. Although Sherill did not keep accurate records of the corporation's activities, there is no evidence that Wright believed it was doing business with Sherill rather than with the Shop corporation. Wright sold its account receivable (the right to receive payment from the shop) to Commonwealth Financial Corporation. That corporation sued Sherill individually for the corporation's debt. Can it collect?

2. Gartner sued Westerlind Enterprises for a breach of contract when it failed to deliver a home contracted for by a certain date. Enterprises was one of three corporations owned by Snyder. It had no capital, books, files, or office distinct from Snyder's. Gartner claimed that these facts showed that Enterprise was being used in a fraudulent manner by Snyder to get a higher price for houses sold. Was the fact that Enterprise was undercapitalized grounds for piercing the corporate veil and holding Snyder personally liable?

3. Principle (franchisee) sued McDonald's (franchisor) for tying its willingness to lease its stores and use its

brand name to a $15,000 security deposit and 8.5 percent of its gross sales or rent. Principle argues that McDonald's is selling three distinct products: franchise, leases, and security deposit. It argues that this is a violation of the antitrust laws because a prospective franchisee must agree to all three to obtain the franchise, thus restricting its ability, for example, to lease another building not built by McDonald's or to build its own stores. McDonald's argues that it is not selling three distinct products but one system of selling hamburgers, using its name in exchange for royalties. It seeks to bring quality control to the location of its stores, their management, and the products

sold by virtue of its franchise agreements. Is the requirement by McDonald's in its franchise agreements a violation of Section 1 of the Sherman Act? Explain.

4. In 1959 Philip Miller asked the plaintiff to marry him, move to his hometown, and help him run his failing nursery business. She agreed, and when Mr. Miller died in 1974, the business was prospering. There was never any formal written partnership agreement between the Millers. Also, on some occasions, including tax returns, Mr. Miller described his business as a sole proprietorship. The trial court held that Mrs. Miller had not proved that a partnership existed. Explain.

38

Nature and Formation of Partnerships

Nature of Partnerships   Partnership Formation

Nature of Partnerships

Known to the ancients, the partnership is the oldest form of business association. The partnership concept is traceable from Babylonian sharecropping through classical Greece and Rome to the enterprise of the Renaissance. Today the partnership still is an important form of business organization, especially in areas outside manufacturing.

Sources of Partnership Law

The primary source of partnership law is the **Uniform Partnership Act** (UPA). The UPA has been enacted in virtually every state.

Partnership Defined

The UPA defines a **partnership** as "an association of two or more persons to carry on as co-owners of a business for profit" (Section 6[1]). This statutory definition governs whether a partnership exists. Anyone entering a relation satisfying this definition incurs the liability of a partner to the firm's creditors. A partnership is to be distinguished from a joint venture, in which two or more persons associate to carry on a single transaction or a limited series of transactions for profit.

Aggregate and Entity Nature of Partnerships

There are two competing conceptions of a partnership: (1) it is an aggregate of people who associate to share its profits and losses, owning its property and liable for its debts and (2) it is an artificial being, a distinct entity, separate in rights and responsibility from the partners who compose it. The first conception is referred to as the aggregate theory of partnership, and the second is called the entity theory. Note that under either theory, each partner is personally liable for the partnership's debts.

Aggregate Theory The *aggregate theory* considers the partners to be co-owners of the enterprise and the property used in it, each owning an individual interest in the partnership. Creditors can reach each partner's personal assets if partnership assets are insufficient to discharge a debt.

Entity Theory The *entity theory* treats the partnership as a separate legal entity, distinct from the individual partners. This theory holds that the partnership is a "person" for legal purposes. Because the partnership is a separate legal person, individual partners may enter into transactions with the firm, such as lending it money or

680

ISSUES AND TRENDS

The Revised Uniform Partnership Act

A new uniform state law governing partnerships has been written by the National Conference of Commissioners on Uniform State Laws (NCCUSL), the same folks who brought you the original partnership law. The NCCUSL consists of representatives from each state who have been appointed by their governor or state legislature. The organization drafts uniform and model laws, which it proposes that the states adopt.

The NCCUSL now recommends that the states adopt the new partnership law, known as the Revised Uniform Partnership Act (RUPA), which it adopted in 1993. The new law, however, is controversial.

For example, one of RUPA's controversial features is a section that allows partners to change or eliminate their fiduciary duty in a partnership agreement. RUPA's critics claim that the law is poorly written and needs wider public review and study.

Each state will now take up the issue of whether to adopt the new law, and the controversy is expected to continue as each state takes up the proposal. Because only two states (Montana and Wyoming) have adopted the new law as of this writing, the discussion of partnership law in this chapter and the next is based on the original partnership law, the UPA.

---

equipment. Accountants and businesspeople generally regard and treat a partnership as a business, separate and distinct from its individual partners.

UPA Approach   The UPA strikes a balance between the two theories. Generally speaking, under the UPA a partnership is an aggregate, but in certain limited circumstances it is treated as an entity. For example, the UPA recognizes the partnership as an entity for owning its own property by authorizing conveyances of real estate to or by the partnership in the partnership name and by creating the presumption that all property acquired with partnership finds is partnership property. Thus the UPA adopts both the aggregate and entity theories of partnership, depending upon the particular problem involved.

In the following case the court considers whether a partnership is to be treated as an entity or as an aggregate.

McKINNEY V. TRUCK INSURANCE COMPANY

Court of Appeals of Missouri
324 S.W.2d 773 (1959)

BACKGROUND: Truck Insurance Company (defendant) issued a workers' compensation policy to "Ralph McKinney & Paul McKinney dba Acme Glass Co.," which was described in the policy as a "co-partnership" whose "operations" were classified as "glass merchants." Davis, a man employed by Paul McKinney (plaintiff) in connection with McKinney's 167-acre farm, was injured while working on activities wholly unrelated to the business conducted by Acme Glass. Davis filed a claim for benefits against McKinney, as employer, and Truck Insurance, as his insurer. After successfully defending against Davis' claim, Paul sued Truck Insurance to recoup his expenses incurred in the defense. Paul theorized that "a partnership cannot be considered a separate entity." It is an aggregate of individuals, and the effect of the policy was to insure fully all workers' compensation obligations of both Paul and Ralph whether or not relating to Acme Glass Co.

Stone, Presiding Judge

Cut to the quick by the indignity inflicted upon him, a bull calf being castrated by one Davis, "sort of an expert" at such matters, rebelled and grievously injured his tormentor, by reason of which Davis filled a claim for benefits under the Missouri Workmen's Compensation Law against Paul McKinney, as employer, and Truck Insurance Exchange (hereinafter referred to as the Exchange), his alleged insurer. The Exchange theretofore had issued a "standard workmen's compensation and employers' liability policy" to "Ralph McKinney & Paul McKinney dba Acme Glass Co., 1647 St. Louis, Springfield, Missouri," as "employer," described in the policy declarations as a "co-partnership"; but, claimant Davis having been employed by Paul in connection with operation of a 167-acre farm in another county owned by Paul and his wife and Davis' castration of the calf having been wholly unrelated to the business conducted by Acme Glass Company (even though the castrated calf had wreaked as much havoc as the proverbial bull in a china closet), the Exchange insisted that its Policy issued to Acme afforded no coverage to Paul with respect to his farm operation and refused to defend him in the compensation proceeding instituted by Davis, although Davis' joinder of the Exchange as a party to the proceeding necessitated a defense on its own behalf. After counsel employed by Paul personally and counsel for the Exchange, presenting a united front against their common antagonist, had concluded upon appeal to this court a successful defense of Davis' claim . . . and thus had put out of the way (if not out of mind) the castrated calf and the contentious claimant, Paul turned on the Exchange and brought the instant suit to recoup the expenses (primarily attorney's fees) incurred by him personally in such defense. Cast in the trial court on the Exchange's motion to dismiss his petition, Paul appeals from the adverse judgment.

Although other jurisdictions reflect a sharp conflict of authority as to whether or not a partnership is a legal or juristic entity separate and distinct from the individuals who compose it, the courts of this state usually have regarded a partnership as a mere ideal entity with no legal existence apart from its members, and have followed the so-called aggregate or common-law theory of partnership rather than the entity theory. There may be a judicial tendency toward the entity theory; and, as counsel for the Exchange assert, the Uniform Partnership Act adopted in Missouri in 1949 may have "wrought decided changes in the common-law conception" of a partnership. However, the persuasive opinion of informed scholars is that the Uniform Partnership Act does not transform a partnership into a separate legal or juristic entity but adopts the common-law approach with modifications relating to partnership property so that the Act is consistent with the entity approach for the purposes of facilitating transfers of property, marshalling assets, and protecting the business operation against the immediate impact of personal involvements of the partners. Accordingly, we cannot agree with counsel for the Exchange that the Uniform Partnership Act "makes a partnership a legal entity."

But, grave danger lurks in unquestioning acceptance and unguarded application of potentially deceptive generalities; and although our Missouri courts usually follow the aggregate or common-law theory as to partnership, we think that it should not and cannot be announced, as an arbitrary, absolute, unqualified and unyielding rule, that under no circumstances and for no purposes may a partnership be considered and treated as an entity. We read that the partnership entity sometimes is recognized with reference to its contracts with third persons; and we like and adopt the logical, forthright, common-sense reasoning of the Supreme Court of Tennessee in *United States Fidelity & Guaranty Co. v. Booth*, a case involving a workmen's compensation policy, where it was said that, in construing and giving effect to contracts made by and with partnerships, it may appear from the subject-matter or otherwise that the parties dealt with and treated the partnership as if it were an entity, separate and distinct from the individuals composing it; and, to the extent that this is so, the intention of the parties can only be given effect, in the enforcement of the contract, by judicial recognition of the partnership entity as contemplated by the parties.

Thus, in jurisdictions where, as in Missouri, the aggregate or common-law theory as to partnerships usually is followed, the courts have given effect to the intention of contracting parties by treating a partnership as an entity in determining and delimiting the coverage afforded by insurance policies issued to the partnership.

Since the unambiguous provisions of the policy contract establish beyond room for reasonable doubt that the parties thereto intended and undertook to provide workmen's compensation coverage for Acme Glass Company, and since nothing in the policy suggests that thereby such coverage would be provided for any employee of either individual partner engaged in work wholly unrelated to the partnership operation, we believe that we should recognize the partnership entity of Acme Glass Company as the employer with whom the Exchange contracts, thereby giving effect to the plain intent of the contracting parties and following the general rule that an insurer may afford workmen's compensation coverage for a partnership and its business activities without exposing itself to liability for all of the unrelated business operations of each individual partner.

DECISION: The Court of Appeals affirmed the trial court's judgment against Paul McKinney.

Partnership Formation

No particular steps are required to form a general partnership. Although customarily each partner's rights and responsibilities are established in an instrument called the **partnership agreement** or the *articles of partnership*, usually this is not required. A partnership may result from any arrangement of facts fulfilling UPA Section 6(1)'s definition of a partnership.

Factors Establishing Partnership Existence

To understand how UPA Section 6(1) determines partnership existence, the meaning of each phrase of the definition must be examined. The following paragraphs dissect the definition of a partnership and explain the reasons for the words used.

"An Association" *Association* denotes the voluntary nature of the partnership arrangement. Because a partnership arrangement is a voluntary association, the participants must intend to enter into a partnership. Whether or not a partnership is created depends on the intent of the participants to create one. Their intent is the primary test of a partnership existence. This intent may be expressed by either a written or an oral agreement, or it may be inferred from conduct. As with contractual intent, partnership intent is measured objectively. Subjective intent is not material.

"Of Two or More Persons" One person alone cannot form a partnership. A sole proprietor cannot convert his or her sole proprietorship into a partnership by drafting articles of partnership or otherwise conducting the business as a partnership. It takes two to tango, and it takes at least two to form a partnership. Although a minimum number of two is required, the UPA imposes no maximum limit on the number of people who may form a partnership. A thousand people may create a partnership.

The intention of one person alone cannot create a partnership. When someone wishes to join an existing partnership, all the partners must consent to the new member's admission.

UPA Section 2 states that a *person* "includes individuals, partnerships, corporations, and other associations." Thus the definition of a partnership provides that any of these entities may form a partnership. Any individual having contractual capacity may become a partner. By including partnerships as persons in Section 2, the UPA permits one partnership to be a member of another partnership. Similarly, a corporation may be a partner.

"To Carry On" It is often said that "the carrying on" of a business, not an agreement to carry on business at a future date, is the test of partnership existence. The official comment to UPA Section 6 indicates that this is not the intended meaning of the phrase "to carry on." Section 6(1) does not provide that persons are not partners until they participate in the carrying on of the business. The words "to carry on," not "carrying on," are used.

"As Co-Owners" To form a partnership, the associates must *co-own* the business. Co-ownership distinguishes partnership from nonpartnership relations such as employment. For example, if a general manager is not a co-owner of the enterprise, he or she is an employee, not a partner.

Co-ownership describes the community of interest each partner shares in the firm's operations. It includes the power of ultimate control each partner possesses in the firm's management. For an association to consist of co-owners, the associates must have equal rights in the decision-making process. Section 18(e) of the UPA states that "all partners have equal rights in the management and conduct of the partnership business." Factors reflecting co-ownership include giving instructions, hiring and firing employees, and determining how money is spent. But Section 18 permits partners to agree to delegate their managerial rights to a managing partner.

"A Business" Co-ownership of property by itself does not establish a partnership. The co-ownership required by Section 6(1) is co-ownership of a *business*. A partnership must be formed as a business. Section 2 states that a business includes "every trade, occupation, or profession." If two people together inherit real estate that remains unimproved and idle, they are co-owners, but not of a business. However, if they improve the property by erecting an apartment complex, their actions constitute a business.

"For Profit" A partnership must be formed as a business for *profit*. Nonprofit organizations cannot be formed as partnerships under the UPA. Courts require only an expectation, not the actual making, of profit for the existence of a partnership. Profit motive, not profit making, is the test.

The importance of profit sharing to the determination of partnership existence is reflected in UPA Section 7(4)'s declaration:

> The receipt by a person of a share of the profits of a business is prima facie evidence that he is a partner in the business.

Questions concerning the existence of a partnership can arise in a variety of situations. In the following case, the answer to the question of partnership existence determined whether Barbara Campbell would go to jail for stealing from her local little league.

COMMONWEALTH V. CAMPBELL
Supreme Judicial Court of Massachusetts
616 N.E.2d 430 (1993)

BACKGROUND: Barbara A. Campbell (defendant) was convicted of presenting false financial reports concerning the financial condition of the Greenfield Minor League (league), of which she was the treasurer. The league was a baseball league for young boys. The statute under which she was convicted, G.L.c. 266, Section 92, subjects to criminal liability "whoever wilfully and with intent to defraud makes . . . any . . . report . . . concerning the . . . financial condition . . . of any partnership." Campbell admitted that she wilfully presented inaccurate financial reports on various occasions throughout her tenure, from 1980 to 1988. At the close of the Commonwealth's case, Campbell moved for a finding of not guilty on the ground that the Commonwealth had failed to present any evidence that the league was a partnership. The trial judge denied her motion. Campbell appealed to the Supreme Judicial Court of Massachusetts.

Liacos, Chief Justice

The sole question before us is whether the then unincorporated league fell within the ambit of c. 266, Section 92, that is, whether it was a partnership.

We hold that the Commonwealth failed to present evidence that the league was a partnership, and therefore, that the motion for a required finding of not guilty ought to have been granted.

Our conclusion rests on the meaning of the word "partnership" in G.L.c. 266, Section 92. We begin by reciting the well-settled principle that criminal statutes are to be strictly construed. The Uniform Partnership Act, G.L.c. 108A (1990 ed.) (UPA), defines a "partnership" as "an association of two or more persons to carry on as co-owners a business for profit." The Commonwealth presented no evidence and makes no argument that the league satisfies this statutory definition. Additionally, the judge, in his instructions, affirmed that the jury "are considering an organization not carried on as a business for profit."

The Commonwealth argues that neither the UPA's definition of partnership nor the common law definition of partnership, developed prior to the adoption of the UPA, applies to G.L.c. 266, Section 92. Instead, the Commonwealth contends, "partnership" must be defined "nonstatutorily," and by its "common definitions." This so-called "nonstatutory" definition of "partnership" is "an association of persons working toward a common goal." According to the Commonwealth, the league meets this definition because the league's officers, coaches, assistant coaches, and managers worked toward the desired goal of teaching young men baseball through which they would develop "ideals of good sportsmanship, honesty, loyalty, courage and reverence leading to healthy adult lives" (citing art. 2 of the league's Constitution). In denying Campbell's motion for a required finding, the judge agreed with the Commonwealth's formulation. He stated: "I think the intent of the statute is to prevent publishing of false statements, to someone who is a member of an association, or a society or something like that. . . ." Additionally, during deliberations, the judge responded, "No," to the jury's question whether "the 'for profit' [component is] necessary to qualify an association as a partnership."

Both the Commonwealth and the judge relied on a definition of partnership that was mistakenly broad. When a statute does not define its words we give them their usual and accepted meanings, as long as these meanings are consistent with the statutory purpose. We derive the words' usual and accepted meaning from sources presumably known to the statute's enactors, such as their use in other legal contexts and dictionary definitions.

In 1907, when the Legislature enacted c. 266, Section 92 (St. 1907, c. 383), "partnership" was well understood as descriptive of legal, business-for-profit relationships. While the word "partner" has also been known to describe other kinds of relationships, as diverse as husband and wife or two people who dance together—see *Webster's Third New Int'l Dictionary* 1648 (2d ed. 1959)—we must credit the Legislature, in drafting a criminal statute, to have considered the well-settled legal meaning of the term it chose.

The Commonwealth argued in opposition to Campbell's motion for a required finding that, if the Legislature had intended to include an organization like the league, there was no term other than "partnership" to describe it. We cannot agree. The Legislature could have used the term "voluntary association." It could have used the term "organization," "society," "club," or "group united for a common purpose," any of which would have described the league more accurately than "partnership."

The record reflects, in the Commonwealth's words, that the league was "an association of individuals organized for the purpose of teaching young boys sportsmanship and life skills through baseball." There was no evidence that the league was organized as a profit-making venture. We believe this is a necessary component of a "partnership" for purposes of G.L.c. 266, Section 92.

Therefore, even though the evidence may have been sufficient to permit a reasonable trier of fact to conclude that Campbell knowingly presented false financial reports, her actions did not violate the statute and her motion for a required finding of not guilty should have been allowed.

DECISION: The Supreme Judicial Court of Massachusetts reversed Campbell's conviction and ordered the trial court to enter a finding of not guilty.

Protected Relations

While providing that profit sharing presumes partnership existence, UPA Section 7(4) enumerates certain situations in which profit sharing does not create a partnership. These include situations in which profits are:

1. Received to discharge a debt
2. Received as wages or rent
3. Paid to a widow or an estate as an annuity
4. Paid for the purchase of a partnership asset

This protection against the risk of unwanted partnership formation can be lost if the protected party becomes too involved in the firm's operation. In the following case the court considers whether the parties created a partnership.

LUPIEN V. MALSBENDEN

Supreme Court of Maine
477 A.2d 749 (1984)

BACKGROUND: On March 5, 1980, Robert Lupien (plaintiff) entered into a written agreement with Stephen Cragin, doing business in the town of York, Maine, as York Motor Mart, for the construction of a Bradley automobile. (A Bradley automobile is a "kit car" constructed on a Volkswagen chassis.) Lupien made a deposit of $500 toward the purchase price of $8,020 upon signing the contract, and made a further payment of $3,950 one week later on March 12. Both the purchase order of March 5, 1980, and a later bill of sale, although signed by Cragin, identified the seller as York Motor Mart. After he signed the contract, Lupien visited York Motor Mart on an average of once or twice a week to check on the progress being made on his car. During those visits he dealt with Frederick Malsbenden (defendant) because Cragin was seldom present. On one visit in April, Malsbenden told Lupien that it was necessary for Lupien to sign over ownership of his pickup truck, which would constitute the balance of the payment due under the contract, so that the proceeds from the sale of the truck could be used to complete construction of the Bradley. When Lupien complied, Malsbenden provided him with a rental car, and later with a "demo" model of the Bradley, for his use pending the completion of the vehicle he had ordered. When it was discovered that the demo actually belonged to a third party who had entrusted it to York Motor Mart for resale, Malsbenden purchased the vehicle for Lupien's use. Lupien never received the Bradley he had contracted to purchase.

Lupien sued both Cragin and Malsbenden, claiming that they were liable as partners for the breach of contract. Because Cragin had "disappeared" several months before the lawsuit, Cragin was never served with process, and the trial judge dismissed Lupien's claim against him. However, the trial judge entered judgment against Malsbenden, holding him to partnership liability on the contract with Lupien. Malsbenden appealed to the Supreme Court of Maine.

McKusick, Chief Justice

The sole issue asserted on appeal is whether the Superior Court erred in its finding that Malsbenden and Cragin were partners in the pertinent part of York Motor Mart's business.

In his trial testimony, defendant Malsbenden asserted that his interest in the Bradley operation of York Motor Mart was only that of a banker. He stated that he had loaned $85,000 to Cragin, without interest, to finance the Bradley portion of York Motor Mart's business. The loan was to be repaid from the proceeds of each car sold. Malsbenden acknowledged that Bradley kits were purchased with his personal checks and that he had also purchased equipment for York Motor Mart. He also stated that after Cragin disappeared sometime in late May 1980, he had physical control of the premises of York Motor Mart and that he continued to dispose of assets there even to the time of trial in 1983.

The Uniform Partnership Act, adopted in Maine, defines a partnership as "as association of 2 or more persons . . . to carry on as co-owners a business for profit." Whether a partnership exists is an inference of law based on established facts. A finding that the relationship between two persons constitutes a partnership may be based upon evidence of an agreement, either express or implied, to place their money, effects, labor, and skill, or some or all of them, in lawful commerce or business with the understanding that a community of profits will be shared. No one factor is alone determinative of the existence of a partnership. If the arrangement between the parties otherwise qualifies as a partnership, it is of no matter that the parties did not expressly agree to form a partnership or did not even intend to form one. It is possible for parties to intend no partnership and yet to form one. If they agree upon an arrangement which is a partnership in fact, it is of no importance that they call it something else, or that they even expressly declare that they are not to be partners. The law must declare what is the legal import of their agreements, and names go for nothing when the substance of the arrangement shows them to be inapplicable.

Here the trial justice concluded that, notwithstanding Malsbenden's assertion that he was only a "banker," his "total involvement" in the Bradley operation was that of a partner. The testimony at trial, both respecting Malsbenden's financial interest in the enterprise and his involvement in day-to-day business operations, amply supported the Superior Court's conclusion. Malsbenden had a financial interest of $85,000 in the Bradley portion of York Motor Mart's operations. Although Malsbenden termed the investment a loan, significantly he conceded that the "loan" was not made in the form of a fixed payment or payments, but was made to the business, at least in substantial part, in the form of day-to-day purchases of Bradley kits, other parts and equipment, and in the payment of wages. Furthermore, the "loan" was not to be repaid in fixed amounts or at fixed times, but rather only upon the sale of Bradley automobiles.

The evidence also showed that, unlike a banker, Malsbenden had the right to participate in control of the business and in fact did so on a day-to-day basis. According to Urbin Savaria, who worked at York Motor Mart from late April through June 1980, Malsbenden during that time opened the business establishment each morning, remained present through part of every day, had final say on the ordering of parts, paid for parts and equipment, and paid Savaria's salary. On plaintiff's frequent visits to York Motor Mart, he generally dealt with Malsbenden because Cragin was not present. It was Malsbenden who insisted that plaintiff trade in his truck prior to the completion of the Bradley because the proceeds from the sale of the truck were needed to complete the Bradley. When it was discovered that the demo Bradley [had] given to plaintiff while he awaited completion of his car actually belonged to a third party, it was Malsbenden who bought the car for plaintiff's use. As of three years after the making of the contract now in litigation, Malsbenden was still doing business at York Motor Mart, "just disposing of property."

Malsbenden and Cragin may well have viewed their relationship to be that of creditor-borrower, rather than a partnership. . . . [W]hatever the intent of these two men as to their respective involvements in the business of making and selling Bradley cars, there is no clear error in the Superior Court's finding that the Bradley car operation represented a pooling of Malsbenden's capital and Cragin's automotive skills, with joint control over the business and intent to share the fruits of the enterprise. As a matter of law, that arrangement amounted to a partnership under [section 6 of the UPA].

DECISION: The Supreme Court of Maine affirmed the trial court's decision against Malsbenden.

Partnership Established by Representation

The existence of a true partnership depends on the intent of the parties to associate as partners. But in certain situations people who actually are not partners are liable to third parties as though they were. People who represent themselves to be partners or consent to others' representing them as partners are liable as partners to third parties who rely upon those representations in their dealings with the purported partnership. This arrangement is called **partnership by estoppel**. Represented partners are called *partners by estoppel* or *ostensible partners*. The statutory basis for this doctrine is provided by UPA Section 4(2), and Section 16's more detailed declaration:

> When a person . . . represents himself or consents to another representing him to any one as a partner . . . he is liable to any such person to whom such representation has been made, who has, on the faith of such representation, given credit to the apparent partnership.

Liability is imposed on the represented partner in these situations, because he or she is in a better position to avoid injury to others by correcting the misperception. Liability rests on the person most capable of preventing any loss from occurring. Two elements are the essence of estoppel: representation and reliance.

Representation Partnership by estoppel results either from someone representing himself or herself as a partner or from someone consenting to such a representation by another. A signature on a letter or check can constitute a representation. Liability resulting from someone's own representation simply is another application of the principle, well established in contract law, that a person is responsible for the apparent or objective manifestations of intent. Someone behaving like a partner is liable as a partner. It is not material that a person may secretly deny all connection with the partnership or even be unaware of the significance of the behavior.

Liability also results from someone consenting to being represented as a partner by another. But it is not enough that a person knows that he or she is being portrayed as a partner. UPA Section 16 imposes liability only where there is some consent to the other person's representation.

Reliance Someone seeking to hold another liable as a partner by estoppel must have extended credit in reliance upon the representation of that person as a partner. UPA Section 16 requires that the duped person must have "on the faith of such representation, given credit to the actual or apparent partnership." Thus not every creditor of the purported partnership relation may hold the false partner responsible as a partner by estoppel. Only creditors who have suffered economic loss by relying on the represented partnership may require payment from the ostensible partner.

A creditor's reliance must be reasonable under the circumstances. This requirement of reasonable reliance may impose upon a creditor a duty to investigate the relationship before assuming the existence of a partnership. In certain circumstances—such as when the representations of partnership are made directly to the creditor by one of the purported partners—a creditor may have no obligation to inquire further.

The following case illustrates the nature of the reliance requirement.

SMITH V. NORMAN
Supreme Court of Alabama
495 So. 2d 536 (1986)

BACKGROUND: Two married couples, Glen and Peggy Smith and David and Karlin Wright (plaintiffs), each entered into a contract with Mike Norman, doing business as Norman Construction Company, for the construction of their new home. Construction on both homes was begun, but neither home was completed. Each couple brought suit for breach of contract against Mike Norman, his father, Max Norman, and his brother Keith Norman individually and as partners doing business as Norman Construction Company. The plaintiffs later dropped their claims against Keith Norman. Their claims against Mike Norman were stayed when he filed for bankruptcy. The plaintiffs' suits against Max Norman were consolidated by trial. The plaintiffs alleged that Max Norman was a partner by estoppel in the Norman Construction Company. The trial court granted a directed verdict in favor of Max Norman and denied the plaintiffs' motion for a new trial. The plaintiffs appealed to the Supreme Court of Alabama.

Houston, Judge

The plaintiffs' case against Max Norman is based upon an estoppel theory. The plaintiffs contend that Norman led them to believe he was a partner with his son Mike in Norman Construction Company. They argue that during the construction work on their homes, they made payments to Mike Norman in reliance on Max Norman's representations that he was a partner in the business. Because of this alleged reliance, they assert that Max Norman, although he was in actuality not a partner of his son, should be estopped from denying liability for the losses sustained by the plaintiffs from the alleged poor workmanship and failure to complete their homes. We disagree.

The plaintiffs bore the burden of proving that they relied to their detriment on the defendant's alleged representations. They did not meet this burden.

. . . [T]here is not a scintilla of evidence that the plaintiffs entered into their contracts with Mike Norman based upon any conduct or declaration by his father. Plaintiff Glenn Smith testified that when he entered into the contract with Mike Norman, he did not think Max Norman was a partner in Mike Norman's business. Plaintiff David Wright testified that he likewise dealt only with Mike Norman and knew of no involvement by Max Norman in the business. Although the plaintiffs allege that there was detrimental reliance in that they made payments to Mike Norman based upon Max Norman's alleged representations, their existing contracts clearly obligated them to make those payments. Had the alleged representations by Max Norman been made prior to or at the time the plaintiffs entered into their contracts with Mike Norman, the decision in this case might be different. Because the alleged representations came after the plaintiffs had obligated themselves to make the payments, however, it cannot be said that they relied upon those alleged representations to their detriment.

DECISION: The Alabama Supreme Court affirmed the trial court's verdict in favor of the defendant, Max Norman.

Formalities

Although under the UPA no formalities are required to create a general partnership, some may be required by other statutes. Certificates, licenses, and permits may have to be obtained. A name should be selected and in some cases must be registered. Although not usually required, the execution of a partnership agreement often is advisable. Technical formalities do accompany the formation of limited partnerships, which are the topic of Chapter 40.

License, Permit, and Certificate Requirements Partnerships engaging in certain types of activity usually do need to obtain state or local licenses to do business. Occupational licensing is a well-known fact of professional life among doctors and lawyers. License requirements also fall on those in other callings. Certified public accountants, real estate brokers, and construction contractors are only a few of the many businesspeople required to obtain licenses. Failure to obtain the necessary licenses and permits may deprive a part-

nership of the ability to enforce its contracts. This is another application of the rule of contract law to the nonenforcement of illegal agreements.

Name Selection and Registration It is customary, but not necessary, to use a firm name for a partnership. A partnership should have a business name because of the goodwill that may develop from its use. As a practical matter, a name may be required for the opening of the partnership's bank account.

Unless prohibited by statute, the partners may use any name they desire so long as fraud, trade name infringement, and unfair competition are not involved. Thus the partnership cannot use a

---

PREVENTIVE LAW
Drafting Partnership Agreements

Although not required for most partnerships, entering into a written partnership agreement when forming a partnership is still a good idea. There are advantages to a writing. A written partnership agreement avoids the problems of later proving that the agreement to enter into partnership was actually made. Drafting articles of partnership with the guidance of good legal counsel can focus the parties' attention on potential problem areas in their relationship. The written agreement also helps avoid future disagreements by clarifying the parties' relationship for future reference.

The partnership agreement usually takes the form of a series of numbered paragraphs addressing important aspects of the parties' relationship. Partnership agreements range from fairly simple instruments to rather complex documents, depending on the nature of the business and the number and character of the associates. The following items may be considered when drafting the partnership agreement. The following list is not exhaustive, but it provides a good start.

1. Name of the partnership
2. Names of the partners
3. Date of the agreement
4. Purpose of the partnership
5. Location of the business
6. Duration of the enterprise
7. Investment of each partner—capital, realty, services, and so on
8. Any loans to the partnership of assets or cash
9. Sharing of profits and losses
10. Whether there will be any remuneration to the partners for services rendered to the partnership
11. Management and voting powers of each partner

12. Whether there will be arbitration for the disposition of disagreements
13. Whether there will be voluntary or involuntary retirement
14. The method of disposing of any dead partner's share in the partnership, and the method of evaluation
15. Cross-insurance of the partners
16. Respective duties of the partners
17. How books of account are to be established and maintained, and what the period of accounting will be
18. What the banking arrangements will be
19. Who has the authority to borrow money
20. Method of hiring and firing—who does it and who determines pay

name that is deceptively similar to the name of another business.

Most businesses operate under fictitious names. A fictitious name is one that does not disclose the surnames of all the firm's owners. For example, if Julius Jones and Penelope Smith operate a café under the name of "The Bottoms Up Bar," their business name is fictitious. By statute in most states, fictitious names must be registered so that creditors of the partnership can enforce their rights against all the firm's members. A nonfictitious name is one containing the surnames of all the partners and does not have to be registered. Any form of expression may be used for the fictitious name. But some states prohibit use of the word "Company" or any other word that might confuse the partnership with a corporation.

Registration provides public notice of the names and addresses of all partners. It usually involves the filing of a certificate with the recorder of the county in which the partnership is located and, in some states, in each county in which partnership real estate is situated. A few states require the information supplied on the certificate to be published in a local newspaper for a designated period. A new certificate or amendments to the old certificate must be filed for every change in the firm's composition.

Noncompliance usually results in the partnership's liability to sue on its contracts until the registration requirement is satisfied. Registration is easily done and does not usually result in hardship to the partnership. Fines and penalties are also authorized but seldom levied because prosecutors and police usually have more important matters to look after than pursuing nonregistered partnerships.

Partnership Articles   Although not usually required, it is customary to define the rights and duties of the members of a partnership in the partnership agreement. A written partnership agreement is necessary if the partnership agreement qualifies as a contract coming under the Statute of Frauds, which requires a written memorandum signed by the party against whom enforcement is sought for certain contracts. If a partnership is to continue for longer than 1 year or involves the transfer of an interest in real estate to or by the partnership, a written partnership agreement must be executed.

CONCEPT SUMMARY
Selected UPA Sections on Partnership Liability

Section 6   Defines a partnership as "an association of two or more persons to carry on as co-owners a business for profit."
Relations that satisfy the elements of this definition are considered partnerships, even if the parties actually think they have some other relationship.

Section 7   Establishes profit sharing as the test of partnership existence.
States that profit sharing does not create a partnership where profits are:

- Received to discharge a debt
  (debtor-creditor relations)
- Received as wages or rent
  (employer-employee relations and landlord-tenant relations)
- Paid to a widow or an estate as an annuity
- Paid for the purchase of a partnership asset

However, this protection from partnership liability can be lost if the recipient of profits exercises control over the business.

Section 16   Creates partnership by estoppel. A person who is not actually a partner may incur partnership liability on the basis of a representation of partnership status that was relied on by a third party who dealt with the partnership.

Review Questions and Problems

Key Terms

Uniform Partnership Act

partnership

partnership agreement

partnership by estoppel

Discussion Questions

1. What is a partnership?

2. What is meant by treating the partnership as an entity? As an aggregate? When is a partnership treated as an entity? When is it treated as an aggregate?

3. What are the essential elements of partnership existence under Section 6 of the Uniform Partnership Act? What test of partnership existence is provided in Section 7 of the Uniform Partnership Act?

4. What is required to establish partnership by estoppel (under Section 16 of the Uniform Partnership Act)?

Review Problems

1. Seller operates a store in a building he rents from Owner. Creditor, who dealt with Seller, wants to hold Owner liable for the debt as Seller's partner. May Owner ignore the obligation on the basis that both Seller and Owner had mutually agreed that their relationship was not a partnership? Suppose Owner and Seller had an agreement that read: "The parties do not intend by this agreement to form a partnership of any kind, but rather a landlord-tenant relationship." Is this language conclusive on the issue of partnership liability?

2. Can-Do Corporation and Cannot Corporation wish to form a partnership. Can they?

3. Penelope and Julius inherit joint ownership rights in a house. Are they partners? Suppose they decide to lease the house to Renter. Are they then partners?

4. Penelope and Julius decide to go into the business of making widgets, but instead of making profits they lose money. Are they liable to creditors as partners?

Case Problems

1. United Foods, a food broker, was an authorized buyer of produce from Minute Maid. It realized profits by purchasing Minute Maid inventories at bargain prices. United entered into an agreement with Cold Storage as follows: Cold Storage would lend money to United to purchase produce. The produce would be collateral for the loans. A special account would be established and managed by Cold Storage. The books were to be credited with advances by Cold Storage and debited by advances made by Minute Maid. At the year's end the books were to be closed and the profits divided. Over the year United became overextended and indebted to Minute Maid, which sued Cold Storage rather than United because it was a more attractive defendant, alleging that Cold Storage was United's partner. What is the result?

2. Ralph Presutti approached his father, Claude, in April 1969, saying, "Dad, if you put up the money, we'll go partners in a gas station." However, because the oil company whose station they were to operate frowned on partnership stations, Ralph explained that Claude could not sign any dealer agreements or leases or any other partnership documents, such as tax returns. Claude agreed to the arrangement. He withdrew $8,000 from his bank account, which he and Ralph used to open a joint account under the service station's trade name. From time to time Claude drew checks upon the account for payment of merchandise at the station. In July, Ralph returned $2,000 to Claude. In September, Claude began working at the station and continued for 1 year. For these services Claude drew a salary of $125 each week. Occasionally he received additional sums that were from partnership profits, as well as free gas, tires, and automobile accessories. During his 1-year tenure Claude managed the station whenever Ralph was away and participated in policy decisions such as whether they should buy a truck and whether they should distribute trading stamps. After a year Ralph still refused to sign a written partnership agreement, so Claude stopped working at the station. Despite this, he continued to receive payments of money and car repairs from the station until January 1972. As of January 1972, Claude had received approximately $17,000 as salary, partial return of his capital contribution, and distribution of profits. When Ralph finally refused to affirm the partnership's existence, Claude filed suit for an accounting of his share of the partnership profits. What was the result?

3. A barbershop owner executed two separate but similar partnership agreements with two barbers in his shop. Under the agreements the owner provided the barber chair, supplies, and licenses while the others provided the tools of their trade. Upon dissolution, ownership of these items was to revert to the party providing them. Income was divided 30–70 percent between the owner and one barber and 20–80 percent between the owner and the other barber. The agreements further required the owner to hold and distribute all receipts and stated the work hours and holidays of the two barbers. The agreements provided that all policy was to be decided by the shop owner, and it also forbade any assignment of the agreement without the owner's permission. By state law, employers are to file an assessment report with the state employment com-

mission and to make unemployment compensation contributions. But partnerships are not subject to unemployment compensation assessment when no nonpartner employees are involved. Must the barbershop owner file the forms and make the assessed contributions?

4. Francis and Thelma Gosman were an ambitious and industrious young couple, married in 1945 when he was 21 and she was 18. He drove a milk truck and she was a clerk-typist. After several years of marriage, when their first child was expected and Thelma could no longer keep her job, she began to raise chickens at home and planted a garden to supplement the family income—selling chickens, eggs, and garden produce from the house. The sale proceeds were deposited in the Gosmans' joint bank account, which was subject to the order of either of them. Ultimately Francis gave up his milk route, and his participation in the family business increased while Thelma's decreased. This was followed by the removal of the business from their home to a business complex, where the business ultimately became a grocery store, a liquor store, a restaurant, and a nightclub which grossed almost $500,000 in 1969, close to $600,000 in 1970, and over $600,000 in 1971. Francis managed the enterprise and, although Thelma's duties were less onerous she continued stocking grocery shelves, waiting tables in the restaurant and nightclub, bartending, counting money and making bank deposits, managing the club when Francis was sick or out of town, decorating the building interior, and running errands. In 1972 Francis filed for divorce against Thelma, and she counterclaimed, seeking a divorce alleging that, because she was a "partner" with Francis in the family business, her property rights should be determined pursuant to the Uniform Partnership Act, awarding her 50 percent of the partnership's fair market value and 50 percent of the balance of the checking account. What was the result?

5. Tracey Peoples worked for Trans Texas Properties, which was owned by Richard Filip. While working for Trans Texas, Peoples purchased advertising in the newspaper the *Austin American Statesman*, which is published by Cox Enterprises, Inc. To obtain the advertising on credit for Trans Texas, Peoples represented to Cox Enterprises that Jack Elliott was an owner of the business. Peoples had no authority to make that representation, and Cox Enterprises made no effort to verify it. As for Elliott, he did not hold himself out as having an ownership interest in Trans Texas. Jack Elliott actually had no financial interest in Trans Texas Properties. When Trans Texas did not pay for the advertising, Cox Enterprises sued both Richard Filip and Jack Elliott as partners, doing business as Trans Texas Properties. Cox Enterprises claimed that Jack Elliott was liable as a partner by estoppel because he was negligent in allowing Cox Enterprises to rely on Peoples' representation that he was Filip's partner. Is Cox Enterprises correct? Explain.

39

Operation and Dissolution of Partnerships

Property Rights in Partnerships
Relations among Partners

Relations with Third Parties
Partnership Dissolution

This chapter explores the rights and duties resulting from the operation and dissolution of partnerships. First it focuses on the property rights created by the partnership relation. Next, it examines the rules governing the relations among partners and their relations with persons dealing with the partnership. The chapter concludes with an explanation of how partnerships are dissolved and wound up.

Property Rights in Partnerships

The Uniform Partnership Act (Section 24) defines the property rights of partners as:

1. Their rights in a specific partnership property
2. Their interest in the partnership
3. Their right to participate in the firm's management

The following paragraphs discuss the first two types of property rights. The partner's right to

participate in the firm's management is discussed later in the chapter.

Property rights in partnerships pose two problems:

1. Distinguishing partnership property from an individual partner's personal assets
2. Distinguishing partnership property from the related type of property known as the partner's interest in the partnership.

Partnership Property

Partnership property is property that the partners agree belongs to the partnership and must be used for partnership purposes. It differs from a partner's personal assets because it belongs to all the partners. Partnership property also differs from a partner's interest in the partnership, which is the partner's share of the profits and surplus. In ordinary language, a partner's interest is commonly called a *partner's share*.

Most partnerships require property for their operation. This property may be either *real property* (land) or *personal property* (movable items). Usually the partnership acquires its original property from individual partners as their capital contributions. The partners may contribute specific assets to the firm, such as land, equipment, or patents, or they may contribute money used to purchase assets. These assets, including money, usually become partnership property.

Partners may have property that is not partnership property. This property may remain the sole property of an individual partner even though it is used by the firm. For example, an individual partner's real estate may be used by the firm for its business premises without becoming the partnership's property if the partner providing it intends only to lend it to the firm. Similarly, nothing prevents a partner from lending equipment to the firm while retaining ownership of it.

What Constitutes Partnership Property   Although a partner's personal assets may be vulnerable to partnership obligations, distinguishing partnership property from a partner's personal assets is essential for several reasons. If property belongs to the partnership, its use by individual partners is restricted. If it is sold, any *capital gain* or *loss* is distributed to each partner in the same proportion as profits, unless otherwise agreed. If the property must be applied to satisfy creditor claims, partnership creditors have priority over an individual partner's personal creditors. But if the property is an individual partner's personal asset, his or her use of it is unrestricted. The entire capital gain or loss from its

sale belongs to the partner and is subject to personal income taxes. If the partner dies, the property belongs to his or her estate.

The controlling criterion for deciding if certain property is the partnership's is the partners' *intent* that it belong to the firm and be devoted to its purposes. The partners' intent is the primary consideration. They may decide among themselves what will be owned by all as partnership property and what will be retained by each as his or her own.

One measure of the partners' intent is the way the property is acquired. Property bought with the firm's money is considered the partnership's. If it is bought with individual funds, it is considered that individual's property. Additional factors may strengthen this presumption. Repairing and improving the property at partnership expense, paying insurance premiums from partnership accounts, or listing the property on partnership financial statements may reinforce this presumption. But the presumption can be explained away if an intention of individual ownership appears.

Tenancy in Partnership   Assuming that certain property belongs to the partnership, the UPA describes the nature of a partner's ownership rights in it: "A partner is a co-owner with his [or her] partner of specific partnership property as a tenant in partnership." This **tenancy in partnership** is a unique property concept created by the UPA especially for partnerships. It recognizes that a partner's co-ownership rights in specific partnership property differ from other types of

---

PREVENTIVE LAW
Partnership Property

The UPA creates the presumption that property bought with partnership funds is partnership property. On occasion this may not be what the individual partners intend. One way for the partners to explain away the presumption is to establish their intent at the outset in their partnership agreement. The partnership agreement generally governs, because it is the clearest indication of intent. Usually the statement describes the partnership property and its agreed-upon value in a separate schedule incorporated by reference into the agreement. Property used by the firm but owned by an individual partner also may be identified in this way. When an individual partner's property is loaned to the partnership, a copy of the lease may be attached to the agreement and incorporated by reference. The partnership agreement can provide that acquired property be recorded as partnership property in the partnership accounts. A well-kept set of books will identify the partnership's assets, and the property listed there will be considered partnership property.

co-ownership. For example, many of the details of land ownership do not fit the needs of partnerships. The UPA's tenancy in partnership recognizes that the rights of a partner as a co-owner of specific partnership property should depend on the needs of the partnership relation.

The special needs of the partnership relation require that an individual partner's ownership rights in specific partnership property be restricted. Although the partners are co-owners of partnership property, they have limited ownership rights. Generally a partner cannot sell specific partnership property or dispose of it by will. The theory is that the partnership property is to remain intact. It reflects recognition of the business primacy of the partnership relation.

Under the UPA:

> A partner . . . has an equal right with his partners to possess specific partnership property for partnership purposes, but he has no right to possess such property for any other purpose without the consent of his partners.

A partner's use of partnership property is limited to partnership purposes. He or she may not use partnership property for personal or other nonpartnership purposes unless all the other partners agree. Their agreement may be implied by continued acceptance of the individual partner's personal use of partnership property, or the partners may expressly provide their consent in their partnership agreement.

Because a partner cannot possess partnership property for personal purposes, he or she cannot claim that specific partnership property as part of his or her home and thereby free it from seizure by creditors in a bankruptcy proceeding.

The UPA further restricts a partner's power to assign his or her rights in specific partnership property. A partner cannot assign his or her rights in partnership property unless it is an assignment of the rights of all the partners in the same property. For example, a partner cannot *pledge* specific partnership property as security for a personal obligation. This aspect of the tenancy in partnership is necessary because partnerships are voluntary, personal relations. If the law recognized the possibility of individual assignments, the assignee would become a partner in the firm with the rights to possess the property for part-

nership purposes. But partnerships are voluntary relations, and people cannot have partners forced on them.

Creditors may not force an involuntary assignment through a judicial seizure of the property. Thus a partner's rights to partnership property are not subject to creditor claims, except upon a claim against the partnership.

When a partner dies, his or her ownership of specific partnership property passes to the surviving partners. It is not included in the deceased partner's estate. This is called the **right of survivorship**. It fits nicely the needs of the partnership, because it permits the partnership to be dissolved without interference from the dead partner's estate. Because a deceased partner's ownership rights in specific partnership property is not distributed to the heirs or beneficiaries, a partner may not include it in a will.

Partner's Interest in the Partnership

The UPA states that "a partner's interest in the partnership is his [or her] share of the profits and surplus, and the same as personal property." This interest is an intangible economic right. Its value appears on the partnership's balance sheet as each partner's capital account. Unlike specific partnership property, which belongs to the firm and is collectively held by the partners, each partner's interest belongs to him or her individually. Because it is each partner's individual property, a partner's interest has most of the ownership qualities that are denied to a partner in specific partnership property: It is assignable; it may be seized by creditors; and, when a partner dies, it becomes a part of his or her estate.

Assignment of Partner's Interest Partners may convey their interest to another. An attempted assignment by a partner of his or her ownership in specific partnership property is regarded as valid. The person to whom the partner transfers the interest does not become a partner in the firm but receives only a right to share in the firm's profits. The assignee does not enjoy the usual rights and privileges of partners. He or she may not interfere with the firm's management, require information about the firm's transactions, or inspect the partnership books. But if the partnership is dissolved, the assignee may require an accounting of the interest from the date it was acquired. These restrictions place the assignee of a partner's interest in an insecure position and often make it difficult to find a buyer.

Creditor's Rights   Unlike specific partnership property, which is shielded from attack by a partner's personal creditors, a partner's interest in the partnership may be seized by his or her individual creditors to satisfy a debt resulting from a transaction outside the firm's business. In that a partner may voluntarily assign his or her interest to creditors, it follows that the partner's personal creditors should be able to force an involuntary assignment by a judicial seizure of the interest. The creditors may accomplish this by seeking a **charging order**, which is similar to the garnishment of someone's wages. Under the charging order, a personal creditor may reach the partner's interest without interfering with the firm's business.

The charging order attaching the partner's interest is the exclusive remedy for a partner's personal creditors. It is available only to a partner's personal creditors, those who have obtained a judgment against the partner. UPA Section 28 provides that a court "may charge the interest of the debtor partner with payment of the unsatisfied amount of such judgment debt."

A creditor also may ask a court to appoint a **receiver**, an independent person who receives the partner's share of profits for the creditor. The receiver enters into the partnership and acts as a partner. Under UPA Section 28, the receiver may make "orders, directions, accounts and inquiries which the debtor partner might have made, or which the circumstances of the case may require."

From the other partner's perspective the appointment of a receiver is not desirable. The partners may redeem the charged interest and get rid of the receiver by paying off the judgment creditor. They also can use partnership property to do so, provided there is approval among all the partners whose interests are not subject to the charging order.

As illustrated in the case that follows, a partner might sometimes resort to slippery maneuvers, such as fraudulent transfers of partnership property, in an attempt to protect his or her partnership interest from a creditor's charging order. The law attempts to protect creditors from such schemes.

STAFFORD V. MCCARTHY
Missouri Court of Appeals
825 S.W.2d 650 (1992)

BACKGROUND: Plaintiff Stafford sued Don McCarthy on a debt. Stafford won, and was awarded over $8,000. Stafford tried to collect on this judgment by getting a charging order on Don's partnership interest in McCarthy Drilling, the only assets of which were supposedly a drilling rig and a truck. McCarthy claimed that McCarthy Drilling was not a partnership, and that the drilling rig and truck were not partnership property but rather were owned by Don and his wife as "tenants by the entirety." (In tenancy by the entirety, a form of property ownership available to married couples only, each spouse owns all of the property; the husband's interest and the wife's interest cannot be separated, and creditors generally cannot use the property to satisfy a debt that only one spouse owes.)

However, the Circuit Court of Polk County ruled on January 15, 1988, that McCarthy Drilling was indeed a partnership between Don McCarthy and his wife, Pat, and that Don's interest was subject to Stafford's charging order. Five days after the ruling, the McCarthys executed an "Agreement to Dissolve Partnership," which purported to dissolve the partnership and transfer the rig and truck to Pat McCarthy as consideration for $10,000 that Pat had put into the business earlier. By making this transfer, Don was apparently attempting to render his partnership interest—and hence Stafford's charging order—worthless. Stafford then sued Pat McCarthy, claiming that the property transfer was an attempt to defraud Stafford out of the amount that Don owed him and that Pat should therefore be required to pay the debt. The trial court agreed, and awarded Stafford a money judgment against Pat. Pat appealed.

Crow, Judge

The "Agreement to Dissolve Partnership" signed by Don and Pat on January 20, 1988, recites they commenced a business known as McCarthy Drilling in June, 1986. As this was before the marriage, they obviously could not have owned McCarthy Drilling as tenants by the entirety when they started it. It is equally clear McCarthy Drilling was not a corporation, and there was no evidence suggesting Pat's $10,000 was a gift or a loan to Don. On the contrary, the agreement recites Pat "contributed" $10,000 "to commence said business," and it also recites Don is transferring to Pat all his rights and title in the partnership and its assets "in satisfaction of the partnership obligation to" her. This sounds like a return of a capital contribution to Pat upon dissolution of a partnership.

Where property is owned in tenancy by the entirety, each spouse is seized of the whole or entirety and not of a share, moiety or divisible part. That is, each spouse owns an undivided interest in the whole of the property and no separate interest.

In the "Agreement to Dissolve Partnership," Don purported to transfer to Pat all his rights and title in the partnership and its assets. As noted earlier, Pat concedes in her brief that if the equipment was not partnership property, the partnership had no assets.

Consequently, if the equipment was entirety property, Pat received nothing from the partnership upon its dissolution. Said another way, if the interest of Don and Pat in the equipment was owned by them as tenants by the entirety, Pat owned the whole of such interest, not a share or divisible part. She and Don owned an undivided interest in the whole, not separate interests. It therefore follows that if Pat's and Don's interest in the equipment was held by them as tenants by the entirety, Pat received nothing for her $10,000 contribution upon dissolution of the partnership.

The trial court was obviously persuaded that the interest held by Don and Pat in the equipment was partnership property, not entirety property. It will be recalled that the trial court found the partnership had a value of $40,000 on January 20, 1988, when Don ostensibly transferred all his rights and title in the partnership and its assets to Pat. This finding was apparently based on Don's testimony that the "drill rig" was "worth at least $40,000.00 on January 20th of 1988."

At trial, Pat admitted that in the "Agreement to Dissolve Partnership," she extinguished the $10,000 debt the business owed her "in exchange for the assets of the partnership." In determining whether an asset standing in the names of individuals who are partners is to be treated as partnership property, a court may ascertain from the conduct of such individuals and their course of dealing the understanding and intention of the partners themselves, which, when ascertained, unquestionably should control. The trial court could have reasonably found Don and Pat were treating their interest in the equipment as partnership property; otherwise there was no partnership property for Pat to receive in repayment of her $10,000 contribution.

Don admitted he and Pat signed the "Agreement to Dissolve Partnership" because of the ruling five days earlier that McCarthy Drilling Company was a partnership and Don's interest was subject to a charging order. Had the partnership owned no assets, there would have been no apparent reason to dissolve the partnership, as there would have been nothing to transfer to Pat. Because the partnership admittedly had no assets other than the equipment, the trial court could have reasonably found Don and Pat held their interest in that equipment as partners, not as tenants by the entirety, and that they wanted to place Don's partnership interest in the equipment beyond Plaintiff's reach by dissolving the partnership and transferring Don's interest to Pat.

We hold there is substantial evidence to support the trial court's implicit finding that the drilling rig/truck was partnership property and that such finding is not against the weight of the evidence.

DECISION: The Court affirmed the money judgment against Pat McCarthy.

Inheritance   When a partner dies, his or her interest in the partnership passes to the heirs or beneficiaries of his or her estate. Because a partner individually owned the partnership interest while living, it follows that it should become a part of the estate upon death. A partner may convey the interest by will. This may be done by a specific *bequest* of the interest to a particular beneficiary. But because a partner's interest is personal property, a bequest of all a partner's personal property includes a transfer of the partnership interest.

In addition to transfers by will, a partner may provide in the partnership agreement that his or her interest in the partnership will pass to one or more surviving partners. Usually this is done by a buy-sell provision in the partnership agreement. Under a **buy-sell agreement**, the partners agree that the survivors will buy the deceased partner's interest by paying the representative of the deceased partner the value of the deceased's interest in the firm. This payment may be either in a lump sum or in installments, and it may be backed by insurance. The partnership agreement may state that partnership proceeds be used to purchase life insurance for each partner covering the value of each partner's interest. The insurance proceeds then are used to pay the value of the deceased partner's interest to the deceased's representative.

Relations among Partners

The UPA contains rules governing the relations of the partners to each other. These rules reflect the partners' presumed intent regarding their relationship. In providing general rules for determining the rights and obligations of the partners, the UPA states:

> The rights and duties of the partners in relation to the partnership shall be determined, *subject to any agreement between them*, by the following rules [emphasis added].

The phrase *subject to any agreement between them* lets the partners alter or waive the rules governing their relationship when that is their actual intent. They usually make these changes in the partnership agreement, in that its function is to express the intentions of the partners about law and tax considerations. When no partnership agreement exists, or when an existing agreement is silent, the UPA provisions are implied. Thus the UPA serves as a backdrop and as a point of departure for the drafting of the partnership agreement.

As we have noted earlier, smart businesspeople appreciate the advantages of a written partnership agreement. Because a partnership is an intimate relationship, perhaps the greatest potential problem is the risk of future disagreement

---

PREVENTIVE LAW
Partnership Agreement

Because either majority or unanimous approval usually governs the partnership's operations regardless of each partner's contribution, the partners may prefer to specify a different rule in the partnership agreement. For example, majority rule may be replaced by a provision in the partnership agreement leaving ordinary business decisions to a "majority in interest" of either the earnings or the capital contributions of the partners. The partners who together are entitled to more than half the profits or who together contributed more than half the capital would make ordinary business decisions under this provision. A major contributor may insist on complete control, and the partnership agreement may allow it. When the partners contemplate that one of them will assume most of the managerial duties, the partnership agreement may designate a "managing partner," specifying the responsibilities entrusted to him or her. When a firm has many partners, such as a large, national accounting firm, provisions for centralizing management in an executive committee may be considered. If there is an even number of partners, the agreement may provide for arbitration to resolve deadlocks.

among those who start out with the highest mutual regard. This risk may be diminished by reducing the partners' relation to a written instrument. By focusing attention on potential trouble spots, a carefully drafted partnership agreement may avoid future disagreements and litigation. Because the UPA provides the basic rules governing the partners' relation to each other and also provides that these rules may be varied by the partners, the following paragraphs discuss these rules and the extent to which they may be altered by agreement. In short, the UPA defines the fiduciary duties of partners, their rights to compensation, their management rights, and their right to information.

Partner's Fiduciary Duties

The UPA provides that partners owe a fiduciary duty to each other. The fiduciary duties of agents are discussed in Chapter 35. In that the UPA provides that "every partner is an agent of the partnership for purposes of its business" and further states that "the law of agency shall apply under this act," it follows that partners share fiduciary duties similar to those of agents. A partnership is just a special type of agency, and partnership law is simply the application of agency principles to partnerships.

The intimate nature of the partnership also makes the application of the fiduciary rule to partnerships appropriate. Someone should not have to deal with his or her partners as if they were opposing parties. A partner should be able to trust his or her other partners, to expect that they are pursuing a common goal and not working at cross-purposes.

The partner's fiduciary duty requires loyalty to his or her partners. In a partnership, each partner is the confidential agent of his or her other partners. Therefore, no one may act at another partner's expense. The fiduciary relation prohibits all forms of trickery, secret dealings, and selfishness in matters relating to the partnership. For example, a secret profit may not be made to the exclusion of other partners.

The duty of loyalty resulting from a partner's fiduciary position is such that the severity of a partner's breach is not questioned. The question is whether there has been any breach at all. The required degree of loyalty must be maintained at all times. From the first exploratory discussions, through formal association in partnership, partners are required to exercise scrupulous loyalty and good faith. A partner's duty of loyalty usually operates in two areas:

1. Instances in which a partner engages in transactions with other partners and the firm
2. Instances in which partnership opportunities are presented to a partner

Nothing prohibits partners from dealing with each other at arm's length, as ordinary businesspeople, when negotiating a nonpartnership transaction. But when a transaction concerns any aspect of the partnership relation, the requisite degree of loyalty must be maintained. Transactions of this type include one partner's purchase of the partnership share of another and one partner's sale of personal property to the partnership.

Whenever a person buys the partnership share of another partner, the purchasing partner must inform the selling partner fully of any information he or she has that would affect the value of the partnership share. The purchaser may not conceal or fraudulently represent material facts to his or her partner. Similarly, when a partner sells his or her own property to the partnership, there must be no misrepresentation to the firm or concealment of the seller's identity.

The same high standards of loyalty apply when partners are presented with a partnership opportunity. Occasionally third parties refuse to deal with the partnership and offer a partnership opportunity to a partner in his or her individual capacity. A partner may not accept such an offer while still a member of the firm, unless his or her partners grant permission.

When partners learn of or are offered any opportunity in their capacity as a member of a partnership, they may not appropriate this opportunity for personal benefit without first offering it to the firm. A partner may not, for example, purchase the rights to manufacture a product that would fit into the firm's product line. When the firm is presented with a business opportunity, a partner may take the opportunity for himself or herself if the partnership does not have enough money to take advantage of the opportunity or simply fails to take action on it. Otherwise, a partner may take advantage of a partnership opportunity only when it has been completely abandoned by the firm.

Because a partner is a fiduciary, he or she is held accountable for profits made in competition with the business. But a partner may engage in additional enterprises for personal benefit so long as they are not within the scope of the partnership and are undertaken in good faith. When litigation develops, it is not always easy to determine what the partners intended as the scope of the business. For example, partners in real estate may intend to retain some freedom to deal on their own accounts. Failure to delineate the scope of the partnership business in a partnership agreement invites quarrels. This problem is usually avoided by the inclusion of a purpose clause in the partnership agreement. A closely allied problem is the amount of time each partner must spend on firm business. If outside interests of one or more partners are to be permitted, a partnership agreement can include such a provision.

Profits and Compensation

Unless there is an agreement to the contrary, under the UPA partners share equally in the profits. This equal sharing in profits results regardless of unequal contributions of capital, skills, or services by the partners.

Without an agreement stating otherwise, a partner is not entitled to compensation for services rendered for the firm's business. What a partner does for the firm's business is presumed to be in his or her own interest. It is ordinarily expected that each partner will devote himself or herself to the promotion of the firm's business without compensation. This expectation holds even when one partner performs more than the others. This rule rests on the presumed intent of the partners. If a provision for compensation is included in the partnership agreement, it is enforced.

From an economic perspective, the rules governing profits and compensation are sound when partners have contributed equally to the venture. To the extent that contributions are unequal, different rules are needed. For example, the senior partner in an accounting firm may demand more of the earnings than the other partners on the basis of his or her experience and reputation. Contributions to a manufacturing enterprise may vary widely in terms of equipment, goodwill, and time. By fixing the percentages of each partner's share of the profits in the partnership agreement, some of these differences may be taken into account. If the chief variation in contribution is the amount of capital, the proportion of capital contributed may determine the proportion of the profits received. But in many situations it is wise to base salaries on economic contributions—as, for example, when one partner contributed managerial talent. The important point is that, unless the partners want the UPA's rules governing equal sharing of profits and no compensation to apply, the partnership agreement should specify the partners' intent.

Management

Under the UPA all partners have equal rights in the management and conduct of the partnership business. From this concept of equality it follows that a majority of the partners may decide ordinary partnership matters, provided that no agreement between them makes a different rule. A majority of the partners may determine the firm's action in ordinary affairs regardless of each partner's comparative investment in the firm. A majority governs over a minority in such matters as borrowing money, hiring and firing employees, collecting debts, and determining when and how profits are to be divided.

Individual partners and those in a minority are protected from majority oppression by two exceptions to the general principle of majority rule in management matters:

1. No partner may be excluded from participating in the firm's management.
2. The majority must act in good faith for the firm's interest and not out of self-interest.

Because each partner has an equal right to take part in the management of the firm's business, it makes sense that one partner may not exclude another partner from his or her full share in the management of the partnership. The requirement that the majority act in good faith and not for private advantage springs from the fiduciary duty of loyalty each partner owes to the others. Practically speaking, fairness requires consulting with the minority before taking action.

Individual partners and minorities are also protected by the requirement of unanimous approval on extraordinary matters, admission of incoming partners, and changes in the partnership agreement. Because the UPA permits majority rule regarding *ordinary matters* connected with the partnership business, majority control does not extend to unusual or extraordinary transactions. These require unanimous approval. For example, a majority cannot engage the firm in a different business or change the firm's location if any partner objects.

The UPA provides that no one may become a member of a partnership without the consent of all the partners. This rule reflects the intimate nature of partnership. No person should have a partner forced on him or her. Each partner may choose his or her associates.

Nothing contradicting the partnership agreement may be undertaken without unanimous approval. This rule is just another application of contract law, in that an act contravening the partnership agreement constitutes a breach of contract, and any modification of a contract requires agreement among all parties. Both majority and unanimous actions may be taken with complete informality, such as an exchange of letters or a telephone call.

Information

The UPA provides:

> Partners shall render on demand true and full information of all things affecting the partnership to any partner or to the legal representative of any deceased partner or any partner under legal disability.

Thus each partner has the right to all information concerning partnership affairs. Although the UPA conditions the duty to render information on a demand, the courts hold that partners must perform a duty of disclosure regardless of demand. The duty to inform springs from the partners' fiduciary duty of loyalty. As part of this duty, partners must not conceal information from each other.

A partner's right to information continues even if a partner lets others manage the firm. To protect his or her investment and to guard against exposure to potential liability, a partner needs access to all partnership information whether or not the partner actively participates in the firm's management.

The UPA requires:

> The partnership books shall be kept, subject to any agreement between the parties, at the principal place of business of the partnership, and every partner shall *at all times*, have access to and may inspect and copy *any* of them [emphasis added].

Although the UPA does not specify what types of books and records are to be kept, federal income tax regulations require a detailed balance sheet, statements of partnership income and each partner's share of income and deductions, and a reconciliation of the partners' capital accounts. A partner need not be a bookkeeper or an accountant to maintain the records; nor need he or she follow standard accounting practice. But partners may be wise to hire a competent accountant or bookkeeper when they lack these skills themselves. If keeping partnership records at the principal place of business and making them available at all times seems inconvenient, the partnership agreement may provide for a different location and specify times when records may be inspected.

To protect a partner's right to partnership information further, the UPA gives each partner the right to a formal accounting of partnership affairs. A formal accounting is a comprehensive, court-ordered review of partnership transactions by a court-appointed investigator. The UPA gives the right to an accounting when specific circumstances justify it even though there is no dissolution of the partnership. Under the UPA, a partner may seek an accounting without dissolving the partnership when:

1. He or she is wrongfully excluded from partnership business.
2. A partner withholds profits from a secret transaction.
3. An accounting is provided for in the partnership agreement.
4. Other circumstances render an accounting just and reasonable.

Except in these situations one partner does not have a right to an accounting from his or her partners unless the partnership is dissolved. The partner already has access to the firm's books and property.

A partner's only recourse against his or her partners for breaching a duty owed under either the UPA or the partnership agreement is to bring an action for an accounting. A partner cannot otherwise sue his or her partners or the partnership for claims arising out of the partnership's affairs, because the partner would be both plaintiff and defendant in the case. Outside of an action for an accounting, a partner can sue his or her partners only when the problems at issue have nothing to do with partnership affairs or when an accounting has already taken place and the partner's share has been determined.

Relations with Third Parties

Because a partnership exists to do business, partners need to interact with third parties who deal with the partnership. This interaction may be in making contracts or in committing torts. The problem is to what extent a partner's conduct binds the firm and fellow partners.

As mentioned earlier, partnership law is a particular application of agency law. A partner's power to bind the firm in dealings with third parties is determined by the general rules of agency law as provided in the UPA. Because each partner is an agent of the partnership for the purpose of its business, his or her acts may result in the firm's being:

- Liable for contracts made and torts committed by a partner
- Bound by a partner's admissions
- Charged with the knowledge of or notice to a partner

Agency rules provided in the UPA also apply for determining the liability of incoming and withdrawing partners for obligations incurred by the partnership.

Contracts

The power of a partner to bind the partnership to contracts with third parties may be either actual or apparent. The partner may have actual authority as expressly provided in the partnership agreement. If no actual or express authority is provided there, the partner may have apparent authority. When a partner's acts are unauthorized, they may be ratified by a majority of the partners and made binding on the firm. Thus the power of a partner to bind the firm by contract to third parties may be found either in the partnership agreement or, by implication, in his or her conduct or the conduct of the partners.

The UPA provides that any act of a partner is binding on the partnership if it is "for apparently carrying on in the usual way the business of the partnership." This is just a restatement of the agency rule regarding apparent authority. Partners have apparent authority consistent with the nature of the partnership business. The usual authority possessed by partners in similar businesses is the measure of a particular partner's apparent authority.

The UPA further provides that any "act of a partner which is not apparently for the carrying on of the business of the partnership in the usual way does not bind the partnership unless authorized by the other partners." For acts unrelated to the partnership's business, a partner needs actual authority, whether informal or given in the partnership agreement.

Sometimes a partnership agreement restricts a partner's authority to bind the partnership. For example, a partnership agreement may provide that no partner shall incur any debt for the firm of over $500. What effect should this have on third parties? Under the UPA third parties are not limited or bound by secret restrictions of a partner's authority or by restrictions in a partnership agreement unless they know of them. Thus any contracts made by a partner for the firm and related to its business are binding on the partnership despite any secret restrictions on the partner's authority if they are unknown to the third party.

In the following case the court examines to what extent a partnership is liable on the contracts entered into by the partners.

NATIONAL BISCUIT COMPANY V. STROUD

Supreme Court of North Carolina
106 S.E.2d 692 (1959)

BACKGROUND: In March 1953 C. N. Stroud (defendant) and Earl Freeman entered into a general partnership to sell groceries under the name of Stroud's Food Center. Thereafter the National Biscuit Company (Nabisco) (plaintiff) sold bread regularly to the partnership. In October 1955 Stroud advised an agent of Nabisco that he personally would not be responsible for any additional bread sold by Nabisco to Stroud's Food Center. From February 6, 1956, to February 25, 1956, Nabisco, through this same agent, at the request of Freeman, sold and delivered bread in the amount of $171.04 to Stroud's Food Center. Stroud and Freeman by agreement dissolved the partnership at the close of business on February 25, 1956. Stroud paid all the partnership's obligations, amounting to $12,014.45, except the amount of $171.04 claimed by Nabisco. To pay the obligations, Stroud exhausted all the partnership's assets. Nabisco sued both Stroud and Freeman, seeking to recover the $171.04. Stroud claimed that he was not liable to Nabisco. The trial court awarded judgment for Nabisco, and Stroud appealed to the Supreme Court of North Carolina.

Parker, Justice

In *Johnson v. Bernheim*, this Court said:

A and B are general partners to do some given business; the partnership is by operation of law, a power to each to bind the partnership in any manner legitimate to the business. If one partner goes to a third person to buy an article on time for the partnership, the other partner cannot prevent it by writing to the third not to sell to him on time; or, if one party attempts to buy for cash, the other has no right to require that it shall be on time. And what is true in regard to buying is true in regard to selling. What either partner does with a third person is binding on the partnership. It is otherwise where the partnership is not general, but is upon special terms, as that purchases and sales must be with and for cash. There the power to each is special, in regard to all dealings with third persons at least who have notice of the terms.

The General Assembly of North Carolina in 1941 enacted a Uniform Partnership Act, which became effective 16 March 1941. [The court then quoted the applicable sections of the UPA.]

Freeman as a general partner with Stroud, with no restrictions on his authority to act within the scope of the partnership business so far as the agreed statement of facts shows, had under the Uniform Partnership Act "equal rights in the management and conduct of the partnership business." Under [the UPA] Stroud, his co-partner, could not restrict the power and authority of Freeman to buy bread for the partnership as a going concern, for such a purchase was an "ordinary matter connected with the partnership business." . . . Therefore Freeman's purchases of bread from plaintiff for Stroud's Food Center as a going concern bound the partnership and his co-partner Stroud. The quoted provisions of our Uniform Partnership Act, in respect to the particular facts here, are in accord with the principle of law stated in *Johnson v. Bernheim*.

In *Crane on Partnership*, 2nd Ed., p. 277, it is said:

In cases of an even division of the partners as to whether or not an act within the scope of the business should be done, of which disagreement a third person has knowledge, it seems that logically no restriction can be placed upon the power to act. The partnership being a going concern, activities within the scope of the business should not be limited, save by the expressed will of the majority deciding a disputed question; half of the members are not a majority.

DECISION: The Supreme Court of North Carolina affirmed the trial court judgment in favor of Nabisco.

Torts

Under the UPA the partnership is liable for the torts of any partner acting in the ordinary course of the business of the partnership or with the authority of his or her partners. All members of a partnership are liable for a partner's torts committed within the scope and course of the partnership business. This liability also extends to absent partners who did not participate in, ratify, or know about the tort. The determining factor for invoking partnership liability is whether the tort was committed within the reasonable scope of and on behalf of the partnership business. If the wrongful conduct was clearly outside the scope of the partnership business, the nonparticipating partners may still be liable if they authorize, ratify, or consent to

the tort. Consent, scope, and course of business provide the principal channels through which liability attaches to a partnership for a partner's torts. Liability usually attaches when a partner's negligence injures a third party. In comparison with negligent conduct, a willful and malicious tort is generally held not to be within the scope of an ordinary partnership, and the partnership is not liable unless the nonparticipating partners authorize, ratify, or consent to their partner's willful tort. For example, if a partner in a tavern assaults a customer without provocation, liability would not extend to the absent partner who had neither consented to nor authorized the attack.

The following case demonstrates the potential tort liability of partners.

KELSEY-SEYBOLD CLINIC V. MACLAY

Supreme Court of Texas
466 S.W.2d 716 (1971)

BACKGROUND: For several years John Dale Maclay (plaintiff) and his wife and children had been under the medical care of Kelsey-Seybold Clinic (defendant), including treatment by a pediatrician, Dr. Brewer, who was a partner in the clinic. Claiming that Dr. Brewer was engaging in conduct designed to alienate the affections of his wife, Maclay notified Dr. Kelsey, a senior partner at the clinic, of the alleged tortious relationship. Maclay claimed that despite such notice, the physician's relationship with Maclay's wife continued. Maclay brought suit against Dr. Brewer and the clinic for the tort of alienation of affection. The trial court awarded summary judgment in favor of the clinic. Maclay appealed to the Texas Court of Civil Appeals, which ruled in favor of Maclay and reversed the trial court decision. The clinic then appealed to the Texas Supreme Court.

Walker, Justice

We are unwilling to believe that plaintiff seriously expects to prove in a conventional trial that the acts alleged to have been committed by Dr. Brewer were in the course and scope of the partnership business or were either authorized or ratified by the Clinic. . . . [W]e assume for the purpose of this opinion that Dr. Brewer was not acting in the ordinary course of the

Clinic's business and that his conduct was neither authorized nor ratified by the partnership. This will enable us to reach questions that may well arise at the trial of the case.

The Court of Civil Appeals reasoned that the summary judgment was improper because the Clinic had not conclusively negated consent on its part of the alleged wrongful conduct of Dr. Brewer. In reaching this conclusion, it relied on our opinion in *K&G Oil Tool & Service Co. v. G&G Fishing Tool Service*, where it was stated that:

> A non-participating partner is ordinarily not personally liable for the wrongful tortious or criminal acts of the acting partner unless such acts are within the scope of the partnership's business or were consented to, authorized, ratified or adopted by the non-participating partner.

There was no question of consent in *K&G*, and it was held that the non-participating partner was not liable.

Where a partner proposed to do, in the name or for the benefit of the partnership, some act that is not in the ordinary course of the business, consent by the other partners may constitute his authority to do the act for the partnership. We also recognize that even a wilful or malicious act outside the ordinary scope of the partnership business may be so related to the business that tacit consent of the other partners could fairly be regarded as a grant of authority. In this instance, however, Dr. Brewer was acting solely for his own personal gratification. His conduct could not benefit the Clinic in any way, and no one would have supposed that he was acting for the partnership. It is our opinion that in these circumstances the "consent" that might be inferred from the silence or inaction of the Clinic after learning of his conduct does not render the Clinic vicariously liable for the damages claimed by the plaintiff.

On the basis of the present record and the facts we are assuming in this case, the liability of the Clinic must rest, if at all, upon some theory akin to that recognized by the court in *Williams v. F.&W. Grand Five, Ten and Twenty-five Cent Stores*. The Clinic was under a duty, of course, to exercise ordinary care to protect its patients from harm resulting from tortious conduct of persons upon the premises. A negligent breach of that duty could subject the Clinic to liability without regard to whether the tortious conduct immediately causing the harm was that of an agent or servant or was in the ordinary scope of the partnership business. For example, it might become liable, as a result of its own negligence, for damage done by a vicious employee while acting beyond the scope of his authority.

We are also of the opinion that the Clinic owed a duty to the families of its patients to exercise ordinary care to prevent a tortious interference with family relations. It was not required to maintain constant surveillance over personnel on duty or to inquire into and regulate the personal conduct of partners and employees while engaged in their private affairs. But if and when the partnership received information from which it knew or should have known that there might be a need to take action, it was under a duty to use reasonable means at its disposal to prevent any partner or employee from improperly using his position with the Clinic to work a tortious invasion of legally protected family interests. This duty relates only to conduct of a partner or employee on the premises of the Clinic or while purportedly acting as a representative of the Clinic elsewhere. Failure to exercise ordinary care in discharging that duty would subject the Clinic to liability for damages proximately caused by its negligence.

The rather meager information in the present record does not necessarily indicate that the Clinic was under a duty to act or that it could have done anything to prevent the damage when Dr. Kelsey first learned of the situation. On the other hand, it does not affirmatively and clearly appear that the Clinic could or should have done nothing. Mrs. Maclay's affections may have been alienated from her husband before anyone talked with Dr. Kelsey, but the facts in that respect are not fully developed. There is not proof as to when, where or under what circumstances the misconduct, if any, on Dr. Brewer's part occurred. Dr. Kelsey testified that he did not believe anything improper occurred at the Clinic, but the proofs do not establish as a matter of law that he was justified in not making further inquiry after his conversations with plaintiff and Mr. Maclay's uncle. The record does not show whether there is a partnership agreement that might have a bearing on the case, and we have no way of knowing the extent to which the Clinic might have determined which patients were to be seen by Dr. Brewer or controlled his actions while on duty. Dr. Kelsey's testimony suggests that the partners might have been in a position to prevent improper conduct by one of their number on the premises of the Clinic. In our opinion the Clinic has failed to discharge the heavy, and in a case of this character virtually impossible, burden of establishing as a matter of law at the summary judgment stage that it is not liable under any theory fairly presented by the allegations.

DECISION: The Texas Supreme Court affirmed the appellate court's decision in favor of Maclay and ordered the case to be sent back to the trial court for a trial.

Admissions, Knowledge, and Notice

Agency rules make the partnership responsible for the admissions or representations of any partner about partnership affairs within the scope of his or her authority. As in agency law, knowledge or notice to any partner of matters relating to partnership affairs is assumed to extend to all the partnership. Thus notice to a partner about a matter of firm business is notice to the partnership and all its members. But knowledge or notice is not assumed when the partner acquires it while acting fraudulently or adversely to the firm, or when the knowledge was acquired by the partner before joining the firm.

Withdrawing and Incoming Partners

Partners often withdraw or retire from firms and are replaced by incoming partners. Partners must take care to consider how the change in membership will affect the liabilities of each. A retiring partner remains liable to third parties unless he or she notifies third parties who know of the partnership and have extended credit to it. This notice may be given informally by letter or phone, or by a novation, substituting the incoming partner for the retiring partner as responsible to the partnership's creditors. Constructive notice, such as publication in a newspaper, is essential to notify third parties adequately who know about the partnership but have never extended credit to it.

An incoming partner is liable for all partnership obligations arising before his or her admission, just as if the incoming partner had been a partner when such obligations were incurred. But this liability may be satisfied only out of the partnership property. A judgment for such an obligation may not be satisfied out of the incoming partner's individual property. An incoming partner may promise the partners that old creditors will be paid. When this happens, the promise can be enforced by the creditors as third-party beneficiaries to the contract and may subject the incoming partner's individual property to satisfy the debt. Another way to accomplish the same result is for the creditors to enter into a novation, substituting the incoming partner for any withdrawing partner.

Partnership Dissolution

The day may come when the partnership is dissolved. The partners may wish to withdraw from the firm or simply to change to the corporate form. The partnership may be bankrupt. There are many reasons for *partnership dissolution.* Unlike corporations, partnerships lack continued existence. Like humankind, they are mortal. But with a little wizardry, the partnership business may be born again and continue its commercial course in a new guise. We now visit the deathbed of the partnership, view its "dissolution," and witness its "winding up." However, this discussion concludes on a happier note, with how the business may be continued.

Dissolution, Winding Up, and Termination

The UPA distinguishes among a partnership's dissolution, winding up, and termination, which are the three phases of ending a partnership. The first phase, the partnership's **dissolution**, occurs when the partners cease being associated with one another as partners. It has nothing to do with the discontinuation of the partnership *business* but refers only to a change of *relation* among the partners. The partnership does not automatically stop doing business upon dissolution. A partnership continues after dissolution until the business is liquidated and the partnership terminated, unless continued by agreement or pursuant to the UPA. The second phase is the winding up of partnership affairs. **Winding up** is the process of bringing the partnership business to an end. The third phase is the partnership's termination. Upon **termination** the partnership is legally and functionally dead.

Dissolution The UPA defines dissolution as the change in the relation of the partners caused by any partner's ceasing to be associated in the carrying on, as distinguished from the winding up, of the business. Dissolution is a legal event, a point in time when partners stop doing business together. The partnership has technically dissolved.

Winding Up and Termination The UPA cautions that "on dissolution the partnership is not terminated, but continues until the winding up is completed." The winding up, called **liquidation**, is the process of ending partnership affairs. It is the administration of assets to discharge the firm's obligations to its creditors and members. When that process is complete, the partnership is terminated.

Causes of Dissolution

Partnership dissolution is caused by the acts of the partners or by operation of law.

Acts of the Partners Any partner may dissolve the partnership at any time, and each partner has the power to dissolve the partnership. But the distinction between the *power* to dissolve and the *right* to dissolve should be carefully noted. A power is the ability to affect the legal status of another—for example, a partner's ability to alter his or her associates' status as members of a partnership by dissolving the firm. A person may incur a liability for exercising a power wrongfully. But with a right to do something, there is no liability for its exercise. A partner may have the power to dissolve but not the right. Although a partner can cause a dissolution of the partnership at any time, if the dissolution is wrongful, the guilty partner may be liable to his or her partners for the misconduct.

Whether the partner has the right to dissolve is determined by the agreement among the partners. It may show consent to future dissolution. It may confer, or it may withhold the right under certain circumstances. Any act by a partner that causes the firm's dissolution is rightful if it complies with the agreement. Any act by a partner that causes the firm's dissolution is wrongful if it contradicts the agreement. Under the UPA, dissolution is caused without violating the agreement between the partners in the following circumstances:

1. When the partnership term expires, which may be upon the completion of a specified time period or a particular period
2. If no definite time or particular undertaking is specified, at the express will of any partners
3. By agreement of all the partners or by less than all when one or more of the partners has assigned his or her interest or it has been subjected to a *charging order*
4. By expelling a partner according to the terms of the partnership agreement

When a dissolution contradicts the partnership agreement, the remaining partners may recover damages from the partner who violates the agreement. This provision is another application of the contract law principles regarding the rights of contracting parties in the event of a breach. The UPA also protects the remaining partners from wrongful dissolution by permitting them to continue the partnership without the errant partner. To do so, the remaining partners must pay to the dissolving partner the value of his or her interest in the partnership, less damages, and must *indemnify* (repay) him or her against all partnership liabilities.

Operation of Law Dissolution of a partnership also may be caused by operation of law. Under the UPA dissolution is caused by operation of law in the following ways:

- By any event that makes it unlawful to carry on the partnership business
- By the death of any partner
- By the bankruptcy of any partner or the partnership
- By court decree under the UPA

The UPA allows dissolutions by a court when a partner applies for it on one of the following grounds.

1. When a partner is incapable of performing as a partner
2. When improper conduct of a partner is detrimental to the business, such as continual breaches of the partnership agreement
3. When the business can be carried on only at a loss
4. When circumstances and equities show that dissolution is necessary

Winding Up the Partnership Business

As mentioned, the winding up is the process by which the partnership business is brought to an end. After the partnership relation has dissolved, the partnership's affairs must be wound up if business is to be terminated. This winding up of a firm's affairs is the process of reducing assets to pay creditors and members of the partnership. During winding up all uncompleted transactions are finished, debts are settled or paid, claims and accounts owed are collected or settled, and the remaining assets are either sold or distributed along with any surplus to the partners. During this process the partnership continues for the limited purpose of liquidation, and the partners retain only those powers that are incidental to winding up the business.

Right to Wind Up The surviving partners who are not bankrupt and who have not wrongfully dissolved the partnership have the right to wind up the affairs of the partnership. When the partners agree to a dissolution, or when the partnership's term expires, all the partners have the right to wind up the firm's affairs. Partners often designate a fellow partner to be in charge of winding up the business. This person is usually called the **liquidating partner** or **liquidator**. The partners may appoint the liquidating partner by agreement in the articles of partnership.

If the partnership is dissolved because of the bankruptcy or death of a partner, the remaining or surviving partners are entitled to wind up the partnership. Under the UPA a surviving partner is entitled to reasonable compensation for winding up the business. Only if the last surviving partner dies before the business is wound up does the legal representative of a deceased partner have the right to participate in the winding up. If dissolution is by court order, a court-appointed receiver winds up the firm.

Partners' Powers during Winding Up Two needs arise upon dissolution of the partnership:

1. The need to wind up the firm's affairs
2. The need to protect third parties who do business with the firm without knowing of its dissolution

Both needs are satisfied by two agency law concepts: actual and apparent authority.

To prevent partners from engaging in any new business that might delay winding up, a partner's actual authority upon dissolution is limited to what needs to be done to end the business. A partner may do only what is necessary and incidental to winding up the firm's affairs.

Whether a transaction is necessary and incidental to winding up the partnership depends on the circumstances. Generally the partners who are winding up the firm's partnership may sell partnership property to liquidate the firm's assets, take payment for obligations owed to the partnership, and enter into compromises with creditors to release the partnership from its obligations. Actions that at first seem inappropriate actually may be appropriate if they are necessary and incidental to the partnership's winding up.

The concept of apparent authority protects third parties who deal with a partner without knowing about the partnership's dissolution and winding up. A partner's apparent authority may serve to bind the firm to a transaction that would have been binding before dissolution when a third party deals with a partner without knowledge or notice of the dissolution. The UPA incorporates the concept of apparent authority by providing that after dissolution a partner may still bind the partnership to transactions with those who for-merly extended credit to the firm if the former creditors have no notice of the dissolution. People who never extended credit to the firm are consid-ered to have notice of the dissolution advertised in a newspaper of general circulation.

In the following case the court considers what constitutes the winding up of partnership affairs and the extent of a surviving partner's authority.

KING V. STODDARD
Court of Appeals of California
104 Cal. Rptr. 903 (1972)

BACKGROUND: Lyman Stoddard, Sr., his wife, Alda, and their son, Lyman, Jr., oper-ated a partnership that published a newspaper, the *Walnut Kernel*. After Lyman and Alda died, Lyman, Jr., continued operating the paper as the sole surviving partner. King and White, an accounting firm, had been accountants for the *Walnut Kernel* for about 10 years before Lyman and Alda died and continued to render accounting ser-vices after their deaths. When King and White (plaintiffs) were not paid, they sued Lyman, Jr., and the estates of Lyman and Alda (defendants). The agents of the es-tates argued that the estates were not liable because the son lacked the authority to employ an accounting firm and had the authority to hire one only on behalf of the part-nership. Their reasoning was that the newspaper had continued to preserve its asset value as a going business so it could be sold and that this was part of the winding up of the business. The trial court found the estates liable to King and White, and the es-tates appealed.

Brown, Justice

The partnership was dissolved by operation of law upon the deaths of Alda and Lyman E. Stoddard, Sr. [The UPA] provides that dissolution of a partnership is ". . . caused by any partner ceasing to be associated in the carrying on as distinguished from the winding up of the business." Death is one of the causes of dissolution. Dissolution, however, does not ter-minate the partnership which ". . . continues until the winding up of the partnership affairs is completed." Although the general rule is that a partner has no authority to bind his co-partners to new obligations after dissolution, [the UPA] provides that "[a]fter dissolution a partner can bind the partnership . . . (a) By any act appropriate for winding up partnership af-fairs. . . ."

It is this latter provision upon which the court based its decision that the estates of the deceased partners were liable for the accounting services performed after dissolution. The court found that "LYMAN STODDARD, JR.'S continuation of the WALNUT KERNEL business was an appropriate act for winding up the partnership, since the assets of the business would have substantial value only if it was a going business. It was to the advantage of the partnership that the business be maintained as a going business."

Respondents, as accountants, had performed services both before and after the disso-lution. The services, however, were a continuation of the accounting services pursuant to the ordinary course of the operation of the business. Respondent King testified that he was "doing work for the activity of the newspaper, the financial activity of the newspaper" and that he was doing the same type of work as he had always performed for the *Walnut Kernel*. The exhibits which support his bill for services indicate that he did not, or was not able to, break down his services into categories which would separate ordinary accounting services from those related to the winding up of the partnership. The court, however, found that the continuation of the business itself was an "act appropriate for winding up partnership affairs."

We disagree with this finding. It is probably true that there might have been advantages to the partnership to sell the business as a going business, but the indefinite continuation of the partnership business is contrary to the requirement for winding up of the affairs upon dissolution.

Even if we assume that a situation might exist where continuation of the business for a period would be appropriate to winding up the partnership interest, such a situation did not exist here. The record reflects the fact that the surviving partner was not taking action to wind up the partnership as was his duty, nor did the estates consent in any way to a delay. Rather, their insistence on winding up took the form of an effort to sell the business and a suit to require an accounting. There is nothing in the record upon which to base the argument made by respondents that appellants consented to their continued employment. The fact that they did not object is of no relevance. They had no right to direct and did not participate in the operation of the business. Therefore, the determination that the acts of the accountants were rendered during a winding-up process is not based upon substantial evidence.

DECISION: The California Court of Appeals reversed the trial court's decision and ruled that the estates were not liable to the accounting firm.

Distribution of Assets

Order of Claims   After partnership assets are liquidated, the proceeds are distributed to pay any claims against the firm. Claims against the partnership are paid in the following order:

1. Claims of partnership creditors
2. Claims of partners for loans or advances
3. Partners' capital contributions
4. Remaining assets distributed as profits and surplus to the partners

If the partnership is solvent, no problems are presented because everyone gets paid. But if the partnership's assets are insufficient to pay its debts, the partners must make up the loss in the same proportion as they shared profits. If some of the partners are insolvent but others are able to pay, the firm's creditors are paid by the solvent partners.

Marshaling of Assets   A partnership creditor has a claim against partnership assets. When partnership assets are insufficient to pay the claim, the creditor has a claim against the individual partners' property. A problem arises when there are both individual and partnership creditors. What are their relative rights to a partner's partnership and individual property? Individual creditors have priority to the partner's individual property, but partnership creditors have priority to partnership property. Under the doctrine called marshaling of assets, a partnership creditor must pursue a claim against partnership property before pursuing a partner's individual property. By compelling partnership creditors to exhaust partnership property before pursuing a partner's individual property, the doctrine lets both individual and partnership creditors satisfy their claims if there are substantial assets.

Continuing the Partnership Business

Depending on the particular business involved, dissolution and subsequent liquidation without the right to continue the partnership business can be economically disastrous to the remaining partners. Consequently, one of the major reasons for having a partnership agreement is to provide for the firm's **continuation** by the remaining partners despite dissolution. In large accounting and brokerage firms, for example, partners are continually joining and withdrawing from the firm. Technically, these comings and goings dissolve the partnership. But through carefully considered provisions in their partnership agreements, they

PREVENTIVE LAW
Dissolution of Partnership

A dissolved partnership may be continued by an agreement between the withdrawing and remaining partners at the time of dissolution. It may be provided for in advance by a provision in the partnership agreement. For example, a clause in the partnership agreement may provide:

> In the event of dissolution caused by the retirement of a partner, the remaining partners shall have the right to continue the partnership business under the same name by themselves or with any other persons they may choose; however, they shall pay to the retiring partner the value of his or her interest as of the date of dissolution.

When the dissolution occurs, liquidation will consist of bookkeeping and buying out the withdrawing partner.

Providing for the firm's continuation in the partnership agreement requires foresight and care by the partners. They should determine:

1. Which events, such as death, retirement, bankruptcy, and so on, that cause dissolution may also give rise to the right to continue
2. Which partners have the right to continue
3. The method of disposing of the withdrawing partner's interest—for example, purchase by the remaining partners or by an incoming partner
4. The method of payment for the withdrawing partner's interest, such as cash, insurance proceeds, or payments out of future earnings
5. The method of allocating the price of the withdrawing partner's interest

The partnership provision calling for the purchase of a withdrawing partner's interest is usually referred to as a buy-sell agreement. When the death of a partner is contemplated, the buy-sell agreement usually provides for the purchase of a deceased partner's interest at death and is frequently funded by insurance. In a growing business in which the partners have reinvested their profits, the surviving partners may be without immediate funds to pay the deceased partner's interest. The only source of funds for the deceased partner's interest may be the future profits of the business, which then will not be available for reinvestment. In such a situation the buy-sell provision in the partnership agreement may provide for the funding of the purchase price with insurance. The insurance premiums may be paid by the partners or the partnership. On the death of a partner the insurance policy proceeds are then used to pay the deceased partner's interest.

avoid any termination of activities. A continuation provision in a partnership agreement may allow remaining partners to carry on the partnership by buying out a withdrawing partner. Although this arrangement technically is a dissolution of the partnership, the partnership *business* continues.

Right to Continue Partners may have the right to continue the partnership business although their agreement contains no continuation provision. As we mentioned earlier, when dissolution is caused by an act that contradicts the agreement, the innocent partners may continue the business by

- Paying the dissolving partner the value of his or her interest minus an amount attributable to any damages resulting from the breach
- Repaying the wrongful partner for all partnership liabilities

The value of the partner's interest is generally determined by its market value at dissolution rather than by its book value.

The UPA grants the innocent partners the right to continue when there is a wrongful dissolution, but the partners still should provide for the situation in their partnership agreement. Their continuation agreement should include at least:

1. A method for placing a value on the guilty partner's interest
2. An agreed method of reimbursement
3. An agreed method of payment if other than cash

Continuation's Effect on Existing Liabilities When a partnership continues, creditors of the former partnership remain as creditors of the continuing partnership. The creditors may enforce their claims against a withdrawing partner, who remains liable for any obligations incurred by the partnership before he or she withdrew from the firm. The remaining partners may relieve the withdrawing partner of existing liabilities, but third parties are not bound by the

arrangement unless they agree to the change through a novation.

Continuation's Effect on Later Liabilities Just as it is important to notify third parties of the partnership's dissolution when it is terminated, it is equally important to provide notice when the business continues. Failure to notify third parties of the dissolution when the business continues may increase the liability of the continuing and former partners. If the continuing partners fail to notify third parties of the partnership's dissolution when a partner withdraws from the firm, the continuing partners may be bound by later acts of their former partner. Conversely, if the business is continued as a corporation, failure to notify former creditors may result in the former partners being held personally liable for new obligations as if they were still partners.

CONCEPT SUMMARY
Partner's Rights under the UPA

The following are the rights a partner has under the UPA. A partner can avoid these rules by entering into a partnership agreement that creates different rules. So, unless the partnership agreement provides a different rule, a partner has under the law:

- The right to possess partnership property for partnership purposes
- The right of survivorship in partnership property in the event of a co-partner's death
- The right to transfer his or her partnership interest (the share of profits or surplus) by conveyance, assignment, or inheritance
- The right to undivided loyalty from one's co-partner
- The right to an equal share of profits
- The right to participate equally in the management of the partnership business
- A veto right on extraordinary management matters (such as the admission of new partners or changes in the partnership agreement)
- The right to all information concerning partnership affairs
- The right to inspect and copy partnership records
- The right to a formal accounting under certain circumstances (for example, if the partner has been wrongfully excluded from partnership business or has been denied profits)
- The authority to bind the partnership to contracts that are related to partnership business
- The right to wind up partnership affairs upon dissolution, if the partner is not bankrupt and has not wrongfully dissolved the partnership
- The right to continue the partnership business, if a co-partner has wrongfully dissolved the partnership

Review Questions and Problems

Key Terms

partnership property

tenancy in partnership

right of survivorship

charging order

receiver

buy-sell agreement

dissolution

winding up

termination

liquidation

liquidating partner

liquidator

Discussion Questions

1. What is the difference between partnership property and a partner's interest in a partnership?

2. In the absence of a partnership agreement, how are ordinary partnership matters to be decided by the partners?

3. Compare what is meant by partnership dissolution and winding up of partnership business.

4. What are the rights and powers of the partners during the winding up of the partnership business?

Review Problems

1. Julius and Penelope formed a partnership to operate under the name of the Swish Toilet Company, which would manufacture and sell contour toilet fixtures. Julius applied for a personal loan at the Hard Luck Loan Company. The intended purpose of the loan, as disclosed by Julius to Hard Luck, was to purchase a new car for his wife, Fifi. Hard Luck refused to lend Julius the money unless the firm signed as guarantor, guaranteeing Julius' repayment. Julius signed his name on the loan contract and then signed the Swish Toilet Company name, as guarantor. All this was done in the presence of the Hard Luck agent. If Julius fails to pay back the loan and is insolvent, can Hard Luck hold the Swish Toilet Company liable as guarantor of the loan? Explain. Can Hard Luck obtain Julius' partnership interest in the Swish Toilet Company? Explain. Suppose the same facts, except that Julius has died. What are Penelope's and Fifi's rights with regard to the partnership property? Explain.

2. Doug Whitman, Bill McCarty, and Bartley Brennan formed a partnership, the Ace Cosmetic Company, which manufactured cosmetics for women. They did not enter into either a written or an oral partnership agreement. Whitman and McCarty each contributed $200,000 to the capital of the partnership. Brennan contributed $50,000. For the first year of operation Brennan managed the business. Profits for the first year amounted to $300,000. How should the profits be distributed among the three partners?

Explain. Assume that Brennan now wants the partnership to bring out a new line of cosmetics for the older woman. Whitman and McCarty think that this is a bad idea. How should the issue be decided if the partners maintain their positions? Explain.

3. Julius owned and operated a sawmill. One day his daughter, Penelope, introduced him to Frank, who had recently moved into the area and who had met Penelope at a social function. Frank had previously managed a sawmill in another state. Julius asked Frank if he would be interested in going into the mill business as his partner. Frank looked the sawmill over and agreed to go into partnership with Julius. It was agreed that Frank would pay $60,000 for a half interest. He would pay $20,000 down, $10,000 in 30 days, and the rest at $1,000 a month. Things went smoothly for a month, but the mill was forced to close down when loggers refused to deliver logs because the mill had failed to pay on past accounts. It was then that Frank took his first look at the mill's books. There he discovered that the mill's liabilities exceeded its assets. The only cash in the bank was the money Frank had contributed. The mill owed over $300,000 to creditors. Its chief assets were its premises and its equipment. But Frank discovered that the First National Bank held mortgages on the land, the building, and the equipment. What are Frank's rights and liabilities with regard to the mill's creditors and Julius? Explain.

4. Curtis Cyrus wrote to his brother Cecil in North Dakota asking him to come to Minnesota to form a partnership in a resort venture. Curtis had recently bought 60 acres of land in Minnesota with his own money and in his own name. Cecil, a skilled carpenter, agreed. He moved his family to Minnesota, built a cabin on the property, and moved his family into it. Cecil built six other cabins on the property and operated them as a resort. Each year the brothers divided the profits equally between them. When Cecil died several years later, his wife decided to move back to North Dakota. She asked Curtis to pay her one-half of the value of the resort, including the fair market value of the land. Curtis claimed that the land was his. What are the rights of the parties? Explain.

5. Anderson, Baker, and Chase were partners. Anderson contributed $50,000 in capital and loaned the partnership $40,000. Baker contributed $30,000 in capital. Chase contributed his services. Five years after the partnership was formed, the three partners agreed to dissolve the partnership and wind up the business. The partnership creditors, other than Anderson, have claims of $130,000. After all profits and losses have been recorded, there are $176,000 of assets to be distributed to creditors and partners. How are the proceeds of the partnership to be distributed upon dissolution? Explain.

6. Baker and Corbin were partners doing business as Ace Photographers. When Corbin indicated that she wanted to withdraw from the business, the partners entered into a written dissolution agree-

ment whereby Baker was allowed to continue the business. No notice was given to the firm's creditors. Photo Film, Inc. had sold film to Ace Photographers before the dissolution and continued to do so for several years after the dissolution. Baker ran into financial trouble. He terminated the business and filed for personal bankruptcy. Photo Film had a claim against Ace Photographers for $5,000 for film sold to Ace after the dissolution date. Photo Film sued Corbin, claiming that she was liable on the claim. Who wins and why?

7. McCarty and Brennan are partners. Recently McCarty has noticed that Brennan's memory is slipping more than usual and that he rambles and annoys customers. McCarty has been thinking of dissolving the partnership and continuing the business as sole proprietor. The partnership agreement still has several years to go before its termination. What should McCarty do? Explain.

Case Problems

1. Hugo and Charles were brothers who did business as partners. After several years Hugo died, and Charles was appointed administrator of his estate. Tax returns disclosed that the partnership business was continued just as it had been before Hugo's death. Hugo's estate received the profits and was charged with the losses of the business. Did Charles have the authority to continue the partnership business after the dissolution of the partnership brought on by Hugo's death, and are the assets of Hugo's estate chargeable with the liabilities of the partnership incurred after Hugo's death?

2. Salmon, as lessee, entered into a 20-year lease of a building for the purpose of operating a hotel. The lease required that Salmon alter the hotel to make it suitable for shops and offices. Needing capital to make the required improvements, Salmon turned to Meinhard. The two entered into a joint venture whereby Meinhard would provide one-half the cost of the alteration, upkeep, and repair in return for one-half of the profits. The venture was successful. Four months prior to the end of the 20-year lease term, the lessor renewed the lease with Salmon and made a deal with Salmon to develop the hotel property and adjoining lots and to construct a larger $3 million building. Meinhard was not told of this new deal, and when he learned about it a month later, he demanded that the new lease be held in trust for the joint venture, which had not yet expired. Salmon refused, and Meinhard sued. Is Meinhard entitled to an interest in the new lease? Discuss.

3. Hess was a real estate agent in a real estate brokerage. Unknown to his employer, he opened an account in which he deposited client funds that were temporarily held in connection with real estate transactions that he handled. The firm already had a client trust account for this purpose, but Hess chose to use his own account instead. Hess converted his account to an interest-bearing account and earned over $10,000 in interest on deposits held temporarily on behalf of clients. Hess withdrew about $6,000 of his interest earnings and deposited it in his personal account. When Hess' brokerage found out about his account, Hess was forced to resign. Hess was also brought before the state disciplinary board for real estate agents. Hess claimed that he was justified in doing what he did because his employer did not treat him fairly with respect to the allocation of firm commissions. Assuming that Hess was in fact treated unfairly, was he justified in doing what he did? Discuss.

4. Kelly was a lawyer with the firm of Beckman, Kelly, and Smith, a partnership. Kelly left the partnership, thus causing the partnership to be automatically dissolved. Kelly continued to work on cases that he had started while he was still with the firm. His former partners at the firm sued him, claiming to be entitled to share in any profits that Kelly made on cases begun while he was still with the firm. What was the result?

40

Limited Partnerships

A **limited partnership** carries many of the characteristics of a general partnership except that the liability of some members is limited. It offers some of the benefits of both partnerships and corporations and may be used to attract investors willing to put up money but unwilling to risk personal liabilities. A limited partnership protects a special partner by exempting him or her from personal liability.

A limited partnership consists of one or more **general partners** who conduct the business and are personally liable to creditors, as in an ordinary partnership. It also includes one or more **limited partners** who make contributions to the partnership and share in profits but who do not participate in the control of the business and who assume no liability for the obligations of the partnership beyond that of their investment. (Unless qualified by either "general" or "limited," the term "partner," refers to both general and limited partners.)

You may wonder why someone would choose to do business as a limited partnership rather than as a corporation. As discussed in Chapter 41, limited liability can be obtained by forming a corporation. However, the limited partnership offers flexibility that is not provided in corporate law. Statutes governing corporations contain require-ments that many small businesses find cumbersome, such as requiring that there be a board of directors and an annual shareholders meeting, to name just a couple. Limited partnerships do not have to meet these requirements. In addition to flexibility, limited partnerships require a general partner to obtain the approval of the other partners in situations where a corporation would not need to seek shareholder approval. So in some circumstances, limited partners may have more rights than corporate shareholders.

The Law Governing Limited Partnerships

Limited partnerships were unknown to the common law and are entirely the creatures of statute. The earliest limited partnership statutes were enacted in New York and Connecticut in 1822. Today, each state has its own limited partnership law, and businesspeople wanting to do business through the limited partnership will need to consult a lawyer familiar with the limited partnership law of their state.

State limited partnership laws are based on the **Uniform Limited Partnership Act (ULPA)**. The ULPA was originally written in 1916. However, it was substantially revised in 1976, and again in 1985. As of this writing, thirty-three states have enacted the 1985 revision. The rest of the states have adopted either the 1916 or the 1976 version of the law. There is enough difference among the three versions of the law that it is necessary to consult the law of your particular state to know which version of the ULPA it adopted. Because the majority of the states have adopted the 1985 ULPA, it will be the version discussed in this chapter.

Forming the Limited Partnership: The Certificate of Limited Partnership

You will recall from the discussion in Chapter 38 that the Uniform Partnership Act does not require formalities to form a general partnership. This is not the case with limited partnerships. Technical formalities do accompany the formation of limited partnerships.

In order to form a limited partnership, a **certificate of limited partnership** must be executed and filed with a state authority, usually the office of the Secretary of State.

A limited partnership is formed at the time of the filing of the certificate of limited partnership or at any later time specified in the certificate. Substantial compliance with the filing requirement is sufficient to bring the limited partnership into existence; minor errors in the certificate will not affect the limited partnership's existence.

Filing the certificate of limited partnership serves to mechanically bring the limited partnership into existence. The certificate also serves to provide notice to creditors that the partnership is a limited partnership and serves to notify creditors of the identities of the designated general partners. However, as with general partnerships, the partnership agreement, not the certificate of limited partnership, is the authoritative and comprehensive document for most limited partnerships. Although a **limited partnership agreement** is not required, most limited partnerships have one. Potential creditors of the limited partnership should ask to see the partnership agreement, not the certificate of limited partnership, to obtain information regarding the limited partnership's finances.

A general partner who becomes aware that any statement in the certificate of limited partnership is false must promptly amend the certificate. If a certificate contains a false statement, anyone who suffers a loss by relying on the statement may recover for the loss from any general partner who knew or should have known that the statement was false. The certificate must be amended whenever a general partner is admitted to or withdraws from the firm.

The name of the limited partnership, as set forth in its certificate of limited partnership, must contain the words "limited partnership." The name may not contain the name of a limited partner unless it is also the name of a general partner, or unless the business had been carried on under the name before the admission of that limited partner. Further, the name may not be the same as or deceptively similar to the name of any corporation or limited partnership organized or registered in the state.

Person Erroneously Believing Himself or Herself a Limited Partner

Sometimes a person believes that he or she has invested in a limited partnership when that is not the case. When this happens, the ULPA specifies that a person who has contributed to a business enterprise is not a general partner in the enterprise and is not bound by its obligations if two conditions are met.

CONCEPT SUMMARY
Contents of the Certificate of Limited Partnership

The certificate of limited partnership must include the following items:

- The name of the limited partnership
- The name and address of the statutory agent—the person designated to receive service of process for purposes of a lawsuit
- The name and the business address of each general partner
- The date the limited partnership is to dissolve
- Any other matters the general partners decide to include

First, at the time the person contributes to the business, the person must have a good faith belief that he or she has become a limited partner in the enterprise rather than a general partner. Second, the person must on ascertaining the mistake take one of two courses of action. He or she may correct the mistake by filing a certificate of limited partnership. In the alternative, the person may give notice and withdraw completely from future equity participation in the business. If these conditions are met, the person is liable only as a limited partner with respect to third parties dealing with the enterprise. Personal liability as a general partner is avoided. (However, if the conditions are not met—for example, if the person did not have a good faith basis for believing that the business was a limited partnership—the person would be liable as a general partner, assuming that the existence of a general partnership can be established.)

Personal liability to third parties arises when the third party transacts business with the enterprise before the person files a proper certificate or withdraws. Liability is limited, however, by the requirement that at the time the third party transacts business with the enterprise, he or she actually believed in good faith that the person was a general partner at the time of the transaction. Reliance on the part of the third party on that person's apparent status as a general partner in transacting business with the enterprise is essential before liability is imposed for transactions occurring before withdrawal.

In the following case, Judith Carpenter, an experienced businesswoman, thought she was a limited partner in a business that she and her husband had invested in. When Judith and her husband divorced, she discovered that the partnership was not a limited partnership after all, and that the partnership owed over $100,000 to one of its creditors. As you read the case, consider what you would have done had you been in Judith Carpenter's place.

BRIARGATE CONDOMINIUM ASSOC. INC. V. CARPENTER

U.S. Court of Appeals, Fourth Circuit
976 F.2d 868 (1992)

BACKGROUND: Briargate Homes (the Partnership) was a North Carolina partnership which purchased several units in the Briargate Condominium Association (the Association) complex in Richland County, South Carolina. The Association was entitled to levy assessments against unit owners for maintenance, repair, and replacement of common areas in the complex. As of December 1, 1988, the Partnership failed to pay assessed fees in the amount of $85,106.08, some of which accrued prior to February 1988 and some afterward. The Association sued the Partnership and six individuals, including Judith Carpenter, claiming that as partners they were personally liable for the assessed fees. Five of Carpenter's six individual codefendants settled with the Association for $25,000, which was credited against the indebtedness. The trial court entered judgment against the Partnership and Carpenter for $104,146.75. Carpenter appealed to the Fourth Circuit Court of Appeals.

Hamilton, Circuit Judge

Briargate Homes was formed in the latter part of 1984 when William E. Goodall, Jr., Carpenter's accountant at that time, induced her and other of his clients to invest in the Partnership as a tax shelter. Goodall received funds from Carpenter and her then-husband Hicks to purchase units in the Briargate Condominium complex on behalf of the Partnership. While Carpenter contends that she believed she was investing in a limited partnership, Briargate Homes operated as a general partnership from its inception. No attempt was ever made to achieve actual or substantial compliance with the statutes governing the formation of a limited partnership. The district court concluded that Briargate Homes had never been represented as anything other than a general partnership.

Carpenter did not sign the Briargate Homes partnership agreement. She contends, and the district court so concluded, that she never personally saw copies of the K-1 partnership tax forms, which clearly identified her as a general partner in Briargate Homes. Carpenter claimed deductions respecting partnership losses and profits on her tax returns which were, apparently, only allowable to her if she was a general partner, not a limited partner.

As early as April 1987, incident to her divorce, Carpenter or her attorneys had in their possession documents transferring her husband's share of Briargate Homes to her. The transfer documents explicitly state that Briargate Homes was a general partnership and that the interest transferred was a general partnership interest. Similarly, in June 1987, Carpenter attended a partnership meeting in which she was presented with documents which explicitly identified Briargate Homes as a general partnership. She did not sign these documents, but asserts that she took them to her lawyer for review. In December 1987, Carpenter attended another partnership meeting where she was again made aware that Briargate Homes was a general, not a limited, partnership.

On February 5, 1988, only days after a deposition in another case in which she was informed that she might be liable as a general partner, Carpenter notified the other partners and the Association by mail that she was withdrawing from any equity participation and renouncing any interest in the profits of Briargate Homes. Carpenter is an experienced businesswoman, serves on the board of directors of a bank, and has ready access to legal and other professional advice.

We believe the judgment of the district court must be vacated, and the case remanded to the district court for additional findings.

First, the district court must determine whether or not Carpenter held a "good faith" belief that she was a limited partner at the time she initially joined and contributed to the Briargate Homes venture.

Second, assuming Carpenter demonstrated a good faith belief at the time she invested, then her notice of withdrawal effectively cut off liability for any fees accrued after such notice. To hold Carpenter liable for fees accrued prior to the notice, the district court must determine if and when the Association "actually believed in good faith that the person [Carpenter] was a general partner." Carpenter may be held liable only for those assessments made in reliance on the belief that the Association could look to the assets of Carpenter as a general partner to satisfy the debt. Absent such reliance, no personal liability as a general partner attaches to Carpenter for the debts of the Partnership to the Association.

Carpenter points to statements in the record indicating that agents of the Association apparently believed they were dealing with a limited partnership and were totally unaware of Carpenter's interest in the Partnership until the time of her notice withdrawing from any equity participation and renouncing any interest in the profits of Briargate Homes. To the extent the Association was unaware of Carpenter's participation and believed Briargate Homes was a limited partnership, it would appear impossible to conclude that the Association was misled to believe it could rely on Carpenter's assets in conducting business with Briargate Homes. We decline, however, to rule on the issue in the first instance. It does not appear that this issue received much attention at trial. The district court should, on remand, review the record and may take additional evidence if necessary to aid its fact-finding on this issue.

Decision: The Circuit Court vacated the District Court's decision and sent the case back to the district court for further proceedings.

Foreign Limited Partnerships

A **foreign limited partnership** is one that has been formed under the laws of another state. The laws of the state under which the foreign limited partnership is organized govern its organization and internal affairs as well as the liability of its limited partners. Before transacting business in another state, the foreign limited partnership must register with an administrative authority of the state, usually the secretary of state.

Financing the Limited Partnership: Contributions

The contribution of any partner (general or limited) may be in cash, property, or services. To be enforceable, a limited partner's promise to contribute to the limited partnership must be in a signed writing.

A partner is obligated to perform any enforceable promise to contribute cash, property or services, unless the partnership agreement provides otherwise. This is true even if the partner is unable to perform because of death, disability, or any other reason. If a partner does not make the required contribution, he or she must pay the cash value of the services, unless the partnership agreement states otherwise. A creditor who relies on the promised contribution may enforce it.

Limited Partners

In order to qualify as a limited partnership, the partnership must have at least one limited partner. A limited partner is a person or entity who has been admitted to a limited partnership as a limited partner according to the terms of the partnership agreement. A person becomes a limited partner by being named as one in the partnership records. The obligation is on the limited partnership to maintain in its records the date each limited partner becomes a limited partner. These records establish the fact and the date of a limited partner's admission into the limited partnership. However, a

---

CONCEPT SUMMARY
"Safe Harbor" Activities of a Limited Partner

A limited partner does not participate in the control of the business by doing any of the following:

1. Being a contractor, an agent, or employee of the limited partnership or of a general partner or being an officer, director, or shareholder of a general partner that is a corporation
2. Consulting with and advising a general partner
3. Acting as a guarantor of the limited partnership
4. Bringing a derivative lawsuit on behalf of the limited partnership
5. Requesting or attending a meeting of the partners
6. Voting on the following:

   - Dissolution of the partnership
   - Transfer of the partnership assets
   - Incurrence of indebtedness of the partnership other than in the ordinary course of the business
   - Changing the nature of the business
   - Admitting or removing a partner
   - A transaction involving a conflict of interest between a general partner and the partnership
   - Amending the partnership agreement or the certificate of limited partnership

person cannot become a limited partner before the certificate of limited partnership is filed.

Unanimous written consent of all partners is required for admission of new limited partners unless the partnership agreement provides otherwise. For example, a large business that wishes to do business in the form of a limited partnership can provide that individual investors can acquire a partnership interest directly from the limited partnership. However, if the partnership agreement does not provide for this, written consent of all partners is required for the admission of a limited partner.

Another way a person can become a limited partner is to receive an assignment of a limited partner's interest in the partnership. (Assignment of partnership interests is discussed later in this chapter.)

By becoming a limited partner, an investor risks only his or her investment in the limited partnership. Unlike a general partner, a limited partner is not liable for the obligations of a limited partnership unless he or she is also a general partner. (A person can be both a general and a limited partner in a limited partnership.)

The trade-off for obtaining limited liability is the surrender of any right on the part of a limited partner to participate in the **control of the business.** This arrangement prevents a creditor from mistaking a limited partner for one of the general partners who have full liability.

A limited partner loses the protection of limited liability if he or she participates in the control of the business. However, when this happens, he or she is liable only to persons who transact business with the limited partnership reasonably believing, on the basis of the limited partner's conduct, that the limited partner is a general partner. In a provision known as the "safe harbor" section, the ULPA lists certain activities that a limited partner may perform without being considered to have taken part in the control of the business.

The following case illustrates how involved the limited partners can be in the business of the enterprise without losing their limited liability. Although the case was decided before the ULPA's 1985 revisions, the court's decision is now codified in the ULPA.

FRIGIDAIRE SALES CORPORATION V. UNION PROPERTIES, INC.

Supreme Court of Washington
562 P.2d 244 (1977)

BACKGROUND: Frigidaire Sales Corporation (petitioner) entered into a contract with Commercial Investors (Commercial), a limited partnership. Leonard Mannon and Raleigh Baxter (respondents) were limited partners of Commercial. Respondents were also officers, directors, and shareholders of Union Properties, Inc., the only general partner of Commercial. Respondents controlled Union Properties, and through their control of Union Properties they exercised the day-to-day control and management of Commercial. Commercial breached the contract, and petitioner brought suit against Union Properties and respondents. The trial court concluded that respondents did not incur general liability for Commercial's obligations by reason of their control of Commercial, and the Court of Appeals affirmed. Petitioner appealed to the Supreme Court of Washington.

Hamilton, Justice

Petitioner, Frigidaire Sales Corporation, sought review of a Court of Appeals decision which held that limited partners do not incur general liability for the limited partnership's obligations simply because they are officers, directors, or shareholders of the corporate general partner.

Petitioner's sole contention is that respondents should incur general liability for the limited partnership's obligations under RCW 25.08.070, because they exercised the day-to-day control and management of Commercial. Respondents, on the other hand, argue that

Commercial was controlled by Union Properties, a separate legal entity, and not by respondents in their individual capacities.

[P]etitioner was never led to believe that respondents were acting in any capacity other than in their corporate capacities. The parties stipulated at the trial that respondents never acted in any direct, personal capacity. When the shareholders of a corporation, who are also the corporation's officers and directors, conscientiously keep the affairs of the corporation separate from their personal affairs, and no fraud or manifest injustice is perpetrated upon third persons who deal with the corporation, the corporation's separate entity should be respected.

For us to find that respondents incurred general liability for the limited partnership's obligations under RCW 25.08.070 would require us to apply a literal interpretation of the statute and totally ignore the corporate entity of Union Properties, when petitioner knew it was dealing with that corporate entity. There can be no doubt that respondents, in fact, controlled the corporation. However, they did so only in their capacities as agents for their principal, the corporate general partner. Although the corporation was a separate entity, it could act only through its board of directors, officers, and agents. Petitioner entered into the contract with Commercial. Respondents signed the contract in their capacities as president and secretary-treasurer of Union Properties, the general partner of Commercial. In the eyes of the law it was Union Properties, as a separate corporate entity, which entered into the contract with petitioner and controlled the limited partnership.

Further, because respondents scrupulously separated their actions on behalf of the corporation from their personal actions, petitioner never mistakenly assumed that respondents were general partners with general liability. Petitioner knew Union Properties was the sole general partner and did not rely on respondents' control by assuming that they were also general partners. If petitioner had not wished to rely on the solvency of Union Properties as the only general partner, it could have insisted that respondents personally guarantee contractual performance. Because petitioner entered into the contract knowing that Union Properties was the only party with general liability, and because in the eyes of the law it was Union Properties, a separate entity, which controlled the limited partnership, there is no reason for us to find that respondents incurred general liability for their acts done as officers of the corporate general partner.

DECISION: The Supreme Court of Washington affirmed the decision of the Court of Appeals in favor of the respondents.

A limited partner may also lose the protection of limited liability by allowing his or her name to be used in the name of the limited partnership. A limited partner who knowingly permits his or her name to be used in the name of the limited partnership is liable to creditors who extend credit to the limited partnership without actually knowing that the limited partner is not a general partner.

Although limited partners may not participate in the control of the partnership as fully as general partners without risking loss of their limited liability, their passive position requires that they have access to information to protect their investment. Under the ULPA a limited partner may obtain from the general partners relevant partnership records.

Each limited partner has the right to obtain from the general partners information regarding the state of the business and financial condition of the limited partnership as well as the partnership's tax returns. In this way limited partners may obtain information about the partnership that is useful to them in making decisions concerning the partnership and their investment in it.

The extent of a limited partner's voting rights is determined by the partnership agreement. The partnership agreement may grant to all or a specified group of limited partners to right to vote on a per capita basis or other basis (for example, on an investment basis) on any matter. The partnership agreement may even provide that limited partners have absolutely no voting rights on partnership matters. It is common for limited partners to have different voting rights than do general partners. If the partnership agreement gives the limited partners voting rights that go beyond the "safe harbor" activities provided under the ULPA, the limited partner runs the risk of losing his or her limited liability as a result of having participated in the control of the business.

General Partners

A limited partnership must have at least one general partner. A general partner is a person or an entity who has been admitted to a limited partnership as a general partner according to the terms of the partnership agreement. Additionally, the person must be named in the certificate of limited partnership as a general partner. After the filing of a limited partnership's original certificate of limited partnership, additional general partners may be admitted as provided in the written partnership agreement. If the written partnership agreement does not provide for the admission of additional general partners, all partners must consent in writing to the admission of a new general partner.

A person ceases to be a general partner by withdrawing from the partnership. A general partner may withdraw at any time, regardless of any agreement to the contrary. However, if the withdrawal is a breach of the partnership agreement, the general partner is liable to the other partners for the resulting damages.

The partners may remove a general partner according to the terms of the partnership agreement. Additionally, the partners may get rid of a general partner who is in dire financial straits (for example, if the general partner has declared bankruptcy).

A general partner of a limited partnership has the same rights and obligations of a partner in a general partnership under the Uniform Partnership Act (UPA). All general partners have the right to run the day-to-day operations of the business. Furthermore, general partners are personally liable for the obligations of the partnership. The general partners owe each other and the limited partners the fiduciary duty of loyalty.

The Sharing of Profits, Losses, and Distributions in Limited Partnerships

Profits and Losses

Profits and losses in a limited partnership are allocated on the basis of each partner's capital contribution to the partnership, unless a written partnership agreement provides otherwise. Distributions of the cash or other assets of the limited partnership are shared on the same basis (according to capital contribution, unless a written agreement provides for some other allocation).

Distributions and Withdrawal

A partner (general as well as limited) is entitled to receive distributions from the limited partnership before his or her withdrawal from the limited partnership and before the dissolution of the partnership as specified in the partnership agreement.

A general partner may withdraw from a limited partnership at any time by giving written notice to the other partners. If the withdrawal violates the partnership agreement, the limited partnership may recover from the withdrawing general partner damages for breach of the partnership agreement. The partnership may also offset the damages against the amount that would otherwise be distributed to the partner.

A limited partner may withdraw from a limited partnership as specified in the partnership agreement. If the agreement does not specify in writing when a limited partner may withdraw, a limited partner may withdraw by giving 6 months' written notice to each general partner.

Upon withdrawal, any withdrawing partner is to receive any distribution that he or she is entitled to under the partnership agreement. If the agreement is silent, the partner is entitled to the value of his or her interest in the limited partnership on the withdrawal date, based upon the partner's right to share in distributions. Distributions are to be in the form of cash, unless the partnership agreement provides otherwise. Partners who are entitled to distributions are considered creditors of the limited partnership, and may sue as ordinary creditors and obtain a judgment. A partner may not receive a distribution if the partnership's liabilities exceed the value of the partnership's assets.

If a partner has received the return of his or her capital contribution according to the terms of the partnership agreement, the partner remains liable to the limited partnership for 1 year in order to discharge the partnership's liabilities to creditors who extended credit to the partnership while the contribution was held by the partnership. If the partner's capital contribution was returned to him or her in violation of the partnership agreement, the partner remains liable to the partnership for 6 years.

Assignment of Partnership Interests

A partner's interest in a limited partnership is the same as the interest of a partner in a general partnership—the partner's share of the profits and losses of the limited partnership and the right to receive distributions of partnership assets. Like the interest in a general partnership, it is personal property, assignable and subject to a charging order. When the partner dies, the interest is included in his or her estate.

A partner may assign his or her interest in a limited partnership. An assignment of a partnership interest does not dissolve a limited partnership or entitle the assignee to become a partner. An assignment entitles the assignee to receive the distributions entitled to by the assignor. A partner ceases to be a partner upon assignment of his or her partnership interest, unless the partnership agreement provides otherwise.

An assignee of a partnership interest may become a limited partner. For this to happen, the assignor has to give the assignee the right. Also, the partnership agreement must give the assignor the authority to do so. If the partnership agreement does not provide the authority, all the other partners must consent to the assignee's becoming a limited partner.

An assignee who becomes a limited partner has the same rights and powers of the limited partner who made the assignment. However, the assignee is not obligated for liabilities unknown to the assignee at the time he or she became a limited partner.

A judgment creditor of a partner may obtain from a court an order to charge the partnership interest of a partner with payment of an unpaid judgment. To the extent of the charging order, the judgment creditor has only the rights of an assignee of the partnership interest.

If a partner dies or is adjudicated incompetent, the partner's executor or guardian may exercise all the partner's rights. These include any power the partner had to give an assignee the right to become a limited partner.

Dissolution

The causes of dissolution are fewer for limited partnerships than for general partnerships. For example, you will recall from Chapter 39 that in a general partnership, the ceasing of a partner to carry on the business may bring about dissolution of the general partnership. This is not true with limited partnerships. The death, incapacity, bankruptcy, or withdrawal of one of the limited partners does not dissolve a limited partnership.

Further, the withdrawal of a general partner does not dissolve a limited partnership if there is at least one other general partner and the partnership agreement permits the business to be carried on by the remaining general partners. Even when the agreement is silent on the issue, or the only general partner withdraws from the firm, the limited partnership will not be dissolved if the remaining partners, within 90 days, appoint the necessary additional partners and agree in writing to continue the business.

A limited partnership is dissolved, however, by the completion of its term or the occurrence of events specified in the partnership agreement or the limited partnership certificate, or upon the written consent of all the partners. A partner may obtain a court-ordered dissolution of a limited partnership if it is not reasonably practical to carry on the business in conformity with the partnership agreement.

Except as provided in the partnership agreement, the general partners who have not wrongfully dissolved a limited partnership may wind up the limited partnership affairs. If there are no general partners to wind up the limited partnership business, the limited partners may do so. Further, a court may wind up the limited partnership's affairs upon the application of any partner.

Upon the winding up of a limited partnership, the assets of a limited partnership are distributed as follows:

1. Creditors, including limited partners who are creditors (not including the return of a limited partner's capital contribution)

2. Withdrawing partners receive the return of their capital contributions to the partnership, except where the partnership agreement provides otherwise

3. Remaining partners receive the return of their partnership interest, in proportion to which they share distributions, except when the partnership agreement provides otherwise

In the following case, the limited partners thought they were protected from a sale of the partnership's assets by provisions in the limited partnership agreement. However, that was not the case.

WOODRUFF V. LEIGHTON AVENUE OFFICE PLAZA, LTD.

Supreme Court of Alabama
622 So.2d 304 (1993)

BACKGROUND: Leighton Avenue Office Plaza, Ltd. (Leighton) was organized in October 1980 as a limited partnership to implement architect Julian W. Jenkins' plan to renovate a Victorian house in Anniston, Alabama and convert it into an office complex. The sole general partner was Gulf General Corporation, an Alabama corporation, whose stockholders were Julian W. Jenkins, William J. Davis, and Ian MacKenzie (defendants). Once the Leighton partnership was formed, the property at 1419 Leighton Avenue, Anniston, Alabama, was acquired, and Jenkins, Davis, and MacKenzie set about finding investors to purchase limited partnership interests. Gerald G. Woodruff, Jr. and Jack S. Wallach (plaintiffs) paid $21,300 each and were sold limited partnership interests.

The venture was not successful. On December 31, 1985, Gulf General Corporation, Leighton's general partner, was dissolved by its shareholders, Davis and Jenkins. On June 30, 1986, the assets of the Leighton partnership were sold.

On June 23, 1988, Woodruff and Wallach sued Leighton and Jenkins, Davis, and MacKenzie, seeking monetary damages. Among the claims were that the defendants had breached an agreement with the plaintiffs by disposing of the assets of the partnership without their consent and that the defendants had transferred the assets of the partnership in violation of the limited partnership agreement and had breached a fiduciary duty to the plaintiffs.

The trial judge entered a summary judgment on behalf of Leighton, Jenkins, Davis, and MacKenzie. Woodruff and Wallach appealed to the Supreme Court of Alabama.

Shores, Justice

Woodruff and Wallach contend that the trial court erred in entering the summary judgment. They rely upon Section 6.1(i) of the "Limited Partnership Certificate and Agreement," which concerns the rights and duties of the general partner. Here, the agreement provides that the powers of the general partner include, but are not limited to, the power to:

> . . . sell, lease, trade, exchange or otherwise dispose of any portion of the Limited Partnership property upon . . . such terms and conditions and for such considerations as the General Partner deems appropriate, provided that the General Partner shall not sell substantially all of the assets of the Limited Partnership without the consent of seventy-five percent (75%) of the then Limited Partnership interests of the Limited Partnership, signified in writing. . . .

However, the Limited Partnership Certificate and Agreement also provides in Article X, "Duration of Business: Dissolution," as follows:

> 10.2 . . . the Limited Partnership shall be dissolved upon the occurrence of any of the following events:
>
> (a) the bankruptcy, insolvency, death, retirement, mental incompetency, or dissolution of the last remaining General Partner.
>
>   . . .
>
> 10.5 In the event of dissolution and final termination . . . the General Partner shall wind up the affairs of the Limited Partnership, and shall sell all or such portion of the remaining Limited Partnership assets as promptly as is consistent with obtaining the fair value thereof. . . .
>
> The defendants argue that, while paragraph 6 may have applied while the partnership was a going concern, once Gulf General Corporation, the general partner, was dissolved, Article X took over and those provisions of the Certificate of Limited Partnership governing dissolution, along with the Alabama Business Corporation Act, controlled.
>
> Section 10-9A-140, Alabama Code 1975, provides that a limited partnership is dissolved and its affairs shall be wound up upon the happening of events specified in the Certificate of Limited Partnership or in the event of withdrawal of a general partner. When Gulf General Corporation, the general partner, was dissolved on December 31, 1985, the limited partnership was thereby dissolved under Section 10.2. Once the partnership was dissolved, under Section 10.5 the general partner had a duty to wind up the affairs and "sell all or such portion of the remaining Limited Partnership assets as promptly as is consistent with obtaining the fair value thereof." Under Section 10-9A-143, the creditors of the partnership were entitled to the first proceeds. When the proceeds were insufficient to pay the creditors, they looked to Jenkins and MacKenzie, who personally paid the remaining debt.
>
> Once the limited partnership was dissolved, it had to be liquidated. The limited partners had no authority to liquidate it. This left only the representatives of the general partner to wind up the affairs of the partnership.
>
> **DECISION:** The Supreme Court of Alabama affirmed the trial court's summary judgment in favor of Leighton, Jenkins, Davis, and MacKenzie.

Review Questions and Problems

Key Terms

limited partnership

limited partner

general partner

Uniform Limited
   Partnership Act
   (ULPA)

certificate of limited
   partnership

limited partnership
   agreement

foreign limited partnership

control of the business

Discussion Questions

1. What is the basic difference between a limited partnership and a general partnership?

2. Why would someone choose the limited partnership form of doing business over the corporate form?

3. How is a limited partnership created?

4. Under what circumstances will a limited partner become personally liable for the debts of a limited partnership? What should a limited partner do to avoid liability as a general partner?

Review Problems

1. Owner, Seller, and Dealer want to form a limited partnership. What do they have to do?

2. Suppose that after Owner, Seller, and Dealer form their limited partnership, Owner discovers that the certificate of limited partnership erroneously lists him as a general partner. What should Owner do? If Creditor extends credit to the partnership without knowing that Owner is listed as a general partner, is Owner personally liable to Creditor?

3. If the limited partnership of Owner, Seller, and Dealer is formed in California but intends to do business in other states, what should Owner, Seller, and Dealer do?

4. If Dealer wants to make his contribution to the limited partnership in the form of services, can Dealer do this?

5. Owner, Seller, and Dealer want to form their limited partnership with all three as limited partners and without a general partner. Can Owner, Seller, and Dealer do this?

6. Suppose that Owner, Seller, and Dealer form a limited partnership with all three as limited partners. They then form a corporation to serve as the general partner, and the three of them are the only shareholders in the corporation. Can they do this?

7. Suppose the same facts as in the question above. However, suppose that Dealer acts as the manager of the business of the limited partner. As manager, he is in charge of the daily operations of the partnership business. What are the consequences of this conduct?

8. If Seller decides to withdraw from the limited partnership of Owner, Seller, and Dealer, may Seller do so without causing a dissolution of the partnership? Explain.

41

Introduction to Corporations

Historical Perspective　　　　　　　　　　　**Nature of Corporations**

One of the most important tools of modern business is the corporate form of organization. For some businesses the corporate structure is ideal. That is because the corporation offers two major benefits: (1) it has an identity separate and distinct from its human operatives, who are not held personally liable for the corporation's obligations in most cases; and (2) it may continue to function regardless of the death or departure of its management. If limited liability and business continuity are not important objectives for a firm, however, the corporate form may be inefficient. Corporations are more administratively complex than other types of business organization, they are often expensive to set up, and they are frequently taxed at higher rates than individuals.

This chapter examines the special characteristics that define the corporation and distinguish corporations from other forms of business organizations. The chapters that follow will cover the important issues that arise over the course of a corporation's existence: how the corporation is formed (Chapter 42), how the corporation is financed (Chapter 43), how the corporation is managed (Chapter 44) and, finally, how the corporation may be merged, dissolved, or otherwise terminated (Chapter 45).

Historical Perspective

The corporation as a form of business organization was well known to the Romans. It was Elizabethan England, however, that gave birth to the modern business corporation. Two forerunners of contemporary corporations were the overseas trading company and the joint stock company. (Recall from high school history the role that joint stock companies like the British East India Company played in colonizing America.) Even in their infancy corporations had their critics. In 1720 a panic-stricken British Parliament passed the "Bubble Act," establishing as criminal the "acting or presuming to act as a corporate body or bodies" without being incorporated, which at that time was an expensive and cumbersome process. The act did not stem the corporate tide, however, as imaginative lawyers created new forms of business organization to circumvent the law. It was not until 1825 that Parliament officially recognized the reality of corporate existence and repealed its anticorporate law.

The United States has evolved from a mid-nineteenth-century nation of farmers, shopkeepers, and small manufacturers into a highly industrialized society dominated by corporations. During the twentieth century several changes have occurred in the nature of corporations and corporate law. As corporate size has increased, so has the need for capitalization, usually obtained through the sale of securities to investors. The focus of the law in recent decades has been to provide investors with protection in the securities market. At the same time, legislatures have sought to attract corporations to their states by adopting corporate codes that give management more and shareholders less control over corporate activities. Currently the focus of attention is on the problems of small, privately owned corporations (called close corporations), which have different needs from those addressed by state laws directed toward large corporations. For example, one relatively recent change has been the modification of state corporate law to permit the creation of single-shareholder corporations.

Nature of Corporations

As the previous discussion of partnership law made clear, partnerships have two distinct disadvantages: (1) the partners share unlimited personal liability for partnership obligations and (2) a technical dissolution of the partnership may result from any change in the partnership's composition, such as the retirement or death of one of the partners. These features of personal liability and lack of business continuity add risks to partnership ventures that potential investors may be unwilling to assume. This is particularly true when the potential investors do not wish to participate in the management of the business.

Even a limited partnership may be unattractive to such investors, since limited partnership statutes require the filing of information revealing the involvement of each limited partner; thus a publicity-shy investor may have information regarding his or her financial support become part of the public record. Further, a limited partner runs some risk of losing his or her limited liability if there is not strict compliance with the statutory prohibitions concerning participating in the control of the firm.

The corporation was conceived as a means of avoiding the risks and discontinuities of partnership and of achieving business objectives beyond the reach of individuals. When capital needs are great, risks are high and the enterprise's duration is long, the corporation is the preferred form of business organization. The corporation is the legal institution that can hold over a period of time the aggregated capital of many people, unaffected by the death or withdrawal of individuals. Table 41-1 compares partnerships and corporations.

TABLE **41-1**

Concept Summary   Comparison of Partnership and Corporation

Partnership	Corporation
Controlled by partners each with equal vote, unless partnership agreement directs otherwise	Controlled indirectly by shareholders, who elect directors, appoint managers, and have centralized operational control
Unlimited liability except in case of limited partnership, in which only general partners have unlimited liability	Limited liability of shareholders for debts of corporation as well as managers and directors, unless corporate veil is "pierced"
Interest of partnership can be assigned but not partnership rights unless approved by partners	Shares of stock in a corporation can be transferred
Partners pay pro rata share of income taxes on net profits of partnership, whether or not distributed; partnership does not pay federal income tax, but some states levy taxes	Corporation income tax paid at federal and state levels; dividends of shareholders taxed at federal and state levels (but see discussion on S corporations at the end of this chapter)
Not a separate legal entity in most states; dissolved upon death of a partner unless partnership agreement states otherwise	A separate legal entity with perpetual existence in the event of death of a shareholder, an officer, or a director

Corporate Characteristics

The chief attributes of a **corporation** are (1) its status as a separate entity, sometimes called juristic or corporate personality; (2) the limited liability of its owners; (3) its continued existence, meaning that a corporation may be established in perpetuity; (4) the transferability of its ownership; and (5) the centralization of its management in its officers and directors rather than in its shareholder-owners. These corporate characteristics are descriptive only. They are not generally "tests" of corporate existence and are not necessarily found in all corporations. However, most corporations share these characteristics. Furthermore, for federal income tax purposes the presence or absence of these characteristics determines whether an enterprise is taxed as a corporation.

Juristic Personality   The principal characteristic of a corporation that distinguishes it from all other business organizations is its status as a legal entity. Because of that status, the law treats the corporation as a person. This convenient fiction permits the corporation to enter into and execute contracts, own and convey property, and sue and be sued as a separate entity distinct from its owners and managers.

To the uninitiated, the concept of the corporation as a legal person separate from its members may seem mysterious. But in fact it is a very practical solution to an important societal problem. Because human beings must be the subjects of the law's commands, it is necessary for the law to personify the corporation—treat it like a person—in order to regulate it for beneficial social and economic purposes. One such purpose is to permit the efficient conduct of business. To imagine life without the concept of the corporation as a legal entity, consider a transaction between the Ford Motor Company and B.F. Goodrich. Treating the transaction as involving two partnerships would involve millions of people as "partners" with hundreds changing every day. Keeping track of the potentially liable people would be a burdensome task even in a computer society.

Limited Liability   A major consequence of the corporation's entity status is the limited liability it accords to its shareholders. Corporate rights and liabilities are not to be confused with those of its owners. Generally shareholders are not liable for corporate debts beyond the amount of their investment, and the corporation is not liable for the debts of its shareholders. The limited liability includes tort and criminal as well as contractual liability. This is a major business incentive for investors, because they can avoid personal liability for corporate activities. Similarly, personal creditors of shareholders cannot reach the corporate property, although they may reach the shares of the debtor shareholder.

Continued Existence   Another key advantage of the corporation that stems from its separateness from the shareholders is its capacity for continuous life, sometimes called perpetual succession. In his *Commentaries*, Blackstone described corporations as "artificial persons who enjoy a kind of legal immortality," and compared them with the River Thames as it flows with constantly changing water but continues as the same stream. Similarly, shareholders may come and go with no effect upon the corporate entity. A corporation such as the Ford Motor Company can continue long after its founder and major stockholder has died. As Peter Drucker wrote, "The corporation is permanent, the shareholder is transitory."

Although in most states corporations enjoy continuous existence, a few jurisdictions, such as Mississippi and Oklahoma, limit the life of a corporation to a certain number of years. Furthermore, the corporation's articles of incorporation and bylaws, which are its governing instruments, may limit its duration if that is deemed desirable by its incorporators. Thus the Revised Model Business Corporation Act (RMBCA) provides, "Unless its articles of incorporation provided otherwise every corporation . . . has without limitation power to have perpetual duration and succession in its corporate name."

Transferability of Ownership   Ownership interest in a corporation, which generally takes the form of shares of corporate stock, can be traded readily. This permits investors to place a value on their investment and to liquidate it if their investment objectives change. Because ownership interest in a corporation may be transferred by a shareholder while living, upon his or her death it is possible to distribute the interest to the shareholder's beneficiaries or heirs. Thus a shareholder may convey by will his or her corporate stock to another, just as he or she could have given that stock away while alive. When the stockholder dies without leaving a will, the shares pass to the heirs as a part of the estate.

Restrictions on the transferability of shares provided in the corporate governing instruments are permitted if they are reasonable. This usually occurs in corporations having only a few shareholders who wish to limit the corporation's ownership to themselves. Such restrictions are discussed later in this chapter.

Centralized Management and Control

The final characteristic of a corporation is the separation of its management from its ownership. Shareholders have no direct control over the daily business of the corporation. While this may not be as true of those corporations that have only a few shareholders, individual shareholders are generally powerless to affect corporate affairs in the case of large organizations in which the ownership of stock is dispersed. This is because shareholder control is generally limited to electing the corporation's directors and approving major changes in the corporation's structure and operation.

The corporation's management rests with its officers and directors. By statute in most states the management function is centralized in the board of directors. The board of directors often delegates its duties to several officers, such as a president and vice presidents, whom the board appoints to manage the daily corporate business and to report to the directors for guidance. The only control usually possessed by the shareholders is the power to elect and remove the directors. Shareholders, of course, can achieve power if they join together, but in many large corporations this is often difficult and involves large-scale organization.

There are obvious efficiencies in centralized management, since direct participation of shareholders in management decision making is likely to create more problems than it solves. Thus the centralized management promotes large-scale organization, not individual rights. The result has been the emergence in recent years of an increasingly professionalized and frequently self-perpetuating class of corporate managers who merely go through the formalities of accounting to shareholders. It would not be unfair to characterize the government of a large corporation as "oligarchical" in the sense that the small group running it accounts only to itself or to a few large shareholders.

Considering, however, that management selection is often meritocratic and that there is a community of interest and outlook in most instances between management and shareholders, the virtual disenfranchisement of the shareholder is not so oppressive as it appears. In partial recognition of these realities corporate law in recent times has sought to protect the shareholder—viewed primarily as investor rather than owner—against fraud and has substantially strengthened the obligations of management to act honestly and to disclose all material facts.

Corporations and the Constitution

The legal personification of the corporation raises questions as to whether and how the rights and protections that the U.S. Constitution extends to "persons," "people," and "citizens" apply to corporations. For example, the Fifth and Fourteenth Amendments provide that no "person" shall be "deprived of life, liberty or property, without due process of law," and the Fourteenth Amendment prohibits any state to "deny to any person within its jurisdiction the equal protection of the laws." The Fifth Amendment also provides that no person "shall be compelled in any criminal case to be a witness against himself . . .," and the Fourth Amendment guarantees "the right of the people to be secure in their persons, houses, papers, and effects against unreasonable searches and seizures. . . ." Furthermore, Article IV and the Fourteenth Amendment secure the privileges and immunities of the "citizens" of each state and the United States.

Are corporations "persons" and "citizens" under these constitutional provisions? Is a corporation one of the "people" entitled to the Fourth Amendment's protection against unreasonable searches and seizures? The answer to these questions depends not on semantics but on the purposes underlying these various constitutional provisions.

The U.S. Supreme Court has specifically held that a corporation is a "person," entitled to the equal protection of the law, whose property cannot be taken without legal due process. However, a corporation is not a "person" entitled to the Fifth Amendment's privilege against self-incrimination, although it is considered one of the "people" entitled to the Fourth Amendment's protection against unreasonable searches.

This apparent inconsistency rests on the different purposes underlying these constitutional guarantees. The constitutional provision against self-incrimination is considered essentially a personal one, applying only to natural persons. It is not applicable to corporations because its original purpose was to protect individuals against the use of legal process to obtain self-incriminating testimony. Thus a corporation cannot oppose the subpoenaing of its books and records by asserting the privilege. Further, an officer or employee of a corporation cannot withhold testimony or documents on the ground that the corporation would be incriminated, although it would be permissible for such an officer or employee to refuse such evidence on the ground that he or she might be incriminated by its production.

Unlike the privilege against self-incrimination, the Fourth Amendment's protection against unreasonable searches and seizures applies to corporations as well as to individuals. However, the protection is not absolute; only *unreasonable* governmental searches are prohibited. Hence the protection yields in the face of a valid search warrant or subpoena.

Thus under the Fourth and Fifth Amendments the books and records of a corporation cannot be insulated from governmental inspection unless the scope of the governmental intrusion is unreasonable under the Fourth Amendment. The determina-tion of which governmental intrusions are reasonable and which are not is a judicial function. In appraising the reasonableness of an intrusion, the courts attempt to balance the expectation of privacy with the government's need for information before issuing warrants or subpoenas.

Although the word "person" impliedly includes "citizen," a corporation is not considered to be a citizen entitled to the protection of the privileges and immunities clauses of the U.S. Constitution, since these also apply only to natural persons. The consequence of a corporation not being a citizen under these clauses is that it may be compelled to comply with the corporation laws of a state in which it intends to do business but in which it is not incorporated. It may even be kept out of the state entirely if the state so wishes, unless the corporation is an interstate business. A state's "doing business" requirements cannot burden interstate commerce because of overriding provisions in the U.S. Constitution. Thus a state may usually require out-of-state corporations to register and pay fees for the privilege of doing business within the state or to designate an agent within the state for the acceptance of service of legal process.

The U.S. Supreme Court in the case that follows resolved the question of whether the corporation possesses freedom of expression under the First Amendment.

FIRST NATIONAL BANK OF BOSTON V. BELLOTTI
U.S. Supreme Court
435 U.S. 765 (1978)

BACKGROUND: First National Bank and other corporations (appellants) brought suit against Bellotti, attorney-general of the Commonwealth of Massachusetts (appellee), to have Section 8 of the state's criminal statute declared unconstitutional. Section 8 forbade expenditures by banks and business corporations for purposes of influencing or affecting the vote on any question submitted to the voters other than one materially affecting any of the property, business, or assets of the corporation. Further, the statute specifically stated that "questions submitted to the voters solely concerning taxation of income, property or transaction of individuals shall not be considered to materially affect the property, business or assets of corporation." Violations of the statute were punishable by a maximum fine of $50,000 to be levied against each corporation, and a fine of $10,000 and/or 1 year in prison for corporate officers, directors, or agents of the corporation.

When First National Bank and other corporations sought to spend money to publicize their opposition to a referendum proposed to amend Massachusetts' constitution to authorize the legislature to enact a graduated personal income tax, the appellee,

Attorney-General Bellotti, informed appellants that he intended to enforce the statute. The Massachusetts courts held Section 8 to be constitutuional. First National and other corporations appealed to the U.S. Supreme Court.

Powell, Justice

The court below framed the principal question in this case as whether and to what extent corporations have First Amendment rights. We believe that the court posed the wrong question. The constitution often protects interests broader than those of the party seeking their vindication. The First Amendment, in particular, serves significant societal interests. The proper question therefore is not whether corporations "have" First Amendment rights and, if so, whether they are coextensive with those of natural persons. Instead, the question must be whether § 8 abridges expression that the First Amendment was meant to protect. . . .

The speech proposed by appellants is at the heart of the First Amendment protection. In appellants' view, the enactment of a graduated personal income tax, as proposed to be authorized by constitutional amendment, would have a seriously adverse effect on the economy of the State. The importance of the referendum issue to the people and government of Massachusetts is not disputed. Its merits, however, are the subject of sharp disagreement.

As the Court said in *Mills v. Alabama,* "there is practically universal agreement that a major purpose of [the First] Amendment was to protect the free discussion of governmental affairs." If the speakers here were not corporations, no one would suggest that the State could silence their proposed speech. It is the type of speech indispensable to decision making in a democracy, and this is no less true because the speech comes from a corporation rather than an individual. The inherent worth of the speech in terms of its capacity for informing the public does not depend upon the identity of its source, whether corporation, association, union, or individual. . . .

Section 8 permits a corporation to communicate to the public its views on certain referendum subjects—those materially affecting its business—but not others. It also singles out one kind of ballot question—individual taxation—as a subject about which corporations may never make their ideas public. The legislature has drawn the line between permissible and impermissible speech according to whether there is a sufficient nexus, as defined by the legislature, between the issue presented to the voters and the business interests of the speaker.

In the realm of protected speech, the legislature is constitutionally disqualified from dictating the subjects about which persons may speak and the speakers who may address a public issue. If a legislature may direct business corporations to "stick to business," it also may limit other corporations—religious, charitable, or civic—to their respective "business" when addressing the public. Such power in government to channel the expression of views is unacceptable under the First Amendment. Especially where, as here, the legislature's suppression of speech suggests an attempt to give one side of a debatable public question an advantage in expressing its views to the people, the First Amendment is plainly offended. . . .

DECISION: The Supreme Court ruled in favor of First National Bank and other corporations.

Classes of Corporations

The corporate form of organization has many dimensions. A corporation may be either public or private, profit or nonprofit, publicly issued or closely held, professional or nonprofessional, and foreign or domestic. Thus there are many different kinds of corporations, each bearing a generally accepted label. Because a court may refer to a corporation by its label, familiarity with the common types of corporations and the terminology used to describe them is useful. Moreover, comparison of various kinds of corporations that at first appear to be dissimilar often reveals certain commonly shared characteristics.

ETHICS
Moral Accountability of Corporations

Can a corporation be unethical? If one says that a corporation is unethical, what does that mean? There are various answers. It could mean that the abstract entity of the corporation is somehow unethical. Or that the senior managers, or directors, or shareholders, or some combination are unethical. If you worked for Beech-Nut and the company was found to have sold a synthetic substance as apple juice, would that mean that you were unethical? Would your answer be influenced by whether you were a truck driver or a quality control manager for juice?

Those who argue that a corporation cannot be unethical note that a corporation can't think and can't have an unethical intent. Further, they accuse those who attribute morality to the corporate entity of assessing guilt by association on corporate members. Advocates of the moral accountability of corporations point out that corporations do have distinct cultures that influence employee behaviors. They reason that if the corporation, or the law, recognizes something as an "official" corporate act, then the corporation should bear full responsibility for its consequences.

The issue is not merely an abstraction. The concept of moral accountability supports the idea of liability of the corporate entity for specific-intent crimes such as homicide.

Public and Private Corporations   A corporation may be broadly classified as either public or private. The distinction refers to its purposes and powers. A **public corporation** is created and funded by the government to act as its instrumentality for the carrying out of some public purpose. Examples of public corporations include municipal, school, and water districts and various public-benefit corporations such as the U.S. Legal Services Corporation. Many state colleges and universities are organized as public corporations.

Private corporations are all corporations other than those that are public. They are created for private rather than public purposes. The General Motors Corporation is an example of a private corporation.

You should be aware that in common business language, the distinction between public and private corporations has a second meaning. "Public corporation" commonly refers to a corporation whose shares are traded among the general public, and "private corporation" typically denotes a corporation whose shares are owned by a small, tightly knit group. To avoid confusion, we will refer to this second type of public corporation as a *public-issue corporation* and to this second type of private corporation as a *close corporation* or a *closely held corporation*. Public-issue corporations and close corporations are discussed below.

Profit and Nonprofit Corporations   A **corporation for profit** is primarily a business corporation, one engaged in commercial enterprises. Thus a corporation for profit is organized to conduct a business with a view to realizing gains to be distributed as dividends among its shareholders. A **nonprofit corporation** is not organized to make a profit for its members and does not conduct a business. Because they are not organized with a view to distributing gains, nonprofit corporations are usually expressly forbidden by statute to issue certificates of shares. They may issue membership certificates, if they so desire. Thus they are sometimes characterized as membership rather than shareholder corporations. Social, philanthropic, religious, and cultural corporations are examples of nonprofit corporations.

Public-Issue and Closely Held Corporations.   A **public-issue corporation** is one whose stock ownership is diffused and whose management is divorced from its owners. "Going public" is a phrase frequently used to describe the process by which a privately owned firm issues stock to the public. This process is usually accompanied by increased governmental regulation, most notably from the Securities and Exchange Commission (SEC), which administers federal legislation regulating the issuance and trading of corporate securities.

In contrast to a public-issue corporation, in which stock is often widely held and management is normally unrelated to stock ownership, a **close corporation** or **closely held corporation** is one whose stock is not publicly traded and whose stock ownership and management usually intertwine. A close corporation usually has only a few shareholders, most or all of whom participate in its management. Thus there is a striking resemblance to a partnership.

Many corporate concepts and principles created with public-issue corporations primarily in mind are ill-adapted to close corporations. Although the nature and methods of operation of the two kinds of corporations are different, in the past, and especially before 1960, state corporate codes generally established the same rules for governing both corporations. Great Britain and some countries of continental Europe have long had special statutes governing the "private company."

Since World War II, strong pleas have been made to enact in this country similar comprehensive statutes to govern close corporations. Since 1960 a legislative breakthrough has occurred, with many states adding to their corporation statutes provisions designed to meet the problems of close corporations. Even now, however, only a handful of states, most notably Florida, Delaware, and Maryland, have adopted separate statutes for close corporations.

The owners of a close corporation usually attempt to ensure that the ownership stays within a tightly knit group. A close corporation typically places restrictions on the right of shareholders to sell their shares to outsiders. Generally this takes the form of a right of first refusal conferred upon the corporation or the other shareholders in the event of any sale of corporate stock. A right of first refusal generally means that before any stock may be sold, it must first be offered to the corporation or other stockholders who have the right to purchase the stock for fair value, thereby preventing outsiders from obtaining an ownership interest in the corporation. Close corporations often attempt to require outsiders who stand to acquire shares through inheritance, marriage dissolutions, or other means to offer to sell those shares to the corporation or the other shareholders. The restrictions discussed above are typically set forth in a **shareholders agree-ment**, an agreement executed by all the shareholders that spells out their rights and obligations with respect to their shares and, in some cases, by the management of the corporation.

Restrictions on the sale of shares will be enforced only if they are reasonable. In order to be reasonable, such restrictions must not unduly interfere with the shareholder's right to dispose of his or her property as he or she sees fit. Courts have interpreted this to mean that if the corporation or the other shareholders refuse to purchase a shareholder's shares, then that shareholder must be allowed to sell the shares to anyone. Courts have refused to enforce requirements that the board of directors or other shareholders approve any sale, since this could effectively prevent a shareholder from selling his or her property.

Problems occur with close corporations when minority shareholders come to believe that the majority shareholders are managing the corporation to benefit the majority shareholders only. A close corporation is more vulnerable than a public-issue corporation to this type of abuse, because a close corporation is typically managed by its majority shareholders. There have been numerous cases in which majority shareholders have attempted to "squeeze out" minority shareholders by retaining all the management authority and using it to increase managers' salaries, decrease dividends, or steer corporate business to companies owned by the majority. Without special legal protections, minority shareholders, faced with a "squeeze out," would likely face a difficult situation: They would be powerless to protect their interests as shareholders (the majority could always outvote them) and would have a hard time selling their shares for an acceptable price (potential buyers would be wary of the oppressive majority).

Minority shareholders often try to protect themselves through shareholder agreements that give them the power to veto certain corporate decisions that could be used to squeeze them out. Additionally, courts generally impose a duty on majority shareholders to manage the corporation in the best interests of *all* the shareholders, including the minority shareholders. The case that follows is a good example of a dispute between minority and majority shareholders of a close corporation.

EX PARTE BROWN

Supreme Court of Alabama

562 So.2d 485 (1990)

BACKGROUND: Plaintiffs were minority owners of Greene Group, Inc., a close corporation that ran a racetrack. Plaintiffs sued majority owners Bryant, Phelps, and May for attempting to "squeeze out" the minority shareholders. The minority shareholders claimed that the defendants used corporate resources to set up opportunities for the majority shareholders to manage other racetracks in Georgia and Iowa. Also, the minority shareholders claimed that the majority shareholders increased their own salaries and failed to pay dividends. The defendants argued that because of their management, the value of all the shares, including the minority shares, had greatly increased. The trial court ruled for the defendants and the minority shareholders appealed.

Per Curiam

In *Galbreath v. Scott*, this Court discussed the opportunities that majority shareholders in a closely held corporation have to "squeeze out" the minority's voice in the operation of the business:

> When majority stockholders personally assume the multiple roles of owners, board of directors, and managing officers, they can not only deprive minority shareholders of a voice in the operation of the business, but they can also siphon off corporate income and deprive minority owners of income from their interest in the business. Minority shareholders can find themselves holding stock which pays no dividends and which cannot, as a practical matter, be sold. Majority shareholders can "squeeze out" minority shareholders.
>
> There is a trend among courts to adopt attitudes toward close corporations which reflect the realities of the situation and which recognize a distinction between closely and widely held corporations. In *Burt v. Burt Boiler Works, Inc.*, this Court ruled that "majority stockholders owe a duty to at least act fairly to minority interests. . . ."

The minority stockholders make a number of factual claims that they assert show the majority's attempt to squeeze out the minority. The majority stockholders contend there has been no "squeeze out" and that the minority wants to substitute its business judgment for that of the majority. They argue that they have met the "reasonable expectations" for the minority stockholders by the increase in the value of the stock. Each minority shareholder paid $25.00 per share of stock in Greene Group, Inc., when it was formed in 1977. The corporation purchased stock from some of the minority shareholders in December 1986, for an average price of $4,583 per share. . . . The majority's contention seems to be that the minority has no cause to complain of a "squeeze out," and should not care whether there are dividends, since the stock has increased so greatly in value. The fact, however, that the stock has increased in value is no answer to the charge of systematic squeeze out of the minority.

An examination of the record shows that the majority stockholders have systematically moved to squeeze out the minority stockholders, in that the majority stockholders have removed all minority stockholders from all positions as officers and directors; have . . . voted a raise for Bryant, Phelps, and May in 1987 which was a marked increase from previous years; have sought for themselves individually corporate opportunities in Macon County, Alabama, and in Iowa; have paid inadequate dividends or failed to pay dividends; [and] have cancelled the minority stockholders' right to use the recreational farm, Thisildu, in Greene County. . . .

The minority has made an affirmative showing that the majority has systematically sought to squeeze out the minority. The failure to pay adequate dividends when so much income is being made by the corporation and the salaries for Bryant, Phelps, and May are being raised is prima facie evidence of a squeeze out. The board of directors of a corporation, acting through the officers, is entitled to conduct the business of the corporation for the mutual profit of all of the stockholders. The minority is not entitled to any special privilege, but it is entitled to fair treatment in the corporate decision-making process. We direct the trial court on remand to determine whether the majority has acted in the best interest of all the stockholders or whether its decisions were made for the purpose of squeezing out the minority, as the bare facts seem to suggest. If the trial judge determines that the rights and interests of the minority stockholders have been prejudiced by the actions of the majority stockholders, he shall determine and fix an amount necessary to compensate the minority for this breach of duty owed them by the majority.

Decision: The Supreme Court of Alabama reversed the decision and remanded the case to the trial court.

Professional Corporations Until recently every state prohibited professionals, such as accountants, architects, doctors, and lawyers, from incorporating their professional practices. Today some states do authorize professionals to practice their professions in the corporate form of organization. An individual or group of persons licensed in some kind of professional service may now organize as a **professional corporation** in these states. However, restrictions are imposed to protect the public. Thus stock may usually be issued only to duly licensed professionals engaged in the service for which the corporation has been organized.

S and C Corporations One of the major disadvantages of the corporate form is the "double taxation" of corporate income. This occurs because a corporation's income is taxed both at the corporate level and at the shareholder level. Double taxation works as follows: When a corporation earns income, it has to pay taxes on the amount of that income (minus expenses). Then, when the corporation pays dividends out of its earnings left over, each shareholder has to pay tax on the amount of the dividend. Corporate earnings that eventually are used to pay dividends are thus taxed twice—once as the corporation's income, and again as the shareholder's income.

Partnership income, on the other hand, is not taxed twice. The federal government does not impose a partnership tax in the way that it imposes a corporate tax. The net income of a partnership is allocated among the individual partners, and is taxed only as income to the individual partners.

The federal Internal Revenue Code recognizes a hybrid called an *S Corporation*, which allows small firms and certain other businesses to enjoy the advantages of the corporate form without the disadvantage of double taxation. An **S corporation** is a corporation that may avoid the corporate tax and be taxed at the shareholder level only, similar to the way that a partnership is taxed. A corporation must satisfy several requirements in order to qualify as an S corporation, including the following: (1) the corporation must not be organized under the laws of a foreign country: (2) the corporation must have 35 or fewer shareholders; (3) only individuals, estates, and certain types of trusts may be shareholders; (4) no shareholder may be a nonresident alien; and (5) the corporation must have no more than one class of stock.

S corporations are so named because they are governed by Subchapter S of the Internal Revenue Code. The taxation of all other corporations is governed by Subchapter C of the Internal Revenue Code; these other corporations are sometimes referred to as C corporations.

Foreign and Domestic Corporations A corporation is domestic to the state where it is created. It is considered foreign in all other states and countries where it does business. Thus a corporation incorporated in Delaware is considered a "foreign" corporation in Ohio. This is true even if the corporation's principal place of business is in Ohio. Foreign corporations doing business in another state are usually required to register with the agency that regulates corporations in that state. The court in the next case had to determine whether the activities of an Arizona professional corporation in Georgia were enough to constitute "doing business" in Georgia.

REISMAN V. MARTORI, MEYER, HENDRICKS AND VICTOR
Court of Appeals of Georgia
271 S.E.2d 685 (1980)

BACKGROUND: A law firm incorporated in Arizona (plaintiff), sued Reisman (defendant), a surgeon practicing in Georgia, for the balance of a debt owed for professional service in the amount of $6,438.14. The defendant had hired a member of the plaintiff law firm, Hendricks, in order to represent him in a dispute with a Georgia hospital. Hendricks flew to Atlanta, and with local counsel brought about a negotiated compromise with the hospital. The defendant argued that the plaintiff's action should have been dismissed because the Arizona law firm failed to register as a foreign corporation under Georgia corporation laws. The trial court ruled in favor of the law firm. Dr. Reisman appealed.

Banke, Judge

Assuming, without deciding, that the appellee professional association was required under Code Ann. § 22–1421 (a) to procure a certificate of authority from the Secretary of State in order to transact business in Georgia, its activities in this state have not been sufficiently extensive to invoke the statute here. "In most jurisdictions it has been held that single or isolated transactions do not constitute doing business within the meaning of such statutes, although they are a part of the very business for [sic] which the corporation is organized to transact, if the action of the corporation in engaging therein indicated no purpose of continuity of conduct in that respect." (*Winston Corp. v. Park Elec. Co.*)

Winston held that "the question of 'doing business' is to be considered a matter of fact to be resolved on an ad hoc or case-by-case basis . . . and . . . the meaning of 'isolated transaction' in our corporation code is to be determined in the same way as the term 'doing business.'" Winston also makes it clear that the purpose of Code Ann. § 22–1401 is to require registration of foreign corporations which intend to conduct business in Georgia on a continuous basis, not as a temporary matter. Activity related to a single transaction or contract is thus not contemplated.

The evidence here showed that the law firm's activities were concentrated in Arizona, although various attorneys in the firm had handled litigation (or "transacted business") outside the state of incorporation. Hendricks had represented clients in Georgia on two prior occasions, but these had nothing to do with his representation of Dr. Reisman. Under these circumstances, there is ample basis for the court's conclusion that the law firm had neither extended its business into Georgia on a continuous basis nor engaged "in the course of a number of repeated transactions of like nature" within the state. The trial court correctly held that the law firm's representation of Dr. Reisman amounted to an isolated transaction and therefore properly denied the motion for directed verdict.

DECISION: The Court of Appeals ruled in favor of the plaintiff law firm.

ETHICS
A Model of Corporate Moral Development

Eric Reidenbach and Donald Robin have proposed a conceptual model of corporate moral development. Working from models of human moral development, particularly those of Lawrence Kohlberg, Reidenbach and Robin developed a scale that characterizes corporations on the basis of their current state of moral development. They envision that corporations can change their culture and thereby change their state of moral development. Their scale, with some of their examples, is as follows:

Stage	Name	Characteristics	Examples
Stage 1	Amoral Organization	Outlaw culture, break law if it profits the firm	Film Recovery Systems
Stage 2	Legalistic Organization	If it's legal it's OK; work the gray areas	Nestlé; Ford (re Pinto)
Stage 3	Responsive Organization	Considers some stakeholders but essentially reactive to pressures	Proctor & Gamble (re Rely); Abbott Labs
Stage 4	Emerging Ethical Organization	More proactive, emerging core values of firm	Boeing; General Mills; Johnson & Johnson
Stage 5	Ethical Organization	Corporate culture is planned and managed to be ethical	Authors could not identify any

See, generally, Reidenbach & Robin, "A Conceptual Model of Corporate Moral Development," 10 *Journal of Business Ethics*, 273–284 (1991).

Review Questions and Problems

Key Terms

corporation
public corporation
private corporation
corporation for profit
nonprofit corporation
public-issue corporation
close corporation
closely held corporation
shareholders agreement
professional corporation
S corporation

Discussion Questions

1. What are the chief characteristics of a corporation?
2. What is the difference between an S corporation and a C corporation?
3. Give second meanings for the terms "private corporation" and "public corporation."

Review Problems

1. Willis and Howard own a convenience store as partners. They are considering adopting a corporate form of ownership instead. What factors might make the corporate form more attractive than a partnership to Willis and Howard? What factors might make the corporate form less attractive than a partnership? Can any of the disadvantages of the corporate form be mitigated by choosing the right type of corporation?

2. Friendly Corp. is being prosecuted for dumping toxic waste near a schoolyard. The government subpoenas documents that it hopes will show that Friendly Corp. engaged in the illegal dumping activity. Friendly Corp. refuses to produce the documents under the corporation's Fifth Amendment right against self-incrimination. Is Friendly Corp.'s objection valid? Explain.

3. Acting on a tip that illegal drugs are being manufactured at an ABC Pharmaceuticals Corp. plant, police search the premises and find incriminating evidence. The police did not have a warrant, nor

were they given permission to enter the plant. At trial, ABC moves to prevent the evidence from being admitted on the grounds that ABC's Fourth Amendment rights have been violated. The prosecution counters that ABC, as a corporation, does not have Fourth Amendment rights. Who's right? Explain.

4. Manny, Moe, Jack, and Jill each own 25 percent of XYZ Co.'s shares. Manny, Moe, and Jack tend to act together, and have appointed themselves to be XYZ's only officers. They have doubled the salaries of the officers, refused to pay dividends, and sold off much of XYZ's property at low prices to a competing firm owned by Manny, Moe, and Jack only. As a result, Jill's stock in XYZ is virtually worthless. How might Jill have protected herself at the outset from the possibility that such a situation would arise? Assuming that Jill did not take steps to protect herself at the outset, are there any legal remedies available to her? Discuss.

5. A, an armored truck company, was charged with maintaining a gambling room in violation of a Florida criminal statute carrying a term of imprisonment up to 3 years or a fine not exceeding $5,000. B, the president of the corporation, sought an injunction to prevent the case from going to trial because he claimed the corporation was not a natural person; therefore, it was not subject to the state gambling law. Who won? Explain.

Case Problems

1. A divorce court awarded a wife one-half of the shares owned by her husband in a close corporation. Following the decree, the wife demanded that the corporation issue stock certificates in her name. The corporation refused, pointing out that its bylaws require anyone wishing to transfer shares to first offer to sell them back to the corporation. What was the result?

2. Before the Bolshevik Revolution in 1917 in Russia, a Russian bank held a balance outstanding to its credit of $66,749.45 in a U.S. bank. When the revolution took place, all the bank's assets in the Soviet Union were confiscated by the Bolsheviks, and its stock was canceled. Years later the Russian bank through its shareholders sued a New York bank for the balance outstanding. The defense of the New York bank was that the corporation had been dissolved under Russian law, and thus there existed no legal person or corporation under U.S. law. It refused to pay the credit balance. What was the result?

3. Carlton owned the stock of ten taxi corporations, each owning two cabs and carrying the minimum insurance required by state law. Walkovszky was injured in an accident as a result of the negligence of one of the drivers of the cabs. Can Walkovszky successfully sue Carlton and hold him personally liable for his injuries, or must he satisfy any claim he has against the assets of the particular two-cab corporation involved in the accident?

42

Forming the Corporation

Regulation of Corporations
Corporate Formation

Disregarding Corporate Personality

I n the last chapter we learned about the special attributes that distinguish corporations from other business organizations. This chapter will discuss the steps that must be followed in order to obtain the benefits of the corporate form. Since the corporation is a creature of statute, we will first cover the statutory codes that govern the formation and conduct of corporations. We will then turn to the incorporation process itself, and discuss the consequences of not properly complying with the requirements of that process. Finally, we will learn about the limited circumstances under which the law will ignore the corporate form in order to impose liability on a corporation's shareholders.

Regulation of Corporations

Since the beginning of the Republic the activities of corporations have been enmeshed in government regulation. Before the middle of the nineteenth century corporations were generally created pursuant to the granting of a corporate charter of franchise by the state in the form of special legislation. However, as the corporate form of organization became popular, the states enacted general corporate codes that governed the creation and operation of corporations.

Although the commerce clause and the necessary and proper clause of the federal Constitution empower the U.S. government to grant corporate charters, the federal government has no corporate code. On occasion, however, the federal govern-

ment has chartered certain corporations, such as the Postal Service Corporation, by the enactment of special legislation. Virtually all corporations are the creations of the states. Various federal laws, such as the securities and exchange laws, the tax code, the labor statutes, and the antitrust laws, are noteworthy for their impact upon corporations. These may be viewed as constituting a "federal law of corporations," even though there is no single comprehensive federal corporate code.

State Corporation Codes

Corporate law is basically statutory. Each state has its own corporation statutes, usually consisting of a general corporation statute for commercial corporations and several supplemental or special statutes governing certain specific corporations, such as banks, insurance companies, nonprofit corporations, and other categories of corporations. Although there is no uniformity among the various state general corporation laws, the **Model Business Corporation Act (MBCA)** has served as the basic guideline for the majority of states, and the corporate law principles employed in the remaining state statutes are sufficiently similar to permit a degree of generalized discussion.

Because it has affected the majority of state statutes, the MBCA will provide our primary statutory basis for discussion. Drafted by the American Bar Association in 1946 and substantially revised in 1969, the MBCA has widely influenced recent statutory revisions. Because it is a "model" statute, states are not discouraged from adopting it with modifications, as opposed to a "uniform" statute such as the Uniform Commercial Code (UCC), which, in the interests of uniformity, is encouraged by its drafters to be adopted by the states in its completed form with only a few suggested alternative provisions. A major revision of the MBCA was set forth in 1983 by the Bar Association. It is entitled the "Revised Model Business Corporation Act" (RMBCA). It will be the primary statutory basis for discussion in this chapter and those that follow.

Federal Regulation of Corporations

State corporate codes are having diminishing effects on corporate management as various federal regulatory laws increasingly impact upon the corporation. There has been a tremendous upsurge of federal law affecting corporate activities in such areas as antitrust, labor-management relations, taxation, the securities markets, civil rights, and consumer protection. The Sherman Antitrust Act has been in existence since the late nineteenth century, but most federal regulation of corporations has occurred since 1933, when the Securities Act was enacted as one response to the Great Depression.

Proposals for federal chartering of corporations date from the creation of the Republic. Federal chartering was advocated early in this century by Louis Brandeis in his book *Other People's Money*. The main contemporary support for the proposal derives from those who most vocally criticize the social performance of corporations, the foremost of whom is Ralph Nader. In his book *Taming the Giant Corporation*, Nader argues that sweeping federal legislation is needed rather than piecemeal reforms of the existing regulatory framework in response to particular problems. Federal chartering proposals vary from proposals for the federal licensing of large corporations to a full-scale federal corporate code complete with an "employee bill of rights." The serious proponents of federal chartering so far have limited their proposals for the most part to larger interstate corporations.

Taxation of Corporations

As discussed in the last chapter, a corporation's income is subject to taxation. It is required to file returns and pay income taxes in a manner similar to that required of individual taxpayers. This produces what is known as a "double-tax effect": Income is taxed to the corporation as earned and taxed again to the shareholders when distributed.

An S corporation, as we learned in the last chapter, may elect special tax treatment and avoid corporate income tax. Instead, its income will be attributed to its shareholders in much the same way that a partnership's income is attributed to its partners. Although there is a limit on the number of shareholders that an S corporation may have, there is no limit on the size of corporate assets. Even large corporations may be S corporations, although S corporations were designed with small businesses in mind. Since corporations and partnerships may not own S corporation shares, an S corporation can never be the subsidiary of another corporation.

Corporate Formation

Modern incorporation procedures are not nearly as cumbersome and time-consuming as they were when incorporators had to shepherd special corporate charters through state legislatures. Today thousands of corporations are formed each year without much intellectual effort on the part of the incorporators and without raising any significant legal issues.

Preincorporation Activity

Corporation formation starts with certain preincorporation activity on the part of those who are promoting the yet-to-be-formed corporation. Before the corporation is formally launched, contracts must sometimes be made, legal relations created, and business activities undertaken with a view to creation of the corporation. Preincorporation problems are not as common as they once were, because modern corporation laws making incorporation relatively easy have all but eliminated the need for much work to be done in advance of actual incorporation. The preincorporation problems that do arise result from the activities of promoters.

The Promoter A **promoter** is someone who undertakes to form a corporation. Corporations do not spring into existence spontaneously. They result from planning and preliminary work by promoters. It is the promoter who transforms an idea into a business. The promoter plans the development of a corporate business venture, brings together people who are interested in the projected enterprise, effectuates its organization and incorporation, and establishes the newly formed corporation as a fully functioning business. Although promoters are sometimes called "preincorporators," their activities often reach beyond the point of formal incorporation.

The promoter's efforts are largely devoted to making contracts on behalf of the proposed corporation. Sometimes these contracts are self-serving—for instance, when the promoter conveys property to the corporation in exchange for shares of the corporation's stock. Frequently the contracts are with third persons for materials and services that are necessary to launch the enterprise. Problems arising from these promoter contracts involve (1) the duties of promoters toward the unborn corporation and (2) the contractual liabilities of both the promoter and the newborn corporation to third parties.

Promoter's Duties to the Corporation

Since at the time of the promoter's activities no corporation is yet in being, the promoter is not the corporation's agent. No agency can be said to exist because there is no principal. Furthermore, someone cannot serve another as a self-appointed agent. Nevertheless, a promoter is under certain obligations.

Because they are joint venturers in forming the corporation, all promoters occupy a fiduciary relationship with any other co-promoters. Promoters also have a fiduciary relationship to the corporation they form. This fiduciary relationship casts upon the promoter an affirmative duty of full disclosure to the corporation regarding any dealings with the corporation in which the promoter has a personal interest and, further, a duty to enter any transactions with the corporation in good faith. Thus the promoter may not obtain any secret profits out of transactions with or on behalf of the corporation to be formed.

A typical case of promoter liability for failing to disclose material information fully to the corporation occurs when, after organizing the new corporation, the promoter sells to it his or her own property. If the promoter conveys property to the corporation, he or she must fully disclose any personal interest, the extent of any profit on the transaction, and any other material factors that might affect the corporation's decision whether to purchase it. This disclosure must be made either to an independent board of directors, meaning a board that is not controlled by the promoter or to all existing shareholders.

The usual case of promoter liability for failing to deal in good faith with the corporation is when "watered stock" has been issued to the promoter. The term **watered stock** refers to stock issued by a corporation in excess of any fair and adequate consideration received in exchange for it. This results in a diminution of the value of the stock held by other shareholders and further damages creditors of the corporation who may have relied on the belief that the corporation had received assets equivalent in value to the value of the issued shares. Stock watering occurs when promoters cause the overvaluation of their contribution to the corporation, resulting in the issuance of stock by the corporation for less than fair consideration.

For example, a promoter may receive shares in the corporation in exchange for the performance of preincorporation services or for property contributed. If the promoter assigns too high a value on his or her services or contributed property, the promoter may receive more stock than the amount to which he or she is legitimately entitled. When there is stock watering, innocent shareholders whose stock has been devalued by the issuance of the watered stock may bring suit on behalf of the corporation to recover the lost value. Further, any injured creditors may force the promoter to pay to the corporation the unpaid value of the shares.

Preincorporation Contracts

A contract made by the promoter with a third party on behalf of the proposed corporation raises the question of whether the promoter, the corporation, or both are contractually liable. Generally the promoter remains liable as a party to the contract unless relieved of the liability by the corporation. On the other hand, the corporation generally is not bound by the contract of the promoter until the corporation affirmatively assents to the contractual obligation.

The usual case of promoter liability on preincorporation contracts occurs when the proposed corporation never comes into existence or the corporation completely disavows the contract. In such a situation the other party to the contract will usually attempt to hold the promoter liable. Because the promoter acts for the corporation before its organization, under the general rules of agency law he or she is the principal on the contract.

Under agency law an agent for an undisclosed or, more aptly, a nonexistent principal becomes a party to any contracts made with third parties. Similarly, the promoter is held bound by his or her contracts. If this were not so, any agreement made by the promoter on behalf of the future corporation would be inoperative until after the corporation was formally organized, thereby depriving the third party of any remedy until that time. Personal liability for the promoter on preincorporation contracts is not unfair, since the promoter is in the best position to bring about incorporation and the adoption of the contract by the corporation. Thus it is only fair that the risk that the corporation may not be formed should be the promoter's and not the third party's, even if the third party is advised of the exact state of affairs.

Nevertheless, it is possible that those dealing with the promoter may be said to be looking to the corporation and not the promoter for performance of the contractual obligation. If the promoter clearly negates liability, the agreement is considered to be a continuing offer to the corporation rather than a contract. Thus if the promoter specifically states that he or she is contracting in the name of the proposed corporation and not individually, the other party must rely entirely on the credit of the proposed corporation and has no claim against the promoter. This is simply a matter of recognizing the intention of the parties.

Generally a corporation is not liable on a contract made by the promoter for its benefit unless it takes some affirmative actions to adopt the contract when it formally comes into existence. Mere incorporation does not of itself render the promoter's contracts binding on the company; there must be some action by the corporation indicating its assent. This adoption may be by express words or writing or may be inferred from the corporation's knowingly accepting the contract's benefits. Thus adoption of the contract need not be express but may be implied.

In the *Coastal Shutters* case below, the court had to determine whether a corporation had impliedly adopted a preincorporation contract.

COASTAL SHUTTERS AND INSULATION, INC. V. DERR

Court of Appeals of Texas
809 S.W.2d 916 (1991)

BACKGROUND: Jimmie Ireland and David and Minnie Fineman entered into an agreement in which each would contribute money or property in exchange for shares of appellant Coastal Shutters and Insulation, Inc., a corporation that wasn't yet formed at the time. The agreement also provided that Ireland would lend the new corporation $25,000. Ireland made the $25,000 loan prior to the incorporation of Coastal Shutters and Insulation, Inc.; the loan was evidenced by a promissory note executed by "Coastal Shutters, a division of Sand 'n Sea Properties," a company owned by the Finemans. Jimmie Ireland died, and subsequent to his death two extensions of the note were executed by Barbara Ireland Derr, the person administering Jimmie Ireland's estate. The loan was never fully repaid, and Derr sued. Coastal Shutters and Insulation, Inc. claimed that it was not liable on the preincorporation promissory note because it never signed it. The trial court ruled in favor of Derr, and the corporation appealed.

Junell, Justice

The issue . . . is whether sufficient evidence was presented to support the court's finding from a preponderance of the evidence that Coastal Shutters and Insulation, Inc. signed the promissory note of August 7, 1979. A review of the record shows that not only was there insufficient evidence, the undisputed evidence showed that Coastal Shutters and Insulation, Inc. did not sign the original promissory note. The note was signed "COASTAL SHUTTERS, a

Division of SAND 'N SEA PROPERTIES, INC. /s/ David R. Feinman." Thus, appellants are correct in their assertion of insufficient evidence; and if the suit was solely on the original promissory note this court would have to reverse the trial court's judgment. However, this is not the case. The suit by Derr also encompasses the two extensions to the original note. The extensions, which were signed by Coastal Shutters and Insulation, Inc., refer to Coastal Shutters and Insulation, Inc. as the "Borrower" of the twenty-five thousand dollars for which the original promissory note was given. Further, both extensions explicitly say, " . . . Coastal Shutters and Insulation, Inc. . . . being legally obligated to pay that one certain promissory note . . ." Coastal Shutters and Insulation, Inc. intended to be responsible for that original promissory note and derived the benefits from this note. In the pre-incorporation subscription agreement between David Feinman, Minnie B. Feinman and Jimmie C. Ireland it was stated that Mr. Ireland was receiving shares in Coastal Shutters and Insulation, Inc. in exchange for cash AND he would also lend the corporation $25,000.00, the loan to be evidenced by a promissory note. So even though the note was executed approximately three weeks before the subscription agreement and any actual incorporation of Coastal Shutters and Insulation, Inc., the intent was for the money secured by the origianal note to be used for the benefit of the new corporation of Coastal Shutters and Insulation, Inc. In Texas an entity not yet incorporated will still be held liable for pre-incorporation acts that are ratified or from which the entity derives benefit. Therefore, as Coastal Shutters and Insulation, Inc. ratified the original note by signing and obligating itself in the extensions and accepted the benefits of the twenty-five thousand dollars, there can be no other conclusion but that Coastal Shutters and Insulation, Inc. is liable for the original promissory note.

DECISION: The Court of Appeals affirmed the trial court's ruling in Derr's favor.

Incorporation Procedure

The modern mechanics of incorporation are much more streamlined than they once were. However, because corporate existence continues to be a privilege conferred by the state, the proper papers must be filed and certain formalities attended to in order to bring about incorporation. Businesspeople will continue to require the assistance of an attorney during this process.

The first step taken in incorporating a business is the selection of the state of incorporation. Once that has been decided the incorporators must prepare and file the **articles of incorporation**, a document which establishes the name of the corporation, its purpose, the amount and type of authorized shares and certain other basic matters depending on the laws of the state and the objectives of the incorporators. If all is in order, the secretary issues a certificate of incorporation, sometimes called the corporate charter. After the issuance of the certificate, an organizational meeting must be held to adopt the corporate bylaws, elect officers, and transact any initial corporate business.

Selecting the State of Incorporation

After the determination to incorporate, the first decision to be made is where to incorporate. Most small corporations usually incorporate in the state where they are to be located. If the business is of an interstate nature, consideration is sometimes given to other states if the local state corporation and tax laws have restrictions. Delaware is often the first state considered because the climate of opinion prevalent in its legislature and courts is generally favorable to corporate management and unfavorable to dissident minority shareholders. Delaware's corporation statute is considered "liberal" because of its flexibility, which enables management to conduct corporate business with few restrictions.

Delaware is not the only state that may be attractive to incorporators. Although early state corporation codes were hostile to the corporation, states later encouraged corporations by enacting unrestrictive legislation. New Jersey and New York competed with Delaware by offering liberal corporation codes. Today many corporations are incorporated in these states even though their principal places of business are elsewhere. Thus the official state residences of many Delaware corporations are mailboxes. This practice has led to the characterization of some state corporation laws as "for export only." On the other hand, California has a corporate code that attempts to limit the discretion of corporate management.

One disadvantage of out-of-state incorporation is that the corporation will incur double taxation in the form of a franchise tax for doing business in the state where its business is done. Out-of-state incorporation also subjects the corporation to liability for suits in a jurisdiction removed from its principal place of business. Furthermore, in the event of litigation, there may be an issue of which state's law applies. The general rule is that the law of the incorporating state will be applied to issues relating to the internal affairs of the corporation. However, there is a trend toward making this determination on the basis of whether the state of incorporation has an interest in having its law applied.

Articles of Incorporation   After the state of incorporation is selected the incorporators must prepare and file the articles of incorporation, which are to be submitted, along with any fees and taxes due, to the secretary of state (Figure 42-1). Among the items to be included in the articles is the corporation's name. This name must include the word "corporation," "company," "incorporated," or "limited" or an abbreviation of one of those words. The

---

ARTICLE I
Name
The name of this corporation is XYZ Corporation.

ARTICLE II
Registered Office and Resident Agent
The registered office of the corporation is 15 Main Street, Kansas City, Kansas.
The resident agent at that address is John Doe.

ARTICLE III
Nature of Business
The nature of the business or purposes to be conducted or promoted are:
To engage in any lawful conduct or activity for which corporations
may be organized under the Kansas Corporation Code.

ARTICLE IV
Capital Stock
This corporation is authorized to issue Ten Thousand (10,000)
shares of common stock without par value.

ARTICLE V
Incorporators
The names and mailing addresses of the incorporators are as follows:
Dennis Jones—100 Main Street, Kansas City, Kansas
Mary Jones—100 Main Street, Kansas City, Kansas

ARTICLE VI
Initial Directors
The powers of the incorporators are to terminate upon the filing of these
Articles of Incorporation, and the names and mailing address of the persons
who are to serve as directors until the first annual meeting of stockholders or
until their successors are elected and qualified are:
Dennis Jones—100 Main Street, Kansas City, Kansas
Mary Jones—100 Main Street, Kansas City, Kansas

ARTICLE VII
The power to adopt, repeal, and amend the bylaws of this corporation
shall reside in the Board of Directors of this corporation.

IN TESTIMONY WHEREOF, we have hereunto set our names this
_____ day of _____

FIGURE 42-1

Articles of Incorporation of XYZ Corporation

Source: Douglas Whitman, F. William McCarty, Frank F. Gibson, Thomas W. Dunfee, Bartley A. Brennan, and John D. Blackburn, *Law and Business* (New York; Random House, 1987), p. 555. Copyright © 1987 by Thomas W. Dunfee, F. William McCarty, Frank F. Gibson, Douglas Whitman, John D. Blackburn, and Bartley A. Brennan.

RMBCA prohibits using any word or phrase that indicates that the corporation is organized for any purpose other than the one stated in its articles. It requires a corporate name to be distinguishable upon the records of the secretary of state from that of other corporations authorized to transact business. If a name is available, the RMBCA permits incorporators to apply to the secretary of state in advance to reserve the name for 120 days while the corporation is being organized.

Additional information regarding the corporation's capital structure must also be provided, such as the number and classes of authorized shares. Although many states require a minimum stated cap-ital for starting the business, the RMBCA does not.

The articles must also state the name and address of the corporation's initial registered agent and initial office and the names and addresses of all incorporators. Although many states still require that there be three incorporators and three directors, the RMBCA permits the corporation to have only one incorporator and one director, thus enabling sole proprietors to incorporate their businesses without needlessly involving others.

Organizational Meeting After issuance of the certificate of incorporation by the secretary of state (see Figure 42-2), an organizational

FIGURE 42-2

Certificate of Incorporation

STATE OF KANSAS

1467645

OFFICE OF SECRETARY OF STATE
JACK H. BRIER • SECRETARY OF STATE

To all to whom these presents shall come, Greeting:

I, JACK H. BRIER, Secretary of State of the State of Kansas, do hereby certify that the following and hereto attached is a true copy of

**ARTICLES OF INCORPORATION
OF
XYZ CORPORATION**

STATE OF KANSAS
COUNTY OF JOHNSON } SS
FILED FOR RECORD

RUBIE M. SCOTT
REGISTER OF RECORDS
BY _____ REP.

Filed:
the original of which is now on file and a matter of record in this office.

IN TESTIMONY WHEREOF:
I hereto set my hand and cause to be affixed my official seal.
Done at the City of Topeka, this _____Thirtieth_____ day of
_____January_____ A.D. _____1982_____

Jack H. Brier
JACK H. BRIER
SECRETARY OF STATE

Willa M. Roe
BY ASSISTANT SECRETARY OF STATE
Willa M. Roe

VOL 2002 PAGE 533

Source: Douglas Whitman, F. William McCarty, Frank F. Gibson, Thomas W. Dunfee, Bartley A. Brennan, and John D. Blackburn, *Law and Business* (New York, Random House, 1987), p. 556. Copyright © 1987 by Thomas W. Dunfee, F. William McCarty, Frank F. Gibson, Douglas Whitman, John D. Blackburn, and Bartley A. Brennan.

meeting of the board of directors must be held for the purpose of adopting the bylaws, electing officers, and transacting initial corporate business, such as the adoption of any preincorporation contract.

The corporate **bylaws** set forth the rules of internal governance for the corporation. Among the issues typically addressed in the bylaws are the number of directors, how directors are elected, the powers of the board of directors, the rights of shareholders, the conduct of the annual meeting, and the selection of officers. The bylaws must not be inconsistent with the articles or state law. Unless the articles provide otherwise, adoption of the initial bylaws as well as any later amendments rests with the board of directors. Many states permit shareholder adoption and amendment of the bylaws.

Incomplete Incorporation

Problems may arise when there has been some defect in the incorporation process, such as a failure by one of the incorporators to sign the articles or a failure to provide sufficient information in the articles as required by statute. Streamlined incorporation procedures make this less of a problem. When it does occur, however, it raises the possibility of personal liability for the shareholders. Because the consequences of failing to comply with the technical requirement of incorporation are potentially so dire, three mitigating doctrines have been developed by the courts to shield shareholders from being treated as partners. These doctrines are (1) de jure incorporation, (2) de facto incorporation, and (3) corporation by estoppel.

De Jure Incorporation In construing the requirements of incorporation statutes, courts have generally held that no useful purpose will be served by a strict technical interpretation that converts every detailed requirement into a prerequisite of corporate existence. Thus, if there has been substantial compliance with the provisions of a statute authorizing the formation of a corporation—that is if the noncompliance is slight—a **de jure corporation** results. A de jure corporation is recognized as a corporation for all purposes and as to all parties, including the state of incorporation. No one, not even the state, may challenge the organization's corporate status, notwithstanding a technical noncompliance with the incorporation procedures.

To obtain de jure status there must be literal compliance with all mandatory requirements of incorporation and substantial compliance with all directive requirements. What constitutes a mandatory as opposed to a directive requirement is a matter of statutory construction and depends on the nature of the incorporation defect. Requirements that are merely formalities, such as the requirement that a seal be affixed on the articles, are considered directive only. Their absence is not sufficient to defeat corporate existence. However, the more important a requirement is, the more likely it will be considered a mandatory require-

---

CONCEPT SUMMARY
The Incorporation Process

Step 1: Choose state of incorporation	Need not be principal place of business; Delaware has long been a favorite state of incorporation because of laws favorable to corporate management.
Step 2: File articles of incorporation	Articles, which set forth corporation's name, purpose, authorized stock, agents for service of process and other matters, are filed with secretary of state along with any fees and taxes due. Secretary generally issues certificate of incorporation or charter.
Step 3: Hold organizational meeting	Initial board of directors must adopt bylaws, elect officers, and address certain other matters (such as ratifying preincorporation contracts).

ment. Thus the requirement that the articles be filed would be mandatory; failure to file the articles could not result in de jure corporate status.

De Facto Incorporation   When there are significant defects in the incorporation to prevent a de jure existence, courts may nevertheless recognize the organization as a **de facto corporation**. In the case of a de facto corporation third persons cannot take advantage of the defects to charge the shareholders with unlimited liability or to void contracts with them. The state, however, can maintain proceedings to attack the corporate existence directly and have its charter revoked. This is because the defect is significant enough that the law cannot ignore it, and the state is permitted to take any necessary steps to remedy the situation. Thus, whereas a de jure corporation cannot be challenged by anyone, a de facto corporation can be challenged by the state.

Generally a de facto corporation results if there is a law in the state under which a corporation might be formed, there has been an apparent attempt in good faith to incorporate under such law, and the organization has conducted business as a corporation. An example of de facto corporate existence might be when articles are drafted in due form and turned over to an attorney who neglects to file them through no fault of the incorporators. Although there is not sufficient compliance for de jure existence, the de facto corporate status thus achieved will nevertheless shield the shareholders from personal liability to third parties.

The statutory trend is to eliminate the de facto doctrine because it is believed that modern incorporation statutes are sufficiently streamlined to justify stricter compliance than the doctrine requires. Further, it is believed that the continued viability of the de facto doctrine at a time when it is not needed only encourages noncompliance with incorporation procedures. Thus the RMBCA has eliminated the doctrine.

Incorporation by Estoppel   When a third person deals with a defectively organized corporation as if it were in fact incorporated, he or she may be estopped to challenge the corporate status of the organization upon later learning of the defective incorporation. It is generally considered to be unfair to allow the third party to hold the shareholders personally liable when he or she originally dealt with the organization as though it were a corporation, knowing that a corporation is an entity of limited liability. Unlike the de facto doctrine, however, which recognizes a corporate status as to all third parties, the corporation by **estoppel** recognizes the corporation only for the particular third-party transaction. The following case discusses the de jure, de facto, and estoppel theories of incorporation.

TIMBERLINE EQUIPMENT CO., INC. V. DAVENPORT, BENNETT ET AL.

Supreme Court of Oregon
514 P.2d 1109 (1973)

BACKGROUND: Timberline (plaintiff-appellee) brought this complaint to recover rentals on equipment leased to Bennett and others (defendant-appellant). In addition to making general denial, Bennett alleged as a defense that the rentals were to a de facto corporation, Aero-Fabb Corp., of which Bennett was an incorporator, director, and shareholder. He also alleged that plaintiff was estopped from denying the corporate character of the organization to whom plaintiff rented the equipment.

On January 22, 1970, Bennett signed articles of incorporation for Aero-Fabb Co. The original articles were not in accord with the statutes and, therefore, no certificate of incorporation was issued for the corporation until June 12, 1970, after new articles were filed. The leases were entered into and rentals earned during the period between January 22 and June 12, 1970. The lower court ruled in favor of the plaintiff. Bennett appealed.

Denecke, Justice

Prior to 1953 Oregon had adopted the common-law doctrine that prohibited a collateral attack on the legality of a defectively organized corporation which had achieved the status of a de facto corporation.

In 1953 the legislature adopted the Oregon Business Corporation Act. Oregon Laws 1953, ch. 549. The Model Business Corporation Act was used as a working model for the Oregon Act.

ORS 57.321 of the Oregon Business Corporation Act provides:

Upon the issuance of the certificate of incorporation, the corporate existence shall begin, and such certificate of incorporation shall be conclusive evidence that all conditions precedent required to be performed by the incorporators have been complied with and that the corporation has been incorporated under the Oregon Business Corporation Act, except as against that state in a proceeding to cancel or revoke the certificate of incorporation or for involuntary dissolution of the corporation.

ORS 57.793 provides:

All persons who assume to act as a corporation without the authority of a certificate of incorporation issued by the Corporation Commissioner, shall be jointly and severally liable for all debts and liabilities incurred or arising as a result thereof.

This is merely an elaboration of § 146 of the Model Act. The Comment states:

This section is designed to prohibit the application of any theory of de facto incorporation. The only authority to act as a corporation under the Model Act arises from completion of the procedures prescribed in sections 53 to 55 inclusive. The consequences of those procedures are specified in section 56 as being the creation of a corporation. No other means being authorized, the effect of section 146 is to negate the possibility of a de facto corporation.

We hold the principle of de facto corporation no longer exists in Oregon.

The defendant also contends that the plaintiff is estopped to deny that it contracted with a corporation. . . . One of the better explanations of the problem and the varied solutions is contained in Ballentine, Manual of Corporation Law and Practice §§§§28-30 (193):

The so-called estoppel that arises to deny corporate capacity does not depend on the presence of the technical elements of equitable estoppel, viz. misrepresentations and change of position in reliance thereon, but on the nature of the relations contemplated, that one who has recognized the organization as a corporation in business dealings should not be allowed to quibble or raise immaterial issues on matters which do not concern him in the slightest degree or affect his substantial rights.

We need not decide whether the doctrine of corporation by estoppel would apply in such a case as this. The trial court found that if this doctrine was still available under the Business Corporation Act defendants did not prove all the elements necessary for its application. . .

Under the explanation stated above for the application of the doctrine of estoppel in this kind of case, it is necessary that the plaintiff believe that it was contracting with a corporate entity. The evidence on this point is contradictory and the trial court apparently found against defendants.

A final question remains: Can the plaintiff recover against Dr. Bennett individually?

* * *

The trial court found that Dr. Bennett "acted in the business venture which was subsequently incorporated on June 12, 1970."

The proposed business of the corporation which was to be formed was to sell airplanes, recondition airplanes and give flying lessons. . . . Equipment was rented from plaintiff. . . .

There is evidence from which the trial court could have found that while Drs. Bennett and Gorman, another defendant, entrusted the details of management to Davenport, they endeavored to and did retain some control over his management. All checks required one of their signatures. Dr. Bennett frequently visited the site and observed the activity and the presence of the equipment rented by plaintiff. He met with the organization's employees to discuss the operation of the business. Shortly after the equipment was rented and before most of the rent had accrued, Dr. Bennett was informed of the rentals and given an opinion that they were unnecessary and ill-advised. Drs. Bennett and Gorman thought they had Davenport and his management "under control."

This evidence all supports the finding that Dr. Bennett was a person who assumed to act for the organization and the conclusion of the trial court that Dr. Bennett is personally liable.

DECISION: Affirmed. The Supreme Court of Oregon ruled in favor of Timberline.

Disregarding Corporate Personality

Once incorporation is complete the shareholders reasonably expect to be insulated from liability for the corporation's debts. One of the main purposes of incorporating is to enable the stockholders to engage in a business without incurring any personal liability beyond the loss of their investments. However, if the recognition of the corporate entity will result in some injustice, such as defrauding creditors, evading statutory obligations, or defeating the interest of the public, the corporate entity will be disregarded. In such a case personal liability will be imposed on the stockholders.

The rapid growth of closely held corporations and diversified corporate organization consisting of a single parent and several subsidiaries has compelled the courts recently to reexamine the entity status of some corporations. Like most statutes the RMBCA confers liability on the corporation for corporate debts. As a legal entity the corporation normally bears sole liability for debts created in its name. However, limited liability protection is a privilege granted to shareholders for the convenience of conducting business in the corporate form. It is a privilege that must be used to promote decent and fair objectives. The corporate entity will be disregarded, resulting in a loss of limited liability, when the privilege is abused. Shareholders will be held personally liable for corporate debts when such a solution is necessary to avoid an injustice.

Courts have used colorful language in holding shareholders liable. The most common phrase is "piercing the corporate veil," meaning that the corporate entity, which is normally an effective veil shielding shareholders from liability on corporate debts, will be "pierced" to reach the shareholders and hold them liable. Another phrase frequently found is that the corporate entity is merely the "alter ego" or "instrumentality" of the shareholder, meaning that there is in reality no distinction between the corporation's and the shareholder's legal personalities. Stripped of this verbiage, and irrespective of any enunciated formulas, the end result is that shareholder liability will be imposed to reach an equitable result.

The question of the status of a corporation often arises when a liability has been incurred in the name of the corporation but the corporation has become insolvent. The creditor, seeking to find a solvent defendant, may sue all or some of the shareholders, arguing that for some reason they should be called upon to pay the corporation's debts. The issue presented is whether the loss should be imposed on third persons or shareholders. A blind application of the entity approach would mean that the creditor inevitably suffers the loss. In most cases this is a reasonable result, since the creditor extended credit to a corporation, which he or she should realize is a creature of limited liability. However, this result often does not occur when it would be unjust to the creditor. This is more likely to be true in cases of involuntary creditors, such as tort victims. Creditors who made contracts with the corporation have greater difficulty in obtaining shareholder liability because they presumably dealt with the corporation voluntarily and should have known whether the corporation lacked substance.

Significant considerations in deciding whether to disregard the corporate entity are whether there has been a lack of observance of corporate formalities resulting in a commingling of shareholder and corporate assets and whether there has been inadequate capitalization of the corporation. When control by the stockholders or a parent corporation is carried out in a normal manner, with due regard for all necessary formalities and for the rights of creditors, separate entity status will normally be recognized. However, when the corporation is totally without any voice in its own affairs, when there is a manipulation of the assets of the corporation and the shareholders, and when corporate and personal activities are so intertwined that no separation is discernible, then the courts will look behind the facade and consider the identities as one. In doing this, the courts sometimes say that the corporate entity is merely a "sham" or a mere shadow of the shareholder's personality. Closely held and parent-subsidiary corporations are particularly vulnerable to this attack because frequently close corporations fail to follow the formalities of corporate existence and subsidiaries often have the same directors as their parents. Undercapitalized corporations are also targets for piercing litigation, because a grossly undercapitalized corporation may be considered a fraud upon creditors.

In the case that follows, the court examined evidence of undercapitalization and several other factors to determine whether to pierce the corporate veil.

W. M. PASSALACQUA BUILDERS, INC. V. RESNICK DEVELOPERS SOUTH, INC.

U.S. Court of Appeals, Second Circuit
933 F.2d 131 (1991)

BACKGROUND: Passalacqua Builders entered into a contract with Resnick Developers South, Inc. (Developers) to construct a project in Florida to be known as the Mayfair House. After numerous contractual disputes between the parties were submitted to arbitration, Passalacqua was awarded over $1.7 million. Passalacqua's right to recover the award was assigned to Safeco and General Insurance (collectively, the plaintiffs). The plaintiffs sued Developers after they were able to recover only $770,000 from Developers. The plaintiffs also sued the individual members of the Resnick family, which owned Developers, as well as several other companies owned by the Resnicks. The plaintiffs argued that the circumstances entitled them to "pierce the corporate veil" to reach the assets of the Resnicks and their other companies. The trial court granted a directed verdict dismissing the complaint against the Resnicks and the other companies, and the plaintiffs appealed.

Cardamone, Circuit Judge

Plaintiffs assert that the Resnick corporations were one whole entity—that is, Developers was dominated by the other corporations—and that Developers was really the agent of the Resnick family members who used it to pursue their own ends. To determine whether these assertions are valid, the triers of fact are entitled to consider factors that would tend to show that defendant was a dominated corporation, such as: (1) the absence of the formalities and paraphernalia that are part and parcel of the corporate existence, i.e., issuance of stock, election of directors, keeping of corporate records and the like, (2) inadequate capitalization, (3) whether funds are put in and taken out of the corporation for personal rather than corporate purposes, (4) overlap in ownership, officers, directors, and personnel, (5) common office space, address and telephone numbers of corporate entities, (6) the amount of business discretion displayed by the allegedly dominated corporation, (7) whether the related corporations deal with the dominated corporation at arms length, (8) whether the corporations are treated as independent profit centers, (9) the payment or guarantee of debts of the dominated corporation by other corporations in the group, and (10) whether the corporation in question had property that was used by other of the corporations as if it were its own. . . .

The Resnick family real estate business consisted of various partnerships and corporations, all controlled either directly or indirectly by family members. Developers was set up specifically in April 1972 to develop real estate in Florida. Throughout its existence it did not establish and maintain corporate indicia. It did not issue its shares timely, it had no employees except its officers—many of whom were also the officers and employees of the other corporate defendants—and neither held regular meetings, nor elected officers and directors as required by its certificate of incorporation. At the same time, Developers had separate books—though they were kept by Jack Resnick & Sons, Inc.—maintained separate bank accounts, and filed separate tax returns (except when consolidated legally with other Resnick-controlled companies).

There was no evidence of any fraud by the Resnicks or any of the corporations they controlled, a fact plaintiffs concede. Yet, Developers were severely undercapitalized during the period the building contract was in effect, having only $10 in capital paid by 90079, Inc.—another Resnick-controlled entity—when it bought all of Developer's shares in 1973. All other funds available to Developers came in the form of loans, made initially by Resnick-controlled companies and eventually by Bankers Trust, the bank which agreed to fund the Mayfair House construction project. . . .

Evidence also showed the lines of corporate control and responsibility among Resnick-controlled entities were often blurred. The Resnick corporations shared a common office in New York City, had the same office staff, and essentially the same officers and directors, albeit in different permutations and combinations. Burton Resnick, Jack Resnick, and Stanley Katz were officers of all the corporate defendants. Employees of one Resnick corporation were sometimes paid as though they actually worked for another corporation, and employees would represent to clients that they were an officer of one of the corporations when in fact they actually occupied that position in another Resnick corporation. For instance, Irving Katz was employed as treasurer of Jack Resnick & Sons, Inc., but he signed letters as the controller of Developers, even though he was not an employee or officer of that corporation.

Financial transactions also revealed a high degree of intermingling among the various corporate entities. The Resnicks shuffled funds from one to another of their corporations frequently with the source of the funds chosen based on which of their corporations had sufficient funds at the time, rather than on any demonstrated business purpose of the corporation that was the source of the funds. Interest was not generally charged by the corporation advancing money to another Resnick entity. Funds were shifted in this fashion into and out of Developers' bank accounts with regularity, but all such sums were duly noted in the corporate books and most loans from other Resnick-controlled corporations or individual family members were repaid. Other proof showed the Resnick corporations paid personal expenses of officers and employees in certain instances, and provided Resnick relatives with below-market deals on real estate.

In addition, the corporations did not deal at arms length with each other. For example, Burton Resnick testified that when Developers was purchased by 90079, Inc. for $10, he anticipated a three million dollar profit on the Mayfair House. Nor were the Resnick corporations treated as individual profit centers. Profit calculations were compiled that suggested that the distinctions between corporations were artificial, and it was actually the profit to the entire collection of Resnick-controlled corporations—as opposed to each separate entity—that was being calculated for the family to review.

Looking at these factors and considering the totality of the evidence . . . we think a jury could find a level of control that was substantial, and could be interpreted as sufficient domination to justify piercing the corporate veil to reach the assets of either the individual Resnick family members or the other Resnick-controlled corporate entities. . . .

DECISION: The Circuit Court of Appeals reversed the trial court's directed verdict and remanded the case for a new trial.

ETHICS
Ethics in Corporate Restructuring

In 1992, Marriott Corporation announced that it would divide the firm into two separate businesses. One, Marriott International Inc., would receive fees for managing the well-known hotel chain and was expected to be basically debt-free. Further, its cash flow was expected to be strong. The second portion of the business, the Host Marriott Corp., would own the hotels, along with additional real estate, and would to be responsible for the firm's nearly $3 billion in debt.

The market reaction to the announcement was dramatic. Moody's immediately downgraded Marriott bonds from investment grade to junk bond grade. Marriott 10 percent bonds dropped $300 from a price of $1,100 in 3 days. The price of Marriott stock rose in response to the announcement.

A Marriott spokesman was quoted as saying: "We have a fiduciary obligation to stockholders, and this transaction is in the best interest of stockholders. Our obligation to bondholders is to make all the bond payments on time and to pay off the principal on time." Essentially Marriott's claim is that the firm has a general obligation to stockholders dominating all others, and that any obligation to bondholders is defined by the contract terms of the bond covenant. The Marriott bond covenants did not contain any restrictive clauses protecting against a reorganization of this type.

Do you agree with the representative of Marriott? What other factors, if any, should a firm consider in a decision of this sort? What impact would you expect this decision to have on future bond offerings by Marriott? What would be the impact of this decision on the market for corporate bonds generally? Should Marriott be concerned with such an impact?

Review Questions and Problems

Key Terms

Model Business Corporation Act	bylaws
promoter	de jure corporation
watered stock	de facto corporation
articles of incorporation	corporation by estoppel

Discussion Questions

1. Does the federal government have the power to charter corporations?

2. What are the steps necessary to start a corporation?

3. What risks does a promoter take by executing a preincorporation contract for the corporation?

4. Under what circumstances may a business organization be treated as a corporation even though it has not complied with proper incorporation procedure?

5. Under what circumstances might a court disregard the corporate status of a duly incorporated company?

Review Problems

1. A, a promoter of a real estate corporation, B, that was not yet formed, entered into a contract with C for real estate services in buying land. Corporation B was later formed. C sued A for a breach of contract when A refused to pay a commission to C. A's defense was that C knew that the corporation had not been formed at the time the contract was entered into. What was the result?

2. A, a cemetery company, owned a cemetery of approximately 60 acres. Part of the cemetery was for stone monuments and part for bronze. A seldom sold stone monuments but did sell a number of bronze markers to customers purchasing burial places. B, a competitor, sued claiming that A's charter did not provide for the sale of bronze markers. A's charter did not expressly mention the bronze markers but did provide that it could "enter into any or all contracts" "proper" to the "conduct of its business." Who won? Explain.

3. A, B, and C signed articles of incorporation in New Jersey whereby the corporation was to engage in the trucking business. Before filing the articles with the secretary of state, one of the association's trucks injured Frawley. At the time of the accident was the company a corporation and liable on that basis, or is there individual liability?

4. The Illinois incorporation statute provided that people wishing to form a corporation must "sign, send, and acknowledge" the articles of incorporation before a notary public. Ford and Fisher filed articles of incorporation with the secretary of state but failed to affix any seal to the document. Later the Illinois attorney general brought legal proceedings against the two men, claiming that they were doing business under an illegal corporate certificate and attempting to revoke the corporate status. What was the result?

Case Problems

1. Seller entered into a contract for the sale of plants to the Denver Memorial Nursery, Inc. The contract was signed by Parr as Denver's president. Seller knew that the corporation was not yet formed, and the contract recited this fact, but Seller insisted that the contract be executed this way rather than wait until the corporation was organized. The corporation was never formed. Seller sued Parr to hold him personally liable on the contract. What result? Explain.

2. Helen Joplin owned a liquor store as a sole propri-

etorship. Later she sold 25 percent to Henderson. They agreed that a new corporation would be formed with Henderson purchasing 25 percent of the stock, becoming an officer, and drawing a salary of $700. The business was incorporated and operated successfully for three years. Then Henderson proposed a buyout. Joplin refused and fired Henderson. Henderson sued based on a breach of contract. Joplin defended, claiming that preincorporation agreements between directors or shareholders are contrary to public policy and thus void. What result? Explain.

3. A restaurant owner, Zechery, entered into a security agreement for a loan of $11,000 on July 24, 1975. A certificate of incorporation for the restaurant, Roseberry Inn, Inc., was executed on July 24 but was not filed with the secretary of state until July 30, 1975. When the restaurant failed the bank sued Roseberry Inn, Inc. and Zechery for repossession of the restaurant equipment, which was security for the loan. Zechery, the defendant, and one of the owners of the Inn argued that the bank could not have acquired a security interest in the equipment because the restaurant was not incorporated, and thus did not exist (de jure) at the time the security agreement was executed. What result? Explain.

43

Financing the Corporation

Kinds of Securities
Stock Subscriptions

Transfer of Securities

A business corporation must raise money in order to finance its operations. Bank loans and lines of credit can meet certain financing needs, especially short-term needs. But the bulk of a corporation's financing, particularly its long-term financing, typically comes from the sale of securities. A **security** is an instrument that evidences either a debt owed by the corporation that issued it or an ownership interest in that corporation. The most well-known types of securities are stocks and bonds, which will be discussed in this chapter.

The initial financing activity of a corporation is **capitalization**, which is the process of assembling funds in exchange for issued shares of stock. The funds so assembled are known as **capital**, although the term "capital" is often used in a broader sense to include accumulated earnings and even certain long-term loans. Since the corporation is owned by its stockholders, the corporation's capitalization represents the money that the corporation's owners have risked on the enterprise. Until a corporation has reached an adequate level of capitalization, third parties will generally be reluctant to extend credit to the corporation.

This chapter focuses primarily on the financing of corporations through the sale of securities. The material falls roughly into three parts: (1) the

kinds of securities and their characteristics, (2) the process of raising initial capital through subscription contracts, and (3) the process of raising additional capital after incorporation.

Kinds of Securities

The sale of securities is the usual method of corporate financing. Most financing comes from investors who receive securities in return for their investments. The security is usually represented by a certificate, such as a share of stock or a bond, that evidences the security holder's rights in the corporate business. However, a security need not necessarily involve this type of formal paper. The two main types of securities are (1) debt securities and (2) equity securities. **Debt securities** represent obligations that must be repaid with interest. An **equity security** represents an ownership interest in the corporation or the right to acquire such an ownership interest.

Debt Securities

The Revised Model Business Corporation Act (RMBCA) authorizes corporations to borrow money, incur liabilities, and issue bonds; none of these expedients needs shareholder approval.

CONCEPT SUMMARY
Characteristics of Equity and Debt Securities

Equity Securities	Debt Securities
1. Those holding stocks elect the board of directors which hire and control management.	1. In general those holding bonds have no control over the board of directors or management, except in bankruptcy situations
2. No maturity date exists for repayment of owners of stock, although corporations can buy back their stock from stockholders.	2. Bonds have a maturity date for repayment to holders of the value of the bond at that time.
3. Returns (dividends) are paid on stocks at the option of the board of directors depending on the profit level of the corporation.	3. Returns (interest) on bonds must be paid whether or not profit level expectations are met.
4. Upon dissolution of a corporation, stockholders' claims against the assets of the corporation are secondary to all creditors including bondholders.	4. Upon dissolution of a corporation, bondholders have a claim against the assets of the corporation prior to shareholders.

The funds generated by this borrowing must be used only for corporate purposes. Debt securities evidence a debt of the corporation and become corporate liabilities.

Types of Debt Securities Debt securities include notes, debentures, and bonds. **Notes** usually represent short-term borrowing of the corporation. They are payable upon order to a bank or person. Interest payments are due periodically. **Debentures** are unsecured corporate obligations backed by the general credit of the corporation and its assets. If the corporation defaults, creditors will attempt to seize the assets. A **bond** (used interchangeably in this chapter with debentures) is usually a long-term debt security secured by a lien or mortgage on corporate property. Bonds are bearer instruments. Interest payments are made periodically upon submission of coupons by the bondholders.

Debt securities have two important characteristics. They are subject to *redemption* and, sometimes, *conversion*. Redemption means the corporation reserves the right to call in and pay off its obligations at any time before they are due, usually at a premium over face value. Debt securities may also be convertible—that is, they may be converted into equity securities (for example, common stock) at a certain ratio.

Tax Advantages of Debt Securities Debt securities offer significant tax advantages for the corporation that issues them. Interest payments on bonds or notes are tax deductible for the corporation, whereas dividend payments on equity securities (such as common stock) are not. Payments of a debt by a corporation may be considered a nontaxable return on capital for the investor, whereas a redemption of equity securities from a shareholder by the corporation may be taxed as ordinary income. The Internal Revenue Service (IRS) has often investigated corporations' debt structures to determine if they are excessive. If the IRS finds that a debt structure is excessive, it attempts to treat the excessive debt as a form of corporate equity for tax purposes. Thus the substantial advantages associated with corporate debt financing have led to considerable litigation. Because the courts have treated each situation as unique, no overriding legal principle has evolved to determine when a corporation's debt is excessive. Courts have considered the ratio of debt to equity as relevant but have rejected a purely quantitative approach.

Equity Securities

Every business corporation must issue equity securities, which represent ownership interests in the corporation. Equity securities are usually called **shares** or **stock** (see Figure 43-1). Stockholders (shareholders) own the corporation. Authorization for the issuance of equity is contained in the corporation's articles of incorporation. Unless authorized, the sale of shares is void.

The money raised by the corporation from the sale of stock is the fund out of which the corporation may meet its obligations to creditors; it represents the corporation's stated capital. The corporation is not bound to return to the shareholders their investment before liquidation of the enterprise. The shares usually have no maturity date. Return on the shareholders' investment takes two forms: **dividends**, which are distributions of earnings to shareholders made at the board of directors' discretion; and **capital gains**, which represent the stock's increase in value from the time the shareholder buys it to the time the shareholder sells it. Shareholders' claims are subordinate to the claims of debt-security holders because debt holders stand as creditors of the corporation, not as its owners. Upon corporate liquidation following dissolution, shareholders receive only those funds available after all corporate creditors have been paid.

Common and Preferred Stock Most states authorize the issuance of more than one class of corporate stock and permit the corporation to vary the rights and restrictions among the different classes. The two classes most frequently issued are (1) common stock and (2) preferred stock.

Common stock is generally the class of stock that carries voting rights, thus allowing common stockholders to participate in corporate management. (See Chapter 41 for a discussion of the shareholders' role in management.) Common stockholders generally do not receive dividends until the preferred shareholders have received the dividends to which they are entitled. If the corporation is dissolved, common stockholders will not receive any of the corporation's assets until the claims of creditors and the other classes of shareholders have been satisfied. Common stockholders assume a greater risk than other corporate investors, but they have the opportu-

nity to receive a higher return on their investment. If a corporation issues only one class of stock, that stock will be common stock.

Preferred stock is stock which carries some sort of preference over common stock. Preferred stock typically carries a dividend preference, which prohibits the corporation from paying any dividends to common shareholders until preferred shareholders have received dividends during the year representing a certain rate of return. Assume that ABC Corp. issues "10 percent preferred stock," its only class of preferred stock. The total face value of ABC's outstanding preferred stock is $1 million. That means that ABC must pay out 10 percent of $1 million—$100,000—in dividends to its preferred shareholders before it may pay any dividends to common shareholders.

The corporation is not required to pay dividends to preferred stockholders, just as it is not required to pay dividends to common stockholders. However, if the corporation chooses to pay dividends during any year, it must satisfy the preference on the preferred stock before it pays any dividends to common shareholders. **Cumulative preferred stock** is stock for which the dividend preference carries over from year to year. Thus, if the corporation had not paid any dividends during 1994, it would not be allowed to pay dividends on common shares during 1995 until it had satisfied its preference for preferred shareholders for 1995 *and* 1994.

Preferred stock generally also carries a liquidation preference, which gives preferred shareholders priority over common shareholders in the event that the corporation's assets are distributed in a liquidation.

Preferred stock may be made redeemable. The RMBCA permits the articles to provide that preferred stock may be redeemed by the corporation at the price fixed by the articles.

Preferred stock may also be convertible into shares of another class or into another type of security, such as a bond. However, the RMBCA provides that the shares of one class of stock may not be converted into those of another class that has superior or prior rights and preferences regarding corporate distributions. Thus preferred stock may be converted into common stock, but not vice versa.

Preferred shareholders generally participate less in corporate management than common

FIGURE 43-1

Stock certificate

Source: Douglas Whitman, F. William McCarty, Frank F. Gibson, Thomas W. Dunfee, Bartley A. Brennan, and John D. Blackburn, *Law and Business* (New York, Random House, 1987), p. 568. Copyright © 1987 by Thomas W. Dunfee, F. William McCarty, Frank F. Gibson, Douglas Whitman, John D. Blackburn, and Bartley A. Brennan.

shareholders. This balances the lower risk assumed by preferred shareholders. Thus preferred stock is generally nonvoting.

Stock Options and Warrants

Certain securities do not give their owners a direct ownership interest in the corporation, but rather they grant the owner the right to purchase such an interest. A **stock option** gives the owner the right to purchase or sell a certain number of a corporation's shares at a specified price on or before a set expiration date. A **call option** gives the holder the right to buy stock, and a **put option** grants the right to sell stock. The holder of a call option benefits if the market price of a stock rises above op-

tion price, since he or she has locked in a cheaper price. Conversely, the holder of a put option benefits if the market price of the stock falls below the option price, since he or she will be entitled to sell the stock for a higher-than-market price.

Stock options are often issued by a corporation to an officer or employee to compensate him or her for work done or to provide an incentive for further effort. Under the RMBCA, if options or warrants are to be issued to the directors, officers, or employees of the corporation, shareholder approval is not required. The following is a well-reasoned decision illustrating the law as applied to stock options granted to executives as part of a compensation package.

LIEBERMAN V. KOPPERS CO., INC.

Court of Chancery of Delaware
149 A.2d 756, affd. sub. nom. Lieberman v. Becker, 155 A.2d 596 (1959)

BACKGROUND: Lieberman (plaintiff), a stockholder of Koppers Co., Inc. brought a derivative action against the company to have declared invalid a deferred-compensation unit plan approved by the stockholders. The purpose of the plan was to attract and retain persons of outstanding competence and to give key employees a stockholder's point of view of the company. The plan provided for the issuance of units in lieu of options to purchase stocks. The value of each unit on the date of issue was that of one share of common stock on the same date. Each unit was subject to being increased in value by the crediting to it of dividends paid on a share of stock as well as any increase in the market value of a single share before a participant's right to a unit occurred. As a condition to the award of units, each participant agreed to remain in the company's employ for 5 years from the date of his award or until retirement and to be available for consultation for a 10-year period after retirement, during which time a participant might not compete with Koppers. The plan was administered by three or more board members declared ineligible to participate. Both parties moved for summary judgment.

Marvel, Vice Chancellor

The complaint alleges that as of December 31, 1957, 89,800 units had been awarded under the plan to various employees and that to the extent that the plan provides for awards to participants based on the increased market value of common stock of the defendant corporation it is invalid for the reason that such awards bear no reasonable relation to the value of services rendered by a participant, and that such awards thus constitute a waste and gift of corporate assets. No complaint, however, is made concerning the provisions of the plan dealing with dividend credits. It is further alleged that since the adoption of the plan the stock of Koppers has fluctuated widely, that such fluctuations bear little or no relation to the services to the corporation and its stockholders and so are invalid.

In addition to the enjoining of the operation of the plan the complaint seeks an accounting for all payments made by Koppers under the plan and for general equitable relief, but admittedly those persons who have become eligible for and received payments under the plan by reason of severance of employment are not before the Court, and no accounting is presently sought.

The answer admits the pleaded facts as to the adoption of the plan, sets forth the vote on stockholder approval and concludes that the plan was adopted and given effect by directors of Koppers in the exercise of their best business judgment as directors and was approved by substantially all of the stockholders who voted thereon in the belief the plan is a fair, reasonable, appropriate and valid plan in furtherance of the welfare and success of Koppers and for the advantage of all its shareholders.

There being no doubt but that the plan here under attack is reasonably calculated to insure the receipt of services by the corporation, it is not subject to the Kerbs ruling (*Kerbs v. California Eastern Airways*).

Furthermore, while it is alleged that certain directors are beneficiaries of the plan, no real attack is made nor could such be made on the basis of director self-dealing in view of the existence of an impartial committee and stockholder approval.

In short, it is my considered opinion that the plan is reasonably and fairly designed to achieve a legitimate business purpose, namely to retain or obtain qualified executive personnel through the medium of deferring compensation until retirement. While a substantial block of stock has been reserved for financing the plan, corporate reserves, if any, may be allocated to the payment of deferred compensation, thereby probably reducing what would have been the stock demands of a comparable stock option plan. Furthermore, while moneys are not paid out by participants for units, there is no reason advanced why a reasonable and impartial committee may not be expected to take this factor into consideration in the award of units, and when need be, in the reduction of units already awarded. Plaintiff also declines to give proper recognition to the dividend credit provision, the most tangible and perhaps the most attractive feature of the plan in the eyes of participants. Finally, the so-called speculative or capital gains features of the plan are by no means absent from conventional option plans and certain types of incentive plans based on earnings, and it would be unrealistic not to recognize that the plan, if fairly operated, will add to job satisfaction and induce added effort on the part of participants with resulting benefits to the corporation.

Admittedly, the market value of stock of any substantial corporation cannot be isolated from broad economic trends, wars, rumours and many other factors both direct and indirect which affect stock prices. However, earnings are the mark of corporate success and the main factor in stock appreciation, and I do not believe it can be dogmatically said that the services of employees given in response to an incentive plan based in substantial part on the appreciation in the market value of their employer's common stock bear no reasonable relation to such appreciation, and I decline to strike down the plan as per se unreasonable and invalid.

While it may be established in the future that the award of specific units under the plan may in an individual case ultimately pose the threat of payment of illegally excessive compensation, such a case is not now before me.

DECISION: The court ruled in favor of Koppers Co., Inc.

CONCEPT SUMMARY
Securities

Debt Securities

Note	Short-term debt security.
Debenture	Unsecured debt security.
Bond	Secured debt security (although term is commonly used loosely to include debentures as well).

Equity Securities

Common stock	Voting stock without preference.
Preferred stock	Stock carrying preference with respect to dividends, liquidation, and/or other matters. Dividend preference generally entitles preferred stock holder to receive a certain percentage of stock's face value in dividends each year before common stock dividends may be declared. With cumulative preferred stock, amount of dividend preference not satisfied in one year carries over to the next year.
Stock option	Security giving holder the right to purchase (in the case of a call option) or sell (in the case of a put option) a certain number of a corporation's shares for a set price on or before a specified date.
Stock warrant	Usually attached to debt security or preferred stock, a warrant gives its holder the right to purchase a certain number of the corporation's shares at a set price on or before a specified date.
Stock right	Usually attached to a class of stock, a stock right gives the holder the right to purchase additional shares of the same class of stock (often on an "as and when issued" basis) for a set price.

A **stock warrant** is a security that gives the holder the right to buy shares of a corporation on or before a certain expiration date. Unlike stock options, stock warrants are typically attached to bonds, preferred stock, or other securities. A corporation thus might issue bonds with warrants that give purchasers the right to buy the corporation's stock at a favorable price. The bondholder has the choice of holding the warrant, exercising it (that is, purchasing stock), or selling it separately. Warrants are traded in the securities markets.

Closely related to a warrant is a **stock right**, which gives existing shareholders the right to buy additional shares of the same type of stock. Rights often grant shareholders the right to subscribe to newly issued shares at a favorable price or to subscribe to future shares as they are issued. Rights are traded in securities markets.

Stock Subscriptions

A method of corporate financing more common with small corporations than with large corporations is the stock subscription. A **stock subscription** is an agreement between a corporation and a prospective shareholder whereby the corporation agrees to issue shares and the subscriber agrees to pay for them. In a majority of states an offer by the prospective shareholder and an acceptance by the corporation must exist in order to bring the stock subscription contract into existence. Stock subscriptions may be executed either before or after incorporation. The issue raised by both preincorporation and postincorporation subscriptions is whether the subscriber attains shareholder status in the corporation. If the subscriber does, he or she will be liable for whatever consideration was promised under the subscription agreement in payment for the shares.

Preincorporation Subscriptions

Persons interested in the formation of a business corporation frequently desire to begin the process of financing the proposed enterprise before the formal steps resulting in the formation of the corporation are complete. One of the devices employed in this process of assembling funds is the **preincorporation subscription**, by which one or more investors make known to the promoter their intention to purchase shares of a designated class and number in the proposed corporation at an agreed-upon sum.

A preincorporation subscription may take many forms. Although a few states, such as Delaware and Kansas, require that stock subscriptions be in writing and signed by the subscriber, most states do not require that a subscription be written. A preincorporation subscription may be an individual transaction or it may be a class of transactions by a number of persons, as when a "subscription list" is signed. The word "subscriber" need not appear, and other language such as "I hereby purchase, etc." may be employed. The agreement may include definite provisions as to the time and manner of payment of the agreed amount, the time when the subscriber is to become entitled to a stock certificate, and the legal relations between the subscriber and other shareholders; but usually it gives little or no indication of the intent of the parties with respect to these matters.

Authorities disagree whether a subscriber may withdraw his or her subscription before the corporation comes into existence. The older rule, which still prevails in many jurisdictions, is that a preincorporation subscription may be withdrawn at any time prior to acceptance by the corporation, which cannot occur until the corporation comes into existence. Because there is no corporation in existence at the time the subscription is executed, the subscription is merely an expression of intent to purchase shares and has no legal effect. Furthermore, under general contract law the subscriber's death, insanity, or bankruptcy will terminate the subscription offer in accordance with the usual rules relating to an unaccepted offer.

In states in which a preincorporation subscription may be revoked, budding corporations face uncertainty as to the amount of funds that they will have available upon incorporation. In states that also have minimum capital requirements, there is the danger that the business will not have sufficient funds to permit its formal incorporation. If a subscriber who happens to be one of the major contributors to the proposed corporation revokes his or her subscription, the whole venture may collapse even before it gets started. These concerns underlie the newer approach taken by the RMBCA and other states. In states adopting this newer approach, preincorporation subscriptions are irrevocable for a certain period of time, typically 6 months, unless the subscription agreement provides otherwise or all the subscribers consent to the revocation.

Although by statute in some states acceptance of the subscription offer is deemed to occur upon incorporation, most statutes, including the RMBCA, require that the corporation act affirmatively to accept the preincorporation subscription offers. Thus, to make a binding subscription contract under these statutes, not only must the corporation be completely organized but there must be an acceptance by the corporation after coming into existence, either expressly by issuing shares to the subscribers or impliedly by recognizing the subscriber as a stockholder.

Postincorporation Subscriptions

A **postincorporation subscription** is a subscription entered into between a subscriber and a corporation already in existence. A postincorporation subscription creates a binding obligation for the subscriber to purchase, and the corporation to sell, shares of the corporate stock. Once a subscription agreement is executed, the subscriber assumes the status of a shareholder immediately. This is true regardless of whether the corporation has issued a stock certificate to the subscriber. By the same token, the subscriber is liable for the subscription payment even if the corporation has not delivered the stock certificate. Although the subscriber becomes a shareholder immediately, some shareholder rights, such as the right to vote and the right to receive dividends, may be suspended until the subscription price is fully paid.

A postincorporation subscription must be distinguished from an executory contract to purchase stock. With an executory contract, the purchaser does not become a shareholder until the shares are paid for and the stock certificate is issued to the purchaser. A purchaser under an executory contract is relieved of the duty to pay in the event of the corporation's bankruptcy, because the corporation cannot perform its duty to deliver shares in a going concern.

How does one distinguish between a subscription and an executory contract to buy shares? The most important factor is the intention of the parties: Did the parties intend for the purchaser to assume shareholder status immediately upon the signing of the contract, or only after the contract is fully performed? A clue to the parties' intentions might be found in the agreement title, with "Purchase Agreement" suggesting an executory contract and "Subscription Agreement" suggesting, of course, a subscription.

Consideration to Be Paid by Subscriber

The issuance of shares by a corporation implies that it has received consideration equal to or greater than some set value. Traditionally, this minimum value has been known as par value. A stock's **par value** is the value of each share as stated in the articles of incorporation or set by the board of directors. A stock's par value usually bears no relation to its market value; stocks generally sell for prices much greater than their par value. Par value does, however, set the minimum original issue price for the corporation's shares. Shareholders who do not contribute an amount at least equal to the par value of the stock are liable to the corporation's creditors for the balance.

In states in which stock is still required to have a par value, the total amount of par value of the corporation's issued shares is known as the corporation's **stated capital**. A corporation's stated capital is designed to serve as a "cushion" to protect creditors; the stated capital provides a fund of money that will be there to satisfy creditors' claims in the event that the corporation's business fails. A corporation may not pay dividends out of its stated capital.

The total amount of money paid for a corporation's shares *in excess of par value* is known as the corporation's **capital surplus**, also referred to as *additional paid-in capital*. Capital surplus is also generally used as part of the cushion for creditors, although a number of states allow the capital surplus to be used to pay dividends.

Par value does not have the significance that it once had. For one thing, most corporations assign a very low par value to their stock—$1 is typical. Also, most states allow corporations to issue **no-par-value stock**, which, as the name implies, is stock with no par value. In many jurisdictions, the corporation assigns a **stated value** to its no-par-value stock. The corporation's stated capital is the total amount of stated value of the corporation's issued shares. (If the corporation issues both par-value stock and no-par-value stock, then its stated capital is total par value plus total stated value.) The total amount paid for the shares in excess of stated value goes into the corporation's capital surplus account. The allocation of no-par-stock proceeds between stated capital and capital surplus is generally driven by accounting and legal considerations that are beyond the scope of this text.

The RMBCA eliminates the distinction between par stock and no-par stock. Under the RMBCA, the board may set a minimum price or establish a formula or other method for determining the price of shares.

The RMBCA provides that payment for shares may be made with money or other property of any description actually transferred to the corporation or with labor or other services actually rendered to the corporation. Also, the RMBCA allows promissory notes and agreements to provide future services to constitute payment for shares. Most state statutes presently will not allow these latter items to serve as consideration. Because shares may be issued for a consideration other than cash, a question sometimes arises over whether the corporation received full value for its stock.

Authorities disagree regarding the valuation of property or services transferred to the corporation in consideration for its shares. A few states follow the "true value" rule. Under this rule, whether a shareholder is liable for any unpaid value depends on whether the assets given in consideration for the shares were actually worth the price of the stock. The shareholder is held liable for any substantial variance between the fair market value of the property or service transferred to the corporation and the price of the stock.

Most states (including those that adopt the RMBCA), follow the "good faith" rule, which is based on the assumption that people may honestly differ about the value of property and service rendered to a corporation in consideration for its stock. Under this rule the valuation made by the corporation will be upheld as long as it was honestly made, no fraud or bad faith exists on the part of the directors, and they have exercised the degree of care that an ordinary, prudent person in their position would exercise. The case that follows is the landmark opinion of the U.S. Supreme Court that originally set forth the good faith rule.

COIT V. AMALGAMATING COMPANY

U.S. Supreme Court
119 U.S.343 (1886)

BACKGROUND: Coit (plaintiff), holder of a judgment for $5,489 against Gold (defendant), brought this suit to compel the stockholders to pay what he claimed to be due and unpaid on the shares of the capital stock held by them. Coit was unable to obtain execution of his judgment against the corporation itself because it was insolvent. The defendant, the North Carolina Gold Amalgamating Company, was incorporated under the laws of North Carolina, on January 30, 1874, for the purpose, among other things, of working, milling, smelting, reducing, and assaying ores and metals, with the power to purchase such property, real and personal, as might be necessary in its business and to mortgage or sell the same. By its charter the minimum capital stock was fixed at $100,000, divided into 1,000 shares of $100 each; the corporation was empowered to increase it from time to time, by a majority vote of the stockholders, to $2.5 million. The charter provided that the subscription to the capital stock might be paid "in such installments, in such manner and in such property, real and personal," as a majority of the corporators might determine, and that the stockholders should not be liable for any loss or damages or be responsible beyond the assets of the company. Previously to the charter, the corporators had been engaged in mining operations, conducting their business under the name and title which they took as a corporation. When the charter was obtained, the capital stock was paid by the property of the former association, which was estimated to be of the value of $100,000, the shares being divided among the stockholders in proportion to their respective interests in the property. Each stockholder placed his estimate upon the property; and the average estimate amounted to $137,500. This sum they reduced to $100,000, inasmuch as the capital stock was to be of that amount. The lower courts ruled in favor of the defendant, and it is from these decisions that plaintiff appealed.

Field, Justice

The plaintiff contends, and it is the principal basis of his suit, that the valuation thus put upon the property was illegally and fraudulently made at an amount far above its actual value, averring that the property consisted only of a machine for crushing ores, the right to use a patent called the Crosby process, and the charter of the proposed organization; that the articles had no market or actual value, and, therefore, that the capital stock issued thereon was not fully paid, or paid to any substantial extent, and that the holders thereof were still liable to the corporation and its creditors for the unpaid subscription. If it were proved that actual fraud was committed in the payment of the stock, and that the complainant had given credit to the company from a belief that its stock was fully paid, there would undoubtedly be substantial ground for the relief asked. But where the charter authorizes capital stock to be paid in property, and the shareholders honestly and in good faith put in property instead of money in payment of their subscriptions, third parties have no ground of complaint. The case is very different from that in which subscriptions to stock are payable in cash, and where only a part of the installments has been paid. In that case there is still a debt due to the corporation, which, if it becomes insolvent, may be sequestered in equity by the creditors, as a trust fund liable to the payment of their debts. But where full paid stock is issued for property received, there must be actual fraud in the transaction to enable creditors of the corporation to call the stockholders to account. A gross and obvious overvaluation of property would be strong evidence of fraud.

But the allegation of intentional and fraudulent undervaluation of the property is not sustained by the evidence. The patent and the machinery had been used by the corporators in their business, which was continued under the charter. They were immediately serviceable, and therefore had to the company a present value. The corporators may have placed too high an estimate upon the property, but the court below finds that its valuation was honestly and fairly made; and there is only one item, the value of the chartered privileges, which is at all liable to any legal objection. But if that were deducted, the remaining amount would be so near to the aggregate capital, that no implication could be raised against the entire good faith of the parties in the transaction. In May, 1874, the company increased its stock, as it was authorized to do so by its charter, to $1,000,000 or 10,000 shares of $100 each. This increase was made pursuant to an agreement with one Howes, by which the company was to give him 2000 shares of the increased stock for certain lands purchased from him. Of the balance of the increased shares, 4000 were divided among the holders of the original stock upon the return and delivery to the company of the original certificates—they thus receiving four shares of the increased capital stock for one of the original shares returned. The other 4000 shares were retained by the company. The land purchased was subject to three mortgages, of which the plaintiff held the third; and the agreement was that, under the first mortgage, a sale should be made of the property, and that mortgages for a like amount should be given to the parties according to their several and respective amounts, and in their respective positions and priorities. The plaintiff was to be placed by the company, after the release of his mortgage, in the same position. Accordingly he made a deed to it of all his interest and title under the mortgage held by him, the trustee joining with him, in which deed the agreement was recited. The company, thereupon, gave him its mortgage upon the same and other property, which was payable in installments. The plaintiff also received at the same time an accepted draft of Howe's on the company for $1000. When the first installment on the mortgage became due, the company being unable to pay it, he took its draft for the amount, $3000, payable in December following. It is upon these drafts that the judgment was recovered in the Court of Common Pleas of Philadelphia, which is the foundation of the present suit. It is in evidence that the plaintiff was fully aware, at the time, of the increase in the stock of the company, and of its object. Six months afterwards, the increase was cancelled, the outstanding shares were called in, and the capital stock reduced to its original limit of $100,000. Nothing was done after the increase to enlarge the liabilities of the company. The draft of the Howes was passed to the plaintiff and received by him at the time the agreement was carried out upon which the increase of the stock was made; and the draft for $3000 was for an installment upon the mortgage then executed. The plaintiff had placed no reliance upon the supposed paid-up capital of the company on the increased shares, and, therefore, has no cause of complaint by reason of their subsequent recall. Had a new indebtedness been created by the company after the issue of the stock and before its recall, a different question would have arisen. The creditor in that case, relying on the faith of the stock being fully paid, might have insisted upon its full payment. But no such new indebtedness was created, and we think, therefore, that the stockholders cannot be called upon, at the suit of the plaintiff, to pay in the amount of the stock, which, though issued, was soon afterwards recalled and cancelled.

DECISION: Affirmed. The U.S. Supreme Court ruled in favor of Amalgamating Company.

Transfer of Securities

Method of Transfer

The transfer of securities is governed by Article 8 of the Uniform Commercial Code (UCC). Generally, owners of securities have the right to transfer those securities.

The proper method of transferring securities depends upon the type of security being transferred. Article 8 classifies securities as either certificated securities or uncertificated securities. A **certificated security** is a security that is evidenced by a certificate. A certificated security may be a **registered certificated security**, which means that the owner's name is recorded both on the security and on the corporation's books; or a **bearer security**, which is evidenced by a certificate payable to "bearer." An **uncertificated security** is a security that is not evidenced by a certificate.

A bearer security is transferred simply by delivery. An uncertificated security is transferred when the corporation records the transfer on its books.

A registered certificated security can be validly transferred only by the delivery of the certificate and its indorsement by the registered owner. The indorsement may be on either the certificate itself or on a **stock power**, which is a separate instrument that provides for the transfer of the security. The signature of the registered owner on the back of the certificate constitutes a valid indorsement. An indorsement alone does not transfer any rights unless the certificate is also delivered to the transferee. When a certificate has been delivered to a purchaser with the intent to transfer it but without the necessary indorsement, a transfer has been completed and the purchaser has a specifically enforceable right to compel any necessary indorsement. The effect of a valid transfer is to make the transferee the complete legal and equitable owner of the shares, and the corporation generally must register the transfer and recognize the transferee as the rightful owner.

UCC 8-313 sets forth rules for determining when the transfer of securities to a purchaser becomes final. This determination depends on a number of factors, including whether the stock certificates are delivered directly from the seller to the buyer or are instead transferred through a "financial intermediary" such as a stockbroker. The *Crawford* case, which follows, hinged on when a transfer of securities became effective.

ESTATE OF CRAWFORD
Court of Appeals of Texas
795 S.W.2d 835 (1990)

BACKGROUND: Jo Ann Crawford had two sons, Bill Morgan and Dick Morgan. Her will left all her shares of stock to Bill and all her cash to Dick. When Crawford was hospitalized shortly before her death, Dick arranged for her to sell her preferred stock in Foremost-McKesson for a price of $94,000. Dick contacted a stockbroker, Pierce of the A. G. Edwards brokerage, to arrange the transaction. On March 9, the shares were offered to and accepted by a purchaser on the New York Stock Exchange floor. On March 11, Pierce received the stock certificates, indorsed by Crawford, in the mail. On March 13, Pierce deposited the stock certificates into a joint account set up for Crawford and Dick pending receipt of the purchase price from the buyer. Crawford died on March 13. On March 16, Pierce received the purchase price from the buyer, sent the stock certificates to the buyer, and deposited the money in the joint account. Dick then took the funds and deposited them into his personal account.

Bill sued Dick for the proceeds of the preferred stock. Bill claimed that at the time of their mother's death on March 13, the preferred shares had not yet been transferred to the purchaser and that the shares should therefore have passed to Bill according to Crawford's will. The trial court agreed with Bill, and Dick appealed.

Reynolds, Chief Justice

Section 8.31(a) contains a total of ten subsections, each containing alternative formalities marking the completion of transfer. To support the judgment in favor of Bill, the record must demonstrate conclusively that none of the formalities of transfer were completed.

Subsections (2) and (6) relate only to uncertificated securities. . . . Therefore, these subsections are not pertinent to the transaction.

Similarly, subsections (8), (9), and (10) apply to the transfer of investment securities which have been made collateral for an obligation of the holder. . . . Consequently, these subsections have no application to the transaction.

Subsection (1) defines completion of the transfer of stock as possession of the certificated security by the purchaser or his designee. The uncontroverted deposition testimony of Steve Pierce, the broker who conducted the sale for Dick, conclusively demonstrates that subsection (1) requisites were not met.

Pierce testified that he received the certificates of stock on March 11th. If he, as a stock broker, were considered to be in possession of the certificates, he held them as a financial intermediary pursuant to section 8.313(d), thereby rendering subsection (1) inapplicable. Further, A.G. Edwards' records show that on March 13, the day of Mrs. Crawford's death, the stock was deposited into account number 55 475-253, the joint account of Jo Ann Crawford and Dick Morgan. Pierce also testified that stock is placed in the buyer's name after the settlement date if the buyer so instructs. In the absence of controverting evidence, it is a permissible inference that the usual practice was not varied in the instant transfer. Therefore, reasonable minds cannot differ in concluding the purchaser had not obtained possession of the certificated securities by the time of Mrs. Crawford's death.

Subsection (3) defines completion of transfer as possession by a financial intermediary of certificated securities "specially indorsed to or issued in the name of the purchaser." Even though A.G. Edwards qualified as a financial intermediary as defined in section 8.313(d), there is no contention or evidential indication that the stock certificates were specially endorsed to or issued in the name of the purchaser. . . .

A subsection (4) completion of transfer occurs when the financial intermediary sends confirmation of the sale to the purchaser and in some way identifies the securities as belonging to the purchaser, as by making a book entry. The record contains two confirmations of sale, requesting remittance of the purchase amounts, which might be presumed to have been sent to the purchaser. But if so, there is no indication, by book entry or otherwise, of any identification of the securities as belonging to the purchaser. The notation "sold" on the A.G. Edwards securities receipt is, without more, insufficient to identify the securities as belonging to a specific purchaser. In the absence of such identification, no transfer was completed under this subsection.

Subsection (5) applies to a situation in which the certificates are in the possession of a third party who is not a financial intermediary. . . . Again, . . . the stock certificates were held by a financial intermediary, A.G. Edwards, in the joint account at the time of Mrs. Crawford's death. Plainly, subsection (5) is inapplicable.

Subsection (7) requires a transfer of certificated securities to be shown by appropriate entries on the books of a clearing corporation. . . . There is, however, no indication that a clearing corporation was utilized in this transaction. . . .

DECISION: The Court of Appeals found that the shares had not yet been transferred at the time of Crawford's death, and therefore affirmed the trial court's judgment for Bill.

Restrictions on Transfer

Since the right to transfer one's property is an important right of ownership, the law does not favor restrictions on an owner's right to transfer his or her securities. However, corporations may sometimes impose transfer restrictions on their securities as long as they are reasonable. To be valid, any such restrictions must generally be noted conspicuously on the certificate in the case of a certificated security. In the case of an uncertificated security, the restriction must generally be noted in the first transaction statement sent by the corporation to the new owner. If the transferee has actual knowledge of the restrictions, however, they will be enforced against the transferee even if the restrictions were not noted as otherwise required.

Most jurisdictions recognize the right of corporations to impose restrictions giving the corporation or other shareholders the option to purchase the shares at an agreed-upon price before the shares are offered to third parties. This type of restriction is known as a "right of first refusal" and is most commonly imposed by close corporations in attempt to restrict control to a homogeneous shareholder group. However, restrictions giving the directors an option to purchase the shares at a price to be fixed at the directors' sole discretion are generally considered to be unreasonable restraints and therefore invalid.

Transfer restrictions are also used to protect corporations from the burdens of certain securities laws. As we will learn in Chapter 46, the Securities Act of 1933 offers certain important exemptions from its cumbersome registration requirements. One important exemption requires that the securities be issued for investment purposes only and not for resale; resale of the securities can result in the loss of the exemption and can expose the corporation to certain types of liability. To protect themselves, corporate issuers often require the issuee to sign a letter indicating his or her investment intent. Stock sold in this fashion is known as **lettered stock**. The letter alone is not an effective transfer restriction; the restriction must still be conspicuously included on the certificate (or, in the case of an uncertificated security, in the first transaction statement). As additional protection, corporate issuers print a legend on the face of the certificate stating that the shares are not transferred until registered, thus notifying potential purchasers that the corporation may refuse to recognize any transfer that will impair this exemption.

The RMBCA authorizes transfer restrictions when imposed by the articles of incorporation, bylaws and agreements among the shareholders. Transfer restrictions are authorized to maintain the corporation's identity, to preserve exemptions under federal or state securities laws, and "for any other reasonable purpose."

Warranties on Transfer

UCC Section 8-306 sets forth various warranties that are deemed to be given upon the transfer of a security. A person who transfers a certificated security for value warrants to the transferee that:

1. The transfer is effective and rightful
2. The security is genuine and has not been materially altered; and
3. He or she knows of no fact that might impair the validity of the security.

Review Questions and Problems

Key Terms

security	stock warrant
capitalization	stock right
capital	stock subscription
debt security	preincorporation subscription
equity security	
note	postincorporation subscription
debenture	
bond	par value
shares	stated capital
stock	capital surplus
dividend	no-par-value stock
capital gains	stated value
common stock	certificated security
preferred stock	registered certificated security
cumulative preferred stock	
	bearer security
stock option	uncertificated security
call option	stock power
put option	lettered stock

Discussion Questions

1. What is the prevailing rule as to whether a preincorporation subscriber to shares of a corporation may withdraw his or her subscription before the corporation comes into existence?
2. Who determines the value of shares to be received as consideration when a corporation issues stocks?
3. Define the "true value" and "good faith" rules governing the valuation of property or services transferred to the corporation in consideration for its shares.

4. What article and statute govern the transfer of stocks and bonds?

Review Problem

1. Henry Molina attended a meeting with Rudy Largosa to discuss the formation of a corporation to engage in selling stereo equipment. At the meeting Molina signed a subscription form for the purchase of forty shares at $50 per share for a total investment of $2,000 in the proposed corporation. The subscription form did not set forth the capital of the proposed corporation or the extent of Molina's proportionate interest in it. Molina later paid Largosa $2,000, which was deposited in a bank account under the name of the proposed corporation. Shortly after the corporation was officially organized, it failed. Molina sued Largosa to recover his $2,000, contending that because the subscription form did not set forth the total capital of the proposed corporation and his proportionate interest in it, there was no valid subscription contract. What result would you expect? Explain.

Case Problems

1. D Corporation was organized by S, who transferred property for preferred stock and then caused $1.5 million in par value common stock to be issued. D and S agreed that there would be no consideration paid for the common stock. D subsequently incurred liabilities, became insolvent, and entered receivership. P, a corporation organized to purchase the assets of D and to carry on the business, bought the claims of creditors and sued to collect from S the par value of the common stock. What will be the result? Explain.
2. The Columbia Straw Paper Company purchased thirty-nine paper mills from Emanuel Stein for $5 million, for which it issued to Stein $1 million of the corporation's bonds, $1 million worth of its preferred stock, and $3 million worth of common stock. The value of the mills was arrived at by analyzing the expected profits to be derived from the property. Columbia later became insolvent, and creditors of the company sued Stein, claiming that the mills he sold to the corporation were not worth $5 million; that the directors acted in bad faith by basing the value of the mills on an extravagant estimation of prospective profits rather than on the appraised value of the mills' property. May a corporation make an exchange for its stock on the basis of an estimation of prospective profits to be derived from that property? Explain.
3. Citizens of Schuyler, Nebraska, sought to form a corporation for the processing of chicory. Lednicky signed a subscription agreement to purchase five shares of stock, par value $50, in the proposed company. Articles of incorporation were obtained.

Lednicky agreed to pay for his five shares at the rate of $10 a month. After paying $80 he refused to continue payment, and the corporation sued for the balance. The defense was that the subscription agreement was not an enforceable contract. What will be the result? Explain.

4. The Clifton Coal Co. was organized with 1,200 shares, par value $100, with power to increase the shares to 2,000 by a majority vote of the stockholders. This increase was later voted, but the corporation was unable to sell the additional 800 shares. The corporation then issued $50,000 worth of bonds and was able to dispose of them by offering the buyers $50,000 worth of stock as a bonus; the remaining $30,000 worth of stock was given to the original stockholders of the corporation. The stock certificates bore the statement that the shares were "fully paid and nonassessable." Stutz and other creditors of the corporation brought an action to compel an assessment on the 800 shares. What should the result be? Explain.

5. Sherman, to whom certain creditors of the Oleum Development Co. had assigned their judgments, sued the stockholders of Oleum to recover amounts alleged due on unpaid subscriptions to the capital stock of the corporation. The stock had a par value of $1 a share and was issued as fully paid-up stock, but in no instance was it actually fully paid for, and in some cases the corporation had received no more than 10 cents a share. These facts were fully known to the creditors when they extended credit to the corporation. What will be the result?

44

Managing the Corporation

Corporate Purposes and Powers

Corporate Management

Management's Fiduciary Obligations

Once the corporation has been formed and financed, it is ready to commence the operation of its business. Just what that business may be depends on the purpose of the corporation as reflected by its charter and articles of incorporation. Thus, in discussing corporate operation, this chapter focuses first on the subject of permissible corporate activity as circumscribed by the corporation's purposes and powers. Then the discussion turns to the three groups who participate in operating the corporation: the shareholders, the board of directors, and the corporate officers or executives. These three groups are examined separately, but their roles are closely interrelated. Generally speaking, those who comprise the corporation's management (the board of directors and the corporate executives) are permitted much flexibility in operating the corporation, and are protected from shareholder involvement in management affairs. This protection against shareholder interference is offset by certain fiduciary obligations imposed upon corporate management for the protection of shareholder interests.

Corporate Purposes and Powers

Both business and legal theory hold that a corporation must have a purpose. Business theorists speak of corporate purpose in terms of "strategy," which is defined as the determination of fundamental long-term goals for the company and the adoption of courses of action and the allocation of resources necessary to achieve them. Strategy includes selecting target markets, defining products or services to address these markets, and determining the distribution system in a manner that is within the corporation's resources and capabilities.

Legal theorists view corporate purpose differently. A corporation's purpose is defined in the articles of incorporation and state statutory law under which the corporation is formed.

Closely related to the subject of proper purposes is the subject of proper powers. State law often sets forth the acts that a corporation may legally perform. These acts should be consistent with proper corporate purposes. If the corporation engages in an improper purpose or exercises an improper power, the purpose or act is declared to be "ultra vires" (beyond the corporation's power) and unenforceable. This is known as the **ultra vires** doctrine. Recent legislative developments have attached a declining role to this doctrine.

Corporate Purposes

The corporation's purpose is the reason for which the corporation is organized. This establishes the nature of its business and circumscribes the range of permissible corporate activities. Corporations need not be formed for a single purpose only; they may be organized to undertake as many purposes as the incorporators deem desirable. Section 3.01 of the Revised Model Business Corporation Act (RMBCA) provides that "Every corporation incorporated under this Act has the purpose of engaging in *any* lawful business unless a narrower purpose is set forth in the articles of incorporation." Implicit in this statement also is the requirement that a corporation formed under the general corporate law must have a profit-making purpose, since nonprofit corporations are usually organized under a separate statute.

Earlier in the evolution of corporation law, detailed descriptions of corporate purposes were required to be included in the articles of incorporation. This reflected the general mistrust of unchecked corporate activity.

Today, most states allow a corporation to state its purpose in its articles of incorporation in the broadest possible terms. The typical corporation might state its purpose to be "to engage in any act or activity for which a corporation may be organized" in the state of incorporation. Corporations tend to favor these "full purpose" clauses, even if they intend only to engage in one line of business; such clauses allow the corporation the flexibility to pursue other profitable opportunities that may present themselves in future without having to amend the articles. Because most companies now use "full purpose" clauses in their articles of incorporation, the issue of what is a proper corporate purpose has greatly diminished in importance.

Sometimes, however, incorporators desire to limit the activities of the corporation to the furtherance of a particular purpose. When this is the case, a narrower purpose clause may be inserted in the articles, or specific prohibitions against certain activities may be stated.

Corporate Powers

Closely related to the subject of corporate purposes is that of corporate powers. Corporate powers are those powers granted to the corporation by articles and statute to implement its overall objectives. Because corporate purposes and powers are to be compatible, the corporation's powers must be consistent with the corporation's stated purpose.

A corporation's powers may be express or implied. A corporation has express power to perform those acts authorized by the general corporation law of the state of incorporation and those acts authorized by its articles. Most states have express statutory provisions allowing corporations to sue and be sued, own property, borrow money, etc. Corporations also have implied powers to do whatever is reasonably necessary to promote their express powers, unless such acts are expressly prohibited by law. The trend is to construe broadly what is meant by reasonably necessary.

The RMBCA codifies most of the permissible powers of a corporation. Two additional powers—the ability to indemnify directors, officers, and other employees, and the ability to purchase and dispose of its own shares—are provided. Many of the powers included in these sections were provided to remove doubt that existed with regard to certain activities. For example, Section 3.02(9) empowers the corporation to lend money and invest its funds. By statute the RMBCA also expands the scope of a corporation's implied powers. As mentioned, a corporation's implied powers usually include whatever is reasonably necessary to effectuate the corporation's express powers. Under RMBCA the corporation is allowed "to . . . do any other act not inconsistent with law, that furthers the business and affairs of the corporation."

The *Ultra Vires* Doctrine Corporate transactions outside the corporation's purposes and powers are *ultra vires* (beyond the power). Under the doctrine of *ultra vires* the corporation is not responsible for transactions that were not authorized by its charter, the articles of incorporation, or the law of the state of incorporation.

The older view was that *ultra vires* acts were void for lack of legal capacity because the state had not given the corporation the power to do the particular act. Under this view the shareholders could not subsequently ratify the unauthorized corporate act because the transaction was void. The present view is that *ultra vires* transactions are merely voidable not void. If completely unperformed on both sides, neither party can bring an action on the contract. However, if the *ultra vires* transaction has been fully performed or executed on both sides, either party can bring an action on the contract. The doctrine does not apply to tortious or criminal conduct, because the lack of authorization is not considered an excuse for such conduct.

Two legal consequences attach to an *ultra vires* transaction: (1) the doctrine may serve as a *basis of liability* asserted by the state or shareholders to enjoin or set aside a corporate act and (2) the doctrine may serve as a *defense to liability* by the corporation arising from an unauthorized transaction, much in the same manner as a minor can defend against a contract claim by raising the defense of lack of contractual capacity. This second consequence has been criticized because it permits a corporation to reap the benefits of an *ultra vires* transaction while avoiding any of its burdens.

Because the use of the doctrine as a defense threatens the security of commercial transactions, the doctrine is in decline. Most statutes, including the RMBCA, severely limit the *ultra vires* doctrine by stating that "corporate action may not be challenged on the ground that the corporation lacks power or lacked power to act" (Section 3.04[a]). The RMBCA limits challenges to the corporation's power to act to suits brought by the state attorney general, suits by the corporation against officers or directors for previously authorizing an *ultra vires* act, and shareholder suits to enjoin *ultra vires* acts (Section 3.04[b]).

Additional Areas of *Ultra Vires* Vitality
As seen earlier, two legislative developments have resulted in the decline of the doctrine of *ultra vires:* (1) the elimination of the doctrine as a defense to creditor claims and (2) the expansion of permissible corporate powers. The doctrine retains vitality where the general corporation statute is silent on the subject. For example, the corporation's right to make charitable contributions is still uncertain in some states. According to the older view, corporations existed solely for the economic benefit of the shareholders; thus corporate charitable contributions were considered *ultra vires* unless a benefit to the corporation could be shown. Under this "corporate benefit rule" a corporate contribution to a business college, for example, would have to be supported by showing that the act was intended to create goodwill between the corporation and the college, which might provide the corporation with a pool of potential employees. Some state corporation codes are still silent on the subject of corporate charitable contributions, thus necessitating this type of analysis. However, present provisions in the federal income tax law allowing deductions for charitable contributions, along with the current concern for corporate social responsibility, have resulted in the amendment of the large majority of states' corporation statutes to allow gifts for "the public welfare or for charitable, scientific or educational purposes."

Another area in which the doctrine of *ultra vires* is applicable is that of corporate political activity, illustrated by the following case. The power to make political contributions is not specifically included in the RMBCA or most corporate statutes.

MARSILI V. PACIFIC GAS AND ELECTRIC COMPANY
Court of Appeals of California
124 Cal. Rptr. 313 (1975)

BACKGROUND: Marsili and two other stockholders (plaintiff) initiated a derivative suit challenging the propriety of a $10,000 contribution made by Pacific Gas and Electric Company (PG&E) (defendants) to Citizens for San Francisco, an unincorporated association that advocated the defeat of Proposition T. Proposition T was a proposal that, if adopted by the voters, would have prohibited construction in San Francisco of any building more than 72 feet high without prior voter approval. Plaintiffs argued that the contribution was *ultra vires* because neither PG&E's articles of incorporation nor the law of California permitted PG&E to make political contributions. They argued that the individual members of the board of directors of PG&E should be compelled to restore the $10,000 contribution to the Corporation. The lower court granted a motion for summary judgment made by the defendants and dismissed the complaint.

Kane, Associate Justice

The articles of PG&E . . . authorize all activities and endeavors incidental or useful to the manufacturing, buying, selling, and distributing of gas and electric power, including the construction of buildings and other facilities convenient to the achievement of its corporate purposes, and the performance of "all things whatsoever that shall be necessary or proper for the full and complete execution of the purposes for which. . . [the] corporation is formed, and for the exercise and enjoyment of all its powers and franchises."

In addition to the exercise of such express powers, the generally recognized rule is that the management of a corporation, "in the absence of express restrictions, has discretionary authority to enter into contracts and transactions which may be deemed reasonably incidental to its business purposes."

No restriction appears in the articles of PG&E which would limit the authority of its board of directors to act upon initiative or referendum proposals affecting the affairs of the company or to engage in activities related to any other legislative or political matter in which the corporation has a legitimate concern. Furthermore, there are no statutory prohibitions in California which preclude a corporation from participating in any type of political activity. In these circumstances, the contribution by PG&E to Citizens for San Francisco was proper if it can fairly be said to fall within the express o implied powers of the corporation.

The crux of the controversy at bench, therefore, is whether a contribution toward the defeat of a local ballot proposition can ever be said to be convenient or expedient to the achievement of legitimate corporate purposes. Appellants take the flat position that in the absence of express statutory authority, corporate political contributions are illegal. This contention cannot be sustained. We believe that where, as here, the board of directors reasonably concludes that the adoption of a ballot proposition would have a direct, adverse effect upon the business of the corporation, the board of directors has abundant statutory and charter authority to oppose it.

The law is clear that those to whom the management of the corporation has been entrusted are primarily responsible for judging whether a particular act or transaction is one which is helpful to the conduct of corporate affairs or expedient for the attainment of corporate purposes. . . . Indeed, a court cannot determine that a particular transaction is beyond the powers of a corporation unless it clearly appears to be so as a matter of law. With respect to the means which the corporation may adopt to further its objects and promote its business, its managers are not limited in law to the use of such means as are usual or necessary to the objects contemplated by their organization, but where not restricted by law, may choose such means as are convenient and adapted to the end, though they be neither the usual means, nor absolutely necessary for the purpose intended. . . .

Neither the court nor minority shareholders can substitute their judgment for that of the corporation "where its board has acted in good faith and used its best business judgment in behalf of the corporation."

Plaintiffs, as mentioned earlier, do not contend that the individual defendants acted in bad faith, or that they acted unreasonably or for an improper purpose. Accordingly, the judgment of the board of directors cannot be disturbed by the court unless it is held, as a matter of law, that the contribution could not be construed as incidental or expedient for the attainment of corporate purposes. For several reasons which we shall set forth, such a holding would simply not be reasonable in the light of the uncontradicted record below.

First, the Executive Committee of PG&E based its decision to authorize the contribution upon its judgment that the adoption of Proposition T would have an adverse impact upon the corporation and, in particular, would increase the tax rate applicable to the company's facilities and interfere with present and future building plans of the company. . .

Second, the Executive Committee considered the adoption of Proposition T to be detrimental to the City and County of San Francisco: specifically, by increasing taxes, it would have depressed business growth. . .

Third, by requiring voter approval for the construction of any building more than 72 feet in height, the decision to construct necessary corporate facilities would depend upon the mood of the electorate rather than upon relevant business considerations. The corporation would thereby become embroiled in a contested political campaign every time it determined that it was in the corporation's interest to construct a building more than 72 feet in height.

Not only would the business judgment of the board of directors be subservient to the vagaries of an election campaign, but the cost of submitting such a proposal to the voters would undoubtedly be considerable. This is demonstrated by the very case at bench where in excess of $68,000 was spent by the supporters of Proposition T, and an even greater sum was spent by its opponents. These figures attest to the high cost of submitting a proposal to the voters and demonstrate the severe economic burden that the proposition would have imposed upon those seeking to comply with its terms.

The members of the Executive Committee of PG&E reasonably sought to avoid these consequences. Their judgment was not arbitrary or capricious but was based upon pertinent business considerations that were of direct and immediate concern to the corporation.

DECISION: The California Court of Appeals ruled in favor of Pacific Gas and Electric Co.

Corporate Management

Three groups participate in operating the corporation: the shareholder, the board of directors, and the corporate officers and executives. The following pages examine the management role of each of these groups. The material begins with a discussion of the role of shareholders, whose involvement in corporate management is indirect and therefore minimal. It proceeds to a discussion of the role of the board of directors, which is charged with the responsibility of setting corporation policy, and concludes with a look at the function of corporate officers and executives, to whom the day-to-day management of the corporation is delegated.

The Role of Shareholders

In a large, public-issue corporation, shareholders have no direct control over corporate operations. They cannot command the board of directors or the corporate executives to undertake an activity or decide a matter in a particular way. Although ultimate control resides with the shareholders, they usually do not participate actively in corporate affairs. They can take action only by voting during a shareholders meeting. Shareholder suffrage at these meetings is usually confined to selecting the membership of the board of directors and approving certain extraordinary transactions. Little more than this minimal involvement is permitted of investors. If they are dissatisfied with their investment, they may sell their stock. However, if the corporate management has violated the corporate documents or otherwise incurred a liability toward the investors, the shareholders may bring suit against the responsible parties to recover any loss on behalf of the corporation or to recoup any loss to their investment.

Areas of Shareholder Involvement There are usually two areas of shareholder involvement in corporate affairs: (1) the election of members of the board of directors and (2) the approval of certain extraordinary corporate transactions. Thus under the RMBCA shareholder participation is restricted to the annual election or removal of corporate directors, loans to employees and directors, sale of the corporation's assets outside the usual course of corporate business, any plan of merger or share exchange, and a voluntary dissolution of the corporation. Although some statutes require shareholder approval of bylaw amendments, the RMBCA does not. Of course, it is always permissible to increase the areas of shareholder involvement by the appropriate provisions in the corporate articles and bylaws.

Shareholders' Meetings   Because they are not agents of the corporation, shareholders cannot act individually; they can act only collectively at shareholders' meetings. The RMBCA requires that an annual shareholders' meeting be held at the times specified in the corporate bylaws. Sometimes it is necessary to have a special meeting of the shareholders for a particular purpose. The RMBCA further permits special meetings to be called by the board of directors, by the holders of more than 5 percent of the shares entitled to vote at the meeting, or by any person authorized to do so in the articles or bylaws.

Most statutes, including the RMBCA, require that notice of any shareholders' meeting be provided to each shareholder of record entitled to vote at such a meeting. The RMBCA stipulates that the notice be in writing, stating the place, day, and hour of the meeting. In the case of a special meeting the notice must also include the purpose or purposes for which the meeting is called (see Figure 44-1). The notice must be delivered not less than 10 days or more than 50 days before the date of the meeting.

Unless the required notice is waived, failure to provide it voids any action taken at the meeting. A waiver may be made by a signed writing or evidenced by conduct, such as attending the meeting without objecting to the lack of notice. The RMBCA permits an action to be taken without a shareholders' meeting if written consent specifying the action to be taken is signed by all of the shareholders who are entitled to vote on the matter.

A quorum of the shares entitled to vote, represented in person or by proxy, must be present before any action can take place at the shareholders' meeting. The RMBCA provides that a majority of the voting shares shall constitute a quorum, unless

---

October 4, 1995

To the Common Stock Shareowners of
The Toledo Edison Company

A special meeting of the Shareowners of The Toledo Edison Company ("Toledo Edison") will be held at the principal office of Toledo Edison, Edison Plaza, 300 Madison Avenue, Toledo, Ohio, on November 26, 1995 at 10:00 a.m., Toledo time, for the purpose of acting on the following matters:

1. To consider and vote upon a proposal to approve and adopt an Agreement and Plan of Reorganization between Toledo Edison and the Cleveland Electric Illuminating Company ("CEI") dated June 25, 1995, as amended, which agreement provides for simultaneous mergers of two subsidiaries of Centerior Energy Corporation (the "Holding Company") into Toledo Edison and CEI, respectively, with the result that Toledo Edison and CEI each will become subsidiaries of the Holding Company as described in the accompanying Joint Proxy Statement/Prospectus and the common stock shareowners of Toledo Edison and CEI will become common stock shareowners of Toledo Edison and CEI will become common stock shareowners of the Holding Company; and to approve and adopt an Agreement of Merger among the Holding Company, Toledo Edison and the West Merger Company, a wholly-owned subsidiary of the Holding Company.

2. Any other matters which may properly come before the meeting. Holders of record of Common Stock at the close of business on September 30, 1995 will be entitled to vote at the meeting.

By order of the Board of Directors,

Stratman Cooke

Stratman Cooke, Secretary

FIGURE 44-1

Notice of Special Meeting of Shareholders

the articles provide otherwise. However, the articles cannot provide for a quorum consisting of less than one-third of the voting shares.

The shareholders' meeting is usually conducted according to the provisions of the corporate articles or bylaws, which generally provide that the board chair or corporate president preside. Minutes of the meeting are customarily recorded by the corporate secretary. Shareholders are entitled to submit and speak upon proposals and resolutions during the meeting. Recently shareholders who are concerned about social issues and politically active have used the shareholders' meeting to submit proposals to limit the involvement of their corporations in certain activities, such as investing in countries that violate human rights.

In the case of large public-issue corporations, most voting is generally done by proxy (one party voting on behalf of many shareholders who have agreed to assign their vote for this purpose). The result of a shareholder vote is thus often a foregone conclusion, and the shareholders' meeting itself is often a well-orchestrated occasion designed to comply with the formalities of corporate law. For this reason some scholars seriously question the continued practice of requiring an annual shareholders' meeting. In what may very well be a harbinger of future development, Delaware no longer requires an annual meeting.

Voting   Shareholders function by voting on matters at the shareholders' meeting. Each share of stock entitles its holder to one vote on each matter submitted to a vote, unless the corporate articles provide for more or less than one vote per share. Thus the holder of fifty shares is generally entitled to cast fifty votes. The RMBCA also authorizes the issuance of nonvoting shares. For example, preferred stock generally has no voting rights. However, even nonvoting stock is entitled to vote on certain extraordinary transactions, such as amendments to the corporate articles, mergers and consolidations, and dissolution of the corporation. To determine who is entitled to vote, the directors may set a date of record, and the person having legal title to the stock on the record date is entitled to vote the shares. A person acquiring legal title to the shares after the record date must obtain the proxy of the record title holder in order to vote them at the shareholders' meeting.

Because a shareholder is entitled to one vote for each share held, the holder of 51 percent of the voting shares will have complete control. To give minority shareholders more power, most states either require or allow corporations to adopt cumulative voting for directors. **Cumulative voting** is a system that gives each share a number of votes equal to the number of directors to be elected, and allows each shareholder to concentrate all of his or her votes to support one director.

Cumulative voting is best explained through an example. Assume that XYZ Corp. will elect all three of its directors at its next annual meeting. Of the 100,000 majority shares of XYZ Corp. outstanding, 60,000 are held by the majority shareholders and 40,000 are held by the minority shareholders. The minority shareholders wish to elect at least one candidate to the board, but the majority wants to fill all three slots with its own people. If each position is voted on separately—that is, if cumulative voting is *not* used—then the majority will be able to vote in all three of its candidates by a margin of 60,000 votes to 40,000 votes.

Now let's see what happens when a cumulative voting system is employed. Each share of stock is given three votes—one for each director to be elected. If a shareholder owns only one share of stock, the shareholder may cast one vote for each of three candidates, or may instead *cumulate* his or her votes by casting all three votes for one candidate and no votes for anyone else. (The shareholder could also, of course, cast two votes for one candidate and one vote for another candidate.) In our example, the minority shareholders would have 120,000 votes (the 40,000 shares they own times the three spots to be filled), which they can allocate however they choose. The majority has 180,000 votes, meaning that 300,000 votes will be cast to elect three directors. Although it may not be obvious to you, this arrangement allows the minority to elect one director by cumulating all its votes for one candidate.

Assume that the majority slate is Anderson, Brennan, and Cohen, and that the minority shareholders wish to elect Dunfee. The candidates with the three highest vote totals will be elected. If the minority casts all 120,000 of its votes for Dunfee, there is no way for the majority to keep Dunfee off the board. The majority could cast almost all 180,000 of its votes for Anderson, but then it would hardly have any votes left to elect Brennan and Cohen. As the second highest vote-getter, Dunfee would be elected. Alternatively, the majority could cast 120,001 votes for Anderson. This would give Anderson one more vote than Dunfee. But then the majority would have only 59,999 votes to allocate between Brennan and Cohen. Again, Dunfee's 120,000 would ensure him a spot on the board. This example is summarized in Table 44-1.

Cumulative voting does not guarantee minority representation if the minority does not own enough shares. The minority shareholders in the above illustration would not have been able to elect Dunfee if, for example, they owned only 20,000 shares and the majority owned 80,000. (Try the calculations yourself.)

Cumulative voting usually applies only to the election of directors. In some states cumulative voting is required by statute and cannot be refused in any election or eliminated in the corporate articles or bylaws. In other states it is permissive, meaning that cumulative voting can be eliminated in the corporate documents. Under the RMBCA cumulative voting is permissive.

Cumulative voting for directors is controversial. Proponents claim that it is necessary to assure a minority voice in corporate affairs. Opponents claim that minority representation means dissent in the boardroom.

A device for diluting the effect of cumulative voting is the staggered election of directors, because the fewer directors there are to be elected, the greater the number of shares that will be necessary to assure representation. As an illustration, consider what would happen in our earlier example if XYZ Corp.'s directors were elected for staggered 3-year terms and only one director came up for election each year. That would neutralize the effect of cumulative voting: In any given year, the majority would have 60,000 votes (60,000 shares times one director to be elected) and the minority would have 40,000 votes. With only one slot to be filled each year, the majority candidate would win each year by a 60,000 to 40,000 margin.

Staggered elections are allowed to a limited extent by the RMBCA, which permits boards consisting of nine or more directors to be divided into two or three classes, with each class being elected

TABLE 44-1

Cumulative Voting

Situation

Number of directors to be elected: 3

Shares owned by majority: 60,000
   Votes that majority may cast: 180,000 (60,000 × 3)

Shares owned by minority: 40,000
   Votes that minority may cast: 120,000 (40,000 × 3)

	Scenario 1	Scenario 2	Scenario 3
	Votes		
Majority Candidates			
Anderson	179,997	120,001	60,001
Brennan	2	50,000	60,000
Cohen	1	9,999	59,999
Minority Candidate			
Dunfee	120,000	120,000	120,000
	Winners		
	Anderson	Anderson	Dunfee
	Dunfee	Dunfee	Anderson
	Brennan	Brennan	Brennan

to a staggered 3-year term. Since the RMBCA is permissive on the subject of cumulative voting, requiring the staggered election of directors in classes poses no problems. However, in states where cumulative voting is mandatory, the staggered election of directors is often prohibited.

A shareholder may vote either in person or by proxy. A **proxy** is a delegation of authority given by a shareholder to another person to vote his or her stock. A proxy is basically a special type of principal-agent relationship and therefore is subject to the rules of agency law as modified by special state statutes or by federal regulations under Section 14 of the Securities Exchange Act of 1934.

The RMBCA requires that a proxy be in writing. A telegram or cablegram should be sufficient. Some states, like California, require that the proxy be filed with the corporation before or at the shareholders' meeting. A few states allow oral proxies.

Because the proxy is an agency, every appointment of a proxy is revocable. One way a shareholder may revoke a proxy is to attend and vote at the shareholders' meeting. A proxy is not revocable if it is coupled with an interest, meaning that some consideration has been received by the shareholder for his or her delegation of voting rights—for example, an option to purchase the stock.

Even when proxies are irrevocable, statutes generally limit their duration. The RMBCA provides that the appointment of a proxy is valid for only 11 months after it is made unless otherwise provided in the proxy. Thus a proxy can extend beyond 11 months only if the writing specifies the date on which it is to expire or the length of time it is to continue in force.

Proxy solicitation by corporate management, insurgent shareholder groups, competing shareholder factions, or even outsiders has become a common and effective method of establishing or maintaining control over a corporation without actually purchasing enough stock to exert control. Section 14 of the Securities Exchange Act of 1934 and Rule 14a of the Securities and Exchange Commission (SEC) regulate proxy solicitation. Their purpose is to protect shareholders from misleading or concealed information in the solicitation of proxies. These proxy rules apply to corporations having more that 500 shareholders and assets of more that $1 million. They are discussed in detail in Chapter 46.

Because proxies are revocable, other devices for combining votes for control of the corporation are frequently used. Two such devices are the pooling agreement and the voting trust. A pooling agreement, sometimes called a voting agreement, is a contract entered into by several shareholders who mutually promise to vote their shares in a certain manner. In most states, and under the RMBCA, such agreements are enforceable.

A voting trust is an agreement among shareholders to transfer their voting rights to a trustee, who is permitted to vote the shares in a block at the shareholders' meeting according to the terms of the trust instrument. Courts are divided as to the legality of voting trusts at common law, but most statutes, including the RMBCA allow them (trusts) if certain requirements are met. Under the RMBCA a voting trust must be in writing. This writing, termed the "voting trust agreement," must specify the terms and conditions of the voting trust, and a copy of it must be deposited with the corporation. The shareholders must transfer their shares to the trustee and receive in return trust certificates, sometimes called certificates of beneficial ownership. The RMBCA also limits the life of a voting trust to 10 years.

Inspection Rights   For a shareholder to exercise his or her voting rights intelligently, it may be necessary to have access to certain corporate information. Most statutes, including the RMBCA, recognize that those opposing corporate management must be able to obtain a list of existing shareholders if they are ever to be successful in ousting management; therefore they grant shareholders an absolute right to examine and copy shareholder lists. Under the RMBCA the shareholder list must be available at the shareholders' meeting.

The shareholder may also be able to obtain information contained in the corporate records. The RMBCA provides that a shareholder has a qualified right to certain corporate information. Section 16.01 requires that the corporation keep records of account, the minutes of shareholders and directors meetings, and a shareholders list, usually at the corporation's principal place of business. Upon written demand 5 business days before the date on which a shareholder wishes to inspect, he or she may examine any of the relevant corporate records during reasonable working hours. The RMBCA permits an attorney or an agent, who could be an accountant, to accompany the shareholder or to make the inspection for the shareholder if the shareholder so wishes. The written demand must be in good faith and for a proper purpose. The right of inspection is limited to three classes of corporate records: minutes of meetings of the board and committees of the board, accounting records, and a record of shareholders.

What is a "proper purpose" or a request made in good faith is an issue to be decided by the courts in cases like the one that follows.

ADVANCE CONCRETE FORM, INC. v. ACCUFORM, INC.

Court of Appeals of Wisconsin
462 N.W.2d 271 (1990)

BACKGROUND: Advance and Accuform were competitors in the manufacture and sale of concrete forms used in construction. Advance convinced Accuform's only full-time salesman to come to work for Advance. That salesman owned 10 percent of the shares of Accuform and sold his shares to Advance when he switched jobs. As a shareholder of Accuform, Advance demanded to inspect Accuform's books and records. Advance contended that it had a valid purpose to make the inspection—namely, to determine the value of its investment in Accuform. Accuform refused to allow the inspection, claiming that Advance was really trying to obtain information that would give it a competitive advantage against Accuform. Advance sued to compel the inspection. The trial court ruled for Accuform, and Advance appealed.

Sundby, Judge

State ex rel. Boldt v. St. Cloud Milk Producers' Ass'n is closely analogous to this case. Petitioner was a member of the respondent dairy cooperative. The cooperative refused petitioner's demand to examine its books and records. The court found that the inference was inescapable that the lawsuit was brought for the benefit of rival dairy companies. In reversing the grant of mandamus, the court said:

> The writ will not be denied merely because the petitioner is hostile to the respondent or because he is a member of a competing corporation. The writ is issued only to protect some right of the petitioner, either as a stockholder or member of the corporation as such, or some right of the corporation in which he is interested as such stockholder or member. The relief sought must be germane to his rights as a stockholder or member. If it is foreign thereto, the writ will be denied even though he otherwise might be entitled to it. Accordingly, it has been held that the writ will not be granted where it appears that the examination is desired for the purpose of obtaining information to be used in crippling the business of the corporation for the benefit of a business rival.

If the circuit court's finding, that Advance's true purpose for its inspection demand was to gain a competitive advantage over Accuform, was an inference it could reasonably draw from the evidence, the court correctly dismissed Advance's complaint. We therefore examine the facts and circumstances of this case.

The circuit court found: (1) Advance and Accuform are direct and fierce competitors. (2) The principals of each corporation have exhibited an intense competitiveness and personal animosity going back many years. (3) Advance's principal stated several times that he wanted to put Accuform's principal out of business. (4) Advance is a much larger corporation than Accuform and was able to woo away Accuform's only full-time sales person and thus acquired its stock in Accuform. (5) Advance's principal investigated whether he could object to the small business loan which helped finance Accuform's start-up and whether the financial disclosures made by Accuform's principal were public records which could be inspected. (6) The information Advance seeks from inspection of Accuform's books and records is highly proprietary and, in the hands of a determined competitor such as Advance, would permit it to underbid Accuform. Continued underbidding could drive Accuform out of business. (7) Nothing in the record suggests that there is any present market for Accuform's stock. Valuing a stock does not create a market for a minority interest with no control. Finding a market for such an interest is very difficult. (8) Advance has a minimal investment in Accuform.

With one exception, Advance does not challenge these findings but instead argues that the facts do not support the inference drawn by the circuit court. The exception is the court's finding that the information which Advance sought would permit Advance to drive Accuform out of business through an extended pattern of underbidding on Accuform's main product lines. Advance argues that the circuit court's finding in this respect is "totally a matter of speculation." We disagree. Had Advance been allowed to examine and extract information from Accuform's books and records, it would have had access to Accuform's general ledgers, payroll ledgers, purchase journals, a description of all assets of the corporation with depreciation schedules, and accounts receivable and accounts payable with aging documentation. In short, Advance would have been able to assess Accuform's ability to withstand repeated underbidding by Advance on jobs in which they were competitors.

DECISION: The Court of Appeals affirmed the decision in Accuform's favor.

Dividends   A dividend, as noted in the last chapter, is a distribution paid to shareholders because of their stock ownership. It may be in cash, property (including the stock of other corporations), or the stock of the corporation itself. This latter type of dividend is referred to as a **stock dividend**.

The RMBCA prohibits the declaration or payment of a dividend when the corporation is insolvent or when such a payment would render the corporation insolvent, meaning that the corporation is unable to pay its debts. Under the traditional rule adopted in most states, dividends can be lawfully declared and paid only out of the corporation's earned surplus. Earned surplus represents the profits realized on operations and investments.

The directors have wide discretion concerning whether or not to declare a dividend. The shareholders ordinarily have no right to a dividend. The directors alone determine the amount of dividends and when they are to be distributed. A shareholder's "right" to a dividend normally materializes only after a dividend has been declared by the board.

Although courts usually do not disturb the discretion of directors with regard to a dividend declaration, there is an exception to this general rule. When there is a bad faith refusal by the board of directors to declare a dividend, a court may use its equitable powers to compel a distribution. However, courts do not possess any equitable power to require a board of directors to declare dividends out of abundant earnings in the absence of fraud or abuse or discretion.

Preemptive Rights   If the articles of incorporation so provide, a shareholder has an option called a **preemptive right** that entitles the shareholder to subscribe to a newly authorized issue of shares in the same proportion that his or her present shares bear to all outstanding shares before new shares are offered to the public. Preemptive rights are aimed at preventing the dilution of the shareholder's equity in the corporation against his or her wishes. Under most state statutes preemptive rights usually do not apply to **treasury shares** (meaning shares previously issued and reacquired by the corporation), previously authorized but unsold and unissued shares, or shares that are issued or agreed to be issued upon the conversion of convertible shares. Preemptive rights to not apply to these shares because such shares are not new issues but are part of previous offerings.

Since preemptive rights often interfere with the disposition of large issues of shares, many corporations restrict or eliminate this right. How preemptive rights may be restricted or eliminated depends on the particular statutory provision governing their application. Some statutes provide that preemptive rights exist unless otherwise provided in the articles. Under these statutes preemptive rights can be eliminated or limited only by an appropriate provision in the corporate articles. Other statutes provide that preemptive rights do not exist unless otherwise provided in the corporate articles. Under this approach for shareholders to have preemptive rights such rights must be expressly included in the articles of incorporation. The RMBCA adopts this latter approach.

Transfer of Shares Generally a shareholder who is dissatisfied with corporate operations may freely transfer his or her shares to someone else. Such transfers traditionally have been governed by Article 8 of the Uniform Commercial Code (UCC) as adopted by most states today.

Appraisal and Buyout Rights of Dissenting Shareholders Certain kinds of extraordinary transactions, even though lawfully authorized and validly effected, entitle dissenting shareholders to have their shares purchased by the corporation at a fair cash value. This is referred to as the shareholder's **appraisal and buyout right**. Its purpose is to effect a compromise between the overwhelming majority who desire a fundamental change in the corporate venture and the insistence of a dissenter not to be forced into a position different from that bargained for when he or she bought the stock.

The RMBCA recognizes five extraordinary transactions that give rise to an appraisal and buyout right:

1. A merger or consolidation
2. A sale or exchange of all or substantially all of the corporate property and assets not in the regular course of business.
3. The acquisition of the corporation by another through the exchange of the corporate stock
4. An amendment to the articles of incorporation that materially and adversely affects rights of a dissenter's shares
5. Any other corporate action that by virtue of the articles of incorporation, bylaws, or board resolution entitles shareholders to dissent, and be paid for their shares.

However, the right does not apply to the shareholders of a surviving corporation in a merger if a vote of that corporation's shareholders is not necessary to authorize the merger. The right also does not apply when the corporation's shares are registered on a national securities exchange. Some states, such as Ohio, additionally grant appraisal rights when certain amendments to the corporate articles change the purpose of the corporation or adversely affect the class of shares owned by the dissenter.

Under the RMBCA the shareholder must take certain procedural steps to effectuate an appraisal and buyout remedy. If one of the transactions noted above is to be voted on, and dissenter rights are created, the dissenting shareholder must notify the corporation prior to the shareholders' meeting that he or she intends to demand payment if the proposed action of management is approved. Then the shareholder must vote against the proposed action at the meeting. After majority approval has been obtained the dissenting shareholder must be notified how to demand payment and then make a written demand on the corporation for payment of the fair value of the shares.

The corporation must respond with an offer to the shareholder of what it considers to be the fair value of the shares plus interest. If no agreement is reached, either party may petition the court in the county where the registered office of the corporation is located for an appraisal of the fair value of the shares. All dissenting shareholders will be made parties to the proceeding and will be bound by any judgment. In such a case the court may appoint one or more appraisers to recommend a fair value of the shares. The costs of the proceeding, including the expenses of the appraisers, will be assessed against the corporation unless the court determines that the shareholders' failure to accept the corporation's offer was arbitrary, vexatious, or not in good faith, in which case the cost and expenses will be apportioned among the dissenting shareholders.

When mergers or consolidations involve proxy offers or tender offers, they are subject to federal and state securities regulations discussed in Chapter 46. When merger combinations of sales or acquisitions of a corporation are contemplated, state and federal antitrust laws discussed in Chapter 54 may become important.

Shareholder Suits   Sometimes in order to enforce a right or to protect his or her investment, a shareholder must resort to legal action in the form of a lawsuit.

Shareholder litigation falls into two broad categories: (1) direct suits by shareholders on their own behalf and (2) derivative suits on behalf of the corporation. Direct actions by shareholders on their own behalf may be further subdivided into two additional categories: (a) individual actions and (b) class actions.

Direct suits by shareholders on their own behalf are limited to the enforcement of claims belonging to the shareholder on the basis of his or her share ownership. When the injury is primarily to the shareholder, the shareholder may bring an action on his or her own behalf. If the injury is peculiar to the shareholder, the action will be an individual one. If the injury affects several shareholders or a class of shares, a class action may be pursued, with the shareholder initiating the action representing the entire class. In a shareholder class action the representative of the class brings suit on behalf of himself or herself individually and on behalf of all other shareholders who are similarly situated. Some examples of shareholder suits that may be brought individually or by way of class action are suits:

1. To enforce the right to vote
2. To sue for breach of a shareholder agreement
3. To enforce the right to inspect corporate books and records
4. To compel the payment of lawfully declared dividends
5. To protect preemptive rights
6. To compel corporate dissolution

When the injury to the shareholder's investment results from a wrong to the *corporation* rather than a wrong directed against the shareholder, a shareholder cannot bring a direct suit on his or her own behalf but must bring a **derivative action** on behalf of the corporation to enforce a right belonging to the corporation. Any judgment will go directly to the corporation, not to the shareholder who brings the action. The reason for this restriction is to avoid a multiplicity of litigation that might otherwise occur if all shareholders were permitted to bring direct actions on their own behalf for wrongs committed against the cor-

porate entity. The restriction also is consistent with the separateness of corporate and shareholder interests recognized by the courts when the corporation is sued as a defendant. Although any remedy belongs to the corporation, theoretically the shareholder will also benefit from the judgment because any corporate remedy should also enhance the shareholder's investment.

The shareholder's derivative suit involves the assertion by a shareholder of a corporate cause of action against persons either in or out of the corporation who have allegedly wronged it. Such suits are brought where the corporation has failed to enforce such claims itself. Some examples of derivative suits would be actions:

1. To recover damages resulting from a consummated *ultra vires* act
2. To enjoin corporate officials from breaching their fiduciary duty to the corporation
3. To recover improperly paid dividends
4. To enjoin outsiders from wronging the corporation or to recover from such a wrong

Certain procedural requirements must be met in a shareholder's derivative suit. The plaintiff must have been a shareholder at the time the wrong was committed against the corporation or have acquired the shares by operation of law (such as through the distribution of a decedent's estate) from someone who was a holder of record at that time. The shareholder must also show that he or she has exhausted internal corporate remedies. He or she must describe with particularity the efforts, if any, made to obtain the desired action from the directors and, if necessary, from the shareholders, and provide the reasons for any failure to obtain the action or for not making the effort. A derivative proceeding, once begun, cannot be discontinued or settled without court approval.

The Role of the Board of Directors

Although the shareholders are the owners of the corporation, the board of directors is the supreme power in the management of the corporation. The following pages examine the nature of the board's authority, the appointment of directors to the board, and the formalities of board functions.

Nature of Board Authority Although the board of directors is charged by statute with the duty of managing the corporation, it is generally recognized that the purpose of the board is only to establish policy and to provide direction to the corporation. Recent legislative developments reflect a trend toward recognizing this reality.

Most state statutes say that the business affairs of the corporation "shall be managed by a board of directors." Recently many commentators have voiced concern that such language may be interpreted to mean that the directors must become involved in the detailed administration of the corporation's affairs. Although requiring such involvement is reasonable in closely held corporations, recent developments make such an expectation unreasonable in today's complex corporations. Noteworthy among these developments is the advent of outside directors, who are individuals from outside the corporate management and not otherwise involved with the corporation. The RMBCA seeks to clarify board responsibility and bring it into accord with the realities of today's corporations, particularly the large diversified enterprise. Section 8.01 now provides that the business and affairs of the corporation shall be managed *"under the direction"* of a board of directors. The RMBCA eliminates any ambiguity regarding the role of the board of directors in formulating major management policy as opposed to direct day-to-day management. Only a few state statutes, such as Delaware's and California's, have similar provisions, although a trend exists toward adopting such language.

Generally the board's responsibility may be broadly described as establishing basic corporate objectives, selecting competent senior executives, monitoring personnel policies and procedures with a view to assuring that the corporation is provided with other competent managers in the future, reviewing the performance of senior executives, and monitoring the corporation's performance. Typical matters over which the board has control include dividends, financing, and corporate policy as to the prices of its products, expansion, and labor relations. More specifically, the board of directors is also required or authorized to: call special shareholders' meetings, elect corporate officers, declare dividends, recommend dissolution, approve any merger or consolidation, change the registered office or registered agent, allocate to capital surplus consideration received for shares having no par value, cancel reacquired shares, and approve amendments to the corporate bylaws.

ETHICS
Ethics and Board of Directors

In recent years Delaware and New York courts, two trend-setting states in the area of corporate law, have ruled that they will accept the findings of litigation committees of boards of directors when a company is sued by shareholders. Usually, but not always, these committees are made up of outside directors. Those in favor of litigation committees argue that they represent the most efficient way for both the company and the shareholders to handle a suit; otherwise both may be faced with several years of discovery proceedings before getting to trial. Those who oppose such committees raise ethical questions posed here:

1. If the members of a litigation committee are picked by the board of directors of the corporation that is being sued, will they be able to make an objective decision?

2. If "outside directors" are picked for a committee, will they be truly independent in light of the fact that they tend to belong to the same clubs, travel in the same professional circles, have similar attitudes, and are chosen by inside management to sit on boards initially?

3. Do members of the litigation committees of a board of directors have conflicting ethical and legal obligations? Is there fiduciary obligation to the majority shareholders of the corporation, or is there a higher obligation to render an independent judgment on a suit brought by shareholders while a member of a litigation committee?

Appointment of Directors Under the RMBCA the initial directors may be named in the articles of incorporation. These directors may be "dummy directors" who serve only until the first shareholders' meeting and then resign. The RMBCA does not require that the number and names of the directors constituting the initial board be stated in the articles. Except for the first board, the number of directors may be established by either the corporate articles or the bylaws. The effect of putting this provision in the bylaws rather than the articles is to permit the directors to retain for themselves the power to change the number of directors without seeking shareholder approval. This is because under Section 2.06 of the RMBCA, the power to amend the bylaws is vested solely in the board unless reserved to the shareholders by the articles, whereas amendments to the articles require shareholder approval.

Until recently most state statutes required a minimum of three directors. However, the trend, as illustrated by Section 8.03 of the RMBCA, is to allow for only one director. This eliminates the need for single-shareholder corporations to enlist superfluous directors.

Although traditionally shareholders elect the directors from among their ranks, most statutes specifically provide that directors need not be shareholders of the corporation. Furthermore, few statutes impose age and residency requirements upon directors. For example, the RMBCA specifically states that "directors need not be residents of this State . . ." (Section 8.02). However, these and other requirements may be prescribed in the corporate articles. Thus, if it is felt that a real financial stake in the success of the enterprise will likely increase both vigilance and diligence, the articles may provide a requirement of substantial stock ownership by directors. Such stock is generally called a **director's qualifying stock**.

Federal legislation affecting board composition may disqualify some individuals from becoming directors. Interlocking directorates of competing corporations are restricted by Section 8 of the Clayton Act. This statute forbids someone from serving as a director of two or more competing corporations if one corporation has capital, surplus, and undivided profits aggregating more than $1 million and if the elimination of competition between them would constitute a violation of federal antitrust laws.

Aside from the members of the initial board, directors are elected at the annual shareholders' meeting and usually hold office until the next annual meeting. However, the RMBCA allows corporations with nine or more members to set staggered 2- or 3-year terms for directors.

Vacancies may occur on the board as the result of the resignation, death, or removal of an incumbent director or as the result of an increase in the number of directors. Many statutes provide that any vacancy on the board must be filled by a vote of the shareholders. The RMBCA allows the shareholders or the remaining directors to fill the vacancy.

Although directors may be removed from the board by failure to obtain reelection at the annual shareholders' meeting, a stickier question is presented when the removal is to occur during the director's term of office. In the absence of a statute or a provision in the articles the courts do not permit shareholders to remove a director without cause. Thus, at common law, directors can be removed during their terms only for cause. Exactly what constitutes cause is often unclear. Today most statutes permit a majority of the voting shareholders to remove a director or the entire board "with or without cause" before the end of his or her term at a special shareholders' meeting called expressly for that purpose.

Formalities of Board Functions The general common law rule is that a director can act as a part of the board of directors only at a proper meeting of the board. Under this approach the board cannot act unless it is formally convened. Informal action is insufficient; the directors have to be physically present at the meeting and cannot vote by proxy. The reason for this is to encourage consultation among board members as a body. Today most statutes establish a contrary rule and allow board members to act informally without a meeting upon the written consent of all board members. The RMBCA also allows board members to participate in board meetings via a telephone conference call.

Board meetings may be held either in or outside the state of incorporation. The time for board meetings is included in the corporate bylaws; therefore, a director is considered to have constructive notice of all regular board meetings. Many statutes provide that if there is no provision to the contrary in the bylaws, the directors must be given notice of the time and topic of all specially called meetings. The RMBCA provides only that such notice as required by the bylaws must be given, and it also states that neither the business to be transacted nor the purpose of any special meeting must be specified in the notice unless required by the bylaws. When notice is required by the bylaws the RMBCA states that a director's attendance at the meeting constitutes a waiver of the required notice, unless the director attends to object to the meeting.

Under the RMBCA, unless the articles or bylaws provide a greater number, a majority of the board members constitutes a quorum for a meeting of the directors. A majority vote of the quorum constitutes a binding act of the board.

The RMBCA permits the articles or bylaws to authorize the board to designate an executive committee or other committees composed of board members to exercise all the authority of the board except in extraordinary matters, such as article amendments, mergers, and so on. Executive committees function between board meetings and are especially useful when the board of directors is large and when consideration of specific matters by the smaller group will facilitate decision making. Finance and audit committees, with duties relating to corporate finance and the selection of auditors, are less common.

The Role of Officers and Executives

It is generally recognized that the board of directors is not expected to operate the corporate business. The board delegates the day-to-day management to the corporate officers and executives, who are elected by the board and serve at the board's discretion. The RMBCA provides that "A corporation has the officers described in its bylaws or appointed by the board of directors . . ." (Section 8.40). Unlike most state statutes today, the RMBCA does not require that there be a president, vice president, and treasurer, but leaves the number and titles of officers to the bylaws of the board. This is especially important for small corporations. The officers are regarded as agents of the corporation, having such authority as is conferred by the bylaws or by a board resolution.

Management's Fiduciary Obligations

As already observed, those who control and manage modern corporations are protected against interference from shareholders in the handling of corporate affairs. Thus individual shareholders are generally powerless to affect corporate affairs in the case of large-scale organizations. However, this virtual disenfranchisement of the shareholder is not so oppressive as it appears. In partial recognition of these realities, corporate and securities law in recent times have substantially strengthened the fiduciary obligations of management and of other controlling persons to both the corporation and to the shareholder.

Fiduciary Duty to the Corporation

Directors and officers owe fiduciary duties to the corporation similar to the fiduciary duties that agents owe their principals. These fiduciary duties fall broadly into two categories: (1) the duty of loyalty and (2) the duty of care.

Duty of Loyalty Corporate directors and officers occupy a fiduciary relationship with the corporation, which requires the exercise of good faith and loyalty in any dealings with and for the corporation. The basic principle is that corporate directors and officers should not use their positions to make personal profits or to gain other personal advantages. In principle, this duty of loyalty is similar to the duty of loyalty exercise by agents and partners; however, this duty is owed to the corporate entity, not to the shareholders. The duty arises most frequently in transactions

---

CONCEPT SUMMARY
Role of Shareholders, Directors, and Officers

Shareholders	Own corporation
	Elect directors
	Approve major transactions, such as mergers
Directors	Manage corporation (or direct management of corporation)
	Appoint officers
Officers	Manage day-to-day affairs of corporation

between the corporation and the corporate official involving possible conflict of interest or when a corporate opportunity comes to the attention of the corporate official.

Conflicts of interest between officers and directors and their corporations can occur whenever a transaction takes place between the corporation and them. The RMBCA does not prohibit a transaction between a director and the corporation in which the director has a financial interest as long as the transaction was fair when authorized, or was ratified by the board of directors. When a transaction is contested the burden of proof to establish fairness falls on the person charged with having a conflict. The person charged has the burden to show there was full disclosure of the conflict and approval by disinterested directors or shareholders.

The general rule is that a corporation has a prior claim to opportunities for business and profits that may be regarded as incidental to its business. Such an opportunity is called a **corporate opportunity**, and directors and officers cannot acquire this business opportunity to the detriment of the corporation. Usurpation of a corporate opportunity is normally dealt with by imposing a **constructive trust** on the wrongful director or officer, meaning that he or she is deemed to hold the benefits of the bargain on behalf of the corporation. When an opportunity that is relevant to the corporation's present or prospective business activities comes to the attention of a corporate director or officer, he or she must first offer it to the corporation. Only after disinterested members of the board determine that the corporation should not pursue the opportunity may the corporate officer or director pursue the matter for his or her own account. However, if the corporation is financially unable to take advantage of the opportunity, the officer or director need not present it to the corporation. The following case illustrates the corporate opportunity doctrine.

GUTH V. LOFT, INC.

Supreme Court of Delaware

5 A.2d 503 (1939)

BACKGROUND: Loft (plaintiff) filed a complaint in the Court of Chancery against Charles Guth, Grace Company, and Pepsi-Cola Company (defendants) seeking to impress a trust in favor of Loft upon all shares of capital stock of Pepsi-Cola registered in the name of Guth and Grace (approximately 91 percent of Pepsi's capital stock).

Guth became the president and general manager of Loft in 1931. Loft manufactured and sold candies, syrups, and beverages. When Pepsi-Cola was adjudicated bankrupt in 1931, one Megargel, an officer and major stockholder of that company, and Guth entered into an agreement whereby 50 percent of the stock of Pepsi-Cola went to Grace, a corporation owned by Guth's family that made syrups for soft drinks and that sold some syrup to Loft. Through several other transactions with Megargel, Guth came to own another 41 percent of Pepsi-Cola stock. During this period, 1931–1935, Guth borrowed heavily from Loft, and Grace became insolvent. Additionally, without the knowledge of the board of directors, Guth used Loft's facilities, materials, credit, executives, and employees at will. Some reimbursement was made for wages to workers. Loft suffered a loss of profits in its retail stores estimated at $300,000. Guth had discarded Coca-Cola and spent $20,000 advertising Pepsi-Cola.

Layton, Chief Justice

Corporate officers and directors are not permitted to use their position of trust and confidence to further their private interests. While technically not trustees, they stand in a fiduciary relation to the corporation and its stockholders. A public policy, existing through the years, and derived from a profound knowledge of human characteristics and motives, has established a rule that demands of a corporate officer or director, peremptorily and inexorably, the most scrupulous observance of his duty, not only affirmatively to protect the interests of the corporation committed to his charge, but also to refrain from doing anything that would work injury to the corporation, or to deprive it of profit or advantage which his skill and ability might properly bring to it, or to enable it to make in the reasonable and lawful exercise of its powers. The rule that requires an undivided and unselfish loyalty to the corporation demands that there shall be no conflict between duty and self-interest. The occasions for the determination of honesty, good faith and loyal conduct are many and varied, and no hard and fast rule can be formulated. The standard of loyalty is measured by no fixed scale.

If an officer or director of a corporation, in violation of his duty as such, acquires gain or advantage for himself, the law charges the interest so acquired with a trust for the benefit of the corporation, at its election, while it denies to the betrayer all benefit and profit. The rule, inveterate and uncompromising in its rigidity, does not rest upon the narrow ground of injury or damage to the corporation resulting from a betrayal of confidence, but upon a broader foundation of a wise public policy that, for the purpose of removing all temptation, extinguishes all possibility of profit flowing from a breach of the confidence imposed by the fiduciary relation. Given the relation between the parties, a certain result follows; and a constructive trust is the remedial device through which precedence of self is compelled to give way to the stern demands of loyalty.

The rule, referred to briefly as the rule of corporate opportunity, is merely one of the manifestations of the general rule that demands of an officer or director the utmost good faith in his relation to the corporation which he represents.

The real issue is whether the opportunity to secure a very substantial stock interest in a corporation to be formed for the purpose of exploiting a cola beverage on a wholesale scale was so closely associated with the existing business activities of Loft, and so essential thereto, as to bring the transaction within that class of cases where the acquisition of the property would throw the corporate officer purchasing it into competition with his company. This is a factual question to be decided by reasonable inferences from objective facts.

The facts and circumstances demonstrate that Guth's appropriation of the Pepsi-Cola opportunity to himself placed him in a competitive position with Loft with respect to a commodity essential to it, thereby rendering his personal interest incompatible with the superior interests of his corporation; and this situation was accomplished, not openly and with his own resources, but secretly and with the money and facilities of the corporation which was committed to his protection.

Although the facts and circumstances disclosed by the voluminous record clearly show gross violations of legal and moral duties by Guth in his dealings with Loft, the appellants make bold to say that no duty was cast upon Guth; hence he was guilty of no disloyalty. The fiduciary relation demands something more than the morals of the market place. Guth's abstractions of Loft's money and materials are complacently referred to as borrowings. Whether his acts are to be deemed properly cognizable in a civil court at all, we need not inquire, but certain it is that borrowing is not descriptive of them. A borrower presumes a lender acting freely. Guth took without limit or stint from a helpless corporation, in violation of a statute enacted for the protection of corporations against such abuses, and without the knowledge or authority of the corporation's Board of Directors. Cunning and craft supplanted sincerity. Frankness gave way to concealment. He did not offer the Pepsi-Cola opportunity to Loft, but captured it for himself. He invested little or no money of his own in the venture, but commandeered for his own benefit and advantage the money, resources and facilities of his corporation and the services of its officials. He thrust upon Loft the hazard, while he reaped the benefit. His time was paid for by Loft. The use of the Grace plant was not essential to the enterprise. In such manner he acquired for himself and Grace ninety-one percent of the capital stock of Pepsi, now worth many millions. A genius in his line he may be, but the law makes no distinction between the wrongdoing genius and the one less endowed.

> Upon a consideration of all the facts and circumstances as disclosed we are convinced that the opportunity to acquire the Pepsi-Cola trademark and formula, goodwill and business belonged to the complainant, and that Guth, as its President, had no right to appropriate the opportunity to himself.
>
> **DECISION:** Affirmed. The Supreme Court of Delaware ruled in favor of Loft.

Duty of Care   The director must conduct the affairs of the corporation using the same degree of care and skill that an ordinary prudent person would exercise in the conduct of his or her own personal business affairs. This means that officers and directors must seek out the information necessary to make an informed decision.

Business Judgment Rule   Even though officers and directors have a duty of care with regard corporate transactions, they will not be subject to liability every time something goes wrong. Under the **business judgment rule**, an officer or director will not be held liable for a corporate decision if the decision was made in (1) good faith, (2) with the care that an ordinary prudent person in a similar situation would exercise, and (3) with the belief, premised on a ratio-

nal basis, that the decision is in the best interests of the corporation. An officer or director who acts in good faith and who otherwise fulfills the fiduciary duties of loyalty and care will be shielded from liability, even if the decision turns out to have disastrous consequences for the corporation. Unless the director or officer breaches his or her fiduciary duties, the court will not substitute its business judgment (or the business judgment of dissenting shareholders) for the business judgment of the officer or director.

The business judgment rule is an important defense for officers or directors who are sued by shareholders for mismanaging the corporation. The rule has generally been interpreted to give officers and directors a very wide degree of latitude in making corporate decisions. The following case might be read as a very important departure to the traditional approach to the business judgment rule.

SMITH V. VAN GORKOM
Supreme Court of Delaware
488 A.2d 858 (1985)

BACKGROUND: Smith (plaintiff) initiated a class action suit on behalf of the shareholders of Trans Union Corporation ("Trans Union" or "the Company") against Van Gorkom, the Chief Executive Officer (CEO), members of the Board of Directors ("Board"), and others (defendants) seeking a rescission of a cash buyout merger of Trans Union into a new corporation. Alternatively, money damages were sought against the board of directors of Trans Union and the newly merged corporation. Van Gorkom, a certified public accountant and lawyer, had been CEO for 17 years and chairman of the board for 2 years. He was familiar with acquisition procedures, valuation methods, and negotiations in merger situations. Beginning September 5, 1980, he held several private meetings with one Jay Pritzker, a well-known acquirer of corporations, and convinced Pritzker to make a cash buyout merger offer for Trans Union at $55 per share. On September 18 Pritzker advised his attorney to begin drafting merger documents. Pritzker insisted on September 19 that Trans Union's Board of Directors act by September 21 on his proposal. After obtaining financing from Trans Union's lead bank on September 19 Van Gorkom called for a meeting of senior management and scheduled a Board meeting the next day. Trans Union's investment bankers (Solomon Brothers) were not present at the Senior Management meeting.

Donald Romans, Chief Financial Officer of Trans Union, reported that a study he prepared showed the price range of a leveraged buyout by management would be between $55 and $65 per share. Van Gorkom never saw the study and did not make it available to the Board.

Senior management's reaction to the Pritzker proposal was negative on the basis of the $55 price, the adverse tax consequences to many shareholders, and the closing out of potential higher bids if an auction took place. Nevertheless, the Board met the following day to discuss the proposal. After a 20-minute oral presentation by Van Gorkom and a brief statement by the Chief Financial Officer, the directors approved the merger agreement. Neither Van Gorkom nor any member of the Board had seen copies of the merger agreement prior to voting as they were delivered too late. The total length of the meeting was 2 hours. The Board claimed that several conditions were attached to its acceptance, including that Trans Union reserved the right to accept any better offer during a 90-day period following its acceptance. The minutes of the Board meeting do not reflect this. Nonetheless, after amending the merger agreement with Pritzker, Solomon Brothers solicited offers from October 21, 1980 to January 21, 1981 producing only one serious suitor, General Electric Credit Corporation, which was unwilling to make an offer unless Trans Union rescinded the agreement it had with Pritzker. Shareholder approval of Pritzker's offer took place on February 10, 1981. The Delaware Court of Chancery found that the Board's approval of the Pritzker merger proposal fell within the protection of the business judgment rule, and that the Board was not reckless or imprudent, but informed. The plaintiffs appealed.

Horsey, Justice

The standard of care applicable to a director's duty of care has been recently restated by this Court. In *Aronson,* we stated:

> While the Delaware cases use a variety of terms to describe the applicable standard of care, our analysis satisfies us that under the business judgment rule director liability is predicated upon concepts of gross negligence. (footnote omitted)

We again confirm that view. We think the concept of gross negligence is also the proper standard for determining whether a business judgment reached by a board of directors was an informed one.

On the record before us, we must conclude that the Board of Directors did not reach an informed business judgment on September 20, 1980 in voting to "sell" the Company for $55 per share pursuant to the Pritzker cash-out merger proposal. Our reasons, in summary, are as follows:

The directors (1) did not adequately inform themselves as to Van Gorkom's role in forcing the "sale" of the Company and in establishing the pershare purchase price; (2) were uninformed as to the intrinsic value of the Company; and (3) given these circumstances, at a minimum, were grossly negligent in approving the "sale" of the Company upon two hours' consideration, without prior notice, and without the exigency of a crisis or emergency.

As has been noted, the Board based its September 20 decision to approve the cash-out merger primarily on Van Gorkom's representations. None of the directors, other than Van Gorkom and Chelberg, had any prior knowledge that the purpose of the meeting was to propose a cash-out merger of Trans Union. No members of Senior Management were present, other than Chelberg, Romans and Peterson; and the latter two had only learned of the proposed sale an hour earlier. Both general counsel Moore and former general counsel Browder attended the meeting, but were equally uninformed as to the purpose of the meeting and the documents to be acted upon.

Without any documents before them concerning the proposed transaction, the members of the Board were required to rely entirely upon Van Gorkom's 20-minute oral presentation of the proposal. No written summary of the terms of the merger was presented; the directors were given no documentation to support the adequacy of $55 price per share for sale of the Company; and the Board had before it nothing more than Van Gorkom's statement of his understanding of the substance of an agreement which he admittedly had never read, nor which any member of the Board had ever seen. . . .

Here, the record establishes that the Board did not request its Chief Financial Officer, Romans, to make any valuation study or review of the proposal to determine the adequacy of $55 per share for sale of the Company. On the record before us: The Board rested on Romans' elicited response that the $55 figure was within a "fair price range" within the context of a leveraged buy-out. No director sought any further information from Romans. No director asked him why he put $55 at the bottom of his range. No director asked Romans for any details as to his study, the reason why it had been undertaken or its depth. No director asked to see the study; and no director asked Romans whether Trans Union's finance department could do a fairness study within the remaining 36-hour period available under the Pritzker offer.

Had the Board, or any member, made an inquiry of Romans, he presumably would have responded as he testified: that his calculations were rough and preliminary; and that the study was not designed to determine the fair value of the Company, but rather to assess the feasibility of a leveraged buy-out financed by the Company's projected cash flow, making certain assumptions as to the purchaser's borrowing needs. Romans would have presumably also informed the Board of his view, and the widespread view of Senior Management, that the timing of the offer was wrong and the offer inadequate.

DECISION: Reversed. The Supreme Court of Delaware ruled in favor of the plaintiffs, Smith and other shareholders.

Fiduciary Duty to Shareholders

In early court decisions the directors and officers of a corporation were said to have no fiduciary duty to existing or potential stockholders but solely to the corporation. More recently there has been a trend in decisions finding a duty on the part of officers, directors, employees of the corporation, as well as employees of investment banking firms retained by the corporation, to disclose information obtained as a result of being insiders. At the federal level, the Securities Exchange Act addressed itself to disclosure requirements for officers and directors and to what constitutes insider trading. Chapter 46 discusses these and other topics in detail.

While the business judgment rule has given officers and directors wide latitude in managing a corporation, minority shareholders have recently been filing suits alleging that they have been "frozen out" of the corporation. As discussed earlier, minority shareholders often seek injunctions or damages in cases where corporate boards have ratified high salaries for majority or controlling shareholders who are also officers of the corporation. A minority shareholder suit may also result when the board fails to declare dividends and it can be shown that there was not a "good faith" reason. For example, if the controlling shareholders seek to force the minority to sell their stock by not declaring a dividend, or to depress the price of the stock to serve the interest of officers or directors, the courts will see a wrongful purpose and a violation of the business judgment rule.

Other circumstances in which minority shareholders have charged "oppression" involve mergers and amendments to the corporate charter altering voting rights of a class of stock.

ISSUES AND TRENDS

Following *Smith v. Van Gorkom* examined here, the Delaware Supreme Court and the federal courts have scrutinized carefully board of directors' decisions in what are referred to as "control" situations; that is, where control of the corporation is threatened by investors outside the corporation such as in *Smith*, or when officers of the corporation seek to gain control by a leveraged buyout (using the assets of the corporation to finance a buyout and take the company private). With the number of mergers and leveraged buyouts that have taken place in the 1980s and 1990s, the courts in these situations no longer presume boards of directors have correctly applied the business judgment rule. The courts have offered guidelines for directors, officers, and shareholders to follow in "control" situations:

1. The board of directors should have a preponderance of outside directors, or at minimum a committee of outside directors that weighs a takeover or leveraged buyout proposal and any defensive measures that are to be taken.

2. Defensive measures should generally be enacted only when there is a specific pending threat, or the industry environment is such that takeovers are frequent.

3. When a board of directors is involved in the takeover process it should seek advice from in-house counsel, as well as retained counsel, investment bankers, and others who can show that they have some expertise in valuating the assets of the corporation. A valuating report should be prepared by the board taking into consideration the definition of a "report" in *Smith*.

4. Boards of directors should plan on being sued when making decisions in control situations, and thus develop a legal and management strategy that is perceived by courts of law as having the interests of shareholders as its primary goal.

Review Questions and Problems

Key Terms

ultra vires	appraisal and buyout right
cumulative voting	derivative action
proxy	director's qualifying stock
stock dividend	corporate opportunity
preemptive right	constructive trust
treasury shares	business judgment rule

Discussion Questions

1. Why do corporations generally choose to state their purpose broadly rather than narrowly in their articles of incorporation?

2. Why is the *ultra vires* doctrine less important than it once was?

3. How does cumulative voting help minority stockholders? How can the effect of cumulative voting be countered?

4. For what reasons do minority shareholders in a corporation bring suits against the corporation, its board of directors, and officers?

Review Problems

1. X Corporation was organized with an authorization of 1,000 shares of stock. The adopted bylaws of the corporation contained provisions limiting the number of shares available to each stockholder and restricting stock transfers during both the life of the stockholder and in case of death. According to the bylaws, if a stockholder wanted to sell or transfer shares, he or she had to give the corporation or other stockbrokers the chance to purchase the stock from the stockholder at the price paid when the stock was originally purchased. If the option was not exercised within 90 days, the stockholder then was free to sell the stock. Y had purchased shares with restrictions of sale and transfer, as detailed previously, printed on the stock certificates. When Y died, the board of directors of X voted to exercise its option to repurchase the shares from Y's estate and agreed to pay a sum greater than Y paid for the stock. Those administering the estate declined to sell and wanted the stock transferred to the estate. They brought a lawsuit to compel the corporation to transfer the stock according to the estate's wishes, claiming that the limitation on sale and transfer was an unreasonable restraint. The corporation argued that because of the restriction of sale and transfer of the stock, it was not prohibiting the transfer of stock, but merely putting a reasonable restriction on the transfer. Does the

provision in the corporate bylaws, giving the corporation a right or first option to purchase the stock at the price that it originally received for it, amount to an unreasonable restraint on the transfer of the stock?

2. A, who owned stock in a gold-mining company, B, made a contract with the company to sell his stock. For financial reasons A later refused to sell and breached his contract. The bylaws of the corporation allowed the executive committee to "conduct the corporation's business." When B sued A, the latter's defense was that the contract was invalid because B's articles of incorporation did not expressly allow the company to purchase its stock from stockholders. Was A's defense valid? Explain.

3. A, president of B company, made a contract with an employee, C, by which C was promised certain retirement benefits. A owned 80 percent of the stock of B and had managed the company independent of the board of directors. When C retired, the board refused to pay the benefits promised him. C sued based on a breach of contract. B company's defense was that the contract was invalid because it was not approved by the board of directors. What was the result? Explain.

Case Problems

1. Gilbert, the owner of record of seventeen shares of Transamerica Corporation, wrote the management of the company and submitted four proposals that he wanted to be presented for action by shareholders at the next annual stockholders meeting. The Securities and Exchange Commission (SEC) demanded that Transamerica comply with Gilbert's request, but the company refused. The SEC brought an action to forbid Transamerica from making use of any proxy solicited by it for use at the annual meeting, from making use of the mails or any instrumentality of interstate commerce to solicit proxies, or from making use of any soliciting material without complying with the SEC's demands. Transamerica claimed that the shareholder may interest himself only in a subject in respect to which he is entitled to vote at a stockholders' meeting when every requirement of state law and of the provisions of the charter and bylaws has been fulfilled. State law states that a certificate of incorporation may set forth provisions that limit, regulate, and define the powers and functions of the directors and stockholders.

   A bylaw of Transamerica vested in the board of directors the power to decide whether any proposal should be voted on at an annual meeting of stockholders. Three of Gilbert' proposals were: (1) to have independent public auditors of the books of Transamerica elected by the stockholders, (2) to eliminate from a bylaw the requirement that notice of any proposed alteration or amendment of the bylaws be contained in the notice of meetings, and (3) to require an account or a report of the proceedings at the annual meetings to be sent to all stockholders. Is Gilbert entitled to make such demands? What are the reasons for and against the proposals made by Gilbert? Will the power of shareholders go to an extreme if small shareholders like Gilbert can exert so much pressure? Explain.

2. The directors of Acoustic Products Company concluded that it was essential for the success of the company to purchase the rights to manufacture under certain patents held by the DeForest Radio Company. Acoustic was already involved in the manufacture of phonographs and radios. A contract was entered into between an agent of Acoustic and the major shareholder of DeForest providing that Acoustic could purchase one-third of the DeForest stock. This would increase the possibility for Acoustic to obtain the needed patent rights. The directors of Acoustic were not able to acquire enough funds for Acoustic to perform the contract. Thus they personally purchased the DeForest stock. When Acoustic later went bankrupt, the trustee in bankruptcy brought this action against the directors, claiming that by purchasing the DeForest shares they had violated the fiduciary duty owed to the corporation. The parties agreed that the acquisition of the rights under the DeForest patents was essential for Acoustic's success. Conceding that there existed a close relation between Acoustic and DeForest, the directors argued that since the company did not have the money to purchase the shares, the directors had violated no duty by purchasing the shares themselves. Who should win? Should the directors suffer financially even though they made their effort to help Acoustic? Or is this possibility for suffering by the directors part of the game in order to prompt directors to use their best efforts in uncovering financial resources to be used by their companies in acquiring an attractive opportunity?

3. Emerson Electric Company acquired 13.2 percent of the outstanding common stock of Dodge Manufacturing Company through a tender offer made in an unsuccessful attempt to take over Dodge. Shortly thereafter, the shareholders of Dodge approved a merger with Reliance Electric Company. Emerson decided to dispose of enough of its shares to bring its holding below 10 percent in order to immunize the disposal of the remainder of its shares from liability under Section 16(b) of the Securities Exchange Act of 1934. Section 16(b) provides that a corporation may recover for itself the profits realized by an owner of more than 10 percent of its shares from a purchase and sale of its stock within any 6-month period, provided the owner held more than 10 percent at the time of both purchase and sale. Emerson sold some shares of Dodge, reducing its holdings in Dodge to 9.96 percent of the outstanding shares. Several weeks later Emerson sold the remainder of the Dodge shares to Dodge. Reliance demanded the profits realized on both sales, since the purchase and two sales all occurred within a 3-month period. Emerson does not dispute

the fact that the profits from the first sale should now be turned over. It contends that after the first sale it no longer held more than 10 percent and should not be treated as an "insider" but like any other investor, and consequently, should be able to keep its profit. Who should prevail? If Emerson should lose, is there any time it can keep its profit, or will it always be penalized, since it once held more than 10 percent of Dodge's stock?

4. Pillsbury had long opposed the Vietnam War. He learned that Honeywell, Inc. had a substantial part of its business in the production of munitions used in the war and also that Honeywell had a large government contract to produce antipersonnel fragmentation bombs. Pillsbury was determined to stop this production. He bought one share of Honeywell in his name in order to get himself a voice in Honeywell's affairs so he could persuade the company to cease producing munitions. Pillsbury submitted demands to Honeywell requesting that it produce its original shareholder ledger, current shareholder ledger, and all corporate records dealing with weapons and munitions manufacture. Honeywell refused. Pillsbury brought suit to compel Honeywell to let him inspect the requested records. Pillsbury claimed that he wished to inspect the records in order to correspond with other shareholders, with the hope of electing to the board one or more directors who represented his particular viewpoint. Should the court let Pillsbury inspect the records? Does Pillsbury have a proper purpose germane to his interest as a shareholder? Should a shareholder be allowed to persuade a company to adopt his social and political views?

5. Cole Real Estate Corporation was a closely held corporation that owned, managed, and rented residential apartment properties. Helen Cole was the majority stockholder, owning all but 86 of the 4,120 outstanding shares of common stock. Peoples Bank & Trust Company of Indianapolis held the remaining 86 shares in a trustee capacity. Mrs. Cole had been a director, the president, and the treasurer of the corporation since its organization in 1935. Cole Corporation was a "one-woman corporation," and little evidence of corporate identity was maintained. The most recent board of directors meeting was held in 1954, when the corporation was reorganized. At that meeting the last stock dividend was declared on previously outstanding preferred shares. Mrs. Cole testified that a shareholder meeting had not been held because of lack of interest, even though she knew Indiana law required annual shareholder meetings. As the corporation's sole employee, Mrs. Cole lived in a home owned and operated by the Corporation. The home also was the corporate office, and she paid no rent or utilities. Two automobiles—owned, operated, and maintained by the corporation—provided Mrs. Cole with her only means of transportation. She set

her own salary during the years 1964–1970 without consulting the board of directors. Peoples Bank & Trust, as minority shareholder, brought a lawsuit for an accounting, recovery of corporate assets, and a declaration of dividends. Mrs. Cole argues that a close corporation should be justifiably distinguished from a public corporation when questions of corporate formality and internal operations are at issue. Peoples Bank contends that corporate law prevents an officer and a director of a corporation from using the assets of a corporate entity for their personal gain. Who should win? Was there excessive compensation and/or converted corporate assets? Should a dividend be declared?

6. Wiberg, a director of Gulf Coast Land and Development Company, and another director contracted with the corporation to devote their full time to selling a new line of its stock, for which they were to receive a commission on sales. The corporate resolution creating this contract was passed by the votes of these two directors and by a third director. The resolution was later ratified by holders of a majority of the shares at a special meeting in which the three directors, who were the majority shareholders, voted to ratify their action as directors. After 2 years the corporation terminated the contract and refused to pay Wiberg his commission. Wiberg sued to recover his commission. The defendant contends that the contract was void as against public policy because two of the three directors who had voted for it had personal interest in the transaction and because it had not been ratified by 100 percent of the shareholders. Wiberg argues that the contract is enforceable even even when the corporation makes a contract with a director; that the director's vote is necessary to authorize the contract if the contract appears to be fair, just, and beneficial to the corporation; and that the director personally made a full disclosure and the contract was then ratified by a majority of the stockholders. Assuming that the contract is what Wiberg contends it is—that is, fair, just, and beneficial to the corporation—should Wiberg prevail? Even though Wiberg has a personal interest in the contract, do you think he will act fairly and honestly in the corporation's interests?

7. Jan Schakowsky and the National Consumers Union (NCU) sought to examine the books and records of National Tea Company, purportedly for the purpose of soliciting proxies. Schakowsky and NCU each owned one share of the corporation. Schakowsky and NCU admitted that they hoped to "sensitize" National Tea Company to NCU's "consumer" demands. NCU had, in the past, complained about certain of National Tea Company's practices and had urged consumers not to purchase the corporation's products. The corporation refused to allow the inspection, and Schakowsky and NCU sued. What was the result?

45

Corporate Mergers, Dissolution, and Termination

Mergers and Acquisitions

Dissolution and Termination of the Corporation

This chapter covers changes in corporate structure, such as those that occur when two corporations merge into one. Over the last several years, especially in the 1980s, major corporate mergers and acquisitions have captured headlines and changed the face of the business world. Some mergers have been between direct competitors, as when Bank of America purchased Security Pacific National Bank. Some mergers have been between companies at different stages of a particular distribution chain, as when Sony, a manufacturer of entertainment hardware, acquired Columbia Studios. And some mergers have been between firms in separate markets, as when the tobacco company Philip Morris purchased General Foods. The 1980s saw the rise to prominence of the "corporate raider," a high-stakes investor whose specialty was acquiring corporations—or threatening to acquire corporations—over the objections of the target companies' managers.

Mergers and acquisitions often raise antitrust law issues—mergers that may tend to create a monopoly or otherwise lessen competition in a particular market are prohibited under the federal Clayton Act.

This chapter does not include a full discussion of corporate takeovers or the Clayton Act. To properly understand these topics, one must become familiar with securities law (Chapter 46) and antitrust law (Chapter 54). This chapter does, however, cover the basics of corporate structural changes that are essential to understand those later chapters. This chapter also discusses the ultimate change in corporate structure: dissolution and termination of the corporation.

Mergers and Acquisitions

Mergers

A **merger** occurs when one or more corporations are absorbed into another existing corporation. In a merger, as opposed to a *consolidation* (discussed below), one of the merging corporations survives. A merger occurs after the board of directors for each merging corporation agrees on a plan of merger. The plan details the terms of the merger, including the compensation that shareholders of the nonsurviving corporation or corporations will receive in exchange for their shares. Typically, such shareholders receive shares or other securities of the surviving corporation and/or cash.

Mergers must generally be approved by the shareholders of each merging corporation. Some jurisdictions require that shareholders representing a mere majority of shares outstanding vote to approve the merger, but most states require a higher percentage to approve the transaction. (A two-thirds requirement is most common; some states require approval of four-fifths of the outstanding shares.) It is common to require approval from holders of all classes of stock.

Many states provide for a **short-form merger** procedure in which shareholders do not have to approve a merger if certain conditions are met. In order to qualify for a short-form merger, the nonsurviving corporation must be a subsidiary of the surviving corporation and the surviving corporation must own a certain percentage of the subsidiary's stock. The Revised Model Business Corporation Act (RMBCA) makes the short-form merger procedure available to parent corporations that own at least 90 percent of the outstanding shares of all classes of the nonsurviving corporation's securities. Other states set the minimum ownership level at 95 percent.

In order for a merger to become effective, *articles of merger* must be filed with the secretary of state of the state in which the surviving corporation is incorporated. The secretary of state then issues a *certificate of merger* to document that the merger has been accomplished. The surviving corporation's articles of incorporation are amended by the articles of merger.

Consolidations

A **consolidation** occurs when one or more corporations combine to form a *new* corporation—that is, none of the merging corporations survives. Corporations might choose to consolidate rather than merge when they can't agree on which corporation should be the surviving corporation. Consolidations are much less common than mergers.

In a consolidation, *articles of consolidation* are filed with the secretary of state. These articles replace the articles of incorporation of each consolidated corporation. Like mergers, consolidations must be approved by the directors and shareholders of each corporation.

Rights and Obligations of Disappearing Corporations

In either a merger or a consolidation, all the rights and obligations of the disappearing corporations pass automatically to the surviving corporation. If, for example, Disappearing Corp. merges into Surviving Corp., Surviving Corp. automatically assumes title to all Disappearing Corp.'s property. Surviving Corp. would also benefit from any legal rights, such as the right to sue certain third parties, that Disappearing Corp. enjoyed. But Surviving Corp. would also be liable for all Disappearing Corp.'s debts and other liabilities.

Purchase of Stock

Mergers are often accomplished through the purchase of the target company's stock. If the target company is a closely held corporation, the purchase of stock can be negotiated directly with the target company's shareholders. Otherwise, the purchase can be accomplished by means of a *tender offer*, in which the purchaser announces its intention to buy the target company's shares at a stated price. Target company shareholders who wish to sell their shares at that price may accept the offer by tendering their shares to the purchaser. If enough of the target company's shareholders agree to sell their shares at the price offered, then the purchaser can take control of the target company and cause a merger. A tender offer may be friendly or hostile—that is, it can be made with or without the blessing of the target company's management. Tender offers are subject to extensive federal regulation. A number of states indirectly regulate tender offers as well. Tender offers are discussed in more detail in Chapter 46.

Appraisal Rights

As noted above, mergers and consolidations generally require shareholder approval. Most states allow shareholders who do not support the merger to receive "fair value" for all shares held at the time of the merger or consolidation. This right is known as the shareholder's **appraisal right**. A shareholder must comply with certain procedures in order to qualify for the appraisal right. The requirements vary from state to state. Generally, however, the shareholder must (1) file a written notice of opposition to the merger prior to the shareholder vote and (2) issue a written demand for payment of fair value for the shareholder's shares after the merger or consolidation has been approved.

The most important issue arising from the appraisal right is how to determine the "fair value" of the dissenting shareholder's shares. This problem is discussed in the case that follows.

SPINNAKER SOFTWARE CORP. v. NICHOLSON

Court of Appeals of Minnesota
495 N. W. 2d 441 (1993)

BACKGROUND: Nicholson owned both common and preferred shares of Springboard Software, Inc. Springboard agreed to merge with Spinnaker Software Corp. Nicholson opposed the merger and took steps to exercise his appraisal right. Spinnaker offered Nicholson $0.90 per common share and $1.575 per preferred share. Nicholson rejected this offer, and estimated the fair value of his shares to be $1.75 per common share and $3.00 per preferred share. Spinnaker brought an action to seek a judicial valuation of Nicholson's shares. The trial court awarded Nicholson $2.16 per common share and $3.00 per preferred share. Spinnaker appealed.

Davies, Presiding Judge

Upon a fundamental corporate change, such as merger, Minn. Stat. § 302A.471 subd. 1 (Supp. 1991), allows a minority shareholder to dissent from the corporate action. The dissenting shareholder is entitled to receive the "fair value" of shares held if the shareholder follows the appropriate procedures for dissenting and is further entitled ultimately to have the trial court make a binding determination of fair value.

In determining "fair value" of the shares, Minn. Stat. § 302A.473, subd. 7, provides:

> The court . . . shall determine the fair value of the shares, taking into account any and all factors the court finds relevant, computed by any method or combination of methods that the court, in its discretion, sees fit to use, whether or not used by the corporation or by a dissenter.

Spinnaker argues that the trial court's valuation of Nicholson's shares must be reversed in light of this court's holding in *MT Properties, Inc. v. CMC Real Estate Corp.* Spinnaker argues that *MT Properties* mandates that Nicholson's shares be valued as a pro rata share of the purchase price of Springboard negotiated by Springboard and Spinnaker in their merger agreement.

In *MT Properties*, this court reviewed whether "fair value" could include a discount of the dissenting shareholder's shares to reflect their minority status. Because it was a case of first impression, this court examined cases from other jurisdictions.

Spinnaker relies on language in *MT Properties* that "valuing a dissenter's shares involves valuing the corporation as a whole rather than the individual shares." Spinnaker claims that this supports its assertion that this court has chosen to follow the American Law Institute's Tentative Draft No. 11 of the Principles of Corporate Governance § 7.22 (the "ALI standard") and the rule of the Massachusetts Court of Appeals in *BNE Mass. Corp. v. Sims*. These authorities establish the principle that, in valuing the corporation as a whole, a court ought to use the purchase price of the company when the price has been negotiated in an arms-length transaction. The ALI standard is, however, somewhat qualified.

The ALI standard states:

§ 7.22 Standards for Determining Fair Value

(b) In the case of a business combination that gives rise to appraisal rights, . . . the aggregate price accepted by the board of directors of the subject corporation should be presumed to represent the fair value of the corporation, . . . unless the plaintiff can prove otherwise by clear and convincing evidence.

The Massachusetts Court of Appeals gave credence to this standard in *BNE*, finding that the trial court could appropriately determine the blended cash value of the merger price for the company (assuming it was negotiated in an arms-length transaction) in arriving at the fair value of the dissenter's shares.

Despite Spinnaker's assertion to the contrary, *MT Properties* does not go so far; it does not stand for the rule that the purchase price of a corporation is presumed to be its fair value for purposes of determining the fair value of a dissenting shareholder's shares. It holds only that minority discounts are inappropriate. And, even were we to apply the ALI presumption, Spinnaker's argument would fail here. Spinnaker argues that the purchase price for Springboard was $5.4 million, based on the footnote to Spinnaker's financial records attached to the prospectus. The evidence shows that the merger transaction involved an exchange of shares for a percentage of ownership in the merged entity and that the $5.4 million was merely the amount that Spinnaker's accountants used to represent the transaction for accounting purposes. We are not persuaded that a preponderance of the evidence shows the $5.4 million was the purchase price or fair value of Springboard as negotiated in an arms-length transaction.

Valuation of property is a finding of fact which an appellate court will reverse only if clearly erroneous. We conclude that the trial court's findings in support of its valuation are supported by the evidence and the testimony of Nicholson's expert witness. The method of valuation used by Nicholson's expert and adopted by the trial court in determining the value of Nicholson's common shares falls within the broad discretion accorded the trial court under Minn. Stat. § 302A.473. The evidence also supports the trial court's finding regarding the value of Nicholson's preferred shares.

DECISION: The Court of Appeals affirmed the trial court's valuation of Nicholson's shares.

Purchase of Assets

Rather than affecting a merger or consolidation, an acquiring corporation may elect to purchase all (or substantially all) the assets of the target corporation. Once the acquiring and selling corporations agree on terms, the selling corporation's shareholders must approve the transaction. Most states do not require shareholder approval from the acquiring corporation; however, acquiring corporations whose shares are traded on a national stock exchange are sometimes required by stock exchange rules to obtain shareholder approval. Most states also give appraisal rights to shareholders of the selling corporation who oppose the asset sale. After the sale, the selling corporation can either remain in existence or dissolve itself. If the corporation chooses to dissolve itself, it would liquidate the proceeds of the asset sale. Any funds remaining after all creditors are paid would be distributed to the shareholders.

By purchasing assets rather than effecting a merger or consolidation through the purchase of stock, the acquiring company can avoid assuming the liabilities of the target company. This is the major advantage of an asset purchase. The purchaser of assets is not liable for the debts and other liabilities of the selling corporation if:

1. The purchaser does not expressly or impliedly agree to assume the debts and liabilities.

2. The transaction does not amount to a merger or consolidation.

3. The purchasing corporation is not merely a continuation of the selling corporation.

4. The transaction is not entered into fraudulently to escape debts and liabilities.

CONCEPT SUMMARY
Mergers, Consolidations, and Asset Purchases

Merger	Consolidation	Asset Purchase
One corporation survives	New corporation replaces consolidating corporations	Selling corporation may continue in existence or dissolve
Shareholder approval is generally required from each corporation	Shareholder approval is generally required from each corporation	In most states, shareholder approval is required from selling corporation only (subject to stock exchange rules)
Dissenting shareholders have appraisal rights	Dissenting shareholders have appraisal rights	In most states, dissenting shareholders have appraisal rights
Surviving corporation assumes all debts and other liabilities of merged corporation(s)	New corporation assumes all debts and other liabilities of consolidated corporations	Purchasing corporation does not assume debts and other liabilities of selling corporation, unless certain conditions apply

---

Typically, the acquiring corporation *will* agree to assume all known debts and other liabilities of the selling corporation. The asset purchase is designed to protect the acquiring corporation against *contingent* liabilities—liabilities that may arise in the future, such as product liability suits. However, the asset purchase does not always protect the acquiring corporation from the selling corporation's contingent liabilities. If a court finds that any of the four factors listed above are missing, it can, in the interests of fairness, declare an asset purchase to be a **de facto merger** (or consolidation). If a transaction is ruled to be a de facto merger or consolidation, then the acquiring company is liable for all debts and other liabilities of the selling corporation. The de facto merger doctrine is discussed in the case that follows.

COUNTY OF COOK v. MELLON STUART CO.
U.S. District Court, N.D. Illinois
812 F.Supp. 793 (1992)

BACKGROUND: Mellon Stuart Co. won a contract to build a jail in Cook County. After Mellon Stuart completed its work, serious cracks and other defects were discovered at the new facility. Mellon Stuart undertook to remedy its defective work, but its attempt to remedy the situation created additional structural problems. Around this time, Mellon Stuart changed its name to Federal Street and transferred substantially all its valuable assets to three corporations: MBC, Baker Engineering, and MSCI. Cook County sued Mellon Stuart/Federal Street for damages resulting from its failure to meet proper standards in constructing the jail. Cook County also sued MBC, Baker Engineering, and MSCI. In the excerpt below the U.S. District Court rules on a procedural motion that turns on whether Cook County might have a case against Baker Engineering.

Aspen, District Judge

Under Illinois law, a corporation that purchases the assets of another corporation is generally not liable for the debts and liabilities of the transferor. The Illinois courts, however, have recognized several exceptions that serve to impute liability to the purchasing company, including:

(1) Where there is an express or implied agreement of assumption;

(2) Where the transaction amounts to a consolidation or merger, including a *de facto* merger, of the purchaser and seller corporations;

(3) Where the purchaser is merely a continuation of the seller; or

(4) Where the transaction is for the fraudulent purpose of escaping liability for the seller's obligations.

In the instant case, the County contends that the September 1991 transfer of Mellon Stuart assets to MBC constitutes a *de facto* merger. Further, the County argues that Baker Engineering, operating as part of a common enterprise to deliver combined services, can be held liable for the obligations of Mellon Stuart. Under Illinois law, a *de facto* merger occurs in the following circumstances:

(1) The seller corporation ceases its ordinary business operations, liquidates, and dissolves as soon as legally and practically possible;

(2) The purchasing corporation assumes those liabilities and obligations of the seller ordinarily necessary for the uninterrupted continuation of normal business operations of the seller;

(3) There is a continuation of shareholders which results from the purchasing corporation paying for the acquired assets with shares of its own stock, this stock ultimately coming to be held by shareholders of the seller corporation so that they become a constituent part of the purchasing corporation; and

(4) There is a continuation of the enterprise of the seller corporation, so that there is continuity of management, personnel, physical location, assets, and general business operation.

To support its position, the County, in its verified complaint and exhibits appended to its current motion, assert the following: MBC acquired substantially all of Mellon Stuart's valuable assets and on-going projects in consideration for a promise to make payments totaling $4 million, the first payment being due on March 1, 1993. Defendant MBC created MSCI to receive the Mellon Stuart assets and to conduct its ongoing projects, absorbing Mellon Stuart's employees. With the addition of MSCI, MBC embodies three functional work groups (*i.e.,* engineering, operation and maintenance, and construction), organized to provide one integrated product. Baker Engineering is a division of MBC's engineering group, and is closely related to MSCI. Baker Engineering shares directors, officers and common management with both MBC and MSCI. Defendant Federal Street was created by MBC in order to liquidate Mellon Stuart's losing projects. Indeed, Federal Street, purportedly a shell company for the affiliated Baker defendants, was burdened with such enormous liabilities that it was forced to seek protection under Chapter 11 of the Bankruptcy Code. MSCI, through its President, who is also the Executive Vice President of MBC, and other officers and employees, directed and continued the operations of Federal Street throughout the time when serious damage was caused to the County's new jail. Baker Engineering worked out of the same address, 118 South Clinton Street in Chicago, Illinois, as did Federal Street and MSCI. Further, Baker Engineering pursued design business with Mellon Stuart, a/k/a Federal Street, on public sector projects in Chicago during the time when Federal Street was controlled and directed by MBC.

In order to rebut the County's allegations regarding Baker Engineering's role in the alleged common enterprise, defendants rely on the affidavit of Harry R. Hanley, President of Baker Engineering. In this affidavit, Hanley states "Baker Engineering, Inc. does not now, nor has it ever controlled or directed the operations of Mellon Stuart Company/Federal Street Construction Company." Hanley also denied that it ever shared or maintained common offices with Mellon Stuart or Federal Street. The assertions of the Hanley affidavit, however, at best create a factual dispute regarding the interrelationship of the Baker defendants. Resolving all questions of law and fact in favor of the County, we find a reasonable possibility that an Illinois court would conclude that the transfer of assets from Mellon Stuart to MBC constitutes a *de facto* merger and, as such, Baker Engineering, acting as an integral part of a common enterprise with MBC and MSCI, would be liable for Mellon Stuart's purportedly deficient work on the new jail. Moreover, these same allegations support the County's assertion that the creation of Federal Street by MBC, acting in a common enterprise with Baker Engineering, was for the fraudulent purpose of escaping liability for Mellon Stuart's obligations.

DECISION: The U.S. District Court ruled that Baker Engineering was properly made a party to Cook County's lawsuit.

Dissolution and Termination of the Corporation

One of the advantages of the corporate form of doing business is that the corporation lives on in perpetuity despite the death of any manager, director, or shareholder. However, perpetual existence does not prevent *dissolution* and *termination* of the corporation. Corporate **dissolution** occurs—that is, the corporation *dissolves* itself—when the corporation stops doing business and begins to wind up its affairs and liquidate its business. **Termination** occurs when all assets have been liquidated and creditors and shareholders have received the proceeds. The RMBCA provides for both voluntary and involuntary dissolutions, as discussed below.

Voluntary Dissolution

The RMBCA allows for voluntary dissolution of a corporation either before or after a corporation begins business. A vote of a majority of its incorporators or initial directors dissolves a corporation before it commences business. After business has been commenced, the RMBCA allows a corporation to dissolve itself through (1) the adoption of a dissolution resolution by the board of directors and (2) the approval of the resolution by holders of a majority of the shares outstanding. In order for the dissolution to be effective, the corporation must file *articles of dissolution* with the secretary of state of the state in which the corporation is chartered. Articles of dissolution should include the date that the dissolution resolution was approved and the number of voters who opposed and supported the resolution.

If the corporation's certificate of incorporation lists an expiration date for the corporation's existence, then voluntary dissolution of the corporation occurs on that expiration date. Voluntary dissolution may also occur when all existing shareholders decide to dissolve the corporation.

Involuntary Dissolution

Involuntary dissolution of a corporation may take place through court action or administrative decree. The secretary of state of the corporation's state of incorporation may have the corporation involuntarily dissolved if it can be proved that the articles of incorporation were obtained through fraud or that the corporation exceeded or abused its authority under the law. In some states a corporation found guilty of certain antitrust violations may be subject to dissolution.

Shareholders may also obtain court-ordered dissolution when (1) the directors are deadlocked in a manner that's harmful to the corporation, (2) the shareholders are deadlocked and cannot elect directors, or (3) the directors are acting contrary to the best interests of the corporation.

Additionally, creditors of a corporation may obtain a judicial order to dissolve the corporation if the corporation is proved to be insolvent. In the case that follows, a deadlock between a corporation's two shareholders leads one to seek involuntary dissolution.

MARTIN V. MARTIN'S NEWS SERVICE, INC.
Appellate Court of Connecticut
518 A.2d 951 (1986)

BACKGROUND: Albert and Raymond Martin each owned 50 percent of the shares of Martin's News Service, Inc., a retail newsstand. The two began to have trouble working together, and eventually stopped communicating with one another. Albert stopped working in the store, but Raymond continued to operate the store profitably. Albert sued to have the corporation dissolved. A trial court granted Albert's request for dissolution and appointed a receiver. The trial court relied upon Connecticut General Statutes Section 33-382(b) (1), which allows the court to dissolve a corporation and appoint a receiver when (1) the corporation has wilfully exceeded its powers; (2) there has been fraud or gross mismanagement in the operation of the corporation; (3) the corporation's assets are in danger of being squandered; (4) the corporation has abandoned its business but neglected to wind up its affairs; or (5) any good or sufficient reason exists for winding up the corporation. Raymond (the defendant) appealed.

Hull, Judge

The defendant claims that the present situation does not fall within any of the specifically enumerated grounds for dissolution in the statute. In support of this claim, he states that the business is being run profitably and effectively, that there has been no finding of depletion of corporate assets, that business debts are being paid off, and that the liquidity of the corporation has increased.

The plaintiff cites *Krall v. Krall* in support of his position. The discussion in *Krall* revolves around the language of General Statutes § 33-382(b)(1)(v). That section provides that upon institution of proceedings by a 10 percent voting shareholder, the Superior Court can order dissolution of a company if "any good and sufficient reason exists." In *Krall,* the court was faced with a ten year paralysis of corporate functions during which time the business was operated profitably but under the sole direction of the defendant. Neither the plaintiff nor the board of directors had any control over corporate activities. In holding that the appointment of a receiver was proper, the court stated that "[i]t is generally true that disagreement and dissension among stockholders is not in itself sufficient ground for a corporate receivership. . . . Nevertheless, the statute is broad in its purpose and intent. It confers extensive equitable powers. It gives considerable latitude to the exercise of judicial discretion and does not hold the court to the stark letter of the law."

The court went on to state that "[a] receiver is properly appointed when there are such dissensions in the governing body of a corporation . . . that the corporation ceases to function in the manner provided for by its own by-laws and in accordance with the statutes relating to corporations."

We find *Krall v. Krall* authoritative in this case. Although Martin's is being run profitably and successfully, it is being run as a sole proprietorship. The corporate functions have been paralyzed since the late 1970s, almost equal to the ten year paralysis in *Krall*. There have been no corporate meetings during this time, and there has been no input from one of the two 50 percent shareholders. This scenario is sufficient under the rule set forth in *Krall* to be "good and sufficient reason" to order appointment of a receiver pursuant to General Statutes § 33-382.

The individual defendant attempts to distinguish the *Krall* case from the present one. He claims that there was no deadlock, but rather that the plaintiff voluntarily abdicated his role in corporate affairs. The plaintiff claims to the contrary, however, that he did voice his objections concerning corporate management, and offered to sell his shares of the corporate stock only after his objections went unaddressed.

DECISION: The appeals court affirmed the trial court's decision to appoint a receiver.

Termination

Upon dissolution, the corporation must begin to wind up its business and liquidate its assets. In a voluntary dissolution, the board of directors or someone appointed by the board collects, sells, and distributes the proceeds of all the assets. In an involuntary dissolution, a court-appointed receiver carries out the liquidation of assets and other wind-up activities.

The proceeds from the sale of assets are paid in the following order of claims: (1) creditors, (2) preferred shareholders, and (3) common shareholders. Termination of the corporation's existence occurs when (1) all the affairs of the corporation have been wound up and (2) all the assets of the corporation have been liquidated and their proceeds distributed.

Review Questions and Problems

Key Terms

merger	de facto merger
short-form merger	dissolution
consolidation	termination
appraisal right	

Discussion Questions

1. Suggest a policy reason for allowing short-form mergers to proceed without shareholder approval.

2. What factors should a company consider in deciding whether to acquire another company through a stock purchase or an asset purchase?

3. What factors might lead a court to hold a company that has purchased all the assets of another company liable for the selling company's debts?

4. Under what conditions can a shareholder obtain involuntary dissolution of a corporation?

Review Problems

1. ABC Corporation launches a hostile tender offer for the shares of DEF Corporation. The tender offer is successful, allowing ABC to take control of DEF. The shareholders of both corporations agree to combine the two into XYZ Corporation. What type of transaction has occurred?

2. The boards of Buyer, Inc. and Target, Inc. agree to merge. Under the agreement, Buyer will pay $50 for each share of Target. Target will then be merged into Buyer. Fred is a Target shareholder who believes that his shares are worth more than $50. What options are available to Fred?

3. Harry is the sole shareholder of Sleazeco, which publishes a tabloid newspaper. Faced with the threat of an expensive libel lawsuit from a famous celebrity, Harry forms another corporation named Slimeco. Slimeco purchases all the assets of Sleazeco and specifically refuses to assume any of Sleazeco's contingent liabilities. The famous celebrity sues both Sleazeco and Slimeco. If the celebrity can prove libel, can he recover damages from Slimeco? Discuss.

4. Moe and Joe are the only two shareholders of MoJoCo. Moe owns 51 percent of the company and Joe owns the other 49 percent. Moe uses his control of the corporation to authorize transactions that, in Joe's opinion, benefit his friends and family at the corporation's expense. Joe argues against these transactions, but is always outvoted in accordance with MoJoCo's bylaws. Discuss what options might be available to Joe.

Case Problems

1. American Tredex manufactured treadmills, one of which was purchased by Dr. Brandt. After Dr. Brandt bought his treadmill, Nissen Corp. purchased all the assets of American Tredex. Dr. Brandt injured his finger when he tried to adjust the treadmill. He sued Nissen. Discuss what factors would determine whether Dr. Brandt could recover from Nissen.

2. Cust-O-Fab, an Oklahoma corporation, built gas condensers. In 1986, the shareholders and directors of Cust-O-Fab ceased doing business and sold all the corporation's assets to a new corporation, also named Cust-O-Fab. The new corporation, which was formed by two former employees of the original Cust-O-Fab, immediately notified customers of the change in ownership, opened new bank accounts, and obtained a new federal employer identification number. The two corporations did not have any common directors, officers, or shareholders. The new Cust-O-Fab continued the business of the old Cust-O-Fab at the same location. A person was injured when a gas condenser built by the old Cust-O-Fab exploded. Can the new Cust-O-Fab be held liable for the injuries? Discuss.

3. Thomas owned 70 percent of Weldon Corporation and Elmer owned the other 30 percent. Thomas and Elmer began to argue about how to operate the corporation. Elmer was fired as an employee of the corporation, although he retained his minority ownership interest. Elmer was unable to sell his stake in the corporation, and Thomas refused to declare dividends. Elmer sued to dissolve the corporation. What was the result?

4. Pickett suffered asbestos-related lung problems, and sued the Philip Carey Corporation for negli-

gence in manufacturing asbestos products. After the events that led to Pickett's lawsuit, Philip Cary Corporation consolidated with Briggs Manufacturing Company to form Panacon Corporation. Celotex purchased Panacon and merged it into Celotex. The jury ruled that Pickett was entitled to $500,000 in compensatory damages, and further ruled that Philip Carey's conduct warranted punitive damages in the amount of $100,000. Should Celotex be held liable to Pickett for the compensatory damages? For the punitive damages?

46

Securities Regulation

The Securities Act of 1933
The Securities Act of 1934

The Foreign Corrupt Practices Act of 1977
State Securities Laws

I n Chapter 43 two types of securities (stocks and bonds) were described and their roles in raising capital for corporate financing were analyzed. The importance of securities to our society cannot be overemphasized. Not only are they a means of raising capital for corporate expansion, but they also serve as instruments by which individual citizens accumulate wealth through interest received on bonds and dividends paid on stocks. This wealth is often passed on to heirs or contributed to nonprofit organizations such as universities to be used for student scholarship funds and faculty research. Additionally, securities are an integral part of the private sector of our economy with its emphasis on individual decision making in the marketplace.

Individual investors, by themselves or through their pension and mutual funds, determine which segments of the economy and which industries within segments will grow. For example, if investors believe that solar power rather than nuclear power will be the energy source of the future, they will move their capital in that direction, stimulating the growth of the solar industry. Further, security holders are the owners of corporations. Through their election of boards of directors they determine which officers will govern and what direction the corporations will take. For example, stockholders through derivative suits may force officers and directors to personally return to the corporation funds illegally spent or wasted. When over 400 corporations in the

mid–1970s confessed to the Securities and Exchange Commission that they had made questionable payments overseas and illegal political contributions in this country, many stockholder derivative suits were filed.

This chapter discusses the role of government in regulating securities. Initially the Securities Act of 1933 (1933 Act) is examined. It sets forth rules governing the *issuance* of securities and their registration. While the 1933 Act prescribes requirements for registration, it does not seek to evaluate the worth of a particular stock or bond offering made to the investing public. Its primary purpose is to force publicly held corporations to disclose all material information to potential investors so the latter can make prudent judgments on whether or not to invest. Second, the chapter examines the 1934 Securities Exchange Act (Exchange Act). This act sets forth rules governing the *trading* in securities once issued. With the Exchange Act, Congress established the Securities and Exchange Commission (SEC) to protect the securities market from fraudulent conduct and to ensure full disclosure for investors trading in securities (see Figure 46-1). The 1933 Act and the Exchange Act are often referred to as the "Securities Acts." While they are the most significant federal legislation regulating securities, Congress has passed additional specialized security statutes. This chapter concludes with an analysis of the role of state legislation in regulating securities issued and traded in intrastate commerce.

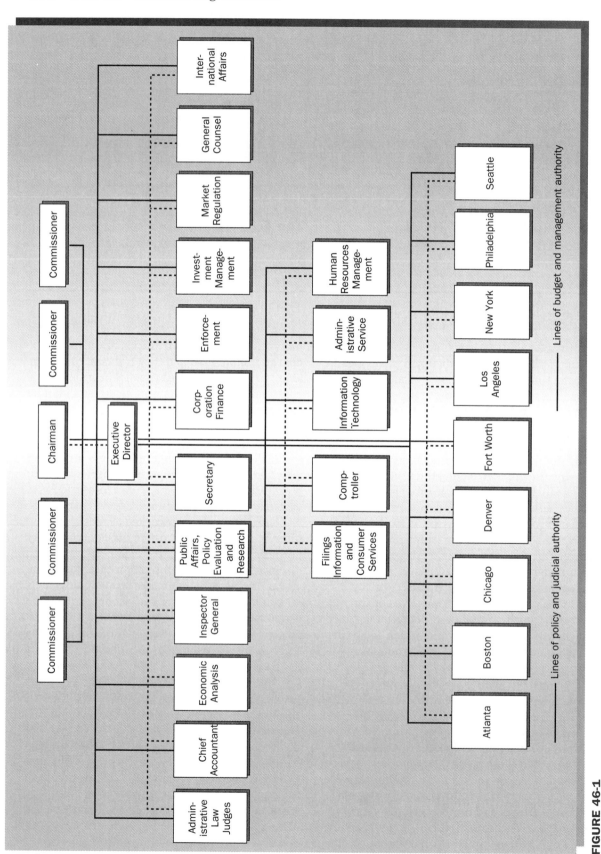

FIGURE 46-1

Securities and Exchange Commission

Source: U.S. Government Manual, 1992–1993 (Washington, D.C.: U.S. Government Printing Office).

The Securities Act of 1933

Definition of a Security

Section 2(1) of the 1933 Act defines a **security** as

> any note, stock, treasury stock, bond, debenture, evidence of indebtedness, certificate of interest or participation in any profit-sharing agreement, collateral-trust certificate, preorganization certificate or subscription, transferable share, investment contract, voting-trust certificate, certificate of deposit for a security, fractional undivided interest in oil, gas, or other mineral rights, or, in general, any interest or instrument commonly known as a "security," or any certificate of interest or participation in, temporary or interim certificate for, receipt for, guarantee of, or warrant or right to subscribe to or purchase, any of the foregoing.

The interpretation of this definition has been left to the SEC, through its rule-making power and advisory releases, as well as to the courts in individual decisions. In a landmark 1946 case, *SEC v. W. J. Howey Co.*, the U.S. Supreme Court outlined a test that is presently used in determining whether a particular instrument or transaction can be termed a "security" and thus falls within the federal security statutes. The Court stated that:

1. A contract or scheme must exist in which a person invests money in a common enterprise.
2. The investors must have some expectation of profits.
3. The profits must be derived *solely* from the efforts of a promoter or third party but not the investors themselves.

The third element in this test has been the focus of further court concern. It has been interpreted to mean that notes formalizing a debt incurred in a business or shares of stock entitling a purchaser to lease an apartment in a state-subsidized nonprofit housing cooperative are *not* securities. More recently the courts have modified their interpretation of the words "solely from the efforts of those other than investors." This is particularly true when the efforts made by noninvestors are the significant ones. The following case involving a fraudulent pyramid sales scheme illustrates this trend.

SEC v. GLENN W. TURNER ENTERPRISES

U.S. Court of Appeals, Ninth Circuit
474 F .2d 476 (1973)

BACKGROUND: This is an action by the Securities and Exchange Commission (plaintiff) to enjoin Glenn W. Turner (defendant) from violating the securities law by selling securities that were not registered. Dare To Be Great (Dare) was a subsidiary of Glenn W. Turner Enterprises, Inc. It offered courses in self-motivation that were entitled Adventures I, II, III. The initial course (Adventure I) included a portable tape recorder, twelve tape-recorded lessons, and some printed material. The purchaser also was entitled to attend a twelve-to-sixteen-hour series of group meetings. The initial cost was $300. For Adventure II, which included more tapes and an additional eighty hours of meetings, the purchaser paid $700. If he or she paid $2,000 more, Adventure III was made available with more tape recordings, more group sessions, and a notebook called "The Fun of Selling." The purchaser of Adventure III could also become an "independent sales trainee" for the purpose of selling Adventures I, II, and III. For an additional $5,000, he or she also received Adventure IV and the right to sell Adventure IV. The purchaser also had the option of selling a $1,000-plan that was similar to Adventure II. The SEC claimed that all these plans were "securities" within the meaning of the 1933 and 1934 Securities Acts. The federal district court decided in favor of the SEC. Defendant, Turner Enterprises, Inc. appealed.

Duniway, Justice

The trial court's findings, which are fully supported by the record, demonstrate that Turner Enterprises' scheme is a gigantic and successful fraud. The question presented is whether the "Adventures" or "Plans" enjoined are "securities" within the meaning of the federal securities laws.

It is apparent from the record that what is sold is not of the usual "business motivation" type of courses. Rather, the purchaser is really buying the possibility of deriving money from the sale of the plans by Dare to individuals whom the purchaser has brought to Dare. The promotional aspects of the Plans, such as seminars, films, and records, are aimed at interesting others in the Plans. Their value for any other purpose is, to put it mildly, minimal.

Once an individual has purchased a Plan, he turns his efforts toward bringing others into the organization, for which he will receive a part of what they pay. His task is to bring prospective purchasers to "Adventure Meetings."

These meetings are like an old-time revival meeting, but directed toward the joys of making easy money rather than salvation. Their purpose is to convince prospective purchasers, or "prospects," that Dare is a sure route to great riches. Films are shown, usually involving the "rags-to-riches" story of Dare founder, Glenn W. Turner. The goal of all this is to persuade the prospect to purchase a plan, especially Adventure IV, so that he may become a "salesman," and thus grow wealthy as part of the Dare organization. It is intimated that as Glenn W. Turner Enterprises, Inc., expands, high positions in the organization, as well as lucrative opportunities to purchase stock, will be available. After the meeting, pressure is applied to the prospect by Dare people, in an effort to induce him to purchase one of the Adventures or the Plan. In *SEC v. W. J. Howey Co.,* the Supreme Court set out its by now familiar definition of an investment contract: "The test is whether the scheme involves an investment of money in a common enterprise with profits to come solely from the efforts of others."

In *Howey* the Court held that a land sales contract for units of a citrus grove, together with a service contract for cultivating and marketing the crops, was an investment contract and hence a security. The Court held that what was in essence being offered was "an opportunity to contribute money and to share in the profits of a large citrus-fruit enterprise managed and partly owned by respondents." The purchasers had no intention themselves of either occupying the land or developing it; they were attracted only "by the prospects of a return on their investment." It was clear that the profits were to come "solely" from the efforts of others.

For purposes of the present case, the sticking point in the *Howey* definition is the word "solely," a qualification which of course exactly fitted the circumstances in *Howey*. All the other elements of the *Howey* test have been met here. There is an investment of money, a common enterprise, and the expectation of profits to come from the efforts of others. Here, however, the investor, or purchaser, must himself exert some efforts if he is to realize a return on his initial cash outlay. He must find prospects and persuade them to attend Dare Adventure Meetings, and at least some of them must then purchase a plan if he is to realize that return. Thus it can be said that the returns or profits are not coming "solely" from the efforts of others.

We hold, however, that in light of the remedial nature of the legislation, the statutory policy of affording broad protection to the public, and the Supreme Court's admonitions that the definition of securities should be a flexible one, the word "solely" should not be read as a strict or literal limitation on the definition of an investment contract, but rather must be construed realistically, so as to include within the definition those schemes which involve in substance, if not form, securities. Within this context, we hold that Adventures III and IV and the $1,000 Plan are investment contracts within the meaning of the 1933 and 1934 Acts.

DECISION: Affirmed. The Court of Appeals ruled in favor of the SEC.

Securities Markets

Securities markets are not easily defined because, unlike goods (for example, clothes) that are manufactured, distributed, and consumed by the public, securities as defined earlier are not consumed directly by the purchaser/investor. Securities become a form of currency in which an initial investor may trade for other securities in what are known as "securities markets." These may have a physical location, such as the New York Stock Exchange (NYSE) with its trading floor, or none, such as the over-the-counter (OTC) market. There is a marked contrast to their operations. The NYSE acts in a very formal manner, determining who will be allowed to trade on the exchange (who has a "seat") and the function of each member. Until 1975 it prescribed the commissions to be charged.

In a NYSE transaction a buyer or seller goes to an investment firm, which acts as a **broker**—a party that buys or sells a security on behalf of another party. Sometimes, an investment firm sells securities to a client from its own inventory or buys securities from a client to hold in its own inventory. When an investment firm buys or sells securities in this manner for its own account, it is acting as a **dealer**. Getting back to our typical NYSE transaction, the broker transmits the customer's order to the exchange floor, where only certain parties are authorized to buy or sell the particular security as dealers. These exchange-floor dealers are known as **specialists**. The broker's firm charges the customer a commission.

In contrast, the OTC market has no physical facilities and no specialists. Most work is done by a computer network or phone, and anyone can act as a dealer. If a customer orders a particular stock on the OTC market and the firm is not a dealer in the stock, it will purchase it as a broker from another dealer, making a market in the stock.

With satellite communication and data transmission networks, some have argued that there is no longer a need for physical facilities like the NYSE. In effect they argue that computerized national and international marketing systems for securities will soon be in place and that stock exchanges will be outmoded.

Registration of Securities

Before discussing the registration process, certain players should be defined. The **issuer** is the corporation that issues the securities. The securities are generally sold to the public through the efforts of an investment banking firm acting as an *underwriter*. An **underwriter** generally sells the securities to the public in one of two ways: (1) by purchasing the securities outright from the issuer and then selling them to the public; or (2) by undertaking to use its best efforts to sell the securities, without guaranteeing that the securities will be sold. The underwriter generally sells the securities to the public through a network of dealers.

The 1933 Act generally forbids a corporation from offering or selling any security unless the security has been registered with the SEC. Certain securities and certain transactions are exempt from registration; these exemptions are discussed in the sections that follow.

The issuer starts the registration process by filing a *registration statement* with the SEC. The **registration statement** is a document that includes material information required by the SEC regarding the securities and the company. Such information generally includes certified financial statements, a summary of the corporation's business, the background and qualifications of the corporation's management, the corporation's business prospects and other relevant material. The registration statement must be signed by the issuer, a majority of its board of directors, its principal executive officer, its chief financial officer, and its principal accounting officer. As discussed later in the chapter, all these parties may incur liability for misstatements contained in the registration statement.

The purpose of the registration statement is to provide public disclosure of material information to potential investors so they will have an adequate basis for determining whether to invest in an issuer's security offering. The SEC does not evaluate the merit or worth of the securities registered and to be issued. The material information of the registration statement is summarized in a **prospectus**, a copy of which must be delivered to each buyer.

The registration process is separated into three stages: (1) the *prefiling period*, which lasts until the registration statement is filed; (2) the *waiting period*, which runs from the time the registration statement is filed until the time the registration becomes effective; and (3) the *posteffective period*, which takes effect as soon as the registration becomes effective.

Securities may not be offered or sold during the prefiling period. The most important of the three stages is the waiting period, during which the SEC examines the registration statement. If the SEC takes no action, registration automatically becomes effective 20 days after a registration statement has been filed. However, the SEC has authority to request additional information or to issue a *refusal order*—that is, an order preventing the registration from becoming effective—if the registration statement contains serious deficiencies. Usually a letter of comment (a *deficiency letter*) by the SEC staff is sufficient to correct deficiencies.

Oral offers by underwriters to dealers and the public are permitted during the waiting period, but written offers and sales are forbidden. During the waiting period the SEC allows notices of potential offerings by the issuer to appear in newspapers as long as such notices clearly specify that they are not offers to sell securities.

Although the waiting period can last 20 days, it is typical for the SEC to accelerate the effective date of the registration. An issuer will generally request that the effective date be accelerated as soon as it is notified that the registration statement has been approved or that the registration statement will not be thoroughly reviewed. (The SEC completely reviews the registration statements of all first-time issuers, but does not thoroughly examine most registration statements filed by other issuers.)

Since securities markets can fluctuate significantly from day to day, it is important to maintain flexibility in setting the price of securities. It would be very risky, for example, for an issuer to

---

CONCEPT SUMMARY
The Securities Registration Process

1. **Prefiling Period: Prior to Filing Registration Statement with SEC**
   - Securities may not be offered or sold.

2. **Waiting Period: From Time Registration Statement Is Filed with SEC until Time Registration Becomes Effective**
   - Oral offers to sell are permitted, but sales may not be finalized.
   - Written offers to sell are not permitted.
   - Registration becomes effective if SEC takes no action within 20 days.
   - SEC may request additional information or may refuse registration outright.
   - Notice of potential offering may appear in newspaper, so long as it is made clear that such notice is not an offer to sell securities.
   - Issuer may request that effective date be accelerated to before the twentieth day if SEC indicates that registration statement is satisfactory or if SEC declines to perform thorough review of registration statement
   - Issuer (on advice of underwriter) typically sets price of securities by filing a last-minute "pricing amendment."

3. **Posteffective period: From Time Registration Becomes Effective**
   - Securities may be offered for sale, either orally or in writing.
   - Sales may be finalized.
   - Seller must deliver prospectus to buyer on or before time that written confirmation of sale is delivered to buyer.

set a price for securities upon filing the registration statement, since market conditions might change drastically by the time the securities can actually be sold. For this reason, the SEC allows the price of the securities to be set in a pricing amendment to the registration statement. The pricing amendment is generally filed just before the effective date, together with a request to accelerate the approval of the pricing amendment to the time that the registration statement is to otherwise become effective.

As soon as the registration becomes effective, the securities may be offered orally or in writing and may be sold.

In an attempt to cut red tape and help issuers raise capital at opportune moments, the SEC allows certain large, publicly traded corporations to avail themselves of a procedure known as *shelf registration*. Under **shelf registration**, the issuer files a single registration statement designating the amount of bonds and stocks it wants to put on the "shelf" for a 2-year period. This statement covers all potential sales of the designated securities, so the issuer does not have to publish a new, detailed prospectus each time it wants to raise capital. It can simply refer investors to data published in its annual and quarterly reports and enter the market with its "shelf securities" at an appropriate time.

Exempted Securities

Section 3 of the 1933 Act, and regulations implementing it, exempt from the registration provision certain types of securities. It should be noted that the Section 3 securities discussed here are *not* exempted from the antifraud provisions of either the 1933 or 1934 Securities Acts.

Section 3(a) exempts from registration commercial paper such as drafts, notes, and bankers' acceptance provided they arise out of current transactions, have maturity dates of not more than 9 months, and are not advertised for sale to the public.

Section 3(b) authorizes the SEC to exempt relatively small offerings of securities that do not exceed $5 million. Also, Section 3(b) exempts small public offerings of securities that do not exceed $1.5 million over a 12-month period. The issuing company must file a notification and offering circular with a regional SEC office 10 days before each proposed offering of securities. The SEC

may follow with some informal comments similar to the regular registration process.

Section 3(b) also provides an exemption for a public offering of "any security which is part of an issue sold only *within the border of a single state* and to residents of that state." The issuer must be a resident or a corporation incorporated or doing business in that state. The courts and the SEC under Rule 147 have emphasized that *all* purchasers must be residents of the state. If one is not, the securities offering will not be exempted. Additionally, Rule 147 requires that 80 percent of the gross revenues of the issuer must come from operations within the state; 80 percent of its assets must be within the state; and 80 percent of the proceeds of the securities must be used within the state.

Certain other securities are also exempt from registration by virtue of Section 3 of the 1933 Act and SEC interpretations of that section—for example, securities issued by the U.S. government, nonprofit organizations, and domestic banks, as well as securities regulated by agencies other than the SEC. Securities are exempted if they are issued pursuant to mergers or reorganizations in which no cash is involved and the issuer offers securities solely in exchange for other securities.

Exempted Transactions

Section 4(1) of the 1933 Act exempts transactions by persons other than an issuer, underwriter, or dealer. Sections 4(3) and 4(4) allow qualified exemptions for dealers and brokers. In reality, underwriters are the only ones not exempted. Rule 144 promulgated by the SEC sets forth the conditions that determine when a person is not an underwriter and not involved in selling restricted securities and is therefore exempt.

Section 4(2) involves transactions that are exempt because they do *not* involve any public offering of securities. Approximately 25 percent of all corporate securities fall under this exemption. An offering that meets this exemption is known as a **private placement**. There are several factors that are considered in determining whether a transaction qualifies as a private placement. These factors are set forth in Regulation D, an SEC regulation comprising Rules 501 through 506, as summarized below.

Rule 501 defines the terms used in Regulation D. Of most significance is the definition of "accredited investors," which are generally investors that do not need the protection afforded by the 1933 Act registration process. They include banks; insurance companies; investment companies; employee benefit plans; business development companies; charitable or educational institutions with assets of more than $5 million; individuals with a net worth of over $1 million, or with an annual income of over $200,000 for 3 years; or a person who buys $150,000 of securities at one time.

Under Rule 504 an issuer can sell an aggregate of up to $500,000 of securities in any 12-month period to accredited or nonaccredited purchasers with no requirement for the furnishing of any information to such purchasers. This exemption is available to any issuer except an investment company or an issuer disqualified by Rule 252 from using Regulation A.

Under Rule 505 an issuer can sell up to $5 million of securities in a 12-month period to any number of accredited investors and up to thirty-five other nonaccredited investors. However, the $5 million will be reduced by amounts sold and exempted under other provisions. Investment companies are not eligible for this exemption.

Rule 506 seeks to clarify Section 4(2) dealing with the private placement exemptions. It allows an issuer to sell an unlimited amount of securities to any number of accredited investors and up to thirty-five nonaccredited investors. However, the rule states that an issuer must believe, prior to sale, that each nonaccredited investor or "purchaser representative" (as defined by Rule 501) has enough knowledge or experience in business or financial matters to evaluate the merits and risks of the investment.

Rule 502 sets forth certain conditions and information that must be given nonaccredited investors when purchasing pursuant to Rules 505 and 504.

Integration

In cases in which companies may seek to qualify for a small business exemption of dividing a large issuance of securities into smaller units, the SEC has adopted *integration* and *aggregation* rules. These rules prohibit companies from making two or more exempt offerings of similar shares at approximately the same times. The SEC will integrate and aggregate otherwise exempt offerings if:

1. The offerings are part of a unitary plan of financing by an issuing company
2. The offerings concern the same class of securities
3. The offerings are made for the same general purpose, and about the same level of pricing

Additionally, the SEC has adopted a rule which in effect states that any offering made 6 months before or 6 months after an offering will not be integrated.

Liability under the 1933 Act

The 1933 Act seeks to ensure full disclosure for potential investors. The registration process, as noted previously, is the major tool for carrying out this statutory policy. Congress provided civil liability for the failure of issuing corporations to meet the provisions of the 1933 Act in Sections 11, 12, and 17. It should be noted that both private and public remedies are provided.

Section 11 provides for a statutory cause of action allowing purchasers who have relied on material misstatements or incorrect data in the registration statement to sue and obtain civil damages. Since Section 11 was enacted, case law has pointed to certain individuals as most likely to be held liable. For example, losses have been recouped from

1. The issuer
2. All who signed the registration statement
3. Lawyers, engineers, and accountants who participated in the preparation of the registration statement
4. Every director
5. Every underwriter

The issuing corporation and all those involved in the preparation of a registration statement should therefore exercise great care. It should be noted that all but the issuer are allowed a **due diligence defense**, which allows an individual defendant to escape liability by showing that he or she had reasonable grounds to believe that there were no misstatements or material omissions. In the landmark 1968 case *Escott v. Bar Chris Corp.*, the court treated each of the defendants' pleas of due diligence individually, considering their relationship to the issuing corporation and their areas of expertise. Based on *Bar Chris*, an "inside" director of a corporation who is also a lawyer will have greater difficulty establishing a due diligence defense than will an outside director, especially if he or she is a nonlawyer.

Section 12(1) imposes liability for the sale of an unregistered security that fails to meet any of the Section 3 or 4 exemptions. The sale of securities prior to the filing of a registration statement or before the effective date subjects the issuer to liability from the person who purchased the securities. The standard for recovery set out by the courts is the purchase price paid for the security,

plus interest, less income received. The purchaser must return the security to the seller.

Section 17 imposes liability on all those who aid and abet any fraud in connection with the offer or sale of securities. It is a general fraud section, bolstered by Section 24, which imposes criminal sanctions where it can be shown that there were any *willful* violations of any provision of the 1933 Act or rules and regulations made by the SEC pursuant to that statute. An individual convicted can be imprisoned for up to 5 years and/or fined up to $10,000. The reach of Section 17 is illustrated in the case that follows.

UNITED STATES V. NAFTALIN

U.S. Supreme Court
441 U.S. 768 (1979)

BACKGROUND: Naftalin (defendant) was president of a registered broker-dealer firm. In July and August 1969, he selected stocks that had peaked in price and were entering declines. He placed five broker orders to sell shares of these stocks, although he did not own the shares he pretended to sell. Gambling that the price of securities would decline before he was requested to deliver them to the broker, he planned to make offsetting purchases through other brokers at lower prices. His profit would be the difference between the price at which he sold and the price at which he covered. Naftalin was aware, however, that had the brokers who executed his sell orders known that he did not own the securities, they would either not have accepted the orders or would have required a margin deposit. He therefore falsely represented that he owned the shares he directed them to sell.

Unfortunately for Naftalin, the market prices of the securities he "sold" did not fall prior to the delivery date but instead rose sharply. Naftalin was unable to make covering purchases and never delivered the promised securities. Consequently, the five brokers were unable to deliver the stock they had "sold" to investors and were forced to borrow stock to keep their delivery promises. Then, in order to return the borrowed stock, the brokers had to purchase replacement shares in the open market at the now-higher prices. The five brokers suffered substantial losses, although the persons to whom the stocks were sold suffered no losses.

The brokers reported the scheme to the SEC, which in turn reported it to the Department of Justice. The Justice Department instituted criminal proceedings against Naftalin for violating Section 17 of the Securities Act of 1933. Naftalin was found guilty, but the Court of Appeals reversed, citing that the act was designed to protect investors rather than brokers. The government appealed to the Supreme Court.

Brennan, Justice

Section 17 of the Securities Act of 1933 states: "It shall be unlawful for any person in the offer or sale of any security by the use of any means or instruments of transportation or communication in interstate commerce or by the use of the mails, directly or indirectly:

  (1) to employ any device, scheme, or artifice to defraud, or

> (2) to obtain money or property by means of any untrue statement of a material fact or any omission to state a material fact necessary in order to make the statements made in the light of the circumstances under which they were made not misleading, or
>
> (3) to engage in any transaction, practice or course of business which operates or would operate as a fraud or deceit upon the purchaser."

Naftalin claims he did commit fraud but the fraud was against the brokers, not the investors who purchased the securities. He claims brokers are not investors under the Act. Nothing in the Act supports this view. Subsection (1) makes it unlawful for any person in the offer or sale of any securities directly or indirectly to employ any device to defraud. This language does not require that the victim of the fraud be an investor—only that the fraud occur in an offer or sale.

An offer and sale occurred here. Naftalin placed orders to sell with the brokers, the brokers acted as his agent and executed the orders and the results were contracts of sale. The fraud can occur at any stage of the selling transaction. Section 17 of the Act applies not only to the issuance of new securities but to the subsequent resale of those securities. This section was intended to cover any fraudulent scheme in an offer or sale of securities, whether in the course of an initial distribution or in the course of ordinary market trading.

DECISION: Reversed. The U.S. Supreme Court ruled in favor of the United States.

The Securities Act of 1934

Purpose and Scope

As stated in the introduction to this chapter, the Securities Exchange Act of 1934 established the SEC to ensure fair trading practices for investors and others in the securities market. It sets forth rules governing the trading of securities, not initial offerings, that are governed by the 1933 Act.

Registration and Reporting Requirements

Section 12 of the Exchange Act requires all publicly held companies regulated by the SEC to register two classes of securities: debt and equity. This requirement pertains to all companies with assets of $1 million or more and a class of equity securities having at least 500 shareholders of record. Such securities must be registered or they will not be allowed to be traded on a national securities exchange. Registration of a class of securities under the Exchange Act should not be confused with the registration of an initial offering of nonexempt securities within a class under the 1933 Act. A company registering a class of securities under the Exchange Act will always have to meet the requirements of the 1933 Act when making an initial public offering that does not meet any of the exemptions noted previously in this chapter. The 1933 Act regulates the initial sale of securities, whereas the Exchange Act governs its trading on national exchanges.

Over the years since 1934 the SEC has promulgated rules and prescribed forms for registering classes or securities. Much of the information requested is similar to that required by the 1933 Act. The Exchange Act registration requirements supplement and extend the requirements of the 1933 Act.

The SEC through its rule-making power has also devised periodic refiling requirements for corporate registrants to ensure that the potential investor has continuing access to information about securities that are being traded on the exchanges. Annual reports (Form 10-K) and quarterly reports (Form 10-Q) have been updated to provide increasing amounts of information for potential investors. Additionally, current reports (Form 8-K) can be requested and must be filed by the registering company within fifteen days if the SEC perceives that a material event has taken place that a reasonably prudent investor should know about in order to make an investment decision. A significant change in a company's assets or a potential merger have been considered material events.

Section 18 of the Exchange Act makes a registering company liable for civil damages to anyone who buys or sells securities and relies on misleading statements contained in the registration statement or any of the reports noted earlier.

Proxy Solicitations

A *proxy solicitation* is a request for some shareholder's vote; a *proxy* is a writing whereby a holder of registered securities gives permission to another person to vote the stockholder's shares at a stockholders' meeting. In many cases inside management seeks proxies from its shareholders to defeat a particular issue that has been placed before the board by dissident shareholders. Proxies are also given by shareholders who will not be present for the purpose of electing new directors or preventing a takeover of a company. Since the proxy solicitation process often involves the future direction of the corporation, full disclosure is required by the Exchange Act and the SEC. Ten days prior to mailing a proxy statement to shareholders, the issuing company must file it with the SEC. The Commission often issues informal letters of comment requiring some changes before proxies are mailed. SEC rules require the solicitor of proxies to furnish shareholders with all material information concerning the matter being submitted to them for their vote. A form by which shareholders may indicate their agreement or disagreement must be provided as well. In the case of proxies solicited for the purpose of voting for directors, shareholders must be furnished an annual report.

Often shareholders will request that a certain proposal be placed on the agenda at an annual meeting. Under the Exchange Act and SEC rules, if timely notice is given by the shareholder(s), management must include such proposals in its proxy statement and allow shareholders to vote for or against it. If management opposes the proposal, it must include a statement in support of the shareholder's proposal, not to exceed 200 words, along with its statement of opposition. This shareholder prerogative has been used to oppose the making of napalm, to force companies to deal with forms of discrimination, and to deal with company-caused environmental problems. SEC rules allow management to exclude shareholder proposals for the following reasons:

1. The matter is moot.
2. The matter is not significantly related to the issuing company's business.
3. The matter relates to ordinary business operations.
4. The matter would violate state or federal law if included in a proxy proposal passed by the board of directors.

Any issuing company that supplies a proxy statement that is misleading to its shareholders may be held civilly liable under Section 18 of the Exchange Act to any person who relies on such statements in the buying or selling of registered securities. The SEC is authorized to force compliance with proxy rules by invoking injunctive relief. Additionally the U.S. Supreme Court had held that private citizens have a right of action for damages and other relief under Section 14 in light of Section 27, which grants federal district courts jurisdiction over actions "to enforce any liability or duty rendered by the Exchange Act."

Tender Offers

A **tender offer** is an offer by an individual or a corporation to the shareholder of another corporation to purchase a number of shares at a specified price. Tender offers are sometimes referred to as "takeover bids" and are usually communicated through newspaper advertising.

In the 1960s, following a large number of conglomerate mergers, many of which involved bitter struggles between acquiring and targeted corporations, Congress became concerned with charges of fraud, insider trading, and manipulation of markets. As a result, it passed the Williams Act, which amended the Exchange Act by adding provisions giving the SEC authority over tender offers, particularly those involving cash. The three most important provisions governing tender offers are set out in Sections 13(d), 14(d), and 14(e).

Under Section 13(d) any person or group that acquires more than 5 percent of a class of securities registered under the Exchange Act is required to file a statement with the SEC and the issuing company within 10 days. It must include:

1. The person or group background and the number of share owners
2. Its purpose in acquiring the stock
3. The source of funds used to acquire the securities
4. Its plans for the targeted company
5. Any contracts or understandings with individuals or groups relevant to the targeted company

It should be noted that if there is a hostile tender offer or takeover bid, the targeted company must also file a statement in its attempt to defeat the takeover.

Section 14(d) sets forth procedural and substantive requirements that must be met in making a tender offer. For example, no tender offer that would result in the ownership of 5 percent or more of a class of securities may be made unless the offeror furnishes each offeree a statement concerning the information required by Section 13(d). Certain substantive requirements dealing with the term of the tender offer are also provided for, as well as such matters as the right of withdrawal of a tender offer, terms of its acceptance, and payment of consideration.

Section 14(e) makes it a criminal offense for any person to misstate or omit a material fact or to engage in fraudulent or deceptive practice in connection with a tender offer. Both civil action by shareholders who have relied on such statements and can show injury as well as SEC-initiated administrative proceedings can be brought. The following case interprets the meaning of Section 14(e).

SCHREIBER V. BURLINGTON NORTHERN, INC.
U.S. Supreme Court
472 U.S. 1 (1985)

BACKGROUND: Schreiber (petitioner) on behalf of herself and other shareholders of El Paso Gas Company sued Burlington Northern (respondent) claiming that the company violated Section 14(e) of the Securities Exchange Act of 1934. In December 1982 Burlington issued a hostile tender offer for El Paso Gas Company. Burlington did not accept the shares traded by a majority of shareholders of El Paso, but rather, rescinded the December tender offer and substituted a January offer for El Paso. The rescission of the first tender offer caused a lesser payment per share to shareholders who retendered following the January offer. The petitioners claim that Burlington's withdrawal of the December tender offer, and the substitution of the January offer, was a "manipulative" distortion of the market for El Paso Stock and a violation of 14(e). The respondent argued that "manipulative" acts under 14(e) require misrepresentation or nondisclosure. They argued that no such acts took place in this case, and moved for dismissal of the case on the basis of a failure to state a cause of action. The U.S. District Court granted the motion for dismissal. The Court of Appeals affirmed. Schreiber appealed.

Burger, Justice

We are asked in this case to interpret §14(e) of the Securities Exchange Act. The starting point is the language of the statute. Section 14(e) provides:

It shall be unlawful for any person to make any untrue statement of a material fact or omit to state any material fact necessary in order to make the statements made, in the light of the circumstances under which they are made, not misleading, or to engage in any fraudulent, deceptive or manipulative acts or practices, in connection with any tender offer or request or invitation for tenders, or any solicitation of security holders in opposition to or in favor of any such offer, request, or invitation. The Commission shall, for the purposes of this subsection, by rules and regulations define, and prescribe means reasonably designed to prevent, such acts and practices as are fraudulent, deceptive, or manipulative.

Our conclusion that "manipulative" acts under §14(e) require misrepresentation or nondisclosure is buttressed by the purpose and legislative history of the provision. Section 14(e) was originally added to the Securities Exchange Act as part of the Williams Act.

It is clear that Congress relied primarily on disclosure to implement the purpose of the Williams Act. Senator Williams, the Bill's Senate sponsor, stated in the debate:

> Today, the public shareholder in deciding whether to accept or reject a tender offer possesses limited information. No matter what he does, he acts without adequate knowledge to enable him to decide rationally what is the best course of action. This is precisely the dilemma which our securities laws are designed to prevent. 113 Cong. Rec. 24664 (1967) (Remarks of Sen. Williams).

The expressed legislative intent was to preserve a neutral setting in which the contenders could fully present their arguments. To implement this objective, the Williams Act added §§13(d), 13(e), 14(e), and 14(f) to the Securities Exchange Act. Some relate to disclosure; §§13(d), 14(d), and 14(f) all add specific registration and disclosure provisions. Others—§§13(e) and 14(d)—require or prohibit certain acts so that investors will possess additional time within which to take advantage of the disclosed information.

To adopt the reading of the term "manipulative" urged by petitioner would not only be unwarranted in light of the legislative purpose but would be at odds with it. Inviting judges to read the term "manipulative" with their own sense of what constitutes "unfair" or "artificial" conduct would inject uncertainty into the tender offer process. An essential piece of information—whether the court would deem the fully disclosed actions of one side or the other to be "manipulative"—would not be available until after the tender offer had closed. This uncertainty would directly contradict the expressed congressional desire to give investors full information.

Congress' consistent emphasis on disclosure persuades us that it intended takeover contests to be addressed to shareholders. In pursuit of this goal, Congress, consistent with the core mechanism of the Securities Exchange Act, created sweeping disclosure requirements and narrow substantive safeguards. The same Congress that placed such emphasis on shareholder choice would not at the same time have required judges to oversee tender offers for substantive fairness.

We hold that the term "manipulative" as used in §14(e) requires misrepresentation or nondisclosure. It connotes "conduct designed to deceive or defraud investors by controlling or artificially affecting the price of securities." Without misrepresentation of nondisclosure, §14(e) has not been violated.

Applying that definition to this case, we hold that the actions of respondents were not manipulative. The amended complaint fails to allege that the cancellation of the first tender offer was accompanied by any misrepresentation, nondisclosure or deception.

DECISION: The U.S. Supreme Court affirmed for Burlington Northern.

Short Swing Profits

Section 16(b) of the Exchange Act seeks to further the goal of full disclosure for potential investors by preventing certain insiders from realizing profits solely by virtue of their access to material information. It prevents directors, officers, and owners of 10 percent of the securities of an issuing corporation that has securities registered with the SEC or a national exchange from realizing profits on stocks by buying and selling within a 6-month period. Any such profits must be returned to the corporation. If the corporation fails to sue for recovery of profits, shareholders may file on behalf of the corporation. The SEC seeks to monitor insider short swing profits by requiring officers, directors, and 10 percent owners to file forms with the SEC within 10 days of a sale or purchase. It should be noted that major newspapers such as the *Wall Street Journal* also report such buying or selling by insiders.

Securities Fraud

Section 10(b) and Rule 10b–5   As stated in the introduction to this chapter, the Securities Act seeks to ensure full disclosure of material information for potential investors. Therefore, it is important that any form of fraudulent conduct that would distort the free flow of information to investors in the securities market be made unlawful.

Section 10(b) of the Exchange Act is referred to as a "catchall" provision to deal with securities fraud. It makes illegal the use of the mails or other facilities of interstate commerce to do the following:

> To use or employ, in connection with the purchase of sale of any security, any manipulative or deceptive device or contrivance

in contravention of such rules and regulations as the Commission may prescribe as necessary or appropriate in the public interest or for the protection of investors.

The case that follows concerns a famous scheme that involved a former reporter for the *Wall Street Journal*. It is not a typical case under Section 10(b) and Rule 10b-5. For one thing, the defendants did not have access to corporate "inside" information. The secret information that the defendants did possess, however, was just as valuable.

CARPENTER V. UNITED STATES
U.S. Supreme Court
484 U.S. 19 (1987)

BACKGROUND: A *Wall Street Journal* reporter and others were charged with violating securities laws as well as mail and wire fraud statutes. The activities that led to these charges are detailed below in the excerpt from the opinion. The defendants were convicted, and their convictions were, with a minor exception, upheld on appeal. The U.S. Supreme Court agreed to review the case.

White, Justice

In 1981, Winans became a reporter for the Wall Street Journal (the Journal) and in the summer of 1982 became one of the two writers of a daily column, "Heard on the Street." That column discussed selected stocks or groups of stocks, giving positive and negative information about those stocks and taking "a point of view with respect to investment in the stocks that it reviews." Winans regularly interviewed corporate executives to put together interesting perspectives on the stocks that would be highlighted in upcoming columns, but, at least for the columns at issue here, none contained corporate inside information or any "hold for release" information. Because of the "Heard" column's perceived quality and integrity, it had the potential of affecting the price of the stocks which it examined. The District Court concluded on the basis of testimony presented at trial that the "Heard" column "does have an impact on the market, difficult though it may be to quantify in any particular case."

The official policy and practice at the Journal was that prior to publication, the contents of the column were the Journal's confidential information. Despite the rule, with which Winans was familiar, he entered into a scheme in October 1983 with Peter Brant and petitioner Felis, both connected with the Kidder Peabody brokerage firm in New York City, to give them advance information as to the timing and contents of the "Heard" column. This permitted Brant and Felis and another conspirator, David Clark, a client of Brant, to buy or sell based on the probable impact of the column on the market. Profits were to be shared. The conspirators agreed that the scheme would not affect the journalistic purity of the "Heard" column, and the District Court did not find that the contents of any of the articles were altered to further the profit potential of petitioners' stocktrading scheme. Over a 4-month period, the brokers made prepublication trades on the basis of information given them by Winans about the contents of some 27 "Heard" columns. The net profits from these trades were about $690,000.

In November 1983, correlations between the "Heard" articles and trading in the Clark and Felis accounts were noted at Kidder Peabody and inquiries began. Brant and Felis denied knowing anyone at the Journal and took steps to conceal the trades. Later, the Securities and Exchange Commission began an investigation. Questions were met by denials both by the brokers at Kidder Peabody and by Winans at the Journal. As the investigation progressed, the conspirators quarreled, and on March 29, 1984, Winans and Carpenter went to the SEC and revealed the entire scheme. This indictment and a bench trial followed. Brant, who had pleaded guilty under a plea agreement, was a witness for the Government.

The District Court found, and the Court of Appeals agreed, that Winans had knowingly breached a duty of confidentiality by misappropriating prepublication information regarding the timing and contents of the "Heard" column, information that had been gained in the course of his employment under the understanding that it would not be revealed in advance of publication and that if it were, he would report it to his employer. It was this appropriation of confidential information that underlay both the securities laws and mail and wire fraud counts. With respect to the § 10(b) charges, the courts below held that the deliberate breach of Winans' duty of confidentiality and concealment of the scheme was a fraud and deceit on the Journal. Although the victim of the fraud, the Journal, was not a buyer or seller of the stocks traded in or otherwise a market participant, the fraud was nevertheless considered to be "in connection with" a purchase or sale of securities within the meaning of the statute and the rule. The courts reasoned that the scheme's sole purpose was to buy and sell securities at a profit based on advance information of the column's contents. The courts below rejected petitioners' submission, which is one of the two questions presented here, that criminal liability could not be imposed on petitioners under Rule 10b-5 because "the newspaper is the only alleged victim of fraud and has no interest in the securities traded."

In affirming the mail and wire fraud convictions, the Court of Appeals ruled that Winans had fraudulently misappropriated "property" within the meaning of the mail and wire fraud statutes and that its revelation had harmed the Journal. It was held as well that the use of the mail and wire services had a sufficient nexus with the scheme to satisfy §§ 1341 and 1343. The petition for certiorari challenged these conclusions.

The Court is evenly divided with respect to the convictions under the securities laws and for that reason affirms the judgment below on those counts. For the reasons that follow, we also affirm the judgment with respect to the mail and wire fraud convictions. . . .

Both courts below expressly referred to the Journal's interest in the confidentiality of the contents and timing of the "Heard" column as a property right, and we agree with that conclusion. Confidential business information has long been recognized as property. The Journal had a property right in keeping confidential and making exclusive use, prior to publication, of the schedule and contents of the "Heard" column. As the Court has observed before:

> [N]ews matter, however little susceptible of ownership or dominion in the absolute
> sense, is stock in trade, to be gathered at the cost of enterprise, organization, skill,
> labor, and money, and to be distributed and sold to those who will pay money for it, as
> for any other merchandise. *International News Service v. Associated Press* (1918).

Petitioners' arguments that they did not interfere with the Journal's use of the information or did not publicize it and deprive the Journal of the first public use of it, miss the point. The confidential information was generated from the business, and the business had a right to decide how to use it prior to disclosing it to the public. Petitioners cannot successfully contend based on *Associated Press* that a scheme to defraud requires a monetary loss, such as giving the information to a competitor; it is sufficient that the Journal has been deprived of its right to exclusive use of the information, for exclusivity is an important aspect of confidential business information and most private property for that matter.

DECISION: The Supreme Court affirmed the defendants' convictions.

Defensive Strategies

The **business judgment rule** is based principally on the fifty states' case law and the Revised Model Business Corporations Act. It allows management in targeted companies wide latitude, as long as they act in good faith in the best interests of the shareholders, do not waste the corporate assets, or enter into conflict of interest situations. Defensive tactics to prevent hostile takeovers include (1) awarding large compensation packages ("golden parachutes") to target company management when there is a rumored takeover, (2) issuing new classes of securities before or during a takeover battle that require a tender offerer to pay much more than the market rate ("poison pill"), (3) buying out a "hostile" shareholder at a price far above the current market price of the target company's stock in exchange for the hostile shareholders' agreement not to buy more shares for a long time ("greenmail").

Other defensive strategies include (1) writing supermajority requirements into the bylaws and corporation articles for merger approval ("porcupine provisions"), (2) issuing treasury shares (stock repurchased by the issuing corporation) to friendly parties, (3) moving to states with strong antitakeover ("shark repellent") laws, (4) bankrupting a company ("scorched earth" policy), and (5) attempting to find a friendly acquiror ("white knight") to outbid the would-be hostile acquiror of a target company. This statutory provision's broad language encompasses all possible forms of fraud that the Commission may proscribe using its rule-making powers. In 1942 the Commission set forth Rule 10b-5, which has been the foundation for most SEC and private enforcement action dealing with fraudulent conduct. It states:

> It shall be unlawful for any person, directly or indirectly, by the use of any means or instrumentality of interstate commerce, or of the mails, or of any facility of any national securities exchange,
>
> (1) to employ any device, scheme, or artifice to defraud,
>
> (2) to make any untrue statement of a material fact necessary in order to make the statements made, in the light of circumstances under which they were made, not misleading, or
>
> (3) to engage in any act, practice, or course of business which operates or would operate as a fraud or deceit upon any person, in connection with the purchase or sale of any security.

The reader should be aware that the rule applies to *any* purchase or sale by *any* person of *any* securities in interstate commerce. Whether or not a company is registered under the Exchange Act is unimportant. Thus all the exempted securities and transactions previously set forth in this chapter are *not* exempted from Rule 10b-5. Privately held corporations, as well as those publicly held, can be held liable under the rule. It should be noted that the conduct of the purchaser as well as the seller is covered by Rule 10b-5. Further, there must be a misrepresentation or deceptive omission of a material fact with intent shown.

The rule is basically an antifraud provision designed to prohibit manipulative or deceptive practices. Both the SEC and private parties alleged to have been injured may bring actions because no specific standards for determining fraud under Rule 10b-5 were set out by the Commission. It was left to the federal courts to develop criteria. In the 1960s and early 1970s federal district and appellate courts developed a broad interpretation of fraud under 10b-5, imposing liability for negligent conduct as well as for intended or deliberate acts. With a change in the makeup of the Supreme Court in the mid-1970s, private and SEC actions alleging fraud were held to a narrower *intent* (scienter) standard, with some federal courts imposing liability for knowing or reckless behavior. An illustration of the present standard of liability for fraud under Rule 10b-5 is provided by the following case. This case has special importance for the accounting profession.

ERNST & ERNST V. HOCHFELDER

U.S. Supreme Court
425 U.S. 185 (1976)

BACKGROUND: Ernst & Ernst (defendant-appellant) was a Big Eight accounting firm retained by First Securities Company (First Securities), a small brokerage firm, to audit its books and records, to prepare annual reports for SEC filing, and to respond to questionnaires from the Midwest Stock Exchange.

Plaintiff-respondents were customers of First Securities who invested in a fraudulent securities scheme perpetrated by Leston B. Nay, president of the firm and owner of 92 percent of its stock. Nay induced the respondents to invest funds in "escrow" accounts that he represented would yield a high rate of return. Respondents did so from 1942 through 1966, with the majority of the transactions occurring in the 1950s. In fact, there were no escrow accounts, since Nay converted respondents' funds to his own use immediately upon receipt. These transactions were not in the customary form of dealings between First Securities and its customers. The respondents drew their personal checks payable to Nay or a designated bank for his account. No such escrow accounts were reflected on the books and records of First Securities, and none was shown on its periodic accounting to respondents in connection with their other investments. Nor were they included in First Securities' filings with the SEC or the Exchange.

The fraud came to light in 1968 when Nay committed suicide, leaving a note that described First Securities as bankrupt and the escrow accounts as "spurious." Respondents subsequently filed this action for damages against Ernst & Ernst in the U.S. District Court for the Northern District of Illinois under Section 10(b) of the 1934 Act. The complaint charged that Nay's escrow scheme violated Section 10(b) and Commission Rule 10b-5, and that Ernst & Ernst had "aided and abetted" Nay's violations by its "failure" to conduct proper audits of First Securities. As revealed through discovery, respondents' cause of action rested on a theory of negligent nonfeasance. The premise was that Ernst & Ernst had failed to utilize "appropriate auditing procedures" in its audits of First Securities, thereby failing to discover internal practices of the firm said to prevent an effective audit. The practice principally referred to was Nay's rule that only he could open mail addressed to him at First Securities or addressed to First Securities to his attention, even if it arrived in his absence. Respondents contended that if Ernst & Ernst had conducted a proper audit, it would have discovered this "mail rule." The existence of the rule then would have been disclosed in reports to the Exchange and to the SEC by Ernst & Ernst as an irregular procedure that prevented an effective audit. This would have led to an investigation of Nay that would have revealed the fraudulent scheme. Respondents specifically disclaimed the existence of fraud or intentional misconduct on the part of Ernst & Ernst.

The District Court granted Ernst & Ernst's motion for summary judgment and dismissed the action. The Court of Appeals for the Seventh Circuit reversed and remanded, holding that one who breaches a duty of inquiry and disclosure owed another is liable in damages for aiding and abetting a third party's violation of Rule 10b-5 if the fraud would have been discovered or prevented but for the breach. The court stated in its reasoning that Ernst & Ernst had both a common law and statutory duty of inquiry into the adequacy of First Securities' internal control system by virtue of its contractual duties to audit and prepare filings with the SEC. The U.S. Supreme Court agreed to review the case.

Powell, Justice

Although the extensive legislative history of the 1934 Act is bereft of any explicit explanation of Congress' intent, we think the relevant portions of that history support our conclusion that § 10(b) was addressed to practices that involve some element of scienter and cannot be read to impose liability for negligent conduct alone.

The section was described rightly as a "catch all" clause to enable the Commission "to deal with new manipulative (or cunning) devices." It is difficult to believe that any lawyer, legislative draftsman, or legislator would use these words if the intent was to create liability for merely negligent acts or omissions. Neither the legislative history nor the briefs supporting respondents identify any usage or authority for construing "manipulative (or cunning) devices" to include negligence.

We have addressed to this point, primarily the language and history of §10(b). The Commission contends, however, that subsections (b) and (c) of Rule 10b-5 are cast in language which—if standing alone—could encompass *both intentional* and *negligent* behavior. These subsections respectively provide that it is unlawful "[t]o make any untrue statement of a material fact or to omit to state a material fact necessary in order to make the statements made, in the light of the circumstances under which they were made, not misleading . . ." and "[t]o engage in any act, practice, or course of business which operates or would operate as a fraud or deceit upon any person. . . ." Viewed in isolation the language of subsection (b), and arguably that of subsection (c), could be read as proscribing, respectively, any type of material misstatement or omission, and any course of conduct, that has the effect of defrauding investors, whether the wrongdoing was intentional or not.

We note first that such a reading cannot be harmonized with the administrative history of the Rule, a history making clear that when the Commission adopted the Rule, it was intended to apply only to activities that involved scienter. More importantly, Rule 10b-5 was adopted pursuant to authority granted the Commission under §10(b). The rule-making power granted to an administrative agency charged with the administration of a federal statute is not the power to make law. Rather, it is "'the power to adopt regulations to carry into effect the will of Congress as expressed by the statute.'" Thus, despite the broad view of the Rule advanced by the Commission in this case, its scope cannot exceed the power granted the Commission by Congress under §10(b).For the reasons stated above, we think the Commission's original interpretation of Rule 10b-5 was compelled by the language and history of §10(b) and related sections of the Acts. When a statute speaks so specifically in terms of manipulation and deception, and of implementing devices and contrivances—the commonly understood terminology of intentional wrongdoing—and when its history reflects no more expansive intent, we are quite unwilling to extend the scope of the statute to negligent conduct.

DECISION: Reversed. The U.S. Supreme Court ruled in favor of Ernst & Ernst.

Over the past 40 years Rule 10b-5 has been most frequently applied to three forms of conduct: (1) insider trading, (2) corporate misstatements, (3) corporate mismanagement.

Insider Trading   Charges of *insider trading* have led to the convictions of some of the most prominent players in the securities business—Michael Milken, Ivan Boesky, Dennis Levine and others. **Insider trading** may be defined as the buying or selling of securities of a corporation by individuals who have access to nonpublic material information and have a fiduciary obligation to shareholders and potential investors. In most cases the courts have also required a showing that the insider or a tippee to whom the nonpublic material information was given benefited from trading on that information. The SEC and courts originally defined "insiders" as corporate officers, directors, and major stockholders. Over the years Rule 10b-5 has been interpreted to include anyone who receives nonpublic material information from a corporate source. Courts have found insider trading by partners in a brokerage firm, broker-dealers acting as underwriters, and even an employee of a financial printing firm who worked on documents that involved a contemplated tender offer (see Figure 46-2).

FIGURE 46-2

Insider Traders

Wall Street's Army of Insider Traders

THE INSIDERS
As part of their jobs, hundreds of people help to arrange mergers and buybacks that will push up stock prices once the deals become public. The process often begins in the executive suite, when chairmen talk merger and bring in their top associates.

Vice Chairmen   General Counsel   Board of Directors

INVESTMENT BANKS Any company involved in a merger hires a Wall Street bank, with
its numerous specialists.

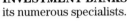  

Financial Experts   Research Analysts   Merger and Aquisition Teams

THE SUPPORTING CAST

Law Firms   Public Relations Advisers   Banks, Bond Dealers, Lenders

ON THE EDGE
Many others get insider information from the key players. These are the friends and relatives of the deal makers. Arbitragers, who speculate on mergers, can end up as well-informed as the key players through constant sleuthing.

Proxy Solicitors   Printers   Secretaries

Source: New York Times, May 18, 1986, Section 3, p. F-1. (Reprinted with permission of *The New York Times.*)

In the financial printing firm case, which is set out below, the U.S. Supreme Court appeared to limit the scope of the rule by defining "insiders" as those who "have a relationship of trust and confidence with shareholders."

CHIARELLA V. UNITED STATES

U.S. Supreme Court
445 U.S. 222 (1980)

BACKGROUND: In 1975 and 1976, Chiarella (defendant), a printer, worked as a "markup man" in the composing room of Pandick Press, a New York financial printer. Among documents that the defendant handled were five announcements of corporate takeover bids. When these documents were delivered to the printer, the identities of the acquiring and target corporations were concealed by blank spaces or false names. The true names were sent to the printer on the night of the final printing.

The defendant, however, was able to deduce the names of the target companies before the final printing from other information contained in the documents. Without disclosing his knowledge, the defendant purchased stock in the target companies and sold the shares immediately after the takeover attempts were made public. By this method, the defendant realized a gain of slightly more than $30,000 in the course of 14 months. Subsequently, the SEC began an investigation of his trading activities. In May 1977 the defendant entered into a consent decree with the Commission in which he agreed to return his profits to the sellers of the shares. On the same day he was discharged by Pandick Press.

In January 1978 the defendant was indicted on seventeen counts of violating Section 10(b) of the Securities Exchange Act of 1934 (1934 Act) and SEC Rule 10b-5. After the defendant unsuccessfully moved to dismiss the indictment, he was brought to trial and convicted on all counts. The Court of Appeals affirmed his conviction.

Powell, Justice

The question in this case is whether a person who learns from the confidential documents of one corporation that it is planning an attempt to secure control of a second corporation violates §10(b) of the Securities Exchange Act of 1934 if he fails to disclose the impending takeover before trading in the target company's securities.

In this case, the defendant was convicted of violating §10(b) although he was not a corporate insider and he received no confidential information from the target company. Moreover, the "market information" upon which he relied did not concern the earning power or operations of the target company, but only the plans of the acquiring company. Defendant's use of that information was not a fraud under §10(b) unless he was subject to an affirmative duty to disclose it before trading. In this case, the jury instructions failed to specify any such duty. In effect, the trial court instructed the jury that defendant owed a duty to everyone; to all sellers, indeed, to the market as a whole. The jury simply was told to decide whether defendant used material nonpublic information at a time when "he knew other people trading in the securities market did not have access to the same information."

The Court of Appeals affirmed the conviction by holding that "anyone—corporate insider or not—who regularly received material nonpublic information may not use that information to trade in securities without incurring an affirmative duty to disclose." Although the court said that its test would include only persons who regularly receive material, nonpublic information, its rationale for that limitation is unrelated to the existence of a duty to disclose. The Court of Appeals, like the trial court, failed to identify a relationship between defendant and the sellers that could give rise to a duty. Its decision thus rested solely upon its belief that the federal securities laws have "created a system providing equal access to information necessary for reasoned and intelligent investment decisions." The use by anyone of material information not generally available is fraudulent, this theory suggests, because such information gives certain buyers or sellers an unfair advantage over less informed buyers and sellers.

This reasoning suffers from two defects. First, not every instance of financial unfairness constitutes fraudulent activity under §10(b). Second, the element required to make silence fraudulent—a duty to disclose—is absent in this case. No duty could arise from petitioner's relationship with the seller of the target company's securities, for petitioner had no prior dealings with them. He was not their agent, he was not a fiduciary, he was not a person in whom the sellers had placed their trust and confidence. He was in fact, a complete stranger who dealt with the sellers only through impersonal market transactions.

In this case, as we have emphasized before, the 1934 Act cannot be read "'more broadly than its language and the statutory scheme reasonably permits.'" Section 10(b) is aptly described as a catch-all provision, but what it catches must be fraud. When an allegation of fraud is based upon nondisclosure, there can be no fraud absent a duty to speak. We hold that a duty to disclose under §10(b) does not arise from the mere possession of nonpublic market information. The contrary result is without support in the legislative history of §10(b) and would be inconsistent with the careful plan that Congress has enacted for regulation of the securities markets.

DECISION: Reversed. The Supreme Court ruled in favor of Chiarella.

Following this decision the SEC adopted Rule 14e-3, which makes it illegal for "any person to purchase or sell a security while in possession of material nonpublic information about a prospective tender offer, if he or she knows or has reason to know that such information emanates from either the offering person or the issuer or person acting on their behalf."

In September 1982 the SEC extended its enforcement scope with regard to insider trading in American stocks to individuals who use Swiss bank accounts to trade in stocks illegally. In a memorandum of understanding negotiated with Swiss officials, a system was established in Switzerland to process SEC requests for information about bank clients suspected of insider trad-

TABLE 46-1

A Sample of Major Criminal Cases Brought by the U.S. Attorney's Office Related to Insider Trading

Michael Milken	Director	Drexel Burnham	10 years imprisonment (paroled after 2 years)
Ivan Boesky	Private investor		3 years imprisonment
Dennis Levine	Managing director	Drexel Burnham	4 concurrent 2-year prison terms, $362,000 fine
Ira Sokolow	Investment banker	Shearson Lehman Brothers	1 year and 1 day imprisonment, 3 years probation
Ilan Reich	Attorney	Wachtel Lipton	1 year and 1 day imprisonment
Robert Wilkis	Investment banker	Lazard Freres	1 year and 1 day imprisonment
David Brown	Investment banker	Goldman Sachs	30 days imprisonment, 3 years probation, 300 hours of community service, $10,000 fine

ing. A special three-member Swiss commission was set up to review these inquiries. Upon receipt of a SEC request for information the Swiss bank involved freezes assets in a client's account equal to his or her alleged trading profits, studies the SEC allegations, and reports to the Swiss special commission. That panel then makes a decision as to whether the bank should honor the SEC request. If the SEC loses, it may appeal to the Swiss Federal Banking Commission. Prior to this agreement, bank secrecy legislation in Switzerland provided insiders with a shield against disclosure of trading in American stocks on the basis of nonpublic information. The SEC sees this agreement as a model for future understandings with other countries that have bank secrecy laws.

Corporate Misstatements In addition to disclosure required by the Securities Act of 1933 (Sections 13 and 14) when dealing with proxies and other documents filed with the SEC, Rule 10b-5 prohibits misstatements in the form of overoptimistic profit reports or press releases as to earnings if they would affect the prudent judgment of potential investors. In the landmark 1968 case of *SEC v. Texas Gulf Sulfur*, executives were held liable for releasing pessimistic, not overoptimistic, statements concerning the possible success of Texas Gulf's (TGS) exploration for ore. After denying the company's success in its Timmens, Ontario, operation, executives purchased stock, or calls on the stock, knowing of a potential ore discovery. The same information was undisclosed to the investing public, sellers, the stock option committee of TGS, or the TGS board of directors. TGS argued that the press release denying ore discoveries was not issued "in connection with the purchase or sale of securities." Since the company was not engaged in buying or selling securities at the time of the release, there was no violation of Rule 10b-5.

The Second Circuit Court of Appeals rejected this argument, stating that prices of TGS stock had been artificially held down by the pessimistic press release, enabling the executives and their tippees, acting on information not available to potential investors, to purchase stock and options at low prices. The court, basing its decision on the legislative history of Rule 10(b), found that the SEC was correct in stating that there was a connection between the press release and the investing public's transactions if it "would cause reasonable investors to rely thereon, and in connection therewith, so relying, cause them to purchase or sell a corporation's security." In that case the court deemed that a misleading statement needed a "wrongful purpose" for it to be a violation of Section 10(b) and Rule 10b-5.

When a large, publicly traded corporation makes a material misstatement to the public, literally thousands of current and potential shareholders can be affected. In order to recover for fraud, plaintiffs have traditionally had to prove that they relied to their detriment on the defendant's misstatement. In a typical securities transaction, the buyer or seller may not be specifically aware of misstatements that have been made by the issuer. However, most investors trust that the market price of the security reflects all relevant information available to the public. By buying or selling a security at the market price, is one not at least indirectly relying on all public statements made by the issuer that might affect the value of the security? Yes, according to the *fraud-on-the-market theory*, which holds that by accepting the market price for a security, the buyer or seller presumably is relying on the accuracy of all information supplied by the issuer that may have affected that market price. This theory is discussed in the important case that follows.

BASIC, INC. V. LEVINSON

U.S. Supreme Court
485 U.S. 224 (1988)

BACKGROUND: Combustion Engineering, Inc. expressed interest in acquiring Basic, Inc. Beginning in 1976, the two companies discussed the possibility of a merger. During 1977 and 1978, Basic made three public statements denying that it was engaged in merger negotiations. On December 18, 1978, Basic released a statement that it had been approached by another company regarding a possible merger. Basic immediately asked the New York Stock Exchange to suspend trading in its securities. On December 20, 1978, Basic announced that its board had approved Combustion Engineering's tender offer for all Basic's outstanding shares. Basic was sued in a class action by former shareholders who had sold off their shares after Basic publicly denied that it was discussing a merger. The District Court ruled in favor of Basic, and the Court of Appeals affirmed in part and reversed in part. The U.S. Supreme Court agreed to review the case. In the excerpt below, the Court discusses whether each plaintiff must specifically prove reliance upon Basic's statements that no merger discussions were taking place.

Blackmun, Justice

We turn to the question of reliance on the fraud-on-the-market theory. Succinctly put:

> The fraud on the market theory is based on the hypothesis that, in an open and developed securities market, the price of a company's stock is determined by the available material information regarding the company and its business. . . . Misleading statements will therefore defraud purchasers of stock even if the purchasers do not directly rely on the misstatements. . . . The causal connection between the defendants' fraud and the plaintiffs' purchase of stock in such a case is no less significant than in a case of direct reliance on misrepresentations. *Peil v. Speiser*.

Our task, of course, is not to assess the general validity of the theory, but to consider whether it was proper for the courts below to apply a rebuttable presumption of reliance, supported in part by the fraud-on-the-market theory.

Petitioners and their *amici* complain that the fraud-on-the-market theory effectively eliminates the requirement that a plaintiff asserting a claim under Rule 10b-5 prove reliance. . . .

We agree that reliance is an element of a Rule 10b-5 cause of action. See *Ernst & Ernst v. Hochfelder*. Reliance provides the requisite causal connection between a defendant's misrepresentation and a plaintiff's injury. There is, however, more than one way to demonstrate the causal connection. . . .

The modern securities markets, literally involving millions of shares changing hands daily, differ from the face-to-face transactions contemplated by early fraud cases, and our understanding of Rule 10b-5's reliance requirement must encompass these differences.

> In face-to-face transactions, the inquiry into an investor's reliance upon information is into the subjective pricing of that information by that investor. With the presence of a market, the market is interposed between seller and buyer and, ideally, transmits information to the investor in the processed form of a market price. Thus the market is performing a substantial part of the valuation process performed by the investor in a face-to-face transaction. The market is acting as the unpaid agent of the investor, informing him that given all the information available to it, the value of the stock is worth the market price." *In re LTV Securities Litigation*. . . .

The presumption is also supported by common sense and probability. Recent empirical studies have tended to confirm Congress' premise that the market price of shares traded on well-developed markets reflects all publicly available information, and, hence, any material misrepresentation. It has been noted that "it is hard to imagine that there ever is a buyer or seller who does not rely on market integrity. Who would knowingly roll the dice in a crooked crap game?" *Schlanger v. Four-Phase Systems Inc.* Indeed, nearly every court that has considered the proposition has concluded that where materially misleading statements have been disseminated into an impersonal, well-developed market for securities, the reliance of individual plaintiffs on the integrity of the market price may be presumed. Commentators generally have applauded the adoption of one variation or another of the fraud-on-the-market theory. An investor who buys or sells stock at the price set by the market does so in reliance on the integrity of that price. Because most publicly available information is reflected in market price, an investor's reliance on any public material misrepresentations, therefore, may be presumed for purposes of a Rule 10b-5 action.

DECISION: The Supreme Court vacated the decision of the lower court and remanded the case for further proceedings. The Court specifically ruled that the plaintiffs were entitled to the presumption that they relied on Basic's misstatements, although Basic would be given the opportunity to rebut those presumptions.

Corporate Mismanagement The *Hochfelder* case previously set out in this chapter is an obvious illustration of corporate mismanagement and fraud upon shareholders. Shareholder derivative suits or minority stockholders' actions have become common in attacking transactions dealing with mergers and reorganizations, and sales and purchases of corporations of their own securities. State incorporation laws provide for a fiduciary duty between shareholders and a corporation's officers and directors. Suits have been based on breaches of this duty. When attempts have been made by shareholders to avoid state corporation law and to sue on the basis of fraud under Section 10(b), the Supreme Court has been reluctant to "federalize" state corporate law. The courts have refused to allow actions for mismanagement under Rule 10b-5 unless the plaintiffs (shareholders) have bought or sold securities in the transactions under question and there exists some connection between the alleged fraud and the transactions.

Insider Trader Sanctions Act Following the *Hochfelder* decision and *Dirks v. United States*, in which the SEC was unable to persuade the U.S. Supreme Court to broaden its definition of insider trading, Congress enacted the Insider Trader Sanctions Act of 1984. The Act leaves the definition of insider trading to the courts. It does, however, provide for treble damages ("three times the profits gained or avoided") to be levied against "any person who has violated any provision [of the 1934 Act] or rules or regulations while in possession of material nonpublic information. . . ." The treble damage provision does not apply to aiders and abettors, but other provisions of the Act do.

The 1984 Act provides for civil penalties which increase in severity with the seriousness of the violation. The most costly penalties are for violations that involve fraud, deceit, manipulation, or deliberate or reckless disregard of a regulatory requirement *and* result in substantial losses (or the risk of substantial losses to others). In such cases, the defendant is subject to a maximum penalty equal to the greater of (1) $500,000 (if the defendant is a business) or $100,000 (if the defendant is an individual) or (2) the gross amount of gain realized by the defendant as result of the transaction.

The Foreign Corrupt Practices Act of 1977

Background

In 1973, during the Watergate hearings, Americans learned for the first time about illegal domestic political contributions made by corporations to President Nixon's 1972 reelection campaign. The SEC undertook a study in 1974 of these secret payments, viewing the companies' failures to disclose as violations of the Exchange Act of 1934. The SEC found upon further investigation that corporations had made questionable payments overseas as well. The Commission's staff concluded that there were clear patterns of illegal or questionable payments both domestically and overseas. The SEC considered these payments *material* information under the Securities Acts because they affected the integrity of both management and the record-keeping procedures of the companies involved. This undisclosed information, in the

ETHICS
Ethics and International Issues

Many have argued that insider trading should not be illegal and is not unethical. They argue that insiders' ability to trade on nonpublic information is good for the marketplace in that it shows that officers or directors have confidence in their own firm because they trade in their own stocks and that others will then follow. Others argue that it is part of the "perks" of being an officer or director. It is an incentive device, particularly when applied to stock options awarded managers as compensation. Still others believe the cost of enforcing insider trading rules far outweighs the benefits. They argue that insider trading is simply so far-reaching and indefinable that no particular governmental agency can regulate it.

Some of these arguments are supported by looking at Japanese and European markets in which little effort is made to control insider trading. When the Tokyo Stock Exchange does discover insider trading, it issues warnings to violators that remain confidential, thus denying investors the chance to know who the "bad guys" are. In 38 years Japan has prosecuted only five securities law violations. This may be explained in some part by the Japanese cultural aversion to adversary processes and to court systems in general. Only in late 1986 after a major scandal has Great Britain shown some concern over insider trading. Prior to that time, of the 100 cases the London Stock Exchange turned over to the British government, only a handful were prosecuted. In Germany trading on nonpublic material information is not illegal.

Of course, the fact that some argue insider trading should not be criminally sanctioned and that some foreign countries do not have strictly enforced laws cannot justify engaging in insider trading. So long as it is illegal in the United States, insider trading is unethical to engage in. The arguments that the law is inefficient or erratically enforced do not make a sufficient case, on ethical grounds, for disobeying the law.

eyes of the Commission, would in all likelihood have altered the judgment of a reasonably prudent investor. The corporations argued that disclosure was not required because the amounts involved were small compared with sales or earnings and thus not material. The SEC interpretation of materiality was accepted by the Supreme Court in 1976. In *TSC Industries, Inc. v. Northrup* the Court defined "material information" as that which a "reasonable investor would consider important in deciding how to vote or whether to buy, sell or hold securities." The SEC brought thirty-nine enforcement actions prior to passage of the Foreign Corrupt Practices Act, alleging violations of the Exchange Act. The Commission also set up in 1975 a volunteer disclosure program whereby companies were encouraged to conduct investigations of their operations and, upon finding questionable payments, to discuss appropriate disclosure methods with the SEC staff. More than 450 companies admitted making questionable or illegal payments totaling more than $300 million; 117 of the Fortune 500 companies were involved. Payments had been made to high-level officials for the purpose of obtaining contracts. In the enforcement actions, as well as in the voluntary disclosure program, corporate officials testified that these "bribes" or "commissions" were a means of doing business. They were "facilitating" or "grease" payments that were often necessary to meet the competition of other American firms as well as foreign multinationals. In many cases it was learned that the payments were treated by corporate accountants as expense items and illegally deducted as business expenses on income tax returns filed with the Internal Revenue Service.

Although the Justice Department was able to prosecute some payments under currency transaction regulations and mail or wire fraud statutes, statutory authority to reach questionable payments overseas for foreign political bribery was only indirect. The SEC had forced disclosure under Exchange Act provisions, but by 1977 Congress felt a need to take further action.

Provisions

The Foreign Corrupt Practices Act (FCPA) was enacted because Congress considered corporate bribes to foreign officials to be (1) unethical, (2) harmful to our relations with foreign governments (Korean and Japanese officials were forced to resign after disclosure of payments from American-based multinational corporations), and (3) unnecessary to American companies doing business overseas.

Passed in 1977 and amended in 1988, the Act applies to all "domestic concerns" whether or not doing business overseas and whether or not registered with the SEC. The Act's antibribery provisions prohibit all domestic concerns, whether or not registered with SEC, from offering or authorizing corrupt payments to:

1. A foreign official (or someone acting in an official capacity for a foreign government)
2. A foreign political party official or a foreign political party
3. A candidate for political office in a foreign country
4. Any person, if the party making the payment knows that the money will be passed along, directly or indirectly, to any of the above

A payment is "corrupt" if its purpose is to get the recipient to act or refrain from acting so the American firm can retain or get business.

A U.S. business that violates the FCPA can be fined up to $2 million and is subject to a civil penalty of up to $10,000. Any officer, director, stockholder, employee, or agent of a U.S. business that willfully violates the Act can be fined up to $100,000, imprisoned for up to 5 years, or both. Additionally, such a person is subject to a civil penalty of up to $10,000. The Act does not prohibit "facilitating or expediting payments" to foreign officials to expedite or ensure performance of a routine governmental action. Also, a defendant can escape liability by proving that any payments made were legal in the foreign country.

Enforcement

The SEC and the Justice Department share responsibility for enforcing the Foreign Corrupt Practices Act. The SEC is charged with investigating suspected violations of the bribery and accounting provisions. The SEC can bring only civil actions, but it may recommend criminal enforcement to the Justice Department. The Justice Department has authority to proceed civilly and criminally against domestic concerns alleged to have violated the antibribery provisions.

State Securities Laws

State regulation of securities began in 1911 when Kansas enacted a securities statute. The U.S. Supreme Court, in the 1917 case of *Hall v. Geiger Jones Co.*, called such regulations of securities "blue sky" laws, describing their purposes as "the prevention of speculative schemes which have no more basis than so many feet of blue sky." In enacting the 1933 Securities Act, Congress specifically preserved the power of the states to regulate securities transactions of an *intrastate* nature. All fifty states, the District of Columbia, and Puerto Rico have enacted securities statutes. A corporation issuing securities in interstate commerce must meet the registration requirements of each of the states in which its securities are sold as well as the federal requirements. The cost and time involved in meeting various state requirements have led to the adoption of the Uniform Securities Act (USA), in whole or in part, by most states.

Common Provisions

Almost all state statutes contain provisions covering: registration of securities, broker-dealer registration, and fraud in issuance and trading of securities.

Registration of Securities The 1933 Securities Act has served as a model for state statutes with regard to types of information required for registration. There are generally three methods of registration: notification, qualification, and coordination. Unlike the federal securities acts, state laws provide that securities may be registered by notification when the issuing corporation meets certain tests of reliability and earnings. In most states notification is effective if the state administrator of the securities law does not take action within a number of days after filing. When an issuing company registers in a "coordination" state, the same procedure is followed except that generally a prospectus is all that is required. In "qualification" states, following the filing of information, registration of the securities is not effective until the state administrator has approved. It should be noted that this power is in sharp contrast to that of the SEC under the 1933 Act. The SEC has no power to determine the worth of a particular filing. The sole purpose of the federal securities acts is to provide full disclosure of material information for potential investors. State administrators, however, may evaluate the securities being issued as well as the issuing corporation. Most states exempt from registration those securities exempted by the 1933 Securities Act—for example regulatory statutes. Additionally, state securities legislation exempts securities listed on major stock exchanges.

Broker-Dealer Registration and Fraud

Almost every state statute requires registration by brokers and agents. Some establish licensing requirements and reserve the right to deny or revoke licenses. Issuers or broker-dealers must post surety bonds in many states.

Most states have adopted antifraud provisions similar to those set forth in Section 10b of the Exchange Act and Rule 10b-5. States generally use some form of injunctive relief as a remedy for fraud, but many also have criminal provisions in their statute. The USA would permit individual investors to recover money damages.

Conflict between Federal and State Security Statutes

As noted earlier, fifty-two separate jurisdictions in addition to the federal government have statutes governing securities registration and trading. Often securities statutes apply to any offer or sale of securities in a state, but many transactions involve a seller or securities-issuing company incorporated or doing business in one state and a buyer located in another state.

State securities statutes can raise serious constitutional questions regarding the relationship between federal and state law. Recall from our discussion of constitutional law earlier in the book that the U.S. Congress, through the U.S. Constitution's Commerce Clause, is given the power to regulate interstate commerce. That does not mean that states cannot enact laws that affect interstate commerce. But because the federal government's power to regulate interstate commerce takes priority, a state law that affects interstate commerce is valid only if the state law does not (1) discriminate against interstate commerce, (2) unduly burden interstate commerce, or (3) conflict with a valid federal law. This third point is derived not only from the Commerce Clause but also from the U.S. Constitution's Supremacy Clause, which provides that a valid federal law preempts a conflicting state law.

In *CTS Corporation v. Dynamics Corporation of America*, the landmark case that follows, the U. S. Supreme Court discusses the constitutional ramifications of a state law designed to protect corporations from hostile tender offers. The *CTS* court refers to another important case, the *MITE* case: (*Edgar v. MITE Corporation*, 457 U.S. 624 [1982]).

In that case the trial court struck down an Illinois statute that required the secretary of state to review all tender offers made to Illinois corporations in order to determine their fairness. When the secretary determined that a tender offer was not fair, and was about to issue a cease and desist order, the tender offeror went to federal district court and obtained an injunctive order. The Court of Appeals and the U.S. Supreme Court affirmed stating that the Illinois statute violated the Commerce Clause of the U.S. Constitution, and that the federal Williams Act preempted the statute. Please note carefully how the *CTS Corporation* case distinguishes *Edgar v. MITE*.

CTS CORPORATION V. DYNAMICS CORPORATION OF AMERICA

U.S. Supreme Court
1075 S-Ct 1637 (1987)

BACKGROUND: The state of Indiana enacted a law to protect Indiana corporations from hostile takeovers. The Indiana act provided that if a would-be acquirer purchased a certain percentage of stock in a target corporation, the preexisting shareholders essentially got to veto any attempt by the would-be acquirer to take over the corporation. The Indiana act accomplished this by denying voting rights to the would-be acquirer unless a majority of all preexisting disinterested shareholders voted to grant voting rights to the would-be acquirer. The shareholder vote would normally come at the next regularly scheduled annual meeting, but the would-be acquirer could require a shareholder vote within 50 days by following certain procedures. The appellee, Dynamics Corporation, announced a tender offer that would have raised its ownership interest in CTS Corporation above the Indiana act's threshold. Dynamics also filed suit in U.S. District Court alleging federal securities violations by CTS. After CTS opted into the Indiana act, Dynamics amended its complaint to challenge the act's validity. The District Court granted Dynamics' motion for declaratory relief, ruling that the act is preempted by the federal Williams Act and violates the Commerce Clause. The Court of Appeals affirmed, adopting the holding of the plurality opinion in *Edgar v. MITE Corp.*, 457 U.S. 624 (1982), that the Williams Act preempts state statutes that upset the balance between target company management and a tender offeror. The court based its preemption finding on the view that the Indiana act, in effect, imposes at least a 50-day delay on the consummation of tender offers and that this conflicts with the minimum 20-day hold-open period under the Williams Act. The court also held that the state act violates the U.S. Constitution's Commerce Clause, since it deprives nonresidents of the valued opportunity to accept tender offers from other nonresidents.

Powell, Justice

In implementing its goal, the Indiana Act avoids the problems the plurality discussed in *MITE*. Unlike the *MITE* statute, the Indiana Act does not give either management or the offeror an advantage in communicating with the shareholders about the impending offer. The Act also does not impose an indefinite delay on tender offers. Nothing in the Act prohibits an offeror from consummating an offer on the 20th business day, the earliest day permitted under applicable federal regulations. Nor does the Act allow the state government to interpose its views of fairness between willing buyers and sellers of shares of the target company. Rather, the Act allows *shareholders* to evaluate the fairness of the offer collectively.

The principal objects of dormant Commerce Clause scrutiny are statutes that discriminate against interstate commerce.

Dynamics . . . contends that the statute is discriminatory because it will apply most often to out-of-state entities. This argument rests on the contention that, as a practical matter, most hostile tender offers are launched by fearers outside Indiana. But this argument avails Dynamics little. "The fact that the burden of a state regulation falls on some interstate companies does not, by itself, establish a claim of discrimination against interstate commerce." Because nothing in the Indiana Act imposes a greater burden on out-of-state fearers than it does on similarly situated Indiana fearers, we reject the contention that the Act discriminates against interstate commerce.

This Court's recent Commerce Clause cases also have invalidated statutes that adversely may affect interstate commerce by subjecting activities to inconsistent regulations. The Indiana Act poses no such problem. So long as each State regulates voting rights only in the corporations it has created, each corporation will be subject to the law of only one State. No principle of corporation law and practice is more firmly established than a State's authority to regulate domestic corporations, including the authority to define the voting rights of shareholders. Accordingly, we conclude that the Indiana Act does not create an impermissible risk of inconsistent regulation by different States.

The Court of Appeals did not find the Act unconstitutional for either of these threshold reasons. Rather, its decision rested on its view of the Act's potential to hinder tender offers.

We think the Court of Appeals failed to appreciate the significance for Commerce Clause analysis of the fact that state regulation of corporate governance is regulation of entities whose very existence and attributes are a product of state law. Every State in this country has enacted laws regulating corporate governance. By prohibiting certain transactions, and regulating others, such laws necessarily affect certain aspects of interstate commerce. This necessarily is true with respect to corporations with shareholders in States other than the State of incorporation. Large corporations that are listed on national exchanges, or even regional exchanges, will have shareholders in many States and shares that are traded frequently. The markets that facilitate this national and international participation in ownership of corporations are essential for providing capital not only for new enterprises but also for established companies that need to expand their businesses. This beneficial free market system depends at its core upon the fact that a corporation—except in the rarest situations—is organized under, and governed by, the law of a single jurisdiction, traditionally the corporate law of the State of its incorporation.

These regulatory laws may affect directly a variety of corporate transactions. Mergers are a typical example. In view of the substantial effect that a merger may have on the shareholders' interests in a corporation, many States require supermajority votes to approve mergers. By requiring a greater vote for mergers than is required for other transactions, these laws make it more difficult for corporations to merge. State laws also may provide for "dissenters' rights" under which minority shareholders who disagree with corporate decisions to take particular actions are entitled to sell their shares to the corporation at fair market value. By requiring the corporation to purchase the shares of dissenting shareholders, these laws may inhibit a corporation from engaging in the specified transactions.

It thus is an accepted part of the business landscape in this country for States to create corporations, to prescribe their powers, and to define the rights that are acquired by purchasing their shares. A State has an interest in promoting stable relationships among parties involved in the corporations it charters, as well as in ensuring that investors in such corporations have an effective voice in corporate affairs.

There can be no doubt that the Act reflects these concerns. The primary purpose of the Act is to protect the shareholders of Indiana corporations. It does this by affording shareholders, when a takeover offer is made, an opportunity to decide collectively whether the resulting change in voting control of the corporation, as they perceive it, would be desirable. A change of management may have important effects on the shareholders' interests; it is well within the State's role as overseer of corporate governance to offer this opportunity. The autonomy provided by allowing shareholders collectively to determine whether the takeover is advantageous to their interests may be especially beneficial where a hostile tender offer may coerce shareholders into tendering their shares.

DECISION: Reversed. The Supreme Court ruled in favor of the CTS Corporation.

Review Questions and Problems

Key Terms

security

broker

dealer

specialist

issuer

underwriter

registration statement

prospectus

shelf registration

private placement

due diligence defense

proxy

tender offer

business judgment rule

insider trading

Discussion Questions

1. What is the major difference in purpose between the Securities Act of 1933 and the Securities Exchange Act of 1934?

2. What criteria are used by the courts to determine

whether an instrument or transaction is a "security" within the meaning of the 1933 Act?

3. Which securities are exempt from registration under the 1933 Act?

4. What defenses may be used by target companies in an effort to prevent a hostile takeover?

5. How do state securities statutes differ from the federal securities laws?

Review Problems

1. Sleazeco borrowed $5 million by selling bonds to the public. The registration statement filed in connection with the bonds stated Sleazeco's net worth to be $10 million. In reality, Sleazeco was insolvent. Which parties may be held liable for this inaccuracy under Section 11 of the 1933 Act? What defense might be available to some of these parties? What would each party have to prove in order to successfully assert this defense?

2. ABC Corp. is incorporated in the State of California and has its principal place of business there. It wishes to issue $30 million worth of securities to about 300 investors who are residents of California. What should ABC Corp. be able to demonstrate in order to avoid having to register these securities under the 1933 Act?

3. A owned oil and gas leases in Ohio. Because he needed cash, he sought to sell interests in the leases. He organized three separate corporations for this purpose, and each sold $1 million in securities over a 12-month period. Do the corporations need to register under the 1933 Securities Act, or are they exempt? Explain.

4. A was a journalist for the *Wall Street Journal*. He wrote a column telling of rumors on Wall Street about various companies' health or lack of it. His roommate, B, traded on this information before it was published, because he found drafts of A's columns in the wastebasket in the room where A wrote. B also passed information on to C. The SEC charged A with being a tipper under Section 10(b) of the Exchange Act and B and C with being tippees. Should A, B, and C be found guilty of insider trading under Section 10(b)(5) of the 1934 Exchange Act? Explain.

Case Problems

1. Maresh, a geologist, owned some oil and gas leases on land in Nebraska. He entered into an oral agreement with Garfield whereby the latter would provide some investment funds for Maresh to drill for oil. Garfield, a businessman, knew a great deal about oil stocks and the securities market. He promised to wire the money to Maresh, who began drilling immediately. Maresh found out that the land was dry before he received Garfield's money. Garfield refused to invest as he had promised, claiming that the offered lease investment was a "security" within the meaning of the Securities Act of 1933 and that it had not been registered. What was the result?

2. Continental Tobacco Company, a manufacturer of cigarettes, sold some unregistered 5-year debentures, paying 6 percent common stock, to thirty-eight persons between June 1969 and October 1970. All investors prior to purchase signed an agreement with Continental that acknowledged receipt of unaudited financial statements, other information about the corporation, access to officers of the company, knowledge of the risk involved, and that they were experienced investors. Purchasers went to meetings in a room where telephones were staffed and orders for securities continually came in. One investor called the meetings a "boiler plate operation" in which high-pressure tactics were used to sell the securities. The SEC brought suit against Continental claiming that it was selling unregistered securities. The company claimed that its sale of securities was a private offering and thus was exempt from registration under the 1933 Act. What was the result?

3. Truckee Showboat, a California corporation, offered to sell its common stock to residents of California through the U.S. mail. Its offer to sell was advertised in the *Los Angeles Times* on June 18, 1957, and the offer was made exclusively to residents of the State of California. The proceeds of the sale of the stock, minus commission, were to be used to acquire the El Cortez Hotel in Las Vegas, Nevada. Truckee Showboat, Inc. was incorporated and kept all its records in California. All its directors and officers were Californians. The SEC charged the company with issuing unregistered nonexempt securities under the 1933 Act. Truckee Showboat claimed an intrastate exemption. What was the result?

4. Livingston was a 20-year employee of Merrill Lynch, a large securities investment firm. Livingston was a securities salesman who was given the title "account executive." In January 1972 the company gave Livingston and forty-seven other account executives the title "vice president" as a reward for outstanding sales records. All their duties and responsibilities were the same as before this recognition. Livingston never acquired any executive duties and never attended board of directors meetings. In November and December 1972 Livingston sold 1,000 shares of Merrill Lynch stock. In March 1973 he repurchased the same number of shares, making a profit of $14,836.37. The company sued for the profits, claiming that Livingston by virtue of his inside information made short-swing profits in violation of Section 16(b) of the Securities Exchange Act of 1934. The defendant denied this charge. What was the result?

5. Mills was a minority shareholder of Electric Auto-Lite Company. Prior to the merger of Auto-Lite and Mergenthaler into the Mergenthaler Linotype Co., Mergenthaler owned 50 percent of Auto-Lite and

dominated its board of directors. American Manufacturing Company in turn had control of Mergenthaler and through it controlled Auto-Lite. Auto-Lite's management at the time of the merger sent out a proxy statement to shareholders of Auto-Lite telling them that their board of directors recommended that they vote for approval of the merger. They failed to include in the proxy statement information concerning the fact that Morgenthaler dominated the board and that American Manufacturing through Morgenthaler controlled Auto-Lite. Mills and other minority shareholders filed a class action and derivative suit claiming that management had sent out a misleading proxy in violation of Section 14 of the Exchange Act of 1934 and that the merger should be set aside. Management and the board of directors of the merged company claimed that there was no material omission in the proxy statement. What was the result?

6. Lakeside Plastics and Engraving Company (LPE) was a closed corporation incorporated in the State of Minnesota in 1946. It suffered losses until 1952, when it showed a yearly profit but still a large overall deficit. Fields and King in 1946 had each purchased thirty shares, which they held. Myzel, a relative of the Levine family, founders of the company, advised Fields and King in 1954 that the company stock was not worth anything and the company was going out of business. Both sold their shares to Myzel, who sold them to the Levine family at a substantial profit. Myzel failed to disclose before purchasing the shares that there were increased sales in 1953, a new Blatz contract, and profits of $30,000, along with the potential of 1954 sales. Fields, King, and others in separate actions sought damage for violation of Section 10(b) of the Exchange Act of 1934. What was the result?

47

Personal Property

Types of Personal Property

Fixtures

Bailments

Transfer of Title to Property

Abandoned, Lost, and Mislaid
Property

Changing Concepts of Property

W hen we speak of *property*, we usually refer to something we own—a compact disk player, a car, a house. From the standpoint of property law, however, the things themselves are not important; rather, it is the *rights* the individual has in them. Property rights—the *bundle of rights* a person has in something—may include the right to use, sell, lease, or even destroy the thing in question. Figure 47-1 illustrates some of the property rights recognized by the law.

Property rights exist only with respect to things that may be *owned*. Thus one may have property rights in a house, since a house is subject to ownership. Similarly, one may have property rights in something intangible like a patent or trademark, since the government has created a system that allows such things to be owned (and hence sold or traded, just like tangible property). The right to travel, however, is not a property right. Like the right to vote and other civil rights, the right to

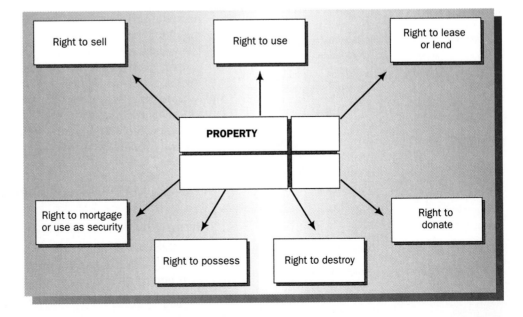

FIGURE 47-1

Property: A
Bundle or
Package of
Rights

Right to sell

Right to use

Right to lease
or lend

PROPERTY

Right to mortgage
or use as security

Right to possess

Right to destroy

Right to
donate

travel is a right that one exercises with respect to *oneself* and not with respect to some separately owned thing. Whether something is considered as property is important because both federal and state constitutions prohibit the government from taking "property" without due process of law.

The existence of property depends on government. Some societies do not allow individuals to own certain types of property; only the government is permitted to own mineral rights, strategic resources (for example, oil), or key industries (for example, banks). It is the legal system that creates and protects a person's property rights. In countries which, like the United States, have a common law legal system, the importance of land ownership was recognized and protected by allowing property owners to bring "real actions" against anyone who sought to throw the owner off his or her land. Today, land is known as **real property** while movable items, such as automo-

biles, furniture, and even bank accounts, are known as **personal property**.

People have property rights in things because the government will protect those rights. If you have a contract with a firm that agrees to pay you $1,000 in exchange for your agreement to paint a building, your contract is property because the society will enforce your right to collect the money due you under the contract.

In the United States, both federal and state constitutions protect property. The "due process" clause provides that the government cannot deprive a person of life, liberty, or *property* without due process of law. It can therefore be important to determine if you have a recognized property right to attend a school, to be a part of a team, or to receive certain government benefits. If you do have a property right, you cannot be deprived of that right by the government (federal, state, or local) without first meeting the due process requirements imposed by the Constitution. If your right is not recognized as a property right (such as the right to travel to another country) but instead is regarded as a privilege, the due process protection does not apply.

Historically, the law first protected personal property items that had substance; these *tangible* items are referred to as chattels or goods. **Chattels** include farm equipment, household furniture, and tools of the trade because they, like land, were forms of wealth. **Goods** are items of inventory which are to be sold, such as a bicycle shop's bicycles, tires, bicycle seats, and helmets. As the nature of the economy changed, the law also extended property protection to *intangible* items, such as trademarks or patents. The concept of personal property is still expanding. People now may have rights in water, gas, or cable television transmissions; taking of this property without proper permission and payment deprives the owner of his or her property. Licenses to practice a profession and a person's status or reputation are being recognized by some courts as property interests. Table 47-1 provides an overview of how various property interests are classified.

Types of Personal Property

Tangible Personal Property

Tangible personal property—goods and chattels—generally refers to movable property. You probably own hundreds of items of tangible personal property: textbooks, notebooks, pencils, pocket calcu-

TABLE **47-1**

Classification of Property

Type	Example
Real Estate	40 acres of Iowa farmland; one-half acre of land with attached house and garage in Columbus, Ohio; Condominium in New York City
Real Property Fixtures	Built-in dishwasher in residence;
Trade Fixtures	Display case used by tenant in retail store
Tangible Personal Property	
Chattels	Farm equipment, office computers
Goods	Inventory of store's unsold bicycles
Intangible Personal Property	Bank account, stocks
Intellectual Property	Patent, copyright, trademark
Emerging Interests	License to practice law; status and reputation

lators, clothing, magazines, cassette tapes—and maybe even a television, a VCR, a stereo system, a microwave oven, an automobile.

Intangible Personal Property

Consider the example of a stock certificate. The certificate is evidence of value, although it has no worth itself. The owner of the stock has a "bundle of rights" in the stock: he or she can sell it, use it as security, or give it away. The owner also has numerous rights in relation to the firm, creditors, and other owners. Because it possesses all of these attributes, a share of corporate stock is property—and since the rights associated with the stock don't relate directly to land, the stock is *personal* property. But while a textbook, television, or VCR is tangible, a share of stock is intangible.

Today, a significant amount of wealth is in the form of intangible personal property. Other than corporate stock, intangible personal property includes bank accounts, bonds, and other financial instruments. An item of intangible personal property is often referred to as a **chose in action** (from the French: *chose* which means "thing").

One form of intangible property that has grown rapidly in importance is *intellectual property,* which is discussed in Chapter 50. Intellectual property includes patents, trademarks, copyrights, and trade secrets.

Fixtures

The classification of property as real or personal can have important legal consequences. For example, an oral contract to sell an interest in real property is not enforceable under the statute of frauds, whereas an oral contract to sell personal property may be enforceable. The classification of an item of property as real or personal can also impact numerous tax, insurance, financing, and inheritance issues.

For example, real property taxes are often based on the assessed value of the property. If machines or appliances in the factory or home are regarded as real property, their value is included in determining the tax due on the real property. If instead these items are considered personal property, their value is not considered when taxing real property.

In many situations conflicting arguments exist for classifying property one way or the other. Naturally, individuals and firms wish to have property classified in the manner most beneficial to them. This classification problem is further complicated by the fact that the property's designation can change, depending on how it is used.

A common example is items used in home construction, such as a built-in oven. The oven would be personal property when part of a building supplier's inventory. But as part of a dwelling, the built-in oven becomes real property. As we mentioned in Chapter 24, personal property that becomes real property through attachment to land or a building is called a *fixture.*

In some instances real property is transformed into personal property. This change is often referred to as severance. Trees growing in a forest are real property, but if a tree is cut to be milled into lumber or stacked as firewood it becomes personal property. In some states courts recognize the doctrine of constructive severance. In these states trees standing in a forest are considered personal property as soon as a contract is made selling them to be logged.

Determination of Fixtures

The chief test in determining whether personal property has become a fixture is the intention of the party who attached the item to real property. This intention is not the secret intention of that person, but the intention determined by how the person acted. Other factors that courts consider are how the item is attached and its application and use as a permanent part of the real property. Often attachment and use are considered only as evidence of what was intended. The case that follows indicates the importance of intention.

GEORGE V. COMMERCIAL CREDIT CORP.

U.S. Court of Appeals
440 F.2d 551 (7th Cir. 1971)

BACKGROUND: George (petitioner-appellant), a trustee in bankruptcy for Foskett, claimed an interest in a mobile home owned by the bankrupt, Foskett. Commercial Credit Corp. (respondent-appellee) was the assignee of a mortgage that Foskett had taken out on the property. George claimed the mobile home was an item of personalty (that is, personal property) and thus not a part of the real estate on which the mortgage had been given. Commercial Credit argued that the mobile home was a fixture, attached to the realty, and thus had become a part of it.

The bankruptcy referee found the mobile home to be a fixture and rejected George's claim for the property. George appealed.

Duffy, Senior Circuit Judge

Foskett owned five acres of land in Jefferson County, Wisconsin. On December 6, 1968, he purchased a Marshfield Mobile Home, No. 9090, from Highway Mobile Home Sales, Inc. He signed an installment contract and paid $880 on the purchase price of $8,800. Added was a sales tax and interest covering a ten-year period.

Sometime in December 1968, Foskett executed a real estate mortgage to Highway Mobile Home Sales, Inc. The mortgage recites the sum of $14,277.70 and described the real estate in metes and bounds. The mortgage was assigned to Commercial Credit Corporation, the respondent-appellee herein.

The mobile home here in question could not move under its own power. It was delivered to Foskett's real estate property by Mobile Sales. This mobile home was never again operated on or over the highways as a motor vehicle.

The mobile home here in question was 68 feet in length, 14 feet in width, and 12 feet in height. It contained six rooms and weighed 15,000 pounds.

The bankrupt owned no other home and he and his wife occupied the mobile home continuously from December 6, 1968 until forced to vacate same by order of the Trustee in Bankruptcy.

The home was set on cement cinder blocks three courses high. It was connected with a well. It was hooked up to a septic tank. It also was connected with electric power lines.

The bankrupt never applied for a certificate of title from the Wisconsin Motor Vehicle Department. However, he did apply for a homeowner's insurance policy and he asked the seller to remove the wheels from his home. He also applied for a building permit and was told he had to construct a permanent foundation for the home. The permit was granted upon condition that the foundation he constructed within one year. However, within that period, the petition for bankruptcy was filed.

The issue before us can be thus stated: Commercial Credit Corporation argues that the mobile home was a fixture under applicable law and is not personalty. The trustee insists that the mobile home was and still is a "motor vehicle" and is personalty.

The mobile homes industry has grown rapidly in the last few years. There has been a great demand for relatively inexpensive housing by middle income families. In Wisconsin, a distinction is now recognized between mobile homes (those used as homes) and motor homes (those often used as vehicles).

The Wisconsin law on the question is found in *Auto Acceptance and Loan Corp. v. Kelm*, where the Wisconsin Supreme Court reaffirmed its decision in *Standard Oil Co. v. LaCrosse Super Auto Service, Inc.* That case held that the three tests for determining whether facilities remain personalty or are to be considered part of the realty are (1) actual physical annexation to the realty; (2) application or adaptation to the use or purpose to which the realty is devoted, and (3) intention of the person making annexation to make a permanent accession to the freehold.

In the *Standard Oil Company* case, the Court pointed out that "physical annexation" is relatively unimportant and "intention" of the parties is the principal consideration.

In *Premonstratensian Fathers v. Badger Mutual Insurance Co.,* the Court reaffirmed its adherence to the three-fold test saying, "It is the application of these tests to the facts of a particular case which will lead to a determination of whether or not an article, otherwise considered personal property, constitutes a common-law fixture, and hence takes on the nature of real property."

Viewed in light of these Wisconsin tests, the finding of the referee and the District Court that this mobile home had become a fixture must clearly stand. The bankrupt's actual intention pointed definitely toward affixing the mobile home to the land as a permanent residence, as seen in his application for a building permit (which, by law, required him to erect a concrete slab as a permanent foundation within one year), his purchase of a homeowner's insurance policy, and his requests made to the seller to have the wheels of the home removed. Moreover, the home was clearly adapted to use as the permanent residence of the bankrupt and was never moved off of his five-acre plot.

The fact that it may have been physically possible for this mobile home to have been more securely attached to the ground should not alter our position. Physical attachment did occur by means of cinder blocks and a "C" clamp, while connections for electricity, sewage and natural gas were provided as well. Finally, we note that the very size and difficulty in transporting this mobile home further highlight the fact that this was a vehicle which was intended primarily to be placed in one position for a long period of time and to be used as an intended permanent home.

DECISION: The court of appeals affirmed the referee's decision.

Trade Fixtures

The rule that once personal property is permanently annexed to real estate it becomes a part of it has serious consequences to tenants. Unless the tenant and owner agree, a tenant making permanent additions to real property may not remove a fixture at the end of the term. This greatly hampers a business from leasing a building if the firm needs to add items—such as display cases or machinery—to operate effectively. Because of this, the legal system differentiates between fixtures and personalty attached to real estate to carry on a trade or business.

Items of this latter nature are called **trade fixtures** and generally may be taken by the tenant at the end of the term. Agricultural fixtures are treated in a similar manner. To remove a trade or agricultural fixture, the tenant must restore the premises to its original condition and must remove the item while in possession.

Allowing tenants to remove trade fixtures has social benefits. It encourages both the use of land and efficiency in business. Tenants are more likely to invest in new and improved equipment if they can remove these items. In a number of states, statutes establish tenants' rights to remove trade fixtures.

Because the doctrine of trade fixtures is important to tenants, parties to a commercial lease should include provisions clearly expressing their intentions. They might agree that the tenant may remove items that ordinarily would be trade fixtures. A lease provision stating the tenant's right to remove items added to carry out its business or trade would clearly show the intention of the parties and would lessen possibilities of disagreement.

Bailments

As we have seen, the determination as to whether personal property has become a fixture causes problems in some business transactions. Other legal problems may arise when one person holds an item of property that is owned by another. This practice is common in many business relationships. Generally if an owner places an item of personal property in the holder's control to accomplish something about which both have agreed, a legal relationship called **bailment** exists. The owner who has surrendered the property is called the **bailor**; the person who holds and controls it is called the **bailee**.

Examples of bailment in commercial transactions include leasing an automobile or equipment, storing goods in a warehouse, or delivering goods to a trucker for shipment. A bailment is also created when a person takes an automobile to a garage for repairs, checks a coat in a restaurant, or borrows a friend's golf clubs.

Since bailments are important in business, the business manager must know the rights and duties of the parties to a bailment and be able to distinguish bailments from other transactions.

Essential Elements

The essential elements of the relationship are as follows:

1. A bailment's subject matter is *personal property*.
2. The bailee must have *possession* of the property.
3. There must be an *agreement*, either express or implied, to create a bailment.
4. The property must be *returned or accounted for* when the bailment is completed.

Personal Property The subject matter of a bailment must be personal property. The property can be either tangible or intangible, but it must be in existence at the time the bailment is created. The promise of a company to deliver stock to an employee is not a bailment if that stock does not exist. However, if the stock has been issued, but the company retains the certificates until the employee obtains the money to pay for it, the relationship is a bailment.

Possession Possession of the property by the bailee is a major element in any bailment. Possession is generally determined by the control that the bailee exercises over the property. In most bailments the property is actually in the bailee's possession. However, constructive possession is also sufficient. For example, a bank

that supplies safe deposit facilities generally is considered as a bailee in spite of the fact that the bank as bailee does not have actual control of the bailor's property. The bank's control of admission to the vault where the property is stored is the basis for considering the bank to be in control of the property.

Agreement A bailment may be created by an express agreement (such as an agreement I make with a business firm that agrees to store my boat in their winter storage sheds) or by actions indicating that the parties intended to make such an agreement (I leave my boat in my neighbor's garage again this year as I have done for the last three years).

Return of Property Ordinarily the item bailed, or a substitute for it, usually money, is to be returned or accounted for by the bailee. This aspect of the bailment clearly distinguishes it from a sale or a gift. In both a sale and a gift the title to the personal property in question passes to the recipient. That is not true with the bailment. As a result of this important distinction, the legal rights and obligations of the bailee are significantly different from those of the buyer of property. For this reason the business manager should be able to determine clearly if a given transaction is a bailment or a sale.

Consider the conditional sale and the consignment. If an item of property is delivered to another, who is to pay for the item over a period of time, with title to the property passing to the recipient once the item is paid for, the transaction is considered a conditional sale, not a bailment. This transaction is a sale rather than a bailment because the parties do intend for the title to the property to be transferred, even though that transfer generally comes well after the transfer of the possession of the property.

On the other hand, if an item of property is delivered to another and the recipient has the option of purchasing the property or selling it to others, no sale has yet taken place. Instead, the transaction, known as a consignment, is a type of bailment. All that is being transferred at the present time is the possession of the property. At the time of the consignment the parties do not intend for title to pass to the recipient. In fact, in most consignments, the title to the property never passes to the bailee-recipient, but passes from the seller only after the bailee has found a buyer to purchase the property. Gasoline is often consigned to service stations by the major gasoline producers, and works of art are frequently consigned to art galleries for sale from the artist or owner to the purchaser.

Legal Principles

Before discussing some common legal problems involving bailors and bailees, two fundamental legal principles need to be reviewed. First, as in other legal relationships, a bailment results from the way in which the parties act. A bailment is not created merely because the parties label their transaction as a bailment. If the essential elements we have discussed exist, a bailment is created, regardless of the name given by the parties to their transaction. If those elements are not present, no bailment exists.

Second, subject to a few specific statutory provisions, the rights and duties of a bailor and a bailee are determined by their agreement. The parties can settle on almost any terms they find desirable. Courts will first look to the agreement of the parties to determine their respective rights and duties. Of course, as noted in Chapter 16, any agreement that violates public policy will not be enforced.

Classification

In many bailments the parties fail to indicate adequately how their duties and obligations will be divided between them. In such cases courts have to determine how to divide the duties between the parties equitably. One method that has been used to assist in making that determination is based on looking at the benefits received by both the bailor and the bailee.

A threefold method of classification of bailments has developed. The most common type of bailment in business is one in which both parties benefit. This is referred to as a **mutual benefit bailment**. An example of a mutual benefit bailment is where a company pays the owner of a warehouse to store goods there.

A bailment in which the bailee furnishes no consideration for the property he or she possesses is referred to as a **bailment for the sole benefit of the bailee** or a gratuitous bailment. In this situation someone lends an item to another, expecting no payment in return. If only the owner of the property benefits, the bailment is said to be a **bailment for the sole benefit of the bailor**. This type of bailment exists if someone who is not paid holds another's property for safekeeping. Not all courts look to these classifications to assist them in solving problems involving bailments, but they are helpful in some cases.

Bailor's Responsibility for Defective Goods

In bailments for the sole benefit of the bailee, courts traditionally have required only that the bailor warn the bailee of known dangers that expose the borrower to an unreasonable risk of harm. In either a mutual benefit bailment or a bailment for the sole benefit of the bailor the bailor's responsibility for defects in the property is more extensive.

The law in most states is that the bailor must use reasonable care in inspecting the property and seeing that it is safe for the purposes for which it is being used. For example, if Hertz does not conduct a reasonable inspection of a rental car after it has been returned, it would be liable if the vehicle had defective brakes and that defect caused injury to a subsequent user of the car.

Some states go even further and impose an implied warranty of fitness for goods that are rented to or loaned by a bailor. Courts in these states impose this warranty in cases where the bailee must rely on the bailor's expertise to determine that the property is fit for use. When such a warranty is implied, a bailor can be held liable even if it acted reasonably. Suppose that Hertz does indeed conduct a reasonable inspection of all of its cars and trucks after they are returned. If one of its vehicles is found to have a defect which causes the bailee to be injured, Hertz would be liable under such a warranty. This is true even though Hertz acted reasonably and was not negligent. Like the seller of goods warranted to be fit for a particular purpose, the bailor generally is allowed to disclaim this specific warranty. The opinion that follows is a case in point.

MERCEDES-BENZ CREDIT CORPORATION V. SHIELDS
Court of Appeals of Georgia
403 S.E.2d 891 (1991)

BACKGROUND: Shields (defendant-appellee) leased a Mercedes-Benz automobile from Mercedes-Benz Credit Corporation (the plaintiff-appellant). Shields defaulted on his payments several times, and eventually the car was repossessed. The car was sold at an auction, with the proceeds applied to the debt owed by Shields to the lessor. The proceeds weren't enough to cover Shields's entire debt, however, and the lessor sued to recover the deficiency. Shields contended that the lessor had breached an implied warranty of fitness because the car was defective. The trial court ruled in favor of Shields, and the lessor appealed.

Cooper, Judge

On January 27, 1984, appellee entered into an agreement with appellant for the lease of a 1984 Mercedes-Benz, imported, sold and warranted by Mercedes-Benz of North America, Inc. The evidence is undisputed that over the course of the lease, appellee developed an inconsistent payment history, repeatedly falling behind and having to catch up past due payments months at a time, each missed payment constituting a default under the lease. Moreover, for a time, appellee's insurance was cancelled for non-payment, also a default under the lease. In a modification letter, appellee declared that the car would be primarily used for personal, family or household purposes. However, Ralph McClure ("McClure"), a real estate agent in appellee's employ, admitted using the car "95% of the time" to show properties and in performance of his duties as "office manager" of appellee's real estate business. In March, 1985, while driving the car, McClure detected the smell of gasoline. He opened the trunk and discovered gasoline floating in the trunk, one quarter of an inch deep. The car was returned to the original dealership, in accordance with the lease, where repair technicians discovered that the underside was thickly covered with a large amount of mud and dirt, in a quantity never before seen on a car and so thick it could be chiseled away in huge chunks with a screwdriver. Cakes of mud were also in the engine compartment. The car had to be cleaned before the source of the problem could be determined. The charcoal canister located under the hood, which ventilated the gas tank, was clogged with mud resulting in a buildup of pressure in the tank causing the trunk to rupture. The canister and the gas tank were replaced under the warranty at no cost to appellee. Two weeks later, the car was brought back, heavily encrusted with mud, with the same problem. The car was cleaned, and the tank and canister were again replaced at no cost to appellee. After another two weeks the car was again returned for repair, the ventilation system blocked with mud. The car was repaired; however, appellee never returned for the car and did not make the April payment on the lease. Appellee made no further payments on the lease. . . .

Appellee relied on OCGA § 44–12–63(3), as a defense to his suspension of payments on the lease, which requires a bailor, such as appellant, "[t]o warrant the right of possession and that the thing bailed is free from any secret fault rendering it unfit for the purposes for which it is hired." Appellee contended that the "flooding of gasoline in the trunk area" was a secret fault and that a representation by a mechanic that the car could not be repaired justified his action. However, the lease agreement provided that appellee acknowledged that appellant "[made] no express warranties regarding the vehicle as to its condition, merchantability or fitness for use, that [appellant] disclaim[ed] any implied warranties, and that [appellee was] leasing [the vehicle] from [appellant] 'as is.'" The agreement also stated that "[t]he monthly rent shall be paid for the full term of the lease without notice or demand and without setoff, counterclaim, reduction, abatement, suspension, deferment or any other defense because of the disappearance, theft, destruction, levy, judicial seizure or *unsatisfactory performance* of the vehicle or for any other reason whatever, unless this lease is terminated under an express provision of this agreement." (Emphasis supplied.)

"'[P]arties are free to contract and may by express agreement enlarge, abridge, qualify, or supersede obligations that otherwise would arise from the bailment by implication of law—so long as the contract does not violate statutory law or contravene public policy—and, so long as such restrictions are expressed in clear and unambiguous language.'

A contract in which a lessor or bailor exculpates himself from liability with a disclaimer clause, as in the instant case, is not prohibited by law or public policy.

Moreover, the disclaimer and abatement clauses were "explicit, prominent, clear and unambiguous," evidencing an intentional waiver of the statutory warranties of OCGA §44–12–63.

DECISION: The court of appeals reversed the trial court's decision and ruled in the lessor's favor.

Bailee's Responsibility for Care and Use

Although the bailee is in possession of the bailor's property, the bailee does not guarantee the safety of the property against loss or injury. Almost all courts have stated that a bailee is not an insurer. A bailee is, however, responsible for any loss caused by its negligence, but traditionally the courts have measured the degree of care that must be exercised by the type of bailment.

In a mutual-benefit bailment the general rule requires the bailee to take ordinary and reasonable care of the property. Liability occurs if the bailee does not exercise the same degree of care that an ordinarily prudent person would use in caring for his or her own property.

Some jurisdictions allow the bailee to escape or limit its liability by agreement with the bailor; however, in a number of states an agreement of this nature is against public policy and not enforceable. These kinds of agreements are especially apt to be unenforceable if the bargaining power of the bailee is substantially greater than that of the bailor. As it is possible for the bailee to limit its liability by agreement, the bailor, too, can increase the bailee's responsibility by contract. A common example would be a requirement that the bailee insure the property for the bailor's benefit.

Negligence or the absence of due care is also the standard in a bailment for the sole benefit of the bailor or one that solely benefits the bailee. In each case, however, the degree of care that the bailee must exercise in order to escape liability differs. In a situation where only the bailor benefits, the bailee needs to exercise only slight diligence. Thus the bailee is liable only if its neglect of duty amounts to willfulness and evidences a reckless disregard for the rights of others. Conversely, if the bailment is for the sole benefit of the bailee, slight negligence is enough to establish the bailee's responsibility for injury or loss. Courts feel that it is reasonable to expect that a person who borrows another's property will take extraordinary care to protect it. This degree of care has been defined as that which the prudent person would exercise in his or her own affairs of great importance.

Although classification of bailments based on benefit has traditionally aided courts in determining liability, the current trend is to consider the type of bailment as only one factor in measuring whether conduct is reasonable under the circumstances. Whether a bailee has exercised the proper degree of care is determined by this and factors such as the type of property, the reason for the bailment, custom of the trade, and prior dealings between the parties.

As the following case illustrates, the bailee is also required to exercise due care when returning the bailed property to the bailor.

FIREMAN'S FUND INSURANCE CO. v. WAGNER FUR, INC.

U.S. District Court (S.D. N.Y.)

760 F. Supp. 1101 (1991)

BACKGROUND: Mr. and Mrs. Cullman paid Wagner to store three of their furs at a facility that Wagner operated. When it was time to return the furs to the Cullmans, Wagner arranged for them to be shipped to the Cullmans' residence by United Parcel Service (UPS). The Cullmans lived at 784 Park Avenue, but the furs were mistakenly delivered to 785 Park Avenue. It was not clear whose fault the mistake was. A porter at 785 Park Avenue accepted the furs and put them in a service elevator, from which they disappeared. Fireman's Fund, the Cullmans' insurer, paid the Cullmans' claim and then sued Wagner for, among other things, the tort of conversion. Wagner moved for summary judgment. The case was submitted to a U.S. magistrate, who recommended that the federal district court grant the motion for summary judgment with respect to the conversion claim.

Lowe, District Judge

On the claims of conversion against Wagner, Magistrate Francis found that the record revealed "no evidence that [Wagner] converted the furs for its own use," and thus that it was entitled to summary judgment. Plaintiff objects that Magistrate Francis improperly applied the law of conversion in considering whether the evidence showed any benefit to Wagner from the misdelivery of the furs. We agree.

The tort of conversion commonly refers to "the act of wrongfully converting (something) to one's own use." More precisely, however, a conversion is any "intentional exercise of dominion or control over a chattel which so seriously interferes with the right of another to control it that the actor may justly be required to pay the other the full value of the chattel." ALI, Restatement (second) of Torts, §222A(1) (1964).

The requisite interference with an owner's right of control will readily be found where bailed property is misdelivered. *Any* unauthorized delivery of bailed property by a bailee—even delivery to the wrong person resulting from the bailee's good faith mistake—constitutes a conversion. Thus, in *Jacobson v. Richards & Hassen Enterprises, Inc.*, the Second Circuit, applying New York law, held the operator of a coat-check in a hotel restaurant liable for conversion of a fur coat where the defendant's employee turned the coat over to an imposter posing as its owner. See also *Wabco Trade Co. v. S.S. Inger Skou.* ("The absence of benefit to [the defendant-bailee] does not preclude liability. An action for conversion may be based on transferring possession of the owner's property to one not authorized to receive it. In particular, a bailee who transfers goods in a manner inconsistent with an owner's instructions is liable for conversion to his bailor."); *David Crystal, Inc. v. Cunard Steam-ship Co.* (reviewing New York cases standing for the proposition that bailees are "'not only liable for losses occasioned by their negligence, but for those which arise from innocent mistakes in the delivery of goods to persons not entitled to receive them.' [*Bank of Oswego v. Doyle*]").

Under these principles, Wagner could be found liable for conversion if it misaddressed the furs, and thus caused them to be misdelivered and lost, even if, as it appears, this was merely a mistake and Wagner received no benefit from the misdelivery. In other words, plaintiff need not prove that Wagner converted the furs "for its own use" in order to succeed on this claim. Accordingly, summary judgment for Wagner on the conversion claim is inappropriate.

DECISION: The court refused to grant Wagner's motion for summary judgment.

Bailee's Use of Property

A bailee who treats the property in a manner not authorized by the agreement becomes absolutely liable for any loss or damage. This responsibility exists in spite of the bailee's exercise of due care even if the result actually benefits the bailor. A bailee who uses the property in an unauthorized manner, stores it some place other than that agreed upon, or fails to return it according to the contract is liable to the bailor even though injury or loss is caused by an accident or act of God.

In many transactions the bailee's authority to deal with the property is not clearly expressed by the parties. In these cases the court usually considers the following factors to determine the bailee's liability:

1. The purpose of the transaction
2. The type of property
3. The relationship between the parties
4. The custom of the business

Transfer of Title to Property

Sale

Sale is the most important method of transferring title to property. Although the methods of selling both real and personal property have developed along somewhat different lines, both are governed extensively by statute and case law. The sale of goods is the subject of Article 2 of the Uniform Commercial Code, which is discussed in detail in Chapters 21, 22, and 23. Some of the legal problems inherent in the transfer of title to real property by sale are discussed in Chapter 48.

In general the process involved in selling real property is much more formal than that involved in the sale of goods. Statutes in all states require public recording of the transfer of title to real property if the owner's title is to be valid against claims of third parties who might acquire an interest in that property.

Gift

Title to property frequently is transferred by gift. In dollar value the vast majority of gifts are made through the testamentary disposition of a deceased person. Gifts by living persons, however, are very important.

A gift that is to be conveyed while the donor is still living is an **inter vivos gift**, unless the gift is made by the donor in the expectation that he or she is about to die. A **causa mortis gift** is one given by a donor in the expectation of his or her impending death.

In an inter vivos gift the recipient or donee receives an irrevocable title. In a causa mortis gift the gift may be revoked if the donor does not die.

For a gift by a living person to be valid the donor must intend to make a gift, and delivery of the item must take place. In addition, the donee must be willing to accept the gift. While this last requirement causes few problems, the other essential elements of a gift sometimes result in litigation, as the following case illustrates. The role of joint property in estate planning is discussed in Chapter 51.

IN RE THE ESTATE OF ALFRED V. SIPE, DECEASED

Supreme Court of Pennsylvania
422 A.2d 826 (1980)

BACKGROUND: Eleanor Sipe (petitioner-appellee), executrix of the estate of Alfred V. Sipe, petitioned the court for an order directing Mary Drabik (respondent-appellant) to turn over to the estate the money she withdrew after the decedent's death from a joint savings account opened by the decedent in his name and her name. The trial court found that since Ms. Drabik had never signed the card opening the savings account the decedent had not made an effective gift to her during his lifetime.

Ms. Drabik appealed, claiming the requirements for a valid gift had been met.

Flaherty, Justice

The trial court concluded that a gift had not been made because the decedent, when he opened the account, filled out the entire signature card himself by signing both his name and the appellant's name and their Social Security numbers on the card. Appellant's failure to sign the joint signature card was "fatal to her case" according to the trial court. We do not agree.

Although this Court has held on numerous occasions that the "[e]xecution of a signature card creating a joint savings account with a right of survivorship is *sufficient* to establish an inter vivos gift to the joint tenant by the depositor of the funds" . . . , it is not the law and we have never held that such proof is the only proof which can establish a gift. All of the circumstances must be considered in determining whether a gift was made or whether the joint account was established for some other purpose.

Sometime prior to September 17, 1975, decedent opened a savings account in his own name at a branch of the Union National Bank. On the above date, decedent went to the bank and told an employee of the bank that he wanted to close the account in his own name and open a new account in his name and the name of the appellant into which was deposited approximately $8,000.00, which included the $3,000.00 balance in his old account. Decedent signed a temporary signature card for the account and was given a permanent signature card to be signed by himself and the appellant and returned to the bank. The court found that decedent, not appellant, signed appellant's name on the signature card.

About eighteen months later, on February 20, 1977, decedent, who was about to enter the hospital for surgery, gave the passbook for the joint account to appellant. After his discharge from the hospital about a month later, decedent, who needed care, went to the residence of his nephew Vernon Sipe, which was next door. Decedent died about six weeks later on April 30, 1977. After his discharge from the hospital, decedent was not confined to bed. Although he could not drive himself, he visited the hospital for treatments, went shopping on various occasions and was in the bank where the joint account existed sometime in early April, although he did not transact any business, but was there in the company of his nephew Vernon Sipe, who had business at the bank.

The requirements for a gift are intent, delivery and acceptance in all cases. This is so whether we are concerned with monies, a bank account, a stock certificate, or a horse. Accepting the trial judge's conclusion that the appellant did not sign the signature card herself, the issue remains whether or not a valid gift was established.

As to the first requirement for a valid gift—intent—there is no question that the evidence satisfies that requirement. Decedent was not opening a savings account for the first time. He specifically asked that that account be closed and a new joint account be opened in his name and the name of appellant. He was given an explanation of the account and a signature card which he signed and returned to the bank. That signature card clearly states that a joint account is being established with the right of either party to withdraw and with the right of survivorship. The only conclusion possible is that the decedent intended to make a gift.

Appellee seems to attach great significance to the lower court's finding that appellant did not sign the signature card. . . . Signing the card would have shifted the burden of proof to the challenger that joint ownership was not created. Not signing the card merely means that we must consider all the circumstances in determining whether a joint account was intended to exist, whether the requirements of the law pertaining to the creation of gifts have been met. . . .

In addition to donative intent, the law of gifts also requires acceptance of the gift, but acceptance is presumed. The acceptance requirement was met when appellant received the passbook from decedent. It has never been required that a donee sign a document acknowledging acceptance, which is what appellee's position would dictate.

Finally, the law of gifts also requires a delivery. Without reaching the question of whether a delivery was effected when decedent gave the signature card to the bank, it is clear that delivery was made when decedent gave the passbook to appellant.

The only conclusion warranted on the basis of the undisputed facts, coupled with the facts as found by the trial court, is that the decedent made a valid gift to the appellant.

DECISION: The court of appeals reversed the trial court's decision.

In addition to sale or gift, title to property is transferred in several other ways. Some of these, such as adverse possession and eminent domain, are more commonly associated with real property and are discussed in Chapter 48.

Judicial Sale

Most courts have the power to order the sale of a defendant's real or personal property in order to satisfy a judgment. Sometimes the court's order is based on an agreement in which one of the parties has used specific property as a security. Usually the property secures a loan or is used to finance the purchase of the property. A real estate mortgage (Chapter 49) or a security agreement (Chapter 32) executed by the purchaser of goods are examples. In addition, many states allow designated officials to seize various assets of a defendant and to sell them to satisfy a money judgment. As has been noted in Chapter 34, state statutes usually exempt from seizure the property which is necessary to earn a livelihood or sustain life. Table 47-2 depicts the different requirements for transferring real and personal property by sale, gift, or judicial sale.

Table **47-2**

Concept Summary		Transferring Title to Property by Sale, Gift, or Judicial Sale
Method	**Real Property**	**Personal Property**
Sale	Transfer by deed and public recording (for a house or a vacant lot)	Transfer by bill of sale (stereo), certificate of title (auto), possession (textbook)
Gift	Transfer by deed and public recording	Transfer during life (inter vivos) requires intent and delivery (savings account); transfer at death (testamentary) is done by valid will or according to interstate law
Judicial sale	Transfer of property used as security (purchaser of home gives mortgage to lender; if purchaser doesn't pay, home can be sold at judicial sale and proceeds used to pay lender)	Transfer of property used as a security (if car is used as security for loan, nonpayment by buyer may lead to transfer of car to lender)

Abandoned, Lost, and Mislaid Property

Abandoned property is that which the owner has voluntarily given up with the intention of surrendering any interest that he or she has. In the event of litigation over supposedly abandoned property, the person claiming title must be able to prove that the owner intended to abandon the property. Merely not using property even for an extended time is not abandonment, although nonuse may be used as evidence showing an intention to abandon. The first person to acquire abandoned property gets title to it.

Lost property and abandoned property are not the same. **Lost property** is that which the owner had no intention of giving up but has parted with through carelessness or accident. Loss of a diamond that falls out of a ring setting would be an example.

Acquisition of title to lost property differs from the acquisition of title to abandoned property. In most cases the person who finds lost property acquires an interest that is good against everyone but the true owner. But before the finder acquires title, certain conditions must be met. These conditions vary from state to state.

Some states continue to follow the common law rule. At common law, before the finder of lost property acquired title, he or she was required to make a reasonable search for the true owner. Most states by statute require a finder to notify a designated public official of the finding. If the property is not claimed within a specified period of time—usually 6 months to 1 year—the finder acquires the property.

The law considers mislaid property and lost property differently. **Mislaid property** is property that an owner has intentionally placed somewhere and then forgotten. Supposedly when the owner remembers the item, he or she knows where to look for it. As a result, the owner of the place where the property is found and not the finder has the right to the property if it is not claimed by the rightful owner. The law assumes that the owner will return to the place where the item was mislaid. Entrusting the owner of that place with property makes it easier for the true owner to recover his or her property.

For example, Sam, a customer of First Bank, finds a woman's purse on a counter in the lobby. If unclaimed, the purse and its contents become the property of the bank, because the purse apparently was mislaid. If the property had been lost and not mislaid, the result probably would differ. Assume that Sam found the purse on the floor of the lobby and not on the counter. In that event, Sam would acquire title if he took the proper steps, because the purse apparently was lost. But if Sam were an employee of the bank, the bank would be entitled to the purse. An employee who finds lost property while on the job has no right to it as long as the employer has a policy of accepting responsibility for it.

Changing Concepts of Property

Property is a dynamic concept continually being reshaped by society to meet new economic and social needs. In the United States today two movements modifying traditional rights associated with property are worth noting. One of these involves the restructuring of property rights in their relationship to civil rights. This is illustrated by legislation and cases that attempt to ensure the fundamental interests of minorities. In most instances, where traditional property rights conflict with basic civil rights, property rights have been limited.

The 1948 U.S. Supreme Court opinion in *Shelly v. Kramer* exemplifies this trend. This case involved an agreement by certain owners of real estate not to sell or lease their homes to "any person not of the Caucasian race." When Shelly, an African American, purchased a parcel covered by this restriction, Kramer and others sued to restrain him from taking possession. The Supreme Court held that state courts could not enforce a private agreement depriving a person of a constitutional right. In effect, the Supreme Court limited the right of Kramer and the others to restrict the use of their real estate in this manner.

A second direction that the law is taking is to extend property rights to a person's employment or to the degrees and licenses that are necessary to practice. Although the movement in this direction is slow, the trend is clear. Recently courts have been urged to treat status and reputation as property, as the following case illustrates.

MEMPHIS DEVELOPMENT FOUNDATION V. FACTORS ETC., INC.
U.S. Court of Appeals, Sixth Circuit
616 F.2d 959 (1980)

BACKGROUND: Memphis Development Foundation (Foundation) (plaintiff-appellant) sued in U.S. District Court to enjoin Factors Etc. Inc. (defendant-appellee) from interfering with Foundation's attempt to erect a large bronze statue of Elvis Presley in downtown Memphis. Foundation solicited public contributions to pay for the sculpture. Donors of $25 or more received an 8-inch pewter replica of the proposed statue.

During his lifetime Presley had conveyed the exclusive right to exploit the commercial value of his name to Boxcar Enterprises in exchange for royalties. These rights had been assigned to Factors Etc., Inc. (Factors) 2 days after Presley's death. Factors by counterclaim sought damages and an injunction against distribution of the replicas by Foundation.

The district court granted Foundation's injunction prohibiting interference with its efforts to erect the statue but the court also prohibited the Foundation from distributing any statue bearing the image or likeness of Elvis Presley. Foundation appealed.

Merritt, Circuit Judge

This appeal raises the interesting question: Who is the heir of fame? The famous have an exclusive legal right during life to control and profit from the commercial use of their name and personality. We are called upon in this diversity case to determine whether, under Tennessee law, the exclusive right to publicity survives a celebrity's death. We hold that the right is not inheritable. After death the opportunity for gain shifts to the public domain, where it is equally open to all.

At common law, there is a right of action for the appropriation or unauthorized commercial use of the name or likeness of another. An individual is entitled to control the commercial use of these personal attributes during life. But the common law has not heretofore widely recognized this right to control commercial publicity as a property right which may be inherited.

Tennessee courts have not addressed this issue directly or indirectly, and we have no way to assess their predisposition. Since the case is one of first impression, we are left to review the question in the light of practical and policy considerations, the treatment of other similar rights in our legal system, the relative weight of the conflicting interests of the parties, and certain moral presuppositions concerning death, privacy, inheritability and economic opportunity. These considerations lead us to conclude that the right of publicity should not be given the status of a devisable right, even where as here a person exploits the right by contract during life.

Recognition of a post-mortem right of publicity would vindicate two possible interests: the encouragement of effort and creativity, and the hopes and expectations of the decedent and those with whom he contracts that they are creating a valuable capital asset. Although fame and stardom may be ends in themselves, they are normally by-products of one's activities and personal attributes, as well as luck and promotion. The basic motivations are the desire to achieve success or excellence in a chosen field, the desire to contribute to the happiness or improvement of one's fellows and the desire to receive the psychic and financial rewards of achievement. . . .

The desire to exploit fame for the commercial advantage of one's heirs is by contrast a weak principle of motivation. It seems apparent that making the right of publicity inheritable would not significantly inspire the creative endeavors of individuals in our society.

On the other hand, there are strong reasons for declining to recognize the inheritability of the right. A whole set of practical problems of judicial line-drawing would arise should the courts recognize such an inheritable right. How long would the "property" interest last? In perpetuity? For a term of years? Is the right of publicity taxable? At what point does the right collide with the right of free expression guaranteed by the first amendment? Does the right apply to elected officials and military heroes whose fame was gained on the public payroll, as well as to movie stars, singers and athletes? Does the right cover posters or engraved likenesses of, for example, Farah Fawcett Majors or Mahatma Gandhi, kitchen utensils ("Revere Ware"), insurance ("John Hancock"), electric utilities ("Edison"), a football stadium ("RFK"), a pastry ("Napoleon"), or the innumerable urban subdivisions and apartment complexes named after famous people? Our legal system normally does not pass on to heirs other similar personal attributes even though the attributes may be shared during life by others or have some commercial value. Titles, offices and reputation are not inheritable. Neither are trust or distrust and friendship or enmity descendible. An employment contract during life does not create the right for heirs to take over the job. Fame falls in the same category as reputation; it is an attribute from which others may benefit but may not own. . . .

Heretofore, the law has always thought that leaving a good name to one's children is sufficient reward in itself for the individual, whether famous or not. Commercialization of this virtue after death in the hands of heirs is contrary to our legal tradition and somehow seems contrary to the moral presuppositions of our culture.

There is no indication that changing the traditional common law rule against allowing heirs the exclusive control of the commercial use of their ancestor's name will increase the efficiency or productivity of our economic system. It does not seem reasonable to expect that such a change would enlarge the stock or quality of the goods, services, artistic creativity, information, invention or entertainment available. Nor will it enhance the fairness of our political and economic system. It seems fairer and more efficient for the commercial, aesthetic, and political use of the name, memory and image of the famous to be open to all rather than to be monopolized by a few. An equal distribution of the opportunity to use the name of the dead seems preferable. The memory, name and pictures of famous individuals should be regarded as a common asset to be shared, an economic opportunity available in the free market system.

DECISION: The court of appeals reversed the district court's decision.

Review Questions and Problems

Key Terms

real property

personal property

chattels

goods

chose in action

trade fixtures

bailment

bailor

bailee

mutual benefit bailment

bailment for the sole benefit of the bailee

bailment for the sole benefit of the bailor

inter vivos gift

causa mortis gift

abandoned property

lost property

mislaid property

Discussion Questions

1. Explain the difference between real and personal property, and indicate some of the legal consequences of this difference.

2. Define intangible personal property and provide some examples of it.

3. Indicate the tests courts use to determine if an item is a fixture.

4. What are the essential elements necessary for making a valid gift?

5. Explain the different legal consequences of classifying an item as a trade fixture as compared with a fixture.

Review Problems

1. Tillotson purchased a drying bin from the B. C. Manufacturing Company. The bin was erected on property owned by the Newman Grove Grain Company. The bin was anchored to a concrete base and became an integral part of the grain corporation's elevator, to which it was attached with loading and unloading ducts, electrical wiring, and so on. The Newman Grove Grain Company mortgaged the real estate to the Battle Creek State Bank. Is the bin a fixture? What difference does this make? Explain.

2. Anne P. Graham and Dennis J. Graham were husband and wife. During their 6-year marriage Anne Graham was employed full time. Her husband worked part time, although his main pursuit was his education. He attended school for approximately 3 1/2 years, acquiring a bachelor of science degree and a master's degree in business. Approximately 70 percent of the family funds were supplied by the wife.

   The Grahams filed a petition for dissolution of marriage. As part of this action, Anne Graham claimed that the master's degree was marital property and subject to division by the court. She asked for $33,134 as her share of this property. Should the degree be treated as property? Discuss.

3. Health Clubs, Inc., contracted to purchase an indoor swimming pool from Stanton. The pool was heated and had a large filtering unit. The heater and filter were easily removable once disconnected. Before Health Clubs, Inc., took possession, Stanton removed both units. When sued, Stanton contended that the units were personal property. Health Clubs, Inc., argued that the units were fixtures. Who is correct? Support your answer.

4. Fishbien purchased a small motel from January. He was to take possession in 30 days. The day after he received a deed to the property, he noticed that January was removing all the furniture. Fishbien sued for a court order to prevent this. He argued that the motel was worthless without the furniture. Would he be successful? Discuss.

5. Milligan owned a farm in Iowa, which he sold to Meyers. Milligan moved into town from the farm, but he left a well drilling rig on the property with the permission of Meyers. The rig was in poor condition, and two of its tires were flat. Milligan told Meyers that the rig was for sale. Several people did come to examine the rig in the weeks following the sale. But the rig was never moved. About 2 years later Meyers learned that Milligan had moved to California. The following year Meyers repaired the rig and began to use it. Has Meyers acquired title to the rig? Discuss.

Case Problems

1. Cogliano owned a nursery business on land taken by the state to build a highway. The nursery stock consisted principally of young trees of varying ages and heights, some shrubbery, rose bushes, and perennials. The value of the land apart from the stock was $10,000. The value of the nursery stock was $40,000. The state Department of Public Works awarded Cogliano $10,000 for the land. This award did not include the nursery stock, which Cogliano was given 30 days to remove.

   (a) Indicate the legal basis that the Department of Public Works might use in support of the limited award.

   (b) On what grounds might Cogliano argue that he was entitled to $50,000?

   (c) Who has the best argument? Why?

2. Amerson wished to borrow an electric drill from Howell. Howell was aware that the drill had previously shocked three people, none of whom was injured. This information was conveyed to Amerson. In addition, before giving the drill to Amerson, Howell changed the plug and tested the drill, receiving no shock. When Amerson used the drill, he suffered a fatal shock. Would Amerson's estate be able to recover from Howell? Discuss.

3. Boyd entered State University on a 1-year football scholarship that was renewable at the University's option. State University offered to renew Boyd's scholarship for the next year, but he decided to transfer to Central College which played in the same football conference with State University. The conference, Gulf South Conference, had a rule that prohibited a player who had received a scholarship to play from one college in the conference from playing for another college unless the first college did not offer to renew that player's scholarship and the player waited 2 years after his first college scholarship was not renewed. Boyd claims the rules of Gulf South Conference deprive him of a property right, the right to play football, with a possible scholarship for him if he did so, at Central College. Do you agree with Boyd?

4. Evans rented a safe deposit box and stored his valuables in it. When he went in the hospital, Evans gave the keys to the box to his niece whom he had been close to for many years. Just before he died, Evans told his minister he was giving the church $10,000 and the rest of his things to his niece.

The executor of Evans's estate claims Evans did not make a gift of the contents of the safe deposit box (worth about $80,000) to his niece because he didn't give her the things in the box and he didn't put her name on the box. Evans did visit the safe deposit box about a month before his death. Even though his niece had the keys to the box, the bank would not let her have access to it after Evans's death because her name was not on it. Has Evans made a valid gift to his niece? Why?

5. Rhodes parked his car in a parking lot owned by Pioneer Parking Lot, Inc. There was no attendant at the lot. He took a ticket from a ticket meter when entering the lot which read NOTICE. THIS CONTRACT LIMITS OUR LIABILITY—READ IT. WE RENT SPACE ONLY. NO BAILMENT IS CREATED. Rhodes parked his own car, locked it and kept the keys. When he returned to the lot, he found his car had been stolen. Rhodes claims Pioneer Parking Lot breached its duty as a bailee to use reasonable care. Pioneer, referring to its ticket, said there was no bailment relationship created with Rhodes. Do you agree with Pioneer?

48

Interests in Real Property

Estates in Land
Leasehold Estates

Nonpossessory Interests in Real Property
Co-ownership

Real property law deals with ownership of land and those things permanently attached to it. Because land is an unusual commodity and for centuries has been of great economic importance in the Western world, the legal relationships involving real property are extensive and complicated. This chapter discusses some of the many interests that exist in real estate. As traditionally defined by courts and commentators, land ownership encompasses the surface of the earth, and everything above and below the surface. The space over which the surface owner has dominion is compared to a pyramid extending upward indefinitely into space and downward to the center of the earth. As air travel became an important means of transportation, the traditional rule gradually has been modified. Today the general rule is that the surface owner's air rights are limited to the space that can be reasonably used and enjoyed.

Both the air space above and the natural resources such as oil or minerals below the surface of the land can be separated from the land and treated as independent commodities. In cities some landowners retain ownership of the land's surface and sell the air space above it for the construction of commercial buildings. In mining regions the right to extract natural resources is frequently separated from ownership of the surface and leased or sold. In the arid areas of the West water rights are very often separated from surface ownership of land.

Estates in Land

Interests in land may be divided in many different ways. One way, as the previous section indicates, is to divide use and enjoyment of the land itself horizontally in relation to space. Another way is to separate the land from possible rights in it and allow numerous interests to exist simultaneously. This is the basis of the doctrine of estates. This doctrine was important in the historic development of English and American land law and continues to influence real property law today.

The word **estate** as used in real property law indicates the nature, quantity, and quality of an ownership interest. As an estate refers to an ownership interest, it is or must have the potential for becoming possessory. The extent of an estate is determined by the duration of the interest and the time when the right to possess and enjoy the land begins.

For example, a wife might provide by will that her real property go to her husband for the duration of his life and then to her daughter. Upon the wife's death, both husband and daughter would have existing estates. The husband's estate would be measured by the duration of his life; the daughter's estate could last forever, but it does not begin until her father dies.

Fee Simple Estates

A **fee simple estate**, also called a fee simple absolute or simply a fee, is the most extensive inter-

---

ETHICS
Spying on Property

Du Pont built a new plant in Beaumont, Texas, incorporating a novel technique for manufacturing methanol. Before the plant's roof was installed, a plane—presumably hired by a competitor—flew over the plant and took pictures. It would be possible for a chemical engineer to figure out the new manufacturing process by looking at the pictures of the partially constructed plant.

This case of industrial spying for hire raises numerous ethical and legal questions. Was the flying over the property a trespass? Does it depend on the height of the plane or the intent of the pilot? If Du Pont claimed a trade secret in the process, did it take adequate care to make sure that the secret process was not discoverable?

In the era of spy satellites it might be argued that a company in the position of Du Pont should take care to protect its innovations from being viewed from above. If the property was out of the way and unlikely to be flown over in the normal course of activity, then that might change the situation.

Another view is that the actions of the competitor went beyond the bounds of proper competition. It might be very expensive for Du Pont to protect its properties from viewing from above, and if all firms have to incur such costs, society is worse off. The actions in this case vary little from hiring someone to find a way to be invited into the plant and then surreptitiously take pictures from within.

---

est that a person can have in land. This is the type of estate held by most owners of real property. The estate is potentially infinite in duration. It may be transferred to others during the lifetime of the owner. Upon the owner's death, his or her interest does not end but passes by will or the laws of intestate succession, if the owner dies without leaving a will. This is the type of estate held by the wife in the previous example. In most states, the only restrictions or conditions that can be imposed on this estate are those imposed by government. If a question exists as to the type of estate that is transferred, the courts presume that a fee simple is intended.

Fee Simple Defeasible

A **defeasible fee** is an estate that terminates if certain events occur; a defeasible fee is thus less extensive than a fee simple. Until these events occur, however, the owner of the defeasible fee possesses essentially the same interests as those possessed by the owner of a fee simple. For example, a defeasible fee might be used if a person wished to give land to a municipality for recreational purposes. The grantor might execute a deed with the following language: "to the City of Columbus, Georgia, and its successors and as-

signs so long as the property is used for recreational purposes."

If the land is not used for the stated purpose, the city's interest terminates automatically and reverts to the grantor or the grantor's heirs. Not all defeasible fees terminate automatically. Some require the grantor or the grantor's successors to take steps to terminate them. Although the defeasible fee is not used extensively today, it has played a significant role historically in property law.

Life Estates

A **life estate** is one whose duration is measured by the life of a person, typically the owner but possibly some other person. A life estate measured by the life of a person other than the owner is known as an *estate per autre vie*. The person who holds a life estate is known as the **life tenant**. A person whose possessory interest in the property commences after the expiration of the life estate is known as the **remainderman**. Life estates may be created by deed or will. They are also created by statute and case law. A life estate may be sold or mortgaged, but the acquiring party's interest is terminated by the life tenant's death. The following case illustrates one of the limitations placed on a life tenant. While the life tenant has a recognizable interest in real property, that tenant's rights are limited because remaindermen also have rights in property. One of the most important obligations that a life tenant owes to the remaindermen is to avoid committing *waste*, which occurs when one in rightful possession of the property abuses or neglects the property in a way that diminishes the value of interests held by others in the property.

SAULS V. CROSBY

District Court of Appeals of Florida
258 So.2d 326 (1972)

BACKGROUND: Sauls (plaintiff-appellant) sold real property she owned in Florida to Crosby (defendant-appellee), retaining for herself a life estate in that property. After she cut some of the timber from the land, Crosby objected. He claimed that as a life tenant, Sauls had no right to cut the timber. Sauls sued to enforce her right to cut the timber from the land she had sold to Crosby.

 The trial court determined that because Sauls had only a life estate in the Florida property, she had no right to cut timber from that land unless the proceeds were used for the benefit of the remaindermen (such as Crosby). Sauls appealed to the court of appeals.

Rawls, Judge

On the 9th day of October 1968, appellant (Sauls) conveyed to appellees (Crosby) certain lands situated in Hamilton County, Florida, with the following reservation set forth in said conveyance: "The Grantor herein, reserves a life Estate in said property." By this appeal appellant now contends that the trial court erred in denying her, as a life tenant, the right to cut merchantable timber and enjoy the proceeds.

 The English common law, which was transplanted on this continent, holds that it is waste for an ordinary life tenant to cut timber upon his estate when the sole purpose is to clear the woodlands. American courts today as a general rule recognize that an ordinary life tenant may cut timber and not be liable for waste if he uses the timber for fuel; for repairing fences and buildings on the estate; for fitting the land for cultivation; or for use as pasture if the inheritance is not damaged and the acts are conformable to good husbandry; and for thinning or other purposes which are necessary for the enjoyment of the estate and are in conformity with good husbandry.

 In this jurisdiction a tenant for life or a person vested with an ordinary life estate is entitled to the use and enjoyment of his estate during its existence. The only restriction on the life tenant's use and enjoyment is that he not permanently diminish or change the value of the future estate of the remainderman. This limitation places on the "ordinary life tenant" the responsibility for all waste of whatever character.

 An instrument creating a life tenancy may absolve the tenant of responsibility for waste, unless it is wanton or malicious, by stating that the life tenant has the power to consume or that the life tenant is without impeachment for waste. Thus, there is a sharp distinction in the rights of an ordinary life tenant or life tenant without impeachment for waste or life tenant who has the power to consume. An ordinary life tenant has no right to cut the timber from an estate for purely commercial reasons and so to do is tortious conduct for which the remainderman may sue immediately. . . . In the cause sub judice (under review), the trial court was concerned with the rights of an ordinary life tenant and correctly concluded that appellant "does not have the right to cut merchantable timber from the land involved in this suit unless the proceeds of such cutting and sale are held in trust for the use and benefit of the remaindermen."

DECISION: The court of appeals affirmed the judgment of the trial court.

Legal Life Estates

Despite potential legal problems, life estates have been used to provide financial security for one spouse upon the death of the other. At common law, dower and curtesy were estates that widows and widowers enjoyed in their spouse's real property by virtue of the marriage.

At common law, a **dower** interest gave to a wife, upon the death of her husband, a one-third life interest in land that he had owned during the marriage. Although most states have abolished dower, it continues to exist in a few of them.

Similarly, at common law, the concept of **curtesy** gave to a widower a life interest in all his wife's real property if a child had been born of the marriage. While curtesy has been abolished in most states, a few still allow the surviving husband a life interest in his deceased wife's realty.

Statutes modifying common law dower and curtesy have been enacted in many states. Typically these **elective share** statutes give to a surviving spouse a distributive share in the assets, both real and personal property, of the decedent. Thus the interest of the surviving spouse in the real property owned by the decedent is not limited to a life estate. Instead, full title to a fixed share of the personal and real property is provided by law. If the decedent leaves property to the surviving spouse by a will, the survivor may choose between taking the property passing by the will or the elective share which the statutory law provides. It is likely that these statutory reforms may completely abolish the common law concepts of dower and curtesy.

Leasehold Estates

Leasehold estates are among the most significant interests that exist today in real property. In business, the lease provides a method for obtaining an interest in land with far less capital than fee simple ownership requires. In housing, a lease requires less immediate money to be paid than does the purchase of a fee simple ownership. Further, since the lessee's interest terminates once the lease expires, he or she can easily select a different type of housing without concern about recouping the original housing investment.

A **leasehold interest** is created when the owner of real property, usually referred to as the landlord or **lessor**, conveys possession and control of property to another, called the tenant or **lessee**, in exchange for a payment known as rent. The possessory right granted by the owner is temporary. Upon termination of the leasehold interest, possession and control revert to the owner.

Both real property and contract law apply to leases. In the past courts generally applied real property principles to the lease, treating it primarily as a transfer of land ownership. That treatment generally favored the owner of the property. However, as the country became more urbanized, the condition of the building or unit rented took on more importance to the lessee than the land.

Thus, by the middle of this century, the balance of power began to shift in favor of the tenant instead of the landlord. The form leases prepared for the owner no longer were automatically enforced. Statutes and court decisions began to emphasize the contractual and warranty terms implied in a lease in order to provide increased protection for the tenant. The following case illustrates this trend.

SOLOW V. WELLNER
Civil Court of the City of New York
569 N.Y.S.2d 882 (1991)

BACKGROUND: About eighty tenants (including Wellner) of a luxury apartment building on the upper east side of Manhattan joined a rent strike to protest unsatisfactory living conditions. The landlord (Solow) initiated proceedings to recover the rent. The tenants' defense was based on their contention that the landlord had breached the implied warranty of habitability.

York, Judge

The testimony of C. Scott Smith who, as residential property manager from January 4, 1988, through October 11, 1988, was responsible for the day-to-day and long-term operations of the building, substantially confirmed the tenants' testimony about the conditions described in the public areas by the tenants.

On the second day of his employment, he conducted a roof-to-base inspection of the property. . . . He observed numerous occasions where one or more elevators were out of service . . . Smith's inspection also revealed a collapsing ceiling in the 46th floor laundry room, missing sections of acoustical tile, an overflowed sink and roach infestation. . . .

He observed 60–70 bags of garbage piled inside the main entrance inside the building. The compactor room on the ground floor had garbage all over the floor and was heavily infested with mice and roaches. Standing in front of the valet station, a mouse ran across his foot. The electronically operated security door at the valet station had an inoperative lock, thereby allowing anyone to walk into the building. The boiler room in the sub-basement had four to five inches of standing water. . . .

During the entire period that Smith was employed, the air conditioners for the public area never functioned. He observed that the chilled water cooling coil which provides conditioned air from the outside was cracked in about 20 places. There was no air conditioning in the public areas to the end of the period being litigated—May 31, 1988. . . .

There were soiled carpets in the public hallways, trash in the rear stairwells, unemptied ashtrays, graffiti on some walls caused by a lack of cleaning supplies and a lack of cleaning equipment (one operable vacuum cleaner for the entire building!) and mismanagement of manpower. . . .

Section 235-b of the Real Property Law creating an implied warranty of habitability in residential housing is the starting point in the evaluation of the tenants' main defense. . .

"In every written or oral lease or rental agreement for residential premises the landlord or lessor shall be deemed to covenant and warrant that the premises so leased or rented and all areas used in connection therewith, in common with other tenants or residents are fit for human habitation and for the uses reasonably intended by the parties and that the occupants of such premises shall not be subjected to any conditions which would be dangerous, hazardous or detrimental to their life, health or safety."

The seminal decision on the Warranty was written by then Chief Judge Cook in *Park West Management v. Mitchell.*

There he wrote on behalf of the Court that a breach of warranty occurs where there are conditions which are a threat to the health and safety of the tenants. Illustrations of such a breach, he stated, were the existence of insect and rodent infestation, insufficient heat and plumbing facilities, significantly dangerous electrical outlets, inadequate sanitation facilities or similar lack of services which impact directly on health and safety. . . .

Although each case must turn on its own individual facts, one criterion to evaluate whether there has been a breach of the implied warranty's guarantee of freedom from conditions detrimental to life, health or safety is examination of the various housing codes.

These codes while a starting point, however, are not exclusive determinants of actual threats to life, health, or safety. "Threats to the health and safety of the tenants—not merely violations of the codes—determines the reach on the implied warranty." *Park West Management v. Mitchell*

No one will dispute that health and safety are adversely affected by insect or rodent infestation, insufficient heat and plumbing facilities, significantly dangerous electrical outlets or wiring, inadequate sanitation facilities or similar services which constitute the essence of the modern dwelling unit.

This criterion establishes that the conditions in the public areas establish the failure of the landlord to maintain the premises free of conditions threatening to the lives, safety and welfare of the tenants, thereby breaching the warranty.

DECISION: The court ruled in favor of the tenants.

Classification by Duration of Term

Leased estates are classified in several different ways. A traditional classification is by the duration of the term. Major legal differences exist between leases that are for fixed terms and those that are of indefinite duration. A second method of classifying leases is by how rent is determined; thus commercial or income-producing leases are differentiated from residential leases.

Term Tenancy A **term tenancy**, sometimes called an estate for years, is a leasehold estate that exists for a fixed period of time.

The agreement creating the term establishes particular beginning and ending dates. A lease beginning on February 1, 1996, and terminating on January 31, 1997, would be a term tenancy. The term may be as short as a week or a month, but most are for a year or more. Some commercial leases are written with terms of 99 years.

A term tenancy ends automatically at the time designated in the agreement. The owner is not required to notify the tenant of the termination of the lease. Generally in the United States a term tenancy for more than a year must be in writing to be enforceable.

Periodic Tenancy A **periodic tenancy**, also referred to as a tenancy from month to month or year to year, is a rental agreement that continues to successive periods until terminated by property notice from either party. A periodic tenancy, which is usually oral rather than in writing, may be created in several ways. If a tenant is in possession under a term tenancy that is unenforceable because it is not in writing, courts generally hold that a periodic tenancy exists. More commonly the periodic tenancy is created by the express agreement of the parties to enter into an agreement of this type. Periodic tenancies are also created when a tenant holds over after a term tenancy. The *holdover tenancy* is discussed later in the chapter. The major factor distinguishing the periodic tenancy from the term tenancy is that the periodic tenancy continues until one of the parties gives proper notice of its termination.

The determination of the time period for proper notice varies considerably from state to state.

Many states have adopted the Uniform Residential Landlord and Tenant Act which requires a written notice of 10 days for a week-to-week tenancy and 60 days for a month-to-month tenancy. While year-to-year tenancies are not mentioned in the act, the prevailing rule for year-to-year tenancies is the requirement of 6 months notice.

Tenancy at Will A **tenancy at will** is created when the owner of property gives someone permission to occupy it for an unspecified period of time. This type of tenancy may be created by express agreement or by implication. The key factors are that the tenant is lawfully in possession of the property but the duration of possession is uncertain. An example of a tenancy at will would be a situation in which the landlord allows a tenant to remain in possession of space in a building scheduled to be torn down until the actual demolition begins.

A tenancy at will ends when either party indicates he or she no longer wishes to continue the tenancy. A number of states have passed legislation requiring the person wishing to terminate the tenancy to give proper notification to the other party. Generally the time required for notification is 30 days. The death of either party or the sale or lease of the property also terminates a tenancy at will.

Tenancy at Sufferance A **tenancy at sufferance** exists when someone who was once a lawful occupant unlawfully occupies another's property. The landlord owes this tenant no duties other than not to injure him or her wantonly or willfully. The most common example of the tenancy at sufferance is when a person holds over after the expiration of his or her term. This person becomes a holdover tenant if the landlord elects to treat him as such; however, until this decision is made and acted upon, the tenancy is at sufferance.

Holding Over   When a term tenant remains on the premises at the expiration of the term without the owner's consent, the owner has the option of either evicting the tenant or treating the tenant as a holdover. If the owner decides to treat the tenant as a holdover, in most states a periodic tenancy is created. If the original tenancy was for a year or more, almost all states treat the new term as a periodic tenancy for a year. If the original term was for less than a year, the term of holdover tenancy is for a similar period. For example, a month-to-month tenancy is created if the original term tenancy was for a month. When a tenant holds over after being notified of a rent increase, most states will hold the tenant responsible for the increased rent.

Classification by Method of Determining Rent

A wide range of methods exists for determining the amount of the rent the tenant must pay. In residential leases the rent is usually a fixed amount, but in commercial leases different arrangements are often used to establish the tenant's obligation. These arrangements are primarily the result of the lessor's desire to shift as many economic risks as possible to the tenant. A lessor leasing property for a long term naturally wishes to limit the effect of inflation on rental income. If the rent is a fixed amount and property expenses increase, the owner's income from the property can be drastically reduced. Rental payments can be negotiated that protect the owners from this possibility. In other situations an owner might wish to share in the increased productive use of a parcel of real estate without assuming the risk of investing in a building or a business to utilize the property.

This objective too can be attained through various types of rental payments. A few of the types of leases used to accomplish the objectives set forth above are the percentage lease, the net lease, and the revaluation or appraisal lease. Many variations and combinations of these basic patterns are also frequently used.

Percentage Leases   A *percentage lease* provides the lessor with a rent determined by a fixed percentage of the gross sales or net profits from a business operated on the leased premises. Some percentage leases are written with a fixed minimum rental. Percentage leases protect the lessor against inflation and also provide him or her with a share in the productive use of the property.

Net Leases   A *net lease* is a lease in which the tenant pays a fixed rent and in addition agrees to pay the taxes, insurance, and maintenance expenses. A variation of the net lease is the net-net lease. In the net-net lease the tenant agrees to pay all costs attributed to the property. The net lease protects the lessor against inflation.

Revaluation or Appraisal Leases   Some long-term leases provide for adjustment of rental payments based on periodic revaluation of the property. Several different methods of revaluation are used. Revaluation allows the lessor to share in any increase in the value of the land.

Rights and Duties of the Parties

Most problems that arise in a tenancy can be solved by the parties if they have a well-drafted lease. In the lease, landlord and tenant may allocate rights and duties in any manner that they choose as long as what they do is not illegal or against public policy (see Chapter 16). Sometimes parties who enter into a lease do not anticipate a problem that occurs during the term. If a dispute arises that is not settled by the lease, the solution must be found in state statutory or case law.

Understanding how the law allocates the rights and duties of the parties absent agreement in the lease is complicated by the dual nature of the lease and by developments in landlord-tenant law during the past 50 years. The case of *Solow v. Wellner* illustrates a trend in American law to provide residential tenants with rights that are not generally available to commercial tenants. This increased protection for residential tenants is also reflected in the statutory law, since many states have expanded the duties of landlords of residential property.

Duty to Repair and Maintain   The allocation of the duty to repair and maintain the premises illustrates the different treatment states sometimes afford commercial and residential leases. At common law, in the absence of agreement, the landlord had a limited duty to repair and maintain the property. If he or she knew of a latent defect, this had to be corrected before the lease began. No duty existed to maintain the premises except for the common areas of multi-unit buildings. A number of states retain the common law rule for commercial leases, but in most states the rule has been modified for residential property. In these states, if residential property is not maintained in habitable condition, tenants have various remedies against landlords. These remedies can include revoking the lease or not paying the rent as it becomes due. In some states, tenants are permitted to make necessary repairs and deduct the cost from the rent.

Use of the Premises Because a lease is a transfer of property as well as a contract, during the term the lessee has the right to possession and control of the property. Generally this means the lessor may not enter the premises unless the parties have agreed to the contrary. Thus, at common law the landlord's right of access to inspect, to make alterations or repairs, or to show the premises is limited.

Three principal exceptions exist to the rule limiting the landlord's right of access. First, he or she may enter to collect the rent if the lease fails to state where rent shall be paid. Next, the Uniform Residential Landlord-Tenant Act and similar state statutes extend the landlord's right of access to inspect the condition of the property and to make necessary repairs in emergencies. Inspec-

tion requires notice to the tenant and must be done at reasonable times and intervals. Finally, the landlord has a right of access to prevent material damage or loss to the property resulting from the tenant's negligence or misconduct.

The tenant may use the property for any reasonable purpose in view of the surrounding circumstances. But the tenant cannot use the property for an illegal purpose, for a purpose that violates public policy, or in a manner that would result in substantial or permanent damage to the property. Most commercial leases limit the use that the tenant can make of the property.

Rent Control Laws

Rent control laws were enacted at the federal and state levels during World War I and World War II. While many of these controls were removed in the late 1940s, some rent control laws still exist. The best known law is the rent control laws that are applicable to selected real property in the city of New York. In 1962 the state of New York transferred to the city of New York the authority to impose and administer rent controls in the city. The city was also permitted to adopt and amend local laws regarding rent control.

The basis of the protection granted to the tenant by the New York law is the statutory provision restricting the right of the landlord to remove the tenant from possession. If the tenant continues to pay the rent, only specified acts of the tenant (for example, negligently damaging the property, using

---

ISSUES AND TRENDS
Rent Control: Does It Help Create Affordable Housing?

According to an August 19, 1993, *Wall Street Journal* guest editorial, roughly 150 cities and counties currently have some form of rent control, covering an estimated 10 percent of the nation's housing stock. The editorial's author, John Gilderbloon, a professor of economics and urban policy at the University of Louisville, says "New York City is typically cited as the textbook example of why rent controls do not work. . . The law, entirely one-sided in favor of tenants, discourages investment in rental housing. . . . But making a generalization about rent control based on the New York City example is like trying to argue that all cars are bad by pointing to the Edsel. Most of the laws guarantee landlords a "fair and reasonable return." Typically, the laws exempt new construction, require adequate maintenance as a condition of rent increases, and guarantee annual increases to cover operating and improvement costs. Rent controls are most effective as temporary measures, intended to create a better balance of power between tenant and landlord. A concerted effort to create more home ownership is the only long-term solution to providing affordable housing.

the property for illegal purposes, or committing a nuisance) will justify an eviction of the tenant.

The second critical provision in the rent control law is the limitation on the maximum statutory rent. The rent established March 1, 1950, pursuant to federal law, was adopted by the state of New York, and applied by the city after the transfer of power to it from the state, as the maximum statutory rent. Increases are permitted only if the landlord falls within one of the contemplated situations justifying an increase. These situations include an increase in service, an increase in rental value due to substantial rehabilitation of the building, a voluntary agreement between lessor and lessee, and the maximum rent being substantially lower than prevailing rents in the same area. Although the New York City law is the best known of the rent control laws, it may not be typical.

Transfer of Leased Premises

A tenant transfers his or her interest in leased property by assignment or sublease. Because the legal consequences of the two types of transfer differ, the parties to a transfer should be certain that their documents clearly indicate which type they intend.

A transfer is an **assignment** if the tenant conveys all of his or her remaining interest. If this is the case, both the new tenant and the landlord are liable to each other according to the terms of the original lease. The original tenant becomes a guarantor that the provisions of the lease will be carried out.

A transfer is a **sublease** if the tenant transfers less than his or her remaining interest. An example would be a tenant with a lease running from January 1 to December 31. If that tenant wants to allow someone else (a subtenant) to lease the premises during June and July, the transfer is a sublease. As the following case indicates, if the original lessee keeps any interest in the property itself, its transfers will be a sublease not an assignment. Neither the subtenant nor landlord can sue the other directly for breach of the original lease. If the landlord breaches a lease provision, the subtenant must seek relief by bringing an action against the original tenant on the sublease. If the rent is not paid, the landlord must look to the original tenant with whom the lease was made. The court in the *Bostonian Shoe Co.* case indicates the distinction between an assignment and a sublease.

BOSTONIAN SHOE CO. v. WULWICK ASSOCIATES

Supreme Court, Appellate Division
501 N.Y.S.2d 393 Supreme Court, Appellate Division (1986)

BACKGROUND: Bostonian Shoe Co. (plaintiff) was a tenant in premises it leased in Brooklyn for 15 years ending July 31, 1986. Its lease with Wulwick Associates (defendant) as landlord included a provision that the tenant could not assign its lease without prior approval from the landlord. In 1983 Bostonian entered into an agreement with Genesco subletting the leased premises to it until July 30, 1986, one day prior to the expiration of Bostonian's lease with Wulwick.

Bostonian sued to have the court declare its sublease with Genesco valid and the trial court found in its favor. Landlord Wulwick appealed, claiming the nonassignment provision prohibited Bostonian's sublease of the premises for all but one day of its tenancy.

Memorandum by the Court

The instant appeal involves a written lease between the plaintiff, as tenant, and the defendant, as landlord, which provides for the lease of the premises located at 453 Fulton Street, Brooklyn, for a 15-year period ending July 31, 1986. The lease specifically prohibits the assignment of the lease by the plaintiff without the defendant's prior approval. The lease does not, however, restrict in any way the plaintiff's right to sublet the premises.

On or about April 18, 1983 the plaintiff entered into an agreement with one Genesco, Inc. (hereinafter Genesco), whereby the latter agreed to rent the demised premises for the period beginning May 1, 1983 and ending July 30, 1986, one day prior to the expiration of the lease between the parties hereto. Under that agreement, the plaintiff retained the right of re-entry upon Genesco's default, and Genesco was precluded from assigning . . . the premises without the prior written approval of the plaintiff.

Shortly after the plaintiff entered into the agreement with Genesco, the defendant contacted the plaintiff through a series of notices, stating that the agreement with Genesco constituted an invalid assignment of the parties' lease. As a result, the defendant declared the lease terminated and demanded that the plaintiff cure the breach or vacate the premises and remove Genesco therefrom.

The plaintiff subsequently commenced the instant action seeking declaratory and injunctive relief. Special Term declared, that the agreement between the plaintiff and Genesco constituted a valid sublease, and, that as a result, the plaintiff was not in breach of the provision of the lease which prohibited its assignment without the defendant's consent. We affirm.

"The essential distinction between an assignment and a sublease is simply this: If a lessee, by any instrument whatever, whether reserving conditions or not, parts with his entire interest, he has made a complete assignment, . . . If he retains a reversion in himself, he has made a sublease."

Significantly, the retained reversionary interest need not be for a substantial period of time in order for an agreement to be considered a sublease. Thus, agreements calling for the surrender of possession one day or, in one case, 12 hours short of the expiration of the term of the main lease, have been held to be a sublease rather than an assignment.

Judged by these standards, it is clear that the plaintiff's agreement with Genesco is a sublease rather than an assignment. By the terms of that agreement, Genesco is required to surrender possession of the demised premises to the plaintiff on July 30, 1986, one day prior to the expiration of the plaintiff's lease with the defendant. Thus, since the plaintiff retained a reversionary interest in the demised premises, albeit one short in duration, the subject agreement is a valid sublease. Moreover, given the absence of any provision in the parties' lease restricting the plaintiff's ability to sublease the premises, the plaintiff's actions did not constitute a breach of the provision thereof regarding assignment.

Decision: The appellate division held the sublease agreement valid and affirmed the trial court's decision.

Termination of Lease

Most leases end at a certain time or by agreement of the parties. Many leases contain provisions providing for their termination under certain conditions. A common example is a provision terminating the lease if the premises are destroyed. In the absence of that type of provision the tenant remains responsible for the rent. Another example would be a provision terminating the lease if the tenant files for bankruptcy. Without this provision the tenant remains responsible for the rent until a judgment is entered.

A lease is also terminated by condemnation, the acquiring of private property for a public purpose by the government. In some instances statutes provide for the termination of a lease. Generally death does not terminate the obligations of either party, but a few states allow the estate of a decedent to cancel a lease covering the deceased's residence.

Nonpossessory Interests in Real Property

Easements

An **easement** is an example of a nonpossessory interest in land possessed by another party. The easement grants a limited use or enjoyment of that land to its owner. The requirement that the land on which the easement exists, known as the *servient tenement*, be in possession of someone other than the owner of the easement frequently occurs in situations in which there is an easement appurtenant.

An *easement appurtenant* involves two parcels of land, usually, but not necessarily, adjoining. The easement allows the possessor of one parcel to benefit by using the other parcel of land. The parcel that benefits is referred to as the *dominant tenement* whereas the property that is subject to the easement is known as the servient tenement. If an easement is appurtenant, any transfer of the dominant tenement includes the easement. The easement cannot be separated and transferred independently of the dominant estate. Further, the use of the servient tenement is limited to the terms of the easement. Easements appurtenant run with the land. The easement, allowing the owner of the dominant property to make a limited use of the

servient property, passes automatically to the succeeding owner of that dominant property.

Unless the document creating the easement indicates that the easement is exclusive, the owner of the servient property may also use the land upon which the easement has been dedicated. The servient owner's use must not conflict with the purpose and character of the easement. Similarly, the holder of the easement may not use the property in a manner not permitted by the easement. The *Bijou Irrigation District* case, which follows, illustrates that neither the easement holder nor the owner of the servient estate may use the property in a way that infringes on the other's rights.

BIJOU IRRIGATION DISTRICT V. EMPIRE CLUB
Supreme Court of Colorado
804 P.2d 175 (1991)

BACKGROUND: The Bijou Irrigation District (the "District") used the Empire Reservoir to store irrigation water diverted from the South Platte River. Much of the land underlying the reservoir was owned by private parties, but Colorado law gave the District an easement in that land for irrigation purposes. Several of those private landowners (the "Landowners"), as well as the District, had historically used the reservoir for recreational and piscatorial (*i.e.,* fishing) purposes. The District sued the Landowners to prevent the Landowners from using the reservoir for recreation. The trial court ruled in favor of the Landowners, holding that the District's easement was not exclusive and hence did not prohibit the Landowners from using the reservoir for recreational purposes.

Later, the District filed a separate action in a special state water court requesting that its water rights be changed to expressly permit the District to use the reservoir for recreational and piscatorial purposes. The water court granted the District's request, but ruled that its decision did not affect any rights that the Landowners might have to also use the reservoir for recreational purposes.

The district appealed the trial court's ruling that the Landowners could use the reservoir for recreational purposes, and the Landowners appealed the water court's ruling that the District could use the reservoir for recreational purposes. The two appeals are consolidated in the opinion excerpted below.

Lohr, Justice

The scope of the District's rights as defined by the easement's nature and purpose necessarily includes construction and maintenance of the reservoir and storage of water appropriated for irrigation. The critical question is whether the District's right to store water in the reservoir is exclusive of any right by the Landowners to use the reservoir for recreational purposes.

The practical considerations incident to administration of a reservoir and application of these waters to irrigation use support recognition of the right of the appropriator to control the stored water. In administering water stored in a reservoir to maximize beneficial use, it is sometimes necessary to lower or raise the water level significantly in a short period of time. These rapid fluctuations in water level can create hazards for users of the reservoir. This makes it essential that the reservoir owner have control of use of the reservoir in order to protect the reservoir users. A reservoir owner also is liable for damage caused by waters escaping from a reservoir as the result of negligence. It is essential for purposes of public protection and liability control, therefore, that the reservoir owner carefully monitor the condition of the dams, maintain only that amount of water in storage consistent with safety, and assure that the processes of filling and discharging from the reservoir do not create hazards for reservoir users. These considerations undoubtedly provide the rationale for our long established acceptance of the principle that reservoir companies have the right to control the water that they have diverted. We conclude as a matter of law that use of Empire Reservoir for recreational purposes by owners of the servient estate is inconsistent with the right of the District under its easement to store water over which it has the right of control and would unreasonably interfere with the exercise of that right.

We next consider the challenges to the decree of the water court granting the District's application for a change of water rights to recognize recreational and piscatorial uses of the stored water by the District.

The Act of May 11, 1898, listed three specific uses of canal and reservoir rights of way: water transportation, domestic purposes, and development of power, each "subsidiary to the main purpose of irrigation." In addition it authorized rights of way "for purposes of a public nature."

This public purposes authorization is also subject to the dominant purpose of irrigation. The statute makes no provision for a private use other than the ones specifically mentioned. . . .

Accordingly, for the District to make such uses of the stored water would overburden the easement and would intrude on the rights of the Landowners as owners of the servient estate. Under these circumstances, we believe that the District was precluded from obtaining a change of its water storage rights in Empire Reservoir to recognize the additional and incidental use of the water for recreational and piscatorial purposes. For this reason, we reverse the judgment of the water court recognizing a right in the District to apply the stored water to these uses.

DECISION: The Supreme Court of Colorado held that the Landowners were not entitled to use the reservoir for recreation and fishing, because that would conflict with the Bijou Irrigation District's rights under its easement. The court also held, however, that the District could not use the reservoir for recreation and fishing because that would be beyond the scope of its easement.

Easement in Gross   An *easement in gross* exists independently of a dominant tenement. The privileges given by the easement belong to an individual or firm independently of ownership or possession of any specific land. Telephone and electric transmission lines are examples of easements in gross. The right of access over property in such cases does not benefit any particular piece of property.

Easements, such as those granted to gas and electric utility companies, are used extensively in the development of land. The easement of the utility company typically gives it the right to lay cable in a part of the land of a homeowner. In this case the property owner's land is the servient tenement, because the easement allows another to use a portion of its property, and there is no dominant tenement.

Because of the personal nature of the easement in gross, many American jurisdictions do not allow a noncommercial easement in gross to be transferred. However, commercial easements in gross, because of their importance to the public, are transferable.

Creation of Easements

Easements can be created by express agreement or implied by law. An easement may arise because of an agreement between the developer of property and the utilities that provide hookups to the lots being developed. Similarly, in the absence of an express agreement the law will declare an easement exists if a purchaser of land acquires land that has no access to public roads, except over lands retained by the seller. Courts will imply that the seller meant to grant an easement over the retained land to the purchaser. This type of easement is known as a *way of necessity.*

Profit and License

Two other important nonpossessory interests are the profit and the license. A **profit,** or *profit à prendre* is an interest in real property similar in many ways to an easement in gross. The distinguishing difference is that the owner of a profit has the right to take something of supposed value from the land. The right to cut and remove timber or to quarry and take gravel are examples of a profit. The profit carries with it the right to enter upon the land. Since a profit is an interest in land, it is irrevocable.

A **license** differs from a profit in that the license is merely a personal privilege to enter upon the land of another for a particular purpose. A license is not an interest in real property. Holding a ticket to an athletic event or occupying a motel room are examples of license. Most licenses are revocable at the will of the owner of the property on which the license is exercised; however, if a license is coupled with an interest in the land, license may not be revoked.

Liens

A **lien** is a very important nonpossessory interest in land. It is a right existing in the property of another to secure payment of a debt or performance of some obligation. Some liens are created by statute, others by agreement of the parties. Liens can exist in both real and personal property. One real property lien with which most people are familiar is the mortgage. Mortgages are discussed in the following chapter. Each of the nonpossessory interests in land is portrayed in Figure 48-1.

Co-ownership

A third method of dividing rights in land exists when several people own undivided interests in a parcel of land at the same time. Generally in this type of ownership each person is entitled to a specific fraction of the parcel but also shares with others a single right to possession and profits from the land. This is generally referred to as concurrent ownership or *co-ownership.* Co-ownership is often used for holding investment real estate.

Co-ownership was important to the common law, and the various concurrent estates that developed at common law remain important today. A number of legal problems are associated with these common-law concurrent estates. These problems are reduced or eliminated if multiple owners use a partnership, corporation, or other arrangement (such as a trust, discussed later in this chapter) to hold title to the property. These devices are becoming increasingly important in real estate, replacing the common law forms of multiple ownership.

Joint Tenancy

A **joint tenancy** is a form of property co-ownership that includes the right of survivorship. This means that upon the death of one of the co-owners, that person's interest passes automatically to the surviving joint owners.

Many people today own both personal property (automobiles and bank accounts) and real property as joint tenants. While some states prohibit the creation of a joint tenancy with the right of survivorship, most states permit it. Still the person establishing a joint tenancy should clearly indicate that this is the form of co-ownership that he or she intended to create.

Rights of Joint Tenants   Each co-owner who holds a joint tenancy has an equal right to possession of the entire property. This is referred to as an *undivided interest.* Although a joint tenant may not exclude other joint tenants from possession, the law considers occupancy by one as occupancy by all. If each tenant is to benefit, all must agree to share the property. Where agreement cannot be reached, the tenancy must be terminated.

FIGURE 48-1

Nonpossessory Interests in Land

1. **Easement Appurtenant** This allows an owner of a dominant tenement (A) to use a part of a servient tenement (B) for a specific purpose; for example, to have access to the lake.

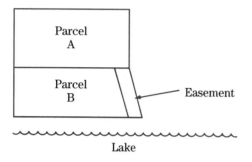

2. **Easement in Gross** This allows an independent owner, ABC utilities, to use the land of another owner (servient tenement—parcel C) for specific purpose; for example, to place telephone transmission lines. Here, the owner of the easement does not have a dominant tenement.

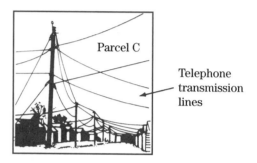

3. **License** This is the privilege to enter the land of another owner for a particular purpose; for example, attending an athletic event or occupying a motel room.

Vacation Inn
Budget Motel

4. **Profit** The owner of the profit, XYZ lumber company, has a right to come on the land of another owner, owner of parcel D, and to remove something of value, for example, to cut and remove timber.

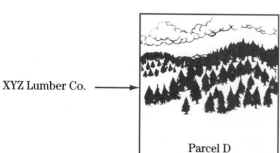

5. **Lien** This is a right existing in the property of another to secure payment of a debt, such as a mortgage.

House

Termination of Joint Tenancy A joint tenancy is terminated if one of the owners sells his or her interest. In some states a joint tenancy is terminated if an owner's interest is mortgaged. The joint tenancy is also terminated if the interest of a joint tenant is sold to satisfy a debt. In any case a person who acquires the interest of a joint tenant becomes a tenant in common with the remaining co-owners.

Tenancy in Common

A **tenancy in common** is a form of co-ownership in which each owner possesses an individual interest in a parcel of land, but other than that, each owner's rights are the same as those possessed by a sole owner. In almost all states where co-ownership of property is concerned, a tenancy in common is implied unless a joint tenancy is clearly indicated by the instrument creating the concurrent estate.

Rights of Tenants in Common Like joint tenants, each tenant in common has an undivided right to possession of the entire parcel. Normally a tenant in common will not be responsible to the co-owners for any benefits obtained through exclusive occupancy. At the same time no tenant in common is entitled to the exclusive use of any part of the land. The result is that problems arise when one co-tenant wrongfully excludes the others or when the property can be practically occupied only by a single tenant. Under these circumstances, in a number of states, the co-tenants not in occupancy will be entitled to a fair compensation for the use of the property. Similar problems arise where a co-tenant not in possession receives benefits from the property exceeding those of his or her co-owners. These types of problems can best be solved by agreement among the parties, as can problems involving liability of co-tenants for upkeep and improvements. When agreement cannot be reached, *partition* of property may be the only solution.

Partition By *partition* a co-owner divides property and ends any interest of other co-owners in the divided portion. Although courts traditionally ordered partition, even when no statute authorized them to do so, today partition exists in some form by statute in every state. In a few states the wording of the statute is broad enough to include partition when owners are divorced. Many states also make partition available to certain holders of future interests. Under the law of almost all states co-owners of personal property enjoy the right to partition to the same degree as do co-owners of realty. The *Milian* case, which follows, is a partition case in which the court first had to determine whether an unmarried man and woman were co-owners of a house.

MILIAN V. DELEON
California Court of Appeal, Fourth District
226 Cal.Rptr. 831 (1986)

BACKGROUND: Arthur Milian (plaintiff) and Sylvia Sanchez Deleon (defendant, hereafter Sanchez) began dating in 1970. In late 1977 they purchased a house as joint tenants. Sanchez claims Milian and she bought the house with plans to marry in a year or two. Milian asked Sanchez to move into the house with him but she refused. The couple separated in late 1978 and Milian sued to have the property declared his. Sanchez, claiming she owned one-half of the house, sought a partition of the property. The trial court agreed with her.

Milian appealed, saying the trial court wrongly relied on *Marvin v. Marvin*, which concerned the division of property by two people who lived together.

Kaufman, Associate Justice

Milian and Sanchez began dating in 1970. Their relationship continued for eight years but ended without marriage. Sanchez testified the two became engaged in 1976 and set a marriage date for approximately one year later.

Sanchez stated repeatedly at trial that the couple's sharing of financial resources during their dating relationship proceeded upon the shared contemplation that the two would eventually marry. Milian denied ever proposing marriage or otherwise discussing plans to get married. Milian stated he asked Sanchez to live with him in order to discover whether the relationship was "going to work out or not." Sanchez, however, refused to live with him outside of marriage.

In late 1977, the couple jointly purchased a house which is the subject real property in the partition action. . . . Milian paid the $500 deposit required to reserve the vacant lot upon which the house was to be constructed and testified he made the loan application in his own name. Sanchez testified both parties provided financial statements to obtain the loan.

The eventual grant deed was taken in the names of both parties as joint tenants. Sanchez testified that to her "joint tenancy" meant the two would be partners in the property prior to marriage, while Milian testified he did not understand the significance of such designation and believed only that Sanchez would live with him and share expenses.

Only Milian occupied the house after its purchase. Although Sanchez fully participated in furnishing, decorating and landscaping the house and provided funds for these purposes, she refused to move in without marriage and never did occupy the house as a full-time resident. She had a key to the house and was there almost every weekend until the couple separated in late 1978.

Most of the couple's testimony concerned numerous exhibits which showed the extent to which they had commingled their property and collectively incurred expenses on the house and otherwise. The monthly mortgage payments were paid by Milian out of his savings account. However, Sanchez also testified that over eight months in 1978 she deposited to that savings account at least $4,300, including a $2,100 annual bonus from her employer and an $1,100 tax refund.

In respect to other decoration and improvement, Sanchez paid $560 on drapes and incurred a $900 charge on her credit card for upgrading the quality of carpet for the house. . . . Sanchez also made considerable nonfinancial contribution to the decoration of the house, spending many weekends landscaping and weeding, shopping with Milian for various home improvements, and purchasing the large patio slab for behind the house. Sanchez frequently stated at trial that the couple's extensive financial entanglement was based upon an agreement that the two would be equal partners in owning the home, sharing all of their property and resources, and preparing for marriage. . . .

It is of course correct that a cotenant who pays taxes, trust deed payments or other charges against the property or expends money for the preservation of the property or who, with the assent of his cotenant, makes improvements to the property is entitled to contribution from the cotenant, and on partition by sale is entitled to reimbursement for those expenditures before division of the proceeds among the property owners. However, what Milian fails to deal with is that the court ultimately declined to make an accounting and order reimbursement in this case because it found an agreement between the parties to own and divide the property equally irrespective of the exact dollar contributions of each party to the purchase price or to the subsequent improvement, maintenance, or preservation of the property.

Of course, if one joint tenant has advanced funds on behalf of the other and there is an agreement between them for reimbursement in the event of sale of the property, that agreement can be enforced by the court. However, by definition joint tenancy ownership means equal ownership, and in the absence of an agreement for reimbursement we are unaware of any authority which authorizes reimbursement on account of unequal contributions to the down payment.

If a tenancy in common rather than a joint tenancy is found, the court may either order reimbursement or determine the ownership interests in the property in proportion to the amounts contributed. It appears to be otherwise in respect to true joint tenancies, however, where by definition ownership of the property is equal.

The burden of all this is twofold; first, there is no inconsistency in the court's finding of joint tenancy and its ordering equal division of the property. Secondly, when the contributions to the down payment on the property are disregarded, the disparity in the potentially reimbursable contributions of these parties is not nearly so great as Milian contends.

We come then to the question whether the court's finding that the parties agreed to own and divide the property equally irrespective of the exact dollar amounts each contributed to the acquisition, improvement, maintenance and preservation of the property is supported by substantial evidence. We conclude it is.

DECISION: The appellate court held that since the two parties were co-owners of the property, each was entitled to one-half the proceeds of the sale.

Tenancy by the Entirety

Nearly half the states recognize **tenancy by the entirety**, a type of co-ownership existing only between husband and wife. This type of co-ownership is based on an ancient legal fiction by which the common law regarded husband and wife as a single legal person. One result was that if the two acquired equal interests in real estate by the same instrument, the property was considered owned as an indivisible legal unit. Upon the death of either, the survivor remained as the parcel's sole owner. This result has also been accepted by modern law. Today a right of survivorship exists for the tenancy by the entirety similar to that existing for the joint tenancy.

A tenancy by the entirety is a more stable type of co-ownership than the joint tenancy. Because the marital partners are considered as a single unit, neither husband nor wife can break the tenancy without the other's consent. Unlike the joint tenancy, a sale by either husband or wife does not terminate the tenancy nor end the right of survivorship.

In many jurisdictions a tenancy by the entirety cannot be terminated by the forced sale of the husband's or wife's interest. If either spouse refuses to pay an individually incurred debt, the creditor cannot attach his or her interest in the property. This rule has been criticized for permitting the debtor to escape responsibility while owning an interest in a valuable asset. In a few states creditors of the husband, but not of the wife, may reach the income, profits, and title of the property. Other states permit the separate creditors of either spouse to sell the share of the debtor, whether husband or wife. If the creditor holds a joint judgment against both spouses, the creditor can attach the estate held by the entirety.

Tenancies by the entireties are terminated primarily by divorce, when the parties become tenants in common.

Community Property

Community property is a form of co-ownership between husband and wife in which each has a half interest in property acquired by the labor or skill of either spouse during marriage. A number of jurisdictions in the United States apply the doctrine of community property to property owned by a husband or wife, including Arizona, California, Idaho, Louisiana, Nevada, New Mexico, Texas, and Washington. Since community property ownership is statutory, each state varies the characteristics of the system to fit its own needs.

Community property is based on the marital relationship. In community property jurisdictions the husband and wife are regarded as partners. Each becomes a co-owner with the other in all property acquired by the labor or skill of either while the two are married. This rule applies even though title to the property is individually held by the husband or wife.

Property owned by the husband or wife prior to marriage and property acquired during marriage by gift, inheritance, or will does not become community property. In addition, any real property purchased with the separate property of one spouse who takes title in his or her name remains separate property.

Table 48-1 depicts the distinctive features of the forms by which property is commonly co-owned.

TABLE 48-1

Types of Co-ownership

Type	Distinctive Features	Example
Joint Tenancy	Rights of survivorship; equal right of each tenant to possess entire property.	Bill and Susan own a farm together. If Bill dies, Susan automatically owns the farm. While both live each has the right to live on the farm. If Bill sells his interest to Doug, the joint tenancy between Bill and Susan terminates.
Tenancy in common	Each tenant's share is transferred on death to that tenant's heirs; each tenant has a right to possess entire property.	Bill and Susan own a farm as tenants in common. If Bill dies, Bill's heirs own his share of the property and Susan still owns her share. While both live, each has the right to live on the farm. If Bill sells his interest to Doug, Doug and Susan will be cotenants if Susan agrees. Otherwise, the property will be partitioned.
Tenancy by the entirety	This form of ownership, which is available only to married couples, is recognized in approximately twenty-five states. Upon death of one spouse the survivor owns the property. Property is owned by the two people as if they were one person.	If Bill and Susan are married, they can own the farm as tenants by the entirety. If Bill dies, Susan automatically owns the farm. While both live, the farm is neither Bill's nor Susan's separate property, but it is owned by the two of them (as one person).
Community property	Community property is recognized in approximately ten states. Both a husband and wife have a half interest in property acquired by either spouse during marriage.	If Bill and Susan are married and living in a community property state, when they decide to purchase a farm, it will become their community property. Even if Susan's money is used and the title to the farm is only in Bill's name, it is community property, not the separate property of either spouse. If Bill dies, the property is automatically owned by Susan.

Tenancy in Partnership

The Uniform Partnership Act, adopted in most states, creates the tenancy in partnership. The **tenancy in partnership** is a form of property ownership by a partnership; it permits a partnership to buy, hold, and sell real estate in the partnership name. Individual partners share ownership in particular property only as members of the firm. Spouses, heirs, and creditors of individual partners have no rights in partnership property. Although an individual partner can transfer partnership real property, any transfer is made only as an agent for the firm. Upon the death of any partner, that person's share passes to surviving partners.

Condominiums and Cooperatives

Condominiums and cooperatives are forms of co-ownership that have become significant factors in the real-estate market since World War II. In both cooperatives and condominiums owners enjoy individual control over designated units in a facility, usually an apartment or office building, while sharing portions of the facility with other owners. This type of ownership is generally found in urban and resort areas where land values have increased because of the concentration of population. Condominium and cooperative ownership is based on statutes, which vary considerably from state to state.

PREVENTIVE LAW
Co-Ownership of Real Property

There are several common methods by which a person can own joint property with another person. If you refer to property merely as joint property, you are not clearly indicating the way in which you want the ownership, rights, and duties regarding that property to be shared between the owners. Thus when you are contemplating sharing the ownership of a vacant lot, residence, or business building jointly, be sure you are clear in indicating whether the parties are: (1) joint tenants with the right of survivorship, (2) tenants in common, (3) tenants by the entirety, or (4) owners of community property. In most states a joint ownership of land between parties who are not spouses is presumed to be shared as tenants in common. Consult Table 48-1 for characteristics of each of the major methods by which real property can be "jointly" owned.

Condominiums A **condominium** is a multifamily housing property in which persons individually own their residential units but share certain common areas as tenants in common. Such common areas generally include the land, walls, halls, lobbies, and service facilities such as elevators and heating and plumbing systems. Because each unit is owned separately and the owner possesses an undivided interest in the common elements, a person may sell, mortgage, or lease an individual unit.

The condominium is created by a *declaration*, a document describing the parcel, units in the structure, and the rights and duties of condominium owners. A set of bylaws regulates the operation and maintenance of the building. Owners of the units share in the costs of maintaining the common elements of the real estate. The case that follows illustrates one type of problem that arises in condominium ownership.

RITCHEY V. VILLA NUEVA CONDOMINIUM ASSOCIATION

Court of Appeals of California
146 Cal.Rptr. 695 (1978)

BACKGROUND: Joe B. Ritchey (plaintiff-appellant) purchased a two-bedroom unit in the Villa Nueva condominium project. He rented the unit to Dorothy Westphal, a woman with two young children. This violated a bylaw of the condominium restricting occupancy to persons 18 years of age and older. The Villa Nueva Condominium Association (defendant-respondent) sued to remove Westphal, who moved out before an answer could be filed. Ritchey then sued seeking an injunction and declaratory relief, as well as damages.

The trial court found the association's regulation reasonable and decided in its favor. Ritchey appealed.

Caldecott, Justice

Appellant challenges the validity of an amendment to the bylaws of the Villa Nueva Condominium project which restricts occupancy in the high-rise portion of the project to persons 18 years of age and older. . . .

Appellant urges that an age restriction is patently unreasonable in that it discriminates against families with children. Age restrictions in condominium documents have not been specifically tested in our courts. Nevertheless, we conclude on the basis of statutory and case authority that such restrictions are not per se unreasonable.

In *Flowers v. John Burnham & Co.,* an apartment house restriction limiting tenancy to adults, female children of all ages, and male children under the age of five was held not to violate the Unruh Act guaranteeing equal access to "accommodations, advantages, facilities, privileges, or services in all business establishments of every kind whatsoever." The court noted that arbitrary discrimination by a landlord is prohibited by the act, but held: "Because the independence, mischievousness, boisterousness and rowdyism of children vary by age and sex . . . [the defendant], as landlord, seeks to limit the children in its apartments to girls of all ages and boys under five. Regulating tenants' ages and sex to that extent is not unreasonable or arbitrary."

Similarly, in *Riley v. Stoves*, the Arizona Court of Appeals upheld a covenant in a deed restricting occupancy of a subdivision to persons 21 years of age or older: "The restriction flatly prevents children from living in the mobile home subdivision. The obvious purpose is to create a quiet, peaceful neighborhood by eliminating noise associated with children at play or otherwise. . . .

"We do not think the restriction is in any way arbitrary. It effectively insures that only working or retired adults will reside on the lots. It does much to eliminate the noise and distractions caused by children. We find it reasonably related to a legitimate purpose and therefore decline to hold that its enforcement violated defendants' rights to equal protection."

It should also be noted that the United States Congress has adopted several programs to provide housing for the elderly, setting an age minimum of 62 years for occupancy. As the Riley court observed, "These sections represent an implicit legislative finding that not only do older adults need inexpensive housing, but also that their housing interests and needs differ from families with children."

Under Civil Code section 1355, reasonable amendments to restrictions relating to a condominium project are binding upon every owner and every condominium in that project "whether the burdens thereon are increased or decreased thereby, and whether the owner of each and every condominium consents thereto or not." Whether an amendment is reasonable depends upon the circumstances of the particular case.

The amendment of the bylaws here in issue operates . . . as a restraint upon the owner's right . . . of occupancy. However, for the reasons hereinafter discussed, we conclude that under the facts of this case the amendment is reasonable.

Appellant purchased his condominium unit approximately 16 months prior to the [amendment] of the bylaws. At that time, the enabling declaration establishing a plan for condominium ownership, the model form of subscription and purchase agreement, and the report issued to the public by HUD, consistently referred to units in the condominium project as "family home units" or "family units" located in "multi-family structures," and emphasized their suitability for families with children. Appellant states that he relied upon these representations when he purchased his unit.

Appellant, however, does not claim that any of these representations were false or were made to mislead him. As far as the record shows, appellant, at the time of his purchase and for several months thereafter, could lease the premises to a person with children under 18 years of age. Furthermore, appellant does not contend that it was represented to him that the conditions of occupancy would not be changed. In fact, at the time of his purchase, the enabling declaration specifically provided that the bylaws could be amended, and that he would be subject to any reasonable amendment that was property adopted.

The authority of a condominium association necessarily includes the power to issue reasonable regulations governing an owner's use of his unit in order to prevent activities which might prove annoying to the general residents. Thus, an owners' association can prohibit any activity or conduct that could constitute a nuisance, regulate the disposition of refuse, provide for the maintenance and repair of interiors of apartments as well as exteriors, and prohibit or regulate the keeping of pets.

Therefore, a reasonable restriction upon occupancy of the individually owned units of a condominium project is not beyond the scope of authority of the owners' association.

DECISION: The court of appeals affirmed the trial court's judgment in favor of the association.

Cooperatives   A **cooperative** (often called a "co-op") is a multifamily housing property in which persons control—but do not own—their units. Instead, a corporation or their association owns the entire property.

The corporation's shareholders are the building's tenants. An individual's right to a particular unit is based on a lease from the association, available only because he or she is a shareholder. The bylaws of the corporation detail the rights and duties of the tenants. Although the building is maintained by the association, maintenance expenses are shared by the shareholder-tenants. Because the individual does not own the unit to which he or she is entitled, individual financing is usually much harder to come by than in the case of a condominium.

Most bylaws restrict the individual's right to transfer his or her lease.

Real-Estate Investment Trusts

The trust is a device that has been used in the United States and England for centuries. In a trust one person or an institution has the legal title to specific property that is to be managed for the benefit of others. The property may be real or personal. The trust has been an important instrument for law reform and the legal basis for some significant economic innovations. One trust that is frequently used for real property is the **real-estate investment trust (REIT)**.

A REIT is an organization in which the trustees own real estate, or loans secured by real estate, that is managed for beneficiaries (at least 100 persons must be beneficial owners of the trust) who hold transferable shares representing their respective interests. REITs developed in the 1960s because they enjoyed tax advantage over the corporate form of business organization. They remain a popular form of investment today, particularly for individuals who can use them as "tax losses."

REITs are regulated by both federal and state laws. They exist as a form of business organization that differs from the partnership or corporation referred to in Chapters 38 and 42. The REIT is generally regarded as a Massachusetts business trust specializing in a particular field of operations.

Review Questions and Problems

Key Terms

estate	assignment
fee simple estate	sublease
defeasible fee	easement
life estate	profit
life tenant	license
remainderman	lien
dower	joint tenancy
curtesy	tenancy in common
elective share	tenancy by the entirety
leasehold interest	community property
lessor	tenancy in partnership
lessee	condominium
term tenancy	cooperative
periodic tenancy	real-estate investment
tenancy at will	trusts
tenancy at sufferance	

Discussion Questions

1. Explain the difference between a fee simple absolute and a fee simple defeasible. How are they similar?

2. What is the principle difference between a term tenancy and a periodic tenancy?

3. Compare and contrast a joint tenancy and a tenancy in common.

4. What is the difference between a sublease and an assignment?

Review Problems

1. The pipe under Tanya's kitchen sink leaks, causing frequent flooding. Tanya has attempted to get her landlord to fix the leak, to no avail. Tanya refuses to pay her next month's rent. Her landlord institutes proceedings to recover the rent and have her evicted. There is nothing stated in the lease that requires the landlord to make repairs. What might be the basis of Tanya's defense?

2. Mom and Pop own and operate a grocery store. They rent their storefront under the terms of a net lease. A leak develops in the pipe under the store's bathroom sink, causing frequent flooding. Mom and Pop demand that their landlord repair the leak. When the landlord refuses, Mom and Pop have the leak repaired at their own expense and deduct the cost of the repair from the next month's rent. The landlord sues to recover the rent. Mom and Pop's defense is based on the theory that the landlord breached an implied warranty. Who is likely to win? Why?

3. Melvin signs a 2-year lease but continues to occupy the premises after the expiration of the lease. What are the landlord's options? If the landlord decides to allow Melvin to remain in the property without signing a new lease, when will Melvin's new tenancy expire?

4. Pete Brangs and his son, Al, owned real estate as joint tenants. Pete had been involved in a business deal and accumulated a large debt, which he refused to pay because he felt that the creditor had defrauded him. The creditor threatened to attach the real estate if the debt was not paid. Pete believed the creditor could not attach the property because Al had had nothing to do with Pete's business and he and Al were co-owners of the real estate. Was Pete correct? Discuss.

5. Jim and Lucy Monroe, a married couple, lived in a community property state. Jim had not worked for many years because he hated to get up in the morning. Lucy was the sole support of the family. Lucy bought a house and took title in her own name. Six years later, she died, leaving the house to her son. What rights, if any, did Jim have in the property? Support your answer.

6. Anne Crowley purchased a house from Alex Baldwin. The house adjoined an apartment complex that Baldwin was developing. Baldwin promised Crowley that she and future owners of the property would have the use of the pool. Crowley lived in the house for several years. During this period she used the pool each summer. When she sold the property, she told the new owners of Baldwin's promise. But Baldwin would not allow them to use the pool. Describe Crowley's interest in the use of the pool. Could Baldwin prevent the new owners from using the pool? Support your answer.

Case Problems

1. Cushman is developing Blackacre as a residential subdivision. Prior to Cushman's acquisition of the property, Blackacre had been an apricot orchard. A roadway based on an easement ran from the orchard to a public street. This property subject to the roadway easement was owned by Davis. The road had existed for many years. Its primary use was to move spraying and picking equipment into the orchard. This was done about ten times each year. Davis also used the road for access to his home and to a water tank. From time to time others used the road to reach the orchard. Cushman seeks to quiet title to the easement for access to the subdivision and Davis strenuously objects. Will Cushman be successful in his quiet title action? Discuss.

2. The will of Alma H. Rand contained the following provision: "3rd. That the share of the Estate of Henry Rand of the town of Southport, Lincoln County, State of Maine, shall be left to John Freeman Rand in fee simple *with the proviso that he shall never deny access or occupation to the several heirs hereinafter named during their lifetime.*" What kind of estate did John Rand have as a result of this provision? Explain.

3. The Chelsea Yacht Club owned a clubhouse that had been erected on piles driven into the bed of the Mystic River. The land was owned by the state, but the club had secured a license to construct the building. The only access to the clubhouse was over the Chelsea North Bridge. Both clubhouse and bridge were over 60 years old. Because of the age of the bridge, the state constructed a new bridge several miles away. The old bridge was removed. This left the clubhouse surrounded by water. The club sued the bridge authority for damages occasioned by the loss of access over the bridge. On what theory might the club sue the bridge authority? Would the club be successful? Discuss.

4. Luithle and his wife owned real estate as joint tenants. Luithle purchased cattle from Schlichenmayer, paying for the cattle with a worthless check. Luithle immediately sold the cattle. Part of the proceeds were used to make a $1,100 mortgage payment on the

49

Acquisition, Financing, and Control of Real Property

Purchase and Sale of Real Property
Other Methods of Acquiring Real
  Property

Real Property as Security
Foreclosure
Control of Land Use

The previous chapter outlined the various interests that can exist in real property. This chapter begins by discussing how those interests can be transferred—voluntarily or involuntarily—from one party to another. The most common method of acquiring real property is for a buyer to purchase it from a willing seller. But we shall see that property can also be acquired under certain circumstances without the consent of the owner, through adverse possession or, when the government wishes to acquire property, through eminent domain.

Since real property tends to be relatively expensive, most real property purchases are secured transactions—that is, they are financed in part by loans secured by the purchased property. In Chapter 32 we learned about secured transactions involving personal property; as we shall see in this chapter, the procedures for securing loans with real property are quite different.

In the final section of the chapter, the government's control of real property is examined. Al-though an owner of real estate has significant rights, local, state, and federal governments can and do impose regulations that restrict the use of real property.

Purchase and Sale of Real Property

The purchase and sale of real property should be of special interest to business students because they will probably participate in several such transactions during their lifetime. The large amounts of money, long-term financial commitments, and technical legal procedures that are a part of most real estate sales make knowledge of these transactions particularly important. Buying and selling real estate involves several legal areas. Agency and contract law are especially important. Many real estate sales are negotiated by brokers who are agents. Brokers are also involved in leasing, property management, and real estate appraisal. The contract is the critical document in a real estate sale; it governs the relationship between brokers and clients and also between landlords and tenants.

Anatomy of a Real Estate Sale

Purchase Contract   The typical real estate sale in the United States is usually the result of negotiations between the buyer and seller, often with the help of a real estate broker. In some areas, especially for residential real estate, a person desiring to buy property will submit a purchase offer to the seller. Buyers should realize that this document's terms become the contract if the seller accepts the offer. However, the seller can reject or make a counteroffer if he or she is not satisfied with the purchase offer terms. In this case the negotiations often continue and a contract on different terms may result.

Another procedure, more frequently used in commercial transactions, is for the parties to negotiate until an agreement appears to have been reached. Then the parties will have a document drafted; they will then review and sign it as their agreement. Whatever procedure is used, all states require that a contract for the sale of real property be in writing to be enforceable.

Interim before Closing   The real estate purchase contract does not transfer title to the real property; it is simply a contract whereby the seller agrees to transfer title for the agreed-upon purchase price. There is generally an interval of time between the date that the contract is signed and the date of the title closing. The *title closing* is an event where the buyer obtains legal title by deed and the seller gets the purchase price.

During the interval between the execution of the purchase contract and the title closing, the buyer typically arranges financing for the transaction. The buyer's ability to get suitable financing is usually a condition precedent to the obligation of both parties to perform the contract.

Another typical condition precedent is that the seller have good title to the property. The buyer uses this interval period to examine the seller's title. The buyer will generally commission a search of public records to confirm that the seller owns the property, and to identify any liens or other interests that others might have in the property. All states maintain records of real property interests; these recording systems will be discussed later in the chapter. If the seller's title is defective, the seller will have an opportunity to cure the defects before the date set for title closing.

Equitable Title   When a contract for the sale of real estate is completed, the buyer acquires *equitable title*. This gives the buyer the right to sue for damages or specific performance if the seller refuses to perform. Simultaneously, the seller acquires a right to enforce the contract.

Risk of Loss   As the buyer has equitable title during the period between the contract signing and title closing, in some states the buyer bears the risk of loss or damage to the property. Thus if the property is damaged by fire, the buyer still must complete the transaction as agreed. Other states reject this rule as unfair, especially when the buyer is not in possession. These states allow the buyer an adjustment in the price to compensate for loss. Parties to real estate contract need not leave the allocation of the risk of loss to state law. Instead, this problem can and should be settled by the parties in their contract.

Title Closing   Two types of title closing are common in the United States. In residential transactions, the parties involved in the transaction meet as a group and exchange the funds and documents required to complete the transfer. Ordinarily the buyer, the seller, brokers, a representative of the institution financing the sale, and perhaps attorneys for each party are present.

In commercial transactions, real estate sales generally close through a third party, called an escrow agent. In an *escrow closing*, the buyer and seller submit the necessary documents and funds to the escrow agent, who is responsible for seeing that the transaction closes on the terms agreed upon in the contract. When the seller delivers a properly executed deed to the escrow agent and the agent is assured that the seller is passing a good title, the funds and mortgage documents are turned over to the proper parties, and the transaction is completed.

Deeds

Ownership of real property is transferred by an instrument called a **deed**. A deed is a two-party instrument; the person conveying the property is called the **grantor** and the person to whom the property is conveyed, the **grantee**. Several types of deeds are in common use in the United States. Generally the type of deed a seller will use is agreed upon in the sales contract.

Warranty Deed   The most common type of deed used in a real-estate transaction is the warranty deed. A **warranty deed** conveys title and warrants that the title is good and free of liens and encumbrances. The warranties are also referred to as covenants. They provide the purchaser with some protection against claims that might interfere with ownership.

Although the use and wording of particular covenants vary from one jurisdiction to another, four covenants are common in the United States. One of these is called the covenant of seisin or **covenant of right to convey**. By this covenant the seller guarantees that he or she has a good title and the right to transfer it. A second covenant used in many jurisdictions is the **covenant against encumbrances**. In making this covenant, the seller affirms that no encumbrances exist against the property. The **covenant of quiet enjoyment** and the **covenant of general warranty** are guarantees that the buyer will not be evicted from the property by someone with a title superior to the seller's. As a result of these two covenants, the seller agrees to defend the buyer's title against all lawful claims.

Warranty deed covenants do not assure the buyer that the seller has title, but they do provide a right to sue if a covenant is broken. This is a valuable right if the seller is solvent and still within the jurisdiction.

Bargain and Sale Deed   A **bargain and sale deed** conveys title but contains no warranties. Although no formal guarantees of title are made, the bargain and sale deed is by nature contractual, and the seller implies that he or she has a title to convey. It will sometimes contain covenants which guarantee that the seller has done nothing that might adversely affect the title.

Quitclaim Deed   A **quitclaim deed** merely releases whatever interest the grantor has. Unlike the warranty deed and bargain and sale deed, the transferor by a quitclaim does not purport to convey title. But if the grantor has title, this interest is conveyed as effectively as it would be by a warranty or bargain and sale deed. Quitclaim deeds are commonly used to correct defective titles.

Table 49-1 summarizes the essential characteristics of the three types of deeds: the warranty deed, the bargain and sale deed, and the quitclaim deed.

Essential Elements of a Deed   A deed is a complicated legal instrument that should be drafted by an attorney. To be valid, a deed must contain words of conveyance that indicate an

TABLE 49-1

Concept Summary	Characteristics of Deeds
Type	**Characteristics**
Warranty deed	Covenant of seisin or right to convey: grantor has good title and the right to transfer it
	Covenant against encumbrances: there are no encumbrances against the property
	Covenant of quiet enjoyment: grantee will enjoy the property without disturbance from others claiming an interest in the property
	Covenant of general warranty: grantee's use of the property will not be interrupted by someone with superior title
Bargain and sale deed	Generally contains no covenants, but may contain covenants that grantor has done nothing that might adversely affect title
	Grantor implies that he or she has title to convey
Quitclaim deed	Merely releases whatever interest the grantor may have
	Grantor does not purport to convey title

intention to convey title. The deed also must identify a competent grantor and grantee, contain a legal description, and be properly signed and executed. A final requirement is a valid delivery and

acceptance. Most legal problems involving deeds arise because someone claims the deed has not been properly delivered. The case that follows is an example.

JORGENSEN V. CROW
Supreme Court of North Dakota
466 N.W.2d 120 (1991)

BACKGROUND: John and Beulah Jorgensen arranged to sell ranch land to their nephew, Leslie Crow, and his wife. The total purchase price was $150,000, of which $85,000 was to be borrowed from a bank and paid up front and $65,000 was to be paid in six yearly installments of $10,128.31. The terms of the purchase were spelled out in a document entitled Contract for Deed, which provided that the Jorgensens would convey title to the Crows *when the Crows had satisfied all of their obligations under the contract.* Prior to the closing, the Jorgensens executed both the contract for deed and a warranty deed to the property. The warranty deed was on the table at the closing; Leslie Crow picked it up, took it with him, and later recorded it. Following a dispute as to whether Beulah Jorgensen had the right to use the property, she sued. The trial court ruled in favor of the Crows, and Jorgensen appealed.

Levine, Justice

Beulah Jorgensen attended the loan closing and sat at a conference table with the Crows and a FLB [bank] loan officer. The warranty deed was on the table at the closing. Leslie Crow picked it up, examined it, and put it with his loan papers. Crow took the deed when he left the closing.

In 1985, Jorgensen used the property to pasture her cattle, and in exchange, the Crows asked for and were given a receipt for the 1985 land payment of $10,128.31. The Crows recorded the warranty deed in February 1986. In 1986 and 1987, Jorgensen pastured her cattle on the ranchland, but she did not give the Crows receipts showing satisfaction of the yearly contract installment payment.

In May 1988, Jorgensen put her cattle on the property. The Crows attempted to remove the cattle, claiming that Jorgensen had no right to use the property. Jorgensen brought this action, asking that the recorded warranty deed be set aside. Jorgensen also sought, and received, a temporary restraining order preventing the Crows from interfering with her use of the land.

The interest transferred by a deed does not vest until there is a delivery of the deed. Absent a delivery of the deed, the deed is of no effect. The recording of a deed may create a rebuttable presumption of its delivery to, and its acceptance by, the grantee. The presumption must be rebutted with clear and convincing evidence. However, the fact a grantee has possession of a deed does not mean that there was a delivery, unless the grantor intended delivery. There must be some act or declaration from which an intent to pass title may be inferred.

Leslie Crow testified that he picked up the signed warranty deed during the loan closing, examined it, and placed it with his papers. Jorgensen, however, testified that she did not give the warranty deed or intend to deliver it to the Crows at the loan closing. There was also written evidence that Jorgensen did not intend to deliver the deed. The contract for deed that the Crows signed at the loan closing stated that the warranty deed would be conveyed "[w]hen the contract is completed and the provisions are fulfilled. . . ." When two instruments have been executed at the same time, by the same parties, in the course of the same transaction, and covering the same subject matter, they must be read and construed together. Under the terms of the contract for deed and the warranty deed, the Crows were not entitled to the deed until full consideration had been given. In addition to the $85,000 paid to Jorgensen at the closing, the contract called for yearly installments of $10,128.31, until a balance of $65,000 had been paid with interest. None of the payments had been made when Leslie Crow took possession of the deed. The trial court's finding that a lawful delivery had been made necessarily includes a finding that Jorgensen intended to deliver the deed at the loan closing. There was, however, no act or declaration from which an intent to pass title could be inferred. Reviewing this record, we are left with a definite and firm conviction that it was a mistake for the trial court to find a "lawful delivery" when the manual transfer of a deed was accompanied by written evidence that no present delivery was intended.

DECISION: The Supreme Court of North Dakota reversed the trial court's decision and ruled in favor of Jorgensen.

Recording Statutes

All states have statutes requiring that important instruments affecting the title to real property be entered into the public record. In addition to deeds and mortgages, the statutes generally require that long-term leases, easements, assignments, and other similar instruments be recorded. The purpose of these statutes is to notify third parties of interests that might exist in a particular piece of land. This notice protects the third party from loss that might occur if he or she were to acquire an interest in land subject to unknown claims of others.

Recording statutes are based on the idea that if a real property interest is not recorded, a person acquiring a conflicting interest will have superior rights in the land. For example, if X conveys real property to Y, Y is required to record the deed. If Y does not and X fraudulently conveys to Z, Z may acquire an ownership interest superior to Y's. In order for this to occur, Z must be a good-faith purchaser. This means that Z must not have knowledge of the sale to Y and must give value for the property. The person who has recorded an interest in property is favored by the law over others who later acquire some interest in that same property.

Constructive Notice

Constructive notice is knowledge that the law implies a person has. Constructive notice exists if a person without actual knowledge is in a position to have acquired that knowledge by reasonably investigating available sources. If a person acquiring an interest in realty knows something that would induce a reasonable person to make further inquiry, and none is made, the law presumes actual knowledge exists. In addition, any information that might be discovered by a careful check of the record is presumed known. A person with actual or constructive knowledge of a prior conflicting interest does not acquire his or her interest in good faith. Thus the result is that a person who does not examine the record is penalized and the recording statutes operate effectively. Since several documents granting interests to different parties may be recorded for the same property, the time of recording can affect the priority given to the owner of the interest being recorded. In the following case the Supreme Court of Kansas had to determine whether higher priority should be given to the person holding a mechanic's lien, an interest given for labor performed or materials furnished in the construction or improvements made to real property, or to the holder of a valid mortgage on the property.

DAVIS-WELLCOME MORTGAGE CO. v. LONG-BELL LUMBER CO.

Supreme Court of Kansas
336 P.2d. 463 (1959)

BACKGROUND: Durham owned several parcels of land in the city of Newton on which he intended to build homes that would then be sold. On June 28, 1955 he obtained a loan from the plaintiff, Davis-Wellcome Mortgage Co. (Davis) and delivered to it his promissory note and mortgage. On June 30, 1955 the mortgage was recorded. On June 29, 1955 the defendant Long-Bell Lumber Company (Long-Bell) agreed to furnish lumber to Durham for use in the construction of the homes.

Durham failed to pay the amount due to either Long-Bell or to Davis. Plaintiff Davis then sued to foreclose on its loan to Durham. The trial court found that defendant Long-Bell commenced work on June 29, 1955, and that Long-Bell thus obtained a statutory mechanic's lien that became effective on that date. The court rendered judgment in favor of both Davis and Long-Bell against Durham. It also determined that because the statutory mechanic's lien of Long-Bell arose before the mortgage of Davis was recorded, Long-Bell's lien was entitled to priority over the mortgage interest of Davis.

Davis appealed the trial court's decision granting Long-Bell's lien priority over its mortgage interest.

Fatzer, Justice

The principal question presented is the priority of liens of a mortgagee and a mechanic's lien holder where construction of houses on real estate covered by the mortgage was begun the day after the mortgage was executed and delivered, but the day before it was recorded. . . .

[P]laintiff asserts the trial court erred in holding that the recording of plaintiff's mortgage on June 30, 1955, determined the date on which its lien became effective as against the lien of Long-Bell. The assertion requires an examination of our so-called recording statutes. G.S.1957 Supp. 67–221 provides in effect that every instrument in writing that conveys real estate or whereby any real estate may be affected, proved or acknowledged, may be recorded in the office of the register of deeds of the county in which such real estate is situated. . . . The following sections of General Statutes 1949 provide:

> 67–222. Every such instrument in writing, certified and recorded in the manner hereinbefore prescribed, shall, from the time of filing the same with the register of deeds for record, impart notice to all persons of the contents thereof; and all subsequent purchasers and mortgagees shall be deemed to purchase with notice.
>
> 67–223. *No such instrument in writing shall be valid*, except between the parties thereto, and such as have actual notice thereof, *until the same shall be deposited with the register of deeds for record.* (Emphasis supplied.)

There is nothing in the record which suggests that Long-Bell had actual notice of plaintiff's mortgage prior to its recordation on June 30, 1955, and the clear and unambiguous language of 67–223 would seem to decide this controversy. But, plaintiff contends it does not, and . . . argues that the sections above quoted have application to and protect only subsequent purchasers and mortgagees in good faith; further, that a judgment creditor is not a subsequent purchaser or mortgagee in good faith and for a valuable consideration. . . .

There is a basic distinction between a judgment creditor and a mechanic's lien holder. A judgment creditor is not a bona fide purchaser and parts with nothing to acquire his lien which is subject to the equities of all other persons in the property of the judgment debtor.

On the other hand, a mechanic's lien holder parts with a valuable consideration in the form of labor or materials for which the statute gives a lien upon the property improved; it is not acquired by an adverse proceeding after the debt has been incurred but it accrues as the debt accrues, being incident to the improvements, and the owner of the land to which it is attached consents to it when he consents to the improvements.

We can see no fundamental difference between a statutory lien [such as a mechanic's lien] and a lien created by a mortgage. Each arises as a result of a contract with the owner of the property. Under G.S.1949, 60–1401 a mechanic's lien is security for a debt and is an encumbrance in the nature of a statutory mortgage founded upon consent, under which the holder parts with a valuable consideration. In the language of the statute, the lien for materials and labor furnished or performed in the erection or improvement of land,

> shall be preferred to all other liens or encumbrances which may attach to or upon said land, building, or improvement, or either of them, subsequent to the commencement of such building, the furnishing or putting up of such fixtures, or machinery, the planting of trees, vines, plants or hedge, the building of such fence, footwalk, as sidewalk, or the making of any such repairs or improvements. (Emphasis supplied.)

Although plaintiff's mortgage was executed and delivered prior to the commencement of work and created a valid lien upon the property as between the parties, it was invalid under the clear and unambiguous terms of G.S.1949, 67–223 as to Long-Bell's statutory mortgage which attached upon the real estate on June 29, 1955, the day before plaintiff's mortgage was recorded.

Under the facts in this case Long-Bell perfected and filed its mechanic's lien in accordance with the terms of the statute which was protected by the recording statutes. Long-Bell was a stranger to the mortgage, and the trial court did not err in holding that its statutory mortgage was prior in right to the mortgage lien of the plaintiff.

DECISION: The Supreme Court of Kansas, finding that the mortgage interest of Davis was not valid as to Long-Bell until the date of its recording, affirmed the trial court's decision.

Other Methods of Acquiring Real Property

Purchase is the most common way that real property is acquired, but it is not the only way. Real property also be acquired by gift. (The discussion of gifts in Chapter 47, dealing with personal property, may be applied to real property as well.) Real property may also be inherited, as discussed in Chapter 51.

There are also ways, discussed below, that real property can be acquired without the owner's consent. Table 49-2 summarizes the various methods of acquiring ownership of real property.

Adverse Possession

Obtaining title by adverse possession is a legal oddity. Under the doctrine of **adverse possession**, a person occupying land as a trespasser can, by satisfying certain requirements, defeat the rights of the

TABLE **49-2**

Methods of Acquiring Real Property

Purchase

  Warranty deed: Seller guarantees title.
  Bargain and sale deed: No guarantee of title.
  Quitclaim deed: Seller transfers his or her interest.

Obtain title through adverse possession

  Possession must be continuous, open and notorious, hostile, actual, and exclusive.

Eminent domain

  Government acquisition of private property for public purposes. Compensation is required.

Gift

  Discussed in Chapter 47.

Inheritance

  Discussed in Chapter 51.

PREVENTIVE LAW
Purchase of Real Property—Points for Purchasers

Because the purchase of a home is generally the largest monetary transaction a person makes, it is important for that purchaser to be sure that his or her legal rights in the property are protected. In most cases the best advice is to hire a real estate attorney who will look after your interests. The points noted here are general comments and should not be regarded as complete or appropriate for every purchase.

1. Inspect the property for obvious problems with the land (sewer, water drainage) or the building's roof, furnace, cracking walls, and so on.

2. Before having a purchase offer prepared,
   a. Discuss what personal property is to be included.
   b. Make inquiries with financial institutions to determine if you are likely to obtain financing.
   c. Establish a tentative time for possession and closing.
   d. Include any special terms and conditions in your offer.
   e. Limit the time for the offer to be accepted.
   f. Specify you want a warranty deed.

3. After agreeing on the terms of purchase, find out what you have to do and what the seller must do before closing.
   a. Seller: Provide survey, deed, discharge of existing mortgage, evidence of tax payments, evidence of title.
   b. Purchaser: Obtain financing, review seller's evidence of title, tax payments and other documents, make plans for taking possession.

4. At closing, transfer documents and money based on closing statement, obtain documents (deed and bill of sale) showing title to real and personal property, and plan for recording of deed and safekeeping of title policy.

---

true owner. The justification for this unusual policy is that society benefits when idle land is put to use. The legal system encourages the use of land by providing a trespasser with a means to establish clear title to the property he or she is using.

Balanced against the policy of encouraging land use is concern with the protection of private property rights. Because of the importance of protecting private property, a trespasser acquires title only if prescribed conditions are met and certain acts occur. These acts and conditions exist to ensure that the owner has a opportunity to discover challenges to his or her title and a reasonable chance to protect it.

Statutes of Limitations Basic to all adverse possession claims are state *statutes of limitations*. These statutes establish a period of time during which the rightful owner of land must bring an action to oust the trespasser.

At common law the owner had to bring suit within 20 years; several states have adopted this as the limitation period. Although only a handful of states allow the owner more than 20 years to act, a substantial number apply shorter periods, ranging from 5 to 18 years. Many of the states with short limitation periods are in the sparsely populated western United States. This reflects the public policy underlying adverse possession, which is to encourage land use. In some states the limitation period is reduced if the adverse possessor has paid taxes or occupies the land on the basis of a document such as an invalid deed or will.

Elements of Adverse Possession Generally five elements must exist for title to be acquired by adverse possession. The claimant must prove his or her possession is: (1) continuous for the statutory period, (2) open and notorious, (3) hostile, (4) actual, and (5) exclusive.

A number of states allow occupancy of two or more successive adverse possessors to be added together to establish possession for the necessary period. This is called *tacking*, since the periods are "tacked" together. Although tacking is probably permitted in a minority of states, some jurisdictions limit it to cases involving heirs, spouses, or blood relatives.

CONTINUOUS   A person seeking title to property must prove that his or her possession has been continuous for the statutory period.

OPEN AND NOTORIOUS   Open and notorious acts are those that will alert the true owner to claims that are adverse to his or her rights. Although the true owner does not have to know what is taking place, the acts must be such that a diligent owner would become aware of them.

HOSTILE   Facts that are open and notorious are often hostile. The requirement that possession be hostile does not require ill will or evil intent but merely that the person in possession of the property claims to occupy it as the owner. Most state courts accept that possession is hostile for purposes of adverse possession if the oc-cupant claims ownership either by mistake or willfully. A person who enters into property with the owner's permission cannot claim title by adverse possession unless he or she later repudiates the owner's title.

ACTUAL POSSESSION   Actual possession consists of exercising dominion over land, making ordinary use of it, and taking the ordinary profit the land is capable of yielding. Courts determine actual possession by looking at the character of the land that is involved. Residing on the property is not necessary unless that use would be expected. In a few states the adverse possessor must enclose the land to establish a claim.

EXCLUSIVE USE   Exclusive use means that the claimant possesses the land for his or her own use. Total exclusion of others is not required, but the adverse possessor must exclude others as would be expected of an owner under the circumstances. Occasional use by others, even the rightful owners, does not negate exclusiveness if the use permitted by the adverse possessor is consistent with his or her claims of ownership. The following case involves the element of exclusive use and several other aspects of adverse possession.

PORTER V. POSEY
Missouri Court of Appeals
592 S.W.2d 844 (1979)

BACKGROUND: The Porters (plaintiffs) purchased property from the Engelmeyers. In addition to the property conveyed to them by deed, the plaintiffs also took possession of a 0.18-acre tract of land that had been maintained and used by the Englemeyers but that was owned by the Poseys (defendants). The parcel in question was used by the Engelmeyers for 20 years; they built a graveled turnaround on it and used the property for parking and for access by them to other adjoining property they owned. At all times the Engelmeyers believed they owned the disputed parcel.

Just prior to the Porter's purchase from the Engelmeyers, the Poseys had the property surveyed. They then discovered that the turnaround was on their land. They threatened Mr. Engelmeyer and told him to get off the property and blocked the access to the turnaround. The Porters sued to clear title to the land; they claimed the Englemeyers had title through adverse possession. The trial court found the possession by the Englemeyers of the disputed parcel satisfied the requirements for adverse possession. Accordingly, it found the plaintiffs, who purchased from them, had title to the parcel. The defendants appealed to the court of appeals.

Satz, Judge

The crucial questions in this case are: (1) was title to the tract in dispute vested in the Engelmeyers; (2) if so, was their title subsequently extinguished or divested; and (3) if not divested or extinguished, was their title properly transferred to plaintiffs.

In order for the trial court to have vested title in plaintiffs on the present record, it must have found that title first vested in the Englemeyers by adverse possession. Thus, implicit in the court's ultimate decision is a finding that . . . the Engelmeyers occupied or used the tract and their occupation or use of the tract was (1) actual (2) open and notorious (3) hostile (4) exclusive and (5) continuous for ten years. Defendants limit their attack on these implicit findings to an attack on the open and notorious, hostile and exclusive elements of the Engelmeyers' adverse possession.

Open and notorious occupancy or possession is an essential element of adverse possession because the openness and notoriety of the occupancy or possession gives the owner cause to know that an adverse claim of ownership is being made by another. . . . The element of open and notorious is satisfied by a showing that the occupancy or possession manifested a claim of ownership and was conspicuous, widely recognized and commonly known.

In the instant case, the Engelmeyers entered the disputed tract with a bulldozer, cleared the land, built the turnaround, then maintained it and the land surrounding it. The family also played volleyball and parked on this land. . . . Changing the physical structure of the land by clearing it, building a turnaround and then using and maintaining the turnaround was sufficient evidence to support the court's finding that the Engelmeyers' acts were acts of ownership, sufficient to give the then existing owner notice of this claim and were commonly known so as to constitute open and notorious occupancy or possession. . . .

Defendants next argue that the Englemeyers' use and possession was not hostile. Hostility of possession does not imply ill will or acrimony. . . . Hostile possession is simply an assertion of ownership adverse to that of the true owner and all others; i.e., "the claimant must occupy the land with the intent to possess it as his own and not in subservience to a recognized, superior claim of another." . . .

In the present case, as we have previously noted, there was sufficient evidence for the trial court to find that the Engelmeyers occupied and used the disputed tract with the intent to possess it as their own and, thus, clearly their use and occupancy was hostile.

Defendants' next attack on adverse possession is that the Engelmeyers' possession was not exclusive because others occasionally used the turnaround and, thus, defendants contend, plaintiffs' evidence, at best, merely established a common easement by prescription. . . .

Possession or use is exclusive when the claimant occupies or uses the land for his own use and not for that of another. The present record reveals that the Engelmeyers built the turnaround believing it to be on their property. The fact that travelers occasionally also used this roadway to turn around does not imply nor indicate that the Engelmeyers occupied the land for the benefit of these travelers. Indeed, even occasional use of disputed property by the record owner will not of itself negate the exclusive use by an adverse claimant, if the record owner's knowledge or notice of the adverse claim is not otherwise altered. For these reasons, defendants' argument against exclusivity is not persuasive.

The remaining question, then, is whether the Engelmeyers properly transferred title to plaintiffs. As noted, the principle urged by plaintiffs to support the Engelmeyers' transfer of title to plaintiffs, in effect, permits title to property acquired by adverse possession to be transferred without a written conveyance, and simply requires the title owner to intend to transfer the property so acquired and the transferee to receive or take possession of that property.

In the present case, Mrs. Engelmeyer's unrefuted testimony was that she and her husband intended to convey the disputed tract to plaintiffs. Moreover, this was plaintiffs' understanding, and the fact that plaintiff Eugene Porter sought legal advice to carry out that intention merely enforces the weight to be given to Mrs. Engelmeyer's testimony. Further, there was sufficient explicit testimony and inferential evidence for the trial court of find that, after the transfer, plaintiffs took possession of the disputed tract. Thus, the Engelmeyers transferred their title to the disputed tract to plaintiffs.

DECISION: The court of appeals affirmed the trial court's decision.

Prescription   The previous chapter described the easement, a nonpossessory right to use the land of another for a particular purpose. Most easements are created by written instruments; however, an easement may be created by *prescription*, a legal doctrine similar in several ways to adverse possession. Both are based on wrongful invasion of the property rights of the true owner, but prescription is based on adverse use, not occupancy. As a result, a person acquiring a prescriptive easement merely acquires a *right to use another's land*, while the successful adverse possessor actually acquires title. Another common difference between the two is that the time necessary to acquire an easement by prescription is frequently less than the time required to acquire title by adverse possession.

Eminent Domain

Eminent domain is the power of the government to acquire private property without the owner's consent. Both the United States and the individual states may delegate the power of eminent domain. They often delegate this power to cities, counties, state colleges and universities, and public service corporations. The federal and state constitutions limit the government's power by requiring that:

- The property must be taken for a public purpose.
- The owner must be adequately compensated.
- The property cannot be taken without due process of law.

There can be problems with each of these requirements. The first problem—concerned with taking for a public purpose—occurs in situations where private owners benefit from the government-taking. Clearly, if the taking is for the purpose of building an interstate highway, a state prison or local civic center, a public purpose is involved. However, where private property is taken for urban development, condemned private property is taken by the government and then generally resold to a private developer. In these cases the public purpose—to improve and develop the city—seems less clear when the property is ultimately returned to private ownership.

The second problem concerns when a "taking of property" occurs. Government regulation of private property is permitted even when that regulation interferes with the owner's use of the property. For example, if the state or local government through the exercise of its police power regulates the use of property but does not take it, there is no obligation to compensate the owner. On the other hand, if there has been a "taking" of property, the government is obligated to compensate the owner. **Inverse condemnation** occurs if there is a significant interference with the private property owner's use and enjoyment of his or her property. Many recent cases have discussed this aspect of the government's use of its power of eminent domain. The *Seawall Associates* case that follows illustrates the application of this concept.

The third problem concerns the process used by the government exercising its eminent domain power. The owner of the property is guaranteed the opportunity to have a trial focusing on public use being made of the property and on the amount of compensation to be paid. The owner of the property is entitled to the fair market value of the property. Is that determined by the current use of the property or the highest and most expensive use to which the property could be put? Should the amount of compensation reflect the emotional attachment of a person who has long occupied the property as a home? These and other related questions concern the process surrounding the government's eminent domain power.

SEAWALL ASSOCIATES V. CITY OF NEW YORK
Court of Appeals of New York
542 N.E.2d 1059 (1989)

BACKGROUND: The city of New York (defendant) had long encouraged the demolition of low-rent single-room occupancy (SRO) residence buildings, thus enticing many investors to purchase SRO buildings for the purpose of tearing them down and redeveloping the property. In the face of a low-cost housing shortage during the 1980s, the city reversed this policy and enacted Local Law No. 9, which placed a moratorium on the conversion, alteration, or demolition of SRO buildings. That law also contained an "antiwarehousing" provision to prevent owners from neglecting vacant units: Owners were required to rehabilitate and make habitable every SRO unit in their buildings. Also, the law included a "rent-up" obligation requiring the owners to lease every unit in their buildings to a "bona fide tenant." If any unit was left vacant for more than 30 days, the building owner was presumed to have violated the law and was subject to stiff penalties. SRO building owners (plaintiffs) challenged the law as an unconstitutional taking of their property without compensation. The owners won at the trial court level, but the city appealed and won a reversal in appeals court. The owners then appealed to New York's highest court, the court of appeals.

Hancock, Judge

Whether the mandatory "rent-up" obligations of the antiwarehousing provision effect a physical taking depends upon the nature and extent of their interference with certain essential property rights. Here, the claimed physical taking is the City's forced control over the owners' possessory interests in their properties, including the denial of the owners' rights to exclude others. Local Law No. 9 requires the owners to rent their rooms or be subject to severe penalties; it compels them to admit persons as tenants with all of the possessory and other rights that that status entails; it compels them to surrender the most basic attributes of private property, the rights of possession and exclusion. . . . Defendants argue that a physical taking must entail . . . palpable invasion . . . and, therefore, that the deprivation of intangible property rights alone, such as that resulting from coerced tenancies, is not enough. We disagree. Where, as here, owners are forced to accept the occupation of their properties by persons not already in residence, the resulting deprivation of rights in those properties is sufficient to constitute a physical taking for which compensation is required.

Under the traditional conception of property, the most important of the various rights of an owner is the right of possession which includes the right to exclude others from occupying or using the space (*see, Loretto v. Teleprompter Manhattan CATV Corp.*). As the court noted in *Loretto*, "an owner suffers a special kind of injury when a *stranger* directly invades and occupies the owner's property", and "property law has long protected an owner's expectation that he will be relatively undisturbed at least in the possession of his property." . . .

Moreover, to constitute a physical taking, the occupation need not be by the government itself, but may be by third parties under its authority.

Even if Local Law No. 9 were not held to effect a physical taking, it would still be facially invalid as a regulatory taking. "Suffice it to say that government regulation—by definition—involves the adjustment of rights for the public good. Often this adjustment curtails some potential for the use or economic exploitation of private property" (*Andrus v. Allard*). But the constitutional guarantee against uncompensated takings is violated when the adjustment of rights for the public good becomes so disproportionate that it can be said that the governmental action is "forcing some people alone to bear public burdens which, in all fairness and justice, should be borne by the public as a whole" (*Armstrong v. United States*). There is no "set formula" for determining in all cases when an adjustment of rights has reached the point when "justice and fairness" require that compensation be paid. It is basic, however, that such a burden-shifting regulation of the use of private property will, without more, constitute a taking: (1) if it denies an owner economically viable use of his property, *or* (2) if it does not substantially advance legitimate State interests.

Either would be sufficient to invalidate a property-use regulation. In our opinion, Local Law No. 9 fails on both counts. We turn first to whether the law denies owners the economically viable use of their properties. . . .

If analyzed with respect to its effect on property owners' basic rights "'to possess, use and dispose'" of their buildings, it is evident that Local Law No. 9 abrogates or substantially impairs each of the three rights. As previously discussed, the coerced rental provisions deprive owners the fundamental *right to possess* their properties. Moreover, these mandatory rental provisions—together with the prohibition against demolition, alteration and conversion of the properties to other uses, and the requirement that uninhabitable units be refurbished—deny owners of SRO buildings any *right to use* their properties as they see fit. Unquestionably, the effect of the law is to strip owners of SRO buildings—who may have purchased their properties solely to turn them into profitable investments by tearing down and replacing the existing structures with new ones (as plaintiffs claim they have)—of the very right to use their properties for any such purpose. Owners are forced to devote their properties to another use which, albeit one which might serve the City's interests, bears no relation to any economic purpose which could be reasonably contemplated by a private investor.

Finally, Local Law No. 9, particularly in those provisions prohibiting redevelopment and mandating rental, inevitably impairs the ability of owners to sell their properties for any sums approaching their investments. Thus, the local law must also negatively affect the owners' *right to dispose* of their properties. By any test, we think these restrictions deny the owners "economically viable use" of their properties.

We agree with plaintiffs, moreover, that Local Law No. 9 does not pass the other threshold test for constitutional validity of regulatory takings: that the burdens imposed substantially advance legitimate State interests.

Of course, the end sought to be furthered by Local Law No. 9 is of the greatest societal importance—alleviating the critical problems of homelessness. The question here, however, concerns the means established by the local law purportedly to achieve this end. In other words, can it be said, that imposing the burdens of the forced refurbishing and rent-up provisions on the owners of SRO properties *substantially* advances the aim of alleviating the homelessness problem? Is there a sufficiently close nexus between these burdens and "the end advanced as the justification for [them]"?

Defendants contend that by increasing the availability of SRO units the antiwarehousing and moratorium measures will provide more available low-cost housing and, thereby, further the aim of alleviating homelessness; this relationship between means and ends, they argue, supplies the required "close nexus". The City's own Blackburn study, however, acknowledges that a ban on converting, destroying and warehousing SRO units would do little to resolve the homeless crisis. Indeed, the SRO units are not earmarked for the homeless or for potentially homeless low-income families, and there is simply no assurance that the units will be rented to members of either group. While, of course, any increase in the supply of low-cost housing would benefit some prospective tenants, it is by no means clear that it would actually benefit the homeless.

DECISION: The court of appeals reversed the lower court's decision and ruled in favor of the property owners.

Real Property as Security

People often must borrow money for their purchases of a home or commercial real estate. When people have to borrow money the loan ordinarily is secured by an interest in the property. This security interest gives the lender the right to sell the property and apply the proceeds against the debt if the borrower defaults. Security interests in real estate are established by mortgages and deeds of trust.

The Mortgage Transaction

A **mortgage** is a written instrument that gives a party a security interest in real estate. The party who receives the security interest is known as the **mortgagee**; the party who pledges the real estate is known as the **mortgagor**.

A mortgage financing transaction generally involves, in addition to the mortgage, a promissory note or bond; the note or bond contains the terms of the loan and establishes the borrower's personal obligation to pay.

The mortgage and promissory note give the lender alternative remedies in the event of default. Suit may be brought on the note and a personal judgment obtained against the debtor, or the real property may be sold and the proceeds applied against the debt. The latter remedy, called *foreclosure*, is discussed later in this chapter.

If the lender wins a judgment on the note, the judgment may be collected by attaching other property or by garnishing the debtor's wages. If the security when sold does not bring enough to pay the debt, the lender may sue for the difference, using the note. A few states require the lender to choose either to foreclose against the collateral to pay the debt or to sue on the note.

Lien and Title Theories of Mortgages

Modern mortgage law can be traced to the early use of the mortgage in England. At common law a borrower who mortgaged real property as security actually transferred title to the lender. The lender obtained a deed just as if he had purchased the property. As the mortgage was given as security, the title that the lender acquired was not absolute. A provision in the mortgage, called the defeasance clause, provided that if the debt was paid when due, transfer of title to the lender was voided. Title reverted to the borrower.

The historical theory that the mortgage conveys title to the mortgagee continues to be used in some states, referred to as *title theory* states. Even in these states, however, although the lender acquires title, the lender does not acquire the right of possession unless the mortgagor defaults.

Most states recognize that in reality a mortgage is a lien. It is a device used by debtors and creditors to secure a debt. The creditor is primarily interested in having the security sold and the proceeds applied to the debt if the debtor fails to pay or violates some other mortgage provision. States taking this position are called *lien theory* states.

Deed of Trust

In a number of states the typical real estate security instrument involves three parties and is based on the law of trusts. Instead of executing a mortgage, the borrower transfers title to a trustee by a deed of trust. The important difference between a mortgage and a deed of trust is that in the latter, legal title to the real estate passes to the trustee.

The trustee holds the property for the benefit of both the borrower and the lender. When the debt secured by the deed of trust is repaid the trustee must reconvey title to the borrower.

One of the principal differences between a deed of trust and most mortgages is that the trustee under a deed of trust generally has the right, upon the borrower's default, to sell the property without initiating a judicial action. This difference will be discussed in greater detail later in the chapter.

Mortgage Provisions

Interest Payments Although many mortgages establish a fixed annual rate of interest to be paid by the borrower over the life of the mortgage, in recent years variable-rate mortgages have also become available. In a variable-rate mortgage the note and mortgage documents provide for interest payments at a rate that fluctuates based on prevailing interest rates at the time the payments are being made. Frequently the prime rate, the interest rate charged by a lender to its prime or best corporate customers, is the benchmark against which the interest rate due on the mortgage loan is to be tied. Thus a variable-rate mortgage may

ISSUES AND TRENDS
Lender Liability for Environmental Cleanup

A cornerstone of the federal government's effort to clean up hazardous waste sights has been the Comprehensive Environmental Response, Compensation, and Liability Act (CERCLA). CERCLA provides that any party that has ever owned or operated contaminated property can be held liable for its cleanup, even if all of the contamination occurred prior to that party's tenure as owner or operator. CERCLA imposes joint and several liability on owners and operators of contaminated property, which means that a subsequent owner who did nothing to cause a property's contamination could be required to pay the entire cost of the cleanup. For some properties, the cleanup costs can run well into the millions of dollars.

CERCLA has long made real property lenders nervous. For one thing, a lender can become an owner of real property through foreclosure. CERCLA exempts from liability lenders whose control over property relates exclusively to the protection of a security interest; however, some courts have interpreted this exemption to be lost whenever the lender participates in the property's management. A commercial real estate lender usually includes language in the loan that, in the event of a default by the borrower, grants the lender broad powers to control what the borrower does with the property. These powers can amount to participation in the property's management, leaving the lender exposed to CERCLA liability.

The potential for CERCLA liability has caused lenders to change their practices. Before agreeing to accept a security interest in real property, most lenders now require a thorough "environmental audit" of the property to make sure that there is no hazardous waste problem. What has long been a problem for lenders became a big headache for the federal government when the savings and loan crisis struck in the late 1980s. When the government was forced to take over hundreds of failed savings institutions, it became the owner of thousands of properties that the failed institutions had acquired through foreclosure. Would the federal government face CERCLA liability for any contaminated properties that it now owned?

In response to these problems, in 1991 the federal Environmental Protection Agency passed regulations that (1) gave lenders wider latitude in dealing with distressed properties without giving rise to CERCLA liability and (2) protected the government from CERCLA liability relating to properties acquired through the takeover of savings and loans and other financial institutions. There is a continuous struggle on CERCLA liability between environmentalists, who want to avoid creating loopholes in the law, and lenders, who believe that they are unfairly burdened because they are most often the party with the greatest financial resources even if their management of the property was not significant.

A 1993 Illinois law exemplifies an attempt to clarify the level of inquiry necessary to establish an "innocent purchaser" liability defense. The law requires two phases of environmental audits to be performed; phase II activities are required only if the phase I audit discloses the likely presence of a hazardous substance or pesticide. The Illinois law illustrates that state laws, as well as federal laws, must be consulted to determine potential liability for environmental cleanup.

provide for an interest rate that is "2 percent above the prime rate charged by this institution."

Usually variable-rate mortgages also provide some limit to the amount of annual increase in the interest rate. For example, assume that a variable-rate mortgage that is set at 2 percent above the prime rate also has a 2 percent annual cap.

Now let's assume that in one year the prime lending rate increases from 9 to 13 percent. Would the mortgage rate, which was 11 percent the year before, jump to 15 percent the next year? No, the 2 percent cap would hold the rate for that year to 13 percent. Of course, if the prime interest rate for the following year was still 13 percent, the mortgage interest rate for that year would then rise to 15 percent.

Due-on-Sale Clause Because the term of mortgage is typically 15, 20, or 30 years, the lender will seek some protection against rising interest rates. The variable rate mortgage was devised to provide such protection for the lender. Another form of protection is available through the use of the due-on-sale clause.

A **due-on-sale clause** in a mortgage provides that when the property that is the security for the loan is sold, the full amount of the loan made by the mortgage lender is due. Suppose a purchaser of a $65,000 home borrows $50,000 from a mortgage lender. Let's assume the mortgage and note is for 20 years and it provides that annual interest at the fixed rate of 10 percent will be due with each payment. Even though the loan is for 20 years, let's assume that 4 years later the purchaser decides to sell the original home and move into another one. Because the note and mortgage has a due-on-sale clause in it, the purchaser now owes the mortgage lender the full amount that is unpaid on the loan (probably about $48,000).

If during those four years the prevailing interest rate on fixed-rate mortgages has increased from 10 to 13 percent, the lender will receive the $48,000, which was lent out at 10 percent, and will be able to lend it out to another borrower at the higher 13 percent rate. The homeowner will find that he or she will not be able to borrow money for the new home at the 10 percent rate in effect 4 years ago. Thus the homeowner, who borrowed at a time when interest rates were lower than they are at the time his or her home is being sold, does not want the due-on-sale clause to be enforced. Lenders, of course, do want such clauses to be enforced.

During the 1970s and early 1980s, several states had laws that prohibited the enforcement of due-on-sale clauses. These states justified the policy by arguing that due-on-sale clauses unreasonably restricted the transfer of real property. Lenders, on the other hand, argued that due-on-sale clauses were necessary to protect them from rising interest rates. Congress eventually stepped in to settle the matter in favor of the lenders. The Garn-St. Germain Depository Institutions Act of 1982 provided that states did not have the power to prohibit the enforcement of due-on-sale clauses.

Installment Land Contracts

An alternative to using mortgages or deeds of trust is the **installment land contract**. In this agreement the buyer contracts to purchase the property and to pay for it over a period of time. Until the buyer makes all the required payments the title to the property remains with the seller. The buyer, however, has the right to possess the property and to collect rents and profits from it.

Installment land contracts are often used by a buyer who cannot acquire the mortgage financing needed to purchase property. Such a buyer can agree to make a down payment and have the seller receive periodic payments over a period of time. While the seller who sells the property does not receive the full purchase price until all contractual payments are made, the buyer has agreed to buy the property and the seller still retains title if the buyer defaults. Statutes in many states regulate the use of land contracts. A maximum interest rate that can be charged is specified and provisions requiring the seller to give a defaulting buyer a certain time to make up missed payments are common features in such laws.

Foreclosure

A **foreclosure** occurs when a lender, who has advanced funds with real property as security, recovers in the event of default. A foreclosure may lead to the sale of the property with the sale proceeds applied to pay the debt. Any balance remaining after paying the expenses of the sale and the debt is turned over to the borrower. If the sale does not bring enough to pay the debt, in most states the lender can sue for the remainder.

Judicial Foreclosure

In the United States foreclosure generally is accomplished by a judicial decree ordering the mortgaged real estate sold to pay the debt. This process is known as judicial foreclosure and is what most people have in mind when they use the term "foreclosure." Judicial foreclosure requires a complicated and costly legal action. Because the procedure results in a court order, the procedural requirements of litigation designed to protect the parties must be observed. In obtaining the court order and selling the premises, the lender must strictly follow the law.

Power-of-Sale Foreclosure

Legal complications, expenses, and delays associated with judicial foreclosure have encouraged alternative methods of foreclosure. Most deeds of trust and many mortgages have **power-of-sale** provisions which give the trustee (in the case of a deed of trust) or the mortgagor (in the case of a mortgage) the right to sell the property after the borrower's default without initiating a separate judicial action. In jurisdictions where the power of sale is allowed, lenders can generally foreclose on property more rapidly and economically.

Most states have statutes that protect a borrower whose property is subject to a power-of-sale foreclosure. These statutes generally require that the borrower be notified of the sale and that the sale be public, advertised and conducted fairly in order to bring the best price. In addition, trustees under a deed of trust must conform to an extensive body of law that regulates all fiduciaries.

Control of Land Use

An owner's rights in real property are not absolute. Often these rights are subject to restrictions imposed by government and/or by private agreements. The most common type of public control of land use is *zoning*. Private agreements limiting land use are called **restrictive covenants**.

Restrictive Covenants

Restrictive covenants are usually placed in a deed by the seller when conveying land to a buyer. The buyer, of course, must have agreed to accept these limitations on the use of the land. Restrictive covenants can be made part of a plan for the development of real property. Such covenants are included in the plot plan, which must be filed with the proper authorities.

In developing real property restrictive covenants are used to ensure that property owners do not suffer a loss in property value because of a neighbor's activity. Restrictive covenants in a residential development might limit the use of land to single family dwellings or require houses to exceed a minimum square footage. Restrictive covenants also are used when an individual sells a portion of his or her property to ensure that the buyer will not use the land in a way that the seller, who remains a neighbor, finds objectionable.

Restrictive covenants run with the land. This means that the limitations on the use of the land are not dependent on the continued ownership of the buyer who originally agreed to the restriction. In general, enforcement of restrictive covenants has not been favored by courts because they interfere with the free transferability of property. In order for a restrictive covenant to run with the land it must have been the intention of the original grantor and grantee, and the covenant must substantially affect the essential nature of the land. The idea that property, both real and personal, should be freely transferable is an important concept in Anglo-American law.

Courts will refuse to enforce some restrictive covenants on public policy grounds. In some parts of the country, it was once common to have restrictive covenants that prohibited the property from being sold to African Americans or members of other minority groups. Such covenants are no longer enforced.

Restrictive covenants can be terminated in several ways. All concerned parties may agree in writing to the termination. This method of termination is very difficult if the number involved is large. Covenants can also be terminated by condemnation or by not being enforced when they are violated. The longer violations of covenants are ignored, the less likely a court is to enforce them.

Zoning

Zoning is the division of an area, usually a municipality, into districts to control land use. Zoning ordinances regulate such things as the structure and design of buildings, lot size, set-back requirements, and uses to which land may be put. Limitations on the use of land through zoning are of recent vintage. Comprehensive control of land use is a product of the twentieth century. The notion of comprehensive zoning was first approved by the U.S. Supreme Court in 1926.

Today zoning is based on the states' police power. On the basis of this power, land use can be regulated to protect the health, safety, and welfare of the public. Like all regulation based on police power, zoning ordinances to be valid must not be unreasonable or arbitrary. The case that follows is a rather colorful example of a zoning ordinance that was challenged on such grounds.

ELYSIUM INSTITUTE, INC. V. COUNTY OF LOS ANGELES
California Court of Appeal
283 Cal.Rptr. 688 (1991)

BACKGROUND: Elysium Institute (appellant) operated a nudist camp in Los Angeles County (respondent). The area where the camp was located was zoned "A-1-1," a designation primarily designed for light agriculture. Prior to 1971, nudist camps were permitted in zone A-1-1. In 1971, Los Angeles County passed an ordinance that specifically excluded nudist camps from zone A-1-1. However, the county gave Elysium permission to continue to operate its nudist camp, subject to periodic renewals. When Elysium's permission to operate a nudist camp came up for renewal in 1986, the county refused to approve it. Elysium challenged the county's action on several grounds, including that the definition of "nudist camp" in the county zoning ordinance violated the California constitution. The trial court ruled in favor of Los Angeles County, and Elysium appealed.

Lillie, Presiding Justice

Relying on *City of Santa Barbara v. Adamson* appellants contend that the zoning regulation as to nudist camps should be struck down because the definition of nudist camp violates the right of privacy afforded by article 1, section 1 of the California Constitution.

According to the ordinance, "nudist camp" means "any place where three or more persons not all members of the same family congregate, assemble, associate or engage in any activity while without clothing or covering or with partial clothing or covering but with any pubic area or any portion of the crease of the buttocks exposed in the presence of others or of each other, other than an occasional gathering in, or on the premises of a private home. 'Nudist camp' includes growth center." (Los Angeles County Code, § 22.08.140.)

"Family" is defined by the ordinance as "a person or persons related by blood, marriage or adoption living together as a single housekeeping unit in a dwelling unit. 'Family' shall also include a group of not more than five persons, including roomers but not servants, unrelated by blood, marriage or adoption, when living together as a single housekeeping unit in a dwelling unit." (Los Angeles County Code, § 22.08.060.)

In *City of Santa Barbara v. Adamson*, a substantially similar definition of "family" was incorporated into an ordinance which required that in the zone where Adamson lived with 11 other adults, all occupants of houses like that in which they reside be members of a family. The trial court granted the request of the City of Santa Barbara for a preliminary injunction and concluded that Adamson and the other residents of the house could not reside in the particular zone because they were not within the ordinance's definition of "family." The California Supreme Court reversed the order granting the preliminary injunction, recognizing that article 1, section 1 of the California Constitution ensures "a right of privacy, not only in one's family but also in one's home," and that any incursion into individual privacy must be justified by a compelling public interest. The Court impliedly answered "no" to the question it posed: "Has Santa Barbara demonstrated that, in fact, such an interest does underlie its decision to restrict communal living?" In light of the privacy interest at stake and the lack of a compelling public interest to justify the distinctions drawn by the ordinance, the Court held "invalid the distinction effected by the ordinance between (1) an individual or two or more persons related by blood, marriage, or adoption, and (2) groups of more than five other persons."

Although respondent argues that "there is no authority for the contention that California's more liberal privacy concept as enunciated in *Adamson* extends to appellants' activities," respondent does not dispute the contention that the right of privacy under the

California Constitution comprehends the right of three nudists, not members of the same family, to assemble together in a *home*. If "more than an occasional gathering," such activities inside a private home would bring that home within the definition of "nudist camp" under the instant ordinance!

The ordinance's stated purpose for the designation of certain zones is to "classify regularly and restrict the location of trades and industries and the location of buildings for special uses, and the use and area of premises for the general welfare of the county of Los Angeles." This language hardly provides the compelling public interest which would justify the ordinance's broad definition of nudist camp. . . .

Our record reveals no compelling interest to justify the inclusion of a private home within the definition of "nudist camp." We thus conclude that the definition of nudist camp in County Code section 22.08.140 violates article 1, section 1 of the California Constitution.

DECISION: The court ruled that the County's zoning ordinance violated California's constitution. However, the court upheld on other grounds the County's denial of Elysium's application to continue operating a nudist camp on the property.

Traditional zoning ordinances divide the municipality into districts for residential, commercial, and industrial uses. Over the years these basic zoning classifications have expanded considerably. As a result, many localities now have fifteen to twenty or more zones. Because use within these zones is restricted, multiplication of zones promotes inflexibility in land use and gives rise to criticism of the traditional zoning process. In response to criticism of the zoning process, other techniques for controlling land use have developed since World War II.

Planned unit development (PUDs) are an example of innovative use of the zoning power. In a PUD zoning regulations are applied to an area larger than the traditional subdivision. The objective of a PUD is to permit mixed use of an area within a development while providing a maximum amount of land for open space. Various types of housing such as townhouses, apartments, and single family dwellings are permitted within the same tract. In some instances the zoning plan permits commercial as well as residential use. In addition, the plan provides for extensive open areas. A major advantage of the PUD is the flexibility it provides in planning for community growth.

The extension of public control of real property through zoning is illustrative of major changes that have occurred in real property law. Other changes include the development of new forms of ownership such as condominiums and cooperatives, major modifications in financing and investing techniques, and limits on the rights of owners to deal with their property in a manner interfering with the civil rights of others. In spite of such changes, traditional legal concepts and terminology remain important factors in the real property field.

Review Questions and Problems

Key Terms

deed	eminent domain
grantor/grantee	inverse condemnation
warranty deed	mortgage
covenant of right to convey	mortgagee/mortgagor
covenant against encumbrances	due-on-sale clause
	installment land contract
covenant of quiet enjoyment	foreclosure
covenant of general warranty	power-of-sale provision
bargain and sale deed	restrictive covenant
quitclaim deed	zoning
adverse possession	planned unit development (PUD)

Discussion Questions

1. Explain the difference between a warranty deed and a bargain and sale deed.
2. What is constructive notice? Explain how constructive notice is related to the operation of the recording statutes.

3. Compare and contrast the lien and title theories of mortgages.

4. What is the difference between a judicial foreclosure and power of sale foreclosure? How are they similar?

5. List some of the uses of restrictive covenants.

Review Problems

1. McNaughten's deed contained a restrictive covenant barring the use of the land for purposes such as a "bar, tavern, alehouse, or the like." McNaughten wants to open a restaurant that serves alcoholic beverages. Will he be prohibited from doing so by the restrictive covenant? Support your answer.

2. Fox bought a $90,000 home in a newly developed area. To finance the purchase, he borrowed $80,000 from Central Savings, executing the customary note and mortgage in Central's favor. Some time later a major highway was proposed for the area, and real estate values fell sharply. At about this time Fox accepted a job in another state. Unable to sell the house or keep up payments, Fox defaulted on the loan. Central Savings then foreclosed. Discuss Fox's potential liability if the home sells at the foreclosure sale for $60,000, with $72,000 remaining on the debt.

3. Cordes, who died in 1946, owned a 420-acre farm in western Illinois. His will divided the farm between his sons, Isaac and James. James built a home on his portion. Isaac's portion contained the family residence. The easiest way to reach James's home was over a lane along the edge of a field belonging to Isaac. This lane was used until 1975, when Isaac died. Isaac's farm was sold to Von Schied, who blocked the lane. James contended that he had an easement by prescription over the land. Do you agree? Discuss.

4. General Motors wished to expand its Detroit plant. The economy of the area was depressed, and the city wanted to help GM get the properties necessary to expand. The city council used the power of eminent domain to acquire several pieces of property in the neighborhood. Local landowners who did not want the plant expanded tried to prevent the transfer of title to GM on grounds that the city did not have the right to acquire this land by eminent domain. Explain on what basis this argument might be made. Do you agree? Discuss.

5. In 1935 Malone gave an easement to his brother Ted. The easement allowed Ted to cross a corner of Malone's land so that Ted could make repairs to a windmill. The easement was recorded, but little use was made of it, and both parties forgot that it existed. In 1972 Malone sold the property to Cudy. Title was transferred by warranty deed. What warranty, if any, has Malone breached? Support your answer.

Case Problems

1. Linmont purchased a corner lot from Amoco in order to construct and operate a filling station. At the time of the purchase, Linmont and Amoco entered into an agreement by which Linmont agreed to take all its requirements of gas and oil from Amoco. The agreement also obligated subsequent owners and tenants of the station to purchase all requirements of petroleum products from Amoco. This agreement and the deed were properly recorded in the office of the county clerk. Linmont sold the property to Chock Full of Power, which refused to comply with the agreement. Amoco sues. Would Amoco be successful? Discuss.

2. Smith owned one of three contiguous parcels of wetlands situated in low-lying and partially submerged peninsula in upper Tampa Bay known as Cooper's Point. The city had zoned the land in a general business district, permitting single-family or multiple-dwelling uses with limited residental use. In 1974, development plans for the parcel, which was to be combined with others in the same area, were submitted. The following year, the city applied its "aquatic lands" zone, which limited property use to recreational purposes, to over 50 percent of Smith's property. Smith claims the rezoning of its property to aquatic lands constitutes a taking. Do you agree?

3. Stephens and his wife had two sons. They quarreled with the older son and as a result wished to deny him any interest in a farm they owned. In order to accomplish this, they conveyed the farm to their younger son, retaining a life estate for themselves. The younger son gave no consideration for the farm. A few months later Stephens and his wife wished to vacate the deed to the younger son because they believed he had conspired against them with his brother. They brought an action to cancel the deed on grounds that no consideration had been paid. Would they be successful? Discuss.

4. The village of Northbrook approved a zoning ordinance permitting the construction of a large shopping center in an area along its boundary with Highland Park. Residents of Highland Park and the municipality of Highland Park sued to block construction of the shopping center on grounds that it would cause massive congestion in the area, destroying the quiet residential character of their community. They argued that this violated the equal protection clause of the Constitution since the shopping center actually protected much of the residential character of Northbrook. The reason for this was that the chief highway leading to the site ran through Highland Park. Would the suit be successful? Support your answer.

50

Intellectual Property and Computer Law

Types of Intellectual Property   Computer Law

Intellectual **property** is intangible property created primarily by mental rather than physical effort. The most common types of intellectual property are copyrights, patents, trademarks, and trade secrets. The first three are governed primarily by federal law, whereas trade secrets are regulated mostly by state laws. Today, it is important for almost all companies to protect their rights to intellectual property. Just as the ownership of the land and attached buildings that constituted real property was critical to many firms in the nineteenth century and tangible property such as cars, planes, and machines became significant in the twentieth century, the various forms of intellectual property are likely to dominate the concern of business firms in the twenty-first century.

Each of these forms of intellectual property is important to the designers, producers, and users of computers. Computers are used by hundreds of millions of people worldwide in performing tasks ranging from word processing to data storage to product scanning. Both legislatures and courts have had to modify existing laws or make new laws to govern situations which have arisen as a result of the computer. The term **computer law** is used to designate this emerging body of law. The unique aspects of computer law that are discussed in this chapter deal primarily with *software*, the programs of instruction that control the operation of computers. The computer *hardware*

equipment includes the monitors, terminals, printers, and other attachments. Computer hardware generally is a form of tangible personal property, discussed in Chapter 47.

The four major types of intellectual property are discussed first in the chapter. The legal protection given to computer programs is then reviewed. Several computer-specific legislative provisions are then noted. Finally, some possible applications of criminal law to computers are evaluated.

Types of Intellectual Property

A **trademark** is a mark on goods or services that distinguishes them from the goods or services of competitors. The owner of a tradename, mark, or unique design can prevent others from using similar forms of expression on their goods or services. A **copyright** grants the right to exclude others from using the original words or compositions of authors, painters, or musicians. A **patent** protects inventions by giving to its owner the right to make, sell, and use the product or process. A **trade secret** is a valuable formula, pattern, or information used in a business that is not known to competitors. Table 50-1 depicts the legal protection available for intellectual property.

899

TABLE 50-1

Intellectual Property

Type of Property	What Is Protected	Period of Protection	How It Is Infringed
Patent	Right to make, sell, and use product	17 years	Making a product that is the same or a substantial equivalent
Trademark	Use of mark by other manufacturers or sellers of similar products or services	20 years plus 20 years if still in use	Use of mark that is likely to cause confusion, mistake, or deception regarding origin of product
Copyright	Unauthorized copying of words, music, or artistic work of creator	Life of creator plus 50 years	Copying work and distributing copies or using material without permission if beyond its fair use
Trade secret	Wrongful appropriation of valuable and secret information such as customer list, special manufacturing process, or unique recipe	As long as information is secret	Unauthorized acquisition of confidential information or public disclosure of secret information

Trademarks

A trademark is a picture, word, or design that identifies a manufacturer's or merchant's goods, and distinguishes them from those of the competitors. The golden arches of McDonald's are trademarked; they are used on packages and advertisements to show the consumer that the products originate from that firm instead of from competitors. Although most people refer to all marks as trademarks, in fact four different types of marks are protected by federal law:

1. *Trademarks:* IBM and Coca-Cola are trademarks used to identify goods originating from a specific company.

2. *Service marks:* Holiday Inn and McDonald's are service marks because the mark identifies the user's services.

3. *Certification marks:* Napa Valley wines or grade A meats are certification marks because they certify that goods come from a particular region or that certain standards have been met by the manufacturer of the goods.

4. *Collective marks:* Girls Scouts of America is a collective mark used by an association to identify and distinguish its goods, such as cookies, or services from those offered by nonmembers.

The Lanham Act establishes a system of federal registration for all such marks (we refer to them hereafter as trademarks). Registered trademarks are valid for 20 years, and if the mark is still in use in commerce after that period, it can be renewed for an additional 20 years. The act also makes unauthorized use of that mark illegal. Both Pepsi and Coke are registered trademarks of competing soft drink manufacturers. Thus, if you order a Coke in a restaurant that serves only Pepsi, you will likely be asked if Pepsi is okay. If the restaurant does not ask, it could be accused of trying to pass off another product when you have ordered one from a certain source.

Because a trade mark seeks to identify protected products, the marks must be distinctive. Marks generally fall into four categories of distinctiveness.

1. *Arbitrary or fanciful mark:* Marks such as "Kodak" or "Exxon" do not describe the product being protected; these marks are "made-up" names that cannot be confused with the marks of their competitors. They are granted the widest protection.

2. *Suggestive marks:* A mark like "Crest" is not suggestive for toothpaste unless you use imagination or thought to make the connec-

tion. Suggestive marks are likely to be protected against those of competitors.

3. *Descriptive marks:* A descriptive mark can be protected only if it acquires secondary meaning. A term that has a general primary meaning may acquire a protected secondary meaning if, through long use, the public has come to identify the particular mark with its product. The term "Philadelphia" has acquired a secondary meaning with cream cheese because the public associates that name with a particular brand. Thus, if you were to make competing cream cheese in Philadelphia, you couldn't use the Philadelphia name because it would be confusing to the public.

4. *Generic marks:* A mark like "diamond" ring or "pick-up" truck refers to the general class of goods, not to those from a specific source. These marks cannot be registered under the federal law.

The *Levi Strauss* case that follows illustrates these distinct categories and details the court's analysis of the factors to be reviewed in a trademark infringement case.

LOIS SPORTSWEAR, U.S.A., INC. V. LEVI STRAUSS & CO.

Circuit Court of Appeals
799 F.2d 867 (2d Cir. 1986)

BACKGROUND: Lois Sportswear, U.S.A., Inc. and Textiles Y Confecciones Europeas, S.A. (collective appellants) appealed from a summary judgment enjoining them from using a back-pocket stitching pattern similar to the trademark jean back-pocket stitching pattern of Levi Strauss & Company (appellee) on appellants' jeans. The question presented by this appeal is whether summary judgment for the trademark owner is appropriate on claims of trademark infringement and unfair competition when the trademark owner has shown that a rival jeans manufacturer is using the trademark owner's registered back-pocket stitching pattern trademark on its competing jeans, and the undisputed evidence shows that the trademark is intimately associated with the trademark owner's products in the minds of jeans consumers.

Timbers, Circuit Judge

Appellee is a world-famous clothing manufacturer. One of its most popular products is a line of casual pants known as Levi Jeans. Appellee began manufacturing its denim jeans in the 1850s. Each pair of jeans contains numerous identifying features. One such feature is a distinct back-pocket stitching pattern. This pattern consists of two intersecting arcs which roughly bisect both pockets of appellee's jeans. Appellee has an incontestable federal trademark in this stitching pattern. Appellee has used this pattern on all its jeans continuously since 1873. In many ways the back-pocket stitching pattern has become the embodiment of Levi Jeans in the minds of jeans buyers. The record is replete with undisputed examples of the intimate association between the stitching pattern and appellee's products in the buying public's mind.

Appellant Lois Sportswear, U.S.A., Inc ("Lois") imports into the United States jeans manufactured in Spain by Textiles Y Confecciones Europeas, S.A. ("Textiles"). The instant litigation was commenced because appellants' jeans bear a back-pocket stitching pattern substantially similar to appellee's trademark stitching pattern. On appeal, appellants do not challenge the district court's conclusion that the two stitching patterns are substantially similar. Nor could they; the two patterns are virtually identical when viewed from any appreciable distance. In fact, the results from a survey based on showing consumers videotapes of the back pockets of various jeans, including appellants', indicate that 44 percent of those interviewed mistook appellants' jeans for appellee's jeans. Appellants instead rely on their use of various labels, some permanent and some temporary, to distinguish their jeans and defeat appellee's trademark infringement and unfair competition claims.

The parties have clashed over appellants' use of a back-pocket stitching pattern continuously since 1979. The evidence is undisputed that appellants and appellee manufacture and sell a similar product. While stratifying the jeans market with various styles and grades seems to be the current rage, there can be no dispute that the parties before us compete to sell their jeans to the public. . . .

In short, the uncontested facts show that appellants' jeans exhibit a back-pocket stitching pattern substantially similar to appellee's incontestable registered trademark back-pocket stitching pattern. The record also makes plain that the stitching pattern is closely associated with appellee's jeans, and that appellants' use of the stitching pattern on arguably competing jeans at least presents the possibility that consumers will be confused as to the source of appellants' jeans or the relationship between appellants and appellee.

Appellants' arguments, for the most part, focus only on the likelihood that consumers will buy appellants' jeans thinking they are appellee's jeans due to the similar stitching patterns. Appellants point to their labeling as conclusive proof that no such confusion is likely. We agree with the district court, however, that the two principle areas of confusion raised by appellants' use of appellee's stitching pattern are: (1) the likelihood that jeans consumers will be confused as to the relationship between appellant and appellee; and (2) the likelihood that consumers will be confused as to the source of appellants' jeans when the jeans are observed in the post-sale context. We hold that the Lanham Act, as interpreted by our Court, was meant to prevent such likely confusion.

As a threshold matter, in the past we have found it useful to decide how much protection a particular trademark is to be given by first determining what type of trademark is at issue. In *Abercrombie & Fitch Co. v Hunting World, Inc.*, Judge Friendly set forth what has become the governing law of trademark classification:

> Arrayed in an ascending order which roughly reflects their eligibility to trademark status and the degree of protection accorded, these classes are (1) generic, (2) descriptive, (3) suggestive, and (4) arbitrary or fanciful.

Superimposed on this framework is the rule that registered trademarks are presumed to be distinctive and should be afforded the utmost protection.

It is clear under this framework that appellee's back-pocket stitching pattern deserves the highest degree of protection. First, the mark is registered and incontestable. This, of course, entitles the mark to significant protection. Second, the mark, being a fanciful pattern of interconnected arcs, is within Judge Friendly's fourth category and is entitled to the most protection the Lanham Act can provide. In deciding the likelihood-of-confusion issues, therefore, appellee's mark is entitled to a liberal application of the law.

In deciding the issue of likelihood of confusion in the instant case, the district court relied on the multifactor balancing test set forth by Judge Friendly in *Polaroid Corp. v. Polarad Electronics Corp.* We agree wholeheartedly that Judge Friendly characteristically has provided the controlling law.

At the outset, it must be remembered just what the Polaroid factors are designed to test. The factors are designed to help grapple with the "vexing" problem of resolving the likelihood-of-confusion issue. Therefore, each factor must be evaluated in the context of how it bears on the ultimate question of likelihood of confusion as to the source of the product. . . .

The eighth and final factor—the sophistication of relevant buyers—does not, under the circumstances of this case, favor appellants. The district court found, and the parties do not dispute, that the typical buyer of "designer" jeans is sophisticated with respect to jeans buying. Appellants argue that this sophistication prevents these consumers from becoming confused by nearly identical back-pocket stitching patterns. On the contrary, we believe that it is a sophisticated jeans consumer who is most likely to assume that the presence of appellee's trademark stitching pattern on appellants' jeans indicates some sort of association between the two manufacturers. Presumably it is these sophisticated jeans buyers who pay the most attention to back-pocket stitching patterns and their "meanings."

Our review of the district court's application of the *Polaroid* factors convinces us that the court correctly concluded that consumers are likely to mistakenly associate appellants' jeans with appellee or will confuse the source of appellants' jeans when the jeans are observed in the post-sale context.

DECISION: The court upheld the trial court's decision that Lois Sportswear jeans infringed on the Levi Strauss trademark.

Acquiring Trademark Rights   Trademarks are acquired either by use or by registration. Canada and the Philippines require that a trademark be used; it cannot be registered until it is first used. The use system was in effect in the United States until 1988. Now, the United States and most other countries in the world allow a trademark to be registered before it is put into use. The U.S. law requires the trademark to be used within 6 months of its registration. (Extensions can increase the period to 3 years.)

Some famous trademarks, such as McDonald's or Coca-Cola, may not have to be registered. In several countries, local companies that have sought to register the McDonald's trademark before the McDonald's Corporation began doing business there were denied registration because of possible confusion with the mark that was well known in the country as a result of its use outside the country.[1]

Losing Trademark Rights   Trademark owners may lose the rights of their mark if they abandon it or if the mark becomes generic. Abandonment occurs if a company goes out of business and no longer sells the product. The second way to lose a mark's protection is to become too successful in promoting it. If the public begins to think of the protected mark whenever they think of the product, whether from the trademark owner or from a competitor, the mark may lose its protection. *Saran Wrap* plastic film, *Scotch* cellophane tape, *Tabasco* pepper sauce, *Styrofoam* plastic foam and *Jeep* vehicles exemplify trademark products that are commonly used as generic names. As noted in Figure 50-1, *Xerox* is also fighting to separate its name from other photocopy machines.

Copyrights

A *copyright* protects the original work of authors, painters, and musicians who produce original works of artistic or intellectual merit. This book is copyrighted, so it is illegal for anyone to take the words used by the authors and treat them as their own words. Like the owner of the patent who assigns the patent to a firm that agrees to manufacture and market a novel product, the writer or artist frequently assigns the copyright for his or her work to the publisher that agrees to produce the work for sale. A copyright is effective for the life of the creator plus an additional 50 years. If there is more than one creator, as is true of this book, the copyright lasts for 50 years beyond the life of the longest surviving creator.

A common law copyright exists once a work is created. However, if the work is widely distributed without statutory copyright protection, it becomes part of the public domain and is no longer protected by copyright law. Statutory protection is available if the work is published and distributed with a copyright notice. The notice can take the form of the word, "copyright," the abbreviation, "copr," or a symbol "©," followed by the year and the name of the copyright holder. The copyright for this text is located on the back side of the title page.

FIGURE 50-1

Trademark Protection: The Xerox Corporation

There are two R's in Xerox.

One is right in the middle.

But the really important one is the one you probably never notice.

It's the little R in a circle—like the one you see at the bottom of this ad—that tells you that Xerox is a registered trademark.

And it reminds you that our name—which is also our trademark—should only be used in connection with the products and services of our corporation.

Including everything from Xerox copiers to information processors to electronic printers.

So as you can see, our trademark is a very valuable one.

To us. And to you, too.

Because it ensures that when you ask for something you can be sure of what you're going to get.

Of course, we don't expect you to use the second R every time you use our name.

But we do hope you'll give it a second thought.

XEROX

XEROX® is a trademark of XEROX CORPORATION.

The Fair Use Doctrine The **fair use doctrine** constitutes a major exception to the exclusive rights given to a copyright owner. If the use is "fair," anyone may use some material from a copyrighted work. There are several areas in which the application of the fair use exception remains unclear. Two of these that are familiar to many college students concern legal parodies and making copies from textbooks and academic journals.

What constitutes a legal parody has been the focus of a recent case decided by the U.S. Supreme Court. The case concerns the song "Oh Pretty Woman" which is played on radio stations and television commercials and was the title song

---

PREVENTIVE LAW
Protecting Trademarks

1. Use a descriptive term along with the trademark. For example, the jar of Vaseline refers to the contents as petroleum jelly.
2. Protest generic uses of the mark in publications. For example, Xerox has taken out advertisements to let offenders and the general public know that they don't want their name used for generic products.
3. Follow up by writing suspected infringers and requesting they change their practices. Coca-Cola has dozens of trademark examiners who check to see if retailers are selling another cola and calling it Coke. After testing the product at the company's headquarters, it sends a representative to remind the retailer that the Coca-Cola name cannot be used with other colas. If necessary, legal action, even against a small mom-and-pop store, will follow.
4. Put the words "trademark" or "registered trademark" next to the mark itself.
5. Check the laws of any country where you might use the mark. Generally, you are able to register the mark before you begin using it. If you register early, you may save significant expense later.

---

of a 1990 hit movie. Acuff-Rose Music Inc. owns the copyright to this 1964 Roy Orbison-William Dees hit. In 1989, 2 Live Crew and rap musician Luther Campbell came out with a parody version using the same title and similar words and music. The copyright owners, who considered the rap version to be an exploitation of their original tune, sued to enforce their copyright.

Campbell claimed the rap version was protected under the fair use doctrine because his song consisted of "material used for criticism, comment, news reporting, or scholarship." Campbell argued his song is protected as criticism or commentary because he intended to mock the banality of white-centered rock and roll music by attacking one of its time-honored ballads.

In *Campbell v. Acuff-Rose Music, Inc.*, 114 S.Ct.1164 (1994), the Supreme Court sided with the parody version. It found that the 2 Live Crew version departed markedly from the Orbison lyrics and produced otherwise distinctive music. It noted too that the 2 Live Crew version was unlikely to substitute for the original as the two works serve different market functions.

A second concern with the fair use provision of the copyright laws arises with regard to copying materials from textbooks or academic journals. The 1976 Copyright Act states that making multiple copies of certain works for classroom use constitutes a fair use. But when the material copied is extensive and is compiled and sold separately, the fair use doctrine does not seem to apply. Although the extent of protection offered to the person or firm making "fair use" of copyrighted material still needs clarification, administrative guidelines from the Copyright Office and court decisions do provide some direction.

Soon after the 1976 Copyright Act took effect, the Copyright Office suggested that making anthologies or course-packs of collected readings generally would not be an acceptable fair use. Loud protests immediately arose from copy shops, which claimed the increased cost of paying fees to copyright owners would destroy their business. Publishers of textbooks and journals sought to enforce their right to collect royalties for unauthorized copies.

The *Kinko's* case that follows is the federal district court's decision regarding this controversy.

BASIC BOOKS, INC., ET AL. V. KINKO'S GRAPHICS

U.S. District Court

758 F.Supp.1522 (S.D.N.Y. 1991)

BACKGROUND: Plaintiffs, all major publishing houses in New York City, alleged that Kinko's infringed their copyrights when Kinko's copied excerpts from books, whose rights are held by the plaintiffs, without permission and without payment of required fees, and sold the copies for a profit. Plaintiffs requested relief in the form of statutory damages, injunction, declaratory judgment, and attorney's fees and costs.

Kinko's admitted that it copied the excerpts in suit without permission, compiled them into course "packets," and sold them to college students. Kinko's claims their use of the excerpts was "fair use," specifically provided for in section 107 of the Copyright Act.

Motley, District Judge

There are 12 instances of copyright infringement alleged in this case. The 12 excerpts, which vary in length from 14 to 110 pages, were copied from books previously published by the plaintiffs, compiled in five numbered packets ("anthologies") with excerpts from other books and distributed by Kinko's. Kinko's neither sought nor obtained permission to copy any of these works. There are two stores from which Kinko's sold the excerpts included in this suit: one at 24 E. 12th Street (which services, among others, students at New York University and the New School for Social Research) and a second at 2872 Broadway (which services Columbia University students).

Coined as an "equitable rule of reason," the fair use doctrine has existed for as long as the copyright law. It was codified in section 107 of the Copyright Act of 1976, Article 17 of the United States Code. The section reads in its entirety:

Notwithstanding the provisions of section 106, the fair use of a copyrighted work, including such use by reproduction in copies of phonorecords or by any other means specified by that section, for purposes such as criticism, comment, news reporting, teaching (including multiple copies for classroom use), scholarship, or research, is not an infringement of copyright. In determining whether the use made of a work in any particular case is a fair use the factors to be considered shall include—

(1) the purpose and character of the use, including whether such use is of a commercial nature or is for nonprofit educational purposes;

(2) the nature of the copyrighted work;

(3) the amount and substantiality of the portion used in relation to the copyrighted work as a whole; and

(4) the effect of the use upon the potential market for or value of the copyrighted work.

For almost 300 years, American law has protected intellectual property rights through the copyright law. Section 106 of the 1976 Copyright Act provides that "subject to Section 107 . . . the owner of copyright under this title has the exclusive right to reproduce the copyrighted work." Justice Story set forth the meaning of fair use to which we adhere today. "In short, we must often . . . look to the nature and objects of the selections made, the quantity and value of the materials used, and the degree in which the use may prejudice the sale, or diminish the profits, or supersede the objects, or the original work." . . .

A. The 4 Factors of Fair Use

1. Purpose and Character of the Use

Section 107 specifically provides that under this factor we consider "whether [the] use is of a commercial nature or is for nonprofit educational purposes." Kinko's work cannot be categorized as anything other than a mere repackaging.

Commercial Use   The use of the Kinko's packets, in the hands of the students, was no doubt educational. However, the use in the hands of Kinko's employees is commercial. Kinko's claims that its copying was educational and, therefore, qualifies as a fair use. Kinko's fails to persuade us of this distinction.

Kinko's has not disputed that it receives a profit component from the revenue it collects for its anthologies. The amount of that profit is unclear; however, we need only find that Kinko's had the intention of making profits. Its Professor Publishing promotional materials clearly indicate that Kinko's recognized and sought a segment of a profitable market, admitting that "tremendous sales and profit potential arise from this program."

Although Kinko's tries to impress this court with its purportedly altruistic motives, the facts show that Kinko's copying had "the intended purpose of supplanting the copyright holder's commercially valuable right."

"The crux of the profit/nonprofit distinction is not whether the sole motive of the use is monetary gain but whether the user stands to profit from exploitation of the copyrighted material without paying the customary price." This is precisely the concern here and why this factor weighs so strongly in favor of plaintiffs.

2. The Nature of the Copyrighted Work

The second factor concerns the nature of the copyrighted work. Courts generally hold that "the scope of fair use is greater with respect to factual than non-factual works." Fictional works, on the other hand, are often based closely on the author's subjective impressions, and, therefore, require more protection. These are general rules of thumb. The books infringed in suit were factual in nature. This factor weighs in favor of defendant.

3. The Amount and Substantiality of the Portion Used

"There are no absolute rules as to how much of a copyrighted work may be copied and still be considered a fair use." This third factor considers not only the percentage of the original used but also the "substantiality" of that portion to the whole of the work; that is, courts must evaluate the qualitative aspects as well as the quantity of material copied.

This factor, amount, and substantiality of the portions appropriated weighs against defendant. In this case, the passages copied range from 14 to 110 pages, representing 5.2% to 25.1% of the works. In one case Kinko's copied 110 pages of someone's work and sold it to 132 students. Even for an out-of-print book, this amount is grossly out of line with accepted fair use principles.

In almost every case, defendant copied at least an entire chapter of a plaintiff's book. This is substantial because they are obviously meant to stand alone, that is, as a complete representation of the concept explored in the chapter. This indicates that these excerpts are not material supplemental to the assigned course material but the assignment. Therefore, the excerpts, in addition to being quantitatively substantial, are qualitatively significant.

4. The Effect of the Use on Potential Markets for or Value of the Copyrighted Work

The fourth factor, market effect, also fails the defendant. This factor has been held to be "undoubtedly the single most important element of fair use." "To negate fair use one need only show that if the challenged use 'should become widespread, it would adversely affect the potential market for the copyrighted work.'"

Kinko's confirms that it has 200 stores nationwide, servicing hundreds of colleges and universities which enroll thousands of students. The potential for widespread copyright infringement by defendant and other commercial copiers is great. In this case, Kinko's had admitted that its market for these anthologies or packets is college students. The packets were compiled as a result of orders placed by professors at Columbia University, New York University, and the New School for Social Research as to what readings they needed to supply their courses. In this case, the competition for "student dollars" is easily won by Kinko's, which produced 300- to 400-page packets including substantial portions of copyrighted books at a cost of $24.00 to the student. Packet #34 contained excerpts from 20 different books. While it is possible that reading the packets whet the appetite of students for more information from the authors, it is more likely that purchase of the packets obviates purchase of the full texts. This court has found that plaintiffs derive a significant part of their income from textbook sales and permissions. This court further finds Kinko's copying unfavorably impacts upon plaintiffs' sales of their books and collections of permission fees. This impact is more powerfully felt by authors and copyright owners of the out-of-print books, for whom permissions fees constitute a significant source of income. This factor weighs heavily against defendant.

5. Other Factors

In this case an important additional factor is the fact that defendant has effectively created a new nationwide business allied to the publishing industry by usurping plaintiffs' copyrights and profits. This cannot be sustained by this court as its result is complete frustration of the intent of the copyright law which has been the protection of intellectual property and, more importantly, the encouragement of creative expression. Because of the vastness and transitory nature of its business (Kinko's has 200 stores nationwide which are typically located near colleges), it has become difficult for plaintiffs to challenge defendant.

Anthologies   In addition to these tests, most of which defendant has failed, Kinko's conduct appears to violate a specific mandate of the Classroom Guidelines:

III. Prohibitions as to I and II Above. Notwithstanding any of the above, the following shall be prohibited: (A) Copying shall not be used to create or to replace or substitute for anthologies, compilations or collective works. . . . (C) Copying shall not: (a) substitute for the purchase of books, publishers' reprints or periodicals. (D) No charge shall be made to the student beyond the actual cost of the photocopying.

An injunction is not the automatic consequence of infringement but the result of suitable consideration. When liability has been determined, and a history of continuing infringement and a significant threat of future infringement exists, a court must enjoin infringement of future copyrighted works.

In this case, liability has been determined and there remains a significant threat that Kinko's will continue to infringe plaintiffs' copyrights given the nature of Professor Publishing, and Kinko's historic willful blindness to the copyright law. . . . The nature of Professor Publishing makes it particularly susceptible to infringement because of the large volume of copying it conducts and the added threat created by anthologizing. Additionally, the willfulness defendant exhibited in this case persuades this court that "there is a strong possibility that defendant will engage in continuing copyright violations unless an injunction is issued."

* * *

A copyright owner may elect to recover statutory damages instead of actual damages and profits. Plaintiffs have made that election. Once the plaintiff elects statutory damages, that remedy is generally exclusive.

Kinko's instructions to its workers possessed little of the nuance of the copyright law. They provided no hypothetical situations nor any factual summary of the state of the law presently. There was no mention of the facts of the Sony case, the Salinger case, the Harper & Row case or other which may illustrate some of the complexities of this doctrine. This can hardly be considered a "good faith" effort on Kinko's part to educate their employees. To the contrary, it appears more to be a way to "cover" themselves while Kinko's remained willfully blind to the consequences of their activity.

This court also finds and concludes that substantial damages are necessary to deter Kinko's from repeating the conduct proved in this case. . . . Therefore, this court will assess statutory damages in the amount of $50,000 for nine of the 12 infringements, and $20,000 for three of the infringements for a total of $510,000. Here we are not attempting to measure the financial loss to the plaintiff but to deter the defendant from future infringing copying. . . .

***

DECISION: This court finds the excerpts copied by defendant Kinko's are not a fair use of plaintiffs' copyrights and, therefore, constitute infringement. Further, Kinko's defenses of copyright misuse, unclean hands, and estoppel fail. Plaintiff is granted statutory damages, injunctive relief, and attorneys' fees and costs.

Electronic Copying   A rather new issue that copyright law has had to deal with concerns electronic copying. Copyrighted newsletters and specialized journals provide timely and specific information to subscribers that is often of significant value. Newsletters provide investment advice, status reports on legislative or administrative issues, and discussion of medical or legal trends culled from numerous sources. Although it is clear that these publications are protected by copyright laws, some firms have purchased a single newsletter and then stored that newsletter electronically for use by numerous people within the firm. This electronic copying also apparently violates the fair use exception to the copyright laws.

In 1993, Atlas Telecom Inc. paid $100,000 to settle a lawsuit brought by Phillips Business Information Inc. after Atlas admitted electronically distributing within its firm about a dozen newsletters from Phillips.[2] The electronic copying of information from copyrighted sources is certain to be subject to further litigation.

Obtaining a Copyright   Although generally only the author may hold the initial copyright, he or she may assign or license some or all of its protected rights to others. Thus, an author of a book might assign the right to copy the material and publish the book in North America to a publisher. Note that this author still retains both the right to have the book published in other parts of the world and the right to make a movie based on the book. Only a portion of the rights of the author were transferred by the assignment to the firm publishing the book in North America.

Any person who is employed to write, such as a newspaper reporter, an advertiser, or a writer for a law reporter, is writing for his or her employer. The work of this person is known as *work for hire*; the employer, not the author, owns the copyright.

In order to copyright a work, notice must be given to the public that copyright protection is being claimed. Such notice must include:

1. Use of the word "copyright" or use of the abbreviation "copr.," or use of the symbol ©

2. The date of the first publication

3. The name of the copyright owner

Patents

A *patent* protects an invention by giving to its owner the exclusive right to make, sell, and use the product or process for a limited time. Any "new and useful, process, machine, manufacture, or composition of matter, or any new and useful improvement thereof" may be patented. Thus a new process for making steel and a sewing machine are both patentable. A manufacture is an article or product such as a ballpoint pen, light bulb, or television. A composition of matter is a new arrangement of elements such that the resulting compound is not found in nature; new disease-fighting drugs are thus patentable.

In the United States, a patent is issued by the Patent Office for products or processes that are original, novel, useful, and nonobvious. If the product is not new, has no usefulness, or is obvi-

ISSUES AND TRENDS
What Is Fair Use?

The fair use doctrine is deceptive to many people. A common perception is that significant copying of musical recordings, television programs, books, magazines, or newspaper articles is permitted. The current fair use exemption from copyright law protection for the owner or creator or protected works in fact appears to be much narrower.

As electronic publishing and private database storage increases, the digitization (electronic storage) of information is certain to become a common practice. If a firm purchases one book or one newsletter and places information from that source in its in-house database, it could save the trouble and expense associated with making dozens or hundreds of copies. However, that is not fair to the creator of the work and the copyright holder. When hundreds of people make use of a particular work, royalties should be paid for each use. In most **site licenses**, a copyright holder authorizes multiple copies to be made at one site. The copyright fee paid for a site license usually reflects a significant volume discount from the fees due for numerous individual licenses to different users.

Publishers who invest heavily in copyrighted works say that those who copy their works, through either photocopies or electronic distributions, should expect lawsuits if permission to use the work and appropriate fees for doing so are not paid. The October 6, 1993, *Wall Street Journal* quoted one publisher, Tod Sedgwick of Pasha Publication, "Unless we protect our copyright, we're going to lose it." It is likely that as businesses increase their use of electronic copying, a clearer borderline between fair use and copyright infringement will emerge. Perhaps by the year 2000, the law will clarify for the business manager what will be an appropriate use of technology regarding copyrighted material.

ous to a person of ordinary skill in a particular field, it will not be patentable. As is noted in Chapter 57, not all countries follow these same standards.

In Belgium, Austria, and Switzerland there is little or no examination as to the novelty of an invention. In Japan, a new method of doing business could be patentable if it meets the requirement of being useful in industry. Although national laws vary greatly regarding the regulation of patents, over ninety nations, including the United States, are members of the International Convention for the Protection of Industrial Property, known as the Paris Union. The convention allows applicants in one country to apply subsequently for protection in other countries without losing their priority.

Unlike most of the other types of intellectual property, the process for obtaining a patent is often time-consuming and expensive. In the United States most patents are granted for a period of 17 years. In exchange for the novel and useful invention of the inventor the government gives the patent owner an exclusive monopoly for a limited time.

While patents are issued to the person inventing the product or process, the patent holder may assign his or her rights to others. Thus an inventor may, in exchange for royalty payments, assign a patent to a firm that agrees to manufacture and market the new product. Frequently corporations will require as a condition of employment that scientists or engineers employed by it agree that any patents developed within the scope of the employee's job belong to the corporation. In such cases the patent will be issued to the corporation instead of to the employees who worked on the invention.

During this period anyone who uses the patented product without the consent of the patent holder may be committing patent infringement. A person who infringes a patent can be held liable for damages caused to the patent holder and stopped from committing future infringements. After the term of the patent has expired, other firms or individuals are free to use the information about the patented product to make and sell their own products.

Acquiring a Patent   A patent office (the U.S. Office is the U.S. Patent and Trademark Office; it is a part of the U.S. Department of Commerce) must approve a request for a patent. As the patent approval process is lengthy and expensive, a patent attorney is usually hired by the applicant. The patent attorney conducts a search to determine the nature of existing patents so that the application can be described and differentiated from inventions already protected. The description must be in sufficient detail so that one skilled in the art will be able to make and use the subject invention. Once the patent office examiner concludes his or her search of the record and accepts the description from the applicant, the patent office allows the inventor to put "Patent Pending" on the invention. Those words put others on notice that the patent owner's application is on file. If someone else makes an infringing product, even if made before the patent is granted, the owner may sue to stop the infringement. Of course, if the patent application is denied, there is no infringement. The Stiffel lamp case involving the ubiquitous pole lamp illustrates this concept.

STIFFEL CO. V. SEARS, ROEBUCK & CO.
U.S. Court of Appeals
313 F.2d 115 (7th Cir. 1963)

BACKGROUND: Stiffel obtained a design patent for a pole lamp in 1957. Later that year, it found a similar lamp in a Sears catalog. Stiffel charged Sears with infringement of its patent and unfair competition in violation of Illinois law. Sears asserted that Stiffel's patent was not valid because the pole lamp was neither new nor nonobvious. The district court found for Sears as to the patent infringement and for Stiffel on the unfair competition claim. Both parties appealed.

Kiley, Circuit Judge

The patents in suit are Stiffel Patents . . . relating to floor to ceiling pole lamps. The patents were issued to Theophile Stiffel in May 1957 and subsequently assigned to plaintiff (Stiffel Co.). The lamp was first shown to the public in 1956. Plaintiff learned from a Sears, Roebuck & Co. catalog in 1957 that pole lamps were being sold by Sears. It purchased a Sears lamp in Greensboro, North Carolina, and this suit followed.

The vital questions are upon the findings and conclusions with respect to patent invalidity and unfair competition. . . .

The Stiffel pole lamp consists of a plurality of detachable tubular members, of small diameter, joined together to form a single pole longer than the distance between floor and ceiling of a room. It carries three lamps, with swivel brackets, on the exterior of one of the sections. The lamps are served by wires "extending interiorly" down through and out the lower section of the pole. In use it is supported between floor and ceiling under compression of a spring contained in the uppermost section. The upper and lower ends are small round felt or rubber covered discs to protect ceiling and floor. The lower disc is at the end of an adjustable leg for making fine adjustments to the length of the pole.

The District Court found that the Stiffel pole lamp was anticipated in the prior art more than one year prior to the Stiffel patent application in January, 1956, by Sears' public use and sale of the Deca pole lamp; and in printed publications. The question is whether the court erred in concluding, on these findings, that Stiffel Patent No. 2,739,286 is invalid.

The findings underlying the conclusion have substantial basis in the admitted use of the Deca poles by Sears in 1953 and 1954, and the evidence of their published illustrations, sketches and descriptions more than one year prior to the Stiffel patent application, and were sufficient to overcome the presumption of validity of the patent. We hold the conclusion of invalidity of Patent No. 2,793,286 is not clearly erroneous.

The Deca pole included all the essential elements of the Stiffel pole except the adjustable leg. Instead of the adjustable leg, the Deca pole employed an equivalent, i.e., sections of various lengths for adjusting height. The court was not required to find on the evidence that the adjustable leg was novel or was functionally different than the various sized sections of Deca pole which have the same purpose. This is true also of the Stiffel spring unit and the Deca pole sliding section and spring which have the same effect. And there is substantial evidence that Deca pole had the wire run "extending interiorly" within the pole.

The District Court's conclusion of invalidity of Design Patent No. 180,251 rests on findings that the Deca pole Exhibit No. 55 does not differ in ornamental design aspects from the Stiffel patented design, and that the Miller "Lamp Tree" was disclosed in several magazines in 1950 and 1954. . . .

We hold the conclusion of the invalidity of Design Patent No. 180,251 is not erroneous.

Because the District Court's conclusions with respect to the patents are not erroneous, it follows that the court did not err in its conclusion of non-infringement.

There is substantial basis in the evidence to support the findings underlying the conclusion that Sears was guilty of unfair competition. The evidence is: the lamp had a decided impact on the market in 1956 as something revolutionary in lighting fixtures. In four years (1956–1960) Stiffel shipped about $3,250,000 in pole lamps. They were widely advertised in national magazines. Sears "moved in" when they saw the Stiffel pole lamp was moving toward a mass market. Sears lamps are not labeled, and the Sears lamp retails at the wholesale price of the Stiffel lamp.

The Stiffel pole lamps and that of Sears made from a copy of a picture of the Stiffel lamp are before us as exhibits. A comparison of the two gives substantial support for the finding that the lamps have a remarkable sameness of appearance. And there is testimony of buyers for Marshall Field and Company and John M. Smyth Company of customer confusion. The finding that there is a likelihood of confusion and some actual confusion, as to the source of the lamps, is not clearly erroneous. The conclusion of unfair competition, based on the finding, is not erroneous.

DECISION: The court found for Sears on Stiffel's claim of patent infringement and for Stiffel on its claim of unfair competition. It affirmed the trial court's judgment.

Trade Secrets

Trade secrets are valuable formulas, patterns, or information used in a business that are not known to competitors. Thus two elements must be present in order to have a trade secret. First, there must be some valuable information such as a customer list, a process for making a certain product, or a special recipe. Second, the information must be kept secret. If the information is widely known to other competitors or to the public in general, it cannot be a trade secret.

Employees working in sensitive positions are often asked to sign agreements to keep certain information confidential. Although employees with access to such information have that duty anyway, since as Chapter 30 notes they are agents of the employer, a written agreement may help to ensure that the information is intended to be kept secret. Unlike the other types of intellectual property, trade secrets are not protected for a specific period of time. Instead, it is the duration of the information as being valuable and secret that determines the period of protection granted to its owner.

The owner of a trade secret is protected from its wrongful appropriation. If someone reverse-engineers a product or figures out through trial and error your secret recipe, no wrongful appropriation has occurred. On the other hand, if an employee of your firm is bribed to give the customer list or unique manufacturing process wrongfully to a competitor, a wrongful appropriation of your trade secret has occurred.

Patents and trade secrets can both protect ideas. If the inventor of the idea believes he or she can keep the idea secret for longer than the term for which a patent is granted, he or she may want to make it into a trade secret rather than patent it. This is what the owners of the Coca-Cola syrup formula have done; they have kept secret their method of making the syrup and have never patented that process. Conversely, the patent guarantees protection for an established time period, and even if others were about to discover the same idea you discovered when you patented its use on a particular type of product, your protection continues for 17 years after the patent is applied for. Table 50-1 portrays the different types of intellectual property and the protection available to owners.

As new forms of wealth have been created, personal property has become more like real property in economic significance. This trend has led to a narrowing of the legal distinction between the two, but differences continue to exist and to influence decisions that businesspeople must make. The distinction between real and personal property raises numerous insurance, tax, financing, and inheritance questions. In the case that follows the distinction between the two types of property influenced the outcome of the litigation.

One of the most common problems with regard to trade secrets occurs when an employee is hired by a competitor. Hertz has charged Avis with unfairly hiring away managers who took with them knowledge of secret operations and financial information. In 1993, General Motors accused Volkswagen of hiring away a key purchasing manager who it alleged took with him cartons of confidential information and then made copies of them for use at Volkswagen. Businesses in the United States spend billions on security, much of that to safeguard secret information from their competitors.

Business competitors often "spy" on one another in many ways. They buy and reverse-engineer competing products, visit retail outlets to see how competing products are packaged, interview customers who purchase competing products, and make use of the Freedom of Information Act to obtain from government agencies product performance or liability data. If a company has information it wants to keep secret, it must take specific steps to protect that information.

Employees must be reminded that the information is confidential; written agreements expressly mentioning trade secrets should be used. Publically distributed catalog descriptions cannot provide details that are to be protected. Some firms that used to allow plant tours no longer do so because of concerns about competitors learning about production techniques and capabilities. Of course, even if a firm takes steps to protect its information, it may be possible to find out those secrets. Sometimes, as in the *Du Pont* case, the method used to find out about secret information is illegal.

E. I. Du Pont de Nemours and Company v. Christopher et al.

U.S. Court of Appeals
431 F.2d 1012 (5th Cir. 1970)

BACKGROUND: Du Pont (plaintiff) brought suit alleging that Christopher et al. (defendants) had wrongfully obtained photographs revealing the plaintiff's trade secrets which they then sold to an undisclosed third party. Du Pont sued, asking for damages and temporary and permanent injunctions. The U.S. District Court denied the defendants' motion to dismiss for failure to state a claim. The defendants appealed.

Goldberg, Circuit Judge

This is a case of industrial espionage in which an airplane is the cloak and a camera the dagger. The defendants-appellants, Rolfe and Gary Christopher, are photographers in

Beaumont, Texas. The Christophers were hired by an unknown third party to take aerial photographs of new construction at the Beaumont plant of E. I. Du Pont de Nemours & Company, Inc. Sixteen photographs of the Du Pont facility were taken from the air on March 19, 1969, and these photographs were later developed and delivered to the third party. . . .

Du Pont subsequently filed suit against the Christophers, alleging that the Christophers had wrongfully obtained photographs revealing Du Pont's trade secrets which they then sold to the undisclosed third party. Du Pont contended that it had developed a highly secret but unpatented process for producing methanol, a process which gave Du Pont a competitive advantage over other producers.

This process, Du Pont alleged, was a trade secret developed after much expensive and time-consuming research, and a secret which the company had taken special precautions to safeguard. The area photographed by the Christophers was the plant designed to produce methanol by this secret process, and because the plant was still under construction parts of the process were exposed to view from directly above the construction area. Photographs of that area, Du Pont alleged, would enable a skilled person to deduce the secret process for making methanol. Du Pont thus contended that the Christophers had wrongfully appropriated Du Pont trade secrets by taking the photographs and delivering them to the undisclosed third party.

This is a case of first impression, for the Texas courts have not faced this precise factual issue, and sitting as a diversity court we must sensitize our *Erie* antennae to divine what the Texas courts would do if such a situation were presented to them. The only question involved in the interlocutory appeal is whether Du Pont has asserted a claim upon which relief can be granted. The Christophers argued both at trial and before this court that they committed no "actionable wrong" in photographing the Du Pont facility and passing these photographs on to their client because they conducted all of their activities in public airspace, violated no government aviation standard, did not breach any confidential relation, and did not engage in any fraudulent or illegal conduct. In short, the Christophers argue that for an appropriation of trade secrets to be wrongful there must be a trespass, other illegal conduct, or breach of a confidential relationship. We disagree.

It is true, as the Christophers assert, that the previous trade secret cases have contained one or more of these elements. However, we do not think that the Texas courts would limit the trade secret protection exclusively to these elements. On the contrary, in *Hyde Corporation v. Huffines,* 1958, the Texas Supreme Court specifically adopted the rule found in the Restatement of Torts which provides:

> One who discloses or uses another's trade secret, without a privilege to do so, is liable to the other if (a) he discovered the secret by improper means, or (b) his disclosure or use constitutes a breach of confidence reposed in him by the other in disclosing the secret to him. . . .

Restatement of Torts § 757 (1939)

Thus, although the previous cases have dealt with a breach of a confidential relationship, a trespass, or other illegal conduct, the rule is much broader than the cases heretofore encountered. Not limiting itself to specific wrongs, Texas adopted subsection (a) of the Restatement which recognizes a cause of action for the discovery of a trade secret by any "improper" means.

The question remaining, therefore, is whether aerial photography of plant construction is an improper means of obtaining another's trade secret. We conclude that it is and that the Texas courts would so hold. The Supreme Court of that state has declared that "the undoubted tendency of the law has been to recognize and enforce higher standards of commercial morality in he business world." Hyde Corporation v. Huffines. That court has quoted with approval articles indicating that the *proper* means of gaining possession of a competitor's secret process is "through inspection and analysis" of the product in order to create a duplicate. . . .

We think, therefore, that the Texas rule is clear. One may use his competitor's secret process if he discovers the process by reverse engineering applied to the finished product; one may use a competitor's process if he discovers it by his own independent search; but one may not avoid these labors by taking the process from the discoverer without his permission at a time when he is taking reasonable precautions to maintain its secrecy. To obtain knowledge of a process without spending the time and money to discover it independently is *improper* unless the holder voluntarily discloses it or fails to take reasonable precautions to ensure its secrecy.

In the instant case the Christophers deliberately flew over the Du Pont plant to get pictures of a process which Du Pont had attempted to keep secret. The Christophers delivered their pictures to a third party who was certainly aware of the means by which they had been acquired and who may be planning to use the information contained therein to manufacture methanol by the Du Pont process. The third party has a right to use this process only if he obtains this knowledge through his own research efforts, but thus far all information indicates that the third party has gained this knowledge solely by taking it from Du Pont at a time when Du Pont was making reasonable efforts to preserve its secrecy. In such a situation Du Pont has a valid cause of action to prohibit the Christophers from improperly discovering its trade secret and to prohibit the undisclosed third party from using the improperly obtained information. . . .

In taking this position we realize that industrial espionage of the sort here perpetrated has become a popular sport in some segments of our industrial community. However, our devotion to free wheeling industrial competition must not force us into accepting the law of the jungle as the standard of morality expected in our commercial relations. Our tolerance of the espionage game must cease when the protections required to prevent another's spying cost so much that the spirit of inventiveness is dampened. Commercial privacy must be protected from espionage which could not have been reasonably anticipated or prevented. We do not mean to imply, however, that everything not in plain view is within the protected vale, nor that all information obtained through every extra optical extension is forbidden. Indeed, for our industrial competition to remain healthy there must be breathing room for observing a competing industrialist. A competitor can and must shop his competition for pricing and examine his products for quality, components, and methods of manufacture. Perhaps ordinary fences and roofs must be built to shut out incursive eyes, but we need not require the discoverer of a trade secret to guard against the unanticipated, the undetectable, or the unpreventible methods of espionage now available.

In the instant case Du Pont was in the midst of constructing a plant. Although after construction the finished plant would have protected much of the process from view, during the period of construction the trade secret was exposed to view from the air. To require Du Pont to put a roof over the unfinished plant to guard its secret would impose an enormous expense to prevent nothing more than a school boy's trick. We introduce here no new or radical ethic since our ethos has never given moral sanction to piracy. The market place must not deviate far from our mores. We should not require a person or corporation to take unreasonable precautions to prevent another from doing that which he ought not do in the first place. Reasonable precautions against predatory eyes we may require, but an impenetrable fortress is an unreasonable requirement, and we are not disposed to burden industrial inventors with such a duty in order to protect the fruits of their efforts. . . .

DECISION: The court held for Du Pont and remanded the case to the trial court.

ETHICS
Ethics and Information

Many firms systematically obtain information about their competitors' strategies and products. In the process, they may employ consulting firms that are specialists in gathering competitor information.

Techniques for gathering information include going through public records such as journal articles and trade magazine reports, talking to consultants familiar with the industry, and talking to former employees of the competitors. More problematic activities include paying large consulting fees to former employees of the targeted competitors and sending out their own employees to "interview" for jobs with the competitors. Other questionable strategies involve sending out employees to pose as prospective customers of competitors to obtain information on pricing and financing strategies or to claim to be journalists in order to interview their competitors' managers.

In one recent case, a contract employee at 3M sent samples of a product under development to four competitors. What would you do if you received the samples?

In the actual incident, none of the four competitors reported the information to 3M. Instead, the word got around generally, and another firm in the industry told 3M, who then contacted the FBI. The 3M employee was arrested and eventually jailed. It turned out that one of the four competitors actually made use of the samples and ultimately was held liable to 3M. In the initial decision in the case, the competitor was ordered to pay $116.3 million to 3M.

Computer Law

A variety of legal problems has arisen since the advent of computers. Computer hardware (computer unit, monitor, printer, etc.) and software (operating system, word processing, spreadsheet, and graphics packages) components are often sold together with servicing packages (contracts agreeing to install, modify, and repair any part that becomes defective). What governs here—the Uniform Commercial Code's provisions regarding the sale of goods or the common law's contract provisions regarding sale of services? What if there is a lease rather than a sale? Are these same questions relevant? Do the warranty provisions discussed in Chapter 24 also apply?

Another problem arises because computers can be used to accomplish criminal objectives. While some of the general criminal laws are used to prosecute criminal activities, the states and the federal government have also enacted statutes that specifically address criminal activities involving the computer.

Finally, how are intellectual property laws being applied to the development of computer programs and hardware?

Computers and the Uniform Commercial Code

It is clear that the sale of computer hardware is subject to the Uniform Commercial Code. Computers are goods just like items of furniture or briefcases or bookshelves. Similarly, the code applies to either a lease or a sale of computer equipment; both are regarded as a transaction in goods.

The problem of determining whether a sale of hardware, software, and technical services involves a sale of goods rather than a sale of services is more difficult to resolve. Generally, the courts look to the primary factor in the contract. If the services are incidental to the sale of goods, the code applies. If the sale of services is more important, the common law applies. The method used by the court to make these determinations is discussed in the following case.

RRX Industries, Inc. v. Lab-Con, Inc.

U.S. Court of Appeals
772 F.2d 543 (9th Cir. 1985)

Background: TEKA agreed to supply RRX with a computer software system for use in its medical laboratory. The contract obligated TEKA to service the software package. RRX claims TEKA breached its contract and sought both compensatory and consequential damages (the latter being allowed under the Uniform Commercial Code). TEKA argues the Uniform Commercial Code's provisions do not apply because this contract was for services, not goods.

The trial court found for RRX, and TEKA appealed.

Wright, Circuit Judge

This action arises out of a computer software contract negotiated between RRX and TEKA. TEKA agreed to supply RRX with a software system for use in its medical laboratories. The contract obligated TEKA to correct any malfunctions or "bugs" that arose in the system, but limited TEKA's liability to the contract price.

TEKA began installing the software system in January 1981 and completed it in June 1981. Bugs appeared in them soon after installation. TEKA attempted to repair the bugs by telephone patching. Subsequently, TEKA upgraded the system to make it compatible with more sophisticated hardware. The system, however, remained unreliable because defects continued to exist.

After contracting with RRX, Kelly formed Lab-Con, Inc. in order to market TEKA's software system. Lab-Con was a successor corporation to TEKA. TEKA assigned the RRX software contract to Lab-Con.

In September 1982, RRX instituted this diversity action against TEKA, Lab-Con, Kelly, and other defendants alleging breach of contract and fraud. . . .

Appellants contend that the district court's breach of contract finding was clearly erroneous because RRX also breached the contract. This contention lacks merit.

The contract obligated TEKA to timely install an operational software system, to repair malfunctions, and to train RRX employees. The record reflects that the software never functioned as intended. TEKA failed to correct adequately programming errors. Further, TEKA did not provide RRX employees with sufficient training. The evidence thus supports the district court's finding of a contract breach.

1. California Commercial Code

The district court relied on the California Commercial Code to award RRX consequential damages. Such reliance was proper only if the computer software system may be characterized as a "good" rather than a service.

The California Commercial Code defines a good as "all things (including specially manufactured goods) which are movable at the time of identification to the contract for sale other than the money in which the price is to be paid, investment securities (Division 8) and things in action." Cal. Com.Code § 2105 (West 1964).

In determining whether a contract is one of sale or to provide services we look to the essence of the agreement. When a sale predominates, incidental services provided do not alter the basic transaction. Because software packages vary depending on the needs of the individual consumer, we apply a case-by-case analysis.

Here, the sales aspect of the transaction predominates. The employee training, repair services, and system upgrading were incidental to sale of the software package and did not defeat characterization of the system as a good.

Under the Code, a plaintiff may pursue all of the remedies available for breach of contract if its exclusive or limited remedy fails of its essential purpose. Cal.Com.Code § 2719(2) (West 1985 Supp.). Appellants argue that the award of consequential damages was nevertheless improper because the contract limited damages to the amount paid.

In *S.M. Wilson & Co. v. Smith Int'l., Inc.,* this court held that the failure of a repair remedy does not require permitting the recovery of consequential damages. The court reasoned that where parties agree to a limitation of damages provision, courts should not alter the bargained-for risk allocation unless a breach of contract is so fundamental that it causes a loss which is not part of that allocation.

The district court's award of consequential damages is consistent with *S.M. Wilson.* The court concluded that "since the defendants were either unwilling or unable to provide a system that worked as represented, *or* to fix the 'bugs' in the software, *these* limited remedies failed of their essential purpose." (emphasis added). This is a finding that *both* limited remedies failed of their essential purpose. The trial judge did not state that *because* the repair remedy failed, the limitation of damages provision should not be enforced.

The district court's choice of language and supporting authority creates an ambiguity. However, it properly found the default of the seller so total and fundamental that its consequential damages limitation was expunged from the contract. . . .

The facts here justify the result. Neither bad faith nor procedural unconscionability is necessary under California Commercial Code § 2719(2). It provides an independent limit when circumstances render a damages limitation clause oppressive and invalid. The award of consequential damages was proper.

DECISION: The court of appeals affirmed the trial court's decision to award compensatory and consequential damages to RRX.

Computers and Criminal Laws

General Criminal Laws The term *computer law* generally refers to a crime that can only be committed by a person who knows something about how computers operate. Some of the traditional criminal laws do apply to computer-related crimes. If the computer is used to embezzle funds, the defendant could be charged with committing the crime of embezzlement. If hardware or software equipment is taken, a larceny or theft of property may have occurred. Fraud or the taking of property through false pretenses may be committed where a person invades a computer file by passing as a legitimate user of the stored data.

Specific State Statutes Almost all states have also passed specific statutes concerned with the unauthorized access of a computer system, the tampering or causing damage to a system, or the invasion of database records. The unauthorized copying of computer programs or intentionally introducing a computer virus (one that will injure or destroy computer files) into any computer resource are also usually addressed by these statutes. For example, Michigan computer crime law makes it illegal to

1. Access a computer (statutory definition includes computer system or network) to defraud money, property, or service
2. Access, damage, alter, or destroy a computer, a software program, or data in a computer
3. Use a computer to commit violations of other criminal laws (theft, larceny, conversion, etc.)

Violations involving more than $100 are felonies.

Federal Statutes The Computer Fraud and Abuse Act is the primary federal statute that specifically addresses computer-assisted crimes. The act focuses on the use of computers to gain certain information or the unauthorized access to "federal interest computers." These computers include those used by or for the federal government, by financial institutions, and by those that operate in interstate commerce. Acts prohibited by the Computer Fraud and Abuse Act include

1. Unauthorized use of a computer to obtain specific information such as
   a. Restricted government information
   b. Information in a financial record of a financial institution
   c. Information in a consumer's record of a consumer reporting agency
2. Access to a computer of a U.S. department or agency that affects the government's use of a computer
3. Access of a federal interest computer when anything of value is obtained
4. Unauthorized access of a federal interest computer that alters or destroys information causing $1,000 of loss or potentially impairing medical diagnosis, treatment, or care of another
5. Trafficking in passwords and access information that affects interstate or international commerce or use of the computer by government

The *Riggs* case, which follows, illustrates how both a general federal criminal law (interstate transportation of stolen property) and the Computer Fraud and Abuse Act could apply to an unauthorized invasion of a computer system.

U.S. v. RIGGS

U.S. District Court
739 F.Supp. 414 (N.D. Ill. 1990)

BACKGROUND: Over the course of the past decade, advances in technology and growing respect and acceptance for the powers of computers have created a true explosion in the computer industry. Quite naturally, the growth of computer availability and application has spawned a host of new legal issues. This case requires the court to wrestle with some of these novel legal issues which are a product of the marriage between law and computers.

The indictment charges that defendants Robert J. Riggs and Craig Neidorf, through the use of computers, violated the federal wire fraud statute and the federal statute prohibiting interstate transportation of stolen property. Neidorf argues that the wire fraud statute and the statute prohibiting interstate transportation of stolen property do not apply to the conduct with which he is charged.

Bua, District Judge

In about September 1988, Neidorf and Riggs devised and began implementing a scheme to defraud Bell South Telephone Company ("Bell South"), which provides telephone services to a nine-state region including Alabama, Georgia, Mississippi, Tennessee, Kentucky, Louisiana, North Carolina, South Carolina, and Florida. The objective of the fraud scheme was to steal Bell South's computer text file which contained information regarding its enhanced 911 (E911) system for handling emergency calls to policy, fire, ambulance, and other emergency services in municipalities. The text file which Riggs and Neidorf planned to steal specifically details the procedures for installation, operation, and maintenance of E911 services in the region in which Bell South operates. Bell South considered this file to contain valuable proprietary information and, therefore, closely guarded the information from being disclosed outside of Bell South and its subsidiaries. . . .

In about December 1988, Riggs began the execution of the fraud scheme by using his home computer in Decatur, Georgia, to gain unlawful access to Bell South's computer system located at its corporate headquarters in Atlanta, Georgia. After gaining access to Bell South's system, Riggs "downloaded" the text file, which described in detail the operation of the E911 system in Bell South's operating region. Riggs then disguised and concealed his unauthorized access to the Bell South system by using account codes of persons with legitimate access to the E911 text file.

Pursuant to the scheme he had devised with Neidorf, Riggs then transferred the stolen computer text file to Neidorf by way of an interstate computer data network. Riggs stored the stolen text on a computer bulletin board system located in Lockport, Illinois, so as to make the file available to Neidorf. . . . Neidorf, a twenty-year-old student at the University of Missouri in Columbia, Missouri, used a computer located at his school to access the Lockport computer bulletin board and thereby receive the Bell South E911 text file from Riggs. At the request of Riggs, Neidorf then edited and retyped the E911 text file in order to conceal the fact that it had been stolen from Bell South. Neidorf then "uploaded" his revised version of the stolen file back onto the Lockport bulletin board system for Riggs' review. To complete the scheme, in February 1989, Neidorf published his edited edition of Bell South's E911 text file in his PHRACK newsletter. . . .

The current indictment asserts seven counts. Count I charges that Riggs committed wire fraud by transferring the E911 text file from his home computer in Decatur, Georgia to the computer bulletin board system in Lockport, Illinois. Count II charges both Riggs and Neidorf with violating § 1343 by causing the edited E911 file to be transferred from a computer operated by Neidorf in Columbia, Missouri, to the computer bulletin board system in Lockport, Illinois.

Counts III and IV assert that . . . Riggs and Neidorf violated the National Stolen Property Act, which prohibits interstate transfer of stolen property. Finally, Counts V–VII charge Riggs and Neidorf with violating the Computer Fraud and Abuse Act of 1986, which prohibits knowingly, and with intent to defraud, trafficking in information through which a computer may be accessed without authorization.

II. Discussion

A. Motion to Dismiss Count II

[1] Neidorf claims that Count II of the indictment is defective because it fails to allege a scheme to defraud, one of the necessary elements for a wire fraud claim. . . . The indictment plainly and clearly charges that Neidorf and Riggs concocted a fraud scheme, the object of which was to steal the E911 text file from Bell South and to distribute it to others via the PHRACK newsletter. The indictment also clearly alleges that both Riggs and Neidorf took action in furtherance of the fraud scheme. . . . Both Neidorf and Riggs allegedly used coded language, code names, and other deceptive means to avoid the detection of their fraud by law enforcement officials. These allegations sufficiently set forth the existence of a scheme to defraud, as well as Neidorf's participation in the scheme. . . .

The government charges Riggs and Neidorf with scheming to defraud Bell South out of *property*—the confidential information contained in the E911 text file. The indictment specifically alleges that the object of defendants' scheme was the E911 text file, which Bell South considered to be valuable, proprietary, information. The law is clear that such valuable, confidential information is "property," the deprivation of which can form the basis of a wire fraud charge under § 1343. . . .

Counts III and IV charge Riggs and Neidorf with violating 18 U.S.C. § 2314, which provides, in relevant part:

> Whoever transports, transmits, or transfers in interstate or foreign commerce any goods, wares, merchandise, securities or money, of the value of $5000 or more, knowing the same to have been stolen, converted or taken by fraud . . . [s]hall be fined not more than $10,000 or imprisoned not more than ten years, or both.

The government concedes that charging Neidorf under § 2314 plots a course on uncharted waters. No court has ever held that the electronic transfer of confidential, proprietary business information from one computer to another across state lines constitutes a violation of

§ 2314. However, no court has addressed the issue. Surprisingly, despite the prevalence of computer-related crime, this is a case of first impression. The government argues that reading § 2314 as covering Neidorf's conduct in this case is a natural adaptation of the statute to modern society. Conversely, Neidorf contends that his conduct does not fall within the purview of § 2314 and that the government is seeking an unreasonable expansion of the statute. He urges the court to dismiss the charge on two grounds.

Neidorf's first argument is that the government cannot sustain a § 2314 charge in this case because the only thing which he allegedly caused to be transferred across state lines was "electronic impulses." Neidorf maintains that under the plain language of the statute, this conduct does not come within the scope of § 2314 since electronic impulses do not constitute "goods, wares, or merchandise."

The court is unpersuaded by Neidorf's disingenuous argument that he merely transferred electronic impulses across state lines. Several courts have upheld § 2314 charges based on the wire transfer of fraudently obtained money, rejecting the arguments of the defendants in those cases that only electronic impulses, not actual money, crossed state lines. . . . In all of these cases, the courts held that money was transferred across state lines within the meaning of § 2314 because funds were actually accessible in one account prior to the transfer, and those funds were actually accessible in an out-of-state account after the transfer. The courts refused to accept the superficial characterization of the transfers as the mere transmittal of electronic impulses.

Similarly, in the instant case, Neidorf's conduct is not properly characterized as the mere transmission of electronic impulses. Through the use of his computer, Neidorf allegedly transferred proprietary business information—Bell South's E911 text file. Like the money in the case dealing with wire transfers of funds, the information in the E911 text file was accessible at Neidorf's computer terminal in Missouri before he transferred it, and the information was also accessible at the Lockport, Illinois computer bulletin board after Neidorf transferred it. Therefore, the mere fact that the information actually crossed state lines via computer-generated electronic impulses does not defeat a charge under § 2314.

The question this case presents, then, is not whether electronic impulses are "goods, wares, or merchandise" within the meaning of § 2314, but whether the proprietary information contained in Bell South's E911 text file constitutes a "good, ware, or merchandise" within the purview of the statute. This court answers that question affirmatively. It is well-settled that when proprietary business information is affixed to some tangible medium, such as a piece of paper, it constitutes "goods, wares, or merchandise" within the meaning of § 2314.

In order to sustain a charge against Neidorf under § 2314, however, the government cannot simply allege that Neidorf transferred "goods, wares, or merchandise" across state boundaries; the government must also allege that Neidorf executed the transfer knowing the goods were "stolen, converted or taken by fraud." This requirement forms the basis for Neidorf's second challenge to Counts III and IV. This case involves the transfer of confidential, proprietary business information, not copyrights. . . . The owner of confidential, proprietary business information . . . possesses something which has clearly been recognized as an item of *property.* As such, it is certainly capable of being misappropriated, which, according to the indictment, is exactly what happened to the information in Bell South's E911 text file.

In his final gasp, Neidorf . . . notes that Congress has enacted a statute—the Computer Fraud and Abuse Act ("CFAA"), which is specifically designed to address computer-related crimes, such as unauthorized computer access. Neidorf claims that the enactment of the CFAA precludes a finding that § 2314 reaches his alleged conduct in this case.

The problem with Neidorf's argument, however, is that he does not cite, and this court is unable to find, anything in the legislative history of the CFAA which suggests that the statute was intended to be the exclusive law governing computer-related crimes, or that its enactment precludes the application of other criminal statutes to computer-related conduct.

Therefore, the court rejects Neidorf's claim that applying § 2314 to the instant case would undermine the Congressional intent behind the CFAA. Similarly, the court rejects Neidorf's bald assertion that the legislative history behind § 2314 supports his argument. Nothing in the legislative history of § 2314 prevents the court from finding that the information in Bell South's E911 text file was "stolen, converted or taken by fraud" as that term is used in the statute prohibiting the interstate transportation of state property.

DECISION: The court denied Riggs's motion to dismiss the charges against him.

Another statute, the Electronic Funds Transfer Act, makes it a crime to use any counterfeit control device to obtain money or goods through an electronic funds transfer system. Thus, obtaining money from a bank by adding a name to allow funds to be withdrawn from a savings account or by transferring funds from someone's account to a fictitious account violates the law. Ordering goods from a retailer and charging someone else's account or diverting delivery of goods intended for a legitimate purchaser to a different address exemplifies illegally obtaining goods through an electronic funds transfer.

The law also forbids shipping such devices or goods obtained in interstate commerce. Finally, knowingly receiving goods that have been obtained (such as by your friend) by means of fraudulent use of the system also violates the law.

Two other federal statutes are also aimed at improper uses of computer resources. The Computer Matching and Privacy Act of 1988 regulates computer programs that compare two or more automated systems of records. Such matches are used to determine eligibility for and compliance with federal benefit programs such as social security or student financial aid. The law imposes requirements aimed at protecting privacy and ensuring due process.

The Semiconductor Chip Protection Act (SCPA) of 1984 protects for a 10-year period "mask works" and the "semiconductor chip" products where they are found. A **mask work** is a form of expression used in a chip design; it includes stencils used in the manufacturing of the chips. **Semiconductor chip** products include analog chips, microprocessors, and RAM or ROM memory chips. These products are placed in an established pattern on a semiconductor material so as to perform electrode circuitry functions.

The act requires mask work owners to register within 2 years of a work's first commercial exploitation. Unlike copyrighted works, the SCPA does not grant the mask work owner the right to prevent others from copying its product. Instead, some copying is allowed; the mask work can be reverse-engineered and used in other semiconductor chip products so long as the new products are the result of substantial study and not mere copying. Infringement can result in actual damages and loss of profits or statutory damages up to $250,000.

Review Questions and Problems

Key Terms

intellectual property	trade secret
computer law	fair use doctrine
trademark	site license
copyright	mask works
patent	semiconductor chip

Discussion Questions

1. What are the four major types of trademarks protected by U.S. law?
2. Discuss the differences among arbitrary, suggestive, descriptive, and generic marks. Give an example of each.
3. Explain the fair use exemption in the copyright laws. Give two examples of fair use problems.
4. What requirements must be met to obtain a patent? Compare the process for obtaining a patent with the process for obtaining a copyright or a trademark.
5. Does the Federal Computer Fraud and Abuse Act preempt and displace state criminal laws that involve theft or destruction of computer data?

Review Problems

1. Griffin holds a valid patent in the United States and in Italy for a composting machine. He grants an exclusive license to Long to allow Long (along with

Griffin) to make and sell it in the United States and to Carmine in Italy. Keystone, a U.S. firm, purchased three machines from Carmine in Italy and brought them back to be used in the United States. He sold two of the machines, which Griffin claims violates the patent rights he has regarding the sale of the machine in the United States. Do you agree?

2. Selden has copyrighted a particular method of bookkeeping; the system uses lined pages with headings indicating the manner in which the system operates. Baker used a system with a substantially similar ledger system; the ruled lines and headings used were almost the same as Selden's. Selden asserts Baker infringed his copyright; Baker says Selden's copyright is invalid. Who is correct?

3. Coca-Cola sells its cola beverages in bottles of a distinctive shape. Although it has a trademark on the name and artistic depiction of that name on its bottle, Coca-Cola also wants to obtain a trademark on the bottle itself. The Trademark Office where it sought this protection claims that the trademark distinguishes the goods, not the container used. It refused Coca-Cola's request for trademark protection. Coca-Cola appeals to your court. How would you decide this case? Why?

4. American Packaging Co. wants to keep a list of its customers secret. Although it refuses to provide that information to any individuals or business firms, it does supply customer information to its trade association. As the trade association maintains customer list information for firms and periodically discloses general statistical information as to the number of customers in the industry, average dollar amount purchased, size of customer firms, and an overall list of customers of the industry (not segregated by firms), Kirgan argues that the customer list information of American Packaging is not a trade secret. Do you agree?

Case Problems

1. Nintendo's home video game system, the NES, includes a monitor, console, and controls. Nintendo game cartridges are used with the system and Nintendo designed a program, the 10NES, to prevent its system from accepting unauthorized game cartridges. For several years, Atari sought unsuccessfully to break Nintendo's 10NES program code. Later, it obtained a copy of the program from the Copyright Office by falsely asserting it was in litigation with Nintendo. (Copyright law authorizes access to copyright records for litigants.) Finally, through its own reverse-engineering efforts, Atari wrote its own program, Rabbit, to access the NES with its own cartridges. Nintendo claims Atari infringed its copyright; Atari claims the fair use exception authorizing "copying for research purposes" allows companies to legally reverse-engineer its competitors' copyrighted property. Do you agree with Nintendo? Why?

2. Lotus produced and marketed Lotus 1-2-3, a highly successful spreadsheet program. Paperback Software also produced VP-Planner. Paperback copied the nonliteral elements of the 1-2-3 program, its user interface system, menu structure, and the way in which information is presented on the monitor. Paperback claims those elements are not protected by copyright; only the source code and object codes are protected. Do you agree?

3. Starting about 1950, Volkswagenwerk imported almost 7 million "Beetle" cars into the United States. It had trademarks and servicemarks on the term "VW" and "Beetle." By 1968, it was also using the term "beetle" in publications relating to the servicing of its cars. In 1972, the Wheelers began operating an auto sales and service firm described as "The Beetle Barn." The Wheelers has no association with Volkswagenwerk, but much of their repair work was on Volkswagens. Volkswagenwerk wants to enjoin Wheeler from using the term "Beetle Barn." What factors would the court examine to determine whether to grant the relief? How would you decide the case?

4. Diamond developed a computerized process for curing rubber based on a mathematical formula. He obtained a patent allowing him to exclude others in using the formula in the process of curing rubber. Diehr claims that mathematical formulas, used in solving many types of scientific work, cannot be patented. Is Diamond's patent valid?

Footnotes

[1] See references cited by *Ray August in International Business Law: Text, Readings, and Cases* (Englewood Cliffs, N.J.: Prentice-Hall, 1993, pp. 614–615).

[2] Junda Woo, "Electronic Copying May Bring Lawsuits," *The Wall Street Journal*, October 6, 1993, p. B-4.

51

Wills, Trusts, and Estates

State Intestacy Laws

Wills and Testamentary Laws

Estate Administration

Estate Planning

I n this chapter we discuss the laws affecting the disposition of property when the owner of that property dies. The word **estate** means the interest a person has in property, both real and personal property. Thus estate planning occurs during a person's life when he or she arranges for the future distribution of his or her estate. It concerns the distribution of a person's property not only after death, but also during his or her lifetime.

This chapter first focuses on the state laws that govern the descent and distribution of the property of the **decedent**, the person who has died. Those laws determine who is entitled to receive that property if the decedent did not make a valid will. However, since by making a valid will a person can specify, with certain limitations, who shall inherit his or her property, the laws governing wills are also examined.

The chapter then briefly describes the process, known as **estate administration**, by which property is transferred from the decedent to those entitled to receive it. Finally, some of the techniques used in estate planning—such as the creating of a trust or the transfer of property to children, parents, or a charity during a person's lifetime—are discussed.

State Intestacy Laws

Two sets of state laws govern the inheritance of property. The first set comes into effect if the person did not make a valid will and is referred to as the **intestacy laws**. The second set of laws, those affecting the *testate* distribution of property, comes into effect when a person has made a valid "last will and testament."

There are significant differences in state inheritance laws, particularly as they relate to community property of married persons. There are no federal laws governing the inheritance of property (of course, federal tax laws certainly affect estate planning). A uniform law, the Uniform Probate Code, governing the descent and distribution of property has been adopted in whole or in part in at least 15 states. Our discussion of intestacy laws focuses on the general provisions found in most state statutes.

State intestacy laws govern the disposition of the decedent's real and personal property. Since real property *descends* to a person's heirs while personal property is *distributed* according to state statutes, these laws are generally referred to as *statutes of descent and distribution*.

The law of the state where the decedent's real estate is located determines the heirs to whom the real estate descends. Consequently, if an Indiana decedent owned a Michigan summer cottage, the statutory descent and distribution laws of Michigan will determine who inherits that real estate. But since the decedent's personal property is distributed according to the laws of the state where the decedent was domiciled, the furniture in that summer cottage will be distributed according to the Indiana descent and distribution statutes.

As a general rule, state intestacy laws provide that a decedent's estate, both real and personal property, shall be shared by the surviving spouse and children. The spouse's share will typically be from one-third to one-half if there are descendants of the decedent, such as children or grandchildren. If no children or grandchildren survive the decedent, the surviving spouse usually takes the entire estate.

Per Stirpes and Per Capita Distribution

If children and grandchildren survive the decedent, the question arises as to how each of them will share in the decedent's estate. If there is no surviving spouse, the entire estate will usually be split among the *lineal descendants* (children and grandchildren) of the decedent. In determining a descendant's share, the law provides that any children of a deceased child generally will take the share that the deceased child would have been entitled to inherit. This method of dividing property is known as **per stirpes distribution**. Consider the following example. John Adams is married to Jane Adams and they have three children, Al, Bonnie, and Carl. If Carl predeceases (dies before) his father John, then Carl's children (George, Harold, and Irene) inherit Carl's share of John Adams's estate. According to typical intestacy laws, John Adams's estate would be distributed as follows (see Figure 51-1 for illustration):

1. Jane Adams as the surviving spouse would receive a certain share, usually one-third.

2. The remaining two-thirds would be divided among John's descendants. In a per stirpes distribution, an equal share of this amount is given to each child. If a child has died before the decedent, then the share that would have gone to that child is instead divided equally among the predeceased child's children.

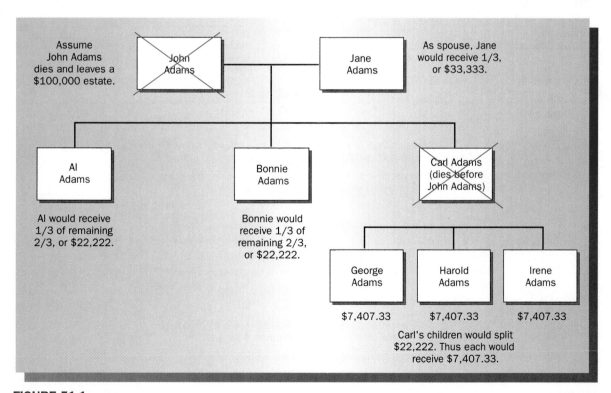

FIGURE 51-1

Intestacy Laws—Per Stirpes Distribution

a. Thus, Al, Bonnie, and Carl would each have received one-third of the remaining two-thirds (two-ninths). Al and Bonnie actually get their two-ninth shares because they're still alive.

b. Since Carl is dead, his three children divide Carl's two-ninth share equally among themselves. George, Harold, and Irene thus each receive two twenty-sevenths of John's estate.

Another method by which property may be divided is known as **per capita distribution**. This means that each person who is to receive a share of the estate as a descendant of the deceased would receive the same amount. Usually the per capita distribution system, if followed, is used for persons of the same generation rather than for persons of different generations. Thus it would probably not be used in dividing John Adams's property among his children and grandchildren.

However, if neither Jane Adams nor any children survived John Adams, his estate would then

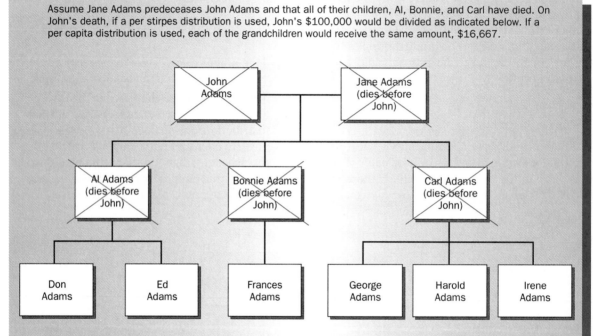

Assume Jane Adams predeceases John Adams and that all of their children, Al, Bonnie, and Carl have died. On John's death, if a per stirpes distribution is used, John's $100,000 would be divided as indicated below. If a per capita distribution is used, each of the grandchildren would receive the same amount, $16,667.

Al's Children

Per stirpes: Al, as one of three siblings, would have received a 1/3 share, or $33,333. Splitting their father's share, **Don and Ed each receive $16,667.**

Per capita: Don and Ed each receive $16,667, the same as the other grandchildren (and, coincidentally, the same amount that they would receive under a per stirpes distribution).

Bonnie's Child

Per stirpes: Bonnie would have received a 1/3 share, or $33,333. Since she has no siblings with whom to split her mother's share, daughter **Frances receives $33,333**.

Per capita: Frances receives $16,667, the same as the other grandchildren.

Carl's Children

Per stirpes: Carl would have received a 1/3 share, or $33,333. Since this amount must be divided equally among three siblings, **George, Harold, and Irene each receive $11,111**.

Per capita: George, Harold, and Irene each receive $16,667, the same as the other grandchildren.

FIGURE 51-2

Intestacy Laws—Per Stirpes vs. Per Capita Distribution

be distributed to his grandchildren. Assume there are six grandchildren, two who are Al's children, one who is Bonnie's child, and the three who are Carl's children. In this case, as Figure 51-2 indicates, a grandchild's share under a per stirpes system of distribution could vary from $33,333 to $11,111. This can be contrasted with a per capita system of distribution, which would provide each grandchild with the same amount, $16,667.

Distributions to Others

In most states, if the decedent leaves neither a spouse nor descendants, the estate will be divided in some way among the decedent's parents, if living (known as **ascendants**), and surviving brothers and sisters, whereas in other states one or more parents may take the entire estate. If there are no people in these categories, the estate will usually be distributed to nephews and nieces since they are blood relatives of the decedent. It should also be noted that most statutes of descent and distribution make no provision for relatives by marriage. The spouse of a child, brother, or parent who is not a blood relative of the decedent usually takes no share of a decedent's estate. Similarly, stepchildren, unless they have been legally adopted, are usually excluded as heirs since they are not blood relatives. Adopted children are generally regarded as children and heirs of a decedent.

Finally, if there are no descendants, ascendants, or collateral relatives of the decedent, the intestacy laws provide that the property goes to the state. This provision, known as **escheat**, is rarely applied.

As stated above, intestacy laws generally distinguish between blood relatives and relatives by marriage. The *Warpool* case, which follows, involves the interpretation of intestacy laws as they relate to an in-between case: half-blood relatives.

WARPOOL v. FLOYD
Supreme Court of Tennessee
524 S.W.2d 247 (1975)

BACKGROUND: The decedent, Warpool, was one of three children. He was predeceased by his parents and his brother and sister. His sister left no children, whereas his brother's sole surviving child, James Warpool, is the administrator of the estate and the defendant-appellant.

The decedent's father had children and grandchildren of a previous marriage, and one of those surviving grandchildren, plaintiff-appellee, Ida Mae Floyd, asked the trial court to rule that the children of half-brothers and half-sisters were to share with the child of a brother of the whole blood in Warpool's estate.

The trial court held that Floyd and the other children of the decedent's half-brothers and half-sisters were entitled to share equally with the children of the decedent's brother of the whole blood. James Warpool appealed.

Harbinson, Judge

Decedent, who never married, was predeceased by both parents. His father, however, by a previous marriage had ten children, all of whom had predeceased the decedent. Eight of these, however, left surviving children, representatives of whom were named as defendants in the court below. There are some twenty-eight of these nephews and nieces of the half blood.

Under the law of intestate distribution in this state, . . . children of brothers and sisters, however, do take by representation, and it has been held that they take the intestate's personal property *per stirpes*, rather than *per capita*.

The statutes governing distribution of intestate personal property give priority to the surviving spouse and/or children of a decedent. Where there are no persons in these categories, however, the parents are preferred. The statutes then provide as follows:

If no father or mother, to brothers and sisters, or the children of such brothers and sisters representing them, equally.

The statutes provide that if there are neither brothers, sisters, nieces nor nephews, then the personal estate is distributed "to every of the next of kin of the intestate who are in equal degree, equally."

In the case of *Kyle v. Moore* (1855), this Court expressly held that brothers and sisters of half blood shared equally in intestate personal property with brothers and sisters of the whole blood.

The Court noted that in the computation of the degrees of kinship, there was no distinction between the half blood and the whole blood. The Court said:

There is no law giving preference to the half blood on the side of the transmitting ancestor, to the exclusion of the other line, in the distribution of personalty.

The Court in that case took note of express provisions in the statutes governing the descent of real property, which had altered the feudal policy of earlier English law, excluding persons of the half blood entirely. Statutes in effect at the time of the decision of the *Kyle* case, and still in effect today, do make certain distinctions between acquired and inherited realty, insofar as inheritance by half-brothers or half-sisters are concerned.

These "ancestral property" provisions were not part of the law of distribution of personal property when the *Kyle* case was decided, nor have they since been included therein.

The *Kyle* case has not been overruled or modified by any subsequent decision of this Court, and appellant concedes that it would be controlling here except for certain changes in the statutes of distribution which occurred in the revision and codification of the state law, resulting in the Code of 1858. For the first time, in that code, there were included provisions for inheritance by brothers and sisters and their children, if the decedent did not leave a surviving spouse, child or parent.

It is insisted that because the words "brothers and sisters" were used in the Code of 1858, without qualification and without reference to relatives of the half blood, the Legislature intended to prefer brothers and sisters of the whole blood to those of the half blood.

This Court is unable to find such a legislative intent in the Code of 1858. It is true that the "ancestral property" statutes governing real estate were then in force, and that they contained explicit reference to half-brothers and half-sisters. The argument before us is that if the legislature had intended for siblings of the half blood to share fully with those of the whole blood, the legislature would have so provided.

It is equally plausible to assume, however, that if the legislature had intended to exclude half-brothers and half-sisters or to put them in a less-preferred category than full siblings, it could easily have so provided. Since it did not do so, it is the opinion of the Court that the legislature did not so intend, and that the holding in the *Kyle* case was not intended to be modified.

Finding no legislative history which would lead us to believe that the General Assembly intended to prefer siblings of the whole blood over those of the half blood, we hold that half-brothers and half-sisters share equally with full brothers and sisters in the distribution of intestate personalty, and that their children, taking by representation, take equally with the children of full brothers and sisters.

Decision: The trial court's decision was affirmed by the Supreme Court of Tennessee.

Wills and Testamentary Laws

If a person does not make a will expressing his or her own desires regarding the distribution at death, state intestacy laws determine who inherits the property and how it will be divided. Thus the basic reason for preparing a will is to establish one's own plan for the distribution of property owned at death.

A will is also used to indicate to the courts the decedent's choice of the person who will care for and look after one's children and estate. The naming of a guardian for minor children and of a personal representative for administrating one's property accomplish this purpose. Gifts to charities or the creation of trusts to split the use of property among several people also can be provided for when a will is used. Finally, a will usually clarifies the rights of possible claimants to the decedent's property, thereby making possible the settlement of the estate. For these reasons it is sound business practice for a person to prepare a will and review its provisions periodically throughout his or her lifetime.

Terminology

A **will** is a written declaration stating its maker's desires for the disposition of his or her property or estate after death. The person making a will is called a **testator** if male and a **testatrix** if female; in this chapter the term *testator* refers to both a testator and a testatrix. The person named by the testator to look after and administer the estate of the decedent is referred to as the **executor**, **administrator**, or **personal representative**; this chapter uses the term *personal representative*. Finally, the term **probate** refers to the process by which the will is legally approved as valid and through which the estate is administered until all its property is distributed. If a will is found to be invalid, it will be denied probate; in that case it has no legal effect and does not control the distribution of the testator's estate.

In the *Kenney* case the court looks at the decedent's will to see what he intended to do with his property. Where the court is unable to determine what the decedent intended with regard to some of his property, the will does not control who is to receive that property. Instead, the laws of intestacy govern.

KENNEY V. PASIEKA

Appellate Court of Illinois
260 N.E.2d 766 (1970)

BACKGROUND: Frank Pasieka, the decedent, had two relatives who were also named Frank Pasieka; one was a cousin living in Chicago and the other a nephew living in Peoria. The decedent's will left to the children of "Frank Pasieka" part of the *residue* of the estate—that is, the property left in the estate after the payment of debts and the distribution of property specifically designated in the will. Kenney, the executor of the decedent's estate, sought to have the will admitted to probate and asked the court to determine who was the decedent referred to as Frank Pasieka. Mary Pasieka, the surviving wife of the decedent, claimed that since the will was ambiguous, it was ineffective.

The trial court admitted the will to probate and determined that the decedent was referring to himself when his will referred to the children of "Frank Pasieka." Mary Pasieka appealed that decision to the court of appeals.

Moran, Justice

This case involves three men with the same name—Frank Pasieka. The first is the deceased testator who lived at Tonica, Illinois and was, in the argument before this Court, called "Tonica Frank"; the second, a nephew of the testator, who resided in Peoria and was called "Peoria Frank"; and the third, a cousin of the testator, who resided in Chicago and was called "Chicago Frank."

Tonica Frank died on October 5, 1966, leaving a last will which was executed November 24, 1962. Tonica Frank was twice married and left surviving him his second wife. He had one child by his first marriage, Theodore Pasieka, and none by his second marriage. Theodore died on October 11, 1964, after the making of the will in question but before the death of his father.

During his lifetime, Tonica Frank took into his home two boys, Walter and Joseph, both of whom changed their last name to his and lived with him as his sons. Walter never married and has no children. Joseph, on the other hand, is married and is the father of three children.

Tonica Frank's will is relatively simple but the problems it creates are substantial. After providing for the payment of his debts and funeral expenses, he bequeathed all of his personal property to his second wife. He then devised all of his real estate to his son, Theodore, for life and provided that, upon the death of Theodore, the real estate would become part of the residue of his estate. The residue was then devised "one-third thereof to the children of Walter Pasieka, share and share alike; one-third thereof to the children of Joseph Pasieka, share and share alike; and one-third thereof to the children of Frank Pasieka, share and share alike." The will then provided, "In the event any child shall not be living at the time of the death of my son, Theodore Pasieka, but shall leave brothers and sisters him surviving, said brothers and sisters shall take the share of such deceased child." . . .

The executor filed suit for a proper construction. There is no dispute as to the one-third share to the children of Joseph Pasieka. They do exist and are entitled to that portion. The difficulty, however, arises in determining which "Frank Pasieka" the testator intended, since there were three, and what happens to the share devised to the children of Walter Pasieka, since he has no children.

The trial court, after considerable deliberation and effort, wrote a memorandum of decision which concluded that the testator meant himself when he devised a one-third share to the children of "Frank Pasieka" and, therefore, this share was to be divided equally between Joseph and Walter, and finally that the one-third share to the children of Walter did not fail but passed one-half to the children of Joseph and one-fourth each to Joseph and to Walter.

This appeal followed raising the issues that the trial court erred in ruling that the testator meant himself and that the disposition of the one-third interest to the children of Walter was erroneous since there were no such children. . . .

In construing a will the guiding principle is the intention of the testator. . . .

In determining who is the right "Frank Pasieka" it appears clear to us that it cannot be Peoria Frank. Peoria Frank had not seen the decedent for twenty-eight years before his death and they had no communication.

Similarly, it would seem clear that the Frank in question cannot be Chicago Frank because they were not close and saw each other only about once each year.

We are hard pressed to find that the decedent referred to himself because the gift, of course, is not to himself but to his children and he had already provided for his only natural child by giving him a life estate in all of his property.

Likewise, we cannot determine what the decedent meant by the gift to the "children" of Walter, since Walter never had and does not now have any children.

The sad thing about this case is that the decedent went to an attorney and made an attempt to write a will. Unfortunately, he did not make a will which completely disposed of his property and the only way there can be complete disposition is for this Court to write his will for him or for the property to be administered as though the decedent had no will. While there is a presumption against intestacy and the Court should make an effort to construe the will if that is possible, this Court has no power to write a new will for a decedent if it cannot determine his intention. As our Supreme Court said in Hampton v. Dill, the testator's "intention must be determined by the language of the will itself and not from any surmise that he used the language to express an intention or meaning he had in his mind which he failed to express. If he has overlooked a condition which he probably would have provided against had he thought of it, the court cannot guess which provision he would have made and read it into his will on the presumption that he would naturally have made such a provision if he had thought of it." Where a testator in disposing of his property overlooks a particular event, which, had it occurred to him, he would have in all probability provided against, the court will not supply a provision by intendment, on a presumption of what the testator would naturally have done. . . .

We conclude that the two-thirds of the residue of the decedent's estate which were devised to the children of "Frank Pasieka" and to the children of Walter Pasieka, go as intestate under the statute.

The case is, therefore, reversed and remanded to the trial court with instructions to enter an order consistent with this opinion.

DECISION: The appellate court found the phrase ambiguous and ineffective and reversed the trial court's decision. Thus the property that was to be distributed under the will to the children of Frank Pasieka would have to be distributed according to the intestacy laws.

Requirements for a Valid Will

The requirements for a valid will are established by a state's testamentary statutes. The law of the state where a person lives or is a legal resident at the time of his death must be met in order to dispose of personal property by will. The law of the state where a person's real property is located must be complied with to dispose of it by will.

Some states have **statutory wills**, which are wills that can be filled in by any person choosing to use them. Statutory wills provide a person who does not want to consult an attorney with a model that can be used and that will be given effect if completed according to the requirements of the statute.

Since statutes vary from state to state, the person who drafts a will must be familiar with the law of the state where the will is to be effective. If the statutory requirements are not complied with, the will is usually not valid and the decedent's property then passes according to the intestacy laws.

While state statutes do vary, there are three general requirements that must be met in almost every state in order for a will to be valid. First, the person making the will must have proper testamentary capacity. A person's capacity to make valid contracts was discussed in Chapter 15. The testamentary capacity required by inheritance laws, while similar to contractual capacity, differs from it in several important respects. Second, testamentary intent is required to make a valid will. The testator must clearly intend that the document offered as a will be effective to transfer property at death. Thus, if a person intends to transfer property during his or her lifetime and writes a statement giving stock, jewelry, or personal property to another, that statement cannot be a will; it does not indicate the intent to transfer the property effective only with the testator's death. Third, the testator must comply with the statutory requirements relating to the execution or signing of the will. Certain formalities in writing, signing, and witnessing a will must be complied with for the will to be valid. If these requirements are not strictly adhered to, the proposed will is not valid and legally effective.

Testamentary Capacity   There are two elements of the requirement of testamentary capacity. The statutes require that the person making a will have attained a certain age (usually 18) before signing the will. A person who has not attained that age cannot leave his or her property to another by a will. A will executed or signed by a person who is under the statutory age is invalid for lack of testamentary capacity.

The second element of testamentary capacity is the testator's being of "sound mind." The test of a "sound mind" is expressed by courts in different terms, but usually it requires that the testator be aware of three different matters. The testator must know who are the "natural objects of his or her bounty." Usually this means the testator's family members, but it could also include close friends for whom the testator has special concerns. Second, the testator must realize the kind and extent of property that he or she is proposing to distribute by the will. Finally, the testator must be able to plan for the disposition of that property.

Each of these requirements is generally reviewed in a case where the testator's testamentary capacity is questioned. Usually, less mental capacity is required to make a valid will than is necessary to manage business affairs or enter into contracts. A person may be feeble, aged, or of low intelligence and still have the required testamentary capacity. In the *Lockwood* case the court is asked to determine whether a **codicil** (an addition to or alteration of an existing will) is valid. The claim is that it is not valid because the testatrix, Mrs. Lockwood, lacked testamentary capacity at the time she signed the codicil.

IN RE ESTATE OF LOCKWOOD
California Court of Appeals
62 Cal. Rptr. 230 (1967)

BACKGROUND: The decedent, Annie Lockwood, executed a valid will in 1958. Then 4 days before her death in 1964 when she was 89 years of age, she executed a codicil to that will. The codicil was executed 8 days after the decedent entered the hospital and during the time she was suffering her last illness.

The decedent's heirs at law who were to receive most of her estate under the provisions of the codicil sought to admit it to probate, but the probate court held the decedent lacked testamentary capacity at the time it was executed.

The heirs at law appealed the decision of the probate court to the court of appeals.

Salsman, Associate Justice

This is an appeal from a judgment entered on a jury verdict denying probate of a codicil to the will of Annie L. Lockwood on the ground that the testatrix lacked testamentary capacity on February 28, 1964 when the codicil was executed, four days before her death. The will itself was admitted to probate, there being no question of Mrs. Lockwood's testamentary capacity on July 28, 1958 when it was executed.

The codicil revoked the testatrix's gift of her entire estate to William and Irene Rolfe, close friends for many years, who had rendered personal services to her at various times, and substituted a gift of $5,000 to May Delaney and gave the remainder of her estate to her heirs at law, Alan, Audrie and Sharon Swanson, who are appellants here.

The sole issue on appeal is whether there is any substantial evidence to support the verdict of the jury, which found . . . that the testatrix was not mentally competent at the time she executed the codicil. . . .

The testatrix was 89 years of age at the time of her death on March 3, 1964. An autopsy report gave the cause of death as cardiac failure due to arteriosclerotic heart disease, but the report also catalogued the many physical miseries from which the testatrix suffered at the end of her life. . . .

The testatrix was brought to the hospital on February 20, 1964, eight days before the execution of the codicil. Up to that date there was no serious question as to her mental competency. Her condition while in the hospital, that is, from February 20th to the date of her death on March 3rd, is described by numerous witnesses, and . . . their testimony is in conflict as to the mental competency of the testatrix during that interval. . . .

The trial court gave accurate, full and complete instructions to the jury.

They were instructed that the contestants had the burden of proving that the testatrix was not mentally competent to execute her codicil on the 28th of February, and that proof had to be by a preponderance of the evidence. . . . The court then gave the jury the test by which it was to measure mental competency.

The instruction declared that: "The determinants of testamentary capacity are whether or not the decedent had sufficient mental capacity to be able to understand the nature of the act she was doing, and to understand and recollect the nature and situation of her property, and to remember and understand her relations to the persons who have claim upon her bounty and whose interests are affected by the provisions of the instrument." The jury was further instructed that the contestants were required to prove testamentary incapacity at the very moment of the execution of the will, and that a contestant must prove that the will was not made at a lucid interval. The court also instructed that: "Not every weakness and impairment of the faculties of a testatrix will invalidate a will or codicil. Even where a testatrix is feeble in health, suffering from disease and aged and infirm, yet if she was sufficiently of sound mind to be capable of understanding the nature and situation of her property, and disposing thereof intelligently, without any delusions affecting her actions, she had sufficient capacity to make a will or codicil." . . .

Upon submission, as we have related, the jury found the testatrix mentally incompetent to execute the codicil to her will. . . .

The proponents of the codicil did produce evidence through the testimony of the subscribing witnesses to the instrument to show that at the time it was executed the testatrix was of sound mind. But there was contrary evidence. Thus Mrs. King, one of the hospital nurses who cared for the testatrix from the 25th of February to the 29th, including the day upon which the codicil was executed, testified that Mrs. Lockwood showed no recognition or understanding during that period of time, and did not realize or understand her surroundings. Other witnesses, however, were able only to testify as to Mrs. Lockwood's testamentary capacity before and after the date the codicil was executed. There was testimony that both before and after February 28th the testatrix was often in deep coma, unable to be aroused, unable to recognize old friends or to remember who such friends were even for brief moments after being told. Several witnesses testified that conversation and communication with the testatrix while she was in the hospital was virtually impossible. Thus the evidence shows that both before and after the 28th the testatrix, overcome both physically and mentally by the extremities of age and her many physical ailments, was unable to communicate with her nurses and old friends and was often, if not continuously, in a semi-coma, from which she could not be aroused. It may be inferred from this evidence that, before the codicil was executed, and afterwards to the time of her death a few days later, the condition of the testatrix remained the same. . . .

We think the jury by its verdict, and the trial judge by denying the motion for judgment notwithstanding the verdict, and also in denying appellants' motion for a new trial, were justified in concluding that the decedent, weakened by age, illness and disease, lacked testamentary capacity both before and after she executed the codicil to her will, and in inferring that such lack of capacity existed at the very moment the codicil was executed.

DECISION: The court of appeals affirmed the probate court's decision denying probate to the codicil.

Testamentary Intent   The testator must (1) intend to transfer the property and (2) intend that the transfer occur only upon his or her death. Thus a document that does not clearly show the testator's intent to transfer property will be lacking in testamentary intent. Suppose I have a valuable diamond ring in an envelope and write on the envelope "This ring is for my sister Susan Sleaford." If the other requirements for a valid will are met, would this document indicate my intent to transfer the property and to have the property transferred at my death? Review the *Brown* case that follows as it relates to this question.

The case involves a holographic document, which, as we will discuss in greater detail later in the chapter, is a document wholly written in the handwriting of the person who drafted it.

IN RE ESTATE OF BROWN

Court of Civil Appeals of Texas
507 S.W.2d 801 (1974)

BACKGROUND: The decedent, Ada Brown, wrote a short note to Josephine May Benton on an envelope containing a certificate of deposit. Ms. Benton filed in the county court to have the note declared to be a valid holographic codicil to a will the decedent had made several years before her death. Josephine Brown, a beneficiary under the will of the decedent, contested the probate of the note as a codicil to the decedent's will.

The county court ordered the note to be probated as a codicil and on appeal the district court agreed with the county court. That court's decision was appealed to the court of civil appeals.

Claude Williams, Chief Justice

This appeal is from a judgment admitting to probate a writing offered as a codicil to the will of Ada B. Brown, deceased. Miss Brown executed a formal and witnessed will in 1965. Following Miss Brown's death in 1970 this will was duly probated by the County Court of Collin County, Texas, without contest. Thereafter Josephine May Benton filed her application in the County Court of Collin County to probate a written instrument as a codicil to Miss Brown's will. The writing tendered as a codicil was a cryptic note written on an envelope. The envelope contained a certificate of deposit dated July 2, 1968, from the First Savings and Loan Association of McKinney, Texas, in the principal sum of $10,000 payable to Ada B. Brown and reciting that the holder thereof would be paid earnings at the rate of five and one-half percent interest per annum. The writing on the envelope was as follows:

> This certafice [sic] from
> Ada B. Brown—
> Goes to Josephine May Benton

Josephine Brown, a beneficiary under the 1965 will, filed a contest to the probate of the alleged codicil. The County Court ordered the tendered codicil to be probated. Appeal from this judgment was timely made to the District Court.

Trial was had before the court, without a jury. The proponent of the codicil offered in evidence the writing on the envelope, together with its contents. Two witnesses testified that the writing was entirely in the handwriting of Ada B. Brown. Sally Lou Brown Benton, the mother of Josephine May Benton and the other beneficiary under the original will, testified that in July 1968 she took Ada B. Brown to the First Savings and Loan Association in McKinney where she transacted some business. Mrs. Benton testified that at that time she saw the envelope and that Ada B. Brown said to her: "This is for Josephine if anything happens to me, and I don't need it." The witness said that she did not see the envelope again until Miss Brown died in 1970. At that time she gathered up all of Miss Brown's papers which the deceased had given her to keep at the time the deceased went to the hospital, and took these instruments, including the envelope with the writing thereon, to the office of Miss Brown's attorney, Mr. Truett, who is executor under the original will. On cross-examination the witness testified that the envelope, together with its writing, was not attached to the original will in any way; that Mr. Truett had possession of the will in his office.

Based upon evidence the District Judge decided that the writing tendered was a valid holographic codicil to the 1965 will and decreed that it be admitted to probate. It is from this order that appellant-contestant appeals.

The principal question to be resolved is whether the instrument in question is testamentary in character. . . .

It is established law in Texas that whether there was testamentary intent on the part of the maker is a proper question in a proceeding to probate or in a contest of an application to probate. . . . While the actual words utilized by the maker of an instrument are the primary subject of inquiry to resolve the question of testamentary intent the rule concerning the admissibility of extrinsic evidence to resolve any doubt created by the actual words used seems to be well settled. This rule is but a refinement of the long-followed principle of Texas law that the extrinsic evidence is inadmissible to supply something necessary in, but totally missing from, the instrument itself. . . .

Applying the rule announced to the factual situation presented to the trial court we conclude that it was not error for the trial court to receive and consider extrinsic evidence relating to the circumstances which surrounded the preparation of the writing in question as well as declarations on the part of the writer of the instrument wherein she definitely clarified the meaning of the words "from" and "goes to." These words could possibly express the intent of the writer to make a gift *inter vivos* of the certificate. Clearly the statement of the decedent to the effect that she wanted Josephine to have the certificate "if anything happens to me and I don't need it" clearly negates any intention on the part of the writer to give the certificate to Josephine prior to the time that "anything happens to me." The words "if I don't need it" clearly indicate the revocability of the instrument during the lifetime of the writer. The words "goes to" have been held to indicate testamentary intent, i.e., to give property upon death, especially when there are no findings of fact and conclusions of law. These words of the writer, when taken in connection with the fact that the writer did not deliver the certificate to Josephine but kept the same in her private papers where it remained until after her death, constitute adequate evidence of testamentary intent to support the trial court's findings and judgment ordering probate of the instrument.

DECISION: The court of civil appeals affirmed the admission to probate of the note as a codicil to the decedent's will.

Recall from Chapter 14 that fraud, duress, mistake, and undue influence can defeat the genuine assent required for an enforceable contract. These same factors can defeat the testamentary intent required for a valid will.

Undue influence is the most common basis for challenging a will for lack of testamentary intent. Undue influence occurs when one person's influence effectively subjugates the will of the testator and causes the testator to make a disposition of property contrary to what he or she would have done if permitted to follow his or her own judgment.

A court might find undue influence if (1) the will doesn't properly provide for the natural objects of the decedent's bounty, such as close relatives; (2) the will doesn't reflect the intentions expressed by the decedent; (3) the primary beneficiaries of the will were in a position to control or strongly influence the contents of the will and were active in procuring the will; and (4) the decedent was mentally and physically vulnerable to acts of undue influence.

The following scenario might fit the requirements to invalidate a will on the basis of undue influence. An elderly widower in failing health hires a nurse to care for him in his home. The nurse also helps the man look after his personal affairs. The man has three children, with whom he has always enjoyed good relationships. As the man's health continues to deteriorate, the nurse takes more and more control over the man's life. The nurse convinces the man that his children are out to get him and, at the nurse's urging, the man executes a will that leaves everything to the nurse. In this scenario, the man's children have a strong basis to challenge the will.

Execution of a Will Most states require that a will be written, signed, and witnessed. A written document is generally required. The writing usually does not need to be on a particular kind of material nor made by particular instruments. A will can be written on a paper bag, a scrap of paper, or a piece of wallpaper. It can be typed or written in ink or crayon. No particular language is required as long as the testator's intentions can be determined.

A will generally must be signed by the testator. In some states, statutes specify that the signature be at the end of the will in order to assure that no pages are later added to the document that was signed. In most states the statute specifies only that the will be signed but does not state where the signature is to appear.

Similarly, each state by statute and court decision indicates the type of signature that will be effective. Use of nicknames ("Junior"), marks ("X"), or other designations ("Mom") usually will be acceptable. As long as the testator has indicated by some mark or sign on the document that he or she approves and intends it to dispose of property at his death, the signature will be valid. A person who is unable to sign his or her name or make a mark may by state statute usually have another person, at the testator's request and in his presence, place the testator's signature on the document.

Finally, a will generally must be witnessed in order to be valid. Most states require two witnesses, but a few states require three. Witnesses are there to verify that the testator actually signed the document and that, according to the witnesses, he or she had the require testamentary intent and capacity at that time. A witness does not have to read the will in order to witness it.

Some states require that the witnesses actually see the testator sign the document; others require only that the testator in some way acknowledge to the witnesses that the signature is his or her signature. Some states also require that the witnesses sign their names to the document in the presence of the testator and in the presence of the other witnesses. The statutes may also require that the will be *published*, which means that the witnesses must be told that the paper they are signing is a will.

The witnesses to a will usually need not be of legal age as long as they can understand that they are witnessing a signature. If a witness is an interested person who will receive some property by the will (a beneficiary), some statutes require an additional witness to verify the testator's signature or limit the witness's legacy to the amount he or she would have received had there been no valid will.

While other requirements may be imposed by some statutes, the writing, signing, and witnessing of the will are usually the only formalities that must be met to make a valid will.

Many states allow exceptions to the general requirements for will execution in certain limited circumstances. Over twenty states recognize some form of **holographic will**, traditionally defined as a will signed by and written entirely in the handwriting of the testator. Because the testator's handwriting is thought to guaranty the genuineness of the will, witnesses generally are not required for a holographic will. Some states require that a holographic will, in order to escape the witness requirement, be *entirely* in the testator's handwriting and contain no printed material at all. The Uniform Probate Code relaxes this rule somewhat and requires only that the "material provisions" of the will be in the testator's writing. The *Brown* case earlier in the chapter dealt with a holographic codicil to a regular will.

Some states recognize **noncupative wills**, or wills made orally. Those jurisdictions that allow noncupative wills invariably place tight restrictions on when they are allowed, because of the obvious danger of fraud and failure of memory. Generally, the person making the will must be suffering from his or her last illness (i.e., the illness that immediately precedes death) and/or must be an active soldier or seaman. Noncupative wills must be witnessed by a certain number of people (the number varies from state to state), and those witnesses must reduce the will to writing and sign the writing within a certain number of days after the will is made. Noncupative wills may not be used to distribute real property, and most states put a maximum dollar value on the personal property that is disposed of through a noncupative will.

Table 51-1 shows the different types of wills.

While a will does not have to be prepared by an attorney, the preparation of a simple will by an attorney usually is not very costly. The will does not generally have to be notarized, although a notary can be a witness. The will does not have to be filed in a specific place in the county of a person's residence or handed over to an attorney. Each of those alternatives exists in some states but usually they are not requirements. Whoever has the will of a person at the time that person dies is required by law to file it with a court (usually the

TABLE 51-1

	Concept Summary **Types of Wills**	
Type	**Characteristics**
Standard will	Must be written, signed, and witnessed and must otherwise be executed in accordance with the relevant state statute; requires testamentary intent and testamentary capacity.
Holographic will	Must be either entirely in the testator's handwriting (common law) or the "material provisions" must be in the testator's handwriting (Uniform Probate Code); need not be witnessed; requires testamentary intent and testamentary capacity; not recognized in most states.
Noncupative will	An oral will, generally allowed only for testators suffering their last illness and/or soldiers or seamen on active duty; may be used to dispose of personal property only, subject to limits on the value of distributed property that vary from state to state; must be witnessed, and must be reduced to writing and signed by the witnesses within a statutory deadline; requires testamentary intent and testamentary capacity; not recognized in most states.
Statutory will	Simplified form of will prescribed by some states that allows maker to "fill in the blanks"; designed for persons who wish to execute a will without hiring attorney; requires testamentary intent and capacity.
Living will	*Not* a means of distributing property; statement by person that he or she does not want life extended by artificial means in the event of incapacity coupled with terminal sickness or injury; recognized in a growing number of states; requires capacity.

probate court). Once the will or wills of a person are on file, admission to probate and the validation of the document as the last will and testament of the decedent can be sought.

Revocation of a Will

Since a will is without legal effect until the testator dies, a testator may revoke a will at any time prior to death. A person usually revokes a will when he or she desires to make a different distribution of the estate. The new will generally includes a clause stating that all prior wills made by the testator are revoked. In other situations the testator may simply tear up or burn an existing will, leaving property to be distributed under the intestacy laws. In addition to these methods of revoking a will by the act of the testator, the law specifies several circumstances under which revocation of an existing will occurs.

If a person subsequently executes a new will or a codicil but does not state that the new revokes the old, the law generally presumes there was the intent to revoke the old will if the new one is totally inconsistent with it. If the new will and the old will are not totally inconsistent, both are read together.

If a person who has written a will changes his or her marital status, some state statutes provide that the will is automatically revoked. In these states the marriage of a person who was single or the divorce of a person who was married automatically revokes that person's will.

In most states a divorce does not revoke the entire will. It only cancels that portion of the will providing for the former spouse. Most states also provide that a person cannot totally disinherit a spouse. By common law a wife (and less frequently also a husband) had an interest in the real property acquired during the marriage by her spouse. This interest, known as dower (which is discussed in Chapter 42), gives the wife a life estate in her spouse's land. Today most states have replaced dower with an elective share. Under these laws a surviving spouse can elect the portion of the total assets of the decedent's estate provided by law, often one-third of the estate, if she or he prefers them to the assets left to that spouse by the decedent's will.

The birth of a child usually does not revoke a will, but most states provide that a child born after a will has been executed will receive that portion of the estate of the testator that he or she would have received had no will been made.

However, if it appears from the terms of a will that a person does not want that child (or other children born before execution of the will) to inherit property, the testator's intentions will be honored. Statutes usually do not provide for a forced share for the children of a decedent in the same way they provide for the surviving spouse.

Estate Administration

Whether or not the decedent makes a valid will, there still must be some method by which the decedent's property can be collected, debts and taxes paid, and the estate distributed among those people who are entitled to receive it. The rules and procedures for administering or probating a decedent's estate determine what happens to the property from the moment of the decedent's death until the property and title of it are distributed according to law.

Probate of an Estate

Estates are usually administered according to statutory law and rules of procedure developed and overseen by probate courts. The first step in the administration or probate of a decedent's estate is to determine if the decedent had a valid will. If there is a will, the will should contain the name of the person who the decedent desired to be responsible for administering the estate—the personal representative. If there is no will, one of the decedent's heirs, usually a surviving spouse or child, will petition the probate court to be named the personal representative. The court will usually appoint a close heir as personal representative although in some states the person appointed to administer the estate must live within the state where the court being petitioned is located.

If there is a will, the will must be admitted to probate before it is considered valid. Persons interested in the will or in the decedent's estate must be notified that there is a petition to admit the will to probate. At the court hearing proof that the will was executed according to the statutory requirements will be given. If anyone questions the execution of the will or either the testamentary intent or the capacity of the decedent, a will contest may develop. In extraordinary cases, such as occurred when billionaire Howard Hughes died, the will contests may take years to resolve. In the usual case the hearing of the court

to probate the will and appoint the personal representative (whether or not there is a will) will be simple, uncontested, and quick. If more than one person seeks to be the personal representative, statutory provisions giving preference to close relatives will have to be consulted and interpreted by the court.

Once the personal representative has been appointed, the actual administration of the estate begins. Creditors of the decedent are notified, usually by publication in a local newspaper, that they must present their claims against the estate of the decedent within a specified time period (generally 6 months or less). A monetary award for the support of a surviving spouse while the estate is being administered is then made; this temporary support or allowance paid to the spouse generally takes precedence over all other claims.

Next, the personal representative must inventory all the assets in the estate and establish the value of the property. If there are sufficient assets, the funeral and burial expenses, expenses of the decedent's last illness, estate administration costs, and debts of the decedent are then paid.

Taxes that may be due the state or the federal government must be determined and paid. Estate taxes due to the federal government are assessed against the estate based on its value. Sizable exemptions from the estate taxes are incorporated in the estate tax laws. Additionally, transfers from one spouse to the other are generally deductible. Accordingly, most estates today do not have significant estate tax liability.

Inheritance taxes due to the state government are assessed on the property received from the decedent. The amount of tax depends not only on the value of the property received but also on the relationship between the decedent and the inheritor; the closer the relationship is, the lower the rate of inheritance tax will be. These taxes are then due not from the decedent giver, but rather, from the living recipient. However, since the testator may have provided by will that the estate was to pay the inheritance tax, it can become liable for this tax. In any event the taxing authorities can ensure that their taxes are paid before the title to any property is transferred from the estate.

After all administration expenses, taxes, and valid claims or debts have been paid, the personal representative furnishes an accounting to the court and, once it is approved, distributes the remaining property and money to the beneficiaries.

Alternative Methods of Estate Administration

Statutes in a number of states provide several alternatives to administering an estate through the probate procedure. A very simple procedure can usually be used for small estates that do not contain unusual amounts or types of property. Often these estates are exempt from the normal probate procedures. Other statutes provide for a probate procedure that can be used if the persons interested in the estate have no objections to it. Usually, the beneficiaries and heirs of the decedent are allowed to administer the estate independently with only minimal review by probate court authorities. Some of these alternative procedures are sometimes referred to as "family settlement agreements" or "summary procedures."

Finally, there are a number of estate planning techniques that can be used to minimize the need for estate administration under the probate court. Trusts, life insurance policies, custodial accounts, and joint tenancy agreements are often used. These techniques are discussed in the concluding pages of this chapter. Not every method is suitable in every situation, but alternatives to the formalized probate method of estate administration exist and should be considered in formulating an estate plan.

Estate Planning

Estate planning is the process of planning for the future distribution of a person's estate. The distribution of property during a person's life as well as after death can be planned to achieve various objectives. An estate plan cannot be simply chosen and then put aside; it requires periodic review and revision as a person's assets increase, marital status changes, and expenses such as those related to rearing and educating children or caring for elderly parents fluctuate.

There are often numerous objectives around which the estate must be planned. Generally the primary objective is to ensure that the testator's property is distributed to those persons he or she wants to provide for, at the time and in the portion and manner most desirable to the testator. The estate plan also seeks to minimize the taxes and fees that will have to be paid from the estate. The payment of substantial taxes not only would interfere with the primary objective, but also could force the sale of valuable property, such as a business, that the testator may prefer to pass along intact to the chosen beneficiaries.

Estate Planning and Taxation

The desire to avoid or minimize taxes due at one's death should not be the primary purpose of estate planning. A person's estate plan should seek instead to meet objectives regarding the distribution of the estate and the care and support of those who are to benefit from it. Only after the objectives of the plan have been determined and the means for attaining them have been examined should attention be focused on the taxation of the estate.

There are several taxes that affect an estate plan. The two that are of central concern are usually the federal estate tax and the state inheritance tax. As discussed above, both must be paid before the decedent's property can be transferred to heirs or named beneficiaries.

Income taxes also must be paid from the estate for income received by the decedent prior to death. If the estate receives income while it is being administered, further income taxes may be due. The federal income tax on estates is set at rates that are comparable to the income tax rates for a married couple.

Estate Planning and Trusts

A **trust** is an arrangement for holding property in which the person who has legal title to the property must manage it for the benefit of others. The person with legal title to the property is the **trustee**. The persons for whose benefit the property must be managed are the **beneficiaries**. The trustee has a *fiduciary relationship* with the beneficiaries (fiduciary relationships were discussed in Chapter 35). The trustee therefore owes several duties to the beneficiaries, including a duty of loyalty, and must manage the property exclusively to promote the best interests of the beneficiaries.

The person who creates the trust is the **settlor**, who typically contributes the property to the trust. The settlor executes a **trust agreement** or trust deed, which instructs the trustee on how to utilize and manage the trust property. If the settlor creates the trust and transfers property to it while he or she is living, the trust is referred to as a **living trust** or *inter vivos trust.*

If the trust is established by the terms of a person's will, it is referred to as a **testamentary trust**.

The settlor who creates a living trust may want to retain the power to change the trust agreement to name a new trustee or totally revoke the trust. This type of living trust is a **revocable trust**, and since the settlor can change it, the property in trust will usually be taxed as part of his or her estate. On the other hand, since the property has been transferred during the settlor's lifetime, it would not be property that is transferred at the settlor's death. Accordingly, the assets in the trust will usually not be subject to probate on the settlor's death.

If a person creates an **irrevocable trust** during his or her lifetime, the property in the trust is legally owned by the trustee. The trust, not the person who created it, now must pay taxes on income earned by the trust property. If the creator of the trust dies after having transferred property to the trustee, generally no estate taxes are assessed against that property and no probate fees are due for its administration. The property is not in the estate of the decedent at his or her death since he or she earlier transferred it to another person (the trustee). However, since the trust property is managed and administered by the trustee from the date the trust is established, fees are usually charged for those services. Most major banks have trust departments staffed by a variety of people who provide professional service to the property that the bank holds as trustee.

A testamentary trust found in a will does not become effective until the death of the testator. This means of course that the testamentary trust can be revoked or modified at any time during its creator's lifetime. Since the trust assets are in the control of the testator until death, the trust is actually created by transfer from the personal representative of the decedent's estate to the trustee. In many cases the creator of a testamentary trust will name a bank to act as both the personal representative of the estate and as trustee of the trust. Its powers and directions are those specified by the will creating the trust (as well as some statutory and common law provisions).

One of the benefits of a trust is that it provides for professional property management by the trustee instead of by the person for whom the property is to be used. Another benefit is that the income from property can be given to one person for a limited time (10 years, 20 years, or a lifetime) with instructions that after that time another person is to become owner of the property. In this way a trust can "skip" a generation, and the person in the skipped generation, who never owned the property, would not have that property subject to estate taxes or probate fees at his or her death.

In the following example George's children, Alice and Bill, are the skipped generation:

George Smith has $500,000 that he wants to give to his children and grandchildren. Since George's children are adults and have good jobs and reasonable incomes, George, by means of a trust, will primarily provide for his grandchildren. Assume that George has two children, Alice and Bill, and that each of them has two children; George then has four grandchildren. His inter vivos trust agreement would:

1. Give $500,000 to the First National Bank as trustee of the George Smith Trust

2. Provide that the income from the trust be paid annually in equal amounts to his children, Alice and Bill

3. Provide that on the death of either Alice or Bill, their share of the trust (one-half for each) should be kept in trust for the benefit of their children (grandchildren 1, 2, 3, and 4) until the youngest grandchild attains age 30 and then given to the grandchildren as their own property. (If one of the grandchildren dies before attaining age 30, that share could go to that grandchild's brothers or sisters. If both grandchildren of the same parent die before reaching age 30, their shares would go to the surviving grandchildren.)

With a testamentary trust, as with a will, courts often must struggle to determine the intent of the testator. In the case that follows, the court faced the difficult task of determining whether the testator intended to benefit grandchildren adopted into his family years after his death.

CONNECTICUT NATIONAL BANK AND TRUST CO. V. CHADWICK

Supreme Court of Connecticut
585 A.2d. 1189 (1991)

BACKGROUND: Edwin Fickes's will, executed 3 years before his death in 1943, established a testamentary trust. The trust agreement provided that upon the death of his last surviving child, one-half of the trust property would be divided equally among all of his grandchildren then living. Years later, when Fickes's last surviving child died, Fickes had four living biological grandchildren and four living adopted grandchildren. Two of the adopted grandchildren were grandsons adopted before Fickes's death. The other two were granddaughters who were adopted several years after Fickes's death. The trustee brought an action to determine whether the adopted grandchildren were entitled to share in the trust distribution. The trial court ruled that the adopted grandsons were entitled to distributions but that the granddaughters were not. The trial court ruling was appealed by both the adopted granddaughters (because they were not awarded shares of the trust property) and the biological grandchildren (because the adopted grandsons *were* awarded shares of the trust property).

Hull, Associate Justice

Significantly, the common law presumed that an adopted child is not within the intended bounty of a settlor who, as a nonadopting parent, is a stranger to the adoption. *Mooney v. Tolles.* In 1959, the legislature enacted Public Act No. 106, which reversed this common law presumption; it expressly restricted the application of the act, however, to any will or trust instrument executed after October 1, 1959. Since the will of the testator was executed on November 19, 1940, the common law presumption applies in this case.

[C]ommon law presumptions do not invariably govern interpretation of the terms of a will. Because the touchstone of trust interpretation is the intent of the settlor, the presumptions in favor of ancestral blood give way when an intent to include adoptees 'definitely appears from a reading of the instrument in light of the circumstances surrounding the settlor at the time of execution.' *Connecticut Bank & Trust Co. v. Bovey.*

Therefore, although the common law presumption against including adoptees as beneficiaries of a will applies in this case, the intent of the testator is dispositive of whether his adopted grandchildren are "grandchildren" within the meaning of his will. . . .

The testator . . . was acquainted with the twin boys. The trial court found that he showed a sincere affection and concern for them. . . . He also showed an interest in the financial welfare of the boys. He advised his son to establish a trust fund for the adopted twins and stated that "the income from this trust fund, to which your mother and I may be able to make some further contributions, would provide for their education." The testator attended their christening even though he was not a regular churchgoer. He also regularly spoke with the twins' mother about their health and welfare and was known to have inquired specifically about their eating habits and medications.

The testator also had ample time to change his will in order to rule out his adopted grandsons as "grandchildren," if he so desired, which he did not do. This fact provided further evidence that he approved of the adoptions and wanted the boys to share in his estate.

The fact that the adopted granddaughters were adopted nineteen and twenty-two years respectively after the testator's death would, standing alone, militate strongly against their being found to be "grandchildren" within the meaning of the testator's will. In other cases we have upheld the trial court's finding excluding persons adopted after the testator's death as beneficiaries of a testator's will because in considering the rights of an adoptee to take under a will, the fact that the adoption occurred after the death of the testator is a factor to be given great weight. These cases, however, do not control this case.

Although Holmes' aphorism that the life of the law is not logic but experience has been oft-quoted, we have not on this court by any means abandoned logic in our reasoning. This court has recognized that "[p]erhaps there is no class of cases where precedents have so little weight as in the construction of wills." *Lyon v. Acker.* The position of the adopted granddaughters is a good example of this, for this case is unique among previous cases in that there are here two adopted grandsons of whom the testator had knowledge and approved, and two granddaughters adopted much later of whom the testator obviously had not an inkling. Under this unusual scenario the trial court, in construing the testator's will, incorrectly applied the customary adopted after death presumption without considering the unbreakable logical link between the two groups of adoptees. In construing the term "grandchildren" as it applied to his twin grandsons, the court properly interpreted his intent, at the time of execution of his will, as including the adopted grandsons whom he later knew and approved before his death. On the basis of this conclusion, we conclude that the testator's use of the term "grandchildren" also included his two adopted granddaughters—also the children of Charles.

So far as this record shows, Charles had no natural children. It is likely, therefore, that the testator recognized that any of his grandchildren through Charles would be adopted, rather than biological. Thus, when he drew his will and intended "grandchildren" to include adopted grandchildren, he must be regarded as intending to include not only those adopted prior to his death, but also those adopted thereafter, because the taking class was designated as "grandchildren . . . living" at the death of his last remaining child. Under these circumstances, it is unlikely that the testator intended to include the children of Charles adopted before his death but to exclude those adopted after his death. He must have intended to include both.

DECISION: The Supreme Court of Connecticut ruled that both the adopted grandsons and the adopted granddaughters were entitled to share in the trust property.

While trusts generally must be managed for the benefit of one or more designated persons (beneficiaries), there is one exception to that rule. A **charitable trust** is created when a settlor arranges for property to be managed in trust not for the benefit of specific persons, but to promote some charitable purpose. Charitable trusts have been established for a variety of purposes, including to finance schools, hospitals, parks, and charitable organizations.

Estate Planning and Joint Property

Joint property is used in estate planning to transfer property from one person to another by an agreement made during a person's life. Thus joint property is usually not in the *probate estate* of the first of the two persons to die; that property has been transferred by agreement prior to that person's death to the second person. However, joint property is usually a part of the *taxable estate* of the first person to die.

There are several legal arrangements for sharing property among two or more people. These were discussed in the context of real property in Chapter 48. These methods can also be applied to personal property and will be quickly reviewed here.

The first arrangement is to establish the two or more persons as joint tenants with rights of survivorship; the second is to establish them as tenants in common. The first method is probably the most common; most states have statutes that provide that bank accounts or securities held in two names are usually held as joint tenants with the right of survivorship. For example, Tom and Jane have a $1,000 savings account in their joint names. If Tom dies before Jane, the

$1,000 is owned by Jane. It is not transferred to her by Tom's will or by the intestacy laws but by the agreement they made while they were both alive.

If Tom and Jane instead hold the savings account as tenants in common, both of them own one-half or $500. When Tom dies, $500 is transferred by his will or by the intestacy laws to his heirs or beneficiaries. Thus Jane would still have her $500, but the $500 owned by Tom might be transferred to her or to someone else.

If Tom and Jane are husband and wife, their joint property is sometimes referred to as being owned by them as *tenants in the entirety*. This is simply a special term for joint tenants who are spouses and who want the survivor by virtue of the agreement they made (or which the law assumes they made) to inherit all their jointly held property.

A husband and wife often hold title to property jointly. This allows each access to the property during his or her lifetime and automatically provides that the property passes to the survivor on the death of either. Property that is held by joint tenants with right of survivorship (or by tenants in the entirety) avoids probate fees but usually not estate taxes. Often, because of the size of the estate and the marital deduction that the estate tax laws allow for transfers at death to one's spouse, estate taxes are not a consideration in the estate plan. Thus joint property is a viable estate planning device for many people.

Estate Planning and Insurance

Life insurance can be used in a variety of ways in estate planning. Ownership of an insurance policy may be established in such a way that the proceeds from the policy at the insured's death will not be subject to federal estate taxes. Life insurance is usually not subject to probate expenses since the benefits are due pursuant to the policy and not by virtue of any provision in a will or the intestacy laws. In many states some of the proceeds from insurance policies on the decedent's life are also exempt from state inheritance taxes.

Life insurance is thus often used as a means of providing security for the average person. A variety of policies—whole life, term, endowment, annuity—are available to serve different needs and desires. Persons who have significant assets in a business often use insurance as a means for transferring those assets to the surviving business associates. The business owns the insurance policy on the partner or key employee, and on that person's death the proceeds from the policy are used by the surviving business associates to purchase the decedent's share and to compensate the estate of the deceased for the decedent's ownership interest in the business.

Estate Planning and Custodial Accounts

A **custodial account** is a type of trust account. One person, the custodian, holds money that belongs to someone else, the beneficiary. While the custodian oversees the money, he or she can use it only for the benefit of the beneficiary to whom it belongs. Many custodial accounts are established by parents for their minor children. When a custodial account is used, once the child attains the age of majority (usually 18), the money in the account then belongs to the child and no longer is administered by the parent.

Custodial accounts are often established by parents for their minor children. When a custodial account is used, the money in the account is to be used for the child during his or her minority. Once the child attains the age of majority, the money in the account belongs to the child.

The tax laws (kiddie tax) provide that children under the age of 14 are taxed on their earned income and on their investment or unearned income at their parent's marginal tax rate, if that rate is higher than what the child would pay. The tax applies whether the income earned is from work or services performed by the child (earned income) or from assets transferred by the parents or others to the child.

The kiddie tax does not apply to the income derived from property in a custodial account established for children who are 14 years of age. The income from such an account is taxable at the tax rate applicable for the child, not the tax rate of the parent.

Finally, custodial accounts that are established for young minor children would still remove the property transferred from the parent's estate. Since the property in a custodial account is owned by the beneficiary (child), not the custodian, any estate or inheritance tax due on property owned by the custodian (parent) would not affect property owned by the beneficiary.

Tax laws allow a parent to transfer $10,000 per year to any recipient (including their children) without any gift tax liability. Thus if George and Mary Smith have three children, each year George can give $30,000 to them and Mary can give $30,000 to them. While such gifts made to minor children under the age of 14 will not save George or Mary income taxes due on the income from the transferred property, the property given will not incur the estate tax or inheritance tax due if they were transferred at their death. Thus the transfer of property from parent to child during the parent's lifetime can still minimize the tax burden due on that property.

Table 51-2 summarizes various estate planning documents.

Planning for Incapacity

As part of the estate planning process, one often makes arrangements for what to do in the event that one becomes incapacitated.

Power of Attorney   A **power of attorney** is a document that gives one person the authority to act on behalf of another with respect to specified matters. A person may execute a power of attorney, for example, to allow his or her agent to sign contracts on the person's behalf.

A power of attorney generally expires automatically upon the incapacity of the person granting the power. But there is a special type of power of attorney, known as a **durable power of attorney**, that does not terminate in the event of the grantor's incapacity. A person can thus use a

TABLE 51-2

Concept Summary	**Estate Planning Documents**
Document	**Purpose**
Will	States who is to receive decedent's property.
	Allows for specific bequests of family heirlooms.
	Names *personal representative* to administer estate until property is distributed.
Trust	Provides that one or more persons (*trustees*) will have legal title to property while others (*beneficiaries*) will benefit from use of property through payment of its income and/or principal at later date.
	A trust may be revocable or irrevocable and effective during its creator's life (inter vivos) or at death (testamentary).
Power of attorney	Gives another person the right to act on behalf of the person who may be out of town or unable to act for himself or herself. It may grant broad general powers or only narrow specific ones.
	A durable power of attorney does not terminate if the grantor becomes incapacitated.
Living will	A document detailing a person's wishes regarding medical treatment to be given (or denied) during a terminal and incapacitating illness.
Life insurance policy	Names a beneficiary who will receive stated benefits on death of insured (see Chapter 52).
Contract with joint property with survivorship provisions	A contract allowing either named party to own the stated property after the death of the joint tenant.
Custodial account agreement	An agreement by a custodian to hold and use money for a child during the child's minority; once the child attains the age of majority, the fund belongs to the child.

PREVENTIVE LAW
Estate Planning for Younger Individuals

Estate planning concerns the planning for the future distribution of an estate. The answers to several common questions may provide some guidance regarding the appropriate degree of estate planning for younger individuals.

1. *Do I need to be concerned with estate planning?*

   This depends on several things. First, what is the size of your "estate"? Total the value of your assets—both real and personal property, insurance policies, and pension benefits. If this value is significant to you or exceeds $100,000, you need an estate plan. Second, who are you concerned about if you were to die? Do you have parents, children, brothers, or sisters whom you want to inherit your property? Both the number of people and the intensity of your concern about providing for them, as well as the value of your estate, affect the need for an estate plan.

2. *Do I have to be concerned with wills, trusts, custodial accounts, and taxes? It sounds too complicated and expensive.*

   Not necessarily. If you have a normal-sized estate and are concerned about providing for several people, you probably need a will. The other items referred to only affect those people with sizable estates. A simple will usually can be prepared for several hundred dollars and a review of your overall estate may not be much more expensive.

3. *If I make a will and prepare an estate plan when I'm 25 or 30 years old, how long will it be good for?*

   Again, there is not one answer. If your situation does not change a lot, it could be good for a decade or more. However, if you get married, have children, buy a house, purchase life insurance policies, and begin to acquire stocks or inherit money from someone, a review should occur. A good rule of thumb would be to review your estate plan yourself every 5 years and note what is different in your life. If there are major differences in your circumstances or in your estate, you probably want to schedule a meeting with an estate planning attorney.

durable power attorney to designate who will be authorized to manage his or her affairs in the event of the person's incapacity. For example, a person might execute a durable power of attorney granting his younger sister broad authority to manage his property and sign documents on his behalf in the event of his incapacity. By so doing, the person can ensure that his affairs will be managed by someone whom he trusts, and can save his family the time and expense of petitioning a court for the right to manage his affairs.

Living Will   In a number of highly publicized cases, families of terminally sick or injured comatose patients have petitioned courts to allow the patients to be disconnected from artificial life support systems. The court must often confront the dilemma of trying to determine the wishes of a patient who has no hope of recovering from a coma. These cases typically pit doctors, who believe that they have a duty to keep the patient alive if at all possible, against families who sincerely believe that the patient would have wanted to "die with dignity." Most states now recognize **living wills**, documents in which a person states in advance that he or she does not want his or her life to be prolonged by artificial means in the event of a terminal and incapacitating illness or injury. The requirements for a living will vary from state to state.

Review Questions and Problems

Key Terms

estate

decedent

estate administration

intestacy laws

per stirpes distribution

per capita distribution

ascendants

escheat

will

testator/testatrix

executor/administrator/
   personal representative

probate

statutory will

codicil

holographic will

noncupative will

estate planning

trust

trustee

beneficiary

settlor

living trust

testamentary trust

revocable trust

irrevocable trust

charitable trust

custodial account

power of attorney

durable power of
   attorney

living will

Discussion Questions

1. Under what circumstances will you get more money than your first cousin under a per stirpes distribution than under a per capita distribution?
2. Which basic laws govern the inheritance of property?
3. Which requirements must be met for a will to be valid?
4. Is there more to estate planning than the drafting of a valid will? Explain.

Review Problems

1. The Hunts, a married couple, were both admitted to a nursing home on June 4, 1979. A few days later, Mrs. Hunt died. Mr. Hunt, who was terminally ill with cancer, was hospitalized on July 5, 1979. Two days later, on July 7, he executed a will. He died the next day, July 8, 1979. Mr. Hunt had been taking a variety of medication since his cancer had been discovered in October 1978. He had pain medicine available to him every 4 hours, if needed. He had taken the medicine several times on the day he executed his will. Usually after taking this medicine, Mr. Hunt was incoherent for several hours. Mr. Hunt's doctor saw him several times on the day he died. He testified that at 9:00 A.M. Mr. Hunt was very ill but that by noon he had improved. When the doctor saw him at 5:00 P.M., one hour before the will was signed, he was sitting up on a chair. Did Mr. Hunt have the testamentary capacity needed to make a valid will?

2. Bass died in March 1975, leaving a will dated May 2, 1974, in which he gave all his property to the local Baptist Church, to the exclusion of his wife. His widow objected to the probate of his will, claiming that he lacked testamentary capacity due to his use of drugs and alcohol. The testator had been a heavy drinker for several years and was known in the community as a habitual drunkard. Does the testimony on Bass's alcoholism prove that he lacked testamentary capacity to make a valid will?

3. Ritcheson died in July 1971, in Arkansas. In January of that year he asked his close friend, Peevy, to help him make his will. But Peevy refused and suggested that Ritcheson see a lawyer. In March 1971 Ritcheson was involved in an automobile accident. He remained in poor health from that time until his death. Ritcheson went to Peevy about a week before his death and asked Peevy to call his attorney so that he could have his will made. Ritcheson made some notes on a yellow legal pad for the proposed will. When Peevy found the lawyer out of the office, Ritcheson left the yellow pad of notes with Peevy. These notes were never again found. A week later, Peevy found Ritcheson dead at his home. On the table beside him, Peevy found a note, entirely in Ritcheson's handwriting, which claimed to dispose of all of Ritcheson's property. In fact, the note did not dispose of some of Ritcheson's property. The note was not signed at the end, nor was it dated. But it did include the decedent's name in the body of the note. Does the document qualify as a holographic will?

4. Ruth Evans claims that her father's will is valid. Other relatives assert that it is not, because Ruth used undue influence over her father. Ruth did arrange for her father to make a will, found an attorney, and accompanied him to the attorney's office for its signing. But the attorney testified that she did not participate in any discussion regarding the terms of the will. The father was found to have acted "senile" at times, but he was also referred to as "stubborn." He insisted on driving his own car and managing some of his own affairs. He confided in his daughter Ruth and frequently followed her suggestions on things he should do. Should the will of Ruth Evans's father be voided due to her undue influence?

Case Problems

1. On January 12, 1962, Thomas Jackson, an attorney, wrote to several of his clients, "As I am rather ill, I am discontinuing my active practice." Four months later Jackson signed a will that his attorney had prepared for him. The will left Jackson's property to his wife and nothing to his two sons by a prior marriage. The two sons contended that the letter and other evidence showed that during the period just prior to the date on which their father signed the will Jackson was forgetful, less talkative and communicative, unable to drive a car, and prone to sit and stare for long periods of time. The decedent was 72 when he

died on July 9, 1962. Do you think the decedent lacked testamentary capacity to make a will?

2. William Birkeland died in 1972. In 1970 he had a document stated to be a will drafted by an attorney. However, contrary to the attorney's instructions, he did not sign it in the attorney's office. He had it sent to him and he signed it alone. Then, on separate occasions, it was witnessed by two witnesses. Birkeland did not tell either witness that the document was a will, and neither saw him sign his name. One witness said Birkeland had already signed it, and the other said he didn't recall if there was any other signature on it. The state statute requires that a will (1) be signed by the testator (2) in the presence of two attesting witnesses and (3) be acknowledged by the testator to the witnesses as his will. Is this will validly executed?

3. A father wrote a letter to his son containing the following language: "I want to inform you that I bequeathed to you by my last Will the farm in Converville, Virginia, after my wife's death and my own death. I have the Will in my safe here and it nullifies the one which is in the bank. Be sure and keep this letter." The son says the letter is a valid holographic will. The state statute says a will totally in the handwriting of the testator and signed by him can be given effect even if it is not witnessed. Does the letter constitute a will? Can it revoke a prior will (the one in the bank)?

4. The decedent executed a will approximately one year before death. In the will she expressly excluded her husband because "he is financially well off" and her daughter because "she is financially well off and has not visited me for many years." The decedent was 82 when she died. Toward the end of her life she expressed hostility toward her husband and voiced delusions about his attempts to poison her (which the facts show he did not do). The husband claims the decedent was unduly influenced by her son, who: (1) took his mother to a lawyer's office to arrange for her to make a will; (2) asked the family doctor to witness his mother's will, but when the doctor refused unless the mother was examined by a psychiatrist, declined to take his mother to a psychiatrist; (3) was present with his mother in the lawyer's office when she conferred about the will and also when she signed it. Do you think these facts constitute undue influence sufficient to set aside the will?

5. Decedent died intestate in Buffalo, New York. Surviving him were six brothers and sisters. Also surviving him was a person who claimed to be his daughter. She claimed that the decedent had lived with her mother in Florida, where she now resided, for 15 years prior to the decedent's move to Buffalo 3 years before his death. The person who claimed to be his daughter said that under Florida law she would be considered the decedent's daughter and as such should be chosen to be the personal representative of his estate. Under New York law she would not be considered his daughter and would not have a claim to be his personal representative. Should the laws of Florida be referred to in order to determine her legal status and claim to be his personal representative?

52

Insurance Law

Kinds of Insurance

Nature of Insurance Contracts

Defenses of the Insurer

Interpretation of Insurance Contracts

Insurance Firms

The term **insurance** describes a contractual arrangement by which one party agrees to pay another party a sum of money or something of value upon the happening of some event that is beyond the control of the contracting parties. The party who agrees to pay upon the happening of the event is known as the **insurer**; the party who purchases the insurance (or on whose behalf the policy is purchased) is known as the **insured**. The insurance contract is referred to as an **insurance policy**. The insurance policy is purchased with payment known as **premiums**. Insurance sales and contracts are regulated by state law pursuant to the terms of the McCarran Act, a federal law enacted in 1945.

Each state has its own statutes and administrative regulations establishing standards that both its own domestic and foreign (those that are situated either in other states in the United States or in foreign countries) insurance companies must meet in order to do business in the state. Most of the state laws are concerned with the solvency of the firms that can be incorporated or licensed in the state. Other provisions specify the conditions under which insurance agents and brokers can be licensed to conduct business.

Because the insurance relationship arises from a contract between the insurer and the insured, insurance law is best viewed as a subpart of contract law. Thus the concepts of offer and acceptance as well as the other rules relating to contracts generally apply to the insurance contract. Of course, since there are special terms, conditions, and practices that affect insurance contracts, this chapter highlights some of the unique aspects of this important field of law.

Kinds of Insurance

There are many kinds of insurance and the listing that follows is not necessarily comprehensive. Nevertheless, the descriptions found in this section refer to those insurance agreements that are most frequently encountered by the individual business person, in either a personal or a business capacity.

Life Insurance

A **life insurance** policy is one in which the insurer agrees to pay a specific sum of money upon the death of the insured, provided that the premiums due to keep the policy in force have been paid. The insurer pays the money to the person designated by the insured, the **beneficiary**, or, if no such person is named, to the estate of the insured. As long as the insured is alive, he or she generally retains the right to change the beneficiary on the insurance policy. There are several different types of life insurance policies; the most common are whole life, term life, and universal life policies.

Whole Life Insurance

Whole life insurance provides coverage that runs for the entire life of the insured. As the insured pays in premiums, some of the money goes to pay for the death benefits and some goes into what is essentially a savings account for the insured. This savings portion of the policy, known as the **cash surrender value**, may not be withdrawn outright but the insured may borrow against it. A whole life policy is thus a savings or investment vehicle as well as an insurance policy.

Whole life policies are generally classified by how the premiums are paid. **Ordinary life insurance** is whole life insurance for which premiums are paid throughout the life of the insured or until he or she reaches a specific age. If the insured is unable to continue to pay the premiums due on the policy, it is generally possible, without any further payment being made, to convert the policy to an extended term insurance policy (term insurance is discussed below) or to have a smaller amount of ordinary life insurance. The amount of ordinary life insurance that the insured would qualify for in such an event is known as the **paid-up amount**.

Another type of whole life is **limited-payment life insurance**, for which premiums are paid for a certain number of years or until a specified event, such as retirement. Finally, there is **single-premium life insurance**, for which the entire premium is paid in one payment.

Term Insurance

Term life insurance is issued for a limited number of years or terms; beyond that date it provides no insurance or benefits for the insured or for the named beneficiary. Term insurance is the least expensive form of insurance because it grants no loan or cash surrender value to the insured. Thus it provides protection but no savings. Some term insurance policies have provisions allowing the owner to convert at some later date to ordinary life or endowment insurance. Term insurance is a popular alternative for people who want to separate the investment portion of ordinary life insurance from its death benefits or who cannot afford the equivalent protection provided by an ordinary life plan. Frequently this type of insurance may be provided by an employer to a group of employees for the term of each individual employee's employment.

Universal Life

A **universal life insurance policy** combines the benefits of the term and the ordinary life insurance policies. Essentially these policies give the insured an opportunity to receive market rate increases in the cash value, rather than in the smaller guaranteed company rate. Only the portion of premium necessary to support death benefits is withheld from the investment program; the remainder is available for cash value growth. It is also possible to vary the premium and in so doing to vary the amount of death protection provided by the policy.

Endowment and Annuity Contracts

Endowment and annuity contracts are similar to the ordinary life insurance contract. They generally obligate the insurer to pay either a lump sum of money or a fixed sum for a period of time to the insured. The payments are to be made when the insured reaches a specified age or after a set period of time. If the insured dies prior to the date established in the policy, the insured's beneficiary receives the sum of money. The **endowment policy** generally pays the insured a lump sum of money at a specified date, whereas the **annuity contract** pays specific sums to the insured at periodic intervals after the insured reaches a specified age. These policies are often used to fund a child's education or to provide some additional security during a person's retirement years.

Although annuity contracts are not technically regarded as pure insurance agreements, they are similar and therefore are subject to regulation by state insurance departments. Under a **fixed annuity** the insured or his beneficiary receives a set sum of money for a set term or for the life of the insured. A **variable annuity** obligates the insurer to pay a variable sum of money to the insured. The amount to be paid varies with the rate of inflation or with the rate of return on the insurance company's investments. The assumption is that investment return will parallel the cost of living so that the varying payment will provide the insured with a stable amount of purchasing power.

Accident and Health Insurance

Accident and health insurance protects the insured against losses suffered due to accidents or sickness. These policies provide for the payment of benefits or the reimbursement of specified expenses if the insured becomes ill from an accident or illness. These policies generally limit the amount of benefits to be paid. Furthermore, certain health problems or illnesses may be either excluded by the terms of a health insurance policy or covered only after a waiting period. This type of insurance is also referred to as *medical insurance*, since it provides the insured with benefits for medical expenses, hospital fees, and doctor bills.

Employers often provide some group-based health or accident insurance to employees. In group insurance the insurer offers one master contract for the employer. Further, since many group policies base some of the premium cost on previous claims experience of the group, its cost per person may be at significantly lower rates than would be true for similar individually based contracts.

Disability Insurance

Disability insurance provides income to those who become too ill to continue work in their occupation. While medical insurance covers a person's hospital and medical expenses during an illness, disability insurance provides a source of income for the person during the time of the disability. Generally, disability insurance does not completely replace a person's former income. Because disability insurance benefits are not taxable, a smaller amount of income usually allows the person to continue to meet normal household and living expenses.

Casualty and Fire Insurance

Casualty insurance protects the insured from loss due to the damage or destruction of personal property by causes other than fire or the elements. This type of insurance is frequently applied to loss or injury due to accident. Fire insurance protects the policyholder against loss of insured real or personal property from fire. While the terms of fire insurance policies are standardized by law, additional coverage is generally available for other forms of damage or to benefit the insured in ways that are not provided by the standard policy.

Liability Insurance

Liability insurance provides the insured with money to cover losses suffered by others, whether for personal or property damages, for which the insured is held liable. Liability insurance is commonly carried by owners of automobiles and by people who own or lease real property. A related type of insurance covers a professional person who could be held liable for injuries caused to his or her clients, patients, or students. The insurance company agrees to indemnify or repay the insured for the amount of his or her liability up to an amount specified in the policy.

Homeowner's and Renter's Insurance

People who own houses or condominiums generally purchase **homeowner's insurance**, which protects the homeowner's property against loss. The property covered generally includes the structures on the homeowner's property as well as the homeowner's personal possessions. The property is protected against a variety of perils, including fire and natural hazards, accidents, theft, and vandalism. People who live in apartments or other rented dwellings can purchase **renter's insurance**, which insures personal possessions in the same manner that homeowner's insurance does.

Automobile Insurance

Automobile insurance generally insures the car owner against both damage to his or her car and liability. The damage coverage includes *collision insurance*, which covers losses to the insured's own car as a result of a collision with another vehicle or object, as well as protection against hazards and theft. *Liability coverage* protects the insured from liability for personal injury or property damage resulting from the insured's operation of his or her vehicle.

People across the country complain about high auto insurance premiums. Some blame the high premiums on excessive damages that have been awarded to people who have been injured in car accidents. Large awards often include a very substantial amount of damages for "pain and suffering," which is awarded in addition to compensation for such tangible costs as medical expenses and lost wages. Some argue that these large recoveries lead to soaring insurance premiums because they greatly increase the insurers' costs; others contend that the frequency and effect of excessive damage awards is greatly exaggerated by insurers.

In an effort to control auto insurance premiums and other costs associated with car accidents, some states have adopted no-fault insurance plans. Under a **no-fault auto insurance** system, each party's own insurance company pays his or her own personal injury costs (and, under some systems, property damage costs). Unlike the standard system, where the insurance company of the party at fault pays each party's costs, the no-fault system generally eliminates the litigation and settlement procedures required to determine which party was at fault. Most no-fault plans also tightly restrict the ability of an injured party to recover for pain and suffering. Under most no-fault plans, an injured party still may bring an action against the other party or his or her insurer in cases where the person has suffered serious injury and incurred large medical expenses.

Supporters of no-fault say that the system saves money by reducing litigation costs and by preventing excessive pain and suffering awards. Opponents say that the system unfairly restricts the rights of people who are injured in auto accidents because of the negligence of others.

Credit Insurance

Credit insurance protects both the creditor and the debtor by providing for the payment of an indebtedness of the insured in the event of death before the indebtedness has been paid. It is most commonly used to cover a mortgage indebtedness on a home or for a debt due by a business that might be forced out of business to pay creditors if a key officer or partner dies.

Title Insurance

Title insurance repays the insured for a loss arising from defects in the title to real estate. Title policies for an owner of a home generally are written to cover the purchase price of the property. Similar policies for the amount of a mortgage are written for the mortgagee's benefit (usually the mortgagee is a bank or other financial institution). If the seller of the property does not provide a clear title to the property, the purchaser has a right to recover damages either from the seller or from the title insurance company.

Business Interruption Insurance

A **business interruption insurance** policy provides benefits to cover losses due to interruptions in business operations caused by an insured peril. An interruption might be caused by a strike, fire, or storm or because of construction near the place of business that prevents customers from reaching the business.

Worker's Compensation Insurance

State laws generally require employers to compensate workers who are accidentally injured while on the job. Even if an employee was injured because of an act of another employee, the employer must compensate the injured employee. These laws are not based on negligence or fault by the employer. Instead, they hold the employer strictly liable for injuries occurring in the workplace. Employers purchase **worker's compensation insurance** to pay claims resulting from their employees' injuries.

In most states policies can be purchased either from a state fund or from private insurance companies. Sometimes, rather than purchase an insurance policy, an employer uses company assets to pay for any claims. This method of providing insurance coverage is called **self insurance** and is used in a variety of situations.

Table 52-1 lists most of the types of insurance.

Nature of Insurance Contracts

Because insurance companies generally deal in volume and in spreading their covered risks among a pool of people, their contracts must be standardized. In fact, laws in many states require substantial standardization in policies covering the same risk for different people. For this reason insurance contracts are not subject to the same bargaining between parties as are most other contracts.

TABLE 52-1

Concept Summary   Types of Insurance

Type	Characteristic
Life insurance	
Ordinary life	Provides coverage for life of insured; some cash savings (cash surrender value) and death benefit. Premiums paid for insured's life or until set age
Limited-payment life or single-premium life	Provides same coverage as with ordinary life. Premiums paid for a set number of years or only once
Term	Provides death benefit but no savings. Often provided by employer; may be convertible to ordinary life
Universal life	Provides death benefits and savings; amount of savings portion and death benefit varies with market increases
Endowment and annuity contracts	
Endowment	Pays insured a lump sum at a specific date
Annuity	Pays insured a specific sum at periodic intervals (variable annuity pays amount that varies with inflation rate or investment return rate)
Accident and health insurance	Protects insured against losses due to sickness or accident. Pays by reimbursing for specific expenses (hospitals, doctors, drugs, etc.)
Disability insurance	Provides income to those who become too ill to continue working in their occupation
Casualty and fire insurance	Protects insured against loss of insured real or personal property due to a casualty other than fire or the elements
Liability insurance	Provides insured with money to cover losses suffered by other persons for which insured is held liable. Automobile and professional malpractice insurance are examples of liability insurance
Homeowner's and renter's insurance	Provides owner of property (real or personal for homeowners, and personal for renters) with protection against loss due to perils such as fire, accident, or theft
Automobile insurance	Provides insured with protection against damage to her car. Auto insurance includes collision (loss to insured's car as a result of a collision) and liability coverage for personal injury or property loss suffered by others
Credit insurance	Pays an indebtedness of the insured (such as a mortgage) in the event of death or disability
Title insurance	Pays insured for a loss arising from defects in the title to real estate
Business interruption insurance	Provides benefits to cover loss due to interruption in business operations caused by an insured peril (such as storms, fire, nearby construction)
Worker's compensation insurance	Provides benefits to workers accidentally injured on the job; employers purchase to cover their liability

Offer and Acceptance

While insurance agents frequently contact customers to try to sell insurance policies, by law it is the customer, not the insurance agent, who makes the offer. Thus the contract occurs only after the company accepts the offer, not after the customer has signed approval of the policy terms.

If a customer seeks health insurance, the company may condition its acceptance on the results of an up-to-date physical examination. If the examination reveals a history of disease or other physical problems, the company may reject the offer. It could, of course, make a counteroffer and agree to write a different or more expensive policy.

Many insurance problems relate to the authority of the agent to bind the company. If the customer signs an offer, can the agent sign and accept that offer on behalf of the company or must someone else in the company's home office accept any offers made to the company? An agent generally has authority to bind the company that issues fire or casualty insurance through offering a **binder**, a document that commits the company even before a person in the home office issues the actual policy. However, that same agent does not have similar authority to bind the company to issue most life insurance policies. Because the agent represents the company, the agent's statements can and do affect the terms of the insurance contract made between the company and the insured. The *Phillips* case raises issues about the effect of an agent's statement on the terms of an insurance policy.

RANGER INSURANCE COMPANY V. PHILLIPS

Arizona Court of Appeals
544 P.2d 250 (1976)

BACKGROUND: Boyle was a passenger in a small plane owned by Phillips (defendant-appellee) that crashed while being piloted by Bruner, a student pilot. Ranger (plaintiff-appellant) had issued a liability insurance policy to Phillips that contained a standard clause, as specified by Federal Aviation Administration (FAA) regulations, limiting those who were qualified to pilot the insured aircraft. The policy did not cover student pilots. In fact Bruner had a note affixed to his student pilot's license that expressly prohibited him from carrying passengers.

However, Phillips proved that he told Ranger's agent that he wanted insurance coverage that covered student pilots. The agent assured Phillips of the requested coverage and sent Phillips a handwritten note to that effect. Later, the coverage for the student pilot was deleted from the policy by the agent without informing Phillips of the change. The actual policy was not delivered to Phillips until after the crash causing Boyle's death.

The insurance company argues that the written insurance policy, not the oral or written statement of its agents, specifies the terms of its coverage. Further, it notes that the premium charged to Phillips was not based on the higher cost associated with student pilot coverage. Thus Ranger claims it is not obligated to pay claims for the accident involving the student pilot. The trial court found for Phillips and the insurance company appealed.

Froeb, Judge

This suit was filed by appellant Ranger Insurance Company (Ranger) to obtain a judicial declaration of the extent of its duties and obligations under a contract of aircraft insurance. After a non-jury trial, the trial court found the company had a duty to defend appellees Robert W. Phillips (Phillips) and Ivadelle Bruner, administratrix of the estate of Marvin L. Bruner, deceased, against a claim asserted by Inez Boyle, individually and as executrix of the estate of Gayle Boyle, deceased, and to indemnify them against any judgment not exceeding $100,000.

Gayle Boyle was a passenger in a small two-seat aircraft (known as a Lark 95) when he died in a crash near Willcox, Arizona, on April 20, 1967. The plane was piloted by Marvin L. Bruner (Bruner), student pilot, whose total experience and flight time consisted of approximately 70 hours. Phillips, the owner of the plane, conducted a flight service business at Falcon Field in Mesa, Arizona, from which the fatal flight originated. As this case involves only the question of insurance coverage, we are not here concerned with the cause of the crash.

Ranger issued a liability policy covering the aircraft (referred to as Lark 9502) in which the two men were killed. Both Phillips and Ivadelle Bruner claim liability coverage for the wrongful death claim arising out of the crash. . . .

As written, the policy does not cover a student pilot. "Student pilot" is a separate category of pilot under Federal Air Regulations, and flight conducted by a student "pilot" is authorized only after the issuance of a student pilot "certificate." . . .

The trial court could reasonably have found that there was an oral contract between Phillips and Ranger (through its agents) by which a student pilot was insured. The general rule is that a parol contract of insurance is valid and enforceable. This is true where there is a showing that the parties have agreed on all the essential terms of the contract, including the subject matter, the risk insured against, the time of commencement and duration of the risk, the amount of insurance and the amount of the premium. . . .

Turning now to the evidence in the case, Phillips testified that student instruction was one of the services he provided and that he would not have considered insurance without such coverage. Initially he contacted his own insurance agent, Sabatelli Insurance Agency. Not being familiar with aircraft insurance, Sabatelli contacted John Sanderson who was employed by American Underwriters Agencies, Inc. (American). . . .

The product of these communications was a written "set-up" sheet in Alderman's handwriting, whereby coverage was arranged for "student, private or commercial pilots" on five aircraft, including Lark 9502, the one which crashed. The words "student, private or commercial pilots" were thereafter crossed out on the "set-up" sheet by Alderman without Phillips' knowledge or consent. The written policy, absent an endorsement for student pilot coverage, was thereafter issued on February 27, 1967, but, as has been pointed out, the policy was not delivered to Phillips until after April 20, 1967, the date of the accident, nor was Phillips informed that the written policy did not provide student pilot coverage. We find that this evidence was sufficient for the trial court to find that student pilot coverage had been sought by Phillips and contracted for by Ranger through its agents.

Appellant argues that Phillips was neither charged nor did he pay a premium for student pilot coverage. This is not, however, controlling as to the issue of whether coverage was provided by Ranger. If by not charging the higher premium Ranger intended not to cover student pilots, contrary to the mutual understanding of the parties, that fact was never communicated to Phillips. No policy had ever been delivered which would have indicated to Phillips the extent of coverage provided and a breakdown of premiums charged. . . .

In conclusion, the true contract of insurance in this case was found by the trial court to be that which arose out of the oral agreement between the parties and not that as evidenced by the written policy. . . .

DECISION: The court of appeals affirmed the trial court's decision.

Insurable Interest

To eliminate gambling and immoral activities, the law allows only certain people to obtain insurance covering specific risks. If anyone could purchase a large life insurance policy on a stranger's life or personal property, people might be tempted to purchase such insurance and cause that death or property damage just to collect the insurance benefits. Thus the law requires a person to have an *insurable interest*, such that another person's loss or injury would result in a direct loss or injury to that person.

If you own property or even lease property, you have an insurable interest in it. Shareholders in a closely held corporation would have such an interest in the property of the corporation. In life insurance a close relative, business associate, or creditor of another person would have an insurable interest enabling him or her to take out life insurance on that person's life. For the purchase of life insurance the insurable interest must exist at the time the policy is taken out. For other forms of insurance the insurable interest must exist at the time of the loss.

An insured may take out a life insurance policy on his own life and assign the benefits due under the policy to any person, even if that person does not have an insurable interest in the insured's life. Fire and casualty insurance policies can be assigned only with the approval of the insurer.

The concept of an insurable interest is discussed in the following case.

ERIE-HAVEN, INC. V. TIPPMANN REFRIGERATION CONSTRUCTION
Court of Appeals of Indiana
486 N.E.2d 646 (1985)

BACKGROUND: Erie-Haven leased a building to Tippmann Refrigeration Construction. The building was destroyed by fire. Erie-Haven maintained an insurance policy on the building and was paid $79,594.14 in proceeds after the fire. Tippmann sued, claiming that it was entitled to share in the proceeds. Tippmann did not have an ownership interest in the building, although the lease did give Tippmann the option to buy the building. Tippmann argued that most of the building's value derived from improvements made by Tippmann. The trial court awarded Tippmann $57,546.56 out of the proceeds, and Erie-Haven appealed.

Hoffman, Judge

In order to maintain a valid insurance policy, the insured must have an insurable interest in the property. An insurable interest exists when one obtains a benefit from the existence of the property or would suffer a loss from destruction of the property. It is not essential that the insured hold title of any kind to the property. Both the lessor and the lessee have an insurable interest in the property which is the subject of the lease. The extent of the interest of each and thus the right to insurance proceeds is determined as of the time of the fire.

Although the holding of an unexercised option does not create a present interest in property in the lessee, a lessee has an interest in the property to the extent of the unexpired term of the lease. In addition, a lessee who makes improvements on the leased property, has an insurable interest in those improvements.

Here Tippmann had made improvements and occupied the premises in a continuous and uninterrupted manner from the time of the improvements until the destruction of same. The lease was still unexpired as was the option to purchase at the time of the destruction. Tippmann therefore had a pecuniary interest in the improvements at the time of the destruction regardless of the contract provisions for ownership of the improvements at expiration or cancellation of the lease since neither had yet transpired.

While the risk of eventual loss of an interest in the improvements at time of cancellation or expiration or exercise of option was placed on lessee by the lease in Paragraph 4, the risk of destruction of or damage to same during the interim was covered by the provisions for insurance at lessor's expense in Paragraph 8 and entitles lessee to recover the proceeds applicable to his interest.

The trial court determined the lessee was entitled to $57,546.56. Considering the extent of the improvements by lessee, the increased value of the property due to those improvements and the use of the value of those improvements by Erie-Haven to establish its loss, the award is within the evidence and consistent with the principles established in *Loving v. Ponderosa Systems, Inc.*, preventing a windfall to a lessor who has not suffered a loss to the extent of available proceeds and allowing equitable relief to a lessee who has complied with the terms of the lease and been injured substantially.

DECISION: The appeals court affirmed the trial court's award of $57,546.56 to Tippmann.

Premiums

Premiums for life insurance coverage generally are paid by the insured over a long time period, whereas payments for casualty, fire insurance, health, and accident insurance are usually paid over short time periods. The premiums charged on a life insurance policy are determined on the basis of mortality rates, guaranteed interest, and expenses. The mortality rates are based on the experience of insurance companies in the past with the rate of death. Premiums also reflect the rate of interest the company expects to earn on the money it receives in premiums and the expenses it incurs for medical examinations, commission payments to its agents, and operating expenses.

The premiums charged for many kinds of business and casualty insurance are based primarily on the company's evaluation of the risks it is assuming. Rates charged for certain kinds of casualty and business insurance are regulated by state law. The regulating authority seeks to allow the company to charge rates that are high enough to provide the company with a reasonable return on its assets and low enough so that people and businesses desiring insurance will not find its cost prohibitive.

Allocation of Costs between Insurer and Insured

Insurance policies often provide that the insured will have to bear some of the cost of an insured event. Costs are allocated between the insurer and the insured through the use of deductibles and coinsurance. When a **deductible** is in place, the insured must pay the first part of any insured cost up to the amount of the deductible.

Assume, for example, that Harry's health insurance policy has a $500 annual deductible. That means that Harry will have to pay the first $500 of insured health expenses that he incurs each year. The insurer will only have to reimburse Harry for insured expenses incurred that year in excess of $500. In this example, Harry's deductible is applicable for a period of time (1 year). Once Harry has incurred $500 in insured medical expenses during a given year, all of his additional health expenses will be reimbursed (in full or in part, depending upon the policy) until the end of the year. When the next year begins, Harry will again have to pay his first $500 of insured medical expenses until the insurer is required to pay its share.

A deductible may also, on the other hand, apply to each insured event. Assume that Harry's auto insurance policy includes a $1,000 deductible per occurrence. That means that each time Harry has an accident, he will have to pay the first $1,000 in damages before the insurer becomes obligated to pay. If Harry has two accidents in 1 year, the amount that he had to pay toward his deductible after the first accident will not count toward his deductible for the second accident. However, some policies combine a deductible per occurrence with a limit on the total deductible that the insured will be required to pay in any given year.

A person shopping for insurance can generally get lower premiums if he or she is willing to accept a higher deductible.

Another way of allocating costs between the insured and the insurer is through coinsurance. **Coinsurance** is a percentage limit on the amount of an insured cost that the insurer is required to bear. A health plan, for example, might provide that only 80 percent of the cost of doctor visits will be paid for by the insurer.

Coinsurance is commonly used in fire insurance policies and in other policies that protect property against hazards. Coinsurance clauses in such policies generally limit the amount of insurance that can be collected for a partial loss. The typical coinsurance clause works as follows: In the event of a partial loss, the insurer will compare the amount of coverage with the current value of the property. If the amount of coverage is less than some stated percentage (typically 80 percent) of the property's value, then the insured will not be fully compensated for the loss. The lower the amount of coverage as a percentage of the current property value, the lower the percentage of the loss that the insurer will cover. A coinsurance clause is thus designed to encourage property owners to purchase insurance that fully covers, or nearly covers, the full market value of their property. Property owners who underinsure their property will have to bear a greater percentage of the cost if property damage occurs.

Subrogation

When a person suffers a loss as a result of another person's negligent or intentionally tortious behavior, the person may generally recover the amount of his or her loss from the tortfeasor. But what if a person's loss is covered by his or her own insurance? If we allow the person to recover from the tortfeasor as well as from the insurer, the person would receive double compensation for the loss. And what about the insurer, who has to pay for the tortfeasor's damage? Shouldn't the insurer be able to recover its loss directly from the tortfeasor?

To prevent the insured from receiving a windfall and to allow the insurer to recover its loss from the tortfeasor, the insurer in many types of insurance is given the right of *subrogation*. The doctrine of **subrogation**, as applied to insurance, provides that an insurer who has paid for its insured's loss steps into the shoes of the insured with respect to any claim relating to the loss that the insured may have had against third parties.

Suppose that Merv is speeding around a tight curve, loses control of his car, veers off the road, and smashes into Wanda's house. Merv causes $10,000 worth of damage to the house, all of which is covered by Wanda's insurance. Once Wanda's insurance company has paid Wanda the cost of repairing her house, the insurance company becomes *subrogated* to Wanda's claim against Merv. This means that Wanda's claim against Merv for negligence (or maybe even gross negligence) passes to Wanda's insurance company. The insurance company now steps into

Wanda's shoes, may assert any claim that Wanda had and is subject to any defense that Merv may have had against Wanda. Thus Wanda's insurance company will presumably recover $10,000 from Merv (or Merv's insurance company), and the loss will be allocated to the party responsible for it.

The insurer is generally given the right of subrogation as a matter of law when the insurer pays for property damage that was caused by a third party.

Defenses of the Insurer

People who purchase insurance may believe that the insurance contract is filled with fine print and that thousands of different defenses are asserted by companies refusing to pay claims against the policy. In fact, in addition to the ordinary defenses used in contract cases, only three defenses are generally used by insurance companies seeking to avoid paying an otherwise valid claim. The three defenses commonly asserted by the insurer are concealment, misrepresentation, and breach of warranty.

Concealment

Concealment is the intentional failure of the insured to disclose a material fact to the insurer that would affect the insurer's willingness to accept the risk. For example, a driver who fails to reveal convictions for drunken driving when applying for an automobile insurance policy is committing concealment. The essence of concealment is the intentional nondisclosure of a material fact. However, if an insurance application specifically asks the applicant for information and the applicant provides false information, misrepresentation, not concealment, occurs.

Misrepresentation

Misrepresentation occurs when a prospective insured intentionally or innocently misrepresents a material fact that leads an insurer to enter into an insurance contract. The misrepresentation may be oral or written. It may be made on the insurance application form or in written or oral statements made while discussing the possible insurance contract. A person who states that she or he is in perfect health when in fact she or he has been under recent treatment for a heart condition makes a misrepresentation.

Only a material misrepresentation provides the insurer with a defense. Further, if the insurer investigates and learns the truth before issuing the insurance policy, it cannot rely on the representation made by the applicant. In that case, because the applicant's statement did not induce the insurer to enter into the contract (the insurer knew the statement to be false), the insurer would not have a valid defense to payment of the insurance benefits.

Finally, whether the misrepresentation is innocent or intentional, the insurer would have a defense. The principal difference between the innocent and intentional misrepresentation concerns the effect of the misrepresentation on the remedy available to the insurer. The principal remedy available to the insurer is rescission, but damages are available if the misrepresentation was intentional instead of innocent. Rescission returns the parties to their places prior to the making of the contract. Thus the insurer must return all un-

used premiums and the insured is without the insurance coverage that the policy provided.

To be effective, the rescission by the insurer must be made as soon as the misrepresentation is discovered. Statutes generally require that life insurance contracts include an **incontestability clause**. Typically, this clause provides that after the passage of a set period of time (usually 1 or 2 years) the insurer may not contest the representations of the insured. One exception to the incontestability clause exists for a life insurance applicant who misrepresents his or her age. Even if the 2-year period of incontestability has passed, a contract provision usually limits the amount of benefits payable on the insured's death to the amount that the paid premiums would have purchased for a person of the insured's actual age.

The opinion that follows illustrates a classic case of misrepresentation. Note the creative argument made by the attorney for the party that made the misrepresentation.

MUTUAL BENEFIT LIFE INSURANCE CO. V. JMR ELECTRONICS CORP.

U.S. Court of Appeals
848 F.2d 30 (2d Cir. 1988)

BACKGROUND: JMR bought from Mutual a $250,000 "key man" life insurance policy on its president, Joseph Gaon. ("Key man" policies insure companies against the loss of their president or other top officers.) In the application, Gaon claimed to be a nonsmoker; the company was thus allowed to purchase the policy at the low rates available for nonsmokers. Actually, Gaon was a heavy smoker and had been one for several years. Gaon died within the policy's period of contestability, and Mutual discovered that Gaon was a smoker. Mutual sued to rescind the policy, and JMR counterclaimed for the proceeds. The federal district court, Judge Sweet presiding, ruled in favor of Mutual. JMR appealed.

Per Curiam

Under New York law, which governs this diversity suit, "[i]t is the rule that even an innocent misrepresentation as to [the applicant's medical history], if material, is sufficient to allow the insurer to avoid the contract of insurance or defeat recovery thereunder." *Process Plants Corp. v. Beneficial National Life Insurance Co.* A "misrepresentation" is defined by statute as a false "statement as to past or present fact, made to the insurer . . . at or before the making of the insurance contract as an inducement to the making thereof." N.Y. Ins. Law § 3105(a). A misrepresentation is "material" if "knowledge by the insurer of the facts misrepresented would have led to a refusal by the insurer to make such contract." § 3105(b). Case law has somewhat broadened the materiality inquiry: "The question . . . is not whether the company *might have issued* the policy even if the information had been furnished; the question in each case is whether the company has been induced to accept an application which it *might otherwise have refused."* Geer v. Union Mutual Life Insurance Co.

In the present case JMR has stipulated that Gaon's smoking history was misrepresented in the insurance application. However, JMR disputes that this misrepresentation is material as a matter of law. JMR argues that under New York law a misrepresentation is not material unless the insurer can demonstrate that, had the applicant provided complete and accurate information, coverage either would have been refused or at the very least withheld pending a more detailed underwriting examination. In JMR's view summary judgment was inappropriate on the facts of this case because a jury could reasonably have found that even "had appellee been aware of Gaon's smoking history, a policy at the smoker's premium rate would have been issued." JMR takes the position that the appropriate remedy in this situation is to permit recovery under the policy in the amount that the premium actually paid would have purchased for a smoker.

We agree with Judge Sweet that this novel theory is without basis in New York law. The plain language of the statutory definition of "materiality," found in section 3105(b), permits avoidance of liability under the policy where "knowledge of . . . the facts misrepresented would have led to a refusal by the insurer to make *such contract."* (Emphasis added.) Moreover, numerous courts have observed that the materiality inquiry under New York law is made with respect to the particular policy issued in reliance upon the misrepresentation. . . .

There is no doubt that Mutual was induced to issue the non-smoker, discounted-premium policy to JMR precisely as a result of the misrepresentation made by Gaon concerning his smoking history. That Mutual might not have refused the risk on *any* terms had it known the undisclosed facts is irrelevant. Most risks are insurable at some price. The purpose of the materiality inquiry is not to permit the jury to rewrite the terms of the insurance agreement to conform to the newly disclosed facts but to make certain that the risk insured was the risk covered by the policy agreed upon. If a fact is material to the risk, the insurer may avoid liability under a policy if that fact was misrepresented in an application for that policy whether or not the parties might have agreed to some other contractual arrangement had the critical fact been disclosed. As observed by Judge Sweet, a contrary result would reward the practice of misrepresenting facts critical to the underwriter's task because the unscrupulous (or merely negligent) applicant "would have everything to gain and nothing to lose" from making material misrepresentations in his application for insurance. Such a claimant could rest assured not only that he may demand full coverage should he survive the contestability period, but that even in the event of a contested claim, he would be entitled to the coverage that he might have contracted for had the necessary information been accurately disclosed at the outset. New York law does not permit this anomalous result.

DECISION: The circuit court of appeals affirmed the district court's ruling in favor of Mutual.

Warranties and Other Conditions

Insurance policies invariably include a number of conditions to the insurer's obligation to pay. The insurer will typically warrant that a number of conditions are true at the time the policy is issued, or will be true during the life of the policy. If the condition specified fails to occur, the insurer is not obligated to pay. A condition may express the limits of the insurer's liability. For example, the following clause specifies the time period and the locations of accidents that are or are not covered by an automobile insurance policy:

This automobile policy applies only to accidents occurring during the policy period while the automobile is within the United States, its territories, or Canada.

Similarly, a liability policy may provide time limits affecting the insurer's obligation to pay policy claims. A common clause is one that states:

The insurer shall not be liable unless suit is brought within 12 months from the date of the occurrence of the loss or of the event giving rise to a claim.

Generally the trend is away from allowing an insurer to avoid liability on the policy for any breach of a warranty made by the insured. Instead, as in the case of misrepresentation, the breach of warranty must be regarded as material to be given effect. Statutes in some states provide that all statements made by an applicant for life insurance will be considered to be representations and not warranties. Thus the materiality requirement must be met for the insurer's defense to be valid.

Table 52-2 lists the major defenses available to an insurer.

Interpretation of Insurance Contracts

Waiver, Estoppel, and Unconscionability

The doctrines of waiver, estoppel, and unconscionability, discussed earlier in the book in the context of contract law and sales law, can be invoked to prevent an insurer from asserting a defense that would otherwise be available. These concepts will be reviewed briefly here in the context of insurance law.

A *waiver* is the voluntary relinquishment of a known right. Actions by an insurance agent that waive, on behalf of the company, some factual concealment by the applicant exemplify the waiver.

Estoppel, as we have noted in earlier chapters, is the prevention of a person from asserting a position that is inconsistent with his or her actions or conduct when such actions or conduct have been justifiably relied on by the other party. Thus a company that periodically accepts premium payments from an insured that are late by several weeks is estopped later from asserting that a similar late payment of premiums is a defense to its obligation to continue the insurance coverage. The prior conduct of accepting the payments in earlier months estops the company from asserting the warranty defense (payments must be made before the policy is in effect) for similar subsequent late payments.

Both waiver and estoppel are specific legal concepts that prevent an insurance company from assessing a defense to the payment of benefits. However, the general concept of unconscionability also affects the defenses available to the insured. *Unconscionability* is the quality of being shocked to the conscience. As we noted in Chapter 16, when one party has little bargaining power and is faced with a standard contract that cannot be altered and that has been prepared by the other party, the courts may declare the contract or particular parts of it unconscionable and unenforceable.

Performance and Termination

As with contracts generally, most insurance contracts are performed according to their terms. The

TABLE **52-2**

	Concept Summary Insurer's Defenses
Concealment	Insured's intentional failure to disclose a material fact.
	Example: Applicant for life insurance fails to disclose a rare serious illness not detectable by the insurer's physical examination.
Misrepresentation	Insured intentionally or innocently misrepresents a material fact. Most states require life insurance contracts to include an incontestability clause which prohibits insurer from contesting insured's representations (other than age) after a certain date.
	Example: Applicant states, in response to a question on an auto insurance application that she has not been involved in an auto accident in the last 3 years. Actually, she was involved in a recent accident that was never reported to the police or the state authorities.
Failure of condition	Insured's obligation to fulfill conditions of the policy is not met.
	Example: Auto insurance policy requires insured to notify insurer promptly in the event of an accident. Insured fails to report an accident for 1 year, making it impossible for the insurer to properly investigate the accident.

payment of premiums by the insured and the payment of benefits due by the insurer usually constitute performance of the insurance contract. Full performance terminates the obligations of both the insured and the insurer under the contract.

Cancellation   A policy of insurance may also provide that the insurer has the option to cancel the policy after the happening of an insured event. If cancellation occurs before the end of the effective date for which premiums have been paid, the unearned premiums must be returned by the insurer. Thus cancellation is another way of terminating the insurance contract. The *Spindle* case shows how a cancellation clause in an insurance contract may be interpreted.

SPINDLE V. TRAVELERS INSURANCE COS.
Court of Appeals of California
136 Cal.Rptr. 404 (1977)

BACKGROUND: Spindle, a neurosurgeon in California, had malpractice liability insurance coverage by virtue of the agreement between Travelers (along with Phoenix Insurance Co., hereinafter the insurer) and the Southern California Physicians Council, a nonprofit association of 7,000 physicians and surgeons (including Spindle) in Southern California. Spindle claims the insurer agreed to provide liability insurance for the council members beginning in January 1974 and continuing as long as those members did not have excessive claims filed against them. Despite that agreement, and even though no malpractice claims were filed against Spindle, the insurer notified Spindle of its intent to cancel his insurance as of August 1975.

Spindle (plaintiff) sued Travelers and Phoenix (defendants) for breaching their agreement and warranty not to cancel his insurance except for excessive claims. Defendant insurers claimed their insurance policy clearly gave them the right to cancel plaintiff's malpractice liability insurance simply by providing 30 days notice of the cancellation. The trial court dismissed Spindle's suit. Spindle appealed.

Jefferson, Associate Judge

It is plaintiff's contention that defendant was seeking a premium increase of 141 percent while members of the Council were resisting this percentage increase and contending that the Master Contract between the Council and defendant Phoenix limited such increase during the period from January 2, 1975 to January 1, 1976, to 15 percent. In effect, plaintiff alleges that his malpractice insurance policy was cancelled to serve as an example to other members so they would agree to the greater premium increase sought by defendant, the only insurer in a position to insure them.

Plaintiff alleges that he was informed by Norman Aronson, head of the Professional Claims Department of defendant Travelers, that his insurance would not have been cancelled had the Council agreed to the 141 percent premium increase.

Plaintiff further alleges that, at the time of cancellation, defendant Phoenix was aware that plaintiff would be unable to practice medicine and surgery in hospitals without malpractice insurance. He also states that the wrongful cancellation of his insurance was "intended as a threat and a warning" to every member of the Council, *i.e.,* that the members could each expect similar treatment if they opposed the premium increase. . . .

In asserting by their demurrer that plaintiff's amended complaint fails to state a cause of action, defendants rely on what they regard as their "absolute" right, set forth in the contract with the Council and in the contract with plaintiff, to cancel the policy of insurance for any reason upon which they chose to act. We note that the Master Contract . . . provides: "No provision of this Agreement . . . shall restrict the rights of cancellation specified in the policies of insurance issued pursuant to this Agreement." We note also that plaintiff's particular policy provides: ". . . This policy may be cancelled by the *Company* by *mailing* to the *named insured* at the address shown in this policy, written *notice stating when,* not less than 30 days thereafter, such *cancellation shall be effective."* (Emphasis added except for "named insured.") . . .

It is the plaintiff's contention that public policy requires the rule of law that precludes an insurance carrier from possessing the right to cancel a policy for a malicious reason such as the wrongful objective of making an "example" of plaintiff, the insured, during the struggle between the Council and its members and defendant Phoenix over the problem of premium increases. Defendants reject the notion that public policy requires, as plaintiff contends, that the legal principle of good faith and fair dealing between an insurer and its insured be extended to include a limitation on insurer's right to cancel malpractice insurance policies issued to its insured. . . .

Despite the absence of an expressed "public policy" basis pursuant to existing California decisional law, it is clear that the right of insurers to cancel insurance policies is not absolute in this state. Sections 660 through 679.73 of the Insurance Code deal with the subjects of cancellation and failure to renew particular kinds of insurance policies such as automobile liability policies and property loss policies. Section 661 sets forth and limits specifically the grounds upon which an automobile liability or collision policy may be cancelled, and section 676 specifies and limits the grounds for cancellation of property loss policies. . . .

In addition, there is the area of developed case law in California which pertains to the matter of bad faith in carrying out the terms of a contract. While defendants term plaintiff's allegations of bad faith as "absurd," we note again that in a demurrer situation, we are compelled to accept plaintiff's allegation as true for the purpose of weighing the sufficiency of the amended complaint against a demurrer thereto, and need not concern ourselves with any problems of proof that plaintiff Spindle may encounter in a trial.

"There is an implied covenant of good faith and fair dealing in *every contract* that neither party will do anything which will injure the right of the other to receive the benefits of the agreement.

"This principle is applicable to policies of insurance." . . .

We are unable to discern any logical basis for distinguishing between an insurer's conduct in settling a claim made pursuant to the policy and that involved in an insurer's cancelling a policy if bad-faith conduct is the basis for the cancellation. The situations are similar in that the ultimate result of the conduct of the insurer effectively deprives the insured of the benefit of his bargain, *i.e.,* the coverage for the period for which he paid a premium. Cancellation provisions of a contract are subject to the covenant of good faith and fair dealing just as are other provisions of a contract. No plausible reason exists why cancellation provisions of a contract should be treated differently from other contractual provisions insofar as application of the implied covenant of good faith and fair dealing is concerned. . . .

In the instant case, the deprivation to the insured of the benefit of his bargain is greater than average due to the lack of competition in the field of malpractice insurance alleged in the amended complaint.

DECISION: The court of appeals reversed the trial court's dismissal and remanded the case to the trial court.

Notice Provisions The nonperformance by one party of material terms of a contract generally excuses the other party's duty to perform. Clearly, nonpayment of premiums terminates any performance obligation of the insurer. On the other hand, many insurance contracts have notice clauses that require the insured to notify the insurer within a specified time of a claim that the insurer is obligated to pay. If the insured does not give this notice, the obligation to perform by the insurer may be discharged or excused. But these notice provisions usually are not strictly enforced. Instead, a reasonable time requirement is imposed. Of course, because the notice provision allows the insurance company to begin its investigation regarding its liability in a timely manner, such provisions benefit both the insurer and the insured. In the *Milam* case the court is faced with interpreting the notice provisions found in an automobile policy.

STATE FARM MUTUAL AUTOMOBILE INSURANCE COMPANY V. MILAM

U.S. District Court
438 F. Supp.227 (S.D.W.VA., 1977)

BACKGROUND: Carlos Milam (defendant) was the insured on a policy of automobile liability insurance issued by State Farm (plaintiff). On June 17, 1973, Andrew Milam, Carlos's 19-year-old son, was driving a truck owned by Jarrell. The truck veered off the road and struck three pedestrians, killing one and injuring two others.

Andrew Milam was arrested and charged with negligent homicide while under the influence of drugs. He pleaded guilty and was sentenced to a year in jail and a $100.00 fine. On January 29, 1974 a civil case was filed against both Andrew and Carlos Milam by one of the persons who was injured. Soon after the suit was filed, Carlos learned that Andrew perhaps was covered by the insurance policy issued by State Farm. He then notified State Farm of the accident and asked it to defend Andrew in the civil case. State Farm refused, claiming it first learned of the January 17, 1973, accident and the January 29, 1974, civil suit on April 29, 1974. State Farm sought a declaratory judgment. It argued that Milam's failure to give it timely and adequate notice of the accident, as required by its insurance policy, was grounds for it to refuse to defend Andrew Milam in the civil suit brought against him.

Knapp, Chief Judge

Trooper W. W. Walker of the West Virginia State Police was the investigating officer of the tragic occurrence. By all accounts, including that of State Farm, Trooper Walker made a very thorough investigation of all the ascertainable circumstances surrounding the accident. . . .

This declaratory action was commenced on January 17, 1975. In paragraph 12 of the complaint, State Farm states that it has never denied coverage to Andrew Milam but has refused to defend him. On October 14, 1976, State Farm filed a motion for summary judgment. . . .

Affidavits of Carlos and Andrew Milam were filed in opposition to the summary judgment motion. These counter-affidavits were to the effect that the Milams were not aware that the accident should be reported to State Farm inasmuch as no State Farm insured vehicle was involved in the accident; that notice was given State Farm within a reasonable time and that in any event, State Farm suffered no prejudice in receiving notice of the accident when it did. . . .

Carlos Milam's testimony was that he . . . was unaware that his State Farm policy would provide Andrew with coverage and that no one even suggested this to him until April 29, 1974. . . .

* * *

The State Farm policy contained the following provision:

1. Notice. In the event of an accident or loss, written notice containing particulars sufficient to identify the insured and also reasonably obtainable information respecting the

time, place and circumstances of the accident, and the names and addresses of injured *persons* and available witnesses, shall be given by or on behalf of the *insured* to the company or any of its authorized agents as soon as practicable. If claim is made or suit is brought against the *insured,* he shall immediately forward to the company every demand, notice, summons or other process received by him or his representative. (Emphasis in original).

The purpose of a notice provision in policies of automobile liability insurance is to give the insurer an opportunity to make a timely and adequate investigation of the circumstances *surrounding the event* which resulted in the claim being made against an insured. . . .

In the case at bar we feel that whether or not State Farm was prejudiced by the 10 months' delay is a question of fact that the trier of the facts must decide.

It must be remembered, too, that in all of these "lack of notice" cases, the insurer, sooner or later, does receive notice of the occurrence. In order then for the insurer to successfully avail itself of the "lack of notice" defense, it must show that it was prejudiced by reason thereof. The test to apply is whether the insurer would be in a better position with regard to the investigation of the circumstances surrounding the event which resulted in the claim being made either against it or its insured had it been furnished notice within a reasonable time of the occurrence which gave rise to such claim.

Thus, the focal point of the test is with regard to how the accident occurred, or, more simply stated, "what happened?" In the instant case, State Farm does not seriously contend that the circumstances surrounding the accident were other than as set forth in Trooper Walker's report. That report, included in which was the statement of Andrew regarding the use of marijuana and how he felt as a result therefrom and a finding of lack of mechanical failure of the vehicle involved, taken together with Andrew's plea of guilty to the negligent homicide charge (i.e., an admission of such negligence), constitute beyond any peradventure as to "what happened."

Furthermore, there was no evidence adduced at the trial which showed or even tended to show that additional salient facts as to the events surrounding the accident could have been uncovered if notice had been received even at the earliest possible moment after the accident. There were no skid marks to observe, thus making a view of the scene of the accident a perfunctory act. . . .

In view of all of the foregoing, the Court, as trier of the facts in the case, accordingly finds as a fact that State Farm's rights were not prejudiced by the delay in receiving notice of the June 17, 1973 accident.

As quoted, supra, the "notice" provision of the State Farm policy required that written notice of an accident or loss be given "as soon as practicable." The West Virginia courts have interpreted the phrase "as soon as practicable" to mean "within a reasonable time, having regard to all of the circumstances." . . .

The explanation or excuse of the Milams for not reporting the accident was that neither had any idea that Carlos Milam's State Farm policy would afford coverage to Andrew while the latter was driving the Jarrell vehicle. We think that as a result of that tendered explanation, the issue of the timeliness of the notice is one of fact. Considering all of the circumstances in this case, we resolve this issue in favor of the defendants. Thus, we find and hold that notice was given "as soon as practicable."

DECISION: The U.S. District Court found for the defendants.

Insurance Firms

Forms of Organization

There are two major types of insurance organizations: stock companies and mutual companies. A **stock insurance company** is an insurance company organized in corporate form. The corporation is organized like other businesses. It generally has a board of directors, officers, employees, and shareholders. The shareholders may receive corporate profits in the form of dividends declared by the corporation's board of directors. The shareholders are not necessarily customers of the corporation.

A **mutual insurance company** is owned by the policyholders. By purchasing insurance from the company, the policyholders obtain the right to elect the directors and they in turn select the officers. Only policyholders may have an ownership interest in a mutual insurance company. A mutual insurance company does not have shareholders, and therefore it does not distribute any profit in the form of dividends.

Agents and Brokers

Because both the agent and the broker are agents of other parties in sales of insurance, you may find it helpful to review Chapter 35. Under the law of agency, an agent is a person who represents another person, the principal, and who is subject to control by the principal.

The **insurance agent** represents the insurance company (the insurer) that acts as the principal in the selling of insurance to third persons (the insured). The insurance agent who contracts with an applicant for insurance does so on behalf of the principal and not in his or her own right. The agent for an insurance company must be appointed by

---

ETHICS
An Ethical Problem for an Insurance Agent or Broker

An insurance agent is negotiating products liability coverage for a manufacturing firm with an insurance company underwriter. The agent knows that the Consumer Product Safety Commission (CPSC) is considering investigating the safety of one of the firm's products. If the commission does conduct such an investigation and recommends the client recall its product, the recall expenses of the client would be covered by the products liability insurance policy. The insurance company underwriter does not ask the insurance agent about any possible commission action against the firm. Does the agent have an ethical obligation to divulge the information he knows about the firm and its products to the insurance underwriter? Would the ethical obligation be the same for a broker?

Based on the Code of Professional Ethics of the American Institute for Property and Liability Underwriters, there appears to be no ethical obligation for an agent to volunteer information in his or her possession except when the information is specifically requested in the application, or by the underwriter, or if the agent knows the information is material to insurers and the agent has good reason to believe the insurer cannot readily discover the information. Here, the latter of these exceptions is applicable. The agent must have known that an investigation by the CPSC is material to insurers whose insurance covers recall expenses. Thus the agent is concealing a material fact, one that the insurer cannot readily discover. This is ethically wrong, and perhaps also illegal (if the omission was intentional, there might be fraud).

Legally the agent is a representative of the insurer, whereas the broker is a representative of the insured. While the legal obligations of the two differ, both have ethical obligations to their clients and to the public interest. The agent who represents the insurer (insurance company), of course, has the clearest obligation to divulge the information to his or her principal. However, even the broker, who represents the insured (manufacturing firm), has an ethical obligation not to conceal knowingly material information from an insurer.

the company he or she represents and must be licensed as a sales agent by the state. An independent agent represents more than one insurer and thus can select from those companies for the insurance needs of the insured.

An **insurance broker** represents the buyer of insurance, by placing an order with an insurance company on behalf of that buyer. The broker is the representative or agent for the insured, and, like the insurance agent, generally is compensated through commissions paid by the insurance companies. Unlike an agent, the broker does not represent one insurance company but chooses the company to write policies needed by the insured. The state licensing requirements imposed on brokers are generally higher than those on insurance agents. Some states allow only agents, not brokers, to write insurance within their boundaries.

Review Questions and Problems

Key Terms

insurance	homeowner's insurance
insurer/insured	renter's insurance
insurance policy	automobile insurance
premiums	no-fault automobile insurance
life insurance	credit insurance
beneficiary	title insurance
whole life insurance	business interruption insurance
cash surrender value	worker's compensation insurance
ordinary life insurance	self insurance
paid-up amount	binder
limited-payment life insurance	deductible
single-premium life insurance	coinsurance
term life insurance	subrogation
universal life insurance	concealment
endowment policy	misrepresentation
annuity contract	incontestability clause
fixed/variable annuity	stock insurance company
accident and health insurance	mutual insurance company
disability insurance	insurance agent
casualty insurance	insurance broker
liability insurance	

Discussion Questions

1. Describe the primary features and typical uses for whole life insurance, term life insurance, and endowment or annuity life insurance.

2. What type of coverage is generally provided in a health insurance policy? How does a group health insurance policy differ from an individual policy?

3. Why are the rules of offer and acceptance especially important in insurance contracts?

4. Describe the insurer's defenses of breach of warranty. What is the significance of an insurance policy's incontestability clause?

5. Explain how the insurer can use the defenses of concealment, misrepresentation, and breach of warranty against paying claims.

Review Problems

1. Jim Johnson just purchased an office building. He informs his agent at 10:00 A.M that he wants the building insured immediately. The agent represents only one company and tells him, "no problem, you are covered." The agent intends to begin processing the paperwork but is interrupted several times and decides to do the paperwork after lunch and relay the information to the insurer. When the insurance agent returns from lunch, he is informed that the building caught fire at 11:00 A.M. Is there an enforceable contract?

2. An application for property insurance explicitly stated that the building was to be used only as a center for teenagers. This was reiterated in the terms of the policy, giving it the effect of a warranty. The center for teenagers was a front for a legal, but unpopular dissident group. The group was subject to threats of violence and the building was burned down by a rival group. Can the insurer be allowed to avoid the terms of the policy?

3. The general agent of an insurer learned that an insured materially lied on an insurance application. The agent collects premiums on the policy, but doesn't report the discrepancy. The company has "knowledge" as imputed by the general agent. Does the insurer have a right to rescission when it accepts the premium and has knowledge of the discrepancy?

4. Sarah has been named in the will of her uncle, as he willed his mansion to "my daughter Joan for life, and then to Sarah in fee simple." The uncle had several operations before he died, and the hospital obtained a $40,000 judgment against him for bills due from his last illness. The savings and loan held a mortgage on the mansion and rented it to an attorney on a 2-year lease. Who would suffer a pecuniary (legally recognized) loss if the mansion was damaged or destroyed?

Case Problems

1. Moore's wife applied to the Palmetto Insurance Co. for accident insurance on her husband. Several weeks later, she asked Palmetto's agent as to the status of her application. He said he hadn't heard from Palmetto. Unknown to the agent, it had rejected her application. Mrs. Moore inquired again and the agent said he thought perhaps the policy had came in and that he'd check and if the policy was not in, he'd notify her. Mrs. Moore heard nothing for 2 weeks. Her husband was then accidentally killed. Several days later, Palmetto informed Mrs. Moore that her application had been rejected. Mrs. Moore sued Palmetto for breach of contract. Should she recover?

2. Cook purchased a life insurance policy from plaintiff, New York Life Insurance Co., and named as beneficiary defendant Baum, who was an agent of the plaintiff, and had lent Cook money for Cook's business. Some of the money had been lent before Cook purchased insurance from plaintiff, but most of it was lent after the policy went into effect. When New York Life found Baum was Cook's beneficiary, it required Cook to designate another beneficiary because its corporate policy prohibited one of its agents (such as Baum) from being a beneficiary. Cook named a corporation, which was to be created solely for that purpose. The corporation was not completely created. After Cook died, Baum claimed to be the legitimate beneficiary of the policy. New York Life claimed he did not have an insurable interest. Do you agree?

3. Armstrong purchased a fire insurance policy from the Travelers Insurance Co. The policy promised to pay the insured "the actual cash value" if the property being insured, a farmhouse, was totally destroyed by fire. After a fire destroyed Armstrong's farmhouse, Travelers asserted that the "actual cash value" as used in the policy meant the replacement cost of the farmhouse, less depreciation. Armstrong claims that since the policy provides it will indemnify him from loss, the actual cash value means the replacement cost, unaffected by depreciation. Who is correct?

4. In August, Mrs. Englert applied for automobile insurance with the American Family Insurance Co. A policy was issued effective August 9. Then, on September 1, Mrs. Englert received notice that due to the poor driving record of her husband, who would be a potential driver of the car being insured, her policy would be cancelled effective September 16. After Mrs. Englert was involved in an accident on September 3, the insurer discovered that Mrs. Englert's application contained misrepresentations regarding her own and her husband's driving record. Has the insurer waived the right to cancel her policy effective August 9, instead of September 16?

5. Daniel Corrales, a minor, and Andrea Behrens were waterskiing in the Corrales family boat when Andrea was injured. She sued Daniel's parents claiming they were negligent in failing to supervise Daniel's operation of the boat. The Corrales asked their homeowner's insurer, Aetna, to defend them because their policy covered "injury to another away from home" and the suit against them was based on their "negligent supervision" not their son's operation of the boat.

   Aetna refused their request because the policy excluded "bodily injury or property damage arising out of the . . . operation . . . of any water craft. Andrea won her suit against the Corrales; she seeks to recover against Aetna. Do you think Aetna's policy makes them liable?

53

Government Regulation and the Role of Administrative Agencies

History of Government Regulation

Administrative Agencies

Administrative Agencies and Constitutional Separation of Powers

Work of Administrative Agencies

Government Regulation and Administrative Agencies: An Evaluation

Government regulation is a fact of life for every business in America. Depending on the industry, government regulation may determine who may participate in the industry, what activities the business may engage in, how the business must go about hiring and promoting employees, how the workplace must be designed, how the firm's products must be labeled and handled, how much of the business's earnings must be paid to government, and a whole host of other issues. Businesspeople have long complained that there is simply too much government regulation, and that the productivity and competitiveness of American business has been stifled as a result. Others argue that the current level of government regulation is necessary to achieve desirable social objectives.

This chapter explains the process of government regulation and introduces its primary vehicle: the administrative agency. As we shall see, federal administrative agencies must satisfy a number of requirements in the performance of their regulatory function—in other words, the process of government regulation itself is highly regulated. After the basic principles of government regulation are laid down in this chapter, the chapters that follow will focus on the work of specific regulatory agencies.

History of Government Regulation

In the eighteenth century the royal governments of Europe regulated and sometimes monopolized all forms of commerce. Their fear of such centralized government and economic regulation led the founders of the United States to espouse private property concepts and a laissez-faire theory of government. Eventually, however, political leaders decided that at least certain forms of government regulation could be in the public interest. The Interstate Commerce Act (1887) was passed in response to farmers' complaints that the railroads were charging discriminatory rates. The Sherman Antitrust Act (1890) was passed in response to the growth of combinations or trusts in oil, whiskey, sugar, lead, and beef. Federal regulation grew with the passage of the Clayton Act (1914) and the Federal Trade Commission Act (1914).

The administration of Franklin D. Roosevelt, with its New Deal program designed to fight the Great Depression, created a host of new government agencies. The creation of such agencies as the Federal Communications Commission (FCC), the National Labor Relations Board (NLRB), and the Securities and Exchange Commission (SEC) initiated unprecedented federal regulation of business. With the advent of civil rights, environmental, and worker safety legislation in the 1960s and 1970s, new areas of regulation, along with new administrative agencies, came into being. In the federal government today we have over 150 regulatory agencies that affect all aspects of individual and business activity.

Administrative Agencies

Definition and Nature

Every type of business enterprise in the United States falls within the area of concern of one or more administrative agencies. Our political system operates so extensively through administrative agencies that they have been called a "fourth branch of government" and the United States has been described as an "administrative state." **Administrative agencies** can be defined as governmental bodies, other than the courts and legislatures, that carry out the administrative tasks of government and affect the rights of private parties through adjudication or rule making.

Administrative agencies are found at every level of government. Often they are called boards, commissions, or agencies; but department, bureau, division, office, or authority also frequently designate an administrative agency. A municipal health board, a county zoning commission, a state public utilities commission, and federal organizations such as the NLRB and the Internal Revenue Service are but a few of the many agencies that directly influence American life.

Administrative agencies differ considerably in size. In general, federal agencies are highly structured and staffed with hundreds or thousands of employees; state and local agencies tend to be smaller and more loosely organized. As a result, state and local agencies are more informal, and much important business is carried out behind the scenes by people who are personally acquainted with the problems and the parties or their representatives. People in state and local agencies are also usually acquainted with others in government and can interact with them informally. Frequently they work in the same office building, share other facilities, and have a background of common participation in state and local party politics.

Administrative agencies affect the rights of private parties in many ways. Some, such as parole boards and the Immigration and Naturalization Service of the U.S. Department of Justice, are concerned with matters involving rights as basic as liberty itself. Others, such as state workers' compensation boards, make determinations that involve substantial monetary claims. The Interstate Commerce Commission (ICC) and state public utility commissions fix rates that influence profits in sizable segments of the economy. A principal function of other agencies is to police certain types of activities, such as the sale of liquor, by granting licenses and permits. Many of these same agencies also attempt to protect the public by prohibiting certain actions under threat of fine or suspension of license.

Sometimes an agency has the power to bring criminal actions against those who violate a statute that the agency has been authorized to enforce. The fields in which agencies operate are extensive and their influence in our society is far-reaching.

Reasons for Growth

With the growth of federal legislation noted previously, Congress found it necessary to set up agencies to carry out the details of the statutes enacted. Congress is composed of 435 members of the House of Representatives and 100 senators. Collectively they could not realistically regulate the radio and television industry, for example, on a daily basis. Thus when passing the Federal Communications Act of 1933, they created the FCC. A second reason for creating the agencies was the need for expertise to deal with complex and technical details that demand attention. For example, imagine a new senator or representative attempting to deal with the daily regulation of satellite communications. Members of the FCC staff have the training and experience to perform that task. A third reason Congress created administrative agencies was to keep a large number of complex cases out of the already overcrowded federal courts. To the extent that the ICC can settle disputes over trucking routes, for example, it keeps trucking cases out of court.

Administrative Procedure Act and Related Statutes

The operations of federal administrative agencies are governed by the **Administrative Procedure Act** (APA), which sets forth rules that agencies must follow when they promulgate regulations and when they adjudicate disputes. Specific provisions of the APA are discussed throughout the chapter. Most states have enacted legislation to govern the operation of state administrative agencies, and many of these state statutes are modeled at least in part on the APA.

The APA was amended in 1966 by the Freedom of Information Act, which entitles any person to records and other information possessed by any federal agency. The agency generally must respond to a request for information within 10 working days. There are certain categories of information that the agency is not required to release. For example, the public is not entitled to information on matters affecting national security. However, the burden is on the agency to establish that the information requested falls within a specific exemption to the Act.

The APA was amended again in 1976 by the government's Sunshine Act, which generally requires meetings of federal agencies to be announced in advance and open to the public. The Act does not apply to staff meetings—only to meetings of the actual members of the commission or board in which agency business is transacted. The Act also allows closed meetings to be held in certain situations.

Administrative Agencies and Constitutional Separation of Powers

Historically our government has been viewed as composed of three independent branches: the executive, the legislative, and the judicial. Each possesses certain powers that enable it to restrain, but not entirely control, the actions of the others. The relationships between administrative agencies and the traditional branches of government influence to a large degree what agencies can accomplish. A working knowledge of these relationships is important to businesspeople, for they can use this knowledge to modify the impact of agency activity.

Before examining the relationships, we need to consider an important difference in the lines of authority between certain agencies and the executive branch. Several of the largest and most influential federal agencies are not part of any department of the executive branch. The ICC, FTC, SEC, and NLRB are examples of **independent agencies** that are very important to the business community. In some states major administrative agencies are independent of the chief executive. Many state constitutions provide for the election of important administrative officers, such as the attorney general and the state treasurer, and deny the governor the right to remove even appointive department heads except for cause.

On the other hand, some well-known federal agencies are parts of **executive departments**. For example, both the Food and Drug Administration and the Social Security Administration are parts of the U.S. Department of Health and Human Services. The Federal Aviation Administration (FAA) is a part of the U.S. Department of Transportation. Most local agencies and a majority of state agencies are also organized within larger executive departments. On a day-to-day basis this does not make much difference because the agencies operate without interference from the other components of the executive branch, but when agencies are organized within the executive branch greater potential for direct control exists. Many major policy decisions within the jurisdictional power of the agencies may be influenced by the chief executive and his staff. Table 53-1 presents a sample of independent and executive agencies.

TABLE 53-1

Illustrative Independent and Executive Federal Administrative Agencies

Independent	Executive
Interstate Commerce Commission (ICC)	Small Business Administration (SBA)
Federal Trade Commission (FTC)	Occupational Safety and Health Administration (OSHA)
Securities and Exchange Commission (SEC)	National Science Foundation (NSF)
National Labor Relations Board (NLRB)	Office of Personnel Management (OPM)
Commodities Futures Trading Commission (CFTC)	Federal Aviation Administration (FAA)
Federal Reserve Board (FRB)	Department of Transportation (DOT)

Executive Branch and Independent Agencies

Although many federal agencies are structurally independent of the executive branch, the President, with the advice and consent of the Senate, does appoint the chief agency officials. Once the appointment is confirmed, however, the President has no direct control over the appointee. He cannot remove the individual from office. In addition, the enabling act that creates a commission generally requires that the commission itself be politically balanced within practical limits. The Federal Trade Commission Act, for example, provides as follows:

[A] commission is hereby created and established, to be known as the Federal Trade Commission, which shall be composed of five commissioners, who shall be appointed by the President by and with the advice and consent of the Senate. Not more than three of the commissioners shall be members of the same political party.

The terms of commissioners tend to be quite lengthy—7 years is typical—and thus considerable time may elapse before a newly elected President is able to put his personal "stamp" on one of the commissions. In addition, the length of the terms tends to make even a President's own appointees somewhat independent. But in spite of this and of their structural independence from the executive branch, the major regulatory agencies are in reality subject to considerable executive influence. A member of the presidential staff sometimes attempts directly to persuade a commissioner to adopt the President's position. Because the independent regulatory agencies presumably make their decisions without interference from the executive branch, this type of influence is generally viewed with disapproval. More frequently a presidential memorandum or the report of a presidential task force studying the matter also being investigated by a commission may be released to the public in a manner designed to sway the commission. Finally, executive influence may be asserted through the budgetary process. Agency requests for funds go through the Office of Management and Budget (OMB) and so are subject to executive surveillance. Executive orders 12291 and 12498, issued in 1980 and 1985, require all agencies in the executive branch to provide a yearly agenda to OMB of all proposed rulemaking.

Judicial Review and Administrative Agencies

Although the scope of judicial review of particular administrative agency decisions is limited, most state and federal administrative agency decisions are subject to review by the courts. The logic underlying the limitations on judicial review is that the agency, rather than the court, is the expert in those fields in which it has been empowered to act. The courts can reverse any action taken by an agency that is outside the scope of the agency's jurisdiction.

As will be discussed later, administrative agencies may perform two separate functions: (1) to issue rules and regulations and (2) to adjudicate cases. The criteria used by the courts in reviewing the actions of an agency may vary according to the functions involved. When an agency acts in a *legislative manner* the courts will review the agency action to make sure that:

1. The congressional delegation of legislative authority to the agency is constitutional in that Congress sufficiently limited the area within which the agency can act

2. The action of the agency was within the powers granted it by Congress

3. The agency action did not violate another constitutional limitation or disregard a prohibitory provision of an applicable federal statute

When an administrative agency acts in an *adjudicative context*, the courts review its procedures to ensure that

1. They are constitutionally valid

2. The agency had proper jurisdiction

3. The statutory rules controlling procedures have been observed

The courts may also review the agency's interpretation of substantive law in its adjudication, but they exercise substantial restraint in this area and their powers are limited.

Generally courts have accepted agency determinations of fact as final, provided that substantial evidence supporting the findings is shown by the record. Substantial evidence has been described as the kind of evidence on which responsible persons are accustomed to rely in serious affairs and as more than a mere scintilla. It means such relevant evidence as a reasonable mind might accept to support a conclusion. Courts also have refused to consider suits brought by those who question the wisdom of the agency's discretionary decisions. If an administrative agency decides to apply a greater portion of its resources, such as funds and personnel, to a particular segment of the industry over which it has jurisdiction than it has previously done, an individual adversely affected by this new policy is not entitled to judicial review. Businesspeople should object, however, to those discretionary agency decisions that appear to be clearly arbitrary or capricious, for courts will not allow these to stand even though the agency is the expert.

In spite of its limitations, judicial review of administrative agency actions is important to the business community. It provides a safeguard against administrative excesses and the unfair or arbitrary actions of overzealous officials. A court will be most likely to set aside an agency ruling when the agency has erred in the interpretation of a statute, has acted outside the scope of its authority, or appears to have denied due process by unfair agency procedures. The case that follows discusses the limits of judicial review for actions by agencies—and for the failure of agencies to act.

HECKLER V. CHANEY
U.S. Supreme Court
470 U.S. 821 (1985)

BACKGROUND: Death row inmates who were sentenced to die by lethal injection petitioned the federal Food and Drug Administration (FDA) to prevent the toxic drugs from being used in their executions. The prisoners argued that use of the drugs for executions was a violation of the Food, Drug, and Cosmetic Act (FDCA). After the FDA refused to take enforcement action, the prisoners sued the Secretary of Health and Human Services, who oversaw the FDA. The U.S. District Court granted summary judgment for the government, and the prisoners appealed. The Court of Appeals reversed, ruling that the FDA's refusal to take enforcement action was subject to judicial review under the Administrative Procedure Act (APA) and that the FDA's failure to take enforcement action was an abuse of discretion. The U.S. Supreme Court granted certiorari.

Rehnquist, Justice

This Court has recognized on several occasions over many years that an agency's decision not to prosecute or enforce, whether through civil or criminal process, is a decision generally committed to an agency's absolute discretion. This recognition of the existence of discretion is attributable in no small part to the general unsuitability for judicial review of agency decisions to refuse enforcement.

The reasons for this general unsuitability are many. First, an agency decision not to enforce often involves a complicated balancing of a number of factors which are peculiarly within its expertise. Thus, the agency must not only assess whether a violation has occurred, but whether agency resources are best spent on this violation or another, whether the agency is likely to succeed if it acts, whether the particular enforcement action requested best fits the agency's overall policies, and, indeed, whether the agency has enough resources to undertake the action at all. An agency generally cannot act against each technical violation of the statute it is charged with enforcing. The agency is far better equipped than the courts to deal with the many variables involved in the proper ordering of its priorities. Similar concerns animate the principles of administrative law that courts generally will defer to an agency's construction of the statute it is charged with implementing, and to the procedures it adopts for implementing that statute.

In addition to these administrative concerns, we note that when an agency refuses to act it generally does not exercise its *coercive* power over an individual's liberty or property rights, and thus does not infringe upon areas that courts often are called upon to protect. Similarly, when an agency *does* act to enforce, that action itself provides a focus for judicial review, inasmuch as the agency must have exercised its power in some manner. The action at least can be reviewed to determine whether the agency exceeded its statutory powers. Finally, we recognize that an agency's refusal to institute proceedings shares to some extent the characteristics of the decision of a prosecutor in the Executive Branch not to indict—a decision which has long been regarded as the special province of the Executive Branch, inasmuch as it is the Executive who is charged by the Constitution to "take Care that the Laws be faithfully executed."

We of course only list the above concerns to facilitate understanding of our conclusion that an agency's decision not to take enforcement action should be presumed immune from judicial review. . . . For good reasons, such a decision has traditionally been "committed to agency discretion," and we believe that the Congress enacting the APA did not intend to alter the tradition. In so stating, we emphasize that the decision is only presumptively unreviewable; the presumption may be rebutted where the substantive statute has provided guidelines for the agency to follow in exercising its enforcement powers. Thus, in establishing this presumption in the APA, Congress did not set agencies free to disregard legislative direction in the statutory scheme that the agency administers. Congress may limit an agency's exercise of enforcement power if it wishes, either by setting substantive priorities, or by otherwise circumscribing an agency's power to discriminate among issues or cases it will pursue.

* * *

The danger that agencies may not carry out their delegated powers with sufficient vigor does not necessarily lead to the conclusion that courts are the most appropriate body to police this aspect of their performance. That decision is in the first instance for Congress, and we therefore turn to the FDCA. . . . If it has indicated an intent to circumscribe agency enforcement discretion, and has provided meaningful standards for defining the limits of that discretion, . . . courts may require that the agency follow that law; if it has not, then an agency refusal to institute proceedings is a decision "committed to agency discretion by law" within the meaning of that section.

To enforce the various substantive prohibitions contained in the FDCA, the Act provides for injunctions, 21 U.S.C. § 332, criminal sanctions, §§ 333 and 335, and seizure of any offending food, drug, or cosmetic article, § 334. The Act's general provision for enforcement, § 372, provides only that "[t]he Secretary is *authorized* to conduct examinations and investigations . . ." (emphasis added). . . . [S]ection 332 gives no indication of when an injunction should be sought, and § 334, providing for seizures, is framed in the permissive—the offending food, drug, or cosmetic "shall be liable to be proceeded against." The section on criminal sanctions states baldly that any person who violates the Act's substantive prohibitions "shall be imprisoned . . . or fined." Respondents argue that this statement mandates criminal prosecution of every violator of the Act but they adduce no indication in case law or legislative history that such was Congress' intention in using this language. . . . We are unwilling to attribute such a sweeping meaning to this language, particularly since the Act charges the Secretary only with recommending prosecution; any criminal prosecutions must be instituted by the Attorney General. The Act's enforcement provisions thus commit complete discretion to the Secretary to decide how and when they should be exercised.

DECISION: The Supreme Court reversed the Court of Appeals decision, ruling that the FDA's failure to take enforcement action was not subject to judicial review.

Legislatures and Administrative Agencies

Agencies acquire their authority to act from the legislature. For a legislative grant of authority to be constitutional, it must set standards to guide the agency's actions because the legislature is either delegating some of its power to a nonelected body or authorizing it to perform a judicial function. The legislation creating an agency is called an **enabling act**. Since the 1930s very few respondents have successfully challenged the action of either state or federal agencies on the constitutional grounds that the act creating the agency did not include sufficient standards. Most modern enabling acts that allow an agency considerable discretion to act have been approved by the courts. Thus very broad and general standards may be constitutional. The Federal Trade Commission Act authorized the FTC to commence an action in a deceptive practice or false advertising case "if it shall appear to the Commission that a proceeding . . . would be in the interest of the public." The only standard is the Commission's own belief that an action is in the public interest.

Administrative agencies that have been created by the legislature can also be terminated by the legislature; however, the threat of termination has not been taken seriously in the past. Most legislative influence on agencies is the result of the agencies' dependence on the legislature for financial support. For example, much of the early history of the FTC was dominated by congressional refusal to finance the agency adequately. This was especially true in the early 1920s when the Commission planned an aggressive attack against the structure of American industry. Adverse congressional reaction to the Commission's investigation of the meat-packing industry led to a reduction in funds for the agency. Agency personnel had to be discharged, and Congress transferred jurisdiction over meat-packing to the U.S. Department of Agriculture. In addition, the agency was denied appropriations for other investigations that it had planned. More recently, after receiving harsh criticism in the late 1960s and early 1970s for being a "do nothing" agency, the FTC became active on behalf of consumers in such areas as deceptive advertising and antitrust. By 1980 the FTC, with its aggressive investigations and rule making, had alienated a large number of businesses, which then lobbied Congress for a cutback in the authority of the agency as well as in its level of funding. In response to this lobbying effort Congress enacted the FTC Improvement Act of 1980. The Act provided for some clear restraints on FTC operations and much closer scrutiny by Congress through the House and Senate commerce committees, which are responsible for overseeing the agency. For example, one provision forced the FTC to reconsider any order previously issued upon the request of the corporation or person involved if it can be shown that changed conditions of law or fact require an altering, modifying, or setting aside of the order. Additionally, the Act subjected any new FTC rule to a veto by a concurrent resolution of the House and Senate. The FTC was required to submit advance notice of rulemaking to the oversight committees in both the House and Senate. In its notice the FTC had to provide an explanation of the need for the new rule and its potential benefits and adverse effects. The Commission was barred from using any funds to issue or propose a regulation affecting the funeral industry similar to ones it had previously drafted. The 1980 Act forbade the use of funds for initiating or conducting an investigation of the insurance industry. It also put a 3-year moratorium on existing FTC authority to promulgate rules for unfair commercial advertising. When one reviews the 1980 Act, it is clear that Congress intended the FTC to be a less activist agency. It also explains why all administrative agencies tend to be solicitous of congressional views before launching investigations or proposing new rules.

Work of Administrative Agencies

Administrative agencies do much of the day-to-day work of government. As a consequence, they make many significant policy decisions. Businesspeople who fail to recognize this will lose an opportunity to influence governmental changes that might benefit them and society. Some businesspeople find that the record-keeping requirements of the various agencies that directly affect their business operations add significantly to costs and even adversely affect their competitive positions. Nevertheless, regulatory agencies perform many needed services and assist businesspeople by working to control potentially harmful market conditions.

The work done by a single administrative agency may encompass a broad range of activities. In addition, the general nature and scope of operations often vary significantly from agency to agency. Thus a broad generalization regarding the work of administrative agencies is almost impossible. Some agencies, such as draft boards, were created to accomplish very limited objectives; others have very extensive assignments. The FTC, for example (see Figure 53-1), has primary responsibility for enforcing the antitrust provi-

sions of the Clayton Act and the unfair business practices sections of the Federal Trade Commission Act. The Commission also has responsibility for carrying out all or some of the provisions of several other federal statutes.

An additional complication exists because agencies operate at all levels of government. As a result, they focus on problems and needs that are very different. In fact, arms of government sometimes appear to be working in opposition to each other. For example, at a time when the FCC was attempting to limit the sale of cigarettes by restricting television advertising, the U.S. Department of Agriculture continued to encourage the production of tobacco by paying price-supporting subsidies to tobacco growers.

The powers of those agencies that have the greatest impact on the business community are broad. Those agencies, which include the ICC, FTC, SEC, NLRB, and FCC, generally have the authority to make rules that have the force of law. Many agencies also function like courts. They settle disputes and hear and decide on violations of statutes or of their own rules. Finally, much of the work of agencies is administrative in nature. This covers a wide variety of duties: investigating firms in the regulated industry, determining if formal action should be brought, and negotiating settlements. A substantial number of agencies have administrative responsibilities but do not have adjudicatory or rulemaking powers.

Adjudication

One of the most important powers that most agencies have is to adjudicate claims and disputes that fall within the particular agency's jurisdiction. When exercising such power, the agency functions in a manner similar to a judicial body. In many instances, both state and federal agencies find facts and apply rules and regulations to these facts just as a court would. In carrying out this adjudicatory function, the federal agencies generally employ procedures similar to those used by the courts. This is probably due to the influence of the large number of legally trained people who are involved in some way with agency adjudication. In addition, the Administrative Procedure Act requires almost all federal agencies to meet certain standards in their procedures. As a result of these factors, generally there is considerable similarity in the enforcement procedures of fed-

FIGURE 53-1

The Federal Trade Commission

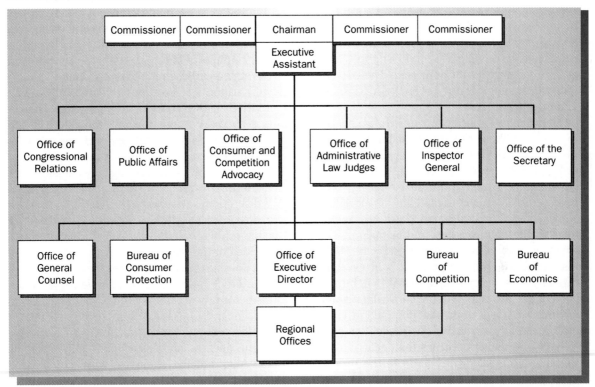

eral agencies, and state agencies frequently follow similar patterns. Thus we can examine the procedures of an agency such as the FTC and obtain an idea of how the adjudicatory function is performed in agencies in general.

In adjudication proceedings the FTC, like most administrative agencies, follows a procedure of "investigation–complaint–hearing–order." However, because of limited resources, the Commission makes a determined effort to prevent disputes from reaching the hearing stage; as a result, more than 90 percent of the investigations of violations do not result in hearings.

Many cases are administratively "closed" by the Commission because investigation fails to turn up sufficient evidence to substantiate a violation or because the public interest does not warrant the lengthy and costly investigation needed to develop the facts necessary to establish a prima facie case. In a substantial number of cases where evidence of a violation does exist, the Commission is able to dispose of the case before a hearing by a *consent decree* procedure. A **consent decree** is a document entered into by the

FTC and the respondent (corporation, partnership, or individual) which allows the respondent to avoid admitting any violation of the law, but which commits the respondent to stop engaging in the behavior that the Commission has challenged.

Both the Commission and the respondent benefit from the consent decree procedure. The FTC obtains a binding **cease-and-desist order**—that is, an order that prohibits the respondent from engaging in the activities that have been challenged—with minimal cost and without having to worry about appeal. Respondents benefit because the agreement is for settlement purposes only and does not constitute an admission of guilt. As a result, the order cannot be used in a triple-damage action brought against them, and respondents avoid the cost of litigation and the possible public disclosures that would stem from a formal hearing.

If settlement attempts are unsuccessful, an initial hearing is conducted by an *administrative law judge*. An **administrative law judge** (ALJ) is an impartial hearing officer within the agency who presides over administrative adjudications. The Administrative Procedure Act includes provisions designed to ensure that ALJs are impartial. For one thing, the ALJ may not be subject to supervision by anyone involved in the investigation or prosecution of violations of the statute that the agency is charged with enforcing. The APA also limits the agency's control over the ALJ's tenure, assignments, and salary.

The procedures used in administrative hearings are similar to those used by the federal courts, although the rules of evidence are relaxed. The parties have the rights of due notice, cross-examination, presentation of evidence, objections, motions, argument, and any other right essential to a fair trial. This does not include, however, the right to a jury, and factual questions as well as legal issues are resolved by the ALJ. In most instances, the respondent will be represented by an attorney who ordinarily will be a specialist in the law related to the particular agency.

Within 90 days after the completion of the hearing, the administrative law judge files an initial decision, which becomes the decision of the FTC unless appealed. Any party to the proceeding, but not everyone who might be interested, may appeal the ALJ's decision to the Commission; or the Commission may review the decision of its ALJ upon its own motion. In the event of appeal or review, briefs are generally submitted by the parties and oral arguments are heard unless the Commission feels they are not necessary. In rendering its decision, the Commission has broad power to modify the ALJ's decision, including his or her findings of fact.

As stated earlier in this chapter, limited judicial review of the FTC's order to cease and desist is permitted in the Court of Appeals. The facts as found by the Commission are conclusive if supported by evidence. Most appeals are taken on questions of law, although the Administrative Procedure Act allows review of agency decisions that are arbitrary, capricious, or an abuse of the agency's discretion, as well as those decisions or procedures that violate the Constitution or exceed the agency's statutory authority. A final review may be requested of the Supreme Court, but the Supreme Court does not have to consider the case.

The procedures described above for adjudications before the FTC are similar to those used by other federal agencies. For example, federal agencies generally have the power to formulate consent decrees and issue cease-and-desist orders. Also federal agencies with adjudicative powers employ administrative law judges. The case that follows, involving the Department of Agriculture, explores the independence of those who preside over agency adjudications.

UTICA PACKING CO. V. BLOCK

U.S. Court of Appeals, Sixth Circuit
781 F.2d 71 (1976)

BACKGROUND: Fenster, president and part owner of Utica Packing Company, was convicted of bribing a meat inspector in 1978. Thereafter, the U.S. Department of Agriculture (USDA) brought an administrative action against Utica. After a hearing, an administrative law judge ruled that Utica would be ineligible to receive the USDA's meat-inspection services unless Fenster severed his ties to the company. The decision effectively would have prevented Utica from continuing its meat-services business as long as Fenster was connected to the firm. The ALJ's decision was appealed to USDA Judicial Officer Campbell, who affirmed it. Fenster and Utica obtained judicial review but lost in the U.S. District Court. On appeal, however, the Court of Appeals ruled that Judicial Officer Campbell had erred in refusing to consider mitigating circumstances present in the case. The Court of Appeals remanded the case to Campbell "to afford the Judicial Officer an opportunity to consider the mitigating circumstances advanced by Fenster." On remand, Campbell restored Utica's meat-inspection privileges. Among the mitigating circumstances considered by Campbell were possible misconduct by the USDA inspectors, virulent anti-Semitic remarks by one inspector (Fenster was Jewish and a Holocaust survivor), Fenster's poor health at the time, and evidence that the bribe resulted from a misunderstanding.

The Secretary of Agriculture "violently disagreed" with Campbell's second ruling. The Secretary revoked Campbell's authority to preside over any further proceedings in the Utica case and vested such authority in Deputy Assistant Secretary Franke. Franke was not a lawyer and had never performed any adjudicatory work before. USDA attorney Davis was assigned to assist Franke. Once Campbell had been replaced by Franke, the Secretary filed a motion with Franke to reconsider the Utica case. Franke granted the motion and ruled that in spite of the mitigating circumstances, Utica should be stripped of its meat-inspection privileges until it severed ties to Fenster. Fenster and Utica again sought judicial review, and the District Court again ruled in the USDA's favor. Fenster and Utica appealed to the Court of Appeals.

Lively, Chief Judge

The Supreme Court affirmed in *Withrow v. Larkin* that the due process requirement of a fair trial in a fair tribunal "applies to administrative agencies which adjudicate as well as to courts." Nevertheless, the Court distinguished cases where the probability of actual bias is "too high to be constitutionally tolerable" from normal administrative adjudication:

> The contention that the combination of investigative and adjudicative functions necessarily creates an unconstitutional risk of bias in administrative adjudication has a much more difficult burden of persuasion to carry. It must overcome a presumption of honesty and integrity in those serving as adjudicators; and it must convince that, under a realistic appraisal of psychological tendencies and human weakness, conferring investigative and adjudicative powers on the same individuals poses such a risk of actual bias or prejudgment that the practice must be forbidden if the guarantee of due process is to be adequately implemented.

> There can be no doubt that the requirement of separation of functions is relaxed in administrative adjudication. However, the requirement of a fair trial before a fair tribunal has not been eliminated. This concept requires the appearance of fairness and the absence of a probability of outside influences on the adjudicator; it does not require proof of actual partiality.

* * *

We believe this is a case where the plaintiffs have shown the risk of unfairness to be "intolerably high." Every disappointed litigant would doubtless like to replace a judge who in the regular course of his or her duties has decided a case against the litigant and present a motion for a new trial or for reconsideration to a different judge of his own choosing. All notions of judicial impartiality would be abandoned if such a procedure were permitted.

There is no guarantee of fairness when the one who appoints a judge has the power to remove the judge before the end of proceedings for rendering a decision which displeases the appointer. Yet that is exactly what occurred in this case. Campbell was appointed Judicial Officer long before the Utica case arose, and considered the case in the normal course of his duties. When Campbell rendered a decision in the case with which USDA "violently disagreed," officials of the department unceremoniously removed him and presented a petition for reconsideration to their handpicked replacement.

It is of no consequence for due process purposes that Fenster and Utica were unable to prove actual bias on the part of Franke or Davis. The officials who made the revocation and redelegation decision chose a non-career employee with no background in law or adjudication to replace Campbell. They assigned a legal advisor to the new Judicial Officer who worked under an official who was directly involved in prosecution of the Utica case. Such manipulation of a judicial, or quasi-judicial, system cannot be permitted. The due process clause guarantees as much. As the court stated in *D.C. Federation of Civic Ass'ns v. Volpe:*

> With regard to judicial decisionmaking, whether by court or agency, the appearance of bias or pressure may be no less objectionable than the reality.

Nothing in this opinion should be perceived as minimizing the seriousness of Fenster's criminal activities. Bribing an inspector does strike at the heart of the meat inspection program and cannot be tolerated. . . .

Judicial Officer Campbell properly concerned himself with the nature of Fenster's criminal activities and the possible harm to the public which could flow from them. It is not certain that Campbell properly construed this court's remand order in considering mitigating circumstances. However, that is not the issue presently before us. Whether the Judicial Officer was correct or incorrect in his application of the law, the Secretary's efforts to change the result by the methods described in this opinion cannot be permitted to succeed.

DECISION: The Court of Appeals reversed the District Court's decision and ordered the Secretary of Agriculture to reinstate Campbell, ruling in favor of Fenster and Utica.

Rulemaking

When a pronouncement affecting the rights and duties of a number of people is made by an agency, the agency acts in the same manner as a legislature. The power to make rules and regulations of this kind, which may be as binding as laws passed by legislative bodies, has been delegated to the agency by the legislature. The only important difference between an agency rule and a "law" enacted by a legislative body is that the former may be slightly more susceptible to attack in the courts because the rule was not made by elected officials. Let us consider examples of the rulemaking authority that some administrative agencies possess.

There are two major types of rulemaking carried on by administrative agencies: (1) **formal rulemaking** and (2) **informal rulemaking**. Both types of rulemaking make use of the *Federal Register*, which is published every business day by the federal government and contains the texts of proposed and newly approved regulations, notices of government meetings that are open to the public, and other information.

Formal Rulemaking   Section 553(c) of the Administrative Procedure Act requires formal rulemaking when an enabling statute or other legislation requires that all regulations or rules be enacted by an agency as part of a formal hearing process that includes a complete transcript. This procedure is as follows: (1) a notice of proposed rulemaking to the public by the agency is published in the *Federal Register*; (2) a public hear-

---

CONCEPT SUMMARY
Formal and Informal Rulemaking

Formal	Informal
1. Notice of proposed rule in *Federal Register*	1. Notice of proposed rule in *Federal Register*
2. Public hearing, at which there are witnesses, cross-examination of witnesses, and formal rules of evidence	2. All interested parties may submit written comments
3. Formal findings are made and published with final rule in the *Federal Register*	3. Publications of final rule with statement of its basis and purpose in *Federal Register*

ing is held at which witnesses give testimony on the pros and cons of the proposed rule, cross-examination of each witness takes place, and formal rules of evidence are applied; (3) formal findings are made and published by the agency; and (4) on the basis of these findings, an agency may or may not promulgate a regulation. Because of the expense and time involved in obtaining a formal transcript and record, most enabling statutes do not require a formal rulemaking procedure when regulations are promulgated.

Informal Rulemaking   Informal rulemaking is provided in Section 553 of the APA and applies in all situations where the agency's enabling legislation or other congressional directives do not require another form. The APA requires that the agency (1) give prior notice of the proposed rule by publishing it in the *Federal Register*; (2) provide an opportunity for all interested parties to submit written comments; and (3) publish the final rule, with a statement of its basis and purpose, in the *Federal Register*. This type of rulemaking is most often used because it is more efficient in terms of time and cost to the agency. No formal public hearing is required and no formal record need be established, as in formal rulemaking.

With both formal and informal rulemaking, parties adversely affected by the rule often seek to persuade the courts from enforcing the rule or regulation by showing that the agency did not follow APA procedures. The case that follows illustrates such an attempt.

FLORIDA POWER & LIGHT CO. v. UNITED STATES

U.S. Court of Appeals, D.C. Circuit

846 F.2d 765 (1988)

BACKGROUND: The Nuclear Regulatory Commission (NRC) promulgated a rule that imposed a uniform annual fee on all parties licensed by the NRC to operate a nuclear reactor. The NRC published a "cost base statement" that set forth the cost of NRC services that the fee was designed to cover. Several NRC licensees sued to challenge the rule.

Nies, Circuit Judge

Petitioners challenge the validity of the final rule because of alleged violations of the Administrative Procedure Act (APA). The APA requires the Commission to provide notice of its proposed rulemaking adequate to afford "interested parties a reasonable opportunity to participate in the rulemaking process." Such notice must not only give adequate time for comments, but also must provide sufficient factual detail and rationale for the rule to permit interested parties to comment meaningfully.

On the latter point, petitioners assert that the NRC cost base statement is merely conclusory and that no explanation is given with respect to the criteria used to include or exclude particular items. They point, for example, to the dollar amount of the cost of reactor-related research in the proposed rule and to the reduction, purportedly without explanation, made in that cost figure in the notice promulgating the final rule.

In the final notice the Commission had explained that between the proposed and final rule it had reviewed the research costs "to ensure that only generic costs associated with *all* power reactors, with operating licenses, regardless of type, were included in the cost basis." . . . It is essentially irrelevant . . . that some costs were removed from the base as long as the remaining costs meet, first, the statutory criteria that they be reasonably related to the regulatory services provided by the NRC and, second, the notice's criteria that the costs be associated with *all* operating licenses. Petitioners do not identify any included programs which do not fall into that category. We conclude that the Commission's explanation was adequate.

Petitioners also argue that the fifteen-day period for comment was too short. On that issue, the Commission notes that Congress gave it only ninety days to report and forty-five more days to enact a final rule. Given Congress' deadline, the Commission maintains that the fifteen days for comment were reasonable.

We find no evidence that petitioners were harmed by the short comment period. The Commission received sixty-one comments, some of them lengthy, addressing its proposed rule. Those comments had a measurable effect on the final rule. Petitioners have had a substantial period of time since publication of the final rule to consider the rule and the supporting data. No substantive challenges which differ in kind from the original comments have been raised. In this instance, the short length of the comment period appears to be no more than a technical argument, which we do not find meritorious. In sum, we conclude that the Commission's rulemaking process did not violate the APA.

DECISION: The court upheld the NRC rule.

Administrative Activities

The acts of administrative agencies of most interest from the legal standpoint are those that involve rulemaking or adjudication. Agencies, however, act in many ways that are neither judicial nor legislative in nature. They carry out a myriad of statutory directives and have countless functions that defy classification. Many of these acts are purely administrative, although they may involve the rights and duties of many citizens, thousands of transactions, and millions of dollars. In many cases, these acts are informal in nature and are usually not reviewed by a court.

Even when the possibility of judicial review of intra-agency actions exists, the person affected often does not, for many reasons, believe that review is practical, and the agency's action is accepted without formal protest.

Many examples of administrative acts of this nature can readily be cited. Agencies are often responsible for the allocation of funds and the granting of licenses; they make tests, manage government property, and supervise inmates in institutions. Different agencies carry out tasks as varied as clearing vessels to leave port and classifying grain. Agencies grant patents, collect taxes, and oversee educational institutions. Agencies frequently conduct investigations. Sometimes this is done at the request of the executive or the legislature, but many agencies have the power to initiate their own investigations. Some agencies are responsible for the business of law enforcement and prosecution. The principal function of others is to plan or to approve or disapprove the plans of others. Most of the countless jobs that are necessary in the administration of government are done by people in administrative agencies.

Many of these administrative acts are politically, economically, and socially significant and clearly relate to important issues of public policy. The SEC decision in the late 1960s to investigate the selling of mutual funds was an administrative act of this type. As a result of this investigation, the Commission proposed sweeping legislation curtailing certain practices in the industry.

In carrying out its administrative activities, the agency involved employs many people who have frequent informal contacts with businesses and individuals whom they are supposed to regulate. These informal agency activities do not fall within the rulemaking and adjudicative models for decision making discussed in this chapter. They often involve *ex parte* communications (with only one side present) between agency decision makers or representatives of decision makers when only one interested party is present. Some would do away with all *ex parte* communications, claiming they bias decisions in favor of one party over the other. The Administrative Conference, which sets forth procedural rules for administrative agencies, disagrees, noting that flexibility is needed to help rulemaking procedures and *ex parte* contacts are needed by the agencies. It does, however, believe that such contacts should be banned when agencies are involved in adjudication of a specific dispute. One court's approach to this question is shown in the following case.

HOME BOX OFFICE INC. V. FEDERAL COMMUNICATIONS COMMISSION
U.S. Court of Appeals
567 F.2d 9 (D.C. Cir. 1977)

BACKGROUND: In March 1975 the Federal Communications Commission (defendant-respondent) adopted amendments to its rules governing the programs that could be shown by paid television services. If contemporary films on sports could be shown over these services, the networks were afraid they would be at a disadvantage, and viewers who could not afford the cost of paid television would be injured. The informal rulemaking process resulted in neither the paid television carriers nor the commercial networks being satisfied. There were many *ex parte* contacts in the informal rulemaking process, all of which formed one of the bases for parties on both sides to appeal.

Per Curiam

. . . In an attempt to clarify the facts this court ordered the Commission to provide "a list of all of the *ex parte* presentations, together with the details of each, made to it, or to any of its members or representatives, during the rulemaking proceedings." In response to this order the Commission filed a document over 60 pages long which revealed, albeit imprecisely, widespread *ex parte* communications involving virtually every party before this court. It is apparently uncontested that a number of participants before the Commission sought out individual commissioners or Commission employees for the purpose of discussing *ex parte* and in confidence the merits of the rules under review here. In fact, the Commission itself solicited such communications in its notices of proposed rulemaking. . . .

[T]he possibility that there is here one administrative record for the public and this court and another for the Commission and those "in the know" is intolerable.

As a practical matter, . . . the public record must reflect what representations were made to an agency so that relevant information supporting or refuting those representations may be brought to the attention of the reviewing courts by persons participating in agency proceedings. This course is obviously foreclosed if communications are made to the agency in secret and the agency itself does not disclose the information presented. Moreover, where, as here, an agency justifies its actions by reference only to information in the public file while failing to disclose the substance of other relevant information that has been presented to it, a reviewing court cannot presume that the agency has acted properly, . . . but must treat the agency's justifications as a fictional account of the actual decisionmaking process and must perforce find its actions arbitrary.

The failure of the public record in this proceeding to disclose all the information made available to the Commission is not the only inadequacy we find here. Even if the Commission had disclosed to this court the substance of what was said to it *ex parte,* it would still be difficult to judge the truth of what the Commission asserted it knew about the television industry because we would not have the benefit of an adversaries discussion among the parties. The importance of such discussion to the proper functioning of the agency decisionmaking and judicial review processes is evident in our cases. We have insisted, for example, that information in agency files or consultants' reports which the agency has identified as relevant to the proceeding be disclosed to the parties for adversaries comment. Similarly, we have required agencies to set out their thinking in notices of proposed rulemaking. This requirement not only allows adversaries critique of the agency but is perhaps one of the few ways that the public may be apprised of what the agency thinks it knows in its capacity as a repository of expert opinion. From a functional standpoint, we see no difference between assertions of fact and expert opinion tendered by the public, as here, and that generated internally in an agency: each may be biased, inaccurate, or incomplete—failings which adversary comment may illuminate.

Equally important is the inconsistency of secrecy with fundamental notions of fairness implicit in due process and with the ideal of reasoned decisionmaking on the merits which undergirds all of our administrative law. . . . In the Government in the Sunshine Act, for example, Congress has declared it to be "the policy of the United States that the public is entitled to the fullest practicable information regarding the decisionmaking processes of the Federal Government," . . . and has taken steps to guard against *ex parte* contacts in formal agency proceedings. . . .

From what has been said above, it should be clear that information gathered *ex parte* from the public which becomes relevant to a rulemaking will have to be disclosed at some time. On the other hand, we recognize that informal contacts between agencies and the public are the "bread and butter" of the process of administration and are completely appropriate so long as they do not frustrate judicial review or raise serious questions of fairness. Reconciliation of these considerations in a manner which will reduce procedural uncertainty leads us to conclude that communications which are received prior to issuance of a formal notice of rulemaking do not, in general, have to be put in a public file. Of course, if the information contained in such a communication forms the basis for agency action, then, under well established principles, that information must be disclosed to the public in some form. Once a notice of proposed rulemaking has been issued, however, any agency official or employee who is or may reasonably be expected to be involved in the decisional process of the rulemaking proceeding, should "refus[e] to discuss matters relating to the disposition of a [rulemaking proceeding] with any interested private party, or an attorney or agent for any such party, prior to the [agency's] decision." If *ex parte* contacts nonetheless occur, we think that any written document or a summary of any oral communication must be placed in the public file established for each rulemaking docket immediately after the communication is received so that interested parties may comment.

DECISION: The U.S. Court of Appeals remanded the case to the FCC with instructions that it appoint a hearing examiner to determine the nature and source of all *ex parte* approaches to the Commission and its employees during the informal rulemaking process.

Government Regulation and Administrative Agencies: An Evaluation

As stated at the beginning of this chapter, there exists a debate between those who advocate deregulation and the abolition of administrative agencies and those who argue that the wider public interest would suffer if there were no regulation. The work of administrative agencies in carrying out the statutory responsibilities that Congress and the President have given them is subject to criticism by industry, consumer, environmentalist, and other groups. Over the past 50 years, administrative agencies have probably been subject to more criticism than praise. One frequently expressed charge is that there is just too much regulation. The result is that the individ-

ual, the economy—in fact, society as a whole—is stifled. Often this general condemnation is given added weight because critics are able to point to specific instances in which agencies have not performed well. Many times agencies, which supposedly are the experts, have erred in major decisions that have hurt both the regulated business and the general public. For example, long after it became clear in the 1930s that the nineteenth-century concept of the common carrier responsibility of the railroads to provide a complete transportation service to every locality along every mile of track had become obsolete, the ICC only reluctantly allowed railroads to abandon unprofitable passenger service. This policy forced the railroads to continue passenger service, often when losing money, to the detriment of their competitive position. This eventually led to a deterio-

---

ETHICS
Ethics and Government Regulation

The vice president for government relations (Jones) of Teletalk Communications, Inc., the second largest communications common carrier in the United States, frequently plays golf with a commissioner (Abbott) of the Federal Communications Commission (FCC) on Saturday mornings at a posh country club. They are also neighbors and talk over FCC business at social functions. The agency forbids all *ex parte* communications during business hours and requires that each office log in the name of any individual who is not an employee and engages in such communications, and the subject matter discussed. While playing golf one Saturday morning, Jones indicates to Abbott that a present rulemaking procedure that would deregulate all long-distance telephone rates would drive his company into bankruptcy. He notes that the company cannot show this in its financial statement or the capital markets will dry up immediately for the company. If the FCC turns down this proposal, the company will be able to stay in business and prosper. Abbott shows Jones financial statements that have not been made public to any administrative agency inclusive of the FCC. In a 4-to-3 vote turning down the proposal for complete deregulation of long-distance telephone rates, Abbott is the swing vote. He does not mention his conversation with Jones or the fact that he has seen the true financial statements of Teletalk Communications, Inc. Later, he fails to disclose that shortly after this decision his club dues were paid anonymously for the next 5 years.

The Ethics in Government Act of 1978, as well as FCC rules, forbid Abbott from participating in the FCC vote, and require disclosure of all information received by Abbott from Jones. Abbott must disclose the payment of his country club dues even if he does not know the source. A potential bribery and statute violation exists for Jones and Teletalk Communications, Inc. if the paying of Abbott's dues can be traced to either.

---

ration in the ability of the railroads to provide the type of transportation that the economy actually needed.

Although some critics charge that agencies regulate too much, others claim that regulation is either insufficient or frequently oriented to the needs of the industry rather than to the needs of the public. Because most agencies operate in only one field, their members often acquire a sympathetic knowledge of the industry they are supposed to regulate. As a result, they forget their duty to regulate for the public welfare. This condemnation has been made by groups initiated by consumer advocate Ralph Nader that have reviewed the operations of the ICC and the FTC.

Industry Influence

The close ties that develop between the agencies and industry stem from a natural tendency of people to be interested in the problems of others with whom they have a common background. Few deliberate instances of industry–agency collusion can be documented. Commissioners and other agency executives frequently receive their appointments because they have employment backgrounds in the industry regulated by their agency. Often they intend to return to the industry after government service. Personnel who have not been hired from the industry may regard the industry as a potential employer; agency lawyers may think of it as a source of future fees. As a result of these and other considerations, regulators perhaps unconsciously curtail their activities.

Legislative Influence

Administrative agencies have been accused of being overly susceptible to legislative as well as executive influence. Pressures that would never be countenanced by the courts are part of the everyday experience of many federal and state regulatory authorities. Pressures from legislative sources are highly effective because the legislatures control agency funds. Almost every state can point to at least one scandal in which legislative leverage has influenced a state agency. At the federal level, congresspeople and members of their immediate staffs have been exposed as sources of influence peddling. The power that some agencies have to grant the right to engage in certain types of highly profitable business makes them particularly susceptible to attempts to influence them. For a long time the right to operate a television station was so valuable that the granting of such licenses by the FCC was thought to be similar to the granting of licenses to print money.

Other criticisms of a more esoteric nature have been directed against agencies. In several agencies rulemaking and adjudicatory functions are not separated. In other instances not only do agency personnel establish the rules and serve as the judges, but the decision to bring an action is also made within the agency. One of the highly esteemed American political traditions is the separation of legislative, judicial, and executive powers; this tradition would seem to be violated when the decision to bring an action is not separated from adjudication. During the 1940s the NLRB was subjected to considerable criticism because its general counsel was controlled by the Board. Eventually, as a result of public pressure, Congress adopted legislation separating the office of the general counsel for the NLRB from the Board, which was responsible for deciding cases initiated by the general counsel. At the present time staff personnel of the FTC adjudicate cases that are brought by the agency and that involve, in many instances, purported violations of agency rules.

Another charge against some agencies, including several of the most important federal agencies, is that the commissioners, who make the ultimate decisions in many cases, are removed from the actual fact-finding. Thus, the critics argue, the commissioners never really know what is going on because they see only a record when they make their decisions. They act on the basis of facts found by an administrative law judge, and they do not hear the actual testimony themselves.

Many of these criticisms are partially valid, and most authorities agree that steps should be taken to improve the performance of the administrative agencies. In spite of their problems, they have performed an important function in our system of government, and they have unquestionably taken much of the burden from courts and legislatures, as noted earlier in this chapter. Without them in this age of rapidly increasing population, expanding technology, and specialization, the traditional branches of government would long ago have come to a standstill. Agencies appear to be the most practical method of administering the complex statutes necessary to regulate activities effectively in our society. If some form of government regulation is desired by society, institutions of this type are inevitable. They have developed in all the heavily industrialized nations of the West and will continue to be important as technology expands and our economy becomes more complex.

Administrative Agency Reform

Recently a number of proposals have been made to improve the effectiveness of administrative agencies. These proposals range widely in nature and in the extent to which they advocate change. The modifications suggested include changes in the alignment of responsibilities of several agencies as well as in their internal structures and processes.

During recent administrations a number of proposals to reorganize major federal agencies responsible to the President were carried out. These changes were the outcome of broad authority granted by Congress to the President to reorganize the executive branch. This authority allows the Chief Executive to submit proposals for reorganization of executive agencies to Congress. If Congress does not veto a proposal within 60 days, it automatically goes into effect. The presidential authority to modify agency organization and responsibility does not apply to the independent federal regulatory agencies.

Over the years numerous presidential, congressional, and private committees have studied the federal regulatory agencies and made suggestions for change. The most recent detailed proposal was submitted in 1971 by the President's Advisory Council on Executive Reorganization. The Council recommended major realignment of responsibility within the independent agencies. One proposal would have combined the ICC, the Civil Aeronautics board, and the Federal Maritime Commission into a single transportation agency. The chief argument for this proposal was that the nation's transportation systems increasingly are becoming an integrated network, and overall regulation of all elements of the system is necessary for effective control.

A second proposal recommended dividing the FTC into two agencies. One would concentrate on antitrust matters, the other on consumer protection. The Council also considered combining the Justice Department's antitrust function with those recommended for separation from the present FTC. Antitrust activities would then be carried out within either the Justice Department or a new separate agency. A Reagan administration proposal to do away with FTC antitrust authority met with opposition from Congress.

In addition to proposals realigning agency responsibility, the Council recommended modifications in internal organization and functions for some agencies. The most farreaching proposal suggested replacing boards or commissions with single administrators. The rationale struck at the heart of the concept of having several governmental functions included in a single organization. Council members felt that a number of agencies would operate more effectively if policy or rulemaking were separated from adjudication. A single administrator would have final responsibility in these agencies, as in the vast majority of executive department agencies. This person would be more accountable to Congress than to the NLRB or FTC. Administrative courts would be created to carry out the current adjudicatory functions of the agency.

Opinions vary as to what is necessary to improve the regulatory system. On the one hand, there are numerous authorities who propose the creation of new, powerful independent agencies to solve society's problems. Congress has considered bills creating an independent Consumer Protection Agency, an independent Federal Elections Committee, an independent public prosecutor, and even an independent commission to review classified material. On the other hand, both in Congress and in many of the states, proposed legislation calls for the automatic termination of agencies after they have been in operation for a number of years. In some industries deregulation will lighten the workload of agencies.

A different approach to agency reform has been "sunshine" or "open government" legislation. Several states have adopted laws requiring governmental bodies to meet regularly in announced sessions open to the public. Bills introduced in Congress would require all agencies headed by two or more persons, a majority of whom were appointed by the President and con-

firmed by the Senate, to open all meetings to the public unless a majority voted to close. These bills also specifically set the types of meetings that could be closed by vote. These include meetings dealing with national defense, foreign policy, company trade secrets, and reviews of agency personnel rules and practices. This type of legislation may force administrative agencies to be more aware of the needs of the public.

Congress enacted the Regulatory Flexibility Act of 1980, which seeks to force all agencies to fit regulations and information requirements made by the agency to the size of the business. The Act was a result of agencies making regulations that burdened small businesses within an industry with high costs. Whereas large businesses were able to pass on the costs of regulation to consumers, small businesses often could not. Under the Act, an agency must show each October and April the areas of regulation it will be concerned with. The agency must present its agenda to the Small Business Administration, which will publish it for small businesses. Each agency must solicit comments from small businesses and periodically review all rules in order to assess their impact on small companies.

Additional reforms of administrative agencies have been making their way through both houses of Congress.

Review Questions and Problems

Key Terms

administrative agency	consent decree
Administrative Procedure Act	cease-and-desist order
independent agency	administrative law judge
executive departments	formal rulemaking
enabling act	informal rulemaking
	Federal Register

Discussion Questions

1. For what reasons have administrative agencies grown?
2. How does the executive branch control administrative agencies?
3. What are the grounds for a court to review an administrative agency action when the agency acts in an adjudicative context?

4. What broad standard of delegation of power does congress use when it authorizes an administrative agency to act in a regulatory manner?

5. What are the two most important functions performed by administrative agencies? Explain each.

Review Problems

1. The Federal Trade Commission (FTC) has brought an administrative action against a local chapter of the U.S. Business Lawyers Association for violating the price-fixing provisions of the Clayton Act. The specific activity challenged by the FTC is an annual survey sponsored by the association in which members disclose the fees that they charge for different types of business law cases. The association is reluctant to admit its guilt, fearing that it and its members might be sued for treble damages by parties who claim to have been injured by the alleged price fixing. The FTC, on the other hand, is determined to put an end to the annual survey. What options are available to both parties?

2. The National Widget Commission (NWC), a federal agency charged with regulating commerce in the widget industry, has promulgated a new rule that imposes a $1,000 annual fee on all licensed widget traders. The NWC did not hold any hearings before promulgating the rule, but it did give prior notice of the proposed rule in the *Federal Register* and allowed interested parties 90 days to comment. The National Widget Act, the NWC's enabling legislation, provides that the NWC may utilize the informal rulemaking procedure "unless the proposed rule or regulation will have an adverse financial impact on one or more licensees." Licensed widget traders bring a class action suit against the NWC, seeking to invalidate the annual fee. What is the result? Discuss.

3. The Office of the Comptroller of the Currency (OCC), one of the agencies that regulates national banks, proposes a new regulation that would drastically alter accounting practices of national banks. The regulation, which is 138 pages long, would effectively make it easier for the federal government to seize troubled banks. The OCC publishes the proposed regulation in the *Federal Register* and gives interested parties 24 hours to comment. After the regulation goes into effect, a banking trade association sues to invalidate it. What is the result? Why?

4. The Federal Communications Commission (FCC) moves to revoke Marlon's radio broadcast license on the grounds that Marlon's station has "consistently broadcast obscene and profane material." Wilson, an FCC attorney responsible for investigating Marlon's case, suddenly is selected to fill an ALJ vacancy. Wilson hears Marlon's case and orders that Marlon's license be revoked. Marlon challenges the FCC's action in federal court. What is the result? Discuss.

Case Problems

1. In September 1969 the State of Tennessee, following agreement with local Memphis city officials, acquired a right-of-way inside Overton Park. The right-of-way was to be used to extend Interstate 40 into Memphis. If this was done, the park would have been cut in two, with the zoo on one side of the highway and all other facilities on the other. The U.S. Secretary of Transportation (Volpe), after consulting with state and local officials, approved the plan without indicating whether a "feasible" alternative existed. A citizen's group sued to enjoin the U.S. Department of Transportation from financing this extension of Interstate 40, claiming that Congress, in creating the Department of Transportation, prohibited the use of funds for highway construction through a park if "feasible" alternatives existed. The Citizens to Preserve Overton Park claimed that the Secretary of Transportation had failed to show that he had investigated and considered "feasible" alternatives or design changes that might have brought less harm to the park, with the result that his order approving the new route was invalid. What standards would a court have used in determining whether Secretary Volpe had met the statutory requirement? Who would win?

2. The Federal Communications Commission set forth rules prohibiting cable television systems from broadcasting first-run feature films (shown on over-the-air television) that were less than 3 but more than 10 years old. Home Box Office (HBO) appealed this rule and other restrictions to the District of Columbia Circuit Court of Appeals, claiming that this exercise of the Commission's rulemaking authority was arbitrary and capricious and that it restricted competition. The Commission claimed that the regulations were needed to prevent siphoning by cable companies of copyrighted material broadcast over the air. Were the regulations arbitrary and capricious? Who wins?

3. The Endangered Species Act of 1973 invested the Secretary of the Interior with exclusive authority to determine whether a species is "endangered" or "threatened" and to ascertain the factors that have led to the problem. The Secretary is also commanded by Congress under the 1973 Act to issue regulations to provide for the conservation of the endangered species. The Secretary of Interior set forth regulations that declared the snail darter as an endangered species whose habitat would have been destroyed by the creation of the Tellico Reservoir on the Little Tennessee River. The dam creating the reservoir was almost completed ($100 million having been spent) when environmental groups and others brought suit under the 1973 Act to enjoin the Tennessee Valley Authority from completing the dam. Would the court be usurping the power of the Secretary of the Interior and Congress if it failed to enforce the 1973 Act? What about the $100 million spent on the dam? Is it significant in terms of the court's decision? Who wins?

4. The Emergency Price Control Act established an Office of Price Administration with authority to promulgate rules and orders fixing maximum prices of commodities and rents during World War II. The administrator of the OPA was given two standards by Congress to fix prices: (a) he had to consult with the industries and promulgate regulations that were "fair and equitable" and (b) due consideration had to be given to prices prevailing between October 1 and October 15, 1941. When Yakus and other defendants sold beef in excess of the wholesale price set by the regulations, they were prosecuted under a criminal section of the act and sentenced to 6 months in jail and fined $1,000 each. The defendants argued that the standards set by Congress for the OPA administrator were so broad that they failed to give adequate notice and thus violated the Fifth Amendment's due process requirements. Were the standards too broad? Who wins?

5. In 1972 the National Highway Traffic Safety Administration issued a standard requiring that all pneumatic passenger tires retreaded after February 1974 contain information (permanently molded into one side of the tire) as to size, inflation pressure, load, and whether the tire was bias-belted or radial. This rule was promulgated pursuant to the National Traffic and Motor Safety Vehicle Act of 1966, which required that rules be "practical" and "meet the need for motor vehicle safety." The National Tire Dealers and Retreaders Association opposed the rule, claiming that it was arbitrary and capricious in that it was not "practicable" and that the Administrator of Traffic Safety had failed to show that the information required by the rule met "the need for vehicle safety" only if it was permanently molded onto a tire. The Administrator of Traffic Safety argued that safety could be provided only through permanent labeling because tires are often transferred from wheel to wheel or car to car. Was the rule economically "feasible" and did it "meet the need for vehicle safety"? Who wins?

6. An association of fishermen represented by the National Resources Defense Council sued U.S. Secretary of the Interior Morton, challenging the Secretary's decision to open a large part of the outer continental shelf off the Louisiana coast to oil and gas exploration. Under the National Environmental Policy Act of 1969, Congress directed all governmental agencies to file environmental impact statements (EIS) noting "any adverse environmental effects of the proposed action" and "alternatives to the proposed action." The Secretary filed an EIS but failed to consider in any detailed way alternative methods for meeting the energy needs of the nation. The Secretary argued that he failed to consider alternatives (for example, removal of oil import quotas, development of oil shale, and coal liquefaction) because they were outside his statutory duty or had no prospect for increasing energy in 1970. The fishermen argued that the Secretary had failed to meet the statutory mandate and that his decision should be overturned. Who wins?

54

Antitrust Laws: Enforcement and Control

Law and Economics in Setting
  Antitrust Policy
Enforcement of the Antitrust Laws

Exemptions from the Antitrust Laws
Sherman Act
Clayton Act

This chapter discusses **antitrust laws**, which are designed to prevent businesses from engaging in behavior harmful to commercial competition. Antitrust laws exist at both the federal and state levels; this chapter focuses on federal antitrust laws.

Historically this nation's economy was founded on the concept of laissez-faire—that is, government would not interfere in the activities of individual sellers freely competing in the marketplace. Underlying this classical economic theory was the assumption that there would be many sellers in the marketplace and a free flow of information between sellers and buyers. In the latter half of the nineteenth and the early twentieth century business power in several industries (particularly oil) became concentrated in one or two companies. Public demand to break up these "trusts" resulted in the passage of federal antitrust laws and some state statutes. (See page 993 for a summary of these statutes and the business behavior they regulate. They will frequently be referred to through-

out the chapter.) While concentrating on such business conduct as price fixing, conspiracies to restrain trade, and other anticompetitive behavior, this chapter also looks at how the number and size of sellers in an industry affect competition. If an industry has only four domestic sellers, like the auto industry, is it more or less competitive? Should we look further and include Volkswagen and Nissan when we talk about the number of sellers and how competitive the industry may be?

In some industries (including many of our most important national industries) a few firms account for all or sizable portions of production. Other industries are composed of a large number of relatively small firms with no single firm having a significant share of the market.

This chapter identifies important federal antitrust statutes, describes their enforcement, and explains certain exemptions. It then discusses business behaviors regulated under these acts, with particular emphasis on monopolies, mergers, and price discrimination.

CONCEPT SUMMARY

Selected Federal Antitrust Statutes

Sherman Act (1890), Sec. 1	Condemns combinations and conspiracies in restraint of trade including vertical and horizontal price fixing, group boycotts, and division of markets. Applies to interstate or foreign commerce.
Sherman Act (1890), Sec. 2	Prohibits monopolies and attempts or conspiracies to monopolize. Applies to interstate and foreign commerce.
Clayton Act (1914), Sec. 2	Prohibits price discriminations, substantially lessening sellers' level competition (primary line violations). *Amended (1936). Robinson–Patman Act* prohibits price discriminations, substantially lessening buyers' (and below) level competition (secondary line violations).
Clayton Act (1914), Sec. 3	Prohibits exclusive dealing and tying arrangements, the effect of which may be to lessen competition substantially.
Clayton Act (1914), Sec. 7	Prohibits mergers, the effect of which may be substantially to lessen competition or to tend to create a monopoly. *Amended (1950). Celler–Kefauver Act* clarified application of Sec. 7 to acquisitions of assets.

Law and Economics in Setting Antitrust Policy

In examining the enforcement and content of antitrust statutes, we need to know that two major schools of thought have arisen in the last 30 years. They analyze antitrust statutes in the belief that Congress had distinctly different goals in mind when enacting these laws.

The Chicago School approach believes that all antitrust decisions by courts should be based on the sole criterion of economic efficiency; that is, the decision should promote the maximization of consumer welfare. Consumer welfare is defined as an improvement in the allocation of resources without an impairment to productive efficiencies. Reagan administration Justice Department officials argued successfully in many cases that by encouraging the efficient allocation of resources, antitrust enforcement can make sure consumers are provided goods at the lowest possible prices. Also, efficiency criteria when used in antitrust decision making helps U.S. firms compete with large state-subsidized and privately owned foreign multinational corporations. This approach to antitrust enforcement will become evident to the reader when analyzing the present merger guidelines as well as the vertical restraint cases, such as *Continental T.V., Inc.* and *Jefferson Hospital*, that are set out in this chapter.

In contrast, the Harvard School approach to setting antitrust policy would emphasize goals such as:

1. The preservation of small businesses and an economy in which many sellers compete with each other

2. The prevention of the concentration of economic and political power in the hands of a few large industries

3. The prevention of labor dislocation by keeping control of businesses in the hands of local people

This approach calls for the breakup of large corporations such as General Motors, the nonparticipation of large corporations in the political process, and the prevention of economic concentration through strict enforcement of our antitrust statutes. Adherents to this approach also advocate plant-closing legislation that would mandate that companies give 6 months or more notice before they close a plant, as well as the return of all tax abatements previously received from the state in which the plant is located.

An approach that emphasizes these criteria is set forth for the reader in this chapter in *United States v. Du Pont & Co.* and *Brown Shoe Co. v. United States.*

Enforcement of the Antitrust Laws

As we examine several forms of business conduct prohibited by the antitrust laws, it should be remembered that their major purpose is to preserve a competitive industry structure and economy.

Actions under the antitrust laws may be initiated in one of the following three ways:

1. By the Department of Justice in the regular court system
2. By administrative agencies through specially established procedures
3. By private citizens to obtain compensation for injuries they have suffered as a result of violations of the antitrust laws

The Department of Justice has a special Antitrust Division, headed by an Assistant Attorney General, responsible for enforcing the Sherman Act and, together with the Federal Trade Commission (FTC), for enforcing the Clayton Act. In addition, the Antitrust Division has special powers relating to the antitrust actions of federal administrative agencies. The FTC is the most important agency in this field. It has exclusive jurisdiction to enforce the Federal Trade Commission Act and has concurrent jurisdiction with the Department of Justice to enforce the Clayton Act. In addition, the FTC has authority to enforce a number of other statutes relating to labeling and export trade. In jointly enforcing the Clayton Act, the Department of Justice and the FTC attempt to coordinate their efforts to prevent wasteful duplication. For example, the FTC has taken primary responsibility for enforcing the Robinson–Patman Act; the Department of Justice rarely litigates under that statute.

These public agencies make use of three basic remedies:

- Injunctions
- Criminal sanctions
- Fines

An **injunction** is a court order prohibiting a specified action (for example, dissemination of pricing information by a trade association) or requiring affirmative action on the part of the party against whom the order applies (for example, the divestiture of certain designated assets).

Violation of the Sherman Act is a felony and may result in imprisonment for up to 3 years. Although the imposition of jail terms in Sherman Act proceedings has received considerable publicity when it has occurred, the number of instances in which jail terms have actually been imposed on businesspeople is relatively small. The Sherman Act also provides for fines of $350,000 per count for an individual and $10 million per count for a corporation.

Both the Clayton Act and the Sherman Act provide for civil treble-damage suits by private citizens as well as by the federal government. Although victims of an electrical equipment price-fixing conspiracy in the 1950s were able to recover hundreds of millions of dollars, private plaintiffs found that antitrust litigation was costly and time-consuming. In addition, there is often an imbalance of economic interest in the lawsuit. An extreme example will emphasize the latter point. Suppose the manufacturers of a mass-distributed product such as legal pads were to engage in a price-fixing conspiracy unlawfully raising the price 5 cents per pad. Even the most prolific purchasers of legal pads would find it hardly worth their while to bring suit. If they were to bring suit, they would find that the outcome of the case would be substantially more important to the manufacturers than it would be to them. There are two possible solutions to this dilemma. A state government might bring suit on behalf of all its citizens and then spend whatever monies it obtained in the public interest. Or a class action might be allowed, whereby a sufficiently homogeneous group, having substantially the same claim, would bring action as though it were a single person. The courts may allow a class action in an antitrust suit if they are convinced that it is practicable and that there are no other realistic alternatives available to the plaintiffs comprising the class. The courts determine whether class actions will be allowed on a case-by-case basis.

The 1974 decision of the U.S. Supreme Court in *Eisen v. Carlisle & Jacquelin* had the effect of limiting the use of class actions under the federal antitrust laws. In *Eisen* the Court held that the plaintiff must bear the costs of notifying all the members of the class of their rights during the progress of the suit. The costs of notifying a large class that may involve tens of thousands (or, in some cases, even millions) are prohibitively high (postage alone would be staggering) and operate as a practical matter to discourage the very large class action.

In 1972 the Supreme Court held in *Hawaii v. Standard Oil of California* that a state could not bring a civil antitrust action for damages against a defendant on behalf of all the citizens of the state. Ironically, in the *Hawaii* decision the Supreme Court suggested that a class action was the better way to deal with this problem. Hawaii had tried to bring an action as *parens patriae* (legal guardian) on behalf of its citizens.

In reaction to the *Eisen* and *Hawaii* decisions, Congress passed the Antitrust Improvements Act (1976), which established a statutory *parens patriae* right of action that would allow state attorneys general to bring civil treble-damage suits on behalf of all natural persons within the state against defendants who had committed violations of the antitrust laws. At the direction of the federal court, the proceeds of a successful suit would be either distributed to injured citizens or added to the state's general revenues. Damages would be calculated from the losses suffered by the natural citizens of the state. Sampling and aggregation techniques could be used to make the calculation if price fixing was involved.

In *Illinois Brick v. Illinois* (1977), the Supreme Court refused to allow Illinois and some 700 Illinois government entities to recover treble damages as indirect purchasers. The state had alleged that it and others had been overcharged $3 million for concrete blocks sold by Illinois Brick and other manufacturers that had engaged in price fixing. The manufacturers sold blocks to masonry contractors who in turn passed on the extra costs to general contractors who passed them on to the state when building office buildings. Illinois taxpayers were the injured citizens. To support its refusal, the Court cited the evidentiary complexity involved in analyzing price and output decisions based on economic models; it also pointed to problems associated with apportionment of damages. This decision has been criticized by Congress, the federal courts, and legal scholars. The *Illinois Brick* decision, the easing of Justice Department merger guidelines in 1982 and 1984, and a pro-business Supreme Court may be reasons for a decline in private antitrust filings from 1,528 in 1977

ISSUES AND TRENDS

Sections 1 and 2 of the Sherman Act apply to "trade or commerce . . . with foreign nations." The courts on a case-by-case basis have interpreted the language of these statutes to determine what activities of U.S. companies operating abroad come within this jurisdiction of the Sherman Act. The general principle that has evolved on a case-by-case basis has been that if U.S. or foreign private companies enter into an *agreement* forbidden by Section 1, and it *affects* the foreign commerce of the United States, American courts have jurisdiction. The Department of Justice has issued foreign antitrust enforcement guidelines in which it requires business practices to have a "substantial and foreseeable effect" on U.S. commerce. The business practices must have a direct and intended effect. For example, if two companies based in the United States were able to fix the prices of widgets in three Eastern European countries because they were the sole licensed producers there, and then use the profits to force out competitors in the United States, the Justice Department might be willing to step in.

Another issue is whether nations that do not have a competitive model of private entrepreneurs are subject to the jurisdiction of U.S. courts. For example, when the International Association of Machinists sued the Organization of Petroleum Exporting Countries (OPEC) for price fixing under Section 1 of the Sherman Act, the federal court said it lacked jurisdiction under the Act of State doctrine, which states that U.S. courts will not evaluate the lawfulness of acts of nation-states or state-owned companies performed within their own territory even if the foreign commerce of the United States is affected.

to 452 in 1990 (according to the annual reports of the Director of the Administrative Office of the United States Courts).

Historically a higher percentage of the antitrust cases initiated by the Department of Justice have been settled by agreement between the government and the defendants. This is an impressive fact, because it is more difficult for the government to settle a case than it is for a private litigant. Before a settlement may be judicially approved, the government must publish the terms of the proposed agreement along with a Competitive Impact Statement that details its likely economic effect. This is done to ensure that the interests of the public are served by the settlement. If the judge approves, a consent decree is filed with the court. Violation of the terms of the decree puts the violating party in contempt of court. If a criminal action has been filed, the same basic process is followed to obtain a decree of nolo contendere.

Settling of cases saves the government time and money and allows the Department of Justice to deal with more antitrust violations. Nevertheless, the settlement of antitrust cases has several drawbacks. For example, if the government litigates and wins, that victory constitutes prima facie evidence of the antitrust violation and may be used by a private plaintiff in a civil treble-damages suit. It is then necessary for the private plaintiff only to prove the injuries that he or she suffered and that they resulted from the proven antitrust violation. On the other hand, a consent settlement entered into and accepted prior to the taking of any testimony carries no implications for a private suit. The private litigant will have to prove both the fact of the antitrust violation and his or her injuries resulting therefrom. In addition, it may be questioned whether an "I'll promise not to do it again if you won't prosecute" approach effectively deters others from engaging in similar practices.

Exemptions from the Antitrust Laws

Certain types of businesses and certain business and labor union activities are specifically exempted from the antitrust laws. In some instances, exemptions are based on recognition of the fact that competition is not desirable in all market situations. Other exemptions, like the exempt status of professional baseball, are based on nothing more than historical legal quirks. Two of the most important exemptions—regulated industries and labor unions—are briefly discussed here. In addition to these two, there are other important exemptions (see Table 54-1).

Regulated Industries

A number of important industries are closely regulated by federal and state agencies to protect the public interest. These include transportation, electricity, gas, telephone service, and broadcasting. Because intervention by antitrust enforcement agencies would be redundant, these industries enjoy a qualified exemption from direct application of the antitrust laws. In addition, some of these industries are thought to involve so-called natural monopolies, thus making competitive considerations irrelevant. The exemptions, however, are not absolute, and the Justice Department has the authority to review antitrust-related decisions by federal regulatory agencies.

Labor Unions

Over the years Congress has exempted the organizational and operational activities of labor unions from the antitrust laws. Today labor unions retain their exempt status so long as they do not combine with nonlabor groups to effect restraints of trade. Thus, if a firm enters into a conspiracy with a labor union for the purpose of economically handicapping a competing firm, the antitrust laws will apply. There have been few examples of such outright labor–nonlabor conspiracies. Instead, the courts have had to deal with the question of the applicability of the antitrust laws to more ordinary and more subtle labor–management relationships. For example, labor in a sense combines with a nonlabor group every time a collective bargaining agreement is signed. Yet the peaceful resolution of labor disputes through collective bargaining is encouraged by federal labor law. In view of these countervailing policies, can an anticompetitive provision contained in a collective bargaining agreement in and of itself be considered a conspiracy in restraint of trade? The courts have yet to effectively resolve this difficult question.

TABLE 54-1
_____

Activities Wholly or Partially Exempt from the Federal Antitrust Statutes

Activities	Examples and/or Bases for Exemptions
Regulated industries	Transportation, electricity, gas, and telephone service are closely regulated.
Labor union activities	Collective bargaining is encouraged for the peaceful resolution of disputes.
Intrastate activities	Intrastate telephone calls are regulated by state public utility commissions.
Agricultural activities	Farmers may belong to cooperatives that legally set prices.
Baseball	The U.S. Supreme Court declared baseball a sport, not a trade. No other professional sport has been exempted by the Congress or the courts.
Activities falling within the Act of State doctrine	In *Parker v. Brown* (1943) the U.S. Supreme Court held a state marketing program that was clearly anticompetitive to be exempt from the federal antitrust statutes because the program obtained its authority from a "clearly articulated legislative command of the state." The Court looks at the degree of involvement before exempting any *activity* under this doctrine.
Activities of cities, towns, and villages	The *Local Government Antitrust Act of 1984* prohibits monetary recovery under the federal antitrust laws from any of these local subdivisions or from local officials, agents, or employees.
Export activities	The *Webb–Pommerce Act of 1918* and the *Export Trading Act of 1982* made the formation of selling cooperatives of U.S. exporters exempt. The *Joint Venture Trading Act of 1983* exempted certain joint ventures of competing companies when seeking to compete with foreign companies that are private and/or state-controlled. Approval of the Justice Department is required. The *Shipping Act of 1984* allowed shipping lines to enter into joint ventures and to participate in international shipping conferences that set worldwide rates and divide routes and shipments.

Sherman Act

Price Fixing and Conspiracies in Restraint of Trade

Section 1 of the Sherman Act prohibits contracts, combinations, and conspiracies that restrain interstate trade. The Supreme Court has interpreted this provision to prohibit only those restraints of trade that are *unreasonable*. Thus, for most cases brought under Section 1, the courts apply a **rule-of-reason standard** in which the procompetitive effects of a trade restraint are weighed against its anticompetitive effects in order to determine its reasonableness. Such factors as the nature of the business, the history of the restraint, the reason that businesses have adopted it, and factors peculiar to the industry are considered.

While the rule-of-reason standard is applied to determine the legality of most types of trade restraints, certain types of commercial behavior have been deemed to be so inherently anticompetitive that they cannot be justified under any circumstances. These types of trade restraints are evaluated under the **per se standard**: Engaging in the behavior is an antitrust violation per se (in and of itself). Unlike the rule-of-reason standard, the per se standard does not allow the defendant to escape liability by showing that its behavior did not substantially threaten competition. When the per se standard applies, it need be proved only that the defendant actually engaged in the behavior as alleged.

Horizontal price fixing, which occurs when direct competitors in an industry collude on pricing policy, is the classic example of activity which is per se illegal under the antitrust laws. Agreements fixing prices have always appealed to businesspeople because they reduce, even eliminate, the risks of economic loss. Suppose competitors A, B, and C, the major manufacturers of generators, agree to take turns offering low bids. Each is assured a portion of the available market, and each knows that price competition with its attendant potential for monetary losses will be eliminated. Artificially high prices can safely be charged and greater profits made because those who buy generators will pay more than they would in a competitive market. Similar results would follow in a broader-based industry if the majority of firms were to agree to charge the same price, or at least that no one would charge less than a specified price.

The judicial rationalization for treating horizontal price fixing as a per se violation of the antitrust laws is provided by the following quotation from *United States v. Trenton Potteries Co.*, a 1927 Supreme Court case:

> The aim and result of every price-fixing agreement, if effective, is the elimination of one form of competition. The power to fix prices, whether reasonably exercised or not, involves power to control the market and to fix arbitrary and unreasonable prices. The reasonable price fixed today may through economic and business changes become the unreasonable price of tomorrow. Once established, it may be maintained unchanged because of the absence of competition secured by the agreement for a price reasonable when fixed.

In addition to horizontal price fixing, price fixing occurs between firms at different levels of the distribution chain for a particular product. This is known as **vertical price fixing**. Price agreements between wholesalers and retailers, manufacturers and dealers, franchisors and franchisees, are examples of vertical price fixing. For example, a television manufacturer, worried that unwise dealer pricing policies might hurt demand for its product, might contractually require its dealers to sell the televisions at a certain price. This would affect competition in the retail market for televisions, since the dealers would not be free to adjust the price of the television sets to reflect competitive pressures.

Antitrust experts have grappled with the question of whether vertical price fixing, like horizontal price fixing, should be a per se antitrust violation. The U.S. Supreme Court in *Monsanto v. Spray-Rite Service Corporation* (1984) continued to apply the per se standard to vertical price fixing even though the Justice Department argued that a rule-of-reason standard would better promote economic efficiencies. In its 1985 *Vertical Restraint Guidelines*, the Justice Department stated that it would hold vertical price restraints per se illegal only when "there is direct or circumstantial evidence of an explicit agreement to establish specific resale prices."

Horizontal Territorial Limitation and Customer Allocation

One device for reducing competition is an agreement between business rivals to divide markets on a geographic basis. Each of two or more competi-

---

ETHICS
Matching Prices

You have surely seen ads in the paper in which a retailer states a "low price guarantee" such as the following:

> We'll match any local competitor's price on an identical item, or we'll cheerfully refund the difference if the item was purchased from us within 7 days of the competitor's ad.

Some have questioned whether such an ad is really aimed at customers or, instead, whether it is a coded public message to competitors. The translated message to competitors would be "don't lower your prices below ours, because if you do we will match your price and it won't do you any good."

If you were an advertising manager for a retailer, would you offer a "low price guarantee"?

tors agrees not to sell in a designated territory. Courts have frequently referred to these agreements as **horizontal territorial limitations.** Similarly, business competitors sometimes agree to allocate customers. When horizontal territorial limitations and/or customer allocations are carried out, the seller that is left in the market can generally obtain higher prices and provide less service because of its monopoly position. Since territorial sales restrictions and customer allocation have few redeeming features, they have consistently been held to be per se violations of antitrust laws. In *United States v. Topco Associates, Inc.*, (1972) the Supreme Court ruled that market allocations were per se illegal even when a group of small- and medium-size grocery chains with 6 percent of the market created a joint subsidiary to market private-label products in competition with large supermarket chains such as A&P and Safeway. The Topco participants divided markets for the sale of Topco brand products so they could compete more efficiently with large rival chains. Competition among sellers of Topco pri-

vate-label products in the same market was eliminated following the market division. This decision has been criticized in light of the *Sylvania* case, cited later in this chapter. Critics argue that Topco had so little market power (6 percent) that it could not adversely affect interbrand competition—that is, between A&P and Topco or Safeway and Topco. Also, it is often argued that if Topco did not allocate exclusive territories to the participants, they would have no incentive to compete with A&P or Safeway. Sellers of Topco labels in adjoining areas would undercut a participant's prices and also have a "free ride" on their promotions or advertising. Critics suggest that some joint ventures may be procompetitive and thus horizontal or vertical restraints might be best judged by a rule of reason. In *NCAA v. Board of Regents of the University of Oklahoma*, the U.S. Supreme Court rejected the per se approach in determining whether the NCAA was the exclusive agent to sell all college football games to the television networks and to fix prices for those broadcasts. This case is excerpted below.

NATIONAL COLLEGIATE ATHLETIC ASSOCIATION, PETITIONER V. BOARD OF REGENTS OF THE UNIVERSITY OF OKLAHOMA AND UNIVERSITY OF GEORGIA ATHLETIC ASSOCIATION

U.S. Supreme Court
468 U.S. 85 (1984)

BACKGROUND: In 1981 petitioner-defendant National Collegiate Athletic Association (NCAA) adopted a plan for the televising of college football games of its member institutions for the 1982–1985 football seasons. The plan stated that its purpose was to reduce the adverse effects of live television on football game attendance. The plan limited the total amount of televised intercollegiate football games and the number of games that any one college might televise. No member of the NCAA was permitted to make any sale of television rights except in accordance with the plan. The NCAA had separate agreements with the two carrying networks, ABC and CBS, granting each network the right to telecast the live "exposures" described in the plan. Each network agreed to pay a specified "minimum aggregate compensation" to the participating NCAA members, and was authorized to negotiate directly with the members for the right to televise their games. Respondent-plaintiff universities, in addition to being NCAA members, were members of the College Football Association (CFA), which was originally organized to promote the interests of major football-playing colleges within the NCAA structure, but whose members eventually claimed that they should have a greater voice in the formulation of football television policy than they had in the NCAA. The CFA negotiated a contract with NBC that would have allowed a more liberal number of television appearances for each member college and increased the revenues realized by CFA members. In response, the NCAA announced that it would take disciplinary action against any CFA member that complied with the CFA–NBC contract. Respondents then commenced an action in U.S. District Court, which, after an extended trial, held that the controls exercised by the NCAA over televising college football games violated Section 1 of the Sherman Act. Accordingly, the court granted injunctive relief. The Court of Appeals affirmed. The NCAA appealed.

Stevens, Justice

The plan adopted in 1981 for the 1982–85 seasons is at issue in this case. This plan recites that it is intended to reduce, insofar as possible, the adverse effects of live television upon football game attendance. It provides that "all forms of television of the football games of NCAA member institutions during the Plan control periods shall be in accordance with this Plan."

There can be no doubt that the challenged practices of the NCAA constitute a "restraint of trade" in the sense that they limit members' freedom to negotiate and enter into their own television contracts. In that sense, however, every contract is a restraint of trade, and as we have repeatedly recognized, the Sherman Act was intended to prohibit only unreasonable restraints of trade.

It is also undeniable that these practices share characteristics of restraints we have previously held unreasonable. The NCAA is an association of schools which compete against each other to attract television revenues, not to mention fans and athletes. As the District Court found, the policies of the NCAA with respect to television rights are ultimately controlled by the vote of member institutions. By participating in an association which prevents member institutions from competing against each other on the basis of price or kind of television rights that can be offered to broadcasters, the NCAA member institutions have created a horizontal restraint—an agreement among competitors on the way in which they will compete with one another. A restraint of this type has often been held to be unreasonable as a matter of law (per se). Because it places a ceiling on the number of games member institutions may televise, the horizontal agreement places an artificial limit on the quantity of televised football that is available to broadcasters and consumers. By restraining the quantity of television rights available for sale, the challenged practices create a limitation on output; our cases have held that such limitations are unreasonable restraints of trade. Moreover, the District Court found that the minimum aggregate price, in fact, operates to preclude any price negotiation between broadcasters and institutions, thereby constituting horizontal price fixing, perhaps the paradigm of an unreasonable restraint of trade.

Horizontal price-fixing and output limitation are ordinarily condemned as a matter of law under an "illegal per se" approach because the probability that these practices are anticompetitive is so high; a per se rule is applied when "the practice facially appears to be one that would always or almost always tend to restrict competition and decrease output." In such circumstances a restraint is presumed unreasonable without inquiry into the particular market context in which it is found. Nevertheless, we have decided that it would be inappropriate to apply a per se rule to this case.

Our decision not to apply a per se rule rests in large part on our recognition that a certain degree of cooperation is necessary if the type of competition that petitioner and its member institutions seek to market is to be preserved. It is reasonable to assume that most of the regulatory controls of the NCAA are justifiable means of fostering competition among amateur athletic teams and therefore procompetitive because they enhance public interest in intercollegiate athletics. The specific restraints on football telecasts that are challenged in this case do not, however, fit into the same mold as do rules defining the conditions of the contest, the eligibility of participants, or the manner in which members of a joint enterprise shall share the responsibilities and the benefits of the total venture.

The interest in maintaining a competitive balance that is asserted by the NCAA as a justification for regulating all television of intercollegiate football is not related to any neutral standard or to any readily identifiable group of competitors. The television plan is not even arguably tailored to serve such an interest. There is no evidence that this restriction produces any greater measure of equality throughout the NCAA than would a restriction on alumni donations, tuition rates, or any other revenue producing activity.

Perhaps the most important reason for rejecting the argument that the interest in competitive balance is served by the television plan is the District Court's unambiguous and well supported finding that many more games would be televised in a free market than under the NCAA plan. The hypothesis that legitimates the maintenance of competitive balance as a procompetitive justification under the Rule of Reason is that equal competition will maximize consumer demand for the product. The finding that consumption will materially increase if the controls are removed is a compelling demonstration that they do not in fact serve any such legitimate purpose.

Today we hold only that the record supports the District Court's conclusion that by curtailing output and blunting the ability of member institutions to respond to consumer preference, the NCAA has restricted rather than enhanced the place of intercollegiate athletics in the nation's life.

DECISION: Affirmed. The Supreme Court ruled in favor of the University of Oklahoma and University of Georgia.

Vertical Territorial Limitation and Customer Allocation

Agreements that limit territories in which sales can be made are frequently entered into by manufacturers and dealers or by distributors who sell the manufacturer's product. These **vertical territorial limitations** generally provide an exclusive territory for a single dealer or small number of dealers in a particular product. Both the manufacturer and the dealer-distributor benefit from these territorial restraints. Many argue that limitations of this kind benefit society as well because they increase *interbrand* competition even though they clearly curtail *intrabrand* competition. For example, franchise agreements frequently contain provisions limiting the territory in which a franchisee can operate.

Because under certain circumstances benefits can be shown as a result of market divisions of this nature, the Supreme Court has generally examined each case individually and weighed the reasons for the restrictions against the value of the general policy of fostering competition. Territorial restraints are important to successful quality merchandising. A manufacturer that wishes to keep dealers who are financially sound and able to provide high-grade distribution and service facilities frequently has to guarantee that the dealer will enjoy an exclusive right to market the product in a particular territory. Without such assurances, some dealers might be reluctant to invest the capital necessary to develop and maintain quality facilities.

Another argument used to support the imposition of territorial restraints by a manufacturer on a distributor is that these restraints facilitate the distributor's ability to compete with other brands because the distributor is not forced to spend resources competing with others selling the same brand. This, the argument goes, is one reason that small businesses sometimes survive in highly competitive markets. Preventing intrabrand competition also has social utility in a market in which a company competes with a much stronger rival as well as for enterprises that depend for their success on personal relationships between the buyer and seller.

Territorial restraints that eliminate intrabrand competition, however, are not always in the best interests of the public. Many generically similar products sold under different brand names may be highly differentiated in the buyer's mind. Thus the buyer might consider purchasing only one brand and would look for price competition among different dealers in that brand. Much competition in the automobile industry is actually intrabrand. Were the antitrust laws to permit territorial arrangements that allocated exclusive territories to dealers in a particular brand, the ability of automobile buyers to compare prices among different dealers in that brand would be eliminated and a substantial reduction in competition would result. Another argument against intrabrand territorial restrictions is that the elimination of competitors often increases concentration in markets in which far too little competition already exists.

In the case that follows, the manufacturer attempted to maintain control over territory by limiting locations from which retailers sold. Here the U.S. Supreme Court overruled a previous case in which it had used a per se standard to judge nonprice vertical restrictions illegal. Using a rule-of-reason standard, the Court came to a different conclusion as to the legality of vertical territorial restraints.

CONTINENTAL T.V., INC. v. GTE SYLVANIA
U.S. Supreme Court
433 U.S. 36 (1977)

BACKGROUND: GTE Sylvania (plaintiff-respondent) manufactures and sells television sets. Prior to 1962 Sylvania sold its televisions to independent or company-owned distributors, who resold to a large and diverse group of retailers. Prompted by a decline in its market share to 1 to 2 percent of the national market, Sylvania adopted a franchise plan.

Sylvania phased out its wholesale distributors and sold directly to a smaller and more select group of franchised retailers. In order to attract aggressive, competent retailers, Sylvania limited the number of franchises in any area and required each franchisee to sell only from the location at which he was franchised. A franchise did not constitute an exclusive territory. Sylvania retained the right to modify the number of franchises in an area.

The revised marketing strategy was successful, and by 1965 Sylvania's share of national television set sales had increased to approximately 5 percent. Dissatisfied with its sales in the city of San Francisco, Sylvania decided to establish an additional San Francisco retailer (Young Brothers), which would be in competition with Continental (defendant-petitioner-appellant in this case), since the proposed new franchisee would be only 1 mile away. Continental protested that the location of the new franchise violated Sylvania's marketing policy, but Sylvania persisted in its plan. Continental then canceled a large Sylvania order and placed an order with Phillips, one of Sylvania's competitors.

During this same period, Continental expressed a desire to open a store in Sacramento, a desire Sylvania attributed at least in part to Continental's displeasure over the Young Brothers decision. Sylvania believed that the Sacramento market was adequately served by existing Sylvania retailers and denied the request. In the face of this denial, Continental advised Sylvania in September 1965 that it was moving Sylvania merchandise from its San Jose warehouse to a new retail location that it had leased in Sacramento. Two weeks later, allegedly for unrelated reasons, Sylvania's credit department reduced Continental's credit line from $300,000 to $50,000. In response to the reduction in credit and the generally deteriorating relations with Sylvania, Continental withheld all payments owed to John P. Maguire & Co., Inc. (Maguire), the finance company that handled the credit arrangements between Sylvania and its retailers. Shortly thereafter, Sylvania terminated Continental's franchise, and Maguire filed this diversity action in the U.S. District Court seeking recovery of money owed and of secured merchandise held by Continental. Continental filed cross-claims against Sylvania and Maguire, claiming that Sylvania had violated Section 1 of the Sherman Act by entering into and enforcing franchise agreements that prohibited sale of Sylvania products by Continental and other franchises except from specific locations. At the District Court level, the jury found in favor of Continental, awarding treble (triple) damages totaling $1,774,515 for violations of Section 1 of the Sherman Act. The Court of Appeals reversed in favor of Sylvania. Continental appealed.

Powell, Justice

We turn first to Continental's contention that Sylvania's restriction on retail locations is a *per se* violation of §1 of the Sherman Act as interpreted in *Schwinn*. (*United States v. Arnold Schwinn*, 338 U.S. 365(1967)).

Schwinn came to this Court on appeal by the United States from the District Court's decision. . . . [T]he Court (in *Schwinn*) proceeded to articulate the following "bright line" *per se* rule of illegality for vertical restrictions: "Under the Sherman Act, it is unreasonable without more for a manufacturer to seek to restrict and confine areas or persons with whom an article may be traded after the manufacturer has parted with dominion over it." But the Court expressly stated that the rule of reason governs when "the manufacturer retains title, dominion, and risk with respect to the product and the position and function of the dealer in question are, in fact, indistinguishable from those of an agent or salesman of the manufacturer."

In the present case, it is undisputed that title to the televisions passed from Sylvania to Continental. Thus, the *Schwinn per se* rule applies unless Sylvania's restriction on locations falls outside *Schwinn's* prohibition against a manufacturer attempting to restrict a "retailer's freedom as to where and to whom it will resell the products."

Sylvania argues that if *Schwinn* cannot be distinguished, it should be reconsidered. Although *Schwinn* is supported by the principle of *stare decisis*, we are convinced that the need for clarification of the law in this area justifies reconsideration. *Schwinn* itself was an abrupt and largely unexplained departure from *White Motor Co. v. United States*, where only four years earlier the Court had refused to endorse a *per se* rule for vertical restrictions. Since its announcement, *Schwinn* has been the subject of continuing controversy and confusion, both in the scholarly journals and in the federal courts. The great weight of scholarly opinion has been critical of the decision, and a number of the federal courts confronted with analogous vertical restrictions have sought to limit its reach. In our view, the experience of the past 10 years should be brought to bear on this subject of considerable commercial importance.

In essence, the issue before us is whether *Schwinn's per se* rule can be justified under the demanding standards of *Northern Pac. R. Co.* The Court's refusal to endorse a *per se* rule in *White Motor Co.* was based on its uncertainty as to whether vertical restrictions satisfied those standards. Addressing this question for the first time, the Court stated:

> We need to know more than we do about the actual impact of these arrangements on competition to decide whether they have such a 'pernicious effect on competition and lack . . . any redeeming virtue' and therefore should be classified as *per se* violations of the Sherman Act.

Only four years later the Court in *Schwinn* announced its sweeping *per se* rule without even a reference to *Northern Pac. R. Co.* and with no explanation of its sudden change in position. We turn now to consider *Schwinn* in light of *Northern Pac. R. Co.*

The question remains whether the *per se* rule stated in *Schwinn* should be expanded to include nonsale transactions or abandoned in favor of a return to the rule of reason. We have found no persuasive support for expanding the rule. As noted above, the *Schwinn* Court recognized the undesirability of "prohibit[ing] all vertical restrictions of territory and all franchising. . . ." And even Continental does not urge us to hold that all such restrictions are *per se* illegal.

We revert to the standard articulated in *Northern Pac. R. Co.*, and reiterated in *White Motor*, for determining whether vertical restriction must be "conclusively presumed to be unreasonable and therefore illegal without elaborate inquiry as to the precise harm they have caused or the business excuse for their use." Such restrictions, in varying forms, are widely used in our free market economy. As indicated above, there is substantial scholarly and judicial authority supporting their economic utility. There is relatively little authority to the contrary. Certainly, there has been no showing in this case, either generally or with respect to Sylvania's agreements, that vertical restrictions have or are likely to have a "pernicious effect on competition" or that they "lack . . . any redeeming virtue." Accordingly, we conclude that the *per se* rule stated in *Schwinn* must be overruled. In so holding, we do not foreclose the possibility that particular applications of vertical restrictions might justify *per se* prohibition under *Northern Pac. R. Co.* But we do make clear that departure from the rule of reason standard must be based upon demonstrable economic effect rather than—as in *Schwinn*—upon formalistic line drawing.

In sum, we conclude that the appropriate decision is to return to the rule of reason that governed vertical restrictions prior to *Schwinn*. When competitive effects are shown to result from particular vertical restrictions they can be adequately policed under the rule of reason, the standard traditionally applied for the majority of anticompetitive practices challenged under §1 of the Act.

DECISION: Affirmed. The Supreme Court ruled in favor of Sylvania.

Trade Associations

A **trade association** is a loosely knit combination of business firms operating in the same industry. Frequently the members are either competitors or potential competitors. Most associations are supported by dues and governed by directors elected by members. The relationship is often an informal one, and members can usually resign at will. Daily operations of the association generally are the responsibility of a paid executive director and his or her staff. In most instances the purpose of the association is to promote the common interests of the members by providing services, supplying information, and engaging in promotional activities such as institutional advertising. Many activities of trade associations are beneficial not only to the members but also to the economic system.

Trade associations sometimes promote more effective competition. When participants in a particular industry have some idea of industrywide inventories, sales, and costs of production, they can plan more efficiently. This reduces costs, prevents waste, and improves services to the public. Trade associations have often been leaders in the standardization and development of products. In addition, they may establish general rules for the industry, carry out market surveys, provide a means for exchanging credit information, and supply arbitrators to aid in settling disputes. Some trade associations have also been instrumental in developing and improving ethical standards within their industry.

The opportunity provided competitors by trade association contacts, however, sometimes leads to activities that may violate the antitrust statutes. Activities that have resulted in antitrust prosecutions usually have involved some covert effort to control prices. When members report prices to their association, pressures can be used to force those firms charging lower prices (firms that are now clearly identified) to get into line with the industry. In several cases, trade associations have been used by dominant members to enforce desired price levels by denying certain benefits of the association to recalcitrants. These activities have reduced competition and increased profit levels for association members at the expense of the buying public.

In general, the courts attempt to distinguish between legitimate and illegitimate activities of trade associations. Price reports by members for the use of the membership are usually permitted if the association does not identify the prices with the names of the reporting firms and if the information is also available to nonmembers, customers, and the government. Just as knowledge of prices charged by competitors can be used to attain common industrywide prices, so other types of data sometimes supplied by members of a trade association may be used to restrict competition. Nevertheless, the compilation of cost data and the circulation of information about inventories, unused production capacity, unfilled orders, and sales can also encourage more realistic competition. As long as this type of information is disclosed in general terms, it is not subject to government restraints. If, however, such information is used solely by the membership and is not available to the public, the courts will closely scrutinize those activities.

Boycotts

Another business practice that is permissible if done individually but illegal if done in collusion is the **boycott**. A single business firm may withhold its patronage or refuse to sell in order to accom-

plish some self-serving end, but a concerted group refusal to deal has been held to violate Section 1 of the Sherman Act. Courts have generally applied a per se prohibition to this type of activity when it is carried out in a commercial context. Boycotts unrelated to the profits of the group refusing to deal have generally not been held violations of Section 1 of the Sherman Act. For example, in *Missouri v. National Organization of Women* (8th Cir., 1980), the National Organization of Women (NOW) organized a boycott of states that refused to endorse the proposed Equal Rights Amendment. Missouri sued NOW, claiming a violation of Section 1 of the Sherman Act. The Eighth Circuit Court of Appeals termed the Sherman Act inapplicable to this situation and the Supreme Court denied Missouri's petition for review.

In the case that follows, the U.S. Supreme Court considered another boycott that appeared, at first blush, to raise some of the issues posed by the NOW case.

FTC v. SUPERIOR COURT TRIAL LAWYERS ASSOCIATION

U.S. Supreme Court
58 LW 4145 (1990)

BACKGROUND: Respondents were a group of lawyers who frequently acted as court-appointed counsel for indigent criminal defendants in the District of Columbia. The lawyers were compensated for their services pursuant to D.C.'s Criminal Justice Act (CJA), and were commonly referred to as "CJA lawyers." The CJA lawyers had been attempting for some time to increase their hourly compensation, which many observers agreed was far too low. In 1983, the lawyers staged a boycott designed to convince the D.C. government to raise their hourly compensation to $35. The boycott created chaos in D.C.'s criminal justice system, and the D.C. government soon agreed to the increase demanded. The FTC filed a complaint against the lawyers for engaging in an illegal price-fixing scheme and boycott. The case was first heard by an administrative law judge (ALJ), who ruled that the complaint should be dismissed. The FTC reversed the ALJ's decision, ruling that the boycott was per se illegal and ordering the lawyers to refrain from engaging in such boycotts in the future. The lawyers obtained a review from the U.S. Court of Appeals, which ruled that the boycott was not illegal under the antitrust laws because it was designed to convey a political message. The U.S. Supreme Court then agreed to review the case.

Stevens, Justice

As the ALJ, the FTC, and the Court of Appeals all agreed, respondents' boycott "constituted a classic restraint of trade within the meaning of Section 1 of the Sherman Act." . . . Prior to the boycott CJA lawyers were in competition with one another, each deciding independently whether and how often to offer to provide services to the District at CJA rates. The agreement among the CJA lawyers was designed to obtain higher prices for their services and was implemented by a concerted refusal to serve an important customer in the market for legal services and, indeed, the only customer in the market for the particular services that CJA regulars offered. "This constriction of supply is the essence of 'price-fixing,' whether it be accomplished by agreeing upon a price, which will decrease the quantity demanded, or by agreeing upon an output, which will increase the price offered." The horizontal arrangement among these competitors was unquestionably a "naked restraint" on price and output.

It is of course true that the city purchases respondents' services because it has a constitutional duty to provide representation to indigent defendants. It is likewise true that the quality of representation may improve when rates are increased. Yet neither of these facts is an acceptable justification for an otherwise unlawful restraint of trade. As we have remarked before, the "Sherman Act reflects a legislative judgment that ultimately competition will produce not only lower prices, but also better goods and services." *National Soc. of Professional Engineers v. United States* (1978). This judgment "recognizes that all elements of a bargain—quality, service, safety, and durability—and not just the immediate cost, are favorably affected by the free opportunity to select among alternative offers." *Ibid.* That is equally so when the quality of legal advocacy, rather than engineering design, is at issue.

The social justifications proffered for respondents' restraint of trade thus do not make it any less unlawful. The statutory policy underlying the Sherman Act "precludes inquiry into the question whether competition is good or bad." *Ibid.* Respondents' argument, like that made by the petitioners in *Professional Engineers*, ultimately asks us to find that their boycott is permissible because the price it seeks to set is reasonable. But it was settled shortly after the Sherman Act was passed that it "is no excuse that the prices fixed are themselves reasonable." *Catalano, Inc. v. Target Sales, Inc.*, (1980). Respondents' agreement is not outside the coverage of the Sherman Act simply because its objective was the enactment of favorable legislation. . . .

The lawyers' association argues that if its conduct would otherwise be prohibited by the Sherman Act and the Federal Trade Act, it is nonetheless protected by the First Amendment rights recognized in *NAACP v. Claiborne Hardware* (1982). That case arose after black citizens boycotted white merchants in Claiborne County, Miss. The white merchants sued under state law to recover losses from the boycott. We found that the "right of the States to regulate economic activity could not justify a complete prohibition against a nonviolent, politically motivated boycott designed to force governmental and economic change and to effectuate rights guaranteed by the Constitution itself." We accordingly held that "the nonviolent elements of petitioners' activities are entitled to the protection of the First Amendment."

The lawyers' association contends that because it, like the boycotters in *Claiborne Hardware*, sought to vindicate constitutional rights, it should enjoy a similar First Amendment protection. It is, of course, clear that the association's efforts to publicize the boycott, to explain the merits of its cause, and to lobby District officials to enact favorable legislation—like similar activities in *Claiborne Hardware*—were activities that were fully protected by the First Amendment. But nothing in the FTC's order would curtail such activities, and nothing in the FTC's reasoning condemned any of those activities.

The activity that the FTC order prohibits is a concerted refusal by CJA lawyers to accept any further assignments until they receive an increase in their compensation; the undenied objective of their boycott was an economic advantage for those who agreed to participate. It is true that the *Claiborne Hardware* case also involved a boycott. That boycott, however, differs in a decisive respect. Those who joined the *Claiborne Hardware* boycott sought no special advantage for themselves. They were black citizens in Port Gibson, Mississippi, who had been the victims of political, social, and economic discrimination for many years. They sought only the equal respect and equal treatment to which they were constitutionally entitled. They struggled "to change a social order that had consistently treated them as second class citizens." As we observed, the campaign was not intended "to destroy legitimate competition." Equality and freedom are preconditions of the free market, and not commodities to be haggled over within it.

The same cannot be said of attorney's fees. As we recently pointed out, our reasoning in *Claiborne Hardware* is not applicable to a boycott conducted by business competitors who "stand to profit financially from a lessening of competition in the boycotted market." *Allied Tube Corp. v. Indian Head.* No matter how altruistic the motives of respondents may have been, it is undisputed that their immediate objective was to increase the price that they would be paid for their services. Such an economic boycott is well within the category that was expressly distinguished in the *Claiborne Hardware* opinion itself.

Only after recognizing the well-settled validity of prohibitions against various economic boycotts did we conclude in *Claiborne Hardware* that "peaceful, political activity such as that found in the [Mississippi] boycott" are entitled to constitutional protection. We reaffirmed the government's "power to regulate [such] economic activity." This conclusion applies with special force when a clear objective of the boycott is to economically advantage the participants.

DECISION: Reversed. The U.S. Supreme Court ruled that the lawyers had violated the antitrust laws.

Tying Agreements

Business managers who control the sale of a product in limited supply because of some natural advantage, or possibly because of a patent, have sometimes tried to increase the sale of another product by tying purchase of the two together. The buyer is not permitted to purchase one item without also purchasing the other. Arrangements of this kind are called **tie-ins** or **tying agreements**. In one well-known case, the International Salt Company, which had patents on two salt-dispensing machines, leased the machines (the *tying* product) only if the lessee would agree to buy all the salt (the *tied* product) to be used in the machines from International Salt. The Supreme Court, in *International Salt Co. v. United States* (1947), held this to be an unlawful restraint of trade. Tying agreements have also been used by sellers who, for one reason or another, are convinced that the "leverage" of one of their products will enable them to sell another, less marketable product.

Tying agreements have been used extensively in sales to consumers, but most litigation has arisen out of transactions at the producer level. Economically, the device is objectionable because it limits other sellers of the tied product (the second good or service) from competing in that particular market. This is considered an artificial barrier to competition and has been the subject of considerable judicial censure.

At one time the Supreme Court argued that the effects of a tie-in were so pernicious that mere proof of the agreement established violation of the antitrust laws (Section 1 of the Sherman Act, Section 3 of the Clayton Act). That is, such agreements were to be condemned per se. This, however, does not appear to be the present state of the law. Tie-in agreements will almost invariably be struck down if the tying product is either a natural or a legal monopoly, such as a patented product. Even when the seller of the tying product does not have monopoly control, tying contracts will be unenforceable (1) if control of the tying product has given the seller sufficient economic power to lessen competition in the market in which the tied product is sold and (2) if a substantial amount of interstate commerce is affected. This is true even if no actual injury to competition can be proved.

On the other hand, tying agreements have been allowed by the courts using a rule of reason, by which the seller is able to prove that the tied product or service is necessary to maintain the utility and reputation of the desired product. Sellers have successfully defended also by showing that the tying product is only of minor importance in the market and that the buyer was not forced by economic pressures to accept the tied product. In addition, tie-ins are economically beneficial when they are used by new competitors to facili- tate entry into markets dominated by established sellers. The case excerpted below illustrates a rule-of-reason approach.

JEFFERSON PARISH HOSPITAL DISTRICT NO. 2 V. EDWIN G. HYDE

U.S. Supreme Court
468 U.S. 2 (1984)

BACKGROUND: Jefferson Parish Hospital (petitioner-defendant) was sued by Hyde, an anesthesiologist (plaintiff-respondent), who claimed that the hospital violated Section 1 of the Sherman Act. The defendant entered into an exclusive contract between itself and a firm of anesthesiologists (Roux & Associates), whereby the firm would provide all the anesthesiological services required by the hospital's patients. When the plain- tiff applied for admission to the hospital staff, the credentials committee and the medical staff's executive committee recommended approval of his application. The hospital board denied the application because of its exclusive contract with Roux & Associates. The District Court held for the defendants. The Court of Appeals held for the plaintiff. The hospital appealed.

Stevens, Justice

At issue in this case is the validity of an exclusive contract between a hospital and a firm of anesthesiologists. We must decide whether the contract gives rise to a *per se* violation of §1 of the Sherman Act because every patient undergoing surgery at the hospital must use the services of one firm of anesthesiologists, and, if not, whether the contract is neverthe- less illegal because it unreasonably restrains competition among anesthesiologists.

Certain types of contractual arrangements are deemed unreasonable as a matter of law. The character of the restraint produced by such an arrangement is considered a sufficient basis for presuming unreasonableness, without the necessity of any analysis of the market contest in which the arrangement may be found. A price fixing agreement between competi- tors is the classic example of such an arrangement. It is far too late in the history of our an- titrust jurisprudence to question the proposition that certain tying arrangements pose an unacceptable risk of stifling competition and therefore are unreasonable "per se."

Any inquiry into the validity of a tying arrangement must focus on the market or markets in which the two products are sold, for that is where the anticompetitive forcing has its im- pact. Thus, in this case our analysis of the tying issue must focus on the hospital's sale of services to its patients, rather than its contractual arrangements with the providers of anes- thesiological services. In making that analysis, we must consider whether petitioners are selling two separate products that may be tied together, and, if so, whether they have used their market power to force their patients to accept the tying arrangement.

The hospital has provided its patients with a package that includes the range of facilities and services required for a variety of surgical operations. At East Jefferson Hospital the package includes the services of the anesthesiologist. Petitioners argue that the package does not involve a tying arrangement at all—that they are merely providing a functionally in- tegrated package of services. Therefore, petitioners contend that it is inappropriate to apply principles concerning tying arrangements to this case.

Our cases indicate, however, that the answer to the question whether one or two prod- ucts are involved, turns not on the functional relation between them, but rather on the char- acter of the demand for the two items. Thus, in this case no tying arrangement can exist unless there is a sufficient demand for the purchase of anesthesiological services separate from hospital services to identify a distinct product market in which it is efficient to offer anesthesiological services separately from hospital services.

Unquestionably, the anesthesiological component of the package offered by the hospital could be provided separately and could be selected either by the individual patient or by one of the patient's doctors if the hospital did not insist on including anesthesiological services in the package it offers to its customers. As a matter of actual practice, anesthesiological services are billed separately from the hospital services petitioners provide. There is ample and uncontroverted testimony that patients or surgeons often request specific anesthesiologists to come to a hospital and provide anesthesia, and that the choice of an individual anesthesiologist separate from the choice of a hospital is particularly frequent in respondent's specialty, obstetric anesthesiology. The record amply supports the conclusion that consumers differentiate between anesthesiological services and the other hospital services provided by petitioners.

The question remains whether this arrangement involves the use of market power to force patients to buy services they would not otherwise purchase.

Seventy percent of the patients residing in Jefferson Parish enter hospitals other than East Jefferson. Thus East Jefferson's "dominance" over persons residing in Jefferson Parish is far from overwhelming. The fact that a substantial majority of the parish's residents elect not to enter East Jefferson means that the geographic data does not establish the kind of dominant market position that obviates the need for further inquiry into actual competitive conditions. The Court of Appeals acknowledged as much; it recognized that East Jefferson's market share alone was insufficient as a basis to infer market power, and buttressed its conclusion by relying on "market imperfections" that permit petitioners to charge noncompetitive prices for hospital services: the prevalence of third party payment for health care costs reduces price competition, and a lack of adequate information renders consumers unable to evaluate the quality of the medical care provided by competing hospitals. While these factors may generate "market power" in some abstract sense, they do not generate the kind of market power that justifies condemnation of tying. The record therefore does not provide a basis for applying the *per se* rule against tying to this arrangement.

In order to prevail in the absence of *per se* liability, respondent has the burden of proving that the Roux contract violated the Sherman Act because it unreasonably restrained competition. That burden necessarily involves an inquiry into the actual effect of the exclusive contract on competition among anesthesiologists.

Petitioners' closed policy may raise questions of medical ethics, and may have inconvenienced some patients who would prefer to have their anesthesia administered by someone other than a member of Roux & Associates, but it does not have the obviously unreasonable impact on purchasers that has characterized the tying arrangements that this Court has branded unlawful. There is no evidence that the price, the quality, or the supply or demand for either the "tying product" or the "tied product" involved in this case has been adversely affected by the exclusive contract between Roux and the hospital. It may well be true that the contract made it necessary for Dr. Hyde and others to practice elsewhere, rather than at East Jefferson. But there has been no showing that the market as a whole has been affected at all by the contract. There is simply no showing here of the kind of restraint on competition that is prohibited by the Sherman Act.

DECISION: Reversed. The U.S. Supreme Court ruled in favor of Jefferson Parish Hospital.

Monopoly Behavior

Monopoly in its purest economic sense involves a single firm without any effective competition. This means not only that no other firm produces the same product, but that no other firm produces a product that consumers could switch to if the monopolist's prices are too high. The foregoing definition is far too restrictive for an antimonopoly statute, because a firm could have the ability to act unilaterally and create market restraints without falling within the economic definition of a monopoly. Consequently, a legal definition of monopoly has been developed by the courts as they have interpreted the language of Section 2 of the Sherman Act. Section 2 reads as follows:

> Every person who shall monopolize, or attempt to monopolize, or combine or conspire with any other person or persons, to monopolize any part of the trade or commerce among the several States, or with foreign nations, shall be deemed guilty of a felony, and, on conviction thereof, shall be punished by fine not exceeding $10 million if a corporation, or, if any other person, $350,000, or by imprisonment not exceeding three years. . . .

As its language clearly indicates, Section 2 prohibits three types of activities: (1) monopolization, (2) attempts to monopolize, and (3) combinations or conspiracies to monopolize. Most actions under Section 2 have been against single firms charged with monopolization. Suits based on attempts or conspiracies to monopolize are much more difficult to win because they require proof of a specific intent to achieve the unlawful result of monopoly power.

The most difficult problem arising from the language of Section 2 is how the term *monopolize* should be legally defined. A variety of definitions is available to the courts. The courts could determine, for example, that only firms in single-firm industries are monopolies. They might alternatively decide that any firm capable of realizing specified "excess" profits by its pricing ability is a monopoly. They could take yet another approach and conclude that any firm controlling a certain percentage of an industry's total sales or assets is a monopoly. Unfortunately, the actual words of the statute provide little guidance in choosing among alternative definitions.

Relevant Product Market

To determine whether a firm has overwhelming market power, we must first determine the specific market in respect to which the firm's market power is to be judged. Assume, for example, that Tipsi Cola sues Croak-a-Cola for monopolizing the cola market. In deciding the case, should the court consider Croak-a-Cola's market power in the cola market? Or should Croak-a-Cola's power be considered in the broader market for all soft drinks, or perhaps all beverages? In order to decide a monopolization case, a court must define the **relevant product market**—that is, the court must decide which product or set of products shall be considered in evaluating the defendant's market power. The following well-known case established the basic test of cross-elasticity or interchangeability that the courts use in defining relevant markets.

UNITED STATES V. DU PONT & CO.

U.S. Supreme Court
351 U.S. 377 (1956)

BACKGROUND: The government instituted suit under Section 2 of the Sherman Act alleging that Du Pont (defendant) had monopolized and attempted and conspired to monopolize the cellophane market. The government asked the court to issue an injunction to prevent further monopolization and to order the divestiture of plants and assets, if necessary. At the time of the suit, Du Pont produced approximately 75 percent of all cellophane sold in the United States. This in turn represented 17.9 percent of all flexible wrapping material. The U.S. District Court found that the relevant product market was all flexible wrapping materials and entered a judgment for Du Pont on all counts. The government appealed directly to the Supreme Court.

Reed, Justice

During the period that is relevant to this action, du Pont produced almost 75 percent of the cellophane sold in the United States, and cellophane constituted less than 20 percent of all "flexible packaging materials" sales. Du Pont . . . contends that the prohibition of §2 against monopolization is not violated because it does not have the power to control the price of cellophane or to exclude competitors from the market in which cellophane is sold. The court below found that the "relevant market for determining the extent of du Pont's market control is the market for flexible packaging materials," and that competition from those other materials prevented du Pont from possessing monopoly powers in its sales of cellophane.

The Government asserts that cellophane and other wrapping materials are neither substantially fungible nor like priced. For these reasons, it argues that the market for other wrappings is distinct from the market for cellophane and that the competition afforded cellophane by other wrappings is not strong enough to be considered in determining whether du Pont has monopoly powers. . . . Every manufacturer is the sole producer of the particular commodity it makes, but its control, in the above sense of the relevant market, depends upon the availability of alternative commodities for buyers: i.e., whether there is a cross-elasticity of demand between cellophane and the other wrappings. This interchangeability is largely gauged by the purchase of competing products for similar uses considering the price, characteristics and adaptability of the competing commodities. The court below found that the flexible wrappings afforded such alternatives.

If cellophane is the "market" that du Pont is found to dominate, it may be assumed it does have monopoly power over that "market." Monopoly power is the power to control prices or exclude competition. It seems apparent that du Pont's power to set the price of cellophane has been limited only by the competition afforded by other flexible packaging materials. Moreover, it may be practically impossible for anyone to commence manufacturing cellophane without full access to du Pont's technique. However, du Pont has no power to prevent competition from other wrapping materials. It is inconceivable that price could be controlled without power over competition or vice versa. . . .

Determination of the competitive market for commodities depends on how different from one another are the offered commodities in character or use, how far buyers will go to substitute one commodity for another. For example, one can think of building materials as in commodity competition, but one could hardly say that brick competed with steel or wood or cement or stone in the meaning of Sherman Act litigation; the products are too different. . . . [T]here are certain differences in the formulae for soft drinks but one can hardly say that each one is an illegal monopoly.

Cellophane costs more than many competing products and less than a few.

Cellophane differs from other flexible packaging materials. From some, it differs more than from others.

It may be admitted that cellophane combines the desirable elements of transparency, strength and cheapness more definitely than any of the others. . . .

But, despite cellophane's advantages, it has to meet competition from other materials in every one of its uses. The Government makes no challenge to Finding 283 that cellophane furnishes less than seven percent of wrappings for bakery products, 25 percent for candy, 32 percent for snacks, 35 percent for meats and poultry, 27 percent for crackers and biscuits, 47 percent for fresh produce, and 34 percent for frozen foods. 75 to 80 percent of cigarettes are wrapped in cellophane. Finding 292. Thus, cellophane shares the packaging market with others. The overall result is that cellophane accounts for 17.9 percent of flexible wrapping materials, measured by the wrapping surface.

An element for consideration as to cross-elasticity of demand between products is the responsiveness of the sales of one product to price changes of the other. . . . The court below

> held that the "[g]reat sensitivity of customers in the flexible packaging markets to price or quality changes" prevented du Pont from possessing monopoly control over price. . . .
>
> We conclude that cellophane's interchangeability with the other materials mentioned suffices to make it a part of this flexible packaging material market.
>
> **DECISION:** Affirmed. The U.S. Supreme Court ruled in favor of Du Pont.

Relevant Geographic Market

In addition to defining the relevant product market, the courts must also decide the geographic boundaries within which to evaluate the defendant's market power. Have the effects of the defendant's alleged anticompetitive behavior been nationwide, or have they been limited to a specific region or locality? By defining the **relevant geographic market**, the courts determine the territory within which a defendant's activities should be examined.

Basically the courts define the relevant geographic market in terms of the area of the defendant firm's effective competitive presence in regard to sales of the relevant product. This determination has not represented an important issue in Section 2 proceedings because generally only national producers have been challenged as monopolies. However, the *Grinnell* case, appearing later in this chapter, did involve the issue of whether the national relevant geographic market found to exist by a lower court should be broken down into local markets.

Overwhelming Market Power

The development of a legally practical and economically meaningful test of monopoly power within a particular relevant competitive market has been a major task of the federal judiciary. The difficulties encountered by the federal courts in their search for an appropriate test have been due, in part, to the fact that a variety of tests could be considered consistent with the very general language of Section 2. Reasonable alternative approaches might include basing the determination of illegality on

1. The achievement of a particular absolute or relative size
2. The existence of a specified "monopolistic" intent

3. The actual commission of specified anticompetitive acts

The question of the competitive effect of sheer physical size is central to determining which alternative test is most appropriate for application by the courts in Section 2 cases. We often hear the term *big business* used in a derogatory sense. Noted judges have written that "bigness is bad." Unfortunately, economic theorists have yet to answer definitively, by empirical findings, the question of whether large firm size is necessary to realize productive efficiencies from the viewpoint of the economy as a whole.

Proponents of large firm size argue that large firms are more efficient by virtue of their ability to realize economies of scale in production and promotion, attract top talent, obtain capital market advantages, effectively conduct research, and introduce advanced technology. Opponents of large firm size argue that many firms become unmanageable beyond an optimum size, economies of scale are often not effectively realized, large size (which is likely to result in just a few firms in a particular industry) encourages collusive pricing and other harmful market practices, and the resulting lack of competition deters research. Opponents further argue that the promotion economies and capital-market power of large firms permit these less efficient firms to survive and even dominate their industries.

In applying Section 2 of the Sherman Act, the courts have been unable to rely directly on the economic model of monopoly, which posits a single firm in its market protected from entry of new firms and from the competition of substitute products. Because this is an exceedingly rare phenomenon in our modern economy, it does not afford a practical *legal* standard. The *Grinnell* case that follows dramatizes the generally analytical, nontechnical approach that the courts have used in determining the presence of the overwhelming market power necessary to violate the statute.

The first major monopoly case was the famous *Standard Oil of New Jersey v. United States* (1911). That decision, which broke up the Standard Oil of New Jersey holding company, established a rule-of-reason approach—the Supreme Court looked for an intent to monopolize and actual instances of conduct manifesting that intent. Thus, if such elements were present, an illegal monopoly would be found to exist. That case was quickly followed by the *United States Steel Corporation* case in 1920, in which the Supreme Court stated that "the law does not make mere size an offense, or the existence of unexerted power an offense." The Court found that United States Steel did not have the power to control prices, even though at times it had controlled 50 percent of the market, and refused to break up the company. This resulted in the so-called abuse theory under which the courts for the next 20 years looked for specific abuses and analyzed the actions of alleged monopolists to determine whether they were "good" or "bad" trusts. During this period the courts applied essentially behavioral criteria to determine whether Section 2 had been violated.

The case establishing the modern interpretation of Section 2, and perhaps the most important monopoly case decided to date, is the circuit court opinion of Judge Learned Hand in *United States v. Aluminum Co. of America* (Alcoa) (1945). In *Alcoa* the court used a structuralist approach and focused mainly on the percentage of the market controlled by Alcoa. Judge Hand found that Alcoa had 90 percent of the relevant competitive market and concluded that "that percentage is enough to constitute a monopoly; it is doubtful whether 60 or 64 percent would be enough; and certainly 33 percent is not." On the basis of the monopolization cases decided to date, it can be said that when a firm controls more than 80 percent of a relevant competitive market it is likely to be found in violation of Section 2 of the Sherman Act. This "big is bad" approach by Judge Hand has been severely criticized because the monopoly position of a firm could have been gained by patents or internal efficiencies. Are innovative and efficient firms to be punished because they have obtained more than 80 percent of their market? Will a firm fail to expand and meet buyer demand for fear of obtaining too large a share of its market and becoming a "monopoly"? What effect does this have on production, output, and employment? An equity standard that opposes "bigness" seems to be in conflict with an efficiency standard that is concerned with consumer welfare. The meaning of *Alcoa* is still debated.

Intent to Monopolize

The existence of market power by itself does not constitute monopolization. The defendant must be shown to have a *general intent* to exercise that power. General intent exists if acts are performed leading to the prohibited result regardless of whether that particular result was actually desired. It is not necessary to show specific intent—that is, the defendant wanted to monopolize. Often general intent to monopolize can be inferred from common and usual methods of doing business.

The case that follows outlines the elements of monopoly and identifies conduct that may show an intent to monopolize. Additionally, the Court defines what constitutes a relevant product market.

UNITED STATES V. GRINNELL CORP.

U.S. Supreme Court
384 U.S. 563 (1966)

BACKGROUND: The United States charged Grinnell with monopolizing the accredited central station protection business by using its subsidiaries (identified in the opinion) to obtain a dominant market position. Grinnell manufactured plumbing supplies and fire sprinkler systems. It also owned 76 percent of the stock of ADT, 89 percent of the stock of AFA, and 100 percent of the stock of Holmes. ADT provided both burglary and fire protection services; Holmes provided burglary services alone; AFA supplied only fire protection service. Each offered a central station service under which hazard-detecting devices installed on the protected premises automatically transmitted an electric signal to a central station. The three companies that Grinnell controlled had over 87 percent of the business. The U.S. District Court found for the government and ordered Grinnell to prepare a plan for divestiture of certain of its subsidiaries. The government felt that the relief granted was inadequate, and both parties appealed to the Supreme Court.

Douglas, Justice

The offense of monopoly under §2 of the Sherman Act has two elements: (1) the possession of monopoly power in the relevant market and (2) the willful acquisition or maintenance of that power as distinguished from growth or development as a consequence of a superior product, business acumen, or historic accident. In the present case, 87 percent of the accredited central station service business leaves no doubt that the congeries of these defendants have monopoly power—power which, as our discussion of the record indicates, they did not hesitate to wield—if that business is the relevant market. The only remaining question therefore is, what is the relevant market?

In case of a product, it may be of such a character that substitute products must also be considered, as customers may turn to them if there is a slight increase in the price of the main product. That is the teaching of the *du Pont* case . . . viz., that commodities reasonably interchangeable make up that "part" of trade or commerce which §2 protects against monopoly power.

The District Court treated the entire accredited central station service business as a single market and we think it was justified in so doing. Defendants argue that the different central station services offered are so diverse that they cannot, under *du Pont*, be lumped together to make up the relevant market. For example, burglar alarm services are not interchangeable with fire alarm services. They further urge that *du Pont* requires that protective services other than those of the central station variety be included in the market definition.

But there is here a single use, *i.e.*, the protection of property, through a central station that receives signals. It is that service, accredited, that is unique and that competes with all the other forms of property protection. . . .

[W]e deal with services, not with products; and . . . we conclude that the accredited central station is a type of service that makes up a relevant market and that domination or control of it makes out a monopoly and a "part" of trade or commerce within the meaning of §2 of the Sherman Act. The defendants have not made out a case for fragmentizing the types of services into lesser units.

There are, to be sure, substitutes for the accredited central station service. But none of them appears to operate on the same level as the central station service so as to meet the interchangeability test of the *du Pont* case.

Watchman service is far more costly and less reliable. Systems that set off an audible alarm at the site of a fire or burglary are cheaper but often less reliable. They may be inoperable without anyone's knowing it. Moreover, there is a risk that the local ringing of an alarm will not attract the needed attention and help. Proprietary systems that a customer purchases and operates are available; but they can be used only by a very large business or by government and are not realistic alternatives for most concerns.

The accredited, as distinguished from nonaccredited service, is a relevant part of commerce. Virtually, the only central station companies in the status of the nonaccredited are those that have not yet been able to meet the standards of the rating bureau. The accredited ones are indeed those that have achieved, in the eyes of underwriters, superiorities that other central stations do not have. These standards are important, as insurance carriers often require accredited central station service as a condition to writing insurance. There is indeed evidence that customers consider the unaccredited service as inferior.

As the District Court found, the relevant market for determining whether the defendants have monopoly power is not the several local areas which the individual stations serve, but the broader national market that reflects the reality of the way in which they build and conduct their businesses.

Grinnell was ordered to file, not later than April 1, 1966, a plan of divestiture of its stock in each of the other defendant companies. It was given the option either to sell the stock or distribute it to its stockholders or combine or vary those methods.

The defendants object to the requirements that Grinnell divest itself of its holdings in the three alarm company defendants, but we think that provision is wholly justified. Dissolution of the combination is essential as indicated by many of our cases, starting with *Standard Oil Co. v. United States*.

DECISION: Affirmed. The U.S. Supreme Court ruled in favor of the federal government.

The few large American firms that control 40 to 60 percent of their identifiable relevant competitive markets react with extreme caution to changes in their market shares to make sure they will not be charged with monopolization. The restraint exercised by such firms directly affects their marketing and advertising strategies. These strategies often emphasize maintaining rather than increasing *relative* market shares, and steps are taken to make sure that the company does not have even the appearance of engaging in anticompetitive activities. Following the *Grinnell* case, one can imagine the reaction of the board of directors and top officers at General Motors to a proposal by a young marketing vice president for an aggressive long-run marketing strategy whose aim would be to obtain an 85 percent share of domestic auto sales within 10 years. On occasion the dominant firm in an industry has even provided marketing and research assistance to weak or marginal competitors to keep them in business.

Two important monopolization cases were settled in January 1982. If one or the other had been carried to the U.S. Supreme Court, we might have had a redefinition of the law of monopolization. The Justice Department suits against American Telephone and Telegraph (AT&T) and International Business Machines (IBM) charged both firms with monopolizing and attempting to monopolize services and equipment in the telecommunications and computer industries, respectively. After the cases were filed (in the early 1970s) more competitors entered both fields, domestically and abroad, and technology revolutionized the two industries. Also, congressional pressure, in the form of proposed legislation, was brought to bear on the companies and the Justice Department. All these factors led to an agreed modification of a 1956 consent decree (AT&T case) and a stipulated dismissal (IBM case).

From these cases and several cases reaching federal courts of appeal, it has become clear that some monopolistic conduct will be considered permissible. When a monopolist seeks to protect its position against rivals entering the market with new products, aggressive pricing policies, and innovative products, these actions will be considered legitimate as long as the monopolist does not subsidize one product with revenue from others. In addition to the intent to monopolize, it now appears that efficiency and consumer welfare criteria will be considered by some federal courts in examining Section 2 monopoly charges against firms that have large shares of a market.

Attempts to Monopolize

Section 2 of the Sherman Act forbids *attempts* to monopolize as well as monopolization. In other words, a company does not have to be successful in monopolizing a market. Conduct that brought a corporation close to monopolization and showed an intent to monopolize was all that was required by the Supreme Court in early cases. Today most authorities agree that an attempt to monopolize requires

1. Specific intent

2. Predatory or anticompetitive conduct to attain the purpose

3. A dangerous probability of success

A "dangerous probability of success" is usually shown through direct proof of the market power that the firm has attained.

Attempts to monopolize are typically characterized by **predatory pricing**, in which the would-be monopolist charges artificially low prices in order to drive out competitors. Once the competitors leave the industry, the monopolist is free to raise prices above the level that the market would allow in a competitive situation. But how do courts determine when prices are "predatory"? Academics Phillip Areeda and Donald Turner have devised a test that has been adopted by many courts. Under the Areeda-Turner test, a firm is engaged in predatory pricing when its price is less than its marginal cost. You might recall from economics that a product's marginal cost is the cost of producing the last unit of the product, including both fixed and variable costs. Areeda and Turner reason that if a firm sets a price that doesn't even cover its production costs, its intention cannot be to maximize profit but rather must be to eliminate competition. Critics of this standard argue that those not trained in economic analysis have a difficult time understanding terms such as marginal, variable, and fixed costs. They point out that accountants and economists who regularly use these terms define them differently. Because of the imprecision of economic analysis (particularly in a litigation context), critics argue that definitions of predatory pricing that include economic cost terminology should be received with some skepticism by the courts.

Clayton Act

Mergers

A **merger** is the acquisition by one corporation of the assets or stock of another independent corporation wherein the acquired corporation comes to be controlled by the acquirer. Mergers have had an important effect on the nature of industrial organization. They have accounted for a substantial degree of the current concentration in many industries. Numerous mergers take place in the United States each year.

On the basis of the economic interrelationships between the firms involved, mergers may be classified into three basic types—horizontal, vertical, and conglomerate. A **horizontal merger** is a merger between direct competitors. For example, the merger between Chevron and Standard Oil was a horizontal merger. A **vertical merger** is one between two firms at different levels of the production or distribution chain for the same basic product or process. A vertical merger occurs, for example, if an automobile manufacturer that regularly purchases steel merges with a steel manufacturer. One might also cite Sony's purchase of Columbia Studios as a vertical merger, since Sony produces entertainment "hardware" (cameras, video equipment, VCRs, and the like) and Columbia Studios produces entertainment "software" (movies). A **conglomerate merger** results when noncompeting, nonrelated firms merge. Conglomerate mergers include all mergers that are neither horizontal mergers nor vertical mergers. The acquisition of Hertz Rental Car Company by RCA is an example of a conglomerate merger.

Relevant Competitive Market   To evaluate the effect of a merger for regulatory purposes, we need to define the product and geographic dimensions of a relevant competitive market. This is mandated by amended Section 7 of the Clayton Act, which provides:

No person engaged in commerce or in any activity affecting commerce shall acquire, directly or indirectly, the whole or any part of the stock or other share capital and no person subject to the jurisdiction of the Federal Trade Commission shall acquire the whole or any part of the assets of another person engaged also in commerce or in any activity affecting commerce, where *in any line of commerce* or *in any activity affecting commerce in any section of the country*, the effect of such acquisition may be substantially to lessen competition, or to tend to create a monopoly.

The determination of the relevant competitive market in a merger case often establishes whether the postmerger firm is relatively a whale or a minnow. It often is *the* critical factor in the lawsuit's ultimate outcome.

In defining "line of commerce"—that is, the relevant product market—the courts have used the same basic standards of cross-elasticity of demand and marketplace treatment discussed earlier in reference to monopoly. When considering mergers, the courts are concerned with the treatment accorded products by consumers and industry representatives. They have shown a willingness to break product lines into submarkets or to combine product lines into aggregate markets whenever the circumstances in a particular case justified either approach.

After having defined the relevant product market, the courts must determine the relevant geographic market. Section 7 condemns mergers whose effects may be to lessen competition substantially "in any section of the country." On its face, that language raises an important question. If a lessening of competition can be found to exist in any single market area, is it then necessary to define a relevant geographic market? For example, could an acquisition by General Motors of a small custom-car manufacturer in Maine (one that sells interstate) be found to violate Section 7 because of its combined market share in Bangor? The implications of this question are particularly bothersome if we assume that in no other city of the United States would its combined market share represent a violative figure. To date, with one confusing exception, all the cases have involved delineation of a relevant geographic market even if that were only a single metropolitan or commercial area.

As should be apparent, the determination of the boundaries of the relevant geographic market may significantly influence the final outcome of a particular case. For example, assume that a twenty-five-store discount chain selling throughout Ohio were to acquire an even smaller discount chain selling only in southern Ohio. For jurisdictional purposes, further assume that both are interstate firms. If the relevant geographic market were found to be the nation as a whole, there would be little chance that the merger would be in violation of Section 7. If, on the other hand, the state of Ohio were found to comprise the relevant geographic market, the chances of the merger's being set aside would be substantially increased. In general, the smaller the relevant geographic market is, the more likely the government will prevail. The larger the geographic market is, the more likely the defendant firm will prevail.

In defining a relevant geographic market, the courts have sought to determine the boundaries of the geographic area of effective competition of the business involved in terms of the relevant product(s). When mergers at the manufacturing level are involved, the relevant geographic market is likely to be the nation as a whole, or at least several contiguous states. Retailing presents more complex questions, and a single large city (for supermarket retailing) or a contiguous four-county area (for commercial banking) may constitute the relevant geographic market. In the *Brown Shoe* case, excerpted later in this chapter, the court found the relevant geographic market to consist of those cities with populations of 10,000 or more in which both merging firms (Brown Shoe and Kinney Shoe) had outlets. Thus the courts have not required that the geographic market be defined as one unitary, contiguous area.

Potential Effect on Competition   Once a court has defined the boundaries of the relevant competitive market and has thereby implicitly determined the type of merger involved, it must then evaluate the potential effect of the proposed merger on competition within that market. Section 7 indicates, in general terms, the anticompetitive effect necessary in order to condemn a merger. The language "effect of such acquisition *may be* substantially to lessen competition" and "tend to create a monopoly" seems to indicate that it is not necessary for the government to prove an actual, existing competitive restraint. Instead, the language is concerned with future probabilities. Thus in the past the government was required to demonstrate only that a proposed merger would probably result in prohibited anticompetitive effects in order to obtain a judgment striking down the merger. More recently (as discussed at the end of this section) the courts have required stricter proof of anticompetitive effects by the government.

In developing the criteria by which to apply the general language of Section 7 to actual mergers, the courts have found it necessary to distinguish between the different types of mergers. Such distinctions are proper and logical because horizontal, vertical, and conglomerate mergers may have significantly different economic effects. Thus, even though the same language of the same statute is applied to each type of merger, the specific questions to be answered in applying the statute will vary. These distinctions will become evident in the following discussion.

HORIZONTAL MERGERS Of the three types of mergers, a horizontal merger involves the most direct and immediate competitive effect. Unless a firm's acquisition of a competitor is offset by a new entry into the industry, an immediate result of the merger will be increased concentration. Because horizontally merging firms already have identifiable market shares in their industry, the courts have specific, objective criteria from which to draw initial conclusions concerning the competitive effect of the merger. Consequently, the courts have had to resolve the following two questions concerning the use of market share information:

1. What postacquisition market shares, if any, are so insignificant that the merger may be found to be clearly legal without further questions?

2. What market shares, if any, are probably so anticompetitive that the merger may be found to be illegal without further investigation?

In *United States v. Philadelphia National Bank* (1963), the Supreme Court determined that a postacquisition market share of 30 percent or more was prima facie illegal and thus resolved the second question. Note that the *Philadelphia Bank* opinion indicated that a share smaller than 30 percent could be prima facie illegal, but no lower limit has yet been established by the Supreme Court.

The question of whether an identifiable minimum postacquisition market share could be clearly legal was faced by the Supreme Court in the first important merger case reaching it under Section 7. *Brown Shoe v. United States*, set out subsequently, is particularly instructive because it clearly outlines the relevant product and geographic markets as well as the merger's potential effect on competition.

In evaluating the competitive effect of a proposed horizontal merger, the Justice Department uses a device known as the **Herfindahl-Hirschman Index** (HHI), which is computed by summing the squares of each firm's market share in an industry. For example, an industry with two competitors that each have 50 percent of the market would have an HHI of 5,000: 50 squared

(2,500) plus 50 squared (2,500). On the other hand, an industry with five competitors each with 20 percent of the market would have an HHI of 2,000: 20 squared (400) times 5. The higher the HHI, the higher the concentration in an industry. The Justice Department compares the premerger HHI for an industry with the HHI that would result from the merger. According to joint merger guidelines issued by the Justice Department and the FTC in 1992, any postmerger HHI below 1,000 will be considered to be an unconcentrated market; an HHI between 1,000 and 1,800 will be considered a moderately concentrated market and will be challenged only when the merger produces an increase in the HHI of more than 100 points; a postmerger HHI of more than 1800 will be challenged depending on the following: (1) whether a leading firm in an industry is involved; (2) the ease of entry into the relevant market; (3) the nature of the product; (4) market performance; and (5) other factors.

VERTICAL MERGERS Vertical mergers are more difficult to evaluate because they do not involve combinations of direct competitors. Thus the courts cannot avail themselves of easily applied criteria such as market share or percentage of total productive assets controlled. Instead, the courts must analyze the resulting market structure and the probable market behavior of the postacquisition firm to determine if an actual or potential competitor is likely to be foreclosed from important markets. Ordinarily, the exclusion is of a direct competitor of one of the merging firms.

The *Brown Shoe* case, below, presents the Supreme Court's concern that independent shoe manufacturers should not be denied access to retail outlets because of the number of retail stores that Brown-Kinney would control after the acquisition; and because of the established tendency of retail stores acquired by Brown to sell a much higher percentage of Brown's shoes after acquisition. Typically, the foreclosure is of a manufacturer from retail outlets or from a needed source of supply. As in this case, it is most likely to occur in an industry in which a few large firms are vertically integrated and a large number of smaller competitors are not.

BROWN SHOE CO. V. UNITED STATES

U.S. Supreme Court
370 U.S. 294 (1962)

BACKGROUND: The government challenged the acquisition of the G. R. Kinney Company by Brown Shoe (defendant) on the grounds that the merger violated Section 7 of the Clayton Act. Brown was the third largest retail shoe seller (over 1,230 outlets) and the fourth largest shoe manufacturer, whereas Kinney was the eighth largest seller (over 350 outlets) and the twelfth largest manufacturer. The U.S. District Court found for the government and Brown appealed to the Supreme Court.

Warren, Chief Justice

This case is one of the first to come before us in which the Government's complaint is based upon allegations that the applicants have violated Section 7 of the Clayton Act, as that section was amended in 1950.

The dominant theme pervading congressional consideration of the 1950 amendments was a fear of what was considered to be a rising tide of economic concentration in the American economy. Other considerations cited in support of the bill were the desirability of retaining "local control" over industry and the protection of small businesses. Throughout the recorded discussion may be found examples of Congress' fear, not only of accelerated concentration of economic power on economic grounds, but also of the threat to other values a trend toward concentration was thought to pose.

Congress neither adopted nor rejected specifically any particular tests for measuring the relevant markets, either as defined in terms of product or in terms of geographic locus of competition, within which the anticompetitive effects of a merger were to be judged. Nor did it adopt a definition of the word "substantially," whether in quantitative terms of sales or assets or market shares or in designated qualitative terms, by which a merger's effects on competition were to be measured.

Congress used the words "*may* tend substantially to lessen competition" (emphasis supplied), to indicate that its common concern was with probabilities, not certainties. Statutes existed for dealing with clear-cut menaces to competition; no statute was sought for dealing with ephemeral possibilities. Mergers with a probable anticompetitive effect were to be proscribed by this Act.

The Vertical Aspects of the Merger

Economic arrangements between companies standing in a supplier-customer relationship are characterized as "vertical." The primary vice of a vertical merger or other arrangement tying a customer to a supplier is that, by foreclosing the competitors of either party from a segment of the market otherwise open to them, the arrangement may act as a "clog on competition," . . . which "deprive(s) . . . rivals of a fair opportunity to compete."

The "area of effective competition" must be determined by reference to a product market (the "line of commerce") and a geographic market (the "section of the country").

The Product Market

The outer boundaries of a product market are determined by the reasonable interchangeability of use or the cross-elasticity of demand between the product itself and substitutes for it. However, within this broad market, well-defined submarkets may exist which, in themselves, constitute product markets for antitrust purposes. The boundaries of such a submarket may be determined by examining such practical indicia as industry or public recognition of the submarket as a separate economic entity, the product's peculiar characteristics and uses, unique production facilities, distinct customers, distinct prices, sensitivity to price changes, and specialized vendors.

Applying these considerations to the present case, we conclude that the record supports the District Court's finding that the relevant lines of commerce are men's, women's, and children's shoes. The product lines are recognized by the public; each line is manufactured in separate plants; each has characteristics peculiar to itself rendering it generally noncompetitive with the others; and each is, of course, directed toward a distinct class of customers.

Appellant, however, contends that the District Court's definitions fail to recognize sufficiently "price/quality" distinctions in shoes. Brown argues that the predominantly medium-priced shoes which it manufactures occupy a product market different from the predominantly low-priced shoes which Kinney sells. But agreement with that argument would be equivalent to holding that medium-priced shoes do not compete with low-priced shoes. We think the District Court properly found the facts to be otherwise.

The Geographic Market

We agree with the parties and District Court that insofar as the vertical aspect of this merger is concerned, the relevant geographic market is the entire Nation.

The Probable Effect of the Merger

. . . (I)t is apparent from both past behavior of Brown and from testimony of Brown's president, that Brown would see its ownership of Kinney to force Brown shoes into Kinney stores.

Another important factor to consider is the trend toward concentration in the industry.

. . . The necessary corollary of these trends is the foreclosure of independent manufacturers from markets otherwise open to them. And because these trends are not the product of accident but are rather the result of deliberate policies of Brown and other leading shoe manufacturers, account must be taken of these facts in order to predict the probable future consequences of this merger.

The Horizontal Aspects of the Merger

An economic arrangement between companies performing similar functions in the production or sale of comparable goods or services is characterized as "horizontal." Where the arrangement effects a horizontal merger between companies occupying the same product and geographic market, whatever competition previously may have existed in that market between the parties to the merger is eliminated. The 1950 amendments made plain Congress' intent that the validity of such combinations was to be gauged on a broader scale: Their effect on competition generally in an economically significant market.

Thus, again, the proper definition of the market is a "necessary predicate" to an examination of the competition that may be affected by the horizontal aspects of the merger. The acquisition of Kinney by Brown resulted in a horizontal combination at both the manufacturing and retailing levels of their businesses. (T)he District Court found that the merger of Brown's and Kinney's *manufacturing* facilities was economically too insignificant to come within the prohibition of the Clayton Act.

The Product Market

Shoes are sold in the United States in retail shoe stores and in shoe departments of general stores. These outlets sell: (1) men's shoes, (2) women's shoes, (3) women's or children's shoes, or (4) men's, women's, and children's shoes.

The Geographic Market

The criteria to be used in determining the appropriate geographic market are essentially similar to those used to determine the relevant product market. Moreover, just as a product submarket may have Section 7 significance as the proper "line of commerce," so may a geographic submarket be considered the appropriate "section of the country." . . . Congress prescribed a pragmatic, factual approach to the definition of the relevant market and not a formal, legalistic one. The geographic market selected must, therefore, both "correspond to the commercial realities" of the industry and be economically significant. Thus, although the geographic market in some instances may encompass the entire Nation, under other circumstances it may be as small as a single metropolitan area.

We believe, however, that the record fully supports the District Court's findings that shoe stores in the outskirts of cities compete effectively with stores in central downtown areas, and that while there is undoubtedly some commercial intercourse between smaller communities within a single "standard metropolitan area," the most intense and important competition in retail sales will be confined to stores within the particular communities in such an area and their immediate environs.

We therefore agree that the District Court properly defined the relevant geographic markets in which to analyze this merger as those cities with a population exceeding 10,000 and their environs in which both Brown and Kinney retailed shoes through their own outlets.

The Probable Effect of the Merger

Having delineated the product and geographic markets within which the effects of this merger are to be measured, we turn to an examination of the District Court's finding that, as a result of the merger, competition in the retailing of men's, women's, and children's shoes may be lessened substantially in those cities in which both Brown and Kinney stores are located.

In 118 separate cities, the combined shares of the market of Brown and Kinney in the sale of one of the relevant lines of commerce exceeded 5%. In 47 cities, their share exceeded 5% in all three lines.

The market share which companies may control by merging is one of the most important factors to be considered when determining the probable effects of the combination on effective competition in the relevant market. In an industry as fragmented as shoe retailing, the control of substantial shares of the trade in a city may have important effects on competition. If a merger achieving 5% control were now approved, we might be required to approve future merger efforts by Brown's competitors seeking similar market shares. The oligopoly Congress sought to avoid would then be furthered and it would be difficult to dissolve the combinations previously approved. Furthermore, in this fragmented industry, even if the combination controls but a small share of a particular market, the fact that this share is held by a large national chain can adversely affect competition. It is competition, not competitors, which the Act protects. But we cannot fail to recognize Congress' desire to promote competition through the protection of viable, small, locally owned businesses. Congress appreciated that occasional higher costs and prices might result from the maintenance of fragmented industries and markets. It resolved these competing considerations in favor of decentralization. We must give effect to that decision.

Other factors to be considered in evaluating the probable effects of a merger in the relevant market lend additional support to the District Court's conclusion that this merger may substantially lessen competition. One such factor is the history of tendency toward concentration in the industry. As we have previously pointed out, the shoe industry has, in recent years, been a prime example of such a trend.

On the basis of the record before us, we believe the Government sustained its burden of proof. We hold that the District Court was correct in concluding that this merger may tend to lessen competition substantially in the retail sale of men's, women's, and children's shoes in the overwhelming majority of those cities and their environs in which both Brown and Kinney sell through owned or controlled outlets.

DECISION: Affirmed for the United States.

Trends in Horizontal and Vertical Mergers Since *United States v. General Dynamics* (1974), the Supreme Court has moved away from the aggregate numbers/relative percentage approach and begun to evidence a willingness to consider the competitive consequences or the specific economic characteristics of the market involved. The Court has looked not only at the conduct of the merging firms and the structure of their market but at the economic consequences of the merger for their industry. For example, in *United States v. Marine Bancorporation, Inc.* (1974), the Court refused to allow the Justice Department to claim that the potential effect of a merger of one national bank and a bank in the Seattle area would be to decrease competition because the acquired bank would have expanded internally or merged with smaller banks if it were not acquired. The Court also rejected the claim that the acquiring bank was seeking to eliminate a "potential competitor." After examining the regulated nature of the banking industry and its effect on ease of entry into the Seattle banking market, the Court approved the merger. Following this decision, the federal courts have required the Justice Department and FTC to show the actual anticompetitive effects of a merger they oppose. The government must demonstrate by objective facts that the acquiring firm would enter the market via internal expansion if the merger were disallowed. How near the firm was to entering the market on its own prior to the merger is a question that must be answered by the plaintiffs. Contentions based on subjective intent, or looking into the company's mind, are not acceptable. As noted earlier, *conglomerate mergers* are generally mergers between two firms in unrelated industries. For example, General Electric's acquisition of RCA could be considered a conglomerate merger. They have been considered illegal under Section 7 of the Clayton Act if the acquiring firm is a perceived potential entrant into the market. For example, if antitrust enforcers had perceived that General Electric had some special incentive to enter the broadcasting market, and this market was an "extension" of its own, they might have objected. Also, if General Electric had been on the "edge" of the broadcast market itself, and could have entered without acquiring, the antitrust enforcement agencies might have taken a closer look.

Price Discrimination

In an economy based on freedom and competition, neophyte business managers, not unnaturally, might expect that they would be permitted to price their products as the economics of production, distribution, and profit dictate. This, however, is not the case. Management responsible for determining prices must make its decisions within the framework of extensive federal and state regulations that restrict choices.

One of the most important statutory provisions influencing pricing decisions is Section 2 of the Clayton Act, as amended by the Robinson–Patman Act. This legislation attempts to foster competition by prohibiting price discrimination in certain instances. Selling physically identical products at different prices can be anticompetitive in many situations. To be found illegal, price discrimination must occur in *interstate commerce* between a seller and different purchasers of commodities of *like grade and quality*, and the effect of such discrimination by the seller must be to *substantially lessen competition* or *tend* to create a monopoly. Congress enacted the law in 1936 to protect small businesses from huge sellers coming into a market and cutting prices on a product below cost for the sole purpose of driving out small sellers.

One situation, frequently referred to as "primary" or "seller's level" competition, involves competition between sellers and their rivals. The primary or seller's level competitive strategy that is likely to violate Section 2 of the Clayton Act is *whipsawing*. When, for example, the price-cutting seller operates in several geographic markets, it can cut prices in one while maintaining its prices in another. This gives it an unfair advantage when competing with a seller that operates only in a single geographic market. Unable to maintain its price, the latter has no way of keeping up its profits; the former, however, can make up at least a portion of its losses by profits earned in other areas. After eliminating one regional competitor by selective price-cutting, the firm functioning in several regions can then turn its attention to another region and so on until all regional competitors have been eliminated.

Cases of blatant whipsawing are rare, and selective price cutting can be done for legitimate economic motives—for example, when a firm wishes to secure a market share in a new geographic market area. The courts have had some difficulty balancing legitimate economic interests with the price discrimination laws in the situation where a national firm invades a market area that is dominated by a regional firm.

The major defenses of large sellers for their selective price cutting or discrimination among purchasers are (1) cost justification, (2) changing conditions in the market, and (3) meeting the competition. The "meeting the competition" defense is most controversial. Those who view the act as being noncompetitive argue that this defense should be widened by the courts to allow the marketplace to dictate price. They argue that many inefficient small businesses are kept in existence if this defense is narrowed, and consumers lose in the form of higher prices.

The Supreme Court considers price discrimination in the case that follows.

TEXACO V. HASBROUCK

U.S. Supreme Court
58 LW 4807 (1990)

BACKGROUND: Texaco sold its gasoline directly to retailers and also to distributors, who in turn sold the gasoline to retailers. Texaco charged a much lower price to distributors than to retailers. Texaco justified this price difference as a "functional discount": Distributors are entitled to a discount because they perform a different function than do retailers and must bear marketing costs that retailers do not have to bear. A number of retailers who purchased gasoline directly from Texaco sued Texaco, alleging price discrimination. The retailers won a jury verdict of $449,900, which was trebled. The decision was affirmed by the Ninth Circuit Court of Appeals, and the U.S. Supreme Court agreed to hear the case. Additional facts are set forth in the opinion excerpt.

Stevens, Justice

Respondents are 12 independent Texaco retailers. They displayed the Texaco trademark, accepted Texaco credit cards, and bought their gasoline products directly from Texaco. Texaco delivered the gasoline to respondents' stations.

The retail gasoline market in Spokane was highly competitive throughout the damages period, which ran from 1971 to 1981. Stations marketing the nationally advertised Texaco gasoline competed with other major brands as well as with stations featuring independent brands. Moreover, although discounted prices at a nearby Texaco station would have the most obvious impact on a respondent's trade, the cross-city traffic patterns and relatively small size of Spokane produced a city-wide competitive market.

* * *

The respondents tried unsuccessfully to increase their ability to compete with lower priced stations. Some tried converting from full service to self-service stations. Two of the respondents sought to buy their own tank trucks and haul their gasoline from Texaco's supply point, but Texaco vetoed that proposal.

While the independent retailers struggled, two Spokane gasoline distributors supplied by Texaco prospered. Gull Oil Company (Gull) had its headquarters in Seattle and distributed petroleum products in four western States under its own name. In Spokane it purchased its gas from Texaco at prices that ranged from six to four cents below Texaco's RTW [retail tank wagon, that is the delivered price to retail service stations] price. Gull resold that product under its own name; the fact that it was being supplied by Texaco was not known by either the public or the respondents. . . . Its policy was to price its gasoline at a penny less than the prevailing price for major brands.

* * *

The Dompier Oil Company (Dompier) started business in 1954 selling Quaker State Motor Oil. In 1960 it became a full line distributor of Texaco products, and by the mid-1970's its sales of gasoline represented over three-quarters of its business. Dompier purchased Texaco gasoline at prices of 3.95¢ to 3.65¢ below the RTW price. Dompier thus paid a higher price than Gull, but Dompier, unlike Gull, resold its gas under the Texaco brand names.

* * *

The stations supplied by Dompier regularly sold at retail at lower prices than respondents'. . . . Dompier's sales volume increased continuously and substantially throughout the relevant period.

* * *

Texaco's first argument would create a blanket exemption for all functional discounts. Indeed, carried to its logical conclusion, it would exempt all price differentials except those given to competing purchasers. The primary basis for Texaco's argument is the following comment by Congressman Utterback, an active sponsor of the Act:

> In its meaning as simple English, a discrimination is more than a mere difference. Underlying the meaning of the word is the idea that some relationship exists between the parties to the discrimination which entitles them to equal treatment, whereby the difference granted to one casts some burden or disadvantage upon the other. If the two are competing in the resale of the goods concerned, that relationship exists. . . . But where no such relationship exists, where the goods are sold in different markets and the conditions affecting those markets set different price levels for them, the sale to different customers at those different prices would not constitute a discrimination within the meaning of this bill.

We have previously considered this excerpt from the legislative history, and have refused to draw from it the conclusion which Texaco proposes. Although the excerpt does support Texaco's argument, we remain persuaded that the argument is foreclosed by the text of the Act itself. In the context of a statute that plainly reveals a concern with competitive consequences at different levels of distribution, and carefully defines specific affirmative defenses, it would be anomalous to assume that the Congress intended the term "discriminate" to have such a limited meaning.

* * *

Since we have already decided that a price discrimination within the meaning of §2(a) "is merely a price difference," we must reject Texaco's first argument.

* * *

In *FTC v. Morton Salt Co.*, (1948), we held that an injury to competition may be inferred from evidence that some purchasers had to pay their supplier "substantially more for their goods than their competitors had to pay." Texaco, supported by the United States and the Federal Trade Commission as amici curiae (the Government), argues that this presumption should not apply to differences between prices charged to wholesalers and those charged to retailers. Moreover, they argue that it would be inconsistent with fundamental antitrust policies to construe the Act as requiring a seller to control his customers' resale prices. The seller should not be held liable for the independent pricing decisions of his customers.

* * *

In this case, however, both the District Court and the Court of Appeals concluded that even without viewing the evidence in the light most favorable to the respondents, there was no substantial evidence indicating that the discounts to Gull and Dompier constituted a reasonable reimbursement for the value to Texaco of their actual marketing functions.

* * *

"Only to the extent that a buyer actually performs certain functions, assuming all the risks and costs involved, should he qualify for a compensating discount. The amount of the discount should be reasonably related to the expenses assumed by the buyer."

* * *

Both Gull and Dompier received the full discount on all their purchases even though most of their volume was resold directly to consumers. The extra margin on those sales obviously enabled them to price aggressively in both their retail and their wholesale marketing.

* * *

The evidence indicates, moreover, that Texaco affirmatively encouraged Dompier to expand its retail business and that Texaco was fully informed about the persistent and marketwide consequences of its own pricing policies. Indeed, its own executives recognized that the dramatic impact on the market was almost entirely attributable to the magnitude of the distributor discount and the hauling allowance. Yet at the same time that Texaco was encouraging Dompier to integrate downward, and supplying Dompier with a generous discount useful to such integration, Texaco was inhibiting upward integration by the respondents: two of the respondents sought permission from Texaco to haul their own fuel using their own tankwagons, but Texaco refused. The special facts of this case thus make it peculiarly difficult for Texaco to claim that it is being held liable for the independent pricing decisions of Gull or Dompier.

* * *

At the least, a functional discount that constitutes a reasonable reimbursement for the purchasers' actual marketing functions will not violate the Act. When a functional discount is legitimate, the inference of injury to competition recognized in the *Morton Salt* case will simply not arise. Yet it is also true that not every functional discount is entitled to a judgment of legitimacy, and that it will sometimes be possible to produce evidence showing that a particular functional discount caused a price discrimination of the sort the Act prohibits. When such anticompetitive effects are proved—as we believe they were in this case—they are covered by the Act.

DECISION: The U.S. Supreme Court affirmed the ruling against Texaco.

Review Questions and Problems

Key Terms

antitrust laws	tying agreement
injunction	monopoly
rule-of-reason standard	relevant product market
per se standard	relevant geographic market
horizontal price fixing	predatory pricing
vertical price fixing	merger
horizontal territorial limitation	horizontal merger
vertical territorial limitation	vertical merger
trade association	conglomerate merger
boycott	Herfindahl-Hirschman Index
tie-in	

Discussion Questions

1. What three remedies does the Justice Department make use of most in enforcing the antitrust laws? Explain.

2. What is the difference between horizontal and vertical price fixing? Explain.

3. Do the courts use a rule-of-reason or per se standard when determining the legality of nonprice vertical territorial restraints? Explain.

4. What guidelines do the courts use in analyzing monopoly cases under Section 2 of the Sherman Act?

5. What three defenses do companies most commonly use when charged with price fixing?

Review Problems

1. ABC Medical Society, comprising a group of doctors, established foundations to provide an alternative to existing health insurance plans. The foundations, by agreement of their member doctors, would establish maximum fees that the doctors could claim for health services provided to policyholders of specified insurance plans. An insurance company not allied with ABC Medical Society sued, claiming that the plan amounted to price fixing that was per se illegal. ABC Medical Society argued that its plan was not per se illegal, because it set *maximum* prices rather than minimum prices. What was the result?

2. Cancerlungs, Inc., which manufactures cigarettes, sues Wheez Corp. for attempting to monopolize the

cigarette market. Cancerlungs' complaint indicates that Wheez controls 60 percent of the U.S. cigarette market. Wheez argues that the relevant product market should include all tobacco products, including pipe tobacco, cigars, and chewing tobacco. Wheez points out that its share of the market for all tobacco products is considerably smaller than its share of the cigarette market. How should the relevant product market be defined? Discuss.

3. Beginning in 1959, four major distributors of stainless steel pipe and tubing who sold in Washington, Oregon, California, Idaho, and Utah began to experience substantial price competition from eastern mills and from small local jobbers who sold but did not stock pipe and tubing. Upon the invitation of Tubesales Corporation, the dominant and largest distributor, a series of meetings was held to discuss mutual problems.

The government claimed that at these meetings the parties agreed to reduce discounts to nonstocking jobbers from 10 to 5 percent and to reduce the freight factor in their prices; as a result, new price lists embracing lower freight rates were drawn up by Tubesales and hand delivered to the others. All four distributors were charged with violations of Section 1 of the Sherman Act. What was the result?

4. In 1864 and 1870 Congress granted the Northern Pacific Railway Company approximately 40 million acres of land to facilitate financing and constructing a railroad to the Northwest. The grant consisted of alternate sections of land in a belt 20 miles wide on each side of the track. The granted lands were of various kinds.

By 1949 the railroad had sold about 37 million acres of its holdings and leased most of the rest. In a large number of sales and leases, the railroad had inserted "preferential routing" clauses that compelled the owner or lessee to ship over Northern Pacific lines all commodities produced on the land. The preferential routing clause applied only if Northern Pacific's rates were equal to those of competing carriers.

In 1949 the government sued under Section 1 of the Sherman Act seeking a declaration that the preferential routing clauses were unlawful as unreasonable restraints of trade because they constituted tying arrangements. What was the result?

Case Problems

1. A group of Carvel franchisees operating stores selling soft ice cream products sued Carvel Corporation for treble damages. They alleged that Carvel engaged in illegal exclusive dealing and tying arrangements by requiring the franchisees (1) to refrain from selling non-Carvel products, (2) to purchase from Carvel or its designatees certain supplies that ultimately would be part of the final product sold (the franchisees were allowed to purchase equipment and paper goods from other sources subject to quality control specifications), and (3) to follow "suggested" resale prices. What was the result?

2. From 1958 until 1961 Utah Pie Company, a local producer, was the leading seller of frozen pies in the Salt Lake City market. Because of the advantage of its location, the company usually was able to maintain the lowest prices in a market in which the major competitive weapon was price. During a 4-year period Utah Pie was challenged at one time or another by each of three major competitors, all of which operated in several other markets. Evidence showed that each of these competitors sold frozen pies in the Salt Lake market at prices lower than they charged for pies of like grade and quality in other markets considerably closer to their plants. Evidence also indicated that in several instances one or more of them had sold at prices below actual cost and that one of the competitors had sent an industrial spy into Utah's plant.

During the period, price levels deteriorated substantially. In 1958 Utah had been selling pies for $4.15 per dozen. Some 44 months later, Utah was selling similar pies for $2.75 per dozen. As a result of the actions of Pet Milk, Carnation, and Continental, the three major competitors, Utah Pie brought an action for treble damages charging each with a violation of Section 2(a) of the Clayton Act as amended by the Robinson–Patman Act. What was the result?

3. The Philadelphia National Bank and Girard Trust Bank were the second and third largest of the forty-two commercial banks with head offices in the metropolitan area consisting of the city of Philadelphia and three adjoining counties. Philadelphia National had assets over $1 billion; Girard had assets of over $750 million. The boards of directors of the banks approved a merger. If they merged, the resulting bank would be the largest in the four-county Philadelphia area. The two banks viewed the merger as strengthening their hand in competing with other large banks in the northeastern United States. The government filed suit alleging that the proposed merger was in violation of Section 7 of the Clayton Act and asking that the court enjoin it. What was the result?

4. Reynolds Metal Company was the largest producer of aluminum foil in the world. In 1956 it acquired Arrow Brands, Inc., then engaged in converting aluminum and selling it nationally to wholesale florist supply houses. Arrow purchased its "raw" aluminum from Reynolds, converted it, and, prior to its acquisition by Reynolds, accounted for 33 percent of the converted foil sold to the florist industry. Eight other firms also supplied converted aluminum to the florist industry, and some bought from Reynolds. The FTC sued under Section 7, claiming that aluminum foil in the florist

trade was the relevant market. Reynolds argued that all trades that require specialized use of aluminum are the relevant product market. What was the result?

5. Kennecott Copper Corporation, holding 33 percent of the copper market, acquired Peabody Coal Company, which held 10 percent of the coal market. Both were leaders in their respective markets. Kennecott also owned a small coal company. There were high barriers to entry in the coal industry, and copper supplies were dwindling for Kennecott at the time of purchase. The FTC charged Kennecott with a violation of Section 7 of the Clayton Act, noting that Kennecott would have entered the coal industry on its own because of dwindling copper reserves. The FTC charged that a potential entrant into the coal industry was eliminated when this acquisition took place. What was the result?

6. United Shoe Machinery Corporation produced 75 percent of all shoe machines. The company *leased* these machines for 10-year periods and provided free maintenance and repair. It refused to *sell* machines and required all its lessees to operate the leased machines at full capacity. The Justice Department sued United Shoe, charging that it monopolized the shoe machinery market in violation of Section 2 of the Sherman Act. The company claimed that its market share was gained from its superior business acumen and attempts to protect its patents and reputation. What was the result?

55

Consumer Protection Law

The Federal Trade Commission as an Administrative Agency

Unfair Trade Practices
Consumer Protection Laws

Consumers shopping for products often feel as if they're making their way through a jungle, full of hazards and traps for the unwary. This is especially true for consumers shopping for expensive, "big ticket" items. Where do consumers acquire the information that they need to make informed purchasing decisions? How does a consumer sort through the competing claims that sellers make about their products— and about one another's? Buying on credit brings on another set of problems. How can a consumer evaluate the complicated provisions of a credit agreement to make sure that the terms are really acceptable? And safety is often a concern: Is the product a fire hazard or is it otherwise likely to cause injury?

Historically, consumers have had to grapple with these issues on their own. *Caveat emptor*, or "let the buyer beware," was the reigning philosophy. With the development of our consumer society and the emergence of consumers as an interest group, however, the law has evolved to give greater importance to the rights of consumers. Consumers are now protected by numerous statutes designed to prevent businesses from selling unsafe products, making false claims and playing "hardball" with consumers. There are also consumer protection statutes that impose affirmative obligations on sellers to provide con-

sumers with important information in a manner that is clear and not misleading.

Earlier chapters of this book covered certain aspects of consumer protection law, such as products liability and warranties. This chapter discusses several federal statutes that are designed to protect consumers. This chapter emphasizes the role of the Federal Trade Commission (FTC or Commission), which is charged with enforcing some of the most important consumer protection statutes. Keep in mind that virtually every state has consumer protection statutes, and that these statutes sometimes have at least as much impact on business practices as the federal statutes. Many states, for example, have "lemon laws" that are designed to protect consumers who purchase defective automobiles. Because state consumer protection law is varied and difficult to summarize, this chapter will focus on federal law.

Historically, the vigor with which the FTC and other federal agencies have enforced consumer protection laws appears to have increased and decreased in cycles. This probably reflects the ebb and flow in the running battle between interest groups seeking to increase government regulation to protect consumers and interest groups seeking to relieve business of the burden of overregulation. In the late 1960s, some consumer advocates accused the FTC of being a "do nothing" agency and called for its reorganization and a more activist stance in carrying out its duties under the antitrust statutes and the Federal Trade Commission Act of 1914. The Commission responded to these criticisms by upgrading its staff and organizing its bureaus by functions. Major procedural changes, granting the Commission specific authority to prescribe enforceable rules for the first time, were initiated by Congress with passage of the Magnuson–Moss Warranty Federal Trade Commission Improvement Act of 1975 (Magnuson–Moss Act). Subsequent to the passage of this legislation, the Commission, using its rulemaking authority, eliminated the "holder in due course" doctrine in consumer transactions and issued rules governing the advertisement of eyeglasses. It also proposed rules to regulate diverse areas such as the funeral industry, vocational schools, and children's advertising. Additionally, a proconsumer environment in the 1970s led Congress to pass numerous consumer-oriented statutes delegating regulatory authority and enforcement duties to the FTC. This increased authority and responsibility ultimately led to calls from affected private-sector interests for limits on the FTC. After being criticized for being a "do nothing" agency in the late 1960s, an activist Commission, 10 years later, was "reined in" by Congress with passage of the 1980 Federal Trade Commission Improvement Act, which limited the FTC's rulemaking authority and made the agency more accountable to Congress.

The Federal Trade Commission as an Administrative Agency

History, Purpose, Jurisdiction

The Federal Trade Commission Act of 1914 created a five-member bipartisan Commission to enforce the antitrust laws discussed in Chapter 54. The Commission was particularly charged with enforcement of Sections 2, 3, 7, and 8 of the Clayton Act and Section 5 of the Federal Trade Commission Act. Section 5 of the Federal Trade Commission Act forbids "unfair methods of competition." Congress sought to use this broad language to reach anticompetitive practices not covered by the Sherman and Clayton acts. Only civil remedies may be sought and no private treble-damage suits can be brought under Section 5 of the Federal Trade Commission Act. In 1938 the Wheeler-Lea amendment to Section 5 added a prohibition of "unfair or deceptive acts or practices," providing the Commission with broad authority to regulate business practices that may not violate the antitrust statutes but that are considered "unfair" or "deceptive." With this statutory language and a congressional mandate, the FTC ventured into the marketplace as a consumer protector.

Following the growth of a proconsumer environment in the late 1960s and 1970s, Congress passed additional statutes delegating administrative and enforcement authority to the FTC beyond the original antitrust laws. Some of these statutes are the Export Trade Act, Packers and Stockyard Act, Wool Products Labeling Act, Lanham Trade Mark Act, Fur Products Labeling Act, Textile Fiber Product Identification Act, Federal Cigarette and Advertising Act, Fair Packaging and Labeling Act, Truth-in-Lending Act, Fair Credit Reporting Act, Fair Credit Billing Act, Equal Credit Opportunity Act, Hobby Protection Act, Magnuson–Moss Warranty Federal Trade Improvement Act, Energy Policy and Conservation Act, Hart–Scott–Rodino Antitrust Improvement Act, and the Federal Drug and Cosmetic Act. Congress has given the FTC exclusive authority under some statutes, and in other instances the Commission shares authority with other agencies. For example, it shares enforcement authority with the Food and Drug Administration under the Federal Drug and Cosmetic Act.

Structure

The structure of the FTC is diagrammed in Figure 55-1. The chairman and four commissioners are appointed for 5-year terms by the President of the United States with the advice and consent of the Senate. No more than three of the five may be from a single political party. The chairman is the executive and administrative head of the agency. He or she presides at Commission meetings and hearings conducted by the Commission.

Other officers of the Commission include the executive director, who supervises regional

FIGURE 55-1

Federal Trade Commission

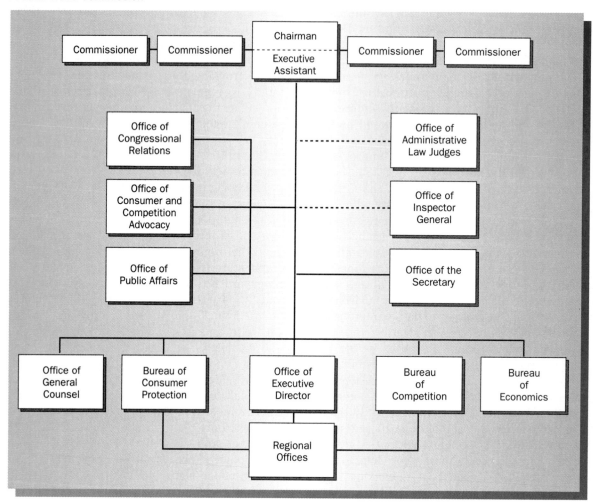

offices and coordinates bureaus, and the general counsel, who is the chief law officer and advisor to the Commission, and who represents the Commission in federal and state courts. An important role played by the general counsel is to assist businesspeople in obtaining advice from the Commission as to the legal propriety of a proposed course of action.

Three bureaus carry out the FTC's mandated functions. The Bureau of Competition investigates potentially unfair or deceptive acts or practices under Section 5 of the FTCA and prosecutes cases before administrative law judges after issuance of a formal complaint. These adjudicatory proceedings are described in Chapter 53. As an alternative to adjudication, the Bureau may obtain negotiated consent orders, which must be ap-

proved by the full Commission. The Bureau also conducts rulemaking proceedings in order to define specific acts that may be violations of statutes enforced by the FTC.

The Bureau of Consumer Protection is significant to the business community and consumers because it is the initiator of litigation in specific cases as well as the source of proposed rules that may affect an entire industry. Also, it makes public efforts to educate all parties as to the laws that it is charged with enforcing.

The Bureau of Economics advises the Commission on the economic aspects of all its functions. Its work has become more important as the Commission has begun to rely on cost-benefit analyses in proposing new rules and evaluating present regulations.

Functions

Adjudication   The FTC has used its authority under Section 5 to investigate various types of unfair or deceptive business practices. The FTC staff seeks to bring about a voluntary admission of wrongdoing or a consent order from the firm involved in a questionable practice before issuing a formal complaint. If this negotiating procedure fails, the FTC initiates litigation before an administrative law judge. Following a hearing and initial decision of the judge, either the staff of the FTC or the corporation may appeal. On appeal the case is heard by the full Commission. The Commission's decision becomes final if it is not appealed to a federal court of appeals within 60 days. The Commission issues cease-and desist orders.

Advisory Opinions   Additionally, the Commission, when asked, issues advisory opinions on the legality of a firm's proposed activity, assuming that such activity falls under one of the statutes enforced by the FTC. Advisory opinions are *not* binding on the Commission.

Rulemaking   As discussed earlier, the FTC can issue rules for an entire industry. The FTC can also obtain temporary restraining orders or preliminary injunctions from courts in order to prevent violations or threatened violations of Commission-administered laws. The Magnuson-Moss Act provides that the Commission may bring civil actions in federal or state courts upon behalf of consumers if they have been injured by unfair or deceptive practices that violate Commission regulations.

The FTC's rulemaking authority has come under closer scrutiny by Congress since passage of the 1980 Federal Trade Commission Improvement Act. The Act provided Congress with the power to override an FTC rule by majority votes of the Senate and the House. This "legislative veto" was applied in 1982 to an FTC regulation that required used-car dealers to list a car's major defects on the car before it was sold. Of the 286 House members who voted to kill the FTC regulation, 242 had received contributions to their 1980 campaigns totaling $675,000 from the Used Car Dealers Association's political action committees. A Federal Court of Appeals in October 1982 unanimously overturned the "legislative veto" of the FTC used-car regulation, claiming that such a veto of regulatory action violated the constitutional principle of separation of powers.

Unfair Trade Practices

Section 5 of the Federal Trade Commission Act

As previously noted, Section 5 of the Federal Trade Commission Act allocates broad consumer protection powers to the FTC because it forbids "unfair or deceptive acts or practices." While deceptive practices have a long history of common law definition, court and FTC interpretations of "unfair" now permit the FTC to investigate a practice that is neither deceptive nor a violation of the antitrust statutes under Section 5 if it (1) offends public policy, (2) is immoral, unethical, or unscrupulous, and (3) causes material or substantial harm to the consumer. The Commission has investigated false or misleading labeling, palming off, misleading product names, disparagement of competition, violations of warranties (see Chapter 53 for the FTC role), and many other practices using these standards; however, few practices affecting the consuming public have been so closely monitored by the FTC as deceptive and unfair advertising and product labeling.

Deceptive Advertising

As previously stated, the Wheeler–Lea Act amended Section 5 of the Federal Trade Commission Act to include "unfair or deceptive trade practices." In passing the amendment, Congress made it clear that the FTC had broad power to "cover every form of advertisement deception over which it would be humanly practical to exercise governmental control." It was to reach every case, from inadvertent or uninformed to the most subtle or vicious advertising. Through a case approach to enforcement, the FTC prior to 1983 evolved a standard by which the advertiser did not have to *intend* deception as in the common law definition of deceit to be guilty of unfair or deceptive practices. All that was required was a misrepresentation and a tendency to deceive an ordinary purchaser at whom the advertisement was directed or by whom it was expected to be read or viewed. The FTC did not have to demonstrate that specific consumers relied on or believed the advertisement.

Following a change in makeup of the Commission, the FTC by a 3–to–2 vote issued a policy statement in October 1983 offering guidelines as to what it would consider to be "deceptive" advertising under Section 5 for the future.

Specifically, the advertising would have to contain (1) a *material* misrepresentation or omission that (2) would *likely mislead* a consumer acting *reasonably* under the circumstances.

The *Kraft* case, which follows, provides an example of advertising that the FTC has found to be deceptive.

KRAFT, INC. V. FTC

U.S. Court of Appeals, Seventh Circuit
970 F.2d 311 (1992)

BACKGROUND: The FTC ordered Kraft, Inc., a producer of cheese and other food products, to stop running certain television advertisements that the Commission found to be deceptive. The FTC found, among other things, that the ads were designed to give consumers the false impression that one slice of Kraft Singles cheese contained as much calcium as 5 ounces of milk. Kraft appealed the order.

Flaum, Circuit Judge

Three categories of cheese compete in the individually wrapped process slice market: process cheese food slices, imitation slices, and substitute slices. Process cheese food slices, also known as "dairy slices," must contain at least 51% natural cheese by federal regulation. Imitation cheese slices, by contrast, contain little or no natural cheese and . . . are as a whole considered "nutritionally inferior" and must carry the label "imitation." Substitute slices fit somewhere in between. . . .

Kraft Singles are process cheese food slices. In the early 1980s, Kraft began losing market share to an increasing number of imitation slices that were advertised as both less expensive and equally nutritious as dairy slices like Singles. Kraft responded with a series of advertisements, collectively known as the "Five Ounces of Milk" campaign, designed to inform consumers that Kraft Singles cost more than imitation slices because they are made from five ounces of milk rather than less expensive ingredients. The ads also focused on the calcium content of Kraft Singles in an effort to capitalize on growing consumer interest in adequate calcium consumption. . . .

. . . The FTC Act makes it unlawful to engage in unfair or deceptive commercial practices, or to induce consumers to purchase certain products through advertising that is misleading in a material respect. . . . In implementing this standard, the Commission examines the overall net impression of an ad and engages in a three-part inquiry: (1) what claims are conveyed in the ad; (2) are those claims false or misleading; and (3) are those claims material to prospective consumers.

Two facts are critical to understanding the allegations against Kraft. First, although Kraft does use five ounces of milk in making each Kraft Single, roughly 30% of the calcium contained in the milk is lost during processing. Second, the vast majority of imitation slices sold in the United States contain 15% of the U.S. Recommended Daily Allowance (RDA) of calcium per ounce, roughly the same amount contained in Kraft Singles. Specifically then, the FTC complaint alleged that the challenged advertisements made an untrue implied claim that a slice of Kraft Singles contains the same amount of calcium as five ounces of milk (the "milk equivalency" claim. . . .

The . . . ads at issue in this case, referred to as the "Skimp" ads . . . , ran nationally in print and broadcast media between 1985 and 1987. The Skimp ads were designed to communicate the nutritional benefit of Kraft Singles by referring expressly to their milk and calcium content. The broadcast version of this ad on which the FTC focused contained the following audio copy:

Lady (voice over): I admit it, I thought of skimping. Could you look into those big blue eyes and skimp on her? So I buy Kraft Singles. Imitation slices use hardly any milk. But Kraft has five ounces per slice. Five ounces. So her little bones get calcium they need to grow. No, she doesn't know what that big Kraft means. Good thing I do.
Singers: Kraft Singles. More milk makes 'em . . . more milk makes them good.
Lady (voice over): Skimp on her? No way.

Kraft asserts that the milk equivalency . . . claims, even if made, are not material to consumers. A claim is considered material if it "involves information that is important to consumers and, hence, likely to affect their choice of, or conduct regarding a product." *Cliffdale Assocs.* . . .

In determining that the milk equivalency claim was material to consumers, the FTC cited Kraft surveys showing that 71% of respondents rated calcium content an extremely or very important factor in their decision to buy Kraft Singles, and that 52% of female, and 40% of all respondents, reported significant personal concerns about adequate calcium consumption. The FTC further noted that the ads were targeted to female homemakers with children and that the 60 milligram difference between the calcium contained in five ounces of milk and that contained in a Kraft Single would make up for most of the RDA calcium deficiency shown in girls aged 9–11. Finally, the FTC found evidence in the record that Kraft designed the ads with the intent to capitalize on consumer calcium deficiency concerns.

Significantly, the FTC found further evidence of materiality in Kraft's conduct: despite repeated warnings, Kraft persisted in running the challenged ads. Before the ads even ran, ABC television raised a red flag when it asked Kraft to substantiate the milk and calcium claims in the ads. Kraft's ad agency also warned Kraft in a legal memorandum to substantiate the claims before running the ads. Moreover, in October 1985, a consumer group warned Kraft that it believed the Skimp ads were potentially deceptive. Nonetheless, a high-level Kraft executive recommended that the ad copy remain unaltered because the "Singles business is growing for the first time in four years due in large part to the copy." Finally, the FTC and the California Attorney General's Office independently notified the company in early 1986 that investigations had been initiated to determine whether the ads conveyed the milk equivalency claims. Notwithstanding these warnings, Kraft continued to run the ads and even rejected proposed alternatives that would have allayed concerns over their deceptive nature. From this, the FTC inferred—we believe, reasonably—that Kraft thought the challenged milk equivalency claim induced consumers to purchase Singles and hence that the claim was material to consumers.

DECISION: The Court of Appeals enforced the order of the FTC.

Deceptive Price Advertising   Some examples of deceptive advertising are false price comparisons (if the advertisement claims a price is reduced, it must be reduced from the regular price), bait and switch, and offers of a free good or service to a customer who buys one. The case that follows illustrates the "free good" type of deceptive price advertising.

FEDERAL TRADE COMMISSION V. MARY CARTER PAINT CO., ET AL.

U.S. Supreme Court
382 U.S. 46 (1965)

BACKGROUND: Mary Carter Paint Company (respondent) manufactured and sold paint and related products. The FTC ordered the respondent to cease and desist from the use of certain representations found by the Commission to be deceptive and in violation of Section 5 of the Federal Trade Commission Act. The representations appeared in advertisements that stated in various ways that, for every can of respondent's paint purchased by a buyer, the respondent would give the buyer a "free" can of equal quality and quantity. The Court of Appeals for the Fifth Circuit set aside the Commission's order. The Supreme Court agreed to review the case.

Brennan, Justice

Although there is some ambiguity in the Commission's opinion, we cannot say that its holding constituted a departure from Commission policy regarding the use of the commercially exploitable word "free." Initial efforts to define the term in decisions were followed by "Guides Against Deceptive Pricing." These informed businessmen that they might advertise an article as "free," even though purchase of another article was required, so long as the terms of the offer were clearly stated, the price of the article required to be purchased was not increased, and its quality and quantity were not diminished. With specific reference to two-for-the-price-of-one offers, the Guides required that either the sales price for the two be "the advertiser's usual and customary retail price for the single article in the recent, regular course of his business," or where the advertiser has not previously sold the article, the price for the two be the "usual and customary" price for one in the relevant trade areas. These, of course, were guides, not fixed rules as such, and were designed to inform businessmen of the factors which would guide Commission decisions. Although Mary Carter seems to have attempted to tailor its offer to come within these terms, the Commission found that it failed; the offer complied in appearance only.

The gist of the Commission's reasoning is in the hearing examiner's finding, which it adopted, that "the usual and customary retail price of each can of Mary Carter paint was not, and is not now, the price designated in the advertisement [$6.98] but was, and is now, substantially less than such price. The second can of paint was not, and is not now, 'free,' that is, was not, and is not now, given as a gift or gratuity. The offer is, on the contrary, an offer of two cans of paint for the price advertised as or purporting to be the list price or customary and usual price of one can." In sum, the Commission found that Mary Carter had no history of selling single cans of paint; it was marketing twins, and in allocating what is in fact the price of two cans to one can, yet calling one "free," Mary Carter misrepresented. It is true that respondent was not permitted to show that the quality of its paint matched those paints which usually and customarily sell in the $6.98 range, or that purchasers of paint estimate quality by the price they are charged. If both claims were established, it is arguable that any deception was limited to a representation that Mary Carter has a usual and customary price for single cans of paint, when it has no such price. However, it is not for courts to say whether this violates the Act. "[T]he Commission is often in a better position than are courts to determine when a practice is 'deceptive' within the meaning of the Act."

The Commission advises us in its brief that it believes it would be appropriate here "to remand the case to it for clarification of its order." The judgment of the Court of Appeals is therefore reversed and the case is remanded to that court with directions to remand to the Commission for clarification of its order.

DECISION: The Supreme Court ruled in favor of the FTC.

ETHICS
Infomercials

You turn on the TV and you see what appears to be a talk show. Four people sit around and chat with a media star such as Cher. The conversation is witty and humorous. Yet the conversation seems to keep coming around to positive comments about a particular product. And that is the whole point. Although not labeled as commercials, these "infomercials" are actually designed with a single purpose: to sell specific products. They are quite effective, since nearly $1 billion in merchandise is sold through infomercials. For certain types of products, advertisers believe that infomericals are more effective than the traditional 15- to 30-second commercial spots.

Some infomercials featuring an audience watching a demonstration of a product's attributes have been successfully challenged for being deceptive. For example, the FTC obtained a $550,000 settlement from the sellers of a hand-held mixer demonstrated as capable of grinding up an "uncut" pineapple. In fact, the pineapple had been cut prior to the demonstration of its use in the infomercial.

Assuming that there is no deception in the display of products in infomercials, do you see any ethical problems in their use? If you were an advertising manager, under what circumstances would you approve of their use?

Advertising and Product Quality and Quantity   There is often a fine line between "puffing" and deception. The FTC and the courts have recognized that certain types of claims by advertisers do not violate Section 5 of the Federal Trade Commission Act. A car salesman's claim that "this car is the best that ever came out of Detroit" is an example of "puffing," but when an advertisement claims that "this car will run for 50,000 miles without a mechanical breakdown" it goes beyond puffing and approaches deception. A famous example of deception arose in the case of a Firestone Tire and Rubber Company ad that stated: "When you buy a Firestone tire—no matter how much or little you pay—you get a safe tire." It should be noted that a claim does not have to be expressly deceptive; it may deceive by implication. The FTC must also show that there was no basis for the claim. The Commission argued that the Firestone ad could have been interpreted to mean that, regardless of road conditions or usage, the tire was absolutely safe. This would obviously be false. In this case the FTC was found to be correct in its position. The Commission requires that an advertiser keep data on file to support its claims as to quality, performance, and comparative price.

Sometimes advertisers are accused of deception by their competitors. Seven-Up, for example, accused Pepsi-Cola of false, misleading, and deceptive ads because Pepsi did not say clearly in its television ads that regular, sugared Pepsi Free wasn't completely caffeine free—only 99 percent. In two cases brought under the Lanham Act, Section 43(a), which forbids "false description or representation," McDonald's and Wendy's accused Burger King of falsely portraying its hamburger as superior on the basis of an alleged "taste test." Both plaintiffs challenged the method and results of the taste test and sought injunctions and corrective advertising. The cases were settled out of court. The FTC can receive complaints from competitors as well as consumers, but it is not required to act on the complaints. The FTC generally takes the position that the government should not be involved when two or more private parties want to fight it out as to comparative advertising claims dealing with quality and quantity.

Deceptive Advertising and Testimonials   The FTC forbids endorsement of products by well-known personalities who either don't use the product or don't actually prefer it over another product. The Bureau of Consumer Protection also monitors claims by well-known personalities that they have superior knowledge of a product. In a negotiated consent order, entertainer Pat Boone agreed to pay damages to purchasers of Acne Stain. Boone represented the product as a cure for acne when in fact there was

---

ETHICS
Ethics and Advertising

P, a cereal company, spends one-third of its annual budget on television advertising. One-half of that amount is spent on sponsoring Saturday morning children's television programming. Critics contend that this is unfair advertising because it "brainwashes" children who cannot distinguish between the claims that are made in the advertising and reality. P has recently commissioned a study by a marketing research professor at a college of business administration to determine what ill effects, if any, its advertising has on children who watch television programs on Saturday morning. The marketing research professor (who was paid $50,000) found that the study did influence children between the ages of 4 and 10, and this age group was not able to differentiate between the claims made in ads and reality. For example, the professor pointed out that one of P's advertisements claimed that its cereal provided extra protein and children grew to be healthier, faster. P was able to substantiate its claim of more protein, but not that children grew faster as visually shown in the advertisement. The professor, under previous agreement with P, is about to publish his results, which are based on scientific research:

1. What ethical problems, if any, does P face?
2. What ethical problems, if any, do the television networks that carry the Saturday morning ads have?
3. What ethical problems, if any, does the marketing professor have?
4. What ethical problems, if any, do the parents of the children watching the ads have?

---

no scientific basis for such a claim. Boone also failed to reveal that he had a commercial interest in Acne Stain.

Unfair Advertising

Section 5 forbids "unfair" as well as deceptive advertising. As discussed earlier in this chapter, advertising is considered "unfair" if it (1) offends public policy; (2) is immoral, unethical, or unscrupulous; and (3) causes material or substantial harm to the consumer.

The failure of the FTC to provide a precise definition of "unfair" has led to calls by some at the Commission for more specificity from Congress. As an alternative, others have argued that "unfair and deceptive practices" should be deleted from

Section 5 of the Federal Trade Commission Act. Others have used the vagueness of definition as grounds for requesting an exemption from FTC authority under Section 5.

Remedies for Deceptive and Unfair Advertising

In adjudicative proceedings the FTC has the power to issue cease-and-desist orders. It has also ordered firms to disclose their deceptive or unfair advertising to the public through corrective advertising. Under this remedy, the firm is usually ordered to allocate a portion of its advertising budget to correct the long-held impression it has created in the public mind. In the following case, corrective advertising was approved by a federal appeals court.

WARNER LAMBERT V. FEDERAL TRADE COMMISSION
U.S. Court of Appeals, D.C. Circuit
562 F.2d. 49 (1977)

> **BACKGROUND:** Warner Lambert (petitioner) advertised that the product Listerine prevented, cured, or alleviated the common cold. Listerine had been on the market since 1879, and its formula and advertising (begun in 1921) had never changed. The FTC

ordered the company to cease and desist advertising this claim and to devote $10 million to corrective advertising that included the following: "Contrary to prior advertising Listerine will not help prevent colds or sore throats or lessen their severity." The petitioner challenged this order. The administrative law judge (ALJ) ruled in favor of the FTC staff. Petitioner appealed to the full Commission. The Commission affirmed essentially all the findings of the ALJ. Petitioner appealed to the Court of Appeals.

Wright, Judge

Both the ALJ and the Commission carefully analyzed the evidence. They gave full consideration to the studies submitted by petitioner. The ultimate conclusion that Listerine is not an effective cold remedy was based on . . . specific findings of fact.

Petitioner contends that even if its advertising claims in the past were false, the portion of the Commission's order requiring "corrective advertising" exceeds the Commission's statutory power. The argument is based upon a literal reading of Section 5 of the Federal Trade Commission Act, which authorizes the Commission to issue "cease and desist" orders against violators and does not expressly mention any other remedies. The Commission's position, on the other hand, is that the affirmative disclosure that Listerine will not prevent colds or lessen their severity is absolutely necessary to give effect to the prospective cease and desist order; a hundred years of false cold claims have built up a large reservoir of erroneous consumer belief which would persist, unless corrected, long after petitioner ceased making the claims.

The need for the corrective advertising remedy and its appropriateness in this case are important issues. But the threshold question is whether the Commission has the authority to issue such an order. We hold that it does [based on the legislative history of the Federal Trade Commission Act of 1914, the Wheeler–Lea Act Amendments of 1938, and the 1975 amendments, along with case precedents interpreting the Act].

Having established that the Commission does have the power to order corrective advertising in appropriate cases, it remains to consider whether use of the remedy against Listerine is warranted and equitable. We have concluded that part 3 of the order should be modified to delete the phrase "Contrary to prior advertising." With that modification, we approve the order. . . .

The Commission has adopted the following standard for the imposition of corrective advertising:

> [I]f a deceptive advertisement has played a substantial role in creating or reinforcing in the public's mind a false and material belief which lives on after the false advertising ceases, there is clear and continuing injury to competition and to the consuming public as consumers continue to make purchasing decisions based on the false belief. Since this injury cannot be averted by merely requiring respondent to cease disseminating the advertisement, we may appropriately order respondent to take affirmative action designed to terminate the otherwise continuing ill effects of the advertisement.

We think this standard is entirely reasonable. It dictates two factual inquiries: (1) Did Listerine's advertisements play a substantial role in creating or reinforcing in the public's mind a false belief about the product? and (2) Would this belief linger on after the false advertising ceases? It strikes us that if the answer to both questions is not yes, companies everywhere may be wasting their massive advertising budgets. Indeed, it is more than a little peculiar to hear petitioner assert that its commercials really have no effect on consumer belief.

DECISION: The U.S. Court of Appeals ruled in favor of the FTC with modifications.

Deceptive Packaging and Labeling

Closely related to the problems associated with advertising are questions involved in packaging and labeling. Studies have indicated that consumers tend to rely more heavily on labeling than on other forms of advertising. Labeling and packaging came under fire when a 1965 study by the Food and Drug Administration indicated that it was not uncommon to find packages with as little as 20 percent of the inner container filled with a food product.

Against this background Congress in 1966 passed the Fair Packaging and Labeling Act. Congress ordered the Secretary of Health, Education, and Welfare (HEW, now Health and Human Services) and the FTC to develop mandatory and discretionary rules governing the labeling and packaging of products. HEW was authorized to regulate packaging of foods, drugs, and cosmetics, whereas the FTC was given jurisdiction over other consumer commodities.

The rules require that a packaged or labeled consumer commodity bear the following information.

1. The name and address of the manufacturer, packer, and distributor of the product
2. The net quantity, which must be conspicuously placed on the package front
3. An accurate description of the contents

These requirements were intended to enable consumers to compare prices of competing products on the basis of uniform measures. This seemed necessary because of the wide variety of package weights and volumes used by manufacturers.

In passing the Fair Packaging and Labeling Act, Congress authorized discretionary regulations to:

1. Set up standards for size characterization (for example, "small," "medium," "large")
2. Control "cents off" promotions
3. Regulate additional ingredient information on containers of drugs and cosmetics
4. Prevent nonfunctional slack fill of packages

The Fair Packaging and Labeling Act provides that any violation of the act is also a violation of Section 5 of the Federal Trade Commission Act.

Thus the FTC has used the same enforcement measures for violations of both acts.

Consumer Protection Laws

Consumer Product Safety Act

The Consumer Product Safety Act, passed in 1972, sets up a framework for regulating potentially unsafe consumer products. The Act established the Consumer Product Safety Commission (CPSC), which is empowered to set safety standards for consumer products and to ban certain products that pose an unreasonable risk of injury. The CPSC also sponsors research on the safety of various products. The Act does not apply to certain products, including tobacco products, motor vehicles and related equipment, pesticides, boats, food, and drugs. These exempted products are regulated by other statutes.

Consumer Leasing Act

The Consumer Leasing Act of 1976 imposes various requirements on lessors of consumer products, such as automobiles. The Act applies only to products leased primarily for personal, family, or household purposes; the lease of a car for business purposes, then, would not be subject to the Act. Additionally, the Act applies only to leases made to natural persons (which is usually the case for products leased for personal, family, or household purposes) for whom the total obligation does not exceed $25,000.

Lessors are required to disclose items of information to lessees, including a brief description of the leased property; the amount of any payments required at the onset of the lease; the amount payable by the lessee in addition to the periodic payments; the method of determining any liabilities imposed upon the lessee at the end of the lease term; a description of any security interest held by the lessor; the number, amount, and due dates or periods of payments; and the total amount of periodic payments to be made under the lease. These disclosures must be in writing and delivered to the lessee before the transaction is consummated.

The Act also prohibits lessors from imposing excessive liability upon the lessee upon the expiration of the lease or in the event of delinquent payments, default, or early termination.

If a lessor advertises, the advertisement must disclose, among other things, that the advertised transaction is in fact a lease; the amount of payment, if any, required at the inception of the lease; the schedule of payments under the lease; and any liability that may be imposed upon the lessee when the lease expires.

A lessor who violates the Consumer Leasing Act incurs civil liability as provided in the Truth-in-Lending Act, discussed below.

Consumer Credit Protection Act

In 1968 Congress passed the Consumer Credit Protection Act, which addresses problems associated with consumer buying on credit. This comprehensive act comprises the Truth-in-Lending Act (Title I), the Fair Credit Reporting Act (Title IV), the Equal Credit Opportunity Act (Title VI), and the Fair Debt Collection Practices Act. Basically the Act requires disclosure of information concerning the cost of credit transactions and prohibits unfair treatment of consumers in credit applications and debt collections.

The Truth-in-Lending Act

Title I of the Consumer Credit Protection Act is commonly known as the Truth-in-Lending Act.

The main thrust of the Truth-in-Lending Act is to require disclosure by creditors of the terms and conditions of consumer credit before extending such credit to consumer-debtors. In theory, as a result of these disclosures, the creditor and the consumer-debtor should have equal knowledge of the terms of the transaction, and the consumer should be able to shop for the cheapest price (interest rate or finance charge) in the credit marketplace. Competition in the consumer-credit markets should thus be enhanced.

Under the Truth-in-Lending Act, the board of governors of the Federal Reserve Board is given the power to prescribe regulations. Regulation Z and its interpretations are given deference by the courts and thus are important in daily business transactions.

Regulation Z provides, among other things, that a consumer may be reimbursed for disclosure errors with regard to finance or other charges by creditors, when these result from a clear and consistent pattern of negligence or a willful violation intended to mislead. Additionally, the Department of Justice, upon referral from an enforcement agency, can bring criminal actions under the Truth-in-Lending Act against creditors who "willfully and knowingly" give false information or fail to make proper disclosures as required by the Act. If convicted, a creditor is subject to a fine of not more than $5,000 or imprisonment for not more than one year or both.

A consumer has a right to bring an individual action for damages if he or she can show that the transaction comes within the Truth-in-Lending Act and that the creditor failed to comply with the requirements of Regulation Z. It is *not* necessary for the consumer to show that the creditor's noncompliance was substantial, that it was relied on, or that any injury resulted. The measure of damages is actual damages plus a statutory penalty, usually twice the amount of the finance charges imposed when dealing with open-end transactions (for example, installment credit where one can pay in full or partially, as in the case of VISA or department store accounts). The statutory penalty cannot exceed $1,000. Closed-end transactions (for example, mortgages) limit creditors' liability for a statutory penalty to certain types of nondisclosure.

Scope of the Truth-in-Lending Act   The Truth-in-Lending Act affects a substantial number of credit transactions. Under the Act those who in the ordinary course of business regularly extend consumer credit must make proper disclosures. Basically consumer credit transactions are those in which credit of less than $25,000 is extended to a natural person for personal, family, or household use. Natural persons borrowing for business or commercial purposes, or those borrowing over $25,000 for any purpose, are not entitled to the Truth-in-Lending disclosures. Congress reasoned that people in these categories should be able to protect themselves. Disclosures also do not have to be made to organizations such as corporations, partnerships, trusts, estates, and associations, nor do the required disclosures have to be made to governments or units of government. Institutional debtors are not protected because they, like the businessperson and the wealthy individual, are assumed to be sophisticated borrowers with sufficient economic and legal resources to protect their interests. Transactions in real property exceeding $25,000 in which security interests are acquired are also exempt. Items of personal property used or expected to be used at the principal dwelling place of a consumer to which a security interest attaches are also excluded if their value exceeds $25,000. Finally, the consumer credit granted must involve a finance charge or be payable in four or more installments.

Finance Charges For disclosure of the costs of credit to be meaningful, each offer or extension of credit to a consumer should include all the charges to be paid for the credit. If one potential lender includes in the cost of credit the premium on credit life insurance and a second does not (even though the latter also requires credit life insurance), the quoted costs to the consumer in the second instance will be misleading. The Truth-in-Lending Act and Regulation Z require all who extend credit to include certain costs if they are charged to the consumer.

The Truth-in-Lending Act and Regulation Z use the term **finance charge** when referring to dollar charges that make up the cost of credit. Basically, any charge paid by a debtor that he or she would not have had to pay except for the grant of credit is to be included in the finance charge. Many of these charges are obvious, but in some instances the creditor must look to both Regulation Z and the Federal Reserve Board's interpretations to determine if a particular amount must be included in the finance charge.

Annual Percentage Rate The **annual percentage rate** (APR) is similar to "simple annual interest." The requirement that the APR be disclosed allows consumers to compare finance charges on a common basis. The importance of this is illustrated by the following example.

Suppose that a consumer is interested in buying a combination stereo and color television unit that costs $500. The consumer's account with a large retail store allows him or her to pay all the bill or a specified minimum portion of it based on the size of the balance. He or she may also pay any sum in between and may have a number of days within which to pay without incurring a finance charge. If the consumer does not pay the entire account, monthly carrying charges are 1½ percent on the average daily balance. The APR that the retailer must disclose is 18 percent.

A second alternative open to this consumer is to borrow the $500 from a bank, which may charge 7 percent if the loan is repaid in twenty-four monthly installments. The consumer is also required to pay $6, which includes charges for a credit report and credit life insurance. The bank would have to show finance charges of $76 and an APR of 14 percent. Without knowing the APR, this consumer would have difficulty comparing the two sources of credit.

General Disclosure Provisions The Truth-in-Lending Act is solely a disclosure statute. It does not prescribe interest rates or finance charges. What must be disclosed will depend on whether the consumer credit transaction is classified as open-end or closed-end. However, there are some general requirements imposed by the Act and Regulation Z, including the following:

1. All disclosure of terms and conditions of credit must be made "clearly and conspicuously in meaningful sequence"
2. Additional nonrequired information may be disclosed if it does not confuse customers
3. A creditor must furnish the consumer with a copy of the disclosure requirements at the time of disclosure

Closed-End Credit **Closed-end credit** includes both loans to consumers and sales made on credit, where the credit is for a specific period of time and the total amount, number of payments, and due dates are agreed upon by the buyer and seller. Typically closed-end credit is used in buying or financing "big ticket" items like automobiles, washing machines, television sets, or other major appliances. Closed-end credit also includes a single-payment loan.

If the credit is closed-end, in addition to an explanation of the "finance charge" and the "APR," the consumer is entitled upon written request to an itemization of the "amount financed." The creditor must affirmatively disclose this right to the consumer. Also, such terms as "total of payments" and "total sale price" must be described by the creditor. The Federal Reserve Board has prepared forms for creditors' use.

Open-End Credit Regulation Z defines **open-end credit** as credit extended on an account pursuant to a plan under which

1. The creditor may permit the customer to make purchases or obtain loans from time to time

2. The customer has the privilege of paying the balance in full or in installments

3. A finance charge may be computed from time to time on an outstanding unpaid balance

An open-end credit plan as defined by the Reform Act includes a requirement that the creditor "reasonably contemplated repeated transactions." Common examples of this type of consumer credit are revolving charge accounts of retail stores, oil company and bank credit cards, and bank plans that permit limited overdrafts with finance charges periodically imposed on any unpaid balances.

For consumer credit of this type an initial statement by the creditor must be given at the time the account is opened. It must indicate the conditions under which the finance charge may be imposed, the method of computing it, and the means of determining the balance subject to the finance charge. The periodic rates as well as the corresponding annual percentage rates must also be disclosed in the initial statement.

At the end of each billing period the creditor must provide the customer with a statement if the customer's account has an outstanding balance. Regulation Z requires certain disclosures to appear on the face of the periodic statement.

Credit Advertising and Solicitation
The Truth-in-Lending Act and Regulation Z impose restrictions on advertising as it relates to credit terms. The definition of advertising in Regulation Z is very broad. All the usual channels—newspapers, radio, television, and direct mail—are specifically mentioned. The provisions also cover almost any "commercial message" made available to the public if the message "aids, promotes, or assists" an extension of consumer credit. Although a statement made by a salesperson to a particular client is not considered to be an advertisement, a similar statement promoting a sale or loan posted in writing at the store or delivered over a store's public-address system would be an advertisement.

Both the Act and Regulation Z prohibit lenders and sellers from advertising terms of credit that are not usually or regularly extended to cus-

tomers. For example, a creditor who advertises "no down payment" or a seller who advertises "$5 down, $5 per month" must regularly extend credit on those terms. This provision helps to eliminate the practice of enticing customers by advertising generous credit terms that are seldom, if ever, granted. It does not require that every customer be offered the advertised terms, only that the terms be "usually and customarily" those upon which credit is granted.

The basic philosophy of the credit advertising section of the Truth-in-Lending Act is *if* creditors advertise credit terms they must disclose (1) down payment, if any, (2) terms of repayment, and (3) finance charges expressed as an annual percentage rate. Additionally, an advertisement of consumer credit payable in four installments without a finance charge must clearly and conspicuously state: "THE COST OF CREDIT IS INCLUDED IN THE PRICE QUOTED FOR THE GOODS AND SERVICES."

The Truth-in-Lending Act and Regulation Z have special, detailed rules governing advertising and solicitation of some of the most popular forms of consumer credit: credit cards, charge cards, and home equity loans and lines of credit.

Right of Rescission   Regulation Z provides an important protection for those who put up their homes as security for consumer credit. A consumer basically has 3 days to rescind such a transaction. The 3-day period starts from the time that the lender delivers to the consumer written notice of the right to rescind and other material disclosures that are required by law. If the lender fails to properly notify the consumer of the right to rescind or fails to make other required disclosures, the consumer's right to rescind lasts for 3 years or until the property is sold, whichever comes first. The right to rescind does not apply to a first mortgage on the consumer's home. However, the right does apply to other extensions of credit secured by the consumer's principal dwelling, such as home equity lines of credit and home improvement loans.

Some problems arising from the right of rescission are discussed in the *Williams* case below.

WILLIAMS V. HOMESTAKE MORTGAGE CO.

U.S. Court of Appeals, Eleventh Circuit
968 F.2d 1137 (1992)

BACKGROUND: Annie Mae Williams borrowed money from Homestake Mortgage Company, which secured the loan with a lien on Williams' house. Williams sought legal advice after the monthly payments turned out to be more than she expected them to be. Williams sued Homestake for failing to make required disclosures under the Truth-in-Lending Act (referred to below as TILA or the Act) and Regulation Z. One month after she filed the lawsuit and a year after she had taken out the loan, Williams delivered a letter to Homestake purporting to rescind the transaction pursuant to Regulation Z. The U.S. District Court ruled for Williams, requiring Homestake to terminate its security interest in Williams' home and to pay statutory damages in the amount of $1,000. Homestake's obligation was *not* made conditional upon Williams' return of the $12,917.79 that she had borrowed. Homestake appealed.

Fay, Circuit Judge

In 1968, Congress enacted TILA "to assure a meaningful disclosure of credit terms so that the consumer will be able to compare more readily the various credit terms available to him and avoid the uninformed use of credit." As part of the Act, Congress provided the consumer with the right to rescind a credit transaction under § 1635(a) solely by notifying the creditor within set time limits of his intent to rescind. Once the consumer exercises his right to rescind, the effect of that decision and the subsequent exchange of property is then governed by 15 U.S.C. § 1635(b), which provides:

> When an obligor exercises his right to rescind under subsection (a) of this section, he is not liable for any finance or other charge, and any security interest given by the obligor, including any such interest arising by operation of law, becomes void upon rescission. Within 20 days after receipt of a notice of rescission, the creditor shall return to the obligor any money or property given as earnest money, downpayment, or otherwise, and shall take any action necessary or appropriate to reflect the termination of any security interest created under the transaction. If the creditor has delivered any property to the obligor, the obligor may retain possession of it. Upon the performance of the creditor's obligations under this section, the obligor shall tender the property to the creditor, except that if return of the property in kind would be impracticable or inequitable, the obligor shall tender its reasonable value. Tender shall be made at the location of the property or at the residence of the obligor, at the option of the obligor. If the creditor does not take possession of the property within 20 days after tender by the obligor, ownership of the property vests in the obligor without obligation on his part to pay for it. The procedures prescribed by this subsection shall apply except when otherwise ordered by a court.

The sequence of rescission and tender set forth in § 1635(b) is a reordering of common law rules governing rescission. Under common law rescission, the rescinding party must first tender the property that he has received under the agreement before the contract may be considered void. Once the rescinding party has performed his obligations, the contract becomes void and the rescinding party may then bring an action in replevin or assumpsit to insure that the non-rescinding party will restore him to the position that he was in prior to entering into the agreement, i.e., return earnest money or monthly payments and void all security interests. Under § 1635(b), however, all that the consumer need do is notify the creditor of his intent to rescind. The agreement is then automatically rescinded and the creditor must, ordinarily, tender first. Thus, rescission under § 1635 "place[s] the consumer in a much stronger bargaining position than he enjoys under the traditional rules of rescission." Furthermore, because rescission is such a painless remedy under the statute (placing all burdens on the creditor), it acts as an important enforcement tool, insuring creditor compliance with TILA's disclosure requirements.

Though one goal of the statutory rescission process is to place the consumer in a much stronger bargaining position, another goal of § 1635(b) is to return the parties most nearly to the position they held prior to entering into the transaction. The addition of the last sentence of § 1635(b), stating that "[t]he procedures prescribed by this subsection shall apply except when otherwise ordered by a court," was added by the Truth in Lending Simplification and Reform Act and is a reflection of this equitable goal. Prior to the statute's amendment, the majority of circuit courts that addressed this issue permitted judicial modification of the statutory rescission process. Despite a lack of Congressional sanction for such action, these courts relied on their equity powers to fashion rescission procedures not contemplated by the Act. . . .

Where the "intent of Congress is clear, that is the end of the matter; for the court, as well as the agency, must give effect to the unambiguously expressed intent of Congress." *Chevron U.S.A. v. Natural Resources Defense Council* (1984). In this instance, Congress, through its legislative history, has made it quite clear that "the courts, *at any time during the rescission process*, may impose equitable conditions to insure that the consumer meets his obligations after the creditor has performed his obligations as required by the act." S.Rep. No. 368, 96th Cong., 2d Sess. 29 (1980) (emphasis added). Furthermore, the plain language of § 1635(b) leaves little room for narrowing the court's ability to modify the process of effecting rescission, as Congress' grant of authority covers all "procedures prescribed by [the] subsection."

DECISION: The Circuit Court reversed the decision of the District Court and remanded the case for a determination of whether Williams should be required to return all or part of the loan proceeds.

The Fair Credit Reporting Act

Purpose The Fair Credit Reporting Act of 1970 was enacted by Congress to require consumer credit-reporting agencies to adopt reasonable procedures for meeting the needs of lenders while maintaining the confidentiality, accuracy, and relevancy of their records. This legislation was aimed at several problems:

1. Inaccurate and sometimes misleading information in the files of credit-reporting agencies

2. Irrelevant information in such files (for example, the name of a credit applicant's dog)

3. Lack of standards to maintain the confidentiality of credit files

Scope The Fair Credit Reporting Act regulates the **consumer reporting agency**, which is defined as any entity that "regularly" engages in the practice of assembling or evaluating consumer credit or other information on consumers for the purpose of furnishing "consumer reports to third parties." A business can escape the coverage of the Act if it disseminates information *infrequently* or if it collects it solely for its own use and does not transmit it to third parties. The Act's provisions contain:

• Requirements for consumer reporting agencies

• Requirements for users of consumer reports

• Rights of consumers

• Remedies for violations

ETHICS
Ethics and Bank Lending

Jones and Mary Smith earn together approximately $70,000 as elementary school teachers. Their monthly disposable income after mortgage payments, credit cards, utilities, and so on is $600 per month. They have a 1-year-old-house with $10,000 equity. An ad from a local bank urged them to use their home equity for a loan to consolidate their debts on "easy terms." In asterisk form at the bottom of the ad all the terms were outlined as required by the Truth-in-Lending Act. They were disclosed again to Mr. and Mrs. Smith by First National Bank's lending officer when they borrowed $7,000 at a variable rate of 14 percent, with no cap, which was based on the monthly Treasury bill rate. No lawyer was present when this loan was taken out to advise the Smiths, and the bank's lawyers drafted the documents they signed. Now, 2 years later, the variable rate has risen to 22 percent and they cannot make the monthly payments. The bank forecloses.

There are several ethical issues involved in this case. The bank has more experience and information about the capacity of individuals to handle mortgage payments than do the schoolteachers. The bank should gather this information in the course of the application and inform the borrowers about the risks. Further, when there is a new financial mechanism, as in the case of the variable-rate home equity loan, the bank has an obligation to make sure that the borrowers understand how this arrangement differs from the more traditional forms.

Advertising performs many useful and important functions. It reduces consumer search costs for significant information about products and can inform prospective buyers about new products. As is true of many things, advertising can also have a dark side. Providing incorrect or misleading information is a major problem. There may also be a question of advertising being manipulative when it is designed to overcome critical judgment and induce people to act in a manner that they later regret.

The requirements for consumer reporting agencies include a directive that all agencies must maintain "reasonable procedures" to avoid making a consumer report that contains obsolete information. Such information is "obsolete" under the Act if it is older than 7 years (10 years in the case of information relating to bankruptcy). The time limitation is inapplicable if the report is to be used in conjunction with a credit or life insurance transaction involving $50,000 or more. If the consumer reporting agency is reporting to a prospective employer, it cannot use materials that are not up to date. Further, the act requires that a consumer reporting agency maintain "reasonable" procedures to ensure that its report will be furnished only to those designated or qualified under the Act. They include:

1. A consumer who requests the reporting agency to furnish information

2. A court of law, or someone authorized by a valid court order

3. A person or entity whom the credit reporting agency has "reason to believe" intends to use such information to determine if a consumer is eligible for credit, employment, government license, or other business purposes

The Fair Credit Reporting Act also prescribes certain regulations for users of reports received from credit-reporting agencies. Among the obligations users have is to notify a consumer in advance if they intend to order an investigative report from a reporting agency. They must also notify the consumer of the probable content of the report. If the user relies "wholly or partly" on the report in rejecting a consumer for credit, insurance, or employment, it must notify the consumer and provide the name and address of the reporting agency. If a consumer reporting agency as defined by the Act is *not* involved, the user of a report that is the basis for the denial of credit must make all such information available upon request and must advise the consumer of his or her right to make that request.

Consumers have rights under the Act, as noted earlier. Inaccurate and obsolete information cannot be used in their credit reports. They have a right to be notified of a reporting agency's reliance on adverse information when they are denied credit. The Act gives the consumer a right of disclosure upon request. The reporting agency must disclose:

1. Nature and substance of all information (except medical)
2. Source of all information (except when it is used solely in preparing "investigative reports")
3. Names of any users of the report who have received the consumer's file in the last 2 years when employment was involved (the last 6 months for all other reasons)

The consumer has a right to correct information in his or her file once it is received. Following notification of errors, the reporting agency must investigate the matter in the file that the consumer disputes, assuming that the correction is not frivolous or irrelevant. The agency must note the dispute and provide a consumer statement for the file or a summary of the consumer's views. Upon request, the reporting agency must notify any users of the file of the disputed information.

Remedies   The FTC has the principal responsibility for administering the Act, and does so through cease-and-desist orders. Other agencies share enforcement authority when applicable to matters subject to their regulatory jurisdictions. Some of the same agencies are involved in enforcement of both the Fair Credit Reporting Act and the Truth-in-Lending Act. Criminal liability is involved if a user obtains information from a consumer reporting agency "knowingly and willfully" under false pretenses. Officers and employees of an agency are also subject to a penalty of up to $5,000 and 1 year imprisonment for willfully providing information from an agency file to unauthorized persons. Civil liability is also provided for if there is a *willful* violation of the Act by the reporting agency or user. Compensatory (actual) and punitive damages can be awarded to a consumer, along with attorney's fees and court costs. In case of *negligence* by a reporting agency or user, only compensatory damages are available. The major defense for a reporting agency in a civil suit is that "reasonable procedures" were used as required by the Act.

The Equal Credit Opportunity Act

Purpose   Following a study by the National Commission on Consumer Finance which showed blatant discrimination against women in the granting of credit, Congress in 1974 enacted the Equal Credit Opportunity Act (ECOA) to prohibit discrimination against a person applying for credit on the basis of sex or marital status. In 1976 Congress amended the Act to include age, race, color, national origin, recipients of public assistance, and those who exercise their rights under any section of the Consumer Credit Protection Act. The Act empowers the Federal Reserve Board to prescribe regulations and allows the Board to exempt "any classes of transaction not primarily for personal, family or household purposes." Regulation B has been issued by the Board as a basis for interpreting and enforcing the Act. Several administrative agencies share enforcement authority depending on the type of credit involved. Overall enforcement is entrusted to the FTC.

Scope   The ECOA covers all phases of a credit transaction and all groups noted previously. A creditor may not ask for information about race, age, sex, religion, or national origin. The Act prohibits asking for information about marital status, alimony, child support, use of birth control pills, and former spouses. A model application form has been issued by the Federal Reserve Board. Use of this form by the creditor offers a presumption of compliance with these provisions.

The Act requires that a creditor give an applicant notification of action it has taken on his or her completed application for credit within 30 days. If the application is incomplete, a 90-day notice period is required if the application is denied. The notification must include:

- A statement of the action taken
- Basic provisions of ECOA
- Name and address of compliance agency
- A statement of the specific reasons for the action taken, or a disclosure of the applicant's right to receive a statement of reason

Remedies   The FTC, as well as individuals, may sue to enforce the Act. A person injured may recover actual and punitive damages. In individual actions such punitive damages may not exceed $10,000, whereas in class actions $500,000 or

1 percent of the net worth of the creditors (whichever is less) is the maximum.

The Fair Debt Collection Practices Act

Purpose   Up to this point, discussion has centered on federal laws that seek to protect consumers in obtaining credit. A consumer's problems might not be over, of course, once the credit has been obtained. Thousands of debt collection agencies exist to try to collect from consumers who have defaulted on their debts. Because many of these agencies were found to engage in abusive practices, including threats of violence, obscene language, and anonymous phone calls in the middle of the night, Congress in 1977 passed the Fair Debt Collection Practices Act. As noted previously, this and other pieces of consumer protection legislation are included as separate titles under the Consumer Credit Protection Act. The FTC is charged with its administration and enforcement. A violation of this Act is considered to be an unfair or deceptive practice under Section 5 of the Federal Trade Commission Act.

Scope   Because laws preventing abuses in debt collection have been passed in many states, the Fair Debt Collection Practices Act allows exemptions for states that meet federal standards. Also, the Act covers only those debt collectors who collect for someone other than themselves. Large companies that do their own debt collecting are not covered by the Act but may be covered by state legislation. The Act forbids the following practices:

1. A debt collector may contact someone other than the consumer debtor, his or her family, or his or her attorney only for purposes of finding the debtor. This section seeks to prevent a collector from ruining the good name of a debtor with his employer or neighbors.

2. Debt collectors may not contact a debtor at inconvenient times (9 p.m.–8 a.m.), or at all if the collector is aware that the consumer is represented by an attorney.

3. Any conduct by debt collectors that is abusive, deceptive, misleading, or unfair is forbidden. Posing as lawyers or police officers to collect debts, for example, is forbidden.

4. Collections that require liens on real property may be brought only where the property is located. Other collection actions must be brought where the debtor resides.

Attorneys and law firms that participate in debt collection also fall within the Act, as a result of a 1986 amendment passed by Congress.

Remedies   Action can be brought by the FTC and individuals. Any violator of the Act is liable for actual damages and "additional damages" up to $1,000. Attorney's fees and court costs also may be assessed.

The *Bloom* Case, which follows, involves an informal loan between friends that was mistakenly reported to a debt collection agency. The case raises issues under both the Fair Debt Collection Practices Act and the Fair Credit Reporting Act.

■ BLOOM v. I.C. Systems, Inc.

U.S. Court of Appeals, Ninth Circuit
972 F.2d 1067 (1992)

Background: Michael Bloom borrowed $5,000 from his friend, Steven Parker. Bloom used the money to invest in a software company. Parker's company mistakenly reported the debt to I.C. System, a debt collection agency. I.C. started debt collection efforts against Bloom. Bloom notified Parker of the mistake, and Parker attempted through phone calls and letters to explain that the debt was reported in error. I.C. responded by requesting documentation to verify that no debt was owed. I.C. thereafter continued to list the debt on Bloom's credit report, although it listed the debt as "contested." Bloom sued I.C. for violations of the Fair Debt Collection Practices Act (FDCPA) and the Fair Credit Reporting Act. The U.S. District Court ruled in favor of I.C., and Bloom appealed.

Goodwin, Circuit Judge

The FDCPA protects consumers from unlawful debt collection practices. Consequently, the Act applies to consumer debts and not business loans. The term "debt" is defined as:

> [A]ny obligation or alleged obligation *of a consumer* to pay money arising out of a transaction in which the money, property, insurance, or services which are the subject of the transaction are *primarily for personal, family, or household purposes* . . .

15 U.S.C. § 1692a(5) (emphasis added.) . . .

Bloom urges us to characterize the loan as personal rather than commercial because the loan was informal in nature, with none of the trappings of a commercial loan, and because Parker's motivation in lending the money was personal rather than business in nature. We are not persuaded. The fact that a loan is informal or that the lender may have loaned the money for personal reasons does not make it a personal loan under the FDCPA. The Act characterizes debts in terms of end uses, covering debts incurred "primarily for personal, family or household purposes." Neither the lender's motives nor the fashion in which the loan is memorialized are dispositive of this inquiry.

How Bloom actually spent the money is not disputed. Bloom invested the proceeds of the loan as venture capital in a software company with which he was closely associated. . . .

The Fair Credit Reporting Act ("FCRA") requires credit reporting agencies to disclose extensive credit information to consumers. To limit the potential scope of liability for these agencies, Congress preempted state common law defamation claims.

> Except as provided in §§ 1681n and 1681o of this title, no consumer may bring any action or proceeding in the nature of defamation . . . with respect to the reporting of information against any consumer reporting agency, any user of information, or any person who furnishes information to a consumer reporting agency, based on information disclosed pursuant to 1681g . . ., *except as to false information furnished with malice or willful intent to injure such consumer.*

15 U.S.C. § 1681h(e) (emphasis added).

Bloom argues that I.C. acted with malice because it refused to delete information regarding the debt. A collection agency does not have a duty to delete all references to a debt whenever such debt is contested. I.C. reported the debt as disputed when it learned of the controversy. Moreover, the record demonstrates that I.C. took reasonable steps to verify the information in the report.

The following facts are not in dispute. In late 1988, under a contract with Parkwest which provided that "[a]ll accounts submitted to I.C. . . . will be deemed assigned and set over to I.C. for collection, and will be validly due and owing by the debtor," I.C. received a debt naming Bloom as the debtor. Upon Bloom's prompting, Parker made phone calls and wrote letters stating that no debt existed. In March 1989, I.C. requested further written verification that no debt was owed. Thereafter, I.C. informed credit reporting agencies that the debt was disputed. In May 1989, Bloom filed suit.

Bloom argues that it was "false" to report the debt as disputed because both Bloom and Parker represented that no debt existed. The representations of the parties do not explain, from I.C.'s perspective, how or why such a loan was submitted for collection in the first place. The debt had been properly submitted under a valid contract. Under the circumstances, I.C.'s decision to list the debt as disputed and to seek written verification that no debt was in fact owed was not unreasonable. Such conduct does not constitute malice or the willful intent to injure.

DECISION: The Court of Appeals affirmed the decision of the District Court.

CONCEPT SUMMARY
Major Consumer Protection Statutes

Federal Trade Commission Act	Section 5 prohibits "unfair or deceptive acts or practices," including deceptive or unfair advertising.
Fair Packaging and Labeling Act	Imposes uniform disclosure requirements for information contained on labels and packages.
Consumer Product Safety Act	Empowers Consumer Product Safety Commission to regulate or, in some cases, ban hazardous consumer products.
Consumer Leasing Act	Imposes disclosure requirements on lessors in consumer transactions and regulates certain consumer lease terms.
Truth-in-Lending Act	Imposes uniform disclosure requirements for providers of consumer credit; also regulates solicitation and advertising.
Fair Credit Reporting Act	Prohibits credit-reporting agencies from including obsolete or inaccurate material in credit reports. Gives consumers access to credit reports and regulates who may use those reports.
Equal Credit Opportunity Act	Prohibits discrimination in the provision of credit on the basis of sex, marital status, age, race, color, and national origin. Also prohibits discrimination against recipients of public assistance and those who exercise their rights under the Consumer Credit Protection Act.
Fair Debt Collection Practices Act	Regulates activities of debt collection agencies to prevent abusive practices.
Real Estate Settlement Procedures Act (RESPA)	Provides uniform disclosure procedures for real estate settlement costs.
Interstate Land Sales Full Disclosure Act	Provides uniform disclosure procedures for property subject to interstate land sales.

Real Estate Sales

Two important federal acts require certain disclosures in connection with real estate sales: the Real Estate Settlement Procedures Act (RESPA) and the Interstate Land Sales Full Disclosure Act.

RESPA RESPA is designed to enable consumers to understand the often confusing array of charges and expenses incurred in connection with the purchase of a home or other real estate. Escrow fees, title search fees, title insurance fees, credit life insurance premiums, taxes, and several other expenses are generally included in the cost of closing a real estate purchase. RESPA requires that these costs be disclosed to the buyer clearly according to uniform standards.

RESPA also prohibits the payment of referral fees for business in connection with the settlement process; these fees are typically called *kickbacks*.

Interstate Land Sales Full Disclosure Act The Interstate Land Sales Act was passed in 1968 for people who purchase property outside their state of residence. The Act was designed to remedy the classic "swampland in Florida" problem, in which people were deceived into buying worthless property that they had never seen. The Act requires interstate sellers of land to file a detailed information statement with the Department of Housing and Urban Development. The process is designed to enable prospective buyers to obtain all the information that they would want to know prior to purchasing the property. A seller who violates the Act may be fined up to $10,000, imprisoned for up to 5 years, or both. The Act also provides that violators may incur civil liability.

Review Questions and Problems

Key Terms

finance charge

annual percentage rate

closed-end credit

open-end credit

consumer reporting agency

Discussion Questions

1. What three areas of deceptive price advertising does the FTC most concern itself with?

2. When does the court consider advertising to be "unfair"?

3. What remedies can the FTC invoke against deceptive and unfair advertising?

4. What is the main purpose of the Truth-in-Lending Act?

5. What is the scope of the Truth-in-Lending Act?

6. Distinguish between open-end and closed-end credit.

7. What is the purpose of the Fair Credit Reporting Act?

8. What is the purpose of the Equal Credit Opportunity Act?

Review Problems

1. In a television ad singing the praises of Wonder-Gro Plant Food, Myron appears as a "satisfied customer." He reports that Wonder-Gro has greatly improved the condition of his garden. Myron does not disclose that he is an attorney whose major client is Wonder-Gro. However, Myron genuinely is impressed with the product. Each factual statement that Myron makes during the commercial is true, and each opinion is offered with sincerity. Does the Wonder-Gro ad violate Section 5 of the Federal Trade Commission Act? Discuss.

2. Melvin owned a store that sold jewelry in a low-income area. Melvin ran ads that frequently mentioned the "easy credit" available at his store. In fact, it was Melvin's practice to offer credit without determining the customer's credit status or ability to make payments. However, it was also Melvin's practice to seek, frequently with success, garnish-

ments against the wages of customers who defaulted. Is it misleading for Melvin to advertise the "easy credit" offered at his store? Discuss.

3. Your grandfather, who lives in Iowa, tells you that a nice young man knocked on his door and offered to sell him some wonderful retirement property in Florida. After seeing pictures of the property, your grandfather has decided to buy it. You advise your grandfather not to purchase the land without inspecting it first. He tells you that he won't be able to travel to Florida for the next several months, but that the salesperson wants to close the deal within a few weeks because "the land is going fast." What steps would you advise your grandfather to take to protect himself in this situation?

4. Mark wants to add an enclosed patio to his house. He applies for a home improvement loan from Friendly Federal Savings & Loan. Friendly Federal approves the loan and, on March 6, delivers all the requisite Regulation Z disclosures to Mark just before he signs the loan documents. On the very next day, Mark learns that Fast Federal Savings Bank is willing to make him a home improvement loan on substantially better terms, including a lower interest rate. Mark wants to take the Fast Federal loan, but he has already signed the Friendly Federal loan documents. What are Mark's options?

Case Problems

1. The Colgate-Palmolive Company, manufacturer of a shaving cream, "Rapid Shave," sought to test the effectiveness of its cream on men's beards. In an advertisement broadcast on television, Colgate sought to show that its product could soften even sandpaper. However, when the advertisement was run, a sheet of Plexiglas with sand sprinkled on it was used in place of sandpaper. The FTC claimed that the commercial was deceptive and violated Section 5 of the FTC Act. Colgate claimed there was no deception because the viewer was simply being given a visual presentation of the test on sandpaper that had actually been made. Was there a violation of Section 5?

2. Kathleen Carroll, a single working woman, applied for an Exxon credit card in August 1976 and was advised by mail shortly thereafter that her application for credit was denied. No reason for the denial was given. Fourteen days after the denial she asked to be advised of the specific reasons. In an undated letter she was told by Exxon that a local reporting agency had not been able to supply sufficient information. The name of the credit bureau used by Exxon was not included in any of their communications. Upon filing the present lawsuit, Carroll was given the name and address of the credit bureau. Carroll did not have a major credit card, or a savings account, and had been employed for 1 year. Would Carroll win the suit? If so, on the basis of what consumer protection statute(s)?

3. For the price of $408 Linda Glaire obtained a 7-year membership in a health club owned and operated by LaLanne. The $408 was paid by Glaire over a 2-year period at the rate of $17 monthly. The installment contract stated that there were no finance charges. The contract was sold to Universal Guidance Acceptance Corporation. LaLanne and Universal are in reality owned by the same shareholders, with Universal assisting LaLanne in financing. Glaire filed suit against LaLanne alleging violation of the Truth-in-Lending Act. Is there a violation of the Truth-in-Lending Act?

4. Rutyna was a 60-year-old widow and social security retiree, suffering from high blood pressure and epilepsy. In late December 1976 and early 1977, she incurred a debt for services performed by a doctor that were not covered by Medicare or private insurance. Rutyna assumed it had been paid or would be paid by her insurance. When the defendant, a collection agency, notified her of $56 that remained unpaid to a medical group, she denied the existence of the debt. Rutyna claimed that she received telephone calls and a letter from the collection agency (defendant) notifying her of a neighborhood investigation that was to be undertaken. The letter, with the defendant's return address on it, required immediate payment or a visit by her to the defendant's office to prevent any further embarrassment. Upon receipt of this communication, Rutyna claimed she became very nervous and upset because of the embarrassment that might be caused by the defendant. The defendant claimed a lack of knowledge concerning Rutyna's reaction to their letter, denied the phone calls, and insisted that the plaintiff called many times. What consumer protection statute is the basis for Rutyna's claim? Will she win?

56

Fair Employment Practices

E qual employment opportunity law is one of the major concerns of business. The laws that govern this area affect the daily operation of business firms of all types. It is important not only to business executives but to employees, to union leaders, and—because it deals with questions of fundamental fairness and economic opportunity—to all citizens. This chapter examines the various federal statutes that prohibit discriminatory employment practices.

An Overview of Federal Statutory Law

Several federal laws prohibit discriminatory employment practices. The most comprehensive of the equal employment opportunity laws is Title VII of the Civil Rights Act of 1964. Title VII prohibits discrimination in employment on the basis of race, color, sex, religion, and national origin. The statute covers private and public employers that have at least fifteen employees. It also covers employment agencies and labor organizations. The statute is enforced by the Equal Employment Opportunity Commission (EEOC) and by private lawsuits. Parties seeking redress under this statute must first file a charge with the EEOC. Upon getting a "right to sue" letter from the EEOC, parties may file suit in federal court.

The Civil Rights Act of 1866 prohibits racial discrimination in employment contracts. Parties seeking to enforce their rights under this law may go directly to federal court to file suit.

Executive Order 11246 is an order by the President prohibiting federal contractors from discriminating against any employee or applicant on the basis of race, sex, religion, or national origin. The order also requires employers to take "affirmative action" to ensure that applicants are employed, and that employees are treated during employment without regard to their race, sex, religion, or national origin.

The Equal Pay Act prohibits discrimination on the basis of sex when the parties are performing jobs of equal skill, effort, and responsibility and

> ## CONCEPT SUMMARY
> ### Selected Federal Civil Rights Laws
>
> | | |
> |---|---|
> | **Title VII of the Civil Rights Act of 1964** | Makes it unlawful for employers, unions, or employment agencies to make any decision concerning the employment status of an individual on the basis of race, sex, religion, or national origin. |
> | **Civil Rights Act of 1866** | Forbids racial discrimination in the making, performance, termination, and terms and conditions of employment contracts. |
> | **Executive Order 11246** | Prohibits federal contractors from discriminating against employees or applicants because of race, sex, religion, or national origin. Also requires affirmative action by federal contractors to ensure that applicants are employed without regard to race, sex, religion, or national origin. |
> | **Age Discrimination in Employment Act** | Prohibits discrimination in employment against people over 40. |
> | **Americans with Disabilities Act** | Prohibits employment discrimination against otherwise qualified disabled persons who can perform the essential functions of a job. Also requires employers to make reasonable accommodations to allow for the employment of disabled persons. |
> | **Family and Medical Leave Act** | Provides employees with up to 12 weeks unpaid leave from their employment in the event of the birth or adoption of a child, the serious health condition of a family member, or their own serious health condition. |

under similar working conditions. The statute is enforced by the EEOC.

The Age Discrimination in Employment Act forbids discrimination on the basis of age for people who are older than 40. This law is also enforced by the EEOC and through private lawsuits.

The Americans with Disabilities Act prohibits discrimination against qualified workers on the basis of disability. In addition, employers are required to undertake efforts to reasonably accommodate a qualified employee with a disability. This law is also administered by the EEOC and through private litigation.

The Family and Medical Leave Act provides employees with 12 weeks of unpaid leave for reasons of childbirth or for serious medical conditions affecting the employee or the employee's family. Employees are entitled to return to their old jobs.

The rest of this chapter discusses in more detail the provisions of the federal equal employment opportunity laws. However, first it is necessary to look at the concept that these laws forbid: discrimination.

The Meaning of Discrimination: Disparate Treatment and Disparate Impact

The laws that forbid discrimination in employment generally are limited to certain types of prohibited discrimination. For example, Title VII forbids discrimination on the basis of race, color, sex, national origin, and religion. And the Age Discrimination in Employment Act prohibits discrimination against workers over the age of 40. The antidiscrimination laws do not forbid "discrimination" in general, only certain types of discrimination. For example, although Title VII forbids discrimination on the basis of sex, federal law does not prohibit discrimination on the basis of sexual orientation. (However, some state and local laws forbid this form of discrimination.) Therefore, the first question that a business must answer is whether some law prohibits the type of discrimination that is in question.

Many of the equal employment opportunity statutes simply state that a type of discrimination is forbidden without defining what is meant by "discrimination." For example, Title VII forbids discrimination on the basis of race, but it does not define the term "discrimination." Questions such as whether the statute forbids only intentional discrimination or also encompasses unintentional forms of discrimination have been left for the courts to decide.

The U.S. Supreme Court has developed two analytical models for determining whether unlawful discrimination has occurred under Title VII. These models are referred to as the *disparate treatment model* and the *disparate impact model*. The models have also been used in deciding cases under other antidiscrimination laws, such as the Age Discrimination in Employment Act. The **disparate treatment** model reaches intentional forms of discrimination. The **disparate impact** model determines whether unintentional discrimination violates the statute.

The Disparate Treatment Model of Discrimination

Discrimination that takes the form of overt, intentional discriminatory treatment is addressed by the disparate treatment model of analysis. For example, when an employer treats individuals of one race differently from another, the employer has engaged in the disparate treatment form of discrimination. Determination requires comparing how the employer treats members of one group versus those of another group. In cases involving hiring or promotion, the Supreme Court has said that an individual establishes a case of unlawful discrimination under the disparate treatment model when the individual proves four elements: (1) that he or she is a member of a protected group, (2) that he or she applied for and was qualified for the job the employer had open, (3) that despite his or her qualifications, the individual was rejected for the job, and (4) that the employer continued looking for others with the individual's qualifications after the individual was rejected for the job.

If an individual job applicant can establish these four requirements, he or she has made out what is called a prima facie case of discriminatory treatment. The employer is then required to state a legitimate nondiscriminatory reason for

rejecting the individual applicant or employee. If such a reason can be stated, the individual charging discrimination is required to show that the employer's stated reason is a pretext for discrimination. If the individual can meet the four prima facie case requirements and the employer can state a legitimate nondiscriminatory reason for its decision, the case then turns on the pretextuality of the employer's statement—that is, the employer's intent.

An example of how the model is applied may be helpful at this point. Suppose that an employer, Acme Financial Services, has a job opening for a "financial analyst." In advertising the job opening, Acme states that the minimum qualifications for the job require that the applicant have an undergraduate college degree in accounting. Three people apply for the job. One applicant, Bill, is an African-American with an undergraduate degree in accounting from State University. Another applicant, Susan, has an undergraduate degree in accounting from Selective University. A third applicant, Lance, a Caucasian, has an undergraduate degree in accounting from State University and a master's in business administration (MBA) from Selective University. All are interviewed by managers of Acme, who provide written reports to Acme's human resources department. In one of the reports a manager states that Bill's credentials are impressive, but he questions whether Bill will be able to join certain private clubs which do not admit African-Americans into their membership. Another manager's report describes Susan as smart but needing to go to charm school. All the managers recommend hiring Lance because of his additional graduate business degree, which in their opinion gives him flexibility to undertake additional tasks that might lead to advancement in the company. Who should be hired?

Whoever is hired, the company faces the possibility of a charge of discrimination under the disparate treatment model. Regardless of whom Acme hires, the other two candidates can establish that they are members of a protected group—racial or sexual. (Title VII prohibits discrimination on the basis of race and sex; it does not protect only members of a particular race or sex.) All the applicants can establish that they are qualified for the job, because they possess an undergraduate degree in accounting, which was what Acme advertised as the job qualification for the position of

Part IX   Government Regulation

financial analyst. Whoever is not hired can establish that he or she was rejected for the position despite his or her qualifications, and that Acme continued looking for candidates from another protected group, and in this case hired that candidate. Therefore, the rejected candidates can establish a prima facie case of disparate treatment.

Let's assume that Acme acts on the managers' recommendations and hires Lance. Will Acme be able to state a legitimate, nondiscriminatory reason for selecting Lance? If Acme states that it selected Lance because his additional degree made him the most qualified person for the job, Acme will have stated a legitimate, nondiscriminatory reason for selecting Lance over Susan or Bill. Hiring the most qualified person is a legitimate, nondiscriminatory reason.

However, if Susan and Bill can persuade a jury that Acme's stated reason is a pretext for discrimination, she or he will prevail against Acme. The managers' comments, reflecting stereotypical views of the employment capabilities of women and minorities, are evidence of the pretextuality of Acme's stated reason. Susan and Bill will have the burden of persuading the court that Acme's decision was a pretext for discrimination. If they can show that Acme took into consideration the stereotypical remarks contained in the managers' reports, then Acme will have to show that it would have made the same decision regardless of the statements in the managers' reports.

The Disparate Impact Model of Discrimination

Unlawful employment discrimination is not limited to instances of overt, intentional discriminatory treatment. Title VII prohibits "discrimination." The statute, as well as other antidiscrimination laws, does not prohibit only "intentional discrimination." Therefore, employment practices that outwardly do not appear to be discriminatory, and may not have been developed with any discriminatory intent, may nevertheless be unlawful if the effect or impact of the practice is to discriminate against members of protected groups. The Supreme Court developed the disparate impact model of discrimination to ferret out the discreet discriminator who uses practices which, although fair in form, nevertheless have a discriminatory effect.

Applying the disparate impact model, an indi-

vidual makes a case of unlawful employment discrimination if he or she shows that an employer's policy or practice disproportionately excludes members of a protected group. For example, suppose that an employer refuses to hire individuals who have an arrest record. Courts have consistently held that an employer's reliance on arrest records has a disparate impact on the employment opportunities of African-Americans, pointing to national statistics showing that although African-Americans make up 11 percent of the population, they account for 27 percent of arrests. Unlike conviction records, arrest records do not reflect formal prosecution and trial.

If an applicant or individual employee can show that an employer's practice has a disparate impact, the employer can avoid liability if it can persuade the court that its practice is justified by business necessity. A job-related reason that is required for safe or efficient job performance will qualify as a business necessity. For example, suppose that an employer refuses to hire anyone with a felony larceny conviction within the last 5 years for a job involving the collection of money. Even if the applicant can show that the practice will disproportionately exclude members of a protected group, the employer may be able to persuade the court that its practice is justified as a business necessity.

Even when an employer has a business necessity justification for its practice, the employer will be liable if the applicant or employee can show that there is a less discriminatory alternative reasonably available to the employer that will accomplish the employer's objective. For example, suppose that a bank has an antinepotism policy— a policy of refusing to hire family members—as tellers in the bank. The bank justifies its policy because of its concerns over security. The bank maintains that a teller is to report on another teller if he or she observes another teller stealing money from the bank. The bank believes that a family member will be less willing to report the stealing of another family member. Suppose that the effect of the bank's policy is to discriminate against men because more male tellers than female tellers are likely to quit their jobs and seek alternative employment upon getting married to a co-worker. The bank's security concerns might constitute a business necessity justification. However, if the individual could show that there is a less discriminatory alternative reasonably available to the bank—such as transferring the married employee to another branch, relying on security cameras in the bank, or instituting auditing procedures to detect stealing—the bank may be liable under the disparate impact model.

The following case is the first one that the Supreme Court decided involving Title VII of the Civil Rights Act. Although decided in 1971, it is the landmark case in employment discrimination law.

GRIGGS V. DUKE POWER CO.
U.S. Supreme Court
401 U.S. 424 (1971)

BACKGROUND: A group of African-American employees (plaintiffs) brought a suit against Duke Power Co. (defendant) alleging violations of Title VII, Section 703(a), in requiring a high school diploma and a passing score on a standardized general intelligence test for employment or for transfer between departments. The U.S. District Court found for Duke Power Co., and the Court of Appeals affirmed. The plaintiffs appealed to the Supreme Court of the United States.

Burger, Chief Justice

The District Court found that prior to July 2, 1965, the effective date of the Civil Rights Act of 1964, the Company openly discriminated on the basis of race in the hiring and assigning of employees at its Dan River plant. The plant was organized into five operating departments: (1) Labor, (2) Coal Handling, (3) Operations, (4) Maintenance, and (5) Laboratory and Test. Negroes were employed only in the Labor Department where the highest paying jobs paid less than the lowest paying jobs in the other four "operating" departments in which only whites were employed. Promotions were normally made within each department on the basis of job seniority. Transferees into a department usually began in the lowest position.

In 1955 the Company instituted a policy of requiring a high school education for initial assignment to any department except Labor, and for transfer from the Coal Handling to any "inside" department (Operations, Maintenance, or Laboratory). When the Company abandoned its policy of restricting Negroes to the Labor Department in 1965, completion of high school also was made a prerequisite to transfer from Labor to any other department.

The Company added a further requirement for new employees on July 2, 1965, the date on which Title VII became effective. To qualify for placement in any but the Labor Department it became necessary to register satisfactory scores on two professionally prepared aptitude tests, as well as to have a high school education. Completion of high school alone continued to render employees eligible for transfer to the four desirable departments from which Negroes had been excluded if the incumbent had been employed prior to the time of the new requirement. In September 1965 the Company began to permit incumbent employees who lacked a high school education to qualify for transfer from Labor or Coal Handling to an "inside" job by passing two tests—the Wonderlic Personnel Test, which purports to measure general intelligence, and the Bennett Mechanical Comprehension Test. Neither was directed or intended to measure ability to learn to perform a particular job or category of jobs. The requisite scores used for both initial hiring and transfer approximated the national median for high school graduates.

The objective of Congress in the enactment of Title VII is plain from the language of the statute. It was to achieve equality of employment opportunities and remove barriers that have operated in the past to favor an identifiable group of white employees over other employees. Under the Act, practices, procedures, or tests neutral on their face, and even neutral in terms of intent, cannot be maintained if they operate to "freeze" the status quo of prior discriminatory employment practices.

The Act proscribes not only overt discrimination but also practices that are fair in form, but discriminatory in operation. The touchstone is business necessity. If an employment practice which operates to exclude Negroes cannot be shown to be related to job performance, the practice is prohibited.

On the record before us, neither the high school completion requirement nor the general intelligence test is shown to bear a demonstrable relationship to successful performance of the jobs for which it was used. Both were adopted, as the Court of Appeals noted, without meaningful study of their relationship to job performance ability. Rather, a vice president of the Company testified, the requirements were instituted on the Company's judgment that they generally would improve the overall quality of the work force.

The evidence, however, shows that employees who have not completed high school or taken the tests have continued to perform satisfactorily and make progress in departments for which the high school and test criteria are not used.

The Company's lack of discriminatory intent is suggested by special efforts to help the undereducated employees through Company financing of two-thirds the cost of tuition for high school training. But Congress directed the thrust of the Act to the *consequences* of employment practices, not simply the motivation. More than that, Congress has placed on the employer the burden of showing that any given requirement must have a manifest relationship to the employment in question.

DECISION: Reversed. The U.S. Supreme Court ruled in favor of Griggs and the other African-American employees.

Exceptions to the Nondiscrimination Rule

Title VII provides that it is not unlawful for an employer to rely upon the results of a professionally developed ability test, if it is not designed, intended, or used to discriminate on the basis of race, sex, religion, or national origin. This exception was involved in the *Griggs* decision. Because Title VII's language states that an employer may rely on an ability test if it is not "used to discriminate," tests that have an adverse impact are unlawful unless they are related to job performance. The business necessity or job-relatedness requirement means that employers are required to validate tests that have an adverse impact on members of protected groups.

Title VII also exempts bona fide seniority systems. Collective bargaining contracts negotiated between employers and unions representing employees typically provide that employment benefits (salary, vacations, promotions, and the like) are based on seniority—that is, on the time an employee has spent on a given job or at a particular location. So long as the se-

niority system is not created with the intent to discriminate on the basis of race, sex, religion, or national origin, an employer may rely on a seniority system.

Title VII (and also the Age Discrimination in Employment Act) permits an employer to discriminate on the basis of sex, national origin, or religion, when sex, national origin, or religion is a bona fide occupational qualification (BFOQ) reasonably necessary for the normal operation of the employer's business. The **BFOQ** exception allows an employer to intentionally discriminate where sex, religion, or national origin is a job requirement. The BFOQ exception does not apply to racial discrimination.

In interpreting the BFOQ the Supreme Court has stressed the narrowness of the exception. For example, ordinarily, customer preference cannot be the basis of a BFOQ. An employer cannot say that its customers prefer men to women, or members of a particular religion or nationality to do the job. For a BFOQ to apply to justify an employer's discrimination, the employer must be able to show that all or substantially all the members of a protected group who are excluded from the job cannot perform the essential job duties.

Other EEO Principles: Affirmative Action and Reasonable Accommodation

EEO law includes two other principles that go beyond the requirement of nondiscrimination. They are the principles of affirmative action and reasonable accommodation. **Affirmative action** requires that an employer undertake positive efforts to hire members of protected groups. The principle of **reasonable accommodation** requires an employer to oblige an employee's circumstances and adapt the workplace to the employee's condition.

Affirmative Action

Many companies rely on affirmative action plans to achieve their EEO goals. Affirmative action plans are required for government contractors. Many companies who are not federal contractors also use affirmative action plans.

An affirmative action plan establishes **goals** and **timetables** for hiring women and minorities. Affirmative action plans represent the application of strategic planning to the hiring of groups who are underrepresented in the work force.

An affirmative action plan is usually prepared by someone with responsibility for the company's human resources management. The first step in preparing the plan is to undertake a *utilization analysis*. This is an analysis of how the company is currently utilizing members of protected groups. Jobs within the company will be grouped according to a system of classification. (The EEOC has a job classification system that employers can use.) For example, a secretarial position may fall under the classification for clericals, and an accounting job may fall under the classification for administrative personnel. Statistics will be compiled regarding the number of women and minorities who are employed in each job classification.

In order to determine whether the company is underutilizing women and minorities, the company must compare its employment statistics with statistics regarding the availability of women and minorities in the relevant work force. For example, if 20 percent of engineers in the area are women and women make up 5 percent of the employer's engineering staff, the employer would be underutilizing women in the engineering classification.

The employer would next establish hiring goals and timetables (usually 1 to 3 years) for achieving those goals when women or minorities are underutilized. For example, suppose the employer knows that three men will be retiring from the engineering department, one each year over the next 3 years. Suppose further that by hiring two more women the employer's engineering staff would have 20 percent women. Under these circumstances the employer could make a goal of hiring two women over the 3-year period. If the employer is a federal contractor, the employer will be required to make a good faith effort to achieve its goal.

Companies often use affirmative action plans even though they do not fall under the affirmative action requirements for federal contractors. In the following case, the Supreme Court considered whether such an affirmative action plan violates Title VII.

JOHNSON V. TRANSPORTATION AGENCY, SANTA CLARA COUNTY, CALIFORNIA

U.S. Supreme Court
480 U.S. 616 (1987)

BACKGROUND: The Transportation Agency of Santa Clara County, California (respondent) issued an affirmative action plan applicable to promotions of employees. In selecting applicants for promotion to road dispatcher, the Agency, pursuant to the plan, passed over Paul Johnson (petitioner), a male employee, and promoted a female employee applicant, Diane Joyce. Johnson filed a complaint with the EEOC alleging that he had been denied promotion on the basis of sex in violation of Title VII. After receiving a right-to-sue letter from the EEOC, Johnson filed suit in U.S. District Court, which ruled that the Agency had violated Title VII. The Circuit Court of Appeals reversed. Johnson appealed to the Supreme Court of the United States.

Brennan, Justice

In reviewing the composition of its work force, the Agency noted in its Plan that women were represented in numbers far less than their proportion of the county labor force in both the Agency as a whole and in five of seven job categories. Specifically, while women constituted 36.4% of the area labor market, they composed only 22.4% of Agency employees. Furthermore, women working at the Agency were concentrated largely in EEOC job categories traditionally held by women. As for the job classification relevant to this case, none of the 238 Skilled Craft Worker positions was held by a woman.

The Agency stated that its Plan was intended to achieve "a statistically measurable yearly improvement in hiring, training and promotion of minorities and women throughout the Agency in all major job classifications where they are underrepresented." As a benchmark by which to evaluate progress, the Agency stated that its long-term goal was to attain a work force whose composition reflected the proportion of minorities and women in the area labor force. Thus, for the Skilled Craft category in which the road dispatcher position at issue here was classified, the Agency's aspiration was that eventually about 36% of the jobs would be occupied by women.

The Agency's Plan set aside no specific number of positions for minorities or women, but authorized the consideration of ethnicity or sex as a factor when evaluating qualified candidates for jobs in which members of such groups were poorly represented.

Nine of the applicants, including Joyce and Johnson, were deemed qualified for the job, and were interviewed by a two-person board. Seven of the applicants scored above 70 on this interview, which meant that they were certified as eligible for selection by the appointing authority. The scores awarded ranged from 70 to 80. Johnson was tied for second with a score of 75, while Joyce ranked next with a score of 73. A second interview was conducted by three Agency supervisors, who ultimately recommended that Johnson be promoted. Prior to the second interview, Joyce had contacted the County's Affirmative Action Office because she feared that her application might not receive disinterested review. The Office in turn contacted the Agency's Affirmative Action Coordinator, whom the Agency's Plan makes responsible for, inter alia, keeping the Director informed of opportunities for the Agency to accomplish its objectives under the Plan. At the time the Agency employed no women in any Skilled Craft position, and had never employed a woman as a road dispatcher. The Coordinator recommended to the Director of the Agency, James Graebner, that Joyce be promoted.

Graebner, authorized to choose any of the seven persons deemed eligible, thus had the benefit of suggestions by the second interview panel and by the Agency Coordinator in arriving at his decision. After deliberation, Graebner concluded that the promotion should be given to Joyce.

The assessment of the legality of the Agency Plan must be guided by our decision in *Steelworkers v. Weber*. In that case, the Court addressed the question whether the employer violated Title VII by adopting a voluntary affirmative action plan designed to "eliminate manifest racial imbalances in traditionally segregated job categories."

We upheld the employer's decision to select less senior black applicants over the white respondent, for we found that taking race into account was consistent with Title VII's objective of "break[ing] down old patterns of racial segregation and hierarchy."

In evaluating the compliance of an affirmative action plan with Title VII's prohibition on discrimination, we must be mindful of "this Court's and Congress' consistent emphasis on 'the value of voluntary efforts to further the objectives of the law.'" The Agency in the case before us has undertaken such a voluntary effort, and has done so in full recognition of both the difficulties and the potential for intrusion on males and nonminorities. The Agency has identified a conspicuous imbalance in job categories traditionally segregated by race and sex. It has made clear from the outset, however, that employment decisions may not be justified solely by reference to this imbalance, but must rest on a multitude of practical, realistic factors. It has therefore committed itself to annual adjustment of goals so as to provide a reasonable guide for actual hiring and promotion decisions. The agency earmarks no positions for anyone; sex is but one of several factors that may be taken into account in evaluating qualified applicants for a position. As both the Plan's language and its manner of operation attest, the Agency has no intention of establishing a work force whose permanent composition is dictated by rigid numerical standards.

We therefore hold that the Agency appropriately took into account as one factor the sex of Diane Joyce in determining that she should be promoted to the road dispatcher position. The decision to do so was made pursuant to an affirmative action plan that represents a moderate, flexible, case-by-case approach to effecting a gradual improvement in the representation of minorities and women in the Agency's work force. Such a plan is fully consistent with Title VII, for it embodies the contribution that voluntary employer action can make in eliminating the vestiges of discrimination in the workplace.

DECISION: The U.S. Supreme Court affirmed the judgment of the Court of Appeals in favor of the Agency.

Accommodation

Another concept that is found in Title VII and the Americans with Disabilities Act (ADA) is the concept of reasonable accommodation. An employer has the duty to accommodate an employee's religious practice or belief under Title VII. Under the ADA the employer has the duty to make reasonable accommodation to allow qualified disabled applicants and employees to perform a job. Under both Title VII and the ADA, the employer is required to undertake "reasonable" accommodation, unless the company can show that such steps would pose an "undue hardship" on its operations. Under both statutes the burden is on the employer to show that it has undertaken reasonable accommodations or to prove that the required accommodations would produce an undue hardship.

In a Title VII case involving religious accommodation, the Supreme Court held that an employer satisfies its duty once it makes an offer of reasonable accommodation, and that the employer is not under a duty to undertake another, perhaps more reasonable accommodation, offered by the employee. The Supreme Court has also applied what is called the *de minimis* test of undue hardship with regard to Title VII's duty to accommodate religion. Under this test, an employer can avoid the accommodation requirement if it can show that the required accommodation would be more than a minimal hardship on the operation of its business.

Although the ADA's accommodation requirement also contains an "undue hardship" exception, the statute's wording rejects the *de minimis* test used in cases involving religious discrimination under Title VII. The ADA lists several factors that are to be taken into consideration in determining whether a given accommodation would be an undue hardship on the business. An example is the cost of the accommodation in relation to the size of the employer's business facility. The language of the ADA indicates that it will be more difficult for an employer to claim that an accommodation will be an undue hardship for purposes of accommodating a qualified individual with a disability than it will be to establish an undue hardship with regard to religious practices or beliefs.

Specific Protections: Race, National Origin, Religion, Sex, Age, Disability, and the Family and Medical Leave Act

Race

Both Title VII and the Civil Rights Act of 1866 forbid racial discrimination in employment. The Civil Rights Act of 1866 is limited to intentional discrimination, whereas Title VII is not. A major difference between the two laws is that someone charging racial discrimination under Title VII must file a charge with the EEOC, but a person may sue directly in federal court under the Civil Rights Act of 1866.

An employee's attire and grooming sometimes are linked to the employee's racial or cultural identification. Courts have generally allowed employers to set reasonable dress and grooming standards even when they infringe on an employee's cultural or racial identification. However, courts have struck down grooming policies which were a pretext for intentional discrimination on the basis of race.

Racial harassment is forbidden by both Title VII and the Civil Rights Act of 1866. A pattern of racial slurs would violate these statutes. For example, an employer that permitted racially derogatory notes to be posted on a company bulletin board would be engaging in racial harassment.

National Origin

Title VII prohibits employer discrimination on the basis of national origin. "National origin" refers to the country a person came from or the country his or her forebears came from. It includes members of all national groups and groups of persons of common ancestry, heritage, or background. It does not refer to citizenship. Thus, generally speaking an employer can discriminate against an applicant or an employee on the basis of his or her lack of citizenship.

The Immigration Reform and Control Act prohibits an employer from knowingly employing aliens who are not authorized to work in the United States. The employer must verify that its employees are not illegal aliens. Applicants and employers must complete an I-9 form verifying that the applicant is not an illegal alien. The employer attests that the employer has examined appropriate documents (for example, a passport or resident alien card) verifying the applicant's identity and authorization for work.

Title VII's protection in relation to national origin also forbids discrimination on the basis of an applicant or employee's marriage or association with a person of a specific national origin, membership in organizations promoting national groups, and attendance at schools or places of worship generally used by people of a particular national origin.

Requiring that employees speak a particular language on the job may discriminate on the basis of national origin. When such a policy has a disparate impact, the employer must justify its policy by proof that it is job-related.

Employers must also be careful with height and weight requirements. Requiring that employees be of a minimum height and weight may discriminate against certain nationalities. Under these circumstances the employer will need to prove that the policy is job-related.

Harassment that takes the form of derogatory remarks or epithets also violates Title VII. Insults, name calling, and ethnic slurs are prohibited.

Religion

As mentioned earlier, employers are prohibited from discriminating on the basis of religion, and employers are further required to make reasonable accommodation to an employee's religious practice or belief unless doing so would cause an undue hardship on the employer's business operations. Courts and the EEOC take a broad view of what constitutes a religious belief. All that is required is that the employee hold a sincere and meaningful belief with the strength of traditional religious views. Under this approach, an atheist's views would constitute a religious belief so long as they were sincerely held.

Title VII exempts a religious corporation, association, and school with respect to hiring individuals of a particular religion to perform work connected with the carrying on of its activities. Also, the BFOQ exception permits an employer to hire employees of a particular religion when religion is reasonably necessary to the operation of the business.

The most extensively litigated area has dealt with work-scheduling issues regarding an employer's duty to accommodate an employee's religious practices. The typical situation involves an employee requesting Saturdays off when that day is the employee's Sabbath. EEOC guidelines include a list of proposed accommodations, including job swapping, flexible scheduling, and lateral job transfers. In *Trans World Airlines v. Hardison*, the U.S. Supreme Court held that such practices constituted an undue hardship on the employer when such practices would have violated the employer's collective bargaining contract with the union representing the employees.

Sex

Both Title VII and the Equal Pay Act forbid employment discrimination on the basis of sex. The Equal Pay Act is limited to discrimination in compensation when employees of the opposite sex are paid less for doing essentially the same job. Title VII forbids discrimination on the basis of sex in virtually all aspects of employment, including compensation.

The Equal Pay Act provides that an employer shall not engage in sex-based wage discrimination when employees of the opposite sex are working on jobs that require equal skill, effort, and responsibility and are performed under similar working conditions. The statute provides exemptions for wage differences that are the result of a seniority system, a merit system, a system which measures earnings by quantity or quality of production, or a wage differential based on any factor other than sex.

The Equal Pay Act provides for equal pay for equal work. Title VII makes it unlawful to discriminate in compensation on the basis of sex. Under Title VII, it is not necessary to prove that the employees were performing substantially equal jobs. So, if an employer decided to pay men market-rate salaries, but paid women only 90 percent of the market rate, the employer would be violating Title VII even if the women were not performing the same jobs as the men.

Under Title VII, discrimination on the basis of sex extends to pregnancy, childbirth, or related medical conditions. Women affected by pregnancy, childbirth, or related medical conditions must be treated the same for all employment-related purposes, including receipt of benefits, as persons not so affected.

The BFOQ exemption applies to sex discrimination. However, as mentioned earlier, courts and the EEOC narrowly interpret the exception.

A closely related issue involves discrimination against women not because they are pregnant, but because they have the potential to become pregnant. Certain jobs, for example, require the employee to come in contact with chemicals that could harm a woman's fetus were she to become pregnant. Is it reasonable, for the protection of the woman and her potential unborn child, to keep women of childbearing age from such jobs? The U.S. Supreme Court grappled with this issue in the landmark case that follows.

UNITED AUTO WORKERS V. JOHNSON CONTROLS, INC.

U.S. Supreme Court
111 S.Ct. 1196 (1991)

BACKGROUND: Johnson Controls (respondent) manufactured batteries. A primary component in the battery-manufacturing process is lead. Exposure to lead could be harmful to any fetus carried by a pregnant employee. After several of its employees became pregnant while maintaining blood lead levels above those recommended by the Occupational Health and Safety Administration, Johnson Controls announced a policy barring all women, except those who could document their infertility, from jobs requiring high exposure to lead. A group of employees filed a class action suit against the policy, claiming that it amounted to unlawful sex discrimination. The U.S. District Court granted Johnson Controls' motion for summary judgment, and the Circuit Court of Appeals affirmed.

Blackmun, Justice

The bias in Johnson Controls' policy is obvious. Fertile men, but not fertile women, are given a choice as to whether they wish to risk their reproductive health for a particular job. Respondent's fetal protection policy explicitly discriminates against women on the basis of their sex. The policy excludes women with childbearing capacity from lead-exposed jobs and so creates a facial classification based on gender.

Nevertheless, the Court of Appeals assumed, as did the two appellate courts that already had confronted the issue, that sex-specific fetal-protection policies do not involve facial discrimination. These courts analyzed the policies as though they were facially neutral, and had only a discriminatory effect upon the employment opportunities of women. Consequently, the courts looked to see if each employer in question had established that its policy was justified as a business necessity. The business necessity standard is more lenient for the employer than the statutory BFOQ defense. The court assumed that because the asserted reason for the sex-based exclusion (protecting women's unconceived offspring) was ostensibly benign, the policy was not sex-based discrimination. That assumption, however, was incorrect.

First, Johnson Controls' policy classifies on the basis of gender and childbearing capacity, rather than fertility alone. Respondent does not seek to protect the unconceived children of all its employees, despite evidence in the record about the debilitating effect of lead exposure on the male reproductive system. Johnson Controls is concerned only with the harms that may befall the unborn offspring of its female employees. Johnson Controls' policy is facially discriminatory because it requires only a female employee to produce proof that she is not capable of reproducing.

Our conclusion is bolstered by the Pregnancy Discrimination Act of 1978 (PDA), in which Congress explicitly provided that, for purposes of Title VII, discrimination "on the basis of sex" includes discrimination "because of or on the basis of pregnancy, childbirth, or related medical conditions." "The Pregnancy Discrimination Act has now made clear that, for all Title VII purposes, discrimination based on a woman's pregnancy is, on its face, discrimination because of her sex." *Newport News Shipbuilding & Dry Dock Co. v. EEOC.* In its use of the words "capable of bearing children" in the 1982 policy statement as the criterion for exclusion, Johnson Controls explicitly classified on the basis of potential for pregnancy. Under the PDA, such a classification must be regarded, for Title VII purposes, in the same light as explicit sex discrimination. Respondent has chosen to treat all its female employees as potentially pregnant; that choice evinces discrimination on the basis of sex.

Under Section 703(e)(1) of the Title VII, an employer may discriminate on the basis of "religion, sex, or national origin in those certain instances where religion, sex, or national origin is a bona fide occupational qualification reasonably necessary to the normal operation of that particular business or enterprise." We therefore turn to the question whether Johnson Controls' fetal-protection policy is one of those "certain instances" that come within the BFOQ exception.

The BFOQ defense is written narrowly, and this Court has read it narrowly.

The wording of the BFOQ defense contains several terms of restriction that indicate that the exception reaches only special situations. The statute thus limits the situations in which discrimination is permissible to "certain instances" where sex discrimination is "reasonably necessary" to the "normal operation" of the "particular" business. Each one of these terms—certain, normal, particular—prevents the use of general subjective standards and favors an objective, verifiable requirement. But the most telling term is "occupational"; this indicates that these objective, verifiable requirements must concern job-related skills and aptitudes.

The PDA's amendment to Title VII contains a BFOQ standard of its own; unless pregnant employees differ from others "in their ability or inability to work," they must be "treated the same" as other employees "for all employment-related purposes." This language clearly sets forth Congress' remedy for discrimination on the basis of pregnancy and potential pregnancy. Women who are either pregnant or potentially pregnant must be treated like others "similar in their ability . . . to work." In other words, women as capable of doing their jobs as their male counterparts may not be forced to choose between having a child and having a job.

We conclude that the language of both the BFOQ provision and the PDA which amended it, as well as the legislative history and the case law, prohibit an employer from discriminating against a woman because of her capacity to become pregnant unless her reproductive potential prevents her from performing the duties of her job. We reiterate our holding that an employer must direct its concerns about a woman's ability to perform her job safely and efficiently to those aspects of the woman's job-related activities that fall within the "essence" of the particular business.

DECISION: The U.S. Supreme Court reversed the decision of the Circuit Court of Appeals and remanded the case for further proceedings.

Another issue that has received a lot of attention is sexual harassment. Title VII's prohibition against discrimination on the basis of sex has been interpreted by the U.S. Supreme Court to include sexual harassment.

EEOC guidelines provide the following definition of sexual harassment:

Unwelcome sexual advances, requests for sexual favors, and other verbal or physical conduct of a sexual nature constitute sexual harassment when (1) submission to such conduct is made either explicitly or implicitly a term or condition of an individual's employment, (2) submission to or rejection of such conduct by an individual is used as the basis for employment decisions affecting such individual, or (3) such conduct has the purpose or effect of unreasonably interfering with an individual's work performance or creating an intimidating, hostile, or offensive working environment.

There are two types of sexual harassment: (1) quid pro quo sexual harassment (the first two items in the EEOC guidelines), and (2) harassment stemming from a hostile work environment (the third item in the EEOC guidelines). Quid pro quo sexual harassment arises when an employee's job or job benefits are conditioned on the employee's acceding to the employer's sexual demands. (For example, "Date me or lose your job.") Hostile environment cases involve a workplace that has a hostile climate as a result of a pattern of conduct that is harassing to members of one sex. In the following case, the Supreme Court dealt with the issue of what is required to establish a hostile work environment.

HARRIS V. FORKLIFT SYSTEMS, INC.

U.S. Supreme Court
1993 U.S. Lexis 7155 (1993)

BACKGROUND: Teresa Harris (petitioner) worked as a manager at Forklift Systems, Inc. (respondent), an equipment rental company, from April 1985 until October 1987. Charles Hardy was Forklift's president. Throughout Harris' time at Forklift, Hardy often insulted her because of her gender and often made her the target of unwanted sexual innuendos. Hardy told Harris on several occasions, in the presence of other employees, "You're a woman—what do you know?" and "We need a man as the rental manager." At least once, he told her she was "a dumb ass woman." Again in front of others, he suggested that the two of them "go to the Holiday Inn to negotiate [Harris'] raise." Hardy occasionally asked Harris and other female employees to get coins from his front pants pocket. He threw objects on the ground in front of Harris and other women, and asked them to pick the objects up. He made sexual innuendos about Harris' and other women's clothing.

In mid-August 1987, Harris complained to Hardy about his conduct. Hardy said he was surprised that Harris was offended, claimed he was only joking, and apologized. He also promised he would stop, and on the basis of this assurance Harris stayed on the job. But in early September, Hardy began anew: While Harris was arranging a deal with one of Forklift's customers, he asked her, again in front of other employees, "What did you do, promise the guy . . . some [sex] Saturday night?" On October 1, Harris collected her paycheck and quit.

Harris then sued Forklift, claiming that Hardy's conduct had created an abusive work environment for her because of her gender. The U.S. District Court found this to be "a close case," but held that Hardy's conduct did not create an abusive environment. The court found that some of Hardy's comments offended Harris, and would offend the reasonable woman, but that they were not so severe as to be expected to seriously affect Harris' psychological well-being. The Circuit Court of Appeals affirmed. Harris appealed to the U.S. Supreme Court.

O'Connor, Justice

In this case we consider the definition of a discriminatorily "abusive work environment" (also known as a "hostile work environment") under Title VII of the Civil Rights Act of 1964.

Title VII of the Civil Rights Act of 1964 makes it "an unlawful employment practice for an employer . . . to discriminate against any individual with respect to his compensation, terms, conditions, or privileges of employment, because of such individual's race, color, religion, sex, or national origin." As we made clear in *Meritor Savings Bank v. Vinson*, this language "is not limited to 'economic' or 'tangible' discrimination. The phrase 'terms, conditions, or privileges of employment' evinces a congressional intent 'to strike at the entire spectrum of disparate treatment of men and women' in employment," which includes requiring people to work in a discriminatorily hostile or abusive environment. When the workplace is permeated with "discriminatory intimidation, ridicule, and insult" that is "sufficiently severe or pervasive as to alter the conditions of the victim's employment and create an abusive working environment," Title VII is violated.

This standard, which we reaffirm today, takes a middle path between making actionable any conduct that is merely offensive and requiring the conduct to cause a tangible psychological injury. As we pointed out in *Meritor*, "mere utterance of an . . . epithet which engenders offensive feelings in an employee" does not sufficiently affect the conditions of employment to implicate Title VII. Conduct that is not severe or pervasive enough to create an objectively hostile or abusive work environment—an environment that a reasonable person would find hostile or abusive—is beyond Title VII's purview. Likewise, if the victim does not subjectively perceive the environment to be abusive, the conduct has not actually altered the conditions of the victim's employment, and there is no Title VII violation.

But Title VII comes into play before the harassing conduct leads to a nervous breakdown. A discriminatorily abusive work environment, even one that does not seriously affect employees' psychological well-being, can and often will detract from employees' job performance, discourage employees from remaining on the job, or keep them from advancing in their careers. Moreover, even without regard to these tangible effects, the very fact that the discriminatory conduct was so severe or pervasive that it created a work environment abusive to employees because of their race, gender, religion, or national origin offends Title

VII's broad rule of workplace equality. The appalling conduct alleged in *Meritor*, and the reference in that case to environments "'so heavily polluted with discrimination as to destroy completely the emotional and psychological stability of minority group workers,'" merely present some especially egregious examples of harassment. They do not mark the boundary of what is actionable.

We therefore believe the District Court erred in relying on whether the conduct "seriously affected plaintiff's psychological well-being" or led her to "suffer injury." Such an inquiry may needlessly focus the factfinder's attention on concrete psychological harm, an element Title VII does not require. Certainly Title VII bars conduct that would seriously affect a reasonable person's psychological well-being, but the statute is not limited to such conduct. So long as the environment would reasonably be perceived, and is perceived, as hostile or abusive, there is no need for it also to be psychologically injurious.

This is not, and by its nature cannot be, a mathematically precise test. But we can say that whether an environment is "hostile" or "abusive" can be determined only by looking at all the circumstances. These may include the frequency of the discriminatory conduct; its severity; whether it is physically threatening or humiliating, or a mere offensive utterance; and whether it unreasonably interferes with an employee's work performance. The effect on the employee's psychological well-being is, of course, relevant to determining whether the plaintiff actually found the environment abusive. But while psychological harm, like any other relevant factor, may be taken into account, no single factor is required.

DECISION: The U.S. Supreme Court reversed the judgment of the Circuit Court of Appeals, and remanded the case for further proceedings.

ETHICS
Ethics and Sexual Harassment

As more women enter the work force and obtain managerial positions, the extent of male–female interaction naturally increases. Surveys indicate that many women think they have been subjected to unwanted sexual behavior in the workplace. This is true of most professions and extends beyond the United States. In a 1993 survey published in the *New England Journal of Medicine*, 73 percent of women medical residents reported having been sexually harassed at least once. In a 1990 survey, 82 percent of female Japanese office workers reported being subjected to "seku-hara."

Although the law is increasingly important in regulating behavior of this type, the ethical values of managers will probably still be the dominant factor in curtailing problematic behavior in the workplace. If you were a senior manager, with complete discretion to deal with the problem, how would you respond to the following cases?

- A female administrative assistant complains of a peer who constantly tells her that she "has great legs" and "a nice figure" and who constantly comments on "how nice she looks today."

- A female mailroom clerk objects that her supervisor constantly refers to all the women in the department as "babes" and "broads" and constantly interrupts women, but not men, during departmental meetings. The supervisor allows pinups of scantily clad females to be posted in the mailroom.

- A female blackjack dealer in a casino complains that the customers make lewd remarks and tell her dirty jokes in a loud voice. She also states that some customers stare at her. Her uniform is designed to be sexy but not excessively revealing. She notes that she is treated in a professional and appropriate manner by her fellow employees.

Age

The Age Discrimination in Employment Act (ADEA) prohibits discrimination against workers who are over 40 years of age. Courts have used the disparate treatment and disparate impact models developed under Title VII in deciding cases under the ADEA. The statute provides four defenses when (1) age is a BFOQ, (2) the employer used reasonable factors other than age, (3) the employer followed a bona fide seniority system, and (4) the employee was discharged or disciplined for good cause.

Reductions in force (RIFs) occur when an employer chooses to downsize its operations in order to cut costs. Because many older workers earn more than younger workers, it is tempting for employers to lay off older workers. If the employer were to do so, the ADEA would be violated, unless the employer could show that its decision was based on a reasonable factor other than age.

In deciding whether an individual layoff decision was based on a reasonable factor other than age, courts rely heavily upon whether the employer used ordinary, objective, and valid criteria, such as employee performance appraisals that are part of an established system of evaluating the qualifications of employees.

Employers sometimes seek to hire younger workers in order to reach a younger market. This practice would violate the ADEA if the employer refused to hire applicants over the age of 40. An employer can avoid liability if it can establish that hiring younger employees is a BFOQ, but that requires showing that all or substantially all applicants over the age of 40 cannot perform the job. The courts have refused to use customer preference as a basis for a BFOQ under both Title VII and the ADEA.

Disability

The Americans with Disabilities Act (ADA) is the most sweeping statute dealing with the rights of the disabled. The ADA has provisions relating to public accommodations as well as employment. The employment provisions are addressed here.

The ADA applies to employers with fifteen or more employees. It prohibits employment discrimination against qualified individuals with dis-

---

ETHICS
The Incompetent Prof

Professor William Smith is a tenured faculty member at a state university in its Management Department. In 1998 he will be 70 years old and does not have to retire at any future age under the ADEA. He lectures to his class by reading from his coauthored textbook, which covers materials outlined in the college catalog. The head of the Management Department receives complaints each semester from a number of students who enroll in his class. The complaints systematically indicate that Professor Smith is often forgetful, is an arbitrary and capricious grader, continually talks about his experiences 30 years ago, treats women students "different" from men, and does not disguise his contempt for students. He holds 2 hours a week of office hours. If students come to consult him, he lectures them on their inadequacies and refuses to answer their questions. The university hiring manual that is incorporated in Professor Smith's contract requires that he attend classes and hold office hours. The state statute covering this employment, as interpreted by the courts, indicates that he can be fired only for reasons of "moral turpitude." The head of the department has discussed this matter with Professor Smith frequently. The dean of the College of Business and the provost of the university have asked the department head to find a way to fire Professor Smith.

1. What ethical question(s), if any, face Professor Smith?
2. What ethical question(s), if any, face the head of the Management Department?
3. What ethical question(s), if any, face the dean and the provost?

abilities. The ban against discrimination extends to all aspects of employment: job applications, hiring, promotion, termination, compensation, training, benefits, and other terms and conditions of employment.

Employers are required to make reasonable accommodation to the needs of disabled employees. Such accommodation may include the renovation of facilities, the alteration of work schedules, the provision of readers and special equipment, and other steps to enable disabled persons to function at a workplace.

An employer is not required to hire an individual whose disability prevents him or her from performing the essential aspects of a job, even with reasonable accommodation. However, any employment requirements that tend to screen out disabled persons must be justified as a business necessity.

The Family and Medical Leave Act

The Family and Medical Leave Act provides employees with temporary leave from their employment in the event of the birth or adoption of a child, the serious health condition of a family member, or their own serious health condition.

The Act applies to employers with fifty or more employees. In order to be eligible for the Act's protection, an employee must be employed by the employer for at least 12 months, for not fewer than 1,250 hours.

The Act provides that employees are entitled to unpaid family leave of 12 weeks in any 12-month period, providing that the employee gives his or her employer 30 days' advance notice and the employer does not deny the leave under one of the Act's exceptions. While an employee is on leave, the employer is required to maintain whatever health care coverage the employee would have received. An employer can require an employee, or the employee may elect, to substitute accrued paid vacation leave, personal leave, or family leave for any leave under the Act, other than leave for the employee's own illness. An employee who returns to work after a leave is entitled to be restored to the position which he or she had prior to the leave, or to an equivalent position.

An employer may deny job restoration to an employee under limited circumstances. The employee must be salaried and among the top 10 percent of the employees employed within 75 miles of the facility at which the employee is employed. The denial of restoration must be necessary to prevent substantial and grievous economic injury to the employer's operation. Further, the employer must notify the employee of its intent to deny the restoration once the employer determines that the denial is necessary.

Review Questions and Problems

Key Terms

disparate treatment	reasonable accommodation
disparate impact	goals
BFOQ	timetables
affirmative action	

Discussion Questions

1. What are the prohibited forms of discrimination outlawed by federal antidiscrimination statutes?
2. What is the purpose of the Age Discrimination in Employment Act?
3. What do affirmative action programs require employers to do?
4. What statutory provisions exist to protect the employment rights of disabled Americans?
5. What are some of the ways in which sexual discrimination law is different from law prohibiting other types of discrimination?

Review Problems

1. Acme Lumber Company requires all its truck drivers to have a high school diploma. Jones, an employee who was denied a job at Acme, is challenging this requirement in court. Jones claims that the high school diploma requirement has the effect of discriminating against members of minority groups who, in the area where Acme operates, are less likely than others to have a high school diploma. What would Jones have to establish as his prima facie case? If Jones is successful in establishing his prima facie case, what would Acme Lumber then be required to establish in order to avoid liability?

2. Smith is the first woman hired to work at Fire Station No. 711. The firehouse is full of pinup posters of naked women, which offend Smith. She complains to her supervisor, Johnson, who tells her the following: "If anyone makes any lewd remarks to

you, let me know and he'll be fired right away. If anyone ever tries to pressure you to do anything social that you don't want to do, let me know and I'll make him stop. You'll be promoted on the basis of your on-the-job performance only. But these pinup posters are sort of a tradition around here, and it would destroy morale if I made the guys take them down. The pinups stay." Smith continues to be offended by the pinups, but is not otherwise treated improperly by her co-workers. Does Smith have a claim for sexual discrimination? Discuss.

3. Handy Dan's Barber Shop employed fifteen barbers. Eleven were Spanish-surnamed Americans, two were African-Americans, and two were white. Handy Dan's maintained a longstanding rule forbidding its Spanish-surnamed barbers from speaking Spanish to each other in the presence of English-speaking patrons. Three Spanish-surnamed barbers were discharged pursuant to this policy. Did Handy Dan's violate Title VII?

4. Sanchez is a 50-year-old African-American female worker in a large department store. She is a fitter in the women's wear department. She earns $400 a week. Cranchford, a white male, worked as a fitter in the men's wear department for $450 a week. Both Sanchez and Cranchford joined the company on the same day. Cranchford was fired for refusing on religious grounds to work on Saturdays. Sanchez requested a transfer to Cranchford's vacant position. Sanchez was the applicant with the most experience, which under company rules governed who received a transfer. Sanchez was denied the transfer. Discuss the legal issues involved in this case.

Case Problems

1. Jellef Associates was a women's specialty store that catered to mature women. It began reducing personnel because of poor business conditions and excessive payroll expenses. By discharging its older employees (those over 40) and expanding its product line, the company hoped to appeal to a younger market. In terminating one employee, the company gave as its reason the fact that "business was falling off." Another was terminated after being advised that "business was slow." The terminated employees sued Jelleff Associates, claiming that it had violated the Age Discrimination in Employment Act. What was the result? Explain.

2. Employer's pay policy provides that its employees will be paid on the basis of their value in the labor market as well as their productivity. According to the policy, an employee's salary will be based on a survey of the salaries of Employer's competitors. Employees may receive additional compensation by earning up to 10 points in each of four cate-

gories. Three categories relate to productivity measures. A fourth category is labeled "diversity." Women and minorities automatically receive 10 points for being members of protected groups. Are there any legal problems with Employer's pay policy? Explain.

3. Phillips applied for a job as assembly trainee with Martin Marietta Corporation. She was denied the position because the company was not hiring women with preschool children. At the time she applied, 75 percent of those applying were women, and 80 percent of those hired were women. The company employed men with preschool children. Has Martin Marietta violated Title VII? Explain.

4. Western Airlines required that its flight engineers, who are members of the cockpit crew but do not operate flight controls unless the pilot and copilot are incapacitated, retire at age 60. A Federal Aviation Administration regulation prohibits pilots and copilots from serving after age 60. A group of flight engineers forced to retire at age 60 and pilots who at age 60 were denied reassignment as flight engineers brought suit against Western Airlines, contending that the age 60 retirement requirement for flight engineers was in violation of the Age Discrimination in Employment Act. The airline defended, arguing that a BFOQ existed because its age 60 retirement requirement was "reasonably necessary" for the safe operation of the airline. Who should win? Explain.

5. Marie Fernandez was employed by the Wynn Oil Company. She held various positions, including that of administrative assistant to the executive vice president reporting directly to Wynn's director of worldwide marketing. Wynn has extensive operations outside the United States. Much of its business takes place in Latin America and Southeast Asia. Fernandez applied for and was denied a promotion to the position of director of international marketing. She sued Wynn, alleging that it discriminated against her on the basis of sex, in violation of Title VII. Wynn defended by claiming that it was legally entitled to discriminate on the basis of sex in hiring for the position of director of international marketing because sex is a BFOQ for the position. It argued that it would not consider any woman for the position because of the feeling among Wynn's customers and distributors that it would be undesirable to deal with a woman in a high management position. Will Wynn be successful in establishing sex as a BFOQ? Explain.

6. An employer is concerned with the underrepresentation of women and minorities in its work force. It is considering developing an affirmative action plan. Can the employer develop an affirmative action plan without running the risk of violating Title VII? Explain.

57

Environmental Law

Throughout most of this nation's history, Americans have not been very concerned about the quality of the environment. When thick smoke billowed into the air, we regarded the resultant smog as a sign of progress. The rivers and land were seen as convenient and cheap dumping grounds for waste. Since the 1970s, however, we began to realize that degradation of our air, water, and land need not be a necessary consequence of progress. During the past two decades our nation has adopted and begun enforcing a body of regulations referred to as *environmental law*—regulations designed to clean up and protect the environment.

Environmental laws have a significant impact on how business operates today. This chapter will explain those laws and their implications for business.

History

Nuisance

The first attempts to control pollution were made through the tort action of nuisance. A *nuisance* is an unreasonable interference with someone else's use and enjoyment of his or her land. If a factory were emitting black particles that settled on a person's property every day, depositing a layer of dirt on everything in the vicinity, that person might bring an action against the factory on the basis of nuisance. He or she would ask the court to enjoin the emission of the particulates. Prior to the attempted use of nuisance to stop pollution, an injunction was always granted when a nuisance was found. It sounds as if nuisance should therefore be the perfect solution to the problem of pollution. The following case, however, demonstrates why nuisance was not the panacea it initially appeared to be.

BOOMER V. ATLANTIC CEMENT COMPANY
New York State Court of Appeals
257 N.E. 2d 870 (1970)

BACKGROUND: Defendant Atlantic Cement Company operated a large cement plant that emitted considerable amounts of dirt and smoke into the air. These emissions, combined with vibrations from the plant, caused damage to the plaintiffs, Boomer and other owners of property located close to the plant. The trial court ruled in favor of the defendants, finding a nuisance, but denying plaintiffs an injunction. Plaintiffs appealed to the intermediate appellate court, and the judgment of the trial court was affirmed in favor of the defendant. Plaintiffs then appealed to the state's highest appellate court.

Bergan, Justice

The public concern with air pollution arising from many sources in industry and in transportation is currently accorded ever wider recognition accompanied by a growing sense of responsibility in state and federal governments to control it. Cement plants are obvious sources of air pollution in the neighborhoods where they operate.

But there is now before the court private litigation in which individual property owners have sought specific relief from a single plant operation. The threshold questions raised by the division of view on this appeal is whether the court should resolve the litigation between the parties now before it as equitably as seems possible, or whether, seeking promotion of the general public welfare, it should channel private litigation into broad public objectives.

A court performs its essential function when it decides the rights of parties before it. Its decision of private controversies may sometimes greatly affect public issues. Large questions of law are often resolved by the manner in which private litigation is decided. It is a rare exercise of judicial power to use a decision in private litigation as a purposeful mechanism to achieve direct public objectives greatly beyond the rights and interests before the court.

Effective control of air pollution is a problem presently far from solution even with the full public and financial powers of government. In large measure adequate technical procedures are yet to be developed and some that appear possible may be economically impracticable.

It seems apparent that the amelioration of air pollution will depend on technical research in great depth, on a carefully balanced consideration of the economic impact of close regulation, and on the actual effect on public health. It is likely to require massive public expenditure and to demand more than any local community can accomplish and to depend on regional and interstate controls.

A court should not try to do this on its own as a by-product of private litigation and it seems manifest that the judicial establishment is neither equipped in the limited nature of any judgment it can pronounce nor prepared to lay down and implement an effective policy for the elimination of air pollution. This is an area beyond the circumference of one private lawsuit. It is a direct responsibility for government and should not thus be undertaken as an incident to solving a dispute between property owners and a single cement plant—one of many—in the Hudson River Valley.

The cement making operations of defendant have been found by the Court at Special Term to have damaged the nearby properties of plaintiffs in these two actions. That court, as it has been noted, accordingly found defendant maintained a nuisance and this has been affirmed at the Appellate Division. The total damage to plaintiff's properties is, however, relatively small in comparison with the value of defendant's operation and with the consequences of the injunction which plaintiffs seek.

The ground for the denial of injunction, notwithstanding the finding both that there is a nuisance and that plaintiffs have been damaged substantially, is the large disparity in economic consequences of the nuisance and of the injunction.

The parties could settle this private litigation at any time if defendant paid enough money and the imminent threat of closing the plant would build up the pressure on defendant. If there were no improved techniques found, there would inevitably be applications to the Court at Special Term for extensions of time to perform on showing of good faith efforts to find such techniques.

On the other hand, to grant the injunction unless defendant pays plaintiffs such permanent damages as may be fixed by the court seems to do justice between the contending parties. All of the attributions of economic loss to the properties on which plaintiffs' complaints are based will have been redressed.

The nuisance complained of by these plaintiffs may have other public or private consequences, but these particular parties are the only ones who have sought remedies and the judgment proposed will fully redress them. The limitation of relief granted is a limitation only within the four corners of these actions and does not foreclose public health or other public agencies from seeking proper relief in a proper court.

It seems reasonable to think that the risk of being required to pay permanent damages to injured property owners by cement plant owners would itself be a reasonable effective spur to research for improved techniques to minimize nuisance.

The damage base here suggested is consistent with the general rule in those nuisance cases where damages are allowed. "Where a nuisance is of such a permanent and unabatable character that a single recovery can be had, including the whole damage past and future resulting therefrom, there can be but one recovery." It has been said that permanent damages are allowed where the loss recoverable would obviously be small compared with the cost of removal of the nuisance.

Thus it seems fair to both sides to grant permanent damages to plaintiffs which will terminate this private litigation. The theory of damage is the "servitude on land" of plaintiffs imposed by defendant's nuisance.

The judgment, by allowance of permanent damages imposing a servitude on land, which is the basis of the actions, would preclude future recovery by plaintiffs or their grantees.

DECISION: Reversed. The Court ordered payment of damages to the plaintiff in lieu of the issuance of an injunction.

Thus, in *Boomer v. Atlantic Cement Company* the court decided that before it would apply the traditional nuisance remedy—an injunction to halt the pollution—it would look at the harms that would result from the injunction against the benefits of the injunction. Because of a lack of scientific knowledge, judges at the time did not see the true costs that the polluting behavior was imposing on the community.

The 1970s: The Protection Decade

Even though nuisance law proved to be an ineffective means of controlling pollution, the *Boomer* case heralded a new era. It was decided in the year when some of the first major legislative initiatives toward environmental protection were enacted: 1970.

Three books had a significant impact on people's attitudes during the early 1970s: Rachel Carson's *Silent Spring*, which alerted the public to the potential hazards created by pesticides; Paul Ehrlich's *Population Bomb*, which warned of potential problems caused by an ever-increasing population; and Barry Commoner's *The Closing Circle*, which made ecological principles understandable to everyday people. These books, along with some cataclysmic events such as the 1969 Santa Barbara Oil Spill, and the first Earth Day Celebration in 1970, led to at least a perception on the part of lawmakers that there was strong public support for new laws to protect the environment. This public pressure led to the passage of twenty-seven environmental statutes between 1969 and 1979. Among these statutes are most of the laws you will read about in this chapter. With the passage of these laws, as well as many similar state initiatives, vast improvements were made in the quality of our air, water, and land.

Most of the 1970s laws are known as "command and control" or "end of pipe" regulations. That is, they mandate standards, expressed as either technology that must be installed or limits on the amounts of pollutants that can be emitted. Failure to comply results in the imposition of fines.

The 1980s: The Deregulation Decade

The 1980s saw the election of presidents who perceived themselves as being elected with a mandate to deregulate. And one way to deregulate is to reduce agencies' budgets and staffs. The budget of Environmental Protection Agency (EPA)—the primary federal agency responsible for controlling environmental problems—was slashed by over a third (when adjusted for inflation) between 1981 and 1983. EPA personnel were cut by 20 percent. Sensing the reduction in funding for enforcement, businesses felt less constrained by environmental regulations.

At first Congress went along with the new deregulatory agenda, but by the second half of the decade, Congress began to oppose the administration's policies. When several environmental laws came up for reauthorization, Congress chose to strengthen them. Thus, the decade ended with what appeared to be renewed environmental vigor, at least on the part of Congress.

The 1990s: The Prevention Decade

With the 1990s, there appears to be increased pressure from the public to strengthen environmental laws and enforcement. As you will see, however, this decade also reflects a growing awareness of a need to shift away from relying on command and control strategies to clean up pollution toward attempts to harness market forces to encourage pollution prevention. There is also a greater emphasis on voluntary programs.

Enforcement of Environmental Law and Policy

Like other areas of administrative law, environmental law is primarily made up of regulations passed by a federal agency operating under the guidance of congressional mandates. As noted above, the primary agency responsible for promulgation and enforcement of environmental regulations is the Environmental Protection Agency.

The EPA is the largest federal agency, having over 17,000 employees by the year 1992. The agency was created by executive order in 1972 to control and regulate pollution in relation to air, water, solid waste, pesticides, radiation, and toxic substances—a rather substantial mandate for any agency! The reason for placing control of all types of environmental problems within one agency was to ensure that the attack on pollution would be an integrated, coordinated effort. In other words, Congress wanted to be certain that regulations reducing, say, air pollution would not simply lead to increased water pollution. Unfortunately, for two decades such integration did not occur. Within the agency, separate offices were established for each of the areas of pollution, and there was very little interaction among the various offices.

Recognizing the inefficiency of the EPA's organizational structure, in July of 1993, EPA administrator Carol Browner took one of the first major steps toward trying to give the agency a truly integrated focus. She announced her decision to move all enforcement actions from the various program offices into one main enforcement office. Environmentalists applauded this change because it would make multimedia enforcement a routine practice, rather than an extraordinary undertaking.

In October of 1993, Browner reified her idea of unification. She established an Office of Compliance, which has as its primary focus "providing industry with coherent information about compliance requirements." The office is divided into groups of regulators who will focus on separate sectors of the economy—energy and transportation, agriculture, and manufacturing. She also created a new Office of Regulatory Enforcement to take on the tough responsibility of deciding which pollutors would be taken to court.

The Policy Acts

Two pieces of legislation set forth our nation's policies for protection of the environment. The first policy act, the National Environmental Policy Act (NEPA) of 1970, has been regarded by many as the most influential piece of environmental legislation. The second act, the Pollution Prevention Control Act (PPCA), was passed 20 years later and is seen by many as an attempt to redirect our nation's environmental policies.

National Environmental Policy Act (NEPA)

NEPA is viewed as an extremely powerful piece of legislation because its primary effect has been to

PREVENTIVE LAW
Corporate Compliance with Environmental Regulations

Immediately following the election of President Bill Clinton, numerous articles began appearing in business and law publications warning corporate managers that they should prepare for a period of increased scrutiny of their compliance with federal regulations. Environmental regulations are extremely complex and fines for their violation can be stiff. Here are a few ways to help encourage corporate compliance with environmental regulations:

1. Appoint one person to be a compliance officer, a person who is familiar with all environmental regulations and who will review the actions of all other managers to ensure that regulations are being followed.

2. Establish regular procedures, including internal or external compliance and management audits, to evaluate, detect, prevent, and remedy circumstances that might lead to noncompliance.

3. Make environmental compliance a standard by which employee and departmental performance are judged.

4. Establish an effective internal disciplinary procedure for those who violate environmental compliance standards.*

* Paul Wallach and Dan Levin, "Using Government's Guidance to Structure Compliance Plan," *National Law Journal*, August 30, 1993.

reform the process by which regulatory agencies make decisions. Title II of the Act requires the preparation of an **environmental impact statement** (EIS) for every major legislative proposal or agency action that would have a significant impact on the quality of the human environment. A substantial number of these statements are filed every year, over which a significant amount of litigation results. Table 57-1 details the litigation under NEPA from 1984 to 1991.

Threshold Considerations An EIS is required when three elements are present. First, the action in question must be federal, such as the grant of a license, the extension of a loan, or the lease of property by a federal agency. Second, the proposed activity must be major—that is, requiring a substantial commitment of resources. Finally, the proposed activity must have a significant impact on the human environment.

Following the passage of NEPA, the question of what constituted a significant impact engendered a great deal of litigation. But guidelines established in 1979 resolved some of the questions by providing that the significance of an impact re-

quires consideration of both the context of the action and its intensity. Looking at the context requires consideration of both long- and short-term impacts. It also means looking at the impact of the act on the society as a whole, the affected region, and the locality.

Intensity refers to the severity of the impact. In an evaluation of intensity, ten factors are to be considered:

1. Both beneficial and detrimental effects

2. The degree to which the public health or safety will be affected

3. Unique characteristics of the geographic area

4. The degree to which the effects of the action on the human environment are likely to be controversial

5. The degree to which the effects on the human environment are highly uncertain or unique

6. The degree to which the action may set a precedent for future actions

7. Whether the Act is related to other acts with insignificant individual impacts but significant cumulative impacts

TABLE 57-1

NEPA Litigation Survey, 1984–1991

Year*	Cases Filed	Number of Injunctions	Most Frequent Defendant	Most Frequent Plaintiff	Most Common Complaint	Second Most Common Complaint
1984	89	14	USDA, DOI, DOT	Environmental groups; individuals or citizen groups	Inadequate EIS	No EIS
1985	77	8	DOT, DOI, COE, FERC	Environmental groups; individuals or citizen groups	No EIS	Inadequate EIS
1986	71	16	DOT, DOI, USDA	Individuals or citizen groups; environmental groups	No EIS	Inadequate EIS
1987	69	3	DOI, DOT, USDA	Environmental groups; individuals or citizen groups	No EIS	Inadequate EA and EIS
1988	91	7	COE, USDA, DOI, DOT	Environmental groups; individuals or citizen groups	No EIS	Inadequate EIS
1989	57	5	USDA, DOT	Individuals or citizen groups; environmental groups	No EIS	Inadequate EIS
1990	85	11	DOT, COE, EPA	Environmental groups; individuals or citizen groups	No EIS	Inadequate EIS
1991	94	14	DOT, DOI, ARMY	Individuals or citizen groups; environmental groups	No EIS	Inadequate EIS

*1970–1975: A cumulative survey on these years was published in the 1976 CEQ Annual Report. By June 30, 1975, 332 NEPA cases had been completed, resulting in 54 injunctions; 322 cases were still pending with 65 injunctions. The most frequent defendants were the Department of Transportation and Housing and Urban Development.

Source: Council on Environmental Quality, *Environmental Quality*, 23rd Annual Report on Environmental Quality, 1993, p. 165.

8. The degree to which the Act may affect places of historical, cultural, or scientific significance

9. The degree to which the Act may adversely affect an endangered species

10. Whether the Act threatens any law designed to protect the environment

Content of the EIS   Once an agency has determined that an EIS is necessary, it must gather the information necessary to prepare the document. The NEPA requires that the EIS include a detailed statement of:

1. The environmental impact of the proposed action

2. Any adverse environmental effects that cannot be avoided should the proposal be implemented

3. Alternatives to the proposed action

4. The relationship between local short-term uses of the human environment and the maintenance and enhancement of long-term productivity

5. Any irreversible and irretrievable commitments of resources that would be involved in the proposed activity should it be implemented

A continuing problem under NEPA, however, is interpreting what is meant by environmental impacts. Clearly, they extend beyond the effects on the natural environment and in some cases have been held to include noise, increased traffic and congestion, the overburdening of public facilities such as sewage and mass transportation systems, increased crime, increased availability of illegal drugs, and in a small number of cases damage to the psychological health of those affected by the agency action. Other cases, however, have not allowed all such damages. The loss of business profits resulting from a proposed agency action has not been considered an environmental impact.

One of the more controversial issues is the potential impact of the proposed action on the psychological health of members of the community. Whether such an impact must be included in an EIS is addressed in the following case.

METROPOLITAN EDISON COMPANY V. PEOPLE AGAINST NUCLEAR ENERGY

U.S. Supreme Court
103 S.Ct. 1556 (1983)

BACKGROUND: After the near disaster at Pennsylvania's Three Mile Island (TMI) nuclear plant, the Metropolitan Edison Company petitioned the Nuclear Regulatory Commission (NRC) to resume operations of the TMI-1 nuclear reactor. People Against Nuclear Energy (PANE) sought to enjoin the operation on the ground that the EIS was insufficient because it failed to include a discussion of whether the risk of an another accident at TMI-1 might cause psychological harm to the residents. The Circuit Court of Appeals found in favor of PANE. Metropolitan appealed.

Rehnquist, Justice

PANE is an association of residents of the Harrisburg area who are opposed to further operation of either TMI reactor. PANE contended that restarting TMI-1 would cause both severe psychological health damage to persons living in the vicinity, and serious damage to the stability, cohesiveness, and well-being of the neighboring communities.

The Court of Appeals concluded that the Atomic Energy Act does not require the NRC to address PANE's contentions. It did find, however, that NEPA requires the NRC to evaluate "the potential psychological health effects of operating" TMI-1 which have arisen since the original EIS was prepared. It also held that, if the NRC finds that significant new circumstances or information exist on this subject, it shall prepare a "supplemental {EIS} which considers not only the effects on psychological health but also effects on the well-being of the communities surrounding Three Mile Island." We granted certiorari. All the parties agree that effects on human health can be cognizable under NEPA, and that human health may include psychological health. The Court of Appeals thought these propositions were enough to complete a syllogism that disposes of the case: NEPA requires agencies to consider effects on health. An effect on psychological health is an effect on health. Therefore, NEPA requires agencies to consider the effects on psychological health asserted by PANE.

To paraphrase the statutory language in light of the facts of this case, where an agency action significantly affects the quality of the human environment, the agency must evaluate the "environmental impact" and any unavoidable adverse environmental effects of its proposal. The theme of 102 is sounded by the adjective "environmental": NEPA does not require the agency to assess every impact or effect of its proposed action, but only the impact or effect on the environment. If we were to seize the word "environmental" out of its context and give it the broadest possible definition, the words "adverse environmental effects" might embrace virtually any consequence of a governmental action that someone thought "adverse." But we think the context of the statute shows that Congress was talking about the physical environment—the world around us, so to speak. NEPA was designed to promote human welfare by alerting governmental actors to the effect of their proposed actions on the physical environment.

Some effects that are "caused by" a change in the physical environment in the sense of "but for" causation, will nonetheless not fall within 102 because the causal chain is too attenuated. For example, residents of the Harrisburg area have relatives in other parts of the country. Renewed operation of TMI-1 may well cause psychological health problems for these people. They may suffer "anxiety, tension and fear, a sense of helplessness," and accompanying physical disorders . . . because of the risk that their relatives may be harmed in a nuclear accident. However, this harm is simply too remote from the physical environment to justify requiring the NRC to evaluate the psychological health damage to these people that may be caused by renewed operation of TMI-1.

Our understanding of the congressional concerns that led to the enactment of NEPA suggests that the terms "environmental effect" and "environmental impact" in 102 be read to include a requirement of a reasonably close causal relationship between a change in the physical environment and the effect at issue. This requirement is like the familiar doctrine of proximate cause from tort law.

PANE argues that the psychological health damage it alleges "will flow directly from the risk of {a nuclear} accident." But a risk of an accident is not an effect on the physical environment. A risk is, by definition, unrealized in the physical world. In a causal chain from renewed operation of TMI-1 to psychological health damage, the element of risk and its perception by PANE's members are necessary middle links. We believe that the element of risk lengthens the causal chain beyond the reach of NEPA.

It is difficult for us to see the differences between someone who dislikes a government decision so much that he suffers anxiety and stress, someone who fears the effects of that decision so much that he suffers similar anxiety and stress, and someone who suffers anxiety and stress that "flow directly" from the risks associated with the same decision. It would be extraordinarily difficult for agencies to differentiate between "genuine" claims of psychological health damage and claims that are grounded solely in disagreement with a democratically adopted policy. Until Congress provides a more explicit statutory instruction than NEPA now contains, we do not think agencies are obliged to undertake the inquiry.

DECISION: Reversed. The Supreme Court agreed with defendant Metropolitan Edison that the EIS need not include a discussion of the psychological effects of the risk of another nuclear accident.

Factors other than changes in the physical environment have sometimes been required in court cases involving environmental impact. However, in most of the cases, there has been a link to some actual, physical change.

Another problem regarding the scope of the EIS pertains to the requirement of a detailed statement of alternatives to the proposed actions. What alternatives must be discussed and how detailed must the discussion be? Generally, any reasonable alternatives, including taking no action, must be discussed. The more likely the alternative is to be implemented, the more detailed the statement must be.

Effectiveness of the EIS Process   The EIS requirement has clearly changed the *process* of agency decision making, but many wonder whether the requirement has likewise improved the *quality* of the decision making.

Critics of NEPA argue that the EIS process is only one more piece of bureaucratic red tape that must be untangled before the agency implements an action that it was going to take all along. Some environmentalists point out that NEPA requires only that the statement be prepared and considered by the agency. A court can merely make sure that the agency follows the proper procedures; it cannot decide that the agency did not give proper weight to certain environmental effects and then force the agency to alter its course of action.

If an EIS is found deficient, the agency may be forced to redo it. This revision of the EIS may result in huge time delays and increased costs for a project. Also, detractors of the process say, after an agency has filled out a number of such statements, it learns what must and must not be included in order for an EIS to pass judicial scrutiny. Thus, in these people's view, the preparation of an EIS is simply an expensive, time-consuming procedure that must be followed even though it has almost no influence on the agency's ultimate course of action.

Another perceived problem with the EIS requirement is that the information contained in the statement may not be credible, since it is provided by parties who want to undertake the action. For example, if the owner of a ski resort wanted to expand business and therefore needed to lease more land from the U.S. Forest Service, an EIS would be required. The developer would hire a consulting firm to gather the needed information to prepare the EIS for the U.S. Forest Service. Will the data be unbiased? This type of data gathering is so expensive that most private parties opposed to the action could probably not afford to contribute data for use by the agency, so the party providing data will be the developer.

Not everyone criticizes the EIS process, however. Supporters of the EIS argue that it has made a modest, but important contribution to the protection of the environment. At minimum, possible effects are out in the open for interested parties to examine. In fact, before the passage of NEPA, many agencies did not have the statutory authority to take environmental factors into account when deciding on an appropriate course of action, even if they had wished to do so. Supporters of the process cite numerous instances in which the EIS has had an impact on agency decision making, causing agencies to modify or drop projects that might have created environmental problems.

Pollution Prevention Control Act

Twenty years after the passage of the National Environmental Policy Act, Congress recognized that end of pipe regulations were not going to be sufficient to stop pollution and clean up the environment; we were going to have to find ways to not pollute in the first place. The Pollution Prevention Control Act was designed to encourage businesses to focus on pollution prevention.

The policy set forth in this act was that:

Pollution should be prevented or reduced at the source whenever feasible; pollution that cannot be prevented should be recycled in an environmentally safe manner, whenever feasible; pollution that cannot be prevented or recycled should be treated in an environmentally safe manner whenever feasible; and disposal or other release into the environment should be employed only as a last resort and should be conducted in an environmentally safe manner.

The main thing the act does is provide matching grants to states for programs to promote the use of source reduction by firms. The act also implemented a number of voluntary programs designed to encourage waste reduction.

It is too early to know whether this law will have any significant impact. Many doubt whether it will because it does not have any mandatory provisions.

Regulating Water Quality

Water pollution is controlled today primarily by two pieces of legislation: the Federal Water Pollution Control Act (FWPCA)—particularly its 1972 amendments—and the Safe Drinking Water Act (SDWA). The first concentrates on the quality of water in our waterways, while the second ensures that the water we drink is not harmful to our health.

Federal Water Pollution Control Act

When Congress passed the 1972 amendments to the FWPCA, it established two goals: (1) "fishable" and "swimmable" waters by 1983 and (2) total elimination of pollutant discharges into navigable waters by 1985. These goals were to be achieved through a system of permits and limitations on pollutant discharges from specific sources. Obviously, these goals were not attained. Many, in fact, argue that no one really expected their attainment. However, the amendments set a high standard to aspire to and work toward.

Point-Source Effluent Limitations One of the primary tools for meeting the goals of the 1972 FWPCA amendments was the establishment and enforcement of point-source effluent limitations. Point sources are distinct places from which pollutants can be discharged into water. Factories, refineries, and sewage treatment facilities are a few examples of point sources. Effluents are the outflows from a specific source. Effluent limitations, therefore, are the maximum allowable amounts of pollutants that can be discharged from a source within a given time period. Different limitations were established for different pollutants.

Under the National Pollutant Discharge Elimination System (NPDES), every point source that discharges pollutants must obtain a discharge permit from the EPA or from the state if the state has an EPA-approved plan at least as strict as the federal standards. The permits specify the types and amounts of effluent discharges allowed. The discharger is required to continually monitor its discharges and report any excess discharges to either the state or the federal EPA. Discharges without a permit or in amounts in excess of those allowed by the permit may be subject to criminal penalties. Enforcement is left primarily to the states in which there is an approved program for regulation. However, the FWPCA provides for federal monitoring, inspection, and enforcement. Citizens may also bring suit to enforce the effluent limits.

Under Section 301 of the amended FWPCA, effluent limitations for all existing point sources except public sewage treatment facilities were to reflect the "best practicable control technology currently available" (BPT) by 1977. By 1983, they were to reflect the "best available technology economically achievable" (BAT), a more stringent standard. In 1977, amendments delayed these deadlines for many pollutants. They required that by 1987, all existing point sources were to meet BAT standards for toxic pollutants and meet the "best conventional pollutant control standard" (BCT) for nontoxic pollutants.

Much litigation ensued over how these standards were to be established. The case below illustrates how the paper industry challenged the BCT standard set by the EPA. The case also provides some insight into how the EPA established its standards.

AMERICAN PAPER INSTITUTE V. ENVIRONMENTAL PROTECTION AGENCY

U.S. Court of Appeals, Fourth Circuit
660 F.2d 954 (1981)

BACKGROUND: The American Paper Institute objected to the BCT standards established by the EPA. The petitioners claimed that Congress, in Section 304(b)(4)(B) of the amended FWPCA, required the EPA to incorporate two factors into its methodology for determining BCT: an industry cost-effectiveness test and a test that compares the cost for private industry to reduce its effluent levels with that incurred by publicly owned treatment works (POTWs) for a similar purpose. The petitioners asserted that the EPA considered only the latter factor and that EPA's benchmark for this latter factor was arbitrary and capricious. The trial court upheld the regulation, and the petitioners appealed, arguing again that the use of the second test was arbitrary.

Ervin, Circuit Judge

While the parties disagree over precisely what Congress intended to do when it enacted the 1977 amendments to the Act and draw markedly different conclusions from the language of the amendments and the legislative history, it is clear that Congress felt that the results produced by the BPT have provided a high degree of water quality improvement, and that in some instances, BAT for conventional pollutants about which much was known might require treatment not deemed necessary to meet the 1983 water quality goals of the Act. Concern was expressed about requiring "treatment for treatment's sake," and there was much discussion about comparing the cost of treatment with the benefits obtained from the reductions achieved.

Out of this came the development of a new standard, best conventional pollutant control technology (BCT). The new requirement was described by one Senate–House conferee as "the equivalent of best practical technology or something a little bit better, even as far as best available technology in some circumstances."

In addition, in section 73 of the 1977 amendments, Congress directed EPA to "review every effluent guideline promulgated prior to the enactment of this Act which is final or interim final." This required review of all outstanding BAT limitations for conventional pollutants for all secondary industrial sources within 90 days after the effective date of the amendments.

EPA's position is that Congress did not require it to utilize [the] industry cost-effectiveness test, but instead only mandated a POTW cost comparison standard in arriving at BCT regulations for industry. In interpreting section 304(b)(4)(B), EPA concludes that the proposed effluent guidelines are not required to pass two reasonableness tests. In support of its position, EPA reads the seemingly dual requirements of section 304(b)(4)(B) as one, commanding only a consideration of reasonableness. It contends that the second clause in the relevant portion of section 304(b)(4)(B) sets forth the benchmark of reasonableness—a comparison of the proposed BCT cost and level of effluent reduction for industry to the cost and level of reduction from the discharge of POTWs.

We are unable to accept this suggested statutory interpretation. When faced with such a question, our starting point for discerning congressional intent is the words of the statute itself. The law which empowers EPA to act directs that EPA's effluent regulations "shall . . . specify factors to be taken into account in determining the best conventional pollutant control technology measures and practices to comply with section 301(b)(2)(E) of this title to be applicable to any point source (other than publicly owned treatment works) within such categories or classes." Congress did not leave EPA free to select these factors.

EPA's construction of section 304(b)(4)(B) is contrary to the plain meaning of the words contained therein. EPA ignores the mandatory language of the law ("shall"), disregards the conjunctive ("and"), and completely eliminates the first factor. By its own admission, the agency made no effort to determine what it would cost an affected industry to remove a pound of pollutant past the BPT level nor did it compare the costs of such removal with the benefits derived from the removal, as specifically required by statute.

Where, as here, the language of the Act is unambiguous and EPA has failed to comply with its directives, we must grant the petitions to set aside the regulations involved and remand the regulations to EPA for reconsideration. On remand EPA is to develop an industry cost-effectiveness test in accordance with the provisions of section 304(b)(4)(B), employ

> that test in a manner consistent with the statute, and re-examine all existing BCT regulations to ensure that they are not inconsistent with the proper employment of this industry cost-effectiveness test.
>
> EPA has rationally justified its use of the AST increment. AST is the "knee-of-the-curse" point, the maximum cost-effective level of control for POTWs. The increment from secondary treatment to AST for POTWs was also determined by EPA to be roughly analogous to the industrial increment from BPT to BAT.
>
> **DECISION:** Affirmed, in part, reversed in part, and remanded. The Appellate Court agreed with the American Paper Institute that Section 304(b)(4)(B) required the EPA to take into account two distinct factors when calculating the BAT standard. Failure of the EPA to do so rendered the agency's rulemaking arbitrary and capricious. With respect to the way the EPA evaluated the factor that it did take into account, the court found that the EPA did so in a reasonable manner.

Although plants were expected to meet the BPT effluent standards by the established deadlines, the administrator of the EPA was given the authority to grant individual sources variances from the BAT standards. To be granted a variance, the point-source owner must establish that the modified requirements under the variance (1) represent the maximum use of technology within the economic capability of the owner or operator and (2) will result in reasonable further progress toward elimination of the discharge pollutants.

Additional Provisions of the FWPCA
In addition to the scheme of regulating effluent discharges, the FWPCA attempts to encourage the cleanup of the waterways by establishing a subsidy program for the construction of publicly owned water treatment plants that meet a state-of-the-art standard and are cost-effective.

The Safe Drinking Water Act

The FWPCA seeks to ensure that the waterways are clean, but "clean" does not mean "fit to drink."

ETHICS
The CERES (*Valdez*) Principles

In response to the environmental impact of the oil spill resulting from the grounding of the tanker *Exxon Valdez* in Alaska in 1989, the Coalition for Environmentally Responsible Economies (CERES) adopted a set of standards which could be voluntarily adopted by corporations. Initially only small, closely held firms like Ben & Jerry's adopted the *Valdez* Principles, as they were then called. However, in 1993 the principles became known as the CERES Principles, and the Sun Oil Company became the first major firm to support them. The original principles are printed below. Would you recommend that a large corporation adopt them?

The *Valdez* Principles

1. Protection of the Biosphere
We will minimize and strive to *eliminate* the release of any pollutant that may cause environmental damage to the air, water, or earth or its inhabitants. We will safeguard habitats in rivers, lakes, wetlands, coastal zones, and oceans and will minimize contributing to the greenhouse effect, depletion of the ozone layer, acid rain, or smog.

2. Sustainable Use of Natural Resources

We will make sustainable use of renewable natural resources, such as water, soils, and forests. We will conserve nonrenewable natural resources through efficient use and careful planning. We will protect wildlife habitat, open spaces, and wilderness, while preserving biodiversity.

3. Reduction and Disposal of Waste

We will minimize the creation of waste, especially hazardous waste, and wherever possible recycle materials. We will dispose of all wastes through safe and responsible methods.

4. Wise Use of Energy

We will make every effort to use environmentally safe and sustainable energy sources to meet our needs. We will invest in improved energy efficiency and conservation in our operations. We will maximize the energy efficiency of products we produce or sell.

5. Risk Reduction

We will minimize the environmental, health, and safety risks to our employees and the communities in which we operate by employing safe technologies and operating procedures and by being constantly prepared for emergencies.

6. Marketing of Safe Products and Services

We will sell products or services that minimize adverse environmental impacts and that are safe as consumers commonly use them. We will inform consumers of the environmental impacts of our products or services.

7. Damage Compensation

We will take responsibility for any harm we cause to the environment by making every effort to fully restore the environment and to compensate those persons who are adversely affected.

8. Disclosure

We will disclose to our employees and to the public incidents relating to our operations that cause environmental harm or pose health or safety hazards. We will disclose potential environmental, health, or safety hazards posed by our operations, and we will not take any action against employees who report any condition that creates a danger to the environment or poses health and safety hazards.

9. Environmental Directors and Managers

We will commit management resources to implement the *Valdez* Principles, to monitor and report upon our implementation efforts, and to sustain a process to ensure that the Board of Directors and Chief Executive Officer are kept informed of and are fully responsible for all environmental matters. We will establish a Committee of the Board of Directors with responsibility for environmental affairs. At least one member of the Board of Directors will be a person qualified to represent environmental interests to come before the company.

10. Assessment and Annual Audit

We will conduct and make public an annual self-evaluation of our progress in implementing these Principles and in complying with all applicable laws and regulations throughout our worldwide operations. We will work toward the timely creation of independent environmental audit procedures which we will complete annually and make available to the public.

The Safe Drinking Water Act (SDWA) therefore sets standards for drinking water supplied by a public water supply system. A public water supply system is defined by the SDWA as a water supply system that has at least fifteen service connections or serves twenty-five or more people.

The original SDWA, passed in 1974, required the EPA to establish two levels of drinking water standards for potential drinking water contaminants. Primary standards were to protect human health and secondary standards were to protect the aesthetic quality of drinking water. These standards were to have been established by September 1977, but by 1986 standards had been adopted for only twenty-three of the hundreds of potential drinking water contaminants.

The SDWA was amended in 1986, requiring the EPA to establish maximum contaminant level goals (MCLGs) and maximum contaminant levels (MCLs) for all contaminants that had the potential to have an adverse effect on human health. MCLGs are the levels at which there are no potential adverse health effects. These are unenforceable, health-based goals. They are the high standards to which we aspire. The MCLs are the enforceable standards. They are based on the MCLGs, but also take into account the feasibility and cost of meeting the standard. By 1991, the EPA was to have set MCLs for 108 of the hundreds of contaminants found in our drinking water, and MCLs for 25 more contaminants every 3 years thereafter.

As you might guess, keeping up with the ever-increasing MCLs is a difficult task for public drinking water suppliers. Monitoring these systems is also a chore. Most states do monthly monitoring. Violations may be punished by administrative fines or orders.

Regulating Air Quality

The Clean Air Act of 1970 was designed to protect human health and the human environment by regulating the amount of pollutants in the air. Air pollutants are those gases and particles in the air that are viewed as undesirable because they are harmful to human health or the environment. The major air pollutants include carbon monoxide, nitrogen dioxide, sulfur dioxide, hydrocarbon compounds, ozone, lead, and suspended particulates. Table 57-2 illustrates some of the most common health problems caused by these pollutants. In addition to these enumerated health problems, nitrogen oxides and sulfur dioxide contribute to the formation of acid rain, which defaces buildings and causes the ph levels of lakes to rise to such a level that most fish can no longer survive. These pollutants, frequently referred to as *criteria pollutants*, have been regulated primarily through national air-quality standards.

National Ambient Air Quality Standards (NAAQS)

NAAQS provide the focal point for air pollution control. Under the Clean Air Act, the administrator of the EPA established primary and secondary **ambient air quality standards** for carbon monoxide, particulates, sulfur dioxide, nitrogen dioxide, hydrocarbons, and ozone. Lead was later added to this list. Primary standards are those that the administrator determined were necessary to protect the public health, including an adequate margin of safety. Secondary standards are more stringent, since they are the standards that would protect the public welfare

TABLE 57-2

Criteria Pollutants and Associated Health Problems

Pollutant	Associated Problems
Carbon monoxide	Angina, impaired vision, poor coordination, and lack of alertness
Lead	Neurological system and kidney damage
Nitrogen oxides	Lung and respiratory tract damage
Ozone	Eye irritation, increased nasal congestion, reduction of lung functions, and reduced resistance to infection
Particulates	Reduced resistance to infection and eye, ear, and throat irritation
Sulfur dioxide	Lung and respiratory tract damage

(crops, buildings, and animals) from any known or anticipated adverse affect associated with the air pollutant for which the standard is being established. The administrator of the EPA retains the authority to establish new primary and secondary standards if scientific evidence indicates that the present standards are inadequate or that such standards must be set for currently unregulated pollutants.

Under the 1970 Act, after each NAAQS was established, every state had 9 months to establish a state implementation plan (SIP) that explained how the state was going to ensure that the pollutants in the air within its boundaries would not exceed the NAAQS. Under the state SIPs, primary NAAQS had to be achieved within 3 years of their creation, and secondary standards had to be met within a reasonable time. The administrator of the EPA had to approve all SIPs. When an SIP was found inadequate, the administrator had the power to amend it or could send it back to the state for revision. Numerous challenges were made to these SIPs. One issue that arose is the role of economic and technological considerations in the establishment of standards. That issue is discussed in the following case.

UNION ELECTRIC COMPANY v. ENVIRONMENTAL PROTECTION AGENCY, ET AL.

U.S. Supreme Court
427 U.S. 246 (1976)

BACKGROUND: Union Electric Company filed a petition for review of the EPA administrator's approval of the state implementation plan's emission standards for sulfur dioxide. The petition was filed over 30 days past the date on which the standards were promulgated. The primary ground for Union Electric's challenge was that technological and economic difficulties in meeting SIP standards arose over 30 days after approval of the SIP.

The U.S. Court of Appeals dismissed the petition on the grounds that challenges more than 30 days after approval of the plan had to be based on new evidence not available at the time of approval. The Supreme Court agreed to review the case.

Marshall, Justice

Section 307(b)(1) allows petitions for review to be filed in an appropriate court of appeals more than 30 days after the Administrator's approval of an implementation plan only if the petition is "based solely on grounds arising after such 30th day." Petitioner claimed to meet this requirement by asserting, inter alia, that various economic and technological difficulties had arisen more than 30 days after the Administrator's approval and that these difficulties made compliance with the emission limitations impossible.

We reject at the outset petitioner's suggestion that a claim of economic or technological infeasibility may be considered upon a petition for a review based on new information and filed more than 30 days after approval of an implementation plan even if such a claim could not be considered by the Administrator in approving a plan or by a court in reviewing a plan challenged within the original 30-day appeal period.

As we have previously recognized, the 1970 Amendments to the Clean Air Act were a drastic remedy to what was perceived as a serious and otherwise uncheckable problem of air pollution. The Amendments place the primary responsibility for formulating pollution control strategies on the States, but nonetheless subject the States to strict minimum compliance requirements. The requirements are of a "technology-forcing character," and are expressly designed to force regulated sources to develop pollution control devices that might at the time appear to be economically or technologically infeasible.

This approach is apparent on the face of § 110(a)(2). The provision sets out eight criteria that an implementation plan must satisfy, and provides that if these criteria are met and if the plan was adopted after reasonable notice and hearing, the Administrator "shall approve" the proposed state plan. The mandatory "shall" makes it quite clear that the Administrator is not to be concerned with factors other than those specified, and none of the eight factors appears to permit consideration of technological or economic infeasibility. Nonetheless, if a basis is to be found for allowing the Administrator to consider such claims, it must be among the eight criteria.

Section 110(a)(2)(A)'s three-year deadline for achieving primary air quality standards is central to the Amendments' regulatory scheme and, as both the language and the legislative history of the requirement make clear, it leaves no room for claims of technological or economic infeasibility. The 1970 congressional debate on the Amendments centered on whether technology forcing was necessary and desirable in framing and attaining air quality standards sufficient to protect the public health, standards later termed primary standards. The House version of the Amendments was quite moderate in approach, requiring only that health-related standards be met "within a reasonable time." The Senate bill, on the other hand, flatly required that, possible or not, health-related standards be met "within three years."

• • •

In sum, we have concluded that claims of economic or technological infeasibility may not be considered by the Administrator in evaluating a state requirement that primary ambient air quality standards be met in the mandatory three years. And, since we further conclude that the States may submit implementation plans more stringent than federal law requires and that the Administrator must approve such plans if they meet the minimum requirements of § 110(a)(2), it follows that the language of § 110(a)(2)(B) provides no basis for the Administrator ever to reject a state implementation plan on the ground that it is economically or technologically infeasible. According, a court of appeals reviewing an approved plan under § 307(b)(1) cannot set it aside on those grounds, no matter when they are raised.

Our conclusion is bolstered by recognition that the Amendments do allow claims of technological and economic infeasibility to be raised in situations where consideration of such claims will not substantially interfere with the primary congressional purpose of prompt attainment of the national air quality standards. Thus, we do not hold that claims of infeasibility are never of relevance in the formulation of an implementation plan or that sources unable to comply with emission limitations must inevitably be shut down.

Perhaps the most important forum for consideration of claims of economic and technological infeasibility is before the state agency formulating the implementation plan. So long as the national standards are met, the State may select whatever mix of control devices it desires, and industries with particular economic or technological problems may seek special treatment in the plan itself.

DECISION: Affirmed. The Supreme Court upheld the state's determination of the most effective mix of controls.

Initially, all NAAQS were to be achieved by 1977. This goal was not met. Hence, the 1977 amendments extended the deadlines. In 1982, the hydrocarbons standard was eliminated, ostensibly because it was unnecessary. By 1985, the NAAQS for four of the six criteria air pollutants had been met in most areas of the country. Since that time, ozone has remained the most pervasive problem, and the carbon monoxide standard is still unmet in a number of urban areas. But there has been a significant decline in the amount of emissions of these two pollutants over the past decade.

In addition to establishing the NAAQS, the EPA administrator is required to determine national, uniform emission standards for new motor vehicles, as well as for new and major expansions of existing stationary sources of pollutants. The standards for the new stationary sources are to reflect the best available control technology (BCT), taking into account the costs of compliance. Like the NAAQS, the initial emission standards for automobiles and new stationary sources were not all met within the original timetables. Some deadlines have been extended, and many individual sources of pollutants have received short-term exemptions.

Prevention of Significant Deterioration

One problem that arose under the Clean Air Act of 1970, and that was subsequently addressed by the 1977 amendments, involved establishing standards for areas in which the air was already cleaner than the 1970 Act required. Should the air quality in these areas be allowed to deteriorate as long as it did not fall below the NAAQS? Congress said no. It committed the country to the principle of the prevention of significant deterioration (PSD) in air quality. Under this principle, every area that had met the NAAQS was originally designated Class I or II. A third classification, Class III, is now available on request of the governor.

The amount of deterioration of air quality allowable in the area now depends on an area's class designation. Class I areas include primarily national parks and wilderness preserves. Very little deterioration is allowed in these areas. Degradation down to the secondary NAAQS is *not* allowed in Class I areas. All other areas that had met the NAAQS were originally designated Class II. Moderate increases in concentrations of pollutants are allowed in these areas. Larger increases in pollutant concentration are allowed in Class III areas to provide for industrial development. However, even in Class III regions, the increased concentrations may not be so significant that the air quality no longer meets the NAAQS.

Effectiveness of the Clean Air Act

Ever since its enactment, there has been debate over the effectiveness of the Clean Air Act. Critics have repeatedly charged that the Act does not properly take into account the cost of air pollution control technology. Others argue that the Act is impossible to enforce because sufficient technology does not exist to monitor sources and determine whether they are in compliance with the Act. Still others argue that so many exemptions are granted that the standards are not taken seriously by industrial polluters who do not actually have to comply with the standards set by the EPA. Finally, some argue that it is too costly to comply with many of the Act's regulations.

Supporters of the Act defend its effectiveness. They point out that the air quality has been steadily improving since its enactment. Between 1970 and 1988, the estimated total emissions of sulfur dioxide, hydrocarbons, and carbon monoxide were substantially reduced. The amount of suspended particulates emitted annually was cut almost in half during this time.

Part of the problem in evaluating the effectiveness of the Clean Air Act is that causal factors external to the Act also play a role in shaping the number of pollutants emitted. For example, during a recession, when industrial output is low, there is naturally less pollution than when industrial output is high. When gasoline is in short supply or is inordinately expensive, travel by individual vehicles may be substantially less than when gasoline is plentiful and inexpensive. When vehicular use declines, the total amount of emissions from nonstationary sources is reduced. Weather conditions also have a significant impact. When large masses of air are stagnant over urban areas, the concentration of pollutants in the air increases.

The 1990 Clean Air Act Amendments

Congress was faced with a challenging problem when it came time to reauthorize the Clean Air Act. On the one hand, as noted above, there was considerable evidence that air quality had improved significantly under the Clean Air Act. On the other hand, it was becoming clear to many people that further incremental gains were going to become much more costly per unit of pollution reduced. So Congress decided to try a new approach, one in line with the newly articulated policy of trying to take greater advantage of market forces.

Under the 1990 Clean Air Act amendments, Congress required the EPA to establish an emissions trading program that would cut the emissions of sulfur dioxide in half by the year 2000. Under the program, the EPA would auction a given number of sulfur dioxide allowances each year. A holder could emit one ton of sulfur dioxide for each allowance. Firms holding the allowances would be able to use them to emit pollutants and could "bank" unused allowances for the next year or sell those allowances to other firms. The idea behind the program was that those firms for which emission reduction was the cheapest would reduce their emissions extensively, whereas those firms for which emission reduction was extremely expensive would find it more efficient to buy allowances. Total emissions would fall, because every succeeding year the number of allowances issued would be reduced.

It is too early to really know how successful the program will be. The first auction of allowances was held in the fall of 1992. There were no major problems with the initial auction.

Regulating Hazardous Waste and Toxic Substances

When people think about pollution, they often think of air and water pollution. Yet the land can be polluted too, often with tragic results. Perhaps the most dramatic instance of land pollution was the Love Canal incident.

In 1978, state officials ordered the emergency evacuation of 240 families from the Love Canal area of Niagara Falls, New York. This residential area had been built over the site of a Hooker Chemical Company dump that contained over 300 million tons of industrial waste. The sharply increased incidences of asthma, urinary tract disease, miscarriages, and birth defects among the residents were attributed to exposure to the waste.

Most of us want to enjoy the products that technology has developed during the last 50 years. But what price are we willing to pay for these amenities? Most of us do not wish to pay

the price paid by the former residents of Love Canal. Nor would any of us want to be the businessperson whose decisions were partially responsible for such a tragedy.

Until the mid-1970s, most people were content to take advantage of newly available products without giving much thought to the by-products engendered by their manufacture. Most businesspeople were primarily concerned about creating new products and using new technology to increase production and profits. Then came a growing awareness of the potential health and environmental risks posed by the waste created in the production process. In addition to the problems of waste, some of the new products themselves and their newly created chemical components were proving to be harmful.

The health risks from these chemicals and waste include a plethora of cancers, respiratory ailments, skin diseases, and birth defects. Environmental risks include not only pollution of the air and water but also unexpected explosions and soil contamination. Species of plants and animals may be threatened with extinction.

During the mid-1970s, Congress began to take a closer look at regulating waste and toxic materials. One of the problems regulators face in this area, however, is a lack of scientific knowledge concerning the impact of many chemicals on human health. We know that exposure to many chemicals causes cancer in laboratory animals. We are unable, however, to ascertain the marginal impact of each increment of exposure. For example, we know that saccharin in some quantity can cause cancer in humans, but we do not know what quantity or whether especially sensitive people may be affected by substantially smaller amounts. Given the limited knowledge we have, should we ban such substances altogether? Should they be produced with warning labels required in conjunction with their sale? As the reader will see, Congress has responded to these and related problems in a variety of ways.

Four primary acts are designed to control hazardous waste and toxic substances: (1) the Resource Conservation and Recovery Act (RCRA); (2) the Comprehensive Environmental Response, Compensation, and Liability Act (CERCLA) as amended by the Superfund Amendment and Reauthorization Act (SARA); (3) the Toxic Substance Control Act (TSCA), and (4) the Federal Insecticide, Fungicide, and Rodenticide Act (FIFRA).

Resource Conservation and Recovery Act

In 1976, Congress enacted the Resource Conservation and Recovery Act. While RCRA regulates both hazardous and nonhazardous waste, its primary emphasis is on controlling **hazardous waste**.

When Congress enacted RCRA, it could have focused on encouraging reductions in the volume of waste generated. Such reductions might have been achieved by taxation, by a permit system, or by the imposition of direct limits on the amount of waste a firm could generate. Instead of attempting to force a reduction in the volume of waste, however, Congress decided to regulate the treatment, storage, and disposal of hazardous waste. The reason for the decision was the belief that it was not necessarily the creation of waste that was the problem, but rather the improper disposal of such waste. Also, some believed that making firms pay the true costs of safe disposal would provide the financial incentive for them to generate less waste.

The Manifest Program The most well-known component of the RCRA is its manifest program, which is designed to provide "cradle to grave" regulation of hazardous waste. A waste material may be considered hazardous, and thus fall under the manifest program, in one of three ways. First, it may be listed by the EPA as a hazardous waste. Second, the generator may choose to designate the waste as hazardous. Finally, according to RCRA, a hazardous waste may be "garbage, refuse, or sludge or any other waste ma-

terial that has any one of the four defining characteristics: ignitability, corrosivity, reactivity, or toxicity."

Once a waste is designated as hazardous, it falls under RCRA's manifest program. Under this program, generators of hazardous waste must maintain records called *manifests*. These manifests contain the amount and type of waste produced, how it is to be transported, and how it will ultimately be disposed of. Some wastes cannot be disposed of in landfills at all. Others must receive chemical or biological treatment to reduce toxicity or stabilize them before they can be landfilled. If the waste is transported to a landfill, both the transporter and the owner of the disposal site must certify their respective sections of the manifest and return it to the creator of the waste. The purpose of these manifests is to provide a record of the location and amount of all hazardous wastes and to ensure that such waste will be properly transported and disposed of.

All those involved in the transportation and disposal of hazardous waste must be certified by the EPA in accordance with standards established under RCRA. These standards are very stringent, as evidenced by the fact that there has been only one hazardous waste landfill licensed since 1980.

RCRA Amendments of 1984 Congress amended RCRA in 1984. The amendments demonstrate a lack of confidence in the EPA's ability to enforce broad, policy-oriented legislation. The amendments resemble administrative rules rather than statutes because they are very specific and leave the agency only small amounts of discretion. The primary effect of the amendments is to make landfills, or hazardous waste dumps, a last resort for the disposal of many types of waste. Advanced treatment, recycling, incineration, and other forms of hazardous waste treatment are all assumed to be preferable to land disposal. To implement this preference for alternative waste disposal methods, some wastes were banned from landfill disposal after 1988. The EPA is also required to study other types of waste to determine whether their disposal in landfills should be prohibited.

Enforcement of RCRA RCRA is enforced by the EPA. However, states may set up their own programs as long as these programs are at least as stringent as the federal program. If a state takes responsibility for regulating its hazardous wastes, the EPA gives the state the first opportunity to prosecute violators. This procedure is consistent with the EPA's enforcement of other environmental laws.

If the state fails to act within 30 days, the EPA takes action to enforce the state's requirements. The EPA may issue informal warnings; seek temporary or permanent injunctions, criminal penalties, and/or civil penalties of up to $25,000 per day for the violation of an administrative order; or announce other penalties that the EPA administrator finds appropriate.

Comprehensive Environmental Response Compensation and Liability Act, as Amended

If the RCRA manifest program is followed, waste will be disposed of properly and there will be no more incidents like Love Canal. However, prior to RCRA's enactment, there was extensive unregulated dumping. Something needed to be done to take care of cleaning up the sites created by improper disposal.

To alleviate the problems created by improper waste disposal, Congress passed the Comprehensive Environmental Response and Liability Act of 1980. CERCLA authorized the creation of a **superfund**, derived primarily from taxes on corporations in industries that create significant amounts of hazardous waste. The money in the superfund was to be used by the EPA or state and local governments to cover the cost of cleaning up leaks from hazardous waste disposal sites when their owners cannot be located or are unable or unwilling to pay for a cleanup.

The superfund also provides money for emergency responses to hazardous waste spills other than oil spills. When an owner is found after a cleanup, or initially displays an unwillingness to pay for it, the EPA may sue to recover the costs of the cleanup. Under CERCLA, liability for cleanup extends beyond the immediate owner. So-called *potentially responsible parties* may also be held liable. They include (1) present owners or operators of a facility in which hazardous materials have been stored, (2) owners or operators of the facility at the time the waste was deposited, (3) hazardous waste generators, and (4) parties that transported the hazardous waste to the site.

Initially, it was unclear whether lenders that foreclosed on a property could be potentially responsible parties. Then, especially after the 1990 case of *United States v. Fleet Factors*, the courts appeared to be taking a very broad interpretation of CERCLA and seemed willing to hold lenders that foreclosed on such property liable. Then, in 1992, the EPA issued a rule clarifying lender liability to some extent, making it appear that if lenders foreclosed and quickly divested themselves of property, they would not be held liable under CERCLA, as long as the lenders never participated in any management decisions with respect to use of the land.

After several years of debate over the effectiveness of the superfund, CERCLA was amended in late 1986 by the Superfund Amendment and Reauthorization Act of 1986 (SARA). These amendments provided more stringent cleanup requirements and increased the superfund to $8.5 billion—an amount to be generated primarily by taxes on petroleum, chemical feedstocks, imported chemical derivatives, and a new "environmental tax" on corporations. The remainder of the money was to come from general revenues, recoveries, and interest.

Successful actions under CERCLA to recover costs have been less frequent than originally hoped. The superfund was originally intended to be self-replenishing, but the subsequent addition of funds through SARA made the lack of self-replenishment apparent. However, a substantial amount of money has still been recovered. Between 1980 and 1989, potentially responsible parties agreed to contribute over $642 million toward cleanups at 441 sites. In 1990, the EPA recovered over $1 billion in private-party contributions to cleanups of superfund sites!

Sites earmarked for cleanup with superfund resources are placed on the National Priorities List (NPL), a compilation of the most contaminated waste sites. As of November 1992, 1252 sites had been listed. During fiscal year 1992, cleanup was completed at 86 sites, more than the total number of sites cleaned up during the first 11 years of the superfund's existence.[1]

The cleanup of hazardous waste sites presents a tremendous challenge, not only because of the cost but also because there is a need for further development of cost-effective cleanup technology. Whether we can meet that challenge remains to be seen.

Toxic Substance Control Act

As mentioned earlier, toxic substances are found not only as by-products of hazardous waste but also as integral parts of products that we use daily. Because these products greatly enhance our lives, toxic substances will probably remain a part of the environment. Neither RCRA nor CERCLA regulates these substances. The Toxic Substance Control Act (TSCA) attempts to fill this regulatory gap. TSCA attempts to ensure that the least amount of damage will be done to human health and the environment while allowing the greatest possible use of chemical substances in commerce.

The term *toxic substances* has not been clearly defined by Congress. However, a review of the types of substances regulated under TSCA suggests that a toxic substance is any chemical or mixture whose manufacture, processing, distribution, use, or disposal may present an unreasonable risk of harm to human health or the environment. That is a broad definition and encompasses a large number of substances. Thus, control of these substances is a major undertaking.

Regulating Existing Chemicals   TSCA provides a system for reviewing "old" chemicals—those in use in commerce at the time the Act was passed. All those chemicals will eventually be reviewed to ensure that they do not present an unreasonable risk to human health or the environment. Reviewing these chemicals, however, is not a high priority of the EPA, to a large extent because many people believe that if a chemical used in commerce today poses a problem, we will soon have some indication of that problem. Once a chemical seems to be causing a risk, it will receive review by the EPA.

Regulating New Chemicals   The primary impact of TSCA comes from those provisions that apply to future production. The Act establishes a procedure for the evaluation of the environmental impact of all chemicals, except those regulated under other statutes such as the Food, Drug, and Cosmetic Act.

Under TSCA, every manufacturer of a new chemical must give the EPA a premanufacturing notice (PMN) at least 90 days before the first use of the substance in commerce. The PMN contains data and test results showing the risk posed by the chemical. The EPA then determines whether the substance presents an unreasonable risk to health or whether further testing is required to establish the substance's safety. The manufacture of the product is banned when the risk of harm is unacceptable. If more testing is required, a manufacturer of the product must wait until the tests have been satisfactorily completed. Otherwise, manufacture may begin as scheduled.

The chemicals industry often argues that TSCA establishes a costly, burdensome set of procedures. Many new and potentially useful chemicals will never reach the market because it is more cost-effective for the firm to invest its capital in projects other than new-product development.

Some environmentalists are critical of the law for another reason. Those seeking to produce the chemical are the ones responsible for providing the test data that the EPA reviews to determine the chemical's safety. Thus, producers might have an incentive not to transmit all relevant data to the EPA. Despite the existence of the potential of nondisclosure, most observers agree that from a financial perspective it makes sense to place the burden of providing safety data on the manufacturer. The EPA has neither the financial nor the human resources to provide such data.

Federal Insecticide, Fungicide, and Rodenticide Act

One category of toxic substances that has been singled out for special regulatory treatment is pesticides. *Pesticides* are defined as substances designed to prevent, destroy, repel, or mitigate any pest, or to be used as plant regulators or defoliants. Insecticides, fungicides, and rodenticides are all forms of pesticides.

Pesticides are obviously highly important. Their use results in increased crop yields. Some pesticides kill disease-carrying insects. Others eradicate pests, such as mosquitoes, that simply cause us discomfort. Yet many pesticides have harmful side effects. Some may cause damage to all species of life. When a pesticide does not degrade quickly, it may be consumed along with the crops on which it was used, potentially resulting in damage to the consumer's health. Or the pesticide may get washed into a stream to contaminate marine life and animals that drink from the stream. Once the pesticide gets into the food chain, it may do inestimable harm.

CONCEPT SUMMARY
Focal Points of Environmental Law

Environmental Impact Statement

A statement filed any time there is a major federal activity that may have a significant impact on the environment. The EIS is an important decision-making tool because it reveals the significant environmental impact that may result if an action is undertaken, as well as alternative actions and their potential consequences.

National Ambient Air Quality Standards

A two-tiered set of standards developed for the primary conventional air pollutants. Primary standards are designed to protect human health and secondary standards protect the human environment.

Superfund

A theoretically self-replenishing fund generated initially by taxes on corporations that generate hazardous waste. The fund is used to clean up hazardous waste sites and emergency spills.

In 1972, Congress passed the Federal Insecticide, Fungicide, and Rodenticide Act to control pesticide use. Under FIFRA, in order for a pesticide to be sold in the United States, it must first be registered and properly labeled. A pesticide will be registered when (1) its composition warrants the claims made for it, (2) its label complies with FIFRA, and (3) the manufacturer provides data to demonstrate that the pesticide can perform its intended function, in accordance with commonly accepted practice, without presenting unreasonable risks to human health and the environment.

A pesticide will receive general-use registration if it can be sold without any restrictions. Restricted-use registration will be granted if the pesticide will not cause an unreasonable risk only if its use is restricted in some manner. Typical restrictions include allowing the pesticide to be used only by certified applicators, allowing the pesticide to be sold only during certain times of the year, or limiting sales to certain regions of the country or to certain quantities.

Registration is good for only 5 years, at which time the manufacturer must apply for a new registration. If at any time prior to the end of the registration period, the EPA obtains evidence that a pesticide poses a risk to human health or the environment, the agency may institute proceedings to cancel or suspend the registration.

The EPA believes that progress under FIFRA has been significant, although some are critical of the Act. Since FIFRA's enactment, thirty-four pesticide registrations have been canceled and about sixty harmful chemicals have been eliminated from use as active ingredients in pesticides.[2]

Review Questions and Problems

Key Terms

environmental impact
  statement
ambient air quality
  standard

hazardous waste
superfund

Discussion Questions

1. Why is tort law an ineffective means for controlling pollution?

2. Why is the RCRA manifest program referred to as a "cradle to grave" system of protection?

3. If a manufacturer wants to use a new chemical in commerce, what must it do to be in compliance with the Toxic Substance Control Act?

Review Problems

1. The Army Corps of Engineers wants to deepen an 11-foot-long natural drainage ditch along its complete length. The cost is estimated at $10,000. Must an EIS be filed before the action is taken?

2. The Zardus Bank loaned money to Malmon Corporation for the purchase of a 10-acre plot of land. Zardus held a mortgage on the property. Malmon went bankrupt shortly thereafter. Zardous foreclosed on the property and resold it within 15 days. Some 5 years later, when the property became a candidate for cleanup with CERCLA superfund dollars, the EPA tried to join Zardus Bank as a potentially responsible party. Do you believe the bank can be held liable?

3. Maxtell Corporation uses about 50 gallons a day of a highly corrosive battery acid as a cleaning agent in its production process. It collects the used acid and funnels it through a pipe out into a pond located entirely on company property. The pond, in fact, was dug to serve as a place in which to dispose of the acid and other wastes that could not be incinerated or recycled. Is Maxtell violating any federal environmental regulations?

4. Ajax Corporation was required under an SIP to reduce its particulate emissions by 10 percent by the end of the year. It failed to make such a reduction and defended its behavior on the ground that it was economically not feasible to install the necessary technology to meet the standard. Is Ajax's defense valid?

Case Problems

1. At approximately the same time that a homeowner began construction of her home, Exxon began construction of a plant 700 feet north of the home. Both were completed at approximately the same time. The plant was noisy and emitted noxious odors that gave the homeowner headaches and kept her friends from visiting her. Did the homeowner have any recourse against Exxon?

2. The Texas Department of Transportation proposed two highway projects to complete a beltway around a city. While considerable state money and time were spent on the project, no federal funds were requested or federal permits sought. Federal officials stated that they had no interest in the project. A community group opposed the project because of a fear of adverse environmental consequences. The group sought an injunction pending filing of an EIS. Did the court grant the injunction? Why or why not?

3. As the U.S. Secretary of Defense prepared to close certain military bases, an action was brought to compel the filing of an environmental impact statement. Was the EIS required?

4. The Frezzo brothers operated a mushroom farm. As part of their business, they maintained a compost heap to provide a growing base for their mushrooms. The compost consisted mostly of hay and horse manure mixed with water for fermentation. Runoff from the heap flowed into a holding tank for recycling. Another runoff system carried rainwater through a pipe to a channel box on an adjoining property and on into a tributary of White Creek. Water samples taken from the channel box showed high concentrations of pollutants characteristic of manure. The Frezzo brothers had no discharge permit. Were they in violation of the FWPCA?

Footnotes

1. Council on Environmental Quality, *Environmental Quality*, 23rd Annual Report of the Council on Environmental Quality, 1993, p. 127.

2. Nancy Kubasek and Gary Silverman, *Environmental Law*, Englewood Cliffs, N.J.: Prentice-Hall, 1990, p. 180.

PART **X**

SPECIAL TOPICS

58

International Business

The International Environment

Sources of Law

International Business: Trade

International Business: Investments

The International Environment

Because international business has become so important both to individual nations and to the business firms that manufacture products or provide services, some study of its scope and character is essential for today's business student. This chapter examines the laws and legal environment affecting both international trade and international investing.

After briefly noting the current status of foreign trade and investment in and by the United States, we review the different sources of law affecting the conduct of international business. The chapter then discusses in detail the laws affecting both international trade, such as export controls and licensing restrictions, and international investing, whether conducted through joint ventures or direct investing.

International Trade

Despite a great deal of talk about protectionism, the most recent figures show that the value of world trade continues to increase. As Figure 58-1 depicts, according to the International Monetary Fund, global trade (exports and imports) peaked at a level of $3.67 trillion in 1992—approximately double the 1985 total. Note too that the industrial countries consistently account for approximately 75 percent of the dollar value of world trade.

Even though the United States remains the world's largest trader, its role in the world's trade is significantly different from what it was several decades ago. In 1960, it accounted for approximately 18 percent of world exports and 12.5 percent of world imports. Three decades later, its position had practically flip-flopped. In 1990, it accounted for almost 12 percent of world exports and over 15 percent of world imports. Germany and Japan are the second and third largest exporters, together accounting for over 20 percent of the world's total.

Figure 58-2 depicts the changing relationship between the United States and its trading partners over a period of 25 years. Since the late 1960s, the share of trade between the United States and the nations of the Pacific Rim has nearly doubled. The countries of the Pacific Rim—stretching from New Zealand and Australia on the south through Singapore, Malaysia, and Thailand to Hong Kong, China, South Korea, and Japan in the north—accounted for 35 percent of the total U.S. trade in 1992.

International Investment

While there are continuing opportunities to conduct international business through trade, in recent years many businesses have focused on investments rather than on trade. These firms do so for several reasons. First, there is a more or less logical progression from trade to investment.

FIGURE 58-1

Trends in World Trade (In trillions of dollars)

Source: Direction of Trade Statistics Yearbook, 1992 (Washington, D.C.: U.S. International Monetary Fund).

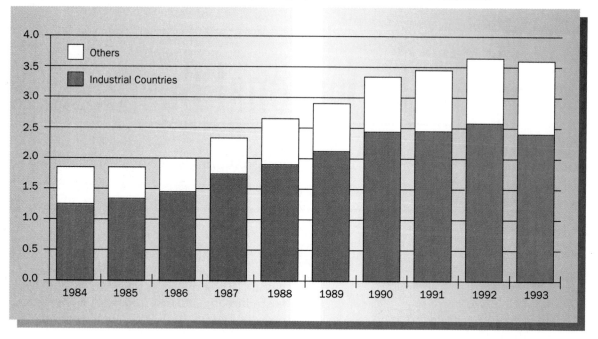

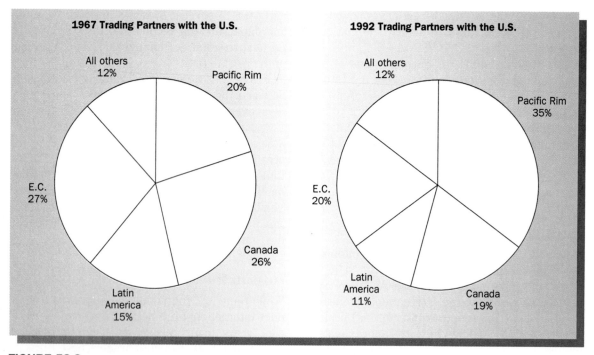

FIGURE 58-2

U.S. Trading Partners: 1967 and 1992

Source: U.S. Department of Commerce (Washington, D.C.: U.S. Government Printing Office).

Once a firm does enough trade volume, it may find that investment in the new market area has become more economical than export trade. Second, once enough sales are made in a market to obtain a competitive position with local firms, a foreign firm may find that to keep its market share, it needs to be continually present in that market. Finally, investing inside a country or region may be a way of avoiding protectionist measures aimed at those whose products originate outside a country's borders.

Foreign investment can include both portfolio investment and direct investment. **Portfolio investment** is the purchase of stocks, bonds, and notes for the purpose of obtaining a return on the investment. Portfolio investment in the United States by individuals, corporations, and governments from outside the United States provides a very significant source of funds flowing into the country.

Direct investment occurs when an investor not only invests funds, but also participates in the management of the firm in which the investment has been made. Further, when an investment in the stock of a particular firm reaches the stage where it accounts for at least 25 percent of that firm's total stock, most scholars would characterize the investment as a direct investment rather than as a portfolio investment. Our focus in this chapter is on direct investment rather than on portfolio investments.

Although figures on the total amount of worldwide direct investment abroad are difficult to determine, The *Economist* found the 1990 total to be over $200 billion.[1] Investment by U.S.-based corporations accounted for more than 40 percent of that total. While most of the foreign direct investment is placed in industrialized countries, the largest increase in direct investment in recent years has occurred in Mexico, Central American countries, and Pacific Rim countries.

Twenty-five of the 500 largest U.S. corporations derive at least half of their total profits from outside the United States. Coca-Cola, IBM, American Standard, and International Harvester exemplify this group of multinational corporations with significant foreign investments.

The United States is also an attractive place for foreign-based corporations to expand their operations. According to *Forbes* magazine, seven of the top ten private sources of direct foreign investment in the United States in 1993 were from European firms. The top ten also included one firm from Canada, one from Venezuela, and one from Japan.[2]

Although the annual amount of new investments has declined significantly since the peak years of 1988 and 1989, the total book value of all foreign investment in the United States exceeded $400 billion in 1990, almost five times the 1980 total of $83 billion. Figure 58-3 illustrates the changing composition of that investment since 1980.

We know that firms engaged in international business encounter significant legal, financing, and marketing problems. Why do businesses go into other countries? Comments made over two decades ago by the chairman of the board of the RCA Corporation provide both a glimpse of the degree to which a company can be internationalized and some reasons that the conduct of international business has become so important:

RCA is stepping up its activities in the Far East in a number of significant ways and is also evaluating business opportunities in Eastern Europe and the Middle East. Among the solid reasons for seeking to expand abroad is our conviction that it would be unwise not to do so. Except in rare instances, national economies tend to grow at different rates and fluctuate at different frequencies. In seeking sustained growth and profitability, geographical diversification can be just as important as product diversification to a company like RCA.

Moreover, there are no natural boundaries for such RCA businesses as electronics, communications, car rentals, and prepared foods. Competition is worldwide. We must face our competitors abroad as well as at home if we expect to remain a leader. Finally, we increase our competence by operating internationally. This country is by no means the sole repository of technological skill or business capability. There is a constant exchange of ideas and experience with associates and customers abroad. We benefit from this give-and-take by gaining greater insight to apply to our operations elsewhere, including domestic market. Beyond considerations of self-interest, your management is committed to liberalized trade and international cooperation. Companies like ours can play a constructive part in furthering

FIGURE 58-3

Source of Foreign Direct Investment in the United States: 1980 and 1990

Source: Chart prepared by U.S. Bureau of the Census, *Statistical Abstract of the United States: 1991* (Washington, D.C.: U.S. Bureau of the Census).

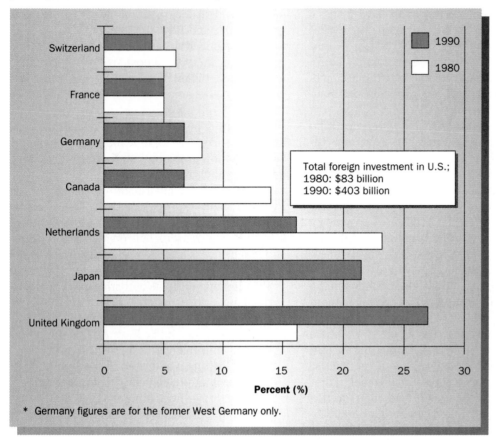

* Germany figures are for the former West Germany only.

these objectives. They serve as vehicle for the free flow of goods and capital, the evolution of living standards, and the wider distribution of managerial skills and advanced technology.[3]

Nations and International Business Firms

The increasing role of foreign firms in the economic life of a nation has led to a loss of power for the host national government. As early as the 1950s governments began to realize that local businesses that were subsidiaries of foreign corporations could pursue objectives that were in conflict with those of the governments. This realization led to the imposition of a variety of laws, administrative rules, and investment codes by some national governments. Other national governments wanted to welcome the foreign in-

vestors who held out the promise of additional jobs and improved economic conditions. These nations modified their tax laws, currency exchange regulations, and administrative regulations to attract the multinational enterprise.

Thus different nations have different policies and laws that affect the conduct of business in their country by foreign-based firms. Countries also seek to regulate how firms in their own country conduct international business activities. At times exports are encouraged, whereas at other times they are restricted. Foreign investment may be promoted or subjected to significant legal controls. Even within one country, some laws may promote international business, whereas others seek to control it. Some countries have banded together in regional associations, granting to those regional authorities some of their lawmaking authority. A few international organizations, such as the International Monetary Fund (IMF) or the United Nations (UN) also can have significant effect on the legal environment affecting firms conducting international business.

Sources of Law

Whenever a firm engages in international business, that firm's activity is regulated by international, regional, and national laws. International laws are developed by international organizations such as the IMF, the World Trade Organization (WTO)—formerly the General Agreement on Tariffs and Trade (GATT)—or the World Bank. Regional laws, on the other hand, are developed by a specific group of nations (such as the European Community, now known as the European Union or EU), whereas national laws emanate from lawmakers within one nation. On the international level, recent international conferences on the law of the sea, environmental problems, and monetary matters provide examples of the continuing international development of new rules, regulations, and laws that affect international business.

International laws also are based in the customs and practices agreed to by countries of the world. The following quote about international law, and its role in the U.S. legal system, is taken from the court's decision in *Zenith Radio Corporation v. Matsushita Electric Industries Company*, 404 F.Supp. 1161, 1178-79 (1980):

> Essentially, international law is a body of consensual principles which have evolved from the customs and practices civilized nations utilize in regulating their relationships. These customs have great moral force, and are often cited approvingly by domestic courts. The United States, for example, adheres to the frequently quoted view that "[i]nternational law is part of our law." However, international law must give way when it conflicts with or is superseded by a federal statute or treaty, made supreme under Article VI of the Constitution, to the extent permitted by the due process clause of the Fifth Amendment. It is therefore possible that the United States might find it necessary, in order to enforce domestic law, to violate international principles. In order to avoid such conflict to the extent possible, it has been said that "an act of Congress ought never to be construed to violate the law of na-

tions, if any other possible construction remains."

Much of international law is concerned with delineating the respective jurisdictional spheres of nations. Five principles govern the exercise of jurisdiction by a nation: the territorial principle, by which jurisdiction is based on the place where the offense was committed; the nationality principle, based on the nationality of the offender; the protective principle, which covers conduct which threatens the national security or operation of governmental functions, such as counterfeiting and falsification of official documents; the universality principle, under which the custody of a perpetrator of a crime of universal interest, such as piracy, provides jurisdiction; and the passive personality principle, based on the nationality of the victim. As to jurisdiction over economic regulatory matters, only the territorial principle is applicable. That principle, however, admits of two interpretations. Viewed subjectively, a state may extend its jurisdiction over persons found within its borders who violate its laws there. Under what the law styles an "objective interpretation," however, a state has jurisdiction over acts which take effect within its borders, regardless of the location of the actor.

On a regional level, we find an increasing number of regional institutions with legal authority in or affecting that region. The European Community (now known as the European Union), which began in 1957, is the oldest, best known and most comprehensive of the regional organizations. The Andean Common Market (referred to as the Andean Group) and the Mercado Commun del Ser Mercosur (Mercosur) are regional integration associations in South America. The Caricom alliance of thirteen Caribbean nations, the Association of South East Asian Nations (ASEAN), the Gulf-Cooperation Council and the North American Free Trade Area exemplify other attempts to attain some level of regional economic integration. While the regional organizations provide a larger forum than the nation-state institutions, they are also more manageable and cohesive than international bodies.

The business enterprise conducting an international venture soon realizes that instead of dealing with the laws of one nation, it may have to deal with several overlapping and conflicting national laws that attempt to control or regulate a transaction. Thus the expansion of business abroad is accompanied by increasingly complex legal problems. The transition from doing business domestically to doing business internationally involves a change from dealing with sources of law that are generally quite stable and well known (the national and state or local rules of one county) to dealing with legal sources that may be ever-changing and unfamiliar. These sources include the national laws of a foreign country, regional rules enforced in several countries in specified geographical areas, and international standards from international organizations and institutions.

National and International Problems

A national legal problem is approached by attempting to fit the facts into a known legal framework. While doing business within the United States, a business manager assumes the existence of rules and principles established by a legislature or an administrative body and interpreted by a court with the power to resolve disputes. The international community has few such institutions that are organized for solving business disputes. The national (and perhaps regional) rules and principles that govern a transaction occurring in a foreign country may be based on social, political, and economic values with which the U.S. businessperson is unfamiliar. The role of law and the legal system itself may be totally different from that of the domestic environment with which the business is familiar.

Prior to the disintegration of the former Soviet Union, there was a stark contrast in the way that business was done in the Soviet bloc and in free market economies. In countries which were once part of the Soviet bloc, the situation has changed and continues to change drastically. Recent years have witnessed the passage of new foreign investment laws, changing concepts regarding ownership of property, and the emergence of private firms and entrepreneurs now entering spheres of economic activity that were once controlled by state monopolies. The structure of the legal systems in new republics, such as Latvia and Lithuania, and in countries with new leadership, such as Hungary and Poland, is still in flux. In the Czech Republic, Slovakia, and what was once Yugoslavia, the instability of the legal system constitutes a major deterrent to foreign investment. The evolving situation must be closely monitored by firms engaged in international business activities.

Classifications of World's National Legal Systems

The national laws of the country in which a firm does business usually have the greatest impact on that firm's activities. While there are variations among the laws of many countries, most laws can be considered to belong to one of three major legal systems:

1. The Romano–Germanic system (the civil law or code law found in countries such as France and Germany)
2. The Islamic system (found in Pakistan and many Mideast countries)
3. The common law system (found in countries such as the United States, England, and Australia).

Despite the different legal systems found throughout the world, most laws are found in custom, judicial decisions, or legislative sources. Although similar sources of law are found in the different legal systems, there are significant differences in how each legal system makes use of those sources. In the common law legal system found in the United States the judicial decisions are clearly recognized as a source of law. Further, the courts are vested with the power to interpret acts of the legislative branch and to declare them to be null and void if they conflict with the Constitution. In a civil law or code law legal system, such as that found in France, the role of the courts in interpreting legislation is much more restrictive. There, it is the administrators, not the court judges, who initially interpret legislative enactments. Additionally, the court decisions are not given the same status as are the legislative enactments that are based on provisions in the code.

There are also important differences in many of the basic substantive law fields. In most of the civil and common law legal systems international business contracts generally are made by privately owned business firms, not by the government. Consequently, public law concepts such as sovereign immunity and the act of state doctrine (both discussed near the end of the chapter) do not intrude into contract law.

In a common law legal system, such as that found in the United States, means are available to change the law as conditions change. New legislation amends outdated statutes, and courts generally are flexible in following or rejecting prior cases that do not apply to current problems. By contrast, in a country with a legal system based primarily on a code or on religious teachings found in a specific source (such as the Koran in the Islamic law or the Talmud in Jewish law), existing laws may be more rigid and less adaptable to change. Finally, the legal institutions in different countries may have varying degrees of independence and authority. The courts may be subservient to the head of the country's government. The legislative body may be composed of people from different political parties or it may be packed with loyal supporters of the government. Even where the letter of the law seems to be similar from country to country, its interpretation, application, and enforceability can differ greatly from a similar law in another country.

National Laws and Extraterritoriality

In addition to encountering national laws that originate in a different legal system from that with which the domestic business is familiar, in some cases more than one nation may have laws that seek to regulate the same transaction. This conflict between laws of different nations usually occurs when the laws of one of the nations seek to have some effect beyond its own territory or boundary; for this reason these laws are referred to as **extraterritorial laws**. Two examples of the extraterritorial reach of national laws are found in provisions of the U.S. income tax laws and antitrust laws.

For example, if a corporation incorporated in a state in the United States derives income from export sales to Germany, license royalties from Brazil, and dividend income from a branch opera-

tion in Japan, all three sources of income will be subject to taxation by the United States. This occurs because the United States asserts worldwide (extraterritorial) jurisdiction over the income earned by corporations located within its territory. Thus the U.S. position is that the income earned by these corporations is subject to U.S. taxation, even if the income was earned outside its territory.

Of course, the country where the income is earned, known as the country of source, generally also seeks to tax this same income. The result is that the income of U.S. corporations can be subject to double taxation, once from the United States and once from the country of source. There are, however, credit provisions in the U.S. tax laws and bilateral treaty agreements between the United States and many other countries that are designed to reduce or eliminate this possible double taxation.

Another example of an extraterritorial law is found in the Sherman Act, which is the keystone of the U.S. antitrust laws. Section 1 of the Sherman Act reads:

> Every contract, combination or conspiracy in restraint of trade or commerce . . . with foreign nations is declared to be illegal.

In 1945 Judge Learned Hand made it clear that the Sherman Act applied to restrictive practices of non-U.S. firms acting abroad if their practices were intended to and did affect imports into the United States. "It is settled law . . . that any state may impose liabilities, even upon persons not within its allegiance for conduct outside its borders which the state reprehends." *United States v. Aluminum Co. of America* 148 F.2d 416, 419 (2d Cir. 1945). In determining whether the United States can assert jurisdiction over acts occurring outside its territory, courts apply the "effects doctrine"; they look at the effect a foreign transaction will have within the United States. In the following case, the court reviews that concept in considering a dispute between a British mining company and a Luxembourg corporation.

CONSOLIDATED GOLD FIELDS PLC V. MINORCO, S.A.

U.S. Court of Appeals, Second Circuit
871 F.2d 252 (1989)

BACKGROUND: Minorco, a Luxemborg corporation, launched a hostile takeover of Gold Fields, a British mining company with significant holdings in the United States. Gold Fields sought a preliminary injunction of the takeover. Gold Fields claimed, among other things, that Minorco violated the antifraud provisions of U.S. securities laws when it failed to disclose to Gold Fields shareholders that Minorco was controlled by individuals and companies from South Africa. Gold Fields contended that this information was material because Minorco's South African ties might prevent Gold Fields from doing business in the several countries which, at the time of this action, were participating in the boycott against South Africa. Minorco argued that U.S. securities antifraud provisions should not be applied in this case because the transaction did not have substantial effects in the United States—only 2.5 percent of Gold Fields shareholders were American residents. The U.S. District Court granted the preliminary injunction against Minorco but ruled that it did not have jurisdiction to rule on the U.S. securities law claim. Minorco appealed.

Newman, Circuit Judge

The antifraud laws of the United States may be given extraterritorial reach whenever a predominantly foreign transaction has substantial effects within the United States. *See Schoenbaum v. Firstbrook; Restatement (Third) of the Foreign Relations Law of the United States* § 402(1)(c) (1987) [hereinafter "Third Restatement"]. In determining whether certain effects qualify as "substantial," courts have been reluctant to apply our laws to transactions that have only remote and indirect effects in the United States, since "it would be . . . erroneous to assume that the legislature always means to go to the full extent permitted" by a literal reading of the anti-fraud laws. *Leasco Data Processing Equipment Corp. v. Maxwell.* As Judge Friendly observed: "When, as here, a court is confronted with transactions that on any view are predominantly foreign, it must seek to determine whether Congress would have wished the precious resources of United States courts and law enforcement agencies to be devoted to them rather than leave the problem to foreign countries." *Bersch v. Drexel Firestone, Inc.*

In applying the so-called "effects" test enunciated in *Schoenbaum*, the District Court determined that the number of Americans holding stock in the allegedly defrauded British company was "insignificant" and that Minorco had taken "whatever steps it could to assure that the tender offer documents would not reach Gold Fields ADR holders." Because Minorco had sent the offering documents to British nominees of American shareholders, the District Court concluded that the transaction between Minorco and Gold Fields had only indirect effects on a relatively small number of Americans. However, the District Court's analysis cannot be reconciled with this Court's prior holding in *Bersch*. In that case, purchasers of common stock of I.O.S., Ltd., a Bahamian corporation, brought a class action for damages, alleging that fraudulent financial statements were included in prospectuses that were used in offerings of 3.95 million shares of I.O.S. stock. The prospectus stated that the shares were not being offered in the United States. Nevertheless, at least 22 United States residents purchased 41,936 shares. Although the record did not indicate how the Americans came to purchase the shares, Judge Friendly assumed that the allegedly misleading documents must have been sent into the United States, and he asserted subject matter jurisdiction on the basis of that assumption.

In this case, the District Court should have asserted jurisdiction once it noted that Minorco knew that the British nominees were required by law to forward the tender offer documents to Gold Fields' shareholders and ADR depository banks in the United States. This "effect" (the transmittal of the documents by the nominees) was clearly a direct and foreseeable result of the conduct outside the territory of the United States. If in *Bersch* we could say that Congress intended American antifraud laws to apply to a transaction involving 41,936 shares owned by 22 American residents, then surely we must come to the same conclusion here, where American residents representing 2.5% of Gold Fields' shareholders owned 5.3 million shares with a market value of about $120 million.

In rejecting subject matter jurisdiction, the District Court relied on *Plessey Co. PLC v. General Electric Co. PLC.* In *Plessey*, the target company sought to compel the bidder to make certain filings with the Securities and Exchange Commission (SEC) under the Williams Act. No allegations of fraud were made. As we observed in *Bersch*, however, the antifraud provisions of American securities laws have broader extraterritorial reach than American filing requirements.

The SEC, which filed a brief as *amicus curiae* supporting subject matter jurisdiction over the fraud claims, nevertheless urges us to direct the District Court to abstain from granting a remedy for reasons of international comity. We decline this suggestion and instead remand the fraud claims to the District Court for further proceedings. It is a settled principle of international and our domestic law that a court may abstain from exercising enforcement jurisdiction when the extraterritorial effect of a particular remedy is so disproportionate to harm within the United States as to offend principles of comity. In determining whether a particular enforcement measure is "reasonably related to the laws or regulations to which they are directed," the American court may take note, for example, of "connections . . . between the regulating state and the person principally responsible for the activity to be regulated" as well as "the extent to which another state may have an interest in regulating the activity." We decline to conduct this inquiry, however, because the record in the District Court is insufficiently developed for us to determine whether plaintiffs' requested remedy for the fraud violations—corrective disclosure of Minorco's ties to South African interests— is warranted. Now that we have determined that the District Court has jurisdiction over the fraud claims, Judge Mukasey should proceed to the merits and, if plaintiffs prevail, conduct additional fact-finding to determine whether an appropriate remedy, consistent with comity principles, may be fashioned in this case.

DECISION: The Circuit Court of Appeals ruled that the federal courts did have jurisdiction to hear Gold Fields' securities law claim against Minorco.

Once a court determines it has the right to assert its jurisdiction, that it can hear and decide a dispute involving actions by foreign corporations occurring outside its territory, the court must then determine whether it should assert its jurisdiction. This is a matter of judicial comity. In the *Timberlane* case that follows, the court considers the comity question as it applies to actions that the plaintiff, a Honduras corporation, said the defendant, a U.S. corporation, did in Honduras to interfere with the foreign commerce of the United States.

Under the principle of **judicial comity**, the courts of one nation may choose to give effect to the laws, judicial decisions, or other government actions of another nation, not as a matter of obligation, but out of deference and respect. For example, a U.S. court might decide that U.S. antitrust laws allow it to assert jurisdiction over a foreign party charged with violating those laws. On the other hand, the court might decide that bringing the foreign party before a U.S. court in a given circumstance might harm fragile international relationships, based on mutual respect, that are necessary for the conduct of international affairs. The court could therefore decide not to hear the case as a matter of judicial comity. *Timberlane* discusses the factors that courts weigh in deciding whether to invoke the doctrine of judicial comity.

TIMBERLANE LUMBER CO. V. BANK OF AMERICA
U.S. Court of Appeals, Ninth Circuit
749 F.2d 1378 (1984)

BACKGROUND: Timberlane Lumber Co. (plaintiff) claimed that soon after it began lumber operations in Honduras, a competing lumber business in Honduras and Bank of America (defendants) conspired to disrupt its efforts. Since Timberlane's business in Honduras was operated in part to export lumber from there to the East Coast of the United States, it claimed that the defendants violated the U.S. antitrust law by interfering with the foreign commerce of the United States. The court had to determine whether the antitrust laws prohibiting acts and conspiracies that restrain foreign commerce applied to conduct occurring outside U.S. borders.

The District Court dismissed the plaintiff's claim because it determined that the actions of the defendants, which took place in Honduras, did not have sufficient effect on the foreign commerce of the United States for its antitrust laws to apply. Timberlane appealed and the Court of Appeals (Timberlane I) vacated the dismissal of the lower court and remanded the case back to it. The District Court again dismissed the case and Timberlane again appealed.

Sneed, Judge

Timberlane I's test undertakes three separate inquiries: (1) the effect or intended effect on the foreign commerce of the United States; (2) the type and magnitude of the alleged illegal behavior; and (3) the appropriateness of exercising extraterritorial jurisdiction in light of considerations of international comity and fairness.

. . . The district court applied *Timberlane's* analysis and, on the basis of its third part, concluded that jurisdiction should not be exercised in this case. Although we agree with the district court's conclusion regarding each part of the *Timberlane I* test, we do not expressly approve all of its analysis. Therefore, we discuss each part of the inquiry as set forth in *Timberlane I.*

[The court went on to find that (1) the defendant's alleged actions would have an effect on the foreign commerce of the United States and (2) the alleged actions were of the type and magnitude to be cognizable as a violation of the Sherman Act—in other words, that the first two prongs of the *Timberland I* test were satisfied. The court went on to consider the third prong of the test:]

3. *As a matter of international comity and fairness, should the extraterritorial jurisdiction of the United States be asserted to cover it?*

Under the third part of *Timberlane I's* analysis, the district court must determine "whether the interests of, and links to, the United States—including the magnitude of the effect on American foreign commerce—are sufficiently strong, vis-a-vis those of other nations, to justify an assertion of extraterritorial authority." This determination requires that a district court consider seven factors. The district court here found that the undisputed facts required that jurisdiction not be exercised in this case. We agree. To support our conclusion each factor will be examined.

a. *The degree of conflict with foreign law or policy*

We must determine whether the extraterritorial enforcement of United States antitrust laws creates an actual or potential conflict with the laws and policies of other nations. Timberlane argues that no conflict exists between United States and Honduran law. We disagree. The application of United States antitrust law in this case creates a potential conflict with the Honduran government's effort to foster a particular type of business climate.

Although Honduras does not have antitrust laws as such, it does have definite policies concerning the character of its commercial climate. To promote economic development and efficiency within its relatively undeveloped economy, the Honduran Constitution and Commercial Code guarantee freedom of action. The Code specifically condemns any laws prohibiting agreements (even among competitors) to restrict or divide commercial activity. Under Honduran law, competitors may agree to allocate geographic or market territories, to restrict price or output, to cut off the source of raw materials, or to limit credit financing to obtain enterprises as long as the contracting parties are not de facto monopolists.

On balance, we believe that the enforcement of United States antitrust laws in this case would lead to a significant conflict with Honduran law and policy. This conflict, unless outweighed by other factors in the comity analysis, is itself a sufficient reason to decline the exercise of jurisdiction over this dispute.

b. *The nationality or allegiance of the parties and the locations of principal places of business of corporations*

Next we should consider the citizenship of the parties and witnesses involved in the alleged illegal conduct. In this case, with only one exception, all of the named parties are United States citizens or nationals. But it is also true that "[a]ll of the crucial percipient witnesses to the incidents were either Honduran citizens or residents." We believe, therefore, that the citizenship of the parties weighs slightly in favor of the exercise of jurisdiction.

c. *The extent to which enforcement by either state can be expected to achieve compliance*

The weighing of this factor yields no clear answer. Of course, any judgment against Bank of America could easily be enforced in a United States court. Whether such a judgment could be enforced as easily in Honduras is less certain. We believe that the enforcement factor tips slightly in favor of the assertion of jurisdiction in this case.

d. *The relative significance of effects on the United States as compared with those elsewhere*

A more definitive answer emerges when we compare the effect of the alleged illegal conduct on the foreign commerce of the United States with its effect abroad. The insignificance of the effect on the foreign commerce of the United States when compared with the substantial effect in Honduras suggests federal jurisdiction should not be exercised.

A comparison of Honduran lumber imports to both United States imports and total United States lumber consumption is instructive.

. . .

The actual effect of Timberlane's potential operations on United States foreign commerce is insubstantial, even in the narrow pine lumber market. In comparison, the effects of its activity on the considerably smaller Honduran lumber markets would have been much greater. . . . We believe that the relative significance of effects in this case weighs strongly against the exercise of jurisdiction.

e. *The extent to which there is explicit purpose to harm or affect American commerce*

Timberlane has not demonstrated that Bank of America had any particular interest in affecting United States commerce.

f. *The foreseeability of such effect*

A court should also consider whether, at the time of the alleged illegal behavior, the defendant should have foreseen an effect on the foreign commerce of the United States. Aside from the fact that American commerce has not been substantially affected, Timberlane has not shown that Bank of America should have foreseen the consequences of its actions. We do not believe that a reasonable investor would have foreseen the minimal effect that has occurred here. This weighs against the exercise of jurisdiction.

g. *The relative importance to the violations charged of conduct within the United States as compared with conduct abroad*

Finally, a court should consider the location of the alleged illegal conduct in order to assess the appropriateness of the exercise of extraterritorial jurisdiction. In this case both parties agree that virtually all of the illegal activity occurred in Honduras. This factor clearly weighs against the exercise of jurisdiction.

h. *Resolving the Seven Factor Test*

It follows that all but two of the factors in *Timberlane I's* comity analysis indicate that we should refuse to exercise jurisdiction over this antitrust case.

DECISION: In this opinion the Court of Appeals upheld the dismissal of the plaintiff's claim.

Legal Problems in Doing Business with Foreign Governments

In the United States most domestic and international business activities are conducted primarily by private corporations. These corporations, owned by institutional and individual shareholders and managed by company officers and directors, are recognized as legally separate from the government. In other countries of the world, particularly those that still have socialistic or communistic governments, most international business transactions are performed by the governments or by separate corporations that are totally owned and operated or controlled by the government.

Thus, the U.S. business manager often finds that the "business manager" with whom he or she deals in conducting international business is a representative of a foreign government. Several unique legal problems occur when one or more of the parties to an international business transaction are agents or representatives of a government. Such problems often involve two important doctrines: the *doctrine of sovereign immunity* and the *act of state doctrine.*

The **doctrine of sovereign immunity**, developed by international custom, holds that the courts of one nation generally do not have jurisdiction to adjudicate suits against another nation. An important exception to this doctrine exists for controversies involving commerce. Under the **act of state doctrine**, courts are to refrain from adjudicating politically sensitive controversies that would require the court to rule on the legality of a foreign nation's actions. Although the two doctrines sound very similar, they are different in their scope and effect. These differences are explained in the *OPEC* case, which follows.

INTERNATIONAL ASSOCIATION OF MACHINISTS, ETC. v. OPEC

U.S. Court of Appeals, Ninth Circuit
649 F.2d 1354 (1981)

BACKGROUND: The International Association of Machinists and Aerospace Workers (IAM) felt that its members were adversely affected by the high price of petroleum in the United States. Believing the high prices were caused by the price-fixing activities of the Organization of Petroleum Exporting Countries (OPEC), the IAM as plaintiffs brought suit against OPEC and its member nations (defendants), alleging that the price-fixing activities violated U.S. antitrust laws. Even though the defendants did not appear in court or recognize its jurisdiction to hear the case, the District Court ordered various parties to provide it with information and to argue the case on their behalf. At the close of the trial the District Court granted judgment in favor of the defendants and the plaintiffs appealed.

Choy, Circuit Judge

A. Sovereign Immunity

In the international sphere each state is viewed as an independent sovereign, equal in sovereignty to all other states. It is said that an equal holds no power of sovereignty over an equal. Thus the doctrine of sovereign immunity: the courts of one state generally have no jurisdiction to entertain suits against another state. This rule of international law developed by custom among nations. Also by custom, an exception developed for the commercial activities of a state. The former concept of absolute sovereign immunity gave way to a restrictive view. Under the restrictive theory of sovereign immunity, immunity did not exist for commercial activities since they were seen as non-sovereign.

The court below defined OPEC's activity as follows:

[I]t is clear that the nature of the activity engaged in by each of these OPEC member countries is the establishment by a sovereign state of the terms and conditions for the removal of a prime natural resource—to wit, crude oil—from its territory.

. . . The trial judge reasoned that, according to international law, the development and control of natural resources is a prime governmental function. . . . The opinion cites several resolutions of the United Nations' General Assembly, which the United States supported, and the United States Constitution, Art. 4, §3, cl. 2, which treat the control of natural resources as governmental acts.

B. The Act of State Doctrine

The act of state doctrine declares that a United States court will not adjudicate a politically sensitive dispute which would require the court to judge the legality of the sovereign act of a foreign state. This doctrine was expressed by the Supreme Court in *Underhill v. Hernandez*, 168 U.S. 250, 252 (1897):

Every sovereign State is bound to respect the independence of every other sovereign State, and the courts of one country will not sit in judgment on the acts of the government of another done within its own territory.

The doctrine recognizes the institutional limitations of the courts and the peculiar requirements of successful foreign relations. To participate adeptly in the global community, the United States must speak with one voice and pursue a careful and deliberate foreign policy. The political branches of our government are able to consider the competing economic and political considerations and respond to the public will in order to carry on foreign relations in accordance with the best interests of the country as a whole. . . .

When the courts engage in piecemeal adjudication of the legality of the sovereign acts of states, they risk disruption of our country's international diplomacy.

The act of state doctrine is similar to the political question doctrine in domestic law. It requires that the courts defer to the legislative and executive branches when those branches are better equipped to resolve a politically sensitive question. . . .

The Supreme Court has stated that the act of state doctrine arises out of the basic relationships between branches of government in a system of separation of powers. . . . The doctrine as formulated in past decisions expresses the strong sense of the Judicial Branch that its engagement in the task of passing on the validity of foreign acts of state may hinder rather than further this country's pursuit of goals both for itself and for the community of nations as a whole in the international sphere. . . .

The doctrine of sovereign immunity is similar to the act of state doctrine in that it also represents the need to respect the sovereignty of foreign states. The two doctrines differ, however, in significant respects. The law of sovereign immunity goes to the jurisdiction of the court. The act of state doctrine is not jurisdictional. Rather, it is a prudential doctrine designed to avoid judicial action in sensitive areas. Sovereign immunity is a principle of international law, recognized in the United States by statute. It is the states themselves, as defendants, who may claim sovereign immunity. The act of state doctrine is a domestic legal principle, arising from the peculiar role of American courts. It recognizes not only the sovereignty of foreign states, but also the spheres of power of the co-equal branches of our government. . . . The record in this case contains extensive documentation of the involvement of our executive and legislative branches with the oil question. IAM does not dispute that the United States has a grave interest in the petro-politics of the Middle East, or that the foreign policy arms of the executive and legislative branches are intimately involved in this sensitive area. It is clear that OPEC and its activities are carefully considered in the formulation of American foreign policy.

The remedy IAM seeks is an injunction against the OPEC nations. The possibility of insult to the OPEC states and of interference with the efforts of the political branches to seek favorable relations with them is apparent from the very nature of this action and the remedy sought. . . .

DECISION: The Court of Appeals affirmed the judgment of the District Court in favor of OPEC. It found the OPEC countries immune from suit due to their sovereign immunity, and also indicated that the act of state doctrine would lead the court to decline to exercise any jurisdiction it might have against OPEC.

International Business: Trade

While there are several methods of conducting international business, the least complex method is exporting and importing. **Exporting** is the selling of a product manufactured in one country to a purchaser in another country; **importing** is the purchase in one country of a product manufactured in another country. Different laws affect both the export and import of the product and each will be dealt with subsequently. A second method commonly used in conducting international business is licensing. A **license**, which is generally a certificate or document that gives permission, may be used to permit a foreign manufacturer or distributor to make or distribute a product in a certain territory or country. The basic legal framework of licensing agreements is briefly examined. The more complex international direct investments are discussed in the next section. We look at both the laws affecting a firm deciding to enter into a joint venture with a foreign firm and the laws governing the establishment of a wholly owned office or manufacturing plant in a foreign country.

Laws Affecting Exports

Laws affecting exports may be directed at either encouraging or discouraging such exports; this section examines some legal provisions of each type. Those laws that are directed at discouraging exports may be imposed because of the scarcity of the products domestically (U.S. export quotas have been imposed on wheat and soybean commodities during periods of crop shortages) or as a result of the concern over the use of the product by the importer (such as is true for military equipment and technologically advanced computer hardware). On the other hand, exports are often stimulated and encouraged to take markets away from foreign competitors and to ease the balance of trade problems. Our analysis of the laws affecting exports first focuses on laws seeking to control, restrict, or regulate exports.

License Regulations for Exports Each nation's government is usually careful about what it exports, particularly during wartime or periods of economic crisis. Thus it is important that a business attempting to export should investigate its own laws to see if the goods in question require prior approval before they are allowed to leave the country. Sometimes a law restricts particular goods from being sent to another country, whereas in other cases a law may restrict certain products from some countries while allowing them to be shipped to other destinations.

A U.S. exporter may determine whether a commodity requires a license by consulting the U.S.

Department of Commerce. All commodities to be exported carry a designation number known as a Schedule B number. These numbers, published by the Bureau of the Census, make it possible to record the dollar value and volume of all commodities leaving the country. A typical Schedule B listing would be: steel sheets, galvanized, 60340.

The Export Administration Act provides for three types of licenses: (1) the *general license*, which authorizes the export without any application by the exporter—no specific documentary approval is required for the export of goods under this license; (2) a *validated license*, which authorizes a specific export and is issued pursuant to an application by the exporter; and (3) a *qualified license*, which authorizes multiple exports and is also issued pursuant to the exporter's application.

The export of certain goods, technology, or industrial techniques developed in part, directly or indirectly, from federally financed research and development must be approved by the Secretary of Defense. If the Secretary of Defense determines that the export of such goods, technology, or techniques would significantly increase the present or potential military capacity of a potentially hostile country, he can recommend that the application for the validated or qualified license be denied.

Any individual, corporation, or partnership acting as an exporter under the jurisdiction of the United States may apply for an export license. The license requires information such as the quantity of the commodity, the description, the Schedule B number, the processing code, the unit price, the total value, the end use of the material, and the identity of the foreign importer.

Governmental Assistance for Exports

A variety of governmental programs are designed to assist the exporter. Since tax incentives, credits, and rebates are often a pivotal part of such governmental assistance, those laws will be examined separately in the next section of this chapter. In addition to providing tax assistance, a government frequently provides valuable information to the potential exporter.

In the United States the Department of Commerce has several publications available that are of significant value to any potential exporter. In addition to providing brochures and pamphlets, the Department of Commerce conducts searches for agents to represent a U.S. firm in foreign countries. The Department also organizes various exhibits and trade fairs in U.S.-owned trade centers located throughout the world so that U.S. goods can be shown to potential foreign purchasers.

Another type of assistance given to U.S. firms is provided by the Export Trading Company Act of 1982. This law is designed to assure exporting firms that they will not be prosecuted for violations of U.S. antitrust laws. Essentially the company files information regarding its activities and applies for a certificate of antitrust immunity. If the firm meets appropriate conditions and does in fact perform according to the terms outlined in the certificate, the company will be immune from antitrust prosecution by the government. Another section of this law also permits U.S. banks to invest capital in and make loans to export trading companies.

Financial assistance is available for the exporter from several governmental organizations. For example, the Export–Import Bank (Eximbank) offers both medium- and long-term loans and credit guarantees for the exporter. While some direct loans are made by Eximbank, it primarily provides credit guarantees to commercial banks that in turn lend money to the exporting business.

Tax Assistance for Exports Although exports are frequently encouraged because of the jobs they provide to a nation's employees and the money added to its economy, when a country experiences a serious balance of trade problem, additional tax assistance to exporters is frequently also made available. The U.S. Congress took such steps in the early 1970s when it passed the Revenue Act of 1971. That law provided tax benefits when U.S. products were marketed overseas through a Domestic International Sales Corporation (DISC). Over a decade later, after some of the trading partners of the United States claimed that law violated the international General Agreement on Tariffs and Trade, the DISC provisions of the U.S. tax laws were replaced in 1984 by the Foreign Sales Corporation (FSC) rules.

A Foreign Sales Corporation must be located outside the United States, either in a U.S. possession or in a foreign country that has a tax information exchange agreement with the United States. Meetings of the corporation's shareholders and board of directors also must be maintained outside the United States. The principal benefit of the FSC is the exemption from U.S. taxation of about 15 percent of the corporation's income that is derived from qualified export transactions. Thus if a corporation has $1 million of income from qualified export transactions, only $850,000 of it will be subject to U.S. income taxes.

Laws Affecting Imports

In international trade a business may encounter legal controls imposed on products by the country into which a product is imported, as well as by the country from which it is exported. The country from which the product is exported may not want to lose the resource to governments or consumers of other nations. A country into which a product is imported may not want foreign products to compete with products manufactured by local firms, or it simply may lack the capital necessary to pay for the import. There are a number of means by which a country seeks to prohibit, restrict, or regulate imports into it from outside its borders.

Such legal restrictions could include an outright prohibition against importing certain products, a limitation on the amount of a product that can be imported, taxes on imported products, and various other forms of discrimination against foreign goods in favor of domestic items. Each of these types of restrictions will be discussed below.

While each nation can and does adopt its own import policy, international institutions, such as the World Trade Organization and the International Monetary Fund, limit some policies that member countries may impose. While different nations use various means of restricting or encouraging imports, an examination of some U.S. laws affecting imports should illustrate the type of legal measures often used.

Prohibitions on Imports

A **prohibition** is a law that makes it illegal to import certain specified products into the country. The United States has enacted several such laws. Among these are laws prohibiting the import of undesirable products (drugs and guns) or agricultural items that could cause disease. The Trading with the Enemy Act also grants to the President the power to restrict all imports from the countries considered to be enemies. For example, two businessmen and the company they created pleaded guilty to trading with the enemy when

they sent 90 used cars from Honolulu to Vietnam in 1992 and 1993. The cars were sent initially to Hong Kong but from there went to a company in Vietnam.[4] Although modifications have been made in the U.S. policy regarding trading with Vietnam, until recently violators of the Act continued to face possible prosecution.

Many developing nations also prohibit imports on goods that otherwise might overwhelm their own infant industries. Brazil prohibits the import of small computers and light passenger airplanes, whereas Taiwan keeps out chemicals used in making drugs if those chemicals can be produced domestically. Japan's import laws are frequently cited as being among the most restrictive among industrialized countries.

Quotas   A **quota** limits the number of items that may be imported. While a quota is less restrictive than an outright prohibition, it generally is more restrictive than a policy that merely taxes the product to be imported. Since 1964 the United States has had a quota on the import of meat products.

Quotas are widely regarded as one of the most effective forms of laws restricting imports. Quotas are frequently disguised as "voluntary" agreements between trading partners. The Commission of the European Union has pressured Japan to limit its shipments of quartz watches, stereo equipment, and computer-controlled machine tools. The United States has similar promises from steel-exporting countries in Europe and in South America.

Tariffs   **Tariffs** are taxes assessed on imported goods but not on domestic goods; thus such taxes are invariably discriminatory. Usually these taxes are levied to protect infant industries against the industrial force possessed by foreign competitors. The tariffs may be levied on an ad valorem basis (the tariff represents a percent of the value or price of the item imported) or on a flat rate basis (the tariff being levied on each barrel of oil, foot of pipe, or pound of nails). An examination of customs duties would disclose page after page of tariff rates applicable to various classifications of goods. As the next case indicates, the placing of goods within a particular classification is often a critical factor in determining whether importing an item is economically feasible.

CHILDCRAFT EDUCATION CORP. V. UNITED STATES

U.S. Court of International Trade

572 F.Supp. 1275 (1983)

BACKGROUND: Childcraft (plaintiff) imported from Japan a Teaching Typewriter and Touch to Learn machine, which were made for use by children. The United States (defendant) classified the items as toys, subject to a 21 percent ad valoren tariff, instead of educational machines, subject to a 6 or 6.5 percent tariff. The plaintiff claimed that since the chief use of the merchandise was for the education of the children, the items should not have been classified as toys.

Landis, Judge

This action involves merchandise known as "Teaching Typewriters," "Touch to Learn," and "Touch to Match," manufactured in Japan and entered at the port of New York between May 28, 1971 and October 1, 1971.

The pertinent statutory provisions are as follows:

2. For the purposes of the tariff schedules, a "toy" is any article chiefly used for the amusement of children or adults.

The primary issue is whether the merchandise in issue is chiefly used for the *education* of pre-school children or whether it is used chiefly for the *amusement* of adults or children and thereby classifiable as a "toy."

Plaintiff's witness, Mr. Saul Cohen, was at the time of the trial Senior Vice-President of Merchandising for plaintiff corporation. His testimony indicated that he has been employed by plaintiff for twenty-eight (28) years. According to the witness, approximately eighty (80) percent of plaintiff's business is generated by sales to schools and other educational systems.

Mr. Cohen's testimony and actual demonstration indicated that the merchandise known as "Teaching Typewriter" and the related programmed cards were designed for educational purposes. According to the witness, the machine functions by introducing a programmed card containing a mathematical, spelling or other educational type problem. The merchandise user then presses one of the typewriter keys that completes a word or answers a mathematical problem. If the user engages the wrong key the programmed card is immobilized and new problems are not presented to the user. If the user selects a correct answer the programmed card advances presenting a new problem. The process is repeated each time the user gives a correct answer.

Subsequently, the witness described and illustrated the "Touch to Learn" merchandise and its related cassette.

According to the witness, "Touch to Learn" operates in the same manner as the "Teaching Typewriter," except that it uses programmed cassettes instead of programmed cards. Basically, when the user engages the machine it presents a problem. If the correct response is made, the cassette automatically moves to the next problem. If the wrong answer is made, the cassette will not present a subsequent problem. The problems on the cassette are in different combinations to teach the child, for example, that two and one equal three, etc. The sequence of problems increases in degree of difficulty as the cassette progresses. The principles behind the "Touch to Learn" and the "Teaching Typewriter" are the same.

Mr. Cohen's testimony further indicates that the imported machines could not function without a programmed card or cassette and that the particular programs were progressive in degree of learning difficulty. . . .

The witness stated that the articles in question were merchandised through a school catalog and through a force of sales representatives who conducted workshops in schools and with teachers to demonstrate the merchandise. Additionally, Childcraft attempted to sell these articles through its stores, a consumer catalog, and by public distribution through retail stores. . . .

Plaintiff has failed to demonstrate by the evidence of record that the imported merchandise is chiefly used for educational purposes and not chiefly used for the amusement of children.

Under TSUS, a "toy" for the purposes of the tariff schedules is any article chiefly used for the amusement of children or adults. Thus, plaintiff's burden is to prove that the chief purpose of the merchandise in issue is not amusement.

Plaintiff's case ultimately relies upon the theory that the chief utilitarian purpose of the imported merchandise is that of education of children and that any amusement derived therefrom is merely incidental to its chief use. When amusement and utility become locked in controversy, the question becomes one of determining whether the amusement is incidental to the utilitarian purpose, or the utilitarian purpose incidental to the amusement.

Plaintiff's only witness at the trial did not have a background as an educator or in educational psychology although he did indicate that he worked with teachers and educational consultants as well as people who are engaged in the field of education of pre-school children.

While the testimony of the witness indicated that in his belief the main purpose of the merchandise in issue was to teach children he also stated that he had observed children using the merchandise in school and that the children were enjoying themselves.

Thus, the witness admitted that the basis of the merchandise was amusement of a young child with the hopeful purpose that the child would learn something while being amused. An article that has some incidental educational value or is used in school does not remove it from the toy category.

Moreover, in toy cases especially, a sample is a potent witness. The court in viewing a demonstration of the merchandise at trial and reviewing the exhibits in chambers is of the solid conclusion that the main effect thereof is the amusement of children and any educational value is merely incidental thereto. Moreover, if plaintiff's position were sustained then almost any toy could be deemed educational in nature as most experiences are new to the young child's receptive mind and he learns by the new experiences.

DECISION: The Court of International Trade upheld the classification of the plaintiff's imported items as toys.

Nontariff Barriers

It is impracticable, if not impossible, to attempt to enumerate even the dominant forms of nontariff barriers. They would include import licensing controls, foreign exchange controls, deposits required of importers, and fees other than tariffs levied by custom officials. The definition of **nontariff barriers** generally includes all references to import restrictions of any kind, except for tariffs.

Our discussion of nontariff barriers first focuses on those that affect the goods as they come into a country; these are known as *nontariff barriers effective upon entry*. The second category consists of programs, practices, and policies within a country that discriminate against imported goods, but that are not effective on the entry of goods into a country. These practices are referred to as *nontariff barriers effective subsequent to the entry* of the goods.

Effective upon Entry Import licensing controls require importers to obtain a license through a governmental agency. The license may require payment of a fee, completion of extensive documentation, or approval by several different agencies. An import license may be available only if a business also has certain export "credits" with which to purchase the imported goods. In some

Latin American countries the required license may take months to process; often almost complete discretion as to the approval of the license is given to chosen officials.

Standards, procedures, and guidelines for determining the likelihood of receiving a license may be nonexistent. In most communist countries, import licenses are granted only if the imported item is required pursuant to governmental plans. Imports that do not fit into the plan are effectively, although perhaps not expressly, prohibited.

Foreign exchange controls are measures that are adopted to regulate payments in or transfers of local or foreign currencies or both. Usually these controls restrict the conversion of local currency into foreign currency and the movement of local or foreign currencies into or out of the country. France imposed exchange controls in 1983 limiting the amount of French francs that individuals could take out of the country.

Laws may specify through what institutions and under what circumstances exchanges between local and foreign currency take place. While different schemes can become extremely complex, all such controls seek to restrict the import or export of some commodities, goods, or services or limit the possibility of acquiring certain foreign currencies. In extreme cases the only currency that can be used to pay for imported goods is the local currency. Thus, in Russia, where the currency is not freely traded on the world market, a foreign seller would have difficulty in converting rubles into a marketable currency.

Effective Subsequent to Entry These nontariff barriers include governmental procurement policies, internal tax policies, subsidy programs, and other practices that accord an advantage to domestic industries. The "Buy America" Act prohibits the purchase by federal agencies of foreign goods when domestic equivalents are available at comparable prices or when national security interests are involved.

Since late in the nineteenth century the United States has required all imported items to be marked with a legend identifying the foreign country from which it originated. The purpose of the requirement is to insure that the consumer or user of the item in the United States knows the item is a product of a particular foreign country. If there is no marking, no import is permitted. As a result, this law is effective on the entry of an imported item. However, if there is a marking, given the choice, the consumer may choose the American-made product. Thus the law imposing the "country of origin" requirement is also a nonentry barrier.

Licenses

A second method of conducting international business trade is by licensing agreements. A **license**, as discussed earlier, is a certificate or document that gives permission. Thus a **patent license** gives written authority from the owner of a patent to another person to make or use the patented article for a limited time in a designated territory. License arrangements are particularly advantageous in providing an entry into foreign markets without direct investment. A company may be able to add income to its balance sheet without incurring added research or development expenditures. Some companies that are not willing or able to commit large amounts of capital abroad in fact seem to specialize in licensing.

Usefulness of Licenses

Licensing arrangements may be entered into for patents, copyrights, trademarks, or know-how and technical assistance. A license usually grants to the licensee the right to use, lease, or sell a product that the licensor manufactures domestically. Anyone who has traveled abroad is aware of the franchise type of license agreements used in the hotel (Hilton or Holiday Inns), fast food (McDonald's), and soft drink (Coca-Cola) industries.

Property rights that can be licensed arise from statutory or nonstatutory sources. Statutory sources include patents, trademarks, designs, and copyrights, whereas nonstatutory examples include know-how, technical data, and nonpatentable inventions. Usually more protection is available for the licensing of property rights based on statutory sources, such as patents, than for nonstatutory products or services.

Special Legal Concerns with Licensing Agreements

In addition to a concern with taxation, discussed in the next section, international licensing agreements should be particularly concerned with the governing law, the resolution of disputes, and the effect of the licensing agreement on competition.

The rules for determining the law that will govern the licensing agreement vary from country to country. Frequently the choice of the governing law depends on the place in which any legal action is brought. Most countries enforce a contract provision in which the parties specify in their licensing agreement the law governing any contract dispute.

Disputes between the licensor and the licensee may arise regarding the obligation to disclose new techniques affecting the manufacture of a product or the need to maintain quality production standards. Differences regarding the level of support in advertising or expertise given by the licensor to the licensee may occur. While we might expect such differences between parties to a contract to be resolved in courts, most parties to international licensing agreements instead prefer the use of arbitration.

The effect of the licensing agreement on competition may be of concern to both the country of the licensor and the country of the licensee. For example, if a U.S. licensor grants to a foreign licensee an exclusive right to manufacture a product that is protected by patent or trademark laws, the licensor should be concerned with U.S. antitrust laws and the effect the agreement has on the foreign commerce of the United States. Conversely, the laws where the licensee is located may prohibit certain provisions in a licensing agreement. Provisions that restrict the flow of technology into the country or that impose on the licensee the obligation to share with the licensor new technologies learned by the licensee are among those that might be prohibited by the country of the licensee.

Taxation of Licenses

The tax effect of a licensing agreement is of significant concern to both the licensor and licensee. The country in which the licensor has a place of business and the country in which the licensee manufactures, uses, or sells the licensed product both will try to obtain a share of the royalty payments provided for by the licensing agreement. In the absence of tax treaties, royalties for licenses are usually subject to income tax in the country of the licensee since the income came from the manufacture, use, or sale of the product in that country (known as the country of source). The tax authorities of the country of source normally require that the licensee withhold the tax due to it

prior to any payment of the royalty to the licensor.

After the royalties have been received by the licensor, the royalty income generally is taxed in the country in which the licensor resides (the country of origin since the product or process licensed and for which a royalty is paid originates there). Some countries have sought to avoid such double taxation by concluding tax treaties that either exempt royalty payments from taxation in one of the two countries involved or at least give credit for the tax paid in the country of source. Generally if the licensor is doing business in the country of source or origin by way of permanent establishment (branch, office, factory, warehouse, or other fixed place of business), the royalty is taxed only in the country of source.

International Business: Investments

While exporting and licensing arrangements allow a company to derive income from foreign trade without substantial investment, critical legal restraints on those methods of operation may tend to make international investment a more desirable means of conducting international business. Thus in the face of severe import restrictions or local laws that discriminate against foreign products, the only way in which a product may be sold is by directly establishing plants and equipment in those countries.

Similarly, critical business factors affect the need for direct investment as opposed to the international trade options of exporting or licensing. Many U.S. enterprises began direct investment in European countries not only to get inside the tariff walls of the European Union's common market but also to be able to market their goods more effectively through onsite locations. Transportation expenses often make trade arrangements prohibitively costly; thus investment becomes the most profitable means of selling internationally.

Joint Ventures

For whatever reason, international investments through joint ventures and direct participation are significant methods by which businesses engage in international transactions.

International joint venture investments are those investments with two or more active partners; generally, one partner is located in the country where the business activity takes place and the other partner is based in some other country. Direct investments are those undertaken by a single firm. In the joint venture there is a sharing of contributions by each party as well as a sharing of ownership. For example, a foreign firm may contribute capital and management experience, whereas a local firm may contribute raw material resources and local marketing expertise.

Particular legal problems accompany all such international investments. The laws of the countries in which the operations are conducted, as well as certain aspects of international law, must be closely examined to determine the benefits of international investment.

Whether investing through direct investment or via a joint venture, the laws of the country in which the investment is made are of crucial importance in the organization and operation of the business enterprise.

Other legal sources are superimposed on those national laws. Certain rules of international law, extraterritorial aspects of the laws of the business'

country of origin, treaty obligations between the two nations, and relevant rules of international institutions also affect the international investment ventures. Our analysis of some of the laws affecting international investments begins with a review of some of the unique legal problems associated with investing in a joint venture.

A joint venture is a common form used by companies engaged in international business. It involves a sharing of the ownership of a business enterprise among two or more parties. Unlike the joint venture the direct investment generally places all of the control and management of the new investment operations with one business enterprise. Even if the direct investment involves less than 100 percent ownership of another firm, if the effective management and control of the subsidiary is vested in one parent firm, it can be regarded as a direct investment rather than a joint venture. A comparison of these two methods of investment is shown in Figure 58-4.

A joint venture can be compared to a partnership. Each of the parties to the business agrees to cooperate with the other in pursuit of a profitable

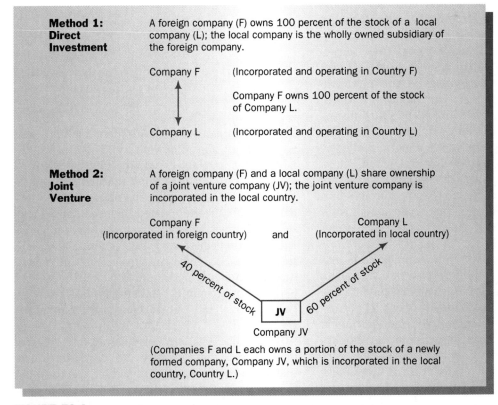

FIGURE 58-4

Comparison of Joint Venture and Direct Investment

business that will benefit both parties. However, unlike a partnership, a joint venture is generally limited in scope. The parties are not agreeing to merge all of their activities and ventures into one combined business. Instead, each agrees to do certain things and to cooperate in some areas while still competing as separate firms in other activities.

The General Motors–Toyota agreement to produce cars in California is a joint venture. It is neither a direct investment nor a partnership. If Toyota was purchasing the California plant and running it as a branch or as a subsidiary of Toyota, it would be a direct investment. On the other hand, if Toyota and General Motors agreed to drop their other activities and to work together not only in building these cars, but as partners on other products, they could form a partnership or merge their corporations into one. This venture is more limited in scope. They are to produce one type of car in one plant; the other operations of both Toyota and General Motors are to be kept separate.

While direct investment into wholly owned subsidiaries once was the prevalent method for establishing manufacturing facilities in a foreign country, today rising nationalism has brought about legal restrictions that often prohibit such direct investments. This trend away from participation by direct investment and toward joint ventures with foreign enterprises is not limited to countries in the former communist bloc or to those in Latin America. In recent years investment laws in Chile, China, France, and to some extent in England have made joint ventures the normal mode for foreign investments in those countries. Conducting international business through joint ventures allows the foreign firm some of the advantages of direct investment without acceptance of all the risks that such direct participation may bring.

Many countries have an investment code that details rather extensively the type of investments welcomed or permitted. Such an investment code generally establishes the degree of capital participation allowed and specifies the required training of local personnel that must accompany any approved investment. In these instances the joint venture is the only permitted form of investment by foreign enterprises in many countries.

Even in the absence of legal restraints that have the effect of forcing the foreign investor to use joint ventures, this method of international investing may be selected. More involved participation by the firm may be too expensive. The political or business risk may be so great, it can only be accepted if shared with some other business. There may be some critical ingredient or assistance that only a partner can provide, such as access to local capital, political contacts, easier recruitment of personnel, broader access to local suppliers, or faster penetration of local or regional markets.

The organization of a joint venture usually requires the parties to prepare and exchange a number of legal documents. A typical list of the documents that might be used would include:

1. A contract between the parties entering into the joint venture

2. Documents necessary to establish a joint corporation, such as the articles of incorporation, bylaws, and shareholder agreements

3. A loan agreement to provide for payment of funds lent by one party to the other to establish the joint venture

4. Patent, trademark, or know-how licensing agreements

5. Management assistance or know-how agreements

6. An export agreement for one party to export supplies, machinery, or parts the venture may need

In some countries, the government itself is often an owner of any joint venture. There are both advantages and disadvantages to having a foreign government as a joint venture partner. A clear advantage is that the venture is now very likely to obtain the needed licenses and necessary regulatory approval from the governmental agencies that must approve certain of the venture's actions. Disadvantages are found when the governmental participants lack business experience or are subject to being replaced simply because they fall out of favor with the ruling government.

The unique legal problems associated with the international joint venture are primarily those that affect the venture's organization and the relations with the firms that have created it. Whether investing by joint venture or by direct investment, a number of legal sources must be consulted to determine the profitability of the venture. The most prominent legal sources are the laws of the country in which the venture is to operate (the country of source). Since a review of the laws of the country of source is also important to the firm engaged in direct investments, the next section of the text highlights some of the concerns with such laws for both the joint venture and the direct investment in international business.

Direct Investments

The most involved method of conducting international business is by direct investment. Nations have mixed views about granting to foreign firms the right to participate directly in economic activities within their borders. The attitudes toward private foreign investment vary from country to country. The policies adopted are shaped by and reflective of political and economic considerations. A country's historical experiences with foreign investors, the relative state of development of its economy, its need for foreign capital and technology, as well as its political ideology are important considerations in the formation of a country's national policy toward foreign investment. Significant segments of a country's legal system are relevant to a firm's judgment as to the desirability of engaging in international business through either a joint venture or direct foreign investment.

Of course, economic regulations are a primary consideration. What is the taxation policy of the source country? Are there different labor laws requiring worker representation on a company's board of directors or demanding a certain percentage of the labor force to be from that country? What are the antitrust policies and how are they developing? In direct investment possibilities the entire legal climate must be evaluated. Is expropriation or nationalization a possibility? Are the courts independent of the political framework of the government? Highlights from several legal areas that particularly affect international direct investments will be examined to illustrate the overall concern with the legal system in the source country.

Investment Laws and Policies   Probably the first area for investigation when contemplating international investment is the controlling foreign investment law. In many countries legisla-

tion has been enacted to attract foreign investors. Incentives to invest in particular industries, in stipulated depressed geographical locales, or in special programs are common in numerous countries. The devices used are often tax incentives such as tax holidays, increased depreciation, or other benefits aimed at making the tax rate of the country favorable for foreign investors. Several computer hardware manufacturing operations located in Ireland due largely to the existence of such tax incentives.

Form of Business Organization   Corporations, rather than partnerships or proprietorships, are the dominant form of business organization for international investments. While state laws in the United States generally do not distinguish between a closely held corporation (with only a few shareholders) and a publicly held corporation (with many shareholders), laws in many countries do have different requirements for those seeking to organize such corporations. In France and Germany, for example, only the limited liability company (the closely held corporation) can impose restrictions on the transfer of shares by corporate shareholders. The role of limited liability companies now recognized by most states in the United States is discussed in Chapter 37.

Before any final decision is made concerning the specific corporate form to use, the firm seeking to organize such a corporation needs to consider the relationship between the organization used for conducting international activities and the organizing firm itself. This choice normally involves some comparison of the advantages and disadvantages of the branch and subsidiary relationships. One choice would be to organize a separate foreign corporation. When this choice is selected, the foreign corporation is generally established as a subsidiary of the parent firm since the parent firm will own all or most of the shares of stock of the foreign firm.

A second choice would be to forgo the establishment of a separate foreign corporation. If this choice is selected, the foreign operations are treated like the domestic operations and all are performed by and on behalf of the parent corporation. Since the foreign activities are conducted in a different location from that for the corporation's domestic activities, the foreign activities are generally seen as a branch of the domestic ones. Unlike the subsidiary, the branch is not an independent legal entity. Instead, like a branch bank, it is a part of the overall activities of the parent corporation. It will have its own managers and different operations than the parent firm, but is legally seen as a part of the parent corporation.

Figure 58-5 provides a comparison of these two basic methods by which corporate units can be organized.

Exchange Controls An investment decision is not only concerned with applicable legal provisions regarding investing money in a foreign country, but also with exchange controls that may seek to limit the right to withdraw profits, interest, dividends, or portions of the invested capital. The IMF's Twenty-third Annual Report on exchange restrictions lists 123 countries that have exchange controls and regulations of varying kinds and intensities. Some protection against the most severe restrictions is available to U.S. corporations through treaty provisions and through insurance protection that generally protects business in certain countries against the risk of inability to convert investment receipts from the local currency into dollars.

Tax Considerations As we have noted, the tax laws in the context of the investment incentives or the form in which to organize a firm should be reviewed. A comprehensive review of both foreign and U.S. tax laws affecting the business's operations, as well as its initial organization, is also necessary. In reviewing the foreign tax laws, the investor must examine not only direct taxes but also indirect taxes. In many countries the indirect taxes, such as the sales tax, turnover tax, or excise tax, account for most of the country's income. Indirect taxes are easier to collect and are not so dependent on a high level of per capita income of the taxpayers as are direct taxes. For example, 67 percent of France's income from taxes is from indirect taxes (turnover tax, tobacco, gas, liquor, and customs).

Municipal or state taxes, as well as national taxes, must be taken into account to determine the real tax burden; in Switzerland, for example, the municipal tax on corporate income is far more significant than is the federal tax. Finally, tax treaties often play an important role in determining the tax burden in effect for a particular transaction. Often such treaties do much to alleviate double taxation that each country might otherwise impose and to simplify conflicting or overlapping tax provisions of the country of

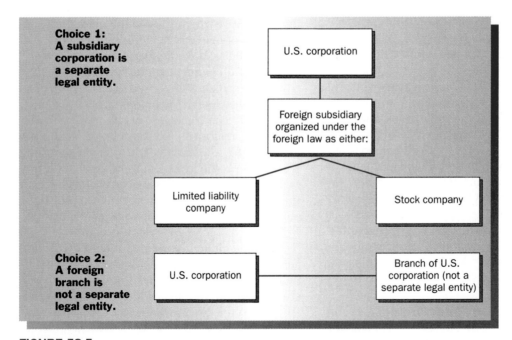

FIGURE 58-5

Comparison of a Branch and a Foreign Subsidiary of a U.S. Corporation source (the country where the income will be produced) and the country of origin (the country that invested the capital to make the income possible).

Labor Laws   Labor laws influence any foreign investment, as they affected the decision of some domestic companies once operating in northern states to move into southern states that had fewer labor unions and lower wage rates. The labor laws that affect the investment deal not only with any minimum or prevailing wage laws, but also with provisions regarding hours of work, workmen's compensation, retirement benefits, and vacation bonuses. Bonuses of approximately one month's salary are required by legislation or practice in most European countries for both salaried and hourly workers. In Japan, bonuses are awarded to most Japanese workers in July and December and are usually equal to as much as two to six months in pay. Severance payments required to accompany notice of termination are expected or legislated in many countries.

A worker may have a vested right to his or her job; Mexican and Italian laws restrict the right of an employer to discharge a worker except for carefully prescribed conditions. Local laws often require all foreign workers to obtain work permits. Further, a minimum percentage of the labor force may be required to be local nationals. Saudi Arabian law requires all foreigners working in the country to obtain work permits; the law also requires all companies employing foreigners to employ 75 percent Saudi nationals, with a total of 51 percent of the total payroll being paid to nationals.

Safety of Investment from Expropriation or Nationalization   Expropriation or nationalization occurs when a country takes over the ownership and management of private firms. While the terms are often used interchangeably, **nationalization** generally refers to situations where the government pays compensation to the former owner, whereas **expropriation** occurs where no such compensation is paid. In 1982 France nationalized many banks operating in France, both foreign and domestically owned, whereas in the 1960s and 1970s Cuba expropriated many banks operating in Cuba.

Available legal protection against risk of expropriation may be a consideration where a sizable

investment is contemplated. Such protection may be available from a variety of sources. The local investment code may have express nonexpropriation guarantees. Treaties signed by some foreign countries and by the United States indicate agreement as to the standard for "reasonable compensation." Certainly insurance protection offered through U.S. agencies such as the Export–Import Bank, the Foreign Credit Insurance Association, and the Office of Private Investment Controls should be examined if there is any danger regarding the safety of one's investment from expropriation or nationalization.

Antitrust Laws   Firms operating in the United States, whether of domestic or foreign origin, have long been aware of the possible effect of antitrust laws on their business operations. Antitrust laws aim at preserving a relatively free system of competition by controlling anticompetitive practices and attempting to regulate the growth and use of economic power. The basic provisions of the key U.S. statute, the Sherman Act, are as follows:

> Section 1: Every contract, combination in the form of trust or otherwise, or conspiracy, in restraint of trade or commerce among the several states, or *with foreign* nations, is declared to be illegal. . . .
>
> Section 2: Every person who shall monopolize, or attempt to monopolize, or combine or conspire with any other person or persons, to monopolize any part of the trade or commerce among the several States, or *with foreign* nations, shall be deemed guilty of a felony. . . .

It is clear from the italicized references both in Sections 1 and 2 that the U.S. antitrust law has an extraterritorial reach; that is, it applies not only to transactions taking place within the United States but also to contracts ". . . in restraint of trade or commerce . . . with foreign nations." Most of the cases, such as the *Timberlane* case found earlier in the chapter, which have applied U.S. antitrust law in international transactions, have involved allegations of restraints on competition occurring, at least in part, outside the United States. Those activities violate U.S. law if they have had an adverse effect on competition and commerce in the United States.

Although U.S. antitrust law has had the most

influence on international business transactions, antitrust laws were enacted in most major European countries after World War II. Those national laws subsequently have been supplemented and to some extent replaced by Article 85–90 of the Rome Treaty creating the European Community. Article 85 of the Treaty of Rome prohibits practices and agreements that restrict or distort competition within the community between member states. Furthermore, the European Court of Justice has clearly indicated that the Article also applies to extraterritorial activities that affect trade or commerce in the member states even if one of the parties is located outside the community.

Trademarks and Patents   Intimately connected with antitrust provisions is the legal protection afforded trademarks and patents. It is not surprising that these legal areas often overlap. Whereas antitrust law is antimonopolistic, patent law gives a limited monopoly to a certain process, product, or design, and trademark law gives a limited monopoly to a symbol or word.

Recall from Chapter 50 that trademarks designate the source or origin of a product, whereas patents give to the owner a monopoly over its manufacture, sale, or use. The consumer of trademarked goods often does not know the name of the manufacturer of a trademarked item; the mark merely identifies that all goods with that mark have come from the same source. The golden arches, Ronald McDonald, the "Big Mac," and other names and symbols are all trademarks and trade names used by one producer. Obviously with the expansion of international business operations, an owner of a trademarked item (McDonald's, Coca-Cola, Hilton Hotel) or of a patent will seek to have that legal protection extended internationally. A patent confers rights that are protected only within the boundaries of the country issuing the patent. Thus a U.S. and a Canadian patent, even when granted for the same invention, create separate and distinct rights that may differ in scope and effect in each country.

In the same manner, U.S. courts have held that a foreign patent confers upon its owner no rights or protection with respect to acts done in the United States. Today every country has its own distinct set of patent laws and regulations.

Some of these differences can be noted briefly. Under U.S. patent laws, inventors are not required to use or permit others to use their patent; they do not have to pay taxes to maintain it; they are not compelled to grant licenses to others unless they misuse their patents. In some other nations many of these obligations must be performed to maintain a patent's validity.

Germany, Great Britain, and the Netherlands require a thorough examination as to the novelty and patentability of an invention. In Austria and

---

ETHICS
International Ethics

Do ethical standards vary between nations? If Italians take a different approach to paying taxes, does that mean that while in Italy behaving as the Italians behave constitutes ethical behavior? The issue is one of ethical relativism. To what extent can each society define for itself what is ethical?

Certainly it makes sense to follow local customs such as removing shoes when entering a Japanese house, or not serving alcoholic beverages at business gatherings in Saudi Arabia. But, as discussed in Chapter 8, if the local practice violates universal or fundamental ethical principles, then it can be condemned as unethical even though it is accepted by the society. Thus apartheid can be condemned because it violates fundamental principles.

Complying with Italian tax law presents a very difficult question. Here the law on the books says that the tax must be paid. But the actual practice is not to report all of the income and thus not to pay the full amount owing. Legal realists might support not paying the full tax on the grounds that the actual law is determined by the way in which it is enforced. Under that approach, having accurate information about what constitutes acceptable practice becomes critically important.

Switzerland there is little or no examination and the validity is left for the courts to determine. In Japan, in order to be patentable, an invention must be capable of being used in industry; thus patents are available for typical methods of doing business, such as methods of advertising. In the United States no taxes are imposed to maintain the patent. In many nations a tax or annuity fee must be paid to maintain the patent. If the taxes are not paid when due, the patent is considered abandoned.

The United States is planning to make its patent system more like the Japanese and European systems. Patents are published 18 months after they are granted. Patent life in the United States will also be extended from 17 to 20 years to make it conform to emerging international standards.

The principal international agreement relating to patents is the International Convention for the Protection of Industrial Property (Paris Union). Over ninety nations, including the United States, are members of the International Convention. While the Paris Union contains no provisions that directly affect the substantive aspects of national patent law, it does create uniformity by allowing applicants in one country to apply subsequently for protection in other countries. If a person in one nation files an application in another country, within 12 months of the original filing that person is entitled to priority on the basis of the original filing date. Such protection is granted to any person domiciled in one country or any firm having a place of business in a member country.

Review Questions and Problems

Key Terms

portfolio investment	license
direct investment	prohibition
extraterritorial laws	quota
judicial comity	tariff
doctrine of sovereign immunity	nontariff barrier
	patent license
act of state doctrine	nationalization
exporting	expropriation
importing	

Discussion Questions

1. Describe the four methods of conducting international business and explain how each differs.

2. Give an example of a U.S. law, other than the antitrust laws, that can be applied to conduct occurring outside the United States.

3. Assume your company manufactures parts for certain industrial machinery and you are considering establishing a manufacturing plant in Germany. What specific German laws would you examine before you committed to make such an investment?

4. If you were to consider a joint venture with a Polish company rather than a direct investment in Germany, what special legal concerns other than those mentioned in your answer in Question 3 would you want to examine?

5. Explain the differences and similarities in the act of state and the doctrine of sovereign immunity. Give one example of the possible application of each concept.

Review Problems

1. Eurim is a small Korean firm that distributes worldwide brand name drugs manufactured by multinational pharmaceutical manufacturers. Pfizer is a multinational pharmaceutical corporation headquartered in the United States. It had a patent on one of the drugs it manufactured and after its patent expired, Pfizer granted an exclusive license to several manufacturers in each of its major foreign markets to produce that drug.

   The manufacturers agreed to restrict their sales to specific geographic areas assigned by Pfizer and to sell the drug at prices Pfizer established. Eurim claims Pfizer's practices have increased the worldwide price of its drug and made it difficult for Eurim to sell that drug either in Korea or in the United States. Eurim claims Pfizer's price-fixing agreements violate U.S. antitrust law. Do you think Eurim can prove the antitrust case against Pfizer?

2. A German helicopter firm (Hifly) made a contract with a Kuwait firm (Oil Bucks) to provide transportation during the reconstruction of several oil wells in Kuwait. Hifly negotiated the contract while it and Oil Bucks were in the United States (New Mexico). Hifly was paid by funds Oil Bucks had in banks in the United States. Hifly also trained some of its pilots in the New Mexico desert to simulate the conditions in Kuwait.

   One of Hifly's helicopters crashed in Kuwait, killing three U.S. citizens who had been employed by Oil Bucks to work on the oil well reconstruction. The heirs of the deceased oil workers brought suit against Hifly in New Mexico. Hifly claimed New Mexico did not have jurisdiction to hear the case. Do you agree? Why? What if the helicopters were manufactured in the U.S.? What provisions in the Hifly–Oil Bucks contract could affect your answer?

3. Group Bull, a French computer firm, receives an offer in the mail from Furniture One, a Grand Rapids, Michigan, furniture manufacturing firm seeking to purchase 100 computers. The offer was sent from the U.S. firm on March 1 and it arrives in

France on March 5. On March 10, the French firm sends its acceptance by Federal Express mail. That acceptance is received in Grand Rapids by the furniture firm on March 12. Having found a better price from a Chicago firm, the U.S. furniture manufacturer sends a revocation of its offer to the French firm. The revocation arrives at that firm on March 11. Discuss why there is or is not a valid contract.

4. The U.S. enacted a law to establish a trust fund to pay for the cleanup of toxic waste sites. The payment for the cleanup is financed by taxes on oil. Congress levied a 20 cents per barrel tax on imported oil and a 14 cents per barrel tax on U.S. oil. The 6 cents difference was intended to aid the economics of oil-producing firms in the United States. Several countries with firms which export oil into the United States complain the U.S. law violates WTO. The United States argues that (1) the 6 cents difference in the tax on a barrel of oil is so small (.0012 cents per gallon) that commercially it is insignificant, (2) the tax has not caused a decrease in the demand for oil and did not affect the export of oil into the United States. What principle of WTO would the oil exporters argue is being violated? How would you decide this case?

Case Problems

1. Nippondensa U.S.A. is a Delaware corporation which is a wholly owned subsidiary of Nippondensa Inc., a Japanese automobile parts manufacturing company. Maxine the manager and Susan the salesperson work at Nippondensa U.S.A.'s main office for 3 years until November 7, 1992. On that day, Maxine and Susan were fired and Nippondensa U.S.A. hired two male Japanese citizens, Terry Toyota and Larry Yoshida, to replace Maxine and Susan. Maxine and Susan claim their firing violates the U.S. civil rights law because Nippondensa U.S.A. discriminates in who it hires based on sex (only males) and national origin (only Japanese citizens). Nippondensa U.S.A. says the 1964 civil rights law does not apply to it because the U.S.–Japan Friendship, Commerce, and Navigation (FCN) Treaty of 1974 takes precedence. That treaty has a clause that says:

> Nationals and companies of either Party shall be permitted to engage within the territories of the other Party, accountants and other technical experts, executive personnel, attorneys, agents and other specialists of their choice.

Does this clause of the FCN treaty allow Nippondensa U.S.A. to give preference in its hiring to Japanese citizens despite the civil rights law? Why?

2. The United States has entered into a tax treaty with Switzerland that provides that an individual resident of Switzerland is exempt from U.S. tax on compensation received for labor or personal services performed in the United States if he or she is temporarily present in the United States for less than 183 days and received compensation for labor or services performed as an employee or agent of a corporation or other entity of Switzerland.

Ingemar Johansson, a Swedish citizen, fought Floyd Patterson three times for the heavyweight championship of the world, each time in the United States. All three fights occurred between December 1, 1959 and March 1, 1961. When the IRS claimed Johansson owed it approximately one million dollars in tax payments, Johansson claimed he was a resident of Switzerland and thus was exempt from U.S. taxes. Johansson argues:

a. Switzerland has classified him as a resident.

b. He entered into a contract on December 1, 1959 with a Swiss corporation and was employed by it for the entire period through March 1961.

The IRS argues:

a. Johansson resided in Switzerland only 80 days compared to the 120 days he spent in Sweden and 217 days he spent in the United States during this period.

b. Johansson was the sole employee of the Swiss corporation and his revenue was its sole source of income.

Who is correct and why?

3. Taca International Airlines, a San Salvador corporation, sued Rolls-Royce of England, Ltd., a British corporation, for negligence causing damage to its airplanes. Taca brought suit against the English corporation in New York by serving a summons on Rolls-Royce, Inc., a U.S. subsidiary corporation incorporated in and doing business in the United States. Rolls-Royce Ltd. maintains that the New York court does not have jurisdiction over it since its products in the United States, including the engine sold to Taca, are sold and serviced only by its subsidiary, R.R. Inc. Do you agree?

4. What relationship or activities performed by a U.S.-based multinational chemical corporation, such as Union Carbide Inc., would make it liable for damages to persons killed or seriously injured from an explosion in a foreign country from a factory owned by one of its foreign subsidiary corporations?

Footnotes

[1] "World Economy Survey," *The Economist*, September 19, 1992, p. 17.

[2] "The 100 Largest Foreign Investments in the U.S.—The Deal Flow Dries Up" *Forbes*, July 19, 1993, p. 174.

[3] Robert W. Sarnoff, Chairman of the Board of Directors, RCA Corporation, *1974 Annual Meeting of Shareholders*, p. 4. New York, May 7, 1974.

[4] As reported in the *Honolulu Star-Bulletin*, October 19, 1993. p. A-4.

59

Accountants and Professional Liability

Professional Standards
The Accountant–Client Relationship

Liability to Third Parties
Statutory Liability

Business firms rely on certified public accountants (CPAs) to perform a number of important functions, including preparing financial statements (which summarize the company's current financial condition and recent financial performance), auditing the company's finances, valuing the company's assets, preparing tax returns, advising the company on how to reduce its tax burden, and assisting the company in complying with governmental requirements. Third parties also rely on the work of accountants: for example, a party deciding whether to purchase a target company is likely to rely on financial statements prepared by the target company's accountants. Clients and others who rely on the work of accountants have a strong interest in ensuring that the work is done with care and skill.

In recent years, accountants have had to be concerned as never before about their potential liability to clients, third parties, and the government. When a savings and loan collapses or when a corporate acquisition goes sour, aggrieved investors often seek to hold the accountants liable for failing to prepare accurate financial statements. This chapter traces the legal developments affecting accountants and their profession. Other licensed professionals, such as architects, engineers, and even ministers, also must be concerned

with the imposition of liability on accountants and other professional service providers.

There are several ways in which public accountants can incur liability in the practice of their profession. Failure to meet the standards of an employment contract will expose an accountant to contract liability (see the general discussion of contractual liability in Part III of this text). Theories of intentional tort and negligence (discussed in Chapters 6 and 7) can also provide the basis for a suit against an accountant who has performed improperly. In addition to common-law actions, there are various federal and state statutes that impose both civil and criminal liability on accountants.

An accountant's potential liability to third parties, once tightly restricted by the privity-of-contract requirement, has been expanded in recent years. An accountant's exposure to criminal liability has also expanded. This chapter traces the legal developments affecting accountants and their profession.

Professional Standards

Accountants are expected to comply with standards set forth by a number of professional bodies. The American Institute of Certified Public

Accountants (AICPA), the professional association of CPAs, has promulgated many of these standards. The most important guidelines applicable to accountants are **generally accepted accounting principles (GAAP)**, a compilation of conventions that accountants are expected to follow. Also important are **generally accepted auditing standards (GAAS)**, which set forth standards to be used in the performance of audits.

The standards included in GAAP are derived from a variety of sources. The Financial Accounting Standards Board (FASB) issues guidelines and interpretations applicable to accounting practices; many of these are reflected in GAAP. GAAP also reflects some of the accounting regulations promulgated by the Securities and Exchange Commission (SEC) applicable to financial statements prepared in connection with SEC filings. Pronouncements by the AICPA also help to shape GAAP.

While compliance with GAAP and GAAS can substantially reduce the likelihood that an accountant will be subject to liability, compliance is not in itself a complete defense. Thus the court in *U.S. v. Simon*, 425 F.2d 796 (1970), in affirming the convictions of accountants who had apparently adhered to GAAP, stated:

> Generally accepted accounting principles instruct an accountant what to do in the usual case where he has no reason to doubt that the affairs of the corporation are being honestly conducted. Once he has reason to believe that this basic assumption is false, an entirely different situation confronts him.

Accountants' common law civil liability to clients can be grounded in contract or in tort. In many contract suits and in all tort actions the plaintiff will be required to show that the defendant accountant failed to satisfy a required standard of care. Accountants are expected to exercise "reasonable care and competence." In *Kemmerlin v. Wingate*, the Supreme Court defined this standard as the care and competence normally exercised by accountants in the particular locality, according to accepted professional standards. Since laypersons generally do not possess knowledge of this standard, a plaintiff must produce expert testimony to establish the standard of care allegedly breached.

The Accountant–Client Relationship

Confidentiality

The confidentiality of the relationship between an attorney and his or her client is protected by law. No such protection applies to the accountant–client relationship. Thus, in *Couch v. United States*, 409 U.S. 322 (1973), the Supreme Court ruled that the Internal Revenue Service (IRS) could summon from an accountant records owned by a client even though the client objected.

Despite the *Couch* ruling, the U.S. Court of Appeals for the Second Circuit devised a doctrine providing that an accountant's work-product could be immune from forced disclosure. In *U.S. v. Arthur Young and Co.*, 677 F.2d 211 (1982), the court reasoned that protecting the confidentiality of accountants' records was necessary to promote full disclosure by clients to accountants. This disclosure, according to the court, was necessary to protect the integrity of the securities markets, which depend on complete and accurate information from their participants. The court thus developed a confidentiality doctrine for accountants similar to the work-product immunity that applies to attorneys.

The Court of Appeals ruling in *Arthur Young* was controversial, because it seemed to conflict with the Supreme Court's decision in *Couch*. In the case that follows, the Supreme Court reviewed the *Arthur Young* decision to settle whether an accountant–client privilege exists under law.

UNITED STATES V. ARTHUR YOUNG AND CO.

U.S. Supreme Court
465 U.S. 805 (1984)

BACKGROUND: The IRS sued the accounting firm of Arthur Young and Co. (respondent), an independent auditor for the Amerada Hess Corporation, to obtain files and workpapers relating to Amerada's tax returns. One of Young's functions was to evaluate the adequacy of Amerada's reserve account for contingent tax liabilities. The reserve account was required to cover tax liabilities that might later be assessed by the IRS over and above those reflected on the corporation's return.

After a routine IRS audit revealed questionable financial practices on the part of the corporation, the IRS initiated a criminal investigation of its tax returns. The IRS issued a summons to Young commanding that it hand over its Amerada files, including workpapers. At Amerada's request, Young refused to honor the summons. The IRS sued in federal District Court to enforce the summons.

The District Court ruled in favor of the IRS. The Court of Appeals for the Second Circuit, in reversing the lower court's decision with regard to the workpapers, fashioned a doctrine of work-product immunity for accountants.

Burger, Chief Justice

The Court of Appeals . . . concluded that "substantial countervailing policies" required the fashioning of a work-product immunity for an independent auditor's tax accrual workpapers. To the extent that the Court of Appeals, in its concern for the "chilling effect" of the disclosure of tax accrual workpapers, sought to facilitate communication between independent auditors and their clients, its remedy more closely resembles a testimonial accountant–client privilege than a work-product immunity for accountants' workpapers. But as this Court stated in *Couch v. United States*, "no confidential accountant–client privilege exists under federal law, and no state-created privilege has been recognized in federal cases." In light of *Couch*, the Court of Appeals' effort to foster candid communication between accountant and client by creating a self-styled work-product privilege was misplaced, and conflicts with what we see as the clear intent of Congress.

Nor do we find persuasive the argument that a work-product immunity for accountants' tax accrual workpapers is a fitting analogue to the attorney work-product doctrine established in *Hickman v. Taylor*. The *Hickman* work-product doctrine was founded upon the private attorney's role as the client's confidential advisor and advocate, a loyal representative whose duty it is to present the client's case in the most favorable possible light. An independent certified public accountant performs a different role. By certifying the public reports that collectively depict a corporation's financial status, the independent auditor assumes a *public* responsibility transcending any employment relationship with the client. The independent public accountant performing this special function owes ultimate allegiance to the corporation's creditors and stockholders, as well as to investing public. This "public watchdog" function demands that the accountant maintain total independence from the client at all times and requires complete fidelity to the public trust. To insulate from disclosure a certified public accountant's interpretations of the client's financial statements would be to ignore the significance of the accountant's role as a disinterested analyst charged with public obligations.

We cannot accept the view that the integrity of the securities markets will suffer absent some protection for accountants' tax accrual workpapers. The Court of Appeals apparently feared that, were the IRS to have access to tax accrual workpapers, a corporation might be tempted to withhold from its auditor certain information relevant and material to the proper evaluation of its financial statements. But the independent certified public accountant cannot be content with the corporation's representations that its tax accrual reserves are adequate; the auditor is ethically and professionally obligated to ascertain for himself as far as possible whether the corporation's contingent tax liabilities have been accurately stated. If the auditor were convinced that the scope of the examination had been limited by management's reluctance to disclose matters relating to the tax accrual reserves, the auditor would be unable to issue an unqualified opinion as to the accuracy of the corporation's financial statements. Instead, the auditor would be required to issue a qualified opinion, an adverse opinion, or a disclaimer of opinion, thereby notifying the investing public of possible potential problems inherent in the corporation's financial reports. Responsible corporate management would not risk a qualified evaluation of a corporate taxpayer's financial posture to afford cover for questionable positions reflected in a prior tax return. Thus, the independent auditor's obligation to serve the public interest assures that the integrity of the securities markets will be preserved, without the need for a work-product immunity for accountants' tax accrual workpapers.

Congress has granted to the IRS "broad latitude to adopt enforcement techniques helpful in the performance of [its] tax collection and assessment responsibilities." Recognizing the intrusiveness of demands for the production of tax accrual workpapers, the IRS has demonstrated administrative sensitivity to the concerns expressed by the accounting profession by tightening its internal requirements for the issuance of such summonses.

Beyond question it is desirable and in the public interest to encourage full disclosures by corporate clients to their independent accountants; if it is necessary to balance competing interests, however, the need of the Government for full disclosure of all information relevant to tax liability must also weigh in that balance. This kind of policy choice is best left to the Legislative Branch. Accordingly, the judgment of the Court of Appeals is reversed in part, and the case is remanded.

DECISION: The Supreme Court ruled that the IRS summons seeking the accountant's files and workpapers pertaining to a client's tax returns was enforceable.

Accountant's Liability to Client

Contract Liability An accountant's liability to a client is usually based in some way on the contract with the client. Violation of the agreement's terms can give rise to an action for breach of contract. A breach-of-contract action can be based on violations of either the express or implied terms of the contract.

If an accountant expressly agrees to prepare and file a client's tax returns by April 15 and then misses the deadline, an express term of the agreement has been violated. The accountant can be held liable to the client for any penalties resulting from the late filing.

If the accountant commits careless errors that cause the client to suffer losses, the client again has an action in breach of contract. This is true even though the contract is silent regarding the standard of care to which the accountant must adhere. Every accountant is impliedly bound, in the performance of a contract, to exercise that degree of skill and competence commonly exercised by members of the profession.

Tort Liability In a contract action against an accountant the parties' rights and obligations are primarily determined by their own agreement. The parties' rights and liabilities in a tort action are determined by the common law or by statute. Recall from Chapter 6 that tort liability is founded upon the breach of duties imposed by society. The breach can be unintentional, as in the case of negligence, or deliberate, as with fraud.

Negligence As in other negligence actions, a client suing an accountant for negligence must establish (1) that the accountant owed the client a *duty of care*, (2) that the accountant *breached this duty*, (3) that the client suffered an *injury*, and (4) that the accountant's breach was the *proximate cause* of the client's injury.

ETHICS
Ethical Dilemmas Facing Professionals

All types of professional practitioners face similar ethical dilemmas. Doctors, engineers, lawyers, and accountants encounter problems concerning determining who is the real client, how much should be disclosed to clients, who should make certain decisions, and what information should be kept confidential. For example, all these professionals may encounter clients who are engaged in wrongdoing where the professional possesses key information relating to the wrongful acts. Under what circumstances should a professional blow the whistle using confidential information?

Consider the following short case problems.

- An accountant conducts an audit for a client. In the process of the audit the accountant discovers that the client is using unsafe procedures in pasteurizing its product. There have been several recent outbreaks of salmonella poisoning in the area, but they have not been associated with the client. The accountant reports the information to the client, but no action is taken. What should the accountant do?

- An accounting firm provides a full range of services for both the Alpha Brokerage Company and the Modern Industrial Bank. In the process of auditing Alpha, the firm discovers that Alpha is engaged in practices that have the effect of creating negative balances in its checking accounts with Modern Industrial. From their work for Modern Industrial the accounting firm realizes that the bank is not aware of Alpha's practices. The legality of Alpha's action is ambiguous, but it clearly breaches the implied understanding with the bank concerning the operation of the checking accounts. Should the firm notify the bank of what is going on?

- An accountant discovers that a manager at one of its clients is embezzling large sums. The accountant discloses this and the manager is removed from all financial responsibility. The accountant then discovers that the manager is being hired by another client, having received a strong positive recommendation from the first client. What, if anything, should the accountant do?

The accountant's duty of care to a client generally originates in the contract between them. The accountant's obligations in tort law are thus organically linked to obligations in contract law. As with other professionals, accountants have a general duty to perform services with the level of "skill, care, knowledge and judgment usually possessed and exercised by members of that profession in the particular locality, in accordance with accepted professional standards and in good faith. . . ."

Fraud Accountants can also be held liable to their clients for intentional torts. Perhaps the most common action is one alleging fraud. Recall from Chapter 14 that fraud generally involves a material misrepresentation of fact, made with knowledge of its falsity and with intent to deceive. To collect damages for fraud, a plaintiff must prove personal reliance on the misrepresentation and that the reliance caused injury. Since accountants' opinions are representation, they can be used as the basis for fraud actions.

An accountant may be held liable for fraud even in cases in which he or she does not issue a formal opinion. Because an accountant is assumed to have a certain level of expertise in business matters, a person might be justified in relying on a statement made by an accountant regarding the value of an investment. This is true even if the exact same statement, if made by someone without comparable expertise, could be dismissed as an "opinion" that could not form the basis of a fraud action. The case that follows illustrates this point.

HALL V. EDGE
Supreme Court of Oklahoma
782 P.2d 122 (1989)

BACKGROUND: Hall was an investor in certain limited partnerships sponsored by Edge Energies. Each limited partnership owned an oil or gas project. Hall lost his investment, and sued the general partner in the partnerships as well as Jackson, the accountant for Edge Energies. Hall claimed that Jackson defrauded Hall by claiming, before Hall made the investment, that Edge Energies' limited partnerships were a "good deal," that they were "good moneymakers," and that "they were expecting something like a two-year payoff." The trial court judge ordered summary judgment for Jackson and the appeals court affirmed. The Supreme Court of Oklahoma granted certiorari.

Summers, Justice

Generally, the false representation [in a fraud action] must be a statement of existing fact and not a mere expression of opinion. For example, a seller's opinion which is nothing more than "puffing" will not give rise to an action based on misrepresentation. However, courts have fashioned several exceptions to this general rule and will allow, under certain circumstances, a cause of action based on a false representation which was in the form of an opinion.

One court explained three exceptions to this general rule as follows:

Where circumstances indicate that the parties did not stand in a position of parity and normal wariness with respect to the subject of the representation, however, exceptions have been carved out of the general rule. Most of these exceptions derive their legitimacy from circumstances that would lead the reasonable person to believe that implicit in the prediction or opinion is an assertion of fact upon which the recipient of the representation might prudently rely. Where the person making the representation occupies a fiduciary or other position of trust for the recipient of his remarks, for instance, the recipient may be justified in assuming the correctness not only of factual representations but also of opinions. . . . Since partners as to partnership matters are fiduciaries *inter se*, it is often found that partners were entitled to rely on the opinions of their colleagues.

Another exception to the general requirement that the misrepresentation be one of existing fact appears in the situation where the speaker may reasonably be understood as having based an opinion or prediction on facts that are unavailable to the listener either because he does not have access to them or because he is obviously incapable of interpreting them. Still a third exception is based upon the logical assumption that one who asserts that a future event will come to pass impliedly warrants that he knows of no fact that will prevent its occurrence. *Day v. Avery.*

These exceptions are expressed in the *Restatement (Second) of Torts*. Professors Prosser and Keeton have explained this principle as follows:

[I]t has been recognized very often that the expression of an opinion may carry with it an implied assertion, not only that the speaker knows no facts which would preclude such an opinion, but that he does know facts which justify it. There is quite general agreement that such assertion is to be implied where the defendant holds himself out or is understood as having special knowledge of the matter which is not available to the plaintiff, so that his opinion becomes in effect an assertion summarizing his knowledge.

Thus, the ordinary man is free to deal in reliance upon the opinion of an expert jeweler as to the value of a diamond, of an attorney upon a point of law, of a physician upon a matter of health, of a banker upon the validity of a signature, or the owner of land at a distance as to its worth, even though the opinion is that of his antagonist in a bargaining transaction. W. Keeton, and W. Prosser, *Prosser and Keeton on the Law of Torts*.

* * *

In today's case Hall alleged that Jackson stated that the partnerships were a "good deal," that they were "good moneymakers," and "they were expecting something like a two-year payoff." The phrase "expecting something like a two-year payoff" is significant. This phrase quantifies the terms "good deal" and "good moneymakers" and thus, may be found to be a representation of the quality of the investment. A representation of the quality of property bought unseen may be the basis for fraud inducing a contract for sale. Finefrock v. Carney, 263 P.2d 744 (Okl. 1953).

Jackson responded to this argument on summary judgment by arguing that Edge drilling ventures were good "because at the time the statement was made the drilling ventures of Edge Energies were often profitable." Jackson's argument is that his opinion concerned all of the Edge partnerships generally and not the specific partnerships invested in by Hall. Hall responded that he understood Jackson to be making a representation that each and all of the limited partnerships would have a two-year payback. These issues are properly left for resolution by a jury.

DECISION: The Supreme Court of Oklahoma reversed the order of summary judgment against Jackson, allowing Hall to attempt to prove his fraud claim at trial.

The Effect of Accountants' Opinions

After auditing a company's financial statement, an accountant will issue an **opinion**. An accountant's opinion is a representation to those who can reasonably be expected to rely on the financial statements.

By expressing an **unqualified opinion**, an accountant represents that the company's financial statements fairly reflect the company's financial picture; that is, the balance sheet properly presents the firm's financial position, the income statement fairly represents the results of the firm's operations, and changes in financial position are accurately depicted. An unqualified opinion requires that the financial statements reflect the consistent application of GAAP.

An accountant who is unable to express an unqualified opinion is required to issue one of the following: a **qualified opinion**, which can be necessitated by material uncertainty or deviations from GAAP; an **adverse opinion**, which states that the financial statements do not fairly present the firm's position in conformance with GAAP; or a **disclaimer of opinion**, which is issued when there is insufficient information to form an opinion on the accuracy of the audited statements.

Accountants may sometimes prepare or analyze financial documents without conducting a full-blown audit. In such circumstances accountants rely on the client's financial records without investigating their accuracy. The AICPA has developed the concepts of *compilations* and *reviews* to protect accountants from unwarranted reliance on such documents by clients and third parties. In a **compilation** the accountant puts information supplied by the client into the form of financial statements. The compilation should be accompanied by a report explaining that no audit has been performed and that the accuracy of the information cannot be assured. Each page of the compiled financial statements should contain a printed reference directing the reader to the disclaiming report. A **review** involves a limited analysis of financial statements that have been prepared by the client. In a review the accountant expresses limited assurance that the financial statements are not materially misleading. In an accompanying report, which must be referred to on each page of the statements, the accountant states that the analysis conducted in the review was substantially less than that for a proper audit.

Although qualifications and disclaimers may limit an accountant's liability in certain tort actions, they do not themselves relieve the accountant of contractual obligations.

Liability of Tax Preparers

Accountants can expose themselves to contract or tort liability in the preparation of clients' tax returns. Accountants can be held liable for damages resulting from the late filing of clients' returns, from negligent misstatement of tax liability, and from erroneous tax advice. In *Whitlock v. PKW Supply Co.*, 269 S.E.2d 36 (Ga. Ct. App. 1980), an accountant was held liable for breach of contract for refusing to either file or return the client's tax returns until the bill was paid. The court noted that the accountant could also have been held liable for the tort of nonfeasance, for failing to attempt to perform as promised.

In preparing taxes, as in an accountant's other duties, an accountant is required to exercise the degree of care, skill, and competence exercised by others in the profession. Breach of this duty can leave the accountant liable for compensatory damages, which are commonly penalties and interest assessed against the client because of the tax preparer's mistake. Tax preparers are sometimes also required to compensate clients for fees paid to attorneys and/or other accountants to straighten out the tax preparer's error.

A tax preparer can also be subject to civil and criminal liability under the provisions of the Internal Revenue Code. This will be discussed later in the chapter.

Liability to Third Parties

Clients are not the only parties that rely on accountants' work. A potential creditor will rely on a company's financial statements to evaluate the riskiness of a contemplated loan. A potential purchaser of a firm will examine its balance sheet to determine the value of the assets and the extent of the liabilities that would be assumed. A potential buyer of a firm's securities will use the firm's prospectus and other financial data to make the purchase decision. A potential assignee of a debt

---

ETHICS
Accountants' Professional Responsibility

The practice of accountancy is a recognized profession. Entry into the accounting field is controlled through educational requirements and an exam. Standards are developed and enforced by the profession, and the license to practice may be revoked under certain circumstances.

As with all professions, the question may be raised whether the minimal levels for professional conduct should be determined primarily by the profession itself. On the pro side is the argument that the professionals themselves better understand the technical intricacies of their field and have greater depth of knowledge. They also have a strong incentive to self-regulate because the public is often unable to judge the quality of individual practitioners, and incompetents and wrongdoers must be weeded out in order to maintain the reputation of the accounting profession.

On the other hand, the practice of a profession is a business and the professionals may often be accused of looking out for themselves in assuming all the power of regulation of their practice. Critics of professional self-regulation point to "ethics" rules that formerly prohibited competition in fees (these have been struck down by antitrust actions brought against the profession itself) and still do restrict advertising.

As emphasized in this chapter, the law poses an outer bound on the actions of accountants. Yet the law is not entirely independent in that many cases make reference to and rely on the self-created standards of the profession in deciding to impose liability. At times the courts have been handicapped by a "conspiracy of silence" in which the most qualified professionals refused to step forward and testify against colleagues.

will want to determine the collectibility of that debt before exchanging something of value for the assignment.

In deciding how far to extend an accountant's liability to third parties, the law must reconcile conflicting policy interests. On the one hand, it would appear that the efficient operation of credit markets, securities markets, and other markets would require that participants be entitled to rely on the relevant information available to them. If participants in these markets are forced to assume the risks associated with inaccurate information, they will demand compensation for that risk in the marketplace. An economist would argue that it is most efficient to place the risk on the party with the power to control the risk. In our case the accountant would be one of the parties best able to control the risks to third parties of inaccurate information.

On the other hand, the accountant might not be able to bear the risk of liability to every third party that could conceivably be hurt by reliance on a financial document prepared by the accountant. For one thing there is no clear way to control the number of people who rely on particular financial documents since clients are the ones that distribute the documents. If a negligent mistake could leave an accountant liable to thousands of unknown third parties, the accountant would clearly be assuming an unreasonable risk. Accountants could, of course, insure against such

risk, but the cost of such extensive coverage— whether borne by accountants or their clients— might be prohibitive.

For many years the law placed more emphasis on the need to limit accountants' liability to third parties than on the need to protect third parties from the negligent mistakes of accountants. Thus an accountant's liability for negligence was limited to those with contractual relationships with the accountant—those in **privity of contract** with the accountant. Over the last several decades the privity requirement has been steadily eroded in most areas of law. Since the 1960s the privity doctrine has been weakened with regard to accountants.

The scope of potential liability is dramatized by Figure 59-1. The figure does not actually represent the state of the law as it is today. As we shall see in the pages that follow, every jurisdiction imposes some sort of limitation on the right of a third party—that is, someone other than the client—to sue an accountant. The figure is designed merely to demonstrate the massive exposure to liability that could result if everyone who happens to rely on the work of an accountant could hold the accountant liable for errors in his or her work. As discussed below, some jurisdictions have expanded the scope of accountant's liability to third parties to the point where it approaches the extreme scenario illustrated by Figure 59-1.

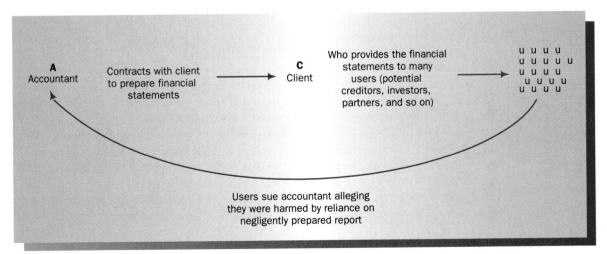

FIGURE 59-1

Open-Ended Scope of Accountant's Potential Liability

Privity and the Ultramares Doctrine

The proposition that an accountant's negligence liability is limited to those in privity with the accountant was set forth in the classic case of *Ultramares Corporation v. Touche*. In an often-quoted phrase from his opinion, Chief Justice Cardozo stated that an accountant's negligent error should not result in exposure to liability "in an indeterminate amount for an indeterminate time to an indeterminate class." Cardozo's opinion is excerpted here.

ULTRAMARES CORPORATION V. TOUCHE

Court of Appeals of New York

174 N.E. 441 (1931)

BACKGROUND: Ultramares Corporation (plaintiff) sued Touche, Niven & Company (defendant) for losses sustained in lending money to a Touche client whose Touche-certified balance sheet misrepresented its solvency. Touche performed accounting services for Fred Stern and Co., a rubber dealer. In February 1924 Touche issued a balance sheet that showed Stern's net worth to be over a million dollars. Touche certified that the balance sheet presented "a true and correct view" of Stern's financial position as of December 31, 1923. In reality, Stern was insolvent. The firm's net worth was misrepresented by falsified entries in Stern's books. The Ultramares Corporation loaned a large amount of money to Stern, relying on the balance sheet. Although Touche was not specifically aware that Ultramares would rely on the balance sheet, it was aware that Stern would use the balance sheet for the purpose of securing credit. Stern went bankrupt in January 1925. Ultramares sued Touche for both fraud and negligence in the preparation of Stern's balance sheet.

The trial court judge dismissed the fraud action and sent the negligence action to the jury. After the jury returned a verdict for Ultramares for $187,576. 32 on the negligence action, the trial judge dismissed the cause of action for negligence. The case was appealed to the Supreme Court, Appellate Division (an intermediate appeals court in New York), which affirmed the dismissal of the fraud action but restored the jury verdict with regard to the negligence action.

Cardozo, Chief Justice

We are brought to the question of duty, its origin and measure.

The defendants owed to their employer a duty imposed by law to make their certificate without fraud, and a duty growing out of contract to make it with the care and caution proper to their calling. Fraud includes the pretense of knowledge when knowledge there is none. To creditors and investors to whom the employer exhibited the certificate, the defendants owed a like duty to make it without fraud, since there was notice in the circumstances of its making that the employer did not intend to keep it to himself. A different question develops when we ask whether they owed a duty to these to make it without negligence. If liability for negligence exists, a thoughtless slip or blunder, the failure to detect a theft or forgery beneath the cover of deceptive entries, may expose accountants to a liability in an indeterminate amount for an indeterminate time to an indeterminate class. The hazards of a business conducted on these terms are so extreme as to enkindle doubt whether a flaw may not exist in the implication of a duty that exposes to these consequences.

* * *

The assault upon the citadel of privity is proceeding these days apace. How far the inroads shall extend is now a favorite subject of judicial discussion. [The court then reviewed case law dealing with privity of contract.]

* * *

Liability for negligence if adjudged in this case will extend to many callings other than an auditor's. Lawyers who certify their opinion as to the validity of municipal or corporate bonds, with knowledge that the opinion will be brought to the notice of the public, will become liable to the investors, if they have overlooked a statute or a decision, to the same extent as if the controversy were one between client and adviser. Title companies insuring titles to a tract of land, with knowledge that at an approaching auction the fact that they have insured will be stated to the bidders, will become liable to purchasers who may wish the benefit of a policy without payment of a premium. These illustrations may seem to be extreme, but they go little, if any, farther than we are invited to go now. Negligence, moreover, will have one standard when viewed in relation to the employer, and another and at times a stricter standard when viewed in relation to the public. Explanations that might seem plausible, omissions that might be reasonable, if the duty is confined to the employer, conducting a business that presumably at least is not a fraud upon his creditors, might wear another aspect if an independent duty to be suspicious even of one's principal is owing to investors. "Every one making a promise having the quality of a contract will be under a duty to the promisee by virtue of the promise, but under another duty, apart from contract, to an indefinite number of potential beneficiaries when performance has begun. The assumption of one relation will mean the involuntary assumption of a series of new relations, inescapably hooked together."

Our holding does not emancipate accountants from the consequences of fraud. It does not relieve them if their audit has been so negligent as to justify a finding that they had no genuine belief in its adequacy, for this again is fraud. It does no more than say that, if less than this is proved, if there has been neither reckless misstatement nor insincere profession of an opinion, but only honest blunder, the ensuing liability for negligence is one that is bounded by the contract, and is to be enforced between the parties by whom the contract has been made. We doubt whether the average business man receiving a certificate without paying for it, and receiving it merely as one among a multitude of possible investors, would look for anything more.

DECISION: The Court of Appeals, New York's highest court, refused to allow a recovery based on negligence, but granted a new trial with regard to the allegation of fraud.

Gross Negligence and Fraud

In the second part of his *Ultramares* opinion, Cardozo noted that the lack of privity was no defense to a fraud action. As for the relationship between negligence and fraud, Cardozo wrote: "negligence or blindness, even when not equivalent to fraud, is none the less evidence to sustain an inference of fraud. At least this is so if the negligence is gross."

Since the *Ultramares* opinion, many courts have used gross negligence theories to circumvent the privity requirement. Although the accepted legal doctrine allows gross negligence to raise only an inference of fraud, many courts have treated it as being tantamount to fraud. Courts have thus allowed recovery against accountants to third parties who have established gross negli-

gence, without requiring any other evidence to support the inference of fraud. Some of these courts have not made it clear that the recovery is based on fraud and not on gross negligence. This manipulation of the relationship between fraud and gross negligence has been harshly criticized by legal scholars.

Extension of Liability

Since the late 1960s the "assault on the citadel of privity" has spread into the area of accountant's liability. Courts in many jurisdictions will now allow a third-party plaintiff to recover against an accountant for ordinary negligence.

Such recoveries generally are limited to circumstances in which the plaintiff's reliance on the accountant's work was actually foreseen by the accountant. Through the requirement that the reliance be foreseen, the courts limit liability to a small, well-defined group. An example of such an extension of liability occurred in *Rusch Factors, Inc. v. Levin*, where a federal court in Rhode Island upheld an action by a financier who relied on financial statements prepared by an accountant for a corporation seeking a loan. The credit application required the financial statements and the accountant understood the purpose of the statements. The *Rusch* court, in support of its argument for broader accountants' liability to third parties, cited tentative drafts of the *Restatement (Second) of Torts*. This *Restatement* has since been finalized. Section 552, dealing with information negligently supplied for the guidance of others, provides:

(1) One who, in the course of his business, profession or employment, or in any other transaction in which he has a pecuniary interest, supplies false information for the guidance of others in their business transactions, is subject to liability for pecuniary loss caused to them by their justifiable reliance upon the information, if he fails to exercise reasonable care or competence in obtaining or communicating the information.

(2) Except as stated in Subsection (3), the liability stated in Subsection (1) is limited to loss suffered

(a) by the person or one of a limited group of persons for whose benefit and guidance he intends to supply the information or knows that the recipient intends to supply it; and

(b) through reliance upon it in a transaction that he intends the information to influence or knows that the recipient so intends or in a substantially similar transaction.

(3) The liability of one who is under a public duty to give the information extends to loss suffered by any of the class of persons for whose benefit the duty is created, in any of the transactions in which it is intended to protect them.

Some jurisdictions have extended the scope of an accountant's liability to third parties even further than that prescribed by Section 552. The supreme courts of California and New Jersey, for example, have held that an accountant can be held liable to a third party who relies on the accountant's work if the reliance was *reasonably foreseeable*—even if the reliance wasn't actually foreseen. Under such a standard, for example, an accountant might conceivably be held liable to a third party, not specifically known to the accountant, who relies on financial statements prepared in connection with a Securities and Exchange Commission filing.

Although some jurisdictions have completely abandoned the *Ultramares* privity requirement, others still follow *Ultramares*. In *Credit Alliance Corporation v. Arthur Andersen & Co.*, 493 N.Y.S.2d 435 (1985), New York's highest court ruled that an accountant may not be held liable to a third party absent privity of contract or a relationship that approaches privity. An example of a relationship that approaches privity would be if the accountant was hired by the client for the express purpose of preparing financial statements for the third party's use.

The law regarding an accountant's liability to third parties is still evolving in most jurisdictions. The case that follows summarizes the various approaches adopted in different states.

FIRST FLORIDA BANK V. MAX MITCHELL & CO.

Supreme Court of Florida
558 So.2d 9 (1990)

BACKGROUND: Mitchell, a CPA, prepared financial statements for C.M. Systems for the 1983 and 1984 fiscal years. In 1985, Mitchell delivered those financial statements to an officer of First Florida Bank and negotiated with the bank to provide a $500,000 unsecured line of credit to C.M. Systems. The bank approved the line of credit on the basis of the financial statements and several oral statements made by Mitchell regarding the financial condition of C.M. Systems. C.M. Systems thereafter borrowed the entire amount of the line of credit and never repaid it. The bank subsequently discovered that the financial statements prepared by Mitchell overstated C.M. Systems' assets and net income and understated its liabilities. The bank sued Mitchell. The trial court dismissed the suit because the bank was not in privity of contract with Mitchell. The appeals court affirmed, but specifically requested the Supreme Court of Florida to rule on whether an accountant may be held liable to a third party for negligence in the absense of privity.

Grimes, Judge

In the more than fifty years which have elapsed since *Ultramares*, the question of an accountant's liability for negligence where no privity exists has been addressed by many courts. There are now essentially four lines of authority with respect to this issue.

(1) Except in cases of fraud, an accountant is only liable to one with whom he is in privity or near privity.

(2) An accountant is liable to third parties in the absence of privity under the circumstances described in section 552, *Restatement (Second) of Torts* (1976), which reads in pertinent part:

§ 552. Information Negligently Supplied for the Guidance of Others

(1) One who, in the course of his business, profession or employment, or in any other transaction in which he has a pecuniary interest, supplies false information for the guidance of others in their business transactions, is subject to liability for pecuniary loss caused to them by their justifiable reliance on the information, if he fails to exercise reasonable care or competence in obtaining or communicating the information.

(2) Except as stated in Subsection (3), the liability stated in Subsection (1) is limited to loss suffered

(a) by the person or one of a limited group of persons for whose benefit and guidance he intends to supply the information or knows that the recipient intends to supply it; and

(b) through reliance upon it in a transaction that he intends the information to influence or knows that the recipient so intends or in a substantially similar transaction.

(3) An accountant is liable to all persons who might reasonably be foreseen as relying upon his work product.

(4) An accountant's liability to third persons shall be determined by the balancing of various factors, among which are the extent to which the transaction was intended to affect the plaintiff, the foreseeability of harm to him, the degree of certainty that the plaintiff suffered injury, the closeness of the connection between the defendant's conduct and the injury suffered, the moral blame attached to the defendant's conduct, and the policy of preventing future harm. *Biakanja v. Irving.*

Most significant, however, to the instant case is this Court's decision in *First American Title Insurance Co. v. First Title Service Co.*, 457 So.2d 467 (Fla. 1984), which modified the *Sickler* requirement of privity for abstracters' negligence which had been relied upon in *Buchman*. In *First American Title Insurance*, we said:

The effect of our holding in this case will be to change the law of abstracter's liability, but not so drastically as the petitioner would have us change it. Where the abstracter knows, or should know, that his customer wants the abstract for the use of a prospective purchaser, and the prospect purchases the land relying on the abstract, the abstracter's duty of care runs, as we have said, not only to his customer but to the purchaser. Moreover, others involved in the transaction through their relationship to the purchaser—such as lender-mortgagees, tenants and title insurers—will also be protected where the purchaser's reliance was known or should have been known to the abstracter. But a party into whose hands the abstract falls in connection with a subsequent transaction is not among those to whom the abstracter owes a duty of care.

The opinion in *First American Title Insurance* is also important for the arguments which this Court rejected. We declined to approve the principle that an abstracter is liable in negligence to all persons who might foreseeably use and rely on the abstract. We also found unpersuasive the asserted analogy to cases of products liability, and we distinguished *A.R. Moyer, Inc.* on its facts.

* * *

It is contended by those favoring such liability that accountants, due to their professional status and the respect they command, invite reliance on their work by the business community, and that investors and creditors do, in fact, rely upon their accuracy and integrity; on the other hand, it is pointed out that unlike members of other professions, accountants have no control over the identity or number of those who rely on their work, and that imposition of liability, in negligence, to third parties would place an enormous potential burden on the profession.

Those in favor of expanding liability argue that the accounting profession no longer needs the protection of nonliability in this area, due to its wealth, and contend that the cost of insurance protection could be passed on to the client, stating that the innocent relier should not be damaged because of the error of the negligent accountant. In reply, it is observed that the cost of such insurance protection is prohibitive and, in many cases, that such coverage is not available at any price; furthermore, it is said, such higher costs would tend to lead to dominance of the profession by the large national accounting firms and to a curtailment of the availability of accountancy services to small businesses. Nor, it is contended, does the argument for extended liability take into consideration the ever more acute shortage of qualified public accountants in private practice. Those in favor of expanding liability argue that liability could easily be limited by the increased use of disclaimers and limited certifications, pointing to the success of the British experience in this area. Opponents, however, observe that the use of such devices is a commercial impossibility unless all accountants follow this practice, since it tends to dissatisfy the client, who will then turn to the use of other accountants not following this practice.

Upon consideration, we have decided to adopt the rationale of section 552, *Restatement (Second) of Torts* (1976), as setting forth the circumstances under which accountants may be held liable in negligence to persons who are not in contractual privity. The rule shall also apply to allegations of gross negligence, but the absence of privity shall continue to be no bar to charges of fraud.

* * *

Because of the heavy reliance upon audited financial statements in the contemporary financial world, we believe permitting recovery only from those in privity or near privity is unduly restrictive. On the other hand, we are persuaded by the wisdom of the rule which limits liability to those persons or classes of persons whom an accountant "knows" will rely on his opinion rather than those he "should have known" would do so because it takes into account the fact that an accountant controls neither his client's accounting records nor the distribution of his reports.

* * *

There remains the need to apply this rule to the facts at hand. At the time Mitchell prepared the audits for C.M. Systems, it was unknown that they would be used to induce the reliance of First Florida Bank to approve a line of credit for C.M. Systems. Therefore, except for the unusual facts of this case, Mitchell could not be held liable to the bank for any negligence in preparing the audit. However, Mitchell actually negotiated the loan on behalf of his client. He personally delivered the financial statements to the bank with the knowledge that it would rely upon them in considering whether or not to make the loan. Under this unique set of facts, we believe that Mitchell vouched for the integrity of the audits and that his conduct in dealing with the bank sufficed to meet the requirements of the rule which we have adopted in this opinion.

DECISION: The Supreme Court of Florida remanded the case to trial court.

Statutory Liability

In addition to common law theories of liability, there are various federal and state statutes that can provide the basis for accountants' liability. We confine our discussion to the federal statutes.

Civil Liability

Securities Laws The statutes with the greatest effect on accountants are the Securities Act of 1933 and the Securities and Exchange Act of 1934, both of which were discussed in detail in Chapter 46. Accountants can be brought under the jurisdiction of these acts through their work on financial statements, annual reports, registration statements, and proxy statements.

Recall that Section 11 of the 1933 Act provides a civil remedy for securities buyers who have been injured by their reliance on misinformation in the registration statement. Accountants can be held liable under this section for materials that they prepare or certify. Accountants who aid and abet a securities fraud are subject to liability under Section 17.

Accountants who make misstatements in proxy statements can be held liable under Section 14(a) of the 1934 Act or under SEC Rule 14a–9. Accountants who make false statements in tender offers can be held liable under Section 14(e) of the 1934 Act. Courts have held that *scienter*—knowledge of falsity with intent to deceive—is required to hold an accountant liable under both sections.

Accountants' liability under the 1934 Act is typically founded on Section 10(b), which grants an implied civil remedy to buyers or sellers of securities who have been damaged by fraud. In the landmark case of *Ernst & Ernst v. Hochfelder*, excerpted in Chapter 46, the Supreme Court ruled that a plaintiff would have to establish that the defendant acted with scienter in order to prevail in a Section 10(b) action. This standard also applies to SEC Rule 10b–5, which fills in gaps left open by Section 10(b). In the absence of guidance from the Supreme Court many circuits have held that reckless conduct is sufficient to satisfy the scienter requirement of *Ernst*.

In *Ernst* the Court did not rule on whether a party could be held liable for aiding and abetting violations of Section 10(b) or Rule 10b–5. Aiding and abetting, along with other potential sources of liability under the securities laws, is discussed in the *Resnick* case.

RESNICK V. TOUCHE ROSS AND CO.

U.S. District Court, Southern District of New York

470 F.Supp. 1020 (1979)

BACKGROUND: A group of investors (plaintiffs) sued the accounting firm Touche Ross (defendant) for securities law violations after their investments in Touche Ross's client went sour. The plaintiffs purchased securities of Weis Securities, Inc., before the latter's collapse in 1973. The plaintiffs claimed that in purchasing the securities they relied on misinformation in the financial statements. The statements were certified by Touche Ross and Co., the defendant accounting firm. The plaintiffs sued Touche Ross on a number of grounds, including violations of Section 10(b) of the Securities and Exchange Act of 1934, aiding and abetting violations of Section 10(b) and

Rule 10b–5, and violations of the antifraud provisions of Section 17 of the Securities Act of 1933. The federal District Court denied the defendant accountant's motion to dismiss the aforementioned claims.

Knopp, District Judge

Scienter and the 10(B) and 17(A) Claims

Defendants argue that plaintiffs' claims under 10(b) and 17(a) should be dismissed because they fail to satisfy the *scienter* standard enunciated by the Supreme Court in *Ernst & Ernst v. Hochfelder* (1976). Although that decision held that negligent action or inaction was not sufficient to support a 10b–5 claim, in a footnote the Court left open the question of whether recklessness would suffice. Prior to *Hochfelder*, it was established in this Circuit that the standard of *scienter* required in an action under Rule 10b–5 was "willful or reckless disregard for the truth." Several recent cases have confirmed that, in the absence of further word from the Supreme Court, reckless conduct will continue to meet the requirements of *scienter* for 10b–5 actions. Thus, the *scienter* standard we will apply is one of recklessness.

The amended complaint alleges that the statements certified by defendant were "materially false and misleading" in twenty-four specified respects, and that "defendant knew, should have known or was on notice of or recklessly disregarded" facts relating to these misstatements. The amended complaint further alleges that "the defendant obtained actual knowledge of the materially false and misleading entries . . . or, in the alternative conducted its examination and audit with reckless disregard for the truth." Finally, the amended complaint sets forth the circumstances, with respect to each alleged misstatement, that are said to constitute "defendant's knowing and/or reckless conduct."

Defendant argues, with some force, that the amended complaint in essence alleges no more than several instances of negligent conduct. However, we cannot say as a matter of law that if plaintiffs prove all their allegations the recklessness standard will not be met. As we thus cannot say as a matter of law that the *scienter* requirement has not been satisfied, plaintiff's claim under Rule 10b–5 must survive this motion to dismiss.

Aiding and Abetting

In addition to their allegations of primary violations under the securities laws by defendant, plaintiffs argue that the defendant is secondarily liable as an aider and abettor of the violations of Weis. In this Circuit, Section 10(b) and Rule 10b–5 may give rise to aiding and abetting liability.

Three elements must be established in order to impose such liability. First, it must be shown that the primary party (Weis), as distinguished from the alleged aider and abettor (Touche Ross), violated the securities laws. Second, it must be established that the aider and abettor knew of the violation. Third, the aider and abettor must have rendered substantial assistance in effecting the violation.

As to the first element, the parties do not dispute that Weis engaged in violations of the securities laws. Knowledge of the violation, the second element, has been pleaded by the plaintiffs. Once again, the *Rolf* court indicates that the *scienter* element will be satisfied by a showing of recklessness. We cannot say, as a matter of law, that plaintiffs would be unable to meet that standard at trial. Finally, the plaintiffs allege that defendant gave substantial assistance in effecting the primary securities laws violation. While it is not clear what sort of conduct is included within the term "substantial assistance," plaintiffs' allegations are sufficient for purposes of this motion. Therefore plaintiffs' cause of action for aiding and abetting under Section 10(b) and Rule 10b–5 survives this motion to dismiss.

DECISION: The court ruled that the plaintiffs had stated claims for which relief could be granted, but did not rule on the substance of those claims.

The Internal Revenue Code   The Internal Revenue Code (IRC) is an important source of liability for accountants who prepare their clients' tax returns. Section 6694 of the IRC imposes a $250 fine on preparers who underestimate a client's tax liability on the basis of unrealistic positions and a $1000 fine on preparers who willfully or recklessly make such a misstatement. Section 6695 provides penalties for tax preparers who fail to furnish a copy of the return to the client, who fail to sign the return, or who fail to retain the return (or a proper listing of it) for a period of 3 years after the return is due.

Section 7407 of the IRC authorizes the federal government to seek injunctions to prevent violations of Sections 6694 and 6695. Injunctions are also available to prevent tax preparers from engaging in other types of conduct, such as guaranteeing to clients the payment of any tax refund or the allowance of any tax credit. Tax preparers who have repeatedly violated the IRC can be enjoined from preparing taxes.

The IRC and the securities acts also contain criminal provisions, which will be discussed in the next section.

Criminal Liability

The federal securities statutes contain criminal as well as civil sanctions. Section 24 of the 1933 Act, as amended, provides for a maximum $10,000 fine or 5-year jail sentence, or both, for persons who willfully violate any section of the act. The penalties also apply to anyone who willfully makes an untrue statement of material fact—or omits pertinent information—in a registration statement. Section 32(a) of the 1934 Act provides for a fine of up to $1 million and a maximum jail sentence of 10 years for willful violators of the statute. Criminal liability for accountants can derive from their preparation and filing of annual reports, quarterly reports, and proxy statements.

Accountants can also be subject to criminal liability under the Internal Revenue Code, the federal mail fraud statute, and the conspiracy statute.

Accountants who assist in the fraudulent preparation of a tax return can be subject to a $100,000 fine under Section 7206(2) of the Internal Revenue Code. The section also provides for a maximum prison term of 3 years.

The federal mail fraud statute makes it a crime

CONCEPT SUMMARY
Sources of Accountant's Liability

Source	Liability To
Common Law	
Contract	Client
Fraud	Client, third parties
Negligence	Client, third parties (in some states third party must be in privity of contract with accountant; other states allow reasonably foreseeable users to sue; still other states take a middle ground)
Statutory Law (Civil Liability)	
Securities Act of 1933	Buyers and sellers of securities
Securities Exchange Act of 1934	Buyers and sellers of securities
Statutory Law (Criminal Liability)	Statutes listed are enforced by the federal government
Securities Act of 1933	
Securities Exchange Act of 1934	
Internal Revenue Code	
Mail fraud statute	
Conspiracy statute	

to use the postal service to perpetrate a fraudulent scheme. The law carries a maximum $1000 fine, 5-year prison sentence, or both.

In the wake of the savings and loan crisis that occurred in the late 1980s and early 1990s, Congress imposed even tougher penalties for mail fraud that affects a financial institution. In such cases, the violator can be fined up to $1 million, imprisoned for up to 30 years, or both.

Courts have interpreted the statute to allow for each mailing to constitute a separate offense. An accountant can be exposed to liability under this statute by certifying financial statements that he or she knows (or should know) to be false and when he or she knows that the statements will be mailed for the purpose of fraud.

Conspiracy liability can be incurred when parties agree to violate any of the preceding statutes. To be convicted of conspiracy, one need only be party to a criminal agreement in which one of the parties overtly acts to further the crime. The crime need not have been successful nor have been completed by the time it was discovered. A convicted conspirator can face a fine of up to $10,000, a jail term of up to 5 years, or both.

Review Questions and Problems

Key Terms

GAAP	adverse opinion
GAAS	disclaimer of opinion
opinion	compilation
unqualified opinion	review
qualified opinion	privity of contract

Discussion Questions

1. What different types of opinions can an accountant express?
2. To whom besides clients can an accountant be held liable? Under what circumstances?
3. What is the privity requirement in regard to accountant liability? How has the requirement been altered in recent years?
4. What acts can expose an accountant to criminal liability?

Review Problems

1. Accountants prepared and certified a financial statement for their client, which used the statement to induce a bank to lend it money. The accountants made several major errors in the statement. In addition, they delayed sending out an explanatory letter—which they believed should be read by anyone using the statement—for about 30 days. The bank, which was not in privity of contract with the accountants, claimed to have suffered damages as a result of the accountants' negligence. Assume that you have been hired to represent the bank in a lawsuit against the accountants. If your jurisdiction recognizes the lack of privity as a bar to accountants' negligence actions, what theory should you pursue?

2. Your tax accountant has agreed to file your income tax return and supporting documents by April 15 of this year. In October you receive notice that the tax payment sent is insufficient, because the return did not arrive at IRS headquarters until July, and interest payments are due. In addition, you discover in going over the forms filed by the accountant that he failed to minimize your tax burden through taking certain deductions for which you are eligible. Is your accountant liable to you? Under what theory of law? How might the accountant defend himself against your claim?

3. In preparing Ann's tax return, her accountant intentionally inflated the value of certain real estate listed in order to minimize income realized upon sale of the land in the future. Ann provided these inflated documents to Herbert Finance, which gave Ann a loan based on an assumption that collateral of the inflated value existed. Ann defaulted on the loan and moved to South America. Herbert Finance sued Ann's tax accountant for the amount of the unpaid debt. What decision should the court reach? What legal doctrines should be used to reach this decision?

4. Smith and Jones, CPAs, signed an unqualified opinion on the financial statements of New Firm, a company that sold its stock in an offering governed by the 1933 Securities Act. An investor who purchased New Firm's stock in a public offering brings suit against Smith and Jones because of false statements made in New Firm's financial statement. Does the investor have to prove the intentional tort of fraud or only negligence? What would be the CPA firm's best defense?

Case Problems

1. Herzfeld purchased securities issued by FGL, a real estate dealer, after reading its financial statements for the period ending November 30, 1969. Those statements, audited by Laventhol, presented FGL as a very profitable company. Crucial to that impres-

sion was Laventhol's treatment of two contemplated transactions: FGL's purchase of nursing homes from Monterey for $13.4 million and the resale of those properties to Continental for $15.4 million. Laventhol knew that Continental's net worth was only $100,000; that FGL had yet to acquire title to the homes; and that recognizing the revenue would turn a loss of almost $800,000 to a gain of over $1.2 million. Nonetheless, Laventhol recorded the balance of the expected profit in the income statement as "deferred gross profit." Laventhol qualified the opinion letter accompanying the report, stating that the financial statements represented FGL's position "subject to the collectibility of the balance receivable on the contract to sell the homes." FGL's contracts to purchase and resell the homes both fell through. About a year later FGL went bankrupt. Assuming that he can show injury, does Herzfeld have a cause of action against Laventhol?

2. Guarante-Harrington Associates was a limited partnership engaged in trading securities. According to the partnership agreement, partners could withdraw portions of their interest only at the end of a fiscal year upon 30 days' notice. Guarante and Harrington, the general partners, withdrew $2 million of their capital investment in violation of the agreement. From examining the partnership's audit report and tax returns, which were prepared by Anderson, one could not discover that the $2 million withdrawal was made in violation of the agreement. White, a limited partner, claimed to have suffered damages resulting from his use of the partnership's negligently prepared tax returns to prepare his own tax returns. He sued Anderson. Can Anderson avoid liability by claiming that it did not foresee that White would rely on the partnership's tax returns to prepare his own?

3. The accounting partnership of James, Guinn and Head audited the financial statements of Buddy Paschal, who owned various automobile glass businesses. James knew that the Shatterproof Glass Corporation would rely on the audited statements in deciding whether to loan money to Paschal's enterprises. James issued an unqualified opinion that the financial statements, which showed Paschal's businesses to be solvent, were accurate. The businesses were actually insolvent. Shatterproof loaned money to Paschal and lost $400,000. How do you think the court in *Rusch Factors, Inc. v. Levin* would have ruled if Shatterproof sued James? Do you think the court in *Ultramares Corp. v. Touche* would have ruled differently?

4. Credit Alliance agreed to loan money to L. B. Smith after reviewing a certified financial statement audited by Arthur Andersen & Co. After Smith went bankrupt, Credit Alliance sued Arthur Andersen claiming it should have known that Alliance was relying on the financial statement because Credit Alliance was one of only eight firms that could provide Smith with the massive and specialized funding it required. Arthur Andersen claimed that, since it had no knowledge of Credit Alliance's reliance on the financial statements, it was not liable. Is Arthur Andersen liable?

APPENDIXES

The Constitution of the United States of America

PREAMBLE

We the People of the United States, in Order to form a more perfect Union, establish Justice, insure domestic Tranquility, provide for the common defence, promote the general Welfare, and secure the Blessings of Liberty to ourselves and our Posterity, do ordain and establish this Constitution for the United States of America.

ARTICLE I

Section 1. All legislative Powers herein granted shall be vested in a Congress of the United States, which shall consist of a Senate and House of Representatives.

Section 2. [1] The House of Representatives shall be composed of Members chosen every second Year by the People of the several States, and Electors in each State shall have the qualifications requisite for electors of the most numerous Branch of the State Legislature.

[2] No Person shall be a Representative who shall not have attained to the Age of twenty five Years, and been seven Years a Citizen of the United States, and who shall not, when elected, be an Inhabitant of that State in which he shall be chosen.

[3] [Representatives and direct Taxes shall be apportioned among the several States which may be included within this Union, according to their respective Numbers, which shall be determined by adding to the whole Number of free Persons, including those bound to Service for a Term of Years, and excluding Indians not taxed, three fifths of all other Persons.] The actual Enumeration shall be made within three Years after the first Meeting of the Congress of the United States, and within every subsequent Term of ten Years, in such Manner as they shall by Law direct. The Number of Representatives shall not exceed one for every thirty Thousand, but each State shall have at Least one Representative; and until such enumeration shall be made, the State of New Hampshire shall be entitled to chuse three, Massachusetts eight, Rhode Island and Providence Plantations one, Connecticut five, New York six, New Jersey four, Pennsylvania eight, Delaware one, Maryland six, Virginia ten, North Carolina, five, South Carolina five, and Georgia three.

Note: *The clause of this paragraph inclosed in brackets was amended, as to the mode of apportionment of representatives among the several states, by the Fourteenth Amendment, Section 2, and as to taxes on incomes without apportionment, by the Sixteenth Amendment.*

[4] When vacancies happen in the Representation from any State, the Executive Authority thereof shall issue Writs of Election to fill such Vacancies.

[5] The House of Representatives shall chuse their Speaker and other Officers; and shall have the sole Power of Impeachment.

Section 3. [1] The Senate of the United States shall be composed of two Senators from each State, [chosen by the Legislature thereof,] for six Years; and each Senator shall have one Vote.

Note: *This paragraph and the clause of following paragraph inclosed in brackets were susperseded by the Seventeenth Amendment.*

[2] Immediately after they shall be assembled in Consequence of the first Election, they shall be divided as equally as may be into three Classes. The Seats of the Senators of the first Class shall be vacated at the Expiration of the Second Year, of the second Class at the Expiration of the fourth Year, and of the third Class at the Expiration of the sixth Year, so that one third may be chosen every second Year; [and if Vacancies happen by Resignation, or otherwise, during the Recess of the Legislature of any State, the Executive thereof may make temporary Appointments until the next Meeting of the Legislature, which shall then fill such Vacancies.]

[3] No Person shall be a Senator who shall not have attained to the Age of thirty Years, and been nine Years a Citizen of the United States, and who shall not, when elected, be an Inhabitant of that State for which he shall be chosen.

[4] The Vice President of the United States shall be President of the Senate, but shall have no Vote, unless they be equally divided.

[5] The Senate shall chuse their other Officers, and also a President pro tempore, in the Absence of the Vice President, or when he shall exercise the Office of President of the United States.

[6] The Senate shall have the sole Power to try all Impeachments. When sitting for that Purpose, they shall be an Oath or Affirmation. When the President of the United States is tried, the Chief Justice shall preside; And no Person shall be convicted without the Concurrence of two thirds of the Members present.

[7] Judgment in Cases of Impeachment shall not extend further than to removal from Office, and disqualification to hold and enjoy an Office of honor, Trust, or Profit under the United States; but the Party convicted shall nevertheless be liable and subject to Indictment, Trial, Judgment, and Punishment, according to Law.

Section 4. [1] The Times, Places and Manner of holding Elections for Senators and Representatives, shall be prescribed in each State by the Legislature thereof; but the Congress may at any time by Law make or alter such Regulations, except as to the Places of chusing Senators.

[2] The Congress shall assemble at least once in every Year, and such Meeting shall [be on the first Monday in December,] unless they shall by Law appoint a different Day.

Note: *The part included in brackets was changed by Section 2 of the Twentieth Amendment.*

Section 5. [1] Each House shall be the Judge of the Elections, Returns, and Qualifications of its own Members, and a Majority of each shall constitute a Quorum to do Business; but a smaller Number may adjourn from day to day, and may be authorized to compel the Attendance of absent Members, in such Manner, and under such Penalties as each House may provide.

[2] Each House may determine the Rules of its Proceedings, punish its Members for disorderly Behavior, and, with the Concurrence of two thirds, expel a Member.

[3] Each House shall keep a Journal of its Proceedings, and from time to time publish the same, excepting such Parts as may in their Judgment require Secrecy; and the Yeas and Nays of the Members of either House on any question shall, at the Desire of one fifth of those Present, be entered on the Journal.

[4] Neither House, during the Session of Congress, shall, without the Consent of the other, adjourn for more than three days, nor to any other Place than that in which the two Houses shall be sitting.

Section 6. [1] The Senators and Representatives shall receive a Compensation for their Services, to be ascertained by Law, and paid out of the Treasury of the United States. They shall in all Cases, except Treason, Felony and Breach of the Peace, be privileged from Arrest during their Attendance at the Session of their respective Houses, and in going to and returning from the same; and for any Speech or Debate in either House, they shall not be questioned in any other Place.

[2] No Senator or Representative shall, during the Time for which he was elected, be appointed to any civil Office under the Authority of the United States, which shall have been created, or the Emoluments whereof shall have been increased during such time; and no Person holding any Office under the United States, shall be a Member of either House during his Continuance in Office.

Section 7. [1] All Bills for raising Revenue shall originate in the House of Representatives; but the Senate may propose or concur with Amendments as on other Bills.

[2] Every Bill which shall have passed the House of Representatives and the Senate, shall, before it become a Law, be presented to the President of the United States; If he approves he shall sign it, but if not he shall return it, with his Objections to the House in which it shall have originated, who shall enter the Objections at large on their Journal, and proceed to reconsider it. If after such Reconsideration two thirds of that House shall agree to pass the Bill, it shall be sent together with the Objections, to the other House, by which it shall likewise be reconsidered, and if approved by two thirds of that House, it shall become a Law. But in all such Cases the Votes of both Houses shall be determined by

Yeas and Nays, and the Names of the Persons voting for and against the Bill shall be entered on the Journal of each House respectively. If any Bill shall not be returned by the President within ten Days (Sundays excepted) after it shall have been presented to him, the Same shall be a Law, in like Manner as if he had signed it, unless the Congress by their Adjournment prevent its Return in which Case it shall not be a Law.

[3] Every Order, Resolution, or Vote, to Which the Concurrence of the Senate and House of Representatives may be necessary (except on a question of Adjournment) shall be presented to the President of the United States; and before the Same shall take Effect, shall be approved by him, or being disapproved by him, shall be repassed by two thirds of the Senate and House of Representatives, according to the Rules and Limitations prescribed in the Case of a Bill.

Section 8. [1] The Congress shall have Power To lay and collect Taxes, Duties, Imposts and Excises, to pay the Debts and provide for the common Defence and general Welfare of the United States; but all Duties, Imposts and Excises shall be uniform throughout the United States:

[2] To borrow money on the credit of the United States;

[3] To regulate Commerce with foreign Nations, and among the several States, and with the Indian Tribes;

[4] To establish an uniform Rule of Naturalization, and uniform Laws on the subject of Bankruptcies throughout the United States;

[5] To coin Money, regulate the Value thereof, and of foreign Coin, and fix the Standard of Weights and Measures;

[6] To provide for the Punishment of counterfeiting the Securities and current Coin of the United States;

[7] To Establish Post Offices and Post Roads;

[8] To promote the Progress of Science and useful Arts, by securing for limited Times to Authors and Inventors the exclusive Right to their respective Writings and Discoveries;

[9] To constitute Tribunals inferior to the Supreme Court;

[10] To define and punish Piracies and Felonies committed on the high Seas, and Offenses against the Law of Nations;

[11] To declare War, grant Letters of Marque and Reprisal, and make Rules concerning Captures on Land and Water;

[12] To raise and support Armies, but no Appropriation of Money to that Use shall be for a longer Term than two Years;

[13] To provide and maintain a Navy;

[14] To make Rules for the Government and Regulation of the land and naval Forces;

[15] To provide for calling forth the Militia to execute the Laws of the Union, suppress Insurrections and repel Invasions;

[16] To provide for organizing, arming, and disciplining the Militia, and for governing such Part of them as may be employed in the Service of the United States, reserving to the States respectively, the Appointment of the Officers, and the Authority of training the Militia according to the discipline prescribed by Congress;

[17] To exercise exclusive Legislation in all Cases whatsoever, over such District (not exceeding ten Miles square) as may, by Cession of particular States, and the Acceptance of Congress, become the Seat of the Government of the United States, and to exercise like Authority over all Places purchased by the Consent of the Legislature of the State in which the Same shall be, for the Erection of Forts, Magazines, Arsenals, dock-Yards, and other needful Buildings;—And

[18] To make all Laws which shall be necessary and proper for carrying into Execution the foregoing Powers, and all other Powers vested by this Constitution in the Government of the United States, or in any Department or Officer thereof.

Section 9. [1] The Migration or Importation of Such Persons as any of the States now existing shall think proper to admit, shall not be prohibited by the Congress prior to the Year one thousand eight hundred and eight, but a Tax or duty may be imposed on such Importation, not exceeding ten dollars for each Person.

[2] The privilege of the Writ of Habeas corpus shall not be suspended, unless when in Cases of Rebellion or Invasion the public Safety may require it.

[3] No Bill of Attainder or ex post facto Law shall be passed.

[4] No Capitation, or other direct, Tax shall be laid, unless in Proportion to the Census or Enumeration herein before directed to be taken.

Note: *See also the Sixteenth Amendment.*

[5] No Tax or Duty shall be laid on Articles exported from any State.

[6] No Preference shall be given by any Regulation of Commerce or Revenue to the Ports of one State over those of another; nor shall Vessels bound to, or from, one State be obliged to enter, clear, or pay Duties in another.

[7] No money shall be drawn from the Treasury, but in Consequence of Appropriations made by Law; and a regular Statement and Account of the Receipts and Expenditures of all public Money shall be published from time to time.

[8] No Title of Nobility shall be granted by the United States; And no Person holding any Office of Profit or Trust under them, shall, without the Consent of the Congress, accept of any present, Emolument, Of-

fice, or Title, of any kind whatever, from any King, Prince, or foreign State.

Section 10. [1] No State shall enter into any Treaty, Alliance, or Confederation; grant Letters of Marque and Reprisal; coin Money; emit Bills of Credit; make any Thing but gold and silver Coin a Tender in Payment of Debts; pass any Bill of Attainder, ex post facto Law, or law impairing the Obligation of Contracts, or grant any Title of Nobility.

[2] No State shall, without the Consent of the Congress, lay any Imposts or Duties on Imports or Exports, except what may be absolutely necessary for executing its inspection Laws; and the net Produce of all Duties and Imposts, laid by any State on Imports or Exports, shall be for the Use of the Treasury of the United States; and all such Laws shall be subject to the Revision and control of the Congress.

[3] No State shall, without the Consent of Congress, lay any Duty of Tonnage, keep Troops, or Ships of War in time of Peace, enter into any Agreement or Compact with another State, or with a foreign Power, or engage in War, unless actually invaded, or in such imminent Danger as will not admit of delay.

ARTICLE II

Section 1. [1] The executive Power shall be vested in a President of the United States of America. He shall hold his Office during the Term of four Years, and, together with the Vice President, chosen for the same Term, be elected, as follows:

[2] Each State shall appoint, in such Manner as the Legislature thereof may direct, a Number of Electors, equal to the whole Number of Senators and Representatives to which the State may be entitled in the Congress; but no Senator or Representative or Person holding an Office of Trust or Profit under the United States, shall be appointed an Elector.

[3] [The Electors shall meet in their respective States, and vote by Ballot for two Persons, of whom one at least shall not be an Inhabitant of the same State with themselves. And they shall make a List of all the Persons voted for, and of the Number of Votes for each; which List they shall sign and certify, and transmit sealed to the Seat of Government of the United States, directed to the President of the Senate. The president of the Senate shall, in the presence of the Senate and House of Representatives, open all the Certificates, and the Votes shall then be counted. The Person having the greatest Number of Votes shall be the President, if such Number be a Majority of the whole Number of Electors appointed; and if there be more than one who have such Majority, and have an equal Number of Votes, then the House of Representatives shall immediately chuse by Ballot one of them for President; and if no Person have a Majority, then from the five highest on the List the said House shall in like Manner chuse the Presi-

dent. But in chusing the President, the Votes shall be taken by States, the Representation from each State having one Vote; A quorum for this Purpose shall consist of a Member or Members from two thirds of the States, and a Majority of all the States shall be necessary to a Choice. In every Case, after the Choice of the President, the Person having the greatest Number of Votes of the Electors shall be the Vice President. But if there should remain two or more who have equal Votes, the Senate shall chuse from them by Ballot the Vice President.]

Note: *This paragraph, enclosed in brackets, was superseded by the Twelfth Amendment.*

[4] The Congress may determine the Time of chusing the Electors, and the Day on which they shall give their Votes; which Day shall be the same throughout the United States.

[5] No person except a natural born Citizen, or a Citizen of the United States, at the time of the Adoption of this Constitution, shall be eligible to the Office of President; neither shall any Person be eligible to that Office who shall not have attained to the Age of thirty five Years, and been fourteen Years a Resident within the United States.

[6] In case of the removal of the President from Office, or of his Death, Resignation or Inability to discharge the Powers and Duties of the said office, the Same shall devolve on the Vice President, and the Congress may by law provide for the Case of Removal, Death, Resignation or Inability, both of the President and Vice President, declaring what Officer shall then act as President, and such Officer shall act accordingly, until the Disability be removed, or a President shall be elected.

[7] The President shall, at stated Times, receive for his Services, a Compensation, which shall neither be increased nor diminished during the Period for which he shall have been elected, and he shall not receive within that Period any other Emolument from the United States, or any of them.

[8] Before he enter on the Execution of his Office, he shall take the following Oath or Affirmation: "I do solemnly swear (or affirm) that I will faithfully execute the Office of President of the United States, and will to the best of my Ability, preserve, protect and defend the Constitution of the United States."

Section 2. [1] The President shall be Commander in Chief of the Army and Navy of the United States, and of the militia of the several States, when called into the actual Service of the United States; he may require the Opinion, in writing, of the principal Officer in each of the Executive Departments, upon any Subject relating to the Duties of their respective Offices, and he shall have Power to grant Reprieves and Pardons for Offenses against the United States, except in Cases of Impeachment.

[2] He shall have Power, by and with the Advice and Consent of the Senate, to make Treaties, provided two thirds of the Senators present concur; and he shall nominate, and by and with the Advice and Consent of the Senate, shall appoint Ambassadors, other public Ministers and Consuls, Judges of the supreme Court, and all other Officers of the United States, whose Appointments are not herein otherwise provided for, and which shall be established by Law; but the Congress may by Law vest the Appointment of such inferior Officers, as they think proper, in the President alone, in the Courts of law, or in the Heads of Departments.

[3] The President shall have Power to fill up all Vacancies that may happen during the Recess of the Senate, by granting Commissions which shall expire at the End of their next Session.

Section 3. He shall from time to time give to the Congress Information of the State of the Union, and recommend to their Consideration such Measures as he shall judge necessary and expedient; he may, on extraordinary Occasions, convene both Houses, or either of them, and in Case of Disagreement between them, with Respect to the Time of Adjournment, he may adjourn them to such Time as he shall think proper; he shall take Care that the laws be faithfully executed, and shall Commission all the Officers of the United States.

Section 4. The President, Vice President and all civil Officers of the United States, shall be removed from Office on Impeachment for, and Conviction of, Treason, Bribery, or other high Crimes and Misdemeanors.

ARTICLE III

Section 1. The judicial Power of the United States, shall be vested in one supreme Court, and in such inferior Courts as the Congress may from time to time ordain and establish. The Judges, both of the supreme and inferior Courts, shall hold their Offices during good Behaviour, and shall, at stated Times, receive for their Services a Compensation, which shall not be diminished during their Continuance in Office.

Section 2. [1] The judicial Power shall extend to all Cases, in Law and Equity, arising under this Constitution, the laws of the United States, and Treaties made, or which shall be made, under their Authority;—to all Cases affecting Ambassadors, other public Ministers and Consuls;—to all Cases of admiralty and maritime Jurisdiction;—to Controversies to which the United States shall be a Party;—to Controversies between two or more States;—between a State and Citizens of another State;*—between Citizens of different States;—

between Citizens of the same State claiming Lands under the Grants of different States, and between a State, or the Citizens thereof, and foreign States, Citizens or Subjects.

[2] In all Cases affecting Ambassadors, other public Ministers and Consuls, and those in which a State shall be a Party, the supreme Court shall have original Jurisdiction. In all the other Cases before mentioned, the supreme Court shall have appellate Jurisdiction, both as to Law and Fact, with such Exceptions, and under such Regulations as the Congress shall make.

[3] The Trial of all Crimes, except in Cases of Impeachment, shall be by Jury; and such Trial shall be held in the State where the said Crimes shall have been committed; but when not committed within any State, the Trial shall be at such Place or Places as the Congress may by Law have directed.

Section 3. [1] Treason against the United States, shall consist only in levying War against them, or, in adhering to their Enemies, giving them Aid and Comfort. No Person shall be convicted of Treason unless on the Testimony of two Witnesses to the same overt Act, or on Confession in open Court.

[2] The Congress shall have Power to declare the Punishment of Treason, but no Attainder of Treason shall work Corruption of Blood, or Forfeiture except during the Life of the Person attained.

ARTICLE IV

Section 1. Full Faith and Credit shall be given in each State to the public Acts, Records, and judicial Proceedings of every other State. And the Congress may by general Laws prescribe the Manner in which such Acts, Records and Proceedings shall be proved, and the Effect thereof.

Section 2. [1] The Citizens of each State shall be entitled to all Privileges and Immunities of Citizens in the several States.

[2] A Person charged in any State with Treason, Felony, or other Crime, who shall flee from Justice, and be found in another State, shall on demand of the executive Authority of the State from which he fled, be delivered up, to be removed to the State having Jurisdiction of the Crime.

[3] [No Person held to Service or Labour in one State, under the Laws thereof, escaping into another, shall, in Consequence of any Law or Regulation therein, be discharged from such Service or Labour, but shall be delivered up on Claim of the Party to whom such Service or Labour may be due.]

Note: *This paragraph has been superseded by the Thirteenth Amendment.*

* This Clause has been affected by the Eleventh Amendment.

Section 3. [1] New States may be admitted by the Congress into this Union; but no new State shall be formed or erected within the Jurisdiction of any other State; nor any State be formed by the Junction of two or more States, or Parts of States, without the Consent of the Legislatures of the States concerned as well as of the Congress.

[2] The Congress shall have Power to dispose of and make all needful Rules and Regulations respecting the Territory or other Property belonging to the United States; and nothing in this Constitution shall be so construed as to Prejudice any Claims of the United States, or of any particular State.

Section 4. The United States shall guarantee to every State in this Union a Republican Form of Government, and shall protect each of them against Invasion; and on Application of the Legislature, or of the Executive (when the Legislature cannot be convened) against domestic Violence.

ARTICLE V

The Congress, whenever two thirds of both Houses shall deem it necessary, shall propose Amendments to this Constitution, or, on the Application of the Legislature of two thirds of the several States, shall call a Convention for proposing Amendments, which, in either Case, shall be valid to all Intents and Purposes, as part of this Constitution, when ratified by the Legislatures of three fourths of the several States, or by Conventions in three fourths thereof, as the one or the other Mode of Ratification may be proposed by the Congress; Provided that no Amendment which may be made prior to the Year One thousand eight hundred and eight shall in any Manner affect the first and fourth Clauses in the Ninth Section of the first Article; and that no State, without its Consent, shall be deprived of its equal Suffrage in the Senate.

ARTICLE VI

[1] All Debts contracted and Engagements entered into, before the Adoption of this Constitution, shall be as valid against the United States under this Constitution, as under the Confederation.

[2] This Constitution, and the Laws of the United States which shall be made in Pursuance thereof; and all Treaties made, or which shall be made, under the Authority of the United States, shall be the supreme Law of the Land; and the Judges in every State shall be bound thereby, any Thing in the Constitution or Laws of any State to the Contrary notwithstanding.

[3] The Senators and Representatives before mentioned, and the Members of the several State Legislatures, and all executives and judicial Officers, both of the United States and of the several States, shall be bound by Oath or Affirmation, to support this Constitution; but no religious Test shall ever be required as a Qualification to any Office or public Trust under the United States.

ARTICLE VII

The Ratification of the Conventions of nine States shall be sufficient for the Establishment of this Constitution between the States so ratifying the Same.

Done in Convention by the Unanimous Consent of the States present the Seventeenth Day of September in the Year of Our Lord one thousand seven hundred and Eighty seven and of the Independence of the United States of America the Twelfth. IN WITNESS whereof We have hereto subscribed our Names,

Go. Washington—Presidt.
and deputy from Virginia

New Hampshire

John Langdon	Nicholas Gilman

Massachusetts

Nathaniel Gorham	Rufus King

Connecticut

Wm. Saml. Johnson	Roger Sherman

New York

Alexander Hamilton

New Jersey

Wil: Livingston	Wm. Paterson
David Brearley	Jona: Dayton

Pennsylvania

B. Franklin	Thos. FitzSimons
Thomas Mifflin	Jared Ingersoll
Robt. Morris	James Wilson
Geo. Clymer	Gouv Morris

Delaware

Geo: Read	Richard Bassett
Gunning Bedford Jun	Jaco: Broom
John Dickinson	

Maryland

James McHenry	Danl. Carroll
Dan of St. Thos. Jenifer	

Virginia

John Blair	James Madison, Jr.

North Carolina

Wm. Blount	Hu Williamson
Richd. Dobbs Spaight	

South Carolina

J. Rutledge	Charles Pinckney
Charles Cotesworth Pinckney	Pierce Butler

Georgia

William Few	Abr Baldwin
	William Jackson
Attest	Secretary

AMENDMENTS TO THE CONSTITUTION OF THE UNITED STATES

Amendment I [1791]

Congress shall make no law respecting an establishment of religion, or prohibiting the free exercise thereof; or abridging the freedom of speech, or of the press; or the right of the people peaceably to assemble, and to petition the Government for a redress of grievances.

Amendment II [1791]

A well regulated Militia being necessary to the security of a free State, the right of the people to keep and bear Arms, shall not be infringed.

Amendment III [1791]

No Soldier shall, in time of peace be quartered in any house, without the consent of the Owner, nor in time of war, but in a manner to be prescribed by law.

Amendment IV [1791]

The right of the people to be secure in their persons, houses, papers, and effects, against unreasonable searches and seizures, shall not be violated, and no Warrants shall issue, but upon probable cause, supported by Oath or affirmation, and particularly describing the place to be searched, and the persons or things to be seized.

Amendment V [1791]

No person shall be held to answer for a capital, or otherwise infamous crime, unless on a presentment or indictment of a Grand Jury, except in cases arising in the land or naval forces, or in the Militia, when in actual service in time of War or public danger; nor shall any person be subject for the same offence to be twice put in jeopardy of life or limb, nor shall be compelled in any criminal case to be a witness against himself, nor be deprived of life, liberty, or property, without due process of law; nor shall private property be taken for public use, without just compensation.

Amendment VI [1791]

In all criminal prosecutions, the accused shall enjoy the right to a speedy and public trial, by an impartial jury of the State and district wherein the crime shall have been committed; which district shall have been previously ascertained by law, and to be informed of the nature and cause of the accusation; to be confronted with the witnesses against him; to have compulsory process for obtaining witnesses in his favor, and to have the Assistance of Counsel for his defence.

Amendment VII [1791]

In Suits at common law, where the value in controversy shall exceed twenty dollars, the right of trial by jury shall be preserved, and no fact tried by jury shall be otherwise reexamined in any Court of the United States, than according to the rules of the common law.

Amendment VIII [1791]

Excessive bail shall not be required, nor excessive fines imposed, nor cruel and unusual punishments inflicted.

Amendment IX [1791]

The enumeration in the Constitution, of certain rights, shall not be construed to deny or disparage others retained by the people.

Amendment X [1791]

The powers not delegated to the United States by the Constitution, nor prohibited by it to the States, are reserved to the States respectively, or to the people.

Amendment XI [1798]

The Judicial power of the United States shall not be construed to extend to any suit in law or equity, commenced or prosecuted against one of the United States by Citizens of another State, or by Citizens or Subjects of any Foreign State.

Amendment XII [1804]

The electors shall meet in their respective states and vote by ballot for President and Vice-President, one of whom, at least, shall not be an inhabitant of the same state with themselves; they shall name in their ballots the person voted for as President, and in distinct ballots the person voted for as Vice-President, and they shall make distinct lists of all persons voted for as President, and of all persons voted for as Vice-President, and of the number of votes for each, which lists they shall sign and certify, and transmit sealed to the seat of the government of the United States, directed to the President of the Senate;—The President of the Senate shall, in the presence of the Senate and House of Representatives, open all the certificates and the votes shall then be counted;—The person having the greatest number of votes for President, shall be the President, if such number be a majority of the whole number of Electors appointed; and if no person have such majority, then from the persons having the highest numbers not exceeding three on the list of those voted for as

President, the House of Representatives shall choose immediately, by ballot, the President. But in choosing the President, the votes shall be taken by states, the representation from each state having one vote; a quorum for this purpose shall consist of a member of members from two-thirds of the states, and a majority of all the states shall be necessary to a choice. [And if the House of Representatives shall not choose a President whenever the right of choice shall devolve upon them before the fourth day of March next following, then the Vice-President shall act as President, as in the case of the death or other constitutional disability of the President.] The person having the greatest number of votes as Vice-President, shall be the Vice-President, if such number be a majority of the whole number of electors appointed, and if no person have a majority, then from the two highest numbers on the list, the Senate shall choose the Vice-President; a quorum for the purpose shall consist of two-thirds of the whole number of Senators, and a majority of the whole number shall be necessary to a choice. But no person constitutionally ineligible to the office of President shall be eligible to that of Vice-President of the United States.

Note: *The part included in brackets has been superseded by Section 3 of the Twentieth Amendment.*

Amendment XIII [1865]

Section 1. Neither slavery nor involuntary servitude, except as a punishment for crime whereof the party shall have been duly convicted, shall exist within the United States, or any place subject to their jurisdiction.

Section 2. Congress shall have power to enforce this article by appropriate legislation.

Amendment XIV [1868]

Section 1. All persons born or naturalized in the United States, and subject to the jurisdiction thereof, are citizens of the United States and of the State wherein they reside. No State shall make or enforce any law which shall abridge the privileges or immunities of citizens of the United States; nor shall any State deprive any person of life, liberty, or property, without due process of law; nor deny to any person within its jurisdiction the equal protection of the laws.

Section 2. Representatives shall be apportioned among the several States according to their respective numbers, counting the whole number of persons in each State, excluding Indians not taxed. But when the right to vote at any election for the choice of electors for President and Vice President of the United States, Representatives in Congress, the Executive and Judicial officers of a State, or the members of the Legisla-

ture thereof, is denied to any of the male inhabitants of such State, being twenty-one years of age, and citizens of the United States, or in any way abridged, except for participation in rebellion, or other crime, the basis of representation therein shall be reduced in the proportion which the number of such male citizens shall bear to the whole number of male citizens twenty-one years of age in such State.

Section 3. No person shall be a Senator or Representative in Congress, or elector of President and Vice President, or hold any office, civil or military, under the United States, or under any State, who, having previously taken an oath, as a member of Congress, or as an officer of the United States, or as a member of any State legislature, or as an executive or judicial officer of any State, to support the Constitution of the United States, shall have engaged in insurrection or rebellion against the same, or given aid or comfort to the enemies thereof. But Congress may by a vote of two-thirds of each House, remove such disability.

Section 4. The validity of the public debt of the United States, authorized by law, including debts incurred for payment of pensions and bounties for services in suppressing insurrection or rebellion, shall not be questioned. But neither the United States nor any State shall assume or pay any debt or obligation incurred in aid of insurrection or rebellion against the United States, or any claim for the loss or emancipation of any slave; but all such debts, obligations and claims shall be held illegal and void.

Section 5. The Congress shall have power to enforce, by appropriate legislation, the provisions of this article.

Amendment XV [1870]

Section 1. The right of citizens of the United States to vote shall not be denied or abridged by the United States or by any State on account of race, color, or previous condition of servitude.

Section 2. The Congress shall have power to enforce this article by appropriate legislation.

Amendment XVI [1913]

The Congress shall have power to lay and collect taxes on incomes, from whatever source derived, without apportionment among the several States, and without regard to any census or enumeration.

Amendment XVII [1913]

The Senate of the United States shall be composed of two Senators from each State, elected by the people thereof, for six years; and each Senator shall have one vote. The electors in each state shall have the qualification requisite for electors of the most numerous branch of the State legislatures.

When vacancies happen in the representation of any State in the Senate, the executive authority of such State shall issue writs of election to fill such vacancies: Provided, That the legislature of any State may empower the executive thereof to make temporary appointments until the people fill the vacancies by election as the legislature may direct.

This amendment shall not be so construed as to affect the election or term of any Senator chosen before it becomes valid as part of the Constitution.

Amendment XVIII [1919]

Section 1. [After one year from the ratification of this Article the manufacture, sale, or transportation of intoxicating liquors within, the importation thereof into, or the exportation thereof from the United States and all territory subject to the jurisdiction thereof for beverage purposes is hereby prohibited].

Section 2. [The Congress and the several States shall have concurrent power to enforce this article by appropriate legislation].

Section 3. [This article shall be inoperative unless it shall have been ratified as an amendment to the Constitution by the legislatures of the several States, as provided in the Constitution, within seven years from the date of the submission hereof to the States by the Congress].

Note: *The Eighteenth Amendment was repealed by the Twenty-first Amendment to the Constitution of the United States.*

Amendment XIX [1920]

The right of citizens of the United States to vote shall not be denied or abridged by the United States or by any State on account of sex.

Congress shall have the power to enforce this Article by appropriate legislation.

Amendment XX [1933]

Section 1. The terms of the President and Vice President shall end at noon on the 20th day of January, and the terms of Senators and Representatives at noon on the 3d day of January, of the years in which such terms would have ended if this article had not been ratified; and the terms of their successors shall then begin.

Section 2. The Congress shall assemble at least once in every year, and such meeting shall begin at noon on the 3d day of January, unless they shall by law appoint a different day.

Section 3. If, at the time fixed for the beginning of the term of the President, the President-elect shall have died, the Vice President-elect shall become President. If the President shall not have been chosen before the time fixed for the beginning of his term, or if the President-elect shall have failed to qualify, then the Vice President-elect shall act as President until a President shall have qualified; and the Congress may by law provide for the case wherein neither a President-elect nor a Vice President-elect shall have qualified, declaring who shall then act as President, or the manner in which one who is to act shall be selected, and such person shall act accordingly until a President or Vice President shall have qualified.

Section 4. The Congress may by law provide for the case of the death of any of the persons from whom the House of Representatives may choose a President whenever the right of choice shall have devolved upon them, and for the case of the death of any of the persons from whom the Senate may choose a Vice President whenever the right of choice shall have devolved upon them.

Section 5. Sections 1 and 2 shall take effect on the 15th day of October following the ratification of this article.

Section 6. This article shall be inoperative unless it shall have been ratified as an amendment to the Constitution by the legislatures of three-fourths of the several States within seven years from the date of its submission.

Amendment XXI [1933]

Section 1. The eighteenth article of amendment to the Constitution of the United States is hereby repealed.

Section 2. The transportation or importation into any State, Territory, or possession of the United States for delivery or use therein of intoxicating liquors, in violation of the laws thereof, is hereby prohibited.

Section 3. This article shall be inoperative unless it shall have been ratified as an amendment to the Constitution by conventions in the several States, as provided in the Constitution, within seven years from the date of the submission hereof to the States by the Congress.

Amendment XXII [1951]

Section 1. No person shall be elected to the office of the President more than twice, and no person who has held the office of President, or acted as President, for more than two years of a term to which some other person was elected President shall be elected to the office of President more than once. But this Article shall not apply to any person holding the office of President when this Article was proposed by the Congress, and shall not prevent any person who may be holding the office of President, or acting as President, during the term within which this Article becomes operative from holding the office of President or acting as President during the remainder of such term.

Section 2. This Article shall be inoperative unless it shall have been ratified as an amendment to the Constitution by the legislatures of three-fourths of the several States within seven years from the date of its submission to the States by the Congress.

Amendment XXIII [1961]

Section 1. The District constituting the seat of Government of the United States shall appoint in such manner as the Congress may direct:

A number of electors of President and Vice President equal to the whole number of Senators and Representatives in Congress to which the District would be entitled if it were a State, but in no event more than the least populous state; they shall be in addition to those appointed by the States, but they shall be considered, for the purposes of the election of President and Vice President, to be electors appointed by a State; and they shall meet in the District and perform such duties as provided by the twelfth article of amendment.

Section 2. The Congress shall have power to enforce this article by appropriate legislation.

Amendment XXIV [1964]

Section 1. The right of citizens of the United States to vote in any primary or other election for President or Vice President, for electors for President or Vice President, or for Senator or Representative in Congress, shall not be denied or abridged by the United States or by any State by reason of failure to pay any poll tax or other tax.

Section 2. The Congress shall have power to enforce this article by appropriate legislation.

Amendment XXV [1967]

Section 1. In case of the removal of the President from office or of his death or resignation, the Vice President shall become President.

Section 2. Whenever there is a vacancy in the office of the Vice President, the President shall nominate a Vice President who shall take office upon confirmation by a majority vote of both Houses of Congress.

Section 3. Whenever the President transmits to the President pro tempore of the Senate and the Speaker of

the House of Representatives his written declaration that he is unable to discharge the powers and duties of his office, and until he transmits to them a written declaration of the contrary, such powers and duties shall be discharged by the Vice President as Acting President.

Section 4. Whenever the Vice President and a majority of either the principal officers of the executive departments or of such other body as Congress may by law provide, transmit to the President pro tempore of the Senate and the Speaker of the House of Representatives their written declaration that the President is unable to discharge the powers and duties of his office, the Vice President shall immediately assume the powers and duties of the office as Acting President.

Thereafter, when the President transmits to the President pro tempore of the Senate and the Speaker of the House of Representatives his written declaration that no inability exists, he shall resume the powers and duties of his office unless the Vice President and a majority of either the principal officers of the executive department or of such other body as Congress may by law provide, transmit within four days to the President pro tempore of the Senate and the Speaker of the House of Representatives their written declaration that the President is unable to discharge the powers and duties of his office. Thereupon Congress shall decide the issue, assembling within forty-eight hours for that purpose if not in session. If the Congress, within twenty-one days after receipt of the latter written declaration, or, if Congress is not in session, within twenty-one days after Congress is required to assemble, determines by two-thirds vote of both Houses that the President is unable to discharge the powers and duties of his office, the Vice President shall continue to discharge the same as Acting President; otherwise, the President shall resume the powers and duties of his office.

Amendment XXVI [1971]

Section 1. The right of citizens of the United States, who are eighteen years of age or older, to vote shall not be denied or abridged by the United States or by any State on account of age.

Section 2. The Congress shall have the power to enforce this article by appropriate legislation.

Amendment XXVII [1992]

No law, varying the compensation for the services of the Senators and Representatives, shall take effect, until an election of Representatives shall have intervened.

B

Uniform Commercial Code, 1978 Text with 1990 Amendments

Note: The 1978 text of the UCC has been updated to reflect the 1990 amendments of Article 3. So, in this appendix you can read either the 1978 version of the UCC or the 1991 version.

To update the UCC, the drafters used brackets ([ ]) to indicate deleted words, and underscoring (___) to indicate added words. If you want to use the 1978 text, read the ordinary type plus the bracketed words. If you want to use the 1991 text, read the ordinary type plus the underscored words (but minus the bracketed words).

ARTICLE 1: GENERAL PROVISIONS

Part 1: Short Title, Construction, Application and Subject Matter of the Act

§1-101. Short Title. This Act shall be known and may be cited as Uniform Commercial Code.

§1-102. Purposes; Rules of Construction; Variation by Agreement.

(1) This Act shall be liberally construed and applied to promote its underlying purposes and policies.

(2) Underlying purposes and policies of this Act are

(a) to simplify, clarify and modernize the law governing commercial transactions;

(b) permit the continued expansion of commercial practices through custom, usage and agreement of the parties;

(c) to make uniform the law among the various jurisdictions.

(3) The effect of provisions of this Act may be varied by agreement, except as otherwise provided in this Act and except that the obligations of good faith, diligence, reasonableness and care prescribed by this Act may not be disclaimed by agreement but the parties may by agreement determine the standards by which the performance of such obligations is to be measured if such standards are not manifestly unreasonable.

(4) The presence in certain provisions of this Act of the words "unless otherwise agreed" or words of similar import does not imply that the effect of other provisions may not be varied by agreement under subsection (3).

(5) In this Act unless the context otherwise requires

(a) words in the singular number include the plural, and in the plural include the singular;

(b) words of the masculine gender include the feminine and the neuter, and when the sense so indicates words of the neuter gender may refer to any gender.

§1-103. Supplementary General Principles of Law Applicable. Unless displaced by the particular provisions of this Act, the principles of law and equity, including the law merchant and the law relative to capacity to contract, principal and agent, estoppel, fraud, misrepresentation, duress, coercion, mistake, bankruptcy, or other validating or invalidating cause shall supplement its provisions.

§1-104. Construction Against Implicit Repeal. This Act being a general act intended as a unified coverage of its subject matter, no part of it shall be deemed to be impliedly repealed by subsequent legislation if such construction can reasonably be avoided.

§1-105. Territorial Application of the Act; Parties' Power to Choose Applicable Law.

(1) Except as provided hereafter in this section, when a transaction bears a reasonable relation to this state and also to another state or nation the parties may agree that the law either of this state or of such other state or nation shall govern their rights and duties. Failing such agreement this Act applies to transactions bearing an appropriate relation to this state.

(2) Where one of the following provisions of this Act specifies the applicable law, that provision governs and a contrary agreement is effective only to the extent permitted by the law (including the conflict of laws rules) so specified:

Rights of creditors against sold goods. Section 2-402.

Applicability of the Article on Bank Deposits and Collections. Section 4-102.

Bulk transfers subject to the Article on Bulk Transfers. Section 6-102.

Applicability of the Article on Investment Securities. Section 8-106.

Perfection provisions of the Article on Secured Transactions. Section 9-103.

§1-106. Remedies to Be Liberally Administered.

(1) The remedies provided by this Act shall be liberally administered to the end that the aggrieved party may be put in as good a position as if the other party had fully performed but neither consequential or special nor penal damages may be had except as specifically provided in this Act or by other rule of law.

(2) Any right or obligation declared by this Act is enforceable by action unless the provision declaring it specifies a different and limited effect.

§1-107. Waiver or Renunciation of Claim or Right After Breach. Any claim or right arising out of an alleged breach can be discharged in whole or in part without consideration by a written waiver or renunciation signed and delivered by the aggrieved party.

§1-108. Severability. If any provision or clause of this Act or application thereof to any person or circumstances is held invalid, such invalidity shall not affect other provisions or applications of the Act which can be given effect without the invalid provision or application, and to this end the provisions of this Act are declared to be severable.

§1-109. Section Captions. Section captions are parts of this Act.

Part 2: General Definitions and Principles of Interpretation

§1-201. General Definitions (1987 and 1990 Amendments). Subject to additional definitions contained in the subsequent Articles of this Act which are applicable to specific Articles or Parts thereof, and unless the context otherwise requires, in this Act:

(1) "Action" in the sense of a judicial proceeding includes recoupment, counterclaim, set-off, suit in equity and any other proceedings in which rights are determined.

(2) "Aggrieved party" means a party entitled to resort to a remedy.

(3) "Agreement" means the bargain of the parties in fact as found in their language or by implication from other circumstances including course of dealing or usage of trade or course of performance as provided in this Act (Sections 1-205 and 2-208). Whether an agreement has legal consequences is determined by the provisions of this Act, if applicable; otherwise by the law of contracts (Section 1-103). (Compare "Contract".)

(4) "Bank" means any person engaged in the business of banking.

(5) "Bearer" means the person in possession of an instrument, document of title, or certificated security payable to bearer or indorsed in blank.

(6) "Bill of lading" means a document evidencing the receipt of goods for shipment issued by a person engaged in the business of transporting or forwarding goods, and includes an airbill. "Airbill" means a document serving for air transportation as a bill of lading does for marine or rail transportation, and includes an air consignment note or air waybill.

(7) "Branch" includes a separately incorporated foreign branch of a bank.

(8) "Burden of establishing" a fact means the burden of persuading the triers of fact that the existence of the fact is more probable than its non-existence.

(9) "Buyer in ordinary course of business" means a person who in good faith and without knowledge that the sale to him is in violation of the ownership rights or security interest of a third party in the goods buys in ordinary course from a person in the business of selling goods of that kind but does not include a pawnbroker. All persons who sell minerals or the like (including oil and gas) at wellhead or minehead shall be deemed to be persons in the business of selling goods of that kind. "Buying" may be for cash or by exchange of other property or on secured or unsecured credit and includes receiving goods or documents of title under a preexisting contract for sale but does not include a transfer in bulk or as security for or in total or partial satisfaction of a money debt.

(10) "Conspicuous": A term or clause is conspicuous when it is so written that a reasonable person against whom it is to operate ought to have noticed it. A printed heading in capitals (as: NON-NEGOTIABLE BILL OF LADING) is conspicuous. Language in the body of a form is "conspicuous" if it is in larger or other contrasting type or color. But in a telegram any stated term is "conspicuous". Whether a term or clause is "conspicuous" or not is for decision by the court.

(11) "Contract" means the total legal obligation which results from the parties' agreement as affected by this Act and any other applicable rules of law. (Compare "Agreement".)

(12) "Creditor" includes a general creditor, a secured creditor, a lien creditor and any representative of creditors, including an assignee for the benefit of creditors, a trustee in bankruptcy, a receiver in equity and an executor or administrator of an insolvent debtor's or assignor's estate.

(13) "Defendant" includes a person in the position of defendant in a cross-action or counterclaim.

(14) "Delivery" with respect to instruments, documents of title, chattel paper, or certificated securities means voluntary transfer of possession.

(15) "Document of title" includes bill of lading, dock warrant, dock receipt, warehouse receipt or order for the delivery of goods, and also any other document which in the regular course of business or financing is treated as adequately evidencing that the person in possession of it is entitled to receive, hold and dispose of the document and the goods it covers. To be a document of title a document must purport to be issued by or addressed to a bailee and purport to cover goods in the bailee's possession which are either identified or are fungible portions of an identified mass.

(16) "Fault" means wrongful act, omission or breach.

(17) "Fungible" with respect to goods or securities means goods or securities of which any unit is, by nature or usage of trade, the equivalent of any other like unit. Goods which are not fungible shall be deemed fungible for the purposes of this Act to the extent that under a particular agreement or document unlike units are treated as equivalents.

(18) "Genuine" means free of forgery or counterfeiting.

(19) "Good faith" means honesty in fact in the conduct or transaction concerned.

(20) "Holder" [means a person who is in possession of a document of title or an instrument or a certificated investment security drawn, issued, or indorsed to him or his order or to bearer or in blank] with respect to a negotiable instrument, means the person in possession if the instrument is payable to bearer or, in the case of an instrument payable to an identified person, if the identified person is in possession. "Holder" with respect to a document of title means the person in possession if the goods are deliverable to bearer or to the order of the person in possession.

(21) To "honor" is to pay or to accept and pay, or where a credit so engages to purchase or discount a draft complying with the terms of the credit.

(22) "Insolvency proceedings" includes any assignment for the benefit of creditors or other proceedings intended to liquidate or rehabilitate the estate of the person involved.

(23) A person is "insolvent" who either has ceased to pay his debts in the ordinary course of business or cannot pay his debts as they become due or is insolvent within the meaning of the federal bankruptcy law.

(24) "Money" means a medium of exchange authorized or adopted by a domestic or foreign government [as a part of its currency] and includes a monetary unit of account established by an intergovernmental organization or by agreement between two or more nations.

(25) A person has "notice" of a fact when

(a) he has actual knowledge of it; or

(b) he has received a notice or notification of it; or

(c) from all the facts and circumstances known to him at the time in question he has reason to know that it exists.

A person "knows" or has "knowledge" of a fact when he has actual knowledge of it. "Discover" or "learn" or a word or phrase of similar import refers to knowledge rather than to reason to know. The time and circumstances under which a notice or notification may cease to be effective are not determined by this Act.

(26) A person "notifies" or "gives" a notice or notification to another by taking such steps as may be reasonably required to inform the other in ordinary course whether or not such other actually comes to know of it. A person "receives" a notice or notification when

(a) it comes to his attention; or

(b) it is duly delivered at the place of business through which the contract was made or at any other place held out by him as the place for receipt of such communications.

(27) Notice, knowledge or a notice or notification received by an organization is effective for a particular transaction from the time when it is brought to the attention of the individual conducting that transaction, and in any event from the time when it would have been brought to his attention if the organization had exercised due diligence. An organization exercises due diligence if it maintains reasonable routines for communicating significant information to the person conducting the transaction and there is reasonable compliance with the routines. Due diligence does not require an individual acting for the organization to communicate information unless such communication is part of his regular duties or unless he has reason to know of the transaction and that the transaction would be materially affected by the information.

(28) "Organization" includes a corporation, government or governmental subdivision or agency, business trust, estate, trust, partnership or association, two or more persons having a joint or common interest, or any other legal or commercial entity.

(29) "Party", as distinct from "third party", means a person who has engaged in a transaction or made an agreement within this Act.

(30) "Person" includes an individual or an organization (See Section 1-102).

(31) "Presumption" or "presumed" means that the trier of fact must find the existence of the fact presumed unless and until evidence is introduced which would support a finding of its non-existence.

(32) "Purchase" includes taking by sale, discount, negotiation, mortgage, pledge, lien, issue or re-issue, gift or any other voluntary transaction creating an interest in property.

(33) "Purchaser" means a person who takes by purchase.

(34) "Remedy" means any remedial right to which an aggrieved party is entitled with or without resort to a tribunal.

(35) "Representative" includes an agent, an officer of a corporation or association, and a trustee, executor or administrator of an estate, or any other person empowered to act for another.

(36) "Rights" includes remedies.

(37) "Security interest" means an interest in personal property or fixtures which secures payment or performance of an obligation. The retention or reservation of title by a seller of goods notwithstanding shipment or delivery to the buyer (Section 2-401) is limited in effect to a reservation of a "security interest". The term also includes any interest of a buyer of accounts or chattel paper which is subject to Article 9. The special property interest of a buyer of goods on identification of such goods to a contract for sale under Section 2-401 is not a "security interest", but a buyer may also acquire a "security interest" by complying with Article 9. Unless a [lease or] consignment is intended as security, reservation of title thereunder is not a "security interest", but a consignment [is] in any event is subject to the provisions on consignment sales (Section 2-326).

Whether a [lease is intended as] <u>transaction creates a lease or</u> security <u>interest</u> is [to be] determined by the facts of each case; however, [(a) the inclusion of an option to purchase does not of itself make the lease one intended for security, and (b) an agreement that upon compliance with the terms of the lease the lessee shall become or has the option to become the owner of the property for no additional consideration or for a nominal consideration does make the lease one intended for security.] <u>A transaction creates a security interest if the consideration the lessee is to pay the lessor for the right to possession and use of the goods is an obliga-</u>

<u>tion for the term of the lease not subject to termination by the lessee, and</u>

(a) <u>the original term of the lease is equal to or greater than the remaining economic life of the goods,</u>

(b) <u>the lessee is bound to renew the lease for the remaining economic life of the goods or is bound to become the owner of the goods,</u>

(c) <u>the lessee has an option to renew the lease for the remaining economic life of the goods for no additional consideration or nominal additional consideration upon compliance with the lease agreement, or</u>

(d) <u>the lessee has an option to become the owner of the goods for no additional consideration or nominal additional consideration upon compliance with the lease agreement.</u>

<u>A transaction does not create a security interest merely because it provides that</u>

(a) <u>the present value of the consideration the lessee is obligated to pay the lessor for the right to possession and use of the goods is substantially equal to or is greater than the fair market value of the goods at the time the lease is entered into,</u>

(b) <u>the lessee assumes risk of loss of the goods, or agrees to pay taxes, insurance, filing, recording, or registration fees, or service or maintenance costs with respect to the goods,</u>

(c) <u>the lessee has an option to renew the lease or to become the owner of the goods,</u>

(d) <u>the lessee has an option to renew the lease for a fixed rent that is equal to or greater than the reasonably predictable fair market rent for the use of the goods for the term of the renewal at the time the option is to be performed, or</u>

(e) <u>the lessee has an option to become the owner of the goods for a fixed price that is equal to or greater than the reasonably predictable fair market value of the goods at the time the option is to be performed.</u>

<u>For purposes of this subsection (37):</u>

(x) <u>Additional consideration is not nominal if (i) when the option to renew the lease is granted to the lessee the rent is stated to be the fair market rent for the use of the goods for the term of the renewal determined at the time the option is to be performed, or (ii) when the option to become the owner of the goods is granted to the lessee the price is stated to be the fair market value of the goods determined at the time the option is to be performed. Additional consideration is nominal if it is less than the lessee's reasonably predictable cost of per-</u>

forming under the lease agreement if the option is not exercised;

(y) "Reasonably predictable" and "remaining economic life of the goods" are to be determined with reference to the facts and circumstances at the time the transaction is entered into; and

(z) "Present value" means the amount as of a date certain of one or more sums payable in the future, discounted to the date certain. The discount is determined by the interest rate specified by the parties if the rate is not manifestly unreasonable at the time the transaction is entered into; otherwise, the discount is determined by a commercially reasonable rate that takes into account the facts and circumstances of each case at the time the transaction was entered into.

(38) "Send" in connection with any writing or notice means to deposit in the mail or deliver for transmission by any other usual means of communication with postage or cost of transmission provided for and properly addressed and in the case of an instrument to an address specified thereon or otherwise agreed, or if there be none to any address reasonable under the circumstances. The receipt of any writing or notice within the time at which it would have arrived if properly sent has the effect of a proper sending.

(39) "Signed" includes any symbol executed or adopted by a party with present intention to authenticate a writing.

(40) "Surety" includes guarantor.

(41) "Telegram" includes a message transmitted by radio, teletype, cable, any mechanical method of transmission, or the like.

(42) "Term" means that portion of an agreement which relates to a particular matter.

(43) "Unauthorized" signature [or indorsement] means one made without actual, implied, or apparent authority and includes a forgery.

(44) "Value". Except as otherwise provided with respect to negotiable instruments and bank collections (Sections 3-303, 4-208 and 4-209) a person gives "value" for rights if he acquires them

(a) in return for a binding commitment to extend credit or for the extension of immediately available credit whether or not drawn upon and whether or not a chargeback is provided for in the event of difficulties in collection; or

(b) as security for or in total or partial satisfaction of a preexisting claim; or

(c) by accepting delivery pursuant to a pre-existing contract for purchase; or

(d) generally, in return for any consideration sufficient to support a simple contract.

(45) "Warehouse receipt" means a receipt issued by a person engaged in the business of storing goods for hire.

(46) "Written" or "writing" includes printing, typewriting or any other intentional reduction to tangible form.

§1-202. Prima Facie Evidence by Third-Party Documents. A document in due form purporting to be a bill of lading, policy or certificate of insurance, official weigher's or inspector's certificate, consular invoice or any other document authorized or required by the contract to be issued by a third party shall be prima facie evidence of its own authenticity and genuineness and of the facts stated in the document by the third party.

§1-203. Obligation of Good Faith. Every contract or duty within this Act imposes an obligation of good faith in its performance or enforcement.

§1-204. Time; Reasonable Time; "Seasonably".

(1) Whenever this Act requires any action to be taken within a reasonable time, any time which is not manifestly unreasonable may be fixed by agreement.

(2) What is a reasonable time for taking any action depends on the nature, purpose and circumstances of such action.

(3) An action is taken "seasonably" when it is taken at or within the time agreed or if no time is agreed at or within a reasonable time.

§1-205. Course of Dealing and Usage of Trade.

(1) A course of dealing is a sequence of previous conduct between the parties to a particular transaction which is fairly to be regarded as establishing a common basis of understanding for interpreting their expressions and other conduct.

(2) A usage of trade is any practice or method of dealing having such regularity of observance in a place, vocation or trade as to justify an expectation that it will be observed with respect to the transaction in question. The existence and scope of such a usage are to be proved as facts. If it is established that such a usage is embodied in a written trade code or similar writing the interpretation of the writing is for the court.

(3) A course of dealing between parties and any usage of trade in the vocation or trade in which they are engaged or of which they are or should be aware give particular meaning to and supplement or qualify terms of an agreement.

(4) The express terms of an agreement and an applicable course of dealing or usage of trade shall be construed wherever reasonable as consistent with each other; but when such construction is unreasonable express terms control both course of dealing and usage of trade and course of dealing controls usage of trade.

(5) An applicable usage of trade in the place where any part of performance is to occur shall be used in interpreting the agreement as to that part of the performance.

(6) Evidence of a relevant usage of trade offered by one party is not admissible unless and until he has given the other party such notice as the court finds sufficient to prevent unfair surprise to the latter.

§1-206. Statute of Frauds for Kinds of Personal Property Not Otherwise Covered.

(1) Except in the cases described in subsection (2) of this section a contract for the sale of personal property is not enforceable by way of action or defense beyond five thousand dollars in amount or value of remedy unless there is some writing which indicates that a contract for sale has been made between the parties at a defined or stated price, reasonably identifies the subject matter, and is signed by the party against whom enforcement is sought or by his authorized agent.

(2) Subsection (1) of this section does not apply to contracts for the sale of goods (Section 2-201) nor of securities (Section 8-319) nor to security agreements (Section 9-203).

§1-207. Performance or Acceptance Under Reservation of Rights.

(1) A party who, with explicit reservation of rights, performs or promises performance or assents to performance in a manner demanded or offered by the other party does not thereby prejudice the rights reserved. Such words as "without prejudice", "under protest" or the like are sufficient.

(2) Subsection (1) does not apply to an accord and satisfaction.

§1-208. Option to Accelerate at Will.

A term providing that one party or his successor in interest may accelerate payment or performance or require collateral or additional collateral "at will" or "when he deems himself insecure" or in words of similar import shall be construed to mean that he shall have power to do so only if he in good faith believes that the prospect of payment or performance is impaired. The burden of establishing lack of good faith is on the party against whom the power has been exercised.

§1-209. Subordinated Obligations.

An obligation may be issued as subordinated to payment of another obligation of the person obligated, or a creditor may subordinate his right to payment of an obligation by agreement with either the person obligated or another creditor of the person obligated. Such a subordination does not create a security interest as against either the common debtor or a subordinated creditor. This section shall be construed as declaring the law as it existed prior to the enactment of this section and not as modifying it.

Note: *This new section is proposed as an optional provision to make it clear that a subordination agreement does not create a security interest unless so intended.*

ARTICLE 2: SALES

Part 1: Short Title, General Construction, and Subject Matter

§2-101. Short Title. This Article shall be known and may be cited as Uniform Commercial Code—Sales.

§2-102. Scope; Certain Security and Other Transactions Excluded from This Article. Unless the context otherwise requires, this Article applies to transactions in goods; it does not apply to any transaction which although in the form of an unconditional contract to sell or present sale is intended to operate only as a security transaction nor does this Article impair or repeal any statute regulating sales to consumers, farmers or other specified classes of buyers.

§2-103. Definitions and Index of Definitions.

(1) In this Article unless the context otherwise requires

> **(a)** "Buyer" means a person who buys or contracts to buy goods.
> **(b)** "Good faith" in the case of a merchant means honesty in fact and the observance of reasonable commercial standards of fair dealing in the trade.
> **(c)** "Receipt" of goods means taking physical possession of them.
> **(d)** "Seller" means a person who sells or contracts to sell goods.

(2) Other definitions applying to this Article or to specified Parts thereof, and the sections in which they appear are:

"Acceptance"	Section 2-606
"Banker's credit"	Section 2-325
"Between merchants"	Section 2-104
"Cancellation"	Section 2-106(4)
"Commercial unit"	Section 2-105
"Confirmed credit"	Section 2-325
"Conforming to contract"	Section 2-106
"Contract for sale"	Section 2-106
"Cover"	Section 2-712
"Entrusting"	Section 2-403
"Financing agency"	Section 2-104
"Future goods"	Section 2-105
"Goods"	Section 2-105
"Identification"	Section 2-501
"Installment contract"	Section 2-612
"Letter of credit"	Section 2-325
"Lot"	Section 2-105
"Merchant"	Section 2-104
"Overseas"	Section 2-323
"Person in position of seller"	Section 2-707
"Present sale"	Section 2-106
"Sale"	Section 2-106
"Sale on approval"	Section 2-326
"Sale or return"	Section 2-326

"Termination"   Section 2-106

(**3**) The following definitions in other Articles apply to this Article:

"Check"   Section 3-104
"Consignee"   Section 7-102
"Consignor"   Section 7-102
"Consumer goods"   Section 9-109
"Dishonor"   Section 3-507
"Draft"   Section 3-104

(**4**) In addition Article 1 contains general definitions and principles of construction and interpretation applicable throughout this article.

§2-104. Definitions: "Merchant"; "Between Merchants"; "Financing Agency".

(**1**) "Merchant" means a person who deals in goods of the kind or otherwise by his occupation holds himself out as having knowledge or skill peculiar to the practices or goods involved in the transaction or to whom such knowledge or skill may be attributed by his employment of an agent or broker or other intermediary who by his occupation holds himself out as having such knowledge or skill.

(**2**) "Financing agency" means a bank, finance company or other person who in the ordinary course of business makes advances against goods or documents of title or who by arrangement with either the seller or the buyer intervenes in ordinary course to make or collect payment due or claimed under the contract for sale, as by purchasing or paying the seller's draft or making advances against it or by merely taking it for collection whether or not documents of title accompany the draft. "Financing agency" includes also a bank or other person who similarly intervenes between persons who are in the position of seller and buyer in respect of the goods (Section 2-707).

(**3**) "Between merchants" means in any transaction with respect to which both parties are chargeable with the knowledge or skill of merchants.

§2-105. Definitions: Transferability; "Goods"; "Future" Goods; "Lot"; "Commercial Unit".

(**1**) "Goods" means all things (including specially manufactured goods) which are movable at the time of identification to the contract for sale other than the money in which the price is to be paid, investment securities (Article 8) and things in action. "Goods" also includes the unborn young of animals and growing crops and other identified things attached to realty as described in the section on goods to be severed from realty (Section 2-107).

(**2**) Goods must be both existing and identified before any interest in them can pass. Goods which are not both existing and identified are "future" goods. A purported present sale of future goods or of any interest therein operates as a contract to sell.

(**3**) There may be a sale of a part interest in existing identified goods.

(**4**) An undivided share in an identified bulk of fungible goods is sufficiently identified to be sold although the quantity of the bulk is not determined. Any agreed proportion of such a bulk or any quantity thereof agreed upon by number, weight or other measure may to the extent of the seller's interest in the bulk be sold to the buyer who then becomes an owner in common.

(**5**) "Lot" means a parcel or a single article which is the subject matter of a separate sale or delivery, whether or not it is sufficient to perform the contract.

(**6**) "Commercial unit" means such a unit of goods as by commercial usage is a single whole for purposes of sale and division of which materially impairs its character or value on the market or in use. A commercial unit may be a single article (as a machine) or a set of articles (as a suite of furniture or an assortment of sizes) or a quantity (as a bale, gross, or carload) or any other unit treated in use or in the relevant market as a single whole.

§2-106. Definitions: "Contract"; "Agreement"; "Contract for Sale"; "Sale"; "Present Sale"; "Conforming" to Contract; "Termination"; "Cancellation".

(**1**) In this Article unless the context otherwise requires "contract" and "agreement" are limited to those relating to the present or future sale of goods. "Contract for sale" includes both a present sale of goods and a contract to sell goods at a future time. A "sale" consists in the passing of title from the seller to the buyer for a price (Section 2-401). A "present sale" means a sale which is accomplished by the making of the contract.

(**2**) Goods or conduct including any part of a performance are "conforming" or conform to the contract when they are in accordance with the obligations under the contract.

(**3**) "Termination" occurs when either party pursuant to a power created by agreement or law puts an end to the contract otherwise than for its breach. On "termination" all obligations which are still executory on both sides are discharged but any right based on prior breach or performance survives.

(**4**) "Cancellation" occurs when either party puts an end to the contract for breach by the other and its effect is the same as that of "termination" except that the cancelling party also retains any remedy for breach of the whole contract or any unperformed balance.

§2-107. Goods to Be Severed From Realty: Recording.

(**1**) A contract for the sale of minerals or the like (including oil and gas) or a structure or its materials to be removed from realty is a contract for the sale of goods within this Article if they are to be severed by the seller but until severance a purported present sale thereof which is not effective as a transfer of an interest in land is effective only as a contract to sell.

(2) A contract for the sale apart from the land of growing crops or other things attached to realty and capable of severance without material harm thereto but not described in subsection (1) or of timber to be cut is a contract for the sale of goods within this Article whether the subject matter is to be severed by the buyer or by the seller even though it forms part of the realty at the time of contracting, and the parties can by identification effect a present sale before severance.

(3) The provisions of this section are subject to any third party rights provided by the law relating to realty records, and the contract for sale may be executed and recorded as a document transferring an interest in land and shall then constitute notice to third parties of the buyer's rights under the contract for sale.

Part 2: Form, Formation and Readjustment of Contract

§2-201. Formal Requirements; Statute of Frauds.

(1) Except as otherwise provided in this section a contract for the sale of goods for the price of $500 or more is not enforceable by way of action or defense unless there is some writing sufficient to indicate that a contract for sale has been made between the parties and signed by the party against whom enforcement is sought or by his authorized agent or broker. A writing is not insufficient because it omits or incorrectly states a term agreed upon but the contract is not enforceable under this paragraph beyond the quantity of goods shown in such writing.

(2) Between merchants if within a reasonable time a writing in confirmation of the contract and sufficient against the sender is received and the party receiving it has reason to know its contents, it satisfies the requirements of subsection (1) against such party unless written notice of objection to its contents is given within 10 days after it is received.

(3) A contract which does not satisfy the requirements of subsection (1) but which is valid in other respects is enforceable

(a) if the goods are to be specially manufactured for the buyer and are not suitable for sale to others in the ordinary course of the seller's business and the seller, before notice of repudiation is received and under circumstances which reasonably indicate that the goods are for the buyer, has made either a substantial beginning of their manufacture or commitments for their procurement; or

(b) if the party against whom enforcement is sought admits in his pleading, testimony or otherwise in court that a contract for sale was made, but the contract is not enforceable under this provision beyond the quantity of goods admitted; or

(c) with respect to goods for which payment has been made and accepted or which have been received and accepted (Sec. 2-606.)

§2-202. Final Written Expression: Parol or Extrinsic Evidence.
Terms with respect to which the confirmatory memoranda of the parties agree or which are otherwise set forth in a writing intended by the parties as a final expression of their agreement with respect to such terms as are included therein may not be contradicted by evidence of any prior agreement or of a contemporaneous oral agreement but may be explained or supplemented

(a) by course of dealing or usage of trade (Section 1-205) or by course of performance (Section 2-208); and

(b) by evidence of consistent additional terms unless the court finds the writing to have been intended also as a complete and exclusive statement of the terms of the agreement.

§2-203. Seals Inoperative.
The affixing of a seal to a writing evidencing a contract for sale or an offer to buy or sell goods does not constitute the writing a sealed instrument and the law with respect to sealed instruments does not apply to such a contract or offer.

§2-204. Formation in General.

(1) A contract for sale of goods may be made in any manner sufficient to show agreement, including conduct by both parties which recognizes the existence of such a contract.

(2) An agreement sufficient to constitute a contract for sale may be found even though the moment of its making is undetermined.

(3) Even though one or more terms are left open a contract for sale does not fail for indefiniteness if the parties have intended to make a contract and there is a reasonably certain basis for giving an appropriate remedy.

§2-205. Firm Offers.
An offer by a merchant to buy or sell goods in a signed writing which by its terms gives assurance that it will be held open is not revocable, for lack of consideration, during the time stated or if no time is stated for a reasonable time, but in no event may such period of irrevocability exceed three months; but any such term of assurance on a form supplied by the offeree must be separately signed by the offeror.

§2-206. Offer and Acceptance in Formation of Contract.

(1) Unless otherwise unambiguously indicated by the language or circumstances

(a) an offer to make a contract shall be construed as inviting acceptance in any manner and by any medium reasonable in the circumstances;

(b) an order or other offer to buy goods for prompt or current shipment shall be construed as inviting acceptance either by a prompt promise to ship or by the prompt or current shipment of conforming or nonconforming goods, but such a shipment of nonconforming goods does not constitute an acceptance if the seller seasonably notifies the buyer that the shipment is offered only as an accommodation to the buyer.

(2) Where the beginning of a requested performance is a reasonable mode of acceptance an offeror who is not notified of acceptance within a reasonable time may treat the offer as having lapsed before acceptance.

§2-207. Additional Terms in Acceptance or Confirmation.

(1) A definite and seasonable expression of acceptance or a written confirmation which is sent within a reasonable time operates as an acceptance even though it states terms additional to or different from those offered or agreed upon, unless acceptance is expressly made conditional on assent to the additional or different terms.

(2) The additional terms are to be construed as proposals for addition to the contract. Between merchants such terms become part of the contract unless:

(a) the offer expressly limits acceptance to the terms of the offer;

(b) they materially alter it; or

(c) notification of objection to them has already been given or is given within a reasonable time after notice of them is received.

(3) Conduct by both parties which recognizes the existence of a contract is sufficient to establish a contract for sale although the writings of the parties do not otherwise establish a contract. In such case the terms of the particular contract consist of those terms on which the writings of the parties agree, together with any supplementary terms incorporated under any other provisions of this Act.

§2-208. Course of Performance or Practical Construction.

(1) Where the contract for sale involves repeated occasions for performance by either party with knowledge of the nature of the performance and opportunity for objection to it by the other, any course of performance accepted or acquiesced in without objection shall be relevant to determine the meaning of the agreement.

(2) The express terms of the agreement and any such course of performance, as well as any course of dealing and usage of trade, shall be construed whenever reasonable as consistent with each other; but when such construction is unreasonable, express terms shall control course of performance and course of performance shall control both course of dealing

and usage of trade (Section 1-205).

(3) Subject to the provisions of the next section on modification and waiver, such course of performance shall be relevant to show a waiver or modification of any term inconsistent with such course of performance.

§2-209. Modification, Rescission and Waiver.

(1) An agreement modifying a contract within this Article needs no consideration to be binding.

(2) A signed agreement which excludes modification or rescission except by a signed writing cannot be otherwise modified or rescinded, but except as between merchants such a requirement on a form supplied by the merchant must be separately signed by the other party.

(3) The requirements of the statute of frauds section of this Article (Section 2-201) must be satisfied if the contract as modified is within its provisions.

(4) Although an attempt at modification or rescission does not satisfy the requirements of subsection (2) or (3) it can operate as a waiver.

(5) A party who has made a waiver affecting an executory portion of the contract may retract the waiver by reasonable notification received by the other party that strict performance will be required of any term waived, unless the retraction would be unjust in view of a material change of position in reliance on the waiver.

§2-210. Delegation of Performance; Assignment of Rights.

(1) A party may perform his duty through a delegate unless otherwise agreed or unless the other party has a substantial interest in having his original promisor perform or control the acts required by the contract. No delegation of performance relieves the party delegating of any duty to perform or any liability for breach.

(2) Unless otherwise agreed all rights of either seller or buyer can be assigned except where the assignment would materially change the duty of the other party, or increase materially the burden or risk imposed on him by his contract, or impair materially his chance of obtaining return performance. A right to damages for breach of the whole contract or a right arising out of the assignor's due performance of his entire obligation can be assigned despite agreement otherwise.

(3) Unless the circumstances indicate the contrary a prohibition of assignment of "the contract" is to be construed as barring only the delegation to the assignee of the assignor's performance.

(4) An assignment of "the contract" or of "all my rights under the contract" or an assignment in similar general terms is an assignment of rights and unless the language or the circumstances (as in an assignment for security) indicate the contrary, it is a delegation of performance of the duties of the assignor and its acceptance by

the assignee constitutes a promise by him to perform those duties. This promise is enforceable by either the assignor or the other party to the original contract.

(5) The other party may treat any assignment which delegates performance as creating reasonable grounds for insecurity and may without prejudice to his rights against the assignor demand assurances from the assignee (Section 2-609).

Part 3: General Obligation and Construction of Contract

§2-301. General Obligations of Parties. The obligation of the seller is to transfer and deliver and that of the buyer is to accept and pay in accordance with the contract.

§2-302. Unconscionable Contract or Clause.

(1) If the court as a matter of law finds the contract or any clause of the contract to have been unconscionable at the time it was made the court may refuse to enforce the contract, or it may enforce the remainder of the contract without the unconscionable clause, or it may so limit the application of any unconscionable clause as to avoid any unconscionable result.

(2) When it is claimed or appears to the court that the contract or any clause thereof may be unconscionable the parties shall be afforded a reasonable opportunity to present evidence as to its commercial setting, purpose and effect to aid the court in making the determination.

§2-303. Allocation or Division of Risks. Where this Article allocates a risk or a burden as between the parties "unless otherwise agreed", the agreement may not only shift the allocation but may also divide the risk or burden.

§2-304. Price Payable in Money, Goods, Realty, or Otherwise.

(1) The price can be made payable in money or otherwise. If it is payable in whole or in part in goods each party is a seller of the goods which he is to transfer.

(2) Even though all or part of the price is payable in an interest in realty the transfer of the goods and the seller's obligations with reference to them are subject to this Article, but not the transfer of the interest in realty or the transferor's obligations in connection therewith.

§2-305. Open Price Term.

(1) The parties if they so intend can conclude a contract for sale even though the price is not settled. In such a case the price is a reasonable price at the time for delivery if

(a) nothing is said as to price; or

(b) the price is left to be agreed by the parties and they fail to agree; or

(c) The price is to be fixed in terms of some agreed market or other standard as set or recorded by a third person or agency and it is not so set or recorded.

(2) A price to be fixed by the seller or by the buyer means a price for him to fix in good faith.

(3) When a price left to be fixed otherwise than by agreement of the parties fails to be fixed through fault of one party the other may at his option treat the contract as cancelled or himself fix a reasonable price.

(4) Where, however, the parties intend not to be bound unless the price be fixed or agreed and it is not fixed or agreed there is no contract. In such a case the buyer must return any goods already received or if unable so to do must pay their reasonable value at the time of delivery and the seller must return any portion of the price paid on account.

§2-306. Output, Requirements and Exclusive Dealings.

(1) A term which measures the quantity by the output of the seller or the requirements of the buyer means such actual output or requirements as may occur in good faith, except that no quantity unreasonably disproportionate to any stated estimate or in the absence of a stated estimate to any normal or otherwise comparable prior output or requirements may be tendered or demanded.

(2) A lawful agreement by either the seller or the buyer for exclusive dealing in the kind of goods concerned imposes unless otherwise agreed an obligation by the seller to use best efforts to supply the goods and by the buyer to use best efforts to promote their sale.

§2-307. Delivery in Single Lot or Several Lots. Unless otherwise agreed all goods called for by a contract for sale must be tendered in a single delivery and payment is due only on such tender but where the circumstances give either party the right to make or demand delivery in lots the price if it can be apportioned may be demanded for each lot.

§2-308. Absence of Specified Place for Delivery. Unless otherwise agreed

(a) The place for delivery of goods is the seller's place of business or if he has none his residence; but

(b) in a contract for sale of identified goods which to the knowledge of the parties at the time of contracting are in some other place, that place is the place for their delivery; and

(c) documents of title may be delivered through customary banking channels.

§2-309. Absence of Specific Time Provisions; Notice of Termination.

(1) The time for shipment or delivery or any other

action under a contract if not provided in this Article or agreed upon shall be a reasonable time.

(**2**) Where the contract provides for successive performances but is indefinite in duration it is valid for a reasonable time but unless otherwise agreed may be terminated at any time by either party.

(**3**) Termination of a contract by one party except on the happening of an agreed event requires that reasonable notification be received by the other party and an agreement dispensing with notification is invalid if its operation would be unconscionable.

§2-310. Open Time for Payment or Running of Credit; Authority to Ship Under Reservation. Unless otherwise agreed

(**a**) payment is due at the time and place at which the buyer is to receive the goods even though the place of shipment is the place of delivery; and

(**b**) if the seller is authorized to send the goods he may ship them under reservation, and may tender the documents of title, but the buyer may inspect the goods after their arrival before payment is due unless such inspection is inconsistent with the terms of the contract (Section 2-513); and

(**c**) f delivery is authorized and made by way of documents of title otherwise than by subsection (b) then payment is due at the time and place at which the buyer is to receive the documents regardless of where the goods are to be received; and

(**d**) where the seller is required or authorized to ship the goods on credit the credit period runs from the time of shipment but post-dating the invoice or delaying its dispatch will correspondingly delay the starting of the credit period.

§2-311. Options and Cooperation Respecting Performance.

(**1**) An agreement for sale which is otherwise sufficiently definite (subsection (3) of Section 2-204) to be a contract is not made invalid by the fact that it leaves particulars of performance to be specified by one of the parties. Any such specification must be made in good faith and within limits set by commercial reasonableness.

(**2**) Unless otherwise agreed specifications relating to assortment of the goods are at the buyer's option and except as otherwise provided in subsections (1)(c) and (3) of Section 2-319 specifications or arrangements relating to shipment are at the seller's option.

(**3**) Where such specifications would materially affect the other party's performance but is not seasonably made or where one party's cooperation is necessary to the agreed performance of the other but is not seasonably forthcoming, the other party

(**a**) is excused for any resulting delay in his own performance; and

(**b**) may also either proceed to perform in any reasonable manner or after the time for a material part of his own performance treat the failure to specify or to cooperate as a breach by failure to deliver or accept the goods.

§2-312. Warranty of Title and Against Infringement; Buyer's Obligation Against Infringement.

(**1**) Subject to subsection (2) there is in a contract for sale a warranty by the seller that

(**a**) the title conveyed shall be good, and its transfer rightful; and

(**b**) the goods shall be delivered free from any security interest or other lien or encumbrance of which the buyer at the time of contracting has no knowledge.

(**2**) A warranty under subsection (2) will be excluded or modified only by specific language or by circumstances which give the buyer reason to know that the person selling does not claim title in himself or that he is purporting to sell only such right or title as he or a third person may have.

(**3**) Unless otherwise agreed a seller who is a merchant regularly dealing in goods of the kind warrants that the goods shall be delivered free of the rightful claim of any third person by way of infringement or the like but a buyer who furnishes specifications to the seller must hold the seller harmless against any such claim which arises out of compliance with the specifications.

§2-313. Express Warranties by Affirmation, Promise, Description, Sample.

(**1**) Express warranties by the seller are created as follows:

(**a**) Any affirmation of fact or promise made by the seller to the buyer which relates to the goods and becomes part of the basis of the bargain creates an express warranty that the goods shall conform to the affirmation or promise.

(**b**) Any description of the goods which is made part of the basis of the bargain creates an express warranty that the goods shall conform to the description.

(**c**) Any sample or model which is made part of the basis of the bargain creates an express warranty that the whole of the goods shall conform to the sample or model.

(**2**) It is not necessary to the creation of an express warranty that the seller use formal words such as "warrant" or "guarantee" or that he have a specific intention to make a warranty, but an affirmation merely of the value of the goods or a statement purporting to be merely the seller's opinion or commendation of the goods does not create a warranty.

§2-314. Implied Warranty: Merchantability; Usage of Trade.

(1) Unless excluded or modified (Section 2-316), a warranty that the goods shall be merchantable is implied in a contract for their sale if the seller is a merchant with respect to goods of that kind. Under this section the serving for value of food or drink to be consumed either on the premises or elsewhere is a sale.

(2) Goods to be merchantable must be at least such as

(a) pass without objection in the trade under the contract description; and

(b) in the case of fungible goods, are of fair average quality within the description; and

(c) are fit for the ordinary purposes for which such goods are used; and

(d) run, within the variations permitted by the agreement, of even kind, quality and quantity within each unit and among all units involved; and

(e) are adequately contained, packaged, and labeled as the agreement may require; and

(f) conform to the promises or affirmations of fact made on the container or label if any.

(3) Unless excluded or modified (Section 2-316) other implied warranties may arise from course of dealing or usage of trade.

§2-315. Implied Warranty: Fitness for Particular Purpose.

Where the seller at the time of contracting has reason to know any particular purpose for which the goods are required and that the buyer is relying on the seller's skill or judgment to select or furnish suitable goods, there is unless excluded or modified under the next section an implied warranty that the goods shall be fit for such purpose.

§2-316. Exclusion or Modification of Warranties.

(1) Words or conduct relevant to the creation of an express warranty and words or conduct tending to negate or limit warranty shall be construed wherever reasonable as consistent with each other; but subject to the provisions of this Article on parol or extrinsic evidence (Section 2-202) negation or limitation is inoperative to the extent that such construction is unreasonable.

(2) Subject to subsection (3), to exclude or modify the implied warranty of merchantability or any part of it the language must mention merchantability and in case of a writing must be conspicuous, and to exclude or modify any implied warranty of fitness the exclusion must be by a writing and conspicuous. Language to exclude all implied warranties of fitness is sufficient if it

states, for example, that "There are no warranties which extend beyond the description on the face hereof."

(3) Notwithstanding subsection (2)

(a) unless the circumstances indicate otherwise, all implied warranties are excluded by expressions like "as is", "with all faults" or other language which in common understanding calls the buyer's attention to the exclusion of warranties and makes plain that there is no implied waranty; and

(b) when the buyer before entering into the contract has examined the goods or the sample or model as fully as he desired or has refused to examine the goods there is no implied warranty with regard to defects which an examination ought in the circumstances to have revealed to him; and

(c) an implied warranty can also be excluded or modified by course of dealing or course of performance or usage of trade.

(4) Remedies for breach of warranty can be limited in accordance with the provisions of this Article on liquidation or limitation of damages and on contractual modification of remedy (Sections 2-718 and 2-719).

§2-317. Cumulation and Conflict of Warranties Express or Implied.

Warranties whether express or implied shall be construed as consistent with each other and as cumulative but if such construction is unreasonable the intention of the parties shall determine which warranty is dominant. In ascertaining that intention the following rules apply:

(a) Exact or technical specifications displace an inconsistent sample or model or general language of description.

(b) A sample from an existing bulk displaces inconsistent general language of description.

(c) Express warranties displace inconsistent implied warranties other than an implied warranty of fitness for a particular purpose.

§2-318. Third Party Beneficiaries of Warranties Express or Implied.

Note: *If this Act is introduced in the Congress of the United States this section should be omitted. (States to select one alternative.)*

Alternative A—A seller's warranty whether express or implied extends to any natural person who is in the family or household of his buyer or who is a guest in his home if it is reasonable to expect that such person may use, consume or be affected by the goods and who is injured in person by breach of the warranty. A seller may not exclude or limit the operation of this section.

Alternative B—A seller's warranty whether express or implied extends to any natural person who may reasonably be expected to use, consume or be affected by the goods and who is injured in person by breach of the warranty. A seller may not exclude or limit the operation of this section.

Alternative C—A seller's warranty whether express or implied extends to any person who may reasonably be expected to use, consume or be affected by the goods and who is injured by breach of the warranty. A seller may not exclude or limit the operation of this section with respect to injury to the person of an individual to whom the warranty extends. As amended 1966.

§2-319. F.O.B. and F.A.S. Terms.

(**1**) Unless otherwise agreed the term F.O.B. (which means "free on board") at a named place, even though used only in connection with the stated price, is a delivery term under which

> (**a**) when the term is F.O.B. the place of shipment, the seller must at that place ship the goods in the manner provided in this Article (Section 2-504) and bear the expense and risk of putting them into the possession of the carrier; or
>
> (**b**) when the term is F.O.B. the place of destination, the seller must at his own expense and risk transport the goods to that place and there tender delivery of them in the manner provided in this Article (Section 2-503);
>
> (**c**) when under either (a) or (b) the term is also F.O.B. vessel, car or other vehicle, the seller must in addition at his own expense and risk load the goods on board. If the term is F.O.B. vessel the buyer must name the vessel and in an appropriate case the seller must comply with the provisions of this Article on the form of bill of lading (Section 2-323).

(**2**) Unless otherwise agreed the term F.A.S. vessel (which means "free alongside") at a named port, even though used only in connection with the stated price, is a delivery term under which the seller must

> (**a**) at his own expense and risk deliver the goods alongside the vessel in the manner usual in that port or on a dock designated and provided by the buyer; and
>
> (**b**) obtain and tender a receipt for the goods in exchange for which the carrier is under a duty to issue a bill of lading.

(**3**) Unless otherwise agreed in any case falling within subsection (1) (a) or (c) or subsection (2) the buyer must seasonably give any needed instructions for making delivery, including when the term is F.A.S. or F.O.B. the loading berth of the vessel and in an appropriate case its name and sailing date. The seller may treat the failure of needed instructions as a failure of cooperation under this Article (Section 2-311). He may

also at his option move the goods in any reasonable manner preparatory to delivery or shipment.

(**4**) Under the term F.O.B. vessel or F.A.S. unless otherwise agreed the buyer must make payment against tender of the required documents and the seller may not tender nor the buyer demand delivery of the goods in substitution for the documents.

§2-320. C.I.F. and C.&F. Terms.

(**1**) The term C.I.F. means that the price includes in a lump sum the cost of the goods and the insurance and freight to the named destination. The term C.&F. or C.F. means that the price so includes cost and freight to the named destination.

(**2**) Unless otherwise agreed and even though used only in connection with the stated price and destination, the term C.I.F. destination or its equivalent requires the seller at his own expense and risk to

> (**a**) put the goods into the possession of a carrier at the port for shipment and obtain a negotiable bill or bills of lading covering the entire transportation to the named destination; and
>
> (**b**) load the goods and obtain a receipt from the carrier (which may be contained in the bill of lading) showing that the freight has been paid or provided for; and
>
> (**c**) obtain a policy or certificate of insurance, including any war risk insurance, of a kind and on terms then current at the port of shipment in the usual amount, in the currency of the contract, shown to cover the same goods covered by the bill of lading and providing for payment of loss to the order of the buyer or for the account of whom it may concern; but the seller may add to the price the amount of the premium for any such war risk insurance; and
>
> (**d**) prepare an invoice of the goods and procure any other documents required to effect shipment or to comply with the contract; and
>
> (**e**) forward and tender with commercial promptness all the documents in due form and with any indorsement necessary to perfect the buyer's rights.

(**3**) Unless otherwise agreed the term C.&F. or its equivalent has the same effect and imposes upon the seller the same obligations and risks as a C.I.F. term except the obligation as to insurance.

(**4**) Under the term C.I.F. or C.&F. unless otherwise agreed the buyer must make payment against tender of the required documents and the seller may not tender nor the buyer demand delivery of the goods in substitution for the documents.

§2-321. C.I.F. or C.&F.: "Net Landed Weights"; "Payment on Arrival"; Warranty of Condition on Arrival. Under a contract containing a term C.I.F. or C.&F.

(1) Where the price is based on or is to be adjusted according to "net landed weights", "delivered weights", "out turn" quantity or quality or the like, unless otherwise agreed the seller must reasonably estimate the price. The payment due on tender of the documents called for by the contract is the amount so estimated, but after final adjustment of the price a settlement must be made with commercial promptness.

(2) An agreement described in subsection (1) or any warranty of quality or condition of the goods on arrival places upon the seller the risk of ordinary deterioration, shrinkage and the like in transportation but has no effect on the place or time of identification to the contract for sale or delivery or on the passing of the risk of loss.

(3) Unless otherwise agreed where the contract provides for payment on or after arrival of the goods the seller must before payment allow such preliminary inspection as is feasible; but if the goods are lost delivery of the documents and payment are due when the goods should have arrived.

§2-322. Delivery "Ex-Ship".

(1) Unless otherwise agreed a term for delivery of goods "ex-ship" (which means from the carrying vessel) or in equivalent language is not restricted to a particular ship and requires delivery from a ship which has reached a place at the named port of destination where goods of the kind are usually discharged.

(2) Under such a term unless otherwise agreed

(a) the seller must discharge all liens arising out of the carriage and furnish the buyer with a direction which puts the carrier under a duty to deliver the goods; and

(b) the risk of loss does not pass to the buyer until the goods leave the ship's tackle or are otherwise properly unloaded.

§2-323. Form of Bill of Lading Required in Overseas Shipment; "Overseas".

(1) Where the contract contemplates overseas shipment and contains a term C.I.F. or C.&F. or F.O.B. vessel the seller unless otherwise agreed must obtain a negotiable bill of lading stating that the goods have been loaded on board or, in the case of a term C.I.F. or C.&F., received for shipment.

(2) Where in a case within subsection (1) a bill of lading has been issued in a set of parts, unless otherwise agreed if the documents are not to be sent from abroad the buyer may demand tender of the full set; otherwise only one part of the bill of lading need be tendered. Even if the agreement expressly requires a full set

(a) due tender of a single part is acceptable within the provisions of this Article on cure of improper delivery (subsection (1) of Section 2-508); and

(b) even though the full set is demanded, if the documents are sent from abroad the person tendering an incomplete set may nevertheless require payment upon furnishing an indemnity which the buyer in good faith deems adequate.

(3) A shipment by water or by air or a contract contemplating such shipment is "overseas" insofar as by usage of trade or agreement it is subject to the commercial, financing or shipping practices characteristic of international deep water commerce.

§2-324. "No Arrival, No Sale" Term.
Under a term "no arrival, no sale" or terms of like meaning, unless otherwise agreed,

(a) the seller must properly ship conforming goods and if they arrive by any means he must tender them on arrival but he assumes no obligation that the goods will arrive unless he has caused the nonarrival; and

(b) where without fault of the seller the goods are in part lost or have so deteriorated as no longer to conform to the contract or arrive after the contract time, the buyer may proceed as if there had been casualty to identified goods (Section 2-613).

§2-325. "Letter of Credit" Term; "Confirmed Credit".

(1) Failure of the buyer seasonably to furnish an agreed letter of credit is a breach of the contract for sale.

(2) The delivery to seller of a proper letter of credit suspends the buyer's obligation to pay. If the letter of credit is dishonored, the seller may on seasonable notification to the buyer require payment directly from him.

(3) Unless otherwise agreed the term "letter of credit" or "banker's credit" in a contract for sale means an irrevocable credit issued by a financing agency of good repute and, where the shipment is overseas, of good international repute. The term "confirmed credit" means that the credit must also carry the direct obligation of such an agency which does business in the seller's financial market.

§2-326. Sale on Approval and Sale or Return; Consignment Sales and Rights of Creditors.

(1) Unless otherwise agreed, if delivered goods may be returned by the buyer even though they conform to the contract, the transaction is

(a) a "sale on approval" if the goods are delivered primarily for use, and

(b) a "sale or return" if the goods are delivered primarily for resale.

(2) Except as provided in subsection (3), goods held on approval are not subject to the claims of the buyer's creditors until acceptance; goods held on sale

or return are subject to such claims while in the buyer's possession.

(3) Where goods are delivered to a person for sale and such person maintains a place of business at which he deals in goods of the kind involved, under a name other than the name of the person making delivery, then with respect to claims of creditors of the person conducting the business the goods are deemed to be on sale or return. The provisions of this subsection are applicable even though an agreement purports to reserve title to the person making delivery until payment or resale or uses such words as "on consignment" or "on memorandum". However, this subsection is not applicable if the person making delivery

(a) complies with an applicable law providing for a consignor's interest or the like to be evidenced by a sign, or

(b) establishes that the person conducting the business is generally known by his creditors to be substantially engaged in selling the goods of others, or

(c) complies with the filing provisions of the Article on Secured Transactions (Article 9).

(4) Any "or return" term of a contract for sale is to be treated as a separate contract for sale within the statute of frauds section of this Article (Section 2-201) and as contradicting the sale aspect of the contract within the provisions of this Article on parol or extrinsic evidence (Section 2-202).

§2-327. Special Incidents of Sale on Approval and Sale or Return.

(1) Under a sale on approval unless otherwise agreed

(a) although the goods are identified to the contract the risk of loss and the title do not pass to the buyer until acceptance; and

(b) use of the goods consistent with the purpose of trial is not acceptance but failure seasonably to notify the seller of election to return the goods is acceptance, and if the goods conform to the contract acceptance of any part is acceptance of the whole; and

(c) after due notification of election to return, the return is at the seller's risk and expense but a merchant buyer must follow any reasonable instructions.

(2) Under a sale or return unless otherwise agreed

(a) the option to return extends to the whole or any commercial unit of the goods while in substantially their original condition, but must be exercised seasonably; and

(b) the return is at the buyer's risk and expense.

§2-328. Sale by Auction.

(1) In a sale by auction if goods are put up in lots

each lot is the subject of a separate sale.

(2) A sale by auction is complete when the auctioneer so announces by the fall of the hammer or in other customary manner. Where a bid is made while the hammer is falling in acceptance of a prior bid the auctioneer may in his discretion reopen the bidding or declare the goods sold under the bid on which the hammer was falling.

(3) Such a sale is with reserve unless the goods are in explicit terms put up without reserve. In an auction with reserve, the auctioneer may withdraw the goods at any time until he announces completion of the sale. In an auction without reserve, after the auctioneer calls for bids on an article or lot, that article or lot cannot be withdrawn unless no bid is made within a reasonable time. In either case a bidder may retract his bid until the auctioneer's announcement of completion of the sale, but a bidder's retraction does not revive any previous bid.

(4) If the auctioneer knowingly receives a bid on the seller's behalf or the seller makes or procures such a bid, and notice has not been given that liberty for such bidding is reserved, the buyer may at his option avoid the sale or take the goods at the price of the last good faith bid prior to the completion of the sale. This subsection shall not apply to any bid at a forced sale.

Part 4: Title, Creditors and Good Faith Purchasers

§2-401. Passing of Title; Reservation for Security; Limited Application of This Section.

Each provision of this Article with regard to the rights, obligations and remedies of the seller, the buyer, purchasers or other third parties applies irrespective of title to the goods except where the provision refers to such title. Insofar as situations are not covered by the other provisions of this Article and matters concerning title become material the following rules apply:

(1) Title to goods cannot pass under a contract for sale prior to their identification to the contract (Section 2-501), and unless otherwise explicitly agreed the buyer acquires by their identification a special property as limited by this Act. Any retention or reservation by the seller of the title (property) in goods shipped or delivered to the buyer is limited in effect to a reservation of a security interest. Subject to these provisions and to the provisions of the Article on Secured Transactions (Article 9), title to goods passes from the seller to the buyer in any manner and on any conditions explicitly agreed on by the parties.

(2) Unless otherwise explicitly agreed title passes to the buyer at the time and place at which the seller completes his performance with reference to the physical delivery of the goods, despite any reservation of a security interest and even though a document of title is to be delivered at a different time or place; and in particular and despite any reservation of a security interest by the bill of lading

   (a) if the contract requires or authorizes the seller to send the goods to the buyer but does not require him to deliver them at destination, title passes to the buyer at the time and place of shipment; but

   (b) if the contract requires delivery at destination, title passes on tender there.

   (3) Unless otherwise explicitly agreed where delivery is to be made without moving the goods.

   (a) if the seller is to deliver a document of title, title passes at the time when and the place where he delivers such documents; or

   (b) if the goods are at the time of contracting already identified and no documents are to be delivered, title passes at the time and place of contracting.

   (4) A rejection or other refusal by the buyer to receive or retain the goods, whether or not justified, or a justified revocation of acceptance revests title to the goods in the seller. Such revesting occurs by operation of law and is not a "sale".

§2-402. **Rights of Seller's Creditors Against Sold Goods.**

   (1) Except as provided in subsections (2) and (3), rights of unsecured creditors of the seller with respect to goods which have been identified to a contract for sale are subject to the buyer's rights to recover the goods under this Article (Section 2-502 and 2-716).

   (2) A creditor of the seller may treat a sale or an identification of goods to a contract for sale as void if as against him a retention of possession by the seller is fraudulent under any rule of law of the state where the goods are situated, except that retention of possession in good faith and current course of trade by a merchant-seller for a commercially reasonable time after a sale or identification is not fraudulent.

   (3) Nothing in this Article shall be deemed to impair the rights of creditors of the seller

   (a) under the provisions of the Article on Secured Transactions (Article 9); or

   (b) where identification to the contract or delivery is made not in current course of trade but in satisfaction of or as security for a pre-existing claim for money, security or the like and is made under circumstances which under any rule of law of the state where the goods are situated would apart from this Article constitute the transaction a fraudulent transfer or voidable preference.

§2-403. **Power to Transfer; Good Faith Purchase of Goods; "Entrusting".**

   (1) A purchaser of goods acquires all title which his transferor had or had power to transfer except that a purchaser of a limited interest acquires rights only to the extent of the interest purchased. A person with voidable title has power to transfer a good title to a good faith purchaser for value. When goods have been delivered under a transaction of purchase the purchaser had such power even though

   (a) the transferor was deceived as to the identity of the purchaser, or

   (b) the delivery was in exchange for a check which is later dishonored, or

   (c) it was agreed that the transaction was to be a "cash sale", or

   (d) the delivery was procured through fraud punishable as larcenous under the criminal law.

   (2) Any entrusting of possession of goods to a merchant who deals in goods of that kind gives him power to transfer all rights of the entruster to a buyer in ordinary course of business.

   (3) "Entrusting" includes any delivery and any acquiescence in retention of possession regardless of any condition expressed between the parties to the delivery or acquiescence and regardless of whether the procurement of the entrusting or the possessor's disposition of the goods have been such as to be larcenous under the criminal law.

   (4) The rights of other purchasers of goods and of lien creditors are governed by the Articles on Secured Transactions (Article 9), Bulk Transfers (Article 6) and Documents of Title (Article 7).

Part 5: Performance

§2-501. **Insurable Interest in Goods; Manner of Identification of Goods.**

   (1) The buyer obtains a special property and an insurable interest in goods by identification of existing goods as goods to which the contract refers even though the goods so identified are non-conforming and he has an option to return or reject them. Such identification can be made at any time and in any manner explicitly agreed to by the parties. In the absence of explicit agreement identification occurs

   (a) when the contract is made if it is for the sale of goods already existing and identified;

   (b) if the contract is for the sale of future goods other than those described in paragraph (c), when goods are shipped, marked or otherwise designated by the seller as goods to which the contract refers;

   (c) when the crops are planted or otherwise become growing crops or the young are conceived if the contract is for the sale of unborn young to be born within twelve months after contracting or for the sale of crops to be harvested within twelve months or the next normal harvest season after contracting whichever is longer.

(2) The seller retains an insurable interest in goods so long as title to or any security interest in the goods remains in him and where the identification is by the seller alone he may until default or insolvency or notification to the buyer that the identification is final substitute other goods for those identified.

(3) Nothing in this section impairs any insurable interest recognized under any other statute or rule of law.

§2-502. Buyer's Right to Goods on Seller's Insolvency.

(1) Subject to subsection (2) and even though the goods have not been shipped a buyer who has paid a part or all of the price of goods in which he has a special property under the provisions of the immediately preceding section may on making and keeping good a tender of any unpaid portion of their price recover them from the seller if the seller becomes insolvent within ten days after receipt of the first installment on their price.

(2) If the identification creating his special property has been made by the buyer he acquires the right to recover the goods only if they conform to the contract for sale.

§2-503. Manner of Seller's Tender of Delivery.

(1) Tender of delivery requires that the seller put and hold conforming goods at the buyer's disposition and give the buyer any notification reasonably necessary to enable him to take delivery. The manner, time and place for tender are determined by the agreement and this Article, and in particular

(a) tender must be at a reasonable hour, and if it is of goods they must be kept available for the period reasonably necessary to enable the buyer to take possession; but

(b) unless otherwise agreed the buyer must furnish facilities reasonably suited to the receipt of the goods.

(2) Where the case is within the next section respecting shipment tender requires that the seller comply with its provisions.

(3) Where the seller is required to deliver at a particular destination tender requires that he comply with subsection (1) and also in any appropriate case tender documents as described in subsections (4) and (5) of this section.

(4) Where goods are in the possession of a bailee and are to be delivered without being moved

(a) tender requires that the seller either tender a negotiable document of title covering such goods or procure acknowledgement by the

bailee of the buyer's right to possession of the goods; but

(b) tender to the buyer of a non-negotiable document of title or of a written direction to the bailee to deliver is sufficient tender unless the buyer seasonably objects, and receipt by the bailee of notification of the buyer's rights fixes those rights as against the bailee and all third persons; but risk of loss of the goods and of any failure by the bailee to honor the non-negotiable document of title or to obey the direction remains on the seller until the buyer has had a reasonable time to present the document or direction, and a refusal by the bailee to honor the document or to obey the direction defeats the tender.

(5) Where the contract requires the seller to deliver documents

(a) he must tender all such documents in correct form, except as provided in this Article with respect to bills of lading in a set (subsection (2) of Section 2-323); and

(b) tender through customary banking channels is sufficient and dishonor of a draft accompanying the documents constitutes non-acceptance or rejection.

§2-504. Shipment by Seller. Where the seller is required or authorized to send the goods to the buyer and the contract does not require him to deliver them at a particular destination, then unless otherwise agreed he must

(a) put the goods in the possession of such a carrier and make such a contract for their transportation as may be reasonable having regard to the nature of the goods and other circumstances of the case; and

(b) obtain and promptly deliver or tender in due form any document necessary to enable the buyer to obtain possession of the goods or otherwise required by the agreement or by usage of trade; and

(c) promptly notify the buyer of the shipment. Failure to notify the buyer under paragraph (c) or to make a proper contract under paragraph (a) is a ground for rejection only if material delay or loss ensues.

§2-505. Seller's Shipment under Reservation.

(1) Where the seller has identified goods to the contract by or before shipment:

(a) his procurement of a negotiable bill of lading to his own order or otherwise reserves in him a security interest in the goods. His procurement of the bill to the order of a financing agency or of the buyer indicates in addition only the seller's expectation of transferring that interest to the person named.

(b) a non-negotiable bill of lading to himself or his nominee reserves possession of the goods as security but except in a case of conditional delivery (subsection (2) of Section 2-507) a non-negotiable bill of lading naming the buyer as consignee reserves no security interest even though the seller retains possession of the bill of lading.

(2) When shipment by the seller with reservation of a security interest is in violation of the contract for sale it constitutes an improper contract for transportation within the preceding section but impairs neither the rights given to the buyer by shipment and identification of the goods to the contract nor the seller's powers as a holder of a negotiable document.

§2-506. Rights of Financing Agency.

(1) A financing agency by paying or purchasing for value a draft which relates to a shipment of goods acquires to the extent of the payment or purchase and in addition to its own rights under the draft and any document of title securing it any rights of the shipper in the goods including the right to stop delivery and the shipper's right to have the draft honored by the buyer.

(2) The right to reimbursement of a financing agency which has in good faith honored or purchased the draft under commitment to or authority from the buyer is not impaired by subsequent discovery of defects with reference to any relevant document which was apparently regular on its face.

§2-507. Effect of Seller's Tender; Delivery on Condition.

(1) Tender of delivery is a condition to the buyer's duty to accept the goods and, unless otherwise agreed, to his duty to pay for them. Tender entitles the seller to acceptance of the goods and to payment according to the contract.

(2) Where payment is due and demanded on the delivery to the buyer of goods or documents of title, his right as against the seller to retain or dispose of them is conditional upon his making the payment due.

§2-508. Cure by Seller of Improper Tender or Delivery; Replacement.

(1) Where any tender or delivery by the seller is rejected because non-conforming and the time for performance has not yet expired, the seller may seasonably notify the buyer of his intention to cure and may then within the contract time make a conforming delivery.

(2) Where the buyer rejects a non-conforming tender which the seller had reasonable grounds to believe would be acceptable with or without money allowance the seller may if he seasonably notifies the buyer have a further reasonable time to substitute a conforming tender.

§2-509. Risk of Loss in the Absence of Breach.

(1) Where the contract requires or authorizes the seller to ship the goods by carrier

(a) if it does not require him to deliver them at a particular destination, the risk of loss passes to the buyer when the goods are duly delivered to the carrier even though the shipment is under reservation (Section 2-505); but

(b) if it does require him to deliver them at a particular destination and the goods are there duly tendered while in the possession of the carrier, the risk of loss passes to the buyer when the goods are there duly so tendered as to enable the buyer to take delivery.

(2) Where the goods are held by a bailee to be delivered without being moved, the risk of loss passes to the buyer

(a) on his receipt of a negotiable document of title covering the goods; or

(b) on acknowledgement by the bailee of the buyer's right to possession of the goods; or

(c) after his receipt of a non-negotiable document of title or other written direction to deliver, as provided in subsection (4) (b) of Section 2-503.

(3) In any case not within subsection (1) or (2), the risk of loss passes to the buyer on his receipt of the goods if the seller is a merchant; otherwise the risk passes to the buyer on tender of delivery.

(4) The provisions of this section are subject to contrary agreement of the parties and to the provisions of this Article on sale on approval (Section 2-327) and on effect of breach on risk of loss (Section 2-510).

§2-510. Effect of Breach on Risk of Loss.

(1) Where a tender or delivery of goods so fails to conform to the contract as to give a right of rejection the risk of their loss remains on the seller until cure or acceptance.

(2) Where the buyer rightfully revokes acceptance he may to the extent of any deficiency in his effective insurance coverage treat the risk of loss as having rested on the seller from the beginning.

(3) Where the buyer as to conforming goods already identified to the contract for sale repudiates or is otherwise in breach before risk of their loss has passed to him, the seller may to the extent of any deficiency in his effective insurance coverage treat the risk of loss as resting on the buyer for a commercially reasonable time.

§2-511. Tender of Payment by Buyer; Payment by Check.

(1) Unless otherwise agreed tender of payment is a condition to the seller's duty to tender and complete any delivery.

(2) Tender of payment is sufficient when made by

any means or in any manner current in the ordinary course of business unless the seller demands payment in legal tender and gives any extension of time reasonably necessary to procure it.

(**3**) Subject to the provisions of this Act on the effect of an instrument on an obligation (Section 3-802), payment by check is conditional and is defeated as between the parties by dishonor of the check on due presentment.

§2-512. Payment by Buyer Before Inspection.

(**1**) Where the contract requires payment before inspection non-conformity of the goods does not excuse the buyer from so making payment unless

(**a**) the non-conformity appears without inspection; or

(**b**) despite tender of the required documents the circumstances would justify injunction against honor under the provisions of this Act (Section 5-114).

(**2**)   Payment pursuant to subsection (1) does not constitute an acceptance of goods or impair the buyer's right to inspect or any of his remedies.

§2-513. Buyer's Right to Inspection of Goods.

(**1**) Unless otherwise agreed and subject to subsection (3), where goods are tendered or delivered or identified to the contract for sale, the buyer has a right before payment or acceptance to inspect them at any reasonable place and time and in any reasonable manner. When the seller is required or authorized to send the goods to the buyer, the inspection may be after their arrival.

(**2**) Expenses of inspection must be borne by the buyer but may be recovered from the seller if the goods do not conform and are rejected.

(**3**) Unless otherwise agreed and subject to the provisions of this Article on C.I.F. contracts (subsection (3) of Section 3-221), the buyer is not entitled to inspect the goods before payment of the price when the contract provides

(**a**) for delivery "C.O.D." or on other like terms; or

(**b**) for payment against documents of title, except where such payment is due only after the goods are to become available for inspection.

(**4**)   A place or method of inspection fixed by the parties is presumed to be exclusive but unless otherwise expressly agreed it does not postpone identification or shift the place for delivery or for passing the risk of loss. If compliance becomes impossible, inspection shall be as provided in this section unless the place or method fixed was clearly intended as an indispensable condition failure of which avoids the contract.

§2-514. When Documents Deliverable on Acceptance; When on Payment. Unless otherwise agreed documents against which a draft is drawn are to be de-

livered to the drawee on acceptance of the draft if it is payable more than three days after presentment; otherwise, only on payment.

§2-515. Preserving Evidence of Goods in Dispute. In furtherance of the adjustment of any claim or dispute

(**a**) either party on reasonable notification to the other and for the purpose of ascertaining the facts and preserving evidence has the right to inspect, test and sample the goods including such of them as may be in the possession or control of the other; and

(**b**) the parties may agree to a third party inspection or survey to determine the conformity or condition of the goods and may agree that the findings shall be binding upon them in any subsequent litigation or adjustment.

Part 6: Breach, Repudiation and Excuse

§2-601. Buyer's Rights on Improper Delivery. Subject to the provisions of this Article on breach in installment contracts (Section 2-612) and unless otherwise agreed under the sections on contractual limitations of remedy (Sections 2-718 and 2-719), if the goods or the tender of delivery fail in any respect to conform to the contract, the buyer may

(**a**) reject the whole; or

(**b**) accept the whole; or

(**c**) accept any commercial unit or units and reject the rest.

§2-602. Manner and Effect of Rightful Rejection.

(**1**)   Rejection of goods must be within a reasonable time after their delivery or tender. It is ineffective unless the buyer seasonably notifies the seller.

(**2**) Subject to the provisions of the two following sections on rejected goods (Section 2-603 and 2-604),

(**a**) after rejection any exercise of ownership by the buyer with respect to any commercial unit is wrongful as against the seller; and

(**b**) if the buyer has before rejection taken physical possession of goods in which he does not have a security interest under the provisions of this Article (subsection (3) of Section 2-711), he is under a duty after rejection to hold them with reasonable care at the seller's disposition for a time sufficient to permit the seller to remove them; but

(**c**) the buyer has no further obligations with regard to goods rightfully rejected.

(**3**) The seller's rights with respect to goods wrongfully rejected are governed by the provisions of this Article on Seller's remedies in general (Section 2-703).

§2-603. Merchant Buyer's Duties as to Rightfully Rejected Goods.

(1) Subject to any security interest in the buyer (subsection (3) of Section 2-711), when the seller has no agent or place of business at the market of rejection a merchant buyer is under a duty after rejection of goods in his possession or control to follow any reasonable instructions received from the seller with respect to the goods and in the absence of such instructions to make reasonable efforts to sell them for the seller's account if they are perishable or threaten to decline in value speedily. Instructions are not reasonable if on demand indemnity for expenses is not forthcoming.

(2) When the buyer sells goods under subsection (1), he is entitled to reimbursement from the seller or out of the proceeds for reasonable expenses of caring for and selling them, and if the expenses include no selling commission then to such commission as is usual in the trade or if there is none to a reasonable sum not exceeding ten per cent on the gross proceeds.

(3) In complying with this section the buyer is held only to good faith and good faith conduct hereunder is neither acceptance nor conversion nor the basis of an action for damages.

§2-604. Buyer's Options as to Salvage of Rightfully Rejected Goods.
Subject to the provisions of the immediately preceding section on perishables if the seller gives no instructions within a reasonable time after notification of rejection the buyer may store the rejected goods for the seller's account or reship them to him or resell them for the seller's account with reimbursement as provided in the preceding section. Such action is not acceptance or conversion.

§2-605. Waiver of Buyer's Objections by Failure to Particularize.

(1) The buyer's failure to state in connection with rejection a particular defect which is ascertainable by reasonable inspection precludes him from relying on the unstated defect to justify rejection or to establish breach

(a) where the seller could have cured it if stated seasonably; or

(b) between merchants when the seller has after rejection made a request in writing for a full and final written statement of all defects on which the buyer proposes to rely.

(2) Payment against documents made without reservation of rights precludes recovery of the payment for defects apparent on the face of the documents.

§2-606. What Constitutes Acceptance of Goods.

(1) Acceptance of goods occurs when the buyer

(a) after a reasonable opportunity to inspect the goods signifies to the seller that the goods are conforming or that he will take or retain them

in spite of their non-conformity; or

(b) fails to make an effective rejection (subsection (1) of Section 2-602), but such acceptance does not occur until the buyer has had a reasonable opportunity to inspect them; or

(c) does any act inconsistent with the seller's ownership; but if such act is wrongful as against the seller it is an acceptance only if ratified by him.

(2) Acceptance of a part of any commercial unit is acceptance of that entire unit.

§2-607. Effect of Acceptance; Notice of Breach; Burden of Establishing Breach After Acceptance; Notice of Claim or Litigation to Person Answerable Over.

(1) The buyer must pay at the contract rate for any goods accepted.

(2) Acceptance of goods by the buyer precludes rejection of the goods accepted and if made with knowledge of a nonconformity cannot be revoked because of it unless the acceptance was on the reasonable assumption that the non-conformity would be seasonably cured but acceptance does not of itself impair any other remedy provided by this Article for non-conformity.

(3) Where a tender has been accepted

(a) the buyer must within a reasonable time after he discovers or should have discovered any breach notify the seller of breach or be barred from any remedy; and

(b) if the claim is one for infringement or the like (subsection (3) of Section 2-312) and the buyer is sued as a result of such a breach he must so notify the seller within a reasonable time after he receives notice of the litigation or be barred from any remedy over for liability established by the litigation.

(4) The burden is on the buyer to establish any breach with respect to the goods accepted.

(5) Where the buyer is sued for breach of a warranty or other obligation for which his seller is answerable over

(a) he may give his seller written notice of the litigation. If the notice states that the seller may come in and defend and that if the seller does not do so he will be bound in any action against him by his buyer by any determination of fact common to the two litigations, then unless the seller after seasonable receipt of the notice does come in and defend he is so bound.

(b) if the claim is one for infringement or the like (subsection (3) of Section 2-312) the original seller may demand in writing that his buyer turn over to him control of the litigation including settlement or else be barred from any remedy over and if he also agrees to bear all expense and to satisfy any adverse judgment, then unless the buyer after seasonable receipt of the demand does turn over control the buyer is so barred.

(**6**) The provisions of subsection (3), (4) and (5) apply to any obligation of a buyer to hold the seller harmless against infringement or the like (subsection (3) of Section 2-312).

§2-608. Revocation of Acceptance in Whole or in Part.

(**1**) The buyer may revoke his acceptance of a lot or commercial unit whose non-conformity substantially impairs its value to him if he has accepted it

(**a**) on the reasonable assumption that its non-conformity would be cured and it has not been seasonably cured; or

(**b**) without discovery of such non-conformity if his acceptance was reasonably induced either by the difficulty of discovery before acceptance or by the seller's assurances.

(**2**) Revocation of acceptance must occur within a reasonable time after the buyer discovers or should have discovered the ground for it and before any substantial change in condition of the goods which is not caused by their own defects. It is not effective until the buyer notifies the seller of it.

(**3**) A buyer who so revokes has the same rights and duties with regard to the goods involved as if he had rejected them.

§2-609. Right to Adequate Assurance of Performance.

(**1**) A contract for sale imposes an obligation on each party that the other's expectation of receiving due performance will not be impaired. When reasonable grounds for insecurity arise with respect to the performance of either party the other may in writing demand adequate assurance of due performance and until he receives such assurance may if commercially reasonable suspend any performance for which he has not already received the agreed return.

(**2**) Between merchants the reasonableness of grounds for insecurity and the adequacy of any assurance offered shall be determined according to commercial standards.

(**3**) Acceptance of any improper delivery or payment does not prejudice the aggrieved party's right to demand adequate assurance of future performance.

(**4**) After receipt of a justified demand failure to provide within a reasonable time not exceeding thirty days such assurance of due performance as is adequate under the circumstances of the particular case is a repudiation of the contract.

§2-610. Anticipatory Repudiation. When either party repudiates the contract with respect to a performance not yet due the loss of which will substantially impair the value of the contract to the other, the aggrieved party may

(**a**) for a commercially reasonable time await performance by the repudiating party; or

(**b**) resort to any remedy for breach (Section 2-703 or Section 2-711), even though he has notified the repudiating party that he would await the latter's performance and has urged retraction; and

(**c**) in either case suspend his own performance or proceed in accordance with the provisions of this Article on the seller's right to identify goods to the contract notwithstanding breach or to salvage unfinished goods (Section 2-704).

§2-611. Retraction of Anticipatory Repudiation.

(**1**) Until the repudiating party's next performance is due he can retract his repudiation unless the aggrieved party has since the repudiation cancelled or materially changed his position or otherwise indicated that he considers the repudiation final.

(**2**) Retraction may be by any method which clearly indicates to the aggrieved party that the repudiating party intends to perform, but must include any assurance justifiably demanded under the provisions of this Article (Section 2-609).

(**3**) Retraction reinstates the repudiating party's rights under the contract with due excuse and allowance to the aggrieved party for any delay occasioned by the repudiation.

§2-612. "Installment Contract"; Breach.

(**1**) An "installment contract" is one which requires or authorizes the delivery of goods in separate lots to be separately accepted, even though the contract contains a clause "each delivery is a separate contract" or its equivalent.

(**2**) The buyer may reject any installment which is non-conforming if the non-conformity substantially impairs the value of that installment and cannot be cured or if the non-conformity is a defect in the required documents; but if the non-conformity does not fall within subsection (3) and the seller gives adequate assurance of its cure the buyer must accept that installment.

(**3**) . Whenever non-conformity or default with respect to one or more installments substantially impairs the value of the whole contract there is a breach of the whole. But the aggrieved party reinstates the contract if he accepts a non-conforming installment without seasonably notifying of cancellation or if he brings an action with respect only to past installments or demands performance as to future installments.

§2-613. Casualty to Identified Goods. Where the contract requires for its performance goods identified when the contract is made, and the goods suffer casualty without fault of either party before the risk of loss

passes to the buyer, or in a proper case under a "no arrival, no sale" term (Section 2-324) then

   (**a**) if the loss is total the contract is avoided; and

   (**b**) if the loss is partial or the goods have so deteriorated as no longer to conform to the contract the buyer may nevertheless demand inspection and at his option either treat the contract as avoided or accept the goods with due allowance from the contract price for the deterioration or the deficiency in quantity but without further right against the seller.

§2-614. Substituted Performance.

(**1**) Where without fault of either party the agreed berthing, loading, or unloading facilities fail or an agreed type of carrier becomes unavailable or the agreed manner of delivery otherwise becomes commercially impracticable but a commercially reasonable substitute is available, such substitute performance must be tendered and accepted.

(**2**) If the agreed means or manner of payment fails because of domestic or foreign governmental regulation, the seller may withhold or stop delivery unless the buyer provides a means or manner of payment which is commercially a substantial equivalent. If delivery has already been taken, payment by the means or in the manner provided by the regulation discharges the buyer's obligation unless the regulation is discriminatory, oppressive or predatory.

§2-615. Excuse by Failure of Presupposed Conditions.
Except so far as a seller may have assumed a greater obligation and subject to the preceding section on substituted performance:

   (**a**) Delay in delivery or non-delivery in whole or in part by a seller who complies with paragraphs (b) and (c) is not a breach of his duty under a contract for sale if performance as agreed has been made impracticable by the occurrence of a contingency the non-occurrence of which was a basic assumption on which the contract was made or by compliance in good faith with any applicable foreign or domestic governmental regulation or order whether or not it later proves to be invalid.

   (**b**) Where the causes mentioned in paragraph (a) affect only a part of the seller's capacity to perform, he must allocate production and deliveries among his customers but may at his option include regular customers not then under contract as well as his own requirements for further manufacture. He may so allocate in any manner which is fair and reasonable.

   (**c**) The seller must notify the buyer seasonably that there will be delay or non-delivery and, when allocation is required under paragraph (b), of the estimated quota thus made available for the buyer.

§2-616. Procedure on Notice Claiming Excuse.

(**1**) When the buyer receives notification of a material or indefinite delay or an allocation justified under the preceding section he may by written notification to the seller as to any delivery concerned, and where the prospective deficiency substantially impairs the value of the whole contract under the provisions of this Article relating to breach of installment contracts (Section 2-612), then also as to the whole,

   (**a**) terminate and thereby discharge any unexecuted portion of the contract; or

   (**b**) modify the contract by agreeing to take his available quota in substitution.

(**2**) If after receipt of such notification from the seller the buyer fails so to modify the contract within a reasonable time not exceeding thirty days the contract lapses with respect to any deliveries affected.

(**3**) The provisions of this section may not be negated by agreement except in so far as the seller has assumed a greater obligation under the preceding section.

Part 7: Remedies

§2-701. Remedies for Breach of Collateral Contracts Not Impaired.
Remedies for breach of any obligation or promise collateral or ancillary to a contract for sale are not impaired by the provisions of this Article.

§2-702. Seller's Remedies on Discovery of Buyer's Insolvency.

(**1**) Where the seller discovers the buyer to be insolvent he may refuse delivery except for cash including payment for all goods theretofore delivered under the contract, and stop delivery under this Article (Section 2-705).

(**2**) Where the seller discovers that the buyer has received goods on credit while insolvent he may reclaim the goods upon demand made within ten days after the receipt, but if misrepresentation of solvency has been made to the particular seller in writing within three months before delivery the ten day limitation does not apply. Except as provided in this subsection the seller may not base a right to reclaim goods on the buyer's fraudulent or innocent misrepresentation of solvency or of intent to pay.

(**3**) The seller's right to reclaim under subsection (2) is subject to the rights of a buyer in ordinary course or other good faith purchaser under this Article (Section 2-403). Successful reclamation of goods excludes all other remedies with respect to them. As amended 1966.

§2-703. Seller's Remedies in General.
Where the buyer wrongfully rejects or revokes acceptance of goods or fails to make a payment due on or before delivery or repudiates with respect to a part or the whole, then with respect to any goods directly affected and, if the breach is of the whole contract (Section 2-612),

then also with respect to the whole undelivered balance, the aggrieved seller may

(**a**) withhold delivery of such goods;

(**b**) stop delivery by any bailee as hereafter provided (Section 2-705);

(**c**) proceed under the next section respecting goods still unidentified to the contract;

(**d**) resell and recover damages as hereafter provided (Section 2-706);

(**e**) recover damages for non-acceptance (Section 2-708) or in a proper case the price (Section 2-709);

(**f**) cancel.

§2-704. Seller's Right to Identify Goods to the Contract Notwithstanding Breach or to Salvage Unfinished Goods.

(**1**) An aggrieved seller under the preceding section may

(**a**) identify to the contract conforming goods not already identified if at the time he learned of the breach they are in his possession or control;

(**b**) treat as the subject of resale goods which have demonstrably been intended for the particular contract even though those goods are unfinished.

(**2**) Where the goods are unfinished an aggrieved seller may in the exercise of reasonable commercial judgment for the purposes of avoiding loss and of effective realization either complete the manufacture and wholly identify the goods to the contract or cease manufacture and resell for scrap or salvage value or proceed in any other reasonable manner.

§2-705. Seller's Stoppage of Delivery in Transit or Otherwise.

(**1**) The seller may stop delivery of goods in the possession of a carrier or other bailee when he discovers the buyer to be insolvent (Section 2-702) and may stop delivery of carload, truckload, planeload or larger shipments of express or freight when the buyer repudiates or fails to make a payment due before delivery or if for any other reason the seller has a right to withold or reclaim the goods.

(**2**) As against such buyer the seller may stop delivery until

(**a**) receipt of the goods by the buyer; or

(**b**) acknowledgement to the buyer by any bailee of the goods except a carrier that the bailee holds the goods for the buyer; or

(**c**) such acknowledgement to the buyer by a carrier by reshipment or as warehouseman; or

(**d**) negotiation to the buyer of any negotiable document of title covering the goods.

(**3**)

(**a**) To stop delivery the seller must so notify as to enable the bailee by reasonable diligence to prevent delivery of the goods.

(**b**) After such notification the bailee must hold and deliver the goods according to the directions of the seller but the seller is liable to the bailee for any ensuing charges or damages.

(**c**) If a negotiable document of title has been issued for goods the bailee is not obliged to obey a notification to stop until surrender of the document.

(**d**) A carrier who has issued a non-negotiable bill of lading is not obliged to obey a notification to stop received from a person other than the consignor.

§2-706. Seller's Resale Including Contract for Resale.

(**1**) Under the conditions stated in Section 2-703 on seller's remedies, the seller may resell the goods concerned or the undelivered balance thereof. Where the resale is made in good faith and in a commercially reasonable manner the seller may recover the difference between the resale price and the contract price together with any incidental damages allowed under the provisions of this Article (Section 2-710), but less expenses saved in consequence of the buyer's breach.

(**2**) Except as otherwise provided in subsection (3) or unless otherwise agreed resale may be at public or private sale including sale by way of one or more contracts to sell or of identification to an existing contract of the seller. Sale may be as a unit or in parcels and at any time and place and on any terms but every aspect of the sale including the method, manner, time, place and terms must be commercially reasonable. The resale must be reasonably identified as referring to the broken contract, but it is not necessary that the goods be in existence or that any or all of them have been identified to the contract before the breach.

(**3**) Where the resale is at private sale the seller must give the buyer reasonable notification of his intention to resell.

(**4**) Where the resale is at public sale

(**a**) only identified goods can be sold except where there is a recognized market for a public sale of futures in goods of the kind; and

(**b**) it must be made at a usual place or market for public sale if one is reasonably available and except in the case of goods which are perishable or threaten to decline in value speedily the seller must give the buyer reasonable notice of the time and place of the resale; and

(**c**) if the goods are not to be within the view of those attending the sale the notification of sale must state the place where the goods are located and provide for their reasonable inspection by prospective bidders; and

(d) the seller may buy.

(5) A purchaser who buys in good faith at a resale takes the goods free of any rights of the original buyer even though the seller fails to comply with one or more of the requirements of this section.

(6) The seller is not accountable to the buyer for any profit made on any resale. A person in the position of a seller (Section 2-707) or a buyer who has rightfully rejected or justifiably revoked acceptance must account for any excess over the amount of his security interest, as hereinafter defined (subsection (3) of Section 2-711).

§2-707. "Person in the Position of a Seller".

(1) A "person in the position of a seller" includes as against a principal an agent who has paid or become responsible for the price of goods on behalf of his principal or anyone who otherwise holds a security interest or other right in goods similar to that of a seller.

(2) A person in the position of a seller may as provided in this Article withhold or stop delivery (Section 2-705) and resell (Section 2-706) and recover incidental damages (Section 2-710).

§2-708. Seller's Damages for Non-acceptance or Repudiation.

(1) Subject to subsection (2) and to the provisions of this Article with respect to proof of market price (Section 2-723), the measure of damages for non-acceptance or repudiation by the buyer is the difference between the market price at the time and place for tender and the unpaid contract price together with any incidental damages provided in this Article (Section 2-710), but less expenses saved in consequence of the buyer's breach.

(2) If the measure of damages provided in subsection (1) is inadequate to put the seller in as good a position as performance would have done then the measure of damages is the profit (including reasonable overhead) which the seller would have made from full performance by the buyer, together with any incidental damages provided in this Article (Section 2-710), due allowance for costs reasonably incurred and due credit for payments or proceeds of resale.

§2-709. Action for the Price.

(1) When the buyer fails to pay the price as it becomes due the seller may recover, together with any incidental damages under the next section, the price

(a) of goods accepted or of conforming goods lost or damaged within a commercially reasonable time after risk of their loss has passed to the buyer; and

(b) of goods identified to the contract if the seller is unable after reasonable effort to resell them at a reasonable price or the circumstances reasonably indicate that such effort will be unavailing.

(2) Where the seller sues for the price he must hold for the buyer any goods which have been identified to the contract and are still in his control except that if resale becomes possible he may resell them at any time prior to the collection of the judgment. The net proceeds of any such resale must be credited to the buyer and payment of the judgment entitles him to any goods not resold.

(3) After the buyer has wrongfully rejected or revoked acceptance of the goods or has failed to make a payment due or has repudiated (Section 2-610), a seller who is held not entitled to the price under this section shall nevertheless be awarded damages for non-acceptance under the preceding section.

§2-710. Seller's Incidental Damages.

Incidental damages to an aggrieved seller include any commercially reasonable charges, expenses or commissions incurred in stopping delivery, in the transportation, care and custody of goods after the buyer's breach, in connection with return or resale of the goods or otherwise resulting from the breach.

§2-711. Buyer's Remedies in General; Buyer's Security Interest in Rejected Goods.

(1) When the seller fails to make delivery or repudiates or the buyer rightfully rejects or justifiably revokes acceptance then with respect to any goods involved, and with respect to the whole if the breach goes to the whole contract (Section 2-612), the buyer may cancel and whether or not he has done so may in addition to recovering so much of the price as has been paid

(a) "cover" and have damages under the next section as to all the goods affected whether or not they have been identified to the contract; or

(b) recover damages for non-delivery as provided in this Article (Section 2-713).

(2) Where the seller fails to deliver or repudiates the buyer may also

(a) if the goods have been identified recover them as provided in this Article (Section 2-502); or

(b) in a proper case obtain specific performance or replevy the goods as provided in this Article (Section 2-716).

(3) On rightful rejection or justifiable revocation of acceptance a buyer has a security interest in goods in his possession or control for any payments made on their price and any expenses reasonably incurred in their inspection, receipt, transportation, care and custody and may hold such goods and resell them in like manner as an aggrieved seller (Section 2-706).

§2-712. "Cover"; Buyer's Procurement of Substitute Goods.

(1) After a breach within the preceding section the buyer may "cover" by making in good faith and without unreasonable delay any reasonable purchase of or contract to purchase goods in substitution for those due from the seller.

(2) The buyer may recover from the seller as damages the difference between the cost of cover and the contract price together with any incidental or consequential damages as hereinafter defined (Section 2-715), but less expenses saved in consequence of the seller's breach.

(3) Failure of the buyer to effect cover within this section does not bar him from any other remedy.

§2-713. Buyer's Damages for Non-Delivery or Repudiation.

(1) Subject to the provisions of this Article with respect to proof of market price (Section 2-723), the measure of damages for non-delivery or repudiation by the seller is the difference between the market price at the time when the buyer learned of the breach and the contract price together with any incidental and consequential damages provided in this Article (Section 2-715), but less expenses saved in consequence of the seller's breach.

(2) Market price is to be determined as of the place for tender or, in cases of rejection after arrival or revocation of acceptance, as of the place of arrival.

§2-714. Buyer's Damages for Breach in Regard to Accepted Goods.

(1) Where the buyer has accepted goods and given notification (subsection (3) Section 2-607) he may recover as damages for any non-conformity of tender the loss resulting in the ordinary course of events from the seller's breach as determined in any manner which is reasonable.

(2) The measure of damages for breach of warranty is the difference at the time and place of acceptance between the value of the goods accepted and the value they would have had if they had been as warranted, unless special circumstances show proximate damages of a different amount.

(3) In a proper case any incidental and consequential damages under the next section may also be recovered.

§2-715. Buyer's Incidental and Consequential Damages.

(1) Incidental damages resulting from the seller's breach include expenses reasonably incurred in inspection, receipt, transportation and care and custody of goods rightfully rejected, any commercially reasonable charges, expenses or commissions in connection with effecting cover and any other reasonable expense incident to the delay or other breach.

(2) Consequential damages resulting from the seller's breach include

(a) any loss resulting from general or particular requirements and needs of which the seller at the

time of contracting had reason to know and which could not reasonably be prevented by cover or otherwise; and

(b) injury to person or property proximately resulting from any breach of warranty.

§2-716. Buyer's Right to Specific Performance or Replevin.

(1) Specific performance may be decreed where the goods are unique or in other proper circumstances.

(2) The decree for specific performance may include such terms and conditions as to payment of the price, damages, or other relief as the court may deem just.

(3) The buyer has a right of replevin for goods identified to the contract if after reasonable effort he is unable to effect cover for such goods or the circumstances reasonably indicate that such effort will be unavailing or if the goods have been shipped under reservation and satisfaction of the security interest in them has been made or tendered.

§2-717. Deduction of Damages From the Price.
The buyer on notifying the seller of his intention to do so may deduct all or any part of the damages resulting from any breach of the contract from any part of the price still due under the same contract.

§2-718. Liquidation or Limitation of Damages; Deposits.

(1) Damages for breach by either party may be liquidated in the agreement but only at an amount which is reasonable in the light of the anticipated or actual harm caused by the breach, the difficulties of proof of loss, and the inconvenience or nonfeasibility of otherwise obtaining an adequate remedy. A term fixing unreasonably large liquidated damages is void as a penalty.

(2) Where the seller justifiably withholds delivery of goods because of the buyer's breach, the buyer is entitled to restitution of any amount by which the sum of his payments exceeds

(a) the amount to which the seller is entitled by virtue of terms liquidating the seller's damages in accordance with subsection (1), or

(b) in the absence of such terms, twenty per cent of the value of the total performance for which the buyer is obligated under the contract or $500, whichever is smaller.

(3) The buyer's right to restitution under subsection (2) is subject to offset to the extent that the seller establishes

(a) a right to recover damages under the provisions of this article other than subsection (1), and

(b) the amount or value of any benefits received by the buyer directly or indirectly by reason of the contract.

(4) where a seller has received payment in goods their reasonable value or the proceeds of their resale shall be treated as payments for the purposes of subsection (2); but if the seller has notice of the buyer's breach before reselling goods received in part performance, his resale is subject to the conditions laid down in this Article on resale by an aggrieved seller (Section 2-706).

§2-719. Contractual Modification or Limitation of Remedy.

(1) Subject to the provisions of subsections (2) and (3) of this section and of the preceding section on liquidation and limitation of damages,

(a) the agreement may provide for remedies in addition to or in substitution for those provided in this Article and may limit or alter the measure of damages recoverable under this Article, as by limiting the buyer's remedies to return of the goods and repayment of the price or to repair and replacement of non-conforming goods or parts; and

(b) resort to a remedy as provided is optional unless the remedy is expressly agreed to be exclusive, in which case it is the sole remedy.

(2) Where circumstances cause an exclusive or limited remedy to fail of its essential purpose, remedy may be had as provided in this Act.

(3) Consequential damages may be limited or excluded unless the limitation or exclusion is unconscionable. Limitation of consequential damages for injury to the person in the case of consumer goods is prima facie unconscionable but limitation of damages where the loss is commercial is not.

§2-720. Effect of "Cancellation" or "Rescission" on Claims for Antecedent Breach. Unless the contrary intention clearly appears, expressions of "cancellation" or "rescission" of the contract or the like shall not be construed as a renunciation or discharge of any claim in damages for an antecedent breach.

§2-721. Remedies for Fraud. Remedies for material misrepresentation or fraud include all remedies available under this Article for non-fraudulent breach. Neither rescission or a claim for rescission of the contract for sale nor rejection or return of the goods shall bar or be deemed inconsistent with a claim for damages or other remedy.

§2-722. Who Can Sue Third Parties for Injury to Goods. Where a third party so deals with goods which have been identified to a contract for sale as to cause actionable injury to a party to that contract

(a) right of action against the third party is in either party to the contract for sale who has title to or a security interest or a special property or an insurable interest in the goods; and if the goods have been destroyed or converted a right of action is also in the party who either bore the risk of loss under the contract for sale or has since the injury assumed that risk as against the other;

(b) if at the time of the injury the party plaintiff did not bear the risk of loss as against the other party to the contract for sale and there is no arrangement between them for disposition of the recovery, his suit or settlement is, subject to his own interest, as a fiduciary for the other party to the contract;

(c) either party may with the consent of the other sue for the benefit of whom it may concern.

§2-723. Proof of Market Price: Time and Place.

(1) If an action based on anticipatory repudiation comes to trial before the time for performance with respect to some or all of the goods, any damages based on market price (Section 2-708 or Section 2-713) shall be determined according to the price of such goods prevailing at the time when the aggrieved party learned of the repudiation.

(2) If evidence of a price prevailing at the times or places described in this Article is not readily available the price prevailing within any reasonable time before or after the time described or at any other place which in commercial judgment or under usage of trade would serve as a reasonable substitute for the one described may be used, making any proper allowance for the cost of transporting the goods to or from such other place.

(3) Evidence of a relevant price prevailing at a time or place other than the one described in this Article offered by one party is not admissible unless and until he has given the other party such notice as the court finds sufficient to prevent unfair surprise.

§2-724. Admissibility of Market Quotations. Whenever the prevailing price or value of any goods regularly bought and sold in any established commodity market is in issue, reports in official publication or trade journals or in newspapers or periodicals of general circulation published as the reports of such market shall be admissible in evidence. The circumstances of the preparation of such a report may be shown to affect its weight but not its admissibility.

§2-725. Statute of Limitations in Contracts for Sale.

(1) An action for breach of any contract for sale must be commenced within four years after the cause of action has accrued. By the original agreement the parties may reduce the period of limitation to not less than one year but may not extend it.

(2) A cause of action accrues when the breach occurs, regardless of the aggrieved party's lack of knowledge of the breach. A breach of warranty occurs when tender of delivery is made, except that where a war-

ranty explicitly extends to future performance of the goods and discovery of the breach must await the time of such performance the cause of action accrues when the breach is or should have been discovered.

(3) Where an action commenced within the time limited by subsection (1) is so terminated as to leave available a remedy by another action for the same breach such other action may be commenced after the expiration of the time limited and within six months after the termination of the first action unless the termination resulted from voluntary discontinuance or from dismissal for failure or neglect to prosecute.

(4) This section does not alter the law on tolling of the statute of limitations nor does it apply to causes of action which have accrued before this Act becomes effective.

ARTICLE 2A: LEASES

Part 1: General Provisions

§2A-101. Short Title. This Article shall be known and may be cited as the Uniform Commercial Code—Leases.

§2A-102. Scope. This Article applies to any transaction, regardless of form, that creates a lease.

§2A-103. Definitions and Index of Definitions.

(1) In this Article unless the context otherwise requires:

(a) "Buyer in ordinary course of business" means a person who in good faith and without knowledge that the sale to him[or her] is in violation of the ownership rights or security interest or leasehold interest of a third party in the goods buys in ordinary course from a person in the business of selling goods of that kind but does not include a pawnbroker. "Buying" may be for cash or by exchange of other property or on secured or unsecured credit and includes receiving goods or documents of title under a pre-existing contract for sale but does not include a transfer in bulk or as security for or in total or partial satisfaction of a money debt.

(b) "Cancellation" occurs when either party puts an end to the lease contract for default by the other party.

(c) "Commercial unit" means such a unit of goods as by commercial usage is a single whole for purposes of lease and division of which materially impairs its character or value on the market or in use. A commercial unit may be a single article, as a machine, or a set of articles, as a suite of furniture or a line of machinery, or a quantity, as a gross or carload, or any other unit treated in use or in the relevant market as a single whole.

(d) "Conforming" goods or performance under a lease contract means goods or performance that are in accordance with the obligations under the lease contract.

(e) "Consumer lease" means a lease that a lessor regularly engaged in the business of leasing or selling makes to a lessee, except an organization, who takes under the lease primarily for a personal, family, or household purpose, if the total payments to be made under the lease contract, excluding payments for options to renew or buy, do not exceed $25,000.

(f) "Fault" means wrongful act, omission, breach, or default.

(g) "Finance lease" means a lease in which (i) the lessor does not select, manufacture or supply the goods, (ii) the lessor acquires the goods or the right to possession and use of the goods in connection with the lease, and (iii) either the lessee receives a copy of the contract evidencing the lessor's purchase of the goods on or before signing the lease contract, or the lessee's approval of the contract evidencing the lessor's purchase of the goods is a condition to effectiveness of the lease contract.

(h) "Goods" means all things that are movable at the time of identification to the lease contract, or are fixtures (Section 2A-309), but the term does not include money, documents, instruments, accounts, chattel paper, general intangibles, or minerals or the like, including oil and gas, before extraction. The term also includes the unborn young of animals.

(i) "Installment lease contract" means a lease contract that authorizes or requires the delivery of goods in separate lots to be separately accepted, even though the lease contract contains a clause "each delivery is a separate lease" or its equivalent.

(j) "Lease" means a transfer of the right to possession and use of goods for a term in return for consideration, but a sale, including a sale on approval or a sale or return, or retention or creation of a security interest is not a lease. Unless the context clearly indicates otherwise, the term includes a sublease.

(k) "Lease agreement" means the bargain, with respect to the lease, of the lessor and the lessee in fact as found in their language or by implication from other circumstances including course of dealing or usage of trade or course of performance as provided in this Article. Unless the context clearly indicates otherwise, the term includes a sublease agreement.

(l) "Lease contract" means the total legal obligation that results from the lease agreement as affected by this Article and any other applicable rules of law. Unless the context clearly indicates otherwise, the term includes a sublease contract.

(m) "Leasehold interest" means the interest of the lessor or the lessee under a lease contract.

(n) "Lessee" means a person who acquires the right to possession and use of goods under a lease. Unless the context clearly indicates otherwise, the term includes a sublessee.

(o) "Lessee in ordinary course of business" means a person who in good faith and without knowledge that the lease to him[or her] is in violation of the ownership rights or security interest or leasehold interest of a third party in the goods, leases in ordinary course from a person in the business of selling or leasing goods of that kind but does not include a pawnbroker. "Leasing" may be for cash or by exchange of other property or on secured or unsecured credit and includes receiving goods or documents of title under a pre-existing lease contract but does not include a transfer in bulk or as security for or in total or partial satisfaction of a money debt.

(p) "Lessor" means a person who transfers the right to possession and use of goods under a lease. Unless the context clearly indicates otherwise, the term includes a sublessor.

(q) "Lessor's residual interest" means the lessor's interest in the goods after expiration, termination, or cancellation of the lease contract.

(r) "Lien" means a charge against or interest in goods to secure payment of a debt or performance of an obligation, but the term does not include a security interest.

(s) "Lot" means a parcel or a single article that is the subject matter of a separate lease or delivery, whether or not it is sufficient to perform the lease contract.

(t) "Merchant lessee" means a lessee that is a merchant with respect to goods of the kind subject to the lease.

(u) "Present value" means the amount as of a date certain of one or more sums payable in the future, discounted to the date certain. The discount is determined by the interest rate specified by the parties if the rate was not manifestly unreasonable at the time the transaction was entered into; otherwise, the discount is determined by a commercially reasonable rate that takes into account the facts and circumstances of each case at the time the transaction was entered into.

(v) "Purchase" includes taking by sale, lease, mortgage, security interest, pledge, gift, or any other voluntary transaction creating an interest in goods.

(w) "Sublease" means a lease of goods the right to possession and use of which was acquired by the lessor as a lessee under an existing lease.

(x) "Supplier" means a person from whom a lessor buys or leases goods to be leased under a finance lease.

(y) "Supply contract" means a contract under which a lessor buys or leases goods to be leased.

(z) "Termination" occurs when either party pursuant to a power created by agreement or law puts an end to the lease contract otherwise than for default.

(2) Other definitions applying to this Article and the sections in which they appear are:

"Accessions"	Section 2A-310(1)
"Construction mortgage"	Section 2A-309(1)(d)
"Encumbrance"	Section 2A-309(1)(e)
"Fixtures"	Section 2A-309(1)(a)
"Fixture filing"	Section 2A-309(1)(b)
"Purchase money lease"	Section 2A-309(1)(c)

(3) The following definitions in other Articles apply to this Article:

"Accounts"	Section 9-106
"Between merchants"	Section 2-104(3)
"Buyer"	Section 2-103(1)(a)
"Chattel paper"	Section 9-105(1)(b)
"Consumer goods"	Section 9-109(1)
"Documents"	Section 9-105(1)(f)
"Entrusting"	Section 2-403(3)
"General intangibles"	Section 9-106
"Good faith"	Section 2-103(1)(b)
"Instruments"	Section 9-105(1)(i)
"Merchant"	Section 2-104(1)
"Mortgage"	Section 9-105(1)(j)
"Pursuant to commitment"	Section 9-105(1)(k)
"Receipt"	Section 2-103(1)(c)
"Sale"	Section 2-106(1)
"Sale on approval"	Section 2-326
"Sale or return"	Section 2-326
"Seller"	Section 2-103(1)(d)

(4) In addition Article 1 contains general definitions and principles of construction and interpretation applicable throughout this Article.

§2A-104. Leases Subject to Other Statutes.

(1) A lease, although subject to this Article, is also subject to any applicable:

(a) statute of the United States;

(b) certificate of title statute of this State: (list any certificate of title statutes covering automobiles, trailers, mobile homes, boats, farm tractors, and the like);

(c) certificate of title statute of another jurisdiction (Section 2A-105); or

(d) consumer protection statute of this State.

(2) In case of conflict between the provisions of this Article, other than Sections 2A-105, 2A-304(3) and 2A-305(3), and any statute referred to in subsection (1), the provisions of that statute control.

(3) Failure to comply with any applicable statute has only the effect specified therein.

§2A-105. Territorial Application of Article to Goods Covered by Certificate of Title. Subject to the provisions of Sections 2A-304(3) and 2A-305(3), with respect to goods covered by a certificate of title issued under a statute of this State or of another jurisdiction, compliance and the effect of compliance or noncompliance with a certificate of title statute are governed by the law (including the conflict of laws rules) of the jurisdiction issuing the certificate until the earlier of (a) surrender of the certificate, or (b) four months after the goods are removed from that jurisdiction and thereafter until a new certificate of title is issued by another jurisdiction.

§2A-106. Limitation on Power of Parties to Consumer Lease to Choose Applicable Law and Judicial Forum.

(1) If the law chosen by the parties to a consumer lease is that of a jurisdiction other than a jurisdiction in which the lessee resides at the time the lease agreement becomes enforceable or within 30 days thereafter or in which the goods are to be used, the choice is not enforceable.

(2) If the judicial forum chosen by the parties to a consumer lease is a forum that would not otherwise have jurisdiction over the lessee, the choice is not enforceable.

§2A-107. Waiver or Renunciation of Claim or Right After Default. Any claim or right arising out of an alleged default or breach of warranty may be discharged in whole or in part without consideration by a written waiver or renunciation signed and delivered by the aggrieved party.

§2A-108. Unconscionability.

(1) If the court as a matter of law finds a lease contract or any clause of a lease contract to have been unconscionable at the time it may enforce the remainder of the lease contract without the unconscionable clause, or it may so limit the application of any unconscionable clause as to avoid any unconscionable result.

(2) With respect to a consumer lease, if the court as a matter of law finds that a lease contract or any clause of a lease contract has been induced by unconscionable conduct or that unconscionable conduct has occurred in the collection of a claim arising from a lease contract, the court may grant appropriate relief.

(3) Before making a finding of unconscionability under subsection (1) or (2), the court, on its own motion or that of a party, shall afford the parties a reasonable opportunity to present evidence as to the setting, purpose, and effect of the lease contract or clause thereof, or of the conduct.

(4) In an action in which the lessee claims unconscionability with respect to a consumer lease:

(a) If the court finds unconscionability under subsection (1) or (2), the court shall award reasonable attorney's fees to the lessee.

(b) If the court does not find unconscionability and the lessee claiming unconscionability has brought or maintained an action he [or she] knew to be groundless, the court shall award reasonable attorney's fees to the party against whom the claim is made.

(c) In determining attorney's fees, the amount of the recovery on behalf of the claimant under subsections (1) and (2) is not controlling.

§2A-109. Option to Accelerate at Will.

(1) A term providing that one party or his[or her] successor in interest may accelerate payment or performance or require collateral or additional collateral "at will" or "when he [or she] deems himself [or herself] insecure" or in words of similar import must be construed to mean that he[or she] has power to do so only if he[or she] in good faith believes that the prospect of payment or performance is impaired.

(2) With respect to a consumer lease, the burden of establishing good faith under subsection (1) is on the party who exercised the power; otherwise the burden of establishing lack of good faith is on the party against whom the power has been exercised.

Part 2: Formation and Construction of Lease Contract

§2A-201. Statute of Frauds.

(1) A lease contract is not enforceable by way of action or defense unless:

(a) the total payments to be made under the lease contract, excluding payments for options to renew or buy, are less than $1,000; or

(b) there is a writing, signed by the party against whom enforcement is sought or by that party's authorized agent, sufficient to indicate that a lease contract has been made between the parties and to describe the goods leased and the lease term.

(2) Any description of leased goods or of the lease term is sufficient and satisfies subsection (1)(b), whether or not it is specific, if it reasonably identifies what is described.

(3) A writing is not insufficient because it omits or incorrectly states a term agreed upon, but the lease contract is not enforceable under subsection (1)(b) beyond the lease term and the quantity of goods shown in this writing.

(4) A lease contract that does not satisfy the requirements of subsection (1), but which is valid in other respects, is enforceable:

(a) if the goods are to be specially manufactured or obtained for the lessee and are not suitable for lease or sale to others in the ordinary course of the lessor's business, and the lessor, before notice of repudiation is received and under circumstances that reasonably indicate that the goods are for the lessee, has made either a substantial beginning of their manufacture or commitments for their procurement;

(b) if the party against whom enforcement is sought admits in that party's pleading, testimony or otherwise in court that a lease contract was made, but the lease contract is not enforceable under this provision beyond the quantity of goods admitted; or

(c) with respect to goods that have been received and accepted by the lessee.

(5) The lease term under a lease contract referred to in subsection (4) is:

(a) if there is a writing signed by the party against whom enforcement is sought or by that party's authorized agent specifying the lease term, the term so specified;

(b) if the party against whom enforcement is sought admits in that party's pleading, testimony, or otherwise in court a lease term, the term so admitted; or

(c) a reasonable lease term.

§2A-202. Final Written Expression: Parol or Extrinsic Evidence. Terms with respect to which the confirmatory memoranda of the parties agree or which are otherwise set forth in a writing intended by the parties as a final expression of their agreement with respect to such terms as are included therein may not be contradicted by evidence of any prior agreement or of a contemporaneous oral agreement but may be explained or supplemented:

(a) by course of dealing or usage of trade or by course of performance; and

(b) by evidence of consistent additional terms unless the court finds the writing to have been intended also as a complete and exclusive statement of the terms of the agreement.

§2A-203. Seals Inoperative. The affixing of a seal to a writing evidencing a lease contract or an offer to enter into a lease contract does not render the writing a sealed instrument and the law with respect to sealed instruments does not apply to the lease contract or offer.

§2A-204. Formation in General.

(1) A lease contract may be made in any manner sufficient to show agreement, including conduct by both parties which recognizes the existence of a lease contract.

(2) An agreement sufficient to constitute a lease contract may be found although the moment of its making is undetermined.

(3) Although one or more terms are left open, a lease contract does not fail for indefiniteness if the parties have intended to make a lease contract and there is a reasonably certain basis for giving an appropriate remedy.

§2A-205. Firm Offers. An offer by a merchant to lease goods to or from another person in a signed writing that by its terms gives assurance it will be held open is not revocable, for lack of consideration, during the time stated or, if no time is stated, for a reasonable time, but in no event may the period of irrevocability exceed 3 months. Any such term of assurance on a form supplied by the offeree must be separately signed by the offeror.

§2A-206. Offer and Acceptance in Formation of Lease Contract.

(1) Unless otherwise unambiguously indicated by the language or circumstances, an offer to make a lease contract must be construed as inviting acceptance in any manner and by any medium reasonable in the circumstances.

(2) If the beginning of a requested performance is a reasonable mode of acceptance, an offeror who is not notified of acceptance within a reasonable time may treat the offer as having lapsed before acceptance.

§2A-207. Course of Performance or Practical Construction.

(1) If a lease contract involves repeated occasions for performance by either party with knowledge of the nature of the performance and opportunity for objection to it by the other, any course of performance accepted or acquiesced in without objection is relevant to determine the meaning of the lease agreement.

(2) The express terms of a lease agreement and any course of performance, as well as any course of dealing and usage of trade, must be construed whenever reasonable as consistent with each other; but if that construction is unreasonable, express terms control course of performance, course of performance controls both course of dealing and usage of trade, and course of dealing controls usage of trade.

(3) Subject to the provisions of Section 2A-208 on modification and waiver, course of performance is relevant to show a waiver or modification of any term inconsistent with the course of performance.

§2A-208. Modification, Rescission and Waiver.

(1) An agreement modifying a lease contract needs no consideration to be binding.

(2) A signed lease agreement that excludes modification or rescission except by a signed writing may not be otherwise modified or rescinded, but, except as between merchants, such a requirement on a form sup-

plied by a merchant must be separately signed by the other party.

(**3**) Although an attempt at modification or rescission does not satisfy the requirements of subsection (2), it may operate as a waiver.

(**4**) A party who has made a waiver affecting an executory portion of a lease contract may retract the waiver by reasonable notification received by the other party that strict performance will be required of any term waived, unless the retraction would be unjust in view of a material change of position in reliance on the waiver.

§2A-209. Lessee Under Finance Lease as Beneficiary of Supply Contract.

(**1**) The benefit of the supplier's promises to the lessor under the supply contract and of all warranties, whether express or implied, under the supply contract, extends to the lessee to the extent of the lessee's leasehold interest under a finance lease related to the supply contract, but subject to the terms of the supply contract and all of the supplier's defenses or claims arising therefrom.

(**2**) The extension of the benefit of the supplier's promises to the lessee does not: (a) modify the rights and obligations of the parties to the supply contract, whether arising therefrom or otherwise, or (b) impose any duty or liability under the supply contract on the lessee.

(**3**) Any modification or rescission of the supply contract by the supplier and the lessor is effective against the lessee unless, prior to the modification or rescission, the supplier has received notice that the lessee has entered into a finance lease related to the supply contract. If the supply contract is modified or rescinded after the lessee enters the finance lease, the lessee has a cause of action against the lessor, and against the supplier if the supplier has notice of the lessee's entering the finance lease when the supply contract is modified or rescinded. The lessee's recovery from such action shall put the lessee in as good a position as if the modification or rescission had not occurred.

§2A-210. Express Warranties.

(**1**) Express warranties by the lessor are created as follows:

(**a**) Any affirmation of fact or promise made by the lessor to the lessee which relates to the goods and becomes part of the basis of the bargain creates an express warranty that the goods will conform to the affirmation or promise.

(**b**) Any description of the goods which is made part of the basis of the bargain creates an express warranty that the goods will conform to the description.

(**c**) Any sample or model that is made part of the basis of the bargain creates an express war-

ranty that the whole of the goods will conform to the sample or model.

(**2**) It is not necessary to the creation of an express warranty that the lessor use formal words, such as "warrant" or "guarantee," or that the lessor have a specific intention to make a warranty, but an affirmation merely of the value of the goods or a statement purporting to be merely the lessor's opinion or commendation of the goods does not create a warranty.

§2A-211. Warranties Against Interference and Against Infringement; Lessee's Obligation Against Infringement

(**1**) There is in a lease contract a warranty that for the lease term no person holds a claim to or interest in the goods that arose from an act or omission of the lessor, other than a claim by way of infringement or the like, which will interfere with the lessee's enjoyment of its leasehold interest.

(**2**) Except in a finance lease there is in a lease contract by a lessor who is a merchant regularly dealing in goods of the kind a warranty that the goods are delivered free of the rightful claim of any person by way of infringement or the like.

(**3**) A lessee who furnishes specifications to a lessor or a supplier shall hold the lessor and the supplier harmless against any claim by way of infringement or the like that arises out of compliance with the specifications.

§2A-212. Implied Warranty of Merchantability.

(**1**) Except in a finance lease, a warranty that the goods will be merchantable is implied in a lease contract if the lessor is a merchant with respect to goods of that kind.

(**2**) Goods to be merchantable must be at least such as

(**a**) pass without objection in the trade under the description in the lease agreement;

(**b**) in the case of fungible goods, are of fair average quality within the description;

(**c**) are fit for the ordinary purposes for which goods of that type are used;

(**d**) run, within the variation permitted by the lease agreement, of even kind, quality, and quantity within each unit and among all units involved;

(**e**) are adequately contained, packaged, and labeled as the lease agreement may require; and

(**f**) conform to any promises or affirmations of fact made on the container or label.

(**3**) Other implied warranties may arise from course of dealing or usage of trade.

§2A-213. Implied Warranty of Fitness for Particular Purpose. Except in a finance of lease, if the lessor at the time the lease contract is made has reason to

know of any particular purpose for which the goods are required and that the lessee is relying on the lessor's skill or judgment to select or furnish suitable goods, there is in the lease contract an implied warranty that the goods will be fit for that purpose.

§2A-214. Exclusion or Modification of Warranties.

(1) Words or conduct relevant to the creation of an express warranty and words or conduct tending to negate or limit a warranty must be construed wherever reasonable as consistent with each other; but, subject to the provisions of Section 2A-202 on parol or extrinsic evidence, negation or limitation is inoperative to the extent that the construction is unreasonable.

(2) Subject to subsection (3), to exclude or modify the implied warranty of merchantability or any part of it the language must mention "merchantability", be by a writing, and be conspicuous. Subject to subsection (3), to exclude or modify any implied warranty of fitness the exclusion must be by a writing and be conspicuous. Language to exclude all implied warranties of fitness is sufficient if it is conspicuous and states, for example, "There is no warranty that the goods will be fit for a particular purpose".

(3) Notwithstanding subsection (2), but subject to subsection (4),

(a) unless the circumstances indicate otherwise, all implied warranties are excluded by expressions like "as is" or "with all faults" or by other language that in common understanding calls the lessee's attention to the exclusion of warranties and makes plain that there is no implied warranty, and is conspicuous;

(b) if the lessee before entering into the lease contract has examined the goods or the sample or model as fully as desired or has refused to examine the goods, there is no implied warranty with regard to defects that an examination ought in the circumstances to have revealed; and

(c) an implied warranty may also be excluded or modified by course of dealing, course of performance, or usage of trade.

(4) To exclude or modify a warranty against interference or against infringement (Section 2A-211) or any part of it, the language must be specific, be by a writing, and be conspicuous, unless the circumstances, including course of performance, course of dealing, or usage of trade, give the lessee reason to know that the goods are being leased subject to a claim or interest of any person.

§2A-215. Cumulation and Conflict of Warranties Express or Implied.
Warranties, whether express or implied, must be construed as consistent with each other and as cumulative, but if that construction is unreasonable, the intention of the parties determines

which warranty is dominant. In ascertaining that intention the following rules apply:

(a) Exact or technical specifications displace an inconsistent sample or model or general language of description.

(b) A sample from an existing bulk displaces inconsistent general language of description.

(c) Express warranties displace inconsistent implied warranties other than an implied warranty of fitness for a particular purpose.

§2A-216. Third-Party Beneficiaries of Express and Implied Warranties.
Alternative A

A warranty to or for the benefit of a lessee under this Article, whether express or implied, extends to any natural person who is in the family or household of the lessee or who is a guest in the lessee's home if it is reasonable to expect that such person may use, consume, or be affected by the goods and who is injured in person by breach of the warranty. This section does not displace principles of law and equity that extend a warranty to or for the benefit of a lessee to other persons. The operation of this section may not be excluded, modified, or limited, but an exclusion, modification, or limitation of the warranty, including any with respect to rights and remedies, effective against the lessee is also effective against any beneficiary designated under this section.

Alternative B

A warranty to or for the benefit of a lessee under this Article, whether express or implied, extends to any natural person who may reasonably be expected to use, consume, or be affected by the goods and who is injured in person by breach of the warranty. This section does not displace principles of law and equity that extend a warranty to or for the benefit of a lessee to other persons. The operation of this section may not be excluded, modified, or limited, but an exclusion, modification, or limitation of the warranty, including any with respect to rights and remedies, effective against the lessee is also effective against the beneficiary designated under this section.

Alternative C

A warranty to or for the benefit of a lessee under this Article, whether express or implied, extends to any person who may reasonably be expected to use, consume, or be affected by the goods and who is injured by breach of the warranty. The operation of this section may not be excluded, modified, or limited with respect to injury to the person of an individual to whom the warranty extends, but an exclusion, modification, or limitation of the warranty, including any with respect to rights and remedies, effective against the lessee is also effective against the beneficiary designated under this section.

§2A-217. Identification. Identification of goods to which a lease contract refers may be made at any time and in any manner explicitly agreed to by the parties. In the absence of explicit agreement, identification occurs:

(**a**) when the lease contract is made if the lease contract is for a lease of goods that are existing and identified;

(**b**) when the goods are shipped, marked, or otherwise designated by the lessor as goods to which the lease contract refers, if the lease contract is for a lease of goods that are not existing and identified; or

(**c**) when the young are conceived, if the lease contract is for a lease of unborn young of animals.

§2A-218. Insurance and Proceeds.

(**1**) A lessee obtains an insurable interest when existing goods are identified to the lease contract even though the goods identified are nonconforming and the lessee has an option to reject them.

(**2**) If a lessee has an insurable interest only by reason of the lessor's identification of the goods, the lessor, until default or insolvency or notification to the lessee that identification is final, may substitute other goods for those identified.

(**3**) Notwithstanding a lessee's insurable interest under subsections (1) and (2), the lessor retains an insurable interest until an option to buy has been exercised by the lessee and risk of loss has passed to the lessee.

(**4**) Nothing in this section impairs any insurable interest recognized under any other statute or rule of law.

(**5**) The parties by agreement may determine that one or more parties have an obligation to obtain and pay for insurance covering the goods and by agreement may determine the beneficiary of the proceeds of the insurance.

§2A-219. Risk of Loss.

(**1**) Except in the case of a finance lease, risk of loss is retained by the lessor and does not pass to the lessee. In the case of a finance lease, risk of loss passes to the lessee.

(**2**) Subject to the provisions of this Article on the effect of default on risk of loss (Section 2A-220), if risk of loss is to pass to the lessee and the time of passage is not stated, the following rules apply:

(**a**) If the lease contract requires or authorizes the goods to be shipped by carrier.

(**i**) and it does not require delivery at a particular destination, the risk of loss passes to the lessee when the goods are duly delivered to the carrier; but

(**ii**) if it does require delivery at a particular destination and the goods are there duly tendered while in the possession of the carrier, the risk of loss passes to the lessee when the goods are there duly so tendered as to enable the lessee to take delivery.

(**b**) If the goods are held by a bailee to be delivered without being moved, the risk of loss passes to the lessee on acknowledgment by the bailee of the lessee's right to possession of the goods.

(**c**) In any case not within subsection (a) or (b), the risk of loss passes to the lessee on the lessee's receipt of the goods if the lessor, or, in the case of a finance lease, the supplier, is a merchant; otherwise the risk passes to the lessee on tender of delivery.

§2A-220. Effect of Default on Risk of Loss.

(**1**) Where risk of loss is to pass to the lessee and the time of passage is not stated:

(**a**) If a tender or delivery of goods so fails to conform to the lease contract as to give a right of rejection, the risk of their loss remains with the lessor, or, in the case of a finance lease, the supplier, until cure or acceptance.

(**b**) If the lessee rightfully revokes acceptance, he [or she], to the extent of any deficiency in his[or her] effective insurance coverage, may treat the risk of loss as having remained with the lessor from the beginning.

(**2**) Whether or not risk of loss is to pass to the lessee, if the lessee as to conforming goods already identified to a lease contract repudiates or is otherwise in default under the lease contract, the lessor, or, in the case of a finance lease, the supplier, to the extent of any deficiency in his [or her] effective insurance coverage may treat the risk of loss as resting on the lessee for a commercially reasonable time.

§2A-221. Casualty to Identified Goods. If a lease contract requires goods identified when the lease contract is made, and the goods suffer casualty without fault of the lessee, the lessor or the supplier before delivery, or the goods suffer casualty before risk of loss passes to the lessee pursuant to the lease agreement or Section 2A-219, then:

(**a**) if the loss is total, the lease contract is avoided; and

(**b**) if the loss is partial or the goods have so deteriorated as to no longer conform to the lease contract, the lessee may nevertheless demand inspection and at his[or her] option either treat the lease contract as avoided or, except in a finance lease that is not a consumer lease, accept the goods with due allowance from the rent payable for the balance of the lease term for the deterioration or the deficiency in quantity but without further right against the lessor.

Part 3: Effect of Lease Contract

§2A-301. Enforceability of Lease Contract. Except as otherwise provided in this Article, a lease contract is effective and enforceable according to its terms between the parties, against purchasers of the goods and against creditors of the parties.

§2A-302. Title to and Possession of Goods. Except as otherwise provided in this Article, each provision of this Article applies whether the lessor or a third party has title to the goods, and whether the lessor, the lessee, or a third party has possession of the goods, notwithstanding any statute or rule of law that possession or the absence of possession is fraudulent.

§2A-303. Alienability of Partsy's Interest Under Lease Contract or of Lessor's Residual Interest in Goods; Delegation of Performance; Assignment of Rights.

(1) Any interest of a party under a lease contract and the lessor's residual interest in the goods may be transferred unless

 (a) the transfer is voluntary and the lease contract prohibits the transfer; or
 (b) the transfer materially changes the duty of or materially increases the burden or risk imposed on the other party to the lease contract, and within a reasonable time after notice of the transfer the other party demands that the transferee comply with subsection (2) and the transferee fails to comply.

(2) Within a reasonable time after demand pursuant to subsection (1)(b), the transferee shall:

 (a) cure or provide adequate assurance that he[or she] will promptly cure any default other than one arising from the transfer;
 (b) compensate or provide adequate assurance that he [or she] will promptly compensate the other party to the lease contract and any other person holding an interest in the lease contract, except the party whose interest is being transferred, for any loss to that party resulting from the transfer;
 (c) provide adequate assurance of future due performance under the lease contract; and
 (d) assume the lease contract.

(3) Demand pursuant to subsection (1)(b) is without prejudice to the other party's rights against the transferee and the party whose interest is transferred.

(4) An assignment of "the lease" or of "all my rights under the lease" or an assignment in similar general terms is a transfer of rights, and unless the language or the circumstances, as in an assignment for security, indicate the contrary, the assignment is a delegation of duties by the assignor to the assignee and acceptance by the assignee constitutes a promise by him[or her] to perform those duties. This promise is enforceable by either the assignor or the other party to the lease contract.

(5) Unless otherwise agreed by the lessor and the lessee, no delegation of performance relieves the assignor as against the other party of any duty to perform or any liability for default.

(6) A right to damages for default with respect to the whole lease contract or a right arising out of the assignor's due performance of his [or her] entire obligation can be assigned despite agreement otherwise.

(7) To prohibit the transfer of an interest of a party under a lease contract, the language of prohibition must be specific, by a writing, and conspicuous.

§2A-304. Subsequent Lease of Goods by Lessor.

(1) Subject to the provisions of Section 2A-303, a subsequent lessee from a lessor of goods under an existing lease contract obtains, to the extent of the leasehold interest transferred, the leasehold interest in the goods that the lessor had or had power to transfer, and except as provided in subsection (2) and Section 2A-527(4), takes subject to the existing lease contract. A lessor with voidable title has power to transfer a good leasehold interest to a good faith subsequent lessee for value, but only to the extent set forth in the preceding sentence. When goods have been delivered under a transaction of purchase the lessor has that power even though:

 (a) the lessor's transferor was deceived as to the identity of the lessor;
 (b) the delivery was in exchange for a check which is later dishonored;
 (c) it was agreed that the transaction was to be a "cash sale"; or
 (d) the delivery was procured through fraud punishable as larcenous under the criminal law.

(2) A subsequent lessee in the ordinary course of business from a lessor who is a merchant dealing in goods of that kind to whom the goods were entrusted by the existing lessee before the interest of the subsequent lessee became enforceable against the lessor obtains, to the extent of the leasehold interest transferred, all of the lessor's and the existing lessee's rights to the goods, and takes free of the existing lease contract.

(3) A subsequent lessee from the lessor of goods that are subject to an existing lease contract and are covered by a certificate of title issued under a statute of this State or of another jurisdiction takes no greater rights than those provided both by this section and by the certificate of title statute.

§2A-305. Sale or Sublease of Goods by Lessee.

(1) Subject to the provisions of Section 2A-303, a buyer or sublessee from the lessee of goods under an existing lease contract obtains, to the extent of the interest transferred, the leasehold interest in the goods that the lessee had or had power to transfer, and except as provided in subsection (2) and Section 2A-511(4), takes subject to the existing lease contract. A lessee with a voidable leasehold interest has power to transfer a good leasehold interest to a good faith buyer for value or a good faith sublessee for value, but only to the extent set forth in the preceding sentence. When goods have been delivered under a transaction of lease the lessee has that power even though:

(a) the lessor was deceived as to the identify of the lessee;

(b) the delivery was in exchange for a check which is later dishonored; or

(c) the delivery was procured through fraud punishable as larcenous under the criminal law.

(2) A buyer in the ordinary course of business or a sublessee in the ordinary course of business from a lessee who is a merchant dealing in goods of that kind to whom the goods were entrusted by the lessor obtains, to the extent of the interest transferred, all of the lessor's and lessee's rights to the goods, and takes free of the existing lease contract.

(3) A buyer or sublessee from the lessee of goods that are subject to an existing lease contract and are covered by a certificate of title issued under a statute of this State or of another jurisdiction takes no greater rights than those provided both by this section and by the certificate of title statute.

§2A-306. Priority of Certain Liens Arising by Operation of Law. If a person in the ordinary course of his[or her] business furnishes services or materials with respect to goods subject to a lease contract, a lien upon those goods in the possession of that person given by statute or rule of law for those materials or services takes priority over any interest of the lessor or lessee under the lease contract or this Article unless the lien is created by statute and the statute provides otherwise or unless the lien is created by rule of law and the rule of law provides otherwise.

§2A-307. Priority of Liens Arising by Attachment or Levy on, Security Interests in, and Other Claims to Goods.

(1) Except as otherwise provided in Section 2A-306, a creditor of a lessee takes subject to the lease contract.

(2) Except as otherwise provided in subsections (3) and (4) of this section and in Sections 2A-306 and 2A-308, a creditor of a lessor takes subject to the lease contract:

(a) unless the creditor holds a lien that attached to the goods before the lease contract became enforceable, or

(b) unless the creditor holds a security interest in the goods that under the Article on Secured Transactions (Article 9) would have priority over any other security interest in the goods perfected by a filing covering the goods and made at the time the lease contract became enforceable, whether or not any other security interest existed.

(3) A lessee in the ordinary course of business takes the leasehold interest free of a security interest in the goods created by the lessor even though the security interest is perfected and the lessee knows of its existence.

(4) A lessee other than a lessee in the ordinary course of business takes the leasehold interest free of a security interest to the extent that it secures future advances made after the secured party acquires knowledge of the lease or more than 45 days after the lease contract becomes enforceable, whichever first occurs, unless the future advances are made pursuant to a commitment entered into without knowledge of the lease and before the expiration of the 45-day period.

§2A-308. Special Rights of Creditors.

(1) A creditor of a lessor in possession of goods subject to a lease contract may treat the lease contract as void if as against the creditor retention of possession by the lessor is fraudulent under any statute or rule of law, but retention of possession in good faith and current course of trade by the lessor for a commercially reasonable time after the lease contract becomes enforceable is not fraudulent.

(2) Nothing in this Article impairs the rights of creditors of a lessor if the lease contract (a) becomes enforceable, not in current course of trade but in satisfaction of or as security for a pre-existing claim for money, security, or the like, and (b) is made under circumstances which under any statute or rule of law apart from this Article would constitute the transaction a fraudulent transfer or voidable preference.

(3) A creditor of a seller may treat a sale or an identification of goods to a contract for sale as void if as against the creditor retention of possession by the seller is fraudulent under any statute or rule of law, but retention of possession of the goods pursuant to a lease contract entered into by the seller as lessee and the buyer as lessor in connection with the sale or identification of the goods is not fraudulent if the buyer bought for value and in good faith.

§2A-309. Lessor's and Lessee's Rights When Goods Become Fixtures.

(1) In this section:

(a) goods are "fixtures" when they become so related to particular real estate that an interest in them arises under real estate law;

(**b**) a "fixture filing" is the filing, in the office where a mortgage on the real estate would be recorded or registered, of a financing statement concerning goods that are or are to become fixtures and conforming to the requirements of subsection (5) of Section 9-402;

(**c**) a lease is a "purchase money lease" unless the lessee has possession or use of the goods or the right to possession or use of the goods before the lease agreement is enforceable;

(**d**) a mortgage is a "construction mortgage" to the extent it secures an obligation incurred for the construction of an improvement on land including the acquisition cost of the land, if the recorded writing so indicates; and

(**e**) "encumbrance" includes real estate mortgages and other liens on real estate and all other rights in real estate that are not ownership interests.

(**2**) Under this Article a lease may be of goods that are fixtures or may continue in goods that become fixtures, but no lease exists under this Article of ordinary building materials incorporated into an improvement on land.

(**3**) This Article does not prevent creation of a lease of fixtures pursuant to real estate law.

(**4**) The perfected interest of a lessor of fixtures has priority over a conflicting interest of an encumbrancer or owner of the real estate if:

(**a**) the lease is a purchase money lease, the conflicting interest of the encumbrancer or owner arises before the goods become fixtures, the interest of the lessor is perfected by a fixture filing before the goods become fixtures or within ten days thereafter, and the lessee has an interest of record in the real estate or is in possession of the real estate; or

(**b**) the interest of the lessor is perfected by a fixture filing before the interest of the encumbrancer or owner is of record, the lessor's interest has priority over any conflicting interest of a predecessor in title of the encumbrancer or owner, and the lessee has an interest of record in the real estate or is in possession of the real estate.

(**5**) The interest of a lessor of fixtures, whether or not perfected, has priority over the conflicting interest of an encumbrancer or owner of the real estate if:

(**a**) the fixtures are readily removable factory or office machines, readily removable equipment that is not primarily used or leased for use in the operation of the real estate, or readily removable replacements of domestic appliances that are goods subject to a consumer lease, and before the goods become fixtures the lease contract is enforceable; or

(**b**) the conflicting interest is a lien on the real estate obtained by legal or equitable proceedings after the lease contract is enforceable; or

(**c**) the encumbrancer or owner has consented in writing to the lease or has disclaimed an interest in the goods as fixtures; or

(**d**) the lessee has a right to remove the goods as against the encumbrancer or owner. If the lessee's right to remove terminates, the priority of the interest of the lessor continues for a reasonable time.

(**6**) Notwithstanding paragraph (a) of subsection (4) but otherwise subject to subsections (4) and (5), the interest of a lessor of fixtures is subordinate to the conflicting interest of an encumbrancer of the real estate under a construction mortgage recorded before the goods become fixtures if the goods become fixtures before the completion of the construction. To the extent given to refinance a construction mortgage, the conflicting interest of an encumbrancer of the real estate under a mortgage has this priority to the same extent as the encumbrancer of the real estate under the construction mortgage.

(**7**) In cases not within the preceding subsections, priority between the interest of a lessor of fixtures and the conflicting interest of an encumbrancer or owner of the real estate who is not the lessee is determined by the priority rules governing conflicting interests in real estate.

(**8**) If the interest of a lessor has priority over all conflicting interests of all owners and encumbrancers of the real estate, the lessor or the lessee may (a) on default, expiration, termination, or cancellation of the lease agreement by the other party but subject to the provisions of the lease agreement and this Article, or (b) if necessary to enforce his [or her] other rights and remedies under this Article, remove the goods from the real estate, free and clear of all conflicting interests of all owners and encumbrancers of the real estate, but he [or she] must reimburse any encumbrancer or owner of the real estate who is not the lessee and who has not otherwise agreed for the cost of repair of any physical injury, but not for any diminution in value of the real estate caused by the absence of the goods removed or by any necessity of replacing them. A person entitled to reimbursement may refuse permission to remove until the party seeking removal gives adequate security for the performance of this obligation.

(**9**) Even though the lease agreement does not create a security interest, the interest of a lessor of fixtures is perfected by filing a financing statement as a fixture filing for leased goods that are or are to become fixtures in accordance with the relevant provisions of the Article on Secured Transactions (Article 9).

§2A-310. Lessor's and Lessee's Rights When Goods Become Accessions.

(1) Goods are "accessions" when they are installed in or affixed to other goods.

(2) The interest of a lessor or a lessee under a lease contract entered into before the goods became accessions is superior to all interests in the whole except as stated in subsection (4).

(3) The interest of a lessor or a lessee under a lease contract entered into at the time or after the goods became accessions is superior to all subsequently acquired interests in the whole except as stated in subsection (4) but is subordinate to interests in the whole existing at the time the lease contract was made unless the holders of such interests in the whole have in writing consented to the lease or disclaimed an interest in the goods as part of the whole.

(4) The interest of a lessor or a lessee under a lease contract described in subsection (2) or (3) is subordinate to the interest of

(a) a buyer in the ordinary course of business or a lessee in the ordinary course of business of any interest in the whole acquired after the goods became accessions; or

(b) a creditor with a security interest in the whole perfected before the lease contract was made to the extent that the creditor makes subsequent advances without knowledge of the lease contract.

(5) When under subsections (2) or (3) and (4) a lessor or a lessee of accessions holds an interest that is superior to all interests in the whole, the lessor or the lessee may

(a) on default, expiration, termination, or cancellation of the lease contract by the other party but subject to the provisions of the lease contract and this Article, or

(b) if necessary to enforce his[or her] other rights and remedies under this Article, remove the goods from the whole, free and clear of all interests in the whole, but he[or she] must reimburse any holder of an interest in the whole who is not the lessee and who has not otherwise agreed for the cost of repair of any physical injury but not for any diminution in value of the whole caused by the absence of the goods removed or by any necessity for replacing them. A person entitled to reimbursement may refuse permission to remove until the party seeking removal gives adequate security for the performance of this obligation.

Part 4: Performance of Lease Contract—Repudiated, Substituted, and Excused

§2A-401. Insecurity: Adequate Assurance of Performance.

(1) A lease contract imposes an obligation on each party that the other's expectation of receiving due performance will not be impaired.

(2) If reasonable grounds for insecurity arise with respect to the performance of either party, the insecure party may demand in writing adequate assurance of due performance. Until the insecure party receives that assurance, if commercially reasonable the insecure party may suspend any performance for which he[or she] has not already received the agreed return.

(3) A repudiation of the lease contract occurs if assurance of due performance adequate under the circumstances of the particular case is not provided to the insecure party within a reasonable time, not to exceed 30 days after receipt of a demand by the other party.

(4) Between merchants, the reasonableness of grounds for insecurity and the adequacy of any assurance offered must be determined according to commercial standards.

(5) Acceptance of any nonconforming delivery or payment does not prejudice the aggrieved party's right to demand adequate assurance of future performance.

§2A-402. Anticipatory Repudiation. If either party repudiates a lease contract with respect to a performance not yet due under the lease contract, the loss of which performance will substantially impair the value of the lease contract to the other, the aggrieved party may:

(a) for a commercially reasonable time, await retraction of repudiation and performance by the repudiating party;

(b) make demand pursuant to Section 2A-401 and await assurance of future performance adequate under the circumstances of the particular case; or

(c) resort to any right or remedy upon default under the lease contract or this Article, even though the aggrieved party has notified the repudiating party that the aggrieved party would await the repudiating party's performance and assurance and has urged retraction. In addition, whether or not the aggrieved party is pursuing one of the foregoing remedies, the aggrieved party may suspend performance or, if the aggrieved party is the lessor, proceed in accordance with the provisions of this Article on the lessor's right to identify goods to the lease contract notwithstanding default or to salvage unfinished goods (Section 2A-524).

§2A-403. Retraction of Anticipatory Repudiation.

(1) Until the repudiating party's next performance is due, the repudiating party can retract the repudiation unless, since the repudiation, the aggrieved party has cancelled the lease contract or materially changed the aggrieved party's position or otherwise indicated that the aggrieved party considers the repudiation final.

(2) Retraction may be by any method that clearly indicates to the aggrieved party that the repudiating party intends to perform under the lease contract and includes any assurance demanded under Section 2A-401.

(3) Retraction reinstates a repudiating party's rights under a lease contract with due excuse and allowance to the aggrieved party for any delay occasioned by the repudiation.

§2A-404. Substituted Performance.

(1) If without fault of the lessee, the lessor and the supplier, the agreed berthing, loading, or unloading facilities fail or the agreed type of carrier becomes unavailable or the agreed manner of delivery otherwise becomes commercially impracticable, but a commercially reasonable substitute is available, the substitute performance must be tendered and accepted.

(2) If the agreed means or manner of payment fails because of domestic or foreign governmental regulation:

(a) the lessor may withhold or stop delivery or cause the supplier to withhold or stop delivery unless the lessee provides a means or manner of payment that is commercially a substantial equivalent; and

(b) if delivery has already been taken, payment by the means or in the manner provided by the regulation discharges the lessee's obligation unless the regulation is discriminatory, oppressive, or predatory.

§2A-405. Excused Performance. Subject to Section 2A-404 on substituted performance, the following rules apply:

(a) Delay in delivery or nondelivery in whole or in part by a lessor or a supplier who complies with paragraphs (b) and (c) is not a default under the lease contract if performance as agreed has been made impracticable by the occurrence of a contingency the nonoccurrence of which was a basic assumption on which the lease contract was made or by compliance in good faith with any applicable foreign or domestic governmental regulation or order, whether or not the regulation or order later proves to be invalid.

(b) If the causes mentioned in paragraph (a) affect only part of the lessor's or the supplier's capacity to perform, he [or she] shall allocate production and deliveries among his [or her] customers but at his [or her] option may include regular customers not then under contract for sale or lease as well as his[or her] own requirements for further manufacture. He [or she] may so allocate in any manner that is fair and reasonable.

(c) The lessor seasonably shall notify the lessee and in the case of a finance lease the supplier seasonably shall notify the lessor and the lessee, if known, that there will be delay or nondelivery and, if allocation is required under paragraph (b), of the estimated quota thus made available for the lessee.

§2A-406. Procedure on Excused Performance.

(1) If the lessee receives notification of a material or indefinite delay or an allocation justified under Section 2A-405, the lessee may by written notification to the lessor as to any goods involved, and with respect to all of the goods if under an installment lease contract the value of the whole lease contract is substantially impaired (Section 2A-510):

(a) terminate the lease contract (Section 2A-505(2)); or

(b) except in a finance lease that is not a consumer lease, modify the lease contract by accepting the available quota in substitution, with due allowance from the rent payable for the balance of the lease term for the deficiency but without further right against the lessor.

(2) If, after receipt of a notification from the lessor under Section 2A-405, the lessee fails so to modify the lease agreement within a reasonable time not exceeding 30 days, the lease contract lapses with respect to any deliveries affected.

§2A-407. Irrevocable Promises: Finance Leases.

(1) In the case of a finance lease that is not a consumer lease the lessee's promises under the lease contract become irrevocable and independent upon the lessee's acceptance of the goods.

(2) A promise that has become irrevocable and independent under subsection (1):

(a) is effective and enforceable between the parties or against third parties including assignees of the parties, and

(b) is not subject to cancellation, termination, modification, repudiation, excuse, or substitution without the consent of the party to whom the promise runs.

Part 5: Default A. In General

§2A-501. Default: Procedure.

(1) Whether the lessor or the lessee is in default under a lease contract is determined by the lease agreement and this Article.

(2) If the lessor or the lessee is in default under the lease contract, the party seeking enforcement has rights and remedies as provided in this Article and, except as limited by this Article, as provided in the lease agreement.

(3) If the lessor or the lessee is in default under the lease contract, the party seeking enforcement may reduce the party's claim to judgment, or otherwise enforce the lease contract by self-help or any available judicial procedure or nonjudicial procedure, including administrative proceeding, arbitration, or the like, in accordance with this Article.

(4) Except as otherwise provided in this Article or the lease agreement, the rights and remedies referred to in subsections (2) and (3) are cumulative.

(5) If the lease agreement covers both real property and goods, the party seeking enforcement may proceed under this Part as to the goods, or under other applicable law as to both the real property and the goods in accordance with his[or her] rights and remedies in respect of the real property, in which case this Part does not apply.

§2A-502. Notice After Default. Except as otherwise provided in this Article or the lease agreement, the lessor or lessee in default under the lease contract is not entitled to notice of default or notice of enforcement from the other party to the lease agreement.

§2A-503. Modification or Impairment of Rights and Remedies.

(1) Except as otherwise provided in this Article, the lease agreement may include rights and remedies for default in addition to or in substitution for those provided in this Article and may limit or alter the measure of damages recoverable under this Article.

(2) Resort to a remedy provided under this Article or in the lease agreement is optional unless the remedy is expressly agreed to be exclusive. If circumstances cause an exclusive or limited remedy to fail of its essential purpose, or provision for an exclusive remedy is unconscionable, remedy may be had as provided in this Article.

(3) Consequential damages may be liquidated under Section 2A-504, or may otherwise be limited, altered, or excluded unless the limitation, alteration, or exclusion is unconscionable. Limitation of consequential damages for injury to the person in the case of consumer goods is prima facie unconscionable but limitation of damages where the loss is commercial is not.

(4) Rights and remedies on default by the lessor or the lessee with respect to any obligation or promise collateral or ancillary to the lease contract are not impaired by this Article.

§2A-504. Liquidation of Damages.

(1) Damages payable by either party for default, or any other act or omission, including indemnity for loss or diminution of anticipated tax benefits or loss or damage to lessor's residual interest, may be liquidated in the lease agreement but only at an amount or by a formula that is reasonable in light of the then antici-

pated harm caused by the default or other act or omission.

(2) If the lease agreement provides for liquidation of damages, and such provision does not comply with subsection (1), or such provision is an exclusive or limited remedy that circumstances cause to fail of its essential purpose, remedy may be had as provided in this Article.

(3) If the lessor justifiably withholds or stops delivery of goods because of the lessee's default or insolvency (Section 2A-525 or 2A-526), the lessee is entitled to restitution of any amount by which the sum of his [or her] payments exceeds:

(a) the amount to which the lessor is entitled by virtue of terms liquidating the lessor's damages in accordance with subsection (1); or

(b) in the absence of those terms, 20 percent of the then present value of the total rent the lessee was obligated to pay for the balance of the lease term, or, in the case of a consumer lease, the lesser of such amount or $500.

(4) A lessee's right to restitution under subsection (3) is subject to offset to the extent the lessor establishes:

(a) a right to recover damages under the provisions of this Article other than subsection (1); and

(b) the amount or value of any benefits received by the lessee directly or indirectly by reason of the lease contract.

§2A-505. Cancellation and Termination and Effect of Cancellation, Termination, Rescission, or Fraud on Rights and Remedies.

(1) On cancellation of the lease contract, all obligations that are still executory on both sides are discharged, but any right based on prior default or performance survives, and the cancelling party also retains any remedy for default of the whole lease contract or any unperformed balance.

(2) On termination of the lease contract, all obligations that are still executory on both sides are discharged but any right based on prior default or performance survives.

(3) Unless the contrary intention clearly appears, expressions of "cancellation", "rescission", or the like of the lease contract may not be construed as a renunciation or discharge of any claim in damages for an antecedent default.

(4) Rights and remedies for material misrepresentation or fraud include all rights and remedies available under this Article for default.

(5) Neither rescission nor a claim for rescission of the lease contract nor rejection or return of the goods may bar or be deemed inconsistent with a claim for damages or other right or remedy.

§2A-506. Statute of Limitations.

(1) An action for default under a lease contract, including breach of warranty or indemnity, must be commenced within 4 years after the cause of action accrued. By the original lease contract the parties may reduce the period of limitation to not less than one year.

(2) A cause of action for default accrues when the act or omission on which the default or breach of warranty is based is or should have been discovered by the aggrieved party, or when the default occurs, whichever is later. A cause of action for indemnity accrues when the act or omission on which the claim for indemnity is based is or should have been discovered by the indemnified party, whichever is later.

(3) If an action commenced within the time limited by subsection (1) is so terminated as to leave available a remedy by another action for the same default or breach of warranty or indemnity, the other action may be commenced after the expiration of the time limited within 6 months after the termination of the first action unless the termination resulted from voluntary discontinuance or from dismissal for failure or neglect to prosecute.

(4) This section does not alter the law on tolling of the statute of limitations nor does it apply to causes of action that have accrued before this Article becomes effective.

§2A-507. Proof of Market Rent: Time and Place.

(1) Damages based on market rent (Section 2A-519 or 2A-528) are determined according to the rent for the use of the goods concerned for a lease term identical to the remaining lease term of the original lease agreement and prevailing at the time of the default.

(2) If evidence of rent for the use of the goods concerned for a lease term identical to the remaining lease term of the original lease agreement and prevailing at the times or places described in this Article is not readily available, the rent prevailing within any reasonable time before or after the time described or at any other place or for a different lease term which in commercial judgment or under usage of trade would serve as a reasonable substitute for the one described may be used, making any proper allowance for the difference, including the cost of transporting the goods to or from the other place.

(3) Evidence of a relevant rent prevailing at a time or place or for a lease term other than the one described in this Article offered by one party is not admissible unless and until he[or she] has given the other party notice the court finds sufficient to prevent unfair surprise.

(4) If the prevailing rent or value of any goods regularly leased in any established market is in issue, reports in official publications or trade journals or in newspapers or periodicals of general circulation published as the reports of that market are admissible in evidence. The circumstances of the preparation of the report may be shown to affect its weight but not its admissibility.

B. Default by Lessor

§2A-508. Lessee's Remedies.

(1) If a lessor fails to desliver the goods in conformity to the lease contract (Section 2A-509) or repudiates the lease contract (Section 2A-402), or a lessee rightfully rejects the goods (Section 2A-509) or justifiably revokes acceptance of the goods (Section 2A-517), then with respect to any goods involved, and with respect to all of the goods if under an installment lease contract the value of the whole lease contract is substantially impaired (Section 2A-510), the lessor is in default under the lease contract and the lessee may:

(a) cancel the lease contract (Section 2A-505(1));

(b) recover so much of the rent and security as has been paid, but in the case of an installment lease contract the recovery is that which is just under the circumstances;

(c) cover and recover damages as to all goods affected whether or not they have been identified to the lease contract (Sections 2A-518 and 2A-520), or recover damages for nondelivery (Sections 2A-519 and 2A-520).

(2) If a lessor fails to deliver the goods in conformity to the lease contract or repudiates the lease contract, the lessee may also:

(a) if the goods have been identified, recover them (Section 2A-522); or

(b) in a proper case, obtain specific performance or replevy the goods (Section 2A-521).

(3) If a lessor is otherwise in default under a lease contract, the lessee may exercise the rights and remedies provided in the lease contract and this Article.

(4) If a lessor has breached a warranty, whether express or implied, the lessee may recover damages (Section 2A-519(4)).

(5) On rightful rejection or justifiable revocation of acceptance, a lessee has a security interest in goods in the lessee's possession or control for any rent and security that has been paid and any expenses reasonably incurred in their inspection, receipt, transportation, and care and custody and may hold those goods and dispose of them in good faith and in a commercially reasonable manner, subject to the provisions of Section 2A-527(5).

(6) Subject to the provisions of Section 2A-407, a lessee, on notifying the lessor of the lessee's intention to do so, may deduct all or any part of the damages resulting from any default under the lease contract from any part of the rent still due under the same lease contract.

§2A-509. Lessee's Rights on Improper Delivery; Rightful Rejection.

(1) If a lessee elects not to cover or a lessee elects to cover and the cover does not qualify for treatment under Section 2A-518(2), the measure of damages for non-delivery or repudiation by reject or accept the goods or accept any commercial unit or units and reject the rest of the goods.

(2) Rejection of goods is ineffective unless it is within a reasonable time after tender or delivery of the goods and the lessee seasonably notifies the lessor.

§2A-510. Installment Lease Contracts: Rejection and Default.

(1) Under an installment lease contract a lessee may reject any delivery that is nonconforming if the nonconformity substantially impairs the value of that delivery and cannot be cured or the nonconformity is a defect in the required documents; but if the nonconformity does not fall within subsection (2) and the lessor or the supplier gives adequate assurance of its cure, the lessee must accept that delivery.

(2) Whenever nonconformity or default with respect to one or more deliveries substantially impairs the value of the installment lease contract as a whole there is a default with respect to the whole. But, the aggrieved party reinstates the installment lease contract as a whole if the aggrieved party accepts a nonconforming delivery without seasonably notifying of cancellation or brings an action with respect only to past deliveries or demands performance as to future deliveries.

§2A-511. Merchant Lessee's Duties as to Rightfully Rejected Goods.

(1) Subject to any security interest of a lessee (Section 2A-508(5)), if a lessor or a supplier has no agent or place of business at the market of rejection, a merchant lessee, after rejection of goods in his [or her] possession or control, shall follow any reasonable instructions received from the lessor or the supplier with respect to the goods. In the absence of those instructions, a merchant lessee shall make reasonable efforts to sell, lease, or otherwise dispose of the goods for the lessor's account if they threaten to decline in value speedily. Instructions are not reasonable if on demand indemnity for expenses is not forthcoming.

(2) If a merchant lessee (subsection (1)) or any other lessee (Section 2A-512) disposes of goods, he [or she] is entitled to reimbursement either from the lessor or the supplier or out of the proceeds for reasonable expenses of caring for and disposing of the goods and, if the expenses include no disposition commission, to such commission as is usual in the trade, or if there is none, to a reasonable sum not exceeding 10 percent of the gross proceeds.

(3) In complying with this section or Section 2A-512, the lessee is held only to good faith. Good faith conduct hereunder is neither acceptance or conversion nor the basis of an action for damages.

(4) A purchaser who purchases in good faith from a lessee pursuant to this section or Section 2A-512 takes the goods free of any rights of the lessor and the supplier even though the lessee fails to comply with one or more of the requirements of this Article.

§2A-512. Lessee's Duties as to Rightfully Rejected Goods.

(1) Except as otherwise provided with respect to goods that threaten to decline in value speedily (Section 2A-511) and subject to any security interest of a lessee (Section 2A-508(5)):

(a) the lessee, after rejection of goods in the lessee's possession, shall hold them with reasonable care at the lessor's or the supplier's disposition for a reasonable time after the lessee's seasonable notification of rejection;

(b) if the lessor or the supplier gives no instructions within a reasonable time after notification of rejection, the lessee may store the rejected goods for the lessor's or the supplier's account or ship them to the lessor or the supplier or dispose of them for the lessor's or the supplier's account with reimbursement in the manner provided in Section 2A-511; but

(c) the lessee has no further obligations with regard to goods rightfully rejected.

(2) Action by the lessee pursuant to subsection (1) is not acceptance or conversion.

§2A-513. Cure by Lessor of Improper Tender or Delivery; Replacement.

(1) If any tender or delivery by the lessor or the supplier is rejected because nonconforming and the time for performance has not yet expired, the lessor or the supplier may seasonably notify the lessee of the lessor's or the supplier's intention to cure and may then make a conforming delivery within the time provided in the lease contract.

(2) If the lessee rejects a nonconforming tender that the lessor or the supplier had reasonable grounds to believe would be acceptable with or without money allowance, the lessor or the supplier may have a further reasonable time to substitute a conforming tender if he [or she] seasonably notifies the lessee.

§2A-514. Waiver of Lessee's Objections.

(1) In rejecting goods, a lessee's failure to state a particular defect that is ascertainable by reasonable inspection precludes the lessee from relying on the defect to justify rejection or to establish default:

(a) if, stated seasonably, the lessor or the supplier could have cured it (Section 2A-513); or

(b) between merchants if the lessor or the supplier after rejection has made a request in writing for a full and final written statement of all defects on which the lessee proposes to rely.

(2) A lessee's failure to reserve rights when paying rent or other consideration against documents precludes recovery of the payment for defects apparent on the face of the documents.

§2A-515. Acceptance of Goods.

(1) Acceptance of goods occurs after the lessee has had a reasonable opportunity to inspect the goods and

(a) the lessee signifies or acts with respect to the goods in a manner that signifies to the lessor or the supplier that the goods are conforming or that the lessee will take or retain them in spite of their nonconformity; or

(b) the lessee fails to make an effective rejection of the goods (Section 2A-509(2)).

(2) Acceptance of a part of any commercial unit is acceptance of that entire unit.

§2A-516. Effect of Acceptance of Goods; Notice of Default; Burden of Establishing Default After Acceptance; Notice of Claim or Litigation to Person Answerable Over.

(1) A lessee must pay rent for any goods accepted in accordance with the lease contract, with due allowance for goods rightfully rejected or not delivered.

(2) A lessee's acceptance of goods precludes rejection of the goods accepted. In the case of a finance lease, if made with knowledge of a nonconformity, acceptance cannot be revoked because of it. In any other case, if made with knowledge of a nonconformity, acceptance cannot be revoked because of it unless the acceptance was on the reasonable assumption that the nonconformity would be seasonably cured. Acceptance does not of itself impair any other remedy provided by this Article or the lease agreement for nonconformity.

(3) If a tender has been accepted:

(a) within a reasonable time after the lessee discovers or should have discovered any default, the lessee shall notify the lessor and the supplier, or be barred from any remedy;

(b) except in the case of a consumer lease, within a reasonable time after the lessee receives notice of litigation for infringement or the like (Section 2A-211) the lessee shall notify the lessor or be barred from any remedy over for liability established by the litigation; and

(c) the burden is on the lessee to establish any default.

(4) If a lessee is sued for breach of a warranty or other obligation for which a lessor or a supplier is answerable over:

(a) The lessee may give the lessor or the supplier written notice of the litigation. If the notice states that the lessor or the supplier may come in and defend and that if the lessor or the supplier does not do so he [or she] will be bound in any action against him [or her] by the lessee by any determination of fact common to the two litigations, then unless the lessor or the supplier after seasonable receipt of the notice does come in and defend he [or she] is so bound.

(b) The lessor or the supplier may demand in writing that the lessee turn over control of the litigation including settlement if the claim is one for infringement or the like (Section 2A-211) or else be barred from any remedy over. If the demand states that the lessor or the supplier agrees to bear all expense and to satisfy any adverse judgment, then unless the lessee after seasonable receipt of the demand does turn over control the lessee is so barred.

(5) The provisions of subsections (3) and (4) apply to any obligation of a lessee to hold the lessor or the supplier harmless against infringement or the like (Section 2A-211).

§2A-517. Revocation of Acceptance of Goods.

(1) A lessee may revoke acceptance of a lot or commercial unit whose nonconformity substantially impairs its value to the lessee if he [or she] has accepted it:

(a) except in the case of a finance lease, on the reasonable assumption that its nonconformity would be cured and it has not been seasonably cured; or

(b) without discovery of the nonconformity if the lessee's acceptance was reasonably induced either by the lessor's assurances or, except in the case of a finance lease, by the difficulty of discovery before acceptance.

(2) Revocation of acceptance must occur within a reasonable time after the lessee discovers or should have discovered the ground for it and before any substantial change in condition of the goods which is not caused by the nonconformity. Revocation is not effective until the lessee notifies the lessor.

(3) A lessee who so revokes has the same rights and duties with regard to the goods involved as if the lessee had rejected them.

§2A-518. Cover; Substitute Goods.

(1) After default by a lessor under the lease contract (Section 2A-508(1)), the lessee may cover by making in good faith and without unreasonable delay any purchase or lease of or contract to purchase or lease goods in substitution for those due from the lessor.

(2) Except as otherwise provided with respect

to damages liquidated in the lease agreement (Section 2A-504) or determined by agreement of the parties (Section 1-102(3)), if a lessee's cover is by lease agreement substantially similar to the original lease agreement and the lease agreement is made in good faith and in a commercially reasonable manner, the lessee may recover from the lessor as damages (a) the present value, as of the date of default, of the difference between the total rent for the lease term of the new lease agreement and the total rent for the remaining lease term of the original lease agreement and (b) any incidental or consequential damages less expenses saved in consequence of the lessor's default.

(3) If a lessee's cover does not qualify for treatment under subsection (2), the lessee may recover from the lessor as if the lessee had elected not to cover and Section 2A-519 governs.

§2A-519. Lessee's Damages for Non-Delivery, Repudiation, Default and Breach of Warranty in Regard to Accepted Goods.

(1) If a lessee elects not to cover or a lessee elects to cover and the cover does not qualify for treatment under Section 2A-518(2), the measure of damages for non-delivery or repudiation by the lessor or for rejection or revocation of acceptance by the lessee is the present value as of the date of the default of the difference between the then market rent and the original rent, computed for the remaining lease term of the original lease agreement together with incidental and consequential damages, less expenses saved in consequence of the lessor's default.

(2) Market rent is to be determined as of the place for tender or, in cases of rejection after arrival or revocation of acceptance, as of the place of arrival.

(3) If the lessee has accepted goods and given notification (Section 2A-516(3)), the measure of damages for non-conforming tender or delivery by a lessor is the loss resulting in the ordinary course of events from the lessor's default as determined in any manner that is reasonable together with incidental and consequential damages, less expenses saved in consequence of the lessor's default.

(4) The measure of damages for breach of warranty is the present value at the time and place of acceptance of the difference between the value of the use of the goods accepted and the value if they had been as warranted for the lease term, unless special circumstances show proximate damages of a different amount, together with incidental and consequential damages, less expenses saved in consequence of the lessor's default or breach of warranty.

§2A-520. Lessee's Incidental and Consequential Damages.

(1) Incidental damages resulting from a lessor's default include expenses reasonably incurred in inspection, receipt, transportation, and care and custody of goods rightfully rejected or goods the acceptance of which is justifiably revoked, any commercially reasonable charges, expenses or commissions in connection with effecting cover, and any other reasonable expense incident to the default.

(2) Consequential damages resulting from a lessor's default include:

(a) any loss resulting from general or particular requirements and needs of which the lessor at the time of contracting had reason to know and which could not reasonably be prevented by cover or otherwise; and

(b) injury to person or property proximately resulting from any breach of warranty.

§2A-521. Lessee's Right to Specific Performance or Replevin.

(1) Specific performance may be decreed if the goods are unique or in other proper circumstances.

(2) A decree for specific performance may include any terms and conditions as to payment of the rent, damages, or other relief that the court deems just.

(3) A lessee has a right of replevin, detinue, sequestration, claim and delivery, or the like for goods identified to the lease contract if after reasonable effort the lessee is unable to effect cover for those goods or the circumstances reasonably indicate that the effort will be unavailing.

§2A-522. Lessee's Right to Goods on Lessor's Insolvency.

(1) Subject to subsection (2) and even though the goods have not been shipped, a lessee who has paid a part or all of the rent and security for goods identified to a lease contract (Section 2A-217) on making and keeping good a tender of any unpaid portion of the rent and security due under the lease contract may recover the goods identified from the lessor if the lessor becomes insolvent within 10 days after receipt of the first installment of rent and security.

(2) A lessee acquires the right to recover goods identified to a lease contract only if they conform to the lease contract.

C. Default by Lessee

§2A-523. Lessor's Remedies.

(1) If a lessee wrongfully rejects or revokes acceptance of goods or fails to make a payment when due or repudiates with respect to a part or the whole, then, with respect to any goods involved, and with respect to all of the goods if under an installment lease contract the value of the whole lease contract is substantially impaired (Section 2A-510), the lessee is in default under the lease contract and the lessor may:

(a) cancel the lease contract (Section 2A-505(1));

(b) proceed respecting goods not identified to the lease contract (Section 2A-524);

(c) withhold delivery of the goods and take possession of goods previously delivered (Section 2A-525);

(d) stop delivery of the goods by any bailee (Section 2A-526);

(e) dispose of the goods and recover damages (Section 2A-527), or retain the goods and recover damages (Section 2A-528), or in a proper case recover rent (Section 2A-529).

(2) If a lessee is otherwise in default under a lease contract, the lessor may exercise the rights and remedies provided in the lease contract and this Article.

§2A-524. Lessor's Right to Identify Goods to Lease Contract.

(1) A lessor aggrieved under Section 2A-523(1) may:

(a) identify to the lease contract conforming goods not already identified if at the time the lessor learned of the default they were in the lessor's or the supplier's possession or control; and

(b) dispose of goods (Section 2A-527(1)) that demonstrably have been intended for the particular lease contract even though those goods are unfinished.

(2) If the goods are unfinished, in the exercise of reasonable commercial judgment for the purposes of avoiding loss and of effective realization, an aggrieved lessor or the supplier may either complete manufacture and wholly identify the goods to the lease contract or cease manufacture and lease, sell, or otherwise dispose of the goods for scrap or salvage value or proceed in any other reasonable manner.

§2A-525. Lessor's Right to Possession of Goods.

(1) If a lessor discovers the lessee to be insolvent, the lessor may refuse to deliver the goods.

(2) The lessor has on default by the lessee under the lease contract the right to take possession of the goods. If the lease contract so provides, the lessor may require the lessee to assemble the goods and make them available to the lessor at a place to be designated by the lessor which is reasonably convenient to both parties. Without removal, the lessor may render unusable any goods employed in trade or business, and may dispose of goods on the lessee's premises (Section 2A-527).

(3) The lessor may proceed under subsection (2) without judicial process if that can be done without breach of the peace or the lessor may proceed by action.

§2A-526. Lessor's Stoppage of Delivery in Transit or Otherwise.

(1) A lessor may stop delivery of goods in the possession of a carrier or other bailee if the lessor discovers the lessee to be insolvent and may stop delivery of carload, truckload, planeload, or larger shipments of express or freight if the lessee repudiates or fails to make a payment due before delivery, whether for rent, security or otherwise under the lease contract, or for any other reason the lessor has a right to withhold or take possession of the goods.

(2) In pursuing its remedies under subsection (1) the lessor may stop delivery until

(a) receipt of the goods by the lessee;

(b) acknowledgment to the lessee by any bailee of the goods, except a carrier, that the bailee holds the goods for the lessee; or

(c) such an acknowledgment to the lessee by a carrier via reshipment or as warehouseman.

(3) (a) To stop delivery, a lessor shall so notify as to enable the bailee by reasonable diligence to prevent delivery of the goods.

(b) After notification, the bailee shall hold and deliver the goods according to the directions of the lessor, but the lessor is liable to the bailee for any ensuing charges or damages.

(c) A carrier who has issued a nonnegotiable bill of lading is not obliged to obey a notification to stop received from a person other than the consignor.

§2A-527. Lessor's Rights to Dispose of Goods.

(1) After a default by a lessee under the lease contract (Section 2A-523(1)) or after the lessor refuses to deliver or take possession of goods (Section 2A-525 or 2A-526), the lessor may dispose of the goods concerned or the undelivered balance thereof in good faith and without unreasonable delay by lease, sale or otherwise.

(2) If the disposition is by lease contract substantially similar to the original lease contract and the lease contract is made in good faith and in a commercially reasonable manner, the lessor may recover from the lessee as damages (a) accrued and unpaid rent as of the date of default, (b) the present value as of the date of default of the difference between the total rent for the remaining lease term of the original lease contract and the total rent for the lease term of the new lease contract, and (c) any incidental damages allowed under Section 2A-530, less expenses saved in consequence of the lessee's default.

(3) If the lessor's disposition is by lease contract that for any reason does not qualify for treatment under subsection (2), or is by sale or otherwise, the lessor may recover from the lessee as if the lessor had

elected not to dispose of the goods and Section 2A-528 governs.

(4) A subsequent buyer or lessee who buys or leases from the lessor in good faith for value as a result of a disposition under this section takes the goods free of the original lease contract and any rights of the original lessee even though the lessor fails to comply with one or more of the requirements of this Article.

(5) The lessor is not accountable to the lessee for any profit made on any disposition. A lessee who has rightfully rejected or justifiably revoked acceptance shall account to the lessor for any excess over the amount of the lessee's security interest (Section 2A-508(5)).

§2A-528. Lessor's Damages for Non-Acceptance or Repudiation.

(1) Except as otherwise provided with respect to damages liquidated in the lease agreement (Section 2A-504) or determined by agreement of the parties (Section 1-102(3)), if a lessor elects to retain the goods or a lessor elects to dispose of the goods and disposition is by lease agreement that for any reason does not qualify for treatment under Section 2A-527(2), or is by sale or otherwise, the lessor may recover from the lessee as damages for non-acceptance or repudiation by the lessee (a) accrued and unpaid rent as of the date of default, (b) the present value as of the date of default of the difference between the total rent for the remaining lease term of the original lease agreement and the market rent at the time and place for tender computed for the same lease term, and (c) any incidental damages allowed under Section 2A-530, less expenses saved in consequence of the lessee's default.

(2) If the measure of damages provided in subsection (1) is inadequate to put a lessor in as good a position as performance would have, the measure of damages is the profit, including reasonable overhead, the lessor would have made from full performance by the lessee, together with any incidental damages allowed under Section 2A-530, due allowance for costs reasonably incurred and due credit for payments or proceeds of disposition.

§2A-529. Lessor's Action for the Rent.

(1) After default by the lessee under the lease contract (Section 2A-523(1)), if the lessor complies with subsection (2), the lessor may recover from the lessee as damages:

(a) for goods accepted by the lessee and for conforming goods lost or damaged within a commercially reasonable time after risk of loss passes to the lessee (Section 2A-219), (i) accrued and unpaid rent as of the date of default, (ii) the present value as of the date of default of the rent for the remaining lease term of the lease agreement, and (iii) any inci-

dental damages allowed under Section 2A-530, less expenses saved in consequence of the lessee's default; and

(b) for goods identified to the lease contract if the lessor is unable after reasonable effort to dispose of them at a reasonable price or the circumstances reasonably indicate that effort will be unavailing, (i) accrued and unpaid rent as of the date of default, (ii) the present value as of the date of default of the rent for the remaining lease term of the lease agreement, and (iii) any incidental damages allowed under Section 2A-530, less expenses saved in consequence of the lessee's default.

(2) Except as provided in subsection (3), the lessor shall hold for the lessee for the remaining lease term of the lease agreement any goods that have been identified to the lease contract and are in the lessor's control.

(3) The lessor may dispose of the goods at any time before collection of the judgment for damages obtained pursuant to subsection (1) and the lessor may proceed against the lessee for damages pursuant to Section 2A-527 or Section 2A-528.

(4) Payment of the judgment for damages obtained pursuant to subsection (1) entitles the lessee to use and possession of the goods not then disposed of for the remaining lease term of the lease agreement.

(5) After a lessee has wrongfully rejected or revoked acceptance of goods, has failed to pay rent then due, or has repudiated (Section 2A-402), a lessor who is held not entitled to rent under this section must nevertheless be awarded damages for non-acceptance under Sections 2A-527 and 2A-528.

§2A-530. Lessor's Incidental Damages.
Incidental damages to an aggrieved lessor include any commercially reasonable charges, expenses, or commissions incurred in stopping delivery, in the transportation, care and custody of goods after the lessee's default, in connection with return or disposition of the goods, or otherwise resulting from the default.

§2A-531. Standing to Sue Third Parties for Injury to Goods.

(1) If a third party so deals with goods that have been identified to a lease contract as to cause actionable injury to a party to the lease contract (a) the lessor has a right of action against the third party, and (b) the lessee also has a right of action against the third party if the lessee:

(i) has a security interest in the goods;

(ii) has an insurable interest in the goods; or

(iii) bears the risk of loss under the lease contract or has since the injury assumed that risk as against the lessor and the goods have been converted or destroyed.

(2) If at the time of the injury the party plaintiff did not bear the risk of loss as against the other party to the lease contract and there is no arrangement between them for disposition of the recovery, his[or her] suit or settlement, subject to his [or her] own interest, is as a fiduciary for the other party to the lease contract.

(3) Either party with the consent of the other may sue for the benefit of whom it may concern.

ARTICLE 3: COMMERCIAL PAPER

Part 1: Short Title, Form and Interpretation

§3-101. Short Title. This Article shall be known and may be cited as Uniform Commercial Code—Commercial Paper.

§3-102. Definitions and Index of Definitions.

(1) In this Article unless the context otherwise requires

(a) "Issue" means the first delivery of an instrument to a holder or a remitter.

(b) An "order" is a direction to pay and must be more than an authorization or request. It must identify the person to pay with reasonable certainty. It may be addressed to one or more such persons jointly or in the alternative but not in succession.

(c) A "promise" is an undertaking to pay and must be more than an acknowledgement of an obligation.

(d) "Secondary party" means a drawer or endorser.

(e) "Instrument" means a negotiable instrument.

(2) Other definitions applying to this Article and the sections in which they appear are:

"Acceptance"	Section 3-410
"Accommodation party"	Section 3-415
"Alteration"	Section 3-407
"Certificate of deposit"	Section 3-104
"Certification"	Section 3-411
"Check"	Section 3-104
"Definite time"	Section 3-109
"Dishonor"	Section 3-507
"Draft"	Section 3-104
"Holder in due course"	Section 3-302
"Negotiation"	Section 3-202
"Note"	Section 3-104
"Notice of dishonor"	Section 3-508
"On demand"	Section 3-108
"Presentment"	Section 3-504
"Protest"	Section 3-509
"Restrictive indorsement"	Section 3-205
"Signature"	Section 3-401

(3) The following definitions in other Articles apply to this Article:

"Account"	Section 4-104
"Banking day"	Section 4-104
"Clearing house"	Section 4-104
"Collecting bank"	Section 4-105
"Customer"	Section 4-104
"Depositary bank"	Section 4-105
"Documentary draft"	Section 4-104
"Intermediary bank"	Section 4-105
"Item"	Section 4-104
"Midnight deadline"	Section 4-104
"Payor bank"	Section 4-105

(4) In addition Article 1 contains general definitions and principles of construction and interpretation applicable throughout this Article.

§3-103. Limitations on Scope of Article.

(1) This Article does not apply to money, documents of title or investment securities.

(2) The provisions of this Article are subject to the provisions of the Article on Bank Deposits and Collections (Article 4) and Secured Transactions (Article 9).

§3-104. Form of Negotiable Instruments; "Draft"; "Check"; "Certificate of Deposit"; "Note".

(1) Any writing to be a negotiable instrument within this Article must

(a) be signed by the maker or drawer; and

(b) contain an unconditional promise or order to pay a sum certain in money and no other promise, order, obligation or power given by the maker or drawer except as authorized by this Article; and

(c) be payable on demand or at a definite time; and

(d) be payable to order or to bearer.

(2) A writing which complies with the requirements of this section is

(a) a "draft" ("bill of exchange") if it is an order;

(b) a "check" if it is a draft drawn on a bank and payable on demand.

(c) a "certificate of deposit" if it is an acknowledgement by a bank of receipt of money with an engagement to repay it;

(d) a "note" if it is a promise other than a certificate of deposit.

(3) As used in other Articles in this Act, and as the context may require, the terms "draft", "check", "certificate of deposit" and "note" may refer to instruments which are not negotiable within this Article as will as to instruments which are so negotiable.

§3-105. When Promise or Order Unconditional.

(1) A promise or order otherwise unconditional is not made conditional by the fact that the instrument

(a) is subject to implied or constructive conditions; or

(b) states its consideration, whether performed or promised, or the transaction which gave rise to the instrument, or that the promise or order is made or the instrument matures in accordance with or "as per" such transaction; or

(c) refers to or states that it arises out of a separate agreement or refers to a separate agreement for rights as to prepayment or acceleration; or

(d) states that is drawn under a letter of credit; or

(e) states that it is secured, whether by mortgage, reservation of title or otherwise; or

(f) indicates a particular account to be debited or any other fund or source from which reimbursement is expected; or

(g) is limited to payment out of a particular fund or the proceeds of a particular source, if the instrument is issued by a government or governmental agency or unit; or

(h) is limited to payment out of the entire assets of a partnership, unincorporated association, trust or estate by or on behalf of which the instrument is issued.

(2) A promise or order is not unconditional if the instrument

(a) states that it is subject to or governed by any other agreement; or

(b) states that it is to be paid only out of a particular fund or source except as provided in this section. As amended 1962.

§3-106. Sum Certain.

(1) The sum payable is a sum certain even though it is to be paid

(a) with stated interest or by stated installments; or

(b) with stated different rates of interest before and after default or a specified date; or

(c) with a stated discount or addition if paid before or after the date fixed for payment; or

(d) with exchange or less exchange, whether at a fixed rate or at the current rate; or

(e) with costs of collection or an attorney's fee or both upon default.

(2) Nothing in this section shall validate any term which is otherwise illegal.

§3-107. Money.

(1) An instrument is payable in money if the medium of exchange in which it is payable is money at the time the instrument is made. An instrument payable in "currency" or "current funds" is payable in money.

(2) A promise or order to pay a sum stated in a foreign currency is for a sum certain in money and, unless a different medium of payment is specified in the instrument, may be satisfied by payment of that number of dollars which the stated foreign currency will purchase at the buying sight rate for that currency on the day on which the instrument is payable or, if payable on demand, on the day of demand. If such an instrument specifies a foreign currency as the medium of payment the instrument is payable in that currency

§3-108. Payable on Demand.
Instruments payable on demand include those payable at sight or on presentation and those in which no time for payment is stated.

§3-109. Definite Time.

(1) An instrument is payable at a definite time if by its terms it is payable

(a) on or before a stated date or at a fixed period after a stated date; or

(b) at a fixed period after sight; or

(c) at a definite time subject to any acceleration; or

(d) at a definite time subject to extension at the option of the holder, or to extension to a further definite time at the option of the maker or acceptor or automatically upon or after a specified act or event.

(2) An instrument which by its terms is otherwise payable only upon an act or event uncertain as to time of occurence is not payable at a definite time even though the act or event has occured.

§3-110. Payable to Order.

(1) An instrument is payable to order when by its terms it is payable to the order or assigns of any person therein specified with reasonable certainty, or to him or his order, or when it is conspicuously designated on its face as "exchange" or the like and names a payee. It may be payable to the order of

(a) the maker or drawer; or

(b) the drawee; or

(c) a payee who is not maker, drawer or drawee; or

(d) two or more payees together or in the alternative; or

(e) an estate, trust or fund, in which case it is payable to the order of the representative of such estate, trust or fund or his successors; or

(f) an office, or an officer by his title as such in which case it is payable to the principal but the incumbent of the office or his successors may act as if he or they were the holder; or

(g) a partnership or unincorporated association, in which case it is payable to the partnership or association and may be indorsed or transferred by any person thereto authorized.

(2) An instrument not payable to order is not made so payable by such words as "payable upon return of this instrument properly indorsed."

(3) An instrument made payable both to order

and to bearer is payable to order unless the bearer words are handwritten or typewritten.

§3-111. Payable to Bearer. An instrument is payable to bearer when by its terms it is payable to

(a) bearer or the order of bearer; or

(b) a specified person or bearer; or

(c) "cash" or the order of "cash", or any other indication which does not purport to designate a specific payee.

§3-112. Terms and Omissions Not Affecting Negotiability.

(1) The negotiability of an instrument is not affected by

(a) the omission of a statement of any consideration or of the place where the instrument is drawn or payable; or

(b) a statement that collateral has been given to secure obligations either on the instrument or otherwise of an obligor on the instrument or that in case of default on those obligations the holder may realize on or dispose of the collateral; or

(c) a promise or power to maintain or protect collateral or to give additional collateral; or

(d) a term authorizing a confession of judgment on the instrument if it is not paid when due; or

(e) a term purporting to waive the benefit of any law intended for the advantage or protection of any obligor; or

(f) a term in a draft providing that the payee by indorsing or cashing it acknowledges full satisfaction of an obligation of the drawer; or

(g) a statement in a draft drawn in a set of parts (Section 3-801) to the effect that the order is effective only if no other part has been honored.

(2) Nothing in this section shall validate any term which is otherwise illegal. As amended 1962.

§3-113. Seal. An instrument otherwise negotiable is within this Article even though it is under a seal.

§3-114. Date, Antedating, Postdating.

(1) The negotiability of an instrument is not affected by the fact that it is undated, antedated or postdated.

(2) Where an instrument is antedated or postdated the time when it is payable is determined by the stated date if the instrument is payable on demand or at a fixed period after date.

(3) Where the instrument or any signature thereon is dated, the date is presumed to be correct.

§3-115. Incomplete Instruments.

(1) When a paper whose contents at the time of signing show that it is intended to become an instrument is signed while still incomplete in any necessary respect it cannot be enforced until completed, but when it is completed in accordance with authority given it is effective as completed.

(2) If the completion is unauthorized the rules as to material alteration apply (Section 3-407), even though the paper was not delivered by the maker or drawer; but the burden of establishing that any completion is unauthorized is on the party so asserting.

§3-116. Instruments Payable to Two or More Persons. An instrument payable to the order of two or more persons

(a) if in the alternative is payable to any one of them and may be negotiated, discharged or enforced by any of them who has possession of it;

(b) if not in the alternative is payable to all of them and may be negotiated, discharged or enforced only by all of them.

§3-117. Instruments Payable With Words of Description. An instrument made payable to a named person with the addition of words describing him

(a) as agent or officer of a specified person is payable to his principal but the agent or officer may act as if he were the holder;

(b) as any other fiduciary for a specified person or purpose is payable to the payee and may be negotiated, discharged or enforced by him;

(c) in any other manner is payable to the payee unconditionally and the additional word are without effect on subsequent parties.

§3-118. Ambiguous Terms and Rules of Construction. The following rules apply to every instrument:

(a) Where there is doubt whether the instrument is a draft or a note the holder may treat it as either. A draft drawn on the drawer is effective as a note.

(b) Handwritten terms control typewritten and printed terms, and typewritten control printed.

(c) Words control figures except that if the words are ambiguous figures control.

(d) Unless otherwise specified a provision for interest means interest at the judgment rate at the place of payment from the date of the instrument, or if it is undated from the date of issue.

(e) Unless the instrument otherwise specifies two or more persons who sign as maker, acceptor or drawer or indorser and as a part of the same transaction are jointly and severally liable even though the instrument contains such words as "I promise to pay."

(f) Unless otherwise specified consent to extension authorizes a single extension for not longer than the original period. A consent to extension, expressed in the instrument, is binding on secondary parties and accommodation makers. A holder may not exercise his option to extend an instrument over the objection of a maker or acceptor or other party who in accordance with Section 3-604 tenders full payment when the instrument is due.

§3-119. Other Writings Affecting Instrument.

(1) As between the obligor and his immediate obligee or any transferee the terms of an instrument may be modified or affected by any other written agreement executed as a part of the same transaction, except that a holder in due course is not affected by any limitation of his rights arising out of the separate written agreement if he had no notice of the limitation when he took the instrument.

(2) A separate agreement does not affect the negotiability of an instrument.

§3-120. Instruments "Payable Through" Bank.
An instrument which states that is is "payable through" a bank or the like designates that bank as a collecting bank to make presentment but does not of itself authorize the bank to pay the instrument.

§3-121. Instruments Payable at Bank.

Note: *If this Act is introduced in the Congress of the United States this section should be omitted. (States to select either alternative.)*

> **Alternative A**—A note or acceptance which states that it is payable at a bank is the equivalent of a draft drawn on the bank payable when it falls due out of any funds of the maker or acceptor in current account or otherwise available for such payment.
> **Alternative B**—A note or acceptance which states that it is payable at a bank is not of itself an order or authorization to the bank to pay it.

§3-122. Accrual of Cause of Action.

(1) A cause of action against a maker or an acceptor accrues

(a) in the case of a time instrument on the day after maturity;

(b) in the case of a demand instrument upon its date or, if no date is stated, on the date of issue.

(2) A cause of action against the obligor of a demand or time certificate of deposit accrues upon demand, but demand on a time certificate may not be made until on or after the date of maturity.

(3) A cause of action against a drawer of a draft or an indorser of any instrument accrues upon demand following dishonor of the instrument. Notice of dishonor is a demand.

(4) Unless an instrument provides otherwise, interest runs at the rate provided by law for a judgment

(a) in the case of a maker, acceptor or other primary obligor of a demand instrument, from the date of demand;

(b) in all other cases from the date of accrual of the cause of action. As amended 1962.

Part 2: Transfer and Negotiation

§3-201. Transfer: Right to Indorsement.

(1) Transfer of an instrument vests in the transferee such rights as the transferor has therein, except that a transferee who has himself been a party to any fraud or illegality affecting the instrument or who as a prior holder had notice of a defense or claim against it cannot improve his position by taking from a later holder in due course.

(2) A transfer of a security interest in an instrument vests the foregoing rights in the transferee to the extent of the interest transferred.

(3) Unless otherwise agreed any transfer for value of an instrument not then payable to bearer gives the transferee the specifically enforceable right to have the unqualified indorsement of the transferor. Negotiation takes effect only when the indorsement is made and until that time there is no presumption that the transferee is the owner.

§3-202. Negotiation.

(1) Negotiation is the transfer of an instrument in such form that the transferee becomes a holder. If the instrument is payable to order it is negotiated by delivery with any necessary indorsement; if payable to bearer it is negotiated by delivery.

(2) An indorsement must be written by or on behalf of the holder and on the instrument or on a paper so firmly affixed thereto as to become a part thereof.

(3) An indorsement is effective for negotiation only when it conveys the entire instrument or any unpaid residue. If it purports to be of less it operates only as a partial assignment.

(4) Words of assignment, condition, waiver, guaranty, limitation or disclaimer of liability and the like accompanying an indorsement do not affect its character as an indorsement.

§3-203. Wrong or Misspelled Name.
Where an instrument is made payable to a person under a misspelled name or one other than his own he may indorse in that name or his own or both; but signature in both names may be required by a person paying or giving value for the instrument.

§3-204. Special Indorsement; Blank Indorsement.

(1) A special indorsement specifies the person to whom or to whose order it makes the instrument payable. Any instrument specially indorsed becomes payable to the order of the special indorsee and may be further negotiated only by his indorsement.

(2) An indorsement in blank specifies no particular indorsee and may consist of a mere signature. An instrument payable to order and indorsed in blank becomes payable to bearer and may be negotiated by delivery alone until specially indorsed.

(3) The holder may convert a blank indorsement into a special indorsement by writing over the signature of the indorser in blank any contract consistent with the character of the indorsement.

§3-205. Restrictive Indorsements. An indorsement is restrictive which either

(a) is conditional; or
(b) purports to prohibit further transfer of the instrument; or
(c) includes the words "for collection", "for deposit", "pay any bank", or like terms signifying a purpose of deposit or collection; or
(d) otherwise states that it is for the benefit or use of the indorser or of another person.

§3-206. Effect of Restrictive Indorsement.

(1) No restrictive indorsement prevents further transfer or negotiation of the instrument.

(2) An intermediary bank, or a payor bank which is not the depositary bank, is neither given notice nor otherwise affected by a restrictive indorsement of any person except the bank's immediate transferor or the person presenting for payment.

(3) Except for an intermediary bank, any transferee under an indorsement which is conditional or includes the words "for collection", "for deposit", "pay any bank", or like terms (subparagraphs (a) and (c) of Section 3-205) must pay or apply any value given by him for or on the security of the instrument consistently with the indorsement and to the extent that he does so he becomes a holder for value. In addition such transferee is a holder in due course if he otherwise complies with the requirements of Section 3-302 on what constitutes a holder in due course.

(4) The first taker under an indorsement for the benefit of the indorser or another person (subparagraph (d) of Section 3-205) must pay or apply any value given by him for or on the security of the instrument consistently with the indorsement and to the extent that he does so he becomes a holder for value. In addition such taker is a holder in due course if he otherwise complies with the requirements of Section 3-302 on what constitutes a holder in due course. A later holder for value is neither given notice nor otherwise affected by such restrictive indorsement unless he has knowledge that a fiduciary or other person has negotiated the instrument in any transaction for his own benefit or otherwise in breach of duty (subsection (2) of Section 3-304).

§3-207. Negotiation Effective Although It May Be Rescinded.

(1) Negotiation is effective to transfer the instrument although the negotiation is

(a) made by an infant, a corporation exceeding its powers, or any other person without capacity; or
(b) obtained by fraud, duress or mistake of any kind; or
(c) part of an illegal transaction; or
(d) made in breach of duty.

(2) Except as against a subsequent holder in due course such negotiation is in an appropriate case subject to rescission, the declaration of a constructive trust or any other remedy permitted by law.

§3-208. Reacquisition. Where an instrument is returned to or reacquired by a prior party he may cancel any indorsement which is not necessary to his title and reissue or further negotiate the instrument, but any intervening party is discharged as against the reacquiring party and subsequent holders not in due course and if his indorsement has been cancelled is discharged as against subsequent holders in due course as well.

Part 3: Rights of a Holder

§3-301. Rights of a Holder. The holder of an instrument whether or not he is the owner may transfer or negotiate it and, except as otherwise provided in Section 3-603 on payment or satisfaction, discharge it or enforce payment in his own name.

§3-302. Holder in Due Course

(1) A holder in due course is a holder who takes the instrument

(a) for value; and
(b) in good faith; and
(c) without notice that it is overdue or has been dishonored or of any defense against or claim to it on the part of any person.

(2) A payee may be a holder in due course.

(3) A holder does not become a holder in due course of an instrument:

(a) by purchase of it at judicial sale or by taking it under legal process; or
(b) by acquiring it in taking over an estate, or
(c) by purchasing it as part of a bulk transaction not in regular course of business of the transferor.

(4) A purchaser of a limited interest can be a holder in due course only to the extent of the interest purchased.

§3-303. Taking for Value. A holder takes the instrument for value

(a) to the extent that the agreed consideration

has been performed or that he acquires a security interest in or a lien on the instrument otherwise than by legal process; or

(b) when he takes the instrument in payment of or as security for an antecedent claim against any person whether or not the claim is due; or

(c) when he gives a negotiable instrument for it or makes an irrevocable commitment to a third person.

§3-304. Notice to Purchaser.

(1) The purchaser has notice of a claim or defense if

(a) the instrument is so incomplete, bears such visible evidence of forgery or alteration, or is otherwise so irregular as to call into question its validity, terms or ownership or to create an ambiguity as to the party to pay; or

(b) the purchaser has notice that the obligation of any party is voidable in whole or part, or that all parties have been discharged.

(2) The purchaser has notice of a claim against the instrument when he has knowledge that a fiduciary has negotiated the instrument in payment of or as security for his own debt or in any transaction for his own benefit or otherwise in breach of duty.

(3) The purchaser has notice that an instrument is overdue if he has reason to know

(a) that any part of the principal amount is overdue or that there is an uncured default in payment of another instrument of the same series; or

(b) that acceleration of the instrument has been made; or

(c) that he is taking a demand instrument after demand has been made or more than a reasonable length of time after its issue. A reasonable time for a check drawn and payable within the states and territories of the United States and the District of Columbia is presumed to be thirty days.

(4) Knowledge of the following facts does not of itself give the purchaser notice of a defense or claim

(a) that the instrument is antedated or postdated;

(b) that it was issued or negotiated in return for an executory promise or accompanied by a separate agreement, unless the purchaser has notice that a defense or claim has arisen from the terms thereof;

(c) that any party has signed for accomodation;

(d) that an incomplete instrument has been completed, unless the purchaser has notice of any improper completion;

(e) that any person negotiating the instrument is or was a fiduciary;

(f) that there has been default in payment of interest on the instrument or in payment of any other instrument, except one of the same series.

(5) The filing or recording of a document does not of itself constitute notice within the provisions of this Article to a person who would otherwise be a holder in due course.

(6) To be effective notice must be received at such time and in such manner as to give a reasonable opportunity to act on it.

§3-305. Rights of a Holder in Due Course. To the extent that a holder is a holder in due course he takes the instrument free from

(1) all claims to it on the part of any person; and

(2) all defenses of any party to the instrument with whom the holder has not dealt except

(a) infancy, to the extent that it is a defense to a simple contract; and

(b) such other incapacity, or duress, or illegality of the transaction, as renders the obligation of the party a nullity; and

(c) such misrepresentation as has induced the party to sign the instrument with neither knowledge nor reasonable opportunity to obtain knowledge of its character or its essential terms; and

(d) discharge in insolvency proceedings; and

(e) any other discharge of which the holder has notice when he takes the instrument.

§3-306. Rights of One Not Holder in Due Course. Unless he has the rights of a holder in due course any person takes the instrument subject to

(a) all valid claims to it on the part of any person; and

(b) all defenses of any party which would be available in an action on a simple contract; and

(c) the defenses of want or failure of consideration, nonperformance of any condition precedent, non-delivery, or delivery for a special purpose (Section 3-408); and

(d) the defense that he or a person through whom he holds the instrument acquired it by theft, or that payment or satisfaction to such holder would be inconsistent with the terms of a restrictive indorsement. The claim of any third person to the instrument is not otherwise available as a defense to any party liable thereon unless the third person himself defends the action for such party.

§3-307. Burden of Establishing Signatures, Defenses and Due Course

(1) Unless specifically denied in the pleading each signature on an instrument is admitted. When the effectiveness of a signature is put in issue

(a) the burden of establishing it is on the party claiming under the signature; but

(b) the signature is presumed to be genuine or authorized except where the action is to enforce the obligation of a purported signer who has died or become incompetent before proof is required.

(2) When signatures are admitted or established, production of the instrument entitles a holder to recover on it unless the defendant establishes a defense.

(3) After it is shown that a defense exists a person claiming the rights of a holder in due course has the burden of establishing that he or some person under whom he claims is in all respects a holder in due course.

Part 4: Liability of Parties

§3-401. Signature.

(1) No person is liable on an instrument unless his signature appears thereon.

(2) A signature is made by use of any name, including any trade or assumed name, upon an instrument, or by any word or mark used in lieu of a written signature

§3-402. Signature in Ambiguous Capacity. Unless the instrument clearly indicates that a signature is made in some other capacity it is an indorsement.

§3-403. Signature by Authorized Representative.

(1) A signature may be made by an agent or other representative, and his authority to make it may be established as in other cases of representation. No particular form of appointment is necessary to establish such authority.

(2) An authorized representative who signs his own name to an instrument

(a) is personally obligated if the instrument neither names the person represented nor shows that the representative signed in a representative capacity;

(b) except as otherwise established between the immediate parties, is personally obligated if the instrument names the person represented but does not show that the representative signed in a representative capacity, or if the instrument does not name the person represented but does show that the representative signed in a representative capacity.

(3) Except as otherwise established the name of an organization preceded or followed by the name and office of an authorized individual is a signature made in a representative capacity.

§3-404. Unauthorized Signatures.

(1) Any unauthorized signature is wholly inoperative as that of the person whose name is signed unless he ratifies it or is precluded from denying it; but it operates as the signature of the unauthorized signer in favor of any person who in good faith pays the instrument or takes it for value.

(2) Any unauthorized signature may be ratified for all purposes of this Article. Such ratification does not of itself affect any rights of the person ratifying against the actual signer.

§3-405. Imposters; Signature in Name of Payee.

(1) An indorsement by any person in the name of a named payee is effective if

(a) an impostor by use of the mails or otherwise has induced the maker or drawer to issue the instrument to him or his confederate in the name of the payee; or

(b) a person signing as or on behalf of a maker or drawer intends the payee to have no interest in the instrument; or

(c) an agent or employee of the maker or drawer has supplied him with the name of the payee intending the latter to have no such interest.

(2) Nothing in this section shall affect the criminal or civil liability of the person so indorsing.

§3-406. Negligence Contributing to Alteration or Unauthorized Signature. Any person who by his negligence substantially contributes to a material alteration of the instrument or to the making of an unauthorized signature is precluded from asserting the alteration or lack of authority against a holder in due course or against a drawee or other payor who pays the instrument in good faith and in accordance with the reasonable commercial standards of the drawee's or payor's business.

§3-407. Alteration.

(1) Any alteration of an instrument is material which changes the contract of any party thereto in any respect, including any such change in

(a) the number or relations of the parties; or

(b) an incomplete instrument, by completing it otherwise than as authorized; or

(c) the writing as signed, by adding to it or by removing any part of it.

(2) As against any person other than a subsequent holder in due course

(a) alteration by the holder which is both fraudulent and material discharges any party whose contract is thereby changed unless that party assents or is precluded from asserting the defense;

(b) no other alteration discharges any party and the instrument may be enforced according to its original tenor, or as to incomplete instruments according to the authority given.

(3) A subsequent holder in due course may in all cases enforce the instrument according to its original tenor, and when an incomplete instrument has been completed, he may enforce it as completed.

§3-408. Consideration.

Want or failure of consideration is a defense as against any person not having the rights of a holder in due course. (Section 3-305), except that no consideration is necessary for an instrument or obligation thereon given in payment of or as security for an antecedent obligation of any kind. Nothing in this section shall be taken to displace any statute outside this Act under which a promise is enforceable notwithstanding lack or failure of consideration. Partial failure of consideration is a defense pro tanto whether or not the failure is in an ascertained or liquidated amount.

§3-409. Draft Not an Assignment.

(1) A check or other draft does not of itself operate as an assignment of any funds in the hands of the drawee available for its payment, and the drawee is not liable on the instrument until he accepts it.

(2) Nothing in this section shall affect any liability in contract, tort or otherwise arising from any letter of credit or other obligation or representation which is not an acceptance.

§3-410. Definition and Operation of Acceptance.

(1) Acceptance is the drawee's signed engagement to honor the draft as presented. It must be written on the draft, and may consist of his signature alone. It becomes operative when completed by delivery or notification.

(2) A draft may be accepted although it has not been signed by the drawer or is otherwise incomplete or is overdue or has been dishonored.

(3) Where the draft is payable at a fixed period after sight and the acceptor fails to date his acceptance the holder may complete it by supplying a date in good faith.

§3-411. Certification of a Check.

(1) Certification of a check is acceptance. Where a holder procures certification the drawer and all prior indorsers are discharged.

(2) Unless otherwise agreed a bank has no obligation to certify a check.

(3) A bank may certify a check before returning it for lack of proper indorsement. If it does so the drawer is discharged.

§3-412. Acceptance Varying Draft.

(1) Where the drawee's proffered acceptance in any manner varies the draft as presented the holder may refuse the acceptance and treat the draft as dis-

honored in which case the drawee is entitled to have his acceptance cancelled.

(2) The terms of the draft are not varied by an acceptance to pay at any particular bank or place in the United States, unless the acceptance states that the draft is to be paid only at such bank or place.

(3) Where the holder assents to an acceptance varying the terms of the draft each drawer and indorser who does not affirmatively assent is discharged. As amended 1962.

§3-413. Contract of Maker, Drawer and Acceptor.

(1) The maker or acceptor engages that he will pay the instrument according to its tenor at the time of his engagement or as completed pursuant to Section 3-115 on incomplete instruments.

(2) The drawer engages that upon dishonor of the draft and any necessary notice of dishonor or protest he will pay the amount of the draft to the holder or to any indorser who takes it up. The drawer may disclaim this liability by drawing without recourse.

(3) By making, drawing or accepting the party admits as against all subsequent parties including the drawee the existence of the payee and his then capacity to indorse.

§3-414. Contract of Indorser; Order of Liability.

(1) Unless the indorsement otherwise specifies (as by such words as "without recourse") every indorser engages that upon dishonor and any necessary notice of dishonor and protest he will pay the instrument according to its tenor at the time of his indorsement to the holder or to any subsequent indorser who takes it up, even though the indorser who takes it up was not obligated to do so.

(2) Unless they otherwise agree indorsers are liable to one another in the order in which they indorse, which is presumed to be the order in which their signatures appear on the instrument.

§3-415. Contract of Accommodation Party.

(1) An accommodation party is one who signs the instrument in any capacity for the purpose of lending his name to another party to it.

(2) When the instrument has been taken for value before it is due the accommodation party is liable in the capacity in which he has signed even though the taker knows of the accommodation.

(3) As against a holder in due course and without notice of the accommodation oral proof of the accommodation is not admissible to give the accommodation party the benefit of discharges dependent on his character as such. In other cases the accommodation character may be shown by oral proof.

(4) An indorsement which shows that it is not in the chain of title is notice of its accommodation character.

(5) An accommodation party is not liable to the

party accommodated, and if he pays the instrument has a right of recourse on the instrument against such party.

§3-416. Contract of Guarantor.

(1) "Payment guaranteed" or equivalent words added to a signature mean that the signer engages that if the instrument is not paid when due he will pay it according to its tenor without resort by the holder to any other party.

(2) "Collection guaranteed" or equivalent words added to a signature mean that the signer engages that if the instrument is not paid when due he will pay it according to its tenor, but only after the holder has reduced his claim against the maker or acceptor to judgment and execution has been returned unsatisfied, or after the maker or acceptor has become insolvent or it is otherwise apparent that it is useless to proceed against him.

(3) Words of guaranty which do not otherwise specify guarantee payment.

(4) No words of guaranty added to the signature of a sole maker or acceptor affect his liability on the instrument. Such words added to the signature of one of two or more makers or acceptors create a presumption that the signature is for the accommodation of the others.

(5) When words of guaranty are used presentment, notice of dishonor and protest are not necessary to charge the user.

(6) Any guaranty written on the instrument is enforcible notwithstanding any statute of frauds.

§3-417. Warranties on Presentment and Transfer.

(1) Any person who obtains payment or acceptance and any prior transferor warrants to a person who in good faith pays or accepts that

(a) he has a good title to the instrument or is authorized to obtain payment or acceptance on behalf of one who has a good title; and

(b) he has no knowledge that the signature of the maker or drawer is unauthorized, except that this warranty is not given by a holder in due course acting in good faith

    (i) to a maker with respect to the maker's own signature; or

    (ii) to a drawer with respect to the drawer's own signature, whether or not the drawer is also the drawee; or

    (iii) to an acceptor of a draft if the holder in due course took the draft after the acceptance or obtained the acceptance without knowledge that the drawer's signature was unauthorized; and

(c) the instrument has not been materially altered, except that this warranty is not given by a holder in due course acting in good faith

    (i) to the maker of a note; or

    (ii) to the drawer of a draft whether or not the drawer is also the drawee; or

    (iii) to the acceptor of a draft with respect to an alteration made prior to the acceptance if the holder in due course took the draft after the acceptance, even though the acceptance provided "payable as originally drawn" or equivalent terms; or

    (iv) to the acceptor of a draft with respect to an alteration made after the acceptance.

(2) Any person who transfers an instrument and receives consideration warrants to his transferee and if the transfer is by indorsement to any subsequent holder who takes the instrument in good faith that

(a) he has a good title to the instrument or is authorized to obtain payment or acceptance on behalf of one who has a good title and the transfer is otherwise rightful; and

(b) all signatures are genuine or authorized; and

(c) the instrument has not been materially altered; and

(d) no defense of any party is good against him; and

(e) he has no knowledge of any insolvency proceeding instituted with respect to the maker or acceptor or the drawer of an unaccepted instrument.

(3) By transferring "without recourse" the transferor limits the obligation stated in subsection (2)(d) to a warranty that he has no knowledge of such a defense.

(4) A selling agent or broker who does not disclose the fact that he is acting only as such gives the warranties provided in this section, but if he makes such disclosure warrants only his good faith and authority.

§3-418. Finality of Payment or Acceptance.

Except for recovery of bank payments as provided in the Article on Bank Deposits and Collections (Article 4) and except for liability for breach of warranty on presentment under the preceding section, payment or acceptance of any instrument is final in favor of a holder in due course, or a person who has in good faith changed his position in reliance on the payment.

§3-419. Conversion of Instrument; Innocent Representative.

(1) An instrument is converted when

(a) a drawee to whom it is delivered for acceptance refuses to return it on demand; or

(b) any person to whom it is delivered for payment refuses on demand either to pay or to return it; or

(c) it is paid on a forged indorsement.

(2) In an action against a drawee under subsection (1) the measure of the drawee's liability is the face amount of the instrument. In any other action under subsection (1) the measure of liability is presumed to be the face amount of the instrument.

(3) Subject to the provisions of this Act concerning restrictive indorsements a representative, including a depositary or collecting bank, who has in good faith and in accordance with the reasonable commercial standards applicable to the business of such representative dealt with an instrument or its proceeds on behalf of one who was not the true owner is not liable in conversion or otherwise to the true owner beyond the amount of any proceeds remaining in his hands.

(4) An intermediary bank or payor bank which is not a depositary bank is not liable in conversion solely by reason of the fact that proceeds of an item indorsed restrictively (Sections 3-205 and 3-206) are not paid or applied consistently with the restrictive indorsement of an indorser other than its immediate transferor.

Part 5: Presentment, Notice of Dishonor, and Protest.

§3-501. When Presentment, Notice of Dishonor, and Protest Necessary or Permissible.

(1) Unless excused (Section 3-511) presentment is necessary to charge secondary parties as follows:

(a) presentment for acceptance is necessary to charge the drawer and indorsers of a draft where the draft so provides, or is payable elsewhere than at the residence or place of business of the drawee, or its date of payment depends upon such presentment. The holder may at his option present for acceptance any other draft payable at a stated date;

(b) presentment for payment is necessary to charge any indorser;

(c) in the case of any drawer, the acceptor of a draft payable at a bank or the maker of a note payable at a bank, presentment for payment is necessary, but failure to make presentment discharges such drawer, acceptor or maker only as stated in Section 3-502(1)(b).

(2) Unless excused (Section 3-511)

(a) notice of any dishonor is necessary to charge any indorser;

(b) in the case of any drawer, the acceptor of a draft payable at a bank or the maker of a note payable at a bank, notice of any dishonor is necessary, but failure to give such notice discharges such drawer, acceptor or maker only as stated in Section 3-502(1)(b).

(3) Unless excused (Section 3-511) protest of any dishonor is necessary to charge the drawer and indorsers of any draft which on its face appears to be drawn or payable outside of the states, territories, dependencies and possessions of the United States, the District of Columbia and the commonwealth of Puerto Rico. The holder may at his option make protest of any dishonor of any other instrument and in the case of a foreign draft may on insolvency of the acceptor before maturity make protest for better security.

(4) Notwithstanding any provision of this section, neither presentment nor notice of dishonor nor protest is necessary to charge an indorser who has indorsed an instrument after maturity. As amended 1966.

§3-502. Unexcused Delay; Discharge.

(1) Where without excuse any necessary presentment or notice of dishonor is delayed beyond the time when it is due

(a) any indorser is discharged; and

(b) any drawer or the acceptor of a draft payable at a bank or the maker of a note payable at a bank who because the drawee or payor bank becomes insolvent during the delay is deprived of funds maintained with the drawee or payor bank to cover the instrument may discharge his liability by written assignment to the holder of his rights against the drawee or payor bank in respect of such funds, but such drawer, acceptor or maker is not otherwise discharged.

(2) Where without excuse a necessary protest is delayed beyond the time when it is due any drawer or indorser is discharged.

§3-503. Time of Presentment.

(1) Unless a different time is expressed in the instrument the time for any presentment is determined as follows:

(a) where an instrument is payable at or a fixed period after a stated date any presentment for acceptance must be made on or before the date it is payable;

(b) where an instrument is payable after sight it must either be presented for acceptance or negotiated within a reasonable time after date or issue whichever is later;

(c) where an instrument shows the date on which it is payable presentment for payment is due on that date;

(d) where an instrument is accelerated presentment for payment is due within a reasonable time after the acceleration;

(e) with respect to the liablility of any secondary party presentment for acceptance or payment of any other instrument is due within a reasonable time after such party becomes liable thereon.

(2) A reasonable time for presentment is determined by the nature of the instrument, any usage of banking or trade and the facts of the particular case. In the case of an uncertified check which is drawn and payable within the United States and which is not a draft drawn by a bank the following are presumed to be reasonable periods within which to present for payment or to initate bank collection:

(a) with respect to the liability of the drawer, thirty days after date or issue whichever is later; and

(b) with respect to the liability of an indorser, seven days after his indorsement.

(3) Where any presentment is due on a day which is not a full business day for either the person making presentment or the party to pay or accept, presentment is due on the next following day which is a full business day for both parties.

(4) Presentment to be sufficient must be made at a reasonable hour, and if at a bank during its banking day.

§3-504. How Presentment Made.

(1) Presentment is a demand for acceptance or payment made upon the maker, acceptor, drawee or other payor by or on behalf of the holder.

(2) Presentment may be made

(a) by mail, in which event the time of presentment is determined by the time of receipt of the mail; or

(b) through a clearing house; or

(c) at the place of acceptance or payment specified in the instrument or if there be none at the place of business or residence of the party to accept or pay. If neither the party to accept or pay nor anyone authorized to act for him is present or accessible at such place presentment is excused.

(3) It may be made

(a) to any one of two or more makers, acceptors, drawees or other payor; or

(b) to any person who has authority to make or refuse the acceptance or payment.

(4) A draft accepted or a note made payable at a bank in the United States must be presented at such bank.

(5) In the cases described in Section 4-210 presentment may be made in the manner and with the result stated in that section. As amended 1962.

§3-505. Rights of Party to Whom Presentment Is Made.

(1) The party to whom presentment is made may without dishonor require

(a) exhibition of the instrument; and

(b) reasonable identification of the person making presentment and evidence of his authority to make it if made for another; and

(c) that the instrument be produced for acceptance or payment at a place specified in it, or if there be none at any place reasonable in the circumstances; and

(d) a signed receipt on the instrument for any partial or full payment and its surrender upon full payment.

(2) Failure to comply with any such requirement invalidates the presentment but the person presenting has a reasonable time in which to comply and the time for acceptance or payment runs from the time of compliance.

§3-506. Time Allowed For Acceptance or Payment.

(1) Acceptance may be deferred without dishonor until the close of the next business day following presentment. The holder may also in a good faith effort to obtain acceptance and without either dishonor of the instrument or discharge of secondary parties allow postponement of acceptance for an additional business day.

(2) Except as a longer time is allowed in the case of documentary drafts drawn under a letter of credit, and unless an earlier time is agreed to by the party to pay, payment of an instrument may be deferred without dishonor pending reasonable examination to determine whether it is properly payable, but payment must be made in any event before the close of business on the day of presentment.

§3-507. Dishonor; Holder's Right of Recourse; Term Allowing Re-Presentment.

(1) An instrument is dishonored when

(a) a necessary or optional presentment is duly made and due acceptance or payment is refused or cannot be obtainedwithin the prescribed time or in case of bank collections the instrument is seasonably returned by the midnight deadline (Section 4-301); or

(b) presentment is excused and the instrument is not duly accepted or paid.

(2) Subject to any necessary notice of dishonor and protest, the holder has upon dishonor an immediate right of recourse against the drawers and indorsers.

(3) Return of an instrument for lack of proper indorsement is not dishonor.

(4) A term in a draft or an indorsement thereof allowing a stated time for re-presentment in the event of any dishonor of the draft by nonacceptance if a time draft or by nonpayment if a sight draft gives the holder as against any secondary party bound by the term an option to waive the dishonor without affecting the liability of the secondary party and he may present again up to the end of the stated time.

§3-508. Notice of Dishonor.

(1) Notice of dishonor may be given to any person who may be liable on the instrument by or on behalf of the holder or any party who has himself received notice, or any other party who can be compelled to pay the instrument. In addition an agent or bank in whose hands the instrument is dishonored may give notice to his principal or customer or to another agent or bank from which the instrument was received.

(2) Any necessary notice must be given by a bank before its midnight deadline and by any other person before midnight of the third business day after dishonor or receipt of notice of dishonor.

(3) Notice may be given in any reasonable manner. It may be oral or written and in any terms which identify the instrument and state that it has been dishonored. A misdescription which does not mislead the party notified does not vitiate the notice. Sending the instrument bearing a stamp, ticket or writing stating that acceptance or payment has been refused or sending a notice of debit with respect to the instrument is sufficient.

(4) Written notice is given when sent although it is not received.

(5) Notice to one partner is notice to each although the firm has been dissloved.

(6) When any party is in insolvency proceedings instituted after the issue of the instrument notice may be given either to the party or to the representative of his estate.

(7) When any party is dead or incompetent notice may be sent to his last known address or given to his personal representative.

(8) Notice operates for the benefit of all parties who have rights on the instrument against the party notified.

§3-509. Protest; Noting for Protest.

(1) A protest is a certificate of dishonor made under the hand and seal of a United States consul or vice consul or a notary public or other person authorized to certify dishonor by the law of the place where dishonor occurs. It may be made upon information satisfactory to such person.

(2) The protest must identify the instrument and certify either that due presentment has been made or the reason why it is excused and that the instrument has been dishonored by nonacceptance or nonpayment.

(3) The protest may also certify that notice of dishonor has been given to all parties or to specified parties.

(4) Subject to subsection(5) any necessary protest is due by the time that notice of dishonor is due.

(5) If, before protest is due, an instrument has been noted for protest by the officer to make protest, the protest may be made at any time thereafter as of the date of the noting.

§3-510. Evidence of Dishonor and Notice of Dishonor.
The following are admissible as evidence and create a presumption of dishonor and of any notice of dishonor therein shown:

(a) a document regular in form as provided in the preceding section which purports to be a protest;

(b) the purported stamp or writing of the drawee, payor bank or presenting bank on the instrument or accompanying it stating that acceptance or payment has been refused for reasons consistent withdishonor:

(c) any book or record of the drawee, payor bank, or any collecting bank kept in the usual course of business which shows dishonor, even though there is no evidence of who made the entry.

§3-511. Waived or Excused Presentment, Protest or Notice of Dishonor or Delay Therein.

(1) Delay in presentment, protest or notice of dishonor is excused when the party is without notice that it is due or when the delay is caused by circumstances beyond his control and he exercises reasonable diligence after the cause of the delay ceases to operate.

(2) Presentment or notice or protest as the case may be is entirely excused when

(a) the party to be charged has waived it expressly or by implication either before or after it is due; or

(b) such party has himself dishonored the instrument or has countermanded payment or otherwise has no reason to expect or right to require that the instrument be accepted or paid; or

(c) by reasonable diligence the presentment or protest cannot be made or the notice given.

(3) Presentment is also entirely excused when

(a) the maker, acceptor or drawee of any instrument except a documentary draft is dead or in insolvency proceedings instituted after the issue of the instrument; or

(b) acceptance or payment is refused but not for want of proper presentment.

(4) Where a draft has been dishonored by nonacceptance a later presentment for payment and any notice of dishonor and protest for nonpayment are excused unless in the meantime the instrument has been accepted.

(5) A waiver of protest is also a waiver of presentment and of notice of dishonor even though protest is not required.

(6) Where a waiver of presentment or notice of

protest is embodied in the instrument itself it is binding upon all parties; but where it is written above the signature of an indorser it binds him only.

Part 6: Discharge

§3-601. Discharge of Parties.

(1) The extent of the discharge of any party from liability on an instrument is governed by the sections on

    (a) payment or satisfaction (Section 3-603); or

    (b) tender of payment (Section 3-604); or

    (c) cancellation or renunciation (Section 3-605); or

    (d) impairment of right of recourse or of collateral (Section 3-606); or

    (e) reacquisition of the instrument by a prior party (Section 3-208); or

    (f) fraudulent and material alteration (Section 3-407); or

    (g) certification of a check (Section 3-411); or

    (h) acceptance varying a draft (Section 3-412); or

    (i) unexcused delay in presentment or notice of dishonor or protest (Section 3-502).

(2) Any party is also discharged from his liability on an instrument to another party by any other act or agreement with such party which would discharge his simple contract for the payment of money.

(3) The liability of all parties is discharged when any party who has himself no right of action or recourse on the instrument

    (a) reacquires the instrument in his own right; or

    (b) is discharged under any provision of this Article, except as otherwise provided with respect to discharge for impairment of recourse or of collateral (Section 3-606).

§3-602. Effect of Discharge Against Holder in Due Course.
No discharge of any party provided by this Article is effective against a subsequent holder in due course unless he has notice thereof when he takes the instrument.

§3-603. Payment or Satisfaction.

(1) The liability of any party is discharged to the extent of his payment or satisfaction to the holder even though it is made with knowledge of a claim of another person to the instrument unless prior to such payment or satisfaction the person making the claim either supplies indemnity deemed adequate by the party seeking the discharge or enjoins payment or satisfaction by order of a court of competent jurisdiction in an action in which the adverse claimant and the holder are parties. This subsection does not, however, result in the discharge of the liability

    (a) of a party who in bad faith pays or satisfies a

holder who acquired the instrument by theft or who (unless having the rights of a holder in due course) holds through one who so acquired it; or

    (b) of a party (other than an intermediary bank or a payor bank which is not a depositary bank) who pays or satisfies the holder of an instrument which has been restrictively indorsed in a manner not consistent with the terms of such restrictive indorsement.

(2) Payment or satisfaction may be made with the consent of the holder by any person including a stranger to the instrument. Surrender of the instrument to such a person gives him the rights of a transferee (Section 3-201).

§3-604. Tender of Payment.

(1) Any party making tender of full payment to a holder when or after it is due is discharged to the extent of all subsequent liability for interest, costs and attorney's fees.

(2) The holder's refusal of such tender wholly discharges any party who has a right of recourse against the party making the tender.

(3) Where the maker or acceptor of an instrument payable otherwise than on demand is able and ready to pay at every place of payment specified in the instrument when it is due, it is equivalent to tender.

§3-605. Cancellation and Renunciation.

(1) The holder of an instrument may even without consideration discharge any party

    (a) in any manner apparent on the face of the instrument or the indorsement, as by intentionally cancelling the instrument or the party's signature by destruction or mutilation, or by striking out the party's signature; or

    (b) by renouncing his rights by a writing signed and delivered or by surrender of the instrument to the party to be discharged.

(2) Neither cancellation or renunciation without surrender of the instrument affects the title thereto.

§3-606. Impairment of Recourse or of Collateral.

(1) The holder discharges any party to the instrument to the extent that without such party's consent the holder

    (a) without express reservation of rights releases or agrees not to sue any person against whom the party has to the knowledge of the holder a right of recourse or agrees to suspend the right to enforce against such person the instrument or collateral or otherwise discharges such person, except that failure or delay in effecting any required presentment, protest or notice of dishonor with respect to any such person does not discharge any party as to whom presentment, protest or notice of dishonor is effective or unnecessary; or

(b) unjustifiably impairs any collateral for the instrument given by or on behalf of the party or any person against whom he has a right of recourse.

(2) By express reservation of rights against a party with a right of recourse the holder preserves

(a) all his rights against such party as of the time when the instrument was originally due; and

(b) the right of the party to pay the instrument as of that time; and

(c) all rights of such party to recourse against others.

Part 7: Advice of International Sight Draft

§3-701. Letter of Advice of International Sight Draft.

(1) A "letter of advice" is a drawer's communication to the drawee that a described draft has been drawn.

(2) Unless otherwise agreed when a bank receives from another bank a letter of advice of an international sight draft the drawee bank may immediately debit the drawer's account and stop the running of interest pro tanto. Such a debit and any resulting credit to any account covering outstanding drafts leaves in the drawer full power to stop payment or otherwise dispose of the amount and creates no trust or interest in favor of the holder.

(3) Unless otherwise agreed and except where a draft is drawn under a credit issued by the drawee of an international sight draft owes the drawer no duty to pay an unadvised draft but if it does so and the draft is genuine, may appropriately debit the drawer's account.

Part 8: Miscellaneous

§3-801. Drafts in a Set.

(1) Where a draft is drawn in a set of parts, each of which is numbered and expressed to be an order only if no other part has been honored, the whole of the parts constitutes one draft but a taker of any part may become a holder in due course of the draft.

(2) Any person who negotiates, indorses or accepts a single part of a draft drawn in a set thereby becomes liable to any holder in due course of that part as if it were the whole set, but as between different holders in due course to whom different parts have been negotiated the holder whose title first accrues has all rights to the draft and its proceeds.

(3) As against the drawee the first presented part of a draft drawn in a set is the part entitled to payment,

or if a time draft to acceptance and payment. Acceptance of any subsequently presented part renders the drawee liable thereon under subsection (2). With respect both to a holder and to the drawer payment of a subsequently presented part of a draft payable at sight has the same effect as payment of a check notwithstanding an effective stop order (Section 4-407).

(4) Except as otherwise provided in this section, where any part of a draft in a set is discharged by payment or otherwise the whole draft is discharged.

§3-802. Effect of Instrument on Obligation for which It Is Given.

(1) Unless otherwise agreed where an instrument is taken for an underlying obligation

(a) the obligation is pro tanto discharged if a bank is drawer, maker or acceptor of the instrument and there is no recourse on the instrument against the underlying obligor; and

(b) in any other case the obligation is suspended pro tanto until the instrument is due or if it is payable on demand until its presentment. If the instrument is dishonored action may be maintained on either the instrument or the obligation; discharge of the underlying obligor on the instrument also discharges him on the obligation.

(2) The taking in good faith of a check which is not postdated does not of itself so extend the time on the original obligation as to discharge a surety.

§3-803. Notice to Third Party.
Where a defendant is sued for breach of an obligation for which a third person is answerable over under this Article he may give the third person written notice of the litigation, and the person notified may then give similar notice to any other person who is answerable over to him under this Article. If the notice states that the person notified may come in and defend and that if the person notified does not do so he will in any action against him by the person giving the notice be bound by any determination of fact common to the two litigations, then unless after seasonable receipt of the notice the person notified does come in and defend he is so bound.

§3-804. Lost, Destroyed or Stolen Instruments.
The owner of an instrument which is lost, whether by destruction, theft or otherwise, may maintain an action in his own name and recover from any party liable thereon upon due proof of his ownership, the facts which prevent his production of the instrument and its terms. The court may require security indemnifying the defendant against loss by reason of further claims on the instrument.

§3-805. Instruments Not Payable to Order or to Bearer.
This Article applies to any instrument whose terms do not preclude transfer and which is otherwise

negotiable within this Article but which is not payable to order or to bearer, except that there can be no holder in due course of such an instrument.

REVISED ARTICLE 3: NEGOTIABLE INSTRUMENTS (1991 TEXT)

Part 1: General Provisions and Definitions

Rev. §3-101. Short Title. This Article may be cited as Uniform Commercial Code—Negotiable Instruments.

Rev. §3-102. Subject Matter.

(a) This Article applies to negotiable instruments. It does not apply to money, to payment orders governed by Article 4A, or to securities governed by Article 8.

(b) If there is conflict between this Article and Article 4 or 9, Articles 4 and 9 govern.

(c) Regulations of the Board of Governors of the Federal Reserve System and operating circulars of the Federal Reserve Banks supersede any inconsistent provision of this Article to the extent of the inconsistency.

Rev. §3-103. Definitions.

(a) In this Article:

(1) "Acceptor" means a drawee who has accepted a draft.

(2) "Drawee" means a person ordered in a draft to make payment.

(3) "Drawer" means a person who signs or is identified in a draft as a person ordering payment.

(4) "Good faith" means honesty in fact and the observance of reasonable commercial standards of fair dealing.

(5) "Maker" means a person who signs or is identified in a note as a person undertaking to pay.

(6) "Order" means a written instruction to pay money signed by the person giving the instruction. The instruction may be addressed to any person, including the person giving the instruction, or to one or more persons jointly or in the alternative but not in succession. An authorization to pay is not an order unless the person authorized to pay is also instructed to pay.

(7) "Ordinary care" in the case of a person engaged in business means observance of reasonable commercial standards, prevailing in the area in which the person is located, with respect to the business in which the person is engaged. In the case of a bank that takes an instrument for processing for collection or payment by automated means, reasonable commercial standards do not require the bank to examine the instrument if the failure to examine does not violate the bank's prescribed procedures and the bank's procedures do not vary unreasonably from general banking usage not disapproved by this Article or Article 4.

(8) "Party" means a party to an instrument.

(9) "Promise" means a written undertaking to pay money signed by the person undertaking to pay. An acknowledgment of an obligation by the obligor is not a promise unless the obligor also undertakes to pay the obligation.

(10) "Prove" with respect to a fact means to meet the burden of establishing the fact (Section 1-201(8)).

(11) "Remitter" means a person who purchases an instrument from its issuer if the instrument is payable to an identified person other than the purchaser.

(b) Other definitions applying to this Article and the sections in which they appear are:

"Acceptance"	Section 3-409
"Accommodated party"	Section 3-419
"Accommodation party"	Section 3-419
"Alteration"	Section 3-407
"Anomalous indorsement"	Section 3-205
"Blank indorsement"	Section 3-205
"Cashier's check"	Section 3-104
"Certificate of deposit"	Section 3-104
"Certified check"	Section 3-409
"Check"	Section 3-104
"Consideration"	Section 3-303
"Draft"	Section 3-104
"Holder in due course"	Section 3-302
"Incomplete instrument"	Section 3-115
"Indorsement"	Section 3-204
"Indorser"	Section 3-204
"Instrument"	Section 3-104
"Issue"	Section 3-105
"Issuer"	Section 3-105
"Negotiable instrument"	Section 3-104
"Negotiation"	Section 3-201
"Note"	Section 3-104
"Payable at a definite time"	Section 3-108
"Payable on demand"	Section 3-108
"Payable to bearer"	Section 3-109
"Payable to order"	Section 3-109
"Payment"	Section 3-602
"Person entitled to enforce"	Section 3-301
"Presentment"	Section 3-501
"Reacquisition"	Section 3-207
"Special indorsement"	Section 3-205
"Teller's check"	Section 3-104
"Transfer of instrument"	Section 3-203
"Traveler's check"	Section 3-104

"Value"   Section 3-303

(c) The following definitions in other Articles apply to this Article:

"Bank"	Section 4-105
"Banking day"	Section 4-104
"Clearing house"	Section 4-104
"Collecting bank"	Section 4-105
"Depositary bank"	Section 4-105
"Documentary draft"	Section 4-104
"Intermediary bank"	Section 4-105
"Item"	Section 4-104
"Payor bank"	Section 4-105
"Suspends payments"	Section 4-104

(d) In addition, Article 1 contains general definitions and principles of construction and interpretation applicable throughout this Article.

Rev. §3-104. Negotiable Instrument.

(a) Except as provided in subsections (c) and (d), "negotiable instrument" means an unconditional promise or order to pay a fixed amount of money, with or without interest or other charges described in the promise or order, if it:

(1) is payable to bearer or to order at the time it is issued or first comes into possession of a holder;

(2) is payable on demand or at a definite time; and

(3) does not state any other undertaking or instruction by the person promising or ordering payment to do any act in addition to the payment of money, but the promise or order may contain (i) an undertaking or power to give, maintain, or protect collateral to secure payment, (ii) an authorization or power to the holder to confess judgment or realize on or dispose of collateral, or (iii) a waiver of the benefit of any law intended for the advantage or protection of an obligor.

(b) "Instrument" means a negotiable instrument.

(c) An order that meets all of the requirements of subsection (a), except paragraph (1), and otherwise falls within the definition of "check" in subsection (f) is a negotiable instrument and a check.

(d) A promise or order other than a check is not an instrument if, at the time it is issued or first comes into possession of a holder, it contains a conspicuous statement, however expressed, to the effect that the promise or order is not negotiable or is not an instrument governed by this Article.

(e) An instrument is a "note" if it is a promise and is a "draft" if it is an order. If an instrument falls within the definition of both "note" and "draft," a person entitled to enforce the instrument may treat it as either.

(f) "Check" means (i) a draft, other than a documentary draft, payable on demand and drawn on a bank or (ii) a cashier's check or teller's check. An instrument may be a check even though it is described on its face by another term, such as "money order."

(g) "Cashier's check" means a draft with respect to which the drawer and drawee are the same bank or branches of the same bank.

(h) "Teller's check" means a draft drawn by a bank (i) on another bank, or (ii) payable at or through a bank.

(i) "Traveler's check" means an instrument that (i) is payable on demand, (ii) is drawn on or payable at or through a bank, (iii) is designated by the term "traveler's check" or by a substantially similar term, and (iv) requires, as a condition to payment, a countersignature by a person whose specimen signature appears on the instrument.

(j) "Certificate of deposit" means an instrument containing an acknowledgment by a bank that a sum of money has been received by the bank and a promise by the bank to repay the sum of money. A certificate of deposit is a note of the bank.

Rev. §3-105. Issue of Instrument.

(a) "Issue" means the first delivery of an instrument by the maker or drawer, whether to a holder or nonholder, for the purpose of giving rights on the instrument to any person.

(b) An unissued instrument, or an unissued incomplete instrument that is completed, is binding on the maker or drawer, but nonissuance is a defense. An instrument that is conditionally issued or is issued for a special purpose is binding on the maker or drawer, but failure of the condition or special purpose to be fulfilled is a defense.

(c) "Issuer" applies to issued and unissued instruments and means a maker or drawer of an instrument.

Rev. §3-106. Unconditional Promise or Order.

(a) Except as provided in this section, for the purposes of Section 3-104(a), a promise or order is unconditional unless it states (i) an express condition to payment, (ii) that the promise or order is subject to or governed by another writing, or (iii) that rights or obligations with respect to the promise or order are stated in another writing. A reference to another writing does not of itself make the promise or order conditional.

(b) A promise or order is not made conditional (i) by a reference to another writing for a statement of rights with respect to collateral, prepayment, or acceleration, or (ii) because payment is limited to resort to a particular fund or source.

(c) If a promise or order requires, as a condition to payment, a countersignature by a person whose specimen signature appears on the promise or order, the condition does not make the promise or order conditional for the purposes of Section 3-104(a). If the person whose specimen signature appears on an instrument fails to counter-sign the instrument, the failure to countersign is a defense to the obligation of the issuer, but the failure does not prevent a transferee of the instrument from becoming a holder of the instrument.

(d) If a promise or order at the time it is issued or first comes into possession of a holder contains a statement, required by applicable statutory or administrative law, to the effect that the rights of a holder or transferee are subject to claims or defenses that the issuer could assert against the original payee, the promise or order is not thereby made conditional for the purposes of Section 3-104(a); but if the promise or order is an instrument, there cannot be a holder in due course of the instrument.

Rev. §3-107. Instrument Payable in Foreign Money. Unless the instrument otherwise provides, an instrument that states the amount payable in foreign money may be paid in the foreign money or in an equivalent amount in dollars calculated by using the current bank-offered spot rate at the place of payment for the purchase of dollars on the day on which the instrument is paid.

Rev. §3-108. Payable on Demand or at Definite Time.

(a) A promise or order is "payable on demand" if it (i) states that it is payable on demand or at sight, or otherwise indicates that it is payable at the will of the holder, or (ii) does not state any time of payment.

(b) A promise or order is "payable at a definite time" if it is payable on elapse of a definite period of time after sight or acceptance or at a fixed date or dates or at a time or times readily ascertainable at the time the promise or order is issued, subject to rights of (i) prepayment, (ii) acceleration, (iii) extension at the option of the holder, or (iv) extension to a further definite time at the option of the maker or acceptor or automatically upon or after a specified act or event.

(c) If an instrument, payable at a fixed date, is also payable upon demand made before the fixed date, the instrument is payable on demand until the fixed date and, if demand for payment is not made before that date, becomes payable at a definite time on the fixed date.

Rev. §3-109. Payable to Bearer or to Order.

(a) A promise or order is payable to bearer if it:

(1) states that it is payable to bearer or to the order of bearer or otherwise indicates that the person in possession of the promise or order is entitled to payment;

(2) does not state a payee; or

(3) states that it is payable to or to the order of cash or otherwise indicates that it is not payable to an identified person.

(b) A promise or order that is not payable to bearer is payable to order if it is payable (i) to the

order of an identified person or (ii) to an identified person or order. A promise or order that is payable to order is payable to the identified person.

(c) An instrument payable to bearer may become payable to an identified person if it is specially indorsed pursuant to Section 3-205(a). An instrument payable to an identified person may become payable to bearer if it is indorsed in blank pursuant to Section 3-205(b).

Rev. §3-110. Identification of Person to Whom Instrument Is Payable.

(a) The person to whom an instrument is initially payable is determined by the intent of the person, whether or not authorized, signing as, or in the name or behalf of, the issuer of the instrument. The instrument is payable to the person intended by the signer even if that person is identified in the instrument by a name or other identification that is not that of the intended person. If more than one person signs in the name or behalf of the issuer of an instrument and all the signers do not intend the same person as payee, the instrument is payable to any person intended by one or more of the signers.

(b) If the signature of the issuer of an instrument is made by automated means, such as a check-writing machine, the payee of the instrument is determined by the intent of the person who supplied the name or identification of the payee, whether or not authorized to do so.

(c) A person to whom an instrument is payable may be identified in any way, including by name, identifying number, office, or account number. For the purpose of determining the holder of an instrument, the following rules apply:

(1) If an instrument is payable to an account and the account is identified only by number, the instrument is payable to the person to whom the account is payable. If an instrument is payable to an account identified by number and by the name of a person, the instrument is payable to the named person, whether or not that person is the owner of the account identified by number.

(2) If an instrument is payable to:

(i) a trust, an estate, or a person described as trustee or representative of a trust or estate, the instrument is payable to the trustee, the representative, or a successor of either, whether or not the beneficiary or estate is also named;

(ii) a person described as agent or similar representative of a named or identified person, the instrument is payable to the represented person, the representative, or a successor of the representative;

(**iii**) a fund or organization that is not a legal entity, the instrument is payable to a representative of the members of the fund or organization; or

(**iv**) an office or to a person described as holding an office, the instrument is payable to the named person, the incumbent of the office, or a successor to the incumbent.

(**d**) If an instrument is payable to two or more persons alternatively, it is payable to any of them and may be negotiated, discharged, or enforced by any or all of them in possession of the instrument. If an instrument is payable to two or more persons not alternatively, it is payable to all of them and may be negotiated, discharged, or enforced only by all of them. If an instrument payable to two or more persons is ambiguous as to whether it is payable to the persons alternatively, the instrument is payable to the persons alternatively.

Rev. §3-111. Place of Payment. Except as otherwise provided for items in Article 4, an instrument is payable at the place of payment stated in the instrument. If no place of payment is stated, an instrument is payable at the address of the drawee or maker stated in the instrument. If no address is stated, the place of payment is the place of business of the drawee or maker. If a drawee or maker has more than one place of business, the place of payment is any place of business of the drawee or maker chosen by the person entitled to enforce the instrument. If the drawee or maker has no place of business, the place of payment is the residence of the drawee or maker.

Rev. §3-112. Interest.

(**a**) Unless otherwise provided in the instrument, (i) an instrument is not payable with interest, and (ii) interest on an interest-bearing instrument is payable from the date of the instrument.

(**b**) Interest may be stated in an instrument as a fixed or variable amount of money or it may be expressed as a fixed or variable rate or rates. The amount or rate of interest may be stated or described in the instrument in any manner and may require reference to information not contained in the instrument. If an instrument provides for interest, but the amount of interest payable cannot be ascertained from the description, interest is payable at the judgment rate in effect at the place of payment of the instrument and at the time interest first accrues.

Rev. §3-113. Date of Instrument.

(**a**) An instrument may be antedated or postdated. The date stated determines the time of payment if the instrument is payable at a fixed period after date. Except as provided in Section 4-401(c), an instrument payable on demand is not payable before the date of the instrument.

(**b**) If an instrument is undated, its date is the date of its issue or, in the case of an unissued instrument, the date it first comes into possession of a holder.

Rev. §3-114. Contradictory Terms of Instrument. If an instrument contains contradictory terms, typewritten terms prevail over printed terms, handwritten terms prevail over both, and words prevail over numbers.

Rev. §3-115. Incomplete Instrument.

(**a**) "Incomplete instrument" means a signed writing, whether or not issued by the signer, the contents of which show at the time of signing that it is incomplete but that the signer intended it to be completed by the addition of words or numbers.

(**b**) Subject to subsection (c), if an incomplete instrument is an instrument under Section 3-104, it may be enforced according to its terms if it is not completed, or according to its terms as augmented by completion. If an incomplete instrument is not an instrument under Section 3-104, but, after completion, the requirements of Section 3-104 are met, the instrument may be enforced according to its terms as augmented by completion.

(**c**) If words or numbers are added to an incomplete instrument without authority of the signer, there is an alteration of the incomplete instrument under Section 3-407.

(**d**) The burden of establishing that words or numbers were added to an incomplete instrument without authority of the signer is on the person asserting the lack of authority.

Rev. §3-116. Joint and Several Liability; Contribution.

(**a**) Except as otherwise provided in the instrument, two or more persons who have the same liability on an instrument as makers, drawers, acceptors, indorsers who indorse as joint payees, or anomalous indorsers are jointly and severally liable in the capacity in which they sign.

(**b**) Except as provided in Section 3-419(e) or by agreement of the affected parties, a party having joint and several liability who pays the instrument is entitled to receive from any party having the same joint and several liability contribution in accordance with applicable law.

(**c**) Discharge of one party having joint and several liability by a person entitled to enforce the instrument does not affect the right under subsection (b) of a party having the same joint and several liability to receive contribution from the party discharged.

Rev. §3-117. Other Agreements Affecting Instrument. Subject to applicable law regarding exclusion of proof of contemporaneous or previous agreements, the obligation of a party to an instrument to pay the instrument may be modified, supplemented, or nullified by a separate agreement of the obligor and a person entitled to enforce the instrument, if the instrument is issued or the obligation is incurred in reliance on the agreement or as part of the same transaction giving rise to the agreement. To the extent an obligation is modified, supplemented, or nullified by an agreement under this section, the agreement is a defense to the obligation.

Rev. §3-118. Statute of Limitations.

(a) Except as provided in subsection (e), an action to enforce the obligation of a party to pay a note payable at a definite time must be commenced within six years after the due date or dates stated in the note or, if a due date is accelerated, within six years after the accelerated due date.

(b) Except as provided in subsection (d) or (e), if demand for payment is made to the maker of a note payable on demand, an action to enforce the obligation of a party to pay the note must be commenced within six years after the demand. If no demand for payment is made to the maker, an action to enforce the note is barred if neither principal nor interest on the note has been paid for a continuous period of 10 years.

(c) Except as provided in subsection (d), an action to enforce the obligation of a party to an unaccepted draft to pay the draft must be commenced within three years after dishonor of the draft or 10 years after the date of the draft, whichever period expires first.

(d) An action to enforce the obligation of the acceptor of a certified check or the issuer of a teller's check, cashier's check, or traveler's check must be commenced within three years after demand for payment is made to the acceptor or issuer, as the case may be.

(e) An action to enforce the obligation of a party to a certificate of deposit to pay the instrument must be commenced within six years after demand for payment is made to the maker, but if the instrument states a due date and the maker is not required to pay before that date, the six-year period begins when a demand for payment is in effect and the due date has passed.

(f) An action to enforce the obligation of a party to pay an accepted draft, other than a certified check, must be commenced (i) within six years after the due date or dates stated in the draft or acceptance if the obligation of the acceptor is payable at a definite time, or (ii) within six years after the date of the acceptance if the obligation of the acceptor is payable on demand.

(g) Unless governed by other law regarding claims for indemnity or contribution, an action (i) for conversion of an instrument, for money had and received, or like action based on conversion, (ii) for breach of warranty, or (iii) to enforce an obligation, duty, or right arising under this Article and not governed by this section must be commenced within three years after the [cause of action] accrues.

Rev. §3-119. Notice of Right to Defend Action.

In an action for breach of an obligation for which a third person is answerable over pursuant to this Article or Article 4, the defendant may give the third person written notice of the litigation, and the person notified may then give similar notice to any other person who is answerable over. If the notice states (i) that the person notified may come in and defend and (ii) that failure to do so will bind the person notified in an action later brought by the person giving the notice as to any determination of fact common to the two litigations, the person notified is so bound unless after seasonable receipt of the notice the person notified does come in and defend.

Part 2: Negotiation, Transfer, and Indorsement

Rev. §3-201. Negotiation.

(a) "Negotiation" means a transfer of possession, whether voluntary or involuntary, of an instrument by a person other than the issuer to a person who thereby becomes its holder.

(b) Except for negotiation by a remitter, if an instrument is payable to an identified person, negotiation requires transfer of possession of the instrument and its indorsement by the holder. If an instrument is payable to bearer, it may be negotiated by transfer of possession alone.

Rev. §3-202. Negotiation Subject to Rescission.

(a) Negotiation is effective even if obtained (i) from an infant, a corporation exceeding its powers, or a person without capacity, (ii) by fraud, duress, or mistake, or (iii) in breach of duty or as part of an illegal transaction.

(b) To the extent permitted by other law, negotiation may be rescinded or may be subject to other remedies, but those remedies may not be asserted against a subsequent holder in due course or a person paying the instrument in good faith and without knowledge of facts that are a basis for rescission or other remedy.

Rev. §3-203. Transfer of Instrument; Rights Acquired by Transfer.

(a) An instrument is transferred when it is delivered by a person other than its issuer for the purpose of giving to the person receiving delivery the right to enforce the instrument.

(b) Transfer of an instrument, whether or not the transfer is a negotiation, vests in the transferee any right of the transferor to enforce the instrument, including any right as a holder in due course, but the transferee cannot acquire rights of a holder in due course by a transfer, directly or indirectly, from a holder in due course if the transferee engaged in fraud or illegality affecting the instrument.

(c) Unless otherwise agreed, if an instrument is transferred for value and the transferee does not become a holder because of lack of indorsement by the transferor, the transferee has a specifically enforceable right to the unqualified indorsement of the transferor, but negotiation of the instrument does not occur until the indorsement is made.

(**d**) If a transferor purports to transfer less than the entire instrument, negotiation of the instrument does not occur. The transferee obtains no rights under this Article and has only the rights of a partial assignee.

Rev. §3-204. Indorsement.

(**a**) "Indorsement" means a signature, other than that of a signer as maker, drawer, or acceptor, that alone or accompanied by other words is made on an instrument for the purpose of (i) negotiating the instrument, (ii) restricting payment of the instrument, or (iii) incurring indorser's liability on the instrument, but regardless of the intent of the signer, a signature and its accompanying words is an indorsement unless the accompanying words, terms of the instrument, place of the signature, or other circumstances unambiguously indicate that the signature was made for a purpose other than indorsement. For the purpose of determining whether a signature is made on an instrument, a paper affixed to the instrument is a part of the instrument.

(**b**) "Indorser" means a person who makes an indorsement.

(**c**) For the purpose of determining whether the transferee of an instrument is a holder, an indorsement that transfers a security interest in the instrument is effective as an unqualified indorsement of the instrument.

(**d**) If an instrument is payable to a holder under a name that is not the name of the holder, indorsement may be made by the holder in the name stated in the instrument or in the holder's name or both, but signature in both names may be required by a person paying or taking the instrument for value or collection.

Rev. §3-205. Special Indorsement; Blank Indorsement; Anomalous Indorsement.

(**a**) If an indorsement is made by the holder of an instrument, whether payable to an identified person or payable to bearer, and the indorsement identifies a person to whom it makes the instrument payable, it is a "special indorsement." When specially indorsed, an instrument becomes payable to the identified person and may be negotiated only by the indorsement of that person. The principles stated in Section 3–110 apply to special indorsements.

(**b**) If an indorsement is made by the holder of an instrument and it is not a special indorsement, it is a "blank indorsement." When indorsed in blank, an instrument becomes payable to bearer and may be negotiated by transfer of possession alone until specially indorsed.

(**c**) The holder may convert a blank indorsement that consists only of a signature into a special indorse-

ment by writing, above the signature of the indorser, words identifying the person to whom the instrument is made payable.

(**d**) "Anomalous indorsement" means an indorsement made by a person who is not the holder of the instrument. An anomalous indorsement does not affect the manner in which the instrument may be negotiated.

Rev. §3-206. Restrictive Indorsement.

(**a**) An indorsement limiting payment to a particular person or otherwise prohibiting further transfer or negotiation of the instrument is not effective to prevent further transfer or negotiation of the instrument.

(**b**) An indorsement stating a condition to the right of the indorsee to receive payment does not affect the right of the indorsee to enforce the instrument. A person paying the instrument or taking it for value or collection may disregard the condition, and the rights and liabilities of that person are not affected by whether the condition has been fulfilled.

(**c**) If an instrument bears an indorsement (i) described in Section 4–201(b), or (ii) in blank or to a particular bank using the words "for deposit," "for collection," or other words indicating a purpose of having the instrument collected by a bank for the indorser or for a particular account, the following rules apply:

(**1**) A person, other than a bank, who purchases the instrument when so indorsed converts the instrument unless the amount paid for the instrument is received by the indorser or applied consistently with the indorsement.

(**2**) A depositary bank that purchases the instrument or takes it for collection when so indorsed converts the instrument unless the amount paid by the bank with respect to the instrument is received by the indorser or applied consistently with the indorsement.

(**3**) A payor bank that is also the depositary bank or that takes the instrument for immediate payment over the counter from a person other than a collecting bank converts the instrument unless the proceeds of the instrument are received by the indorser or applied consistently with the indorsement.

(**4**) Except as otherwise provided in paragraph (3), a payor bank or intermediary bank may disregard the indorsement and is not liable if the proceeds of the instrument are not received by the indorser or applied consistently with the indorsement.

(**d**) Except for an indorsement covered by subsection (c), if an instrument bears an indorsement using words to the effect that payment is to be made to the indorsee as agent, trustee, or other fiduciary for the benefit of the indorser or another person, the following rules apply:

(1) Unless there is notice of breach of fiduciary duty as provided in Section 3–307, a person who purchases the instrument from the indorsee or takes the instrument from the indorsee for collection or payment may pay the proceeds of payment or the value given for the instrument to the indorsee without regard to whether the indorsee violates a fiduciary duty to the indorser.

(2) A subsequent transferee of the instrument or person who pays the instrument is neither given notice nor otherwise affected by the restriction in the indorsement unless the transferee or payor knows that the fiduciary dealt with the instrument or its proceeds in breach of fiduciary duty.

(e) The presence on an instrument of an indorsement to which this section applies does not prevent a purchaser of the instrument from becoming a holder in due course of the instrument unless the purchaser is a converter under subsection (c) or has notice or knowledge of breach of fiduciary duty as stated in subsection (d).

(f) In an action to enforce the obligation of a party to pay the instrument, the obligor has a defense if payment would violate an indorsement to which this section applies and the payment is not permitted by this section.

Rev. §3–207. Reacquisition. Reacquisition of an instrument occurs if it is transferred to a former holder, by negotiation or otherwise. A former holder who reacquires the instrument may cancel indorsements made after the reacquirer first became a holder of the instrument. If the cancellation causes the instrument to be payable to the reacquirer or to bearer, the reacquirer may negotiate the instrument. An indorser whose indorsement is canceled is discharged, and the discharge is effective against any subsequent holder.

Part 3: Enforcement of Instruments

Rev. §3–301. Person Entitled to Enforce Instrument. "Person entitled to enforce" an instrument means (i) the holder of the instrument, (ii) a nonholder in possession of the instrument who has the rights of a holder, or (iii) a person not in possession of the instrument who is entitled to enforce the instrument pursuant to Section 3–309 or 3–418(d). A person may be a person entitled to enforce the instrument even though the person is not the owner of the instrument or is in wrongful possession of the instrument.

Rev. §3–302. Holder in Due Course.

(a) Subject to subsection (c) and Section 3–106(d), "holder in due course" means the holder of an instrument if:

(1) the instrument when issued or negotiated to the holder does not bear such apparent evidence of forgery or alteration or is not otherwise so irregular or incomplete as to call into question its authenticity; and

(2) the holder took the instrument (i) for value, (ii) in good faith, (iii) without notice that the instrument is overdue or has been dishonored or that there is an uncured default with respect to payment of another instrument issued as part of the same series, (iv) without notice that the instrument contains an unauthorized signature or has been altered, (v) without notice of any claim to the instrument described in Section 3–306, and (vi) without notice that any party has a defense or claim in recoupment described in Section 3–305(a).

(b) Notice of discharge of a party, other than discharge in an insolvency proceeding, is not notice of a defense under subsection (a), but discharge is effective against a person who became a holder in due course with notice of the discharge. Public filing or recording of a document does not of itself constitute notice of a defense, claim in recoupment, or claim to the instrument.

(c) Except to the extent a transferor or predecessor in interest has rights as a holder in due course, a person does not acquire rights of a holder in due course of an instrument taken (i) by legal process or by purchase in an execution, bankruptcy, or creditor's sale or similar proceeding, (ii) by purchase as part of a bulk transaction not in ordinary course of business of the transferor, or (iii) as the successor in interest to an estate or other organization.

(d) If, under Section 3–303(a)(1), the promise of performance that is the consideration for an instrument has been partially performed, the holder may assert rights as a holder in due course of the instrument only to the fraction of the amount payable under the instrument equal to the value of the partial performance divided by the value of the promised performance.

(e) If (i) the person entitled to enforce an instrument has only a security interest in the instrument and (ii) the person obliged to pay the instrument has a defense, claim in recoupment, or claim to the instrument that may be asserted against the person who granted the security interest, the person entitled to enforce the instrument may assert rights as a holder in due course only to an amount payable under the instrument which, at the time of enforcement of the instrument, does not exceed the amount of the unpaid obligation secured.

(f) To be effective, notice must be received at a time and in a manner that gives a reasonable opportunity to act on it.

(g) This section is subject to any law limiting status as a holder in due course in particular classes of transactions.

Rev. §3–303. Value and Consideration.

(a) An instrument is issued or transferred for value if:

(1) the instrument is issued or transferred for a promise of performance, to the extent the promise has been performed;

(2) the transferee acquires a security interest or other lien in the instrument other than a lien obtained by judicial proceeding;

(3) the instrument is issued or transferred as payment of, or as security for, an antecedent claim against any person, whether or not the claim is due;

(4) the instrument is issued or transferred in exchange for a negotiable instrument; or

(5) the instrument is issued or transferred in exchange for the incurring of an irrevocable obligation to a third party by the person taking the instrument.

(b) "Consideration" means any consideration sufficient to support a simple contract. The drawer or maker of an instrument has a defense if the instrument is issued without consideration. If an instrument is issued for a promise of performance, the issuer has a defense to the extent performance of the promise is due and the promise has not been performed. If an instrument is issued for value as stated in subsection (a), the instrument is also issued for consideration.

Rev. §3–304. Overdue Instrument.

(a) An instrument payable on demand becomes overdue at the earliest of the following times:

(1) on the day after the day demand for payment is duly made;

(2) if the instrument is a check, 90 days after its date; or

(3) if the instrument is not a check, when the instrument has been outstanding for a period of time after its date which is unreasonably long under the circumstances of the particular case in light of the nature of the instrument and usage of the trade.

(b) With respect to an instrument payable at a definite time the following rules apply:

(1) If the principal is payable in installments and a due date has not been accelerated, the instrument becomes overdue upon default under the instrument for nonpayment of an installment, and the instrument remains overdue until the default is cured.

(2) If the principal is not payable in installments and the due date has not been accelerated, the instrument becomes overdue on the day after the due date.

(3) If a due date with respect to principal has been accelerated, the instrument becomes overdue on the day after the accelerated due date.

(c) Unless the due date of principal has been accelerated, an instrument does not become overdue if there is default in payment of interest but no default in payment of principal.

Rev. §3–305. Defenses and Claims in Recoupment.

(a) Except as stated in subsection (b), the right to enforce the obligation of a party to pay an instrument is subject to the following:

(1) a defense of the obligor based on (i) infancy of the obligor to the extent it is a defense to a simple contract, (ii) duress, lack of legal capacity, or illegality of the transaction which, under other law, nullifies the obligation of the obligor, (iii) fraud that induced the obligor to sign the instrument with neither knowledge nor reasonable opportunity to learn of its character or its essential terms, or (iv) discharge of the obligor in insolvency proceedings;

(2) a defense of the obligor stated in another section of this Article or a defense of the obligor that would be available if the person entitled to enforce the instrument were enforcing a right to payment under a simple contract; and

(3) a claim in recoupment of the obligor against the original payee of the instrument if the claim arose from the transaction that gave rise to the instrument; but the claim of the obligor may be asserted against a transferee of the instrument only to reduce the amount owing on the instrument at the time the action is brought.

(b) The right of a holder in due course to enforce the obligation of a party to pay the instrument is subject to defenses of the obligor stated in subsection (a)(1), but is not subject to defenses of the obligor stated in subsection (a)(2) or claims in recoupment stated in subsection (a)(3) against a person other than the holder.

(c) Except as stated in subsection (d), in an action to enforce the obligation of a party to pay the instrument, the obligor may not assert against the person entitled to enforce the instrument a defense, claim in recoupment, or claim to the instrument (Section 3–306) of another person, but the other person's claim to the instrument may be asserted by the obligor if the other person is joined in the action and personally asserts the claim against the person entitled to enforce the instrument. An obligor is not obliged to pay the instrument if the person seeking enforcement of the instrument does not have rights of a holder in due course and the obligor proves that the instrument is a lost or stolen instrument.

(d) In an action to enforce the obligation of an accommodation party to pay an instrument, the accommodation party may assert against the person entitled to enforce the instrument any defense or claim in recoupment under subsection (a) that the accommodated party could assert against the person entitled to enforce the instrument, except the defenses of discharge in insolvency proceedings, infancy, and lack of legal capacity.

Rev. §3–306. Claims to an Instrument. A person taking an instrument, other than a person having rights of a holder in due course, is subject to a claim of a property or possessory right in the instrument or its proceeds, including a claim to rescind a negotiation and to recover the instrument or its proceeds. A person having rights of a holder in due course takes free of the claim to the instrument.

Rev. §3–307. Notice of Breach of Fiduciary Duty.

(a) In this section:

(1) "Fiduciary" means an agent, trustee, partner, corporate officer or director, or other representative owing a fiduciary duty with respect to an instrument.

(2) "Represented person" means the principal, beneficiary, partnership, corporation, or other person to whom the duty stated in paragraph (1) is owed.

(b) If (i) an instrument is taken from a fiduciary for payment or collection or for value, (ii) the taker has knowledge of the fiduciary status of the fiduciary, and (iii) the represented person makes a claim to the instrument or its proceeds on the basis that the transaction of the fiduciary is a breach of fiduciary duty, the following rules apply:

(1) Notice of breach of fiduciary duty by the fiduciary is notice of the claim of the represented person.

(2) In the case of an instrument payable to the represented person or the fiduciary as such, the taker has notice of the breach of fiduciary duty if the instrument is (i) taken in payment of or as security for a debt known by the taker to be the personal debt of the fiduciary, (ii) taken in a transaction known by the taker to be for the personal benefit of the fiduciary, or (iii) deposited to an account other than an account of the fiduciary, as such, or an account of the represented person.

(3) If an instrument is issued by the represented person or the fiduciary as such, and made payable to the fiduciary personally, the taker does not have notice of the breach of fiduciary duty unless the taker knows of the breach of fiduciary duty.

(4) If an instrument is issued by the represented person or the fiduciary as such, to the taker as

payee, the taker has notice of the breach of fiduciary duty if the instrument is (i) taken in payment of or as security for a debt known by the taker to be the personal debt of the fiduciary, (ii) taken in a transaction known by the taker to be for the personal benefit of the fiduciary, or (iii) deposited to an account other than an account of the fiduciary, as such, or an account of the represented person.

Rev. §3–308. Proof of Signatures and Status as Holder in Due Course.

(a) In an action with respect to an instrument, the authenticity of, and authority to make, each signature on the instrument is admitted unless specifically denied in the pleadings. If the validity of a signature is denied in the pleadings, the burden of establishing validity is on the person claiming validity, but the signature is presumed to be authentic and authorized unless the action is to enforce the liability of the purported signer and the signer is dead or incompetent at the time of trial of the issue of validity of the signature. If an action to enforce the instrument is brought against a person as the undisclosed principal of a person who signed the instrument as a party to the instrument, the plaintiff has the burden of establishing that the defendant is liable on the instrument as a represented person under Section 3–402(a).

(b) If the validity of signatures is admitted or proved and there is compliance with subsection (a), a plaintiff producing the instrument is entitled to payment if the plaintiff proves entitlement to enforce the instrument under Section 3–301, unless the defendant proves a defense or claim in recoupment. If a defense or claim in recoupment is proved, the right to payment of the plaintiff is subject to the defense or claim, except to the extent the plaintiff proves that the plaintiff has rights of a holder in due course which are not subject to the defense or claim.

Rev. §3–309. Enforcement of Lost, Destroyed, or Stolen Instrument.

(a) A person not in possession of an instrument is entitled to enforce the instrument if (i) the person was in possession of the instrument and entitled to enforce it when loss of possession occurred, (ii) the loss of possession was not the result of a transfer by the person or a lawful seizure, and (iii) the person cannot reasonably obtain possession of the instrument because the instrument was destroyed, its whereabouts cannot be determined, or it is in the wrongful possession of an unknown person or a person that cannot be found or is not amenable to service of process.

(b) A person seeking enforcement of an instrument under subsection (a) must prove the terms of the instrument and the person's right to enforce the instrument. If that proof is made, Section 3–308 applies to the case as if the person seeking enforcement had produced the instrument. The court may not enter judgment in favor of the person seeking enforcement unless it finds that the person required to pay the instrument is adequately protected against loss that might occur by reason of a claim by another person to enforce the instrument. Adequate protection may be provided by any reasonable means.

Rev. §3–310. Effect of Instrument on Obligation for Which Taken.

(a) Unless otherwise agreed, if a certified check, cashier's check, or teller's check is taken for an obligation, the obligation is discharged to the same extent discharge would result if an amount of money equal to the amount of the instrument were taken in payment of the obligation. Discharge of the obligation does not affect any liability that the obligor may have as an indorser of the instrument.

(b) Unless otherwise agreed and except as provided in subsection (a), if a note or an uncertified check is taken for an obligation, the obligation is suspended to the same extent the obligation would be discharged if an amount of money equal to the amount of the instrument were taken, and the following rules apply:

(1) In the case of an uncertified check, suspension of the obligation continues until dishonor of the check or until it is paid or certified. Payment or certification of the check results in discharge of the obligation to the extent of the amount of the check.

(2) In the case of a note, suspension of the obligation continues until dishonor of the note or until it is paid. Payment of the note results in discharge of the obligation to the extent of the payment.

(3) Except as provided in paragraph (4), if the check or note is dishonored and the obligee of the obligation for which the instrument was taken is the person entitled to enforce the instrument, the obligee may enforce either the instrument or the obligation. In the case of an instrument of a third person which is negotiated to the obligee by the obligor, discharge of the obligor on the instrument also discharges the obligation.

(4) If the person entitled to enforce the instrument taken for an obligation is a person other than the obligee, the obligee may not enforce the obligation to the extent the obligation is suspended. If the obligee is the person entitled to enforce the instrument but no longer has possession of it because it was lost, stolen, or destroyed, the obligation may not be enforced to the extent of the amount payable on the instrument, and to that extent the obligee's rights against the obligor are limited to enforcement of the instrument.

(c) If an instrument other than one described in subsection (a) or (b) is taken for an obligation, the effect is (i) that stated in subsection (a) if the instrument is one on which a bank is liable as maker or acceptor, or (ii) that stated in subsection (b) in any other case.

Rev. §3–311. Accord and Satisfaction by Use of Instrument.

(a) If a person against whom a claim is asserted proves that (i) that person in good faith tendered an instrument to the claimant as full satisfaction of the claim, (ii) the amount of the claim was unliquidated or subject to a bona fide dispute, and (iii) the claimant obtained payment of the instrument, the following subsections apply.

(b) Unless subsection (c) applies, the claim is discharged if the person against whom the claim is asserted proves that the instrument or an accompanying written communication contained a conspicuous statement to the effect that the instrument was tendered as full satisfaction of the claim.

(c) Subject to subsection (d), a claim is not discharged under subsection (b) if either of the following applies:

(1) The claimant, if an organization, proves that (i) within a reasonable time before the tender, the claimant sent a conspicuous statement to the person against whom the claim is asserted that communications concerning disputed debts, including an instrument tendered as full satisfaction of a debt, are to be sent to a designated person, office, or place, and (ii) the instrument or accompanying communication was not received by that designated person, office, or place.

(2) The claimant, whether or not an organization, proves that within 90 days after payment of the instrument, the claimant tendered repayment of the amount of the instrument to the person against whom the claim is asserted. This paragraph does not apply if the claimant is an organization that sent a statement complying with paragraph (1)(i).

(d) A claim is discharged if the person against whom the claim is asserted proves that within a reasonable time before collection of the instrument was initiated, the claimant, or an agent of the claimant having direct responsibility with respect to the disputed obligation, knew that the instrument was tendered in full satisfaction of the claim.

Part 4: Liability of Parties

Rev. §3–401. Signature.

(a) A person is not liable on an instrument unless (i) the person signed the instrument, or (ii) the person is represented by an agent or representative who signed the instrument and the signature is binding on the represented person under Section 3–402.

(b) A signature may be made (i) manually or by means of a device or machine, and (ii) by the use of any name, including a trade or assumed name, or by a word, mark, or symbol executed or adopted by a person with present intention to authenticate a writing.

Rev. §3–402. Signature by Representative.

(a) If a person acting, or purporting to act, as a representative signs an instrument by signing either the name of the represented person or the name of the signer, the represented person is bound by the signature to the same extent the represented person would be bound if the signature were on a simple contract. If the represented person is bound, the signature of the representative is the "authorized signature of the represented person" and the represented person is liable on the instrument, whether or not identified in the instrument.

(b) If a representative signs the name of the representative to an instrument and the signature is an authorized signature of the represented person, the following rules apply:

(1) If the form of the signature shows unambiguously that the signature is made on behalf of the represented person who is identified in the instrument, the representative is not liable on the instrument.

(2) Subject to subsection (c), if (i) the form of the signature does not show unambiguously that the signature is made in a representative capacity or (ii) the represented person is not identified in the instrument, the representative is liable on the instrument to a holder in due course that took the instrument without notice that the representative was not intended to be liable on the instrument. With respect to any other person, the representative is liable on the instrument unless the representative proves that the original parties did not intend the representative to be liable on the instrument.

(c) If a representative signs the name of the representative as drawer of a check without indication of the representative status and the check is payable from an account of the represented person who is identified on the check, the signer is not liable on the check if the signature is an authorized signature of the represented person.

Rev. §3–403. Unauthorized Signature.

(a) Unless otherwise provided in this Article or Article 4, an unauthorized signature is ineffective except as the signature of the unauthorized signer in favor of a person who in good faith pays the instrument or takes it for value. An unauthorized signature may be ratified for all purposes of this Article.

(b) If the signature of more than one person is required to constitute the authorized signature of an organization, the signature of the organization is unauthorized if one of the required signatures is lacking.

(c) The civil or criminal liability of a person who makes an unauthorized signature is not affected by any provision of this Article which makes the unauthorized signature effective for the purposes of this Article.

Rev. §3–404. Imposters; Fictitious Payees.

(a) If an impostor, by use of the mails or otherwise, induces the issuer of an instrument to issue the instrument to the impostor, or to a person acting in concert with the impostor, by impersonating the payee of the instrument or a person authorized to act for the payee, an indorsement of the instrument by any person in the name of the payee is effective as the indorsement of the payee in favor of a person who, in good faith, pays the instrument or takes it for value or for collection.

(b) If (i) a person whose intent determines to whom an instrument is payable (Section 3–110(a) or (b)) does not intend the person identified as payee to have any interest in the instrument, or (ii) the person identified as payee of an instrument is a fictitious person, the following rules apply until the instrument is negotiated by special indorsement:

(1) Any person in possession of the instrument is its holder.

(2) An indorsement by any person in the name of the payee stated in the instrument is effective as the indorsement of the payee in favor of a person who, in good faith, pays the instrument or takes it for value or for collection.

(c) Under subsection (a) or (b), an indorsement is made in the name of a payee if (i) it is made in a name substantially similar to that of the payee or (ii) the instrument, whether or not indorsed, is deposited in a depositary bank to an account in a name substantially similar to that of the payee.

(d) With respect to an instrument to which subsection (a) or (b) applies, if a person paying the instrument or taking it for value or for collection fails to exercise ordinary care in paying or taking the instrument and that failure substantially contributes to loss resulting from payment of the instrument, the person bearing the loss may recover from the person failing to exercise ordinary care to the extent the failure to exercise ordinary care contributed to the loss.

Rev. §3–405. Employer's Responsibility for Fraudulent Indorsement by Employee.

(a) In this section:

(1) "Employee" includes an independent contractor and employee of an independent contractor retained by the employer.

(2) "Fraudulent indorsement" means (i) in the case of an instrument payable to the employer, a forged indorsement purporting to be that of the employer, or (ii) in the case of an instrument with respect to which the employer is the issuer, a forged indorsement purporting to be that of the person identified as payee.

(3) "Responsibility" with respect to instruments means authority (i) to sign or indorse instruments on behalf of the employer, (ii) to process instruments received by the employer for bookkeeping purposes, for deposit to an account, or for other disposition, (iii) to prepare or process instruments for issue in the name of the employer, (iv) to supply information determining the names or addresses of payees of instruments to be issued in the name of the employer, (v) to control the disposition of instruments to be issued in the name of the employer, or (vi) to act otherwise with respect to instruments in a responsible capacity. "Responsibility" does not include authority that merely allows an employee to have access to instruments or blank or incomplete instrument forms that are being stored or transported or are part of incoming or outgoing mail, or similar access.

(b) For the purpose of determining the rights and liabilities of a person who, in good faith, pays an instrument or takes it for value or for collection, if an employer entrusted an employee with responsibility with respect to the instrument and the employee or a person acting in concert with the employee makes a fraudulent indorsement of the instrument, the indorsement is effective as the indorsement of the person to whom the instrument is payable if it is made in the name of that person. If the person paying the instrument or taking it for value or for collection fails to exercise ordinary care in paying or taking the instrument and that failure substantially contributes to loss resulting from the fraud, the person bearing the loss may recover from the person failing to exercise ordinary care to the extent the failure to exercise ordinary care contributed to the loss.

(c) Under subsection (b), an indorsement is made in the name of the person to whom an instrument is payable if (i) it is made in a name substantially similar to the name of that person or (ii) the instrument, whether or not indorsed, is deposited in a depositary bank to an account in a name substantially similar to the name of that person.

Rev. §3–406. Negligence Contributing to Forged Signature or Alteration of Instrument.

(a) A person whose failure to exercise ordinary care substantially contributes to an alteration of an instrument or to the making of a forged signature on an instrument is precluded from asserting the alteration or

the forgery against a person who, in good faith, pays the instrument or takes it for value or for collection.

(b) Under subsection (a), if the person asserting the preclusion fails to exercise ordinary care in paying or taking the instrument and that failure substantially contributes to loss, the loss is allocated between the person precluded and the person asserting the preclusion according to the extent to which the failure of each to exercise ordinary care contributed to the loss.

(c) Under subsection (a), the burden of proving failure to exercise ordinary care is on the person asserting the preclusion. Under subsection (b), the burden of proving failure to exercise ordinary care is on the person precluded.

Rev. §3–407. Alteration.

(a) "Alteration" means (i) an unauthorized change in an instrument that purports to modify in any respect the obligation of a party, or (ii) an unauthorized addition of words or numbers or other change to an incomplete instrument relating to the obligation of a party.

(b) Except as provided in subsection (c), an alteration fraudulently made discharges a party whose obligation is affected by the alteration unless that party assents or is precluded from asserting the alteration. No other alteration discharges a party, and the instrument may be enforced according to its original terms.

(c) A payor bank or drawee paying a fraudulently altered instrument or a person taking it for value, in good faith and without notice of the alteration, may enforce rights with respect to the instrument (i) according to its original terms, or (ii) in the case of an incomplete instrument altered by unauthorized completion, according to its terms as completed.

Rev. §3–408. Drawee Not Liable on Unaccepted Draft.

A check or other draft does not of itself operate as an assignment of funds in the hands of the drawee available for its payment, and the drawee is not liable on the instrument until the drawee accepts it.

Rev. §3–409. Acceptance of Draft; Certified Check

(a) "Acceptance" means the drawee's signed agreement to pay a draft as presented.
It must be written on the draft and may consist of the drawee's signature alone. Acceptance may be made at any time and becomes effective when notification pursuant to instructions is given or the accepted draft is delivered for the purpose of giving rights on the acceptance to any person.

(b) A draft may be accepted although it has not been signed by the drawer, is otherwise incomplete, is overdue, or has been dishonored.

(c) If a draft is payable at a fixed period after sight and the acceptor fails to date the acceptance, the holder may complete the acceptance by supplying a date in good faith.

(d) "Certified check" means a check accepted by the bank on which it is drawn. Acceptance may be made as stated in subsection (a) or by a writing on the check which indicates that the check is certified. The drawee of a check has no obligation to certify the check, and refusal to certify is not dishonor of the check.

Rev. §3–410. Acceptance Varying Draft.

(a) If the terms of a drawee's acceptance vary from the terms of the draft as presented, the holder may refuse the acceptance and treat the draft as dishonored. In that case, the drawee may cancel the acceptance.

(b) The terms of a draft are not varied by an acceptance to pay at a particular bank or place in the United States, unless the acceptance states that the draft is to be paid only at that bank or place.

(c) If the holder assents to an acceptance varying the terms of a draft, the obligation of each drawer and indorser that does not expressly assent to the acceptance is discharged.

Rev. §3–411. Refusal to Pay Cashier's Checks, Teller's Checks, and Certified Checks.

(a) In this section, "obligated bank" means the acceptor of a certified check or the issuer of a cashier's check or teller's check bought from the issuer.

(b) If the obligated bank wrongfully (i) refuses to pay a cashier's check or certified check, (ii) stops payment of a teller's check, or (iii) refuses to pay a dishonored teller's check, the person asserting the right to enforce the check is entitled to compensation for expenses and loss of interest resulting from the nonpayment and may recover consequential damages if the obligated bank refuses to pay after receiving notice of particular circumstances giving rise to the damages.

(c) Expenses or consequential damages under subsection (b) are not recoverable if the refusal of the obligated bank to pay occurs because (i) the bank suspends payments, (ii) the obligated bank asserts a claim or defense of the bank that it has reasonable grounds to believe is available against the person entitled to enforce the instrument, (iii) the obligated bank has a reasonable doubt whether the person demanding payment is the person entitled to enforce the instrument, or (iv) payment is prohibited by law.

Rev. §3–412. Obligation of Issuer of Note or Cashier's Check.

The issuer of a note or cashier's check or other draft drawn on the drawer is obliged to pay the instrument (i) according to its terms at the time it was issued or, if not issued, at the time it first came into possession of a holder, or (ii) if the issuer signed an incomplete instrument, according to its terms when completed, to the extent stated in Sections 3–115 and 3–407. The obligation is owed to a person entitled to enforce the instrument or to an indorser who paid the instrument under Section 3–415.

Rev. §3–413. Obligation of Acceptor.

(a) The acceptor of a draft is obliged to pay the draft (i) according to its terms at the time it was accepted, even though the acceptance states that the draft is payable "as originally drawn" or equivalent terms, (ii) if the acceptance varies the terms of the draft, according to the terms of the draft as varied, or (iii) if the acceptance is of a draft that is an incomplete instrument, according to its terms when completed, to the extent stated in Sections 3–115 and 3–407. The obligation is owed to a person entitled to enforce the draft or to the drawer or an indorser who paid the draft under Section 3–414 or 3–415.

(b) If the certification of a check or other acceptance of a draft states the amount certified or accepted, the obligation of the acceptor is that amount. If (i) the certification or acceptance does not state an amount, (ii) the amount of the instrument is subsequently raised, and (iii) the instrument is then negotiated to a holder in due course, the obligation of the acceptor is the amount of the instrument at the time it was taken by the holder in due course.

Rev. §3–414. Obligation of Drawer.

(a) This section does not apply to cashier's checks or other drafts drawn on the drawer.

(b) If an unaccepted draft is dishonored, the drawer is obliged to pay the draft (i) according to its terms at the time it was issued or, if not issued, at the time it first came into possession of a holder, or (ii) if the drawer signed an incomplete instrument, according to its terms when completed, to the extent stated in Sections 3–115 and 3–407. The obligation is owed to a person entitled to enforce the draft or to an indorser who paid the draft under Section 3–415.

(c) If a draft is accepted by a bank, the drawer is discharged, regardless of when or by whom acceptance was obtained.

(d) If a draft is accepted and the acceptor is not a bank, the obligation of the drawer to pay the draft if the draft is dishonored by the acceptor is the same as the obligation of an indorser under Section 3–415(a) and (c).

(e) If a draft states that it is drawn "without recourse" or otherwise disclaims liability of the drawer to pay the draft, the drawer is not liable under subsection (b) to pay the draft if the draft is not a check. A disclaimer of the liability stated in subsection (b) is not effective if the draft is a check.

(f) If (i) a check is not presented for payment or given to a depositary bank for collection within 30 days after its date, (ii) the drawee suspends payments after expiration of the 30-day period without paying the check, and (iii) because of the suspension of payments, the drawer is deprived of funds maintained with the drawee to cover payment of the check, the drawer to the extent deprived of funds may discharge its obligation to pay the check by assigning to the person entitled to enforce the check the rights of the drawer against the drawee with respect to the funds.

Rev. §3–415. Obligation of Indorser.

(a) Subject to subsections (b), (c), and (d) and to Section 3–419(d), if an instrument is dishonored, an indorser is obliged to pay the amount due on the instrument (i) according to the terms of the instrument at the time it was indorsed, or (ii) if the indorser indorsed an incomplete instrument, according to its terms when completed, to the extent stated in Sections 3–115 and 3–407. The obligation of the indorser is owed to a person entitled to enforce the instrument or to a subsequent indorser who paid the instrument under this section.

(b) If an indorsement states that it is made "without recourse" or otherwise disclaims liability of the indorser, the indorser is not liable under subsection (a) to pay the instrument.

(c) If notice of dishonor of an instrument is required by Section 3–503 and notice of dishonor complying with that section is not given to an indorser, the liability of the indorser under subsection (a) is discharged.

(d) If a draft is accepted by a bank after an indorsement is made, the liability of the indorser under subsection (a) is discharged.

(e) If an indorser of a check is liable under subsection (a) and the check is not presented for payment, or given to a depositary bank for collection, within 30 days after the day the indorsement was made, the liability of the indorser under subsection (a) is discharged.

Rev. §3–416. Transfer Warranties.

(a) A person who transfers an instrument for consideration warrants to the transferee and, if the transfer is by indorsement, to any subsequent transferee that:

(1) the warrantor is a person entitled to enforce the instrument;

(2) all signatures on the instrument are authentic and authorized;

(3) the instrument has not been altered;

(4) the instrument is not subject to a defense or claim in recoupment of any party which can be asserted against the warrantor; and

(5) the warrantor has no knowledge of any insolvency proceeding commenced with respect to the maker or acceptor or, in the case of an unaccepted draft, the drawer.

(b) A person to whom the warranties under subsection (a) are made and who took the instrument in good faith may recover from the warrantor as damages for breach of warranty an amount equal to the loss suffered as a result of the breach, but not more than the amount of the instrument plus expenses and loss of interest incurred as a result of the breach.

(c) The warranties stated in subsection (a) cannot be disclaimed with respect to checks. Unless notice of a claim for breach of warranty is given to the warrantor within 30 days after the claimant has reason to know of the breach and the identity of the warrantor, the liability of the warrantor under subsection (b) is discharged to the extent of any loss caused by the delay in giving notice of the claim.

(d) A [cause of action] for breach of warranty under this section accrues when the claimant has reason to know of the breach.

Rev. §3–417. Presentment Warranties.

(a) If an unaccepted draft is presented to the drawee for payment or acceptance and the drawee pays or accepts the draft, (i) the person obtaining payment or acceptance, at the time of presentment, and (ii) a previous transferor of the draft, at the time of transfer, warrant to the drawee making payment or accepting the draft in good faith that:

(1) the warrantor is, or was, at the time the warrantor transferred the draft, a person entitled to enforce the draft or authorized to obtain payment or acceptance of the draft on behalf of a person entitled to enforce the draft;

(2) the draft has not been altered; and

(3) the warrantor has no knowledge that the signature of the drawer of the draft is unauthorized.

(b) A drawee making payment may recover from any warrantor damages for breach of warranty equal to the amount paid by the drawee less the amount the drawee received or is entitled to receive from the drawer because of the payment. In addition, the drawee is entitled to compensation for expenses and loss of interest resulting from the breach. The right of the drawee to recover damages under this subsection is not affected by any failure of the drawee to exercise ordinary care in making payment. If the drawee accepts the draft, breach of warranty is a defense to the obligation of the acceptor. If the acceptor makes payment with respect to the draft, the acceptor is entitled to recover from any warrantor for breach of warranty the amounts stated in this subsection.

(c) If a drawee asserts a claim for breach of warranty under subsection (a) based on an unauthorized indorsement of the draft or an alteration of the draft, the warrantor may defend by proving that the indorsement is effective under Section 3–404 or 3–405 or the drawer is precluded under Section 3–406 or 4–406 from asserting against the drawee the unauthorized indorsement or alteration.

(d) If (i) a dishonored draft is presented for payment to the drawer or an indorser or (ii) any other instrument is presented for payment to a party obliged to pay the instrument, and (iii) payment is received, the following rules apply:

(1) The person obtaining payment and a prior transferor of the instrument warrant to the person making payment in good faith that the warrantor is, or was, at the time the warrantor transferred the instrument, a person entitled to enforce the instrument or authorized to obtain payment on behalf of a person entitled to enforce the instrument.

(2) The person making payment may recover from any warrantor for breach of warranty an amount equal to the amount paid plus expenses and loss of interest resulting from the breach.

(e) The warranties stated in subsections (a) and (d) cannot be disclaimed with respect to checks. Unless notice of a claim for breach of warranty is given to the warrantor within 30 days after the claimant has reason to know of the breach and the identity of the warrantor, the liability of the warrantor under subsection (b) or (d) is discharged to the extent of any loss caused by the delay in giving notice of the claim.

(f) A [cause of action] for breach of warranty under this section accrues when the claimant has reason to know of the breach.

Rev. §3–418. Payment or Acceptance by Mistake.

(a) Except as provided in subsection (c), if the drawee of a draft pays or accepts the draft and the drawee acted on the mistaken belief that (i) payment of the draft had not been stopped pursuant to Section 4–403 or (ii) the signature of the drawer of the draft was authorized, the drawee may recover the amount of the draft from the person to whom or for whose benefit payment was made or, in the case of acceptance, may revoke the acceptance. Rights of the drawee under this subsection are not affected by failure of the drawee to exercise ordinary care in paying or accepting the draft.

(b) Except as provided in subsection (c), if an instrument has been paid or accepted by mistake and the case is not covered by subsection (a), the person paying or accepting may, to the extent permitted by the law governing mistake and restitution, (i) recover the payment from the person to whom or for whose benefit payment was made or (ii) in the case of acceptance, may revoke the acceptance.

(c) The remedies provided by subsection (a) or (b) may not be asserted against a person who took the instrument in good faith and for value or who in good faith changed position in reliance on the payment or acceptance. This subsection does not limit remedies provided by Section 3–417 or 4–407.

(d) Notwithstanding Section 4–215, if an instrument is paid or accepted by mistake and the payor or acceptor recovers payment or revokes acceptance

under subsection (a) or (b), the instrument is deemed not to have been paid or accepted and is treated as dishonored, and the person from whom payment is recovered has rights as a person entitled to enforce the dishonored instrument.

Rev. §3-419. Instruments Signed for Accommodation.

(a) If an instrument is issued for value given for the benefit of a party to the instrument ("accommodated party") and another party to the instrument ("accommodation party") signs the instrument for the purpose of incurring liability on the instrument without being a direct beneficiary of the value given for the instrument, the instrument is signed by the accommodation party "for accommodation."

(b) An accommodation party may sign the instrument as maker, drawer, acceptor, or indorser and, subject to subsection (d), is obliged to pay the instrument in the capacity in which the accommodation party signs. The obligation of an accommodation party may be enforced notwithstanding any statute of frauds and whether or not the accommodation party receives consideration for the accommodation.

(c) A person signing an instrument is presumed to be an accommodation party and there is notice that the instrument is signed for accommodation if the signature is an anomalous indorsement or is accompanied by words indicating that the signer is acting as surety or guarantor with respect to the obligation of another party to the instrument. Except as provided in Section 3-605, the obligation of an accommodation party to pay the instrument is not affected by the fact that the person enforcing the obligation had notice when the instrument was taken by that person that the accommodation party signed the instrument for accommodation.

(d) If the signature of a party to an instrument is accompanied by words indicating unambiguously that the party is guaranteeing collection rather than payment of the obligation of another party to the instrument, the signer is obliged to pay the amount due on the instrument to a person entitled to enforce the instrument only if (i) execution of judgment against the other party has been returned unsatisfied, (ii) the other party is insolvent or in an insolvency proceeding, (iii) the other party cannot be served with process, or (iv) it is otherwise apparent that payment cannot be obtained from the other party.

(e) An accommodation party who pays the instrument is entitled to reimbursement from the accommodated party and is entitled to enforce the instrument against the accommodated party. An accommodated party who pays the instrument has no right of recourse against, and is not entitled to contribution from, an accommodation party.

Rev. §3-420. Conversion of Instrument.

(a) The law applicable to conversion of personal property applies to instruments. An instrument is also converted if it is taken by transfer, other than a negotiation, from a person not entitled to enforce the instrument or a bank makes or obtains payment with respect to the instrument for a person not entitled to enforce the instrument or receive payment. An action for conversion of an instrument may not be brought by (i) the issuer or acceptor of the instrument or (ii) a payee or indorsee who did not receive delivery of the instrument either directly or through delivery to an agent or a co-payee.

(b) In an action under subsection (a), the measure of liability is presumed to be the amount payable on the instrument, but recovery may not exceed the amount of the plaintiff's interest in the instrument.

(c) A representative, other than a depositary bank, who has in good faith dealt with an instrument or its proceeds on behalf of one who was not the person entitled to enforce the instrument is not liable in conversion to that person beyond the amount of any proceeds that it has not paid out.

Part 5: Dishonor

Rev. §3-501. Presentment.

(a) "Presentment" means a demand made by or on behalf of a person entitled to enforce an instrument (i) to pay the instrument made to the drawee or a party obliged to pay the instrument or, in the case of a note or accepted draft payable at a bank, to the bank, or (ii) to accept a draft made to the drawee.

(b) The following rules are subject to Article 4, agreement of the parties, and clearing-house rules and the like:

(1) Presentment may be made at the place of payment of the instrument and must be made at the place of payment if the instrument is payable at a bank in the United States; may be made by any commercially reasonable means, including an oral, written, or electronic communication; is effective when the demand for payment or acceptance is received by the person to whom presentment is made; and is effective if made to any one of two or more makers, acceptors, drawees, or other payors.

(2) Upon demand of the person to whom presentment is made, the person making presentment must (i) exhibit the instrument, (ii) give reasonable identification and, if presentment is made on behalf of another person, reasonable evidence of authority to do so, and (iii) sign a receipt on the instrument for any payment made or surrender the instrument if full payment is made.

(3) Without dishonoring the instrument, the party to whom presentment is made may (i) return the instrument for lack of a necessary indorsement, or (ii) refuse payment or acceptance for failure of the presentment to com-ply with the terms of the instrument, an agreement of the parties, or other applicable law or rule.

(4) The party to whom presentment is made may treat presentment as occurring on the next business day after the day of presentment if the party to whom presentment is made has established a cut-off hour not earlier than 2 p.m. for the receipt and processing of instruments presented for payment or acceptance and presentment is made after the cut-off hour.

Rev. §3-502. Dishonor.

(a) Dishonor of a note is governed by the following rules:

(1) If the note is payable on demand, the note is dishonored if presentment is duly made to the maker and the note is not paid on the day of presentment.

(2) If the note is not payable on demand and is payable at or through a bank or the terms of the note require presentment, the note is dishonored if presentment is duly made and the note is not paid on the day it becomes payable or the day of presentment, whichever is later.

(3) If the note is not payable on demand and paragraph (2) does not apply, the note is dishonored if it is not paid on the day it becomes payable.

(b) Dishonor of an unaccepted draft other than a documentary draft is governed by the following rules:

(1) If a check is duly presented for payment to the payor bank otherwise than for immediate payment over the counter, the check is dishonored if the payor bank makes timely return of the check or sends timely notice of dishonor or nonpayment under Section 4-301 or 4-302, or becomes accountable for the amount of the check under Section 4-302.

(2) If a draft is payable on demand and paragraph (1) does not apply, the draft is dishonored if presentment for payment is duly made to the drawee and the draft is not paid on the day of presentment.

(3) If a draft is payable on a date stated in the draft, the draft is dishonored if (i) presentment for payment is duly made to the drawee and payment is not made on the day the draft becomes payable or the day of presentment, whichever is later, or (ii) presentment for acceptance is duly made before the day the draft becomes payable and the draft is not accepted on the day of presentment.

(4) If a draft is payable on elapse of a period of time after sight or acceptance, the draft is dishonored if presentment for acceptance is duly made and the draft is not accepted on the day of presentment.

(c) Dishonor of an unaccepted documentary draft occurs according to the rules stated in subsection (b)(2), (3), and (4), except that payment or acceptance may be delayed without dishonor until no later than the close of the third business day of the drawee following the day on which payment or acceptance is required by those paragraphs.

(d) Dishonor of an accepted draft is governed by the following rules:

(1) If the draft is payable on demand, the draft is dishonored if presentment for payment is duly made to the acceptor and the draft is not paid on the day of presentment.

(2) If the draft is not payable on demand, the draft is dishonored if presentment for payment is duly made to the acceptor and payment is not made on the day it becomes payable or the day of presentment, whichever is later.

(e) In any case in which presentment is otherwise required for dishonor under this section and presentment is excused under Section 3-504, dishonor occurs without presentment if the instrument is not duly accepted or paid.

(f) If a draft is dishonored because timely acceptance of the draft was not made and the person entitled to demand acceptance consents to a late acceptance, from the time of acceptance the draft is treated as never having been dishonored.

Rev. §3-503. Notice of Dishonor.

(a) The obligation of an indorser stated in Section 3-415(a) and the obligation of a drawer stated in Section 3-414(d) may not be enforced unless (i) the indorser or drawer is given notice of dishonor of the instrument complying with this section or (ii) notice of dishonor is excused under Section 3-504(b).

(b) Notice of dishonor may be given by any person; may be given by any commercially reasonable means, including an oral, written, or electronic communication; and is sufficient if it reasonably identifies the instrument and indicates that the instrument has been dishonored or has not been paid or accepted. Return of an instrument given to a bank for collection is sufficient notice of dishonor.

(c) Subject to Section 3-504(c), with respect to an instrument taken for collection by a collecting bank, notice of dishonor must be given (i) by the bank before midnight of the next banking day following the banking day on which the bank receives notice of dishonor of the instrument, or (ii) by any other person within 30 days following the day on which the person receives notice of dishonor. With respect to any other instrument, notice of dishonor must be given within 30 days following the day on which dishonor occurs.

Rev. §3-504. Excused Presentment and Notice of Dishonor.

(a) Presentment for payment or acceptance of an instrument is excused if (i) the person entitled to present the instrument cannot with reasonable diligence make presentment, (ii) the maker or acceptor has repudiated an obligation to pay the instrument or is dead or in insolvency proceedings, (iii) by the terms of the instrument presentment is not necessary to enforce the obligation of indorsers or the drawer, (iv) the drawer or indorser whose obligation is being enforced has waived presentment or otherwise has no reason to expect or right to require that the instrument be paid or accepted, or (v) the drawer instructed the drawee not to pay or accept the draft or the drawee was not obligated to the drawer to pay the draft.

(b) Notice of dishonor is excused if (i) by the terms of the instrument notice of dishonor is not necessary to enforce the obligation of a party to pay the instrument, or (ii) the party whose obligation is being enforced waived notice of dishonor. A waiver of presentment is also a waiver of notice of dishonor.

(c) Delay in giving notice of dishonor is excused if the delay was caused by circumstances beyond the control of the person giving the notice and the person giving the notice exercised reasonable diligence after the cause of the delay ceased to operate.

Rev. §3-505. Evidence of Dishonor.

(a) The following are admissible as evidence and create a presumption of dishonor and of any notice of dishonor stated:

(1) a document regular in form as provided in subsection (b) which purports to be a protest;

(2) a purported stamp or writing of the drawee, payor bank, or presenting bank on or accompanying the instrument stating that acceptance or payment has been refused unless reasons for the refusal are stated and the reasons are not consistent with dishonor;

(3) a book or record of the drawee, payor bank, or collecting bank, kept in the usual course of business which shows dishonor, even if there is no evidence of who made the entry.

(b) A protest is a certificate of dishonor made by a United States consul or vice consul, or a notary public or other person authorized to administer oaths by the law of the place where dishonor occurs. It may be made upon information satisfactory to that person. The protest must identify the instrument and certify either that presentment has been made or, if not made, the reason why it was not made, and that the instrument has been dishonored by nonacceptance or nonpayment. The protest may also certify that notice of dishonor has been given to some or all parties.

Part 6: Discharge and Payment

Rev. §3-601. Discharge and Effect of Discharge.

(a) The obligation of a party to pay the instrument is discharged as stated in this Article or by an act or agreement with the party which would discharge an obligation to pay money under a simple contract.

(b) Discharge of the obligation of a party is not effective against a person acquiring rights of a holder in due course of the instrument without notice of the discharge.

Rev. §3-602. Payment.

(a) Subject to subsection (b), an instrument is paid to the extent payment is made (i) by or on behalf of a party obliged to pay the instrument, and (ii) to a person entitled to enforce the instrument. To the extent of the payment, the obligation of the party obliged to pay the instrument is discharged even though payment is made with knowledge of a claim to the instrument under Section 3-306 by another person.

(b) The obligation of a party to pay the instrument is not discharged under subsection (a) if:

(1) a claim to the instrument under Section 3-306 is enforceable against the party receiving payment and (i) payment is made with knowledge by the payor that payment is prohibited by injunction or similar process of a court of competent jurisdiction, or (ii) in the case of an instrument other than a cashier's check, teller's check, or certified check, the party making payment accepted, from the person having a claim to the instrument, indemnity against loss resulting from refusal to pay the person entitled to enforce the instrument; or

(2) the person making payment knows that the instrument is a stolen instrument and pays a person it knows is in wrongful possession of the instrument.

Rev. §3-603. Tender of Payment.

(a) If tender of payment of an obligation to pay an instrument is made to a person entitled to enforce the instrument, the effect of tender is governed by principles of law applicable to tender of payment under a simple contract.

(b) If tender of payment of an obligation to pay an instrument is made to a person entitled to enforce the instrument and the tender is refused, there is discharge, to the extent of the amount of the tender, of the obligation of an indorser or accommodation party having a right of recourse with respect to the obligation to which the tender relates.

(c) If tender of payment of an amount due on an instrument is made to a person entitled to enforce the instrument, the obligation of the obligor to pay interest after the due date on the amount tendered is discharged. If presentment is required with respect to an instrument and the obligor is able and ready to pay on the due date at every place of payment stated in the instrument, the obligor is deemed to have made tender of payment on the due date to the person entitled to enforce the instrument.

Rev. §3-604. Discharge by Cancellation or Renunciation.

(a) A person entitled to enforce an instrument, with or without consideration, may discharge the obligation of a party to pay the instrument (i) by an intentional voluntary act, such as surrender of the instrument to the party, destruction, mutilation, or cancellation of the instrument, cancellation or striking out of the party's signature, or the addition of words to the instrument indicating discharge, or (ii) by agreeing not to sue or otherwise renouncing rights against the party by a signed writing.

(b) Cancellation or striking out of an indorsement pursuant to subsection (a) does not affect the status and rights of a party derived from the indorsement.

Rev. §3-605. Discharge of Indorsers and Accommodation Parties.

(a) In this section, the term "indorser" includes a drawer having the obligation described in Section 3-414(d).

(b) Discharge, under Section 3-604, of the obligation of a party to pay an instrument does not discharge the obligation of an indorser or accommodation party having a right of recourse against the discharged party.

(c) If a person entitled to enforce an instrument agrees, with or without consideration, to an extension of the due date of the obligation of a party to pay the instrument, the extension discharges an indorser or accommodation party having a right of recourse against the party whose obligation is extended to the extent the indorser or accommodation party proves that the extension caused loss to the indorser or accommodation party with respect to the right of recourse.

(d) If a person entitled to enforce an instrument agrees, with or without consideration, to a material modification of the obligation of a party other than an extension of the due date, the modification discharges the obligation of an indorser or accommodation party having a right of recourse against the person whose obligation is modified to the extent the modification causes loss to the indorser or accommodation party with respect to the right of recourse. The loss suffered by the indorser or accommodation party as a result of the modification is equal to the amount of the right of recourse unless the person enforcing the instrument proves that no loss was caused by the modification or that the loss caused by the modification was an amount less than the amount of the right of recourse.

(e) If the obligation of a party to pay an instrument is secured by an interest in collateral and a person entitled to enforce the instrument impairs the value of the interest in collateral, the obligation of an indorser or accommodation party having a right of recourse against the obligor is discharged to the extent of the impairment. The value of an interest in collateral is impaired to the extent (i) the value of the interest is reduced to an amount less than the amount of the right of recourse of the party asserting discharge, or (ii) the reduction in value of the interest causes an increase in the amount by which the amount of the right of recourse exceeds the value of the interest. The burden of proving impairment is on the party asserting discharge.

(f) If the obligation of a party is secured by an interest in collateral not provided by an accommodation party and a person entitled to enforce the instrument impairs the value of the interest in collateral, the obligation of any party who is jointly and severally liable with respect to the secured obligation is discharged to the extent the impairment causes the party asserting discharge to pay more than that party would have been obliged to pay, taking into account rights of contribution, if impairment had not occurred. If the party asserting discharge is an accommodation party not entitled to discharge under subsection (e), the party is deemed to have a right to contribution based on joint and several liability rather than a right to reimbursement. The burden of proving impairment is on the party asserting discharge.

(g) Under subsection (e) or (f), impairing value of an interest in collateral includes (i) failure to obtain or maintain perfection or recordation of the interest in collateral, (ii) release of collateral without substitution of collateral of equal value, (iii) failure to perform a duty to preserve the value of collateral owed, under Article 9 or other law, to a debtor or surety or other person secondarily liable, or (iv) failure to comply with applicable law in disposing of collateral.

(h) An accommodation party is not discharged under subsection (c), (d), or (e) unless the person entitled to enforce the instrument knows of the accommodation or has notice under Section 3-419(c) that the instrument was signed for accommodation.

(i) A party is not discharged under this section if (i) the party asserting discharge consents to the event or conduct that is the basis of the discharge, or (ii) the instrument or a separate agreement of the party provides for waiver of discharge under this section either specifically or by general language indicating that parties waive defenses based on suretyship or impairment of collateral.

ARTICLE 4: BANK DEPOSITS AND COLLECTIONS (1990 AMENDMENTS)

Part 1: General Provisions and Definitions

§4-101. Short Title. This Article shall be known and may be cited as Uniform Commercial Code—Bank Deposits and Collections.

§4-102. Applicability.

[(1)] (a) To the extent that items within this Article are also within [the scope of] Articles 3 and 8, they are subject to [the provisions of] those Articles. [In the event of] If there is conflict, [the provisions of] this Article [govern those of] governs Article 3, but [the provisions of] Article 8 [govern those of] governs this Article.

[(2)] (b) The liability of a bank for action or non-action with respect to [any] an item handled by it for purposes of presentment, payment, or collection is governed by the law of the place where the bank is located. In the case of action or non-action by or at a branch or separate office of a bank, its liability is governed by the law of the place where the branch or separate office is located.

§4-103. Variation by Agreement; Measure of Damages; [Certain] Action Constituting Ordinary Care.

[(1)] (a) The effect of the provisions of this Article may be varied by agreement[except that no agreement can], but the parties to the agreement cannot disclaim a bank's responsibility for its [own] lack of good faith or failure to exercise ordinary care or [can] limit the measure of damages for [such] the lack or failure[; but]. However, the parties may determine by agreement [determine] the standards by which [such] the bank's responsibility is to be measured if [such] those standards are not manifestly unreasonable.

[(2)] (b) Federal Reserve regulations and operating [letters] circulars, [clearing house] clearing-house rules, and the like[,] have the effect of agreements under subsection [(1)] (a), whether or not specifically assented to by all parties interested in items handled.

[(3)] (c) Action or non-action approved by this Article or pursuant to Federal Reserve regulations or operating [letters constitutes] circulars is the exercise of ordinary care and, in the absence of special instructions, action or non-action consistent with [clearing house] clearing-house rules and the like or with a general banking usage not disapproved by this Article, is prima facie [constitutes] the exercise of ordinary care.

[(4)] (d) The specification or approval of certain procedures by this Article [does not constitute] is not disapproval of other procedures [which] that may be reasonable under the circumstances.

[(5)] **(e)** The measure of damages for failure to exercise ordinary care in handling an item is the amount of the item reduced by an amount [which] that could not have been realized by the [use] exercise of ordinary care [, and where]. If there is also bad faith it includes any other damages[, if any, suffered by] the party suffered as a proximate consequence.

§4-104. Definitions and Index of Definitions.

[(1)] **(a)** In this Article, unless the context otherwise requires:

[(a)] **(1)** "Account" means any deposit or credit account with a bank [and includes], including a [checking, time, interest or savings account] demand, time, savings, passbook, share draft, or like account, other than an account evidenced by a certificate of deposit;

[(b)] **(2)** "Afternoon" means the period of a day between noon and midnight;

[(c)] **(3)** "Banking day" means [that] the part of [any] a day on which a bank is open to the public for carrying on substantially all of its banking functions;

[(d)] **(4)** "Clearing house" means [any] an association of banks or other payors regularly clearing items;

[(e)] **(5)** "Customer" means [any] a person having an account with a bank or for whom a bank has agreed to collect items [and includes], including a bank [carrying] that maintains an account [with] at another bank;

[(f)] **(6)** "Documentary draft" means [any negotiable or nonnegotiable draft with accompanying documents, securities or other papers to be delivered against honor of the draft] a draft to be presented for acceptance or payment if specified documents, certificated securities (Section 8-102) or instructions for uncertificated securities (Section 8-308), or other certificates, statements, or the like are to be received by the drawee or other payor before acceptance or payment of the draft;

(7) "Draft" means a draft as defined in Section 3-104 or an item, other than an instrument, that is an order.

(8) "Drawee" means a person ordered in a draft to make payment.

[(g)] **(9)** "Item" means [any instrument for the payment of money even though it is not negotiable but does not include money] an instrument or a promise or order to pay money handled by a bank for collection or payment. The term does not include a payment order governed by Article 4A or a credit or debit card slip;

[(h)] **(10)** "Midnight deadline" with respect to a bank is midnight on its next banking day following the banking day on which it receives the relevant item or notice or from which the time for taking action commences to run, whichever is later;

[(i)] "Properly payable" includes the availability of funds for payment at the time of decision to pay or dishonor;]

[(j)] **(11)** "Settle" means to pay in cash, by [clearing house] clearing-house settlement, in a charge or credit or by remittance, or otherwise as [instructed] agreed. A settlement may be either provisional or final.

[(k)] **(12)** "Suspends payments" with respect to a bank means that it has been closed by order of the supervisory authorities, that a public officer has been appointed to take it over, or that it ceases or refuses to make payments in the ordinary course of business.

[(2)] **(b)** Other definitions applying to this Article and the sections in which they appear are:

"Agreement for electronic presentment"	Section 4-110
"Bank"	Section 4-105
"Collecting bank"	Section 4-105
"Depositary bank"	Section 4-105
"Intermediary bank"	Section 4-105
"Payor bank"	Section 4-105
"Presenting bank"	Section 4-105
"Presentment notice"	Section 4-110
["Remitting bank"	Section 4-105]

[(3)] **(c)** The following definitions in other Articles apply to this Article:

"Acceptance"	Section [3-410] 3-409
"Alteration"	Section 3-407
"Cashier's check"	Section 3-104
"Certificate of deposit"	Section 3-104
["Certification"	Section 3-411]
"Certified check"	Section 3-409
"Check"	Section 3-104
"Good faith"	Section 3-103
"Holder in due course"	Section 3-302
"Instrument"	Section 3-104
"Notice of dishonor"	Section [3-508] 3-503
"Order"	Section 3-103
"Ordinary care"	Section 3-103
"Person entitled to enforce"	Section 3-301

"Presentment"	Section [3-504] 3-501
"Promise"	Section 3-103
["Protest"	Section 3-509]
"Prove"	Section 3-103
["Secondary party	Section 3-102]
"Teller's check"	Section 3-104
"Unauthorized signature"	Section 3-403

[(4)] (d) In addition, Article 1 contains general definitions and principles of construction and interpretation applicable throughout this Article.

§4-105. "Bank"; "Bank"; "Depositary Bank"; "Payor Bank"; "Intermediary Bank"; "Collecting Bank"; "Presenting Bank" [; "Remitting Bank"]. In this Article [unless the context otherwise requires]:

(1) "Bank" means a person engaged in the business of banking, including a savings bank, savings and loan association, credit union, or trust company.

[(a)] (2) "Depositary bank" means the first bank to [which] take an item [is transferred for collection] even though it is also the payor bank, unless the item is presented for immediate payment over the counter;

[(b)] (3) "Payor bank" means a bank[by which an item is payable as drawn or accepted] that is the drawee of a draft;

[(c)] (4) "Intermediary bank" means [any] a bank to which an item is transferred in course of collection except the depositary or payor bank;

[(d)] (5) "Collecting bank" means [any] a bank handling [the] an item for collection except the payor bank;

[(e)] (6) Presenting bank" means [any] a bank presenting an item except a payor bank[;].

[(f)   "Remitting bank" means any payor or intermediary bank remitting for an item.]

§4-106. Payable Through or Payable at Bank; Collecting Bank.

(a) If an item states that it is "payable through" a bank identified in the item, (i) the item designates the bank as a collecting bank and does not by itself authorize the bank to pay the item, and (ii) the item may be presented for payment only by or through the bank.

Alternative A

(b) If an item states that it is "payable at" a bank identified in the item, the item is equivalent to a draft drawn on the bank.

Alternative B

(b) If an item states that it is "payable at" a bank identified in the item, (i) the item designates the bank as a collecting bank and does not by itself authorize the bank to pay the item, and (ii) the item may be presented for payment only by or through the bank.

(c) If a draft names a nonbank drawee and it is unclear whether a bank named in the draft is a co-drawee or a collecting bank, the bank is a collecting bank.

§ [4-106] 4-107. Separate Office of Bank.

A branch or separate office of a bank [[maintaining its own deposit ledgers]] is a separate bank for the purpose of computing the time within which and determining the place at or to which action may be taken or notice or orders [shall] must be given under this Article and under Article 3.

§ [4-107] 4-108. Time of Receipt of Items.

[(1)] (a) For the purpose of allowing time to process items, prove balances, and make the necessary entries on its books to determine its position for the day, a bank may fix an afternoon hour of 2 P.M. or later as a [cut-off] cutoff hour for the handling of money and items and the making of entries on its books.

[(2)] (b) [Any] An item or deposit of money received on any day after a [cut-off] cutoff hour so fixed or after the close of the banking day may be treated as being received at the opening of the next banking day.

§ [4-108] 4-109. Delays.

[(1)] (a) Unless otherwise instructed, a collecting bank in a good faith effort to secure payment [may, in the case] of a specific [items] item drawn on a payor other than a bank, and with or without the approval of any person involved, may waive, modify, or extend time limits imposed or permitted by this [Act] for a period not [in excess of an] exceeding two additional banking [day] days without discharge of [secondary parties and without] drawers or indorsers or liability to its transferor or [any] a prior party.

[(2)] (b) Delay by a collecting bank or payor bank beyond time limits prescribed or permitted by this [Act] or by instructions is excused if (i) the delay is caused by interruption of communication or computer facilities, suspension of payments by another bank, war, emergency conditions, failure of equipment, or other circumstances beyond the control of the bank[provided it], and (ii) the bank exercises such diligence as the circumstances require.

§4-109. Process of Posting. The "process of posting" means the usual procedure followed by a payor bank in determining to pay an item and in recording the payment including one or more of the following or other steps as determined by the bank:

(a) verification of any signature;

(b) ascertaining that sufficient funds are available;

(c) affixing a "paid" or other stamp;

(d) entering a charge or entry to a customer's account;

(e) correcting or reversing an entry or erroneous action with respect to the item.]

§4-110. Electronic Presentment.

(a) "Agreement for electronic presentment" means an agreement, clearing-house rule, or Federal Reserve regulation or operating circular, providing that presentment of an item may be made by transmission of an image of an item or information describing the item ("presentment notice") rather than delivery of the item itself. The agreement may provide for procedures governing retention, presentment, payment, dishonor, and other matters concerning items subject to the agreement.

(b) Presentment of an item pursuant to an agreement for presentment is made when the presentment notice is received.

(c) If presentment is made by presentment notice, a reference to "item" or "check" in this Article means the presentment notice unless the context otherwise indicates.

§4-111. Statute of Limitations.

An action to enforce an obligation, duty, or right arising under this Article must be commenced within three years after the [cause of action] accrues.

Part 2: Collection of Items—Depositary and Collecting Banks

§4-201. [Presumption and Duration of Agency] Status of Collecting [Banks] Bank as Agent and Provisional Status of Credits; Applicability of Article; Item Indorsed "Pay Any Bank".

[(1)] (a) Unless a contrary intent clearly appears and [prior to] before the time that a settlement given by a collecting bank for an item is or becomes final, [(subsection (3) of Section 4-211 and Sections 4-212 and 4-213)] the bank, with respect to the item, is an agent or sub-agent of the owner of the item and any settlement given for the item is provisional. This provision applies regardless of the form of indorsement or lack of indorsement and even though credit given for the item is subject to immediate withdrawal as of right or is in fact withdrawn; but the continuance of ownership of an item by its owner and any rights of the owner to proceeds of the item are subject to rights of a collecting bank, such as those resulting from outstanding advances on the item and [valid] rights of recoupment or setoff. [When] If an item is handled by banks for purposes of presentment, payment [and], collection, or return, the relevant provisions of this Article apply even though action of the parties clearly establishes that a particular bank has purchased the item and is the owner of it.

[(2)] (b) After an item has been indorsed with the words "pay any bank" or the like, only a bank may acquire the rights of a holder until the item has been:

[(a)] (1) [until the item has been] returned to the customer initiating collection; or

[(b)] (2) [until the item has been] specially indorsed by a bank to a person who is not a bank.

§4-202. Responsibility for Collection or Return; When Action [Seasonable] Timely.

[(1)] (a) A collecting bank must [use] exercise ordinary care in:

[(1)] (a) presenting an item or sending it for presentment; [and]

[(b)] (2) sending notice of dishonor or nonpayment or returning an item other than a documentary draft to the bank's transferor [[or directly to the depositary bank under subsection (2) of Section 4-212] (see note to Section 4-212)] after learning that the item has not been paid or accepted, as the case may be; and

[(c)] (3) settling for an item when the bank receives final settlement; and

[(d)] making or providing for any necessary protest; and]

[(e)] (4) notifying its transferor of any loss or delay in transit within a reasonable time after discovery thereof.

[(2) A collecting bank taking proper action before its midnight deadline following receipt of an item, notice or payment acts seasonably; taking proper action within a reasonably longer time may be seasonable but the bank has the burden of so establishing.]

(b) A collecting bank exercises ordinary care under subsection (a) by taking proper action before its midnight deadline following receipt of an item, notice, or settlement. Taking proper action within a reasonably longer time may constitute the exercise of ordinary care, but the bank has the burden of establishing timeliness.

[(3)] (c) Subject to subsection [(1)(a)] (a)(1), a bank is not liable for the insolvency, neglect, misconduct, mistake, or default of another bank or person or for loss or destruction of an item in the possession of others or in transit [or in the possession of others].

§4-203. Effect of Instructions.
Subject to [the provisions of] Article 3 concerning conversion of instruments (Section [3-419] 3-420) and [the provisions of both Article 3 and this Article concerning] restrictive indorsements (Section 3-206), only a collecting bank's transferor can give instructions [which] that affect the bank or constitute notice to it, and a collecting bank is not liable to prior parties for any action taken pursuant to [such] the instructions or in accordance with any agreement with its transferor.

§4-204. Methods of Sending and Presenting; Sending [Direct] Directly to Payor Bank.

[(1)] (a) A collecting bank [must] shall send items by a reasonably prompt method, taking into consideration[any] relevant instructions, the nature of the item, the number of [such] those items on hand, [and] the cost of collection involved, and the method generally used by it or others to present [such] those items.

[(2)] (b) A collecting bank may send:

[(a)] (1) [any] an item [direct] directly to the payor bank;

[(b)] (2) [any] an item to [any] a nonbank payor if authorized by its transferor; and

[(c)] (3) [any] an item other than documentary drafts to [any] a nonbank payor, if authorized by Federal Reserve regulation or operating [letter] circular, [clearing house] clearing-house rule, or the like.

[(3)] (c) Presentment may be made by a presenting bank at a place where the payor bank or other payor has requested that presentment be made.

§4-205. [Supplying Missing Indorsement; No Notice from Prior Indorsement] Depositary Bank Holder of Unindorsed Item. If a customer delivers an item to a depositary bank for collection:

(1) the depositary bank becomes a holder of the item at the time it receives the item for collection if the customer at the time of delivery was a holder of the item, whether or not the customer indorses the item, and, if the bank satisfies the other requirements of Section 3-302, it is a holder in due course; and

(2) the depositary bank warrants to collecting banks, the payor bank or other payor, and the drawer that the amount of the item was paid to the customer or deposited to the customer's account.

[(1) A depositary bank which has taken an item for collection may supply any indorsement of the customer which is necessary to title unless the item contains the words "payee's indorsement required" or the like. In the absence of such a requirement a statement placed on the item by the depositary bank to the effect that the item was deposited by a customer or credited to his account is effective as the customer's indorsement;

(2) An intermediary bank, or payor bank which is not a depositary bank, is neither given notice nor otherwise affected by a restrictive indorsement of any person except the bank's immediate transferor.]

§4-206. Transfer Between Banks. Any agreed method [which] that identifies the transferor bank is sufficient for the item's further transfer to another bank.

§4-207. Warranties of Customer and Collecting Bank on Transfer or Presentment of Items; Time for Claims.

(1) Each customer or collecting bank who obtains payment or acceptance of an item and each prior customer and collecting bank warrants to the payor bank

or other payor who in good faith pays or accepts the item that

(a) he has a good title to the item or is authorized to obtain payment or acceptance on behalf of one who has a good title; and

(b) he has no knowledge that the signature of the maker or drawer is unauthorized, except that this warranty is not given by any customer or collecting bank that is a holder in due course and acts in good faith

(i) to a maker with respect to the maker's own signature; or

(ii) to a drawer with respect to the drawer's own signature, whether or not the drawer is also the drawee; or

(iii) to an acceptor of an item if the holder in due course took the item after the acceptance or obtained the acceptance without knowledge that the drawer's signature was unauthorized; and

(c) the item has not been materially altered, except that this warranty is not given by any customer or collecting bank that is a holder in due course and acts in good faith

(i) to the maker of a note; or

(ii) to the drawer of a draft whether or not the drawer is also the drawee; or

(iii) to the acceptor of an item with respect to an alteration made prior to the acceptance if the holder in due course took the item after the acceptance, even though the acceptance provided "payable as originally drawn" or equivalent terms; or

(iv) to the acceptor of an item with respect to an alteration made after the acceptance.

(2) Each customer and collecting bank who transfers an item and receives a settlement or other consideration for it warrants to his transferee and to any subsequent collecting bank who takes the item in good faith that

(a) he has a good title to the item or is authorized to obtain payment or acceptance on behalf of one who has a good title and the transfer is otherwise rightful; and

(b) all signatures are genuine or authorized; and

(c) the item has not been materially altered; and

(d) no defense of any party is good against him; and

(e) he has no knowledge of any insolvency proceeding instituted with respect to the maker or acceptor or the drawer of an unaccepted item.

In addition each customer and collecting bank so

transferring an item and receiving a settlement or other consideration engages that upon dishonor and any necessary notice of dishonor and protest he will take up the item.

(3) The warranties and the engagement to honor set forth in the two preceding subsections arise notwithstanding the absence of indorsement or words of guaranty or warranty in the transfer or presentment and a collecting bank remains liable for their breach despite remittance to its transferor. Damages for breach of such warranties or engagement to honor shall not exceed the consideration received by the customer or collecting bank responsible plus finance charges and expenses related to the item, if any.

(4) Unless a claim for breach of warranty under this section is made within a reasonable time after the person claiming learns of the breach, the person liable is discharged to the extent of any loss caused by the delay in making claim.]

§4-207. Transfer Warranties.

(a) A customer or collecting bank that transfers an item and receives a settlement or other consideration warrants to the transferee and to any subsequent collecting bank that:

(1) the warrantor is a person entitled to enforce the item;

(2) all signatures on the item are authentic and authorized;

(3) the item has not been altered;

(4) the item is not subject to a defense or claim in recoupment (Section 3-305(a)) of any party that can be asserted against the warrantor; and

(5) the warrantor has no knowledge of any insolvency proceeding commenced with respect to the maker or acceptor or, in the case of an unaccepted draft, the drawer.

(b) If an item is dishonored, a customer or collecting bank transferring the item and receiving settlement or other consideration is obliged to pay the amount due on the item (i) according to the terms of the item at the time it was transferred, or (ii) if the transfer was of an incomplete item, according to its terms when completed as stated in Sections 3-115 and 3-407. The obligation of a transferor is owed to the transferee and to any subsequent collecting bank that takes the item in good faith. A transferor cannot disclaim its obligation under this subsection by an indorsement stating that it is made "without recourse" or otherwise disclaiming liability.

(c) A person to whom the warranties under subsection (a) are made and who took the item in good faith may recover from the warrantor as damages for breach of warranty an amount equal to the loss suffered as a result of the breach, but not more than the amount of the item plus expenses and loss of interest incurred as a result of the breach.

(d) The warranties stated in subsection (a) cannot be disclaimed with respect to checks. Unless notice of a claim for breach of warranty is given to the warrantor within 30 days after the claimant has reason to know of the breach and the identity of the warrantor, the warrantor is discharged to the extent of any loss caused by the delay in giving notice of the claim.

(e) A cause of action for breach of warranty under this section accrues when the claimant has reason to know of the breach.

§4-208. Presentment Warranties.

(a) If an unaccepted draft is presented to the drawee for payment or acceptance and the drawee pays or accepts the draft, (i) the person obtaining payment or acceptance, at the time of presentment, and (ii) a previous transferor of the draft, at the time of transfer, warrant to the drawee that pays or accepts the draft in good faith that:

(1) the warrantor is, or was, at the time the warrantor transferred the draft, a person entitled to enforce the draft or authorized to obtain payment or acceptance of the draft on behalf of a person entitled to enforce the draft;

(2) the draft has not been altered; and

(3) the warrantor has no knowledge that the signature of the purported drawer of the draft is unauthorized.

(b) A drawee making payment may recover from a warrantor damages for breach of warranty equal to the amount paid by the drawee less the amount the drawee received or is entitled to receive from the drawer because of the payment. In addition, the drawee is entitled to compensation for expenses and loss of interest resulting from the breach. The right of the drawee to recover damages under this subsection is not affected by any failure of the drawee to exercise ordinary care in making payment. If the drawee accepts the draft (i) breach of warranty is a defense to the obligation of the acceptor, and (ii) if the acceptor makes payment with respect to the draft, the acceptor is entitled to recover from a warrantor for breach of warranty the amounts stated in this subsection.

(c) If a drawee asserts a claim for breach of warranty under subsection (a) based on an unauthorized indorsement of the draft or an alteration of the draft, the warrantor may defend by proving that the indorsement is effective under Section 3-404 or 3-405 or the drawer is precluded under Section 3-406 or 4-406 from asserting against the drawee the unauthorized indorsement or alteration.

(d) If (i) a dishonored draft is presented for payment to the drawer or an indorser or (ii) any other item is presented for payment to a party obliged to pay the item, and the item is paid, the person obtaining payment and a prior transferor of the item warrant to the person making payment in good faith that the warrantor is, or was, at the time the warrantor transferred the item, a person entitled to enforce the item or authorized to obtain payment on behalf of a person entitled to enforce the item. The person making payment may recover from any warrantor for breach of warranty an amount equal to the amount paid plus expenses and loss of interest resulting from the breach.

(e) The warranties stated in subsections (a) and (d) cannot be disclaimed with respect to checks. Unless notice of a claim for breach of warranty is given to the warrantor within 30 days after the claimant has reason to know of the breach and the identity of the warrantor, the warrantor is discharged to the extent of any loss caused by the delay in giving notice of the claim.

(f) A cause of action for breach of warranty under this section accrues when the claimant has reason to know of the breach.

§4-209. Encoding and Retention Warranties.

(a) A person who encodes information on or with respect to an item after issue warrants to any subsequent collecting bank and to the payor bank or other payor that the information is correctly encoded. If the customer of a depositary bank encodes, that bank also makes the warranty.

(b) A person who undertakes to retain an item pursuant to an agreement for electronic presentment warrants to any subsequent collecting bank and to the payor bank or other payor that retention and presentment of the item comply with the agreement. If a customer of a depositary bank undertakes to retain an item, that bank also makes this warranty.

(c) A person to whom warranties are made under this section and who took the item in good faith may recover from the warrantor as damages for breach of warranty an amount equal to the loss suffered as a result of the breach, plus expenses and loss of interest incurred as a result of the breach.

§ [4-208] 4-210. Security Interest of Collecting Bank in Items, Accompanying Documents and Proceeds.

[(1)] **(a)** A collecting bank has a security interest in an item and any accompanying documents or the proceeds of either:

[(a)] **(1)** in case of an item deposited in an account, to the extent to which credit given for the item has been withdrawn or applied;

[(b)] **(2)** in case of an item for which it has given credit available for withdrawal as of right, to the extent of the credit given, whether or not the credit is drawn upon [and whether] or [not] there is a right of chargeback; or

[(c)] **(3)** if it makes an advance on or against the item.

[(2)] **(b)** [When] If credit [which has been] given for several items received at one time or pursuant to a single agreement is withdrawn or applied in part, the security interest remains upon all the items, any accompanying documents or the proceeds of either. For the purpose of this section, credits first given are first withdrawn.

[(3)] **(c)** Receipt by a collecting bank of a final settlement for an item is a realization on its security interest in the item, accompanying documents, and proceeds. [To the extent and so] So long as the bank does not receive final settlement for the item or give up possession of the item or accompanying documents for purposes other than collection, the security interest continues to that extent and is subject to [the provisions of] Article 9, [except that] but:

[(a)] **(1)** no security agreement is necessary to make the security interest enforceable ([subsection (1)(a) of] Section [9-203] 9-203(1)(a)); [and]

[(b)] **(2)** no filing is required to perfect the security interest; and

[(c)] **(3)** the security interest has priority over conflicting perfected security interests in the item, accompanying documents, or proceeds.

§ [4-209] 4-211. When Bank Gives Value for Purposes of Holder in Due Course.
For purposes of determining its status as a holder in due course, [the] a bank has given value to the extent [that] it has a security interest in an item, [provided that] if the bank otherwise complies with the requirements of Section 3-302 on what constitutes a holder in due course.

§ [4-210] 4-212. Presentment by Notice of Item Not Payable by, Through, or at Bank; Liability of [Secondary Parties] Drawer or Indorser.

[(1)] **(a)** Unless otherwise instructed, a collecting bank may present an item not payable by, through, or at a bank by sending to the party to accept or pay a written notice that the bank holds the item for acceptance or payment. The notice must be sent in time to be received on or before the day when presentment is due and the bank must meet any requirement of the party to accept or pay under Section [3-505] 3-501 by the close of the bank's next banking day after it knows of the requirement.

[(2)] **(b)** [Where] If presentment is made by notice and [neither honor nor] payment, acceptance, or request for compliance with a requirement under Section [3-505] 3-501 is not received by the close of business on the day after maturity or, in the case of demand items, by the close of business on the third banking day after notice was sent, the presenting bank may treat the item as dishonored and charge any [secondary party] <u>drawer or indorser</u> by sending [him] <u>it</u> notice of the facts.

§ [4-211] <u>4-213.</u> [Media of Remittance; Provisional and Final Settlement in Remittance Cases] <u>Medium and Time of Settlement by Bank.</u>

[(1)] A collecting bank may take in settlement of an item

(a) a check of the remitting bank or of another bank on any bank except the remitting bank; or

(b) a cashier's check or similar primary obligation of a remitting bank which is a member of or clears through a member of the same clearing house or group as the collecting bank; or

(c) appropriate authority to charge an account of the remitting bank or of another bank with the collecting bank; or

(d) if the item is drawn upon or payable by a person other than a bank, a cashier's check, certified check or other bank check or obligation.

(2) If before its midnight deadline the collecting bank properly dishonors a remittance check or authorization to charge on itself or presents or forwards for collection a remittance instrument of or on another bank which is of a kind approved by subsection (1) or has not been authorized by it, the collecting bank is not liable to prior parties in the event of the dishonor of such check, instrument or authorization.

(3) A settlement for an item by means of a remittance instrument or authorization to charge is or becomes a final settlement as to both the person making and the person receiving the settlement

(a) if the remittance instrument or authorization to charge is of a kind approved by subsection (1) or has not been authorized by the person receiving the settlement and in either case the person receiving the settlement acts seasonally before its midnight deadline in presenting, forwarding for collection or paying the instrument or authorization,—at the time the remittance instrument or authorization is finally paid by the payor by which it is payable;

(b) if the person receiving the settlement has authorized remittance by a non-bank check or obligation or by a cashier's check or similar primary obligation of or a check upon the payor or other remitting bank which is not of a kind approved by subsection (1)(b),—at the time of the receipt of such remittance check or obligation; or

(c) if in a case not covered by sub-paragraphs (a) or (b) the person receiving the settlement fails to seasonably present, forward for collection,

pay or return a remittance instrument or authorization to it to charge before its midnight deadline,—at such midnight deadline.

(a) With respect to settlement by a bank, the medium and time of settlement may be prescribed by Federal Reserve regulations or circulars, clearinghouse rules, and the like, or agreement. In the absence of such prescription:

(1) the medium of settlement is cash or credit to an account in a Federal Reserve bank of or specified by the person to receive settlement; and

(2) the time of settlement, is:

(i) with respect to tender of settlement by cash, a cashier's check, or teller's check, when the cash or check is sent or delivered;

(ii) with respect to tender of settlement by credit in an account in a Federal Reserve Bank, when the credit is made;

(iii) with respect to tender of settlement by a credit or debit to an account in a bank, when the credit or debit is made or, in the case of tender of settlement by authority to charge an account, when the authority is sent or delivered; or

(iv) with respect to tender of settlement by a funds transfer, when payment is made pursuant to Section 4A-406(a) to the person receiving settlement.

(b) If the tender of settlement is not by a medium authorized by subsection (a) or the time of settlement is not fixed by subsection (a), no settlement occurs until the tender of settlement is accepted by the person receiving settlement.

(c) If settlement for an item is made by cashier's check or teller's check and the person receiving settlement, before its midnight deadline:

(1) presents or forwards the check for collection, settlement is final when the check is finally paid; or

(2) fails to present or forward the check for collection, settlement is final at the midnight deadline of the person receiving settlement.

(d) If settlement for an item is made by giving authority to charge the account of the bank giving settlement in the bank receiving settlement, settlement is final when the charge is made by the bank receiving settlement if there are funds available in the account for the amount of the item.

§ [4-212] <u>4-214.</u> <u>Right of Charge-Back or Refund; Liability of Collecting Bank; Return of Item.</u>

[(1)] (<u>a</u>) If a collecting bank has made provisional settlement with its customer for an item and [itself] fails by reason of dishonor, suspension of payments by a bank, or otherwise to receive [a] settlement for the item which is or becomes final, the bank may revoke the settlement given by it, charge back the amount of any credit given for the item to its customer's account, or obtain refund from its customer, whether or not it is able to return the [items] item, if by its midnight deadline or within a longer reasonable time after it learns the facts it returns the item or sends notification of the facts. If the return or notice is delayed beyond the bank's midnight deadline or a longer reasonable time after it learns the facts, the bank may revoke the settlement, charge back the credit, or obtain refund from its customer, but it is liable for any loss resulting from the delay. These rights to revoke, charge back, and obtain refund terminate if and when a settlement for the item received by the bank is or becomes final [(subsection (3) of Section 4-211 and subsections (2) and (3) of Section 4-213).]

[[(2) Within the time and manner prescribed by this section and Section 4-301, an intermediary or payor bank, as the case may be, may return an unpaid item directly to the depositary bank and may send for collection a draft on the depositary bank and obtain reimbursement. In such case, if the depositary bank has received provisional settlement for the item, it must reimburse the bank drawing the draft and any provisional credits for the item between banks shall become and remain final.]]

(b) A collecting bank returns an item when it is sent or delivered to the bank's customer or transferor or pursuant to its instructions.

[(3)] (c) A depositary bank [which] that is also the payor may charge back the amount of an item to its customer's account or obtain refund in accordance with the section governing return of an item received by a payor bank for credit on its books (Section 4-301).

[(4)](d) The right to charge back is not affected by:

[(a)] (1) [prior] previous use of [the] a credit given for the item; or

[(b)] (2) failure by any bank to exercise ordinary care with respect to the item, but [any] a bank so failing remains liable.

[(5)] (e) A failure to charge back or claim refund does not affect other rights of the bank against the customer or any other party.

[(6)] (f) If credit is given in dollars as the equivalent of the value of an item payable in [a] foreign [currency] money, the dollar amount of any charge-back or refund [shall] must be calculated on the basis of the [buying sight] bank-offered spot rate for the foreign [currency] money prevailing on the day when the person entitled to the charge-back or refund learns that it will not receive payment in ordinary course.

§ [4-213] 4-215. **Final Payment of Item by Payor Bank; When Provisional Debits and Credits Become Final; When Certain Credits Become Available for Withdrawal.**

[(1)] (a) An item is finally paid by a payor bank when the bank has first done any of the following [,whichever happens first]:

[(a)] (1) paid the item in cash;[or]

[(b)] (2) settled for the item without [reserving] having a right to revoke the settlement and without having such right] under statute, [clearing house] clearing-house rule, or agreement; or

[(c)] completed the process of posting the item to the indicated account of the drawer, maker or other person to be charged therewith; or]

[(d)] (3) made a provisional settlement for the item and failed to revoke the settlement in the time and manner permitted by statute, [clearing house] clearing-house rule, or agreement. [Upon a final payment under subparagraph (b), (c) or (d) the payor bank shall be accountable for the amount of the item.]

(b) If provisional settlement for an item does not become final, the item is not finally paid.

[(2)] (c) If provisional settlement for an item between the presenting and payor banks is made through a clearing house or by debits or credits in an account between them, then to the extent that provisional debits or credits for the item are entered in accounts between the presenting and payor banks or between the presenting and successive prior collecting banks seriatim, they become final upon final payment of the items by the payor bank.

[(3)] (d) If a collecting bank receives a settlement for an item which is or becomes final, [(subsection (3) of Section 4-211, subsection (2) of Section 4-213)] the bank is accountable to its customer for the amount of the item and any provisional credit given for the item in an account with its customer becomes final.

[(4)] (e) Subject to (i) applicable law stating a time for availability of funds and (ii) any right of the bank to apply the credit to an obligation of the customer, credit given by a bank for an item in [an account with its customer] a customer's account becomes available for withdrawal as of right:

[(a)] (1) [in any case where] if the bank has received a provisional settlement for the item, when [such] the settlement becomes final and the bank has had a reasonable time to [learn that the settlement is final] receive return of the item and the item has not been received within that time;

[(b)] (2) [in any case where] if the bank is both [a] the depositary bank and [a] the payor bank, and the item is finally paid, at the opening of the bank's second banking day following receipt of the item.

[(5)] (f) [A deposit of money in a bank is final when made but, subject] Subject to applicable law stating a time for availability of funds and any right of [the] a bank to apply [the] a deposit to an obligation of the [customer] depositor, [the] a deposit of money becomes available for withdrawal as of right at the opening of the bank's next banking day [following] after receipt of the deposit.

§ [4-214] 4-216. Insolvency and Preference.

[(1)] (a) [Any] If an item is in or [coming] comes into the possession of a payor or collecting bank [which] that suspends payment and [which] the item [is] has not been finally paid, the item must [shall] be returned by the receiver, trustee, or agent in charge of the closed bank to the presenting bank or the closed bank's customer.

[(2)] (b) If a payor bank finally pays an item and suspends payments without making a settlement for the item with its customer or the presenting bank which settlement is or becomes final, the owner of the item has a preferred claim against the payor bank.

[(3)] (c) If a payor bank gives or a collecting bank gives or receives a provisional settlement for an item and thereafter suspends payments, the suspension does not prevent or interfere with the [settlement] settlement's becoming final if [such] the finality occurs automatically upon the lapse of certain time or the happening of certain events [(subsection (3) of Section 4-211, subsections (1)(d), (2) and (3) of Section 4-213).]

[(4)] (d) If a collecting bank receives from subsequent parties settlement for an item, which settlement is or becomes final and the bank suspends payments without making a settlement for the item with its customer which settlement is or becomes final, the owner of the item has a preferred claim against [such] the collecting bank.

Part 3: Collection of Items—Payor Banks

§4-301. Deferred Posting; Recovery of Payment by Return of Items; Time of Dishonor; Return of Items by Payor Bank.

[(1)] (a) [Where an authorized settlement] If a payor bank settles for a demand item [(] other than a documentary draft[)] received by a payor bank] presented otherwise than for immediate payment over the counter[has been made] before midnight of the banking day of receipt, the payor bank may revoke the settlement and recover [any payment] the settlement if,

before it has made final payment [(subsection (1) of Section 4-213)] and before its midnight deadline, it

[(a)] (1) returns the item; or
[(b)] (2) sends written notice of dishonor or nonpayment if the item is [held for protest or is otherwise] unavailable for return.

[(2)] (b) If a demand item is received by a payor bank for credit on its books, it may return [such] the item or send notice of dishonor and may revoke any credit given or recover the amount thereof withdrawn by its customer, if it acts within the time limit and in the manner specified in [the preceding] subsection (a).

[(3)] (c) Unless previous notice of dishonor has been sent, an item is dishonored at the time when for purposes of dishonor it is returned or notice sent in accordance with this section.

[(4)] (d) An item is returned:

[(a)] (1) as to an item [received] presented through a clearing house, when it is delivered to the presenting or last collecting bank or to the clearing house or is sent or delivered in accordance with clearing-house rules;
[(b)] (2) in all other cases, when it is sent or delivered to the bank's customer or transferor or pursuant to [his] instructions.

§4-302. Payor Bank's Responsibility for Late Return of Item.

[In the absence of a valid defense such as breach of a presentment warranty (subsection (1) of Section 4-207), settlement effected or the like, if]

(a) If an item is presented to on and received by a payor bank, the bank is accountable for the amount of:

[(a)] (1) a demand item, other than a documentary draft, whether properly payable or not, if the bank, in any case [where] in which it is not also the depositary bank, retains the item beyond midnight of the banking day of receipt without settling for it or,[regardless of] whether or not it is also the depositary bank, does not pay or return the item or send notice of dishonor until after its midnight deadline; or
[(b)] (2) any other properly payable item unless, within the time allowed for acceptance or payment of that item, the bank either accepts or pays the item or returns it and accompanying documents.

(b) The liability of a payor bank to pay an item pursuant to subsection (a) is subject to defenses based on breach of a presentment warranty (Section 4-208) or proof that the person seeking enforcement of the liability presented or transferred the item for the purpose of defrauding the payor bank.

§4-303. When Items Subject to Notice, [Stop-Order] Stop-Payment Order, Legal Process, or Setoff; Order in Which Items May Be Charged or Certified.

[(1)] (a) Any knowledge, notice, or [stop order] stop-payment order received by, legal process served upon, or setoff exercised by a payor bank[, whether or not effective under other rules of law] comes too late to terminate, suspend, or modify the bank's right or duty to pay an item or to charge its customer's account for the item [, comes too late to so terminate, suspend or modify such right or duty] if the knowledge, notice, [stop order] stop-payment order, or legal process is received or served and a reasonable time for the bank to act thereon expires or the setoff is exercised after the [bank has done any] earliest of the following:

[(a)] (1) [accepted or certified] the bank accepts or certifies the item;

[(b)] (2) [paid] the bank pays the item in cash;

[(c)] (3) [settled] the bank settles for the item without [reserving] having a right to revoke the settlement [and without having such right] under statute, [clearing house] clearing-house rule, or agreement;

[(d) completed the process of posting the item to the indicated account of the drawer, maker or other person to be charged therewith or otherwise has evidenced by examination of such indicated account and by action its decision to pay the item; or]

[(e)] (4) [become] the bank becomes accountable for the amount of the item under[subsection (1)(d) of Section 4-213 and] Section 4-302 dealing with the payor bank's responsibility for late return of items [.]; or

(5) with respect to checks, a cutoff hour no earlier than one hour after the opening of the next banking day after the banking day on which the bank received the check and no later than the close of the next banking day or, if no cutoff hour is fixed, the close of the next banking day after the banking day on which the bank received the check.

[(2)] (b) Subject to [the provisions of] subsection [(1)] (a), items may be accepted, paid, certified, or charged to the indicated account of its customer in any order [convenient to the bank].

Part 4: Relationship Between Payor Bank and Its Customer

§4-401. When Bank May Charge Customer's Account.

[(1)] (a) [As against its customer, a] A bank may charge against [his] the account [any] of a customer an item [which] that is [otherwise] properly payable from that account even though the charge creates an overdraft. An item is properly payable if it is authorized by the customer and is in accordance with any agreement between the customer and bank.

(b) A customer is not liable for the amount of an overdraft if the customer neither signed the item nor benefited from the proceeds of the item.

(c) A bank may charge against the account of a customer a check that is otherwise properly payable from the account, even though payment was made before the date of the check, unless the customer has given notice to the bank of the postdating describing the check with reasonable certainty. The notice is effective for the period stated in Section 4-403(b) for stop-payment orders, and must be received at such time and in such manner as to afford the bank a reasonable opportunity to act on it before the bank takes any action with respect to the check described in Section 4-303. If a bank charges against the account of a customer a check before the date stated in the notice of postdating, the bank is liable for damages for the loss resulting from its act. The loss may include damages for dishonor of subsequent items under Section 4-402.

[(2)] (d) A bank [which] that in good faith makes payment to a holder may charge the indicated account of its customer according to:

[(a)] (1) the original [tenor] terms of [his] the altered item; or

[(b)] (2) the [tenor] terms of [his] the completed item, even though the bank knows the item has been completed unless the bank has notice that the completion was improper.

§4-402. Bank's Liability to Customer for Wrongful Dishonor; Time of Determining Insufficiency of Account.

(a) Except as otherwise provided in this Article, a payor bank wrongfully dishonors an item if it dishonors an item that is properly payable, but a bank may dishonor an item that would create an overdraft unless it has agreed to pay the overdraft.

(b) A payor bank is liable to its customer for damages proximately caused by the wrongful dishonor of an item. [When the dishonor occurs through mistake liability] Liability is limited to actual damages proved. [If so proximately caused and proved damages] and may include damages for an arrest or prosecution of the customer or other consequential damages. Whether any consequential damages are proximately caused by the wrongful dishonor is a question of fact to be determined in each case.

(c) A payor bank's determination of the customer's account balance on which a decision to dishonor for insufficiency of available funds is based may be made at any time between the time the item is received by the payor bank and the time that the payor bank returns the item or gives notice in lieu of return, and no more than one determination need be made. If, at the election of the payor bank, a subsequent balance determination is made for the purpose of reevaluating the bank's decision to dishonor the item, the account balance at that time is determinative of whether a dishonor for insufficiency of available funds is wrongful.

§4-403. Customer's Right to Stop Payment; Burden of Proof of Loss.

[(1)] (a) A customer [may by order to his bank stop payment of any item payable for his account but the order must be] or any person authorized to draw on the account if there is more than one person may stop payment of any item drawn on the customer's account or close the account by an order to the bank describing the item or account with reasonable certainty received at [such] a time and in [such] a manner [as to afford] that affords the bank a reasonable opportunity to act on it [prior to] before any action by the bank with respect to the item described in Section 4-303. If the signature of more than one person is required to draw on an account, any of these persons may stop payment or close the account.

[(2)] An oral order is binding upon the bank only for fourteen calendar days unless confirmed in writing within that period. A written order is effective for only six months unless renewed in writing.]

(b) A stop-payment order is effective for six months, but it lapses after 14 calendar days if the original order was oral and was not confirmed in writing within that period. A stop-payment order may be renewed for additional six-month periods by a writing given to the bank within a period during which the stop-payment order is effective.

[(3)] (c) The burden of establishing the fact and amount of loss resulting from the payment of an item contrary to a [binding stop payment] stop-payment order or order to close an account is on the customer. The loss from payment of an item contrary to a stop-payment order may include damages for dishonor of subsequent items under Section 4-402.

§4-404. Bank Not [Obligated] **Obliged** to Pay Check More Than Six Months Old. A bank is under no obligation to a customer having a checking account to pay a check, other than a certified check, which is presented more than six months after its date, but it may charge its customer's account for a payment made thereafter in good faith.

§4-405. Death or Incompetence of Customer.

[(1)] (a) A payor or collecting bank's authority to accept, pay, or collect an item or to account for proceeds of its collection, if otherwise effective, is not rendered ineffective by incompetence of a customer of either bank existing at the time the item is issued or its collection is undertaken if the bank does not know of an adjudication of incompetence. Neither death nor incompetence of a customer revokes [such] the authority to accept, pay, collect, or account until the bank knows of the fact of death or of an adjudication of incompetence and has reasonable opportunity to act on it.

[(2)] (b) Even with knowledge, a bank may for 10 days after the date of death pay or certify checks drawn on or [prior to] before that date unless ordered to stop payment by a person claiming an interest in the account.

§4-406. Customer's Duty to Discover and Report Unauthorized Signature or Alteration.

[(1) When a bank sends to its customer a statement of account accompanied by items paid in good faith in support of the debit entries or holds the statement and items pursuant to a request for instructions of its customer or otherwise in a reasonable manner makes the statement and items available to the customer, the customer must exercise reasonable care and promptness to examine the statement and items to discover his unauthorized signature or any alteration on an item and must notify the bank promptly after discovery thereof.]

(a) A bank that sends or makes available to a customer a statement of account showing payment of items for the account shall either return or make available to the customer the items paid or provide information in the statement of account sufficient to allow the customer reasonably to identify the items paid. The statement of account provides sufficient information if the item is described by item number, amount, and date of payment.

(b) If the items are not returned to the customer, the person retaining the items shall either retain the items or, if the items are destroyed, maintain the capacity to furnish legible copies of the items until the expiration of seven years after receipt of the items. A customer may request an item from the bank that paid the item, and that bank must provide in a reasonable time either the item or, if the item has been destroyed or is not otherwise obtainable, a legible copy of the item.

(c) If a bank sends or makes available a statement of account or items pursuant to subsection (a), the customer must exercise reasonable promptness in examining the statement or the items to determine whether any payment was not authorized because of an alteration of an item or because a purported signature by or on behalf of the customer was not authorized. If, based on the statement or items provided, the customer should reasonably have discovered the unauthorized payment, the customer must promptly notify the bank of the relevant facts.

[(2)] **(d)** If the bank [establishes] proves that the customer failed, with respect to an item, to comply with the duties imposed on the customer by subsection [(1)] (c), the customer is precluded from asserting against the bank:

[(a)] **(1)** [his] the customer's unauthorized signature or any alteration on the item, if the bank also [establishes] proves that it suffered a loss by reason of [such] the failure; and

[(b)] **(2)** [an] the customer's unauthorized signature or alteration by the same wrongdoer on any other item paid in good faith by the bank [after the first item and statement was available to the customer for a reasonable period not exceeding fourteen calendar days and before the bank receives notification from the customer of any such unauthorized signature or alteration] if the payment was made before the bank received notice from the customer of the unauthorized signature or alteration and after the customer had been afforded a reasonable period of time, not exceeding 30 days, in which to examine the item or statement of account and notify the bank.

[(3) The preclusion under subsection (2) does not apply if the customer establishes lack of ordinary care on the part of the bank in paying the item(s).]

(e) If subsection (d) applies and the customer proves that the bank failed to exercise ordinary care in paying the item and that the failure substantially contributed to loss, the loss is allocated between the customer precluded and the bank asserting the preclusion according to the extent to which the failure of the customer to comply with subsection (c) and the failure of the bank to exercise ordinary care contributed to the loss. If the customer proves that the bank did not pay the item in good faith, the preclusion under subsection (d) does not apply.

[(4)] **(f)** Without regard to care or lack of care of either the customer or the bank, a customer who does not within one year from the time after [from the time] after the statement [and] or items are made available to the customer (subsection [(1)] (a)) discover and report [his] the customer's unauthorized signature on or any alteration[on the face or back of the item or does not within 3 years from that time discover and report any unauthorized indorsement] on the item is precluded from asserting against the bank [such] the unauthorized signature [or indorsement] or [such] alteration. If there is a preclusion under this subsection, the payor bank may not recover for breach of warranty under Section 4-208 with respect to the unauthorized signature or alteration to which the preclusion applies.

[(5)] If under this section a payor bank has a valid defense against a claim of a customer upon or resulting from payment of an item and waives or fails upon request to assert the defense the bank may not assert against any collecting bank or other prior party presenting or transferring the item a claim based upon the unauthorized signature or alteration giving rise to the customer's claim.]

§4-407. Payor Bank's Right to Subrogation on Improper Payment.

If a payor bank has paid an item over the [stop payment] order of the drawer or maker to stop payment, or after an account has been closed, or otherwise under circumstances giving a basis for objection by the drawer or maker, to prevent unjust enrichment and only to the extent necessary to prevent loss to the bank by reason of its payment of the item, the payor bank [shall be] is subrogated to the rights

[(a)] **(1)** of any holder in due course on the item against the drawer or maker; [and]

[(b)] **(2)** of the payee or any other holder of the item against the drawer or maker either on the item or under the transaction out of which the item arose; and

[(c)] **(3)** of the drawer or maker against the payee or any other holder of the item with respect to the transaction out of which the item arose.

Part 5: Collection of Documentary Drafts

§4-501. Handling of Documentary Drafts; Duty to Send for Presentment and to Notify Customer of Dishonor.
A bank [which] that takes a documentary draft for collection [must] shall present or send the draft and accompanying documents for presentment and, upon learning that the draft has not been paid or accepted in due course, [must] shall seasonably notify its customer of [such] the fact even though it may have discounted or bought the draft or extended credit available for withdrawal as of right.

§4-502. Presentment of "On Arrival" Drafts.
[When] If a draft or the relevant instructions require presentment "on arrival", "when goods arrive" or the like, the collecting bank need not present until in its judgment a reasonable time for arrival of the goods has expired. Refusal to pay or accept because the goods have not arrived is not dishonor; the bank must notify its transferor of [such] the refusal but need not present the draft again until it is instructed to do so or learns of the arrival of the goods.

§4-503. Responsibility of Presenting Bank for Documents and Goods; Report of Reasons for Dishonor; Referee in Case of Need.
Unless otherwise

instructed and except as provided in Article 5, a bank presenting a documentary draft:

[(a)] (1) must deliver the documents to the drawee on acceptance of the draft if it is payable more than three days after presentment; otherwise, only on payment; and

[(b) (2) upon dishonor, either in the case of presentment for acceptance or presentment for payment, may seek and follow instructions from any referee in case of need designated in the draft or, if the presenting bank does not choose to utilize [his] the referee's services, it must use diligence and good faith to ascertain the reason for dishonor, must notify its transferor of the dishonor and of the results of its effort to ascertain the reasons therefor, and must request instructions.

[But] However the presenting bank is under no obligation with respect to goods represented by the documents except to follow any reasonable instructions seasonably received; it has a right to reimbursement for any expense incurred in following instructions and to prepayment of or indemnity for [such] those expenses.

§4-504. Privilege of Presenting Bank to Deal with Goods; Security Interest for Expenses.

[(1)] (a) A presenting bank [which] that, following the dishonor of a documentary draft, has seasonably requested instructions but does not receive them within a reasonable time may store, sell, or otherwise deal with the goods in any reasonable manner.

[(2)] (b) For its reasonable expenses incurred by action under subsection [(1)] (a), the presenting bank has a lien upon the goods or their proceeds, which may be foreclosed in the same manner as an unpaid seller's lien.

ARTICLE 5: LETTERS OF CREDIT

§5-101. Short Title. This Article shall be known and may be cited as Uniform Commercial Code—Letters of Credit.

§5-102. Scope.

(1) This Article applies

(a) to a credit issued by a bank if the credit requires a documentary draft or a documentary demand for payment; and

(b) to a credit issued by a person other than a bank if the credit requires that the draft or demand for payment be accompanied by a document of title; and

(c) to a credit issued by a bank or other person if the credit is not within subparagraphs (a) or (b) but conspicuously states that it is a letter of credit or is conspicuously so entitled.

(2) Unless the engagement meets the requirements of subsection (1), this Article does not apply to engagements to make advances or to honor drafts or demands for payment, to authorities to pay or purchase, to guarantees or to general agreements.

(3) This Article deals with some but not all of the rules and concepts of letters of credit as such rules or concepts have developed prior to this act or may hereafter develop. The fact that this Article states a rule does not by itself require, imply or negate application of the same or a converse rule to a situation not provided for or to a person not specified by this Article.

§5-103. Definitions.

(1) In this Article unless the context otherwise requires

(a) "Credit" or "letter of credit" means an engagement by a bank or other person made at the request of a customer and of a kind within the scope of this Article (Section 5-102) that the issuer will honor drafts or other demands for payment upon compliance with the conditions specified in the credit. A credit may be either revocable or irrevocable. The engagement may be either an agreement to honor or a statement that the bank or other person is authorized to honor.

(b) A "documentary draft" or a "documentary demand for payment" is one, honor of which is conditioned upon the presentation of a document or documents. "Document" means any paper including document of title, security, invoice, certificate, notice of default and the like.

(c) An "issuer" is a bank or other person issuing a credit.

(d) A "beneficiary" of a credit is a person who is entitled under its terms to draw or demand payment.

(e) An "advising bank" is a bank which gives notification of the issuance of a credit by another bank.

(f) A "confirming bank" is a bank which engages either that it will itself honor a credit already issued by another bank or that such a credit will be honored by the issuer or a third bank.

(g) A "customer" is a buyer or other person who causes an issuer to issue a credit. The term also includes a bank which procures issuance or confirmation on behalf of that bank's customer.

(2) Other definitions applying to this Article and the sections in which they appear are:

"Notation of credit"   Section 5-108
"Presenter"   Section 5-112(3)

(3) Definitions in other Articles applying to this Article and the sections in which they appear are:

"Accept" or "Acceptance"	Section 3-410
"Contract for sale"	Section 2-106
"Draft"	Section 3-104
"Holder in due course"	Section 3-302
"Midnight deadline"	Section 4-104
"Security"	Section 8-102

(4) In addition, Article 1 contains general definitions and principles of construction and interpretation applicable throughout this Article.

§5-104. Formal Requirements; Signing.

(1) Except as otherwise required in subsection (1)(c) Section 5-102 on scope, no particular form of phrasing is required for a credit. A credit must be in writing and signed by the issuer and a confirmation must be in writing and signed by the confirming bank. A modification of the terms of a credit or confirmation must be signed by the issuer or confirming bank.

(2) A telegram may be a sufficient signed writing if it identifies its sender by an authorized authentication. The authentication may be in code and the authorized naming of the issuer in an advice of credit is a sufficient signing.

§5-105. Consideration.
No consideration is necessary to establish a credit or to enlarge or otherwise modify its terms.

§5-106. Time and Effect of Establishment of Credit.

(1) Unless otherwise agreed a credit is established

(a) as regards the customer as soon as a letter of credit is sent to him or the letter of credit or an authorized written advice of its issuance is sent to the beneficiary; and

(b) as regards the beneficiary when he receives a letter of credit or an authorized written advice of its issuance.

(2) Unless otherwise agreed once an irrevocable credit is established as regards the customer it can be modified or revoked only with the consent of the customer and once it is established as regards the beneficiary it can be modified or revoked only with his consent.

(3) Unless otherwise agreed after a revocable credit is established it may be modified or revoked by the issuer without notice to or consent from the customer or beneficiary.

(4) Notwithstanding any modification or revocation of a revocable credit any person authorized to honor or negotiate under the terms of the original credit is entitled to reimbursement for or honor of any draft or demand for payment duly honored or negotiated before receipt of notice of the modification or revocation and the issuer in turn is entitled to reimbursement from its customer.

§5-107. Advice of Credit; Confirmation; Error in Statement of Terms.

(1) Unless otherwise specified an advising bank by advising a credit issued by another bank does not assume any obligation to honor drafts drawn or demands for payment made under the credit but it does assume obligation for the accuracy of its own statement.

(2) A confirming bank by confirming a credit becomes directly obligated on the credit to the extent of its confirmation as though it were its issuer and acquires the rights of an issuer.

(3) Even though an advising bank incorrectly advises the terms of a credit it has been authorized to advise, the credit is established as against the issuer to the extent of its original terms.

(4) Unless otherwise specified the customer bears as against the issuer all risks of transmission and reasonable translation or interpretation of any message relating to a credit.

§5-108. "Notation Credit"; Exhaustion of Credit.

(1) A credit which specifies that any person purchasing or paying drafts drawn or demands for payment made under it must note the amount of the draft or demand on the letter or advice of credit is a "notation credit".

(2) Under a notation credit

(a) a person paying the beneficiary or purchasing a draft or demand for payment from him acquires a right to honor only if the appropriate notation is made and by transferring or forwarding for honor the documents under the credit such a person warrants to the issuer that the notation has been made; and

(b) unless the credit or a signed statement that an appropriate notation has been made accompanies the draft or demand for payment the issuer may delay honor until evidence of notation has been procured which is satisfactory to it but its obligation and that of its customer continue for a reasonable time not exceeding thirty days to obtain such evidence.

(3) If the credit is not a notation credit

(a) the issuer may honor complying drafts or demands for payment presented to it in the order in which they are presented and is discharged pro tanto by honor of any such draft or demand;

(b) as between competing good faith purchasers of complying drafts or demands the person first purchasing has priority over a subsequent purchaser even though the later purchased draft or demand has been first honored.

§5-109. Issuer's Obligation to Its Customer.

(1) An issuer's obligation to its customer includes

good faith and observance of any general banking usage but unless otherwise agreed does not include liability or responsibility

    (a) for performance of the underlying contract for sale or other transaction between the customer and the beneficiary; or

    (b) for any act or omission of any person other than itself or its own branch or for loss or destruction of a draft, demand or document in transit or in the possession of others; or

    (c) based on knowledge or lack of knowledge of any usage of any particular trade.

(2) An issuer must examine documents with care so as to ascertain that on their face they appear to comply with the terms of the credit but unless otherwise agreed assumes no liability or responsibility for the genuineness, falsification or effect of any document which appears on such examination to be regular on its face.

(3) A non-bank issuer is not bound by any banking usage of which it has no knowledge.

§5-110. Availability of Credit in Portions; Presenter's Reservation of Lien or Claim.

(1) Unless otherwise specified a credit may be used in portions in the discretion of the beneficiary.

(2) Unless otherwise specified a person by presenting a documentary draft or demand for payment under a credit relinquishes upon its honor all claims to the documents and a person by transferring such draft or demand or causing such presentment authorizes such relinquishment. An explicit reservation of claim makes the draft or demand non-complying.

§5-111. Warranties on Transfer and Presentment.

(1) Unless otherwise agreed the beneficiary by transferring or presenting a documentary draft or demand for payment warrants to all interested parties that the necessary conditions of the credit have been complied with. This is in addition to any warranties arising under Articles 3, 4, 7 and 8.

(2) Unless otherwise agreed a negotiating, advising, confirming, collecting or issuing bank presenting or transferring a draft or demand for payment under a credit warrants only the matters warranted by a collecting bank under Article 4 and any such bank transferring a document warrants only the matters warranted by an intermediary under Articles 7 and 8.

§5-112. Time Allowed for Honor or Rejection; Withholding Honor or Rejection by Consent; "Presenter".

(1) A bank to which a documentary draft or demand for payment is presented under a credit may without dishonor of the draft, demand or credit

    (a) defer honor until the close of the third banking day following receipt of the documents; and

    (b) further defer honor if the presenter has expressly or impliedly consented thereto. Failure to honor within the time here specified constitutes dishonor of the draft or demand and of the credit [except as otherwise provided in subsection (4) of Section 5-114 on conditional payment].

Note: *The bracketed language in the last sentence of subsection (1) should be included only if the optional provisions of Section 5-114(4) and (5) are included.*

(2) Upon dishonor the bank may unless otherwise instructed fulfill its duty to return the draft or demand and the documents by holding them at the disposal of the presenter and sending him an advice to that effect.

(3) "Presenter" means any person presenting a draft or demand for payment for honor under a credit even though that person is a confirming bank or other correspondent which is acting under an issuer's authorization.

§5-113. Indemnities.

(1) A bank seeking to obtain (whether for itself or another) honor, negotiation or reimbursement under a credit may give an indemnity to induce such honor, negotiation or reimbursement.

(2) An indemnity agreement inducing honor, negotiation or reimbursement

    (a) unless otherwise explicitly agreed applies to defects in the documents but not in the goods; and

    (b) unless a longer time is explicitly agreed expires at the end of ten business days following receipt of the documents by the ultimate customer unless notice of objection is sent before such expiration date. The ultimate customer may send notice of objection to the person from whom he received the documents and any bank receiving such notice is under a duty to send notice to its transferor before its midnight deadline.

§5-114. Issuer's Duty and Privilege to Honor; Right to Reimbursement

(1) An issuer must honor a draft or demand for payment which complies with the terms of the relevant credit regardless of whether the goods or documents conform to the underlying contract for sale or other contract between the customer and the beneficiary. The issuer is not excused from honor of such a draft or demand by reason of an additional general term that all documents must be satisfactory to the issuer, but an issuer may require that specified documents must be satisfactory to it.

(2) Unless otherwise agreed when documents appear on their face to comply with the terms of a credit but a required document does not in fact conform to the warranties made on negotiation or transfer of a document of title (Section 7-507) or of a certificated security (Section 8-306) or is forged or fraudulent or there is fraud in the transaction

(a) the issuer must honor the draft or demand for payment if honor is demanded by a negotiating bank or other holder of the draft or demand which has taken the draft or demand under the credit and under circumstances which would make it a holder in due course (Section 3-302) and in an appropriate case would make it a person to whom a document of title has been duly negotiated (Section 7-502) or a bona fide purchaser of a certificated security (Section 8-302); and

(b) in all other cases as against its customer, an issuer acting in good faith may honor the draft or demand for payment despite notification from the customer of fraud, forgery or other defect not apparent on the face of the documents but a court of appropriate jurisdiction may enjoin such honor.

(3) Unless otherwise agreed an issuer which has duly honored a draft or demand for payment is entitled to immediate reimbursement of any payment made under the credit and to be put in effectively available funds not later than the day before maturity of any acceptance made under the credit.

[(4) When a credit provides for payment by the issuer on receipt of notice that the required documents are in the possession of a correspondent or other agent of the issuer

(a) any payment made on receipt of such notice is conditional; and

(b) the issuer may reject documents which do not comply with the credit if it does so within three banking days following its receipt of the documents; and

(c) in the event of such rejection, the issuer is entitled by charge back or otherwise to return to the payment made.]

[(5) In the case covered by subsection (4) failure to reject documents within the time specified in subparagraph (b) constitutes acceptance of the documents and makes the payment final in favor of the beneficiary.]

Note: *Subsections (4) and (5) are bracketed as optional. If they are included the bracketed language in the last sentence of Section 5-112(1) should also be included.*

§5-115. Remedy for Improper Dishonor or Anticipatory Repudiation.

(1) When an issuer wrongfully dishonors a draft or demand for payment presented under a credit the person entitled to honor has with respect to any documents the rights of a person in the position of a seller (Section 2-707) and may recover from the issuer the face amount of the draft or demand together with incidental damages under Section 2-710 on seller's incidental damages and interest but less any amount realized by resale or other use or disposition of the subject matter of the transaction. In the event no resale or other utilization is made the documents, goods or other subject matter involved in the transaction must be turned over to the issuer on payment of judgment.

(2) When an issuer wrongfully cancels or otherwise repudiates a credit before presentment of a draft or demand for payment drawn under it the beneficiary has the rights of a seller after anticipatory repudiation by the buyer under Section 2-610 if he learns of the repudiation in time reasonably to avoid procurement of the required documents. Otherwise the beneficiary has an immediate right of action for wrongful dishonor.

§5-116. Transfer and Assignment.

(1) The right to draw under a credit can be transferred or assigned only when the credit is expressly designated as transferable or assignable.

(2) Even though the credit specifically states that it is nontransferable or nonassignable the beneficiary may before performance of the conditions of the credit assign his right to proceeds. Such an assignment is an assignment of an account under Article 9 on Secured Transactions and is governed by that Article except that

(a) the assignment is ineffective until the letter of credit or advice of credit is delivered to the assignee which delivery constitutes perfection of the security interest under Article 9; and

(b) the issuer may honor drafts or demands for payment drawn under the credit until it receives a notification of the assignment signed by the beneficiary which reasonably identifies the credit involved in the assignment and contains a request to pay the assignee; and

(c) after what reasonably appears to be such a notification has been received the issuer may without dishonor refuse to accept or pay even to a person otherwise entitled to honor until the letter of credit or advice of credit is exhibited to the issuer.

(3) Except where the beneficiary has effectively assigned his right to draw or his right to proceeds, nothing in this section limits his right to transfer or negotiate drafts or demands drawn under the credit.

§5-117. Insolvency of Bank Holding Funds for Documentary Credit.

(1) Where an issuer or an advising or confirming bank or a bank which has for a customer procured issuance of a credit by another bank becomes insolvent

before final payment under the credit and the credit is one to which this Article is made applicable by paragraphs (a) or (b) of Section 5-102(1) on scope, the receipt or allocation of funds or collateral to secure or meet obligations under the credit shall have the following results:

(**a**) to the extent of any funds or collateral turned over after or before the insolvency as indemnity against or specifically for the purpose of payment of drafts or demands for payments drawn under the designated credit, the drafts or demands are entitled to payment in preference over depositors or other general creditors of the issuer or bank; and

(**b**) on expiration of the credit or surrender of the beneficiary's rights under it unused any person who has given such funds or collateral is similarly entitled to return thereof; and

(**c**) a charge to a general or current account with a bank if specifically consented to for the purpose of indemnity against or payment of drafts or demands for payment drawn under the designated credit falls under the same rules as if the funds had been drawn out in cash and then turned over with specific instructions.

(**2**) After honor or reimbursement under this section the customer or other person for whose account the insolvent bank has acted is entitled to receive the documents involved.

ARTICLE 6: BULK TRANSFERS

§6-101. Short Title. This Article shall be known and may be cited as Uniform Commercial Code—Bulk Transfers.

§6-102. "Bulk Transfers"; Transfers of Equipment; Enterprises Subject to This Article; Bulk Transfers Subject to This Article.

(**1**) A "bulk transfer" is any transfer in bulk and not in the ordinary course of the transferor's business of a major part of the materials, supplies, merchandise or other inventory (Section 9-109) of an enterprise subject to this Article.

(**2**) A transfer of a substantial part of the equipment (Section 9-109) of such an enterprise is a bulk transfer if it is made in connection with a bulk transfer of inventory, but not otherwise.

(**3**) The enterprises subject to this Article are all those whose principal business is the sale of merchandise from stock, including those who manufacture what they sell.

(**4**) Except as limited by the following section all bulk transfers of goods located within this state are subject to this Article.

§6-103. Transfers Excepted From This Article. The

following transfers are not subject to this Article:

(**1**) Those made to give security for the performance of an obligation;

(**2**) General assignments for the benefit of all the creditors of the transferor, and subsequent transfers by the assignee thereunder;

(**3**) Transfers in settlement or realization of a lien or other security interests;

(**4**) Sales by executors, administrators, receivers, trustees in bankruptcy, or any public officer under judicial process;

(**5**) Sales made in the course of judicial or administrative proceedings for the dissolution or reorganization of a corporation and of which notice is sent to the creditors of the corporation pursuant to order of the court or administrative agency;

(**6**) Transfers to a person maintaining a known place of business in this State who becomes bound to pay the debts of the transferor in full and gives public notice of that fact, and who is solvent after becoming so bound;

(**7**) A transfer to a new business enterprise organized to take over and continue the business, if public notice of the transaction is given and the new enterprise assumes the debts of the transferor and he receives nothing from the transaction except an interest in the new enterprise junior to the claims of creditors;

(**8**) Transfers of property which is exempt from execution. Public notice under subsection (6) or subsection (7) may be given by publishing once a week for two consecutive weeks in a newspaper of general circulation where the transferor had its principal place of business in this State an advertisement including the names and addresses of the transferor and transferee and the effective date of the transfer.

§6-104. Schedule of Property, List of Creditors.

(**1**) Except as provided with respect to auction sales (Section 6-108), a bulk transfer subject to this Article is ineffective against any creditor of the transferor unless:

(**a**) The transferee requires the transferor to furnish a list of his existing creditors prepared as stated in this section; and

(**b**) The parties prepare a schedule of the property transferred sufficient to identify it; and

(**c**) The transferee preserves the list and schedule for six months next following the transfer and permits inspection of either or both and copying therefrom at all reasonable hours by any creditor of the transferor, or files the list and schedule in (a public office to be here identified).

(**2**) The list of creditors must be signed and sworn to or affirmed by the transferor or his agent. It must contain the names and business addresses of all creditors of the transferor, with the amounts when known, and also the names of all persons who are known to the transferor to assert claims against him even though such claims are disputed. If the transferor is the obligor of an outstanding issue of bonds, debentures or the like as to which there is an indenture trustee, the list of creditors need include only the name and address of the indenture trustee and the aggregate outstanding principal amount of the issue.

(3) Responsibility for the completeness and accuracy of the list of creditors rests on the transferor, and the transfer is not rendered ineffective by errors or omissions therein unless the transferee is shown to have had knowledge.

§6-105. Notice to Creditors. In addition to the requirements of the preceding section, any bulk transfer subject to this Article except one made by auction sale (Section 6-108) is ineffective against any creditor of the transferor unless at least ten days before he takes possession of the goods or pays for them, whichever happens first, the transferee gives notice of the transfer in the manner and to the persons hereafter provided (Section 6-107).

§6-106. Application of the Proceeds. In addition to the requirements of the two preceding sections:

(1) Upon every bulk transfer subject to this Article for which new consideration becomes payable except those made by sale at auction it is the duty of the transferee to assure that such consideration is applied so far as necessary to pay those debts of the transferor which are either shown on the list furnished by the transferor (Section 6-104) or filed in writing in the place stated in the notice (Section 6-107) within thirty days after the mailing of such notice. This duty of the transferee runs to all the holders of such debts, and may be enforced by any of them for the benefit of all.

(2) If any of said debts are in dispute the necessary sum may be withheld from distribution until the dispute is settled or adjudicated.

[(3) If the consideration payable is not enough to pay all of the said debts in full distribution shall be made pro rata.]

Note: *This section is bracketed to indicate division of opinion as to whether or not it is a wise provision, and to suggest that this is a point on which State enactments may differ without serious damage to the principle of uniformity.*

In any State where this section is omitted, the following parts of sections, also bracketed in the text, should also be omitted, namely:

Section 6-107(2) (e).
6-108(3) (c).
6-109(2).

In any State where this section is enacted, these other provisions should be also.

Optional Subsection (4)

[(4) The transferee may within ten days after he takes possession of the goods pay the consideration into the (specify court) in the county where the transferor had its principal place of business in this state and thereafter may discharge his duty under this section by giving notice by registered or certified mail to all the persons to whom the duty runs that the consideration has been paid into that court and that they should file their claims there. On motion of any interested party, the court may order the distribution of the consideration to the persons entitled to it.]

Note: *Optional subsection (4) is recommended for those states which do not have a general statute providing for payment of money into court.*

§6-107. The Notice.

(1) The notice to creditors (Section 6-105) shall state:

(a) that a bulk transfer is about to be made; and
(b) the names and business addresses of the transferor and transferee, and all other business names and addresses used by the transferor within three years last past so far as known to the transferee; and
(c) whether or not all the debts of the transferor are to be paid in full as they fall due as a result of the transaction, and if so, the address to which creditors should send their bills.

(2) If the debts of the transferor are not to be paid in full as they fall due or if the transferee is in doubt on that point then the notice shall state further:

(a) the location and general description of the property to be transferred and the estimated total of the transferor's debts;
(b) the address where the schedule of property and list of creditors (Section 6-104) may be inspected;
(c) whether the transfer is to pay existing debts and if so the amount of such debts and to whom owing;
(d) whether the transfer is for new consideration and if so the amount of such consideration and the time and place of payment;[and]
[(e) if for new consideration the time and place where creditors of the transferor are to file their claims.]

(3) The notice in any case shall be delivered personally or sent by registered or certified mail to all the persons shown on the list of creditors furnished by the transferor (Section 6-104) and to all other persons who are known to the transferee to hold or assert claims against the transferor.

Note: *The words in brackets are optional. See Note under §6-106.*

§6-108. Auction Sales; "Auctioneer".

(1) A bulk transfer is subject to this Article even though it is by sale at auction, but only in the manner and with the results stated in this section.

(2) The transferor shall furnish a list of his creditors and assist in the preparation of a schedule of the property to be sold, both prepared as before stated (Section 6-104).

(3) The person or persons other than the transferor who direct, control or are responsible for the auction are collectively called the "auctioneer". The auctioneer shall:

(a) receive and retain the list of creditors and prepare and retain the schedule of property for the period stated in this Article (Section 6-104);

(b) give notice of the auction personally or by registered or certified mail at least ten days before it occurs to all persons shown on the list of creditors and to all other persons who are known to him to hold or assert claims against the transferor;[and]

[(c) assure that the net proceeds of the auction are applied as provided in this Article (Section 6-106).

(4) Failure of the auctioneer to perform any of these duties does not affect the validity of the sale or the title of the purchasers, but if the auctioneer knows that the auction constitutes a bulk transfer such failure renders the auctioneer liable to the creditors of the transferor as a class for the sums owing to them from the transferor up to but not exceeding the net proceeds of the auction. If the auctioneer consists of several persons their liability is joint and several.

Note: *The words in brackets are optional. See Note under §6-106.*

§6-109. What Creditors Protected;[Credit for Payment to Particular Creditors].

(1) The creditors of the transferor mentioned in this Article are those holding claims based on transactions or events occurring before the bulk transfer, but creditors who become such after notice to creditors is given (Sections 6-105 and 6-107) are not entitled to notice.

[(2) Against the aggregate obligation imposed by the provisions of this Article concerning the application of the proceeds (Section 6-106 and subsection (3)(c) of 6-108) the transferee or auctioneer is entitled to credit for sums paid to particular creditors of the transferor, not exceeding the sums believed in good faith at the time of the payment to be properly payable to such creditors.]

Note: *The words in brackets are optional. See Note under §6-106.*

§6-110. Subsequent Transfers. When the title of a transferee to property is subject to a defect by reason of his noncompliance with the requirements of this Article, then:

(1) a purchaser of any of such property from such transferee who pays no value or who takes with notice of such noncompliance takes subject to such defect, but

(2) a purchaser for value in good faith and without such notice takes free of such defect.

§6-111. Limitation of Actions and Levies. No action under this Article shall be brought nor levy made more than six months after the date on which the transferee took possession of the goods unless the transfer has been concealed. If the transfer has been concealed, actions may be brought or levies made within six months after its discovery.

ARTICLE 7: WAREHOUSE RECEIPTS, BILLS OF LADING AND OTHER DOCUMENTS OF TITLE

Part 1: General

§7-101. Short Title. This Article shall be known and may be cited as Uniform Commercial Code—Documents of Title.

§7-102. Definitions and Index of Definitions.

(1) In this Article, unless the context otherwise requires:

(a) "Bailee" means the person who by a warehouse receipt, bill of lading or other document of title acknowledges possession of goods and contracts to deliver them.

(b) "Consignee" means the person named in a bill to whom or to whose order the bill promises delivery.

(c) "Consignor" means the person named in a bill as the person from whom the goods have been received for shipment.

(d) "Delivery order" means a written order to deliver goods directed to a warehouseman, carrier or other person who in the ordinary course of business issues warehouse receipts or bills of lading.

(e) "Document" means document of title as defined in the general definitions in Article 1 (Section 1-201).

(f) "Goods" means all things which are treated as movable for the purposes of a contract of storage or transportation.

(g) "Issuer" means a bailee who issues a document except that in relation to an unaccepted delivery order it means the person who orders the possessor of goods to deliver. Issuer includes any person for whom an agent or employee purports to act in issuing a document if the agent or employee has real or apparent authority to issue documents, notwithstanding that the issuer received no goods or that the goods were misdescribed or that in any other respect the agent or employee violated his instructions.

(h) "Warehouseman" is a person engaged in the business of storing goods for hire.

(2) Other definitions applying to this Article or to specified Parts thereof, and the sections in which they appear are:

"Duly negotiate"   Section 7-501
"Person entitled under
  the document"   Section 7-403(4)

(3) Definitions in other Articles applying to this Article and the sections in which they appear are:

"Contract for sale"   Section 2-106
"Overseas"   Section 2-323
"Receipt" of goods   Section 2-103

(4) In addition Article 1 contains general definitions and principles of construction and interpretation applicable throughout this Article.

§7-103. Relation of Article to Treaty, Statute, Tariff, Classification or Regulation. To the extent that any treaty or statute of the United States, regulatory statute of this State or tariff, classification or regulation filed or issued pursuant thereto is applicable, the provisions of this Article are subject thereto.

§7-104. Negotiable and Non-Negotiable Warehouse Receipt, Bill of Lading or Other Document of Title

(1) A warehouse receipt, bill of lading or other document of title is negotiable

(a) if by its terms the goods are to be delivered to bearer or to the order of a named person; or

(b) where recognized in overseas trade, if it runs to a named person or assigns.

(2) Any other document is non-negotiable. A bill of lading in which it is stated that the goods are consigned to a named person is not made negotiable by a provision that the goods are to be delivered only against a written order signed by the same or another named person.

§7-105. Construction Against Negative Implication. The omission from either Part 2 or Part 3 of this Article of a provision corresponding to a provision made in the other Part does not imply that a corresponding rule of law is not applicable.

Part 2: Warehouse Receipts: Special Provisions

§7-201. Who May Issue a Warehouse Receipt; Storage Under Government Bond.

(1) A warehouse receipt may be issued by any warehouseman.

(2) Where goods including distilled spirits and agricultural commodities are stored under a statute requiring a bond against withdrawal or a license for the issuance of receipts in the nature of warehouse receipts, a receipt issued for the goods has like effect as a warehouse receipt even though issued by a person who is the owner of the goods and is not a warehouseman.

§7-202. Form of Warehouse Receipt; Essential Terms; Optional Terms.

(1) A warehouse receipt need not be in any particular form.

(2) Unless a warehouse receipt embodies within its written or printed terms each of the following, the warehouseman is liable for damages caused by the omission to a person injured thereby:

(a) the location of the warehouse where the goods are stored;

(b) the date of issue of the receipt;

(c) the consecutive number of the receipt;

(d) a statement whether the goods received will be delivered to the bearer, to a specified person, or to a specified person or his order;

(e) the rate of storage and handling charges, except that where goods are stored under a field warehousing arrangement a statement of that fact is sufficient on a non-negotiable receipt;

(f) a description of the goods or of the packages containing them;

(g) the signature of the warehouseman, which may be made by his authorized agent;

(h) if the receipt is issued for goods of which the warehouseman is owner, either solely or jointly or in common with others, the fact of such ownership; and

(i) a statement of the amount of advances made and of liabilities incurred for which the warehouseman claims a lien or security interest (Section 7-209). If the precise amount of such advances made or of such liabilities incurred is, at the time of the issue of the receipt, unknown to the warehouseman or to his agent who issues it, a statement of the fact that advances have been made or liabilities incurred and the purpose thereof is sufficient.

(3) A warehouseman may insert in his receipt any other terms which are not contrary to the provisions of this Act and do not impair his obligation of delivery (Section 7-403) or his duty of care (Section 7-204). Any contrary provisions shall be ineffective.

§7-203. Liability for Non-Receipt or Misdescription.

A party to or purchaser for value in good faith of a document of title other than a bill of lading relying in either case upon the description therein of the goods may recover from the issuer damages caused by the non-receipt or misdescription of the goods, except to the extent that the document conspicuously indicates that the issuer does not know whether any part or all of the goods in fact were received or conform to the description, as where the description is in terms of marks or labels or kind, quantity or condition, or the receipt or description is qualified by "contents, condition and quality unknown." "said to contain" or the like, if such indication be true, or the party or purchaser otherwise has notice.

§7-204. Duty of Care; Contractual Limitation of Warehouseman's Liability.

(1) A warehouseman is liable for damages for loss of or injury to the goods caused by his failure to exercise such care in regard to them as a reasonably careful man would exercise under like circumstances but unless otherwise agreed he is not liable for damages which could not have been avoided by the exercise of such care.

(2) Damages may be limited by a term in the warehouse receipt or storage agreement limiting the amount of liability in case of loss or damage, and setting forth a specific liability per article or item, or value per unit of weight, beyond which the warehouseman shall not be liable; provided, however, that such liability may on written request of the bailor at the time of signing such storage agreement or within a reasonable time after receipt of the warehouse receipt be increased on part or all of the goods thereunder, in which event increased rates may be charged based on such increased valuation, but that no such increase shall be permitted contrary to a lawful limitation of liability contained in the warehouseman's tariff, if any. No such limitation is effective with respect to the warehouseman's liability for conversion to his own use.

(3) Reasonable provisions as to the time and manner of presenting claims and instituting actions based on the bailment may be included in the warehouse receipt or tariff.

(4) This section does not impair or repeal . . .

Note: *Insert in subsection (4) a reference to any statute which imposes a higher responsibility upon the warehouseman or invalidates contractual limitations which would be permissible under this Article.*

§7-205. Title Under Warehouse Receipt Defeated in Certain Cases.

A buyer in the ordinary course of business of fungible goods sold and delivered by a warehouseman who is also in the business of buying and selling such goods takes free of any claim under a warehouse receipt even though it has been duly negotiated.

§7-206. Termination of Storage at Warehouseman's Option.

(1) A warehouseman may on notifying the person on whose account the goods are held and any other person known to claim an interest in the goods require payment of any charges and removal of the goods from the warehouse at the termination of the period of storage fixed by the document, or, if no period is fixed, within a stated period not less than thirty days after the notification. If the goods are not removed before the date specified in the notification, the warehouseman may sell them in accordance with the provisions of the section on enforcement of a warehouseman's lien (Section 7-210).

(2) If a warehouseman in good faith believes that the goods are about to deteriorate or decline in value to less than the amount of his lien within the time prescribed in subsection (1) for notification, advertisement and sale, the warehouseman may specify in the notification any reasonable shorter time for removal of the goods and in case the goods are not removed, may sell them at public sale held not less than one week after a single advertisement or posting.

(3) If as a result of a quality or condition of the goods of which the warehouseman had no notice at the time of deposit the goods are a hazard to other property or to the warehouse or to persons, the warehouseman may sell the goods at public or private sale without advertisement on reasonable notification to all persons known to claim an interest in the goods. If the warehouseman after a reasonable effort is unable to sell the goods he may dispose of them in any lawful manner and shall incur no liability by reason of such disposition.

(4) The warehouseman must deliver the goods to any person entitled to them under this Article upon due demand made at any time prior to sale or other disposition under this section.

(5) The warehouseman may satisfy his lien from the proceeds of any sale or disposition under this section but must hold the balance for delivery on the demand of any person to whom he would have been bound to deliver the goods.

§7-207. Goods Must Be Kept Separate; Fungible Goods.

(1) Unless the warehouse receipt otherwise provides, a warehouseman must keep separate the goods covered by each receipt so as to permit at all times identification and delivery of those goods except that different lots of fungible goods may be commingled.

(2) Fungible goods so commingled are owned in common by the persons entitled thereto and the warehouseman is severally liable to each owner for that owner's share. Where because of overissue a mass of fungible goods is insufficient to meet all the receipts which the warehouseman has issued against it, the per-

sons entitled include all holders to whom overissued receipts have been duly negotiated.

§7-208. Altered Warehouse Receipts. Where a blank in a negotiable warehouse receipt has been filled in without authority, a purchaser for value and without notice of the want of authority may treat the insertion as authorized. Any other unauthorized alteration leaves any receipt enforceable against the issuer according to its original tenor.

§7-209. Lien of Warehouseman.

(1) A warehouseman has a lien against the bailor on the goods covered by a warehouse receipt or on the proceeds thereof in his possession for charges for storage or transportation (including demurrage and terminal charges), insurance, labor, or charges present or future in relation to the goods, and for expenses necessary for preservation of the goods or reasonably incurred in their sale pursuant to law. If the person on whose account the goods are held is liable for like charges or expenses in relation to other goods whenever deposited and it is stated in the receipt that a lien is claimed for charges and expenses in relation to other goods, the warehouseman also has a lien against him for such charges and expenses whether or not the other goods have been delivered by the warehouseman. But against a person to whom a negotiable warehouse receipt is duly negotiated a warehouseman's lien is limited to charges in an amount or at a rate specified on the receipt or if no charges are so specified then to a reasonable charge for storage of the goods covered by the receipt subsequent to the date of the receipt.

(2) The warehouseman may also reserve a security interest against the bailor for a maximum amount specified on the receipt for charges other than those specified in subsection (1), such as for money advanced and interest. Such a security interest is governed by the Article on Secured Transactions (Article 9).

(3)

(a) A warehouseman's lien for charges and expenses under subsection (1) or a security interest under subsection (2) is also effective against any person who so entrusted the bailor with possession of the goods that a pledge of them by him to a good faith purchaser for value would have been valid but is not effective against a person as to whom the document confers no right in the goods covered by it under Section 7-503.

(b) A warehouseman's lien on household goods for charges and expenses in relation to the goods under subsection (1) is also effective against all persons if the depositor was the legal possessor of the goods at the time of deposit. "Household goods" means furniture, furnishings and personal effects used by the depositor in a dwelling.

(4) A warehouseman loses his lien on any goods which he voluntarily delivers or which he unjustifiably refuses to deliver. (As amended in 1966.)

§7-210. Enforcement of Warehouseman's Lien.

(1) Except as provided in subsection (2), a warehouseman's lien may be enforced by public or private sale of the goods in block or in parcels, at any time or place and on any terms which are commercially reasonable, after notifying all persons known to claim an interest in the goods. Such notification must include a statement of the amount due, the nature of the proposed sale and the time and place of any public sale. The fact that a better price could have been obtained by a sale at a different time or in a different method from that selected by the warehouseman is not of itself sufficient to establish that the sale was not made in a commercially reasonable manner. If the warehouseman either sells the goods in the usual manner in any recognized market therefor, or if he sells at the price current in such market at the time of his sale, or if he has otherwise sold in conformity with commercially reasonable practices among dealers in the type of goods sold, he has sold in a commercially reasonable manner. A sale of more goods than apparently necessary to be offered to insure satisfaction of the obligation is not commercially reasonable except in cases covered by the preceding sentence.

(2) A warehouseman's lien on goods other than goods stored by a merchant in the course of his business may be enforced only as follows:

(a) All persons known to claim an interest in the goods must be notified.

(b) The notification must be delivered in person or sent by registered or certified letter to the last known address of any person to be notified.

(c) The notification must include an itemized statement of the claim, a description of the goods subject to the lien, a demand for payment within a specified time not less than ten days after receipt of the notification, and a conspicuous statement that unless the claim is paid within that time the goods will be advertised for sale and sold by auction at a specified time and place.

(d) The sale must conform to the terms of the notification.

(e) The sale must be held at the nearest suitable place to that where the goods are held or stored.

(f) After the expiration of the time given in the notification, an advertisement of the sale must be published once a week for two weeks consecutively in a newspaper of general circulation where the sale is to be held. The advertisement must include a description of the goods, the name of the person on whose account they are being held, and the time and place of the sale. The sale must take place at least fifteen days after the first publication. If there is no newspaper of general circulation where the sale is to be held, the advertisement must be posted at least ten days before the sale in not less than six conspicuous places in the neighborhood of the proposed sale.

(3) Before any sale pursuant to this section any person claiming a right in the goods may pay the amount necessary to satisfy the lien and the reasonable expenses incurred under this section. In that event the goods must not be sold, but must be retained by the warehouseman subject to the terms of the receipt and this Article.

(4) The warehouseman may buy at any public sale pursuant to this section.

(5) A purchaser in good faith of goods sold to enforce a warehouseman's lien takes the goods free of any rights of persons against whom the lien was valid, despite noncompliance by the warehouseman with the requirements of this section.

(6) The warehouseman may satisfy his lien from the proceeds of any sale pursuant to this section but must hold the balance, if any, for delivery on demand to any person to whom he would have been bound to deliver the goods.

(7) The rights provided by this section shall be in addition to all other rights allowed by law to a creditor against his debtor.

(8) Where a lien is on goods stored by a merchant in the course of his business the lien may be enforced in accordance with either subsection (1) or (2).

(9) The warehouseman is liable for damages caused by failure to comply with the requirements for sale under this section and in case of willful violation is liable for conversion. As amended in 1962.

Part 3: Bills of Lading: Special Provisions

§7-301. Liability for Non-Receipt or Misdescription; "Said to Contain"; "Shipper's Load and Count"; Improper Handling.

(1) A consignee of a non-negotiable bill who has given value in good faith or a holder to whom a negotiable bill has been duly negotiated relying in either case upon the description therein of the goods, or upon the date therein shown, may recover from the issuer damages caused by the misdating of the bill or the non-receipt or misdescription of the goods, except to the extent that the document indicates that the issuer does not know whether any part or all of the goods in fact were received or conform to the description, as where the description is in terms of marks or labels or kind, quantity, or condition or the receipt or description is

qualified by "contents or condition of contents of packages unknown", "said to contain", "Shipper's weight, load and count" or the like, if such indication be true.

(2) When goods are loaded by an issuer who is a common carrier, the issuer must count the packages of goods if package freight and ascertain the kind and quantity if bulk freight. In such cases "shipper's weight, load and count" or other words indicating that the description was made by the shipper are ineffective except as to freight concealed by packages.

(3) When bulk freight is loaded by a shipper who makes available to the issuer adequate facilities for weighing such freight, an issuer who is a common carrier must ascertain the kind and quantity within a reasonable time after receiving the written request of the shipper to do so. In such cases "shipper's weight" or other words of like purport are ineffective.

(4) The issuer may be inserting in the bill the words "shipper's weight, load and count" or other words of like purport indicate that the goods were loaded by the shipper; and if such statement be true the issuer shall not be liable for damages caused by the improper loading. But their omission does not imply liability for such damages.

(5) The shipper shall be deemed to have guaranteed to the issuer the accuracy at the time of shipment of the description, marks, labels, number, kind, quantity, condition and weight, as furnished by him; and the shipper shall indemnify the issuer against damage caused by inaccuracies in such particulars. The right of the issuer to such indemnity shall in no way limit his responsibility and liability under the contract of carriage to any person other than the shipper.

§7-302. Through Bills of Lading and Similar Documents.

(1) The issuer of a through bill of lading or other document embodying an undertaking to be performed in part by persons acting as its agents or by connecting carriers is liable to anyone entitled to recover on the document for any breach by such other persons or by a connecting carrier of its obligation under the document but to the extent that the bill covers an undertaking to be performed overseas or in territory not contiguous to the continental United States or an undertaking including matters other than transportation this liability may be varied by agreement of the parties.

(2) Where goods covered by a through bill of lading or other document embodying an undertaking to be performed in part by persons other than the issuer are received by any such person, he is subject with respect to his own performance while the goods are in his possession to the obligation of the issuer. His obligation is discharged by delivery of the goods to another such person pursuant to the document, and does not include liability for breach by any other such persons or by the issuer.

(3) The issuer of such through bill of lading or other document shall be entitled to recover from the connecting carrier or such other person in possession of the goods when the breach of the obligation under the document occurred, the amount it may be required to pay to anyone entitled to recover on the document therefor, as may be evidenced by any receipt, judgment, or transcript thereof, and the amount of any expense reasonably incurred by it in defending any action brought by anyone entitled to recover on the document therefor.

§7-303. Diversion; Reconsignment; Change of Instructions.

(1) Unless the bill of lading otherwise provides, the carrier may deliver the goods to a person or destination other than that stated in the bill or may otherwise dispose of the goods on instructions from

(a) the holder of a negotiable bill; or

(b) the consignor on a non-negotiable bill notwithstanding contrary instructions from the consignee; or

(c) the consignee on a non-negotiable bill in the absence of contrary instructions from the consignor, if the goods have arrived at the billed destination or if the consignee is in possession of the bill; or

(d) the consignee on a non-negotiable bill if he is entitled as against the consignor to dispose of them.

(2) Unless such instructions are noted on a negotiable bill of lading, a person to whom the bill is duly negotiated can hold the bailee according to the original terms.

§7-304. Bills of Lading in a Set.

(1) Except where customary in overseas transportation, a bill of lading must not be issued in a set of parts. The issuer is liable for damages caused by violation of this subsection.

(2) Where a bill of lading is lawfully drawn in a set of parts, each of which is numbered and expressed to be valid only if the goods have not been delivered against any other part, the whole of the parts constitute one bill.

(3) Where a bill of lading is lawfully issued in a set of parts and different parts are negotiated to different persons, the title of the holder to whom the first due negotiation is made prevails as to both the document and the goods even though any later holder may have received the goods from the carrier in good faith and discharged the carrier's obligation by surrender of his part.

(4) Any person who negotiates or transfers a single part of a bill of lading drawn in a set is liable to holders of that part as if it were the whole set.

(5) The bailee is obliged to deliver in accordance with Part 4 of this Article against the first presented part of a bill of lading lawfully drawn in a set. Such delivery discharges the bailee's obligation on the whole bill.

§7-305. Destination Bills.

(1) Instead of issuing a bill of lading to the consignor at the place of shipment a carrier may at the request of the consignor procure the bill to be issued at destination or at any other place designated in the request.

(2) Upon request of anyone entitled as against the carrier to control the goods while in transit and on surrender of any outstanding bill of lading or other receipt covering such goods, the issuer may procure a substitute bill to be issued at any place designated in the request.

§7-306. Altered Bills of Lading. An unauthorized alteration or filling in of a blank in a bill of lading leaves the bill enforceable according to its original tenor.

§7-307. Lien of Carrier.

(1) A carrier has a lien on the goods covered by a bill of lading for charges subsequent to the date of its receipt of the goods for storage or transportation (including demurrage and terminal charges) and for expenses necessary for preservation of the goods incident to their transportation or reasonably incurred in their sale pursuant to law. But against a purchaser for value of a negotiable bill of lading a carrier's lien is limited to charges stated in the bill or the applicable tariffs, or if no charges are stated then to a reasonable charge.

(2) A lien for charges and expenses under subsection (1) on goods which the carrier was required by law to receive for transportation is effective against the consignor or any person entitled to the goods unless the carrier had notice that the consignor lacked authority to subject the goods to such charges and expenses. Any other lien under subsection (1) is effective against the consignor and any person who permitted the bailor to have control or possession of the goods unless the carrier had notice that the bailor lacked such authority.

(3) A carrier loses his lien on any goods which he voluntarily delivers or which he unjustifiably refuses to deliver.

§7-308. Enforcement of Carrier's Lien.

(1) A carrier's lien may be enforced by public or private sale of the goods, in block or in parcels, at any time or place and on any terms which are commercially reasonable, after notifying all persons known to claim an interest in the goods. Such notification must include a statement of the amount due, the nature of the proposed sale and the time and place of any public sale. The fact that a better price could have been obtained by a sale at a different time or in a different method from that selected by the carrier is not of itself sufficient to establish that the sale was not made in a commercially reasonable manner. If the carrier either sells the goods in the usual manner in any recognized market therefor or if he sells at the price current in such market at the time of his sale or if he has otherwise sold in conformity with commercially reasonable practices among dealers in the type of goods sold he has sold in a commercially reasonable manner. A sale of more goods than apparently necessary to be offered to ensure satisfaction of the obligation is not commercially reasonable except in cases covered by the preceding sentence.

(**2**) Before any sale pursuant to this section any person claiming a right in the goods may pay the amount necessary to satisfy the lien and the reasonable expenses incurred under this section. In that event the goods must not be sold, but must be retained by the carrier subject to the terms of the bill and this Article.

(**3**) The carrier may buy at any public sale pursuant to this section.

(**4**) A purchaser in good faith of goods sold to enforce a carrier's lien takes the goods free of any rights of persons against whom the lien was valid, despite noncompliance by the carrier with the requirements of this section.

(**5**) The carrier may satisfy his lien from the proceeds of any sale pursuant to this section but must hold the balance, if any, for delivery on demand to any person to whom he would have been bound to deliver the goods.

(**6**) The rights provided by this section shall be in addition to all other rights allowed by law to a creditor against his debtor.

(**7**) A carrier's lien may be enforced in accordance with either subsection (1) or the procedure set forth in subsection (2) of Section 7-210.

(**8**) The carrier is liable for damages caused by failure to comply with the requirements for sale under this section and in case of willful violation is liable for conversion.

§7-309. Duty of Care; Contractual Limitation of Carrier's Liability.

(**1**) A carrier who issues a bill of lading whether negotiable or non-negotiable must exercise the degree of care in relation to the goods which a reasonably careful man would exercise under like circumstances. This subsection does not repeal or change any law or rule of law which imposes liability upon a common carrier for damages not caused by its negligence.

(**2**) Damages may be limited by a provision that the carrier's liability shall not exceed a value stated in the document if the carrier's rates are dependent upon value and the consignor by the carrier's tariff is afforded an opportunity to declare a higher value or a value as lawfully provided in the tariff, or where no tariff is filed he is otherwise advised of such opportunity; but no such limitation is effective with respect to the carrier's liability for conversion to its own use.

(**3**) Reasonable provisions as to the time and manner of presenting claims and instituting actions based on the shipment may be included in a bill of lading or tariff.

Part 4: Warehouse Receipts and Bills of Lading: General Obligations

§7-401. Irregularities in Issue of Receipt or Bill or Conduct of Issuer.
The obligations imposed by this Article on an issuer apply to a document of title regardless of the fact that

(**a**) the document may not comply with the requirements of this Article or of any other law or regulation regarding its issue, form or content; or

(**b**) the issuer may have violated laws regulating the conduct of his business; or

(**c**) the goods covered by the document were owned by the bailee at the time the document was issued; or

(**d**) the person issuing the document does not come within the definition of warehouseman if it purports to be a warehouse receipt.

§7-402. Duplicate Receipt or Bill; Overissue.
Neither a duplicate nor any other document of title purporting to cover goods already represented by an outstanding document of the same issuer confers any right in the goods, except as provided in the case of bills in a set, overissue of documents for fungible goods and substitutes for lost, stolen or destroyed documents. But the issuer is liable for damages caused by his overissue or failure to identify a duplicate document as such by conspicuous notation on its face.

§7-403. Obligation of Warehouseman or Carrier to Deliver; Excuse.

(**1**) The bailee must deliver the goods to a person entitled under the document who complies with subsections (2) and (3), unless and to the extent that the bailee establishes any of the following:

(**a**) delivery of the goods to a person whose receipt was rightful as against the claimant;

(**b**) damage to or delay, loss or destruction of the goods for which the bailee is not liable [, but the burden of establishing negligence in such cases is on the person entitled under the document];

Note: *The brackets in (1) (b) indicate that State enactments may differ on this point without serious damage to the principle of uniformity.*

(**c**) previous sale or other disposition of the goods in lawful enforcement of a lien or on warehouseman's lawful termination of storage;

(**d**) the exercise by a seller of his right to stop

delivery pursuant to the provisions of the Article on Sales (Section 2-705);

(**e**) a diversion, reconsignment or other disposition pursuant to the provisions of this Article (Section 7-303.) or tariff regulating such right;

(**f**) release, satisfaction or any other fact affording a personal defense against the claimant;

(**g**) any other lawful excuse.

(**2**) A person claiming goods covered by a document of title must satisfy the bailee's lien where the bailee so requests or where the bailee is prohibited by law from delivering the goods until the charges are paid.

(**3**) Unless the person claiming is one against whom the document confers no right under Sec. 7-503(1), he must surrender for cancellation or notation of partial deliveries any outstanding negotiable document covering the goods, and the bailee must cancel the document or conspicuously note the partial delivery thereon or be liable to any person to whom the document is duly negotiated.

(**4**) "Person entitled under the document" means holder in the case of a negotiable document, or the person to whom delivery is to be made by the terms of or pursuant to written instructions under a non-negotiable document.

§7-404. No Liability for Good Faith Delivery Pursuant to Receipt or Bill. A bailee who in good faith including observance of reasonable commercial standards has received goods and delivered or otherwise disposed of them according to the terms of the document of title or pursuant to this Article is not liable therefor. This rule applies even though the person from whom he received the goods had no authority to procure the document or to dispose of the goods and even though the person to whom he delivered the goods had no authority to receive them.

Part 5: Warehouse Receipts and Bills of Lading: Negotiation and Transfer

§7-501. Form of Negotiation and Requirements of "Due Negotiation".

(**1**) A negotiable document of title running to the order of a named person is negotiated by his indorsement and delivery. After his indorsement in blank or to bearer any person can negotiate it by delivery alone.

(**2**)

(**a**) A negotiable document of title is also negotiated by delivery alone when by its original terms it runs to bearer.

(**b**) When a document running to the order of a named person is delivered to him the effect is the same as if the document had been negotiated.

(**3**) Negotiation of a negotiable document of title after it has been indorsed to a specified person requires indorsement by the special indorsee as well as delivery.

(**4**) A negotiable document of title is "duly negotiated" when it is negotiated in the manner stated in this section to a holder who purchases it in good faith without notice of any defense against or claim to it on the part of any person and for value, unless it is established that the negotiation is not in the regular course of business or financing or involves receiving the document in settlement or payment of a money obligation.

(**5**) Indorsement of a non-negotiable document neither makes it negotiable nor adds to the transferee's rights.

(**6**) The naming in a negotiable bill of a person to be notified of the arrival of the goods does not limit the negotiability of the bill nor constitute notice to a purchaser thereof of any interest of such person in the goods.

§7-502. Rights Acquired by Due Negotiation.

(**1**) Subject to the following section and to the provisions of Section 7-205 on fungible goods, a holder to whom a negotiable document of title has been duly negotiated acquires thereby:

(**a**) title to the document;

(**b**) title to the goods;

(**c**) all rights accruing under the law of agency or estoppel, including rights to goods delivered to the bailee after the document was issued; and

(**d**) the direct obligation of the issuer to hold or deliver the goods according to the terms of the document free of any defense or claim by him except those arising under the terms of the document or under this Article. In the case of a delivery order the bailee's obligation accrues only upon acceptance and the obligation acquired by the holder is that the issuer and any indorser will procure the acceptance of the bailee.

(**2**) Subject to the following section, title and rights so acquired are not defeated by any stoppage of the goods represented by the document or by surrender of such goods by the bailee, and are not impaired even though the negotiation or any prior negotiation constituted a breach of duty or even though any person has been deprived of possession of the document by misrepresentation, fraud, accident, mistake, duress, loss, theft or conversion, or even though a previous sale or other transfer of the goods or document has been made to a third person.

§7-503. Document of Title to Goods Defeated in Certain Cases.

(**1**) A document of title confers no right in goods against a person who before issuance of the document had a legal interest or a perfected security interest in them and who neither

(a) delivered or entrusted them or any document of title covering them to the bailor or his nominee with actual or apparent authority to ship, store or sell or with power to obtain delivery under this Article (Section 7-403) or with power of disposition under this Act (Sections 2-403 and 9-307) or other statute or rule of law; nor

(b) acquiesced in the procurement by the bailor or his nominee of any document of title.

(2) Title to goods based upon an unaccepted delivery order is subject to the rights of anyone to whom a negotiable warehouse receipt or bill of lading covering the goods has been duly negotiated. Such a title may be defeated under the next section to the same extent as the rights of the issuer or a transferee from the issuer.

(3) Title to goods based upon a bill of lading issued to a freight forwarder is subject to the rights of anyone to whom a bill issued by the freight forwarder is duly negotiated; but delivery by the carrier in accordance with Part 4 of this Article pursuant to its own bill of lading discharges the carrier's obligation to deliver.

§7-504. Rights Acquired in the Absence of Due Negotiation; Effect of Diversion; Seller's Stoppage of Delivery.

(1) A transferee of a document, whether negotiable or non-negotiable, to whom the document has been delivered but not duly negotiated, acquires the title and rights which his transferor had or had actual authority to convey.

(2) In the case of a non-negotiable document, until but not after the bailee receives notification of the transfer, the rights of the transferee may be defeated

(a) by those creditors of the transferor who could treat the sale as void under Section 2-402; or

(b) by a buyer from the transferor in ordinary course of business if the bailee has delivered the goods to the buyer or received notification of his rights; or

(c) as against the bailee by good faith dealings of the bailee with the transferor.

(3) A diversion or other change of shipping instructions by the consignor in a non-negotiable bill of lading which causes the bailee not to deliver to the consignee defeats the consignee's title to the goods if they have been delivered to a buyer in ordinary course of business and in any event defeats the consignee's rights against the bailee.

(4) Delivery pursuant to a non-negotiable document may be stopped by a seller under Section 2-705, and subject to the requirement of due notification there provided. A bailee honoring the seller's instructions is entitled to be indemnified by the seller against any resulting loss or expense.

§7-505. Indorser Not a Guarantor for Other Parties. The indorsement of a document of title issued by a bailee does not make the indorser liable for any default by the bailee or by previous indorsers.

§7-506. Delivery Without Indorsement: Right to Compel Indorsement. The transferee of a negotiable document of title has a specifically enforceable right to have his transferor supply any necessary indorsement but the transfer becomes a negotiation only as of the time the indorsement is supplied.

§7-507. Warranties on Negotiation or Transfer of Receipt or Bill. Where a person negotiates or transfers a document of title for value otherwise than as a mere intermediary under the next following section, then unless otherwise agreed he warrants to his immediate purchaser only in addition to any warranty made in selling the goods

(a) that the document is genuine; and

(b) that he has no knowledge of any fact which would impair its validity or worth; and

(c) that his negotiation or transfer is rightful and fully effective with respect to the title to the document and the goods it represents.

§7-508. Warranties of Collecting Bank as to Documents. A collecting bank or other intermediary known to be entrusted with documents on behalf of another or with collection of a draft or other claim against delivery of documents warrants by such delivery of the documents only its own good faith and authority. This rule applies even though the intermediary has purchased or made advances against the claim or draft to be collected.

§7-509. Receipt or Bill: When Adequate Compliance With Commercial Contract. The question whether a document is adequate to fulfill the obligations of a contract for sale or the conditions of a credit is governed by the Articles on Sales (Article 2) and on Letters of Credit (Article 5).

Part 6: Warehouse Receipts and Bills of Lading: Miscellaneous Provisions

§7-601. Lost and Missing Documents

(1) If a document has been lost, stolen or destroyed, a court may order delivery of the goods or issuance of a substitute document and the bailee may without liability to any person comply with such order. If the document was negotiable the claimant must post security approved by the court to indemnify any person who may suffer loss as a result of non-surrender of the document. If the document was not negotiable, such security may be required at the discretion of the court. The court may also in its discretion order payment of the bailee's reasonable costs and counsel fees.

(2) A bailee who without court order delivers goods to a person claiming under a missing negotiable

document is liable to any person injured thereby, and if the delivery is not in good faith becomes liable for conversion. Delivery in good faith is not conversion if made in accordance with a filed classification or tariff or, where no classification or tariff is filed, if the claimant posts security with the bailee in an amount as least double the value of the goods at the time of posting to indemnify any person injured by the delivery who files a notice of claim within one year after the delivery.

§7-602. Attachment of Goods Covered by a Negotiable Document. Except where the document was originally issued upon delivery of the goods by a person who has no power to dispose of them, no lien attaches by virtue of any judicial process to goods in the possession of a bailee for which a negotiable document of title is outstanding unless the document be first surrendered to the bailee or its negotiation enjoined, and the bailee shall not be compelled to deliver the goods pursuant to process until the document is surrendered to him or impounded by the court. One who purchases the document for value without notice of the process or injunction takes free of the lien imposed by judicial process.

§7-603. Conflicting Claims; Interpleader. If more than one person claims title or possession of the goods, the bailee is excused from delivery until he has had a reasonable time to ascertain the validity of the adverse claims or to bring an action to compel all claimants to interplead and may compel such interpleader, either in defending an action for nondelivery of the goods, or by original action, whichever is appropriate.

ARTICLE 8: INVESTMENT SECURITIES

Part 1: Short Title and General Matters

§8-101. Short Title. This Article shall be known and may be cited as Uniform Commercial Code—Investment Securities.

§8-102. Definitions and Index of Definitions

(1) In this Article, unless the context otherwise requires:

(a) A "certificated security" is a share, participation, or other interest in property of or an enterprise of the issuer or an obligation of the issuer which is

   (i) represented by an instrument issued in bearer or registered form:

   (ii) of a type commonly dealt in on securities exchanges or markets or commonly recognized in any area in which it is issued or dealt in as a medium for investment; and

   (iii) either one of a class or series or by its terms divisible into a class or series of shares, participations, interest, or obligations.

(b) An "uncertificated security" is a share, participation, or other interest in property or an enterprise of the issuer or an obligation of the issuer which is

   (i) not represented by an instrument and the transfer of which is registered upon books maintained for that purpose by or on behalf of the issuer;

   (ii) of a type commonly dealt in on securities exchanges or markets; and

   (iii) either one of a class or series or by its terms divisible into a class or series of shares, participations, interests, or obligations.

(c) A "security" is either a certificated or an uncertificated security. If a security is certificated, the terms "security" and "certificated security" may mean either the intangible interest, the instrument representing that interest, or both, as the context requires. A writing that is a certificated security is governed by this Article and not by Article 3, even though it also meets the requirements of that Article. This Article does not apply to money. If a certificated security has been retained by or surrendered to the issuer or its transfer agent for reasons other than registration of transfer, other temporary purpose, payment, exchange, or acquisition by the issuer, that security shall be treated as an uncertificated security for purposes of this Article.

(d) A certificated security is in "registered form" if

   (i) its specifies a person entitled to the security or the rights it represents, and

   (ii) its transfer may be registered upon books maintained for that purpose by or on behalf of the issuer, or the security so states.

(e) A certificated security is in "bearer from" if it runs to bearer according to its terms and not by reason of any indorsement.

(2) A "subsequent purchaser" is a person who takes other than by original issue.

(3) A "clearing corporation" is a corporation registered as a "clearing agency" under the federal securities laws or a corporation:

(a) at least 90 percent of whose capital stock is held by or for one or more organizations, none of which other than a national securities exchange or association, holds in excess of 20 percent of the capital stock of the corporation, and each of which is

   (i) subject to supervision or regulation pursuant to the provisions of federal or state banking laws or state insurance laws,

(ii) a broker or dealer or investment company registered under the federal securities laws, or

(iii) a national securities exchange or association registered under the federal securities laws; and

(b) any remaining capital stock of which is held by individuals who have purchased at or prior to the time of their taking office as directors of the corporation and who have purchased only so much of the capital stock as is necessary to permit them to qualify as directors.

(4) A "custodian bank" is a bank or trust company that is supervised and examined by state or federal authority having supervision over banks and is acting as custodian for a clearing corporation.

(5) Other definitions applying to this Article or to specified Parts thereof and the sections in which they appear are:

"Adverse claim"	Section 8-302
"Bona fide purchaser"	Section 8-302
"Broker"	Section 8-303
"Debtor"	Section 9-105
"Financial intermediary"	Section 8-313
"Guarantee of the signature"	Section 8-402
"Initial transaction statement"	Section 8-408
"Instruction"	Section 8-308
"Intermediary bank"	Section 4-105
"Issuer"	Section 8-201
"Overissue"	Section 8-104
"Secured party"	Section 9-105
"Security agreement"	Section 9-105

(6) In addition Article 1 contains general definitions and principles of construction and interpretation applicable throughout this Article.

§8-103. Issuer's Lien. A lien upon a security in favor of an issuer thereof is valid against a purchaser only if:

(a) the security is certificated and the right of the issuer to the lien is noted conspicuously thereon; or

(b) the security is uncertificated and a notation of the right of the issuer to the lien is contained in the initial transaction statement sent to the purchaser or, if his interest is transferred to him other than by registration of transfer, pledge, or release, the initial transaction statement sent to the registered owner or the registered pledgee.

§8-104. Effect of Overissue; "Overissue".

(1) The provisions of this Article which validate a security or compel its issue or reissue do not apply to the extent that validation, issue, or reissue would result in overissue; but if:

(a) an identical security which does not constitute an overissue is reasonably available for purchase, the person entitled to issue or validation may compel the issuer to purchase the security

for him and either to deliver a certificated security or to register the transfer of an uncertificated security to him, against surrender of any certificated security he holds; or

(b) a security is not so available for purchase, the person entitled to issue or validation may recover from the issuer the price he or the last purchaser for value paid for it with interest from the date of his demand.

(2) "Overissue" means the issue of securities in excess of the amount the issuer has corporate power to issue.

§8-105. Certificated Securities Negotiable; Statements and Instructions Not Negotiable; Presumptions.

(1) Certificated securities governed by this Article are negotiable instruments.

(2) Statements (Section 8-408), notices, or the like, sent by the issuer of uncertificated securities and instructions (Section 8-308) are neither negotiable instruments nor certificated securities.

(3) In any action on a security:

(a) unless specifically denied in the pleadings, each signature on a certificated security, in a necessary indorsement, on an initial transaction statement, or on an instruction, is admitted;

(b) if the effectiveness of a signature is put in issue, the burden of establishing it is on the party claiming under the signature, but the signature is presumed to be genuine or authorized;

(c) if signatures on a certificated security are admitted or established, production of the security entitles a holder to recover on it unless the defendant establishes a defense or a defect going to the validity of the security;

(d) if signatures on an initial transaction statement are admitted or established, the facts stated in the statement are presumed to be true as of the time of its issuance; and

(e) after it is shown that a defense or defect exists, the plaintiff has the burden of establishing that he or some person under whom he claims is a person against whom the defense or defect is ineffective (Section 8-202).

§8-106. Applicability. The law (including the conflict of law rules) of the jurisdiction of organization of the issuer governs the validity of a security, the effectiveness of registration by the issuer, and the rights and duties of the issuer with respect to:

(a) registration of transfer of a certificated security;

(b) registration of transfer, pledge, or release of an

uncertificated security; and

(**c**) sending of statements of uncertificated securities.

§8-107. Securities Transferable; Action for Price.

(**1**) Unless otherwise agreed and subject to any applicable law or regulation respecting short sales, a person obligated to transfer securities may transfer any certificated security of the specified issue in bearer form or registered in the name of the transferee, or indorsed to him or in blank, or he may transfer an equivalent uncertificated security to the transferee or a person designated by the transferee.

(**2**) If the buyer fails to pay the price as it comes due under a contract of sale, the seller may recover the price of:

(**a**) certificated securities accepted by the buyer:

(**b**) uncertificated securities that have been transferred to the buyer or a person designated by the buyer; and

(**c**) other securities if efforts at their resale would be unduly burdensome or if there is no readily available market for their resale.

§8-108. Registration of Pledge and Release of Uncertificated Securities. A security interest in an uncertificated security may be evidenced by the registration of pledge to the secured party or a person designated by him. There can be no more than one registered pledge of an uncertificated security is the person in whose name the security is registered, even if the security is subject to a registered pledge. The rights of a registered pledgee of an uncertificated security under this Article are terminated by the registration of release.

Part 2: Issue—Issuer

§8-201. "Issuer".

(**1**) With respect to obligations on or defenses to a security, "issuer" includes a person who:

(**a**) places or authorizes the placing of his name on a certificated security (otherwise than as authenticating trustee, registrar, transfer agent, or the like) to evidence that it represents a share, participation, or other interest in his property or in an enterprise, or to evidence his duty to perform an obligation represented by the certificated security;

(**b**) creates shares, participations or other interests in his property or in an enterprise or undertakes obligations, which shares, participations, interests, or obligations are uncertificated securities;

(**c**) directly or indirectly creates fractional interests in his rights or property, which fractional interests are represented by certificated secu-

rities; or

(**d**) becomes responsible for or in place of any other person described as an issuer in this section.

(**2**) With respect to obligations on or defenses to a security, a guarantor is an issuer to the extent of his guaranty, whether or not his obligation is noted on a certificated security or on statements of uncertificated securities sent pursuant to Section 8-408.

(**3**) With respect to registration of transfer, pledge, or release (Part 4 of this Article), "issuer" means a person on whose behalf transfer books are maintained.

§8-202. Issuer's Responsibility and Defenses; Notice of Defect or Defense.

(**1**) Even against a purchaser for value and without notice, the terms of a security include:

(**a**) if the security is certificated, those stated on the security;

(**b**) if the security is uncertificated, those contained in the initial transaction statement sent to such purchaser, or if his interest is transferred to him other than by registration of transfer, pledge, or release, the initial transaction statement sent to the registered owner or registered pledgee; and

(**c**) those made part of the security by reference, on the certificated security or in the initial transaction statement, to another instrument, indenture, or document or to a constitution, statute, ordinance, rule, regulation, order or the like, to the extent that the terms referred to do not conflict with the terms stated on the certificated security or contained in the statement. A reference under this paragraph does not of itself charge a purchaser for value with notice of a defect going to the validity of the security, even though the certificated security or statement expressly states that a person accepting it admits notice.

(**2**) A certificated security in the hands of a purchaser for value or an uncertificated security as to which an initial transaction statement has been sent to a purchaser for value, other than a security issued by a government or governmental agency or unit, even though issued with a defect going to its validity, is valid with respect to the purchaser if he is without notice of the particular defect unless the defect involves a violation of constitutional provisions, in which case the security is valid with respect to a subsequent purchaser for value and without notice of the defect. This subsection applies to an issuer that is a government or governmental agency or unit only if either there has been substantial compliance with the legal requirements governing the issue or the issuer has received a substantial consideration for the issue as a whole or for the particular security and a stated purpose of the issue is one for which the issuer has power to borrow money or issue the security.

(3) Except as provided in the case of certain unauthorized signatures (Section 8-205), lack of genuineness of a certificated security or an initial transaction statement is a complete defense, even against a purchaser for value and without notice.

(4) All other defenses of the issuer of a certificated or uncertificated security, including nondelivery and conditional delivery of a certificated security, are ineffective against a purchaser for value who has taken without notice of the particular defense.

(5) Nothing in this section shall be construed to affect the right of a party to a "when, as and if issued" or a "when distributed" contract to cancel the contract in the event of a material change in the character of the security that is the subject of the contract or in the plan or arrangement pursuant to which the security is to be issued or distributed.

§8-203. Staleness as Notice of Defects or Defenses.

(1) After an act or event creating a right to immediate performance of the principal obligation represented by a certificated security or that sets a date on or after which the security is to be presented or surrendered for redemption or exchange, a purchaser is charged with notice of any defect in its issue or defense of the issuer if:

(a) the act or event is one requiring the payment of money, the delivery of certificated securities, the registration of transfer of uncertificated securities, or any of these on presentation or surrender of the certificated security, the funds or securities are available on the date set for payment or exchange, and he takes the security more than one year after that date; and

(b) the act or event is not covered by paragraph

(c) and he takes the security more than 2 years after the date set for surrender or presentation or the date on which performance became due.

(2) A call that has been revoked is not within subsection (1).

§8-204. Effect of Issuer's Restrictions on Transfer.

A restriction on transfer of a security imposed by the issuer, even though otherwise lawful, is ineffective against any person without actual knowledge of it unless:

(a) the security is certificated and the restriction is noted conspicuously thereon; or

(b) the security is uncertificated and a notation of the restriction is contained in the initial transaction statement sent to the person or, if his interest is transferred to him other than by registration of transfer, pledge, or release, the initial transaction statement sent to the registered owner or the registered pledgee.

§8-205. Effect of Unauthorized Signature on Certificated Security or Initial Transaction Statement.

An unauthorized signature placed on a certificated security prior to or in the course of issue or placed on an initial transaction statement is ineffective, but the signature is effective in favor of a purchaser for value of the certificated security or a purchaser for value of an uncertificated security to whom such initial transaction statement has been sent, if the purchaser is without notice of the lack of authority and the signing has been done by:

(a) an authenticating trustee, registrar, transfer agent, or other person entrusted by the issuer with the signing of the security, of similar securities, or of initial transaction statements or the immediate preparation for signing of any of them; or

(b) an employee of the issuer, or of any of the foregoing, entrusted with responsible handling of the security or initial transaction statement.

§8-206. Completion or Alteration of Certificated Security or Initial Transaction Statement.

(1) If a certificated security contains the signatures necessary to its issue or transfer but is incomplete in any other respect:

(a) any person may complete it by filling in the blanks as authorized; and

(b) even though the blanks are incorrectly filled in, the security as completed is enforceable by a purchaser who took it for value and without notice of the incorrectness.

(2) A complete certificated security that has been improperly altered, even though fraudulently, remains enforceable, but only according to its original terms.

(3) If an initial transaction statement contains the signatures necessary to its validity, but is incomplete in any other respect:

(a) any person may complete it by filling in the blanks as authorized; and

(b) even though the blanks are incorrectly filled in, the statement as completed is effective in favor of the person to whom it is sent if he purchased the security referred to therein for value and without notice of the incorrectness.

(4) A complete initial transaction statement that has been improperly altered, even though fraudulently, is effective in favor of a purchaser to whom it has been sent, but only according to its original terms.

§8-207. Rights and Duties of Issuer With Respect to Registered Owners and Registered Pledgees.

(1) Prior to due presentment for registration of transfer of a certificated security in registered form, the issuer or indenture trustee may treat the registered owner as the person exclusively entitled to vote, to receive notifications, and otherwise to exercise all the rights and powers of an owner.

(2) Subject to the provisions of subsections (3), (4), and (6), the issuer or indenture trustee may treat the registered owner of an uncertificated security as the person exclusively entitled to vote, to receive notifications, and otherwise to exercise all the rights and powers of an owner.

(3) The registered owner of an uncertificated security that is subject to a registered pledge is not entitled to registration of transfer prior to the due presentment to the issuer of a release instruction. The exercise of conversion rights with respect to a convertible uncertificated security is a transfer within the meaning of this section.

(4) Upon due presentment of a transfer instruction from the registered pledgee of an uncertificated security, the issuer shall:

(a) register the transfer of the security to the new owner free of pledge, if the instruction specifies a new owner (who may be the registered pledgee) and does not specify a pledgee;

(b) register the transfer of the security to the new owner subject to the interest of the existing pledgee, if the instruction specifies a new owner and the existing pledgee; or

(c) register the release of the security from the existing pledge and register the pledge of the security to the other pledgee, if the instruction specifies the existing owner and another pledgee.

(5) Continuity of perfection of a security interest is not broken by registration of transfer under subsection (4)(b) or by registration of release and pledge under subsection (4)(c), if the security interest is assigned.

(6) If an uncertificated security is subject to a registered pledge:

(a) any uncertificated securities issued in exchange for or distributed with respect to the pledged security shall be registered subject to the pledge;

(b) any certificated securities issued in exchange for or distributed with respect to the pledged security shall be delivered to the registered pledgee; and

(c) any money paid in exchange for or in redemption of part or all of the security shall be paid to the registered pledgee.

(7) Nothing in this Article shall be construed to affect the liability of the registered owner of a security for calls, assessments, or the like.

§8-208. Effect of Signature of Authenticating Trustee, Registrar, or Transfer Agent.

(1) A person placing his signature upon a certificated security or an initial transaction statement as authenticating trustee, registrar, transfer agent, or the like, warrants to a purchaser for value of the certificated security or a purchaser for value of an uncertificated security to whom the initial transaction statement has been sent, if the purchaser is without notice of the particular defect, that:

(a) the certificated security or initial transaction statement is genuine;

(b) his own participation in the issue or registration of the transfer, pledge, or release of the security is within his capacity and within the scope of the authority received by him from the issuer; and

(c) he has reasonable grounds to believe that the security is in the form and within the amount the issuer is authorized to issue.

(2) Unless otherwise agreed, a person by so placing his signature does not assume responsibility for the validity of the security in other respects.

Part 3: Transfer

§8-301. Rights Acquired by Purchaser

(1) Upon transfer of a security to a purchaser (Section 8-313), the purchaser acquires the rights in the security which his transferor had or had actual authority to convey unless the purchaser's rights are limited by Section 8-302 (4).

(2) A transferee of a limited interest acquires rights only to the extent of the interest transferred. The creation or release of a security interest in a security is the transfer of a limited interest in that security.

§8-302. "Bona Fide Purchaser"; "Adverse Claim"; Title Acquired by Bona Fide Purchaser.

(1) A "bona fide purchaser" is a purchaser for value in good faith and without notice of any adverse claim:

(a) who takes delivery of a certificated security in bearer form or in registered form, issued or indorsed to him or in blank;

(b) to whom the transfer, pledge or release of an uncertificated security is registered on the books of the issuer; or

(c) to whom a security is transferred under the provisions of paragraph (c) (d) (i), or (g) of Section 8-313(1).

(2) "Adverse claim" includes a claim that a transfer was or would be wrongful or that a particular adverse person is the owner of or has an interest in the security.

(3) A bona fide purchaser in addition to acquiring the rights of a purchaser (Section 8-301) also acquires his interest in the security free of any adverse claim.

(4) Notwithstanding Section 8-301(1), the transferee of a particular certificated security who has been a party to any fraud or illegality affecting the security, or who as a prior holder of that certificated security had notice of an adverse claim, cannot improve his position by taking from a bona fide purchaser.

§8-303. "Broker". "Broker" means a person engaged for all or part of his time in the business of buying and selling securities, who in the transaction concerned acts for, buys a security from, or sells a security to, a customer. Nothing in this Article determines the capacity in which a person acts for purposes of any other statute or rule to which the person is subject.

§8-304. Notice to Purchaser of Adverse Claims.

(1) A purchaser (including a broker for the seller or buyer, but excluding an intermediary bank) of a certificated security is charged with notice of adverse claims if:

(a) the security, whether in bearer or registered form, has been indorsed "for collection" or "for surrender" or for some other purpose not involving transfer; or

(b) the security is in bearer form and has on it an unambiguous statement that it is the property of a person other than the transferor. The mere writing of a name on a security is not such a statement.

(2) A purchaser (including a broker for the seller or buyer, but excluding an intermediary bank) to whom the transfer, pledge, or release of an uncertificated security is registered is charged with notice of adverse claims as to which the issuer has a duty under Section 8-403(4) at the time of registration and which are noted in the initial transaction statement sent to the purchaser or, if his interest is transferred to him other than by registration of transfer, pledge, or release, the initial transaction statement sent to the registered owner or the registered pledge.

(3) The fact that the purchaser (including a broker for the seller or buyer) of a certificated or uncertificated security has notice that the security is held for a third person or is registered in the name of or indorsed by a fiduciary does not create a duty of inquiry into the rightfulness of the transfer or constitute constructive notice of adverse claims. However, if the purchaser (excluding an intermediary bank) has knowledge that the proceeds are being used or the transaction is for the individual benefit of the fiduciary or otherwise in breach of duty, the purchaser is charged with notice of adverse claims.

§8-305. Staleness as Notice of Adverse Claims. An act or event that creates a right to immediate performance of the principal obligation represented by a certificated security or sets a date on or after which a certificated security is to be presented or surrendered for redemption or exchange does not itself constitute any notice of adverse claims except in the case of a transfer:

(a) after one year from any date set for presentment or surrender for redemption or exchange; or

(b) after 6 months from any date set for payment of money against presentation or surrender of the security if funds are available for payment on that date.

§8-306. Warranties on Presentment and Transfer of Certificated Securities; Warranties of Originators of Instructions.

(1) A person who presents a certificated security for registration of transfer or for payment or exchange warrants to the issuer that he is entitled to the registration, payment, or exchange. But, a purchaser for value and without notice of adverse claims who receives a new, reissued, or re-registered certificated security on registration of transfer or receives an initial transaction statement confirming the registration of transfer of an equivalent uncertificated security to him warrants only that he has no knowledge of any unauthorized signature (Section 8-311) in a necessary indorsement.

(2) A person by transferring a certificated security to a purchaser for value warrants only that:

(a) his transfer is effective and rightful;

(b) the security is genuine and has not been materially altered; and

(c) he knows of no fact which might impair the validity of the security.

(3) If a certificated security is delivered by an intermediary known to be entrusted with delivery of the security on behalf of another or with collection of a draft or claim against delivery, the intermediary by delivery warrants only his own good faith and authority, even though he has purchased or made advances against the claim to be collected against the delivery.

(4) A pledgee or other holder for security who redelivers a certificated security received, or after payment and on order of the debtor delivers that security to a third person makes only the warranties of an intermediary under subsection (3).

(5) A person who originates an instruction warrants to the issuer that:

(a) he is an appropriate person to originate the instruction; and

(b) at the time the instruction is presented to the issuer he will be entitled to the registration of transfer, pledge, or release.

(6) A person who originates an instruction warrants to any person specially guaranteeing his signature (subsection 8-312 (3)) that:

(a) he is an appropriate person to originate the instruction; and

(b) at the time the instruction is presented to the issuer

(i) he will be entitled to the registration of transfer, pledge, or release; and

(ii) the transfer, pledge, or release requested in the instruction will be registered by the issuer free from all liens, security interests, restrictions, and claims other than those specified in the instruction.

(7) A person who originates an instruction warrants to a purchaser for value and to any person guaranteeing the instruction (Section 8-312(6)) that:

(a) he is an appropriate person to originate the instruction;

(b) the uncertificated security referred to therein is valid; and

(c) at the time the instruction is presented to the issuer

(i) the transferor will be entitled to the registration of transfer, pledge, or release;

(ii) the transfer, pledge, or release requested in the instruction will be registered by the issuer free from all liens, security interests, restrictions, and claims other than those specified in the instruction; and

(iii) the requested transfer, pledge, or release will be rightful.

(8) If a secured party is the registered pledgee or the registered owner of an uncertificated security, a person who originates an instruction of release or transfer to the debtor or, after payment and on order of the debtor, a transfer instruction to a third person, warrants to the debtor or the third person only that he is an appropriate person to originate the instruction and at the time the instruction is presented to the issuer, the transferor will be entitled to the registration of release or transfer. If a transfer instruction to a third person who is a purchaser for value is originated on order of the debtor, the debtor makes to the purchaser the warranties of paragraphs (b), (c)(ii) and (c)(iii) of subsection (7).

(9) A person who transfers an uncertificated security to a purchaser for value and does not originate an instruction in connection with the transfer warrants only that:

(a) his transfer is effective and rightful; and

(b) the uncertificated security is valid.

(10) A broker gives to his customer and to the issuer and a purchaser the applicable warranties provided in this section and has the rights and privileges of a purchaser under this section. The warranties of and in favor of the broker acting as an agent are in addition to applicable warranties given by and in favor of his customer.

§8-307. Effect of Delivery Without Indorsement; Right to Compel Indorsement. If a certificated security in registered form has been delivered to a purchaser without a necessary indorsement he may become a bona fide purchaser only as of the time the indorsement is supplied; but against the transferor, the transfer is complete upon delivery and the purchaser has a specifically enforceable right to have any necessary indorsement supplied.

§8-308. Indorsements; Instructions.

(1) An indorsement of a certificated security in registered form is made when an appropriate person signs on it or on a separate document an assignment or transfer of the security or a power to assign or transfer it or his signature is written without more upon the back of the security.

(2) An indorsement may be in blank or special. An indorsement in blank includes an indorsement to bearer. A special indorsement specifies to whom the security is to be transferred, or who has power to transfer it. A holder may convert a blank indorsement into a special indorsement.

(3) An indorsement purporting to be only of part of a certificated security representing units intended by the issuer to be separately transferable is effective to the extent of the indorsement.

(4) An "instruction" is an order to the issuer of an uncertificated security requesting that the transfer, pledge, or release from pledge of the uncertificated security specified therein be registered.

(5) An instruction originated by an appropriate person is:

(a) a writing signed by an appropriate person; or

(b) a communication to the issuer in any form agreed upon in a writing signed by the issuer and an appropriate person.

If an instruction has been originated by an appropriate person but is incomplete in any other respect, any person may complete it as authorized and the issuer may rely on it as completed even though it has been completed incorrectly.

(6) "An appropriate person" in subsection (1) means the person specified by the certificated security or by special indorsement to be entitled to the security.

(7) "An appropriate person" in subsection (5) means:

(a) for an instruction to transfer or pledge an uncertificated security which is then not subject to a registered pledge, the registered owner; or

(b) for an instruction to transfer or release an uncertificated security which is then subject to a registered pledge, the registered pledgee.

(8) In addition to the persons designated in subsections (6) and (7), "an appropriate person" in subsections (1) and (5) includes:

(a) if the person designated is described as a fiduciary but is no longer serving in the described capacity, either that person or his successor;

(b) if the persons designated are described as more than one person as fiduciaries and one or more are no longer serving in the described capacity, the remaining fiduciary or fiduciaries, whether or not a successor has been appointed or qualified;

(c) if the person designated is an individual and is without capacity to act by virtue of death; incompetence, infancy, or otherwise his executor, administrator, guardian, or like fiduciary;

(d) if the persons designated are described as more than one person as tenants by the entirety or with right of survivorship and by reason of death all cannot sign the survivor or survivors;

(e) a person having power to sign under applicable law or controlling instrument; and

(f) to the extent that the person designated or any of the foregoing persons may act through an agent, his authorized agent.

(9) Unless otherwise agreed, the indorser of a certificated security by his indorsement or the originator of an instruction by his origination assumes no obligation that the security will be honored by the issuer but only the obligations provided in Section 8-306.

(10) Whether the person signing is appropriate is determined as of the date of signing and an indorsement made by or an instruction originated by him does not become unauthorized for the purposes of this Article by virtue of any subsequent change of circumstances.

(11) Failure of a fiduciary to comply with a controlling instrument or with the law of the state having jurisdiction of the fiduciary relationship, including any law requiring the fiduciary to obtain court approval of the transfer, pledge, or release, does not render his indorsement or an instruction originated by him unauthorized for the purposes of this Article.

§8-309. Effect of Indorsement Without Delivery. An indorsement of a certificated security, whether special or in blank, does not constitute a transfer until delivery of the certificated security on which it appears or, if the indorsement is on a separate document, until delivery of both the document and the certificated security.

§8-310. Indorsement of Certificated Security in Bearer Form. An indorsement of a certificated security in bearer form may give notice of adverse claims (Section 8-304) but does not otherwise affect any right to registration the holder possesses.

§8-311. Effect of Unauthorized Indorsement or Instruction. Unless the owner, or pledgee has ratified an unauthorized indorsement or instruction or is other-

wise precluded from asserting its ineffectiveness:

(a) he may assert its ineffectiveness against the issuer or any purchaser, other than a purchaser for value and without notice of adverse claims, who has in good faith received a new, reissued, or re-registered certificated security on registration of transfer or received an initial transaction statement confirming the registration of transfer, pledge, or release of an equivalent uncertificated security to him; and

(b) an issuer who registers the transfer of a certificated security upon the unauthorized indorsement or who registers the transfer, pledge, or release of an uncertificated security upon the unauthorized instruction is subject to liability for improper registration (Section 8-104).

§8-312. Effect of Guaranteeing Signature, Indorsement or Instruction.

(1) Any person guaranteeing a signature of an indorser of a certificated security warrants that at the time of signing:

(a) the signature was genuine;

(b) the signer was an appropriate person to indorse (Section 8-308); and

(c) the signer had legal capacity to sign.

(2) Any person guaranteeing a signature of the originator of an instruction warrants that at the time of signing:

(a) the signature was genuine;

(b) the signer was an appropriate person to originate the instruction (Section 8-308) if the person specified in the instruction as the registered owner or registered pledgee of the uncertificated security was, in fact, the registered owner or registered pledgee of such security, as to which fact the signature guarantor makes no warranty;

(c) the signer had legal capacity to sign; and

(d) the taxpayer identification number, if any, appearing on the instruction as that of the registered owner or registered pledgee was the taxpayer identification number of the signer or of the owner or pledgee for whom the signer was acting.

(3) Any person specially guaranteeing the signature of the originator of an instruction makes not only the warranties of a signature guarantor (Subsection (2)) but also warrants that at the time the instruction is presented to the issuer:

(a) the person specified in the instruction as the registered owner or registered pledgee of the uncertificated security will be the registered owner or registered pledgee; and

(b) the transfer, pledge, or release of the uncertificated security requested in the instruction will be registered by the issuer free from all liens, security interests, restrictions, and claims other than those specified in the instruction.

(4) The guarantor under subsections (1) and (2) or the special guarantor under subsection (3) does not otherwise warrant the rightfulness of the particular transfer, pledge, or release.

(5) Any person guaranteeing an indorsement of a certificated security makes not only the warranties of a signature guarantor under subsection (1) but also warrants the rightfulness of the particular transfer in all respects.

(6) Any person guaranteeing an instruction requesting the transfer, pledge, or release of an uncertificated security makes not only the warranties of a special signature guarantor under subsection (3) but also warrants the rightfulness of the particular transfer, pledge, or release in all respects.

(7) No issuer may require a special guarantee of signature (subsection (3)), a guarantee of indorsement (subsection (5)), or a guarantee of instruction (subsection (6)) as a condition to registration of transfer, pledge, or release.

(8) The foregoing warranties are made to any person taking or dealing with the security in reliance on the guarantee, and the guarantor is liable to the person for any loss resulting from breach of the warranties.

§8-313. When Transfer to Purchaser Occurs: Financial Intermediary as Bona Fide Purchaser; "Financial Intermediary".

(1) Transfer of a security or a limited interest (including a security interest) therein to a purchaser occurs only:

(a) at the time he or a person designated by him acquires possession of a certificated security;

(b) at the time the transfer, pledge, or release of an uncertificated security is registered to him or a person designated by him:

(c) at the time his financial intermediary acquires possession of a certificated security specially indorsed to or issued in the name of the purchaser;

(d) at the time a financial intermediary, not a clearing corporation, sends him confirmation of the purchase and also by book entry or otherwise identifies as belonging to the purchaser

(i) a specific certificated security in the financial intermediary's possession;

(ii) a quantity of securities that constitute or are part of a fungible bulk of certificated securities in the financial intermediary's possession or of uncertificated securities registered in the name of the financial intermediary; or

(iii) a quantity of securities that constitute or are part of a fungible bulk of securities shown on the account of the financial intermediary on the books of another financial intermediary;

(e) with respect to an identified certificated security to be delivered while still in the possession of a third person, not a financial intermediary, at the time that person acknowledges that he holds for the purchaser;

(f) with respect to a specific uncertificated security the pledge or transfer of which has been registered to a third person, not a financial intermediary, at the time that person acknowledges that he holds for the purchaser;

(g) at the time appropriate entries to the account of the purchaser or a person designated by him on the books of a clearing corporation are made under Section 8-320;

(h) with respect to the transfer of a security interest where the debtor has signed a security agreement containing a description of the security, at the time a written notification, which, in the case of the creation of the security interest, is signed by the debtor (which may be a copy of the security agreement) or which, in the case of the release or assignment of the security interest created pursuant to this paragraph, is signed by the secured party, is received by

(i) a financial intermediary on whose books the interest of the transferor in the security appears:

(ii) a third person, not a financial intermediary, in possession of the security, if it is certificated;

(iii) a third person, not a financial intermediary, who is the registered owner of the security, if it is uncertificated and not subject to a registered pledge; or

(iv) a third person, not a financial intermediary, who is the registered pledgee of the security, if it is uncertificated and subject to a registered pledge;

(i) with respect to the transfer of a security interest where the transferor has signed a security agreement containing a description of the security, at the time new value is given by the secured party; or

(j) with respect to the transfer of a security interest where the secured party is a financial intermediary and the security has already been transferred to the financial intermediary under paragraphs (a), (b), (c), (d), or (g), at the time the transferor has signed a security agreement containing a description of the security and value is given by the secured party.

(**2**) The purchaser is the owner of a security held for him by a financial intermediary, but cannot be a bona fide purchaser of a security so held except in the circumstances specified in paragraphs (c), (d)(i), and (g) of subsection (1). If a security so held is part of a fungible bulk, as in the circumstances specified in paragraphs (d)(ii) and (d)(iii) of subsection (1), the purchaser is the owner of a proportionate property interest in the fungible bulk.

(**3**) Notice of an adverse claim received by the financial intermediary or by the purchaser after the financial intermediary takes delivery of a certificated security as a holder for value or after the transfer, pledge, or release of an uncertificated security has been registered free of the claim to a financial intermediary who has given value is not effective either as to the financial intermediary or as to the purchaser. However, as between the financial intermediary and the purchaser the purchaser may demand transfer of an equivalent security as to which no notice of adverse claim has been received.

(**4**) A "financial intermediary" is a bank, broker, clearing corporation or other person (or the nominee of any of them) which in the ordinary course of its business maintains security accounts for its customers and is acting in that capacity. A financial intermediary may have a security interest in securities held in account for its customer.

§8-314. Duty to Transfer, When Completed.

(**1**) Unless otherwise agreed, if a sale of a security is made on an exchange or otherwise through brokers:

(**a**) the selling customer fulfills his duty to transfer at the time he:
  - (**i**) places a certificated security in the possession of the selling broker or of a person designated by the broker;
  - (**ii**) causes an uncertificated security to be registered in the name of the selling broker or a person designated by the broker;
  - (**iii**) if requested, causes an acknowledgment to be made to the selling broker that a certificated or uncertificated security is held for the broker; or
  - (**iv**) places in the possession of the selling broker or of a person designated by the broker a transfer instruction for an uncertificated security, providing the issuer does not refuse to register the requested transfer if the instruction is presented to the issuer for registration within 30 days thereafter; and

(**b**) the selling broker, including a correspondent broker acting for a selling customer, fulfills his duty to transfer at the time he:
  - (**i**) places a certificated security in the possession of the buying broker or a person designated by the buying broker;
  - (**ii**) causes an uncertificated security to be registered in the name of the buying broker or a person designated by the buying broker;
  - (**iii**) places in the possession of the buying broker or of a person designated by the buying broker a transfer instruction for an uncertificated security, providing the issuer does not refuse to register the requested transfer if the instruction is presented to the issuer for registration within 30 days thereafter; or
  - (**iv**) effects clearance of the sale in accordance with the rules of the exchange on which the transaction took place.

(**2**) Except as provided in this section and unless otherwise agreed, a transferor's duty to transfer a security under a contract of purchase is not fulfilled until he:

(**a**) places a certificated security in form to be negotiated by the purchaser in the possession of the purchaser or of a person designated by the purchaser;

(**b**) causes an uncertificated security to be registered in the name of the purchaser or a person designated by the purchaser; or

(**c**) if the purchaser requests, causes an acknowledgment to be made to the purchaser that certificated or uncertificated security is held for the purchaser.

(**3**) Unless made on an exchange, a sale to a broker purchasing for his own account is within subsection (2) and not within subsection (1).

§8-315. Action Against Transferee Based Upon Wrongful Transfer.

(**1**) Any person against whom the transfer of a security is wrongful for any reason, including his incapacity, as against anyone except a bona fide purchaser, may:

(**a**) reclaim possession of the certificated security wrongfully transferred;

(**b**) obtain possession of any new certificated security representing all or part of the same rights:

(**c**) compel the origination of an instruction to transfer to him or a person designated by him an uncertificated security constituting all or part of the same rights; or

(**d**) have damages.

(**2**) If the transfer is wrongful because of an unauthorized indorsement of a certificated security, the owner may also reclaim or obtain possession of the security or a new certificated security, even from a bona fide purchaser, if the ineffectiveness of the purported indorsement can be asserted against him under the provisions of this Article on unauthorized indorsements (Section 8-311).

(3) The right to obtain or reclaim possession of a certificated security or to compel the origination of a transfer instruction may be specifically enforced and the transfer of a certificated or uncertificated security enjoined and a certificated security impounded pending the litigation.

§8-316. Purchaser's Right to Requisites for Registration of Transfer, Pledge, or Release on Books. Unless otherwise agreed, the transferor of a certificated security or the transferor, pledgor, or pledgee of an uncertificated security on due demand must supply his purchaser with any proof of his authority to transfer, pledge, or release or with any other requisite necessary to obtain registration of the transfer, pledge, or release of the security; but if the transfer, pledge, or release is not for value, a transferor, pledgor, or pledgee need not do so unless the purchaser furnishes the necessary expenses. Failure within a reasonable time to comply with a demand made gives the purchaser the right to reject or rescind the transfer, pledge, or release.

§8-317. Creditors' Rights.

(1) Subject to the exceptions in subsections (3) and (4), no attachment or levy upon a certificated security or any share or other interest represented thereby which is outstanding is valid until the security is actually seized by the officer making the attachment or levy, but a certificated security which has been surrendered to the issuer may be reached by a creditor by legal process at the issuer's chief executive office in the United States.

(2) An uncertificated security registered in the name of the debtor may not be reached by a creditor except by legal process at the issuer's chief executive office in the United States.

(3) The interest of a debtor in a certificated security that is in the possession of a secured party not a financial intermediary or in an uncertificated security registered in the name of a secured party not a financial intermediary (or in the name of a nominee of the secured party) may be reached by a creditor by legal process upon the secured party.

(4) The interest of a debtor in a certificated security that is in the possession of or registered in the name of a financial intermediary or in an uncertificated security registered in the name of a financial intermediary may be reached by a creditor by legal process upon the financial intermediary on whose books the interest of the debtor appears.

(5) Unless otherwise provided by law, a creditor's lien upon the interest of a debtor in a security obtained pursuant to subsection (3) or (4) is not a restraint on the transfer of the security, free of the lien, to a third party for new value; but in the event of a transfer, the lien applies to the proceeds of the transfer in the hands of the secured party or financial intermediary, subject to any claims having priority.

(6) A creditor whose debtor is the owner of a security is entitled to aid from courts of appropriate jurisdiction, by injunction or otherwise, in reaching the security or in satisfying the claim by means allowed at law or in equity in regard to property that cannot readily be reached by ordinary legal process.

§8-318. No Conversion by Good Faith Conduct. An agent or bailee who in good faith (including the observance of reasonable commercial standards if he is in the business of buying, selling, or otherwise dealing with securities) has received certificated securities and sold, pledged, or delivered them or has sold or caused the transfer or pledge of uncertificated securities over which he had control according to the instructions of his principal, is not liable for conversion or for participation in breach of fiduciary duty although the principal had no right so to deal with the securities.

§8-319. Statute of Frauds. A contract for the sale of securities is not enforceable by way of action or defense unless:

(a) there is some writing signed by the party against whom enforcement is sought or by his authorized agent or broker, sufficient to indicate that a contract has been made for sale of a stated quantity of described securities at a defined or stated price;

(b) delivery of a certificated security or transfer instruction has been accepted, or transfer of an uncertificated security has been registered and the transferee has failed to send written objection to the issuer within 10 days after receipt of the initial transaction statement confirming the registration, or payment has been made, but the contract is enforceable under this provision only to the extent the delivery, registration, or payment;

(c) within a reasonable time a writing in confirmation of the sale or purchase and sufficient against the sender under paragraph (a) has been received by the party against whom enforcement is sought and he has failed to send written objection to its contents within 10 days after its receipt; or

(d) the party against whom enforcement is sought admits in his pleading, testimony, or otherwise in court that a contract was made for the sale of a stated quantity of described securities at a defined or stated price.

§8-320. Transfer or Pledge Within Central Depository System

(1) In addition to other methods, a transfer, pledge, or release of a security or any interest therein may be effected by the making of appropriate entries on the books of a clearing corporation reducing the account of the transferor, pledgor, or pledgee and increasing the account of the transferee, pledgee, or pledgor by the amount of the obligation, or the number of shares or rights transferred, pledged, or released, if the security is shown on the account of a transferor, pledgor, or pledgee on the books of the clearing corporation; is subject to the control of the clearing corporation; and

>   (a) if certificated,
>   >   (i) is in the custody of the clearing corporation, another clearing corporation, a custodian bank or a nominee of any of them; and
>   >   (ii) is in bearer form or indorsed in blank by an appropriate person or registered in the name of the clearing corporation, a custodian bank, or a nominee of any of them; or
>   (b) if uncertificated, is registered in the name of the clearing corporation, another clearing corporation, a custodian bank, or a nominee of any of them.

(2) Under this section entries may be made with respect to like securities or interests therein as a part of a fungible bulk and may refer merely to a quantity of a particular security without reference to the name of the registered owner, certificate or bond number, or the like, and, in appropriate cases, may be on a net basis taking into account other transfers, pledges, or releases of the same security.

(3) A transfer under this section is effective (Section 8-313) and the purchaser acquires the rights of the transferor (Section 8-301). A pledge or release under this section is the transfer of a limited interest. If a pledge or the creation of a security interest is intended, the security interest is perfected at the time when both value is given by the pledgee and the appropriate entries are made (Section 8-321). A transferee or pledgee under this section may be a bona fide purchaser (Section 8-302).

(4) A transfer or pledge under this section is not a registration of transfer under Part 4.

(5) That entries made on the books of the clearing corporation as provided in subsection (1) are not appropriate does not affect the validity or effect of the entries or the liabilities or obligations of the clearing corporation to any person adversely affected thereby.

§8-321. Enforceability, Attachment, Perfection, and Termination of Security Interests.

(1) A security interest in a security is enforceable and can attach only if it is transferred to the secured party or a person designated by him pursuant to a provision of Section 8-313(1).

(2) A security interest so transferred pursuant to agreement by a transferor who has rights in the secu-

rity to a transferee who has given value is a perfected security interest, but a security interest that has been transferred solely under paragraph (i) of Section 8-313(1) becomes unperfected after 21 days unless, within that time, the requirements for transfer under any other provision of Section 8-313(1) are satisfied.

(3) A security interest in a security is subject to the provisions of Article 9, but:

>   (a) no filing is required to perfect the security interest; and
>   (b) no written security agreement signed by the debtor is necessary to make the security interest enforceable, except as otherwise provided in paragraph (h), (i), or (j) of Section 8-313(1).

The secured party has the rights and duties provided under Section 9-207, to the extent they are applicable, whether or not the security is certificated, and, if certificated, whether or not it is in his possession.

(4) Unless otherwise agreed, a security interest in a security is terminated by transfer to the debtor or a person designated by him pursuant to a provision of Section 8-313(1). If a security is thus transferred, the security interest, if not terminated, becomes unperfected unless the security is certificated and is delivered to the debtor for the purpose of ultimate sale or exchange or presentation, collection, renewal, or registration of transfer. In that case, the security interest becomes unperfected after 21 days unless, within that time, the security (or securities for which it has been exchanged) is transferred to the secured party or a person designated by him pursuant to a provision of Section 8-313(1).

Part 4: Registration

§8-401. Duty of Issuer to Register Transfer, Pledge, or Release.

(1) If a certificated security in registered form is presented to the issuer with a request to register transfer or an instruction is presented to the issuer with a request to register transfer, pledge, or release, the issuer shall register the transfer, pledge, or release as requested if:

>   (a) the security is indorsed or the instruction was originated by the appropriate person or persons (Section 8-308);
>   (b) reasonable assurance is given that those indorsements or instructions are genuine and effective (Section 8-402);
>   (c) the issuer has no duty as to adverse claims or has discharged the duty (Section 8-403);
>   (d) any applicable law relating to the collection of taxes has been complied with; and
>   (e) the transfer, pledge, or release is in fact rightful or is to a bona fide purchaser.

(2) If an issuer is under a duty to register a transfer, pledge, or release of a security, the issuer is also liable to the person presenting a certificated security or an instruction for registration or his principal for loss resulting from any unreasonable delay in registration or from failure or refusal to register the transfer, pledge, or release.

§8-402. Assurance that Indorsements and Instructions Are Effective.

(1) The issuer may require the following assurance that each necessary indorsement of a certificated security or each instruction (Section 8-308) is genuine and effective:

(a) in all cases, a guarantee of the signature (Section 8-312(1) or (2)) of the person indorsing a certificated security or originating an instruction including, in the case of an instruction, a warranty of the taxpayer identification number or, in the absence thereof, other reasonable assurance of identity:

(b) if the indorsement is made or the instruction is originated by an agent, appropriate assurance of authority to sign;

(c) if the indorsement is made or the instruction is originated by a fiduciary, appropriate evidence of appointment or incumbency;

(d) if there is more than one fiduciary, reasonable assurance that all who are required to sign have done so; and

(e) if the indorsement is made or the instruction is originated by a person not covered by any of the foregoing, assurance appropriate to the case corresponding as nearly as may be to the foregoing.

(2) A "guarantee of the signature" in subsection (1) means a guarantee signed by or on behalf of a person reasonably believed by the issuer to be responsible. The issuer may adopt standards with respect to responsibility if they are not manifestly unreasonable.

(3) "Appropriate evidence of appointment or incumbency" in subsection (1) means:

(a) in the case of a fiduciary appointed or qualified by a court, a certificate issued by or under the direction or supervision of that court or an officer thereof and dated within 60 days before the date of presentation for transfer, pledge, or release; or

(b) in any other case, a copy of a document showing the appointment or a certificate issued by or on behalf of a person reasonably believed by the issuer to be responsible or, in the absence of that document or certificate, other evidence reasonably deemed by the issuer to be appropriate. The issuer may adopt standards with respect to the evidence if they are not manifestly unreasonable. The issuer is not charged with notice of the contents of any document obtained pursuant to this paragraph (b) except to the extent that the contents relate directly to the appointment or incumbency.

(4) The issuer may elect to require reasonable assurance beyond that specified in this section, but if it does so and, for a purpose other than that specified in subsection (3)(b), both requires and obtains a copy of a will, trust, indenture, articles of co-partnership, by-laws, or other controlling instrument, it is charged with notice of all matters contained therein affecting the transfer, pledge, or release.

§8-403. Issuer's Duty as to Adverse Claims.

(1) An issuer to whom a certificated security is presented for registration shall inquire into adverse claims if:

(a) a written notification of an adverse claim is received at a time and in a manner affording the issuer a reasonable opportunity to act on it prior to the issuance of a new, reissued, or reregistered certificated security, and the notification identifies the claimant, the registered owner, and the issue of which the security is a part, and provides an address for communications directed to the claimant; or

(b) the issuer is charged with notice of an adverse claim from a controlling instrument it has elected to require under Section 8-402(4).

(2) The issuer may discharge any duty of inquiry by any reasonable means, including notifying an adverse claimant by registered or certified mail at the address furnished by him or, if there be no such address, at his residence or regular place of business that the certificated security has been presented for registration of transfer by a named person, and that the transfer will be registered unless within 30 days from the date of mailing the notification, either:

(a) an appropriate restraining order, injunction, or other process issues from a court of competent jurisdiction; or

(b) there is filed with the issuer an indemnity bond, sufficient in the issuer's judgment to protect the issuer and any transfer agent, registrar, or other agent of the issuer involved from any loss it or they may suffer by complying with the adverse claim.

(3) Unless an issuer is charged with notice of an adverse claim from a controlling instrument which it has elected to require under Section 8-402(4) or receives notification of an adverse claim under subsection (1), if a certificated security presented for registration is indorsed by the appropriate person or persons the issuer is under no duty to inquire into adverse claims. In particular:

(a) an issuer registering a certificated security in the name of a person who is a fiduciary or who is described as a fiduciary is not bound to inquire into the existence, extent, or correct description of the fiduciary relationship; and thereafter the issuer may assume without inquiry that the newly registered owner continues to be the fiduciary until the issuer receives written notice that the fiduciary is no longer acting as such with respect to the particular security;

(b) an issuer registering transfer on an indorsement by a fiduciary is not bound to inquire whether the transfer is made in compliance with a controlling instrument or with the law of the state having jurisdiction of the fiduciary relationship, including any law requiring the fiduciary to obtain court approval of the transfer; and

(c) the issuer is not charged with notice of the contents of any court record or file or other recorded or unrecorded document even though the document is in its possession and even though the transfer is made on the indorsement of a fiduciary himself or to his nominee.

(4) An issuer is under not duty as to adverse claims with respect to an uncertificated security except:

(a) claims embodied in a restraining order, injunction, or other legal process served upon the issuer if the process was served at a time and in a manner affording the issuer a reasonable opportunity to act on it in accordance with the requirements of subsection (5);

(b) claims of which the issuer has received a written notification from the registered owner or the registered pledgee if the notification was received at a time and in a manner affording the issuer a reasonable opportunity to act on it in accordance with the requirements of subsection (5);

(c) claims (including restrictions on transfer not imposed by the issuer) to which the registration of transfer to the present registered owner was subject and were so noted in the initial transaction statement sent to him; and

(d) claims as to which an issuer is charged with notice from a controlling instrument it has elected to require under Section 8-402(4).

(5) If the issuer of an uncertificated security is under a duty as to an adverse claim, he discharges that duty by:

(a) including a notation of the claim in any statements sent with respect to the security under Sections 8-408(3), (6), and (7); and

(b) refusing to register the transfer or pledge of the security unless the nature of the claim does not preclude transfer or pledge subject thereto.

(6) If the transfer or pledge of the security is registered subject to an adverse claim, a notation of the claim must be included in the initial transaction statement and all subsequent statements sent to the transferee and pledgee under Section 8-408.

(7) Notwithstanding subsections (4) and (5), if an uncertificated security was subject to a registered pledge at the time the issuer first came under a duty as to a particular adverse claim, the issuer has no duty as to that claim if transfer of the security is requested by the registered pledgee or an appropriate person acting for the registered pledgee unless:

(a) the claim was embodied in legal process which expressly provides otherwise;

(b) the claim was asserted in a written notification from the registered pledgee;

(c) the claim was one as to which the issuer was charged with notice from a controlling instrument it required under Section 8-402(4) in connection with the pledgee's request for transfer; or

(d) the transfer requested is to the registered owner.

§8-404. Liability and Non-Liability for Registration.

(1) Except as provided in any law relating to the collection of taxes, the issuer is not liable to the owner, pledgee, or any other person suffering loss as a result of the registration of a transfer, pledge, or release of a security if:

(a) there were on or with a certificated security the necessary indorsements or the issuer had received an instruction originated by an appropriate person (Section 8-308); and

(b) the issuer had no duty as to adverse claims or has discharged the duty (Section 8-403).

(2) If an issuer has registered a transfer of a certificated security to a person not entitled to it, the issuer on demand shall deliver a like security to the true owner unless:

(a) the registration was pursuant to subsection (1);

(b) the owner is precluded from asserting any claim for registering the transfer under Section 8-405(1); or

(c) the delivery would result in overissue, in which case the issuer's liability is governed by Section 8-104.

(3) If an issuer has improperly registered a transfer, pledge, or release of an uncertificated security, the issuer on demand from the injured party shall restore

the records as to the injured party to the condition that would have obtained if the improper registration had not been made unless:

   (a) the registration was pursuant to subsection (1); or

   (b) the registration would result in overissue, in which case the issuer's liability is governed by Section 8-104.

§8-405. Lost, Destroyed, and Stolen Certificated Securities.

   (1) If a certificated security has been lost, apparently destroyed, or wrongfully taken, and the owner fails to notify the issuer of that fact within a reasonable time after he has notice of it and the issuer registers a transfer of the security before receiving notification, the owner is precluded from asserting against the issuer any claim for registering the transfer under Section 8-404 or any claim to a new security under this section.

   (2) If the owner of a certificated security claims that the security has been lost, destroyed, or wrongfully taken, the issuer shall issue a new certificated security or, at the option of the issuer, an equivalent uncertificated security in place of the original security if the owner:

   (a) so requests before the issuer has notice that the security has been acquired by a bona fide purchaser;

   (b) files with the issuer a sufficient indemnity bond; and

   (c) satisfies any other reasonable requirements imposed by the issuer.

   (3) If, after the issue of a new certificated or uncertificated security, a bona fide purchaser of the original certificated security presents it for registration of transfer, the issuer shall register the transfer unless registration would result in overissue, in which event the issuer's liability is governed by Section 8-104. In addition to any rights on the indemnity bond, the issuer may recover the new certificated security from the person to whom it was issued or any person taking under him except a bona fide purchaser or may cancel the uncertificated security unless a bona fide purchaser or any person taking under a bona fide purchaser is then the registered owner or registered pledgee thereof.

§8-406. Duty of Authenticating Trustee, Transfer Agent, or Registrar.

   (1) If a person acts as authenticating trustee, transfer agent, registrar, or other agent for an issuer in the registration of transfers of its certificated securities or in the registration of transfers, pledges, and releases of its uncertificated securities, in the issue of new securities, or in the cancellation of surrendered securities:

   (a) he is under a duty to the issuer to exercise good faith and due diligence in performing his functions; and

   (b) with regard to the particular functions he performs, he has the same obligation to the holder or owner of a certificated security or to the owner or pledgee of an uncertificated security and has the same rights and privileges as the issuer has in regard to those functions.

   (2) Notice to an authenticating trustee, transfer agent, registrar or other agent is notice to the issuer with respect to the functions performed by the agent.

§8-407. Exchangeability of Securities.

   (1) No issuer is subject to the requirements of this section unless it regularly maintains a system for issuing the class of securities involved under which both certificated and uncertificated securities are regularly issued to the category of owners, which includes the person in whose name the new security is to be registered.

   (2) Upon surrender of a certificated security with all necessary indorsements and presentation of a written request by the person surrendering the security, the issuer, if he has no duty as to adverse claims or has discharged the duty (Section 8-403), shall issue to the person or a person designated by him an equivalent uncertificated security subject to all liens, restrictions, and claims that were noted on the certificated security.

   (3) Upon receipt of a transfer instruction originated by an appropriate person who so requests, the issuer of an uncertificated security shall cancel the uncertificated security and issue an equivalent certificated security on which must be noted conspicuously any liens and restrictions of the issuer and any adverse claims (as to which the issuer has a duty under Section 8-403(4)) to which the uncertificated security was subject. The certificated security shall be registered in the name of and delivered to:

   (a) the registered owner, if the uncertificated security was not subject to a registered pledge; or

   (b) the registered pledgee, if the uncertificated security was subject to a registered pledge.

§8-408. Statements of Uncertificated Securities.

   (1) Within 2 business days after the transfer of an uncertificated security has been registered, the issuer shall send to the new registered owner and, if the security has been transferred subject to a registered pledge, to the registered pledgee a written statement containing:

   (a) a description of the issue of which the uncertificated security is a part;

   (b) the number of shares or units transferred;

   (c) the name and address and any taxpayer identification number of the new registered owner and, if the security has been transferred subject to a registered pledge, the name and address and any taxpayer identification number of the registered pledgee;

(d) a notation of any liens and restrictions of the issuer and any adverse claims (as to which the issuer has a duty under Section 8-403(4)) to which the uncertificated security is or may be subject at the time of registration or a statement that there are none of those liens, restrictions, or adverse claims; and

(e) the date the transfer was registered.

(2) Within 2 business days after the pledge of an uncertificated security has been registered, the issuer shall send to the registered owner and the registered pledgee a written statement containing:

(a) a description of the issue of which the uncertificated security is a part;

(b) the number of shares or units pledged;

(c) the name and address and any taxpayer identification number of the registered owner and the registered pledgee;

(d) a notation of any liens and restrictions of the issuer and any adverse claims (as to which the issuer has a duty under Section 8-403(4)) to which the uncertificated security is or may be subject at the time of registration or a statement that there are none of those liens, restrictions or adverse claims; and

(e) the date the pledge was registered.

(3) Within 2 business days after the release from pledge of an uncertificated security has been registered, the issuer shall send to the registered owner and the pledgee whose interest was released a written statement containing:

(a) a description of the issue of which the uncertificated security is a part;

(b) the number of shares or units released from pledge;

(c) the name and address and any taxpayer identification number of the registered owner and the pledgee whose interest was released;

(d) a notation of of any liens and restrictions of the issuer and any adverse claims (as to which the issuer has a duty under Section 8-403(4)) to which the uncertificated security is or may be subject at the time of registration or a statement that there are none of those liens, restrictions or adverse claims; and

(e) the date the release was registered.

(4) An "initial transaction statement" is the statement sent to:

(a) the new registered owner and, if applicable, to the registered pledgee pursuant to subsection (1);

(b) the registered pledgee pursuant to subsection (2); or

(c) the registered owner pursuant to subsection (3).

Each initial transaction statement shall be signed by or on behalf of the issuer and must be identified as "Initial Transaction Statement."

(5) Within 2 business days after the transfer of an uncertificated security has been registered, the issuer shall send to the former registered owner and the former registered pledgee, if any, a written statement containing:

(a) a description of the issue of which the uncertificated security is a part;

(b) the number of shares or units transferred.

(c) the name and address and any taxpayer identification number of the former registered owner and of any former registered pledgee; and

(d) the date the transfer was registered.

(6) At periodic intervals no less frequent than annually and at any time upon the reasonable written request of the registered owner, the issuer shall send to the registered owner of each uncertificated security a dated written statement containing:

(a) a description of the issue of which the uncertificated security is a part;

(b) the name and address and any taxpayer identification number of the registered owner.

(c) the number of shares or units of the uncertificated security registered in the name of the registered owner on the date of the statement;

(d) the name and address and any taxpayer identification number of any registered pledge and the number of shares or units subject to the pledge; and

(e) a notation of any liens and restrictions of the issuer and any adverse claims (as to which the issuer has a duty under Section 8-403(4)) to which the uncertificated security is or may be subject or a statement that these are none of those liens, restrictions, or adverse claims.

(7) At periodic intervals no less frequent than annually and at any time upon the reasonable written request of the registered pledgee, the issuer shall send to the registered pledgee of each uncertificated security a dated written statement containing;

(a) a description of the issue of which the uncertificated security is a part;

(b) the name and address and any taxpayer identification number of the registered owner;

(c) the name and address and any taxpayer identification number of the registered pledgee;

(d) the number of shares or units subject to the pledge; and

(e) a notation of any liens and restrictions of the issuer and any adverse claims (as to which the issuer has a duty under Section 8-403(4)) to which the uncertificated security is or may be subject or a statement that there are none of these liens, restrictions, or adverse claims.

(8) If the issuer sends the statements described in subsections (6) and (7) at periodic intervals no less frequent than quarterly, the issuer is not obliged to send additional statements upon request unless the owner or pledgee requesting them pays to the issuer the reasonable cost of furnishing them.

(9) Each statement sent pursuant to this section must bear a conspicuous legend reading substantially as follows: "This statement is merely a record of the rights of the addressee as of the time of its issuance. Delivery of this statement, of itself, confers no rights on the recipient. This statement is neither a negotiable instrument nor a security."

ARTICLE 9: SECURED TRANSACTIONS, SALES OF ACCOUNTS AND CHATTEL PAPER
Part 1: Short Title, Applicability and Definitions

§9-101. Short Title This Article shall be known and may be cited as Uniform Commercial Code—Secured Transactions.

§9-102. Policy and Subject Matter of Article.

(1) Except as otherwise provided in Section 9-104 on excluded transactions, this Article applies:

(a) to any transaction (regardless of its form) which is intended to create a security interest in personal property or fixtures including goods, documents, instruments, general intangibles, chattel paper or accounts, and also

(b) to any sale of accounts or chattel paper.

(2) This Article applies to security interests created by contract including pledge, assignment, chattel mortgage, chattel trust, trust deed, factor's lien, equipment trust, conditional sale, trust receipt, other lien or title retention contract and lease or consignment intended as security. This Article does not apply to statutory liens except as provided in Section 9-310.

(3) The application of this Article to a security interest in a secured obligation is not affected by the fact that the obligation is itself secured by a transaction or interest to which this Article does not apply.

Note: *The adoption of this Article should be accompanied by the repeal of existing statues dealing with conditional sales, trust receipts, factor's liens where the factor is given a non-possessory lien, chattel mortgages, crop mortgages, mortgages on railroad equipment, assignment of accounts and generally statues regulating security interests in personal property.*

Where the state has a retail installment selling act or small loan act, that legislation should be carefully examined to determine what changes in those acts are needed to conform them to this Article. This Article primarily sets out rules defining rights of a secured party against persons dealing with the debtor; it does not prescribe regulations and controls which may be necessary to curb abuses arising in the small loan business or in the financing of consumer purchases on credit. Accordingly there is no intention to repeal existing regulatory acts in those fields by enactment or re-enactment of Article 9. See Section 9-203(4) and the Note thereto.

§9-103. Perfection of Security Interests in Multiple State Transactions.

(1) Documents, instruments and ordinary goods.

(a) This subsection applies to documents and instruments and to goods other than those covered by a certificate of title described in subsection (2), mobile goods described in subsection (3), and minerals described in subsection (5).

(b) Except as otherwise provided in this subsection, perfection and the effect of perfection or non-perfection of a security interest in collateral are governed by the law of the jurisdiction where the collateral is when the last event occurs on which is based the assertion that the security interest is perfected or unperfected.

(c) If the parties to a transaction creating a purchase money security interest in goods in one jurisdiction understand at the time that the security interest attaches that the goods will be kept in another jurisdiction, then the law of the other jurisdiction governs the perfection and the effect of perfection or non-perfection of the security interest from the time it attaches until thirty days after the debtor receives possession of the goods and thereafter if the goods are taken to the other jurisdiction before the end of the thirty-day period.

(d) When collateral is brought into and kept in this state while subject to a security interest perfected under the law of the jurisdiction from which the collateral was removed, the security interest remains perfected, but if action is required by Part 3 of this Article to perfect the security interest.

(i) if the action is not taken before the expiration of the period of perfection in the other jurisdiction or the end of four months after the collateral is brought into this state, whichever period first expires, the security interest becomes unperfected at the end of that period and is thereafter deemed to have been unperfected as against a person who became a purchaser after removal.

(ii) if the action is taken before the expiration of the period specified in subparagraph (i), the security interest continues perfected thereafter;

(iii) for the purpose of priority over a buyer of consumer goods (subsection (2) of Section 9-307), the period of the effectiveness of a filing in the jurisdiction from which the collateral is removed is governed by the rules with respect to perfection in subparagraphs (i) and (ii).

(2) Certificate of title.

(a) This subsection applies to goods covered by a certificate of title issued under a statute of this state or of another jurisdiction under the law of which indication of a security interest on the certificate is required as a condition of perfection.

(b) Except as otherwise provided in this subsection, perfection and the effect of perfection or non-perfection of the security interest are governed by the law (including the conflict of laws rules) of the jurisdiction issuing the certificate until four months after the goods are removed from that jurisdiction and thereafter until the goods are registered in another jurisdiction, but in any event not beyond surrender of the certificate. After the expiration of that period, the goods are not covered by the certificate of title within the meaning of this section.

(c) Except with respect to the rights of a buyer described in the next paragraph, a security interest, perfected in another jurisdiction otherwise than by notation on a certificate of title, in goods brought into this state and thereafter covered by a certificate of title issued by this state is subject to the rules stated in paragraph (d) of subsection (1).

(d) If goods are brought into this state while a security interest therein is perfected in any manner under the law of the jurisdiction from which the goods are removed and a certificate of title is issued by this state and the certificate does not show that the goods are subject to the security interest or that they may be subject to security interests not shown on the certificate, the security interest is subordinate to the rights of a buyer of the goods who is not in the business of selling goods of that kind to the extent that he gives value and receives delivery of the goods after issuance of the certificate and without knowledge of the security interest.

(3) Accounts, general intangibles and mobile goods.

(a) The subsection applies to accounts (other than an account described in subsection (5) on minerals) and general intangibles and to goods which are mobile and which are of a type normally used in more than one jurisdiction, such as motor vehicles, trailers, rolling stock, airplanes, shipping containers, road building and construction machinery and commercial harvesting machinery and the like, if the goods are equipment or inventory leased or held for lease by the debtor to others, and are not covered by a certificate of title described in subsection (2).

(b) The law (including the conflict of laws rules) of the jurisdiction in which the debtor is located governs the perfection and the effect of perfection or non-perfection of the security interest.

(c) If, however, the debtor is located in a jurisdiction which is not a part of the United States, and which does not provide for perfection of the security interest by filing or recording in that jurisdiction, the law of the jurisdiction in the United States in which the debtor has its major executive office in the United States governs the perfection and the effect of perfection or non-perfection of the security interest through filing. In the alternative, if the debtor is located in a jurisdiction which is not a part of the United States or Canada and the collateral is accounts or general intangibles for money due or to become due, the security interest may be perfected by notification to the account debtor. As used in this paragraph, "United States" includes its territories and possessions and the Commonwealth of Puerto Rico.

(d) A debtor shall be deemed located at his place of business if he has one, at his chief executive office if he has more than one place of business, otherwise at his residence. If, however, the debtor is a foreign air carrier under the Federal Aviation Act of 1958, as amended, it shall be deemed located at the designated office of the agent upon whom service of process may be made on behalf of the foreign air carrier.

(e) A security interest perfected under the law of the jurisdiction of the location of the debtor is perfected until the expiration of four months after a change of the debtor's location to another jurisdiction, or until perfection would have ceased by the law of the first jurisdiction, whichever period first expires. Unless perfected in the new jurisdiction before the end of that period, it becomes unperfected thereafter and is deemed to have been unperfected as against a person who became a purchaser after the change.

(4) Chattel paper.

The rules stated for goods in subsection (1) apply to a possessory security interest in chattel paper. The rules stated for accounts in subsection (3) apply to a nonpossessory security interest in chattel paper, but the security interest may not b perfected by notification to the account debtor.

(5) Minerals.

Perfection and the effect of perfection or non-perfection of a security interest which is created by a debtor who has an interest in minerals or the like (including oil and gas) before extraction and which attaches thereto as extracted, or which attaches to an account resulting from the sale thereof at the wellhead or minehead are governed by the law (including the conflict of laws rules) of the jurisdiction wherein the wellhead or minehead is located.

§9-103. Perfection of Security Interests in Multiple State Transactions *(1977 Amendments)*.

* * *

(3) Accounts, general intangibles and mobile goods.

(a) This subsection applies to accounts (other than an account described in subsection (5) on minerals) and general intangibles (other than uncertificated securities) and to goods.

* * *

(6) Uncertificated securities.

The law (including the conflict of laws rules) of the jurisdiction of organization of the issuer governs the perfection and the effect of perfection or non-perfection of a security interest in uncertificated securities.

§9-104. Transactions Excluded From Article. This Article does not apply

(a) To a security interest subject to any statute of the United States to the extent that such statute governs the rights of parties to and third parties affected by transactions in particular types of property; or

(b) to a landlord's lien; or

(c) to a lien given by statute or other rule of law for services or materials except as provided in Section 9-310 on priority of such liens; or

(d) to a transfer of a claim for wages, salary or other compensation of an employee; or

(e) to a transfer by a government or governmental subdivision or agency; or

(f) to a sale of accounts, or chattel paper as part of a sale of the business out of which they arose, or an assignment of accounts or chattel paper which is for the purpose of collection only, or a transfer of a right to payment under a contract to an assignee who is also to do the performance under the contract or a transfer of a single account to an assignee in whole or partial satisfaction of a preexisting indebtedness; or

(g) to a transfer of an interest in or claim in or under any policy of insurance, except as provided with respect to proceeds (Section 9-306) and priorities in proceeds (Section 9-312); or

(h) to a right represented by a judgment (other than a judgment taken on a right to payment which was collateral); or

(i) to any right of set-off; or

(j) except to the extent that provision is made for fixtures in Section 9-313, to the creation or transfer of an interest in or lien on real estate, including a lease or rents thereunder; or

(k) to a transfer in whole or in part of any claim arising out of tort; or

(l) to a transfer of an interest in any deposit account (subsection (1) of Section 9-105), except as provided with respect to proceeds (Section 9-306) and priorities in proceeds (Section 9-312).

§9-105. Definitions and Index of Definitions.

(1) In this Article unless the context otherwise requires:

(a) "Account debtor" means the person who is obligated on an account, chattel paper or general intangible;

(b) "Chattel paper" means a writing or writings which evidence both a monetary obligation and a security interest in or a lease of specific goods, but a charter or other contract involving the use or hire of a vessel is not chattel paper. When a transaction is evidenced both by such a security agreement or a lease and by an instrument or a series of instruments, the group of writings taken together constitutes chattel paper;

(c) "Collateral" means the property subject to a security interest, and includes accounts and chattel paper which have been sold;

(d) "Debtor" means the person who owes payment or other performance of the obligation secured, whether or not he owns or has rights in the collateral, and includes the seller of accounts or chattel paper. Where the debtor and the owner of the collateral are not the same person, the term "debtor" means the owner of the collateral in any provision of the Article dealing with the collateral, the obligor in any provision dealing with the obligation, and may include both where the context so requires;

(e) "Deposit account" means a demand, time savings, passbook or like account maintained with a bank, savings and loan association, credit union or like organization, other than an account evidenced by a certificate of deposit;

(f) "Document" means document of title as defined in the general definitions of Article 1 (Section 1-201), and a receipt of the kind described in subsection (2) of Section 7-201);

(g) "Encumbrance" includes real estate mortgages and other liens on real estate and all other rights in real estate that are not ownership interests.

(h) "Goods" includes all things which are movable at the time the security interest attaches or which are fixtures (section 9-313), but does not include money, documents, instruments, accounts, chattel paper, general intangibles, or minerals or the like (including oil and gas) before extraction. "Goods" also includes standing timber which is to be cut and removed under a conveyance or contract for sale, the unborn young of animals, and growing crops.

(i) "Instrument" means a negotiable instrument (defined in Section 3-104), or a security (defined in Section 8-102) or any other writing which evidences a right to the payment of money and is not itself a security agreement or lease and is of a type which is in ordinary course of business transferred by delivery with any necessary indorsement or assignment;

(j) "Mortgage" means a consensual interest created by a real estate mortgage, a trust deed on real estate, or the like;

(k) An advance is made "pursuant to commitment" if the secured party has bound himself to make it, whether or not a subsequent event of default or other event not within his control has relieved or may relieve him from his obligation.

(l) "Security agreement" means an agreement which creates or provides for a security interest;

(m) "Secured party" means a lender, seller or other person in whose favor there is a security interest, including a person to whom accounts or chattel paper have been sold. When the holders of obligations issued under an indenture of trust, equipment trust agreement or the like are represented by a trustee or other person, the representative is the secured party;

(n) "Transmitting utility" means any person primarily engaged in the railroad, street railway or trolley bus business, the electric or electronics communications transmission business, the transmission of goods by pipeline, or the transmission or the production and transmission of electricity, steam, gas or water, or the provision of sewer service.

(2) Other definitions applying to this Article and the sections in which they appear are;

"Account"	Section 9-106
"Attach"	Section 9-203
"Construction mortgage"	Section 9-313 *1)
"Consumer goods"	Section 9-109 (1)
"Equipment"	Section 9-109 (2)
"Farm products"	Section 9-109 (3)
"Fixture"	Section 9-313
"Fixture filing"	Section 9-313
"General intangibles"	Section 9-106
"Inventory"	Section 9-109 (4)
"Lien creditor"	Section 9-301 (3)
"Proceeds"	Section 9-306 (1)
"Purchase money security interest"	Section 9-107
"United States"	Section 9-103

(3) The following definitions in other articles apply to this Article:

"Check"	Section 3-104
"Contract for sale"	Section 2-106
"Holder in due course"	Section 3-302
"Note"	Section 3-104
"Sale"	Section 2-106

(4) In addition Article 1 contains general definitions and principles of construction and interpretation throughout this Article.

§9-105. Definitions and Index of Definitions *(1977 Amendments).*

(1)   In this Article unless the context otherwise requires:

* * *

(i) "Instrument" means a negotiable instrument (defined in Section 3-104), or a certificated security (defined in Section 8-102) or . . .

* * *

§9-106. Definitions: "Account"; "General Intangibles". "Account" means any right to payment for goods sold or leased or for services rendered which is not evidenced by an instrument or chattel paper, whether or not it has been earned by performance. "General intangibles" means any personal property (including things in action) other than goods, accounts, chattel paper, documents, instruments, and money. All rights to payment earned or unearned under a charter or other contract involving the use or hire of a vessel and all rights incident to the charter or contract are accounts.

§9-107. Definitions: "Purchase Money Security Interest". A security interest is a "purchase money security interest" to the extent that it is

(a) taken or retained by the seller of the collateral to secure all or part of its price;

(b) taken by a person who by making advances or incurring an obligation gives value to enable the debtor to acquire rights in or the use of collateral if such value is in fact so used.

§9-108. When After-Acquired Collateral Not Security for Antecedent Debt. Where a secured party makes an advance, incurs an obligation, releases a perfected security interest, or otherwise gives new value which is to be secured in whole or in part by after-acquired property his security interest in the after-acquired collateral shall be deemed to be taken for new value and not as security for an antecedent debt if the debtor acquires his rights in such collateral either in the ordinary course of his business or under a contract of purchase made pursuant to the security agreement within a reasonable time after new value is given.

§9-109. Classification of Goods; "Consumer Goods"; "Equipment"; "Farm Products"; "Inventory". Goods are

(1) "consumer goods" if they are used or bought for use primarily for personal, family or household purposes;

(2) "equipment" if they are used or bought for use primarily in business (including farming or a profession) or by a debtor who is a non-profit organization or a governmental subdivision or agency or if the goods are not included in the definitions of inventory, farm products or consumer goods;

(3) "farm products" if they are crops or livestock or supplies used or produced in farming operations or if they are products of crops or livestock in their unmanufactured states (such as ginned cotton, wool-clip, maple syrup, milk and eggs), and if they are in the possession of a debtor engaged in raising, fattening, grazing or other farming operations. If goods are farm products they are neither equipment nor inventory;

(4) "inventory" if they are held by a person who holds them for sale or lease or to be furnished under contracts of service or if he has so furnished them, or if they are raw materials, work in process or materials used or consumed in a business. Inventory of a person is not to be classified as his equipment.

§9-110. Sufficiency of Description. For the purposes of this Article any description of personal property or real estate is sufficient whether or not it is specific if it reasonably identifies what is described.

§9-111. Applicability of Bulk Transfer Laws. The creation of a security interest is not a bulk transfer under Article 6 (see Section 6-103).

§9-112. Where Collateral Is Not Owned by Debtor. Unless otherwise agreed, when a secured party knows that collateral is owned by a person who is not the debtor, the owner of the collateral is entitled to receive from the secured party any surplus under Section 9-502 (2) or under Section 9-504 (1), and is not liable for the debt or for any deficiency after resale, and he has the same right as the debtor

(a) to receive statements under Section 9-208;

(b) to receive notice of and to object to a secured party's proposal to retain the collateral in satisfaction of the indebtedness under Section 9-505;

(c) to redeem the collateral under Section 9-506;

(d) to obtain injunctive or other relief under Section 9-507 (1); and

(e) to recover losses caused to him under Section 9-208 (2).

§9-113. Security Interests Arising Under Article on Sales. A security interest arising solely under the Article on Sales (Article 2) is subject to the provisions of this Article except that to the extent that and so long as the debtor does not have or does not lawfully obtain possession of the goods

(a) no security agreement is necessary to make the security interest enforceable; and

(b) no filing is required to perfect the security interest; and

(c) the rights of the secured party on default by the debtor are governed by the Article on Sales (Article 2).

§9-114. Consignment.

(1) A person who delivers goods under a consignment which is not a security interest and who would be required to file under this Article by paragraph (3) (c) of Section 2-326 has priority over a secured party who is or becomes a creditor of the consignee and who would have a perfected security interest in the goods if they were the property of the consignee, and also has priority with respect to identifiable cash proceeds received on or before delivery of the goods to a buyer, if

(a) the consignor complies with the filing provision of the Article on Sales with respect to consignments (paragraph (3) (c) of Section 2-326) before the consignee receives possession of the goods; and

(b) the consignor gives notification in writing to the holder of the security interest if the holder has filed a financing statement covering the same types of goods before the date of the filing made by the consignor; and

(c) the holder of the security interest receives the notification within five years before the consignee receives possession of the goods; and

(d) the notification states that the consignor expects to deliver goods on consignment to the consignee, describing the goods by item or type.

(2) In the case of a consignment which is not a security interest and in which the requirements of the preceding subsection have not been met, a person who delivers goods to another is subordinate to a person who would have a perfected security interest in the goods if they were the property of the debtor.

Part 2: Validity of Security Agreement and Rights of Parties Thereto

§9-201. General Validity of Security Agreement. Except as otherwise provided by this Act a security agreement is effective according to its terms between the parties, against purchasers of the collateral and against creditors. Nothing in this Article validates any charge or practice illegal under any statute or regulation thereunder governing usury, small loans, retail installment sales, or the like, or extends the application of any such statute or regulation to any transaction not otherwise subject thereto.

§9-202. Title to Collateral Immaterial. Each provision of this Article with regard to rights, obligations and remedies applies whether title to collateral is in the secured party or in the debtor.

§9-203. Attachment and Enforceability of Security Interest; Proceeds; Formal Requisites.

(1) Subject to the provisions of Section 4-208 on the security interest of a collecting bank and Section 9-113 on a security interest arising under the Article on Sales, a security interest is not enforceable against the debtor or third parties with respect to the collateral and does not attach unless

(a) the collateral is in the possession of the secured party pursuant to agreement, or the debtor has signed a security agreement which contains a description of the collateral and in addition, when the security interest covers crops growing or to be grown or timber to be cut, a description of the land concerned; and

(b) value has been given; and

(c) the debtor has rights in the collateral.

(2) A security interest attaches when it becomes enforceable against the debtor with respect to the collateral. Attachment occurs as soon as all of the event specified in subsection (1) have taken place unless explicit agreement postpones the time of attaching.

(3) Unless otherwise agreed a security agreement gives the secured party the rights to proceeds provided by Section 9-306.

(4) A transaction, although subject to this Article, is also subject to . . . . *, and in the case of conflict between the provisions of this Article and any such statute, the provisions of such statute control. Failure to comply with any applicable statue has only the effect which is specified therein.

Note: *At * in subsection (4) insert reference to any local statute regulating small loans, retail installment sales and the like.*

The foregoing subsection (4) is designed to make it clear that certain transactions, although subject to this Article, must also comply with other applicable legislation.

This Article is designed to regulate all the "security" aspects of transactions within its scope. There is, however, much regulatory legislation, particularly in the consumer field, which supplements this Article and should not be repealed by its enactment. Examples are small loan acts, retail installment selling acts and the like. Such acts may provide for licensing and rate regulation and may prescribe particular forms of contract. Such provisions should remain in force despite the enactment of this Article. On the other hand if a retail installent selling act contains provisions on filing, rights on default, etc., such provisions should be repealed as inconsistent with this Article except that inconsistent provisions as to deficiencies, penalities, etc., in the Uniform Consumer Credit Code and other recent related legislation should remain because those statutes were drafted after the substantial enactment of the Article and with the intention of modifying certain provisions of this Article as to consumer credit.

§9-203. Attachment and Enforceability of Security Interest; Proceeds; Formal Requisites *(1977 Amendments).*

(1) Subject to the provisions of Section 4-208 on the security interest of a collecting bank, Section 8-321 on security interests in securities and Section 9-113 on a security interest arising under the Article on Sales, a security interest in not enforceable against the debtor or third parties with respect to the collateral and does not attach unless:

(a) the collateral is in the possession of the secured party pursuant to agreement, or the debtor has signed a security agreement which contains a description of the collateral and in addition, when the security interest covers crops growing or to be grown or timber to be cut, a description of the land concerned;

(b) value has been given; and

(c) the debtor has rights in the collateral.

§9-204. After-Acquired Property; Future Advances.

(1) Except as provided in subsection (2), a security agreement may provide that any or all obligations covered by the security agreement are to be secured by after-acquired collateral.

(2) No security interest attaches under an after-acquired property clause to consumer goods other than accessions (Section 9-314) when given as additional security unless the debtor acquires rights in them within ten days after the secured party gives value.

(3) Obligations covered by a security agreement may include future advances or other value whether or not the advances or value are given pursuant to commitment (subsection (1) of Section 9-105).

§9-205. Use or Disposition of Collateral Without Accounting Permissible. A security interest is not invalid or fraudulent against creditors by reason of liberty in the debtor to use, commingle or dispose of all or part of the collateral (including returned or repossessed goods) or to collect or compromise accounts or chattel paper, or to accept the return of goods or make repossessions, or to use, commingle or dispose of proceeds, or by reason of the failure of the secured party to require the debtor to account for proceeds or replace collateral. This section does not relax the requirements of possession where perfection of a security interest depends upon possession of the collateral by the secured party or by a bailee.

§9-206. Agreement Not to Assert Defenses Against Assignee; Modification of Sales Warranties Where Security Agreement Exists.

(1) Subject to any statute or decision which establishes a different rule for buyers or lessees of consumer goods, an agreement any claim or defense which he may have against the seller or lessor is enforceable by an assignee who takes his assignment for value, in good faith and without notice of a claim or defense, except as to defenses of a type which may be asserted against a holder in due course of a negotiable instrument under the Article on Commercial Paper (Article 3). A buyer who as part of one transaction signs both a negotiable instrument and a security agreement makes such an agreement.

(2) When a seller retains a purchase money security interest in goods the Article on Sales (Article 2) governs the sale and any disclaimer, limitation or modification of the seller's warranties. Amended in 1962.

§9-207. Rights and Duties When Collateral is in Secured Party's Possession.

(1) A secured party must use reasonable care in the custody and preservation of collateral in his possession. In the case of an instrument or chattel paper reasonable care includes taking necessary steps to preserve rights against prior parties unless otherwise agreed.

(2) Unless otherwise agreed, when collateral is in the secured party's possession

(a) reasonable expenses (including the cost of any insurance and payment of taxes or other charges) incurred in the custody, preservation, use or operation of the collateral are chargeable to the debtor and are secured by the collateral;

(b) the risk of accidental loss or damage is on the debtor to the extent of any deficiency in any effective insurance coverage;

(c) the secured party may hold as additional security any increase or profits (except money) received from the collateral, but money so received, unless remitted to the debtor, shall be applied in reduction of the secured obligation;

(d) the secured party must keep the collateral indentifiable but fungible collateral may be commingled;

(e) the secured party may repledge the collateral upon terms which do not impair the debtor's right to redeem it.

(3) A secured party is liable for any loss caused by his failure to meet any obligation imposed by the preceding subsections but does not lose his security interest.

(4) A secured party may use or operate the collateral for the purpose of preserving the collateral or its value or pursuant to the order of a court of appropriate jurisdiction or, except in the case of consumer goods, in the manner and to the extent provided in the security agreement.

§9-208. Request for Statement of Account or List of Collateral.

(1) A debtor may sign a statement indicating what he believes to be the aggregate amount of unpaid indebtedness as of a specified date and may send it to the secured party with a request that the statement be approved or corrected and returned to the debtor. When the security agreement or any other record kept by the secured party identifies the collateral a debtor may similarly request the secured party to approve or correct a list of the collateral.

(2) The secured party must comply with such a request within two weeks after receipt by sending a written correction or approval. If the secured party claims a security interest in all of a particular type of collateral owned by the debtor he may indicate that fact in his reply and need not approve or correct an itemized list of such collateral. If the secured party without reasonable excuse fails to comply he is liable for any loss caused to the debtor thereby; and if the debtor has properly included in his request a good faith statement of the obligation or a list of the collateral or both, the secured party may claim a security interest only as shown in the statement against persons misled by his failure to comply. If he no longer has an interest in the obligation or collateral at the time the request is received he must disclose the name and address of any successor in interest known to him and he is liable for any loss caused to the debtor as a result of failure to disclose. A successor in interest is not subject to this section until a request is received by him.

(3) A debtor is entitled to such a statement once every six months without charge. The secured party may require payment of a charge not exceeding $10 for each additional statement furnished.

Part 3: Rights of Third Parties; Perfected and Unperfected Security Interests; Rules of Priority

§ 9-301. Persons Who Take Priority Over Unperfected Security interests; Right of "Lien Creditor".

(1) Except as otherwise provided in subsection (2), an unperfected security interest is subordinate to the rights of

(a) persons entitled to priority under Section 9-312;

(b) a person who becomes a lien creditor before the security interest is perfected;

(c) in the case of goods, instruments, documents, and chattel paper, a person who is not a secured party and who is a transferee in bulk or other buyer not in ordinary course of business, or is a buyer of farm products in ordinary course of business, to the extent that he gives value and receives delivery of the collateral without knowledge of the security interest and before it is perfected;

(d) in the case of accounts and general intangibles, a person who is not a secured party and who is a transferee to the extent that he gives value without knowledge of the security interest and before it is perfected.

(2) If the secured party files with respect to a purchase money security interest before or within ten days after the debtor receives possession of the collateral, he takes priority over the rights of a transferee in bulk or of a lien creditor which arise between the time the security interest attaches and the time of filing.

(3) A "lien creditor" means a creditor who has acquired a lien on the property involved by attachment, levy or the like and includes an assignee for benefit of creditors from the time of assignment, and a trustee in bankruptcy from the date of the filing of the petition or a receiver in equity from the time of appointment.

(4) A person who becomes a lien creditor while a security interest is perfected takes subject to the security interest only to the extent that it secures advances made before he becomes a lien creditor or within 45 days thereafter or made without knowledge of the lien or pursuant to a commitment entered into without knowledge of the lien.

§9-302. When Filing Is Required to Perfect Security Interest; Security Interests to Which Filing Provisions of This Article Do Not Apply.

(1) A financing statement must be filed to perfect all security interests except the following:

(a) a security interest in collateral in possession of the secured party under Section 9-305;

(b) a security interest temporarily perfected in instruments or documents without delivery under Section 9-304 or in proceeds for a 10 day period under Section 9-306;

(c) a security interest created by an assignment of a beneficial interest in a trust or a decedent's estate;

(d) a purchase money security interest in consumer goods; but filing is required for a motor vehicle required to be registered; and fixture filing is required for priority over conflicting interests in fixtures to the extent provided in Section 9-313;

(e) an assignment of accounts which does not alone or in conjunction with other assignments to the same assignee transfer a significant part of the outstanding accounts of the assignor;

(f) a security interest of a collecting bank (Section 4-208) or arising under the Article on Sales (see section 9-113) or covered in subsection (3) of this section;

(g) in assignment for the benefit of all the creditors of the transferor, and subsequent transfers by the assignee thereunder.

(2) If a secured party assigns a perfected security interest, no filing under this Article is required in order to continue the perfected status of the security interest against creditors of and transferees from the original debtor.

(3) The filing of a financing statement otherwise required by this Article is not necessary or effective to perfect a security interest in property subject to

(a) a statute or treaty of the United States which provides for a national or international registration or a national or international certificate of title or which specifies a place of filing different from that specified in this Article for filing of the security interest; or

(b) the following statutes of this state; [[list any certificate of title statute covering automobiles, trailers, mobile homes, boats, farm tractors, or the like, and any central filing statute.*.]]; but during any period in which collateral is inventory held for sale by a person who is in the business of selling goods of that kind, the filing provisions of this Article (Part 4) apply to a security interest in that collateral created by him as debtor; or

(c) a certificate of title statute of another jurisdiction under the law of which indication of a security interest on the certificate is required as a condition of perfection (subsection (2) of Section 9-103).

(4) Compliance with a statute or treaty described in subsection (3) is equivalent to the filing of a financing statement under this Article, and a security interest in property subject to the statute or treaty can be perfected only by compliance therewith except as provided in Section 9-103 on multiple state transactions. Duration and renewal of perfection of a security interest perfected by compliance with the statute or treaty are governed by the provisions of the statute or treaty; in other respects the security interest is subject to this Article.

§9-302. When Filing is Required to Perfect Security Interest; Security Interests to Which Filing Provisions of This Article Do Not Apply *(1977 Amendments).*

(1) A financing statement must be filed to perfect all security interests[s] except the following:

* * *

(f) a security interest of a collecting bank (Section 4-208) or in securities (Section 8-321) or arising under the Article on Sales (see Section 9-113) or covered in subsection (3) of this section;

* * *

§9-303. When Security Interest is Perfected; Continuity of Perfection.

(1) A security interest is perfected when it has attached and when all of the applicable steps required for perfection have been taken. Such steps are specified in Section 9-304, 9-305, and 9-306. If such steps are taken before the security interest attaches, it is perfected at the time when it attaches.

* Note: It is recommended that the provisions of certificate of title acts for perfection of security interests by notation on the certificates should be amended to exclude coverage of inventory held for sale.

(2) If a security interest is originally perfected in any way permitted under this Article and is subsequently perfected in some other way under this Article, without an intermediate period when it was unperfected, the security interest shall be deemed to be perfected continuously for the purposes of this Article.

§9-304. Perfection of Security Interest in Instruments, Documents, and Goods Covered by Documents; Perfection by Permissive Filing; Temporary Perfection Without Filing or Transfer of Possession.

(1) A security interest in chattel paper or negotiable documents may be perfected by filing. A security interest in money or instruments (other than instruments which constitute part of chattel paper) can be

perfected only by the secured party's taking possession, except as provided in subsections (4) and (5) of this section and subsections (2) and (3) of Section 9-306 on proceeds.

(2) During the period that goods are in the possession of the issuer of a negotiable document therefor, a security interest in the goods is perfected by perfecting a security interest in the document, and any security interest in the goods otherwise perfected during such period is subject thereto.

(3) A security interest in goods in the possession of a bailee other than one who has issued a negotiable document therefor is perfected by issuance of a document in the name of the secured party or by the bailee's receipt of notification of the secured party's interest or by filing as to the goods.

(4) A security interest in instruments or negotiable documents is perfected without filing or the taking of possession for a period of 21 days from the time it attaches to the extent that it arises for new value given under a written security agreement.

(5) A security interest remains perfected for a period of 21 days without filing where a secured party having a perfected security interest in an instrument, a negotiable document or goods in possession of a bailee other than one who has issued a negotiable document therefor

(a) makes available to the debtor the goods or documents representing the goods for the purpose of ultimate sale or exchange or for the purpose of loading, unloading, storing, shipping, transshipping, manufacturing, processing or otherwise dealing with them in a manner preliminary to their sale or exchange, but priority between conflicting security interests in the goods is subject to subsection (3) of Section 9-312; or

(b) delivers the instrument to the debtor for the purpose of ultimate sale or exchange or of presentation, collection, renewal or registration of transfer.

(6) After the 21 day period in subsections (4) and (5) perfection depends upon compliance with applicable provisions of this Article.

§9-304. Perfection of Security Interest in Instruments, Documents, and Goods Covered by Documents; Perfection by Permissive Filing; Temporary Perfection Without Filing or Transfer of Possession *(1977 Amendments).*

(1) A security interest in chattel paper or negotiable documents may be perfected by filing. A security interest in money or instruments (other than certificated securities or instruments which constitute part of chattel paper) can be perfected only by the secured party's taking possession, except as provided in subsections (4) and (5) of this section and subsections (2) and (3) of Section 9-306 on proceeds.

* * *

(4) A security interest in instruments (other than certificated securities) or negotiable documents is perfected without filing or the taking of possession for a period of 21 days from the time it attaches to the extent that it arises for new value given under a written security agreement.

(5) A security interest remains perfected for a period of 21 days without filing where a secured party having a perfected security interest in an instrument (other than a certificated security), a negotiable document or goods in possession of a bailee other than one who has issued a negotiable document therefor:

* * *

(b) delivers the instrument to the debtor for the purpose of ultimate sale or exchange or of presentation, collection, renewal, or registration of transfer.

(6) After the 21 day period in subsections (4) and (5) perfection depends upon compliance with applicable provisions of this Article.

§9-305. When Possession by Secured Party Perfects Security Interest Without Filing. A security interest in letters of credit and advices of credit (subsection (2) (a) of Section 5-116), goods, instruments, money, negotiable documents or chattel paper may be perfected by the secured party's taking possession of the collateral. If such collateral other than goods covered by a negotiable document is held by a bailee, the secured party is deemed to have possession from the time the bailee receives notification of the secured party's interest. A security interest is perfected by possession from the time possession is taken without relation back and continues only so long as possession is retained, unless otherwise perfected as provided in this Article before or after the period of possession by the secured party.

§9-305. When Possession by Secured Party Perfects Security Interest Without Filing *(1977 Amendments).* A security interest in letters of credit and advices of credit (subsection (2)(a) of Section 5-116), goods, instruments (other than certificated securities), money, negotiable documents, or chattel paper may be perfected by the secured party's taking possession of the collateral. If such collateral other than goods covered by a negotiable document is held by a bailee, the secured party is deemed to have possession from the time the bailee receives notification of the secured party's interest. A security interest is perfected by possession from the time possession is taken without relation back and continues only so long as possession is retained, unless otherwise specified in this Article. The security interest may be otherwise per-

fected as provided in this Article before or after the period of possession by the security party.

§9-306. "Proceeds"; Secured Party's Rights on Disposition of Collateral.
(1) "Proceeds" includes whatever is received upon the sale, exchange, collection or other disposition of collateral or proceeds. Insurance payable by reason of loss or damage to the collateral is proceeds, except to the extent that it is payable to a person other than a party to the security agreement. Money, checks, deposit accounts, and the like are "cash proceeds". All other proceeds are "non-cash proceeds".

(2) Except where this Article otherwise provides, a security interest continues in collateral notwithstanding sale, exchange or other disposition thereof unless the disposition was authorized by the secured party in the security agreement or otherwise, and also continues in any identifable proceeds including collections received by the debtor.

(3) The security interest in proceeds is a continuously perfected security interest if the interest in the original collateral was perfected but it ceases to be a perfected security interest and becomes unperfected ten days after receipt of the proceeds by the debtor unless

(a) a filed financing statement covers the original collateral and the proceeds are collateral in which a security interest may be perfected by filing in the office or offices where the financing statement has been filed and, if the proceeds are acquired with cash proceeds, the description of collateral in the financing statement indicates the types of property constituting the proceeds; or

(b) a filed financing statement covers the original collateral and the proceeds are identifiable cash proceeds; or

(c) the security interest in the proceeds is perfected before the expiration of the ten day period.

Except as provided in this section, a security interest in proceeds can be perfected only by the methods or under the circumstances permitted in this Article for original collateral of the same type.

(4) In the event of insolvency proceedings instituted by or against a debtor, a secured party with a perfected security interest in proceeds has a perfected security interest only in the following proceeds:

(a) in identifiable non-cash proceeds and in separate deposit accounts containing only proceeds;

(b) in identifiable cash proceeds in the form of money which is neither commingled with other money nor deposited in a deposit account prior to the insolvency proceedings;

(c) in identifiable cash proceeds in the form of checks and the like which are not deposited in a deposit account prior to the insolvency proceedings; and

(d) in all cash and deposit accounts of the debtor in which proceeds have been commingled with other funds, but proceeds have been commingled with other funds, but the perfected security interest under this paragraph (d) is

(i) subject to any right of set-off; and

(ii) limited to an amount not greater than the amount of any cash proceeds received by the debtor within ten days before the institution of the insolvency proceedings less the sum of (i) the payments to the secured party on account of cash proceeds received by the debtor during such period and (ii) the cash proceeds received by the debtor during such period to which the secured party is entitled under paragraphs (a) through (c) of this subsection (iv).

(5) If a sale of goods results in an account or chattel paper which is transferred by the seller to a secured party, and if the goods are returned to or are repossessed by the seller or the secured party, the following rules determine priorities:

(a) If the goods were collateral at the time of sale, for an indebtedness of the seller which is still unpaid, the original security interest attaches again to the goods and continues as a perfected security interest if it was perfected at the time when the goods were sold. If the security interest was originally perfected by a filing which is still effective, nothing further is required to continue the perfected status; in any other case, the secured party must take possession of the returned or repossessed goods or must file.

(b) An unpaid transferee of the chattel paper has a security interest in the goods against the transferor. Such security interest is prior to a security interest asserted under paragraph (a) to the extent that the transferee of the chattel paper was entitled to priority under Section 9-308.

(c) An unpaid transferee of the account has a security interest in the goods against the transferor. Such security interest is subordinate to a security interest asserted under paragraph (a).

(d) A security interest of an unpaid transferee asserted under paragraph (b) or (c) must be perfected for protection against creditors of the transferor and purchasers of the returned or repossessed goods.

§9-307. Protection of Buyers of Goods.

(1) A buyer in ordinary course of business (subsection (9) of Section 1-201) other than a person buying farm products from a person engaged in farming operations takes free of a security interest created by his seller even though the security interest is perfected and even though the buyer knows of its existence.

(2) In the case of consumer goods a buyer takes free of a security interest even though perfected if he buys without knowledge of the security interest, for value and for his own personal, family or household purposes unless prior to the purchase the secured party has filed a financing statement covering such goods.

(3) A buyer other than a buyer in ordinary course of business (subsection (1) of this section) takes free of a security interest to the extent that it secures future advances made after the secured party acquires knowledge of the purchase, or more than 45 days after the purchase, whichever first occurs, unless made pursuant to a commitment entered into without knowledge of the purchase and before the expiration of the 45 day period.

§9-308. Purchase of Chattel Paper and Instruments.
A purchaser of chattel paper or an instrument who gives new value and takes possession of it in the ordinary course of his business has priority over a security interest in the chattel paper or instrument

(a) which is perfected under Section 9-304 (permissive filing and temporary perfection) or under Section 9-306 (perfection as to proceeds) if he acts without knowledge that the specific paper or instrument is subject to a security interest; or

(b) which is claimed merely as proceeds of inventory subject to a security interest (Section 9-306) even though he knows that the specific paper or instrument is subject to the security interest.

§9-309. Protection of Purchasers of Instruments and Documents.
Nothing in this Article limits the rights of a holder in due course of a negotiable instrument (Section 3-302) or a holder to whom a negotiable document of title has been duly negotiated (Section 7-501) or a bona fide purchaser of a security (Section 8-301) and such holders or purchasers take priority over an earlier security interest even though perfected. Filing under this Article does not constitute notice of the security interest to such holders or purchasers.

§9-309. Protection of Purchasers of Instruments, Documents and Securities *(1977 Amendments)*.
Nothing in this Article limits the rights of a holder in due course of a negotiable instrument (Section 3-302) or a holder to whom negotiable document of title has been duly negotiated (Section 7-501) or a bona fide purchaser of a security (Section 8-302) and such holders or purchasers take priority over an earlier security inter-

est even though perfected. Filing under this Article does not constitute notice of the security interest to such holders or purchasers.

§9-310. Priority of Certain Liens Arising by Operations of Law. When a person in the ordinary course of his business furnishes services or materials with respect to goods subject to a security interest, a lien upon goods in the possession of such person given by statute or rule of law for such materials or services takes priority over a perfected security interest unless the lien is statutory and the statute expressly provides otherwise.

§9-311. Alienability of Debtor's Rights: Judicial Process. The debtor's rights in collateral may be voluntarily or involuntarily transferred (by way of sale, creation of a security interest, attachment, levy, garnishment or other judicial process) notwithstanding a provision in the security agreement prohibiting any transfer or making the transfer constitute a default.

§9-312. Priorities Among Conflicting Security Interests in the Same Collateral.

(1) The rules of priority state in other sections of this Part and in the following sections shall govern when applicable: Section 4-208 with respect to the security interests of collecting banks in items being collected, accompanying documents and proceeds; Section 9-103 on security interests related to other jurisdictions; Section 9-114 on consignments.

(2) A perfected security interest in crops for new value given to enable the debtor to produce the crops during the production season and given not more than three months before the crops become growing crops by planting or otherwise takes priority over an earlier perfected security interest to the extent that such earlier interest secures obligations due more than six months before the crops become growing crops by planting or otherwise, even though the person giving new value had knowledge of the earlier security interest.

(3) A perfected purchase money security interest in inventory has priority over a conflicting security interest in the same inventory and also has priority in identifiable cash proceeds received on or before the delivery of the inventory to a buyer if

(a) the purchase money security interest is perfected at the time the debtor receives possession of the inventory; and

(b) the purchase noney secured party gives notification in writing to the holder of the conflicting security interest if the holder had filed a financing statement covering the same types of inventory (i) before the date of the filing made by the purchase money secured party, or (ii) before the beginning of the 21 day period where the purchase money security interest is

temporarily perfected without filing or possession (subsection (5) of Section 9-304); and

(c) the older of the conflicting security interest receives the notification within five years before the debtor receives possession of the inventory; and

(d) the notification states that the person giving the notice has or expect to acquire a purchase money security interest in inventory of the debtor, describing such inventory by item or type.

(4) A purchase money security interest in collateral other than inventory has priority over a conflicting security interest in the same collateral or its proceeds if the purchase money security interest is perfected at the time the debtor receives possession of the collateral or within ten days thereafter.

(5) In all cases not governed by other rules stated in this section (including cases of purchase money security interests which do not qualify for the special priorities set forth in subsections (3) and (4) of this section), priority between conflicting security interests in the same collateral shall be determined according to the following rules:

(a) Conflicting security interests rank according to priority in time of filing or perfection. Priority dates from the time a filing is first made covering the collateral or the time the security interest is first perfected, whichever is earlier, provided that there is no period thereafter when there is neither filing nor perfection.

(b) So long as conflicting security interests are unperfected, the first to attach has priority.

(6) For the purposes of subsection (5) a date of filing or perfection as to collateral is also a date for filing or perfection as to proceeds.

(7) If future advances are made while a security interest is perfected by filing or the taking of possession, the security interest has the same priority for the purposes of subsection (5) with respect to the future advances as it does with respect to the first advance. If a commitment is made before or while the security interest is so perfected, the security interest has the same priority with respect to advances made pursuant thereto. In other cases a perfected security interest has priority from the date the advance is made.

§9-312. Priorities Among Conflicting Security Interests in the Same Collateral *(1977 Amendments).*

(7) If future advances are made while a security interest is perfected by filing, the taking of possession, or under Section 8-321 on securities, the security interest has the same priority for the purposes of subsection (5) with respect to the future advances as it does with respect to the first advance. If a commitment is made

before or while the security interest is so perfected, the security interest has the same priority with respect to advances made pursuant thereto. In other cases a perfected security interest has priority from the date the advance is made.

* * *

§9-313. Priority of Security Interests in Fixtures.

(1) In this section and in the provisions of Part 4 of this Article referring to fixture filing, unless the context otherwise requires

(a) goods are "fixtures" when they become so related to particular real estate that an interest in them arises under real estate law

(b) a "fixture filing" is the filing in the office where a mortgage on the real estate would be filed or recorded of a financing statement covering goods which are or are to become fixtures and conforming to the requirements of subsection (5) of Section 9-402

(c) a mortgage is a "construction mortgage" to the extent that it secures an obligation incurred for the construction of an improvement on land including the acquisition cost of the land, if the recorded writing so indicates.

(2) A security interest under this Article may be created in goods which are fixtures or may continue in goods which become fixtures, but no security interest exists under this Article in ordinary building materials incorporated into an improvement on land.

(3) This Article does not prevent creation of an encumbrance upon fixtures pursuant to real estate law.

(4) A perfected security interest in fixtures has priority over the conflicting interest of an encumbrance or owner of the real estate where

(a) the security interest is a purchase money security interest, the interest of the encumbrancer or owner arises before the goods become fixtures, the security interest is perfected by a fixture filing before the goods become fixtures or within ten days thereafter, and the debtor has an interest of record in the real estate or is in possession of the real estate; or

(b) the security interest is perfected by a fixture filing before the interest of the encumbrancer or owner is of record, the security interest has priority over any conflicting interest of a predecessor in title of the encumbrancer or owner, and the debtor has an interest of record in the real estate or is in possession of the real estate; or

(c) the fixtures are readily removable factory or office machines or readily removable replacements of domestic appliances which are consumer goods, and before the goods become fixtures the security interest is perfected by any method permitted by this Article; or

(d) the conflicting interest is a lien on the real estate obtained by legal or equitable proceedings after the security interest was perfected by any method permitted by this Article.

(5) A security interest in fixtures, whether or not perfected, has priority over the conflicting interest of an encumbrancer or owner of the real estate where

(a) the encumbrancer or owner has consented in writing to the security interest or has disclaimed an interest in the goods as fixtures; or

(b) the debtor has a right to remove the goods as against the encumbrancer or owner. If the debtor's right terminates, the priority of the security interest continues for a reasonable time.

(6) Notwithstanding paragraph (a) of subsection (4) but otherwise subject to subsections (4) and (5), a security interest in fixtures in subordinate to a construction mortgage recorded before the goods become fixtures if the goods become fixtures before the completion of the construction. To the extent that it is given to refinance a construction mortgage, a mortgage has this priority to the same extent as the construction mortgage.

(7) In cases not within the preceding subsections, a security interest in fixtures is subordinate to the conflicting interest of an encumbrancer or owner of the related real estate who is not the debtor.

(8) When the secured party has priority over all owners and encumbrancers of the real estate, he may, on default, subject to the provisions of Part 5, remove his collateral from the real estate but he must reimburse any encumbrancer or owner of the real estate who is not the debtor and who has not otherwise agreed for the cost of repair of any physical injury, but not for any diminution in value of the real estate caused by the absence of the goods removed or by any necessity of replacing them. A person entitled to reimbursement may refuse permission to remove until the secured party gives adequate security for the performance of this obligation.

§9-314. Accessions.

(1) A security interest in goods which attaches before they are installed in or affixed to other goods takes priority as to the goods installed or affixed (called in this section "accessions") over the claims of all persons to the whole except as stated in subsection (3) and subject to Section 9-315(1).

(2) A security interest which attaches to goods after they become part of a whole is valid against all persons subsequently acquiring interests in the whole except as stated in subsection (3) but is invalid against any person with an interest in the whole at the time the security interest attaches to the goods who has not in writing consented to the security interest or disclaimed an interest in the goods as part of the whole.

(3) The security interests described in subsections (1) and (2) do not take priority over

(a) a subsequent purchaser for value of any interest in the whole; or

(b) a creditor with a lien on the whole subsequently obtained by judicial proceedings; or

(c) a creditor with a prior perfected security interest in the whole to the extent that he makes subsequent advances

if the subsequent purchase is made, the lien by judicial proceedings obtained or the subsequent advance under the prior perfected security interest is made or contracted for without knowledge of the security interest and before it is perfected. A purchaser of the whole at a foreclosure sale other than the holder of a perfected security interest purchasing at his own foreclosure sale is a subsequent purchaser within this section.

(4) When under subsections (1) or (2) and (3) a secured party has an interest in accessions which has priority over the claims of all persons who have interests in the whole, he may on default subject to the provisions of Part 5 remove his collateral from the whole but he must reimburse any encumbrancer or owner of the whole who is not the debtor and who has not otherwise agreed for the cost of repair of any physical injury but not for any diminution in value of the whole caused by the absence of the goods removed or by any necessity for replacing them. A person entitled to reimbursement may refuse permission to remove until the secured party gives adequate security for the performance of this obligation.

§9-315. Priority When Goods are Commingled or Processed.

(1) If a security interest in goods was perfected and subsequently the goods or a part thereof have become part of a product or mass, the security interest continues in the product or mass if

(a) the goods are so manufactured, processed, assembled or commingled that their identity is lost in the product or mass; or

(b) a financing statement covering the original goods also covers the product into which the goods have been manufactured, processed or assembled. In a case to which paragraph (b) applies, no separate security interest in that part of the original goods which has been manufactured processed or assembled into the product may be claimed under Section 9-314.

(2) When under subsection (1) more than one security interest attaches to the product or mass, they rank equally according to the ratio that the cost of the goods to which each interest originally attached bears to the cost of the total product or mass.

§9-316. Priority Subject to Subordination. Nothing in this Article prevents subordination by agreement by

any person entitled to priority.

§9-317. Secured Party Not Obligated On Contract of Debtor. The mere existence of a security interest or authority given to the debtor to dispose of or use collateral does not impose contract or tort liability upon the secured party for the debtor's acts or omissions.

§9-318. Defenses Against Assignee; Modification of Contract After Notification of Assignment; Term Prohibiting Assignment Ineffective; Identification and Proof of Assignment.

(1) Unless an account debtor has made an enforceable agreement not to assert defenses or claims arising out of a sale as provided in Section 9-206 the rights of an assignee are subject to

(a) all the terms of the contract between the account debtor and assignor and any defense or claim arising therefrom; and

(b) any other defense or claim of the account debtor against the assignor which accrues before the account debtor receives notification of the assignment.

(2) So far as the right to payment or a part thereof under an assigned contract has not been fully earned by performance, and notwithstanding notification of the assignment, any modification of or substitution for the contract made in good faith and in accordance with reasonable commercial standards is effective against an assignee unless the account debtor has otherwise agreed but the assignee acquires corresponding rights under the modified or substituted contract. The assignment may provide that such modification or substitution is a breach by the assignor.

(3) The account debtor is authorized to pay the assignor until the account debtor receives notification that the amount due or to become due has been assigned and that payment is to be made to the assignee. A notification which does not reasonably identify the rights assigned is ineffective. If requested by the account debtor, the assignee must seasonably furnish reasonable proof that the assignment has been made and unless he does so the account debtor may pay the assignor.

(4) A term in any contract between an account debtor and an assignor is ineffective if it prohibits assignment of an account or prohibits creation of a security interest in a general intangible for money due or to become due or requires the account debtor's consent to such assignment or security interest.

Part 4: Filing

§9-401. Place of Filing; Erroneous Filing; Removal of Collateral.

First Alternative Subsection (1)

(1) The proper place to file in order to perfect a security interest is as follows:

(a) when the collateral is timber to be cut or is minerals or the like (including oil and gas) or accounts subject to subjection (5) of Section 9-103, or when the financing statement is filed as a fixture filing (Section 9-313) and the collateral is goods which are or are to become fixtures, then in the office where a mortgage on the real estate would be filed or recorded;

(b) in all other cases, in the office of the [[Secretary of State]]

Second Alternative Subsection (1)

(1) The proper place to file in order to perfect a security interest is as follows:

(a) when the collateral is equipment used in farming operations, or farm products, or accounts or general intangibles arising from or relating to the sale of farm products by a farmer, or consumer goods, then in the office of the . . . . in the county of the debtor's residence or if the debtor is not a resident of this state then in the office of the . . . . in the county where the goods are kept, and in addition when the collateral is crops growing or to be grown in the office of the . . . . in the county where the land is located;

(b) when the collateral is timber to be cut or is minerals or the like (including oil and gas) or accounts subject to subsection (5) of Section 9-103, or when the financing statement is filed as a fixture filing (Section 9-313) and the collateral is goods which are or are to become fixtures, then in the office where a mortgage on the real estate would be filed or recorded;

(c) in all other cases, in the office of the

Third Alternative Subsection (1)

(1) The proper place to file in order to perfect a security interest is as follows:

(a) when the collateral is equipment used in farming operations, or farm products, or accounts or general intangibles arising from or relating to the sale of farm products by a farmer, or consumer goods, then in the office of the . . . . . . in the county of the debtor's residence or if the debtor is not a resident of this state then in the office of the . . . . . . in the county where the goods are, kept, and in addition when the collateral is crops growing or to be grown in the office of . . . . . . in the county where the land is located;

(b) when the collateral is timber to be cut or is minerals or the like (including oil and gas) or accounts subject to subsection (5) of Section 9-103, or when the financing statement is filed as a fixture filing (Section 9-313) and the col-

lateral is goods which are or are to become fixtures, then in the office where a mortgage on the real estate would be filed or recorded;

(c) in all other cases, in the office of the . . . . . and in addition, if the debtor has a place of business in only one county of this state, also in the office of . . . . . . of such county, or, if the debtor has no place of business in this state, but resides in the state, also in the office of . . . . . . of the county in which he resides.

Note: *One of the three alternatives should be selected as subsection (1).*

(2) A filing which is made in good faith in an improper place or not in all of the places required by this section is nevertheless effective with regard to any collateral as to which the filing complied with the requirements of this Article and is also effective with regard to collateral covered by the financing statement against any person who has knowledge of the contents of such financing statement.

(3) A filing which is made in the proper place in this state continues effective even though the debtor's residence or place of business or the location of the collateral or its use, whichever controlled the original filing, is thereafter changed.

Language in double brackets is Alternative Subsection (3).

[[(3) A filing which is made in the proper county continues effective for four months after a change to another county of the debtor's residence or place of business or the location of the collateral, whichever controlled the original filing. It becomes ineffective thereafter unless a copy of the financing statement signed by the secured party is filed in the new county within said period. The security interest may also be perfected in the new county after the expiration of the four-month period; in such case perfected dates from the time of perfection in the new county. A change in the use of the collateral does not impair the effectiveness of the original filing.]]

(4) The rules stated in Section 9-103 determine whether filing is necessary in this state.

(5) Notwithstanding the preceding subsections, and subject to subsection (3) of Section 9-302, the proper place to file in order to perfect a security interest in collateral, including the fixtures, of a transmitting utility is the office of the [[Secretary of State]]. This filing constitutes a fixture filing (Section 9-313) as to the collateral described therein which is or is to become fixtures.

(6) For the purposes of this section, the residence of an organization is its place of business if it has one or its chief executive office if it has more than one place of business.

Note: *Subsection (6) should be used only if the state chooses the Second or Third Alternative Subsection (1).*

§9-402. Formal Requisites of Financing Statement; Amendments; Mortgage as Financing Statement.

(1) A financing statement is sufficient if it gives the names of the debtor and the secured party, is signed by the debtor, gives an address of the secured party from which information concerning the security interest may be obtained, gives a mailing address of the debtor and contains a statement indicating the types, or describing the items, of collateral. A financing statement may be filed before a security agreement is made or a security interest otherwise attaches. When the financing statement covers crops growing or to be grown, the statement must also contain a description of the real estate concerned. When the financing statement covers timber to be cut or covers minerals or the like (including oil and gas) or accounts subject to subsection (5) of Section 9-103, or when the financing statement is filed as a fixture filing (Section 9-313) and the collateral is goods which are or are to become fixtures, the statement must also comply with subsection (5). A copy of the security agreement is sufficient as a financing statement if it contains the above information and is signed by the debtor. A carbon, photographic or other reproduction of a security agreement or a financing statement is sufficient as a financing statement if the security agreement so provides or if the original has been filed in this state.

(2) A financing statement which otherwise complies with subsection (1) is sufficient when it is signed by the secured party instead of the debtor if it is filed to perfect a security interest in

(a) collateral already subject to security interest in another jurisdiction when it is brought into this state, or when the debtor's location is changed to this state. Such a financing statement must state that the collateral was brought into this state or that the debtor's location was changed to this state under such circumstances; or

(b) proceeds under Section 9-306 if the security interest in the original collateral was perfected. Such a financing statement must describe the original collateral; or

(c) collateral as to which the filing has lapsed; or

(d) collateral acquired after a change of name, identity or corporate structure of the debtor (subsection (7)).

(3) A form substantially as follows is sufficient to comply with subsection (1):

Name of debtor (or assignor)....................................
Address ....
Name of secured party (or assignee) ....
Address..
    1. This financing statement covers the following types (or items) of property:

(Describe)..
2. (If collateral is crops) The above described crops are growing or are to be grown on:
(Describe Real Estate) ....
3. (If applicable) The above goods are to become fixtures on (Describe Real Estate) .
. . . . and this financing statement is to be filed [[for record]] in the real estate records.
(If the debtor does not have an interest of record)
The name of a record owner is
4. (If products of collateral are claimed) Products of the collateral are also covered.

(use whichever is applicable) { Signature of Debtor (or Assignor)

Signature of Secured Party (or Assignee)

(4) A financing statement may be amended by filing a writing signed by both the debtor and the secured party. An amendment does not extend the period of effectiveness of a financing statement. If any amendment adds collateral, it is effective as to the added collateral only from the filing date of the amendment. In this Article, unless the context otherwise requires, the term "financing statement" means the original financing statement and any amendments.

(5) A financing statement covering timber to be cut or covering minerals or the like (including oil and gas) or accounts subject to subsection (5) of Section 9-103, or a financing statement filed as a fixture filing (Section 9-313) where the debtor is not a transmitting utility, must show that it covers this type of collateral, must recite that it is to be filed [[for record]] in the real estate records, and the financing statement must contain a description of the real estate [[sufficient if it were contained in a mortgage of the real estate to give constructive notice of the mortgage under the law of this state]]. If the debtor does not have an interest of record in the real estate, the financing statement must show the name of a record owner.

(6) A mortgage is effective as a financing statement filed as a fixture filing from the date of its recording if (a) the goods are described in the mortgage by item or type, (b) the goods are or are to become fixtures related to the real estate described in the mortgage, (c) the mortgage complies with the requirements for a financing statement in this section other than a recital that it is to be filed in the real estate records, and (d) the mortgage is duly recorded. No fee with reference to the financing statement is required other than the regular recording and satisfaction fees with respect to the mortgage.

(7) A financing statement sufficiently shows the name of the debtor if it gives the individual, partnership or corporate name of the debtor, whether or not it adds other trade names or the names of partners. Where the debtor so changes his name or in the case of an organization name, identity or corporate structure that a filed financing statement becomes seriously misleading, the filing is not effective to perfect a security interest in collateral acquired by the debtor more than four months after the change, unless a new appropriate financing statement is filed before the expiration of that time. A filed financing statement remains effective with respect to collateral transferred by the debtor even though the secured party knows of or consents to the transfer.

(8) A financing statement substantially complying with the requirements of this section is effective even though it contains minor errors which are not seriously misleading.

Note: *Language in double brackets is optional.*

Note: *Where the state has any special recording system for real estate other than the usual grantor-grantee index (as, for instance, a tract system or a title registration or Torrens system) local adaptations of subsection (5) and Section 9-403(7) may be necessary. See Mass. Gen. Laws Chapter 106, Section 9-409.*

§9-403. What Constitutes Filing; Duration of Filing; Effect of Lapsed Filing; Duties of Filing Officer.

(1) Presentation for filing of a financing statement and tender of the filing fee or acceptance of the statement by the filing officer constitutes filing under this Article.

(2) Except as provided in subsection (6) a filed financing statement is effective for a period of five years from the date of filing. The effectiveness of a filed financing statement lapses on the expiration of the five year period unless a continuation statement is filed prior to the lapse. If a security interest perfected by filing exists at the time insolvency proceedings are commenced by or against the debtor, the security interest remains perfected until termination of the insolvency proceedings and thereafter for a period of sixty days or until expiration of the five year period, whichever occurs later. Upon lapse the security interest becomes unperfected, unless it is perfected without filing. If the security interest becomes unperfected upon lapse, it is deemed to have been unperfected as against a person who became a purchaser or lien creditor before lapse.

(3) A continuation statement may be filed by the secured party within six months prior to the expiration of the five year period specified in subsection (2). Any such continuation statement must be signed by the secured party, identify the original statement by file number and state that the original statement is still effective. A continuation statement signed by a person other than the secured party of record must be accompanied by a separate written statement of assignment

signed by the secured party of record and complying with subsection (2) of Section 9-405, including payment of the required fee. Upon timely filing of the continuation statement, the effectiveness of the original statement is continued for five years after the last date to which the filing was effective whereupon it lapses in the same manner as provided in subsection (2) unless another continuation statement is filed prior to such lapse. Succeeding continuation statements may be filed in the same manner to continue the effectiveness of the original statement. Unless a statute on disposition of public records provides otherwise, the filing officer may remove a lapsed statement from the files and destroy it immediately if he has retained a microfilm or other photographic record, or in other cases after one year after the lapse. The filing officer shall so arrange matters by physical annexation of financing statements to continuation statements or other related filings, or by other means, that if he physically destroys the financing statements of a period more than five years past, those which have been continued by a continuation statement or which are still effective under subsection (6) shall be retained.

(4) Except as provided in subsection (7) a) filing officer shall mark each statement with a file number and with the date and hour of filing and shall hold the statement or a microfilm or other photographic copy thereof for public inspection. In addition the filing officer shall index the statements according to the name of the debtor and shall note in the index the file number and the address of the debtor given in the statement.

(5) The uniform fee for filing and indexing and for the stamping a copy furnished by the secured party to show the date and place of filing for an original financing statement or for a continuation statement shall be $. . . . . . if the statement is in the standard form prescribed by the . . . . . and otherwise shall be $. . . . . . , plus in each case, if the financing statement is subject to subsection (5) of Section 9-402, $. . . . . . . The uniform fee for each name more than one required to be indexed shall be $. . . . . The secured party may at his option show a trade name for any person and an extra uniform indexing fee of $. . . . . shall be paid with respect thereto.

(6) If the debtor is a transmitting utility (subsection (5) of Section 9-401) and a filed financing statement so states, it is effective until a termination statement is filed. A real estate mortgage which is effective as a fixture filing under subsection (6) of Section 9-402 remains effective as a fixture filing until the mortgage is released or satisfied or record or its effectiveness otherwise terminates as to the real estate.

(7) When a financing statement covers timber to be cut or covers minerals or the like (including oil and gas) or accounts subject to subsection (5) of Section 9-103, or is filed as a fixture filing, [[it shall be filed for record and]] the filing officer shall index it under the names of the debtor and any owner of record shown on the financing statement in the same fashion as if they were the mortgagors in a mortgage of the real estate described, and, to the extent that the law of this state provides for indexing of mortgages under the name of the mortgagee, under the name of the secured party as if he were the mortgagee, thereunder, or where indexing is by description in the same fashion as if the financing statement were a mortgage of the real estate described.

Note: *In states in which writings will not appear in the real estate records and indices unless actually recorded the bracketed language in subsection (7) should be used.*

§9-404. Termination Statement.

(1) If a financing statement covering consumer goods is filed on or after . . . ., then within one month or within ten days following written demand by the debtor after there is no outstanding secured obligation and no commitment to make advances, incur obligations or otherwise give value, the secured party must file with each filing officer with whom the financing statement was filed, a termination statement to the effect that he no longer claims a security interest under the financing statement, which shall be identified by file number. In other cases whenever there is no outstanding secured obligation and no commitment to make advances, incur obligations or otherwise give value, the secured party must on written demand by the debtor send the debtor, for each filing officer with whom the financing statement was filed, a termination statement to the effect that no longer claims a security interest under the financing statement, which shall be identified by file number. A termination statement signed by a person other than the secured party of record must be accompanied by a separate written statement of assignment signed by the secured party of record complying with subsection (2) of Section 9-405, including payment of the required fee. If the affected secured party fails to file such a termination statement as required by this subsection, or to send such a termination statement within ten days after proper demand therefor he shall be liable to the debtor for one hundred dollars, and in addition for any loss caused to the debtor by such failure.

(2) On presentation to the filing officer of such a termination statement he must note it in the index. If he has received the termination statement in duplicate, he shall return one copy of the termination statement to the secured party stamped to show the time of receipt thereof. If the filing officer has a microfilm or other photographic record of the financing statement, and of any related continuation statement, statement of assignment and statement of release, he may remove the originals from the files at any time after receipt of

the termination statement, or if he has no such record, he may remove them from the files at any time after one year after receipt of the termination statement.

(3) If the termination statement is in the standard form prescribed by the . . . . ., the uniform fee for filing and indexing the termination statement shall be $. . . . ., and otherwise shall be $. . . . ., plus in each case an additional fee of $. . . . . . for each name more than one against which the termination statement is required to be indexed.

Note: *The date to be inserted should be the effective date of the revised Article 9.*

§9-405. Assignment of Security Interest; Duties of Filing Officer; Fees.

(1) A financing statement may disclose an assignment of a security interest in the collateral described in the financing statement by indication in the financing statement of the name and address of the assignee or by an assignment itself or a copy thereof on the face or back of the statement. On presentation to the filing officer of such a financing statement the filing officer shall mark the same as provided in Section 9-403(4). The uniform fee for filing, indexing and furnishing filing data for a financing statement so indicating an assignment shall be $. . . . . . if the statement is in the standard form prescribed by the . . . . and otherwise shall be $. . . . . . plus in each case an additional fee of $. . . . . . . for each name more than one against which the financing statement is required to be indexed.

(2) A secured party may assign of record all or part of his rights under a financing statement by the filing in the place where the original financing statement was filed of a separate written statement of assignment signed by the secured party of record and setting forth the name of the secured party of record and the debtor, the file number and the date of filing of the financing statement and the name and address of the assignee and containing a description of the collateral assigned. A copy of the assignment is sufficient as a separate statement if it complies with the preceding sentence. On presentation to the filing officer of such a separate statement, the filing officer shall mark such separate statement with the date and hour of the filing. He shall note the assignment on the index of the financing statement, or in the case of a fixture filing, or a filing covering timber to be cut, or covering minerals or the like (including oil and gas) or accounts subject to subsection (5) of Section 9-103, he shall index the assignment under the name of the assignor as grantor and, to the extent that the law of this state provides for indexing the assignment of a mortgage under the name of the assignee, he shall index the assignment of the financing statement under the name of the assignee. The uniform fee for filing, indexing and furnishing filing data about such a separate statement of assignment shall be $. . . . . if the statement is in the standard form prescribed by the . . . . . and otherwise shall be $. . . . . ., plus in each case an additional fee of $. . . . . . for each name more than one against which the statement of assignment is required to be indexed. Notwithstanding the provisions of this subsection, an assignment of record of a security interest in a fixture contained in a mortgage effective as a fixture filing (subsection (6) of Section 9-402) may be made only by an assignment of the mortgage in the manner provided by the law of this state other than this Act.

(3) After the disclosure or filing of an assignment under this section, the assignee is the secured party of record.

§9-406. Release of Collateral; Duties of Filing Officer; Fees.

A secured party of record may by his signed statement release all or a part of any collateral described in a filed financing statement. The statement of release is sufficient if it contains a description of the collateral being released, the name and address of the debtor, the name and address of the secured party, and the file number of the financing statement. A statement of release signed by a person other than the secured party of record must be accompanied by a separate written statement of assignment signed by the secured party of record and complying with subsection (2) of Section 9-405, including payment of the required fee. Upon presentation of such a statement of release to the filing officer he shall mark the statement with the hour and date of filing and shall note the same upon the margin of the index of the filing of the financing statement. The uniform fee for filing and noting such a statement of release shall be $. . . . . if the statement is in the standard form prescribed by the . . . . . and otherwise shall be $. . . . . ., plus in each case an additional fee of $. . . . . for each name more than one against which the statement of release is required to be indexed.

§[[9-407. Information From Filing Officer.]]

[[(1) If the person filing any financing statement, termination statement, statement of assignment, or statement of release, furnishes the filing officer a copy thereof, the filing officer shall upon request note upon the copy the file number and date and hour of the filing of the original and deliver or send the copy to such person.]]

[[(2) Upon request of any person, the filing officer shall issue his certificate showing whether there is on file on the date and hour stated therein, any presently effective financing statement naming a particular debtor and any statement of assignment thereof and if there is, giving the date and hour of filing of each such statement and the names and addresses of each secured party therein. The uniform fee for such a certificate shall be $. . . . . if the request for the certificate is in the standard form prescribed by the [[Secretary of State]] and otherwise shall be $. . . . . Upon request

the filing officer shall furnish a copy of any filed statement or statement of assignment for a uniform fee of $. . . . . per page.]]

Note: *This section is proposed as an optional provision to require filing officers to furnish certificates. Local law and practices should be consulted with regard to the advisability of adoption.*

§9-408. Financing Statements Covering Consigned or Leased Goods.

A consignor or lessor of goods may file a financing statement using the terms "consignor," "consignee," "lessor," "lessee" or the like instead of the terms specified in Section 9-402. The provisions of this Part shall apply as appropriate to such a financing statement but its filing shall not of itself be a factor in determining whether or not the consignment or lease is intended as security (Section 1-201(37)). However, if it is determined for other reasons that the consignment or lease is so intended, a security interest of the consignor or lessor which attaches to the consigned or leased goods is perfected by such filing.

Part 5: Default

§9-501. Default; Procedure When Security Agreement Covers Both Real and Personal Property.

(1) When a debtor is in default under a security agreement, a secured party has the rights and remedies provided in this Part and except as limited by subsection (3) those provided in the security agreement. He may reduce his claim to judgment, foreclose or otherwise enforce the security interest by any available judicial procedure. If the collateral is documents the secured party may proceed either as to the documents or as to the goods covered thereby. A secured party in possession has the rights, remedies and duties provided in Section 9-207. The rights and remedies referred to in this subsection are cumulative.

(2) After default, the debtor has the rights and remedies provided in this Part, those provided in the security agreement and those provided in Section 9-207.

(3) To the extent that they give rights to the debtor and impose duties on the secured party, the rules stated in the subsections referred to below may not be waived or varied except as provided with respect to compulsory disposition of collateral (subsection (3) of Section 9-504 and Section 9-505) and with respect to redemption of collateral (Section 9-506) but the parties may by agreement determine the standards by which the fulfillment of these rights and duties is to be measured if such standards are not manifestly unreasonable:

(a) subsection (2) of Section 9-502 and subsection (2) of Section 9-504 insofar as they require accounting for surplus proceeds of collateral;

(b) subsection (3) of Section 9-504 and subsection (1) of Section 9-505 which deal with disposition of collateral;

(c) subsection (2) of Section 9-505 which deals with acceptance of collateral as discharge of obligation;

(d) Section 9-506 which deals with redemption of collateral; and

(e) subsection (1) of Section 9-507 which deals with the secured party's liability for failure to comply with this Part.

(4) If the security agreement covers both real and personal property, the secured party may proceed under this Part as to the personal property or he may proceed as to both the real and the personal property in accordance with his rights and remedies in respect of the real property in which case the provisions of this Part do not apply.

(5) When a secured party has reduced his claim to judgment the lien of any levy which may be made upon his collateral by virtue of any execution based upon the judgment shall relate back to the date of the perfection of the security interest in such collateral. A judicial sale, pursuant to such execution, is a foreclosure of the security interest by judicial procedure within the meaning of this section, and the secured party may purchase at the sale and thereafter hold the collateral free of any other requirements of this Article.

§9-502. Collection Rights of Secured Party.

(1) When so agreed and in any event on default the secured party is entitled to notify an account debtor or the obligor on an instrument to make payment to him whether or not the assignor was theretofore making collections on the collateral, and also to take control of any proceeds to which he is entitled under Section 9-306.

(2) A secured party who by agreement is entitled to charge back uncollected collateral or otherwise to full or limited recourse against the debtor and who undertakes to collect from the account debtors or obligors must proceed in a commercially reasonable manner and may deduct his reasonable expenses of realization from the collections. If the security agreement secures an indebtedness, the secured party must account to the debtor for any surplus, and unless otherwise agreed, the debtor is liable for any deficiency. But, if the underlying transaction was a sale of accounts or chattel paper, the debtor is entitled to any surplus or is liable for any deficiency only if the security agreement so provides.

§9-503. Secured Party's Right to Take Possession After Default.
Unless otherwise agreed a secured party has on default the right to take possession of the collateral. In taking possession a secured party may proceed without judicial process if this can be done

without breach of the peace or may proceed by action. If the security agreement so provides the secured party may require the debtor to assemble the collateral and make it available to the secured party at a place to be designated by the secured party which is reasonably convenient to both parties. Without removal a secured party may render equipment unusable, and may dispose of collateral on the debtor's premises under Section 9-504.

§9-504. Secured Party's Right to Dispose of Collateral After Default; Effect of Disposition.

(1) A secured party after default may sell, lease or otherwise dispose of any or all of the collateral in its then condition or following any commercially reasonable preparation or processing. Any sale of goods is subject to the Article on Sales (Article 2). The proceeds of disposition shall be applied in the order following to

(a) the reasonable expenses of retaking, holding, preparing for sale or lease, selling, leasing and the like and, to the extent provided for in the agreement and not prohibited by law, the reasonable attorneys' fees and legal expenses incurred by the secured party;

(b) the satisfaction of indebtedness secured by the security interest under which the disposition is made;

(c) the satisfaction of indebtedness secured by any subordinate security interest in the collateral if written notification of demand therefor is received before distribution of the proceeds is completed. If requested by the secured party, the holder of a subordinate security interest must seasonably furnish reasonable proof of his interest, and unless he does so, the secured party need not comply with his demand.

(2) If the security interest secures an indebtedness, the secured party must account to the debtor for any surplus, and, unless otherwise agreed, the debtor is liable for any deficiency. But if the underlying transaction was a sale of accounts, or chattel paper, the debtor is entitled to any surplus or is liable for any deficiency only if the security agreement so provides.

(3) Disposition of the collateral may be by public or private proceedings and may be made by way of one or more contracts. Sale or other disposition may be as a unit or in parcels and at any time and place and on any terms but every aspect of the disposition including the method, manner, time, place and terms must be commercially reasonable. Unless collateral is perishable or threatens to decline speedily in value or is of a type customarily sold on a recognized market, reasonable notification of the time and place of any public sale or reasonable notification of the time after which any private sale or other intended disposition is to be

made shall be sent by the secured party to the debtor, if he has not signed after default a statement renouncing or modifying his right to notification of sale. In the case of consumer goods no other notification need be sent. In other cases notification shall be sent to any other secured party from whom the secured party has received (before sending his notification to the debtor or before the debtor's renunciation of his rights) written notice of a claim of an interest in the collateral. The secured party may buy at any public sale and if the collateral is of a type customarily sold in a recognized market or is of a type which is the subject of widely distributed standard price quotations he may buy at private sale.

(4) When collateral is disposed of by a secured party after default, the disposition transfers to a purchaser for value all of the debtor's rights therein, discharges the security interest under which it is made and any security interest or lien subordinate thereto. The purchaser takes free of all such rights and interests even though the secured party fails to comply with the requirements of this Part or of any judicial proceedings

(a) in the case of a public sale, if the purchaser has no knowledge of any defects in the sale and if he does not buy in collusion with the secured party, other bidders or the person conducting the sale; or

(b) in any other case, if the purchaser acts in good faith.

(5) A person who is liable to a secured party under a guaranty, indorsement, repurchase agreement or the like and who receives a transfer of collateral from the secured party or is subrogated to his rights has thereafter the rights and duties of the secured party. Such a transfer of collateral is not a sale or disposition of the collateral under this Article.

§9-505. Compulsory Disposition of Collateral; Acceptance of the Collateral as Discharge of Obligation.

(1) If the debtor has paid sixty per cent of the cash price in the case of a purchase money security interest in consumer goods or sixty per cent of the loan in the case of another security interest in consumer goods and has not signed after default a statement renouncing or modifying his rights under this Part a secured party who has taken possession of collateral must dispose of it under Section 9-504 and if he fails to do so within ninety days after he takes possession the debtor at his option may recover in conversion or under Section 9-507(1) on secured party's liability.

(2) In any other case involving consumer goods or any other collateral a secured party in possession may, after default, propose to retain the collateral in satisfaction of the obligation. Written notice of such proposal shall be sent to the debtor if he has not signed after default a statement renouncing or modifying his

rights under this subsection. In the case of consumer goods no other notice need be given. In other cases notice shall be sent to any other secured party from whom the secured party has received (before sending his notice to the debtor or before the debtor's renunciation of his rights) written notice of a claim of an interest in the collateral. If the secured party receives objection in writing from a person entitled to receive notification within twenty-one days after the notice was sent, the secured party must dispose of the collateral under Section 9-504. In the absence of such written objection the secured party may retain the collateral in satisfaction of the debtor's obligation.

§9-506. Debtor's Right to Redeem Collateral.
At any time before the secured party has disposed of collateral or entered into a contract for its disposition under Section 9-504 or before the obligation has been discharged under Section 9-505(2) the debtor or any other secured party may unless otherwise agreed in writing after default redeem the collateral by tendering fulfillment of all obligations secured by the collateral as well as the expenses reasonably incurred by the secured party in retaking, holding and preparing the collateral for disposition, in arranging for the sale, and to the extent provided in the agreement and not prohibited by law, his reasonable attorneys' fees and legal expenses.

§9-507. Secured Party's Liability for Failure to Comply With This Part.

(1) If it is established that the secured party is not proceeding in accordance with the provisions of this Part disposition may be ordered or restrained on appropriate terms and conditions. If the disposition has occurred the debtor or any person entitled to notification or whose security interest has been made known to the secured party prior to the disposition has a right to recover from the secured party any loss caused by a failure to comply with the provisions of this Part. If the collateral is consumer goods, the debtor has a right to recover in any event an amount not less than the credit service charge plus ten per cent of the principal amount of the debt or the time price differential plus 10 per cent of the cash price.

(2) The fact that a better price could have been obtained by a sale at a different time or in a different method from that selected by the secured party is not of itself sufficient to establish that the sale was not made in a commercially reasonable manner. If the secured party either sells the collateral in the usual manner in any recognized market therefor or if he sells at the price current in such market at the time of his sale or if he has otherwise sold in conformity with reasonable commercial practices among dealers in the type of property sold he has sold in a commercially reasonable manner. The principles stated in the two preceding sentences with respect to sales also apply as may be ap-

propriate to other types of disposition. A disposition which has been approved in any judicial proceeding or by any bona fide creditors' committee or representative of creditors shall conclusively be deemed to be commercially reasonable, but this sentence does not indicate that any such approval must be obtained in any case nor does it indicate that any disposition not so approved is not commercially reasonable.

ARTICLE 10: EFFECTIVE DATE AND REPEALER

[omitted]

ARTICLE 11: EFFECTIVE DATE AND TRANSITION PROVISIONS

[omitted]

Uniform Partnership Act, 1992

ARTICLE 1: GENERAL PROVISIONS

§101. Definitions. In this [Act]:

(1) Business" includes every trade, occupation, and profession.

(2) "Debtor in bankruptcy" means a person who is the subject of:

(i) an order for relief under Title 11 of the United States Code or a comparable order under a successor statute of general application; or

(ii) a comparable order under federal or state law governing insolvency.

(3) "Distribution" means a transfer of cash or other property from a partnership to a partner in the partner's capacity as a partner, or to the partner's transferee.

(4) "Partnership agreement" means an agreement, written or oral, among the partners concerning the partnership.

(5) "Partnership at will" means a partnership in which the partners have not agreed to remain partners until the expiration of a definite term or the completion of a particular undertaking.

(6) "Person" means an individual, corporation, business trust, estate, trust, partnership, association, joint venture, government, governmental subdivision, agency, or instrumentality, or any other legal or commercial entity.

(7) "Property" means all property, real, personal, or mixed, tangible or intangible, or any interest therein.

(8) "State" means a state of the United States, the District of Columbia, the Commonwealth of Puerto Rico, or any territory or insular possession subject to the jurisdiction of the United States.

(9) "Statement" means a statement of partnership authority under Section 303, a statement of denial under Section 304, a statement of dissociation under Section 704, a statement of dissolution under Section 806, a statement of merger under Section 906, or an amendment or cancellation of any of the foregoing.

(10) "Transfer" includes an assignment, conveyance, lease, mortgage, deed, and encumbrance.

§102. Knowledge and Notice.

(a) A person knows a fact if the person has knowledge of it.

(b) A person has notice of a fact if the person:

(1) knows of it;

(2) has received a notice of it; or

(3) has reason to know it exists from all of the facts known to that person at the time in question.

(c) A person notifies or gives a notice to another by taking steps reasonably required to inform the other person in the ordinary course of business, whether or not the other person learns of it.

(d) A person is notified or receives a notice of a fact when:

(1) the existence of the fact comes to the person's attention; or

(2) the notice is duly delivered at the person's place of business or at any other place held out by the person as a place for receiving communications.

(e) Except as provided in subsection (f), notice received by a person who is not an individual, including a partnership, is effective for a particular transaction when the notice is brought to the attention of the individual conducting the transaction, or in any event when the notice would have been brought to that individual's attention if the person had exercised due diligence. Such a person exercises due diligence if it maintains reasonable routines for communicating significant information to the individual conducting the transaction and there is reasonable compliance with the routines. Due diligence does not require an individual acting for the person to communicate information unless the communication is part of the individual's regular duties or the individual has reason to know of the transaction and that the transaction would be materially affected by the information.

(**f**) Receipt of notice by a partner of a matter relating to the partnership is effective immediately as notice to the partnership, but is not effective in the case of fraud on the partnership committed by or with the consent of the partner who received the notice.

§103. Effect of Partnership Agreement; Nonwaivable Provisions.

(**a**) Except as provided in subsection (b), a partnership agreement governs relations among the partners and between the partners and the partnership. To the extent the partnership agreement does not otherwise provide, this [Act] governs relations among the partners and between the partners and the partnership.

(**b**) A partnership agreement may not:

(**1**) vary the rights and duties under Section 105 except to eliminate the duty to provide copies of statements to all the partners;

(**2**) unreasonably restrict a partner's right of access to books and records under Section 403(b);

(**3**) eliminate the duty of loyalty under Section 404(b);

(**4**) unreasonably reduce the duty of care under Section 404(d);

(**5**) eliminate the obligation of good faith and fair dealing under Section 404(e);

(**6**) vary the power to withdraw as a partner under Section 601(1), except to require the notice to be in writing;

(**7**) vary the right to expulsion of a partner by a court in the events specified in Section 601(5);

(**8**) vary the requirement to wind up the partnership business in cases specified in Section 801(4), (5), or (6); or

(**9**) restrict rights of third parties under this [Act].

§104. Supplemental Principles of Law.

(**a**) Unless displaced by particular provisions of this [Act], the principles of law and equity supplement this [Act].

(**b**) If an obligation to pay interest arises under this

[Act] and the rate is not specified, the rate is that specified in [applicable statute].

§105. Execution, Filing, and Recording of Statements.

(**a**) A statement may be filed in the office of [the Secretary of State]. A certified copy of a statement that is filed in an office in another state may be filed in the office of [the Secretary of State]. Either filing has the effect provided in this [Act] with respect to partnership property located in or transactions that occur in this State.

(**b**) A certified copy of a statement that has been filed in the office of the [Secretary of State] that is recorded in the office for recording transfers of real property shall have the effect provided for recorded statements in this [Act]. A recorded statement that is not a certified copy of a statement filed in the office of the [Secretary of State] shall not have the effect provided for recorded statements in this [Act].

(**c**) A statement filed by a partnership must be executed by at least two partners. Other statements must be executed by a partner or other person authorized by this [Act]. An individual who executes a statement as, or on behalf of, a partner or other person named as a partner in a statement must personally declare under penalty of perjury that the contents of the statement are accurate.

(**d**) A person authorized by this [Act] to file a statement may amend or cancel the statement by filing an amendment or cancellation that names the partnership, identifies the statement, and states the substance of the amendment or cancellation.

(**e**) A person who files a statement pursuant to this section shall promptly send a copy of the statement to every partner, and to any other person named as a partner in the statement. Failure to send a copy of a statement to a partner or other person does not limit the effectiveness of the statement as to a person not a partner.

(**f**) The [Secretary of State] may collect a fee for filing or providing a certified copy of a statement. The [officers responsible for] recording transfers of real property may collect a fee for recording a statement.

§106. Law Governing Internal Affairs. Laws of the state in which a partnership has its chief executive office govern the partnership's internal affairs.

§107. Partnership Subject to Amendment or Repeal of [Act]. A partnership governed by this [Act] is subject to any amendment or repeal of this [Act].

ARTICLE 2: NATURE OF PARTNERSHIP

§201. Partnership as Entity. A partnership is an entity.

§202. Creation of Partnership.

(a) Except as provided in subsection (b), the association of two or more persons to carry on as co-owners a business for profit creates a partnership, whether or not the persons intend to create a partnership.

(b) An association created under a statute other than this [Act], any predecessor law, or comparable law of another jurisdiction is not a partnership.

(c) In determining whether a partnership is created, the following rules apply:

(1) Joint tenancy, tenancy in common, tenancy by the entireties, joint property, common property, or part ownership does not by itself establish a partnership, even if the co-owners share profits made by the use of the property.

(2) The sharing of gross returns does not by itself establish a partnership, even if the persons sharing them have a joint or common right or interest in property from which the returns are derived.

(3) The receipt by a person of a share of the profits of a business is prima facie evidence that the person is a partner in the business, but that inference may not be drawn if the profits were received in payment:

(i) of a debt by installments or otherwise;

(ii) for services as an independent contractor, or of wages or other compensation to an employee;

(iii) of rent;

(iv) of an annuity or other retirement or health benefit to a beneficiary, representative, or designee of a deceased or retired partner;

(v) of interest or other charge on a loan, even if the amount of payment varies with the profits of the business, including a direct or indirect present or future ownership of the collateral, or rights to income, proceeds, or increase in value derived from the collateral; or

(vi) of consideration for the sale of the goodwill of a business or other property by installments or otherwise.

(d) Except as provided by Section 308, persons who are not partners as to each other are not partners as to other persons.

(e) A partnership created under this [Act] is a general partnership, and the partners are general partners of the partnership.

§203. Partnership Property.

Property transferred to or otherwise acquired by a partnership is property of the partnership and not of the partners individually.

§204. When Property Is Partnership Property.

(a) Property is partnership property if acquired:

(1) in the name of the partnership; or

(2) in the name of one or more partners with an indication in the instrument transferring title to the property of the person's capacity as a partner or of the existence of a partnership, but without an indication of the name of the partnership.

(b) Property is acquired in the name of the partnership by a transfer to:

(1) the partnership in its name; or

(2) one or more partners in their capacity as partners in the partnership, if the name of the partnership is indicated in the instrument transferring title to the property.

(c) Property is presumed to be partnership property if purchased with partnership assets, even if not acquired in the name of the partnership or of one or more partners with an indication in the instrument transferring title to the property of the person's capacity as a partner or of the existence of a partnership.

(d) Property acquired in the name of one or more of the partners, without an indication in the instrument transferring title to the property of the person's capacity as a partner or of the existence of a partnership and without use of partnership assets, is presumed to be separate property, even if used for partnership purposes.

ARTICLE 3: RELATIONS OF PARTNERS TO PERSONS DEALING WITH PARTNERSHIP

§301. Partner Agent of Partnership.

Subject to the effect of a statement of partnership authority pursuant to Section 303:

(1) Each partner is an agent of the partnership for the purpose of its business. Any act of a partner, including the execution of an instrument in the partnership name, for apparently carrying on in the usual way the partnership business or business of the kind carried on by the partnership binds the partnership, unless the partner has no authority to act for the partnership in the particular matter and the person with whom the partner is dealing knows or has received a notice that the partner lacks authority.

(2) An act of a partner which is not apparently for carrying on in the usual way the partnership business or business of the kind carried on by the partnership does not bind the partnership unless authorized by the other partners.

§302. Transfer of Partnership Property.

(a) Subject to the effect of a statement of partnership authority pursuant to Section 303:

(1) Partnership property held in the name of the partnership may be transferred by an instrument of transfer executed by any partner in the partnership name.

(2) Partnership property held in the name of one or more partners with an indication in the instrument transferring the property to them of their capacity as partners or of the existence of a partnership, but without an indication of the name of the partnership, may be transferred by an instrument of transfer executed by the persons in whose name the property is held.

(3) A partnership may recover property transferred under this subsection if it proves that execution of the instrument of transfer did not bind the partnership under Section 301, unless the property was transferred by the initial transferee or a person claiming through the initial transferee to a subsequent transferee who gave value without having notice that the person who executed the instrument of initial transfer lacked authority to bind the partnership.

(b) Partnership property held in the name of one or more persons other than the partnership, without an indication in the instrument transferring the property to them of their capacity as partners or of the existence of a partnership, may be transferred free of any claims of the partnership or the partners by the persons in whose name the property is held to a transferee who gives value without having notice that it is partnership property.

(c) If a person holds all of the partners' interests in the partnership, all of the partnership property vests in that person. That person may execute documents in the name of the partnership to evidence vesting of the property in that person and may file or record those documents.

§303. Statement of Partnership Authority.

(a) A partnership may file a statement of partnership authority, which:

(1) must include:

(i) the name of the partnership;

(ii) the street address of its chief executive office and of an office in this State, if any;

(iii) the names and mailing addresses of all the partners or of an agent appointed and maintained by the partnership for the purpose of subsection (b); and

(iv) a statement specifying the names of the partners authorized to execute an instrument transferring real property held in the name of the partnership; and

(2) may include a statement of the authority, or of

limitations on the authority, of some or all of the partners to enter into other transactions on behalf of the partnership and any other matter.

(b) If a statement of partnership authority names an agent, the agent shall maintain a list of the names and mailing addresses of all of the partners and make it available to any person on request for good cause shown.

(c) If a filed statement of partnership authority is executed pursuant to Section 105(c) and states the name of the partnership but does not contain all of the other information required by subsection (a), the statement nevertheless operates with respect to a person not a partner as provided in subsections (d) and (e).

(d) Except as provided in subsections (e), (f), and (g), a filed statement of partnership authority supplements the authority of a partner to enter into transactions on behalf of the partnership as follows:

(1) Except for transfers of real property, a grant of authority contained in a filed statement of partnership authority is conclusive, in favor of a person who gives value without knowledge to the contrary, so long as and to the extent that a limitation on that authority is not then contained in another filed statement. A filed cancellation of a limitation on authority revives the previous grant of authority.

(2) A grant of authority to transfer real property held in the name of the partnership contained in a certified copy of a filed statement of partnership authority recorded in the office for recording transfers of that real property is conclusive, in favor of a person who gives value without knowledge to the contrary, so long as and to the extent that a certified copy of a filed statement containing a limitation on that authority is not then recorded in the office for recording transfers of that real property. The recording in the office for recording transfers of that real property of a certified copy of a filed cancellation of a limitation on authority revives the previous grant of authority.

(e) A person not a partner is deemed to know of a limitation on the authority of a partner to transfer real property held in the name of the partnership if a certified copy of the filed statement containing the limitation on authority is recorded in the office for recording transfers of that real property.

(f) Except as provided in subsection (e) and Sections 704 and 806, a person not a partner is not deemed to know of a limitation on the authority of a partner merely because the limitation is contained in a filed statement.

(g) Unless earlier cancelled, a filed statement of partnership authority is cancelled by operation of law five years after the date on which the statement, or the most recent amendment, was filed with the [Secretary of State].

§304. Statement of Denial. A partner or other person named as a partner in a filed statement of partnership authority or in a list maintained by an agent pursuant to Section 303(b) may file a statement of denial stating the name of the partnership and the fact that is being denied, which may include denial of a person's authority or status as a partner. A statement of denial is a limitation on authority to the extent provided in Section 303(d) and (e).

§305. Partnership Liable for Partner's Actionable Conduct.

(a) A partnership is liable for loss or injury caused to a person, or for a penalty incurred, as a result of a wrongful act or omission, or other actionable conduct, of a partner acting in the ordinary course of business of the partnership or with the authority of the partnership.

(b) If, in the course of its business, a partnership receives money or property of a person not a partner which is misapplied by a partner while it is in the custody of the partnership, the partnership is liable for the loss.

§306. Partner's Liability. All partners are liable jointly and severally for all obligations of the partnership unless otherwise agreed by the claimant or provided by law.

§307. Actions by and Against Partnership and Partners.

(a) A partnership may sue and be sued in the name of the partnership.

(b) An action may be brought against the partnership and any or all of the partners in the same action or in separate actions.

(c) A judgment against a partnership is not by itself a judgment against a partner. A judgment against a partnership may not be satisfied from a partner's assets unless there is a judgment against the partner.

(d) A judgment creditor of a partner may not levy execution against the assets of the partner to satisfy a judgment based on a claim against the partnership unless:

(1) a judgment based on the same claim has been obtained against the partnership and a writ of execution on the judgment has been returned unsatisfied in whole or in part;

(2) an involuntary case under Title 11 of the United States Code has been commenced against the partnership and has not been dismissed within 60 days after commencement,

or the partnership has commenced a voluntary case under Title 11 of the United States Code and the case has not been dismissed;

(3) the partner has agreed that the creditor need not exhaust partnership assets;

(4) a court grants permission to the judgment creditor to levy execution against the assets of a partner based on a finding that partnership assets subject to execution are clearly insufficient to satisfy the judgment, that exhaustion of partnership assets is excessively burdensome, or that the grant of permission is an appropriate exercise of the court's equitable powers; or

(5) liability is imposed on the partner by law or contract independent of the existence of the partnership.

(e) This section applies to any partnership liability or obligation resulting from a representation by a partner or purported partner under Section 308(a) or (b).

§308. Purported Partner.

(a) If a person, by words or conduct, purports to be a partner, or consents to being represented by another as a partner, in a partnership or with one or more persons not partners, the purported partner is liable to a person to whom the representation is made and who, relying on the representation, enters into a transaction with the actual or purported partnership. If the representation, either by the purported partner or by a person with the purported partner's consent, is made in a public manner, the purported partner is liable to a person who relies upon the purported partnership even if the purported partner is not aware of being held out as a partner to the claimant. If partnership liability results, the purported partner is liable as if the purported partner were a partner. If no partnership liability results, the purported partner is liable jointly and severally with any other person consenting to the representation.

(b) If a person is thus represented to be a partner in an existing partnership, or with one or more persons not partners, the purported partner is an agent of persons consenting to the representation to bind them to the same extent and in the same manner as if the purported partner were a partner, with respect to persons who enter into transactions in reliance upon the representation. If all the partners of the existing partnership consent to the representation, a partnership act or obligation results. If fewer than all the partners of the existing partnership consent to the representation, the person acting and the partners consenting to the representation are jointly and severally liable.

(c) A person is not a partner in a partnership solely because the person is named by another in a statement of partnership authority.

(d) A person does not continue to be a partner solely because of a failure to file a statement of dissociation or to amend a statement of partnership authority to indicate the partner's dissociation from the partnership.

§309. Liability of Incoming Partner. A person admitted as a partner into a partnership is liable for all obligations of the partnership arising before the person's admission as if the person had been a partner when the obligations were incurred, but this liability may be satisfied only out of partnership property.

ARTICLE 4: RELATIONS OF PARTNERS TO EACH OTHER AND TO PARTNERSHIP

§401. Partner's Rights and Duties.

(a) A partnership shall establish an account for each partner which must be credited with an amount equal to the cash plus the value of any other property, net of the amount of any liabilities, the partner contributes to the partnership and the partner's share of the partnership profits. Each partner's account must be charged with an amount equal to the cash plus the value of any other property, net of the amount of any liabilities, distributed by the partnership to the partner and the partner's share of the partnership losses.

(b) A partnership shall credit each partner's account with an equal share of the partnership profits and shall charge each partner with a share of the partnership losses, whether capital or operating, in proportion to the partner's share of the profits.

(c) A partnership shall indemnify each partner for payments reasonably made and liabilities reasonably incurred by the partner in the ordinary and proper conduct of the business of the partnership or for the preservation of its business or property.

(d) A partnership shall repay a partner who, in aid of the partnership, makes a payment or advance beyond the amount of capital the partner agreed to contribute.

(e) A payment made by a partner which gives rise to a partnership obligation under subsection (c) or (d) constitutes a loan to the partnership. Interest accrues from the date of the payment or advance.

(f) Each partner has equal rights in the management and conduct of the partnership business.

(g) A partner may use or possess partnership property only on behalf of the partnership.

(h) A partner is not entitled to remuneration for services performed for the partnership, except for reasonable compensation for services rendered in winding up the business of the partnership.

(i) A person may become a partner only with the consent of all the partners.

(j) A difference arising as to a matter in the ordinary course of business of a partnership may be decided by a majority of the partners. An act outside the ordinary course of business of a partnership and an amendment to the partnership agreement may be undertaken only with the consent of all the partners.

(k) This section does not affect the obligations of a partnership to other persons under Section 301.

§402. Distributions in Kind. A partner has no right to receive, and may not be required to accept, a distribution in kind.

§403. Partner's Right to Information.

(a) A partnership shall keep its books and records, if any, at its chief executive office.

(b) A partnership shall provide partners and their agents and attorneys access to its books and records. It shall provide former partners and their agents and attorneys access to books and records pertaining to the period during which they were partners. The right of access provides the opportunity to inspect and copy books and records during ordinary business hours. A partnership may impose a reasonable charge, covering the costs of labor and material, for copies of documents furnished.

(c) Each partner and the partnership, on demand, shall furnish to a partner, and the legal representative of a deceased partner or partner under legal disability, to the extent just and reasonable, complete and accurate information concerning the partnership.

§404. General Standards of Partner's Conduct.

(a) The only fiduciary duties a partner owes to the partnership and the other partners are the duty of loyalty and the duty of care set forth in this section.

(b) A partner's duty of loyalty to the partnership and the other partners is limited to the following:

(1) to account to the partnership and hold as trustee for it any property, profit, or benefit derived by the partner, without the consent of the other partners, in the conduct and winding up of the partnership business or from a use or appropriation by the partner of partnership property or opportunity;

(2) to refrain from dealing with the partnership in the conduct or winding up of the partnership business, as or on behalf of a party having an interest adverse to the partnership without the consent of the other partners; and

(3) to refrain from competing with the partnership in the conduct of the partnership business without the consent of the other partners before the dissolution of the partnership.

(c) A partner's duty of loyalty may not be eliminated by agreement, but the partners may by agreement identify specific types or categories of activities that do not violate the duty of loyalty, if not manifestly unreasonable.

(d) A partner's duty of care to the partnership and the other partners in the conduct and winding up of the partnership business is limited to refraining from engaging in grossly negligent or reckless conduct, intentional misconduct, or a knowing violation of law.

(e) A partner shall discharge the duties to the partnership and the other partners under this [Act] or under the partnership agreement, and exercise any rights, consistent with the obligation of good faith and fair dealing. The obligation of good faith and fair dealing may not be eliminated by agreement, but the partners may by agreement determine the standards by which the performance of the obligation is to be measured, if the standards are not manifestly unreasonable.

(f) A partner does not violate a duty or obligation under this [Act] or under the partnership agreement merely because the partner's conduct furthers the partner's own interest. A partner may lend money to and transact other business with the partnership. The rights and obligations of a partner who lends money to or transacts business with the partnership are the same as those of a person who is not a partner, subject to other applicable law.

(g) This section applies to a person winding up the partnership business as the personal or legal representative of the last surviving partner as if the person were a partner.

§405. Partner's Liability to Partnership. A partner is liable to the partnership for a breach of the partnership agreement, or for the violation of any duty to the partnership, causing harm to the partnership.

§406. Remedies of Partnership and Partners.

(a) A partnership may maintain an action against a partner for a breach of the partnership agreement, or for the violation of any duty to the partnership, causing harm to the partnership.

(b) A partner may maintain an action against the partnership or another partner for legal or equitable relief, including an accounting as to partnership business, to:

(1) enforce a right under the partnership agreement;

(2) enforce a right under this [Act], including:

    (i) the partner's rights under Sections 401, 403, and 404;

    (ii) the partner's right on dissociation to have the partner's interest in the partnership purchased pursuant to Section 701 or enforce any other right under Article 6 or 7; or

    (iii) the partner's right to compel a dissolution and winding up of the partnership business under Section 801 or enforce any other right under Article 8; or

(3) enforce the rights and otherwise protect the interests of the partner, including rights and interests arising independently of the partnership relationship.

(c) The accrual of, and any time limitation on, a right of action for a remedy under this section is governed by other law. A right to an accounting upon a dissolution and winding up does not revive a claim barred by law.

§407. Continuation of Partnership Beyond Definite Term or Particular Undertaking.

(a) If a partnership for a definite term or particular undertaking is continued, without an express agreement, after the expiration of the term or completion of the undertaking, the rights and duties of the partners remain the same as they were at the expiration or completion, so far as is consistent with a partnership at will.

(b) A continuation of the business by the partners or those of them who habitually acted in the business during the term or undertaking, without any settlement or liquidation of the partnership business, is prima facie evidence of an agreement that the business will not be wound up.

ARTICLE 5: TRANSFEREES AND CREDITORS OF PARTNER

§501. Partner's Interest in Partnership Property Not Transferable. A partner is not a co-owner of partnership property and has no interest that can be transferred, either voluntarily or involuntarily, in partnership property.

§502. Partner's Transferable Interest In Partnership.

(a) The only transferable interest of a partner in the partnership is the partner's interest in distributions. The interest is personal property.

(b) A transferee of a partner's transferable interest in the partnership has the right to cause a winding up of the partnership business as provided in Section 801(6).

§503. Transfer of Partner's Transferable Interest.

(a) A transfer, in whole or in part, of a partner's transferable interest in the partnership:

(1) is permissible;

(2) does not by itself cause a winding up of the partnership business; and

(3) does not, as against the other partners or the partnership, entitle the transferee, during the continuance of the partnership, to participate in the management or conduct of the partnership business, to require access to information concerning or an account of partnership transactions, or to inspect or copy the partnership books or records.

(b) A transferee of a partner's transferable interest in the partnership is entitled to receive, in accordance with the transfer, distributions to which the transferor would otherwise be entitled. Upon transfer, the transferor retains the rights and duties of a partner other than the interest in distributions transferred.

(c) If an event causes a dissolution and winding up of the partnership business under Section 801, a transferee is entitled to receive, in accordance with the transfer, the net amount otherwise distributable to the transferor. In a dissolution and winding up, a transferee may require an accounting only from the date of the last account agreed to by all of the partners.

(d) Until receipt of notice of a transfer, a partnership has no duty to give effect to the transferee's rights under this section.

§504. Partner's Transferable Interest Subject to Charging Order.

(a) On application by a judgment creditor of a partner or partner's transferee, a court having jurisdiction may charge the transferable interest of the debtor partner or transferee to satisfy the judgment. The court may appoint a receiver of the debtor's share of the distributions due or to become due to the debtor in respect of the partnership and make all other orders, directions, accounts, and inquiries the debtor might have made or which the circumstances of the case may require.

(b) A charging order constitutes a lien on the judgment debtor's transferable interest in the partnership. The court may order a foreclosure of the interest subject to the charging order at any time and upon conditions it considers appropriate. The purchaser at the foreclosure sale has the rights of a transferee.

(c) At any time before foreclosure, an interest charged may be redeemed:

(1) by the judgment debtor;

(2) with property other than partnership property, by one or more of the other partners; or

(3) with partnership property, by one or more of the other partners with the consent of all the partners whose interests are not so charged.

(d) This [Act] does not deprive a partner of a right under exemption laws with respect to the partner's interest in the partnership.

(e) This section provides the exclusive remedy by which a judgment creditor of a partner or partner's transferee may satisfy a judgment out of the judgment debtor's transferable interest in the partnership.

ARTICLE 6: PARTNER'S DISSOCIATION

§601. Events Causing Partner's Dissociation. A partner is dissociated from a partnership upon:

(1) receipt by the partnership of notice of the partner's express will to withdraw as a partner or upon any later date specified in the notice;

(2) an event agreed to in the partnership agreement as causing the partner's dissociation;

(3) the partner's expulsion pursuant to the partnership agreement;

(4) the partner's expulsion by the unanimous vote of the other partners if:

   (i) it is unlawful to carry on the partnership business with that partner;

   (ii) there has been a transfer of all or substantially all of that partner's transferable interest in the partnership, other than a transfer for security purposes, or a court order charging the partner's interest, which has not been foreclosed;

   (iii) within 90 days after the partnership notifies a corporate partner that it will be expelled because it has filed a certificate of dissolution or the equivalent, its charter has been revoked, or its right to conduct business has been suspended by the jurisdiction of its incorporation, there is no revocation of the certificate of dissolution or no reinstatement of its charter or its right to conduct business; or

   (iv) a partnership that is a partner has been dissolved and its business is being wound up;

(5) on application by the partnership or another partner, the partner's expulsion by judicial decree because:

   (i) the partner engaged in wrongful conduct that adversely and materially affected the partnership business;

   (ii) the partner willfully or persistently committed a material breach of the partnership agreement or of a duty owed to the partnership or the other partners under Section 404; or

   (iii) the partner engaged in conduct relating to the partnership business which makes it not reasonably practicable to carry on the business in partnership with that partner;

(6) the partner's:

   (i) becoming a debtor in bankruptcy;

   (ii) executing an assignment for the benefit of creditors;

   (iii) seeking, consenting to, or acquiescing in the appointment of a trustee, receiver, or liquidator of that partner or of all or substantially all of that partner's property; or

   (iv) failing, within 90 days after the appointment, to have vacated or stayed the appointment of a trustee, receiver, or liquidator of the partner or of all or substantially all of the partner's property obtained without the partner's consent or acquiescence, or failing within 90 days after the expiration of a stay to have the appointment vacated;

(7) in the case of a partner who is an individual:
   (i) the partner's death;
   (ii) the appointment of a guardian or general conservator for the partner; or
   (iii) a judicial determination that the partner has otherwise become incapable of performing the partner's duties under the partnership agreement;

(8) in the case of a partner that is a trust or is acting as a partner by virtue of being a trustee of a trust, distribution of the trust's entire transferable interest in the partnership, but not merely the substitution of a successor trustee;

(9) in the case of a partner that is an estate or is acting as a partner by virtue of being a personal representative of an estate, distribution of the estate's entire transferable interest in the partnership, but not merely the substitution of a successor personal representative; or

(10) termination of a partner who is not an individual, partnership, corporation, trust, or estate.

§602. Partner's Wrongful Dissociation.

(a) A partner's dissociation is wrongful only if:

(1) it is in breach of an express provision of the partnership agreement; or

(2) in the case of a partnership for a definite term or particular undertaking, before the expiration of the term or the completion of the undertaking:
   (i) the partner withdraws by express will, unless the withdrawal follows the dissociation of another partner and results in a right to dissolve the partnership under Section 801(2)(i);
   (ii) the partner is expelled by judicial decree under Section 601(5); or
   (iii) in the case of a partner who is not an individual, trust other than a business trust, or estate, the partner is expelled or otherwise dissociated because it willfully dissolved or terminated.

(b) A partner who wrongfully dissociates is liable to the partnership and to the other partners for damages caused by the dissociation. That liability is in addition to any other liability of the partner to the partnership or to the other partners.

§603. Effect of Partner's Dissociation.

(a) A dissociated partner's interest in the partnership must be purchased pursuant to Article 7 unless the partner's dissociation results in a dissolution and winding up of the partnership business under Article 8.

(b) Upon a partner's dissociation, that partner's right to participate in the management and conduct of the partnership business is terminated, except as provided in Section 804, and that partner's duties (i) under Section 404(b)(1) and (2) and (d) continue only with regard to matters or events that occurred before the dissociation, and (ii) under Section 404(b)(3) terminate.

ARTICLE 7: PARTNER'S DISSOCIATED PARTNER'S INTEREST.

§701. Purchase of Dissociated Partner's Interest.

(a) If a partner is dissociated from a partnership without resulting in a dissolution and winding up of the partnership business under Section 801, the partnership shall cause the dissociated partner's interest in the partnership to be purchased for a buyout price determined pursuant to subsection (b).

(b) The buyout price of a dissociated partner's interest is the amount that would have been distributable to the dissociating partner under Section 808(b) if, on the date of dissociation, the assets of the partnership were sold at a price equal to the greater of the liquidation value or the value based on a sale of the entire business as a going concern without the dissociated partner and the partnership were wound up as of that date. In either case, the sale price of the partnership assets must be determined on the basis of the amount that would be paid by a willing buyer to a willing seller, neither being under any compulsion to buy or sell, and with knowledge of all relevant facts. Interest must be paid from the date of dissociation to the date of payment.

(c) Damages for wrongful dissociation under Section 602(b), and all other amounts owing, whether or not presently due, from the dissociated partner to the partnership, must be offset against the buyout price. Interest must be paid from the date the amount owed becomes due to the date of payment.

(d) A partnership shall indemnify a dissociated partner against all partnership liabilities incurred before the dissociation, except liabilities then unknown to the partnership, and against all partnership liabilities incurred after the dissociation, except liabilities incurred by an act of the dissociated partner under Section 702. For purposes of this subsection, a liability not known to a partner other than the dissociated partner is not known to the partnership.

(e) If no agreement for the purchase of a dissociated partner's interest is reached within 120 days after a written demand for payment, the partnership shall pay, or cause to be paid, in cash to the dissociated partner the amount the partnership estimates to be the buyout price and accrued interest, reduced by any offsets and accrued interest under subsection (c).

(f) If a deferred payment is authorized under subsection (h), the partnership may tender a written offer to pay the amount it estimates to be the buyout price and accrued interest, reduced by any offsets under subsection (c), stating the time of payment, the amount and type of security for payment, and the other terms and conditions of the obligation.

(g) The payment or tender required by subsections (e) or (f) must be accompanied by the following:

(1) a statement of partnership assets and liabilities as of the date of dissociation;

(2) the latest available partnership balance sheet and income statement, if any;

(3) an explanation of how the estimated amount of the payment was calculated; and

(4) written notice that the payment is in full satisfaction of the obligation to purchase unless, within 120 days after the written notice, the dissociated partner commences an action to determine the buyout price, any offsets under subsection (c), or other terms of the purchase obligation.

(h) A partner who wrongfully dissociates before the expiration of a definite term or the completion of a particular undertaking is not entitled to payment of any portion of the buyout price until the expiration of the term or completion of the undertaking, unless the partner establishes to the satisfaction of the court that earlier payment will not cause undue hardship to the business of the partnership. A deferred payment must be adequately secured and bear interest.

(i) A dissociated partner may maintain an action against the partnership, pursuant to Section 406(b)(2)(ii), to determine the buyout price of that partner's interest, any offsets under subsection (c), or other terms of the purchase obligation. The action must be commenced within 120 days after the partnership has tendered payment or an offer to pay or within one year after written demand for payment if no payment or offer to pay is tendered. The court shall determine the buyout price of the dissociated partner's interest, any offset due under subsection (c), and accrued interest, and enter judgment for any additional payment or refund. If deferred payment is authorized under subsection (h), the court shall also determine the security for payment and other terms of the obligation to purchase. The court may assess reasonable attorney's fees and the fees and expenses of appraisers or other experts for a party to the action, in amounts the court finds equitable, against any other party, if the court finds that the other party acted arbitrarily, vexatiously, or not in good faith, including the partnership's failure to tender payment or an offer to pay or to comply with the requirements of subsection (g).

§702. Dissociated Partner's Power to Bind and Liability to Partnership.

(a) For two years after a partner dissociates without resulting in a dissolution and winding up of the partnership business, the partnership, including a surviving partnership under Article 9, is bound by an act of the dissociated partner that would have bound the partnership under Section 301 before dissociation only if the other party to the transaction:

(i) reasonably believes when entering the transaction that the dissociated partner is a partner at that time;

(ii) does not have notice of the partner's dissociation; and

(iii) is not deemed to have notice under Section 303(e) or Section 704.

(b) A dissociated partner is liable to the partnership for any loss caused to the partnership arising from an obligation incurred by the dissociated partner after dissociation, for which the partnership is liable under subsection (a).

§703. Dissociated Partner's Liability to Other Persons.

(a) A partner's dissociation does not of itself discharge the partner's liability for a partnership obligation incurred before dissociation. A dissociated partner is not liable for a partnership obligation incurred after dissociation except as provided in subsection (b).

(b) A partner who dissociates without resulting in a dissolution and winding up of the partnership business is liable as a partner to the other party in a transaction entered into by the partnership, or a surviving partnership under Article 9, within two years after the partner's dissociation, only if the other party to the transaction:

(i) reasonably believes when entering the transaction that the dissociated partner is a partner at that time;

(ii) does not have notice of the partner's dissociation; and

(iii) is not deemed to have notice under Section 303(e) or Section 704.

(c) By agreement with the partnership creditor and the partners continuing the business, a dissociated partner may be released from liability for a partnership obligation.

(d) A dissociated partner is released from liability for a partnership obligation if a partnership creditor, with notice of the partner's dissociation but without the partner's consent, agrees to a material alteration in the nature or time of payment of a partnership obligation.

§704. Statement of Dissociation.

(a) A dissociated partner or the partnership may file a statement of dissociation stating the name of the partnership and that the partner is dissociated from the partnership. A statement of dissociation is a limitation on the authority of a dissociated partner for the purposes of Section 303(d) and (e).

(b) For the purposes of Sections 702 and 703(b), a person not a partner is deemed to have notice of the dissociation 90 days after the statement of dissociation is filed.

§705. Continued Use of Partnership Name. Continued use of a partnership name, or a dissociated partner's name as part thereof, by the partners continuing the business does not of itself make the dissociated partner liable for an obligation of the partners or the partnership continuing the business.

ARTICLE 8: WINDING UP PARTNERSHIP BUSINESS

§801. Events Causing Dissolution and Winding Up of Partnership Business. A partnership is dissolved, and its business must be wound up, only upon:

(1) except as provided in Section 802, receipt by a partnership at will of notice from a partner, other than a partner who is dissociated under Section 601(2) to (10), of that partner's express will to withdraw as a partner, or upon any later date specified in the notice;

(2) in a partnership for a definite term or particular undertaking:

(i) except as provided in Section 802, within 90 days after a partner's wrongful dissociation under Section 602 or a partner's dissociation by death or otherwise under Section 601(6) to (10), receipt by the partnership of notice from another partner of that partner's express will to withdraw as a partner;

(ii) the express will of all the partners; or

(iii) the expiration of the term or the completion of the undertaking, unless all the partners agree to continue the business, in which case the partnership agreement is deemed amended retroactively to provide that the expiration or completion does not result in the dissolution and winding up of the partnership business;

(3) an event agreed to in the partnership agreement resulting in the winding up of the partnership business, unless all the partners agree to continue the business, in which case the partnership agreement is deemed amended retroactively to provide that the event does not result in the dissolution and winding up of the partnership business;

(4) an event that makes it unlawful for all or sub-stantially all of the business of the partnership to be continued, but any cure of illegality within 90 days after notice to the partnership of the event is effective retroactively to the date of the event for purposes of this section;

(5) on application by a partner, a judicial decree that:

(i) the economic purpose of the partnership is likely to be unreasonably frustrated;

(ii) another partner has engaged in conduct relating to the partnership business that makes it not reasonably practicable to carry on the business in partnership with that partner; or

(iii) it is not otherwise reasonably practicable to carry on the partnership business in conformity with the partnership agreement; or

(6) on application by a transferee of a partner's transferable interest, a judicial decree that it is equitable to wind up the partnership business:

(i) if the partnership was for a definite term or particular undertaking at the time of the transfer or entry of the charging order that gave rise to the transfer, after the expiration of the term or completion of the undertaking; or

(ii) if the partnership was a partnership at will at the time of the transfer or entry of the charging order that gave rise to the transfer, at any time.

§802. Dissolution Deferred 90 Days.

(a) Except as provided in subsection (b), a partnership of more than two persons is not dissolved until 90 days after receipt by the partnership of notice from a partner under Section 801(1) or (2)(i), and its business may be continued until that date as if no notice were received. Before that date, the partner who gave the notice may waive the right to have the partnership business wound up. If there is no waiver before that date, the partnership is dissolved and its business must be wound up.

(b) A partnership may be dissolved at any time during the 90-day period, and its business wound up, by the express will of at least half of the other partners.

(c) After receipt by the partnership of notice from a partner under Section 801(1) or (2)(i), the partner who gave the notice:

(1) has no rights in the management and conduct of the partnership business if it is continued under subsection (a), but may participate in winding up the business under Section 804 if the partnership is dissolved on or before the expiration of the 90-day period pursuant to subsection (a) or (b);

(2) is liable for obligations incurred during the period only to the extent a dissociated partner would be liable under Section 702(b) or Section 703(b), but is not liable for contributions for, and must be indemnified by the other partners against, any partnership liability incurred by another partner to the extent the liability is not appropriate for winding up the partnership business; and

(3) with respect to profits or losses incurred during the period, shall be credited with a share of any profits but shall be charged with a share of any losses only to the extent of profits credited for the period.

§803. Partnership Continues After Dissolution. A partnership continues after dissolution until the winding up of its business is completed, at which time the partnership is terminated.

§804. Right to Wind Up Partnership Business.

(a) After dissolution, a partner who has not wrongfully dissociated has a right to participate in winding up the partnership's business, but on application of any partner, partner's legal representative, or transferee, the [designate the appropriate court], for good cause, may order judicial supervision of the winding up.

(b) The legal representative of the last surviving partner may wind up a partnership's business.

(c) A person winding up a partnership's business may preserve the partnership business or property as a going concern for a reasonable time, prosecute and defend actions and proceedings, whether civil, criminal, or administrative, settle and close the partnership's business, dispose of and transfer the partnership's property, discharge the partnership's liabilities, distribute the assets of the partnership pursuant to Section 808, and perform other necessary acts, including settlement of disputes by mediation or arbitration.

§805. Partner's Power to Bind Partnership After Dissolution. Subject to Section 806, a partnership is bound by a partner's act after dissolution that:

(1) is appropriate for winding up the partnership business; or

(2) would have bound the partnership under Section 301 before dissolution, if the other party to the transaction does not have notice of the dissolution.

§806. Statement of Dissolution.

(a) After dissolution, a partner who has not wrongfully dissociated may file a statement of dissolution stating the name of the partnership and that the partnership has dissolved and is winding up its business.

(b) A statement of dissolution cancels a filed statement of partnership authority for the purposes of Section 303(d) and is a limitation on authority for the purposes of Section 303(e).

(c) For the purposes of Sections 301 and 805, a person not a partner is deemed to have notice of the dissolution and the limitation on the partners' authority as a result of the statement of dissolution 90 days after it is filed.

(d) After filing and, where appropriate, recording a statement of dissolution, the dissolved partnership may file and, where appropriate, record a statement of partnership authority which will operate with respect to a person not a partner as provided in Section 303(d) and (e) in any transaction, whether or not the transaction is appropriate for winding up the partnership business.

§807. Partner's Liability to Other Partners After Dissolution.

(a) Except as provided in subsection (b) and Section 802(c)(2), after dissolution a partner is liable to the other partners for the partner's share of any partnership liability incurred under Section 805.

(b) A partner who, with knowledge of the winding up, incurs a partnership liability under Section 805(2) by an act that is not appropriate for winding up the partnership business is liable to the partnership for any loss caused to the partnership arising from that liability.

§808. Settlement of Accounts Among Partners.

(a) In winding up the partnership business, the assets of the partnership must be applied to discharge its obligations to creditors, including partners who are creditors. Any surplus must be applied to pay in cash the net amount distributable to partners in accordance with their right to distributions pursuant to subsection (b).

(b) Each partner is entitled to a settlement of all partnership accounts upon winding up the partnership business. In settling accounts among the partners, the profits and losses that result from the liquidation of the partnership assets must be credited and charged to the partners' accounts. The partnership shall make a distribution to a partner in an amount equal to that partner's positive balance. A partner shall contribute to the partnership an amount equal to that partner's negative balance.

(c) To the extent not taken into account in settling the accounts among partners pursuant to subsection (b), each partner shall contribute, in the proportion in which the partner shares partnership losses, the amount necessary to satisfy partnership obligations. If a partner fails to contribute, the other partners shall contribute, in the proportions in which the partners share partnership losses, the additional amount necessary to satisfy the partnership obligations. A partner or partner's legal representative may recover from the other partners any contributions the partner makes to the extent the amount contributed exceeds that partner's share of the partnership obligations.

(d) The estate of a deceased partner is liable for the partner's obligation to contribute to the partnership.

(e) An assignee for the benefit of creditors of a partnership or a partner, or a person appointed by a court to represent creditors of a partnership or a partner, may enforce a partner's obligation to contribute to the partnership.

ARTICLE 9: CONVERSIONS AND MERGERS

§901. Conversion of Partnership to Limited Partnership.

(a) A partnership may be converted to a limited partnership pursuant to this section.

(b) The terms and conditions of a conversion of a partnership to a limited partnership must be approved by all the partners or by a number or percentage specified for conversion in the partnership agreement.

(c) After the conversion is approved by the partners, the partnership shall file a certificate of limited partnership which satisfies the requirements of [Section _____ of the State Limited Partnership Act] and includes:

(1) a statement that the partnership was converted to a limited partnership from a partnership;

(2) its former name; and

(3) a statement of the number of votes cast by the partners for and against the conversion and, if the vote is less than unanimous, the number or percentage required to approve the conversion under the partnership agreement.

(d) The conversion takes effect when the certificate of limited partnership is filed or at any later date specified in the certificate.

(e) A partner who becomes a limited partner as a result of the conversion remains liable as a partner for an obligation incurred by the partnership before the conversion takes effect. If the other party to a transaction with the limited partnership reasonably believes when entering the transaction that the limited partner is a general partner, the partner is liable for an obligation incurred by the limited partnership within 90 days after the conversion takes effect. The partner's liability for all other obligations of the limited partnership incurred after the conversion takes effect is that of a limited partner as provided in the [State Limited Partnership Act].

§902. Conversion of Limited Partnership to Partnership.

(a) A limited partnership may be converted to a partnership pursuant to this section.

(b) Notwithstanding a provision to the contrary in a limited partnership agreement, the terms and conditions of a conversion of a limited partnership to a partnership must be approved by all the partners.

(c) After the conversion is approved by the partners, the limited partnership shall cancel its certificate of limited partnership pursuant to [Section _____ of the State Limited Partnership Act].

(d) The conversion takes effect when the certificate of limited partnership is cancelled.

(e) A limited partner who becomes a partner as a result of the conversion remains liable only as a limited partner for an obligation incurred by the limited partnership before the conversion takes effect. The limited partner is liable as a partner for an obligation of the partnership incurred after the conversion takes effect.

§903. Effect of Conversion; Entity Unchanged.

(a) A partnership or limited partnership that has been converted pursuant to this article is for all purposes the same entity that existed before the conversion.

(b) When a conversion takes effect:

(1) all property owned by the converting partnership or limited partnership remains vested in the converted entity;

(2) all obligations of the converting partnership or limited partnership continue as obligations of the converted entity; and

(3) an action or proceeding pending against the converting partnership or limited partnership may be continued as if the conversion had not occurred.

§904. Merger of Partnerships.

(a) Pursuant to a plan of merger approved as provided in subsection (c), a partnership may be merged with one or more partnerships or limited partnerships.

(b) The plan of merger must set forth:

(1) the name of each partnership or limited partnership that is a party to the merger;

(2) the name of the surviving entity into which the other partnerships or limited partnerships will merge;

(3) whether the surviving entity is a partnership or a limited partnership and the status of each partner;

(4) the terms and conditions of the merger;

(5) the manner and basis of converting the interests of each party to the merger into interests or obligations of the surviving entity, or into cash or other property in whole or part; and

(6) the street address of the surviving entity's chief executive office.

(c) The plan of merger must be approved:

(1) in the case of a partnership that is a party to

the merger, by all the partners, or a number or percentage specified for merger in the partnership agreement; and

(2) in the case of a limited partnership that is a party to the merger, by the vote required for approval of a merger by the law of the state or foreign jurisdiction in which the limited partnership is organized and, in the absence of such specifically applicable law, by all the partners, notwithstanding a provision to the contrary in the partnership agreement.

(d) After a plan of merger is approved and before the merger takes effect, the plan may be amended or abandoned as provided in the plan.

(e) The merger takes effect on the later of:

(1) the approval of the plan of merger by all parties to the merger, as provided in subsection (c);

(2) the filing of all documents required by law to be filed as a condition to the effectiveness of the merger; or

(3) any effective date specified in the plan of merger.

§905. Effect of Merger.

(a) When a merger takes effect:

(1) every partnership or limited partnership that is a party to the merger other than the surviving entity ceases to exist;

(2) all property owned by each of the merged partnerships or limited partnerships vests in the surviving entity;

(3) all obligations of every partnership or limited partnership that is a party to the merger become the obligations of the surviving entity; and

(4) an action or proceeding pending against a partnership or limited partnership that is a party to the merger may be continued as if the merger had not occurred or the surviving entity may be substituted as a party to the action or proceeding.

(b) The [Secretary of State] of this State is the agent for service of process in an action or proceeding against a surviving foreign partnership or limited partnership to enforce an obligation of a domestic partnership or limited partnership that is a party to a merger. The surviving entity shall promptly notify the [Secretary of State] of the mailing address of its chief executive office and of any change of address. Upon receipt of process, the [Secretary of State] shall mail a copy of the process to the surviving foreign partnership or limited partnership.

(c) A partner of the surviving partnership or limited partnership is liable for:

(1) all obligations of a party to the merger for which the partner was personally liable before the merger;

(2) all other obligations of the surviving entity incurred before the merger by a party to the merger, but those obligations may be satisfied only out of property of that entity; and

(3) all obligations of the surviving entity incurred after the merger takes effect.

(d) If the obligations incurred before the merger by a party to the merger are not satisfied out of the property of the surviving partnership or limited partnership, the partners of that party immediately before the effective date of the merger shall contribute the amount necessary to satisfy that party's obligations to the surviving entity, in the manner provided in Section 808(c) as if the merged party were dissolved.

(e) A partner of a party to a merger who does not become a partner of the surviving partnership or limited partnership is dissociated from the entity, of which that partner was a partner, as of the date the merger takes effect. The surviving entity shall cause the partner's interest in the entity to be purchased under Section 701. The surviving entity is bound under Section 702 by an act of a partner dissociated under this subsection, and the partner is liable under Section 703 for transactions entered into by the surviving entity after the merger takes effect.

§906. Statement of Merger.

(a) After a merger, the surviving partnership or limited partnership may file a statement that one or more partnerships or limited partnerships have merged into the surviving entity.

(b) A statement of merger must contain:

(1) the name of each partnership or limited partnership that is a party to the merger;

(2) the name of the surviving entity into which the other partnerships or limited partnership were merged;

(3) the street address of the surviving entity's chief executive office and of an office in this State, if any; and

(4) whether the surviving entity is a partnership or limited partnership.

(c) Except as provided in subsection (d), for the purposes of Section 302, property of the surviving partnership or limited partnership which before the merger was held in the name of another party to the merger is property held in the name of the surviving entity upon filing a statement of merger.

(d) For the purposes of Section 302, real property of the surviving partnership or limited partnership which before the merger was held in the name of another party to the merger is property held in the name of the surviving entity upon recording a certified copy of the statement of merger in the office for recording transfers of that real property.

(e) A filed and, where appropriate, recorded statement of merger, executed and declared to be accurate pursuant to Section 105(c), stating the name of a partnership or limited partnership that is a party to the merger in whose name property was held before the merger and the name of the surviving entity, but not containing all of the other information required by subsection (b), operates with respect to the partnerships or limited partnerships named to the extent provided in subsections (c) and (d).

§907. Nonexclusive. This article is not exclusive. Partnerships or limited partnerships may be converted or merged in any other manner provided by law.

ARTICLE 10: MISCELLANEOUS PROVISIONS

§1001. Uniformity of Application and Construction. This [Act] shall be applied and construed to effectuate its general purpose to make uniform the law with respect to the subject of this [Act] among states enacting it.

§1002. Short Title. This [Act] may be cited as the Uniform Partnership Act (1992).

§1003. Severability. If any provision of this [Act] or its application to any person or circumstance is held in-valid, the invalidity does not affect other provisions or applications of this [Act] which can be given effect without the invalid provision or application, and to this end the provisions of this [Act] are severable.

§1004. Effective Date. This [Act] takes effect. . . .

§1005. Repeals. The following acts and parts of acts are repealed: [the State Partnership Act as amended and in effect immediately prior to the adoption of this [Act]].

§1006. Application to Existing Relationships.

(a) Except as otherwise provided in this section, this [Act] applies to all partnerships in existence on its effective date that were formed under the [State] Partnership Act or any predecessor law providing for the formation, operation, and liquidation of partnerships.

(b) Section 802 does not apply to a partnership in existence on the effective date of this [Act] unless the partners agree otherwise.

(c) This [Act] does not impair the obligations of a contract existing when the [Act] takes effect or affect an action or proceeding begun or right accrued before this [Act] takes effect.

(d) A judgment against a partnership or a partner in an action commenced before the effective date of this [Act] may be enforced in the same manner as a judgment rendered before the effective date of this [Act].

APPENDIX D

Uniform Limited Partnership Act (1976), with 1985 Amendments

ARTICLE I

General Provisions

§101. Definitions. As used in this Act, unless the context otherwise requires:

(1) "Certificate of limited partnership" means the certificate referred to in Section 201, and the certificate as amended or restated.

(2) "Contribution" means any cash, property, services rendered, or a promissory note or other binding obligation to contribute cash or property or to perform services, which a partner contributes to a limited partnership in his capacity as a partner.

(3) "Event of withdrawal of a general partner" means an event that causes a person to cease to be a general partner as provided in Section 402.

(4) "Foreign limited partnership" means a partnership formed under the laws of any state other than this State and having as partners one or more general partners and one or more limited partners.

(5) "General partner" means a person who has been admitted to a limited partnership as a general partner in accordance with the partnership agreement and named in the certificate of limited partnership as a general partner.

(6) "Limited partner" means a person who has been admitted to a limited partnership as a limited partner in accordance with the partnership agreement and named in the certificate of limited partnership as a limited partner.

(7) "Limited partnership" and "domestic limited partnership" mean a partnership formed by 2 or more persons under the laws of this State and having one or more general partners and one or more limited partners.

(8) "Partner" means a limited or general partner.

(9) "Partnership agreement" means any valid agreement, written or oral, of the partners as to the affairs of a limited partnership and the conduct of its business.

(10) "Partnership interest" means a partner's share of the profits and losses of a limited partnership and the right to receive distributions of a partnership assets.

(11) "Person" means a natural person, partnership, limited partnership (domestic or foreign), trust, estate, association, or corporation.

(12) "State" means a state, territory, or possession of the United States, the District of Columbia, or the Commonwealth of Puerto Rico.

§102. Name. The name of each limited partnership as set forth in its certificate of limited partnership:

    (1) shall contain without abbreviation the words "limited partnership";

    (2) may not contain the name of a limited partners unless (i) it is also the name of a general partner or the corporate name of a corporate general partner, or (ii) the business of the limited partnership had been carried on under that name before the admission of that limited partner;

    (3) may not be the same as, or deceptively similar to, the name of any corporation or limited partnership organized under the laws of this State or licensed or registered as a foreign corporation or limited partnership in this State; and

    (4) may not contain the following words [here insert prohibited words].

§103. Reservation of Name. . . .

§104. Specified Office and Agent. Each limited partnership shall continuously maintain in this State:

    (1) an office, which may but need not be a place of its business in this State, at which shall be kept the records required by Section 105 to be maintained; and

    (2) an agent for service of process on the limited partnership, which agent must be an individual resident of this State, a domestic corporation, or a foreign corporation authorized to do business in this State.

§105. Records to Be Kept.

    (a) Each limited partnership shall keep at the office referred to in Section 104(1) the following:

    (1) a current list of the full name and last known business address of each partner, separately identifying the general partners (in alphabetical order) and the limited partners (in alphabetical order);

    (2) a copy of the certificate of limited partnership and all certificates of amendment thereto, together with executed copies of any powers of attorney pursuant to which any certificate has been executed;

    (3) copies of the limited partnership's federal, state, and local income tax returns and reports, if any, for the three most recent years;

    (4) copies of any then-effective written partnership agreements and of any financial statements of the limited partnership for the three most recent years; and

    (5) unless contained in a written partnership agreement, a writing setting out:

        (i) the amount of cash and a description and statement of the agreed value of the other property or services contributed by each partner and which each partner has agreed to contribute;

        (ii) the times at which or events on the happening of which any additional contributions agreed to be made by each partner are to be made;

        (iii) any right of a partner to receive, or of a general partner to make, distributions to a partner which include a return of all or any part of the partner's contribution; and

        (iv) any events upon the happening of which the limited partnership is to be dissolved and its affairs wound up.

    (b) Records kept under this section are subject to inspection and copying at the reasonable request and at the expense of any partner during ordinary business hours.

§106. Nature of Business A limited partnership may carry on any business that a partnership without limited partners may carry on except [here designate prohibited activities].

§107. Business Transactions of Partner with Partnership Except as provided in the partnership agreement, a partner may lend money to and transact other business with the limited partnership and, subject to other applicable law, has the same rights and obligations with respect thereto as a person who is not a partner.

ARTICLE 2

Formation: Certificate of Limited Partnership

§201. Certificate of Limited Partnership.

    (a) In order to form a limited partnership, a certificate of limited partnership must be executed and filed in the office of the Secretary of State. The certificate shall set forth:

    (1) the name of the limited partnership;

    (2) the address of the office and the name and address of the agent for the service of process required to be maintained by Section 104;

    (3) the name and the business address of each general partner;

    (4) the latest date upon which the limited partnership is to dissolve; and

    (5) any other matters the general partners determine to include therein.

    (b) A limited partnership is formed at the time of the filing of the certificate of limited partnership in the office of the Secretary of State or at any later time specified in the certificate of limited partnership if, in either case, there has been substantial compliance with the requirements of this section.

§202. Amendment to Certificate.

(a) A certificate of limited partnership is amended by filing a certificate of amendment thereto in the office of the Secretary of State. The certificate shall set forth:

(1) the name of the limited partnership;
(2) the date of filing the certificate; and
(3) the amendment to the certificate.

(b) Within 30 days after the happening of any of the following events, an amendment to a certificate of limited partnership reflecting the occurrence of the event or events shall be filed:

(1) the admission of a new general partner;
(2) the withdrawal of a general partner; or
(3) the continuation of the business under Section 801 after an event of withdrawal of a general partner.

(c) A general partner who becomes aware that any statement in a certificate of limited partnership was false when made or that any arrangements or other facts described have changed, making the certificate inaccurate in any respect, shall promptly amend the certificate.

(d) A certificate of limited partnership may be amended at any time for any other proper purpose the general partners determine.

(e) No person has any liability because an amendment to a certificate of limited partnership has not been filed to reflect the occurrence of any event referred to in subsection (b) of this section if the amendment is filed within the 30-day period specified in subsection (b).

(f) A restated certificate of limited partnership may be executed and filed in the same manner as a certificate of amendment.

§203 Cancellation of Certificate.

A certificate of limited partnership shall be canceled upon the dissolution and the commencement of winding up of the partnership or at any other time there are no limited partners. A certificate of cancellation shall be filed in the office of the Secretary of State and set forth:

(1) the name of the limited partnership;
(2) the date of filing of its certificate of limited partnership;
(3) the reason for filing the certificate of cancellation;
(4) the effective date (which shall be a date certain) of cancellation if it is not to be effective upon the filing of the certificate; and
(5) any other information the general partners filing the certificate determine.

§204. Execution of Certificates.

(a) Each certificate required by this article to be filed in the office of the Secretary of State shall be exe-cuted in the following manner:

(1) an original certificate of limited partnership must be signed by all general partners;
(2) a certificate of amendment must be signed by at least one general partner and by each other general partner designated in the certificate as a new general partner; and
(3) a certificate of cancellation must be signed by all general partners.

(b) Any person may sign a certificate by an attorney-in-fact, but a power of attorney to sign a certificate relating to the admission, of a general partner must specifically describe the admission.

(c) The execution of a certificate by a general partner constitutes an affirmation under the penalties of perjury that the facts stated therein are true.

§205. Execution by Judicial Act.

If a person required by Section 204 to execute any certificate fails or refuses to do so, any other person who is adversely affected by the failure or refusal, may petition the [designate the appropriate court] to direct the execution of the certificate. If the court finds that it is proper for the certificate to be executed and that any person so designated has failed or refused to execute the certificate, it shall order the Secretary of State to record an appropriate certificate.

§206. Filing in Office of Secretary of State.

(a) Two signed copies of the certificate of limited partnership and of any certificates of amendment or cancellation (or of any judicial decree of amendment or cancellation) shall be delivered to the Secretary of State. A person who executes a certificate as an agent or fiduciary need not exhibit evidence of his or her authority as a prerequisite to filing. Unless the Secretary of State finds that any certificate does not conform to law, upon receipt of all filing fees required by law he or she shall:

(1) endorse on each duplicate original the word "Filed" and the day, month and year of the filing thereof;
(2) file one duplicate original in his or her office; and
(3) return the other duplicate original to the person who filed it or his or her representative.

(b) Upon the filing of a certificate of amendment (or judicial decree of amendment) in the office of the Secretary of State, the certificate of limited partnership shall be amended as set forth therein, and upon the effective date of a certificate of cancellation (or a judicial decree thereof), the certificate of limited partnership is canceled.

§207. Liability for False Statement in Certificate.

If any certificate of limited partnership or certificate of amendment or cancellation contains a false statement, one who suffers loss by reliance on the statement may recover damages for the loss from:

(1) any person who executes the certificate, or causes another to execute it on his behalf, and knew, and any general partner who knew or should have known, the statement to be false at the time the certificate was executed; and

(2) any general partner who thereafter knows or should have known that any arrangement or other fact described in the certificate has changed, making the statement inaccurate in any respect within a sufficient time before the statement was relied upon reasonably to have enabled that general partner to cancel or amend the certificate, or to file a petition for its cancellation or amendment under Section 205.

§208. Scope of Notice. The fact that a certificate of limited partnership is on file in the office of the Secretary of State is notice that the partnership is a limited partnership and the persons designated therein as general partners are general partners, but it is not notice of any other fact.

§209. Delivery of Certificates to Limited Partners. Upon the return by the Secretary of State pursuant to Section 206 of a certificate marked "Filed", the general partners shall promptly deliver or mail a copy of the certificate of limited partnership and each certificate of amendment or cancellation to each limited partner unless the partnership agreement provides otherwise.

ARTICLE 3

Limited Partners

§301. Admission of Limited Partners.

(a) A person becomes a limited partner:

(1) at the time the limited partnership is formed; or

(2) at any later time specified in the records of the limited partnership for becoming a limited partner.

(b) After the filing of a limited partnership's original certificate of limited partnership, a person may be admitted as an additional limited partner:

(1) in the case of a person acquiring a partnership interest directly from the limited partnership, upon compliance with the partnership agreement or, if the partnership agreement does not so provide, upon the written consent of all partners; and

(2) in the case of an assignee of a partnership interest of a partner who has the power, as provided in Section 704, to grant the assignee the right to become a limited partner, upon the ex-

ercise of that power and compliance with any conditions limiting the grant or exercise of the power.

§302. Voting. Subject to Section 303, the partnership agreement may grant to all or a specified group of the limited partners the right to vote (on a per capita or other basis) upon any matter.

§303. Liability to Third Parties.

(a) Except as provided in subsection (d), a limited partner is not liable for the obligations of a limited partnership unless he or she is also a general partner or, in addition to the exercise of his or her rights and powers as a limited partner, he or she participates in the control of the business. However, if the limited partner participates in the control of the business, he or she is liable only to persons who transact business with the limited partnership reasonably believing, based upon the limited partner's conduct, that the limited partner is a general partner.

(b) A limited partner does not participate in the control of the business within the meaning of subsection (a) solely by doing one or more of the following:

(1) being a contractor for or an agent or employee of the limited partnership or of a general partner or being an officer, director, or shareholder of a general partner that is a corporation;

(2) consulting with and advising a general partner with respect to the business of the limited partnership;

(3) acting as surety for the limited partnership or guaranteeing or assuming one or more specific obligations of the limited partnership;

(4) taking any action required or permitted by law to bring or pursue a derivative action in the right of the limited partnership;

(5) requesting or attending a meeting of partners;

(6) proposing, approving, or disapproving, by voting or otherwise, one or more of the following matters:

(i) the dissolution and winding up of the limited partnership;

(ii) the sale, exchange, lease, mortgage, pledge, or other transfer of all or substantially all of the assets of the limited partnership;

(iii) the incurrence of indebtedness by the limited partnership other than in the ordinary course of its business;

(iv) a change in the nature of the business;

(v) the admission or removal of a general partner;

(vi) the admission or removal of a limited partner;

(vii) a transaction involving an actual or a potential conflict of interest between a general partner and the limited partnership or the limited partners:

- **(viii)** an amendment to the partnership agreement or certificate of limited partnership; or
- **(ix)** matters related to the business of the limited partnership not otherwise enumerated in this subsection (b), which the partnership agreement states in writing may be subject to the approval or disapproval of limited partners;
- **(7)** winding up the limited partnership pursuant to Section 803; or
- **(8)** exercising any right or power permitted to limited partners under this [Act] and not specifically enumerated in this subsection (b).

(c) The enumeration in subsection (b) does not mean that the possession or exercise of any other powers by a limited partner constitutes participation by him or her in the business of the limited partnership.

(d) A limited partner who knowingly permits his or her name to be used in the name of the limited partnership, except under circumstances permitted by Section 102(2), is liable to creditors who extend credit to the limited partnership without actual knowledge that the limited partner is not a general partner.

§304. Person Erroneously Believing Himself or Herself Limited Partner.

(a) Except as provided in subsection (b), a person who makes a contribution to a business enterprise and erroneously but in good faith believes that he or she has become a limited partner in the enterprise is not a general partner in the enterprise and is not bound by its obligations by reason of making the contribution, receiving distributions from the enterprise, or exercising any rights of a limited partner, if, on ascertaining the mistake, he or she:

- **(1)** causes an appropriate certificate of limited partnership or a certificate of amendment to be executed and filed; or
- **(2)** withdraws from future equity participation in the enterprise by executing and filing in the office of the Secretary of State a certificate declaring a withdrawal under this section.

(b) A person who makes a contribution of the kind described in subsection (a) is liable as a general partner to any third party who transacts business with the enterprise (i) before the person withdraws and an appropriate certificate is filed to show withdrawal, or (ii) before an appropriate certificate is filed to show that he [or she] is not a general partner, but in either case only if the third party actually believed in good faith that the person was a general partner.

§305. Information. Each limited partner has the right to:

- **(1)** inspect and copy any of the partnership records required to be maintained by Section 105; and
- **(2)** obtain from the general partners from time to time upon reasonable demand (i) true and full information regarding the state of the business and financial condition of the limited partnership, (ii) promptly after becoming available, a copy of the limited partnership's federal, state and local income tax returns for each year, and (iii) other information regarding the affairs of the limited partnership as is just and reasonable.

ARTICLE 4

General Partners

§401. Admission of Additional General Partners. After the filing of a limited partnership's original certificate of limited partnership, additional general partners may be admitted as provided in writing in the partnership agreement or, if the partnership agreement does not provide in writing for the admission of additional general partners, with the written consent of all partners.

§402. Events of Withdrawal. Except as approved by the specific written consent of all partners at the time, a person ceases to be a general partner of a limited partnership upon the happening of any of the following events:

- **(1)** the general partner withdraws from the limited partnership as provided in Section 602;
- **(2)** the general partner ceases to be a member of the limited partnership as provided in Section 702.
- **(3)** the general partner is removed as a general partner in accordance with the partnership agreement;
- **(4)** unless otherwise provided in writing in the partnership agreement, the general partner; (i) makes an assignment for the benefit of creditors; (ii) files a voluntary petition in bankruptcy; (iii) is adjudicated a bankrupt or insolvent; (iv) files a petition or answer seeking for himself or herself any reorganization, arrangement, composition, readjustment, liquidation, dissolution or similar relief under any statute, law, or regulation; (v) files an answer or other pleading admitting or failing to contest the material allegations of a petition filed against him or her in any proceeding of this nature; or (vi) seeks, consents to, or acquiesces in the appointment of a trustee, receiver, or liquidator of the general partner or of all or any substantial part of his or her properties;

(5) unless otherwise provided in writing in the partnership agreement, [120] days after the commencement of any proceeding against the general partner seeking reorganization, arrangement, composition, readjustment, liquidation, dissolution or similar relief under any statute, law, or regulation, the proceeding has not been dismissed, or if within [90] days after the appointment without his or her consent or acquiescence of a trustee, receiver, or liquidator of the general partner or of all or any substantial part of his or her properties, the appointment is not vacated or stayed or within [90] days after the expiration of any such stay, the appointment is not vacated;

(6) in the case of a general partner who is a natural person,

    (i) his or her death; or

    (ii) the entry by a court of competent jurisdiction adjudicating him or her incompetent to manage his or her person or estate;

(7) in the case of a general partner who is acting as a general partner by virtue of being a trustee of a trust, the termination of the trust (but not merely the substitution of a new trustee);

(8) in the case of a general partner that is a separate partnership, the dissolution and commencement of winding up of the separate partnership;

(9) in the case of a general partner that is a corporation, the filing of a certificate of dissolution, or its equivalent, for the corporation or the revocation of its charter; or

(10) in the case of an estate, the distribution by the fiduciary of the estate's entire interest in the partnership.

§403. General Powers and Liabilities. (a) Except as provided in this Act or in the partnership agreement, a general partner of a limited partnership has the rights and powers and is subject to the restrictions of a partner in a partnership without limited partners. (b) Except as provided in this Act, a general partner of a limited partnership has the liabilities of a partner in a partnership without limited partners to persons other than the partnership and the other partners. Except as provided in this Act or in the partnership agreement, a general partner of a limited partnership has the liabilities of a partner in a partnership without limited partners to the partnership and to the other partners.

§404. Contributions by General Partner. A general partner of a limited partnership may make contributions to the partnership and share in the profits and losses of, and in distributions from, the limited partnership as a general partner. A general partner also may make contributions to and share in profits, losses, and distributions as a limited partner. A person who is both a general partner and a limited partner has the rights and powers, and is subject to the restrictions and liabilities, of a general partner and except as provided in the partnership agreement, also has the powers, and is subject to the restrictions of a limited partner to the extent of his or her participation in the partnership as a limited partner.

§405. Voting. The partnership agreement may grant to all or certain identified general partners the right to vote (on a per capita or any other basis), separately or with all or any class of the limited partners, on any matter.

ARTICLE 5

Finance

§501. Form of Contribution. The contribution of a partner may be in cash, property, or services rendered, or a promissory note or other obligation to contribute cash or property or to perform services.

§502. Liability for Contribution.

(a) A promise by a limited partner to contribute to the limited partnership is not enforceable unless set out in a writing signed by the limited partner.

(b) Except as provided in the limited partnership agreement, a partner is obligated to the limited partnership to perform any enforceable promise to contribute cash or property or to perform services, even if he or she is unable to perform because of death, disability, or any other reason. If a partner does not make the required contribution of property or services, he or she is obligated at the option of the limited partnership to contribute cash equal to that portion of the value, as stated in the partnership records required to be kept pursuant to Section 105, of the stated contribution that has not been made.

(c) Unless otherwise provided in the partnership agreement, the obligation of a partner to make a contribution or return money or other property paid or distributed in violation of this Act may be compromised only by consent of all the partners. Notwithstanding the compromise, a creditor of a limited partnership who extends credit, or otherwise acts in reliance on that obligation after the partner signs a writing which reflects the obligation, and before the amendment or cancellation thereof to reflect the compromise, may enforce the original obligation.

§503. Sharing of Profits and Losses. The profits and losses of a limited partnership shall be allocated among the partners, and among classes of partners, in the manner provided in writing in the partnership agreement. If the partnership agreement does not so provide in writing, profits and losses shall be allocated on the basis of the value, as stated in the partnership records required to be kept pursuant to Section 105, of the contributions made by each partner to the extent they have been received by the partnership and have not been returned.

§504. Sharing of Distributions. Distributions of cash or other assets of a limited partnership shall be allocated among the partners, and among classes of partners in the manner provided in writing in the partnership agreement. If the partnership agreement does not so provide in writing, distributions shall be made on the basis of the value, as stated in the partnership records required to be kept pursuant to Section 105, of the contributions made by each partner to the extent they have been received by the partnership and have not been returned.

ARTICLE 6

Distribution and Withdrawal

§601. Interim Distributions. Except as provided in this Article, a partner is entitled to receive distributions from a limited partnership before his or her withdrawal from the limited partnership and before the dissolution and winding up thereof to the extent and at the times or upon the happening of the events specified in the partnership agreement.

§602. Withdrawal of General Partner. A general partner may withdraw from a limited partnership at any time by giving written notice to the other partners, but if the withdrawal violates the partnership agreement, the limited partnership may recover from the withdrawing general partner damages for breach of the partnership agreement and offset the damages against the amount otherwise distributable to him or her.

§603. Withdrawal of Limited Partner. A limited partner may withdraw from a limited partnership at the time or upon the happening of events specified in writing in the partnership agreement. If the agreement does not specify in writing the time or the events upon the happening of which a limited partner may withdraw or a definite time for the dissolution and winding up of the limited partnership, a limited partner may withdraw upon not less than six months' prior written notice to each general partner at his or her address on the books of the limited partnership at its office in this State.

§604. Distribution Upon Withdrawal. Except as provided in this Article, upon withdrawal any withdrawing partner is entitled to receive any distribution to which he or she is entitled under the partnership agreement and, if not otherwise provided in the agreement, he or she is entitled to receive, within a reasonable time after withdrawal, the fair value of his or her interest in the limited partnership as of the date of withdrawal based upon his or her right to share in distributions from the limited partnership.

§605. Distribution in Kind. Except as provided in writing in the partnership agreement, a partner, regardless of the nature of his or her contribution, has no right to demand and receive any distribution from a limited partnership in any form other than cash. Except as provided in writing in the partnership agreement, a partner may not be compelled to accept a distribution of any asset in kind from a limited partnership to the extent that the percentage of the asset distributed to him or her exceeds a percentage of that asset which is equal to the percentage in which he or she shares in distributions from the limited partnership.

§606. Right to Distribution. At the time a partner becomes entitled to receive a distribution, he or she has the status of, and is entitled to all remedies available to, a creditor of the limited partnership with respect to the distribution.

§607. Limitations on Distribution. A partner may not receive a distribution from a limited partnership to the extent that, after giving effect to the distribution, all liabilities of the limited partnership, other than liabilities to partners on account of their partnership interests, exceed the fair value of the partnership assets.

§608. Liability upon Return of Contribution.

(a) If a partner has received the return of any part of his or her contribution without violation of the partnership agreement or this Act, he or she is liable to the limited partnership for a period of one year thereafter for the amount of the returned contribution, but only to the extent necessary to discharge the limited partnership's liabilities to creditors who extended credit to the limited partnership during the period the contribution was held by the partnership.

(b) If a partner has received the return of any part of his or her contribution in violation of the partnership agreement or this Act, he or she is liable to the limited partnership for a period of six years thereafter for the amount of the contribution wrongfully returned.

(c) A partner receives a return of his or her contribution to the extent that a distribution to him or her reduces his or her share of the fair value of the net assets of the limited partnership below the value as set forth in the partnership records required to be kept pursuant to Section 105, of his or her contribution which has not been distributed to him or her.

ARTICLE 7

Assignment of Partnership Interests

§701. Nature of Partnership Interest. A partnership interest is personal property.

§702. Assignment of Partnership Interest. Except as provided in the partnership agreement, a partnership interest is assignable in whole or in part. An assignment of a partnership interest does not dissolve a limited partnership or entitle the assignee to become or to exercise any rights of a partner. An assignment entitles the assignee to receive, to the extent assigned, only the distribution to which the assignor would be entitled. Except as provided in the partnership agreement, a partner ceases to be a partner upon assignment of all his or her partnership interest.

§703. Rights of Creditor. On application to a court of competent jurisdiction by any judgment creditor of a partner, the court may charge the partnership interest of the partner with payment of the unsatisfied amount of the judgment with interest. To the extent so charged, the judgment creditor has only the rights of an assignee of the partnership interest. This Act does not deprive any partner of the benefit of any exemption laws applicable to his or her partnership interest.

§704. Right of Assignee to Become Limited Partner.

(a) An assignee of a partnership interest, including an assignee of a general partner, may become a limited partner if and to the extent that (i) the assignor gives the assignee that right in accordance with authority described in the partnership agreement or (ii) all other partners consent.

(b) An assignee who has become a limited partner has, to the extent assigned, the rights and powers, and is subject to the restrictions and liabilities, of a limited partner under the partnership agreement and this Act. An assignee who becomes a limited partner also is liable for the obligations of his or her assignor to make and return contributions as provided in Articles 5 and 6. However, the assignee is not obligated for liabilities unknown to the assignee at the time he or she became a limited partner.

(c) If an assignee of a partnership interest becomes a limited partner, the assignor is not released from his or her liability to the limited partnership under Sections 207 and 502.

§705. Power of Estate of Deceased or Incompetent Partner. If a partner who is an individual dies or a court of competent jurisdiction adjudges him or her to be incompetent to manage his or her person or his or her property, the partner's executor, administrator, guardian, conservator, or other legal representative may exercise all the partner's rights for the purpose of settling his or her estate or administering his or her property, including any power the partner had to give an assignee the right to become a limited partner. If a partner is a corporation, trust, or other entity and is dissolved or terminated, the powers of that partner may be exercised by its legal representative or successor.

ARTICLE 8

Dissolution

§801. Nonjudicial Dissolution. A limited partnership is dissolved and its affairs shall be wound up upon the happening of the first to occur of the following:

(1) at the time specified in the certificate of limited partnership;

(2) upon the happening of events specified in writing in the partnership agreement;

(3) written consent of all partners;

(4) an event of withdrawal of a general partner unless at the time there is at least one other general partner and the written provisions of the partnership agreement permit the business of the limited partnership to be carried on by the remaining general partner and that partner does so, but the limited partnership is not dissolved and is not required to be wound up by reason of any event of withdrawal, if, within 90 days after the withdrawal, all partners agree in writing to continue the business of the limited partnership and to the appointment of one or more additional partners if necessary or desired; or

(5) entry of a decree of judicial dissolution under Section 802.

§802. Judicial Dissolution. On application by or for a partner the [designate the proper court] court may decree dissolution of a limited partnership whenever it is not reasonably practicable to carry on the business in conformity with the partnership agreement.

§803. Winding Up. Except as provided in the partnership agreement, the general partners who have not wrongfully dissolved a limited partnership, or, if none, the limited partners, may wind up the limited partnership's affairs; but the [designate the proper court] court may wind up the limited partnership's affairs upon application of any partner, his or her legal representative, or assignee.

§804. Distribution of Assets. Upon the winding up of a limited partnership, the assets shall be distributed as follows:

(1) to creditors, including partners who are creditors, to the extent permitted by law, in satisfaction of liabilities of the limited partnership other than liabilities for distributions to partners under Section 601 or 604;

(2) except as provided in the partnership agreement, to partners and former partners in satisfaction of liabilities for distributions under Section 601 or 604; and

(3) except as provided in the partnership agreement, to partners first for the return of their

contributions and secondly respecting their partnership interests, in the proportions in which the partners share in distributions.

ARTICLE 9
Foreign Limited Partnerships

§901. Law Governing. Subject to the Constitution of this State, (i) the laws of the state under which a foreign limited partnership is organized govern its organization and internal affairs and the liability of its limited partners, and (ii) a foreign limited partnership may not be denied registration by reason of any difference between those laws and the laws of this State.

§902. Registration. . . .

§903. Issuance of Registration. . . .

§904. Name. A foreign limited partnership may register with the Secretary of State under any name, whether or not it is the name under which it is registered in its state of organization, that includes without abbreviation the words "limited partnership" and that could be registered by a domestic limited partnership.

§905. Changes and Amendments. . . .

§906. Cancellation of Registration. . . .

§907. Transaction of Business without Registration.

(a) A foreign limited partnership transacting business in this State may not maintain any action, suit, or proceeding in any court of this State until it has registered in this State.

(b) The failure of a foreign limited partnership to register in this State does not impair the validity of any contract or act of the foreign limited partnership or prevent the foreign limited partnership from defending any action, suit, or proceeding in any court of this State.

(c) A limited partner of a foreign limited partnership is not liable as a general partner of the foreign limited partnership solely by reason of having transacted business in this State without registration.

(d) A foreign limited partnership, by transacting business in this State without registration, appoints the Secretary of State as its agent for service of process with respect to [claims for relief] [causes of action] arising out of the transaction of business in this State.

§908. Action by [Appropriate Official.] The [designate the appropriate official] may bring an action to restrain a foreign limited partnership from transacting business in this State in violation of the Article.

ARTICLE 10
Derivative Actions

§1001. Right of Action. A limited partner may bring an action in the right of a limited partnership to recover a judgment in its favor if general partners with authority to do so have refused to bring the action or if an effort to cause those general partners to bring the action is not likely to succeed.

§1002. Proper Plaintiff. . . .

§1003. Pleading. . . .

§1004. Expenses. . . .

ARTICLE 11
Miscellaneous

§1101. Construction and Application. . . .

§1102. Short Title. This Act may be cited as the Uniform Limited Partnership Act.

§1103. Severability. . . .

§1104. Effective Date, Extended Effective Date and Repeal. . . .

§1105. Rules for Cases Not Provided for in This Act. In any case not provided for in this Act the provisions of the Uniform Partnership Act govern.

§1106. Savings Clause. . .

E

Revised Model Business Corporation Act (1984) (Excerpts)

§1.02. Reservation of Power to Amend or Repeal. The [name of state legislature] has power to amend or repeal all or part of this Act at any time and all domestic and foreign corporations subject to this Act are governed by the amendment or repeal. . . .

§1.40. Act Definitions. In this Act:

(1) "Articles of incorporation" include amended and restated articles of incorporation and articles of merger.

(2) "Authorized shares" means the share of all classes a domestic or foreign corporation is authorized to issue. . . .

(4) "Corporation" or "domestic corporation" means a corporation for profit, which is not a foreign corporation, incorporated under or subject to the provisions of this Act. . . .

(8) "Employee" includes an officer but not a director. A director may accept duties that make him also an employee. . . .

(10) "Foreign corporation" means a corporation for profit incorporated under a law other than the law of this state. . . .

(17) "Principal office" means the office (in or out of this state) so designated in the annual report where the principal executive offices of a domestic or foreign corporation are located. . . .

(21) "Share" means the unit into which the proprietary interests in a corporation are divided.

(22) "Shareholder" means the person in whose name shares are registered in the records of a corporation or the beneficial owner of shares to the extent of the rights granted by a nominee certificate on file with a corporation. . . .

(24) "Subscriber" means a person who subscribes for shares in a corporation, whether before or after incorporation. . . .

§2.01. Incorporators. One or more persons may act as the incorporator or incorporators of a corporation by delivering articles of incorporation to the secretary of state for filing.

§2.02. Articles of Incorporation.

(a) The articles of incorporation must set forth:

(1) a corporate name for the corporation that satisfies the requirements of section 4.01;

(2) the number of shares the corporation is authorized to issue;

(3) the street address of the corporation's initial registered office and the name of its initial registered agent at that office; and

(4) the name and address of each incorporator. . . .

§2.03. Incorporation.

(a) Unless a delayed effective date is specified, the corporate existence begins when the articles of incorporation are filed.

(b) The secretary of state's filing of the articles of incorporation is conclusive proof that the incorporators satisfied all conditions precedent to incorporation except in a proceeding by the state to cancel or revoke the incorporation or involuntarily dissolve the corporation.

§2.04. Liability for Preincorporation Transactions.
All persons purporting to act as or on behalf of a corporation, knowing there was no incorporation under this Act, are jointly and severally liable for all liabilities created while so acting.

§2.05. Organization of Corporation.

(a) After incorporation:

(1) if initial directors are named in the articles of incorporation, the initial directors shall hold an organizational meeting, at the call of a majority of the directors, to complete the organization of the corporation by appointing officers, adopting bylaws, and carrying on any other business brought before the meeting;

(2) if initial directors are not named in the articles, the incorporator or incorporators shall hold an organizational meeting at the call of a majority of the incorporators: . . .

§2.06. Bylaws.

(a) The incorporators or board of directors of a corporation shall adopt initial bylaws for the corporation.

(b) The bylaws of a corporation may contain any provision for managing the business and regulating the affairs of the corporation that is not inconsistent with law or the articles of incorporation. . . .

§3.01. Purposes.

(a) Every corporation incorporated under this Act has the purpose of engaging in any lawful business unless a more limited purpose is set forth in the articles of incorporation. . . .

§3.02. General Powers.
Unless its articles of incorporation provide otherwise, every corporation has perpetual duration and succession in its corporate name and has the same powers as an individual to do all things necessary or convenient to carry out its business and affairs, including without limitation power:

(1) to sue and be sued, complain and defend in its corporate name; . . .

(3) to make and amend bylaws, not inconsistent with its articles of incorporation or with the laws of this state, for managing the business and regulating the affairs of the corporation;

(4) to purchase, receive, lease, or otherwise acquire, and own, hold, improve, use, and otherwise deal with, real or personal property, or any legal or equitable interest in property, wherever located;

(5) to sell, convey, mortgage, pledge, lease, exchange, and otherwise dispose of all or any part of its property; . . .

(11) to elect directors and appoint officers, employees, and agents of the corporation, define their duties, fix their compensation, and lend them money and credit; . . .

(15) to make payments or donations, or do any other act, not inconsistent with law, that furthers the business and affairs of the corporation. . . .

§3.04. Ultra Vires.

(a) Except as provided in subsection (b), the validity of corporate action may not be challenged on the ground that the corporation lacks or lacked power to act.

(b) A corporation's power to act may be challenged:

(1) in a proceeding by a shareholder against the corporation to enjoin the act;

(2) in a proceeding by the corporation, directly, derivatively, or through a receiver, trustee, or other legal representative, against an incumbent or former director, officer, employee, or agent of the corporation; or

(3) in a proceeding by the Attorney General under section 14.30. . . .

§4.01. Corporate Name.

(a) A corporate name:

(1) must contain the word "corporation," "incorporated," "company," or "limited," or the abbreviation "corp.," "inc.," "co.," or "ltd.," or words or abbreviations of like import in another language; and

(2) may not contain language stating or implying that the corporation is organized for a purpose other than that permitted by section 3.01 and its articles of incorporation.

(b) Except as authorized by subsections (c) and (d), a corporate name must be distinguishable upon the records of the secretary of state from:

(1) the corporate name of a corporation incorporated or authorized to transact business in this state; . . .

§5.01. Registered Office and Registered Agent.
Each corporation must continuously maintain in this state:

(1) a registered office that may be the same as any of its places of business; . . .

§6.01. Authorized Shares.

(a) The articles of incorporation must prescribe the classes of shares and the number of shares of each class that the corporation is authorized to issue. If more than one class of shares is authorized, the articles of incorporation must prescribe a distinguishing designation for each class, and, prior to the issuance of shares of a class, the preferences, limitations, and relative rights of that class must be described in the articles of incorporation. All shares of a class must have preferences, limitations, and relative rights identical with those of other shares of the same class except to the extent otherwise permitted by section 6.02. . . .

§6.03. Issued and Outstanding Shares.

(a) A corporation may issue the number of shares of each class or series authorized by the articles of incorporation. Shares that are issued are outstanding shares until they are reacquired, redeemed, converted, or cancelled.

(b) The reacquisition, redemption, or conversion of outstanding shares is subject to the limitations of subsection (c) of this section and to section 6.40.

(c) At all times that shares of the corporation are outstanding, one or more shares that together have unlimited voting rights and one or more shares that together are entitled to receive the net assets of the corporation upon dissolution must be outstanding. . . .

§6.20. Subscription for Shares before Incorporation.

(a) A subscription for shares entered into before incorporation is irrevocable for six months unless the subscription agreement provides a longer or shorter period or all the subscribers agree to revocation. . . .

§6.21. Issuance of Shares.

(a) The powers granted in this section to the board of directors may be reserved to the shareholders by the articles of incorporation.

(b) The board of directors may authorize shares to be issued for consideration consisting of any tangible or intangible property or benefit to the corporation, including cash, promissory notes, services performed, contracts for services to be performed, or other securities of the corporation. . . .

§6.22. Liability of Shareholders.

(a) A purchaser from a corporation of its own shares is not liable to the corporation or its creditors with respect to the shares except to pay the consideration for which the shares were authorized to be issued (section 6.21) or specified in the subscription agreement (section 6.20).

(b) Unless otherwise provided in the articles of incorporation, a shareholder of a corporation is not personally liable for the acts or debts of the corporation except that he may become personally liable by reason of his own acts or conduct. . . .

§6.27. Restriction on Transfer of Shares and Other Securities.

(a) The articles of incorporation, bylaws, an agreement among shareholders, or an agreement between shareholders and the corporation may impose restrictions on the transfer or registration of transfer of shares of the corporation. A restriction does not affect shares issued before the restriction was adopted unless the holders of the shares are parties to the restriction agreement or voted in favor of the restriction.

(b) A restriction on the transfer or registration of transfer of shares is valid and enforceable against the holder or a transferee of the holder if the restriction is authorized by this section and its existence is noted conspicuously on the front or back of the certificate or is contained in the information statement required by section 6.26(b). Unless so noted, a restriction is not enforceable against a person without knowledge of the restriction. . . .

§6.30. Shareholders' Preemptive Rights.

(a) The shareholders of a corporation do not have a preemptive right to acquire the corporation's unissued shares except to the extent the articles of incorporation so provide. . . .

§6.31. Corporation's Acquisition of Its Own Shares.

(a) A corporation may acquire its own shares and shares so acquired constitute authorized but unissued shares.

(b) If the articles of incorporation prohibit the reissue of acquired shares, the number of authorized shares is reduced by the number of shares acquired, effective upon amendment of the articles of incorporation. . . .

§6.40. Distributions to Shareholders.

(a) A board of directors may authorize and the corporation may make distributions to its shareholders subject to restriction by the articles of incorporation and the limitation in subsection (c).

(b) If the board of directors does not fix the record date for determining shareholders entitled to a distribution (other than one involving a repurchase or reacquisition of shares), it is the date the board of directors authorizes the distribution.

(c) No distribution may be made if, after giving it effect:

(1) the corporation would not be able to pay its debts as they become due in the usual course of business; or

(2) the corporation's total assets would be less than the sum of its total liabilities plus (unless the articles of incorporation permit otherwise) the amount that would be needed, if the corporation were to be dissolved at the time of the distribution, to satisfy the preferential rights upon

dissolution of shareholders whose preferential rights are superior to those receiving the distribution. . . .

(f) A corporation's indebtedness to a shareholder incurred by reason of a distribution made in accordance with this section is at parity with the corporation's indebtedness to its general, unsecured creditors except to the extent subordinated by agreement.

§7.01. Annual Meeting.

(a) A corporation shall hold a meeting of shareholders annually at a time stated in or fixed in accordance with the bylaws.

(b) Annual shareholders' meetings may be held in or out of this state at the place stated in or fixed in accordance with the bylaws. If no place is stated in or fixed in accordance with the bylaws, annual meetings shall be held at the corporation's principal office.

(c) The failure to hold an annual meeting at the time stated in or fixed in accordance with a corporation's bylaws does not affect the validity of any corporate action.

§7.02. Special Meeting.

(a) A corporation shall hold a special meeting of shareholders:

(1) on call of its board of directors of the person or persons authorized to do so by the articles of incorporation or bylaws; or

(2) if the holders of at least 10 percent of all the votes entitled to be cast on any issue proposed to be considered at the proposed special meeting sign, date, and deliver to the corporation's secretary one or more written demands for the meeting describing the purpose or purposes for which it is to be held. . . .

(d) Only business within the purpose or purposes described in the meeting notice required by section 7.05(c) may be conducted at a special shareholders' meeting.

§7.03. Court-Ordered Meeting.

(a) The [name or describe] court of the county where a corporation's principal office (or, if none in this state, its registered office) is located may summarily order a meeting to be held:

(1) on application of any shareholder of the corporation entitled to participate in an annual meeting if an annual meeting was not held within the earlier of 6 months after the end of the corporation's fiscal year or 15 months after its last annual meeting; . . .

§7.04. Action without Meeting.

(a) Action required or permitted by this Act to be taken at a shareholders' meeting may be taken without a meeting if the action is taken by all the shareholders enti-

tled to vote on the action. The action must be evidenced by one or more written consents describing the action taken, signed by all the shareholders entitled to vote on the action, and delivered to the corporation for inclusion in the minutes or filing with the corporate records. . . .

§7.05. Notice of Meeting.

(a) A corporation shall notify shareholders of the date, time, and place of each annual and special shareholders' meeting no fewer than 10 nor more than 60 days before the meeting date. Unless this Act or the articles of incorporation require otherwise, the corporation is required to give notice only to shareholders entitled to vote at the meeting.

(b) Unless this Act or the articles of incorporation require otherwise, notice of an annual meeting need not include a description of the purpose or purposes for which the meeting is called.

(c) Notice of a special meeting must include a description of the purpose or purposes for which the meeting is called. . . .

§7.06. Waiver of Notice.

(a) A shareholder may waive any notice required by this Act, the articles of incorporation, or bylaws before or after the date and time stated in the notice. The waiver must be in writing, be signed by the shareholder entitled to the notice, and be delivered to the corporation for inclusion in the minutes or filing with the corporate records.

(b) A shareholder's attendance at a meeting:

(1) waives objection to lack of notice or defective notice of the meeting, unless the shareholder at the beginning of the meeting objects to holding the meeting or transacting business at the meeting;

(2) waives objection to consideration of a particular matter at the meeting that is not within the purpose or purposes described in the meeting notice, unless the shareholder objects to considering the matter when it is presented. . . .

§7.20. Shareholders' List for Meeting. . . .

(b) The shareholders' list must be available for inspection by any shareholder, beginning two business days after notice of the meeting is given for which the list was prepared and continuing through the meeting, at the corporation's principal office or at a place identified in the meeting notice in the city where the meeting will be held. A shareholder, his agent, or attorney is entitled on written demand to inspect and, subject to the requirements of section 16.02(c), to copy the list, during regular business hours and at his expense, during the period it is available for inspection.

(c) The corporation shall make the shareholders' list available at the meeting, and any shareholder, his agent, or attorney is entitled to inspect the list at any time during the meeting or any adjournment. . . .

§7.22. Proxies.

(a) A shareholder may vote his shares in person or by proxy.

(b) A shareholder may appoint a proxy to vote or otherwise act for him by signing an appointment form, either personally or by his attorney-in-fact.

(c) An appointment of a proxy is effective when received by the secretary or other officer or agent authorized to tabulate votes. An appointment is valid for 11 months unless a longer period is expressly provided in the appointment form.

(d) An appointment of a proxy is revocable by the shareholder unless the appointment form conspicuously states that it is irrevocable and the appointment is coupled with an interest. . . .

§7.25. Quorum and Voting Requirements for Voting Groups.

(a) Shares entitled to vote as a separate voting group may take action on a matter at a meeting only if a quorum of those shares exists with respect to that matter. Unless the articles of incorporation or this Act provides otherwise, a majority of the votes entitled to be cast on the matter by the voting group constitutes a quorum of that voting group for action on that matter.

(b) Once a share is represented for any purpose at a meeting, it is deemed present for quorum purposes for the remainder of the meeting and for any adjournment of that meeting unless a new record date is or must be set for that adjourned meeting. . . .

§7.27. Greater Quorum or Voting Requirements.

(a) The articles of incorporation may provide for a greater quorum or voting requirement for shareholders (or voting groups of shareholders) than is provided for by this Act. . . .

§7.28. Voting for Directors; Cumulative Voting.

(a) Unless otherwise provided in the articles of incorporation, directors are elected by a plurality of the votes cast by the shares entitled to vote in the election at a meeting at which a quorum is present.

(b) Shareholders do not have a right to cumulate their votes for directors unless the articles of incorporation so provide. . . .

§7.30. Voting Trusts.

(a) One or more shareholders may create a voting trust, conferring on a trustee the right to vote or otherwise act for them, by signing an agreement setting out the provisions of the trust (which may include anything consistent with its purpose) and transferring their shares to the trustee. When a voting trust agreement is signed, the trustee shall prepare a list of the names and addresses of all owners of beneficial interests in the trust, together with the number, and class of shares each transferred to the trust, and deliver copies of the list and agreement to the corporation's principal office. . . .

§8.01. Requirement for and Duties of Board of Directors.

(a) Except as provided in subsection (c), each corporation must have a board of directors.

(b) All corporate powers shall be exercised by or under the authority of, and the business and affairs of the corporation managed under the direction of, its board of directors, subject to any limitation set forth in the articles of incorporation.

(c) A corporation having 50 or fewer shareholders may dispense with or limit the authority of a board of directors by describing in its articles of incorporation who will perform some or all of the duties of a board of directors. . . .

§8.03. Number and Election of Directors.

(a) A board of directors must consist of one or more individuals, with the number specified in or fixed in accordance with the articles of incorporation or bylaws. . . .

(d) Directors are elected at the first annual shareholders' meeting and at each annual meeting thereafter unless their terms are staggered under section 8.06. . . .

§8.08. Removal of Directors by Shareholders.

(a) The shareholders may remove one or more directors with or without cause unless the articles of incorporation provide that directors may be removed only for cause. . . .

§8.10. Vacancy on Board.

(a) Unless the articles of incorporation provide otherwise, if a vacancy occurs on a board of directors, including a vacancy resulting from an increase in the number of directors:

(1) the shareholders may fill the vacancy;

(2) the board of directors may fill the vacancy; or

(3) if the directors remaining in office constitute fewer than a quorum of the board, they may fill the vacancy by the affirmative vote of a majority of all the directors remaining in office. . . .

§8.11. Compensation of Directors.
Unless the articles of incorporation or bylaws provide otherwise, the board of directors may fix the compensation of directors.

§8.20. Meetings.

(a) The board of directors may hold regular or special meetings in or out of this state.

(b) Unless the articles of incorporation or bylaws provide otherwise, the board of directors may permit any or all directors to participate in a regular or special meeting by, or conduct the meeting through the use of, any means of communication by which all directors participating may simultaneously hear each other during the meeting. A director participating in a meeting by this means is deemed to be present in person at the meeting.

§8.21. Action Without Meeting.

(a) Unless the articles of incorporation or bylaws provide otherwise, action required or permitted by this Act to be taken at a board of directors' meeting may be taken without a meeting if the action is taken by all members of the board. The action must be evidenced by one or more written consents describing the action taken, signed by each director, and included in the minutes or filed with the corporate records reflecting the action taken.

(b) Action taken under this section is effective when the last director signs the consent, unless the consent specifies a different effective date.

(c) A consent signed under this section has the effect of a meeting vote and may be described as such in any document. . . .

§8.23. Waiver of Notice.

(a) A director may waive any notice required by this Act, the articles of incorporation, or bylaws before or after the date and time stated in the notice. Except as provided by subsection (b), the waiver must be in writing, signed by the director entitled to the notice, and filed with the minutes or corporate records.

(b) A director's attendance at or participation in a meeting waives any required notice to him of the meeting unless the director at the beginning of the meeting (or promptly upon his arrival) objects to holding the meeting or transacting business at the meeting and does not thereafter vote for or assent to action taken at the meeting.

§8.24. Quorum and Voting.

(a) Unless the articles of incorporation or bylaws require a greater number, a quorum of a board of directors consists of:

(1) a majority of the fixed number of directors if the corporation has a fixed board size: . . .

§8.30. General Standards for Directors.

(a) A director shall discharge his duties as a director, including his duties as a member of a committee:

(1) in good faith;
(2) with the care an ordinarily prudent person in a like position would exercise under similar circumstances; and
(3) in a manner he reasonably believes to be in the best interests of the corporation.

(b) In discharging his duties a director is entitled to rely on information, opinions, reports, or statements, including financial statements and other financial data, if prepared or presented by:

(1) one or more officers or employees of the corporation whom the director reasonably believes to be reliable and competent in the matters presented;

(2) legal counsel, public accountants, or other persons as to matters the director reasonably believes are within the person's professional or expert competence; or

(3) a committee of the board of directors of which he is not a member if the director reasonably believes the committee merits confidence.

(c) A director is not acting in good faith if he has knowledge concerning the matter in question that makes reliance otherwise permitted by subsection (b) unwarranted.

(d) A director is not liable for any action taken as a director, or any failure to take any action, if he performed the duties of his office in compliance with this section.

§8.31. Director Conflict of Interest.

(a) A conflict of interest transaction is a transaction with the corporation in which a director of the corporation has a direct or indirect interest. A conflict of interest transaction is not voidable by the corporation solely because of the director's interest in the transaction if any one of the following is true:

(1) the material facts of the transaction and the director's interest were disclosed or known to the board of directors or a committee of the board of directors and the board of directors or committee authorized, approved, or ratified the transaction;

(2) the material facts of the transaction and the director's interest were disclosed or known to the shareholders entitled to vote and they authorized, approved, or ratified the transaction; or

(3) the transaction was fair to the corporation. . . .

§8.33. Liability for Unlawful Distributions.

(a) Unless he complies with the applicable standards of conduct described in section 8.30, a director who votes for or assents to a distribution made in violation of this Act or the articles of incorporation is personally liable to the corporation for the amount of the distribution that exceeds what could have been distributed without violating this Act or the articles of incorporation.

(b) A director held liable for an unlawful distribution under subsection (a) is entitled to contribution:

(1) from every other director who voted for or assented to the distribution without complying with the applicable standards of conduct described in section 8.30; and

(2) from each shareholder for the amount the shareholder accepted knowing the distribution was made in violation of this Act or the articles of incorporation.

§8.40. Required Officers.

(a) A corporation has the officers described in its bylaws or appointed by the board of directors in accordance with the bylaws. . . .

§8.41. Duties of Officers.
Each officer has the authority and shall perform the duties set forth in the bylaws or, to the extent consistent with the bylaws, the duties prescribed by the board of directors or by direction of an officer authorized by the board of directors to prescribe the duties of other officers.

§8.42. Standards of Conduct for Officers [*See Section 8.30. Same standards.*]

§8.43. Resignation and Removal of Officers.

(a) An officer may resign at any time by delivering notice to the corporation.

(b) A board of directors may remove any officer at any time with or without cause. . . .

§10.01. Authority to Amend Articles of Incorporation.

(a) A corporation may amend its articles of incorporation at any time. . . .

§10.03. Amendment by Board of Directors and Shareholders.

(a) A corporation's board of directors may propose one or more amendments to the articles of incorporation for submission to the shareholders.

(b) For the amendment to be adopted:

(1) the board of directors must recommend the amendment to the shareholders unless the board of directors determines that because of conflict of interest or other special circumstances it should make no recommendation and communicates the basis for its determination to the shareholders with the amendment; and

(2) the shareholders entitled to vote on the amendment must approve the amendment as provided in subsection (e). . . .

§10.20. Amendment of Bylaws by Board of Directors or Shareholders.

(a) A corporation's board of directors may amend or repeal the corporation's bylaws unless:

(1) the articles of incorporation or this Act reserve this power exclusively to the shareholders in whole or part; or

(2) the shareholders in amending or repealing a particular bylaw provide expressly that the board of directors may not amend or repeal that bylaw.

(b) A corporation's shareholders may amend or repeal the corporation's bylaws even though the bylaws may also be amended or repealed by its board of directors. . . .

§11.03. Action on Plan.

(a) After adopting a plan of merger or share exchange, the board of directors of each corporation party to the merger, and the board of directors of the corporation whose shares will be acquired in the share exchange, shall submit the plan of merger . . . for approval by its shareholders.

(b) For a plan of merger or share exchange to be approved:

(1) the board of directors must recommend the plan of merger or share exchange to the shareholders, unless the board of directors determines that because of conflict of interest or other special circumstances it should make no recommendation and communicates the basis for its determination to the shareholders with the plan; and

(2) the shareholders entitled to vote must approve the plan. . . .

§11.04. Merger of Subsidiary.

(a) A parent corporation owning at least 90 percent of the outstanding shares of each class of a subsidiary corporation may merge the subsidiary into itself without approval of the shareholders of the parent or subsidiary. . . .

§12.01. Sale of Assets in Regular Course of Business and Mortgage of Assets.

(a) A corporation may, on the terms and conditions and for the consideration determined by the board of directors:

(1) sell, lease, exchange, or otherwise dispose of all, or substantially all, of its property in the usual and regular course of business; . . .

(b) Unless the articles of incorporation require it, approval by the shareholders of a transaction described in subsection (a) is not required.

§12.02. Sale of Assets Other than in Regular Course of Business.

(a) A corporation may sell, lease, exchange, or otherwise dispose of all, or substantially all, of its property (with or without the goodwill), otherwise than in the usual and regular course of business, on the terms and conditions and for the consideration determined by the corporation's board of directors, if the board of directors proposes and its shareholders approve the proposed transaction.

(b) For a transaction to be authorized:

(1) the board of directors must recommend the proposed transaction to the shareholders unless the board of directors determines that because of conflict of interest or other special circumstances it should make no recommendation and communicates the basis for its de-

termination to the shareholders with the submission of the proposed transaction; and

(2) the shareholders entitled to vote must approve the transaction. . . .

§14.02. Dissolution by Board of Directors and Shareholders.

(a) A corporation's board of directors may propose dissolution for submission to the shareholders.

(b) For a proposal to dissolve to be adopted:

(1) the board of directors must recommend dissolution to the shareholders unless the board of directors determines that because of conflict of interest or other special circumstances it should make no recommendation and communicates the basis for its determination to the shareholders; and

(2) the shareholders entitled to vote must approve the proposal to dissolve as provided in subsection (e). . . .

§16.01. Corporate Records.

(a) A corporation shall keep as permanent records minutes of all meetings of its shareholders and board of directors, a record of all actions taken by the shareholders or board of directors without a meeting, and a record of all actions taken by a committee of the board of directors in place of the board of directors on behalf of the corporation. . . .

§16.02. Inspection of Records by Shareholders.

(a) A shareholder of a corporation is entitled to inspect and copy, during regular business hours at the corporation's principal office, any of the records of the corporation described in section 16.01(e) if he gives the corporation written notice of his demand at least five business days before the date on which he wishes to inspect and copy.

(b) a shareholder of a corporation is entitled to inspect and copy, during regular business hours at a reasonable location specified by the corporation, any of the following records of the corporation if the shareholder meets the requirements of subsection (c) and gives the corporation written notice of his demand at least five business days before the date on which he wishes to inspect and copy: . . .

§16.03. Scope of Inspection Right.

(a) A shareholder's agent or attorney has the same inspection and copying rights as the shareholder he represents.

(b) The right to copy records under section 16.02 includes, if reasonable, the right to receive copies made by photographic, xerographic, or other means.

(c) The corporation may impose a reasonable charge, covering the costs of labor and material, for copies of any documents provided to the shareholder. The charge may not exceed the estimated cost of production or reproduction of the records. . . .

Glossary

A fortiori—With a stronger reason; much more (Latin). A term used to emphasize that because one fact exists, another must logically be true.

A priori—A method of reasoning that starts with general principles and attempts to find specific facts that will flow from them (Latin).

Acceleration clause—A statement in a time instrument that permits the instrument to become due immediately upon the occurrence of some specified event.

Acceptance—The receipt and retention of that which is offered; the assent to a legal offer that is a prerequisite to the formation of a contract.

Acceptor—A person who has agreed to accept a draft.

Accession—The obtaining of a right or an office; the acquisition of property by its addition or incorporation with other property already owned.

Accommodation paper—A note signed by another as a favor without consideration passing between the individuals.

Accommodation party—A person who signs an instrument in any capacity for the purpose of lending his or her name and credit to another party to the instrument.

Acknowledgment—A declaration before a notary that the executor of a document executed such of his or her own free will.

Act of state doctrine—A policy whereby a court agrees to recognize the act of a foreign government, taken in its territory, as valid and causing the court (of another country) not to question the validity of that foreign government's action.

Actionable—Furnishing a basis or legal reason for a lawsuit.

Ad valorem—According to its value (Latin). For example, an *ad valorem* tax will generate revenues based on the percentage value of the item taxed as opposed to a fixed or specific tax, which is imposed regardless of value.

Adjudication—The pronouncing of a formal judgment by a court for one party or the other in a lawsuit.

Administrative agency—Governmental department created by Congress or executive order to regulate some specialized aspect of interstate commerce (e.g., Federal Trade Commission).

Administrative law judge (Hearing examiner)—Officer who presides at initial hearing on matters litigated before a federal agency. He or she is chosen by civil service exam and is independent of the agency staff.

Administrative Procedure Act—A statute setting forth the procedural rules for U.S. regulatory agencies and for parties appearing before such agencies.

Adversary principle—The principle that places the responsibility for developing or defending a case upon the parties and not on some designated legal official.

Adverse possession—Method of acquiring title to real property by occupying property in an open and notorious manner for a statutory period, thus denying title or ownership to anyone else.

Advisory opinion—A formal opinion rendered by a judge or a court on a question of law submitted by the legislative or executive branch; such an opinion will not usually arise out of an adversary proceeding or lawsuit.

Affidavit—A written statement of facts that a person has sworn to before someone qualified to take an oath.

Affirm—To confirm or agree with. A higher court affirms a lower court decision when it declares the decision valid.

Affirmative action—A process by which the public and private sectors are required by executive orders, regulations, and court decisions to take steps to remedy past discrimination in the hiring and promotion of minorities and women.

Affirmative defense—A part of defendant's answer to plaintiff's complaint; sets out new arguments showing why defendant should win even if everything in the complaint is true.

After-acquired property—Property that becomes the subject of a security interest after the parties have made a security agreement.

Agency—A legal relationship in which one person is authorized to act for another, who is called a principal.

Agent—A person authorized to act for another in a legal relationship.

Allonge—A paper firmly attached to an instrument on which indorsements are written.

Altruism, ethical—Giving primacy to the interests of others in one's decisions. The opposite of egoism.

Amend—To revise or correct. For example, the proposed equal rights amendment (ERA) is an attempt to correct past discriminatory patterns against women.

Amicus curiae—Friend of the court (Latin). A person who is not a direct party to the proceeding but, with the permission of the court, is allowed to file a brief and often participate in oral argument on appeal.

Ancilliary—A subordinate or attendant to the main proceeding or process. For example, *ancilliary* administration is a proceeding in a state where a deceased person may have property but did not live there, and thus his or her main estate is not administered there.

Annual percentage—The actual cost of borrowing money for a stated period expressed in yearly terms. Required by federal statute to make it easier for people to understand the terms of a credit agreement and compare rates charged by financial institutions.

Annuity contract—A contract that pays a specific sum to the insured at periodic intervals after the insured reaches a specified age.

Anticipatory breach—A breach of an agreement prior to the duty of performance. Words or actions showing an intention to refuse performance in the future are grounds for immediate suit by a party without waiting for the time of performance.

Apparent authority—The authority of an agent that seems superficially true to a third party because of the words or conduct of such agent in representing his or her principal, and the latter's acquiescence in these representations.

Appeal—A process by which a party asks a higher court to review alleged errors of law made by a lower court or federal-state agency. In the case of new facts that develop following a lower court decision, an appellate court may also be requested to review the decision with the purpose of obtaining a new trial. Appeals from regulatory agencies may also be based on abuse of discretion or arbitrary judgment.

Appellant—The party to a suit who appeals a case to a higher court. Usually the party who loses in a lower court is the one who will appeal. The party who wins below will sometimes appeal, asking for a greater recovery or modification of a court order.

Appellee—The party to a suit against whom an appeal may be brought. This person is usually, but not always, the winner in the court below.

Appurtenance—Something adjoined or attached to a principal. For example, a house or barn is an *appurtenance* to land.

Arbitration—The process of submitting a dispute to an independent expert for decision. This takes place outside the formal court system and is based on an agreement between the parties to the dispute that they will accept the outcome of the process.

Arguendi—"In the course of argument" (Latin). Usually applies to a statement made by a judge, referee, or arbitrator as a matter of illustration but having no direct bearing on the case in dispute.

Assault—An intentional *tort* or *crime* in which force or movement could put the person approached in reasonable fear of bodily harm or contact.

Assignee—A person to whom an assignment has been made. Also called a *grantee*.

Assignment—The process of transferring rights in real or personal property to another person. Such rights are commonly called *choses in action*. For example, *A* sells and assigns his contract right to *C*, to be paid money by *B*. *A* is the assignor, *C* is the assignee.

Assignor—A person who makes an assignment. Also referred to as a *grantor*.

Attachment—The process of bringing property or persons within the jurisdiction of the court by seizing one or both. For example, one may *attach* a bank account in order to be sure that a person pays a debt owed.

Attest—To bear witness to a fact; to act as a witness to a fact.

Automated teller machine—A machine that enables the user to withdraw cash, make deposits, transfer money from one account to another, and carry on other similar transactions with a bank.

Bailee—The person to whom personal property is delivered by a bailor under a contract of bailment.

Bailment—The delivery of personal property by owner to bailee in trust for a specific purpose. Delivery takes place as a result of an expressed or implied agreement between the parties.

Bailor—The person who initiates a contract of bailment and delivers the personal property to the bailee.

Bankruptcy—The process by which a person who is unable to pay his, her, or its (corporation) debts is declared a bankrupt, has its nonexempt debts distributed by a bankruptcy court, and thereafter is released from claims on any balance due to creditors. Bankruptcy is not *insolvency*.

Bargain and sale deed—A deed that conveys title but makes no warranties.

Battery—An intentional physical contact by one individual (or through a thing in the control of that person) with another individual. Can be a basis for criminal and/or tort action.

Bearer—A person possessing a negotiable instrument (e.g., a check) that is payable to any individual and does not specifically designate a payee. The instrument may be made "payable to bearer" or indorsed in blank.

Bearer paper—An instrument that is payable to bearer.

Beneficiary—A person who receives benefit from an insurance policy as a payee, who benefits from a trust, or who inherits under a will. *Creditor beneficiary* is one who is not a direct party to an agreement between a promisor and promisee but receives performance because the promisee wishes to discharge a debt to him or her. A *donee beneficiary* is one who is also not a party to the original agreement but receives benefit from the agreement as a gift (e.g., life insurance policy designated for a child upon the death of parents).

Bequeath—To give personal property to another by a will.

Bid—A legal offer for property at an auction.

Bilateral contract—An agreement in which the oral or written promises of the parties serve as consideration for each other's promises.

Bill of complaints—A formal written declaration of bases for a plaintiff's action against a defendant in a court proceeding.

Bill of lading—A document of title or acknowledgment evidencing receipt of particular goods on board a ship (or by whomever is transporting the goods); the bill of lading also serves to note that the goods were in good order and fit for shipment.

Binder—A document that commits an insurance company prior to a policy being issued.

Blank indorsement—An indorsement that does not specify a particular payee.

"Blue Sky" laws—A common or popular term for state and federal statutes that regulate the sale of securities. These laws seek to protect investors from fraudulent or unethical promoters of investment schemes.

Boiler plate—A standard form contract, or clause in a contract, that is not drafted for the particular client but is generally issued (e.g., insurance contracts and clauses therein).

Bona fide—In good faith (Latin).

Boycott—A conspiracy on the part of individuals, unions, or firms to refuse to do business with someone else, or to prevent others from doing business with, or employing, others.

Bribe—Payment or offer of payment of something of value in return for a breach of duty.

Brief—A written summary for an appellate court setting forth facts, issues, and points of law argued by counsel in a lower court. Also students use a *brief* of a case as a way of summarizing a long published case and thus preparing for class.

Broker—1. A person who carries on negotiations and makes contracts for a principal. 2. A person who buys and sells securities on behalf of a third party.

Bulk transfer—A sale or transfer of major part of the inventory of a business at one particular time, such sale not ordinarily carried on in daily business.

Burden of proof—The process in a lawsuit by which one party has the duty of proving the facts in dispute.

Bylaws—The internal self-made regulations of a corporation adopted for the purpose of governing the company's internal management. Nonprofit organizations and other business associations also have bylaws.

C.I.F.—Shipping agreement in which seller agrees to pay insurance and freight as well as cost of goods.

C.O.D.—Cash on delivery. The buyer must pay for the goods upon receipt before opening goods.

Capacity—The ability or competency to do something at law. For example, a child is capable of entering a contract depending on his or her age; a person is capable of committing a crime depending on his or her state of mind at the time of commission.

Cash dispenser—A machine that dispenses cash.

Cash surrender value—The amount of money that a whole life insurance is worth if surrendered to the company prior to the death of the insured.

Casualty insurance—Insurance that protects the insured from loss due to damage or destruction of personal property by causes other than fire or elements.

Causa mortis gift—A gift given by a living person in contemplation of approaching death.

Cause of action—When a person's legal rights have been invaded, the facts showing that invasion constitutes a *cause of action* and are usually set out in a complaint. The failure to set out these facts by the plaintiff will lead to a motion for dismissal of the case by the defendant, alleging that the plaintiff has failed to state a cause of action.

Caveat emptor—Let the buyer beware (Latin). This idea at common law expressed the view that the buyer could not depend on the seller for any warranties after sale and thus should be careful in making his or her purchase.

Caveat venditor—Let the seller beware (Latin). Present-day maxim that, considering the amount of consumer action legislation and the number of pro-consumer court decisions, it is the seller who should be careful to whom he, she, or it sells.

Cease and desist order—An order by a court or administrative agency requiring an individual or a corporation to stop carrying on a particular act.

Certificate of title—A written opinion by a lawyer that a title to property is valid.

Certification—An acceptance by a bank of a check; it guarantees that the bank will pay the check when it is presented.

Certiorari—The process by which an appellate court exercises discretionary authority to hear appeals.

Chattel mortgage—A transfer of a right in personal property or a lien on such that serves as security for payment of a debt or performance of a promised act.

Chattels—Personal property.

Check—A bank draft that is payable on demand.

Chose in action—A personal right of an owner to recover in a legal action things owned by him or her but not in her possession.

Code of Professional Responsibility—Rules governing the practice of law; drafted by the American Bar Association and adopted by the chief governing authority of each state bar.

Codicil—An addition to a person's will modifying, altering, or revoking provisions.

Collateral action—An attempt to avoid or evade a judicial proceeding or order by instituting a proceeding in another court attacking such.

Common carrier—One who transports goods (e.g., train) or services (e.g., telephone) for hire to the public and is regulated by federal and/or state agencies who insure that the public convenience and necessity are served.

Common law—A law derived from the published opinions of appellate courts as contrasted with law derived from statute.

Compensatory damages—A term used to denote damages that compensate the injured party for the injury suffered and nothing more.

Competent—Describes one who is capable at law. *See* capacity.

Complainant—A person who asks a court of law for redress of an injury allegedly suffered.

Composition—A legal agreement made between a debtor and several creditors whereby the latter agree to accept less from the debtor on a *pro rata* basis in satisfaction of all debts.

Conciliation—An informal method of bringing together parties to a dispute to settle differences before going to court.

Concur—To agree. With reference to appellate court decisions a "concurring opinion" is often written by a judge who may agree with the majority opinion's conclusion, but for differing reasons; thus he or she writes a separate opinion.

Conditional acceptance—A statement by the offeree to a bargain that he or she will enter into an agreement that differs from the original offer. In effect a *conditional acceptance* constitutes a counteroffer as to personal and real property. Often used to qualify or limit offeree's liability on bills of exchange.

Conditional sale—The sale of goods in which buyer obtains possession but seller retains title until the purchase price is paid.

Confession of judgment—The process by which a debtor agrees to submit to the jurisdiction of a court, and the judgment of such court, without extended legal proceedings, in the event that he or she breaches an agreement.

Conflict of interest—When one has a personal interest that contrasts with a duty owed to another; mutually exclusive duties to two or more entities.

Consequential damages—Damages that do not flow directly from the acts of a party (e.g., breach of contract) but only indirectly.

Consignment—1. The delivery of goods to a seller to be sold for the owner's account. 2. Delivery of goods to a common carrier to be shipped as directed by the owner.

Constructive fraud—Acts or omissions that, though having no intent to deceive, by their nature mislead an individual, corporation, or the public at large.

Constructive notice—A legal presumption that a person has knowledge of certain facts.

Consumer-credit contract—A contract for the sale of consumer goods on an installment basis.

Contempt citation—An order issued by a judge holding a person for incarceration following the individual's affront to the judge or his or her attempts to obstruct the court processes.

Conversion—The taking and keeping of personal property or goods without an owner's consent.

Corporate moral accountability—The concept that a corporation, as an independent entity, can be morally accountable for its actions.

Cost-benefit analysis—A measurement technique by which one adds up the total cost of implementation of a regulation(s), then compares it to the benefits accrued to both private and public parties.

Counterclaim—A claim by the defendant in opposition to plaintiff's claim that, if proved true, would tend to diminish, alter, or defeat plaintiff's action.

Counteroffer—An offer made by the offeree to the offeror that would materially alter the original offer and thus demand acceptance by the offeror.

Cover—A remedy for buyer under the Uniform Commercial Code that allows the buyer in good faith to purchase, or make a contract to purchase, goods in substitution for those seller has not been able to deliver.

Credit insurance—Protects both the creditor and the debtor by providing for the payment of an indebtedness of the insured in the event of death before the indebtedness has been paid.

Cross-appeal—A term used to denote a situation where both parties appeal from a lower court decision. Their appeals are said to "cross" each other.

Cross-examination—The examination of a witness provided by the opposition in a civil or criminal trial.

Curtesy—The estate at common law that a husband has in the estate of his wife upon her death.

Custodial account—An account in which one person holds property and uses it for the benefit of another; the person for whom the property is to be used is generally regarded as its owner for tax purposes.

De facto—What has happened *in fact* as opposed to what was ordered or may be ordered at law (Latin).

De jure—An action is taken by *right* or by *law* (Latin).

Debenture—An instrument issued as evidence of unsecured debt. A debenture is usually made payable to bearer with interest to be paid (e.g., a corporate bond).

Debtor—One who is under an obligation to pay a sum of money to another.

Decedent—A deceased person.

Deceit—A fraudulent mispresentation, or device by which one person tricks another who is ignorant of or does not have full knowledge of the facts.

Declaratory judgment—An order of the court that renders an opinion on a question of law but does not order the parties to do any specific act.

Decree—An order of a court in equity determining the rights of both parties.

Deed—An instrument that transfers title to real estate.

Deed of trust—An instrument that conveys title to real estate to a trustee, who holds title as security for a debt owed to a lender who is the beneficiary of the trust.

Default—A failure on the part of a party to perform a legal obligation. For example, the failure of a party to appear to defend against a claim brought against him may result in a *default judgment*.

Defeasible—A term that refers to the capability of title for real property to be revoked.

Defendant—A party who is being sued in a civil action or accused of a crime in a criminal matter.

Defendant in error—A party who receives a favorable judgment in a lower court, which *plaintiff in error* now seeks to reverse.

Delegable duties—Contractual obligations that may be performed by a person who was not a party to the original contract.

Delegatee—A person to whom a *delegator* transfers rights and duties.

Delegation—The process of transferring or assigning authority from one person to another.

Delegator—The person who is responsible for transferring rights and duties.

Demurrer—The equivalent of a motion by defendant to dismiss, because even admitting the facts stated in plaintiff's complaint, they are insufficient for plaintiff to proceed on, and serve as no basis for defendant to form an answer.

Deontology—Concepts of duty that serve as guidelines for moral behavior.

Deposition—The process by which testimony of witnesses is taken in writing prior to a trial for use in the actual court action. The basis for this process may be by court order or statutory rules of procedure.

Depositary bank—The bank in which an instrument is first deposited for purpose of collection.

Derivative action—A suit by shareholder(s) of a corporation to force the corporation to enforce shareholders' rights against a third party (often an officer of the company).

Descent—A term used to denote a receiving of real property by inheritance.

Detriment (legal)—A term used to show a loss or harm suffered to real or personal property or the giving up of a right to take action.

Direct investment—Situation in which an investor participates in the management of a firm in which investment has been made.

Directed verdict—A verdict that the court instructs the jury to bring back, such as a verdict in favor of one party because reasonable minds could not differ as to the facts. This verdict usually results from a motion on the part of counsel for either party in a trial but can be granted by the judge alone as well.

Disability insurance—Provides income to persons too ill or injured to continue to work.

Disaffirm—To revoke or repudiate. For example, an infant may *disaffirm* a contract prior to reaching the age of majority, or within a reasonable time thereafter.

Discharge—To release a party from obligations set forth in a contract. Also, a term used in bankruptcy to denote a release from all obligations. Used after a person is adjudicated a bankrupt.

Disclaimer—A refusal or rejection. For example, a *disclaimer* clause in a contract notes the promises or warranties that will be given and disclaims all other responsibilities or warranties.

Discovery—The pretrial process by which parties to a suit disclose to each other relevant facts that are necessary for framing the issues, correcting them, and expediting trial procedure.

Dishonor—The refusal to pay or accept a negotiable instrument upon presentation for acceptance.

Dismiss—A term used to show a discharge of a cause of action. A *motion* for *dismissal* can be made by either party and will be ruled on by the judge.

Disparagement—The act of discrediting. For example, the tort of disparagement is a basis for a claim for damages when a business can show that a competitor has with intent injured the reputation and product of the business.

Dissolution—A cancellation or breaking up by mutual agreement. For example, the dissolution of a marriage contract.

Distribution—The division of personal property of a person who dies without a will; often also applied to the division of real property of a person who dies without a will.

Diversity of citizenship—One of the bases of jurisdiction for the federal courts; that is, when parties to a suit are citizens from different states.

Document of title to personal property—Any document that in the regular course of business financing is treated as adequately evidencing that the person in possession of it is entitled to receive, hold, and dispose of the document and the goods it covers. To be a document of title, the document must purport to be issued by or addressed to a bailee and purport to cover goods in the bailee's possession, which are either identified or are fungible portions of an identified mass.

Documentary draft—A draft used with an attached bill of lading.

Domain—The absolute and complete ownership of real property. For example, the right of *eminent domain* relates to the primary power of the legislature to control private property when it uses such for public purposes and compensates the owners.

Dominion—The perfect ownership or power over something.

Dower—The right of a wife to the real property of her husband as set forth by state statute.

Draft—A written order to pay money to another on demand or at a stated date.

Drawee—The individual to whom a bill of exchange is addressed and to whom a request for payment is made by a *drawer*.

Drawee bank—A bank that a check or draft is drawn on and that is ordered to pay the instrument when it is presented.

Drawer—The person who draws a bill of exchange.

Due-on-sale clause—A clause in a mortgage allowing the lender to treat sale of the property by the owner as a default.

Due process—Fundamental fairness in the administration of justice.

Duress—An unlawful restraint placed on an individual by another. It does not have to be the use of physical force; it may be any form of coercion that leads an individual to an act contrary to his or her free will.

Duty based ethics—Ethical theories based on principles of duty derived through religion, logic, or some conception of natural law.

Easement—The right of an individual to use the land of another for a limited purpose without obtaining possession or title.

Egoism—Acting solely to maximize one's self-interest.

Egoism, ethical—The idea that everyone has the right to act in his or her own self-interest and that it is the job of the government to place any restrictions on behavior.

Egoism, psychological—The idea that humans are incapable of considering the interests of others in their decisions.

Electronic fund transfer—Any transfer of funds, other than a transaction originated by check draft or similar paper instrument, that is initiated through an electronic terminal, telephonic instrument, computer, or magnetic tape so as to order, instruct, or authorize a financial institution to debit or credit an account.

Embezzlement—Fraudulently taking money or property of another by a person to whom it has been entrusted.

Endorsement—*See* Indorsement.

Entrustment—Leaving goods temporarily in the hands of a third party.

Equalitarism—A theory of social justice based on the premise that everyone should be treated equally.

Equitable estoppel—A term that refers to the inability of an individual based on justice and fairness (equity) to assert legal rights, especially when another individual has been induced to act based on conduct or silence of the former's representation.

Equity—A legal system that developed in England. Today *equity* is used to denote fairness and justice as opposed to statutory or case law as a basis for decisions.

Error of law—Drawing incorrect conclusions of law from known and existing facts. Refers to the basis for appeals from lower courts to appellate courts.

Escheat—A reversion of property rights to the state when there is no individual competent to inherit.

Estate—The interest that anyone has in land. An *estate for life* denotes an interest in land that an individual has for his or her life or the life of another.

Estate administration—The process by which property is transferred from a decedent's estate to those entitled to receive it.

Estate planning—The process of planning for the future distribution of a person's property or estate.

Estate taxes—Taxes due to the government for the transfer of property at death; calculated on the value of the decedent's estate minus applicable exemptions.

Ethics—Standards of behavior based on personal values and external standards. Ethics are principles reflecting what is good or bad and what is acceptable to one's self and to others.

Ex delicto—From a tort or fault (Latin). Refers to a legal action arising out of fault, misconduct, or malfeasance.

Exculpatory—Clearing someone from guilt or excusing a party to a contract from doing something. For example, an *exculpatory clause* may excuse the seller from some warranties on the product sold.

Executed—Denoting a form of contract that has been completely performed and is now in effect.

Execution—The process of completing or carrying out something.

Executor—A man appointed by the deceased to carry out his or her directions as set out in a will.

Executory—Not yet completed because acts are incomplete.

Executrix—A woman appointed by a testator to carry out the terms of his or her will.

Exemplary damages—Damages granted to an injured party to compensate her or him for mental anguish and shame when it is shown that wrong was done with malice or wanton conduct. Often called *punitive damages*.

Exhaustion of administrative remedies—A legal doctrine that requires a party to seek all remedies within an administrative agency or entity if provided for by statute before requesting assistance from a court of law.

Express warranty—A guarantee created by a seller by an afffirmation of fact, a description, a sample, or a model.

Expressed authority—Authority given in writing or by words, as opposed to that given by implication from a principal to an agent.

Expropriation—The taking of another's property, by a private party or for public use by the right of eminent domain.

Extortion—Taking property from another by wrongful threat of force or violence.

Extraterritorial laws—Laws of a nation that have effect beyond its own territory or boundary.

Extrinsic evidence—Those facts obtained from things outside an agreement. For example, the fact that an individual was or was not competent to sign an agreement is *extrinsic* to the terms of the agreement itself.

F.A.S.—The abbreviation for "free alongside ship." Denotes that seller must deliver goods to the correctly designated dock where ship is waiting to be loaded and must assume all expenses and risks up to that point.

FOB—The abbreviation for "free on board." Denotes that seller must ship and bear expenses to the point designated for delivery.

Fair market value—The price at which a willing seller and buyer will trade.

Fee simple—An estate in real property that is limited to an individual and heirs and assigns forever without any limitations on title or ownership.

Felony—A crime that is of a graver nature than a misdemeanor and is punishable by incarceration in a state or federal prison. A *felony* will always be set out by statute.

Fiduciary—A person holding a relationship of trust in which he or she acts primarily for the benefit of another in certain matters.

First instance—A trial court in which a case is first tried, as opposed to an appellate court.

Fixture—A chattel attached to real property. Generally refers to something attached to real property and intended to be permanent.

Forbearance—The giving up of a right by one party to a contract in exchange for a promise by the other.

Foreclosure—The termination of all interests or rights of the mortgagor in property covered by a mortgage.

Fraud—An intentional misrepresentation of facts relied on by another, leading to legal injury.

Full faith and credit rule—Article IV, Section 1, in the United States Constitution, which requires that each state treat as valid and enforceable where appropriate the laws of other states.

Fungible—Describing goods that are equivalent to each other in general mercantile usage; for example, wines and liquors.

Future interests—The present interest in real or personal property that gives the right to future use.

Futures contract—A contract for future delivery of goods.

Garnishee—A person holding money or property of a debtor that a creditor is trying to reach. A garnishee is served with a garnishment order.

Garnishment—The process by which a creditor obtains money or property of a debtor that is in the possession of another (garnishee).

General creditor—A creditor whose debt or claim is not secured by a lien on particular property; that is, it must be paid from the debtor's assets or estate.

General license—A license that authorizes export without application by the exporter.

Good faith—Honesty in fact and the observance of reasonable commercial standards of fair dealing.

Grand jury—A jury that hears evidence presented by the state and determines if sufficient evidence exists to indict a person for a specific crime.

Grantee—An individual to whom a grant is given. Usually refers to the deeding of land or the assignment of real property.

Grantor—An individual who is assigning or granting something.

Gratuitous promise—Promise made as part of an agreement without consideration for such promise being expected.

Guarantor—A person who signs an instrument agreeing to pay the instrument under certain circumstances.

Guaranty—A promise by an individual to answer for the debt of another in the event that the latter cannot pay.

Habeas corpus—Generally refers to any of the common law writs that bring a prisoner before a court (Latin). Used today to determine whether a prisoner was incarcerated in accordance with due process procedure.

Hearing examiner—An individual who is the chief fact finder in most federal administrative agency hearings.

Hearsay—The evidence coming not from a primary source but from an individual who has obtained such information from others, or a secondary source.

Hold harmless—A clause in an agreement in which an individual agrees to hold another party not liable and pay all claims against that party.

Holder—Anyone in possession of an instrument drawn, issued, or indorsed to him or her, to his or her order, to bearer, or in blank.

Holder in due course—An individual holder of a negotiable instrument who has taken it in good faith, for value, complete on its face, without knowledge of the instrument's being dishonored or overdue, and without notice of defect in the title. The holder must not have taken an instrument that was obviously forged, altered, irregular, or incomplete.

Holding company—A corporation that owns other companies' stock but is not responsible for their day-to-day operations.

Illusory contract—An agreement that on its face appears to be binding but in reality lacks mutuality of obligation.

Implied agency rule—A rule in contract law that implies the proper form of communication by offeree in transmitting an acceptance to an offeror, although it may not be clear from words or writings.

Implied authority—A form of authority of an agent inferred from his or her position and conduct in representing a principal. The principal will be bound in contract to a third party based on this authority unless he or she renounces such authority and communicates such to the third party.

Implied warranty—A guarantee automatically created by operation of law when goods are sold.

Impossibility—A doctrine in contract law that allows for a rescission when a contract becomes legally impossible to perform. For example, if the subject matter of an agreement is destroyed by an unforseen tornado, the defendant will plead impossibility of performance.

Impracticability—A doctrine that may allow for rescission of a contract when it becomes commercially impracticable to perform. This excuse for performance has been adopted by the Uniform Commercial Code in the event that a contingency occurs that was not planned for and that affects the complete capacity of the seller to perform.

In camera—In chambers (Latin). A court hearing that is closed to public scrutiny. Often used in cases where matters under consideration affect the national security of the country.

In pari delicto—In equal fault (Latin). Often used as a basis in tort law for joining two parties as defendants in a legal action.

In personam—Against a person (Latin). Basis for jurisdiction in a legal action to enforce rights against a specific person. For example, a suit brought against another person for injuries suffered in an automobile accident is *in personam* because it is against the driver or owner only.

In re—In the matter of (Latin). Often used in the heading of a case to denote that the suit is concerned with a thing rather than a lawsuit between two individuals directly. For example, "In re Brennan's Estate" refers to a title of a legal proceeding to dispose of property of a dead person.

In rem—Against a thing (Latin). Basis for jurisdiction in a legal action against the whole world, as opposed to in personam jurisdiction. For example, a suit to establish title to land. The winner has title against all other claimants or the whole world.

Incontestability—A term used to denote the fact that for the life of an agreement or patent it is not open to any contesting claims.

Incontestability clause—A clause providing that after the passage of a set period of time (usually one or two years) the insurer may not contest representations made by the insured.

Incorporate—To create a formal corporate entity.

Independent contractor—An individual who contracts with a principal to do work by his or her own methods, unsupervised, and not subject to any control of the principal. He or she is solely responsible for the finished work product.

Indictment—Charge by a group of sitting jurors that an individual has committed some crime punishable by incarceration in a prison.

Indorsement—The signing of the back of a negotiable instrument by a drawee, thus assigning such property to another.

Infringement—An encroachment on others' rights in violation of law. For example, the unauthorized use for profit of a patented invention is a basis for a legal action for an *infringement of patent*.

Inheritance taxes—Taxes due a state government assessed on property received from a person who has died. The amount of the tax depends on the relationship between the decedent and the inheritor and on the value of the property inherited.

Injunction—An equitable writ or order directing the defendant to stop doing an act or preventing him or her from continuing a course of conduct.

Insolvency—The inability of an individual legal entity to pay its, his, or her debts when they become due.

Insurable interest—An interest in property protected that would lead to a benefit from property owned, or a loss in case of destruction. Such an interest is usually protected by an insurance policy covering a risk.

Integrated—Describing legal writings that are considered to be final and complete as to all parties having a direct interest.

Inter alia—Among other things (Latin). Often used in pleadings and other legal documents to show that only a portion of a statute or a line of cases is cited.

Inter vivos gift—A gift given by a living person to another living person.

Inter vivos trust—A trust that is established by a person while he or she is alive and that transfers property to the trustee prior to the death of the person establishing it.

Interlocutory—Denoting decisions made by a court during a pending lawsuit; not final as to the substance of the litigation.

Intermediary bank—Any bank to which an instrument is transferred in the course of collection except the depositary bank or payor bank.

Interpleader—The process by which a third party having no ownership in held property brings two adversary claimants into court and asks the judge to decide which claimant is entitled to the property.

Interpretation—The process by which a statute or written document is given meaning.

Intestate—A legal state in which a person dies without a will.

Ipso facto—By the fact itself (Latin).

Irreparable harm—An injury that cannot be measured and for which a court remedy would be insufficient or which a court would be incapable of redressing.

Issue—The voluntary delivery of an instrument by the maker or drawer to the payee.

Joint and several—Referring to a situation in which two parties having a related obligation can be sued jointly or individually.

Joint property—Property owned by two or more persons.

Joint tenancy—An estate in which two co-owners have undivided interests; upon death of one owner his or her interest passes to the other.

Joint venture investments—Investments with two or more active participants.

Judgment debtor—A defendant who has not satisfied a judgment that has been entered against him or her.

Judicial law—Law derived from the opinions of appellate courts; also referred to as common law or case law.

Jurisdiction—The geographic area, persons, and subject matter over which a particular court has the power to make decisions.

Jurisprudence—The philosophy of law. Schools of jurisprudence include positivist, sociological, existential, and natural law.

Larceny—Taking property of another intending to deprive that person of the property or its value.

Legacy—A gift or bequest of personal property.

Legislative veto—The method by which Congress reserves to itself the right to prevent a proposed agency regulation from becoming law.

Lemon laws—State laws designed to protect the purchasers of motor vehicles.

Letter of credit—An instrument issued by a bank that requests payment to bearer or guarantees payment of financial obligation for goods sold on credit.

Levy—To collect, or to seize goods by an officer of the law.

Liability insurance—Insurance that covers losses suffered by others for which the insured is legally responsible.

Libel—A written defamation in which an individual is held up to public contempt and ridicule that injures his or her reputation.

Libertarianism—Theory of social justice that emphasizes individual freedom based on property rights and a minimal role for government.

Lien creditor—A creditor whose debt or claim is secured by a lien on particular property.

Life estate—An estate whose duration is measured by the life of the holder or some other person.

Limited partnership—A partnership of one or more general partners who manage the business and are personally responsible for partnership debts, and one or more limited partners who contribute capital, share in profits, but take no part in running the business and incur no liability for partnership obligations beyond their contribution.

Liquidated damages—A form of damages fixed as part of a contractual relationship. For example, a general contractor agrees with an owner that for every day's delay in completion of a commercial building beyond an agreed date the contractor will pay the owner $1,000 a day.

Litigant—A party to a legal action.

Litigation—A lawsuit.

Maker—A person who makes or first executes a negotiable instrument.

Mandamus—We command (Latin). A term that denotes a court order directing an officer of a private or public corporation to carry out a specified act that is within his or her power by virtue of the office held.

Material—A term describing something essential or significant. For example, a *material* alteration in a contract might be a six-month delay in delivery when the parties agree on a specific date that both knew was important to the buyer.

Material alteration—With respect to negotiable instruments, any alteration of the instrument that changes the contract of any party to the instrument.

Mechanic's lien—A claim on real property that seeks to secure priority of payment on debts owed for value of work completed and materials supplied in constructing or making improvements on debtor-owned building.

Mediation—A method of settling a dispute by bringing in a neutral third party to help resolve differences between the parties.

Mens rea—A guilty mind (Latin). A term used to show criminal intent; an essential element of a crime.

Merchantability—A term used to show the goods sold are fit for the purpose for which they are sold.

Merger guidelines—Specific U.S. Justice Department guidelines for private sector corporate mergers set forth as a warning that the Department *may* challenge companies that violate or plan to violate them. The guidelines are *not* law.

Misappropriation—The act of taking something one does not own and using it for a wrongful purpose. For example, in some states a banker may be accused of *misappropriation* of funds if he or she deals fraudulently with money entrusted to him or her.

Misdemeanor—A crime considered less serious than a felony and punishable by a fine or incarceration in an institution other than a state penitentiary for less than one year.

Misrepresentation—Words or conduct that misleads others as to the material facts of a situation. If such acts or conduct are unintentional, *innocent misrepresentation* has taken place. If done with intent and relied on by a party, and injury can be proven, fraud has been committed.

Mistake—An unintentional act or omission of law or fact. A *bilateral* or *mutual mistake* is an error made by both parties; if material to a contract, it will be grounds for rescission or reformation. A *unilateral mistake* is an error made by a single party and is not usually grounds for rescission.

Mistrial—A fundamental error in procedure that causes a trial judge to end and cancel out the proceedings of a trial. This is done usually without prejudice to a new trial's taking place. For example, an error in selection of jurors may be a basis for *mistrial.*

Mitigation of damages—A lowering or abatement of injury from a wrongful act.

Monopoly—A market structure in which a single seller (monopolist) has virtually complete control over the source of goods as well as the means of production. The monopolist is the sole influence on the price variable in this market.

Mortgage—A contract or conveyance of a lien on real property by a debtor to a creditor to secure the payment of an obligation by the debtor.

Mortgagee—An individual who receives or takes a mortgage, for example, a financial institution.

Mortgagor—The debtor who gives a mortgage for purpose of securing a debt owed by mortgagee.

Mutual insurance company—A company owned by policyholders.

Nationalization—The taking of private property by government, which pays compensation.

Necessaries—Goods and services that are reasonably proper for the maintenance of a minor in light of his or her family's income and position in the community. For example, food, clothing, shelter, and education through high school.

Negligence—A theory of tort law where damages are awarded based on the failure of an individual to exercise reasonable care when there existed such a duty toward another individual. This failure must be the proximate cause of damage to that individual.

Negotiable instrument—A written instrument that is executed containing an unconditional promise to pay a fixed amount of money on demand or at an agreed time to order or to bearer.

Negotiation—The transfer of a negotiable instrument in a manner that makes the transferee a holder.

No-fault insurance—Insurance that compensates victims of motor vehicle accidents regardless of fault or liability of the parties.

No-par value stock—The stock issued with no value amount on its certificate. A subscriber will pay that value as set by the board of directors of the corporation.

Nolo contendere—I will not contest it (Latin). A plea in a criminal action; it is treated by most courts as the equivalent of a guilty plea. It cannot be used to establish liability in a civil suit based on the same cause of action.

Nominal consideration—Consideration passing between parties may be *nominal*, thus inflating a portion of the exchange. For example, John deeds two acres of land to his son Peter in exchange for one dollar.

Nominal damages—A small sum of money awarded to a plaintiff who is unable to prove substantial loss.

Nonfeasance—The failure of one party to attempt performance. Often referred to in agency law when an agent fails to begin performance of agreed upon duties.

Nonsuit—A term used for judgment entered by a court when a plaintiff fails to carry the burden of proof or proceed with a case.

Nontariff barriers—Any factor adversely affecting imports, except for tariffs.

Note—A written promise to pay money to another on demand or at a stated date.

Novation—An agreement to substitute one party for another in a contract.

Nuisance—A legal action in which plaintiff attempts to show that someone is interfering with the use and enjoyment of his or her property.

Obligee—A creditor or promisee.

Obligor—A debtor or promisor.

Offeree—One who accepts an offer or acts upon a legal offer in some manner.

Offeror—One who initiates or makes an offer.

Option contract—A contract in which one party has exchanged consideration for the sole purpose of having the right to buy certain real property or goods at a time of his or her choosing, at a price stated in the option agreement.

Order paper—An instrument that is payable to the order of a specific person.

Ostensible authority—Such authority in agency law that is allowed by a principal to his or her agent as seen from the perspective of a third party dealing with the agent.

Overdraft—A withdrawal of money by a depositor in excess of that which he or she has on account. Can also be used to mean a form of loan to depositor.

Pareto superiority—The condition of welfare maximization in which no action may be taken that will make someone better off without making others less well off.

Parol evidence—Evidence extrinsic or external to that set out in writing.

Partition—Proceedings by which a court divides lands usually held by joint tenants or tenants in common so that parties can hold such real property separately.

Patents—A document that protects inventors by giving the patent owner the exclusive right to make, sell, and use the product or process.

Payee—An individual who is paid, or to whom an instrument is made payable.

Payor bank—A bank on which an instrument is drawn.

Per capita distribution—The distribution of property among a person's descendants whereby each descendant's share is determined pro rata based on the number of beneficiaries.

Per curiam—By the court (Latin). Generally refers to a short statement of decision by the whole court as distinguished from a decision with reasoning written by an individual judge.

Per se—By himself or itself (Latin). A term referring to something forbidden in and of itself because of its pernicious nature, with the court not allowing an argument for the reasonableness of conduct. For example, price fixing in the antitrust area is *per se* illegal.

Per stirpes—The distribution of property among a person's descendants whereby equal shares are granted to the first generation of beneficiaries. If a beneficiary predeceases the testator, the beneficiary's descendants must share his or her portion.

Perfect tender rule—A rule of the law of sale of goods stating that the seller must tender the goods exactly as specified by the contract.

Perjury—The giving of willful false statements under oath in a court of law or in depositions material to

such proceeding. One can also *perjure* oneself before legislative bodies.

Personal representative—The person named by the testator to look after and administer his or her estate after death.

Petit jury—A jury, traditionally of 12 people, used in a civil or criminal trial.

Petitioner—A party that files an appeal with a higher court after losing in a lower court.

Plaintiff-in-error—Generally, a party who is appealing from a lower court decision that has gone against him or her.

Planned unit development—A form of zoning that allows various uses of a site in order to provide maximum land for open space.

Pmsi (Purchase money security interest)—A security interest taken by a seller in items sold to a buyer securing all or a part of the price.

Point-of-sale terminal—A machine that permits the transfer of funds from an individual's account directly into an account maintained by the business in payment for goods or services.

Possession—The dominion or control over property.

Power of attorney—An executed instrument authorizing an agent to represent the individual signing in a general manner or only with reference to a particular transaction or proceeding.

Precedent—A previous decision relied upon by a court for authority in making a current decision.

Prescription—The method of obtaining a right to use another's land through wrongful use for a period of time established by statute.

Presentment—The act of presenting a negotiable instrument to a party for acceptance or payment.

Prima facie—"At first sight" (Latin). Denoting a fact that appears true and will stand as such in the eyes of the court until contradicted.

Principal—In agency law an individual who delegates authority to an agent to represent him or her either generally or only for a specific transaction.

Privileged communication—A term used to denote the right of counsel to refuse disclosure of any communication between the attorney and his or her client to any individual or court of law.

Privity—A contractual relation between parties to a contract as opposed to those affected by the agreement but not parties to it.

Pro rata—"Proportionately, or by share" (Latin).

Probable cause—The existence of sufficient circumstances leading a reasonable person to believe that a person accused of a crime had committed the act.

Probate—A legal process by which a will is proven valid and conflicting claims on the estate are settled. This process takes place in a *probate* court.

Procure—To initiate a proceeding.

Promisee—An individual who receives a promise.

Promisor—An individual who initiates and makes a promise to promisee.

Promissory estoppel—An equitable doctrine often used as a substitute when consideration is not present in a contract and a grave injustice will result if the agreement is not enforced. The doctrine will be specifically invoked when a promise is made by one party that induces justifiable reliance by the other and causes a change in position on the part of the injured party.

Promissory note—A written promise to pay a certain sum to order or bearer within a specific period or at a stated time.

Proximate cause—Used in tort law and negligence theory to denote the direct and natural sequence between the breach of a duty and the injury to an individual.

Proxy—The process by which a shareholder gives another the right to vote his or her stock.

Public affairs management—Techniques that firms use to influence the external environment, for example, lobbying or issues advertising.

Puffing—The favorable statements a seller makes about his or her product.

Punitive damages—Those nonquantifiable damages that do not flow directly from a cause of action but are awarded by the court because of the willful and malicious nature of conduct of the defendant. The court sees such damages as a deterrent to future wrongful conduct.

Qualified indorsement—Indorsement that eliminates the secondary liability of an indorser on the instrument.

Qualified privilege—In tort actions, an exemption for a speaker from liability on a charge of libel or slander unless the defendant can be shown to have had actual malice and knowledge of the falsity of the statement.

Quantum meruit— "As much as he deserved" (Latin). An old common law pleading requesting recovery for materials and services rendered.

Quasi contract—A court-imposed agreement designed to provide equitable relief when one party has received a benefit at the expense of the other. The court imposes a legal relationship on the parties even though all the elements of a contract are not present.

Quid pro quo—Something in exchange for something else.

Quitclaim deed—An instrument of conveyance of the grantor. It passes rights and interests in real property but does not warrant title.

Quota—A legal restriction on the number of items of a particular type that may be imported into a given country.

Ratification—The process by which one adopts the terms of an agreement by silence or affirmative conduct. For example, a minor ratifies agreements made in his or her minority by continuous adherence to the terms for a reasonable period after reaching legal majority.

Rebuttal—An introduction of evidence in a trial that attempts to show that a previous witness's testimony is not credible.

Recoupment—A holding back of an amount of money by a defendant that is owed plaintiff for damages. Defendant may argue that, although he or she breached, plaintiff also failed to comply with obligations arising out of the same agreement.

Regulation Z—A group of rules set forth by the Federal Reserve Board that requires lenders to disclose a number of items to borrowers.

Relativism—Belief that ethical analysis depends on social and economic context in which it occurs and is not universal.

Release—The giving up of a claim or right on the part of one party in exchange for some consideration.

Replevin—A common law term referring to the legal process of obtaining, or taking back, of personal property that is in the hands of another.

Res—A thing or object (Latin).

Res ipsa loquitur—The thing speaks for itself (Latin). Presumption in tort law that defendant is negligent because instrument was in sole control of him or her, and accident would not have happened but for defendant's negligence.

Res judicata—A thing decided (Latin). A legal doctrine that a decision by a court in a suit is final as to future suits on the same cause of action and between the same parties.

Rescission—A remedy in contract law that cancels or abrogates an agreement.

Respondeat superior—The doctrine that the employer is responsible for acts of an employee who is acting within the scope of his or her employment.

Respondent—An appellee or a person who usually has won a verdict in a lower court, and against whom an appeal is being taken.

Restatement of agency—A scholarly work prepared by the American Law Institute summarizing the law of agency; the model the authors recommend be followed for the future.

Restatement of contracts—A scholarly work prepared by the American Law Institute summarizing present contract law; the model the authors recommend be followed for the future.

Restitution—A remedy for breach of a contract in which the court seeks to restore both parties to their original position following rescission of the agreement.

Restrictive indorsement—An indorsement that is conditional, or purports to prohibit the further transfer of the instrument, or includes words that signify a purpose of deposit or collection, or otherwise states that it is for the benefit or use of the indorsee or another person.

Reversion—The returning of an estate left to a grantor after the termination of an estate granted by him or her to another individual.

Revocation—Recall of an offer by an offeror prior to acceptance by offeree.

Rule making—A function of most federal agencies; allows interested parties to comment on proposed binding rules prior to their enactment.

Sale on approval—A sale on terms that allow the buyer to reject the goods after inspecting them.

Satisfaction—The discharge of a debt by payment in full or in part,with agreement of the parties.

Scienter—"Knowingly" (Latin). Generally refers to need for knowledge as an essential element in a tort action for deceit or fraud.

Security interest—A pledge by debtor of property or other matters of value, to make his or her promise of payment under a contract enforceable by a creditor in the event of a breach.

Severable—Capable of being divided and existing independently. For example, a severable contract is one that can be enforced in part, since performance can be divided and apportioned.

Social justice—Manner in which rights and responsibilities are distributed among members of society.

Sovereign immunity—The doctrine that holds that courts of one country have no jurisdiction over suits brought against another country. The doctrine is generally restricted to noncommercial activities of a country.

Special indorsement—An indorsement that specifies the person to whom or to whose order the instrument is payable.

Stakeholder—A person affected by corporate actions who has a claim that the corporation should consider his or her interests.

Stale check—An uncertified check that is presented for payment more than six months after date of issue.

Stare decisis—A legal doctrine stating that decisions of a court should serve as precedent for future legal actions dealing with similar factual situations and points of law.

Statute of frauds—State laws that require certain forms of contracts to be in writing. For example, a promise in consideration of marriage in some states is required to be in writing.

Stay order—A court judgment that prevents a lower court order from being enforced pending an appeal by one of the parties.

Stop-payment order—An order by a customer to the drawee not to pay a check when it is presented for payment.

Strict liability—A concept applied in both civil and criminal law. In criminal law it imposes criminal penalty without proof of intent. In civil law it imposes liability without fault.

Subpoena—The process by which a court orders an individual to appear and testify at a time stated.

Subpoena duces tecum—The process by which, at the request of a party to a suit, the court orders a witness to appear with a relevant document in his or her possession.

Substantial performance—In contract law, the term indicates that all material terms of an agreement have been met, and only insignificant matters remain.

Substantive—Pertaining to essential or basic law that sets out rights. Procedural law is concerned with the legal procedures necessary to obtain these rights in courts or administrative agencies.

Sui generis—One of a kind (Latin).

Supra—Above (Latin). The term refers the reader to a previous part of a book.

Surety—An individual who is originally bound on a debtor–creditor contract to assume primary liability for his or her principal (debtor) in case of a failure of the latter to perform.

Takeover—A process by which an individual or a corporation seeks to obtain control of the management of a corporation by purchasing controlling shares of the stock.

Tariff—A tax assessed on imported goods. The tariff may be based on the value of the goods (ad valorem) or on the number of goods (flat rate) being imported.

Tenancy at will—A leased estate created when the owner of real property allows someone to occupy it for an unspecified period of time.

Tenants in common—The method of holding title to property in which each person owns a certain amount of the property; on the death of one of the parties, that person's property goes to his or her heirs, not to the other tenant.

Tenant by the entirety—Joint tenants who are spouses and who provide that the survivor of them will automatically become the owner of the property held as joint tenants.

Tender—An offer to pay a sum of money without conditions attached.

Testamentary trust—A trust created by a person's will; comes into effect only on that person's death.

Testator—An individual who has died leaving a will.

Title insurance—Insurance that repays the insured for a loss arising from defects in the title to real estate.

Tort-feasor—In law of torts, a wrong-doer, or one guilty of a tort.

Trade acceptance—Time draft drawn by a seller naming the seller as payee and the purchaser of goods as drawee; obligates the buyer to pay the draft upon acceptance of the goods.

Trade fixtures—Articles a tenant attaches to land or buildings to be used in the tenant's trade or business.

Trade secrets—Valuable formulas, patterns, or information used by a business but unknown to competitors.

Transferability—An instrument's assignability or negotiability.

Transferee—An individual to whom a transfer is made.

Transferor—A person who initiates or makes a transfer.

Treasury shares—Generally refers to stock issued by a corporation to shareholders and subsequently acquired by the issuing corporation.

Treble damages—Refers to triple the amount of damages awarded by a jury. The purpose of such is to discourage similar conduct in the future. Such statutory damages are usually awarded by the court on motion of the plaintiff following a jury award.

Trespass—Unlawful violation of another's person or property.

Trust—1. An interest or right in real or personal property by one party for the benefit of another. 2. In antitrust law an unlawful combination seeking to do an act in contravention of federal or state statute.

Trust indorsement—An indorsement that indicates that the proceeds of an instrument should be held in trust for a third party.

Trustee in bankruptcy—An individual who holds title to a bankrupt's property at the direction of the court. His or her function is to defend all assets in suits and to provide an accounting to the court of moneys for distribution to creditors.

Tying agreements—In antitrust law, a refusal by a manufacturer to sell a primary product (tying) unless the retailer or franchisee agrees to buy a secondary product (tied).

Ultra vires—"Beyond its power"(Latin). Pertaining to a corporation's acting beyond the scope of the power set out in its charter or articles of incorporation.

Unconscionable—Denoting a contract that is grossly unfair and shocking to the conscience. For example, the use of small print and technical language in a contract for necessaries with poor, illiterate people while charging prices that are far above normal market prices. The court will generally not enforce such agreement and will order a rescission.

Underwriter—Usually, a firm that markets securities for a corporate registrant. It sells corporate securities as an agent and receives a commission for such work.

Undue influence—The pressure exerted on an individual to sign an agreement. Generally it refers to the misuse of a position of confidential communication (e.g., doctor-patient) to influence an individual.

Unilateral—Pertaining to one side, or to only one party. For example, a *unilateral* mistake by a party to a contract is a misunderstanding of the terms of an agreement by one party but not the other.

Universalism—The view that there are universal principles that transcend local custom or practice.

Utilitarianism—The theory that the morality of actions is determined by their outcome, with an emphasis on the greatest number. It is an example of outcome based ethics.

Utilitarianism, act—Requires an individual analysis of any action that may have moral consequences.

Utilitarianism, rule—The practice of identifying rules that are assumed to maximize utility instead of making an individual assessment of each action's moral consequences.

Unliquidated debt—A debt the exact amount of which cannot be determined by the terms of the obligation.

Usage of trade—Well known manner of conducting transactions in a particular industry or trade.

Usury—The loan of money at an interest rate in excess of that allowed by law.

Valid—Containing all the elements of a contract and thus is operative at law.

Vendee—A purchaser of property.

Vendor—A seller of property.

Vest—To give an immediate fixed right of possession in an estate of real property.

Vicarious liability—Indirect liability. Used in agency law to describe a principal's liability to third party for the acts of an agent.

Void—Having no legal force in the eyes of the law at its inception. A *void* agreement can never be cured of its defect and will always be inoperative.

Voidable—Pertaining to an agreement that becomes inoperative when the parties treat it as effective and binding.

Waive—To relinquish intentionally a legal right that could be exercised.

Warehouse receipt—A receipt, issued by a warehouse supervisor, that enables the person in possession of it to pick up goods from the warehouse.

Warrant—In criminal law a written order directing a law enforcement officer to arrest a person.

Warranty—An undertaking by a seller to guarantee a product against defects. The scope of such warranty as to goods is usually set out in writing. Implied warranties are those established from the nature of goods and their intended purpose.

Warranty deed—A deed that conveys title and warrants that the seller's title to the real estate is marketable.

Watered stock—The issued stock that is represented as fully paid but in fact is not paid up.

Whistle blowing—Reporting the wrongdoing of another person to someone in authority; a type of ethical problem that places one person in a position of telling his or her supervisors that the actions of someone else are illegal, wrongful, or unethical.

White collar crime—The term used to describe nonviolent criminal acts committed in a commercial context by a member of the management or professional class.

Will—A written declaration stating its maker's desires as to the disposition of his or her property or estate after death.

Workable competition—A term used to denote industrial organization economists' yardstick for measuring the effect a merger will have on an industry's competitive framework. Conduct, structure, and performance criteria are used to judge the effectiveness of competition in a market.

Zoning—The division of an area, usually a municipality, into districts to control land use.

Subject Index

Case Index